EXPERIMENTAL PSYCHOLOGY

Contributors

MATHEW ALPERN University of Michigan

ALEXANDER K. BARTOSHUK University of Western Ontario

LINDA BARTOSHUK John B. Pierce Foundation Laboratory

DONALD S. BLOUGH Brown University

ROBERT M. BOYNTON University of Rochester

RUSSELL M. CHURCH Brown University

CHARLES N. COFER The Pennsylvania State University

TRYGG ENGEN Brown University

JULIAN HOCHBERG Columbia University

DAN R. KENSHALO Florida State University

J. W. KLING Brown University

LEWIS P. LIPSITT Brown University

RICHARD B. MILLWARD Brown University

MAXWELL M. MOZELL State University of New York, Upstate Medical Center

LEO POSTMAN University of California, Berkeley

LORRIN A. RIGGS Brown University

ALLAN M. SCHRIER Brown University

CHARLES F. STEVENS University of Washington

WILLARD R. THURLOW University of Wisconsin

WOODWORTH & SCHLOSBERG'S

EXPERIMENTAL
PSYCHOLOGY
Third Edition

J. W. KLING &
LORRIN A. RIGGS
Brown University

and
seventeen contributors

HOLT, RINEHART AND WINSTON, Inc.

New York   •   Chicago   •   San Francisco   •   Atlanta   •   Dallas
Montreal   •   Toronto   •   London   •   Sydney

SBN: 03-068680-6
Printed in the United States of America
1 2 3 4   074   9 8 7 6 5 4 3 2 1

PREFACE

TO THE THIRD EDITION

In 1938, Robert S. Woodworth brought out the first edition of his *Experimental Psychology*. In his preface he remarked on the "youth and immaturity of experimental psychology" in which "the student can rather quickly penetrate the zone of unsettled problems in original investigation." Woodworth traces the beginning of his work on the book to 1910 and states that a preliminary mimeographed edition of the book came out in 1920 with the collaboration of A. T. Poffenburger.

Surely no other psychologist could have made so lucid and comprehensive a presentation of the field as did Woodworth in 1938. He had had experience as a teacher and student in the basic fields of mathematics, philosophy, and physiology. He had also done research in collaboration with the great Sir Charles Sherrington in the study of expressions of anger and defense in the decerebrate cat. He later worked with Thorndike in the more traditionally psychological area of transfer of training and did his own research on voluntary movement, imageless thought, psychophysics, motivation, and tests of emotional stability. All this had brought Woodworth to the age of 70 by the time *Experimental Psychology* first appeared. Prior to that he had written several other books, including a revision of Ladd's *Physiological Psychology*, the widely used *Contemporary Schools of Psychology*, and the best-selling elementary textbook, *Psychology*, of which there were five editions from 1921 to 1947.

v

The second edition of *Experimental Psychology* appeared in 1954 as a collaborative effort by Woodworth, then 85 years of age, and Harold Schlosberg. Schlosberg, like Woodworth, was known for the breadth of his interests in psychology, his eclectic position with regard to the various schools of psychological thought, and a strong concern for the intellectual development of students. In their preface, Woodworth and Schlosberg expressed the conviction that a book such as theirs should be revised at least once every decade. They did, in fact, start the revision of the first edition in 1949, but found as they went along that a new book was required, rather than a mere updating of the old one. Thus the second edition emphasized American psychology while the old one had been concerned to a large degree with European, especially German psychology, and much of the old material was omitted to make room for a greatly expanded coverage of topics of current interest. The new bibliography was larger by forty percent than the old, and over half of the 2,480 items cited had not been used in the old edition.

It is remarkable that two men could achieve in five years the enormous task of bringing out the second edition. With all this, they managed to preserve the easy informality and clarity of the earlier work despite the increasing complexity of the material covered. Both first and second editions were thus able to serve three rather different groups: advanced undergraduates, taking courses in experimental psychology, learning, motivation, sensory psychology or perception; graduate students, seeking a review of selected research areas to complement their study of primary source materials; and instructors, selecting illustrative materials directly within their own areas of specialization.

Before his death in 1964, Harold Schlosberg conceived the idea of bringing out a third edition of *Experimental Psychology* as a collaborative work with his colleagues in the Psychology Department at Brown University. The present edition is an outgrowth of that idea in which the two present editors and seven of the other authors are, indeed, members of that department. Of the remaining ten authors, five studied with Schlosberg and have degrees in psychology from Brown. Obviously, these authors could not aim their chapters equally at undergraduate, graduate, and professional psychologists. We have, instead, concentrated on the needs of the advanced undergraduate students; but we hope that this edition, like its predecessors, will also be found useful by the more advanced readers. Appraisal of the degree to which this edition fills these needs will have to come from our readers.

A good part of the success of the previous editions can be attributed to the avoidance of any preoccupation with jargon and narrowly defined experimentation. Especially to the student making his first explorations of an area, this is an important characteristic. We hope that we have achieved authenticity by having the chapters prepared by persons actively engaged in research in these areas; but we trust that the experience each author has had as a student and a teacher has been reflected in the organization he has given to his materials.

The present editors have found, as did Woodworth and Schlosberg in 1954, that great changes have occurred in the field of psychology since the previous edition. In fact, we estimate that only ten to fifteen percent of the figures, examples, and descriptive material contained in the earlier editions are retained in this one. While many of the chapter headings are carried over, some entirely new ones have been included, namely those on basic mechanisms of neural function, color vision, positive reinforcement, and aversive behavior. To make way for these new chapters and the mass of new material in others, we have necessarily dropped some previous chapters on reaction time, attention, emotion, conditioning, maze learning, and problem solving. In most cases, the experiments in these areas are covered within the other chapters to the extent that they are still active subjects for investigation. But the earlier editions of this work will have to be consulted by those particularly interested in such topics as reaction time and maze learning. We must similarly admit that most of the chapters present an unbalanced sample of species used as experimental subjects, but that is only a reflection of the research in those areas. Most of psychophysics and sensory psychology is based on data gathered with adult human subjects, while many problems in learning and motivation have been studied almost exclusively with the laboratory rat or pigeon. For some problems, of course, the unique characteristics of the octopus or the tree shrew may make it the species of choice, and wherever possible, the authors have tried to include such information. But a textbook, however large, must sacrifice breadth of coverage for depth, and therefore the emphasis in each chapter has been on the problems that have been most thoroughly studied. In that sense, it seems fair to say that the biases shown in the chapters are the biases of experimental psychology in the 1960s.

We make no claim for completeness of coverage of this book. In the sensory chapters, for example, there is a heavy emphasis on vision and only scanty coverage of kinesthesis, static sensitivity, or the common chemical sense. In some measure we reflect a proportionate amount of experimental work in these areas at the present time, and we choose to cover in depth the topics most thoroughly explored with the idea that the methods and principles involved will be found common to areas remaining for future exploration.

We wish to acknowledge most humbly our indebtedness to Woodworth and Schlosberg for defining the area of experimental psychology and bringing it through its years of "youth and immaturity." Our hope is that this multi-author book has not lost the cohesive and elucidative qualities brought to the field by the previous authors.

To the present authors we wish to express

our gratitude for undertaking the task and willingness to take on rather extensive revision where recommended by the editors or by the many readers of early versions of the separate chapters. These readers, colleagues and students, have helped immeasurably by pointing to gaps or errors of coverage.

To our publisher we wish to express our appreciation of tolerance for the repeated delays and changes in plan that have occurred over the years since this undertaking was first begun. We particularly value the cooperation of Mr. Brian Heald in securing the reviews of the chapters by competent experts in each area and in bringing each author to the achievement of a manuscript of quality and attractiveness.

Mrs. Lynn Sullivan and Mrs. Kathryn Huntington have typed—and retyped—the many versions of the manuscript, and Mrs. Dody Giletti has constructed our index. They all have our admiration, affection, and appreciation.

Finally we wish to acknowledge our debt to the following book publishers for permitting us to use illustrations: Academic Press, Inc.; Allyn and Bacon, Inc.; Almqvist & Wiksell Foerlag AB; Appleton-Century-Crofts; Chapman and Hall, Ltd.; Charles C Thomas, Publisher; Clark University Press; Cranbrook Institute of Science; D. C. Heath & Company; Doubleday and Company, Inc.; Dover Publications, Inc.; D. Van Nostrand Co., Inc.; Elsevier Publishing Company; Gyldendalske Bodhandel, Nordisk Forlag A/S; Henry Kimpton, Ltd.; John Wiley & Sons, Inc.; Holden-Day, Inc.; Holt, Rinehart and Winston, Inc.; Houghton Mifflin Company; Institute superière de Philosophie; McGraw-Hill Book Company; Pergamon Press, Inc.; Psychological Institute, University of Helsinki; Stanford University Press; The Clarendon Press, Oxford; The Johns Hopkins Press; The Macmillan Company; University of Chicago Press; W. B. Saunders Company; Yale University Press.

We are also indebted to the following journals, proceedings, and other periodical publications: Acta Physiologica Scandinavica; Acta Psychologica Scandinavica; American Journal of Ophthalmology; American Journal of Physics; American Journal of Physiology; American Journal of Psychology; American Psychologist; Annals of Otolaryngology; Annals of the New York Academy of Science; Archiv fur die Gesamte Psychologie; Archives of Philosophy, Psychology, and Scientific Methods; Archives of Psychology, New York; AV Communication Review; Biological Review; British Journal of Applied Physics; British Journal of Psychology; British Medical Bulletin; Canadian Journal of Psychology; Cold Spring Harbor Symposia on Quantitative Biology; Education Monographs; Illuminating Engineering; Journal of Biophysics, Biochemistry, and Cytology; Journal of Cellular and Comparative Physiology; Journal of Clinical Investigation; Journal of Comparative Psychology; Journal of Comparative and Physiological Psychology; Journal of Experimental Psychology; Journal of General Physiology; Journal of General Psychology; Journal of Neurophysiology; Journal of Physiology; Journal of Psychology; Journal of the Acoustical Society of America; Journal of the Experimental Analysis of Behavior; Journal of the Optical Society of America; Journal of

Verbal Learning and Verbal Behavior: L'Année Psychologique; Optica Acta; Perception and Psychophysics; Perceptual and Motor Skills; Physiological Review; Physiology and Behavior; Proceedings of the National Academy of Science; Proceedings of the Royal Society, London, Series B; Psychological Bulletin; Psychological Monographs; Psychological Reports; Psychological Review; Psychologische Forschung; Psychonomic Science; Quarterly Journal of Experimental Psychology; Scandinavian Journal of Psychology; Science; Scientific American; Vision Research; Zeitschrift fur Psychologie; Zeitschrift fur Sinnesphysiologie.

We have tried to make this a useful book, both for independent study and for help in connection with actual laboratory exercises. Accordingly we have emphasized the headings and subheadings within each chapter, the wide use of cross-references from one chapter to another, and a list of tables and formulas likely to be used by the student and easily available to him at the end of the book. A separate instructor's manual is being prepared by Dr. Stephen Sadowsky.

J.W.K. and L.A.R.
Providence, Rhode Island

CONTENTS

10. COLOR VISION   315
Robert M. Boynton

11. EFFECTOR MECHANISMS IN VISION   369
Mathew Alpern

12. PERCEPTION   395
I. Color and Shape
Julian Hochberg

EXPERIMENTAL PSYCHOLOGY

Lorrin A. Riggs and J. W. Kling

INTRODUCTION

1

Experimental psychology, as a separate field of scientific inquiry, is only a hundred years old. But it did not burst forth, fully formed, when Wundt "founded" the first laboratory at the University of Leipzig in 1879. Much earlier, experimental investigations of distinctly psychological problems had been undertaken by astronomers, physicists, and philosophers. These men were indeed the first to be confronted with the major question of whether psychological processes could ever be studied by experimental methods. Sensory physiology and psychology had already proved to be fertile fields for the experimentalist, but whether the "higher mental processes" (such as learning and memory, judgment, thinking) and such complex phenomena as motivation and emotion could also be probed by these techniques was doubted by many.

The ingenuity of the nineteenth century experimentalists soon provided techniques suitable for the investigation of many of these problems, and it is now possible to claim that it was the success of the experimental part of psychology that finally established the field as a separate discipline, just as it had been the success of the experimentalists in physics, chemistry and biology that validated their claims to independence from the older philosophical inquiries. Experimental psychology gained much needed prestige at the time from the active involvement of such intellectual giants as Helmholtz, Darwin, and Galton,

1

each of whom opened up important fields of psychological inquiry. Then came a succession of men, starting with Wundt, who were self-acknowledged practitioners of experimental psychology, interested in psychological problems per se rather than as adjuncts or incidentals to the investigation of philosophical or physiological questions. Brentano, Ebbinghaus, Binet, James, Titchener, Watson, Skinner—these are some of the best known shapers of the course of experimental psychology, for they have occupied pivotal positions in the evolution of our basic concepts, our methods, and our self-image.

A science, of course, is not just a haphazard collection of experimental observations; early attempts to systematize and theorize gave birth to what we now know as "schools" of psychology: Structuralism, Functionalism, Gestalt Psychology, and Behaviorism. Each had its ardent champions and each left its contributions to method and emphasis on special problems. Today it probably is correct to say that the majority of experimental psychologists have adopted the eclectic viewpoint of Woodworth and Schlosberg: few of us are Behaviorists; rather we are all behaviorists who have accepted the best (the surviving) ideas and methods of the earlier schools of psychology. Whether we deal with programmed learning, perceptual constancy, or payoff matrices, few of us feel called upon to wave the flag for a single basic approach to all the problems of our science.

We find that just as the global schools have disappeared, so also have the broad theories gone from psychology. For example, learning in all its forms is no longer regarded as reducible to the formation of conditioned reflexes according to the models of Pavlov, Guthrie, or Hull. Instead, we have more restricted paradigms for human verbal learning, discrimination learning, or schedule-generated behavior. Similarly, the seemingly contradictory theories of Helmholtz and Hering in color vision are now shown to account for particular stages in the visual process and so have their individual contributions to offer,

just as the quantum and wave theories of light are both fruitful concepts for the contemporary experimental physicist. In short, the present complexity of our field seems to leave little possibility for all-embracing explanations. Instead, the trend of theorizing and systematization in the 1960s has been toward the development of more restricted (and hence more realistic) models or paradigms, and toward the utilization of a greater variety of experimental techniques, many adapted from other laboratory sciences.

Definition of Experimental Psychology

All psychology is based upon observation, but not all observation occurs in experimental settings. For some problems, such nonexperimental techniques as the case history method or observation in naturalistic settings may be the methods of choice. But the pages of any contemporary introductory textbook will attest to the fact that the great majority of the facts of modern psychology are derived from formal experimentation.

Much excellent experimental investigation is being carried on in such fields as social psychology, child psychology, and personality, but these are not ordinarily included within "Experimental Psychology." In part, the restricted application of this label is an historical accident: sensing and perceiving, learning and remembering—these were the earliest problems to be attacked with success by laboratory experimentation; these formed the core of such influential textbooks as Woodworth's 1938 edition of *Experimental Psychology*; these were the topics around which the basic theories grew and for which the most fundamental experimental techniques were developed.

In this edition, we continue to treat Experimental Psychology in its rather narrow sense, but we need not look further back into our history than to the 1954 edition to see that there are continual changes in even so restricted a field. The most noticeable trend seems to be toward an amalgamation of physiological psychology and experimental psychology, with the physiological and anatomical contributions to behavioral phenomena becoming a natural part of the body of psychological knowledge. Another trend is toward a rapid increase in the number of psychological problems in relation to which significant quantitative theorizing can be carried out.

The Experimental Method

Can we define the experimental method in psychology? If we try to do so, we soon find that contemporary methodology has become so highly specific that it is difficult to lay down general rules applicable to all experiments. However, a few characteristics of the experimental method may be mentioned.

1. The experimenter starts with some purpose in mind. Whether he has a rather general question or some quite specific hypothesis to test, he will at the least know what selected aspects of behavior to observe, and when to observe them. Thus, he starts with an immediate advantage of having defined just what it is he will try to study.

2. The experimenter creates his own opportunities and can initiate the procedure for observation when he is fully ready to measure and record the behavior. Thus he is prepared to observe under the best possible conditions. By controlling the occurrence of events, he can also repeat the events under controlled conditions, and thus obtain some idea of how consistent is the phenomenon he is studying.

3. Since the experimenter has established the conditions for observation, he can specify his procedure so that both he and others can repeat the process.

4. Having control of the conditions, the experimenter can usually manipulate them systematically, to the end that he can specify the effects on behavior of making certain changes in the conditions.

Independent and Dependent Variables

In designing an experiment, one attempts to control the situation in such a way that meaningful relationships can be established between antecedents and consequences. Among the antecedents are conditions present in the environment and in the organism, as well as the so-called independent variables, such as stimuli deliberately imposed upon the organism at the time of the experiment. Among the consequences are the so-called dependent variables, in particular the responses of the organism and physiological changes following upon the stimuli. In the simplest case one can distinguish between constants and variables in the situation. Constants are defined as those aspects of the experiment that are not under primary study, typical of which are the immediate environment and the characteristics of the subject such as age, alertness, familiarity with the task, and motivation. Environmental constants may typically include the conditions of lighting, quietness, temperature, and specific provisions for the experiment, such as comfortable seating and adequate communication between subject and experimenter.

In the majority of experiments, it is still possible to follow the old standard "rule of one variable," where the experimenter holds constant all aspects of the situation except the one factor which he makes his "experimental variable." In such cases, it is tempting to conclude that changes in the dependent variable are attributable to manipulations of the independent variable, and while we are all aware that correlation does not prove causation, many an experimenter has discovered to his sorrow that some previously unsuspected factor has really had the immediate controlling influence in his experiment. For example, the "stimulus discriminations" of laboratory animals sometimes prove to be controlled by factors which the unwary investigator may overlook: the noises of programming equipment, or the presence and absence of reinforcement are two common sources of such stimulation. After eliminating all possible stimuli correlated with the independent variable, the cautious experimenter frequently will see what happens if he completely removes the stimulus which he thinks is controlling the behavior of his subject. As Blough (1966, page 370) has pointed out, there is no more convincing argument for such empirical evaluations of experimental conditions than "seeing a pigeon continue to make a difficult 'visual' discrimination after the stimulus lamp has been turned off."

A still more complex task of control and evaluation faces the experimenter who would manipulate two or more antecedent conditions in the same experiment. Statistical techniques by which the effects of each variable and their interactions may be evaluated can be very valuable adjuncts to experimentation, but these techniques assume that the experimenter does indeed know what the true antecedent factors were. Unfortunately, it sometimes seems that the more complex and obscure the experimental problem, the more variables the experimenter decides to include in a single study!

Independent variables are those imposed on the subject by the experimenter, and are all those aspects of the experiment which the experimenter varies systematically. In studying the effects of intensity of light on speed of reaction, for example, light intensity would be the independent variable. By convention, the independent variable is marked off in units of intensity, time, trials, and so forth, and scaled accordingly on the baseline or abscissa of any graph displaying the results of the experiment.

Sometimes what is the independent variable in one experiment will be merely one of many antecedent conditions to be held as nearly constant as possible in another experiment. For example, a great many species show cyclic changes in their responsivity. Sometimes these changes are correlated with the day–night cycle and so are called "circadian rhythms." The experimenter who is not studying such rhythms usually will schedule each subject to be run at the same time every day. Thus, while the state of the organism remains one of the antecedent conditions influencing his behavior, the influence will be relatively constant for each subject throughout the experiment. On the other hand, an experimenter may be primarily interested in such

rhythms, and he may therefore try to hold constant other environmental conditions (such as temperature) and vary the time of day at which his observations are taken.

Typical dependent variables are measures of the response of the organism, whether these be enumerations of errors or correct performance, magnitude or speed of reaction to the stimulus, or physiological changes such as contraction of the pupil, electrophysiological changes evoked by the stimuli, or changes in heart rate. Thus we may consider the observed changes in a dependent variable to be the main result of the experiment and we conventionally plot our data on a graph in which the ordinate is used for an appropriate scaling of the dependent variable.

Having outlined typical or traditional procedures, we must now recognize their limitations for some types of experimental work. Sometimes, for example, one cannot distinguish clearly between independent and dependent variables, and sometimes there may be many of each, rather than a single one, so that the process of graphical description may become much more complex. As one example, the critical frequency of fusion may be observed as a function of intensity of flashes delivered to the eye. In this case, both frequency and intensity are manipulated by the experimenter so that it is only for convenience that we consider frequency of fusion as a dependent variable to be plotted on the ordinate as we see it on page 311 in the chapter on vision. The true dependent variable, of course, is not plotted at all. This is the verbal response of the subject indicating whether the light appears to be steady or flickering at any given time. Similarly, one may cite an operant conditioning paradigm in which the animal is given bits of food when it presses a bar. The schedule of reinforcement in this case is partly an independent variable, since it is set up in advance by the experimenter. Moreover, selection of the reinforcement schedule determines, more than does any other single factor, the rate and pattern of responses emitted. But the reinforcement schedule is also related, as a dependent variable, to the responses of the animal; it is those responses that determine whether any reinforcements will occur. The point is that even seemingly straightforward procedures may include many factors, not all of which can be classified simply as independent or dependent variables. These situations impose special problems for graphical or tabular presentation of results, and the elementary rules do not always apply.

Every field of experimentation has now, of necessity, developed special tricks and precautions to avoid artifacts and spurious conclusions. No living organism remains the same throughout the day, or even during a few minutes of experimentation. Apprehension and excitement at the beginning of the run may give way to boredom and fatigue at the end. Dark adaptation can only be tested by the use of light, and certain perceptual phenomena can only be reported if the subject learns and remembers the appropriate words with which to describe them. Similarly, an overly cooperative subject may report detecting an odor when none is present, while a less alert subject may overlook test stimuli even when they approach moderate strength. The basic remedy in all these situations is so to design the experimental procedure that the uncontrolled variations in performance have a minimal effect on the final conclusions drawn from the experiment. Counterbalancing the order of presentation is one of the most valuable features of experimental design. The comparison of Condition A with Condition B for learning lists of nonsense syllables (see Chapter 21) sometimes may best be made by following an ABBA order to balance out the factors of inexperience at the beginning and boredom at the end of the experiment. Similarly, sensory experiments may be designed in such a way that progressive changes in adaptation or alertness are also counterbalanced. This may often be done by randomizing the order of presentation of stimuli of different strengths.

Single and Repeated Observations

In theory, it would seem that the experimenter's job would be least complicated if he could always work with the same subjects, thus coming to know their characteristics and controlling for their past experiences. While this often proves to be possible, there are some experiments which, by their very nature, can only be carried out once on a given subject. For example, in his studies of double-alternation behavior, Hunter found that once the human subject came upon the solution to the problem, the experiment was over and the subject could not be used again.[1]

If it is the case that a subject can be tested but once, the experimenter is then forced into the use of different subjects for each value of his independent variable. If a great many subjects can be included in each such group, random assignment of subjects to groups may balance individual differences and the groups may be directly compared. Where such large numbers are not feasible, subjects may be matched on the basis of a significant variable, and then so assigned that the groups are balanced before the crucial phase of the procedure is introduced. Finally, there are even some statistical techniques (such as analysis of covariance) that allow the experimenter to estimate the significance of his procedure in spite of having nonmatched groups with which to work. These techniques are discussed in many textbooks of statistics and experimental design.

Performance Criteria

When the experimenter sets out to study the effects of X on Y, he not only must decide which subjects to use, and what antecedent

[1] Hunter referred to such experiments as ones in which "you can only skin a fox once." Whether the experimental problem does indeed have but one pelt must always be determined by experimentation. (See Hunter, W. S., & Bartlett, S. C. Double alternation in young children, *J. exper. Psychol.*, 1948, *38*, 558–567). Other examples of "one-shot" experiments can be found in the study of hidden figures in perceptual patterns. Still others are in several types of experiment on memory where the mere testing of retention may facilitate future performance on retention tests (for example, Brown, 1923).

and consequent conditions to employ, but he must also determine just how he will relate antecedent to consequent in his procedure. In this regard, particular mention should be made of the use of a "constant effect" as the performance criterion. The alternative procedure is to measure the subject's response under a constant set of stimulating conditions. A few examples may make the distinction clear. Suppose first that the problem is to study the learning of nonsense syllables. A constant-effect procedure might require that each subject attempt to recall the nonsense syllables immediately after each reading of the list of syllables, and to keep at this practice until it had produced some constant effect, such as the errorless recall of the list on two successive trials of practice. The subject would then be scored on the number of trials taken to achieve this constant effect, and this number of trials would be the basis for comparing him with other subjects, or comparing the mean performance of subjects using one method with a similar mean of subjects using another method of learning. This is basically the method introduced by Ebbinghaus in his pioneering studies in 1885.

As opposed to the constant-effect procedure, the "constant-treatment" method would allow each subject a fixed number of practice trials in which to learn as many of the correct responses as he could. His score would then be the number of nonsense syllables mastered in that many trials. The chief weakness of the constant-treatment procedure is our ignorance of the characteristics of the units in which the dependent variable is measured. What does it mean to say that a subject has learned eight of twelve words in a list when using one practice procedure, but only six of twelve when using another procedure? At most, we can conclude that the first method is the more efficient, but we cannot carry out such manipulations of the data as are involved when we attempt to say how much better is one method than the other. By way of contrast, the dependent variables in the constant-effect procedure usually are

measured in units whose characteristics are well known, and the experimenter does have some confidence that his manipulations of the data (adding, dividing, and so forth) are valid ones. Of course, many problems in psychology are still at the stage of development where it is necessary to discover whether Treatment A produces any effect at all, or whether A has a greater or lesser effect than Treatment B; in such cases, the constant-treatment procedure will continue to find applications.

The advantages of the "constant-effect" procedure are perhaps even more clear in sensory experiments. In a typical experiment on visual dark adaptation the subject's eyes are first exposed to light for a preliminary interval of time. Then the light is cut off and the increase in visual sensitivity is measured by determining the intensity of a test flash that the subject is just able to see at various intervals of time after the light is cut off. In this case, we assume that when a test light can barely be detected, it is producing a relatively constant level of responding on the part of the visual system, and accordingly we express the visual sensitivity of the organism as the reciprocal of that amount of light. Much less satisfactory would be the "constant-treatment" procedure of using a fixed intensity of test flash throughout the process of dark adaptation and asking the subject to give repeated estimates of its apparent brightness.

Intervening Variables

The design of experiments requires decisions about independent and dependent variables, but the interpretation of results and their implications almost always involves the experimenter with "intervening variables." A few comments about them may help to define this term.

First, it is essential that we recognize that an intervening variable is a concept: it is a product of the experimenter's consideration of his observations and his comparisons of other sets of information. The visual sensitivity mentioned above is such a concept, as is memory or retention. They are called "intervening variables" because they are not directly observed independent or dependent variables of an experiment, but they frequently do help the experimenter think about the relations between such antecedents and consequences, and thus "intervene" between them. They are, to this extent, hypothetical entities and for this reason we must be especially careful in the use of them in drawing conclusions from the experiments. Retention, for example, may turn out to be zero as tested by the method of recall, or 50 percent as measured by a recognition procedure. Similarly, visual sensitivity may seem to reach a maximum value after 15 minutes in the dark as judged by the subject himself, while other more careful psychophysical procedures may show increasing sensitivity out to an hour or longer of dark adaptation. Yet retention and sensitivity are useful concepts and need to be kept in our working vocabulary along with others such as set, bias, deficiency, or preference.

The constant hazard to the experimenter from such concepts as that of the intervening variable is the temptation we all have to reify them. Thus, the beginning student may ask which is the "true" measure of retention or the "best" index of visual sensitivity. Such questions imply that retention or visual sensitivity really is somewhere, if only we could get at it, or that the concepts have some meaning other than that which we abstract from the observed relations of independent and dependent variables. Unfortunately, being verbal creatures with a rich history of associations among words, we frequently compound the situation by letting additional meanings accrue to such concepts, so that a commonly used term such as "preference" may begin to imply desire, pleasure or conscious choice. Properly employed, however, this term simply designates the relative frequency with which a subject approaches or avoids each stimulus among several that are made equally available to him.

Analysis of Results

We have outlined some of the general problems involved in the design and conduct of psychological experiments. We must now say a few words about the way in which results can be analyzed so as to yield valid conclusions. It is customary here to distinguish between descriptive statistics or data processing on the one hand, and the testing of hypotheses, estimating the significance of a given effect for the entire population of subjects, or the establishment of functional relationships, on the other hand. These topics may well form the subject matter of separate courses in quantitative methods in psychology. We may simply mention here that on the descriptive side one needs to have available in the laboratory standard statistical books, various sorts of graph paper, a slide rule, and preferably access to calculators or modern computers for reducing the drudgery and increasing the accuracy of numerical work. The numerical tables and formulae to be found at the end of this book may provide a sort of bare minimum of help to the student in the experimental laboratory.

On the analytical side, the guiding principle would be that of a healthy scientific skepticism. In a very real sense it is true that the body of knowledge in any scientific subject consists of those generalizations and hypotheses that have survived repeated experimental attempts at rejection. The scientist, in fact, does not set out to prove a pet theory of his or to agitate for its acceptance by the rest of the scientific community. Instead he sets himself the task of stating his theory as explicitly and objectively as possible so that it will be testable by those undertaking experiments in his field. It is generally true that no one experiment is ever able to establish the validity of a scientific theory or hypothesis. A single well-conducted experiment, on the other hand, may sometimes yield results that lead to the rejection of an hypothesis at a high level of confidence. The natural history of theories seems to be that ad hoc adjustments in them are made as required by such well-designed disproving experiments, until the burden of these qualifying adjustments becomes so great that the advantages of a simpler explanation become apparent.

Of course, some generally accepted guidelines are needed to help us decide when an experimental effect can be considered of sufficient importance to warrant our serious consideration. This introduces the concepts of *reliability, validity,* and *relevance*. An effect is reliable to the extent that it is repeatable. In many experiments, we actually repeat the procedure dozens or hundreds of times, and observe the degree to which the results vary around some average value. In other cases, where we can only expose each subject to the treatment one time, we use large numbers of subjects and estimate reliability from the variability in the group results.

Validity refers to the degree to which our dependent variable is really measuring that with which we are concerned. Suppose, for example, that we wish to find a valid measure of animal motivation. We may start by training an animal to press a bar in a Skinner box situation (see p. 752). We observe that the animal will not respond very much unless it is well motivated, and we decide to find out whether rate of responding is a suitable dependent variable, that is, whether it is a *valid* measure of motivation.

To answer such questions of validity, we must first agree on a criterion. For example, suppose the motivation in question is "thirst." To find out if response rate measures thirst, we must pick some criterion that defines thirst. Suppose we agree that an animal is thirsty if he drinks water, and that the thirstier he is the more water he will drink. The amount of water consumed is now our *criterion* of thirst. To get different degrees of thirst, we may deprive the animal of water for varying lengths of time. We then give him free access to water for a testing period of, say, ten minutes, and measure the amount he drinks during that interval. Now we can see if rate of bar pressing is a valid measure of

thirst by doing a separate experiment in which we again deprive the animal of water and measure the rate at which he presses the bar (reinforced by drops of water) at various levels of deprivation. The correlation of response rate with the criterion, water consumption, at the same levels of deprivation, indicates the *validity* of the rate measure of thirst motivation.

Much of the work in psychology laboratories is devoted to efforts to obtain "good" measures, by which we mean performance measures that are highly reliable and that vary in a meaningful way as we manipulate conditions in which we are interested. The term "meaningful" introduces the concept of relevance, which obviously is based on value judgments that must be made by the experimenter when he considers how he will spend his time in the laboratory, and by the teacher or writer when he decides which experiments he will cite in a lecture or in a chapter. Fads and fashions exist in science as well as in everyday life, and judgments of relevance are no doubt influenced by them. For the most part, however, we can use as a working criterion, against which to judge the relevance of an experiment, our judgment of whether it makes a contribution to our understanding of behavior. In the broadest sense, we may ask, "would another 10 years of this type of experimentation give us a better appreciation of the factors governing the behavior of organisms?" Unfortunately, every psychologist sometimes completes an experiment that is technically adequate and that meets objective standards of reliability, but that is relegated to the rear of a file drawer because it does not meet his own subjective standards of relevancy. This, of course, is a matter of personal style, and no textbook can provide rules for such judgments!

The Challenge to the Student

We have summarized some of the guidelines and a few of the common precautions which have governed the behavior of the experimenters whose work is cited in the following chapters. Their standards probably are the best basis against which the student may judge his own work. This emphasizing of precautions should not lead the student to conclude that all the fun has gone out of experimental psychology or that one must be an experienced researcher to make a contribution to the field. Far from it! Probably in no other laboratory science are so many undergraduates participating in, and making significant contributions to, the experimental literature. As you study the following chapters, jot down on the back page of your notebook the ideas that come to you for experiments that may fill gaps in our knowledge, or help us evaluate an hypothesis. Don't be too self-critical at this stage of the process; do include the page number so later you can reread the material and see how your idea sounds; if you don't jot down a few key phrases and a page number when the idea strikes you, it may be lost forever! Discussion with your colleagues and instructors will help you sharpen your judgments; some of your ideas may be developed into your own research problem. There is plenty of room in experimental psychology for fresh viewpoints, bright ideas, and clever experimentation.

Trygg Engen

PSYCHOPHYSICS

I. DISCRIMINATION
AND DETECTION

2

When Fechner, one of the chief precursors of experimental psychology, published in 1860 a voluminous treatise on "Psychophysics," he was trying to work out in a scientific manner the relations between mind and body, or between the psychical and physical worlds. Being a scientist with strong interests in mathematics and philosophy, he hoped to discover some definite quantitative relation between the physical stimulus and the resulting conscious sensation. The basic philosophical notion of Fechner's psychophysics was that mind and body actually are identical, or merely different sides of one reality, but appear to be separate entities depending on whether the observer takes an introspective and internal (mind), or an objective and external (body) viewpoint. To solve this problem he had to develop suitable methods of experimentation. A large share of his book was devoted to these psychophysical methods, although they have lost the philosophical significance attached to them by Fechner. However, it should be noted in passing that on the basis of research with these methods Fechner proposed as scientific evidence in support of his philosophy what is now called Fechner's Law, that sensation intensity is proportional to the logarithm of the stimulus intensity. The next chapter will take up this problem of *scaling*. The present chapter is devoted to the problem of *threshold*, beginning with what might be called classical psychophysics based on Fechner's methods and the statistical treatment of the data they yield.

Since the time of Fechner the term "psychophysics" has been used to describe the relationship between sensation and stimulation. It is not necessary to delve into the metaphysics or even into the long and animated debate about "sensation" and whether it can be measured. Operationally the experiments are really straightforward and fit easily into the familiar formula $R = f(S)$. Here R is a *response,* typically the observer's verbal report regarding S, and S is a particular *stimulus* of a defined value or magnitude. The observer is instructed in advance to make a certain kind of report regarding the stimulus. For example, S may be one of a number of tones which differ in physical wave amplitude or wavelength, and the instructions specify the dimension to be observed, as by saying, "This tone is louder than the standard tone," or, "This tone is higher in pitch than the standard tone." Loudness is the psychological attribute that corresponds to wave amplitude, and pitch is the psychological attribute that corresponds to wavelength, but the relationships are by no means simple and linear. They are examples of what "sensation" means in a psychophysical experiment.

The response, R, is not always a verbal report. The instructions may require the observer to adjust one tone to match another in pitch, or to react with his hand as soon as a tone changes its pitch. Pavlov found a way to conduct psychophysical experiments on animals by the conditioning method, and a great deal of progress has been made in this field in recent years (see Chapter 17). In the early days of behaviorism, Watson (1916) suggested that conditioning might well be employed in the human laboratory, for it seemed to him that such terms as "louder" or "yellower" were tainted with subjectivism. He wanted to get rid of the instructions. However, until recently it was the general opinion of psychophysicists that the conditioning procedure would be a waste of time with human subjects who can, they believe, be told what they have to do and if necessary be given

a little preliminary training in responding objectively to such attributes as pitch. The idea is that the observer is merely observing stimuli, just as in a physical experiment, although the data are used for the investigation of the observer's power of discrimination.

The problem of classical psychophysics as first formulated by Fechner was the relation between stimulus and response, but the stimulus variable received most of the emphasis. The basic purpose of the classical method was to determine a threshold, measured as a transition point on the physical dimension. Direct measurements were not made of the response variable in the $R = f(S)$ formula, and classical psychophysics may be said to have been limited to this extent. Contemporary psychophysics differs from classical psychophysics in two *basic* ways: (1) It makes a more detailed psychological analysis of the observer's honesty and objectivity and attempts to correct the threshold values by adjusting them in terms of measures of his response biases. One might say modern psychophysics puts more emphasis on R–R laws than S–R laws. We shall come back to this problem at the end of the chapter. (2) Contemporary psychophysics has made a new attack on the original purpose of psychophysics, as exemplified by Fechner's Law, by devising methods for measuring response magnitude (R), and is thus a more complete psychophysics. These measures will be considered in the next chapter.

As has been noted, the classical methods have an application beyond Fechner's philosophical problem. His methods are devoted to various kinds of threshold, or minimum discriminable physical value, which will now be considered.

Threshold, Uncertainty, and Equality

The word *threshold* and its Latin equivalent, *limen,* mean essentially what one would guess: a boundary value on the stimulus dimension (continuum) separating the stimuli that elicit one response from the stimuli that elicit a different response or no response. For example, let a very light weight be placed gently on the observer's palm. If the weight is below a certain value, his report may be, "No, I don't feel it," but if the weight is increased trial by trial, it eventually reaches a value which gets the positive response, "Yes, now I feel it." The value of the weight has crossed the *absolute threshold*—often called *stimulus threshold* and abbreviated *RL* from the German *Reiz Limen,* psychophysics having begun as a German enterprise. Typically the value of *RL* is defined as that value that can be detected 50 percent of the time.

If the weight in our experiment is increased after crossing the absolute threshold, the observer will report that it feels heavier and heavier. For such supra-threshold weights one can determine a *difference threshold,* abbreviated *DL* for *Differenz Limen,* which is also known as *just noticeable difference (jnd)*. A *DL* is usually measured by presenting the observer with a constant *standard stimulus (St)* and, for comparison, a variable stimulus. Suppose in our weight example that the experimenter begins by presenting the *comparison stimulus (Co)* at a much lower value than *St* and then he increases *Co* in small steps until it can no longer be distinguished from *St*. The value of the weight has crossed the lower difference threshold. If the same experiment is performed by starting with a *Co* of greater value than *St* one can similarly determine the upper threshold by decreasing the *Co* until it is indistinguishable from *St*. The upper and lower thresholds so determined mark the upper and lower limits of the *interval of uncertainty (IU)*. Because this *IU* runs from a *Co* that is just noticeably lighter to one that is just noticeably heavier than *St, IU* includes two jnd units; that is, $DL = IU/2$.

These examples of measuring threshold are typical for the classical psychophysical methods and answer the classical questions about boundary values on the physical stimulus continuum. Only a few more concepts need be considered to complete the list. What is the value of that comparison stimulus which on the average is judged equal to a specified *St?* This value is usually called the *point of subjective equality (PSE)* and is used particularly in the study of perceptual illusions, for example, the Müller-Lyer illusion (see Chapter 12). The extent of the illusion may be defined as the difference between *point of objective equality (POE)*, defined as the exact value of *St,* and the *PSE* established by pair comparisons of stimuli. In other words, the *constant error (CE)* is, for this example, an index of illusion that is defined by the expression $CE = PSE - St$. Finally, the observer's judgments vary from moment to moment as his sensitivity, motivation, or attention to the task varies from moment to moment. Because of this variation, the sources of which will be considered more closely later, a threshold is always a computed average based on a large number of individual judgments. The *variable error* is given by some measure of the variability of the distribution of judgments; for example, the standard deviation of the weights judged equal to the standard in determining the *PSE* above.

THE BASIC PSYCHOPHYSICAL METHODS

Fechner himself contributed three psychophysical methods, and these are the so-called basic methods. Many other methods are reported in the literature, but they are usually modifications of one or another of these three methods. These three methods are alike in certain respects but quite different in others. All of them may be used to define the concepts described above, and a choice of one of them in this respect usually depends on two technical and practical considerations: (1) The nature of the stimulus continuum, that is, whether the stimuli can be varied continuously (or at least in *very* small steps) or can be presented only in discrete steps. The use of discrete steps is often required, for example in the study of taste and smell. (2) The nature of the stimulus configuration as, for example, whether simultaneous or only successive presentation of pairs of stimuli is possible. In this respect more flexibility is possible in vision than hearing. The basic psychophysical methods will first be described briefly and then in detail.

1. *The method of limits* (just noticeable difference, minimal change, or serial exploration). This is the most direct method of locating a threshold. For *DL* the experimenter varies the *Co* in small steps in ascending and descending series, and the observer reports for each step whether the *Co* is smaller, equal, or larger in comparison with the *St*. The data are the physical values of the *Co* where the observer's response shifts from one of these response categories to another. For *RL* there is no *St* and the observer's task is to report whether he does or does not detect the presence of the stimulus.

2. *The method of adjustment* (average error, reproduction, or the equation method). For *DL* the observer himself usually adjusts the value of the *Co*, which can be varied continuously, and sets it to apparent equality with the *St*. He does so repeatedly, and the central tendency and variability of his settings are computed. His average setting is a direct indication of *PSE* and his variability can be used to calculate a *DL*. For *RL* the observer repeatedly sets the variable stimulus to a value that he judges to be the lowest that he can detect; the average of these settings is taken to be the *RL*.

3. *The method of constant stimuli* (right and wrong cases, or frequency method). For *DL*, each of several fixed, discrete values of the *Co* is compared with the *St* many times, and the relative frequency of the different responses, for example, "smaller" and "larger," are counted for each of these fixed values. When only two response categories are used the observer will be right half of the time by just guessing, and his *DL* is therefore usually defined as that increment or decrement he judged correctly 75 percent of the time, that is, halfway between 50 percent (chance performance) and 100 percent. This percentage is located by interpolation or by one of several alternative statistical treatments. If a third response category is added, permitting a response of "equal," "doubtful,"

and the like, the method of constant stimuli becomes very similar to the method of limits. The method of constant stimuli can also be used to find *RL*. In this case no *St* is used, and *RL* is usually specified as the value of the variable stimulus for which there are equal numbers of "Yes" and "No" judgments of detection.

Our aim in the following pages is to enable the student, given suitable apparatus, to conduct an experiment by each basic method and to handle the data statistically. The work of Luce, Bush, and Galanter (1963) may be consulted for a fuller mathematical treatment of the problem.

THE METHOD OF LIMITS

The Absolute Threshold (*RL*)

The procedure and computations for determining the lower pitch threshold by the method of limits are shown in Table 2.1 (taken from Titchener, 1905, II, p. 6). The observer has been instructed to report "Yes" when he hears a tone and "No" when he hears no tone during a certain interval indicated by the experimenter. There should be practice trials preceding the collection of data to ensure that the observer understands the procedure, for verbal instructions are difficult to write briefly and clearly and are often inferior to the preliminary training in the task itself.

The first column of Table 2.1, reading downward, records the observer's responses in a descending series. The experimenter starts the *Co* at 24 cycles per second (Hz) and the observer reports "Yes." The experimenter lowers the *Co* by 1 cycle per trial, and the observer continues to report "Yes" until he reaches 14 cycles when he reports "No." Thus, the threshold lies somewhere between 15 and 14 cycles; it is taken as the midpoint, 14.5, and this *T* (for Threshold) value is entered below this column as one estimate of *RL*.

Next the experimenter starts an ascending series at 10 cycles, well below the observer's threshold as indicated so far, and the report is "No." The experimenter again increases the

TABLE 2.1 DETERMINATION OF STIMULUS THRESHOLD BY THE METHOD OF LIMITS: LOWER LIMIT OF AUDIBLE PITCH

Frequency (Hz)	Alternate descending and ascending series									
24	Y									
23	Y									
22	Y		Y							
21	Y		Y							
20	Y		Y						Y	
19	Y		Y				Y		Y	
18	Y		Y		Y		Y		Y	
17	Y		Y		Y		Y		Y	
16	Y	Y	Y		Y		Y		Y	
15	Y	N	Y	Y	Y	Y	Y		Y	Y
14	N	N	N	N	ª?	N	?	Y	?	N
13		N		N		N		N		N
12		N		N		N		N		N
11		N		N		N		N		
10		N		N		N		N		
9				N				N		
8				N				N		
7				N				N		

(1)	T =	14.5	15.5	14.5	14.5	14.5	14.5	14.5	13.5	14.5	14.5
	M = 14.5;		SD = .45								

(2)	AvT =	15.0		14.5		14.5		14.0		14.5	
	M = 14.5;	SD = .32									

ª? = "Doubtful," and counts as a shift in sign from the previous judgment. See text.
Data from Titchener, 1905, II, p. 6

Co 1 cycle per trial. This time the response shifts from "No" to "Yes" at 16 cycles, yielding a T of 15.5 cycles. As many alternating descending and ascending series are run as are feasible or until the experimenter is satisfied with the relative uniformity of the T values. He varies the starting point of the successive series to prevent the observer from falling into a routine. Near-threshold judgments are difficult, and even a conscientious observer may fall into the habit of utilizing some incidental cue that seems to facilitate his task.

The following procedure is used for the computation of RL from these data. The T values can be averaged (arithmetic mean) in any one of three ways, two of which are shown at the bottom of the table. (1) Below the upper line all the single values of T are added across the page and averaged; the mean, 14.5 Hz, is the RL. The standard devia-

tion of this distribution measures the variability of the observer's performance. (2) Below the second line each pair of T values (one from a descending and one from the following ascending series) is averaged to give a neutral T value, and then these averages are averaged. The final RL remains the same, of course, but the SD is smaller because the variation associated with separate ascending and descending series is reduced. (3) All the descending Ts may be averaged to give a descending RL, and all the ascending Ts similarly. The final neutral RL is the average of these two averages and will be the same, of course, as obtained above. But the ascending and descending RL values may be different because of certain "constant errors." The error of habituation is the tendency to keep on reporting "Yes" in a descending series, or "No" in an ascending series; the error of anticipa-

TABLE 2.2 DETERMINATION OF THE DIFFERENCE THRESHOLD BY THE METHOD OF LIMITS

Values of Co	Responses in alternate descending and ascending series							
8	+	+		+	+	+		
7	+	+	+	+	+	+	+	+
6	+	+	+	=	=	=	+	+
St = 5	=	=	−	+	+	+	=	=
4	=	−	−	−	−	=	+	+
3	−	−		−	−	−	=	=
2	−	−				−	−	−
1	−						−	−
T(+) =	5.5	5.5	5.5	4.5	6.5	4.5	5.5	3.5 Mean T(+) = 5.125
T(−) =	3.5	4.5	5.5	4.5	4.5	3.5	2.5	2.5 Mean T(−) = 3.875

IU = Interval of Uncertainty = T(+) − T(−) = 5.125 − 3.875 = 1.25

DL = Difference Threshold = 1/2 Interval of Uncertainty = 0.625

PSE = Point of Subjective Equality = $\dfrac{T(+) + T(-)}{2} = \dfrac{5.125 + 3.875}{2} = 4.5$

CE = Constant Error = PSE − ST = 4.5 − 5.0 = −.5

tion (or expectation) is just the opposite, a tendency to expect a change and thus change from "Yes to "No" in descending trials and "No" to "Yes" in ascending trials. The primary purpose of alternate ascending and descending series is to balance out either of these constant errors when it is present. Habituation would be indicated by overlap of the T values on the stimulus scale from ascending and descending trials; anticipation would be indicated by a gap on the stimulus scales of the T values from ascending and descending series. Practice and fatigue affect the data in opposite ways; their effects can easily be evaluated by comparing the first and second halves of the total number of series run. Such effects may be studied in a more refined way by analysis of variance (see Guilford, 1954). One can get an estimate of reliability of the RL by calculating the standard error of the mean by the usual formula

$$\sigma_M = \frac{SD}{\sqrt{N - 1}}$$

where SD = the standard deviation of the distribution of T values and N = the number of ascending and descending series. Regarding the observer's task in determining RL with the method of limits, it is well to limit him to two response categories, "Yes" and "No," and to instruct him to guess when not certain in order to avoid the response of "doubtful" which suddenly appeared in Titchener's data in Table 2.1, especially since less practiced observers are likely to be used in contemporary psychophysics.

The Difference Threshold (DL)

The same general procedure is followed as for RL but now three rather than two response categories are used. Fictitious data are given in Table 2.2. On each trial two stimuli are presented for comparison, the St and one Co. Three response categories suitable for the sense modality are prescribed for judging the comparison stimulus in relation to St, such as, "larger" (+), "smaller" (−), and "equal" (=), with the instructions for the observer to guess which category when he is not certain. The recommended procedure for locating the T values in this case is as follows: in a descending series, consider only the first shift from plus to equal, and the first shift from equal to minus; and, similarly, in ascending series, locate the first shift from minus to equal and the first shift from equal to plus.

The experimenter starts with the comparison stimulus well above St, as in the preceding example, and runs a descending series. The observer shifts from plus to equal when the comparison stimulus is 5. The experimenter continues the descending series and the first minus judgment occurs at the value of 3. Splitting the step intervals where the two shifts occur, $T(+) = 5.5$ and $T(-) = 3.5$ for this series. The scoring in the other columns shows how the rule applies to different series.

In order to reduce this table to average values, the means for $T(+)$ and $T(-)$ are determined. These will divide the whole range of comparison values into two parts: an upper part where plus judgments predominate, a lower part where minus judgments predominate, and a middle *interval of uncertainty* (*IU*) where the equal judgments are most frequent. The *IU* obviously covers a range of two *DL*s or jnd's from minus to equal and from equal to plus. A *DL* measured by this method is therefore defined as $IU/2$, which is $1.25/2 = .625$. If there were no constant error this would be the physical difference which must be added to or subtracted from St for the observer to notice it. The midpoint of *IU* (that is, $[T(+) + T(-)]/2$, or $(5.125 + 3.875)/2 = 4.5$) is taken as the best estimate of the *point of subjective equality* (*PSE*). *PSE* is theoretically the point where the comparison stimulus is most likely to appear equal to St, or where plus and minus judgments balance. Strangely enough, *PSE* is rarely identical with St. If it lies above St, there is what is called a positive *constant error* (*CE*); if below, a negative constant error, as in the present illustration where $St = 5$ and $PSE = 4.5$. Note that these constant errors are balanced out in computing a *DL*, but sometimes the constant errors are of interest in themselves in the study of perception (Chapter 12).

Weber's Law

The physical value corresponding to the *DL* is called ΔS or ΔI. Often one is interested in *relative discriminability,* defined as $\Delta S/S$, or the ratio of the minimum noticeable differ-

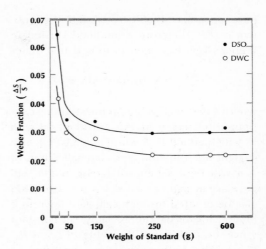

Figure 2.1. Tests of Weber's Law with lifted weights. The weights were lifted successively with one hand. ΔS was determined by using the standard deviation in connection with the method of constant stimuli. See text. The point here is that the Weber fraction may appear to be constant over most of the stimulus range used, but it increases (Weber's Law breaks down) as *RL* is approached.

ence to the stimulus intensity. With the values in our example we obtain $\Delta S/S = 0.625/4.5 = 0.139$. This fraction is called the Weber fraction and should be constant for different values of S according to Weber's Law:

$$\Delta S/S = k, \text{ or } \Delta S = kS$$

$\Delta S/S$ is different for different sense modalities but it tends to be constant within a sense modality for moderate stimulus values. However, it usually increases greatly when S (stimulus magnitude) approaches the observer's stimulus threshold, or *RL*. Note that in calculating the Weber fraction *PSE* is used rather than St, because judgments tend to be distributed more symmetrically about *PSE* than St. In practice it usually makes only a little difference. According to Weber's Law, as S decreases, ΔS decreases and at *RL*, therefore, ΔS would be minute, but the data in Figure 2.1 show that this is not what happens, for ΔS actually increases as one approaches *RL*. Psychophysicists since Fechner (see Stevens, 1951, p. 36) have been aware of this inadequacy and have recognized that it is related to the problem of *RL*. Therefore a modified version of Weber's Law has been proposed that states

$$\frac{\Delta S}{S + a} = k, \text{ or } \Delta S = k(S + a)$$

where *a* is a small value on the stimulus continuum related to *RL* but not identical with it, which added to *S* will make $\Delta S/(S + a)$ a straight-line function of *S*. At small values of *S*, *a* will be a significant factor, but it will decrease in significance as *S* is increased and may be omitted for high values of *S* without influencing the data appreciably. The constant *a* may be considered the value of ΔS at *RL*. It may also be considered as the value of "sensory noise"—a notion of great interest in contemporary detection theory discussed below—which is always present and which is added to the value of *S* presented by the experimenter. Ekman (1959) has shown how the constant *a* may be estimated algebraically and with *a* as the unit "how absolute and differential sensitivity, as well as the relation between stimulus magnitude and subjective magnitude, might be treated within a com-

mon theoretical framework" (p. 350). This is theory rather than fact, but the new form of Weber's Law seems to be a valid description of discrimination data for all sense modalities, and of course lawful relations are desirable. For this reason further empirical work on this problem could prove very useful and particularly in relation to neurophysiological studies of noise (see Chapters 4 and 9).

First of all Weber's Law states that relativity is the principle of sensory intensity according to which *DL* increases with stimulus magnitude. Secondly, the Weber fraction $\Delta S/S$ differs widely from sense to sense and furnishes an important index of power of discrimination. Depending on psychophysical methodology and state of adaptation (McBurney, Kasschau, & Bogart, 1962) the Weber fraction will range from about 1/333 or 0.3 percent for the pitch of pure tones (Shower & Biddulph, 1931) to 1/4 or 25 percent for odor intensity (Stone, 1964). In Table 2.2 above the Weber fraction was 0.139. (The unmodified Weber fraction is used for this illustration.) According to Weber's Law a change in the *St* of 13.9 percent would be

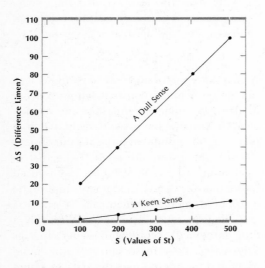

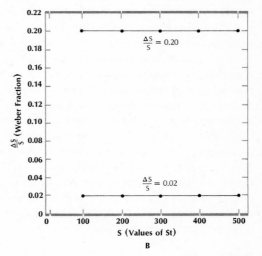

Figure 2.2. Fictitious data illustrating the operation of Weber's Law on two sense modalities, one "dull" (ΔS is relatively large) and the other "keen" (ΔS is relatively small). The figure shows two ways of plotting *DL*s obtained over a wide range of stimulus values. The abscissa represents values of the *St* in both cases. The ordinate in Figure 2.2A is ΔS or the *absolute* change in the physical value of each *St* required for *DL* or jnd. In Figure 2.2B the ordinate is $\Delta S/S$, Weber's fraction, or the *relative* change that is just noticeable.

required for a jnd (*DL*); for example, since ΔS = kS, for St = 10, ΔS would equal 139 × 10.00 = 1.39, which of course is 13.9 percent of 10.00. In other words, a test of Weber's Law means determining ΔS or *DL* or jnd—all are names for the same physical quantity—with at least several values of St spread over as wide a range of the stimulus continuum as possible. Graphically the data should yield a function as the one shown in Figure 2.2A or Figure 2.2B, depending on whether one plots ΔS or $\Delta S/S$ as a function of S. The smaller the Weber fraction the keener the sense, and thus vision and hearing are the keenest senses and taste and smell the dullest, with the other senses ordered in between.

Variations on the Method of Limits

Sometimes, as in measuring *RL* for luminance in the dark-adapted state, a long descending series of stimuli would raise the observer's adaptation level (Chapter 3, p. 59). This difficulty is minimized if the experimenter makes a rough preliminary determination of *IU* and then uses relatively short series extending only a little beyond *IU*. This device is what writers mean when they speak of the "modified method of limits." An alternative in this situation is to use the method of constant stimuli described below.

Another common and useful variation of the method of limits is the so-called *ascending method of limits*, which simply means omitting all descending series. This is used when it is especially desirable to keep the observer's state of adaptation as constant as possible, for example, *RL* for olfactory intensity. Starting with a strong stimulus in a descending series could possibly raise the *RL* considerably.

The forced-choice method is in turn a variation of the ascending method of limits suggested by Blackwell (1953) in research on vision and Jones (1956) for research in taste and smell. The stimulus is presented in small discrete steps as in the regular method, but at each level the observer is forced to choose which of several alternative presentations

actually contains the stimulus when the remaining samples are "blanks." Depending on sense modality and apparatus, one may have *temporal forced-choice,* where the observer must judge which of several marked time intervals contained the stimulus; or *spatial forced-choice,* where he must judge in which of several alternative locations (for example, top, bottom, left, right) the stimulus was presented on a trial. For example, in an *RL* experiment on olfaction (Engen, 1960) the observer was presented four test tubes which were all alike in every respect, but only one of them contained the odorant and diluent while the other three contained only the odorless diluent. The four test tubes were presented side by side on a rack with the position of the tube containing the odorant varied at random as the stimulus series was ascended in small steps. In other respects the *RL* procedure for the ascending method of limits was followed. One can also determine *DL* with this method by using one comparison value and three identical values of St for each trial. Threshold is simply defined in terms of probability of correct choice. The observer's probability of being correct from pure guessing is 1/4 on each trial, 1/16 for two successive trials, 1/64 for three successive trials, and so forth. In the experiment just described it was decided that correct judgments on two successive concentrations of the ascending series would suffice to specify the *RL*; preliminary work had shown that errors on the following (higher) concentrations were unlikely. The size of the step used on the stimulus continuum would of course be one important consideration in such a decision.

It was hoped that this method would tend to produce a more stable judgmental criterion in the observer than do the classical procedures, reduce the effects of errors of expectation and habituation, and thereby yield more valid thresholds. However, our olfactory thresholds are influenced by practice and especially by changes in the observer's criterion; for example, the observer may attempt to detect amyl acetate by attending to the smell of "bananas," which is a typical association to amyl acetate at relatively high concentrations, or he may ignore this psychological attribute and attempt to select by some lower criterion or attribute that is less easily named or popular but by which, nevertheless, he can distinguish better than chance between the odorant and diluent. This criterion problem is similar to the distinction between recognition and detection thresholds. One of the important psychophysical problems is how the experimenter can get control of the observer's criterion. The present forced-choice method is semantically superior to the more phenomenological classical methods where it is difficult to determine the observer's criterion (Blackwell, 1953), but apparently it does not eliminate the problem.

Still another variation of the method of limits is the *up-and-down* or *staircase* method (Dixon & Massey, 1956; Cornsweet, 1962). Only two categories of response are used: Yes or No; and Greater or Smaller. One begins as in the usual method of limits but changes direction (that is, from ascending to descending series or vice versa) each time the observer changes his response. For example, in a *RL* experiment in an ascending series, when the observer changes from saying "No" to "Yes" the experimenter will decrease the stimulus value for the next value and continue in a descending series until the observer says "No", whereupon he will start ascending again. This method saves work and time and is therefore of clinical value. Besides, the regular method of limits may disregard a great many, perhaps most, of the observer's responses and use one or two transition points in each series. However, Dallenbach (1966) reminds us that accuracy in estimating both the observer's biases and other possible constant and variable errors requires the classical approach with as many paired ascending and descending series as necessary. He states that to classical psychophysicists, "Accuracy, not time, was the essence. Researches were continued over days, weeks, months, and even years. Errorless techniques were sought that

facts would be obtained" (p. 654).

The staircase method resembles von Békésy's method of "tracking," the main difference being that in tracking, the stimulus is varied continuously, and in this respect resembles the method of adjustment below. For example, as long as the observer presses a key in von Békésy's audiometer the intensity of the tone decreases until he can no longer hear it, but when the key is released the intensity of the tone increases again. In this manner the observer "tracks" his *RL* (see also Oldfield, 1949). This is a method adapted to animal psychophysics. For example, Blough (1958) first trained pigeons to peck one key when a target was visible and another when it was too dim, and thereafter they tracked their own dark-adaptation curves.

From what has been said, the method of limits is obviously a very flexible one. It can be used with a variety of stimuli and for a wide variety of purposes. It has one final merit; it is the one method that shows clearly what is meant by "threshold." That is, it shows directly where the stimulus passes the boundary separating one response category from another. It is thus the reference experiment for basic psychophysical concepts including the Weber fraction.

THE METHOD OF ADJUSTMENT

As suggested by the name of the method, the observer himself manipulates a continuously variable comparison stimulus. Sometimes it may be better for the experimenter to manipulate the comparison stimulus, but in its most typical form the observer is instructed to adjust the stimulus until it appears equal to a given *St*. He does so repeatedly. The main application of the method is to measure *PSE,* although it can be used to determine *DL*. The method will be illustrated with the use of data from an experiment on the Müller-Lyer illusion with the apparatus shown in Figure 2.3. The lines are equally long but the one on the left, the comparison stimulus, looks longer than the one on the right,

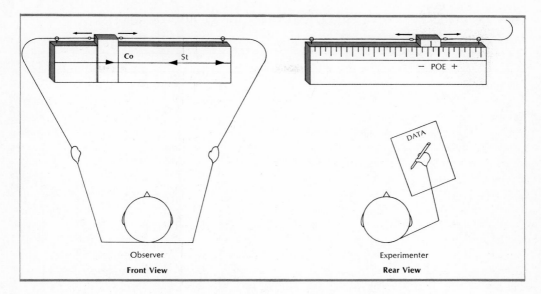

Figure 2.3. Schematic drawing of a simple apparatus for study of the Müller-Lyer illusion.

the *St*. The extent of the illusion can be measured as a constant error (*CE*) in a physical unit of length. The observer was seated about 2 m from the apparatus where he viewed the lines at eye level and was allowed to adjust the length of the variable line and move it back and forth ("bracket") before making a final adjustment. The experimenter sat immediately behind the board where he arranged the presentation of 60 trials and recorded the observer's adjustment to the nearest millimeter. The observer was not informed about his actual settings since the purpose in this experiment is only to determine whether he agrees with or deviates from the physical measure of the line. Half of the adjustments were done with the variable set smaller than the standard line (*St*) and requiring outward movement ("Out" or ascending trial); for the other half, the variable was set larger than the standard so that an inward movement was required ("In" or descending trial). A further necessary variation is to set the variable at different distances from apparent equality at the beginning of each trial. The In and Out trials were balanced for possible effect of practice and fatigue by presenting the first 15 Out, the next 30 In, and the last 15 Out. Other

variables of potential significance might likewise be considered in the design of the adjustment experiment, depending on the generality required of the psychophysical results.

The results are presented in Table 2.3. First it is determined whether the difference between *St* (230.0 mm) and the average adjustment (177.2 mm) is reliable. The *St* is constant and the standard error of only one mean, the average adjustment, need be considered in order to test the difference with a *t* test. $t = 29.3$, which for 59 *df* (degrees of freedom) indicates a reliable difference ($p < .01$). In a similar manner one might test for the effect of trials, direction of movement, orientation of the line, and so forth with a *t* test of more complex design, depending on the number of potentially significant variables and the generality of results desired.

It should of course be realized that with only a few observations one cannot report the size of the illusion very exactly, although in principle any degree of accuracy may be obtained for the individual observer. In order to illustrate the method, the present numerical results will be treated as though they included a much greater number of judgments. Figure 2.4 illustrates the variables in an adjustment

TABLE 2.3 DETERMINATION OF PSE, CE, AND VE[a] BY THE METHOD OF ADJUSTMENT

				Trials				
OUT	mm	IN	mm	IN	mm	OUT	mm
1	181	16	189	31	177	46	166
2	162	17	183	32	180	47	178
3	168	18	194	33	180	48	177
4	168	19	192	34	179	49	184
5	162	20	197	35	181	50	198
6	159	21	180	36	162	51	195
7	168	22	177	37	170	52	191
8	150	23	188	38	164	53	193
9	159	24	179	39	170	54	194
10	152	25	197	40	162	55	196
11	169	26	192	41	154	56	192
12	179	27	188	42	154	57	196
13	176	28	179	43	162	58	187
14	178	29	178	44	148	59	188
15	181	30	185	45	158	60	191

	OUT	IN	TOTAL
M	177.9	176.6	177.2 mm
SD	13.9	13.3	13.6 mm
σ_M	2.6	2.5	1.8 mm

$$PSE = M_{Co} = 177.2 \text{ mm}$$
$$VE = \sigma = 13.6 \text{ mm}$$
$$\sigma_M = 1.8 \text{ mm}$$
$$St = 230.0 \text{ mm}$$
$$CE = PSE - ST = 177.2 - 230.0 = -52.8 \text{ mm}$$

$$t = \frac{230.0 - 177.2}{1.8} = 29.3$$

[a] VE = variable error.
Data obtained in an unpublished undergraduate laboratory exercise.

experiment in which it is assumed that a normal distribution of adjustments would be obtained and that the mean and standard deviation would be proper statistics. The mean of the observer's adjustment, M_{Co}, was 177.2 and that is the PSE. The difference between M_{Co}, or point of subjective equality (PSE), and St defines a constant error, $CE = PSE - St$, which is $177.2 - 230 = -52.8$. In other words, on the average the observer systematically underestimated the standard line length by over 52 mm.

The difference between PSE and the observer's setting at any one specific trial is called a *variable error,* or VE, and varies in magnitude and direction from M_{Co} over trials. VE is thus measured by the standard deviation,

as illustrated in Figure 2.4; since both St and CE are constant and leave the standard deviation unchanged, the distribution of the observer's judgments directly reflects the VE. The standard deviation (13.6 mm) of this distribution could also be used as an index of DL. The ΔS corresponding to the DL thus measured is usually of a different magnitude but linearly related to one obtained by the method of limits. The standard deviation, if used consistently throughout an investigation, serves well as a measure of discrimination or in a test of Weber's Law. For the interval of uncertainty (IU) one might use the interval between the first (Q_1) and third (Q_3) quartiles of the distribution.

This method has several advantages. One

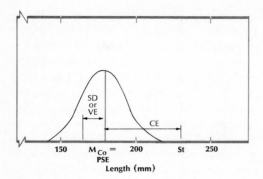

Figure 2.4. Hypothetical distribution of adjustments obtained in study of the Müller-Lyer illusion.

that has been indicated is the conventional statistical treatment of the data. Another is that the experimental procedure is somewhat more appealing to the typical observer as natural and direct, though he would perhaps have preferred to be informed of his performance on each trial. His interest is maintained because he himself manipulates the stimulus, but he may overshoot what seems to him at the moment the equality point, and so motor skills may play an important role in the judgments, as might the amount of time the observer devotes to each judgment. These factors are likely to affect the variability of judgments and hence the *DL* rather than the *PSE*. In general, when the observer is manipulating the stimulus it is somewhat more difficult to maintain constant experimental conditions, as compared with the other two basic psychophysical methods. Finally, as mentioned, many stimuli cannot be varied continuously or in small steps, and the method does not give a direct measure of *DL*, but a measure of the same sort. The essential advantage of the method of adjustment is its simplicity and speed when the proper apparatus is available. The method is difficult to apply in sense modalities where the pair of stimuli to be compared must be presented successively (for example, weights or sounds). At best one would always have to present the comparison stimulus after *St* and would neither be able to counterbalance nor to measure

series effects such as adaptation. (See Kellogg, 1929, for a comparison of the methods of adjustment and of constant stimuli.)

THE METHOD OF CONSTANT STIMULI

This method is concerned with determining stimuli that lie in the transition zone between those that can almost always be perceived and those that can almost never be perceived. When the stimulus or stimulus difference is perceived 50 percent of the time it locates the *RL* and *DL*, respectively. In order to map the whole transition zone, from five to nine stimulus magnitudes increasing by equal small steps are usually chosen over the range from the rarely noticed to the almost always noticed. When measuring *RL* one selects stimuli spanning the stimulus or absolute threshold. See, for example, the "frequency-of-seeing curves" in Figure 2.22. The only response categories are usually "Yes" and "No." "Catch" trials or "blanks" should be included unbeknownst to the observer. The responses to the blanks provide additional data whereby individual *RL*s can be evaluated for guessing and other response biases. *RL* is usually taken as the stimulus value perceived 50 percent of the time, although other arbitrary *p* values can be used.

When the constant stimulus method is used to determine the *DL*, stimulus values decidedly above *RL* are selected and difference judgments relative to a *St* in the middle of the series of comparison stimuli are required. Note that the 50 percent value in the *RL* transition zone corresponds to the *PSE* in the transition zone in the experiment on *DL*, which is based on the value judged greater than *PSE* (as in the method of limits) 75 percent of the time. Since the same stimuli are used throughout the experiment, the method is called the method of constant stimuli or sometimes, when a *St* is used, the method of constant stimulus differences. A trial in the latter case consists of a comparison of a *St* and one of the comparison stimuli. To balance out series effects, for example adaptation, the comparison stimulus is presented first on half of the trials and second on the other half of the trials (or on left versus right, and so on). The comparison stimuli are presented in random order as above and as often as possible, and at least 20 comparisons are made for each stimulus value. The observer's task is to state whether the first or the second stimulus is greater in some attribute of the stimulus; for example, "is the second weight heavier or lighter?" The results are tabulated with respect to the frequency with which the observer perceived it in the RL case (50 percent level) or the frequency with which each comparison stimulus was judged larger than St (75 percent level). As mentioned, there are usually only two response categories available to the observer, although one variation of this method that will be discussed a little later uses three response categories, for example, larger, smaller, and equal.

Because the raw data are frequencies with which the observer applies the response categories to each comparison stimulus, the term frequency method is another name often used in connection with these procedures. Fechner called it the method of right and wrong cases.

Why is this additional method needed? The method of adjustment is impracticable in some fields because many stimuli are not continuously adjustable. The method of limits brings in problems of habituation and anticipation that are avoided in the method of constant stimuli because the stimuli are given in a random order. It may demand a large number of trials, but each trial takes very little time. However, the method of constant stimuli may demand more careful planning; at least one preliminary tryout (and often more) is necessary to show that a series of equally spaced stimuli will adequately cover the observer's transition zone. The method of constant stimuli is flexible, although it is usually applied to the problem of DL, Weber's Law, and related problems. In a sense it typifies classical psychophysics with its emphasis on a statistical and indirect approach to psychological quantities.

Our concern in what follows is with the treatment of the data obtained by the method of constant stimuli. Fuller mathematical discussion of treatments may be found in Guilford (1954) and Luce et al. (Vol. 1, 1963). Here the purpose is merely to provide simple and reasonable ways of handling the data. Unfortunately, perhaps, a great deal of the history of classical psychophysics concerned itself with the problem of what is the best way to treat such data rather than with the problem of perception.

Typical data are shown in Table 2.4, which was taken from an unpublished study of the effect of time and space variables on differential sensitivity for length of lines. The apparatus utilized two commercial projection units with specially designed adapters in place of slide carriers. The function of the adapter was to produce a line of variable length through a projection screen for individual viewing. The change in length of line was accomplished by rotating a cam in desired steps across a pair of parallel knife edges, thus allowing a slit of light to be projected through the system. The line-lengths used in the present study were selected on the basis of preliminary work and were 61, 62, 63, 64, and 65 mm, with a standard of 63 mm (the same as the middle comparison stimulus) viewed at a distance of approximately 2.3 m. The projection systems could be adjusted by a positioning device whereby one projector could be placed in any one of several vertical positions, and the other projector be placed in any one of several horizontal positions. Both the se-

TABLE 2.4 DATA FOR DL FOR APPARENT LENGTH OF LINES WITH METHOD OF CONSTANT STIMULI. $St = 63$ mm.

Co	Frequency "longer"	P	z
61 mm	22	.22	−0.77
62 mm	34	.34	−0.41
63 mm	59	.59	0.23
64 mm	83	.83	0.95
65 mm	93	.93	1.48

Engen, Unpublished data

lection of line length of each projector and the vertical-horizontal relationship between the two projectors could be made from a remote station and displayed for selected presentation durations. The data presented in Table 2.4 were obtained on one observer who judged the lines according to the method of constant stimuli with forced choice for two response categories,—that is, whether the second line was longer or shorter than the first. One of the lines was the *St,* which was presented first on half of the comparisons and second on the other half. The order of presentation of the five comparison stimuli was random. A total of 500 judgments was made, 100 on each of the five comparison stimuli. Table 2.4 gives the number of times each comparison stimulus was judged longer than the standard. (The values in the column under z will be discussed later.) Each experiment required 2–3 days for completion, with several sessions each day and a rest period after each block of 50 trials. Fifty practice trials were given before the start of the experiment; during the practice trials the experimenter indicated whether or not the observer's judgment was correct. During the experiment the experimenter signaled the start of a trial by saying "ready," but gave no information about the observer's performance. Whether or not correction or reinforcement is given depends on the purpose of the experiment.

The data shown in the table are all the results obtained with the method using two response categories, and obviously no further information can be provided by tabulating the "shorter" judgments.

Simple Graphic Interpolation of Median and Q

In Figure 2.5 the *p* values from Table 2.4 have been plotted as a function of the length of the comparison lines. Assuming a reasonably large sample of responses the data usually suggest an s-shaped function. The lower values of the comparison stimulus are judged longer than the standard only occasionally and the higher almost always. The point plot-

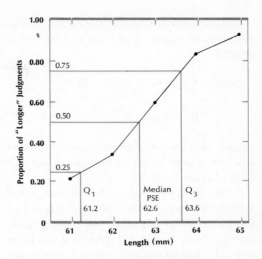

Figure 2.5. Proportion of "longer" judgments as a function of line length obtained with the method of constant stimuli. The standard stimulus (*St*) was 63 mm. See text for further details.

ted for 63 mm (the value of *St*) is the proportion of times this length was judged longer as the second member of the pair of identical values. This is a typical result showing so-called "negative time-order error," a problem of considerable interest in perception. Having connected the data points by straight lines one simply draws horizontal lines from the ordinate at the 25-, 50-, and 75-percent levels, and notices where these cross the data lines. Then one draws vertical lines from those intersections to obtain the physical values corresponding to Q_1, the Median (Q_2), and Q_3 respectively, as shown in Figure 2.5.

The *median* (*mdn*) is the value that would theoretically be judged longer half of the time and shorter half of the time. In this case this is the point of subjective equality (*PSE*), to be compared with the physical value of the *St.* In locating the value of *PSE* it is assumed that the curve is linear between values corresponding to 62 and 63 mm, which is at best only approximately correct. However, depending on the application of the results, the error associated with this may not be of any serious consequence. In the present example the *PSE* or 50 percent level is approximately 62.6 mm.

Algebraic determination of the median is also possible, of course, and gives the following results:

$$Mdn = PSE = 62 + (63 - 62) \frac{.50 - .34}{.59 - .34}$$

$$= 62 + \frac{.16}{.25} = 62.64$$

where .34 is the obtained p value for 62 mm just below and .59 for 63 mm just above the desired p value of .50.

Note that the obtained stimulus value which corresponds to a p value of .50 is almost the same as the one obtained from graphic interpolation. This is not surprising, for both are only approximations subject to the assumption of linearity noted above. As one might expect from such judgments, the value of PSE obtained by either method is close to St. However, the 50 percent level is not usually of great interest here; it is only in experiments on the absolute threshold that this point, defining the RL, is of major importance. The measure of variability or uncertainty is what is desired in the present DL experiment, and the semi-interquartile range, Q, is of primary significance for the present method of analysis.

$$Q = \tfrac{1}{2} (Q_3 - Q_1)$$

where Q_3 and Q_1 are line lengths corresponding to p values of .75 and .25, respectively, obtained from interpolation in the same way as the median in Figure 2.5. With these values

$$Q = \tfrac{1}{2} (63.6 - 61.2) = 1.2$$

This measure of variability is used as an index of differential sensitivity or DL, although it is not numerically identical with DL, as for example measured by the method of limits, but similar to $DL = IU/2$. Assuming the frequency distribution of judgments is normal one could use the standard deviation as a measure of DL by use of the relation

$$\sigma = 1.483 \ Q$$

According to the data in Table 2.4

$$\sigma = 1.483 \times 1.2 = 1.8$$

The standard deviation has well-known and desirable characteristics, and direct determination of it would obviously be a better method. The mean is also more reliable and desirable than the median, assuming the judgmental distribution is normal.

Mean and Standard Deviation of an Unaccumulated Frequency Distribution

The last consideration is the basis of Spearman's (1908) distribution method which computes the mean (as PSE or RL) and the standard deviation (used either as index of DL or simple variability of judgments respectively) from the distribution of judgments. It does this, one should note, by making use of the classical psychophysical assumption that threshold varies from moment to moment. Summation of values (for example, momentary threshold values) will transform a normal distribution into an ogive similar to Figure 2.5 (p. 25). By subtraction therefore one can reverse this and transform the ogive into a normal or symmetrical distribution. In other words, by subtraction one can find the frequency of the observer's thresholds (not only judgments of "longer" or "shorter") which would theoretically fall within each step on our physical scale of length. For example, when the observer gives a response of "longer" to a certain comparison stimulus on a certain trial, Spearman's procedure assumes that his momentary threshold, PSE in our experiment, lies somewhere below the value of the stimulus on that particular trial. In our Table 2.4, the momentary PSE fell below 61 mm on 22 trials and below 62 mm on 34 trials; therefore PSE fell in the 61–62 mm interval $34 - 22 = 12$ times. One would similarly obtain the frequency with which PSE fell in the remaining intervals by subtraction. These frequencies should be symmetrically distributed. Note the different meaning of N, which now refers to the sum of the various frequencies with which PSE falls within the various class intervals. Table 2.5 shows all the computation necessary to determine the mean and standard deviation for the same data used for Table

TABLE 2.5 MEAN AND STANDARD DEVIATION (SPEARMAN'S METHOD)

Co	f "longer"	Co class	Class interval X	f*	fX	d = X-M	d²	fd²
		60–61	60.5	22	1331.0	−2.09	4.3681	96.0982
61	22	61–62	61.5	12	738.0	−1.09	1.1881	14.2572
62	34	62–63	62.5	25	1562.5	− .09	.0081	.2025
63	59	63–64	63.5	24	1524.0	+ .91	.8281	19.8744
64	83	64–65	64.5	10	645.0	+1.91	3.6481	36.4810
65	93	65–66	65.5	7	458.5	+2.91	8.4681	59.2767
				100 = N	6259.0			226.1900

$$M = PSE = \frac{6259.0}{100} = 62.59$$

$$\sigma = \sqrt{\frac{226.1900}{100}} = 1.50$$

$$DL = Q = .67\sigma = 1.01$$

f* is frequency with which *PSE* falls in a certain class interval and $N = \Sigma f$

2.4 (p. 24). The problem with Spearman's method, well illustrated with our data, is that there is some uncertainty at each tail of the distribution. Twenty-two of these momentary *PSE*s would be below 61 mm, but is it reasonable to assume that all of them lie in the 60–61 mm interval? At the other tail, is it reasonable to assume that by adding a stimulus of 66 mm 100 percent "longer" judgments would be obtained? The limitation of the method is that it is fully justified only when the experimenter has extended his stimulus series far enough down to approach closely the 0 percent level, and far enough up to approach the 100 percent level. The analysis itself after converting to the unaccumulated frequency distribution of judgments consists of the simple computation of the mean and standard deviation from grouped data where *N* is the total number of judgments. When the distribution is normal one would of course prefer to compute the mean, unless one is only interested in the *p* value of .50 for *PSE* or *RL*, and especially if the measure of variability is of interest. Fortunately, there is a straightforward method for computing the mean and standard deviation without the limitation of the Spearman method.

The Normal-Graphic and Least-Squares Solution of Mean and Standard Deviation

Experiments with the method of constant stimuli indicate that the ogive describes the results well. Classical psychophysical theory also agrees with the general assumption that whenever a biological function or structure varies, it tends to show an approximately normal distribution of values, as pictured in

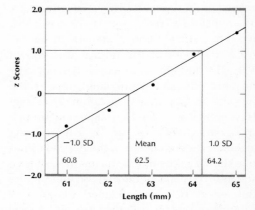

Figure 2.6. Proportion of judgments "longer" expressed as *z* scores as a function of line length. These data are the same as those plotted in Figure 2.5.

the familiar normal distribution curve. As indicated above, the ogive is simply the summated or cumulative form of this curve. In this case, one can use a third method that, in keeping with the assumption of normality, converts the experimentally obtained p values to z scores, and this transformation will simplify our graphic representation of the data. If the normality assumption is correct, z scores, unlike p values, will mark off equal steps on our physical continuum, and a linear plot is obtained depending on sampling error as shown in Figure 2.6. Instead of adjusting the spacing on the ordinate of the graph paper by converting p values to z scores, one may accomplish the same by two methods. One method is to draw a good ogive and interpolate from that, but this is relatively difficult. Therefore it is better to transform the ordinate so that a straight line would be the proper curve to draw. Normal-probability paper with the ordinate divided into proportions according to the normal curve and the abscissa divided into the usual arithmetic steps accomplishes this. Figure 2.6 shows how the same goal is achieved on ordinary graph paper by transforming p values into z scores by use of the normal distribution table, a part of which is reproduced in the reference tables at the end of the book.

The z scores corresponding to our experimental proportions are also listed in Table 2.4. The transformed points seem to lie reasonably close to a straight line as predicted from the classical theory of the normal variation of PSEs. The deviations from linearity seem to be no more than random sampling errors. For the purpose of graphic interpolation, a satisfactory method is to draw a straight line through the points freehand, but for a more exact algebraic determination of the desired values one should fit the line by the method of least squares. The name of the method refers to the differences between obtained values of Y (plotted z scores in Figure 2.6) and values predicted from X (line length) according to the straight line. It is assumed that *the line of*

best fit is the one for which the sum of the squares of these differences is a minimum (see Lewis, 1960).

The normal graphic method involves z scores rather than empirical p values, and therefore PSE corresponds to the p value of .50 and can be read off as the arithmetic mean corresponding to the z score of 0 on the ordinate and the corresponding values on the stimulus dimensions can be read off on the abscissa, as shown in Figure 2.6. The standard deviation is also shown and it is obtained by first following the same procedure for a z score of 1.0 or -1.0, which are associated with stimulus values located one standard deviation above and below the mean, and then simple subtraction.

Due to sampling errors the results from this method will not necessarily agree perfectly with those obtained with other methods, for example Spearman's method above, but if the assumption of normality is appropriate the various methods usually agree quite well. The normal graphic method is useful particularly in the case of the present results which render assumptions about the proportions in the tails

TABLE 2.6 METHOD OF CONSTANT STIMULI—LEAST SQUARES

X (Co)	Y (z)	X^2	XY
61	$-.77$	3721	-46.97
62	$-.41$	3844	-25.42
63	.23	3969	14.49
64	.95	4096	60.80
65	1.48	4225	96.20
$\Sigma 315.00$	1.48	19855	99.10

$$a = \frac{(\Sigma X^2)(\Sigma Y) - (\Sigma X)(\Sigma XY)}{N(\Sigma X^2) - (\Sigma X)^2}$$

$$= \frac{(19855)(1.48) - (315.00)(99.10)}{5(19855) - (315.00)^2} = -36.622$$

$$b = \frac{N(\Sigma XY) - (\Sigma X)(\Sigma Y)}{N(\Sigma X^2) - (\Sigma X)^2}$$

$$= \frac{5(99.10) - (315.00)(1.48)}{5(19855) - (315.00)^2} = \frac{29.3}{50.0} = .586$$

of the distribution debatable. Also, of course, the data obtained with the method of constant stimuli come in the form of cumulative frequencies.

The method of least squares provides a more exact treatment of these data, analogous to graphic or algebraic determination of the median and Q above. In this case, fit a function to the data and determine the values of the constants, and then determine the mean and standard deviation with these constants rather than fitting a straight line by eye and then interpolating. Thus one needs the constants in the equation

$$y = a + bx$$

which describes the regression of y on x. Columns for X^2 and XY have been included in Table 2.6 to compute the parameters of this function, where X represents stimulus values and Y represents z scores, that is, response proportions to different stimulus values (Co) expressed as z scores. Now the equation for the desired function with the constants a and b can be written

$$z = a + b\ (Co)$$
$$= -36.622 + 0.586\ (Co)$$

From this it follows that the mean which corresponds to PSE is obtained by solving the equation for Co when $z = 0$:

$$Co = \frac{z - a}{b}$$

$$M = PSE = \frac{36.622}{0.586} = 62.495$$

The standard deviation which could be used as an index of DL of the data is equal to the distance from $z = 0$ to $z = 1$ (or -1) and is therefore obtained by first solving the equation for Co when $z = 1$:

$$Co = \frac{1.000 + 36.622}{0.586} = 64.201$$

$$\sigma = 64.201 - 62.495 = 1.706$$

This value agrees well with those obtained by other methods above. Assuming a normal distribution, $Q = .674\sigma$, or $.674 \times 1.706$, which gives a value of 1.1 compared to 1.2 obtained with the graphic interpolation from Figure 2.5. If many judgments are made with great care by a few observers for individual analysis, one should probably use the normal-graphic approach or solution of values by the method of least squares. This approach uses all the data in determining the desired values rather than just two adjacent points as in the normal-graphic method. If a few judgments are made by many observers for group analysis, linear interpolation of the median may be refined enough.

Variations on the Method of Constant Stimuli

As mentioned above, the two thresholds RL and DL can be defined in almost the same terms, for in both cases the observer is instructed to respond by using certain prescribed categories. Typically he would be instructed to use only two categories, such as "Yes" and "No," but experimental conditions may demand other alternatives.

Two categories: plus and equal The standard may be a light of steady luminance to which the observer's retina becomes adapted, and the comparison stimulus may be a momentary increment (ΔL) of the light in the center of the field preceded by a signal. If the observer perceives the increase, he says "Yes" (plus); otherwise "No" (equal). The result of interest here is the mean or median transition point between one category and the other, or the DL corresponding to ΔL. Mueller (1951) used this method to determine Weber's fraction over a wide range of light intensities. The "warble" technique in auditory DL determinations is similar (Harris, 1952).

Three categories: plus, equal, minus Suppose the experimenter in a weight-lifting experiment prescribes or allows the three categories: heavier, equal, and lighter. His purpose is probably to determine two transition points,

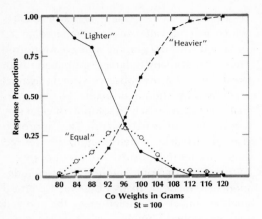

Figure 2.7. Results from weight-lifting experiments with the method of constant stimuli with three response categories, "heavier," "equal," and "lighter." There were 500 trials for each of the five central comparison stimuli from 92–108, with smaller frequencies tapering to 100 trials at each extreme. (In general, constant numbers of trials are desirable.) The curves are regular enough to give almost the same values of the mean and standard deviation by the methods we have described.

			PSE $\dfrac{(T+) + (T-)}{2}$	DL $\dfrac{(T+) - (T-)}{2}$
Method	T+	T−		
Simple interpolation	98.0	92.9	95.4	2.6
Spearman	98.4	93.3	95.8	2.5
Least squares	98.4	93.7	96.0	2.4

PSE as determined by the intersection of the plus and minus curves is 95.5 and the same when taken as the mean of the distribution of "equal" judgments. *CE = PSE − St,* is about -4.5 g, a negative time error since the comparison stimulus was lifted after *St*. (Data from Bressler, 1933, p. 65.)

as in the method of limits, one separating the minus from the equal, and the other the equal from the plus. In using this variation the purpose might merely be to accommodate an observer who insisted on being allowed to say "Equal" or "Doubtful" in certain cases. The experimenter would then have the task of dividing the equals somehow between the plus and minus frequencies to reduce the three categories to two, and he would then

handle the data just as in a two-category experiment. He might follow Fechner and divide the equals equally between plus and minus at each separate value of the comparison stimulus, or he might follow another early suggestion and divide them in proportion to the plus and minus frequencies for each value. For example, if for a certain stimulus value there were 45 judgments of plus, 15 of minus, and 40 of equal, these 40 would be divided 3 to 1, and 30 of them assigned to plus and 10 to minus, so that the corrected percentages would be 75 for plus and 25 for minus. Neither of these schemes is perfect, for if the observer is instructed to guess plus or minus instead of using the equal category, he usually guesses right more often than wrong (Fullerton & Cattell, 1892, p. 132).

If the experimenter wishes to use data from three categories as in Figure 2.7, he will now have two thresholds, $T+$ and $T-$, as in the method of limits used to determine the *DL* above (see p. 16). The difference between the two methods is mainly the order of presentation of stimuli, serial versus random. In this case one takes the plus frequencies alone and determines central tendency and variability by any of the methods already described. For example, the mean for the plus judgments would be an index of $T+$. Between $T+$ and $T-$ is the interval of uncertainty (*IU*) where neither plus nor minus judgments have a clear majority. One half of *IU* is the *DL*. *PSE* is usually taken as the midpoint of *IU*, halfway between $T+$ and $T-$:

$$IU = (T+) - (T-)$$
$$DL = \tfrac{1}{2}\,[(T+) - (T-)]$$
$$PSE = \tfrac{1}{2}\,[(T+) + (T-)]$$

The mean and standard deviation of the equal judgments would provide other estimates of *PSE* and *DL*, as in the method of adjustment. Various determinations of *PSE* and *DL* agree closely in the experiment shown in Figure 2.7, which is based on careful selection of stimulus values and on a large number of trials in the tradition of classical psychophysics.

Instability of the *IU* and the Attitude of the Observer

Whether *IU* shall be large or small is correlated with the total frequency of "equal" judgments. If the observer gives many of them, his *IU* will be relatively large; if few, relatively small. Since *DL* may be defined as half of *IU*, it is similarly related to the number of "equal" judgments; this may produce misleading results. If the observer happens to be a very confident individual, he may use only the plus and minus categories and avoid the equal category as a sign of indecision. This kind of response will probably yield a small *DL* and suggest keen discrimination. At the other extreme is the cautious person who does not give a plus or minus judgment unless he is perfectly sure; he gives a large *DL*, which again reflects his attitude as much as his perceptual ability to discriminate the stimuli. Moreover, the observer's attitude toward the equal category might change in the course of a long experiment and from one experimental condition to another. If discrimination becomes more difficult he may drop the equal category because he feels that guessing between two categories is all he can manage. His *DL* will thus become smaller, and difficult conditions may appear to favor or improve ability to discriminate.

Obviously such results run counter to the purpose of classical psychophysics, discussed above, and make questionable the *validity* of the method of constant stimuli with three categories. One would on the whole do well to limit the observer to two categories, because it gives all the usable results with economy of time and effort. But there is still one unsolved problem.

The Instability of PSE

The *PSE* and thereby *CE*s such as illusions and time errors may be controlled by the observer's response biases rather than his sensory system. Figure 2.8 illustrates this problem by comparing the psychometric functions

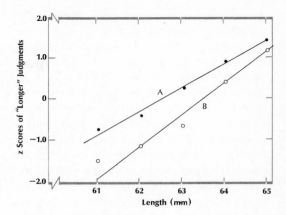

Figure 2.8. Psychometric functions obtained by two observers under the same experimental conditions with the method of constant stimuli. *z* score equivalents of proportions of judgments "longer" are plotted against line length. The standard was 63 mm. The data for the observer plotted as filled circles (●) are also shown in Figures 2.5 and 2.6.

obtained by the method of constant stimuli with two response categories from two paid observers, one of whom produced the results shown in Table 2.4. The observers were students with previous experience in psychophysics who worked in the laboratory during the summer on the same project of discrimination. They were exposed to the same experimental conditions throughout, and their results were similar, with one important exception as shown in Figure 2.8. Observer A has a *PSE* of about 62.5 mm and thus a negative *CE* (*PSE* − *St* = − .5), while observer B has a *PSE* of about 63.5 mm and a positive *CE* (*PSE* − *St* = + .5). The question is whether this difference represents their perception of the lines and thus different modes of operation of the underlying sensory system, perhaps "fading traces" versus "adaptation" (Chapter 9), or is a simpler explanation based on response biases possible? Figure 2.8 indicates that the answer probably is that observer A simply was more likely to say "longer" than was B. Analysis of all 500 judgments of all the values of comparison stimuli in this experiment shows that A used the response category "longer" 58 percent of the time (and "shorter" 42 percent) but B used the "longer" 40 percent of the time (and "shorter" 60 percent). Analysis of the total of 7000 comparisons they made in all the conditions (of standards, and so on) of the experiment support this explanation with results showing A responding "longer" 48 percent of the time and B, 33 percent of the time. In other words, regardless of the physical difference between *St* and *Co,* A was more likely to say "longer" and this is what is meant by a response bias, an important factor in a psychophysical experiment although often irrelevant and even detrimental to its purpose. Of course it may turn out that the desired *DLs,* which are 1.7 mm for A and 1.3 mm for B, are unaffected by this problem, but since the method does not control this response bias one must at least add a cautionary note to our psychophysical conclusions.

Classical psychophysics worked hard to eliminate response biases by carefully training observers, by proper experimental designs, and the like, but the opinion among contemporary psychophysicists grows steadily stronger that the bias is an inherent psychological problem. The most important recent contributions to psychophysics have involved attempts to devise means whereby the experimenter can manipulate and measure the bias, and such research has been successful enough to suggest to some (for example, Swets, 1961) that psychophysical results may be understood better in terms of the psychology of judgments than in terms of the psychophysics of sensory systems.

CLASSICAL CONCEPTS OF THE THRESHOLD

All of the classical methods discussed thus far are based on the following general theory of the nature of the threshold. A stimulus falling on a receptor initiates a train of impulses which produce an effect in brain centers. The size of this central effect will vary with the strength of the stimulus, the sensitivity of the receptor, the efficiency of the connecting paths, and the background level of activity of the center. If the effect on a given trial is greater than a certain minimum, the center will discharge and lead to a response, for example, "Yes, I perceive it." The stimulus which produces that effect represents the *momentary threshold.* The complex of factors listed above will produce random variation from trial to trial, yielding a more or less random distribution of momentary thresholds. The *phi-gamma* hypothesis assumes that the normal cumulative distribution will fit the function obtained when the probability of detection is plotted against stimulus magnitude in linear coordinates. (This curve is similar to Figure 2.5 above, and according to Guilford [1954] the terms *phi* and *gamma* refer to the stimulus and response variables respectively as used in classical psychophysics.) Thurstone (1928) has pointed out that since ΔS increases as a function of S as in Weber's Law or a similar function, the psychometric function would be positively skewed and the skewness would be inversely proportional to the $\Delta S/S$ ratio. Plotting the probability of detection as a function of the logarithm of the stimulus magnitude would normalize the psychometric function, and this is known as the *phi–log gamma hypothesis.* Because there is such a short range of stimuli for these experiments, it is consequently difficult to distinguish between the two hypotheses empirically, although the evidence indicates that Thurstone is correct. In other words, almost the same ogives will result from plotting p as a function of S and of log S.

To return to the general theory, the mean of the distribution of momentary thresholds corresponds to the value of the stimulus threshold. The various psychophysical methods described above were simply different ways of obtaining and treating the data to measure the typical value and its variation. The same line of reasoning was applied to the difference threshold, which was assumed to be related to the distribution of differences in excitation from two stimuli, *St* and comparison stimulus. This variability theory of threshold has been accepted in one form or another since the time of the classical psychophysicists (see Fullerton & Cattell, 1892; Boring, 1917; Guilford, 1927). Apparently it offered no theoretical problems as long as it was believed that the nerve impulse worked like an ordinary current in a circuit, increasing or decreasing its intensity to reflect stimulus changes.

The Quantum Hypothesis

Because neurophysiological research demonstrated that the nerve impulse is all-or-none, the question, "Is discrimination really stepwise?" seemed an obvious one to ask (Stevens, Morgan, & Volkmann, 1941). For example, assume that a brief tactual stimulus is just strong enough to set up a burst of 10 impulses; gradual increase in strength of the stimulus would not increase the strength of the sensation until the stimulus was strong enough to elicit 11 impulses, whereupon the observer would feel a certain finite increase in tactual sensation. (This theory applies to discrimination and *DL,* but not to detection and *RL,* since overall sensitivity of the receptor system is assumed to be continuous.) It

could be assumed that these relatively small discrete steps were not readily evident because of the variability of the receptive system and lack of experimental control of conditions affecting the observer. In 1930, however, von Békésy showed evidence for such steps in auditory thresholds when he minimized variability by giving the observer practice in the observation of a particular stimulus change of short duration. Likewise, each stimulus was judged several times in succession rather than in a random sequence, as in the method of constant stimuli above, in order to prevent temporal variations within the observer that might affect the psychometric function. The resulting quantal psychometric function has three distinguishing characteristics: the probability of detection is a linear function of stimulus magnitude; the slope of this function is inversely proportional to its intercept; and the stimulus increment that is barely sufficient to reach a detection probability of 1.0 is twice as large as the stimulus that is just low enough to yield a detection probability of 0.

Figure 2.9 schematizes the phi–gamma, the phi–log gamma, and the quantal hypotheses and illustrates why it has been difficult to obtain data that would clearly support one hypothesis and reject the other two. The pre-

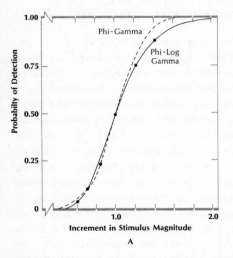

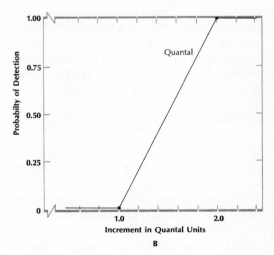

Figure 2.9. Schematic representation of results expected under various hypotheses about the form of the psychometric function. Probability of detection is plotted as a function of *stimulus differences.*

dictions made on the basis of these hypotheses are similar and the proper statistical technique for testing the goodness of fit of the psychometric function is not yet available (Corso, 1956).

It is evident that the quantal hypothesis, even more than the other hypotheses mentioned, demands that the observer in the study of such sensory psychological problems is just another valid and reliable part of the measuring apparatus. However, as Stevens (1961, p. 813) states, "The difference between a human observer and an electron is that the human observer is human. At any moment he may not keep his mind on his work—and thereby spoil the experiment."

General Comments on Classical Psychophysics

A great deal of useful information has been obtained with the classical methods in the study of sensation and perception. However, psychophysicists have long been aware of certain biasing factors (see Guilford, 1954), that must be reckoned with when threshold is used to evaluate the keenness of perception. Classical psychophysics attempted to deal with biases by (1) eliminating them by experimental design—for example, by counterbalancing; (2) by assumption, for example, that fatigue and practice will balance each other in a series of psychophysical judgments; and (3) by correction of judgments. A common formula for obtaining the proportion of judgments corrected for guessing (P_c), or what is now generally called "false alarms" is:

$$P_c = \frac{\text{proportion of hits} - \text{proportion of false alarms}}{1 - \text{proportion of false alarms}}$$

where P_c is the corrected proportion; "hits" refers to correct judgment of the presence of a stimulus or stimulus difference; "false alarms" means that the observer states incorrectly that a stimulus or stimulus difference is present on a so-called "catch trial" or "blank." This formula assumes, as can be shown by rearranging it, that the proportion of hits is a linear function of the proportion

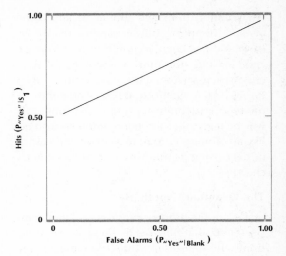

Figure 2.10. Hypothetical relation between the proportion of hits (correct detection) and false alarm (false positives) in classical psychophysical theory. The probability that the observer would respond "Yes" when a certain stimulus, s_1, is actually presented ($p_{\text{"Yes"}}|s_1$) is plotted against the probability that he would respond "Yes" on a blank or catch trial ($p_{\text{"Yes"}}|$blank).

of false alarms obtained, for example, in an experiment with the method of constant stimuli (see Figure 2.10).

DECISION ANALYSIS MODEL OF PSYCHOPHYSICAL THRESHOLD

The main empirical contribution to psychophysics by the theory of signal detectability, which was developed originally in connection with problems in radio and telephone communication and radar (see Swets, Tanner, & Birdsall, 1961) has been that the assumption shown in Figure 2.10 is false. Classical psychophysics, with its carefully trained observers, did not usually obtain large enough proportions of false alarms to make a good test of this assumption. Modern detection theory criticizes this training of observers on two counts, (1) that it forces the observer to make the assumption that there is a real sensory threshold, and (2) that accordingly the observer tends to set high criteria for saying "Yes" and thus high values of *RL*. The modern theory assumes no fixed cutoff for "Yes, I perceive" and "No, I do not perceive," and hence no fixed criterion. For example, the observer's criterion for saying "No" rather than "Yes" may vary depending on whether or not he expects a stimulus to be presented. To obtain a higher proportion of hits the observer must more or less deliberately lower his criterion for saying "Yes," and this means that he is also likely to increase his proportion of false alarms. By comparison, classical psychophysics assumed that increasing proportions of hits and false alarms depended on the observer responding "Yes" on a greater number of trials which he somehow selected at random or by guessing, but that there was nevertheless a real sensory threshold. Detection theory does not assume a sensory threshold and puts the emphasis on judgmental rather than sensory aspects of the psychophysical experiment. It therefore emphasizes the relationship between two kinds of response, hits and false alarms, rather than the relationship between stimulus and response. The sensory effect of a stimulus is continuous, not discrete; and whether or not a response of "Yes" results depends on (1) the effect of the stimulus relative to the effect of noise on the very same sensory continuum, (2) what the observer expects in the situation, and (3) the potential consequence of his decision.

A consequence of this view is the tendency in psychophysical detection theory to deal with only a few, and often with only one stimulus value rather than a series of stimuli. It is not that the stimulus magnitude is unimportant but rather that the effect of the stimulus must be evaluated in relation to the two kinds of response bias. Table 2.7 shows the various stimulus and response alternatives in a typical so-called *"Yes-No" experiment* with one stimulus. It is similar to a trial in the method of limits or constant stimuli in that the observer must judge the effect of *S* or ΔS, but blanks and identical pairs are used frequently. *S* or ΔS is presented on some trials and not on others according to a predetermined random schedule and the observer is required to judge whether indeed the stimulus was On or Off during each trial, a time interval that is indicated by a signal (for example, a light in an experiment on hearing).

TABLE 2.8

		RESPONSE	
		YES	NO
STIMULUS	ON	.50	.50
	OFF	.00	1.00

Table 2.7 shows the four possible events in this experiment. Let us assume that a threshold value has been obtained with the method of limits and that one physical value is used in our detection experiment. One would present this stimulus a large number of times interspersed with an equal number of blanks in a random sequence—at least several hundred trials may be required to obtain stable results. According to classical theory one would expect something close to the probabilities shown in Table 2.8.

TABLE 2.9

		RESPONSE	
		YES	NO
STIMULUS	ON	.66	.34
	OFF	.36	.64

However, results shown in Table 2.9 were actually obtained in such an experiment

TABLE 2.7

		RESPONSE	
		YES	NO
STIMULUS	ON	Hit	Miss
	OFF	False Alarm	Correct Rejection

where the observer's task was to judge "sugar" (Yes) or "water" (No) (Engen, Bartoshuk, & McBurney, 1964, unpublished). The stimulus was a .225 percent (weight/volume) solution of sucrose in distilled water interspersed at random with distilled water, and both were tasted from cups following procedures similar to those used by Linker, Moore, and Galanter (1964). The proportions are based on 60 trials with a water rinse and 30-sec intertrial interval. (Further details of the experiment will be given later). These results indicate that the stimulus was above the observer's 50 percent threshold and the concentration would have to be reduced to obtain equal proportions of "Yes" and "No" but that is a minor problem. What is unexpected is the relatively high false-alarm proportion (.36) of "Yes" when the stimulus was OFF, that is, a strong tendency by the observer to call water "sugar." Such results were hardly obtained in classical psychophysics and probably for the reason that it did not use nearly as many blanks as were used in this detection experiment and therefore did a poor job of sampling the response bias. Of course, the present data were obtained from an experiment in which a difficult judgment was required and the observer was inexperienced in psychophysics, while an important part of classical psychophysics was the training of observers. However, by whatever means such biases are reduced, it may be argued that it is accomplished by manipulation of the observer's criterion for saying "Yes" versus saying "No" and that classical psychophysical theory implicitly promoted a high criterion and thereby high threshold values. False alarms can be reduced by increasing the stimulus magnitude required before the observer is certain enough to say "Yes," but the problem is that it is difficult to change the proportions of false alarms independently of the proportion of hits. Indeed, experiments tend to show that the proportion of hits is a function of the proportion of false alarms. Basically the contribution of detection theory in psychophysics is the determination of the psychophysical

S–R relation in a theoretical frame of reference based on a function called a *receiver-operating-characteristic* (ROC) curve or an *isosensitivity function.* These terms will become clearer as the theory is developed. Only two of the values in our four-fold stimulus response matrix for this function are needed, because when hits and false alarms are known in this binary situation, misses and correct rejections are determined. The treatment of response biases will be considered first.

Bias Related to the Observer's Expectation Regarding the Probability of S

Two kinds of bias form the empirical basis for detection theory in psychophysics. One of these concerns the observer's expectancy that the stimulus will be ON at a particular trial, and this expectancy will be developed by the instructions given by the experimenter, the observer's prior knowledge of the experiment, and his experience during the experiment.

A simple example will demonstrate the effect of expectancy regarding the stimulus presentation probability. Suppose that instead of presenting the stimulus on 50 percent and blanks on 50 percent of the trials as above, the experimenter presents the stimulus on 90 percent and blanks on 10 percent of the trials. After some experience with this condition the observer tends to expect the stimulus on many trials and so is inclined to say "Yes" more often than in the 50-50 condition above. This situation is very similar to the procedures used in classical psychophysics with few if any blanks. The results obtained by Linker et al. (1964) in just this experiment show a high proportion of hits, about .94, *and* a high proportion of false alarms, about .77, as shown in

TABLE 2.10

		RESPONSE	
		YES	NO
STIMULUS	ON	.94	.06
	OFF	.77	.23

Table 2.10. In other words, the tendency to say "Yes" depends at least partly on the probability that a stimulus will be presented, and in addition there is the important fact that the proportions of hits and false alarms are related; this relation defines an isosensitivity curve.

TABLE 2.11

		RESPONSE	
		YES	NO
STIMULUS	ON	.24	.76
	OFF	.06	.94

One more example from Linker et al. may suffice to make this clear. In this case the stimulus was presented only on 10 percent and blanks on 90 percent of the trials. As shown in Table 2.11, this results in low proportions for both hits and false alarms, because under this condition the observer is likely to expect a blank, or water in this case, on each trial. It is not true that the stimulus plays no role, but the problem is that this stimulus is very weak and it is not unusual in psychology that response biases or "sets" (Chapter 12) will be most evident when the situation is ambiguous. In other words, the most reliable S–R relation will begin to falter if the stimulus is reduced to a level where the observer is unable to detect it (at least occasionally). Linker et al. (1964) explored this problem of expectancy systematically with many different probabilities of stimulus presentation, and the results shown in Figure 2.11 have been taken from their paper. The curve drawn by eye through the data represents one isosensitivity function, which means that different points on the curve reflect the same sensitivity, for the experimental points were obtained with the same stimulus but under different conditions of response bias. It is important to realize that this is not at all a standard psychophysical S–R relation but an R–R relation with two dependent variables plotted on the axes and to that extent more

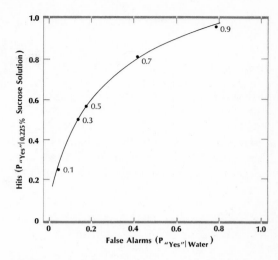

Figure 2.11. The isosensitivity function. Proportion of hits plotted against the proportion of false alarms in an experiment where the observer's task was to detect the presence of sucrose in water. The numbers in the graph show the stimulus presentation probabilities yielding the observed point. These data were adopted from Linker et al. (1964). See text.

purely psychological than psychophysical. For this reason sensitivity cannot be defined in simple terms as, for instance, by locating some point on a stimulus dimension, but instead a less direct and more theoretical approach will be required.

Bias Related to the Effects of Rewards and Punishments

Before discussing this theory, the effect of the consequences of the observer's decision will be illustrated in terms of losses or gains, outcome structure, payoff matrix, or what might more generally be called the effect of motivation on psychophysical judgments. It seems reasonable to assume that a person is more likely to make certain errors of judgment or mistakes, rather than others, depending on the consequences involved; for example, in attempting to detect an enemy one wants most of all to maximize the number of hits and minimize the number of misses, while false alarms and correct rejections are

TABLE 2.12

RESPONSE

		YES	NO
		YES	NO
STIMULUS	ON	+1¢	−1¢
	OFF	−1¢	+1¢

of minor consequence. Such situations might be imitated by payoff matrices of losses and gains in our "Yes–No" experiment. Table 2.12

TABLE 2.13

RESPONSE

		YES	NO
STIMULUS	ON	+25¢	−1¢
	OFF	−1¢	+1¢

shows a symmetrical payoff matrix where the observer must pay 1¢ for each error and where he gets paid 1¢ for each correct judgment. As far as the biases are concerned, this situation would be somewhat analogous to a stimulus presentation probability of .50. Table 2.13 is

TABLE 2.14

RESPONSE

		YES	NO
STIMULUS	ON	+1¢	−1¢
	OFF	−1¢	+25¢

an asymmetrical matrix that pays the observer handsomely (25¢) for hits relative to correct rejections as well as to misses and false alarms. One would expect such payoffs would lead to a tendency to say "Yes" with very high conditional probabilities for both hits and false alarms, analogous to a stimulus presentation probability of .90. Table 2.14 shows another asymmetrical payoff matrix that rewards correct rejections relative to hits, misses, and false alarms and would be expected to encourage the observer to say "No" rather than "Yes," with a relatively low pro-

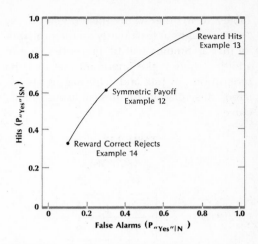

Figure 2.12. Fictitious data on payoff matrices and the isosensitivity function. Proportion of hits are plotted against false alarms under conditions which rewarded responses of "Yes," or "No," differentially or equally (symmetrically).

portion of hits and false alarms, analogous to a low-stimulus presentation probability. If the same stimulus as above is used with a stimulus presentation probability of .50 and applied to the three payoff matrices shown, one should obtain an isosensitivity function as schematized in Figure 2.12. Again the observer's proportion of hits has been manipulated in a psychophysical experiment without varying stimulus magnitude.

Thus far two general ways have been shown in which this might be done and it has been stressed that with stimulus magnitude kept constant the results will fall on the same isosensitivity function whether the results came from experiments on stimulus probabilities or payoffs. Figure 2.13 shows part of the results of an experiment by Galanter and Holman (1967) for one observer whose task was to observe the difference in loudness in a pair of tones. The presentation probabilities were .1, .3, .5, .7, and .9, and the payoff matrices involved losses or gains of 1¢, 1.5¢, or 2.5¢, accumulated over a total of about 10,000 trials following careful preliminary practice of the observer. Different instructions given to instill various biases also produced results

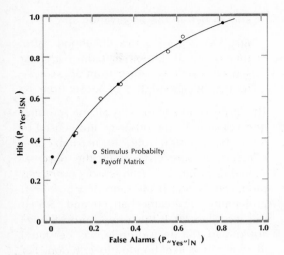

Figure 2.13. The effects of stimulus presentation probabilities and pay-off matrices in an auditory detection experiment involving one stimulus magnitude. All the data seem to be described by the same isosensitivity function. See text.

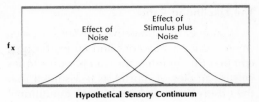

Figure 2.14. Hypothetical effect of noise and stimulation on a sensory continuum in the theory. The distributions are assumed to be density functions.

consistent with this isosensitivity function.

It is against this background of psychological biases that the effect of the stimulus must be evaluated. How this is accomplished in the theory of signal detectability will now be considered. In general, it should be noted that this theory is part of a more general statistical decision theory and conceives the observer's task as one of testing hypotheses.

The Hypothetical Distribution of Sensory Events

It is usually, although not necessarily, assumed that the sensory events resulting from repeated presentation of the same stimulus are normally distributed, an assumption similar to Thurstone's "discriminal dispersion." This underlying hypothetical sensory dimension cannot be observed directly and yet it is there that one must locate our measure of sensitivity and relate it to stimulus magnitude. Furthermore, the theory also assumes that "noise" is ever present as an inherent part of a psychophysical experiment because of external events, variability of the stimulus

source, spontaneous neural firing, or because it has been deliberately introduced by the experimenter. This noise may have an effect on the same hypothetical sensory continuum and, whatever the source, its sensory effect cannot be distinguished from the stimulus effect. It is a problem of signal-to-noise ratio. The sensory effects of noise and stimulus-plus-noise are assumed to produce a normal or Gaussian density function as shown in Figure 2.14. The theory assumes that the observer knows in some sense (possibly from experience with a constant stimulus) that the sensory effect is influenced by noise and thus will vary. His observation is considered analogous to a statistical sample and his "Yes" and "No" therefore do not mean really that he did or did not perceive the stimulus but that he prefers or does not prefer the decision that the stimulus was presented on the basis of the information received from the trial. In other words, there is a sensory event on each trial either due to stimulus-plus-noise (*SN*) or from noise alone (*N*), and the observer must decide which produced it, *N* or *SN*. Although it has been noted that response biases will influence his decision, the effect of the stimulus is to displace the sensory effect away from that produced by *N* alone in proportion to its magnitude as shown in Figure 2.14. Both *N* and *SN* yield a continuously variable effect on the underlying sensory continuum and produce density functions, where the height of the curve indicates the relative frequency of a certain sensory magnitude on the abscissa.

The Likelihood Ratio

Whatever the subjective attributes (tastes, smells, tones, and so on) and no matter how complex the stimulus (for example, pure tones versus samples of music), it is assumed that the observer can and does assign conditional probabilities to each sensory effect (that is, the probability that the effect arose from SN, and the probability that it arose from N), and, thus, that each observation can be treated as an event in probability theory. Assuming the distributions shown in Figure 2.14, the likelihood ratio is the probability that a particular sensory effect, s_1, was produced by stimulus-plus-noise, Ps_1/SN, to the probability that it was produced by noise alone, Ps_1/N. Theoretically, therefore, the underlying sensory continuum shown in Figure 2.14 is translated into a likelihood ratio continuum where the observer's criterion is represented by a particular likelihood ratio that is a point on this axis and that divides it in two. It is assumed that the observer will, on the average, respond "Yes" when his observation on the trial is to the right of this point and "No" when his observation is to the left of this point. That the observer's criterion is influenced by stimulus presentation probabilities and payoffs has been shown, but how does the observer combine into a decision rule the information available to him before a trial with the information obtained on a particular trial? According to the theory, given a sensory event, s_1, the observer can compute the odds in favor of that event arising from SN (that is, the a posteriori probability) according to the following ratio:

$$\frac{P(SN/s_1)}{P(N/s_1)} = \frac{P(SN)}{P(N)} \cdot \frac{P(s_1/SN)}{P(s_1/N)}$$

$P(SN/s_1)/P(N/s_1) =$ the ratio of the a posteriori probabilities and represents the probability that s_1 arose from SN, after observing s_1 and knowing the probability of receiving an SN trial

$P(SN)/P(N) =$ the ratio of a priori probabilities of presentation of SN and N, known before the observation s_1

$P(s_1/SN)/P(s_1/N) =$ the likelihood ratio, that is the likelihood that the particular sensory event, s_1, arose from SN relative to the likelihood that it arose from N.

This expression summarizes all the information available to the observer and is used to form the decision rule. To maximize the number of correct decisions the observer should respond "Yes" (the sensory event was produced by SN) if the ratio of a posteriori probabilities is greater than 1.0, and "No" if it is less than 1.0. If the a priori probabilities are known, the decision rule may be stated in terms of a likelihood-ratio criterion. For example, if $P(SN)$, the stimulus presentation probability, is .50, then the ratio of a priori probabilities is $P(SN)/P(N) = .50/.50 = 1.0$ and the likelihood ratio is the same as the ratio of a posteriori probabilities. The criterion value of the likelihood ratio is also 1.0. However, if $P(SN) = .80$, the a priori ratio is $.80/.20 = 4.0$. In this case, the a posteriori ratio is $P(SN/s_1)/P(N/s_1) = .80/.20 \cdot P(s_1/SN)/P(s_1/N)$, the latter term being the likelihood ratio. If the likelihood ratio exceeds .25 it is clear that the a posteriori ratio will exceed unity; thus the observer responds "Yes" when the likelihood ratio is greater than .25 and "No" when it is less than .25. The likelihood ratio thus has a nonzero numerical value represented on the decision axis, which in turn is a transformation of the sensory axis schematized in Figure 2.14.

The criterion or decision rule is thus determined by the stimulus presentation probability, the values of the observer's decision outcomes, and the stimulus magnitude. The observer might attempt to achieve any number of different goals in a detection situation, but a likelihood-ratio criterion may be calculated to maximize any goal. In theory, the observer's criterion can be compared with that of an *ideal observer*, which is a mathematical abstraction referring to maximal performance computed for the experimental conditions by determining the likelihood criterion that will

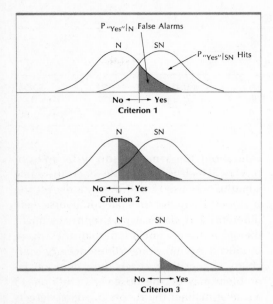

Figure 2.15. The schematic representation of sensory information in the theory of signal detectability. Probability density is plotted against the value of the sensory information expressed as a likelihood ratio on the decision axis. The hypothetical effects of three different criteria are illustrated. The distributions for N and SN are not affected, for it is assumed the stimulus is constant, but the proportions of hits and false alarms do change as the criterion is moved along the decision axis plotted on the abscissa.

maximize payoffs for average or known values of the payoff matrix weighted by known or expected stimulus presentation probabilities. As far as the real observer is concerned this could be a difficult, perhaps impossible task requiring a great deal of practice and understanding. This problem shows signs of bringing psychophysics and the psychology of learning closer together (Atkinson, 1961). Although usually there is the general goal of reporting "Yes" on trials during which the stimulus is presented and "No" otherwise, there is also the notion in detection theory of performing in an optimum manner with respect to the particular payoff matrix and the stimulus presentation probability. Presumably the observer translates the sensory response into a likelihood ratio and then compares this

ratio with the criterion established on this continuum, but no general statement can be made as to how this is done. However, a comparison can be made between the optimal criterion determined theoretically and the observer's criterion as determined by his performance. Three such criteria are illustrated in Figure 2.15. These three pairs of distributions might conceivably have been generated by the *same* stimulus magnitude for the presentation probabilities of .10, .50, and .90 or the three payoff matrices illustrated in Tables 2.12, 2.13, and 2.14. They would yield points that would fall on the same isosensitivity curve, for example, Figure 2.12, which is generated by different criteria as represented theoretically by the cutoffs in Figure 2.15. The curves also show the proportions corresponding to hits and false alarms, which, of course, are empirically determined and define the values on the coordinates of the isosensitivity curve.

The Effect of Stimulus Magnitude

The effect of a constant stimulus is to displace the total sensory effect away from the noise distribution, thus generating two theoretical distributions, N and SN. Assuming that both these distributions are normal and have equal variances, the difference between their means divided by the standard deviation of the distribution for N would provide a parameter d' or

$$d' = \frac{M_{SN} - M_N}{\sigma_N}$$

This is an index of the observer's sensitivity which is independent of the criterion, and hence independent also of payoffs, stimulus presentation probabilities, and instructions. The value of d' may be estimated by converting the experimentally obtained proportions to z scores and subtracting the z score corresponding to false alarms (as an index of the observer's criterion) from the z score corresponding to hits. In the theoretical "ideal observer," d' relates linearly to the common measure of stimulus and noise intensity and

TABLE 2.15 STIMULUS PRESENTATION PROBABILITIES

	.10		.50		.90	
	P	z	P	z	P	z
Hits	.24	−0.71	.66	+0.41	.94	+1.55
False Alarms	.06	−(−1.55)	.36	−(−0.36)	.77	−(+0.74)
$d' =$		.84		.77		.81

"real" and "ideal" observers may be compared (see Green & Swets, 1966, ch. 6). Elliot (1964) has provided tables for the detection experiment considered here so that d' can be looked up directly by means of the probability values of hits and false alarms.

The procedure is illustrated in Table 2.15 for the data on stimulus presentation probabilities presented in Tables 2.9, 2.10, and 2.11. These values of d' are very similar and indi-

cate about the same sensitivity by the observers, which is reasonable since the same stimulus was used in all three cases. Yet the p values listed for hits are of course very different, and classical psychophysics might therefore have concluded that they were produced by individual differences or variability in sensitivity when the source of the problem may be the observer's criterion. In a similar manner the theory of signal detectability has been able to show agreement in results from different psychophysical methods, such as the present method, forced-choice, and rating (see Green & Swets, 1966).

If d' really measures sensitivity, it should vary as a function of stimulus magnitude as shown in Figure 2.16. Figure 2.17 shows the experimentally expected data, namely that

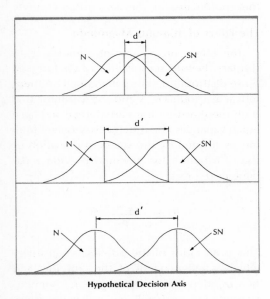

Hypothetical Decision Axis

Figure 2.16. Schematic representation of the effect of stimulus magnitude with other factors constant. Probability density is plotted against likelihood ratio as in Figure 2.15. As stimulus magnitude is increased, the SN distribution is displaced away from the N distribution. We assume the variances remain equal, and the displacement can be expressed as a difference between means or ds.

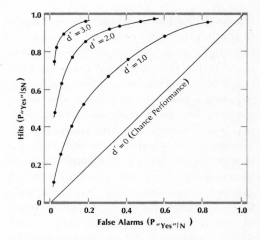

Figure 2.17. Different isosensitivity functions associated with different stimulus magnitudes as indicated by different response criteria with stimulus magnitude constant.

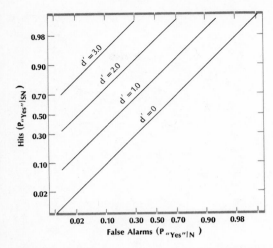

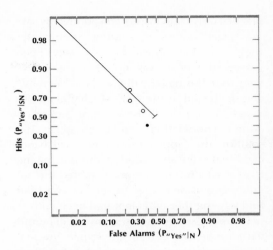

Figure 2.18. Different isosensitivity functions associated with different stimulus magnitudes. This graph is the same as Figure 17 except that the values on both axes have been converted to z scores.

Figure 2.19. The results of a detection experiment in taste measured in terms of d' along the curve drawn along the diagonal in a plot of false alarm as a function of hits. See text for experimental details.

different stimulus magnitudes should be associated with different isosensitivity curves (for example, $d' = 0, 1, 2,$ and 3). The points on each curve represent various possible criteria as discussed above. Note that the d' value of 0 (the straight diagonal line) represents chance performance, while performance worse than chance (as, for example, from confusing the response categories) would be located below this diagonal. Increase in d' is associated with increase in the curvature of the isosensitivity curve as is consistent with the normal curve model. One can make these functions linear with a slope of 1.0 by converting the probability axes to z scores or by plotting the probabilities on normal-normal paper in the first place as in Figure 2.18. The values of d' in Figure 2.16 are located on a scale extending from the diagonal (chance performance) toward the upper left-hand corner of the graph (stimulus magnitudes which are detected all of the time). In this manner d' simply indicates the difficulty of the detection task. Figure 2.19 illustrates this with previously unpublished data in taste referred to above (Engen et al., 1964). The research was concerned with the effect of

deprivation on taste sensitivity, and it has already been shown that the data obtained on the first day agreed with the experiment published by Linker et al. (1964). The observer was an 18-year-old obese woman hospitalized in order to keep her on a strict diet; she did not really eat at all for ten days but received approximately 20 calories per day from liquids such as tea with lemon and dietary colas. Her task was to discriminate between a small (ca. 1 cc) sip of distilled water and a small sip of sucrose dissolved in distilled water (weight/volume). There were two concentrations, .125 percent and .225 percent, which were run in separate sessions each day. The so-called "sip and spit method" was used, meaning that she tasted a liquid and then expectorated. The stimulus presentation probability was always .50. Because of the difficulty of discrimination and shortness of time the .125 percent solution was omitted about halfway into her fast. It was possible to make observations under the same conditions each day, and data on three consecutive days were combined to obtain a more stable performance. There were 70 trials each day of water and sucrose in a random order, but the first 10 trials were used for practice only. The observer responded by saying "sugar" or "water" and the experimenter then told her which had actually been presented. There was no other reinforcement but the patient did seem cooperative and interested in the test, which she understood to be part of the medical procedure done in cooperation with her physician. The solution was sipped from very small paper cups that were discarded at the end of the trial, at which time she expectorated the solution and made her judgment. She was then told whether her judgment had been correct or incorrect, whereupon she rinsed her mouth with distilled water from an ordinary hospital glass, and then waited 30 seconds for the next trial. The results show that as expected the stronger sucrose solution yields the larger d' and also that d' increased over the test period for the .225 percent sucrose solution, and this indicates an increase in sensitivity. In the present case there is relatively little variation in false alarms for the four points plotted, but in another situation there could be, and the point is that d' provides the possibility of measuring sensitivity independently of variations in such factors. Response bias is probably not of primary interest to the sensory psychologist, but the effect of deprivation on sensitivity is. The present data of course are based on only one subject, and the increase in sensitivity in this patient as measured by d' might have resulted from practice rather than sensory physiological effects of deprivation. Further experiments could produce this information in a clearer manner than is possible with classical methods. The effect of practice on sensitivity as well as response bias is another problem of interest to learning psychologists (see Gibson, 1953) and can be studied anew within the theory of signal detectability (Atkinson, 1961).

As expected, d', as defined here, also increases as a function of stimulus magnitude. In a number of "Yes–No" experiments on contrast in brightness, Wuest (1961) found that d' is an approximate power function of luminance, as shown for two observers in the

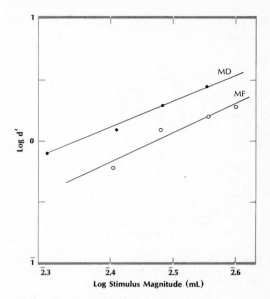

Figure 2.20. The logarithmic values of d' plotted against the logarithm of luminance in a forced choice brightness detection task at a background intensity of .8881 mL and with stimulus duration at 32 msec. Data are shown for two observers. Lines are fitted by the method of least squares. (Wuest, 1961.)

example in Figure 2.20, but more research needs to be done on the form of this type of psychometric function. Recall that in the "ideal observer" d' is a linear function of stimulus magnitude.

Detection theory in psychophysics has been developed to a sophisticated level and has stimulated new interest in the field. The present chapter has only shown how the basic principles relate to classical psychophysics in a simple detection situation and it has made only occasional references to the so-called "ideal observer" and possible applications to problems of sensory physiology. However, two problems appear crucial to the development of the theory in this direction: (1) the nature and empirical determination of noise and (2) the development of tests of the goodness of fit of experimentally obtained data to theoretical isosensitivity curves. The latter has been a continual problem in psychophysics; for example, the attempts to ob-

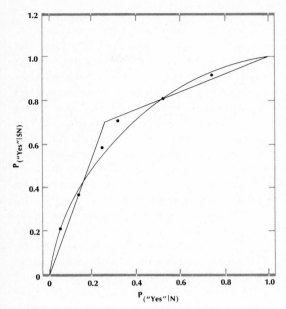

Figure 2.21. Schematic representation and comparison of the isosensitivity function of the multi-state theory of signal detectability and Luce's (1963) two-state threshold theory. Curves fitted by eye.

tain data reliable enough to decide whether the psychometric function would be better described by the phi–gamma or by the quantal hypothesis. Similarly, the classical notion of a threshold, which is a two-state theory in contemporary terms, has not yet been disproven by the data on isosensitivity curves but it has certainly been weakened. Luce (1963) has proposed a threshold theory which assumes that the presentation of the stimulus will place the observer in either a detection state or a nondetection state. The observation he makes *in either state* may be biased by nonsensory factors in such a way that a random portion of the observations are falsified in two mutually exclusive ways, namely, saying "No" when he is in the detection state and "Yes" when he is in the nondetection state. When correct detections, or hits, are plotted as a function of false alarms, this refined threshold theory yields two straight line segments as in Figure 2.21. As can be seen,

the prediction from this theory yields a function very similar to that of the theory of signal detectability. Presently available data and curve fitting methods do not make possible a clear-cut choice between these models, which is reminiscent of the situation with the form of the psychometric function discussed above. Interestingly enough, the sensory criterion proposed by Luce is the number of quantal units required by the observer to define the detection state. However, there is agreement on the very important point that careful measurement must be made of false

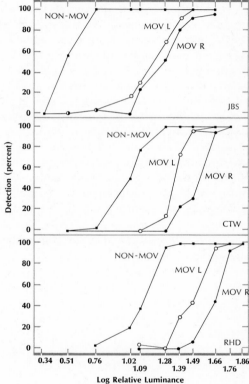

Figure 2.22. Data of Volkmann (1962) for the detection of visual targets during a voluntary saccadic eye movement to the left (MOV L) or to the right (MOV R) as compared with a control condition of no movement (NON-MOV). Method of constant stimuli in which percentage of targets seen is plotted as a function of log relative luminance of the target.

alarms in order to distinguish between the response criterion and sensitivity.

While it is well to be mindful of the limitations of psychophysical thresholds, it would be deceptive to end this methodological chapter without a reminder of some of the more "beautiful" and precise data obtained by classical psychophysical procedures. Figure 2.22 presents one of many possible examples of that kind of data.

The experiment from which the data of Figure 2.22 were obtained is one in which flashes of light were presented to the observer. Flash intensity is displayed on a logarithmic scale on the abscissa. Intensities range over a sufficiently wide domain so that the brightest flashes are nearly always reported as "seen" and the dimmest ones are nearly always "not seen" by an experienced observer. In other words, the brightest flashes are characterized by a stimulus-plus-noise Gaussian density function (see Figure 2.14) that is almost wholly beyond the noise density function; while the dimmest flashes are characterized by a density function that is indistinguishable from that of noise alone. Notice, however, that the various conditions of the experiment with respect to eye movements result in systematic differences in detection.

Thus it is possible to draw the conclusion that these experimental conditions have produced significant changes in the detectability of visual stimuli. In particular, it is clear that for each observer a luminance can be designated such that the stimulus is reported as almost always seen by the nonmoving eye and as almost never seen by the moving eye. This fact, along with appropriate statistical analysis of the data for all subjects, justified the use in this experiment of the traditional method of constant stimuli, and warranted the conclusion that vision is significantly depressed during an eye movement.

Detection theory is one of the few important contributions made to psychophysics since Fechner, and is at least partly responsible for the new interest in psychophysics that led to the translation of Fechner's *Elemente* into English over 100 years after its publication. Another reason for the revival of psychophysics is the effort of S. S. Stevens in psychophysical scaling. As was noted at the outset, Fechner was primarily interested in this problem. Detection and discrimination are important and interesting topics in their own right, but to Fechner they represented a means to solve the more important problem of the law governing the relation between psychological magnitude and stimulus magnitudes over the whole range of values. This is the problem considered in the next chapter.

Trygg Engen

PSYCHOPHYSICS

II. SCALING METHODS

3

Chapter 2 was concerned with methods for determining the acuteness of our senses. It dealt with the smallest perceptible stimuli, that is, absolute and differential thresholds. The present task is to measure the whole range of sensory magnitudes so that one can determine, for example, which gray is halfway between black and white or, more generally, how much visual brightness increases as luminance is increased. Of course, there are physical scales for measuring stimuli, but something else is needed, namely, a psychological scale for measuring the magnitude or intensity of sensation. Suppose a radio engineer wants to design a set that sounds twice as loud as a competing brand. If he merely doubles the physical output, he will be disappointed to find that he has increased loudness by only a trifle. How much will he have to step up the physical output to double the loudness? Questions like this have considerable theoretical and practical importance and involve scaling for the purpose of measuring psychological variables.

Experimental psychologists prefer to work with quantitative data for the basic reason that a thorough study of a dependent variable as a function of an independent variable is possible only when both variables have been measured. Many measurements made by psychologists are not intrinsically psychological or behavioral; for example, latency of response is a behavioral variable, but the measure involved is physical. Such physical measures dominated experimental psychology until about three decades ago.

There are two reasons why physical measures alone are not sufficient, even though they will continue to play an important role in psychological research. One obvious reason is that human and animal subjects are not always able to detect the physical stimuli or stimulus differences that the experimenter presents. A second reason is that, even when the stimulus exceeds the subject's threshold, equal increments or decrements in the physical value of the stimulus are not usually perceived as equal by the subject. Therefore, in order to understand behavior in relation to physical energies which may elicit or control that behavior, it is valuable to know the relationship between perceived (or response) magnitude and physical stimulus magnitude. This is the problem of psychophysical scaling and measuring.

Before going on to outline the actual methods of scaling and measuring, it is necessary to describe four types of scale. In general, measuring means assigning one or more properties of the number scale to attributes of objects. Scaling refers to the methods whereby one determines which properties of the number scale apply to the dimensions of the objects and which transformations leave these properties invariant (Stevens, 1951). Four properties are usually considered, and for each one there is a rule for permissible transformations.

1. *Nominal scales* refer to classifications such as bird–fish–mammal, pleasant and unpleasant odors, and men and women. Because the principle of classification is usually nonquantitative, one cannot properly use the term "measurement" in connection with nominal scales. Although numbers may be used as names for categories of classification or identification, all objects having the same attribute and only those being given the same number, names could be used instead. The transformation rule involves maintaining the identification of the objects and any direct substitution of names which perserves it is permissible; for example, one could call all the men "males" and women "females," or one could substitute the symbols "1" and "2" for "male" and "female" respectively.

2. *Ordinal scales* arrange things in order of magnitude. An example from common experience is found in a foot race; the man who took second place was slower than the winner but faster than the man who took third place. The ranks do not tell how much difference there was in the running times of the three contestants, although it is a rank order and to that extent a quantitative dimension. One can use the rank order of the number system and call the three contestants "1," "2," and "3." This entails more than the arbitrary naming in nominal scaling.

The ordinal scale makes possible comparisons of objects of the type "greater than" and "less than" and mathematically satisfies the condition $1 < 2 < 3$ in time, or $1 > 2 > 3$ in speed. Any transformation that preserves the order is permissible, such as calling the contestants "13," "57," and "148" or just plain "first," "second," and "third," because the size of the steps between the categories is not specified.

3. *Equal-interval scales* go one step further than the ordinal scales and allow statements about how much difference there is between two objects or individuals; they are based on a constant unit and satisfy the condition $2 - 1 = 3 - 2 = n - (n - 1)$. To some scientists this is the first level of quantification where one really talks about measurement, for variables measured on interval scales can be plotted as functions of other variables; for example, average temperature may be plotted as a function of the time of year. However, such numerical values are not absolute magnitudes of the attribute of interest but correspond only to the differences in their values. For example, on the Fahrenheit thermometer there is as much difference between 60° and 70° as there is between 70° and 80°, but because this scale lacks a true zero it is not permissible to say that 80° F is twice as high a temperature as 40° F.

4. *A ratio scale* has a true zero as well as a constant unit. For example, on the physical dimension of length an 8-inch stick has twice the value of a 4-inch stick. Another example of a ratio scale is the Kelvin scale of temperature. With a ratio scale all the operations of arithmetic may be performed, with the numerical values representing absolute values of the object. Only a linear transformation of these values of the form $y = ax$ is permissible. An equal-interval scale permits the use of an additive constant. Thus, $y = ax + b$. In other words, for an interval scale, b may be zero or some other value, but for the ratio scale it must be zero.

How is a psychological scale developed that will have equal intervals and a true zero? Perhaps one can get some hints from physical scales. Consider the problem of measuring the length of some small objects when there is no ruler handy. Find the midpoint of a sheet of paper by folding it in half and continue to divide it into quarters, eighths, and so on, to produce a scale of equal units. After measuring the objects with this arbitrary scale, the lengths can be compared as if a ruler had been used, and these measures in our arbitrary unit can be transformed into inches by the formula $y = ax$. To do so let x = length as measured, y = length in inches, and a = the ratio of the two measures, that is, the number of inches contained in one arbitrary unit.

Can the experiment described above be done with sensations? One can certainly ask the observer to judge whether one sound is twice as loud, or half as loud, as another. The observer can also be asked to choose a series of gray cards that seem to represent equal steps of increasing brightness. This *direct approach* to constructing psychological scales seems plausible, but until recently psychologists viewed it with doubt, and many still consider it too "subjective." Because of such doubts, most psychophysicists resorted to indirect methods of scaling sensory response. Several have been used, such as the *DL*, reaction time, and confidence of judgment methods, but the validity of such indirect measurement has also been questioned. The current tendency seems to be to accept the direct method as the ultimate check, but the issue is by no means dead (see Garner & Creelman, 1967).

INDIRECT SCALING

Scales Based on DL and Fechner's Law

The *DL* and Fechner method for scaling sensation go back to Fechner (1860) who thought that Weber's Law (see pp. 17–19) furnished the key to the measurement of mind. It is an indirect method that uses the *DL* as the unit for an equal-interval scale. Because Weber's law states that the *DL*

TABLE 3.1 EXAMPLE OF WEBER'S LAW

Psychological steps	Stimulus value	Log stimulus	Increment of log
0 (RL)	8.0	0.903	
1	12.0	1.079	0.176
2	18.0	1.255	0.176
3	27.0	1.431	0.176
4	40.5	1.607	0.176
5	60.75	1.784	0.177

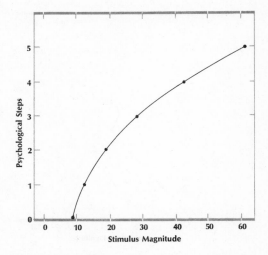

Figure 3.1. An illustration of Fechner's Law. The number of psychological steps (sensory magnitude) as a function of stimulus magnitude in linear coordinates.

is a constant fraction of the standard, $(DL/St) = (\Delta S/S) = k$, the physical steps must be increased as the scale of intensity is ascended, in order that the corresponding subjective increment remain constant or "just noticeably different." Thus, in a hypothetical sense, with an RL of 8.0 physical units and a Weber fraction of $\frac{1}{2}$, the stimulus value required for each successive unit or psychological step would be $1\frac{1}{2}$ times the preceding one; for example, $8.0 \times \frac{1}{2} + 8.0 = 12$, which is the physical intensity that gives us the second step on the psychological scale, as is shown in Table 3.1.

These data are plotted in Figure 3.1, which shows that successive steps require larger and larger increments in stimulus value for equal increments in sensation value. The increase in psychological sensation as a function of stimulus magnitude is described more conveniently with logarithmic than with arithmetic steps because it entails multiplication by a constant. This is accomplished simply by adding the logarithmic value of this constant (0.176) to obtain each successive step on our scale. The log values have been entered in the third column of Table 3.1, and the constancy of the increment in logarithmic value is entered in the fourth column. When the sensation values are plotted as a function of the logarithm of the stimulus values, as in Figure 3.2, a straight line instead of a curve is obtained.

Assuming that Fechner's reasoning is correct, it is obvious that the logarithms are especially convenient when only the relative magnitude of a sensation is of interest. Without going through intermediate steps, one can calculate the log of the intensity of stimulation required to produce any level of sensation (see Reference Tables at the back of this book). Multiply the number of the step by the increment in logarithmic value (which then will be one plus Weber's fraction); add the logarithm of the RL; the result is the logarithm of the desired stimulus. Fechner wrote several formulas for carrying out this operation, but the most familiar is

$$R = k \log S$$

where S is measured in terms of the detection threshold (RL), so that $R = 0$ for $S = 1$. This is Fechner's Law, which states that the magnitude of sensation or response (R) varies directly with the logarithm of the stimulus magnitude (S). Remember that Fechner assumed (1) that jnd or DL was an equal increment in sensation, regardless of the absolute level at which it is taken, and (2) that a sensation is the sum of all the jnd steps that come before it in the scale. Both of these assumptions have been questioned, and they are discussed more fully below. Nevertheless, Fechner's contribution should be recognized, for he gave psychology a way of constructing sensory scales.

The instabilities of classically determined thresholds have been noted in Chapter 2, pages 31–34, but the DL is at least a defined unit. It is ultimately a measure of variability, and because the amount of variability in many biological and psychological processes is a constant fraction of the intensity of the process, many scales in psychology have been based on variability. Examples are the standard or z scores used in psychological testing.

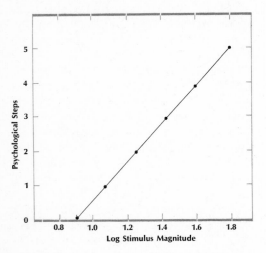

Figure 3.2. Data in Figure 3.1 replotted. The number of psychological steps (sensory magnitude) as a function of the logarithmic value of stimulus magnitude.

A scale based on the *DL* can be obtained either by adding the individual *DL* steps that are obtained by actual measurement or by assuming the validity of the more convenient logarithmic type of formula. The additive method is the more accurate if either extremely weak or strong stimuli are involved, where Weber's Law (unmodified, see p. 17) does not hold well, but the logarithmic transformation may be satisfactory for the middle ranges, which are often of greatest interest. (See Helson's modified Fechnerian function and the comparison of direct and indirect scales below.)

Pair Comparison and the Discriminal Dispersion

The scaling principle used by Fechner was the hypothesis that, regardless of the physical values involved, stimulus differences which are detected equally often are subjectively equal. Thurstone (1927a) started with this principle to promote psychology as a "quantitative and rational science." First, he provided a mathematical model, the Law of Comparative Judgment, which states explicitly the theoretical assumption about the distribution of the effect of stimulation. Second, he devised methodology applicable to the scaling of attributes, such as beauty, for which there are no specifiable physical correlates.

The method of pair comparison was first introduced by Cohn (1894) in his study of color preferences and then developed further by Thurstone. It is often regarded as the most appropriate way of securing value judgments. The observer's task is simplified by giving him only two stimuli to compare. Usually every stimulus is paired with every other stimulus in a randomly presented matrix of pairs. This results in $N(N-1)/2$ pairs; for example, 45 pairs for 10 stimuli. The number of pairs increases rapidly as stimuli are added, but the task can sometimes be shortened by breaking up a series of stimuli into two or more overlapping series.

In Chapter 2 the general psychophysical assumption is stated that repeated presenta-

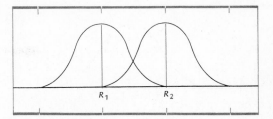

Figure 3.3. Two hypothetical normal frequency distributions of mean response values (R_1 and R_2) corresponding to two stimuli, S_1 and S_2, for a group of observers.

tion of the same stimulus does not produce an identical response each time but rather a distribution of responses that may be described in terms of central tendency and dispersion. In that case, means and standard deviations of physical stimulus values producing the responses were calculated. However, in the present case, calculations will be made on the basis of Thurstone's theory that the sensory or perceptual distribution is a nonobservable and hypothetical continuum. (See the theory of signal detectability in Chapter 2.) Although the discussion is limited to individual differences, which represent the more common application of pair comparisons, Thurstone applied the theory to both individual differences and differences from moment to moment in the same individual.

Theoretically, when the same stimulus S_1 is presented to each member of a group of observers, a distribution of perceptions will result with a mean of R_1. Likewise S_2, which it is assumed is similar to S_1, produces a distribution with a mean of R_2. Figure 3.3 shows the two resulting hypothetical normal distributions where the frequency of different magnitudes of R results from S_1 and S_2. Although both stimuli belong on the same continuum, R_2 (the mean response to S_2) is larger than R_1 (the mean response to S_1). However, some individuals would judge S_1 larger than S_2. The effect of S_1, for example, on observer A can be described as $R_{1A} = R_1 + d_{1A}$, where R_{1A} refers to A's re-

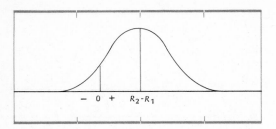

Figure 3.4. Hypothetical normal frequency distribution of differences in response values associated with a pair of stimuli.

sponse to S_1 and d_{1A} to his deviation from R_1, the mean response to S_1 for the group. Likewise, $R_{2A} = R_2 + d_{2A}$ describes observer A's perception of S_2. The important point to note here is that Thurstone's Law of Comparative Judgment made it possible to obtain perceptual scale values associated with the *single* stimulus, S_1 and S_2 in the present example, by starting quantitatively with these individual differences, namely, $D_A = (R_{2A} - R_{1A}) + (d_{2A} - d_{1A})$. By summing the value of D for the N individuals in the group, one obtains the mean $D = R_2 - R_1$ because, by definition, the sum of the individual deviations is zero. The sum of these individual Ds squared and divided by N gives the standard deviation of the differences between the distributions shown in Figure 3.3.

$$\sigma_D = \sqrt{\sigma_2{}^2 + \sigma_1{}^2 - 2r_{21}\sigma_2\sigma_1}$$

where σ_2 and σ_1 are standard deviations for the distributions of R_2 and R_1, the responses associated with stimuli S_2 and S_1, and r_{21} is the correlation between the individual observers' deviations from the means, R_2 and R_1, of the distribution. Figure 3.4 shows the hypothetical distribution of differences and the mean of $R_2 - R_1$. This is Thurstone's theory.

The problem now is to relate Thurstone's theory to actual data. Here Thurstone made use of the known relationship between proportions under the normal curve and the z scores discussed in the previous chapter (*see* Table 2.4). The proportions are simply the number of individual observers, divided by N,

who choose one stimulus over another: this would be S_1 over S_2 in the present example.

Assuming the distributions are normal, as in Figure 3.4, this proportion will correspond to a z score that defines the psychological distance between stimuli S_1 and S_2. Therefore, the experimentally obtained proportions are converted to z scores with the aid of tables of the normal curve (the Reference Table at the back of this book will do for most cases).

In other words, the proportion $R_2 - R_1$ is the only kind of datum obtained, and the rest is theory as is shown in Figure 3.4, in which the zero on the abscissa represents the point at which S_1 is judged equal to S_2. Negative values of $R_2 - R_1$ represent differences for individuals by whom S_1 is judged greater than S_2, but on the average S_2 is judged greater than S_1. The standard deviation of this distribution is σ_D, as defined above.

If we convert the obtained proportion, $R_2 - R_1$, the mean of the distribution of differences, to a z score, z_{21}, and express its value using the standard deviation, σ_D, as the unit of measurement, one then obtains

$$R_2 - R_1 = z_{21} \sqrt{\sigma_2{}^2 + \sigma_1{}^2 - 2r_{21}\sigma_1\sigma_2}$$

This is Thurstone's so-called "*Law of Comparative Judgment*"' of the *psychological* distance between stimuli. Because experimental data on any of the values under the radical are usually not available, this equation cannot be tested directly. However, Thurstone (1927), proposed several simplifying assumptions or "cases," as he called them. One assumption is that the underlying, hypothetical distribution of responses resulting from a given stimulus is the same whether it was obtained from different individuals on one trial or from one individual on different trials. The standard deviation, σ, of this distribution is called the *discriminal dispersion*. The other value under the radical sign, r, refers to the potential correlation between perceptual values of different stimuli. If it is assumed that $\sigma_1 = \sigma_2$ and that $r = 0$, then we obtain $R_2 - R_1 = z_{21}k\sqrt{2}$ where k is a

TABLE 3.2 PROPORTION OF CHOICE OF COMPOSERS BY 308 MUSICIANS IN PAIR COMPARISON

	Bach	Beethoven	Mendelssohn	Mozart	Schumann
Bach	—	.38	.82	.52	.78
Beethoven	.62	—	.94	.79	.94
Mendelssohn	.18	.06	—	.03	.71
Mozart	.48	.21	.97	—	.83
Schumann	.22	.06	.29	.17	—

Each entry is the proportion of musicians preferring the composer listed in the column at the left to the corresponding composer in the row at the top. Data from Folgemann, 1933.

constant corresponding to the value of the discriminal dispersion. If $k\sqrt{2}$ is used as the arbitrary unit of measurement, one can define

$$R_2 - R_1 = z_{21}$$

This is a simplified form ("Case V") of Thurstone's Law of Comparative Judgment. It is theoretically an equal-interval scale.

Much has been written about testing the assumptions that have been made about the form of the distributions and the size of the correlations and dispersions (see Thurstone, 1927b; Guilford, 1954; Torgerson, 1958).

Some data in a large study by Folgemann (1933) of the preference of musicians for the music of different composers illustrate scaling based on pair comparison. The judges were 308 members of the Philadelphia, Boston, Minneapolis, and New York Philharmonic orchestras. For the study, the composers' names were presented in pairs, each name being paired with every other one. The instructions were as follows:

This is an experimental study of preferences of the music of different composers. You are asked to underline the name of the one composer of each pair whose *music you prefer* in general, *not*

taking the personality or greatness of the composer into consideration.

For example, take the pair:

Puccini—Gounod.

If in general you prefer the music of Puccini to that of Gounod, underline *Puccini,* if on the other hand you prefer Gounod, underline *Gounod.* To make this experiment valid, it is absolutely necessary not to omit any pair, even if it is difficult to make a choice. It is also of the greatest importance not to discuss the experiment with anyone before its completion.

Folgemann used 19 different composers. He published tables showing the proportion of the 308 judges who chose each composer when compared with every other one in a total of 190 comparisons, which included 19 control trials. (A smaller sample of five composers has been selected to simplify the illustration of computations which begins with the matrix of proportions in Table 3.2.)

The proportions are obtained by dividing the number of the musicians who preferred Bach to Beethoven, for example, by the total number of judges. This value (118/308 = .38) is entered in the second column of the first row. The proportion who preferred Beethoven over Bach (190/308 = .62) is shown in the first

TABLE 3.3 z-SCORES (PSYCHOLOGICAL DISTANCE) BETWEEN FIVE COMPOSERS AS JUDGED BY 308 MUSICIANS BASED ON PAIR COMPARISON DATA IN TABLE 3.2

	Bach	Beethoven	Mendelssohn	Mozart	Schumann	Σ	Mean R	Linearly transformed R
Bach	—	−0.31	+0.92	+0.05	+0.77	+1.43	+0.38	1.34
Beethoven	+0.31	—	+1.55	+0.81	+1.55	+4.22	+1.06	2.02
Mendelssohn	−0.92	−1.55	—	−1.88	+0.55	−3.80	−0.95	0.01
Mozart	−0.05	−0.81	+1.88	—	+0.95	+1.97	+0.48	1.44
Schumann	−0.77	−1.55	−0.55	−0.95	—	−3.82	−0.96	0.00

column of the second row. Cells in the diagonal, which should theoretically yield proportions of .50, are empty because pairs of identical composers were not used.

The next step in the analysis is to convert the proportion to z scores. Note that a proportion of .50 would yield a psychological distance of zero. The larger the distance between the stimuli, the greater is the z score, as is shown in Table 3.3.

The sign of the z score indicates whether the composer listed in the row or column received a majority ($+$) of the votes. Note that the part above the diagonal is otherwise a mirror image of the part below the diagonal.

Table 3.3 is a matrix of all the distances between the R values (preference) corresponding to the S value (composers), but it does not yet reveal the psychological continuum, where single R values can be located. The question now is how best to accomplish that. Each column or row of the matrix represents a continuum that includes such scale values, but they are relative to only one of the five composers. There are actually four estimates of each distance, one direct one, $A - B$, and three indirect ones, $(A - C) - (B - C) = A - B$, and so on. Therefore, the best estimate of each R value is obtained by taking the mean of the values in each row, for this gives the estimate containing *all* the information about each stimulus in the matrix. These then are scale values with $k\sqrt{2}$ as the arbitrary unit according to Case V.

However, it is awkward to deal with positive and negative values, and because the unit is arbitrary anyway, one can get rid of the sign by adding 0.96 to each R value, as is shown in the last column of Table 3.3. Accordingly, the composers are ordered and the psychological (preferential) distances between them are as follows:

This scale should not be interpreted to imply that Beethoven was judged three times better than Schumann. The numbers only serve to mark off distances along a psychological continuum and show that Schumann and Mendelssohn were located almost in the same place on this continuum, more than a unit below Bach and Mozart, who were placed about a half unit below Beethoven, and so on. Only an arbitrary zero has been defined on this scale.

The method of pair comparison can be applied to any stimulus material for which pairs can be presented. The inclusion of too many pairs may make the task tedious for the observer, and stimulus differences that lead to proportions of 0 or 1.0 only make the computation of scale values more complicated for the experimenter. One usually can overcome such practical problems by using overlapping ranges and making careful preparations.

A more serious problem than the one above is theoretical; that is, will the data actually conform to the model and its strict assumptions? Two checks can be made easily. First, one should compare the mean scale values with each of the scale values in the columns of the matrix of z scores, for these should agree within experimental error. There are such discrepancies, for example, in our matrix between the Mendelssohn and the Beethoven column. Second, one can attempt to reproduce the experimentally obtained proportions by going backwards from our mean scale values. The difference between any two scale values corresponds to a score, and by making the proper subtractions and converting these differences into p values by using Reference Table 1, it should be possible to generate the obtained matrix of proportions in Table 3.2 with only chance variation.

The two sets of data can be evaluated by a chi-square test. Significant differences would indicate that the data do not fit the model and that one or more of its assumptions must be rejected. (See Torgerson, 1958; Bock & Jones, 1968).

Stimulus Rating and Successive Categories

Some of the experiments discussed are called *psychophysical* because they are concerned with the psychological scaling of attributes which can be measured on a physical continuum. The fact the stimuli can be specified in physical terms is a great help in studying various problems in sensation and perception. The last example showed, however, that psychological scales can be constructed even when there is no physical continuum for comparison. Such scales are often called *psychometric,* and perhaps the most familiar example of this type is the rating scale. Rating, pair comparison, and ranking (discussed below) can be applied to both psychophysical and psychometric problems.

Galton (1883) may have been the first to develop rating scales. His purpose was to quantify a strictly psychological attribute, the vividness of memory images. Since then, the rating scale has been used for various purposes in experimental psychology. Most people are familiar with these scales for description of academic achievement, personality characteristics, and the like. Probably no students get through high school without being rated, and the method is widely used in industry, the armed forces, and whenever some simple quantitative description of people is desired. The task of the observer is to judge one attribute of the stimuli by placing it in one of about seven categories reflecting different quantities of the attribute. (Do not confuse rating with methods of interval judgment, partitioning, or the method of equal sense distances, which are considered below.)

The interpretation of facial expression, which is an important aspect of interactions among people, giving clues to feeling or motivations, has been studied seriously with the rating method since the time of Darwin (1872). The typical procedure is to use photographs posed by actors portraying various emotions. The early studies asked the observer to interpret or identify which emotion the

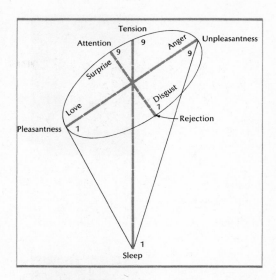

Figure 3.5. Schlosberg's model of the relationship between three dimensions of facial expression: sleep-tension, attention-rejection, and pleasantness–unpleasantness. Each dimension is represented as a nine-point rating scale. The figure illustrates where in this special representation certain emotions, for example, love, would fall.

actor was portraying. The results indicated many confusions in the typical observer, for example, between fear and anger, and seemed to show that emotions are identified in the total situational context rather than in terms of facial expressions alone. However, largely due to Schlosberg (1952, 1954) it came to be realized that the confusion was due to actual similarity in the facial expression associated with different emotions. These similarities, Schlosberg proposed, are the operating psychological dimensions used in judging facial expression, and he showed how these dimensions may be related theoretically by the model shown in Figure 3.5. Rating data along these dimensions are reliable and provide the empirical support for the model (Schlosberg, 1952, 1954).

One procedure employed in Schlosberg's experiments was to present pictures of various emotions, portrayed by the same actress, to a group of observers. Each observer judged

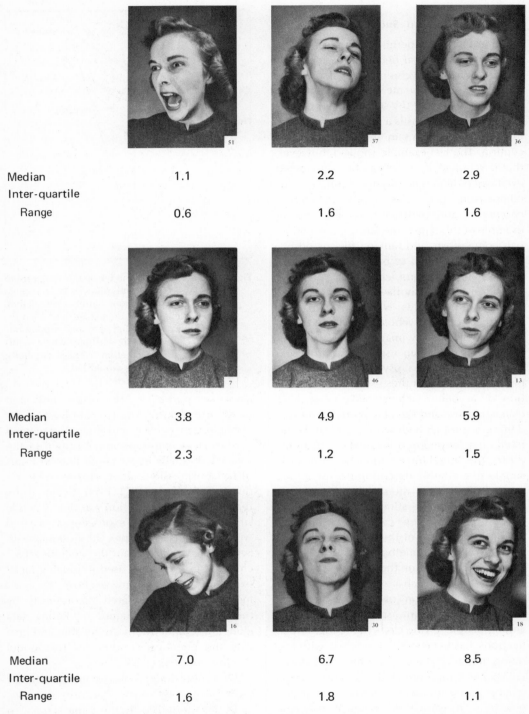

Median	1.1	2.2	2.9
Inter-quartile			
Range	0.6	1.6	1.6
Median	3.8	4.9	5.9
Inter-quartile			
Range	2.3	1.2	1.5
Median	7.0	6.7	8.5
Inter-quartile			
Range	1.6	1.8	1.1

Figure 3.6. Rating scale values for Lightfoot pictures on the Schlosberg dimension of pleasantness–unpleasantness obtained with 96 observers. (Numbers in lower right-hand corner were not visible to the observers and serve only to identify the pictures. See Engen, Schlosberg, & Levy, 1958.)

the pictures along the three Schlosberg dimensions defined by the experimenter and clarified by illustrations. The following instructions were given for the dimension of pleasantness.

> The purpose of this experiment is to see how accurately you can judge the degree of pleasantness in a series of photographs posed by the same actress. Note that you are *not* to judge whether *you* like the picture or not, but the pleasantness *she* is trying to represent. The pictures are arranged in an irregular order. You are to rate each picture on a 9-point scale, where 1 indicates that the actress feels very unpleasant and 9 indicates she feels very pleasant. The facial expressions you will see may fall anywhere on this scale. Your task is to assign a whole number which reflects this degree. Don't worry about whether or not you have seen a picture before— some of them are similar—but judge each picture as independently as you can. There is no right or wrong answer. We want to know how *you* judge the pictures. Any questions?

The instructions quoted above were presented to each observer, along with a table for recording his judgments, and were also read aloud by the experimenter. Usually about 50 pictures representing as varied a sample of the dimensions as possible were presented in one session, but for the present purpose just a few of the so-called "Lightfoot pictures" (Engen, Schlosberg, & Levy, 1958) are shown in Figure 3.6. As can be seen, rating-scale values are simply the measure of the central tendency plus dispersion of the judgment for each stimulus.

Medians are often used, as in the present case, because these distributions are often skewed for stimuli falling at the extremes of the rating scales, that is, extremely pleasant and unpleasant expressions in the present case. (Consult Abelson and Sermat [1962] for a multidimensional analysis of Schlosberg's model.)

The ideal rating scale is one with equal intervals, but the data obtained from the observers are only ordinal. Thus, the problem is how to obtain a possible *latent* equal-interval scale from such *manifestly* ordinal data. If this could be accomplished, one could, for exam-

ple, test Fechner's Law very conveniently with rating data, for ratings can be obtained very quickly for a large number of stimuli as compared with *DL*s and discriminal dispersions.

Those who have been concerned with the construction of interval scales from rating data have usually started with the assumption that the judgments of any object are normally distributed on an interval scale. (See Guilford, 1954, p. 226.) Torgerson (1959) has shown how the theoretical principles of the Law of Comparative Judgment can be applied to rating data and he has thus proposed a *Law of Categorical Judgment.*

The Law of Comparative Judgment assumes that each stimulus of a pair produces a response distribution with certain quantitative attributes. While applying the Law of Categorical Judgment, the same assumption is made about this response distribution, but, in addition, it is assumed that the boundaries between categories on the scale have an effect and a distribution like the one obtained for the stimulus. According to Torgerson (p. 206):

> 1. The psychological continuum of the subject can be divided into a specified number of ordered categories or steps.
> 2. Owing to various and sundry factors, a given *category boundary* is not necessarily always located at a particular point on the continuum. Rather, it also projects a normal distribution of positions on the continuum. Again, different category boundaries may have different mean locations and different dispersions.
> 3. The subject judges a given stimulus to be below a given category boundary whenever the value of the stimulus on the continuum is less

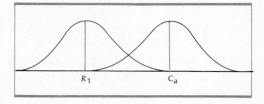

Figure 3.7. Two hypothetical frequency distributions of response values; R_1 corresponds to a stimulus, S_1, and C_a, to the boundary between two categories on the response scale.

than that of the category boundary. Essentially, this amounts to the assumption that the boundaries between adjacent categories behave like stimuli.

To make pair comparisons, the scaling entails converting proportions to z scores that theoretically represent psychological distances between stimuli. In Torgerson's category scaling, the proportion of the time a certain stimulus is placed in a certain category is converted to a z score, which in this case represents the psychological distance between the stimulus and the category boundary. Figure 3.7 is thus analogous to Figure 3.3 except that a category boundary has been substituted for one of the stimuli in a pair. The first and last categories are limited on one side and open on the other.

The experimenter obtains proportions of individuals who put a stimulus S_1 in a certain category. The category scale may be l 2 3 4 5, specific examples, or adjectives, which would then be converted to numerals before scaling. The problem is to determine the numerical values of category boundaries on a hypothetical psychological dimension. For n categories there are $n - 1$ upper category boundaries $(C_a, C_b, \ldots C_{n-1})$. The proportions of raters for whom a certain category boundary lies above a certain stimulus, or P_{CO}, where O is an individual rater and C a certain category boundary are obtained in the experiment. If these proportions are converted to z scores, we may write Torgerson's Law of Categorical Judgment,

$$C_a - R_1 = z_{a1} \sqrt{\sigma_a^2 + \sigma_1^2 - 2r_{a1}\sigma_a\sigma_1}$$

which is directly comparable to Thurstone's Law of Comparative Judgment (p. 51) except that the category boundary has been substituted for one of the stimuli in the pair. Simplifying assumptions must again be considered because the formula contains parameters that are not easily evaluated.

The elegant theory described above ideally should provide a scale with equal intervals for psychological measurement. Unfortunately, great difficulty has been encountered in obtaining stable, useful, and valid ratings at even this ordinal level due to various biases in the observers and variability in the objects or persons rated (see Guilford, 1954). It is apparently almost always necessary to provide the raters with a common anchor or reference point, in order to obtain reliable data.

Another attempt to improve the reliability of the data has involved the use of descriptive adjectives, such as: Very poor—Poor—Fair—Good—Excellent. The rater makes a check on the line above the phrase which best describes the person or object rated. The trouble is that most of the checks seem to land in the central category, unless the rater is consistently optimistic or pessimistic. To spread out and stabilize the ratings, the descriptive phrases are made more specific still, even to the extent of listing typical items of behavior.

In another variation of the method the rater may be told to let each of five successive categories represent 20 percent of the college population. Still another attempt to anchor the scale and prevent context effects uses specific individuals or objects known to all raters as anchors for each category. In spite of all these devices, the raters will tend to produce approximately normal distributions of ratings. One cannot always be sure whether this represents a bias in the rater or the fact that most traits are normally distributed. Unfortunately for both psychophysical and psychometric scaling, there is no *external check* or independent evidence of this kind.

Guilford (1938), Attneave (1949), and Garner and Hake (1951) have developed procedures similar to those described above for equal-interval scaling. The same normality assumption is made, but different data are used to start the procedure. For example, the *method of "absolute" judgments,* which involves essentially the same procedure as the *method of single stimuli,* may be used instead of rating. The latter method was proposed by Wever and Zener (1928) and is in turn similar to the method of constant stimuli

(p. 23), except that no standard stimulus is used; instead each comparison stimulus is to be judged in absolute categories appropriate to the attribute being judged, such as "high," "medium," "low," or on the basis of the observer's previous experience. The first comparison stimulus is judged almost at random, but the observer soon adjusts himself to the range of stimuli encountered and uses the categories consistently and in fair correspondence with the stimuli presented. If the experimenter then shifts the range of the stimuli, by removing the lowest and adding some higher tones for example, the observer soon follows suit by readjusting the category values. This latter observation illustrates the context effect which is of interest in studies of judgment, for example by social psychologists, but which is a nuisance in psychophysical scaling.

Helson (1964) relied on the effect of context on judgments as the starting point for developing a psychological relativity theory much more general than the one suggested above in connection with Weber's Law (p. 17). The basic point in Helson's theory is that there are no absolute quantities in psychology as there are, for example, in physics. Psychology is restricted to relative quantities because the effect of any stimulus is related to the *adaptation level* of the organism, which is determined by all past as well as present stimulation. The value of this neutral point is the mean of the stimuli weighted in terms of their hypothetical psychological effect. To determine the physical value corresponding to this mean in a psychophysical experiment, one needs to know the psychophysical function relating response magnitude to stimulus magnitude, and Helson has assumed that a modified Fechnerian Law is correct. Because this is a logarithmic function, the stimulus distribution corresponding to the hypothetical normal response distribution will be geometric, and the geometric mean is the proper measure of central tendency. In the simple case, adaptation level is determined by taking the mean of the logarithmic values of the

comparison stimuli, and this mean is the psychological origin for the observer's scale.

Helson predicts that ratings can be expressed as differences between the adaptation level and the comparison stimuli weighted in terms of their values, which are determined by curve-fitting methods. Assuming that Fechner's Law is valid, it would provide a more general and powerful statement of the theory.

Fechner's Law (see p. 50) may also be written as $R = k \log (S/S_0)$ where S_0 is the value of S at threshold or RL. Helson obtains a modified logarithmic function by substituting the stimulus value corresponding to the adaptation level for that corresponding to RL.

The formula is compact and the actual calculations can be specified more conveniently in a pair of general formulas. Let $S =$ any value of the stimulus. $S_0 =$ that particular value of the stimulus that is selected as the arbitrary origin or zero. Helson uses the adaptation level (AL) or the geometric mean of the comparison stimuli. This would be the logical measure of central tendency in view of the Fechnerian assumption that the sensory effect of stimuli is proportional to the logarithm of their physical intensity. $d =$ the constant stimulus ratio by which each value of S must be multiplied in order to give the value lying one sensation step or unit higher up the scale. That is, $d =$ the Weber fraction plus 1.0. This sensation unit is defined in terms of the observer's responses and could be defined in some other way as, for example, by rating scale values. If $n =$ the number of psychological units from S_0 to S, then

$$S = S_0 d^n$$
$$\log S = \log S_0 + n \log d$$
$$n = \frac{1}{\log d} (\log S - \log S_0)$$

To adapt this general formula for use in any particular sense modality, one needs a well-defined sensation unit, DL or the numerical value of d, and the arbitrary value of the stimulus, S_0 or AL. For example, to locate in the musical scale any assigned vibration frequency, A of 440 cycles may be defined as S_0 and the octave ($d = 2$) as the sensation unit. The last equation then reduces to

$$n = 3.322 \ (\log S - 2.644)$$

If $S = 10,000$ cycles, the equation gives us $n = 4.505$; in other words, the tone of 10,000 cycles is 4.5 psychological units above A (see Michels & Helson, 1949; Helson, 1964, p. 197).

TABLE 3.4 ABSOLUTE JUDGMENTS OF SINGLE STIMULUS

Very very light	1
Very light	2
Light	3
Medium-light	4
Medium	5
Medium-heavy	6
Heavy	7
Very heavy	8
Very very heavy	9

Helson actually uses a rating method instead of one of the classical methods for determining DL and RL. An example of the kind of rating scale for judgments of weights used by Helson is shown in Table 3.4.

After practicing weight lifting, for example, and becoming familiar with these response categories, the observer may be instructed to lift one weight at a time and apply one of the verbal descriptions to it. These rating categories are considered to have the numerical equivalents shown in Table 3.4 that are used by Helson for numerical computation of scale values. This presupposes that the observer uses the verbal rating scale as though the psychological distance between what he calls "very very light" to "very light" (1 to 2) is the same as the distance from "very light" to "light" (3 to 4) and so on. Furthermore, whatever the range of weights that has been presented, it is assumed that the observer will divide it up into nine psychologically equal intervals. In other words, Helson assumes that the rating scale is a manifest equal-interval scale, as compared with the latent equal-

interval scale assumed in Torgerson's Law of Categorical Judgment.

Two related criticisms have been made of the adaptation level theory. The first, as noted previously, is that ratings are unstable measures. Of special interest here is the observation that rating categories, such as those in Table 3.4, are semantically arbitrary, as well as restricted in number (see Campbell, Lewis, & Hunt, 1958). For example, "very large" can be applied independently to both a flea and an elephant without any link to a common psychological dimension. In using this kind of rating scale the observer might bias his judgments by responding in terms of his expectation of the proper use of the categories in the context. Another criticism of Helson's theory involves the Fechnerian function assumed to govern relations between psychological and physical magnitude. Does a rating scale yield psychologically equal intervals? Can the observer judge only relative magnitude, or is he capable of stating in absolute terms the magnitude of a sensation? These are really problems of direct scaling which we shall consider further after the discussion of indirect scaling has been completed.

The Ranking Method

An older name for the ranking method is *Order of Merit*. The observer arranges a number of stimuli or objects in an ordinal series along a given dimension. The same objects then are either ranked many times by the same observers or once by many observers; the mean rank is computed as a psychological scale value for each object. It is a very convenient method for developing (manifest) ordinal scales directly in psychophysical and psychometric studies. Furthermore, it is an easy procedure for the observer except when the number of objects is very large.

Usually the whole set of objects is presented together, and the observer is allowed to proceed as he wishes as long as he comes through with a single rank order along the dimension specified by the experimenter. If many objects are presented, he may be asked to sort them roughly into grades before he attempts the final ranking. The development of the ranking method was mainly the work of Cattell (1903) and Spearman (1904) who made an important contribution by showing how to use rank order in the measurement of correlation.

Cattell used the ranking method to identify the leaders in each natural science on the basis of judgment by their colleagues. For example, he asked 10 psychologists to rank the 200 people (a very large number) in the United States who were considered psychologists at that time. The 10 judges worked separately and independently. Cattell computed the mean of the 10 ranks assigned by the judges to the psychologists and eventually revealed the names in 1933. The 10 highest ranking men and their mean ranks were:

William James	(1.0)
J. McKeen Cattell	(3.7)
Hugo Munsterberg	(4.0)
G. Stanley Hall	(4.4)
J. Mark Baldwin	(7.5)
Edward B. Titchener	(7.5)
Josiah Royce	(7.6)
George T. Ladd	(9.2)
Joseph Jastrow	(11.6)

In the list of psychologists, numbers 2, 3, and 4 were nearly equal; the same is true for the next three men, and so on. Some of the men on the list were philosophers and the "order of merit" would probably be different if established by a contemporary sample of judges. Cattell's original statement (1903) is clear about the significance of such a list:

> It should be distinctly noted that these figures give only what they profess to give, namely, the resultant opinion of ten competent judges. They show the reputation of the men among experts, but not necessarily their ability or performance. Constant errors, such as may arise from a man's being better or less known then he deserves, are not eliminated. There is, however, no other criterion of a man's work than the estimation in which it is held by those competent to judge.

Why are the mean ranks so close together for the 10 top people listed above? Suppose a group of observers were asked to rank 10 weights differing very noticeably from each other. The chances are good that every observer would rank them in the same order and that the mean ranks would be simply 1, 2, 3, ..., 10. However, if one tried the same experiment with 10 equal weights, the chances are each observer would rank them in a different order, and the mean ranks would all be nearly the same. Finally, let the weights differ by small amounts so that every observer would be likely to make a few errors. The results would lie between the two extremes mentioned, that is, not perfectly ordered according to weight but closely correlated with it. The principle here is that, given competent judges, the mean ranks probably will agree with both the order and the spacing of the objects. In addition, it is possible, of course, to measure the amount of disagreement among the judges (see Siegel, 1956; Hayes, 1963). As a result it can be shown once more that, given variability in the judgments, the same kind of scale can be derived from ranking as from pair comparison by converting rank orders to choice frequencies and then to p values and finally to z scores.

If a judge ranks a certain object No. 1, he obviously prefers it to the others. If he ranks it No. 2, he prefers it to the remaining, and so on. In this manner each rank (r) can be converted into a choice score (c). In general, with n objects, $c = n - r$, and because this equation holds for all the ranks assigned by the judges to the same object, it holds for the mean choice score (M_c) and the mean rank (M_r) of that object. Therefore,

$$M_c = n - M_r$$

The values of M_r are converted into p values according to the formula

$$p = \frac{M_c}{n - 1}$$

TABLE 3.5   RANKS REDUCED TO CHOICE SCORES AND z SCORES

	Astronomers									
	A	B	C	D	E	F	G	H	I	J
Judges										
1	1	2	4	3	9	6	5	8	7	10
2	1	4	2	5	6	7	3	10	8	9
3	1	3	4	5	2	8	9	6	10	7
4	1	3	4	5	2	6	10	8	7	9
5	1	9	2	5	6	3	4	8	10	7
6	1	4	9	2	5	6	7	3	10	8
7	1	3	5	10	2	6	9	7	8	4
8	1	3	5	7	6	4	8	10	2	9
9	1	2	8	4	9	6	3	7	5	10
10	1	2	4	5	9	8	6	3	7	10
Sum of ranks	10	35	47	51	56	60	64	70	74	83
M_r	1.0	3.5	4.7	5.1	5.6	6.0	6.4	7.0	7.4	8.3
$M_c = n - M_r$	9.0	6.5	5.3	4.9	4.4	4.0	3.6	3.0	2.6	1.7
$p = M_c/(n-1)$	1.00	.72	.59	.54	.49	.44	.40	.33	.29	.19
z	?	+.58	+.23	+.10	−.03	−.15	−.25	−.44	−.55	−.88
$R = 5z + 6$		8.90	7.15	6.50	5.85	5.25	4.75	3.80	3.25	1.60

The following are used as checks: the average M_r must $= (n + 1)/2$; the average M_c must $= (n - 1)/2$; the average p must $= 1/2$.

That is, if there are 10 objects in the set, each is compared with the remaining 9. There

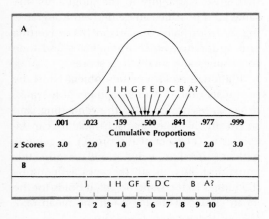

Figure 3.8. *Top.* Psychological scale values (cumulative proportions) for astronomers based on rank ordering of their eminence and an illustration of the assumption of the normal distribution of the psychological distances between them (z scores). *Bottom.* Linearly transformed z scores from data above, with the formula $y = ax + b$, where y is the desired scale value and x the z score. The scale shown here was obtained with $a = 5$ and $b = 6$. See also Table 3.6.

are certain checks on these computations, as is indicated in Table 3.5. The data are taken from Cattell's 1906 study of the 10 leading astronomers of that time; these data were used also in the first edition of this book (p. 373).

The p values have been converted into z scores using Table 3.5. These z scores represent scale values for the astronomers on a psychological scale with equal intervals on the assumption that the rankings are normally distributed, as is illustrated in Figure 3.8A. The reasoning here follows the same general theory discussed in connection with obtaining interval scales from pair comparisons or ratings (also see Guilford, 1954). Unfortunately, astronomer A was invariably ranked No. 1, which means that the scale value for him cannot be determined, which is a limitation of indirect methods.

There must be less than perfect agreement among the judges to obtain an equal-interval scale. The size of the arbitrary unit may be changed, and the negative values may be eliminated by arbitrarily multiplying the z scores by a constant value and then adding a constant, respectively. In the present example $R = 5z + 6$ as is shown in Figure 3.8B. It must be borne in mind that these are at best interval data and that they limit our interpretation to differences between the scale values, for absolute values have no meaning on this scale. Just adding a constant would be enough (see Table 3.3).

Of course, one might object to scale values on the basis that the empirical (manifest) data are merely ordinal numbers, because the judge says nothing about the spacing or distance between them on a psychological interval scale. Yet the theory claims that mean ranks represent something more than ordinal scale positions. One sample of data from an individual judge reflects nothing about the spacing of the objects, for although some may be close together and others far apart, the observer has been asked only to arrange them so that each object has more of a particular quality than those ranked below it. However, mean ranks are not the output of a single judge but of a group of judges. Although the single individual is limited to the ordinal numbers, the group may have a finer (latent) fractional scale of mean ranks at its disposal.

A basic point claimed to support the theory proposed above is that the frequencies of objective (physical) measures of an attribute of different individuals, for example, height measured in inches, are normally distributed, and z scores therefore mark off equal distances on the physical dimension above and below the value corresponding to the mean. It is assumed that the psychological attributes, for example, preferences, would also be normally distributed if they could be measured objectively. A normal distribution of judgments along an arbitrary (subjective) dimension is taken as consistent with this assumption and presumptive evidence supporting the use of z scores as measures on the psychological continuum.

On this basis mean ranks are converted and handled as proportions are handled in the methods of pair comparison and constant stimuli. Even the method of constant stimuli, where the stimuli are measured objectively, relies on the psychological data of ordinal numbers because each comparison stimulus is only judged larger or smaller than the standard stimulus rather than *how much* larger or smaller. If one comparison stimulus is judged larger than the standard 60 percent of the time, while another is judged larger 90 percent of the time, the latter lies above the standard on the psychological continuum by a distance defined in terms of the relationship between z scores and proportions under the normal curve. Thus, this whole group of methods is based on an assumed normal distribution, and the statement of the normality assumption takes different forms depending on the observer's task. The response, whether it be a statement of preference or intensity of sensation, is only considered to be an indirect index of a mechanism mediating between these hypothetical psychological quantities and the stimuli. Guttman's *scalogram analysis* (1950) and Coombs's *unfolding technique* (1964) are methods which emphasize the internal consistency of the judges in ordering the objects in a more direct evaluation of the numerical properties of the scale. Coombs's book, *A Theory of Data,* should be consulted for further study of this topic.

In any case, many investigators are willing to make stronger (equal-interval) assumptions regarding a hypothetical psychological dimension than they are regarding the observer's ability to describe his preference or sensation. They prefer to obtain the equal intervals indirectly or theoretically in the tradition established by Fechner and rationalized by Thurstone. Direct scaling, on the other hand, involves methods which ask the observer for more than ordinal judgments.

DIRECT SCALING

Direct scaling refers to methods for obtaining direct judgments of psychological quantities on an interval or ratio scale. The methods described under the section above on indirect scaling, for example, rank ordering, are direct methods of obtaining psychological ordinal scales and indirect methods of obtaining equal-interval scales. This distinction entails the so-called "latent" versus "manifest" numerical properties of the data. In direct scaling methods the quantitative property desired is stated in the instructions the experimenter gives the observer at the beginning of the experiment, for example, "I want you to tell me for each comparison light *how much* brighter or dimmer it looks than the standard light." Another reason for describing them as direct methods is that the step between the raw data and the final scale is as short as possible. There is really only one assumption involved, namely, that the observer is able to describe his observations at the quantitative level demanded by the instructions. Presumably therefore the data obtained are such that, unlike those obtained with the indirect methods, they need not be supplemented by further theoretical assumptions in order to construct a scale from them.

Operationally the indirect scales may be defined as *confusion scales* (equal intervals obtained from proportions), and direct scales may be defined as *partition scales* (equal intervals based on direct judgment of intervals), or *magnitude scales* (ratio scales based on direct judgment of ratios). Using direct scaling methods, which yield partition scales or magnitude scales, one can distinguish between *estimation methods,* in which the experimenter manipulates the stimuli and the observer judges them, and *production methods,* where the observer manipulates the stimuli so that they reflect a defined subjective relation.

Partition scales involve procedures where the observer works with subjective intervals. These scales are often called *category scales* because the observer works with numerical categories. They should not be confused with rating scales because the instruction given the observer is different—although it is not always clear that the outcome is different.

To use the *category estimation method,*

also called the method of equal-appearing intervals, the observer is usually given one low and one high stimulus as anchors to define the ends of the psychological continuum. The anchors may be included among the comparison stimuli, but usually they are not. Preventing the observer from using a higher or lower category in the event he judges some stimuli more extreme than the anchors, tends to produce skewed response distributions at the extremes of the category scales. The following instructions were used in one study of scaling odor pleasantness (Engen & McBurney, 1964):

> We should like you to judge the pleasantness of odor. The odors will be presented in a random order. In each case your task is to place the odor on a scale by assigning it a whole number. Here is an odor most people find very unpleasant (pyridine). We shall call the odor 2. Here is an odor most people find very pleasant (safrole). We call that 8. The odors we will present next will probably lie somewhere between these two odors in degrees of pleasantness—your task is to assign it a whole number which reflects this degree. Smell number 2 and 8 again and try to remember their relative pleasantness. If you should find an odor even less pleasant than

TABLE 3.6 CATEGORY ESTIMATION SCALE VALUES FOR PLEASANTNESS OF ODORANTS

S (Odorant)	R (Mean judgment)
Safrole	8.0 (as anchor)
Ambre	7.7
Anethol	7.2
Iso-amyl acetate	6.9
Rose double	6.4
Benzaldehyde	6.2
Jasmin	6.0
Citronellol	5.4
Flavor arome chocolate	5.1
Oil of camphor	4.8
Ethyl acetate	4.2
Essence cardamone	4.1
N-Caprylic acid	4.0
Guaiacol	3.7
Heptanal	2.9
Asafoetida	2.8
Pyridine	2.0 (as anchor)
Iso-butyric acid	1.8

number 2, call it 1. And if you should find an odor even more pleasant than number 8 call it 9.

The anchors had been selected as extreme on the basis of preliminary work but were not identified as such or by name to the observer. Many of the 20 observers used in the present experiment actually used both categories 1 and 9. Categories 2 and 8 rather than 1 and 9 were defined in an attempt to avoid the so-called "end effect." This effect refers to the skew of judgmental distributions of stimuli at the extremes of the continuum (Guilford & Dingman, 1955).

The category scale values are obtained by determining the central tendency of the judgments for each stimulus (see Stevens, 1955). The results shown in Table 3.6 are based on the mean. (Note that these scale values depend on the samples of compounds used, and that pleasantness depends on concentration. The present concentrations were matched for psychological intensity, but no attempt was made to maximize the pleasantness or unpleasantness of each odor.)

Except for the instructions, the category estimation method is operationally very similar to the rating scale method discussed above, and it is subject to the same problems noted in that connection and in relation to Helson's work (see p. 59). A particularly important problem is that the observer's results might be influenced by his *expectation* that all the numerical categories should be used equally often regardless of the actual distribution of stimulus values presented. It would have dramatic effects on the form of the psychophysical function if, for example, category scale values for heaviness are plotted as a function of the stimulus weights in grams. (See Johnson, 1944, for a similar experiment.)

Stevens and Galanter (1957) have suggested an *iterative procedure* for eliminating response bias. Their prescription for a "pure" category scale is as follows:

We will assume that the observer expects the series of stimuli to be so arranged that all categories appear equally often. Since at the outset we know nothing about the form of the observer's category scale, we present to the first group of observers a series of stimuli spaced in some arbitrary manner along the continuum. The results of this test give us a first approximation to the category scale. For the second group of observers we space the stimuli so that they reflect equal intervals on the scale obtained from the first group of observers. This is a new curve—a second approximation to the "pure" scale. Using this better approximation we respace the stimuli and repeat the procedure with a third group of observers. We repeat this process until stability is reached, i.e., until the results of a test are such that no further changes in spacing are called for.

With enough homogeneous groups of observers, this iterative procedure could in principle reveal the unadulterated form of the category scale—the form in which the effects of expectation have been neutralized, and discrimination is the only first-order factor left to interact with the observer's intent. (p. 381)

This would eliminate the effect of expectation on the rating scale, but whether it would reveal a valid psychophysical law is still debatable, as will be seen when we compare the results from various direct scaling methods.

The category production method is a much older procedure known as the method of equal sense distances for direct interval scaling and is in a sense estimation in reverse. The observer is now instructed to adjust a continuously variable stimulus, or select one value from a range presented in small steps, to correspond with category scale values of 1, 2, 3, and so on. There are a number of variations of this method but the observer's task is always to adjust or select stimuli so that they mark off subjectively equal distances. *Bisection* was already used by Plateau in the 1850s (see Titchener, 1905, II, ii, pp. 210–214; Boring, 1942). Plateau had eight artists mix a gray which was midway between white and black, so that there was as great a psychological distance between the white and gray as between the gray and black. Plateau's purpose was to test Fechner's logarithmic law, which predicts that the midpoint selected by the artists should correspond to the geometric mean rather than the arithmetic mean. Plateau's results did not verify Fechner's Law.

Instead Plateau found that the relative reflectance of the gray (see Chapter 9) remained approximately constant even with change in illumination. On the basis of these results Plateau suggested that visual brightness grows as the cubic root of the photometric intensity of the stimuli, or $R = cS^{1/3}$ where R is sensation intensity, c a constant, and S the photometric value of the stimulus. This appears to be the first mention of a power function, that is, that sensation intensity is a function of stimulus intensity raised to a power. Plateau's contribution was buried in the methodological and semantic arguments typical of classical psychophysics (see Titchener, 1905, II), but it has been revived as the main alternative to Fechner's Law in contemporary psychophysics.

There is no reason to limit judgments to

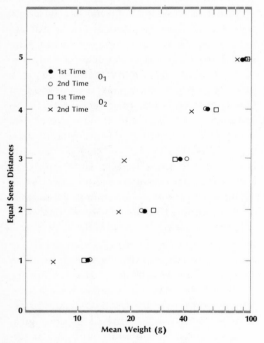

Figure 3.9. Data from an experiment by Titchener (1905). Mean weight in grams assigned to each of five categories representing equal sense distances. It appears that a straight line would describe these data well. Because the coordinate system is semilogarithmic this is consistent with Fechner's law.

bisection, for one can break up a subjective distance into as many equal intervals as desired. This variation of category production also has a long history and is known as the method of *equal-appearing intervals*. In a weight experiment recommended by Sanford for the experimental psychology course of an earlier day (Titchener, 1905, I, p. 33; II, p. 82) the observer was instructed to sort 108 envelopes, ranging in weight from 5 to 100 g, into five piles while keeping the "sense distances" between the piles equal. The average weight placed in each category then defines the psychological scale value of each pile. According to Fechner's Law, if the equal sense distances are plotted against the logarithmic value of these mean weights, one should obtain a linear function. According to Titchener (1905, II, p. 82) results plotted in Figure 3.9 are typical of results obtained from "entirely unpracticed observers." The functions appear linear and represent the kind of results which kept Fechner's Law alive, and for this reason there is still great interest in category scaling in contemporary psychophysics.

However, there is a serious problem with category scaling, namely the problem of the sorter's expectation, which was mentioned above. The distribution of Sanford's weights could also easily have set the stage for this kind of bias. For example, the 26 smallest weights differed from each other by only 0.2 g, whereas the heaviest 25 differed in 2 g steps. In commenting about the data plotted in Figure 3.9 Titchener states that

> . . . the choice of differences recommended by Sanford brings with it a source of error. There is a marked tendency, as well with the observers who are ignorant of the purposes of the experiment, as with those who knew it, to make the piles equal, if possible. Many of the envelopes are so weighted that it is difficult to decide whether they shall be assigned, e.g., to pile 2 or pile 3. Almost invariably, the observer will tend to put them on the pile which contains the smaller number of envelopes. The error cannot be eliminated; it may, in some degree, be counteracted by requiring the observer to revise his first grouping before the measurements are made. The requirement suggests that the in-

structor does not like the look of the piles, as they stand, and so leads to a more objective estimation of the weight of the envelopes.

In other words, the results might have been influenced as much by limiting the observer to a small number of response categories as by the law governing the relation between sensory magnitude and stimulus magnitude. This difficulty was not peculiar to the present method; it is a common problem of response bias. Later, as we have seen, Stevens and Galanter (p. 65) suggested that despite Titchener's pessimism the response bias due to expectancy can be eliminated. In any case, this kind of data and the electrophysiological recording data mentioned below (p. 81) constitute the support for Fechner's Law, which continues to be cited and therefore demands explanation.

There has been a tendency in psychophysics since about the 1950s to develop more and more direct methods in an attempt to maximize the possible variation in the response. The most direct of all would of course be to ask the observer to match numbers to his sensation and eliminate all categories, orderings, or comparisons. This approach to scaling usually requires the observer to make ratio judgments, on the assumption that he is capable of such sophisticated performance.

Direct scaling was derived from production methods which, as is noted above, may only be used when the stimuli can be varied continuously or in very small steps. In direct scaling, the observer is instructed to adjust or select stimuli so that they stand in a prescribed subjective relation to a standard stimulus. One can eliminate the standard and instruct the observer to produce a stimulus which corresponds to various (subjective) numerical values. For example, Ekman, Eisler, and Künnapas (1960) required observers to adjust the visual brightness of a light so that it would correspond to 4, 6, 8, 12, 14, or 16, with a standard designated as 10, and plotted these numbers as a function of the average physical intensity chosen by the observers.

However, the more common method has been *fractionation,* typically halving, with occasional determination of internal consistency of the judgments by doubling. This method received little attention until the 1930s when Stevens (1936) pointed out its value for building a ratio scale for loudness, the well-known *sone scale.* This early work was very successful, and for some time the fractionation method was considered the fundamental method for scaling subjective magnitude. The sone scale was followed by the *mel scale* for pitch (Stevens & Volkmann, 1940), the *veg scale* for heaviness (Harper & Stevens, 1948), the *bril scale* for visual brightness (Hanes, 1949a and b), and others. Some data from an experiment in halving heaviness (Engen & Tulunay, 1956) will be used as an illustration of how psychological scale values are developed.

Thirty-two observers (elementary psychology students) were divided at random into four groups and asked to lift weights, cylinders containing shot, from behind a screen so that the observer could not see them. Each group had a different standard stimulus, 150, 300, 550, or 900 g. The following instructions were given:

> You will be given a container which you will lift with your preferred hand—like this. You will first be given the standard weight. Then you will be given another container which will feel either more or less than half as heavy as the standard. What I want you to do is to tell me to add more weight or to subtract some from this weight until it feels half as heavy as the standard. You may subtract or add to the comparison weight as often as you want before you make your final half-heaviness judgment. We will repeat the procedure several times.

TABLE 3.7 STANDARD WEIGHTS AND MEAN HALF-HEAVINESS VALUES SELECTED BY 8 OBSERVERS

S	$S_{1/2}$
900 g	541.6 g
550 g	325.3 g
300 g	159.0 g
150 g	93.5 g

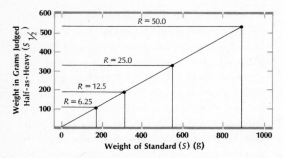

Figure 3.10. Mean half-heaviness judgments in grams plotted as a function of the weight of the standards in grams. The graph illustrates the determination of psychological (*R*) values by interpolation by defining arbitrarily *R* = 100 when *S* = 900 g on an *S-S* relation.

The experimenter used a measuring spoon to add and subtract an amount of shot which varied from more than 1 percent to less than 10 percent of the standard weight. Each observer made eight half-heaviness judgments in counter-balanced ascending and descending trials. The weights judged half as heavy ($S_{1/2}$) as each of the standards (*S*) are shown in Table 3.7, and these average half-heaviness values have been plotted in Figure 3.10 as the first step in obtaining psychological values.

Figure 3.10 shows a linear fit which simplifies the problems of curve fitting (see Harper & Stevens, 1948, and Ekman, 1958, 1961). This is, of course, only a stimulus-stimulus function and not a psychophysical function. The next step is to arbitrarily select a starting point. The highest standard, 900 g, is defined as corresponding to a response value of 100. The response value of 50 will therefore correspond to 541.6 which was judged half as heavy as 900 g. These values have been entered in Table

TABLE 3.8

R	S
100	900 g
50	542 g
25	320 g
12.5	185 g
6.25	110 g

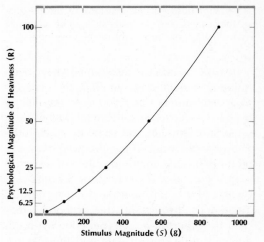

Figure 3.11. Psychological magnitude (*R*) obtained by interpolation in Figure 3.10 as a function of stimulus magnitude (*S*) in grams.

3.8 (rounded to the nearest integers, which is precise enough for the present purpose). From now on one must interpolate on the data

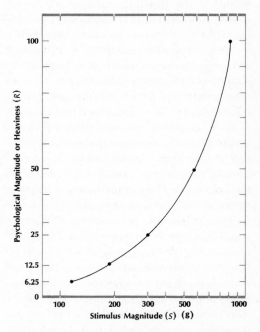

Figure 3.12. Data in Figure 3.11 replotted in semilogarithmic coordinates, that is, psychological (*R*) values as a function of the stimulus magnitude (*S*) on a logarithmic scale.

plotted in Figure 3.10 to determine other pairs of stimulus and response values. Therefore, 542 g (for which $R = 50$) is located on the abscissa and used to find its corresponding response value on the ordinate, namely, 320 g, which corresponds to the response value of 25. *Half of 25 is 12.5 and thus with 320 g, 185 g is located in Figure 3.10.* One proceeds in this manner toward the lower left corner of Figure 3.10 without going too far beyond actual data points.

The data for the positively accelerated psychophysical function plotted in Figure 3.11 were obtained with this procedure. In accordance with Fechner's Law, psychological magnitude should be a linear function of the physical values of stimuli plotted on a logarithmic scale. Data plotted on such coordinates, however, turn out not to be linear. As shown in Figure 3.12, for example, such data are curved even more upwards— and do not confirm Fechner's Law.

Stevens' Power Law

The present results are in agreement with the veg scale and other results obtained from direct scaling mentioned above. It is clear that in ratio production the observer does not behave as though logarithmic steps are psychologically equal. The fact that Figure 3.10 shows that $S_{1/2}$ is a linear function of S suggests a constancy in the ratios of stimuli judged to be in the subjective relation of 2:1 and that physically equal ratios are psychologically equal. The ratios of the obtained values in Table 3.7 are actually very similar; for example, 900/541.6 is almost identical to 541.6/325.3. This is in agreement with the power law proposed by Stevens that equal physical ratios are psychologically equal (Stevens, 1957). According to Fechner's Law the stimuli should be converted to logarithms in order to provide equal distances on a psychological interval scale and thus produce a linear function in semilogarithmic coordinates.

To test the power law in the manner described above, the stimulus values are con-

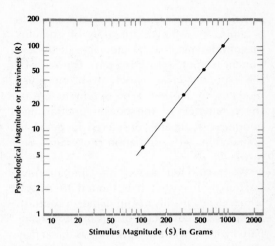

Figure 3.13. Data in Figure 3.12 replotted in double logarithmic coordinates, that is, psychological magnitudes in logarithmic steps as a function of stimulus magnitude in logarithmic steps.

verted to logarithms in order to mark off equal stimulus ratios, but because equal physical ratios should be psychologically equal, one should also mark off the psychological continuum on the ordinate in logarithmic steps in order to obtain a linear plot of the psychophysical function. Thus the arithmetic spacing of our ordinate in Figure 3.11 is converted to logarithmic spacing and we obtain the results shown in Figure 3.13. The latter is obviously a linear function of the form $y = ax + b$ where x and y are logarithmic values of the stimuli and responses. As determined by the method of least squares the line drawn through the data, shown in Figure 3.13, can be stated as

$$\log R = 1.33 \log S - 2.10$$

The line shown will intercept the ordinate at a value (-2.10), which depends on the arbitrary starting point of 100 for the psychological values. The slope of the function (1.33) is the interesting parameter which indicates how heaviness varies as a function of weight. Note that the goodness of the fit of the straight line drawn in Figure 3.13 cannot be evaluated because the values of R were derived from Figure 3.10, which implied a power function. However, psychological magnitude is typically a power function of stimulus magnitude specified by the value of the exponent (slope) in a log-log plot. The value of the exponent varies widely from one sense modality to another. (The determination of the parameters of the power function and goodness of fit are considered in detail in connection with estimation procedures below.)

As mentioned above, one limitation of fractionation is that it is limited to stimuli which can be readily manipulated. In contrast, one possible advantage of this method, compared with other direct methods, is that it may simplify the task of the observer by limiting him to one ratio, and it can readily be checked by plotting halving judgments against doubling judgments on reversed co-ordinates (see Torgerson, 1958). The main problem with the method seems to involve the danger that the observer's selection of a half-value may be determined by the stimulus context and not the sensory system. For example, Garner (1954) questioned the validity of fractionation judgments because his unpracticed observers made half-loudness judgments that seemed to depend entirely on the range of comparison stimuli presented. With the same standard (90 dB) but with different ranges of comparison stimuli (55–65, 65–75, 75–85 dB) three different groups produced half-loudness values which corresponded closely to the midpoint of the range of comparison stimuli, that is, approximately 60, 70, and 80 dB. However, to the contrary, Stevens and Poulton (1956) argue that Garner's conclusions are of limited generality because he *restricted* the observer to fixed comparison stimuli. In other words, Garner used a method that is analogous to the method of constant stimuli rather than adjustment and that deliberately limits variation of response— contrary to the spirit of direct scaling. By allowing the observer to adjust the loudness of a comparison tone himself, Stevens and Poulton obtained results in agreement with the sone scale.

In other experiments it has also been shown that by allowing the observer to adjust the comparison stimulus himself the effect of context is reduced, which may be inevitable with fixed comparison stimuli. Even when the observer makes the adjustments, context effects analogous to "anticipation error" (see p. 15) may be observed. In the weight-lifting experiment described in Table 3.7 the observers tended to select a lower half-heaviness value in the relatively light stimulus context of an ascending series than in the relatively heavy stimulus context of a descending trial. However, practiced psychophysical observers (for example, graduate students in psychology) are decidedly less affected by context than are inexperienced ones (see Engen & Tulunay, 1956).

The fact that psychological scaling rarely works perfectly is often taken as evidence against the validity of psychological scales in general. It seems more probable, however, that such imperfections simply reflect the effect of specific factors in the experimental situation, such as the biases noted, or difficulties in imagining a specific fraction like $\frac{1}{2}$ in specific situations. Hanes (1949a, b) found $\frac{3}{4}$ particularly bad to use in scaling brightness.

It is perhaps more appropriate to conclude that sensory scales based on fractionation are somewhat crude, like the folded paper rule described above, but that the concept of sones, mels, brils, and so on is basically sound. The problem is to eliminate the factors which distort or invalidate the scales; this can best be done by using the most appropriate methods and preferably with a variety of different methods. The restriction of the observer to one ratio is apparently not the best general approach. For example, it became evident during a fractionation experiment ($\frac{1}{2}$) in olfaction (Engen, 1961) that the subjective range of odor intensity is relatively short. The method had been selected because of its successful application in audition and vision, but in olfaction the observers were unable to produce internally consistent half-intensity judgments with different standards, although a wide range of concentrations was provided. Scaling, using estimation methods, indicated that the reason for the problem was that the whole subjective range is only about two or three to one for these odorants. In other words, for many of the standards of lower concentration value, the determination of half-intensity was an unreasonably difficult task. For this and other reasons estimation methods are generally preferred over production methods in direct scaling.

The method for ratio estimation was first suggested by Metfessel (1947), and a procedure for treating the data by Comrey (1950), under the name of the *constant-sum method*. The most popular variation of this method was developed by Ekman (1958). The data analysis suggested by Torgerson (1958) is presented here. Metfessel suggested that the observer be instructed to make "a direct estimate of the ratio between psychological magnitudes" corresponding to each of the

$n(n - 1)$ pairs of stimuli in a set by dividing 100 points between the members of each pair. For example, a division of 75 to 25 would indicate that one member of the pair had three times more of the psychological attribute than the other member. However, division of points makes it difficult for the observer to report large ratios as accurately as small ratios. For example, 94 to 6, 95 to 5, and 96 to 4 correspond to ratios of 15.67:1, 19:1, and 24:1, while 54 to 46, 55 to 45, and 56 to 44 correspond to ratios of 1.17:1, 1.22:1 and 1.27:1 respectively. Ekman's variation of this method reduces this difficulty of judgment by allowing the observer to report the ratio directly as a percentage, for example, "The second weight appears 75 percent as heavy as the first one." This method follows a procedure very similar to that for pair comparison and is subject to some of its advantages and disadvantages. For example, not too many stimuli can be compared in one session; for $n(n - 1)$

TABLE 3.9

Matrix A. Mean ratio estimates of apparent length of pairs of lines are listed above the diagonal and their reciprocals below the diagonal.[a]

Length in inches

	3.00	4.00	6.00	9.00	12.00
3.00		.756	.531	.326	.240
4.00	1.323		.717	.445	.328
6.00	1.884	1.455		.669	.527
9.00	3.069	2.249	1.495		.775
12.00	4.162	3.044	1.893	1.291	

[a] Engen, T., Unpublished data.

Matrix B. Determination of scale values from logarithmic values of the ratio estimates in Matrix A.

Length in inches

	3.00	4.00	6.00	9.00	12.00	Σ	Mean	Antilog of Mean
3.00		−.121	−.274	−.487	−.619	−1.501	−.375	.42
4.00	.121		−.164	−.352	−.483	− .878	−.220	.60
6.00	.274	.164		−.176	−.276	− .014	−.004	.99
9.00	.487	.352	.176		−.111	+ .901	+.226	1.68
12.00	.619	.483	.276	.111		+1.489	+.376	2.36
						00*		

*Check the values in the matrix. They should add to zero.

grows geometrically with n. In contrast, it is a very flexible method, and overlapping ranges can be used to advantage. According to Ekman, "It is possible to obtain two separate scales for stimuli, whether identical or not, which are compared under two different conditions. The two groups may include stimuli presented simultaneously to various parts of the body—weights lifted by the right hand and left hand or pain stimuli applied to one normal and one anesthetized area" (Ekman, 1958, p. 291). Guilford and Dingman (1954) obtained the same results in ratio estimation and fractionation for weights judged to be in ratio of 2/1.

Data from a simple unpublished experiment in judging apparent length of lines with this method are presented in Table 3.9. Pairs of lines were presented horizontally with one line 3 inches above the other but not aligned at the ends. The observer sat 7 feet from the screen and viewed the lines at eye-level. The instructions were as follows:

> Each of a series of slides will project two lines of various lengths just like this one [Example]. In each case tell me which is the longer of the two lines and then report the apparent length of the shorter as a percentage of the longer one. For example, if it is half as long, say 50. Use any number you feel is appropriate and be as accurate as you can. Any questions?

The results are shown in Table 3.9, which shows the mean judgments for a group of observers each of whom judged the 10 pairs of lines twice. The experimentally obtained ratio estimates are presented as proportions above the diagonal in matrix A. The cells in the diagonal are empty because identical pairs were not used. The reciprocals are entered below the diagonal. Following Torgerson's procedure (1958) for computing scale values, the values in matrix A are converted to logarithms, which are entered in matrix B, for equal logarithmic differences correspond to equal ratios. Psychological values are then obtained by computing the mean of each row of matrix B and converting to the antilogarithm of this mean. The psychological scale

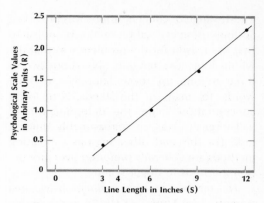

Figure 3.14. Psychological scale values for apparent length (R) obtained by the method of ratio estimation plotted as a function of the length of lines (S) in inches.

value for each stimulus therefore is the geometric mean of the response to each stimulus in comparison with each of the other stimuli in the set. (Note that if identical pairs were used, their ratios would be 1.00, the logarithm of which is 0.) The psychophysical function obtained when these scale values are plotted as a function of the physical values of the stimuli is shown in Figure 3.14. The unit of the

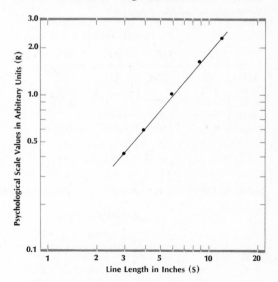

Figure 3.15. Data in Figure 3.14 replotted in double logarithmic coordinates, that is, psychological magnitude in logarithmic steps as a function of line length in logarithmic steps.

psychological scale is arbitrary, and one can multiply the scale values with a constant to obtain any convenient range or magnitude of numbers. However, the actual subjective unit used by each observer is not and cannot be known. This problem will be discussed further in connection with magnitude estimation.

Because the function is linear in arithmetic coordinates, it is obvious that the present psychophysical function does not conform to Fechner's Law, which would require that the function in Figure 3.14 be curved concavely downward or be linear in a semilogarithmic plot. If the data are plotted in such a coordinate system, the function will in fact look like the one in Figure 3.12. Transformation of both axes to logarithmic values in Figure 3.15 results in a linear plot, as required by Stevens' Power Law. Reese et al. (1953) obtained very similar data with the method of fractionation.

The main problem with ratio estimation is that psychophysically naive observers may tend to use a constant range of numbers regardless of the range of stimulus values presented. The results of Table 3.9 illustrate this problem. The psychophysical function obtained has a slope (exponent) greater than 1.00, indicating that the apparent length increases faster than the physical length. Table 3.9 covers a relatively short stimulus range. With a very long range of stimuli, or very large ratios, the results would probably have shown a slope less than unity because of the tendency of the observer to use a constant range of numbers. One can counteract this tendency by training and experience (see Engen & Levy, 1958) or by making the observer's task even more direct.

The Method of Magnitude Estimation

The most direct approach of all would be to ask the observer to match a number directly to the perceived magnitude of each stimulus and eliminate all intervening categories, orderings, comparisons, and theories about the same. This is done in magnitude estimation. Although the so-called "method of sense-ratios" may be traced to Merkel around

1890 (Titchener, 1905, II), the chief contributions to such methodology have been made since the 1950s. As Stevens puts it, "It all started from a friendly argument with a colleague who said, 'You seem to maintain that each loudness has a number and that if someone sounded a tone I should be able to tell him the number.' I replied, 'That's an interesting idea. Let's try it'" (Stevens, 1956, p. 2).

As mentioned above, the basic assumption of direct scaling is that the observer is able to match numbers to his perceptions. The direct methods discussed so far have restricted him to equal intervals, ratios, and pair comparisons, but in magnitude estimation one attempts to avoid all restrictions and encourage the observer to assign the numbers *he* feels are appropriate without any of the biases which may be associated with a response system devised by the experimenter—as has been illustrated amply in this and the previous chapter. Any defined attribute of any set of stimuli may be scaled; for example, visual brightness, intensity of odors, the saltiness of solutions, or the beauty of works of art. It is not a requirement that a corresponding physical continuum be known, although this is necessary in studying the form of the psychophysical law. Usually a fixed set of suprathreshold stimuli covering a wide range of a certain attribute is presented to the observer.

There are two forms of the method. When it was first used it was typical for the experimenter to present the observer with a standard stimulus first and define the subjective value of that as the observer's *modulus*. For example, he might present a weight and tell the observer that it corresponded to a psychological value of 10 and that his task was to judge each of the other weights (presented in an irregular order) in relation to that value. In an experiment on the intensity of odors the observers were given the following instructions, which will define the task in a magnitude estimation experiment with a modulus:

We want you to estimate the intensity of odors. This stimulus defines the standard intensity. The other odors will be presented in an irregular order. They will all be the same quality of smell but the strength will vary.

Call the standard odor before you 10. Your task is then to estimate the intensity or strength of each of the other odors in relation to the standard odor. In other words, the question is: The standard is called 10, what will you call the comparison odor?

Use whatever numbers seem appropriate to you—fractions or whole numbers. For example, if the comparison stimulus smells 7 times as strong as the standard, say 70. If it smells one-fifth as strong, say 2; if a twentieth, say 0.5, etc.

There is no right or wrong answer. We want to know how *you* judge the intensity of odors. Any questions?

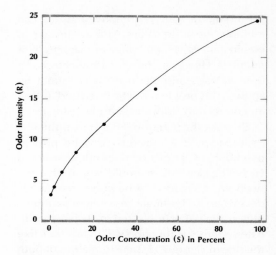

Figure 3.16. Odor intensity (R) obtained by the method of magnitude estimation as a function of the concentration of amyl acetate (S).

TABLE 3.10 GEOMETRIC MEANS (PSYCHOLOGICAL SCALE VALUES) OF 8 CONCENTRATIONS OF AMYL ACETATE DILUTED IN DIETHYL PHTHALATE.[a]

Response value (geometric mean)	Stimulus (concentration)
2.86	1.56
3.81	3.12
5.74	6.25
8.19	12.50
11.57	25.00
15.92	50.00
24.67	100.

[a]The observer was told to assign a scale value of 10 to the modular concentration of 12.5 percent.

Twelve observers were presented each of 7 concentrations twice. The concentration values of the stimuli, obtained by diluting 100 percent amyl acetate in diethyl phthalate, and the geometric means of the observers' judgments are presented in Table 3.10.

One reason for calling the methods "direct" is that there is but a short step between the raw data and the final scale. In this case the step consists of computing the *central tendency judgment* for a group of observers. The appropriate central tendency is usually the geometric mean or the median because occasionally a few unusually high numbers are obtained. For example, while most of the observers described the

weakest stimulus with numbers between 1 and 5, two observers called it 10. In addition, theoretically the distributions of judgments may be assumed to be log normal for reasons discussed further below. (Note also that the value of the standard stimulus was included in the series of comparison stimuli, but it obtained a scale value of less than 10 for

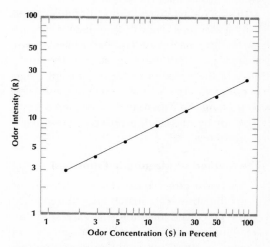

Figure 3.17. Data in Figure 3.16 replotted in double logarithmic coordinates, that is, another so-called "log-log" plot of odor intensity versus odorant concentration.

reasons which will not be considered here.) The data are plotted in linear coordinates, as shown in Figure 3.16, which shows that odor intensity is one of many psychophysical functions exhibiting a negatively accelerated form. Some functions of this kind are linear, and some yield positively accelerated functions in linear coordinates like the one for weight in Figure 3.11 above. This means that in log-log coordinates the slopes (exponents) of many psychophysical functions are less than 1.00, such as for the present data which are replotted in log-log coordinates in Figure 3.17. In other words, all psychological continua scaled by such direct methods seem to be power functions of their respective stimulus continua, and usually stimulus magnitude increases faster than response magnitude.

The main shortcoming of the method of magnitude estimation with a prescribed modulus is that the slope is somewhat influenced by the choice of standard. The highest slope is likely to be obtained for standards in the middle of the series of comparison stimuli, but it decreases as the standard is moved toward either extreme. For example, scaling the odor intensity of the same concentrations as in Table 3.7 using standards of 3.25, 12.5, (as in the present case), and 50 percent concentrations gave the results shown in Figure

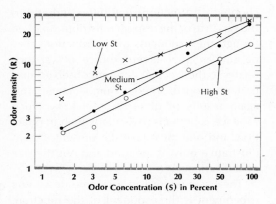

Figure 3.18. Odor intensity obtained by the method of magnitude estimation plotted as a function of log odorant concentration on logarithmic scales of low (3.12%), medium (12.5%), and high (50%) standards.

3.18 (Engen & Lindström, 1963). The value of the intercept on the ordinate reflects the arbitrary choice of modulus, but what is of interest is the slope, which should remain relatively invariant for a perceptual continuum. It is as though the observer spaces the stimuli farther apart when the standard is in the middle of the series than when it is out toward the extreme.

Although this bias appears to be small on a log-log plot and may not change the form of the function, it must at least be considered as a possible contaminating factor when results for the same series of stimuli are being compared and when the slope for a particular perceptual continuum is being specified. The most effective method for reducing this bias seems to be *the free-modulus variation of the method of magnitude estimation*. No standard is presented, and no number is prescribed by the experimenter; instead the observer himself is instructed to select the number he finds appropriate for the first and every subsequent stimulus. Usually the experimenter presents the stimuli in a different random order for each observer in the group. Usually there are about three practice trials although they are often not identified as such for the observer. The instructions may read as follows:

> I am going to present you, in irregular order, a series of test tubes containing the same odor at different intensities. Your task is to tell me how intense or strong they are by assigning numbers to them.
>
> When you have smelled the first stimulus, give its intensity a number—any number you think appropriate. I will then present another to which you will also give a number, and a third, etc.
>
> Try to make the ratios between the numbers you assign to the different odors correspond to the ratios between the intensity of the odors. In other words, try to make the numbers proportional to the intensity of the odor, as you smell it. Remember, you may assign any number and there is no limit on the number that you assign.
>
> There is no right or wrong answer. I want to know how you judge the intensity of the odors. Any questions?

The free-modulus experiment will be illustrated with data obtained by Cain (1968). The

TABLE 3.11A INDIVIDUAL JUDGMENTS OF PENTANOL CONCENTRATIONS

Observer	_Percent concentration_						
	100.	50.00	25.00	12.50	6.25	3.12	1.56
1	20.0	10.0	4.00	10.0	2.5	1.0	.5
1	50.0	7.5	20.0	7.5	5.0	1.5	.5
2	10.0	5.0	5.0	1.0	2.0	3.0	.5
2	8.0	3.0	5.0	1.0	2.0	2.0	2.0
3	30.0	25.0	10.0	5.0	10.0	2.0	5.0
3	50.0	30.0	20.0	5.0	1.0	10.0	1.0
4	140.0	30.0	70.0	85.0	15.0	20.0	8.0
4	70.0	45.0	50.0	10.0	3.0	2.0	3.0
5	20.0	12.0	8.0	2.0	1.0	1.0	1.0
5	25.0	10.0	15.0	4.0	3.0	1.0	2.0
6	20.0	15.0	10.0	12.0	12.0	10.0	7.0
6	30.0	25.0	10.0	25.0	17.0	7.0	5.0
7	25.0	13.0	10.0	10.0	3.0	6.0	3.0
7	20.0	18.0	15.0	4.0	8.0	7.0	5.0
8	40.0	20.0	20.0	15.0	12.0	7.0	10.0
8	60.0	25.0	18.0	10.0	15.0	5.0	15.0
9	30.0	25.0	28.0	15.0	10.0	4.0	2.0
9	35.0	35.0	40.0	25.0	18.0	3.0	1.0
10	10.0	5.0	3.3	5.0	10.0	1.0	1.0
10	7.5	2.0	3.3	2.0	2.0	1.0	1.0
11	150.0	200.0	250.0	100.0	50.0	25.0	10.0
11	125.0	150.0	100.0	80.0	130.0	90.0	75.0
12	30.0	12.0	7.0	15.0	12.0	9.0	2.0
12	25.0	10.0	10.0	5.0	5.0	7.0	10.0
13	80.0	65.0	30.0	20.0	10.0	5.0	1.0
13	85.0	70.0	35.0	10.0	5.0	4.8	1.0
14	20.0	16.0	10.0	6.0	3.0	7.0	2.0
14	18.0	15.0	8.0	5.0	9.0	3.0	1.0
15	60.0	50.0	45.0	40.0	20.0	15.0	15.0
15	85.0	45.0	25.0	30.0	25.0	10.0	10.0

stimuli were presented by an olfactometer in which the odorant (pentanol) was diluted with air and sniffed from a nose piece. Fifteen observers judged each of 7 concentrations twice following the instructions above, and the responses are entered in Table 3.11A.

Geometric means of the responses in each column of the matrix in Table 3.11A may again be used to define scale values, as is done in Table 3.10 above. However, there are two sources of variance which may be eliminated from these data. The first is associated with differences in the modulus chosen by each observer; the overall magnitude of numbers he assigns in the second presentation of the stimuli may be different from that of the first. In that event, the intercepts of the two psy-chophysical functions will differ and add to the variance of the response distribution, even though the exponents of the functions may be similar. The second source of variance relates to the fact that different observers may prefer to work in different number ranges; this again results in different intercepts. (Such variance is perhaps particularly high in olfaction, and one must take the present data as illustrative only of the kind and not the size of the variance.)

The basic interest in a magnitude scaling experiment is the exponent of the function, and what is needed is a transformation of the data which leaves invariant the individual slopes as well as the average of the individual intercepts, while partialing out the

TABLE 3.11B LOGARITHMIC VALUES OF JUDGMENTS AFTER TRANSFORMATION OF JUDGMENTS IN TABLE 3-11A

Observer	Log percent concentration						
	2.00	1.70	1.40	1.10	0.80	0.50	0.20
1	1.84	1.27	1.29	1.27	0.89	0.43	0.04
2	1.54	1.17	1.28	0.59	0.89	0.97	0.59
3	1.68	1.53	1.24	0.79	0.59	0.74	0.44
4	1.70	1.27	1.47	1.17	0.53	0.50	0.39
5	1.74	1.43	1.43	0.85	0.63	0.39	0.54
6	1.28	1.18	0.89	1.13	1.04	0.82	0.66
7	1.42	1.26	1.16	0.87	0.76	0.88	0.66
8	1.50	1.15	1.08	0.89	0.93	0.58	0.89
9	1.43	1.39	1.44	1.20	1.04	0.46	0.07
10	1.42	0.98	1.00	0.98	1.13	0.68	0.83
11	1.20	1.31	1.26	1.02	0.97	0.74	0.50
12	1.47	1.07	0.96	0.97	0.92	0.94	0.69
13	1.78	1.70	1.38	1.02	0.72	0.56	−0.13
14	1.47	1.38	1.14	0.93	0.91	0.85	0.34
15	1.41	1.23	1.08	1.10	0.91	0.65	0.65
Σ	22.88	19.32	18.10	14.78	12.86	10.19	7.15
Mean log	1.53	1.29	1.21	0.99	0.86	0.68	0.47
Antilog (geometric mean)	33.5	19.4	16.2	9.7	7.2	4.8	3.0

variability due to intra- or inter-individual sources of inconsistency. A procedure originated by Lane, Catania, and Stevens (1961) eliminates interobserver variance caused by differing choice of moduli; additional steps are necessary to eliminate intra-observer variability (Kalikow, 1967). The following procedure may be used to accomplish both.

1. Convert each response value to its logarithm.

2. Determine the mean of the logarithms of the two responses made by each observer to each stimulus. This value is the logarithm of the geometric mean of the observer's responses to each stimulus.

3. Determine the mean value of each row. This is the logarithm of the geometric mean of each observer's responses to all the stimuli.

4. Determine the mean of all the values obtained in step 3. This is the logarithmic value of the grand mean of all the responses for all observers to all stimuli in the original data matrix.

5. Subtract the value obtained in step 4, the grand mean log response, from each of the individual mean log responses determined in step 3.

6. Add the value obtained in step 5 to the

TABLE 3.12 THE METHOD OF LEAST SQUARES APPLIED TO MAGNITUDE ESTIMATION DATA

X (log S)	Y (log R)	X²	XY
.20	.47	.04	.09
.50	.68	.25	.34
.80	.86	.64	.69
1.10	.99	1.21	1.09
1.40	1.21	1.96	1.69
1.70	1.29	2.89	2.19
2.00	1.53	4.00	3.06
Σ 7.70	7.03	10.99	9.15

$$a = \frac{N(\Sigma XY) - (\Sigma X)(\Sigma Y)}{N(\Sigma X^2) - (\Sigma X)^2}$$

$$= \frac{7(9.15) - (7.70)(7.03)}{7(10.99) - (7.70)^2}$$

$$= .56$$

$$b = \frac{(\Sigma X^2)(\Sigma Y) - (\Sigma X)(\Sigma XY)}{N(\Sigma X^2) - (\Sigma X)^2}$$

$$= \frac{(10.99)(7.03) - (7.70)(9.15)}{7(10.99) - (7.70)^2}$$

$$= .39$$

Note that $N = 7$, the number of stimuli in the experiment.

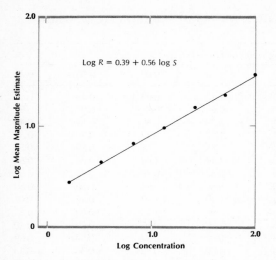

Figure 3.19. Log mean magnitude estimate plotted as a function of log concentration of pentanol.

row of values obtained for each observer in step 2.

These six steps result in a logarithmic matrix, shown in Table 3.11B. The transformation of the data affects only the variability around the main function because none of the six steps affects its exponent or intercept. This problem will be discussed further in deriving the power function from the data, which requires a logarithmic *matrix*. This transformation results in Table 3.12.

The data in Table 3.11 conform to the power function, as can be seen in Figure 3.19, where the mean logarithmic judgments are plotted on Cartesian coordinates as a function of the logarithmic values of the concentrations. The important parameters of the power function have been mentioned occasionally, and now they will be determined more precisely by fitting a function to the data in Table 3.11B. The same procedure will apply to the *R-S* data in Tables 3.8, 3.9 (Matrix B), and 3.10. The curve fitting is simplest when the data are in logarithmic form. Actually, for many purposes the parameters can be estimated from a straight line drawn through the points by eye, but the method of least squares is more precise (see Lewis,

1960). A power function can be described mathematically as

$$R = cS^n \qquad \text{[Eq. 1]}$$

where R is the geometric mean judgment of a stimulus, S the corresponding stimulus magnitude, c a constant reflecting the (arbitrary) unit of measurement used by the observers, and n is the exponent of the function.

If Equation 1 is expressed in logarithmic terms,

$$\log R = n (\log S) + \log c \qquad \text{[Eq. 2]}$$

which is a simple linear equation of the form

$$y = ax + b$$

This equation can be written in this form with $y = \log R$, $a = n$, $x = \log S$, and $b = \log c$. In the coordinates of Equation 2, the exponent n in Equation 1 becomes the slope of the function, and the multiplicative constant c yields the intercept term $\log c$.

The parameters of the power function may be determined graphically, but more precise values are obtained from the computations shown in Table 3.12. The simplest formulas for the method of least squares require that the data approximate a straight line, and Equation 2 satisfies this condition with logarithmic scaling of stimulus and response. Except for the special case where $n = 1$, the power function is nonlinear in Cartesian coordinates. Table 3.12 shows how to determine the values of a and b, which are then converted into a form compatible with Equation 1.

The value of a, .56, is the value of parameter n in Equation 2 and is therefore the slope of the function in logarithmic coordinates. The value b, .39, is the value of parameter ($\log c$) in Equation 2 and is the intercept of the function which states

$$\log R = .56 (\log S) + .39$$

This function describes the line drawn through the data plotted in Figure 3.19. In translating into Equation 1 the value of *n* is unchanged, and the value of *c* becomes the antilog of .39, or 2.45. In linear coordinates the function plotted through the data may then be stated as

$$R = 2.45S^{.56}$$

This is a power function because it states that response magnitude is proportional to stimulus magnitude raised to a power. In the present case that power or exponent is .56, which means that if the stimulus magnitude were increased by a factor of 10:1, or one logarithmic unit, the corresponding increase in response magnitude would only be .56 expressed in these logarithmic units, or a factor of 3.6:1. This conclusion follows, of course, from our previous observation that sensory intensity grows more slowly than does stimulus intensity in olfaction. Exponents have been found to vary from about .33 for visual brightness (in agreement with Plateau's early work mentioned above) to more than 3.00 for electric shock (Stevens, 1961). See also Figure 3.26.

In the six steps outlined above two main operations were made. First, in step 2 each observer's responses to each of the 7 stimuli were averaged. This has no effect on the values derived in Table 3.12. Second, in step 5 factors were added to the values obtained in step 2 to produce a new response matrix. The factors added sum to zero, and therefore the sums of columns used in Table 3.12 are unaffected. It is only necessary to minimize variability associated with the modulus in case of a more detailed analysis of the data. For example, in stating the variance of the original data one might compute the deviations of each observer's responses from that least-squares line. However, this variance would be spuriously high and would obscure the judgmental variance, which is often of interest. Step 5 moves the different observers' functions up or down in the double logarithmic coordinates to minimize the variance around the least-square line without changing the average intercept and slope. This transforma-

tion may present a clearer picture of how well a group of observers approximate the power function despite large differences in the numbers they used. This variability is an index of the goodness of fit and could be useful in comparing sense modalities.

PROBLEMS IN PSYCHOPHYSICAL SCALING

Individual Functions

It should not be assumed that the functions are perfectly stable; for besides effects of specific experimental conditions such as the standard and range used, there are the inevitable individual differences in exponent, as can be observed by inspecting the individual data in Table 3.11B (see also Marks & Stevens, 1966). Keep in mind that the individual slopes are based on few judgments and again that odor judgment is not a psychophysical model for reliability! However, differences in the form of the function are apparently negligible. In a linear plot, for example, all the individual functions for odor intensity are almost invariably negatively accelerated, and those for heaviness positively accelerated. The mean slope in the present odor example is .56 with a standard deviation of .22. Individual exponents (constant *a* in our example) and the parameter represented by the constant *c*, the coefficient of the individual function, can easily be determined. However, the perceptual (subjective) value associated with the latter constant cannot be known. It can be determined that one observer agrees with another in judging the ratio of stimuli 1 and 2, but whether or not observer A's response to stimulus 1 (or 2) is less than, equal to, or greater than observer B's response cannot be revealed. Problems of this sort can only be considered by indirect scaling theory of the kind developed by Thurstone (Björkman & Ekman, 1962). This missing link is the reason for a great deal of criticism and debate about the power function.

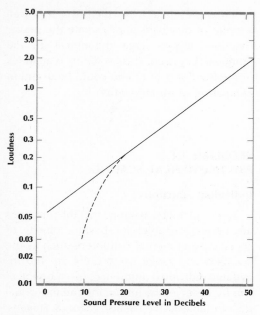

Figure 3.20. Loudness measured by magnitude estimation and ratio production as a function of sound pressure level in decibels. The graph shows how the loudness function becomes steeper near threshold. By correcting for threshold the curvature is eliminated and the obtained data fall along the straight line in a log-log plot. See text. (Data adopted from Scharf & Stevens, 1961.)

Threshold Connection

The most important deviation from the simple power function has been observed for weaker stimulus magnitudes near threshold. Figure 3.20 illustrates this with a psychophysical function for loudness obtained by Scharf and J. C. Stevens (1961). The dotted line represents the obtained function, which seems to be approaching the stimulus threshold value and may therefore reflect a rapidly decreasing effectiveness of stimulus magnitudes at this level. This would suggest a slight modification of the power function, that is,

$$R = c(S - S_0)^n$$

where S_0 is a value roughly corresponding to threshold for the conditions of the particular experiment and may be estimated from scaling

data. Of course, threshold could be measured with any of the methods discussed in the previous chapter, but it must be recalled that such threshold values are also variable and depend on specific experimental procedures. Replotting the response values as a function of each stimulus value minus this threshold value will straighten the function as indicated by the solid line in Figure 3.20. To fit a curve to the data with the method of least squares one would use $\log (S - S_0)$ instead of $\log S$ for X. This "threshold" usually represents a very small quantity; thus it will mostly affect very low stimulus values and may often be excluded. Nevertheless, it cannot be ignored; for example, if Scharf and Stevens (Figure 3.20) had used only the softer stimuli, the loudness function would have appeared steeper and curved. Furthermore, sometimes S_0 is a large quantity compared with S, as in the case of the so-called "physiological zero," which must be considered in scaling warmth (Stevens & Stevens, 1960). Occasionally a more complicated situation arises. In developing a method for estimating the value of S_0, Ekman (1959) discovered that at times its value turned out

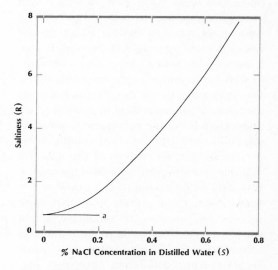

Figure 3.21. Saltiness (R) as measured by magnitude estimation and ratio estimation as a function of NaCl concentration. The constant a represents a positive value of R at $S = 0$. See text. (Data from Ekman, 1961.)

to be negative, which could mean that response magnitude may be greater than zero when S equals zero. Ekman therefore suggested the modified form of the power function be written as

$$R = c(S - a)^n$$

where a was tentatively considered "sensory noise," resulting from spontaneous nervous activity (see the discussion of Weber's Modified Law in Chapter 2, p. 17). For smell and taste one is quite likely to obtain $R > 0$ when $S = 0$. For example, water may be reported as salty because the saliva contains NaCl (Bartoshuk, McBurney, & Pfaffmann, 1964; see Chapter 6). Figure 3.21 illustrates this effect in a psychophysical function estimated from an experiment on taste (Ekman, 1961). Actually, functions of this type may best be described as $R = a + cS^n$, which suggests more complex curve-fitting problems (see Ekman, 1959, 1961; and Fagot & Stewart, 1968).

The constant a may be of considerable interest when weak stimuli or the effect of adaptation on psychophysical functions are being studied (Stevens & Stevens, 1963). The constant c may likewise be of interest when comparing two sets of stimuli in a free-modulus experiment, for it will indicate the overall psychological magnitude involved. In this way the parameters of the power function have begun to define problems of interest to sensory psychologists and appear to be taking over the role which was dominated by Fechner's logarithmic function for over 100 years.

The Usefulness of Fechner's Law

Fechner's psychophysical function is based on Weber's Law, $\Delta S = kS$ (see p. 17), that ΔS tends to increase linearly with stimulus intensity, S. Weber was concerned exclusively with the stimulus dimension, but Fechner assumed that there was a ΔR, a difference in the sensory magnitude associated with the ΔS (the physical value of the DL) and that the value of ΔR was the same size regardless of where ΔS had been determined on the stimulus continuum. Fechner's Law was thus based on an assumption that could not be tested directly because direct scaling methods were not available to classical psychophysics (p. 49).

Taking a direct scaling approach, Fechner's Law can be tested simply by plotting R as a function of the logarithm of the S value, but, as has been shown, when this is done in practice, Fechner's Law almost never holds. Research in vision and hearing has tended to support Weber's Law and by implication Fechner's Law. When these modalities are scaled by direct scaling methods, their power functions have exponents about $\frac{1}{3}$, which means that in linear coordinates the functions are negatively accelerated and similar to an exponential (semilogarithmic) function. Both the exponential function and the power function will provide a better approximation to the changes in psychological magnitude in these two modalities with logarithmic rather than arithmetic spacing of the stimuli. However, results from other modalities where the exponent is greater than 1 support the generality of the power law. (The telephone engineers have found it convenient to use the *decibel*, a logarithmic unit, in specifying the intensity of auditory stimuli [see Chapter 8]; the dB is 1/10 of a log unit of energy and corresponds very roughly to the *DL*. Those who work in photography and optics may use filters calibrated in density, again using a logarithmic scale [see Chapter 9].)

The sensory physiologists also were uncovering relevant facts through the use of electrical recording of the frequency of impulses obtained from sense organs as a function of stimulus intensity. In 1946 Ruch summarized the data by saying that ". . . Fechner's equation appears to express a fundamental feature of sense organ behavior. Over a certain range of intensities, the frequency of discharge is a linear function of the logarithm of the stimulus. This has been shown for the muscle spindle by Matthews, and for the Limulus eye by Hartline and Graham" (p. 314; see also R. Granit, 1955). However, Rosner and Goff have reviewed this, along with more recent evidence, and came to the conclusion that while the Fechnerian logarithmic function may fit the data, a power function fits the data as well. The relationship between peripheral physiological events and central sensory events is still unsettled. Take note of their warning: "Beware of psychophysicists bearing gifts" (Rosner & Goff, 1967, p. 216). The problem is basically a psychophysical one.

Fechner (1860) considered psychophysics a theory about the relation between the psychological and the physical. He divided this problem into *outer* and *inner psychophysics*. Inner psychophysics was concerned with the indirect relationship between sensory physiology and anatomy and sensation, and outer psychophysics is psychophysics in the contemporary sense of the term, that is, the concern with the more direct relationship between sensation and an external stimulus. Fechner acknowledged the importance of inner psychophysics but argued that, "The basic knowledge for all of psychophysics can only be sought in the realm of outer psychophysics since only this is susceptible to direct experience, and therefore, the point of departure must be outer psychophysics" (Fechner, 1860, vol I).

Comparison of Direct and Indirect Scales

Category and magnitude scales are often compared because category scales have provided evidence for Fechner's Law, whereas magnitude scales are power functions. It is assumed then that category scales are equal-interval scales and that magnitude scales are ratio scales.

It was noted in the beginning of this chapter that the formal difference between an interval scale and a ratio scale is essentially the origin of the scales and therefore category scale values should plot as a linear function of magnitude scale values for a set of stimuli, with the slope and intercept of the linear function determined by difference in unit and origin of the two scales. However, the results in a great many experiments on numerous

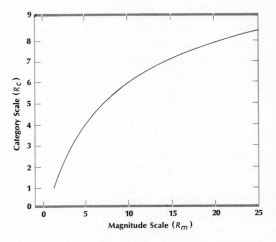

Figure 3.22. Category scale values plotted as a function of magnitude estimation scale values. (Fictitious data.)

continua are almost invariably curved downward, as is shown in Figure 3.22 (see, for example, Stevens, 1957; Stevens & Galanter, 1957; Ekman, 1962; Ekman & Künnapas, 1960, 1962a and b, 1963a and b). Although this is one of the most reliable findings in experimental psychology, the possible reason for the curvature in this function has produced considerable debate and speculation without any

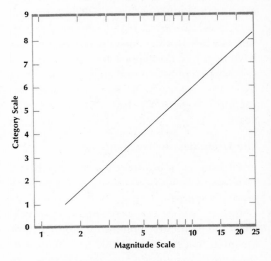

Figure 3.23. Data in Figure 3.22 replotted in semilogarithmic coordinates, that is, category scale values as a function of log magnitude scale values.

definite conclusions (see Eisler, 1962a). Ekman and Künnapas suggest that the category scale (as well as the pair-comparison scale) is closely approximated by a logarithmic transformation of the magnitude scale, shown in Figure 3.23. This transformation can be described mathematically as

$$R_c = a + b \log R_m$$

where R_c is a category scale value and R_m the corresponding magnitude scale value. A theoretical explanation according to what has been called *Ekman's Law* involves traditional and by now familiar psychophysical relations and assumptions. The curvature in Figure 3.22, it is suggested, is caused by the inability of the observer to discriminate constant physical differences equally well along the scale. For example, the difference between lines of 1 and 1.5 inches presented successively will be quite noticeable, and the observer will put these two stimuli in different categories. However, the difference between 20.0 and 20.5 inches often is not detected, and, on these occasions, the observer puts them in the same response category. This is consistent with Weber's Law, $\Delta S = k_s(S + a)$, where k_s and a are constants (see p. 18). Ekman has produced evidence that an analogous relation

seems to apply to the psychological continuum, that is,

$$\Delta R = k_R(R + a),$$

where ΔR is a value on the psychological continuum, for example a magnitude estimation scale, and a and k_R are constants analogous to the Weber fraction and the "threshold" or "noise" factor. The important point is that this contradicts the assumption made by Fechner—whose proposed law is supported by the category scale, which in turn is nonlinear with the magnitude scale—that the discriminal dispersion is constant over the whole psychological continuum. Ekman's relation states that the discriminal dispersion is proportional to stimulus magnitude. In Figure 3.24, Ekman (1956, 1959) has provided evidence for this proportionality on the psychological continuum. The function relates two psychological variables and was obtained by comparing Harper and Stevens' veg scale (1948) with Oberlin's (1936) data on DL for heaviness. ΔR in the present case is estimated, but it may be defined more directly as the intra-individual variance of a certain R value as follows: (1) Obtain several (for example, 10) judgments from each observer for a set of stimuli with the method of magnitude estimation without a prescribed modulus. (2) Multiply the numerical judgments (Rs) for each stimulus magnitude by a factor which renders the sum of the numerical judgments for each stimulus constant (for example, 1.0). (3) The standard deviation of these transformed Rs, or $\sigma_{R'}$, will be analogous to ΔR above (see Eisler, 1962b). Alternative definitions of ΔS are likewise considered in Chapter 2.

The power function implies that both Ekman's Law and Weber's Law should be correct. Fechner apparently considered the power function, and Brentano anticipated Ekman's relation, but it seems that the development of direct methods was required to crystallize the ideas. With respect to the observer's task in category scaling, (Figure 3.21), this means that his categories, or "equal ap-

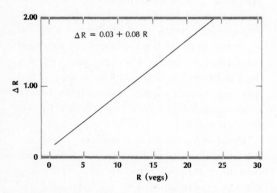

Figure 3.24. Discriminal disperson (ΔR) on the psychological continuum (heaviness measured in vegs) as a function of psychological magnitude. The plot relates two psychological variables and is an R-R rather than the more familiar S-R relation. (Data adapted from Ekman, 1956.)

pearing intervals," are not equal; rather, they are relatively narrow at the low end of the scale and wide at the high end. Therefore, the category scale is steeper at the low end and flatter at the high when plotted against either stimulus magnitude or magnitude estimates. This argues that the bias is in the category scale, which imposes a discrimination that is neither required in magnitude estimation, nor basic to the question concerning the relation between R and S. Consistent with this is the evidence that the spacing of stimuli has a dramatic effect on category scale values while the magnitude scale remains almost invariant. According to Galanter (1962), "In consequence, many psychophysicists have come to believe that the magnitude scale reveals more about the sensory effects of stimuli, and therefore more about the bases of the judgmental process of people when they are called upon to act with respect to stimuli in their environment" (p. 153).

Empirically, the power function is probably as well established as is possible for any quantitative relation involving the whole man, and better than any other in psychology.

The virtue of direct scaling is its simplicity: It makes but one assumption, namely that the observer is able to carry out the instructions to quantify his perceptions. All the criticisms leveled at the power function seem to involve this necessary assumption. Are the numerical judgments valid indicators of perceptual magnitudes? Some think not (for example, Garner, 1954a and b; Graham, 1965), while others propose different interpretations of what the numerical estimates might mean (for example, Warren & Warren, 1963; Treisman, 1964a and b; Savage, 1966). Although the available indirect (or necessary) evidence is undeniably impressive, sufficient evidence of validity can only come from further experience with the practical usefulness of such scales.

Cross-modality Matching

In order to eliminate potential problems with the use of numbers, Stevens has proposed that "cross-modality matching" be used

to test the form of the psychophysical function (Stevens, 1959, 1966). These matching experiments follow the general procedure for determining the point of subjective equality (PSE) with the method of adjustment discussed in Chapter 2 (p. 20). The observers are presented several standards, for example, five weights, well spaced, and in irregular order, under the instruction to adjust the value on the second continuum, for example, loudness, to match the psychological value of each of these standards. If both psychological continua are power functions of their respective stimulus continua, for example, $R_h = W^m$ and $R_l = P^n$, where R_h is heaviness; W physical weight; R_l loudness, P sound pressure; and m and n are exponents. The proportionality constants are not important to the argument. Matching implies that $R_l = R_h$, and the function relating the average sound pressure to the weights of the standards should conform to the function

$$P^n = W^m$$

which in logarithms is

$$\log P = (\log W)\ m/n$$

Therefore the results of the cross-matching should show a linear equal-sensation function in log-log coordinates with an exponent equal to the ratio of the exponents of the psychophysical functions for heaviness and for loudness. Because the exponent for loudness (in decibels) is about .6 and for heaviness 1.5, the predicted slope is .6/1.5 = .4. To test further one would match heaviness to several loudness standards with the predicted result of 1.5/6 = 2.5.

Equal-sensation functions have borne out the power functions because cross-matching functions are well fitted by straight lines in log-log coordinates, and the obtained and predicted slopes have been almost identical. The predicted slopes are sometimes slightly lower due to a possible "regression tendency" (Stevens & Greenbaum, 1966). In general the observer tends to shrink the continuum he adjusts; this has the effect of reducing the slope in estimation experiments and increas-

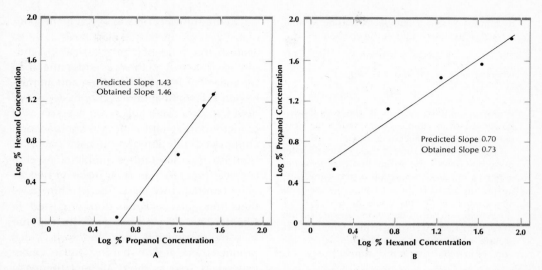

Figure 3.25. Equal sensation function for the odor intensity of hexanol and propanol when (A) hexanol concentration was adjusted to match the intensity of 5 propanol standards and when (B) propanol concentration was adjusted to match the intensity of 5 hexanol standards. The values plotted on the ordinate are median concentrations chosen by 12 observers from a concentration range of .59 to 100 percent in 24 dilution steps. The odors were sniffed from cotton wrapped on a glass rod. When propanol and hexanol had been scaled earlier with the method of magnitude estimation, psychophysical power functions were obtained with a slope of .20 for propanol and .14 for hexanol. From the ratio of these slopes one would predict that the equal-sensation functions obtained when one of these alcohols is matched to the other should be power functions with slopes of .20/.14 = 1.43 and .14/.20 = .70, depending on whether propanol or hexanol is the standard odorant. The lines shown represent the slope obtained as determined by the method of least squares. (From Cain, 1966.)

ing the slope in production experiments. It is necessary therefore to perform a counter-

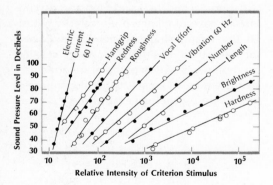

Figure 3.26. Equal-sensation functions obtained by matching 10 other stimuli to loudness. The relative position of each equal-sensation function is arbitrary, but its slope conforms to the prediction made from the ratio of the slopes for psychophysical functions of loudness, electric current, force of handgrip, and so on. (Data by Stevens, 1965.)

balanced cross-matching experiment for the most precise determination of the slope of an equal-sensation function. Examples of a cross-matching experiment are shown in Figures 3.25 and 3.26.

In connection with the problem of matching Ekman (1964) has made the following suggestion.

Let us assume, for the purposes of the present discussion, that Fechner's law is generally valid, so that

$$R_s = a + b \log S, \tag{1}$$

where R_s is a subjective magnitude corresponding to the stimulus magnitude S. Let us further assume that a subject reacts also to *number stimulation* according to Fechner's law. Then

$$R_n = c + d \log N, \tag{2}$$

where R_n is the subjective magnitude corresponding to the stimulus magnitude, i.e., the number N, to which the subject is exposed.

In a typical scaling experiment with a direct method, the subject is instructed to respond to a stimulus S with a number N chosen so that $R_n = R_s$. On this condition the relation

$$\log N = \alpha + n \log S, \qquad (3)$$

where $\alpha = (a - c/d$ and $n = b/d$, or

$$N = \beta S^n,$$

where $\beta =$ antilog α. This is the well-known power law in its simplest form, which has now been derived from Fechner's Law.

The essential feature of the response model presented here is the assumption that a subject reacts to number stimulation in the same way, i.e., according to Fechner's law, as he reacts to any stimulation. In this sense the derivation of the power function is based on a generalization of Fechner's law. According to the model, a direct scaling method is a procedure in which *the subject matches two sets of stimuli.*[1]

Ekman's suggestion highlights the problems associated with the assumption of direct scaling. No clear-cut experiments suggest themselves, but alternative assumptions can always be made about what the observer's numerical responses really mean. On the other hand, there is indirect evidence of the validity of equal-sensation functions and the flexibility of the cross-matching procedure. Abbey (1962) has shown that both linear and nonlinear equal-sensation functions will be obtained in cross-matching experiments, as is predicted from the two contributing individual psychophysical functions. That is, a linear plot of the equal-sensation function is not a necessary consequence of the Fechnerian assumption discussed by Ekman (see also Luce & Galanter, 1963, pp. 278 ff).

[1] G. Ekman. The power law: A specialized case of Fechner's Law? *Perceptual and Motor Skills,* 1964, *19*, 730. Reprinted with permission of author and publisher.

"Methodology can easily become methodolatry," says Stevens (1958), who warns against the tendency of classical psychophysicists to treat methods as ends rather than the means of learning how men and animals respond to stimulation. Psychophysics is evidently still characterized as a "necessary evil" of methodology, although contemporary psychophysics undoubtedly will make contributions to this substantive problem. Psychophysical progress has been made in two almost contradictory ways. The psychology of detection and discrimination discussed in Chapter 2 has attempted to deal with response bias by maximizing the conditions which produce them, and this has resulted in a more general as well as more abstract theory of detection. This in turn has brought psychology into closer contact with the study of learning and animal behavior. Psychophysical scaling, in contrast, in an attempt to eliminate or reduce response bias, has produced simpler and more direct methods for dealing with problems of perception that could not be considered as long as only measurement on the physical continuum was considered. This has widened the applicability of psychophysical scaling, so that it is no longer limited to sensory problems for which the relevant physical correlates are well understood. These two approaches to contemporary psychophysics have in common a greater emphasis on the relationship between psychological variables than was the case with classical psychophysics. We may therefore anticipate an increasing influence of modern psychophysics on psychology as a whole.

Charles F. Stevens

BASIC MECHANISMS
OF NEURAL FUNCTION

4

Chapter 4 presents the basic information necessary for a preliminary understanding of the electrophysiological method as an analytic tool for studying the mechanism of neural function, and as a procedure for enlarging the classes of behavior that can be observed. Experimental psychologists have come to depend more and more heavily upon the concepts and tools of neurophysiology. Thus a chapter on neurophysiology not only serves the practical purpose of indicating to the student of psychology how these tools are applied but also acquaints him with the concepts necessary for the interpretation of results obtained with them. Along with the chapters on psychophysics, then, this chapter provides a background for the later chapters on sensation, perception, and the more complex topics of experimental psychology.

Associated with the activity of nerve and muscle are certain voltage changes that may often be recorded without great difficulty. Because these voltage changes are so intimately involved with the functioning of nerve and muscle, the physiologist studies electrical concomitants of function in an effort to unravel the mechanisms that ultimately underlie behavior. For the psychologist, however, recording voltage changes associated with the operation of the nervous and in particular muscular systems has the additional advantage of extending the range of "behavior" that can be observed and studied (for example, see Hefferline, Keenan, & Harford, 1959).

ANATOMICAL SUBSTRATE
FOR BEHAVIOR

The analysis of behavior often proceeds by identifying stimuli and responses and then by discovering orderly relations between them. When we are dealing with the structural basis for behavior, it is useful to follow an analogous system by considering organs for gathering information about the environment, organs for acting on the environment, and the neural machinery responsible for relations between stimulus and response. This section introduces the anatomical concepts necessary for understanding the function of the neural and muscular elements underlying gross behavior. We first develop certain notions about the structure of the nervous sys-

tem proper—the central organization responsible for relations between stimulus and response—and then briefly consider in turn structures that gather information from the environment and those that act upon the environment.

The natural functional and anatomical unit of the nervous system is the nerve cell. Although neurons may be classified into a considerable number of structural types, virtually all of these types share certain anatomical properties which have proved to be of significance for the physiologist. We therefore describe a typical neuron in order to illustrate the most important of these common features and then present some of the frequent variations in structure.

The typical neuron may be described as

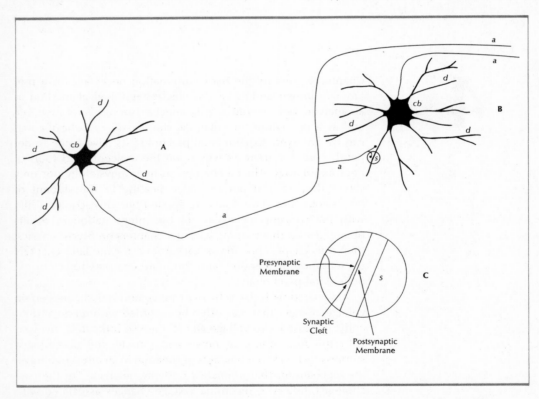

Figure 4.1. Two neurons, A and B, are illustrated schematically. The soma is labeled *cb,* some dendrites are labeled *d,* and the axon is labeled *a.* Neuron A sends its axon to synapse with neuron B, and one of the synapses is marked with *s.* C gives a much magnified and highly schematic view of synapse *s.* The synaptic cleft is about 200 Å in diameter, and the axon terminal may be from half to 10 μ in diameter.

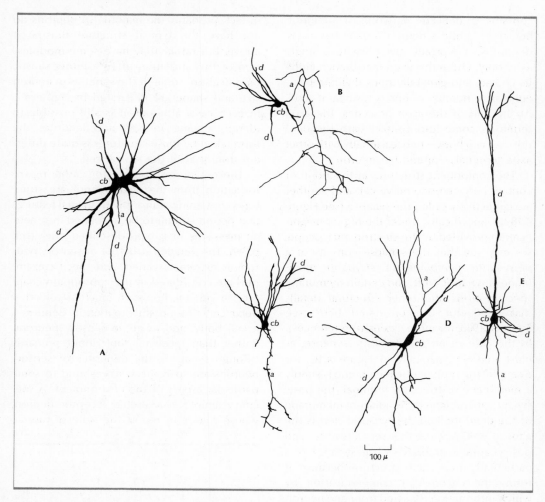

Figure 4.2. Five neurons from various areas of the brain are illustrated. These nerve cells were drawn from ones stained by a special technique, the Golgi method; it should be noted that the actual neuron processes were not all in one plane, but rather they radiated from the cell body in all directions. Neuron A is a motoneuron from the spinal cord and is the type of cell involved in the reflex behavior to be described later. Most of the axons have not been included in the drawings from cells A, C, D, and E, but much of cell B's axon has been drawn to illustrate the complicated branching pattern typical of axons. Cell E is termed a pyramidal cell and is the type of neuron characteristically found in the cortex; because so much of the human brain is taken up by the cortex, this particular type of neuron may be the most common. As in Figure 4.1, *cb* denotes cell body, *d* dendrite, and *a* axon.

having an approximately spherical cell body (or soma, *cb* in Figure 4.1A) with numerous protrusions known as the axon (*a*) and dendrites (*d*). A thin (100 Å)[1] membrane, called the *plasma membrane*, defines the boundary

[1]See index for definition of Å (Ångstrom), μ (micron), and other units.

of the neuron and forms a sharp separation between the cell and its surroundings. The main dendrites, of which there may be a half dozen, divide into smaller branches; these in turn divide again, so that the immediate vicinity of the cell (within a sphere with a radius of perhaps several hundred microns) contains a delicate network of dendritic branches. While a neuron usually has many dendrites, it typically gives rise to a single axon only. Often this axon may branch along its course, and generally does divide repeatedly into a number of fine twigs near its end. At the end of the axon branches, the axon terminals come into contact with the dendrites or cell body—or occasionally with other axon terminals—of another neuron.

The component structures at this point of contact between one nerve cell and another are collectively called the *synapse* (see Figure 4.1B, *s*). Specifically, under the higher magnification provided by the electron microscope, we may see that the synapse consists of a *presynaptic membrane,* a *postsynaptic membrane,* a *synaptic cleft,* and certain membrane specializations and other structural details that need not be considered here (see Stevens, 1968, for more extensive references). In the case of an axo-dendritic synapse, as illustrated schematically in Figure 4.1C, for example, the presynaptic membrane is simply a membrane of the axon terminal, the postsynaptic membrane is the adjacent membrane of the dendrite, and the synaptic cleft is the gap, 200–400 Å wide, that separates pre- and postsynaptic membranes. The synapse is a particularly important structure because it forms the channel of communication by which information is passed from one neuron to the next.

The approximately 10 billion neurons of the human brain are interconnected in fantastically complicated networks. Thus, each neuron receives thousands of synaptic contacts from perhaps hundreds of other neurons, and in turn sends its axon to synapse with many different nerve cells. These interconnecting networks form the anatomical substrate for behavior. Standard neuroanatomy books (Crosby, Humphrey, & Lauer, 1962, for example) summarize our knowledge about brain structure and the principal connections between neurons in different areas.

The neurons that have been described thus far have been ones with "typical" structure.

In fact, probably the majority of neurons do not have the typical structure illustrated above, but rather they have some modification of this structure, often a rather drastic modification. Some of the varieties in neuron size and shape are illustrated in Figure 4.2. In each case, although it is still possible to identify a soma, an axon, and dendrites, the form taken by these structures is quite different from that of the typical cell.

The organs responsible for gathering information from the environment are structures containing neurons with special features that permit stimuli to be translated into neural messages of a type described later (see p. 99). The detailed structure of sensory neurons is extremely varied, and specific examples are considered in the appropriate chapters. In general, however, much as for other nerve cells, it is possible to identify dendrites, a cell body, and axons in sensory neurons. Rather than receiving their input primarily through synapses, the dendrites of sensory neurons are specialized to respond to some particular aspect of the environment. A specific example is a stretch receptor neuron, whose role is to report the state of muscle

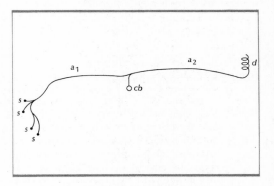

Figure 4.3. The neuron illustrated schematically is a bipolar receptor neuron. *cb* denotes the cell body, *s* denotes axon terminals, which form synapses within the animal's nervous system, a_1 and a_2 are the two branches of the axon, and *d* is a sensory dendrite that is located in muscle. The segment of axon a_2 would in general be much longer than has been illustrated here; in fact it could be a meter in length.

stretch to the central nervous system (see Figure 4.3). The dendrites of this neuron, which are responsive to deformation in a way to be described later (see p. 96), intertwine among special muscle cells; furthermore, the cell body is not in its normal position in proximity to the dendrite. Nerve cells of this general type, known as *bipolar neurons* because the axon divides into two branches after leaving the cell body, are quite commonly employed by the nervous system to receive and transmit sensory information.

The most important effector system (that is, a system which has an effect on the environment) from the point of view of gross behavior is the skeletal musculature. Although the details of muscle structure are beyond the scope of this chapter (see articles in Bourne, 1960), information about certain basic anatomic features is required for the discussion in the following chapters. A muscle is constructed of many small muscle cells arranged in parallel. Each muscle cell may be thought of as a long tube, on the order of 100 μ in diameter, running for the length of the muscle. These muscle cells attach at both ends to strong tendons which in turn usually fasten onto bone. The muscle cell is, like nerve cells, bounded by a very thin (100 Å) plasma membrane and has an internal structure consisting of fibers which are responsible for the ability of these cells to shorten or exert force on their attachments. Just as one neuron forms a synapse with other neurons, so do neurons synapse with muscle cells; the neuron which sends its axon to synapse with a muscle cell is called a *motoneuron,* and the synapse between motoneuron and muscle cell is known as the *myoneural junction.*

Although the most readily observed effects of nervous system operation are mediated through the skeletal musculature, neuronal signals can also produce glandular secretion. Glandular secretions are, of course, sometimes viewed as behavior, but more frequently this effector system is studied in the separate field of neuroendocrinology (see Martini & Ganong, 1966).

NEURON FUNCTION

The properties of neurons and their interconnections ultimately underlie all behavior, and so the most natural context for a discussion of neuron function is as the substrate for behavior. Even a simple behavior is characteristically quite complicated in its own right, however, and in only relatively few

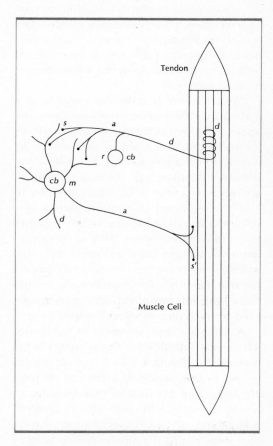

Figure 4.4. This figure presents a schematic representation of the neuronal network responsible for a stretch reflex that operates on a hypothetical three-muscle cell muscle. The bipolar receptor neuron *r* has its stretch-sensitive dendrite wrapped around a special muscle cell and sends its axon to synapse *s* with the motoneuron *m.* The motoneuron *m* sends its axon *a* to form a myoneural junction *s'* with one of the two remaining muscle cells. The innervation of the third muscle cell is not illustrated.

instances can the orderliness of behavior be traced in great detail to the underlying neural function. To minimize complications, then, neuron function is described in the context of a particularly simple form of behavior, the *reflex*. Although more complicated behavior can seldom, if ever, be analyzed into simple component reflexes, it is true that most of the properties of neurons now known do appear in a description of the reflex. Thus it must be remembered that although a simple reflex is used for illustration, the neuronal properties to be discussed are general ones, and are believed to form the substrate for more complicated behavior.

The knee jerk is a familiar example of a particularly simple reflex; when muscles in the upper leg (the quadriceps, a knee extensor) are subjected to a rapid passive stretch by tapping the muscle tendon just below the knee cap (the stimulus)[2], the muscles contract actively after a brief delay, causing the leg to kick (the response). The following discussion will introduce the basic functional properties of neurons in the context of this simple reflex. Before embarking upon a study of neuronal mechanisms, however, we must first outline the anatomical basis for the reflex and provide some basic information about the technique used for recording bioelectric signals.

A schematic representation of the neuroanatomical substrate for the stretch reflex is presented in Figure 4.4. Two neurons are involved in this simplified example (see page 103 and Figure 4.14 for a more realistic representation of the reflex substrate in terms of populations of two neuron types). The receptor neuron (*r*) is a bipolar neuron with its dendrites intertwined with certain special muscle cells and its axon traveling to form a synapse (*s*) with the second neuron (*m*). This second neuron, a motoneuron, in turn sends its axon back to the same muscle, where it forms a neuromuscular junction (*s'*). The task now is to understand the operation

of each link in the chain of events between the stimulus (passive stretch of the muscle) and the response (active contraction of the muscle). Because the neural activity is associated with voltage changes within the neurons, an understanding of nerve-cell properties requires some knowledge of the technique for measuring each of these voltage changes.

Basic Recording Techniques

The general experimental arrangement used for measuring nerve and muscle voltages is illustrated in Figure 4.5. An electrode that makes contact with the tissues being studied is held in a micromanipulator which, because nerve and muscle cells are small, must permit movements of the electrode tip to an accuracy that is on the order of 1 to 10 μ. For reasons to be described later, signals from the electrode are usually led through a special input circuit and then into a preamplifier, which provides output voltages of convenient amplitude. The signals are then usually displayed by making a graph of voltage as a function of time; this is done either with a special ink writing device, or more frequently with an oscilloscope. Whitfield (1959) has provided a readable and more detailed account of the electronic apparatus used in electrophysiology, and the book edited by Nastuk (1964) contains excellent articles on electrodes, micromanipulators, and electronic equipment and its use.

A variety of different electrode types are used for recording the electrical activity of nerve and muscle. In some instances, for recording the EEG (see p. 114) cardiac (see p. 834) and other potentials from the body surface, the recording electrodes are simply silver, platinum, or stainless steel buttons or bands taped or glued to the skin. Stainless steel needles, insulated except for the tip, are inserted into muscles to monitor the electrical activity associated with muscle movements. For recording gross electrical activity from within the brain (see p. 113, for example), satisfactory electrodes may be constructed

---

[2] By tapping the muscle tendon, the tendon is briefly indented and the attached muscle quickly stretched by a small amount.

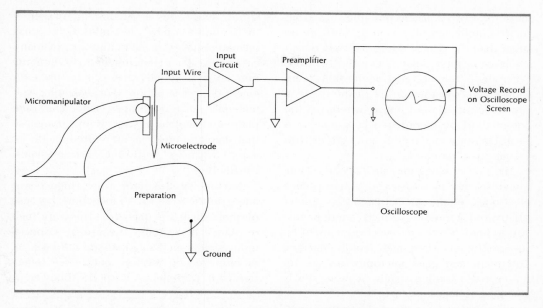

Figure 4.5. The basic arrangement for recording signals from neural tissues involves a micromanipulator to position an electrode on the preparation, a microelectrode to connect the recording apparatus to the preparation, and appropriate equipment for amplifying and displaying the voltages originating in the neural tissue.

from stainless steel, platinum-iridium, or tungsten wire about 200–400 μ in diameter, coated, except for the tip, with varnish or some other insulating material; also, fine insect pins similarly insulated are often used.

The electrodes described in the preceding paragraph are all used for recording the activity of simultaneous active groups of cells; for recording from a single cell, electrodes with particularly small tips, known as *microelectrodes,* are required. Although there is a variety of types of microelectrode, it is convenient to divide them into two classes, the metal microelectrodes and fluid-filled glass micropipettes. Metal microelectrodes are most commonly constructed by electrolytically sharpening stainless steel insect pins or fine tungsten wire which is then coated with insulating varnish. Metal microelectrodes are frequently employed for recording extracellular signs of activity in single cells (see p. 112).

Glass micropipettes used for intracellular recording (that is, for recording potential differences between the inside of the cell and the bathing solution; see p. 95) are made by drawing out glass capillary tubing (with a 1 mm outside diameter, for example) to an extremely fine tip and filling it with a concentrated salt solution. Such electrodes are drawn by heating a short stretch of the capillary tubing until the glass becomes soft, and then pulling rapidly. With this technique it is possible to construct hollow microneedles with an external tip diameter of 0.25 μ or less. The electrodes are then filled by boiling them in concentrated salt solution, 2.8 molar KCl for example, under reduced pressure. The construction of various types of electrode is well described in Nastuk (1964).

Several general principles govern the design and manufacture of electrodes used for recording bioelectric potentials. These principles pertain to the electrical, mechanical, and biological properties of the electrodes. Because different voltages occur in neighboring regions of the brain at the same time, there is a danger that an electrode will record the sum of two adjacent potentials. To avoid such summing, an electrode tip must be no larger than the size of the region over which a voltage is approximately constant. Thus, if a certain potential variation in time were widespread over the surface of the tissue, a large electrode would suffice, whereas if the potential to be recorded occurs only in a small, circumscribed region, an electrode with a small tip is required.

The smaller electrodes are made, the more their resistance increases, and high resistance electrodes require special circuits (see later discussion). For reasons which cannot be discussed here, metal microelectrodes are often superior for recording small, rapidly changing potentials, and glass micropipettes are required for recording steady or more slowly changing voltages.

An essential property of electrodes is that they do not damage the tissue in which they are being used. When recording is to be made from the depth of the brain, one uses an electrode with as small a diameter as possible in order to minimize trauma to the surrounding tissues. If a cell is to survive penetration by an electrode, the electrode tip must be very small indeed; this is why microelectrodes are required for intracellular recording. Although any metal will do for recording electrical activity in the brain, the ions from certain materials tend to be toxic to the tissues. Thus, stainless steel, silver, platinum, or other relatively inert metals are preferred, and metals such as copper and zinc are avoided. If fluid-filled electrodes are used, either electrodes are manufactured with a tip so small that diffusion of the contained salt solution is minimal, or, if a larger tip diameter is used, the electrode is filled with a physiological salt solution.

As is stated above, to obtain finely localized recordings, and to minimize damage to the tissues, it is generally desirable to use an electrode with as small a diameter as possible. However, one often wishes to insert these electrodes through tough material, or into the depth of the brain. Thus, large, or at least

strong, electrodes are required. Altogether then, one must have electrodes with a small diameter but with great rigidity and mechanical stability. These requirements also limit the number of materials that can be used for electrode construction. For example, soft materials such as copper, zinc, and pure platinum generally are not strong enough, so that stainless steel, platinum-iridium alloy, or glass—which is surprisingly strong—must usually be used.

Microelectrodes have a very high resistance, on the order of 10 megohms, because of their small tip diameter. This very high resistance necessitates the use of a special input circuit such as a *cathode follower*, or, of more recent development, a *field effect transistor* amplifier. A cathode follower or

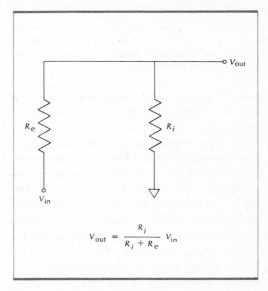

Figure 4.6. The recording situation established after a microelectrode is employed may be represented by the circuit containing an electrode resistance R_e and an input resistance for the amplifier R_i. If the V_{in} is the voltage measured at some point in the neural tissue with respect to some neutral point outside the tissue and V_{out} is the voltage measured with respect to the same neutral point, the relation between these two voltages is given by the equation above. If R_i is very large compared to R_e, the output voltage will be very nearly equal to the input voltage.

$$V_{out} = \frac{R_i}{R_i + R_e} V_{in}$$

some similar device is necessary because any amplifier has a resistance between input and ground, known as the *input resistance*. The resistance may be 1 megohm, although in special amplifiers it may be thousands of megohms. If an electrode with a resistance of say 9 megohms were used with an amplifier with an input resistance of 1 megohm (see Figure 4.6), the electrode and input resistances would form a voltage divider that would attenuate the input signal to one tenth of its true value. Thus, it is clear that the input resistance of the input amplifier must be very high compared to the electrode resistance. For example, if a special circuit with an input resistance of 1000 megohms (such as a cathode follower) were used, the input signal would be attenuated by only 1 percent.

There is another reason why a special input circuit must be employed. In an ordinary amplifier, a certain amount of current flows out of the amplifier through the input. This input circuit current is very low by ordinary standards, on the order of 10^{-9} amps, but it is sufficient to have a marked effect on the nerve cells from which the signals are being recorded. Therefore an appropriate amplifier for electrophysiological investigations must have input current (or *grid current,* as it is often called) that remains much less than 10^{-9} amps.

Elementary Neuron Properties

With the background of the preceding discussion, we may now follow information through the neural circuit subserving the stretch reflex by presenting the schematic intracellular recordings that might be obtained at a number of points along the way. Because the neural mechanisms of the stretch reflex are thought to be typical of nervous system operation in general, tracing information through this neural circuit will serve to introduce important functional properties of nerve cells.

After outlining the sequence of events that starts with muscle stretch (the stimulus) and ends with the muscle contraction (the re-

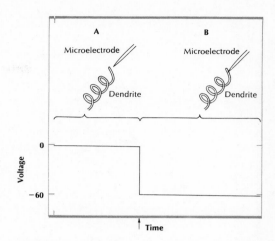

Figure 4.7. A. A microelectrode tip is placed in the bathing solution outside of the bipolar neuron dendrite, and the voltage measured is 0 volts (the bathing solution is grounded). B. The microelectrode is inserted into the sensory neuron dendrite at the time indicated by the arrow, and at once a potential of −60 millivolts is recorded; this is the resting potential.

sponse), we return to several reflex properties for a more detailed consideration. It must be emphasized that the approach here is primarily descriptive and does not deal with the mechanism of the events described. Certain points about mechanism are discussed later in the chapter, but for more detail the reader may refer—in order of increasing difficulty—to Stevens (1966), Ochs (1965), and Ruch and Patton (1965). Further, a number of simplifications will be made for the sake of convenience; some of these simplifications will also be discussed at a later point.

If a microelectrode were advanced toward the dendrite of a bipolar neuron (see Figure 4.7) until the cell is penetrated, that is until the microelectrode tip entered the interior of the dendrite, the recording apparatus would register a steady voltage difference relative to the bathing fluid of approximately −60 millivolts. This constant voltage or inside-outside *polarization* of the cell is known as the *resting potential,* and it is a characteristic of all inactive neurons as well as of other cells. During any activity of the neuron, the voltage re-

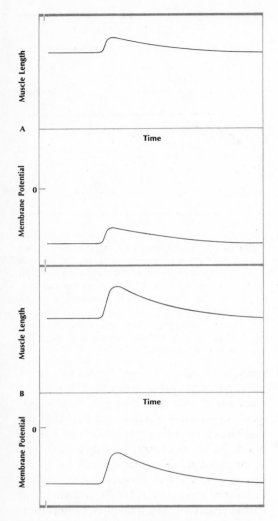

Figure 4.8. Graphs of muscle length as a function of time are presented here with corresponding graphs of membrane potential as a function of time. In A, a slight stretch was applied to the muscle resulting in the lower membrane potential recording. In B a larger muscle stretch produced a larger depolarization.

corded with the microelectrode varies, rather than remaining constant, and for this reason it is useful as well as traditional to have a general term for the voltage inside the cell relative to the outside solution. Because voltage differences exist across the cell membrane, the inside-outside potential difference

is called the *membrane potential.* The resting potential, then, is the particular membrane potential that is recorded in the resting cell. The remainder of this section describes variations in membrane potential that are observed during neuron function.

When the muscle is subjected to a brief stretch, the receptor neuron dendrite is deformed and a change in membrane potential is produced within the dendrite. This voltage change, called the *generator potential,* is the characteristic response of the dendrites to deformation (see Figure 4.8A). If the muscle is stretched more intensely, the generator potential is of greater magnitude (see Figure 4.8B). Altogether, then, by a mechanism which is considered later, the dendrites contain an electrical representation of the muscle stretch within the neuron; the magnitude of the stretch is represented by the magnitude of the membrane potential change.

At this point, it will be convenient to introduce some descriptive terminology widely used in discussions of neuron function. In the resting neuron, the membrane potential is approximately −60 millivolts, that is, the inside is 60 millivolts negative with respect to the outside of the neuron. In the case of the dendrites just described, stretching the muscle caused dendritic deformation and produced a change in the membrane potential toward zero volts. Specifically, the membrane potential changed from −60 millivolts in the resting state to −20 millivolts at the peak of the stretch. Such a change is called a *depolarization.* More generally, any change in the membrane potential that causes the interior of the neuron to become less negative than the resting potential is a depolarization, so that the effect of the stimulation of sensory neuron dendrites can be described by saying that stretch causes a dendritic depolarization the magnitude of which reflects the magnitude of the stimulus. Similarly, changes in the membrane potential that cause the inside of the neuron to become more negative than the resting potential are termed *hyperpolarizations.* The terms *de-* and *hyperpolarization*

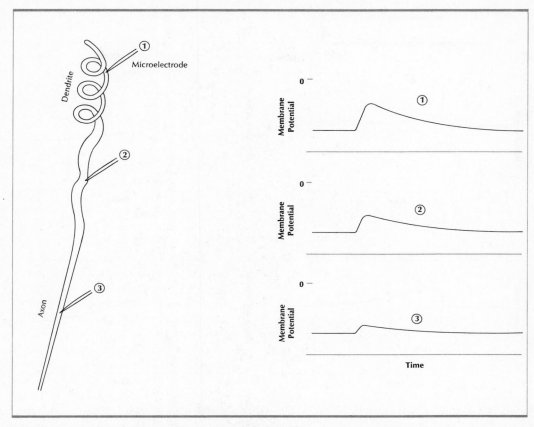

Figure 4.9. Three microelectrodes inserted into the dendrite are indicated by the numbers 1, 2, and 3. When a small stretch is applied to the muscle, the depolarizations that might hypothetically be recorded from each electrode are indicated in the graphs numbered 1, 2, and 3, corresponding to the electrodes with the same number. All three graphs have the same time axis.

arise, of course, because they describe changes in the cell's natural polarization.

With muscle stretch represented as dendritic depolarization, the next problem facing the nervous system is the transmission of this information about stretch to other nerve cells. If a second microelectrode ([2] in Figure 4.9) is inserted into the dendrite at a greater distance from the muscle than the first microelectrode, the generator potential at this more distant point is observed to be smaller than at the closer recording site (see Figure 4.9). If a third microelectrode ([3] in Figure 4.9) is inserted still further away from the muscle, the generator potential at this point is still smaller. A more detailed examination reveals

that the generator potential magnitude falls off quite rapidly with distance from the region of the dendrites where the dendritic membrane is deformed, that is, where the generator potential originates. If a larger stretch is applied to the muscle, thus producing a larger generator potential, this larger generator potential is also seen to decay in magnitude from its site of origin in the dendrite. The phenomenon of a depolarization in one region of a dendrite spreading to neighboring regions is termed *passive spread*. Passive spread of a depolarization along a dendrite is quite analogous to the spread of heat along an iron bar when one region of the bar is heated. Similarly, just as cold will spread

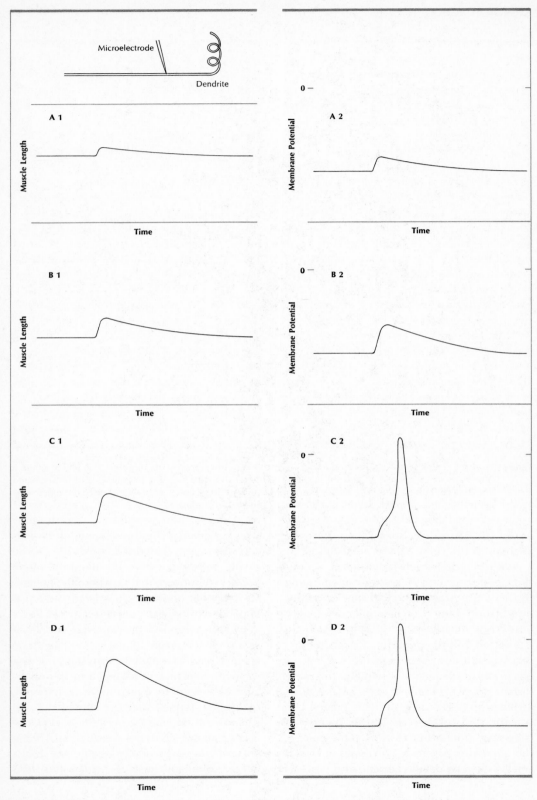

Figure 4.10. Pairs of graphs plotting muscle length and membrane potential as a function of time are presented for muscle stretches of various magnitudes. The recordings are hypothetical ones obtained from a stretch receptor axon near the dendrites.

along an iron bar from a cooled region, so will a hyperpolarization spread passively along a dendrite. In summary, then, a generator potential influences neighboring regions of the dendrite by a process called passive spread, and through this mechanism information about stretch of the muscle is transmitted over several millimeters.

Although the generator potential spreads passively for several millimeters, it is apparent that some further mechanism must be responsible for the transmission of information over the relatively long distances spanned by neuron axons; if passive spread were the only mechanism, the depolarization would decrease to undetectable levels long before the signal reached the axon terminal. Indeed, axons exhibit a particular type of response, the *action potential,* that permits transfer of information over the entire axon length; to see how axons can transmit information we must consider the action potential in detail. Figure 4.10 shows intracellular recordings from a site in the axon near its junction with the dendrite. The magnitude of the stretch applied to the muscle was increased for each of the succeeding records A through D. Only the generator potential, which has spread passively from its site of origin in the dendrite, appears in A and B. In C, the slightly larger stretch has produced not only a somewhat larger generator potential at the site of

recording, but, in addition, a new response of the axon consisting of a 90 millivolt depolarization lasting approximately 1 millisecond. This brief explosive depolarization, the characteristic response of axons, is the action potential. The graphs in Figure 4.10 are hypothetical results of the experiment described; Figure 4.11 is taken from a photograph of the oscilloscope trace of the action potential in an actual experiment.

It is important to emphasize a fundamental difference in the properties of the generator potential and the action potential. The generator potential was caused by an external stimulus—deformation of the dendritic membrane in the example above—whereas the action potential was caused by a depolarization. Thus, in one case a mechanical stimulus produced a neuronal voltage change (the generator potential), and in the other case one voltage change (the generator potential) produced another (the action potential). The adequate stimulus for an action potential, then, is a depolarization.   148634

Two additional differences in the properties of generator potentials and action potentials deserve special mention. It will be recalled that no threshold was apparent in the production of the generator potential; the very slightest stretch produced some detectable generator potential. In contrast, threshold behavior was apparent in the case of the action potential discussed in the preceding paragraph. The two smaller generator potentials A and B in Figure 4.10 produced no action potential, whereas both of the larger generator potentials in that figure gave rise to an action potential. The existence of a threshold, then, is a conspicuous property of action potentials not exhibited by generator potentials. A second difference between generator potentials and action potentials is that while increasing stimulus magnitude produced increasingly larger responses in the case of the generator potential, as is illustrated in C and D in Figure 4.10, an increase in the size of the generator potential did not cause larger action potentials. (Increasing the size of a

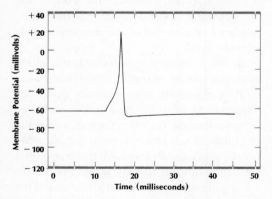

Figure 4.11. A tracing from an oscilloscope record from an experiment illustrates the form of the nerve action potential.

generator potential does have an effect on the *rate* at which action potentials occur, however. See page 108.) This property of action potentials is usually referred to as the *all-or-none law* which states that no action potential results from a below-threshold stimulus (that is, generator potential), whereas the action potentials produced by above-threshold depolarizations are all identical in size regardless of the magnitude of the depolarization.

It is now possible to describe how action potentials permit the transmission of information over long distances in the nervous system. Axons, like dendrites, exhibit the phenomenon of passive spread, so that an action potential will spread to neighboring regions of the axons much as the generator potential spreads to neighboring regions of the dendrite. Thus the action potential will cause a large, brief depolarization of the axon region immediately adjacent to the site of origin of the action potential. This depolarization will itself give rise to an action potential, which will in turn spread to the neighboring region of the axon where again it will cause a depolarization, and still another action potential. Much as the flame sweeps along a firecracker fuse, the action potential sweeps along the axon.

One might ask why an action potential does not spread backwards and re-excite the region which was just previously active. Re-excitation is prevented from occurring because of another property of axons termed the *refractory period.* An axon which has just generated an action potential is temporarily inexcitable, that is, it will not produce another action potential until there has been adequate time for recovery. Thus depolarizations that spread passively back into a previously active region of the axon cannot stimulate this region to produce an action potential. Passive spread of depolarization, the all-or-none phenomenon, and the refractory period thus combine to permit the nervous system to transmit information over long distances.

For the reasons described in the preceding paragraph, action potentials normally travel in only one direction along an axon, from the axon's origin toward the axon terminals which form synapses with the next cell. The impressive term *orthodromic* is used to describe this normal direction of action potential propagation; thus one would say, "Normal action potentials are orthodromic" which would simply mean that normal action potentials conduct in the normal direction. For a variety of reasons, it is often useful in experiments to excite an axon near the terminal end and cause an action potential to travel in the reverse of the normal direction. This reverse direction is called *antidromic,* and one would say, for example, "Exciting an axon near its terminal causes an antidromic action potential."

A modification of the transmission process just described occurs in many axons in the vertebrate nervous system. Although some axons may be considered to be a long cylinder with uniform properties, other axons, termed *myelinated axons,* have small patches of membrane capable of generating action potentials. These patches are separated by long stretches of axon over which the excitable membrane is covered by an insulating *myelin sheath.* The excitable patches are termed *nodes of Ranvier.* In these myelinated axons, the action potential does not spread continuously along as previously discussed, but rather hops from node to node. This specialization of the axon saves energy for the organism. It also serves to speed up the conduction process, for it is not necessary for the action potential to excite all of the membrane, only selected parts.

By the process just described, the action potential sweeps along the myelinated axon until it comes to the synapses upon the motoneuron (*s'* in Figure 4.4). Whenever an action potential reaches terminals, a quantity of chemical substance, termed a *transmitter substance,* is rapidly released. This transmitter substance diffuses quickly across the narrow 200 Å gap between the axon terminal and the motoneuron dendrite, where it is broken down to an inactive form, often in less than

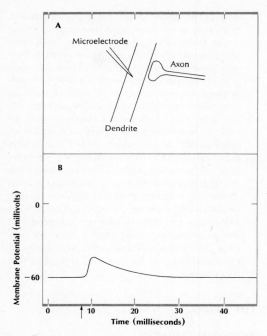

Figure 4.12. A illustrates the recording situation with the microelectrode inserted into the motoneuron dendrite. The result of an action potential invading the axon terminal, an EPSP, is shown in B. Note that the duration of the EPSP is 10 or more times that of an action potential. The action potential reached the axon terminal at the time indicated by the arrow.

is transmitted over the motoneuron's dendrites by passive spread and decreases in amplitude with distance from its origin.

Just as the generator potential spreads down the receptor neuron's dendrites to the axon, where it generates an action potential, so does the EPSP spread along the motoneuron's dendrites, through the soma, and into the axon where, as in the receptor neuron, an action potential is generated, provided the EPSP is above threshold. This action potential then sweeps along the motoneuron axon until it reaches the axon terminals on the muscle, the myoneural junction (s' in Figure 4.4).

The synaptic contact between motoneuron axons and the muscle, the myoneural junction, is essentially like the synapse already

a millisecond. During the period before its inactivation, however, the transmitter substance has a very marked effect upon the dendrite of the motoneuron. This effect is illustrated in Figure 4.12. A microelectrode inserted into the dendrite near the axon terminal would record a depolarization which rises rapidly and lasts for approximately 10 milliseconds or more. Further investigation would reveal that this rapid depolarization, called the *excitatory postsynaptic potential* or EPSP, shares many properties with the generator potential. It has no threshold, for even the smallest amount of transmitter produces an effect; the size of the EPSP reflects the concentration of transmitter applied to the dendritic membrane. Furthermore, the EPSP

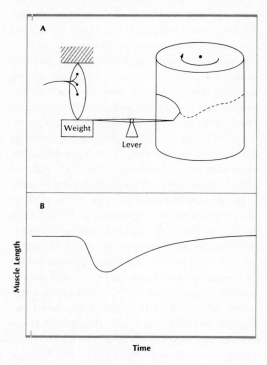

Figure 4.13. A. The muscle is fixed at one end and is provided with a weight to lift at the other end. When an action potential is produced by the muscle cell membrane, the muscle lifts the weight and contracts, as is illustrated in the graph in B.

described. When an action potential reaches the axon terminal, transmitter substance is released and a depolarization with the appearance of an EPSP occurs within the muscle. Although this depolarization has the same general appearance as an EPSP, it has been called, for historical reasons, an *end-plate potential,* abbreviated EPP. The muscle membrane is much like the axon membrane; it also generates action potentials when depolarized. Thus when the EPP occurs, an action potential is generated within the muscle cell. Muscle cells are specialized to contract, and the event which triggers their contraction is a large depolarization. Then when an action potential occurs in a muscle cell, a brief contraction results. This is termed a *muscle twitch* (see Figure 4.13).

We have now traced the chain of events between the stimulus (muscle stretch) and the response (muscle contraction). Stretching the muscle produces a generator potential in the dendrites of the bipolar neuron, and this generator potential spreads passively to the axon of the neuron. In the axon, action potentials are generated, and these sweep along the axon to the terminals upon a motoneuron. An EPSP is produced in the motoneuron as a result of the transmitter release from the axon terminal of the bipolar neuron, and this EPSP causes the motoneuron in turn to generate an action potential. The motoneuron's action potential is propagated along the axon to the myoneural junction, where it causes an EPP; the EPP triggers an action potential in the muscle cell, and this muscle action potential in turn results in contraction of the muscle. It must be emphasized that the properties of nerve cells which have been described in connection with the stretch reflex are not peculiar to this reflex, but indeed are common to neurons throughout the nervous system.

Before returning to a more thorough consideration of certain aspects of the stretch reflex, it is well to make explicit a distinction between the properties of axons and dendrites that has only been implied in the preceding discussion. Note that axons have been described as giving action potentials, whereas dendrites have been described as producing graded depolarizations, generator potentials, or EPSPs. Although there is still controversy regarding the extent to which action potentials can invade dendrites, we shall continue to maintain a sharp distinction between the properties of axons and dendrites. Specifically, it is assumed that a response typical of axons is the action potential and that action potentials do not occur in dendrites. Similarly, EPSPs, or generator potentials, are considered the sole property of dendrites. Although such a sharp distinction between axon and dendrite properties breaks down in fact, a less dogmatic version of the same distinction is generally accepted, and for our present purposes we may therefore continue to maintain a clear separation between characteristics of the axonal and dendritic membranes.

THE REFLEX

Behavioral Properties

Viewed as a simple form of behavior, the reflex has a number of characteristic properties, most of which now have a reasonably satisfactory neurophysiological explanation. Because the neural correlates of many of these properties serve to elucidate general mechanisms operating in the nervous system, an abbreviated listing of reflex properties is presented here preliminary to a discussion of their neuronal basis. Our classification of reflex properties follows Skinner's (1938) discussion of what he termed the static and dynamic laws of reflex behavior.

A conspicuous property of reflexes is the existence of threshold, or, in Skinner's terminology, the Law of Threshold. This law refers to the fact that the stimulus must reach a certain critical amplitude before the response is elicited; in the case of the stretch reflex, then, a passive stretch of the muscle of a certain critical size would be required in order to produce an active contraction of that muscle, and smaller passive stretches would be without effect. A second characteristic of reflexes is that they have a nonzero, and usually quite noticeable, latency (the Law of

Latency). For example, a delay of approximately 25 milliseconds is observed between the stretch of the muscle (the stimulus) and the active contraction of that muscle (the response), and in other reflexes the latency can be quite long, up to a number of seconds. A third property of reflexes relates to the reflex magnitude; this is Skinner's Law of the Magnitude of the Response. As one presents stronger and stronger stimuli—larger muscle stretches in the case of the stretch reflex—a parallel increase in the response magnitude— the muscle contraction—is typically observed.

Stimuli that do not themselves elicit a particular reflex can, however, affect the size of the response when they are paired with stimuli which do elicit the response. Thus, certain stimuli make themselves felt only indirectly, but not directly. If an indirectly effective stimulus causes a larger response, that stimulus is said to *facilitate* the reflex; in contrast, if an indirectly effective stimulus causes the response magnitude to diminish, or causes the response to be absent, that stimulus is said to cause *inhibition*. Skinner referred to these reflex properties as the "Laws of Facilitation and Inhibition." These fourth and fifth properties of reflex action, namely the properties of inhibition and facilitation, are illustrated by the stretch reflex: A muscle that has the same action as the particular test muscle is termed a *synergist*, or synergistic muscle, while a muscle which has an opposing action to the test muscle is called an *antagonist*, or antagonistic muscle. For example, if the test muscle bends the elbow, another muscle which also bends the elbow is a synergist, and one which straightens the elbow is an antagonist. A brief stretch of a synergistic muscle or of an antagonistic muscle does not cause a contraction of the test muscle. However, if a brief stretch of a synergist is paired with a subthreshold stretch of the test muscle, an active contraction of the test muscle may result; the stretch reflex has been facilitated by a simultaneous stretch of a synergist. Alternatively, if a brief stretch of an antagonistic muscle is paired with a suprathreshold stretch

of the test muscle, the contraction of the test muscle may be absent or diminished; stretch of an antagonist causes reflex inhibition.

The five laws just described identify important behavioral properties of the reflex; we now outline the current neurophysiological explanations for these laws, and in doing so we discuss mechanisms of neural interaction thought to be central to much of neuronal function.

Neural Integration

Although a complete analysis of the factors responsible for reflex latency is beyond the scope of the present discussion, it is important to identify several neuronal properties

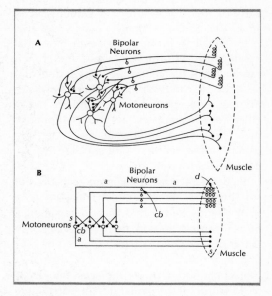

Figure 4.14. The dotted lines indicate the boundaries of the muscle (the individual muscle cells are not illustrated). In A, a group of four bipolar sensory neurons sense the stretch of the muscle and send their axons to a group of four motoneurons. These motoneurons in turn send their axons back to muscle cells within the muscle body. Part B shows the same type of circuit in a still more schematic form. The degree of simplification in this figure can be appreciated from the fact that an actual muscle would be supplied by perhaps 1000 motoneurons rather than 4.

which set the minimum latency of such a reflex. An action potential does not spread instantaneously from one end of an axon to another, but rather is conducted at velocities between 0.1 and 100 m/sec depending on the axon. Furthermore, there is a delay, called the *synaptic delay,* of approximately 0.5 millisecond between the time when the action potential reaches the axon terminals and the appearance of the EPSP in the motoneuron. The conduction delay over axons and the synaptic delay thus establish the minimum latency for a reflex because they determine the minimum time required for information to travel from the sense organ back to the muscle responsible for the response.

An obvious explanation for the minimum threshold of a reflex is contained in earlier parts of this discussion: If a stimulus is so weak that the resulting generator potential is too small to produce an action potential in the axon, information about the stretch cannot reach the central nervous system and no response can result. In actuality, however, the factors determining threshold are rather more complicated, and an understanding of them requires a somewhat more detailed picture of the neuronal interconnections underlying the stretch reflex.

Figure 4.14 presents a more realistic, but still highly schematic circuit diagram of a stretch reflex. Rather than there being a single bipolar sensory neuron, there is a large population of these neurons (represented by only four in the figure), and a pool of perhaps a thousand motoneurons replaces the single motoneuron of the earlier description (Figure 4.4). Each sensory neuron sends its axon to synapse with a number of different motoneurons, and each motoneuron receives synaptic contacts from a number of different sensory neurons. To see how reflex threshold is determined by this interconnecting neural circuit, it is necessary to investigate the effect of several simultaneously active axons on a single motoneuron.

When separate synapses on a motoneuron are simultaneously active, the total effect is,

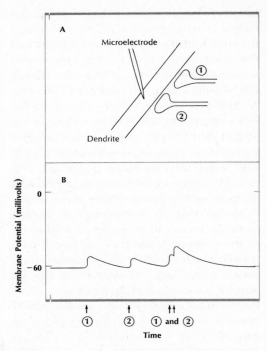

Figure 4.15. A. The microelectrode is inserted into a dendrite near two synapses, 1 and 2. B. Recordings from the dendrite reveal the EPSPs produced by stimulating the axons leading to synapses 1 and 2. The numbers below the arrows indicate which synapses were responsible for production of the EPSP. Note that the size of the EPSP is not the same for both synapses; this illustrates the natural variation that occurs between the effects of different synapses. Spatial summation results when both synapses are simultaneously active (arrows denote 1 and 2).

to a first approximation, simply the sum of the separate effects. The interaction of synchronously occurring EPSPs is illustrated in Figure 4.15; the first EPSP is the result of an action potential arriving at synapse No. 1, the second EPSP is the effect of an action potential arriving at synapse No. 2, and the third EPSP is the result of simultaneous activity of both synapses 1 and 2. This phenomenon of summation of effects from separate synapses is termed *spatial summation.* Note that the designation *EPSP* applies both to the effect of a single synapse, and to the sum effect of a number of synchronously active synapses.

The magnitude of an EPSP produced by a single axon is on the order of .1 to .2 millivolt, and, because approximately a 10 millivolt depolarization is required to produce an action potential in a motoneuron, we may estimate that some 50 or more receptors must be stimulated in order to activate motoneurons. The stretch receptors in a muscle generally have a range of thresholds, and the magnitude of a stimulus adequate to excite a number of these receptors is therefore considerably above the minimum required to excite the most sensitive receptor. Because a response can result only if at least one motoneuron is activated, the reflex threshold requires stimulation of a number of muscle stretch receptors. The precise number required will depend on details of the distribution of axon synapses among the motoneuron population, and on the distribution of receptor thresholds. It should be noted that whereas a single EPSP generally has a peak amplitude of only .1 to .2 millivolt, a single EPP is much larger. In fact, one EPP is sufficiently large to be above threshold for the muscle cell. Once a motoneuron sends an action potential to a muscle cell, that muscle cell will give a twitch contraction.

Just as individual EPSPs can add together to produce a larger depolarization, so can the twitch contraction of individual muscle cells sum to give a larger muscle contraction. This summation of contractions occurs because the individual muscle fibers exert their effect through a common attachment to bone, so that the total force exerted is the sum of the individual forces. Each motoneuron sends its axon to form myoneural junctions with a limited number of muscle cells, and thus the amplitude of a response depends upon the number of motoneurons activated.

It is now possible to see why increasing the stimulus magnitude causes an increased response magnitude. Consider the stretch reflex: As we apply larger brief stretches to the muscle, we increase the stimulus above the threshold for greater numbers of receptors, and consequently the motoneuron pool

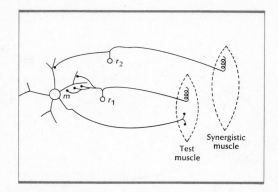

Figure 4.16. The neuroanatomical basis for the effect of synergistic muscle stretch upon the stretch reflex is illustrated by including neuron r_2 in the stretch reflex circuit made up of neurons r_1 and m.

receives a larger number of action potentials. As an increased number of synapses is activated in the motoneuron pool, spatial summation of the individual EPSPs produces an above-threshold depolarization in greater numbers of motoneurons. Therefore, more muscle cells are activated, and the increased number of individual twitches sum to give a larger total contraction. The precise details of the relationship between stimulus intensity and response magnitude, of course, depend on the exact neural circuit arrangement and upon the range of thresholds of the individual elements involved. Nevertheless, the general notion of the cooperative activity of the elements in a pool of neurons is a valid one and illustrates a general principle of nervous system functioning.

Not all axons synapsing with a motoneuron have a single source. Rather many neurons within the nervous system and many different receptors send their axons to form synapses on a given motoneuron. In addition to stretch receptors in the test muscle, stretch receptors in synergistic muscles send their axons to terminate upon the motoneuron, as is illustrated in Figure 4.16. Intracellular recording reveals that stretch of synergistic muscles causes EPSPs in the test motoneuron, but that these EPSPs are generally smaller than those produced by stretch of the receptors in the

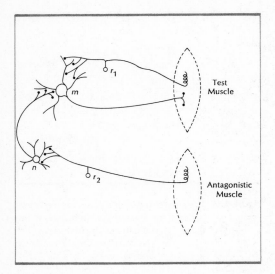

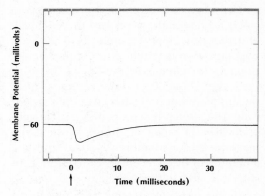

Figure 4.17. The effects of antagonistic muscle stretch on the stretch reflex are mediated through an interneuron *n* as illustrated in this figure. The stretch reflex circuit consists of the receptor (r_1) and the motoneuron (*m*); stretches of the antagonistic muscle are detected by the receptor r_2.

Figure 4.18. At the point indicated by the arrow, an action potential arrives at the axon terminal producing the illustrated IPSP. Note that the form and duration of the IPSP are generally similar to those of the EPSP but that the IPSP is hyperpolarizing, rather than depolarizing.

test muscle. In fact, EPSPs produced by stretching synergistic muscles are not sufficiently large to cause the test motoneurons to produce action potentials. However, subthreshold EPSPs arising from slight stretches of the test muscle can sum with EPSPs from the synergistic muscle and produce a depolarization sufficiently large to activate the motoneurons, thus producing a response. This, then, is the explanation for reflex facilitation.

Figure 4.17 presents a schematic neural circuit for a stretch reflex that includes the contributions from antagonistic muscles. Axons from stretch receptors in the antagonistic muscle terminate upon a neuron within the nervous system, which in turn sends its axon to the test motoneuron; this intermediate neuron is termed an *interneuron,* or *internuncial neuron.* Intracellular recording reveals that stretching the antagonistic muscle produces EPSPs in the interneuron and that these EPSPs can be sufficiently large to cause action potentials to be produced.

Recording from the motoneuron, one finds that stretching the antagonistic muscles produces a brief hyperpolarization, which has the same general form as an EPSP but is, of course, inverted (see Figure 4.18). This hyperpolarization is a second type of synaptic event, called an *inhibitory postsynaptic potential,* or IPSP. Generally speaking, IPSPs have the same properties as EPSPs in that they show spatial summation and spread passively along the dendrite. Furthermore, IPSPs and EPSPs occurring simultaneously show a type of spatial interaction in which the IPSP subtracts from the EPSP. If a stretch of the test muscle just to the threshold is paired with a nearly simultaneous stretch of an antagonistic muscle, the sum of the IPSP and EPSP may cause the depolarization to fall below threshold for producing an action potential in the motoneuron and thus prevent a response from occurring. These neural circuits, then, provide an explanation for reflex inhibition.

In the preceding discussion we give what is believed to be an essentially correct explanation for a number of the behavioral properties of reflexes. However, additional behavioral properties that are not discussed here also have generally satisfactory, although less completely understood explanations in terms of the properties of neurons and their inter-actions. It should be said, however, that the neuronal basis for two of the reflex laws—Conditioning and Extinction—is at present completely unknown. In fact, the neural basis for information storage is considered by many as neurophysiology's central problem and is currently coming under intensive investigation.

Furthermore, human behavior seldom can be analyzed into single reflexes or even groups of reflexes. The central neurons are in a continuous state of activity, as are also certain integrating centers of afferent and efferent systems. Stimuli do not so much initiate activity as modify existing activity, and responses are generally as dependent on the alertness, previous experience, and other complex aspects of the central nervous system as on immediate sensory input. Thus another of neurophysiology's central problems is to understand the principle of the neural interconnections responsible for these more subtle phenomena.

Temporal Aspects of Neural Interaction

In order to simplify the preceding description of neuron properties, the discussion has been limited to one very special type of stimulation, namely the application of very brief stretches to a stretch-receptor neuron. Most stimuli experienced by the organism in real life, however, are of much longer duration, and the nervous system must transmit information about these longer stimuli. To see how the nervous system handles stimuli of longer duration, we will follow the effects of a long stretch as they proceed around the stretch reflex circuit.

Intracellular recording from the sensory neuron dendrites during a prolonged stretch reveals that, as before, the stretch is represented within the neuron as a depolarization (see Figure 4.19). The duration of the depolarization reflects the duration of the stretch, and the depolarization amplitude represents the magnitude of the stretch. For many receptors, it appears that the relationship between generator potential magnitude and stimulus intensity (assuming the proper

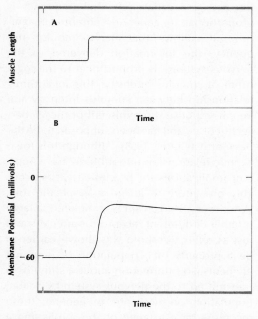

Figure 4.19. The upper graph (A) illustrates muscle length as a function of time during a stretch, and the lower graph (B) shows the generator potential that results from this stretch.

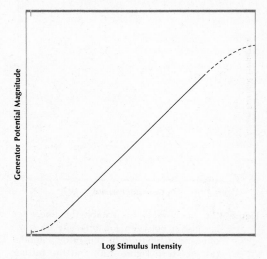

Figure 4.20. Plots of generator potential amplitude as a function of log stimulus intensity are linear over a wide range of stimulus intensities for a number of different receptors, as shown here.

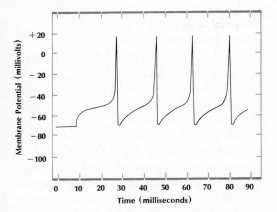

Figure 4.21. This drawing from a photograph of an oscilloscope trace illustrates the repetitive firing produced by a maintained depolarization.

measure of stimulus intensity is used) often is a logarithmic one, as is illustrated in Figure 4.20.

If one compares stretch magnitude with generator potential magnitude, however, some differences may be noted: Most striking is the fact that the generator potential usually

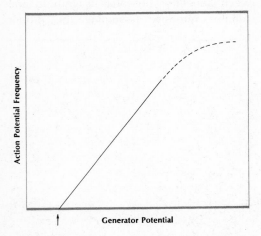

Figure 4.22. Many receptors exhibit the linear relationship between log intensity of stimulus and magnitude of generator potential (as shown in Figure 4.20) and the further linear relationship between magnitude of generator potential and frequency of nerve impulses. The threshold depolarization required to produce an action potential is indicated by the arrow.

declines in the face of a maintained stimulus, a phenomenon known as *adaptation*.

Recording from the axon of a sensory neuron during prolonged stimulation reveals, as might be expected, an action potential at the onset of the generator potential. With a maintained above-threshold generator potential, moreover, a second action potential follows the first after a delay. Furthermore, in many types of neuron, action potentials are produced repeatedly for the duration of an above-threshold depolarization, a phenomenon termed *repetitive discharge* (see Figure 4.21). The frequency of this discharge depends upon the amplitude of the generator potential; for many neurons, action potential frequency (that is, the number of action potentials per second) is proportional to depolarization (see Figure 4.22). Stimulus intensity, then, is first coded logarithmically by the receptor and then transmitted within the nervous system as nerve impulse frequency.

Because generator potential amplitude is proportional to the logarithm of stimulus intensity and action potential frequency is proportional to generator potential magnitude, it follows that nerve impulse frequency—the information delivered to the nervous system—is proportional to the logarithm of stimulus intensity. This logarithmic relationship between stimulus intensity and neural response is reminiscent of the Weber-Fechner Law and has been supposed to be the basis of it (Granit, 1955). Although this logarithmic relationship undoubtedly has important implications for psychology, it is probably premature to assign it a specific role. Whenever an organism is stimulated, a large number of different receptors is affected, and just as reflex threshold was shown earlier to be a property of a population of neuronal elements, so information about a stimulus is transmitted to the nervous system by a large population of receptors. In general, these receptors have a range of thresholds and a variety of proportionality constants by which action potential frequency is related to the logarithm of stimulus intensity. How the sum

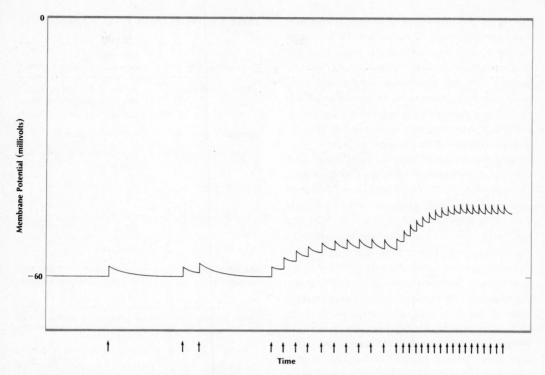

Figure 4.23. This figure illustrates the phenomenon of temporal summation. Each arrow indicates the arrival of an action potential at the axon terminal, and, as can be seen, a steady though rather jagged depolarization is the result of constant frequency of action potential arrivals. It is evident from the figure that a larger average depolarization results from a highter action potential frequency.

total of information carried over all of these receptor channels, with their different properties, is used by the nervous system depends upon the details of the synaptic connections between neurons processing the information. The situation is a very complicated one, then, and it is difficult to assess the significance of any stimulus intensity-action potential frequency relationship without a detailed study of the system under consideration.

Just as EPSPs occurring simultaneously at two separate synapses add together in a neuron, it is reasonable that an EPSP should add to any depolarization remaining from previously occurring EPSPs at the same or other synapses. This phenomenon of an EPSP adding onto the tails of preceding EPSPs is called *temporal summation* (see Figure 4.23) and is extremely important in the functioning of the nervous system. If one records from a moto-

neuron during the stretching of its muscle, the repetitive discharge of the bipolar neuron will cause a rapid sequence of EPSPs to be produced in the motoneuron, and these EPSPs will exhibit temporal summation. Assuming that a second EPSP is produced before the first has died away, the second EPSP will add to what remains of the first; similarly, the third EPSP will sum with the remainder of the first and second, and so on. After an interval equal to the decay time of a single EPSP, this process will reach a steady state, and the mean depolarization will remain constant. This steady (average) depolarization will, by spatial summation, add to the inputs over any other synapses. In this way, then, a replica, although perhaps a distorted one, of the sensory neuron generator potential will have been transmitted to the motoneuron.

The maintained depolarization thus generated by the processes of temporal and spatial summation will be transmitted to the axon by means of passive spread, where, if the depolarization is above threshold, action potentials will be generated repetitively. The process in motoneurons by which a maintained depolarization produces a train of action potentials is strictly analogous to the one already discussed in receptor neurons. Thus, an adequately large muscle stretch will lead first to a maintained generator potential in sensory dendrites, next repetitive firing of sensory axons, then a maintained depolarization of motoneurons, and finally a repetitive discharge over motoneuron axons leading to the muscle cells. In a manner quite analogous to the temporal summation of EPSPs, successive muscle twitches may sum to produce a maintained contraction, the average magnitude of which is approximately proportional to action potential frequency in the motoneuron axons. Thus, in our simplified situation, stretch of a muscle will excite stretch receptors, and these will cause a repetitive discharge of the motoneurons that will result in a maintained contraction of the muscle. Altogether, then, the stretch reflex acts to oppose passive stretches of the muscle by causing active contractions, thus maintaining a constant muscle length in the face of outside disturbances.

Summary of Neuronal Function

The preceding discussion of the stretch reflex has illustrated the types of neural interaction believed to be typical of the function of the nervous system. It is a general rule that receptors act by representing some feature of the environment as a generator potential, and information about this generator potential is, as a rule, transmitted to other neurons in terms of action potential frequency. Furthermore, spatial and temporal summation of EPSPs and IPSPs are of central importance in integrating information within the nervous system. Generator potential magnitude, in general, reflects stimulus intensity, and information about stimulus in-

TABLE 4.1   FREQUENTLY USED EQUIVALENT TERMS*

Term used here	Synonym or approximate equivalent
action potential	spike; spike potential; nerve impulse; impulse; nerve spike
generator potential	receptor potential
myoneural junction	neuromuscular junction; end plate
passive spread	electrotonic spread; electrotonus
electroencephalogram	electrocorticogram (ECG); brain waves
axon terminal	bouton terminal
action potential frequency	nerve impulse frequency; impulse frequency; firing rate

*Although many of the terms are not precisely synonymous, they are frequently used interchangeably.

tensity is carried in terms of action potential frequency and the number of active neurons. Information about the quality of the stimulus, however, as opposed to stimulus magnitude, is represented by the type of neuron or neurons active: Some receptors are maximally sensitive to the deformation of their dendrites, while other neurons respond best, for example, to photic stimulation. Thus by keeping track of which neuron is sending information, the nervous system may know the quality of the stimulus. Finally, although the situation is more complicated, the complex patterns of muscle contractions responsible for gross behavior are produced by mechanisms essentially similar to those involved in the production of a simple stretch reflex.

A number of synonyms for neurophysiological terms are in common use; some of the more important ones appear in Table 4.1.

MECHANISMS OF NERVE ACTIVITY

Although understanding the mechanisms underlying the phenomena described earlier has been a primary concern of students of the nervous system, a detailed presentation of information about these mechanisms is beyond the scope of the present discussion. The following paragraphs deal only briefly with the ionic mechanisms for the action potential and for EPSPs and IPSPs; the reader interested in further details may consult the references cited on page 95.

By the expenditure of metabolic work, nerve cells maintain concentration differences of certain ions across their membranes: Sodium ions are in higher concentration on the outside than on the inside, and potassium ions have a greater concentration inside than outside. The nerve membrane has the ability to increase its permeability to sodium or to potassium independently; and when it does so, sodium, because of its concentration difference, tends to enter the cell, whereas potassium tends to leave the cell. Associated with these ionic flows are changes in membrane potential. The flow of sodium tends to depolarize a neuron while the potassium outflow tends to cause a hyperpolarization.

The event that triggers an increase in sodium permeability is a depolarization, such as that arising from a generator potential. If a nerve cell is depolarized, it rapidly increases its sodium permeability and sodium flows in, causing still further depolarization. This extra depolarization again causes a further increased sodium permeability, increased sodium inflow, additional depolarization, and so on until the cell is quite strongly depolarized. The events just described account for the rising phase of the action potential.

The return of the membrane potential from its peak to the resting potential depends upon two mechanisms. First, after sodium permeability has increased, it then decreases in spite of a depolarization; this phenomenon is termed *sodium inactivation* and is to be contrasted with the increased sodium permeability called *sodium activation*. With the cessation of sodium inflow resulting from sodium inactivation, the membrane potential returns to its resting value. The second mechanism accelerating this return to the resting level is an increase in potassium permeability. Although *potassium activation*, like sodium activation, is a consequence of neuron depolarization, the increase in permeability occurs less rapidly for potassium than for sodium. Thus when the neuron is depolarized by the sodium inflow, potassium permeability increases gradually to a value that is sufficient, when combined with the sodium inactivation, to return the membrane potential to its resting level.

The ionic flows that occur during EPSPs and IPSPs are rather more complicated than those that occur during the action potential in the sense that many different ions may be involved. For our purposes, however, we shall consider the EPSP to be the result of an increase in sodium permeability, and the IPSP to be the result of an increase in potassium permeability. In contrast to the increases in permeability during the action potential, which are triggered solely by a depolarization, the increases in permeability for EPSPs and IPSPs are the result of the transmitter action on the postsynaptic membrane and are independent of the postsynaptic membrane potential. Thus, arrival of an action potential in an axon terminal results in the liberation of a transmitter substance that diffuses to the dendritic membrane; this transmitter then causes an increase in sodium permeability and a consequent depolarization. The transmitter does not continue to act indefinitely, however, because an enzyme transforms it to an inactive form. This destruction occurs very rapidly in many cases, so that the permeability increase producing an EPSP or an IPSP is very short-lived.

OTHER ELECTROPHYSIOLOGICAL TECHNIQUES

Although the intracellular recording technique described in the previous section is in principle the most appropriate one to use for studying the electrical activity of nerve cells, in practice technical difficulties limit its applicability. Fortunately a number of alternative techniques are available for use in situations where intracellular recording is not practicable. Because these techniques involve recording voltages in the fluids surrounding nerve cells, a brief discussion of how voltages arise in a conducting medium is required.

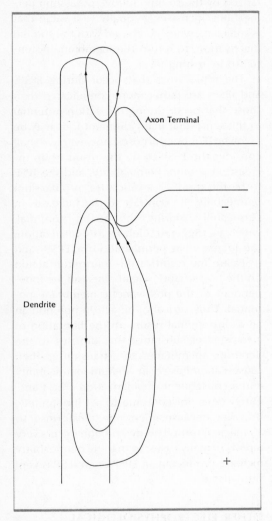

Figure 4.24. Current flows into the dendrite at the site of an EPSP synapse because of the increase of sodium permeability; thus it must flow out through the membrane to make closed loops of current flow of the type illustrated above. Because current flows from + to −, the voltage in the surrounding fluids near the EPSP is negative and is positive at a distance from the synapse.

Nerve cells are surrounded by a fluid that contains, among other things, a relatively high concentration of sodium chloride, and which therefore has a relatively low resistance to the flow of electrical currents. When current flows into a neuron at the site of an EPSP, for example, that current must flow through the neuron interior and out again through the external medium (see Figure 4.24). The activity of nerve cells is therefore associated with currents flowing through the surrounding salt solution, and, because the flow of current through a conductor is associated with voltage differences, the activity of neurons produces voltage differences in the fluid around the cells. Thus by recording the voltage changes in the medium surrounding neurons one can often detect their activity. A detailed explanation of how these extracellular voltages are produced is quite difficult and is beyond the scope of this discussion.

When a neuron discharges action potentials, voltage changes are produced in the surrounding tissue fluids. The amplitude of these voltage changes, which typically ranges from one-tenth to several millivolts, varies inversely with distance from the active soma, and frequently falls to undetectable levels at a distance of several cell-diameters.

Extracellular signs of action potentials are termed, for historical reasons, *extracellular unit potentials*. The term *unit* has its origin in one of the criteria used to identify the activity of one single cell: Often it happens that an extracellular electrode will detect the activity of two adjacent neurons simultaneously, and because the amplitude of the signals recorded from both cells seldom are of the same size, one can distinguish between the responses of the two cells. In contrast if a record reveals signals of a uniform size, it can be concluded that those voltages were generated by a single cell; these "unitary voltages" are now referred to as *unit voltages* or simply *units*. The advantage of extracellular unit recording over the intracellular technique described previously is that extracellular recording is much less difficult, and is even possible in waking, freely moving organisms (see, for example, Evarts, 1968).

Unlike the extracellular signs of a single action potential, the current flows resulting from activation of one or a few synapses are usually too small to produce detectable voltage changes in the fluids surrounding the cell. However, if a large number of synapses are synchronously active and if the shape and orientation of the cells is such that the current from these synapses flows in the same direction and therefore sums, it is possible to record quite large voltage changes. The voltage changes produced by synchronously occurring EPSPs and IPSPs form the basis for an electrophysiological technique termed the *evoked potential method*. Using a brief stimulus, it is possible to produce synchronous action potentials in a bundle of axons that form synapses on cells in a certain region. Because all of the action potentials arrive simultaneously, the postsynaptic potentials are produced simultaneously, and it is possible to record a relatively large voltage change in the region; this voltage change is termed the *evoked potential*. Because evoked potentials are usually the product of a population of cells, it is often quite difficult to infer from them events occurring at the level of the single cell. Nevertheless, simply demonstrating a connection between one brain area and another by demonstrating that stimulation at one location causes an evoked potential to occur at another may be very valuable. Furthermore, even without an understanding of the mechanism of the evoked potential in terms of events occurring in single neurons, increases or decreases in size concomitant with variations in other conditions can in some instances give insight into function.

Although many evoked potentials are sufficiently large to be easily recorded, in some instances—particularly when the stimulus is a weak one—the evoked potential has a small amplitude and is obscured by electrical noise of neural and artifactual origin. Modern developments in data handling have provided a method for detecting such evoked

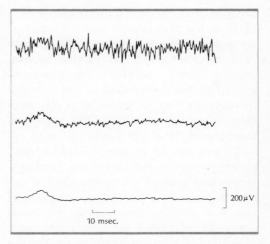

Figure 4.25. Evoked potentials recorded without averaging (top trace), after averaging 10 responses (middle trace) and after averaging 100 responses (bottom trace).

potentials obscured by noise. The basic idea is as follows: Each time a stimulus is presented, it produces a sequence of voltage changes that are always about the same, and these voltage changes are added to the random voltage changes constituting the electrical noise. Whereas the form of the evoked potential is about the same from trial to trial, the noise is constantly changing, so that if a positive noise voltage occurs on one trial, a negative voltage is likely to occur on another. If successive records are added together, the invariant evoked potentials tend to add, while the noise, being out of phase from trial to trial, tends to cancel. The effect of averaging is illustrated by the data presented in Figure 4.25; these data are typical of the type obtained, for example, by recording from the region of cat cortex that receives input from a forepaw that can be stimulated with a weak electrical shock of short duration (0.1 msec). Although the evoked potential is difficult to detect with a single trial, it becomes apparent after 10 responses are averaged and quite clear and noise-free if 100 responses are averaged.

Several difficulties limit the application of the averaging technique described in the preceding paragraph. First, the response must occur with a fixed latency after the stimulus, for otherwise the separate trials will not produce responses which add together. Second, because there is variation in the form of an evoked potential from trial to trial, the sum of many such evoked potentials may bear little resemblance to any of the individual components. Finally, the very power of the technique can be a serious disadvantage; potentials can spread over very large distances, and voltages can be recorded in one area that actually occurred at quite a distant site. It is possible, for example, to record potentials generated by contracting neck muscles over a region which one might expect to record visual potentials, and therefore to mistakenly attribute to the brain evoked potentials which were in fact a result of a gross but not noticeable motor response.

In order to study the function of some brain regions, it is necessary to have a technique that permits the accurate positioning of electrodes within the desired structures. Because brain structure is very similar from animal to animal, brain locations bear a fixed relationship to certain landmarks on the skull, and by using these landmarks for reference, an electrode may be inserted through a small hole in the skull to a predetermined location within the depths of the brain (Horsley & Clarke, 1908). An animal is suspended in a special frame by bars that fit firmly in the ear canals, and by a bite bar that holds the snout in position. When the animal is placed symmetrically in this apparatus, structures within the brain may be located by reference to an arbitrary zero: the most common reference point is the intersection of the line connecting the two ear bars and the animal's midline. For example, to reach the cat hypothalamus, one would move the electrode to a position 11 mm in front of the reference point, 1 mm to the side, and 5 mm down.

The method of locating specific brain areas described above is called the *stereotaxic technique,* and brain maps, known as *stereotaxic atlases* (for example, Jasper & Ajmone-Marsan, 1955) are available for many of the commonly used species. The stereotaxic technique, combined with microelectrode and evoked potential recording, has proved a very fruitful approach to understanding brain function, for by using the appropriate type of stimulation, it is possible to produce evoked potentials in almost any region of the brain.

The evoked potentials from certain neural tissues have been given special names, both for historical reasons and for the reason that these potentials have been of particular significance. Examples are the electroretinogram (ERG) and the electro-olfactogram (EOG). The ERG is generated by photic stimulation of the retina and arises as a result of neural and photochemical activity in retinal cells, although it may be recorded from the cornea and other locations; it has been used, for example, in investigations of light-receptor mechanisms (see p. 307 in Chapter 9). The EOG is an analogous potential generated in the olfactory system and has been used in the study of receptor processes in olfaction (see p. 221 in Chapter 7).

In some areas of the brain it happens, for reasons that are not entirely clear, that the EPSPs and IPSPs are spontaneously synchronous in a large population of cells. Whatever the reason for the synchronization of activity, its result is that spontaneously occurring potentials from the brain reach sufficiently high voltages that they may often be recorded by the use of gross electrodes applied to the scalp. These potentials are referred to as the brain's *electroencephalogram,* abbreviated EEG. Because there are certain differences between normal EEG records and those seen in some pathological conditions, the EEG has proved very valuable in clinical medicine as a diagnostic tool. As a research technique, analysis of the EEG has depended mainly on demonstrating changes in electrical activity with manipulation of experimental conditions.

Just as the activity of nerve cells produces measurable voltage changes in the fluids surrounding them, so may one record voltage changes produced by muscle cell activity. This technique, called *electromyography,* abbreviated EMG, has been of considerable clinical use and is of particular interest to psychologists because it provides a way for recording muscle activity too small to produce gross movements. By inserting small needles into the muscle, or by placing small disc electrodes on the skin over a muscle to be studied, muscle potential may be quite conveniently measured (see Hefferline, Keenan, & Harford, 1959, and p. 379 in Chapter 11).

The heart is a muscular organ, and, like other muscles, it has voltages which produce a record, called the *electrocardiogram* (EKG), associated with its contraction. From the point of view of the psychologist, recording the electrical signs of heartbeats offers a way to measure heart rate in the waking and freely moving animal. Thus if an investigator wishes to use heart rate as a measure of the animal's "emotional state," or if he is interested in heart rate conditioning, he may conveniently record the electrocardiogram. In the study of autonomic conditioning, for example, EKG has proved to be a useful measure of heart rate (see p. 711 in Chapter 16).

The preceding discussion is primarily concerned with recording the voltage changes within and around nerve cells during their activity. An inverse problem, in a certain sense, is concerned with producing activity in neurons by changing their membrane potential. This may be accomplished, for reasons which are quite complicated, by passing current through the fluids surrounding nerve cells. By placing stimulating electrodes stereotaxically, *electrical stimulation of the brain* (ESB) may be accomplished with considerable precision. This technique may be employed in waking, freely moving animals and has proved useful in a number of areas of psychology. For example, stimulation of certain brain areas can act as a reinforcer, and this stimulation has been relied upon in the study of reinforcement *per se* (see Chapter 15). Despite the usefulness of ESB, a number of

sources of error can make results difficult to interpret in terms of normal brain function: ESB tends to cause synchronous activity in the population of stimulated neurons as opposed to the normal asynchronous activity; neurons with opposing actions may be simultaneously stimulated; larger neurons tend to be more affected than smaller ones; it is difficult to know whether neuron somas or passing axon bundles are stimulated; and it is generally impossible to discover whether the observed effects are mediated through the activation of excitatory neurons (those which produce EPSPs) or inhibitory neurons. Nevertheless, used with care, ESB is a valuable research tool.

NEURAL SOURCES OF VARIABILITY

Although behavior can be very predictable, one of its striking attributes is its randomness. The variability of gross behavior appears at first to contrast sharply with the constancy of neuron properties described in the preceding sections. In fact, however, neuronal properties themselves vary somewhat with time, and even if they did not, a nervous system constructed of elements of the type described would be expected to show con-

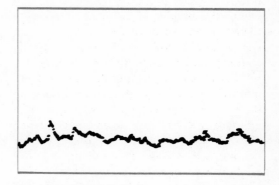

Figure 4.26. The recording of a neuron's membrane potential, photographed from an oscilloscope plot of voltage as a function of time, illustrates the synaptic noise so frequently seen when recording from neurons in the central nervous system. The amplitude of the noise illustrated is approximately 3 mv peak-to-peak.

siderable variability in its behavior. This variability has two main sources. First, even a completely deterministic system that is sufficiently complex can give the appearance of random behavior. If the behavior of a system depends on a sufficiently large number of variables, the inevitable uncontrolled changes in some of these variables can give the appearance of capriciousness to the system. Second, a type of noise can creep into any system, such as the nervous system, in which the individual elements are richly interconnected. In fact, the nervous system is not analogous to a telephone switchboard in which electrical activity is confined to the lines that are busy. Instead, the neurons in the brain are spontaneously active. Stimuli do not serve to initiate activity but to modify existing activity. Responses are governed not only by stimuli but by existing patterns of activity. An individual neuron receives thousands of synaptic contacts, and when large numbers of these synapses are asynchronously activated, the membrane potential exhibits haphazard fluctuations around its mean value. These fluctuations, termed *synaptic noise* by the physiologist (see Figure 4.26), are a ubiquitous property of neurons and can become so large that they dominate the behavior of a nerve cell. (Some implications of noise within the nervous system have already been discussed in relation to signal detection in Chapter 2.)

Dan R. Kenshalo

THE CUTANEOUS SENSES*

5 This chapter is concerned with sensations aroused by stimulation of the skin, *somesthesis*. One of the most remarkable characteristics of the organism is its possession of receptors that are sensitive (or "tuned") only to certain characteristics of various physical and chemical stimuli including those within its body. Most receptors, however, especially those of the skin, are not as specific in their sensitivity to certain aspects of the stimulus as was once thought. It becomes clear how the early impressions of receptor specificity arose when the physiological, anatomical, and psychological data are considered historically.

We experience different sensations, in part because of the selective sensitivity of the receptors. We also experience different sensations in part because the nervous activity initiated by the receptors travels through the nervous pathways to different parts of the brain.

We cannot confine our consideration of the skin senses, or the other senses for that matter, to data obtained by psychophysical methods only. To do so deprives us of the store of information that has been amassed by the physiologists, the anatomists, and the physicists about the characteristics of skin and the other sensory systems. That is, we must be able to describe not only the way in which thresholds and sensations

*Preparation of this chapter was facilitated by USPHS Grant No. NB-02992 and NSF Grant No. GB-2473.

117

change when the conditions of stimulation are changed, but we must also know the mechanical and thermal properties of skin (physics), what structures are available to respond to a particular stimulus (anatomy), and how these structures translate a stimulus into patterns of nerve impulses along relatively specific neural pathways (neurophysiology).

DELIMITATION OF THE SENSES

More than 2000 years ago Aristotle spoke of five senses—sight, hearing, taste, smell, and feeling (as in touch). Then, and in the centuries that followed, the way in which the human organism obtained accurate information about its environment and how the information was conveyed to the brain was of primary concern. In the philosophical period, during the development of the sciences of physiology and psychology, it was generally held that pictures or images—*eidola*—of objects were conveyed to the brain by way of the nerves (Boring, 1942). Thus, red was thought to appear red because a neural image of the color red was directly conveyed to the brain.

The Doctrine of Specific Energies of Nerves

The image theory of sensations persisted to the turn of the nineteenth century. Then in 1826, at the very beginnings of experimental investigations of nervous system functions, the great physiologist Johannes Müller proposed a theory that has become known as the *doctrine of specific nerve energies* (Dennis, 1948). He said that the brain is directly aware of the activity in the sensory nerves, not of the objects that excite them, and that the sensory nerves convey nerve impulses to the brain which are not, in themselves, different in their ability to produce specific sensations. Different sensations arise because each sensory nerve has its characteristic type of activity. Thus, optic nerve activity signals light and color; auditory nerve activity

signals sounds; olfactory nerve activity signals odors; and so on. The theory is vividly expressed by the statement that, if the auditory nerve and visual nerve were crossed, we could see thunder and hear lightning. The experiment is impractical, of course, but there are other ways to identify the source of this specificity. Thus, when the same stimulus, for example, electric current, is applied to the different nerves, or if different stimuli, for example, mechanical, chemical, electrical, and so on, are applied to the same nerve, sensations are produced according to the special properties of the nerve stimulated. Müller thought these special properties might be in the nerves themselves or in the parts of the brain to which they are connected. There is some evidence for the latter view. A blow on the back of the head, over the occipital lobe of the brain where the visual pathways terminate, makes one see a flash of light. This atypical form of stimulation has been called *inadequate stimulation*. Thus, for the sense of sight, the *adequate* stimulus is light, but inadequate ones include an electric current or a beam of x-rays passed through the eyeball.

Sensory Modalities

Why do we say that sight is one sense and hearing is another? There are at least five criteria which set them off as separate or primary sensory modalities (Neff, 1960). They have (1) *markedly different receptive organs* that (2) respond to *characteristic stimuli*. Each set of receptive organs has its (3) *own nerve* that goes to a (4) *different part of the brain*, and the (5) *sensations are different*. With these criteria, we can identify 9 or perhaps 11 different senses: vision, audition, kinesthesis (joint sense), vestibular sense (one or two?), tactile sense, temperature sense (one or two?), pain, taste, and smell. If we insist that all of the criteria for a primary sensory modality be fulfilled in each case, our knowledge of the structure and function of several of the senses disqualifies them as primary sensory modalities. For example, we do not yet know the receptive organs for temperature and pain, nor the specific parts of the brain for them. If we insist that each primary sensory modality has its own nerve pathway, the tactile, pain, and temperature senses fail to qualify as different modalities because their nerves are intermingled, at least in the peripheral nerve bundles. Nor do we have at present a satisfactory account of the chemical characteristics of the stimuli required to stimulate taste and smell.

Within a primary sensory modality, a number of unique sensory experiences can be described. These are classified on a psychological basis according to the different primary qualities of sensation experienced, for example, sweet, bitter, red, blue, cold, warm, and so on. Physiological classifications have also been used in which the number of elementary physiological processes required to account for different psychological qualities of sensation that can be discriminated were determined. Structures that could be morphologically identified were then assigned to each physiological process. For example, Helmholtz knew the physics of light mixing when he accepted Young's trichromatic theory of color vision. He also knew that any pure spectral hue could be matched approximately by blending any three wavelengths of light provided the wavelengths were widely separated in the spectrum. On this basis he suggested that there were red-, green-, and violet-sensitive nerve fibers (receptors) which when differentially stimulated could account for all of the discriminably different hues of the light spectrum. Hering, on the other hand, started with a knowledge of the psychologically primary hues: red, yellow, green, and blue. He proposed that two reversible chemical reactions could account for color vision. A shift in the equilibrium of one reaction toward one side or the other resulted in the sensations of red or green. Shifts in the equilibrium of the other reaction gave yellow or blue sensations.

Unfortunately, these types of classification are as confusing when applied to other sense modalities as they are when used in vision. The confusion is a result of the assumption that there is a one-to-one correlation between elementary psychological qualities of sensation and the elementary physiological and morphological properties of receptors (Melzack & Wall, 1962).

Extension of the "Doctrine"

The doctrine of specific nerve energies is a theory of how an organism can differentiate between the five traditional primary sensory modalities. Müller tried to explain how stimulus objects, which become encoded into nerve impulses, are represented to the brain so that they yield sensations that are clearly different in their essential nature. Müller's theory was effective, for it successfully combatted the earlier notion that pictures of stimulus objects are conveyed to the brain by the nerves.

It is clear, however, that within each of the primary sensory modalities there occur differences in the qualities of sensation, which also must be taken into account. What are the primary qualities in each of the primary sense modalities? That is, if differences between visual and auditory sensations might be accounted for by the part of the brain in which their nerves terminate, how are differences between red and green or between various pitches to be explained? Most researchers think that the peripheral receptor mechanism is responsible for the differentiation of the qualities of sensation within each sensory modality. In order to determine the specific mechanisms within the receptors for such differentiations, the primary qualities of sensations that occur within each primary sensory modality must be defined.

The search for the primary qualities of cutaneous sensations was begun by three physiologists: Blix, a Swede; Goldscheider, a German; and Donaldson, an American, who independently published accounts maintaining that the skin is not uniformly sensitive to tactile, warm, or cold stimuli but shows spots of sensitivity to each of these stimuli.

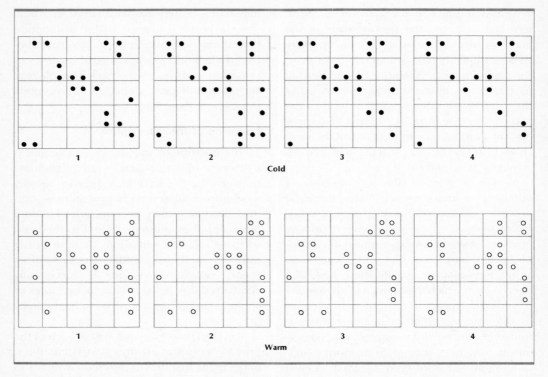

Figure 5.1. Distribution of cold and warm spots found on the upper arm. An area of 1 cm² was mapped four times for cold spots and four times for warm spots on four days within about a week. Each square of the grid contains four tested points. Note most spots on the skin are insensitive to either warm or cold, that cold and warm spots seldom coincide, and that day-to-day reliability is fairly good but by no means perfect for either the cold spots or the warm. (Data from Plate II of Dallenbach, 1927.)

By stamping a grid of ink lines on the skin at 2 mm intervals and exploring each square with appropriate stimuli they found, as have others since, that some squares gave clear tactile sensations when prodded with a stiff hair, for example, but other squares did not. Similarly, when the grid of squares was explored using warm or cool stimuli (delivered by the small tip of a brass cylinder heated or cooled by water) some squares gave rise to clear sensations of cold. Warm sensations were also produced by stimulation of some of the squares with a heated brass cylinder, but these warm spots usually did not coincide with the cold spots found in the same grid, as is shown in Figure 5.1. Sharp, "bright" pain could also be registered by most of the squares in the grid when a needle was stuck into the skin over each square. Thus, the

foundation was laid to establish touch, warmth, and cold as the primary qualities of cutaneous sensation. The establishment of pain as the fourth primary somesthetic quality, however, was not achieved until the work of von Frey was published in 1895, some seven years later.

Von Frey extended Müller's theory of specific nerve energies to the periphery by proposing a particular type of receptive structure for each of the four primary cutaneous sensations. Considering the trends in physiology and psychology of those times, it is not surprising that von Frey proposed, on meager evidence, specific "types" of structure within the skin as receptors for each of the primary qualities of somesthesis, for Helmholtz had proposed three and Hering two specific channels to account for hue discriminations.

Helmholtz had also proposed a large number of specific receptors in the form of resonators in the inner ear to account for the tonal qualities of pitch.

Von Frey's proposition was simple. He proposed that certain histologically identifiable structures associated with the terminals of sensory nerves were responsible for the specificity of response exhibited by the sensory mapping experiments. The correlations between structure and sensation that he drew were that Meissner corpuscles in hairless skin and hair follicle receptors in hairy skin signaled touch, Krause end bulbs signaled cold, and Ruffini cylinders signaled warmth, but only the free nerve endings of the dermal nerve net were widely enough distributed to account for pain. Other cutaneous sensations, such as wetness, oiliness, tickle, and roughness, were held to be blends of these four primary qualities of sensation. It was natural for von Frey to expect to find a particular type of nerve terminal beneath a skin spot that gave a particular quality of sensation. These structures should be different from the nerve terminal structures found beneath other skin spots that gave other qualities of sensation.

Despite its apparent simplicity, von Frey's proposal makes at least three major assumptions (Melzack & Wall, 1962):

1. a physiological assumption that receptors are specific in their responses to a particular stimulus dimension,

2. an anatomical assumption that a morphologically discrete type of receptor lies beneath each sensory spot on the skin,

3. a psychological assumption that an identifiable quality of sensation bears a one-to-one relationship to a single stimulus dimension, and therefore, to a given type of skin receptor.

We next examine each of these assumptions to determine its basis in fact.

1. There can be little doubt that receptive structures have a great deal to do with selecting the characteristics of the stimulus to which their associated nerve fibers will respond. The tendency is so great that the great physiologist Sherrington defined the function of a receptor as increasing the sensitivity of a sensory nerve fiber to one aspect of the stimulus and decreasing it to all others (Sherrington, 1906). This selectivity, as compared to specificity of response, is clearly demonstrated in the spectral light absorption curves of the red-, green-, and blue-sensitive cones of the retina (see Chapter 10). Retinal cones of each type show a selectivity of response in the broad peaks of response at the long, medium, and short wavelengths of visible light. They do not show a specificity of response to particular wavelengths or even narrow bands of wavelengths.

As is discussed later, some cutaneous receptors show a high degree of selectivity by responding either to mechanical or thermal stimuli, but others show considerable activity when stimulated by either. Furthermore, a continuous gradation of intensity of stimulation, from weak to strong enough to cause actual tissue damage, may be required to make the receptors discharge their associated nerve fibers. There is apparently no clear-cut demarcation between the intensity of stimulation required to elicit a mechanical or a thermal sensation and that required to elicit a painful sensation.

These lines of evidence lead to a rejection of the first assumption of von Frey's theory, that receptors of the skin are highly specific in their responses to a particular stimulus dimension. They may be selective, but they are not specific, for there are too many receptor units that fail to fall exclusively into the catagories responding only to tactile, temperature, or pain stimuli.

2. Von Frey's assumption that there are specific types of receptor beneath each characteristically sensitive spot of skin is most in error. The crucial experiment of making histological examinations of the tissue beneath carefully mapped temperature spots has been carried out at least a dozen times (Kenshalo & Nafe, 1962). With one exception (von Frey, 1895), neither Krause end bulbs nor Ruffini cylinders have been found beneath cold or

warm spots. Furthermore, encapsulated endings do not occur in hairy skin except for the Pacinian corpuscles, which lie deep in the dermis. Yet hairy skin shows a sensitivity to mechanical and thermal stimuli at least as high as that of hairless skin (Hagen et al., 1953). Whatever the function of the specialized, encapsulated, nerve endings found in hairless skin, it appears *not* to be that of specific sensitivities to increases or decreases in the temperature of the skin or its mechanical deformation.

3. The psychological assumption that there are four primary qualities to somesthesis, each bearing a one-to-one correlation to a single stimulus characteristic and to a given type of skin receptor, is the most questionable part of von Frey's theory. It proposes a concept of the nervous system in which information is carried from the skin to the brain by a system of nerves that bear a functional resemblance to the differently colored wires of a telephone cable; that is, distinct nerves in separate pathways run from the skin to specific receiving areas of the brain. Although this type of conceptual nervous system was acceptable in von Frey's time, it is totally inconsistent with the modern concepts of neurophysiology. The activity of peripheral sensory nerve fibers passes through several synapses on its way to the brain. At each synapse the patterns of activity undergo temporal and spatial modifications. When they finally arrive at the brain, they bear little resemblance to the patterns of activity that started at the peripheral receptors.

A one-to-one correlation between the physical dimensions of the stimulus and the psychological dimensions of the sensation cannot be assumed for somesthesis. Although skin spots have been described whose stimulation produces one of the four primary qualities of sensation, the variety of somesthetic sensations is much richer than can be accounted for by combinations of these four primary qualities. The data indicate that activity in many sensory fibers supplying the skin shows a high degree of selectivity in response to mechanical or thermal stimulation. However, because there are, for example, warm spots separate from cold spots, it should not be assumed that there are also separate warm and cold receptors or specific warm-sensitive and cold-sensitive, peripheral sensory nerve fibers. If so, it would be the exception rather than the rule in sensory processes.

STRUCTURE OF HUMAN SKIN

The skin is the largest, and, from the standpoint of its diverse functions, the most versatile structure of the body. It has no equal among the other body organs in its regenerative powers. It provides a flexible elastic covering for the body machinery; it provides protection against infrared and ultraviolet radiation, invasions of microorganisms, toxic substances and chemicals; and it prevents the escape of the body's vital juices. The skin contains the mechanisms (cutaneous vascular system and sweat glands) to cool the body effectively when the body core temperature has become too high and to minimize body heat loss when the body core temperature is too low. The cutaneous vascular system also aids in regulating blood pressure (Montagna, 1962).

As a sense organ the skin is the most extensive of the body, and its value to the survival of the individual is clearly demonstrable. For example, the skin serves an important function in the development of affectional systems in lower primates (Harlow & Harlow, 1965) and presumably man. Also, individuals who have no sense of pain usually die early (Sternbach, 1968). In spite of the importance of the skin as an organ of sense, there is little agreement among investigators as to the critical variables of stimulation, the neurological and associated structures that are responsible for its sensitivity, or the nature of the neural code that allows the differentiation of sensations resulting from mechanical, thermal, or painful stimulation.

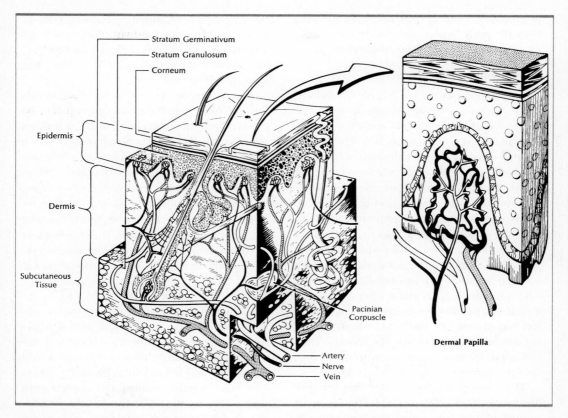

Figure 5.2. A schematic representation of human hairy skin. Sensory nerve fibers terminate around the hair follicles, close to the border of the dermis and epidermis, and among the smooth muscle fibers of the arterioles and venules, especially in the dermal papillae. Encapsulated sensory nerve terminals of the Pacinian corpuscle type are frequently found in the vicinity of the dermis-subcutis boundary as well as in the subcutis proper.

The Basic Skin Structure

Human skin consists of three main layers: The most superficial layer is called the *epidermis;* the *dermis* is the central layer; and underlying these, but external to the fascia, is the *subcutis,* which is composed of fat and loose connective tissue. As may be seen in Figure 5.2, the epidermis may be subdivided into several more or less distinct layers. The main ones, starting with the most superficial, are the *stratum corneum,* the *stratum granulosum,* and the *stratum germinativum.* Apparently cells that originate in the stratum germinativum are continually displaced upward by newly developed cells. They die in the process and become flat and cornified.

These dead cells form the corneum. The epidermis varies in thickness from 0.07 mm over most of the body to as much as 1.4 mm on the soles of feet.

The line of demarcation between the epidermis and the dermis is distinct. It is marked by a basement cell layer and the stratum germinativum. The demarcation is usually irregular and the dermal hillocks, where the dermis pushes into the epidermis, are called *dermal papillae.*

The distinction between the dermis and the subcutis is much less distinct. Although measurements of the dermal thickness are difficult to make, it averages between 1 to 2 mm in thickness over most of the body; it is thinner on the eyelids and prepuce (less than 0.6 mm), but it may reach a thickness of 3 mm or more on the palms and the soles.

The Cutaneous Vascular System

The cutaneous blood supply is derived from a plexus of small arteries lying in the deepest part of the dermis and in the more superficial layers of the subcutis. This plexus of large arterioles and small arteries is usually referred to as the *deep cutaneous vascular plexus*. From the deep plexus, single more or less straight arterioles ascend to the region of the dermal papillae. They branch throughout their course especially as they approach the dermal papillae, where they form the *superficial vascular plexus*. Papillary arterioles send off branches into the individual papillae, which terminate in a capillary net high in the top of the papillae. From there, venules collect blood and join the venous limbs of the superficial vascular plexus. The blood is then collected in the larger veins of the subcutaneous tissue.

The walls of arterioles extending into the dermal papillae contain encircling layers of smooth muscle cells throughout their length. Arterioles lying deeper in the dermis usually possess several layers of smooth muscle fibers. Venules and veins are also muscularized although not as extensively as the arterioles.

In addition to supplying nutrients to the dermis and the epidermis and assisting in the regulation of the blood pressure, the cutaneous vascular system serves an important role in the regulation of body temperature when the skin temperature is between 30° C and 35° C. Certain areas of the brain adjust the amount of heat that is lost from the skin surface in order to maintain body temperature at a relatively constant 37° C by regulating the caliber of the arterioles in the superficial vascular plexus. When the environmental temperature is low and excessive heat loss threatens to reduce the body temperature below normal, the cutaneous arterioles constrict, forcing the blood away from the surface of the skin. When heat loss is too low and

body temperature might rise above normal, as in a warm environment, the cutaneous arterioles dilate, allowing the blood to circulate close to the surface of the skin, thus increasing the heat loss.

Regulation of the arteriole caliber in this type of heat regulation is accomplished by the sympathetic innervation of the arterioles and venules. However, smooth muscle of the cutaneous vascular system may also respond directly to temperature changes. When warmed the smooth muscle elements relax, allowing more blood to flow in the outer layers of the skin. Thus, the hands become red when held in hot water. The direct effect of cooling constricts the smooth muscle elements and causes the skin to appear pallid.

The Cutaneous Nerve Supply

All skin and visceral organs receive sensory innervation from myelinated nerve fibers (usually 5 to 8 μ in diameter) whose terminations are not encapsulated or of a specialized structure (Weddell & Miller, 1962). The fibers lose their myelin sheaths, and branch until they finally terminate in the *free nerve endings* that are too small to be seen, even under the most high-powered light microscope. They most frequently end among the cells of the superficial layers of the dermis and perhaps also in the lower layers of the epidermis. The endings appear to form a dense network of fine branches—the *dermal nerve network*. Branches and collaterals of a single fiber may innervate an area of from 3 to 800 mm^2. Branches from many other nerve fibers may end in the same area, so there is a considerable overlap of the terminal branches of fibers that end in this fashion.

Other myelinated fibers (1.5 to 3.0 μ in diameter) follow the course of the cutaneous arterioles, sending collaterals into the vessel walls at intervals to terminate as a dense nerve net among the smooth muscle cells (Weddell & Pallie, 1954).

Recent evidence indicates that unmyelinated fibers also terminate in the dermis. They appear to end for the most part in the upper part of the neural net formed by myelinated fibers, around the hair shaft in hairy skin, on the piloerector muscle elements of the hair shaft, and among the smooth muscle elements of the cutaneous vascular system (Winkelmann, 1958). Some of the terminals of these fibers show a threshold of response to mechanical or to thermal stimulation that is as low or lower than many of the terminals of the larger fibers supplying the skin.

One variety of encapsulated ending, the *Pacinian corpuscle,* is found deep in the dermis and the subcutis of almost all skin. Pacinian corpuscles are also found in the immediate vicinity of the tendons, around joints, and in the mesentery of the viscera.

The innervation of skin, just described, applies to all skin whether hairy or hairless. However, hairy and hairless skin exhibit some differences. These differences are emphasized in the following sections.

In hairy skin each hair follicle is innervated by 5 to 12 sensory nerve fibers whose diameters vary between 8 and 12 μ—some of the largest myelinated sensory fibers. A single fiber may also send branches to several hairs. These fibers form a dense network around the shaft of the hair follicle so they are ideally placed to be stimulated when the hair shaft is moved.

Hairless skin has the same innervation characteristics as hairy skin, except that it lacks hair follicle receptors. In their place are nerve terminals that have a variety of organized epithelial capsules about them, for example, Krause end bulbs, Ruffini cylinders, Golgi-Mazzoni endings, and so on. They are found in the conjunctiva, lips, breast nipple, the plantar surfaces of the hands and feet, and the genitalia.

More than 100 different varieties of encapsulated endings have been described, each named for its discoverer. The profusion of types has led many histologists to suggest that, rather than each being a discrete type, they constitute a continuum of complexity from the simplest to the most complex organization of epithelial investments. The current

trend in histology is to emphasize the similarities among them rather than the differences. Of the numerous end organs described, only a few have morphological features sufficiently constant and distinctive to justify separating them into types. Among them are the dermal nerve network, the hair follicle networks, Pacinian corpuscles, and Meissner corpuscles (Montagna, 1962). All of these have been discussed except the Meissner corpuscles, which are found primarily and in profusion in the dermal ridges of the plantar surfaces of the palms and soles, especially at the tips of the fingers.

One cannot help but wonder what functions are performed by the varieties of encapsulations. Whatever their function, it appears certain that they do not provide nerve terminals with selective devices to permit differentiation of mechanical, thermal, or painful stimuli. Comparisons of the sensitivities of hairless and hairy skin to tactile, thermal, or painful stimuli fail to reveal any differences (Hagen et al., 1953). This fact, considered along with the limited distribution of encapsulated endings, indicates that they cannot function as the sole receptors for any particular primary quality of cutaneous sensation.

SOMATIC SENSORY PATHWAYS

The nervous system of vertebrate animals is composed of two main parts—the *central* and *peripheral* nervous systems. The central nervous system is further subdivided into the brain and the spinal cord. The brain, consisting largely of the cerebral and cerebellar hemispheres, is contained within the skull case. The spinal cord in adult man extends down the vertebral column in the spinal canal for as much as 40 cm (16 in.) and up into the central part of the brain case, where it is known as the brain stem. The upper part of the brain stem is connected to the cerebral and cerebellar hemispheres by large bundles of nerve fibers. These bundles carry to and from the hemispheres impulses that result in

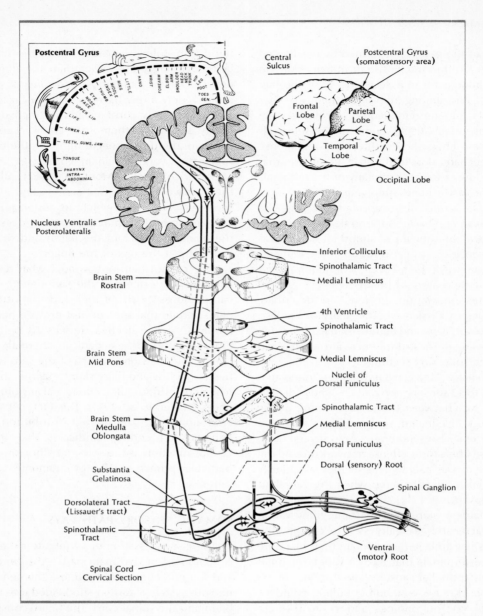

Figure 5.3. The somatosensory neural pathways. Three main pathways exist in the central nervous system for the transmission of impulses from the skin of the body to the upper levels of the central nervous system and the cerebral cortex. Two of these are believed to be involved in conveying impulses to the brain that are aroused by mild mechanical stimulation of the skin. The third pathway is believed to convey impulses that result from thermal and painful skin stimulation. See the text for a detailed description of these pathways.

The nervous system is bilaterally symetrical; thus structures and nerve pathways that exist on one side of the body have a similar representation on the other side of the body. In this figure only those of one side are shown for simplicity.

A uniform dimension scale has not been used throughout this figure. The scale for the section through the cerebral hemispheres is only about one-fourth that used for the sections through the brain stem and spinal cord. (Adapted from Figure 2 of Rasmussen, 1947; and Figure 17 of Penfield & Rasmussen, 1950.)

sensation and also in action (muscular movements) by the organism.

The peripheral nervous system is composed of a large number of bundles of nerve fibers which serve two functions. Some nerves carry *sensory* impulses from receptors located in outlying parts of the body towards the central nervous system. Other nerves carry *motor* impulses from the central nervous system to muscles for movement and, in the *autonomic system,* to internal organs to help regulate the internal environment of the body (heart rate, respiration rate, digestion, glandular secretions, and so on.)

The nerves of the peripheral nervous system enter and leave the spinal cord by 31 pairs of *spinal nerves* and the brain stem by 12 pairs of *cranial nerves.* One member of each pair serves a limited area of one side of the body; the other member of the pair serves a similar area of the opposite side of the body. The area of the body served by a particular spinal nerve is called a *dermatome.* In the human adult each dermatome is irregular in shape; furthermore, the boundaries between dermatomes are not distinct but overlapping.

In general, the cranial nerves serve the olfactory receptors, the eyes and their muscles, the taste buds and muscles of the tongue, the skin and muscles of the face, and the receptors of the ear. Discussion of these pathways will be taken up in the appropriate chapters. Of primary concern here are the nervous pathways between the skin and the cerebral hemispheres.

Spinal Roots

Both the motor and sensory nerves of the peripheral nervous system group together into larger and larger bundles as they approach their connection with the spinal cord. The largest bundle is the spinal nerve. The *sensory* (dorsal root) *ganglion* is composed of the cell bodies of each sensory neuron entering the cord from the dorsal side. The motor fibers leave the cord from the ventral side; their cell bodies are located within the spinal cord itself. The anatomical relationships are shown in Figure 5.3.

Spinal Pathways

The sensory branch of the spinal nerve contains fibers that carry impulses associated with tactile, temperature, and pain sensations from both the skin and the deep structures of the body, as well as those associated with joint movement and muscle stretch. In the peripheral sensory nerve these fibers are intermingled, but once they enter the spinal cord they tend to separate themselves according to function, at least in a gross way. As a result fibers carrying tactile information follow spinal pathways that are separate from that taken by fibers carrying temperature or pain information.

Tactile pathways There are at least two pathways in the spinal cord by which tactile information reaches the brain. In the first pathway, the primary fibers (or first-order neurons—those that enter the spinal cord) turn upward in the *dorsal funiculus* immediately upon entering the spinal cord and continue to the lower margin of the brain stem where they end in the dorsal funiculus *nuclei.* The terminal ends of these primary fibers synapse with the cell bodies of secondary (second-order) fibers that cross to the opposite side of the brain stem and continue in the *medial lemniscus* to the thalamus, at the head of the brain stem. There they end in a specific part of the thalamus—the nucleus *ventralis posterolateralis.* A second synapse is formed here. The axons of the tertiary neurons leave the region of the thalamus and continue on to the cerebral cortex where they end in the *postcentral gyrus* of the parietal lobe.

In the second tactile pathway, primary fibers enter the cord and end in the gray matter of the spinal cord close to their point of entry. The terminals of these primary fibers synapse with the cell bodies of secondary neurons whose axons cross to the opposite side of the spinal cord where they turn toward the brain in the *spinothalamic* tract. In the brain stem, the spinothalamic tract runs close to the medial lemniscus and continues on to the thalamus where these secondary fibers end in the nucleus ventralis posterolateralis, along with the secondary fibers of the dorsal funiculus—this is the medial lemniscus tactile pathway. Terminals of the fibers of the spinothalamic pathways also synapse with the cell bodies of tertiary neurons in the thalamus, whose axons continue on to the postcentral gyrus of the cerebral cortex.

Why two pathways have evolved to carry tactile information to the brain, can only be surmised. There is evidence, however, that the spinothalamic pathway is mainly concerned with general tactile sensibility whereas the dorsal funiculus pathway is concerned with the fine localizing and discriminatory aspects of tactile sensibility (Everett, 1965).

Temperature and pain pathways The primary fibers that carry information about temperature and pain are supposedly smaller in diameter and less heavily myelinated than those that convey tactile information. As these primary fibers enter the spinal cord, they send branches up and down the spinal cord for three or four segments. The short branches form the *dorsolateral* (Lissauer's) tract. Terminals of these branches and the cell bodies of secondary neurons form an immediately adjacent structure—the *substantia gelatinosa*. Secondary axons cross to the opposite side of the spinal cord where they ascend toward the thalamus in the lateral part of the spinothalamic tract. Where these secondary fibers terminate is not known; it is questionable that tertiary fibers reach the cerebral cortex. Only a few reports have been made of electrical activity in the cortex evoked by thermal or painful skin stimulation. However, Rose and Mountcastle (1959) state that all sensory input to the thalamus is relayed to the cortex.

A word of caution should be injected at this point. The somatic pathways from the skin have been drawn as though they were wires in a cable with fixed connections at each synapse. Actually, the nervous system does not have that functional configuration at all. At each synapse the terminals of many fibers, some exciting and others inhibiting, end on the cell bodies of successive neurons. The pattern of neural activity is not merely relayed but may be drastically changed at each synapse.

Somatic Cortical Projection Area

It should be clear from Figure 5.3 that the entire surface of the body is represented along the postcentral gyrus of the cerebral cortex. The fibers that carry impulses from the skin to the cortex cross from one side of the spinal cord or brain stem to the other so that the left half of the body is represented in the right cerebral hemisphere and the right side of the body in the left hemisphere.

Furthermore, the amount of cortex devoted to a particular site on the skin varies from one part of the body to another. As will be shown later, there is a high correlation between point localization and two-point discrimination on a particular skin site and the amount of cortex devoted to the site.

In general, electrical activity observed in the postcentral gyrus or sensations produced by electrical stimulation of the postcentral gyrus are of a tactile quality. Only rarely have thermal sensations been reported to result from electrical stimulation of the cortex; pain never has been.

TACTILE SENSITIVITY

One of the reasons given for neglect of the study of the cutaneous senses is that the receptors are so readily available for stimulation that their investigation does not carry the challenge afforded by the elaborate receptor machinery of the special senses— vision and audition. However, it is clear from Figure 5.2 that getting the stimulus to the skin receptor involves no fewer problems than stimulation of the eye or the ear. Manipulations carried out at the skin surface will be modified by the mechanical properties of the tissue between the stimulator and the receptors. Pushing a probe into the skin, for example, will cause the tissue to be displaced laterally, as well as downward in front of the probe. Tissue will also be displaced upward around the probe, as when a finger is poked into soft mud. The extent to which these mechanical events influence tactile sensation depends on many factors. Among them are the thickness of the corneum, the plasticity of the tissue of the epidermis and dermis, and the character of the substrate—whether bone, tendon, muscle, or a vascular bed.

Tactile Receptors

The principal receptor organs for arousing tactile sensations are the hair follicle endings in hairy skin and, probably, Meissner corpuscles in hairless skin. One need only move a hair slightly to be satisfied that a tactile sensation is aroused. The evidence that Meissner corpuscles are involved in touch is indirect. Their density in the finger tips agrees with the small two-point limen reported there. Also, Cauna (1968) has described their relationship with the surrounding tissue such that each corpuscle is discretely sensitive to stimuli applied to only one point on the skin.

Stimulation of the dermal nerve network is also perceived as touch. Tactile sensations as well as pain can be elicited from mechanical stimulation of the cornea of the eye (Kenshalo, 1960) and from mucous membranes where the only nerve terminals present are those of the dermal nerve network. There is evidence to suggest that both the dermal nerve network and the Pacinian corpuscles located in the subcutis are the receptive organs involved in sensations of vibration. Whether other endings, especially the other encapsulated ones of hairless skin, are involved in tactile sensations is not known.

Some authors have ascribed deep pressure sensitivity to Pacinian corpuscles or muscle spindle endings (nerve terminals wrapped around striate muscle fibers which discharge when the muscle fiber is stretched). Present evidence does not justify these correlations. The term "pressure sensation" implies a continued sensation in the presence of a maintained pressure on the skin. The Pacinian corpuscle induces activity in its attached axon only while its capsule is being distorted. Neural activity ceases almost as soon as movement of the capsule stops, even though the distortion is maintained (Loewenstein, 1959). Other evidence indicates that the activity from stimulation of the muscle spindle endings does not play a part in the appreciation of limb position (Gardner, 1967) or the sensation of deep pressure sensitivity (Gelfan & Carter, 1967).

Stimulation and Adaptation

During a so-called "mechanical event," force is applied to a substance in order to move it from one position to another. In the case of fluids, or semifluids such as the skin, it is usual to express force in terms of the force per unit dimension, for example, grams per millimeter (tension), grams per unit area (pressure), or simply in terms of the work accomplished, for example, force times distance (the distance a substance has been moved or displaced). These are the static aspects of work. When time is involved, dynamic characteristics of the mechanical event are added. These are velocity or the rate at which the work is accomplished (the first temporal derivative of displacement) and acceleration and deceleration (the second temporal derivative of displacement). The question is, which of these stimulus dimensions best describes the events associated with tactile thresholds and sensations?

Psychophysical studies For many years it was thought that the static aspect (pressure, tension, or displacement) of a force applied to the skin was the stimulus characteristic to which tactile receptors responded. Weber (1846) and his predecessors maintained that the perception of pressure was caused by pressure; thus the sensation could be named for its stimulus. In 1859, Meissner (who first described the capsule in hairless skin) pointed out that pressure itself was imperceptible;

thus when the finger was dipped in a thermally neutral pool of fluid, such as mercury, no sensation was experienced except where the finger emerged from the fluid. For this reason, Meissner contended that tactile receptors responded to a gradient of pressure rather than to pressure per se. The gradient theory was perpetuated by von Frey and Kiesow (1899) when they reported that tactile thresholds appeared to be more closely related to tension than to pressure. They emphasized the tensions that are set up at the edge of the deforming stimulus, where tension gradients are the steepest. Von Frey found further support for his tension hypothesis after he discovered that pulling the skin outward was as good a tactile stimulus as pushing it inward.

In spite of the invention of several devices for the application of tactile stimuli, no one thought to provide a means to record the response of the skin to the application of mechanical forces. Thus, the question of the nature of the stimulus parameter best suited to elicit tactile sensations is not yet settled, even though the evidence so far implicates

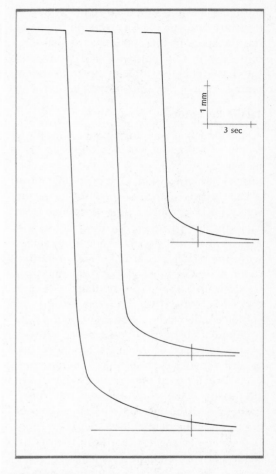

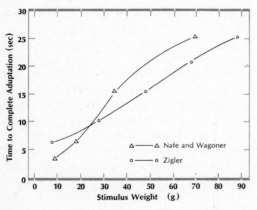

Figure 5.4. Time for complete tactile adaptation as it depends on the weight of the stimulus. Zigler's values (Carleton and Singleton data) were obtained on the hand and forearm using a stimulator surface area of 470 mm² whereas Nafe and Wagoner's were taken from 7.5 cm above the knee and with a stimulator surface area of 200 mm². Differences in the surface area of the skin involved in stimulation do not appear to be an important variable in determining adaptation nor, as Nafe and Wagoner showed, the rate of stimulus movement at complete adaptation. (Modified from Figure 11-A from Nafe & Wagoner, 1941b.)

Figure 5.5. Records of the tactile stimuli as they sank into the skin when 35, 17.5, and 8.75 g of weight were applied to 12.5 mm² area of the skin of the web between the thumb and index finger. The vertical marks toward the end of each record represent the points where the subject reported that tactile adaptation was complete; he no longer felt the stimulator even though it was still sinking slowly into the skin. This point on each record represents the critical minimum rate of tissue movement required to produce a tactile sensation. (Modified from Figure 14 of Nafe & Wagoner, 1941a.)

movement of the skin tissue rather than maintained pressure or tension.

The tactile sense is subject to adaptation. If you put on a glove and hold the hand still, the strong tactile sensation will diminish rapidly and almost disappear unless the glove pressure becomes intermittent as a result of blood pulsing through the arteries beneath the skin of the hand. The term *adaptation,* used in this way, refers to the reduction in intensity or the disappearance of the sensation when the stimulus is constant. The time necessary for complete adaptation (complete disappearance of a tactile sensation) to the application of various weights when the area of the skin being stimulated is held constant is shown in Figure 5.4. In both experiments, it is clear that the heavier the weight, the longer is the time required for complete adaptation.

Although tactile receptors take a long time to adapt to heavy weights, there is reason to believe that most of the receptors adapt almost instantly to a completely steady stimulus. In other words, most cutaneous receptors apparently respond only to the movement of the stimulator. From some clearcut results, Nafe and Wagoner (1941a, b) concluded that the necessary stimulus for tactile sensations is movement of the tissue. To show this, they obtained simultaneous records of the movement of a weight as it sank into the skin of the web between the thumb and index finger or on the thigh, 7.5 cm above the knee cap, and the tactile sensations experienced by the subject. As may be seen from Figure 5.5, the weight sank rapidly into the tissue but slowed as the tissue began to push back. During this time, the subject experienced a tactile sensation. As the rate of the fall continued to slow, the subject signaled that tactile adaptation was complete. He could no longer detect the presence of a tactile stimulator, even though the stimulator was still sinking slowly into the skin.

The results indicate that adaptation in the tactile sense is a stimulus phenomenon and not a receptor property. The data indicate that

the stimulus characteristic necessary to arouse a tactile sensation is movement of the tissue at a rate greater than a critical minimum. The data also suggest that adaptation of a tactile sensation is the result of a failure of the stimulus to stimulate the tactile receptors rather than failure of the receptors to respond to the stimulus because they have become less sensitive to it. In other words, the stimulus is changing from a dynamic to a static state, and the critical rate of movement represents the transition point as far as the tactile sensation is concerned.

Neurophysiological studies Information obtained from observing neural activity in single peripheral sensory axons provides extremely useful information concerning the functioning of a sense modality, especially when it is used with psychophysical data from the same modality. The usual method involves exposing a peripheral nerve, stripping away the connective tissue surrounding the nerve bundle, and then dissecting out single axons that show activity to stimulation of the area of skin in which they terminate. These are called *single-unit preparations.* Preparations of this type from frogs and higher organisms, including man, provide information about the following: (1) the stimulus dimension(s) to which the units are sensitive; (2) the size of the area of skin to which the unit is responsive—its *receptive field*; (3) differences in the activity of sensory nerves that supply hairy and hairless skin in response to identical stimulations; and (4) different thresholds and patterns of response in different units to mechanical, thermal, and pain stimuli.

Although the technique is powerful, interpretation of the results is difficult, for activity in a peripheral afferent nerve does not necessarily mean that it makes a contribution to the sensory experience. Such activity is used as indirect evidence. Thus, the fact that the stimulus dimension for many of the tactile units is movement of the tissue supports the conclusion of the psychophysical study by

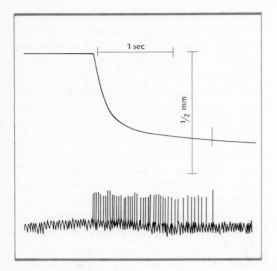

Figure 5.6. A record of a tactile stimulus as it sank into the tongue of a rat. The stimulus weighed 8.75 g and covered 12.5 mm² of the tongue. A simultaneous record of the nerve action potentials from a single tactile fiber terminating in the skin beneath the stimulator was made. Activity in the tactile unit stopped even though the weight was still sinking slowly into the skin. The rate of stimulus movement at the cessation of the nerve activity corresponds roughly to the critical rate of movement shown in Figure 5.5 for the 8.75 g weight. (Modified from Figure 3 of Nafe & Kenshalo, 1958.)

Nafe and Wagoner that tissue movement is the critical stimulus dimension for tactile sensations.

In an effort to extend the Nafe and Wagoner study to animals, peripheral neural activity was relied upon by Nafe and Kenshalo (1958) instead of verbal reports from human subjects. They obtained simultaneous records of various weights (8.75 to 70 g) sinking into the tongues of anesthetized rats or the dorsal skin of frogs and the neural activity in single tactile units supplying the areas. As shown in Figure 5.6, the frequency of neural activity was high at first when the rate of stimulus movement was high, but it decreased as the rate of movement slowed, ceasing altogether as the rate of movement approached zero.

Fibers that show activity only during the

time that the stimulus is producing a movement of the tissue are referred to as *rapidly adapting*. Receptors that are rapidly adapting, mechanically sensitive, and presumed to have a relationship with tactile sensations include the Pacinian corpuscles, hair follicle receptors (except those of vibrissae), and the dermal nerve network.

There are also *slowly adapting* receptors found in the skin of some mammals. Not only do the nerve fibers of these receptors show an initial burst of activity while the stimulator is moving, but they continue to discharge at a slow rate for long periods of time (minutes) after the stimulus has apparently stopped moving. It is not definitely known whether slowly adapting receptors exist in human skin.

Both rapidly and slowly adapting mechanoreceptors have receptive fields that range from a single spot of less than 1 mm² on the skin to areas of up to 800 mm². Mechanical stimulation of any part of the receptive field will produce a train of impulses in the fiber, but the sensitivity of the field appears to be greater at its center than toward its margins.

The receptive fields of single fibers innervating the skin overlap considerably. When a point on the skin is stimulated mechanically it is almost inevitable that activity will be produced in a number of individual fibers. The threshold intensity required to activate the fiber varies so that the stronger the stimulus, within limits, the greater the number of fibers that are discharged.

Another relationship exists between the strength of the stimulus and the response of individual fibers; that is, the stronger the stimulus, within limits, the greater is the frequency of impulses in the individual fiber. When these relationships are considered together, a mechanical stimulus of increasing strength will increase the number of nerve fibers responding and will also increase the frequency of activity within each nerve fiber.

The primary difference in the innervation of hairy and hairless skin is that the latter is innervated by Meissner corpuscles rather than hair follicle receptors. Nevertheless, neurophysiological investigations of the mechano-receptors of primate hairy and hairless skin provide no evidence of a difference in the response to identical stimuli applied to the two types of skin that cannot be accounted for by differences in the thickness of the corneum (Iggo, 1963).

There is a marked selectivity of response of most mechanically sensitive units to mechanical stimuli. Pacinian corpuscles, hair follicle receptors other than vibrissae, and the dermal nerve network terminals, which respond to mechanical stimulation, are not readily excited by even large changes in the temperature of the skin. Slowly adapting mechanoreceptors tend to show responses to changes in skin temperature, but these changes in activity are small compared to their responses to mechanical stimulation.

Touch Thresholds

The sensitivity to touch varies with the mechanical properties of both the skin and the stimulator, as well as the particular site on the skin chosen for stimulation. Touch sensitivity may be demonstrated by use of a

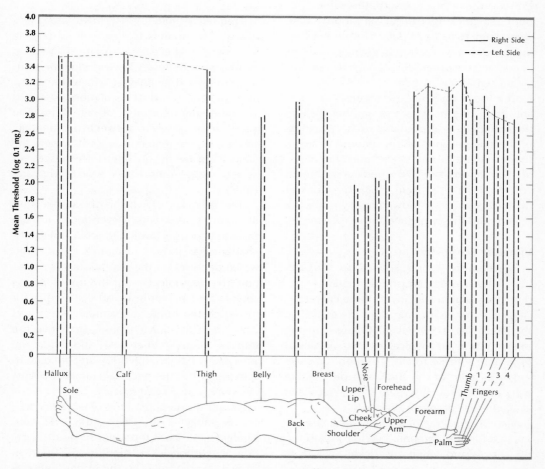

Figure 5.7. Regional variations in the tactile sensitivity of males. Females show a similar distribution of tactile sensitivity but were slightly more sensitive than the males. The measurements were made with a set of modified von Frey-type nylon filaments calibrated on a chemical balance for the force exerted. (Figure 10-2 from Weinstein, 1968.)

series of calibrated hairs (von Frey hairs) of varying stiffness fastened perpendicularly to the ends of light wooden handles. The force that will just bend the hair can be measured by pressing the free end of the hair on the pan of a sensitive balance. The diameter of the hair is also measured, with the aid of a microscope, so that thresholds can be expressed in terms of g/mm^2. Von Frey explored an inked grid on the leg and found 15 points within the grid that responded to 33 g/mm^2, or less. An increase in the force did not yield an increase in the number of touch spots, until the force was increased to about 200 g/mm^2. Above this pressure, the subject reported a pricking painful sensation. There were, then, two sets of points within the grid, one set with low thresholds, giving sensations of contact, the other set with high thresholds, giving sensations of pain.

The touch threshold (*RL*) varies considerably from one body site to another. Part of this variability is attributable to the thickness of the skin and part to the amount of nerve supply. Figure 5.7 shows the touch *RL*s measured on various parts of the body by calibrated von Frey hairs (Weinstein, 1968). The face was the most sensitive, followed by the trunk, the fingers, and the upper and lower extremities.

Vibratory Sensitivity

Mechanical stimuli applied to the skin have intensive, spatial, and temporal characteristics. Variations in any of these characteristics will produce a change in the quality of the sensation experienced. Changes in the intensity of a mechanical stimulus will lead to a more intense touch sensation. Changes in the location of the stimulator on the skin will cause the touch sensation to be localized at a different point on the body.

Certain qualities of a touch sensation are notable for their temporal features, for example, tickle and vibration. Tickle sensations may be aroused by moving a hair to and fro or by touching adjacent points on the skin in an appropriate temporal sequence (Nafe, 1927). Vibratory sensitivity is a special case of

the tactile sense rather than a sense system in its own right (Geldard, 1940a, b, c, d).

Sensitivity to vibration, like that to touch, is not evenly distributed over the skin surface. If one uses a phonograph needle, inserted in a phonograph cutting head and driven by an oscillator and a powerful amplifier, to explore a small area of skin systematically, some patches of skin will give rise to a lively whirring sensation, whereas others will show little sensation. These spots that are sensitive to vibration usually coincide with spots sensitive to touch (as determined with a von Frey hair).

Frequency limits   What, in vibratory sensitivity, corresponds to the 16 to 20,000 Hz sensitivity of the ear? The critical factor in establishing the lower limit of vibratory sensitivity is the frequency at which the sensations of the individual oscillations fuse into a continuous sensation of vibration. The question is not easy to answer experimentally and all experimenters have not meant the same thing by "lower limit." The values reported range from 10 to 80 Hz (Geldard, 1940c).

The question of what is the upper limit of vibratory sensitivity is even more obscure than that of the lower limit. No one really knows what it is. Unlike the lower limit, which depends on the definition of a sensation, the determination of the upper limit is complicated primarily because it is difficult to design the proper apparatus. Mechanical vibrators with sufficient mass (to move the skin at high frequencies) and structural strength (to hold together) are difficult to activate with the necessary amplitudes of vibration at high frequencies.

Values of the upper limit of vibratory sensitivity range from 640 to 8192 Hz, and Geldard (1953) has reported bursts of vibration at frequencies as high as 10,000 Hz. In each instance, however, the upper limit was imposed by the mechanical characteristics of the stimulator and not by the ability of the subject to detect the vibration.

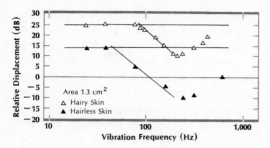

Figure 5.8. Comparison of vibrotactile absolute thresholds (*RL*s) measured on hairy and hairless skin for a stimulator surface area of 1.3 cm². Hairy skin was less sensitive than hairless skin to all frequencies of vibration, and the frequency at which frequency of vibration became important in determining the *RL* was lower in hairless than in hairy skin. Relative displacement is reported on the vertical axis in decibels. In this instance a decibel is 20 times the logarithm of the ratio of the displacement to a reference displacement of 1 μ. (Figure 3 from Verrillo, 1966.)

Thresholds, absolute and differential The absolute vibratory threshold (*RL*), as measured by the displacement of the stimulator probe, depends on the frequency of the vibration, the site of the stimulation, and the temperature of the skin. As shown in Figure 5.8, the vibratory *RL* was relatively high at frequencies up to 40 Hz in hairless skin and 90 Hz in hairy skin (Verrillo, 1966). At higher frequencies the *RL* decreased, reached a minimum at about 250 Hz in both types of tissue, then increased at still higher frequencies. The curve is clearly not a monotonic (result of a single continuous variable) function but appears to have at least two components. For hairy skin, it appears that one component operates up to about 90 Hz, followed by the second that takes over at 90 Hz and beyond. The same holds true for hairless skin except that the transition point is at about 40 Hz. Other evidence, given below, shows that the vibratory *RL* is the result of two different types

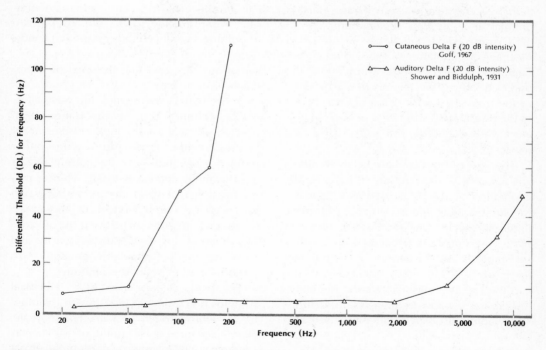

Figure 5.9. Comparison of cutaneous and auditory differential thresholds (*DL*s). The skin and the ear are about equal in their ability to discriminate between frequencies up to 50 Hz. At higher frequencies the ear is vastly superior to the skin. (Modified from Figure 5 of Goff, 1967.)

of receptor—one that functions at a relatively high threshold for low frequencies and a second, of greater sensitivity, that takes over at higher frequencies.

There is an obvious difference between hairy and hairless skin in the vibratory *RL*s shown in Figure 5.8 (in which the sites of stimulation were the hand and the volar surface of the forearm). The reasons for this difference in the *RL*s in hairy and hairless skin and the differences in the frequency at which the frequency of vibration became a variable (90 and 50 Hz) are not clear. Comparisons of vibratory *RL*s with histological and neurophysiological evidence have not yet been done systematically.

Skin temperature is a third variable that affects the vibratory *RL*. When the skin was maintained at a temperature about 4° C above normal (about 36° to 37° C) the vibratory *RL* was at a minimum for a 256 Hz vibration. Either a decrease or an increase in skin temperature resulted in an increase in the *RL*. Perhaps a chemical reaction whose speed is optimal at about this temperature (36° to 37° C) is involved in the process of translating mechanical stimulation of the skin into nerve impulses (Weitz, 1941). Considering the duplex nature of the vibratory *RL* as a function of the frequency of vibration, what happens to the threshold as a function of skin temperature when frequencies other than 256 Hz are used?

The skin can discriminate between different frequencies of vibration. If, for example, a vibration of 100 Hz is used as a standard, the subject feels one of 150 Hz as having a different "pitch." The differential threshold (*DL*), when other frequencies were used as the standard, and the auditory *DL*s are shown in Figure 5.9 (Goff, 1967). Compared to the ear, the skin is a reasonably good frequency discriminator at low frequencies but deteriorates rapidly at high frequencies (see also Figure 8.20, page 249).

Adaptation During prolonged exposure to a local vibration, adaptation has been found to occur in vibratory sensitivity (Hahn,

1966). In order to measure the amount of adaptation that occurs, vibratory *RL*s were measured before and immediately after the skin had been exposed for 25 minutes to an adapting stimulus of 60 Hz. After exposure to the adapting stimulus, the vibratory *RL* was increased by 20 dB (tenfold). Recovery from adaptation was almost complete within 10 minutes after the adapting stimulus ceased. These data are surprising because vibration applied to the skin stimulates the tactile sense and adaptation to tactile stimuli involves stimulus failure (see p. 131). Several considerations may explain this discrepancy. First, the adaptation effect may be purely mechanical. Prolonged vibration may compact the tissue so that it fails to recover promptly to its normal position after each impact. A second possibility, exclusive of or in combination with the first, is that an adaptive process may occur in the central nervous system.

Electrical stimulation of the skin Electrical currents are the great "inadequate stimuli." When applied to the skin they excite everything. Under carefully controlled conditions, however, they can be used to produce sensations that feel like the taps of a mechanical stimulator.

In the initial experiments sine wave alternating currents were used. Hahn (1958) pointed out that the rise time of the current in the individual cycles varies when either frequency or intensity of the current (measured in milliamperes) is varied. Hence, it is not possible to assess the effect of these two variables, each independent of the other. However, if square electrical pulses of variable duration are used, pulse intensity and frequency may be varied independently. Also a third variable is added—duration.

The temporal properties of an electrical stimulus determine, at least in part, whether it will arouse touch or pain. For example, electrical square pulse stimuli of 100 Hz may produce only painful sensations even at threshold intensities, but when the frequency is raised to 1000 Hz, they may produce tactile sensations even at intensities considerably above threshold. Short pulses (less than 0.5 msec duration) tend to be more painful than longer ones, probably because the shorter pulses require higher intensities to produce a sensation. The pain that occurs with high pulse intensities is associated with a breakdown of the electrical resistance of the skin at a small point, causing a high current density at that point (Gibson, 1968). The lowest electrically induced tactile *RL*, in terms of the pulse duration necessary to arouse a tactile

sensation, has been found with pulses of about 2 msec duration, regardless of their frequency, as is shown in Figure 5.10 (Hahn, 1958).

Another interesting aspect of the results appearing in Figure 5.10 is that the electrically aroused vibratory *RL* is not a function of pulse frequency. These results are contrary to those achieved if vibratory sensations are mechanically induced, where frequency markedly influences the mechanical vibratory threshold. This difference suggests an interesting hypothesis: Mechanical stimulation has its principal effect on the tactile receptive structures, whereas the electrical stimulus has its principal effect directly on the sensory nerve fibers. That is, electrical stimulation by-passes the receptive structure.

Receptors The receptors responsible for mechanical vibratory sensitivity have been the subject of both psychophysical and neurophysiological investigations. The mechanical vibratory *RL*, shown in Figure 5.8, appears to be a duplex function of the frequency of vibration. It is as though two receptive elements, each with different sensitivities to mechanical vibration, combine to form the *RL* curve. An analogy is the visual dark-adaptation curve in which cone function determines the early part of the curve and rod function the latter part (see p. 284).

In order to identify the possible nerve terminal configurations responsible for the duplex vibratory *RL* curve, psychophysical measurements of the vibratory *RLs* of skin tissues at various sites of the body were compared (Verrillo, 1968). Verrillo found that tissues gave a duplex curve when the dermal nerve network and Pacinian corpuscles were the sole nerve terminal configurations. When a tissue was used that lacked Pacinian corpuscles (the topside of the tongue tip) the vibration *RL* did not decrease at frequencies between 90 to 300 Hz, as it did in the other tissues.

Neurophysiological studies have also implicated the Pacinian corpuscle with mechanical vibratory sensitivity at the higher

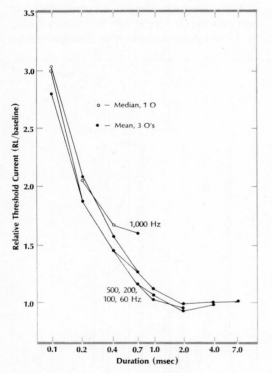

Figure 5.10. The strength and duration of electrical pulses required to produce absolute thresholds (*RLs*) of vibration. The ordinate is the ratio of the intensity of pulses of various durations required to produce *RLs*, to the intensity of a 2.0 msec duration pulse *RL* (baseline). Thus, almost three times the intensity was required to produce an *RL* when the pulse duration was 0.1 msec as when it was 2.0 msec. Unlike the mechanical vibration *RL* shown in Figure 5.8, the electrical vibration *RL* was independent of the frequency but depended on the duration of the individual pulses. (Figure 1 from Hahn, 1958.)

frequencies. The Pacinian corpuscle has a high threshold to vibration at frequencies below 60 Hz, a low threshold at 250 Hz, and an elevated threshold at still higher frequencies (Mountcastle et al., 1967).

Localization and Two-point Threshold

We frequently speak of an object touching our hand or coming in contact with our face. How do we know which part of our body has been contacted? How accurate is this localization? As in vision, where each small area of the retina is represented in a particular part of the visual cortex of the brain, so in somesthesis each part of the body surface is repre-

sented in a particular part of the somesthetic cortex. There is a topographical arrangement of loci so that the skin is represented in an orderly fashion in the somesthetic cortex (see Figure 5.3). Some areas of skin, such as the fingers, lips, and tongue, are much more densely innervated than others. These areas of denser innervation are represented by larger areas of somesthetic cortex.

A partial answer to the question of what body part has been touched is that the activity in a particular part of the somesthetic cortex resulting from stimulation of a particular body part provides the local sign and makes stimulus localization possible. This is supported by

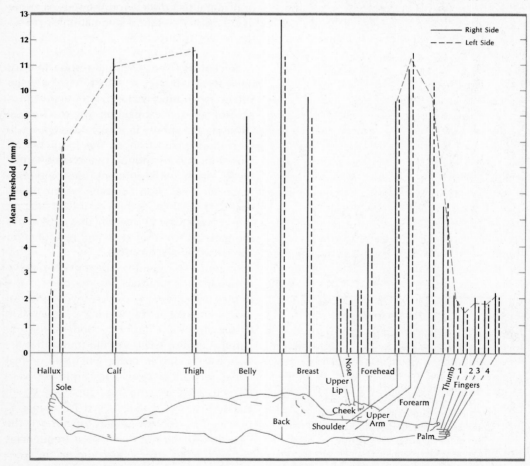

Figure 5.11. Regional variations in point localization of males. The height of each bar represents the size of the difference, in mm, between the reference stimulus and the test stimuli that the subject would accept as located at the reference stimulus. (Figure 10-6 from Weinstein, 1968.)

the fact that mild electrical stimulation of a point on the somesthetic cortex will cause a sensation, usually tingling, which is localized in the body part served by that part of the cortex. If stimulation is applied to the hand area of the cortex, the sensation is localized in the hand, not in the cortex.

The accuracy of point localization is not evenly distributed over the body surface. Figure 5.11 shows that localization is most accurate in the area of the nose and mouth and least accurate on the back. The correlation between accuracy of localization at various skin sites and the amount of area of somesthetic cortex representing that body part is about +0.76 (Weinstein, 1968).

Another kind of tactile acuity, like point localization, is the ability to resolve tactile stimuli separated by very small distances along the skin. The minimum spatial separation of the two points that is judged as two is called the *two-point limen* (threshold). A low two-point limen is essential to such activities as reading Braille, judging fabrics, or determining the texture of objects by feel. Like point localization, the two-point limen varies at different skin sites, and there is a high correlation between two-point sensitivity and the amount of the cortex devoted to the representation of the body part. In contrast to point localization (the nose and mouth yield the smallest errors), the fingers are most acute in two-point discriminations, followed by the areas around the mouth and nose.

Another feature of the two-point discrimination, and somewhat less apparent in point localization, is the proximodistal gradient of two-point sensitivity on all limbs. Thus, the fingers show greater tactile acuity than the forearm, upper arm, and shoulder, and the toes show greater tactile acuity than the calf and thigh.

Interaction of Tactile Stimuli

Tactile stimulation of skin areas adjacent to a main stimulus area produces a variety of modifications in the sensation of the main stimulus. The stimulus may appear to move from one location to another—cutaneous *phi phenomenon;* the sensation of an adjacent stimulus may diminish or completely cancel the sensation produced by the main stimulus—*inhibition;* an adjacent stimulus may enhance the effects of the main stimulus—*summation;* and summation and inhibition may occur simultaneously in the tactile sense—*funneling.* Whether such interactions are phenomena of the peripheral or central nervous system is not clear, although present facts implicate both locations.

Phi phenomenon The cutaneous phi phenomenon is like the visual phi phenomenon (see p. 526) in many respects. It depends upon the interval between the onsets of the stimuli (interstimulus onset interval, ISOI), their duration, and the distance between them. For example, one vibrator can be placed at the wrist and another on the forearm, 15 to 20 cm away. If single pulses with an ISOI of approximately 100 msec are used, a sensation is produced that appears to move from one site of stimulation to the other (Sherrick, 1968). Other combinations of ISOI and dura-

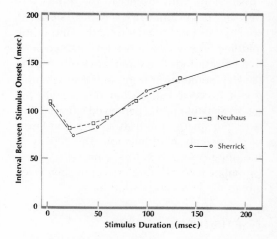

Figure 5.12. The interstimulus interval and stimulus durations required for optimal movement (phi phenomenon). The squares are the data of Neuhaus for visual movement. The circles are the data for tactile movement. (Figure 5 from Sherrick & Rogers, 1966.)

tions that produce good movement are shown in Figure 5.12.

An interesting comparison is made in Figure 5.12 between ISOIs and stimulus duration for tactile and visual movement. The conditions that maximize the visual and tactile apparent movement are similar enough to suggest that they are not specific to a modality, but result from the operation of a common set of neurological principles.

Inhibition, summation, and funneling
When a vibrating needle is brought in contact with the skin of the arm, traveling waves are set up in the skin that involve the whole arm (von Békésy, 1959). However, the sensation is felt only at the point of the stimulator contact. The sensations that should be experienced from the traveling waves in the skin do not occur. Apparently, the effect of the neural activity set up at areas other than the point of contact is somehow blocked (inhibited).

Funneling (simultaneous inhibition and summation) occurs when an array of vibrators placed on the forearm are started simultaneously (von Békésy, 1959). When each is equally loud with respect to the others, and they are set to vibrate in one-octave steps (20, 40, 80, 160, and 320 Hz), only the one in the middle of the array is felt, with a judged pitch that corresponds to its frequency of vibration (80 Hz). Stimulation from the other vibrators is not perceived and does not modify the pitch sensation of the perceived vibrator. This is not so for the intensity aspect (loudness) of the perceived stimulation. The activity of the unperceived vibrators appears to add to (summate with) the loudness of the perceived vibration, increasing its loudness.

TEMPERATURE SENSITIVITY

One of the vital processes of any organism is the regulation of its body temperature. This is particularly true in those organisms that maintain a constant body temperature (homotherms). Two general mechanisms have

evolved which help the organism maintain a set body temperature regardless of the environmental temperature conditions. The first, an automatic process, controls processes such as heat production by changes in metabolism, peripheral thermal conductance (regulation of the cutaneous vascular system), shivering and sweating. The second, primarily in man, is the use of external devices such as clothing and air conditioning to help control the demands placed upon the automatic temperature regulating system. The proper operation of both mechanisms depends, to a considerable extent, upon information provided by the cutaneous temperature sensing mechanism. The available evidence seems to indicate that there is one common temperature-sensing mechanism, which contributes both to the process of body temperature regulation and to the awareness of the environmental thermal conditions.

Receptors

In spite of intensive histological examinations of skin over the past one hundred years, there is no evidence that clearly implicates specific structures in the reception of thermal stimuli. Examinations of the tissue beneath warm and cold spots with light microscopes have failed to reveal structures other than the terminals of the dermal nerve network and clusters of arterioles and capillaries.

In spite of the lack of a specific structure to associate with temperature reception, it is possible to locate the depth of thermal receptors beneath the skin surface by either one of two means. Both methods require information about the rate at which temperature changes are transmitted through skin tissue. The depths of the receptive elements for both warm and cool sensations have been calculated to be 150 to 200 μ beneath the skin surface (Hensel, Ström, & Zotterman, 1951; Hendler & Hardy, 1960). The older notion that warm receptors are located deeper within the skin than the cold receptors is in error.

The important variable in thermal stimulation is the temperature of the tissue at the site of the receptor, approximately 150 to 200 μ beneath the surface. This is difficult to measure directly but may be approximated by calculation if the temperature of the skin surface is known (Hensel, 1952). However, uncontrolled factors may affect the calculations, for example, the rate of blood flow through the cutaneous vascular system, which is also about 150 to 200 μ beneath the surface, and the thickness of the corneum.

Physical Considerations in Thermal Stimulation

The reports on the sensitivity of human skin to changes in its temperature have not been even in general agreement. This can be attributed, at least in part, to the diverse methods that have been employed experimentally to manipulate skin temperature and the equally diverse methods of recording and reporting the stimulus temperatures—either of the stimulus object or the skin surface.

Two primary methods for experimentally controlling skin temperature are the application of conducted heat, as when a temperature controlled object is brought in contact with the skin, and radiant heat, as when the infrared wavelengths from a heater or the sun are directed at the skin.

Two techniques using conducted heat to change skin temperature have involved dipping the fingers or arms into thermostatically controlled water baths, and covering various areas of skin (less than 1 mm² to larger than 20 cm²) with a hollow metallic chamber through which temperature controlled water is circulated (a *thermode*). Recently, the Peltier effect has been incorporated in a new type of conducted heat stimulator. Heating or cooling can be produced, relying on the Peltier effect, when direct current is passed through the junctions of two dissimilar electrical conductors. The amount of current determines the rate and extent, and the polarity of the current determines the direction of the temperature change. Kenshalo (1963) has described an electrical circuit which will permit the Peltier device to maintain any skin

temperature within the physiological range, to an accuracy of ±0.012° C. The device will also produce changes in skin temperature of as little as 0.05° C up to 20° C at rates up to 2° C/sec.

In many experiments the stimulus temperature reported is that of the water bath, the water circulating through the thermode, or the surface of the thermode, apparently on the assumption that these reflect the temperature of the skin. It is a false assumption. Skin temperature is affected not only by the temperature of the stimulating surface, but also by the *specific heat* and the *thermal conductivity* of the surface material. Specific heat is the heat required to raise a unit volume of a substance by 1° C, and thermal conductivity is the ability of a substance to transfer heat energy through itself. Thus, wood and brass, each at 15° C, do not feel equally cool, and water and air each at 40° C do not feel equally warm.

Radiant heat energy from electric lamps has been used to change skin temperature and to produce warm sensations. Dry ice has been used to absorb heat and produce cool sensations. These methods have the advantage that they can be used to stimulate very large or very small areas of skin. They have the disadvantage that the intensity of the radiation must be reported in cal/sec–cm² and as yet there is no convenient method of measuring skin temperature directly during radiant stimulation. The change in skin temperature (ΔT) produced by a particular intensity of radiation for a specified interval of exposure can be calculated (Lipkin & Hardy, 1954). In order for the calculation to be accurate, factors such as the amount of radiation absorbed by the skin and the thermal inertia of the skin must be taken into account.

Another important variable to consider, in addition to methods of stimulation, when quantitative measurements of temperature sensitivity are sought is the size of the skin surface to which a ΔT is applied. A ΔT applied over a small area (less than 1 cm²) does not produce the same change in the temperature of the subsurface tissue as the same ΔT applied to a larger skin surface area. For example, a brass cylinder tapered at one end so as to contact a skin surface of 2 mm² and heated to 40° C will produce only a slight temperature rise in the tissue 200 μ beneath the surface. Another brass cylinder, at the same temperature, but having a 100 mm² stimulating area, produces a larger temperature rise beneath the surface. Similar effects occur with variations in the surface area to which radiant energy is applied.

Adaptation

Thermal adaptation is the reduction in the intensity of the thermal sensation with continued exposure to a constant temperature. When we first step into a hot bath the sensation of warmth is usually intense. As we sit down in the bath water and remain there quietly, we notice that the warm sensation has diminished. This is, of course, due in part to the cooling of the bath water, but it is also due to adaptation of the temperature receptors. To demonstrate this, slide farther down in the bath. A warmer sensation is experienced in the newly immersed skin than in the adapted area.

Adaptation to mild temperatures may become complete; that is, the warm or cool sensation may disappear completely with continued exposure to that temperature. A number of questions should immediately occur to us about thermal adaptation, such as: (1) What are the limits of skin temperature to which complete adaptation can occur? (2) What is the rate of adaptation? (3) Are the temperature limits for complete adaptation fixed or can they be changed? (4) How does the initial skin temperature affect the rate of adaptation to higher or lower temperatures? Answers to these questions are important in describing one aspect of human temperature sensitivity and the operation of temperature receptors.

The usual method used to investigate thermal adaptation has been to place thermodes on the skin at various extreme temperatures and then to note the time required for the thermal sensations to disappear. Using this method, Holm (1903) found that adaptation was complete to an applied temperature of 45° C after 152 seconds and to 5° C after 210 seconds. Less extreme temperatures required less time. Gertz (1921) has reported a narrower range for complete adaptation, namely from 15° C to 40° C, whereas Hensel (1950) was unable to obtain complete adaptation to temperatures lower than 19° C. Several difficulties are inherent in the procedures used by these investigators. The most important is that subjects have difficulty attending to the stimulus for 1 minute, let alone 30 to 40 minutes.

Kenshalo and Scott (1966) adapted the Peltier stimulator so that the up and down method (see p. 20) might be used to investigate the temporal course of adaptation. Thoroughly trained subjects were instructed to maintain the temperature of the stimulator on the forearm at a "just detectably warm"

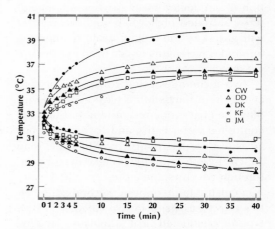

Figure 5.13. The temporal course of thermal adaptation to just perceptably warm and cool stimuli starting from a T_0 of about 32.5° C. The temperature limits of complete adaptation were about 29° to 37° C although some individuals adapted completely to temperatures as high as 40° C. The differences between individuals appear to be due to unique characteristics of the individual rather than variability of the measurements. (Figure 1 from Kenshalo, 1970a.)

or "just detectably cool" sensation by moving a two-way switch. As the subjects adapted to a given temperature, they changed the stimulator to a new temperature, so that the rate of change of the stimulator temperature could be used as an index of the rate of change of adaptation. As shown in Figure 5.13, the subjects started with a normal skin temperature (T_o) of approximately 32.5° C; they changed the temperature of the stimulator rapidly toward either warm or cool during the first 10 minutes or less of adaptation. Beyond that time, the rate of adaptation was slow. After 30 to 40 minutes, the subjects made no further changes in the temperature of the stimulator. The temperature extremes of about 29° and 37° C therefore represent the temperature limits of complete adaptation. Although the range of complete adaptation generally lies between 29° and 37° C, there is evidence, from studying Figure 5.13, that each subject has a different range. For example, the range for CW (filled circles) is 30° to 40° C, but is only 30° to 35° C for JM (open squares). It is not likely that this difference represents different criteria for "just detectably warm" or "just detectably cool" because the warm and cool RLs of these thoroughly trained subjects did not vary by more than 0.1° C.

The data indicate that the range of complete thermal adaptation is from about 29° to about 37° C for most subjects. Outside of this range, persisting cool and warm sensations occur no matter how long the stimulator is left in place on the skin.

Physiological Zero and the Neutral Zone

It should now be apparent that the human thermal receptive system does not respond like a good absolute thermometer. It adapts, and within a narrow range of temperatures, it adapts completely. This leads to another concept, that of *physiological zero* (T_o). As usually defined, T_o is a skin temperature that is thermally indifferent, that is, a temperature to which the subject reports neither warm nor cool. On either side of T_o is a narrow range

of temperatures through which the skin temperature may be changed, even rapidly, without evoking a thermal sensation. This is called the *neutral zone*. The size of the neutral zone may be as little as 0.01° C or as large as 8° C depending upon the particular value of T_o, the size and location of the surface stimulated, and the rate of change of the stimulus temperature.

There may be considerable variation in T_o over the body surface at any one time. For example, the ear lobe may have a T_o of 28° C whereas the forehead or cheek may have a T_o of 35° C. In both instances, the subject feels neither warm nor cool at these particular body locations.

On the forearm T_o may be shifted through a narrow range of temperatures, generally 29° C to 37° C. It is not known whether similar limits exist at other locations of the body. The range of skin temperatures within which complete thermal adaptation occurs represents the range of temperatures through which T_o may be shifted provided sufficient time for adaptation is allowed, or the imposed change in temperature is sufficiently slow (less than about 0.007° C/sec on 20 cm² of the forearm).

Thermal Thresholds

No one value suffices as the RL for warm or cool sensations because thermal RLs vary with the conditions under which they are measured. In this section, the effect of three major conditions of measurement are considered: (1) skin temperature; (2) the rate of change of the stimulus temperature; and (3) the size of the area stimulated.

The smallest RL yet reported for warm sensations is an increase in skin temperature ($+\Delta T$) of 0.003° C and for cool sensations, a decrease ($-\Delta T$) of 0.004° C (Hardy & Oppel, 1937, 1938). In both measurements the entire ventral surface of the body above the waist was exposed to the radiant energy. Exposure of smaller areas results in larger RLs because of the powerful spatial summation capabilities of the temperature-receptive system (see p. 146).

Skin temperature The temperature to which the skin is adapted determines the sensation experienced when a ΔT occurs. Within the T_o zone, and after adaptation is complete, a small $+\Delta T$ or $-\Delta T$ in temperature is felt as warm or cool. When the skin has been adapted to temperatures outside the

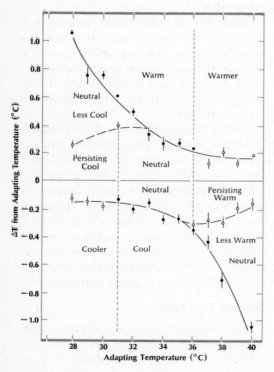

Figure 5.14. The change in the warm and cool *RL*s and *DL*s as a function of the temperature to which the skin of the forearm was adapted. Warm and cool *RL*s are shown by the filled circles. The open circles show *DL*s. When the adapting temperature of the stimulator was low the subject experienced a persisting cool sensation. A detectably cooler sensation occurred when the temperature of the stimulator was lowered by 0.15° C (*DL*). When the warm *RL*s were measured from a low adapting temperature there was first a detectable decrease in the persisting cool sensation, a *DL*, then thermal neutrality, and finally a warm *RL* occurred. A similar series of sensations occurred when the skin had been adapted to high temperatures and measurements of the cool *RL*s were made. (Modified from Figure 3 of Kenshalo, 1970a.)

range of T_o, the warm or cool sensation persists indefinitely, although some adaptation occurs. At these adapting temperatures, a small ΔT increases or decreases the persisting sensation. For example, if the skin has been adapted to 40° C, a warm sensation is experienced no matter how long adaptation is allowed. A small $-\Delta T$ (0.5° C) is felt as a decrease in the persisting warm sensation, not as a cool sensation. A small $+\Delta T$ intensifies the persisting warm sensation.

The temperature to which the skin has been adapted has profound influence upon the warm and cool *RL*s outside of the T_o zone. Both Hensel (1950) and Lele (1954) have reported that the warm *RL* is increased by adapting the skin to low temperatures whereas the cool *RL* is increased by adapting it to high temperatures.

Similar results, reported by Kenshalo (1970a), are shown in Figure 5.14. These measurements of the thermal thresholds were obtained after setting the Peltier stimulator at the desired adapting temperature for a specific period of time and then changing its temperature by various amounts for short intervals (10 seconds). For example, when the cool threshold was to be measured at an adapting temperature of 28° C, the subject was seated in a chair and the stimulator, set to maintain 28°, was placed on the skin of his forearm. After a 40-minute adaptation period, measurements of the cool threshold were made according to the psychophysical method of limits (see p. 14). The temperature of the stimulator was decreased by regular amounts at 1-minute intervals. The stimulus temperature was maintained for a period of 10 seconds or until the subject reported a cool sensation, whichever was shorter; after that the stimulator was returned to the adapting temperature. The threshold for a cooler sensation at this adapting temperature was about −0.15° C or a reduction in skin temperature from 28° to 27.85° C.

It is immediately apparent from Figure 5.14 that the thresholds of the thermal sense are indeed unusual when compared to those of the other senses. What are *RL*s and what are

*DL*s? Further refinement of the definitions of these terms is required in order to apply them to the thermal sense. As discussed in Chapter 2, a *DL* is the smallest change in a stimulus dimension that can be detected on an arbitrary percent of the presentations (usually 50 percent). The *RL* is the limiting case of the *DL*, for it represents the smallest quantity of a stimulus dimension that can be detected as compared to its absence. If intensity thresholds are viewed from the standpoint of the change in the intensity of the stimulus energy required to excite the receptor, all of the thresholds shown in Figure 5.14 are *DL*s, for zero thermal energy is about $-273.63°$ C (absolute zero), and there are only increasing amounts of thermal energy from there on up the temperature scale. However, we measure thresholds of sensation, not thresholds of the quantity of the stimulus dimension, and it is a characteristic of the temperature-sensing system that the absence of thermal sensations occurs at skin temperatures between 29° and 37° C. The zero point for the cutaneous thermal sense is T_0, and T_0 may assume values between 29° and 37° C. At skin temperatures below the T_0 zone a cool sensation persists no matter how much time is allowed for adaptation. After adaptation to these temperatures below T_0 a small $-\Delta T$ is detected as being cooler, so this is a *DL*. A small $+\Delta T$ is detected as less cool, and this also is a *DL*; however, a $+\Delta T$ that is felt as warm is an *RL* because of the transition from thermal neutrality to warm. At high adapting temperatures a similar condition exists, except that the persisting sensation is warm and a small $+\Delta T$ is sensed as warmer, a *DL*. A small $-\Delta T$ is sensed as less warm and is also a *DL*, but a larger $-\Delta T$ that is felt as cool is an *RL*, for the sensations were first less warm and then neutral before becoming cool. All thresholds measured in the T_0 zone are *RL*s.

Rate of temperature change   The rate at which the temperature is changed during the process of measuring a warm or cool *RL* has a pronounced effect upon the size of the *RL*. Hensel (1950), for example, found that the

warm *RL* at T_0 (33.3° C), increased when the rate of warming of the thermode was less than 0.02° C/sec. A further reduction in the rate of warming resulted in a further increase in the *RL* until, starting from a skin temperature of 33.3° C and using a rate of warming of 0.0083° C/sec, an *RL* was obtained only after the skin temperature had reached 36° C, close to the upper limit of T_0. The effect of the rate of ΔT on the cool *RL* is that rates of cooling of 0.007° C/sec become just noticeable only after the skin has been cooled to 29° C, close to the lower limit of T_0.

The effects of the rate of ΔT on warm and cool *RL*s are shown in Figure 5.15. Warm and cool *RL*s were measured for skin at normal temperatures ($T_0 = 31°$ to 32° C), and the rate of warm or cool ΔT's was varied between 0.01° and 0.3° C/sec. Neither the warm nor

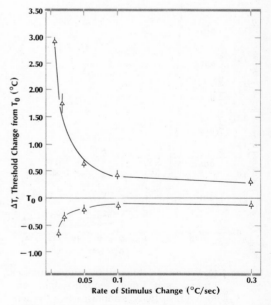

Figure 5.15. The effect of rate of the stimulus temperature change upon the warm and cool *RL*s measured from a T_0 of about 32.5° C on the forearm. The effect of the rate of temperature change on both the warm and cool *RL*s was small when the rates were greater than 0.1° C/sec. At slower rates of temperature change both the warm and the cool *RL*s increased, the effect being larger on the warm *RL*. (Modified from Figure 1 of Kenshalo, Holmes, & Wood, 1968.)

the cool *RL* was markedly affected by rates of Δ*T* of 0.1° C/sec and faster. At rates of Δ*T* slower than 0.1° C/sec, there was a marked increase in the warm *RL*. When a rate of 0.01° C/sec for Δ*T* was used, the *RL* was almost 3° C above normal skin temperature, as is shown in Figure 5.15.

Spatial summation   It is a common observation that our sensitivity to Δ*T*s increases with an increase in the size of the exposed surface. For example, it is difficult to determine whether an object is cool, warm, or indifferent if we touch it with a fingertip. However, if the whole hand is placed in contact with the object, we may experience the entire gamut of thermal sensations. Little

work has been done to quantify the relationship between the surface area of stimulation and the thermal *RL*. The implication of the effect of spatial summation on *RL* is that the activity of individual thermal receptors adds together to increase the intensity of the sensation. For example, suppose two adjacent skin areas each have 10 receptive elements. When one area alone is stimulated, the warm *RL* = +0.5° C. When both areas are simultaneously stimulated, the neural activity from the 10 additional receptive elements is somehow added to that of the original 10 and now perhaps *RL* = +0.25° C.

Quantitative functions of spatial summation for both warm and cool stimuli have been described using radiant energy stimulation (Hardy & Oppel, 1937, 1938). The results for the spatial summation of warm stimuli are similar to those shown in Figure 5.16 (Kenshalo, Decker, & Hamilton, 1967). The formula describing these data is

$$I = kA^{-b} + c$$

in which *I* is the threshold intensity of stimulation for warm sensations in cal/sec–cm² applied to area *A* in cm²; *k* is a constant whose values change with the site of stimulation (back, forehead, or forearm); *c* is the warm threshold in cal/sec–cm² for very large areas of exposure (greater than 2000 cm²); and *b* is a constant which represents the degree to which spatial summation takes place. Because *b* ~ 1 for these data, it indicates that spatial summation is complete and that *A* × *I* = a constant. In other words, as the number of receptive elements doubles, the intensity of stimulation required to produce an *RL* is halved for areas of exposure up to 14 cm².

In Figure 5.16, warm *RL*s were also obtained using conducted energy for areas of 1.7, 7.1, and 14.4 cm². The *RL*s obtained using conducted energy are related to the *RL*s obtained using radiant energy by calculating the elevation in skin temperature produced by various intensities of infrared radiation (Lipkin & Hardy, 1954). The *RL*s obtained by

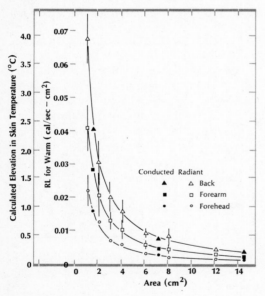

Figure 5.16. Warm *RL*s obtained by nonpenetrating infrared heat (open symbols) and conducted heat (filled symbols) when the surface area of the skin exposed on the back, forearm, and forehead was varied. The elevation in skin temperature produced by various intensities of radiation were computed by the formula given by Lipkin and Hardy (1954). It was possible to compare the thresholds obtained by radiant and conducted energy in this way. (Modified from Figure 1 of Kenshalo, Decker, & Hamilton, 1967.)

using conducted energy agree with those obtained by radiant energy, which demonstrates that there is no unique characteristic in either form of thermal stimulation and that warming of the skin tissue is the necessary factor to produce a warm sensation.

Because the stimulator rests on the skin surface, thermal stimulation by conducted energy involves tactile stimulation as well. Radiant energy, however, involves only thermal stimulation. The close agreement between the RLs from conducted and radiant energy suggests a lack of interaction between tactile and thermal stimulation, a suggestion supported by several investigators (Jones, Singer, & Twelker, 1962; Vendrik & Eijkman, 1968).

A second type of spatial summation, involving widely separated areas of stimulation, has also been shown to occur (Hardy & Oppel, 1937). Simultaneous stimulation of the backs of both hands with radiant energy gave a warm RL with approximately 30 percent less energy than was required to obtain a warm RL from similar stimulation of either hand, individually.

At first glance this type of thermal summation appears similar to the apparent summation encountered in vision when monocular RLs were found to be larger than binocular RLs (see p. 296). The reason for the apparent visual summation is purely statistical. The probability of detecting a flash of light at near-threshold intensity is greater when the flash is presented to both eyes than when it is presented to either eye, individually. However, the evidence suggests that thermal spatial summation involving widely separated areas of skin is of nervous rather than statistical origin. Simultaneous stimulation of the hand and the forehead failed to show the summation effect.

In what part of the nervous system might spatial summation of thermal stimuli take place? Herget, Granath, and Hardy (1941) have suggested that the data could be explained if spatial summation were assumed to occur at two sites in the nervous system. They sup-

posed that the terminal branches of single temperature-sensitive fibers may innervate areas of skin of up to perhaps 6 cm². The most peripheral point at which spatial summation could occur is the point at which the terminal branches join to form the stem axon.

In confirmation of Herget's theory, it has been found that a single temperature-sensitive axon (an axon insensitive to other forms of stimulation), in which the activity can be changed by warming or cooling its terminals, may innervate up to 8 individual spots on the skin of rhesus monkeys (Kenshalo & Gallegos, 1967). The spots, each less than 1 mm in diameter, may be separated by as much as 16 mm. When any one of the spots is cooled, an increase in the frequency of nerve impulses is observed in the axon. When several spots are simultaneously cooled by the same amount, the increase in impulse frequency is found to be proportional to the number of spots cooled.

The second locus at which spatial summation of thermal stimuli may occur is at the first or subsequent synapses in the central nervous system. Summation probably occurs at both loci, for warm and cool stimuli may summate over areas of up to about 2000 cm² and from widely separated areas, for example, the backs of both hands.

Other variables   There are factors other than the three primary ones already discussed that affect thermal RLs (Kenshalo, 1970a). Women show smaller cool RLs during the postovulatory phase of the menstrual cycle than for the period from the onset of menses to ovulation, but only when the skin has been adapted to temperatures above 36° C. No change in the warm RLs has been found at any adapting temperature. Both males and females give smaller cool RLs in the afternoon than in the morning. A change in the warm RLs with a change in the time of day of the measurement has not been demonstrated. Psychological stress, such as the anticipation of a major examination, increased the cool RL, but only when the skin had been adapted to temperatures greater than 36° C. Adrenalin infused into the skin produced cutaneous vasoconstriction, among other things, and caused an increase in the cool RL at adapting temperatures above 35° C and an increase in the warm RL at adapting temperatures below 31° C.

Paradoxical Cold, Warmth, and the Heat Sensation

An interesting phenomenon has been reported in which some cold spots, identified by previous mapping, give a sensation of cold when touched with a hot stimulator (45° C). Von Frey (1895), thinking that arousal of a cold sensation by a hot stimulus represented a paradox, labeled the sensation *paradoxical cold.*

Paradoxical warmth, the arousal of a warm sensation by stimulation of a warm spot with a cold stimulator, would be the opposite of paradoxical cold. The necessary and sufficient conditions for the arousal of this phenomenon have been sought by many investigators with little success. Its existence as a bona fide phenomenon of temperature sensitivity is open to question, although Jenkins and Karr (1957) seem to think that it may occur when the repeated stimulation of a warm spot by a warm stimulus preceeds the application of a cold stimulus.

Paradoxical cold cannot be aroused by applying a hot stimulus to a large area. The closest approximation is a momentary confusion of cold and hot that sometimes occurs when a hand or a foot is plunged into hot water.

Many early investigations of temperature sensitivity sought the necessary conditions for the arousal of the "heat" sensation. This sensation is said to be uniquely different in quality from that of warm and pain. The uniqueness of the heat sensation, as compared with that of intense warm, apparently lies in the addition of a slight stinging sensation, which soon adapts. The threshold of the heat sensation has been reported to range from 40° to 46° C with an average at 42° to 43° C. The threshold for burning heat (pain?) ranges from 43° to 51° C with an average at about 46° to 47° C (Lowenstein & Dallenbach, 1930). These are the temperatures of the water circulating through the stimulator; because perfect heat conduction is never attained, skin temperatures should be expected to be somewhat lower.

Two theories dealing with the mechanism of the heat sensation have been advanced. The older (Alrutz, 1908) suggests that the heat sensation is synthesized by the simultaneous stimulation of warm and cold receptors. The second (Herget & Hardy, 1942) maintains that the unique quality of the heat sensation that differentiates it from warmth—the adapting sting—is mediated by its own receptor type.

The basis of the Alrutz theory is that a hot stimulator arouses a warm sensation and paradoxically arouses a simultaneous cold sensation. The synthesis of heat should therefore be possible by simultaneously stimulating warm and cold spots with mild warm and cool stimuli. One of the clearer demonstrations of synthetic heat is that of the heat grill. Water from two tanks, one at 10° C, the other at 43° C, is circulated through copper tubes so that their temperatures alternate— W C W C W C. The subject places his forearm on the grill; the first sensation reported is usually that of cool, followed by heat, which often disappears after a few seconds and gives way to cold again. Warmth is often experienced at some time during a 10 to 15 second stimulus (Burnett & Dallenbach, 1927). Others have reported that they have synthesized heat by simultaneously applying cold and warm (not hot) stimuli to cold and warm spots on the forearm separated by as much as 15 cm (Alston, 1920). The same effect has also been produced by warm and cold spot stimulation plus mild electric shock (Ferrall & Dallenbach, 1930).

In spite of the impressive evidence presented above, the issue is by no means settled. Others (Jenkins, 1938) have tried to reproduce the results of earlier reports without success. Apparently, the experimental results depend upon the knowledge, attitude, and instructions of the subject, and the conditions of stimulation and the procedures employed. Furthermore, the heat threshold (42° to 43° C) appears to be low compared to the temperature required to stimulate cold spots paradoxically (45° C).

The evidence favoring the second theory of heat—that it is due to its own receptor type—arose primarily from studies of the spatial summation of threshold warm, heat, and cool sensations (Herget & Hardy, 1942.) There was less spatial summation for heat than for either threshold warm or cool sensations. Were cool and warm receptors producing the sensation of heat, as is suggested by the Alrutz theory, the spatial summation rate for threshold heat sensations should have fallen between those of threshold warm and cool sensations. It did not.

Physiological Mechanisms of Temperature Sensitivity

Investigations of temperature sensitivity have taken two different routes in recent years. Psychologists have conducted numerous experiments on the effects of various conditions of thermal stimulation on thermal sensations. Meanwhile physiologists, with the development of neurophysiological methods, have studied changes in peripheral neural activity produced by thermal stimulation. Neither approach can provide a complete picture of the functions of the system. The psychological approach cannot tell us anything about how neural messages of the environmental thermal conditions originate in the nervous system and are conveyed to the brain, and the neurophysiological approach cannot tell us how sensations change when a change occurs in the pattern of neural activity in peripheral afferent fibers. The two methods must be used in close coordination so that a more complete description of the system may be obtained.

How can closer coordination be achieved? The work discussed so far has been concerned with the changes in human temperature sensations that result from changes in the conditions of thermal stimulation. Human subjects cannot, usually, be subjected to the procedures necessary to obtain neurophysiological data. The answer lies in the use of subhuman species to obtain both behavioral measurements of sensation and neurophysiological measures of changes in neural activity.

Behavioral investigations Psychophysical measurements of sensory capacities, conducted on subhuman organisms, involve devising a language, comparable to the human "yes" or "no," by which the animal subject and human experimenter may communicate (see p. 753). The usual method has been to employ an avoidance conditioning method in which the animal is trained to avoid a mild electric shock (*UCS*) if it detects a stimulus (*CS*). As the *CS* becomes less intense, failures to detect it increase until at some arbitrarily determined frequency of failures a threshold is said to be reached.

Investigations of the temperature sense of subhuman species have lagged far behind the investigations of the other senses, perhaps because of the technical difficulties involved in the control of skin temperature. The success of any behavioral technique to measure the thermal sensory capacities of subhuman animals depends on how well the experimenter can present the stimulus without providing simultaneous extraneous cues, a click, a touch, or vibration. The development of the Peltier stimulator (Kenshalo, 1963) has made it possible to maintain and to change the temperature of a patch of skin without extraneous cues.

There is good reason to believe that the temperature sense of cats is not generally distributed over their body surface, yet they can select locations of higher environmental temperature in which to bask, for example. How this discrimination is made is shown in Figure 5.17. The procedure used to measure the cats' sensitivity to warm and cool stimuli was made as nearly like that used to measure human warm and cool *RL*s as was possible.

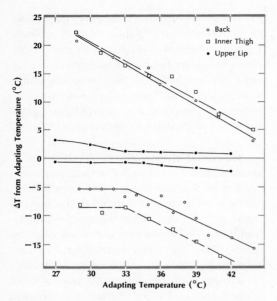

Figure 5.17. The thresholds of a conditioned avoidance response to warm and cool stimuli applied to the shaved skin of the back, inner thigh, and upper lip of cats as a function of the temperature to which the skin was adapted. The cats were insensitive to mild warm stimuli applied to the back and inner thigh. At these sites the skin temperature had to be raised to about 50° C regardless of the adapting temperature before the cats could use skin warming as a cue to avoid electric shock. Somewhat smaller thresholds to cool stimuli were found on the back and inner thigh. These appeared to depend on adapting temperatures above about 33° C. However, they are 40 to 70 times larger than human cool thresholds. Similar measurements, not shown, were obtained from the footpad. In contrast, the upper lip was much more sensitive than either the back or inner thigh to both warm and cool stimuli. Here sensitivity approximates that of the human forearm, considering that the area of skin exposed on the cat's upper lip was smaller than that of the human's forearm. (Modified from Figure 4 of Kenshalo, 1964; Kenshalo, Duncan, & Weymark, 1967; and Brearley & Kenshalo, 1970.)

The stimulator was placed on the shaved skin of different body parts, and the skin was allowed to adapt to temperatures between 27° and 44° C for 40 minutes. After the adaptation period, ΔTs of increasing intensity were presented for 10 second durations at irregular intervals until they were sufficiently intense for the cat to use as a cue to avoid electric shock by lifting its leg (Kenshalo, 1964; Kenshalo, Duncan, & Weymark, 1967).

The upper part of Figure 5.17 shows avoidance conditioned response thresholds to $+\Delta T$s. When the site of temperature stimulation was on the shaved skin of the back, the inner thigh or the footpad, the stimulus temperature had to be raised to almost 50° C, regardless of the adapting temperature (for example, an adapting temperature of 29° C plus an increase in the stimulator temperature of 21° C) before the cats could sense the $+\Delta T$ as a cue to avoid electric shock. (Other evidence also indicates that this 50° C temperature is noxious to cats.) Furthermore, the human pain threshold remains constant at a skin temperature of about 45° C, regardless of the temperature to which the skin has been adapted (Hardy, Goodell, & Wolff, 1951). Given these two facts, it is reasonable to surmise that the cats were responding to pain rather than warmth. The cats could detect much smaller $+\Delta T$s when the stimulator was applied to the shaved upper lip and the measurements of warm sensitivity were repeated (Brearley & Kenshalo, 1970).

Much the same picture of sensitivity to $-\Delta T$s is shown in the lower part of Figure 5.17. When the stimulator was placed on the back, inner thigh, or footpad the thresholds were on the order of $-5°$ to $-9°$ C for low (29° to 33° C) adapting temperatures; larger $-\Delta T$s were required (10° to 18° C) for higher adapting temperatures (35° to 40° C). The upper lip was at least 10 times more sensitive to $-\Delta T$s than the other sites of stimulation.

The sizes of the avoidance thresholds for warm and cool stimuli of the upper lip are sufficiently like those of the human RLs to lead one to believe that these resulted from the stimulation of the feline temperature sense.

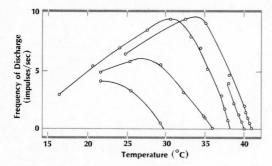

Figure 5.18. The steady-state frequencies of discharge of 5 cold fibers from the lingual nerve of cats measured after 5 minutes of adaptation of the skin of the tongue to temperatures between 16° and 41° C. (Figure 5 from Hensel & Zotterman, 1951.)

The next question concerns the form of the peripheral nerve activity which may account for the behavioral measurements described above.

Thermally sensitive nerves   Peripheral afferent nerve fibers that show changes in activity exclusively to changes of skin temperature are referred to here as "warm" or "cold" fibers. It is a short-hand way of referring to the receptor, its attached sensory

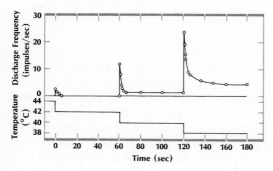

Figure 5.19. The change in discharge frequency of a single cold fiber in the lingual nerve of the cat that resulted from cooling its tongue in 2° C steps from 44° to 38° C. Temperature changes of equal size produced different frequencies of discharge depending on the temperature to which the skin had been adapted. (Figure 9 from Hensel & Zotterman, 1951.)

nerve fiber, and the form of energy specific for its stimulation.

Temperature-sensitive fibers have been found both among the myelinated fibers of 1 to 6 μ in diameter and the very thinly myelinated or unmyelinated fibers.

Myelinated temperature fibers show a regular discharge whose frequency is a function of the static temperature of the skin (the steady-state discharge). Figure 5.18 shows the relationship between skin temperature and the frequency of the steady-state discharge in five different cold fibers. In response to cooling the skin, the myelinated cold fibers show a transient increase in the frequency of their discharge to skin cooling, the amount of which depends on the intensity of cooling and the temperature to which the skin was adapted (Figure 5.19). When the skin is warmed, these fibers show a reduction or complete suppression of their steady-state discharge.

Myelinated cold fibers have been found in the infraorbital and lingual nerves (supplying the face and tongue) of rats, cats, and dogs. They have not been seen in other nerves of these animals, for example, the saphenous, femoral, or clunium nerves of cats (supplying the leg, foot, and inner thigh). Cold fibers have been found, however, in the median and saphenous nerves (supplying the arm, hand, leg, and foot) of rhesus monkeys and the radial nerve (supplying the thumb and back of the hand) of man.

Myelinated warm fibers that show responses opposite to those of cold fibers (that is, an increase in the frequency of activity to warming and a decrease in frequency to cooling) have been found only in specialized areas of skin such as the tongue and bridge of the cat's nose (Hensel & Kenshalo, 1969), and the rat's scrotum (Iggo, 1969).

There are specific temperature fibers among the unmyelinated fiber group as well. In general, these respond like the temperature fibers of the myelinated group. They show a steady-state discharge whose frequency depends on skin temperature, and the cold unmyelinated fibers show an increase in frequency of activity when the skin is cooled and a decrease in frequency when it is warmed. Unmyelinated warm fibers show an increase in frequency when the skin is warmed, and a decrease in frequency when it is cooled. Unmyelinated temperature fibers have been found in the saphenous nerves of cats and the infraorbital nerves of rats, cats, and dogs.

A correlation of behavioral thresholds and neural activities will be made to show how behavioral and neurophysiological methods can be used to complement one another in the interpretation of data. Behavioral evidence shows that responses can be conditioned to mild thermal stimuli applied to the upper lips of cats. The size and form of the threshold curves obtained in these experiments are similar to those found on the human forearm. Responses cannot be conditioned to mild thermal stimuli applied to the inner thigh, footpad, or back of cats. Cold fibers, of the myelinated class, have been found in the nerves supplying the upper lip of cats, but warm fibers have not been found in these nerves. Neither cold nor warm myelinated fibers have been found in the nerves supplying the inner thigh or footpad. Unmyelinated cold and warm fibers have been found in both nerves. Because responses cannot be conditioned to thermal stimuli applied to the inner thigh or footpad and can be conditioned to thermal stimuli of the upper lip and because unmyelinated temperature fibers exist in the nerves supplying both areas of skin, it is doubtful that the unmyelinated fibers contribute in any appreciable way to the experiences of temperature stimulation. Because the upper lip is sensitive to mild temperature changes and the inner thigh and footpad are not, it may be possible that myelinated cold fibers carry the temperature information to which the responses are conditioned. If so, the cold fibers can carry information not only about skin cooling but also about warming. Recall that the steady-

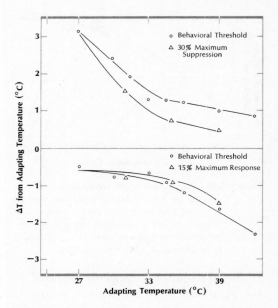

Figure 5.20. Comparison of the behaviorally measured warm and cool thresholds of the cat's upper lip and a constant percent of change in the integrated records of neural activity in small twigs of the infraorbital nerve that innervates the lip. It was assumed that skin warming was signaled to the brain by a reduction in the neural activity (suppression) and that skin cooling was signaled by an increase in neural activity. (Figure 2 from Kenshalo & Brearley, 1970.)

state response of cold fibers is enhanced when the skin is cooled, and suppressed when it is warmed.

In order to test the hypothesis proposed above, measurements were made of the neural response magnitude of fibers supplying the upper lip to warm and cool stimuli of various intensities after the skin had been adapted to temperatures between 27° and 39° C (Kenshalo & Brearley, 1970). The neural code for cooling the skin was assumed to be an increase in neural activity whereas that for warming was assumed to be suppression of activity in the same nerves. Thresholds at each adapting temperature were computed from these response curves to see if they matched the behavioral data shown in Figure 5.17. The result is shown in Figure 5.20. The behavioral warm and cool threshold curves are matched if a 30 percent maximum decrease and 15 percent maximum increase in neural activity, respectively, are assumed to represent the neurophysiological threshold. It is possible that a single temperature-sensing system of cold fibers can convey all of the necessary information to the brain concerning changes in skin temperature.

Because we are at the very edge of scientific progress here, these tentative conclusions may be wrong. More important than the conclusions, however, is the demonstration of the value of using both behavioral and neurophysiological measurements to complement each other in providing answers to common questions.

Specificity of response The specific temperature-sensitive fibers have come to be looked on as the archetype for cutaneous thermal receptors. However, many fibers are encountered, especially in the saphenous nerves of cats, the median nerves of rhesus monkeys, and the radial nerves of man that show responses to both temperature and tactile stimuli. It is difficult to determine what role these multimodal fibers play in sensation, although there is a tendency to regard them as basically mechanoreceptors that may have their activity altered by changes in temperature (Iggo, 1963).

Theoretical Points of View

Temperature sensitivity and the doctrine of specific nerve energies Traditionally, the temperature-sensing system is perceived to be composed of two relatively independent systems—one for sensing warm, the other for sensing cold. This point of view arose from the doctrine of specific nerve energies and was given strong support by the discovery of warm and cold spots that exist independent of each other on the skin. However, like the failure of studies using histological methods to demonstrate a morphologically different structure beneath the spots to which temperature-receptive functions could be assigned, studies using neurophysiological methods have generally failed to demonstrate two functionally different sets of nerve units, one each for warm and cool stimuli (see p. 151). Whether temperature sensitivity is the result of a single or a dual system is still open to debate. The strongest evidence for two systems is still the independent existence of spots sensitive to warm and cool on the skin, but other explanations may account for these.

Stimulation of thermoreceptors Various theories have been advanced to explain the initiation of thermal sensations. The earliest (Weber, 1846) postulated a temporal thermal gradient to excite thermal sensations; that is, the receptors must be subjected to a changing temperature. However, we have already seen that some thermal sensations may persist indefinitely outside of the range of T_o and that specific temperature fibers may discharge at a steady rate for several hours even though skin temperature is constant.

Spatial thermal gradients have also been proposed as the necessary requisite to stimulate thermal receptors (Ebbecke, 1917; Bazett, 1941; Lele, Weddell, & Williams, 1954). Each investigation, in a different way, relied on the fact that tissues are at different temperatures at various depths. Thus, if the skin surface is at 32° C, the temperature 300 μ beneath the surface may measure 32.5° C. The receptors were believed to be activated by an alteration in this spatial thermal gradient. Theories which propose that thermal receptor stimulation is made by spatial thermal gradients do not work for the same reasons that the temporal thermal gradient theory will not work. Furthermore, Hensel and Witt (1959) demonstrated that thermal receptors are stimulated by cooling, independent of the intracutaneous temperature gradient. Hensel and Witt used preparations in which a specific temperature fiber innervated a spot on the upper surface of a cat's tongue. Cooling either the upper or lower surfaces of the tongue, or injecting cold saline into the lingual artery, all produced an increase in the activity of the cold fiber. Moreover, Vendrik and Vos (1958) and Hendler and Hardy (1960) have compared threshold warm sensations resulting from nonpenetrating infrared heat with those obtained by heating the skin with radar pulses. Although they do not agree on the effects of the radar stimulation (it is supposed to heat the tissue uniformly throughout its depth), they do agree that spatial thermal gradients could not account for their results.

Another major theory was proposed by Hering (1877). He suggested that the amount of heat conducted to the receptor was the sole stimulus condition necessary to arouse a thermal sensation. He thought of warm and cold as belonging to a single temperature sense and theorized that the receptive organ was capable of a reversible reaction. Heat is always being conducted outward at normal environmental temperatures, and at this rate of heat conduction, the reaction is at equilibrium. Decreasing the outward heat conduction (warming the skin) drives the reaction in one direction whereas increasing outward heat conduction (cooling the skin) drives it in the opposite direction. Both processes adapt so that within a narrow band of skin temperatures the reaction can again achieve equilibrium. A change in heat conduction upsets the equilibrium, and the predominant process engenders a thermal sensation.

Theories of the thermal receptor   It is now generally accepted that encapsulated endings of the Krause and Ruffini types play little, if any role in temperature reception. The histological studies of Weddell and his collaborators (Weddell, 1955) leave little doubt that encapsulated endings exist only in hairless skin and cannot be found in hairy skin. Furthermore, Hagen and his coworkers (1953) were convincing in their demonstrations that hairy and hairless skin show no significant differences in comparisons of their warm and cool thresholds.

If not morphologically different nerve terminal structures, then what? Weddell and his coworkers have argued that because a variety of sensations may be aroused by activation of free nerve endings with a variety of stimuli, these are not modality-specific. As evidence for this argument, they report having experienced touch, warm, and cool sensations, as well as pain, from appropriate stimulation of the cornea, which contains only free nerve endings (Lele & Weddell, 1956). Kenshalo (1960) agrees with their reports of producing touch sensations in the cornea but challenges their report of arousing thermal sensations with thermal stimulation of the cornea. Furthermore, the repeated demonstrations of specific temperature-sensitive fibers that innervate either one or a few small spots on the skin argues strongly for specificity of modality, at least for thermal stimulation.

Nonspecificity plus an ill-defined pattern of activity does not appear to be the way to account for the data of temperature reception. Hence the question remains: What are the differences in nerve terminals such that one will discharge when it is distorted by mechanical means and another only when its thermal environment is changed? Two hypotheses seem worthy of consideration, although there is as yet no direct evidence in support of either. The first, the "specific terminal hypothesis," assumes a molecular configuration or other specific feature of the terminal membrane that governs differential responsiveness to thermal and mechanical stimuli. The second, known as the "specific tissue hypothesis," assumes that afferent nerves are essentially alike, but they end in non-neural tissues whose characteristics are responsible for the stimulus specificities observed in the activity of the associated axon. An example of this type of hypothesis is the *vascular theory,* proposed by Nafe (1934) and reviewed by Kenshalo (1970b), in which the smooth muscles of the cutaneous vascular system contract when cooled and relax when warmed. The movement of the vessels initiates activity in the afferent nerves that terminate in the vessel walls.

PAIN

Since the days of von Frey (1895) pain has generally been regarded as a separate sense of the skin, as are those of temperature and touch. However, if it is considered strictly as a sensory system, measurements of the pain sensation behave in unexpected ways. The *RL*s, for example, in the visual and auditory systems or even of temperature and touch are not greatly affected by attitudinal variables of the subject. However, pain thresholds are markedly affected by the attitude of the subject toward the experiment and experimenter, his attention and suggestibility. Obviously some strong influence must be feeding into the pain system from the central nervous system to account for these profound effects.

Two different approaches to the study of pain have done little to clarify the issues. On the one hand are the investigators who induce pain experimentally in normal subjects and attempt to measure the effects of analgesic agents (pain relievers) on thresholds of pain. Generally, they find the analgesic has little or no effect upon the intensity of stimulation required to produce a threshold pain sensation, when carefully controlled procedures are used. On the other hand, the physician is faced daily with the problem of alleviating pain in his patients. It is here that analgesics are known to work. What is the difference between experimentally induced pain and that which accompanies pathological conditions? The answer is not easy, although the difference appears to be the presence of anxiety, a state not readily produced by experimental methods (Beecher, 1966).

Pain varies along a sensory-discrimination and a motivational-affective dimension. The intensity of the pain is influenced by the patient's own evaluation of the seriousness of the damage he has sustained, a cognitive process. If tissue damage does not evoke an aversive drive, it cannot be called pain, and by the same token, anxiety not accompanied by a sensory input is not pain. Pain must, therefore, be a combination of all three processes: a discriminatory, a motivational, and a cognitive (evaluative) process (Melzack & Casey, 1968; Sternbach, 1968). The importance of these variables is best exemplified by a report of Beecher (1956) of responses of soldiers to war wounds. Of the soldiers who suffered grievous, but not fatal wounds, only about one-third wanted medication to relieve their pain. Two-thirds refused it, yet many of them complained bitterly about the discomfort experienced if an inept corpsman failed to make a successful venous puncture. According to Beecher, the wounded soldier experienced relief, thankfulness to escape alive from the battlefield, and even euphoria (feeling his wound was a good thing).

There appears to be no direct relationship between the extent of the wound and the pain experienced. The intensity of the pain is dependent, to a considerable extent, on how the patient views the wound from the standpoint of the anxiety produced, its seriousness, and what it means in terms of his future existence.

With full knowledge that the motivational and cognitive aspects of pain are being ignored, pain will be considered here as a sensory process. Reference is made to investigators such as Beecher (1959), Melzack and Casey (1968), and Sternbach (1968) to supply information on the processes related to the motivational and cognitive aspects of pain.

The Definition of Pain

The definition of pain may be made in terms of the stimulus, in which case both its intensity and locus are important. It may also be defined in terms of the response to a stimulus, for example, verbal responses, motor reflexes, or changes in cardiovascular responses.

Painful stimuli Methods to produce pain for experimental purposes may be divided into two categories, according to the locus of stimulus application—cutaneous pain and deep pain. These are not necessarily different pains, although the deep visceral or muscular pains tend to have the long persistent aching quality associated with pathologically induced pain in contrast to the fleeting, sharp quality of cutaneous pain.

The methods of stimulation employed to produce pain are numerous. Almost any violence done to the body, either internally or externally, is likely to produce pain. One cannot conclude, however, that tissue damage and pain are always associated. For example, x-radiation can cause tissue destruction that may not be accompanied by pain, and pain may be felt where no evident tissue damage has occurred, as when an exposed tooth nerve is lightly touched.

Whatever the stimulus used to produce experimental pain, it must be amenable to quantification. Also it should be remembered that most methods of producing experimental pain have a common defect: that repeated exposure to such stimulation usually damages tissue so that succeeding trials fall on tissue that has been altered, at least slightly, by previous exposure.

Experimental production of cutaneous pain was considerably advanced by the introduction of infrared radiation techniques (Hardy, Wolff, & Goodell, 1940). Radiation from a high-intensity lamp was collected by a lens and directed toward the skin through a shutter. The current to the lamp was increased until the subject experienced a sharp stab of pain just before the shutter closed at the end of a 3 second exposure.

Electrical stimulation of the skin has also been used, but the pin-prick sensation experienced usually accompanies the electrical breakdown of the resistance of the skin, and hence, the electrical quantity is associated with the dielectric properties of the skin rather than a threshold of the receptive process (Mueller, Loeffel, & Mead, 1953).

Mechanical methods of producing pain have varied from making gross blows on the fingers (Wells, 1947) and applying pressure on the styloid process of the mastoid bone (Libman, 1934) to driving carefully sharpened needles into the skin with blows of varying intensity (Jones, 1956). However, little success has been attained in producing reliable stimuli.

Arousal of pain with chemical agents has been more successful (Armstrong et al., 1951). A skin blister is produced by cantharidin. After the blister is formed, the top is carefully cut away and chemical solutions, for example, potassium chloride or acetylcholine, of known concentrations are applied to the blister base. The area remains sensitive for about 48 hours during which 50 to 60 applications of the chemicals can be made.

Several methods of producing deep pain have been explored. Distension of the esophagus (Chapman & Jones, 1944) or the bile duct (Gaensler, 1951) with small rubber balloons have been used in studies on the effectiveness of analgesic agents on pain. The results were not generally satisfactory because the methods do not yield clear-cut end-points between the point where there is or is not any pain. Another method, involving muscle ischemia (blocking arterial blood flow to the muscles) induced by the pressure of a blood-pressure cuff, shows considerably more promise. If the subject exercises the muscles below the tourniquet at a regular rate, for example making a fist every second, the onset of pain occurs with a prompt and clear-cut end-point (Harrison & Bigelow, 1943).

Other more radical or drastic procedures employed to induce pain in man include applying electric shocks to the teeth through amalgam fillings (Goetzl, Burrill, & Ivy, 1943), applying shocks to the exposed digital nerve of the index finger (Pattle & Weddell, 1948), to the saphenous nerve, which is sensory to the medial skin of the leg (Heinbecker, Bishop, & O'Leary, 1933), and the sural nerve sensory to the lateral skin of the leg (Collins, Nulsen, & Randt, 1960). Methods of stimulating the gasserian ganglion electrically in awake and active rhesus monkeys have also been developed (Weitzman et al., 1961). (The gasserian ganglion contains the cell bodies of the nerve fibers of the trigeminal nerve which is, in part, sensory to the face.)

Response definitions　Methods by which pain is induced are of importance in investigations of this sensory process. Of at least equal importance are the response criteria employed. They may be divided into categories of verbal responses, behavioral responses including reflexes, and physiological indices employed with both man and animals.

Language is rich in adjectives that can be used to describe painful sensations. Dallenbach (1939) catalogued 44 of them, from "achey" to "thrilling" to "vicious." There is obvious overlap in the meaning of many of these adjectives, but their profusion suggests many subtle, qualitative differences in the sensations of pain. Furthermore, a number of them imply a spatial characteristic whereas others suggest a temporal characteristic.

Measurements of the stimulus intensity required to produce changes in behavior or reflex withdrawal in both man and animals have been employed. Thus, the intensity of a stimulus that causes the animal to escape from the situation has been used as one behavioral criterion of pain. Rice and Kenshalo (1962) defined the heat-induced pain of cats as that intensity of heat required to cause the cat consistently to initiate a response to terminate it. Others, such as Weitzman et al. (1961), defined pain as the intensity of electric shock administered to the gasserian ganglion that would cause the rhesus monkey to press a lever to reduce the intensity of the shock.

Two reflexes used extensively to mark a nociceptive (painful) threshold response to radiant stimulation are the tail flick of the rat and the contraction of the *cutaneous maximus* muscle of the rat, guinea pig, and dog. Also, the leg flexor reflex may be used as an index of painful stimulation in both man and animals. For example, the intensity of radiant stimulation required to produce a flexor reflex in paraplegic man is about the same intensity as that required to produce a pain sensation in normal man (Rice & Kenshalo, 1962).

Physiological indices of pain have consisted mainly of measures of the activity of the sympathetic nervous system. These include changes in systolic and diastolic blood pressure, pulse pressure, heart rate, salivary flow rate, palmar skin resistance (galvanic skin response), finger pulse volume, and respiration rate (Sternbach, 1968).

When we consider the variety of methods that have been used to induce pain, the variety of descriptive adjectives used in the verbal report of pain, as well as the other behavioral and reflex indices, it is not surprising that so little headway has been made in the study of pain as a sensation. This is exclusive of the factors of anxiety and cognition which ultimately must also be considered! A more unified attack on the problems of pain would likely yield more certain knowledge.

Behavioral Analysis

Pain may be aroused in a variety of ways, but it is not easy to find a way that permits quantification of the stimulus intensity. Mechanical devices have been used, but usually they must produce radical deformations of the tissue before pain is aroused. Neither chemical nor electrical stimulation is suitable because it is practically impossible to control the spatial boundaries of their action. Thermally aroused pain appears to be more controllable, and Hardy, Wolff, and Goodell (1940) have made extensive use of it to measure both the *RL*s and *DL*s of pain.

When radiant energy is to be used to cause pain, the energy delivered to the skin surface by the radiant source is measured in millicalories/sec–cm². The elevation in the surface temperature of the skin produced by a 3 second exposure to radiation of various intensities may then be calculated. Direct measurements of skin temperature with thermocouples or thermistors during the time of the exposure to radiation do not suffice because their thermal properties differ from those of skin. Thus, the readings may be in error by a degree or more. More recently, however, the development of rapid response radiometers have made possible direct readings of skin temperature immediately following radiation (Hendler & Hardy, 1960). A radiometer detects changes in the temperature of an object by responding to changes in its rate of infrared emission—in this case, the skin. When the mass of the radiation sensing element is large, however, seconds or even minutes are required for it to complete its response to a change in the temperature of the skin. Rapid response to temperature changes (a few milliseconds) has been made possible by the development of extremely small sensing elements that can change temperature rapidly.

Thresholds and scaling The *RL* of pain produced by thermal stimulation has been reported to be as high as 48.6° C (McKenna, 1958). At skin temperatures as low as 36° C a transient pain may be experienced (Lele, Weddell, & Williams, 1954). Measurements of the pain *RL* show a single individual is fairly consistent in his reports of pain, but the differences between individuals are so great that generalizations of the stimulus intensity required to evoke pain are difficult to make.

The pain *RL* reported at the lower skin temperatures may be synonymous with the slight sting that characterizes the heat threshold (see p. 148), but the sting might be construed as the *RL* by a relatively naive or timorous subject. Trained subjects usually report threshold pain after a 3 second exposure to a radiation intensity of 0.206 gcal/sec–cm² (206 millicalories, for short) (Schumacher et al., 1940). This intensity of radiation produces an elevation in skin temperature of about 12.5° C above normal, so that the pain *RL* is a skin temperature of about 44.5° C. Starting from other skin temperatures, greater or smaller intensities of radiation are required to reach the pain threshold. Unlike the warm

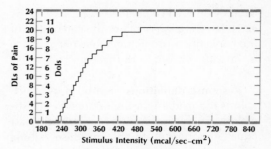

Figure 5.21. The dol scale of pain sensitivity. Although 480 millicalories/sec-cm² may not produce the most intense pain possible, it does represent the approximate practical upper limit for experimental purposes. Higher intensities of radiation produce protracted reddening of the skin and even blistering which makes the effects of repeated applications of the stimulus questionable. (Figure 3 from Hardy, Wolff, & Goodell, 1947.)

threshold, which changes with the adapted skin temperature (see Figure 5.14), a pain *RL* occurs when the skin is heated to 44.5° to 45° C, regardless of the initial skin temperature (Hardy, Goodell, & Wolff, 1951).

The radiant heat method has also permitted measurements of the pain *DL*s. Hardy, Wolff, and Goodell (1947) first determined that the highest intensity of radiation that could be used repeatedly, without inducing hours of long-lasting consequences, was about 480 millicalories during a 3 second exposure (an elevation in skin temperature to about 61° C). Between the limits of 210 and 480 millicalories, they found 21 jnd's (just noticeable differences) of intensity. As shown in Figure 5.21, at intensities up to about 360 millicalories, the *DL* increased, so that the Weber fraction, $\Delta I/I$, was roughly constant at 0.03. The ratio increased at higher intensities. Pain can therefore be scaled, and accordingly Hardy et al. have suggested a unit of pain, the dol, which is equal to 2 jnd's.

Adaptation There is no general agreement on whether or not pain adapts or ceases to be felt even though the cause of the pain is still present. On the one hand, it is held not to adapt, for to do so would be counter to its important function in the survival of the organism. On the other hand, there is considerable evidence to suggest that it does adapt, and in some circumstances it does adapt completely. Yet, we can all think of pains we have experienced that seemed to last for interminable periods of time, such as severe sunburn, an inflamed appendix, a headache, or a toothache. Those who contend that pain adapts point out that these pains involve constantly changing conditions at the pain site, usually rhythmic ones based on circulatory events. As we mention below, many contend that there is a chemical step between painful stimulation and the arousal of peripheral, afferent, neural activity. The adaptation of pain would then be linked to the amount of the responsible chemical substance present.

Complete adaptation of pain induced by heat, for example after an arm and hand has been dipped into thermostatically controlled water baths, occurs when a large area of skin is exposed to temperatures from 40° C up to 45.5° C and may occur infrequently at temperatures up to 47° C (Hardy, Stolwijk, & Hoffman, 1968). The sensation builds rapidly to a maximum for 5 to 10 seconds after immersion, followed by adaptation and generally a complete disappearance of the pain within 15 to 20 seconds. The sensations experienced at these temperatures may be akin to, or even identical with, the sensation of heat described earlier (see p. 148). At higher temperatures (46° to 48° C), pain occurs with little delay and increases to a peak or temporary plateau 4 to 12 seconds after immersion; this is generally followed by a further increase in the pain sensation during the 30 second immersion period. At temperatures above 47° C, pain is nonadapting. The most intense pain is frequently that experienced at the end of the 30 second exposure period. In one subject, the intensity of the pain continued to increase over a 3 minute period. This agrees with the earlier work of Greene and Hardy (1962) in which subjects were required to

maintain a threshold pain sensation by adjusting the intensity of radiation for periods of up to 60 minutes. Once the pain threshold was reached, the subject made no further increases in the radiation intensity, as would have been expected had adaptation occurred.

Pain, produced by radiant energy, may adapt completely if the energy is applied to small areas of skin. Stone and Dallenbach (1934) reported that pain, aroused by radiant heat applied to a 2 mm² area of the forearm, adapted completely. During the course of adaptation the initial sensation was intense heat, followed by warmth, and finally indifference, all within a span of 20 to 30 seconds following onset of the warming of the skin. These findings do not necessarily invalidate those of Hardy et al. that pain induced in large areas of skin does not adapt. Adaptation of small areas to pain stimuli may indeed be as complete as that of small areas to warm and cold stimuli. It is also possible, in view of the fact that Stone and Dallenbach failed to report the skin temperatures produced by their stimuli, that they were within the temperature range where Hardy et al. also reported adaptation of pain.

Complete adaptation of pain produced by cold stimuli is generally agreed to occur within about 5 minutes, even when the whole hand is immersed in a water bath maintained at 0° C (Wolff & Hardy, 1941). The initial sensation experienced is one of ache that becomes progressively stronger for the first minute of exposure but then diminishes and disappears in 4 to 5 minutes. If smaller areas are exposed to cold, the pain adapts completely in shorter times (Edes & Dallenbach, 1936).

The results of various experiments generally agree that the pain produced by mechanical or cold stimuli adapts completely. It is likely that cold pain adapts because of the physiological consequences of the tissue cooling. Cooling nervous tissue blocks stimulation of receptors and conduction of impulses in the peripheral neurons. Mechanically induced pain is not a fatigue phenomenon, as is shown by the fact that once the pain of a needle jabbed into the skin has adapted, pain is again produced when it is withdrawn. This pain sensation fails because of failure of stimulation rather than because of failure of the ability of the receptor to respond—similar to touch adaptation as suggested by Nafe and Wagoner (see p. 131). The pulsations of pain sensations may have a mechanical basis in tissue movement produced by arterial pulsations. Pain produced by heat may adapt when heating is not intense or is not applied over a large area of skin. However, pain engendered by intense heating of the entire forearm does not adapt but frequently becomes more intense with time. These findings suggest that adaptation of heat-pain, as that of tactile and thermal sensations, is a characteristic of the stimulus conditions rather than a characteristic of the neurological processes involved in the transmission or perception of pain.

Spatial summation   There appears to be no clear-cut answer to the question of whether or not spatial summation of the pain sensation exists. In any event, if spatial summation of pain occurs at all, it is much less pronounced than that encountered for warmth, cold, and heat sensations. Pain induced by radiant heat (Greene & Hardy, 1958) or by conducted heat (Benjamin, 1968) applied over areas of 2.5 to 70 cm² shows a slight but reliable summation effect. That is, threshold pain is produced at lower skin temperatures as the area of skin heated is increased. Spatial summation of the aching pain produced by cold does not occur, nor has spatial summation of mechanically induced pain been successfully demonstrated (Bishop, 1949).

Double pain   Two kinds of pain arising from a single stimulation may frequently be distinguished. One is bright and sharp like the pain from the prick of a needle, whereas the other is dull like deep bodily aches. In addition to their qualitative differences they are also distinguished by the length of time it

takes to arouse each kind of pain to the maximum. The sharp pain is relatively rapidly aroused, whereas the dull pain is more slowly aroused; it is also more persistent.

Two lines of evidence support the existence of "double" pain sensations. The first is provided by sensory dissociation experiments in which the order of disappearance of qualities of cutaneous sensations is noted after various nerve blocking agents are used. Arrest in blood flow to the nerves results in progressive loss of function in the small myelinated fibers, and then in the larger ones. After all the myelinated fibers have failed, the unmyelinated fibers finally become blocked. When the order of sensory loss is recorded as a function of onset of limb asphyxia, the sharp pain disappears first, leaving the delayed, persistent dull pain (Zotterman, 1933). Cocaine, in contrast, blocks activity in unmyelinated fibers first, followed later by a loss of function of the myelinated ones. Cocaine has been found to abolish the second pain response before it affects the first (Lewis & Pochin, 1937).

The second line of evidence in support of the existence of double pain is derived from measurements of the reaction time to painful stimuli applied to different body loci. Lewis and Pochin (1937) showed that the time interval between the occurrence of the first and the second pain was greater when the toe rather than the thigh was pricked.

Several considerations dictate caution in accepting the evidence as proof that double pain results from differences in conduction velocities of the fibers carrying the information or that the phenomenon even exists at all. First, even the protagonists of the double pain sensation advise caution in interpreting evidence obtained by the use of nerve blocks. Gasser (1943) has pointed out "it is misleading to state that asphyxia blocks large fibers first, while cocaine blocks small fibers first." Further, critical evaluations on the use of nerve blocks in support of the reality of double pains has been offered by Sinclair and Hinshaw (1951). Second, Jones (1956) has criticized the techniques used to measure reaction time in previous experiments and has suggested that the second pain may well be an artifact of these methods. Rebuttals have been made by Libet (1957) and Pieron (1959). Third, if two pains occur as the result of transmission of information in two types of nerve fiber, why, then, are there not two touches or two thermal sensations? Certainly, it should be most obvious in the case of touch where the information is conducted over both types of fiber as well as in the case of temperature where both types have also been shown to be active. Perhaps the existence of double pain depends on processes that are more central in the nervous system (see p. 165).

Visceral and referred pain   An excellent summary of the problem of visceral and referred pain, from a physiological point of view, is given by Ruch (1965). Pains that arise from deep within the muscles and the viscera show some characteristics different from those pains that arise from the skin stimulation. Surgeons, operating under local anesthesia, have noted that the visceral organs can be crushed, cut, or burned without arousing any sensation. However, a tug on the mesentery (the membranes that hold the gut in place) or stimulation of the lining of the body wall will induce sensations that include pain and nausea. The fact that pathologic states may be accompanied by pain shows that visceral organs are sensitive to stimulation. However, the viscera are not normally exposed to the conditions of stimulation to which the skin is exposed; thus, sensitivity to these conditions may not have evolved. Stimulation of the viscera that results in sensations, usually painful, include (1) spasms or strong muscular contractions, for example, childbirth pains; (2) sudden or extreme distension, for example, a full urinary bladder; (3) chemical irritants, for example, gastric juices in the esophagus, heartburn; (4) mechanical stimulation, especially when the organ is congested with blood. These pains are not often the result of mesentery traction alone. Normal contractions and relaxations of

the viscera are not accompanied by pain, although they may become so when the blood supply is inadequate.

Pains from visceral organs can usually be correctly localized, although at times the pain may appear to arise from the skin surface instead. Such pains are called referred pains. The best known example of a referred pain is from the heart (angina pectoris) in which the pain seems to come from the chest and a narrow strip of skin on the inner surface of the upper arm.

Several theories have been advanced to account for referred pain. One, the convergence-facilitation theory, suggests that afferent impulses from the viscera associated with painful stimulation cannot pass directly to the brain because the visceral afferent fibers have no direct connection with the spinothalamic tract, but they create an "irritable focus" in the part of the spinal cord they enter. Afferent impulses from the skin that enter in the same part of the spinal cord are thereby magnified and cause a pain sensation that is referred to the skin rather than the viscera. A second, the convergence-projection theory, maintains that nerve impulses associated with pain in both the viscera and the afferent fibers of the skin converge on the same cell bodies at some point in the sensory pathways—spinal cord, thalamus, or cortex—so that the origin (whether from the viscera or skin) of the pain is lost. The evidence is conflicting. It indicates that both facilitation and information on the origin are of importance in explaining referred pain.

Physiological Mechanism

Here we consider the evidence for specific pain receptors, a possible chemical link between stimulation and peripheral neural activity, and the evidence that specific types of fiber are involved in the peripheral mediation of pain.

Receptors   The search for the end organs of pain has failed to reveal any distinctive structures that might serve that function. Histological examination of abnormal skin, in which pain is the only sensation that can be evoked, has shown that the ubiquitous free-nerve endings (like those of the dermal nerve network) are the only neurological element present (Sweet, 1959).

Most anatomists find that the cornea of the eye is innervated only by free-nerve terminals. Thus, this tiny bit of tissue has become a veritable battleground over what cutaneous sensory qualities can be aroused by its appropriate stimulation. Certainly pain is one of them and many have shown that touch or sensations of contact can also be experienced. Whether thermal sensations are experienced from appropriate stimulation of the cornea is open to question (Lele & Weddell, 1956; Kenshalo, 1960). From such findings, it seems likely, at least, that the free-nerve endings of the cornea are capable of setting up impulses that allow man to distinguish between light touch, and pain.

Research on deep somatic and visceral pain is at an elementary stage. Free-nerve endings occur in the peritoneum, tendon surfaces, periosteum of the bone, and in the inter-muscular connective tissue of the viscera. Appropriate stimulation of any of these tissues will evoke pain (White & Sweet, 1955). Furthermore, afferent nerve plexuses develop in the adventitial and muscular walls of arteries, and arterial puncture in man usually results in severe pain, in contrast to veno-puncture. Likewise, distention of the cerebral arteries with histamine is a standard method of experimentally inducing a headache. Fine terminal endings have been described in close relation to the capillary walls (Weddell, Palmer, & Pallie, 1955) and may account for the pain Landis (1930) produced in man when his micropipette penetrated these tiny blood vessels. It appears, then, that free-nerve endings are involved in the reception of pain as well as other sensations. Furthermore, the free-nerve endings are the only ones sufficiently generally distributed throughout the body to mediate pain. They must be implicated in pain though that is not their exclusive function.

Chemical link   There is considerable speculation and much research to indicate that there is a chemical step intermediate to the action of a painful stimulus on tissue and the appearances of impulses in afferent nerve fibers. Among the possible chemicals might be (1) intracellular potassium, released by tissue damage (Benjamin, 1968); (2) brady-kinin, an enzyme frequently found at the site of tissue injury and inflammation (Lim, 1968); (3) histamine, both because it is found at the site of painful stimulation and because anti-histamines have been shown to elevate the pain threshold (Rosenthal, 1968); and (4) a more direct effect, modification of molecular configurations in the receptor membrane by thermal agitation (Hardy et al., 1968).

Specific pain fibers   Correlations between the primary qualities of cutaneous sensation and the diameter of peripheral afferent nerve fibers have been attempted many times through the years. Bishop (1960) has reviewed the literature and concluded that there is no clear separation of the cutaneous senses according to fiber size. However there is abundant evidence, reviewed by Douglas and Ritchie (1962), that the unmyelinated fibers exhibit action potentials when noxious (both mechanical and thermal) as well as mild stimuli are applied to the skin. In studies in which exposed peripheral nerves of awake human patients were stimulated electrically, pain was experienced when the recorded compound action potential included fibers of the finer myelinated group (Heinbecker, Bishop, & O'Leary, 1933; Collins, Nulsen, & Randt, 1960).

In other experiments, many fibers in the cat's saphenous nerve have been examined that respond only to pinching of a skin fold. Characteristically, these fibers have conduction velocities between 6 and 30 m/sec and do not respond to strong heating, acid, or the application of bradykinin to the abraded skin (Burgess & Perl, 1967). The implication is that these fibers, covering the range of conduction velocities of the finer myelinated group, convey impulses signaling only mechanically induced skin injury.

Investigations of the activity in fibers that show a response only to strong stimulation of one type or another lead to another question about which there is very little information. That is, when a strong stimulus is applied to the skin, what happens to the response of fibers that show a vigorous response to less intense stimulation? Cold fibers, for example, cease activity altogether at temperatures above about 42° C, except for the few that show a paradoxical discharge at 45° C and above. Furthermore, recordings may be made from the cell bodies of neurons in the ventral medial nucleus of the thalamus that respond to mild mechanical stimulation. Activity in these neurons ceases altogether when a stimulus, judged to be noxious, is applied to the receptive fields of the skin (Poggio & Mountcastle, 1960). Sketchy as it is, the evidence seems to suggest that neurological elements which show a response to mild stimulation are blocked or inhibited from responding during intense stimulation. Furthermore, there appears to be a degree of specificity of response shown by the fibers in that those responding to intense mechanical stimulation do not respond to other noxious agents.

The Management of Pain

It is not the intention here to present a comprehensive review concerning the clinical management of pain but only to provide a brief overview of some of the research, including the effects of some analgesics on experimentally induced pain.

Analgesics With the development of radiant heat as a stimulus amenable to quantification in the production of experimental pain, the effects of standard analgesics, for example, aspirin, morphine, and so on, came under investigation. Many investigators reported that morphine sulfate, for example, affected the experimentally induced pain threshold in a manner similar to its effects

on clinical pain. The pain threshold, in terms of radiant heat units, increased for 3 hours when the effect of the 30 mg injection of morphine sulfate reached a maximum, after which it decreased and returned to a normal level 4 hours later. Lesser doses had a less pronounced effect on the pain threshold, and for a shorter period of time. A similar effect was reported for acetylsalicylic acid (aspirin), although it was less profound and lasted for a shorter period (Hardy, Wolff, & Goodell, 1940).

In many of the early measurements, both the subject and the experimenter were fully aware of the nature of the experiment and when and what analgesic was administered. When measurements of analgesic effectiveness were repeated, however, using the stringent experimental control of a *double-blind procedure*,[1] the effects of the analgesics on the pain thresholds could not be reproduced (Beecher, 1959).

Another factor of considerable importance in the effect of analgesics on experimental pain has been emphasized by Beecher and his colleagues (Smith et al., 1966). This factor is the presence of anxiety, a state not readily produced by the fleeting pain of skin stimulation at threshold. In their experiment, Smith and his coworkers induced ischemia to produce pain. A blood-pressure cuff was placed around the arm of the subject and inflated to interrupt the blood flow. This was followed by periods of exercise of the hand interrupted by rest periods. Pain was judged in five categories from slight to unbearable. Only for the two most intense pain categories were they able to show dose-effect curves after injections of morphine sulfate using the double-blind procedure. Whatever the rea-

---

[1] In this procedure, neither the experimenter nor the subject knows the treatment condition until after the measurements have all been completed. Furthermore, a placebo (an inert substance like lactose) is also given in random order with the analgesics. Thus, this procedure controls both the subject variables which involve subject attitude and expectation as well as experimenter variables which may induce unintentional biases. This control is perhaps more necessary in this type of experiment because of the profound effects of subjective variables on pain sensation.

sons, whether because of the anxiety involved or something else, they concluded that there are qualitative differences between threshold pain and severe pain.

It has long been known that counterirritants may reduce the intensity of pain already being perceived by a subject. For example, pain induced in a limb by the tourniquet method may act as a counterirritant to reduce the intensity of the pain of a tooth ache (Beecher, 1959). Very loud sounds also may be used to reduce dental pain. Gardner, Licklider, and Weisz (1961) have reported that stereophonic music and white noise served as effective analgesics during more than 65 percent of the dental operations and minor skin surgery in which they were used. The authors note that they allowed the subject to control both the intensity and the choice of music or noise, so that subjective factors associated with a partial control of the situation may play a major role in the effectiveness of the auditory stimulation. Vibratory stimuli applied to the skin also seem to reduce the effects of painful stimulation (Wall & Cronly-Dillon, 1960). Thus, although cross-modality masking (one sense modality interfering with action of another) may be a factor in audio-analgesia, it does not appear likely (Carlin et al., 1962). Rather, its success appears to depend on both distraction and suggestion.

Causalgia and neuralgia Causalgia and neuralgia are general terms applied to abnormal sensations, usually intensely painful, that are associated with injury to the peripheral nerve bundles; for example, from cuts, lacerations, crushing, and puncture wounds. There may be such an identifiable injury associated with the onset of the causalgia (defined as a neurally produced sensation of burning) or neuralgia ("nerve pain") or as in the instance of trigeminal neuralgia (see below), no reason may be apparent for the appearance of the pain.

Peripheral nerve causalgias may be of two general forms: those associated with injury, including the peripheral nerve fiber bundle, and those associated with amputation of a limb. In causalgias that involve injury of a peripheral nerve, a peculiar burning pain is produced by light tactile stimulation. The pain sensation is of long latency, poorly localized, and outlasts the stimulation. It spreads to a wide area and causes vigorous protective movements of the member involved. The skin becomes shiny and glossy smooth and may become discolored. Relief from this type of pain usually involves an exploratory operation to determine and clear the peripheral nerve of its involvement with its surrounding tissues (White & Sweet, 1955).

Phantom limb causalgia is one of the most interesting and baffling sequels to the amputation of a limb. Frequently, but not always, the patient seems to experience phantom sensations that he attributes to the limb in the position that he last remembers it. There are frequently profound psychological experiences associated with the phantom. For example, although a young tank soldier had his arm blown off at the elbow, he tried to reenlist after recovery and was rejected. When the request was refused he wanted to strike out with the limb, now amputated, and clench his missing fist. At that moment, he became aware of his phantom limb, the fist of which seemed to remain clenched and painful, until finally he was accepted and sent overseas as a Red Cross Field Director (White & Sweet, 1955).

Sensations such as those described above are frequently attributed to stimulation of the regenerating fibers of the nerve stump. However, injections of alcohol or procaine (to kill or block the regenerating nerve fiber tips) usually have no effect on the sensation. Even cutting the nerve farther up in the limb or even at its entry into the spinal cord has no lasting effect. Removal of the area of the cortex that served the phantom is of such questionable value that it is not a recommended procedure (White & Sweet, 1955).

Another variety of pathological pain that is so far of unknown origin is trigeminal neuralgia or *tic douloureux*. Pains of tic douloureux are confined to the area of the face innervated by branches of the trigeminal nerve; they are usually localized on one side of the face. These pains are paroxysmal (lasting only a few seconds or minutes followed by periods of no pain or a dull ache). There is usually a trigger zone, stimulation of which is followed by pain. Triggering stimuli may be a touch, a draft of air, a facial movement, as involved in talking, chewing, swallowing, yawning, or any jarring of the body that moves the face. The paroxysms of pain may occur only briefly and may be separated by days, weeks, months, or even years, but they may occur with such regularity that they seriously impair eating, thus producing a condition of starvation in the patient. Treatment usually involves killing branches of the trigeminal nerve by alcohol injection, which provides up to 24 months of relief, or cutting the trigeminal branch involved. A new technique for the relief of causalgia and tic douloureux is that of electrically stimulating the larger sensory nerve fibers (Shelden, 1966; Wall & Sweet, 1967) (see p. 166).

Theories of Pain

The varying definitions of pain, the indeterminate role of attitudes and perceptions upon its intensity, and the various approaches to its investigation (behavioral, psychophysical, and neurophysiological) have all created a wealth of literature with little in the way of a central theme. This state of affairs makes the task of theory building and testing exceedingly difficult.

Many questions are posed by the literature on the topic of pain. One of the first is whether pain is really a separate skin sense or whether it is merely a result of intense stimulation of other receptive systems. Few follow the intensive theory now, for there is too much evidence opposed to it, including the fact that stimulation of certain areas of skin (the pain spots) causes only pain. Also, intense stimulation of tactile receptors may yield high frequencies of nerve discharge with no evidence of a painful sensation, for ex-

ample, vibratory stimuli (Geldard, 1953) or puffs of air (Cattell & Hoagland, 1931). Certainly, the fact that pains occur and continue after nerve section to treat causalgia, neuralgia, tic douloureux, and phantom limb, is difficult to explain by an intensity of stimulation theory.

If pain is not simply an extension of normal sensitivity to mechanical and thermal stimuli, then it appears to be a separate sense system. To most investigators, a separate sense system implies a distinct set of receptors, fiber tracts, and brain centers. Whereas many investigators have started with this assumption, it has remained little more than an assumption, and there is little evidence for its support. To contend that the system reporting pain is a separate sense system with its own receptors implies that the skin contains receptors that respond only to intense stimulation; that the receptor is specialized to respond to a particular kind of stimulus—an intense thermal or mechanical stimulus. There is convincing evidence that such receptors exist within the somesthetic system (Maruhashi, Mizuguchi, & Tasaki, 1952; Hunt & McIntyre, 1960a, b; Burgess & Perl, 1967). To maintain that these are pain receptors, however, is a psychological assumption which implies that pain will always be experienced when that receptor, or the nerve to which it is attached, is stimulated. There is no direct evidence to support this implication.

It should be obvious that neither the intensity nor the specificity theories of pain can successfully accommodate the forms of pain and the conditions of stimulation that lead to its experience. A third general theory of pain, the gate control theory, has been proposed by Melzack and Wall (1965). It is, in part, a specificity theory and, in part, a pattern theory in which the frequency of nerve impulses in the small and large axons that arrive at the spinal cord nerve cells is assumed to determine whether pain will be experienced.

In the awake, behaving animal (human or otherwise) a continuous flow of afferent impulses travel from the receptors in the skin, viscera, and elsewhere (*primary* fibers) to the spinal cord. Some of these axons (usually those of a large diameter) continue, uninterrupted, up the spinal cord to specific brain centers where the information that they carry receives further processing. Other peripheral afferent fibers end in the spinal cord, there to synapse with the cell bodies of other neurons. These *secondary* or *transmission* neurons (*T* cells) may have long axons that then convey afferent impulses to other brain centers. It is at this first synapse of the afferent fiber pathways that Melzack and Wall propose a gate. When the gate is open, activity in the endings of the primary neurons induces activity in the *T* cells. *T* cells activate neural mechanisms that are responsible for the pain phenomena. When the gate is closed, however, pain will not be experienced.

Control of the gate comes from at least two sources. The first source of gate control is the relative amounts of activity in the small as compared to the large fibers. If more small fibers are active, the gate is opened and the *T* cells can be stimulated. If the reverse is the case, the gate is shut and activity in the *T* cells is diminished. A second source of gate control is the brain, for impulses in the efferent fibers (those traveling from the brain to the spinal cord) are known to influence the afferent activity at this earliest synapse in the afferent pathway. A mechanism is provided here by which perceptions, attitudes, and so on, may also control the gate.

The sensation of pain, according to the gate theory, is not the responsibility of a single and separate system of receptors and peripheral nerve fibers. Rather pain occurs as a result of interaction at the *T* cells between three sources of neural activity. These are (1) activity in peripheral nerve fibers of a small diameter that are usually activated only by relatively high intensities of stimulation; (2) activity in fibers with large diameters that are activated by mild stimulation; and (3) activity in fibers carrying information from the brain concerned with the affective state of the organism.

In order to be of value, a theory must be testable. Wall and Sweet (1967) have provided one such test of the gate control theory. In patients with chronic cutaneous pain, the sensory nerves or roots supplying the painful area were stimulated by electrical pulses of low intensity. Low intensities of electrical stimulation will produce impulses in only the fibers of large diameter, for these have lower thresholds to electrical stimulation than do the small fibers. During the stimulation, pressure on the previously sensitive areas failed to evoke pain; half of the patients reported relief of their pain for more than half an hour after receiving 2 minutes of electrical stimulation. A similar technique has been used to relieve the pain of tic douloureux (Shelden, 1966). In this instance, a small radio receiving unit was implanted on the skull and platinum wires were connected to the trigeminal nerve. A transistor oscillator was built which, when held close to the receiver, caused electrical stimulation of the nerve and immediate relief of the pain paroxism. A similar device has also been used successfully to relieve chronic heart pains.

THE NATURE OF QUALITY IN SOMESTHESIS

Many different qualities of sensation can be aroused by stimuli that are rough, smooth, wet, dry, oily, ticklish, and itchy, to name but a few. According to the specific receptor theory of the late nineteenth and early twentieth centuries, these qualities result from the simultaneous activity of several different specific receptors blending to form a unitary sensation quality. Thus, wet was analyzed into stimulation of tactile and cold receptors, whereas oily was thought to result from the simultaneous stimulation of tactile and warm receptors (Bershansky, 1922). Itch was held, and still is by many, to result from stimulation of pain receptors (Arthur & Shelley, 1959).

Some of the shortcomings of the specific receptor theory have been discussed earlier in this chapter. The lack of structures in the skin that might serve as receptors for the four primary psychological qualities, the lack of evidence in support of a one-to-one correlation between a physical dimension of a stimulus and a psychological dimension of the sensation, and the inaccurate concept of a nervous system in which neural activity, from specific receptors of one or another type, travels in its own pathway to arrive at its own cortical location have all weakened the specificity theory. Furthermore, were it true, why should cold and touch be expected to blend into a single qualitatively different sensation of wet when we do not expect visual and auditory sensations to blend into a single qualitatively different sensation?

The pendulum of somesthetic theory was driven hard to the opposite extreme when, after an intensive and extensive series of investigations of the morphology and sensitivity of skin, Weddell was unable to find support for the specific receptor theory. He stated, ". . . that sensory experience is now being considered in terms of a spatio-temporal pattern of nervous activity rather than a series of discrete connections within a limited number of modes" (Weddell, 1955, p. 132). Accordingly, there are no specific receptors or specific fibers, but rather spatially and temporally dispersed patterns of activity leaving the skin that are somehow decoded and interpreted by the brain (Sinclair, 1955). No hypothesis is given to explain how the patterns originated or how the brain decoded and interpreted the patterns.

Both theories described above are unacceptable in their present form, yet both have concepts of use to any new theory to be proposed. There must be some degree of specificity or selectivity of response to stimulation at the receptor or fiber terminal because, as is shown above, there is evidence that the terminals of tactually excited fibers do not respond readily to temperature changes and vice versa. Temporal patterns of neural activity must also be part of the neural code, for otherwise how could the smoothness of an object be determined when a

finger tip is moved across its surface, or the textures of silk or burlap cloth be discriminated?

Melzack and Wall (1962) have proposed a theory that synthesized some of the concepts from both the specific receptor and pattern theories. Furthermore, they suggest the probable origin of the neural patterns and the manner in which the brain might decode and interpret the patterns. Spatio-temporal patterns of neural activity originate at the receptive structure in the skin. They occur because of variations in the physiological properties of the receptors or nerve terminals themselves. We have already seen that some receptors respond almost exclusively to mild mechanical stimuli and that others respond predominantly to mild thermal stimuli. Hence, two different populations of fibers in a nerve bundle show activity—the one when mechanical stimuli are involved, and the other when thermal stimuli are involved. Painful stimuli apparently involve a third group of fibers in peripheral nerve bundles. Here it is important to know what happens in the receptors or terminals that respond to mild stimuli when a painful stimulus occurs. Is their activity blocked in some way by intense stimulation or do they also respond, even more vigorously, to the painful stimuli? Such considerations are important in the control of the pain gate proposed by Melzack and Wall (1965).

In addition to the peripheral units that specialize in their responsiveness to particular stimulus characteristics, other peripheral units exist that respond to several forms of stimulation, as those that respond to both mechanical and thermal stimuli. This further complicates both the temporal and spatial dimensions of the neural activity pattern.

Variations in both the temporal and spatial dimensions of neural activity are also introduced by variations in sensitivity to stimulation of the individual receptive units within each broad class of specialization. These variations in sensitivity of the individual receptive units include (1) variations in the threshold to mechanical or thermal stimuli; (2) peak sensitivity to temperature change (in Figure 5.18 five cold fibers are shown, each with a different temperature for peak steady-state responses); (3) variations in speed of adaptation; and (4) differences in the magnitude of response (frequency of nerve impulses) to changes in the strength of stimulation.

On the basis of currently available information, it is safe to say that every different cutaneous sensation that can be discriminated is the result of a unique pattern of neural activity arriving at the points in the brain where it is interpreted. It should also be added that the pattern of neural activity that arrives at the brain will not resemble the pattern in the peripheral afferent nerve because of modifications that occur at each synapse in the pathways from the receptors to the brain. This, in the cutaneous and other sensory channels, is a part of the central decoding and interpreting system.

Linda Bartoshuk

THE CHEMICAL SENSES

I. TASTE

6

In order to survive, an organism must avoid substances that are harmful, and must consume necessary nutrient substances. The chemical senses of gustation and olfaction play a major part in allowing the organism to make these responses in an efficient manner, and the taste or smell of an object often leads at once to its acceptance or rejection without appeal to the other senses. The chemical senses, in addition, have strong hedonic overtones and are intimately involved in satisfying the basic drives of hunger, thirst, and sex.

In this chapter on taste, and in the following one on olfaction, we attempt to "break" the sensory code; that is, to determine by what means the organism translates contact with a chemical substance into neural events that ultimately lead to behavioral responses of approach or avoidance of the substance. We find substantial differences in the encoding of taste and smell, even though we must recognize the difficulties, already enumerated in Chapter 5, that lie in the way of sharply distinguishing one sense modality from another. The sense of taste, at least in the higher animals, originates mainly from contact of substances with the specialized gustatory receptors located on the tongue. The sense of smell, on the other hand, arises mainly from the effects of substances on olfactory receptors lying within the nasal passages. Exceptions to these generalizations are considered in the introductory paragraphs of Chapter 7. Thus two channels of

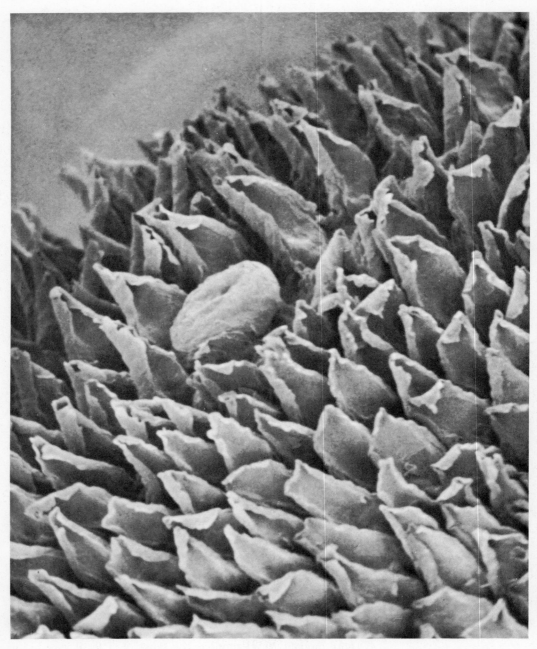

Figure 6.1. Electron scanning microscope picture of the surface of the rabbit tongue. The mushroom shaped structure is a fungiform papilla and the surrounding structures are filiform papillae. (Photograph furnished by L. M. Beidler.)

chemical analysis are open to the organism, and two separate chapters are needed to do justice in this book to the chemical senses.

The study of taste begins with neural responses in the specialized receptor cells at the periphery and continues with responses through the central nervous system. At each point in the nervous system that the investigator studies, he attempts to determine what information is available to the organism. In particular, he looks for properties of the neural message that correlate with intensity and quality as well as more complex taste phenomena such as adaptation and mixture effects. However, the presence of certain correlates does not necessarily mean that a particular organism makes use of them. Psychophysical data, either human or from other species, are necessary to demonstrate that the organism actually uses the information observed in the nervous system.

The latter part of this chapter deals with the hedonic properties of tastes, which Pfaffmann (1960) has described as motivating behavior for the "pleasures of sensation." As an example of hedonic behavior, animals not only can distinguish between such substances as sugar and quinine but they also show a preference for sugar and an aversion to quinine. That is, organisms respond hedonically to the information provided by the taste system. Much of the research directed toward this motivational function of taste has been oriented toward clarifying its exact role in the regulation of food intake and determining whether the hedonic properties of tastes are produced or influenced by learning.

ANATOMY AND PHYSIOLOGY

The Tongue

Four morphologically distinct kinds of projections or papillae are found on the human tongue. The most numerous of these are the *filiform papillae*, which, unlike the other three, contain no taste buds. These filiform papillae are conical in shape and are found over the entire dorsal surface of the tongue.

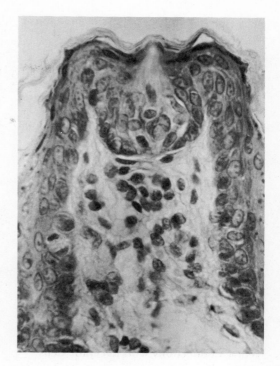

Figure 6.2. Histological cross-section of a fungiform papilla in the rat tongue showing the taste bud near the top surface. (Beidler, 1965.)

In some species, for example the cat, these papillae are somewhat rigid in structure, providing a rough surface which appears to aid in lapping up foods. The other three kinds of papillae differ in appearance and distribution. The *fungiform papillae* are shaped like button mushrooms (see Figure 6.1) and are found mainly on the tip and sides of the tongue. The *foliate papillae* in some mammals consist of a set of folds on the sides near the back of the tongue but are vestigial in man. The *circumvallate papillae* are larger than the others and are shaped like a flat mound surrounded by a trench. They are arranged in an inverted "V" at the back of the tongue.

The taste buds contain the taste receptor cells (see Figure 6.2). In the fungiform papillae the location of the taste buds is still in question. Most sources suggest that the taste buds are on the upper surfaces (Amerine, Pangborn, & Roessler, 1965) but one investigator has suggested that in man taste buds may appear on the sides of fungiform papillae (von Békésy, 1966). Taste buds are found in the folds of the foliate papillae and on both sides of the circular trenches in the circumvallate papillae. Taste buds can occasionally be found in other parts of the mouth, especially in children. Each fungiform papilla contains only a few taste buds, 3 or 4 in man, but the other papillae contain many more, making the total number of taste buds in man about 10,000.

A taste bud is goblet-shaped, with several receptor cells arranged much like the segments of an orange. Slender apical portions of the tops of each cell (microvilli) project into a "taste pore" at the top of the bud and thus are in contact with whatever taste stimuli are present on the tongue. The microvilli presumably contain the sites at which the physicochemical events giving rise to the neural activity take place.

Neural Connections with Receptor Cells

The receptor cells are innervated by nerve fibers which interdigitate to form a plexus beneath the taste bud and extend upward toward the receptor cells. The fibers terminate close to the receptor cell forming a synapse between the cell and the sensory fiber. A single nerve fiber may branch and innervate more than one taste cell. In addition, more than one nerve fiber may send branches to the same taste cell. These taste fibers run from the receptor cells to the brain via three cranial nerves. Fibers from the front of the tongue enter the chorda tympani nerve, which is a branch of the facial or seventh nerve. Fibers from the back of the tongue enter the glossopharyngeal or ninth nerve and fibers from the larynx and pharynx enter the vagus or tenth nerve.

The projections of these fibers to the central nervous system can be studied with several different techniques. Stimulating the taste nerves electrically or the tongue electrically or chemically produces responses that can be recorded from the areas of the brain to which the nerves project. Placing lesions in these areas of the brain causes degeneration along the projections that can be observed histologically. Since lesions also interfere with normal functioning, areas in the brain mediating taste can be located by observing which lesion placements produce impaired taste behavior.

Studies made by using the methods described above have provided the following information about the central projections of the taste nerves. The taste fibers of the seventh, ninth, and tenth cranial nerves meet in the solitary nucleus of the medulla. The taste tract then extends to the thalamus near the area containing tactile input from the face and tongue (Pfaffmann et al., 1961). The localization of taste in the cortex has proved to be most difficult. Benjamin and his coworkers have found two cortical taste projection areas in the squirrel monkey. One of these areas is located in somatosensory area 1 (S1), which contains the cortical projection area for tactile input from the tongue. This area is not exclusively concerned with taste but contains units responsive to tactile and temperature stimulation as well (Landgren, 1961; Benjamin et al., 1968). The other area is located a short distance away in the anterior opercular-insular cortex which is within the sylvian fissure. This area in the sylvian fissure may be responsive only to taste (Benjamin & Burton, 1968).

Taste Cell Replacement

The life span of the taste cells was studied by Beidler (1963). By radioactively "labeling" the chromosomes of newly dividing epithelial cells, he demonstrated that some of these new cells move into the taste bud and become taste cells. These taste cells have an average life span of about 10 days in the rat (Beidler & Smallman, 1965). As the taste cell ages, it moves toward the center of the taste bud and presumably becomes innervated by different fibers. Beidler suggested that the sensitivity of a taste cell to various stimuli may change with the age of the cell. In this case, constancy would be maintained in the taste system because fibers near the edge of the taste bud would always innervate young taste cells while those near the center would innervate old ones.

The maintenance of the taste bud is apparently dependent on the taste nerves because the taste buds degenerate when the taste nerves are cut and regenerate as the nerves grow back. Oakley (1967) has shown, however, that the sensitivity of taste cells to different stimuli does not appear to be determined by the type of taste nerve innervating them. He cut the chorda tympani and glossopharyngeal nerves and crossed them, so that, after growing back, each nerve innervated the part of the tongue normally innervated by the other. These two nerves normally are maximally sensitive to different taste stimuli; for example, the glossopharyngeal nerve is more sensitive to quinine than the chorda tympani. After crossing, the sensitivities of the nerves changed. Thus sensitivity to different tastes appears to be determined by the tongue area that is innervated by the nerve and not the nerve itself.

TASTE PHENOMENA

The following sections are concerned with the kinds of taste phenomena that have been studied in man and other animals. The studies on human subjects were psychophysical for the most part, although some electrophysiological recordings are available. The studies on other animals were both psychophysical and electrophysiological.

Electrophysiological recording methods have made possible the study of the neural correlates of taste-directed behavior in receptor cells, peripheral nerve fibers, and the cells and fibers of central nervous system structures connected with taste. One study involved the recording of receptor potentials through a microelectrode that had been inserted into a single taste cell. After the microelectrode had been placed in the interior of the taste cell, a negative potential change (30 to 50 mV) was produced with respect to the tissues outside the cell (Kimura & Beidler,

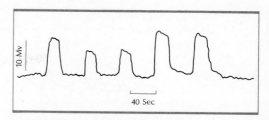

Figure 6.3. Receptor potential of a rat taste cell in response to 0.1 M of NaCl, KCl, NH_4Cl, $CaCl_2$, and $MgCl_2$ applied to tongue surface with water rinses between stimuli. (Kimura & Beidler, 1961.)

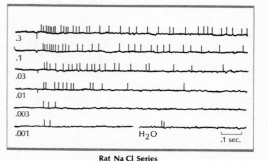

Rat Na Cl Series

Figure 6.4. Responses of a single rat chorda tympani fiber sensitive to NaCl. Responses of this fiber are shown by profile D in Figure 6.7 (Pfaffmann, 1955.)

1961). When taste solutions were flowed over the tongue, slow, positive deflections of this steady potential resulted (see Figure 6.3). The magnitude of these graded deflections depends on the concentration[1] and the solution used.

Another recording technique yields action potentials from single nerve fibers. These potentials consist of a series of "spikes" of negative potential rather than graded potential changes like those of the receptor cell (see Figures 6.4 and 6.11). To apply this technique, the nerve must be dissected, under high visual magnification, into small strands of only one or a few functioning single fibers each. These small strands are then placed on electrodes

[1]A solution has a concentration of 1 mole if the molecular weight of the substance, in grams, is added to enough water to make one liter of solution.

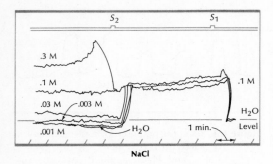

NaCl

Figure 6.5. (Read from right to left) Several super-imposed, averaged whole chorda tympani responses from the rat. 0.1 M NaCl (S_1) was applied for 5 minutes followed by water or one of several other NaCl concentrations (S_2). The magnitude of the whole nerve response is proportional to the average impulse frequency across all fibers. (Pfaffmann & Powers, 1964.)

and the potential changes that take place at the electrodes are amplified so that they can be displayed on an oscilloscope or recorded on magnetic tape for storage. Action potentials vary in frequency with the concentration and the solution used. In general, the frequency is highest when the solution is first applied to the tongue and then it decreases to a steady average value, although some solutions, in particular sugars, produce responses that gradually increase over the first few seconds.

Still another technique involves placing the whole nerve on a relatively large electrode. This provides information about the average responses from a population of fibers. Responses from whole nerves appear on an oscilloscope as a large number of single fiber responses superimposed. For data analysis such responses are usually "averaged" electronically with an "integrator" or summator so that a potential is produced that is proportional to the frequencies of the spikes and the number of fibers stimulated in the whole nerve (see Figure 6.5).

Recordings from the central nervous system are obtained both with microelectrodes that record from one or a few neural units and with larger electrodes that record from populations of units.

In the following section the data on each taste phenomenon will be divided into two sections; the human studies, which are primarily psychophysical, and the animal studies, which are primarily electrophysiological. Ideally, psychophysical and electrophysiological data should be obtained from the same species to allow the best determination of the neural correlates of taste. In a few cases direct comparisons are possible.

Some neural recordings have been made from man during ear surgery. The studies were made during the surgery because the chorda tympani passes across the ear drum, on its way from the tongue to the medulla, and is exposed during the procedure. Consequently it can be readily cut and placed on an electrode, and neural responses to various solutions applied to the tongue can be recorded (Diamant et al., 1963).

In addition, several techniques have provided behavioral measures in species other than man that can be compared to the information available in the nervous system of these species. Even though direct comparisons between the results obtained from psychophysical and electrophysiological studies on the same species are not always available, the similarities in taste mechanisms across species allow many meaningful cross-species comparisons between human psychophysics and animal electrophysiology as long as these comparisons are made with caution.

Intensity

Human data As the concentration of a taste solution is increased above threshold, the intensities of the resulting sensations increase in magnitude. This increase can be measured by both indirect and direct scaling methods. The indirect methods (see Chapter 3) have been used to establish thresholds and to provide jnd scales for some taste solutions (Pfaffmann, 1959). More recently, the direct methods have been used to scale taste intensity Lewis (1948) used the fractionation method (see Chapter 3) to construct intensity scales for sucrose, quinine sulfate, tartaric acid, and sodium chloride (NaCl). Beebe-

Center and Waddell (1948) generalized these scales by having subjects make intensity matches between different concentrations of the four solutions. They arbitrarily defined a unit called a "gust" as the perceived intensity of a 1 percent sucrose solution. Thus the intensity of any of the four solutions used could be expressed in terms of gusts by comparing it with the sucrose standard. Stevens (1960) constructed scales for saccharine, sucrose, and NaCl using a simpler direct method, that of magnitude estimation (see Chapter 3). These taste scales, like the scales he constructed for other modalities, suggest that the mathematical relationship between stimulus intensity and sensation intensity is a power function, although other results suggest limitations for this generalization (Ekman, 1961; Ekman & Akesson, 1964; McBurney, 1966). Deviations from the power law are important to the theory of scaling but do not invalidate the direct methods as a means of investigating a particular sensory system.

The magnitude estimation procedure has proved to be of great utility in taste psychophysics because of the convenience and speed with which data can be collected, which in turn minimizes subject fatigue and boredom that can seriously distort results.

The size of the tongue area stimulated has an effect on taste intensity. Camerer (1870) demonstrated that concentrations of NaCl that are near threshold were identified correctly less often if the concentrations were placed on a small area of the tongue than they were if placed on a larger one. When extremely small areas or single papillae are stimulated, quality itself may be difficult to identify (Öhrwall, 1891; Kiesow, 1898; von Békésy, 1966; Harper, Jay, & Erickson, 1966). Systematic investigations have confirmed that the concentration must be increased as the area stimulated is decreased before the threshold can be reached (Bujas & Ostojčić, 1941; Hara, 1955; McBurney, 1969). One interesting exception to this was reported by von Békésy (1966). He reported optimal concentrations for the stimulation of single papillae which are near threshold for stimulation of

the entire tongue. The techniques used to apply stimuli differed considerably between experiments, and this may explain the different results. Stimulating a single papilla is such a delicate operation that many more data on the anatomy and physiology of the taste papillae as well as on different methods of stimulation are required in order to reconcile the contradictory results.

A few data are available which directly compare human psychophysics and electrophysiology. For the few stimuli tested, the thresholds derived from recording experiments are similar to those derived from psychophysical experiments (Diamant et al., 1963). In addition, the magnitudes of the whole chorda tympani nerve responses were found to be directly proportional to direct magnitude estimates of intensity (Borg et al., 1967). The agreement between electrophysiological responses, which primarily reflect average action potential frequency, and psychophysical estimates of intensity strongly supports the theory that the average frequency of action potentials is the correlate of intensity.

Comparative data on other species
As concentration is increased, the average frequency of the action potentials increases (see Figure 6.4). Just as in the human data, this suggestion, that intensity is coded by the frequency of action potentials, can be tested behaviorally by comparing neural and behavioral thresholds and neural and behavioral suprathreshold responses. If the neural and behavioral thresholds are similar and if the frequency of action potentials varies over the same concentration range as the behavioral responses, average frequency would appear to be the probable correlate of intensity.

The two-bottle preference test has provided threshold data for a number of species. This test consists simply of giving an animal access to two solutions, usually water and a taste solution. The concentration of the taste solution is varied and relative intake of the taste solution above 50 percent indicates preference over water and that below 50 per-

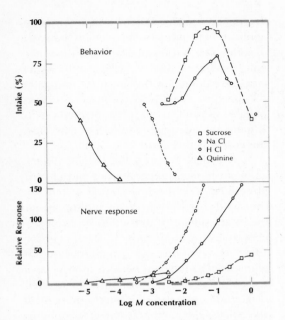

Figure 6.6. Composite graph of preference functions and whole chorda tympani responses from the rat. The upper figure shows the percentage intake of the taste solution as a function of concentration. The lower figure shows chorda tympani responses in arbitrary units. (Pfaffmann, 1960.)

cent indicates aversion in favor of water. Preference functions and whole chorda tympani nerve responses in rats are compared in Figure 6.6. Preference thresholds can be higher than sensory thresholds if the animal has no preference for or if it has an aversion to weak concentrations. For example, for the rat the neural threshold for NaCl appears to be lower than the preference threshold. The rat may simply be indifferent to very weak NaCl solutions even though it can discriminate the solution from water.

Techniques that do not depend on preferences may in some cases determine thresholds more accurately. Carr (1952) and Harriman and MacLeod (1953) used forced taste discrimination methods to obtain NaCl thresholds in rats. Carr presented both water and a NaCl solution to water-deprived rats and shocked them for drinking water. When the rats avoided water the NaCl concentration was

lowered. Threshold was defined as the concentration below which choices did not differ from chance. Harriman and MacLeod used a similar procedure, but they shocked the animals for drinking the salt solution rather than water. The thresholds at which salt in a solution could be detected in both studies were lower than the preference thresholds.

Koh and Teitelbaum (1961) developed a technique based on using taste as a cue for other behavior to obtain thresholds for sucrose, NaCl, hydrochloric acid (HCl), and quinine hydrochloride (QHCl). They trained rats to lick one of two solutions (either water or a taste solution) to obtain food pellets (or in some experiments to avoid shock). If the animal licked the correct solution, the concentration of solute was lowered, and if it licked the incorrect solution the concentration was raised. Under these circumstances the rat's choices varied around a particular concentration, which was defined to be the threshold.

In general, it was found that the levels at which taste can be detected are among the lowest behavioral values and are very similar to those derived from chorda tympani recordings. However, the levels of concentration at which HCl and QHCl can be detected are actually lower than the electrophysiological values. This finding may be explained by referring to the electrophysiological thresholds in the rat glossopharyngeal nerve (Pfaffmann et al., 1967). The HCl and QHCl thresholds are about one log unit lower in the glossopharyngeal than the chorda tympani nerve.

Behavioral and electrophysiological suprathreshold responses cannot be compared as easily as absolute thresholds because a method must be found to enable the animal to display differential responses over a range of concentrations. If an organism uses all the information available to it, the concentration range which produces different frequencies for different concentrations in the taste nerves should also produce differential behavioral responses. Preference functions give us information about the distinctiveness of different concentrations as well as about thresholds. Figure 6.6 shows preference functions and whole chorda tympani nerve responses to four taste solutions in the rat. These two sets of data indicate that the discriminations based on preference take place in the concentration range which produces changes in the average impulse frequency.

Morrison and Norrison (1966) devised a technique to scale suprathreshold concentrations in rats that does not depend on preference behavior. The rats were trained to lick at a tube containing a fairly high concentration of NaCl in water or of water alone. Five licks turned on a tone that signaled that a food reinforcement would be presented if the rat then pressed the correct one of two bars. The rat gradually learned that if he tasted NaCl, he was to press one bar; if he did not taste NaCl, he had to press the other bar for food. After training, the concentration was decreased successively until discrimination just failed. The procedure was then repeated using sucrose, tartaric acid, and quinine sulfate.

The data Morrison and Norrison used for constructing the scales consisted of the probability of a "hit," that is, choosing the taste solution bar when the solution had been in the tube, and a "false alarm," that is, choosing the taste solution bar when water had been in the tube. Morrison and Norrison applied signal detection theory (see pp. 41–46) to combine the two measures to produce an index of detectability, d'. When d' is plotted against concentration, an increasing function results that is a power function. These functions show that detectability increases with concentration over the same range in which average frequency does for NaCl and sucrose. Unfortunately there are no neural data for quinine sulfate and tartaric acid with which the detectability scales can be compared. The concentrations of minimum detectability obtained from the rat agree generally with the absolute thresholds obtained in the experiments reported above. This correspondence

of the animal behavioral and neural response functions agrees with the correspondence found for the human and strongly supports impulse frequency as the peripheral neural correlate of intensity.

Quality

Human data The existence of the four basic tastes (sweet, sour, bitter, and salty) has not been universally accepted throughout the history of taste research and is still very controversial. The very early lists of basic tastes were considerably longer. Linnaeus in 1751, for example, suggested the following list of tastes: sweet, acid, astringent, sharp, viscous, fatty, bitter, dry, aqueous, saline, and nauseous (Hollingworth & Poffenberger, 1917). Suggested lists underwent many changes but by the late nineteenth century tastes which had tactile and olfactory components had been eliminated and the familiar sweet, sour, bitter, and salty were left. For many early taste investigators one of the important questions connected with the four basic tastes was whether or not these should be considered independent modalities. Careful observation demonstrated that different areas of the tongue are differentially sensitive to different tastes. Bitter sensitivity is greatest at the back of the tongue, sweet at the tip, and sour on the sides, while salt sensitivity is more evenly distributed but greatest at the tip.

Additional observation demonstrated that some drugs have differential effects on the four tastes. One of the more prominent effects is the suppression of the sweet taste after chewing on leaves from the plant *Gymnema sylvestre* (Warren & Pfaffmann, 1959; Bartoshuk et al., 1969). Sugar on the tongue has no taste and feels like sand. The fruit of *Synsepalum dulcificum*, more commonly called miracle fruit, appears to change sour to sweet-sour (Inglett et al., 1965; Bartoshuk et al., 1969). Cocaine differentiates between the four tastes by abolishing sensations in a particular order: bitter first, then sweet, salt, and finally sour (Moncrieff, 1967). Since these four tastes appeared to be relatively independent of one another in some ways, they have often been regarded as primary taste qualities, which combine to produce all other tastes.

Observations like those described above have encouraged the search for four types of taste receptor, but the search has been generally unsuccessful. Allen and Weinberg (1925) reported data from electrical stimulation of the human tongue that for many years were considered evidence for the existence of four distinct receptor types (Moncrieff, 1967). Their results, however, were not confirmed by later studies (Jones & Jones, 1952; Ross & Versace, 1953; Pierrel, 1955). Öhrwall (1891) and Kiesow (1898) attempted to stimulate individual papillae by applying small amounts of highly concentrated taste solutions from the tip of a fine brush in order to determine whether each papilla was responsive to only one of the four tastes. Although a few such papillae were indeed found, most of them responded to two or more solutions. These data imply that if sensors specific to the four tastes exist they must consist of smaller units than papillae, for example, taste buds, receptor cells, or even particular sites on receptor cells. However, applying solutions from a brush may allow solutions to spread to adjacent areas and stimulate additional papillae. Von Békésy (1964, 1966) reported data which he felt supported the existence of four different types of papilla. When individual papillae were electrically stimulated with positive current, subjects reported tasting only one of the four tastes although the tastes reported "were a bit different from the tastes produced by chemical substances." Von Békésy reported that his experimenters could visually identify papillae of four different types under 30–60 power magnification and predict quite accurately the taste to be elicited from each. Von Békésy also stimulated single papillae chemically by touching them with small drops of solutions and found that most papillae responded to only one of the four tastes. In two subjects tested with electrical and chemical stimulation the taste qualities were the same. How-

ever, von Békésy concluded that the results do not provide a final answer to the question of whether papillae are specific to one quality partly because of difficulties involved in doing such experiments. Harper and his colleagues (1966) tested the chemical sensitivities of single papillae with a different technique and higher stimulus concentrations than von Békésy used. They used slight suction to elevate individual papillae into a chamber through which solutions could be flowed. The results corroborated those of Öhrwall and Kiesow and contradicted those of von Békésy. Most of the papillae were not specific to one of the four tastes.

In summary, the stimulation techniques and concentrations used by various researchers into taste differ extensively. Furthermore, the fact that the location of taste buds in human fungiform papillae is still uncertain suggests that much more research is needed to determine the sensitivity of single papillae. It would be interesting if human papillae turned out to be highly specific because the data to be discussed below indicate that the individual receptor cells of other mammals respond to several substances and a single papilla contains several taste buds, each one containing several receptor cells.

The adequate stimuli for the four tastes that have in the past been considered basic can be generally grouped. Sourness is primarily due to the hydrogen ion in acids, although this does not entirely account for the sour taste because an organic acid tends to taste more sour than an inorganic acid with an equal hydrogen ion concentration. Saltiness appears to be produced by both chlorides and sulfates (Dzendolet & Meiselman, 1967a). The most typical salty taste is that of NaCl. Other salts tend to have additional tastes, and in some cases the additional taste is predominant, for example, some iodide and bromide salts are bitter, and some inorganic salts of lead and beryllium are sweet. Both sweet and bitter tend to be produced by organic substances. Some of the classes of stimuli producing sweet tastes are aliphatic hydroxy compounds (which include sugars), aldehydes, ketones, amides, esters, amino acids, sulfonic acids, and halogenated hydrocarbons. The best known of the classes that taste bitter are the alkaloids (Pfaffmann, 1959).

The generalizations made above are complicated by the shifts in the quality of the taste that occur when the concentration of some chemicals is changed (Dzendolet & Meiselman, 1967b). Dzendolet (1968) has suggested a common property for substances tasting

sweet to man but no theory available suggests a common property for substances tasting bitter to man.

Comparative data The development of single-fiber recording techniques allowed a new approach to the question of the four basic tastes. If the four tastes that man reports were present in other species and if they were produced by four different types of receptors, this specificity should be observable in the

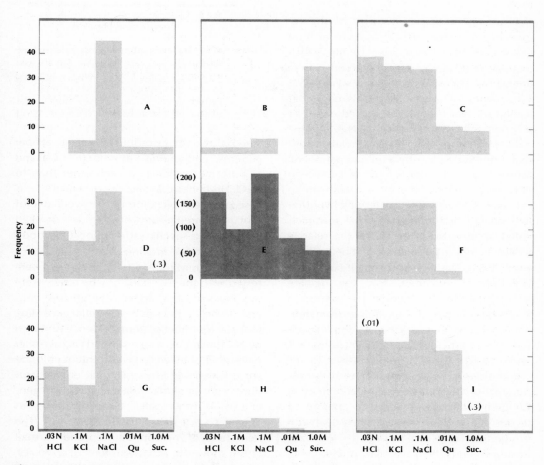

Figure 6.7. Histograms summarizing frequency of impulses during the first second to five standard taste solutions in nine different single fiber preparations in the rat. Sucrose of 0.3 M was used as the test solution in elements D and I, 0.01 M HCl, in element I. In all other cases concentrations are as shown on the abscissa. The darker histogram superimposed on the figure for element E shows the relative magnitude of whole chorda tympani responses for test solutions. Figures in parentheses give magnitudes in arbitrary units. Note that only elements D and G resemble the response of the total nerve. (Pfaffmann, 1955.)

peripheral nervous system. However, Pfaffmann (1941), by recording action potentials
from single fibers in the cat chorda tympani,
found that the fibers of the peripheral nervous
system were not specifically sensitive to the
four basic tastes. Rather, most fibers responded to many different taste stimuli. In
addition, Pfaffmann (1955) showed that the
fibers cannot even be classified into a few
single types, a fact that has been confirmed
by subsequent investigations on cats as well
as several other species (Oakley & Benjamin,
1966).

Figure 6.7 shows histograms of the responses to a series of taste stimuli for 9 rat
fibers. Each fiber has its own profile, which
suggests that quality cannot be coded by a
single fiber. For example, looking at Figure 6.7,
a frequency of action potentials of 30 per
second in fiber C could be caused either by
HCl, potassium chloride (KCl), or NaCl. Unless
information from other fibers were also available, there would not be a unique peripheral
correlate for each stimulus. This lack of specificity in peripheral fibers led Pfaffmann to
suggest the "across-fiber patterning hypothesis"; quality discrimination in all mammals
tested appears to be based on the relative
activity across a population of fibers (Pfaffmann, 1955). The lack of specificity observed
in peripheral taste fibers does not originate
from the fact that a single fiber is connected
to several cells because recordings from individual receptor cells also fail to show specificity for a particular taste quality (Kimura &
Beidler, 1961; Tateda & Beidler, 1964). In any
case the central nervous system receives only
that environmental information contained in
the peripheral nerves and any attempt to
decode the sensory message must deal with
this peripheral lack of specificity. We have
already noted (p. 166) a similar situation with
regard to specificity in cutaneous receptors.

Erickson (1963) elaborated the across-fiber
patterning hypothesis and provided behavioral tests. He constructed profiles of fibers
responsive to salts in order to determine
which salts were electrophysiologically similar

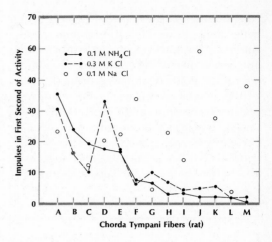

Figure 6.8. Across-fiber patterns of response to three
salts in the rat. Each letter on the abscissa
indicates a single fiber. Fibers are arranged
in order of responsiveness to 0.1 M NH$_4$Cl.
Patterns for NH$_4$Cl and KCl are more similar
to each other than to NaCl. (Erickson, 1963.)

(see Figure 6.8). According to the across-fiber
patterns, ammonium chloride (NH$_4$Cl) and
KCl are more similar to each other than to
NaCl. His behavioral measure of similarity was
based on generalization of the avoidance of
drinking. Three groups of rats were shocked
for drinking a specific salt solution. One group
was shocked for drinking NH$_4$Cl, a second for
KCl, and a third for NaCl. When the rats were
tested with the two salts for which they were
not shocked, they showed the greatest generalization for the salt most similar according
to the across-fiber pattern. Evidence provided
by Nachman (1963) also supports across-fiber
patterning. Rats were given lithium chloride
(LiCl) which, because of its toxic effects, produces subsequent avoidance which will generalize to other salts. Generalization was
greater to NaCl than to NH$_4$Cl or KCl. The
neural data of Erickson, Deutsch, and Marshall
(1965) show similar patterns for LiCl and NaCl,
which differ from those for NH$_4$Cl and KCl.

Morrison (1967) devised a behavioral technique to measure how similar a variety of salts
tasted to the rat, based on using taste as a cue
for other behavior. He trained rats to press
one of two bars in a Skinner box after a NaCl

solution was presented and to respond to the other bar after a second solution was presented. The solution used was sucrose for one group, quinine sulfate for a second, and HCl for a third. When a test salt was introduced, the percentage of responses to the non-salt bar was taken to represent that component of the taste of the test salt. For example, if a rat had been trained to respond to bar 1 after tasting NaCl and bar 2 after tasting quinine, the responses to bar 2 after tasting KCl would represent a component in the taste of KCl similar to quinine. The percentage of responses to the non-NaCl bar across the three groups varied for the different test salts. Similarity of these percentages for test salts is assumed to represent perceptual similarity of these salts. Similarity as measured by this test and similarity determined from the data of Erickson et al. show remarkable agreement.

Evidence for the across-fiber patterning hypothesis also has been obtained, using the opossum, by Marshall (1967). He used a discrimination technique in which the taste of the solution was a cue for the presence of a water reinforcement for water-deprived opossums. In any single trial, three drinking tubes were available. One tube contained a solution of a given taste quality which was defined as correct; that is, licking this tube gave the opossum access to water. Two tubes contained a solution of a different taste quality which was incorrect; that is, licking these tubes did not give the opossum access to water. Successful discrimination was taken to be 5 seconds of licking the correct solution after sampling and rejecting one or both incorrect solutions. Nine solutions were tested and the discriminability of each pair compared to the correlation between these two solutions across all fibers tested. The more similar the solutions, as reflected by low discriminability, the more similar the across-fiber pattern. These behavioral data strongly support the across-fiber pattern as the peripheral neural correlate for quality in mammals.

Experiments on chemoreception in insects have revealed a different sensory code for quality based on highly specific receptors. Dethier and his co-workers investigated the sensory hairs on the mouth parts of the blowfly. A single sensory hair may contain 3 to 5 receptor cells, one of these responding to mechanical stimulation and the remaining cells responding to chemicals. The chemoreceptive cells respond to sugars, cations, anions, and water (Hodgson, 1967).

Von Békésy (1964) has proposed a quality code for man based on specificity. Von Békésy supports the existence of four types of receptor in man, specific to the four basic tastes. He explains the failure to find specificity in the single fibers of other mammals by suggesting that these mammals have different basic tastes so that solutions commonly used in electrophysiological experiments would not be "monogustatory." According to this view, if animals were tested with appropriate monogustatory stimuli, the single fibers would show specificity. Even if this were to be demonstrated (and so far no such stimuli have been found), the pattern across fibers would still be critical for the discrimination of all solutions tested up to now in infrahuman mammals. In von Békésy's theory these solutions would be "mixtures." All solutions other than the basic tastes in human subjects would also be mixtures. Thus even if human papillae were specifically sensitive to four tastes, this would not suggest any alternative for the across-fiber patterning hypothesis for available animal data; or any alternative to across-fiber patterning for the coding of tastes other than these four tastes in man.

The sensory code for quality is complicated by the sensitivity of taste neurons to temperature. Recordings from single chorda tympani fibers in both the rat and cat show that many taste fibers respond to thermal, as well as chemical stimulation (Sato, 1963; Yamashita, Ogaiva, & Sato, 1967). The significance of this in the sensory coding of taste is still unclear.

The way in which taste information is coded may change as that information moves from the periphery to the central nervous system. Multiunit responses from the medulla and thalamus in general appear to be similar to whole chorda tympani recordings, and single units show nonspecificity similar to that found in the periphery (Pfaffmann et al., 1961; Halpern, 1963; Makous et al., 1963). However, there is evidence for some spatial separation of taste centers in both the thalamus and the projection area for the anterior tongue in the medulla; that is, taste areas of the thalamus and the medulla may be organized somewhat chemotopically (Frommer, 1961; Halpern, 1967a; Ishiko, Amatsu, & Sato, 1967). In addition, the posterior tongue area projects to a location in the medulla that is different from that of the anterior tongue and shows sensitivities to taste solutions that differ from those of the anterior tongue area. This suggests an additional spatial separation of tastes that may be important in coding.

Halpern and Nelson (1965) recorded multiunit responses from the medulla while applying taste solutions to the posterior as well as the anterior parts of the tongue in the rat. A quinine hydrochloride solution moving from the front to the back of the tongue produced a small response in one part of the solitary nucleus of the medulla and a larger response slightly later in a different area. A NaCl solution initially produced a large response and later a smaller response. These spatiotemporal patterns of response magnitude could be one means of coding taste information in the nervous stystem.

Taste Variations within and across Species

Human data Some substances taste different to different individuals. Phenylthiocarbamide (PTC) provides a dramatic example of such an effect. Thresholds for the taste of PTC fall in a bimodal distribution so that some individuals can be classified as "tasters" and others as "nontasters." The inability to taste PTC is generally believed to be a simple Mendelian recessive characteristic (Fischer, 1967) and is dependent in part on differences in the saliva of tasters and nontasters (Fischer & Griffin, 1964). Substances more commonly

encountered than PTC also produce different responses in different individuals, although these are not generally reflected by the striking bimodal distribution found for PTC. These individual differences are reflected primarily in variations in the thresholds but secondarily also in quality judgments. Skude (1960), for example, found some subjects who reported that sucrose was bitter.

Fischer (1967) reported some results from a cooperative twin research project on the genetics of taste thresholds. Thresholds for quinine, HCl, and 6-n-phenylthiouracil (PROP), which is an odorless compound similar to PTC, were determined in identical and nonidentical twins. The greatest differences between the two kinds of twins were found for PROP thresholds, indicating a strong genetic influence. Quinine produced a slight difference and HCl produced little difference at all.

Species differences Members of the same species have generally not been studied for individual differences by animal psychophysics or electrophysiology. However, whole nerve recordings are available from more than 20 species. Perhaps the most prominent finding of the study of so many species is the inter-species variation with regard to the most effective stimuli. For example, in some species (hamster, guinea pig, monkey, man) the chorda tympani produces large responses to solutions which taste sweet to man, while in others (cat, rat) the corresponding chorda tympani responses are relatively small.

Contrast Phenomena between Different Tongue Areas

Human data For taste, the term *contrast* has been variously defined. Following von Skramlik (1926) and Dallenbach and Dallenbach (1943) we use the term here to describe the enhancement of tastes on one tongue area produced by exposing another area to various solutions. If the taste is decreased rather than enhanced, the phenomenon is called *suppression*. In general when the two stimuli have different tastes, contrast has been reported (Kiesow, 1894; von Skramlik, 1926; Bujas, 1937). For example, if sucrose is placed in one area of the tongue, this lowers the threshold for NaCl on another area; and enhances the intensity of suprathreshold concentrations of NaCl. However, these effects were dependent on stimulus concentration (Bujas, 1937). Low concentrations of sucrose enhance the sensitivity to NaCl but concentrations over 6 percent actually depress the sensitivity to NaCl. In at least one case, when the two stimuli have the same taste, suppression results. Bujas (1937) showed that if NaCl is put on one area of the tongue, the sensitivity of the tongue to NaCl is decreased in another area, as measured by an elevation in the threshold. Unfortunately, more recent data have not confirmed some of the early results (Pfaffmann et al., 1969). Contrast and suppression phenomena clearly need reexamination, particularly since they may be essential to a thorough understanding of taste mixtures.

Neural interaction   An experiment on the frog suggests that the branching of taste fibers to more than one papilla may provide pathways for contrast effects (Rapuzzi & Casella, 1965). When a papilla was stimulated electrically, impulses traveled from the papilla into the nerve fiber branches that innervated that papilla and on into the central nervous system as usual, but the impulses also traveled backward (antidromically) along the other branches of the innervating fibers and on toward the other papillae contacted by those branches. Presumably, when the frog tongue is stimulated chemically the antidromic impulses coming toward a papilla could prevent impulses originating in that papilla from proceeding toward the central nervous system. Mammalian nerve fibers also branch to more than one receptor, but interactions like those in the Rapuzzi and Casella study have not been demonstrated with either electrical or chemical stimulation in mammals.

Adaptation

Human data   If the tongue is exposed to a taste solution for around one minute, the taste will decrease in intensity and finally disappear, with the possible exception of stimulation by highly concentrated solutions. This decrement in taste intensity during prolonged stimulation is called *adaptation*. The tastes of foods do not ordinarily disappear when we are eating because chewing and tongue movements cause different receptors to be stimulated at different times and thus prevent prolonged, constant stimulation. The first demonstration of complete adaptation in taste unconfounded with dilution of the solution by saliva was provided by Kiesow (1898) in his investigations of the sensitivity of single papillae. The subsequent research focused on the following:

(1) The time required for the sensation to disappear; (2) The changes in absolute threshold during adaptation; (3) The changes in absolute threshold during recovery, that is, after stimulation has been stopped.

The results were as follows: The intensity

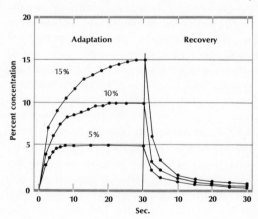

Figure 6.9. Adaptation and recovery curves for NaCl. The ordinate indicates threshold concentrations and the abscissa indicates time of adaptation or recovery. The curves show the temporal course of shifts in the absolute threshold for NaCl during adaptation and recovery for three concentrations of NaCl. The unadapted threshold was 0.24%. (Modified from Hahn, 1934.)

of most taste sensations is greatest when the solution is first applied and begins to decline very rapidly (Abrahams, Krakauer, & Dallenbach, 1937; Krakauer & Dallenbach, 1937). However, for some substances there may be an initial period where the intensity actually increases (Bujas, 1953). During adaptation, the absolute threshold increases until it is at a concentration slightly higher than that of the adapting solution. When the adapting solution is removed, the threshold begins to fall until it returns to its initial value (see Figure 6.9). As concentration increases, the time required for the sensation to disappear increases, the time required for the absolute threshold to arrive at a value slightly above that of the adapting solution increases, and the time required to recover the original threshold increases (Hahn, 1934; Abrahams, Krakauer, & Dallenbach, 1937; Krakauer & Dallenbach, 1937). McBurney and Pfaffmann (1963) demonstrated that the "unadapted" threshold for salt is itself a consequence of adaptation to salt in the saliva. When saliva is removed with a distilled water rinse, the threshold drops to about $\frac{1}{30}$ of the value obtained when saliva is present on the tongue.

The experiments mentioned above focus on the decremental effects of prolonged stimulation on sensitivity, that is, the loss of sensation originally produced by the adapting stimulus and the increase in absolute threshold. Prolonged stimulation has other effects, however, and can actually increase the information available to the nervous system (Keidel, Keidel, & Wigand, 1961). McBurney, Kasschau, and Bogart (1967) measured the size of the jnd near 0.1 M NaCl. The jnd was half as large after the tongue had become adapted to 0.1 M NaCl than the jnd was after the tongue was adapted to water. Thus a smaller change could be detected after adaptation to 0.1 M NaCl.

The association of adaptation with increasing information concerning taste is also supported by experiments on quality shifts. The classic experiments on adaptation mentioned above were concerned with the re-

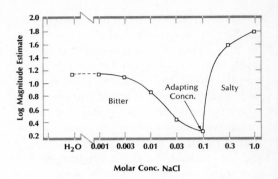

Figure 6.10. Estimated magnitude of sodium chloride solutions after adaptation to sodium chloride. The quality labels reflect the predominant qualities reported for the subadapting and supra-adapting concentrations (Modified from Bartoshuk et al., 1964; Bartoshuk, 1968; and McBurney, 1966.)

sponses to concentrations equal to or greater than the adapting concentration (supra-adapting concentrations) and assumed that concentrations lower than the adapting concentration (sub-adapting concentrations) would be ineffective. However, these sub-adapting concentrations undergo quality as well as intensity changes. Bartoshuk, McBurney and Pfaffman (1964) showed that after adaptation to NaCl, sub-adapting concentrations of salt tasted either bitter or sour. Furthermore, McBurney (1966) showed that the magnitude of the sub-adapting bitter or sour taste increased as the concentration decreased, with a maximum at water (see Figure 6.10). In fact, the bitter taste ascribed to distilled water by many investigators is apparently the result of adaptation to salivary salt. The fact that water can take on discriminable taste qualities if it follows exposure to appropriate solutions was noted anecdotally in the early literature about taste research (von Skramlik, 1926). These observations have been substantiated for HCl, QHCl, and sucrose (Bartoshuk, 1968). For most observers, adaptation to QHCl or HCl makes sub-adapting concentrations taste sweet and adaptation to sucrose makes sub-adapting concentrations taste bitter.

In the discussion above, the term "adaptation" was used to refer to the decrement in sensation reported by a human observer during prolonged taste stimulation. Unfortunately, there is no universally accepted definition of "adaptation." The term has been used to refer to changes in sensation measured psychophysically, to refer to the physiological mechanisms underlying these changes in sensation, or both. In addition there are different sensation changes, for example, the disappearance of taste and the increase in absolute threshold. The only feature these definitions share is dependence on prolonged stimulation. (In fact, in some cases the operation of prolonged stimulation itself is called "adaptation.")

The problem of definition is complicated still further in animal work, where behavioral responses paralleling the psychophysical reports of human subjects are extremely difficult to obtain; information about taste depends heavily on studies made using electrophysiology.

The use of the same term in the study of all the senses has also provided some confusion. It has been established that prolonged stimulation of most if not all the senses decreases their sensitivity to the applied stimulus. However, the mechanisms and the significance of this decrease vary considerably in the different senses. Using one term for such varied phenomena has emphasized some interesting similarities between the senses; however, the differences between them may be even more interesting. Occasionally the decrease in sensitivity has been described as "fatiguelike." This is rarely justified not only because "fatigue" itself is usually undefined but also because "fatigue" fails to suggest the shifts in quality and differential sensitivity that result from prolonged stimulation. Thus, restricting the use of "adaptation" to the reported decrease in taste sensation with prolonged stimulation avoids implicitly grouping phenomena which may or may not prove to be closely related. For example, Bujas (1939) showed that the increase in the absolute threshold does not keep exact pace with the decrease in sensation. The different taste phenomena that accompany prolonged stimulation probably are produced by very different mechanisms and may even be mediated by widely separated parts of the nervous system. Hopefully, as the effects of stimulation are studied further, the relations between the various phenomena will suggest a more precise usage for "adaptation" or a better term.

Electrophysiology of adaptation Not all of the taste phenomena described above have been systematically studied with electrophysiological methods; however, some neural activity changes in animals are analogous to human adaptation. When a given taste solution is applied to the tongue, an initial transient increment usually occurs in the activity of the whole nerve. This is followed by a decline to a steady-state rate of activity that is characteristic of the given concentration (see Figure 6.5). If a higher concentration is applied, a new transient increment and subsequent decline to the corresponding steady-state results. If a lower concentration is applied, a transient decrement and subsequent increase to the steady-state level results. This is especially clear in the rat, which tends to have high steady-state rates. Some species, in particular the cat, show much lower steady-state rates so that most of their responses tend to be transients. In the rat, the steady-state responses to most salts continue until the salt is removed. However, in man, taste sensations disappear rapidly during prolonged stimulation. If man's peripheral neural responses were like those of the rat, some additional mechanism would be necessary to account for the rapid disappearance of sensation. However, recordings from the human chorda tympani indicate that a steady-state rate is not maintained (Borg et al., 1967). During continuous stimulation the peripheral neural response appears to decline in much the same way as does the sensation.

The generalizations made above are complicated by responses to water. The "water" response was originally discovered by Zotterman, first in the frog (Zotterman, 1950) and then in the cat and other species (Liljestrand & Zotterman, 1954; Zotterman, 1956). This response was originally thought to result from a type of fiber responsive to water which was present in some species (for example, cat, rabbit, monkey) and absent in others (for example, rat, man). However, if the tongue is rinsed with appropriate solutions, water produces a peripheral neural response even in the rat, analogous to the water tastes produced in man with appropriate adapting solutions. In addition, if different rinsing solutions are used, different fibers respond to water in species supposedly having a unitary "water" response; for example, one cat fiber may respond to water following exposure to a salt solution, but it may not respond to water following exposure to acid; another fiber may do the reverse (Bartoshuk & Pfaffmann, 1965). The responses to water are contingent on the concentration as well as the chemical nature of the preceding stimulus. A fiber responsive to water following salt will also respond to salts weaker than the concentration of the "adapting" salt. Thus, while sub-adapting concentrations produce decreases in some fibers, they produce increments in some others. The role of these positive responses to sub-adapting concentrations and water is still obscure. Presumably if the pattern across fibers produced by water is similar to the pattern produced by some other taste solution, the water would taste similar to that other solution. This may be the explanation of the bitter, sweet, and sour tastes of water reported in man (Bartoshuk, 1968).

Cross-adaptation

Human data *Cross-adaptation,* like "adaptation," has not been precisely defined; in general it refers to the effects on the taste of one substance by previous adaptation to a different substance. The presence of cross-adaptation can be established by demonstrating an increase in threshold or a decrease in intensity for suprathreshold concentrations of the second solution. However, the adapting

solution may also enhance the taste of the second stimulus. Experiments have tested for cross-adaptation or enhancement among groups of substances that have different as well as similar tastes. In general, enhancement has been reported for tastes that are not similar (Kiesow, 1894; Mayer, 1927; Dallenbach & Dallenbach, 1943; Meiselman, 1968). When a change in threshold is used as the measure for substances with similar tastes, cross-adaptation is found among many but not all sweet substances and bitter substances but among all acids. Hahn (1949) found no cross-adaptation among 24 salts with a salty taste; however, his subjects responded to total intensity. When Smith and McBurney (1969) instructed subjects to divide total intensity among appropriate qualities they found that adaptation to NaCl removed the salty taste from other salts.

Cross-adaptation phenomena have been considered important for theories of receptor mechanisms. The decreased effectiveness of the second substance is assumed to mean that the two substances stimulate at least in part the same receptor sites. The second substance is less effective presumably because the first substance has already produced some adaptation.

Neural data Few electrophysiological data analogous to human cross-adaptation or enhancement data have been reported. Most of the observations have been on salts. Beidler (1961) made recordings from the rat chorda tympani and found that exposing the tongue to 0.1 M calcium chloride for nearly 4 minutes had only a small effect on the response to 0.1 M NaCl. Halpern (1967b) obtained similar results from the medulla using calcium chloride and NaCl also; however, for some other salt pairs, he found results analogous to the human cross-adaptation results achieved by McBurney and Lucas. Analysis of single unit data at different levels in the nervous system would be particularly interesting.

Andersen, Funakoshi, and Zotterman (1963) demonstrated that NaCl depressed chorda tympani responses to sucrose in the dog. Thus fibers responsive to sucrose after the tongue had been rinsed with water were much less responsive to sucrose after the tongue had been rinsed with NaCl. However, fibers responsive to NaCl were not inhibited by prior rinsing with sucrose. These results are in the opposite direction from the enhancement usually found between NaCl and sucrose in human psychophysical experiments (Kiesow, 1894; Mayer, 1927), although this particular comparison may have little meaning. The early human data, although very interesting, are so sketchily described that a great deal of additional work is necessary to accurately determine the facts about cross-adaptation as well as its role in sensory coding.

Mixtures

Human data Early opinion held that, in general, a mixture of taste solutions produced "competition." That is, the overall sensation was produced by tasting each component separately at different times and on different parts of the tongue (Luciani, 1917). However, Kiesow (1896) provided one example of a "compensatory" interaction. He mixed weak solutions of sucrose and salt and found that the resulting solution had little taste at all. Later work (Fabian & Blum, 1943) demonstrated that other taste mixtures can also produce compensation as defined by an enhancement or depression of a taste by the addition of another substance. A considerable amount of work has been done on these interactions both with taste substances dissolved in water and other natural mixtures such as fruit nectars and tomato juice (Amerine, Pangborn, & Roessler 1965). In general, when two substances are mixed the intensities of both components appear to be suppressed. However, when one or both components are weak, some are enhanced rather than suppressed.

Neural data Mixtures applied to tongues of rats, dogs, and cats appear to produce chorda tympani nerve responses that are an algebraic summation of the responses to the components in the mixture if the magnitudes of the component responses are equated (Halpern, 1967b). This holds true, however, only when the responses to the individual components are not near the maximum response. In addition, if a mixture contains components that stimulate the same receptor sites, the response to the mixture will not necessarily be an algebraic sum. For example, 0.1 M NaCl added to 0.1 M LiCl produces a response equivalent to 0.2 M NaCl in the rat (Beidler, 1953). Because the response to 0.2 M NaCl is not twice the response to 0.1 M NaCl, 0.1 M NaCl and 0.1 M LiCl would not sum algebraically.

Halpern (1967b) has compared response magnitudes in the medulla with those in the chorda tympani. Responses to mixtures in the medulla are smaller than the sum of the responses to the components. This suggests the possibility of interactions between responses to different chemicals in the medulla (Halpern, 1967b), which could mean that some of the complex effects of mixtures that have been reported by human subjects may be produced centrally.

Taste Enhancers

Human data Monosodium glutamate (MSG) is said to enhance whatever other tastes are present. Human subjects are only in partial agreement on this point, but, in general, the enhancement by MSG does not appear to occur with simple test solutions (Amerine, Pangborn, & Roessler, 1965). Foods to which MSG has been added are often reported to be more palatable, but this may be due to the addition of the taste of the salt itself. The 5'-nucleotides are used as taste enhancers in Japan. These substances appear to combine with MSG to produce what is known as a synergistic action, that is, their combined effect is greater than the sum of their separate effects. For example, Yamaguchi (1967) reported a synergistic effect for sodium inosinate (IMP) and MSG by demonstrating that the taste intensity of a mixture of the two was greater than the sum of the intensities of the components.

Neural effects   Adachi (1964) studied responses of the cat chorda tympani to solutions formed by adding IMP or MSG to sodium chloride, quinine, sucrose, or acetic acid. IMP and MSG added to solutions of NaCl or acetic acid appeared to have little effect but when added to quinine or sucrose, produced smaller responses than those produced by either quinine or sucrose alone. These data certainly do not support the conclusion that

MSG enhances the tastes of simple solutions.

Adachi, Funakoshi, and Kawamura (1967) also examined the effects of MSG, IMP, and sodium guanylate (GMP) on the taste system of the cat (see Figure 6.11). MSG, IMP, and GMP alone produced very little response, and IMP added to GMP also produced very little response. However, MSG added to either IMP or GMP produced large responses, demonstrating that the synergistic effect does occur in the cat.

The phenomena of adaptation, contrast, and suppression, and the taste interactions resulting from mixtures, are undoubtedly related. However, they must be carefully distinguished, for the mechanisms of the different effects are very likely to be different. Contrast and suppression are phenomena that involve spatially separated receptors, while adaptation involves temporal effects on the same receptors as well. Interactions in mixtures involve all of these effects as well as the simultaneous presence of two or more substances.

Effects of Bodily Needs

Human deprivation effects   Wilkins and Richter (1940) reported that a boy with a tumor of the adrenal gland developed a craving for NaCl. Because the adrenal gland is responsible for salt balance, the boy was presumably in a state of salt deprivation. A correlation of this type between a bodily need and a "specific hunger" for the needed substance led some investigators to suggest that taste sensitivity varies under conditions of need. Several studies with man and other species have examined thresholds as a function of fasting and deprivation of specific substances, such as NaCl. The human experiments have produced conflicting results. Some investigators found that absolute thresholds are elevated after eating while others studying fasting found no changes (Moore et al., 1965). Furthermore, one investigator (Yensen, 1959) found that when the amount of sodium in the blood decreased, the NaCl threshold decreased, while others

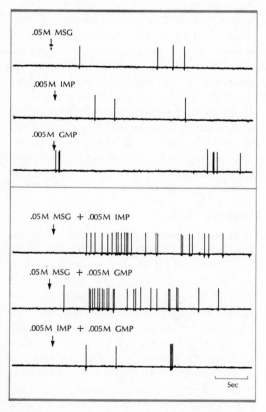

Figure 6.11. Responses of a single chorda tympani fiber from a cat to 0.05M MSG, 0.005M IMP, and 0.005M GMP solutions and to the mixed solutions of 0.05M MSG and 0.005M IMP; 0.05M MSG and 0.005M GMP; and 0.005M IMP and 0.005M GMP. (Adachi, Funakoshi, & Kawamura, 1967.)

(De Wardener & Herxheimer, 1957; Henkin & Solomon, 1962; Pfaffmann, 1964) found no change in the threshold for the detection of salt with changes in blood sodium. In two studies, no relation was found between blood sugar levels and sucrose thresholds (Barto-lović, 1964; Yensen, 1964). At this time there is no convincing evidence that large threshold shifts take place following deprivation.

Comparative data Electrophysiological data give a much clearer description of the influence of bodily needs on taste perception than do the human psychophysical data discussed above. Pfaffmann and Bare (1950) showed that neural thresholds for salt are the same both for adrenalectomized and normal rats; Nachman and Pfaffmann (1963) showed that the neural thresholds are the same for normal rats and those deprived of NaCl; Pfaffmann and Hagstrom (1955) showed that the neural thresholds for sucrose are the same for hamsters given an injection of insulin and those that were not. This evidence suggests that the lowered preference thresholds shown for NaCl by adrenalectomized rats and for sucrose by hamsters injected with insulin reflect a change not in peripheral taste sensitivity but rather in an increased preference for weak solutions. Complicating the results, however, the chorda tympani had been cut in order to place it on the recording electrode in these experiments. Thus, any possible sensitivity changes mediated by efferent fibers in this nerve could not have been observed. Sensitivity changes mediated by changes in salivary constituents could not be observed either, because saliva is rinsed from the tongue during electrophysiological experiments, and the possibility certainly exists that changes in salivary constituents could produce threshold variations via changes in the state of adaptation (see the discussion above on the effects of changes in the adaptation level). However, just as with the human data there is no convincing evidence now available that threshold changes do result from deprivation.

THEORIES OF TASTE RECEPTOR MECHANISMS

The complete sequence of events leading from the application of a taste stimulus to the graded potential in the receptor cell and ultimately to the action potentials in the sensory axon is still unknown. The initial interaction between the stimulus and the receptor site has received the most attention. The presence of enzymes in the area of the taste bud led Baradi and Bourne (1951) to suggest an enzyme theory of taste. According to this theory the action of enzymes could lead to ionic changes which would ultimately give rise to action potentials. This enzyme activity would be differentially influenced by taste substances. For example, one taste could inhibit the activity of a specific enzyme, enhance that of another, and leave a third unchanged. A second taste substance might enhance all three. Baradi and Bourne localized enzymes in six main sites in and around the taste papillae of the rabbit. The pattern of enhancement, inhibition, or no change across these six sites was presumed to code taste quality. Beidler (1961) criticized this theory on several points. In particular, he pointed out that the data concerning the enzyme localizations are themselves in question. Furthermore, the theory contradicts some established neurophysiological evidence, for taste neurons do not fire at moderate rates in the absence of stimulation and then vary their rate of fire with stimulation, as Bourne theorized.

Beidler's more recent work on the initial stimulus-receptor interaction establishes the position that the responsive sites are located on the microvilli of the taste cells and that the molecules of the taste stimulus are bound to the outside of the cell membrane by weak physical forces. This hypothesis is consistent with much of the data from mammals as well as insects (Beidler, 1954; Evans & Mellon, 1962).

The nature of the receptor sites responding to sugars has been studied in two species. Dastoli and Price (1966) isolated from cow tongues a protein fraction that formed complexes with substances sweet to man. Although these results are not conclusive, this material may be the component of the taste bud which interacts with sugars. Evans (1963) has suggested some requirements for the sugar sites in the blowfly based on both electrophysiological and behavioral data. At least two different sites are necessary, because the relative sensitivity to two different sugars was differentially affected by rearing the larva in the presence of one sugar or the other. These sites appear to be associated with a single receptor cell. Evans investigated the requirements of the receptor site for D-glucose by testing compounds with small structural changes and was able to determine what part of the glucose molecule interacts with the receptor site. The manner in which the receptor membrane is depolarized by the physical combination of one part of a stimulus molecule and the receptor site is not known.

HEDONIC PROPERTIES OF TASTE STIMULI

The discussion above has dealt mainly with the processing of information by the taste system; however, tastes have hedonic properties also. Some tastes appear to elicit approach or avoidance very generally across species. Substances tasting sweet to man are usually important nutrients in the environments of most organisms, and are readily accepted by most species (Frings, 1951; Maller & Kare, 1967), whereas substances tasting bitter to man, which are often poisonous alkaloids, are rejected (Fisher & Griffin, 1964). These hedonic responses apparently begin to be made very early in the life of an individual organism; furthermore, they are relatively unchanged by subsequent learning. Jacobs (1964) measured the acceptability of saccharine, water, and quinine in neonate rats by rating the acceptance or rejection of drops applied to the tongue. Maximum acceptance of saccharine together with avoidance of

quinine was reached 9 days after birth, which control experiments showed was related to maturation and not to simple trial and error learning (Jacobs & Sharma, 1968). Warren and Pfaffmann (1958) raised newborn guinea pigs on a solution of sucrose octaacetate, which is bitter to man and avoided by guinea pigs, and which served as the only source of water for three weeks. Later these animals showed the typical rejection of sucrose octaacetate.

The NaCl preference displayed by most species is another example of an apparently biologically determined hedonic response. However, preference for NaCl appears to depend on species and concentration. The hamster, for example, shows no preference for NaCl (Carpenter, 1956). The rat, which has been extensively studied, shows a peak preference for salt when it is in a solution of about 0.1 M and begins to avoid it in solutions near 0.3 M. The preference of rats for NaCl was challenged by Deutsch and Jones (1960). They suggested, on the basis of neural data reported by Zotterman (1956), that the intake of weak salts resulted from the similarity of the sensory codes for weak salt and water. Rats would drink more weak salt than water because the neural signal was diluted by the salt. Additional evidence, both neural and behavioral, does not support the diluted water hypothesis (Benjamin et al., 1965; Stearns, 1965).

The preference of rats for NaCl is dramatically demonstrated with the so-called "contingent lick procedure" developed by Fisher (1965). The rat is required to lick at one tube a specified number of times to get access to a second tube. When the first tube contains salt the rat does not shift to the water in the second tube. However, when the first tube contains water, the rat shifts to the salt as soon as it is made available.

Although these taste-directed preferences can be clearly demonstrated when a choice of solutions is offered, taste is obviously not the sole cue controlling food intake. A number of experiments show that rats will adjust their total food intake to maintain a constant caloric intake when the caloric density of the diet is varied. For example, they increase intake when the diet is diluted with cellulose, which contains no calories, and decrease intake when the diet is calorically enriched with corn oil (Jacobs & Sharma, 1969).

Taste may play a role in the regulation of food intake by inducing some of the metabolic changes (in the absence of ingestion) that usually occur postingestionally. Nicolaidis (1969) demonstrated several direct effects of oral stimulation on metabolic events. One of the most striking of these was the rise in blood glucose after either sucrose or saccharine was applied to the tongues of deprived rats.

The neural correlates of the hedonic properties of taste stimuli have not been studied as extensively as those of the informational content. As electrophysiological techniques improve, these very complex hedonic properties will probably receive more attention. Hopefully, the information obtained about taste will be helpful in understanding other sensory experiences, for example, pain, which also possess affective properties.

Maxwell M. Mozell

THE CHEMICAL SENSES

II. OLFACTION

7

Substances give off some of their molecules. These are then transported to the animal through the medium—air or water—in which he lives. Higher organisms are supplied with receptors of several types, each with its own afferent neural pathway, that can respond to at least some chemical molecules. In vertebrates these receptors include the olfactory and gustatory together with many free nerve endings apparently supplied by the trigeminal, glossopharyngeal, and vagus nerves.

Because any or all of the sensory receptors may, under some set of circumstances, respond to the molecules of a particular chemical stimulus it is very difficult to differentiate or define any of the chemical senses precisely by simply referring to the characteristics of their stimuli. For instance, in terrestrial animals one may be able to distinguish smell from taste by saying that the molecules underlying the former are in the form of vapors and are thus transmitted to the animal through the air. However, this does not hold true for aquatic animals, where all the molecules (those affecting both gustatory and olfactory receptors) are in aqueous solutions. Neither, in view of these aquatic forms, can an iron-clad distinction be made on the basis that olfaction involves the detection of molecules emanating from distant sources whereas gustation seems more like a contact sense. Since in these forms the gustatory and olfactory receptors are stimulated with molecules dispersed in an aqueous solution, the source of the molecules for either sense may be either near or far from the animal.

Note, too, that even in the air-breathers one cannot dogmatically say that olfaction is definable as the sense that responds to air-borne vapors, for, as we shall see, the free nerve endings also respond to such stimuli. In addition, it has recently been shown (Tucker & Shibuya, 1965) that the olfactory receptors of an air-breather can respond quite well to odorous molecules in an aqueous solution, provided that the solution is properly intro-duced into the nasal cavity. Thus, in the final analysis, the chemical senses are distinguished from each other not by the stimuli that im-pinge upon them nor by the way the stimulus is presented. Rather they can only be dis-tinguished by their structure. That is, each chemoreceptor has a different morphology and a different afferent neural input to the central nervous system.

The very maintenance of life for many animal species depends upon the olfactory system. On the one hand, the detection of olfactory cues is essential in foraging for prey, whereas, on the other hand, the detection of such olfactory cues is the first line of defense against the animal's own predators. In many species the finding of a mate depends upon olfaction. A species of moth, for instance, is reputed to be able to find his mate by olfac-tory cues from a distance of up to $2\frac{1}{2}$ miles (Moncrieff, 1967). Many animals use odorous secretions and excretions to mark off terri-tories and to designate places they have been. Among the ants and social insects the whole society appears to communicate through olfactory stimuli called pheromones (Wilson, 1965). The adult salmon, swimming inland from the sea, relies heavily upon olfaction in his quest for the stream in which he was spawned (Wisby & Hasler, 1954).

To civilized man olfaction no longer has the life-or-death significance that it still has for lower species, although it has some im-portance—the smell of smoke signifying fire, for example. Rather, civilized man has taken advantage of the strong affective tone the

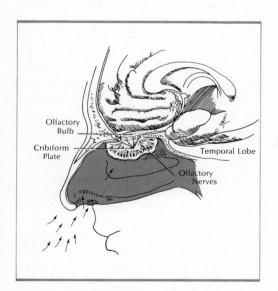
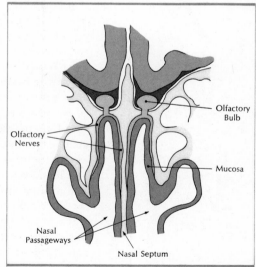

Figure 7.1. The gross anatomy of the olfactory system in man. *Left.* A saggital section through the head showing a lateral view of the position of the olfactory receptive area, the cribiform plate, and the olfactory bulb. The receptor layer of the mucosa has been stripped away showing the underlying bundles of olfactory nerve axons. *Right.* Cross-sectional view of the uppermost nasal passageway lined with the receptor-bearing mucosa. Also shown is the course of the olfactory nerves toward the bulb.

olfactory stimuli can generate by using them for esthetic or hedonic purposes. Thus, rather than merely relying upon odors to forage for a meal, he adds such odors as those of herbs and spices to his food, so that eating is not only a necessity but a pleasurable experience as well. For other hedonic reasons he douses himself with perfumes, grows honeysuckle in his backyard, burns incense in his church, or puts his clothes in a cedar chest.

Not all odors are pleasurable to man, and several large industries have been developed to produce deodorants that protect man from the displeasure generated by certain odors which otherwise are not particularly harmful.

FUNCTIONAL NEUROANATOMY

In man the patch of mucosa that bears olfactory receptor cells lines the lateral, medial, and superior walls of the uppermost passageway of the nasal cavity (Figure 7.1). As the axons of the olfactory receptor cells course centrally they combine into larger and larger nerve bundles and enter the cranium through a series of perforations in the bone (the cribiform plate), which forms the superior wall of the passageway. They then con-

tinue to the surface of the olfactory bulb.

The olfactory neuron is a bipolar cell which simultaneously serves as the end organ and the primary afferent fiber (Figure 7.2). The distal or dendritic end, called the *olfactory rod*, is 20–90 μ long and 1 μ in diameter (LeGros Clark & Warwick, 1946). For most of its length the olfactory rod is wrapped by supporting cells. However, near the surface of the olfactory epithelium, which is bathed in mucus, the rod ends in an unsheathed swelling called the *olfactory knob* (Bloom, 1954). This swelling supports 6 to 12 cilia, which are believed (without direct evidence) to bear the sites that are stimulated by the odorant molecules. In the frog these cilia are as long as 200 μ; their diameters are 0.25 μ proximally and 0.15 μ distally (Reese, 1965). The distal ends of the supporting cells bear a large number of microvilli which appear to become entangled with some of the cilia (de Lorenzo, 1957). This suggests a possible interrelationship between these two structures.

Of considerable interest in conceptualizing the mechanisms of olfactory stimulation and discrimination is the enormous number of receptors involved. In the rabbit there are about 50,000,000 olfactory cells on one side of the nose; about 150,000/mm² (Le Gros Clark & Warwick, 1946). Perhaps these large numbers reflect the necessity of having selectively tuned receptors for each of the vast number of odorants that can be discriminated. Perhaps the large number of olfactory cells is needed to increase the redundancy in an otherwise noisy system (that is, by replicating the same stimulation process and by increasing the number of channels transmitting the same information, momentary distortions at some points will be offset by the fidelity at other points). Perhaps the large number of receptors is needed to amplify certain aspects of the input by summating their synaptic effects on the succeeding neurons. Perhaps this vast number of closely packed receptors with their many cilia might play a role in the differentiation of vapors by providing a large, very finely divided surface area that can adsorb the

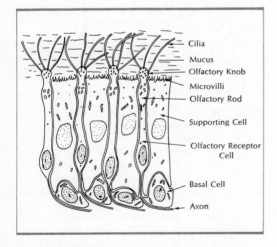

Cilia
Mucus
Olfactory Knob
Microvilli
Olfactory Rod

Supporting Cell

Olfactory Receptor
Cell

Basal Cell

Axon

Figure 7.2. Simplified diagram of the olfactory epithelium. (Moulton & Beidler, 1967, slightly modified.)

incoming molecules of different chemicals in a variety of regional patterns.

Also of much theoretical interest is the mucus bathing the epithelium. In the frog this mucus is 20–35 μ thick (Reese, 1965) and covers the cilia which lie below and parallel to the surface (Reese, 1965). This suggests that odorant solubility may play a key role in determining the distribution of the incoming molecules across the receptor sheet even before the receptors themselves are triggered. Indeed, it appears probable that the number of molecules reaching the receptor and the time it takes them to do so depend upon their interaction with the constituents of the mucus. However, the number of molecules of an odor that usually can be detected is often so small that even compounds classified as insoluble might put a sufficient number of

molecules into solution to be detected. Therefore, perhaps solubility is being over-emphasized as a limiting factor in the access of the molecules to the receptors lying beneath the surface of the mucus.

The thin (0.2 μ diameter) axons of the bipolar olfactory cells are sheathed for their entire length although they themselves are unmyelinated C-fibers. Initially they are surrounded by supporting cells and basal cells (Figure 7.2). Later, where they meet below the epithelium to form a series of longitudinal bundles, groups of them are sheathed by the plasma membranes of Schwann cells, as

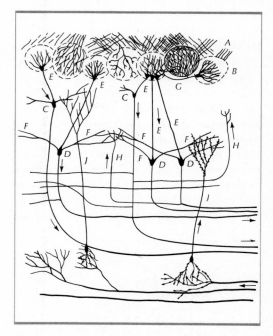

Figure 7.4. Schematic diagram showing how the neural elements of the mammalian olfactory bulb are anatomically related. *A*, primary olfactory nerves; *B*, olfactory glomeruli; *C*, tufted cells; *D*, mitral cells; *E*, primary dendrites; *F*, accessory dendrites; *G*, cells that interconnect nearby glomeruli; *H*, recurrent collateral axons; *I*, fibers passing into the bulb from both the opposite bulb and from more central brain areas; *J*, interneurons which connect the incoming fibers to the mitral and tufted cells. Arrows show the direction of information flow. (Allison, 1953b; the letter designations have been modified.)

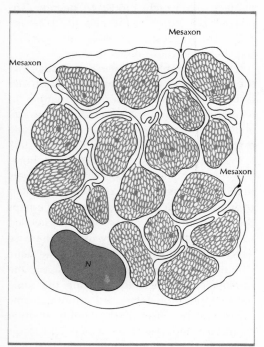

Figure 7.3. Schematic representation of the relationship of the olfactory nerve axons to the Schwann cells. Bundles of olfactory nerve cell axons are enveloped by the invaginations (called mesaxons) of the Schwann cell plasma membrane. The nucleus of the Schwann cell is denoted by *N*. (de Lorenzo, 1957.)

shown in Figure 7.3 (Gasser, 1956; de Lorenzo, 1957). This common sheath raises the possibility that the firing patterns of the axons in a given group influence each other such that the whole group can be considered a type of functional single unit.

In the olfactory bulb the axons of the primary olfactory cells synapse with the dendrites of the secondary olfactory cells, the tufted and mitral cells (Figure 7.4). These synapses are not diffusely scattered but are instead aggregated into very dense packets called the *olfactory glomeruli*. In the rabbit 26,000 primary fibers enter each glomerulus and about 100 secondary fibers leave (Allison, 1953a). Because this 260 to 1 reduction affords an excellent opportunity for summation, the final output of the glomerulus reflects the interplay of a rather large amount of incoming information.

Each receptor in the epithelium is represented directly in only one glomerulus, and, in mammals, each mitral and tufted cell also emanates from only one (Figure 7.4). Thus it might be expected that the group of secondary fibers leaving a given glomerulus carries information from only those receptors which feed into it. However, such an insulated "direct line" from periphery to central nervous system appears unlikely. In the first place "cross-talk" could occur through the cells that connect nearby glomeruli. Second, the mitral cells and the tufted cells of neighboring glomeruli appear to communicate through their accessory dendrites and recurrent axon collaterals. Finally, there are fibers passing into the bulb from more central brain areas as well as from the opposite bulb, which, through interneurons, impinge upon the secondary olfactory cells. Thus, there is an anatomical basis for believing that the output signals of a given secondary olfactory neuron may reflect information gathered from several areas of the ipsilateral olfactory mucosa, from the contralateral olfactory mucosa, and from more central areas of the brain. This last contribution probably represents processed information from other systems as well as from the olfactory system itself.

There is a regional isomorphism in the projection of the epithelium upon the bulb, but its degree of precision differs from region to region. The upper and back parts of the epithelium project quite precisely to the glomeruli on the upper surface of the bulb. Other epithelial regions, although they project to localizable areas of the bulb, do so more diffusely (LeGros Clark, 1951, 1957). Thus, there appears to be an anatomical substrate for a central nervous system analysis of the activity spatially spread across the olfactory mucosa.

Receptors other than olfactory are present in the nasal passageways. First, there are trigeminal nerve fiber endings. Second, in many species, there are the receptors lining the vomeronasal organ. This organ is a sac, tube, or slit lying on the floor of the nasal cavity. Its exact morphology varies widely between species. As we shall see, these two systems can respond to vapors, and their inputs may add further dimensions to olfactory experiences.

In addition, the pharynx also is supplied with receptors that apparently detect at least some odorous molecules. This information seems to be transmitted via the ninth and tenth cranial nerves (Henkin, 1967).

ODOR STIMULATION TECHNIQUES

As is discussed below, the concentration of any given odorant in a carrier medium is one of the primary determinants of the olfactory response. Likewise, the procedures for introducing the odorant to the olfactory mucosa also influence the responses. Unfortunately, perhaps because of the difficulties encountered in trying to control these parameters, they are often either inadequately controlled or overlooked.

Control of Concentration

Several authors have gained at least some knowledge concerning the olfactory effect of stimulus intensity by diluting the odorants with predetermined amounts of inodorous liquid solvents (Beck, Kruger, & Calabresi, 1954). These solutions are kept such that they only partially fill their containers. Although these containers can be anything from a volumetric flask to a pickle jar, they are often referred to as "sniff bottles." The use of liquid dilutions for controlling the odorant intensity coming from a "sniff bottle" is based upon an idealized system described by Raoult's and Henry's Laws. When an ideal liquid solution reaches equilibrium with its vapor in a closed container, the number of molecules of each of the constituent chemicals in that vapor phase can be calculated if two factors are known: (1) the number of molecules of the chemical which would have been in the vapor phase at the existing temperature if, as an undiluted liquid, its molecules were the only ones available for vaporization at the liquid surface; (2) the decrease in the number of these available molecules brought about by their competition with the molecules of the diluent for positions on the surface of the liquid. The first factor can be measured by the chemical's vapor pressure, which is the pressure exerted on the walls of a closed container by its molecules in the vapor phase. The vapor pressure for each chemical at a given temperature must be independently determined, and the greater the value of the vapor pressure, the greater is the concentration of molecules in the vapor phase. The second factor is measured by the mole fraction which represents the fraction of the total number of molecules in the liquid phase of the solution which is contributed by the chemical in question.[1] This is given by the following ratio:

$$\frac{\text{number of moles of the chemical}}{\begin{array}{l}\text{number of moles of the chemical} + \\ \qquad \text{number of moles of the diluent}\end{array}}$$

Thus, in the ideal system, dilution in known steps will decrease the mole fraction proportionately, and, therefore, the pressure contributed by the vapor of the odorant (and thus

[1] It will be recalled that the number of moles of a chemical is expressed as the ratio of its weight in grams to its molecular weight and that every mole, regardless of the chemical, contains the same number of molecules.

its concentration) will be reduced proportionately.

However, in olfactory research a dilution series is often prepared with no heed either to the vapor pressure of the chemicals or to their molecular weights. Thus, because these are constants for any one chemical (at any given set of conditions) but differ among chemicals, a series of vapor concentrations in known ratios to each other might be prepared for any one chemical by simple dilution ratios but nothing can be said about the relative concentrations between different chemicals. Diluting different chemicals the same amount does not produce the same vapor concentration unless their vapor pressures and molecular weights happen to be the same. That is, chemicals can be compared only when the calculations are based on both the mole fraction and the vapor pressure.

As is noted above the procedure to determine stimulus concentration is actually valid only for ideal solutions. An ideal solution is one in which the molecules all act individually (that is, the molecules of each chemical are attracted neither to each other nor to the molecules of the other chemical in the solution). In the vast majority of solutions, however, the molecules do attract each other; they form molecular structures that, to varying degrees, affect the accuracy with which the actual molecular concentration of the vapor phase can be predicted from the vapor pressure and the mole fraction (Stone, 1963b). Nevertheless, this method of estimating concentration can still be quite useful as an approximation. Indeed, this approximation becomes progressively more accurate as the mole fraction of the odorant is made smaller by dilution because the more dilute the solution is made, the more it approaches the ideal system.

Finally, it should be re-emphasized that even with ideal solutions the calculation of concentration described above can be strictly applied only when the solution and its vapor phase are in equilibrium. The moment the container holding the odorant is opened this

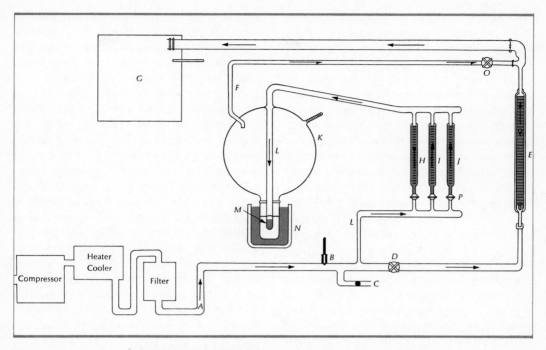

Figure 7.5. An example of a simple but useful flow-dilution olfactometer. Air is supplied by a compressor. It is temperature-regulated and the thermometer, *B*, is used as a monitor. Unwanted odors are removed from the air by filtering it through activated charcoal. This supply of air, *A*, is then split into two streams: one to provide deodorized air and the other to provide odorized air. The latter, *L*, is saturated by bubbling it through the odorant, *M*. The odorant is contained in a diffusion bulb, *K*, which is kept at a known constant temperature by a water bath, *N*. The concentration in the air leaving the diffusion bulb in stream *F* can be calculated from the vapor pressure of the odorant which in turn depends upon its temperature (that is, the temperature maintained by the water bath). This concentration of odorized air can then be diluted to any desired value by recombining it with the pure air in appropriate proportions. The proportion of each stream in the final mixture is controlled by varying its respective flow rate. This is achieved by adjusting valves *C*, *D*, *O*, and *P* in accordance with the flow rates monitored by the flow meters in each stream (*H*, *I*, and *J* allowing fine control through different ranges for the odorized stream and *E* for the deodorized stream). The final mixture reaches the subject whose head is enclosed within a plexiglass hood, *G*. (Stone, 1964, slightly modified.)

requirement is no longer fulfilled. Nevertheless, by using partially closed containers equilibrium may be approached, and the concentration may at least be estimated for each dilution (Moulton & Eayrs, 1960). It is, of course, necessary in this liquid dilution technique to find a diluent which simultaneously is odorless to the animal to be tested and is also a solvent for the odorants to be used (Jones, 1953, 1955; Engen & Pfaffmann, 1959; Moulton & Eayrs, 1960).

In order to gain more precise control of the stimulus intensity and in order to quantify it more accurately in physical units of concentration, a variety of "olfactometers" have been developed. One widely used type is the flow dilution olfactometer (Figure 7.5), which odorizes a previously purified air stream by passing it at known volume flow rates over or through a given odorant. The concentration of this odorant in the air stream is then given by the volume of air passed through it and its consequent weight loss (Allison & Katz, 1919). An alternative to measuring weight loss directly, is to compute the amount of odorant in the air stream, assuming saturation, from its vapor pressure at the ambient temperature (Woodrow & Karpman, 1917; Ough & Stone, 1961).[2] Lower concentrations can then be obtained by diluting this odorized air stream with another air stream containing only purified air. The ratio of the two flow rates, that of the pure air stream and that of the odorized air stream, defines the final concentration.

Control of the volume flow rates is based on the Poiseulle equation, which describes the flow of a gas through a tube as follows:

$$V = \pi r^4 (P_1 - P_2)/8yL$$

where V is the volume per unit time (that is, the volume flow rate), $P_1 - P_2$ is the pressure difference between the two ends of the tube, y is the viscosity of the carrier gas, L is the length of the tube, and r is the radius of the tube. The Poiseulle equation may be used directly to quantify volume flow rates by passing the air through capillaries of fixed diameters and lengths (Stuiver, 1958; O'Connell, 1967; O'Connell & Mozell, 1969), or the air may be passed through stopcocks which afford continuously varying diameters. Because it is difficult to know the exact diameter of the stopcock apertures, investigators using this latter system generally dispense with calculating the flow rates from the Poiseulle equation and instead read them directly on some type of flow meter (Mozell, 1958; Tucker, 1963a). The flow rate may also be controlled by infusion pumps which act by pushing air out of containers with constant velocity pistons (Mozell, 1966).

Another type of olfactometer incorporates the principle of successive air dilutions. In this method a known amount of odorant is allowed to evaporate in a container of given

volume filled with pure air. A small amount of the resulting concentration is then injected into another container of given volume, and the procedure is repeated until the desired concentration is achieved (Goff, 1961).

No matter what the basic design, it is of course important that the olfactometer should be constructed from materials which are themselves odorless. Also these materials should not readily adsorb odors, which could then be given off into the air stream. Thus, rubber tubing and many plastics including Tygon and polyethylene have been found to be inappropriate. Glass and Teflon appear satisfactory but there should be provision for deodorizing or discarding contaminated pieces. Stopcock grease, even the silicone variety, should be used cautiously. Teflon-coated stopcocks are a better choice. Since olfactory sensitivity is so great, any slight contamination is likely to be crucial.

Odorant Presentation

The simplest technique of odorant presentation is normal sniffing, and in man it is often regarded as the only practical technique. Nevertheless, the consistency of the results obtained by this method between subjects and for any given subject has been questioned. In recent years this problem has become particularly troublesome because one of the variables of a sniff is its flow rate, and, as is discussed at length later, the flow rate with which an odorant approaches the mucosa is now known to be one of the primary determinants of the olfactory response.

An attempt has been made to standardize the sniff by Le Magnen (1942–1943) who made constant sniffing a matter of pitch discrimination. He attached a whistle to his olfactometer which changed pitch with the force of the subject's sniff. Thus the subject had to maintain a constant sniff in order to maintain a constant pitch.

However, several authors have found normal sniffing to be quite satisfactory in their experiments, and thus they did not resort to such special procedures (Beck, Kruger, & Calabresi, 1954; Jones, 1955; Engen, 1964).

[2] This calculation depends upon the ideal behavior of gases just as the liquid dilution method, discussed earlier, depends upon the ideal behavior of solutions. Ordinarily, the assumption of "ideal gas" does not introduce much error because it is generally applied to gases with small simple molecules such as oxygen and carbon dioxide. However, we should keep in mind that when the assumption is applied to the large complex molecules of odorants it could, perhaps, introduce an error.

Presumably this is a highly learned motor response which has become quite constant for any given subject. Jones (1955), using "sniff bottles," found that for the determination of thresholds sniffing yielded results with rather high reliability within subjects. On the other hand, between subjects there were large differences. This controversy may have been somewhat resolved by Stone (1963b) who compared the results of sniffing odors from "sniff bottles" to the results of sniffing odors from an olfactometer. He found greater reliability between subjects when they sniffed from the olfactometer. This suggests that any variability observed with sniffing may arise not from the sniffing *per se* but rather from the "sniff bottle" technique of preparing stimulus concentrations which, of course, depends upon the ideality of solutions.

A major problem in normal sniffing is the possible interference of ambient odors. Many authors consider it sufficient merely to ventilate and exhaust the experimental area with the usual commercially available equipment. However, other authors have felt it necessary to go to great lengths in order to enclose either the whole subject or just his head in elaborate odor-controlled compartments (Foster, Scofield, & Dallenbach, 1950; Schneider & Wolf, 1955).

Even though natural sniffing may be an adequate method for presenting stimuli, some investigators have preferred a still more rigid control. This has been especially true in animal experiments where surgical techniques can be used. A glass cannula can be passed into the nasopharynx of an anesthetized, tracheotomized animal (Adrian, 1942). By pulling back on a syringe connected to this cannula the animal is given an artificially produced sniff of controlled flow rate, duration, and volume. An artificially produced sniff for human subjects can be achieved by fitting the subject with two nose pieces: one attached to the olfactometer and the other to a suction pump. During a Valsalva maneuver[3] this pump can draw air in through one nostril and out

the other at any desired flow rate, volume, and duration.

Occasionally the continuous flow method of presentation is still used. In this method, as its name implies, odorized air is made to flow continuously through the nose. The effect of such continuous flow, even when one controls for the possibility of mucosal drying, is still unresolved.

FIRST-ORDER DETERMINANTS OF OLFACTORY EFFICACY

Tucker (1963) has classified three variables as first-order determinants of olfactory efficacy: (1) the particular odorant used, (2) the concentration of the odorant in the carrier gas, (3) the flow rate of the odorant at the mucosa. The measures of efficacy to be discussed will include the absolute threshold, the relative threshold, and the total stimulus-response curve.

The Particular Odorant and Its Concentration

Absolute threshold Allison and Katz (1919), using a flow-dilution olfactometer with human subjects, found the "just detectable" (that is, absolute threshold) concentration for 24 chemicals. The range was quite wide; the highest (5.833 mg/liter) for ether being 100,000 times greater than that for the smallest (4×10^{-5} mg/liter) for artificial musk. Five of these substances were also tested by Bach (1937) who, using the successive-dilution technique, found the absolute thresholds to be about 10,000 times smaller than did Allison and Katz. However, there was some tendency in the two studies for the chemicals to hold about the same rank in their respective ranges. Here we have a difficulty seen all too often in most areas of olfaction, namely, a problem in comparing the data from various laboratories. Comparison is difficult because each uses different odorants, different animal species, different odorant presentation techniques, and different units of concentration.

Occasionally the claim is made that human absolute thresholds are not too different from

---

[3] Forcibly breathing against a closed glottis as when straining to empty the bowels.

the thresholds of other animals. For instance, human thresholds for clove oil and anethole do not appear very different from dog thresholds for the same substances (Becker, King, & Markee, 1962). It has been suggested that the difference in the olfactory prowess between man and lower animals is not due to a difference in the ability to detect minute quantities but rather to a difference in ability to discriminate a large number of qualities (Adrian, 1953). Perhaps then, it is not the sensitivity of the dog's nose that allows it to track a man (Kalmus, 1955), but rather its ability to differentiate that man's body odor from all the other odors that must be on and around the trail. Nevertheless, there are several studies that show that lower mammals, especially dogs, do indeed seem to have greater olfactory sensitivity than humans. For instance, the dog's sensitivity for butyric acid is reported to be 100 times greater than man's (Moulton, Ashton, & Eayrs, 1960).

It is generally agreed that olfaction is very sensitive, but what this assertion actually means is unclear. From Stuiver's data (1958) we can compute that his own absolute threshold for ethyl mercaptan was 1.6×10^{-12} moles/liter. Although this sounds like a minute concentration, it should be emphasized that a single 1-milliliter sniff of this mixture still contains 10^9 molecules of odorant. This is certainly not a small number. Thus, by referring to the great sensitivity of olfaction, one probably refers to the fact that the olfactory system can detect the presence of a smaller number of molecules than can most laboratory methods used for the same purpose. The nose even challenges the great sensitivity of the flame ionization detector, which can detect 10^{-12} grams per second. In 1 ml of a concentration of ethyl mercaptan that a human subject can just detect there is 10^{-13} grams.

According to Stuiver (1958) the nose is even more sensitive than the discussion above suggests because, although these values indicate the number of molecules entering the nares, only a small fraction of these molecules ever actually reaches the receptors. This is the case because (1) many molecules entering the nose are adsorbed by the mucous lining of the non-olfactory epithelium; (2) many of those molecules not so adsorbed will pass through the nose in air streams that are ventral to the olfactory mucosa; (3) many of those that do reach the level of the olfactory mucosa will continue through the region without striking it. Thus in a normal inspiration only about 2 percent of the odorous molecules entering the nose actually reach the olfactory epithelium. Because the approximate number of receptors is known and because the number of molecules needed to reach threshold is also known, the average number of molecules per receptor can be calculated for a threshold stimulation. The probability of a sense cell receiving more than this average may be computed statistically. By comparing this with the actual probability of detection at this concentration, the number of molecules needed to excite a single receptor may be estimated. This number is at most 9 and perhaps as little as 1 for mercaptans. At least 40 receptors must be excited to reach threshold.

Although the analysis above makes many assumptions which require validation, the approach, reminiscent of a similar approach in vision (see p. 284), does emphasize anew the exquisite sensitivity of the olfactory system when it is compared to physical systems.

Difference thresholds   At long last in recent years there have been a few studies concerning olfactory differential thresholds and Weber fractions (see p. 17), in which modern olfactometers and sophisticated stimulus presentation techniques have been used. In general, the Weber fractions determined by these studies showed only minor variations as a function of concentration (Stone, Ough, & Pangborn, 1962; Stone, 1963a; Stone & Bosley, 1965). However, they did differ to some degree between chemicals. For instance, a Weber fraction of 0.36 was found for propionic acid, 0.26 for acetic acid, 0.31 for ethyl-*n*-valerate, and about 0.20 for 4 other chemicals. Consequently the Weber Law holds about as well for olfaction as it does for the other senses, but, as can be seen from the size of the fractions, the differential thresholds are relatively poorer in olfaction than in most other senses. This latter observation may just be another manifestation of what may be a basic attribute of the olfactory system, that is, low information capacity concerning stimulus intensity. In the succeeding discussion concerning olfactory stimulus-response curves other manifestations of this attribute will become apparent.

Stimulus response curves Mozell (1958) electrophysiologically recorded the multi-unit discharge strength from the olfactory bulb of rabbits as a function of stimulus concentration. As is true with most of the other senses, equal stimulus increments yielded diminishing response increments as the stimulus intensity was increased. However, the asymptotes of the curves recorded for the 4 chemicals used were reached after a concentration increase of only 10 to 33 times, that is, about 1 to 1.5 log units. This range, over which the stimulus intensity can increase and still yield an increasing electrophysiological response, is considerably smaller for olfaction than that determined for vision (Hartline, 1938) and audition (see p. 230).

It is questionable whether we can legitimately expect support from behavioral experiments for this electrophysiologically determined concept that only a comparatively small increase in olfactory stimulation is necessary to account for the major part of the increase of the olfactory response. First, the electrophysiological recordings only sample, at best, a small percentage of the total number of the receptors the animal has. It is possible then that this electrophysiological sample, especially if the sample were small, would exclude the particularly sensitive or the particularly insensitive receptors. This would reduce the width of the electrophysiologically determined range compared to that of the behaviorally determined range. Second, the

behaving animal has the advantage of using other sensory nerves that also respond to chemical vapors, notably the trigeminal nerve (see later). Thus these extraolfactory inputs would give an apparently wider stimulus range when it is determined behaviorally than when it is determined by recording from the olfactory nerve alone. Notwithstanding these problems, some parallels can still be drawn between results obtained by using the behavioral and the electrophysiological techniques, albeit with several reservations.

Allison and Katz (1919) reported data from studies using behavioral techniques that can be used to support the apparent narrow range of stimulus intensity increase. Their subjects were instructed to rank various concentrations into five categories ranging from (1) "detectable" to (5) "very strong." Assuming that the scale of 1–5 gives a complete stimulus-response curve, one can compute the stimulus increase in log units necessary to go from the least response to the greatest response for each chemical. These ranged from .8 to 2.3 log units for 21 chemicals with 14 of them ranging from .9 to 1.5 log units (Mozell, 1958). Moulton (1960) reported similar results from his studies with rats. The percentage of correct choices made by rats trying to discriminate several acetates increased asymptotically over a range of only 2 to 3 log units of stimulus increase. It has been suggested that perhaps this narrow intensity coordinate is related to the apparent lack of fine intensity discrimination in olfaction.

There is not universal agreement that the range of the stimulus concentration coordinate in olfactory stimulus-response curves is a narrow one. As could be expected from the previous discussion, this is especially true of behavioral experiments. In one study, using an operant discriminative procedure with rats, olfactory discrimination appeared to improve linearly over a concentration increase of 6 or more log units (Goff, 1961). In another study a similar effect was noted with human subjects (Moncrieff, 1957). However, multiunit recordings from the olfactory nerve (Tucker,

1963) suggest, even beyond the behavioral and electrophysiological methodological differences, that this disagreement concerning the width of the stimulus range might be resolved by considering the water solubility of the odorants. At a constant flow rate the responses to increasing concentrations of amyl acetate level off, whereas the responses to benzyl amine over an equally wide concentration range do not. Because amyl acetate is only slightly soluble in water, whereas benzyl amine is infinitely soluble, one may assume that the amyl acetate will saturate the mucus at a lower concentration than will the benzyl amine. Thus, the range of concentrations over which increasing numbers of mole-

cules can be dissolved in the mucus, in order that they can then reach the receptors, is less for the amyl acetate. After scanning the literature it appears that every odorant reported by all the investigators mentioned above (Allison & Katz, 1919; Moncrieff, 1957; Mozell, 1958; Moulton, 1960; Goff, 1961; Tucker, 1963) that has infinite solubility in water also has a wide range of intensity increase. In many but not all cases where the odorant was not very soluble, a narrow range is reported. Direct confirmatory evidence of this solubility relation would have far-reaching theoretical implications for any model of olfactory stimulation.

There is now experimental confirmation of

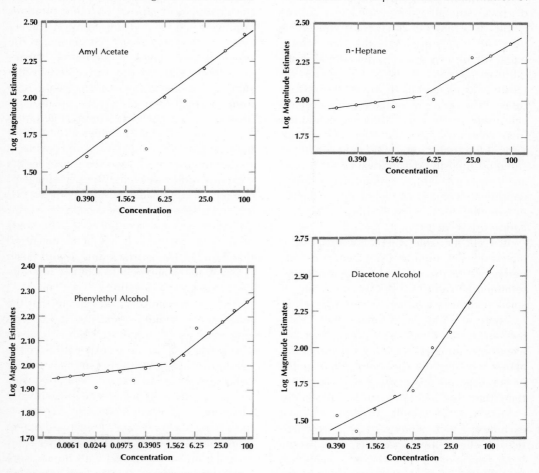

Figure 7.6. Human olfactory magnitude estimates as a function of concentration. The concentration series was prepared by diluting the odorants in benzyl benzoate. Concentration is denoted as the percentage of odorant in the solution. (Engen, 1961.)

the heretofore anecdotal observation that the range of subjective odor magnitude in olfaction is rather short. Engen (1961, 1964) had his subjects estimate the magnitude of the odors given off by chemicals that had been diluted in a geometric series with benzyl benzoate. He found that by raising the concentration of the stimulus from its absolute threshold dilution all the way up to its being completely undiluted, he could increase the perceived magnitude by as little as a factor of 2 (Figure 7.6). With such a narrow range of perceived odor magnitude it is no wonder that his subjects were unable to use fractionation methods as a scaling technique since for many intensities they could not find another that appeared half as intense.

Another type of study also suggests that the salient characteristic of the olfactory system is not its detection or storage of intensity information. Subjects were asked to learn the position of each of five stimulus concentrations ranked according to their intensity, and later the same subjects were asked to identify those ranks when each of those concentrations was presented separately (Engen & Pfaffmann, 1959). They did less well than did subjects in similar studies made of vision and audition (Miller, 1956). Therefore, it may be concluded that intensity in olfaction is somewhat less distinctive than it is in other sensory systems.

Engen's magnitude estimation studies, discussed above, as well as similar studies by other authors (Jones, 1958; Reese & Stevens, 1960) show that the perceived odor magnitude increases as a function of the stimulus intensity raised to some power (Figure 7.6). The power varies considerably around 0.5, depending upon the study quoted and the chemical tested, but in all cases it is considerably less than 1.0. Thus, sensory magnitude in olfaction seems to be "compressed"; that is, successive equal increases in stimulus intensity yield progressively decreasing additions to the perceived sensory magnitude.

Although, as may be expected for power functions, a plot of the log of the estimated magnitude as a function of the log of the stimulus intensity yielded a straight line for amyl acetate, such plots for n-heptane, phenyl ethyl alcohol, and diacetone alcohol did not yield simple straight lines (Figure 7.6). Instead the slopes were smaller at low concentrations and greater at high concentrations. One reason for this change in slope may be the previously discussed difficulty in predicting the vapor phase concentration of an odorant from its percentage in a solution if the solution is not ideal. Thus, the actual stimulus concentration presented to these subjects at each dilution could have been quite different from that expected.

Another reason that the slopes varied with concentration may be that in each graph the two slopes may represent two entirely separate functions. If such is the case, one function, as expected, might depend upon the olfactory input, but the other function, somewhat unexpectedly, might depend upon another input such as that from the trigeminal nerve, for it has been shown electrophysiologically in subhuman species that most odorants can routinely stimulate the trigeminal system as well as the olfactory (Beidler & Tucker, 1956). Previously it had been thought that those odorants yielding a pungent or stinging odor probably stimulated trigeminal receptors; however, it now seems that even mild odorants such as phenyl ethyl alcohol (a rose odor) can likewise do so (Beidler, 1960). In addition, the vomeronasal fibers of the tortoise also respond to vapors. In general, the olfactory and vomeronasal thresholds are lower than the trigeminal threshold for any given odorant. It is therefore possible that the two different slopes in the magnitude estimation curves represent the changing contribution of the olfactory input and the trigeminal input to the subjectively perceived magnitude as the intensity of the stimulus is increased. Of course, it is still to be demonstrated that there is as much overlap between olfactory and trigeminal stimuli in man as in lower animals. That there is at least some overlap has been demonstrated by patients who have lost their olfactory input but have retained their trigeminal, glossopharyn-

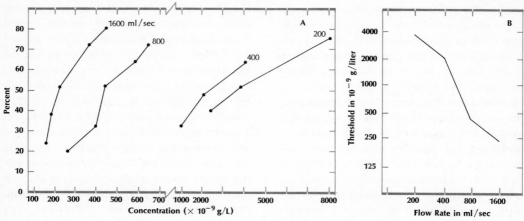

Figure 7.7. A. The effect of concentration and flow rate upon the ability of human subjects to detect the odor of eucalyptol. The ordinate is given as the percentage of stimulus presentations responded to affirmatively. The abscissa gives the concentration in 10^{-9} g/liter. The curves represent the effect of varying the concentration of eucalyptol while the flow rate of the inspiration is held constant at any one of the 4 values designated, in milliliters per second, by the number at the top of the curve to which it refers. The volume of all inspirations was held constant at 600 ml. Note that at any given flow rate the ability to detect an odor increases with concentration. Likewise, where concentrations are equal, the ability to detect an odor increases with the flow rate of the inspiration. B. The human olfactory threshold as a function of the flow rate of inspiration. Threshold is given in 10^{-9} g of eucalyptol per liter of air. The threshold is taken as the concentration at which 50 percent of the presentations are responded to affirmatively. The volume of the inspiration is held constant at 600 ml.

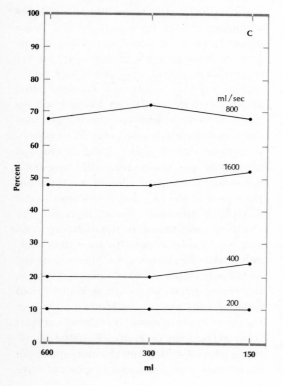

C. The effect of volume upon the ability to detect an odor when the flow rate is held constant. The ordinate is the same as above. Volume is given along the abscissa. The flow rate is indicated by the number, in milliliters per second, near the curve to which it refers. Note that there is no effect of volume upon detection ability; that is, the curves are all essentially horizontal.

It is necessary to point out that this set of curves by itself offers no information concerning the effect of flow rate upon the ability to detect an odor because for each flow rate the author had to use a different concentration (not shown on figure). Consequently, the effect of flow rate is confounded with the effect of concentration. However, the conclusion made above concerning volume is still valid because for any one curve the only variable is the volume. (Le Magnen, 1944–1945; part B has been redrawn.)

geal, and vagal inputs (Henkin, 1967). These patients can still discriminate several vapors, and these discriminations can only be mediated by one or more of the remaining systems.

Volume Flow Rate[4]

Concentration has not been the only variable used to control the strength of olfactory responses. In various studies flow rate and volume also have been varied. It still remains necessary, however, to determine whether flow rate and volume are meaningful, independent measures of olfactory stimuli.

Le Magnen (1944–1945) described a method in which concentration, volume, and volume flow rate could all be varied independently. The frequency with which his human subjects could smell the stimulus was determined for several values of each variable. As expected, the percentages derived from these frequencies increased as a function of concentration at all flow rates (Figure 7.7A). Less expected was the observation that at any given concentration the percentage of affirmative responses varied quite decidedly with the flow rate (Figure 7.7A). In addition threshold decreased as the flow rate increased (Figure 7.7B). In contrast, the percentage of affirmative responses did not appear to vary with the volume when the flow rate and the concentration were held constant (Figure 7.7C).

The importance of flow rate has also been observed electrophysiologically in lower animals (Tucker, 1963 a, b). The summated neural discharges increased with the flow rate when the concentration was held constant. Perhaps the sniffing behavior of lower animals and man, when they suspect the presence of an odor, takes advantage of this enhancement of the olfactory response by increasing the flow rate through the nose.

One of the common explanations for this dependency of olfaction upon flow rate assumes that eddy currents in the nose facilitate the movement of odorous molecules toward

the olfactory epithelium which is, after all, situated a considerable distance from the main nasal air stream. Presumably, the greater the flow rate the greater the eddy currents and consequently the greater the number of molecules reaching the mucosa. This explanation was tested by placing a plastic tube through the naris directly to the olfactory epithelium (Beidler, 1958) so that odors could be brought into contact with the epithelium without the aid of eddy currents. The responses were still found to depend on the flow rate.

Tucker (1963a, b) gave a better explanation of this flow rate dependency. He suggested that the effectiveness of the stimulus depends upon the number of molecules that can be established at the receptors within a certain period of time depending upon the receptor response properties. Thus, for any given stimulation the number of molecules will be dependent upon both the flow rate and the concentration of the odorant. Both of these variables control the number of molecules available at the receptor in any specified period of time. Therefore, both flow rate and concentration are primary determinants of the olfactory response.

SECONDARY VARIABLES CONCERNING THE OLFACTORY RESPONSE

There are many other variables besides those directly associated with the stimulus that have been shown to affect the subject's olfactory report both qualitatively and quantitatively. Only a few of these can be discussed here.

Instructions

There has been a long-standing controversy concerning the possible existence of two olfactory thresholds, that is, one at which the subject merely detects the presence of an odor and another at which the subject can identify the odor. Engen (1960) demonstrated that such a dual threshold is indeed present in olfaction and that one must specify, in determining the absolute threshold, whether the subjects are to identify an odor or merely

[4]Throughout this chapter the term "flow rate" will often be used to refer to the volume flow rate, that is, the volume of gas moving through a given plane per unit time. It will never refer to the linear flow rate, that is, the distance a gas is moved per unit time.

detect the presence of one. He presented his subjects with four test tubes only one of which contained an odorant at some given dilution. He asked his subjects either to detect the test tube that smelled different or to identify the test tube containing a given, named odorant. The first set of instructions yielded considerably lower absolute thresholds. In addition, once the subject operated under the "smelled different" instructions, he found it difficult to go back to the "named odorant" criterion.

The fact that there appear to be two thresholds in olfaction (detection and identification) has far-reaching theoretical implications. For example, are there two sets of receptors, or receptor sites, analogous to a similar duality in vision where the low threshold rods detect the presence of a light and the higher threshold cones permit the identification of its color? Or is it simply that a certain amount of summation of the peripheral events is necessary at some central locus for positive identification?

Effect of Food Consumption

The assertion that hunger increases olfactory sensitivity while food ingestion decreases it fits our teleological notions about food foraging by animals and, therefore, is readily accepted. However, in applying the same type of teleological reasoning to the protection of the animal, one should predict that no changes would occur. Why, for instance, should the animal be hindered in his detection of predators because he himself has eaten?

Several groups of investigators, using a variety of different procedures, have attempted to determine whether eating affects olfactory ability, but unfortunately their results do not agree very closely. One group found a decrease in olfactory sensitivity after eating (Schneider & Wolf, 1955). Another group found no statistically significant change after eating, although there was a little tendency (statistically not significant) toward reduced sensitivity (Furchtgott & Friedman,

1960). Still another group actually showed olfactory ability to be greater after eating than before eating (Berg et al., 1963). Thus, although we may like to think that our olfactory thresholds increase after eating, it is not yet agreed that they do so.

The Effects of the Status of the Mucous Membranes

Recording from the olfactory nerve of the rabbit, Tucker (1961) noted that the strength of the discharge for a given concentration of a given chemical could be increased considerably if he simultaneously either pinched a toe, clapped his hands, shined a light in the rabbit's eye, or electrically stimulated the cervical sympathetic nerves. There are no known feedback loops to the receptors themselves to change their sensitivity, so another explanation is needed.

By direct optical observation of the nasal interior Tucker noted that pinching the foot, shining a light, clapping the hands, and electrically stimulating the cervical sympathetic nerves all produced a blanching of the nasal mucosa and an increase in the width of the nasal passageways. Both of these effects are probably related to a reduction in the engorgement of the nasal tissue with blood, which may produce a less obstructed air flow path leading to the receptor areas. This in turn may allow more molecules of any given stimulant to reach the receptor area.

In addition, Tucker noted that electrical stimulation of parasympathetic outflows to the mucosa decreased the response to a given odorant and simultaneously increased the flow of nasal mucus. Such an increase in mucus probably "stuffs" the nose. Therefore, it appears that the accessibility of the molecules to the receptors is significantly impaired in these animals and that the degree of impairment is controlled by the autonomic nervous system.

Human olfactory thresholds have also been observed to depend upon the state of the epithelium, but the effects vary somewhat from those observed with the lower species.

Again, obstruction was the most important reducer of olfactory sensitivity but short of frank obstruction the highest sensitivities in man were attained when the tissues were considerably swollen, red, and wet (Schneider & Wolf, 1960). Given the contour of the human nasal passageways, these conditions probably increase the efficiency with which the olfactory mucosa traps the available molecules as they pass by. This would produce an apparent reduction in threshold because fewer molecules need now enter the naris to achieve the same olfactory effect.

Sex and Olfaction

Anecdotal evidence and the advertisements of the perfume and cosmetic industries testify to a supposed connection between olfaction and sexual arousal. However, only in comparatively recent years has this connection, together with its underlying neuro-humoral mechanisms, been clearly demonstrated experimentally.

The usual evidence employed to demonstrate the relationship between sex and olfaction is a change in the olfactory threshold during a period when the levels of the various hormones also are varying. This hormonal variation could be due either to normal events or to outside intervention. The sensitivity for certain substances (especially a lactone called exaltolide) varies in such a way with the course of the human female's menstrual cycle that it suggests that this sensitivity is positively correlated with her estrogen production (Le Magnen, 1953). This involvement of estrogen is also suggested by the raised threshold for exaltolide found in women who have been deprived of estrogen by the removal of their ovaries and by the restoration of the threshold to within a normal range after the administration of exogenous estrogen. In addition, prepubic females and both prepubic and adult males are less sensitive to these odorants than are adult females.

It appears, then, that the level of a hormone may affect the olfactory thresholds but the site of this action is still in doubt. One mechanism may depend upon the state of the olfactory mucosa, as discussed in the previous section. Thus, the administration of estrogen to hypogonadal women increased their sensitivity for citral as it concomitantly tended to decrease their nasal obstruction. On the other hand, androgen decreased the sensitivity in one woman and at the same time tended to increase obstruction (Schneider et al., 1958). Thus the hormonal recipe may not be affecting olfactory thresholds by direct action upon the olfactory system itself, but rather indirectly through systems which in turn affect olfaction. This cannot be the only explanation, since the administration of androgen to men increases the sensitivity to some chemicals while reducing it to others (Le Magnen, 1953).

The discussion thus far has been concerned with the effect of the hormonal status upon olfaction; however, there is a reverse relationship, that is, olfaction has an effect on the hormone recipe. Of course, the olfactory system is not unique in this regard, for it has long been known that other sensory systems can also affect the hormonal balance.

The most dramatic example of the regulation of sex hormones by olfactory stimuli is the pregnancy block brought about in female mice by the odor of strange males as reported by Parkes and Bruce (1961). They showed that if female mice are mated, about 8 percent ordinarily do not become pregnant and go back into estrus. However, if soon after mating these females are confronted with the smell of strange males, about 80 percent of them return to estrus. The mechanism of this pregnancy block by an odor appears to be a reduction in the secretion of prolactin,[5] for if they are fortified with exogenous doses of this hormone, the block is prevented (Parkes, 1961). In the mouse, prolactin maintains the corpus luteum which in turn is necessary for the maintenance of a uterine endometrium suitable to support a fertilized ovum. Thus, by interfering with the secretion of a hormone, the odor forces the mouse to abort.

[5] An adenohypophyseal gonadotropin.

As has been mentioned earlier, olfactory cues are important for some animal species to find their mates. When a male rat is faced with the choice of an estrous or a diestrous female, he makes his choice on the basis of olfactory cues (Le Magnen, 1951). Castrated and prepubic males showed no preference until given an injection of androgen (Le Magnen, 1953). Carr and Caul (1962) investigated whether the differences in the choices of castrated and normal rats depended merely upon their differing preferences or whether their choices depended upon their differing abilities to detect and discriminate the odors given off by receptive females. Because castrated and normal rats showed no difference in learning to discriminate the odors of estrous and diestrous females in a choice box situation, the authors concluded that the hormonal state of these animals affected only their preferences and not their sensitivities.

Another body of evidence also suggests a hormonal effect upon olfaction. Patients with adrenal insufficiency tend to have very low olfactory thresholds for aqueous solutions of NaCl, KCl, and $NaHCO_3$ (Henkin and Powell, 1962).[6] Treating these patients with hydrocortisone brings their thresholds back to normal. Likewise, an increased olfactory sensitivity for the same chemicals occurs in patients with cystic fibrosis.

Adaptation

Olfactory adaptation is an everyday experience. Most people have noticed that after being in an odorous environment for some time the odor seems to disappear.[7] For instance, the odor of your impending evening meal is quite clear when you first enter your home, but soon you no longer smell it. Ol-

factory adaptation is here defined as a decrease in responsiveness and sensitivity to odorants as a result of being exposed to them. Recovery from adaptation is used here to mean an increased responsiveness and sensitivity after the removal of the odorous stimuli.

There are two major behavioral methods of studying adaptation. The first is to measure the time needed for a continuously presented odor to disappear. The second is to measure the threshold before and after a subject has been exposed to an odor for a given amount of time.

Most of the studies using the first, simpler, method show that as the concentration of the odorant is increased, the time needed for its smell to disappear is also increased. In addition, equal increments in concentration yield

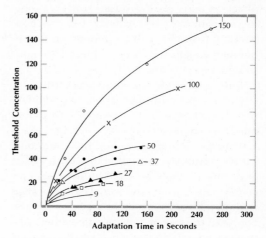

Figure 7.8. Curves showing human adaptation to several different concentrations of d-octanol. Each curve shows the effect of a different concentration (the concentration is noted at the right). Note that at any given concentration the threshold increases as the exposure time increases. Likewise, for any given exposure time the adaptation increases (that is, there are higher thresholds) as the adapting concentration increases.

The notation of concentrations in this figure is a bit unusual. The threshold concentration for the completely unadapted subject was first determined. Then, all other concentrations are given as multiples of this unadapted threshold concentration. (Stuiver, 1958.)

---

[6]Notwithstanding the obvious importance of these observations from an olfaction-hormone point of view, there is another interesting aspect of these studies, that is, the chemicals used are not typical olfactory stimuli and in the non-aqueous state they may even be classified as nonodorous. Perhaps in the aqueous solution some odorous contaminant is released.

[7]However, it is necessary to note Cain's (1968) recent evidence which suggests that a smell is not likely to disappear unless the subject is told that it will do so.

equal increments in the disappearance time, although in one study this linearity did not occur until after the first 100 seconds (Woodrow & Karpman, 1917; Stuiver, 1958).

The second behavioral method of measuring adaptation is exemplified by a study by Stuiver (1958), who measured thresholds as a function of the intensity and duration of an adapting stimulus (Figure 7.8). His procedure was to present low intensity test concentrations at specified intervals throughout the course of the subject's adaptation and to record whether these interspersed test concentrations were above or below the subject's threshold. Stuiver found that the threshold increases as either the concentration or the exposure time of the adapting stimulus is increased, but, contrary to some earlier work (Zwaardemaker, 1925), he believed that the relationship between threshold and exposure time was not linear. However, for at least the first 100 seconds, his curves are actually not very far from straight lines. Only after 100 seconds, and therefore beyond the exposure times used in the earlier work, does it become quite apparent that the curves are not linear; in fact, the thresholds reach a final constant level after prolonged exposure. An important observation is that prior to reaching this constant threshold value the decrease in sensitivity appears to be a function of the total amount of odorous material inspired (Figure 7.8). For example, 40 seconds of exposure to a concentration 100 times the absolute threshold will decrease the sensitivity about the same amount as 80 seconds of exposure to a concentration 50 times the threshold. It was also noted that recovery from adaptation is at first quite rapid and then quite slow. The rapid phase accounts for most of the recovery.

It is easy to demonstrate the phenomenon of olfactory adaptation; however, to elucidate its physiological mechanism has proved to be difficult. Even the locus of adaptation has proved elusive. One's initial supposition, that adaptation is an olfactory receptor phenomenon, has not been verified by recordings from primary olfactory receptor cell axons. At each inspiration, a burst of activity is recorded from the rabbit's olfactory fibers, but at low stimulus intensities these bursts are all of the same strength (Beidler & Tucker, 1956). Thus, there appears to be no neural effect which parallels the human behavioral effect, at least up to this level of the olfactory nervous system. Beidler (1957) has therefore concluded that the locus of adaptation is more centrally located in the nervous system. Human behavioral data also supported the same conclusion when it was demonstrated that both sides of the nose adapted even though only one side had been exposed to a continuous stream of odorant (Stuiver, 1958). Beidler (1957) also noted that at medium stimulus intensities the bursts of neural activity do decline with successive inspirations, but even here they reach a steady size, and do not decline to zero as one might expect from the behavioral reports. Only at the highest concentrations do the bursts disappear altogether. Note that these medium and high concentrations are within the range necessary to evoke the autonomic nasal reflexes which, as discussed previously, alter the nasal swelling and mucus flow. Therefore, Beidler suggested that the response decrements observed at medium to high concentrations are not due to olfactory receptor mechanisms per se but are rather due to changes in the accessibility of the receptors to the molecules.

There is still some reason to believe that the olfactory receptors do play some part in adaptation. This is based upon observations of a slow potential change (called an electroolfactogram) which can be recorded directly from the mucosa and which is believed by some investigators to be the electrical sign of olfactory receptor activity (Ottoson, 1956). After 15 seconds of a continuous flow of odorous air over the mucosa, the electroolfactogram decreased as much as 60 percent from its initial size at the beginning of stimulation. Thus at least some part of the process of adaptation may be occurring in the mucosa.

In summary, it appears that the greater part of adaptation occurs in central areas; the process includes feedback to nasal accessory organs via the autonomic nervous system. However, it is still too early to discount the part played by peripheral olfactory elements completely.

Odor Mixture

Several types of sensory report are conceivable when two or more odorants are mixed together. First, the subject may be able to discriminate each odor separately. Second, an entirely new odor may develop which resembles the components but does not smell exactly like any of them. Third, one odor may predominate making it impossible to discriminate the others. This effect is generally called *masking*. A fourth possibility, neutralization, was described by Zwaardemaker (1925). He claimed that for a few combinations of odors no sensation at all can be perceived if they are presented simultaneously. However, Henning (Woodworth & Schlosberg, 1954) denied the existence of neutralization as a physiological phenomenon but conceded that it could occur by a chemical or physical interaction between the molecules before they enter the nose (Pfaffmann, 1951).

There is a great lack of modern reliable work concerning odor mixture; indeed, a good deal of the information available borders on being anecdotal evidence. As for the first three possible reactions to odor mixing mentioned above, it is generally accepted that olfaction is analytical like pitch discrimination, where one note in a chord may be singled out from the others. Olfaction is generally not considered synthetic like color vision, where the individual hues in a mixture of hues are seen not separately but rather as a totally new hue. However, this exclusively analytic nature of olfaction may be too readily accepted. Its main support is that some experts, such as perfume chemists, are capable of identifying each of about a dozen chemicals in a mixture. However, perhaps these trained chemists only appear to be discriminating all the individual components, for, when they smell a fragrance, they would

know from experience the ingredients needed to approximate it. In color vision even non-experts give similar apparent analyses, yet color vision is not considered analytical. For instance, most people, believing that orange looks more like yellow and red than like blue and green, would likely suggest that orange is composed of the former pair. However, the important issue in this context would be the ability of subjects to determine whether a given orange light is composed of one narrow band of wavelengths in the orange range of the visual spectrum or whether it is composed of a mixture of several wavelengths, none of which is in the orange range of the visual spectrum. With well controlled conditions subjects cannot do this, and thus color vision is considered synthetic. Whether subjects can perform the analogous task with smells (namely determine which odorants contain more than one type of molecule and which do not) has not yet been given adequate experimental testing.

The things we smell in the course of our daily lives are almost always composed of the molecules of several different chemicals, yet we do not often smell them as several simultaneously presented individual odorants. Likewise, we most often smell chemicals purchased from manufacturers as totalities even though, as gas chromatographic analysis tells us, they contain many contaminants. On the other hand, in some instances olfaction has more in common with the perception of pitch, which is analytical, than it does with the perception of hue, which is synthetic. For instance, the perceived intensity of a mixture of pure odorants is less than the sum of the perceived intensities of the same two odorants taken separately (Jones & Woskow, 1964).

At the present time it is probably safest to say that depending upon the circumstances, odorant mixtures may result in any of the possibilities mentioned above. They may continue to be smelled separately. They may combine to yield a new odor (Johnston, 1963). Finally, one of the odorants may mask the others. This last effect is evidenced by the large number of companies manufacturing "odor destroyers," some of which simply lay down such a strong pine or floral scent that the other odorants present can no longer be appreciated.

Deodorization

Deodorizing techniques have taken several forms (Kulka, 1964). First, they may not really deodorize at all but actually only replace an unpleasant odor with a supposedly more pleasant one. As discussed above, this can be done either by masking or by synthesizing a new odor. True deodorization takes place when the odorous molecules themselves are removed from the environment. This can be accomplished by passing the contaminated air over adsorbants such as activated charcoal. Alternatively, the odorant molecules may be made to react with other chemicals to form odorless products. Still another technique is to prevent the production of odorous molecules in the first place. For example, many under-arm deodorants prevent the bacterial activity that converts essentially odorless sweat into its several highly odorous breakdown products.

There are two other techniques that presumably operate on the olfactory system itself. One is the selective adaptation of the receptors to certain unpleasant odorants so that they are no longer annoying. The other is to render the receptors or their axons inoperative by the introduction of certain vapors. For example, several aldehydes are said to anesthetize the receptors (Kulka, 1964).

QUALITY DISCRIMINATION

Attempts to Understand Quality Discrimination by Behavioral Techniques

There appears to be a countless number of discriminable odors, and, indeed, probably the most salient feature of olfaction is the variety of its quality discriminations. However, there are very few generic terms to describe this vast number of odors. Rather they are generally described by the name of the sub-

stance or the article with which they are associated (for example, rose or gasoline) (Harper, 1966). In order to obtain a concise descriptive vocabulary of odor qualities, many investigators have attempted to categorize odors. Perhaps an even more important motivation for categorization has been the hope that if odors could be properly grouped together into categories or placed side by side along some continuum, an insight into the basic mechanisms of quality discrimination could be gained.

Odor categories The most famous of these category systems is Henning's smell prism (Woodworth & Schlosberg, 1954). The corners of the prism were labeled "putrid," "ethereal," "resinous," "spicy," "fragrant," and "burnt." Although Henning's subjects were able to place each odorant on the prism, depending upon how closely it fulfilled the corner descriptions, other authors have had difficulty reproducing the results.

Another classification scheme described odorants numerically rather than by location on a figure (Crocker, 1947). Four basic odor receptor types presumably corresponding to four basic odor qualities were arbitrarily assumed: (1) fragrant; (2) acidic; (3) burnt; (4) caprylic. Subjects were instructed to decide how much of each quality they could find in any given odorant and to assign numbers from 0 to 8 accordingly. Thus, an acid may finally be designated as 4813 meaning that it smells halfway fragrant (4), very acidic (8), slightly burnt (1), and moderately caprylic (3).

Such classification systems have had only limited success in describing odors and even less success in giving insight into the basic discrimination mechanisms. One of the major problems has been that it is difficult to have all odors conform to such arbitrarily chosen categories.

A more promising categorization scheme, with attendant suggestions for the mechanism of discrimination, has been proposed (Amoore, 1962a, b). First, it was assumed that the terms most frequently used to describe the odors of chemicals with rigid molecular configurations defined the so-called "primary odors." These were ethereal, camphoraceous, musky, floral, minty, pungent, and putrid. Odorants particularly exemplifying each of these categories were chosen and a detailed inspection was made of scale models of their molecules. On the basis of the dimensions of these models Amoore suggested that corresponding to each of these first five primary categories there is a corresponding distinct molecular size or shape. Electrical charges were the common features of the remaining two categories. For each of the first five molecular groups it was hypothesized that there was a receptor site with a shape congruent to that of the molecule. The molecules of those chemicals that have only pure "primary odors" were presumed to fit snugly into only one type of receptor site, whereas the vast majority of molecules were presumed to fit into several types and were said to produce compound odors, that is, odors composed of more than one "primary odor." Although this categorization and theory of discrimination has had some early moderate success in correctly predicting the results of a few simple experiments (Amoore, Johnson, & Rubin, 1964), the results obtained from more recent work have forced a rather drastic revision of some of its major tenets. Amoore himself (1965) was unable to demonstrate that the ability of chemical molecules to fit the prescribed primary sites correlated well with human judgments of their odor similarity. Also to be noted here are the recent electrophysiological recordings from single olfactory receptor units (see p. 217) that show that chemicals drawn from the same category may not stimulate the same units in the same way (Gesteland, Lettvin, & Pitts, 1965). Because of the results of his later work, Amoore (1965) abandoned the concept that odorant molecules with particular shapes fit into correspondingly shaped sites. However, if he did not require the molecules to possess rigidly specified configurations, then the human judgments of odor similarity appeared to

correlate reasonably well with molecular shape. Accordingly, Amoore has still retained the concept that the shape of the molecule determines odor quality, but he no longer requires that the molecule have a given shape or that it conform to a set of prescribed primary receptor sites.

Cross-adaptation Adaptation has been used as a basis to classify olfactory stimuli. The rationale for doing this is that a subject's adaptation to one odorant often will increase the subject's threshold to another odorant (cross-adaptation), and it is assumed that odorants that do cross-adapt have some common characteristic or property for the stimulation of the olfactory receptors. In this way some property of the molecule such as its water solubility, its dipole moment, or its shape, among other characteristics, may eventually be identified as the basic physical correlate of olfaction.

Cheesman and Townsend (1956) measured the change in their subjects' thresholds for several test odorants after they had smelled various concentrations of several adapting odorants. The authors found a linear relation between the log of the intensity of the adapting odorant and the log of the threshold concentration for the test odorant. The slope of these curves differed for different combinations of the test odorant and adapting odorant. The results were interpreted to mean that the greater the slope the more the two chemicals were similar in some property for the stimulation of the olfactory system and the more they could be classified together. So far this approach is more noteworthy for the potential of its general concept than for the information it has produced.

It is also possible to reverse the procedure described above by determing whether chemicals known to be very similar in some property also show more cross-adaptation than those chemicals that are less similar. In this way it may be possible to gauge the importance of any given property of a chemical as a basis for its discrimination by the olfactory receptors. Engen (1963) has made a modest start in this direction. He took advantage of the fact that in an homologous series of odorants many physical properties vary in an orderly fashion with the length of the carbon chains in their molecules. One might therefore expect that the closer members in a homologous series will cross-adapt each other more than will the members that are farther apart. However, Engen found that for a homologous series of aliphatic alcohols the amount of cross-adaptation was not related to the closeness of the members. One cannot immediately conclude from this experiment that none of the physical properties of chemicals which vary within an homologous series play a role in the basic process of discrimination. This reluctance to draw such a conclusion is necessary because, as Engen suggests, several properties may be operating simultaneously. Each of these may affect olfaction in a somewhat different and perhaps opposing manner. On the other hand, one could question whether such cross-adaptation studies could ever materially aid our understanding of olfactory receptor discrimination mechanisms. This skepticism is engendered by the previously discussed findings showing: (1) that adaptation may depend more upon the central nervous system than upon the receptors, and (2) that other sensory systems in addition to the olfactory system also contribute to the subjects' perception of vapors.

Continua of the olfactory impression It is becoming increasingly apparent that the olfactory sensory impression is so complex that no single stimulus continuum is likely to account for it. Indeed, Engen (1962) has shown that the olfactory subjective response varies along several dimensions at once. He presented his subjects with an homologous series of alcohols and had them estimate the similarity in quality of each odorant to every other odorant. Three factors were then extracted by a multidimensional analysis of the data. One decreased with chain length and appeared by introspective analysis to be related to an "alcohol" smell. Another, increasing with chain length, appeared to be a "musty" smell. The third factor seemed to vary along a "pleasantness" dimension.

As the subjects went from chemical to chemical in the above study, the stimulus intensity as well as the stimulus quality varied because vapor pressures are inversely related to chain lengths in an homologous series. Therefore, it is possible that one of the dimensions, perhaps the "alcohol" dimension, was actually an intensity dimension. However, it is still quite apparent that smells vary along more than one dimensional continuum. One of the several possible physiological bases for this is the trigeminal input which may add one or more subjective dimensions.

Special notice should be taken of the "pleasantness" dimension in Engen's study. It is clear from everyday life that many odors produce a definite affect, and it is, indeed, difficult to feel serenely indifferent to the presence of most of them. Nevertheless, there are very few controlled experimental studies primarily concerned with the hedonic effects of olfaction.

As a start, several authors have asked subjects to rank odors on some sort of pleasantness-unpleasantness scale. There is a fairly high correlation ($r = .80$) for successive rankings of the same odors by the same subjects over a period of months. However, the correlation between different subjects for the same odors is at best only moderate ($r = .42$) (Beebe-Center, 1931). A partial explanation for this lower correlation between subjects may be the finding that subjects are very much affected by their own past experiences when they are ranking odorants (Young, 1923; Kniep, Morgan, & Young, 1931). For example, phenol recalled medical situations for many subjects, and it was, therefore, often classified as unpleasant. In addition, the order in which the odorants are presented plays an important role in their ranking because the affect they engender shows definite contrast; that is, an unpleasant odor is more unpleasant after a series of pleasant odors and vice versa (Kniep,

Morgan, & Young, 1931). The affective tone generated by an odorant appears to be an integral part of its impression (Eysenck, 1944; Hsü, 1946; Yoshida, 1964), although it may play a lesser role for professional expert perfumers (Yoshida, 1964). Even when subjects were asked not to judge odorants on such a dimension, they were apparently unable to refrain from doing so (Engen, 1962). Thus, this hedonic effect may be such an indelible concomitant of smells that it cannot be disregarded.

The importance of affect to olfaction is also demonstrated by the rather wide range over which odors differ in their pleasantness as compared to the narrower ranges of other olfactory subjective dimensions. For instance, odor pleasantness can increase about 125-fold over its whole range (Engen & McBurney, 1964) whereas the range of subjective odor magnitude can show an increase of as little as twofold. Thus, it is quite possible that odors are in part discriminated from each other by the affective tone they engender.

Attempts to Understand Quality Discrimination by Electrophysiological Techniques

On the basis of behavioral odor discriminations alone, it is very difficult either to determine the receptor mechanisms basic to olfactory discrimination or to classify odors according to some stimulus property relevant to the olfactory discrimination mechanism. The difficulty arises because behavioral judgments use information from other systems in addition to the olfactory system. Consequently, these judgments vary along several perceptual dimensions, some of which may not depend solely upon the olfactory input. A method which circumvents these problems is to classify odorants according to the neural discharges that they produce in the peripheral olfactory system. Chemicals yielding similar neural responses are presumed to have similar properties and to be mediated by similar mechanisms.

Single-unit studies   Because of the technical difficulty in recording from the very small single units in the mucosa, the first recordings from single units in the olfactory system were taken from the second-order neurons in the bulb (Adrian, 1953, 1954). On the basis of these recordings chemicals were grouped together according to the units they excited. All those that excited any given unit were placed in the same group. Although within each group there often was one chemical which stimulated only that particular unit, the other chemicals in that group would excite one or more of the other units. Each chemical, therefore, excited different combinations of single units. Although no single bulbar unit could be discharged by only one odorant, the population of single units would be fired in different patterns depending upon the stimulus used. Extrapolation of these findings peripherally to the mucosa suggested to Adrian receptor types corresponding to the bulbar units. Thus, the mechanism of olfactory discrimination at the level of the mucosa was believed to depend upon receptors that are also selectively sensitive to overlapping groups of stimuli and that would consequently respond together in different patterns to encode different odorants.

However, the hope of discovering the stimulus properties basic to olfactory discrimination by classifying together those odorants that stimulate the same neuron was never quite realized by Adrian's single-unit recordings from the bulb. Perhaps, in order to make the trends apparent, a more detailed quantification should have been made of the frequency with which each odorant stimulated a given unit. In a series of more recent papers Döving (1965, 1966a, b) has offered the necessary quantification. Every odorant he used, working with frogs, was classified as to whether it excited, inhibited, or had no effect upon a given bulbar neuron. Each odorant was then compared to every other odorant to determine whether both fell into the same or different classifications. This was repeated on many cells and a statistical analysis allowed

Döving to determine the degree to which both members of any given pair of odorants were alike in the responses they produced. For instance, in a homologous chemical series the chemicals that had nearly the same molecular weights were more likely to be classified together than those with more variant molecular weights. This suggests that it is some physical property of the molecule, rather than the chemical reactions of its functional group per se, that determines its olfactory effect.

Considering the whole spectrum of neural discharge frequencies that can be observed when a unit responds to stimulation, it may appear that Döving's three-category system is a rather gross matrix upon which to measure the similarity of odorant effects. In addition, there is some question about the precision with which the information taken from these secondary olfactory units can be extrapolated back across a rather complex synapse to explain the mechanism of discrimination by the primary receptor cells. Nevertheless, Döving's method holds much promise.

Only recently have investigators been able to record from the single receptor neurons of the olfactory mucosa (Shibuya & Shibuya, 1963; Gesteland, Lettvin, & Pitts, 1965; O´Connell & Mozell, 1969). Gesteland and his coworkers appeared to confirm Adrian's contention concerning the selective sensitivity of the receptors to overlapping groups of stimuli. However, when the chemicals were ordered according to their ability to affect the single receptor neurons, these same investigators (Lettvin & Gesteland, 1965) found that for each neuron there appeared to be a different order. This result prompted the authors to discuss the possibility of "utter chaos" where no two receptors are alike in all of their sensitivities (Gesteland, Lettvin, & Pitts, 1965). Such a system could, of course, still encode the presence of different chemicals by the pattern of activity of all the receptors to-

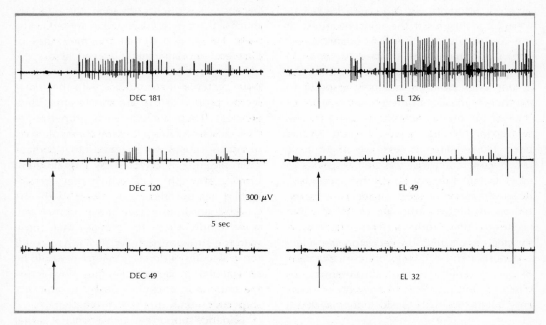

Figure 7.9. The response of a single unit in the olfactory mucosa of a frog to several concentrations of two chemicals, ethyl lactate (EL) and diethyl carbonate (DEC). Because the responses of two different units can be seen on these traces, the reader is asked to concentrate upon the unit giving the larger amplitude action potentials. It will be seen that this unit can respond to both chemicals but at a lower concentration of EL than DEC. Concentration is given in micromoles per liter. (O'Connell & Mozell, 1969.)

gether. However, this finding makes it difficult to predict which molecular properties are basic to olfactory discrimination.

Recent evidence has shown, as Lettvin and Gesteland had earlier suspected (1965), that "utter chaos" is too extreme a term to describe the responses of different units to olfactory stimuli. O'Connell and Mozell (1969) recorded the responses of a large number of single units to the same four chemicals and then ranked the chemicals according to their efficacy in exciting each unit. They found that although the rank orders were not the same for every unit, certain orders were more prevalent than others, and some theoretically possible orders were not observed at all. Thus, although not all units respond in exactly the same way to a battery of odorants, neither are they completely chaotic.

Before leaving this topic a word of caution is necessary. When we are studying the selective sensitivity of the olfactory receptors for different odorants we can easily be led to wrong conclusions if the concentrations of the chemicals are neither quantitatively known nor quantitatively varied. As shown in Figure 7.9, a unit may respond to one chemical at one concentration and may respond to another chemical at a different concentration. Thus, if the only concentration used for the unit giving the large spikes in Figure 7.9 had been 120 μM/liter or less, we might have falsely concluded that this unit responds to ethyl lactate but not to diethyl carbonate. However, as can be seen, raising the concentration of diethyl carbonate to 181 μM/liter excites the unit. Studies that try to determine the degree to which the receptors are selective must be suspect if only one concentration of each chemical is used. In summary, an olfactory unit responds to a variety of odorants, but its sensitivity to each odor may differ.

Multiunit studies Multifiber recordings from the olfactory bulb and olfactory nerve have also suggested mechanisms which, operating at the level of the mucosa, may be basic to olfactory discrimination. It was observed in the rabbit that some chemicals such as amyl acetate, ethyl acetate, and ether were more efficient in exciting the anterior part of the olfactory bulb than were other chemicals such as pentane, heptane, and coal gas; these, in contrast, were more efficient in exciting the posterior areas of the bulb (Adrian, 1950, 1953; Mozell & Pfaffmann, 1954). In addition to this spatial differentiation of odorants there was also noted a temporal differentiation, namely, the multiunit discharges to esters had shorter durations and were more abrupt in their growth and decay than were responses to hydrocarbons. Thus, in the bulb there appeared to be a spatio-temporal encoding of odorants.

In order to account for this bulbar code, Adrian (1950, 1953) reasoned that it reflects a spatio-temporal encoding of odorants that began at the level of the mucosa. He had a good anatomical basis for this contention because, as is discussed earlier, the olfactory mucosa is topographically represented in the bulb. He suggested that the molecules of different odorants might spread across the olfactory mucosa in different spatial and temporal patterns in accordance with those molecular properties that are able to affect their progress. These include such properties as their diffusion rates in air and their solubility in mucus. Later it was suggested that perhaps their progress is affected by the different binding strengths with which they are adsorbed to the receptors; those with the weakest adsorption may move farther and more rapidly across the mucosa than those with the strongest (Beidler, 1957). As a result the molecules of different odorants would be separated from each other as they move across the mucosa in a manner similar to that of a sorption column in a gas chromatograph.

Evidence supporting such a concept as that described above has been reported (Mozell, 1966). Recordings were taken from the olfactory nerve branches of frogs subserving two widely separated regions of the olfactory

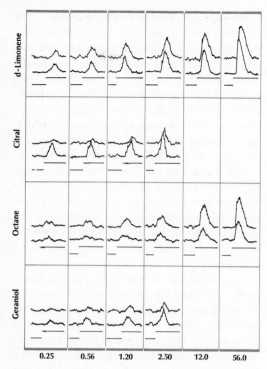

Figure 7.10. These traces are electronically summated multifiber responses taken from two frog olfactory nerve branches; the upper trace in each couplet is the response of the branch supplying the mucosal region near the internal naris and the lower trace is the response of the branch supplying the region of the external naris. The size of the trace reflects the magnitude of the multifiber discharge. This in turn reflects the magnitude of the activity occurring in that region of the mucosa which is supplied by the particular nerve branch in question. Concentration is given along the bottom in terms of the partial pressure ($\times 10^{-2}$ mm Hg). The odorants are noted along the side. The stimulus marker shows only the onset of the stimulus, but in each case the stimulus lasts 3 sec and has a volume of .4 ml. The vertical time lines occur once every 10 seconds. Note that at any given concentration the size of the upper trace relative to the size of the lower trace (that is, their ratio) differs among chemicals. Note also that the magnitude of the time lapse between the onset of the discharges on the two nerve branches likewise differs among chemicals. (Mozell, 1966.)

mucosa, one near the external naris and the other near the internal naris. (If the olfactory mucosa is conceived of as a sorption column, these two regions would be comparable to the areas around its entrance and exit respectively.) The size of the neural discharge recorded from the exit region relative to the size of the neural discharge recorded from the entrance region differed for different odorants and was found to be quite characteristic of each odorant (Figure 7.10). In addition, the time lapse between the onset of the discharges on the two nerve branches also differed for different chemicals.

When the direction of the odorant flow across the mucosa was reversed, the nerve branch that originally gave the larger discharge now gave the smaller. This result would not have been expected if the different activity patterns across the mucosa were merely reflecting a topographical gradient of receptor sensitivity to each chemical. On the other hand, this reversal of activity patterns with the reversal of flow direction is quite consistent with the gas chromatographic model; namely, as a result of their differential attraction to the media of the olfactory mucosa, the molecules of some chemicals progress more rapidly and in greater numbers along the mucosal sheet than do the molecules of other chemicals. The receptors could then simply signal these molecular movements, just as the auditory receptors signal the movements of the basilar membrane, without necessarily having any selective sensitivities of their own. It should be noted that the gas chromatographic concept of olfactory discrimination does not necessarily preclude selective sensitivity of individual receptors as an additional, superimposed mechanism for discrimination; it only precludes such sensitivity as the mechanism basic to the spatio-temporal activity patterns recorded multicellularly.

In summary, evidence is now at hand to support the possibility of two mucosal mechanisms upon which olfactory discrimination may be based: (1) a loose selective sensitivity of the receptors themselves; (2) a spatio-temporal encoding based upon the relative distribution and speed of travel of the molecules across the mucosa.

EXCITATION OF THE OLFACTORY RECEPTOR BY THE ODORANT MOLECULES

At least two tasks emerge as we try to explain how the olfactory receptor is excited: (1) we must identify the molecular property that does the triggering, and (2) we must describe the ensuing depolarization of the receptor.

Identification of the Triggering Property

At the outset one should be warned against confusing some aspects of the previously discussed process of discrimination with some similar aspects of the process of receptor excitation. It is not necessary, for instance, that the property of the molecule that triggers the receptor be the same property that is basic to its discrimination. For example, as an early step in the discrimination process, the shape of the molecule, according to one theory, may allow it to occupy only certain receptor sites, but then some other property of the molecule, which acts at all sites regardless of shape, may actually do the triggering of the receptor.

So far, attempts to identify the triggering property have not been successful. Where evidence is sparse, contradictory theories abound, of course, and this has been all too true in the study of olfaction. With varying amounts of empirical evidence and logical argument a long line of properties have been proposed as the trigger. Almost every property that chemicals possess has at one time or another been implicated. Reviews of olfaction have almost compulsively incorporated a summary of these theories (Gerebtzoff, 1953; Jones & Jones, 1953; Ottoson, 1963; Benjamin et al., 1965; Wenzel & Sieck, 1966; Moncrieff, 1967; Moulton & Beidler, 1967). Because there are so many reviews, it is only necessary here to emphasize a few points.

Theories ascribing the stimulating ability of odorants strictly to chemical properties other than enzyme action have become quite unpopular. Even enzyme theories, in reality neochemical theories, have also lost their earlier glitter. A once-popular theory hypothesized a series of enzymatically catalyzed reactions in the olfactory receptors which were supposed to be inhibited by odorants (Kistiakowsky, 1950). Although several enzymes have indeed been reported in the olfactory area (Baradi & Bourne, 1951), their relation to the olfactory process is problematical, for they are not only in receptors but also in some of the other structures of the epithelium as well; in fact, they are found throughout the body.

Special attention has been paid to intramolecular vibrations as the physical correlates of odors. Both the infrared absorption of the molecules (Beck & Miles, 1947) and their Raman shifts (Dyson, 1938) were proposed as measures of the underlying trigger property. More recently attention has been called to the low-frequency vibrations rather than the high-frequency vibrations (Wright & Michels, 1964). Although these vibrational measures have been used with some success to predict odors, several embarrassing contradictions always arose when chemicals with similar spectra smelled differently and vice versa. In addition, the infrared absorption theory has been refuted by a variety of experimental procedures and by theoretical, thermodynamic considerations (Beets, 1964).

However, Dravnieks (1964) noted that at certain frequencies the Raman spectrum is related to the dipoles of the molecules. The dipole of a molecule is related to its shape. It is also one of the properties of a chemical which would determine its selective adsorption or absorption across the mucosa. Thus, all of these properties may be correlated with each other, and it may be difficult, if not futile, to try to isolate the "basic" trigger. Each of the measures emphasized by the different theories depends upon the fundamental organization of the molecule itself, and this may account for the partial success of each of these theories in predicting the odors of chemicals. One sometimes wonders whether there is a similarity between the factions supporting these different theories and the proverbial six blind men who happened to feel different parts of the same elephant and hence "saw" the same animal in six different ways.

Receptor Depolarization

At some point along the chain of events that begins with the impingement of the necessary molecular property upon the receptor and culminates in the propagation of action potentials along the primary olfactory axon, the molecular energy involved must be transduced into electrical energy. In many other sensory systems this transduction has been shown to involve a sustained depolarization of the receptor, called the *generator potential*. These generator potentials increase in amplitude with increasing stimulus intensity. Their most important attribute is that they provide the immediate drive for the development of action potentials. The generally accepted explanation is that a sustained depolarization of the receptor membrane brings about a potential difference between the receptor and the axon which in turn results in a current flow from the receptor, through the cell, and out through the axon membrane. This outward flowing current depolarizes the axon membrane, and when a certain threshold level of depolarization is reached, an action potential is produced. As the generator potential grows so does the current density depolarizing the axon, and consequently the axon's firing rate increases (see Chapter 4, pp. 95–99).

A potential change, which has many of the characteristics of a classical generator potential, has been recorded with electrodes placed directly upon or in the mucosa (Ottoson, 1956). When odorous air is puffed onto the surface, a slow, negative, potential shift can then be recorded. (The record of this potential shift has been named the electro-olfactogram

[the EOG]. See page 114.) It has been suggested that it is actually the summation of many small generator potentials produced by many single olfactory receptors. However, the work of several authors has cast some doubt upon the role of the EOG as a generator potential. It has been observed that under certain conditions the EOG and the action potentials do not parallel each other as one would expect if the former generated the latter. For example, repeated stimulation reduced the magnitude of the EOG, but the magnitude of the neural discharge was not reduced. More cogent is the observation that by removing a piece of absorbent filter paper which had been placed on the mucosa, one could obliterate the EOG but not the neural response (Shibuya, 1964). This would be quite unexpected if the EOG is really needed to generate the action potentials.

How seriously these studies should be taken as evidence for denying that the EOG is a reflection of olfactory generator potentials is still debatable. Indeed, for the most part, the EOG and neural discharge are well correlated. In addition, because the EOG is recorded extracellularly in volume, changes in the direction of current flow may greatly reduce its magnitude as recorded by the electrodes. Therefore, local damage (caused by removing filter paper, for example) may short-circuit these currents in such a way that the EOG will no longer be detected by the electrodes even though they may still be present.

Gesteland and his coworkers (1965) believe that the EOG does, indeed, represent many generator potentials, but they have shown that the EOG includes positive potential shifts as well as the negative ones. Using the Hodgkin-Huxley formulation of the nature of the nerve impulse, Gesteland suggested that the odorant molecules depolarize the receptor by increasing its permeability to sodium ions. The resulting inward flowing current, recorded as a negative shift, is one side of the circuit which is completed by outward flowing current at the axon. By analogy to the crustacean stretch receptor (Kuffler & Eyza-guirre, 1955) the positive shift in potential was interpreted as an increase in the permeability to outward flow of potassium ions. This shunts the current through the receptor rather than allowing it to pass through the axon, thus, presumably, reducing the production of action potentials.

Although most authors of olfactory theories are quite explicit in designating a particular molecular property as the trigger, they are far less explicit when they try to describe just how this property alters the receptor membrane so that sodium ions can enter the receptor and thus depolarize it. An exception is Davies (1965) who suggested that a molecule adsorbed to the receptor membrane leaves a hole through which ions may flow when it is desorbed. It should be obvious to the reader that our knowledge concerning the excitation of the olfactory receptor by the odorant molecule is abysmally meager.

Willard R. Thurlow

AUDITION

8

The general term "audition" may appear somewhat abstract. To clarify the term, we shall list here some of the questions we shall try to answer in this chapter.

How well can we detect auditory signals?

In what ways does our auditory system fail to be a perfect "high-fidelity" analyzer of signals that are put into it?

How much do loud sounds interfere with our hearing and annoy us?

How are we able to make judgments of musical pitch and of loudness?

What cues are of importance in enabling us to discriminate different speech sounds? Can intelligible speech sounds be synthesized from these cues?

How do we localize sound sources? How well can blind people locate objects by means of echoes? (Bats and porpoises can use echoes. Can people?)

Before we can deal effectively with the questions posed above, we must review the characteristics of auditory stimuli—characteristics you will need to know about (if you do not already) to understand experiments we describe later on in the chapter. Then we will discuss "basic biological mechanisms" of the auditory system. These mechanisms are not only of great interest in themselves, but furnish important clues to how

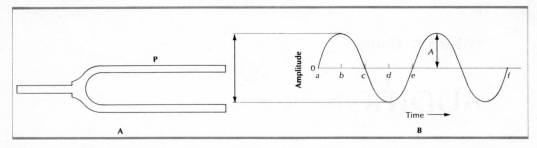

Figure 8.1. A. Tuning fork. B. Limits of the up-and-down vibration of prong P shown, in enlarged view, by vertical arrows. Sine-wave motion of P is also shown as it vibrates in time.

people react to sounds (as you will note in later sections of the chapter).

THE AUDITORY STIMULUS

The auditory stimulus is produced by some vibrating object, which causes vibrations in the surrounding medium (typically air). Finally, the vibrations of the air molecules cause the eardrum of the observer to vibrate.

A simple type of vibration, shown for example by a vibrating tuning fork, is called *simple sine-wave motion*. Figure 8.1 shows a tuning fork, with the limits of the displacement of prong P amplified and indicated by the vertical arrows. If we photographed this motion with a moving-picture camera, we could then plot out how the displacement of the prong varies with time after it is set into vibration. We would obtain a graph as shown in Figure 8.1B. This graph portrays what can be described mathematically as a sine function.

The graph shows that the prong starts from rest (time *a*), moves in an upward direction until it comes to rest (time *b*), moves back to the starting position (time *c*), then moves in a downward direction until it comes to rest (time *d*), and then moves back to the starting position (time *e*). By this time it has finished one complete *cycle* of motion and is ready to start another similar cycle. The frequency of vibration is defined as the number of such cycles of vibration per second. (The abbreviation cps is often used for cycles per second; or Hz, an abbreviation for *Hertz*.)

The vibrating tuning fork causes the surrounding air molecules to vibrate, and the amplitude of their vibration can also be shown to be a sine wave. The variation in pressure from moment to moment at any point in the surrounding air is also a sine-wave function, and so the variations in air pressure that push our eardrum back and

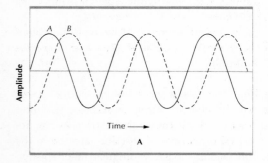

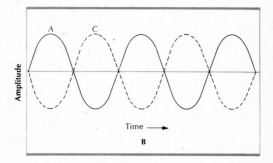

Figure 8.2. A. Diagram of 2 sine waves, *A* and *B*, which differ in phase by a quarter of a cycle. B. Two sine waves that differ in phase by half a cycle.

forth cause the eardrum to move in a simple sinusoidal function. The magnitude of variations in pressure at the eardrum will obviously be related to the amplitude of movement of the prong of the tuning fork back and forth. The letter *A* in Figure 8.1B designates the amplitude of the displacement of the prong of the tuning fork from its rest position.

In order to specify such a simple auditory stimulus adequately, we need to specify not only the frequency, and amount of sound pressure variation, but also the *phase* of the sound wave. Figure 8.2A portrays 2 sine waves, *A* and *B*. Sine wave *B* starts upward from the baseline a quarter of a cycle later than wave *A*; it is said to lag by one-quarter cycle. Often, the phase difference is expressed in terms of degrees, where 360 degrees equals one full cycle. A lag of one-quarter cycle then would be $(\frac{1}{4})$ (360), or 90 degrees. In Figure 8.2B, wave *C* is 180 degrees out of phase with wave *A*. In this case, wave *C* is said to have the "reverse" phase of wave *A*.

The characteristics of a sound-wave stimulus in air can be determined by placing a microphone in the sound field. The *frequency* of the stimulus can be determined by leading the electrical output of the microphone to an electronic counter, which can count the number of cycles per second with great accuracy. If the microphone has been calibrated, it is possible to compute from the voltage of the electrical output from the microphone the sound pressure produced at the location of the microphone in space. The computed sound pressure (actually a measure of amount of pressure change associated with vibrations of the air molecules) is typically expressed as the number of *decibels* above some reference level. The pressure reference level most commonly used is .0002 dynes per square centimeter. The formula for calculating the number of decibels is

$$N_{dB} = 20 \log_{10}\frac{p_1}{p_0}$$

where p_1 is the sound pressure we are trying to describe in terms of decibels, p_0 is the

reference pressure (such as .0002 dyn/cm²), and *N* is the number of decibels. (Decibels are often expressed in the notation, dB re .0002 dyn/cm².) From the formula it can be seen that a sound 10 times the reference pressure corresponds to 20 dB [because 20 $\log_{10}$ (10) = 20]. A sound 100 times the reference pressure corresponds to 40 dB [because 20 $\log_{10}$ (100) = 40]. In other words, for each successive multiplication of sound pressure by a factor of 10, we add 20 dB. Because, in a plane sound wave, energy, *E*, is proportional to the square of pressure, number of decibels can also be calculated from the energy ratio by the formula:

$$N_{dB} = 20 \log_{10}\frac{p_1}{p_0} = 10 \log_{10}\frac{(p_1)^2}{(p_0)^2}$$
$$= 10 \log\frac{E_1}{E_0}$$

E_0 would usually be taken as 10^{-16} watt per square centimeter.

To gain a more concrete idea of the dB scale (when the reference pressure is .0002 dyn/cm²), note that a tone of 1000 Hz reaches threshold at about zero dB; ordinary conversation averages about 60 dB; and sounds become painful to many listeners when the sound pressure reaches 120 to 130 dB.

Simple sine-wave stimuli used in the laboratory are typically produced as electrical sine-wave stimuli by an instrument known as an oscillator. The electrical sine wave then is led through an attenuator, which can be used to decrease the voltage of the signal in decibel steps. From the attenuator the signal passes through an electrical transformer to the subject's earphone. If the attenuator is properly matched to the oscillator and transformer in its electrical impedance characteristics, then a change of *N* dB in the voltage of the electrical signal produces a change of *N* dB in the sound pressure produced by the earphone in the ear canal of the subject. It is thus possible in many experiments to specify the auditory stimulus to be used in terms of the number of dB of sound pressure above the absolute threshold of the subject. This measure is defined as the *sensation level*. For example, if the average threshold setting on the attenuator for the subject is 90 dB for a 1000 Hz stimulus, and we wish to use a 1000 Hz tone at 40 dB above threshold in the experiment, we would set the attenuator at a 50 dB reading (90 minus 40). The stimulus then would be at a sensation level of 40 dB. It is important to note that the attenuator setting gives the ratio, in dB, by which the tone has been weakened (attenuated) in sound pressure. It does not indicate the amount of sound pressure directly.

Specifying the sound pressure produced by the earphone may be preferred unless there is some reason to believe that the phenomenon being investigated is more a function of sensation level than of sound pressure level. With suitable equipment, it is possible to measure the sound pressure level at the eardrum of the subject by means of a probe tube. Alternatively (and with less difficulty) if a specification of pressure produced for an average ear is sufficient, it is possible to measure the output of the earphone in a coupler (or cavity), in which the pressure produced is similar to that produced at the entrance to the ear canal of an average ear. The pressure measured in such a coupler is not exactly the same as that which would be produced at the eardrum of the subject. Pollack (1949) has gathered together data showing relations between pressure measurements made in various ways; he includes data showing the relation between sound pressure produced at the eardrum (for an average ear) by an earphone, and sound pressure produced in a 6 cubic centimeter coupler by that earphone.

You may wonder why we have been talking about using an earphone in laboratory experiments rather than a loudspeaker. It is certainly possible to use a loudspeaker, but in this case the prediction of what sound pressure will reach the ear of the listener is considerably complicated because of reflections of the sound from the walls, floor, and ceiling

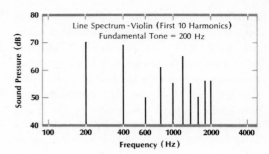

Figure 8.3. First 10 frequency components in a violin tone. (Davis & Silverman, 1960; after Fletcher, 1946.)

of the room. (The term *reverberation* is used to refer to the presence of such reflected sounds in a room.) Furthermore, slight changes in the position of the subject's head may result in sizable changes in sound pressure.

In order to avoid these difficulties, some psychologists use an *anechoic* room, which means a room free of reflection from the walls, floor, and ceiling. These rooms are typically constructed with large wedges of fiberglass mounted on all surfaces in such a way that they absorb practically all of the sound which strikes them. Thus the stimulus used in such a room is not complicated by additional reflected sound waves.

So far we have talked about only simple sine-wave stimuli. Obviously, we can use more complex stimuli. It is possible to analyze complex sounds that have a recurring wave pattern into component frequencies. Instruments for accomplishing this are called wave analyzers.

Figure 8.3 shows the first 10 frequency components in a violin tone. For this complex musical stimulus, the fundamental or lowest tone is 200 Hz, but there are additional frequencies called *harmonics* at multiples of the fundamental (400, 600, 800, and so on).

Not all complex sounds have their frequency components arranged as simple multiples of the lowest frequency.

"Thermal" noise (or "white" noise) is often used in the laboratory as a masking stimulus. To get an idea of what white noise sounds like, say "sh." The "sh" sound is not perfectly "white," that is, certain frequencies have greater energies than others. The thermal noise produced in the laboratory, however, can be thought of as being composed of an infinite number of different frequencies of the same amplitude with no systematic relation between the phases of the components. It is often desirable (as in masking experiments) to produce the thermal noise in restricted frequency regions. Typically we may use low-pass, high-pass, or band-pass noise. For example, we could use 1000 Hz, low-pass noise, that is noise with frequencies only below 1000 Hz, or 1000–2000 band-pass noise with frequencies in the band of 1000–2000 Hz only. It should be noted that the transition from frequencies that do pass the filter to frequencies that do not pass is never perfectly sharp. It is necessary to refer to the description of filters in any given experiment to find what the precise nature of the transition is.

The intensity of noise, in regions of uniform average amplitude, is often expressed in terms of intensity per cycle, or "spectrum level." This figure is obtained by dividing the total intensity measured over a given frequency band by the size of the frequency band in cycles. The resulting intensity can then be expressed in decibels.

For certain complex sounds it may be very important to take into account not only the

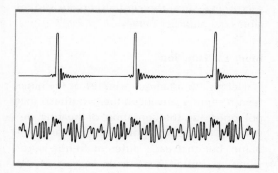

Figure 8.4. Wave forms of 2 sound stimuli with components of the same frequency and amplitude but different phases. (Bergeijk, Pierce, & David, 1960.)

frequency components and the amplitude of each, but also phase relations. Particularly we should examine the total stimulus to see whether it has a pulselike character. Figure 8.4 shows the wave forms for two complex sounds. Each is composed of 32 component sine waves. The frequencies and the intensities of the components are the same for the two sounds, but the phase relations are different. The sound shown in the upper part of the figure has a pulselike character and is perceived by the listener as harsher, somewhat louder, and of lower pitch than the sound shown in the lower part of the figure.

BASIC BIOLOGICAL MECHANISMS IN HEARING

The Auditory Receptive Apparatus

Figure 8.5 shows a semidiagrammatic representation of the ear structures. Sound enters the external auditory canal and sets the ear drum in motion. The vibrations are transferred by the bones of the middle ear (malleus, incus, and stapes) to the fluid of the inner ear or *cochlea*. Figure 8.6 shows how these three middle ear bones (in black) are displaced as sound pressure pushes the drum membrane in. Figure 8.6 also shows a diagram of the inner ear or cochlea "unrolled." (The fluid-filled ducts of the inner ear are actually arranged in a spiral, like the passages in a snail's shell, but for purposes of visualization it is convenient to portray these ducts as straightened out.) The third of the middle ear bones, the stapes, conducts vibrations into a duct or tube called the *scala vestibuli*. A membrane at the *oval window* to which the stapes is attached, allows the stapes to vibrate. When the stapes is pushed in (see Figure 8.6), pressure is exerted through the *scala media* and *scala tympani,* and pushes out a flexible membrane in another opening to the middle ear, the *round window*.

A cross section of these ducts (scala vestibuli, scala media, and scala tympani) is shown in Figure 8.7. The scala vestibuli and scala tympani are filled with a fluid called *peri-*

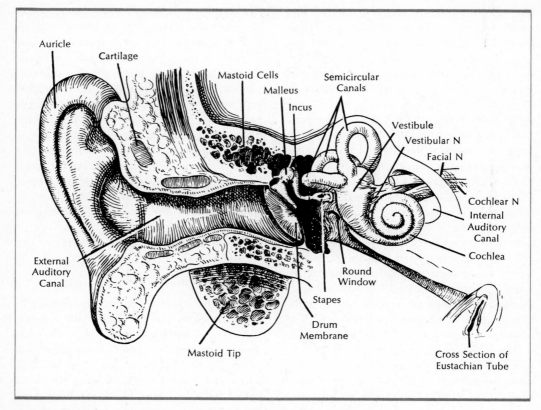

Figure 8.5. A semidiagrammatic drawing of the ear. (Davis & Silverman, 1960.)

lymph, and the scala media is filled with *endolymph.* The inner and outer *hair cells* sit on the *basilar membrane* which is pushed up and down by pressure variations caused by the vibrating stapes. The hair cells are the receptors for auditory stimuli and are stimulated by movements of the basilar membrane. Nerve fibers of the spiral ganglion are connected to the hair cells, and when fired off send signals into the central nervous system along the auditory nerve.

Inner Ear Function

Helmholtz, a famous scientist of the nineteenth century, advanced the hypothesis that not only was the sensation of hearing dependent on the vibration of the basilar membrane, but that each different frequency of vibration caused a particular region of the basilar membrane to vibrate. This theory is known as a "place" theory of frequency analysis. (See Wever [1949] for a review of early hearing theories.)

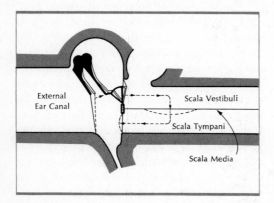

Figure 8.6. Schematic diagram of middle ear bones, and ducts (or scalae) of inner ear. (Modified from Stevens & Davis, 1938.)

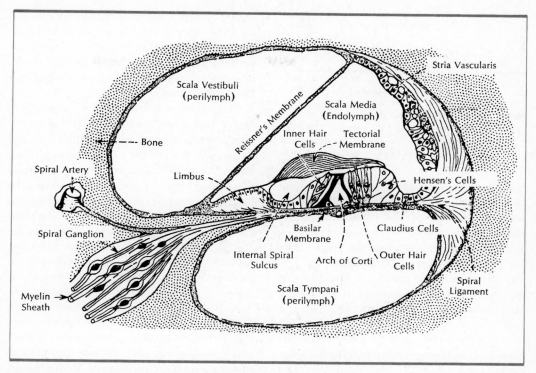

Figure 8.7. Schematic cross section of some details of the ducts of the inner ear. (Flanagan, 1965; adapted from Davis, 1957.)

In more recent years von Békésy (see von Békésy and Rosenblith, 1951) has made direct observations of the displacements of the membranes of the inner ear. These observations had to be made with the aid of a microscope. Measurement of the amplitude of the vibration of the transparent membranes was made possible by scattering tiny light-reflecting crystals of silver over the membranes. Von Békésy was able to show that the basilar membrane was not under tension as Helmholtz had supposed. He showed, however, that it did vary systematically in *stiffness.* (Stiffness is inversely related to the volume of fluid displaced by the membrane when a given pressure difference is exerted across it.) The stiffness was greatest in the portion of the basilar membrane nearest the stapes end of the membrane. Furthermore, he was able to show by means of a model (von Békésy, 1956) that variation in *stiffness* of the membrane and the degree of *coupling* between adjacent portions of the membrane determined the pattern of vibrations produced by the membrane of the model. (No coupling would correspond in the model to having separate elastic fibers side by side, not connected to each other; the strands in the model could be coupled by applying a thin sheet of rubber over the whole set of fibers. Coupling could be increased by increasing the thickness of the rubber sheet.) When the stiffness and the coupling of the membrane of the model were made the same as that which had been measured on the basilar membrane of animal and human ears, the pattern of vibration to a tone shown by the model was the same as that shown by the basilar membrane: There was a *travelling wave* which proceeded down the basilar membrane from the stapes end. Perhaps most important, the maximum amplitude of this wave occurred at *different places* along the basilar membrane for different frequencies of

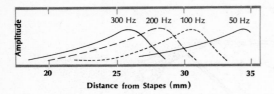

Figure 8.8. Amplitude of displacement of the basilar membrane at various distances from the stapes for several frequencies of stimulation. (von Békésy, 1947.)

tone. Figure 8.8 shows the relative amplitude of displacement of the human basilar membrane for frequencies of stimulation of 50, 100, 200, and 300 Hz as a function of distance along the membrane from the stapes. The higher the frequency of stimulation, the further the location of maximum displacement moves toward the stapes end of the basilar membrane. Thus it is evident that there is a "place" analysis of frequency. (Dr. von Békésy received the Nobel prize in 1961 for his discoveries concerning the dynamics of the inner ear.)

Electrical Potentials of the Inner Ear

Wever and Bray (1930) discovered an electrical potential in the vicinity of the inner ear which followed the input stimulus in frequency. At first this potential ("cochlear microphonic") was thought to be from the auditory nerve, but later work clearly differentiated it from the nerve potentials (Stevens & Davis, 1938). The wave form of the cochlear microphonic tends to be very similar to that of the stimulus, while that of the nerve response is a brief "spike" potential which occurs only at a certain phase of the stimulating wave. The nerve potential is much more affected by anesthetics.

Further experiments, in which potentials were recorded as a microelectrode was pushed slowly up through the basilar membrane, indicated that the principal source of cochlear microphonics was near the boundary between scala media and structures on the basilar membrane (von Békésy, 1952a; Tasaki, Davis, & Eldredge, 1954; Lawrence,

1965). Evidence gathered earlier had associated the hair cells with production of microphonics—for injury to the cells by loud noise or by drugs had been found to lead to depression of cochlear microphonics (Stevens & Davis, 1938; Davis, 1960).

The cochlear microphonic response from the normal internal ear of an animal can be used as an index to study the effect of modifications in the middle ear conduction apparatus (Wever & Lawrence, 1954). Thus variables important in human conduction hearing loss can be studied. The microphonic can also be used as an electrical indicator of mechanical wave motion taking place in the inner ear (Tasaki, Davis, & Legouix, 1952; Teas, Eldredge, & Davis, 1962). It is presumed that the electrical microphonic triggers off the nerve impulses in the auditory nerve. However, there is no direct proof of this hypothesis yet.

Other potentials have been found within the cochlea (see Wever, 1966). A steady positive potential has been observed to exist in the scala media (von Békésy, 1952b; Tasaki, Davis, & Eldredge, 1954). It is as if there were a direct current ("d.c.") battery located in the scala media. The source of this potential has been identified (Davis, 1960) as the *stria vascularis* (see Figure 8.7)—a structure in the scala media. There are also steady negative potentials in and near the cells on the basilar membrane. The relations of the positive and negative steady potentials to the cochlear microphonic and to the nerve impulse are not yet fully worked out.

Potentials Recorded in the Auditory Nervous System

Differential response to stimulus frequency One method of recording electrical activity from nerve fibers and cells of the auditory nervous system involves use of a microelectrode, the tip of which is of the order of 1 μ in diameter. In a pioneering study, Galambos and Davis (1943) recorded from single cells of the *cochlear nucleus* of the cat. The cochlear nucleus is the first nucleus in the brain stem to which fibers of the

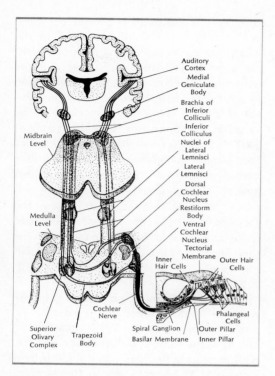

Figure 8.9. A simplified diagram of the ascending auditory pathways. (Flanagan, 1965; adapted from drawings by Netter.)

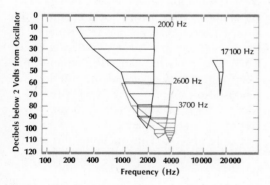

Figure 8.10. The "response areas" obtained from four separate neural units in the cochlear nucleus of the cat. The vertical scale shows how much attenuation was required at each frequency to produce just a threshold response in each unit. Note that a large number on the vertical scale represents a weak intensity tone, and a small number represents a strong intensity tone. (Galambos & Davis, 1943.)

auditory (or cochlear) nerve connect (see Figure 8.9). Galambos and Davis found that each cell was most sensitive to a narrow band of frequencies, though it responded to other frequencies when these were presented at higher intensity. Figure 8.10 shows the triangle-shaped "response areas" they obtained. For instance, in recording from a cell that was most sensitive to tones having frequencies near 2000 Hz, the response area labelled "2000 Hz" on the graph was obtained. The graph shows that it took the least amount of sound pressure (the greatest attenuation of the signal) to produce a threshold response (minimal firing of the cell) when a stimulus of 2000 Hz was used. Frequencies higher and lower than this, however, required more sound pressure in order to produce a threshold response in this cell. The other "response areas" in Figure 8.10 represent cells most sensitive to frequencies in the region of 2600, 3700 and 17,100 Hz. More recent experiments (see Rasmussen & Windle, 1960; Katsuki, 1961) have found cells at various higher levels of the auditory nervous system—inferior colliculus, medial geniculate body, auditory cortex (Figure 8.9)—with response areas for both low and high stimulus frequencies, of the same general shape as those found in the cochlear nucleus. Single nerve fibers in the cochlear nerve also show such "response areas" (Katsuki, 1961). These "response areas" have a much sharper peak than would be expected on the basis of the mechanical analysis of frequencies in the inner ear. The mechanisms by which this "sharpening" is accomplished are not yet fully understood. Von Békésy (1967) and Huggins and Licklider (1951) have discussed several possible mechanisms.

We would infer from the systematic "place" analysis of frequency in the inner ear—where the maximum displacement takes place at a position progressively nearer the stapes as the frequency of stimulation is raised—that there might be a systematic arrangement of cells in the auditory nervous system, so that cells sensitive to progressively higher frequencies would be arranged in

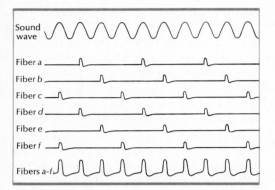

Figure 8.11. Schematic diagram of the volley principle. At this particular stimulus intensity, each nerve fiber is portrayed as firing at every third cycle of the stimulating wave. The combined action of many such fibers produces a summed response (represented at bottom) which is synchronized with the stimulus frequency. (Wever, 1949.)

some linear array from low to high. Evidence has been found for such "tonotopic" organization (Rose, 1960; Tunturi, 1960; Woolsey, 1960; Rose et al., 1963). These results indicate clearly that a possible cue for distinguishing one frequency from another is the difference in the *place* at which the disturbance due to each frequency occurs in the nervous system.

Another *possible* cue for discriminating low frequencies is the rate at which the nerve impulses are discharged (Wever & Bray, 1930). If we make records with a larger size electrode (larger than a microelectrode), from the auditory nerve, the recorded potentials reflect the action of a large number of nerve fibers. It has been found that if a low-frequency stimulating tone is used, nerve impulses occur at a certain phase of the stimulating wave. A volley of nerve impulses occurs once for each cycle of the stimulating wave. As the stimulating frequency is raised, the individual nerve fibers cannot fire at each cycle because of the refractory period of the fiber. However, a given fiber may fire every second cycle, or every third cycle. Figure 8.11 shows schematically how volleys of impulses are produced at each cycle and how they are synchronized

with the stimulus tone. As a result, the number of volleys per second is equal to the number of cycles per second in the stimulating tone. Recent studies of single auditory nerve fibers (see Rose et al., 1967) have shown in great detail that the response of the individual auditory nerve fiber is "locked" to the cycles of the stimulating wave up to at least 5000 cycles per second. (The upper frequency limit is lower in higher centers of the auditory nervous system.) By "locked" we mean that a nerve impulse occurs only at a certain portion of the cycle of the stimulating wave; and time intervals between successive nerve impulses are equal to, or some multiple of, the time necessary for one cycle of the stimulating wave.

Complex influences on neural response
At lower levels in the auditory nervous system, the typical neural unit continues to fire as long as the stimulation continues, and fires with increasing frequency as the intensity is increased. At higher levels in the auditory system, relations of responses to the stimulus may be less simple. For instance, at the cerebral cortex, some units respond when the tonal stimulation comes on, or when it ceases (Galambos, 1960; Hind, 1960). Some units respond to a small *change* in frequency or intensity (Galambos, 1960; Whitfield & Evans, 1965). Sensitivity to change in frequency has been noted at the level of the inferior colliculus also (Thurlow et al., 1951; Grinnell & McCue, 1963; Nelson, Erulkar, & Bryan, 1966). Ability to detect change in stimulation is probably important in order for the animal to respond to sounds in the natural environment.

A good deal of interest has been excited in recent years by experiments showing that attentional variables can modify the magnitude of responses in the nervous system to auditory (and other) stimuli. For example, certain cells in the auditory cortex respond only when the animal's attention is directed to the source of sound (Hubel et al., 1959). Some components in the human cortical response to clicks are greater when the subject pays attention to the clicks (Spong, Haider, & Lindsley, 1965).

What causes the neural response to change in magnitude? We do not know precisely. We do know, however, that the reticular activating system, which is involved in changing states of arousal of the organism, can affect the size of cortical responses to acoustic stimuli (Desmedt, 1960; Bremer, 1961). Some of these effects can be inhibitory. (By an *inhibitory effect*, we mean an effect in which a given response is decreased from what it was originally.)

Another kind of important inhibitory effect occurs very early in the input to the auditory nervous system. One tone can inhibit the firing of an auditory nerve fiber to another tone (Sachs & Kiang, 1967).

A whole system of "efferent" inhibitory mechanisms has been discovered, which may involve control of sensitivity to sound (Rasmussen, 1960; Desmedt, 1962; Rossi & Cortesina, 1965). One of these "efferent" control mechanisms involves nerve connections that come from the cerebral cortex and extend to the cochlear nucleus. When these fibers are stimulated electrically, they inhibit, or block,

responses in the cochlear nucleus to auditory stimuli. Another set of inhibitory fibers (believed to be part of the same general system) travels from the olivary nucleus back down to the cochlea. Electrical stimulation of these fibers causes a decrease in the response of the auditory nerve to acoustic stimuli. Fex (1962) has shown that the olivo-cochlear nerve fibers can be activated by sound. The role of the stapedius and tensor tympani muscles in decreasing responses to sounds of high intensity is discussed below (page 236).

DETECTABILITY THRESHOLDS

Sensitivity to Stimuli of Different Frequency

Figure 8.12 shows the minimum audible pressure (in dB above .0002 dyn/cm^2) necessary for threshold at frequencies from 125 to 8000 Hz. The data combine the results from a number of studies, reviewed by the International Organization for Standardization (ISO), that evaluate the thresholds of normal human hearing. Young adults who showed no signs of disease of the auditory system served as subjects; listening conditions were optimal. The human auditory system is extremely sensitive, for in the most sensitive frequency region, the displacement of the eardrum at threshold is considerably less than the diameter of a hydrogen molecule (Stevens & Davis, 1938).

Many studies show that the pressure required at very high frequencies rises rapidly (Licklider, 1951). Some young people can hear frequencies up to about 24,000 Hz (Wever, 1949; Corso, 1967). Most cannot hear frequencies that high. However, if vibrations with a high intensity are applied to the mastoid bone of the head, subjects can perceive a high-pitch sound at much higher stimulus frequencies (Corso, 1963).

The hearing of low frequencies by humans has been recorded down to a few cycles per second (Corso, 1958). More and more sound pressure is required as frequency is lowered.

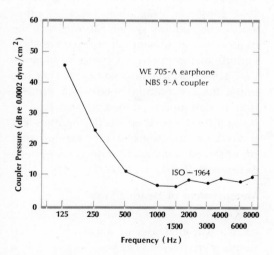

Figure 8.12. Minimum audible pressure for absolute threshold of hearing, as a function of stimulus frequency. (Davis & Krantz, 1964.)

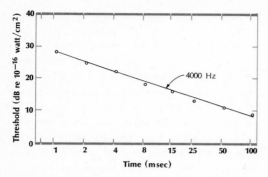

Figure 8.13. Threshold intensity required to hear a 4000 Hz tone as a function of duration of the tone. (Garner, 1947b.)

Summation Effects at Threshold

Numerous studies have shown that, as is the case for other senses (see pp. 136, 303, and 306), the auditory system appears to be capable of temporal summation, in which the effects of a stimulus are added up over short periods of time (Zwislocki, 1960). Figure 8.13 shows that less energy is required for threshold as the duration of a tonal stimulus (4000 Hz) is increased. At longer durations (near .2 seconds) the curve would become parallel with the baseline. The equation $(I - I_0)(t) = K$, a constant, has been found to fit the data (Garner & Miller, 1947; Olsen & Carhart, 1966). I represents the intensity of the stimulus; I_0 represents a constant minimal intensity, and t represents time. (It is of course necessary to specify the largest value for t within which the equation holds.) You can think of I_0 as being the very small stimulus intensity of a tone which, even if continued forever, will not produce an effect beyond the small residual noise present in the auditory system. Any excess in intensity over I_0 will lead to proportionate neural effects that will be summed up over time by the auditory system. A constant total effect is required to reach the subject's criterion for threshold. If the experimenter obtains detection with a stimulus intensity I_1 at duration t_1, and then doubles the stimulus duration (t_1), he only needs to use half as large a value of $(I_1 - I_0)$ to obtain the same total neural effect required for threshold. The equation above tells us that the product of the intensity and time factors again will be equal to K:

$$\frac{I_1 - I_0}{2} (2t_1) = K$$

The simple type of relation described above is not obtained for all stimuli. The energy in a pure tone spreads out increasingly into other frequency regions as the duration is made shorter (Garner, 1947b). If these regions have markedly different sensitivities, the neural effect will not be so easily predictable. Another complication arises from the fact that maximum summation effects occur only when the frequency components in a complex stimulus are not separated very much from each other (Scharf, 1961). They must be contained within a "critical band" of frequencies. If, at very short durations, the stimulus energy of a tone spreads out beyond the critical band, then it is not integrated perfectly. Thus there may be a *lower* duration limit for perfect integration as well as an upper duration limit (Sheeley, 1964).

Temporal summation can also be shown to take place when a series of bursts of tone or noise is presented (Garner, 1947a; Harris, 1958; Zwislocki, 1960; Small, 1963a). In other words, the auditory system can summate the effects of stimuli even when there are short periods of time between bursts of stimulation. However, the summation effect is less under these conditions than when stimulation is continuous, apparently because of dissipation of neural effects during the silent periods. Theories to explain the various types of observed summation effect have been developed (Zwislocki, 1960).

Measurement of Hearing Loss

A pure-tone *audiometer* is calibrated in such a way that *loss* in sensitivity to each frequency in decibels can be determined with respect to normal hearing. [It has been recommended by the International Organization for Standardization that "normal" hearing be defined in terms of the data of Figure 8.12 (Davis & Krantz, 1964).] Tests of the ability to recognize speech (which we discuss in a later section) are also used to evaluate the degree of hearing loss. They are especially valuable in supplementing the pure-tone threshold tests because threshold tone tests do not always indicate completely the degree of impairment present. For example, some patients do fairly well with tones, but very poorly when asked to discriminate speech sounds at above-threshold levels (Hirsh, 1955; Davis & Silverman, 1960). Patients with cerebral damage may often have trouble in integrating and understanding minimal speech cues presented to both ears simultaneously (Bocca & Calearo, 1963).

In order to test very young children, nonverbal indicators of hearing have been developed (Davis & Silverman, 1960; Jerger, 1963). Some of these depend upon the conditioning of a response to tonal stimuli. At the present time there is considerable research being done to explore the possibilities of utilizing electrical brain potentials, recorded from the scalp and averaged by a computer (Davis & Zerlin, 1966; Ward, 1966; Davis et al., 1967).

SOME HARMFUL EFFECTS OF LOUD SOUNDS

In discussing measurements of auditory threshold, we have just been describing measurement of hearing loss. It seems appropriate now to turn to a discussion of the harmful effects of loud sounds—effects ranging from annoyance to permanent loss of hearing.

Temporary Threshold Shift (TTS)

Although many studies have been carried out to investigate the effects of continued auditory stimulation on various kinds of auditory discrimination (see Small, 1963b), perhaps most interest has centered on the effects of continued stimulation on auditory threshold. Probably this interest has arisen from

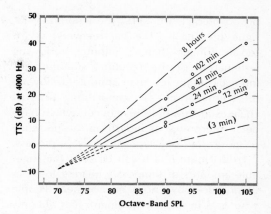

Figure 8.14. Temporary threshold shift (TTS) as a function of sound pressure level and duration of octave-band noise (1200–2400 Hz). (Ward, Glorig, & Sklar, 1959.)

concern with the possibility of permanent hearing loss.

The effects of brief prior stimulation on auditory threshold disappear rapidly; terms such as "residual masking" and "short-duration fatigue" have been used to categorize these effects (Small, 1963b; Ward, 1963). We present some data on residual masking later in the chapter.

Longer durations of exposure with higher intensity stimuli lead to cumulative effects, which have been generally referred to as "temporary threshold shift" (TTS). The amount of TTS produced is a complex function of such variables as the intensity and duration of the stimulation, the duration of intervals between exposures, and stimulus frequency. Despite this complexity, considerable progress has been made in working out predictions of the amount of TTS to be expected as a result of certain types of stimulation. Figure 8.14, for instance, shows the amount of threshold shift measured 2 minutes after a fatiguing noise stimulus was terminated (TTS_2). It is apparent that there is a lawful relation between intensity level of the fatiguing stimulus and TTS_2. The effect produced is also systematically related to the duration of the fatiguing stimulus. TTS_2 is a useful index of fatigue produced because it is possible to predict from TTS$_2$ the amount of fatigue present (as the ear recovers) at intervals longer than 2 minutes following termination of the fatiguing stimulus. For intervals of time less than 2 minutes following the termination of stimulation, unusual changes in threshold may occur, which have been interpreted as indicating the presence of more than one type of recovery process.

From Figure 8.14 it can be seen that sizeable amounts of temporary hearing loss can be produced by a noisy environment. People who work in such environments may not only suffer large elevations of thresholds after a day's work, but may suffer permanent loss of hearing if exposed daily to high noise levels for long periods of time without protection for their ears. It is possible to predict the amount of permanent hearing loss that would be produced by daily exposure for about 10 years to a sound, from the TTS$_2$ produced by this sound (Nixon & Glorig, 1961). Making use of this relationship, as well as other data, it has been possible to set up "damage risk contours" for certain noises (Kryter, 1963; Kryter et al., 1966). These contours state the levels of the steady noises which, if exceeded, will lead eventually to significant hearing loss. Much further work remains to be done in improving the accuracy of prediction of hearing loss produced by different types of sound, and different durations of exposure, as well as in predicting individual differences in susceptibility to hearing loss (see Ward, 1969).

Two muscles, which modify the action of the chain of middle-ear bones, are capable of providing significant protection to the ear, particularly against low-frequency sounds: the *stapedius* muscle, attached to the stapes, and the *tensor tympani* muscle, attached to the malleus. High-intensity sounds cause contraction of these muscles, which in turn decreases the intensity of sound transmitted to the inner ear. In man, the stapedius muscle may have the more important protective action (Jepsen, 1963). These muscles have a latency (or reaction time) to sound stimulation of about 10 msec. On a firing range, pro-

tection against shock waves can be given, however, by presenting a tone just prior to the firing of the gun. The tone elicits the muscle reflex and helps to protect the ear from the noise-impact of the gun (Fletcher & Riopelle, 1960).

Annoyance of Noise, "Annoisance"

If the sound pressure level of a tone is high enough, it will produce unpleasant reactions in the listener. It has been found that subjects can reliably judge the degree of "noisiness" of various noises and that the degree of noisiness can be predicted ahead of time from the intensity level of the various frequency components of the noise, and the duration of the noise (Kryter & Pearsons, 1963). Predicted values of noisiness can be used, in turn, to predict what actions people annoyed by noise will take—ranging from complaints to authorities, to legal action (Kryter, 1968).

Noise can cause annoyance in a variety of ways. It can disturb relaxation or sleep; it can startle; it can interfere with conversation. (See Kryter, 1966, for a study of reactions of people in communities exposed to jet aircraft noise.) Will noise interfere with the *performance* of tasks that do not involve speech communication or auditory signals? A number of studies of this problem indicated no difference in the effect of a high noise level as compared to a lower level on performance of a variety of tasks (Kryter, 1950). However, evidence has shown (Broadbent, 1958), that noise does produce a deleterious effect on the performance of tasks that require continuous attention to signals that are difficult to discriminate and unpredictable with respect to their time of occurrence.

LIMITATIONS OF THE EAR AS AN ANALYZING SYSTEM

If the ear were a perfect frequency analyzing system, different frequencies would not interfere with each other, or interact with each other. Obviously, they do. In the next 3 sections, we are going to consider limitations of the ear as a "high-fidelity" analyzing system. We discuss beats, distortion, and masking.

Beats

Beats are heard when 2 tones, which are not too different in frequency, are sounded simultaneously. If the difference in the frequencies of the 2 tones is small, the beats are heard as fluctuations in loudness. For example, with frequencies of 200 and 202 Hz, the loudness fluctuates, and maxima of loudness occur twice a second. If we lead these 2 frequencies to a loudspeaker instead of the ear, then pick up the resulting output of the loudspeaker with a microphone and look at the waveform, it turns out that the amplitude of the resultant wave fluctuates twice a second. So our perception of beats is related to fluctuations in the amplitude of the wave form produced by 2 frequencies simultaneously stimulating the same physical system. If our ear were a perfect analyzer, and each frequency were isolated at a separate place in the inner ear, beats would not occur.

As the difference in frequency between 2 tonal stimuli is made larger, there is a transition to a perception of intermittent pulses, then to a perception of roughness; finally all beat effects vanish (Wever, 1929). The vanishing of beat perception is not simply due to a lack of overlap of the vibrations on the basilar membrane (von Békésy, 1960). Perceptible beats are heard again as the higher frequency approaches simple multiples of the lower (Wever, 1949).

Beats are of importance in music. If the strings for a given note on the piano are not tuned to give the same frequency, beats occur and produce an unpleasant effect. Two beginning violin students playing the same melody together may cause a very dissonant result, for the slightly different tones they produce beat against each other.

Distortion

Those interested in high-fidelity sound equipment are well acquainted with problems of distortion in physical instruments. The ear itself is a complicated mechanical system, and produces some distortion, even if there is no distortion present in the stimulus.

When a mechanical system capable of vibration is displaced by a small force, the displacement is proportional to force. However, when the force becomes much greater, the displacement is no longer proportional to the force applied. This "nonlinearity" can be shown mathematically to lead to the production of additional frequencies of vibration. Thus if a single frequency is applied to the system at high intensity, harmonics arise which are multiples of the original frequency. (If a frequency of 200 Hz is applied, harmonics of 400, 600, and so on may be produced.) If 2 intense frequencies are applied to the system, difference tones and summation tones ("combination tones") will appear in addition to harmonics of each of the frequencies applied. If we represent the lower frequency by L, and the higher frequency by H, the difference tones produced would have frequencies $H - L$, $2L - H$, and so on. Summation tones would have frequencies of $L + H$, $2L + H$, and so on. In general, frequencies of possible "combination tones" would be predicted by the formula $mL \pm nH$, where m and n are any integers. Study of the actual combination tones produced will give information concerning the type of nonlinearity present.

How do we measure the amount of a combination tone present? One method for measuring *audible* distortion is to introduce an additional frequency equal to that of the distortion frequency we wish to evaluate; then the sound pressure and phase of this additional frequency are adjusted until the pitch corresponding to the distortion frequency vanishes, due to cancellation of the distortion frequency (Zwicker, 1955; Goldstein, 1967). (If the basilar membrane is being pushed in one direction, and you introduce a frequency with a phase that pushes the membrane in the opposite direction at the same moment, then the effects will cancel.) Another method is to increase the intensities of the 2 primary frequencies until the distortion frequency (produced by the 2 primary frequencies) can just be detected by the observer (Plomp, 1965). Plomp has recently summarized earlier results and has also discussed experiments of his own. Early investigators found that the combination tones $H - L$, and $2L - H$ were clearly audible. Plomp found that $3L - 2H$, as well as $H - L$ and $2L - H$, was also detectable by all of his observers. $L + H$ was not detected by his observers. It seems quite likely that harmonics and combination tones (such as $L + H$) above the 2 primary frequencies could be masked out by the more intense primaries. (Low tones at a high intensity tend to mask out high tones.) Clack (1968) varied a frequency $2f_1$ (equal to twice the fundamental frequency f_1) in phase and amplitude in such a way that

it added to the distortion harmonic $2f_1$ present in the ear and made it audible. With this method, he was able to study the characteristics of the $2f_1$ harmonic.

Where in the auditory system do these distortion frequencies arise? Helmholtz thought that they arose in the middle ear, in the movements of the eardrum and chain of middle-ear bones (Wever & Lawrence, 1954). In more recent times, von Békésy (1960) was able to show that neither harmonics nor difference tones were generated by the eardrum. However, his experiments showed that difference tones could be produced by non-linearity in the middle ear—most likely in vibrations of the footplate of the stirrup (the small bone which transmits vibrations to the fluids of the inner ear). Harmonics were shown not to arise from middle-ear distortion. Von Békésy supposed that the production of

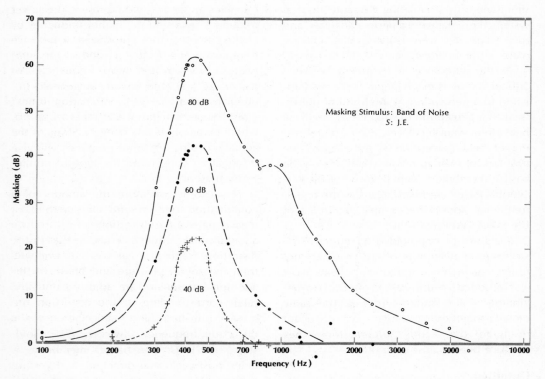

Figure 8.15. Masking produced by three levels (40, 60, 80 dB) of a narrow-band masking noise. Masking is measured by shift in absolute threshold from that measured without noise present. (Egan & Hake, 1950.)

harmonics was related to eddy movements of the fluids of the inner ear. More recently Tonndorf (1958) has been able to show that audible harmonics occur at sound levels at which eddies appear in the fluids of a model of the inner ear. The inner ear has also been implicated in production of combination tones of the type $L - n(H - L)$, where n is a positive integer. The most prominent of these is $2L - H$ (Zwicker, 1955; Goldstein, 1967). In contrast to the combination tone $L - H$, which appears only above a sensation level of about 50 dB, the combination tone $2L - H$ appears at low intensity levels; it is relatively unaffected by changes in the level of the primaries L and H (once it appears) and decreases sharply with frequency separation of the L and H primaries. We would not expect these characteristics if the distortion were produced by a nonlinear system preceding the inner ear.

Masking

Much of our listening in everyday life is done in the presence of various types of noise that interfere with our ability to detect signals. Certain specialized jobs, such as Sonar operator, require detection of a signal in the presence of noise. We shall describe various types of masking situation that have been experimentally investigated and the masking phenomena produced in each of them. (Further information on masking of speech appears later in the chapter.) We should emphasize at the outset that there are undoubtedly a number of different mechanisms operating to produce the masking observed in these various situations.

Masking by tones and bands of noise in the same ear as the signal The most common measure of masking is the threshold shift in the signal (in decibels) caused by the masking sound. That is, we first measure the threshold of the signal by itself; then we remeasure the signal threshold when the masking stimulus is present. The difference in threshold is the amount of masking.

A narrow band of noise was used as a masking stimulus by Egan and Hake (1950), and Ehmer (1959). Figure 8.15 shows one set of results from the study of Egan and Hake. A masking band of noise was used which was 90 Hz wide, and centered at 410 Hz. The amount of masking produced is shown for a number of masked frequencies (horizontal scale). When the noise was at low (40 dB) and medium (60 dB) levels, the amount of masking produced was quite symmetrical. However, at the 80 dB level, the masking noise produced considerably more masking on higher than on lower frequencies.

Some of the earliest experiments on masking were done with tone-on-tone masking (Wegel & Lane, 1924). These indicated clearly that, particularly at high intensity levels, masking was greater on test tones above the frequency of the masking tone than on test tones below it in frequency. Study of tone-on-tone masking is complicated by the presence of beats, and (at higher intensities) by distortion. For instance, if the separations in the frequencies of the masking and masked tones are small, the masked tone can be detected by the presence of beats. The masking effect may involve a neural "inhibition" effect for larger frequency separations between the tones (Galambos & Davis, 1944; Sachs & Kiang, 1967).

"Remote" masking Not only is it possible to obtain a surprising degree of spread in masking effects to frequencies above the band of masking noise, but under special conditions it is possible to obtain masking of *low* frequencies by an intense *high*-frequency noise stimulus. This has been termed "remote" masking (Bilger & Hirsh, 1956; Bilger, 1958). One hypothesis is that the remote masking is caused by distortion processes in the inner ear, which produce interfering vibrations in the low-frequency regions of the inner ear (Deatherage, Bilger, & Eldredge, 1957; Deatherage, Davis, & Eldredge, 1957; Hirsh & Burgeat, 1958). Modulation (variation) of the amplitude of the masking stimulus is an important factor in producing the effect.

Although it was thought that activation of the stapedius muscle reflex might help explain remote masking effects, a recent experiment by Bilger (1966) casts doubt on this hypothesis. Bilger found remote masking even when the stapedius muscle had been removed.

The concept of critical band   Fletcher (1940) pointed out that when a masking noise (such as thermal noise) is used that involves a wide band of frequencies of approximately uniform amplitude, masking of a tone signal is caused by components in the noise close to the tone signal in frequency. Components within certain frequency limits on either side of the signal frequency ("critical band") contribute to the masking, whereas components beyond these limits do not add to the masking. The size of the critical band can be measured directly by taking a broad band of thermal noise, with the signal frequency at the center of the band, and gradually narrowing the size of the band of noise, by successively filtering out high and low frequencies. At first the masked threshold for the tone signal does not change. However, when the noise bandwidth is made narrower than the critical band, the masked threshold starts to decrease; it takes less energy for the signal to be detected (Fletcher, 1940; Scharf, 1961; Swets, 1963).

It turns out that when a tone signal is just detectable in wide-band noise, the energy of noise in the critical band is close to 2.5 times the energy of the tone. (See Scharf, 1961.) Thus it is possible to predict the detectability of a tone signal ahead of time from measurement of the noise intensity present in the critical band (Hawkins & Stevens, 1950). One explanation of what the subject is doing when he detects a signal in noise is that he is listening to input in a restricted frequency region surrounding the signal and is making his judgment in terms of whether the average

energy level present in this region exceeds some criterion level (see Green & Swets, 1966). It is assumed that when the signal is present, it adds to the energy level produced by the noise alone. Discrimination between noise alone and signal plus noise becomes more difficult, however, as noise level increases, probably due to increased variability of neural effects. (Recall Weber's Law, which predicts a proportionality between ΔI, the intensity of a just noticeable "signal," and I, the initial stimulus level—in this case noise. See Chapter 2, p. 39.)

A critical band turns out to correspond to a distance of 1 millimeter along the basilar membrane of the inner ear (Greenwood, 1961). Neurally, the critical band may correspond to a spatial region within which neural effects sum with each other because of lateral neural connections. The critical band mechanism is undoubtedly not the only mechanism involved in integration of information from different frequency regions. The judgment of the loudness of complex sounds, for instance, may involve integration of energy over a frequency range much wider than that of a critical band.

Recruitment   In our discussion of masking so far we have used the shift in the signal threshold caused by the masking stimulus as the criterion of masking. It is important to note at this point that as the signal is increased in intensity *above* its masked threshold, the loudness grows rapidly, until at 15 to 20 dB above the masked threshold, the loudness of a tonal signal is as great in the presence of the masking stimulus as it is alone without any masking stimulus (Steinberg & Gardner, 1937; Small & Thurlow, 1954). Thus the effect of masking on the processing of signals is not always so devastating as might appear from threshold masking curves. A similar "recruitment" or the "gaining-back" of loudness is found in certain cases of deafness in which sensory cells in the inner ear are damaged (Harris, 1953; Egan, 1954).

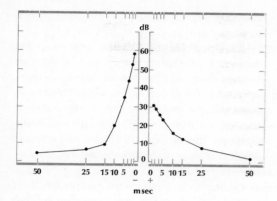

Figure 8.16. The left side of the graph shows backward masking produced by a masking noise burst of 90 dB (re .0002 dyn/cm²) on a probe tone of 5 msec duration and 1000 Hz frequency. The end of the tone burst *preceded* the masking noise burst by intervals of time indicated on the horizontal scale. The right side of the graph shows forward masking produced by this masking noise on the same probe-tone burst when the beginning of the probe tone *followed* the masking burst by intervals of time indicated on the horizontal scale. (Elliott, 1962a.)

Backward masking Although most masking effects involve the simultaneous presence of a masking stimulus and signal, there are some important exceptional situations. It was noted by Miller (1947) in an experiment on the masking effects of short pulses of sound, that a brief sound could be made inaudible by a pulse of sound which *followed* it in time. Since this initial experiment, numerous others have been made on the phenomenon, which is called "backward masking" (Raab, 1963). See also the analogous case of backward visual masking (p. 310).

Figure 8.16 (left side) shows illustrative data from an experiment by Elliott (1962a). A 50 msec burst of thermal noise at 90 dB (re.0002 dyne/cm²) was preceded by a "probe" tone signal of 1000 Hz, 5 msec in duration. Subjects were instructed to indicate whether the addition of the probe tone produced a noticeable change in the sound of the masking thermal noise burst. The ending of the probe tone was made to *precede* the thermal noise burst by different intervals of time, as is indicated in Figure 8.16. The ordinate of the graph shows the number of decibels that the 5 msec probe tone had to be raised above its unmasked threshold in order to be detected. It is apparent that the amount of backward masking is relatively small when the 5 msec tone precedes the masking burst by more than 10 to 15 msec. The amount of backward masking has been found to be less when lower intensities of noise burst are used.

The apparent paradox of masking "backward" in time can possibly be understood by assuming that an intense stimulus causes a burst of neural activity that reaches the central nervous system quickly and "overtakes" neural activity caused by a less intense stimulus (Miller, 1947). There is evidence that the masking stimulus actually shortens the effective and perceived duration of a preceding stimulus (Gol'dburt, 1961; Wright, 1964). It is as if the masking stimulus has overtaken and masked out the last part of the signal.

In some studies of "backward masking" the subject identifies the signal by a distinctive characteristic, such as its pitch (see Elliott, 1962b). In other experiments, however, subjects appear to use as their criterion (of detection of the signal) a change in the total composite of the signal plus the masker. For example, they may use as their criterion the total duration of the composite of a click and burst of masking noise (Osman & Raab, 1963) or the total loudness of the composite of a click plus another masking click (Chistovitch & Ivanova, 1959). In these latter cases is it necessary to assume that there is any diminution of the neural effect of the signal caused by the masker?

Interaural stimulus relations and masking We now turn to masking effects which involve interrelations between the 2 ears.

Sound in 1 ear, if sufficiently intense, can

be conducted physically to the opposite inner ear and cause masking of a sound in the other ear. If precautions are taken to rule out such cross-conduction effects, it is found that "cross-masking" effects can still be obtained, though they are smaller than when masking and masked stimuli are being heard by the same ear; also, the masking effect is restricted more to frequencies near to the masking frequency than in the monaural masking situation (Ingham, 1959; Sherrick & Mangabeira-Albernaz, 1961; Zwislocki et al., 1967). An exception to the last statement is found when one ear is exposed to an intense high-frequency band of noise; it is observed that masking occurs in the low-frequency regions of the other ear. This effect is called "contralateral remote masking" (CRM). Ward (1967) concludes that CRM is due primarily to masking in the central nervous system, part of which is central masking caused by low-frequency distortion originating in the ear listening to the high-frequency noise. The contribution to CRM by the reaction of the ear muscles to the high-frequency noise is considered to be minor.

Far more research effort has been devoted to investigating variations in masking effectiveness that are related to interaural phase relations of noise compared to those of the tone. Early observations by Langmuir and collaborators (Langmuir et al., 1944) showed that detection of a tone signal in masking noise depended on the apparent spatial direction of the tone in relation to the noise. Other researchers have conducted systematic investigations of the phenomenon (Hirsh, 1948; Jeffress et al., 1956; Jeffress, Blodgett, & Deatherage, 1962; Robinson & Jeffress, 1963). The magnitude of the effects depends on the signal frequency used; effects are obtained primarily at low signal frequencies. The following is a brief description of some of the main effects observed:

(1) Start, for example, with a signal tone of 500 Hz, and with thermal noise at an intensity per cycle of 45 dB. Both stimuli are applied to one ear, say the right ear. Determine the threshold SPL for the 500 Hz tone to be detected.

(2) If the identical signal and noise are applied to the other ear (assuming the ears are not different) the threshold for the tone will not be changed appreciably. This result, however, will hold true only if the phase of the tone is the same in each ear, and if the phase of the noise is the same in each ear. This condition is designated as the "homophasic" condition.

(3) If we now determine the threshold for a condition where the tone has been applied to the right ear, and the noise to each ear (with identical phase), the threshold turns out to be about 9 dB lower than for the homophasic condition. A gain in detection over the homophasic condition is termed a "masking level difference" (MLD).

(4) If we start with the homophasic condition and reverse the phase of the signal in the 2 ears (a 180 degree phase difference) we find an MLD of about 14 dB. (There are slight sampling differences in the magnitude of the MLD in different experiments.) If we start from the homophasic condition and reverse the phase of the noise, we obtain a slightly smaller MLD (see Robinson and Jeffress, 1963).

Several types of theory have been proposed to explain MLD effects (Jeffress et al., 1956; Durlach, 1963; Schenkel, 1967). Earlier theorists (Webster and Jeffress; see Jeffress et al., 1956) had pointed out that we should pay attention to the frequency component of the noise in the immediate vicinity of the signal and see what happens to the phase of the composite wave in each ear produced by adding signal to noise. They calculated that adding enough signal intensity to the noise to make the signal detectable should produce a constant shift in the phase between the wave forms at the 2 ears, in the region of the signal frequency. (Studies of sound localization show that such a phase shift should result in a change in the perceived direction of a sound.) Despite some success, this theory was found not to predict

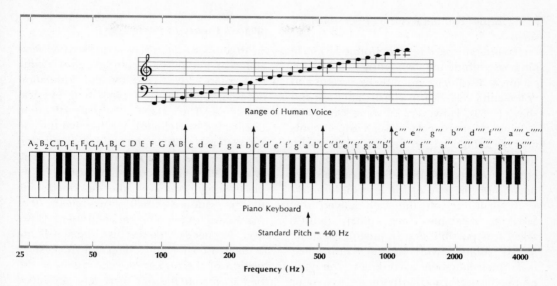

Figure 8.17. Relations between frequency in cycles per second, notes of the piano keyboard, and musical notes that can be sung by the human voice. (Modified from Boring, Langfeld, & Weld, 1948.)

accurately in all cases (Jeffress, Blodgett, & Deatherage, 1962).

The theoretical explanations have become more and more complex as more detailed experiments have been performed on MLD phenomena. For example, investigation of the MLD as a function of differences in the intensity of both signal and noise in each ear have led to elaborations in theory (Colburn & Durlach, 1965; Egan, 1965; Dolan & Robinson, 1967). Green and Henning (1969) have recently reviewed data and theory concerning MLD.

PITCH

Pitch Scales

Psychological pitch is most closely related to the physical dimension of frequency (yet it is by no means identical with physical frequency). Figure 8.17 shows the notes on a piano—with letters corresponding to the musical scale and frequencies in cycles per second below. The note a' corresponds to 440 Hz. You will notice that the sequence of letters repeats. Each sequence is at an *octave* above the one to the left. Thus, in the series

of c's: C_1, C, c, c', c'' . . . , each is an octave above the preceding. The fundamental (lowest) frequency for each c is twice that for the preceding c. Put more generally, the musical interval of the octave, defined *physically*, corresponds to a doubling of fundamental frequency. But do octaves, physically defined as a 2-to-1 frequency ratio, always sound like the same *subjective* interval? The answer is no. Even though subjects' judgments of an octave correspond to a 2-to-1 frequency ratio quite closely over a fairly wide frequency range (Ward, 1954), there may be marked departures from this simple relation at very high frequencies. Not all subjects can judge pitch above about 4000 Hz (the upper range of fundamentals on the piano keyboard). However, some subjects with musical training can judge the pitch of these high frequencies in terms of subjective musical intervals. The judged pitch of these very high frequencies has been shown to be a function of variables that appear to depend on the "arousal" state of the subject (Thurlow, 1946; Elfner, 1964; Thurlow, 1965). Thus, loss of sleep tends to lower judged pitch, while administration of a drug which tends to arouse the subject (benzedrine) counteracts the effect of loss of sleep.

Experiments have been performed to scale pitch magnitude independently of the musical interval scale, for example by Stevens and Volkmann (1940), Harris (1960), and Beck and Shaw (1963). However, in some cases, the judgments of subjects in such experiments may be influenced by their experience with the musical scale. Harris (1960) has pointed out that results with the Method of Bisection depend on the size of the interval bisected. With small intervals, the scale derived from bisection resembles the ordinary musical scale. It is possible that in judging small intervals, subjects with musical training may make their judgment according to the notes on the musical scale. Furthermore, in judging larger frequency intervals, some subjects with musical training may use the octave relationship as a basis for giving numerical estimates of pitch relations (Warren, 1958; Beck & Shaw, 1961). For instance, subjects may assign numbers in such a way that a constant increase in number corresponds to each successive octave increase in pitch (Beck & Shaw, 1961). The use of responses learned in musical training, for judgment of pitch, is not unexpected. However, it is well worth discussing because it serves to emphasize the importance of looking into the mechanisms by which subjects are able to assign numbers to relations between stimuli (see Chapter 3).

Psychological pitch is mainly related to the frequency of the stimulus. However, the pitch of a pure tone can also be affected by intensity. Although there are large individual differences, it has been found that the pitch of low tones tends to go down as the intensity is increased, and the pitch of high frequencies tends to go up (Stevens & Davis, 1938; Morgan, Galambos, & Garner, 1951; Cohen, 1961). Stimulation of the opposite ear can cause similar changes in the pitch of pure tones (Thurlow, 1943). The pitch of a complex musical tone, which contains many low and high harmonics, is not much affected by intensity (Fletcher, 1934).

"Place" Theory of Pitch

Theories of pitch have traditionally been aimed at finding basic physiological events that could serve to explain the correlation between psychological pitch and physical frequency. The "classical" theory of pitch, enunciated by Helmholtz, stated that the cue for pitch was given by the *place* of stimulation in the inner ear and auditory nervous system. (Wever, 1949, has discussed the history of the place theory.) We have earlier described some of the evidence which shows clearly that place cues for pitch height are present. However, we need evidence that these cues are actually used. Recently, direct electrical stimulation of the high-frequency region of the basilar membrane in man has produced pitches that are correlated with place of stimulation (Simmons et al., 1965).

Acceptance of a "place" theory for low frequencies has not been by any means unanimous because there appear to be other possible cues for low pitch. Nevertheless, "place" could be *one* of the cues for low pitch. Zwicker (1964) has found tonal "after-images," following stimulation with bands of noise which have a gap (no acoustical energy) in a certain frequency region. The pitch of the after-image corresponds to the frequency location of the gap. The after-images apparently can be explained in terms of neural "after-discharge" in a particular place in the nervous system. The after-images were obtained in both high- and low-frequency regions.

Convincing evidence for a "place" mechanism for pitch (including low pitch) also comes from observations on "diplacusis." A person with diplacusis hears a different pitch when a given tone stimulates the right ear than when it stimulates the left ear. When the tone stimulates both ears simultaneously, he hears a pitch in between the 2 pitches he hears when the 2 ears are stimulated separately. This phenomenon has been known for years and can be explained by a "place" theory (see von Békésy, 1963). (Can you draw a diagram showing how? Represent each "place" disturbance as a distribution of neural effects with a maximum.)

Time Cues for Low Pitch

In discussing the volleys of nerve impulses produced by a pure low tone, we mentioned that the rate of volleys might act as a cue to the pitch of a low-frequency tone. As the frequency of the tone increases, the number of volleys increases, and pitch increases (Wever, 1949). However, we need to have some more direct evidence that such a cue does operate.

One way of separating this type of cue from a place cue is to use bursts of thermal noise. (At a very slow rate, these would sound approximately like: *sh, sh, sh. . .*). The thermal noise stimulates all frequency regions—so there is no differential place cue. The number of bursts per second can be varied, however, and thus the rate of volleys in the auditory nerve will vary accordingly. Under these circumstances, it has been found that many subjects hear a low pitch that corresponds to the rate of noise pulses (Miller & Taylor, 1948; Licklider, 1959). The upper rate limit for perception of pitch by this cue was originally found to be between 200 to 300 pulses per second. Some later experimenters have tended to put the limit higher (Harris, 1963). In these experiments, there may be difficulty in telling whether the subject is perceiving intermittency or pitch; matching the noise bursts with a non-intermittent oscillator tone provides one method for solving this problem.

It is of interest to note that recently the auditory nerve of a human ear was stimulated electrically with pulses (Simmons et al., 1965). The subject heard a low pitch corresponding to the rate of the pulses, up to an upper limit of about 300 pulses per second. Simmons, Mongeon, Lewis, and Huntington (1964) have reviewed some of the experimental difficulties in such research.

Other experimenters have used acoustic stimuli which create pulses in restricted fre-quency regions (Small, 1955; Licklider, 1959). (See Figure 8.4 for an illustration of a series of pulses.) In these experiments it is important to find out whether the low pitch may be produced within the inner ear by a low-frequency component corresponding to pulse rate (von Békésy, 1963). For if a low physical frequency were produced, the low pitch would be explained as due to the physical stimulus and not due to the pulses of nerve activity produced in another frequency region. Schouten (1940) was the first to show that the low pitch "residue" heard in a series of pulses was not due to the introduction of a low physical frequency equal to the rate of the pulses. (He cancelled out the physical frequency by means of an additional pure tone, varied in phase and intensity.) Several experimenters have used a masking noise in the low-frequency region to mask out any possible low-frequency artifact (Thurlow & Small, 1955; Licklider, 1959; Small & Campbell, 1961; Rosenberg, 1965). They have found that the low pitch remains despite the low-frequency masking.

Further Theoretical Approaches to Low Pitch

In order to take account of the fact that low pitch appears to be related to volleys in the nerve, but also appears to show some "place" characteristics, Licklider (1959) developed a theory of low pitch constructed on the assumption that there is a time-analyzing system in the auditory nervous system that converts the time intervals between volleys of nerve pulses into a "place" cue.

There is another characteristic that might act as a cue to the perception of a low pitch—the pattern of harmonics (Licklider, 1951; de Boer, 1956). It was pointed out earlier in the chapter (see Figure 8.3) that a tone produced by a musical instrument, such as a violin, consists of a fundamental frequency together with many higher frequency harmonics. Fletcher (1934) observed that even when the fundamental was filtered out, his subjects still perceived a low pitch corresponding to the fundamental. Wilson (1969) has recently found a clear correlation between perceived pitch and the pattern of "place" cues in a complex stimulus, analogous to the pattern of harmonics.

If there can be several cues to low pitch, how do these different cues produce a given low pitch perception? We could suppose that a "conditioned pitch perception" might be involved. That is, we suppose that people, especially those with musical training, listen to the pitch produced by a given musical instrument, or singing voice, thousands of times. These stimuli have various cues—which include not only a low fundamental frequency, but also harmonics, and harmonic components which may produce a pulse rate equal to the fundamental frequency. Now, when only one of these cues is presented, it may still be effective in producing the conditioned perception. (Garner, 1952, has spoken of the possibility of a Gestalt "completion" effect in connection with this problem.)

Thurlow and Hartman (1959) noted that subjects often made use of a vocal humming response (or reported they "hummed to themselves" without singing out loud) in matching their perceived pitch to an oscillator tone. Thurlow (1963) has hypothesized that the vocal response may play an important role in perception of the low pitch of complex stimuli. Its role, however, is limited by the vocal range of the subject. Further research is needed on these possibilities.

LOUDNESS

In this section we will look at some of the various ways in which psychological loudness has been measured. When we talk about loudness scales, we will be looking at the data as we look at data from other psychological experiments (Bergman & Spence, 1944). We consider questions such as: How could these responses have been produced? How can different response scales be related?

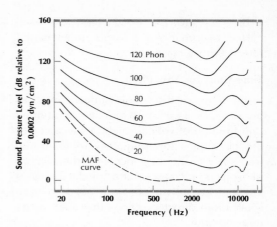

Figure 8.18. Equal-loudness contours. The number associated with each curve represents the loudness in phons for all frequency–intensity combinations of that curve. (Robinson & Dadson, 1956.)

Equal-loudness Contours

Figure 8.18 shows what are called "equal loudness contours" (Robinson & Dadson, 1956). The contour (curve) marked 40, for example, shows the sound pressure level (SPL), in dB at each frequency, that is necessary for a tone of that frequency to sound just as loud as a 1000 Hz tone at 40 dB SPL (SPL with reference to .0002 dynes/cm²). As a more specific example: If you will refer to the graph, you will see that a frequency of 100 Hz must be at an SPL of close to 50 dB in order to sound as loud as a 1000 Hz tone at 40 dB SPL. The loudness of each of the frequencies on the 40 dB contour is said to be 40 "phons."

The contours in Figure 8.18 are called "free-field" contours because of the measuring technique used. The observer faces the source of sound in an anechoic (or "free-field") room, and the sound intensity is adjusted for a given loudness match. The sound intensity is measured after the observer has left, at the position in which the observer's head was located. The curve marked "MAF curve" (meaning "minimum audible field") in Figure 8.18 represents a graph of threshold sensitivity obtained with this same measuring technique. The sensitivity curve shows some differences from that obtained by measuring the minimum audible pressure ("MAP") at the eardrum, due to the influence of the head structures on the sound field.

The technique of measuring the loudness of a sound by equating it to the loudness of a 1000 Hz tone can be applied to various kinds of sounds in addition to pure tones. One disadvantage of the "phon" scale, however, is that it does not tell us anything about psychological loudness relations *between* phon levels. For example, we would be mistaken in believing that the difference between 90 and 100 phons is subjectively the same as the difference between 10 and 20 phons.

Ratio Judgments of Loudness

Stevens (1955) summarized data obtained from estimates of half and double loudness and found that the median value of the change in intensity required for a two-fold* change in loudness was close to 10 dB. He defined one *sone* as the loudness of a 1000 Hz tone of 40 phons. A level of loudness judged to be twice as great would then be 2 sones. If a 10 dB increase in intensity is required to double the loudness, an equation can be derived relating sound intensity to the loudness in sones. For a 1000 Hz tone, $L = .06\ I^{.3}$, where L is the loudness in "sones" and I is intensity. Robinson (1953) proposed a similar equation.

Other data approximating a power law have been found by experimenters who have used methods known as *magnitude estimation* and *magnitude production* (see p. 64). Results obtained vary somewhat depending on the exact procedure followed. For example, if the magnitude estimation method is used, the shape of the function obtained is influenced by the intensity of the stimulus taken as a standard (Stevens, 1956b) and also by the size of the number assigned to the standard stimulus (Hellman & Zwislocki,

1961). Large individual differences in the exponent of the power function have been found by J. C. Stevens, who used the method of magnitude production (Stevens & Guirao, 1964).

Deviations from a simple power law occur at low intensity levels (see Figure 3.19, p. 78). More complex mathematical functions have been proposed in order to describe the loudness judgments at these low intensity levels more adequately. However, it has been difficult to develop a completely satisfactory rationale for these formulations (Ross, 1967).

Why is a power function obtained? Stevens (1961) argues that the power function reflects the neural input into the nervous system from the sense organ. However, other psychologists would worry more about how the numbers get assigned to the neural quantities inside the brain (Attneave, 1962; see also the discussion of cross-modality matching in Chapter 3). Warren has proposed that the

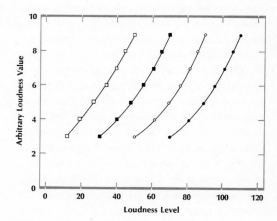

Figure 8.19. A set of data representing equal loudness *intervals* obtained with a 1000 Hz tone. Four different intensity ranges were used: 10 to 50 dB, 30 to 70 dB, 50 to 90 dB, and 70 to 110 dB. On the graph, equal intervals are indicated by 1 unit increase in number on the vertical scale. The horizontal scale is in phons, which in this case is equivalent to decibels with reference to .0002 dyn/cm². (Garner, 1954.)

numbers representing loudness are assigned on the basis of the subject's experience with sound pressure level and physical distance (Warren, Sersen, & Pores, 1958). In free space, the sound pressure level decreases by 6 dB for each doubling of distance. Thus, according to this theory, the number assigned to loudness would double for each 6 dB decrease in the sound pressure level. Most of the data gathered do not agree with this prediction (Stevens, 1963). In the next section we continue our discussion of the question of how numbers are assigned to loudness by the subject.

"Equal-interval" Judgments of Loudness

Figure 8.19 shows results obtained by Garner (1954) when he asked subjects to adjust the intensity of a series of tones (all 1000 Hz) so that the difference in loudness between adjacent tones would be equal. Each curve represents a range of 40 dB—10 to 50, 30 to 70, 50 to 90, and 70 to 110. Seven intensities were presented for each of these ranges. The ends of each range were fixed, and the subject adjusted the remaining 5 intensities to give subjectively equal loudness intervals. The functions obtained show some curvature, but they do not depart greatly from a straight-line relation. Stevens has obtained a function for one of these ranges (55–95 dB) that shows more curvature (Stevens & Guirao, 1962).

The results obtained by using "equal-appearing interval" methods suggest a relation between sensory magnitude and stimulus more of the form $S = k \log I$ where S stands for "sensory" magnitude, and I stands for stimulus intensity. In this case, the "sensation" appears to be increasing by equal units for equal ratio changes in the stimulus. On the other hand, the power law implies that the "sensation" is increasing by equal *ratios* for equal ratio changes in the stimulus. One interpretation to reconcile these results (outlined in the earlier chapter on scaling) is that discriminability of stimuli in the category scaling situation modifies the expected

power-law relation. However, other psychologists have obtained evidence that makes them prefer alternative explanations (Torgerson, 1960; Schneider & Lane, 1963). Torgerson (1961) has suggested that the subject's judgment is based on a single quantitative relation, which is interpreted as a distance or a ratio by the subject, depending on his instructions. Thurlow and Melamed (1967) have tried to indicate what this "quantitative relation" might be, in terms of subject responses in the loudness judgment situation. We might suppose that the subject is using a "measuring response" in both situations involving "equal-interval" and "ratio" scaling—such as that of moving his hand along an imaginary measuring scale in response to a change in stimulus intensity. The increase in the distance he moves his hand would depend on his matching internal kinaesthetic change, associated with hand movement, to an increase in sensory input associated with the change in sound intensity. A given movement along the measuring scale (such as from 1 to 2 inches on the scale) could be interpreted either (1) as an interval—1 to 2—or (2) as a ratio—2/1, depending on the instructions given by the experimenter. The same response would presumably be applied over and over again to enable the subject to make judgments at different intensity levels.

Loudness of Complex Sounds

It would be desirable to be able to predict the loudness of a complex sound from its physical characteristics. Several schemes have been devised which seem to work satisfactorily for certain types of complex sounds (Stevens, 1956a; Zwicker & Scharf, 1965). These schemes involve essentially adding up the contributions to loudness from various frequency regions, making allowance for masking. There are some types of complex stimuli, however, for which the prediction of loudness is difficult. The loudness of impulsive stimuli (produced by typewriters, ham-

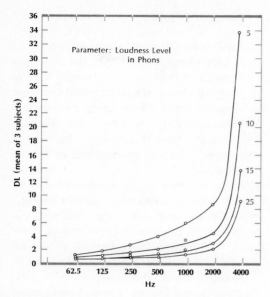

Figure 8.20. Variation of frequency difference threshold as a function of frequency. Vertical and horizontal scales are both in cycles per second. (Harris, 1952.)

mer blows, heel impacts) cannot as yet be predicted satisfactorily (Stevens, 1956a; Corliss & Winzer, 1965).

ACCURACY OF DISCRIMINATIONS OF PURE TONE STIMULI FROM FREQUENCY AND INTENSITY CUES

Frequency Discrimination Threshold

Early studies of frequency discrimination (see Stevens & Davis, 1938) were not completely satisfactory because the frequency was not adequately controlled. It is important in studying frequency discrimination to make sure that the frequency used does not suffer from distortion, and the frequency must be turned on and off slowly enough to avoid introducing transients—which sound like clicks to the subject. The duration of the stimulus also must be controlled (Turnbull, 1944; Sekey, 1963). Figure 8.20 shows data from a more modern study where stimuli were carefully controlled (Harris, 1952). This graph shows how the difference threshold, in

cycles per second, increases as a function of the frequency level at which the difference threshold is measured. The graph also indicates that the difference threshold is higher at low levels of loudness.

In the Harris experiment the subject listened to pairs of tones. He was required to judge whether the second tone was higher or lower in pitch than the first (standard) tone. Systematic changes in the experimental situation lead to different results for threshold measurements. Thus a somewhat different threshold results if a different psychophysical method is used (Rosenblith & Stevens, 1953), or if the stimulus frequency is "warbled" up and down instead of being presented at discrete frequency values (Shower & Biddulph, 1931). These results should serve to remind us that there is no such thing as a simple, single, differential frequency threshold. From the point of view of predicting behavior, this does not cause us any insuperable difficulty. We just have to remember to specify carefully the type of testing situation to which a given set of results applies.

The thresholds shown in Figure 8.20 were obtained with highly trained subjects. These thresholds certainly represent a very fine degree of frequency discrimination. As we might expect from studies of discrimination learning in general, practice produces a lowering of the differential frequency threshold (Campbell & Small, 1963).

Intensity Difference Threshold

If we now consider discrimination of intensity differences, we find that many of the comments in the preceding paragraphs apply. That is: (1) Great care is necessary in the control of the stimulus, especially to prevent transient clicks when the stimulus is turned on and off. (2) Results will vary with the exact nature of the testing method used (Harris, 1963). (3) The degree of training of subjects will be expected to influence the results.

For well-trained subjects, discrimination of

intensity is very acute when a standard is available for comparison. Subjects can detect a change in intensity of the order of .5 dB from a standard intensity under optimal observation conditions.

Frequency and Intensity Discrimination by the Method of Single Stimuli

If the subject is tested for frequency or intensity discrimination by the "Method of Single Stimuli," his ability to discriminate decreases greatly. This loss in discrimination occurs mainly because the subject is not given a standard stimulus on every trial to which to compare the variable stimulus. You will remember that in the Method of Single Stimuli, the subject is given a number of stimuli in succession. Initially each stimulus is labeled with a number. However, on test trials the subject has to recall the number for each stimulus as the stimuli are presented in a random order. Of course, this situation is more like the everyday situation where a stimulus is presented, and a subject classifies it in terms of a scale of numbers or categories he has learned previously. Miller (1956) has pointed out that when a set of stimuli is judged along a single dimension, as in the Method of Single Stimuli, there appears to be an approximate upper limit of 7 stimuli that can be perfectly discriminated. However, we must remember that this conclusion holds only when subjects have had a limited amount of training; also, if more dimensions are introduced, a much greater number of accurate discriminations is possible. Pollack and Ficks (1954) have shown that if auditory stimuli are varied along 6 dimensions—frequency, intensity, rate of interruption, on-time fraction, total duration, and spatial location—about 150 categories can be identified by subjects without error.

Discrimination of Simultaneously Sounding Tones

If 2 or more tones are presented simultaneously, the subject will have very great difficulty in identifying which tones are present,

or even in telling how many tones are present (Thurlow & Rawlings, 1959; Pollack, 1964). It should be emphasized that the inability to detect the components is not due to simple masking. If a component is changed slightly in intensity, then it can be detected (Thurlow & Rawlings, 1959). These results are contrary to the implications of Ohm's Law (Boring, 1942) which states that the ear "hears out" the simple harmonic components in a complex wave.

Some experienced listeners are able to detect a given component if they are first given a cue tone that is in the vicinity of the frequency to be detected (Thurlow & Bernstein, 1957; Plomp, 1964). Other listeners are not assisted by this procedure (Pollack, 1964).

Current signal detection theories (see Chapter 2) are incomplete in that they do not consider this problem. Signal-detection theories deal with situations where there is a change in signal energy, which must be detected. Although the detection of a change in signal energy is more difficult if the subject is not cued as to the frequency region of the signal (Green, 1961), the effects of lack of prior cueing are nowhere near as profound as in the situation of simultaneously sounding tones.

SPEECH

Production of Speech Sounds

The vibration of the vocal folds (or "cords") of the larynx (back of the "Adam's apple"), caused by air pressure from the lungs,

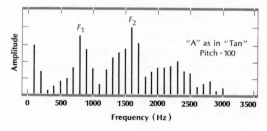

Figure 8.21. Amplitude of the frequency components in the vowel sound *a* as in *tan*. F_1 and F_2 represent first and second formants. (Fletcher, 1953.)

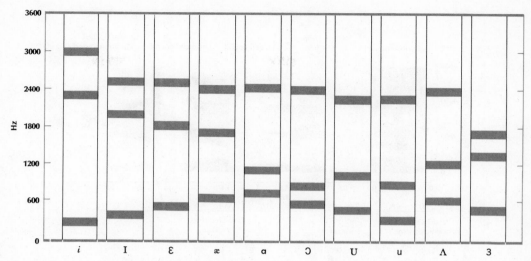

Figure 8.22. Vowel formants. Bars represent frequency regions for formants F_1, F_2, and F_3 of different vowel sounds, produced in an /h — d/ environment. The vowel sounds represented by the symbols are similar to the following vowel sounds: *Eve*, (*i*); *it*, (*I*); *met*, (*ɛ*); *at*, (*æ*); *father*, (*ɑ*); *all*, (*ɔ*); *foot*, (*U*); *boot*, (*u*); *up*, (*ʌ*); *bird*, (*ɜ*). (Flanagan, 1965; after Peterson & Barney, 1952, as plotted by Haskins Laboratories.)

produces the basic "noise" of our voice. This noise consists of a series of pulses of sound at a rate of 100 to 200 per second. Analysis of this series of pulses shows that they contain acoustically a fundamental and a great many harmonics. This noise, however, travels through the cavities of the throat and mouth and is modified in a way that depends on the shape and size of these cavities. Figure 8.21 shows the peaks produced in the spectrum of harmonics for the vowel *a,* as in *tan.* Black lines indicate individual harmonics; height indicates the amplitude of each harmonic. The peaks, labeled by the letters F_1 and F_2,

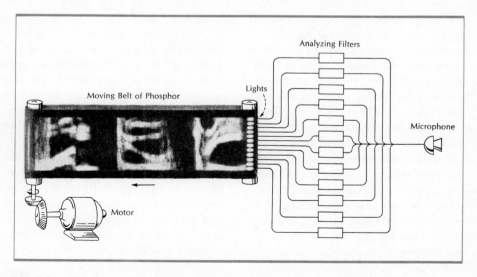

Figure 8.23. Schematic diagram of a sound spectrograph. (Potter, Kopp, & Green, 1947.)

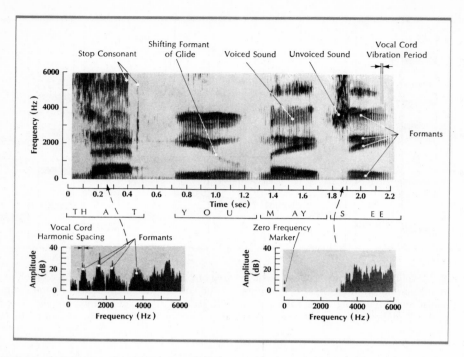

Figure 8.24. A. Sound spectrogram of "That you may see." B. "Amplitude sections": Arrows indicate where the amplitude section was taken from the sound spectrogram. (Flanagan, 1965; after Barney & Dunn, 1957.)

refer to first and second formants, respectively. (A "formant" refers to a concentration of acoustic energy in a restricted frequency region.) The formants of different vowels are at different frequencies; the perceived sound of a vowel depends on the frequency location of the formants. Figure 8.22 shows a chart of the frequency location of the first three formants corresponding to certain English vowels. The lowest bar corresponds to F_1, the next to F_2, the highest to F_3.

Various types of consonant sounds also form an important part of our language. While the vocal tract is left relatively unobstructed when we make the vowel sounds, consonant sounds typically involve narrowing or closing the passageway. For example, the sound of f is produced by turbulent air-flow at a constriction between lips and teeth.

A quantitative representation of all the sounds produced can be obtained by using a *sound spectrograph*. A schematic diagram of this machine is given in Figure 8.23. Speech

sounds picked up by the microphone are analyzed by filters. Each filter passes energy in only a narrow frequency band. Bands represented by the filters cover the frequency range from high to low. The output voltage of each filter determines the brightness of a small light, which in turn leaves a trace on a moving belt of phosphor. Thus a graphical representation of the frequency content of a speech sound is produced on the vertical scale, with brightness representing intensity, and time being indicated along the horizontal scale.

In most commonly used sound spectrographs today, intensity is indicated by the darkness of the trace. Figure 8.24 shows the sound spectrogram for the phrase "that you may see." The concentrations of sound energy at the formants are seen as dark bars on the record. Vibrations of the vocal cords (producing pulses of sound) show up as vertical striations in the record.

Because the darkness of the record gives

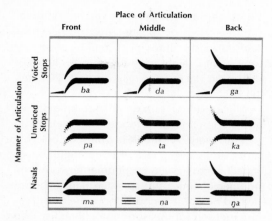

Place of Articulation

Front | Middle | Back

Manner of Articulation

Voiced Stops

ba | da | ga

Unvoiced Stops

pa | ta | ka

Nasals

ma | na | ŋa

Figure 8.25. Pattern playback spectrographic patterns that show the transition cues for the stop and nasal consonants in initial position with the vowel /a/. The dotted portion for unvoiced stops indicates the presence of noise. In each pattern, as in Figure 8.24, the vertical scale represents frequency and the horizontal scale represents time. (Liberman, 1957.)

only a qualitative indication of intensity, other procedures for analysis of intensity are desirable. Figure 8.24 also shows an "amplitude section"—a plot of amplitude in decibels against frequency, which can be obtained at any point in the spectrogram. Arrows show the point in the spectrogram from which the amplitude section was taken. A number of new techniques for analyzing the details of speech signals are currently being investigated (Flanagan, 1965).

Analysis of Cues to Speech Sounds by Synthesis

A machine has been developed that in a sense does the opposite of the sound spectrograph. We start with a visual pattern similar to that produced by a sound spectrograph (see Figure 8.25); the "pattern playback" machine produces speech sounds from it. We can paint patterns of various kinds to see how a modification of the patterns changes the perception of the speech sounds. Thus we can experimentally manipulate determinants of speech sounds. Although other types of speech synthesizers have been developed

(Flanagan, 1965), a great deal of the research on speech sounds up to the present time has been done with the pattern playback machine. In this section we give illustrative findings from research on the synthesis of consonant speech sounds. (See Liberman et al., 1967, for further references.)

Work with the pattern playback has shown that p, t, and k can be discriminated from each other on the basis of the frequency location of the noise burst for each of these sounds and the transition from the consonant to the second formant of the vowel (Cooper et al., 1952). The transitions of the second formant typical of p, t, and k preceding an /a/ sound, as in bah, are shown in Figure 8.25. The transitions are the "hooks" preceding the formant bars.

Liberman, Delattre, Cooper, and Gerstman (1954) showed that the second formant transitions can be important cues for discriminating b, d, and g as well as p, t, and k. The transitions for b, d, g preceding /a/ are also diagrammed in Figure 8.25. Third formant transitions (not shown in Figure 8.25), have also been shown to be important in discrimination of b, d, and g (Harris et al., 1958).

Further research has shown that characteristics of the *first* formant are important in distinguishing b from p, d from t, and g from k. Cutting off initial portions of the first formant transition was found to cause b, d, and g to sound like p, t and k respectively (Liberman, Delattre, & Cooper, 1958).

In the bottom row of illustrations in Figure 8.25 are shown patterns for the nasal consonants m, n, and ŋ (the latter having a sound like the n in sing). Note how similar the second formant transitions are within each column. In addition, however, there are initial lines indicating a "nasal resonance"; your nasal cavity is used as an additional resonator in the production of these sounds. When the transitions for p and b were combined with a nasal resonance, subjects perceived m; transitions for t and d plus nasal resonance were perceived as n; and transitions for k and g plus nasal resonance were heard as ŋ (Liberman et al., 1954).

We have not yet mentioned some of the problems that have arisen in trying to find invariant cues for particular speech sounds. For instance, Liberman found that the direction and extent of the second formant transition for *g* is different when *g* is followed by different vowels. Yet the sound *g* is perceived in all these cases. There was no invariance present in these synthesized speech sounds that could account for the perception of *g*. Liberman suggests that the similarity of sound perception occurs because all of these *g* sounds were originally produced by the same articulatory movement (in this case, movement of the back of the tongue with respect to the soft palate, which is in the upper back region of the mouth cavity); that perhaps the "motor command" for this articulatory movement is the invariant accompaniment of our perception of *g* (Liberman et al., 1962). Other psychologists (Lenneberg, 1962; Lane, 1965) have questioned whether such a "motor" theory is necessary or adequate to account for all of the facts of speech learning. Lenneberg (1962) has discussed the case of a patient who learned to understand speech despite his inability to articulate speech sounds. Liberman's theory, however, is based on *perception* of speech sounds (Liberman et al., 1967). It is possible that normal subjects who are trying to judge whether certain speech sounds *sound* alike, utilize articulatory responses—and these responses may have an important effect on perception. To what extent such articulatory responses (or their representations in the central nervous system) function to facilitate communication in normal subjects remains to be worked out.

Intelligibility of Words

There are many practical situations in which it is desirable to obtain a measure of the intelligibility of samples of speech. We may wish to develop such measures in order to evaluate the hearing of individuals with various types of hearing loss (Hudgins et al., 1947; Egan, 1948; Hirsh et al., 1952; Davis & Silverman, 1960); or we may wish to develop

these measures in order to obtain quantitative measures of the hearing of speech as transmitted by different communication systems, which might introduce various kinds of distortion (Licklider & Miller, 1951; Fletcher, 1953).

The development of an intelligibility or articulation test poses interesting problems in measurement. Although it would be possible to have listeners rate the intelligibility of speech, or to have the experimenter count the number of times the message had to be repeated before it is understood, the most precise method for measuring intelligibility is to count the number of words a listener hears correctly.

One of the first problems that arises is the choice of a speaker. Obviously, the number of words a listener hears depends on how clearly the speaker enunciates. Optimally, if only one speaker can be used, the speaker should represent a typical manner of speaking for the situation being tested. However, the usual procedure adopted in the construction of standardized speech tests has been to make use of an individual who enunciates clearly (such as a radio announcer), and who presumably uses "general American" pronunciation. No attempt has been made to take regional differences in pronunciation into account. (No "Southern accent" is represented!)

Another sampling problem arises with re-

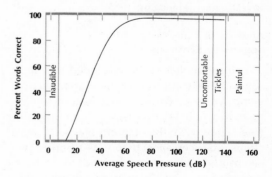

Figure 8.26. Percentage of monosyllabic words that can be recognized correctly as a function of intensity. (Miller, 1951; data from Kryter, 1946, and Silverman, 1947.)

spect to speech materials. Which words should be used? One solution has been to use "phonetically balanced" (PB) monosyllables (Egan, 1948; Hirsh et al., 1952). (Monosyllables are 1-syllable words.) These monosyllables are selected so that the frequency of occurrence of various consonant and vowel sounds is representative of English speech. Figure 8.26 shows how the percentage of monosyllables correctly heard increases as the intensity of the speech sounds is raised. In obtaining data for this graph, a separate list of monosyllables was used at each of a number of intensity levels. A "threshold" value for intelligibility can be taken as the sound pressure level (in decibels) at which 50 percent of the words are correctly received. Although a single threshold value for monosyllables might be useful for subjects considered to hear normally, more extensive information is desirable in the case of subjects with abnormal hearing who may never be able to discriminate between the more difficult words. For these subjects, a useful additional measure is to determine the maximum percentage of words received correctly (Davis & Silverman, 1960).

In constructing syllable lists for practical use, an effort is made to use words that are familiar to the subject population. There is experimental evidence showing precisely how intelligibility is dependent on the frequency with which each word is used. Studies by Rosenzweig and Postman (1957) and Howes (1957) show that threshold for the recognition of a word heard in noise is inversely related to the logarithm of the frequency with which the word occurs. That is, a word that occurs frequently in the English language can be perceived at a lower sound pressure level than one that occurs infrequently; the relationship between frequency and threshold is a simple mathematical function. Similar results have been found for visual recognition (Howes & Solomon, 1951).

Why are frequently used (or more familiar) words more detectable than infrequently used words? A "fragment theory" originally formulated by Solomon and Postman (1952) has been used by a number of researchers to account for the effects of word frequency on detection (see Neisser, 1967). This theory states that a fragment of the stimulus word perceived at a low stimulus intensity can act as a cue to a limited number of complete word responses. Certain word responses in this set will have a higher response strength because they have been used more frequently before the experiment. The word response with the highest response strength will be given by the subject. A fragment from a low-frequency word will be likely to produce a high-frequency word response—which will be an error. Thus, in general, the number of correct responses to low-frequency words will be lower than to high-frequency words at a given intensity level.

Pollack, Rubinstein, and Decker (1959) have shown that if the subject knows the set of words that are to be used in testing threshold, the effects of word frequency noted above do not occur. (According to the theory above, if the message set is known, subjects will not give high-frequency erroneous words from outside the set.) House, Williams, Hecker, and Kryter (1965) have found, in addition, that using a small "closed set" of response alternatives has definite advantages in certain practical evaluations of voice-communication systems where a trained crew of listeners is to be used over and over (see also Black, 1957; Fairbanks, 1958). They have used an intelligibility test where the subject chooses the correct response from 6 alternatives. (Example: bat, bad, back, bass, ban, bath.) The subjects' performance on this test showed great stability over many repetitions of the test. In test situations where the subject is originally uninformed as to the test words, performance tends to show improvement over successive test sessions (see, for example, Egan, 1948; Moser & Dreher, 1955). An extensive training period then is necessary if the listeners are to be used as a "trained crew" for evaluating voice-communication systems.

If subjects know which words are to be used in the test, less intensity is required for correct recognition as number of words in the test vocabulary is decreased (Miller, Heise, & Lichten, 1951; Sumby & Pollack, 1954; Bruner, Miller, & Zimmerman, 1955). In addition, the threshold of recognition is dependent on context: If words are presented in the context of a sentence, they can be perceived more easily (Miller, Heise, & Lichten, 1951; O'Neill, 1957).

Why is recognition of a word presented from a known message set poorer when the message set is larger? One explanation states that the larger the message set, the larger is the number of response alternatives the stimulus must be matched against—with a resulting greater chance for confusion (Pollack, 1959; Garner, 1965). The higher intelligibility of a word presented in the context of a sentence can be understood by supposing that the context reduces the size of the possible set of words from which the correct word must be chosen (Miller, Heise, & Lichten, 1951).

In ordinary conversation visual cues may be given the listener from the speaker's face. Sumby and Pollack (1954) showed that the advantage these visual cues provides is increased as the noise level is increased relative to the speech; O'Neill (1957) showed that the visual cues were more helpful when less auditory information was available. Hard-of-hearing individuals can be trained to make use of these visual cues to aid them in understanding speech (Davis & Silverman, 1960).

Factors Reducing Speech Intelligibility: Single Source

In the preceding section we have discussed primarily cues that will increase the probability that a given word will be perceived correctly when it is spoken. In this section we discuss a number of variables that primarily cause a decrease in intelligibility. These variables have been studied most often by experimenters interested in speech-communication systems. They wished to find how

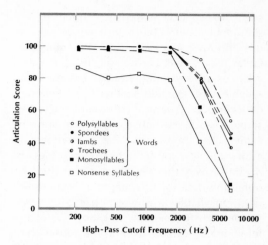

Figure 8.27. Articulation score as a function of low-pass filtering. A *spondee* is a 2-syllable word with an approximately equal accent on each syllable. An *iamb* is a 2-syllable word with accent on the second syllable. A *trochee* is a 2-syllable word with accent on the first syllable. (Hirsh, Reynolds, & Joseph, 1954.)

distortions of various kinds in speech-transmission systems would affect intelligibility of speech (Licklider & Miller, 1951; Fletcher, 1953). Knowledge acquired from these inves-

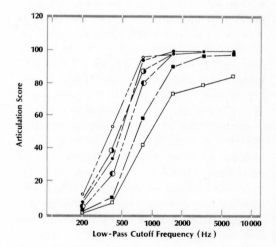

Figure 8.28. Articulation score as a function of high-pass filtering. The different symbols and lines are identified in Fig. 8.27. (Hirsh, Reynolds, & Joseph, 1954.)

tigations can lead to design of speech-communication systems that will meet requirements for efficient speech communication at the least cost.

Filtering A number of experiments have investigated the effects of eliminating various frequency regions from speech (Licklider & Miller, 1951; Fletcher, 1953). Results from one of these experiments (Hirsh, Reynolds, & Joseph, 1954) are shown in Figures 8.27 and 8.28. Six high-pass filter settings, and 6 low-pass filter settings were used. (Recall that a high-pass cut-off frequency of 200 means that all frequencies above 200 Hz were passed by the filter; a low-pass cut-off frequency of 400 means that all frequencies below 400 Hz were passed by the filter.) The articulation score refers to the percentage of each kind of word heard correctly. From Figures 8.27 and 8.28 it is evident how intelligibility deteriorates as more and more of the high frequencies, or more and more of the low frequencies, are eliminated. Study of individual speech sounds in other experiments shows that eliminating high frequencies affects consonant intelligibility more than vowel intelligibility, while the opposite is true for elimination of low frequencies (Fletcher, 1953).

Another way of going about the filtering is to pass only a band of frequencies. For instance, if a band of frequencies ranging from 500 to 2500 Hz is passed by the filter, an articulation score of about 45 percent is obtained (Egan & Wiener, 1946).

Some temporal variables in speech intelligibility If speech is interrupted (pieces "chopped" out of it), the resulting intelligibility depends on the rate of the interruption as well as on the percentage of time the speech is actually sounding. For example, with 50% "on" time, intelligibility is poor for very low rates of interruption—where syllables and even words are chopped out; but intelligibility becomes much better at higher rates of interruption. If we take the pieces of interrupted speech, and place them adjacent to each other, we can achieve a speeded-up communication. Experiments show that words can be made about 2.5 times faster than normal without loss of intelligibility (Garvey, 1953; Fairbanks & Kodman, 1957), provided that the pieces chopped out are not too large. Playing a phonograph record of speech at a higher speed is not a suitable experimental technique for investigating the effects of rate of speech on intelligibility because this procedure also changes the frequencies in the speech sounds by a factor proportional to the change in speed. Shifting the frequencies in speech will in itself cause a decrease in intelligibility (Fletcher, 1929).

Reflection of sound from the walls of a reverberant room causes each sound to persist longer than usual. The sound from one syllable persists and overlaps that of the next syllable, and thus intelligibility is adversely affected (Licklider & Miller, 1951; Lochner & Burger, 1961; Thompson, Webster, & Gales, 1961). Information on the relation between intelligibility and the amount of reverberation is useful in the design of auditoriums.

Noise masking In practical situations, noise of various kinds often interferes with

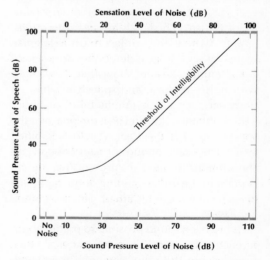

Figure 8.29. Change in threshold for the intelligibility of speech with an increase in the sound pressure level of noise. (Licklider, 1951; after Hawkins & Stevens, 1950.)

speech intelligibility. If noise with a continuous and uniform spectrum is present, the masking effect is reasonably simple to predict. Figure 8.29 shows how the threshold for detectability of speech increases as the level of masking noise increases. It can be seen that at medium and high noise levels a given decibel increase in noise level results in an equal decibel increase in the sound pressure level of the speech required for detectability.

Location of the noise source in space with reference to the location of the speech signal is also an important variable (Hirsh, 1950; Kock, 1950). Speech intelligibility is best when the speech and noise sources are in different locations. The advantage of separating the speech and noise sources is reduced, however, in more reverberant surroundings (Hirsh, 1950; Harvey et al., 1963). Moving the speech source in space leads to changes in the time of arrival (and phase) of the speech signal at both ears, as well as to changes in intensity at both ears. In order to control these variables, analytical studies have been carried out with earphones (Licklider, 1948). These studies are closely related to those on "masking level differences" (MLDs) we discussed earlier in the chapter. Experimenters, however, have not only measured the *detectability* of the speech signal, but also the *intelligibility* (where the subject must recognize words rather than just detect the presence of some sound). Results show that, if we start with noise in-phase and speech in-phase at both ears, a gain in intelligibility of about 6 dB is obtained if we reverse the phase of the speech signal at the 2 ears (Levitt & Rabiner, 1967). The exact amount of gain depends on the stimulus frequencies present that are important in the understanding of the particular speech stimuli used (Carhart, Tilman, & Johnson, 1967).

It has been found possible to predict interference with speech in many practical situations, where the noise spectrum is not uniform, by taking an average of noise levels in certain octave bands, for instance, in bands of 600 to 1200, 1200 to 2400, 2400 to 4800 cycles per second (Beranek, 1956; 1957). Thus it is possible to make recommendations about desirable and permissable noise levels in offices and ships, for example, by knowing how these noises interfere with speech (Beranek, 1957; Kryter et al., 1963; Webster, 1965).

Responding to Speech from Multiple Sources

If the observer has to pay attention to several signal sources and respond to certain relevant messages, a number of new variables enter in to determine performance. For instance, the greater the amount of irrelevant material presented, and the greater the similarity of relevant and irrelevant material, the lower the efficiency of performance (Webster & Thompson, 1954; Poulton, 1956). A control-tower operator at an airport must observe in this type of situation; he may have to pay attention to messages coming from several loudspeakers, and respond to messages from aircraft directed to his control tower only. "Selectivity of attention" was emphasized early in the history of American psychology by William James, but renewed interest in this problem, and especially experimentation, has only occurred in more recent years. Broadbent (1958) has summarized much relevant information and has stressed the conclusion that humans have limited capacities to process information arriving from multiple sources.

A more common type of listening situation in everyday life is one in which the subject is trying to listen to one message and exclude other interfering messages (the "cocktail party" problem). This situation is analogous to those investigated in classical masking experiments, where the subject is trying to detect a particular kind of signal in the presence of an interfering noise. At the same time, listening in the presence of interfering messages is more complex and undoubtedly involves mechanisms beyond those required in the noise-masking situation.

As in the case of noise masking, interference by an irrelevant message is less if this message comes from a loudspeaker or source that is spatially separated from the source of the relevant message to which the subject must listen (Broadbent, 1958). If the irrelevant message is spoken by a different voice, or by a voice that sounds different due to high-pass filtering (removing some of the low frequencies), then reception is improved over the condition where both relevant and irrelevant messages are spoken by the same voice (Broadbent, 1952; Egan, Carterette, & Thwing, 1954).

Further experiments have been performed to find out more about the nature of the attentional mechanisms utilized in rejecting the unwanted material. Cherry (1953) used a technique he called "shadowing," in which the subject was required to repeat aloud a message presented to one ear by earphone. At the same time, irrelevant messages were presented to the other ear by earphone. When subjects were questioned about the irrelevant material, they could report only gross changes from one voice to another, or a change from a voice to a pure tone. They could not report the content of the irrelevant speech or even what language it was in. However, when Moray (1959) included the subject's own name in the "irrelevant" material, he found that this was often noticed by the listener.

Thus, suppression of irrelevant material is by no means complete. The suppressed material can "break through" to the subject's attention under certain special conditions. Treisman (1960) found that if the passages each ear was listening to were suddenly switched to opposite ears, some subjects would repeat 1 or 2 words from the message that was now going to the ear whose word stimuli were not supposed to be repeated.

It has also been found that if messages going to each ear are made the same but the message to the ear *not* attended to is made to lag behind the message to the ear attended to, the subject fails to notice that the messages are the same unless the lag is reduced to

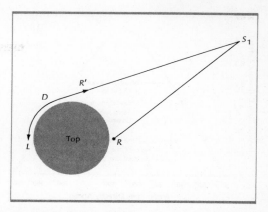

Figure 8.30. Schematic diagram of paths of sound to each ear. Assume that you are looking down from the top at the subject's head and that the source of sound is to the right.

about 4 seconds or less (Cherry, 1953; Treisman, 1964). This effect even occurs with some bilingual subjects when the message to one ear is given in French and the message to the other is given in English, provided that the messages are similar in meaning (Treisman, 1964).

USE OF SOUND CUES IN LOCALIZATION

Available Cues for Localization of Right–Left Direction of a Sound Source

Results of early experiments (Pierce, 1901) which measured the accuracy of sound localization showed that *even if the head was held fixed in position*, discrimination between sources to the left and right of the head was good. Front-back discrimination and up-down discrimination were very poor. What are some possible cues? Let us first consider a source in the horizontal plane—the plane parallel to the ground passing through the ears.

Figure 8.30 indicates schematically the paths of sound from source S to the 2 ears L and R. SR is the distance of the source to the right ear, SL is the distance of the source to the left ear, and $D = SL - SR$, the *difference* in the distance from the source to the left and right ears.

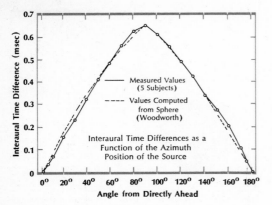

Figure 8.31. Interaural time differences in milliseconds as a function of angular position of source from listener's head. Zero degrees represents a source directly in front of the subject. (Feddersen et al., 1957.)

A sound at *S* will arrive at the left ear later than it will at the right ear. For each centimeter of difference *D* in the distance to the 2 ears, there will be a time difference of about .029 msec. The time difference can give a cue to the left-right location of the source. Figure 8.31 shows the difference in the time of the arrival of a click at the 2 ears measured by a small microphone in each ear canal (Feddersen et al., 1957). An angle of zero degrees represents a click source straight ahead of the subject, and an angle of 180 degrees represents a click source behind the subject. It can be seen that the time difference reaches a maximum (of near .6 msec) when the click source is opposite one ear (90 degrees).

There will also be an intensity difference at the 2 ears, due to the "shadowing" effect of the head, for the head acts as a barrier to attenuate sounds getting to the ear farthest away from the source (ear L in the diagram). Figure 8.32 shows the difference in intensity of sound at the 2 ears for pure tones of various frequencies as the angle of the source is changed. These results, as well as those for time differences, were obtained using a subject placed in an anechoic room, the source being 7 feet from the subject's head. The difference in the intensity of the sound tends to be greatest when the source is nearly opposite one ear. It is greater for high frequencies—reaching 20 dB for frequencies of 5000 and 6000 Hz. However, the variation in the difference in the intensity is such that we would predict—correctly—that determination

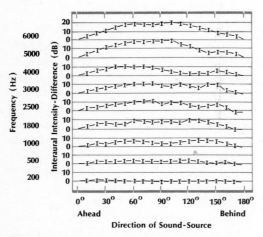

Figure 8.32. Interaural intensity difference in decibels as a function of frequency and direction of sound source. Zero degrees represents a source straight ahead. (Feddersen, et al., 1957.)

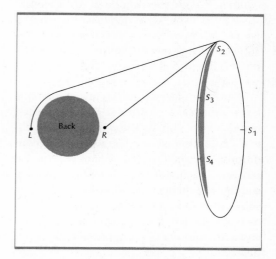

Figure 8.33. S_1, S_2, S_3, S_4, represent sources located so that the differences in the distance to the 2 ears, *L* and *R*, are the same. The head is approximated by a sphere, so the diagram applies only as an approximation to the actual human head. Position S_1 corresponds to the source position shown in Figure 8.30.

of the exact location of the source of a pure tone by means of an intensity cue alone would be rather inaccurate when the tone is in a position to the side of the head.

We have so far been considering cues from sources in the horizontal plane. The concern with sources in this plane is understandable because the majority of the sources we have to locate in everyday life (voices, automobiles) occur in approximately this plane. As soon as the possibility arises that sounds may originate from all three dimensions, however, the problem of localization becomes more difficult—because sources in different positions may produce very similar cues. The circle in Figure 8.33 shows the locations of sources that might be expected to produce very similar intensity and time differences at the two ears. The "shadowing" effect of the auricle (Figure 8.5) helps us to differentiate signals coming from these different directions; and head movements are of especial importance in resolving ambiguities in cues. We discuss the role of the auricle and of head movements in more detail in later sections.

Use of Earphones for Investigation of Right-Left Localization in the Horizontal Plane

If we use earphones to present stimuli to subjects, we can vary the time difference at the 2 ears while holding intensity difference constant, and vice versa. Thus the effects of each of these cues can be determined separately.

If pulse stimuli of equal intensity are led to each ear, and each pulse arrives at the same instant, the subject will perceive a sound in the median plane. (This is the plane through the nose dividing the head into left and right halves). If the pulse to the right ear is made to arrive slightly earlier in time, the perceived composite sound will appear to be coming from a direction more to the right. However, if the intensity of the stimulus to the right ear is increased (even when the time of the arrival of pulses is the same at each ear)

the composite sound will again appear to be coming from a direction to the right of the median plane.

When earphones are used in localization studies, the subject encounters certain problems in indicating where he perceives the sound source. Some subjects perceive the source as traveling inside the head. Others perceive the source as traveling in an arc over, in front of, or behind the head (and close to the head) as the intensity or time difference at the 2 ears is changed. Some experimenters have found it possible for experienced subjects to "project" the sound heard with earphones on to an external scale (von Békésy, 1960; Jeffress & Taylor, 1961; Sayers, 1964).

The term "lateralization" is typically used at the present time to refer to the judgment of the location of sounds when stimuli are produced by earphones worn by the subject, while the term "localization" is reserved for situations where the subject judges the location of a sound coming from some external source not mounted on the head.

Early investigators found that a time difference as small as 30 μsec (microseconds—millionths of a second) between clicks presented to the 2 ears resulted in the perception of a change of location from the median plane. Other investigators (Hornbostel & Wertheimer, 1920; Klemm, 1920) found that time and intensity could compensate for each other within limits. This has been designated a "time-intensity trade." For example, if the right ear received the click 100 μsec earlier than the left, the sound would be localized to the right, but if the intensity of the click in the *left* ear was now increased, the perceived location of the sound could be brought back to the median plane.

Early experimenters also used low-frequency pure tones with earphones and varied the phase relations at the 2 ears. When the tones in the two ears were in phase (zero degrees phase difference) the observer localized the resulting sensation in the median plane. As the phase in one ear was made to

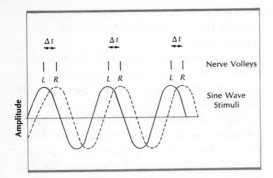

Figure 8.34. Schematic diagram of way in which a *phase* difference in a low-frequency stimulus at the 2 ears gives rise to a *time* difference, Δt in the nerve volleys corresponding to the two waves. Volleys for wave *L* are in the left auditory nerve; for wave *R* they are in the right auditory nerve.

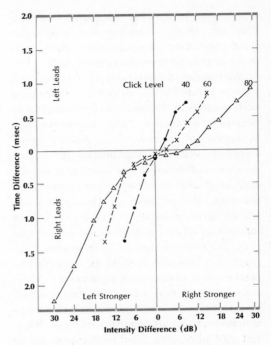

Figure 8.35. Time difference in milliseconds between click stimuli delivered to the 2 ears which will compensate for a given intensity difference between the 2 ears. The parameter is the sound pressure level of a 1000 Hz tone the peak amplitude of which equals the maximum peak of the stronger click. (Deatherage & Hirsh, 1959.)

lead, the tone was localized toward that side. Above about 1500 Hz, no effect of phase shift could be observed (Hughes, 1940). These facts can be understood if we think of the phase difference at both ears as actually presenting a *time* difference to the nervous system. This is possible because of the fact that each cycle of a low pure tone stimulates a volley of nerve impulses (see Figure 8.11). In Figure 8.34 *R* represents schematically a sine-wave stimulus to the right ear, *L* a sine-wave stimulus to the left ear. In this particular example the stimulus to the right ear lags in phase. The volleys sent along each auditory nerve are represented above each wave, and the symbol Δt represents the resulting difference in the time of arrival in the central nervous system of each pair of volleys. Shaxby and Gage (1932) were able to show experimentally that the crucial variable in change of phase was actually a time difference at the 2 ears. They measured the phase difference at the 2 ears necessary to compensate for an opposing intensity difference and to bring the perceived sound image back to center (median plane). They found that the various phase changes necessary at different low frequencies to compensate for a given intensity difference all reduced to a single time differ-

ence (when each phase difference was expressed in terms of a time difference).

Recent Analytic Studies with Earphones

More recent studies have sought to investigate the "time-intensity trade" over a wider range of conditions. Deatherage and Hirsh (1959) set the sound pressure level of a click in one ear at a standard value (40, 60, or 80 dB) and the level of the click in the other ear at a different intensity value. The difference in intensity caused the click image to be perceived toward the ear with the higher intensity click. They found how much the click in this "higher intensity" ear had to be delayed in time in order for the perceived click image to be shifted back to the median plane. Figure 8.35 shows their results. It is evident that the results differ at different click intensity levels (40, 60, or 80 dB). A larger difference in intensity between the ears can be compensated for by a given time difference in the 2 ears at a high intensity level than at a low intensity level.

David, Guttman, and van Bergeijk (1959) have also found that a time difference at the 2 ears was relatively more important at a high intensity level: they found that a much greater time difference (about 5 times) was needed at a low intensity of stimulation than at a high intensity to compensate for a difference in intensity at the 2 ears. Their study, in addition, emphasizes an important point about localization of high-frequency sounds: If high-frequency stimuli come in the form of pulses, the subject can determine the origin of these impulsive, or "transient," high-frequency sounds by utilizing the difference in the time of arrival of the pulses at each ear (David, Guttman, & van Bergeijk, 1958; Leakey, Sayers, & Cherry, 1958; Cherry & Sayers, 1959). A stimulus with sudden onset (with low- or high-frequency content) sets off a large number of nerve impulses that travel as a wave of activity along the auditory nerve into the nervous system. This is similar to the "volley" of impulses caused by a cycle of a sine wave of low frequency.

As more studies were carried out on the time-intensity trade, it became evident that the results depended on frequency content of the signal pulses as well as the intensity level (David, Guttman, & van Bergeijk, 1958; Cherry & Sayers, 1959). A detailed study made by Harris (1960) documented the difference in the trading relation found for low-frequency pulses as compared to high-frequency pulses. The change in time difference between the ears necessary to compensate for each decibel difference in the intensity between the ears was 25 μsec for low-frequency pulses (with a frequency content below 1000 Hz), whereas the figure was 60 μsec for high-frequency pulses (with frequency content above 4000 Hz). In other words, in the operation of the localization system, it requires less time difference at low frequencies to compensate for intensity difference at the 2 ears than at high frequencies.

Further characteristics of the localization system have been revealed by other studies using earphones: Increase in the duration of the stimulation, or in the repetition rate, appears to increase the effectiveness of a stimulus in determining localization (Tobias & Zerlin, 1959; Thurlow & Elfner, 1961; Butler & Naunton, 1964).

Additional experiments have used stimuli of different frequencies in the 2 ears. When 1 pulse is presented to one ear, and 1 to the other, localization interactions may occur even though these pulses are very different in frequency content (Teas, 1962). When 1 pure tone is led to one ear and another pure tone to the other, localization interactions can occur even when these tones do not have the same frequency (Thurlow & Elfner, 1959; Butler, 1962; Butler & Naunton, 1964). The frequency differences for which interaction can be obtained are small, except when the tone in one ear is made much more intense than the tone in the other ear (Thurlow & Elfner, 1959; Butler, 1962; Butler & Naunton, 1964). The interaction observed is a "pulling-over" of the less intense tone toward the perceived location of the other, more intense tone. Low tones will also interact with certain tones in the other ear that are simple multiples in frequency (Thurlow & Elfner, 1959). For example, it has been observed that a tone of 100 Hz in the left ear will cause multiples of 100 Hz up to about 700 Hz to be pulled toward the median plane when the phase relations in the 2 ears are properly adjusted.

Butler (1962) and Butler and Naunton (1964) have found that noise in one ear will cause a pulling over laterally of the perceived location of stimuli in the other ear—including noise, square wave, speech, and tone stimuli. "Pulling over" effects are greater as the intensity of noise used in the opposite ear is increased, and effects are greater when there is an overlap in the frequency content at the 2 ears.

The main purpose of the various analytic

studies we have been discussing is theoretical. The studies seek to find out not only what types of localization effect are possible, but also to understand better what type of system or systems can be responsible for the localization effects.

Physiological and Perceptual Evidence in Relation to Some Theories of Right–Left Sound Localization in the Horizontal Plane

Interaction of neural inputs from the two ears　Our understanding of the mechanisms responsible for sound localization, even in the horizontal plane, is far from complete. However, it will be valuable to discuss some of the current theories and evidence.

Rosenzweig (1954) has gathered data in experiments with cats that show that the amplitude of summated electrical response is larger from the auditory area of the right side of the cerebral cortex when the left ear receives a pulse stimulus slightly ahead of the right ear. When the right ear receives the pulse stimulus earlier, the electrical response is larger in the auditory area of the left side of the cerebral cortex. This result led to the hypothesis that localization is determined by the relative amount of neural activity in the right and left auditory cerebral areas. (A similar type of theory, involving a comparison of the amount of activity coming from 2 lower neural centers, was developed for explaining localization due to intensity differences at the 2 ears. See van Bergeijk, 1962.)

For this hypothesis to be correct, there would have to be some mechanism capable of comparing the amount of neural response in the 2 cortical areas. However, there are other experiments, performed with cats, which show that these animals can still localize sounds even when the interconnections between the higher levels of the 2 sides of the brain are severed (Neff, 1961). Thus, section of the *corpus callosum* (which joins the 2 cerebral hemispheres) and of the neural path which joins the left and right *inferior colliculi* (midbrain region), does not affect sound localization. Finally, Walsh (1957) has

reported the case of a man with only 1 cerebral hemisphere who was able to localize on the basis of time differences between clicks. Hodgson (1967) has recently reported that a female patient with only 1 cerebral hemisphere showed no defect in "centering" the location of a tone (by manipulating the intensity at the two ears). It would appear that localization information can be processed in either cerebral hemisphere. Behavioral experiments with cats show that although some reflex behavioral reactions to sound location may be controlled by cells of the inferior colliculus, other adaptive reactions to sound location require that the analysis of time and intensity differences performed at lower neural centers be somehow coded and transmitted all the way to the cerebral cortex (see Neff, 1961; Masterton, Jane, & Diamond, 1968). It must be remembered that the evidence we have been discussing has been obtained with mammals.

Of course, the neural signals from one ear must cross over and interact at some place in the nervous system with signals from the other ear in order to provide the basis for sound localization. Recent evidence, obtained with cats, indicates that an important center for this interaction is the *accessory nucleus* of the *superior olive*. (This is a nucleus well down in the brain stem; see Figure 8.9.) Galambos, Schwartzkopff, and Rupert (1959) discovered neural cells in the accessory nucleus of the superior olive the responses of which were extremely sensitive to difference in time of arrival of stimuli at the 2 ears. However, different reactions occurred in different types of cells when a click stimulus was delivered to each ear within a short interval of time, or was delivered to one ear alone. *Type 1:* Clicks in both ears produced neural discharge from the unit whereas a click in 1 ear did not. *Type 2:* Clicks in both ears produced a marked increase in latency (the time it takes to react to the stimulus) compared to that produced by a click in 1 ear. *Type 3:* Clicks in both ears inhibited the neural discharge produced by a click in 1 ear.

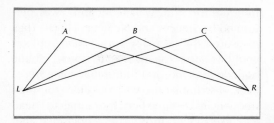

Figure 8.36. Schematic diagram of a "place" theory of sound localization in the horizontal plane. *L* and *R* represent input from left and right auditory nerves respectively. *A, B,* and *C* represent cells where the input from the 2 sides meets. Which cell is fired depends on the time relations between the inputs from *L* and *R*.

Hall (1965) has described a type of cell that responds more to simultaneous stimulation of both ears than to 1 ear alone. This type appears related to type 1 of Galambos, Schwartzkopff, and Rupert. Hall has also made detailed measurements with cells similar to type 3 of Galambos, Schwartzkopff, and Rupert. He found this type much more frequently than other types. The degree to which the firing of these cells was inhibited by binaural stimulation was a function of interaural time difference and interaural intensity difference. A "time-intensity trading relation" was derived from the results which is comparable to that found in experiments with humans.

Other investigators, also using cats, have discovered cells higher up in the nervous system that are sensitive to time differences in stimulation at the 2 ears (Brugge, Dubrovsky, & Rose, 1964; Rose et al., 1966). Cells have also been discovered recently in the inferior colliculus of the cat that are sensitive to small differences in *intensity* at the two ears (Rose et al., 1966).

"Place" theory Some years ago, Jeffress proposed a "place" theory of sound localization for clicks and low-frequency tones that was based on time of arrival of impulses in the neural localization system (Jeffress, 1948). It can be diagrammed very schemati-

cally, as in Figure 8.36. (See also Licklider, 1959.) It essentially proposed that a neural impulse from *L* (left auditory nerve) would travel over pathways *LA, LB, LC* (and many more) the distances of which would increase from left to right. A neural impulse from *R* (right auditory nerve) would travel paths *RC, RB, RA* (and many more). If the impulses started simultaneously from *L* and *R*, they would meet at *B*, and (it is assumed) their effects would summate to cause a cell at *B* to fire, thus signalling a median plane localization. If the pulse at *R* occurred earlier in time, then the *L* and *R* neural pulses would meet at a place such as *A*, the place depending on the difference in starting time of the two pulses. A cell at *A* would fire, and signal that the sound source was a certain distance to the right. (Note that actual localization space and neural localization space would be reversed—but this would be no problem in cueing appropriate reactions. Recall that the image on the retina is upside down!) The "type 1" neural units Galambos, Schwartzkopff, and Rupert found, act in a manner similar to the postulated units at *A, B, C*.

There is evidence from localization experiments with humans that seems to fit in with a "place" theory of the localization processes. Von Békésy (1960) has reported that when bursts of noise are presented alternately at a low rate from 2 positions in space (not too widely separated) only 1 noise is heard, in between the 2 sources. Thurlow and Marten (1962) observed that a steady noise could be heard in between 2 alternating sources, even if the sources were placed at fairly large angular separations, provided the alternation rate of the sources was as high as 7 to 14 per second. These results can be interpreted in terms of interaction between 2 spatially adjacent distributions of neural activity in the localization system. (See also Thurlow, Marten, and Bhatt, 1965.)

Evidence of a separate system for binaural intensity differences At one time it seemed that it was only necessary to assume 1 type of localization system operating for low tones and pulse stimuli—a system operating primarily in terms of time differences at the two ears. The effects of intensity, it was supposed, could be understood in terms of the change in the latency of the nerve discharge (David, Guttman, & van Bergeijk, 1958; Deatherage & Hirsh, 1959). For instance, if a click in one ear was made more intense, the nerve fibers would discharge sooner (latency would decrease), and the neural pulse in the nerve corresponding to this more intense click would arrive in the nervous system earlier. Thus an intensity difference would be converted to a *time* difference.

However, there is mounting evidence from perceptual experiments to indicate that the effects of differences in intensity at the 2 ears can operate through a separate system to influence localization. For instance, in studies described earlier (Thurlow & Elfner, 1959; Butler & Naunton, 1964), it was found that a stimulus in one ear could influence localization of a stimulus in the other ear, in the absence of any systematic temporal relations between these stimuli. Even in the older literature there was evidence that when time and intensity cues of a tone were very different, 2 separately localized tones were heard (Halverson, 1922; Banister, 1926). Harris (1960) has noted an analogous effect more recently. Sayers and Toole (1964) emphasize that in their experiments with pulses, a change in the intensity of the sound at one ear produces effects that are not equivalent to a change in time. We have already seen in a previous section that there is physiological evidence indicating that there are cells specialized for responding to small differences in intensity at the 2 ears.

Experiments on Accuracy of Localization of Direction of Sound Sources at Various Locations in Space

Localization with no head movements allowed An experiment which measured the localization in space of tonal stimuli, without interference from wall reflections, was performed by Stevens and Newman (1936). They measured the accuracy with which subjects could localize the source of sound in the horizontal plane, and found that some front-back discrimination was possible for high frequencies even when the subject's head was fixed in position. They concluded that their subjects were utilizing differences in stimulus intensity correlated with the front and back positions of the source. Burger (1958) has also found some front-back discrimination possible for noise stimuli. This discrimination is mainly due to the presence of the external auricle, or pinna, which blocks sounds coming from the rear more effectively than sounds coming from in front. Kietz (1953) showed how perception of a sound as being in front or behind could be changed by modification of the physical characteristics of the pinna.

Familiarity with the stimulus should increase the accuracy with which a subject can make front-back discriminations. If the subject has learned how the stimulus sounded when it was in front of him, he is better able to notice changes in overall loudness and quality (dependent on high frequencies) when the stimulus is presented from behind him.

Mills (1958) has made measurements, in an anechoic room, of the threshold for *change* in the perceived location of a source of sound in the horizontal plane. He was able to show that thresholds at low frequencies (up to 1400 Hz) for the detection of a change in the position of a source from the median plane were related to thresholds obtained by earphones for the detection of a difference in the phase of stimulation at the 2 ears (Klumpp & Eady, 1956; Zwislocki & Feldman, 1956). An upper limit of 1400 to 1500 Hz was also found by Sandel et al. (1955); we have noted previously a similar upper limit found from work carried out with earphones for the effect of the phase on lateralization.

In a later experiment Mills (1960) demonstrated that thresholds for the detection of a change in the position of a source of *high* frequencies from the median plane were related (at 1500 to 6000 Hz) to thresholds obtained with earphones for the detection of change in the lateral position of a tone from the median plane, when only a difference in the *intensity* at the 2 ears was available as a cue. Mills (1958) also presented detailed data showing how the discrimination of a change in the position of pure tones deteriorates if the tones originate from positions at the side of the head (as compared to straight ahead). This deterioration is particularly marked for high frequencies. It is important to remember that in these experiments carried out by Mills, no head movement was allowed.

Fairly accurate discrimination of the direction of thermal noise in the *vertical* ("up-down") direction has been found for angles of elevation up to 30 to 40 degrees above or below the horizontal plane passing through the 2 ears (Thurlow & Runge, 1967; Roffler & Butler, 1968). Because of the shadowing effect of the head and body, the intensity of high-frequency sound reaching the ear opposite the sound source would be expected to increase with the elevation of the sound source. It is possible that the pattern of intensity differences at the 2 ears, in certain high-frequency regions, may be an important cue to elevation.

Role of head movements in sound localization Observation of subjects trying to locate a source of sound in space shows that they make extensive use of head movements. (See, for example, Thurlow, Mangels, & Runge, 1967.) Analytical experiments are necessary, however, to find out which movements are effective as aids to localization.

Some years ago, Klensch (1948) performed demonstrational experiments that showed the crucial role of head movements in front-back discrimination. (See Young, 1931; Koenig, 1950; Jonkhees and Veer, 1958; for related experiments.) He used 2 funnels, 1 connected to each ear by a tube. The funnels were both

oriented toward a source of sound in *front* of the head. Subjects rotated their heads. (You can produce "rotation" of your head by keeping it upright, and turning it to the left or to the right.) If a subject rotated his head to the right at the same time that the left funnel was advanced toward the source of sound (and the right funnel was moved away from the source) he perceived the source to be in front of his head. (Relatively earlier arrival of sound in the left ear, and increasing intensity in the left ear relative to that in the right ear, are ordinary accompaniments of turning the head to the right when the sound source is in *front* of us.) When the subject rotated his head to the *left* under these conditions, however, he perceived the source in *back* of his head. This result is related to the fact that ordinarily when we rotate our head to the left, and the source is in *back* of us, the left ear receives increasingly greater intensity compared to that received in the right ear, and the sound arrives progressively earlier at the left ear than it does at the right ear. Note that utilization of this information for front-back discrimination does not require previous familiarity with a particular sound stimulus.

Burger (1958) has presented quantitative data on front-back discrimination in the horizontal plane, using filtered thermal noise as a stimulus. Performance was best when head movements were allowed. Thurlow and Runge (1967) showed that if the head of the subject was rotated through a controlled angle (by a motor), errors in location of a source of thermal noise in the horizontal plane were substantially reduced.

Movements of the head would also be expected to help discrimination of the *elevation* of a sound source. Differences in time of arrival and intensity at the 2 ears, produced by a sound source in a given location, should change systematically as the head is rotated, or pivoted, and the type of change should be related to the elevation of the sound source. (A "pivot" movement can be produced by starting with your head upright,

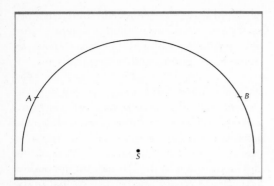

Figure 8.37. Click sources in a "precedence" experiment. One source is indicated at location *A*, and another at location *B*. The subject's head is at *S*.

then tilting your head toward either left or right shoulder.) Wallach (1939, 1940) has emphasized the importance of rotational movements and has pointed out that the changes in time and intensity cues with head rotation are maximal when the source is in the same horizontal plane as the ears, but become less and less as the source elevation is increased until they become zero when the source is directly above the head. Despite these theoretical expectations, Thurlow and Runge (1967) did not find that either induced "rotation" or "pivot" movements aided much in improving elevation discrimination. However, it seems possible that, with special training, subjects might learn to use head movements to obtain more substantial improvements in the discrimination of the elevation of sound sources.

Precedence effects If 2 sounds occur in space, one slightly ahead of the other in time, the first sound appears to dominate in its effects on perception. Figure 8.37 shows schematically a typical location of the subject and click sources *A* and *B*. Let us suppose that 2 clicks, 1 from *A* and 1 from *B*, at equal intensity, are sounded one after the other, *A* then *B*, with a very short time interval between. The following are several of the important phenomena that occur:

For time intervals below 2 msec, only 1 click

is heard, and its location is a compromise between the localizations of *A* and *B*. If they arrive simultaneously, the single click is heard midway between *A* and *B*. As the interval is lengthened (up to about 2 msec), the click heard moves toward *A*. Thus, the effect of the first click stimulus is more important in determining localization. Wallach, Newman, and Rosenzweig (1949) and von Békésy (1960) have studied this problem.

When the time interval between the *A* and *B* clicks is between about 2 and 6 msec, only 1 click is heard, and that is at position *A*. When the time interval between *A* and *B* is greater than about 6 msec, then click *B* can be heard also at its proper location (Wallach, Newman, & Rosenzweig, 1949). This time interval is longer if click *B* is less intense than *A* (Thurlow & Parks, 1961). Could this be masking? It does not appear to be entirely masking because the effect of increasing rate of presentation of click pairs appears to be different for this situation (Thurlow & Parks, 1961), than when click pairs are presented simply to 1 ear alone (Guttman, Bergeijk, & David, 1960).

For time intervals when click *B* is not heard, the loudness of the click heard at *A* is greater than it would be if click *A* were sounded by itself. This is a further reason for believing that click *B* is not simply masked out in the inner ear by *A*. We might describe what is happening as a type of "funneling" in which a stimulus occurring second in time is "funneled" neurally toward the location of the first. Von Békésy has introduced the concept of funneling to describe a number of broadly similar types of interaction in cutaneous as well as in auditory perception (von Békésy, 1959). Thurlow, Marten, and Bhatt (1965) have sketched neural mechanisms that might help to explain several types of precedence effects.

Precedence effects for complex stimuli such as speech and music have been recognized for many years (Haas, 1951; Gardner, 1968). The time intervals over which these precedence effects last are longer than with simple click stimuli. The effects are especially noticeable when we listen to a speaker in an auditorium. The speech appears to be coming from the location of the speaker even though a great deal of sound is being reflected from the walls. The reflected sound enhances the loudness of the speech heard.

In cases where the subject can see the source, there may be an additional effect of vision on auditory localization (a "ventriloquism" effect): If speech sounds from a visible speaker come from a concealed loudspeaker within about 20 degrees of the visible speaker, the sound is perceived as coming from the speaker (Witkin, Wapner, & Leventhal, 1952).

Perception of Source Distance

Perhaps the most obvious cue we can use to determine the source of a sound is sound pressure. In free space, there is a loss of 6 dB in sound pressure for each doubling of distance. Von Békésy (1949) varied the intensity of speech sounds coming from a loudspeaker in an anechoic room and found that the apparent distance of the source increased as the intensity was reduced.

If we are familiar with the source of the sound, pressure magnitude can enable us to estimate the distance of the source. If we are not familiar with the source, we can only make relative judgments of distance on the basis of sound pressure (Coleman, 1962).

Variation in frequency spectrum with distance also can play a role in distance perception (Coleman, 1963). Von Békésy has shown that for distances up to 4 feet, impulsive sounds appear closer as the low-frequency content increases (von Békésy, 1960).

For enclosed spaces there is an additional important factor of reverberation. It has been known for many years in radio broadcasting that a listener can judge the distance of a speaker from the microphone on the basis of amount of reverberation. The greater the distance, the more the reverberation. Von Békésy (1960) reported an experiment in which he systematically varied the amount of reverberation of a speech signal (with an apparatus that kept loudness and frequency spectrum constant). Listeners reported that the speaker was moving farther away as reverberation was increased.

Utilization of Echoes

In the present century man has developed a "sonar" system for detecting underwater targets. In this system (analogous to radar)—a pulse of high-frequency sound is sent out by the source. A target will reflect back sound waves, which then can be picked up at the location of the source, and interpreted to give information about the nature of the target (size, distance, material). Some animals have highly developed sonar or echo-ranging systems. We discuss some of these first before discussing problems of human echo detection.

Bats and porpoises The remarkable ability of bats and porpoises to detect objects at a distance without the aid of vision has been studied extensively.

Spallanzani, before 1800, showed that blinded bats catch as many insects as normal bats. He also showed that plugging the ears of these animals prevented their responding to objects at a distance; they collided with any obstacle in their path. It was not until the twentieth century when equipment was developed to detect and measure frequencies above the range of human hearing, that Griffin discovered that bats were emitting pulses of very high frequencies. If the bats' mouth is covered—thus preventing emission of these high-frequency sounds—the bat is unable to avoid obstacles (Griffin & Galambos, 1941). Thus it is apparent that the bat under normal conditions emits pulses; echoes are then reflected by an obstacle back to the animal's ears, enabling it to detect the obstacle. Frequency, intensity, and duration characteristics of pulses emitted vary with the species of bat. The most studied of the bats—the little brown bat—emits a pulse which lasts for about 2 msec, and sweeps from 90 kilocycles down to 45 kilocycles. Ordinarily these pulses (or chirps) are repeated at rates of 10 to 20 per second. However, if the bat approaches even a small obstacle, the rate of the pulse emission rises greatly. This reaction to an obstacle can be used to measure the distance at which a bat detects an obstacle. When moving pictures of the bat (with sound track) were analyzed, it was found that a wire only 180 μ in diameter was detected at a distance of 110 cm (Griffin, 1959). Wires have to be reduced to a diameter of 70 μ—about the diameter of a human hair—before a bat is unable to detect them. Grinnel has found that the midbrain of the bat has some special neural mechanisms that facilitate the detection of an echo. (See Grinnel, 1963, the first of a consecutive series of articles.)

Kellogg (1961) has described a series of experiments with the porpoise, aimed at demonstrating how this animal utilizes echoes from objects ("echo-ranges") to avoid obstacles and obtain food. Experimentation with these animals is difficult because of their habitat, size, and expense. Consider for example the difficulty of blindfolding a porpoise! C. S. Johnson has found an ingenious solution to this problem by using suction cups, applied over the eyes of the porpoise. (See Stevens and Warshofsky, 1965.)

As a challenge to your ingenuity, try to design a series of experiments which would prove that porpoises make use of echo-ranging in detecting objects. Then refer to Kellogg's account of the experiments he carried out.

Humans Blind people are often able to avoid running into obstacles. There have been numerous theories of how this is accomplished (Hayes, 1935, 1941). One of the most prominent of these theories is the theory of "facial vision," which states that the face is somehow sensitive to stimulation by air currents from obstacles. Supa, Cotzin, and Dallenbach (1944) tested the effectiveness of auditory cues as well as "air-current" cues. They used a Masonite board approximately 4 by 5 feet in size as an obstacle, which could

be moved to various distances from the location of the subject in a large room. The subjects tested were 2 blind people and 2 with normal vision who were blindfolded. The best of the subjects (blind) were able to detect the obstacle when they were 7 to 8 feet from it.

Air currents or pressure waves to the face and hands were ruled out as cues, for it was found that if a heavy felt veil was placed over the head and leather gauntlets on the hands, the detection of the obstacle was only slightly interfered with. In contrast, plugging the ears or interfering with auditory cues by a loud masking tone caused the subjects to fail. Furthermore, when the subject was able to use only auditory cues—when listening with earphones in another room to the experimenter, who walked toward the target with a microphone attached—he did well in detecting the obstacle the experimenter was approaching. It was concluded that auditory cues played a vital role in obstacle detection. It was apparent that noises made by the shoes of the subject interacted with the obstacle to create the cues. Subjects would sometimes try to make additional noises with their feet to provide better cues.

Other similar experiments (Worchel & Dallenbach, 1947) with deaf and blind subjects showed that these subjects could not detect the Masonite obstacle and were not able to learn to detect it. Worchel and Berry (1952) repeated the experiments in an outdoor setting with a group of deaf subjects who were blindfolded, and found that these subjects were incapable of learning to perceive the obstacle. The results of these experiments are of special interest in that they rule out another possible cue—pressure waves on the skin of the external canal of the ear, and on the eardrum.

Ammons, Worchel, and Dallenbach (1953) point out that there are other cues which can conceivably function, but which usually are not present to aid the blind person in detecting obstacles. For instance, odor cues, temperature cues (when the obstacle is between the sun and the subject), and wind pressure cues (if the obstacle intervenes to shield the subject from wind) are possibilities. The limits of effectiveness of these cues remain to be determined.

The experiments so far performed, then, are mainly aimed at showing that auditory cues *can* function importantly in the detection of obstacles by the blind. The next question is: What kinds of auditory cues? Cotzin and Dallenbach (1950) had subjects listen to a sound source approaching the obstacle, and indicate when they detected the obstacle. (Subjects listened with earphones in another room to sound picked up by a microphone which moved on the same carriage as the sound source.) Subjects were not successful in detecting the obstacles if pure tones were used, except when a high frequency of 10,000 Hz was used. Subjects were more successful when they listened to a thermal noise source approaching the obstacle. They reported a rise in pitch as a stimulus approached the obstacle. Bassett and Eastmond (1964) have subsequently shown that when thermal noise is used as a sound source, the pitch heard at a given distance in front of the obstacle is related to the pattern of the sound spectrum at that distance in front of the reflecting obstacle. The pitch is most easily noticed with frequencies from 200 to 2000 Hz; very high frequencies are not required. It cannot be produced with a single pure tone. Thus the cue for obstacle detection with these complex sounds is not the same as that for high frequency pure tones.

Kellogg (1962) has performed experiments with human subjects to find thresholds for the discrimination of the characteristics of objects by means of echoes. His 4 subjects (2 of whom were blind) made various kinds of noise to aid in their discrimination. It was found that the blind subjects were able to do surprisingly well in discriminating depth, size, and the degree of reflectivity of the surface. For example, the better of the blind observers could detect a change in the position of a disc 1 foot in diameter placed 2 feet away when the disc was moved nearer or farther by little more than 4 inches. The blind observers were able to discriminate between hard surfaces (such as sheet metal) and soft, poorly reflecting surfaces of cloth.

Lorrin A. Riggs

VISION

9

This chapter covers some of the main facts about the sense of sight. It starts with the sequence of events that begins when patterns of light enter the eye to act as stimuli for the visual receptors, and goes on to the conduction and integration of information that takes place in the visual pathways. It calls attention to the almost incredible sensitivity and range of the sense of sight. Finally, it describes the evidence, both physiological and psychophysical, that supports our present hypotheses with regard to the visual process. However, because the topic of vision is so important, a broader coverage is needed and therefore the subsequent chapters of this book are designed to present the fields of color vision (Boynton, Chapter 10), the motor aspects of vision (Alpern, Chapter 11) and visual perception (Hochberg, Chapters 12 and 13).

What is the difference between vision, as covered in this chapter, and visual perception? The main difference is in point of view, which a physical analogy may help to clarify. A table may be considered either as a collection of atoms and molecules arranged in certain configurations or as a solid having the more obvious dimensions of length, width, height, and weight. In this chapter we adopt a kind of molecular point of view in trying to understand the basic nature of our responses to light. The perception chapters, in contrast, are concerned with a world of real objects and the way in which we react to them as visual stimuli.

273

THE VISUAL STIMULUS

The typical visual scene contains stationary or moving objects that are characterized by their ability to transmit to the eye distinctive patterns of visible light. For a basic understanding of such patterns we need to consider the physical nature of light and the degree to which it is capable of stimulating the visual receptors (see Riggs, 1965b).

Light Quanta

Light may be said to consist of individual particles. The particles of light are sometimes known as photons, to distinguish them from the many other elementary particles of matter (protons, electrons, neutrons, and so on). More often, however, the particles of light are called *quanta*. These quanta are emitted or radiated from a variety of sources such as very hot objects (the sun, the wire filament of a light bulb, a glowing candle), ionized gas (a neon or mercury tube), and many special materials that are activated by diverse forms of energy (fluorescent lamps, television screens, electroluminescent panels, fireflies, lasers). Once emitted, a quantum travels in a straight line at very high speed (186,000 miles/sec in air, although it travels more slowly in water, glass, or other substances). If it hits the surface of an object, the quantum may be absorbed, it may be reflected from the surface to resume its travel in a different direction, it may be transmitted through the object, or it may possibly undergo more complex events having to do with refraction, fluorescence, diffraction, and so on.

Light Waves

The quantum concept of light is often supplemented by the wave concept, especially when we speak of its effects upon the eye. According to this view, light belongs to a class of electromagnetic radiation that includes radio waves, x rays, and others, each having its own particular spectrum of wavelengths. Visible light is in an intermediate

region between the shorter ultraviolet waves and the longer infrared waves. The eye is most sensitive in the middle part of the visible spectrum, namely over a range of wavelengths from about 400 to 700 nanometers (1 nanometer, nm, = 1 millimicron; mμ is an older equivalent of the same unit).

The quantum and wave concepts of light, though seemingly incompatible, are merged in the theoretical field of quantum mechanics, in which the Einstein equation plays a key role:

$$E = h\nu$$

where E is the energy of a quantum of light, h is Planck's fundamental constant of the theory, and ν is the number of waves per second (that is, frequency) characterizing the particular quantum. The frequency ν is inversely related to the wavelength λ of the light. Thus the equation tells us that a quantum of light having a wavelength of 400 nm, for example, contains more energy than a quantum of 600 nm light. The relative energies are in inverse proportion to the two wavelengths, that is, a 400 nm quantum has 600/400 or 1.5 times as much energy as a 600 nm quantum. Light of shorter wavelengths,

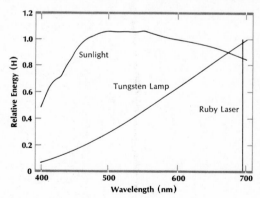

Figure 9.1. Sample energy distributions of sunlight (data of C. G. Abbot in Moon, 1936), a tungsten lamp at a temperature of 2854° K (CIE standard *Illuminant A*), and a ruby laser at various wavelengths of light. Each curve describes the irradiance distribution H of the light source as a function of wavelength λ.

called ultraviolet light, must be very intense to be seen at all. It is absorbed by the cornea or lens of the eye and may damage it if it is present in sufficiently large quantities. Longer waves characterize infrared light, which can also be seen if present in large amounts. These pass more readily through the media of the eye and are therefore potentially harmful to the retina.

Within the 400 to 700 nanometer range over which the eyes operate most efficiently, the wavelength composition of the light is a major determining factor of its hue and saturation (see Chapter 10). Sunlight appears white or achromatic. It has a spectrum that has approximately the same energy overall, that is, the light that it emits contains nearly equal amounts of energy at all wavelengths (see Figure 9.1) within the visible range. Light from a tungsten bulb appears yellowish because it is relatively weak in the short-wave (blue-violet) region, and strong in the longer-wave (yellow-red) region of the spectrum. Light from a ruby laser has its energy all concentrated in a very narrow region (around 694 nm) that typically appears deep red to the eye.

Light from the sun or a light bulb, of course, may be used to illuminate objects, which in turn reflect some of the light into the eye. This is called *irradiance* and is measured in energy units of watts per square meter. The symbol H is used for this dimension. Because a given source generally provides different amounts of energy at each wavelength λ, an instrument known as a spectroradiometer has been developed for measuring H at each value of λ. The resulting relationship of irradiance to wavelength is known as the $H(\lambda)$ distribution of light falling on the surface of an object. Carrying the process one step further, a reflectometer can be used to determine the proportion R of light reflected by the surface of an object at each wavelength. Examples of reflectance distributions determined for various surfaces are shown in Figure 10.1 of Chapter 10. If we know both the irradiance distribution $H(\lambda)$,

and the reflectance distribution $R(\lambda)$, we can designate the product $H(\lambda)R(\lambda)$, as a physical description of the surface as a stimulus for the eye. Thus an object is a strong stimulus if it receives an adequate amount of light from the source, and if its surface reflects a large proportion of the light into the eye of the observer. Conversely, an object is a weak stimulus if it is poorly illuminated or if it absorbs most of the light and its surface reflects only a small proportion of the light into the eye. However there is one more very significant factor that determines the physical effect of light on the receptors, namely the sensitivity of the eye for the particular wavelengths that the object sends back to the eye.

Spectral Sensitivity

The various wavelengths of light differ enormously in the extent to which they stim-

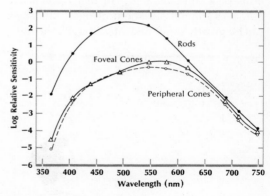

Figure 9.2. The sensitivity of the eye to various wavelengths of light throughout the visible spectrum. The ordinate gives sensitivity, defined as reciprocal of absolute threshold, on a logarithmic scale. Note that the receptors for scotopic vision (rods) are much more sensitive than those for photopic vision (cones), especially for wavelengths below 600 nm. Each curve describes the sensitivity distribution or visibility V as a function of wavelength λ. The rod curve closely resembles the absorption spectrum of the rod photopigment, rhodopsin. The cone curve, however, represents the summed sensitivities of cones containing the various photopic pigments. (Adapted from Wald, 1945.)

ulate the eye. Figure 9.2 presents spectral sensitivity curves (that is, curves showing the relative sensitivity of the eye for each wavelength of light) under scotopic (night vision) and photopic (day vision) conditions. If we call L the luminance or stimulating effect of a given surface illuminated by light, we may deduce from these curves that L depends not only upon the irradiance distribution $H(\lambda)$ of the source of light and the reflectance distribution $R(\lambda)$ of the surface, but also upon the sensitivity distribution $V(\lambda)$ of the eye to the range of wavelengths present in the reflected light. Symbolically,

$$L = H(\lambda) R(\lambda) V(\lambda)$$

Photometry

Calculations of the kind just mentioned are complex and tedious, but they must be used to make the most precise physical specifications of a stimulus field. For many practical purposes the measurement of light intensity can be greatly simplified, however, by the use

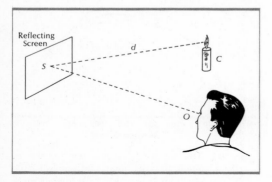

Figure 9.3. A surface S is strongly illuminated by a source of light C if it is close to the source, but it is weakly illuminated if it is far away. Specifically, the illuminance on S in this diagram varies directly with the candlepower, and inversely with the square of the distance, that is, $E = C/d^2$. The luminance L of a screen S, as seen by an observer at O depends on the illuminance times the reflectance R of the screen; thus $L = CR/d^2$. Note that the luminance remains the same regardless of the distance of the observer from the surface. See text for details.

of direct photometry. The original standard for photometric measurement was a candle, manufactured under specified conditions, and used as a source of light. Consider Figure 9.3, in which such a candle is placed at a distance (d) from a white screen (S) that is known to reflect a certain proportion (R) of the light falling upon it. This incident light, known as the illuminance (E) on the screen, is then said to have a value, in footcandles, equal to the candlepower (C) of the source divided by the square of the distance (d) in feet from source to screen. In other words,

$$E = \frac{C}{d^2} \text{ footcandles}$$

Lighting engineers have developed standard levels of illuminance for various visual tasks. A library installation should provide readers with a level above 10 footcandles, for example, whereas street lighting may require less than 1 footcandle. Photoelectric footcandle meters are available to make measurements of this kind.

The appearance of the screen at S to an observer at O depends not only on E, the illuminance of the light falling upon it, but also on R, the reflectance of the screen in the direction of O. If R is defined as the ratio of the light reflected to the light incident on the screen, then L, the luminance of the screen in units called footlamberts, is given by the equation

$$L = ER = \frac{CR}{d^2} \text{ footlamberts}$$

As an example, we may calculate the luminance of a surface that reflects 60 percent of the light reaching it from a 50 candlepower source at a distance of 1.2 feet. Thus

$$L = \frac{50(.60)}{(1.2)^2} = 20.8 \text{ footlamberts}$$

In the practice of photometry, standard tungsten lamps of known candlepower and standard surfaces of measured reflectance are available for laboratory use. In fact, compact

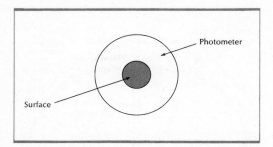

Figure 9.4. The appearance of the photometer field. To measure the luminance of a surface, the observer first points the photometer directly at it so that a portion of the surface fills the central viewing field. He then adjusts the measuring field of the instrument by turning an intensity control until there is a brightness match between the two fields of the instrument. He reads the dial of the control to find the luminance.

instruments (light spot photometers) containing such elements are now available to produce a split visual field of the type shown in Figure 9.4. If we wish to measure the luminance of any particular surface in a visual field, we look directly through the instrument until we can see the surface in question in the central portion of the field. We can then adjust a surrounding part of the field to a brightness that matches the surface in question, using the controls on the instrument for this purpose. The luminance is given directly on the scale that is coupled with these controls. A precision of 1 or 2 percent is possible under the most favorable condition, one in which the two fields have the same color. The method becomes highly unreliable, however, when the observer attempts to match the brightness between a white measuring field, for example, and a red viewing field. For this purpose it may be necessary to use heterochromatic flicker photometry (see p. 312).

In the modern practice of photometry, a glowing platinum source of specified size and temperature has replaced the old standard candle. Furthermore, photoelectric receiving surfaces have been developed that have sensitivity characteristics similar to those of the average human eye at photopic (medium to

high) levels of luminance. Thus light meters, equipped with such photocells, are now used almost exclusively to measure luminance for the practical purposes of industries such as those concerned with lighting, photography, and dyeing.

We have gone into some detail describing the measurement of luminance because, for experimental psychologists, this is the typical way of specifying the intensity dimension of a visual stimulus or a visual environment.

Note that illuminance is a measure that is influenced by distance from the source of light to the surface illuminated (see Figure 9.3). Luminance, however, is independent of the distance from the surface to the eye of the observer. That is why a movie screen, for example, looks equally bright when seen from the back row as from the front row in a theatre. Thus photometry, within the limits imposed by the size of field in the instrument, can be carried out at any convenient distance from the stimulus. This independence from the effects of distance is of course true of the camera as well as the eye; exposure times and lens openings need to be adjusted for the luminance of the object to be photographed but not for the distance from object to camera.

Note also that luminance has been defined physically in footlamberts. The English standard footlambert has been specified in terms of the candlepower of the light source, the distance in feet from source to surface, and the reflectance of the surface. Corresponding metric terms in common use in various countries are based on the millilambert (1 millilambert [mL] = .929 footlambert [ftL] = 3.183 candles per square meter [c/m^2] = 10 apostilbs).

The psychological term that is related to luminance is *brightness,* but we must not make the mistake of assuming that brightness is directly related to or solely dependent on luminance. Brightness, as we see below, is influenced by many factors including the state of the adaptation of the eye, contrast effects, exposure time, and perceptual constancy (see

TABLE 9.1 LUMINANCE VALUES FOR TYPICAL VISUAL STIMULI

	Scale of luminance (mL)	
Sun's surface at noon	10^{10}	⎫
	10^9	Damaging
	10^8	⎭
Tungsten filament	10^7	⎫
	10^6	
	10^5	
White paper in sunlight	10^4	Photopic
	10^3	
	10^2	
Comfortable reading	10	⎭
	1	Mixed
	10^{-1}	⎫
White paper in moonlight	10^{-2}	
	10^{-3}	
White paper in starlight	10^{-4}	Scotopic
	10^{-5}	
Absolute RL	10^{-6}	⎭

Source: Riggs, 1965b

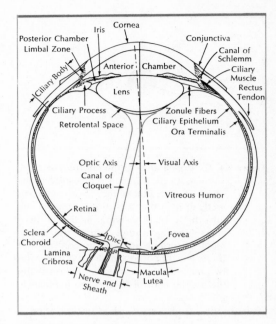

Figure 9.5. Horizontal section of right human eye. Note that two different positions are shown for the posterior surface of the lens. This is because the lens bulges while accommodating for near objects. (Walls, 1942.)

Chapters 12 and 13). However, scaling procedures can be used to attempt a direct estimate of subjective brightness (see Chapter 3). Table 9.1 gives an idea of the wide range of useful luminances over which the eye can function.

For special purposes, still other specifications are sometimes used to describe stimulus intensity. If we consider the stimulus as a patch of light falling on the retina at the back of the eye, we may wish, for example, to note that this light is reduced in proportion to the size of the pupil of the eye. Accordingly, a measure of retinal illuminance, the *troland,* has been arrived at, such that retinal illuminance, E_r in trolands, is given by the expression $E_r = AL$ where L is luminance in c/m^2 of the visual stimulus at which the subject is looking, and A is the area of his pupil in units of square millimeters. Take the example of a person who is looking at a stimulus field of 25 c/m^2, or 7.3 ftL, with eyes having a pupillary radius of 2 mm. The area of his pupil is 4π square millimeters and his retinal illuminance is specified by the equation $E_r = 4\pi(25) = 314$ trolands.

VISUAL ANATOMY

The Eyes

A diagram of a human eye is shown in Figure 9.5. Each eye is about 25 mm in diameter and weighs about 7g. The transparent cornea in front and the tough, fibrous sclera surrounding the rest of the eye serve to protect it from injury and to maintain its shape. The choroid is a middle layer of dark material, richly supplied with blood vessels. The retina is a thin and delicate inner layer containing the photoreceptors and an elaborate network of interconnecting nervous tissue.

The eye, as an optical instrument, is somewhat analogous to a camera. Rays of light from the visual field are focused by the eye in such a way that a fairly accurate, inverted image of the field is formed on the retina at the back of the eye. Most of this optical effect results from the curvature of the cornea, but fine adjustments can be made in focus for far

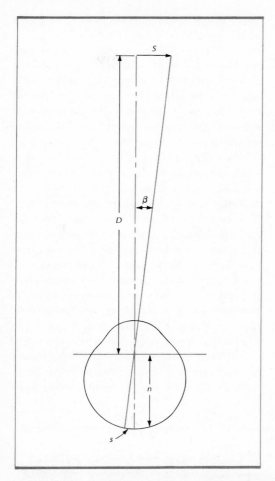

Figure 9.6. Diagram to illustrate the size of a retinal image. (Riggs, 1965c.)

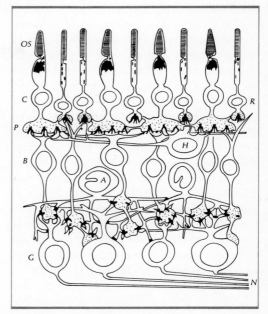

Figure 9.7. Generalized diagram of the retina. See text for details. (After Dowling & Boycott, 1966.)

and near objects. In a camera, focusing is done by moving the lens, but in the human eye it is accomplished by changing the shape of the lens (see Chapter 11). The anterior chamber and posterior chamber on either side of the lens are filled with transparent material (the aqueous and vitreous humors, respectively). The iris is a pigmented structure the central aperture of which, the pupil, contracts and dilates in a manner analogous to the changes in the diaphragm of a camera.

The optical characteristics of the eye are complex, but fairly exact calculations of retinal image size can be made by the use of a schematic eye such as is shown in Figure 9.6.

For simplicity, we draw lines from any points in space crossing each other at a point known as the nodal point of the eye. An object such as the one shown at S in Figure 9.6 is said to subtend a visual angle β at the eye such that $\tan \beta = S/D$ where S is the length or width of the object and D is its distance from the nodal point of the eye. The nodal point is at a distance n of about 17 mm from the image formed on the retina at the back of the eye. The angular size of the retinal image of object S is the same as the visual angle β subtended by that object. Therefore $\tan \beta = s/17$, and the linear size s of the retinal image of S can be calculated, for all small angles, from the equation

$$s = 17 \tan \beta = \frac{17S}{D}$$

The Retina

A schematic view of the retina is presented in Figure 9.7. (Note that in this magnified view the front of the eye lies below.) Light reaches the retina by coming up through the vitreous humor and traversing the various retinal layers before finally reaching the visual receptors, the rods (R) and the cones (C). The outer segments (OS) of the rod receptors are known to contain a photosensitive pigment known as rhodopsin, or visual purple. The rhodopsin is not freely dispersed throughout the segment, however. Instead, it appears organized into hundreds of layers or disks that are oriented transversely to the elongated structure of the rod. It now appears certain that the absorption of a single quantum of light by a molecule of rhodopsin in one of these layers is sufficient to cause a change in the physical structure of that molecule. The change, in turn, acts as a trigger for some sort of signal (chemical, electrical, or both) to travel from the outer segment of the rod receptor to its base or pedicle (P), where the excitation is passed along to the associated neural structures of the bipolar layer of the retina. The bipolars (B) in turn excite the ganglion cells (G), and this causes nerve impulses to travel out of the eye along the optic

nerve fibers (N), which are in fact the axons of the ganglion cells of the retina. The optic nerve fibers from every part of the retina travel along its inner surface and emerge from the eye, as shown in Figure 9.5, at the point known as the blind spot, or optic disk. Within that small region of the retina, there indeed are no rod or cone receptors, so that no visual response can originate from this region.

The rod receptors of the eye function most efficiently at low levels of illumination. They are thus responsible for our scotopic, or nighttime vision. In daylight the cone receptors are most responsible for vision. The typical cone is shorter and thicker than a rod, but it is similar to a rod in having a layered structure in its outer segment. These outer segments of the cones also contain photosensitive pigments and, because color vision is mediated by cone receptors, we may assume that there are at least three different types of photopigment (see Chapter 10). Therefore a cone containing one of the pigments would be most sensitive to wavelengths in the range best absorbed by that pigment. Signals from

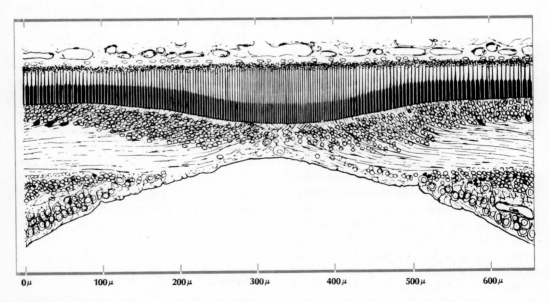

| 0μ | 100μ | 200μ | 300μ | 400μ | 500μ | 600μ |

Figure 9.8. Central fovea of the human retina. The whole diagram includes .65 mm of retinal surface, corresponding to a visual angle of about 2°. Only .1 mm (a visual angle of about 20 minutes) is included in the region of the most slender cone receptors and thinnest neural tissue. (Polyak, 1957.)

the cones are passed along through the bipolar and ganglion cell layers to optic nerve fibers.

The horizontal cells (*H*), also shown in Figure 9.7, provide lateral connections among the receptors, whereas amacrine cells (*A*) interconnect bipolars from one region of the retina to another. As we see below, many visual functions appear to be enhanced by the action of such lateral interconnections at the retinal level.

The human retina is by no means uniform in its structural appearance from one region to another. At its very center, or fovea (see Figure 9.5) there are no rod receptors. The cone outer segments in the fovea are unusually long and slender and very densely packed together, as is shown in Figure 9.8. Note that the neural elements (cone nuclei, bipolar and ganglion cells) appear to be swept aside in this region, thus providing direct access of the light to these receptors. It is significant that this relatively small region (about 2° in diameter) is the only portion of the retina with

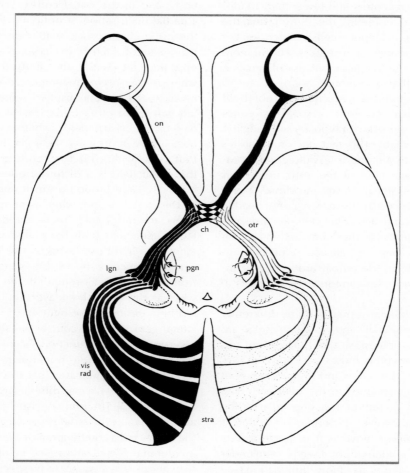

Figure 9.9. Diagram of primary pathways in the human visual system. The optic nerve (*on*) from each retina (*r*) decussates at the chiasma (*ch*) in such a way that each optic tract (*otr*) contains fibers representing one half of the visual field. Each tract terminates in the corresponding lateral geniculate nucleus (*lgn*) from which the visual radiations (*vis rad*) proceed to the striate area (*stra*) in the cortex of the occipital lobe. Some optic tract fibers terminate, however, in the pretectal or pregeniculate (pgn) nucleus (see p. 283). (After Polyak, 1957.)

which we can see very clearly. Look at a single letter on this page and notice that if you do not move your eyes you see very few other letters clearly. The rest of the page is blurred and indistinct. Outside the fovea, rods become mixed with cones, and still farther out in the periphery rods predominate and relatively few cones are present. In the extreme periphery (see Figure 9.5) there are fewer and fewer receptors; the retina finally ends at the *ora terminalis*.

The retina of each eye has more than 100 million rod receptors and fewer than 10 million cones. Considering the entire retina, the total number of bipolar cells is much smaller than the number of receptors. Furthermore the number of ganglion cells is still smaller, being less than 1 million.

The proportions just cited do not hold in the fovea, however. There, the cones are richly supplied with bipolars and ganglion cells. Presumably this fact not only entitles each cone to a more or less direct representation by one fiber of the optic nerve, but also allows signals from individual cones to be influenced by those from cones nearby. Horizontal and amacrine cells are presumably the agents for these interactions within the retina. They are believed to play an important role in the retinal processing of information on color and form (see Chapters 10 and 12).

The peripheral retina is quite differently organized. Bipolar and ganglion cells are sparsely distributed, so that hundreds of rod and cone receptors must excite a given optic nerve fiber. Thus color and form information are not well received in the periphery. The pooling of excitation has one outstanding advantage, however. It permits us to detect the presence or movement of large objects that we are not looking at directly, even under nighttime conditions of low illumination (see p. 285). The optic disk (in Figure 9.5) contains no visual receptors and is thus often called the "blind spot" of each eye. Note that it is the region in which the optic nerve fibers make their way out of the eyeball.

Visual Pathways

Figure 9.9 presents a simplified diagram of the primary visual pathways. The details of structure and function may be found in recent books (Adler, 1959; Brindley, 1960; Granit, 1962). Following is a brief summary of typical features of the organization of the primate visual system including that of man. (1) There is an approximately point-for-point representation of the visual field on each retina, in the various layers of the lateral geniculate body, and in the visual cortex. (2) There is a partial decussation of optic nerve fibers at the optic chiasm such that fibers from the nasal half of each retina cross over to the opposite geniculate and cortical centers, whereas fibers from the temporal do not. This means that the left hemisphere represents the left half-retina of each eye (that is, the right half of the visual field) whereas the right hemisphere represents the right half-retina (left visual field). (3) The "cortical map" of the visual field is a distorted one in that a relatively large proportion of it corresponds to the foveal region, whereas peripheral regions are but poorly represented. (4) The lateral geniculate body has a laminar arrangement such that three layers on the left lateral geniculate receive the axons of ganglion cells from the left hemi-retina of the left eye, whereas the other three layers represent the left hemi-retina of the right eye. In the right lateral geniculate, of course, the situation is reversed. The exact functional significance of the laminar structure is not known, although recent evidence indicates that the encoding of color and pattern may differ from one layer to another. (5) The primary visual projection area (known as the striate area, or area 17) of the cortex has a combination of a laminar and a columnar organization (see below). Again the various layers appear to be specialized for certain types of visual function. Of major significance is the fact that any given column of cells (that is, cells that are found at various depths along a line running perpendicular to the surface) seem to respond selectively to

TABLE 9.2 PHOTOPIC AND SCOTOPIC VISION OF THE HUMAN EYE

	Photopic	Scotopic
Receptor	Cones (ca. 7 million)	Rods (ca. 120 million)
Retinal location	Concentrated at center, fewer in periphery	General in periphery, none in fovea
Neural processing	Discriminative	Summative
Peak wavelength	555 nm	505 nm
Luminance level	Daylight (1 to 10^7 mL)	Night (10^{-6} to 1 mL)
Color vision	Normally trichromatic	Achromatic
Dark adaptation	Rapid (ca. 7 min)	Slow (ca. 40 min)
Spatial resolution	High acuity	Low acuity
Temporal resolution	Fast reacting	Slower reacting

one particular slant or light pattern appearing in a particular region of the visual field. (6) Binocular vision is made possible by the fact that any given column of cortical cells receives axons from cells in the lateral geniculate body that are activated by stimulation of corresponding retinal points in each of the two eyes. (7) There are higher regions of the occipital cortex (known as associative areas 18 and 19) that receive their innervation from area 17 and are presumed to mediate perceptual functions as well as to permit integration with other sensory and motor systems. (8) The parietal and temporal lobes contain centers for visual symbols and language. (9) Outside the primary visual pathways are (a) optic tract fibers that go to the pretectal region rather than the lateral geniculate, and are concerned with regulation of the pupil (see Chapter 11); (b) interhemispheric fibers of the corpus callosum that may perhaps relate to binocular functions such as stereoscopic vision; (c) connections of the primary centers with the cerebellum, having to do with visuo-vestibular coordination and regulation of balance; and (d) connections with the reticular formation or other structures relating to activation or attention.

PHOTOPIC AND SCOTOPIC VISION

We can see from the discussion above that the human retina contains two kinds of photoreceptor, the rods and the cones. We note that the two differ importantly in their distribution and in their functional properties. The duplex nature of vision was clearly pointed out over a century ago (Schultze, 1866). Perhaps the easiest way to summarize the "duplicity theory," as it has come to be called, is to say that cone vision provides acute vision at daytime (photopic) levels of luminance, whereas rod vision provides a high degree of light sensitivity that is essential for seeing at night when light levels are low (scotopic). Nocturnal animals have more rods and relatively few cones in their retinas, and some (deep sea fish, some snakes and bats) are believed to lack cones entirely. Diurnal animals are well provided with cones, and a few species (among the lizards, snakes, birds, and squirrels) lack rods.

Man shares with most other animals the advantages of both photopic and scotopic vision. He is basically a diurnal creature, however (his night life has flourished only in recent times, from the fact that he is able, with bright lights, to turn night into day). Table 9.2 summarizes the properties of human photopic and scotopic vision.

LIGHT AND DARK ADAPTATION

As Table 9.1 shows, the human eye is able to function over a luminance range of more than 13 log units. At any given moment, however, we are seldom confronted with visual stimuli of more than 2 log units, for at any one time, we normally rely on a single source (for example, the sun, moon, or artificial lighting) that illuminates objects which reflect from about 2 to 90 percent of the light falling on them. Few of us must go very often from one light environment rapidly into a very different one, as in going from sunlight into a darkened theatre, tunnel, or mine. When we must, however, the experience takes us out of the immediate dynamic range of visual sensitivity; in other words, we are momentarily blind. Even more disagreeable is the opposite experience of emerging suddenly from darkness into daylight. In this case we normally close the eyes or use dark glasses to allow the eyes to become gradually adapted to the change in light level, after which the eyes can again function efficiently within a new dynamic range of intensities.

Light adaptation is often found to be nearly complete in a minute or two, but dark adaptation may take a half-hour or longer, depending on the previous level of the exposure of the eyes to light. For an understanding of adaptation we need to have experimental data on the exact course it takes, together with measurements of the underlying physiological processes.

Dark-adaptation Curves

In a typical dark-adaptation experiment, the subject is first asked to achieve a high level of light adaptation by fixing his eyes for several minutes on a point at the center of a large bright screen or uniform field of white

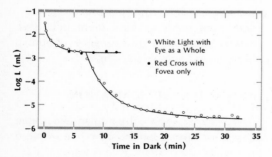

Figure 9.10. The course of dark adaptation in the human eye. On the ordinate is a logarithmic scale of luminance for a test target at the absolute threshold of vision, and on the abscissa is time after exposure of the eye to a high-intensity field of light. (After Hecht, 1934.)

light having a luminance of several hundred footlamberts. The adapting light is then turned off, and the course of dark adaptation is then followed using a test light of variable luminance. The test procedure is to find the absolute threshold as a function of time in the dark, using one of the standard psychophysical methods outlined in Chapter 2.

Figure 9.10 illustrates the course of dark adaptation measured by the method just outlined. Note that a test field of white light must, in this case, be 4 log units (10,000 times) more intense at the beginning of dark adaptation than at the end in order for the subject to report he has seen it. Note also that this curve exhibits two portions, with a "kink" in between. The first, or photopic, portion is due to the cones, as evidenced by the fact that it is the only part of the curve that is shown when the rod-free fovea alone is tested. The second part, after the kink, results from the activity of large numbers of rods; this takes the eye down into scotopic levels of luminance.

The use of a red test light in dark-adaptation experiments deserves some comment. Figure 9.2 shows that rods are scarcely any more sensitive than cones to long wavelengths of light. It is for this reason that a red test light shows no further drop in threshold (Figure 9.10) beyond the photopic portion. The relatively poor sensitivity of rods to red light has also led to the use of red light (Miles, 1953) in situations where it is essential to protect the rods from light adaptation. For example, military men on night lookout duty may be required to wear red goggles or to use red light illumination whenever they must examine charts and instruments immediately before going on watch at night.

After prolonged adaptation to darkness, our vision becomes so sensitive that, under the most favorable conditions, we can see a flash that contains only about a hundred quanta of light. Hecht, Shlaer, and Pirenne (1942) have calculated that a large percentage of these quanta are lost by the various ocular media because of scatter or reflection, among other factors, so that only about 5 to 14 quanta are actually absorbed by the retinal rods. Probability considerations show that this must mean that a single quantum of light is absorbed by a single molecule of the photo-sensitive material, rhodopsin, in each of 5 to 14 rod receptors. In other words, each receptor is functioning at the upper theoretical limit of its own sensitivity, and the simultaneous excitation of several such receptors is necessary for a flash to be seen. It can be shown, furthermore, that with so small a number of quanta involved a supposedly constant series of flashes will actually show a considerable statistical variation in the number of quanta absorbed by the receptors. Thus a part, at least, of the variability of the absolute visual threshold must be attributed to an irreducible variability in the stimulus itself. Indeed, according to Hecht's calculations (based upon small-number, random Poisson distributions) virtually all of the variability is thus accounted for, and we have an additional reason for stating that the receptor system is performing up to the theoretical limit of its capacity.

Scotopic Vision

It is well worth spending an hour or two in the dark in order to experience some of the consequences of completely scotopic vision. One of the most striking effects is the blindness of the central fovea. That is, a very dim test light or star disappears if we look at it directly, because the fovea contains no rod receptors. We can see dim objects much more effectively if we look at them off-center; that is, if we stare a little to the right or left of the object in order to focus it on the region a few degrees outside the fovea where the rods are found to reach their highest density. Off-center viewing is a trick that is easily mastered by amateur astronomers, men on night lookout duty, and others who must take full advantage of the scotopic visual system.

Another effect of night vision is the appearance of the so-called "photochromatic interval." This is easily understood by reference to Figure 9.2. The interval in question is the vertical separation between the photopic and scotopic sensitivity curves. At any given wavelength, such as 450 nm, scotopic vision is much more sensitive than photopic. Thus even a very dim light will exceed the threshold of the dark-adapted rod receptors, but the light must be raised to a much higher level in order to reach the threshold of the cones. During the interval between the two thresholds the light is seen as colorless, but once the cone threshold is reached, the light assumes the appropriate chromatic appearance. The colorless photochromatic interval holds over most of the spectrum, but, in agreement with Figure 9.2, it becomes vanishingly small for the higher wavelengths of light. Thus light of 650 nm or above, if it is seen at all, is seen as red.

Another consequence of Figure 9.2 is the *Purkinje shift*. This effect may be seen most easily by shining a very weak spectrum at the dark-adapted eye, in which all the wavelengths of light are present with approximately equal energy. At the lowest energy levels, the subject will see only a restricted part of the spectrum centered around 505 nm, as a dim colorless field, in accordance with the scotopic curve of Figure 9.2. At higher levels, however, more and more of the spectrum is seen, the various hues are discriminated, and the wavelength providing a maximum brightness shifts from 505 to 555 nm. In other words, the Purkinje shift is the change in wavelength of maximum effectiveness that occurs in going from scotopic to photopic levels of luminance.

While in a fully dark-adapted state we can also readily see certain unique visual phenomena. An example is the "blue-arcs" that are seen with off-center viewing of a rectangular patch of red light. To get the effect, a projector can be used to place a patch of red light about 3° high and 1° wide on a screen in front of the eye. Covering the left eye, fixate with the right on a point about 2° to the right of this rectangle of light. Notice the bluish streaks that appear to emerge from the top and bottom of the rectangle, pass above and below the center of fixation, and curve toward one another in the darkness on the right. Troland (1920) has noted that these arcs appear to follow the course of the optic nerve fibers as they traverse the retina on their way to the blind spot. The blue arcs are explained as an electrical excitation of retinal units that underlie these fibers. This is presumably done by "leakage" to the receptors, or to retinal neural cells, of the activity set up in these fibers by the red stimulus field; however the bluish color and other aspects of the phenomenon have never been adequately explained (Alpern & Dudley, 1966).

Another example of phenomena seen with scotopic vision is that of the "Purkinje tree." This lets you see the outline of your own retinal blood vessels, the ones that supply the neural structures of the retina. More or less sharp shadows of these vessels fall on the rods and cones when a small point source of light is placed in front of the eye. The effect is clearest when you take a small source, such as a flashlight, and shine it into your eye from one side. Moving the flashlight rapidly around in a small arc gives you a vivid picture of the "tree" whose twigs and branches represent the blood vessels of various sizes lying between the vitreous humor and the retina. Notice that the trunk of the tree is at the blind spot, where the blood vessels enter the eye. Notice also the absence of vessels in the central region of the fovea.

It is interesting that we do not notice the blood vessel shadows under ordinary viewing conditions even though they are present all the time. One reason we do not notice them is that they are not present in the region of our clearest vision. Another reason is that they are not sharply outlined except with the use of a point source of light that is off to the side of a uniform dark field. We must also note that these shadows constitute a "stabilized image" on the retina. (We review the evidence later, on pages 306 and 374, that images of this kind tend to disappear from view, due to the fact that they are unaffected

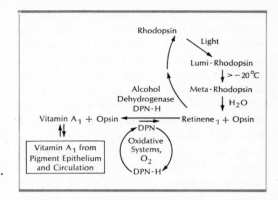

Figure 9.11. Diagram of the molecular basis for responses to light and regeneration of pigment in the rod outer segments. (Wald, 1951.)

by eye movements.) Furthermore, we have become habituated to the continued presence of the images of the blood vessels over the years and do not notice them, any more than we notice the presence of the blind spot in each eye.

Physiological Basis for Visual Adaptation

We have seen that adaptation can be made to a wide range of light levels and that the eye becomes extraordinarily sensitive to dim lights after prolonged dark adaptation. We must now ask whether the adaptation takes place in the brain or in the eye and whether it is due to neuroregulatory processes or to purely photochemical ones.

Dark and light adaptation have a photochemical basis that is well established, especially with respect to the rod receptors. Rhodopsin, the photosensitive substance the molecules of which are arranged in the layers of the rod outer segments, can be bleached by the action of light. Figure 9.11 is a diagram from Wald (1951) that illustrates some of the products of this bleaching at the various stages of this process. The diagram also makes clear the fact that rhodopsin can be restored if the products of the bleaching can use vitamin A. For this reason it is tempting to conclude that light adaptation is equivalent to lowering the concentration of rhodopsin by bleaching it with light, whereas dark adaptation is achieved by removing the light and allowing the restorative processes to raise it again to a high level. Any given level of adaptation would then represent a steady state or balance between the bleaching and restorative reactions, and visual excitation would occur in proportion as the balance was upset, in any given photoreceptor, by increments or decrements in the amount of light falling upon it. Selig Hecht (1937) has given the most extensive and systematic expression to this account of vision as it might apply not only to light and dark adaptation, but also to flicker, acuity, brightness discrimination, and other visual functions.

The classic view, that light and dark adaptation depend exclusively on bleaching and regeneration of the visual pigment, can no longer be entertained. As long ago as 1938, Granit, Holmberg, and Zewi showed that extensive changes in visual threshold can occur as a result of adaptation even when there is very little change in concentration of visual pigment. Crawford (1947) and Baker (1953) have shown that very large threshold changes are presumably neural, rather than chemical in origin, because they are found to occur within an interval of less than 100 μsec after the adapting light is turned on or off. Rushton (1963) has formulated the hypothesis of retinal "pools." According to this hypothesis, adaptation is regulated by a neural feedback action taking place when high intensities of light cause large numbers of receptors to convey signals to a neural regulatory center or pool. These signals are particularly strong when the eye is being stimulated by a high-intensity light; under this condition the photochemical events shown in Figure 9.11 proceed vigorously. However the signals do not cease when the light is turned off. Instead, they continue to be generated by the receptors and delivered to the neural pool. Thus they maintain a relatively

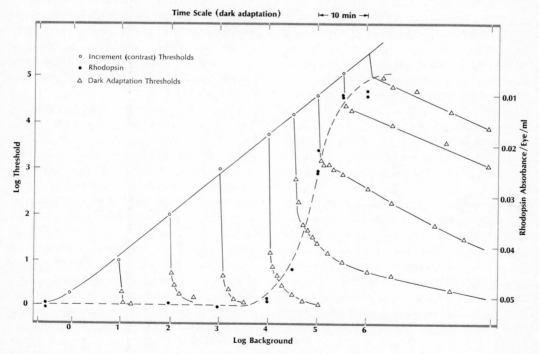

Figure 9.12. Graphical display of the rapid and slow components of dark adaptation, showing the dependence of the latter on the bleaching of rhodopsin. See text for details. (Dowling, 1967.)

high state of activity in the pool that acts to suppress or inhibit responses to test lights until the restorative processes, shown in Figure 9.11, force the receptors to reach their dark-adapted level of equilibrium and thereby stop feeding signals back to the neural pool.

Quantitative data in line with the neural feedback hypothesis of adaptation are shown in Figure 9.12 of Dowling (1967). This is a complicated diagram, but it presents an interesting analysis and deserves careful study. It relates measurements of light and dark adaptation to the concentration of the photopigment (rhodopsin) in the eye of the rat. Considering light adaptation first, we may note the relation between log threshold and log background luminance. We see that there is a nearly straight-line relationship that holds over a range of 6 log units. The open circles are for increment threshold (ΔI) determinations at the various light levels; these thresholds, measured by a technique of electrical recording from the eyeball (the ERG described on pp. 307–308), are notable for demonstrating an approximate agreement with the Weber Law (see Chapter 2) over a very wide range. The dashed-line curve, in the middle of the figure, indicates the rhodopsin concentration (relative concentrations scaled on the right ordinate), measured by photochemical analysis carried out at the same levels of light adaptation. It is apparent that no measurable bleaching of rhodopsin is present over the 4 log unit range from full darkness to moderate levels of background light.

Turning finally to dark adaptation, we see that data on this are given by the $\triangle$ symbols, evaluated against the time scale at the top of Figure 9.12. The curve drawn through each set of $\triangle$ symbols shows the way in which the visual threshold falls, starting when the background light of a particular level is turned off. It is evident that dark adaptation is rapid following the exposure to low or moderate levels of background light. With high levels of light adaptation, however, significant quantities of rhodopsin are bleached, and the

recovery during dark adaptation is very slow.

Dowling's experiments are of particular significance because the various types of measurement (photopigment concentration, increment thresholds at various light levels, and test thresholds taken during dark adaptation) were all conducted on the same species, namely the rat, in which the main pigment is known to be rhodopsin. Experiments by Rushton (1965), using a technique of measuring the absorption of light by receptors in the human eye, have confirmed the relationship of pigment density to visual thresholds determined psychophysically. Johnson and Riggs (1951), using electrical response measurements in the human eye, noted the rapid threshold drop in early dark adaptation, the slow drop following intense light adaptation, and the marked elevation of threshold by relatively weak levels of light adaptation. Barlow (1964) has used the terms "noise" and "dark light" to refer to the signals reaching the neural centers in the human retina from the receptors. Thus a number of investigators are agreed that, during dark adaptation, as the sensitivity of the eye increases, any given adaptational level is equivalent to the level that would be brought about by a real background light of the appropriate intensity (Crawford, 1947).

Several consequences follow from the view of dark adaptation described above. First, as we suddenly go from bright surroundings into darkness, we should continue to "see" the "dark light" as if a real background of light were still present. It is true that people often report the appearance of vivid after-images followed by swirling clouds of "self-light" coming from the retina immediately after going into the dark (Helmholtz, 1909–1911, tr. 1924–1925; Jung, 1961b), but why does this phenomenon not continue as long as dark adaptation proceeds? Barlow and Sparrock (1964) have given a possible answer to this question. They have pointed out that any such after-effect is like an after-image or a stabilized retinal image (see p. 306) in that it disappears quickly and does not reappear unless it is "revived" by some change in the prevailing level of light on the receptors. Indeed they have been able to demonstrate a quantitatively similar effect on visual thresholds if the subject looks at a test light against a background of either the "dark light" that is the after-effect of previous exposure to light, or a stabilized image of real light. In both cases the image has "disappeared" but continues to provide a visually effective background.

A second consequence of the neural "pool" hypothesis is that light falling on one set of visual receptors should produce a generalized state of light adaptation that affects the responses of receptors outside the region directly stimulated by the adapting light. In other words, the visual threshold should rise for neighboring receptors that share the same neural pool. This has indeed been found to occur in experiments made by Lipetz (1961) on the frog and Rushton and Westheimer (1962) on the human eye. Stripes of light falling on the retina caused a marked elevation in threshold for test lights falling on the previously unstimulated receptors lying between the stripes. These effects are much greater than would be caused by light scattering alone.

Finally, the neural-pool hypothesis should be supported by physiological evidence that photoreceptor changes alone are not sufficient to account for changes in light and dark adaptation. Evidence of this kind has already been cited with reference to data on concentration of the photopigment that is found in the receptors. In addition, Dowling (1967) has obtained histological evidence, and evidence from electrical recording, that lead to the conclusion that the main site of visual adaptation is in the bipolar cells of the retina. Dowling's explanation may account in part for the fact that the photopic portion of the human dark-adaptation curve is a small one (Figure 9.10). Not much is known about the bleaching or recovery processes in cone pigments. However, even if they were to behave like rhodopsin, we might expect differences in their rates of dark adaptation. Many more rod receptors than cones typically converge upon a single bipolar; Dowling believes that bipolars are the site of the neural pool, and the opportunity for a strong "dark light" signal may not exist for those bipolars supplied by a relatively small number of cone receptors as it might for those supplied by a much larger number of rods.

SPATIAL ASPECTS OF VISION

So far in this chapter we have considered the way in which light acts upon the retina to initiate the process of seeing. However we have not yet considered one of the main functions of seeing, namely to present us with a spatial representation of the outside world. The chapters on perception will consider the broader aspects of this problem, especially as it relates to the perception of visual depth and the recognition of sizes and shapes of objects. Before doing this, however, we should become acquainted with the more basic mechanisms that transfer to the eye and the rest of the visual system the spatial properties of the visual scene.

The Visual Projection System

We have seen that a more or less accurate optical image is focused upon the retina. Therefore a point-for-point representation of the outer world is impressed on the layer of receptor cells on each retina, each layer of the lateral geniculate bodies, and various layers of the primary visual cortex. We remember, too, that other areas of the brain provide linkages between the main projection system and other systems that control eye movements, pupillary responses, joint activity with the vestibular and other senses, and the general level of activation. With these structural systems in mind we may now turn to such questions as, what kinds of spatial interaction take place between separate points? How accurately is each point localized in relation to other points? How fine is the "grain" of the picture in terms of our discrimination of fine details? What processing of information may occur to enhance the significant features of the visual scene and suppress less significant aspects?

Spatial Interaction

The retina, having an extended photosensitive surface on which an optical image is formed, has been compared to the film of a camera. However, there is abundant evidence that the retina does much more than convert patterns of light into corresponding patterns of optic nerve impulses. Consider, for example, what happens when two small patches of light fall on adjacent groups of receptors. The result may be one of spatial summation, in which small patches of dim light might not be seen when turned on separately but can be seen, when turned on simultaneously, as a single large spot of light. This has been amply shown to be the case for points close to one another in the periphery of the human eye (Graham, 1934), where each optic nerve fiber must pool the excitation it receives from an area containing hundreds of rod receptors. The opposite type of interaction, that of spatial inhibition, is clearly present also. For example, strong stimulation of one region may inhibit the responses of adjacent regions so that they appear less bright, and the contrast between them is enhanced.

Spatial summation Of particular interest here is the case of the absolute threshold for vision. In the earlier description of dark adaptation we found that only a few quanta of light are required to stimulate the eye under the most favorable conditions. One of the conditions is that each quantum be absorbed by a rod receptor within a small enough region of the peripheral retina so that complete spatial summation can occur. This is the situation described by Ricco's Law, or the law of reciprocity of area and intensity of light. In its simplest form, the law states that the absolute threshold for vision is a critical energy of light (E_c), representing the

product of luminance (L) and area (A), or

$$E_c = kAL$$

where k is a constant the value of which depends on the units in which energy, area, and luminance are expressed. Experimental determinations (Abney, 1897; Granit, 1930; Graham, 1934; Graham, Brown, & Mote, 1939) have shown that the area of complete summation as described by the Ricco formula in the periphery may be limited to areas smaller than about 20 minutes of arc in diameter. Much larger areas, however (10° or more in diameter), contribute to partial summation. In other

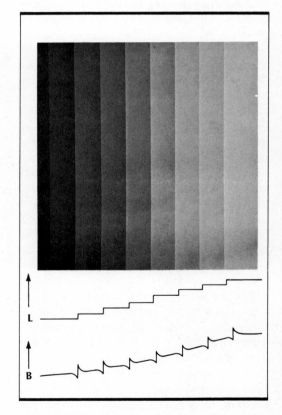

Figure 9.13. Simultaneous brightness contrast. Each strip is actually of uniform luminance (L), as shown in the accompanying graph, but the distribution of perceived brightness (B) is such that the portion of each strip lying near a darker strip appears to be darker, and vice versa.

words, areas up to that size continue to play a part in the visual threshold, and only for still larger areas is the threshold solely determined by intensity.

The functional significance of spatial summation is that, on a dark night, very dim shapes can be seen if they are rather large; similarly, in daylight, we are aware of the presence of large objects such as automobiles on a cross street that appear to the side of us even when we continue to look straight ahead.

A retinal basis for spatial summation was shown in the pioneer experiments of Adrian and Matthews (1928) on the frequency and latency of nerve impulses in the eye of the conger eel, in the work on single optic nerve fibers in the frog by Hartline (1940a, b), and in the cat by Granit (1947), Kuffler (1952), and Barlow, FitzHugh, & Kuffler (1957). Optic nerve impulses were produced more readily

by large patches of light than by small; by patches close together rather than far apart; and by several small patches rather than a single one of the same total area. Interaction effects of this kind were most readily apparent in the fully dark-adapted eye; larger responses were recorded from weak, large-area stimuli than from small-area stimuli of the same luminance. Furthermore, the latency of the response grew shorter as the size of the area illuminated was increased. These facts are consistent with the concept of a receptive field (Hartline, 1940b), the receptive field being the retinal region that includes all the receptors capable of producing a response in a given optic nerve fiber. Neural convergence occurs as the stimulus is passed from the receptors to nerve fibers; the degree of convergence can be enhanced by the application of strychnine, a drug that is known to facilitate synaptic transmission.

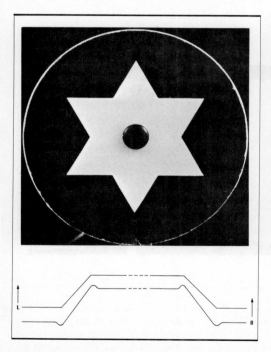
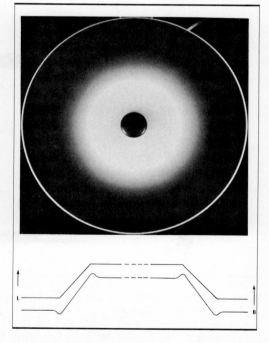

Figure 9.14. *Left:* Star pattern on color wheel used for generating a gradient pattern of luminance. Rapid rotation of the wheel produces the bright and dark Mach bands shown in the right-hand figure. The accompanying graphs show distributions of luminance (*L*) and perceived brightness (*B*) across the horizontal diameter of the color wheel disk (disregarding the black hub of the wheel).

Spatial inhibition Interaction of an inhibitory type is most clearly evident when a relatively high-intensity light is focused at one point on the retina; this acts to depress the activity in a neighboring region. Consider, for example, the series of gray strips in Figure 9.13. The portion of each strip that lies close to a border with a brighter strip looks darker than other portions even though each strip is physically uniform in its composition. Simultaneous contrast and spatial phenomena of greater complexity (see Chapter 13) are undoubtedly dependent in part on the inhibitory effect of strongly excited regions upon less strongly excited ones.

Another example of spatial inhibitory effects is provided by the Mach band phenomenon. This is the subjective appearance of a bright or dark band within a pattern of light that contains no corresponding physical increment or decrement of luminance. A simple procedure for inducing the effect is shown in Figure 9.14. A star-shaped pattern of white paper is placed over a large dark disk and rotated rapidly on a standard color wheel. The resulting physical distribution of light, as shown by line *L* in the accompanying graph, is a solid dark outer ring, a solid white inner ring, and an intermediate zone, produced by the points of the star, in which there is a

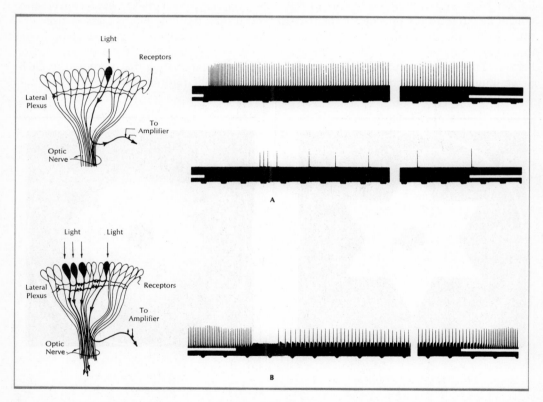

Figure 9.15. Oscillographic records of action potentials in single optic nerve fibers of *Limulus,* the horseshoe crab. A. Response to illumination of a single visual receptor unit with a bright intensity of light (upper record) and with an intensity 4 log units lower (lower record). The signal of exposure to light blackens out the white line above the $\frac{1}{5}$ second time marks. Each record interrupted for about 7 seconds. Records are from Hartline, Wagner, and MacNichol (1952). B. Inhibition of the activity of a steadily illuminated receptor unit produced by illumination of a number of neighboring receptor units. In this record, the blackening of the white line signals the illumination of these neighboring units. The record is from Hartline, Wagner, and Ratliff (1956). (Ratliff, 1965.)

steady change from dark to white. The subjective appearance of the rotating disk is more complex, however. As is shown by line *B* on the graph, it includes a thin, extra-dark ring at the inner edge of the solid dark region and a thin, extra-light ring at the outer edge of the solid bright region.

What causes the dark and light bands? Mach himself (see Ratliff, 1965) pointed out the fact that they occur most readily in regions in which the second derivative of the spatial distribution of luminance has a high value. Such regions are indeed the ones in which the rings mentioned above are seen (see Figure 9.14). The dark outer region of the star has a first derivative (rate of change of luminance over distance) that is zero; the inner white region also has a first derivative of zero. The intermediate zone, however, has a steady change from dark to white. Thus there is an abrupt transition at each edge of this zone, in which the second derivative (change in the rate of change of luminance) is quite large; these are the locations of the two Mach bands.

Mach also speculated on the physiological basis for the bands, believing this to lie in spatial inhibitory effects. However no means were available, at the time he lived, to test this assumption, although a model for explaining spatial inhibition effects now has been provided from the results of experiments on the compound eye of *Limulus,* the horseshoe crab. A single fiber can be dissected free from the rest of the optic nerve (Hartline & Graham, 1932) and records made of its activity (such as that appearing in Figure 9.15). These records illustrate the fact that intensity of excitation is coded as frequency of nerve impulses. This frequency, however, depends not only upon the intensity of light falling on the receptor unit to which the fiber is directly connected, but also upon the activity of neighboring units. In fact. as Figure 9.15 shows, every unit exerts a spatial inhibition over the activity of its neighbors. The effect of this inhibition is to depress the responses of weakly illuminated units more

than those of strongly illuminated ones. An anatomical basis for these inhibitory effects has been found by Hartline, Ratliff, and Miller (1961) in the fact that a plexus of interconnecting neurons lies in the region where the optic nerve fibers emerge from the receptor units.

Ratliff (1962) has shown that the experiments with *Limulus* may serve to explain certain human visual phenomena, if we assume that inhibitory effects take place through the lateral interconnections that are known to be present in the vertebrate retina. This is particularly well illustrated in the Mach band effect. The white inner region in Figure 9.14 illuminates the retina uniformly, so that each retinal region is subjected to direct excitation plus spatial inhibition from neighboring areas. At the outer edge of this white region, however, there is an abrupt drop in the luminance distribution going out into the middle region. At this point, therefore, less spatial inhibition is present. Thus the immediately adjacent portion of the light gray area appears as a bright band, even though no

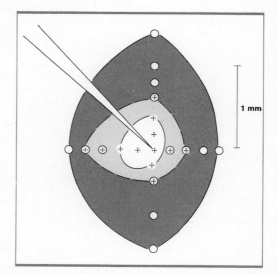

Figure 9.16. Example of a receptive field in a cat retina. A microelectrode placed in contact with a ganglion cell records impulses when a light is turned on at + or off at ○. (Kuffler, 1953.)

physical increase in light intensity can possibly be present. By similar reasoning it is shown that the dark band, appearing even darker than the outer region of uniform darkness, occurs at a point where spatial inhibition is being produced by the higher luminance that is present in the intermediate zone.

Excitatory-inhibitory interactions In the eyes of vertebrates, there appears to be a constant interplay between excitatory and inhibitory neural processes (Granit, 1947). The basis for this lies in the fact that nerve impulses result not only from the action of light on the receptors, but from its cessation as well. Figure 9.16 shows, for example, the receptive field of a ganglion cell in the retina of a cat. This receptive field is defined as including all the receptors that communicate through bipolar cells with the particular ganglion cell in question. A microelectrode in contact with this ganglion cell records nerve impulses when light falls on retinal receptors situated at one of the points marked "+." No response is recorded when light falls

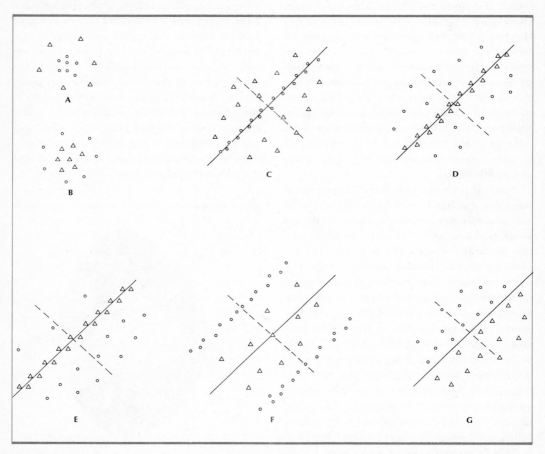

Figure 9.17. Examples of receptive fields of "simple" cells in the lateral geniculate and cortex of the cat. A. *On*-center geniculate receptive field; B. *Off*-center geniculate field; C–G. Various arrangements of "simple" cortical receptive fields: "○" indicates points in the visual field that produce excitatory (*on*) responses in the cell; "△" indicates points in the field that produce inhibitory (*off*) responses. Receptive-field axes are shown by continuous lines through field centers. In the figure these are all oblique, but each arrangement occurs in all orientations. (Hubel & Wiesel, 1962.)

on a spot marked "○" but turning the light off at that spot produces nerve impulses. Furthermore, the "+" and "○" regions inhibit one another; a light directed at a "+" point produces responses that are abolished when a second light is directed at a "○" point. Responses occur each time the light is turned either on or off in the spots marked "⊕." Other ganglion cells are found with the opposite characteristics, namely with "off-sensitivity" at the center and "on-sensitivity" at the outer part of the receptive field. Furthermore, the regions sensitive to the light being on or off inhibit one another; a large patch of light turned on or off over the whole receptive field may therefore stimulate large numbers of receptors but produce little or no response in the ganglion cell to which they are connected. A most effective stimulus is one in which the bright portions of the patch of light fall on regions sensitive to the light's being on at the same time that dark portions fall on regions of the receptive field sensitive to its being off. This, then, is a means of enhancing intensity discrimination; that is, giving the animal a strong visual signal from objects exhibiting a difference in brightness from their backgrounds. Edges and borders, in other words, are emphasized over more uniform visual fields.

A further accentuation of edge and border effects is shown at higher levels in the visual pathways. Hubel and Wiesel (1962) have found that, as in the retina, a single neuron of the lateral geniculate body may respond to the light's being turned on or off at the points defining a concentric pattern (see Figure 9.17A, B). Cortical neurons, most fully explored in the cat, do not show this concentric pattern to a light's being turned on or off. Instead, receptive fields of the kind shown in Figure 9.17C–G are found. These emphasize straight-line borders between the excitatory and inhibitory regions, with various cortical cells showing all possible orientations of the line. It is clear that such an arrangement gives further emphasis to thin lines and sharp borders in the visual field. Furthermore, a line

or edge moving at right angles to its axis of orientation was found to be particularly effective. There is also some specialization, from cell to cell, in the most effective rate and direction of this transverse movement.

Cells of the type just described are called "simple" cortical cells by Hubel and Wiesel. "Complex" and "hypercomplex" cells have also been found, the latter in "associative" areas of the visual cortex. Complex cells are still more specialized, with regard to axis of orientation, than are simple cells. Furthermore, the complex cell has a large receptive field, covering a region of 5 or 10 degrees in width. Thus some complex cells respond to light traveling along lines of a particular orientation, without regard to their specific location within this large receptive field.

A columnar organization of the visual cortex has been found as a result of the Hubel and Wiesel experiments. A microelectrode driven into the cortex to various depths perpendicular to the surface was found to encounter various simple and complex cells with the same axis of orientation. Thus a column of such cells, within a diameter of about 0.5 mm, could be called a functional unit, even though it included cells from six structural layers of the cortex. Furthermore, most of the cells could be excited from either eye, provided that stimuli having the appropriate axis of orientation fell on corresponding points of the two retinas.

There is much evidence that the spatial interactions described above for the cat may hold rather widely for other animals. In lower animals, however, the higher visual centers may not be sufficiently well developed to mediate such activity, and specialization may occur at an earlier (retinal) level. In the octopus, for example, both orientation and direction of movement are preferentially established for single optic nerve fibers (Tomita et al., 1968). Lettvin et al. (1959) attribute to the ganglion cells of the frog a preferential responding to at least five types of stimulus pattern. The goldfish (Wagner, MacNichol, & Wolbarsht, 1960; Cronly-Dillon, 1964; Daw,

1967), the ground squirrel (Michael, 1966), and the pigeon (Maturana & Frenk, 1963) are animals exhibiting highly developed cone vision with elaborate specialization of function in cells of the retina and optic tectum.

Binocular Interaction

The fact that the same cortical cells are activated by stimulation of either eye alone raises many interesting questions. A seemingly simple case is that of binocular summation at the level of the absolute threshold. We have seen that about 100 quanta of 505 nm light are required, under the most favorable conditions, barely to stimulate the dark-adapted eye. If binocular summation were complete, one might expect to reach the same result by delivering 50 quanta to each eye. This is clearly not the case, as many experiments have shown (see Pirenne, 1948; Graham, 1965). However it turns out that there is some advantage to be gained in the use of two eyes, for in this case threshold is reached when fewer than 100 quanta are delivered simultaneously to each of the two eyes. We must not jump to the conclusion, however, that this finding proves that binocular summation is taking place somewhere within the visual pathways. Instead it seems to be true that most of the advantage in using two eyes is a statistical one. In fact, two eyes are better than one even when they are not in the same head!

The statistical advantage of "binocular" vision can easily be seen from the following considerations. Let us say that when one eye is momentarily exposed to a given patch of light about 100 quanta enter the eye and the probability of detecting the flash is 50 percent. The probability of its not being detected is also 50 percent. If the same is true for an exposure of the other eye to the same patch of light, then the combined probability that the light will not be detected by either eye is 50 percent × 50 percent = 25 percent. In other words, the statistical probability that either or both of the two eyes will see the light is 75 percent. We may thus reduce the

number of quanta delivered to each eye until we reach the "binocular" threshold condition in which there will be a 50 percent probability that the flash will be detected. In other words, the *RL* for light is lower when two eyes are used to view a given patch of light than when one alone is used, and this is true whether the detection of the light is reported by one person using both eyes or by two people using one eye apiece.

An experiment by Matin (1962) leads to the conclusion that the binocular probability of seeing is greater than one would expect from the statistical considerations alone that were made above. This the author attributes to true neural summation in a pathway common to the two eyes. The effect is not a large one and comes about only under conditions in which corresponding retinal locations in the two eyes are used and certain statistical requirements are satisfied.

It is certainly true that there is less summation from the responses of the two eyes than there is from the responses of the two ears. Does this mean that there is little advantage in having two eyes instead of one? It is true that persons blind in one eye appear

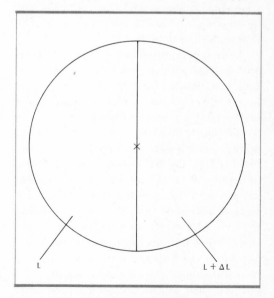

Figure 9.18. Bipartite field for use in determining the increment threshold.

to get along quite well, even to the extent of judging visual directions and distances. However the following points should be kept in mind. (1) Higher animals all have two eyes; lower forms may have six or more. One obvious advantage of having two or more eyes for survival is the fact that the animal can still see if one eye is damaged or destroyed. (2) The field of view is greater (in some animals indeed there is 360° coverage) if one eye is located on each side of the head. (3) Man and a few other animals have true binocular vision in the sense that the visual fields of the two eyes are superimposed in the projection areas of the brain.

Some of the resulting functions of binocular vision are discussed later notably in connection with eye movements (conjugate and vergent, pp. 375–384), stereoscopic depth discrimination (pp. 482–494), and binocular fusion and rivalry (pp. 488–489).

INTENSITY DISCRIMINATION

We can see from the discussion above that the visual system is well equipped to discriminate the edges and borders of various objects that fall within the visual field. The basis for this is intensity discrimination, one of the important functions studied by the methods of psychophysics. A convenient way of studying intensity discrimination is to make use of a bipartite field such as appears in Figure 9.18. The large circular field is presented, having luminance L. While the subject is fixating at the center of the field, a flash of light of luminance ΔL is added to one half of the field. By varying the value of ΔL it is possible to find an increment threshold, ΔL_c, namely the value for which the subject reports that he sees the added flash about 50 percent of the time.[1] The value of ΔL_c represents the difference limen, and $\Delta L_c/L$ is the

[1] A more sophisticated way of doing the experiment would be to use a forced choice procedure, that is, to add the light in random order to the left side or the right side of the field, and to determine the value of ΔL_c for which the subject correctly judges the side about 75 percent of the time (see Chapter 2).

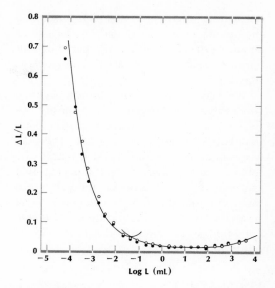

Figure 9.19. Intensity discrimination as a function of luminance. Data from König (open circles) and Brodhun, 1889 (solid circles). Separate curves have been fitted to the high-and low-luminance portions. (After Hecht, 1934.)

Weber ratio. Experiments by König and Brodhun (1889); Hecht, Peskin, and Patt (1938); and Graham and Kemp (1938) have shown that the Weber ratio is not constant, but depends upon numerous parameters such as the size and duration of the increment patch and, most importantly, the value of L, the background intensity (see Figure 9.19). Intensity discrimination is poor in the scotopic range, but the Weber ratio approaches the extraordinarily low value of .01 under the most favorable photopic conditions.

The accuracy of photopic intensity discrimination permits its use in photometry, as is described in connection with Figure 9.4. Accuracy of this kind is only possible, however, with repeated observations by skilled observers, using fields that do not differ greatly in hue or saturation. Flicker photometry (see pp. 312–313) can better be used when qualitative differences in hue and saturation are large. Incidentally, meteorologists have adopted a value of 2 percent as standard for $\Delta L/L$ observations in the field. The meteorological range, for example, is defined as that distance through the atmosphere for which the luminance of a large dark mass (such as a mountain) is 2 percent lower than the luminance of a large bright background (such as the sky).

We may speak of the *contrast* between supra-threshold differences in intensity between two fields. Contrast is conveniently defined by the ratio $\Delta L/(L + \Delta L)$, where ΔL is the intensity difference and $L + \Delta L$ is the intensity of the brighter field. It is clear that this contrast ratio approaches unity for maximum intensity differences, whereas a value of about .01 to .02 is found under favorable conditions as the intensity difference threshold is approached.

VISUAL ACUITY

We have reviewed some of the principles underlying our ability to register spatial aspects of the visual scene. We now turn to the topic of visual acuity, by which is meant the precision with which we can see fine details of the scene. With good acuity we can, for example, see separate stars in the night sky, read signs along a roadway, or identify distant aircraft.

Specification of Acuity

Visual acuity is given a quantitative basis by determining the smallest test object that can be seen by the observer. The familiar eye-test chart, for example, provides letters of various sizes to be read by an observer from a standard distance. In terms of the diagram in Figure 9.6, the width S of lines composing the letters on each line of the chart is reduced until a threshold is reached such that the letters are no longer correctly identified. At this point we may designate the angular threshold β in minutes of arc subtended by S at the eye of the observer. A conventional statement of acuity is then given as the reciprocal of β; for example, a visual acuity of 1.00 designates the ability to see letters having a line width of 1 minute of arc at the standard distance, usually 20 ft. An alternative state-

Figure 9.20. Four types of acuity test. (Riggs, 1965c.)

ment of acuity, based on the same standard, is the ratio between the standard viewing distance and the distance at which the smallest test object would subtend an angle of 1 minute of arc. Thus the eye is said to have an acuity of 20/40 or 50 percent if the observer, at a distance of 20 ft from the chart, can only see letters that would subtend an angle of 1 minute of arc at a distance of 40 ft. Persons with very good vision may have acuity ratings as high as 200 percent, or 20/10. In some states a person is called "legally blind" if his best acuity is as low as 5 percent, or 20/400.

Types of Acuity Task

Although the eye chart is a useful device for clinical purposes, it represents only one particular kind of acuity task. The various forms of acuity may conveniently be designated as those involving the detection, recognition, resolution, or localization of the test object. Figure 9.20 gives samples of these various aspects of acuity.

Detection To detect an object, the observer simply judges its presence or absence in a visual field. It can be shown that this judgment is a form of intensity discrimination, for the effect of such a test object as a dark line or dot (Figure 9.20) is to cause a change ΔL in the luminance of one region of the visual field. Observers are extraordinarily good at the detection of a single dark line, perhaps in part because of the action of cortical cells with straight-line axes of orientation (as in Figure 9.17). The threshold width of such a line is about 0.5 second of arc (Hecht & Mintz, 1939).

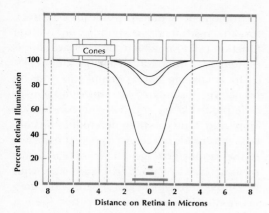

Figure 9.21. Patterns of retinal illumination produced by three widths of black line viewed against a bright field. Actual line widths in units of micrometers (1 $\mu = 10^{-6}$ meter) are shown by solid lines at the base of the figure. Blocks at the top of the figure represent the spacing of the finest cone receptors at the center of the fovea (see Figure 9.8, p. 280). (Hecht & Mintz, 1939.)

The optical phenomenon of diffraction must be considered in relation to problems of detection. Diffraction is an effect due to interference of light waves entering the eye through different parts of the pupil. Because of diffraction, a single point of light is focused on the retina not as a point but as a pattern consisting of a central disk of light surrounded by a series of dark and light rings. The image of a fine line has a width, on the retina, that is typically greater than 30 seconds of arc, no matter how fine the original line used in the test object is. Calculations based on the physical diffraction of light (Byram, 1944) reveal that the retinal image of such a fine line is degraded into a band that is less than 5 percent darker than the surrounding uniform field (Figure 9.21). In other words the line is detected on the basis of intensity discrimination that is nearly as fine as that which is measured with the ideal situation of a bipartite field.

Recognition   Figure 9.20 illustrates the task of recognizing a letter E, such as that which appears in a standard eye chart (Snel-

len, 1862; Cowan, 1928) and a broken ring of the kind used by Landolt (1889). The task involves not only brightness discrimination, but some degree of resolution, and localization as well. It may therefore be considered a sort of overall procedure for testing acuity, particularly convenient in the clinical practice of ophthalmologists and optometrists.

Resolution   By resolution is meant the ability to discriminate a separation between elements of a visual pattern. Resolution may be measured by presenting a subject with two black dots and determining when he can see them as two rather than one (Figure 9.20) (which is a task similar to that used to measure two-point resolution in the sense of touch). The multiple-line grating pattern is perhaps the most widely used device for testing optical performance, not only that of vision but also of instruments such as the camera or telescope. At best, the eye can resolve a grating in which the line widths are about 35 to 40 seconds of arc (Shlaer, 1937), that is, about 70 to 80 times as wide as a single line that can be detected. This kind of performance is only attained at high levels of intensity with light and dark lines of high contrast.

Modulation transfer functions   Engineers have developed methods for measuring the overall efficiency of an optical instrument. The basic principle is to evaluate the image formed by the instrument in comparison with the original test pattern. A camera or telescope, for example, forms a nearly perfect image of a coarse grating. Thus the contrast between the bright and dark lines of the grating is nearly the same in the image as in the original pattern. When tested with a fine grating, however, the optical system forms an image of lower contrast than the original. If an extremely fine grating is used, the performance may become so poor that it fails altogether to transfer the pattern of the original test object to the optical image. The difference in the contrast maintained in the image by the instrument and the contrast that exists in the test pattern may be measured and is referred to as modulation transfer. The fineness of the test pattern is expressed in units of spatial frequency, such as the number of bright lines per angular degree subtended by the test pattern at the location of the

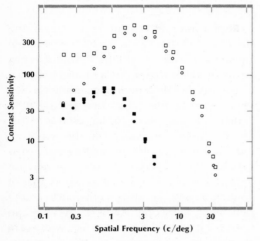

Figure 9.22. Visual acuity defined in terms of contrast sensitivity for bright and dark lines of grating test objects. The ordinate is the contrast sensitivity, defined as the reciprocal of the contrast thresholds determined for subject FWC, where contrast is defined as the modulation (m) of light, that is,

$$m = \frac{L_{\max} - L_{\min}}{2L_{\mathrm{av}}}$$

This definition, based as it is on the maximum, minimum, and average values of luminance in the grating, differs slightly from the earlier definition of contrast given on page 298. The abscissa specifies the fineness of the grating, expressed as the frequency in cycles (or number of dark lines) per degree of visual angle. Data are for square-wave (□, ■) gratings, such as the one appearing in Figure 9.20, and for sine-wave gratings (○,●) having an average luminance of 160 mL (□,○) and .016 mL (■, ●). Compare the effects of luminance with those shown in Figure 9.24. Note also the approximate equivalence of square-wave and sine-wave gratings at all moderate to high spatial frequencies. (Campbell & Robson, 1968.)

instrument. It is then possible to construct, for any instrument, a modulation transfer function (MTF) in which the contrast ratio is plotted as a function of spatial frequency.

To adapt the MTF principle to tests of human visual acuity, test gratings with lines of differing thickness and differing contrast are employed. One can then determine the contrast thresholds of the eye to detect each line of the various gratings. An example of visual contrast data is shown in Figure 9.22. Thus when the lines of the grating are wide, grating resolution can occur even when there is little contrast between the lines. When the lines of the grating are very fine, however, there must be a much greater contrast between them before they can be resolved. As we see below, the effects of optical aberrations and diffraction are such that the retinal image of a fine (high-frequency) grating has a much lower degree of contrast than does the grating itself. Thus diffraction also accounts for the great discrepancy that we have just noted in the threshold widths of line for single-line and multiple-line (grating) tests of visual acuity.

Localization   The relative positions of two lines in space may be judged by the use of the vernier offset test figure shown in Figure 9.20. The task is one of distinguishing whether the upper vertical line is to the right or left of the lower, and the barely discriminable offset is found to be about 2 seconds of arc (Wright, 1942; Berry, 1948). It is evident from vernier acuity data that the observer not only sees very fine details in the visual scene but also is capable of extremely fine discrimination of the relative positions of objects. Binocular displacements of this kind form the basis for stereoscopic depth discrimination, a topic presented in detail in Chapter 13.

Basic Determiners of Acuity

Important factors to consider in relation to visual acuity are the fineness of the mosaic of retinal receptors, the size of the pupil, the luminance and contrast of the test object, the exposure time of the test object, and the effects of eye movements.

The retinal mosaic We have seen that the cone receptors at the center of the human fovea are slender and tightly packed together in a mosaic such as that displayed in Figure 9.8. The distance between cones on the retina is about 2.2 μ and represents a visual angle of about 23 seconds of arc. We may well ask whether this value, small as it is, places a limit on visual acuity. Helmholtz (1909–1911) argued that the lines of a grating could only be resolved if its bright lines were far enough apart so that an unstimulated row of cones could lie between them. Present evidence from a variety of sources suggests, however, that no such simple relationship holds. Indeed, it now seems that acuity would not be greatly improved if the eye were equipped with an even finer receptor mosaic.

We have seen that the eye can detect a single line even when its width is only 0.5 seconds of arc (a small fraction of the inter-cone distance). This is possible because the retinal image of the line is so spread out by diffraction that it causes only a slight darkening to occur on a large number of cone receptors. In this case, then, we may conclude that there would be no advantage in having receptors of smaller diameter.

There may appear to be a problem in accounting for the fact that fine lines appear subjectively to be straight and sharp. Perhaps this is not really a problem, for we may see lines that are physically straight and sharp that way even though an intervening stage in our perception of them may involve a blurred and irregular pattern of stimulation on relatively coarse retinal receptors. For the task of localization, a rather similar situation may hold. A vernier offset of 2 seconds of arc can be observed on the basis of signals from receptors the centers of which are separated by more than 10 times that distance. We know that a large number of receptors must take part, in order for such localization to be

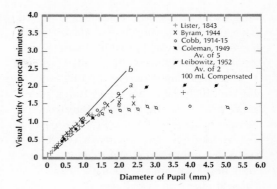

Figure 9.23. The effect of pupil diameter on visual acuity. Lines *a* and *b* are for the predictions made by Rayleigh and Dawes, respectively, with regard to the effects of diffraction of light. (Riggs, 1965c.)

effective. Hering (1899) realized that an "averaging process" might act to fill the gaps between separate receptor elements, and this idea was elaborated into a "retinal mean local sign" hypothesis by Andersen and Weymouth (1923), taking account of the possible effects of diffraction and eye movements. Just as, in statistics, a mean can be determined quite accurately for a large number of relatively variable individual measurements, so a line may appear to have sharpness and a definite location in spite of the irregularity and fuzziness of its image on the retina. For tasks of recognition and resolution, we can show (see below) that visual acuity is approximately as high as would be predicted from the known effects of diffraction in degrading the retinal image. We must therefore conclude that the receptor mosaic is already fine enough so that adequate spatial signaling can occur, and therefore no great improvement in acuity would result if a still finer mosaic were present.

Size of pupil A number of experimental determinations have been made of acuity with various pupillary diameters. Figure 9.23 shows some of the data. Artificial pupils have been placed before the eye to obtain diameters less than 2 mm, and mydriatic drugs have been used to obtain large pupils in some of these experiments. It is clear from the data that acuity is fairly linearly related to pupillary diameter up to a value of about 1 mm. A small improvement occurs if the pupil is opened to somewhat larger diameters, but a nearly constant high value of acuity holds over a range of 2.5 to 5 mm, which is approximately the normal range of the diameter of the pupils for high to moderate photopic levels of luminance. In other words, the diameter of the pupil does not appear to have much of a practical effect on visual acuity.

It may be of interest, however, to inquire into the reasons why acuity bears the relation it does to size of pupil. The nearly constant level of acuity with normal variations in the pupil can in fact be attributed to a balance between favorable and unfavorable consequences of increasing the pupillary aperture. Favorable factors are those of allowing more light to enter the eye and reducing the effects of the diffraction of light. Unfavorable are the effects of optical aberrations, the effects of which are much more serious as the effective diameter of the optical system of the eye is increased.

If the optics of the eye were perfect, diffraction alone would result in a linear increase of acuity with pupillary diameter. This is because the size of a diffraction pattern is inversely related to the diameter of the pupil. This is the major limiting factor for acuity with pupillary diameter of 1 mm or less, as shown by the linear portion of the data at the left of Figure 9.23.

Because the eye is not a perfect optical instrument, it suffers from optical aberrations of various kinds. They all have in common the fact that rays of light emanating from a single point, but entering the eye through different parts of the pupil, are not brought to one point on the retina, causing distortion of the image. The distortion becomes worse as the diameter of the pupil increases; this is probably the main reason why the acuity values in Figure 9.23 do not continue to rise along a straight line throughout the graph.

Perhaps it is surprising, in view of the seriousness of optical aberrations, that acuity does not decline sharply with large increases in pupillary diameter. A possible explanation lies in the Stiles-Crawford effect. Stiles and Crawford (1933) discovered that light rays entering the eye through the center of the pupil (see Figure 9.5) stimulate the cone receptors much more efficiently than do rays entering the eye through the edges of the pupil. They were able to show that the effect is due to a directional sensitivity of the individual receptors. We have seen that the foveal cones are long and slender (Figure 9.8). Also, each cone is typically oriented in the direction of the center of the pupil; thus a ray of light reaching it from that direction is funneled straight through its base and into the outer segment containing the photosensitive pigment of the cone. Rays from the edges of the pupil hit the cone at such an angle that they are less likely to reach the outer segment where they could have an effect. Thus a large-sized pupil has far less influence on acuity than it might have if it were not for the directional sensitivity of the cones. We may therefore regard the Stiles-Crawford effect as maintaining good acuity with large pupillary apertures, in the face of the serious aberrations that are present for rays passing through outer portions of the pupil.

Rod receptors do not appear to show the same directional sensitivity as the cones. Hence, for scotopic vision, the eye receives the full benefit of a dilated pupil at the lowest light levels. The normal pupil exhibits an area change of about 16 to 1, going from a 2 mm diameter at high intensities of light to an 8 mm diameter in complete darkness; this factor contributes to the increased sensitivity of the eye that takes place during dark adaptation, but the contribution of the pupil is small by comparison with the photochemical and neural factors that we have already found to provide a much greater change of sensitivity.

Light intensity One of the most well-known facts about acuity is that it is affected by the intensity of light. By starlight we can

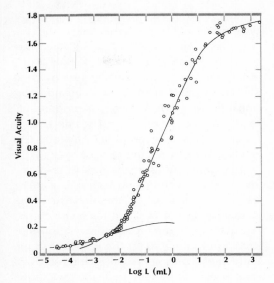

Figure 9.24. Visual acuity as a function of luminance. Separate curves have been fitted to the rod (low-luminance) and cone (high-luminance) portions of the data. (Hecht, 1934.)

see the white page of a book, but not the writing on it; note that this is in the low scotopic luminance range of about .0001 mL (see Table 9.1). Although we can begin to discern separate letters by moonlight, at .01 mL, reading the text does not become comfortable until photopic vision fully predominates, at about 10 mL. Acuity continues to improve as light intensity is further increased, especially when test objects of low contrast are involved.

Figure 9.24 shows the dependence of acuity on intensity, over a wide range of experimental values. In the scotopic range (below .01 millilambert) acuity is poor; it rises only slightly as the intensity of stimulation is increased. This is consistent with the fact that scotopic vision is extrafoveal. The rod receptors, though sensitive to very dim light, are relatively far apart and, as we have seen, combine over a wide region to signal their activity to only a relatively small number of optic nerve fibers. Figure 9.24 shows that acuity improves rapidly as the intensity of the light is increased to the point that photopic

vision can be relied upon and the fovea comes into play. This is easily understood in terms of the fineness in the central fovea of the retinal mosaic and the fact that each cone has ample representation in the fibers of the optic nerve (Polyak, 1941; Vilter, 1949). Less easily interpreted is the fact that acuity continues to rise as intensity is raised far beyond the range of optimal intensity discrimination (compare Figures 9.18 and 9.24). This must mean that stimuli of small dimensions, such as those used for acuity test objects, can be fully discriminated only at intensity levels above those for large test fields such as those used to measure intensity discrimination. One can perhaps assume that optimal discrimination of either type requires the achievement of differentiation of large numbers of excitatory and inhibitory signals; with small test objects this requirement can only be met at high intensity levels, since the number of input channels is limited; larger objects can meet it by supplying fewer signals over each channel, since a larger number of channels are available. Whether or not this hypothesis has any merit, we find it to be consistent with some data of Graham and Bartlett (1940). They show that intensity discrimination in the fovea remains fairly constant over a wide intensity range except for their smallest stimulus patch (of 2 min arc radius), for which intensity discrimination continues to improve as higher and higher intensities are used.

Exposure time   In a later consideration of temporal aspects of vision, we note that a fundamental law of photochemistry, the Bunsen-Roscoe Law, is obeyed if the eye is exposed to light for short periods of time. The data of Sperling and Jolliffe (1965) show, in line with several earlier studies, that the energy of the light necessary for the detection of a small bright disk is constant for all short times (t) of exposure, where energy is the product of time and luminance (L) in agreement with the Bunsen-Roscoe Law. Detection of thin-line targets is similarly in agreement with the law (Niven & Brown,

1944; Bouman, 1953; Keesey, 1960). In each of these studies, however, a critical duration t_c is found above which the law no longer applies. Finally, at very long durations, intensity alone determines the threshold for detection. Values of t_c ranging from .01 sec (Martin, Day, & Kaniowski, 1950) to over .2 sec are found, depending on intensity level and acuity task.

Spatial factors also influence the dependence of acuity on exposure time. In fact, the total energy of light in a test stimulus is governed not only by intensity and exposure time, but also by the area, A, of the test object. For all small area and time values reciprocity extends to the area dimension so that the threshold energy E_c is given by the relation

$$E_c = A \cdot L \cdot t$$

This relationship holds generally for a variety of test objects, as is illustrated in studies by Blackwell (1946), Long (1951), and Davy (1952).

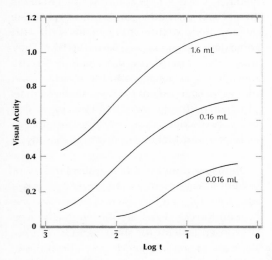

Figure 9.25. Visual acuity as a function of log exposure time (t in seconds). Grating test objects were used and the acuity was defined as a reciprocal of the width of line (minutes of arc of visual angle). Three different luminance values, 1.6, .16, and .016 mL, were used respectively for top, middle and bottom curves. (Graham & Cook, 1937.)

Riggs (1965c) has pointed out that linear dimensions, rather than area, specify the spatial magnitudes of stimuli used for acuity tests. This means, for example, that an acuity score computed for a circular test patch at a given constant intensity (with area proportional to square of diameter) is proportional to $t^{1/2}$ for values of $t < t_c$. For line targets, however, area is proportional to width, and acuity is directly related to t for $t < t_c$.

The complexities of the task of resolving an object are such that no such simple analysis can be made of all the steps involved. Graham and Cook (1937), using high-contrast line gratings, found the sigmoid relationships shown in Figure 9.25 for the influence of log t on acuity. Acuity approaches a high constant level as exposure times are made long; however if the eye is exposed to a light stimulus for a short period of time, acuity becomes as strongly dependent on log t as on log L (compare Figure 9.24).

Schober and Hilz (1965) and Nachmias (1967) have included square-wave grating targets of varying contrast in their studies of resolution in relation to exposure time. This has permitted them to derive threshold contrast functions, as in Figure 9.22, for various values of exposure time.

It is tempting to draw the conclusion (no doubt oversimplified) that one good look at a test target is sufficient for seeing it with maximum acuity. The duration of the best "look" must be greater than t_c, but it need not be longer than one or two tenths of a second at daylight levels of luminance.

Eye movements In Chapter 11 it is made clear that one of the chief functions of eye movements is to direct the gaze onto objects that are of significance in the visual field. The image of an object is thus brought to the center of the fovea. The observer then attempts to keep his eyes fixed on the object, that is, to keep the image at this optimal location long enough to see it with good acuity, which we have just concluded is an interval of .1 or .2 seconds.

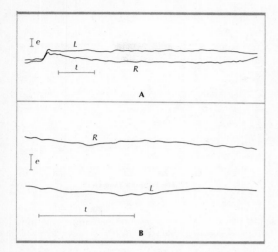

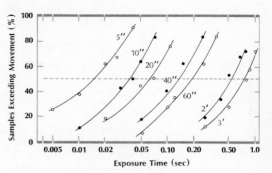

Figure 9.27. Sample data on the extent of involuntary eye movements during various exposure intervals. The ordinate scale is for the percentage of records exhibiting an amount of movement designated beside each curve. The abscissa is the length of record sample (that is, the time interval over which the extent of eye movement was determined). (Riggs, Armington, & Ratliff, 1954.)

Figure 9.26. Involuntary eye movements during attempted steady fixation. Upper records (A) show one "flick" or saccadic movement, well coordinated in the two eyes, and numerous uncoordinated, rapid tremor motions, as well as a slow drift of the eye. Lower records (B) show an enlarged section of A. The length of the line e represents 100 seconds of angular rotation of the eye; length of t is 0.1 second of time. Record L is from the left eye; R is from the right. (Riggs & Ratliff, 1951.)

We must now ask some more questions: Can the eye be held still during this fixational pause, or are there involuntary movements even when steady fixation is attempted? If such movements exist, how large are they and what effect do they have on acuity?

The eye movement records of Ratliff and Riggs (1950), Ditchburn and Ginsborg (1953), Riggs, Armington, and Ratliff (1954), Krauskopf, Cornsweet, and Riggs (1960), Rashbass and Westheimer (1961), and Robinson (1963) are of particular relevance here. In each case, the experimenter attached a tightly fitting contact lens to the eye that supports a mirror or other device that can be used to indicate the extent of the movements of the eye (see Chapter 11). Furthermore, the observer is given a clear fixation point and told to try to keep his eyes fixed on it. The eyes, however, are by no means motionless, as may be seen from the records shown in Figure 9.26. A sampling of measurements on such records gives the information displayed in Figure 9.27. These measurements show, for example, that the retinal image may be considered stationary only for .02 second. During .1 second exposures the image occasionally exhibits a total excursion of 1 minute of arc or more, but typically the image shifts less than half that much. Considered in relation to the data on acuity versus exposure time, given in the preceding section, we therefore have the question: Is acuity importantly affected by image motions of about a half minute of arc?

Various "dynamic" theories of acuity (Andersen & Weymouth, 1923; Marshall & Talbot, 1942) have pointed out that small eye movements permit a given portion of the retinal image to be scanned by the individual cone receptors. They have assumed that such scanning may sharpen the perception of a border or point in much the same way that the moving fingertips of blind people scan the raised pattern of letters in Braille. An opposite assumption is made if we say that the eye, like a camera, must be perfectly steady if blurring due to the motion of the image of the test object is to be prevented. How can we test visual acuity in the absence

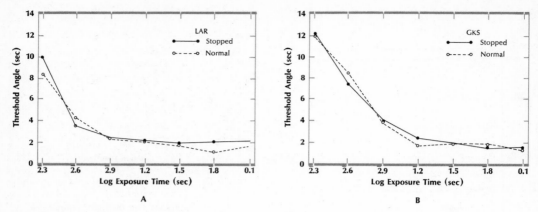

Figure 9.28. Threshold curves for the detection of single black lines under normal viewing conditions and under conditions in which retinal image motion is stopped. (Keesey, 1960.)

of image motion? Can we find a way to clamp the eyeball, or paralyze the eye muscles? Perhaps; but a less hazardous solution to the problem has been developed by applying optical techniques (Ditchburn & Ginsborg, 1952; Riggs & Ratliff, 1952) for producing a *stabilized retinal image*. (These techniques are described in detail in Chapter 11.) They depend for their accuracy on a careful attention to experimental details such as the quality of the optics, clearness of the fixation point, and the careful fitting of a contact lens to support a mirror on the eye. When these conditions are met, the remaining errors of stabilization of the image are not of great visual significance (Riggs & Schick, 1968). It therefore becomes possible to test visual acuity in the absence of image motion.

A direct comparison of acuity with and without motions of the retinal image was made by Keesey (1960). She studied three types of acuity (single-line detection, grating resolution, and vernier offset localization) for exposure times ranging from .02 to 1.28 seconds. A sample of the data is shown in Figure 9.28, where it may be seen that the acuity thresholds are nearly the same whether normal image motion is taking place or whether it is stopped by the technique of optical stabilization. The evidence of these experiments is clearly against any improvement in acuity as a result of scanning of a moving image.

Stereoscopic acuity was found by Shortess and Krauskopf (1961) to be unaffected, also, by normal image motion over a wide range of exposure times.

It is true that the test objects used in the above experiments were all of high contrast, and the possibility exists that vision for low-contrast borders may somehow be improved by image motion. It must also be remembered that image motion is required for the prolonged maintenance of vision; the stabilized image condition results in a sort of functional blindness in which patterns fade and eventually disappear from view (Riggs et al., 1953; see Chapter 11). But we may conclude, on present evidence, that eye movements during a fixational pause are normally too small to have any significant effect on visual acuity as it is usually measured.

TEMPORAL ASPECTS OF VISION

The time dimensions of single and multiple visual stimuli are effective perceptually, and measurements of latent times for visual responses are useful indices of the underlying sensory processes.

Temporal Summation

We have already seen that, in the case of visual acuity, the detectability of a stimulus patch of small area (A), luminance (L), and duration (*t*) is proportional to the total energy (*E*) of the light. Thus

$$E_c = A \cdot L \cdot t$$

where E_c is the critical amount of light needed, for example, for a detection probability of 50 percent. (This is the statement of the Bunsen-Roscoe Law mentioned above.) The equation has been shown to hold for a wide variety of visual functions in addition to acuity, for exposure times shorter than t_c, a value known as the critical duration of the flash. The value of t_c may be as short as a few milliseconds if the object being looked at is well illuminated, or it may be as long as several hundred milliseconds if it is not so well illuminated. In any case, the significance of the equation is that it defines a state of complete temporal summation or integration. In summary, within the time t_c the degree of stimulation of the eye is directly proportional to the duration of the stimulus.

Above t_c temporal summation falls off. Stimulus strength still rises with some further increase in *t*, but finally a duration is reached beyond which there is no further effect of time. At supra-threshold levels, summation holds only for very short flashes. Curiously enough, however, moderately short flashes of light may seem brighter than do longer flashes of the same luminance. This is the Broca-Sulzer effect (1902) discussed by Stainton (1928), Baumgardt and Ségal (1947), Bartley, Paczewitz, and Valsi (1957), Boynton (1961), and Hurvich and Jameson (1966). It furnishes a partial explanation for the fact that a flickering stimulus is particularly effective at rates where the separate flashes are of a duration yielding high brightnesses according to the Broca-Sulzer experiments (see below).

Latency Measurements

The initial effect of light, namely the molecular change that the quanta produce in the photopigment, occurs without measurable latency. Estimates of the time it takes to produce photoproducts (see Figure 9.11) are in the microsecond range. Delays of several milliseconds are presumably associated, how-

ever, with processes that take place in the receptor cell after the photoproducts are formed, whereby the photoproducts act in some way to trigger the signal that is passed along to the bipolar cells. Electrical signs of these events have been recorded. Thus an "early receptor potential" (ERP) is recorded when the retina is exposed to the direct rays of an electronic flash discharge tube (Brown & Murakami, 1964; Cone, 1964). This response, occurring without measurable latency, can be elicited even from an isolated retina that has been removed from the eye and consequently been deprived of its oxygen supply and thereby has lost its neural responses (Goldstein, 1967). Similar potentials can be produced, in chloroplasts taken from plant leaves, by intense flashes of light (Ebrey, 1967). In the eye, therefore, the ERP is presumed to reflect the molecular changes occurring in the outer segment of the receptor.

The electroretinogram (ERG) is a response that is relatively easy to record from any eye

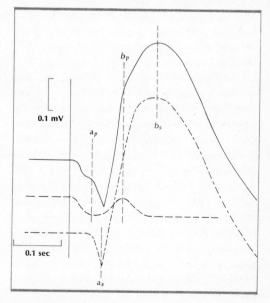

Figure 9.29. Analysis of the photopic (dash line) and scotopic (dot-dash line) components of the electroretinogram of the human eye. The a wave has photopic (a_p) and scotopic (a_s) components, and the b wave similarly has b_p and b_s components. (Armington, Johnson, & Riggs, 1952.)

that is in good metabolic condition (see Granit, 1947, 1955, and 1962; Riggs, 1965a). The ERG can be recorded from a human eye with a contact lens electrode (Riggs, 1941). Figure 9.29 shows an analysis of the human ERG in which an initial a-wave appears with a very short latency, followed by a b-wave that is slower and of opposite polarity. There is considerable evidence to support an early hypothesis of Granit (1947) that the time relations of the a-wave are those of electrical activity in the receptor layer of the retina, whereas the b-waves, which occur later, are the signs of activity at the level of the bipolars. Photopic and scotopic portions of the waves were identified by Adrian (1945, 1946) and later investigators of the human ERG. Modern refinements in technique have permitted the separation of photopic and scotopic ERG activity (Riggs, Johnson, & Schick, 1964, 1966) and have therefore made possible the application of ERG recording to study such photopic functions as spectral sensitivity (Johnson, Riggs, & Schick, 1966), color contrast, and visual acuity.

Judging from the a-wave of the ERG made in response to a moderately bright flash, photopic (cone) receptor activity begins with a latency of only a few milliseconds and reaches a peak in less than 50 msec after the onset of a flash. The scotopic (rod) receptor latency may be 30 msec or longer. Responses at the bipolar level, judging from the b-wave, are some 60 to 100 msec slower than those originating at the receptor level; this is presumably the time consumed by the synaptic delay. At the level of the occipital cortex, electrodes such as those used to record electroencephalograms may be used to pick up potential waves evoked by the activity of neurons in the geniculocalcarine tract or in the various cortical layers. Electrodes used for the recording of human electroencephalograms (EEG) can be used (see Chapter 4) to pick up these responses for latency determinations. Complex wave forms appear that are primarily photopic in origin, with early and late components typically peaking within

about 50 to 150 msec after the onset of moderately strong flash stimulation of the eye (Adrian, 1946).

Experiments on animals have revealed that a major part of the electrical activity of retina and cortex occurs not in the form of nerve impulses (all-or-none spikes) but rather in the form of relatively slow changes (graded membrane potentials) in and around the neurone (see Chapter 4). In the vertebrate retina, for example, microelectrodes have been used to penetrate single cone receptors (Tomita et al., 1967). No evidence is found that the cones are able to generate nerve impulse spikes. Instead the inner portion of each receptor exhibits a generator potential, that is, a change in membrane potential that varies with the intensity of the stimulating light. In other experiments (MacNichol & Svaetichin, 1958) microelectrodes near but outside of receptor cells have been used to record "S-potentials" (see Chapter 10) resulting from the pooled activity of many receptors. These, too, are graded potentials and some of them depend for their size upon the intensity of the stimulus. Others exhibit opposite polarities for contrasting wavelengths of the light. In still other experiments single bipolar and amacrine cells (Werblen, 1968; Kaneko & Hashimoto, 1969) have likewise yielded graded potentials with or without the production of spikes. Finally, the ganglion cells accept the many incoming graded potential forms of response from bipolar and amacrine cells and convert them into true nerve impulses. These are the optic nerve impulses, which travel from the eye to the brain.

One is tempted to compare the retina to an electronic transducer system in which the input signal activates a pattern of 130,000,000 photoreceptor units that feed analog (graded potential) signals into many millions of elements that make up the networks of a miniature computer. The computer analyzes and differentiates these analog signals, enhancing certain of their spatial and temporal properties. Finally, at the output stage, the processed

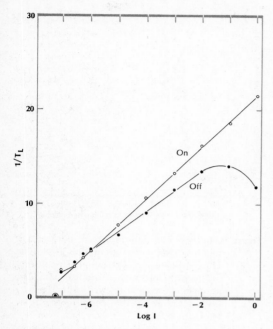

Figure 9.30. The dependence of latency on stimulus intensity in the responses of a single optic nerve fiber of the frog. Reciprocal latencies of on and off responses are plotted as functions of log intensity. (Hartline, 1938.)

analog signals are encoded into digital (nerve impulse) form for efficient transmission along the output cable (optic nerve) to the brain. All of this processing takes place in a sheet of tissue weighing less than a hundredth of an ounce!

Dependence of latency on stimulus parameters The time between the onset of a stimulus and the response recorded from the visual system (the latent time or latency) typically is found to be short if the intensity of the stimulus is high. (Figure 9.30 provides an illustration of the inverse relationship between latent time and log intensity in a single optic nerve fiber of the frog.) The latent time of the response is also inversely related, within limits, to the size of the area stimulated and the duration of the stimulus. Clearly, then, the measurement of latency provides an alternative or supplementary procedure to those psychophysical threshold

procedures used to evaluate the effectiveness of a visual stimulus. In fact it is often true, in the electrical recording of visual responses, that latency measurements are more reliable than measurements of amplitudes of response potential waves or frequencies of nerve impulses.

The simple reaction time of human subjects (see Chapter 4) is one form of latency measure, and like the others, is inversely related to stimulus intensity. Visual reaction times are commonly reported to reach a minimum of about 150 msec for bright flashes of light, whereas strong cutaneous or auditory stimuli yield reaction times that are 30 to 40 msec shorter. From our analysis of the latencies of response at the various levels in the visual pathways, we may conclude that a significant part of the delay occurs as a result of the processing of signals in the retina. This conclusion is confirmed by experiments such as those of Bartley and Bishop (1933) in the rabbit, and Malis and Kruger (1956) in the cat on direct electrical stimulation of the optic tract. They found that cortical response potential waves have latencies of only a few milliseconds. It is evidently true that the superb spatial analysis that takes place in the eye has been achieved at the cost of many milliseconds' delay in the eliciting of visual responses.

An interesting interaction between spatial and temporal signals to the eye is demonstrated by the so-called "Pulfrich pendulum effect." To cause the effect, one eye is covered with a neutral density filter that allows between 10 and 30 percent of the light to pass through. The other eye is left uncovered. A pendulum is then observed binocularly under good illumination as it swings left and right in a vertical plane. The result is that the observer sees the pendulum as swinging in an elliptical path that seems to carry it nearer and farther from him. The explanation offered by Pulfrich (1922), and further explored by Lit (1949), for the effect is that the weaker stimulation of the covered eye results in a delay, with respect to the other eye, of visual signals indicating the position of the pendulum. Thus the uncovered eye sees the pendulum occupying a position at the middle of its swing, for example, at the same time that the covered eye sees it occupying a slightly earlier position. The disparity in the two eyes is therefore interpreted as a spatial one, even though it is actually a disparity in time. Like any spatial disparity it is interpreted as a change in stereoscopic distance (see Chapter 13); hence the pendulum appears to come closer at the middle of its swing in one direction, and to go farther away when the direction is reversed.

Multiple Flashes

We may recall at this point that a large proportion of the research in vision has been concerned either with more or less continuous illumination of the visual field, or with the presentation of a field illuminated by a single flash. There remains, however, a substantial body of work on the effects of multiple stimulation of the eye. We speak now of various two-flash situations in which the effects of the two flashes interact with one another, or of intermittent light stimuli that commonly result in the perception of flicker.

Two-flash situations Typically, research involving two flashes of light has been concerned with the masking effect that the second flash has upon the response to the first. The term "metacontrast" has been used to denote the situation in which the brightness of a flash is reduced by a second flash that is delivered to an adjacent region of the visual field (Alpern, 1953). The degree of suppression has been shown to vary with the intensity of the second flash and with the time interval that separates the two.

The term "visual masking" is used for a situation in which a test flash falls within the same region that is illuminated by a conditioning flash of light. (A more detailed discussion of two-flash experiments is given in Chapter 12).

An experiment of Crawford (1947) is of

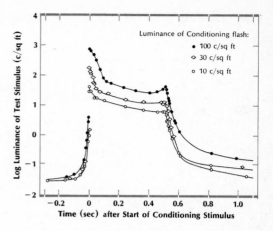

Figure 9.31. Threshold determinations before, during, and after a conditioning flash of light. The ordinate is log luminance threshold for the detection of the test flash. The abscissa is the time relative to the 0.5 second duration of the conditioning flash. (Crawford, 1947.)

particular interest here because it furnishes information about short-term light and dark adaptation. Figure 9.31 presents some of the data. A conditioning stimulus begins at time 0 on the baseline of that figure and remains on for 0.5 sec. A test flash of 0.01 sec duration is presented at various times before, during, and after the conditioning stimulus. On the ordinate is a logarithmic scale of luminance threshold values for the test flash. The various curves show the way in which the threshold value of the test flash is raised by the action of the conditioning stimulus. Paradoxically, the test flash threshold appears to rise *prior* to the onset of the conditioning stimulus. This may be explained, however, by the fact that the conditioning stimulus is so intense that it produces a sensory-neural effect of much shorter latency than that of the weak test flash. Thus the stronger response catches up with the weaker and masks it, even when it was begun at an earlier time. The curves also reveal a large and rapid drop in threshold that takes place at the onset of light adaptation and again at the onset of dark adaptation. These effects have been studied in some detail by Baker (1949, 1963) and by Boynton

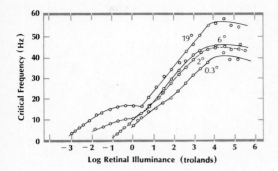

Figure 9.32. The dependence of the critical frequency at fusion on light intensity. (Hecht & Smith, 1936.)

and colleagues (1953, 1954) in the human eye and by Riggs and Graham (1940) in single ommatidia from the eye of *Limulus*.

Flicker: stimulus variables Modern techniques of stimulus control permit an almost limitless variation in temporal pattern of flashes delivered to the eye. Early experiments were conducted on the temporal resolution for intermittent stimulation, in which the major stimulus variables were the frequency (number of flashes per second), intensity, wavelength composition, and duration of the flashes. The critical response variable was the judgment of "flicker" or "fusion." Flicker is perceived for all low rates of intermittence; fusion is perceived as the frequency is raised to some threshold value known as the *cff*, or critical frequency at fusion. At or above this frequency the light is indistinguishable from a steady light having the equivalent mean luminance L_m, as defined by the Talbot-Plateau Law, as follows:

$$L_m = L_1\left(\frac{t_1}{t_1 + t_d}\right)$$

where L_m is the average over time of the luminance of the flickering field, L_1 is the luminance of each separate flash, t_1 is the duration of each separate flash, and t_d is the duration of the dark interval between flashes.

The dependence of *cff* on luminance is illustrated by the data of Figure 9.32. It is clear from this figure that there are two different

portions of the curve if the stimuli are large enough to stimulate both foveal and peripheral regions of the retina. The low-intensity portion of the curve is contributed by the rods. Human photopic resolution rises, at high luminance levels, to approximately 60 flashes per second. Over a middle range of luminances, *cff* rises linearly with log luminance. This is in accordance with the Ferry-Porter Law (see de Lange, 1954; Kelly, 1961), namely that $cff = k \log L + C$, where k and C are constants. At extremely high levels of luminance the Ferry-Porter Law breaks down, and *cff* reaches a plateau or even exhibits a slight decline.

A very extensive literature (see Landis, 1953; Brown, 1965) exists with respect to *cff* under various experimental conditions. Human psychophysical data have been accumulated for the dependence of *cff* on the area of stimulus field, the region of the retina that is stimulated, wavelength composition of the light, and many other stimulus variables. In addition, there have been numerous behavioral and physiological studies of animal vision in which some of the same variables have been explored. Some animals and insects usually active in the daytime are found to have a *cff* well above 120 flashes per second (Autrum, 1958; Devoe, 1962; Kuiper & Leutscher-Hazelhoff, 1965), but nocturnal animals characteristically have a low *cff* (Dodt & Wirth, 1953). In both animal and human subjects, electrical recording at various levels of the visual pathway has shown that the eye itself may respond at higher frequencies than the *cff* determined by behavioral or psychophysical techniques. This leads to the conclusion that temporal resolution is often limited by the brain rather than the eye.

In agreement with the conclusion made above, many studies have shown that *cff* may be used as an index of the physiological functioning of the central nervous system. Fatigue, anoxia, and effects of drugs, state of arousal, and age of the observer are among the factors that have been shown to influence the human *cff* (see Brown, 1965).

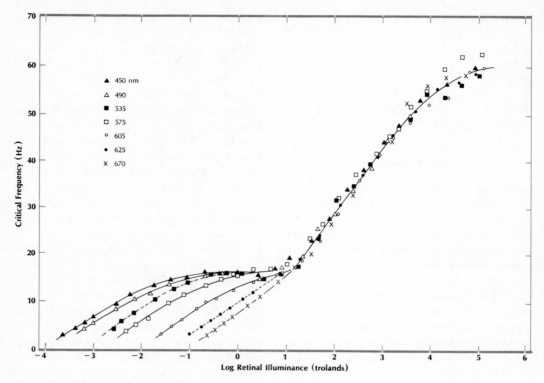

Figure 9.33. The dependence of the critical frequency at fusion on wavelength and the intensity of light. (Hecht & Shlaer, 1936.)

Flicker: wavelength effects Figure 9.33 shows some data of Hecht and Shlaer (1936) in which the *cff* has been determined using light from seven regions of the spectrum. The scale of retinal illuminance was based on a procedure for matching the heterochromatic brightness, carried out at a photopic level of luminance, with comparison fields such as those presented in Figure 9.4. From the figure it is apparent that there is good agreement among the data for various wavelengths, showing that *cff* is primarily dependent on luminance rather than wavelength. The linear portion of the upper curve displays the range over which *cff* is proportional to log luminance, in agreement with the Ferry-Porter Law.

Since the brightness matching was done at photopic levels for Figure 9.33, it is not surprising to find that the various wavelengths have widely differing effectiveness in the low scotopic range. This is in accord with the Purkinje shift (p. 285) whereby the eye becomes relatively much more sensitive, at scotopic levels, to the short wavelengths of light than to the long. Accordingly, we see an extensive rod-receptor portion of each curve except for the data at the longer wavelengths where, as Figure 9.2 has already shown, the rod and cone receptor sensitivities have nearly the same absolute value. In other words, the 670 nm curve may be taken as an indication of cone sensitivity throughout its entire length, while the 450 nm curve most clearly defines the *cff* function for rods in the portion lying below the level of about 10 trolands.

Flicker: photometry In an earlier section on photometry, we observe that the luminance of an visual field could be measured by the use of a photometer designed to permit a match between the brightness of the unknown field and that of a standard field of adjustable luminance provided by the instrument. The method breaks down, however, when the two fields are very different in color because the observer is unable to find any intensity of the standard white field produced by the instrument that makes it resemble the appearance of an unknown that is red, for example, or blue. A solution to this problem of heterochromatic photometry may be provided using a flicker technique.

A flicker photometer consists of a motor-driven shutter device that presents the observer with a small circular patch first of a standard white and then of a color. At a low rate of alternation the subject sees first one and then the other as separate flashes of light; the white standard is still clearly distinguishable from the color. At a rate of about 15 cycles, however (that is, 30 alternations per second from one to the other) the color difference is markedly reduced even though the flicker rate is still far below the *cff*. Now the observer is asked to manipulate the luminance control of the standard until the flicker is reduced to a minimum. This he can usually do with considerable precision because the large color difference between the alternate flashes is almost completely eliminated. Heterochromatic flicker photometry, then, permits us to establish a luminance level that is more or less equivalent for lights of any wavelength throughout the spectrum.

No firm theoretical basis exists for saying that lights equated by the procedure described above are of the same brightness. In fact, some studies have shown small differences in matches made by the flicker technique and those made by other procedures. In practice, however, flicker photometry is a most valuable aid to the quantitative study of color vision. It may also reinforce the conclusion of many color vision experts (see Chapter 10) that chromatic signals are somehow generated separately from brightness signals in the visual system. In any case, the evidence from flicker photometry is that chro-

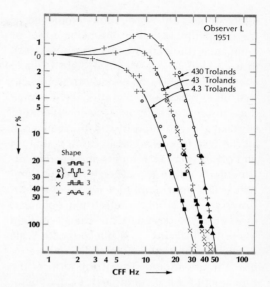

Figure 9.34. Flicker fusion curves defined in terms of the "ripple ratio" at the various frequencies. Note that 4 wave forms were used, as shown in the insert, and that similar functions were found with each of them. (de Lange, 1958.)

matic differences disappear at a lower rate of alternation than do differences in brightness.

Flicker: modulation transfer functions   So far in our consideration of flicker we have confined our discussion to the classic procedure of using rectangular flashes of light, that is, flashes obtained by the use of some sort of shutter that turns the light completely on and off. As early as 1922, however, Ives obtained data on the perception of flicker in response to various nonrectangular wave forms of periodic light stimuli. He came to the conclusion, confirmed by later investigators, that *cff* depends primarily on the frequency rather than the wave form of the stimulating flashes.

Modern work on flicker has greatly benefited from the use of temporal modulation transfer functions (MTF) that are analogous to the spatial MTF that we have already considered on page 299. The application to flicker is illustrated by Figure 9.34, taken from the work of de Lange (1958). The insert in this figure depicts the wave forms employed in these experiments, each one being a plot of luminance (ordinate) versus time (abscissa). In each case, a steady field of light is made alternately brighter or dimmer by some device, other than a simple shutter, that can produce any desired temporal sequence of intensity changes. The intensity variation can range all the way from the classic case of total on and off to small increments and decrements superimposed on the average level of luminance. (The term *amplitude modulation,* borrowed from the field of electronic engineering, is used to designate the change in light intensity.) In Figure 9.34, the ordinate scale designates the degree of modulation in terms of *r*, the *ripple ratio.* This is the ratio of the fundamental wave component of the fluctuation of light, at each frequency, to the mean light intensity. It is therefore analogous in regard to flicker, but not precisely equal, to the Weber ratio $\Delta L/L$ that is used in experiments on brightness discrimination. The abscissa in Figure 9.34 is a logarithmic scale of critical frequency at fusion.

Notice that *r* in Figure 9.34 has a value of about 1.35 percent for very low frequencies of flicker, where the stimulus may be thought of as a series of minimal flashes added to a steady background. This value is in the range of the Weber ratios of 1 to 2 percent that we encountered in Figures 9.19 and 9.22 for brightness discrimination and acuity data.

As the frequency is increased, it is necessary to provide greater and greater amplitudes of modulation in order for the observer to detect the flicker. The value of *r* rises to a level of 100 percent or more for various wave shapes including that of simple on–off flashes of light with no background (shape No. 1 in the insert of the figure). Notice that

the highest ripple ratios permit the *cff* to rise to a value of 30 to 50 flashes per second (see Figure 9.33) depending on retinal illuminance. The curves in Figure 9.34 are photopic temporal resolution threshold functions. They provide a convenient summary of the temporal resolution of the eye, just as its spatial resolution has been displayed by the analogous functions displayed in Figure 9.22 above.

An interesting feature of the temporal resolution curves in Figure 9.34 is the maximum temporal resolution with fluctuation rates of about 8 to 10 cycles per second with sufficiently high intensities of light. This finding is related to the phenomenon of *brightness enhancement* (Brücke, 1864; Ebbecke, 1920; Bartley, 1938), wherein a steady field of light is compared with a light flickering at 10 Hz. The flickering field is usually judged to be brighter even when the average amount of light per second has been made the same for the two fields. Enhanced response has also been demonstrated in single retinal and cortical cells of the cat (Grüsser & Creutzfeldt, 1957) over a similar frequency range. At present the interpretation of brightness enhancement is not clear. Bartley (1939) has called attention to the fact that alpha waves of the EEG occur in the range of 8 to 10 Hz. He has accordingly suggested that enhancement occurs with flashes at this rate because they can most easily evoke responses at a frequency that is already built into a rhythmic spontaneous pattern of activity in the cortex. We must remember, however, that on-off responses represent a major portion of nerve impulse activity at the precortical levels of the ganglion cells and lateral geniculate body, and optic nerve impulse experiments (Enroth, 1952) have shown that intermittent flashes at low to moderate frequencies are strongly effective stimuli.

Robert M. Boynton

COLOR VISION

10

Color vision is a subject that is not the concern of psychologists alone. Among the many other groups interested in it are physicists, physiologists, paint manufacturers, artists, and interior decorators. Such widespread concern over color seems basically attributable to its aesthetic and commercial importance in our daily lives. Color adds immeasurable beauty to our visual world; it can be used to create "atmosphere," and, in the commercial world, to identify and help sell products. (For good reason the Eastman Kodak Company has spent a good deal of money to ensure that the quality of "Kodak yellow" is controlled within very strict and well-defined limits.)

Color creates mood. It is, for example, generally agreed that reds and yellows are "warm" whereas blues are "cool"; it has been demonstrated that people will set a thermostat higher in a blue room than they will in a yellow one, as if to attempt a thermal compensation for coolness that is visually induced.

The richness of chromatic metaphor in our language is great (green with envy, blue note, yellow streak down his back, and so on); it would seem that color experiences, like sensations of taste and smell, are emotionally charged.

In a recent study, Helson and Lansford (1970) studied color preference by placing 125 colored test stimuli against 25 different backgrounds in many hundreds of combinations, and irradiating these with various light sources. His is one of the very few rigorous studies of this sort of problem. He has found that, to assure pleasingness, white is the safest background, certain fluorescent light sources are best avoided, and a color preferred against one background may appear unpleasant against another. He also found that women prefer the "warm" colors (red, orange, and yellow) while men prefer the cool. It is important and significant that a beginning has now been made to put the matter of color preference on a firm experimental basis.

Unfortunately, data from many studies, where global judgments of color preference have been obtained, seem meaningless. In the first place, because color is perceptually attached to objects we do not necessarily have a favorite color that transcends all circumstances: red may be fine for fire engines, but not for the living room wall. Secondly, colors typically exist in more than one part of visual space at a time. The appearance of a color depends upon its surroundings, and so do color preferences. Interior decorators know well that certain colors go together and that others do not. Elaborate descriptive schemes have been worked out to supplement modest rules of thumb, these to help artists, homemakers and architects create environments that are chromatically pleasing.

Because this is a chapter in a textbook of *experimental* psychology we will not deal further with the various fascinating topics just mentioned. Perhaps at some future date, a really solid chapter can be put together in which experimental studies of the affective side of color could be cited and integrated into a theoretical framework capable of accounting for some of the data. But the amount of research on the subjective aspects of color perception is so small, and much of it is of such poor scientific quality, that a good theory cannot now be proposed. This does not therefore seem to be the time to make the attempt. Instead, attention will be focused here upon measurable aspects of the subject of color perception.

In addition to adding beauty to the world,

color also improves visibility. For example, certain types of color-defective individuals cannot find a red ball lying in green grass. The ball is immediately obvious to the normal observer, who would suffer in a way similar to the color-defective person only if the ball were painted green to match the grass. Concerning the discrimation of color, there have been very many good experiments—too many in fact for all of them to be included in one chapter, or even one book. Fortunately the field has advanced far enough that a number of important logical and theoretical concepts can be derived. For this reason, there will be more emphasis upon principles, and somewhat less on raw data than may be the case in other chapters of this book.

Although we are concentrating on the measurable aspects of color vision, the experience of color is really subjective. Such experience lies wholly within the observer. Fortunately these sensations do not occur willy-nilly but are related in definable ways to the characteristics of light sources and reflecting surfaces outside us—surfaces to which the color is so compellingly referred in the process of perception that the color seems to be solely a property of the surface itself. However, color is not exclusively a property of the perceived object; nor is the basis for its meaningful perception wholly within the observer. Rather, color relates both to physical events outside and within the eye, as well as to a subjective state, with the anatomical structure and neurochemical activity of the visual nervous system linking the two.

A guiding principle for the organization of this chapter has been a conviction that it is absolutely necessary to keep the physical, physiological, and psychological aspects of color conceptually separated. A second principle, already referred to, is to stress the discriminative aspects of color, a subject that rests upon a firm scientific footing. Even with this restriction, we shall not include here the entirety of what is encompassed by the expression "color vision." A definition of color given by D. B. Judd in Stevens' (1951) *Hand-*

book of Experimental Psychology states that color consists of "characteristics of light other than spatial and temporal inhomogeneities." Such exclusion specifically fails to rule out brightness differences. Therefore, if two stimuli look different because one is brighter than the other (even if both appear white) then there is by this definition a color difference between them. This definition is not idiosyncratic with Judd, but expresses also a point of view taken by official organizations such as the Optical Society of America, and the International Commission on Illumination. It is also consistent with the use of the concept "color constancy" in perceptual psychophysics, since many experiments dealing with this class of phenomena are actually concerned only with brightness considerations.

Now this is not what color means to the layman. If he were to pay a premium for color television and then receive only a black-and-white image, his irritation would not be reduced by assurances that, in a technical sense, there *are* color differences in the picture. What mainly would be missing, of course, is *hue:* sensations to which we attach the familiar "color" names of red, green, blue, and so forth. It is this hued aspect of color vision which is to be emphasized in this chapter. In order to be perfectly clear about this, the term "chromatic" will be used instead of "color" when the intent is to exclude from consideration that class of visual discriminations which are based upon brightness differences alone.

REQUIREMENTS FOR CHROMATIC VISION

Continuous Spectral Energy Distribution in the Light Source

Because the perception of surfaces and objects is paramount in vision, and most objects are not themselves luminous, we now discuss chromatic vision of surfaces that reflect light. Most people have had the experience of looking at surfaces under a sodium-vapor lamp, which emits almost all of its energy in a very narrow part of the visible

spectrum which appears yellow. If we pay careful attention to what we see in such a circumstance, we will be forced to agree that there is no chromatic vision at all, other than that which may be mediated by memory. To prove this, place an issue of a popular magazine under a sodium-vapor lamp and try to decide whether the advertisements are in color, or in black and white. Again, excluding memory color, this turns out to be impossible.

From the simple demonstration described above we can conclude that although monochromatic light is sufficient for brightness discrimination to take place, chromatic discrimination is not possible when surfaces are illuminated by such a light source. Hues can best be discriminated when objects are illuminated by a source of light that emits a continuous and balanced spectrum. Since the sun is a source of this type, it is perhaps not too much of a leap of faith to suppose that the evolution of chromatic vision has been partly in response to the availability of sunlight throughout evolutionary history.

Incandescent lamps produce the best man-made continuous spectra. When tungsten, which is the most widely used lamp filament, is heated, a perfectly continuous spectrum is produced, meaning that there are no gaps or discontinuities in the function relating emittance to wavelength (see Figure 9.1, p. 274). The relative emission at each wavelength depends upon the temperature of the heated tungsten, being relatively strong in the long visible wavelengths at low temperatures, with short wavelengths contributing relatively more at high levels. Visually, this produces a change in the color of the light from reddish to bluish as temperature is increased.

Some loss in the quality of chromatic vision will result whenever part of the spectrum is missing, or if a part of the spectrum is very low in energy with respect to the remainder. Suppose that a surface reflects light at only one wavelength and completely absorbs all others. A light source that produces a spectrum lacking only that particular wavelength would consequently fail to reveal the chromatic character of the surface, which would look black. In real life, neither surfaces nor sources are anywhere nearly as selective as this, but the problem definitely exists in less exaggerated form, the most common example arising from the use of fluorescent lights. The original ones, marketed in the 1930s, were markedly deficient in long-wavelength light (the "cool white" lamps of today continue to have this deficiency). The result is a relative darkening of surfaces that would appear reddish under light from a tungsten filament or in daylight. Consequently, such sources are particularly uncomplimentary of human complexions and misrender the color of roast beef, which looks well-done even if nearly raw.

Fluorescent sources do not stand alone in their lack of spectral continuity and evenness. Many others, such as gas-discharge tubes (for example, mercury-vapor lamps widely used in street lighting) also tend to emit spectral "lines." That is, the energy tends to be concentrated in certain parts of the spectrum. Curiously, for reasons that are made clear later in this chapter (p. 355), it is possible to produce an acceptable looking "white" light from a source that emits as few as two very narrow spectral lines, provided that they are carefully chosen and their relative intensities are suitably adjusted. However this source in general does not produce the same chromatic appearance of surfaces that it illuminates as does a matching illuminant having a continuous and balanced spectral distribution. This can be understood by imagining a hypothetical surface that reflects all wavelengths excepting the two that happen to be in the source, or which reflects these wavelengths very unequally.

Some degree of chromatic vision is theoretically possible as long as the source is other than "completely" monochromatic. However, no source—not even a laser, which comes closest—is *completely* monochromatic. Complete monochromasy would imply that all emitted quanta must be of *exactly* the same

energy, and this never is the case. In practice, a spectral band as narrow as 5 to 10 nanometers (nm) usually cannot mediate chromatic vision. Such bands are in consequence widely used in vision research, where they are usually—though inexactly—spoken of as "monochromatic," numerically specified in terms of the midpoint of the waveband.

Selective Spectral Reflectance of Surfaces

The appearance of a surface depends to a very important extent upon the way that it reflects light. To a remarkable degree, the color of a surface, as it is viewed subjectively, is not much affected by wide variations in the nature of the illuminant. Much of this type of *color constancy* can be eliminated by viewing the surface through a telescope or reduction screen, causing it to appear as an aperture color having properties that are not relatable either to the illuminant used, nor to the characteristics of the reflecting surface. We can imagine the visual world as being built up from bits and pieces of such areas of aperture color, from which our complex percepts about objects in visual space are derived. (An examination of problems on this higher level of complexity will be given in Chapter 12.)

The property of a surface that is most highly correlated with its perceived color is *diffuse reflectance*. Diffusely reflected light is scattered back from a surface in all possible directions. A perfectly diffuse surface is one that would have the same luminance in all directions and therefore would look equally bright no matter where the observer is positioned with respect to it. A *specularly reflecting* surface, in contrast, is one that reflects incident light in such a manner that the angle of reflection is the same as the angle of incidence. Although no surface can be characterized as being either completely specular or completely diffuse, many surfaces can be approximately so described. For example, a piece of blotting paper comes close to being a perfectly diffuse surface, whereas a plane mirror is almost completely specular.

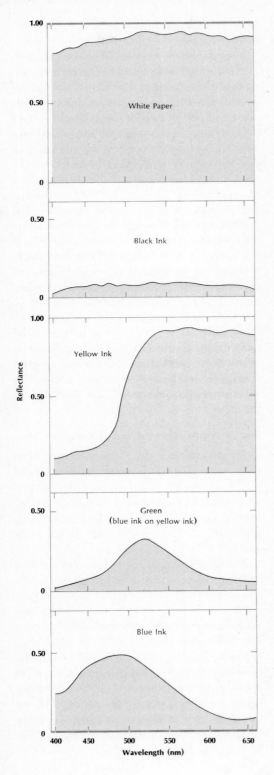

Most surfaces exhibit both specular and diffuse reflection at the same time. The highly polished surface of a new automobile is a good example. In this case, the gloss of the surface is revealed by its specular reflection. Reflected images of objects can be seen in the surface, due to the specular component of its reflectance. However the color of the automobile is determined almost entirely by the diffuse component of reflectance, best seen by looking at the surface at an angle calculated to avoid the specularly reflected component. Another method is to use an extremely large and diffuse source of illumination: even the glossiest surface will look relatively dull under this kind of lighting (see Evans, 1948, for color photographs of this phenomenon).

One of the principal differences between specular and diffuse reflection, apart from directionality, is that specularly reflecting surfaces usually reflect light nonselectively as a function of wavelength. Thus the light of a yellow bulb on a parking lot, reflected from a surface of an automobile, will appear yellow regardless of whether it is reflected from the surface of a red car, a green car, or a black car. If the observer held a reduction screen so that he could see mainly the specularly reflected light from the car, it would be impossible for him to tell what the color of the car really was.

Diffuse reflection, in contrast, is often quite selective with wavelength. In Figure 10.1 are shown spectral reflectance curves of surfaces that appear to most observers, under diffuse white light producing equal energy at all wavelengths, to be yellow, green, blue, white, and black. Each of these curves shows the proportion of incident light, at each

Figure 10.1. Spectral reflection curves of white paper, untreated (top) and covered by inks of various hues as indicated. Each graph shows the percentage of diffusely reflected light measured at each of the wavelengths indicated by the vertical bars. (Adapted from Pirenne, 1948.)

wavelength, which is diffusely reflected to the eye of the viewer.

The proximal optical stimulus for vision is of course the retinal image. All information about the chromatic characteristics of objects in the outside world must be contained in this image; it therefore will profit us to consider at this point the nature of that image relative to the objects that are represented in it.

As is explained in Chapter 9, each object in visual space is imaged on the retina by the optics of the eye. If we consider a given surface of the object, the geometrical distribution of light in the retinal image will approximate the shape of that surface. The chromatic character of that surface is represented in the image by the spectral distribution of the light contained therein. Our problem now is to understand the dependence of this distribution upon the following factors:

(1) the spectral irradiance $H(\lambda)$ of the surface by the light source,
(2) the spectral reflectance $R(\lambda)$ of the surface,
(3) the spectral transmittance $\tau(\lambda)$ of the anterior portions of the eye.

$H'(\lambda)$, representing the spectral irradiance of the retina, is related to these three quantities by the following expression:

$$H'(\lambda) = KH(\lambda)R(\lambda)\tau(\lambda)$$

The equation says that at a given wavelength (λ) the amount of retinal irradiance H' is proportional to the irradiance H of an external object by a light source multiplied by the percentage of light (R) reflected from the object in the direction of the eye at that wavelength, multiplied by the percentage of the light (τ) that is transmitted through the media of the eye before reaching the retina. The constant K does not depend upon wavelength, but rather upon the choice of units used in making the calculation, as well as the dimensions of the eye, which determine the size of the retinal image relative to an external object at a given distance.

When many wavelengths are produced by a light source, as is often the case, the specification of $H'(\lambda)$ must be made for each through repeated application of the equation.

If we view any two surfaces with the same $H'(\lambda)$ through a reduction screen, they will appear to be identical. The same value can be obtained with many combinations of irradiance and reflectance. If we take the reduction screen away, the two areas will not necessarily appear the same, for the color of the surfaces is also affected by their surroundings. Thus, for example, the brighter the surroundings, the darker will be the appearance of the test area. The chromatic appearance of the test area is also affected by the spectral character of the surroundings, and the nature of the light from the illuminant.

From the standpoint of requirements for chromatic vision, the main point to be made here is this: If all surfaces had the same diffuse spectral reflectance curves, there would be no basis for chromatic vision. Thus for chromatic perception of surfaces to be made, there must not only be a reasonably continuous spectral source of illumination, but also a selective and differential absorption and reflection of the light.

Two or More Types of Visual Receptor

So far, we have dealt explicitly only with optical factors outside and inside the observer. However, there is no color at this level—only radiant energy. Not until the incoming energy is analyzed by the receiving organism is it possible to talk about color vision.

In order for chromatic vision to occur, two differing spectral distributions of retinal irradiance, $xH_1'(\lambda)$ and $yH_2'(\lambda)$, must produce different reactions in the visual system, regardless of the values of x and y, at least over the luminance range for which chromatic vision occurs. A subjective corollary is that the corresponding two patches must have an appearance that differs in hue or saturation, regardless of the relative brightnesses of the two fields. For each value of x, there is some value of y that minimizes the difference in appearance.

Logically, there are two possibilities whereby the visual receptors could respond differentially to the spectral character of monochromatic inputs. One possibility is that, although the cone receptors are all alike, the output of each is in some way "tagged," so that it differs in some qualitative way depending upon the wavelength of the light that falls upon it. The simplest receptor of this kind might respond positively to one part of the spectrum, negatively to another. The other possibility is that the quality of the output of any given receptor is entirely nonspecific so far as wavelength is concerned, but that the eye contains at least two classes of receptor that differ in their spectral sensitivities. Thus the relative activation of the two systems would vary depending upon wavelength.

The evidence in favor of the second kind of scheme is overwhelming, as is made evident in the discussion on page 322, and further on pages 350–353. The requisite number of different types of cone receptor turns out to be at least three. (The first scheme, which requires some kind of "tagged" response by the single receptor, has been seriously proposed from time to time, but we shall see that there is no direct evidence whatever to support it.)

Scotopic vision, already defined and described in Chapter 9, provides an excellent example by which we can appreciate the inherent achromatic character of visual experience when it is mediated by receptors all of which have the same spectral sensitivity. What is required is that we look carefully at surfaces at the low illumination levels where only the rods function. There is no chromatic vision. We can test this with the magazine advertisements mentioned above in connection with perception mediated by high levels of sodium-vapor light, with exactly the same negative result. The reason for this is simply that there is no way for a rod to "know about" (that is, respond differentially to) the wavelength of the light that stimulated it.

If the relative intensities of any two lights at scotopic levels are suitably adjusted, they may be made to match exactly because they cause the same rate of light absorption in the rod photoreceptors. This is proof that there is no "tagged" receptor response to be utilized by the scotopic system.

Differentiation of Signal Transmission

A further requirement for chromatic vision is that the messages transmitted to the brain, based upon chromatically separated signals, somehow preserve information about the signal strengths of the component receptor systems. The early thinking about this matter, as embodied in various extensions of the so-called Young-Helmholtz theory of color vision, indicated that signals emanating from each type of receptor might be transmitted by separate pathways all the way from receptor to brain. Such a simple notion is attractive, and dies hard. It is not logically necessary, however, that the three systems of signals be kept separate; modern communication theory shows that in certain cases a higher degree of reliability of transmission, and/or a more efficient use of available channel capacity, can be achieved by the mixing of signals in certain seemingly complicated ways. Of particular importance is the transmission of signals that reflect differences between the outputs of two systems. Evidence that such difference signals are important in human chromatic vision is given later in this chapter (p. 325).

Qualitatively Different Sensations

One additional logical requirement for chromatic vision is that different sensations from different colors can somehow be aroused by the neural messages which transmit the results of receptor activity from the eye. The expression of these differences should be in terms of the whole gamut of chromatic and achromatic sensations, including red, green, yellow, white, black, and certain combinations of these.

Also it is possible to conceive of a visual system that can differentiate between colors at the receptor level and can transmit all the proper signals to the brain, but which nevertheless produces only one quality of sensation in the brain and thus fails to mediate chromatic vision.

It is not possible to describe the various sensations of chromatic vision adequately with words, any more than tastes and odors can be so described. There is, for example, no conceivable way to describe, to a completely color blind individual, what hue sensations are like. Nevertheless it is worthwhile to attempt to measure these sensations, using techniques of psychological scaling; we cannot ignore the need for these chromatically distinct sensations as one of the logical requirements of chromatic discrimination, fully as necessary as any of the four more objective requirements previously described.

THE PHOTOCHEMICAL AND NEUROPHYSIOLOGICAL BASIS OF CHROMATIC VISION

Three Pigments

The initial non-optical event in the visual process is the absorption of light by the visual photopigments contained within the outer segments of photoreceptors located in the retina of the eye. For more than 100 years, there has been strong presumptive evidence to suggest that three classes of photopigment, each with a different spectral sensitivity, must be present in the photoreceptors as the basis of chromatic discrimination. The hypothesis seemed necessary to account for basic facts of color mixture and chromatic adaptation, to be described later in this chapter. These psychophysical experiments also gave strong suggestions concerning what the spectral sensitivity curves of these three pigments should look like.

For a very long time, however, the best efforts of histologists and chemists failed to reveal the three different photopigments hypothesized above, even though the rod pigment, *rhodopsin,* had been extracted in the nineteenth century, and many of its properties had been examined since that time.

Within the last 15 years, the existence of separate classes of cone pigment has definitely been established by two kinds of physical experiment. The first utilizes a technique known as *retinal densitometry.* A beam of light is directed into the eye; some of this light passes through the media of the eye, including the retina, and is diffusely reflected from surfaces behind the retina. A small percentage of this reflected light emerges through the pupil and is delivered to a sensitive photomultiplier tube. The percentages of light absorbed or reflected by most of the eye media are constant, but the percentage absorbed in the double passage through the retina will vary slightly depending upon the concentration of visual photopigments in the receptors illuminated, being relatively high when the eye is dark adapted, and lower when some of the photopigment has been bleached by the action of absorbed light. Such changes are greatest at the wavelength corresponding to the maximum of the spectral sensitivity curve of the pigment being bleached, with proportionally more light being required to produce the same amount of bleaching at other wavelengths. Such measurements define the *action spectrum* of a pigment.

By taking such measurements at a number of wavelengths when the eye is sucessively light- and dark-adapted, it is possible to determine differences in reflectance caused by the bleaching light. The only reasonable cause of such a *difference spectrum* is the bleaching of photopigments of the retinal receptors, for other structures are unlikely to be affected by the bleaching light.

By applying this method to the peripheral retina, which is rich in rod receptors, a difference spectrum which corresponds to the action spectrum of rhodopsin is obtained (Campbell & Rushton, 1955). Because so much is known about rhodopsin, this is an important control experiment. When the method is applied to the fovea of the retina, where cones predominate, a photopic difference spectrum is obtained which is selectively affected by the wavelength of a bleaching light, as would be expected if two or more photopigments were contained in the reflecting area. Moreover, color-defective subjects known as *protanopes* (see p. 363) who are believed to lack all or most of the long-wave-sensitive ("red") pigment show a difference spectrum corresponding to that of the "green" pigment as inferred from the data of normal subjects (Rushton, 1958).

This is a difficult technique to apply to cone vision, for at least the following reasons: (a) only a very small percentage of the incident light is reflected back out through the pupil; (b) only a very small percentage change occurs in this already small amount as a consequence of bleaching. It is not possible to establish the exact shape of the pigment sensitivity curves for each of the pigments by the method described above, but two main peaks have been localized—one at about 530 nm, the other somewhere around 580 nm.

The other physical technique is still more recent, and no less difficult. The technique, known as microspectrophotometry, allows measurement of light passing through a single cell (Liebman, 1962; Marks, Dobelle, & MacNichol, 1964; Wald, 1964). A collection of cone cells is gathered on a microscope cover slip and two equivalent beams of light are directed at them through two optical systems to form tiny images in the slide plane. One image is aimed squarely within a cone outer segment. The other is aimed outside of the cone on the slide itself. The object of the experiment is to measure absorption of light in the outer segment of the cone, using the outside beam for comparison and as a control. This technique is made difficult because the measuring beam must not be too intense, lest it bleach away the pigment that is being measured. The beam with the required intensity level presents a signal so weak that measurements approach the limits of modern technology, close to theoretical limits as well. The most successful experiments have been made with goldfish cones, the latter being huge in comparison to primate ones. The results indicate that there

are definitely three classes of photopigment. For the very small number of primate cones so far measured, peak sensitivities are approximately at 445, 535, and 570 nm.

As a result of the experiments that have been made with retinal densitometry and microspectrophotometry, there can no longer be any doubt about the existence of three or more classes of photopigment in cones. However these experiments have not yet provided hard evidence to indicate exact spectral sensitivities of the photopigments, nor do they provide unequivocal information about the distribution of these pigments within cone types. The evidence to date suggests that a single cone contains only one type of pigment, rather than a mixture.

Opponent-colors Transformation

Red and green cannot be seen in the same place in the visual field at the same time. When mixed together (see p. 349), red and green lights will, if suitably balanced, yield a cancellation of both the red and green sensations, leaving a residual yellow. Blue and yellow bear a similar relation to one another in that they also do not coexist, and when mixed the result is a white that contains not a trace of either component.

Opponent-colors theory was originally based upon such observations as those described above. The German physiologist, Ewald Hering, (1905, 1964) speculated that perhaps a single receptor could act in either of two ways, sometimes to signal red for example, at other times green. This view was challenged by the trichromatic theorists who stressed a viewpoint similar to that stated in the previous section, according to which the response of a single receptor must be nonspecific with respect to the wavelength that produces it. The additional assumption that the trichromatic theorists tended to make was that three separate channels take signals from the location of the photopigment to the visual area of the brain. (See Brindley [1960], for an excellent, brief historical review of this subject.)

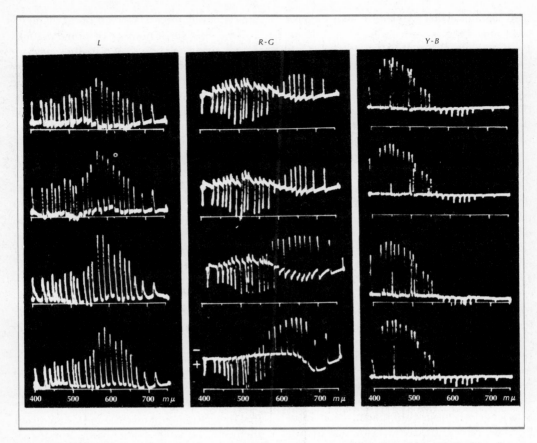

Figure 10.2. Potentials recorded near, but not actually in, the cones of fish (Svaetichin, 1956). Stimuli were 200 msec in duration, and of equal energy, concentrated in the spectral region shown. Some electrode placements give rise to luminosity (L) responses as shown in column 1; others give rise to responses that vary in sign depending upon wavelength as shown in columns 2 and 3. When the neutral wavelength is relatively long, these are called responses from "R-G" units; when it is relatively short, they are called responses from "Y-B" units.

Since the early days of this controversy, a number of writers (Judd, 1951; Hurvich & Jameson, 1955) have correctly pointed out that there is no essential conflict between trichromatic and opponent-colors ideas. The resolution of the contradiction may be made by supposing that the first stage of chromatic vision is trichromatic, but that signals are then recoded into opponent-colors form. There is now a good deal of hard evidence to support this viewpoint, which we review briefly.

It is possible to record electrical activity in the visual system by means of microelectrodes. While attempting to record from single receptors, Svaetichin (1956) discovered responses in the eye of the fish which had very peculiar properties as a function of wavelength. These responses appeared with little latency and remained at maximal strength as long as the stimulating light was left on, returning to the baseline as soon as the light was extinguished. Furthermore—and this is the most important point to be noted here—the electrical *sign* of the response was sometimes found to be wavelength-dependent. An example of this is shown in Figure 10.2. Here the stimulating wavelength was rapidly varied across the spectrum with each light left on for 200 msec, long enough to obtain a maximum response. The time scale has been very much compressed so that the individual responses look like spikes. Although light of the same energy was used at each wavelength tested, note that, for the "R-G" unit, the sign of the response is negative for wavelengths below about 580 nm, whereas it is positive for longer wavelengths. A maximum negative response is reached at about 500 nm, with a maximum positive response being recorded about 650 nm. There is a neutral point at about 580 nm, where no response is recorded, excepting small transients which do not appear on this record.

Svaetichin thought at first that these responses were coming from single cones in the eye of the fish, but further work by MacNichol and himself (1958) proved that this was not so. In this later work, they used a dye-marking technique whereby the exact placement of the microelectrode could be determined histologically at the conclusion of the electrophysiological experiment. It was found that to record this type of response the recording electrode had to be placed very near, but not actually in the receptors. The importance of this finding is the following: If opponent-colors responses actually did come from the receptor, then either the photopigment in the receptor is capable of producing "tagged" responses as a function of wavelength (negative for some, positive for others), or the receptor must contain at least two photopigments that produce responses of opposite sign after they absorb light.

The conclusion of Svaetichin and Mac-Nichol, that the bivalent response does not come directly from the receptor, has been buttressed very recently by Tomita (1966). Tomita also has recorded many responses of the Svaetichin-MacNichol variety and has proposed that these be called "C-responses" (for "color"). He has also succeeded in recording responses from within single cones from a fish eye by using a technique with which the retinal preparation is vibrated onto the delicate recording electrode in a manner that permits intracellular insertion on some lucky occasions. The data from these experiments indicate that the bioelectric responses from individual cones are all of the same sign, varying only in size as a function of the wavelength and intensity of the stimulating light. Different types of cone have been identified by this technique, for each is sensitive to different wavelengths of light. Tomita et al. (1967) have reported that of the first 114 cones they sampled from the eye of a carp, nearly all fell into three classes as defined by maximum spectral sensitivity, which strongly supports the trichromatic theory at the receptor level.

It appears then that the opponent responses recorded originally by Svaetichin result from an interaction between receptor responses. It is far from certain, however, that C-responses are involved in any simple way with the direct chain of events in the visual pathways, which begins with receptors and ends with activity in the visual part of the brain. However this may be, it is nevertheless clear that opponent-color computation is carried out somehow in the primate retina; this is indicated by opponent responses that have been recorded from the lateral geniculate body, a principal relay station between the eye and brain. Here the long neurons of the retinal ganglion cells, which make up the optic tract and optic nerve, synapse with the optic radiation fibers that connect directly to the visual cortex.

In a long series of important experiments on primates, DeValois (1965) has recorded electrical activity from single units in the lateral geniculate body in response to chromatic input. These units exhibit a resting level of activity (spikes per unit time), in the absence of light stimulation, during which firing is rather irregular, and the spike rate is intermediate to low. After the eye is stimulated by light, the response pattern changes. In some cells that were sampled, short wavelengths produce a vigorous response when the stimulus is begun (increased firing rate), which subsides at the termination of the stimulus. Long wavelengths produce a decrease in the spontaneous firing rate, and exhibit another response (increased firing rate) when the light stimulus is turned off. Such a single unit seems to be carrying information of two qualitatively different kinds. The wavelength of stimulation is encoded, within limits, as either an increase or a decrease in firing rate, depending upon whether the light stimulus is of short or long wavelength. (In an approximately equal number of units, the relations are reversed.) Now it is not likely that a particular unit can tell the difference between two short wavelengths (for example, 420 nm and 440 nm), or between two long ones. However DeValois' work shows that, among a sampling of units, the crossover point, where a zero response occurs (separating the opponent effects of long versus short wavelengths) is not always found at the same wavelength. According to the opponent-colors theory, only two classes of mechanisms are required, each with a different crossover point. Although DeValois has found a considerable spread in these values, he has found that they do tend to fall, statistically, into the required two groups.

We are left, then, with the following picture to account for the encoding and transmission of at least some visual information of a chromatic nature: (1) three types of photopic visual photopigments, each contained more or less exclusively within a given type of receptor; (2) an exquisite organization of the receptor types, such that an opponent interaction occurs somehow between the outputs of selective receptor types; (3) the conversion of these intermediate difference signals into a neural message, encoded in terms of a modulation of a resting (dark) level of activity, either upward or downward, depending upon the balance of the opponent activity between receptors. It seems highly probable that some receptor pairs are concerned with the encoding of information about red and green, with the outputs of cones sensitive to long waves and short waves opposing each other and leading to a difference signal that is capable of increasing or decreasing the resting activity level of the nerve fibers to which they connect. Modulation of this activity in one direction leads to some kind of (unspecified) activity in the visual areas of the brain that is correlated with the experience of "red", whereas modulation in the other direction signals "green." Because such modulation cannot occur upward and downward at the same time, impulses transmitted over such pathways signal "red," "green," or "neither" depending upon the balance between receptor outputs. This balance determines the direction of the ensuing nerve fiber modulation in one direction or the other. An analogous argument can be made for the yellow-blue system.

It has not been proved that all activity related to chromatic vision is encoded and transmitted in this opponent-colors fashion. The possibility remains that some chromatic input may be delivered to the brain without such prior interaction.

Nonopponent Spectral Sensitivity Curves

It is frequently observed, in experiments like those just described, that some units exhibit a response the electrical sign of which does not change with wavelength. This was already noted for the case of the single receptor unit, where all responses were found by Tomita to be negative. However the same is found to be true if electrodes are placed elsewhere in the retina or in the lateral geniculate nucleus where opponent-sign responses are also found.

By implication, if a given electrode placement yields responses that do not vary in sign with wavelength, a given response should be achievable with any choice of wavelength, so long as a suitable intensity adjustment is permitted. The substitution of one wavelength for another in this way has been called *silent substitution*, and it is one of several methods that may be used to show whether a given system is mediating chromatic or achromatic information (see p. 345).

If silent substitution is possible, the spectral sensitivity of a given unit may be determined by finding the stimulus radiance required at each wavelength to produce any convenient criterion response. This type of examination has been made at both the retinal and geniculate levels. The resulting spectral sensitivity curve of the geniculate body from primates is identical, within experimental error, to the photopic luminosity curve of these animals as determined by behavioral procedures (DeValois, 1965). A similar interpretation has been made of nonopponent retinal responses from the eye of a fish. By implication, then, these systems seem to be concerned solely with luminosity (brightness) information. A conclusion that has been reached by many workers is that such a nonspecific brightness system coexists with the chromatic ones; that if the chromatic systems were turned off (as can in fact be achieved by balancing the chromatic systems by the use of a "white" light), only achromatic vision would remain. (This point of view is consistent with the discovery by Weale [1953] that there are a few rare individuals who possess perfectly normal photopic vision, except that chromatic vision is entirely lacking.)

If brightness is mediated by a unitary system, luminances of lights of different color should be additive, a condition known as *Abney's Law*. Imagine the following experiment to test the law. On opposite sides of a split field, place red and green lights and adjust the green until it matches the red for brightness, ignoring differences in hue and saturation insofar as possible. Now add an amount of green light to both sides of the field, equal in luminance to that of the original green side. This produces twice the original amount of green on the one side, and a red-green mixture on the other, which will probably look orange. If this experiment were done at scotopic levels, or in an eye in which only one class of mechanism were active, both halves of the field would look exactly alike throughout the experiment. With the complication of chromatic vision, where systems

are being stimulated that give rise to unequal chromatic appearance, it becomes an empirical question whether the achromatic (brightness) component of the complex sensation will behave similarly. The result of this type of experiment is that the match does not hold exactly. In general, when some cancellation of hue occurs (as in the orange half), the brightness will be a bit less than it would be if the same hues are added (the green half). Chromatic cancellation evidently is associated with some brightness cancellation as well. These experiments have been well summarized by LeGrand (1957).

If, in contrast, the same type of experiment as that described above is repeated using flicker photometry as a criterion (see Chapter 9), a photopic sensitivity curve can be deduced that does not seem to be affected by what is going on in chromatic parts of the visual system, inasmuch as Abney's Law holds precisely. A similar result, indicating complete additivity, has been reported by Boynton and Kaiser (1968) in an experiment where subjects minimized the distinctness of the border between heterochromatic fields, ignoring the fact that the more saturated field appeared brighter.

These experiments provide further evidence to support the idea of independent achromatic and chromatic mechanisms. That they are independent has seemed so apparent to some writers that they have proposed separate cone receptors, which supposedly exist for the purpose of handling achromatic information. The direct evidence from microspectrophotometry provides no support for this view. It appears then that the same three receptor types must serve a dual function, that in all probability their outputs are utilized in more than one way, so that summation as well as cancellation of receptor outputs may occur. It will be recalled in this connection that Tomita finds that all receptor potentials are of the same sign; thus an opponent color signal must be generated by reversing the sign of responses from one type of receptor before adding the outputs of the two types together.

There is no reason why the outputs having the same sign cannot also be added together and delivered to the achromatic system.

The Processing of Chromatic Information at Higher Levels of the Visual System

According to any doctrine of psychophysical parallelism, there must be some pattern of activity in the brain that differs when one sees a red rather than a green of equal brightness. The purpose of this short section is to note that no experimental evidence exists on this point. Those few investigators who have looked at the activity of the brain in response to a spectrally selective input have generally contented themselves with attempts to measure spectral sensitivity curves. Without further testing, it is not possible to know whether such curves represent the output of a single class of retinal mechanism (which seems unlikely), or whether they reflect the result of complex interactions (more likely). Further, it is not known whether chromatic information is encoded in terms of which units in the brain are activated (place theory), or the way that they are activated (pattern theory) or both. The place theory would predict that microelectrode stimulation of single units in the visual cortex of conscious humans would lead to different chromatic and/or achromatic experiences depending upon electrode placement. Because color is fairly precisely localized in the visual area of the brain, the place theory alluded to here would be applicable only at the submicroscopic level to allow the blending of different cell activities within approximately the same area. There are many difficult questions for which solutions can be found only after a great deal more work has been completed using microelectrodes on the visual cortex and other brain areas.

A WORKING MODEL OF HUMAN CHROMATIC VISION

In this section, a model is presented that attempts to describe, in a quantitative way, some aspects of the functioning of the human color vision system. It is intended to help in the organization and interpretation of facts to be presented in later sections. It has been extracted from several color theories (especially those of Judd, 1950; Walls and Mathews, 1952; Hurvich and Jameson, 1955; and Boynton, 1960). It is as consistent as possible with the known anatomical, photochemical, and physiological facts, but should not be taken too literally. One fault of the description is the fact that the model goes beyond the direct evidence in some cases. Furthermore, the actual state of affairs in the human visual system is known to be very much more complicated than the model suggests. The model is intended to account only for the appearance of stimuli of intermediate size and duration that are presented at the point of fixation in an otherwise dark field.

Some very important problems, such as chromatic adaptation and induction, are not dealt with here; these will be discussed later as they relate to the model, and we shall then see what kinds of addition to the model must be introduced to account for them.

Photopigment Stage

The physical evidence of microspectrophotometry and retinal densitometry, discussed in the preceding section, indicates that there are three different kinds of photopigment, one of each kind located in the outer segments of one of three different types of retinal cones. (Rushton has given the pigments the names *erythrolabe, chlorolabe,* and *cyanolabe,* meaning [roughly] red-absorbing, green-absorbing, and blue-absorbing, respectively.) These physical experiments show that the absorption peaks of the three pigments occur at approximately 570, 535, and 445 nm in the spectrum. To the spectral absorption curves of these we shall attach the symbols α, β, and γ.

The physical experiments that have been performed to date do not define the lower parts of the spectral absorption curves of these pigments very accurately. This is unfortunate because human color vision, par-

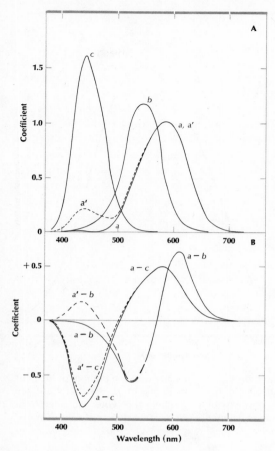

Figure 10.3. A. Fundamental response curves of Thomson and Wright (1953). B. Opponent-color functions calculated from the data of Thomson and Wright: $a' = a + 0.131c$.

ticularly as revealed in color-mixture experiments (to be described below) is critically dependent on light absorbed in small amounts at wavelengths corresponding to the tails of these curves.

When the complication arising from light absorbed in the media of the eye is taken into account, the spectral absorption curves of the cone pigments should be consistent with the many curves derived from color-mixture data obtained from studies made of the human eye (see p. 352). For convenience, we introduce, in Figure 10.3A, the spectral absorption curves of Thomson and Wright (1953): the peaks of these curves agree well with the

physical data, and the shapes agree with color-mixture data. (It is interesting to note that these curves were derived, some years before any direct physical data on cone pigments were available, for the purpose of accounting for certain types of color defect to be described later in this chapter.)

Receptor Stage

Photopigments are contained within the outer segments of the cone receptors. Current evidence suggests, as noted in the previous section, that each of these three types of cone pigment is uniquely contained in one of the three types of cone receptor. Assuming this, we may call the cones that contain the blue-sensitive pigment "blue" cones and speak similarly of "green" and "red" cone receptors. These may be symbolized by the capital letters B, G, and R respectively. Two statements of caution are in order regarding this symbolization. First, sensations do not arise directly in the receptors, so that it is not necessarily true that unique stimulation of, say, an R cone would give rise to a sensation of red (such unique stimulation is impossible anyhow, for all real lights cause absorption in more than one type of cone). Secondly, an R cone does not appear red if you look at it. Indeed, the density of photopigments in the cones leads to selective absorption that is so slight that all cones look alike, being more-or-less colorless when directly viewed under the microscope. However if absorption by the various cones could be intensified, a red cone would not appear red because the part of the spectrum in which red falls would be selectively absorbed by the pigment; it would in fact appear blue-green. We must be careful always to bear in mind that chromatic vision does not arise until the higher centers of the visual system have been activated; the absorption of light in visual photopigments constitutes only the first stage of a complex chain of events between light input and the sensory end result. Thus, although we talk about red, green, and blue cones and sometimes also about red, green, and blue lights,

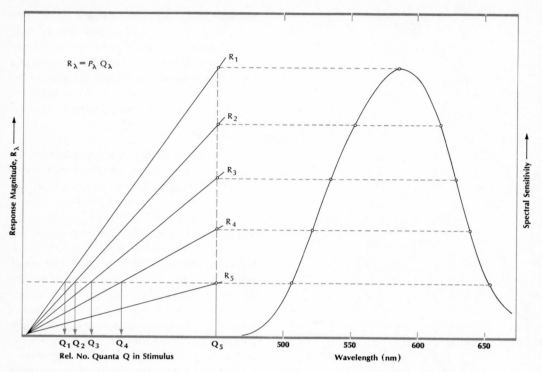

Figure 10.4. *Left:* Functions showing how response magnitude R_λ grows linearly with the number of incident quanta, at a rate which depends upon the probability of quantum absorption p_λ. Spectral sensitivity is defined on a quantum basis. *Right:* Spectral sensitivity of a hypothetical receptor, obtained from response magnitude produced by introducing an equal number of incident quanta at various wavelengths.

such talk is very loose. It does have a mnemonic value, however, so long as we do not lose sight of the fact that visual sensations reside neither in light quanta, visual photopigments, nor cone receptors.

Recently, an electrophysiological response called the "early receptor potential" (ERP) has been measured, which is linearly related to the energy contained in the light stimulus (Brown et al., 1965; Cone, 1965). We may therefore assume, with some justification, that each quantum of light that is absorbed by a receptor gives rise to a tiny element of response. Moreover, these responses appear to summate so that there is a linear relation between the number of quanta absorbed and the magnitude of the initial response of a receptor to a brief flash of light. There is an upper limit to this linearity of response, which

is caused by the bleaching of photopigments by very bright lights; we will not worry about this but will deal only with the normal range of color vision, which takes place at intensity levels below this.

Consider now the action of light upon a single receptor. On the right-hand side of Figure 10.4 is a curve representing the magnitude of response from a cone as a function of wavelength, for a spectrum containing equal numbers of incident quanta at each wavelength. Because response is a linear function of the number of quanta absorbed, this curve is identical in shape to the quantal action spectrum of the pigment contained within the receptor. The latter is obtained by finding how many quanta Q_λ at each wavelength are required to elicit a response R_λ of some particular size. This relation may be clarified by reference to the left-hand side of Figure 10.4. Here we have a set of functions, one for each of five pairs of wavelengths, showing how response magnitude increases with increasing stimulus energy. They are all linear functions, but they have very different slopes. The slope depends upon the probability p_λ that a quantum of light will be absorbed by the receptor under some fixed conditions of delivery to the eye. We may write:

$$R_1 = p_1Q_1$$
$$R_2 = p_2Q_2$$
$$R_3 = p_3Q_3 \qquad (1)$$
$$R_4 = p_4Q_4$$
$$R_5 = p_5Q_5$$

from which it is indicated that in order to generate a response of some fixed size R it is necessary that $p_1Q_1 = p_2Q_2 = p_3Q_3 = p_4Q_4 = p_5Q_5$. Thus the quantum values Q_1 through Q_5 must be reciprocally related to the probabilities p_1 through p_5, respectively, in order for all responses to be equal.

When a stimulus is presented that contains a mixture of light of different wavelengths, the resulting response may be calculated by simple summation. If Q_1 quanta at wavelength λ_1 are delivered to the receptor along with Q_2 quanta at wavelength λ_2, the total response, R_{total}, is given by the equation,

$$R_{\text{total}} = R_1 + R_2 = p_1Q_1 + p_2Q_2 \qquad (2)$$

and in the general case of two or more mixed spectral radiations,

$$R_{\text{total}} = \Sigma p_\lambda Q_\lambda \qquad (3)$$

For the more common case of a continuous spectrum, Equation 3 may be written as a definite integral:

$$R_{\text{total}} = \int p_\lambda Q_\lambda d\lambda \qquad (4)$$

where $Q_\lambda d\lambda$ represents the number of quanta contained in the interval λ to $\lambda + d\lambda$, and the limits of the integration include the wavelengths of the visible spectrum, usually taken as from 380 to 720 nm.

We define the response magnitude from the R receptor as having a units, and those from the G and B receptors as having b and c units respectively. Because each type of receptor has a different spectral absorption characteristic, subscripts will be used to keep them conceptually separated. We shall use $p_{R\lambda}$, $p_{G\lambda}$, and $p_{B\lambda}$ to represent the probabilities that a quantum of light of wavelength λ will be absorbed in each of the three receptor types under fixed conditions of stimulation of the eye. Accordingly, the three equations required to specify the responses generated in the three types of cones are:

$$a = \int p_{R\lambda}Q_\lambda \, d\lambda$$
$$b = \int p_{G\lambda}Q_\lambda \, d\lambda \qquad (5)$$
$$c = \int p_{B\lambda}Q_\lambda \, d\lambda$$

For convenience, response units are defined so that the constant of proportionality is unity for each equation; in other words, if one quantum is absorbed, it produces a response a, b, or c that has a magnitude of one unit by definition. Also, for simplicity, the sign of

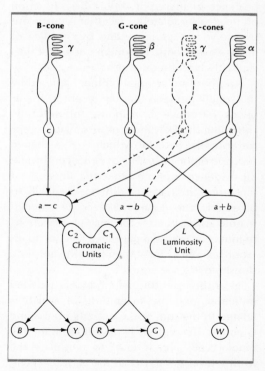

Figure 10.5. Schematic diagram of a model of chromatic visual information processing.

the response is taken to be positive, even though Tomita's experiments indicate that receptor potentials in the fish are negative under his particular conditions of recording, where increasing negativity implies increasing polarization of the cell.

Retinal Interaction Stage

Figure 10.5 shows a schematic diagram of the model under discussion. The outputs of the red, green, and blue cones just discussed are indicated by a, b, and c in the foot of each receptor. These signals become the input to the next stage.

The outputs of the R and G cones summate linearly at a luminosity unit L. Bear in mind here, and for the chromatic interactions to be discussed shortly, that in reality there are many overlapping units forming summation pools, each connected to hundreds or thousands of cones of the appropriate type. This would lead to the expectation that the appearance of the color should be a function of the area stimulated, a fact that is borne out by everyday experience and by the data of many experiments. This model does not deal explicitly with the area problem.

Another fundamental problem ignored by this simple model is that the receptors themselves introduce a response nonlinearity. Following the ERP, there occurs a *late receptor potential* (late RP) which is an **S**-shaped function of the *logarithm* of radiance. The late RP evidence indicates that the linearity of receptor output, assumed here, is unlikely to be exactly true. It can, however, be assumed to hold approximately for small perturbations of intensity around a particular level of adaptation, as well as for stimuli near the absolute thresholds of the cones.

Near the receptor, the L signal is a graded potential, one the magnitude of which is related to the sum of the outputs from R and G cones. This output is passed along by the bipolar cells and is used to modulate the resting level of activity in the ganglion cells, the axons of which make up the optic nerve

fibers that carry information to the lateral geniculate nucleus. There are probably many L units converging upon each ganglion cell, there may be reciprocal overlap, and there are almost certainly inhibitory connections at two or more levels of this system that our model ignores; indeed, no anatomical structures, excepting the cones, are to be implied by Figure 10.5. The main job of the L-system is to maintain or even enhance information pertaining to spatial detail in the light distribution making up the retinal image, but it also must transmit information about the amount of white light in the stimulus.

The output from one stage of a system may be divided and sent to more than one type of structure in the next stage of the nervous system. Here we assume that a second branch of the output from the R cone is delivered to a chromatic cell C_1. A branch of the output from the G cone is also delivered to C_1. The output of C_1 is simply the difference of the two input signals, $a - b$. Therefore, if the outputs from the R and G cones are equal, a zero signal will result from C_1. The output therefore reflects the *imbalance* between the relative stimulation of R and G cones.

In the ganglion cells, information from C_1 is used to modulate nerve impulse frequency in the optic nerve fibers. In the absence of output from C_1, these impulses occur at an intermediate resting frequency. The meaning of this frequency to the brain is "neither red nor green." Positive output from C_1 increases the resting frequency and negative output decreases it.[1] The first of these means "red," the second, "green." In this way, the activity

[1]We ignore here the electrophysiological evidence of DeValois that approximately half of the chromatic units he studied behave in opposite fashion. To include this fact in the model, additional chromatic units C_1' and C_2' should be drawn in, each receiving inputs in the same way as do C_1 and C_2, respectively. However the C_1' difference signal would be $b - a$ instead of $a - b$, and the C_2' difference signal would become $c - a$. Two more chromatic pathways would have to be added, to deliver the outputs of C_1' and C_2' to the cortical units. These additions to the model would not alter its quantitative characteristics; therefore they are deliberately omitted to keep the model as simple as possible. The reader is again cautioned, as he was at the beginning of this section, not to take the model too literally.

in the R–G optic nerve fibers can signal either red or green to the brain at different times, but never both at once. This is why we never see red and green at the same place at the same time.

So far, we have defined a dichromatic system, one that could produce a chromatic world of reds and greens only. There are indeed color-defective observers (see p. 362) whose color vision is well described by those parts of the model covered so far. For them, the saturation of a perceived stimulus is related to the relative signal strength of W to that of R or G. The greater the modulation of the resting activity in directions meaning "red" or "green" relative to that occurring in the "white" fibers, the more saturation the stimulus should appear to have.

When the R- and G-cone systems are in equal balance, the resulting sensation for the normal observer is not white, as the simple dichromatic system would require. It is yellow, because the $a - c$ system, which signals yellow and blue, is unbalanced in the yellow direction at the wavelength which produces an $a - b$ signal of zero.

By reference to the pigment-sensitivity curves in Figure 10.3A, we see that under this condition the value of c, the output from the B cone, is very small. Therefore, the value of $a - c$ is large and positive under this condition. (The difference signal, C_2, is shown in Figure 10.3B.)

The C_2 system is analogous to the C_1 system. It is assumed that when a exceeds c, the modulation of optic nerve fibers resulting therefrom signals "yellow" to the brain; when the reverse is true, the signal means "blue." Thus, when the outputs of the R and G cones are equal, $a - b = 0$, meaning that there are no red and no green sensations, but $a - c$ has a large positive value, which signals yellow. Any stimulus that produces a value $a - b = 0$, with a value of $a - c > 0$ will appear uniquely yellow—that is, a yellow which is neither reddish nor greenish in appearance.

For most spectral stimuli, there will be nonzero contributions from both the C_1 and C_2 systems. When this happens, the result will be the simultaneous activity of brain units: either B or Y units on the one hand, together with either R or G units on the other. This dual activity is assumed to produce composite sensations of four possible types. For example, a stimulus at 590 nm produces a nearly equal response from the C_1 and C_2 systems, both positive, associated with sensations of red and yellow, respectively. The result is a subjective mixture of red and yellow, or orange. In order to make the difference curves, shown in Figure 10.3B, consistent with the appearance of the spectrum (see p. 347), the difference signal produced by the C_2 system, shown in Figure 10.3B, is plotted as $(\frac{1}{2})(a - c)$ in order to account for the fact that the long-wave spectrum appears yellowish-red, not reddish-yellow.

Unique green should appear in the spectrum where the $a - c$ signal equals zero, in the neighborhood of 505 nm. It is found experimentally that unique blue[2] appears in the spectrum in the neighborhood of 460 to 470 nm. The model as so far set forth would not predict this, nor would it account for the reappearance of red (the secondary component of the reddish-blue usually called "violet") in the extreme short-wave end of the visible spectrum.

In order to account for the additional phenomena described above, it is necessary to assume that the $a - b$ signal, which accounts for an excess of green over red to the short-wave side of unique yellow, for some reason becomes zero again at the wavelength of unique blue and then shows a positive value at the short-wave end of the spectrum. A possible mechanism for this is shown in the diagram of Figure 10.5. Here, a minority of the R cones (shown as dotted) contain the γ pigment normally found in the B cone. Because these units are sensitive to short waves,

[2]See p. 346 for definition of this term.

they can account for the excess of *a* over *b* and for the existence of unique blue in the spectrum (as well as for certain other phenomena to be discussed later). The curves in Figure 10.3B labeled $a' - b$ and $a' - c$, make this correction.

Sensation Stage

The final stage of the model indicates the sensations produced by the information-processing networks prior to this final stage, starting with the pigment-containing photoreceptors. Because blue-yellow and red-green are impossible combinations, due to the fact that they share common transmission lines, they cannot exist in the same place in the visual field at the same time. Blue or yellow may coexist with red or green, a matrix of four possible combinations. Any of these may coexist with white, to yield sensations having variable *saturation*. The more intense the subjective chromatic content relative to the achromatic, the more saturated the stimulus is said to be.

This completes the formal exposition of the limited model. As outlined here, it can be set up and dealt with by analog or digital computer. It is consistent with a large body of experimental facts and will be useful for helping to organize these facts in subsequent sections.

CHROMATIC ADAPTATION

Two Effects: Changes in Chromatic Appearance and Changes in Sensitivity

The balances among the chromatic mechanisms of the eye are very delicate and easily can be upset. For example, when the eye is deliberately exposed to intense chromatic fields of light, the phenomenon called *chromatic adaptation* takes place. It has been shown to occur electrophysiologically (Armington & Biersdorf, 1956; Svaetichin & Mac-Nichol, 1958; DeValois, Jacobs, & Jones, 1963; DeValois, Jacobs, & Abramov, 1964), and it has been studied in psychophysical experiments to be described below.

The term "chromatic adaptation" has often been used also to describe or explain the apparent change in the chromatic appearance of light fields when they are presented to the eye following adaptation to chromatic stimuli. This phenomenon can easily be demonstrated by the following experiment, which the reader can do without leaving his chair and without using special equipment. Cover one eye tightly with the hand and stare for a minute or two at any large, bright surface, whether chromatic or white. Following this, alternately view various areas of the visual field, first by shutting one eye and then the other. For a time, considerable differences in chromatic appearance will be noticeable between one eye and the other. (For some people, such differences exist even when the eyes are equally adapted.)

The concept of chromatic adaptation applies also to a second type of experiment wherein sensitivity rather than color appearance is measured (Stiles & Crawford, 1934; Wyszecki & Stiles, 1967). In a typical experiment, the spectral sensitivity of the eye will be measured first in the neutrally adapted state, then following adaptation to colored light. The reciprocal of the energy required for threshold visibility is the most common psychophysical criterion, whereas that required to elicit a criterion height of an electrophysiological response, such as the electroretinogram, has also been used.

Changes in Appearance Described

Visualize a stimulus that appears yellow under the conditions to which the model described above (p. 328) applies—a stimulus presented as a small flash of light at the point of fixation in an otherwise dark visual field. Suppose now that the observer looks away from a series of such yellow flashes—presented, say, once per second—in order to fixate a large, intense red field. Now he looks back at the test flashes, which have not physically been changed. Instead of appearing yellow, the flashes will now appear green. As time goes on, the eye will recover from the adaptive effects of the red field; the yellow content of the test flashes will gradually increase relative to the green, and after a few minutes the flashes will again appear yellow as they did before the adapting field was viewed. The converse experiment can also be made: exposure to a bright green will afterwards alter the appearance of the test toward red. In both cases, there will also be a reduction in brightness and changes in saturation.

Changes in Appearance Related to the Model Described Above

Let us consider the experiment just described in terms of the model described above. The yellow test flashes, prior to adaptation, produce a signal $a - b$ of zero, meaning that there is no output from the C_1 unit, and thus we have sensations of neither red nor green. At the same time, such a stimulus produces a positive value of $a - c$, a positive output from C_2, and an optic nerve fiber signal that means "yellow" when received and interpreted in the visual brain.

Now the adapting field is presented. It produces, while present, a strong excess of a over b, and of a over c, leading to a strong yellowish-red sensation. However we are not interested here in the *appearance* of the adapting field, only in its after-effects upon the test stimulus. So we turn the adapting field off, and once again introduce the yellow test flash.

Prior to adaptation, the test flash presumably appeared yellow because it stimulated the R and G cones equally; this was the basis for the zero value of $a - b$. Afterward, it appears green. This means that the modulation of the red-green optic nerve fibers is for some reason changed to signal green. Unless the adaptive stimulus somehow altered the state of the nerve fibers directly, the change in sensation implies that the output of the C_1 units, formerly zero, has now swung in the negative (green) direction in response to test flashes that were previously neutral so far as red and green were concerned. Why should this be?

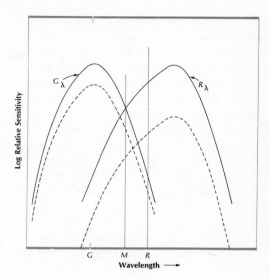

Figure 10.6. Selective chromatic adaptation produced by action of an adapting stimulus of wavelength *R*.

The Receptor Desensitization Hypothesis

The hypothesis most often advanced to explain the changes just described is that the sensitivity of the R cones has been selectively reduced by the stimulus that adapts the eye to bright red; although the adapting stimulus is active upon both the R and G cones, its principal action is upon the former. An attempt to illustrate this is made in Figure 10.6. Prior to adaptation, the yellow test flash at wavelength *M* produced equal stimulation of the red and green cones. The stimulus adapting the eye to red then produced a greater action upon the R cone than the G; as a result the height of the R curve is reduced to a lower position, as is shown by the dotted curve. The G curve is reduced also, but to a lesser degree. In this figure, the curves have all been plotted on a logarithmic ordinate. Because there is reason to believe that the action of an adapting stimulus upon a receptor should be to reduce sensitivity at each wavelength by a constant *ratio*, the ratio shows up as a constant difference on a log plot, which allows us to show the adaptive effect by manipulating the heights of the curves without changing their shapes. This important idea was first explicitly put forth by von Kries (1924), and is known as the *von Kries Coefficient Law*.

With the heights of the curves selectively altered, as shown by the dotted lines, the test flash, which prior to adaptation appeared yellow because it stimulated R and G cones equally, now stimulates the G cones more strongly. The result is a negative output at C_1, and a sensation of green. We may call this idea the *receptor desensitization hypothesis*.

Two questions may be raised with respect to the hypothesis: first, is it true? Second, to the extent that it is true, what is the mechanism of adaptation, or in other words, why is the sensitivity of a system reduced because of prior exposure to an adapting stimulus?

The answer to the first question is that the hypothesis is not exactly true; at best it is incomplete. Very careful experiments have been made using a dichoptic matching technique, where (for example) a yellow test light in the dark-adapted eye is matched to a trichromatic mixture light (see p. 350) presented to the chromatically adapted eye of the same observer. The details of the predictions that the hypothesis makes are beyond the scope of this chapter, but the main idea is this: Assuming that adaptation is solely the result of such a receptor desensitization, it is possible on the basis of such experiments to deduce the spectral sensitivities of the receptors. However, such analyses lead to the conclusion that the shape of the spectral sensitivity curves of at least one of the three types of cone must be altered dramatically—depending upon the wavelength of the adapting field. Now it is very unlikely that this conclusion is correct because there are other conflicting experimental data and purely physical reasons for believing that no such alteration in the shape of any single cone's sensitivity curve can take place. Let us therefore examine the receptor desensitization hypothesis a bit more closely to see what else might be wrong with it.

Implicit in the hypothesis, and in all calculations based upon it, is the following notion. Prior to adaptation, the three types of cone emit signals a, b, and c, respectively. After adaptation, these outputs are altered; signal a is selectively reduced, and so on. However these alterations can be compensated by increasing the inputs to the three types of cone, so that the signals a, b, and c are restored to the same values they had before adaptation. This is done by selectively increasing the amount of red light in a mixture of inputs involving red, green, and blue stimuli. The hypothesis assumes that when this is done, the sensation produced by the test flash will now be the same as it was for the original stimulus prior to adaptation. It is this assumption that appears to be incorrect.

It appears, on the contrary, that the adaptive process also produces temporary changes in the state of the system beyond the receptor level, so that equal values of a, b, and c, adjusted following adaptation to the same values they had before, produce unequal effects in subsequent stages, and thus unequal sensations. In order to produce equal sensations, unequal values of a, b, and c (compared to the preadaptation conditions) must be employed.

There is further experimental evidence to support the idea that the basis of chromatic adaptation is not confined to changes in receptor sensitivity. DeValois and Walraven have shown (1967) that strong adaptation of one eye definitely alters the chromatic appearance of a stimulus presented to the opposite eye, indicating that part of the adaptive effect occurs not in the receptors, nor even in the retina, but in the brain. Boynton and Das (1966) have shown that there is "cross talk" in the adaptive circuitry. Light absorbed, for example, by R cones cannot be limited in its adaptive effect to modifying the R cone sensitivity, but it must alter the sensitivity of other parts of the system as well.

The experiment of DeValois and Walraven has revealed another important fact, that is, that the adaptive effect of a red light that falls on the area of the fovea involved in the test is not primarily, as had been supposed, due to fatigue of the red system by direct action. Rather it appears that the action is mediated by the parts of the adapting field that *sur-*

round the test area. The excess of red activity in the surrounding area induces a relative reduction of the sensitivity to red into the central area. Such effects go beyond the scope included by the model described above (p. 328) and therefore cannot be dealt with explicitly. To do so, the model would need to be complicated by specifically taking lateral interaction effects into account. (A reasonably successful attempt to do this has been made by Hurvich and Jameson [1960].)

Changes in Sensitivity

Let us now consider two examples of changes in the sensitivity of the eye to various colored lights. The first is based on a psychophysical study by Boynton, Kandel, and Onley (1959). This type of study was first done by Stiles and Crawford (1934) and most recently by Wald (1964). First, the spectral sensitivity

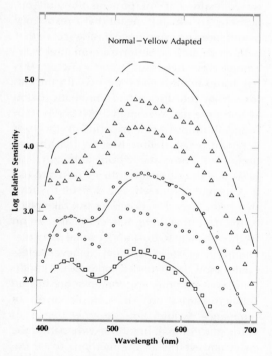

Figure 10.7. Log relative spectral sensitivity as a function of wavelength for foveal flashes. The uppermost curve is for the dark-adapted eye. Lower points, from top to bottom, are for adaptation to a flash of yellow light of 0.8, 2.5, 8.0, 25.0, and 80 mL. (Boynton, Kandel, & Onley, 1959.)

of the eye is measured in the dark-adapted state, by finding the energy required, at each of a number of wavelengths, for threshold visibility at the fovea, where there are only cones. (The reciprocals of these energies are plotted on a log ordinate in Figure 10.7.) The curve of the energies resembles the photopic luminosity function (see Chapter 9). However, if the eye is adapted to yellow light, the shape of the curve is greatly altered. In particular, note the clear emergence of a secondary maximum in the blue end of the spectrum. This particular experiment was repeated using three other chromatic adapting stimuli at various intensity levels, and with color-defective as well as normal subjects. It was found by trial and error that three underlying functions could be found which, when summated, could account fairly well for the experimental data.

Although it was believed at the time of the experiment that the sensitivity curves might be those of the receptors, apparently this is not the case, for the curve indicating the sensitivity of the eye to red in particular does not agree at all with the more modern direct physical evidence. It peaks too far in the long wavelengths, and is too narrow. It may be that the curves represent the peaks of the difference functions of the chromatic units, C_1 and C_2.

Many experiments of the same general type as that described above have been done by taking electro-retinograms from human subjects (see Chapter 9) as a criterion. Most of these, until recently, produced curves that were dominated by results from rod sensitivity and which tended to show little selective chromatic adaptation.

The joint contribution of rods and cones to the perception of color is made clear by many other such studies. For example, it is now possible, through the use of flashing stimuli, average response computers, and appropriate background fields, to eliminate the contribution of the rods to perception completely, but so far the contributions of separate cone systems have not been clearly revealed as humps on the spectral sensitivity curve. A recent experiment by Riggs (1967) used a test field of alternating colored bars. The colors could be changed readily at frequencies too high for the rods to follow. The results suggest that the outputs of the separate cone types summate linearly in the electroretinogram. However they do not seem to be selectively adaptable to a high degree, which suggests that the ERG potentials are recorded at a level of the visual system prior to the site of some of the adaptive mechanisms. (Some additional considerations with respect to chromatic adaptation are dealt with on page 341 of this chapter.)

CRITERIA FOR PROVING THAT ANIMALS AND MAN HAVE CHROMATIC VISION

It is natural to believe that others perceive as we do, and therefore to assume that those aspects of a stimulus configuration that appear most obvious to us are the ones that appear most obvious to the subject of an experiment, even though the subject might be an animal. For example, if a cat is trained to go to a blue dish and to avoid a red one, the uncritical bystander probably will accept this as evidence that the cat has chromatic vision. Actually, the experiment proves nothing of the kind. Although it may be true that the cat *does* have chromatic vision, it is also possible that the two dishes might appear to be chromatically identical to the cat. If so, the cat will base its discrimination upon whatever cues are available. Assuming that cues of position, olfaction, shape of dish, and other factors are controlled, it will seize upon any perceived difference in brightness between the stimuli and respond on this basis. Further, differences in brightness might dominate the cat's perception even though it can perceive chromatic differences.

For an experimenter with normal color vision, brightness differences may seem unimportant in comparison with the vivid chromatic ones that he perceives; moreover, the two stimuli may be equally bright *for him* and

may well have been selected to be so. However it is naive to suppose that equal brightness for man necessarily means equal brightness for the cat.

This chapter is not meant to be a repository for results of experiments concerned with chromatic vision in animals. Many have been done; most of them have had serious methodological flaws. Our purpose here is to summarize methods that can be used to prove or disprove the existence of chromatic vision in man and infra-human subjects, with particular stress upon the logical foundations of these methods.

At the outset, it should be emphasized that the study of color vision is a very difficult subject, for it is logically impossible to prove that chromatic vision does not take place. There are two reasons for this. The first concerns the impossibility—as a statistician would express it—of proving the null hypothesis, by which is meant that a result may be obscured by experimental variance, so that with more data or better experimental techniques, a positive result could show up. This has, for example, been the case with the cat, for whom the disproof of chromatic vision at one time had seemingly been well established. But more recent experiments (Sechzer & Brown, 1964), definitely show that the cat *does* have chromatic vision, although it is weak and the cat seems little disposed to use it. A second reason why it is difficult to prove that color discrimination does not take place is the fact that although chromatic vision might not seem to exist under some particular condition of an experiment, it nevertheless could show itself under some other condition. For example, experiments on human subjects carried out at scotopic levels of luminance would not show evidence of chromatic vision in the short-wave part of the spectrum even if all the methods to be described in this section were tried repeatedly. However, evidence that there is chromatic vision would be easy to obtain by any method carried out at higher luminances. Thus, even when evidence against chromatic vision seems overwhelming, later experiments might be carried out that would prove that chromatic vision is possible. Thus in practice, as negative results continue to accrue for a given species, from many laboratories and by many methods, we come to accept the fact that the species cannot see color, at least very well. This is true, for example, in the case of the dog, although the results from some future study, indicating that the contrary holds, could upset the entire conception for the species.

Five methods will now be reviewed.

Direct Viewing of a Bipartite Field

The first criterion for showing that an organism has chromatic vision has already been discussed in a previous section: this is to show that the two halves of a bipartite (split) field continue to be discriminated over a wide energy range. Even here it is necessary to be very careful. Suppose, for example, that a given animal were entirely blind to long-wave light. If it were, the entire intensity range of such a light, going from that which appears very dark to that which appears dazzlingly red-bright for the normal human, would be completely below the threshold of perception for the animal; thus, even though what might seem to the normal human experimenter to be an inordinately wide range of variation in red intensity were used, the discrimination that the subject might make would be based only upon the perception of visible light, produced by shorter wavelengths compared to darkness in response to longer ones. The only certain solution to this problem is somehow to measure the luminosity function of the subject before beginning the chromatic discrimination experiments. This has been done in many excellent studies, where the luminosity curves obtained are of interest and value in their own right.

Metameric Matching of Bipartite Fields

There are many pairs of lights that are physically different that nevertheless appear identical to an observer. These are called *metamers,* and they will be discussed in detail later (p. 354). Here we consider the probable basis for the phenomenon and its relevance to the question of testing for chromatic vision.

The probable reason that two different lights appear to be the same is that both produce the same amount or rate of light absorption in each of the three classes of visual photopigment. Because a total equivalence of response is established early in the visual nervous system, the equivalence must hold throughout all higher levels as well. Thus the receptor outputs, the opponent colors responses, the optic nerve fiber modulation, the activity of the visual areas of the brain, and the sensations produced by such equivalent action must all be identical.

For a normal subject, a monochromatic yellow light (see p. 346) can be matched by mixing monochromatic red and green lights. We call these "L" and "S" (for long wave and short wave) to remind ourselves that it is wavelength and not hue that is the property of light. In terms of our model (p. 328), yellow will be produced whenever the outputs of the red and green cones are equal ($a = b$). Refer now to Figure 10.3, where the sensitivities of R and G cones are shown. If we have a variable wavelength M (for "medium"), yellow will be produced when M is such that $p_{RM}Q_M = p_{GM}Q_M$. This relation holds only at one wavelength—namely the crossover point of the two curves.

If a mixture of S and L lights is used, their quantum energies[3] can be adjusted so that $a = b$. This relation is expressible as:

$$p_{RL}Q_L + p_{RS}Q_S = p_{GL}Q_L + p_{GS}Q_S \quad (6)$$

---

[3] For brief stimulus flashes, the appearance of a stimulus depends upon the total number of light quanta absorbed during the time of the flash, without regard to how the quanta are distributed during the period of their presentation. The discussion to follow should be considered as related to such a flash mode of presentation. For stimuli that are continuously presented, it is the *rate* of quantum absorption (quantum intensity) that is important. With the substitution of *I* for Q in Equations 1, 2, and 3 the argument to be presented here would apply to the case of continuous stimulus presentation.

Given that a particular amount of red light Q_L is specified, there is a unique solution to the equation, meaning that there is some green light Q_S that will satisfy it and thus produce yellow. Solving Equation 6 shows what this value is

$$Q_S = Q_L \cdot \frac{(p_{RL} - p_{GL})}{(p_{GS} - p_{RS})} \qquad (7)$$

Equation 7 may be stated in these words: A given long-wave stimulus of quantum energy Q_L produces an excess absorption in the R receptor compared to the G, represented by the numerator of the fraction in the right-hand side of the equation. At the same time, a short-wave stimulus of energy Q_S produces an excess absorption in the G receptor compared with the R, represented by the denominator of the fraction. The quantum energy of Q_L required to make the match depends upon the value of the fraction. If it is greater than unity, there is too much absorption in

the R receptor for the equation to hold unless Q_L is reduced to compensate. If the fraction is less than unity, the Q_L must be made greater than Q_S for the equation to hold.

A third way to look at the equation is by the graphical example in Figure 10.8, in which L is a wavelength closer to the crossover point than is wavelength S; thus the difference between the two curves is small. For stimulus S, this difference is larger. In order to obtain the balance required for yellow, the quantum energy of Q_L must be relatively increased to compensate the smaller difference on the right side.

It can be understood from study of Figure 10.8 that Q_M can be increased or decreased to produce the same *absolute* amount of stimulation of the R and G receptor, as that produced by any *absolute* amounts of Q_S and Q_L that themselves produce equal stimulation of R and G. Conversely, to match a monochromatic yellow of energy Q_M, the proper mixture of Q_S and Q_L can be varied in total energy without altering their proportion.

Suppose now that one of the two receptors were missing. Let us assume, for example, that only G remains. It should be clear from Figure 10.8 that, whatever Q_S and Q_L, equal stimulation of the G receptor by the two lights will be possible simply by increasing the energy of one component or reducing that of the other. In more formal terms, this situation corresponds to the simple equation that states that

$$p_{GL}Q_L = p_{GS}Q_S \qquad (8)$$

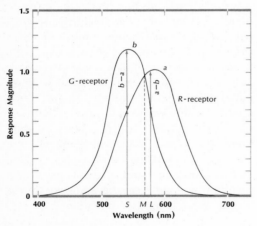

Figure 10.8. Response magnitude curves for the R and G receptors, reproduced from Figure 10.3. Wavelength M, near 570 nanometers, produces equal stimulation of the two receptors, and a signal $a - b = 0$. Two flanking wavelengths, S and L, are also shown. S leads to a large value of $b - a$, L to a smaller value of $a - b$. If mixed, these stimuli would produce an excess of b over a. By keeping the wavelengths the same, but increasing the energy of stimulus L until $a - b$ equals $b - a$, the zero signal can be recovered.

All of the discussion above may have seemed like a long digression, but it is really necessary to understand why the technique of color mixing can be used to diagnose chromatic vision. The reason is that a person with normal color vision, one who has both R and G cones in his eye, is able to match any energy of a monochromatic yellow with a mixture yellow only if he is allowed to vary two stimulus dimensions.

A commercially available instrument is

commonly used for the purpose of studying chromatic vision, called an *anomaloscope*. A split field is used, on one side of which a monochromatic yellow is projected (actually slightly reddish, but this does not matter), the energy of which can be made to seem either brighter or dimmer, as a knob is turned. On the other side of the split field that the instrument provides, a mixture of red and green monochromatic lights is provided. A second knob can be turned to vary their ratio without altering the brightness of the mixture very much (for a normal observer). That is, as light is subtracted from one component, a compensating amount is added to the other. Turning this knob allows the observer to vary the field from red, through yellow, to green in continuous fashion (imagine running across Figure 10.8 from right to left). For the subject who can see color normally, there will be only one setting of the second knob that will produce a yellow that matches the hue of the monochromatic yellow, and only one setting of the first knob that will produce a brightness of the monochromatic yellow that will match that of the mixture yellow. For the observer who cannot see color normally, who, for example, may be lacking either the R or the G receptor, there are very many settings of the two knobs that will produce mixtures each of different brightness. He will however make a unique (brightness) match if one of the knobs is set and he is told to vary only the other. If the monochromatic yellow is fixed in energy and he is allowed to vary the mixture ratio, the subject who cannot see color normally will require a large amount of Q_L relative to Q_S if the R receptor is missing; the converse would be true if the G receptor were missing.

Before leaving the mixture experiment, one additional point should be made. These experiments do not tell anything directly about what colors look like to an observer. They reveal, as we noted at the outset, that equivalent states exist which probably have their basis in the most peripheral stage of the visual system. These equivalences are passed along

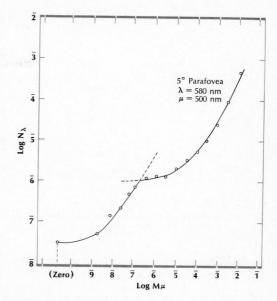

Figure 10.9. Log increment threshold, N_λ versus log field radiance, M_μ for extrafoveal vision. Values are expressed in ergs/sec. deg^2. Note the rod-cone "break" that occurs where log background radiance is about -6.5. (Stiles, 1959.)

through various stages to the brain, finally to produce equivalent senations that permit the match to be made. However the matches tell us nothing whatsoever about what these sensations are.

Demonstration of Selective Chromatic Adaptation

The bottom branch of the curve shown in Figure 10.9 is a so-called "threshold versus radiance" (tvr) curve (Stiles, 1959) of the kind that is found in an eye that contains only rods, or in which rods function over a wide range. To determine the curve experimentally, a subject is presented a background field subtending 10° of visual angle, upon which a 1° test flash is superimposed for 60 msec. The concentric fields are centered 5° extrafoveally. If the background is very dimly lit, the radiance required for the flash just to be perceived is the same as that required when the test flash is projected against a zero background (darkness). As the background is made brighter,

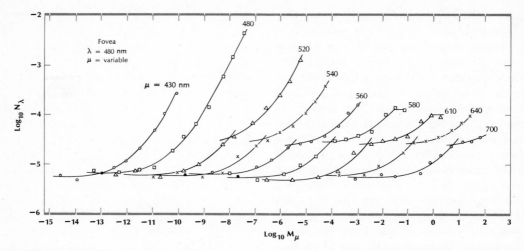

Figure 10.10. Log increment threshold, N_λ versus field radiance M_μ for foveal vision. With test and adapting stimuli both 480 nm, there is no break in the curve. With test stimulus at 480 nm, and as the adapting field is shifted to longer wavelengths there is a pronounced break, which in this case reveals a shift from one photopic mechanism to another. Units same as in Figure 10.9; test stimulus is 1° square, exposed for 63 msec. Horizontal placement of curves is arbitrary. (Stiles, 1953.)

its effectiveness in raising the threshold for perceiving the test flash is at first very slight, and the curve rises gently from the baseline. Its slope gradually increases, so that it rises faster and faster. When the background has been made about 3 log units brighter than it was when the curve began to rise, the curve reaches a slope of 45°, meaning that Weber's Law holds, for the ratio of ΔN (the test radiance) to M (the adapting field) is a constant.

For the scotopic eye, the shape of the tvr curve is independent of the wavelengths of the test and adapting stimuli. Changes in the wavelength (λ) of the test merely cause the curve to shift up and down; changes in the wavelength (μ) of the adapting field cause a shift in the horizontal direction. The curve will have its lowest and leftmost position if wavelengths λ and μ are both set at 505 nm, the wavelength of peak sensitivity for rod vision. The curve will displace itself to the right of this for all other adapting wavelengths, and above this for all other test wavelengths.

For the conditions shown in Figure 10.9, the tvr curve, instead of continuing its upward rise with unit slope, levels off and then rises slowly again before re-achieving unit slope. This is taken as evidence that more than one

mechanism[4] must be at work. The sensitivity of the eye depends, to a first approximation, only upon that mechanism which is most sensitive. At low background radiance, this is of course the rod system unless the test stimulus is confined to the fovea. At higher radiances, one of the cone systems will take over. This produces a rod-cone "break," very evident in Figure 10.9, quite analogous to that already described in Chapter 9, where increasing time in the dark following preadaptation gave the rod system a chance to take over from the cone system which earlier had been more sensitive.

It is possible to obtain "breaks" in the tvr curve at photopic levels using foveal stimuli revealing a changeover from one cone mechanism to another. An example of this is shown in Figure 10.10. The position of the breaks depends upon the particular choice of wavelengths that is made for the test and adapting stimuli. The tvr curve thus has a shape that depends upon stimulus wavelength, and the

[4]The term "mechanism" has been used by Stiles to stress that he is not necessarily referring to pigments or receptors, but to systems containing many of both. A "mechanism," as described by Stiles' technique, has many of the properties of types of cones and may be considered in this way, although inexactly.

eye may be said to have exhibited *selective chromatic adaptation,* in the sense that a given adapting field is shown by the method to have a greater effect on perception when one system of rods or cones is functioning rather than another. Otherwise the breaks in the curve could not occur.

The principle of selective chromatic adaptation is illustrated in another way in Figure 10.6. That is, lowering the sensitivity curve of the G cone at a certain test wavelength is equivalent to raising the tvr curve using the tvr curve method. This is the link between the two approaches.[5] Stiles has deduced the spectral sensitivity of foveal mechanisms by finding the radiance of the adapting field necessary to raise the threshold of a test flash, believed to stimulate uniquely a given mechanism, by a criterion tenfold amount. Of five sensitivity curves obtained by this method, three can be selected which more or less resemble curves of the R, G, and B cones derived by other methods. However there are certain quantitative differences, and it is puzzling that five, rather than just three curves are needed to describe the data.

For purposes of testing color vision, the method of Stiles is too time-consuming to be practical. For this reason, a short-cut method has been developed (Boynton & Wagner, 1961; Boynton et al., 1965) which takes advantage of the fact that, if selective chromatic adaptation has occurred, test flashes should

TABLE 10.1 THE FOUR CONDITIONS REQUIRED TO DETERMINE THE HETEROCHROMATIC THRESHOLD-REDUCTION FACTOR (HTRF); THRESHOLDS FOR THE FOUR CONDITIONS ARE EXPRESSED IN LOGARITHMIC UNITS.

		Background Stimulus	
		R	G
Test	r	r_R	r_G
Stimulus	g	g_R	g_G

[5] From tvr curves for various combinations of test and adapting field wavelength curves like those in Figure 10.6 can be derived immediately; conversely tvr curves for different adapting field radiances, can be obtained. The approach is the same; only the method of displaying various aspects of the results is different.

be more easily seen against backgrounds that differ chromatically than against those that are the same. There is a problem here, one which revolves (as usual) around control of intensity. For example, a red test flash will be harder to see against a very bright green background than against a dim red one. The solution to the problem is to use test and background stimuli in a matrix of four possible combinations that produce a set of four thresholds. An example is given in Table 10.1. The symbols in the matrix represent the logarithmic threshold values for the conditions shown, measured in any convenient units. If the homochromatic condition r_R (red on red) and the heterochromatic condition r_G (red on green) are measured in the same units and for the same test wavelength, the difference between them will be a logarithmic value which corresponds to a dimensionless ratio of the two. Typically, though not always, we can see the combination of red on green more readily.

The heterochromatic threshold reduction factor (HTRF) is defined as the mean of two such differences, one for each wavelength of test stimulus:

$$HTRF = \tfrac{1}{2}[(r_R - r_G) + (g_G - g_R)] \qquad (9)$$

It can be shown that, if this value is reliably greater than zero, selective chromatic adaptation has occurred. The quantitative value shows the factor by which thresholds are lowered specifically as a result of chromatic differences, below what they are for homochromatic conditions.

This test has been applied successfully to human observers (Boynton & Wagner, 1961). It has proved to be useful to detect color-deficient subjects. For example, "red-green blind" subjects (see p. 362) yield HTRF scores of zero when red and green lights are used. Macaque monkeys (Monjan, 1964) show, as do human subjects, a value of about 0.3 (about a factor of 2) for red and green lights of moderate luminance.

It should be noted that the methods used to measure thresholds, unlike all others noted in this section, do not depend upon the

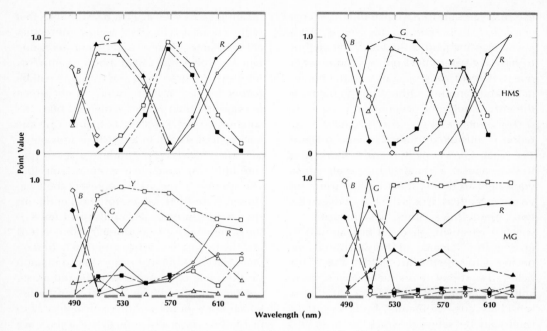

Figure 10.11. Results of a color naming experiment for one normal subject (HMS) and one color-defective subject (MG, a protanope). Filled symbols are for low-luminance stimuli, open symbols are for high-luminance stimuli; stimuli appear equally bright to the subject at a given luminance level. High luminance level matches 1000 trolands of white light, low luminance level, 125. The graph at the left is for dark surround, that at the right is for a white surround of luminance 1000 trolands.

chromatic appearance of the stimuli. The subject is asked only to report the presence or absence of stimuli, not what they look like. It should be noted once again that an organism can indicate that it can tell the difference between one color and another, yet not have true chromatic vision. It is possible also to imagine an eye that shows no adaptation at all, chromatic or otherwise, but which still could exhibit chromatic vision. The methods just described are best considered as revealing the presence or absence of receptor mechanisms that potentially can mediate chromatic vision.

Demonstration of the Reliable Use of Color Names

Outside of the laboratory, people do not spend much time in making color matches, or in demonstrating selective chromatic adaptation with methods like those just described. Most color defective observers first learn of their defect when they attempt to attach *color names* to surfaces, only to find that their efforts yield surprise or even laughter from others. Indeed, if we did not learn to use color vocabularies, it is doubtful that the defective observer would ever learn about his anomaly, since there would be no direct way for him to know what he was missing in the rich normal realm of chromatic sensations.

It is possible to study this commonplace practice of color naming in the laboratory, where it is found that there are very reliable relations between wavelength and color naming, provided that the naming of colors is restricted in certain ways. (The study will be described in detail later, on p. 367.) Sample results from a color-naming experiment for one protanope (a subject suffering defective differentiation of red and green; see p. 364) and one normal subject are shown in Figure 10.11. The exact meaning of these curves will be explained later on page 367, but here it is necessary only to understand that the curves provide an estimate of the amounts of red, green, yellow, and blue that the subject says he sees in stimulus flashes that are presented against a dark surround. Note that the color-defective subject calls all long-wave stimuli "red" when they are dim and "yellow" when they are bright, almost without regard to wavelength. The normal subject shows very little dependence on the intensity of the light; his estimates depend primarily upon the wavelength of the stimulus. Any such dependence, if intensity is controlled, is evidence of chromatic vision. Figure 10.11 shows a slight amount of chromatic vision remaining in the color defective observer.

Stimulus Substitution Methods

We have saved for last a method which is one of the best; at least it is the most sensitive, although technically the most difficult. In the first parts of this section, the notions of color differences and color matches were introduced using the bipartite field, in which the stimuli are compared simultaneously side by side. Such a comparison can also be made successively in time. Imagine that the area of each color used in the bipartite fields is enlarged to fill the full test field. If the fields are slowly alternated with one another, a slow flicker will appear due to the chromatic and achromatic differences between the successive components; luminance adjustment of one component may reduce the appearance of flicker, but it will not eliminate it. Indeed, the point of minimum flicker is used to define photometric equivalence by the method of flicker photometry.

For an observer lacking chromatic vision (including the normal human subject under scotopic conditions) a stimulus having any arbitrary spectral distribution may be substituted for any other spectral stimulus, with the result that, if their relative intensities are suitably adjusted, a steady light should be perceived. For suitable conditions, in an observer who has chromatic vision, no such null point should be achievable, excepting the special case of the metameric match, where the results should agree with those obtained by matching steadily-presented bipartite fields. In practice, the null condition is a very hard condition to achieve—so hard in fact that the method has very seldom been used on human observers. The difficulty is mainly technical and concerns the need for perfect substitution in time of one stimulus for another, for the eye is extremely sensitive to small timing errors. Also, inhomogeneities in the retinal area covered by the alternated test field tend to be smoothed out by the perceptual apparatus during maintained viewing but are much more apparent when short flashes are used. The problem of precise stimulus substitution may be made somewhat easier by using sinusoidal rather than rectangular pulses of flickering light. In experiments using sinusoids, an interesting effect has sometimes been found: in order to minimize flicker, under low-intensity photopic conditions when the wavelengths of the components differ, a phase adjustment of one component must be made with respect to the other. This requirement may reflect differences in response times of the underlying chromatic systems.

THE RELATION BETWEEN WAVELENGTH OF MONOCHROMATIC RADIATION AND COLOR SENSATION

When Newton first dispersed sunlight into a spectrum (1672), he indicated that he saw seven bands of color from short wavelengths toward long: he called these violet-purple, indigo, blue, green, yellow, orange, and red. All but indigo and orange were held to be "primary;" these two (and gradations, such as between blue and green), "derived." The names that he used were arbitrary, but this is still a fairly good description of how a balanced spectrum of moderate intensity looks to persons with normal vision.

The appearance of color depends upon the influence of light fields surrounding the color being examined. Because the spectrum is continuous, it is not possible for us to judge the appearance of an arbitrary section of it without having our perception influenced by the surrounding parts of the spectrum. Thus it is better to present one narrow waveband at a time for a controlled duration and to a particular retinal region. Unless the influence of the surrounding areas is specifically under investigation, it is perhaps best to leave these areas dark.

The normal human subject can judge the dominant hue of a narrow waveband with remarkable reliability. (If this were not so, the use of chromatic signal lights, upon which our very lives depend, would be impossible.) But one hue shades off into the next as wavelength is varied; also the exact hue perceived depends upon many other variables. Our purpose in this section is to look in detail into the relation between the physics of wavelength and the psychology of hue, and then to consider this relation in terms of the model described on page 328.

Sensations are private experiences; about the only way we can get at them is through the use of words. Even so, the common use of color language by two people does not prove that each sees the same colors. No such proof is possible. Each of us must therefore rely upon his own experience with chromatic sensations in order to appreciate what is being discussed here.

Fundamental Hues and Unique Wavelengths

It is often productive to reduce a problem to the smallest number of variables that we can and still describe it adequately. In this spirit, many people have argued that only four color names are needed to describe the chromatic character of bright colors viewed in a dark surround. For a full description, the achromatic term, white, must be added, but we shall ignore this complication for the time being.

The four basic color names are red, yellow, green, and blue. Each of these names is held to describe a unique sensation. This means

for example that a yellow can be produced which is uniquely yellow in the sense that there is no reddishness, greenness, or blueness about it; it cannot be conceived as being made up of a mixture of any of the other sensations. (The fact, to be discussed later, that red and green *lights* can be mixed to produce a yellow light, is irrelevant here. We are talking now about blends of sensations, not of mixtures of lights.)

There are other hues to which color names have been given, which do not meet the criterion of uniqueness. The most widely used of these names is probably orange, with purple not far behind. Orange does not qualify as a unique hue because—to most people at least—it can be appreciated as being made up subjectively of a mixture of red and yellow. That is, the red and yellow components of orange can be seen admixed in the same patch of light and their ratio can be judged accordingly, as being reddish, yellowish, or an equal mixture of each. The same can be said for the simultaneous red and blue component of a purple or violet sensation, and of blue-green and green-yellow blends.

Of considerable interest is the fact that not all possible combinations of the four unique hues can exist in one place at the same time.

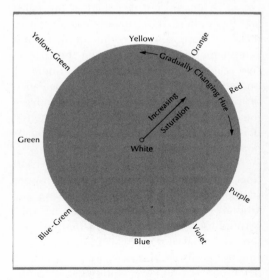

Figure 10.12. Psychological color circle.

For example, mixtures of red and green cannot be seen; we never experience or talk of a "reddish green" or a "greenish red." The same opponent relation exists between yellow and blue, though perhaps it is a little less apparent. The mixtures of chromatic sensations that do or do not occur can be conveniently represented on a diagram such as that of Figure 10.12, which is a "psychological color circle." The hue sensations that lie opposite one another on this diagram are opponent in the sense that they cannot coexist in the same patch of light; adjacent ones can. Intuitively we feel that white should be in the center of the diagram and we place it there. White can mix with any chromatic sensation, simple or complex. Psychological color diagrams such as this have been in use for a very long time, and are based upon pure introspection.

Hue versus Wavelength

Let us now return to the fundamental issue of hue versus wavelength. A convenient way to examine this is by an experiment in which

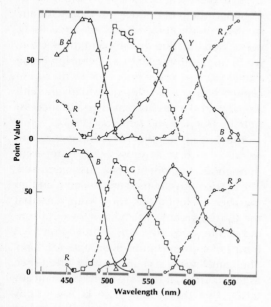

Figure 10.13. Appearance of the spectrum, as gauged by a color-naming technique. (Boynton & Gordon, 1965.)

the subject is restricted to using the names describing the four unique hues to describe a secondary color. In one experiment (Boynton & Gordon, 1965) subjects were instructed to judge spectral hues, one stimulus at a time, and to indicate what they saw with one name (if a unique hue were perceived) or two names (with the name given first describing the dominant component). For example, a reddish orange would be described as red-yellow in that order. A total value of 3 was assigned to each response. When a unique response was given all three points were assigned to it. In the more common double-response case, the first was assigned a weight of two, the second, one. In this way a distribution of response values was built up. The result for one subject is shown in Figure 10.13.

Figure 10.13 provides a good description of the appearance of the spectrum. Consider the upper part of the figure, for stimuli of 100 trolands. The very short wavelengths are reddish blue (violet). Unique blue occurs at about 474 nm, where blue is always the first response, but red and green are given with equal probability as the second response. A balanced blue-green occurs at 496 nm where the blue and green functions cross, and unique green occurs at 513 nm. Following a balanced yellow-green at 565 nm, unique yellow is achieved at 585 nm. This becomes orange at 612 nm where the red and yellow curves cross. The extreme long-wave end of the spectrum still appears as a slightly yellowish red; this is accentuated by raising the luminance to 1000 trolands, as is done in the bottom part of the figure.

Influence of Various Parameters upon the Hue-wavelength Relation

The relation between wavelength and hue is not precisely fixed, even with a dark surrounding field; it depends in detail upon what the exact conditions of the experiment are.

Many experiments, including those of the kinds just described but not limited to these, lead to the following generalizations:

1. As *luminance* is increased, responses of

yellow and blue are made increasingly often relative to those of red and green, although the position of the unique hues in the spectrum is not markedly affected. (This is related to a change in hue with intensity, known as the Bezold-Brücke hue shift.) In particular, the violet end of the spectrum becomes less reddish until at very high luminances the red component disappears; the red end of the spectrum becomes more yellowish. These features can be seen in Figure 10.13. At extremely high luminances under prolonged observation, long-wave stimuli become yellow in appearance—all trace of red disappears.

2. As *area* is increased, responses of yellow and blue increase relative to red and green. Very small areas produce the converse effect; responses of yellow and blue are markedly reduced, particularly in the central fovea, leading to a condition approximating tritanopia (see p. 365).

3. One of the effects of *time* has been alluded to above: prolonged viewing leads to adaptive effects that produce drastic changes in appearance. The effect of very short exposures is similar to that obtained from very dim stimuli of somewhat longer exposure; chromatic appearance depends upon the product of luminance and time for stimuli of about 50 msec duration and shorter (Kaiser, 1968). Small and/or dim stimuli tend to appear white, particularly in the region of the spectrum around 580 nm that normally appears yellow, and also in the region of 400nm.

4. The *region of the retina* stimulated has a powerful effect upon chromatic appearance. Other things being equal, increasing eccentricity of the stimulus relative to the point of fixation leads to relative ascendance of yellow and blue chromatic responses and a reduction of red and green ones (Boynton et al., 1964). Many monochromatic stimuli will be seen as white in the far periphery. Indeed, a safe generalization may be made that yellow sensations tend to be replaced by white ones as viewing conditions are made difficult, whether by reducing luminance, time, or area,

or if the stimulus is perceived in the far periphery of the visual field. The poor quality of chromatic vision in the periphery can be compensated for to a considerable degree by increasing the area and/or the luminance of a stimulus.

5. Chromatic vision is most vivid for large stimulus fields at moderate luminances. Very low luminances lead toward achromatic, scotopic vision whereas very high luminances lead to a "washing out" of chromatic vision with the result that all sensations tend toward white. (The reader is referred to an excellent review by Burnham, Hanes, and Bartleson [1963] for a more detailed description of the effects described above, and for many more detailed and specific references.)

Physiological Bases of These Relations

For stimuli of moderate luminance, duration, and area, centrally fixated, the model discussed on page 328 provides an obvious basis for the chromatic appearance of the spectrum, which depends upon the signs and relative strengths of signals derived from the C_1 (red-green) and C_2 (yellow-blue) units. Although the model does not deal with any of the complicating effects of area, luminance, and duration described in this section, we can point to the kinds of extension in the model that would be necessary to do so. An explicit effort to do this quantitatively with a similar model has been made quite successfully by Hurvich and Jameson (1955).

The linkage of the red with green, and yellow with blue as subsystems, is apparent throughout the phenomena just discussed. These two subsystems seem to come and go together as conditions vary. It appears that the C_1 (red-green) system has a lower threshold and requires less spatial integration from inputs of many receptors in order to function. Thus, small,weak stimuli are most often seen as red or green, if they are seen chromatically at all. That they should also be seen fairly often as white is reasonable; a small sampling of absorbed quanta, even if biased toward wavelengths that would normally be per-

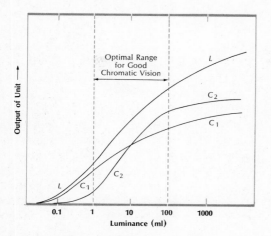

Figure 10.14. Schema to illustrate the shift in dominance of the yellow-blue system (C_1) relative to the red-green (C_2) as stimulus luminance is increased.

ceived as red or green, will sometimes fail statistically to produce the normal imbalance.

It seems clear that, as luminance is raised or area is increased, the effectiveness of the yellow-blue system increases faster than that of the red-green system. Probably the C_1 system also becomes saturated first; that is, the signal from C_1 levels off while the signal from the C_2 system continues to grow.

The L unit, signalling luminosity, has a low threshold, on the same order as that of the C_1 unit, but reaches a much higher level before saturation occurs.[6]

An effort to schematize the notions described above has been made in Figure 10.14, where a qualitative picture of rising output has been given for each of the units as the luminance increases logarithmically.

Saturation

The point of view put forth here is that chromatic and achromatic sensations depend upon signals coming over the pathways leading from the C_1 (red-green), C_2 (yellow-blue) and L (luminosity) pathways. *Saturation* depends upon the relative chromatic-to-achromatic contributions; it is an estimate of the

[6]Note that this use of the term "saturation" is entirely different from that of the next section.

proportion of *chromaticness* in the total sensation. Spectral colors are not equally saturated; saturation is greatest at those wavelengths where the achromatic systems are least active relative to the chromatic ones. This is particularly true at the short-wave end of the spectrum, where the B receptor contributes vigorously to the blue-yellow imbalance, but nothing at all to luminance. The most desaturated stimulus is a white, produced by a balanced spectrum that leads to zero output for C_1 and C_2 together, or any other stimulus producing the same result (see p. 357).

MIXTURES OF RADIATIONS

In order to gain a grasp of fundamentals, we have so far concentrated our attention upon the reaction of the visual system to monochromatic lights. However vision is mainly mediated by surfaces which reflect light continuously throughout the visible spectrum, as is indicated in Figure 10.1. Therefore we must now deal with the problem of how the visual system responds to mixtures of radiant energy that contain such continuous distributions of wavelengths.

Recall that one of the requirements for chromatic vision is that the eye must contain more than one type of visual photopigment. Because all information about the wavelength of light is lost when absorption occurs in the photopigment, any two wavelengths can, if suitably adjusted for intensity, produce identical effects upon any single type of pigment. Therefore, the action of a mixture of wavelengths upon a single pigment comes from the sum of the individual components of the mixture. For example, if 10,000 quanta are absorbed from a flash of light at 600 nm, 5,000 from a flash at 500 nm, and 15,000 from one at 400 nm, a mixture of all three lights would lead to the absorption of 30,000 quanta. However *any* mixture of light leading to the absorption of 30,000 quanta would produce exactly the same effect; for example, the original amount at 400 nm plus 3 times the original amount at 500 nm; or, for another example, 6 times the original amount at 500 nm.

Because the human eye, under photopic conditions, contains not just one, but three different pigments with overlapping spectral sensitivities, the initial basis for chromatic vision lies in the relative absorption of light by each of these three types of pigment. If two physically different stimuli produce the same absorption in all three types of photopigment, it follows that these stimuli should look exactly alike in all respects.

The Basic Colorimetric Experiment and Its Interpretation on the Three-Pigment Hypothesis

We now describe an experiment that is fundamental to *colorimetry*, a science that deals with the specification and measurement of color within a system based upon the experimental operation of *color matching*. The object of the experiment, and the calculations which stem from it, is to attempt a specification of all possible visual stimuli in terms of only three variables. Experimentally, these variables relate to the amounts of three so-called *primary stimuli* which, when mixed together, exactly match the color being specified.

Curiously, although colorimetry is said to specify color, the observer in the basic experiment is not required to judge color appearance. (Color matching has been a favorite visual experiment of the physicist, who often prefers to use the observer only as a null detector.)

In order to carry out the basic experiment, a *colorimeter* is required. First, a means must be provided to produce a *test stimulus* that the subject will try to match. In the experiments that we deal with here, we have chosen to use monochromatic lights as test stimuli, but this need not be so. (Some colorimeters are used to match the color of nonmonochromatic surfaces in the real world.) In our experiment the test stimulus is made to fill one half of a bipartite field uniformly; let us assume that it is the upper half (see Figure

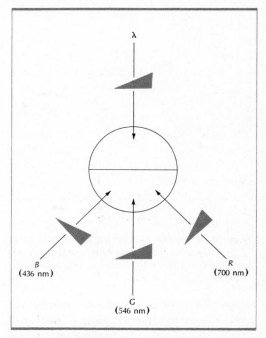

Figure 10.15. Schematic arrangement of stimuli for the color-mixing experiment. A test stimulus (λ) is delivered to the top of a split field, while a mixture of three primaries, B, G, and R, is delivered to the bottom. All are adjustable in intensity by means of neutral wedges. An arrangement must also be provided so that any one of the primaries can, in turn, be added to the test stimulus in the top field.

10.15). Next, a means for obtaining the three primary stimuli must be provided as well as a means for mixing them. (The primary stimuli are likewise monochromatic in the experiment to be described here but, like the test, they need not be.) Mixing is achieved by superposing the three lights on the matching side of the bipartite field uniformly (the bottom half in Figure 10.15). Although it is common to talk of such lights as being "additively mixed," there is in fact no interaction among the light quanta. The situation is analogous to a mixture of sand grains of various sizes which, when poured onto a scale, have a certain weight. Mixture in the eye is a function of the cone receptors that capture the light quanta of various energy values and develop a response that depends upon the rate at which each species of quanta is caught.

Additionally, there must be a means in the apparatus for varying the luminance of the test stimulus, and of each of the three components in the mixture. In Figure 10.15 we have indicated three monochromators, each of which is capable of putting out monochromatic light of any desired wavelength. A *neutral density wedge* is placed in the beam coming from each; this is a variable filter that absorbs light differentially from one end to the other. Some devices of this kind literally are wedge shaped; they absorb more light in the thick positions than in the thin, so that luminance can be varied by sliding the wedge across the beam. For exact work, the bipartite field should be of such good optical quality that the dividing line between its halves should disappear when a perfect match is achieved.

A test wavelength is selected and is placed in the top half of the field at a luminance that is comfortably within the range for good chromatic vision, say about 10 millilamberts. Next the three primary wavelengths are selected, keeping in mind the only requirement that no two of the primaries, when mixed, should match the third. We find that this requirement can only be met when the three are widely separated. Thus we may be sure that each of the three primaries is absorbed preferentially by a different one of the three types of photopigment. Let us select, from an infinity of possibilities, 436, 546, and 700 nanometer wavelengths as blue, green, and red primaries for the experiment. (This particular set was recommended by the International Commission on Illumination [CIE] many years ago, as real reference stimuli in terms of which the properties of the representative eye should be expressed.)

In the remainder of this section we discuss the color matching of an ideal observer, based upon a set of average data selected and slightly smoothed by the CIE in 1931. There are, of course, individual differences even among normal subjects, but the standard data are representative of typical subjects working with centrally-fixated fields subtending about 2° of visual angle.

Three knobs, each connected to one of the neutral wedges in the mixture beams of the optical system, allow the observer to adjust the luminances of the primary components; accordingly, he makes his matches by the method of adjustment. In effect, he acts as an analog computer, finding by trial and error the values of three unknown quantities that yield three simultaneous equations; these equate the amounts of light absorbed in each of the three types of cone photopigment stimulated by the mixture field with those absorbed from the test.

To illustrate the method, we consider only two of the many test stimuli that must be matched in order to build up a full set of color mixture curves. When the test is an orange light of wavelength 600 nm, the observer will discover that he must turn off the blue primary completely in order to make a match. His remaining task is to adjust the amounts of the red and green primaries to achieve an orange field that matches the test field. This is a less difficult match than one requiring all three primaries, yet the subject may experience certain difficulties. For example, if he concentrates on a hue match, he may achieve it only to find that a border remains because of a brightness difference. Both components must then again be adjusted, in which case the hue equality may be thrown off, and so on.

Making a match of blue-green at 500 nm presents a different problem. The observer will discover that the red primary is of no use in the mixture field—any amount of red only makes the match worse. However this time, varying the remaining blue and green primaries presents the complication that, although a match for hue is achievable, the mixture field is always less saturated than the test field. An understanding of why this happens can be grasped by referring once again to Figure 10.3A. A wavelength at 490 nm activates the B and G cones about equally, but it also activates the R cone, although only about 25 percent as much as either of these. However, this activation of the R cone produces some desaturation for two reasons: (1) it reduces the magnitude of the negative values of the C_1 and C_2 signals, reducing the strength of the green and blue signals respectively; (2) it adds to the luminance signal, which increases the white component of the sensation. (If absorption by the R cone could somehow be eliminated, the blue-green sensation provided by the test field would be more saturated than it normally is. This in fact can be accomplished to a degree by prior adaptation to red light.)

When stimuli of mixed colors are used for the test, the blue primary at 436 nm predominately stimulates the B cones. This contributes nothing to luminosity, but it is good for saturation. Because of the great overlap of the sensitivity curves of the R and G cones, the primary at 546 nm stimulates the R cones about 75 percent as much as the G cones. If the B and G cones are again stimulated approximately equally to achieve a hue match, this time by adjusting the components in the mixture, the stimulation of the R cone, due to the green primary, will be about 75 percent that of B or G, compared with the 25 percent produced by the spectral test stimulus. For the reasons stated above, this additional stimulation of the R cone leads to a further decrease in saturation. The match is impossible.

Although it might seem at this point that the mixture experiment is doomed, a solution to the problem is at hand: it is to move the red primary to the same side of the field as the test stimulus. This maneuver allows the subject to desaturate the test stimulus until it matches the mixture field. We will see later that the amount of red light added to the "wrong" side of the field can be legitimately treated as a negative quantity.

A problem that has been ignored so far concerns the units in which the amounts of the three primaries are to be measured. Luminance units normally are not used, al-

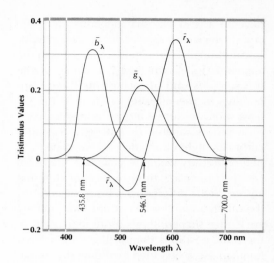

Figure 10.16. Color-matching functions (tristimulus values for an equal energy spectrum) in the primary system where R = 700 nm, G = 546.1 nm, and B = 435.8 nm. (Wyszecki & Stiles, 1967.)

though they could be. Instead, new units are chosen so that when equal amounts of red, green, and blue primaries are mixed, they produce a white (for which an additional experimental operation is required). An amount of white is set into the test field, the subject makes his match, and the settings of the three wedges are marked to indicate that these are so-called *unit trichromatic amounts*. All other quantities are related to these. For example, if the wedge controlling the red primary is adjusted to transmit twice as much light as for the unit setting, the new amount is specified as 2 trichromatic units of the red primary. In making the match, it makes little difference what the absolute amount of white light is, but its spectral distribution is critical, for there are many distributions that will pass for white. The particular white resulting from an equal-energy spectrum, although this is difficult to achieve experimentally, will be assumed here.

The color matching experiment is now continued for each of a large number of test wavelengths throughout the visible spectrum, with the result shown in Figure 10.16. It is not easy to see from the figure that very small positive amounts of the red primary and very small negative amounts of green are present in the short-wave end of the spectrum, to the left of the blue primary at 436 nm. Also, a very small negative amount of the blue primary is necessary to match some colors—more so when large fields are used—throughout the long-wave end of the spectrum. To carry out the full experiment therefore requires apparatus in which any of the three primaries may be shifted to the "wrong" side of the matching field as necessary.

Color Equation

The results of a color match using three spectral primaries may be described by an equation:

$$c(C) + r(R) \equiv g(G) + b(B) \qquad (10)$$

Equation 10 should be read as follows: c units of the test color (C) plus r units of the red primary (R), additively mixed to one half of the field, exactly matches ($\equiv$) g units of the green primary (G) plus b units of the blue primary (B), additively mixed to the other half of the field.

For a test wavelength of 490 nm, the equation reads

$$0.082 \; (C) + 0.058 \; (R)$$
$$\equiv 0.057 \; (G) + 0.083 \; (B) \qquad (11)$$

This is an empirical statement about an experimental operation, not a formal statement of mathematics. The plus sign is borrowed to indicate colorimetric addition by superposition of lights; the symbol "$\equiv$" is deliberately used to make it clear that an experimental match is implied, rather than a mathematical equality. Nevertheless, if the analogous mathematical statement is written and is manipulated in accordance with the rules of algebra, it is found experimentally (within fairly wide limits) that such calculations predict the results of new color matches when translated back into the experimental analog.

As an example, suppose we multiply Equation 11 by a constant factor of 2. It will then read

$$0.164 \; (C) + 0.116 \; (R)$$
$$\equiv 0.114 \; (G) + 0.166 \; (B) \qquad (12)$$

After manipulating our wedges to produce these trichromatic amounts, we can then check to see whether there is still a match between the two halves of the field. There will be. Or we could add a given quantity to both sides of the match—let us call the quantity X. Then, mathematically,

$$0.082 \; (C) + 0.058 \; (R) + X$$
$$\equiv 0.057 \; (G) + 0.083 \; (B) + X \qquad (13)$$

An easy way to check this out is to add a uniform light to the entire field—perhaps reflected off a glass plate in front of the colorimeter. The match will remain.

Generally, the additive, multiplicative, associative, and distributive laws of algebra all work, so that we can predict color matching behavior using the powerful tool of algebra. This is consistent with the model of color vision that has been presented in this chapter, and in fact constitutes one of the primary reasons for believing that equal absorptions in photopigments are responsible for color matches.

There are some algebraic manipulations that cannot be exactly duplicated in the laboratory, namely those that require negative amounts of light. However if a positive quantity is added to the opposite side of the field, as previously explained, the predicted color match will hold.

The values $\bar{r}$, $\bar{g}$, and $\bar{b}$ shown in Figure 10.16 are known as *distribution coefficients* and the curves are called *color mixture functions*. The values have been adjusted so that the area under each of the three functions is 1.0.

In order to provide a colorimetric specification of any stimulus light, it is necessary to evaluate its effectiveness with respect to each of the three color mixture functions. (This is directly related to its effectiveness upon each of the three types of cone photopigment.) For this purpose, the concept of the *tristimulus value* is introduced. There are three of these, defined as follows:

$$R = \int N_\lambda \bar{r} d\lambda$$
$$G = \int N_\lambda \bar{g} d\lambda \qquad (14)$$
$$B = \int N_\lambda \bar{b} d\lambda$$

Here N_λ is the radiance distribution in the stimulus; N must be measured in physical energy units for every wavelength λ throughout the visible range of the spectrum. If we have two stimuli such that $R_1 = R_2$, $G_1 = G_2$, and $B_1 = B_2$, even though physically different values of N had to be used to produce them, they will match for the standard observer. Such matches are called *metameric* and the matching pairs are called *metamers*. (Physical matches are called *isomers*.)

The Chromaticity Diagram

Tristimulus values can have any magnitude, depending upon the radiance levels of the stimuli. Everyday experience tells us that if we double the amount of light (as for example by adding a second light bulb to a lamp) the color appearance of a surface illuminated by the lights changes very little. Because hue and saturation are approximately independent of luminance, it would be convenient to develop a two-variable scheme that deals with relations among trichromatic units, while at the same time factoring luminance out of the system. This is done by specifying *chromaticity coordinates*, defined as follows:

$$r = \frac{R}{R + G + B}$$
$$g = \frac{G}{R + G + B} \qquad (15)$$
$$b = \frac{B}{R + G + B}$$

Tristimulus values, R, G, and B, show the absolute amounts of the three primaries required to make the match being specified. The chromaticity coordinates tell us the ratio of each of the three trichromatic amounts to the sum of the three. (Their sum must total unity and therefore any two of them will provide a complete specification. In practice, a plot of g versus r is most often used.)

A *chromaticity diagram* for this set of pri-

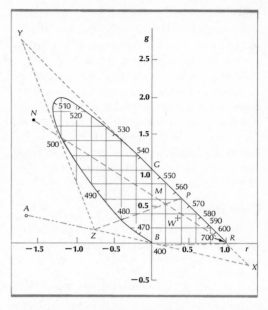

Figure 10.17. Chromaticity diagram based on the spectral primaries of Figure 10.16. X, Y, and Z represent the primaries of the CIE system, as represented in the RGB chromaticity space. (LeGrand, 1957.)

maries is shown in Figure 10.17 in which each spectral stimulus plots as a point. For example if $\lambda = 490$ (for which the tristimulus values were specified in Equation 11), the following chromaticity coordinates are produced:

$$r = \frac{-.058}{.082} = -0.715$$
$$g = \frac{.057}{.082} = +0.700 \qquad (16)$$
$$b = \frac{.083}{.082} = +1.015$$

Other spectral stimuli, calculated and plotted in the same way, form a *spectral locus* connected by a continuous curve that includes all possible intermediate wavelengths.

The diagram in Figure 10.17 has a number of useful properties, the most important of which is that all mixtures of any two stimuli represented on the diagram fall on a straight line connecting the two components of the mixture. The location of the mixture point on this line depends upon the relative number

TABLE 10.2 RELATIONS AMONG LUMINANCE AND TRICHROMATIC UNITS FOR THREE PRIMARY WAVELENGTHS USED IN A COLOR MIXTURE EXPERIMENT

Primary hue	Primary wavelength (nm)	Relative number of trichromatic units	Luminance in mL per relative trichromatic unit	Trichromatic units per luminance unit
Red	700	10	1.00	1.00
Green	546	10	4.59	0.217
Blue	436	10	0.06	16.7
		Sum 30	5.65	17.917

of trichromatic units contained in each of the component stimuli. These may be obtained by the use of equation (14). If these are equal, the mixture point is midway between the two component stimuli on the chromaticity diagram. If one stimulus contains twice the number of trichromatic units as the other, the mixture point will be located two-thirds of the distance from the weaker toward the stronger stimulus, still on the same straight line. If the ratio is 9 to 1, the mixture point will be nine-tenths of the way toward the stronger stimulus, and so on. This has been called the "center-of-gravity" principle. It should be emphasized that if the component stimulus intensities are specified in luminance or radiance units, the center-of-gravity principle cannot be applied, although the mixture point will nevertheless plot somewhere on the line connecting the two stimuli being mixed.

Because the spectrum locus is everywhere convex (although negligibly so for the long wavelengths), it can be seen at a glance that all mixtures of monochromatic lights must fall inside the spectrum locus on the chromaticity chart. Equal-energy white must be located at $r = g = b = 0.333$ because of the manner in which the trichromatic units were defined. Any metamer that matches equal-energy white will plot at the same point.

Any given point on the diagram represents all possible metamers which plot at that point. Excepting the spectral primaries of the system, a color that plots anywhere in the diagram may be obtained in many different ways. Taking the white point as an example,

consider a straight line drawn through it which intersects the spectrum locus at approximately 480 and 580 nm (see Figure 10.17). By rotating this line, all other pairs of spectral stimuli that can produce white can be immediately ascertained. These pairs are said to be *complementary* with respect to this equal-energy white. White could also be made by mixing three stimuli, as is shown in Figure 10.17. (We already know that white can be made from a continuous, equal-energy spectrum.)

The spectral locus does not close upon itself, but leaves a gap between its two ends. Mixtures of spectral stimuli chosen from the extremes of the visible spectrum define a straight line of *extraspectral purples*.

The Relation between Chromaticity and Luminance

The luminances of the three spectral primaries (700, 546, and 436 nm) required to produce equal trichromatic amounts, and thus to match an equal-energy white, are decidedly unequal. Table 10.2 shows this relationship.

From Table 10.2, it can be seen that, if three primaries are mixed together in equal luminance amounts, there would be about 17 times as many trichromatic units of blue as red in the mixture, and an amazing 77 times as many units of blue as green! The resulting mixture would be decidedly blue in appearance, scarcely distinguishable from the blue primary.

If the luminances of the primaries are known, and if Abney's Law is assumed, it should be possible to compute the luminance of any stimulus whatsoever by first matching it with a mixture of the three primaries, and then summing the luminances of the primaries. For example, the stimulus that would be achieved by a mixture of the primary stimuli listed in Table 10.2 would match an equal-energy white and would have a luminance of 56.5 mL. If the tiny amount of blue light (0.6 mL) were removed, the mixture would become yellow in appearance, but its luminance would be reduced by only about 1 percent—hardly a perceptible amount. Thus blue light, which contributes very little to luminance, has powerful coloring powers.

All real light stimuli must have a positive luminance, although we have seen that stimuli can be imagined that have negative amounts. If we could actually produce these, it would be possible to create a series of mixture stimuli having zero luminance. For example, suppose that we could somehow subtract red light from a mixture of 10 trichromatic units of blue and 10 of green. The luminance sum of the blue and green components is 45.9 plus 0.6 = 46.5 mL; to duplicate this luminance with red light would require 4.65 times the 10 mL needed for the 10 trichromatic units, corresponding to 46.5 trichromatic units. From this we can compute the tristimulus values:

$$R = -46.5$$
$$G = 10$$
$$B = 10$$

and the chromaticity coordinates

$$r = -1.755 \qquad g = b = 0.378$$

If we were to increase the energy of the stimulus by any factor, the result would still be a stimulus of zero luminance.

The pair of chromaticity coordinates that we have just calculated falls upon a locus of such points having zero luminance, which Shrödinger (1920) called the *alychne*. In the *g* versus *r* chromaticity diagram of Figure 10.17, the alychne is shown as the dotted line

connecting points labeled *X* and *Z;* the value that we have just computed is at A on an extension of this line.

The CIE System of Imaginary Primaries

The chromaticity system for specifying color, worked out by Maxwell (although in a triangular coordinate system) more than 100 years ago, proved so useful that an international standardizing organization, the Commission Internationale de l'Eclairage (CIE) in 1931 established an international system. A major point to be decided upon was the choice of primaries, for an infinity of chromaticity charts can be prepared, depending upon the colors that are taken as primaries. Whatever the choice, the red primary on an *r* versus *g* chart will plot at $r = 1.0, g = 0$, the green primary will plot at $r = 0, g = 1.0$, and the blue primary at $r = g = 0$ (note that this is the case in Figure 10.17). It works out that the spectral locus defined by one system of primaries is a projective transformation of that defined by any other system of primaries, a projection which places the three primaries in a relation that forms a right triangle with equal sides adjacent to the right angle.

A straight line in one chromaticity chart will transform into a straight line in another chart based on different primaries, but the lengths of such lines relative to one another will change from chart to chart, as will also their angular relations to one another.

In developing the CIE system, a decision was made to utilize a set of imaginary primaries. In essence, this amounts to an extrapolation in the mathematical domain beyond what can be realized physically. Probably the easiest way to visualize what was done is in terms of the chromaticity diagram of Figure 10.17. This diagram, it will be recalled, is based upon a set of real primaries.

The imaginary primaries that were chosen are shown in Figure 10.17 as the points *X, Y,* and *Z.* In this diagram, note that the angle *YZX* is not a right angle, *X* does not plot at an abscissa value of 1.0, *Y* does not plot at

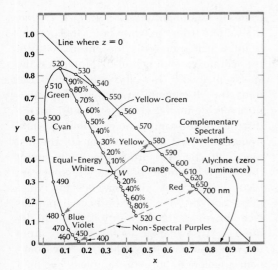

Figure 10.18. Chromaticity diagram based upon the imaginary primaries of the CIE system. (Boynton, 1966.)

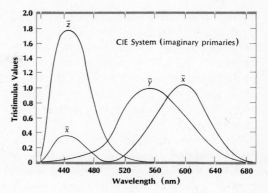

Figure 10.19. Color-matching functions (tristimulus values for an equal-energy spectrum) in the primary system of the CIE. (Boynton, 1966.)

an ordinate value of 1.0, and Z is not at the origin. These positions are accomplished in the diagram of Figure 10.18, which is the appropriate transformation to produce a chromaticity diagram specified in terms of the imaginary primaries X, Y, and Z indicated in the original chromaticity space of Figure 10.17. In both projections, X, Y, and Z are well outside the spectral locus; this is what makes them imaginary. They were deliberately chosen this way so that the chromaticity co-ordinates of all real stimuli would have positive values. In other words, the entire domain of real colors in the transformed diagram falls in the all-positive quadrant.

There are, of course, many sets of three points in the diagram of Figure 10.17 that could accomplish this objective. The ones that were selected have several advantages. In the first place, the lines connecting them just barely graze the spectral locus. This means that there is little waste space near the axes of the transformed diagram. The line X–Y, furthermore, is coincident with the locus of long-wave spectral stimuli from about 550 nm onward. Second, the line X–Z was chosen to

fall on the *alychne*, the zero-luminance line previously discussed. A consequence of this is that both the X and Z primaries in this imaginary system have zero luminance. Cal-culations pertaining to luminance can there-fore be based upon the Y primary alone. To finish the job, the line between Y and Z was drawn to be almost, but not quite, tangent to the spectral locus in the neighborhood of 500 nm.

It will be recalled that the chromaticity diagram in Figure 10.17 was based upon the set of color mixture curves of Figure 10.16. It is possible to go the other way: Given the location of three primaries, such as X, Y, and Z in Figure 10.17, and the luminance of each, a set of color mixture curves can be derived which correspond to these. This has been done for the CIE primaries, and these curves, called $\bar{x}$, $\bar{y}$, and $\bar{z}$, are shown in Figure 10.19. As would be expected, all values are positive. Values of $\bar{z}$ are zero beyond 560 nm. This corresponds to the fact that these stimuli fall on the line where $z = 0$ in the chromaticity chart. Values of $\bar{x}$ form a double-humped curve as a function of wavelength. It reaches close to zero near 500 nm, where the spectral locus of the chromaticity diagram nearly touches the ordinate. The left-hand hump of $\bar{x}$ corresponds to the bending of the spectral locus away from the ordinate in the chromaticity chart as the wavelength is shortened from 500 nm. The $\bar{y}$ function is exactly proportional to the V_λ function discussed in Chapter 9, the luminous efficiency function of the standard observer in the CIE system. As previously noted, this results from a choice of X and Z primaries which puts both of them on the alychne.

The curves of Figure 10.19 are known as the distribution curves for an equal-energy spectrum in the CIE system. These are widely used in order to calculate chromaticities in a standard way, given that the physical characteristics of a stimulus to be evaluated are known; and to predict which stimuli will match other ones.

Suppose that we have two physical samples and we wish to know whether they match. To find out, we determine the tristimulus values X, Y, and Z in the CIE system, defined as follows (see Equation 14):

$$X_1 = \int N_\lambda \bar{x}\, d\lambda$$
$$Y_1 = \int N_\lambda \bar{y}\, d\lambda \qquad (17)$$
$$Z_1 = \int N_\lambda \bar{z}\, d\lambda$$

We do the same for the other sample to obtain X_2, Y_2, and Z_2. If $Y_1 = Y_2$, the two samples have the same luminance, but may not match for hue and/or saturation. If additionally $X_1 = X_2$ and $Z_1 = Z_2$, the two samples will match in all respects.

To determine chromaticity in the CIE system, calculate

$$x' = \frac{X}{X + Y + Z}$$
$$y = \frac{Y}{X + Y + Z} \qquad (18)$$

and plot the result in the standard diagram.

The development of the CIE system has been described here by graphical means. (For a discussion of the corresponding algebra, see LeGrand [1957] or Graham [1965] or Wyszecki and Stiles [1967].)

An alternative scheme for specifying chromaticity may be made in terms of *dominant wavelength* and *excitation purity*. To determine the dominant wavelength of a sample, draw a line from the white point through the point which represents the chromaticity of the sample, extending it until it intersects the spectrum locus. This intersection point defines the dominant wavelength. Excitation purity is defined (see Figure 10.18) as the distance of the sample point from the white point, expressed as a percentage of the distance all the way from the white point through the sample point to the spectrum locus. For samples lying between the white point and the line of extraspectral purples (see above) excitation purity is similarly defined as a percentage of the distance from the white point to the purple line. The dominant wavelength of such a sample is specified

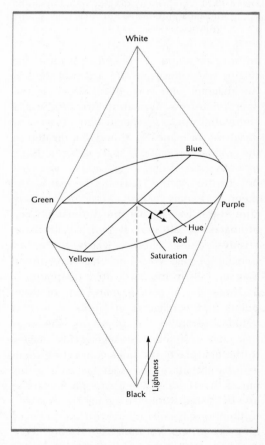

Figure 10.20. Psychological color solid. (After Judd & Wyszecki, 1952.)

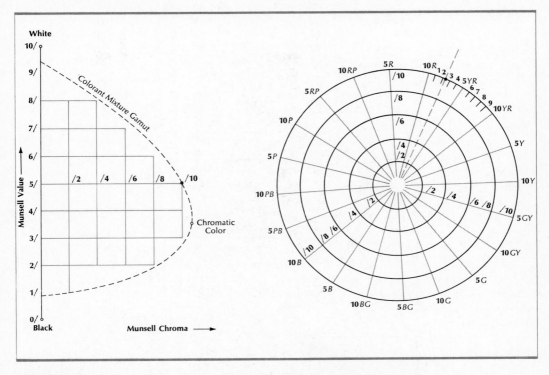

Figure 10.21. Munsell system of color specification. Diagram at the left is for a particular Munsell hue, the one at the right is for a particular Munsell value. If the diagram at the left is for Munsell hue 2.5YR, then the color 2.5YR 5/10 is specified as shown in each part of the diagram. (Wyszecki & Stiles, 1967.)

by the complementary spectral wavelength, followed by a lower-case *c*; for example, $\lambda = 540\ c$.

The Appearance of Mixture Colors: Psychological Color Diagrams and Their Relation to the Chromaticity Diagram

If an individual is given a large collection of chips of colored paper and is asked to arrange them in some reasonable and continuous way, he is likely to order them in a fashion schematized by the psychological color solid depicted in Figure 10.20. The vertical dimension of this solid is a lightness-darkness dimension, which we shall not deal with further here because of the decision to restrict the discussion to chromatic vision and to colors seen against a dark surround. A slice across the diagram yields the familiar color circles previously referred to, with white in the middle, and hues spread around it in the

same order as seen in the spectrum. There is one addition: The circle has been completed in the purple region, which is quite legitimate in this purely psychological diagram, where there is no need to be tied down to what happens to appear in the physical spectrum.

Systems of color specification have been developed, and from these experiments of the kind just described have been carried out. The one most widely known in the United States has led to the publication of the *Munsell Book of Colors,* in which hundreds upon hundreds of color samples are arranged according to their "hue, value, and chroma." (*Value* and *chroma* correspond to lightness and saturation.) Figure 10.21 shows the specification scheme used. To illustrate, taking an example used by Wyszecki and Stiles (1967), "The notation 2.5 YR 5/10 indicates a Munsell hue of 2.5 yellow-red, a Munsell value of 5/

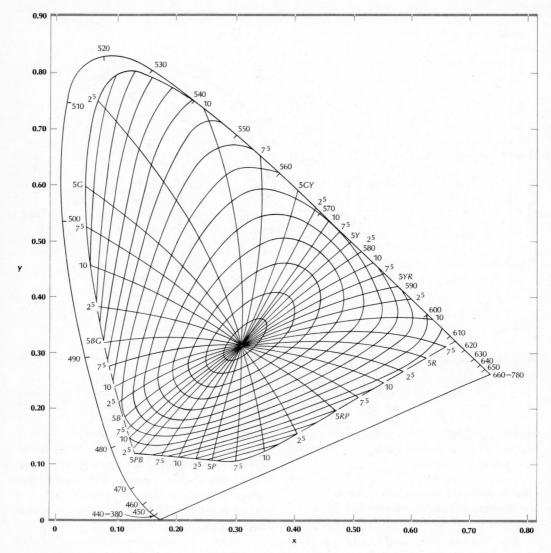

Figure 10.22. Chromaticities of Munsell colors, value 5/, shown on the CIE chromaticity diagram. (Judd & Wyszecki, 1963.)

(which is equally separated from black and white), and a Munsell chroma of /10 (which means 10 steps away from gray (N5/ of the same Munsell value).''

The chromaticity coefficients of all Munsell samples have been calculated (Newhall, Nickerson, & Judd, 1943); this allows the Munsell samples to be plotted on the CIE chromaticity diagram. These plots for Value 5 are shown in Figure 10.22. They reveal the following features:

(1) Because the equal chroma lines emerging from the white point to the spectrum locus are in general curved, stimuli of the same dominant wavelength but variable excitation purity will have a variable hue. For example, if long-wave red at 700 nm is gradually added to equal-energy white, it will first appear as a desaturated bluish red, later as a saturated yellowish red.

(2) The spacings of the closed contours surrounding the white point, each of which

defines a given chroma (saturation) are un-equal, being a function of hue. There are many more chroma steps per unit chromatic-ity change in the lower left-hand part of the diagram than elsewhere.

(3) Real samples of color approach the spectrum locus in the red-yellow-orange part of the spectrum but not elsewhere. This is the result of two factors: (a) Long-wave pig-ments that reflect light have characteristics such as those shown in Figure 10.1. They reflect very little light at the short wave-lengths, and thus avoid desaturation. (b) To a first approximation, only the R and G cones are activated by the long wavelengths that are reflected, so that mixture colors of stimuli containing these wavelengths fall very near to the spectrum locus. Saturated blue-greens, in contrast, are impossible to obtain from reflecting surfaces for analogous reasons: (1) As shown in Figure 10.1, blue-green pigments do not cut out the irrelevant part of the spec-trum so sharply as do red ones. (2) The mix-ture functions of the eye are such that they would produce desaturation in a broad

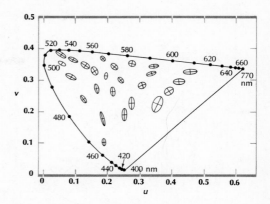

Figure 10.24. MacAdam ellipses plotted in the 1960 CIE-UCS diagram. The new coordinates, u and v, are defined in terms of the standard ones, x and y, as follows: $u = (4x)/(-2x + 12y + 3)$; $v = (6y)/(-2x + 12y + 3)$. (Wyszecki & Stiles, 1967.)

spectral band even if such a sharp cutoff existed.

Many experiments have been made to in-vestigate the lack of uniformity encountered in the CIE chromaticity diagram by other means. Notable among these are the experi-ments of Brown and MacAdam (1949) and of Brown (1957) in which the dispersion of color matches at various sample points in chroma-ticity space was carefully measured. The result is a series of ellipses such as those shown in Figure 10.23. Each of these represents 10 times the standard deviation of the match to a stimulus having a chromaticity located at the point in the center. Where the ellipses are small, very small chromaticity changes are discriminable; where they are large, only very large changes are discriminable. This figure should be compared with Figure 10.22, based on the Munsell scheme. Although the one involves a discrimination experiment, and the other a direct color-ordering experiment, the basic agreement between them is obvious.

The CIE in 1960 adopted a transformation of the chromaticity chart that produces Mac-Adam ellipses of more nearly uniform size. This is shown in Figure 10.24.

MacAdam (1944) has shown that no linear transformation exists that will create perfect uniformity. Farnsworth (1957) worked out an

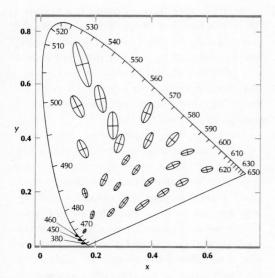

Figure 10.23. MacAdam ellipses. These are plotted as 10 times the standard deviation of attempt-ed isomeric matches, by method of ad-justment, approaching the match point in the directions indicated. (Wyszecki & Stiles, 1967.)

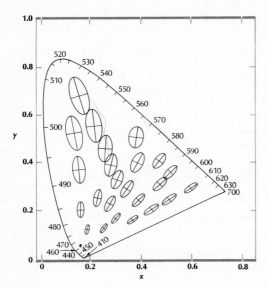

Figure 10.25. Discrimination ellipses derived by Stiles, based upon his line-element theory. These should be compared with the Mac-Adam ellipses of Figure 10.23. (Wyszecki & Stiles, 1967.)

arbitrary nonlinear projection which creates an acceptable uniformity but which lacks all of the other useful properties of a chromaticity diagram. (Many other nonlinear transformations also have been attempted.)

Because color matching experiments do not require judgments of color appearance, or even of color differences, there is no a priori reason why a chromaticity diagram derived from such experiments should provide any reasonable description whatever of chromatic experience. That it does suggests that there are explicit relations between chromatic stimuli and chromatic sensations. Whereas the model discussed on page 328 gives an idea of what some of these relations are, it is a very simple one and does not attempt to deal explicitly with the problem of nonuniformity. Stiles (Wyszecki & Stiles, 1967) has produced a theory that accounts for the nonuniformity of the chromaticity diagram to a remarkable degree (Figure 10.25). His theory is far too complicated to describe here, but one very important feature of it may

be pointed out. It is an elaboration of a "line element" scheme first proposed by Helmholtz: ". . . with . . . three mechanisms in operation, the smallest perceptible difference is obtained by combining the fractional deviations for the three mechanisms in the same way as independent errors are compounded, using the square root of a sum-of-squares relation" (Wyszecki & Stiles, 1967).

ABNORMAL CHROMATIC VISION

In this section we are concerned with what is known in the vernacular as "color blindness." A better expression would be "chromatic deficiency," for if the term "color" is used in its technical sense (see p. 317), one who is considered to be "color blind" would be completely lacking any form of vision.

Only a handful of people have been turned up who are chromatically blind, that is, who possess only black and white vision. Chromatically *defective* people, in contrast, are very common: about 8 percent of the male population is afflicted, along with perhaps 3 females in every 10,000. The disproportionately large percentage of males is accounted for by the fact that the defect is inherited by way of a defect in the x-chromosome. A male, having only one x, is color deficient if that x is defective. A female, having two x chromosomes, is color deficient only if both are defective; the normal one predominates if she has one of each.

Color-matching experiments have provided the principal basis for the classification of color defect. A chief proponent of this approach has been the British physicist, W. D. Wright, whose 1946 volume called *Researches on Normal and Defective Colour Vision* remains today an excellent source of classification criteria and of data on the subject. The physicists' viewpoint appears in modified form in Judd's (1951) chapter in Stevens, *Handbook of Experimental Psychology,* and again in its extreme form in an impressive recent compendium on *Color Science* by Wyszecki and Stiles (1967) which has already been referred to in several places in this chapter.

A limitation of the physicist's approach is that he pays little attention to what the subject actually sees. A vociferous advocate of a more subjective point of view is Arthur Linksz, an ophthalmologist who in his *Essay on Color Vision and Clinical Color-Vision Tests* (1964) is sharply critical of the physical approach and its seeming obsession with difficult mathematical trichromatic concepts. Linksz feels that such concepts ignore a mountain of evidence which seems to support a more direct appeal to sensory experience as it is approached from an opponent-colors viewpoint.

So let the student beware: this is indeed a controversial subject. Color blindness seems to fascinate everyone, even those who have little interest otherwise in vision; it is controversial because of its relation to color theory (itself a controversial subject), because laymen have a tendency to introduce controversy into technical matters, and also because color-defective individuals often do not fit neatly into the pigeonholes that the physically oriented workers have so neatly constructed for them. For every rule, there seem to be exceptions.

The approach to be taken here, to describe defects in color perception, is eclectic. The generally accepted, but clearly oversimplified classification scheme of the physicist will be given; but it would be less than honest to let the subject rest at that point. Therefore, at the end of the section, a few comments will be added to indicate what some of the exceptions are to the statements that have been made.

Color Matching Behavior of Chromatically-Defective Observers

About a quarter of those who are chromatically deficient exhibit the interesting property that they are dichromatic color mixers. Whereas the normal subject, as previously explained, needs three primaries to make a color match, the *dichromat* needs but two,

and this fact defines his condition. For almost all of them, either one of the longwave primaries, the red or the green, can be dispensed with.

On page 341, the *anomaloscope* was described, and the principle of its operation explained. The dichromat evidently has only one longwave-sensitive receptor; both the red and green primary stimuli activate it more than they do the B cone and therefore these cannot be used as independent primaries. When using the anomaloscope, or when making a full trichromatic match, the dichromat finds that there are many combinations of settings of the red and green primaries that will produce the same visual result; thus the matches are not unique. By depriving him of one of the primaries, his unique matching behavior can be examined; the result of this experiment can be plotted on a one-dimensional chromaticity diagram.

It is important to note that, although the dichromat makes matches unacceptable to the normal trichromat, the dichromat will in general accept all matches made by the normal subject. This is theoretically important because it suggests that the dichromat is suffering from a *reduced* form of normal color vision; that which he does have seems to be normal. If the dichromat is made to judge the color matches made by a trichromat, we can plot lines of confusion (called *isochromatic lines*) for the dichromat upon the chromaticity diagram of the normal subject.

The two common forms of dichromatism are known as *protanopia* and *deuteranopia;* those who have these defects are called *protanopes* and *deuteranopes.* The protanope is distinguished by a large insensitivity to stimuli in the long-wave end of the spectrum, requiring five to ten times as much energy to perceive a level of brightness apparently equal to what the normal subject sees. The deuteranope's perception of luminosity, as measured by brightness matching methods, is essentially normal.

Luminosity curves, being arbitrarily set at 1.0 at the value of peak sensitivity, tell us nothing about the differences between normal and defective subjects on an absolute basis. For this purpose, foveal threshold determinations are better, for the absolute radiance levels required are measured throughout the spectrum and can be compared.

In recent studies, Hsia and Graham (1957)

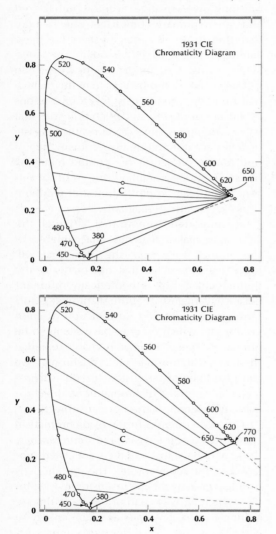

Figure 10.26. Confusion lines for protanopes (top) and deuteranopes (bottom) shown on a standard CIE chromaticity diagram. Any two stimuli the chromaticities of which fall along one of these lines cannot be discriminated by these color-defective observers. (After Wright, 1946.)

worked with 11 dichromats using the threshold method; Wald and Brown (1965) worked with 31. Both agree that the protanope lacks sensitivity in the red end of the spectrum, with average values indicating a loss of sensitivity of a bit more than a factor of 6. Both agree that deuteranopes lack sensitivity to the middle part of the spectrum. Although Hsia and Graham do not show it, Wald and Brown report that deuteranopes are more sensitive than normals to the red end of the spectrum (by a factor of nearly 2) whereas protanopes are more sensitive than normals to the middle of the spectrum (by a factor of nearly 3).

The chromaticity plots of the confusion lines of the protanope and the deuteranope are shown in Figure 10.26. The fact that in each case one of these lines passes through the white point (C) and intersects the spectrum locus suggests that there should be a point in the spectrum that looks white for both classes of observers. This has been confirmed in independent experiments where spectral stimuli have been examined; the deuteranope's neutral point is at a slightly longer wavelength, as would be predicted from the direction of the isochromatic line which for the deuteranope has a steeper slope than it does for the protanope.

The fact that the confusion lines of the protanope seem to converge in the red corner has been interpreted to imply a missing receptor (the point where these lines intersect is known as the *copunctal point* and from it the spectral sensitivity of the missing mechanisms can be derived). Although the deuteranope's confusion lines do not seem to converge as clearly, this is partly a matter of the particular projection of the CIE diagram; they do seem to be converging toward a point outside the diagram, and this can be interpreted to indicate that the deuteranope lacks green receptors.

In terms of the model described on page 328, we may speculate that the protanope lacks R cones containing the red pigment α. If by some genetic mistake, these cones were

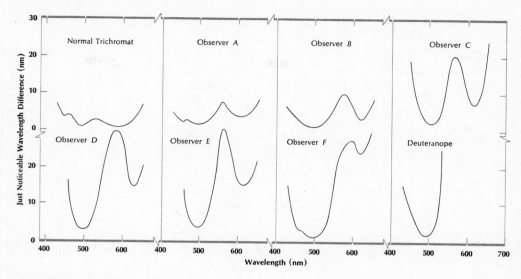

Figure 10.27. Wavelength discrimination functions for subjects ranging from normal (upper left) to the full dichromat (lower right).

to contain the green β pigment instead, this would produce a perpetual zero signal at C_1. The extra β substance would cause an abnormally high sensitivity in the middle part of the spectrum, whereas the loss of α accounts for the sensitivity loss at long wavelengths.

If we assume that the deuteranope lacks the β substance, and that his G cones are filled with the red-sensitive α pigment instead, the basic facts of deuteranopia are accounted for.

A third type of dichromatism exists called *tritanopia,* which is very rare. This seems adequately explained by postulating a loss of B cones.

The largest group of color defective subjects are known as *anomalous trichromats.* As the name implies, they require three controls on the colorimeter in order to make color matches. Their most distinguishing characteristic is that their matches differ from those of a normal subject. If their matches were based upon the use of the same cone photopigments as those possessed by the normal subject, this would be impossible; it is therefore necessary to postulate that at least one of their three pigments has an abnormal spectral sensitivity. The bulk of the evidence

suggests that it is the red-sensitive pigment that is different.

In addition to making atypical matches, anomalous observers usually show visual discrimination of chromatic differences that is poorer than normal. A good way to show this is by measuring their *wavelength discrimination.* A particular wavelength λ is projected into one half of a bipartite matching field, and the other half is adjusted to some other wavelength. The subject is then asked to set a wavelength on each side of the standard which is just barely discriminable. If he attempts to make a match and his dispersions are recorded, this should be recognized as a special case of Brown and MacAdam's method, although it is not possible to generate an ellipse near the spectrum locus.

Results of the wavelength discrimination experiment for a sampling of normal, dichromatic, and anomalous observers are shown in Figure 10.27. Individual differences in this type of experiment are considerable. For the anomalous observers, wavelength discrimination functions range all the way from almost normal to essentially dichromatic in appearance. (Wright [1946] suggests this as a criterion of degree of defect.)

TABLE 10.3 SALIENT PROPERTIES OF COLOR DEFECTIVES

Characteristic	Protanomalous	Deuteranomalous	Protanope	Deuteranope	Tritanope	Rod-Monochromat
Chromaticness discrimination through the spectrum	Materially reduced from red to yellowish-green but to a varying degree in different cases		Absent from the red to about 520 nm	Absent from the red to about 530 nm	Absent in the greenish-blue to blue (445 to 480 nm)	No chromaticness discrimination
Neutral point, that is, wavelength of spectral stimulus that matches white	None	None	494 nm (495.5 nm) Pitt (1935)	499 nm (500.4 nm) Pitt (1935)	(a) 570 nm (b) 400 nm	All wavelengths
Shortening of the red, that is, reduced luminous efficiency of long wavelengths	Yes	No	Yes	No	No	Yes
Wavelength of the maximum of the relative luminous efficiency curve	540 nm	560 nm	540 nm	560 nm	555 nm	507 nm
CIE chromaticity of the confusion point (dichromats only)	—	—	$x_{pc} = 0.747$ $y_{pc} = 0.253$	$x_{dc} = 1.080$ $y_{dc} = -0.080$	$x_{tc} = 0.171$ $y_{tc} = 0$	—
Percentage frequency of occurrence among males among females	1.0 0.02	4.9 0.38	1.0 0.02	1.1 0.01	0.002 0.001	0.003 0.002

From Wyszecki and Stiles (1967)

Anomalous subjects also fall into protan and deutan groupings; they are known as protanomalous if they exhibit a lack of sensitivity for long wavelengths, as evaluated by brightness matching, and as deuteranomalous if they do not. Foveal threshold experiments for anomalous subjects have been done by Wald and Brown (1965).

It is conceivable that the red-sensitive pigment of the anomalous subject constitutes the pigment contained in the second type of R cone in the normal, shown in dotted lines in Figure 10.5. It will be recalled that the reason for introducing this complication was to account for the resurgence, for the normal subject, of red sensations at very short wavelengths, in the violet part of the spectrum. All photopigment absorption curves exhibit a secondary maximum at short wavelengths; for the regular α, β, and γ pigments, this is obliterated by the absorption of ultraviolet light by the eye media. If there were another red-sensitive pigment, with a peak sensitivity at about 625, its secondary short-wave peak would fall within the short-wave end of the visible spectrum and produce a visible effect (Ingling, 1969).

A summary of some of the characteristics of defective chromatic vision is given in Table 10.3, from Wyszecki and Stiles (1967).

At the outset of this section, it was promised that the explanations to be offered of defective chromatic vision would be too pat. One additional experiment will be cited to illustrate this (other complications are spelled out by Linksz, 1964).

In an experiment conducted by Scheibner and Boynton (1968), the color-naming technique was applied to 3 protanopes and 5 deuteranopes. The results for one of the protanopes have already been shown in Figure 10.11, which should be consulted again. In this experiment, the 8 spectral stimuli employed were all equated for brightness for each subject by direct match with a yellow at 580 nm, with the yellow stimulus set at 1000 trolands. Three other sets of stimuli were also used, at 500, 250, and 125 trolands. These were randomly presented, and color naming functions built up by the procedure already described on page 347. Although there were individual differences, no subject exhibited an absolute lack of discrimination in the long-wave end of the spectrum, where all matching experiments and all color theory dictate that a complete confusion should exist. A reasonable conclusion to draw is that there is some red-sensitive α pigment present in the R cones of the protanope, or that there are a few R cones that contain the normal complement of pigment. Either way, the potential exists for a feeble imbalance at the C_1 chromatic unit. Thus the protanopic loss of red-green discrimination is not complete.

THE EFFECT OF SURROUND FIELDS UPON A CENTRALLY VIEWED TEST AREA

We have so far ignored in this chapter most of what would fall under the heading of *color perception,* as distinct from *chromatic vision.* Because color perception will be covered in Chapter 12, we avoid a treatment of object perception, but deal instead only with a few features of a singularly important topic, the effect of a surround field upon the chromatic characteristics of a centrally viewed test area.

Persistence of Color Matches

Over a considerable range, the introduction of a surround field or, for that matter, a change in the state of adaptation of the eye otherwise produced, will not affect a color match. Such a surround field will dramatically alter the *appearance* of both halves of the test field, but equally so on both sides. Thus a red surround will make a central yellow appear green, but all metamers of the original yellow will be affected alike.

It can be shown that this is a logical consequence of the assumption that the shapes of the absorption spectra of the three cone pigments, when plotted on a logarithmic ordinate, do not change with chromatic induction. As previously noted in the discussion of chromatic adaptation, their heights may be altered, and additional adaptive changes may occur further along in the visual system. However all such changes must be mediated initially by what is absorbed in the retinal photoreceptors, so that unless their absorption curves change shape, color matches must hold true. The failure of the color match to change with changes in surround and/or adaptation is known as the *persistence of color matches*.

Like most generalizations, the discussion above has its limits. Color matches do indeed break down under intense conditions of adaptation, although there is some dispute concerning the luminance levels necessary to produce the breakdown. (The data of Brindley [1953] have shown the effect very clearly.) To explain the effect, it is necessary to suppose that the spectral sensitivity of at least one of the receptors has been changed. This could be caused either by a fourth pigment which, for one reason or another, does not contribute sufficiently to prevent trichromatic color mixing but which is bleached relatively little by bright lights. Or it could be the result of a significant change in the density of one of the three regular pigments. Ingling (1969) has marshalled five converging lines of evidence to favor the view that the red receptor contains a small amount of a fourth pigment, which has its peak sensitivity in the neighborhood of 610 nm.

The Dark Colors

When the surround field is brighter than the test area, it induces blackness or grayness into the test area (Evans, 1964). For test areas on the order of one degree of visual angle, subjective black is reached when the test area has a luminance that is 20 percent or so of that of the surround; further reductions in luminance produce no further increase in blackness.

If the test area is already receiving a chromatic stimulus, say an orange one, the effect of a brighter achromatic surround is to induce blackness into the test area; this causes the dark orange that we call "brown." There is no brown in the spectrum—it is solely the result of the induction process and cannot appear in the simple, bright field. "Navy blue" is another example of a color induced by a brighter surround field; especially with large test areas, the blue content can be seen despite an astonishingly high black content. "Maroon" is the term given for reds that are similarly darkened. The effect described above is critically important, for it adds tremendous variation to our color perceptions of real objects.

Another effect of the induction of grayness into the central test area is to increase the saturation of the test stimulus. For this and probably other reasons, surface colors may appear much more saturated in the complex context in which they are normally viewed than would a stimulus of exactly the same chromaticity if viewed with a dark surround.

It has long been suspected (Hering was quite explicit about it) that induction effects revealed lateral interaction effects in the retina. The experiment of DeValois and Walraven (see p. 336) is one of the more recent to confirm this along with electrophysiological evidence. Furthermore, the dramatic experiments of Land (see Chapter 12) have illustrated just how profound these effects can be. Thus, a great many experiments have already been completed on the subject of chromatic induction (see for example the review of Judd, 1960), and it seems likely that this will be a rich area for psychological investigation in the future.

Mathew Alpern

EFFECTOR MECHANISMS IN VISION

11
You have seen that vision involves much more than focusing a sharp optical image on a sensitive retina. But even sharp retinal images are formed only after complex sequences of physiological (and psychological) events take place, which culminate in muscle contractions in the eye. In this chapter, some of the effector mechanisms necessary for seeing are described. Others equally important (for example, the secretion of tears and blinking) are not touched upon at all. An experimental psychology of tear secretion does not yet exist (though it is difficult to understand why). One for blinking has an appreciable literature, but it is largely related to experiments on fatigue and on learning, and therefore more appropriately discussed elsewhere.

INTRODUCTION

Of all the oculomotor mechanisms, the one most exhaustively probed by psychologists has been that of eye movements. This is scarcely surprising, for their study is one of the most accessible ways of analyzing visual behavior in a wide variety of animals. Even man reveals many of his inner secrets in the pattern of his eye movements, a fact appreciated very well by oriental merchants, poets, and policemen at least as long ago as it was by psychologists.

Unlike the photographic film to which we so frequently

compare it, the retina does not have the same spatial sensitivity (visual acuity) throughout. We have already noted, in Chapter 9, that the very center of the retina (the fovea) includes a very small region, a little more than a tenth of a millimeter in diameter (see Figure 9.7) where visual acuity is very high. The visual acuity falls off very quickly the farther away from the fovea the image is made. In the area where the first rods appear, the acuity is already reduced by 50 percent. Eight degrees from the foveal center, the acuity is only 15 percent of the maximum value, and it continues to decrease the farther one progresses into the periphery. Such a photographic film in a perfectly motionless camera would reproduce a "picture" with very sharp detail only in its very center, with less and less detail conveyed the farther away from the center the image falls. The great mass of the picture would be hopelessly blurred.

Such an arrangement is quite unsuitable for the very complex visual requirements of our modern world. It is made remarkably effective, however, merely because of six highly responsive muscles (among the fastest in the human body) attached to each eyeball. These muscles originate in the bony wall of the orbit and are so attached to the globe that upon contraction they rotate the eye around its center (or nearly so). In this way, that part of the retina with the highest acuity can be pointed at different objects in the field of view in rapid succession.

If you were asked what your experience is as you view the world, you would probably describe neither the sequence of eye movements nor the blur of the rest of the visual world around the fixation point. On the contrary, you have the *illusion* of spatial solidity with continuous perception of the entire visual field, all parts of which appear equally sharp and distinct. This is one of many mysteries of the process of vision with moving eyes. How are sharp images of all the successive fixation points fitted together to build this picture of one continuous solid space? How does it happen that all of the fuzzy streaks

of the entire retinal image during the movements and the blurred patterns of that part of the retinal image away from the fixation point are usually not perceived at all?

Of these questions, some await the genius of some future generation either for insightful answers (perhaps by a reader of these pages) or for recognition of the fact that they are not capable of solution. Others are just now beginning to generate the thinking and research from which the answers may be found. We will discuss what is known about them presently.

Muscles

There are six extraocular muscles attached to each globe at various positions. Four of these (the rectus muscles) originate posteriorly at the apex of the orbit and insert into the sclera in the anterior part of the globe, from 5.5 to 7.7 mm back from the junction of the cornea and the sclera. The medial rectus muscle attaches nasally, the lateral rectus temporally, the superior and inferior rectus above and below, respectively. In addition, there are two oblique muscles which effectively originate at the nasal anterior corners of the orbit, one above, the other below the globe. These, the superior and inferior oblique muscles, pass back in each case beneath the relevant rectus muscle and attach to the posterior temporal globe (above in the case of the superior, below in the case of the inferior oblique).

Because of the relations among the muscles described above, individual muscles make distinctively different contributions to globe rotation when the eye is in various positions. However a detailed "switching circuit" in the brain stem produces coordination among these muscles so that signals from higher centers are accurately translated into eye movements. In practice, therefore, it is unnecessary for psychologists to analyze what contributions different muscles make to a given globe rotation, although this is a routine problem for a surgeon confronted with a paralysis of one or more of the eye muscles.

METHODS OF MEASURING EYE MOVEMENTS

The analysis of eye movements is a time-honored pursuit of psychologists. For over 60 years the emphasis has been on the development of better objective methods for indicating eye position. Nevertheless, for many questions very simple methods are often quite satisfactory. The easiest is merely to watch the observer's eyes. An expert eye watcher can detect movements as small as 0.5°, but if you are a beginner, it will take practice before you are that sensitive. Of course, your head will protrude into the observer's field of view, but a judiciously positioned mirror or a small peephole cut in the center of the visual display may suffice to overcome this difficulty in many situations. You can, by this means, make rough estimates of where and how frequently the eyes make different kinds of shifts of gaze; but, if you are interested in more quantitative details, you will have to do something different. Just what depends upon the feature of the shift of gaze you are most interested in measuring precisely. A detailed discussion of many of these methods is available in earlier editions of this book, in a historical review by Carmichael and Dearborn (1947), and in a more recent review (Alpern, 1962). The following contains only a very brief description of the older methods and a summary of some more recent developments.

Afterimages

Assume, for the moment, that accuracy is of prime importance and that you have little or no interest in the time characteristics of the movement as such. The easiest solution is a subjective method, which consists of looking at a bright line (or point) of light long enough to impress a strong afterimage on the foveal cones, after which the light is turned off. It is well known that shifting gaze is accompanied by a movement of the afterimage. You can measure where the foveal cones are pointing by aligning the projected afterimage with a pointer, the position of

which can then be exactly measured with a meter stick. The extent to which the eyes miss any supposed fixation point can be readily determined, assuming that fixation was exact when the afterimage was impressed.

Variations in the technique described above include using various devices for entoptic[1] perception of the fovea, but these are somewhat less satisfactory because they appear only for a few moments and must therefore be periodically reinforced. One modification of this method is to produce afterimages during the eye movement with a high-intensity, stationary, flickering light. The string of afterimages so produced across the retina allows us to estimate not only the duration of the movement but also precisely where the globe was pointing during the moment each of the afterimages was impressed. If more details about time characteristics of the movement are required, however, it is difficult to obtain them by subjective methods.

Objective Methods Without Attachments to the Eye

There is really no completely satisfactory method of measuring eye movements larger than 8° objectively and accurately. The principal difficulty, shared by almost all methods free of globe attachments, is that they do not successfully distinguish between pure rotations that one hopes to record and translational shifts of the globe in the orbit or of the head. These shifts appear as artifacts on the record because they look like eye movements, yet they do not indicate a shift of the retinal image with respect to the fovea. Although there is unequivocal evidence that such translational shifts accompany many eye rotations, it is still far from clear what the relation between the magnitude of the translational shift and the amount of eye rotation is. One disturbing consequence of this is that all systems that require calibration curves for estimating exact eye position may be completely invalid when a different kind of eye

[1] Lying in or originating from the eyeball, rather than the outside world.

movement is used for study than was employed for calibration. (This problem is one of the major difficulties with most of the following methods.)

Electro-oculography There is a small but steady difference in electric potential between the cornea and the retina, which can be recorded by ordinary electrodes placed in pairs on the skin around the orbital rim. As the eye rotates, it moves the electrically positive cornea closer to one electrode and further from its partner at the opposite orbital rim (Schott, 1922; Mowrer, Ruch, & Miller, 1936; Hoffman, Wellman, & Carmichael, 1939). As used ordinarily, the paired electrodes are placed at the inner and outer orbital margins (for study of horizontal rotations) and above and below (for study of vertical rotations) or in all four locations (to study vertical and horizontal movements of both eyes). If all four electrode pairs are used, at least four separate channels are required. The potential differences between the electrodes of each pair must be suitably amplified and recorded, usually with a pen recorder, although a slow-sweep oscilloscope trace may also be used. The amplifiers should be stable, low-noise, and directly coupled if a continuous record of eye position is to be made. Also a means of reducing the potential difference to zero—"zero suppression or bias control"—is desirable to place the record on the zero line when the eye is looking straight ahead. (Care must be taken, by using nonpolarizable electrodes, that potential changes while the eye is steady are not too large.) "Drift" introduced by changes in the galvanic skin responses and other sources of potential may, nonetheless, continue to be annoying; blinks always show up on the records.

The corneal–retinal potential changes with the state of light and dark adaptation of the subject, and therefore periodic recalibration must be made. Byford (1963), moreover, has found certain other nonlinearities that limit the suitability of electro-oculography to study eye movement. He found that in the absence of an independent index there is apparently no way of determining when some nonlinearity is present or its extent at any given time. In spite of its limitations, the method is useful in the laboratory, especially because it allows us to measure eye movements when the lids are closed. (Particularly interesting information comes from electro-oculographic records during sleep which may be associated with dreaming [Dement & Kleitman, 1957].)[2] Electro-oculography also provides an easy way to record nystagmus in both man and animals.

Photographic methods Modern objective recording of eye position was begun by Dodge at about the turn of the century. The method consists of photographing the image of a small light source reflected by the anterior surface of the cornea (as though it were a convex mirror with a radius of about 8 mm). Dodge (1907) employed a film continuously moving vertically so that horizontal eye movements were recorded as lines normal to the direction of film travel and fixations as lines parallel to the direction of film travel. Photographic improvements made possible a device which records the movements of both eyes: the ophthalmograph developed by American Optical Company in 1937. This device, based on the Dodge principle of recording, gives good records of the horizontal movements of the two eyes during reading. It is therefore useful in analyzing certain reading difficulties associated with faulty patterns of coordination and fixation.

Motion picture photography, instead of a continuously moving film, can also be used. Eye position is recorded from changes in position of distinct markings of the iris or a conjunctival blood vessel or a piece of white paraffin placed on the anesthetized cornea.

Modern variations of the techniques described above include a device not only for recording the movements of the eyes but also for superimposing them on the subject's visual field. Two closed-circuit television cam-

---

[2] A "rapid eye movement" (REM) stage of sleep has been identified and explored in this way.

eras are used to provide one composite picture. One television camera gives an image of the subject's visual world, and the other camera superimposes on this same display, but on a second screen, a bright patch from the corneal reflection of a small light which acts as an eye marker to indicate where the eye is looking. The key details being chosen by the eyes at any moment from the complicated picture being viewed are constantly being identified by the eye marker dancing across the screen. The second television screen, which displays both the eye marker and the scene, can in turn be photographed or recorded on video tape and a permanent record made (Mackworth & Mackworth, 1958).

Another variation of the method just described is to mount a small movie camera on a helmet placed on the subject's head. The camera photographs on the same film the corneal reflection of a small light and the field of view immediately in front of the subject. This is a useful way to study eye movement patterns in the field, as when the subject is flying an airplane, driving an automobile, or directing traffic.

Electro-optical methods Lately photoelectric detection methods have been used to study eye movements. In the simplest form an image of an illuminated portion of the junction between the sclera and the iris is focused onto a photomultiplier tube (Smith & Warter, 1960). Because the white sclera is a highly reflective surface and the iris is not, the amount of light focused onto the photomultiplier tube will depend upon the horizontal rotation of the globe. After the voltage has been amplified from the output, it can be used as a measure of eye rotation. In a more sophisticated study, the difference in the diffuse reflectance of the iris and sclera is also recorded by a photomultiplier tube (Rashbass, 1960). The source of light in this case is, however, an oscilloscope spot, and the output of the photomultiplier tube is used to move this oscilloscope spot in such

a way that its image remains at the margin of the iris at all times, even in the presence of eye rotations. The amount of deflector voltage required to do this is a measure of the eye position and can be displayed on the vertical plates of a second cathode-ray oscilloscope, the horizontal plates of which display time.

Recording eye rotations free of translational shifts All of the methods outlined above have the common difficulty that they do not distinguish between rotations and translational shifts of the globe within the orbit.[3] To isolate the factor of eye rotation, Rashbass and Westheimer (1961a) employed two photocells to record the light reflected back from the eye as a scanning light was moved towards the nose from the sclera onto the cornea. During a single scan, the output of one cell undergoes a change when the image crosses from the sclera to the cornea and the output of the other detects the instant a specular reflection of the image from the cornea is formed exactly in its field of view. The time interval of the two changes in the summed output of the two cells is a measure of the rotational eye position. The time interval is isolated electronically, and a signal relative to eye position is produced. Translational shifts are about five times less likely to produce artifacts in the record than if the limbus position alone is recorded and about ten times less so than if the corneal reflex alone is used. The response is linear up to about 8°, but the records of much larger movements become quite nonlinear.

Cornsweet (1958) has devised a method which also avoids the difficulty of separating eye rotations from translations. A spot of light is focused on the retina and made to scan the optic nerve head repeatedly. The light reflected from this spot is focused on a photo-

[3] Translation moves both the retina (particularly the fovea) and the retinal image by the same amount, and therefore translation has little effect on the perception of objects at typical distances from the eye. Rotation, in contrast, moves the fovea with respect to the retinal image; this is what counts in producing visual movement.

multiplier tube connected to the vertical plates of a cathode-ray oscilloscope. The horizontal oscilloscope sweep is synchronized with the scanning spot. Each time the spot passes over a blood vessel on the optic nerve, a deflection appears on the oscilloscope. The distance between the beginning of the scan and this deflection measures the optical position of the retina with respect to a stationary external stimulus. Changes in this distance represent eye rotations.

Objective Methods with Attachments to the Eye

Early objective studies of eye movements involved attaching reflective devices of one sort or another to the eye. In more recent studies either a close-fitting, individually molded, scleral contact lens or a special suction cup cap (Yarbus, 1967) is used. Contact lenses will slip unless they fit very precisely; thus some recent investigators have attached a suction device to the lens so that a negative pressure up to 40 mm Hg holds the lens snugly on the eye. The amount the contact lens slips can be measured by methods outlined by Barlow (1963).

To measure eye rotation, an optical or electrical device must be attached to the contact lens or suction cup cap.

Mirror The reflective device with by far the slightest encumbrance is a small mirror imbedded in the contact lens (Ratliff & Riggs, 1950). A well-fitted lens of this kind can follow globe rotation with slippage of less than $\frac{1}{2}$ minute of arc for all small rotations of the eye (Riggs & Schick, 1968). A light beam can be reflected off the surface of this mirror and focused on a photographic plate or moving film. If the eye (and therefore the mirror) rotates through an angle θ, the light beam will rotate through an angle 2θ. Three mirrors may be employed—one for vertical, one for horizontal, and a third for torsional movements (Fender, 1955). Alternatively, a more elaborate data analysis method can be used in which both vertical and horizontal movements can

be inferred, using a single mirror (Nachmias, 1959).

Coil of wire Recently, experimenters have cemented about ten turns of fine wire in slots in the portion of the contact lens covering the sclera (Robinson, 1963). The subject is exposed to an alternating magnetic field, and the voltage generated in the coil of wire as the eye rotates can be recorded as a measure of the amount of eye rotation. With two uniform alternating magnetic fields, three d.c. voltages (respectively proportional to the horizontal, the vertical, and the torsional components of gaze) can be recorded simultaneously with a sensitivity of 15 seconds of arc.

Stabilizing the Retinal Image

A device which can measure eye movements can sometimes (with further modification) also be used to convert the information it provides about eye rotation into a form which allows the experimenter to control the objects viewed in such a way that they maintain a fixed relation to the rotations of the eye. One particularly informative relation (but by no means the only one) is to have the retinal image of the object move exactly with the eye so that, irrespective of how the eye rotates, the same small group of receptors is always stimulated. A retinal image that achieves this is said to be stabilized. If the output of the eye movement recorder is a voltage, the object being looked at must be one whose position can be made to be voltage-sensitive. A spot on a cathode-ray oscilloscope is one very useful object of this kind. If optical methods are being relied upon, the mirror on the contact lens which rotates with the eye can be used as part of the optical beam that presents the image to be viewed by the eye (Riggs et al., 1953). When this is done, the optical arrangement must provide a compensating path which corrects for the fact that as the eye rotates through an angle θ the light beam reflects through an angle 2θ. Ditchburn and Ginsborg

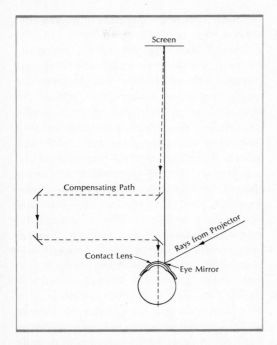

Figure 11.1. Diagram of the method for counteracting the effects of eye movements in order to stabilize the image on the retina. The viewing (compensating) path is effectively double the length of the projection path from the eye mirror to the screen. The compensating path includes an arrangement for providing fixation at the center of a bright annular field. (Riggs et al., 1953.)

(1952), Riggs & Ratliff (1952), Cornsweet (1956), Clowes and Ditchburn (1959), and Keesey (1960) have described various optical systems for achieving this result.

Figure 11.1 illustrates the method employed by Riggs et al. (1953). Light from the target is reflected off the mirror attached to the contact lens and focused on a screen coated with magnesium oxide. With the aid of the additional mirrors in the compensating path, the beam of light used by the eye in viewing this screen is effectively double the distance from the mirror on the contact lens to the screen. As the eye rotates through an angle θ the image on the screen moves through a distance 2θ. However the image, as viewed by the eye, appears to be twice as far away and hence moves only through an angle θ.

When the test object is viewed for an indefinitely long period, however, stabilization of the image produces a very curious phenomenon. The target borders gradually fade away until the entire object disappears; a temporary blindness takes place. First observed by Riggs and Ratliff (1952), Ditchburn and Ginsborg (1952), Riggs et al. (1953) and Yarbus (1957b), this effect has since been studied with many different targets by Pritchard, Heron, and Hebb (1960), and Yarbus (1967). The descriptions of the appearance of stabilized images vary widely with different investigators due, in part, to differences in the degree of stabilization achieved (Barlow, 1963) and in part to variations in the vividness and novelty of the stimulus field (Riggs & Schick, 1968; see also pp. 305–306.)

VARIETY OF EYE MOVEMENTS

Although eye movements can be classified in a number of different ways, the most meaningful classification is based on whether or not the relation of the lines of sight of the two eyes remains constant or changes during the movement. The first kind of movement is called a *version* (or a conjugate movement); the second is called a *vergence* (disjunctive movement).

Version Movements

Version movements are those in which the angle of intersection of the lines of sight of the two eyes remains constant during the movement. Even cursory examination of an eye movement record shows that they can clearly be divided into two types: saccadic movements and pursuit movements.

Saccadic movements During a saccadic eye movement, there is a sudden parallel change in the fixation of both eyes from one point in space to another. This movement can be studied most easily by instructing the subject to hold fixation point A and to shift fixation to a light (which is suddenly turned on at point B) the moment it appears. Westheimer (1954a) showed that the decision concerning the magnitude of the movement is taken before the movement begins and that the movement then follows an inevitable course. Rashbass (1961) found that small displacements of the fixation target less than 0.25° were not immediately followed by a saccade, and he interpreted this result as showing that there was a small dead zone in the error-correction system of the retina within which target displacements could not evoke a saccade. Cornsweet (1956), in contrast, found no such evidence, after studying the small "microsaccades" of steady fixation. Cornsweet found that whenever the eye drifted even a few minutes of arc away from some "optimal" position, the probability that a saccade in the correct direction would occur was significantly greater than if the eye were held exactly on the target. Whether or not these experimental results are contradictory depends upon the extent to which the "voluntary" saccades evoked by large displacements of the object being looked at utilize the same error-monitoring system as the "involuntary" microsaccades of steady fixation.

The latent period of a saccade varies between 180 and 250 msec, although smaller intervals of time than this have been obtained, especially when the subject has prior knowledge of the position of, and/or the moment when, the fixation light will be turned on. The longer values, measured while unpredictable stimuli are being used, are probably more meaningful estimates of the delay in tracking (Saslow, 1967).

The saccadic eye movement is very fast and lasts about $\frac{1}{10}$ of a second for a 40° saccade. Contrary to a popular misconception, the duration is itself a linearly increasing function of the amplitude, increasing about 2 msec for each degree of movement. The peak velocity of the eye also increases with the amplitude of the movement, and for a 90° movement may become as large as 830° per second.

Vision during saccadic movements
Whether or not one sees during an eye movement has long puzzled psychologists. For most kinds of eye movements it is easy enough to demonstrate very clear vision; but when the question is narrowed to "do we see during saccades?" it is more difficult to answer. If in a dark room a neon glow lamp flashing at 120 times a second is seen just nasal to a fixation point, it is seen as a steady, continuous light. If one makes a sudden change in fixation—a saccadic eye movement—to look at a point on the other side of the light, a whole string of interrupted lights are seen between the two fixation points. This shows that the retina is not "turned off" during the movement—that is, that under certain conditions we can see during a saccadic eye movement. How does it happen then that during everyday seeing in a normal environment the fuzzy streaking that the images of the visual world must evoke on the retina is not often noticed? One answer is that it takes time to see. The extremely high velocity of saccadic movements produces a situation in which the intensity of retinal excitation at any given point at any given moment is very weak. This is, however, by no means the whole answer. That this is so may be demonstrated by impressing an afterimage on your fovea and then observing it in the visual field as you move your eyes, say, during optokinetic nystagmus (see below). During the slow phase of the nystagmus the afterimage is clearly visible, but during the quick (saccadic) returns it is not.

Difficulty in carrying out quantitative experiments on the problem discussed above is created because there must be an accurate check on whether the eye is indeed executing a movement or whether it is pausing briefly during the movement. Moreover, we must distinguish between reduced vision due to some "inhibitory" effect of the eye and/or brain and the reduced vision produced by optical smear of the retinal image. Therefore, the target to be detected during the movement should not differ appreciably from that presented to the fixating eye in either sharpness, intensity, duration, or the region of the retina that it excites. This is readily achieved if light flashes of 20 to 50 μsec duration are produced using a system in which the eye movement itself triggers the flash. Using this method and three different visual tasks (flash detection, grating resolution, and word recognition) Volkmann (1962) found that, though vision was never "blanked out" when the eye was moving, thresholds were about three times as high as they were when the eye was not moving (see also p. 46.) The time course of this impairment was similarly studied by Latour (1962). He noted the percentage of flashes that were perceived at various time intervals before, during, and after

eye movement. His results are shown in Figure 11.2. Because his method does not permit us to stimulate exactly the same region of the retina before, during, and after the movement the generality of the results illustrated here is somewhat less than those obtained by Volkmann. Nevertheless, these results show as a first approximation the time course of the impairment in vision obtained when the eye shifts its gaze. Later experiments by Volkmann, Schick, and Riggs (1968) have served to confirm the phenomenon of visual inhibition and the time course followed by the process in relation to an eye movement.

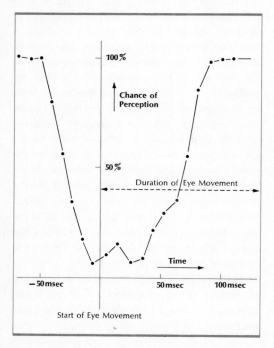

Figure 11.2. The percentage of flashes reported as seen when presented at various times before, during, and after the start of a rapid change of fixation between two lights. The test light is midway between two fixation lights that were alternately flashed on and off at an irregular rate. (Latour, 1962.)

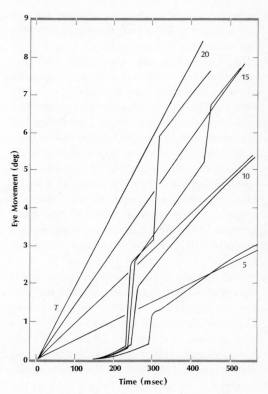

Figure 11.3. Eye movement responses to a smooth target motion of constant velocity of 5, 10, 15, and 20 degrees per second. Each response is the segmental mean of 10 responses of the most common type. The sloping straight lines (*T*) through the origin represent the target position; the other lines, eye position. (After Robinson, 1965.)

Pursuit movements When a subject is confronted with the task of holding his eyes on a moving target, the eyes do not behave in the same way as they do when a subject is required to shift his gaze from one fixed point in space to another. The simplest situation that can be presented is one in which the fixation point is made to start moving with an unpredictable (but constant) velocity in an unpredictable direction. Typical responses of the eyes to four different velocities of this kind of moving stimulus, measured by Robinson (1965), are illustrated in Figure 11.3. In this figure, the sloping straight lines passing through zero show the target position, the other lines indicate the eye position. For any given target velocity two obviously different eye velocities are discernible. A variety of evidence shows that the higher velocity movement is a saccade and has essentially the same characteristics as those in which the eyes shift gaze between two fixed points. The movements with the slower velocities are known as *pursuit movements*. Because of their slow velocity, they are also called *smooth movements* to distinguish them from the "jerky" saccades. Eye following of a given target is much more variable than is the case given a simple saccade between two fixed points. Thus, the illustrated responses are characteristic only of the majority of responses.

Variations occur not only in the moment during the smooth movement that the saccade is made but also in the amplitude as well as in the number of saccades. In a minority of responses, the velocity of the target and eyes will exactly match (provided the target velocity is smaller than 30° per second, according to Westheimer, 1954b); but in the typical response there is a velocity overshoot in the early part of the movement before the eye and target velocity become matched. This overshoot overcomes the viscous nature of the tissues supporting the globe so that the eye reaches its steady-state velocity much quicker than it would otherwise. The amount of this overshoot varies considerably, some of

the variation being related to target velocity. In Fig. 11.3 the velocity overshoot is pronounced at 5° per second but has disappeared at 15° per second. At 20° per second the eye is already approaching velocity saturation.

We have already seen that the stimulus for a saccade is target displacement. Rashbass (1961) found that the major stimulus for the smooth pursuit movement was a steadily moving target and that the pursuit movement maintains the image stationary on the retina irrespective of position errors. If the target is suddenly shifted in one direction and then begins moving with uniform velocity in the opposite direction, a slow smooth pursuit movement can be induced which does not have any saccade superimposed upon it. Robinson (1965) found that the optimal conditions for this effect occur when the displacement (in degrees) is 0.15 to 0.2 times the uniform velocity (in degrees per second). A displacement of this sort is called a *step-ramp*. It evokes a pure smooth pursuit movement uninterrupted by any saccades. The remarkable feature of such a movement is that, as the eye commences its response to the target *velocity*, it moves away from the *position* the target occupied when the eye began its response. This shows that pursuit movements are elicited by target velocity rather than by target position. The pursuit movements in this experiment do, however, match the positions of the eye and target at some finite time after the eyes begin moving. Otherwise a saccade occurs. The latency of a response to a step-ramp—151 ± 19 msec—is considerably longer than that of a response in which no displacement has occurred, proving that the step displacement has been detected.

Independence of pursuit and tracking movements Are saccades and smooth tracking movements different modes of action of the same neurological apparatus or are different pathways involved? Although we know nothing of the details of the connections in the nervous system that regulate these two kinds of movement, a growing body of in-direct evidence suggests that the pathways are quite independent. We have already seen that the stimuli that produce each type of movement are different. Furthermore, electro-myography of the eye muscles shows that the electrophysiological characteristics of the muscle responses are easily distinguishable. Thus to make a saccade, the globe is rotated by a high-frequency burst in the agonist muscle and complete inhibition of firing in the antagonist muscle. However to make a smooth pursuit movement the eye is rotated by high-frequency bursts in both agonist and antagonist muscles; there is only a slight difference in the tension in these two muscles as they rotate the globe. In addition, the saccade has a longer latent period than does the pursuit movement. A saccade might occur in the absence of a stimulus, but a pursuit movement usually does not (Yarbus, 1967). Also the peak velocity of the eye during a saccade is some 50 times greater than that during a pursuit movement.

Many of the distinctions between saccades and tracking movements can be characterized by the statement that a saccade is ballistic while the tracking movements are what Stet-son and McDill (1923) and Hartson (1939) called *slow tension movements*. A ballistic movement acts as a discrete sampled data system, that is, one in which error-detecting activities are carried out at intervals that are interspersed by periods of insensitivity during which no error-detecting activity is carried out.

Westheimer (1954b) has described an ex-periment in which a target is moved to one side and then back to its original position after, say, 40 msec. The eye responds by making a following saccade at 200 msec, de-spite the fact that the movement is at that time wholly inappropriate and takes the eye away from the target. This first movement is then followed 200 msec later by a return to the starting point. The fact that the duration of the inappropriate eye fixation is precisely the duration of the reaction time and not the

appreciably shorter duration of the pulse ar-gues for a sampled data system and not for one in which commands for saccades, once initiated, cannot be canceled. Wheeless, Boynton, and Cohen (1966) have obtained a less clear-cut result when they varied the duration of the pulse. The fact that reaction times to steps in their experiments were sig-nificantly longer than for the pulses suggests their subjects were not tracking normally.

How do pursuit movements behave in the analogous situation? Robinson (1965) varied the time interval between step target dis-placements in two successive step-ramps, either 150, 100, or 75 msec apart. The re-sponses in each case consisted of two distinct smooth pursuit movements which, although delayed in time by the latency, were spaced from each other by 150, 100, and 75 msec respectively, thus indicating that there is no interval in data sampling longer than 75 msec. Smaller intervals produce such small eye movements that the records are not easy to interpret. If smooth pursuit movement is based on a sampled system, it must be one that samples at a rate greater than 13 times per second. Clearly, the simplest hypothesis is that sampling made by a system producing pursuit movements is continuous. In this re-spect it resembles the accommodation and the fusional vergence systems of the eye.

The difference between saccadic and smooth pursuit movements is clearly brought out by altering the normal relationship be-tween eye rotation and the movement of images across the retina. Riggs and Tulunay (1959), Fender and Nye (1961) and Robinson (1965) have developed methods for doing this. Robinson started with a stabilized retinal image, that is, an image that moves with the eye as the eye rotates. (This is the "open loop" case in which any given rotation of the eye results in a corresponding displacement of the retinal image so that no motion occurs be-tween image and receptors.) He used a small point as an image and aimed it at the center of the fovea. Thus, there was little need for a corrective saccade to occur (Cornsweet,

1956). Then the experimenter upset this situation by displacing the image 2° at a time to one side of the fovea. This displacement caused a series of 2° saccades as the subject attempted to catch up with the target as it receded from him as rapidly as he pursued it. This Tantalus-like target motion will lead the subject's eye, in its vain pursuit, right off the edge of the projection screen.

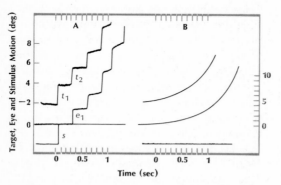

Figure 11.4. The eye movements obtained under positive visual feedback so that the position of the target outpaces the eye position. In each figure, the bottom trace represents the position of the stimulus, controlled by the experimenter; the middle trace represents the eye position; and the top trace represents the position of the target with respect to the eye. In part A the eye is at position zero (fixating on stimulus target) until the moment when the experimenter quickly displaces the stimulus by 2° as shown at s. This causes a corresponding 2° shift t_1 in the position of the target with respect to the center of fixation. Thus t_1 is followed, after a reaction time of about .25 sec, by a saccade e_1, which feeds into the target a displacement t_2 that is slightly larger than e_1 and so on, each eye movement pursuing a target displacement following a reaction time such as is expected in a discrete sampling control system. Part B shows the smooth pursuit system responding by itself to this vain chase when the initial retinal disparity is so small that no saccade is stimulated. Note that the behavior is like a continuous control system with slight positive feedback. The eye movements have a smooth, growing time course with no detectable discrete velocity changes. (Data from Robinson, 1965.)

When the saccadic system engages in this vain pursuit, the result is a staircase pattern of eye movements such as that given in Figure 11.4A, taken from an experiment made by Robinson (1965). This result is typical of a sampled data system.

In the case illustrated in Figure 11.4A, the retinal image was made to move just slightly so that the target not only just kept up with the eye (as with a stabilized image) but actually outpaced it slightly, resulting in the simultaneous development of a growing pursuit velocity between the successive saccades. Figure 11.4B shows how the smooth system by itself responds to this vain chase when the initial retinal disparity is less than 0.1° so that the saccadic system is not stimulated. You can experience a somewhat analogous effect by first producing an afterimage which is just slightly eccentric to the fovea, and then attempting to fixate on it. Thus, Figure 11.4B demonstrates that the smooth pursuit system alone appears to behave like a continuous control system, and under these experimental conditions produces a smooth growing time course with no detectable discrete velocity changes.

There is, moreover, good evidence from experiments made using various drugs that the neural control mechanisms of pursuit and saccadic eye movements are independent. Rashbass (1961) found that barbiturate intoxication produces a pronounced dissociation

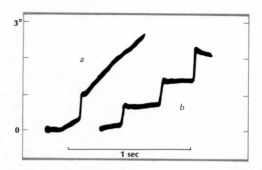

Figure 11.5. Tracking eye movement responses to a target moving with constant velocity (a) before and (b) after administration of a mild barbiturate. (Data from Rashbass, 1961.)

of these two kinds of movements. Figure 11.5 shows eye movements made while tracking a target moving with uniform velocity (3.5° per second) before and after the intravenous administration of sodium thiopentone. The first noticeable effect the drug had was to cause an increase in the number of saccadic movements that occur during the first second of tracking. As the effect of drug increased, the frequency of saccades increased at the expense of smooth movements, until after 8 minutes no smooth tracking could be detected. Similar degradations show if the eye is made to track targets moving sinusoidally after sodium thiopentone has been given to a subject. The behavior of the eye while a subject is tracking sinusoidally moving targets under the influence of barbiturates is very similar to the effect observed when patients with a disease known as myotonic dystrophy try to undertake this task (von Noorden, Thompson, & Van Allen, 1964).

The version movements of the eye that we have just considered result from stimuli that can be presented to the retina of one eye alone. A large variety of animals—even those with eyes on the sides of the head and, consequently, with visual fields that do not overlap—probably display the same kinds of movement, although experimental analysis of versions by behavioral methods on animals is a largely untapped field. Versions have the same characteristics whether one eye is occluded or both are open. There is no change in the angle that the lines of sight make with each other during the course of the movement.

Vergence Movements

In higher primates including man, the eyes, of course, have migrated to the front of the head and the visual fields of the two eyes overlap. One consequence of this is that a second variety of eye movement is required (vergences) to help keep both eyes fixed on the same object. That the vergence system works under normal circumstances can be demonstrated by pressing on one eye through the lower eyelid. If you manage to keep both eyes open, you will have double vision—diplopia—because the eyeball you are pressing on is shifted and the objects in the visual field that stimulate the foveas of the two eyes (as well as other "corresponding retinal points") are different. The technical way of describing this state of affairs is to say that the egocentric localizations of the visual fields of the two eyes differ.

Considering the large variety of factors that can influence the direction in which each eye is pointing, it would be surprising if with only the version system functioning the lines of sight of both eyes exactly intersected at the object being looked at. Moreover, even if by chance the lines of sight did coincide at a given distance from the eye when only the version system was operating, it should be evident that the lines of sight could not then coincide for objects either nearer to or farther away from the observer. To deal with these changing situations, the vergence system has evolved, according to which the angles that the lines of sight make with each other change during the movement. If you look at a pencil and then move it nearer and nearer to your nose along an extension of the median (saggital) body plane, the eyes converge. As you move the pencil away from you, your eyes diverge. (See also pp. 297, 482–494.)

Binocular coordination Clearly then, in ordinary viewing, not only is the globe rotated to point its most sensitive central cones at different parts of the visual field in rapid succession, but the rotations of the two globes are exquisitely synchronized. The neurophysiological investigations of the basis of such control have not yet been carried out in detail, but we know that a muscle, or muscle group, of one eye is "yoked" together with a corresponding muscle, or muscle group, of the other eye; and in any given yoked pair the innervations are always such that the two eyes respond precisely together and to the same extent. In the case of a version, as we have already seen, a simple movement of both eyes to the right, for example, will occur even when one eye is covered. The uncovered eye, after a short latent period, moves quickly to the right to take up its new fixation point, but the eye under the cover moves after the identical latent period just as quickly—and exactly the same amount—as if it too were seeing.

Movement to the right is a result of contraction of both the lateral rectus of the right eye and the medial rectus of the left. This is one example of a yoked muscle pair. In a convergence movement, on the other hand, the yoked muscle pair is the medial rectus of each eye. Thus, depending on the movement, a given muscle can be yoked to either of two muscles of the other eye which are themselves antagonistic. The point is the two

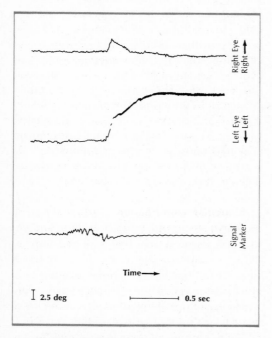

Figure 11.6. Record of the eye movements (by electro-oculography) obtained in binocular fixation from a distant target to one 20 cm from the eye. The near target was carefully aligned on the line of sight of the right eye monocularly. Note that both eyes make two paired movements, a rapid shift to the right and slow convergence onto the target. (Data from Alpern & Ellen, 1956.)

eyes move together. In fact, it is very difficult (but not impossible) to arrange conditions in such a way that only one eye moves, even when that would be the simplest (and most efficient) consequence. For example, close the left eye and bring a near object like the tip of a pencil along the line of sight of the right eye, fixating a distant object. Open the left eye and fixate the distant object binocularly. Since the pencil tip is already along the line of sight of the right eye, it is evident that in order now to shift binocular fixation onto the pencil tip only the left eye needs to move. In fact, it is impossible to shift binocular gaze from the distant to the near object without moving both eyes together.

The movement of the eyes from the distant object to the pencil tip is broken into two parts: a rapid shift of gaze of both eyes to the right (in which the medial rectus of the left eye is yoked to the lateral rectus of the right) and a somewhat slower convergence movement (in which the two medial rectus muscles are yoked together). Because of the differences of time characteristic in the two components, recordings of eye movements during such an experiment clearly reveal this phenomenon (Alpern & Ellen, 1956; Westheimer & Mitchell, 1956; Riggs & Niehl, 1960). Figure 11.6 illustrates a typical record. The bottom line is from a voice microphone, and the irregular deflections on it are caused by the verbal command to look from the far to the near target. The two upper records are of the left (middle line) and right eye. The amplitude of the movement of the right eye is a little less than half of that of the left eye in this record, probably because both component movements begin simultaneously so that for the right eye a fraction of the movement is neutralized even before it can occur. For the left eye (which turns continuously to the right) the two components add together, of course, so that both components are revealed in their entirety.

The details of the control system that allows our eyes to move in this way have not yet been worked out. One theory holds that the eye muscles themselves have two varieties of subunits: slow fibers (perhaps under control of the autonomic nervous system) that are responsible for the vergence, and faster twitch fibers responsible for versions, including the extremely rapid saccades.

Varieties of vergence movements Convergence and divergence are only two examples of vergence movements. Because the eyes may be slightly misaligned by nature, either vertically or with the vertical meridian of one eye not parallel with that of the other, vergence systems exist to correct for both of these kinds of misalignment. (We will say no more about them, but the interested reader will find a thorough discussion of them in Alpern [1962].) The more usual misalignments are those in the horizontal plane.

Insofar as it is now known, the various vergence movements do not differ from one another in time characteristics, for the reaction times of all are about 160 msec. The eyes very quickly achieve maximum velocity and then asymptotically settle into their new positions. The total duration of the movement may be as long as 0.8 to 1.6 sec. The maximum velocity is a simple, linearly increasing function of the amplitude of the movement. Velocities of the order of 20° per second have been reported for movements of 6.6°.

In terms of the absolute value of its velocity, a vergence movement resembles the pursuit movement. However in terms of the way its velocity changes with movement amplitude, it more nearly resembles saccadic eye movements.

Horizontal vergence movements may occur under various conditions. *Fusional* vergences are movements that result when there is a disparity in the egocentric localization of the visual fields of the two eyes with respect to each other. We have already seen that they are nature's way of compensating for minor misalignments of the line of sight of one eye compared to that of its fellow. *Accommodative* vergence is the vergence movement associated with a change in the accommodative

response of the eyes. If you cover one eye and focus sharply on a pencil point as it is brought in along the line of sight of the uncovered eye, the eye underneath the cover converges more and more as the accommodation increases. In addition, vergence movements seem to be evoked by a variety of stimulus variables, including how close the target is to the eyes (independent of changes in accommodation) and to what extent we can evoke "an illusion of nearness" with the target. (This latter may include a number of still poorly defined stimulus parameters, including—among others—familiar, actual, and perceived size.)

Most quantitative data about vergence movements have been obtained on fusional vergence and on accommodative vergence. Rashbass and Westheimer (1961a) have studied horizontal fusional movements under normal viewing conditions as well as under those in which, despite the movements, the disparity in egocentric localization of the two eyes remained fixed. They found that fusional movements are another example of a continuous data sampling process. The movements can be altered during their progress, and information about disparity is continuously sampled during the reaction time as well as during the movements. When the apparatus was arranged in such a way that the movements had no influence on target disparity, any fixed disparity evoked movements that maintained a constant velocity. The velocity was dependent on the amplitude of the disparity. When measuring the phase relation between a sine wave disparity and the movements it evokes, it was found that the control system makes some estimate of what future disparity is to be and that rate of change of disparity is one important factor in this estimate.

Accommodative vergences are related not only to the changes in accommodation of the eyes but also to constriction of the pupil. These three phenomena comprise the *near-focus response*. It is caused principally by changes in the accommodation stimulus, but changes in accommodation response, uncorrelated with changes in the stimulus causing the accommodation, also produce accommodative vergence changes as well as (presumably) pupil size changes.

A variety of evidence supports the view that there are linear relations among the innervations of the accommodation response, the eye rotation, and the pupil constriction. The rate of change of accommodative vergence with a unit of change in accommodation response (within the range where these two are linearly related) is known as AC/A (that is, the ratio of the accommodative convergence to accommodation). AC/A is a quantitative description of the near response of any given individual, which is remarkably stable and insensitive to change either because of age, practice, or drugs (alcohol, amphetamine, and barbiturates are exceptions to this rule) but which is quite different in one individual compared to another. AC/A seems to be correlated with success (or failure) in a variety of different occupations from electronic and camera assemblers to telephone typists and baseball pitchers (Davis & Jobe, 1957). We know nothing about the factors responsible for individual differences in AC/A.

Reflex Movements

In discussing eye movements so far we have made the implicit assumption that the bony structures to which the other ends of the eye muscles are attached remained rigidly fixed with respect to the body and to gravity. In fact, almost all the data described were obtained in a laboratory arrangement designed to hold head and body perfectly still. The best way of doing this is to make impressions of the subject's forehead and teeth in dental wax, and then mount these impressions on a rigid frame to which the subject may be fitted during the experiment. Because in everyday life the head and body move freely about, the characteristics of eye movements discussed above have to be put in the framework of this movement.

Two distinctly different patterns of behavior should be distinguished. In the first, both head and eyes move to pick up the fixation of a new object of regard; the angular distance between the old and the new fixation points is covered partly by the head and partly by the eyes. In contrast, the eyes can move in a direction opposite to that the head may be taking to maintain fixation on one and the same object during the course of the head displacements. In the first kind of movement, the head (as well as the eye) movement is directed by the visual feedback from the retina, but the second kind of eye movement is directed, at least in part, by signals initiated elsewhere in the body. To study these latter kinds of eye movement best in the laboratory, the psychologist may find it appropriate to eliminate all visual feedback by performing the experiments in the dark (or with both eyes tightly patched); just as to study eye movements discussed until now it was convenient to hold the head and body fixed with a forehead rest and biting board. Movements of the eyes which can occur in the absence of retinal feedback have been classified in the literature under the name "reflex" (though we exclude from this category eye movements initiated by "voluntary" events, such as verbal commands, however difficult they may be to define operationally). You should remember that while we are seeing under ordinary circumstances these reflex movements are carried on simultaneously with—indeed, superimposed on—eye movements associated by a variety of signals arising in the retinas.

The end organs that are sensitive to movements of the head from verticality are the hair cells in the macula of the saccule and utricle of the vestibular apparatus of the inner ear. These hair cells have small cilia (steriocilia) projecting into the otoliths (literally "ear stones"—in fact, small crystals of calcium carbonate). Under the influence of changes in position of the head with respect to the earth's gravitational field, the otoliths bend the steriocilia and stimulate the hair cells. Such excitation of the hair cells results in reflex deviation of the eyes. For example, flexing the neck back so that the face points to the sky moves the eyes down. Tilting the head so that the right ear is on the right shoulder causes the right eye to move up higher than the left and to rotate around its line of sight so that the top of the vertical meridian of the cornea moves toward the nose while the left eye rotates so that the top of its vertical corneal meridian moves temporally. In each case, the eye movements tend to maintain the eyeball in the *status quo ante*.

Although the otoliths may of themselves produce these movements, they are by no means uniquely essential. Evidence suggests that stimulation of the proprioceptor end organs in the muscles of the head, neck, and body also produces such effects.

The reflex eye movements are among the most important sources of oculomotor adjustments in lower vertebrates, particularly teleosts. In higher vertebrates they become less and less so as the variety of visual behavior expands. The basic patterns remain, but they become overlaid by the more complicated visually evoked responses already described.

The statokinetic oculomotor reflexes are initiated by the hair cells in the crista ampullaris of the three (on each side) semicircular canals (Magnus, 1924). These cells respond to shearing forces induced by angular acceleration of the head. The oculomotor response, like those induced by stimulation of the utricle and saccule, tends to maintain the eyeball in the *status quo ante*. The easiest way of stimulating hair cells in the crista is to produce a pressure differential in the two halves of a given set of semicircular canals by rotating the head with an angular acceleration about an axis perpendicular to the plane of those canals. During the time that the head is accelerated, the eyes move slowly in the opposite direction to the rotation of the head. When, however, the eyes reach the extreme limit of the field of fixation, they make a quick return to the front before resuming once

more the slow rotation in the direction opposite to the head. Thus, a sequence of rhythmical slow and fast eye movements (known as *nystagmus*) is initiated. If the head is abruptly stopped, shearing forces on the hair cells of the crista in the opposite direction persist for several seconds, even minutes. These cause an after-nystagmus which is opposite in direction to that obtained during the rotation. We specify the direction of the nystagmus by the direction of its quick phase (because when looking at the eyes the saccade is much easier to identify). The rotation nystagmus therefore is in the same direction, the after-nystagmus in the opposite direction, to that of the rotation of the head.

There are a number of ways to produce shearing forces in one or the other of the cristae. A chair which rotates around an axis normal to the floor is commonly used to demonstrate the effect. The subject sits in the chair with his head tilted so that this axis is also normal to the plane of one of the three sets of semicircular canals. By suitable tilting of the head either a horizontal, a vertical, or a rotational nystagmus can easily be produced. Another method consists of placing the head in a position such that the plane of one set of canals is vertical and then injecting cold water into one of the auditory canals. This sets up convection currents (which produce shearing forces mainly, if not exclusively, in the canal in the vertical position) and hence nystagmus.

Although observation of nystagmus is the most common way we study eye responses to stimulation of semicircular canals in the laboratory or in the clinic, nystagmus is rarely found in daily use of the eyes by healthy, normal people. Most accelerations to which the head is subject in the everyday world produce only mild and short duration shearing forces in the crista ampullaris compared to those used to obtain the nystagmus in the laboratory. To these, a slow adjustment of the eyes is the only oculomotor response that is made to semicircular canal excitation.

The majority of the population probably never experiences any very severe accelerations unless they deliberately rotate themselves in a parlor game, although the high-speed complexity of modern life makes this statement apply to an ever-decreasing percentage of the population. As interplanetary travel becomes habitual and the associated severe acceleration to which the head and body must be subjected to transcend the earth's gravitational field becomes commonplace, the experiences of future generations in this respect are going to be quite different from our own. We know virtually nothing about how this repeated and rather severe excitation of these reflex mechanisms may influence the more usual variety of oculomotor performance. We might profitably undertake an investigation of this question by an exhaustive analysis of the characteristics of the eye movements of professional ice skaters or others whose work involves severe acceleration forces applied to the head.

EYE MOVEMENTS AND SEEING IN THE FIELD

We have now analyzed in various, quite artificial laboratory situations the repertoire of eye movements used in carrying on the ordinary work of the world. Naturally, we do not make these various movements in isolation as they have been studied in the laboratory. All of them—vergences and versions, reflex and retinal-induced responses—are intermingled. To analyze how this is done, let us look in some detail at the behavior of the eyes in three very simple tasks which become, however, progressively more complex.

Steady Fixation

You might expect that the simplest of all visual tasks is to maintain fixation on a single point. In fact, it is found that even if you try as hard as you can, it is impossible to maintain the eyes perfectly motionless. During even the steadiest of fixations, the eyes are constantly making extremely fine movements

known collectively as *physiological nystagmus*. Our best measurements of physiological nystagmus have been made with a mirror mounted on a very tight-fitting contact lens. A light beam reflected off the mirror can be photographed for study of movements in the horizontal plane (Ratliff & Riggs, 1950), or by a bit more elaboration of the optics (and more sophisticated treatment of the data) both horizontal and vertical measurements may be obtained (Nachmias, 1959).

Physiological nystagmus is composed of three different kinds of movement, two of which may be only miniature replications of the varieties of version movement already described. The third, only poorly understood, is quite unique to physiological nystagmus. This is a high-frequency tremor having a median amplitude of about 17 seconds of arc. Frequencies from below 30 to above 100 cycles have been reported by various authors, and amplitudes have ranged from near zero to above 1 minute of arc. The other two varieties of movements are: (1) slow drifts occurring in an amplitude range of about 5 minutes of arc and having an average velocity of 1 minute per second, and (2) rapid binocu-

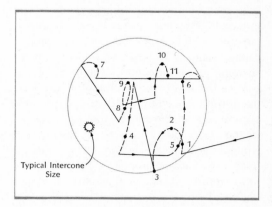

Figure 11.7. Movement of the image of a point object on the retina. The large circle has a radius of 5 minutes of arc. Slow drifts are represented by the dotted, saccades by the solid, lines. The numbered dots indicate the order in which movements are made and are spaced at equal time intervals of $\frac{1}{5}$ of a second. (Ditchburn, 1955.)

lar flicks (or saccades) from 1 to 20 minutes in amplitude, which have a velocity of about 10° per second and occur rather unpredictably. It has been suggested (Cornsweet, 1956) that the saccades act to correct for the drifts which deviate the eyes from some optimum position of fixation. Nachmias (1959) concludes that not only the saccades, but in some degree the drifts as well, serve a corrective function.

The way the drifts and saccades influence the position of the retinal image of a point is illustrated schematically in Figure 11.7, which is due to Ditchburn (1955). The tremor disturbance corresponds to a movement of about 1 to 3 μ on the retina or about the dimension of a single foveal cone (these, however, are not shown in Figure 11.7). The large circle has a radius of about 5 minutes of arc. The dotted lines represent the slow drifts; the solid lines, the rapid saccades. The numbered dots indicate the order in which movements are made and are spaced at equal time intervals 0.2 second apart. On this occasion, all the movements are within the 5-minute radius circle, but records made over longer periods would reveal movements confined to a circle about twice this size. The area, which includes the position of the eye during about 50 percent of the time, is typically an ellipse with a major (horizontal) diameter of around 10 minutes of arc.

It has been suggested that physiological nystagmus plays an important role in improving visual acuity. This appears not to be the case. Ratliff (1952) measured visual acuity during various stages of eye movements, recording the latter with a mirror on a contact lens. Drifts greater than 20 seconds of arc he found were a hindrance, rather than a help, to visual acuity. Keesey (1960) made a systematic study of various forms of visual acuity, comparing the stabilized image condition (see p. 374) with the normal viewing condition in which the physiological nystagmus movements were present. Similar results were obtained in the presence or absence of such movements. These observations strongly sug-

gest that physiological nystagmus plays no role in improving visual acuity (see p. 306).

The brief discussion above shows that the normal movements of physiological nystagmus, although they do not improve visual acuity, have an important function in the visual perception of form. The details of this function and the experiments that relate to them are more appropriately discussed in the chapter on visual perception. For the present, it will suffice to say that continued vision of high-contrast visual forms under steady fixation can occur only because of the eye movements of physiological nystagmus.

Shifts of Gaze

The second degree of complexity in the everyday use of the eyes that we discuss is a simple shift of gaze from an object in one part of the visual field to that in another. If the two points are at the same distance from the observer but have different visual directions, the movement comprises a simple saccade; if the two points have a common visual direction but are at different distances, the movement is a simple vergence movement. What happens if the two points have neither a common visual direction nor a common distance from the observer? The answer seems to be quite simply that the two movements seem to go on virtually simultaneously and apparently quite independently. This kind of movement was studied by Yarbus (1957a, 1967) and by Riggs and Niehl (1960). Because the saccadic movement has a velocity about 20 times that of the vergence movement, it is easy to follow the two kinds of movement even in a single shift of gaze. Yarbus found that the vergence change began a bit sooner and that about 20 percent of the vergence is completed before the saccade appears. During the saccade, the vergence change continues unabated; but, because of the difference in velocity of the saccade and of the vergence, only about 6.5 percent of the vergence is completed between the beginning and the end of the saccadic movement. At the end of a single saccade, the entire shift in visual direction has been achieved and the movement is completed by the unabated continuation of the remaining 73.5 percent of the vergence change. The same basic pattern is found whether one shifts from a far to a near object or in the opposite direction.

Yarbus' study shows a clear separation in the pattern of response of the vergence and version mechanisms when the latter is a simple saccade. Does this same independence persist when the version is a pursuit movement? Rashbass and Westheimer (1961b) asked this question and answered it by recording both the version (tracking) and vergence responses as the stimulus for each was independently manipulated. Both sine wave and square wave stimulus presentations were made. They found that the mean eye position

follows the mean target position according to the characteristics of visual tracking and, simultaneously, the eye vergence response follows the target vergence according to the characteristics of vergence movements. No interaction between the mechanisms was observed. Each can accept and respond to stimuli irrespective of whether the other is being stimulated, is preparing to respond, is

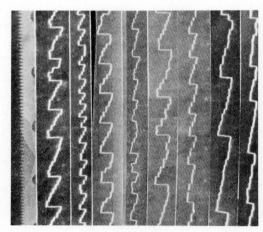

Figure 11.9. Actual photographic records of eye movements obtained by Dearborn (1906). The records are to be read upwards. The short, heavy vertical lines are the fixations, and the lighter oblique lines (almost horizontal) are saccadic eye movements, the long ones to the left carrying the eye from the end of one line to the beginning of the next, and the little ones to the right carrying it from point to point in the reading of a line. Regressive movements can be seen in most of the records.

The records are from four educated adults who differed greatly in reading speed. Each subject is represented by two records, the first from reading material printed in long lines and the second from his reading short newspaper lines. In reading newspaper lines, the complete records, when measured, give the following averages:

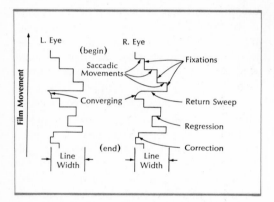

Figure 11.8. Schematic representation of the record of eye movements obtained during reading. Because the film moves upward, the record progresses downward. The length of the vertical lines gives the duration of fixations; that of the horizontal lines, the extent of lateral eye movements. Beginning at the top, the record shows four fixations and three saccadic movements in reading the first line of print. The eyes diverge slightly during the first return sweep and slowly converge to the correct position at the beginning of the second line. There is a regressive movement along this line. The return sweep onto the third line failed to bring the beginning of that line into clear view, and so a corrective movement occurs there. The record was cut off after the next fixation.

Subject	Fixations per line	Average duration of a fixation (msec)
1	3.8	161
2	3.9	216
3	5.5	255
4	5.4	402

responding, or is suffering overload. All target movements were resolved into a vergence and a side-to-side component even when a resolution into right and left eye components would be simpler. This last observation of Rashbass and Westheimer not only confirms the inference we drew from the results illustrated in Figure 11.6 but extends its generality to visual tracking behavior as well.

Eye Movements During Reading

We conclude the discussion of eye movements by considering an even more complex task, namely reading. Now, no doubt, many students may find this, too, much too simple a task. They are interested in much more complicated questions: What do the quarterback's eye movements tell his opponents about the plan of the forthcoming play? How do a guilty man's eye movement responses to incriminating questions differ from those to innocent questions? What characterizes the eye movements to the view of an attractive advertising display as distinct from an ordinary one? And so on. The answers to questions of this sort for the most part still need to be worked out.

The characteristics of eye movements during reading were studied extensively in the first part of the twentieth century (very little new information has been added in the last twenty years). Consequently, previous editions of this text covered this subject more extensively, and those who desire to study the subject in detail should consult them. What follows is an abbreviated summary of this work.

Javal (1879) noted that reading did not consist of smooth tracking of successive rows of letters one after the other. On the contrary, he found that the eyes executed a series of saccadic jumps interspersed by fixations at several different points along each line. These movements have now been extensively studied by photography, using the ophthalmograph. A schematic ophthalmograph record is illustrated in Figure 11.8, which emphasizes certain features. Once the reader is familiar with the phenomena illustrated and explained there, he can find them in the actual records. For example, Figure 11.9 includes several records made by Dearborn over sixty years ago from one eye. They are thus monocular, but because the two eyes work so closely together binocular records would not be very much more informative. Almost all of the features shown in the schematic record can be found in several of Dearborn's photo-

TABLE 11.1   EYE MOVEMENTS IN READING, ACCORDING TO SCHOOL GRADE[a]

School grade	Fixations per line of print	Mean duration of fixation (msec)	Regressive movements per line
I B	18.6	660	5.1
I A	15.5	432	4.0
II	10.7	364	2.3
III	8.9	316	1.8
IV	7.3	268	1.4
V	6.9	252	1.3
VI	7.3	236	1.6
VII	6.8	240	1.5
High school I	7.2	244	1.0
High school II	5.8	248	0.7
High school III	5.5	224	0.7
High school IV	6.4	248	0.7
College	5.9	252	0.5

[a] A sample of 8 to 19 children from each grade, of about medium reading ability, had their eyes photographed while reading, and the mean for each grade is given. From Buswell (1922).

graphs. The average reader shows pretty good coordination of his eyes. They follow the horizontal line pretty well with little vertical movement.

Development of Reading Skill

Reading is a complex skill, and like all skills it develops gradually, improving in both precision and speed. Pencil and paper tests are useful in measuring progress, but eye movement records are of value in analyzing the details of what is happening. By comparing samples of students at various grade levels (see Table 11.1) we see that improvement is made in three ways. In the first place, there is a steady decrease in the number of fixations per line. This holds true even though the reading material increases in difficulty at each grade. Thus, the college student is taking in at least three times as much reading matter per fixation as is the beginning reader. Second, the fixations grow shorter as academic level increases; the advanced reader takes in the material faster. Finally, there is a very marked decrease in regressive movements. This means greater regularity in progressing along the lines of print. It is natural to conclude that the ideal reader would have no regressive movements. Actually, a few regressive movements show that the reader is alert to what he is reading, that he goes back to clear up an obscurity (Buswell, 1937; Bayle, 1942). Sometimes the regressive movement should be blamed on the author rather than on the reader!

Fixations

All reading is done during the fixation pauses, for there is no clear-cut vision during the intervening saccadic movements. Thus, the number and duration of the fixation pauses are two indexes frequently used by psychologists to appraise the quality of reading performance. However, it should always be kept in mind that these are by no means the only relevant variables. The nature of the reading material, as well as the kind of reading the subject ordinarily does, is also important. There is no single rate or style of reading that is appropriate to all types of reading material. The really good reader is the one who adjusts his speed and, indeed, his whole pattern of reading to that required by whatever reading material he is reading at the moment.

The duration of the fixations, as distinguished from their number, is not closely dependent on the difficulty of the material, at least as far as the mode is concerned (Buswell, 1922; Robinson, 1933). Good college freshmen will average around 210 msec, whereas their slower classmates run around 260 msec (Walker, 1933; Anderson, 1937). These fixations are considerably longer than the exposure needed for perception of dots or letters; the usual tachistoscopic exposure is about 100 msec, depending on the illuminance. All of these facts may suggest that the number and duration of fixations, and hence the speed of reading, are limited by central—rather than by peripheral—factors; that is, the subject moves his eyes only as fast as he can absorb the material.

The saccadic movements themselves take very little of the total time. They average around 22 msec for the short jumps and 40 msec for the return sweeps. If we read a line of print with four fixations, there will be three short jumps and one long return, totaling about 100 msec of actual movement. The four fixations will total about 900 msec, indicating that about 90 percent of the total reading time is spent in fixation pauses (Dearborn, 1906; Schmidt, 1917). During slower reading, with longer pauses and larger numbers of pauses per line, the total fixation time may be as high as 95 percent (Tinker, 1936). A poor reader may also fail to progress evenly across the line and down the page; he may exhibit irregular and frequent returns to portions of the material that have already been read. As a matter of fact, the perceptual processes may well be going on during the saccadic movements; we may remember that retinal stimulation is typically discontinuous and is not effective with the moving eye. Reading, in contrast, may well be a continuous process in that the perceptual development of meaning goes on steadily. Perhaps we can think of it as a continuous production process, a machine into which the raw material is tossed by the shovelful. The output will be continuous as long as there is some raw material in the works. This analogy has another similarity to reading—the rate of input will usually be limited by the rate at which the machine processes the raw material. In a similar fashion, the eye movements adjust to the rate at which the subject is digesting the sensory input. The most efficient reader, in short, is the one who can execute the largest number of fixation pauses per minute and the smallest number per line of print.

ACCOMMODATION

The effector mechanisms so far discussed involved the *extraocular* muscles. There are two systems of effector mechanisms related to the *intraocular* muscles: *accommodation,* brought about by contraction of the ciliary muscle, and changes in *pupil* size brought about by changes in the length of the iris muscles.

The eye, like any optical system, can only be sharply focused at one given distance at any given moment of time. Objects at other distances give rise to greater or lesser degrees of defocused images, depending upon how far they are from the plane of sharp focus and (among other things) on the width of the pupil. The eye has a rather remarkable ability to shift its plane of sharp focus by increasing (or decreasing) its refracting power. It does this quickly by changing the length of the ciliary muscle (a band of smooth muscle—capable of graded contractions—which completely surrounds the lens). Contraction of the ciliary muscle relaxes the tensions on the connective tissue fibers that support the lens, and the lens substance becomes molded by its elastic capsule to assume a more convex, that is more highly refracting form (see the diagram of the eye in Figure 9.5). When the

eye is looking at an object far away, the ciliary muscle is relaxed, supporting fibers are taut, and the lens has a less convex spherical shape and therefore a decreased refracting power for the eye as a whole. Although these details are well understood, we know very little about the essential stimulus that releases the sequence of neurophysiological events culminating in this response. Retinal blur, and chromatic and spherical aberration in connection with the fine oscillatory movements of physiological nystagmus, have all been suggested. There is evidence suggesting that each may be sufficient and that no single one is necessary. We only know that the eye controls its focus on an object with a fair degree of accuracy. Focus will change within a reaction time as the distance of the object from the eye is changed and nearly always in the right direction. Apparently the "error" signal—whatever it is—is continuously monitored.

Of all the control systems associated with the effector mechanisms of the eye, the accommodation mechanism is the one the least well understood. We know its reaction time—about 0.36 ± 0.09 second for far-to-near accommodation and about 0.02 second more in the opposite direction (Campbell & Westheimer, 1960). Its precision is a good deal

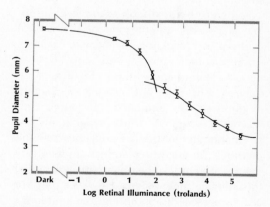

Figure 11.10. Diameter of the pupil as a function of the amount of light stimulating the retina. The plotted points are the means (± one standard error of the mean) of the results of 16 experimental repetitions on a single observer. (ten Doesschate & Alpern, 1967.)

poorer than the systems for saccadic and tracking eye movements. However the depth of focus of the eye is sufficient under many conditions that the eye accommodation may fail to keep up with changes in the distance of the fixated object without appreciable blur. (In earlier literature we read of the "lazy lag" of accommodation.)

One potentially informative way of studying accommodation would be to "change the gain in the feedback loop," that is, to examine the accommodation responses obtained when the normal relation between accommodation and clear focus of the retinal image is altered.

PUPIL SIZE

The pupil of the eye gets smaller and smaller as the amount of light reaching the retina gets larger and larger. The exact relationship is shown in Figure 11.10 according to measurements of ten Doesschate and Alpern (1967). If both eyes are equally illuminated, the pupil is consistently smaller (0.4 to 0.7 mm) than the results illustrated in this figure (which were obtained with only one retina illuminated).

The pupil contraction regulates the amount of light that reaches the retina, and it is therefore a textbook example of a biological control system—one of the earliest studied. This regulatory mechanism has been studied both in the "closed loop" (that is normal fashion) and with the "feedback loop opened" (that is, by not allowing the changes in pupil size to influence how much light reaches the retina). These experiments are fascinating in that they demonstrate how the methods of analyzing automatic feedback control systems can be quantitatively applied to biological phenomena. However they are also somewhat disappointing. The limitations of the theory of linear control systems put severe constraints on the variety of responses that can be quantified by these methods, for most biological phenomena are highly nonlinear. Unfortunately the theory of the non-

linear automatic control system is much less well developed and lacks the elegance and the simplicity of the theory of linear systems.

One way of illustrating the nonlinearity of the pupil reflex is the demonstration (Clynes, 1962) that the pupil contracts whether the retina is exposed to a light flash or to a dark flash (a linear system would contract to a light flash and dilate to a dark flash). For the details of the application of the theory of servo-mechanisms to the human pupil, the reader should examine a paper by Stark (1959) and one by Clynes (1962). In any event, the pupil regulation is highly overrated as a method of controlling the adaptation state of the eye; the retina and the nervous system have developed much more powerful ways of doing this (see Chapter 9).

Although whatever it does when it regulates the amount of light reaching the retina is of trivial importance as a regulator of the adaptation state, the light reflex is a fascinating way of analyzing the sensory mechanisms of the retina.

It might be supposed that for a function of such little moment only an insignificant fraction of retinal photosensitive cells would be capable of exciting a pupil response. Everything we know about the action of the light reflex, on the contrary, suggests that both rods and cones—and, indeed in all likelihood, all rods and all cones—are capable of exciting a pupil contraction. Given sufficiently large fields and sufficiently sensitive detecting methods, the absolute thresholds for rod vision and for photopupillary motility are similar or even identical (Alpern, McCready, and Barr, 1963).

The action spectrum of the light reflex at high light levels is a weighted mean of the logarithm of the rod and cone spectral sensitivities, with both mechanisms given about equal weight. The response of the pupil to light indicates the eye does not easily differentiate between light focused within the geometric retinal image of the test target and light scattered entoptically within the eye, because light focused on the head of the human optic nerve will evoke a somewhat more vigorous response than will light on the surrounding (and hence, sensitive) retina. Thus, to evoke a pupil response by exciting the foveal cones and these alone, the small centrally fixed test flash must be superimposed in the center of a large (at least 15°) and bright blue background. (The background sufficiently adapts the surrounding rods so that the small amount of added light scattered from the test is not capable of exciting them further.) Under such conditions, the action spectrum of the light reflex is the same as that of the psychophysical (foveal) luminosity curve (Alpern & Campbell, 1962). The way the rod and cone signals combine to form suprathreshold pupillary responses at light levels above the cone threshold has yet to be worked out in detail.

Another way of reducing the size of the pupil is to shift the gaze from a distant to a near object, that is to increase accommodation. The miosis (that is, small pupil) associated with increased accommodation and increased accommodative vergence has already been described in the section on vergence movements. Very slight changes in pupil size also occur with fusional movements in about 50 percent of the observers so far examined, but the effect is small. Increased positive fusional convergence evokes almost a 0.087 mm decrease in pupil diameter for each degree of movement. The response to accommodative vergence may be as much as 2.5 times as large as this and occurs in all observers so far examined (Alpern, Mason, & Jardinico, 1961).

THE INFLUENCE OF PSYCHOLOGICAL VARIABLES ON THE INTRAOCULAR MUSCLES

The intraocular muscles that control accommodation and pupil size are smooth muscles. Like all smooth muscles, they are innervated by branches of the autonomic nervous system. Not unnaturally it may be anticipated that relevant psychological varia-

bles that can be expected to influence the autonomic nervous system should prove to be associated with changes in pupil size and accommodation. The matter has been studied only a little if at all in a quantitative way insofar as accommodation is concerned, but recently psychologists have become interested in how the pupil size varies when psychological variables are manipulated. It is very easy to photograph the pupil (with either infrared or ordinary panchromatic film), and when the negatives are magnified to about 10 times the size of the eye, the pupil diameter can easily be measured with a precision of 0.01 mm. Working in this way, Hess (1965) found some evidence that the pupil dilates in association with stimuli thought to be "pleasurable" and constricts to those thought to be "unpleasant." Similarly, while a student is trying to solve a simple arithmetic problem, the pupil seems to dilate and to constrict after the subject reports the solution. The greater the difficulty of the problem, the wider the dilation and subsequent constriction. This has led Kahneman and Beatty (1966) to the idea that pupil dilation is "an indicator of the amount of effort involved in the storing of information for (subsequent) report." Hess also found that intellectually interesting material seemed to be associated with a wide pupil. Evidently, the pupil response can be used to study interest, emotion, and thought processes, as well as attitudes.

The same is probably true of accommodation, but because changes in the refraction of the eye are much more difficult to measure, we know next to nothing about this. Enterprising optometrists (Pheiffer, 1955) have from time to time studied subjects with a retinoscope while they were reading or carrying out other tasks. This technique (so-called book retinoscopy) is a relatively crude one, and the length of time required for any single measurement precludes accurate time resolution of these changes, smaller than a few seconds at best. Nevertheless, there is the suggestion from such work that interest in reading matter and problem solving both produce changes in accommodation. Accurate analysis of such effects awaits the application of a highly sensitive infrared recording optometer by some curious psychologist. Even if the elegant recording devices currently available are used (Campbell & Robson, 1959), the task is difficult, but the potential rewards may in fact be considerably greater than those that can be reaped from studying pupil size changes, which are easier to measure.

Julian Hochberg

PERCEPTION

I. COLOR AND SHAPE

12 The world as we perceive it consists of tridimensional objects, stationary or moving, at various distances in space. Our perception of the world depends on—is *mediated by*—our sense organs. Of these, the most important by far is the eye, in which light waves reflected from (or produced by) the objects around us are focused to form an optical image on the retina, the sensitive tissue at the rear of the eye (p. 278).

The preceding chapters on vision, color vision, and effector mechanisms in vision were concerned with the reception and processing of stimulus information that reaches us through our eyes. These chapters had in common a concern for the physiological bases of vision and for quantitative treatments of such topics as visual sensitivity, color discrimination, and muscular adaptations of the eye to the inspection of visual patterns.

In turning our attention now to visual perception we go far beyond the preceding analyses of sensory events. We concern ourselves with the world of real objects, not only with the images formed by those objects on the retina of the eye. We try to understand how such objects can be perceived as solid visual shapes with characteristic properties of color, size, distance, and movement. For answers to these questions, we must often turn to the broad psychological fields of learning, maturation, thinking, and motivation, proceeding well beyond the processing that occurs in the eye and the visual pathways.

The retinal image is very different from any normal description of the environment. There are no objects in the image, only juxtaposed regions of color. The image is in two dimensions, whereas the environment is in three dimensions. The retinal image of an object changes in size and shape as the observer views the object from different distances and angles, even though the object itself is unchanging. In color, too, the image changes as the object's illumination is changed, whereas the object retains its own characteristic reflectance. Nevertheless, the retinal image must somehow provide good information about such object properties as distances, sizes, shapes, and reflectances, for the observer does see them readily and often quite accurately. It is in trying to discover how the observer extracts and uses the retinal information about object properties that many of the general problems of visual perception arise.

Objects' appearances vary in an immense number of ways. They can appear to be animate or inanimate, light or dark, large or small, threatening or friendly. Most experimental research has centered around 4 of the ways in which objects can differ—their colors, their shapes, their sizes, and their locations (and motions) in space—because these attributes seem to be relatively simple to account for in terms of what is known about the specific nerve energies of the visual sensory system (p. 279), because they seem to be fundamental in understanding how we perceive the world, and because they are relatively easy to study. We shall survey the experimental problems of how we see objects' colors and shapes in this chapter; in the next chapter, we shall consider how we see objects' locations, sizes and motions in space.

PROBLEMS IN THE PERCEPTION OF OBJECT COLORS

Our views of the world normally contain regions of color the appearance of which can differ in many ways. As used in the study of visual perception, "color" includes the attributes of lightness and darkness, hue, and saturation. We have seen in Chapter 9 that a great deal of research has been devoted to explaining how these changes in appearance depend on changes in stimulation. In addition, an expanse of color can be described as looking filmlike and insubstantial, or like a hard surface; it can appear bulky and three-dimensional or it can appear flat and two-dimensional; it can look transparent or opaque, luminous or nonluminous, lustrous or nonlustrous (Katz, 1911, 1935). On the contrary, the appearance of a small homogeneous patch of light viewed in an otherwise dark field varies in only 3 ways: in its hue, its saturation, and its brightness (p. 359). Because we can (theoretically) replace any view of the world whatsoever by a picture that will be indistinguishable from the view itself but that is composed of such small homogeneous patches of light, such stimuli offer a simple starting point for the study of the perception of color. In fact, many of the problems of visual perception originated with the historically influential viewpoint called *structuralism* (p. 402), in which the appearances of homogeneous patches of light were considered to be the elementary units of experience, or *sensations,* of which our perceptions of objects and scenes are assembled. If we attempt to explain the appearance of objects' colors in terms of what we know about the appearance of a small patch of light, 3 sets of problems arise.

The first 2 problems, *color constancy* and *color contrast,* arise because an object's apparent hue or lightness is usually not what we would expect it to be from knowing the light that the object reflects to the eye. The third problem, that of *surface color,* arises because objects' surfaces appear to differ from each other not only in their hue, saturation, and brightness but also in additional ways (they may look more or less lustrous, hard, rough, and so on).

THE PROBLEM OF COLOR CONSTANCY

Early Background

Reflectance is a physical property of substances: the property of absorbing some of the incident light and reflecting the remainder. The reflectance R of a gray surface is equivalent to the ratio of the luminance L to the incident light or illuminance E. Thus, $R = L/E$, or, as pointed out in Chapter 9, $L = ER$. Absolute black would reflect no light under any illumination, but such perfectly black surfaces do not exist. A good black will have a reflectance as low as 3 percent, whereas good whites run about 80 percent.

We know that increasing the amount of light on any part of the retina generally increases the perceived lightness of that region (see pp. 276–278). Yet it is a fact of common observation that coal looks black even in sunlight, and chalk looks white even in shadow, and in these conditions the eye may receive much stronger light from the coal than from the chalk. Thus, even when the illumination of an object's retinal image changes, casual observation seems to show that *the object's color appears to remain relatively constant.*

Interest in the problem of color constancy dates from those early giants of physiological optics, Helmholtz and Hering, who laid out the 2 main kinds of explanation of color constancy, posing between them the central issues of color perception (and perhaps of perceptual inquiry in general).

As Helmholtz first said in 1866 (1962 ed., p. 408):

> Colors are mainly important for us as properties of objects and as means of identifying objects. In visual observation we constantly aim to reach a judgment of the object colors and to eliminate differences of illumination. . . . Seeing the same object under . . . different illuminations, we learn to get a correct idea of the object colors in spite of differences of illumination . . . and since our interest lies entirely in the constant object color, we become unconscious of the sensations on which our judgment rests.

That is, Helmholtz is saying that the light that is reflected to the retina from some object acts as the stimulus to produce a given sensation of brightness but that we usually also have indications of what illumination is falling on the object, and we have learned to allow for the effects of different hues and intensities of illumination without being aware of this correction process. It is *as though* we arrive at our judgments of color by making an inference (unconsciously) about the reflecting properties of the object, an inference based on the brightness of the sensation that we experience and on the various indications of illumination that we have learned to take into account (even though we do not notice them).

Judgment based on unconscious sensations seemed to Hering (1874, 1876, 1879) an unrealistic account of the process of color perception. He pointed to the peripheral factors that compensate for changes of illumination: contraction and dilation of the pupil, retinal adaptation, and contrast. Each of these would tend, normally, to keep the apparent brightness of the object constant, even though the overall illumination on the object and its background increases (see pp. 283–289). Thus, with an increase in illumination, the pupil contracts and lets less light through to the retina. If increased light reaches the retina, the eye adapts to the increase and this adaptation results in a decrease in the retina's sensitivity. Finally, *contrast* has the effect that a bright background darkens the appearance of the object it surrounds. For this reason, if retinal images of object and background do receive more illumination, the increased luminance of the background should result in a greater darkening of the object's appearance, a darkening that will tend to compensate for the increased illumination the object has received. Still, Hering agreed that these peripheral factors were not wholly sufficient to account for all constancy phenomena, and accordingly suggested also a cerebral factor, later elaborated (1907, reprinted 1920) as the concept of "memory color." In his own words, "The color in which we have oftenest seen an external thing impresses itself indelibly on our memory and becomes a fixed characteristic of the memory image. What the layman calls the real color of a thing is a color which has become firmly attached to the thing in his memory; I might call it the memory color of the thing." This "approximate color constancy of seen objects," Hering urged, was one of the most remarkable and important facts in the whole realm of physiological optics.

We shall consider evidence and arguments for these two positions. While we shall see good reason to modify both, we will be able neither to accept nor to reject either of them completely.

Katz (1911), who did a great deal of the early work on the effect of changes in illumination on objects' appearances, argued that neither memory color nor Hering's peripheral factors seemed to provide an adequate explanation of the perception of object colors. However, neither did he accept Helmholtz' notion of a two-stage process, namely sensation followed by judgment. Katz maintained that the correlate of luminance is the experience of *insistence* (the degree to which a color attracts attention), not lightness. Our experiences of the surface color and the illumination of a patch of a given luminance

are inseparably coupled, so that with each impression of illuminance we will perceive a different object color (Katz, 1930; see also Gelb, 1929). A white in one illumination is not the same experience as a white in another illumination. For Katz, the problem is therefore not how illumination is taken into account by an act of judgment, but how a color in one illumination comes to be identified as being the same as some color in another.

Since then, "color constancy," along with "size constancy" and "shape constancy" (pp. 506, 515), has become a familiar psychological term. What it refers to is illustrated in Figure 12.1.

The Measurement of Constancy

The factor of reflectance Suppose the observer is to make a color match between a standard gray surface that is receiving an illumination of E_{st} and a variable gray surface (that is, whose reflectance can be changed) viewed under a different illumination, E_v (Figure 12.1). Let the standard have a reflectance, R_{st}, of 40 percent, and an illumination, E_{st}, of 10 foot-candles. Let the variable receive an illumination E_v of 50 ft-c. What reflectance value of the variable gray R_v will an observer choose to match the standard? A priori, it would seem that an observer could choose either of 2 different reflectances that might be regarded as correct. One "match" is a luminance match. Remember that luminance $L = ER$ (see Chapter 9, p. 276). The gray that would equal the luminance of the standard has a reflectance $R_{VL} = 8$ percent (because 8 percent of 50 ft-c = 40 percent of 10 ft-c = 4 ft-L of luminance in each case). However, the "object's color" may also refer to its *reflectance* (or *albedo*). Therefore, the other possible basis for a "match" is given by a reflectance of the variable which equals that of the standard, or $R_{VA} = R_{st}$. Here, $R_{VA} = 40$ percent.

In actual fact, an observer usually chooses neither R_{VA} nor R_{VL}, but instead chooses a third value, which we may take to lie on a continuum between 2 poles, one conforming to stimulus luminance, the other correspond-

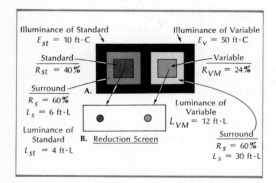

Figure 12.1. A. A simple constancy experiment: the standard and variable are viewed under different levels of illumination. B. Standard and variable are viewed through a reduction screen. See text.

ing to object reflectance:

R_{VL}	R_{VM}	R_{VA}
8 percent	24 percent	40 percent

Brunswik (1929) introduced a method of expressing the results of such a matching procedure as a ratio. He defined perceptual constancy as the ratio

$$\frac{R_{VM} - R_{VL}}{R_{St} - R_{VL}}$$

If the observer were to make a perfect reflectance match, then $R_{VM} = R_{St} = 40$ percent, and the Brunswik ratio = (40 percent − 8 percent)/(40 percent − 8 percent) = 1.0 (that is, the observer achieves perfect constancy). In the case illustrated by Figure 12.1, $R_{VM} = 24$ percent, and the Brunswik ratio = 50 percent. The Brunswik ratio is not the only way of representing the relationship between these measures, of course; several other indices of lightness constancy are described in Woodworth and Schlosberg (1954, page 436; see also Leibowitz, 1956; Landauer, 1962).

It is easy to demonstrate that under *some* circumstances the match between 2 objects is made solely on the basis of their luminances, namely when we use a *reduction screen* (or approximate its use). A reduction screen is a very simple device that merits separate discussion.

The reduction screen or hole screen If you look through a tube or a small hole at a uniformly colored surface, the "surface" vanishes and a mere expanse of color is seen through the hole. This simple piece of apparatus is called the *hole screen* or *reduction screen*. What is seen in an aperture, most appropriately called *aperture color,* appears self-luminous, or internally lit, whereas a surface color appears to be illuminated by an external source. Aperture color ranges from dim to bright, from zero to the maximum brightness. Surface color varies in what is best called *lightness;* in the achromatic series it can also be called *whiteness,* ranging from black through the shades of gray to the

definite upper limit of pure white. Both surface color and aperture color can also vary in hue and saturation.

The hole screen allows the light reflected from a surface to reach the eye but it conceals the surroundings. Clues that the subject might be able to use to discover what the illumination is are thus removed from the field of view. When viewed in a reduction screen, two spots look equally bright only when the stimuli are of equal luminance. Thus, the reduction screen affords a convenient means of matching two stimuli, or of determining their relative brightness, saturation, and hue. When the screen is removed, and the objects are viewed in the unobstructed situation, the subject usually compares the two objects more in terms of their reflectances. Let us survey the experimental results of such experiments in color constancy, and then consider some theories about what these facts imply about the nature of perceptual processes.

Color Constancy Under Normal and Abnormal Conditions of Illumination

Consider a typical experiment by Burzlaff (1931): The observer viewed a set of 48 gray

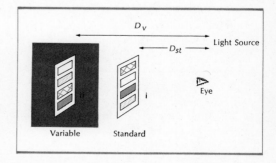

Figure 12.2. Standard and variable at different distances from the light source. Burzlaff (1931) used charts of 48 patches of gray as standard and variable; he obtained Brunswik ratios higher than .90. Brunswik (1929), using one square of gray each for standard and variable, obtained ratios ranging from about .25 to about .65 for adults, and from about .12 to about .50 for young children (ages 3–5).

papers, ranging from the best white to the best black obtainable, placed in irregular order on a large medium-gray cardboard which was set near a window and illuminated by diffuse daylight. A set of identically colored papers, placed in regular graded order from black to white, mounted on a similar piece of medium gray cardboard, was set far back in the room, where it received only $\frac{1}{20}$ of the light that illuminated the irregular set (Fig. 12.2). The subject stood near the window, with his back to it, viewing both charts with the dark rear wall of the room as background. With one gray paper on the near chart designated as the standard, the subject compared each gray in the far chart with the standard, judging whether the variable was the same, lighter, or darker than the standard.

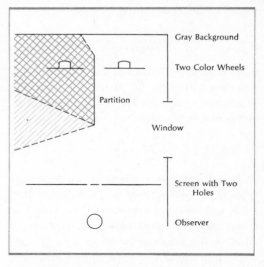

Figure 12.4. The partition between the two color wheels places the left-hand one in shadow. Brunswik ratios for two observers were .31 and .26 for short views; with long inspection periods, they tended more toward luminance matches. (After Katz, 1930.)

Repeating the procedure with several of the standards, and computing the PSEs according to the method of constant stimuli (p. 23), Burzlaff found that the subject matched a given gray on one chart with a gray of almost the same reflectance on the other chart, in spite of the very different illuminations on the two charts. Thus, despite the fact that the light reflected from any particular gray to the eye was only $\frac{1}{20}$ as much in the dim as in the bright illumination, the object color was judged to be nearly the same (see Figure 12.2). The diminution of stimulation had *some* effect, for errors were mostly in one direction; it took a somewhat lighter shade in the dim light to match a given shade in the bright light. The actual match was thus a compromise between a match of object reflectance and a match of luminance but was much closer, in this experiment, to the former, giving us a good example of color constancy (or perhaps we should say *reflectance constancy*).

Color constancy with nonuniform illumination The issue of color constancy arises

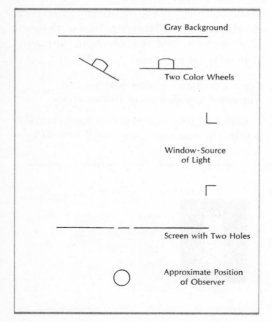

Figure 12.3. Setup for varying angle of incidence. The color wheel on the left had an all white disk. When viewed through the two holes in the reduction screen, the wheel on the right matched the one on the left when the former had a 13 percent white sector and an 87 percent black sector. With a direct view, the two wheels were matched when the right one was 45 percent white and 55 percent black (Katz, 1930). The Brunswik ratio is then .36.

whenever illuminance is changed from one part of the visual field to another (or from one time to another). Several such situations are listed below, and illustrated in Figures 12.2 through 12.6.

One object is at a greater distance from the light source than another (Figure 12.2).

One object is at a more oblique angle to the direction of light than the other, so that the same illuminance is spread over a larger area (Figure 12.3).

One object is viewed through a filter, or other light-reducing device, that covers all or part of the view. For example, Katz used such a device to reduce the overall amount of light coming from a white disk and its surroundings to $\frac{1}{4}$, $\frac{1}{12}$, $\frac{1}{36}$, and $\frac{1}{120}$ of the light coming from a variable color wheel, which was viewed directly. Brunswik ratios were .107, .215, .218, and .224, respectively.

One object is in light, the other in shadow (Figure 12.4) or the 2 objects to be matched are otherwise placed in separately illuminated fields.

The lighting of the entire field of view is different from normal lighting in some respect. The page of this book reflects a much yellower light to the eye under incandescent light than in broad daylight, but it still looks white in both cases.

In all of the circumstances described above, Brunswik ratios are usually greater than 0.0 and less than 1.0. The apparent color of an object viewed under different illuminations is a function not only of its luminance, but of its reflectance as well.

We can readily understand how the subject might match 2 grays as being equal in appearance when the same amount of light reaches his eye from each of them. After all, there are physical light detectors that would respond in just those terms. However, the experiments on color constancy show that the matches subjects make generally are influenced by the objects' reflectances. Because there is no known receptor mechanism that can detect reflectances, a great deal of attention has been devoted to trying to discover the basis of these matches. What information

is there in the retinal image to explain this ability?

If we consider only the luminance L of the local patch of color reflected to the eye by an object whose reflectance is R and which receives illumination E, we see that in order to solve the equation, $R = L/E$, for R, we need to know the value of E. If we view the ability to judge objects' reflectances as the ability to solve the equation for R given L, we see that the subject also must have some indication of E. What information is there in the retinal image concerning E? Does the subject really use this information to solve the equation for R?

Achievement explanations of color constancy Color constancy is an "achievement" (Brunswik, 1952) in this sense: The ability to recognize that the coal is really black, even though it is sending more light to the eye than is the white piece of paper, is *adaptive:* it probably helps one get along in the world. If this ability to judge reflectance rests on anything like the ability to solve the equation, $R = L/E$, for R, given L, then the achievement of color constancy implies the ability to take the illumination E into account, on the basis of whatever indications of E may be available in the retinal image. Because it is hard to see how this ability to take all of the illumination cues into account could be innate (could be built into the organism's nervous system at birth), it seemed reasonable to many psychologists to argue that color constancy is due to the subject's having learned to use the illumination cues (see Helmholtz' explanation, p. 397).

There are, of course, other mechanisms for color constancy that we might postulate, mechanisms that might well be innate, but we shall defer consideration of those mechanisms to a later section (p. 412).

Registering the illumination, E; clues, cues, and unconscious inference The subject might solve the equation, $R = L/E$, in 2 ways. First, he might perceive the illumination and use that as his guide in deciding what the reflectance is. Second, the subject's visual nervous system might process the information about L and E without his being able to judge either of them separately with any degree of accuracy.

As common observation tells us, it is certainly not true that the subject consciously notices the clues to the illumination and consciously deduces from these the nature and magnitude of E. For this reason, Woodworth (1938) proposed that we use the more neutral word, "cue," rather than "clue" for such processes, implying by this that the subject responds to indications of illumination in a well-rehearsed automatic fashion, initiating inference-like processes even though he might be unable to say either what the cues are, or what the subsequent processes of "taking illumination into account" might be. A similar view underlay Katz's (1935) approach to color perception (see p. 398). It is really not all that different from Helmholtz' explanation—that the visual system acts *as though unnoticed* sensations are used as the basis for *unconscious* inferences. It does avoid some of the connotations suggested by Helmholtz' formulation, and it has become standard usage in the study of perception to use the word "cue" to refer to aspects of the sensory stimulus pattern that can *at least potentially* convey information about some aspect of the physical world, and which the observer may or may not be able to report or notice.

Both kinds of explanation assume that the luminance of any patch of light is in fact the starting point from which the subject arrives at the apparent reflectance or object color. As a corollary, both approaches must assume that the subject obtains information about the illumination E from the retinal image (or from some other source of knowledge) and that the apparent color that is produced by L is modified to take E into account. This assumption is inherited from an extremely simple general psychological system, often called *structuralism*, which we should consider briefly here inasmuch as most of the problems with which these chapters are concerned arose in the context of that system.

Theories of Color Constancy

The structuralist theory and its implications: sensations, learned illumination cues, and unconscious inference; can illumination be perceived? The simplest system for analyzing the world of visual perception into simple and fundamental sensory events would be something like the following:

We know that we can reduce all possible patterns of stimulation on the retina to various combinations of small, homogeneous patches of light. We also know that we can match the appearance of any such small patch of light with another dot of light that varies only with respect to the physical energy at each wavelength in the spectrum. We know further that if such a dot of light is viewed against a homogeneous background, and the spectral energy distribution is varied systematically, we see a dot whose appearance also varies systematically (Chapter 10). In terms of the sensory physiology of the eye, it seems reasonable to assume that the visual nervous system analyzes the world in just this way: that the retina consists of a mosaic of receptors, some of which respond maximally to one wavelength, some of which respond maximally to another; that at least ideally each receptor responds to physical stimulation falling on it independently of what the other receptors around it may be doing; and, finally, that a characteristic elementary sensory experience would result from (or accompany) each elementary receptor response.

According to this scheme, we would have 3 sets of analytic units: (1) The elementary physical variables of stimulation (wavelength and intensity distribution). (2) The elementary sensory receptors that are presumably responsive to those physical energies. (3) The simple irreducible experiences of color, called *sensations,* that presumably result from—or accompany—the receptors' activities.

How might we apply this system of analysis to the perception of objects and events? We could assume that the appearance of a particular spot would remain unchanged, regardless of what stimulation was exciting its neighboring receptors. That is, in effect, we could assume that sensations are unchanged by the various combinations into which they enter. We could then extend this analysis to the perception of objects, quite simply: The appearance of any part of an object or scene is (by this theory) the same as the appearance which that colored spot would have when it is observed in isolation. By implication, a finite number of color sensations would, in their different possible combinations, account for all of the immense diversity of different objects and object properties that we perceive in the world.

The attempt to explain the perceived world in terms of such fundamental sensory experiences runs through the thinking of Helmholtz (1866) and Wundt (1902), and is most explicitly pursued by Titchener (1902). It offers a clear, simple and consistent program for psychological research, for relating psychology to the neighboring disciplines of physiology and physics, and for the prediction and explanation of the world we perceive. However, this apparent simplicity is misleading. Color sensations do *not* seem to be independent of the combinations in which they occur. As soon as we turn to the perception of complex and nonhomogeneous scenes, we find that an object's apparent color is not determined simply by the stimulation falling within its retinal image. The fact of color constancy shows us this quite clearly: The assumption that the same retinal stimulation produces the same color experience, regardless of what else is happening, is clearly incomplete, at best; for the subject often reports that two objects have the same apparent color when the 2 objects have equal reflectances in the physical world (that is, $R_1 = R_2$), not when the stimuli each projects to the retina are of equal luminance ($L_1 = L_2$).

This discrepancy might be explained, of course, as originating from a great deal of perceptual learning. Thus, Helmholtz argued (see p. 397) that we learn that objects' reflectances R are usually permanent, even though the illuminance E changes; that we learn to detect the various indications, or

cues, as to what illumination is falling on any object; and that we learn how to take the effects of the illumination into account in order to arrive at the perception of reflectance.

The implications of this theory are these: the value of luminance of some focal region L_f can in fact be correctly sensed regardless of changes in adjacent stimulation, L_a; the illuminance E can be estimated on the basis of its various indications (retinal or otherwise) and can be correctly taken into account in deriving R from L; and these abilities to detect and use E are learned.

Let us consider the experimental status of these various implications.

Can we, in fact, perceive E? There is a problem here. We must know the object color or reflectance in order to deduce the illuminance from the reflected light, whereas we must know the illumination in order to deduce the object color from the reflected light. That is, if all we know is L, we must have R in order to solve the equation $R = L/E$ for E, whereas we must have E in order to solve for R. Hering raised this logical question in 1907. One possible answer is this: In normal scenes, the illumination on a particular object might be gathered from stimuli received from surrounding objects (Kardos, 1929). Moreover, whereas indirect vision indicates little of the object color, it offers the subject a total impression of the general illumination.[1] However, such estimates of general illumination are not enough; parts of the environment often differ in lighting from the overall background, and if those local differences are not "taken into account," reflectance R must be misjudged. Consider a patch of shadow. Taken by itself, it might be perceived as a region of lowered illuminance E, but it might also be seen as a patch of lower reflectance. What indications are there in the retinal image

---

[1] Katz (1935) suggested that the experience of the overall *insistence* (see p. 398) of the whole field of view might be the basis for judging illumination, and that this might be studied quantitatively by the use of the homogeneous visual field. As we shall see (p. 426), however, the homogeneous visual field, or *Ganzfeld*, changes its appearance through adaptation so readily that it is not really suited for this purpose.

that the shadowed region is of lower illuminance?

One cue that a region is in shadow is the *penumbra* or half-shadow along the edges of the region, and an analogous fringe borders on an area of raised illumination. Another indication of shading is given by the three-dimensional arrangement. Thus, if the three-dimensional form of a box is clearly perceived, we might then decide that its darker side is in shadow rather than painted black. If we look beyond the local patch itself, at the *surrounding pattern of stimulation,* such illumination cues can usually be found in the retinal image.

To decide whether or not such indications of illumination indeed affect our object-color perception, we can do two things. First, we can conceal the indications of illumination; this should lead the observer to mistake changes in *E* for changes in *R*. Second, we can try to provide false information about *E;* this should change judgments about *R* appropriately.

Experiments with concealed illumination conditions are diagrammed in Figures 12.5 and 12.6. In a classic experiment, Gelb (1929) presented a background consisting of a wall and several objects illuminated by a rather dim ceiling light (Figure 12.5). In the foreground a textureless black velvet disk received the bright light of a concealed lantern. No penumbra was visible on the disk or on the background. The subject reported seeing a white disk standing in the general illumination (white in the dim light instead of black in the bright light). This represents a complete failure of color constancy. However, the instant a small bit of white paper was held in the bright light, just in front of the disk, the disk was seen to be black. We might say that the bit of white paper was the cue to the extra illumination on the disk. When the white paper was removed, however, the disk returned to its former appearance. We might have expected, from our formula, that once the subject was made aware of the extra illumination of the disk and of its true object color, he would maintain this awareness after the white paper was removed. So he did, no doubt, intellectually; but neither his intellectual knowledge about illumination, nor his knowledge of the true object color was sufficient to maintain color constancy in the absence of the actual white stimulus. We shall see that unequivocal knowledge of the true situation similarly often fails to influence perceptions of size, shape, and distance when we come to discuss experiments with those attributes.

Unqualified claims that perception is the result of knowledge, that is, that we see what we know to be true, are misleading at the very least.

With similar procedures based on concealed illumination, Henneman (1935) showed that if the black disk were replaced by a white one, and only the white disk was placed in the spotlight, the white disk appeared to be *luminous.* This is what we would expect in terms of "taking illumination into account." Because the disk sent more light to the eye than could be accounted for by the dim ceiling light, which was the only visible source of illumination, the disk itself appeared

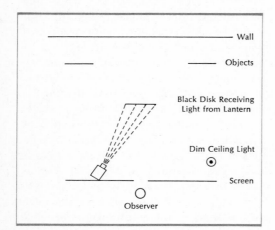

Wall

Objects

Black Disk Receiving Light from Lantern

Dim Ceiling Light

Screen

Observer

Figure 12.5. Gelb's concealed illumination experiment. The lantern at the left is invisible to the observer, and its light is confined to the black disk. The wall and all objects in the room receive the rather dim light from the ceiling lamp. See text.

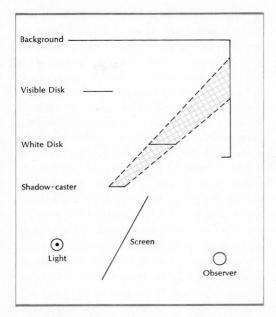

Background ————————

Visible Disk ————

White Disk

Shadow-caster

Light

Screen

Observer

Figure 12.6. The Kardos concealed shadow experiment. The only visible object shaded by the shadow-caster is the white disk, which stands entirely in full shadow. The subject sees this disk as black or gray. Screening the shadow-caster is unnecessary, for even if the subject sees it he gets no suggestion that it is shading the white disk. See p. 404.

to be a source of light; that is, L/E appeared to be greater than 1.00.

Conversely, as shown in Figure 12.6, Kardos (1934) illuminated a field of objects with good light, except for one disk of white paper that was placed in the shadow made by a concealed shadow-caster which covered *only the disk* with shadow. If there is no penumbra (or any other indication of shadow) on the disk, the subject reports a *black* disk standing in good light. Move the shadow a little to the side so that its edge is visible on the disk, and the disk at once appears to be white in shadow instead of black in good light. MacLeod (1932) showed that putting a false shadow on the background made an object in front of it appear lighter and, the larger the background shadow was made, the lighter colored the object appeared.

Thus, by concealing the cues that would

normally show that an object is receiving illumination different from that of its surroundings, or by introducing false cues, the experimenter can influence the subject's perception of object color, much as one would expect from the equation, $R = L/E$.

In all of the experiments that we have described, however, the stimulus conditions have been changed (as by the insertion of the white card in the Gelb experiment) to provide illumination cues. Such experiments can, therefore, show at most that *the stimulus conditions that normally accompany changes in illumination can result also in changes in judgments of surface color.* The experiments cannot show that these stimulus conditions have the effects that they do *because* they are cues or clues, that is, *because* they give the subject information about the illumination which he then takes into account. As we shall see, there are other explanations that can be applied to each of the experiments that we have described. More convincing evidence of the subject's ability to use illumination cues would be direct research on the accuracy with which he makes judgments concerning *illumination* under different conditions. We have as yet only a very little systematic evidence related to this critical point, aside from the information that such judgments can be made (Katz, 1935).

Beck (1959, 1961) had subjects match the illumination falling on a comparison surface to that which appeared to fall on a standard surface, both being viewed in an otherwise dark room. He first explained to the subjects the distinction between a surface's lightness and its illumination. Each pair of surfaces to be compared had texture patterns causing different *average* reflectances; for example, gray with white speckles on one, black with white speckles on the other; gray with white dots on one, black with white dots on the other, and so on. Subjects did make consistent judgments of illumination, setting the illuminance of the comparison surface close to that of the standard. For example, a set of white and gray stripes was used as the standard, receiving an illuminance of 2.88 ft-c, and a set of black and white stripes was used for the comparison, the illuminance of which was varied. The median setting at which subjects judged both surfaces to have the same illuminance was 1.89 ft-c. If both surfaces had appeared to be equally illuminated when the average light that they actually reflected to the eye was equal, the variable illuminance should have been set to 10.4 ft-c. With these alternatives in mind (that is, a retinal match of 10.4 or an illuminance match of 2.88), we can compute an "illumination constancy ratio" $(E_M - E_L)/(E_{st} - E_L)$, by analogy with the Brunswik ratio for brightness constancy. From Beck's data, the illumination constancy is thus $(1.89 - 10.4)/(2.88 - 10.4) = 1.1$.

To what variables are the subjects responding in such illumination-matching experiments? In experiments similar to that described above, Beck (1961) used surfaces with a much finer texture, or *microstructure* (such as fine stippled surfaces, flannel cloth, wood, and so on), rather than clearly discernable patterns of 2 different uniform reflectances. With the stippled and cloth surfaces, illumination constancy was low (Beck's data yield constancy ratios of about 0.10), but when white backgrounds were added to the field of view, the illumination constancy increased considerably (now ranging from 0.4 to 0.8). Beck concludes that subjects' judgments are, in general, close to what we would expect if 2 surfaces were judged to be equally illuminated when equal amounts of light were reflected from their lightest clearly discernible regions.[2]

We can now ask how well judgments of both E and R fit the equation, $R = L/E$, because Beck also had his subjects judge the surfaces' apparent lightnesses. He set the surfaces to the median value at which each sub-

ject had previously judged them to be equally illuminated. The subject then matched the surfaces for lightness against a chart (which was separately illuminated) consisting of pieces of gray paper of various reflectances. If judgments of lightness were made by taking perceived illumination into account, lightness constancy should be poor where illumination judgments were poor. In fact, however, lightness judgments of some of the surfaces (the stipple surfaces, with no white surrounds) were found to produce almost perfect constancy, even though illumination judgments using those surfaces had been very poor.

The discrepancy between illumination constancy and lightness constancy does not necessarily rule out the Helmholtzian theory that lightness judgments depend on unconscious illumination judgments. Perhaps subjects use different cues to form their unconscious judgments of illumination when they explicitly try to match the lightnesses of two surfaces than those they use when they explicitly try to match the illumination of surfaces. After all, the subject has had a lifetime of experience with trying to make correct judgments about reflectance, but he has rarely, if ever, had to concern himself with making explicit responses to illumination as such.

Color constancy in children and animals If color constancy were a learned judgmental ability, it might be less well developed in creatures with less perceptual experience and of less developed intellect. To test such reasoning, color constancy has been studied with human children of different ages to see whether perceptual achievement improves as a function of years of experience, and with animals of different evolutionary level.

Although age differences in color constancy have been found with human subjects in some conditions and not in others (Brunswik, 1929; Burzlaff, 1931; Beck, 1966), it seems clear that at least under *some* judging conditions, if a child is old enough to serve as a

---

[2]Several subjects, who did not fit this generalization, overestimated the illumination for those surfaces that had the greatest difference in reflectance between parts of the pattern. Perhaps these subjects used the degree of brightness difference as a basis for judging the amount of illumination, a possibility that is particularly interesting in terms of Hering's theory of brightness perception, which we discuss shortly (p. 411).

subject at all, he will display color constancy not substantially inferior to that of the adult. Such experiments are not really conclusive, however, because one may argue that even the very young child has had a very large amount of perceptual experience.

Experiments with animals have, in general, shown their color constancy to be as good as (or better than) that of humans. Locke (1935) tested the ability of rhesus monkeys and of human adults to discriminate a white field from a black field that was separated from it by a partition; the white field was sometimes to the right of the black field and sometimes to the left. The monkeys received a raisin when they reached into the white field. Once the discrimination habit was established, extra light was projected on the black field to raise its luminance above that of the white one. With humans, Brunswik ratios (p. 399) ranged from 0.10 to 0.23; with monkeys, from 0.47 to 0.65.

Burkamp (1923) trained fish to seek their food in troughs of a certain color and then tested them to discover whether they could pick this color from among an assemblage of grays and other colors even when the illumination was altered. The fish displayed excellent constancy: Increasing the light did not make them go to the darker shades, nor did colored light send them to the grays or to other colors, not used in training.

Though these results from children and animals indicate that no exalted intellectual process is necessary to "correct for illumination so as to see object colors," they do not show that *no* learning is involved, inasmuch as both children and animals have had perceptual experience before the experimental tests were performed. In order to avoid a training period in which perceptual learning might occur, Gogel and Hess (1951) raised chicks in darkness from the time they were hatched until the time they were tested, and then the chicks were tested to determine whether their innate preference for pecking at lighter grain was affected by local differences in the way the grain was illuminated.

The birds picked the lighter grains even when those grains had the lower luminance, because they were under lower illumination.

Regardless of whether learning *contributes* to color constancy, therefore, we must seriously consider the possibility that in at least some creatures there is an *innate* mechanism that permits some minimum amount of "correction for illumination" to occur. Let us now consider a mechanism that might result in color constancy, but which does not use the illumination cues as sources of information about illumination, and which therefore might be innately given in the nature of the sensory nervous system.

Contrast theories of constancy; simultaneous contrast So far, we have considered explanations of lightness constancy that start with the assumption that an observer first makes some response to the light that the object reflects to his eye and that he then modifies this impression by taking the apparent illumination E into account. This kind of explanation implies that the effects that a stimulus produces in the nervous system are independent of the effects of stimuli that impinge on other parts of the retina, until they are modified by higher processes, and that the observer can correctly identify a given stimulus (whether consciously or unconsciously) regardless of its context. Now, subjects can in fact match 2 stimuli with considerable accuracy and precision when the 2 are presented as small homogeneous targets or test patches side by side on a homogeneous background (Chapter 9). However, if the wavelength or intensity of the field surrounding one such spot is made to be different from that surrounding the other, subjects cannot, in general, judge correctly when both spots are the same, even when neither an object nor a source of illumination is clearly represented in the field of view. This is the familiar phenomenon of *simultaneous contrast,* which is discussed in more detail in Chapter 9. Like *lightness constancy,* contrast refers to a discrepancy between the value of

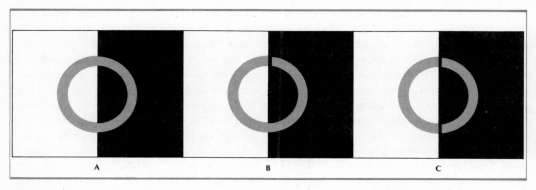

Figure 12.7. Contour and contrast. A. The gray ring appears to be relatively homogeneous at the division between the black and white surrounds. B, C. The gradient of lightness difference between the two halves of the gray ring becomes much more noticeable with the addition of a contour. The configuration of the test region also affects the detectability of the contrast effect (Berman & Leibowitz, 1965; see text). The phenomenon seems to be a relatively local one, and not due to the assimilation of the entire gray region to a single lightness (compare the top and bottom of B).

the local stimulus intensity and the value of the subject's judgment that we would presume to be based on it. Here, however, unlike the case with constancy, the discrepancy seems at first glance not an *achievement*, but rather a *failure* to respond properly to the environment, an "illusion." As a phenomenon, it challenges the assumption that the subject can identify the local stimulus regardless of the context in which it appears.

As a sensory phenomenon, simultaneous contrast usually works to exaggerate the differences between 2 stimuli, speaking loosely. As specific examples of simultaneous contrast, suppose that 2 small identical gray squares or test patches are placed on a variety of different backgrounds or surrounds. The test patch that is surrounded by (or adjacent to) a white background will look darker than one with a black surround; a square with a yellow surround will look bluer than one with a neutral surround; a square with a green surround will look more red, and so on.

An opposite effect, however, may sometimes be observed. This effect is known as *assimilation*. It can be seen in halftone prints and TV screens. Under these conditions, small or narrow regions of color are "diluted" rather than exaggerated, which is what occurs in simultaneous contrast (Newhall, 1942; Burn-

ham, 1953; Helson, 1963). Moreover, even where the conditions are otherwise such that simultaneous contrast should occur, a contour must separate the 2 test patches if the effect is to be clearly observed. Thus, Wundt (Osgood, 1953) noted that a gray test patch placed across the division between a white and a black surround looks uniform in lightness even though we would expect the part in the white surround to look darker. Koffka (1915) and Benussi (1916) are responsible for versions of the demonstration in Figure 12.7. In Figure 12.7A, the gray ring usually appears

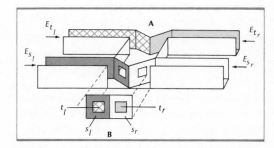

Figure 12.8. A. Apparatus used by Hess and Pretori (1894) to study simultaneous contrast (after Hurvich & Jameson, 1966). The luminance of each of four fields was independently controlled by varying the illuminance each received. B. The appearance of the four fields.

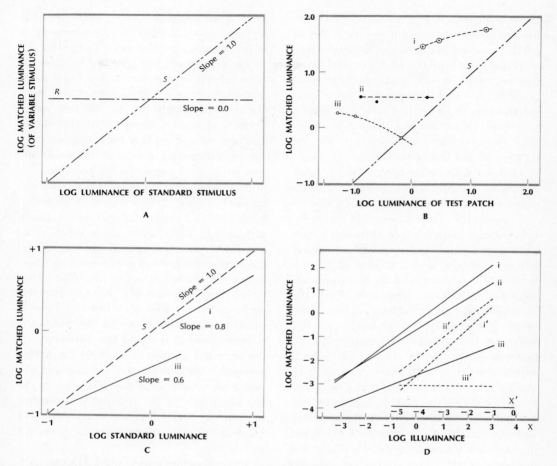

Figure 12.9. Brightness and lightness matches as a function of L_t/L_s.

A. Two theoretical curves representing the values by which an observer might match the appearance of a target and a comparison stimulus. The abscissa shows the luminance to which the target is set. The luminance of the field surrounding the target is varied proportionally, at the same time, so that the ratio, L_t/L_s, is kept fixed. The ordinate represents the values to which a subject might set a comparison stimulus so that it appears equal to the target. If the surround had no effect on the target's appearance, so that for each increase in target luminance, L_t, the luminance must be increased by an equal amount, the subject's judgments would fall on the curve marked S, which has a slope of 1.0. In a constancy experiment, this would have a Brunswik ratio of 0.0 (see p. 399). If the contrast induced by the surroundings, L_s, darkened the appearance of the target by an amount equal to the simultaneous increase in the target's luminance (so that for a given ratio of L_t/L_s the target's appearance remained unchanged), the subject's judgments would fall on the curve marked R, which has a slope of 0.0. In a constancy experiment, these results would yield a Brunswik ratio of 1.0.

In the graphs at B, C, and D, curves marked *i*, *ii* and *iii* represent high, intermediate, and low ratios of L_t/L_s, respectively. Notice that in each case the slopes obtained with the high ratios of L_t/L_s (in which target luminance is high compared to surround luminance) approach 1.0 most closely.

B. Brightness matches made to test patches at different luminances. For each curve (*i, ii, iii*), the luminance of the surround was varied with that of the target to keep a constant ratio of L_t/L_s. (After Jameson & Hurvich, 1961).

C. Hsia (1943) had subjects match the apparent whiteness of standard and variable discs that were presented in separately illuminated booths. Although the rear walls against which the disks uniform in color; in Figure 12.7C the half that has the white surround looks darker. Koffka (1935) proposed that this is so because a part of the field that is perceived as a unified figure will be made to look as homogeneous as possible, and that a figure that has 2 clear subdivisions, like a figure 8, would show contrast effects even without the dividing contour. This prediction was later substantiated by Berman and Leibowitz (1965).

Under a wide range of conditions, however, we can expect simultaneous contrast to occur. How might we measure such effects?

Consider the classic experiment on brightness contrast carried out by Hess and Pretori (1894; as described by Hering, 1907). Right and left test fields, t_r and t_l (Figure 12.8) were set to one luminance, and the two surrounds were set to another luminance. Then the luminance of t_r was changed, so that it no longer looked equal in brightness to the left test patch. The subject's task was to restore the luminance of the right test field to its original appearance (that is, to make t_r again look like t_l). The adjustment was done, however, not by changing the patch's luminance, but by changing the luminance of its surround. To make both test fields again look equal, the luminance of the right surround was adjusted until its contrast effects exactly compensated for the change, ΔL_t, that had been made in the luminance of the right test field.

For certain conditions, these contrast effects follow an extremely simple quantitative relationship: As long as the luminance ratio of the test patch and its surround is kept constant, the test patch maintains the same apparent brightness. Under these conditions, although the apparent brightness of the test patch is not proportional to L_t alone (because it is also being affected by its surround), it *is* proportional to the ratio L_t/L_s. That is, for each increment in L_t (the test luminance), an increase in the surround that maintains the ratio L_t/L_s at some constant level will keep the apparent brightness of the test patch unchanged (curve R, Figure 12.9A). This simple function would explain the occurrence of lightness constancy in most of the conditions that we have discussed in the previous section, a point that we shall elaborate in a moment. However, this simple relationship holds only in a certain range of initial values of L_t and L_s. With higher initial values of L_t and lower values of L_s, a greater change in the surround is needed to counteract a given luminance change ΔL_t in the test patch; that is, the contrast effect of L_s is less when the background is darker and the test field is brighter. If the luminance of the test patch is made much lower and the luminance of the surround is made much higher, a smaller increase in the luminance of the surround will suffice to counteract a given increase ΔL_t in the luminance of the test patch; again the ratio of L_t/L_s that is needed to keep the test patch at the same apparent brightness is not a constant.

Other variables affect contrast per se, such as the separation between the fields (Leibowitz, Mote, & Thurlow, 1953; Fry & Alpern, 1953), their sizes (Diamond, 1955; Kinney, 1962), configurations (Benary, 1924; Mikesell & Bentley, 1930) and many additional factors that influence the response that the visual system makes to a given stimulus (see Chapter 9). Because experiments on brightness contrast have not usually been carried out

---

appeared were black in both booths, the reflectance of the side walls could be changed. Note that curve *i*, which represents the highest level of L_t/L_s that Hsia used, has a slope closer to 1.0 than does curve *iii*, which represents his lowest level of L_t/L_s. (Adapted from Graham & Brown, 1965.)

D. Data from experiments by Leibowitz and his colleagues, using a setup similar to that of Hsia (Figure 12.9C). The solid lines are from Leibowitz, Myers, and Chinetti (1955); the abscissa (*X*) represents the illuminance of the booth containing the standard. The dotted lines are from an experiment by Leibowitz and Chinetti (1957), in which a very short exposure was used (.0002 sec); the abscissa here (*X'*) represents the relative illuminance. Compare with the observation in Figure 12.4 (p. 400) about the effects of viewing time.

under identical conditions, their findings are not always comparable. Those data that are most relevant to the problems of object-color perception, however, and to the issue of lightness constancy, seem to be reasonably well established. *First,* a more luminous region will lower the brightness matches that a subject will make to a less luminous region that is placed nearby, but the less luminous region will induce little or no enhancement of the brightness of the more luminous region (Diamond, 1953; Heinemann, 1955, 1961; Horeman, 1965). *Second,* the amount by which the more luminous region darkens the less luminous region is not simply governed by some effect exerted by the former on the latter; it is a nonlinear function of *both* luminances (Hess & Pretori, 1894). Very similar results to those of Hess and Pretori were obtained by Jameson and Hurvich (1961) using a very different procedure. Jameson and Hurvich used a field containing 5 neighboring test patches at once, for only 3 of which are the results represented in Figure 12.9B. The graph shows what happens to the apparent brightness of a test patch as we increase its luminance L_t and also increase the luminance of the surround, proportionally, at the same time, so as to keep the ratio L_t/L_s constant. For *i,* the ratio of L_t/L_s is high; for *ii,* it is intermediate; for *iii,* it is low. If the apparent brightness of the test patch simply increased with each increase in its luminance, successive judgments would fall on the line marked *s,* where the slope is 1.0. This does not happen. In a middle range, *ii,* the apparent brightness of the test patch does remain constant even though its luminance is increasing. At higher ranges, however, its apparent brightness will increase (*i*) and, at lower ranges, (*iii*), the apparent brightness of the test patch actually decreases as its luminance is increased!

This apparently paradoxical phenomenon, which has been obtained with different procedures by Jameson and Hurvich (1961) and by Stevens and Stevens (1960), may be easier to envision in terms of the following example.

In a totally dark room, everything looks featureless and gray, according to Hering (see below). If we increase the illumination slightly, we can then barely make out a white object as being somewhat lighter, and a dark object as being somewhat darker than the surrounding gloom. As we increase the illumination more, we also increase the separation of dark and light, until the dark object is clearly black and the light object is clearly white. The dark object has become darker because the contrast induced by its surroundings darkened it more than it was brightened by the additional light that it reflected. The apparent brightness of a patch of light is thus highly dependent on the context in which it appears, so much so that the effects of context can make it look darker with each increase in the light that reaches the retina!

How are we to account for these contrast phenomena? Once again, the major opposing explanations were offered most forcefully by Hering and Helmholtz.

According to Hering (1874, 1876), and to several of his predecessors (Brewster, 1833; Müller, 1834–1840; Plateau, 1834), contrast is a retinal phenomenon. The activity of one retinal area induces an opposed activity in the form of a complementary chemical reaction in the adjacent area. When no light at all reaches the eye, only gray is seen. Light in one part of the retinal image makes that part appear bright, and makes the adjacent regions appear dark as part of the same process; as the stimulation increases, the bright region both becomes brighter and induces the adjacent regions to appear darker. This would provide a purely peripheral mechanism to explain contrast, a mechanism that would presumably be innate. There is now a great deal of evidence that just such a process—or a very similar one involving lateral inhibitory connections between adjacent parts of the sensory system—does in fact work at the boundaries between 2 differently stimulated retinal regions (see Chapter 9). Horeman (1965) has recently shown that the effects of an inducing field on a less luminous target occur at retinal or immediately postretinal levels of the nervous system. Diamond (1960) and Jameson and Hurvich (1961, 1964) have recently offered quantitative theories that attempt to predict the interactions between fields of different luminance. The latter theory is particularly simple, and provides a good fit not only to a fair amount of data concerning brightness contrast, but to color contrast phenomena as well.

Against such peripheral explanations as those mentioned above, Helmholtz' theory is sometimes said to attribute the contrast effect to an error of judgment, but this account of his theory is scarcely adequate. His general principle is that clearly perceived differences (whether in hearing, vision, and so on) are enhanced or exaggerated. In the perception of colors, Helmholtz argued that the subject accepts the average color of the field of view temporarily as the *norm* and identifies it as "white" (or as the color of the illumination rather than of objects' surfaces), and makes the appropriate adjustments in arriving at his perceptions of other colors. In yellow illumination, for example, a pale yellow surface appears white or neutral and a neutral gray stimulus "therefore" appears to be tinged with blue, the complementary color. Quite similar to Helmholtz' emphasis on the average color of the field are the conceptions of Gelb (1932), Koffka (1932, 1935), Judd (1941), and Helson (1943, 1964), who think that the viewer takes the general level of the field as a neutral point and that particular bits of the field have apparent color according to their divergence from this level. These writers, however, avoid Helmholtz' intellectualistic phraseology and his references to "illusions of judgment." Helson's *adaptation level theory* comprises a recent attempt to make this approach at once general, objective, and quantitative.

It is not clear at this time that all of the phenomena that contribute to contrast effects are to be subsumed under one set of mechanisms, whether central or peripheral in nature. However, one conclusion seems clear: Sub-

jects do not respond in the same way to a stimulus of a given luminance when the luminances of neighboring regions of stimulation are changed. The phenomena of lightness constancy that were discussed in the previous section referred to judgments of the reflectances of objects made under different conditions of illumination, conditions of illumination that are apparent to the subject. The phenomena of simultaneous brightness contrast that we have outlined here refer to textureless patches of light under conditions of illumination that are not evident to the observer. Even under these latter "impoverished" conditions, as we have just seen, the apparent brightness of a patch of light is not determined by the stimulus that it projects to the retina; it is complexly determined by the luminance of the region itself, by the luminances of the adjacent regions, and by the sizes of and distances between regions of different luminance.

Sensory theories of color constancy; adaptation, hue contrast, and hue constancy: the effects of field diversity In the previous section, we considered the Helmholtzian theory that object-color perception depends on a process something like solving the equation $R = L/E$. Let us call this a *cognitive theory* of object-color perception, for it depends on the subject's knowledge (in some sense of the term) about the conditions under which he is receiving the local stimulation. In order for such an hypothesis to be meaningful, we would have to be able to show (directly or indirectly) that the subject can detect cues to illuminance E with sufficient precision to account for his judgments of R. The evidence we have considered to this point certainly is not encouraging. There is also a very strong secondary implication that such illumination cues must be learned and that therefore lightness constancy must also be learned; we have seen that there is little support for this implication. Finally, there is also the assumption that the subject can, at least in principle, respond to or "register" (whether consciously or unconsciously) the light that falls on each region of his retinal image, regardless of the luminances in neighboring regions. The phenomena of brightness contrast certainly do not support this assumption. At one point, it seemed as though the contrast phenomena could themselves be explained cognitively, as a sort of degenerate case of lightness constancy (see p. 412), but because we now know that at least some of the induction effects are sensory in nature (Horeman, 1965), they are at best an encumbrance to a cognitive theory. Although we cannot completely reject the cognitive type of explanation, we must seriously consider *sensory explanations of color constancy*, explanations that attempt to treat lightness constancy and brightness contrast as manifestations of the same sensory mechanisms.

As we have seen, Hering had argued that brightness contrast arises as a function of the way in which the retina responds to light and that this sensory phenomenon would explain at least some of the facts of lightness constancy. The way in which contrast would account for lightness constancy is most readily illustrated by examining Wallach's (1948) proposal to explain perception of the color of objects by a very simple formula: 2 objects will appear equally light when the ratios of their luminances to those of their surrounds are equal. Consider 2 test objects of luminance L_{t1} and L_{t2} seen against surrounds of luminance L_{s1} and L_{s2}, respectively. Wallach states that the objects will appear equally light under conditions in which the ratios of their luminances to those of their surrounds are equal, that is, $L_{t1}/L_{s1} = L_{t2}/L_{s2}$. In the special case in which the objects that are being matched are presented against the same background, Wallach's formula would, of course, assure perfect lightness constancy, because, regardless of the changes in illumination, the *ratios* of luminance presented to the eye by 2 objects of different reflectance would remain unchanged. In this case $L_{t1} = R_{t1}E$, $L_{t2} = R_{t2}E$ and $L_{t1}/L_{t2} = R_{t1}/R_{t2}$. In fact, for any object of reflectance R_t against

any background whose reflectance is R_s, the light reflected to the eye from the object and the background will be in the ratio $L_t/L_s = R_t/R_s$, regardless of the illumination. Furthermore, no matter how the illumination is changed, the stimulus ratio L_t/L_s will also remain constant as long as the relevant reflectances remain constant. If the subject's visual system were to respond directly to that ratio, as a sensory phenomenon, we need not invent higher cognitive processes that would require him to solve the equation $R = L/E$.

In fact, the conditions described above suggest a way in which the problems of color constancy and color contrast become problems no longer. If we simply assert that the stimulus for perceived lightness is not the luminance L_t of the test object but is rather the ratio of that value to the luminance of the adjacent region, L_t/L_s, all inquiries concerning the cues to illumination described above (p. 404), and concerning unconscious inference, memory colors, and the distinction between sensation and perception, may become unnecessary.

The horizontal line R in Figure 12.9A describes this relationship. The apparent color of the test patch remains unchanged even though its luminance L_t is increased. In fact, as we have seen, research on brightness contrast has shown that just this kind of result occurs under some conditions (Hess & Pretori, 1894; Wallach, 1948; Heinemann, 1955; see Freeman, 1967, for a comprehensive review of this point). Where this relationship occurs, lightness constancy should in fact result from the operation of brightness contrast, regardless of whether or not illumination cues are present.

Test patches do *not* always look equally light when the ratios of their luminances to the luminances of their surrounds are equal. In curve *i* in Figure 12.9B, we see that the brightness of the test patch does not remain constant but increases with increasing luminance, and in curve *iii*, the brightness decreases with increasing luminance, even though in both cases the ratio L_t/L_s is constant for each curve. Wallach's proposal holds for only a restricted range of L_t/L_s ratios, for the data of simultaneous contrast. Therefore, if simultaneous contrast is important in lightness constancy, we should expect corresponding departures from constancy in experiments on object-color perception. When ratios of L_t/L_s are high, matches made to the test patch should come closer to luminance matches, and the Brunswik ratio should come closer to 0.0. That is, if the background is dark compared to the object, lightness constancy should be poorer.

There are several experiments that have given this general form of result. In Hsia's (1943) experiment (Figure 12.9C), subjects looked alternately at gray disks set in separately illuminated chambers. The disks were seen against a distant black background, which separated them visually from the illuminated walls and floors of the chambers. Hsia varied the illumination of one chamber, and the subject tried to adjust the luminance of the disk in the second chamber until both disks seemed equally light. If the results are separated into matches made when the ratio of L_t/L_s was high (as when the object's luminance is greater than that of the booth's walls) from those in which L_t/L_s was low, the responses fall closer to a straight luminance match (curve *i*). If a darker standard and more reflective surroundings are used, the matches are somewhat closer to constancy (curve *iii*). More clear-cut evidence that under these conditions constancy decreases when the relative reflectance of the surroundings is decreased was obtained by Leibowitz, Myers, and Chinetti (1955) and Leibowitz and Chinetti (1957). In these experiments, which were similar to Hsia's except that backgrounds differing in reflectance (white, gray, and black) were placed so that they immediately surrounded gray test objects and a much wider range of illuminations was used, the more reflective (white) backgrounds produced matches close to constancy (Figure 12.9D), whereas the less reflective gray and black backgrounds produced less constancy.

Thus, the object's appearance changed more with changes in its illumination when the background was dark than when it was light. (Note particularly the dotted curves, *i, ii,* and *iii,* which were obtained by Leibowitz and Chinetti in response to very brief exposures.) Other studies, such as those of Kozaki (1963, 1965) and Warren and Poulton (1966), have also found that constancy is better with light than with dark backgrounds. (These latter researchers found that, under their conditions, it made a difference whether or not the test object or the background was more reflective, but the *degree* by which the two differed had no significant effect.)

So at least some of the expected departures from perfect constancy do occur, in at least a qualitative way. However, this does not mean that we can in fact use the data and models of brightness contrast to predict the data on lightness constancy with any degree of precision. This is so for 2 reasons. First, there are some discrepancies between the data of brightness contrast and those produced by experiments with lightness constancy. For example, although brightness contrast experiments fail, in general (see p. 411), to show any enhancement of a more luminous target by a less luminous surround, some constancy experiments have shown clear enhancement of the object's lightness (Kozaki, 1963; Leibowitz, Myers, & Chinetti, 1955). Second, the procedures of the lightness constancy experiments usually differ in several important ways from those used in the brightness contrast research.

Contrast and constancy experiments usually differ in these ways: (1) Whereas test patches and surrounds are small and homogeneously luminous in contrast experiments, in constancy experiments the objects and their backgrounds are usually large and microtextured, and the background scenes are often quite inhomogeneous. (2) The subjects' task is more complex in the constancy experiments than it is in the contrast experiments. In the latter, the subject need only respond to *any* difference in appearance between comparison and standard test patches, while in the former he must, in addition, decide whether the 2 objects have the same reflectance, regardless of whether they look alike in other respects (in other words, there may be *multiple criteria* on which the subject must base his choice). (3) In the constancy experiments, the comparison and test fields are often considerably separated in space, and appear in surroundings that are of different overall luminance. Therefore, the other mechanisms that help adjust the eye to lighting differences (such as pupillary dilation and retinal adaptation) should contribute their effects to the final judgment.

Some of the discrepancies between brightness contrast and lightness constancy data might plausibly be accounted for in terms of all of the procedural differences mentioned above. In order to evaluate such contrast explanations of lightness constancy, therefore, we should consider not whether their success in precise quantitative prediction is better than that of the cognitive theories (which do not really make such predictions, anyway), but whether we can explain away those examples of constancy that seem to be inexplicable on purely sensory grounds, even as gross qualitative phenomena. Before we attempt to do so, we should consider another factor, adaptation, and the theory of *adaptation level*. This theory, although it is not a contrast theory like those considered above, is not a cognitive theory, either, for it attempts to predict perception of the color of an object from measurable aspects of the visual stimulation.

Adaptation to the intensity of the light entering the eye is a familiar and clear example of the eye's adjustment to the illumination (increasing the eye's sensitivity by a factor of over 10,000 after about half an hour in darkness). In Hering's original explanation of lightness constancy, it will be remembered, adaptation was 1 of the 3 main sensory mechanisms that would enable the visual system to make the same response to a scene even though the illumination changes. Also,

the eye adapts to hue, of course: When you first enter a room lit by colored illumination (or put on tinted sunglasses), objects that were white now have the hue of the illuminant; after a while, however, the tint becomes unnoticeable, and the objects appear as they do in normal illumination.

To Hering, adaptation was a physiological mechanism. Helmholtz, in contrast, had proposed that the color of a region is judged by the way in which that region's luminance deviates from the average luminance of the field, which the subject assumes to be the overall illumination. Let us see what the facts are.

Helson (1938) had subjects sit in a light-tight booth, flooded with nearly homogeneous light, all of one wavelength. The walls and the table were covered with paper of a uniform color. The illumination might be either red, green, blue or yellow; the paper lining the booth might be white, gray, or black, with reflectances of 80, 23, or 3 percent, respectively. Consider a session in which the booth was lined with gray paper and flooded with red light. When the subject first entered, everything looked quite red; or at least red-illuminated. After 5 minutes of adaptation to the illumination, the subject judged a set of 19 gray samples, all nonselective reflectors; under normal illumination, the grays were presented in equal-appearing steps running from white to black. The subject's task was to rate the samples in terms of hue, lightness, and saturation, using notation of the Munsell scale (p. 359), with which he had previously practiced in daylight. Samples that had about the same reflectance as the gray walls and background were judged to be gray, of medium brightness. Brighter samples were judged to be red, and the more their reflectance, the greater their apparent saturation. Samples that were darker than the walls were seen as green or blue-green (the afterimage complement of the red illuminant), and the lower the reflectance, the more saturated the blue-green appeared. The lightness ratings of the grays were about the same throughout as in daylight. When, in another session, the walls were covered with white instead of gray paper, the eyes received stronger red stimulation; that is, a higher *adaptation level* was established, in Helson's terms. With this higher level, only the 2 lightest grays appeared red, the next 2 appeared neutral, and the rest appeared blue-green or blue. When the walls were all black, all except the darkest samples appeared red. Experiments with similar results were performed by Helson and Jeffers (1940) and by Judd (1940).

How can we explain these findings? In each case, an adaptation level was established by the prevailing reflectance. Grays near that level appeared neutral, brighter grays appeared to be of the same hue as the illuminant, and darker grays took on the afterimage complement of that hue. When white paper was used to line the walls, the reflectance of the walls was high, the adaptation level was high, and therefore only a few samples appeared red; conversely, when reflectance of the walls was low and, hence, the adaptation level was low, most samples were above the adaptation level, and appeared red. It is tempting to explain the phenomenon cognitively, saying that the subject takes the illumination into account, and "subtracts" the assumed illumination from the level of luminance of any object, thereby inferring its reflectance. However, we should also note what happens in the *Ganzfeld* (see p. 426), in which no objects or cues to illumination exist: When the eye is exposed to an overall homogeneous visual field of some hue, say red, the color soon fades to something approaching a mid-gray, and appears to stay that way unless some change occurs (Hochberg, Triebel, & Seaman, 1951; Cohen 1958). If the light increases in brightness, it will again appear red; if a shadow is imposed, it appears blue-green (Hochberg, Triebel, & Seaman, 1951). The visual system has adapted to the incident light, which has now become homogeneously neutral in appearance, but in this case the explanation cannot be that the subject has separated out what he considers

to be the illumination from what he considers to be surface color: In the *Ganzfeld* no surface color appears, only a space-filling fog (see p. 426). So we can accept Helmholtz' general line of analysis here only if we discard the intellectual connotations suggested by his terms: The conditions of stimulation, rather than any knowledge about surfaces and sources, bring about adaptation.

"Adaptation level" sounds like a physiological concept, something that might correspond to the momentary concentration of photoreceptive substances in the retina (p. 286). Helson (1948, 1964) has since worked out a formula for computing what the adaptation level is. His formula is to be applied not only to the effects of the walls and the stimuli used in the 1938 experiment, but for all manner of judgment situations, ranging from color constancy and contrast to lifted weights (and even to social attitudes). Thus his concept should be viewed more as a matter of judgment scales (Chapter 3) than as a matter of identifiable physiological processes. If we restrict our attention here to color perception, the explanation based on adaptation level does not differ in its gross outlines from the contrast theories of constancy that we have just been considering. There are some differences in prediction; for example, although both contrast and constancy are reduced when targets are more luminous than their surrounds, as we have seen on page 414, Helson (1943) predicts and finds good lightness constancy even when the background is less reflective than the object, as long as the standard and comparison objects are "anchored" by having backgrounds of the same reflectance. Regardless of such differences, the similarity of the theory of adaptation level to one based on contrast, as an explanation of constancy, is much greater than its differences, and we will not try here to separate adaptation level effects from contrast effects. It is not crucial to the present question whether the adaptation mechanism is a matter of central scaling, of changes in retinal sensitivities, or both. It is clear, of course, that adaptation has produced *incorrect* color judgments in the conditions we have discussed thus far. Of greater significance, however, is the fact that a shift of the adaptation level could account for the fact that we tend to see the hues of surfaces correctly even when the wavelength of the illuminant changes.

Hue contrast, or simultaneous color contrast, is very similar in principle to lightness contrast: A region of the visual field of one color induces the complement of that color in an adjacent region (see Chapter 10), without need for an appreciable adaptation period. Thus, a gray patch on a yellow background will look bluish, on a red background it will look greenish, and a yellow patch on a green background will have an orange appearance. To Hering, of course, such contrast was a sensory phenomenon, susceptible to psychophysical analysis and explanation without invoking any cognitive factors. In fact, the quantitative Jameson-Hurvich model, based on Hering's opponent-process theory, has been extended to include hue contrast as well as brightness contrast (1964). Also, like brightness contrast, hue contrast will help explain the constancy of the perception of the color of an object under changing illumination. Let us see how color adaptation and color contrast would work to bring about the perception of true surface color.

When the illumination is confined to a single narrow band of the spectrum, we have very little ability to perceive the true surface color. However, even a small admixture of white light greatly improves the perception of surface colors (Helson & Jeffers, 1940). Consider a green object in a gray surround, both of them receiving yellow light (Wallach & Galloway, 1946). The object reflects yellow-green light to the eye, but the gray surround also reflects some yellow light. The yellow in the surroundings tends to raise the adaptation level for yellow, and to push the yellow-green away from yellow and towards the complementary, blue. That is, the yellow illuminant falling on the object tends to dis-

color the greenish object toward yellow; the yellow illuminant falling on the background tends to induce the complementary of the yellow illuminant, blue, in the object. If the induced blue were equal to the discoloring effect of the yellow illuminant, the resulting apparent hue of the object would remain unchanged even though the hue of the illuminant had changed from white to yellow. More striking are the well-known demonstrations by Land (1954, 1964): If a slide of various colored objects, photographed through a red filter, is projected (through a red filter) in precise superposition with another slide of the same objects that was photographed through a green filter and projected in white (unfiltered) light, subjects see other colors (greens and yellows for example) on the screen, as well as reds. This is a very impressive form of color constancy, considering that only one "color" (the red record) and one "colorless" slide (the white-light projection) is used. We might interpret such findings as evidence for the efficacy of memory color (see pp. 398, 424), except that reversing the 2 records reverses the apparent colors of the objects as well.

In one sense, of course, all of these "colored shadows" are demonstrations of false color perception because the patches of light and shade on the screen, viewed separately, would be seen as varying shades of red, pink or gray. In another sense, however, the constancy is so remarkable that we can argue that the essential stimuli required for perceiving the color of objects have been retained, despite the apparent paucity of the information being given the subject.

In order to account for these phenomena, Land has been developing a theory in which specific wavelengths are not important in determining a region's hue. At present, however, it seems possible to accommodate Land's findings within the more classical theories about how simultaneous contrast occurs in the visual system, and such explanations have indeed been offered (Hurvich & Jameson, 1960; Judd, 1960; Walls, 1960).

However, the surprising efficacy of Land's demonstrations emphasizes the importance of the interactions that occur between regions that receive different stimulation, and the possibility that most of the phenomena of color constancy can follow directly from the nature of such interactions.

The sensory explanations of the perception of objects' colors, then, seem able to account for most of the facts of lightness and hue constancy, at least in principle. In actual research on the constancies, the stimulation consists of complex fields, to which the subject's response is not an immediate match, but involves memory, labeling, and so on (p. 423). Thus, the potential precision of the sensory theories of brightness contrast cannot be directly tested by the much less precise data of the experiments on lightness constancy. The difference between the qualitative cognitive theories and the more quantitative sensory theories is not a trivial one, however, because very different tasks confront the psychologist, depending on which theory he adopts. If some general cognitive principles are involved in the process of turning meaningless sensations into meaningful perceptions of the color of objects, what we learn about color perception will tell us something about cognitive processes in general. This makes problems of color perception the clear concern of the psychologist. On the other hand, if most or all of the perceptual phenomena occur because of the way in which the relatively peripheral sensory nervous system responds to patterns of stimulation to begin with, the phenomena of color contrast and of color constancy may reduce almost to data of sensory physiology, specific to the visual system. This would leave the psychologist with a clearer field of inquiry, which no longer includes the classic problems of color constancy and contrast, but it would also leave the psychologist with one less window into the nature of general cognition.

Sensory explanations of the perception of objects' colors, regardless of the precise nature of the luminance-brightness relationship

they postulate, challenge the cognitive explanations in one major respect. The former assume that the stimulation that falls on the observer's eye is what determines the colors he perceives, after we take his state of adaptation, and so on, into account. The latter do not. This would seem to permit a qualitative confrontation between Hering and Helmholtz to be undertaken, centering on whether or not the distribution of stimulus energies controls the perception of color. Let us next consider what information we have on this point.

Is Perceived Object-Color Stimulus-Determined?

The processes that are responsible for perceived color may be "judgmental" in the Helmholtzian sense, or "physiological" in Hering's sense. In either case they have to start with what is given to the eye. Anything more than the most general sort of "explanation" will have to be able to predict quantitatively what will be seen in response to particular patterns of stimulation.

We can believe, with Helmholtz, that we perceive surface colors as we do because of what we have learned from our experiences with the world, yet still believe that those experiences are themselves lawfully related to measurable aspects of stimulation. After all, the relationships within the physical world are subject to rigorous physical laws (for example, that $R = L/E$), and we would expect most people to learn similar things from their experiences with the physical world (for example, that $R = L/E$, and the various cues about E). However, a theory that explains color constancy as being the result of some process of taking illumination into account has this implication: If we can change the subject's assumption about E without changing the array of luminances in his retinal image, his judgment of R should also change. The cognitive position therefore would not be at all embarrassed by finding that the stimulus does not completely determine the object's apparent color (although, because of the great deal of perceptual learning that has occurred by even a very early age, a Helmholtzian would not be surprised if in fact few such cases of stimulus indeterminacy could be found). To any sensory theory of lightness constancy, on the contrary, to which knowledge of the illumination is irrelevant, a finding that different judgments of lightness are made by subjects, even when the stimulus array remains unchanged, would at first glance seem to pose a very serious challenge. Let us therefore consider what evidence we have on this point.

There have been 2 lines of research concerned with the attempt to change the subject's assumptions about the scene he faces while keeping the stimulus array unchanged. One of these studied the effects of apparent illumination on apparent lightness (some of these have been described above; see p. 404). The other has studied the effect of *memory color*. We consider each of these lines of research in turn.

The effects of space, form and apparent illumination on perceived color   We have already reviewed a number of experiments that seemed to show that the subject takes illumination cues into account in order to arrive at his judgments of reflectance. On closer examination, those experiments fail to support a cognitive theory unequivocally. The cues are themselves components in the distributions of luminance in the stimulus array, and even a sensory theory would expect such components to affect the apparent lightness of the test object, *regardless of the fact that they may also be called "illumination cues."* Consider the Gelb experiment (p. 404). In that case, a black disk appeared to be white when it alone was illuminated in an otherwise dark room. As soon as a small piece of white paper was placed in front of the disk so that the paper also received the spotlight's illumination, the black disk appeared dark or black. At first glance, this appears to be due to the fact that the white paper revealed the true state of illumination, which the subject could then discount.

Against this cognitive explanation, however, are the following considerations.

First, each time the white piece of paper was removed, the disk lost its black appearance and again appeared white: sheer knowledge that the black disk is illuminated by a spotlight, and that it is really black, is not enough to make it look black unless the white paper is actually present. This alone discredits the casual version of the cognitive theory that still pervades college textbooks on psychology: Although it may in some sense be true that "what we know affects what we see," none of the terms in this phrase can mean what they do in common usage.

Second, we have not really left the stimulus unchanged when the piece of white paper was introduced because the white paper would itself be expected to darken the disk by contrast. The white paper is small relative to the black disk, however, and we know that induced brightness contrast decreases when the size of the inducing field is decreased (see Chapter 10). For this reason, it has been argued (Osgood, 1953, p. 283) that although such a small bit of white can act as a cue to the illumination, it must be too small to induce any contrast in the disk. On the contrary Stewart (1959) has shown that the disk's appearance does not simply change from white (with no "cue" present) to black (with the white "cue" present), as we would expect it to in terms of the cognitive theory's explanation of the Gelb effect. In a setup that was essentially similar to Gelb's (see Figure 12.5), Stewart placed small white disks of varying size (0.5, 1.0, 2.0 in.) at different distances from the center of the black disk (which was 12 inches in diameter). The black disk looked darker when the white object was made larger and brought closer to the center of the black disk. Moreover, the darkening effects produced by the white object were not uniform over the entire surface of the black disk but were reported to be greatest in the immediate neighborhood of the white object.

Thus, the Gelb effect can be altered by the same stimulus factors that affect brightness contrast, and it seems evident that contrast contributes to the effect. There are probably other factors at work in the Gelb experiment as well. In Stewart's experiment, there may be some size of the white disk (less than 0.5 in.) below which further size decrements do not reduce the Gelb effect. However, this still would not mean that the apparent lightness is determined by cognitive rather than by sensory factors; even a very small patch of white introduced into Gelb's setup has changed the stimulus display that confronts the eye. For example, the *range* of stimulation in the room has been changed with the introduction of the white paper, and Koffka (1932, 1935) and Judd (1941), proposed (in otherwise quite different theories) that what luminance the subject will see as white, and what he will see as black, is determined by that range.

In short, then, the Gelb experiment may mean the opposite of what it first seems to: It may show that knowledge of illumination is *ineffective* in changing apparent reflectance.

However, there is another method for manipulating the apparent illumination, this time in such a way as to keep the stimulus array effectively unchanged. We can use an ambiguous spatial arrangement—that is, one in which the object can readily be seen in either of 2 very different positions relative to the source of the illumination. For example, imagine a cube, one of whose faces, 1, receives full illumination while the other face, 2, is in partial shadow. Both sides have the same reflectance, say $R = 50$ percent. Let side 1 receive illumination $E = 100$ ft-c, while side 2 receives 60 ft-c. Then side 1 has a luminance of $L_1 = RE_1 = 50$ percent $\times 100 = 50$ ft-L, and side 2 has a luminance of $L_2 = RE_2 = 50$ percent $\times 60 = 30$ ft-L. If the subject should solve the formula $R = L/E$, with adequate cues to the relative illumination that each face receives, he would correctly take the 2 sides to have equal reflectances. Suppose however that his depth perception is in error, and that he takes side 1 to lie in the same plane as side 2. The sides would then appear to receive the same illumination, and if he solved the equation for R with that appearance as his starting point, he would then erroneously decide that the 2 sides had unequal reflectances: $R_1 = L_1/E_1 = 50/100 = 50$ percent, $R_2 = L_2/E_2 = 30/100 = 30$ percent.

There are a few demonstrations and experiments with just such results (Mach, 1914; Katona, 1935). Evans (1948) used apparatus similar to that of Hess and Pretori (Figure 12.8, p. 408) to present 2 sets of background and test fields. The depth cues were sufficiently ambiguous so that the subject could see the 2 background fields as being adjacent parts of a single plane surface, with test and comparison fields t_r and t_l located behind that plane; alternatively, the subject could interpret the view as that of the 2 sides of a cube, with 1 face receiving more illumination than the other, and with t_r and t_l as squares of paper pasted on the cube's faces. The subject was instructed to adopt each interpretation. The 2 different instructions produced very different results when the subject was instructed to match test fields t_r and t_l. Instructions were *not* directly about the illumination, it should be noted, but about which of two *spatial* arrangements the subject should consider.

Similarly, Hochberg and Beck (1954) devised an arrangement to mislead the subject about the target's orientation to the light. Viewed monocularly, the target, which was a trapezoid standing upright on a table, looked like a rectangle lying flat on the table. Good "illumination cues" were offered by large white cubes placed on the black table near the gray target X. The subject was asked to match the apparent color of X by referring to a set of gray papers in the background. The apparent slant of X with respect to the direction of illumination was changed by introducing various depth cues (by switching to binocular vision; by waving a black or a white stick behind the target; or by moving the target from side to side with a wire). Several different depth cues were used because each cue is a change in stimulus conditions, regardless of the fact that it offers information about depth (for example, the total field of view may appear brighter with binocular than with monocular viewing—Katz, 1935). When it appears upright, X should also appear to receive less light than when it appears to lie flat (because its surface would then be receiving only parallel or glancing illumination), so that, in solving for R, the target, when apparently upright, should appear lighter than when it appeared to be flat on the table. Subjects did indeed judge the target to look slightly lighter in that condition. Again, Beck (1965), with a different arrangement, found that the 2 sides of a folded figure, one side of which receives more light than another, look appropriately unequal in lightness when the subject is restricted to monocular viewing and the 2 sides look coplanar, but they look equally light when binocular cues as to their spatial arrangement are provided. We should note, however, that such results have not always been obtained (Epstein, 1961), so that the conditions that produce them are not now clear.

We might interpret these findings as demonstrations that, at least in some cases, "exactly the same stimulation" will produce different apparent surface lightnesses and, therefore, as evidence that surface color is not always stimulus determined. They do show that, but do they therefore clearly support the Helmholtzian view that the perceived illumination is taken into account in arriving at perceived color, and do they clearly oppose those theories that consider color constancy to be an automatic and stimulus-determined consequence of the luminance relationships within the retinal image? No, they do not. In order to see why not, we shall have to consider (1) the limitations on what is meant by an "identical stimulus display" (which, because of possible differences in eye movements, does not mean that the subject has actually received the same set of retinal images under two different instructional conditions); (2) the effects of the object's

surface texture; and (3) the possible implications of the fact that the observer usually must match the standard and variable stimuli when they are widely separated in space.

The possible role of eye movements and of differential attention in constancy experiments In the experiments we have just described, the stimulus displays that confront the observer are indeed identical, or essentially identical, in the different experimental conditions. We do not know, however, that the subject makes the same eye movements when he views what he considers to be different spatial arrangements. Hering had noted long ago (1907) that when the eye makes successive fixations in a field of diverse luminances, the apparent lightness of a given patch will depend on the previous stimulation to which that retinal region has been exposed. Flock, Wilson, and Poizner (1966) have asked a subject to match a standard in one part of the visual field by looking at a set of comparison grays in another region. If he is instructed to do so by following a visual path that takes his eye through a set of grays having a low luminance level, he picks a darker comparison figure as matching the standard than he does when his eye traverses an intervening region of high luminance patches. With the setup used by Hochberg and Beck (p. 420), we might expect the subject to compare the target X and the vertical faces of the cubes when X looks upright, for he will assume that those surfaces are receiving the same illumination as the target; when X looks flat on the table, however, the subject may compare it to the upper faces of the cubes. If he moves his eyes back and forth between those surfaces that he is comparing, the effects of successive adaptation would be different when the subject makes different assumptions about the target's orientation. (Even if eye movements do not occur in accordance with this speculation, the subject might still pay attention to different features of the neighboring cubes to anchor his judgments about X before shifting his gaze to the set of comparison grays to make his lightness match.)

The effects of texture and other inhomogeneities on object color   In the Gelb experiment, a rotating black velvet disk, illuminated by a spotlight, appeared to be white until a piece of white paper was placed next to it, and then it looked black. *However, merely stopping the rotation also made the disk look black.* Why is there this difference between a rotating and stationary disk?

A paper, cloth, or wood surface usually has a fine but definite grain or "microstructure." In the case of the velvet disk, small particles of dust and fibres of the velvet reflect more light than the rest of the disk, and provide a visible microstructure. The rotation of a color wheel blurs or washes out the grain of the paper; when the rotation stops, the microstructure becomes visible. Even though the overall luminance of the disk remained the same in Gelb's experiment, whether or not the disk was spinning, the visibility of the microstructure changed the judgments the subjects made of the disk's lightness. Other observers have noted that there is a relationship between a surface's visible texture and its apparent lightness (Katz, 1935; Judd, 1952).

Why should microtexture improve constancy? In terms of a cognitive theory, it has been argued that the presence of microstructure permits the subject to separate surface color from illumination (Katz, 1935, pp. 90f, 275f; Woodworth & Schlosberg, 1954, p. 435). The few quantitative experiments that have been performed relevant to this question, however, do not support this cognitive interpretation. Beck (1964) performed a series of studies on perceived lightness in which the target was either a smooth matte black paper, or a glossy black tile, whose average or overall luminances were equated. The apparent lightness of the glossy surface remained more constant with changes in illumination than did that of the matte surface. The matte surface is uniform, whereas some parts of a glossy surface reflect more light to the eye

than do others. It follows, therefore, that when both surfaces were equated for overall luminance, parts of the glossy surface must have been darker than the matte surface. The glossy tile was in fact judged to appear darker, even though the overall luminances of both surfaces were equal. In another experiment, when the reflections on the glossy tile were restricted to one part of the tile, and the rest of the tile was kept uniformly equal in luminance to the matte paper, the 2 surfaces were judged to be equally light, even though the glossy surface now had a higher overall luminance. When judging inhomogeneous surfaces, therefore, it seems that subjects do not respond to the average luminance as reflected over the whole surface but make their matches on the basis of some particular selected regions of the surface. In this case, they apparently attempted to avoid the reflections.

The highlights and shadows on a textured surface will therefore affect the surface's apparent lightness in at least 2 ways. First, of course, any small highlight darkens parts of the surface adjacent to it, by contrast. That is, the presence of microstructure results in internal contrast, quite apart from the contrast that is produced by the surround. In fact, the apparent lightnesses of surfaces containing distributed highlights remain more independent of changes in the luminance of the surrounding field than do those of the reflective matte target (Beck, 1964, pp. 56, 60). Second, because subjects seem to base their judgments of lightness on local regions rather than on some average taken across the entire surface, their choice of which regions are selected for this purpose will affect their judgment of lightness. Although there is no experimental evidence to this point, it seems probable that this selection depends on which regions they take to be representative of the "normal" reflectance of the surface and on which regions they take to be "accidental" reflections, highlights and shadows. This, in turn, may be determined by what they assume to be the nature of the surface and its uniformity of color; that is, it may be determined by its perceived *surface quality* (see p. 426) and by what they assume to be the arrangement of the illumination (see Beck, 1965). However, this is very different from the theory that the subject uses the microstructure to take illumination into account in solving the equation $R = L/E$. In fact, because judgments about illumination are probably based on the points of maximum luminance, or the highlights (Beck, 1961, 1962; see p. 406) and because textured surfaces can be manipulated so that the highlights can be varied in luminance independently of the rest of the surface, judgments of illumination and of reflectance can probably be made to be quite independent of each other.

There are thus usually several different criteria on which subjects can base their judgments. They can say, for example, that the standard and variable appear to be equal when the standard's highlights match those of the variable, or they can decide that both are equal when the contrast between the targets and their surroundings seems to be the same. Indeed, the color matches that subjects make can be caused to vary by changing the instructions that they are given (MacLeod, 1932; Henneman, 1935; Katz, 1935; Landauer & Roger, 1964). The fact is that in the constancy experiments, as they have been traditionally performed, we have no explicit knowledge about the criteria by which the subject reaches his decisions about whether or not 2 objects are the same color. Until some techniques are found with which to separate the various criteria available to the subject in the constancy experiments in general, the extent to which apparent lightness is stimulus determined, and in fact, the precise amount of color constancy that has to be explained, remains difficult to evaluate.[3]

[3]Additional demonstrations that factors other than the luminance distributions in the visual field can affect lightness judgments have recently received attention. Thus, Gogel and Mershon (1969) found that the stimulus conditions (specifically, binocular disparity—see Chapter 13, p. 481) which make a test patch and its surround appear to be at different distances from the subject also reduce the

Naming and Remembering Colors in the Constancy Experiment

Time errors In the typical constancy experiment, the subject has to decide whether or not 2 objects that receive different illuminations have the same reflectance. To do this, he usually compares objects that are widely separated in space. This means that he must compare his impression of the object at which he is looking with his memory of what the other object looked like. This introduces a new source of error (the *time error,* see Chapter 2), and it may also provide an opportunity for the subject's attitude and knowledge to influence his psychophysical judgment. Having made some decision about an object's surface color, the subject may remember the decision itself, when he turns to consider the comparison stimulus, rather than the complex visual appearance of the object's surface. Brown and Lenneberg (1954) found that the recognizability of a color, which the subject saw in isolation and then had to identify after a long delay (about 3 minutes) by pointing it out from among a chart of many other colors, was correlated with the *codability* of the color (that is, with how well people agree in naming it). Differences in instruction, or in interpretation of what he is looking at, may perhaps affect the subject's psychophysical judgment by affecting the way in which he categorizes or commits to memory one or both of the stimuli he is comparing, even with considerably shorter delays.

The possibility that the subject may label and remember differently objects that would have looked equally light if he could have

contrast effects that are obtained, even though the two regions remain laterally adjacent and unchanged in their luminances. Again, Coren (1969) showed that a stronger contrast effect is obtained in a test region when it is seen as *figure* (see p. 432) than when it is seen as ground, confirming earlier demonstrations to that point (Benary, 1924; Mikesell & Bentley, 1930; Wertheimer, described in Koffka, 1935, p. 136). The extent to which such demonstrations embarass any theory which holds that the perception of color is stimulus determined, and the degree to which they can be accommodated by the kinds of explanations discussed in pages 421–423, remain to be seen.

compared them simultaneously thus offers still another explanation of why the same stimulus display can elicit different psychophysical judgments under different instructions. It also brings us to a second line of research that *seems* to show that factors that are not contained in the stimulus display can influence the appearance of objects' colors, namely, the work on *memory color*.

Effects of memory and memory color   In addition to the sensory mechanisms that contribute to color constancy, Hering (see p. 398) proposed a nonsensory factor. He held that what we call the real color of any object is the color that we have most often seen on that object, a color that is indelibly impressed on our memory image of it.

Such *memory colors* could only be of limited use in maintaining color constancy, even in the case of familiar objects, because our memory colors are, in general, significantly different from the natural colors of the objects we are remembering. When subjects are asked to match the remembered colors of objects from an array of color chips, they tend to pick chips of greater saturation and lightness (Newhall, Burnham, & Clark, 1957; Bartleson, 1960). However, that still leaves open the question of the extent to which memory colors can influence our perceptions of objects at which we are currently looking.

Duncker (1939) showed subjects two pieces of the same green material, one cut into the shape of a leaf and the other into the shape of a donkey. Both cutouts were viewed under red illumination; although the light was not monochromatic, subjects reported that the green material appeared gray when it was presented to them in the form of a *circular* cutout. A variable color wheel, viewed under normal illumination, was used to match the appearance of either the leaf or the donkey. We would expect that the leaf would appear greener than the donkey, if memory color contributes to the apparent color of the cutouts in this situation, and that is what happened. The color wheel was taken

as matching the donkey when it had a 29° green sector, and as matching the leaf when it had a 60° green sector. Do these results show an absence of stimulus determination of apparent color?

There are 2 reasons why these results don't necessarily rule out stimulus determination. First, because the standard stimulus (donkey or leaf) and the variable stimulus (color wheel) could not be viewed simultaneously; and second, because the stimuli were not in fact identical, but were of different shape, and the shape should have effects on the amount of contrast that would be induced in the figure (by the red illumination on the surrounding field), regardless of the shape's meaning.

Bruner, Postman, and Rodrigues (1951) performed a variation of Duncker's experiment, with a wider variety of shapes and with several conditions of viewing. When the standard cutouts and the variable color wheel were separated from each other (by 80° of visual angle), so that the subject could not see both simultaneously, those standards that should have displayed a memory color did so. When the standard and variable were adjacent to each other, no effects attributable to memory color were obtained. We cannot take these results, therefore, or Duncker's either, to mean that memory colors affect the *perception* of object color, for the effects only appeared when the variable color wheel was matched to the subject's *memory* of the cutout. The results may merely show that a familiar object's characteristic color affects the way we remember it (Hochberg, 1956), not the way we see it. Bolles, Hulicka, and Hanly (1959) pointed out an additional problem with such experiments, in that the standards and variable were such that an exact match could not be made. In an experiment similar to Duncker's, which also precluded an exact match, Duncker's results were confirmed. However, when a black and a white sector were added to the variable color wheel, so that a good match could be achieved, the difference between the donkey and the leaf disappeared. These results support the contention that memory color does not change the actual appearance of a stimulus: when he is unable to make an exact psychophysical match, the subject will resolve the impossible task by making the most reasonable mismatch, namely one that is close to the object's characteristic color.

Harper (1953) introduced a procedure that appeared to be free from both of these flaws. He placed the test figures in front of a differential color mixer, and varied the degree of the redness of the figures. The subject's task was to report when the figure became "indistinguishable" from the background. The test figures were all cut out from the same orange paper, three being shapes of red-associated objects (apple, heart, lobster), and three being neutral shapes (oval, triangle, letter Y). The stimuli were introduced with comments about their color (such as "a reddish apple," or "a yellowish-orange oval") that would identify to the subject the appropriate memory color. Harper found that 71° of red were required to match the nonmeaningful figures, and 134° were needed for the meaningful ones. If the stimuli really became indistinguishable from their backgrounds, and if the effects of memory color on the distinguishabilities of the forms can be unequivocally demonstrated by this kind of procedure, it would be a striking fact indeed, for the processes of contour formation that separate figure from ground are usually thought to depend at least in part on peripheral mechanisms that respond to objective stimulus differences in the retinal image.

Fisher, Hull, and Holtz (1956), using Harper's procedure, found that subjects made no difference in their responses to a cross that was labeled as a "red cross" symbol, and the same figure when it was rotated 45° and called a "letter X." Moreover, in a recent replication and improvement of Harper's experiment by Delk and Fillenbaum (1965), differential instructions as to what the cutouts represented had no effects. It did make a significant difference in the subjects' matches,

however, whether the cutouts were red-associated figures (heart, apple, lips), neutral shapes (oval, circle, and ellipse), or shapes associated with some other color (horse, bell, mushroom). Although all shapes were cut out of the same red-orange paper, and all were of approximately the same area, significantly more red had to be mixed in with the background color in order for subjects to decide that the red-associated figures and the background were of the same color. The cutouts differed among themselves in their shapes, of course, so we might argue that it was the differences in contour per se, not past associations, that influenced the color judgments, but their data make this argument implausible. We still have to ask, however, whether subjects really *saw* a difference in the colors of the cutouts, or whether they were acting in accordance with some sort of *response bias* (see Chapter 2, p. 36). No provision was made to show that the subjects *really could not distinguish* the figures at those settings at which they declared that the cutouts matched their backgrounds. Perhaps a *signal-detection* procedure is in order, which would attempt to separate subjects' *criteria* from their *sensitivity* (see Chapter 2, p. 41). However, this last point is one which, as we have seen (see p. 423), really applies to much of the research on color perception.

In summary: to the question of whether color perception is stimulus-determined, we can answer with a qualified "no." Apparent spatial orientation, attention, memory—all of these cause the subjects to make different judgments in response to one and the same stimulus display. However, it is still possible to maintain a sensory theory which views color constancy as a special case of induced contrast and to explain away these nonsensory effects as *judgmental* phenomena superimposed on the sensory ones.

Does this reject the cognitive theory? Again, a qualified "no"; it may only mean that both Hering and Helmholtz were right, in that the starting point on which judgmental processes are based is itself already corrected (to some degree) for illumination changes, by the nature of the contrast-induction mechanism. This means that what the subject "really perceives" is not a simple matter that can be decided merely by asking him. We shall consider this point in more detail, and confront other conflicts between sensory and cognitive theories of perception, when we consider the problems of space and form perception.

For now, let us turn briefly to some of those aspects of apparent color besides hue, saturation and lightness, that we have so far barely mentioned.

OBJECT COLORS AND THE VARIETIES OF SURFACE QUALITY

So far, we have been asking questions only about objects' lightness and hue. These have mostly been questions that can be answered by manipulating the wavelength or intensity of homogeneous fields of light, and they have therefore been relatively easy to instrument. However, the colors we see in the world may vary in other ways. For example, the same yellow hue may be part of an object's surface, or an attribute of the light that illuminates it; the yellow may appear to be the color of the wine that fills a glass, or it may be the color of the glass that holds the fluid (Hering). These are perceptual qualities that cannot be studied, in general, with single patches of light, but which depend on the *pattern* of light at the eye.

Most of the attempts to list and describe the distinguishable types of color appearance rest at an introspective, phenomenal level. That is, these were, in general, studies in which an observer tried to describe what a particular area of color looked like without paying any attention to his knowledge (or to his guesses) about the stimulus, and without any bias as to what the patch *should* look like. An important distinction between modes of color naming, made by Katz (1911, 1935), who was trying to decide how colors appear to the naive observer, is the difference between *surface color* and *film color*. For example, a

uniform surface viewed through a hole or a reduction screen does not appear to be a surface at all, but rather a mere dimensionless expanse of color which fills the hole (see *aperture color,* p. 399). In an early examination of film color, Martin (1923) decided that this mode of appearance is neither bidimensional nor tridimensional but simply without dimensions in the geometrical sense. Her subjects called the stimulus a film color most frequently when the aperture was small (about 2 cm), and called the stimulus a surface most frequently with larger apertures (30 cm). Metzger (1930), who produced the first *Ganzfeld,* or homogeneous visual field, by placing the subject before a specially curved smooth plaster wall, found that some microstructure (see p. 422) was needed in order to perceive a definitely localized surface under those conditions. If the illumination of the *Ganzfeld* was reduced so that subjects could not focus clearly on the wall's texture, they reported that they saw a bulky, space-filling fog, instead of a definite surface (see Avant, 1965, for a review of *Ganzfeld* research). Outside of the *Ganzfeld,* however, texture is *not* essential in order for a colored area to look like a surface. For example, Fry (1931)

Figure 12.10. Two elementary dimensions of surface quality: glossy–matte, rough–smooth. A, matte, rough; B, glossy, rough; C, matte, smooth; D, glossy, smooth. (After a proposal by Evans, 1951.)

reported that if a rotating color wheel was perfectly uniform in luminance over its entire surface, it appeared to be hard and smooth, but that with even a small gradation of luminance over its surface, the disk tended to be perceived as a soft and bulky color, one that seemed to occupy a volume of space and that varied from fluffy to misty depending on the gradient of luminance.

Given a definite surface, clearly localized in space, there are still several distinctly different appearances it can have. Thus, surfaces can vary from *glossy* (or shiny) to *matte* (or dull); from *rough* to *smooth*; and from *opaque* to *transparent* (Judd, 1951; Evans, 1959). Some of the stimulus conditions that produce these different appearances are easy to identify. In Figure 12.10 (which is modeled after Evans, 1951), a rough matte, a rough glossy, a smooth matte, and a smooth glossy surface are portrayed at A, B, C, and D, respectively. A glossy surface is one which reflects light regularly in localized images (see Bixby, 1926; Hunter, 1937; Judd, 1951); a rough surface is one which has a marked distribution of local shadows cast by glancing light (that is, by illumination that is neither diffuse nor perpendicular to the surface).

A transparent surface is, of course, one that we can see through to some degree, and that means that we see two colors at the same place in space: the color of the surface, and the color that we see behind (or through) the surface. *Bulky color* or volume color implies some degree of transparency, and we have seen that Fry (1931) observed that a smooth gradient of luminance appears to be bulky if the surface is interpreted as being homogeneously illuminated. However, such gradients are certainly *not necessary* in order for a region to appear transparent; a perfectly uniform patch of color (A, C, in Figure 12.18) may or may not appear transparent, depending on the pattern in which it is embedded (Fuchs, 1923; Metelli, 1967).

In each of these surface qualities, the relationship between stimulation and appearance is an ambiguous one. Thus, in Figure 12.10D

the object might not be glossy at all, but might have a white streak painted on it; in Figure 12.18C, the gray rectangle at *i* might have black patches on it. In fact, of course, there really are no object surfaces—glossy, transparent, or otherwise—in Figure 12.10, there is only an inhomogeneous array of pigments on the surface of the page. Why do we see a single surface of uniform reflectance, but with the appropriate surface quality? The perception of the color and quality of an object's surface clearly involves the perception of space and form, and we return to this question about surface quality in the course of discussing these topics.

PROBLEMS IN THE PERCEPTION OF OBJECT SHAPE

Up to this point, we have had little to say about spatial relations in the visual field, or about distances, directions, sizes, and shapes. These characteristics of an object usually appear to be just as directly *seen* as are its color and brightness. It is not as easy to find the stimuli that are responsible for our observations of these properties, however, nor to discern the structures of the retina and of the visual nervous system whose actions are the bases of our experiences. For many years, it was hoped that it would be possible to explain these properties as elaborations or additions that occur after the simpler sensations of brightness and color arise from the direct action of light on the visual nervous system. It has therefore become customary to speak of "perception" of shape, rather than of shape "sensations."

The theory, in its very simplest form, was the Structuralist Theory that underlay the views shared by such physiologists and psychologists as Helmholtz, Wundt, and Titchener (see Boring, 1942; Hochberg, 1962; also pp. 396, 402, 527). According to this view we have a mosaic of independent visual receptors whose responses produce *sensations* (simple elementary experiences) of color. These receptors provide all that we have in the way of *specific nerve energies* (see p. 118) for vision; therefore all visual experience consists only of the sensations that they produce, plus whatever memories have become strongly associated with those sensations as the result of a great deal of experience with the physical world. Thus, the surface looks glossy and smooth in Figure 12.10 not because the visual system responds to "gloss" as such, but because that pattern of lightnesses brings to mind the appropriate tactual memories of what such surfaces feel like. Similarly, a circle looks like a circle because that pattern brings to mind the memories of what eye movements would be needed to follow its contour around (that is, to "trace" its outline with the center of vision, the fovea of the eye), together with the memories of curvature felt by the hand in touching a circular object, and so forth. In short, as far as this theory is concerned, we have discussed *purely visual* experience completely when we have analyzed the distribution of brightness and color within the visual field.

The structuralist approach has been vigorously challenged on several grounds. Historically, the primary challenge came from *Gestalt theory,* a viewpoint shared by such psychologists as Wertheimer, Koffka, and Köhler. They maintained that the basic design of the nervous system was such that it responded to shapes and forms directly, not to individual patches of light. Instead of individual receptors the individual responses of which produced the elementary color sensations, the Gestalt picture of the nervous system rested on broad electrical processes, initiated (but not completely determined) by the *configuration* of the light at the eye. These electrical processes, subject to their own internal laws of organization, were held to be the events in the nervous system to which our perceptions are *isomorphic,* or correspond in form. Much pioneer work on shape and form perception was undertaken by Gestalt psychologists, both to demonstrate various points that they were trying to make against the analytical approach of the structuralists,

and to discover the *laws of organization* of the underlying brain processes.

The stock questions that arose around the opposition of the Structuralist and Gestalt approaches (such as whether or not the elements of experience can be used to explain the properties of the whole, or whether shape perception is innate and not learned) have by no means been resolved, but they have been largely submerged and transformed by new programs and by the sheer pressure of continued research that has often obscured the original purposes of inquiry. A comprehensive review of Gestalt work on shape perception can be found in Koffka (1935) and Metzger (1953). A more eclectic survey was written by Hake in 1957.

BOUNDARIES OF SHAPE: CONTOURS, EDGES AND FIGURES

Contours

To start with, shapes are areas of the visual field that are set off from the rest of the field by a visible *contour.* Thus, if 2 regions of the field differ in luminance, a brightness-difference contour appears to separate the field into regions having different shapes. If the 2 regions appear equal in brightness, and differ only in their hue, the corresponding difference in wavelength does not in general result in clear shape perceptions (Leibman, 1927).[4] Moreover, if the luminance of one region shades off gradually into that of another, the shapes of both are indefinite, so the perception of shape would seem to require a sharp enough contour between regions that differ in luminance.

What produces contour? Mach pointed out in 1865 (see Ratliff, 1965) that a contour occurs with a relatively *abrupt change of gradient:* mathematically, it is a change of a change, that is to say, it is the second deriva-

[4]Bishop (1966) reported that contours can be detected between small regions differing only in hue; he does not say, however, whether the regions were separately matched in apparent brightness for each observer, so the issue is still open.

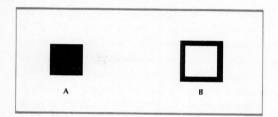

Figure 12.11. Experiment on the development of contour. See text. (Werner, 1935.)

tive of luminance, not the first (d^2L/ds^2, not dL/ds). It belongs in the same class of phenomena as marginal or simultaneous contrast. The neural basis for simultaneous contrast effects has been discussed under the topic of spatial inhibition in Chapter 9, page 292. Because of these effects, the outlines of objects appear sharper and more distinct than they are in the retinal image.

It looks, therefore, as though brightness-difference contours have a sort of unity, in the way in which they are handled by the nervous system, over and above the fact that a particular group of cells in the retinal mosaic is being stimulated. Perceptual research appears to support this view. For example, Fry and Bartley (1953) used threshold methods to study the effect of one contour on another. They determined the minimum luminance-difference necessary to make a contour become visible and found that a contour exerts an inhibitory influence on neighboring parallel contours and exerts a reinforcing influence upon another contour that it approaches at right angles.

Masking contours A phenomenon discovered by Werner (1935) may offer a powerful tool for the study of the processes by which contours are perceived and of their function in the perception of shape. Werner exposed two patterns (Figure 12.11 A, B) successively in the same part of the field. If the presentation of the pattern in A was followed, after a "vacant" (gray) interval of 150 msec by the pattern in B, the black square was not seen at all. The masking figure (A) and the

test figure (B) do not have to be seen by the same eye to obtain these results (Werner, 1940; Kolers & Rosner, 1960). When the sequence was reversed, both squares were seen.

Why was the black square not perceived in the first sequence? Werner proposed that when the pattern in B followed that in A, the latter was obliterated because its contour had insufficient time to establish itself before being wiped out by the opposed luminance-difference of the pattern in B. When the pattern in B was presented first, however, its double contour was too strong to be obliterated. The extent to which the "obliteration" really depends on interactions between contour processes remains to be determined, however, for there are other similar cases in which the explanation based on contour obliteration is not clearly applicable.

There is a wide range of conditions under which the visibility of a test stimulus T is decreased by the presence of a masking stimulus M. Recent reviews of visual masking have been written by Raab (1963) and by Kahneman (1968) (see also Chapter 9). Either or both of the stimuli may be homogeneous patches of light, or patterns with contours; they may be presented simultaneously, or one may follow the other so that some time elapses between the onset of one stimulus and the onset of the other; the retinal image of one may cover that of the other, or their images may fall on disparate retinal regions.

When both stimuli are presented simultaneously in time and do not overlap in space, the darkening of one by the other is, of course, the phenomenon we have already described as *contrast* (pp. 407–412). If the 2 stimuli do not coincide either spatially or temporally, and T precedes M, this backward masking is called *metacontrast*; if M precedes T, the resultant forward masking is called *paracontrast* (Stigler, 1910), although the term metacontrast is often also used for both forward and backward masking. In metacontrast, as in contrast, the brightness of T is reduced by a stimulus M that is presented to an adjacent area (Stigler, 1910; Alpern, 1952, 1953), but under many conditions, *T* is not only darkened—it disappears entirely (Alpern, 1952; Fehrer & Biederman, 1962; Fehrer & Raab, 1962; Fehrer & Smith, 1962; Kahneman, 1967, 1968). This is, of course, very much like the phenomenon described by Werner, in that one shape has been suppressed or obliterated by the successive presentation of another one.

Backward masking has also been found to "erase" briefly presented letters and digits, even when the masking stimulus is a pattern which does not contain contours that are adjacent and parallel to those of the test stimulus (such as a ring, Averbach and Coriell, 1961; or a pattern of irregular line elements, Sperling, 1963). Eriksen and his co-workers (Eriksen & Hoffman, 1963; Eriksen & Lappin, 1964; Eriksen & Steffy, 1964) have argued that at least some of these masking and erasure phenomena are due simply to the fact that the luminance of the white field of the masking stimulus is added to that of the test field, if both fields are presented at a short enough intervening interval. The extra "veil" of luminance added by the masking field would make the test pattern more difficult to see because it lowers the contrast ratio between the black and white regions of the stimulus.

Such luminance summation should reduce the test pattern's visibility regardless of whether the test pattern is submitted before or after the mask. Moreover, because the summation should decrease as the interval between the stimuli increases, the masking effect should be at its maximum when *T* and *M* are simultaneous, decreasing as the interval between *T* and *M* increases. Just such results were found by Eriksen and Collins (1964, 1965), Eriksen, Collins, and Greenspoon (1967), and by Schiller and Smith (1966). On the contrary, other investigators have found masking to be maximal not when the two stimuli were presented simultaneously, but rather after a period of around 50 msec had elapsed between the onset of one and the onset of the other (Averbach & Coriell, 1961;

Mayzner et al., 1964; Weisstein & Haber, 1965). This had also been found using figures like those of Werner (Werner, 1940; Kolers & Rosner, 1960; Kolers, 1962).

To some degree the discrepancies mentioned above may result from differences in experimental conditions. They may also be due to differences in *criterion*—a problem that we shall encounter repeatedly: How can we be sure whether or not the subject *saw* the test stimulus? The question of whether the subject saw the stimulus would seem to be a simple one to answer, but he has to report about a very brief presentation at which he cannot look a second time, and what he decides in retrospect is subject to influences that might bias his answers. Various objective measures may be substituted for the subject's report on what he sees. For example, two masking patterns may be used, and the subject given a forced choice as to whether the test pattern appeared with one or with the other. With this method, if complete masking occurs, the subject should be reduced to chance guesses (Heckenmueller & Dember, 1965). Alternatively, the subject may have to choose which of several letters have been used as the test stimulus (Eriksen and his colleagues; Mayzner et al., 1965; Weisstein & Haber, 1965). But not all measures agree with each other. For example, if subjects are required to respond as quickly as possible when the test stimulus is presented in a backward masking experiment, their reaction times are unaffected by the backward masking (Fehrer & Raab, 1963). This is so even when the subjects report that they do not see the targets at all, and when their guesses about the target's presence or absence are near chance (Fehrer & Biederman, 1962).[5]

[5] The fact that subjects report that they do not see the test stimulus does not mean that the sequence *T-M* looks just like the masking stimulus presented by itself. When 2 masking stimuli flank the test stimulus, for example, the latter are seen as being in motion away from the center, and it is to this that subjects may then respond. The relationship between the conditions under which metacontrast suppression occurs with some patterns, and those under which apparent motion is produced (Chapter 13), has been pointed out by Fehrer and her coworkers (Fehrer & Raab, 1962; Fehrer & Smith, 1962; Fehrer, 1965, 1966), and

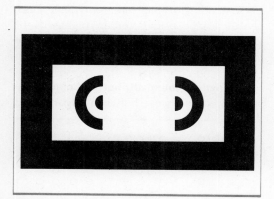

Figure 12.12. Subjective contour. Note the appearance of a vertical white stripe bounded by straight lines at the right and left where it is separated from the semicircular figures. (Schumann, 1904.)

Whether luminance-summation contributes to masking phenomena or not, there are also masking effects that seem to arise from the inhibitory effects of one contour on another. Thus Robinson (1966), using disk patterns as stimuli, showed that if stimulus *b* masked a previously presented test stimulus *a*, *b* could itself be masked by a third stimulus *c*, which in turn masked the masking stimulus *b* and restored visibility to *a*. This has since been replicated, using letters as test stimuli, by Dember and Purcell (1967). Contours also display characteristically inhibitory effects when the two eyes receive different patterns of stimulation (see Ch. 13, page 487).

Subjective contours We have seen that one powerful method for producing definite shapes is by producing a luminance difference

Kahneman (1968). Kahneman suggests that, under the conditions in which masking follows a U-shaped function (that is, in which masking is maximal with a 50 msec interval between the onsets of the two stimuli), the temporal and spatial arrangements would normally result in the perception of movement; with the particular patterns that are used in the masking experiments, however, the resulting movement would be physically impossible (for example, square A expands and becomes outline B, in Figure 12.11). Because the events thus briefly perceived make no sense, they are "lost or suppressed" (see p. 444). Other processes, such as lateral inhibition, also operate in the masking experiments, and contribute the monotonic function that has been obtained in the other experiments to which we have referred.

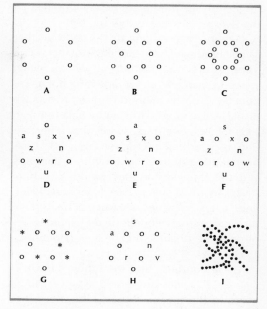

Figure 12.13. Dot figures illustrating the factors of nearness, sameness, continuation, and good figure. The hexagon so clearly visible in A is somewhat obscured in B by the additional dots, but reappears in C as a leftover group when the addition of still more dots in close proximity to each other brings out the interior hexagon. In D, E, and F the sameness of certain items favors grouping them, and the leftovers readily fall into a complementary group, when they make a regular figure, or when, as in G, they are similar; whereas in H, where the leftover items are dissimilar and irregularly arranged, they do not get together readily. I shows the factor of homogeneous continuation, in that the dots are readily seen as lying along straight lines or fairly definite curves.

between two regions. However, there are other ways of producing contours, and hence shapes, that do not involve luminance differences in the same way.

One classic example of "subjective contour" is shown in Figure 12.12, in which the contour is "filled in" or completed across an objectively homogeneous portion of the field. Another is given by the dot-figures in Figure 12.13. Here, you may simply see a set of dots scattered on the page, or the dots may appear to be so grouped as to set off one region of the field from another, depending on factors that we will discuss below (p. 433).

Perhaps most striking are the contours that can be produced by means of binocular vision using 2 displays, neither of which, when viewed separately, shows anything but a random texture. The method for producing such displays, which was devised by Bela Julesz in 1960 for studying stereoscopic depth perception, is described in Chapter 13, p. 483. It has been used to study equal-brightness contours and the shapes that they produce (White, 1962; Lawson & Gulick, 1967; Hochberg, 1968), and to test whether a particular feature of form perception depends on retinal processes or on those of some higher level (Hochberg, 1968; see p. 471, footnote 15).

These contours, and the others shown in Figure 12.13, depend on luminance differences in the retinal image in the sense that each element or dot in the field has luminance-difference contours. Except in this indirect sense, however, we see that luminance-difference contours on the retina are not *necessary* for shape perception.

Figure and Ground

This distinction, first brought out clearly by Rubin (1915, 1921), is fundamental to the

understanding of shape and form perception. Let us first consider certain highlights of Rubin's observations, and then some of the issues that center around this distinction.

The figure-ground attributes   Some of the striking differences between figure and

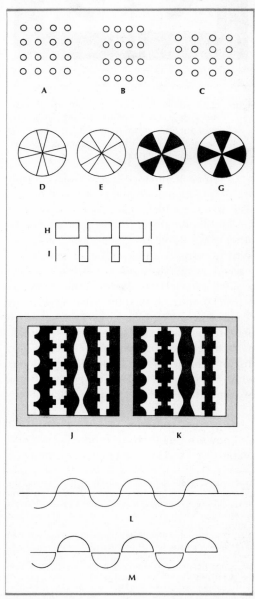

Figure 12.15. Demonstrations of Gestalt organization. See text.

Figure 12.14. Figure and ground. See text and Figure 12.24, page 441.

ground were classified by Rubin as follows. (1) The figure has shape, while the ground is relatively shapeless. For example, in Figure 12.14 you do not see the vase *qua* vase when the black regions are the figures. (2) The ground seems to extend behind the figure's edge. (3) Thus, the figure has some of the character of a *thing*, whereas the ground appears like unformed material. (4) The figure usually tends to appear in front, the ground behind. (5) The figure is more impressive, more apt to suggest meaning, and better remembered.

The first and last points are particularly important. To the limited extent that they are true, an area that is not a figure becomes, in effect, invisible, and even though it is "objectively" present in the world and in the retinal image, it does not provide a stimulus to which the subject can respond.

The determinants of figure-ground organization   In Figures 12.13 and 12.15A–C various aggregates of dots appear to group together to form recognizable shapes. Wertheimer (1923), the founder of the Gestalt school of psychology, used such patterns of dots and simple line drawings (Figure 12.15D–G) to study the factors that determine how the dots are grouped into recognizable figures and that determine which of two areas will be the figure and which will be the ground. Some of these determinants are listed below.

1. *Proximity.* Dots near each other readily group to form contours (Figure 12.13C). In Figure 12.15A the small circles are equally spaced; at B, they are closer horizontally, and we see a pattern of rows; at C, they are closer vertically, and we see columns.

2. *Area.* As a closed region is made smaller, it tends more strongly to be seen as a figure (Figure 12.15D as compared to E), a factor that is obviously closely related to *proximity.*

3. *Orientation.* In at least some kinds of pattern, alignment with the main axes of space seems to be a determining factor. Thus,

Rubin (1921) found that a cross made up of vertical and horizontal limbs (Figure 12.15F) is more likely to be seen as figure than one with oblique limbs (Figure 12.15G).

4. *Closedness.* Regions that are marked off by closed contours tend to be seen as figure more than do those with open or incomplete contours; in Figure 12.15H, the vertical lines belong to horizontal rectangular shapes, whereas in Figure 12.15I, the same lines belong to the upright rectangles, even though in the former case they must overcome the law of *proximity* to do so.

5. *Symmetry.* The more symmetrical a region's shape, the more strongly it tends to be seen as figure; in Figure 12.15J, we tend to see white columns on a black background, but black columns on a white ground in Figure 12.15K (Bahnsen, 1928).

All of the factors listed above refer to features of the physical stimulus pattern, although they are not all equally easy to define objectively, or to submit to experimental test.

Area, proximity, orientation—these are readily varied and measured. Using 6-sector and 8-sector patterns like those in Figure 12.15D–G and varying the width (angle), orientation, contrast, and so on, of one set of sectors relative to the others, Graham (1929), Goldhamer (1934), Oyama and Torii (1955), Künnapas (1957), and Oyama (1960) have shown that objective, quantitative measures of figural dominance can be devised to reflect the subjective and qualitative observations on which these laws had originally been based.

In such ambiguous patterns (Figure 12.15), the figure-ground organization reverses spontaneously while the subject gazes at it, apparently with no effort on his part. A commonly used measure of figural dominance is the relative duration with which the subject reports each shape's appearance (say, by pressing a separate switch when he sees each alternative).

Assuming that suitable response measures are used, these first 5 factors seem to offer ready translation from the intuitive and qual-

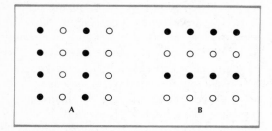

Figure 12.16. Grouping by lightness similarity.

itative form in which they were originally presented, into more quantitative and objective measures. Certainly, a variable such as "proximity" seems like •a straightforward physical measure, and we would think that the only problem is to obtain a valid measure of how it affects organization.[6]

The remaining factors—*similarity, good continuation,* and so on—also seem to be features of the physical stimulus display, but

[6]The task may not be quite that simple, however. Rock and Brosgole (1964) had subjects view an array of dots that was slanted in depth, so that in the retinal image the dots were closer together in one direction (because of perspective foreshortening; see p. 499), whereas both in the physical array and in the way in which subjects perceived the array (because of *shape constancy,* p. 515), they were actually closer together in the other direction. In this experiment, grouping occurred in accordance with *perceived* proximity, rather than with retinal proximity. This seems to imply that attempts to base our predictions about organization on the measured features of the visual field are foredoomed because *perceived* stimulus features, not physically measurable ones, govern perceptual organization. To the contrary, Attneave and Olson (1966), found that the impression of slant in patterns made up of an array of small elements depended on the way in which those elements were grouped into lines, and it was retinal proximity that determined how those elements formed into groups. Helson (1966) attributes the results of the experiment by Rock and Brosgole to an "anchoring effect" produced by the initial grouping, and Bell and Bevan (1968) have indeed shown that anchoring effects can modify the operation of several of the Gestalt organizing principles. For example, when a matrix of dots that is distinctly organized into rows (as in Figure 12.15B) is presented very frequently in the midst of a series of matrices which vary in their spacing, matrices that are normally ambiguous (that is, matrices that can be perceived either as rows or as columns) are perceived as columns. Instead of simply measuring the physical stimulus, therefore, we may have to determine the *effective* stimulus. The effective stimulus would be the difference between the actual level of the variable in the stimulus that is being presented to the subject, and the *adaptation level* (see p. 416) that is computed from the set of patterns to which the subject has been exposed previously. This issue is still therefore open, and we can (with this qualification) consider these first 5 determinants of organization to be susceptible to physical measurement.

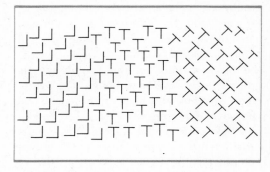

Figure 12.17. Grouping by shape similarity. (Beck, 1966.)

they have not yet been expressed in satisfactory physical measures.

6. Similarity. Dots tend to form groups according to their lightnesses (Figure 12.16A, B), and we can set this factor against that of proximity to assess their relative strengths (Rush, 1937; Hochberg & Silverstein, 1956; Hochberg & Hardy, 1960). This is a very easy kind of similarity to state and to measure. However, similarity of *shape* also appears to affect grouping (Figure 12.13D–H), and how can we measure that?

The problem is not a simple one and has not yet been satisfactorily solved. The displays in Figure 12.17 are part of a series used by Beck (1966) to study the effect of the similarity of shape on perceptual grouping. Each display was made up of 3 sections, and the subject was asked to indicate at which of the 2 boundaries the most natural break occurs. Unfortunately, subjects' judgments of how marked the division between any 2 sets of elements looked to be had little relationship to how other subjects rated the similarity in appearance of those 2 sets of elements.

7. "Common fate." Dots that move simultaneously in the same direction form a single group. Perhaps the strongest factor of all, common fate may be closely related to (or derived from) *motion parallax,* an important factor in depth perception (p. 505).

8. Good continuation. The group of dots follows a uniform direction in Figure 12.13I. We see the particular figure-ground arrange-

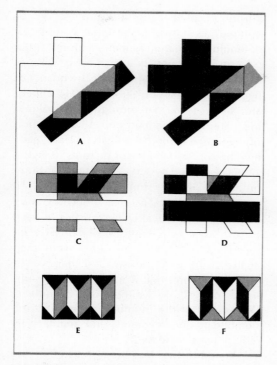

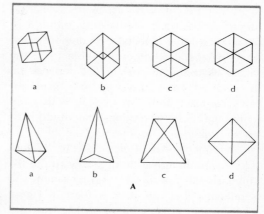

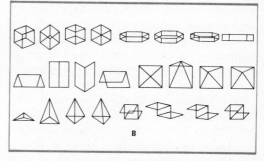

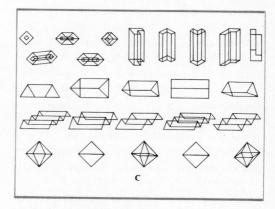

Figure 12.18. Figural organization is as uniform as possible. (A and C are adapted from Fuchs, 1923). In which member of each pair are two overlapping shapes most readily seen?

ment which makes the fewest changes or interruptions in straight or smoothly curving lines or contours. Figure 12.15L is almost always seen as a sine wave superimposed on a line, instead of a set of closed shapes, as shown at *M* (which is what we would expect to see in terms of the law of *closedness*).

9. *Homogeneity or simplicity.* In each example in Figure 12.18, we have alternative ways of seeing: an inhomogeneously colored surface, at some uniform distance and under uniform illumination, is one alternative; a homogeneously colored surface, its parts at varying distances and receiving (or reflecting) nonuniform illumination, is another alternative. In each case, the alternative that *is* seen is the arrangement of edges and distances that will conform to the most homogeneous set of object attributes that is consistent with the stimulus pattern.

Figure 12.19. A. Plane projections of cube and tetrahedron. (Kopfermann, 1930.) B, C. See text. (Hochberg & Brooks, 1960.)

A related set of examples comes from the work with so-called "reversible-perspective pictures" by Kopfermann (1930). She used ambiguous drawings (Figure 12.19), each of which can readily be perceived in either of

3 very different ways (that is, as flat 2-dimensional arrangements or as either 1 of 2 tridimensional objects). She demonstrated that, in general, whether the subject sees the figure as tridimensional or flat depends on how "good" the figure is in 2 dimensions. If it is compact and symmetrical, with good continuation between lines that would have to be broken apart in order to see the figure as tridimensional (for example, Figure 12.19A, *d*), there is little urge toward the tridimensional appearance. As you examine the sequences that run from *a* to *d* in Figure 12.19A notice how tridimensionality decreases and simplicity (as a two-dimensional organization) increases. Within each row, the tridimensional organization is essentially the same (that is, a cube in the top row, a tetrahedron in the bottom row). The strength of the two-dimensional organization seems to increase as its simplicity increases.

Speculations about brain physiology aside, this epitomizes the promise offered by Gestalt psychology. Even ambiguous figures are lawful. Tridimensional space is not built up out of flat sensations (see Chapter 13, p. 503); instead, tridimensionality and flat shape are part of a single organizational process, and whether any line is perceived as being a flat edge or as being a corner between 2 surfaces (that is, as being a dihedral angle) depends on which version results in a simpler overall organization.

The difficulty, of course, is in deciding what ·is "simplest," "good," or "homogeneous." In the following few pages, we outline several approaches to this problem, none of them as yet very successful.

The first few determinants of organization (pp. 433–435) could each be stated in terms of obvious and measurable physical variables. In the case of "simplicity", however, we do not even know which of the many geometrical features, varying within *a* to *d* in Figure 12.19A, are relevant to the fact that *d* looks flatter than *a*.

One picture of some object (Figure 12.19A, *d*) looks more two-dimensional than another

(*a*) presumably because it is more "good" or "simple" as a two-dimensional pattern. By determining what measurable features of the patterns are higher for *a* than for *d*, we may discover the stimulus bases for the quality of figural "goodness" or "simplicity." Hochberg and Brooks (1960) therefore took the following 3 steps to obtain an objective definition of "goodness" or "simplicity." First, each member of the families of pictures in Figure 12.19B was rated by subjects as to its position on a scale running from "apparently flat" to "apparently tridimensional." Second, very many of the physical characteristics of each picture *as a two-dimensional pattern* were measured, and these measures were then analyzed to find the smallest number of physical features that would predict the subjects' ratings. Two-dimensional simplicity decreased as the number of angles, the number of line segments, and angular variability were increased.[7]

The third step was to test whether the measure of simplicity would be correlated with ratings of the apparent tridimensionality that subjects gave to a new set of reversible-perspective pictures (Figure 12.19C). Correlations were high, meaning that the measure did predict subjects' ratings. The selection of pictures was neither random, however, nor governed by explicit rules, and in consequence we cannot estimate how generalizable the measure is; that is, we cannot tell how well it would predict subjects' ratings of other sets of pictures.

The research described above was undertaken with the hope that the complexity of any figural organization (that is, the inverse of its "simplicity" or its "goodness") could be defined objectively in terms of the *amount*

[7] The measure of two-dimensional complexity arrived at with these figures was C = (the total number of angles + the number of different angles/total number of angles + 2 × the number of separate continuous line segments). Populations of reversible-perspective figures can be generated and randomly sampled according to explicit rules (see Figure 12.28, p. 447), but results obtained with such samples can still only be generalized to those populations. This difficulty also applies to the other attempts that have been made to replace the Gestalt principles of organization with more objective formulations (pp. 445–448).

of information needed to specify that organization. In a rough way, this formulation will fit most of the Gestalt phenomena. Hochberg and MacAlister (1953) had proposed that it could be applied to the kinds of measures of organization that we have been describing, while Attneave (1954) had independently proposed that stimulus information (in the more formal sense of *information theory* measures) could be substituted for the intuitive Gestalt terms. We discuss Attneave's informational approach when we consider shape recognition (p. 445).

Summarizing the determinants of organization We have mentioned several factors that appear to determine figure-ground organization (there are others that we have not described). Musatti (1931) combined these principles into one comprehensive law of *homogeneity:* homogeneity as to place (proximity), as to quality (similarity), and so on. Similar generalizations have been offered by others. For example, Koffka, in talking about *symmetry,* says that the figure-ground organization will, other things being equal, be such as to produce shapes as simple as possible (1935, p. 195); that is, we perceive according to some kind of *minimum principle* (Werner & Wapner, 1952; Hochberg, 1957).

Along a somewhat different line, James (1890) has said that we see that which is definite and probable. This position was developed more explicitly by Brunswik (1934, 1952, 1956; see pp. 502f.), who proposed the following relationship to hold between stimulation and perception: The tendency to see a given arrangement of objects and surfaces in response to a particular pattern of stimulation is a function of the frequency with which the observer has received that pattern of stimulation from that physical arrangement. That is, perceptions reflect the probabilities with which situations occur in the environment.

Both of these kinds of formulation (minimum principle and an environmental-probability principle) have in common this virtue: They each summarize a number of very different kinds of observation within a single rubric that not only has intuitive appeal but also seems to suggest underlying explanatory mechanisms. However, they share a drawback in that neither is really specific enough to be of much use in predicting just which shape we will recognize in a given instance. Otherwise, the two kinds of summary statement suggest very different kinds of underlying process.

The minimum principle suggests some underlying physiological process corresponding to the figural organization, a process that can readjust its internal relationships to balance local stresses. This is the *Gestalt* view, in which the effect of any local luminance-difference contour depends on what is happening in the rest of the central nervous system. In other words, the entire system is stimulated by the entire visual field, so that the response to the whole stimulus pattern is not simply the sum of the responses that occur when part of the stimulus is presented separately. In order to apply this approach, we have to be able to identify what comprises a "whole" process, and we have to discover some set of rules by which to predict, from objective measures of the stimulus pattern, what the simplest organization will be.

The environmental-probability principle suggests an explanation based on learning. It is hard to imagine that there are receptors in the visual nervous system that are sensitive to faces or vases, or that there are specific nerve energies for Maltese crosses (Figure 12.15D). Instead, we need merely assert that such perceived shapes are not determined by the sensory processes, taken by themselves, but are elaborated by the effects of our previous experiences with the environment. In short, we see those shapes that our personal history has made most familiar to us. In order to apply this approach, we would have to know what the various shapes are with which each observer has had experience and the relative frequency of those experiences (for example, face or vase in Figure 12.14). In addition, we would have to know the relationship between the frequency with which the subject was exposed to a shape, and the consequent strength of perceptual learning. That is, we would have to know the subject's acquired repertoire of shapes and his relative readiness to use each of them.

The reader will recognize that the 2 alternative formulas that attempt to summarize the determinants of organization are very much like the alternative sensory and cognitive explanations of color constancy and contrast (p. 412). With these alternative approaches to explaining the "laws of organization" in mind, let us mention 2 more factors that appear to operate in determining figure-ground organization, but which refer directly to the expectations and past experience of the observer. These factors are what we may call *nonstimulus determinants of organization,* because neither the subject's attitude nor his past experiences comprises part of the stimulus display in any meaningful sense of these words. Hence it is to the effects of such determinants that we should turn in attempting to evaluate "sensory" and "cognitive" explanations of figure-ground selection.

10. Conformity with the observer's set or Einstellung. *Einstellung* is a German word that means a directed readiness for (or expectation of) a particular perceptual event. Wertheimer distinguished 2 kinds of *Einstellung:* "Subjective" *Einstellung* allows the observer to set himself to see a certain grouping and to do so even though the laws of organization do not particularly favor that grouping, or even if they oppose it. "Objective" *Einstellung* means essentially *figural perseveration,* that is, the tendency to continue seeing a given figural organization even after the conditions no longer favor it. For example, if we were to start out with the matrix of clearly horizontal rows in Figure 12.15B, and decrease the vertical spacing by imperceptible steps, while at the same time increasing the horizontal spacing, objective *Einstellung* would carry us through the point of equal spacing (Figure 12.15A). That is, we would still

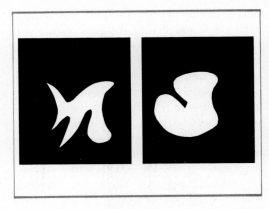

Figure 12.20. Rubin's nonsense shapes. Type of field presented with instructions calling sometimes for taking the enclosed portion as figure, and sometimes for taking the enclosing portion as figure. (Rubin, 1921.)

continue to see horizontal rows even though we otherwise would not have done so with that spacing.

More research has been done on a closely related form of figural persistence. Rubin (1915; see Woodworth, 1938, p. 631) showed a first series of 9 green nonsense figures on black backgrounds. A subject was given 4 exposures of each, with instructions to see the green area as figure, the black as ground (Figure 12.20). This was followed by a second series of 9 similar patterns, but now the instructions were to see the enclosing black areas as figure. After a 30- to 45-minute interval, the subjects were shown a set of 27 patterns consisting of the first 2 sets and 9 new patterns, presented in shuffled, mixed order. They were asked to remain passive as to which part (black or green) should be seen as figure, but to report which part was the figure and whether the field was recognized as one previously seen. Subjects tended to see the same figure on the second exposure as they had in the original series: 64 percent of the figures were reported in the same way as they would have been seen in accordance with the instructions on their previous presentations, 33.5 percent were seen with the reversed organization, and 2.5 percent were seen in both ways. Rubin considered these

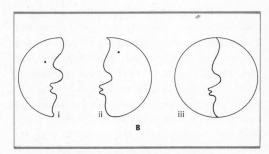

Figure 12.21. Ambiguous figures. A. It can be seen as either a young woman or an old one. (Boring, 1930.) B. Profiles (*i, ii*) and a composite (*iii*). (Schafer & Murphy, 1943.)

results to indicate a carrying over of the same figure-ground organization from one viewing of a pattern to another viewing.

Although the reliability of Rubin's results, and his interpretation of them, have since been questioned on several grounds (see Epstein, 1967), the existence of some such effect seems clear enough. Leeper (1935) showed that subjects who had previously

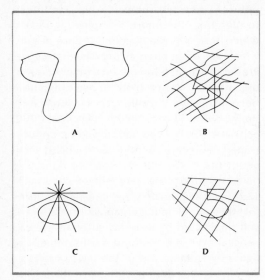

Figure 12.22. The numerals concealed at A and C are revealed at B and D. (Adapted from Köhler, 1929.)

seen an unambiguous version of Boring's ambiguous "wife"-"mother-in-law" pattern (Figure 12.21A), could at first only recognize the version they had previously seen. Again, Epstein and Rock (1960) and Epstein and De Shazo (1961) showed their subjects several unambiguous versions of the Shafer-Murphy faces (Figure 12.21B). The subjects then received brief (tachistoscopic) presentations of the ambiguous composites in each of which 2 of the unambiguous faces were combined. There was a strong tendency for subjects to recognize the particular shape they had most recently been shown.

11. Past experience (familiarity). A series-ofwordslikethisone, which can be separated and read even though neither the configuration nor the spacing would otherwise lead to the appropriate grouping, is one illustration of this factor. Wertheimer urges that this factor of familiarity must not be too readily invoked, and as we can see in the demonstrations in Figure 12.22, the various quite familiar numbers at A and C are there quite well concealed. The numbers are clearly visible at B and D. The fact that they are concealed at A, C cannot be ascribed to "confusion" that is caused by the added lines there because the same shapes are embedded among even more lines at B and D, yet are clearly visible. So much for the simplest form of the *familiarity theory* that we introduced on page 439. The whole patterns in which the shapes are concealed at A, C are certainly no more familiar than the hidden shapes themselves, yet we see the wholes, not the embedded shapes. We shall consider more formal research directed to this issue shortly. For now, we may note that the reasons that the numbers are concealed in A, C and not in B, D are to be found among the first 9 laws of organization (and especially the law of *good continuation*) and, conversely, that the reasons they are visible at B, D are similarly due to those organizational factors, rather than to their familiarity. To prove the reality of the experience factor in any specific case, we must first show that the stimulus factors (and the *Einstellung* variable) do not account for the obtained grouping.

Under some conditions, the association of reward or punishment with one of the two shapes that share a common contour (such as Figures 12.21B *i* and *ii*) affects which shape is identified when the subject is shown an ambiguous pattern (Figure 12.21B *iii*), at an exposure that is too brief for a figure–ground reversal to occur. In general, subjects report seeing the punished shape less often than the nonpunished or rewarded shape (Schafer & Murphy, 1943; Jackson, 1954; Ayllon & Sommer, 1956; Sommer, 1957). Perhaps a partial identification of the punished shape elicits a disruptive emotional response that interferes with the subject's memory of the brief exposure (Hochberg, Haber, & Ryan, 1955; Hochberg & Brooks, 1958; Solley & Murphy, 1960; see also the discussion of tachistoscopic recognition on p. 444). In addition, the subject may really pick up some cues by which he can identify both alternatives, better than by chance guessing, but he may have a response bias (see p. 443) in favor of the rewarded or nonpunished shape (Wallach, 1949; Smith & Hochberg, 1954). In any case, the effects of such differential experience have not always been obtained (Rock & Fleck, 1950; Solley & Long, 1958), and the conditions

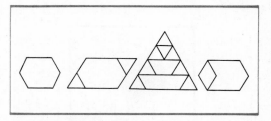

Figure 12.23. A figure hidden in more complex figures. The hidden figure (hexagon) is both familiar and "good." (Gottschaldt, 1926, 1929.)

of their occurrence are not clear. Research on this issue has recently been surveyed by Solley and Murphy (1960) and by Epstein (1967).

In the demonstrations shown in Figure 12.22, familiarity was pitted against good continuation, and the latter won. Gottschaldt (1926) attempted a more formal confrontation between practice or familiarity, on the one hand, and the configurational laws of organization (pp. 433f.), on the other. He showed that simple shapes, like the hexagon in Figure 12.23, with which subjects had received over 500 prior presentations, were not noticed when the subjects were later asked to describe the more complex figures in which they were embedded. These results, which are often cited as proving that figure-ground organization is due to innate laws of organization rather than to learning, have been extensively challenged (Moore, 1930; Braly, 1933; Djang, 1937; Hanawalt, 1942; Schwartz, 1961). Even had they gone unquestioned, however, neither Gottschaldt's experiments (1926, 1929), nor the kinds of demonstrations that are shown in Figure 12.22, can legitimately be enlisted to show that the laws of figural organization are innate and unaffected by learning. After all, we can conceal even the best and most symmetrical figure by suitable use of the laws of organization, yet this does not disprove the advantage of good and symmetrical figures in ordinary perception. Similarly, the fact that we can conceal even the most familiar figures does not disprove the importance of experience in ordinary perception.

Moreover, although the embedding patterns in Figures 12.22 and 12.23 are not familiar ones in the sense that we are likely to have seen each *overall* design before, the *parts* that do the embedding (the uninterrupted lines, the repeated angles, and so on) may be highly familiar units. In other words, some of the factors that we have treated under the heading of "stimulus organization" may in fact be the result of perceptual learning, and may express a more fundamental kind of "familiarity"—a familiarity with edges and corners—

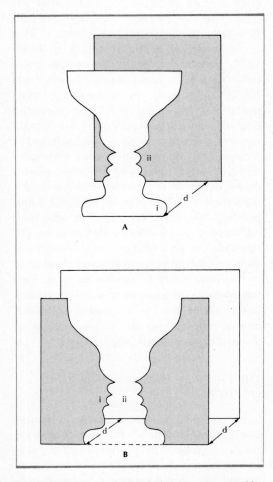

Figure 12.24. The two sets of objects represented by Fig. 12.14 (p. 432). See text. (Adapted from Hochberg, 1962.)

than is tapped by particular shapes or symbols.

Possible fundamental explanations for the figure-ground distinction: figural contours and objects' edges The demonstrations that we have surveyed to this point have suggested that there are laws of figure-ground organization, but have not explained the figure-ground phenomenon. According to Gestalt theory, the laws of organization reflect the self-adjusting nature of the underlying brain processes, but very few attempts have been made to be any more specific about those processes. The few attempts that have been made (pp. 459, 468) have little or nothing to say about figure-ground organization and its laws, nor even about why the ground's shape is less recognizable than that of the figure. If we try to explain the figure-ground distinction in terms of some kind of perceptual learning, the case looks more promising (although still highly sketchy). Consider the properties of figure and ground, on the one hand, and the physical properties of a real object, on the other. The figure has a definite shape, while the ground is formless, and seems to extend somewhat behind the figure's contour. The contour seems to belong only to 1 of the 2 areas that it separates, in the sense that the other area seems to extend behind it. Now consider an actual object (say, the silhouette of a vase as represented by the Rubin pattern, Figure 12.24A). If you move your eye across the object's edge (i), there is an abrupt increase in distance d to the next surface (if there is another surface beyond the edge). Accommodation and convergence (see Chapter 11) will remain appropriate to provide a clear image as long as your gaze moves from one point to another within the bounds set by the object's edge. That is, the object has a surface shape that is determinate and fixed to one side. Past that edge, only empty air or unfocused blur would, in general, meet the gaze. Also, we should remember that saccadic eye movements are scheduled in advance of their execution, so that moving your fovea from one point on a surface to another must be guided, in general, by some "expectation" based on peripheral vision of what the fovea will confront (see Chapter 11, p. 375). In addition, each change in the head's viewing position should cause the object's edge to change the part of the background that it hides from view. The extension of the latter is therefore in fact indeterminate, whereas the parts of the object's surface are not similarly subject to such temporary occlusions (see Hochberg, 1962, in press; Gibson et al., 1969; Kaplan, 1969; Chapter 13, p. 504). There is thus a very good fit between the perceptual properties of figure and ground, on the one hand, and object and background, on the other. It is easy to believe, then, that the figure-ground properties are learned; that they are "expectancies" about the consequences of eye and head movements; and that those expectancies arise in response to contours that normally are produced by object edges but that are in these examples (Figures 12.14, 12.15, 12.21–12.23) produced by print on paper. That is, the main features of the figure-ground phenomenon might be the result of carrying over the perceptual habits formed in looking at objects to the perception of lines on paper.

There are also clear differences, of course, between an object's edge and a figure's outline: The latter bounds 2 equally solid regions at an equal distance from the eye, and in line drawings it does so by a ribbon of pigment. These differences are so considerable that pictures have often been regarded as being more or less arbitrary sets of symbols, which we have learned to associate with objects (see Gibson, 1954; Gombrich, 1960; Hochberg, 1962; for diversely biased discussions of the nature of pictures). If pictures and lines are arbitrarily learned symbols, the determinants of figure-ground organization may merely reflect those arbitrary artistic conventions. However, it is doubtful that such is the case. For one thing, a child who had been raised with no opportunity to associate pictures with objects (or with their names), and who had in fact seen very few

pictures at all, under any circumstances, could nevertheless correctly identify the line drawings of familiar objects (Hochberg & Brooks, 1962). Furthermore, the protective coloration of animals that renders them invisible to other predatory animals seems to express the same principles of masking and organization that conceal familiar shapes from human eyes (Metzger, 1953), and surely the predators have not been exposed to our artistic conventions. To the extent that the determinants of organization are learned, it must be chiefly by way of commerce with objects in the real world.

In this vein, Brunswik and Kamiya (1953) attempted to show that contours that are close together in the visual field tend to belong to the same physical object. If they do, then the Law of Proximity (Figures 12.13, 12.15) might be the result of past experience in an ecology in which visual proximity is a useful *cue* (that is, an indication) of connectedness. Brunswik and Kamiya sampled pairs of adjacent contours from a set of still pictures, each contour pair being classified as to proximity on the one hand, and as to physical connectedness or disconnectedness on the other. There was a low but statistically significant correlation between the 2 variables, showing that there might be some basis for learning the Law of Proximity. This experiment may be criticized in that the sample of contours did not allow us to generalize about the environments to which subjects have habitually been exposed (Hochberg, 1966b), but it remains the only attempt at explaining one of the determinants of organization in a specific and testable manner.

THE PHYSICAL DETERMINANTS OF SHAPE

So far, we have talked about the factors that determine which of 2 shapes that are bounded by a common contour will be seen, but not about *what* shapes are seen. Unfortunately, the questions that arise in this connection are not only very difficult to answer; they are extremely difficult to ask. The last decade has seen much thought and work devoted to some of these problems, but the area remains less well developed than many others with which these chapters deal.

Psychophysics of Shapes

We can describe any stimulus configuration as precisely as we wish in terms of analytic geometry. It would seem, therefore, that we should be able to set up a psychophysics of shape, amassing a body of knowledge that would enable us to predict what shape we will see in response to any stimulus display that confronts the eye. However, this proposition becomes vastly more complicated at second glance, as soon as we start to formulate specific questions that we can ask about how the appearance of a shape is related to the physical stimulus pattern. In what ways can we profitably vary patterns to study apparent shape? In what ways can we measure the resulting changes in shape perception?

Speculating about what the underlying organizational tendencies of the visual system might be, Gestaltists thought that the circle would be the simplest of all physiological configurations and that, the more complex a stimulus pattern might be, the less readily the cortical processes (and the perceived shape) would conform to it (Koffka, 1935; Köhler, 1940). Weakening the strength of the stimulus at the retina might permit the "internal forces" to operate more freely. The stimulus could be weakened by various means: by viewing it with the periphery of the eye; by lowering the luminance or shortening the duration of the stimulus presentation; or, in extreme form, by removing the stimulus entirely and allowing the organizing forces to work on the memory trace of the stimulus. These considerations led to the subsequent research on shape-recognition thresholds in which "stimulus strength" was the independent variable.

Thresholds of Shape Recognition

Early observations (reviewed by Koffka, 1935) led to the generalization that decreasing the "effectiveness" of any given configuration results in simpler and more regular perceived shapes. Since then, however, the validity of this generalization has been restricted almost to the vanishing point. It was found, for example, that stimulus configurations viewed in the periphery of the visual field are not seen as better forms; instead, they are labile, uncertain, and vague (Zigler et al., 1930; Drury, 1933). In other experiments, Helson and Fehrer (1932) determined the lowest luminances at which various geometrical figures were seen as definite shapes, that is, their luminance thresholds. Their results were so inconsistent with different measures and for different subjects that no generalization about the relative ease of seeing their various figures was possible. Hochberg, Gleitman, and MacBride (1948) proposed that figural "goodness" varies inversely with the ratio of a figure's perimeter to its area, P/A, and that the absolute luminance thresholds should thus increase with increasing P/A if the patterns were presented to central vision for brief periods in an ascending order (see Chapter 2, p. 15). Under these conditions, the predicted differences were obtained with a few simple shapes (Hochberg, Gleitman, & MacBride, 1948; Bitterman, Krauskopf, & Hochberg, 1954), but this proposed objective definition of "goodness" turned out to be inadequate when tested with a wide range of patterns (Krauskopf, Duryea, & Bitterman, 1954). Moreover, as Casperson (1950) pointed out, such threshold differences may reflect differences in subjects' readiness to label and report the different shapes rather than differences in what they perceive. This is the problem of *response bias*, which is particularly important in the method of impoverishment that has been most widely used in recent years, namely the method of *tachistoscopic* presentation.

In tachistoscopic experiments, a visual field is exposed for a period of time that is usually too brief to permit the subject to move his eyes or to permit him to respond while the stimulus is still being displayed; for example, the exposure might last 100 msec. After the exposure is terminated, the subject must say what he saw. By increasing the exposure duration until the stimulus is correctly named, a threshold can be obtained. There is now an immense body of literature on tachistoscopic recognition thresholds, obtained, for the most part, using words, numbers or letters as stimuli. Recent reviews are available by Pierce (1963) and Natsoulas (1965). Several characteristics of this method have become clear, in recent years, specific to the method but also revealing more general aspects of the perceptual process. Although the *span of apprehension* in a tachistoscopic experiment seldom goes higher than 6 to 9 items, Sperling (1960, 1963) and Averbach and Coriell (1961) showed that for some brief period after the stimulus was terminated, subjects could be directed to report any one of a much larger matrix of items (such as numbers or letters; see also Eriksen & Lappin, 1967; Keele & Chase, 1967). This demonstrates persistence of the visual information as an "afterimage" or what Neisser (1967) calls an *icon:* If the subject can be instructed to describe what he sees at any portion of the matrix, after the stimulus display is no longer physically present, the entire matrix of items must still be available to him in some form. But even with such persistence (which can be reduced by post-exposure masking; see p. 430), the duration of the effective visual stimulus is less than the time usually needed to scan it and to encode the briefly presented information into some more lasting form, say, to frame the verbal responses with which the subject will report what he saw. The order in which the subject encodes the material is not fixed. For example, Harris and Haber (1963) and Sperling (1963) have shown that subjects tended to encode first what they were asked to report about, and that by the time they came to encoding the features that had not been specifically requested, the immediate (unencoded) memory of the stimulus display was too degraded to be of much use. The primary characteristic of the tachistoscopic experiment thus appears to be that it forces the subject to encode some restricted portion of a stimulus display that fades before his

encoding is complete, and then to make his response on the basis of a memory that he cannot refresh, whose validity he cannot check, and whose detail he cannot extend because the stimulus is no longer present.

Tachistoscopic thresholds should therefore depend on the encoding responses that the subject is ready to make and on the order in which he is prepared to make them. In support of the first point, there is ample evidence that tachistoscopic recognition thresholds are lower for those shapes or words with which the subject is more familiar (Henle, 1942; Solomon & Howes, 1951; Solomon & Postman, 1952); in support of the second point, there is the fact that subjects who are habituated to reading from left to right have lower tachistoscopic thresholds for material displayed in the left part of the field (Anderson & Crosland, 1933; Mishkin & Forgays, 1952; Forgays, 1953; Orbach, 1953; Heron, 1957; Terrace, 1959; Bryden & Rainey, 1963; Harcum & Filion, 1963). Such differences are probably due more to differential readiness to encode the briefly glimpsed pattern than to any differences in sensitivity. Thus, the right-hand differences probably occur because the subject encodes the fading icon in his habitual reading order (Heron, 1957; Sampson & Spong, 1961; Freeburne & Goldman, 1969). Perhaps familiar patterns have lower tachistoscopic thresholds than unfamiliar ones primarily when tasks are used that require the subject to remember and name the stimulus, and have less or no advantage in tasks that do not rely on a naming response. Thus, although Henle (1942) found that mirror images of letters require longer exposures in order to be recognized than do normally oriented letters, Hayes, Robinson, and Brown (1961) found that the thresholds for judging whether or not two patterns are the same were no higher for reversed letters or for letters that are infrequently used than they were for letters that were normally oriented and frequently used (see also Goldiamond & Hawkins, 1958).

This matter of *response bias* (see Chapter

2) also arises in connection with the other techniques that have been used for measuring shape thresholds (Zigler et al., 1930; Krauskopf, Duryea, & Bitterman, 1954; Soltz & Wertheimer, 1959; Pierce, 1963), but the fact that in the tachistoscopic experiment the subject is always confined to describing his memory of the stimulus makes it particularly difficult to determine which tachistoscopic effects, if any, are phenomena of sensory reception, and which are phenomena of memory.[8]

As we noted above, Gestaltists suggested that the same laws of organization would be displayed even more strongly by the memory of the shape than by its percept: The "memory trace" of a good figure would be more stable than that of a poor one, and poor ones either move in the direction of better figures or are lost. The area of *memory for form* is a well worked one in its own right, and is discussed in Chapter 17. Here, let us consider the possibility that by removing the stimulus entirely, we also remove those features that are specific (and, so to speak, accidental or irrelevant) in each method of impoverishment. It might thus be that the "laws of organization" are best revealed by differences in ease of recognizing remembered shapes. To test this possibility, we need objective measures of goodness of organization. The Gestalt "predictions" (such as that a circle with a gap will undergo a change in memory so that the gap gets smaller) were not really made according to formal principles that would permit clear hypotheses and have not in general been substantiated (see Holmes,

1968). Various related attempts have been made to provide such formal principles (see p. 436). As we noted before (p. 437), Attneave (1954) had proposed that the various Gestalt laws are merely expressions of a more general principle that can be stated quantitatively in terms of *information theory* (Attneave, 1959). Consider a matrix of cells, like graph paper. Any scene at all can in principle be duplicated by such a mosaic of cells, if they are sufficiently fine-grained and appropriately colored. If we know that all of the cells are black, there is no uncertainty about how any given cell that we look at will be colored, and it therefore carries no information. *Information theory* offers a mathematical means of stating the uncertainty in such a stimulus display: If each cell's color is independent of any other cell's color, and all colors are equally likely for each cell, the matrix is maximally uncertain. The more cells about which the subject is uncertain, the more information he has to remember, and the various Gestalt laws might make good patterns easier to remember merely because their geometrical order is one way of reducing the overall independence (and uncertainty) of those patterns.

Attneave (1955) chose *symmetry* as the law with which to test this approach and asked whether subjects can remember symmetrical patterns better than irregular ones simply because the former contain less information.

[8] This does not mean that we cannot hope to separate the effects of memory and of verbal response readiness from the effects of more immediate perceptual processes. It does mean that we cannot simply accept subjects' reports of what they see as a direct indication of the latter. Various attempts have been made to separate effects on the response from effects on perception (Neisser, 1954; Eriksen, 1958), and a phenomenon recently reported by Haber and Hershenson (1965) and Dainoff and Haber (1967) may make it possible to study differences in tachistoscopic shape perception with less interference from the subjects' verbal expectations. With repeated presentations at the same exposure duration, subjects report an increasing *clarity* of the stimulus material, a change that cannot be attributed to differences in verbal response readiness because the subjects know what the word is before each presentation of the material.

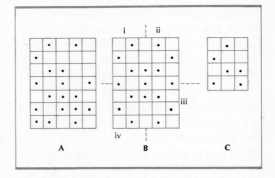

Figure 12.25. Samples of patterns for studying information and memory for shape. (Attneave, 1955.) See text.

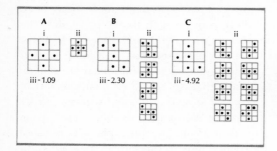

Figure 12.26. Samples of stimuli and their rated goodness. For each stimulus pattern A*i*, B*i*, C*i*, the subset that would be produced by rotation and reflection is shown at *ii*. Subjects' mean goodness ratings are given at *iii*. See text. (Garner & Clement, 1963; Handel & Garner, 1965).

Figure 12.25B, for example, has less information than Figure 12.25A because each of the dots in the parts marked *ii* to *iv* can be predicted from those in the part marked *i*. A critical question is whether symmetrical patterns (Figure 12.25B) remain easier to remember even when they are compared to assymmetrical patterns that have the *same* information (because they have fewer cells; Figure 12.25C). Three measures were used to determine how well subjects could reproduce or identify these patterns from memory, and all of these measures showed that symmetrical patterns were remembered no better (and in fact were worse) than were assymmetrical patterns having the same information content.

With a different information-theoretic approach, Garner (1962, 1966) proposes that "goodness" does not depend on the characteristics of the individual stimulus; in fact, the characteristics that are needed to specify any stimulus themselves depend on the set of alternatives from which that stimulus must be differentiated. A pattern's goodness varies inversely with the number of other equivalent patterns with which the subject classes that stimulus (and which he infers from that stimulus). For example, 5 dots can be arranged in a 3 × 3 matrix (Figure 12.26) to form a total set of 126 different patterns, but the subject

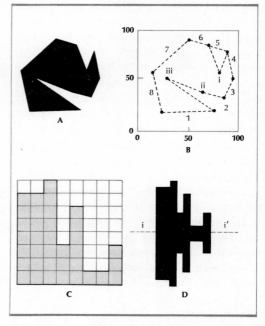

Figure 12.27. Generating populations of patterns. A. A nonsense-figure produced by the method of Attneave and Arnoult (1956). For these figures, *complexity* is a subjective attribute, to be determined empirically from subjects' judgments. B. For details on several methods of generating such figures, see Attneave and Arnoult. As an example, the coordinates for each of the points in Figure 27B may be drawn by pairs from a table of random numbers. The outer points are joined to form the polygon shown by the dashed line. The inner points *i–iii* are joined to the sides (by the dotted lines), again by reference to some arbitrary source such as a random number table. Patterns like these have been the most widely used and studied of the "nonsense shapes." See text, page 449. C. "Metric figures" were constructed by Fitts and his colleagues by assigning a height to each column of the matrix according to various sampling rules. With any given matrix size, the sampling rules determine the number, *N*, of different patterns that can be constructed. For these figures, Fitts and his colleagues defined *complexity* as the number, *N*. Sampling rules that call for a random assignment of heights to the matrix generate the largest *N*. Any limitations or constraints that make the assignment of heights nonrandom reduces *N*, and therefore reduces the complexity of the metric figures that are

treats each pattern as a member of some smaller subset, and the fewer the members of that subset the greater the pattern's goodness. The size of a subset is closely related to the number of different patterns that can be obtained by rotating and reflecting the stimulus. For Figure 12.26A that number is 1.0; for Figure 12.26B*ii*, it is 4; for Figure 12.26C it is 8. With stimuli generated in this fashion, subjects' ratings of "goodness" were predicted well above chance by this measure (Garner & Clement, 1963; Handel & Garner, 1965); the ratings also predict both the ways in which subjects sort the patterns into groups (Garner & Clement, 1963) and what the set of patterns is that any stimulus suggests to subjects (Handel & Garner, 1965).

Such attempts at providing explicit measures of the stimulus (or of the stimulus set) with which we can predict how well subjects remember and discriminate different patterns do not, however, permit us to take up the original task of using impoverished stimuli to discover the determinants of figural organization. First, there is the problem of measuring stimulus information. Various researchers have designed artificial stimuli to make informational measurement relatively easy (see Figures 12.25, 12.26, 12.27 for examples). Unfortunately, however, such stimuli have little in common with those with which the problems of organization were studied, or with those of normal experience. The importance of such properties as *symmetry* or *goodness* for the study of perception lay in their possible value for predicting figural organization (pp. 433–437), and the measures of stimulus information have not been tested in this regard. In fact, it is not clear that those measures can be applied to the problems of figural organization. Perhaps other methods can be devised with which to generate artificial stimuli that will permit information measures to be taken but which will also be more

generated. D. A symmetrical pattern generated from C by reflection around *i–i'*. (Fitts et al., 1956.)

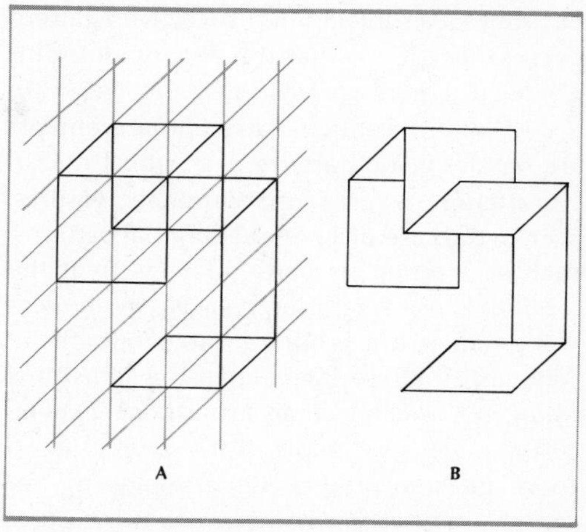

Figure 12.28. A method for generating arbitrary objects. The approach illustrated in Figure 12.27 need not be restricted to flat patterns. For example, one can generate reversible-perspective figures by adding modular surfaces to each others' edges in a three-dimensional matrix, following various arbitrary or random sampling rules. At A: A reversible-perspective figure and its matrix. B. One of the objects represented by A.

relevant to the problems of figural organization; an example of one possible method is shown in Figure 12.28.

Second, there is a difficult problem in determining how much of the stimulus display is actually used by the subject in such experiments. In any recognition or discrimination experiment in which the subject responds to some limited set of stimuli, he can readily select some subset of the features of any stimulus, and respond only to those. If, for example, his task is to decide whether each member of a set of stimuli is a T or an I, the subject need only look for the crossbar at the top in order to class the stimulus one way or the other; he does not even have to see anything else about each stimulus. Similarly, the fact that one part of a pattern is predictable from another (as in Figure 12.25B) does not ensure that the subject will make use of that relationship to obtain the most economical encoding of the stimulus (Attneave, 1955), nor is the subset of alternatives that a subject infers for a given pattern necessarily the set that the experimenter intended (Clement & Varnadoe, 1967). The problem of what the effective perceptual elements are, in any given pattern, is a critical one in any attempt to apply informational measures. Even in the case of simple sequential patterns, such as a series of digits, subjects treat the sequence not as though each event were independent but grouped into a number of "chunks" that are larger than the individual event but smaller than the series (Miller, 1956). Recent attempts (Vitz, 1968; Vitz & Todd, 1969) to predict this grouping or "recoding," and to apply information measures to the recoded elements, seem to be successful at predicting the judged complexities and relative ease of recall for such simple patterns. Nevertheless, this is still very far from being able to apply information measures to the study of two-dimensional shapes and three-dimensional forms.

This leads us to question whether the stimulus measures are really the appropriate independent variables here. For example, Glanzer and his colleagues (Glanzer & Clark, 1963a,b, 1964; Glanzer, Taub, & Murphy, 1968) have shown that the accuracy with which subjects can reproduce or recognize shapes, as measured by a variety of methods, is better predicted from the length of the verbalizations with which subjects describe those shapes, than from information measures taken on the stimuli. Glanzer and Clark propose the *verbal-loop hypothesis*. This is the hypothesis that the differences in recognizability between stimuli are to be accounted for in terms of a *covert verbalization* by which the subject encodes and remembers the stimulus. Hence it is to the characteristics of such verbal encoding that we must ascribe the organizational phenomena. As we saw in our discussion of tachistoscopic recognition, encoding (whether verbal or otherwise) plays a large part in recognition threshold experiments. It may be of course that the lengths of subjects' descriptions, and their recognition errors, reflect a common underlying fig-

ural organization. Glanzer and Clark (1963a) recognize this possibility, and argue that it is unparsimonious, but it is not clear how the nontachistoscopic examples of organization that we discussed on pages 433–436 can depend on covert verbalization to any significant degree. In any case, however, this variable, verbalization length, may turn out to be superior to stimulus information measures, not only because it has been shown to be more predictive in these experiments, but because it can be applied to configurations for which it is difficult or impossible to obtain informational measures. Furthermore, it should remain applicable in those cases in which the subject attends only to selected features of the stimulus.

What Glanzer and Clark have proposed is that the important determinant of shape recognition is the subject's set of verbal responses to any configuration, not the configuration itself. Like any response measure, the verbalization measure has the drawback of not being known before the experiment is performed. A psychophysics of shape would then depend for its predictive power on our ability to decide in advance how people will make such responses to various configurations, and we shall now consider research directed to this question.

Response Dimensions of Shape

Some shapes have specific names, but many more do not. If no name fits exactly, the subject can apply the name that is closest and then add the necessary correction (Woodworth, 1938; Attneave, 1957, 1962). Such qualities as *angular, curved, compact* seem to refer to reasonably measurable geometrical properties, whereas other terms, like *soft, placid, exciting,* may seem harder to pin down to specific physical variables. In any case, the sporadic research that has been done on this topic suffers from an inability to indicate where the patterns that are used in the experiment come from; that is, the results are not generalizable to other stimuli.

Attneave and Arnoult (1956) have offered a convenient means of generating a population of meaningless (nonsense) figures, populations having known statistical parameters, from which random samples of figures could be drawn that would be equivalent in their physical properties (Figure 12.27A,B shows one such figure and indicates the method of generating them). With such populations of stimuli, whatever facts are found out about subjects' responses to the physical variables of one randomly drawn sample of patterns can be tested against another similarly drawn sample.

The configurations are generated according to rules that permit controlled physical variations along certain physical dimensions (for example, number of sides); varying one measure normally changes other physical measures as well (for example, smallest interior angle; total perimeter length). Brown and Owen (1967) have measured and made available a number of these concommitant variations for a total of 1000 configurations, with 200 samples at each of 4,8,12,16, and 20 independent sides.

Figures generated according to the Attneave-Arnoult procedures have been used to study both shape discrimination and paired-associates learning. A population of nonsense shapes has been produced that have known "meaningfulness" as measured by verbal associations (Vanderplas, Sanderson, & Vanderplas, 1965). The area has been reviewed recently by Michels and Zusne (1965). Several studies have pursued the initial purpose of determining the physical correlates of the response dimensions of shape (Attneave & Arnoult, 1956; Arnoult, 1957).

Attneave (1957) found that a weighted combination of the following variables accounted for about 90 percent of subjects' judgments of the complexity of a sample of nonsense shapes: the number of sides, symmetry, angular variability, and P^2/A (where P = perimeter and A = area of the figure; see p. 443). Attneave did not attempt to use this measure of complexity as an independent variable [for example, as complexity measures have been used to predict apparent tridimensionality (p. 436) or luminance thresholds (p. 443)]. It is interesting that a dimension of complexity has also emerged (with 3 others) in a recent study of similarity judgments among random shapes (Stenson, 1966), again with P^2/A a major physical factor in that judgment. Stenson's other dimensions (that appeared to underlie the judged similarities among 20 Attneave-Arnoult shapes) were curvature, curvature-dispersion, and straight-length dispersion.

Whether results obtained with such stimuli can be generalized to other (and more meaningful) stimuli remains, as Attneave and Arnoult (1956) are aware, an unresolved problem of unknown magnitude. In any experiment on shape categorization, how a subject names or classifies a given pattern depends not only on that pattern, but on the entire set of stimuli being considered (see p. 446). The criteria by which a subject decides to call a stimulus pattern by one name rather than another, and how these criteria change as a function of the distinctions that the subject is required to make, are problems that we cannot review here. The reader is referred to Hake, Rodwan, and Weintraub (1966); Imai and Garner (1965); and Forsyth and Brown (1967). However, the difficulties of deciding what shape a subject sees from the names with which he describes them, and of deciding what it means when 2 configurations are given the same name, should be kept in mind in reading the following discussion of transposition.

Transposed and transformed shapes Although the same pattern falling on different parts of the retina (either because the stimulus object or the observer's eye has moved) stimulates very different retinal receptors, to casual observation the shape seems to be unchanged. Similarly, a large square and a small one fall on completely different sets of receptors, yet look alike. This, of course, was one of the major Gestaltist objections to the mosaic theory (p. 427), and is often referred to as the Gestalt problem in attempts to specify the machinery of the visual system. With really familiar items, like letters or other named shapes, the issue can be sidestepped, for it is plausible to say that we have learned to make the same responses to different patterns (thus, we make the same overt response to CAT, to cat, and to either of these displaced to any other locus on the retina even though we see the differences). However, it also seems to some degree to be true that we can recognize unfamiliar, unnamed shapes as being the same when they appear in 2 different retinal locations. Several models of neural function have been devised that would explain how such transposition might be achieved (Lashley, 1942; Deutsch, 1955; Dodwell, 1961, 1964; Uhr, 1963).

When we examine the problem more closely, we see that it is not yet clear what it is that we have to explain. Wallach and Austin (1954) have presented evidence that patterns falling on different parts of the retina are not completely equivalent. Subjects were told that their experiment was one on the peripheral recognition of familiar shapes. Nine silhouettes (whale, tree, car, and so on), varying in size from 3° to 4.6°, were presented singly in 1 of 4 positions, each 2.6° from the fixation point, for a 0.4-second exposure. Subjects were to name the objects. The last silhouette was a pattern which, when it is viewed with its long axis horizontal, is usually recognized as a dog, while with its axis vertical it is recognized as a chef. Inclined 45°, as it was in the final presentation, this pattern is fairly ambiguous. Both the chef version and the dog version were included among the first 9 shapes. For some subjects, the ambiguous version was shown on the position that had previously been occupied by the chef version; for others it was shown on the position previously occupied by the dog version. The ambiguous version was predominantly recognized as that figure (chef or dog) which had previously occupied the same retinal position. There is, thus, at least this limit to the equivalence of the same shape in different locations and different orientations: Recognition on subsequent presentations is, to some extent, specific to both orientation and locus.

Implicit in the description of the experiment of Wallach and Austin is the fact that a change in the orientation with which a pattern falls on the retina may result in a change in the shape that is perceived. The ease and accuracy with which certain shapes

are recognized certainly depends on the orientation of the stimulus pattern. Inverting or reversing a letter of the alphabet, or a map of a continent, or the picture of a face, interferes with its recognition (Gibson & Robinson, 1935; Hochberg & Galper, 1967). We might well argue that such differences are due to the meaningful responses that are made to those patterns, not to shape perception per se. Then, however, we would have to concede that there must be some basis by which the meaningful responses are tied to retinal orientation.

It is often held that children recognize a figure when it is upside down as readily as when it is right side up; and therefore that the differences that adults display in responding to figures in different orientations are due to learning about specific objects. There is little evidence to support the first assertion. If anything, the contrary seems to be true. Younger children give fewer descriptions of the contents of inverted pictures than of upright ones (Hunton, 1955) and recognize significantly more pictures presented with a tachistoscope when these are upright than when they are in other orientations, whereas older children recognize the figures equally well in all positions (Ghent, 1960). Similarly, the fact that young children perform poorly on learning tasks that require them to discriminate between the right and left mirror-images of a shape (Rudel & Teuber, 1963) does not mean that they perceive a shape and its mirror image as being identical. In fact, if all they have to do is report whether two shapes are the same or different, they perform quite well (Rosenblith, 1965; Robinson & Higgens, 1967).

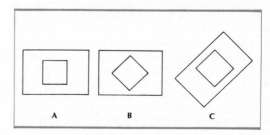

Figure 12.29. Framework and shape. See text.

The effect of orientation on shape recognition may itself be a Gestalt phenomenon, however. The square has become a diamond in Figure 12.29B for example, not necessarily because of the retinal rotation per se; the effect may be due to the pattern's change in relation to the spatial framework that is provided by the page on which it is printed. Any perceived shape would really be a shape-in-relation-to-the-framework, in this view, and the shape that is perceived would change when that relationship changes (Gibson & Robinson, 1935; Koffka, 1935). In Figure 12.29C, the pattern regains much of its appearance as a square (Kopfermann, 1930; in Koffka, 1935, pp. 184 ff.). Using unfamiliar (nonsense) shapes, Rock and his colleagues (Rock, 1956; Rock & Heimer, 1957; Rock & Leaman, 1963) found that the shapes' recognizabilities were not substantially affected by changes in their retinal orientations. On the other hand, changing the shapes' *apparent* orientations (i.e., which part of a pattern appeared to be its "top" with respect to a visual frame of reference, with respect to gravity, and so on), while keeping retinal orientations constant, strongly affected their recognizabilities. This does not mean that patterns were responded to as shapes-in-relation-to-a-visual-framework, however, inasmuch as Rock and Heimer (1957) found that subjects who were merely given verbal information about what the figures' orientations were, recognized the shapes better than did uninformed subjects. The generality of this last point has been questioned by Braine (1965), who argued that the uninformed subjects had been misled because they had automatically assumed that the patterns were in their normal orientation. She showed that subjects who had been told the exact orientation in which briefly presented drawings (horse, elephant, tree, and so on) would appear, recognized them no better than did subjects who were merely informed that the patterns would be disoriented. It remains true, however, that a shape's apparent orientation can be defined in terms of the axis along

which it appears to point, around which symmetry is judged, and with which the shape's recognizability is correlated. So defined, the apparent orientation of a pattern is at least partially independent of its orientation in the retinal image. Thus, as its apparent orientation changes, any stimulus pattern may be perceived as taking on any of several different shapes (Attneave, 1968).

However, the transposition problem as it was raised at the beginning of this section is difficult to state and test with any precision. Even configurations that have not been seen before nevertheless have parts or features that may be very familiar (p. 441), and the subjects may be responding to such features, rather than to entire configurations. Those theories about the nervous system that try to explain transposition may be undertaking an unnecessarily stringent task. Let us consider whether the Gestalt arguments really rule out the possibility that there are units of perception smaller than the entire configuration.

Elementary shapes and features Structuralism sought, in essence, to explain the perception of shapes in terms of 2 different components, namely the elementary point sensations and the associations based on past experience (p. 428). Gestalt theory set the entire figure (with its internal forces of organization, p. 428) as the unit of response. As Hebb has argued very effectively (1949), some middle ground between these extreme

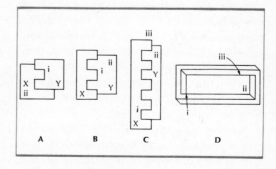

Figure 12.30. Continuous lines serving as inconsistent edges. See text.

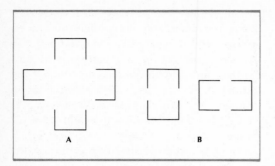

Figure 12.31. Different shapes, same elements.

positions now seems more reasonable than either. Let us here consider some demonstrations that suggest that there are at least 2 components to shape perception, rather than a single process: One component may be designated as the elementary shape feature (which is restricted in extent and sensory in quality). The other component is an integrative *schema* or *map,* which can be much larger than even the contents of the entire retinal image at any moment, and which is less sensory and more conceptual in quality.

First, consider Figure 12.30, which shows a number of shapes in which a contour changes its function from one point to another. In Figure 12.30A, angle *i* is seen predominantly as obtuse (that is, Y is figure), and angle *ii* is a right angle (that is, X is figure). In Figure 12.30B, although the pattern in the immediate vicinity remains as in A, angle *i* looks like a right angle (that is, X is figure). We might say that the overall configuration has determined the function of the contour at *i*. However, in Figure 12.30C, D, as the distances between corners *i*, *ii*, and *iii* increase, their effect on *i* seems to diminish. What these figures suggest is that the figure-ground distinction (that is, the way a contour faces) is not determined for the entire contour, but only for some local extent.

Second, note that it is clear that we can detect and enumerate similarities of features within very different configurations (as long as the contours continue to face the same way). In Figure 12.31, it is easy to see that the

same corners and edges appear in different locations in the two shapes, A and B. Thus it seems plausible to argue that we can recognize elementary features and that these are larger than points but smaller than most figures. Whence would such elementary shapes derive?

Hebb's (1949) speculations provided a very influential theoretical outline of how such units might result from perceptual learning. Because of the way that the world is constructed, some patterns of stimulation are likely to be encountered repeatedly. In essence, this theory proposes that neural groupings (called *cell-assemblies*) will develop in the associative cortex of the brain. These groupings presumably respond as units, each of which is sensitive to some frequently encountered pattern of sensory stimulation, such as a corner or a particular slope of a line in vision, a vowel sound in hearing, a pressure pattern in touch, and so forth.

This theory, although simply stated, is much more complicated when it is made specific and when questions of frequency, timing, and neural interconnection are really spelled out. The attempts to simulate such a model by use of electronic computers have not proved too encouraging (Rochester et al., 1956; see Uhr, 1963). However, receptive fields in the nervous systems of cats, monkeys, and other animals (see Chapter 9) include neural structures which are sensitive to lines and corners of a particular slope, wherever they fall over fairly large regions of the retina. This means that the cell-assemblies would not have to be learned from scratch.

As we have seen, a given contour on the retina does not specify a single elementary shape response but 2 mutually exclusive ones (Figures 12.14, 12.15). Why would we acquire 2 mutually exclusive response systems to the same stimulus? This is the heart of the figure-ground phenomenon, and no theory of shape recognition that fails to offer an explanation for it has accomplished very much. Let us see how a system similar to Hebb's might handle it.

Consider that the eye seldom maintains its fixation for long, but is poised to move again, usually well within a second's time (Chapter 11, p. 386). Because we receive little or no information that guides the eye while it is in motion, its movements must be largely programmed or preset before it starts to move. As we saw earlier (p. 428), shape perception has frequently been explained as being the knowledge of the movements (and especially the eye movements) needed to trace the contour, or to fixate each of its points (Titchener, 1902; Helmholtz, 1910; Washburn, 1916; Taylor, 1962; Festinger et al., 1967). Even without subscribing completely to such proposals, we would expect that the visuomotor system will have acquired a set of plans or programs that will enable the eye to fixate any point on any highly familiar shape's contours. Such an "efferent readiness" (the term is from Festinger et al., 1967), would include a readiness to adjust the eyes to increased depth after moving from *i* to *ii*, with the arrangements of surfaces in Figure 12.24A (page 441), and a readiness for the reverse adjustment, in Figure 12.24B. A layout like that in Figure 12.24A will usually be accompanied by various depth cues (see Chapter 13), or indications of the surface's distance, and those cues would determine what adjustive movements the eye would make. The preparations to move from *i* to *ii* in Figure 12.24A will be the reverse of those in Figure 12.24B, so that the cell-assemblies responsive to the retinal image produced by those 2 sets of surfaces will be mutually exclusive. Now, when we provide the eye with a pattern like that of Figure 12.14 (p. 432), which has no depth cues, the pattern is common to both cell assemblies—the one that has been developed in response to the arrangement of Figure 12.24A and that for Figure 12.24B. Hence, the 2 possible responses, and hence the figure-ground phenomenon (Hochberg, 1970a, b).

Two major questions come immediately to mind, once we accept the possibility that such elementary subshapes may really act as

Figure 12.32. Fragmentation of stabilized images. (After Pritchard, 1961.)

units of shape perception. First, how can we determine a subject's repertory of such elements? Second, how are these elements combined?

We have no well-developed procedures for discovering what such elementary features might be, at present. One possible procedure is based on the long-known fact that if one stares at a pattern steadily, the shape becomes invisible and fades from view (Chapter 9, p. 306). Hebb has proposed that cell-assemblies (and sets of cell-assemblies that share a high proportion of cells in common) tend to act as units, and that, if this is true, under prolonged fixation a shape will tend to reveal the "joints" between its parts by the way it breaks up as it fades. In general, shapes viewed under image stabilization (p. 374) tend to break up in ways that support this. Pritchard, Heron, and Hebb (1960) and Pritchard (1961) studied ways in which several patterns fragmented when they were viewed as stabilized retinal images and found shapes to appear and disappear as meaningful parts rather than in random fragments. For example, if any part of the HB pattern in Figure 12.32A remained, it was usually one of the meaningful segments shown in Figure 12.32B. A similar kind of fragmentation also seems to occur with voluntary fixation of patterns (that is, segments tend to be meaningful, and identical parts tend to appear and to disappear together) whether the observer fixates a luminous figure under low illumination (McKinney, 1963) or at higher illumination levels (Craig & Lichtenstein, 1953; Clarke & Belcher, 1962; Evans & Piggins, 1963). The shape fragments that are reported in these experiments are influenced by learning, as was demonstrated by Donderi and Kane (1965), who found that different stimulus figures to which subjects had learned to make the same response disappeared together more frequently than if the subjects had not learned to give a common response to them.

In reviewing the research on tachistoscopic recognition of shape, we saw that it is difficult to decide whether the effects of meaning or familiarity are attributable to the initial sensory processing, or are due to the set of responses available for recall and report (p. 444). The same problem arises concerning the fragmentation findings, and for similar reasons. As Schuck and Leahy (1966) point out, both retinal stabilization and voluntary fixation often produce rapidly changing apparent shapes, and the subject may be less able to remember and to report fragments that are not easily described. Schuck, Brock, and Becker (1964) showed that assigning simple verbal labels by which subjects could report line segments affected the reports of disappearance. Similarly, Schuck and Leahy (1966) showed that 29 out of 34 subjects who were asked to *describe* the appearance of a fixated luminous HB (Figure 12.32A) reported at least 1 meaningful disappearance (that is, 1 of the segments shown in Figure 12.32B). To the contrary, only 12 out of 34 subjects who were asked to *trace* the fragmented shape on an outline HB figure indicated at least one meaningful disappearance.

This issue is still in question. Tees and More (1967) exposed their subjects repeatedly to a particular 2-digit number (for example, 32) *without requiring them to make any response to that number.* They then presented the subjects with a luminous display containing the 2 numbers (for example, 332) and found that those 2 digits appeared and disappeared together more frequently than was the case when subjects had not received prior exposure to them. It is not clear why mere exposure to a particular set of digits would change the availability of *response* labels.

The units suggested by the fragmentation phenomena may yield valid visual effects and yet may not be general building blocks in the sense of providing the bases of shape recognition, discrimination, and so on. Other techniques can probably be devised that are more closely related to the purposes that such units should serve. For example, Lichtenstein (1961) and MacFarland (1965) have used a procedure in which the parts of a pattern were presented in rapid succession, instead of simultaneously. The subjects' task was to judge when all parts of the shape appeared to be shown at the same time. This technique might be adapted to find out whether breaking a pattern apart in some places and then presenting the pieces successively makes it harder to recognize a shape than breaking it in other places, that is, whether the subject can perceive shapes more readily when some parts of the configuration are available to him as undivided units than when they are not (see Hochberg, 1968). In any case, such elementary units clearly could not account for the whole of shape perception: They are at once too large and too small. They are too large because we can distinguish patterns on the basis of differences between them, down to the limits of our acuity; they are too small because we can distinguish patterns, all of the elements of which are the same but which present those elements in different spatial orders (see for example Figure 12.31A, B).

Schematic maps   Up to this point, we have been considering the retina as though it were a homogeneous mosaic of photoreceptors, and of course it is nothing like that. The acuity falls off very rapidly away from the central fovea (see Chapter 9), so that if a pattern is transposed from one region of the retina to another, the relative acuity of the receptive regions on which its various parts fall is likely to be changed. Similarly, fixating one corner of a large pattern places the other corners so far into the periphery that their detail cannot be discerned. In order to see each corner of a large cross clearly, the eye

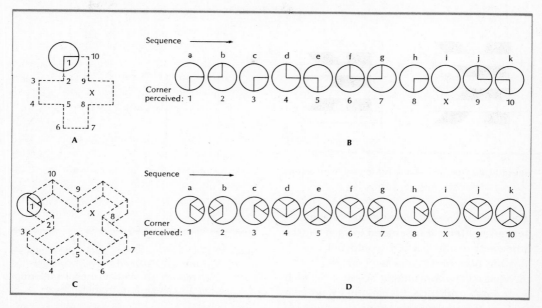

Figure 12.33. Shapes (A, C) presented by successive views (B, D). See text. (After Hochberg, 1968.)

must make at least 4 separate fixations, so that more than a second in time must elapse between the time the first and last corner are fixated. How do we recognize that the shape is a cross, and not one of the other figures that can be built up out of these corners? In some manner, our perceptual system must be able to register and store the relative location of each corner.

The schemas or maps that contain the information of where one has to fixate in order to see some feature are a form of *post-retinal storage*. Parks (1965) proposed that postretinal storage could be demonstrated and studied by moving a pattern behind a stationary slit so that its parts appear successively in the same place. Under the proper conditions, the whole shape is recognizable, even though only a narrow region is exposed at any moment. To Parks, this demonstrates the existence of postretinal visual storage. This phenomenon, which was first noted by Zollner (see Helmholtz, 1866), can be at least partially attributed to eye movements that spread the entire pattern out on adjacent regions of the retina. Explanation of this

phenomenon in terms of such eye movements (Helmholtz, 1866) has been repeatedly challenged (Vierordt, 1868; Rothschild, 1922; Hecht, 1924; Parks, 1965; see Anstis and Atkinson, 1967, for a review of this literature), but it now seems to account for many of the features that Parks described, for example, the compression of the perceived shape that is characteristically reported, and the fact that the entire figure appears to be visible simultaneously (Anstis & Atkinson, 1967; Haber & Nathanson, 1968). However, this factor only provides a source of retinally tied storage that contaminates the study of postretinal storage; the latter is also demonstrated by successive viewing of a figure through an aperture. Thus, if one of the outline patterns shown in Figure 12.33A, C is moved around behind a hole at a reasonably slow pace (about 500–1000 msec. between the corners of Fig. 12.33A, or between the bends of Figure 12.33C), adult subjects can recognize the shapes (Hochberg, 1968). Such storage is unlikely to be due exclusively to any tracking of the pattern by eye movements. Indeed, the patterns shown in Figure 12.33A, C are so large

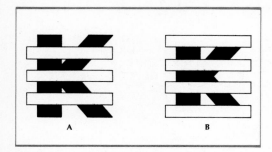

Figure 12.34. The same shape presented by different views. See text.

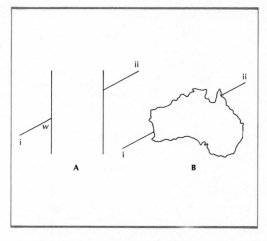

Figure 12.35. The Poggendorf illusion. The diagonals *i–ii* are really aligned. A. With straight-line interruptions. B. With an irregular interruption. (Adapted from Hotopf, 1966.)

that, were the eye to pursue one of the corners even after it disappeared from view, the other end of the pattern would fall too far into the periphery to be seen clearly.

What mechanisms might account for such postretinal storage? Schematic maps are not sensory: When the same shape is recognized in Figure 12.34A, B we do not really see the hidden portions. Similarly, in the aperture viewing of Figure 12.33 (p. 455), there is no real sensory quality either to the shape or its background where these are occluded by the mask. It is as though the *concept* of a cross (perhaps, in the form of a program or plan of the eye movements that would have to be made to trace it out, or to change fixation from one point on it to another, see p. 453), always underlies the perception of this familiar shape, but is only made evident when the sensory overlay in which it is normally clothed has been removed (Hochberg, 1968). A very similar view underlies Neisser's concept of "figural synthesis" (Neisser, 1967). This is thus far only speculation. What should be clear now is that the question of *what* shape is actually *seen* in response to a given retinal configuration is not a simple question with a single answer.

ILLUSIONS AND AFTEREFFECTS

The Geometrical Illusions

Regular vs. irregular patterns If we confine our attention to simple aspects of a given shape, such as its apparent length or curva-

ture, we can often determine with reasonable confidence how that aspect changes with changes in stimulation. When we can do this, we usually find that the relationship of apparent shape to retinal configuration is beyond our present abilities to formulate in general terms or to explain within a single theory. Specific instances in which the apparent curvature or length of a perceived line are not predictable from the curvature or length of its stimulus pattern have long been called the "geometrical illusions," but this does not mean that they occur only with regular lines and patterns; they can also be demonstrated with quite irregular drawings (see Figure 12.35; Hotopf, 1966), and with real objects in normal environments (Chapanis & Mankin, 1967; Zanforlin, 1967). Any theories that dismiss the illusions as being due to the peculiarities of lines on paper (see Gibson) or that explain them as false expectations of rectangularity based on Western man's continuous exposure to a geometrical and "carpentered" world (Segal, Campbell, & Herskovitz, 1963, 1966) are placing unwarranted restrictions on their generality of occurrence. The geometrical character of the traditional illusions is most reasonably re-

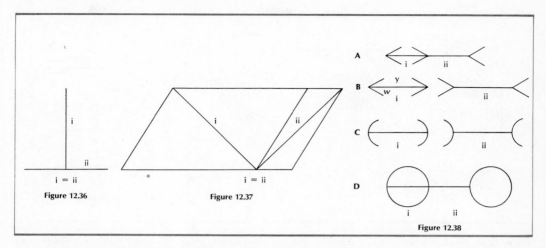

Figure 12.36. Vertical-horizontal illusion.   **Figure 12.37.** Sander parallelogram.   **Figure 12.38.** Variations of the Müller-Lyer illusion. D. is from Zanforlin (1967).

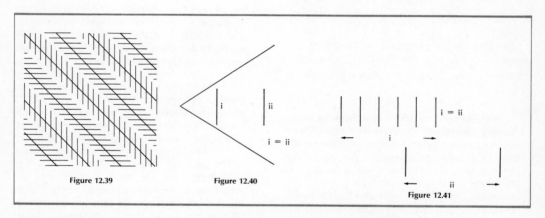

Figure 12.39. Zöllner illusion.   **Figure 12.40.** Ponzo illusion.   **Figure 12.41.** Filled-space illusion.

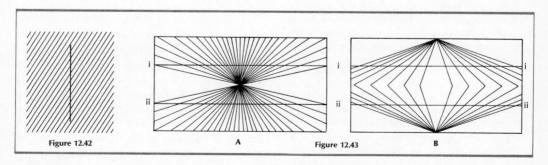

Figure 12.42. The single line is vertical.   **Figure 12.43.** Hering and Wundt illusions. Lines *i* and *ii* are parallel.

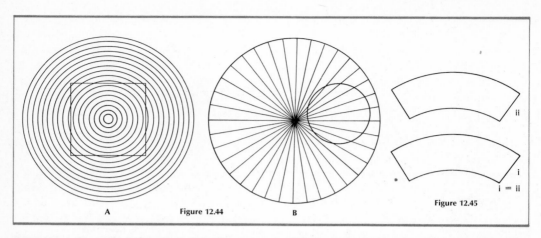

Figure 12.44. Ehrenstein and Orbison illusions. The inscribed figures are perfectly symmetrical.   **Figure 12.45.** The upper and lower areas are equal.

garded as a convenient way in which to make the distortions more easily noticeable than they are in ordinary configurations (Hotopf, 1966).

The illusions are important, therefore, because they may provide clues for our understanding of the processes of shape perception in general.

Measurement of the shape illusions under varying conditions   Quantitative methods used to evaluate the extent of illusions have usually been the adjustment method (p. 20) or the method of constant stimuli, with a fair amount of data accrued by both methods (Thiéry, 1895, Heymans, 1896, 1897; Judd et al., 1899, 1902, 1905). Little application has yet been made of the methods of detection theory (p. 39). Quantitative studies of how the illusions vary with changes in pattern bring out effects that might otherwise have gone unnoticed; for example, Finger and Spelt (1947), showed that the usual **T** form of the vertical-horizontal illusion (Figure 12.36) is contaminated by effects due to the bisected cross-bar and that the illusion is markedly smaller in the form of an **L.** Parametric studies of the horizontal-vertical illusion were performed by Künnapas (1957); of the Sander parallelogram (Figure 12.37) by Ipsen (1926); of the Müller-Lyer figure and its variants by Heymans (1896), who found the illusion to be proportional to the cosine of the angles, w (Figure 12.38), and by Judd (1899), who found that all spatial relations in the immediate neighborhood of the Müller-Lyer figure were distorted,

not only the main lines; of the Poggendorf illusion (Figure 12.35), by Burmeister (1896), who found that the apparent displacement of the 2 diagonal lines, i-ii, followed the formula $v = k\ u \cot w$; of the Zöllner pattern (Figure 12.39), by Heymans (1896), who found the maximum effect when angle w was 30°; of the Ponzo illusion (Figure 12.40), by Sickles (1942); and of Oppel's or Kundt's illusion (Figure 12.41) by Knox (1893), by Lewis (1912), and by Spiegel (1937), all of whom found that there was a maximum number of subdivisions (for each line length) at which the greatest overestimation of the subdivided line occurred. Hofman and Bielschowsky (1909) measured how the orientation of a field of lines affected the apparent slant of a line superimposed on the field (Figure 12.42), a study the data of which should be relevant not only to such illusions of angle as the Hering (Figure 12.43A), Wundt (Figure 12.43B), and Ehrenstein and Orbison patterns (Figure 12.44), but to some of the aftereffects that we discuss on page 466, as well.

These studies are not an end in themselves, of course, but take their importance from the quantitative data that they offer to any theory which is itself definite enough to deal with such facts. As we shall see, few theories can really avail themselves of these resources at present.

Principal Theories of Illusions

The illusions have received a great deal of attention, over the years, and many of them are known by special names. Instead of attempting a full account of the illusions, we state the principal theories that have been suggested to explain them, and give a selection of illusory figures (Figures 12.35 through 12.45) on which the reader can try out these theories.

The eye-movement theory In its simplest form, the eye-movement theory assumes that the impression of length is obtained by moving the eye along from one end of a pattern to the other. This would account for the horizontal-vertical illusion (Figure 12.36) by assuming that the vertical movements require greater effort than horizontal movements over the same distance, and therefore seem longer. In the Müller-Lyer figure (Figure 12.38A), the outward lines in one part might cause eye movements to exceed the length of the included line, whereas in the other part of the figure, the inward pointing lines might act to prevent the eyes from moving so far. The major objection to this theory is that the illusion can be obtained in tachistoscopic presentations, which produce exposures too short to permit the eye to move.

Photographic recordings of eye movements made during examination of the Müller-Lyer illusion show some relationship between the eye movement and the differences in pattern to each side of the illusion but nothing which provides an explanation of the former in terms of the latter (Judd, 1905; Yarbus, 1967).

A less-direct form of this theory assumes only that a *tendency* toward such movement is set up by the stimulus pattern itself, even when no movement can occur, and that this tendency is sufficient to give rise to the impression of length. This kind of theory is not a satisfactory explanation unless we can specify further what such movement tendencies should be and how they are affected by the stimulus pattern. Coren and Festinger (1967) have offered a first step toward such a theory, which we consider later on in another context (p. 467).

The empathy theory Lipps (1897) sought to explain the esthetic effects of architecture on the assumption that the observer responds emotionally in terms of his own actions. A vertical line, in resisting gravity, suggests more effort and thus appears longer than an equally long horizontal line. The right part of the Müller-Lyer pattern in Figure 12.38 suggests expansion, the left, limitation, and therefore the right appears longer. Although there may be circumstances in which this theory might be developed into a predictive one, especially in regard to the expressive arts, it does not really accommodate any of the detailed knowledge of the illusions.

Field factors According to Gestalt theory, illusions are merely cases in which the entire field affects the appearance of any part. Few specific field theories about the illusions have been offered. Of these, the most general is that of Orbison (1939). Following a proposal made earlier by Brown and Voth (1937) in connection with apparent motion (p. 527n), Orbison suggested that forces of attraction might operate between lines in the visual field, and that these would be in conflict with forces of constraint (which would operate to keep the lines fixed in their retinal locations). The 2 sets of forces in concert would generate such illusions as those of Wundt and Hering, and the special figures that were designed to test this theory by Orbison (1939). In any field of lines (Figures 12.43, 12.44) there will be loci of equilibrium at which the forces of attraction and constraint would be equal, and any other lines that are added to the field would be distorted toward the loci of equilibrium. Thus, in Figure 12.44A the radii are the loci of equilibrium, and the sides of the square are accordingly distorted toward those loci. Berliner and Berliner (1948) argued that a more specific and precise explanation of these kinds of illusion can be given by assuming that any line (straight or curved) changes direction wherever it crosses another line at some angle w, with the change in direction being proportional to the quantity $c \sin 4 w$

(see Webster, 1948, however). In any case, neither this formula nor Orbison's balance of forces gives clear predictions for the other classes of illusion.

A general characteristic of most of these illusions is that acute angles look larger than they are and obtuse angles look smaller. This is an observation of long standing, and many theories have been offered to explain it, one of which we consider next.

The perspective or constancy theory   The perspective theory incorporates a general class of theories that imply that the apparent length of lines on paper is affected by the perspective read into the figure and that similar confusions can arise by the mistaken use of cues in the real world, too. Thus a short vertical line in a drawing may represent a relatively long horizontal line extending away from the observer, thus explaining the horizontal-vertical illusion (Figure 12.36). In the Müller-Lyer pattern, the obliques "suggest" perspective, and in terms of the laws of perspective, the horizontal line on the right should, if it appears further away, also appear to represent a line that is longer than the one on the left.

Because, in one form or another, the explanation given above is the most popular explanation of the illusions, at present, let us spell out the general argument in more detail.

Whenever converging lines are present in the retinal image, they are more likely than not to have been projected there by lines that are really not converging, but are extended into distance. We therefore take the left side of the pattern in the Müller-Lyer figure (Figure 12.38A) to be nearer than the right side. The 2 lengths, at *i* and at *ii*, are equal on the page, however, and will also provide images of equal length on the retina of the viewer's eye. In order for this to be so, if *i* is actually nearer than *ii*, *i* must really be shorter than *ii*. Thus, the same mechanisms that enable us to take distance into account and to perceive that an object's size remains constant as it approaches and its retinal image becomes larger

(see *size constancy,* Chapter 13) are reflected in the illusions. The illusions are merely mistaken applications of the distance cues.

This theory has been applied to most of the illusions at one time or another (Thiéry, 1896; Tausch, 1954; von Holzt, 1957; Green & Hoyle, 1963; Gregory, 1963; Segall, Campbell, & Herskovits, 1963). In favor of this theory are the facts of intercultural differences (Rivers, 1901, 1905). Segall, Campbell, and Herskovits (1963, 1966) obtained responses to several illusions from samples of European, African, and other cultures, finding that Europeans showed greater errors on the Müller-Lyer pattern and on the Sander parallelogram (Figure 12.37), whereas most non-European groups showed greater errors on the horizontal-vertical illusion. Their explanation is this: (1) Whenever persons living in "carpentered" or rectangular environments are confronted by lines meeting in nonrectangular junctions, they will perceive the figures in perspective, interpreting them as two-dimensional representations of tridimensional objects having rectangular junctions (hence the tendency to overestimate acute angles and underestimate obtuse angles, mentioned above). (2) Because the horizontal-vertical illusion reflects a tendency to counteract the foreshortening of lines that extend into space away from the observer, people living in open, spacious environments will be more susceptible to the illusion than those dwelling in urban (or rain-forest) surroundings.

The following arguments can be made against the perspective theory. First, there is a question of fact concerning the importance of a "carpentered" environment in determining susceptibility to the various illusions. Jahoda (1966) also found British subjects' judgments to be significantly more susceptible to the Müller-Lyer pattern than were natives of Ghana. The latter subjects, however, had been drawn partly from one population who inhabited open country and lived in round houses devoid of furnishings and partly from another population who lived in dense rain forest and in rectangular dwellings with car-

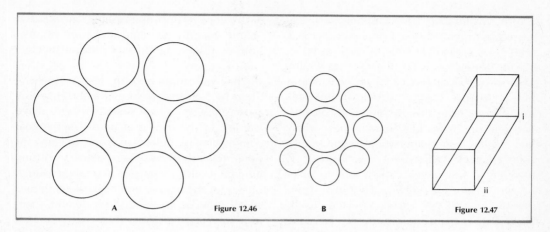

A   Figure 12.46   B   Figure 12.47

Figure 12.46. The inner circles of A and B are equal. p. 462.

Figure 12.47. A version of the Necker cube. See text, p. 462.

pentered furnishings. The 2 groups of Ghanaians failed to show the expected differences in their responses to the illusions. Cultural differences in the measured effects of the illusions may not be due to expectations of rectangularity, therefore, but to other as-yet unknown determinants. These may include differences in perceptual attitudes (p. 464) or they may even depend on sensory differences. For example, Pollack and Silvar (1967) found that subjects whose central region of the retina (the *fundus oculi;* see Chapter 9) is more darkly pigmented showed less of an illusion when they viewed part of the Müller-Lyer pattern briefly under bluish light, than did subjects with lighter pigmentation. Moreover, optical pigmentation differs with race (Ishak, 1952; Pollack & Silvar, 1967; Silvar & Pollack, 1967). It seems quite unlikely that pigmentation differences account for much of the intercultural difference. But with so many other possible sources of difference, it seems premature to conclude that susceptibility to the geometrical illusions reflects the subjects' familiarity with carpentered environments. Moreover, as Zanforlin (1967) points out, even birds display illusions (Warden & Barr, 1929; Winslow, 1933), and their nests are not normally rectangular.

Second: There are illusions whose detailed effects can be explained in terms of other principles (see Figures 12.41, 12.46, 12.47, and p. 459), but which are not as well predicted by size-constancy or perspective explanations (Berliner, 1948; see also Hotopf, 1966; Virsu, 1967).

Third: The illusions to which the perspective theory seems most immediately addressed can themselves be otherwise explained. Thus, Künnapas (1957) attributes the horizontal-vertical illusion to the fact that the shape of our visual field is oval, so that the vertical line is overestimated because it is nearer to the boundary of the field of view. The Müller-Lyer illusion, it has been argued, occurs because the observer confuses the area included between the arrowheads with the length that he is being asked to judge. In some ways, in fact, this explanation seems more readily applicable. Consider, for example, the variations shown in Figure 12.38C and D (C was originally presented by Müller-Lyer in 1889; D is taken from Zanforlin, 1967): What depth cues, perspective or otherwise, contribute to the effects displayed by C and D?

Fourth: There is a question of what it might mean to say that "side *i* looks smaller *because* it looks nearer." This implies a relationship between perceived size and perceived distance that is similar to the possible relationship between perceived reflectance and perceived illumination ($R = L/E$) that we discussed in pages 401–406. Evidence of such a relationship between perceived size and perceived distance will be discussed at length in the next chapter. We can give one example here of such evidence, particularly relevant to the case of the illusions. For many observers, line i in Figure 12.47 looks longer when line ii looks nearer, and when the reversible solid changes its apparent organization so that line i looks nearer, then line ii looks longer (Sanford, 1897; Hotopf, 1966; Hochberg, 1968; Mefferd & Wieland, 1968). These data are uncertain, however, because Gregory reports no size change (1966). According to perspective theory, pretty much the same thing happens in the case of the geometrical illusions caused by the Müller-Lyer pattern, and to this extent the effects in Figure 12.47 buttress the perspective theory. However, there is this clear difference between Figures 12.47 and 12.38: in the former, lines i and ii actually seem in some sense to lie at different distances (even though you know that they are really in the plane of the paper), whereas in the latter the 2 lines seem to lie in the same plane. How can we say that the difference in apparent length is caused by the difference in apparent distance, in Figure 12.38, when there is no difference in apparent distance?

Helmholtz' concept of *unconscious inference* (introduced on page 397) is at its most appealing when it deals with problems of size and distance perception, as we see in the next chapter. In essence, it notes that it often seems *as though* what we perceive results from calculations that were made about objects and about their dispositions in space on the basis of the sensory information that our eyes receive, even though we are aware neither of making the calculations nor of receiving the sensory information. That is, there are 2 levels of processing sensory information, only one of which can be consciously reported, but both of which seem to obey the same or roughly similar laws. In the case of the Müller-Lyer pattern, we might say that we have reached conclusions about the lengths

of the lines by unconscious inferences based on the unconscious (and mistaken) impressions of distance produced by the perspective cues.

This was rephrased in less mentalistic terms by Tolman and Brunswik (1935) and by Tausch (1954). If our visual systems have learned, in the course of normal perceptual commerce with objects in space, to allow for the distorting effects of perspective by setting up counterdistortions (for example, to judge objects at the narrow end of converging perspectives to be larger, at the wide end, smaller), then a two-dimensional configuration that contains depth cues that will trigger off the counterdistorting process will itself be distorted. Gregory (1963, 1967) has labeled 2 processes: (1) *primary scaling* (or *depth cue scaling*), in which the perceptual system automatically corrects size judgments in accordance with whatever distance cues are present, regardless of whether or not those distance cues also produce perceived depth. (2) *secondary scaling* (or *hypothesis scaling*), in which apparent distance determines apparent size. In the case of the illusions, only primary scaling is at work because the various cues available to normal vision serve to localize all of the lines as being in the plane of the paper. Secondary scaling was demonstrated in Figure 12.47 where the changes in apparent length were presumably due to changes in apparent distance. Many questions remain to be answered before we can really evaluate this class of explanation.

Why do some patterns, like those in Figure 12.47, produce apparent depth (and, therefore, secondary scaling), despite the indications given to the eye that all of the lines really rest in the plane of the paper, whereas the illusions in Figures 12.35 through 12.45 remain flat and produce only size change (primary scaling)? Also, if the patterns in Figure 12.38A, B are not seen in depth, how do we know that depth cues are present? Gregory (1963, 1966) had subjects, using 1 eye only, look at luminous versions of the illusion in a dark box, so that such indications of flatness as binocular disparity or surface texture (see Chapter 13, pp. 481f.) would not contradict the perspective cues. He reports that when subjects were instructed to set a binocularly viewed spot of light at the same apparent distance from them as the various parts of the pattern, the binocularly viewed spot (the real distance of which was clear to the subject at all times) was in fact set further away when the subject was matching side *ii* than when he was matching side *i*, and that the magnitude of this apparent depth distance varied in the same way as the magnitude of the illusion varied under normal viewing conditions. Experiments with other illusions under similar conditions have not obtained reliable depth responses, however (Green & Hoyle, 1963; Hotopf, 1966), and, in any case, the fact that some patterns *can* produce apparent depth under certain conditions does not prove that that is *why* they produce size distortions under other conditions. The conditions that determine whether primary or secondary scaling will occur; an independent and quantitative method of identifying the depth cues; a statement of the amount of distortion to be attributed to each cue, separately and in interaction—all of these are needed if the "misapplied constancy" theory is to constitute a serious advance over the old perspective and "unconscious inference" theories.

In summary, the perspective or constancy theories seem plausibly to explain many of the illusions, at least partially and qualitatively. There are illusions to which they do not seem immediately relevant, however, and we shall see that there are other explanations that apply equally well to the illusions to which the perspective theories are relevant.

Contrast and confusion theories   The fact that a subject can judge line lengths does not mean that he is necessarily responding to length as such: the areas of the regions divided by the line are also varying in one-to-one correspondence with the line's length, and he might, for example, be responding to the areas. The way in which the Müller-Lyer illusion varies with the angle (p. 458) is con-

sistent with the interpretation that the subject cannot narrow his attention down to the main lines, but is responding also to the areas included between the fins. However, using only half of the traditional pattern (*i* in Figure 12.38B), Erlebacher and Sekuler (1969) have shown that it is the distance *y* between the ends of the fins that is important: if *y* is held constant (by adjusting the lengths of the fins) while the angle *w* is varied, the illusion ceases to vary with the angle. In other words, the subject may base his length judgments on some compromise between 2 of the cues that are available to him for making "equals" judgments, namely the length of the main line and that of the gap *y* between the fins. This is much like what happens when he makes a judgment in an experiment on color constancy (p. 398), size constancy (p. 509), and so on (see Brunswik, 1956).

The "confusion" theory is similar in some respects to the explanation in terms of *confluence* that was originally proposed by Müller-Lyer. Helmholtz' explanation of many of the geometrical illusions was in terms of *contrast; confluence* (or *confluxion*) is essentially negative contrast. In this connection, the term *contrast* means that perceived differences between similar stimuli, or between those that do not appear to be clearly separate, are diminished. In the case of the geometrical illusions, any parts of a pattern that extend close to other parts, or that are only slightly smaller than the other stimuli to which they are being compared, are overestimated, by confluence. Parts of a pattern that are not close to other parts, or that are compared to other stimuli that are considerably larger than they are (within limits, see Ebbinghaus, 1913), will be underestimated (Virsu, 1967).

Are Illusions Determined by Stimulation?

At present, it seems premature to accept a single explanation for all or any of the illusions, a single "correction," which, when applied to our physical measures of the stimulus configuration, will enable us to predict what shapes will be perceived. In fact, to the de-

TABLE 12.1 ATTITUDE AND OBJECTIVE CONDITIONS FAVORING TOTAL AND PART-ISOLATING PERCEPTION

Main lines of Müller-Lyer	white	white	dark gray
Oblique lines	white	dark gray	white
Background	black	black	black
Average illusion under			
whole-perceiving attitude	4.95	2.20	7.66
part-isolating attitude	1.02	− .50	3.20

Each figure in the table is the average of 20–30 measurements, all on a single subject, but confirmed by results from other subjects. From Benussi, 1904.

gree that nonstimulus factors, such as the subjects' attitudes and the effects of practice, affect the existence and magnitude of illusions, attempts to predict the appearance of these patterns in terms of physical measures alone must be inadequate. Moreover, any theory of the illusion must encompass such effects, if they exist. Let us consider, therefore, the results of research on the roles that attitudes and practice play in the geometrical illusions.

Experimentally controlled attitudes of observation Benussi's subjects (1904) were instructed to observe the Müller-Lyer pattern in one case with a "whole-perceiving" attitude and in another case, with a "part-isolating" attitude. The illusion was greater when the subjects approached the experiment with the whole-perceiving than the part-isolating attitude (see also Brunswik). As the objective conditions made the isolation of the horizontal lines easy or difficult, the

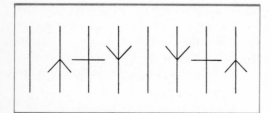

Figure 12.48. Successive positions of the Müller-Lyer element, shown in rapid succession, and giving an appearance of up and down movement of the point of intersection along with the apparent movement of the side lines. (Benussi, 1912.)

illusion itself diminished and increased, respectively, and so did the effectiveness of instructions to overcome it (Table 12.1). In a particularly interesting version of this attitudinal experiment, Benussi (1912) presented the Müller-Lyer figure in rapid succession as in the diagram in Figure 12.48, producing an apparent motion of the "arms." If subjects attend strictly to the lines, and regard the crossing point only as a pivot, the crossing point does not move when the arms do; however, if attention is directed to the changing shape of the total figure, the midpoint seems to glide along the vertical line, upward when the side lines move up and downward when the side lines move down.

It seems plausible at this point to account for the effects of different attitudes in terms of differences in the weight that subjects give to line versus arrowheads (or area) in making their judgments. Because these differential effects of attitude are quite large, even within a culture (Brunswik, 1956), it is difficult to assess how much of the variation in these illusions that has been found between cultures (see p. 460) may be due to differences in attitude and how much to perceptual learning. Changes in attitude may also account for some part of the phenomena we discuss next.

The practice experiments in illusions It has long been known that continued experience with 1 pattern diminishes the amount of the illusion it produces (Heymans, 1896), and several systematic studies of these practice effects have been performed.

Decrements in the magnitude of the illusions due to practice have been studied with the Müller-Lyer pattern (Judd, 1902, 1905; Lewis, 1908; Köhler & Fishback, 1950; Selkin & Wertheimer, 1957; Day, 1962), in the Poggendorf (Cameron & Steele, 1905), in the horizontal-vertical illusion (Seashore et al., 1908), and the Zoellner pattern (Judd & Courten, 1905). In general, the illusions all diminished very greatly, but only if the pattern was in the original position. If the figure were reversed right and left, the illusion returned in full strength, and in some subjects was exaggerated. However, in others the illusion was overcome by a relatively small amount of further practice. The illusion produced by the original figure was revived if the subject stood off and looked at it casually as a whole. Eye movement photographs showed that the subject was by no means passively receptive in viewing the figure. He explored it rather minutely, especially the part with the inward-slanting arrowheads (Judd, 1905). This minute examination of the figure diminished toward the end of practice.

What can account for the decrease in the illusions due to practice? No reinforcement of correct judgments, nor correction of errors, is overtly involved in these experiments. Why then does the illusion decrease with continued inspection? Three major explanations have been suggested.

One plausible explanation is that the subject gradually shifts to an analytic attitude during the practice of judging the illusion (Judd, 1905; Day, 1962), and restricts his attention to the horizontal lines by the use of techniques that are probably adapted to the specific left-right arrangement of the figure with which he is practicing.[9] More challenging explanations have been offered by Köhler and Fishback (1950), based on the assumption of a central "satiation" process, and by Coren

and Festinger (1967), based on a correction of initially erroneous eye movements; we examine both of these explanations in the context of the figural aftereffects, which we consider next.

Shape Adaptation and Figural Aftereffects

The effects of practice on perceived shape have been studied for many years, with increasing diligence and very diverse goals in the last two decades. The aim of most of the research was to test what appeared to be a broad and powerful (if physiologically unorthodox and unconvincing) theory about the isomorphic Gestalt brain processes. The aftereffects thus took on their importance from the breadth of the perceptual theory that they seemed to test, that is, the Köhler-Wallach theory of figural aftereffects. From the beginning, however, many of the same phenomena were studied for quite a different reason, namely to test theories about how the different senses (particularly those of vision, kinesthesis, and proprioception) combine in the perception of space.

Shape adaptation and the learned bases of perceived direction In fact, the study of the effects of practice on shape perception really starts with the question of the relationship between touch and action on the one hand, and the perception of *visual direction* on the other. As we saw on page 427, one might think of a shape as being a set of local signs that identify the two-dimensional spatial location of each retinal element in a stimulus configuration. Wundt (1902) offered the following facts as evidence that the specific two-dimensional spatial meaning of each retinal element is not innate and fixed but rather is learned and changeable. When a subject is first made to wear prismatic glasses, straight lines appear bent and objects' shapes are thus distorted, due to the deformation that the prisms produce in the retinal image. These disturbances gradually disappear if the glasses are worn for some time. After the glasses are removed, distortions appear in the opposite

---

[9]When a subject moves his finger over a raised version of the Müller-Lyer pattern, an illusion is obtained that is similar to the visual one. Rudel and Teuber (1963) found that decrements in the illusion caused by practice obtained with this illusion of active touch—this *haptic* illusion—would transfer to a visual Müller-Lyer illusion, and vice versa. That is, practice with either modality resulted in a decrement not only in the version with which practice had been made (that is, visual or haptic), but in the other version as well. If the decrement is due to a restriction of attention to the horizontal lines, some degree of this restriction of attention would be expected to transfer from visual to haptic judgments, and *vice versa*.

direction even though the retinal image is now again undistorted. Why do these changes occur? Presumably because when a line is curved on the retina but is straight in the physical world, the observer's actions (and his resulting sensations of touch and kinesthesis) inform him of the discrepancy, and a curved configuration of retinal elements now comes to signify the actions by which we define an object's straightness.[10]

The nature of this perceptual learning of the spatial coordinates will concern us again in the next chapter. Before we consider the matter settled, however, let us ponder the issues raised by the following experiments.

Adaptation and aftereffects to curved and tilted lines   In the course of research with prisms, Gibson (1933) noticed that adaptation occurred even without any action on the part of the observer. If the subject inspects a slightly curved line in a vertical position for a few minutes, by the end of the inspection period the line appears less curved than it did at first, and if a straight vertical line is then shown in the same place in the visual field, it appears to be curved in the opposite direction. Similar observations had been made by Verhoeff (1925). The loss of apparent curvature (that is, *the adaptation*) in the curved line being looked at during the inspection period was equal to the opposite apparent curvature (the *negative aftereffect*) that a straight line appeared to have when it was shown to the subject just after the inspection period. (This was measured by having the subject adjust a flexible rod to appear straight.) The aftereffect, strong at first, faded out gradually. The same kinds of aftereffect occur whether the curves are vertical, horizontal, or obliquely presented. Similar effects

[10]In fact, because of the optics of the eye, and of the constraints of the muscle system that moves it, straight lines in the environment do not, in general, project straight lines in the retinal image, even in normal (undistorted) viewing. It seems likely, therefore, that whether a given configuration at some point on the retina results in an impression of straightness or curvature is always determined by what our actions with objects, that are really straight in physical space, have taught us about the meaning of that configuration (see Chapter 13, p. 543; also, Helmholtz, 1866; Lamb, 1918; Roberts & Suppes, 1967).

have been found for lines tilted from the vertical or horizontal. These lose their tilt during prolonged inspection, after which a true vertical appears to tilt in the opposite direction (Vernon, 1934; Gibson, 1937; Gibson & Radner, 1937). We concern ourselves with these tilt effects again in the next chapter. For now, consider the implications of the curvature aftereffects described by Gibson. The aftereffect seemed to be limited to lines that have the same general direction and that are in the same retinal region as was stimulated by the inspection line. (This last restriction has since been shown to be invalid in the case of tilted lines [Morant and Mikaelian, 1960].)

This phenomenon seems to imply exactly the opposite explanation from that given by Wundt (1902); here, the line that is curved on the retina is in reality also curved in physical space. Why should continued inspection then teach the observer to see *unveridically*, that is, to see a curved line as straight? Gibson proposed that shape itself is a sensory response, like temperature or hue or brightness, and that it is merely showing the sensory

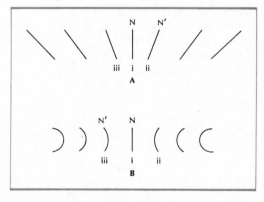

Figure 12.49. Gibson's normalization theory of aftereffects. A. The slant dimension. B. The curvature dimension. After exposure to a line (*ii*), that line tends to be perceived as the neutral point (*N*) on the dimension in question. Because the entire scale of psychophysical correspondence between the physical and perceived dimensions is displaced, the stimulus that was previously seen as neutral (*i*) now has the same appearance that some non-neutral stimulus (*iii*) had before the shift occurred. (Adapted from Gibson, 1950.)

adaptation that is common to such responses (see Chapters 5 and 9). He suggests that a visual line or border has two variable qualities in addition to that of length, namely its place on a continuum that runs from *left-slant* to *right-slant* (Figure 12.49A) and from *convex* to *concave* (Figure 12.49B). These qualities presumably change in the same way as do blue-gray-yellow and warm-neutral-cold during and after prolonged stimulation. That is, adaptation and aftereffects of curvature and tilt result because the neutral point has shifted (Figure 12.49), and what we might call *normalization* of the inspected shape has occurred.

If such normalization occurs with curved lines on the retina seen without distorting prisms, we should expect it to occur as well when the curvature is produced by prisms. Wundt's example would then become a case of adaptation to shape as such, not a proof that visual direction is subject to relearning. We next examine 2 alternative explanations of the curvature adaptation and aftereffects that do not invoke "normalization," but we should note that in any case Held and Rekosh (1963) have found adaptation to distortion of curvature, with prisms, that simply cannot be due to the normalization of curved lines. Indeed, in their procedure, the subject sees no lines at all, either straight or curved: he sees only a random array of spheres (p. 542). Under these conditions, adaptation depends on the subject's being active while wearing prisms, so that Wundt's argument (that the subject can relearn "straightness") remains defensible.

One alternative explanation for the Gibson effect questions the original interpretation, namely that practice leads to illusory perception. Coren and Festinger (1967) showed that the curvature of a line segment is initially *overestimated,* that is, that there is an initial illusion, and that the "normalization" that occurs with continued inspection brings the subject's judgment closer to the actual curvature, not away from it. This is just the kind of practice decrement that we have seen to be characteristic of many of the geometrical

illusions (p. 464). Why should such correction of perceptual error occur when the subject has no way of knowing that he is wrong? The Coren and Festinger explanation is an ingenious one: If the curvature is overestimated (or for that matter, if the lengths are incorrectly estimated in the Müller-Lyer pattern in Figure 12.38) and if eye movements that are made from one point on the pattern to another are guided by these mistaken estimates, such saccades (p. 453) will consistently be found to be in error at their terminal fixation, until suitable recalibration of visual direction is achieved and curvature is correctly seen. The question of why the illusions occur in the first place, and why they are not already corrected by this hypothesized process, long before the subject comes to the experiment, then remains to be answered. Coren and Festinger adopt the perspective theory (that curves act in *primary scaling* [p. 462] as though they were tilted in depth), but in any case, their explanation of the shape aftereffect brings us back to the illusions.[11]

The second explanation for the Gibson effect is the "satiation" theory, an explanation

---

[11] Festinger, White, and Allyn (1968) have in fact shown that subjects' eye movements tend to overshoot the ends of *ii* in Figure 12.38B, and to undershoot the ends of *i*, when they first start to scan the pattern. These errors decrease as scanning continues. Because Festinger and his colleagues maintain that any contour's perceived location in the visual field is given by the eye movements that the subject is prepared to make in order to fixate the contour, the practice decrement in the illusion simply reflects the correction of the scanning errors. McLaughlin, DeSisto, and Kelly (1969) have challenged this interpretation because of the fact that subjects who are experimentally trained to make a 5° eyemovement in order to fixate a target that was presented 10° in the periphery (the target being shifted to a location at 5° after the subject initates the eye movement) fail to show any effects of this training in the way in which they point at the target with their (unseen) hands (McLaughlin et al., 1968). This argument is not conclusive because it tells us only that hand movements and eye movements are not necessarily guided in the same way by the same visual display. It does not tell us what the display looks like (see Chapter 13, p. 537). In any case, however, it now seems plausible that the decrement occurs because the subjects' eye movements provide information about the illusion. However, Bolles (1969) has shown that the illusion is still about 20 percent in initial viewing when the figure is only 0.5° in extent and falls entirely within the fovea. It would be interesting, therefore, to know whether decrements occur with such small figures, inasmuch as the scanning errors involved could not be more than 0.1°, which is within the range in which the eye normally cannot make and hold fixations very well (see Chapter 11, p. 387).

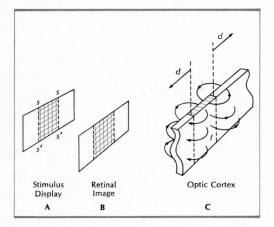

Figure 12.50. The Köhler-Wallach satiation theory of aftereffects. A region of different luminance in the stimulus display, A, produces a region of different bioelectric activity in the optic cortex of the brain, C, causing current flow between the figural region, *f*, and the adjacent tissue. As the current flow continues, the resistance of the adjacent tissue rises, and this process of satiation forces the current further from the original contours. When the stimulus is removed, the persistent satiation will divert the current flow associated with subsequently-viewed stimulus patterns away from that region, as shown by the arrows at *d*.

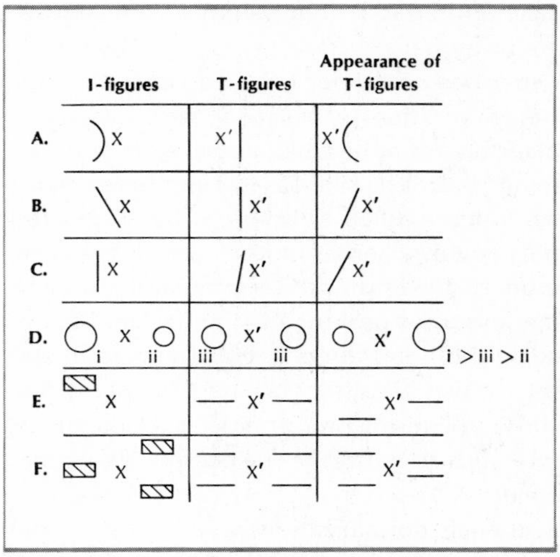

that will also eventually lead us back in a different way to the illusions. This theory has generated a great deal of research in its own right, and offers a very different picture of how shape perception occurs.

The satiation theory of the figural aftereffects Köhler had proposed in 1920 that electrical fields and currents in the visual cortex of the brain are the basis of form perception (see Figure 12.50; also Köhler, 1920, 1940). Both the Gibson effect (in which the same peripheral stimulation comes to produce a changed shape) and the phenomenon of figural reversal (in which different regions of the field alternate as figure even though the stimulus pattern remains unchanged [see p. 433]) seemed to Köhler to be readily explained in terms of such electrical currents (Köhler, 1940; Köhler & Wallach, 1944).

Figure 12.51. Figural aftereffects. The patterns in the first column are *inspection figures,* with fixation points at *X;* the second column shows *test figures* with fixation points at *X;* and the third shows the direction of the aftereffect (exaggerated in magnitude).

These currents would be generated by potential differences between different parts of the visual cortex, potential differences that are in turn produced by differences in excitation of different parts of the retina. Current flow produces *satiation* (an increased resistance to further current flow) in the tissue in the area adjacent to the boundary or contour (Köhler & Wallach, 1944). As satiation increases, current flow is diverted to less satiated regions, so that satiation spreads progressively. In a reversible figure (p. 432), reversal occurs when satiation reaches some level and, as the new region satiates in turn, reversal continues (Köhler, 1944).

Köhler and Wallach (1944) expanded this explanation to include Gibson's results with a broad class of phenomena they called *figural aftereffects.* In general, the subject fixates some point, *X,* on an inspection (*I*) figure, for a few minutes, and then fixates a point *X'* on the test (*T*) figure (Figure 12.51). The satiation of the tissue surrounding the projection of the *I* figure would force the currents generated by any subsequent *T* figure into the less-satiated region. As a consequence of this displacement of figural currents, the perceived locations of the contours change.[12] The contours of the T figure are in general displaced away from the regions that were previously satiated by the contours of the I figure. The amount that the T figure is displaced increases to a maximum at some short distance away from the I figure, and then decreases with a further increase in the distance (this is called the "distance paradox"). A survey of I figures, T figures, and the appearance of the latter after satiation, is given in Figure 12.51. The aftereffects in Figures 12.51C look very much like the normalization effects of Gibson, and of Gibson and Radner, except that they do not seem to follow from normalization (because I is already vertical, it should not affect the neutral point; see Figure 12.49), and they do seem to fit the rubric of contour displacement. The normalization effects might thus simply be instances of the figural aftereffects produced by satiation.

One effect of prolonged viewing remains to be explained by satiation theory, namely the decrement in the geometrical illusions due to practice. Köhler and Fishback (1950) propose that, in the Müller-Lyer pattern, satiation would build up more rapidly within the V than in front of its point. The resulting contour displacement would push the V outward, in effect. Thus, in the example shown in Figure 12.38B, the space between the points of the 2 Vs on the right would be decreased by prolonged inspection, while the space between those on the left would be increased. They demonstrated that the reduction was not due to the subjects' practice in *comparing* the 2 parts of the Müller-Lyer figure with each other, for only one part of the figure was exposed at a time (except during a few test trials), and this separate

inspection procedure seemed to destroy the illusion as quickly as when many simultaneous comparisons of the 2 halves were made. It must therefore be the steady inspection per se, and not the comparison process, that destroys the illusion. Note that the satiation theory only attempts to explain the practice decrement, not the illusion itself.

The *satiation theory* had the appeal of covering a wide range of phenomena: In addition to figure-ground reversal and figural aftereffects, it also seemed to make predictions about shape recognition thresholds (p. 443) and about practice effects in the geometrical illusions. It also seemed to show the kind of nonlocal action (action at a distance, or lateral effects) that Gestalt theory demanded (p. 428). This explanation seemed in some respects to be a real first step in exploring the brain processes that Gestalt theory assumed to underlie all perceptual phenomena and with which it hoped to replace the specific nerve energies of the structuralist theory (p. 428). A great many studies on the figural aftereffects (FAE) have been performed, both in the visual modality and in other senses (for example, by presenting I objects and T objects for the fingers to explore), and we would lose the sense of the purpose of exploring these effects if we attempted to review them in any representative fashion. We shall merely list some areas of inquiry, and otherwise refer the reader to critical reviews by Sagara & Oyama, 1957; McEwen, 1958; Spitz, 1958; Day, Pollack, & Seagrim, 1959.

The size of the FAE depends on the distance between I and T contours, first increasing and then decreasing with distance (Köhler & Wallach, 1944; Sagara & Oyama, 1957). It increases rapidly as the duration of the inspection period is increased up to 1 minute, then tends to level off. In general, the effect decreases as the interval between the I and T figure increases (Bales & Follansbee, 1935), after passing through a maximum shortly after the presentation of the I figure is terminated (Hammer, 1949; Ikeda & Obonai, 1953; Fehrer & Ganchrow, 1963; Farnè, 1965). The shorter the duration of the presentation of the T figure, the greater the aftereffect (Parducci & Brookshire, 1956; Farne, 1965); in fact, Farnè re-

---

[12]Strictly speaking, the cortical locations of the contours are not presumed to move; instead, the density of the "interrelationship" between 2 cortical regions determines their apparent nearness (Köhler & Wallach, 1944), and satiation was thought to change the density distribution in the cortex.

ports that subjects who do not perceive an after-effect with the usual viewing times of 30 seconds to 2 minutes, observe strong aftereffects with exposures of 0.12 second. The FAE increases with an increase in the difference between the luminances of the *I* figure and of its background (Nozawa, 1953; Hochberg & Triebel, 1955; Pollack, 1958; Yoshida, 1960; Graham, 1961; Day, 1962; Gibb, Freeman, & Adam, 1966) and decreases with an increased difference between the *T*-figure and its background (Gibb et al., 1966). It is not affected by the luminance of the *I* figure if the luminance difference is kept at a constant proportion of the luminance (Graham, 1961). Individual differences in FAE (and their relationship to other perceptual measures, such as the ability to detect embedded figures or to set a rod to the vertical when it is surrounded by a tilted framework; see Witkin et al., 1954; and Chapter 13, p. 539n) have been investigated with various purposes, often in hopes of finding general individual differences in cortical functioning (see Immergluck, 1966a, b). Because naive subjects who have not been specifically set to expect FAEs may not even notice them (Dodwell & Gaze, 1965; Gaze & Dodwell, 1965), we cannot tell whether individual differences in reporting FAE reflect differences in the occurrence of the figural aftereffect as such (and in the underlying physiological processes) or differences in the set with which those subjects approach the perceptual task.

Criticisms of the satiation theory The satiation theory must be criticized on several grounds. While it cannot yet be discarded in its entirety, it is now evident that it cannot be retained intact, either as to substance or promise.

First, objections to the physiological explanation have been raised by Smith (1948), Hebb (1949), and most seriously by Lashley, Chow, and Semmes (1951). The latter made explicit the very serious anatomical difficulties that the theory faces (for example, the necessity for an appropriate current to flow across the various distances in the cortex, where there are gross separations). They also showed that after gold foil and gold pins were inserted into monkeys' occipital surfaces to produce tne short-circuits or other rearrangements of figural currents that we would expect from the satiation theory, no impair-

ment of pattern vision was found. Similar conclusions follow from the research of Sperry and Miner (1955) and Sperry, Miner, and Meyers (1955). Various rebuttals may be attempted, but the fact is that each additional bit of information we acquire about the structure of the visual cortex (see Chapter 9) makes the figural current-flow theory less plausible.

We might nevertheless retain the satiation theory, not as an hypothesis about real physiological events, but as a model which seems to account for various perceptual phenomena. However, the satiation theory fails in this respect, too: Consider, in turn, its ability to predict the full range of figural aftereffects; the phenomena of figure-ground reversal; the normalization phenomena; and the practice decrement in the illusions.

Figural aftereffects in visual depth and in other modalities Figural aftereffects occur not only with flat figures, as in Figure 12.51, but in depth as well (Köhler & Emery, 1947; Fernberger, 1948). After subjects have fixated an *I* figure at some distance from them, a subsequently viewed *T* figure that is slightly farther away is displaced so as to appear still farther, and one that is slightly nearer than the *I* figure is displaced still nearer.[13] The electrical model simply cannot be taken seriously in this context. Furthermore, very similar FAEs occur in other modalities that do not permit this kind of cortical projection. These are FAEs which the satiation model cannot explain; see Köhler (1958). Thus one must question the value of the model: too many classes of phenomena are beyond its powers to explain, even though they are very similar to the phenomena for which it does seem able to account.

---

[13] The conditions used by Köhler and Emery may have produced the aftereffects in depth solely as a result of FAEs in the frontal plane (Farnè, 1965a; Osgood & Heyer, 1952). For example, when the *T*-figure was presented nearer than an *I*-figure of the same size, the contours of the *T*-figure would fall outside those of the *I*-figure and cause the latter to appear smaller and hence further than it really was. This kind of explanation is less readily applied to a set of experiments in which the *I*-figures were textured surfaces, viewed at a slant, through windows that concealed the surfaces' edges. Following inspection of such slanted surfaces, *T*-surfaces in the frontal plane appeared to be oppositely slanted (Bergman & Gibson, 1959; Farnè & Giaminoni, 1968).

Figural reversal and perspective reversal If reversal results from the satiation of cortical regions corresponding to each perceptual organization, figural reversal should increase as viewing time is increased, according to Köhler's theory, but results do not clearly support this prediction. Prior inspection of 1 of the 2 figural alternatives should reduce the proportion of the time during which that alternative is seen when the reversible figure is subsequently viewed, and something like that in fact occurs with flat patterns (Hochberg, 1950). On the other hand, a very similar phenomenon occurs in three dimensions: *ambiguous perspective pictures* (such as the "wire objects" in Figure 12.19) also are reversed spontaneously while the subject regards them. With such stimuli, prolonged exposure to one of the alternatives similarly affects subsequent reversals (Carlson, 1953; Howard, 1961; Orbach, Ehrlich, & Heath, 1963). It is unlikely that the electrical theory of satiation could explain such phenomena. We have seen (p. 468) that *I* and *T* patterns must fall on the same retinal regions in order to obtain the aftereffects, but the processes that are responsible for perspective reversal continue to occur even when the patterns are displaced to different regions of the retina and cortex (Orbach, Ehrlich, & Vainstein, 1963; Kolers, 1964), and reversals occur even while the pattern is in the process of being displaced from one region to another (Kolers, 1964). Some form of "fatigue" or other cumulative process may be involved in perceptual reversal, but it does not seem to derive in any specific way from the electrical-satiation model.

Normalization phenomena It remains an open question whether or not the Gibson effect can be completely subsumed under the contour-displacement rubric. Most of the research that is relevant to this issue has been concerned with tilt, not with curvature, and we discuss it in the next chapter (p. 538), merely noting here that it now appears that *both* contour displacement and normalization seem to be demonstrable as tilt aftereffects.

Practice decrement Decrement in the Müller-Lyer illusion due to practice has, as we have noted before (p. 465) also been obtained with haptically inspected stimuli (Rudel & Teuber, 1963), and the electrical-satiation model makes no provision for intermodal transfer. Moreover, the Köhler-Fishback stimulus subtended a visual angle of 3°, whereas Judd's was 26° (p. 465). Although the difference in size may account for the fact that the illusion was de-

creased much more rapidly with the former, we cannot be sure that satiation alone could ever produce a sufficiently strong decrement to account for the reduction of the illusion, in a figure that large, by contour-displacement alone.[14]

The electrical theory of satiation proposed by Köhler and his colleagues does not, in short, provide the general and inclusive explanation of adaptation, aftereffects, and perceptual reversal that it once seemed to offer. Even if this theory had proved to be more successful in dealing with the aftereffects, it still failed even to make a start on the very problems with which Gestalt psychologists had most cogently confronted structuralist explanations of shape perception: The electrical satiation theory deals only with events at specific places on the retina, and in fact the figural aftereffects are determined mostly or entirely by the pattern of retinal stimulation.[15] The problems of transposition, of organization, of the constancy of shape and of size—all of these must be removed to some secondary stage of processing, to some part of the nervous system other than the part that handles the shape and its aftereffects. This picture is not appreciably closer to what the Gestalt theorists held that a systematic theory of perception should be like than were the theories of Wundt and Helmholtz.

Let us briefly consider the alternatives to

[14]Inasmuch as the illusions can be presented without luminance-difference contours (for example, by means of the binocularly produced edges described on page 432 [Hochberg, 1966; Pappert, 1961] and by the successive-aperture viewing procedures described on page 455), and inasmuch as we would expect to obtain little or no satiation or figural aftereffects without luminance-difference contours (Hochberg & Triebel, 1955), such procedures should permit us to estimate how much of the decrement due to practice, if any, can be attributed to satiation.

[15]For example, if 2 objects of the same physical size are viewed at different distances, and their retinal images are therefore of different sizes, their apparent sizes do not differ as much as their retinal sizes do (see size constancy, p. 509). If we take the Gestalt principle of *isomorphism* seriously (p. 428), both the electrical brain processes and the resulting satiation effects should be reflected by the objects' apparent sizes. Nevertheless, if retinal size is varied independently of physical size by changing the relative distance of *I* and *T* figures from the observer, it is the retinal size that determines what aftereffects will result (Prentice, 1950; Hochberg & Bitterman, 1951; Terwilliger, 1961).

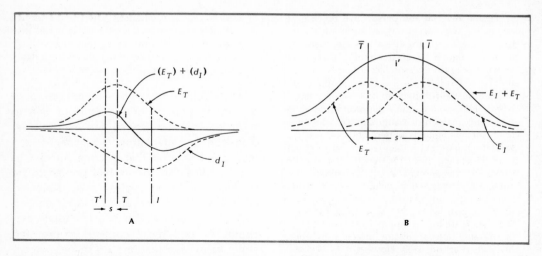

Figure 12.52. Osgood-Heyer theory of the aftereffects. A. The cortical distributions of excitation that would be produced by the T-figure alone is shown by E_T. Because the depression left by the I-figure (shown by d_I) is subtracted from this, the resultant distribution (shown by $i = E_T + d_I$) is displaced so that its peak falls at T' instead of at T. The aftereffect is s. B. Deutsch (1956) pointed out that this would imply that two simultaneously presented contours, separated by the amount s, should not be distinguishable. See text.

the satiation theory, bearing in mind that what made the figural aftereffects most interesting was that they were offered as evidence for a general theory of perception and that none of the alternative theories really fits that description.

Alternatives to the electrical satiation theory These fall into 3 general classes. First, there is the eye-movement and excitation-spread theory proposed by Osgood and Heyer (1952). This theory maintains that each contour that confronts the eye is projected to the optic cortex in a normal distribution of excitation (Figure 12.52A). The cortical projection is spread out partly because rapid involuntary eye movements occur which move the contour around on the retina (see Chapter 11, p. 386) and partly because of the way the nervous system proliferates connections between the retina and the cortex. The contour itself is perceived at the *peak* (*I*) of the cortical distribution. Prolonged inspection of an *I* figure leaves a region of fatigue or depressed excitability in the cortex. This depression subtracts from the distribution of excitation that is later produced by

the *T* figure, and thereby displaces its peak away from that of the *I* figure's distribution.

An empirical criticism of this theory can be made concerning the function it ascribes to eye movements. Eye-movement fluctuation is certainly not essential to obtaining FAE: FAEs (like those of Figure 12.51D) can be obtained·with stimuli that are fixed in their retinal locations (Hochberg & Hay, 1956; Krauskopf, 1960; Ganz, 1964). Similarly, Farnè's report (1964) that stronger FAEs are obtained with *I* and *T* figures exposed at 0.12 second (during which no substantial eye movements can occur) than are obtained with longer exposures is inconsistent with an explanation that depends on eye movements. Moreover, Krauskopf (1954) found contour displacements of almost 13 minutes of arc (visual angle), using a display similar to Figure 12.51F with briefly exposed *T* figures. As he pointed out, eye-movement fluctuation could only be expected to account for something less than 4 minutes of visual angle.

In addition, Deutsch (1956) found a theoretical flaw. Figure 12.52A illustrates the peak shift caused by summation of the *I* figure's excitation and the depression left by the *T* figure, according to the Osgood-Heyer theory. However, if the contour occurs at the distribution peak, and the distributions overlap each other enough to cause a peak shift, as in Figure 12.52A, they also overlap so much that if the *I* and *T* figures had been presented not successively but simultaneously, as in Figure 12.52B, the summing of their distributions of excitation would produce only 1 peak (*i'*), not 2. This means that only 1 contour would be seen. The minimum separation that can be detected between lines is about 1 minute of arc, (see p. 299), yet much larger FAE displacements can be obtained, over much larger separations between *I* and *T* figures: Krauskopf (1954) obtained displacements of 12.6 minutes over a distance of 15.8 minutes, and Heinemann and Marill (1954) obtained what they take to be FAEs over a distance of about 240 minutes. On the other hand, George (1962) showed that subjects cannot distinguish the separation between lines that are as much as 24 minutes of arc apart (at places 13° and 20° away from the fixation point) under "fatigue" conditions like the prolonged fixations usually used in FAE experiments, so that the Osgood and Heyer theory might be salvaged by adding this amendment: Under fatigue conditions, excitation distributions spread much farther from the contour. However, this still leaves unsolved problems. For example, how does the subject resolve the single line itself, and how does he detect that it has been displaced by an amount that is (under these "fatigue" conditions) smaller than the spatial distances he can distinguish between lines? And how are FAEs obtained with short exposures?

Recently, several attempts have been made to explain both the FAE contour displacements and at least some of the geometrical illusions, in terms of *lateral inhibition*—the mechanism by which the excitation of one neural region depresses the activity of adjacent regions (Chapter 9, p. 292). Various models have been proposed by Day (1962), Deutsch, (1964), and Ganz (1965, 1966a, b).

Ganz has offered the most complete and detailed theory of this kind. The FAEs are examples of shape contrast (a proposal made also by Freeman, 1964); that is, they are a class of geometrical illusions that occur as a result of the interaction between the *T* figure and the afterimage of the *I* figure. Both Gibson (1933) and Köhler and Wallach (1944) thought that the FAE could not be due to afterimages or to retinal fatigue because the FAE occurs when the *I* figure is viewed by one eye and the *T* figure is viewed by the other. This conclusion is questionable, however (Day, 1958), because afterimages themselves show interocular transfer (Hansen, 1954). In fact, Terwilliger (1963) demonstrated that afterimages in one eye interact with stimuli presented to the other eye: In the familiar demonstration of the relationship between size and distance (Emmert's Law; see Chapter 13) the apparent size of an afterimage that is produced by a bright light is found to vary directly with the distance from the subject of any surface at which he looks after receiving the afterimage. Terwilliger showed that it makes no difference whether the subject looks at that surface with the eye in which the afterimage was entered, or with the other eye. If an afterimage of the *I* figure interacts with the subsequently viewed *T* figure, so that the displacements are due to a simultaneous rather than a successive interaction between the 2 patterns, the FAEs reduce to a class of the geometrical illusions (Verhoeff, 1925; Ganz, 1965, 1966a, b; Howard & Templeton, 1966).

This is not to say that the FAEs amount simply to the simultaneous viewing of *I* and *T* figures. For one thing, whatever the effects are that produce afterimages, the latter are not always noticeable, even though the effects that underlie them may persist. For another, the eye is in continual motion during both the inspection and the test periods. These movements will decide the distribution of the afterimage left by the *I* figure and will therefore determine the interaction of that distribution with the *T* figure. To the degree that different attitudes toward the *I* figure (for example, whether the pattern is a *B* or a *13*) affect these eye movements, differences in

FAE would be expected, and the fact that such differences occur (Story, 1959) therefore does not constitute an insuperable difficulty for this theory.

An afterimage decays with a characteristic course that is a function of the intensity of stimulation; its onset has definite temporal characteristics, and the FAE must show intensity and onset and decay effects that are consonant with these characteristics if afterimages are to be implicated in the aftereffects. These constraints raise specific and quantitative questions, which Ganz has attempted to answer specifically and quantitatively (1966). For the moment, the case seems well made, as far as it goes. It should be noted, however, that the adequacy of this theory has been challenged on the grounds that the geometrical illusions and the FAEs do not vary in the same way as a function of the subject's age (Pollack, 1967), and it is true that the relation between the simultaneous illusions and successive displacement effects generated by the various illusion patterns has not been systematically explored.

AN OVERVIEW

In this chapter we have reviewed efforts to explain the perception of the colors and shapes of objects. An early and influential approach was one which attempted to explain and predict the appearance of any object or scene in terms of the appearances of each of the small homogeneous patches of stimulation into which the retinal image can be analyzed and to which the visual system was thought to be directly sensitive. That is, the explanation of visual perception started with what we might call the "elementary sensory mosaic." This approach generated a set of classical problems. In general, these problems arose because subjects' judgments about objects' attributes were discrepant with what the mosaic explanation would lead one to expect. With respect to object color, the major problems are those of *color constancy* and *contrast*. With respect to shape, the major

problems of this kind are those of *transposition, figure-ground organization,* the *illusions,* and *shape constancy* (which we discuss in the next chapter). Additional problems arise because of difficulties in identifying the appropriate stimulus and response measures: the problems associated with the attempt to establish a psychophysics of shape perception.

Three general kinds of solution to these problems can be distinguished from each other. (1) A cognitive explanation can be made in which the observer corrects the aggregate of appearances of the sensory mosaic in accordance with his knowledge of the objective physical stimulus situation. That knowledge is presumably based on characteristic features of the stimulus pattern, called *cues,* which the subject's past experiences have taught him to interpret even though he may not be aware of those features. (2) A sensory explanation can be made that seeks to show that the discrepancy occurs because the visual system responds directly to some variable in the stimulation other than the elements of the sensory mosaic. (3) An organizational theory can be proposed in which the entire visual system responds to the entire configuration of sensory stimulation, so that there is no necessary consistent relationship between the characteristics of stimulation at one region of the retinal image and the appearance of the corresponding part of the visual field. The appearance of any portion of the stimulus pattern thus rests on a number of proposed determinants of organization, or on a more general *minimum principle* (that we perceive the simplest arrangement consistent with the pattern of stimulation).

None of these general solutions can be fully accepted nor fully rejected at present. In the set of problems that we have considered, the distinctions between them are often hard to maintain. We shall encounter similar problems and pursue the same general solutions further when we consider the perception of space, motion, and orientation in the next chapter.

Julian Hochberg

PERCEPTION

II. SPACE AND MOVEMENT

13

FORMULATING THE PROBLEMS OF VISUAL DEPTH

Artists, philosophers, and psychologists have long been challenged by the everyday fact of three-dimensional seeing. The problem is set by the very structure of the eye, which forms an optical image on a two-dimensional surface, the *retina*. Such a mechanism can indicate the *direction* from which a beam of light comes, but not, in any obvious way, the distance that extends from the eye to some visible object. The difficulty is made clear by Figure 13.1. That points A_1 and B_1 lie at different directions in space is easily detected by the fact that their retinal images a and b fall on different parts of the retina. But how can the subject possibly tell, of points A_1, A_2, A_3, which is nearest and which is farthest from his eye?

The Use of Depth Cues

Laboratory studies of visual depth and distance perception are often concerned with the stimulus variables that make this possible, the signs or cues (p. 402) of an object's distance. How shall we discover and evaluate these cues? Why not ask the subject to tell us what cues he is using when he judges one object to be more distant than another? The trouble is that he usually cannot tell. He may even assert that he needs no cues,

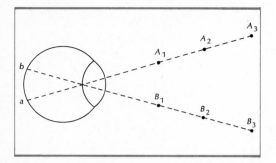

Figure 13.1. The problem of depth perception. The images from all points on a given line, as A_1, A_2, A_3, fall on the retinal point, a. Hence, the retinal point can indicate only the direction of an object, not its distance from the eye.

for he sees the distance of the object directly (he is mistaken here, as our previous analysis has shown). In fact, the training of an artist used to consist, in large part, of learning the rules for portraying depth, which are actually the depth cues themselves.

The depth cues were first studied to help artists portray depth and distance on a flat canvas. Leonardo da Vinci (1452–1519) advised the following experiment:

> Go into the country, select objects situated at distances of 100, 200 yards, etc. . . . place a sheet of glass firmly in front of you, keep the eye fixed in location, and trace the outline of a tree on the glass. . . . Now move the glass to the side just enough to allow the tree to be seen beside

its tracing, and color your drawing to duplicate the color and relief of the object. . . . Follow the same procedure in painting the second and third trees situated at the greater distances. Preserve these paintings on glass as aids and teachers in your work.

Leonardo took note of practically all of the depth and distance cues that can be utilized by the painter. Let us set out the depth and distance cues in a single context:

Figure 13.2A is a side view of a scene. Figure 13.2B is a tracing of the scene shown in part A, drawn on the "picture plane" of glass (P) held between the eye and the scene. An examination of the tracings on the picture plane shows us the cues that might be employed by the painter; some of these are listed below, and discussed briefly. Figure 13.2C is the *retinal image*, which is the point of contact between the visual world and the nervous system.

These illustrations help us make the distinction between *proximal* and *distal stimulus variables*. In Figure 13.2A the various spatial arrangements comprise the *distal* stimulation: objects' physical sizes, shapes, distances, and slants. (In general, we shall use the word *distance* to mean the absolute spatial extent between the observer and the object; *depth* will refer to the relative spatial extent between two points in space, for example, between *4* and *5* in Figure 13.2A). In Figure 13.2B

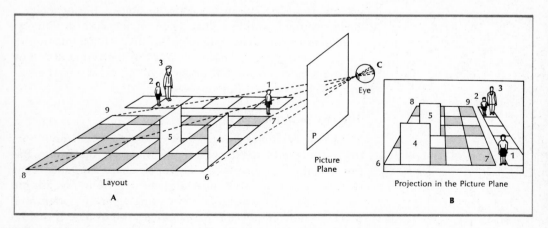

Figure 13.2. Distal layout and its projection in the picture plane and retinal image.

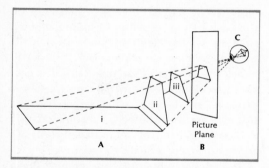

Figure 13.3. Different spatial layouts at *A* all project the same two-dimensional patterns in the picture plane *B* and on the retina *C*.

the tracing (a distal stimulus) provides the eye with the same proximal stimulus pattern as does the layout at A. Note that mathematically the proximal stimulus pattern must be ambiguous because, in each case, as in Figure 13.2A and B (and in any intermediate arrangements, such as the various alternatives at *i*, *ii*, and *iii* in Figure 13.3A), very different *distal* layouts may produce identical visual images on the retina C.

The "tracing" in Figure 13.2B shows us a number of familiar depth and distance cues: *linear perspective* (the fact that the lines converge, so that the distance between *8* and *9* is smaller than between *6* and *7*); *interposition* or covering that occurs because *4* is nearer than, and in front of, *5*; size, the fact that the image of the boy at *1* is about twice as tall as that of the boy at *2*; *texture gradient,* the steady rate of increase of the density in the image of the texture, running from less dense at the bottom (*6–7*) to more dense at the top (*8–9*) of the picture.

Apparent Size and Apparent Distance

Many of these cues follow from the geometry that relates size and distance, as shown in Figure 13.4 (see also Figure 9.6, Chapter 9). There, *S* is the size (length or width) of the object, *D* is the distance of the object, while *s* is the size of the retinal image and *n* is the distance from the optical nodal point of the eye to the retina. Then $s/n = S/D$ and, because *n* depends on the size of the eyeball and is constant, $s = n(S/D)$. In other words, the size of the retinal image is proportional to the ratio of object size to distance, and this ratio for all small angles is the tangent of the visual angle subtended by the object (see p. 279). Relative size, linear perspective, and so on, may all be reduced to the same general formula. For example, on a railroad track, the ties are a series of objects of equal size. Because *S* is constant and *D* increases, each railroad tie must subtend successively smaller visual angles. Although the retinal size changes with changes in distance, the *apparent* or *judged* size tends to remain constant. It is as though the distance were being "taken into account" in judging size.

In this chapter, we shall examine the following: first, the distance cues and their effects; the perception of movement, and of a stationary world; and finally, we survey what is known about the dependence of space perception on past experience.

NONVISUAL CUES OF DEPTH AND DISTANCE

Accommodation

The motor aspects of accommodation and convergence are treated in Chapter 11. Here we discuss them as cues for the judgment of distance.

Berkeley (1709) had pointed out 2 possible muscular cues to the perception of depth, namely convergence and accommodation. The conception was that the subject adjusted his accommodation and convergence until he had a sharp and single image of the object,

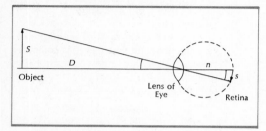

Figure 13.4. The geometry of visual size and depth. See text.

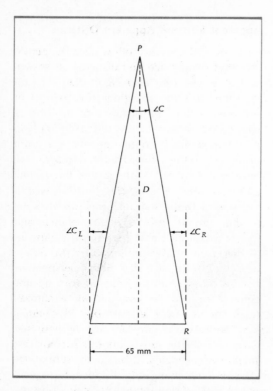

Figure 13.5. The angle of convergence and the distance of the fixated object. *P* is the object; *L* and *R* are the eye positions, assumed to be 65 mm apart (interpupillary distance). In converging upon *P* the left eye turns inward by the angle C_L, the right eye by the angle C_R, and the sum of these angles (which are equal if the observer is facing directly toward the object) is the total convergence and equals the angle *C*. Given the distance *D*, $\angle C$ can be computed; or given this angle the distance can be computed. The computation can use this formula: tan $\angle C/2 = 32.5/D$, 32.5 mm being half the interocular distance. However, it is more convenient and sufficiently accurate for most purposes to treat the interocular distance, *LR*, as the arc of a circle, with *D* in millimeters as the radius, so that $\angle C = 65/D$, when expressed in radian units. A radian = approximately 57.3°, and more exactly 206,265 angular sec. So we have the following formulas:

(1) Given *D* in mm, to find $\angle C$ in sec,

$$\angle C = \frac{65}{D} \times 206,265 = \frac{13,407,225}{D} \text{ sec}$$

(2) Given $\angle C$ in sec, to find *D* in mm,

and then he judged the object's distance on the basis of the sensation of muscular strain from the eye muscles. Can these cues actually be used in distance perception? In order to attack the question experimentally, it is necessary to eliminate the *visual cues* (p. 480), if possible, to discover what impressions of distance are contributed by accommodation and convergence. This requirement turns out to be extremely difficult to meet.

In order to obtain a clear picture of an object, a camera must be focused for the distance of the object, and the same is true of the eye, which focuses on an object by changing the convexity of the lens. This adjustment, called *accommodation,* is accomplished by the ciliary muscle. If the object is relatively distant (more than 2 yards or so), the muscle is relaxed; as the object comes nearer and nearer, the muscle contracts more and more, causing the lens to become more and more convex. Here then is a possible depth cue: the degree of contraction of the ciliary muscle, signaled to the brain by kinesthetic impulses. However, the fact that we ordinarily shift focus from one near object to another without any trial and error shows that other cues have been used first.

Whether accommodation has any actual value as a depth or distance cue can only be determined by experiments in which all other cues of distance are excluded.

$$D = \frac{13,407,225}{C} \text{ mm}$$

For example, when single vision is secured by a total convergence of 10°, the distance of the object $= \frac{13,407,225}{36,000} = 372$ mm (about 15 in.).

In experimental work, *D* is the primary measurement and the angle *C* is computed from *D*. Here are a few corresponding values:

D in mm	$\angle C$ in sec =	approx.
100	134,072	36°
300	44,691	12°
600	22,345	6°
1,000	13,407	3.7°
10,000	1,341	0.37°
50,000	268	0.07°

In the Wundt experiment the subject looked through a short tube into a room at the far end of which was a smooth illuminated wall: nothing else was visible except the middle section of a single thread that was seen as a straight black line. The thread's distance was changed between trials. After some practice, the subject achieved a monocular threshold for detecting a change in the thread's distance of about 7 percent. The threshold with binocular viewing was about 2 percent. Wundt (1862) took the monocular threshold to represent the use of accommodation alone, assuming that (1) convergence is absent in monocular viewing, and (2) all visual cues had been eliminated in both viewing conditions.

With respect to the first assumption, Hillebrand (1894) argued that the sensations provided by convergence might have been the depth cue that was really used, because the eyes attempt to converge upon the object that is fixated even when only monocular vision is employed. With respect to the second assumption, several alternative depth cues remain. For example, the subject might fixate the background and the thread would in consequence produce double images, the separation of which would vary with the distance of the thread from the background (p. 481). In addition, there might be more detailed vision of irregularities on the thread in nearer positions.

Hillebrand and others after him (Peter, 1915; Bappert, 1923; see Woodworth, 1938, pp. 665–674) varied the experimental conditions in an effort to clear up some of these possibilities. Recently, Heinemann, Tulving, and Nachmias (1959) found that subjects who were required to make a successive discrimination as to which of 2 identical disks was nearer, using no cue other than accommodation, actually failed to reach even a chance level of success. They may have been confused because the disks changed in apparent size as accommodation varied (p. 480).

Künnapas (1968) found that subjects were unable to judge the distances of phosphorescent disks, viewed monocularly in a room which was otherwise completely dark, if the sizes of the disks were so varied that their retinal images had a constant size at all distances and the subjects were left with only accommodation as a depth cue. Seventy years of research of this kind leave us with the conclusion that accommodation is, at best, a pretty weak cue to distance even at short distances.

Convergence

Imagine that an observer faces an object at *P* in Figure 13.5 and converges his eyes to obtain single vision by bringing the image of the object to the fovea of each eye. The fixed interocular distance provides a base line, and the amounts of convergence of the right and left eyes, or the sum of these amounts, which is the convergence angle *C* (Figure 13.5) permits the distance to be determined by trigonometry. Not that the subject will know the interocular distance in centimeters or *C* in degrees. However, the interocular distance is a quantity to which he must be thoroughly habituated. This distance, taken together with the record in his nervous system of what degree of convergence his eyes have been ordered to assume, furnishes a possible distance cue. Even if this cue were too imprecise to give the absolute distance *D*, it might enable the subject to tell which of 2 points was farther away.

The mirror stereoscope (p. 482) makes it easy to vary convergence; we merely move the pictures laterally in their holders. The expectation would be that increasing convergence would make the pictured object seem nearer. There should also be a secondary effect: If we apply here the rule suggested earlier, we may predict that decreasing the apparent distance while holding retinal size constant should make the object appear smaller. Wheatstone tried this experiment in 1852, and Judd repeated it with different apparatus in 1897. Both found the expected secondary effect, that is, the decrease of apparent size with increased convergence, retinal size presumably remaining constant. However, the judgments of distance were confused and equivocal. Since then, there have been several further demonstrations that apparent size decreases as convergence increases (Frank, 1930; Hermans, 1954; Adams, 1955).

Because changes in both accommodation and pupil size probably accompany convergence change, and because these in turn may alter the size of the object's retinal image (Brown, 1954), Heinemann, Tulving, and Nachmias (1959) had subjects compare the apparent size of featureless disks, at different distances, under 3 viewing conditions: (1) with monocular viewing (in which accommodation alone provided information about depth, but in which convergence accompanied the accommodation); (2) with binocular viewing, in which both eyes fixated a small point of light at the distance of the disk, but only one eye received the image of the disk (here, information for accommodation and convergence were both potentially available); (3) with conditions the same as in the second condition, except that accommodative information was excluded by use of an artificial pupil (see Chapter 11) and by drugs. At all distances the object subtended 1°. In all conditions, a small but very reliable decrease in apparent size occurred with decreasing distance: notice that this was also true of the first condition, which, as we saw above, did not reveal reliable distance discriminations.

As for convergence as a distance cue, some subjects show some ability to judge the distance of an object to which the eyes are converged, holding accommodation and image size constant (Swenson, 1932; Grant, 1942; Gogel, 1961). At best, however, as with accommodation, convergence itself can only furnish secondary cues of an object's distance, for the correct adjustment of the eyes must first be achieved in response to some other cue. Of the cues that are present *before* the correct ocular response is made, the double images that result from imperfect convergence cannot be eliminated from these experiments by anything that the experimenter can do; they can only be eliminated when the subject adjusts his convergence for

the correct distance, and this he must do on the basis of visual information. Let us consider what visual information he has.

BINOCULAR VISUAL CUES

Let us refer once more to the situation of Figure 13.5 in which the observer looks at the point *P*. He does so by the use of a combination of saccadic and vergent eye movements (see Chapter 11) such that an image of *P* is brought to the foveal center of each retina. These foveal centers are *corresponding points* in the anatomical sense that they are linked by fibers of the optic tract to a common locus in the visual projection areas of the cortex (see Chapter 9). Phenomenally, too, the object

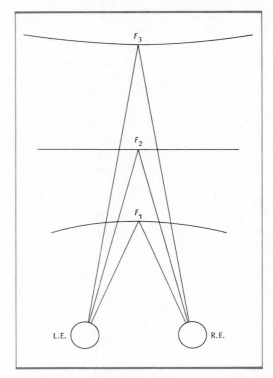

Figure 13.6. The empirical horopter. If the eyes are converged on a rod at F_1, a rod at any other point on the curve passing through F_1 will be seen as single; rods nearer to, or further from, the observer will be seen as double. The actual shape of the horopter changes with fixation distance, as shown by the curves through F_2 and F_3. (Ogle, 1950.)

at P is seen as single rather than double. This is the phenomenon of *binocular fusion* in which the object seems to be located at a single point in space even though two eyes are used for viewing it. In more general terms, the existence of corresponding points is by no means confined to the foveal region. In the discussion that follows, we shall examine the perceptual consequences of corresponding and noncorresponding points as they relate to single and double images received under various conditions of binocular viewing.

Double Images

If a near and a far object are both straight in front and you fixate the near object (F_1 in Figure 13.6) then a far object (F_2 or F_3) is seen by the right eye as lying to the right of F_1 and by the left eye as lying to the left. If you fixate

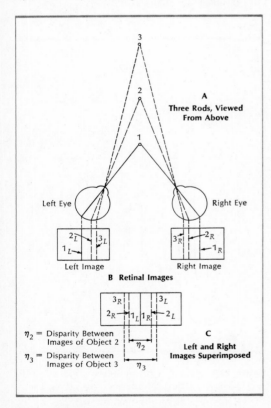

Figure 13.7. Depth and binocular disparity. A. A spatial layout of three rods, viewed from above. B. The images each eye receives. C. The two images superimposed.

the far object, F_3, thus getting double images of the near ones, the right eye sees F_2 or F_1 as lying to the left of F_3 and the left eye sees it to the right.

If you get the latter type of double images (called *crossed disparity*), you can decrease the distance or disparity between them and produce single vision by converging your eyes (see Figure 13.7); this may be used as a cue that the object is nearer than the initial fixation point.

The significance of double images as possible depth cues was noted very early (Hering, 1861–1864) but has often been overlooked since. Some persons cannot notice them at all, and they are certainly not normally observed to the full extent to which they must be present in the combined field of view. While this is no argument against their functional importance, it is hard to see how their contribution could be clearly demonstrated inasmuch as there is no way of eliminating them from binocular vision to find out how much depth perception would be left without them. The *horopter* is the locus of those points in space that, for a given degree of convergence, produce images that fall on corresponding points in the two eyes as shown in Figure 13.6. Geometrically, as Johannes Müller discussed it in 1826, when the eyes are horizontally positioned in the head, the horopter is a circle which passes through the fixated point F and through the centers of rotation of the 2 eyes. However, if we determine the empirical shape of the horopter, by having the subject maintain fixation on one rod while he adjusts other rods until they all look single, it turns out to be quite different, and its actual shape varies with the fixation distance as shown in Figure 13.6. Detailed discussion of the various theoretical horopters, and of empirical measurement procedures and results, may be found in Carr (1935) and Ogle (1950).

Binocular Disparity

Objects that are nearer or further than the horopter project their retinal images on noncorresponding or "disparate" areas of the 2 retinas. *Binocular disparity* is a measurable quantity, which increases with the difference in depth as shown in Figure 13.7. In angular measure, disparity is equal to the convergence angle of the nearer point minus the convergence angle of the farther point; that is, it is equal to the change in convergence in shifting from either point to the other (see Figure 13.5). Because disparity is usually studied in the context of stereoscopy, it is frequently measured pictorially in a projection of the retinal images on a picture plane, as is illustrated in Figure 13.7C; here we are working with the tangents of the convergence angles instead of with these angles measured in degrees. Regardless of how it is measured, however, retinal disparity is a possible depth cue to the distance at which any point lies, nearer or farther than the horopter. As we see in the next section, although there is considerable question about how our visual systems extract the information, there is no question at all about the fact that we can make effective use of this depth cue.

STEREOSCOPIC VISION

The Stereoscope

It was the physicist Charles Wheatstone whose discovery of stereoscopic vision and invention of the stereoscope in 1833 inaugurated the modern era of experimentation on space perception. (For much of this history, see Boring, 1942, pp. 263–311.) Using a diagram similar to the one in Figure 13.7, Wheatstone pointed out in 1838 that the 2 eyes get different views of three-dimensional objects that are located fairly near the observer. The combination of these disparate views, he conjectured, might produce the vivid depth effect of binocular vision. He tested this hypothesis by drawing the view of an object that each eye would receive separately and then presenting each drawing to the appropriate eye. In order to do this with small pictures held close to the eyes, accommodation has to be strong while convergence is relaxed, a trick which is difficult for most people to learn.

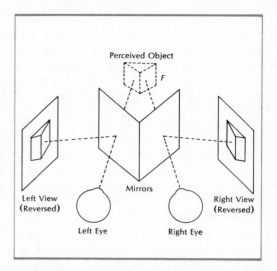

Figure 13.8. Diagram of a mirror stereoscope. The eyes are converged for the distance of the imaginary object at *F*.

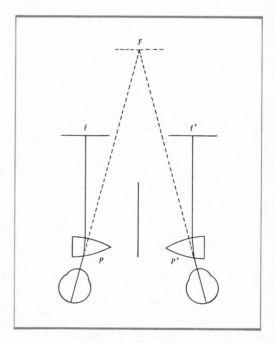

Figure 13.9. Plan of a prism stereoscope. A cardboard slide presents the two views, *f* and *f'*, the rays from which are bent by the prisms *P* and *P'* so as to reach the eyes as if from *F*, the point in space on which the eyes are converged.

Wheatstone therefore invented a device (Figure 13.8) that presents the pictures at the same distance as the objects represented, and that keeps accommodation and convergence in harmony. The 2 retinal images are then those that would be received from the actual object.

The mirror stereoscope is too bulky for any but research and demonstration purposes. More convenient is the *prism* or *lenticular* stereoscope (Figure 13.9) which is usually associated with the name of Brewster (1856), though Wheatstone also developed it independently. This is the gadget that was to be found in almost every home around the turn of the century. Its prisms take the place of the mirrors of Figure 13.8, deflecting the lines of sight outward just enough to center them on right and left pictures mounted on a card and

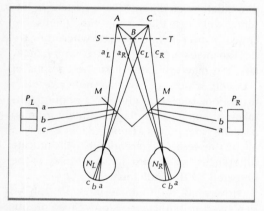

Figure 13.10. The optics of the mirror stereoscope. The eyes are to converge and accommodate as they would in viewing the actual object, here a wedge *ABC*, and the two retinal images are to be the same as in viewing a projection of the wedge on the plane *ST* through the convergence point. With the eyes fixated on the near edge *B*, single foveal vision is obtained of *B*, but there is some (uncrossed) disparity for *A* and also for *C*. This disparity, as present in the projection plane *ST*, is copied in the two drawings to be placed at P_L and P_R and viewed through the mirrors *M* and *M*. If the disparity is not too great, the double images are evidently fused, for the observer sees a single wedge in depth.

placed straight in front of their respective eyes. A thin wooden partition or separator limits each eye to its own picture. The prism is usually ground with a slight convex lens component, so that the picture will be sharp at about 6 inches from the eye, even with accommodation completely relaxed. A large collection of carefully prepared photographic slides was available for these prism stereoscopes, and people could see the Grand Canyon, Niagara Falls, and London Bridge in surprisingly realistic fashion, all in their own parlors.

Binocular disparity in the 2 views, which results from the difference in location of the 2 eyes (approximately 65 mm in interocular distance), is normally horizontal rather than vertical. Only a small amount of vertical disparity can be tolerated. Stereograms can be prepared geometrically by the method illustrated in Figure 13.10; photographically by taking 2 photographs from different positions, separated by the interocular distance (or more in order to increase the depth effect). A particularly useful form of stereogram for laboratory use was recently devised by Julesz (1960, 1964). The stereograms are prepared by a computer, which prints out 2 identical patterns of dots in a random display (or with any other statistical property desired); in one of the patterns an entire region *i* is displaced horizontally relative to the original pattern. Because the original pattern is random, the displacement of region *i* cannot be detected simply by looking at the altered monocular pattern. When the original is viewed by one eye and the altered pattern is viewed by the other, however, the displaced region then becomes visible, floating in space at a different distance than the rest of the pattern. None of the edges that appear to act as contours between surfaces that are seen at different apparent distances in the binocular view are visible when the subject looks with either eye separately. Although such stereograms normally offer cues of convergence (Bridgman, 1964), they are otherwise ideal instruments for the study of the effects of disparity alone on

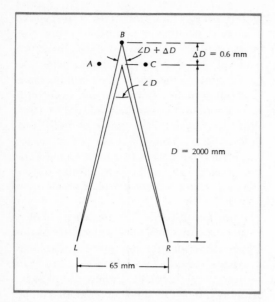

Figure 13.11. The Helmholtz three-needle experiment. The dots *A*, *B*, *C* represent vertical needles, mounted on little blocks that are placed on a level table. Only the needle shafts are visible to the observer, who is represented by the nodal points of his eyes, *L* and *R*. The needles are only a few millimeters apart laterally. The observer must judge whether *B* is lined up accurately with *A* and *C* so that all three are equally far away from him, or whether *B* is a little nearer or farther away. His average error is primarily measured in millimeters (ΔD), but such a measure cannot be compared directly with one taken with a different distance, *D*, from the observer to the plane of the needles, *A* and *C*. A better measure is the *angle of disparity,* or angular measure of disparity, which (see p. 482) is the convergence angle for the nearer object minus that for the farther object. In the figure, then, the angle of disparity equals the angle marked $\angle D$ minus the angle marked $\angle D + \Delta D$. A method for computing these angles has been explained under Figure 13.5 and will be applied here to a result of Bourdon (1902), who found one observer successfully discriminating an offset of 0.6 mm at a distance of 2 m (2,000 mm), as indicated on the figure. We have:

$$\angle D = \frac{13,407,225}{2000} = 6,703.6 \text{ sec}$$

stereopsis because there are no other visual depth cues that contribute to the appearance of depth under these conditions.

Let us survey first the accuracy with which depth differences can be discriminated stereoscopically; second, the main theoretical accounts of the nature of stereopsis; and third, the way in which stereopsis contributes to the perception of objects in space.

Accuracy of Stereoscopic Space Perception

Several equivalent terms are in use: depth or stereoscopic acuity, stereoacuity, stereopsis. Sensitivity to slight disparity is almost incredibly keen; this makes the stereoscope a useful device for comparing 2 very similar objects. For example, a 10 dollar bill that is suspected of being counterfeit can be viewed by the right eye, while a genuine one is viewed by the left. When the 2 are fused binocularly, size differences in pattern or lettering will cause the corresponding figures to appear nearer or farther even when the size discrepancies are as small as .005 mm. Similarly we may evaluate microphotographs of 2 bullets which may or may not have been fired from the same gun, or 2 photographs taken of some camouflaged artillery from an airplane from points a hundred feet apart—in all of these cases, stereodepth will indicate differences which are far too small to be detected by the individual eye.

How small a difference in depth can be perceived in binocular vision? Given an object at a standard distance *D* from the observer, what is the difference in distance ΔD of a comparison object that just can be perceived? The fundamental *three-needle experiment* devised by Helmholtz (1856–1866)

$$\angle D + \Delta D = \frac{13,407,225}{2000.6} = 6,701.6 \text{ sec}$$

$$\text{Angle of disparity} = \overline{ 2.0 \text{ sec}}$$

We usually consider 1° as a pretty small angle, but in this performance an angle of only 1/1800 of a degree was perceptually utilized.

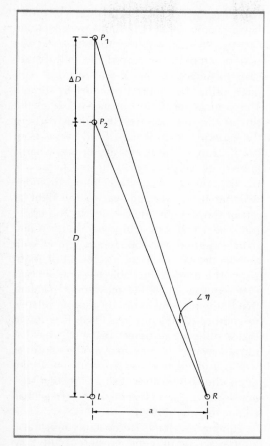

Figure 13.12. Diagram to illustrate the angle of disparity, $\angle\eta$, for points P_1 and P_2 at different distances from the eyes.

and illustrated in Figure 13.11 permits us to measure ΔD and to convert this value into units of visual angle, that is, to compute the smallest amount of disparity that can function as a cue of depth.

Plane geometry can be used to make this conversion, as is shown in Figure 13.12. In this basic diagram the calculations are simplified by the fact that only 2 lines are used and that these far and near lines, at P_1 and P_2, are lined up with the left eye and in a direction perpendicular to the line between the left eye and the right. It is therefore true of the right triangles, P_1LR and P_2LR that $\angle\eta = \angle LP_2R - \angle LP_1R$. If P_1 is a point that is just discriminably farther than P_2 from the observer, then ΔD is the difference threshold at distance D. Then $\angle\eta$ represents the stereoscopic disparity threshold.

Now tan $\angle LP_1R = a/(D + \Delta D)$, and tan $\angle LP_2R = a/D$. Since $\angle\eta = \angle LP_2R - \angle LP_1R$ and since these are all very small angles it is approximately true that they are linearly related to their tangents. Hence tan $\angle\eta =$ tan $\angle LP_2R -$ tan $\angle LP_1R = a/D - a/(D + \Delta D) = a\Delta D/D(D + \Delta D)$. It is also approximately true, since ΔD is very small compared to D, that tan $\angle\eta = a\Delta D/D^2$. Applying this formula to the results of Bourdon, illustrated in Figure 13.11, we see that tan $\angle\eta = 65(.6)/2000)^2 = .00001$ approximately. Now the tangent of one degree is about .018; hence $\eta =$ approximately 1/1800 degree, or 2 seconds of arc. A stereoscopic acuity as fine as this can be obtained only under the best of experimental conditions.

Without pushing the determination to its limit, Helmholtz found that his disparity threshold was certainly less than ±60 seconds of visual angle. Later determinations show that the average threshold is much smaller than even this small amount. A widely used, rather crudely made substitute for the three-needle apparatus is called the *Howard-Dolman apparatus,* devised by Howard in 1919 and taken over as a screening test to eliminate aviation candidates who might have "poor depth perception." Two black vertical rods are mounted side by side on separate blocks that move on parallel tracks so that either rod can be moved forward or away from the subject. All the subject sees is 2 black rods; in the simplest case, his task is to adjust the comparison rod (by pulling on cords) until it looks to be at the same distance as the standard rod set at 20 feet (6.1 m). This is the *method of adjustment* (see Chapter 2) in which the differential threshold for distance ΔD is taken to be .6745 σ_D, where σ_D is the *SD* of the distribution of obtained distances to the comparison rod. In the original experiment, Howard used the method of constant stimuli (see Chapter 2), requiring a judgment of "nearer" or "farther" at each fixed distance and taking as the ΔD threshold half the interpolated distance from the 25 percent to the 75 percent point. Out of 106 subjects, the best 14 had thresholds ΔD of about 5.5 mm corresponding to an angular disparity η of about 2 sec arc.

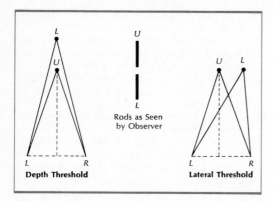

Figure 13.13. Diagram of the observer's task in an experiment comparing depth acuity with lateral (vernier) acuity. The observer saw the two vertical rods, *U* and *L*, as shown in the center. At the right and left are horizontal cross sections suggesting the displacement of the lower rod to one side or the other for determination of the lateral threshold, and forward or back for determination of the depth threshold. (After Berry, 1948.)

In a supplementary experiment with 9 subjects, Howard obtained average binocular thresholds of 14.4 mm as compared to monocular thresholds of 285 mm in the same task. This is a ratio of 20 to 1 in favor of binocular vision. Later experiments that controlled for monocular cues (such as the fact that the width of the image of the further rod will be narrower than that of the near one) have produced substantially the same results (Woodburne, 1934; Matsubayashi, 1937; Hirsch, Horowitz, & Weymouth, 1948); as has research with stereoscopic, as distinguished from "real" depth (Berry, 1948), getting about 2 sec thresholds. Stereoacuity can therefore be at least as sensitive as any other acuity we have. Individual differences are large, however, and some subjects in any unselected population will have little or no stereoscopic vision.

At its best, then, stereoacuity can certainly give exquisitely precise judgments of depth. It is matched only by 2 other kinds of acuity, so similar in both their nature and their magnitude that this may tell us something about the mechanisms that underlie stereoacuity. Berry (1948), using the equipment shown in Figure 13.13, kept the upper rod fixed at a distance of 4.6 m (about 15 feet),

while the lower rod could be displaced either laterally or in depth. The subject's task in one case was to judge whether the lower rod was *right* or *left* of the upper rod and, in the other case, to judge whether it was in *front* or in *back,* using the method of constant stimuli. The vertical separation or gap between the tips of the rods was set, in various parts of the experiment, to various fixed values from 0.5 to 22 mm. The lateral acuity was what is known as *vernier acuity* (see Chapter 9, p. 300), the subject's task being to judge whether the lower rod was to the right or left of the straight line defined by the upper rod. The 2 forms of acuity were both found to be very good, and about equally good, with angular displacement thresholds (η) of about 2 sec. The third comparable level of acuity is that required to detect movement parallax, that is, the movement of one contour relative to another (Graham et al., 1948). It is found that a subject can detect that one object is further away from him than another about as well by moving his head from one viewpoint to another as he can by using binocular stereopsis, as in fact Tschermak-Seysenegg had earlier reported (1939).

Luminance affects stereoacuity much as it affects acuity in general: stereoacuity improves (the threshold becomes smaller) as luminance increases (Mueller & Lloyd, 1948). The familiar rod-cone break (see Chapter 9, p. 303) occurs in the graph of the decrease in acuity; thus some binocular depth discrimination appears even at scotopic levels of illumination (see Berry, Riggs, & Duncan, 1950).

Stereoacuity is highest when the target line (the line whose relative nearness or farness is being judged) is near the reference line, and it falls off regularly as the lateral separation between the 2 lines increases (Matsubayashi, 1937; Graham et al., 1949). These results seem reasonable, for the relative distance of 2 objects ought best to be perceived when they lie nearly in the same line of sight, but no explicit theory has been worked out. Indeed, as we shall see, the theory of binocular stere-

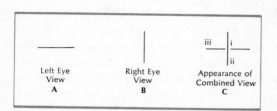

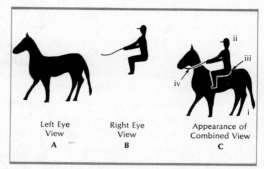

Figure 13.14 (left) and 13.15 (right). Stereograms demonstrating local contralateral suppression at contours. See text. Rivalry occurs at C*i* of Figure 13.14 and C*iii, iv* of Figure 13.15. Otherwise, where one eye's view contains a contour and the other view does not, the contour prevails.

opsis is still, itself, in a rudimentary and speculative state.

Theories of Stereopsis

Each of our eyes usually receives a somewhat different view of the world, but this difference does not normally produce double vision; instead, as we have seen, it produces stereoscopic space perception. The putting together of signals from the 2 eyes to form a single perceptual experience is often so perfectly achieved that the observer is not aware whether, at a given moment, he is using both eyes, his right eye alone or his left eye alone. In some cases, however, the effect can be one of "double vision" or *binocular rivalry*. This can be illustrated by using a stereoscope to present a view to one eye that is markedly different from that of the other. When rivalry occurs, at one moment one eye is dominant for part or even all of the field, so that the view it receives seems to suppress the corresponding portion of the other eye's view. At the next moment, the other eye becomes dominant, and its view prevails. However, rivalry is not commonly noticed outside of the laboratory.

Two distinct questions emerge from these observations: First, by what rules do we see singly instead of doubly? Second, by what rules do we convert binocular disparity into depth?

We really know very little about either of these questions, or about the relationship between them, and all that will be attempted here is to outline the major alternatives.

Combining the monocular fields   Panum offered the following 4 rules in 1858.

1. Rivalry of contours. Where one contour intersects a contour in the other eye's view, there is rivalry in the combined view: at point *i* in Figure 13.14C you see one or the other line, but not both.

2. Prevalence of contours. If a contour in one eye competes with a uniform field in the other, the contour is seen nearly all the time (*iii, iv* in Figure 13.15C). Note that the contour seems to carry some of its immediate background into the combined view.

3. Binocular mixture of colors. Mixing colors binocularly is reported under some conditions (see Chapter 10).

4. Mosaic composition of binocular field. Where contours in the 2 monocular fields do not overlap, they simply appear concurrently in the combined view (*ii, iii* in Figure 13.14C; *i, ii* in Figure 13.15C).

With these in mind, let us consider more general rules, according to one or more of which the 2 eye's views combine.

Summation   This would be equivalent to a simple superposition of the 2 retinal images, so that a horizontal line in one eye and a vertical line in the other would unite to form a cross; and a moderately bright spot of light that falls in one eye should appear brighter if another spot of light, somewhat less bright, is added to the corresponding point in the other eye. As detection thresholds show, a kind of summation does indeed occur under certain conditions, that is, at low luminances (Matin, 1963) or at short exposures (Erikson et al., 1966), but it is not the general case. If a spot of light falls in one eye, and a somewhat dimmer spot is added to the corresponding point in the other eye, in the combined view the spot does not increase in brightness due to the increment it has received—it gets darker. This is known as *Fechner's paradox* (see Helmholtz, 1866) and suggests an averaging, rather than a summation. For a review of research in this area, see Levelt (1965). However, stereopsis depends on contours (or on texture elements that have contours; see page 432), not on expanses of color, and here the summation model fails more dramatically. Consider how each contour that intersects or comes close to another contour that originates in the other eye's view fails to summate in the combined views (Figures 13.14, 13.15). Instead, each contour seems to carry with it a halo of its background, suppressing in its immediate vicinity the contribution that would have been made there by the contralateral eye.

Suppression There may be several very different kinds of suppression, not all of which involve the same mechanisms. The simplest way of avoiding double vision with two eyes would be to suppress one of them. This was a very early proposal (Porta, 1593). A nearly complete suppression of vision in one eye does in fact occur in some cases of strabismus, but it will clearly not account for most of the phenomena (p. 487) that Panum observed in normal subjects. Nor can binocular suppression explain the findings by Crovitz (1964) and by Crovitz and Lipscomb (1963) that short exposures cause the view on the nasal halves of the retinas to suppress the view on the temporal halves. More to the point of Panum's demonstrations are the var-

ious theories of suppression in which a contour in one eye suppresses a corresponding region in the other eye (Verhoeff, 1935; Asher, 1953; Kaufman, 1963; Hochberg, 1964a,b). Where different contours fall on corresponding points in the 2 eyes (see Figures 13.14, 13.15), it is evident that one suppresses the other and *binocular rivalry* occurs (see above, p. 487). Kaufman (1963) has shown that suppression extends for at least 14 minutes of arc around each such rivalrous intersection (and it can be spread further by eye movements). Perhaps the simplest assumption would be that a zone of contralateral suppression (about $\frac{1}{4}$ of a degree wide) surrounds any contour, all of the time, not just when the 2 eyes' views are different (Hochberg, 1964b). Any combined view would then consist of a mosaic made up of bits and pieces of contours from each eye's view (unless contours in one view were spaced so densely and made so strong that their overlapping suppressive fields would completely suppress the other eye's view), but the existence of the suppressive zones that surround each contour would only be manifested when the two views differ (for example, see Figures 13.14, and 13.15). Note that in such a theory of suppression 2 points that originate in different eyes should both be visible in the combined view if they are separated by more than $\frac{1}{4}$ of a degree, but only one should be seen if they are separated by less than that.

Fusion That single vision may be due to fusion is the most widely accepted theory. If 2 points that are perceived in different eyes fall closer together than about $\frac{1}{4}$ of a degree in the combined view, they fall within limits known as *Panum's area,* and "fusion" occurs: only one dot is seen.

This theory is not clearly different from the suppression theory; in terms of the latter, "fusion" would merely mean that 2 eyes' views are so similar that their piecemeal alternation is not discernable as such. The question of whether suppression has occurred during apparent fusion has been explored by Fox and his colleagues. They made the discov-

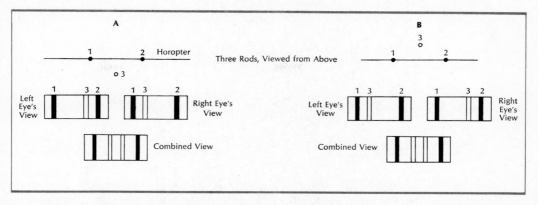

Figure 13.16. The combined view obtained with two rods on the horopter, one off. A. Crossed disparity for the images of rod 3. B. Uncrossed disparity for the images of rod 3. See text.

ery that, in a manifest case of rivalry, a test stimulus that is added to a part of one eye's view while that view is being suppressed is less often perceived than when that view is dominant (Fox & Check, 1966a,b). No interference with test-stimulus recognition was obtained when 2 views containing few contours were "fused" (Fox & Check, 1966a), but interference with test-stimulus recognition was obtained during "fusion" of 2 identical patterns having a high contour density, similar to the interference that occurs during manifest rivalry with dissimilar binocular patterns (Fox & McIntyre, 1967). This is what we would expect if contralateral suppression were generated around each eye's view of a contour in small fields which can summate when they overlap (Hochberg, 1964a,b).

The theory of fusion is not easy to separate from the suppression theory. Because it makes no specific predictions about rivalry, it is relatively unparsimonious with respect to how the two monocular views form a singular binocular field. The fusion theory gains its strongest support in the discussion of the nature of stereopsis, and we shall return to it in that context.

The Nature of Binocular Disparity and Stereopsis

Wheatstone's rule for predicting the stereoscopic effect is a simple one. If the 2 half-views that are paired in a *stereogram* (that is, the pair of views that is to be combined binocularly) are the views of a single solid object as seen by the separate eyes, then the depth effect of the combined binocular view will correspond to that object. Thus, with the 2 half-views shown in Figure 13.16, the combined view will look like 3 rods in depth. Notice that the disparity between the 2 views in Figure 13.16A and in Figure 13.16B is the same in size but opposite in direction; Figure 13.16A has "crossed disparity," Figure 13.16B has "uncrossed disparity." In order to interpret disparity correctly, therefore, the visual system must register which eye each contour in the combined view comes from, an ability that is not reflected directly in awareness. In general, you can only tell which eye is receiving which contour in Figures 13.14, 13.15, and 13.16 by finding secondary clues (for example, by noticing which contour vanishes when you close your right eye, or which one can be occluded by the left side of your nose). As such secondary clues are reduced, it becomes increasingly harder to make that discrimination (Smith, 1945; Pickersgill, 1961). It seems plausible that if secondary clues were eliminated entirely, the ability would be completely lost. The mechanism responsible for producing stereopsis, however, must keep track of this information. Let us sketch some of the suggested mechanisms.

Hering (1861) proposed that each retinal

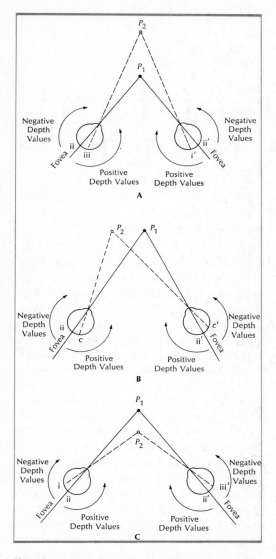

Figure 13.17. Hering's theory of depth-signs. See text.

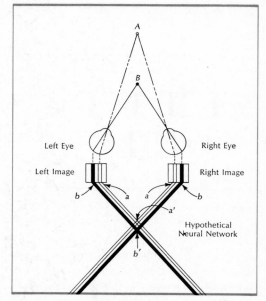

Figure 13.18. One version of a fusion network theory of stereopsis. See text.

point furnishes sensations of light, color, and direction (that is, its position in 2 dimensions) plus a sensation of *depth*. By this theory, these depth sensations are positive (meaning "farther") in the nasal halves of the retinas, negative ("nearer") in the temporal halves. Furthermore, they are identical but opposite in sign at corresponding points (*c* and *c'*, in Figure 13.17B), identical and of the same sign at symmetrically placed retinal points (*iii* and

i' in Figure 13.17A, or *i* and *iii'* in Figure 13.17C). If object P_1 is fixated (Figure 13.17A), its image falls on each eye's fovea (*ii* and *ii'*). P_2 appears farther away than P_1 because *iii* and *i'* both have positive depth values. In Figure 13.17B, P_2 falls on corresponding points *c* and *c'*. These are opposite in sign, and therefore P_2 lies on the horopter with P_1 and the two points seem equally distant. In Figure 13.17C, points *i* and *iii'* are both negative, so P_2 looks nearer than P_1.

Hering proposed that these retinal signs innately provide for stereoscopic depth perception. Against this, Helmholtz argued that this model would predict that if we masked the nasal hemiretinas while looking at a wall, that wall would appear to meet at an angle, which simply does not occur.

An alternative model, related, but not identical, is shown in Figure 13.18. This explanation (which was proposed at various times by Boring, 1933; Charnwood, 1951; Linksz, 1952; Dodwell & Engel, 1963; and is reviewed briefly by Kaufman, 1965) shows a hypothetical network in the brain by means of which

```
patxkrviejlsximudkybfaxkltbdugxlknydjlcx        patxkrbiejlsximudkybfaxkltbdugxlknydjlcx
psfrdcjlgsbmydchksvyfcjkoutrdvgmsckhbkfm        psfrdcjlgsbmydchksvyfcjkoutrdvgmsckhbkfm
utfvnjfxiyjdmeskmrjxugslmgbdxkhrvugsvkgh        utfvnjfxiyjdmeskmrjxugslmgbdxkhrvugsvkgh
ufbsjlbdfvgruojgdxcvlmhsbcuyrjxklyhbrhjv        ufbsjlbdfvgwruojgdxcvlmhsbcurjxklyhbrhjv
lugdxjnrdsulmrcgyxsjhipfsnvwfwyerxiplkmh        lugdxjnrdsuolmrcgyxsjhipfsnvfwyerxiplkmh
gsunxqphedcijmsagckpnyvxrfgenudzkubfxhjn        gsunxqphedcuijmsagckpnyvxrfgnudzkubfxhjn
lumvhdzrtfcynmigkncezyhikmrptcghjfbexdit        lumvhdzrtfcsynmigkncezyhikmrtcghjfbexdit
lhcrsxkybjrvgjurdxuhvkgrsjnxcuokldbvrxyj        lhcrsxkybjrdvgjurdxuhvkgrsjncuokldbvrxyj
lmtvhdubfhubfxkunhdryjkibdenkyhvfjybdcxg        lmtvhdubfhujbfxkunhdryjkibdekyhvfjybdcxg
lmhecshatfbdesupjkinmbghydxesxwzfdghnvrf        lmhecshatfbdesupjkinmbghydxesxwzfdghnvrf
jdhgbcxrdsjhbdxukrdhncsiklrvshbfrchudzlm        jdhgbcxrdsjhbdxukrdhncsiklrvshbfrchudzlm
xlfutgrslnuvcbkfhtdxokmrhbdgcrsklmycidwj        xlfutgrslnuvcbkfhtdxokmrhbdgcrsklmycidwj

                    A                                               B


patxkrviejlsximudkybfaxkltbdugxlknydjlcx        patxkrbiejlsximudkybfaxkltbdugxlknydjlcx
psfrdcjlgsbmydchksvyfcjkoutrdvgmsckhbkfm        psfrdcjlgsbmydchksvyfcjkoutrdvgmsckhbkfm
utfvnjfxiyjdmeskmrjxugslmgbdxkhrvugsvkgh        utfvnjfxiyjdmeskmrjxugslmgbdxkhrvugsvkgh
ufbsjlbdfvgruojgdxcvlmhsbcuyrjxklyhbrhjv        ufbsjlbdfvgwruojgdxcvlmhsbcurjxklyhbrhjv
lugdxjnrdsulmrcgyxsjhipfsnvwfwyerxiplkmh        lugdxjnrdsuolmrcgyxsjhipfsnvfwyerxiplkmh
gsunxqphedcijmsagckpnyvxrfgenudzkubfxhjn        gsunxqphedcuijmsagckpnyvxrfgnudzkubfxhjn
lumvhdzrtfcynmigkncezyhikmrptcghjfbexdit        lumvhdzrtfcsynmigkncezyhikmrtcghjfbexdit
lhcrsxkybjrvgjurdxuhvkgrsjnxcuokldbvrxyj        lhcrsxkybjrdvgjurdxuhvkgrsjncuokldbvrxyj
lmtvhdubfhubfxkunhdryjkibdenkyhvfjybdcxg        lmtvhdubfhujbfxkunhdryjkibdekyhvfjybdcxg
lmhecshatfbdesupjkinmbghydxesxwzfdghnvrf        lmhecshatfbdesupjkinmbghydxesxwzfdghnvrf
jdhgbcxrdsjhbdxukrdhncsiklrvshbfrchudzlm        jdhgbcxrdsjhbdxukrdhncsiklrvshbfrchudzlm
xlfutgrslnuvcbkfhtdxokmrhbdgcrsklmycidwj        xlfutgrslnuvcbkfhtdxokmrhbdgcrsklmycidwj

                    C                                               D
```

Figure 13.19. Stereograms in typescript. A, B. Rivalry can be detected during stereoscopic fusion. (Kaufman, 1965) C, D. An ambiguous stereogram. See text. (Kaufman & Pitblado, 1965.)

images falling in the 2 eyes can be brought to fuse at one place in the nervous system even if they fall at disparate places on the retina. Lines from *a, a* can fuse only at the point *a'* where their respective neurons intersect. Similarly, lines from *b, b* can fuse only at *b'*. In this network, the geometry of the spatial relations that give rise to the disparity in the first place, outside the head, is simply reconstructed inside the head.

The following arguments can be made against such models of binocular fusion, models which are essentially point-by-point in nature.

1. Fusion is not necessary for depth perception. Even when disparities are so large that double images are seen, the appropriate depth is perceived (Hering, 1861; Ogle, 1953). This is not a serious objection, inasmuch as this might comprise a separate class of binocular space perception, depending on a different mechanism. If we start hypothesizing mechanisms that can derive information about

depth from the characteristics of nonfused disparate images, however, then the fusion theory loses some of its special ability to explain stereopsis.[1]

2. The images may not really be fused in stereoscopic "fusion." Stereograms may be prepared with their half-views printed in complementary colors which result in clear rivalry in the combined view (that is, if the left view is red and the right is green, the combined view may display an alternating patchwork of red and green), a fact which does not prevent depth from being perceived

[1] A suppression theory can be extended to accommodate stereopsis by relating the latter to binocular rivalry (see Washburn, 1933; Hochberg, 1964). Eye dominance could then provide a cue as to which is the crossed and which the uncrossed image (Woodworth, 1938, p. 664), and so could changes in convergence that would sort out double images according to their distances from the horopter. The fact that correct judgments of depth can be obtained from the afterimages of very brief exposures (Dove, 1841; Karpinska, 1910; Washburn, 1933; Ogle & Reiher, 1962), and with stabilized retinal images (Shortess & Krauskopf, 1961), however, makes this last explanation necessarily incomplete because convergence changes could not contribute to the depth judgments made in such conditions.

in the combined view (Treisman, 1962; Kaufman, 1964). In fact, in an old method of stereoscopy, the 2 half-views are printed one over the other in complementary colors, and the 2 intermixed scenes (called an *anaglyph*) are sorted out by having each eye look through a filter of the appropriate hue. Moreover, even where there is no obvious rivalry, Asher (1953) claims that alternating suppression, rather than fusion, is usually experienced.

Such observations are very difficult to make with confidence. Kaufman (1965), replacing the dots in the matrix stereograms of Julesz (see p. 483) with letters, has introduced a valuable tool for this purpose. Figure 13.19A,B shows matrices of letters, identical except that the area outlined by the dotted line has been shifted over one column. As with Julesz' patterns, a square of letters is seen at some depth different from the surround: here, the central region appears behind the surround. In some of these letter stereograms, stereopsis occurs even though very dissimilar shapes are superposed; rivalry then also occurs, in which at each moment one or the other eye's view can be discerned.

At least for most of the time (after the initial fraction of a second, and at luminances well above threshold; see page 488), observation seems to support a model of stereopsis that is based on suppression at least as well as one that is based on fusion.

3. The nature of binocular disparity. What is the disparity of the 2 half-views in Figure 13.19C and D? The stereogram there is the same as in A and B, except that the luminances of the letters in the inner regions have been modulated to produce a pattern. The pattern has been shifted one letter to the *right* in the left half-view. In Figure 13.19A and B, responding to the displacement of the letters, subjects report that the inner region appears in depth *behind* the surround. In Figure 13.19 C and D, subjects responding to the displacement of the brightness of the pattern , report that the inner region appears to be *in front of* the surroundings (Kaufman & Pitblado, 1965), even though the letters themselves are displaced with the opposite

disparity. After a while, subjects reverse their response, the surroundings appear to be in front of the inner region, and the stereogram acts like one of the reversible-perspective patterns in Figure 12.19). Kaufman and Pitblado suggest that disparities in the patterns of relative brightnesses are the effective stimuli for binocular stereopsis. Pastore (1932), Koffka (1935), Werner (1937), Woodworth (1938), Linschoten (1956), and Wallach and Lindauer (1962) have suggested that the disparity that is effective for stereopsis is a disparity between *patterns* that are similar in some fashion. The precise nature and limits of the similarity remain to be defined, but a definition of disparity in terms of points alone is clearly insufficient.

Disparity and stereoscopic space The physical space in which we move our eyes and body follows familiar geometrical laws. If the spatial meaning of various convergence angles, and of the various binocular disparities that can occur with each, were faithfully learned as a result of our experiences in physical space, we would expect that the same geometry would be reflected in our judgments about objects and their locations. It should then be possible, for example, to map the relationship between the angles of convergence of the 2 eyes needed to fixate a point of light, on the one hand, and the apparent spatial location of that light in relation to the observer and to any other point of light, on the other hand.

In fact, judgments about apparent space that are based on binocular depth cues are not consistent with physical Euclidean space. Figure 13.6, for example, showed that a horopter that is determined on the basis of subjective judgments has a different shape from the circle that is predicted from purely geometrical considerations. As another example, if a subject is asked to arrange a set of lights in an otherwise dark room so that they appear to line up in 2 parallel rows symmetrically placed around the median plane (straight ahead), and he is also asked to arrange 2 rows of lights so that the distances

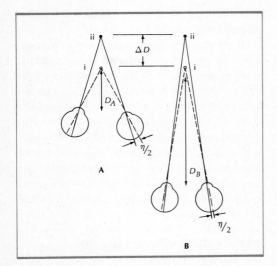

Figure 13.20. Disparity, depth, and distance. The disparity produced by a given depth, ΔD, between two points (i, ii) depends on their distance from the viewer, D. In fact, for large values of D, $\eta = k\,\Delta D/D^2$. See text.

between points of each pair that lie in the same frontal plane are equal, the 2 tasks do not produce equivalent results (Hillebrand, 1902; Blumenfeld, 1913). These inconsistencies need not be unlawful. In fact, Luneberg (1947, 1950) proposed on these and other grounds that visual space is non-Euclidean. The Luneberg theory has been revised and extended by Blank (1953, 1957, 1959) and some of its experimental implications concerning distance matching, aligning, and so on, in binocular space have been tested by Hardy and his colleagues (1953), Zajacskowska (1956), Shipley (1957, 1959), and Foley (1964, 1967).

As a third example, let us consider the apparent depth that is produced by a given disparity. The depth, ΔD, between points i and ii in Figure 13.20 is reflected in the binocular disparity η. As some consideration of Figures 13.12 and 13.20 will show, the relationship between η and ΔD is determined by the object's distance D. However, although the size (s) of the object's retinal image is linearly related to the inverse of the object's distance D (that is, as shown in Figure 13.4, $s = nS/D$),

the disparity (η) is related inversely to the square of that distance. This follows from the facts (see p. 485) that very small angles are linearly related to their tangents, and that $\tan \angle \eta = a\Delta D/D^2$.

Let us assume that a subject perceives distance correctly. If he is also to respond correctly to some binocular disparity η, therefore, the apparent depth that he perceives ($\Delta D'$) should be proportional to the square of the perceived distance. Thus, $\Delta D' = k(D')^2$, where $\Delta D'$ is the apparent depth interval between points i and ii and D' is apparent distance. In various forms, this theory has been held by von Kries (1925), Fry (1950), Ogle (1953), and Wallach and Zuckerman (1963).

In order to alter the apparent distance D' of an object without changing its retinal image, Wallach and Zuckerman (1963) had subjects judge the depth and size of an object while looking through a set of mirrors that required them to converge for half the actual distance. They reasoned that because size decreases with D and depth decreases with D^2, the subject should judge the size to be half what it would be under normal viewing conditions, and the depth to be a quarter. The results turned out to be in reasonably close agreement with the prediction. The same disparity η produced different apparent depths, $\Delta D'$, depending on the distance D to which the convergence (and accommodation) were adjusted. Thus, convergence seems to serve as a cue for the $\Delta D'$ judgment even though it does not do so reliably for distance D' itself (see p. 480). According to these findings, the relationship between disparity and apparent depth reflects the geometry of the physical world.

On the other hand, Gogel (1960a,b,c) had shown experimentally that when normal distance cues are available to indicate the object's distance D, the disparity η must increase linearly with distance if the object's apparent depth $\Delta D'$ is to remain the same. This implies, of course, that $\Delta D'/D'$ is constant, for some fixed disparity, a result also obtained by Foley (1967).

Gogel's thesis is that the apparent depth that is produced by a given disparity depends on how large the parts of the visual field that are adjacent to it appear to be. More specifically, the apparent depth produced by a given disparity is proportional to the perceived *frontal size per unit visual angle* (Gogel, 1960a,b,c). Thus, the perceived size of an adjacent object becomes the "yardstick," or standard, which translates the disparity into a perceived depth, and any cue that causes the subject to change the way he perceives the size of the yardstick will change the perceived depth he attributes to any given disparity, as well (Gogel, 1960c, 1964).

The discrepancy with the earlier data (for example, Wallach & Zuckerman, 1963) remains to be resolved. The differences may in part reflect differences in the mixture of depth cues available in different experimental situations. Jameson and Hurvich (1959), summarizing an earlier investigation by Holway and his colleagues, report that depth discriminations on the basis of retinal disparity alone followed the function $\Delta D = kD^2$. In "commonplace conditions" which afforded additional cues (accommodation, image size, and so on), however, $\Delta D = kD^{1.25}$; very similar data were recently obtained by Vincent and his colleagues (1969).

Increased and reversed disparity   If the disparity produced by a given depth is increased by increasing the distance between the 2 views over that which would have been provided by normal interocular distances, the binocular effect is extended to faraway objects. In this form, the mirror stereoscope becomes a *telestereoscope*. (For a mathematical analysis, see Riggs et al., 1947.)

Wallach, Moore, and Davidson (1963) have shown that after viewing a rotating three-dimensional object through a telestereoscope for only 10 minutes, the normal relationship between binocular disparity (η) and apparent depth ($\Delta D'$) was changed appreciably, the depth associated with a given disparity decreasing by as much as 20 percent. In subsequent experiments, Wallach and Karsh (1963a,b) found evidence suggesting strongly that the factor that changed the spatial meaning of the disparity was the monocular depth cue provided by the rotation, the *kinetic depth effect*, which we discuss on page 505.

If the views perceived by the right and left eye are interchanged in the stereoscope, we obtain a *pseudoscopic* or reversed depth effect because the directions of the disparities have been reversed. This experiment is instructive in that some pictures will reverse their depth with such a reversal of disparity and some will not. Such reversal rarely suc-

ceeds with pictures of concrete objects, like a chair or a human face (see p. 502).

In short, although binocular stereopsis may seem at first to explain our perceptions of objects and space, it cannot be the whole story. Two kinds of sensory information about space remain to be considered: the pictorial cues, and the information about space provided by motion of object and observer. It is well known that people blind in one eye are capable of ordinary space perception. This fact emphasizes the importance of the pictorial and motion cues in comparison with binocular stereopsis.

MONOCULAR VISUAL CUES OF DEPTH AND DISTANCE

The pictorial cues are effective in monocular as well as binocular vision. They are all ambiguous by their nature (p. 477), but they are frequently good indicators of depth and distance. Let us first consider the efficacy of those pictorial cues that have received the most study and then review the assumption that they are learned by association with the primary cues.

Size   If you know the real (*distal*) size of a visible object, and you know the size of the retinal image it subtends at the eye (that is, its *proximal size*), you have a good potential indication of its distance. In Figure 13.4, if S is the size of the object, D is its distance, n is the nodal distance of the eyeball, while s is the size of the retinal image, then $D = nS/s$. There are indeed many demonstrations that proximal size can affect distance judgments, but there are several distinctions that must be drawn with respect to both the definition of the stimulus and the nature of the response.

In Figure 13.2B, the boy at *1* presents a larger proximal stimulus than the boy at *2*. There are 2 cues here that should be distinguished.

Relative size   The proximal stimulus for boy *1* is larger than that for boy *2*. This cue can be defined in terms of stimulus measurements alone: Of 2 similar shapes, presented simultaneously or in close succession, the one with the larger proximal stimulus will appear to be nearer. There is considerable evidence that apparent relative distance or depth is influenced by relative size (that is, that the larger of two objects looks nearer) and that, as its retinal image grows larger, the object appears to approach (Hillebrand, 1894; Calavrezo, 1934; Ittleson, 1951b; Hochberg & Hochberg, 1952; Gogel, Hartman, & Harker, 1957; Epstein, 1961).

Familiar or assumed size If we know the boy's real or distal size, and we can register his proximal or retinal size, then we can tell what his absolute distance is. Boy 1 would thus look nearer than boy 2 because boy 1 is seen as being at distance D_1', boy 2 is seen as being at distance D_2', and $D_1' < D_2'$. By this analysis, the proximal size differences are important only because the observer's visual system assumes that they correspond to objects that have the same distal size. Thus, if we compare man 3 with boy 1, the same apparent difference in distance should arise because, even though the proximal sizes of 1 and 3 are equal, their familiar distal sizes are unequal, and quite different apparent distances (D_1' and D_2', respectively) will be associated by past experiences with their proximal stimuli.

This cue is particularly important to the study of space perception because it is the only one which, *by its very definition*, requires past experience to be invoked, past experience with a particular object, rather than past experience in the sense of learning some rule. Hochberg and Hochberg (1952) argued that the cue of *familiar size* should therefore be disentangled from that of *relative size*, and evaluated separately.

Two types of experiment offer evidence for the efficacy of the familiar size cue: (1) experiments in which stimuli were constructed that were identical in appearance to some familiar object (for example, a playing card) but of an enlarged or reduced physical size; and (2) experiments in

which subjects were given different instructions as to the nature of an otherwise ambiguous stimulus. We shall briefly discuss each type.

In an experiment by Ittelson (1951), each of 3 playing cards (1 was normal in size, 1 was twice normal, and 1 was half the normal in size) was presented singly to the subject under complete *reduction conditions* (that is, it was viewed monocularly, with none of the usual monocular or binocular distance cues available). The distance judgment was made by setting a target to the apparent distance of the playing card; the target, however, was viewed with full binocular vision, with all the usual distance cues present. The results for 5 subjects gave almost precisely the results expected:

Card	Predicted D (ft)	Obtained D (ft)
Normal	7.5	7.5
Half-size	15.0	15.0
Double-size	3.8	4.6

There has been considerable controversy about the generality of the results in the table. Gogel, Hartman, and Harker (1953) had subjects throw a dart (without seeing the results of that action) at either a normal or a double-sized playing card, located either 10 or 20 feet from them in a reduced-cue situation. Epstein (1961) used procedures closer to those of Ittelson. Neither experiment showed results similar to those reported by Ittelson; instead, both found only effects of relative size on relative distance.

In contrast, Epstein (1963) did confirm the Ittelson familiar-size hypothesis, by the use of realistic photographs of coins (dime, quarter, or half-dollar). All photographs were made to have the same physical size regardless of the size of the coin, and all were presented at the same distance so as to present the same proximal size, that is, the same-sized retinal image. Subjects viewed each photograph separately under reduced-cue conditions. Distance matches were obtained by having the subject adjust the distance of a cigarette pack, that was visible with good depth cues, to the distance of the photograph. Gogel (1964) argued that these results might simply reflect relative judgments made between the known size of cigarette packs and the known size of coins, so Epstein (1965) repeated the experiment, but provided no visual comparison. Instead, the subject was made to indicate the apparent distance by telling the experimenter to "stop" when the appropriate length of rope had been pulled through his hand.

The familiar-size hypothesis was again confirmed. Moreover, Epstein and Baratz (1964) found that when a pair of pictures of coins was viewed under reduced conditions, the picture which represented a coin of larger physical size was judged as more distant even when the 2 were identical in actual and in proximal size. Gogel has since shown (1968) that the apparent distance of a familiar object is readily influenced by previous conditions, and that this phenomenon may have affected the outcome of the experiment by Gogel, Hartman, and Harker.

It seems that realistic representations of familiar objects do indeed affect the distance judgments made by subjects who have been instructed to judge distance relationships, in the absence of the usual depth cues, under some circumstances (see also Dinnerstein, 1967; Gogel & Mertens, 1967; Ono, 1969). The circumstances and mechanisms remain to be specified, but the following considerations may be relevant to this point.

Hastorf (1950) found that when subjects were shown a disk of light under reduced conditions, and were told that it was a ping-pong ball, they judged it to be at a closer distance than when they were told that it was a billiard ball. This was so despite the fact that two-thirds of the subjects saw that the disk was not really a ball, and despite the fact that some unspecified number realized that 2 different names had been given to the same stimulus. In another experiment, Baird (1963) showed subjects rectangular strips of light, one at a time, under reduced conditions. Each strip was shown at a distance of 25 feet and varied in length from 6 to 24 inches. The subjects were told, however, that the strips were all the same size as a foot ruler, and were asked to give verbal estimates of the distances of each strip. Estimates differed significantly as a function of the length of the strip, the means of the estimates coming very close to what the distances would have had to be if the strips really had been 1 foot long.

Hastorf's results, and Baird's, seem to show quite clearly that, in the absence of definite distance cues, subjects can decide on a distance that is appropriate to the size that they are told (or decide) to assume some stimulus to be. The incidental observations from Hastorf's experiment show, however, that the subjects do not have to *perceive* (or even to believe) that the stimulus is actually the size they are assuming it to be. This raises the question of whether under such circumstances we can safely accept a sub-

ject's distance judgments as representing his *perceptions* of tridimensional space. As an illustration of the distinction between *relative size* and *familiar size,* Hochberg and Hochberg (1952) had shown that drawings that differ in relative size affected the relative durations with which each face of a reversible perspective figure appeared to be nearer. On the other hand, drawings of a man and boy that differed only in familiar size had no such effect. Ono (1969) has since shown that if subjects are asked questions that direct their attention to the maturity and immaturity of the man and boy, respectively, the familiar size patterns that were otherwise ineffective now do affect the appearance of the reversible pattern, which would certainly seem to reflect changes in the subjects' perceptions of depth and not merely changes in their judgments.

In a recent experiment directed to a somewhat different question—whether knowledge about distance affects the perception of distance—Gruber and Dinnerstein (1965) showed subjects 2 luminous squares in an otherwise dark corridor. One square was 24 feet and the other, 48 feet from the subject, but because the farther one was twice the physical size of the near one, they presented the same proximal size to the subject. In the dark, the subject saw only 2 luminous squares at the same distance. When the corridor was illuminated, he could clearly see the squares' physical distances, sizes, and the apparatus by which they were presented. When the corridor was again darkened, however, most subjects reported with surprise that the squares came together again in about 10 seconds, that is, that their relative depth faded away. Thus, subjects' first-hand knowledge of the true sizes and distances left their perceptions of depth unaffected, but it did modify their absolute distance judgments.[2] Perhaps a clear experience of tridimensionality or of apparent depth depends on relative size differences (or on other indications of depth that may be present), whereas the magnitude of the distances that are associated with that apparent depth (or with completely indeterminate spatial location, as in the experi-

[2] These experiments by Gruber and Dinnerstein reopen the distinction made earlier (p. 476) between relative and absolute apparent distance, inasmuch as the latter was affected by providing the subjects with knowledge about the viewing situation and the former was not. It may be that the judgment of absolute distance is much more labile than that of relative distance, more subject to alternative assumptions. However, it may also be that absolute distance is not really perceived at all, in the absence of a ground plane stretching between the observer and the object and in the absence of motion perspective (see pp. 501, 504) and that the observer assigns some arbitrary distance label to one of the objects and judges the other distances relative to that one.

Figure 13.21. Convexities and concavities on a plane surface, with light coming from one direction. Turn the picture over. (After v. Fieandt, 1938.)

ments of Hastorf and Baird), and the biases (see p. 438) with which the subject views a figure having reversible depth (as in the experiments of Dinnerstein and Ono) can be set by known or familiar size (Dinnerstein, 1967; Gogel & Mertens, 1967; Ono, 1969).

The Gruber and Dinnerstein experiment (like the Gelb experiment that we discussed in Chapter 12) shows that it is possible to get subjects to report appearances that are at variance with their knowledge. It would be very useful to extend a method like this one, with suitable payoff procedures (see p. 37) to the other experiments in which we are dubious about whether subjects' judgments reflect their perceptions.

Shadows

Another indication of depth and relief, much used by the painter, is the shading on a rounded or angular surface. Also the shadow cast by one object upon another can show

which object is further away, provided the source or direction of the light is clearly revealed. Little formal research has been done with this cue, either to define or to test it (see, however, pp. 420, 502).

In the simple example in Figure 13.21, the light seems to come from above, as it usually does. This assumption of overhead lighting seems to be just as strong in young children as in adults (von Fieandt, 1938). This does not mean that it is innate: Hess (1950) has shown that young chicks, 7 weeks of age, who were reared from the time of hatching in cages that were lit from below, through the wire-mesh floor, would then peck at photographs which showed wheat grains lit from below. Control animals reared with overhead lighting would peck only at pictures of grains lit from above. These findings suggest that this cue had been learned from the conditions in which they had

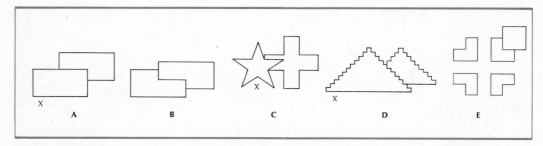

Figure 13.22. Interposition. Helmholtz proposed that the object that does not change direction at the intersection looks nearer. A. An example with consistent cues. B. An example with inconsistent cues. C, D, E. Examples that do not fit Helmholtz' proposal. See text. (A and B from Ratoosh, 1949; C and D from Chapanis & McCleary, 1953; E from Dinnerstein & Wertheimer, 1957.)

been reared. However, a second experiment with samples of chicks tested at 1 to 6 weeks of age was less successful and seemed to show that adjustment to lighting from below was quite difficult, as if overhead lighting were after all more in accordance with the nature of chicks. As we have noted, the question of whether some degree of ability to use the cue is innate or learned can be raised in connection with every one of the depth cues except the one of familiar size; but experimental evidence is very hard to obtain with human subjects because so much spatial learning may occur in the first few months of life.

Aerial Perspective

The distant mountains are blue in the clear country air, and the buildings a few blocks away are gray when seen through the smog of the city. The study of atmospheric optics (see Minnaert, 1940; Eldridge & Johnson, 1958; Duntley & Culver, 1963) has provided the basic physical data and certain generalizations in regard to attentuation and scattering of light. These effects give us a distance cue known as "aerial perspective," that may play an important role over relatively long distances, but neither systematic statement of this cue, nor research on its effectiveness, has been pursued.

Interposition or Covering

The impossibility of seeing around a corner is certainly one of the elementary facts of visual experience, and one which the little child must learn very early in his career. He learns that one object may be hidden behind another, that the hidden one is farther away, and that he can often get to see the hidden object by moving to the right or left. So, by the combined principles of interposition and of motion parallax (which we discuss on p. 504), he can make the acquaintance of the other depth cues.

When a farther object is only partly covered by a nearer one, their common contour may give a pretty good indication of which one is in front, even without any movement on the observer's part and with no familiarity with their shapes. Helmholtz pointed out that the contour line of the covering object usually does not change its direction where it joins the covered object, a fact which might be used to discern which object is nearer even in the absence of any other cues. Ratoosh (1949) proposed that this might be formalized by saying that the continuity of the contour's first derivative at the point of intersection is the feature that determines an object's relative distance, but the examples in Figure 13.22C,D,E show that this is inadequate. In Figure 13.22A and B are 2 examples from Ratoosh, showing objects with unambiguous (a) and ambiguous (b) combinations of intersections; in Figure 13.22C, D, and E are patterns, taken from Chapanis and McCleary (1953), and from Dinnerstein and Wertheimer (1957), in which the interposition cue cannot be fitted into this formulation (because both contours change direction, as

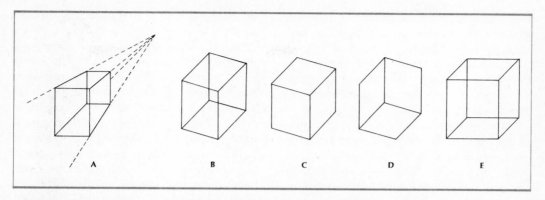

Figure 13.23. The same object in different perspectives. A. Polar projection; B–E. parallel projection. B–D are in isometric perspective; E is in oblique perspective.

in Figure 13.22C or because the formula leads to a false prediction about which object looks nearer). The figure which looked nearer is always labeled *X*. Some overall factor of "simplicity" may be at work here (see p. 435), as well as the local features of the intersection.

Linear Perspective

As an object approaches the eye, the angle that it subtends, its proximal size in the picture plane, and the image that it projects to the retina, all increase as shown in Figure 13.2. The most familiar type of perspective is generated by *polar projection,* with one or more vanishing points at the horizon, as in Figures 13.2 and 13.23A. However, the eye is willing to accept *parallel projections* of various kinds as well, as seen in Figure 13.23B,E. In the latter case, although there is a transformation that compresses the surfaces which are not in the frontal plane, there is no convergence. Such drawings are ambiguous; as you look at them for a while, the depth reverses direction. The solid that you first saw in Figure 13.23B facing one way (say, as in Figure 13.23C) changes the relationship of all of its parts and faces the other way (Figure 13.23D); see p. 519. *Reversible-perspective patterns* provide a research tool in the psychological laboratory, and they have recently attracted the attention of graphic artists (Seitz, 1965). However, such perspective ambiguity is probably not characteristic of nature: As objects increase in size

and their distance decreases, the degree of convergence between near and far edges increases, and the projection of each surface in the picture plane becomes less ambiguous. In fact, when subjects compare the slants of plane rectangles of different sizes, they consistently judge the larger rectangle to have the greater slant (Stavrianos, 1945; Freeman, 1966a). The slants of smaller rectangles are more difficult to judge because the amount of convergence they display is less (Freeman, 1966a,b).

The fact that linear perspective would normally produce foreshortening and convergence in a perspective view of an object means that Figure 13.23B has inconsistent perspective: The object cannot both be seen as a cube (that is, as having equal sides and angles) and still be consistent with the rules of perspective. Attneave and Frost (1969) had subjects view monocularly a number of drawings of cubes having different degrees of inconsistent perspective. The slant in the third dimension that each edge appeared to have was measured by asking the subject to align a rod, which he viewed binocularly, so that it appeared to continue the slant of that edge in space. Given the angles at which the lines met in the drawing, there was only one set of slants that satisfied the condition that all angles and all line lengths and slopes in the perceived object should be maximally homogeneous. The subject's alignments were extremely close to the predicted slant values, lending support to the *minimum principle* that was discussed before in connection with such patterns (Chapter 12, pp. 435, 437). Of particular interest here is the fact that as perspective consistency increased, the apparent extension into the third dimension also increased.

After Western artists discovered the rules of perspective, they followed them to portray depth and distance as faithfully and as compellingly as possible. More recently, with increasing interest in the picture's surface, as such, attempts have been made to explore the effects of using inconsistent and partly in-

verted perspectives to reduce the apparent depth, and to provide incongruities for the viewer to resolve. There is some evidence that the kinds of sketchy perspective that can be used to communicate spatial information to the Western viewer, trained in the interpretation of pictures, do not work with all cultures. Hudson (1960) found that African natives responded to the representations of people and animals as though they were all in the same plane, ignoring the spatial layout portrayed in the pictures. Similar results were obtained by Mundy-Castle (1966) and by Kilbride and Robbins (1968). Because the depth

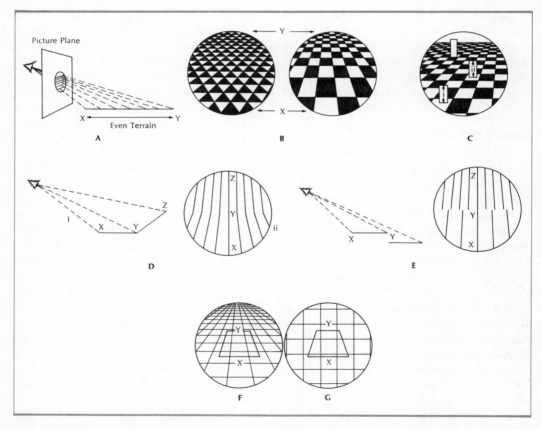

Figure 13.24. Texture density gradients as a possible source of information about the spatial layout. Gibson (1950) has pointed out that terrain that has a statistically homogeneous texture (B) presents the eye with a gradient that is correlated with the slant of the surface. C. Even though objects *i* and *ii* subtend equal visual angles, *ii* covers more units of texture than does *i*, so the observer has been given an indication that *ii* is larger than *i*. D. A change in the slant of the terrain results in a change in the gradient. E. An abrupt change in distance (a "cliff") results in an abrupt change in density. F. *X* and *Y* cover equal amounts of texture, so the pattern is shown to be a rectangle. G. The side *X* covers more texture than does *Y*, so the pattern is shown to be a trapezoid.

was only represented by means of a few sketchy lines of linear perspective, however, we cannot be sure what these results mean; certainly, we cannot assume that subjects who have had little or no experience with pictures will be unable to recognize pictured objects and scenes regardless of the type of picture that is used (see Hochberg & Brooks, 1962, p. 442). The efficacy of more informative perspective displays, such as those in Figure 13.24, has not been tested with pictorially naive viewers.

The effect of linear perspective on the apparent slant of a surface or outline pattern has recently been studied by Clark, Smith, & Rabe (1956), Weinstein (1957), Smith (1959), and Freeman (1966). The effect of perspective on pictorial size constancy was studied by Sonoda (1961), and its effect on represented distance was investigated by Smith, Smith, and Hubbard (1958).

Gradients

When psychologists speak of cues of depth and distance, they are usually thinking of the distance of an isolated object, or of the relative distance (depth) between two objects. In their experiments they are likely to conceal the floors, walls and ceiling of the room in which the objects are located because, with these in plain view, the subject has no difficulty in seeing the distance of any object.

Gibson (1950) calls attention to the importance of such surfaces as the floor or ground over which we walk or creep or drive or fly. He argues that if there is any regular marking or visible texture in the floor, this texture undergoes a perspective transformation such that in the retinal image, or in the *optic array* of light that confronts the eye, there is a *gradient* of texture density. By this he means that there is a specific rate of change in the density of the texture's projection to the eye that is directly correlated with the way objects and surfaces are arranged in the world.

Because any one spatial arrangement of objects and distances can produce the same texture-density gradients under very different

illuminations and with very different textures (Figure 13.24B), Gibson proposed that it is the gradient which is the appropriate stimulus variable to consider, not the points of retinal stimulation, nor the lines in a drawn stimulus. That is, he suggested that a texture gradient is just as truly a stimulus to which the visual system can respond as are the wavelengths and luminances of each part of the retinal image. These gradients in the retinal image are directly correlated with objective arrangements on the one hand and presumably with the subject's perceptions of those arrangements on the other. Thus, he proposed, an all-embracing perception of the immediate environment, and of the surfaces and objects within it, is likely to be achieved before, rather than after, each of the points or shapes into which the scene can be analyzed by a sophisticated observer can be noticed. As the displays in Figure 13.24 show, the gradient of texture-density carries information about the sizes (familiar or otherwise) and distances of objects standing on the surface (C); about the occurrence of a dihedral angle (fold or crease) between surfaces (D); or about the existence of an edge or a cliff between surfaces (E). Even the perception of shape might be accounted for in these terms. In Figure 13.24F, for example, the rear edge of the geometrical figure is the same number of texture-units wide as is the front edge, so that the display may be read as a "square-at-a slant." In Figure 13.24G the top of the figure is a smaller number of texture-units wide than is the bottom, the texture gradient itself is zero (signifying "no slant"), and the figure may be read as "trapezoid-in-the-frontal-plane."

Of these possibilities, the most intensively studied has been that of surface slant, using both regular and irregular textures, with and without outlines. In general, slants have tended to be underestimated when texture is the only cue the subject has to rely on (Gibson, 1950a; Clark, Smith, & Rabe, 1956; Gruber & Clark, 1956; Flock, 1964b). The slants of rectangles, moreover, are judged as well or better without any textures on their surfaces (Clark, Smith, & Rabe, 1955; Freeman, 1966).

Such experiments are difficult to interpret, however, because Gibson has not specified when a texture-density gradient is above threshold, so that we cannot tell whether the gradients involved in those experiments were adequate and comparable to the perspective cues inherent in the outline of a slanted rectangle. Flock (1962, 1964a, b, 1965) has recently undertaken to provide such measures and to reduce the complex pattern of textural stimulation to a single predictive index for slant.

Smith and Smith (1957, 1961) had subjects judge the degree of curvature of a cylinder the ends of which were covered and the surface covering of which could be changed. When the ends were covered, a variety of textures yielded little or no indication of curvature; the same thing was true of some combinations of cues. Texture, linear perspective, convergence, shading, and binocular disparity, all present together, were sufficient for the curvature to be perceived. So was the combination that consisted of seeing the edges (which were insufficient in the absence of other cues) in conjunction with cues that were not sufficient to indicate curvature by themselves. Although texture-density gradients provide *potentially* usable information, it is clear that they are not necessarily used effectively when they are the only cues available (see also Gibson, Purdy, & Lawrence, 1955; Beck, 1960). Gibson no longer rests much of his attempt to devise a psychophysics of space perception on this variable (1966a), as we see shortly (p. 504). However, texture does contribute something to combinations of other cues and can easily be manipulated in demonstrations like those in Figure 13.24. This suggests that it would be worthwhile to devise measures of this visual source of spatial information and to test the limits of its efficacy.

Interaction of Cues

Outside of the laboratory, several cues are nearly always fed into the visual system at once. Normally, they are in agreement, but they will usually differ in the precision with which the observer can use them, and they may occasionally be in conflict. How will they interact?

In some cases, cues seem to combine their effects quite simply. Thus, Jameson and Hurvich (1959; see p. 494) report that subjects' sensitivity to a difference in distance, ΔD, when all cues were available, was close to the arithmetic sum of the sensitivities obtained with each cue alone. That is, $(1/\Delta D) = (1/\Delta D_1 + 1/\Delta D_2 + 1/\Delta D_3 \ldots)$. However, we do not know how general this simple form of cooperation may be. Schriever (1925) used drawings and photographs of solid objects presented in a stereoscope. When the only cue present was binocular disparity, the stereograms produced a good appearance of depth when viewed stereoscopically and a good appearance of reversed depth when viewed pseudoscopically (that is, with the views to each eye interchanged). Other cues were then added. Linear perspective was insufficient as a cue to cause an appearance of depth against disparity: a reversed view of a skeleton cube figure drawn in perspective was seen not as a cube, but as a truncated pyramid with the small end nearer the observer. When the cue of shading was added to that of perspective and both together pitted against binocular disparity, the appearance was unstable, though disparity prevailed in general. However, when interposition (p. 498) was introduced, it could not be overcome by contrary disparity.

The outcome of such experiments on the interaction of cues depends on how we select the cues and the conditions in which we combine them. The way in which we handle this question may itself reveal a theoretical precommitment.

Representative sampling of the kinds of scene to which the organism is normally exposed, is required by the logic of an *empiricist position*. As Brunswik argued effectively (1952, 1956), inasmuch as each cue is ambiguous, it will cause us to interpret what we see incorrectly some of the time. It is a matter of probabilities, and we should expect any cue to be relied on by the subject in proportion to the relative frequency with which it

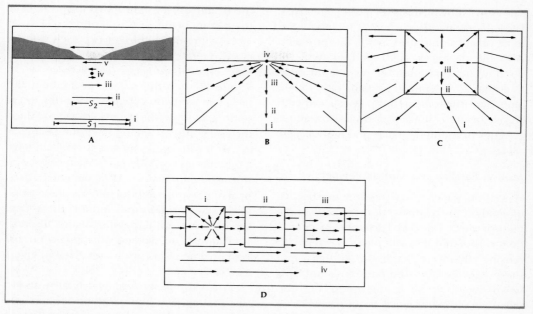

Figure 13.25. Motion perspective and optical flow. These diagrams illustrate the way in which the motion of the observer results in regular transformations of the distribution of points in the visual field in ways that are correlated with the layout and motions of objects in space. If the observer moves his eyes, head, or body, the entire image moves uniformly. In A, the observer is moving to the left and looking in the middle distance, at *iv*. Note that the arrows, which indicate the velocity with which points in the picture plane are moving relative to each other, are distributed in a smooth gradient from *i* to *iv*. B. Locomotion toward the horizon, *iv*. C. Locomotion toward point of contact with a wall, at *iii*. D. The observer is moving to the left, over the ground, *iv*. Object *i* is approaching the observer, object *ii* is upright and stationary on the ground, and object *iii* is moving to the left, but not as fast as the observer is moving. (Adapted from Gibson, 1950a.)

has been right in his past experience. If we wish to estimate the efficacy of any cue or combination of cues, therefore, or to estimate how accurately the organism can judge size, distance, and so on, we should do experiments in which the cues are present in the same combinations as they are in the situations to which the organism has been habitually exposed. That is, our experimental conditions should include *ecologically representative samples*. Only in that way will we be able to predict what the organism will do in some other (similar) situation, and be able to assess the relative contribution to be expected from the various cues in combination.

To the Gestalt psychologist, "cues" do not exist as such. Instead, either as a result of the kinds of rules that we learn about the world, or because of the way in which our perceptual processes are innately organized (see pp. 435, 437), we will see depth when the overall organization favors it. The pictorial "cues" just happen to be features that are common to many patterns that favor a tridimensional organization.[3] They cannot simply be added together, nor can they be exhaustively listed.

To Gibson, as to the Gestalt psychologists, the "cues" are an irrelevancy: the relevant variables are the stimulus gradients and other invariant features of stimulation that confront

[3] Consider the cues that were labeled in Figure 13.2B; they are shown combined in a simple picture. Each one can be seen as a flat pattern (for example, 6, 7, 8, 9 can be seen as a trapezoid in the plane of the paper, 5 can be seen as an inverted **L** adjacent to a square, 4), or each can be seen as the three-dimensional arrangements shown in Figure 13.2A. Note that in each case, the version in Figure 13.2A is somewhat simpler (in terms of number of different angles or line lengths, and so on; see Chapter 12, p. 436) than that in Figure 13.2B.

the normal moving observer (1954, 1957, 1961). These variables of proximal stimulation are, to all practical purposes, perfectly correlated with the distances, sizes, and so forth, of distal events, and therefore provide information that is essentially certain, rather than probable.[4] The force of this proposal can only be felt in the context of a discussion about the cues of motion parallax and motion perspective.

Motion Parallax and Motion Perspective

Motion parallax and motion perspective depend on the relative motion of parts of the field of view. These cues cannot, of course, be incorporated into still pictures. Even with moving pictures we cannot make full use of these cues because the cues arise not only when objects move in the world, but also when we ourselves move about the world in our sensory exploration of it. This factor of sensory exploration may well be the primary source of visual information about space. In Helmholtz' words, "It is only by voluntarily bringing our organs of sense in various relations to the objects that we learn to be sure as to our judgments [of them]. . . . If the objects had simply been passed in review before our eyes . . . probably we should never have found our way about amid such an optical phantasmagoria."

Parallax in general is the change in the visual field resulting from a change in the observer's position. As your head or body moves (or as you are moved in a vehicle), the projections of objects in the picture plane all move about. If you fixate an object in the middle distance (point *iv*, in Figure 13.25A) while you move to the left, the images of all

the nearer objects will move to the right in the picture plane (*i*). The farther objects will move with you to the left (*v*), each velocity in the picture plane being a smoothly graded function of the object's real distance.

Not only do the objects at different distances move with different velocities in the optic array, but the points in each surface, including the very important ground plane on which most objects appear to rest, undergo a differential flow relative to each other. This flow of the points of texture contains a great deal of potentially useful, precise information about the position and motion of the observer. Some of the details of such information have been worked out by Gibson and his coworkers, and are summarized in Figure 13.25A–D.

When the observer moves relative to any textured surface, the resulting motion perspective could, in principle, offer the observer information about slants and distances (Figure 13.25A) and about relative velocities (Figure 13.25D), provided only that the subject can decode the information and that he assumes that the surfaces are themselves rigid and not being deformed at different rates to mimic the flow of motion perspective. In terms of any of the analyses of space that we have been considering up to this point, the scene in the proximal stimulus is one of meaningless confusion, and it is the strength of Gibson's proposal that he attempts to reduce this apparent confusion to simplicity. What Gibson proposes is that space perception is not achieved by restoring the third dimension to the flat proximal stimulus, mediated by the shapes that we see in the latter (such as the shapes that comprise perspective, interposition, and the other cues). Instead, the visual system might respond directly to some features of the continuous transformations due to motion that are confronting the eye, features that are invariant throughout those transformations as long as the distal world itself is invariant, and that therefore contain information about the world.

Figure 13.25 shows the kinds of information available with various kinds of motion.

---

[4] There is good reason to doubt, as we shall see (p. 517) that observers utilize all of this potential information. Furthermore, to the extent that environments differ in the availability of such information, some kind of *ecological sampling,* in Brunswik's sense, will be needed before Gibson's hypotheses can be fully tested or used (Hochberg & Smith, 1955). However, a fundamental difference remains between Gibson's theory and any theory that rests on depth cues. Gibson has shown how one can propose a psychophysics of space perception in which the only use of statistics is to handle errors, not to evaluate the probability that a cue will be a correct indication of distal arrangements.

Analyses of the *optical expansion pattern* and *motion perspective* have been undertaken by Gibson, Olum, and Rosenblatt (1955) and by Purdy (1958); of the rotations and translations of a rigid object, by Hay (1966); and of the occlusion of texture at an object's edge, by Gibson et al. (1969) and Kaplan (1969).

The radical nature of this proposal, and the potential importance of its implications, can hardly be overstated. If Gibson is right, we must replace all previous assumptions about what are the adequate units of stimulation to which we respond (Gibson, 1950, 1960), about what has to be learned in the course of perceptual development, and about how it is learned (Gibson & Gibson, 1957).

Actual research has been very exploratory; at least some of the kinds of transformation shown in Figure 13.25 are indeed seen by subjects as the theory would predict. In other cases, the information is apparently not appropriately used.

In some of the experiments by Gibson and his coworkers, an object or a sheet of clear plastic (with texture or shapes on it) was placed on a turntable, between a point source of light and a translucent screen, so that the light cast the pattern's shadow on the screen. From the other side of the screen, subjects viewed the shadow cast by the pattern. Gibson and Gibson (1957) showed subjects both regular and irregular shapes and textures, rotating the turntable back and forth through an arc of from 15° to 70°, so that the shadows underwent a continuous transformation on the screen. Subjects saw the shadows as being constant shapes at a changing slant, and could make good slant judgments (something that subjects could not do when viewing static shadows of the same objects). Flock (1964, 1965) has extended this experiment, supporting Gibson's supposition that accurate perception of the slant of a moving surface is independent of the particular texture used (within the limits that were tested).

Using a very different method of generating patterns of movement (namely, motion pictures of displays of moving dots, programmed one frame at a time by a computer), Green (1959) and Braunstein (1962) presented subjects with the continuous transformations that would be produced by plane and by spherical surfaces undergoing various rotations or translations: Both found that subjects were able to identify the nature of the surface and its movements.

In a subsequent experiment (Braunstein, 1968), the normal correlation between gradients of texture and gradients of velocity was artificially reduced, and the velocity gradients were found to determine the subjects' judgments of slant much more than did the texture gradients.

There is thus some support for the view that our visual system can extract some kinds of information about surface slant and motion from the transformations of textural elements alone. However, we should note that several experiments have also been performed in which the subjects simply failed to use some or all of the information potentially present in such displays (Gibson & Carel, 1952; Smith & Smith, 1961, 1963; see Epstein and Park, 1964; Kaufman, 1968). Moreover, although there has been some demonstration that even very young animals will respond to an expanding pattern as though it were an approaching object (Schiff, Caviness, & Gibson, 1962; Schiff, 1965), the extent to which the optical flow patterns (Figure 13.25) can actually be used by subjects as a source of information about depth remains to be tested.

There is older work to the same point discussed above: that patterns which look flat when they are stationary will spring into three dimensions when they are moved (see Braunstein, 1962, for a review). The *kinetic depth effect* (KDE), as studied by Wallach and his coworkers, and to which we have referred earlier (p. 494), rested on the same phenomenon. An irregular wire outline figure is placed on a turntable between a screen and a light (with the light far enough away so that its rays are essentially parallel). While the figure is at rest, its shadow looks two dimensional. When the object is rotated around its vertical axis, the shadows snap immediately into three dimensions. At least, this is true for forms meeting certain criteria: the rotations of the figure must result in shadows that change simultaneously in both length and direction. Again, however, there are limits as to how much of the potential information present in such continuous perspective transformations can actually be used, as we see in the next section (p. 517), when we discuss a famous illusion that occurs in perceiving the shape, slant, and motion of a rotating figure.

OBJECTS IN SPACE

What can we infer when a subject reports that he *perceives* depth or distance? That is, what does his report imply beyond the mere fact of this assertion? As we have seen, such reports are hard to interpret, and it is only when further implications can be stated in at least a programmatic fashion that anything is gained by talking about "perception" (see pp. 512, 515; also Garner, Hake, & Eriksen, 1956; Hochberg, 1956, 1968; Natsoulas, 1967). For one thing, we would expect that various of our activities in our environment (reaching, throwing, jumping, among others) would all be appropriate to that report, to the degree that such behaviors are accurate (and to the degree that they do not themselves change the percept). That is, a "perceived distance" refers to some model of spatial arrangement which guides the subject's spatial behaviors, a model which may or may not correspond to the physical reality that confronts the subject and which must be inferred from his spatial behaviors and from what the subject says he sees. In a gross way, it seems clear enough that our spatial behavior is guided by some sort of spatial schema or map of the world that exists only in the subject's nervous system (see pp. 454, 533ff.), and such activities as dart throwing (p. 495), reaching (p. 534), pointing (p. 537), and jumping (p. 548) have been used as measures of a subject's space perception. Unfortunately, these measures do not always agree, either with each other or with the subject's reports, and it is not always easy to infer a consistent underlying percept that we can impute to the subject (pp. 533, 550; see Smith & Smith, 1966).

Second, the concept of "perceived distance" has also been used to explain other attributes or events we perceive. We have considered parallel examples of such "perceptual causation" in connection with color constancy (p. 397) and with the illusions (p. 460). In the former case, the classic example was Helmholtz' suggestion that we take perceived illumination into account when we judge reflectance. Similarly, it has long been argued (p. 477) that we must take an object's distance into account, in order to judge its size, and if for some reason we see it as being farther away than it really is, it will then appear larger; or, conversely, if the object appears nearer than it really is, it looks smaller (Helmholtz, 1866). That is, it is the perceived distance, not the physical distance, that presumably affects the size that will be perceived in response to any given retinal image, and in this sense the perceived distance is one of the determinants of the perceived size. To Helmholtz, this relation between size and distance was something that could only be acquired by experience, and therefore children should be expected to make mistakes in its use. This is one reason for psychologists' interest in the course of size constancy as a function of age.

The relationship between size and distance is physically a very simple one. The size s of the retinal image that is subtended by some object of physical size S, varies inversely with the distance of the object from the eye. That is, s is proportional to S/D. Therefore, for some fixed retinal image, the ratio of size to distance is constant: $S/D = k$ (see p. 477). If this relationship between size and distance were reflected in the observer's perceptual system, the same thing would be true for apparent size S' and apparent distance D', namely that $S'/D' = k$. This has been called the *size-distance invariance hypothesis* (Kilpatrick & Ittelson, 1953). However, we should note that this is only an hypothesis, and that judgments of size and judgments of distance need not be related to each other except to the extent that the stimulus variables on which judgments of size are based, and those on which judgments of distance are based, are normally closely coupled to each other in the physical world (Gruber, 1954; Epstein, 1961; Rump, 1961; Smith & Smith, 1966).

Closely related to the size-distance relationship are those of slant and shape, and of motion and distance. All of the objects (*i-iii*) in Figure 13.3 (p. 477) project the same shape to the eye, and, on the basis of retinal shape alone, the rectangle at *i* may be taken for one of the trapezoids. If the different distances of the near and far edges are accurately taken into account, however, then both the edges should appear to be of equal length, so that the rectangle's shape would be correctly perceived if slant and shape were coupled perceptually as they are physically. Conversely, even if the rectangle were set at different slants to the line of sight, and its proximal stimulus varied with such change, the apparent shape would remain constant if slant were correctly taken into account. Similarly, if points *i* and *ii* in Figure 13.25A move with the same velocity $S_1/t = S_2/t$, the near one will have moved further in the proximal stimulus ($s_1 > s_2$). To the degree that distance is correctly taken into account, and the 2 distances traversed appear equal, we should expect the 2 velocities to appear equal.

Within the explanation presented above, therefore, an entire network of perceptual attributes depends on (and thereby defines what we mean by) perceived distance. To the extent that these other perceptual attributes are in fact predictable from perceived distance, it is important to be able to measure (or to infer) what distances the subject does perceive while looking at some scene.

The physical relationship is so simple that the existence of such relationships between the perceptual variables has been widely accepted as explaining size constancy, shape constancy, and so on (see Epstein, Park, & Casey, 1961; Epstein & Park, 1963, for recent reviews). Let us note, however, that such relationships between perceptual attributes are neither logically required, nor as yet well established by experimental research.

In the discussion of color perception we saw that, as an alternative to Helmholtz' theory that we take illumination into account when judging the lightness of any part of the visual field, we could attempt to explain lightness constancy by assuming that the stimulus for lightness is a *relationship* between local luminances. Similar alternatives exist with respect to the perception of size, shape, and so on. We thus try to account for the phenomena of size constancy by taking the stimulus for an object's apparent size to be some relationship within the retinal image rather than the retinal image size *s* itself. Let us

consider 2 such theories, which we will call *relational* or *stimulus-determined theories of size perception.*

Relational Theories of Size Perception

Objects are generally seen standing on the ground, their distance from the observer being defined by the point on the texture-density gradient at which they intersect the ground. The texture-density gradient may indeed provide information about the object's real distance. However, the ground's texture may provide information about the object's *size,* as well. If, as Gibson suggests, our perceptions of the sizes of objects are a function of the amount of environmental texture the object hides (see Figure 13.24C), that variable of stimulation would remain constant for a given object size, regardless of the distance from which the object is viewed. That is, as the object's distance increases, the number of texture elements that it covers remains constant or invariant; to the extent that the overall gradient of the texture defines the scale of the texture in any region (see p. 501), the object will look to be the same size despite the marked differences in its proximal size. We might call this the *texture-scale size cue.*

Similarly, shape constancy follows this analysis, without any need for "taking slant into account" (see Figure 13.24F and p. 501).

Note that in this theory there is no *necessary* psychological relationship between perceived size and perceived distance. To the extent that distance perception and size perception are both determined by the information in the texture gradient, and to the extent that the texture is in fact homogeneously distributed over the surface of the ground, correct size judgments and correct distance judgments will both be made, regardless of whether or not there is any *internal* (psychological) coupling between the perceived variables. Any degrading of the stimulus display that destroys the texture density gradient will remove both the information about distance and the information about size, and, for this reason, the fact that size constancy and shape constancy both are lost when the depth cues are removed offers no proof that those constancies rest on taking distance into account.

A somewhat similar hypothesis about a relational stimulus for apparent size was offered and tested by Rock and Ebenholtz (1959). Wallach (1948) had proposed that the stimulus for perceiving a particular gray is the ratio of light intensities of neighboring retinal areas (p. 413), and J. F. Brown (1931) had proposed that perceived motion depends not on the rate of displacement in the retinal image but on the rate of displacement relative to the frame of reference in which the movement appears (p. 520). In analogy to these, Rock and Ebenholtz suggested that the stimulus correlate for an object's apparent size is the ratio of its image size to the image size of some neighboring object which serves as a frame of reference. To test this hypothesis, subjects viewed luminous patterns in an otherwise dark room. Each pattern consisted of a rod surrounded by a rectangular frame; subjects were required to report when the lines appeared equal. With the standard a 3-inch line in a 4-inch rectangle, the average setting of the variable line in a 12-inch rectangle at which the subjects reported that it appeared equal in length to the standard was between 6.0 and 7.2 inches—more than twice as long as the standard.[5]

How do these relational theories of size perception differ from the size-distance theory? The former theories propose that an object's apparent size is a direct response to some specific and measurable feature of the pattern of sensory stimulation. That feature (for example, the relationship between retinal size and the adjacent texture scale) is one which is normally in good correspondence to objects' physical sizes, regardless of how the objects' distances may vary. The latter theory

[5]Earlier experiments by Obonai (1954) and Künnapas (1955) were performed with similar displays in order to study context effects in the geometrical illusions (pp. 456–463); these experiments found much smaller effects. They had been performed under full illumination, however, and therefore there was probably a common frame of reference for both rectangles, which would presumably reduce or could even eliminate the relational size effect.

assumes that the visual system makes a response to the size of the retinal image, and then modifies that response by taking distance into account, using any available sources of information about distance.

Regardless of whether either or both of these particular relational-size theories is correct, they represent a class of explanation that is very different from the size-distance theory. The distinction between the 2 explanations here is analogous to the distinction between the sensory and cognitive theories of the perception of lightness that we considered at some length in the previous chapter (see pp. 412–425).

Can we see retinal size? The size-distance theory takes the size of the object's retinal image s as the starting point for size perception, and we might expect, therefore, that subjects would be able to judge s at least as well as S. In fact, as we shall see, when all depth cues are removed, subjects perceive 2 objects as being the same size when the objects subtend equal visual angles (see p. 509). However, this may mean only that in the absence of any cues, subjects assume that the standard and variable are both at some completely arbitrary but specific distance, and make their match in terms of the apparent object sizes that are appropriate to that distance (Gilinsky, 1951; Woodworth & Schlosberg, 1954; Wallach & McKenna, 1960; Epstein, Park, & Casey, 1961; Gogel & Newton, 1969). Note that this explanation assumes a perceptual coupling between size and distance—the size-distance invariance hypothesis (p. 506). The hypothesis that subjects can *not* respond to retinal size as such was supported by the results of an experiment by Wallach and McKenna (1960). They showed that most subjects found it virtually impossible to match a normally viewed variable (which was viewed in the light, with distance cues present) to a standard stimulus, which was viewed under *reduction conditions* (that is, with distance cues removed by presenting the stimuli monocularly and in an otherwise dark room). These results are not surprising if the stimulus for size is relational rather than absolute. On the other hand, Rock and McDermott (1964) found that when both the standard and variable stimuli (which were both luminous equilateral triangles) were presented in an otherwise dark room, and the standard was viewed under completely reduced conditions, subjects could match it reliably with a variable stimulus that subtended the same visual angle. This was so regardless of whether the variable stimulus itself was viewed under completely reduced conditions or with binocular depth cues. When both the standard and the variable are viewed without any *visual* context, therefore, subjects can judge when their retinal images are equal (see also p. 512).

Moreover, even when size judgments are made under daylight conditions, with all depth cues available, subjects who are instructed to match the standard to the variable in terms of visual angle generally succeed in coming quite close to doing so. (Holaday,

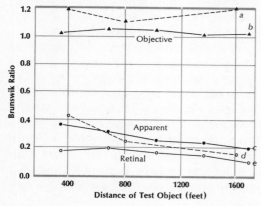

Figure 13.26. Size constancy as a function of instructions. Subjects made size matches of test objects that were located at different distances from them, and each point on the graph shows the Brunswik ratios calculated from those judgments. Lines *a*, *b* were obtained under instructions to make objective matches; lines *d*, *e* were obtained under instructions to make retinal matches; line *c* was obtained under instructions to match the apparent size of the test object. (Lines *b*, *c*, *e* from Leibowitz & Harvey, 1967; lines *a*, *d*, calculated from data of Gilinsky, 1955.)

1933; Gilinsky, 1955; Jenkin & Hyman, 1959; Carlson, 1960, 1962). Figure 13.26 shows how the Brunswik ratios (which we defined in connection with lightness constancy on p. 399 and which are used here as estimates of the percentage of size constancy) vary with distance, under different instructions.[6] The ratios have been computed from the data of Gilinsky (1955), who used triangles as stimuli, and from a graph presented by Leibowitz and Harvey (1967), who used human beings as stimuli. Both experiments were performed out of doors and involved unusually large ranges of distance.

In the closely related case of shape-constancy experiments, in which the standard and variable objects are presented at different slants to the line of sight, instructions have similar effects. If subjects are given instructions to match standard and variable objects, their Brunswik ratios are high; under instructions to match their retinal projections, Brunswik ratios are low (Klimpfinger, 1933; Gottheil & Bitterman, 1951; Epstein, Bontrager, & Park, 1962; Lichte & Borreson, 1967). Thus, subjects can respond at least partially (although not completely) in terms of their retinal images even when depth cues are present.

We really do not need formal experiments to prove the point, however. It is evident that railroad tracks *do* seem to converge to the horizon; that far-off trees *do* look smaller, in some sense, than near ones; that billboards near the highway *do* move faster across the visual field than those that are far back from the road. Thus it is clear that we can see things somewhat as they are in the retinal image.

How can we interpret these facts? Suppose that it had turned out that subjects could *not* make proximal matches. Would this have disproved the Helmholtzian theory? Not at

[6] Here, the Brunswik ratio would be given by the expression $(S' - s)/(S - s)$, where S' is the match that is actually obtained between standard and variable, S is the setting of the variable that is physically equal to the standard, and s is the setting of the variable that subtends the same visual angle (Figure 13.4), as does the standard. A ratio of 1.0 would mean that perfect constancy had been achieved.

all, because Helmholtz (1866) was not arguing that retinal size is consciously reportable: ". . . we are not in the habit of observing our sensations accurately, except as they are useful in enabling us to recognize external objects" (1962 ed., p. 6), and the uncorrected experience of size, in Helmholtz' view, is an unnoticed sensation on the basis of which unconscious inference-like processes operate to produce a conscious judgment of object size.

On the other hand, does the fact that subjects can respond in terms of their proximal stimulus distributions, albeit in a limited fashion, disprove the relational theories? No, because there is no reason why the proponents of such relational theories cannot also admit that there may be several different criteria on which subjects can decide to base their size judgments. "Size" is a word that subjects have learned in the context of a number of very different visual tasks, and there are probably several quite different aspects of perceptual experience to which they can refer in making their judgments. Surely, the railroad tracks occupy a smaller proportion of the total visual field at the horizon than they do at the bottom of the visual field. Even a young subject must have had ample opportunity to learn that in some sense the distance between the railroad tracks does indeed become smaller as they ascend the visual field, and that in some sense the shape of a rectangle viewed at a slant is a trapezoid. Gibson has called these kinds of experience—the pattern of perceptual responses that are more in correspondence with proximal than with distal stimulation—the *visual field,* as opposed to the *visual world.* He takes the latter to be the body of perceptual experiences on which behavior is really based and the former to be a quite different domain (see the debate between Boring, 1952a,b, and Gibson, 1952). To Gibson, then, the visual field is in no sense the basis of the visual world; it is a separate set of experiences that can at best intrude into our perception of the true physical layout (1966, p. 306). But is the visual field really all that useless, and are its effects merely an "intrusion"? If so, it is hard to see why the subject ever identifies proximal size as "size" and maintains any ability to respond to it.

In fact, the relationships within the visual field must guide our activities in the spatial environment, too. To move your eye from 6 to 7 in Figure 13.2B takes a longer excursion of the eye than to move it from 8 to 9; to turn your head so that your nose no longer obscures some object requires a greater rotation when the object is near than far. When 2 objects are at the same distance, "size" as measured by absolute retinal image size coincides with size as measured by relational criteria. When the 2 objects are at different distances, object-oriented behaviors and image-oriented behaviors no longer coincide. The subject may have quite different sensory criteria for judging equality according to each meaning, and unless the experimental conditions can explicitly separate these meanings for him, his actual decision may be some unstable compromise between them.

In any case, the answer to the question of whether we can respond to the retinal image seems to be a qualified "yes", but this fact does not really support the Helmholtzian theory or oppose the relational one. What it does suggest is the need to study object perception with tools like those of signal detection methodology (p. 34) or with reaction-time procedures (see p. 47) that will help to separate the various criteria that subjects may use.

Size-Distance Invariance

If retinal size is fixed, so is the ratio of S/D that will produce it (Figure 13.4). We have already considered (p. 506) the hypothesis that the ratio of perceived size to perceived distance S'/D' is also fixed, for a given image size. For a recent review of evidence concerning this relationship, see Epstein, Park and Casey (1961). At first glance, the evidence for such a relationship is encouraging, and we have seen that it has been used to account for such powerful effects as the geometrical illusions (p. 462), as well as the constancies. So closely related to it that both are often used interchangeably is *Emmert's Law,* which offers a good example both of the implications and difficulties of this hypothesis.

Emmert's Law refers to the fact noted by Emmert in 1881 (Boring, 1942) that an afterimage actually looks bigger if it is projected on a more distant surface, the judged size of the image being proportional to the distance of that surface. As a matter of fact, any physical measure of the projected size of the afterimage must increase with distance because the affected area on the retina has a fixed retinal size s, and the proportion that it covers of the measuring surface is simply proportional to the distance D. This is true, of course, regardless of whether or not there are any distance cues. However, the change in the *apparent* size of the afterimage as a function of distance does depend on the presence of such cues (Helson, 1936; Edwards, 1953; Hastorf & Kennedy, 1957), and it therefore appeared reasonable to propose that the apparent change in the size of an afterimage results from the same mechanisms that produce size constancy. Specifically, perhaps the apparent size of an afterimage is proportional to the apparent distance of the surface on which it is projected: this would then make Emmert's Law a case of the size-distance invariance relationship.

The relationship between Emmert's Law and size perception in general has been discussed by Boring (1940, 1942), Edwards (1950), and Boring and Edwards (1951); the identification of Emmert's Law and size constancy was questioned by Young (1950, 1951) and Crookes (1959). Distinctions between S and D, on the one hand, and S' and D', on the other hand, have not always been kept clear, and there are unresolved measurement problems (for reviews, see Epstein, Park, & Casey, 1961; Onizawa, 1954).

In any case, however, as long as the changes in the apparent distance of the afterimage are produced by varying the distance of the surface against which the afterimage is being judged, the relational determinants of size (and perhaps the effects of binocular convergence, see p. 480) may be responsible for the change in the apparent size of the afterimage, independent of any change in apparent distance.

Let us therefore consider a classical case in which the apparent size of an object undergoes a change, even though the size of its retinal image remains constant and is not projected on a real textured surface.

The moon illusion Most readers will have noticed a phenomenon that has been known and puzzled over for centuries, namely that the moon appears to be much larger when it is low in the sky. It has been shown repeatedly that this is not due to any simple physical effect such as the greater atmospheric scattering or refraction of light when the moon is near the horizon. In fact, the illusion has been demonstrated without the moon at all, so such physical explanations are irrelevant when an artificial image of the moon is presented to the eye against different regions of the sky (Kaufman & Rock, 1962; Rock & Kaufman, 1962), or when an afterimage of fixed retinal size is projected near the horizon or at a 45° elevation (Reimann, 1902; King & Gruber, 1953). It has been thought since Ptolemy that the effect was somehow dependent on apparent distance (Boring, 1942).

> Boring and his associates (1943) worked on the top of a high building, using both the real and mirrored moons. In some cases, they could make the real moon seem to move from zenith to horizon, or vice versa, by mirrors mounted on long supports. Subjects matched the moon's size by means of a nearby disk of variable size. Their final conclusion was that the illusion was largely dependent on the direction of the eyes in relation to the head. If the subject lies on his back, he chooses a larger variable stimulus to match the size of the moon at the zenith, and a smaller one to match the moon at the horizon. The obvious explanation would seem to be that turning the eyes upwards tends to give a slight reflex divergence of the eyes that would increase the

strain to maintain convergence which would, in turn, serve as a cue to decreased distance. If the moon were judged to be nearer at the zenith than at the horizon, it would seem smaller at the zenith, by the size-distance invariance hypothesis, because retinal size is unchanged.

However, the illusion produced by eye direction is small whereas the moon illusion is a large phenomenon, and other factors contribute to it. Kaufman and Rock used two artificial moons optically introduced at different places in the visual field. Under their conditions, eye elevation had no effect, but the presence of terrain adjacent to the horizon was important in causing an increase of from 30 to 100 percent in the apparent size of the moon. Presumably this was so because the distance cues in the terrain made the horizon appear more remote than the zenith sky (Kaufman & Rock, 1962; see also King & Gruber, 1962). The size increase occurs because when the moon is low its proximity to the horizon makes it appear equidistant with the horizon (Gogel, 1965).

There are 2 troubles with these size-distance explanations of the moon illusion. The first is that the illusion may not result from changes in the apparent distance of the moon, but may be a relational size effect produced by the terrain at the horizon. Second, and more troublesome for the size-distance invariance hypothesis: the subject usually reports that the moon *looks* farther away at the zenith, instead of closer. Perhaps size-distance invariance determines the apparent size of the moon in an automatic fashion, but the distance judgment that is the basis of this process is not directly available to introspection. Then the size judgments that the subject has made (once he has encoded them into some stable form; see p. 423) might serve as the basis for another judgment of distance, which may be opposite to the distance judgment that was first arrived at and on which the size judgment was based (Woodworth & Schlosberg, 1954; Kaufman & Rock, 1962a,b).

Inherent in the idea of "allowing for distance," in judging size, is the assumption that some internal representation of distance, D', is a mediating variable. That is, in solving the equation $S'/D' = k$, the effective variable is

D' itself, rather than any of the various stimulus patterns by which the observer arrives at his estimate of D. Yet in each of our 2 classical examples, Emmert's Law and the moon illusion, the size may change because the patterns of stimulation act as relational size determinants (p. 507), not because they provide depth cues. The same objection applies to the many demonstrations, which we next examine, showing that depth cues are necessary to size constancy.

Size constancy depends on the presence of depth cues, as a number of experiments show. Consider a series of experiments performed by Holway and Boring (1941). The

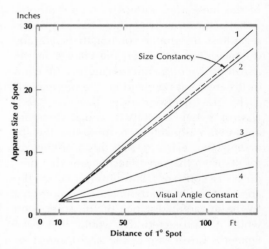

Figure 13.27. Perceived size as a function of depth cues. The standard was a disk of light, displayed at various distances from the observer. Its actual size was increased as the distance was increased to yield a constant retinal angle. The observer varied the comparison disk until it appeared to be the same size as the standard; the distance of the comparison was held constant at 10 ft. There was good size constancy under conditions *1* and *2*, which employed binocular and monocular vision, respectively. In *3* some depth cues were removed by use of an artificial pupil, reducing the constancy. Further reduction of cues by the use of drapes to kill reflections (*4*) forced the observer to make matches almost entirely in terms of visual angle. (Holway & Boring, 1941.)

subject stood at the intersection of 2 long corridors, stretching out like the arms of an L. In one corridor was a variable stimulus, a disk of light that was adjustable in size, placed 10 feet from the subject. At various distances (10 to 120 feet) down the other arm of the L, a standard disk was exposed, its size so chosen that it always subtended exactly 1 degree of visual angle. The subject's task was to set the size of the comparison stimulus so that it looked as large as the standard. The size constancy line (in Figure 13.27) shows the settings that would represent perfect matching of physical size, since an angle of 1° subtends about $8\frac{1}{2}$ inches at 40 feet, 17 inches at 80 feet, and so on. Using normal binocular vision, the subject's results are shown in line 1; they actually overshoot constancy slightly. Line 2 shows the results using monocular observation. When a reduction screen (p. 399) was introduced to reduce depth cues further, the settings fell (to line 3). Some depth cues remained available from faint reflections in the doors that lined the corridor. When these were minimized by black drapes, the settings (line 4) approached still closer to those determined by visual angle. In a later experiment, Lichten and Lurie (1950) reduced these depth cues still further by the use of screens that prevented the subject from seeing anything but the targets. Under these conditions there remained no trace of size constancy.

In more recent experiments in which distance cues were eliminated or reduced (Chalmers, 1952; Hastorf & Way, 1952; Zeigler & Leibowitz, 1957; Rock & McDermott, 1962), similar results were obtained; stimuli were judged to be equal when they subtended equal visual angles. These results might reasonably be taken to mean that the subject can judge the size of an unknown object only to the extent that he has reliable cues as to the object's distance. However, as we have seen, this is not the only plausible interpretation of such results, because impairing vision and removing depth cues not only interferes with the perception of distance, but also eliminates features of stimulation that may be relational

determinants of apparent size, irrespective of the fact that these features may also be depth cues.

How can we change the apparent distance D' of an object without introducing any of the stimulus features which may determine apparent size directly?

When we discussed the "primary" or nonvisual distance cues (p. 479), we noted that as convergence and/or accommodation increased, the apparent size of an object decreased, even though the proximal stimulus remained unchanged (Wheatstone, 1852; Judd, 1897; Hermans, 1954; Bleything, 1957; Roelofs & Zeeman, 1957; Heinemann, Tulving, & Nachmias, 1959; Rock & McDermott, 1962). Inasmuch as convergence normally increases as D decreases, convergence is a potential depth cue, and this decrease in apparent size is what we would expect from the equation $S'/D' = k$. The changes in apparent size, here, which are well attested, cannot be ascribed to the presence of any visual relational determinants, like those proposed by Gibson and by Rock and Ebenholtz (pp. 501, 508), inasmuch as the size s of the retinal image has remained unchanged.

However, this does not necessarily mean that the primary distance cues first produce some response of a perceived distance D' and that this perceived distance then determines a perceived size s'. Of the authors cited, only Roelofs and Zeeman, and Bleything obtained changes in apparent distance that were at all commensurate with the changes in apparent size. In some cases subjects judged that objects that were objectively nearer were further away (Heinemann, Tulving, & Nachmias, 1959). This discrepancy between S' and D' is not a trivial matter, for it makes it difficult to state formally what we mean by "taking distance into account."

Nor is this discrepancy peculiar to the use of the "primary cues." Gruber (1954) had the same subjects make both size and distance judgments, at each of 6 distances (ranging from 200 to 450 cm) and found that while they overestimated the relative size of the standard object, they underestimated its relative distance. Jenkin and Hyman (1959) obtained a similar inverted relationship between estimates of size S and estimates of distance D (in feet) when subjects were instructed to make objective size matches. But surprisingly enough they obtained appropriate size and distance judgments when subjects were instructed to make *analytic* matches (that is, to judge in terms of retinal images).

On the other hand, Blessing and Landauer (1967) instructed their subjects to make objective size and distance judgments of targets that were presented with false perspective cues in order to vary apparent distance; judgments made under these conditions provided a very good fit to the size-distance invariance hypothesis. Coltheart (1969) had subjects view an illuminated triangle with no depth cues in a dark room, and gave them cut-out triangles of different sizes to hold, as haptic information about the visual targets. When subjects were given larger triangles to hold they judged that the targets were at a greater distance (although the distance was significantly underestimated); when both the visual target and the haptic target were doubled in size, the apparent distance of the target remained constant, which is what we would expect under these conditions in terms of the size-distance invariance hypothesis. More indirectly, Künnapas (1968) found that the relation between D' and D varies as a function of the available depth cues in very much the same way as judgments of size varied in the experiment by Holway and Boring.

Nevertheless, subjects often overestimate the size of objects as their physical distance is increased (Holway & Boring, 1941; Chalmers, 1952; Gilinsky, 1955; Jenkin, 1957, 1959), although, using human beings as the stimuli, Leibowitz and Harvey (1967) did not find such overestimation. If we take such judgments to be measures of perceived size S', we must question the efficacy of the relational determinants of size, for these should remain constant regardless of distance. Moreover, if the size-distance invariance hypothesis is to be maintained, we would expect to find that perceived distance D' should also be overestimated as the real distance D is increased; the data do not clearly support this prediction. Gilinsky (1951) had subjects indicate the midpoint of each of 14 distances (ranging from 8 to 200 feet), under normal viewing conditions, and found that subjects set the further sections of each such division too large when comparing them with the nearer ones; that is, far physical distances were *underestimated* in comparison to near ones. Smith (1958) and Harway (1963) found similar results, whereas Purdy and Gibson (1955) found few errors at all. Only in indoor viewing have greater physical distances been overestimated compared to lesser ones (Künnapas, 1960; Luria, Kinney, & Weissman, 1967; Teghtsoonian & Teghtsoonian, 1969).

In short, the overestimation of size with increasing distance cannot be explained by saying that apparent distance increases faster than physical distance, *if we accept subjects' distance estimates as our definition of D'*. There is little reason to do so. Many criteria are available on which the subject can base his response, and with no special training to narrow his use of those criteria, we should not expect that his judgment directly reflects any one of them. In the present case, for example, Carlson (1960) has proposed that the phenomenon of overestimating size occurs because, when the subject is trying to judge actual physical size, he brings to bear all his beliefs about the size-distance relationships, including the belief that an object near by must look larger than one further away in order for the 2 to be equal in physical size. Thus, in terms of this explanation, having arrived at an apparent size that has automatically taken distance into account, he may apply a conscious correction for distance in arriving at his size judgment and thus end up with an erroneous size match. This is the same explanation that was offered earlier for the failure of the hypothesis of the size-distance invariance to predict judgments based on the primary cues (p. 513) and to explain the paradoxes involved in the moon illusion (p. 512). It is an interesting kind of explanation, reminiscent of the Helmholtzian one in this respect: One level of perceived size (what the subject sees before he makes his misguided correction) serves as the basis for a second level of response (the judgments actually made). Presumably these different levels of "perceiving size" differ in ways that the subject could learn to detect under suitable training conditions, and differ also in the speed with which the judgments can be made (permitting, perhaps, their separation by suitable methods of measuring reaction-time).

Certainly, however, indirect methods will be needed to decide the values of S' to put in the formula when solving for D' and vice versa.

Shape Constancy and Shape-Slant Invariance

If an object with a constant physical configuration is viewed from different slants to the line of sight, it produces retinal images of different configurations (Figure 13.3). In the usual experiments to study the judgments of the shape of an object, a subject tries to match the shape of an object (the standard) that is presented to him at one slant, by choosing from among a set of objects having different configurations (the variables), which are viewed at another slant, the one object of the set that has the same apparent shape. The match that he makes under normal viewing conditions usually is intermediate between one in which the 2 objects have the same physical configuration, and one in which their retinal images have the same configurations.

Brunswik or Thouless ratios are often employed to measure the degree to which constancy is "achieved" (although there are inadequacies with these measures here as in the other constancies (see pp. 399, 509; Epstein & Park, 1963).

The first explanation that suggests itself for shape constancy, as for any of the constancies (see pp. 398, 495), is that we know what shape any object really has because of our previous experiences with it. However, most research has found no clear influence of familiarity on shape constancy (Thouless, 1931; Langdon, 1953; Nelson & Bartley, 1956).

Borreson and Lichte (1962) have recently shown that a familiarization session with nonsense shapes (like those of Attneave and Arnoult in Chapter 12, p. 446) that were subsequently used in an experiment, increased the Brunswik ratios that were obtained with one group of subjects. However, the shapes were shown at varying orientations in another familiarization session, yet this specific experience with what these irregular and quite unfamiliar shapes looked like at various slants had no significant effects on the constancy ratios. Perhaps a wider range of experiences would have produced different results. On the other hand, Hake and Myers (1969) have shown that the effects of familiarization that were obtained may be an artifact of the method that was used, and in any case, even with no familiarization at all, average Brunswik ratios for the different shapes that were used varied from 0.19 to 0.77, or 77 percent of constancy in the latter case. Thus, shape constancy does not necessarily arise from one's memory of the true shape, although familiarity *can* contribute to it.

Alternatively, we could explain shape-constancy rather simply in this way. Using depth cues, the subject sees that one edge of the shape is further away than the other; then he automatically makes allowance for this increased distance when he judges the sizes of the near and far edges. Indeed, when viewing conditions are made worse or *impoverished* (for example, by viewing the shapes monocularly instead of binocularly, by eliminating views of the background, by reducing exposure time and intensity, by removing texture, and so on), so that cues as to the object's orientation are likely to be reduced or obliterated, shape constancy decreases as well (Thouless, 1931; Eissler, 1933; Stavrianos, 1945; Langdon, 1951, 1953; Leibowitz, Mitchell, & Angris, 1954; Leibowitz & Bourne, 1956; Nelson & Bartley, 1956; Leibowitz, Bussey, & McGuire, 1957). However, slant cues (or depth cues) are themselves often patterns of stimulation which influence the perception of shapes, regardless of their possible function as depth cues (see Figure 13.24). As with size and color, therefore, we cannot simply assume that because shape judgments are more like the distal than like the proximal patterns when the slant cues are present, this is due to anything like "taking slant into account."

If shape constancy depended on slant being taken into account, we might at first thought expect that shape constancy could be no better than the accuracy with which subjects make judgments of the object's slant.

Stavrianos (1945) performed a series of experiments in which judgments of both slant and shape were obtained, using rectangles and ellipses under 3 conditions of observation. In general, subjects made relatively accurate judgments of the shape of objects under conditions in which they made inaccurate judgments of the slant. We can, of course, argue that the subjects are not responding to the same cues with equal attention when they are making their judgments of shape and slant. As we noted above, the attitudes (objective, retinal, or apparent) with which subjects are instructed to make their matches of the shapes of the objects have marked effects. Subjects instructed to make an analytical or retinal match obtain lower constancy ratios, similar to those obtained with partial removal of the depth cues (Klimpfinger, 1933; Gottheil & Bitterman, 1951; Epstein, Bontrager, & Parks, 1962; Lichte & Borreson, 1967), and although some of the earlier studies could not be unequivocally interpreted to this point, the results now seem to be quite conclusive. Certainly, the fact that a change in instructions can produce a reliable change in the nature of the shape matches that subjects make, and can result in judgments that approach (but do not reach) correspondence to the retinal image, is evidence that there are at least 2 different sets of criteria on which subjects can base their judgments of shapes viewed at some slant.

However, it may also be true that at least some criteria of apparent slant and apparent shape are psychologically coupled to each other. Koffka (1935) proposed that perceived slant and perceived shape are in an invariant relationship, similar to the size-distance relationship we have discussed above (p. 506; see also Chapter 12, p. 460). More specifically, Beck and Gibson (1955) hypothesized that a given retinal projection determines a family of "apparent-shapes-at-apparent-slants." This shape-slant invariance hypothesis does not imply that slant is taken into account to arrive at a shape judgment. It does imply that when different judgments of slant and of shape can be obtained with the same retinal image, the judgments of slant and of shape will be correlated with each other. Although Flock (1964) did not find a systematic relationship between shape and slant judgments, other experiments have yielded judgments of slant and shape that are at least roughly correlated (Stavrianos, 1945; Winnick & Rogoff, 1965). To test the slant-shape invariance hypothesis, however, we must be sure that the slant cues are not acting as relational determiners of shape (see p. 501), rather than as information about the object's slant. In one experiment, Beck and Gibson (1955) presented subjects with a textureless triangle at a

45° slant to a textured vertical background; the subjects viewed the triangle monocularly, keeping their heads motionless. The subjects saw the triangle as being in the plane of the vertical background. Two comparison figures were mounted flat on the same background, one having the same objective shape as the standard, the other having the same projective shape (that is, producing a similar image on the retina). Under these viewing conditions, all subjects chose the latter. When binocular vision was permitted, however, the standard triangle was seen to be slanted out from its background; and now 77 percent of the subjects chose the comparison triangle which was objectively equal to the standard. A modified replication and extension of this experiment, performed by Epstein, Bontrager, and Park (1962), also indicated that subjects made a change toward an objective match when binocular viewing was permitted, although their judgments of slant and shape did not fit each other very well. Kaiser (1967) recently refined and extended this procedure, using 3 trapezoids at different slants to the observer (15°, 45°, and 65°). Each trapezoid was so proportioned that they all projected the same retinal pattern. Subjects were provided with a variable shape, which was viewed in the upright position; the subjects were instructed to adjust the shape to match the judged objective shape of the slanted object. They also rotated a half-black, half-white disk (a procedure previously used by Flock, 1964) to match the object's slant. They were permitted to adjust these variables until they were satisfied with both. Viewing was done under both monocular and binocular conditions, and the way in which the subjects' matches of shape changed between the 2 conditions was compared with the way in which their slant matches changed. Changes in the apparent shape of the trapezoid, as measured by the ratio of height to base, were highly correlated with changes in apparent slant ($r = +.90$); changes in the ratio of top to base were also significantly correlated with changes in slant but somewhat less so ($r = +.68$). In this experiment, therefore, the slant-shape invariance hypothesis was confirmed.

In any case, all 3 studies showed that binocular depth cues which affect perceived slant also affect shape judgments. It is not easy to see how the binocular depth cues could comprise relational size and shape determinants in the sense that we are using this term (see p. 507). Therefore, there does indeed seem to be some coupling between the apparent slant and apparent shape.

Earlier evidence to this point can be obtained

from the experiments of Langdon (1951, 1953, 1955a,b). In one experiment (1951), the standard was a luminous wire circle, and the comparison stimulus was one of 15 luminous ellipses presented in the frontal-parallel plane, both being viewed in an otherwise completely dark room. The circle was rotated around its vertical axis, and the subject's task was to indicate when in the course of its rotation the shape of the rotating circle matched one of the stationary ellipses. In general, the 2 were chosen as being equal when the proximal stimulus projected by the circle was actually narrower than the ellipse. That is, shape constancy was obtained as a result of the spatial information provided by the rotary motion, and by the consequent *motion perspective* (p. 503). Langdon obtained similar results with various modifications of this procedure (1953, 1955a,b), and although he concluded that a simple slant-shape formula is inapplicable (because of marked irregularities in the way that the degree of constancy varied with slant), this is another example of a stimulus variable that cannot plausibly be considered to be a relational shape determinant but which affects judgments of shape by way of the information about slant that it can provide to the visual system.

There thus seems to be evidence to support the existence of a relationship between the stimulus conditions that provide information about slant and the shape that is perceived under those conditions. However, there is little or no support for the proposition that the information must first manifest itself as *perceived* slant before it can work its effects. Indeed, taking the present body of evidence into account, it is not even necessary that the information about slant be reflected in any perception of slant; although not all subjects in Langdon's (1951) experiment experienced tridimensionality as a result of the rotation imparted to the circular standard, this did not appear to interfere with the degree of constancy that they achieved.

Does the achievement of shape constancy imply that the retinal image was corrected by "taking slant into account," supporting the Helmholtzian position? Not necessarily: To Gibson, information about the object's shape is potentially available in those features that remain invariant in the transformations that

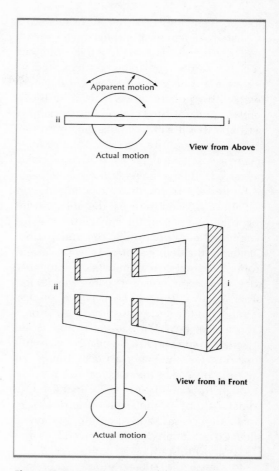

Figure 13.28. Ames' "trapezoidal" window. See text.

its projection undergoes in the optic array (p. 504), and it is only the departures from constancy that require explanation. Let us consider this further in the context of an illusion which seems to show an extremely striking departure from constancy despite the fact that the proximal shape undergoes a continuous rotary transformation.

Perspective reversal

The Ames trapezoidal window produces a phenomenon that has received a great deal of attention in recent years. The subject stands about 20 feet from an object that looks like a window sash mounted on a vertical rod, as an axis (Figure 13.28). The rod is rotated slowly, but the subject does not see the rotation correctly. Instead, the sash seems to oscillate back and forth through an arc of 90° to 100°. The sash is actually a trapezoid, cut from flat cardboard, shaped and painted to resemble a solid window drawn in perspective. A little thought shows that the sash will tend to appear slanted even in frontal-parallel view and that it will seem to swing from this slant to the opposite one as it rotates. Inasmuch as oscillation rather than rotation is perceived, and the longer end always appears to be nearer, we see that the rotary motion has not only failed to reveal the object's true shape; during half of the oscillation, the apparent motion is opposite to the true motion. Of course, the demonstration must be viewed from a fair distance to eliminate contradictory cues from accommodation, convergence, and other sources (one of which we discuss shortly), but the illusion is surprisingly strong. Objects like a card, a ball, or a tube, when attached to the window, appear to make full rotations (as they are actually doing, of course); this makes them appear to pass clear through the "oscillating" sash. If the trapezoidal pattern is replaced by a rectangle, oscillation ceases, and the full rotation is seen. Construction details are given by Ames (1951) and Ittelson (1952).

To Ames, the subject's past experience with rectangular windows was responsible for the phenomenon, and the importance of past experience of some sort is also suggested by cross-cultural differences in the illusion, that were found by Allport and Pettigrew (1957). It has been shown, however, that the pattern need not be a simulated window (Pastore, 1952; Canestrari, 1956), nor even a trapezoid. The illusion of reversal can be obtained with a circle, an ellipse, and a "nonsense figure," none of which contains any linear perspective (Day & Power, 1963, 1965). Various alternative theories have been offered by Pastore (1952); Canestrari (1956); Graham (1963); Day and Power (1965); Guastella (1966); Cook, Mefferd, and Wieland (1967); and Braunstein and Payne (1968). For our present purposes, there are 3 questions to be answered:

1. *Why does the rotary motion fail to be perceived continuously and veridically?* Graham (1963) pointed out that the differential angular velocity between any 2 points on the figure's surface is the same whether that part of the window is approaching or receding, so that the direction of rotation is ambiguous (see also Day & Power, 1965). This is geometrically true, of course, only in the case of parallel projection, such as is approximated when the distance from which the object is viewed is large relative to its size (Hershberger, 1967; see also p. 499). Otherwise, retinal projection is polar projection, and the 2 directions of motion should not give equivalent angular velocities in the optic array. In fact, Zegers (1965) has shown that the reversal rate increases as the viewing distance is increased and the trapezoid size decreased. Braunstein and Payne (1968) find that with parallel projection the rectangle as well as the trapezoid appears to reverse direction, whereas with polar projection, both shapes seem to rotate correctly and continuously.

In short, failure to see the correct motion may occur only when the rotation cues are subliminal. Although Gibson has not seriously addressed himself to the problem of thresholds in connection with the information available in perspective transformations, this is clearly a matter that will have to be taken into account (see pp. 502, 505).

2. *Why does the rectangle appear to rotate as it really does when the trapezoid does not do so, at intermediate ranges of motion perspective?* Perhaps because we are more sensitive to perspective changes in right angles (as Braunstein and Payne suggest), although how this hypothesis might be phrased when we are dealing with continuous perspective transformations has not been specifically spelled out. Perhaps because we respond to the implied linear perspective of the figure (as Pastore, 1952, and Graham, 1963, suggest) when motion perspective is a relatively weak cue. Lending support to the latter interpretation, Canestrari and Farnè (1969) have shown

that the depth cues of interposition (p. 498) and the texture-density gradient (p. 501) also cause continuous rotation to look like oscillation.

Furthermore, Cross and Cross (1969) pointed out that the picture thickness of the Ames window comprises a depth cue that is consistent with oscillatory motion and is inconsistent with rotation; when this cue was removed or reduced, subjects reported a smaller number of reversals.

3. *Why does reversal occur?* The fact that the cues to motion are ambiguous does not explain why the direction of rotation appears to reverse. It seems likely that this problem is related to the other reversal phenomena (pp. 433, 499; see Cook, Mefferd, & Wieland, 1967), and must await a general solution.

As a brief survey of the reversal phenomena, let us note the following points.

Perspective reversal is not restricted to pictures, but will occur while viewing wire objects those pictures represent (Howard, 1961; Cormack & Upchurch, 1969; Price, 1969). Binocular viewing and rotation of the object reduce the reversal rate (Cormack & Upchurch, 1969). Reversal rate for pictured objects appears to be lower with more complex or more difficult forms (Gordon, 1903; Porter, 1938; Ammons, 1954), and the rate generally increases as a result of practice with a given figure (Ammons, Ulrich, & Ammons, 1959; Smith, Imparato, & Exner, 1968). However, a drop in reversal rate also has been reported after more extended observation. (Bruner, Postman, & Mosteller, 1950). Using a rotating reversible object, Price (1969) found that the version that was initially perceived decreased in its duration over the first several reversals (thus increasing the reversal rate) and then became very variable in duration; but the alternative phase remained relatively constant in duration throughout.

The occurrence of the reversals still cannot be explained. At least two components are involved in the reversal of perspective in pictures. One of them seems to be regular and independent of the size of the stimulus, while the other component appears to slow down the first one, has different effects on large than on small figures, and seems to be related to shifts in fixation (Washburn, Mallay, & Naylor, 1931). Washburn and Gillette (1933) showed that although subjects can best control the appearance of an outline cube when they are free to move their fixation point from one region to another, reversals also occur and can be controlled to some degree even when the retinal image is stabilized by viewing it as an afterimage. Moreover, were eye movements responsible for reversals, we should expect adjacent figures to reverse simultaneously and, although neighboring (or nested) outline cubes may reverse at the same time (Adams & Haire, 1959), they may also do so independently (Washburn & Gillette, 1933) as do rotating reversible objects (Mulholland, 1956; Howard, 1961). Changes in fixation are therefore not necessary either to obtain reversals or to control them. The success with which the subject can hold any alternative has been held to be a function of its relative simplicity (defined in terms of the motor actions it suggests) and of the frequency with which the object that it represents is encountered in ordinary life (Washburn, Reagan, & Thurston, 1934).

It is relatively easy to observe reversals in the direction of apparent rotation, or gross changes in the orientation of the object. With each reversal in apparent movement, however, there is associated a large number of more subtle changes in apparent depth relationships and in what Mefferd (1968) has termed "endogeneously-supplied visual attributes of depth." The visual system appears to fit erroneous assumptions about the object's three-dimensional orientation to the changing stimulus patterns that arise as the object rotates. These changes are difficult to study systematically, but are very important to an understanding of the kind of perceptual coupling (pp. 506, 516) that we have been discussing in this chapter.

PERCEPTION OF VISUAL MOVEMENT

Just as the image that falls on the retina is ambiguous as an indicator of the size and distance of the object that projects it, the retinal image is also ambiguous as to the locations and motions of objects in space. An object whose image is tilted on the retina may be tilted in space, or it may be upright and the observer may be tilted. An object whose retinal image is in motion may be moving in space, or the observer may be moving. In order to perceive the location and motion of an object correctly, therefore, the observer must somehow take his bodily positions and movements into account.

There are several sensory systems that respond to the internal state of our joints and muscles, and to the pull of gravity. The information that these systems can provide about the position and motion of the body and of its parts is supplemented by records that are kept in the nervous system concerning the motor impulses that have been sent to move those parts and to change their positions. These sensory systems are discussed in Chapter 11. We shall not attempt to consider them separately here. Instead, we shall usually refer to them indiscriminately as the *position sense*, or as *proprioception*.

Real Movement

Movement is perceived when the image of an object remains stationary on the retina while the eye pursues the object. We may suppose, therefore, that the perception of movement results from sensing the eye movements made while tracking the object. Movement is also perceived, however, when the eye is stationary, and the object's image moves across the retina; in fact, motion in the periphery of the image is what usually initiates eye movements in the pursuit of a moving object. Movement is *not* perceived when the retinal image moves as a result of saccadic eye movements (Chapter 11). We shall also see that movement is perceived under certain conditions in which the eye and its retinal image are both stationary. It is clear that several different processes lead to the same "final common percept" of movement (Kolers, 1963) and that the perception of movement is complexly determined.

Thresholds of displacement Consider an object, the retinal image of which is displaced some distance s in some interval of time t. The minimum velocity (ds/dt) that can be detected is called the *velocity threshold*. The minimum distance over which movement can

be detected is the *displacement threshold*. Because the luminance, duration, uniformity of motion, size of the field over which movement occurs, and the number of moving targets can all be varied, in addition to velocity and displacement, many kinds of thresholds can be studied in the perception of real movement. Threshold research has recently been surveyed by Graham (1965) and by Spigel (1965). In the following discussion, the notation min/sec refers to angular velocity at the eye, that is, to minutes of visual angle of displacement divided by seconds of time. A higher ratio threshold means that a faster movement is needed in order for the movement to be detected than does a lower ratio.

The velocity threshold while fixating a moving stimulus is about 1 to 2 min/sec, when some parts of the visual field are stationary, and about 10 to 20 min/sec when only the moving stimulus is presented (Aubert, 1886; Bourdon, 1902; Grim, 1911). Brown and Conklin (1954) found a threshold of 18 min/sec at an exposure of 0.5 sec in an otherwise homogeneous visual field; with increasing durations, the threshold decreased to a limiting value of 9 min/sec at 16 sec duration. The velocity threshold is higher in peripheral than in central vision (Aubert, 1886); it varies as a function of luminance (Brown, 1955; Leibowitz, 1955a); and it varies with duration up to about 0.3 sec (Brown, 1955). As the velocity of a moving target increases, visual acuity decreases, probably due to failure of the eye to match the motion of the target (Ludvigh, 1948, 1949, 1955, 1965). Smith and Gulick (1956, 1957, 1962) found that although the contour of a small moving square could not be clearly seen at velocities exceeding about 13°/sec, if the stimulus was presented in a fixed position prior to movement, the maximum velocity at which the contours could then be clearly distinguished increased, to an upper limit of about 40°/sec.

The threshold for detecting that 2 stimuli have different velocities was found to be 1 to 2 min/sec by Aubert, and about 30 sec/sec by Graham and his colleagues (1948). Brown (1931) exposed a repetitive pattern of moving targets (for example, a band of small squares on a white background) behind windows of variable size, and found that if the linear dimensions of such a field of movement are increased, the stimulus velocity must also be increased in the same proportion if the motions of the 2 fields are to appear of equal velocity. This "transposition effect" might bring about "velocity constancy," in normal viewing conditions, because the ratio of the retinal displacement rate to the extent of the retinal displacement would remain constant, regardless of the distance of the target from the observer.[7] Smith and Sherlock (1957), however, have shown that subjects in such experiments may be judging the frequency with which moving targets cross the boundaries of the aperture, not the targets' velocities. Perhaps this kind of judgment would also contribute to velocity constancy in normal viewing conditions, in which the ground provides a uniform gradient of texture the elements of which are occluded by the edges of moving objects.

The fact that the velocity threshold is about 10 times as great to perceive a single moving object as it is when a stationary reference stimulus is present suggests that different processes are involved in judging relative and absolute (or *egocentric*) movement. Exner (1875) had proposed that at moderate velocities, displacements are directly sensed as movement, whereas at lower velocities the observer judges that an object is in motion by noting its change in position. Leibowitz (1955b) suggested that at short exposures (.25 sec) only the velocity-sensitive component would operate and that therefore only at longer exposures (16 sec) would velocity thresholds be improved by the presence of a stationary framework. A similar distinction was made by Gregory (1964). Leibowitz' experimental data supported his prediction. Shaffer and Wallach (1966) have reported, however, that displacement thresholds are lower with a framework than without one at all durations, even with exposures as short as 0.011 sec. This finding does not necessarily refute Leibowitz' proposal because Shaffer and Wallach used a framework which closely

surrounded the target, and, at the short exposures, subjects may have used the assymmetrical location within the framework as their criterion for deciding that movement had occurred. In any case, their findings clearly support the hypothesis that the visual system is sensitive to the retinal displacement of a single target, inasmuch as a moving spot can be seen to move even when there is no stationary reference framework at all and when the exposure was too brief for any eye movement to occur, for example, 0.05 sec. This same point is made in a different context by the results of recent research on an old illusion of movement.

Movement aftereffects After looking at a nearby waterfall for a time, look at the bank and you will see the trees swim upward. (For a history of the "waterfall illusion" see Boring [1942].) One plausible explanation was that downward eye movements made in pursuing the water persist when the eyes turn to the bank (Addams, 1834; Helmholtz, 1866). However, a similar aftereffect is obtained after you watch a spiral rotating on a color wheel. If the spiral appears to shrink or recede during

Figure 13.29. A spiral to be rotated for the reverse aftereffect. (Sanford, 1898.)

[7]If 2 objects are at different distances from the observer, D_1 and D_2, and they move through the same physical distance, $(S_1 = S_2)$ at the same rate $(dS_1/t = dS_2/t)$, the motions of the retinal images of the 2 objects will be unequal: $s_1/D_1 \neq s_2/D_2$ (see p. 504). Consequently, the rates of their retinal displacements will also be unequal: $ds/dt \neq ds_2/dt$. However, the ratios $(ds_1/dt)/s_1$ and $(ds_2/dt)/s_2$ will be equal, and if it is on these ratios that perceived velocity depends, the 2 objects should appear to move at the same rate, even though their retinal images are moving at different rates.

rotation (Figure 13.29), it will appear to expand or approach when the rotation is suddenly stopped. It is hard to imagine eye movements that would make an object seem to expand in all directions at once. Perhaps the retina or the visual cortex becomes adjusted to the continued movement and does not recover immediately from this adjustment when the movement in the retinal image ceases (see Wohlgemuth, 1911; Boring, 1942; Woodworth and Schlosberg, 1954, for reviews of such theories). Sutherland (1961) has offered the following more specific explanation: Neural cells which respond to displacement in a single direction in the retinal image have been found in the visual cortex of the cat (Chapter 9). If these exist also in man, and if the effect of prolonged viewing of displacement in one direction is to lower the normal firing rate of the cells which respond to that direction as compared to those which respond to the opposite displacement, this imbalance in the normal firing rate may produce the movement aftereffects.

Supporting this hypothesis, Sekuler and Ganz (1963) showed that after prolonged inspection of stripes moving in one direction, subjects have a higher luminance threshold for stripes moving in that direction than for stripes moving in the opposite direction. In a second experiment, they showed quite clearly that the movement aftereffects occur with conditions of image stabilization (see Chapter 9). These results are consistent with an explanation of the aftereffect in terms of neural units that are sensitive to the direction of displacement in the retinal image. In any case, the second experiment demonstrates that the waterfall illusion can be produced by retinal displacement alone, without eye movements. This point was further supported by Anstis and Gregory (1964), who found that when subjects were instructed to follow, with their eyes, a fixation point that could be moved independently of a set of moving stripes, the aftereffect was determined by the direction of the retinal displacement, not by the direction of eye movements. We shall see,

however, that there are other movement aftereffects to which eye movements do indeed contribute (p. 545).

Sequential patterns of movement The mere fact that a relative displacement is suprathreshold tells us little about what movement is perceived. Consider 2 objects, 1 of which is stationary and 1 of which is moving. The change in the distance between 2 objects' retinal images, considered by itself, is ambiguous. Physically, either one or both of the objects could be in motion and still produce the same retinal image. If you are seated in a smoothly moving train, looking out the window at another train, and proprioceptive information about your own movement is slight, it is a common experience to be uncertain as to which train is moving. Duncker (1938) has shown that there are visual factors that often decide how the relative movement will be distributed between 2 objects, only 1 of which is really moving. The object which is really moving may appear to be completely stationary, and the object which is really stationary will then carry the relative movement. These effects are called *induced movement*. The phenomenon can readily be observed on a cloudy night, in which the moon appears to sail slowly across the sky through apparently stationary clouds.

The smaller of 2 objects generally appears to move, especially if it is enclosed by the larger one. If one of the objects is fixated, that one appears to move (Duncker, 1929). Eye movements are not necessary for induced movement to occur (Shaffer & Wallach, 1966), but that does not mean that eye movements do not normally contribute to it. The objects that we expect from our past experiences to be mobile—cars, planes, people—will appear to move more than the neutral objects that are in fact moving (Duncker, 1929; Comalli, Werner, & Wapner, 1957; Jensen, 1960; Brosgole & Whalen, 1967); however, Brosgole and Whalen (1967) report that enclosing the stationary object in a moving framework obliterates the difference. If the object that is really being displaced is to appear stationary, its absolute velocity may have to fall below the threshold for *egocentric* or "subject-relative" movement

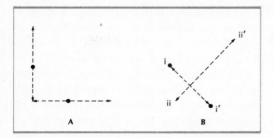

Figure 13.30. Dots moving with the motion shown at A, appear to move as at B. See text. (Johansson, 1950.)

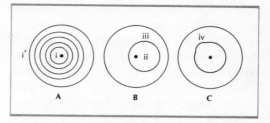

Figure 13.31. Circular patterns mounted on a rotating turntable give rise to illusory motion perception. In all cases, the center of the turntable is marked by the black dot. See text. A. After Benussi (in Musatti, 1924). B, C. After Wallach, Weisz & Adams (1956).

(Wallach, 1959). However, even with more rapid displacements, the physical movements may not be correctly perceived.

Thus, Johansson (1950) found that 2 dots which move toward and away from each other in a homogeneous white field, as shown in Figure 13.30A, are seen to move toward and away from each other on the diagonal *i–i'*; less noticeably, the entire path of movement, *i–i'*, itself appears to move up and down on the diagonal shown at *ii–ii'*. Note that this construction fits the purely visual information as well as the real movement does. For example, if the eyes were following the path marked *ii–ii'*, the diagonal at *i–i'* would in fact represent the movement in the proximal stimulus. Johansson does not give his displacements in visual angles, but by making reasonable assumptions about his viewing distances, the velocity of each dot falls between 1°/sec and 5°/sec, well above the absolute velocity thresholds given above. The visual system has extracted a motion that is common to all parts (*ii = ii'*, in this case), and this motion itself has become the framework against which the residual movement is seen.

The fact that a relative displacement is above threshold, therefore, does not tell us unequivocally what movement will be perceived, because the apparent path of movement is affected by the overall configuration. The situation is similar to that of shape perception (p. 437): Intuitively, it seems that some general principle determines the apparent movement, but none of the general principles or rules that had been proposed in the context of shape perception is specific enough to predict the actual movement illusions that occur.

As an example of such illusory movements, consider the effects that occur when patterns are displayed on a rotating turntable. Musatti (1924) reported that an ellipse that is mounted eccentrically on the turntable tends to appear fluid, and to display amoebalike movements. Benussi (Musatti, 1924) found that eccentrically arranged rings (Figure 13.31A), viewed monocularly, appear to rise up out of the plane of the turntable, forming a three-dimensional cone. Wallach, Weisz, and Adams (1956) have shown similar effects with patterns that look flat when the turntable is stationary but that rise when the turntable revolves. They explain these phenomena as special cases of the kinetic depth effect (p. 505) by the following reasoning. First, they report an exceedingly curious illusion of another kind: that a featureless circle, drawn or pasted on a rotating turntable, does not appear to revolve with the surface. Instead, it seems to undergo just those compound movements that will maintain its orientation. For example, the eccentrically mounted circle in Figure 13.31B seems to revolve not only around the turntable's center, but around its own center, *ii*, as well, in order to keep the imaginary point, *iii*, toward the top of the page. In fact, if a deformed circle is mounted as in Figure 13.31C, it seems to remain fixed in orientation and the bulge, *iv*, travels in a wave around it. If each point on the circle retains its identity in this sense, then in the Benussi figure, points *i* and *i'* are corresponding points on the inner and outer circles. Because the distances between these points change in both length and direction as the pattern revolves, they provide the conditions for depth to be seen in accordance with the rules of the kinetic depth effect.

The phenomena described above were produced at rotation rates of about 20 to 60 revolutions per minute. If luminous patterns rotating at slower rates (for example, 5 to 8 rpm) are viewed in darkness, the range of alternative movements is increased (Mefferd & Wieland, 1967). Even if a naive subject has first seen the object correctly when it was stationary, the illusory movements soon appear when the pattern is rotated.[8]

As with the geometrical illusions (Chapter 12), it is unwarranted to assume that such illusions of movement are confined to these simple patterns and that they therefore reveal nothing about the perception of movement in general. As with the geometrical illusions, also, they cannot now be accounted for by any single explanation. They certainly do not accord with any general rubric of "Gestalt simplicity" (see p. 437). Just as there seem to be different processes contributing to the perception of movement, there may be a number of different sets of rules that govern perceived movement, and the successful formulation of such rules may await the analysis of the perception of movement into its separable components.

Some of the components involved in the perception of movement may involve relatively peripheral mechanisms, such as neural units that respond to specific displacements in the retinal image (p. 522). Other components may depend more on the way the subject encodes and remembers a sequence of events than on any direct sensory response: The fact that movements which take a con-

siderable period of time to run their course can be recognized and compared with each other implies some mechanism of retention by which an entire temporal event can be registered and remembered. Like the experiments on tachistoscopic recognition (p. 444) and on the fragmentation of shapes with stabilized images (p. 454), experiments on movement may call on the subject's memory, on the repertory of temporal events or *schematic sequences* (Hochberg, 1968) with which the subject is familiar. He can use these to identify and store the successive elementary displacements to which the eye

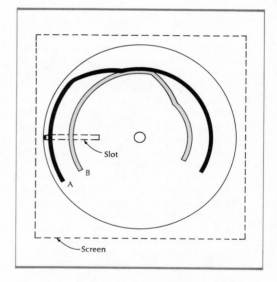

Figure 13.32. Disk for giving kinetic impressions. Through the slot square portions of the stripes *A* and *B* are seen, while the disk rotates in the counterclockwise direction behind the screen. As long as stripe *A* remains at the same distance from the center, the square seen through the slot remains still; but when stripe *A* approaches center the visible part of it approaches *B*. When *A* has reached *B*, *A* becomes stationary and *B* begins to move. The stripes are $\frac{1}{5}$ in. wide, the same as the slot, which is 6 in. long; the subject is 5 ft away. *A* and *B* are 1.6 in. apart at the start, and the speed of the apparent movement is 12 in./sec. These measurements were varied. (Michotte, 1946.)

---

[8] The "coupling" of perceptual attributes (p. 506) is marked, in these cases. If slant is perceived, at least some degrees of slant-shape invariance (p. 516) is displayed; if slant is not perceived, the figures look accordingly nonrigid. There seems to be little doubt that the subjects "really see" the illusory movements reported, in this sense (Mefferd & Wieiand, 1967).

and brain may be more directly sensitive. Only a very few events or actions have actually been studied experimentally.

Apparent Movement

Action and causation We have a few words with which we can identify movements in physical terms, such as "smooth," "abrupt," "erratic"; and we can describe simple movements in terms of their geometrical shapes. These are clearly not the only categories we have with which to identify and remember patterns of displacement. There are many more complex movements to which we are continually exposed in the form of animate and inanimate actions, and to which we make well-practiced responses. Most of these go unclassified and unstudied. Let us merely note here that they seem to be susceptible to disciplined analysis and study. Heider and Simmel (1944) devised an animated cartoon in which triangles and a circle follow complex paths of movement that observers find very difficult to describe in physical terms but which are easy to remember and describe in social terms. The psychophysical relationships involved in such "social perception" have not been further studied. In contrast, the bases for perceiving physical causation have been extensively explored by Michotte (1946) using the apparatus shown in Figure 13.32. As objects, he used small squares seen through a horizontal slot in a screen. When the objects are first shown to the subject, A and B are a short distance apart and both are stationary; then A moves rapidly toward B but stops when it reaches B, and B immediately moves away in the same direction. The observer has a very clear impression of causation, A acting on B and propelling it forward. If A moves along with B, instead of stopping when it reaches B, the impression is that A carries B along. It is interesting to note that slight discontinuities can be tolerated, but when these tolerances are exceeded, the impression received is that of 2 separate events instead of a single causal process. "Causation" seems to be a clear example of a schematic sequence by which a number of successive displacements can be responded to as a single unit.

The simplest example of responding to 2 successive physical events as a single unit is probably the phenomenon of stroboscopic movement, which we shall consider next in some detail.

Stroboscopic movement On the motion picture screen, or on the TV screen, there is of course no actual motion of the figures. The motion picture camera has taken a series of snapshots separated by brief intervals of time, and the projector casts these still views and blank intervals on the screen. The fact that apparent visual motion could be effected under such conditions became known in 1833 with the invention of the stroboscope, a device for illuminating a moving object with intermittent light. The apparent movement is accordingly also called *stroboscopic movement*.

The history of research on stroboscopic movement has been reviewed by Boring (1942). The psychological study of this effect received its major impetus from Wertheimer's paper in 1912. He had a subject look at 2 short vertical lines, 1 cm apart and at reading distance; they were exposed one after the other with a blank interval between them. If the blank interval was about 200 msec or more, the appearance corresponded to the reality: 2 stationary lines, one presented after the other. If the interval was about 30 msec or less, the 2 lines seemed to be presented simultaneously. If the blank interval was adjusted between these limits, various kinds of movement were seen, the kind depending on the arrangement of the lines and on the duration of the interval. There are thus several thresholds that can be measured. The 2 major thresholds are that between succession and movement, and that between movement and simultaneity. The thresholds are in general quite variable and dependent on many factors.

Several kinds of apparent movement have been named. *Optimal movement* is produced with a blank interval of about 60 msec in Wertheimer's arrangement. In this condition, the line clearly appears to move from one place to another. If the intervals are made somewhat longer, *partial movement* seems to occur. Of major interest is what Wertheimer called *phi movement,* or *pure movement.* This is apparent movement between two places even though no object appears to move.

> The following additional names have been offered to distinguish different kinds of apparent movement. In *alpha movement* an object appears to change size (Kenkel, 1913). In *beta* an object appears to move from one place to another (Kenkel, 1913); this is equivalent to Wertheimer's optimal movement. In *gamma movement* (Kenkel, 1913) an apparent expansion and contraction occurs when the stimulus object's luminance is increased and decreased, respectively. In *delta movement* the direction of movement is reversed when the second stimulus is more luminous than the first one (Korte, 1915). *Bow movement* does not follow the shortest path connecting the 2 stimuli; this usually occurs when an obstructing stimulus is introduced between the first and second stimulus; the apparent movement may then curve around the obstruction via the third dimension (Benussi, 1916).
>
> Korte (1915) varied the most obvious stimulus factors, and his results are sometimes called *Korte's Laws.* These relate the threshold values critical to obtaining beta movement in terms of the following variables: the spatial separation of the 2 stimuli, their luminances, the exposure times of the 2 stimuli, and the duration of the interval between them. (Korte's Laws are reviewed in Neff [1936] and Graham [1965].) In summary, these laws mean that it is more difficult to see apparent movement when the illumination is very low, or when the time gap is very short, or when the space gap is very wide. If the space gap is increased, you must increase the time gap to get apparent movement. Subsequent work by Neuhaus (1930) and Sgro (1963) over a larger range of these variables has extended and revised Korte's data.

Although the variables of luminance, distance, and duration are important, and are easy to measure and to specify, they are as insufficient to the prediction of stroboscopic movement in general as they are to real movement. Configurational factors also affect what apparent movement, if any, will be seen,

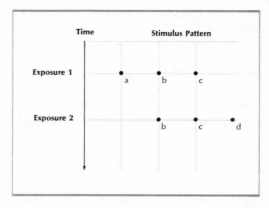

Figure 13.33. The factor of identity in stroboscopic movement. See text. (After Ternus, 1926.)

and as we have noted before, we are not yet prepared to make useful generalizations, wherever configuration is a major factor in perception. Let us simply examine some of the ways in which configuration affects the organization of apparent movement.

> In order for stroboscopic movement to be perceived, the visual system must respond to the second stimulus as being the same object as the first stimulus and must treat the 2 presentations as being at different places in space. In the simplest experiment described above, a single object appears to maintain its identity and change its locus. Ternus (1926) showed that if the 3 spots *a, b, c* in Figure 13.33 comprise the first exposure, followed by 3 spots *b, c, d* for the second exposure, the common points *b* and *c* do not appear twice if beta movement occurs. Instead, *a* moves to *b, b* moves to *c* and *c* moves to *d.* Points *b* and *c* have changed their identity, even though they fall on the same retinal locus. If the common points are not interrupted by the blank period, they retain their identity; as long as the blank period intervenes, however, the identity that a point appears to maintain is determined not by whether it falls on the same retinal region, but where it fits in the overall pattern. The path of the apparent movement tends to be the one which will preserve the identity of 2 successively viewed patterns. The conditions for phenomenal identity are not now clear, but they would seem to be extremely important to the phenomenon of apparent movement, and to the path that the apparent movement takes. When the 2 stimuli are alike, a simple sliding movement along a straight or curved path will usually be seen (Hall, Earle, &

Crookes, 1952), but rotations and translatory movements through the third dimension will occur when these offer simpler "solutions" (see p. 503n), as when an inverted V is followed by a V right-side up and slightly lower in the field. Many examples of three-dimensional apparent movement have been published by Steinig (1929), Fernberger (1934), and Orlansky (1940). The more dissimilar the 2 alternating figures, the more difficult it is to see them as a single figure which is moving and changing form or color as it moves, and the longer the blank interval that is needed to obtain apparent movement (Orlansky, 1940). The interval is therefore not merely a function of spatial separation between the 2 stimuli. Moreover, "spatial separation" is itself not simply a matter of distance in the visual image. When Corbin (1942) measured the time interval required to see movement as a function of the separation between the first and second stimulus, he obtained the same time thresholds whether the 2 stimuli were in the frontal plane or in a plane that was slanted 60° away from the observer, even though the retinal separations were only half as great in the latter case as in the former.

According to structuralist analysis (p. 427), movement is not a simple sensory phenomenon, but a complex perceptual experience compounded of the successive sensations that would normally be provided by a stimulus moving over the retina (Titchener, 1902) or by the eye in pursuing a moving object (Helmholtz, 1866). To Wertheimer, the so-called "phi phenomenon" was of great theoretical importance because it showed that the intervening sensations are unnecessary to the perception of movement. Wertheimer showed also that eye movements are unnecessary to create the effect of stroboscopic movement, inasmuch as 2 movements in opposite directions are seen when 2 suitable pairs of lines are presented. Guilford and Helson (1929) later showed, by eye movement photography, that no significant relation existed between the eye movements and the reports of apparent movement. Nor does the subject need to *infer* movement from an apparent change in position: Experiments have shown that apparent movement is perceived as unequivocally as real movement (Stratton, 1911; Wertheimer, 1925; De Silva,

1929) when 2 dots are shown the observer 1 of which really moves while the other undergoes optimal stroboscopic movement.

Wertheimer therefore held with Exner (1875), Mach, and others (see Boring, 1942) that movement is as direct an experience as is brightness or hue, an experience mediated by its own physiological mechanism rather than by experiences of changes in position. What might that mechanism be? Exner (1875) proposed that the retina is actually stimulated in the region lying between the initial and terminal positions, but against this theory is the fact that apparent movement occurs even if the first stimulus is applied to one eye and the second stimulus to the other. Wertheimer proposed a theory somewhat like Exner's, but he proposed that the hypothetical movement occurs neurally in the visual cortex instead of in the retina. The cortical excitation aroused by the first stimulus could spread and be attracted toward the region excited by the second stimulus, and the movement of excitation along the cortex could give a sensation of movement, a sort of streak.[9] This was the forerunner of the doctrine of *isomorphism,* with which Gestalt psychologists attempted to provide the equivalent of "specific nerve energies" for organized processes like shape and form (pp. 428, 436f.). Against this theory are the following facts. (1) In lower animals, the visual cortex may be removed without interfering with the pursuit movements of the animal's head and eyes that are normally produced by a field of moving stripes, even when those stripes are stroboscopically il-

[9] Brown and Voth (1937) performed a series of experiments to test this "attraction" theory. They exposed lights successively at the corners of a square. If there are long intervals between stimuli, simple succession occurs. As the interval is shortened, so that each light is presented close enough in time to the preceding light to attract it, simple beta movement occurs, and the light is seen to move around the corners of the square. An analysis of the vectors working on each apparent position of the light shows that the path should become circular as the interstimulus interval decreases further, so that lights further apart in space become closer in time and exert cohesive forces on each position. In fact the path does become circular, falling well within the 4 corners of the square. If the interstimulus interval is further reduced, the circle becomes larger again and eventually, of course, the 4 lights are all seen simultaneously.

luminated (Smith, 1940). (2) Although in man, at least, there is a stronger tendency for apparent movement to occur between points whose projections fall in the same cerebral hemisphere than between points that fall in different hemispheres (Gengerelli, 1948), the fact that apparent movement is perceived at all between the 2 hemispheres makes Wertheimer's theory inadequate (Smith, 1948). (3) Apparent movement may occur when the successive presentations fall on the *same* retinal region. Thus, Duncker (1929) caused an objectively stationary dot to appear to move back and forth by presenting it within a rectangular framework for exposures of half a second, the rectangle being displaced to one side or the other on alternate exposures. Perhaps in this experiment the observer's eye followed the center of the rectangle, so that the dot was really projected on disparate retinal locations from one exposure to the next. The results of an experiment by Rock and Ebenholtz (1962) could not be explained in this way. They had subjects look back and forth between 2 places that were physically separated in space. A light flashed at each place as they looked at it. Although the same retinal area—the fovea—was stimulated at each flash, 6 of the 10 subjects reported seeing movement from one position to the other. (4) The existence of tridimensional apparent movements (p. 527) and the fact that objective separation rather than retinal separation determines the time interval needed to produce stroboscopic movement (Corbin, 1942), both seem incompatible with a theory of spreading excitation in the visual cortex.

As Woodworth and Schlosberg said in 1954, we seem left without any acceptable theory to explain apparent movement. It is probably unwarranted to try to lump together under one explanation all the different conditions in which reports of apparent movement are obtained, for the latter may be based on diverse criteria and on very different mechanisms under the different conditions of stimulation. Even though stroboscopic and continuous (real) motion in the stimulus field may produce equally convincing appearances of movement, this does not mean that they do so in the same way. In fact, the visual process must be different for the 2 conditions, if only at the retinal level. Kolers (1963) has shown, for example, that when a target is briefly presented in the path of an objectively moving line, the luminance threshold for detecting the target increases, but this does not happen when the line only appears to move (beta movement).

We have seen that quite different criteria and processes may elicit a judgment that real movement has occurred (pp. 520f.); for example, there may be a direct response mediated by local retinal displacement (Exner, 1875; Leibowitz, 1955a); a response based on relative displacement (p. 521); and a response based on pursuit movements by the eye. Similarly, different processes may contribute to stroboscopic movement. The sort of apparent movement that seems to depend on a change in the egocentric location rather than on retinal displacement may be based on different criteria than is beta or phi movement. In the experiment of Rock and Ebenholtz (1962), the subject looked at successive flashes that were about 7 inches apart at a viewing distance of about 22 inches, or some 17° of visual angle, whereas De Silva (1929, 1935) reported that continuous optimal movement could not be obtained under more ordinary conditions of viewing when the targets appeared successively with separations greater than 4.5°.

In another experiment in the same series, Rock and Ebenholtz (1962) flashed a light successively at the *same* place in space, but this time the subjects moved their eyes from one direction to another in such a way that different parts of the retina were stimulated alternately. No apparent movement was reported in this case. The experimenters concluded that this was so because the light was perceived as being at the same egocentric location even though different retinal regions were stimulated. As we shall see shortly, however, this may reflect a different mechanism; a displacement of the retinal image may simply not result in apparent movement when it occurs in association with a saccadic eye movement. Before we examine this possibility, we consider the more general issue that it implies, namely the question of how we see an object as being stationary in space even when its retinal image is displaced.

PERCEIVING A STATIONARY WORLD

There are 2 questions that arise when we view stationary objects. The first arises from the fact that when we fixate a stationary object in the absence of a well-structured visual field, that object appears to move due to what is called the *autokinetic effect*. The second arises from the fact that when we change our fixation point from one direction to another, the retinal image is displaced but the world appears to remain stationary.

The Autokinetic Phenomenon

Put the subject in a perfectly dark room, and then turn on a pinpoint of light. In a short time, most subjects will report that the point of light is moving or drifting. The phenomenon has a long history, dating back at least to von Humbolt's observation in 1799 that stars seen through a telescope appear to drift about (Howard & Templeton, 1966). Aubert rediscovered it and named it the *autokinetic* (self-moving) phenomenon in 1887. A review of the early literature may be found in Guilford (1928); more recent research and theories are reviewed by Howard and Templeton (1966).

Various measures of autokinetic movement have been attempted, such as drawing it (Guilford & Dallenbach, 1928), having the subject actually control the light to bring it back to the starting point (Bridges & Bitterman, 1954), or having the subject try to touch the point of light (Sandström, 1951). The validity of each of these methods is difficult to assess.

Two general explanations for the phenomenon have received most recent attention, one in terms of eye movements and the other in terms of changes in muscle tonus. Let us consider the explanation based on eye movement first.

Explanations based on eye movements Movements of the eye, made while looking at a stationary distal stimulus, cause movements in the retinal image. Normally, we move our eyes about a great deal, but stationary objects nevertheless appear stationary. However, those eye movements are intentional. Unintentional eye movements, such as can be produced by moving the eye passively by pressing on it through the eyelid, do cause the visual field to appear to move (Helmholtz, 1866). Hoppe suggested in 1879 that involuntary eye movements are responsible for the displacement of the retinal image, which, in turn, results in what we now call *autokinetic movement*. Eye-movement photography (Guilford & Dallenbach, 1928) has not found eye movements to be correlated with autokinetic movement, but the methods used may have been inadequate for the purpose (Skolnik, 1940). Matin and MacKinnon (1964) used image stabilization techniques (see Chapter 9, p. 306) to reduce the displacement in the retinal image that would result from any horizontal eye movements that the subject might make. A normal, unstabilized view of the point of light (35 min in diameter) could be instantaneously substituted for the stabilized view. The subject indicated the direction of autokinetic movement by pressing switches. A much smaller number of horizontal movements was reported under the stabilized condition as compared to the normal viewing condition. This suggests that involuntary eye movements normally contribute to the autokinetic phenomenon.

But how can a point appear to move away from where it first appeared to be, namely straight ahead, yet remain clearly fixated? Something more than involuntary eye movements would also seem to be involved.

Explanations based on muscle tension The eye can change its apparent position even though it has not in fact moved, and remains fixated straight ahead. Subjects often report that their eyes pursue the target as it moves, even though the target really remains fixed (Carr, 1910; Adams, 1912; DeSisto & McLaughlin, 1968). Normally, of course, if the eye moves but a point of light continues to fall on the same part of the retina (for example, the fovea), the point of light will appear to move to a new location. Bruell and Albee (1955) propose that such a perceived change in location occurs *if and only if* the change in tension of the oculomotor muscles, that causes the eye movement, has been voluntarily initiated. If because of postural reflexes (see Chapter 4, p. 103) or because of fatigue, the eye is subjected to tension that would turn it to one side, say the left, a voluntary signal to increase the muscle tension in the opposite direction would be needed to maintain fixation. Because only that voluntary signal would have an effect on the perceived direction, this would be equivalent to having turned the eye to the right; because the object remains fixated on the fovea, it in turn would appear to have moved to the right. The following facts suggest that something like this does occur.[10]

Fixating a stimulus with the eyes held in one direction, which might be expected to fatigue one set of eye muscles, affects the direction of subsequent autokinetic movements (Carr, 1910; Gregory, 1959; Gregory & Zangwill, 1963). Adams (1912) and Luchins (1954) reported that if the subject's head is held so that the light must be fixated eccentrically, autokinetic movement increased in the direction to which the eyes were turned, and Battersby and his coworkers (1956) obtained similar results by turning the head and trunk to one side.

The kind of explanation given above is plausible only if we do not have very good proprioceptive information about the whereabouts of our eyes. There is now considerable

evidence strongly suggesting that that is indeed the case (Ludvigh, 1952; Merton, 1961; Matin & Kibler, 1966). For example, Matin and his colleagues (1966) presented subjects with a fixation target in an otherwise dark room; then they removed the target and had the subjects attempt to maintain their fixation in the same position during a 3-second interval in total darkness. After the 3 seconds had elapsed, a test flash was presented in various horizontal locations, and the subject had to say whether it appeared to the right or to the left of the previously viewed fixation target. Throughout this period, eye movements were monitored by using a technique involving contact lenses (Chapter 11, p. 374). Large involuntary eye movements were found to occur while the subject was trying to hold his fixation in darkness. When the test flash was presented, the subject's judgment of whether the flash was to the right or to the left of the fixation point was determined by whether it was to the right or to the left of wherever the fovea happened to be: no account was taken, apparently, of the fact that the eye had moved from its original position. This is, of course, in contrast with what we have previously said about the effects of *voluntary* eye movement, namely that an object appears to remain stable or stationary when voluntary eye movements are made, even though the retinal image of the object is displaced. Let us now consider how such stability might be achieved.

Stability of the World during Saccadic Eye Movements

The eye normally moves its fixation point several times a second, yet the objects in the world appear to remain fixed in space. This stability may be arrived at by a compensation procedure, in which a record is kept of the direction and amount that the eye is ordered to move, and this record (variously called the sense of innervation, by Helmholtz, 1866; the efferent copy, by von Holst, 1954; and the corollary discharge, by Teuber, 1960) is compared to the subsequent movement in the

---

[10] In order to evaluate such theories, we need more specific bases than have yet been offered for deciding which movements are voluntary and which are involuntary.

retinal image.[11] If the movements of the retinal image are exactly those that would be
produced by the eye movements alone, no
movement of the objects would be seen. We
shall see that something roughly like this does
occur with head movements. It is not now
clear to what extent this kind of compensation actually occurs with saccadic eye
movements, which are by far the most important source of movement in man's retinal
image. But let us briefly consider some of the
factors involved.

As we have seen (p. 521), we are far more
sensitive to relative than to absolute displacements in the retinal image. When a
saccade occurs, the entire visual image is
displaced, so that the parts of the visual field
have remained in an unmoving relationship
to each other. Perhaps this is why the world
remains stable despite the saccades (Duncker,
1929; Koffka, 1935; Gibson, 1954). Against this
argument, however, we can show that apparent movement does occur even when the
entire image is displaced, or when the eye
muscles are ordered to execute a saccade but
the eye movement itself is prevented from
occurring.

One old example is the apparent movement of the scene that occurs when the eyeball is moved passively by pressure through
the eyelid (p. 529). Presumably this happens
because no efferent copy is subtracted from
the retinal movement. It is not clear how
comparable this example is to a saccadic
displacement, however, because the velocity
of the image in this condition is relatively low,
whereas retinal displacement during a saccade might be too rapid to affect the hypothetical velocity-sensitive neural units (p.
522). The range of velocities within which
passive movement of the eye produces apparent movement of the scene is not now
known.

At the other extreme are cases in which

the image remains stationary on the retina,
yet movement is perceived as though a saccade had occurred. Thus, if the eye is immo-
bilized by paralysis of the muscles or by
mechanical means and the subject then tries
to turn his gaze to one side, the entire scene
appears to move in that direction (Helmholtz,
1866; Brindley & Merton, 1960). Some thought
will show that in both cases this is what we
would expect to happen if the saccade had
been executed and no corresponding re-
afference (that is, no visual consequence of
the eye movement) had occurred.

These arguments are not completely conclusive, however. They do suggest very
strongly that voluntary saccadic eye movements normally cause a change in the apparent direction signified by any given place on
the retina and that this change in apparent
direction can result in apparent movement.
However, this does not necessarily imply that
the subtraction of such a change in direction
is the reason why actual retinal displacement
fails to produce apparent movement when
such displacement results from saccadic eye
movements. This logical point must be noted
because there is some evidence that there
may not be any need for compensation, at
least for small saccadic displacements. Wallach and Lewis (1965), using an optical device
that changed the amount that the retinal
image was displaced by any saccade, showed
that subjects failed to notice displacements
that differed from the displacement that the
saccade should have produced. Similarly, in
an experiment by Sperling and Speelman
(1965), in which the onset of a subject's saccade electronically caused a displacement of
the stimulus, subjects failed to notice displacements of as much as 2°. Moreover, if a
light is presented to the eye during a voluntary saccade, in a room that is otherwise
completely dark, the apparent location of the
light shows that only a very small amount of
compensation for the eye movement has occurred (Matin, Matin, & Pearce, 1969).

In short, it is not clear at this time how
much of the stability of the visual world

---

[11] Information about the position of the eyes is now thought
to come only from these efferent records and from the
changes in visual stimulation that result from eye movements (see Chapter 11).

during saccadic eye movements is due to a compensatory mechanism and how much is due to the integrative processes by which successive views are fitted together into a single picture of the world. Almost every motion picture made over the last 30 years has cut back and forth from one camera viewpoint to another, and the observer usually has a good picture of the stable world within which actors move about even though no efferent copies or corollary discharges provide him with compensatory proprioceptive information (see the discussion of "maps" in Chapter 12, p. 454).

A stronger case can be made for the importance of compensatory processes that allow a stationary object to be perceived as stationary despite the movements of its retinal image that occur when the head and body are moving. The relevant experiments involve rearrangements of the relationship between head movement and the resulting movement of the retinal image, and we consider those experiments in the context of optical rearrangement (p. 544f.).

Comparison of Normal and Rearranged Vision

Visual and nonvisual localization of objects Purely visual information about where an object is located in space must, by itself, be ambiguous. We must therefore also use non-visual (proprioceptive) information about the disposition of our eyes, head, and body if our perception of the object's location is to be certain, and if our actions directed toward it are to be successfully executed. The study of how the visual and nonvisual sources of spatial information are fitted together calls quite naturally for experiments that disturb the normal relationship that exists between them. Various optical devices can alter or rearrange the retinal image that is produced by a given visual display and a given arrangement of the eyes, head, and body. These devices therefore have provided an important research tool in the study of perceived loca-

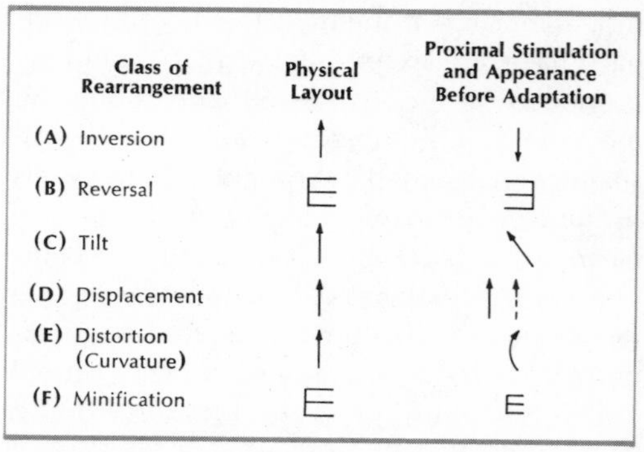

Figure 13.34. Classes of optical rearrangement.

tion, and of the perceptuomotor behaviors associated with this field of inquiry.

Experiments on rearranged vision If the spatial arrangement that we perceive in response to a particular retinal image is the result of what our tactual and kinesthetic experiences with objects in space have taught us (as the classical empiricist position would have it, pp. 465, 477), it may be possible to change our visual perceptions by changing the tactual experiences associated with that retinal image. We may do this by placing some optical device, like a prism or a mirror, in the path of the light entering the eye, to alter the retinal image that is produced by any arrangement of objects in space. Thus, mirrors and lenses can be used to invert, reverse, displace, tilt, curve, break, or "minify" the retinal image that is produced by a given display (Figure 13.34). Inasmuch as the physical arrangement of objects remains unchanged with respect to the observer's body and limbs, the rearranged retinal images will initially mislead any visually guided attempts that we make to touch those objects, and this in turn causes the observer to relearn the spatial meaning of his retinal images.

The hypothesis is that active movement and tactual experience with the world, while wearing devices that produce visual rearrangement, will result in a change in visual appearance that brings the latter into agreement with where things are localized by the sense of touch. We shall examine several attempts at adaptation to rearranged vision with this hypothesis in mind. A trickle of research on adaptation to rearranged vision, going back to 1866 (see Howard & Templeton, 1966), has become a torrent in the last decade, too diverse and unwieldy to review adequately here. Critical reviews by Smith and Smith (1962), Harris (1965), Howard and Templeton (1966), Rock (1966), Epstein (1967), and Taub and Berman (1968) cover much of the recent work.

Stratton (1896, 1897) wore inverting lenses to determine whether the top and bottom of the retinal image are inherently seen as down and up in the visual world, respectively (Figure 13.34A). In that case, he argued, the world would continue to appear inverted no matter how long he wore the lenses. Initially, of course, the world did appear upside down, but Stratton reported that after several days it occasionally appeared "right side up." This result led many psychologists (Carr, 1925, for example) to conclude that adaptation to wearing the prisms had resulted in a change in Stratton's visual perceptions, as such. Since then, Ewert (1930), Peterson and Peterson (1938), and Snyder and Pronko (1952) repeated Stratton's experiment; the latter two used procedures similar to those Stratton used, and obtained improvements in their abilities to behave in tasks that involved vision, but found no clear signs of change in the way the world looked. Thus, when Snyder was asked whether things looked upside down, he replied that although he had been unaware of it until the question was asked, things did look upside down when compared to the way they had looked before he put the glasses on.

A series of investigations by Kohler (1951, 1953, 1964) repeated and extended the rearrangement-adaptation experiments. In general, Kohler's results seemed strongly to support Stratton's conclusion. When rearranging spectacles are first put on, says Kohler, the world seems strange in various ways. Faces look unfamiliar; walking people seem to move mechanically, so that the up-and-down component, normally not noticed, becomes very apparent; and as the subject's head moves, the normally stationary world appears to swing about wildly. Behaviorally, of course, the subject is almost incapacitated.

If he is wearing reversing spectacles, for example, and he wants to touch an object that is objectively to his right, he will reach out toward his left. After some adaptation has occurred, the subject can negotiate streets, can "fence" with the experimenter, can ride a bicycle, and so on. Despite such effective motor performance, however, the visual world remains reversed in appearance. Adaptation does occur eventually in the sense that the world becomes more stable and does not swing around with each head movement, even while the subject performs complicated behavior (bicycling, among other activities). However, visual adaptation in other respects (uprightness as opposed to invertedness, correct left-right orientation as opposed to reversed appearance, and so on) seems to proceed in a curiously piecemeal fashion, judging from subjects' reports. Thus Kohler reports that some parts of the visual field are perceived correctly while other parts remain reversed; vehicles are correctly perceived as driving on the "right" side of the road, but their license numbers are seen as mirror images (1964, p. 155; see also Taylor, 1962). Finally, after many weeks, the subject achieves impressions that are, Kohler claims, almost completely "correct," even when he is viewing letters or numbers. That is, the process of adaptation does not seem to be in any sense a matter of learning to invert (or reverse) the whole visual field at once. This is certainly a bizarre phenomenon, and an explanation of it by Harris (1965) will be important in our further discussion of rearrangement-adaptation. The final stage in these experiments should be noted first, however. This is reached after adaptation has occurred,

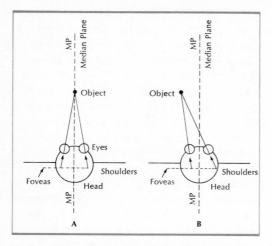

Figure 13.35. Eye movement and the *apparent straight ahead.* See text.

and the spectacles are removed. The visual field now appears rearranged to the unencumbered gaze, rearranged in a way that is complementary to the effects of the adaptation-producing optical devices. For example, after having adapted to reversing prisms (Figure 13.34B), Kohler reports that when these were removed, the subject saw the whole room as though it were reversed. As Rock points out (1966), such aftereffects are impressive evidence that changes have occurred in the *perceptual* system, inasmuch as the subject has no intellectual reason to believe that a correction of any sort is necessary when the device is no longer before his eyes.

Most of the behavioral aspects of the adaptation phenomena described by Kohler have since been replicated, using various kinds of rearrangement. However, it is not at all clear that *visual* perception has been relearned in the service of touch, kinesthesis, and proprioception, as is often inferred. We consider several of these phenomena in more detail.

Perception of "straight ahead" and adaptation to displacement If the eyes, head and trunk are all aligned as in Figure 13.35A, and some object lies in the median plane *MP*, the image falls on the fovea of each retina, and the object appears to be straight ahead. If the

eyes are turned so that the object's image no longer falls on the fovea, some account must be taken of the eyes' rotation if the subject is to continue to see the object as being straight ahead with respect to his body.

The proprioceptive information about the relative position of eye, head, and trunk are not all taken into account with unfailing accuracy. Thus, if the eyes are kept turned to the right, the position at which some object will be judged to be straight ahead (the *apparent straight ahead*) also shifts to the right (Fischer, 1915; Goldstein & Riese, 1923; Werner, Wapner, & Bruell, 1953). Moreover, if a luminous pattern or a pair of spots of light is viewed in the dark, with the leftmost edge of the pattern lying on the *MP* (that is, objectively straight ahead), the pattern appears to be displaced to the left and the apparent straight ahead is now somewhere to the right of the *MP* (Dietzel, 1924; Roelofs, 1935; Akishige, 1951). The apparent straight ahead is therefore shifted toward the pattern's center, and in fact the amount of the shift increases with the width of the pattern (Bruell & Albee, 1955).

Active and passive experience What happens when we change the relationship between proprioception and vision? In 1866, Helmholtz reported that when he looked at an object while wearing prisms which deflected the visual image to the left (as in Figure 13.34D), and then closed his eyes and reached for the object, he initially made a leftwards error. (His eyes were closed during this test so that his reaching would not be guided by continuous vision of his hand approaching the object.) This error was quickly corrected by reaching for the object several times with one hand while he watched that hand through the prism. After having learned to do this, if he removed the prisms, gazed steadily at the object, and then closed his eyes and tried to touch it, he missed the object by reaching too far to the right. Let us reconsider Figure 13.35 in terms of what it implies concerning visually guided actions.

If the eyes, head, and trunk are all aligned as in Figure 13.35A, and the object lies in the median plane *MP,* the image falls on the fovea of the retina, and the hand will touch the object when extended toward the *MP.* However, this does not mean, of course, that any time an object's image is on the fovea that the hand must reach to the median plane to touch it. If the object is displaced to one side, and the eyes or head are turned so that the image still falls on the fovea (Figure 13.35B), the motor system must bring the hand to a position that is no longer on *MP.* Movements that are directed towards objects in space must be guided by some sensorimotor mechanism that combines the information in the retinal image with the information about the relative positions or motions of eye, head and trunk.

In 1961, Held proposed that many kinds of adaptation to rearrangement result from changes in these sensorimotor mechanisms, changes that establish a new correlation between the efferent neural commands that produce the subject's actions, on the one hand, and the visual changes that result from those actions, or *reafference* (von Holst, 1954; see pp. 530f.), on the other hand. For this kind of adaptation to occur, therefore, the subject must engage in active (voluntary) movement while he is wearing the distorting devices and must simultaneously receive the changes in retinal image that result from his movement. Because Held and his colleagues (Held & Bossom, 1961; Held & Freedman, 1963; Held & Hein, 1963; Held & Bauer, 1967) propose that the same process may operate both in the infant's development of these sensorimotor mechanisms and in the adult's adaptation to rearrangement, study of the latter may tell us how the mechanisms that maintain spatially oriented behaviors develop in the first place.

Held's proposal is not the classical empiricist theory. Although active movement is necessary to the kinds of adaptation that he postulates, and although he assumes that the characteristics of such sensorimotor changes

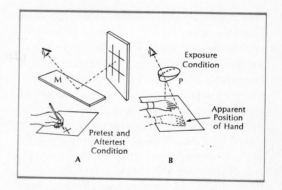

Figure 13.36. Prism adaptation experiment. See text. (After Held & Gottleib, 1958.)

reveal the nature of the processes by which the infant first acquires the ability to perform the spatial behavior in question, Held does not maintain that *all* spatial behaviors are learned, nor that *all* visual adaptation requires active movement. In fact, he and his colleagues have gone to considerable pains in the attempt to remove from their data the effects of those kinds of adaptation that can occur without active movement and without reafference.

Held and his colleagues have used more objective and sensitive versions of Helmholtz' procedure, measuring the effects of the adaptation or exposure period (B, in Figure 13.36) on perceptuomotor tasks that are administered to the subject before and after adaptation (A in Figure 13.36). For example (Held & Gottleib, 1958), the subject looks into the mirror *M* during a pretest and again during an aftertest session. The mirror hides his hand with which he is to mark the apparent location of the target that he sees reflected in the mirror. During the adaptation period, the mirror is removed, and the subject views his arm through the prism *P.* Held and Hein (1958) found that subjects who moved their arms voluntarily while watching them through a prism that produced a lateral displacement (Figure 13.34D) subsequently displayed a considerable degree of adaptation, whereas subjects whose arms were moved for them during the exposure period displayed no adaptation. Subjects' actions and the visual consequences of the actions must be virtually simultaneous if prism adaptation is to occur; a delay of even 0.3 sec between the hand movement and the visual feedback from it prevents adaptation from occurring (Held, Efstathiou, & Greene, 1966).[12]

Using different adaptation and test procedures, Held and Bossom (1961) had a subject walk around while wearing displacing prisms. Subsequently his head was placed in a cylindrical drum, the inner surface of which bore a vertical line, and he was asked to position himself so that the vertical line appeared to be straight ahead. This test revealed a lateral displacement of approximately the predicted amount and direction. Most importantly, however, subjects who had been passively transported over the same path in a wheelchair, so that they were in the same visual environment but were undergoing only *passive* movement, did not obtain the same aftereffects. However, we cannot as yet conclude that active movement and reafference were *necessary,* in a direct sense, for this adaptation to occur, nor that the adaptation that was obtained resulted from recorrelation of the sensorimotor mechanisms.

First, we should note that there are several experiments in which passive subjects adapted to displacement, sometimes as strongly as did active ones (Wertheimer & Arena, 1959; Weinstein et al., 1964; Pick & Hay, 1965; Singer & Day, 1966), and there is some evidence to suggest that if the subject receives adequate information that the visual field is displaced, adaptation will occur even in the absence of any movement. Thus, passive inspection of one's feet through displacing prisms produced some adaptation (presumably because of the information provided

by the discrepancy between the felt and seen locations of the feet), as measured subsequently by a pointing task (Wallach, Kravitz, & Lindauer, 1963). Similarly, Howard, Craske, and Templeton (1965) showed that prodding the subject's lips with a rod, which was made to appear in a displaced position by use of mirrors, also produced adaptation when measured by a pointing task. In other words, it is possible that what is important about active movement is not the action per se, but rather the greater information about the nature of the visual rearrangement that such movement makes available (see p. 540; for further discussion of this viewpoint, see Rock, 1966).

Why did the passive subjects show no adaptation in the experiment of Held and Hein? Perhaps the felt position of a passive hand does not offer the required information that the visual field is displaced. In fact, Hay, Pick, and Ikeda (1965) found that as soon as subjects looked at their hands through a prism, *visual capture* occurred, and the felt position of their hands coincided with the position at which their hands appeared to be in the visual field, not with their actual position in space. There is considerable evidence of this kind to indicate that vision dominates proprioception when the 2 modalities are brought into conflict (Gibson, 1933; Nielsen, 1963; Rock and Victor, 1964; Over, 1966; Rock, 1966; Rock and Harris, 1967). Perhaps, in the experiments of Held and his colleagues, the discrepancy between vision and proprioception made itself felt only when the subject found that an arm movement that normally brought the hand to the median plane in space, for example, and to the fovea of the eye, now failed to do so.

This brings us to the second point, namely that the adaptation that is obtained in these experiments may not result from a recorrelation of sensorimotor mechanisms, but from relatively restricted changes in one modality or the other. The subject has to perform visually guided actions while wearing prisms that change the normal relationship between vision, on the one hand, and action and proprio-

---

[12]This experiment was performed by having the subject move a rod that controlled the motion of the luminous line on an oscilloscope. The line was superimposed on the position of the hand, which was hidden from the direct sight of the subject, by a mirror, and the delay was introduced by means of audio tape recorders. Video tape recorders were first used to study the effects of delays in visual feedback by Smith, McGrary, and Smith (1960); a discussion of such research is to be found in Smith and Smith (1962).

ception, on the other hand. The discrepancy would indeed be resolved if the visual appearance associated with a particular retinal image changed so that it agreed with the information provided by proprioception; this is what one might expect from the classical empiricist viewpoint. Harmony would also be restored, however, if proprioception and the motor system accommodated themselves to vision.[13] Walls (1951a,b,c) pointed out that Stratton's findings were at least as well explained by the second of these alternatives as by the first, and the data obtained by Held and his colleagues have been similarly interpreted as being due to changes in proprioception (McFarland, 1962; Harris, 1963, 1965; Hochberg, 1963; Hamilton, 1964; Hay & Pick, 1964).

Thus, in a review of research on adaptation, Harris (1965) finds most of the data to be consistent with the view that such adaptation consists of changes in the felt position of the subject's arm, head, or eyes. If the adaptation consisted of changes in the visually perceived location of objects a hand-pointing test should reveal those changes regardless of which hand is used. In several experiments, however, in which subjects watched one hand through a displacing prism while pointing with that hand at targets or while moving it back and forth, evidence of adaptation was obtained only when the subject was tested with the hand that had been used during practice (Scholl, 1926; Harris, 1963; Hamilton, 1964). This supports the view that the felt position of the hand, rather than the apparent visual position of the target, is changed by the adaptation. That is, when his arm is really pointing in one direction (for example, straight ahead), the subject feels that it is pointing in another direction (for example, 10° to the right). Additional support for this interpretation was given by the finding that subjects showed the effects of adaptation by

making errors of position when they pointed with their adapted hands at targets even when they could see neither the hand nor the target: this occurred when, with eyes closed, they pointed at a sound-emitting target, at their nonadapted hand, or "straight ahead" (Scholl, 1926; Harris, 1963; Hay & Pick, 1963; McLaughlin & Rifkin, 1965). They also made the appropriate errors in judging the distance between their adapted and their nonadapted hands, while blindfolded (Harris, 1965).

The absence of intermanual transfer occurs only under certain conditions.[14] Thus, in the experiment described by Helmholtz, in which he watched one of his hands while wearing prisms, the effect of adaptation was shown by the other hand as well, even though he had kept it out of sight during the adaptation period. He concluded, therefore, that it was not the felt position of his hand that had changed, but rather his judgment about the direction of his gaze, because a change in the latter should affect all of his visually guided behaviors. In fact, although a subject who is instructed to look straight ahead before adaptation does so without appreciable error, photographic records show that after adaptation his response to the same instruction is to rotate his eyes in the direction of the displacement (Kalil & Freedman, 1966; Craske, 1967; McLaughlin & Webster, 1967). This fact could account for part of the adaptation to displacing prisms, and changes in the felt

---

[13] It is now generally believed (Chapter 11) that the muscles of the oculomotor system provide no proprioceptive information. Instead, "proprioception" and "felt position" here refer to the calibration of the nonvisual systems that guide and execute spatial behaviors, including movements of the head and eyes.

[14] The conditions for obtaining much or little adaptation with the unexposed arm are not clear at present. Harris (1963) and Hamilton (1964) thought that intermanual transfer was due to a change in felt head position, and that this occurred only when the subject was free to move his head during adaptation. In fact, with unrestricted movements, adaptation effects have been obtained with both arms even if *neither* had been visible through the prisms (Bossom & Held, 1957), and subjects described an object as appearing straight ahead when it was actually displaced to one side (Held & Bossom, 1961; Kohler, 1964). But this does not vitiate Harris' thesis: The fact that *some* conditions can be found under which intermanual transfer does not occur suffices to cast doubt on any interpretation of adaptation as a change in vision per se. Those cases in which intermanual transfer does occur may be attributed to changes in judged head or eye position. For example, prism-adaptation can also result in changes in the judgment of the direction in which the eye is pointed, even when the head has been kept fixed during adaptation (Kalil & Freedman, 1966; Craske, 1967; McLaughlin & Webster, 1967), and this, as we shall see, should also result in intermanual transfer.

positions of other parts of the body might well account for the remainder. In fact, Hay and Pick (1966) have obtained separate measures that indicate that the proprioceptive change in the arm, and a change in felt direction of gaze (or eye posture) develop concurrently, but at different rates, during protracted adaptation to displacement by prisms.

The proprioceptive-change hypothesis has not gone unchallenged. The hypothesis predicts that if only one hand is adapted, it will point incorrectly no matter what the task is, and with the same size and direction of error in all cases. This result has been obtained, as we noted above, in pointing at visible targets, at sound-emitting targets, and "straight ahead." Efstathiou, Bauer, Greene, and Held (1967) have described two exceptions, however: They found the error to be smaller when the subject pointed at his unadapted hand, and they found that no significant error was made when the blindfolded subject was asked to mark the remembered locations of four pins for which he had learned to reach, while blindfolded, before adapting. The authors interpret these findings as follows: Proprioception or felt position of the hand has not changed. Instead, what has changed is the correlation between the direction of the hand movement that the subject makes when he wishes to touch any target, and the direction in which his head would face if he were to orient it toward that target.[15]

It is not clear, however, to what extent this interpretation really conflicts with the expla-

nation based on a change in the felt position. "Felt position" cannot be directly observed; it has to be inferred from subjects' behaviors. There may be several criteria for deciding "felt position," only one of which (the relationship between head and hand, for example) is involved in the adaptation that occurred in these experiments. The 2 explanations may yet turn out to be supplementary (or even equivalent), rather than being irreconcilable.

What is important to us here is that in one explanation the motor-proprioceptive system of one arm has changed, and in the other, it is the correlation between the motor-proprioceptive system of the arm and that of the head, in judging visual direction, that has altered. Neither explanation predicates a change in vision itself.

Perception of "upright" and adaptation to tilt A line that is upright with respect to gravity may be tilted in the visual field, and vice versa, depending on the subject's posture and position. Thus, the subject must use information about the orientation both of his head and of the line in his retinal image if he is to judge correctly whether the line is vertical. Howard and Templeton (1966) have recently reviewed research on spatial orientation; here we are concerned only with certain kinds of conflict between visual and proprioceptive information and with the adaptation that results when the relationship between the image's retinal orientation and the subject's posture is changed.

As with the "straight ahead," the compensation for changes in posture is not perfectly maintained. Thus, Aubert (1861) noted that after he tilted his head to one side for a few seconds while looking at a luminous line in an otherwise dark room, the line appeared to be tilted in the opposite direction. Aubert concluded that this occurred because we come to underestimate the tilt of the head after it has been held for some time in the tilted position.[16]

---

[15]By this theory, the direction in which a subject reaches for a target is determined by the actual or potential orientation of his head toward that target. Adaptation to displacement changes the set of reaching movements of the adapted arm that go with a given orientation of the head. In the "remembered locations" task, the subject presumably guides his hand by the arm's proprioception alone, without orienting his head, and so no adaptation effects appear. In pointing at the unexposed hand, if the subject guided his pointing solely by the relationships between each hand and his head, the fact that the correlation between head-hand orientation had been changed for one hand and not for the other would result in a displacement in pointing. But because the subject can also match up the positions of the two hands on the basis of their felt positions (which the authors say remain unchanged), the total effect of adaptation is less in this task than in pointing at a visual target.

[16]We saw that displacement adaptation is in part attributable to changes in the position at which the eyes are felt

Unlike the "straight ahead," we normally have good visual indications of the upright, as in vertical trees and walls, horizontal lakes and floors. We can therefore often rely on vision alone in judging uprightness, taking little account of proprioception. In fact, Koffka (1935) maintained that the main lines of the visual field determine the directions of the apparent vertical and horizontal. When the visual framework is tilted with respect to gravity, and is therefore brought into conflict with proprioception, the visual indications often do determine what is judged to be vertical.[17] Thus, Wertheimer (1912) reported that when he looked into a tilted mirror to see a room in which he was standing, the room soon "righted itself" and looked upright or less tilted.

In more formal versions of this experiment, Asch and Witkin (1948a, b) had subjects judge when a pivoted rod was set vertically in terms of the room in which they were standing. The rod was in a model room which itself was tilted. Using a simpler apparatus, Witkin and Asch (1948b) placed a pivoted rod inside a tilted square frame, and with nothing but the rod and frame in view, the subject had to judge when the rod was vertical. In both experiments, the subject's chair could also be tilted. In general, tilting the visual framework affected subjects' judgments of when the line was vertical more than did tilting the chair. Subsequent research has generally confirmed the finding that the visual framework affects the judgment of uprightness (Curran & Lane, 1962; Mann, 1952), but not all research has done so (Gibson & Mowrer, 1938; Boring, 1952), and subjects vary greatly in their susceptibility to the effects of the visual framework.[18]

Even if the effects of the framework were more complete and more reliable than they are, the framework could not be considered the *necessary* determinant of apparent tilt. Subjects can adjust a luminous line to the vertical in an otherwise dark room without any framework (Neal, 1926), and they can even make a reliable judgment of whether a line is parallel to their bodies when they are lying supine (Rock, 1954). There is thus a relationship between an object's orientation in the retinal image and its apparent uprightness (or its alignment with the subject's body). This relationship can readily be changed by means of prisms that rotate or tilt the visual field, as in Figure 13.34C, providing another means of studying adaptation to rearrangement.

Thus, Mikaelian and Held (1964) had subjects wear prisms that tilted the visual field 20° during the exposure conditions. Before and after wearing the prisms, the subjects had to set a luminous line, viewed in an otherwise dark room, to an apparently vertical position. Two conditions of exposure were used. Subjects who were passively wheeled along a corridor displayed very little adaptation to tilt (1.9°). In the active condition, in which subjects walked back and forth in the same hallway, an adaptation effect of 6.8° was found after an hour of exposure, and 3 selected subjects achieved full compensation (approximately 20°) after an additional 2 hours. Unselected subjects stop short of complete adaptation, with little additional increment occurring after the first hour (Ebenholtz, 1966). The amount of the adaptation to tilt that is obtained under such conditions is a surprisingly simple linear function of the degree of optical tilt that is produced by the adapting prism (Morant & Beller, 1965; Ebenholtz, 1966), and is less when measured with the eye that was covered during adaptation (Ebenholtz, 1966).

The fact that the passive subjects of Mikaelian and Held showed any tilt-adaptation at all raises the same set of issues that we discussed in connection with displacement-adaptation. Because

---

to be looking straight ahead (p. 537). Ogle (1950) suggested that rotation of the eyes about the visual axis (torsion) might account for tilt normalization, but Howard and Templeton (1964b) measured eye torsion photographically under conditions in which tilt adaptation occurred and found no measurable torsion.

[17] In the amusement parks, rooms are sometimes set up in which balls appear to roll uphill (of course, it is the entire room that is tilted), or artificial scenery swings back and forth outside the windows so that the room itself seems to rock, and the people in it feel the appropriate (but illusory) kinesthetic sensations and dizziness.

[18] In fact, individual differences have been used as a measure of "field dependence," a personality variable that has emerged from research correlating performance on these visual orientation tasks with other perceptual and personality tests (Witkin et al., 1954).

Held and his colleagues are primarily concerned with those kinds of adaptation which result from a change in the sensorimotor mechanisms, they have tried to eliminate or to measure separately any adaptation that is due to changes solely in vision or solely in proprioception. Thus, because we know that adaptation to tilt occurs even when a motionless subject views a tilted line (Gibson, 1933; see Chapter 12, p. 466), the Gibson "normalization" effect would be expected to produce some adaptation to the vertical lines in the room, which would be tilted in the subject's retinal image because of the prisms he is wearing. Furthermore, as Mack (1967) has suggested, the "righting" effect of a tilted visual framework noted by Wertheimer and discussed above (p. 539) may also contribute to the adaptation. Mikaelian and Held (1964) therefore went on to eliminate these components by repeating their experiment in a room in which all the subject could see was a set of luminous spheres set in a random arrangement that contained no straight lines. In fact, the random stimulus field gave no clue as to the nature of the rearrangement produced by the prisms, as long as the observer remained motionless. If subjects moved actively during the inspection period, they subsequently displayed adaptation effects of about 2°, 2 selected subjects giving effects of about 5°. Subjects who were wheeled around passively during the exposure period showed no adaptation effects, so that tilt adaptation appears to depend on active movement under these conditions. As in the case of displacement-adaptation (p. 536), however, what might be important about the active movement is the information about the nature of the rearrangement that it offers. Thus, for example, a streaming movement of the spheres across the visual field of the subject who has been passively moved may offer few cues as to the nature of the prism that he is wearing, whereas the active subject would be able to learn, for example, that each horizontal rotation of his head to the left results not in the usual horizontal movement of the visual field to the right, but in a skewed (tilted) movement over the retina (see Held & Bossom, 1961; Rock, 1966).

As to the nature of tilt adaptation, we have seen that there are at least 2 possible components (normalization and frame effects) that do not require active movement. The third component, which was isolated by Mikaelian and Held in their experiments with luminous spheres, may reflect changes in the sensorimotor mechanisms, as Held proposes.

Or the visual appearance that results from a given retinal image may have changed, as the classical empiricist explanation suggests. However, it is just as plausible to assume that a line that appears upright on the retina continues to appear upright with respect to the subject's head, but that his head or body now feels tilted, when it is really upright; that is, that proprioception rather than vision has changed (McFarland, 1962; Hochberg, 1963). The general dominance of vision over proprioception in the perception of the upright (p. 539) makes this last alternative as likely as the others. There is at present no direct evidence to this point.

One may ask whether all of this discussion of proprioceptive change is not irrelevant, anyway, because Stratton and Kohler both reported that the appearance of the world actually changed as a result of adaptation. True, Stratton and Kohler do say, in some places, that the world's visual appearance changed in the course of adaptation, but, as we have seen in connection with problems connected with the perception of color and of shape (pp. 426, 451), perceptual reports cannot in general be taken at face value. Closer examination of Stratton's and Kohler's descriptions of their experiences lends plausibility to the view that it is touch and proprioception that have changed, not vision. For detailed analyses of their reports, see Walls (1951) and Harris (1965). If it seems odd to question these observers' own conclusions about their own experiences, note that they showed considerable uncertainty about the matter themselves.

Left-right and adaptation to reversal   Little is known about the discrimination of right from left. Children can discriminate right from left on their own persons by six years of age, but they cannot discriminate right from left on other people until later (Piaget, 1926; Swanson & Benton, 1955). Piaget considers this difference to be a "development away from egocentric thought." Howard and Templeton (1966) point out, however, that one

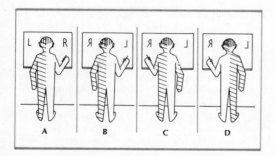

Figure 13.37. A subject's perceptions during the course of adaptation to reversed vision according to the proprioceptive-change hypothesis. In all cases perception of letters is visual; perception for the subject's head and body is proprioceptive. A. The actual physical arrangement. B. The subject's perceptions when he first puts on reversing goggles. C. The subject's perceptions at an intermediate stage of adaptation, with only his arms adapted. D. The subject's perceptions at an advanced stage of adaptation. (Harris, 1965.)

always has the same relation to one's own body, but not to other peoples' bodies, so that the constancy of the former makes the discrimination a much simpler task.

Unlike devices that tilt the visual field, which will normally offer good visual indications to the subject that the field has been tilted (p. 539), an optical device that reverses right for left will present little indication of that reversal to a passive subject. An active subject, of course, obtains visual feedback that reveals the nature of the optical rearrangement. As we have seen (p. 533), Kohler reports that active subjects undergo a curious "piecemeal" adaptation to reversing prisms. Let us now consider Harris' explanation of how this piecemeal adaptation would be accounted for if it is proprioception and not vision that is changing. Imagine a subject looking at the blackboard in Figure 13.37A. When he first puts on reversing prisms, he feels his right hand to be near the side of the blackboard that he sees on the right-hand side of the visual field, namely the side with the reversed L on it (Figure 13.37B). If he now looks at his hand, adaptation begins. When

he moves his hand to the right, he sees it moving to the left, and he soon begins to *feel* it to be moving to the left. In fact, this reversal of his proprioceptive perceptions may even make him write letters backwards while blindfolded, as Harris and Harris found (summarized by Rock & Harris, 1967). Similarly, because his right hand looks nearer to the reversed R on the blackboard than to the L, that hand *feels* nearer to the reversed R than to the L: that is, felt location of the limb comes to match its seen location, as in the experiments on displacement. When the subject is asked at this stage which end of the blackboard appears to be on his right, he should answer that the side with the reversed R does, if he asks himself which side is nearest his right hand (which has changed its felt location). During this stage of adaptation, the reversed writing on the blackboard is illegible, so that we get what looks to the experimenter like piecemeal visual adaptation. In time, the subject also learns to read writing that is reversed, as he would do even without mirrors or prisms, if he were continually confronted by mirror writing. It is easy to see, therefore, why Kohler might conclude that "mirrorwise seeing" had been established as a result of the adaptation, even if the change were primarily proprioceptive and not visual.

The explanation based on proprioceptive change must still be considered a tentative one. For one thing, we have seen that there are displacement-adaptation effects that do not seem to fit it (see Efstathiou et al., p. 538). For another, adaptation to curvature distortion of the retinal image presents a critical problem for a proprioceptive-change hypothesis.

Adaptation to curvature and distortion It is relatively easy to say, of a change in the relationship between vision and proprioception, that proprioception has changed. If the adaptation consists of a rearrangement of relationships within the visual field, however, it would be more difficult to escape the conclusion that it is vision that has changed

(Hochberg, 1963). Adaptation to curvature may provide such a case.

If a subject wears a prism which distorts the visual field in such a way that straight lines initially appear curved, adaptation will occur, and the lines come to look straighter (p. 465). After the prisms are removed, straight lines look curved in the opposite direction (Wundt, 1902; Kohler, 1964; Pick & Hay, 1964). This adaptation might be due, at least in part, to the normalization effect that Gibson (1933) had shown to occur with curved lines (p. 466). To avoid any Gibson normalization effect, Held and Rekosh (1963) used a method similar to that of the second experiment of Mikaelian and Held (1964). Each subject wore prisms while he was exposed to a visual field that was filled with an irregular array of spots. Before and after the exposure period, the subjects adjusted a line of varying curvature until it looked straight. One group of subjects, who had walked around during the exposure period, showed a curvature aftereffect; that is, the line had to be curved in the opposite direction to the distortion produced by the prism in order to look straight. Another group of subjects, who had been moved around in a wheel chair during the exposure period, showed no aftereffect. This demonstrates the existence of a curvature aftereffect which cannot be attributed to a line-normalization phenomenon, for no lines were visible in the field during the exposure period.

> Another demonstration that curvature after-effects can occur without normalization is given in an experiment by Festinger and his colleagues (1967). Taylor (1962) had reported that curvature aftereffects could be obtained after adaptation with a prism that was mounted on a contact lens (that is, on a lens that rides on the front of the eye; see Chapter 11, p. 374). Festinger and his colleagues had their subjects view an apparently straight line while wearing such a distorting contact lens. The optical effect of the prism was such as to make objectively straight lines appear curved, so that the line that the subjects were inspecting had to be objectively curved in order for it to appear straight. The subjects were instructed to look back and forth along the apparently straight line; head movements were pre-

> vented by means of a clamping device. Despite the fact that the line appeared to be straight, of course, the subject's eye would actually have to execute a set of saccadic movements that corresponded to the objective curvature of the line if the line were to be kept on the fovea. These subjects displayed a curvature aftereffect when they removed the contact lens. Inasmuch as the line had been adjusted to compensate for the curvature produced by the prism during the adaptation period, these aftereffects cannot be attributed to normalization.

In the Held-Rekosh experiment, which used prism spectacles, active movements of the head or body were needed to obtain the curvature aftereffects, if only because without such movements the subject had little or no evidence of the optical rearrangement: The eye movements needed to bring one or another part of the retinal image to the fovea are not changed by prism spectacles. With the prisms mounted on contact lenses, as they were in the experiment of Festinger and his coworkers, the relationship between retinal image and eye movements has been rearranged: For example, a curved path of eye movements is needed to scan a line that produces a straight retinal image. Under these conditions, head movements are unnecessary for the aftereffects to occur. Thus, in both experiments, active movements were needed to obtain the aftereffects, but in the second case, movement of the eyes was sufficient.

Not all active movement results in adaptation, however. Festinger and his colleagues (1967) and Burnham (1968) performed a series of experiments to show that only those actions that require the subject to learn to make a new set of movements in response to the pattern of retinal stimulation will produce the curvature aftereffect. In these experiments, subjects wore prism spectacles while shooting (with light beams) at a moving target. The target bore a photocell, and gave an audible signal when the light beam hit it. Adaptation and aftereffects were obtained in the case of subjects who could see neither their hands nor the light beam (because it was infrared light, in that condition). Other subjects shot at the target with visible light beams and could therefore perform the task by purely visual aiming. These subjects showed no adaptation. Only those subjects who were forced to learn to make new pointing arm movements in response to the rearranged retinal image showed adaptation when they were subsequently tested, even though all subjects executed similar overt movements.[19]

It is difficult, but not impossible, to attempt an explanation of curvature adaptation in terms of nonvisual change. For example, Harris (1965) has suggested that perhaps after adaptation the subject feels that his eyes have followed a straight line when they have actually moved along a curve. This would make the change a proprioceptive one, and from this explanation we would expect that the curvature aftereffects would not be obtained if the subject had to make his curvature judgments without moving his eyes. Alternatively, we may note that the visual property of apparent straightness is not uniquely tied to a particular property of the retinal image: A line which appears to be straight when it is fixated with the eyes in one position of the head appears to be curved when fixated with the eyes in another position (Helmholtz, 1866; see Chapter 12, p. 466n). We might argue that in the curvature adaptation experiments the purely visual appearances remain unchanged but that there is a change in the criterion for "straightness," for a given position of the eyes.

It may seem like quibbling to argue in this way about whether the change that occurs in the course of curvature-adaptation is visual or not. There are effects of adaptation to rearrangement that seem unassailably visual, and we consider these next.

Visual changes in adaptation to rearranged vision When prisms are used to achieve optical rearrangement, color fringes are produced at each contour between regions of different luminances in the field of view, and these fringes result in both adaptation and

aftereffects (Hay, Pick, & Rosser, 1964; Kohler, 1964) that must be classed as visual. They do not seem to involve any need for active movement. It seems reasonable to regard them as a different kind of phenomenon from those we have been discussing, an adaptation phenomenon involving relatively peripheral mechanisms such as receptive fields (McCollough, 1965). In any case, they provide no clear implications for the explanation of space perception.

More to the present point is the work on adaptation to minification by Rock and his colleagues. In our earlier discussion of apparent size (p. 509), we saw that there was some evidence that subjects can respond to the absolute size, s, of the retinal image. As Rock points out (1966), if we could respond only to *relationships* within the visual field, any change in the overall size of the retinal image which leaves those relationships unchanged should have no effect on apparent size. Nevertheless, reducing the size of the entire field of view by looking at objects reflected in a convex mirror makes them look smaller, even if one's field of view is restricted to the minified scene. This implies that the visual system maintains some memory or *trace* of the retinal image size that was produced by each object in the scene, at its distance from the eye, before the minifying device was employed. Rock argues that the changes that occur during adaptation in general are in the subject's memories or traces of those features of the retinal image that correspond to the object-property in question (straightness, uprightness, size, and so forth). This is similar to the classical empiricist explanation of perception (see pp. 466, 532, 546). To Rock, however, the primary source of information about the object properties is visual, not kinesthetic. The sight of one's own body, or of familiar objects which have a known shape and size, would therefore be sufficient to bring about adaptation, and active movement would not in principle be necessary to obtain adaptation.

Rock (1965) and his collaborators had sub-

---

[19]Festinger, like Taylor (1962), supports a local sign theory in which the consciousness of any line or shape in the visual field *is* the readiness to perform the movements needed to point the eyes (or the arm) at any point on it (see Chapter 12, p. 467), so to him the distinction between vision and proprioception would be an empty one in this case.

jects view a 12-inch line in a lighted room from a distance of two feet. The subjects then had to match that length from memory, using a luminous line of variable length that they viewed in an otherwise dark room. This comprised the pretest. They were then exposed to a scene whose reflection they viewed in a convex (minifying) mirror. Their view was restricted to their head, trunk, arms, hands, and various objects on a table. After the exposure conditions, they used the luminous line, viewed in darkness, to match their memories of the original 12-inch standard. Subjects who had been in a control condition, in which a plane mirror was used, showed no difference between the pretest and aftertest. Subjects who had viewed a minified image, reflected by a convex mirror, showed a significant decrease in the length of the line that matched their memory of the standard. There was no difference between subjects who had watched the scene while they drew, played checkers, and so on, and those who simply looked at the scene. Thus, we may conclude that active movement is not necessary for adaptation to minification.

But we should reconsider what is meant by the distinction between active and passive adaptation. As was suggested earlier, in the discussion on whether and why subjects are able to respond to retinal size per se (p. 510), the angular size subtended by any part of the visual field has adaptive significance in guiding eye movements, and may be associated with a saccade of corresponding magnitude. Minification increases the proportion of any seen object's extent that is traversed by a given saccade, and the judged size of that saccadic movement might change in consequence of experience with minified images. That is, the essential activity in adaptation to minification may consist of eye movements made in scanning the scene.

As in our similar discussion of curvature-adaptation, this is merely speculation, but in our final example we shall see experimental evidence that a recorrelation between eye movements and apparent motion in the vis-

ual field can be established in the course of adaptation to rearrangement.

Adaptation to rearranged visual effects of head movement   When optical rearranging devices, such as prisms, are first put on, the world appears to swing around wildly. Let us first see why this should happen. Consider an object at some distance from the observer, and 10° to the right of the median plane when he keeps his eyes straight ahead. If the observer turns his head 10° to the right, without wearing any rearranging devices, that object now lies in the median plane and is imaged on his fovea when he looks straight ahead. If he is wearing reversing spectacles, however, after turning to the right the image will now fall still further to the left of the fovea. The direction of retinal movement produced by any head movement has been changed by the prisms, and the eye movements that would normally compensate for the head movement (Chapter 11, p. 384) will no longer do so. Wallach and Kravitz (1965a,b) and Posin (described by Rock, 1966) independently used very similar procedures to demonstrate that adaptation does indeed occur to these rearranged relationships between body movements and retinal image movements, as Stratton and Kohler reported.

As their test condition, Wallach and Kravitz had the subject wear headgear so arranged that it projected a visual target to a curved screen. The subject sat before this screen in an otherwise dark room, and rotated his head. A variable-ratio transmission device was used to vary the relationship between the amount of head rotation that was made and the amount of target movement that this rotation produced. The subject's task was to say whether the target was stationary. In the pretest, the mean setting chosen was one in which the target was in fact stationary. The subject was then given an adapting condition, in which his head movement resulted in a different rate of retinal image movement than normally occurs. Specifically, the subjects were required to wear minifying spectacles for

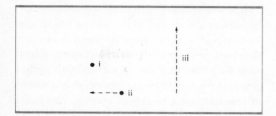

Figure 13.38. Stimulus movement (*ii*) contingent on head movement (*iii*). See text. (After Hay, 1968.)

6 hours, which reduced the rate of image displacement caused by head movement. In the post-test, the amount of movement of the target that the subjects judged to be stationary when the head was moving had changed as a result of exposure to the adapting condition. Both Wallach and Kravitz (1965b) and Posin (Rock, 1966) found such adaptation to occur both with active movement by the subject, and when the subject was moved around by the experimenter.

But what does passive movement mean in this case? Even when the experimenter rotates the subject, compensatory movements of his eyes occur, movements that normally operate to keep the image stable on the retina when the head or body is rotated (Chapter 11, p. 385). Perhaps the major effect of the adaptation to rearranged head-image movements consists of a recorrelation between the direction and magnitude of a head movement, on the one hand, and the compensatory eye movements that it elicits, on the other. Experiments by Hay (1968) suggest that a very similar kind of recorrelation can occur quite rapidly. In his experiments, the subject viewed two spots of light in an otherwise dark room. A bite-board apparatus both registered the subject's head movements, and constrained them to a vertical plane. One of the 2 spots was stationary (Figure 13.38 *i*). The other (*ii*) was moved horizontally each time the subject moved his head vertically, by means of an electronic coupling of spot *ii* with the bite board. In one adapting condition, the subjects were instructed to keep spot *ii*

fixated while they moved their heads. This required them to learn to execute diagonal eye movements correlated with their vertical head movements. During the course of this adaptation, spot *ii* came to appear stationary while spot *i* seemed to make a diagonal movement across the field. In a second adapting condition, the subjects merely fixated the stationary spot, *i*, while they moved their heads vertically. This required them to make only the usual vertical eye movements that are required to compensate for vertical head movements. After adaptation, a test condition was employed in which both spots were held stationary, and the subject moved his head vertically. For subjects who adapted to the first condition, *both* spots now appeared to move in the direction *opposite* to that in which the stationary spot *i* had appeared to move during the adaptation period. For subjects adapted to the second condition, no such aftereffect was obtained. Thus, in the first condition, the subjects seem to have learned to make a set of diagonal eye movements during vertical head movements, in order to compensate for the head movements and keep the spot fixated. This is what we have said may be occurring quite generally in prism-adaptation experiments. Also, as was true in the prism-adaptation experiments, there are at least 2 different kinds of movement aftereffect. The aftereffect that Hay reported seems to depend on the recorrelation of compensatory eye movements and head movements; it obviously requires the subject to make active movements if adaptation is to occur. On the contrary, the aftereffects due to retinal displacement (p. 521), like the "waterfall illusion," can occur with a passive observer and even with stabilized retinal images.

In summary, some forms of adaptation to rearranged vision clearly may occur without active movement. Other forms of such adaptation do require active movement, but a good case can be made for supposing that the changes that occur involve the spatial calibration of the proprioceptive and motor systems, not the visual system. This distinction tends to dissolve, however, when eye movements are closely involved in the visual task, as they so often are. However, the classical interpretation of adaptation to visual arrangement as the re-education of vision to agree with proprioception is certainly not supported. In fact, where vision and proprioception are brought into immediate conflict, proprioception seems to change in order to agree with vision and not vice versa (see p. 536). If visual space is in fact originally learned by early associations between visual and proprioceptive-kinesthetic experiences, as the classical empiricist position maintained, that will have to be demonstrated by research on the origins of space perception, not by the evidence thus far provided by experiments on rearranged vision.

ON THE NATURE-NURTURE QUESTION IN SPACE PERCEPTION

Spatial Perception with Minimal Experience

The question of whether our abilities to perceive the spatial aspects of our environment are completely the result of learning, or whether any of them may be innate, dominated the study of perception from its inception, and remains a challenging issue today, despite some three centuries of controversy.

The issue has been important to different disciplines—to philosophy, to physiology, to art, to psychology—for very different reasons, and the diverse purposes for which this general question was asked cannot always be equally well served by a given answer (Hochberg, 1962). For example, a common assertion in art theory is that if the depth cues required to understand a picture are all learned symbols, then all are arbitrary and subject to change by artistic convention and education. However, this does not follow at all: Instead, we may learn the depth cues during our first few months of visual experience, and they might thereafter be completely

resistant to relearning. A common assumption of sensory physiologists is that if a depth cue is innate, it will be more powerful than any acquired or learned basis for judging depth with which it may be brought into conflict (see Helmholtz, 1896); a considerable amount of research on perceptual change has been motivated by this assumption. Again, however, it does not follow of necessity that what is innate must be stronger than what is learned.

Studies of infants   The most direct experimental attack on the question of whether visual space perception *must* be learned by association with tactual-kinesthetic-proprioceptive experience, as the empiricist position would have it, is to ask whether any degree of this ability can be found in subjects who have had no opportunity whatsoever to form such associations.[20]

Severe methodological difficulties beset such research. We can ask newborn infants only indirectly about what their spatial perceptions may be; that is, only by setting up behavioral tests of depth discrimination. In the higher animals and in man, coordinated motor behavior is very poorly developed at birth, so that few behavioral tests are then available. Nor can we use human infants in control experiments that would deprive them of normal sensorimotor development.

Although eye movements are not well coordinated and the eye's focusing ability is quite limited in earliest infancy (Haynes,

[20] The reasoning that seems to demand an empiricist explanation of space perception, by logic alone, is easily set aside. If space perception were indeed completely learned, the effects of that learning must consist of acquiring particular structures in the nervous system (say, some changes in the synapses in the neural network). At least some of these neural structures might have been acquired during some millions of years of evolutionary selection rather than during the few months or years of an individual's infancy. Thus the baby might be born with all the neural connections he needs for at least some aspects of space perception. Therefore, the question is really one for experimental inquiry, not for logical analysis. However, note that what gave this question its clear theoretical importance was not whether the course of experience with the world modifies or affects spatial behaviors and perception: It was the nature of the underlying general psychological theory of which the empiricist assertion was a part (pp. 428, 437).

White, & Held, 1965; see Hershenson, 1967 for a recent review), some eye-movement behaviors seem to be guided by the spatial features of stimulation shortly after birth. In a unique experiment, Wertheimer (1961) started testing an infant (who had been delivered by natural childbirth and hence was in an undrugged state) 3 minutes after birth. As the infant lay on her back, clicks were sounded next to the right ear or next to the left ear. On most of the trials on which movements occurred, the eyes moved in the direction of the click. Thus, some appropriate visuomotor behavior was elicited by spatially separated auditory stimuli, suggesting strongly that in some degree the discrimination of direction is innate.

Fantz (1961), Hershenson (1964), Hershenson, Munsinger, and Kessen (1965), and Salapatek and Kessen (1966), have demonstrated that different spatial distributions of visual stimulation can evoke different sets of eye movements in infants considerably older than the one used by Wertheimer (see Hershenson, 1967; E. Gibson, 1969). They presented their subjects with patterned visual displays and observed, directly or via motion-picture photography, where the infant appeared to be fixating. The rationale for these studies is that if the subject could not discriminate one stimulus from another, he would have no basis for turning his eye toward one rather than toward the other. Inasmuch as infants' eye movements do appear to be reliably affected by the configuration of the stimulus display, we may attribute to the infants some minimum amount of "pattern vision" (that is, of responses that are controlled by the spatial characteristics of the stimulus, not merely by its overall wavelength and intensity). To go further than that, and to say that we can tell that infants perceive depth because they look more often at a sphere than at a disk (Fantz, 1961) is not yet warranted, inasmuch as it may merely be two-dimensional pattern differences to which they are responding in these cases as well. But is it not true in every case that 2 stimulus displays that

differ in 3 dimensions will necessarily differ as two-dimensional patterns, as well? And if that is so, how can we ever be sure that the infant's response is not simply being given to the two-dimensional differences in pattern?

These questions are simply an extreme form of "How do we know what the subject perceives," which we have encountered before (pp. 426, 505, 540). We can simply note here that, so long as there are features to which the infant might be responding (such as the complexity of a pattern), which are known to attract his gaze even when they are not associated with depth, it seems premature to attribute fixation of those features to "depth perception." To talk profitably about space perception depends on being able to predict the organism's behavior better from the characteristics of objects in space than from the retinal image that falls in the subject's eye. For example, demonstrating the extent to which an infant appears to draw upon his perception of distance to achieve size constancy (pp. 506–510), to reach for objects, and to avoid places, would provide more justification for talking about depth perception.

A major problem, of course, is that the higher organism's response repertory is extremely meager at birth. Perhaps the usefulness of that repertory can be increased by techniques of operant conditioning (p. 595); for example, Bower (1964) reports that infants 70 to 85 days old could be conditioned to perform small head movements in response to the presentation of a 12-inch cube. They showed more generalization to the same cube at 3 times the original distance than to a much larger cube that maintained the original visual angle at the greater distance. Thus, they seemed to be responding to object size, rather than to retinal image size.

The classic solution to this problem, however, is to use older subjects who have been reared under special conditions, such as total darkness, which prevent them from having had any opportunity to associate tactual-kinesthetic experience with the visual stimuli on which they will be tested. Ideally, the subject should be allowed to mature sufficiently to display a full range of responses, but he should not be allowed to attach those responses to any pattern of visual stimulation. The first exposure to visual stimulation would then elicit only those responses (if any) that are innately tied to that pattern.

Dark-rearing can obviously not be carried out with human infants. Fortunately (for the experimenter) certain forms of partial blindness occur very early in life that (fortunately for the child) can often be cured later; these offer the experimenter a substitute for dark-rearing. Although many sight-restoring operations have been performed (Senden, 1932; London, 1960), postoperative visual disturbances (Senden, 1932; Dennis, 1934; Werthelmer, 1951), crudeness of testing, and the fact that varying amounts of visual experience have been available to the preoperative subjects, despite the fact that they were technically blind, make it difficult to draw any firm conclusions from such research. In general, some minimal amount of direction, depth, and even shape recognition seems to have been in evidence (Senden, 1932; Gregory & Wallace, 1963; Ueda, 1967), but it is not safe to build any theoretical structures on these data.

Studies of animals reared in darkness
Animals have been raised in the dark successfully, but the results are difficult to interpret. Negative results (that is, absence of any evidence of innate spatial responses) are inconclusive, inasmuch as the visual nervous system and the perceptuomotor guidance systems may both deteriorate rapidly unless used fairly soon after birth (see Riesen, 1947; Chow & Nissen, 1955; Wiesel & Hubel, 1961, 1963). Moreover, abnormal habits of performance acquired during visual deprivation may interfere with subsequent use of the visual information. For example, Held and Hein (1963) designed an elegant experiment to show the necessity of visuomotor experience for the development of depth discrimination in the cat (which, as we shall see, does not seem to show innate spatial abilities after dark-rearing). They paired kittens in a "carousel" so that an active member wheeled his passive partner around for one hour each day. Both animals were otherwise reared in darkness and both were thus exposed to equal amounts of moving, contoured light. The passive cats showed marked disabilities when confronted with the visual cliff (see below), and in other tasks that require visuomotor coordination and that seem to implicate depth perception. However, we must not infer from these results that the passive cat necessarily has inferior spatial discrimination. An animal (and especially a kitten) that has received visual stimulation only while its limbs were confined, may have started to make movements in response to that stimulation, but, being frustrated by the constraints then felt, may simply have learned not to respond to such stimulation.

In any case, positive findings (that is, evidence of innate spatial responses) are somewhat easier to interpret, although they have their own hazards.[21] Experiments on a variety of species of animals have yielded positive results. (For a recent review, see Walk, 1966.)

> Thus, when chicks that had been raised in darkness since they were hatched are taken into light for the first time, and are placed on platforms of varying height, they display more hesitation in jumping from high platforms than from low ones (Spalding, 1873; Thorndike, 1899; Kurke, 1955). To the extent that the chicks' reluctance to jump is a function of the visual depth cues, their performance must reflect innate depth discrimination. Additional experiments have

[21] The mechanism underlying the innate depth discrimination might have little to do with what we normally think of as depth perception. For example, it might be that some species of animals will not locomote when unfocused images fall on their retinas. In that case, when as infants, with poor accommodation for distance vision, they are confronted by the kind of "visual cliff" that we describe below, they might "freeze" while trying to resolve the blurred images. If this mechanism were responsible for the avoidance of the deep side of such a cliff, flooding the scene with a great deal of light would reduce the size of their pupils, increase the sharpness of focus of the deep side, and eliminate the avoidance behavior.

made use of a "visual cliff" consisting of a horizontal sheet of heavy glass at some height above the floor. A visual pattern, such as a checkerboard design, is attached to the underside of one half of the glass sheet. On the "cliff" side, the same pattern is laid on the floor. Walk, Gibson, and Tighe (1957) and Walk and Gibson (1961) used this device to show that dark-reared rats and light-reared rats both avoided the cliff side when they were placed on the centerboard. This finding was confirmed with additional controls by Nealy and Edwards (1960), who also showed that blinded animals failed to distinguish between the cliff side and the shallow side. This evidence of innate depth discrimination in rats is in line with results obtained with some other species. Thus, chicks show innate depth discrimination (Spalding, 1873; Thorndike, 1899; Gibson & Walk, 1960; Tallarico, 1961) and so may monkeys (Fantz, 1961, 1965; Rosenblum & Cross, 1963) and rabbits (Walk, 1966). Kittens, which normally discriminate depth by 4 weeks of age, do not discriminate on the visual cliff if they have been reared in the dark for that period (Gibson & Walk, 1960), nor do they show other depth-discriminatory behavior (Riesen & Aarons, 1959; Gibson & Walk, 1960), but that may at least in part be due to the fact that prolonged dark-rearing itself interferes destructively with performance on the visual cliff even with species that otherwise display innate depth discrimination (Nealy & Riley, 1963; Walk, Trychin, & Karmel, 1965).

The fact that some species show innate depth discrimination and some do not is interesting from a comparative standpoint. It may be a mistake to think of "space perception," or even of depth discrimination, as a unitary ability. Between species, as we have seen, differences in depth discrimination are gross and can be affected further by dark-rearing. In addition, it has been shown that differences in rearing environments can change the way in which animals behave on the visual cliff within a species (Kaess & Wilson, 1964; Lemmon & Patterson, 1964; Tallarico & Farrell, 1964; Carr & McGuigan, 1965).

However, the fact that differences in environment can effect differences in depth discrimination does not mean that the spatial meaning of visual stimulation is arbitrary, acquired merely by association with tactual-kinesthetic experiences of the world. Hess (1956) found evidence for innate directional cues in experiments with chicks that had been hatched in darkness and had been fitted with hoods containing prisms that displaced the visual field 7° laterally. He observed their initial pecks at a small target and at individual kernels of grain. The main finding was that the average peck was about 7° off target. The initial pecks were deflected as we would expect if their spatial localization were innate. Hess's chicks appeared to show no adaptation to the prisms, but Rossi (1968) has found slight but reliable amounts of such adaptation, together with an aftereffect in the direction opposed to the displacement produced by the prisms. These experiments provide a clear example of a behavior which seems to be innate yet which is subject to adaptation and "relearning."

Developmental Studies

Differences in spatial performance are found not only between members of different species but in the same subject at different ages. As with species differences, these may help us to sort out component abilities that are difficult to separate in adult behavior. However, it is unjustified to infer, from the fact that the performance of some spatial task improves with age, that the underlying perceptual ability was initially learned rather than innate: The fact that an ability continues to improve with age does not imply that it was at one time completely absent. Furthermore, what data we have on the relationship between the sensory systems are not encouraging for the simple empiricist hypothesis that space perception is learned by the association of specific visual patterns with tactual-kinesthetic experiences in space. That hypothesis was the motivation for most research on the development of the constancies, and it will no longer serve that purpose. More specific theories which predict patterns of improvement and of change with age are now needed, and several have been proposed and tested for the various constancies and illusions (Piaget et al., 1942, 1961; Wapner &

Werner, 1957; Pollock et al., 1963, 1967). Developmental studies have recently been reviewed by E. J. Gibson and Olum (1960), Wohlwill (1960), E. J. Gibson (1963, 1969), and by Tanaka (1967), Shinno (1967), and Ueda (1967). The pattern of results is quite complex because whether or not differences between subjects of different ages are found at all is a function of the task. A review of the development of space perception would in consequence be too involved to attempt here. Nevertheless, there are several points that we should note here.

Although age differences have been found in such measures of space perception as size constancy (Beyrl, 1926; Piaget & Lambercier, 1943; Zeigler & Leibowitz, 1957; Tanaka, 1967), these differences only appear with certain tasks and under certain testing conditions. We cannot, therefore, assume that these experiments measure a single homogeneously improving perceptual ability, the development of which would be manifested equally well by all behaviors that depend on space perception: We cannot assume, for example, because a child grossly underestimates the size of a stimulus in a size-constancy experiment, that he will also be unable to throw a ball accurately at that target (Smith & Smith, 1966; Tanaka, 1967). The fact that some perceptual measures change with age, moreover, may mean only that the motivation and the problem-solving strategies with which the subject approaches the experimental task have changed. For example, because the magnitudes of the geometrical illusions change as a function of age, some increasing

and others decreasing at different age levels (Gibson, 1969, pp. 407–409), several attempts have been made to use these developmental differences to sort out separate processes that might underlie the illusions (Pollack & Chaplin, 1963). Such theories suggest cumulative and nonreversible changes. An intriguing demonstration by Parrish, Lundy, and Leibowitz (1968), showed that adults, who had been hypnotically instructed that they were two years old, performed like children on the Ponzo and Poggendorf illusions (pp. 456, 457). This suggests instead that reversible factors (as in attentiveness, judgment attitude, and so on) may underlie some of the age changes.

If the various spatial behaviors were completely independent of each other, and if the effects of the various depth cues on those behaviors were also independent, there would be little systematic interest in measuring any of them; nor would there be much reason to retain the word "perception" in the psychologists' vocabulary. The term is not that empty, however, and there are sets of spatial behaviors that seem to be related to each other as measures of some common underlying perception of space, as we have seen (pp. 499, 505, 511–519). However, the fact that many measures are uncorrelated means that if research on individual and developmental differences is to be profitable past the bare point of testing the Berkeleyan theory of space perception (p. 477), it must rest on other assumptions about what stimulus information, what tasks, and what response measures are related to each other and to our purposes of inquiry.

J. W. Kling

LEARNING

INTRODUCTORY SURVEY

14

In this chapter we survey some of the methods used in the study of learning and consider a few of the persisting problems that face the experimenter. The chapters that follow describe the more specialized techniques of experimentation and data analysis needed for each of their topics. However, there are a few problems which are of general concern to all workers in the experimental psychology of learning, and it is to these that we give our attention.

DEFINITION OF LEARNING

Before plunging into a discussion of the problems facing the experimenter, it would be well to consider some of the ways in which the term *learning* is used. Let us start with a typical definition and then examine some of the phenomena to which such definitions are applied.

Learning is a relatively permanent change in behavior resulting from conditions of practice. The words "relatively permanent" are included in this definition to distinguish learned behavior from changes in behavior that are transient and spontaneously reversible. For example, the effects of becoming adapted to conditions of dim illumination (see pp. 283–289) are reversed by exposure to light, and the entire process may be repeated over and over with no signs that the nature of the

551

TABLE 14.1 RELATIVE PERSISTENCE OF SOME EFFECTS OF EXPERIENCE

Phenomenon	Example	Approx. persistence	Usually considered "learning"?
Short-term memory	If presentation of 3 letters (such as "LRF") is immediately followed by an activity which prevents rehearsal (such as subtracting successive 3s from a number like 698), after just 6 sec correct recall of the letters will occur on only 50% of trials; after 18 sec only 10% correct recall will occur (Peterson & Peterson, 1959).	seconds	yes
Sensory adaptation	A 15% sodium chloride solution applied to the tongue for about 30 sec produces quite complete adaptation (the solution no longer tastes salty). Replacing the salt solution with a water rinse gives rapid recovery from adaptation, with complete recovery requiring something more than 30 sec (Hahn, 1934).	seconds to minutes, depending on sensory modality and stimulus intensity	no
Figural after-effects	A slightly curved vertical line is inspected carefully for 5–10 min. When a straight vertical line is presented, it appears to be curved in the opposite direction (Gibson, 1933).	minutes to days	no
Memory for meaningful verbal materials	A short story is read, and then a complete recall is attempted. With no warning that further recalls will be solicited, subsequent tests are later given (Bartlett, 1932).	days to years	yes

changes are influenced by repetition. However, when behavior is labeled as "learned," the effects, by definition, are both longer lasting and, at least in part, accumulative.

By describing learning as "relatively permanent" we indicate our interest in procedures which have a more long-term influence on behavior. But what does "relatively permanent" mean? When is a behavior change temporary? As we can see from the examples in Table 14.1, there are no hard and fast divisions between temporary and permanent: Some of the experiments in learning are concerned with changes that last only a few minutes, whereas some so-called "temporary" changes—like figural aftereffects (see p. 466)—may last for a day or more.

The definition also includes the phrase "change in behavior," for it is only from such changes that we may infer that learning has taken place. The changes in behavior may be observed directly from the manner in which individual organisms respond to stimuli, or they may be observed indirectly by comparing the behavior of organisms exposed to the experimental conditions with the behavior of other organisms denied the experiences and serving as controls.

The learning process itself is not at this time observable, although most psychologists would agree that such a process is a reasonable inference from behavioral changes. After all, we can see the effects of experience just as clearly as we can see the effects of overeating or fasting; we really do not need an understanding of digestion and metabolic processes to know that food and body weight, ingestion and excretion are somehow related, and we do not need to have a familiarity with the scientific investigation of learning and memory to know that past experiences somehow are coded and stored in the organism and that they can be retrieved to serve as important determinants of behavior. Without any real understanding of metabolism, herdsmen fatten cattle for market and mothers rear more-or-less healthy children, guided by the accumulated "common sense" of centuries, augmented by occasional pieces of new knowledge produced when astute observers note correlations such as that between the presence of fresh fruits and vegetables and the absence of scurvy. Similarly, parents and teachers have had common-sense rules to guide them in the training and education of the youth of the community, and, as with the management of diet, many of the common-sense rules for the government of learning have been found to have at least some degree of validity.

The study of learning processes is now at about the stage of advancement that the study of metabolism and digestion had reached by the late nineteenth century. For example, we know how to manipulate the efficiency of practice, the rate of forgetting, and the persistence of the learner. In the last two decades, rapid advances have been made in the study of learning at the behavioral level; the physiological and anatomical correlates of these processes still remain about as mysterious as they were a generation ago. Yet few would doubt that such processes exist, and all would agree that their discovery will help us understand the behavioral information we already possess and that they will point to variables whose importance we do not yet suspect.

Until such discoveries are made, the process of learning remains just a plausible inference. There are many (for example, Skinner, 1953) who question the utility of explanations couched in the language of such constructs, but the majority of psychologists find "learning" to be a useful concept and have considerable faith that the search for the bodily bases of learning will prove fruitful in the next decade or two.

The term "conditions of practice" ordinarily implies controlled exposure to specific experiences. For example, in the verbal learning laboratory, "practice" may consist of successive presentations of lists of words at a rate determined by the experimenter; in the animal laboratory, "practice" may consist of all the responses up to and including the reinforced response. Of course, not all behavior that takes place under controlled conditions qualifies as practice: a defining characteristic is presentation of knowledge of results, feedback of information, or presentation of reinforcing or punishing stimuli. To allow the important phenomenon of classical conditioning (see p. 554) to be included, the definition of "practice" usually has been extended to include presentation of the conditioned and the unconditioned stimuli in predetermined time orders.

By specifying that the change in behavior must be attributable to practice, we eliminate those relatively permanent changes due to maturation or aging, injury or disease. Where such processes are responsible for rapid changes in behavior, special precautions are required to avoid misinterpretations of the observations. For example, during the first few days or weeks of life, maturation accounts for some major changes in sensory and motor capacities of infants; in these situations, cautious experimenters include a no-practice control group against which the changes shown by the experimental subjects may be evaluated. (See, for example, Wickens and Wickens, 1940.)

Even with all these qualifications, our definition of learning excludes a number of important phenomena which seem to belong in this general category.[1] We are left, then, with the conclusion that "learning" is best thought of as a heading for a set of chapters in a textbook rather than as the description of a psychological process. If it is used as a section heading, we then can define learning as the general term under which are subsumed the effects of certain paradigms (that is, the idealized patterns or diagrams which summarize the essential operations or procedures). It is to these paradigms which we next direct our attention.

---

[1] For example, exposure learning, imprinting, and habituation would be eliminated because they do not involve "practice," as it is usually defined; and short-term memory would be excluded because it is not "relatively permanent."

PARADIGMS OF LEARNING

When we consider the conditions under which learning is studied, we find that although literally thousands of different problems have been investigated, only a small number of paradigms are needed to describe the experimental procedures. By "paradigm" we mean the basic arrangements *used by the experimenter* to produce the phenomenon in which he is interested. We avoid the phrase "types of learning" because this often seems to suggest that the "types" reflect different physiological processes. Knowledge of these processes is fragmentary; it seems equally plausible to assume one or many processes, and although parsimony would argue for the assumption of a single form of change in the nervous system to account for all of the phenomenon with which we are concerned, multiplicity of processes across species and duplication within species is so often found that a single neuronal process for all forms of learning seems unlikely.[2] Certainly we should be cautious, when we are considering possible neuronal mechanisms for learning, that we do not lump together the results of different learning paradigms, or take too firm a posture on how many forms such learning processes might take.

We also should avoid the unprofitable controversy over the relative importance of behavioral or physiological investigations of learning processes. Neither is of primary importance; both will contribute to our understanding of behavior modifications. However, while a study of behavioral processes can be carried on without regard for correlated physiological or anatomical changes, the converse is not true; any study of the physiological or anatomical substrates of learning must of necessity include appropriate behavioral techniques, else how are the effects of the procedures to be seen? Fortunately, in the course of the development of a science of behavior studied at the behavioral level, nu-

merous procedures have been developed which produce just the sort of predictable and highly stable results needed for the analysis of the behavioral effects of physiological or anatomical manipulations. Let us now consider some of the paradigms that are involved in these procedures.

Classical Conditioning

By now, almost everyone is aware that the Russian physiologist, I. P. Pavlov (1849–1936) was led into his studies of conditioning by an interest in "psychic secretions."[3] Briefly, in the course of his investigations of the secretions of digestive glands (for which he was awarded the Nobel Prize in physiology and medicine in 1904), Pavlov was confronted with a fact of nature for which he had no explanation: Not only did his dogs salivate when he provided appropriate stimulation (for example, food in the mouth) for the reflex, but they also salivated when they saw food or a familiar food dish, or heard the steps of the caretaker (Pavlov, 1927, pp. 6, 13–14). Such reactions have probably been observed by everyone who ever kept a dog, and they have probably been accounted "natural" reactions by most who gave them any thought at all. However, Pavlov noted that the salivation could be elicited by a new dish only after the dog had some experience with it. Furthermore, he noted that puppies fed only on milk gave no such reaction when they were first shown meat or bread, although experience with these foods soon established a salivary reaction to the sight of them (pp. 22–23).

What types of experiences were necessary to establish such reactions? In an attempt to answer this question, Pavlov (1927) tells us that his initial investigations consisted of recording "all the external stimuli falling on the animal at the time its reflex reaction was manifested . . . , at the same time recording all changes in the reaction of the animal" (p. 6).

---

[2] In many species, for example, there is more than one mechanism for respiration, or excretion, or other basic life processes.

[3] For additional reading, see Gantt (1965); Pavlov (1928, 1955, 1957); and the summaries of Pavlov's influence on the experimental psychology of learning, in Hilgard and Bower (1966) and Kimble (1961).

As Pavlov described them, the experiments sound unstructured and unsystematic, but it should be remembered that he already was concentrating on a single facet of behavior (secretion from a parotoid or submaxillary gland), and that he had isolated the animal from the uncontrollable flux of stimulation from the real world and substituted the manipulable environment of the laboratory (pp. 21–22). The application of such methods convinced him that "the fundamental requisite is that any external stimulus which is to become the signal in a conditioned reflex must overlap in point of time with the action of an unconditioned stimulus. . . . Further, it is not enough that there should be overlapping between the two stimuli; it is also and equally necessary that the conditioned stimulus should begin to operate before the unconditioned stimulus comes into action" (pp. 26–27).

We see, then, that there are two terms in the description as given by Pavlov: the "stimulus which is to become the signal" and which depends "on very many conditions, both in [its] formation and in the maintenance of [its] physiological activity" (1927, p. 25), and the stimulus which does not depend upon such special conditions for its ability to evoke the reaction. Furthermore, we see that there is a specific temporal relationship necessary for the formation of the conditioned reflex, with the conditioned stimulus (CS) being presented before the unconditioned stimulus (US). These facts may be summarized in a paradigm of the following type:[4]

Initial Tests	Conditioning	Test Trial
CS → OR	CS →	CS → CR
US → UR	US → UR	

The conditioned stimulus There are three essential properties of the conditioned stimulus. First, it must be within the sensory capacities of the organism. Whereas this may seem obvious, there are instances in which this requirement has been overlooked, and "stimuli" have been selected which, while quite obvious to the experimenter, were probably nonexistent as far as the subject was concerned.[5] One way of checking the sensitivity of an organism to a CS is to observe the investigatory or orienting response, since in many cases, the CS elicits an overt and easily recognized reaction of the type which Pavlov labeled "investigatory reflexes" or "What-is-it?" reflexes (1927, p. 12). For example, a dog might prick up his ears to an auditory stimulus, and orient toward the source of the sound. Thus, this type of reaction has come to be known as an *orienting reflex* or OR (Sokolov, 1960; see also Hartman, 1965 for a review of the use of the OR in semantic conditioning). These orienting responses habituate rapidly, and they may disappear before the first conditioned response is seen. Even where no overt reaction occurs, there may be covert responses to the CS which show the same properties of rapid habituation and immediate reappearance as soon as any modification in the stimulus occurs. For example, Sokolov (1960) has shown that such changes in breathing patterns, galvanic skin responses, electroencephalograms, and blood volume reflect the same changes as the more overt orientation responses, such as eye and head movements.[6]

It has also been suggested that a CS will be ineffective if the organism does not attend

---

[4] Abbreviations: CS = conditioned stimulus; OR = orienting response; US = unconditioned stimulus; UR = unconditioned response; CR = conditioned response. Note that CR sometimes is used as the abbreviation for the "conditioned reflex," that is, the behavioral unit CS-CR. Some scholars have urged that the term "conditional" be used when speaking of the stimulus which is initially neutral, since this seems to be a more appropriate translation of Pavlov's term (see Gantt, 1966), but "conditioned" seems to be firmly rooted in English usage.

[5] Indeed, there even has been an auditory "stimulus" generator sold for use with laboratory animals that has as one of its two signals a 100 Hz tone. In all probability, the rats to whom such "stimuli" have been presented heard nothing of the tone, since rats are almost completely deaf to signals with frequencies under 500 Hz, and are maximally sensitive to signals in the region 25–50 KHz (Gourevitch, 1965; Gourevitch & Hack, 1966).

[6] It has been customary to treat "the OR" as a unitary reaction, but some reports (such as Gross & Stern, 1967) have shown that various components of the OR may respond differentially to such variables as the instructions given to subjects.

to it because he has first been trained with a different stimulus, or because the CS is redundant and therefore does not have information value. For example, if a response has been conditioned to a sound and then further conditioning with a sound-light compound is carried out, the light may prove to be quite ineffective where tested alone. (See Egger & Miller, 1962, and pp. 675 ff. See also Pavlov, 1927, on the related problem of "over-shadowing," and Kamin, 1969, on the experimental analysis of these problems.)

A second requirement of the CS is also quite obvious: It must not elicit the same response as the US. Naturally, if both elicit the same UR it will be more difficult to detect changes in the effectiveness of the conditioning procedure. Occasionally it is impossible to avoid this complication, for the organism may be so simple or the observations so difficult that we can measure but one reaction to all stimuli. This has been one of the major problems facing investigators of conditioning in very simple organisms (see reviews by Warden, Jenkins, & Warner, 1936; Thorpe, 1963; and Jensen, 1965) and in very immature organisms (see, for example, Spelt, 1948; also see the discussion of prenatal and neonatal conditioning in Lipsitt, 1963). In studies of possible conditioning in Planaria (flatworms), Thompson and McConnell (1955) found that the body movement characteristically given to electric shock (US) also occurred on about 20 percent of the presentations of the CS (light) to a control group receiving CS only. This immediately raises the possibility that an increase in responses to CS in the experimental group may be attributable to effects other than those of pairing CS and US (see Jensen, 1965; Brown, Dustman & Beck, 1966 for discussions of adequate controls in the design of such experiments). Even in higher organisms, this question is a vexing one, for the CS and US may elicit the same (or highly similar) responses before any pairing has occurred. Human eyelid conditioning—one of the "standard" techniques for the study of classical conditioning—is subject to this problem, inasmuch as a reflexive blink to the

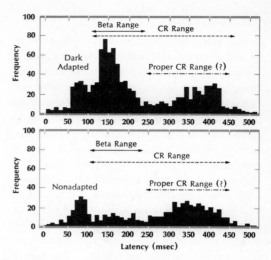

Figure 14.1. Latency distributions of all eyelid responses evoked by a strong light during a conditioning experiment using human subjects. The upper panel represents the results from dark-adapted subjects; the lower panel from subjects not dark adapted. There appear to be two *reflex* responses to the CS: one, with a relatively short latency (approximately 50–110 msec) is present in both dark- and light-adapted subjects; the other, with a longer latency (approximately 120–240 msec), appears primarily during more advanced stages of dark adaptation. It is these latter reflex responses which Grant and Norris called "beta responses" to distinguish them from the previously recognized short-latency "alpha" reflex responses. Present-day experiments usually record eyelid movements with microtorque potentiometers, but many earlier experiments utilized a photographic technique that required a darkened experimental room and that thus produced increasing degrees of dark adaptation as the session proceeded. Under such conditions, beta responses occurred with increasing frequency and could easily be accepted as "true" *conditioned* responses if the range 100–450 msec were taken as the appropriate criterion for CRs. For the data presented in this figure, the range 250–450 msec was suggested as an appropriate one for CRs, but these latency values vary somewhat according to the experimental conditions and must be ascertained for the particular CS, US, interstimulus interval, and instructions given to subjects. The identification of the "true" CRs is further complicated by the presence of voluntary (and suspected voluntary) responses whose latency range often overlaps that of the CRs. (Grant & Norris, 1947.)

CS (for example, light onset) may occur prior to conditioning, especially if the subject is dark adapted (Grant & Norris, 1947). Where problems arising from the similarity of the form of the response to CS and US exist, experimenters frequently utilize differences in latencies or amplitudes of the responses in an attempt to determine whether the response should be called a CR, a UR, or a reaction to the CS alone (Figure 14.1). The distinction is further complicated by the possibility that "voluntary" blinks will occur, and the procedure of discarding certain trials or certain subjects because the latencies or forms of their responses suggest the presence of too many "voluntary" responses seems to account for some of the discrepancies between the results obtained in different laboratories (see discussions by Spence & Ross, 1959; Kimble, 1961; Garmezano, 1965; Ross, 1965).

The third requirement of the CS is an ambiguous and amorphous one: it must not be "too strong." Ordinarily, the OR habituates during the first several presentations of the CS, but if the CS elicits a response which does not habituate, conditioning may be difficult or impossible. Nevertheless, Pavlov (1927, pp. 29–31) was able to demonstrate successful conditioning with conditioned stimuli that originally elicited vigorous unconditioned responses of their own.[7] For example, if electric shocks or mechanical pricking of the skin (which ordinarily elicited struggling and other signs of distress) regularly preceded presentation of food when the dog was hungry, conditioning of the salivary response was successfully accomplished, and all indications of upset in response to the CS disappeared. Pavlov's conclusion was that the stronger reflex must always be in the position of the US-UR (for example, the alimentary reflex in the hungry dog is said to be stronger than the defensive response to painful peripheral stimulation), but which of two stimuli will elicit the stronger response cannot always be foreseen, and the further increase in the intensity of a shock may render it "too strong" for use as a CS even if the dog is very hungry. As a consequence of this uncertainty, experimenters usually select CSs that elicit ORs that habituate readily.

The unconditioned stimulus The most important property of the unconditioned stimulus is that it elicit the UR with a very high degree of reliability. The unit (unconditioned stimulus-unconditioned response) usually is called the "unconditioned reflex" and in many cases the behavior is indeed reflexive. However, as Pavlov's (1927, pp. 33–35) demonstrations of secondary conditioned reflexes[8] indicated, the US-UR need not be a reflex in the physiological sense of the term, but probably need only be a stimulus-response relation that is highly reliable and very resistant to weakening by repeated elicitation.

Temporal relations in conditioning In addition to selecting appropriate stimuli, adequate temporal arrangements of the stimuli must be arranged. As a general rule, the onset of the CS must precede the onset of the US; this is the normal or "forward" order of conditioning. If the US is presented first (that is, the "backward" order), little or no evidence of conditioning will be found. For

---

[7] That aversive stimuli might become CSs for nondefensive CRs is not as surprising as the fact that all signs of the aversive nature of such stimuli sometimes disappear. For example, in experimental studies of morphine addiction, the jab of the syringe is initially a stimulus from which the animals retreat, but as addiction is established, the noxious characteristics of the skin puncture seem to evaporate. Stimuli from the syringe, meanwhile, become CSs for the CR that includes nausea and vomiting, anticipatory salivation, and other components of the UR to the actual injection of the morphine. In spite of this, the animals show strong approach responses to the syringe, choosing the room in which injections are given over rooms in which feeding occurs, or selecting the syringe box when given a choice between it and a food box. This loss of the aversive characteristics of stimuli when they become CSs for nondefensive CRs also occurs in human addiction: opening a vein with a pin and inserting a crude injection device must be highly noxious prior to addiction, but it seems to lose these qualities with repeated pairing of injection and the drug. See, for example, the experimental studies of Kleitman and Crisler, (1927), Pavlov (1927), Spragg (1940), and Weeks (1964).

[8] In generating secondary conditioned reflexes, the CS from one experiment is used as the US in another experiment. A description of this procedure and its relation to secondary reinforcement is given in Chapter 15 (pp. 660–677).

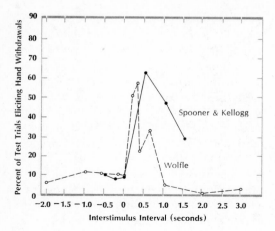

Figure 14.2. Conditioning as a function of interstimulus interval. The subjects were college student volunteers. In both experiments, an auditory CS and electrical shock US were employed. An interstimulus interval of *zero* indicates simultaneous onset of the shock and the sound; negative intervals indicate the onset of the shock before the sound (the "backward" conditioning procedure); positive intervals indicate the onset of sound before shock (the "forward" conditioning procedure). Test trials consisted of the presentation of the sound and omission of the shock. (After Wolfle, 1932; and Spooner & Kellogg, 1947.)

example, Wolfle (1932) compared the effectiveness of various temporal arrangements of CS and US in the conditioning of hand withdrawal from an electric shock. Each group of subjects was exposed to a different CS-US interval, with the CS (sound) for some subjects coming as much as 3 seconds before the US (shock), while for others the US came as much as 2 seconds prior to the CS. The results are summarized in Figure 14-2. Note that the forward order, with CS preceding US by 1/3 to 2/3 seconds, was most favorable for conditioning.

The general pattern of these results has been repeated in several experiments. In addition to the optimal CS-US interval, note that Fig. 14.2 indicates a loss in effectiveness at the longer CS-US intervals, and the inefficiency of both the exactly simultaneous and the backward order of presentation of CS and US. Let us consider first the optimal interval.

This effect will be found whenever a sufficiently wide range of CS-US intervals is explored because there will always be some positive value of the interval which will be superior to simultaneous onset of CS and US, and because the efficiency of the procedure eventually will decline as the interval is lengthened. However, it would be a mistake to assume that there is one interval that will be optimal for all situations. In the first place, the sensory system stimulated by the CS sets a lower limit on the interval, and we should expect that systems that can act relatively rapidly (for example, the cutaneous and auditory) would produce shorter optimal intervals than would slower systems (for example, the chemical senses).

Beyond these relatively small differences attributable to the nature of the CS, much larger effects have been found that are associated with the type of conditioning situation. In human eyelid conditioning, the optimal interval seems to be in the region of 0.25–0.60 sec (McAllister, 1953; Kimble, Mann, & Dufort, 1955; Hartman & Grant, 1962). On the other hand, when conditioned fear responses are examined, longer intervals (2–5 sec or more) seem to be best (see, for example, Vandercar & Schneiderman, 1967). Because blinks of the eye are rapid and the emotional responses presumably involved in conditioned fears are relatively slow, such differences in optimal interstimulus intervals might suggest that the optimal interval for each situation is roughly proportional to the latency of the UR. That this may be incorrect is suggested by the conditioning of the human galvanic skin response (GSR), which is most readily accomplished with a CS-US interval of 0.5 sec (White & Schlosberg, 1952) despite the fact that this reaction requires 2–3 sec to develop after onset of the US.[9]

[9] The galvanic skin response (GSR) is usually measured as a change in resistance or conductance of the skin, especially the palmar or plantar surfaces. GSRs usually occur whenever a sudden change in stimulation occurs, appearing as deflections from the more stable *conductance level*. See Woodworth and Schlosberg (1954), especially pages 137–159 for a description of methodology and typical results; and Prescott (1965) for a critique of studies purporting to condition the GSR.

Of course, it is possible that the GSR is merely one slowly arising component of a general reaction (for example, startle) and that this more rapid general reaction is being conditioned in such experiments. The strongest argument against such dismissal of the conditioned GSR as an artifact comes from experiments in which several different response measures have been monitored in the same organisms during conditioning. Vandercar and Schneiderman (1967), for example, observed three different responses while conditioning rabbits. Different groups of animals were conditioned with interstimulus intervals of 0.25, 0.75, 2.25, and 6.75 sec. The optimal interval for conditioning closure of the nictitating membrane (one of the three "lids" of the rabbit's eye) was 0.25 sec; for conditioning heart rate changes, 2.25 sec was the best interval; and for conditioning changes in breathing patterns, 6.75 sec was best. Such results suggest that, for different situations and types of subjects, different interstimulus intervals are optimal.

In some situations it is impossible to investigate the very shortest interstimulus intervals, for they do not allow sufficient opportunity for the conditioned response to occur before the onset of the US, and they thus preclude the opportunity to observe whether conditioning is, in fact, taking place. One solution to this problem has been the insertion into the procedure of separate test trials, in which the CS-US interval is either very long, or where CS alone is presented. For example, Bitterman (1964) exposed goldfish to pairings of light and shock, with each group of fish having a different CS-US interval. Every tenth trial was a test trial during which all groups were given a long CS-US interval. The effectiveness of the interstimulus intervals on the conditioning trials was estimated from CRs on these test trials. The response monitored was the activity shown by the fish during the CS. The results from this and associated control experiments indicated that no conditioning of activity to the light occurred in the group that had exactly simultaneous onset of CS and US, and that each of the other groups reached its peak in agitated movement approximately 5 seconds after the US would have occurred on regular training trials. Furthermore, the *amount* of conditioned activity was relatively equal among all groups trained with any CS-US interval except exact simultaneity. Hence, to the extent that the amount of activity is an adequate index of the degree of conditioning, there seems to be no evidence for an optimal interval in this situation. In this case, these results could only have been observed during special test trials, since the peak reaction occurred after the normal point of onset of the US.

Theories of classical conditioning Bitterman (1965) suggests that experiments like those described above indicate the importance of the afferent state existing at the moment of US onset and that it is such states which become associated with the sensory consequences of the CS. Such an interpretation of classical conditioning is widely accepted, being essentially the same as that of Pavlov (1927) as well as more recent writers (for example, Woodworth & Schlosberg, 1954; Konorski, 1967). In essence, this viewpoint assumes that classical conditioning procedures create an association of the afferent state of affairs produced by the conditioned stimulus with the afferent activity produced by the unconditioned stimulus. Because the emphasis is entirely upon the association of the two afferent (or sensory) patterns of activity, such interpretations frequently are classified as *S-S* (or, *stimulus-stimulus*) *theories* (Spence, 1951). That is, one stimulus (the CS) is thought to gain the property of initiating the sensory consequences—or the central nervous system activities—that are characteristic of the second stimulus (the US). Because it might be said that the CS serves as a signal that the US is coming, such interpretations also are called *expectancy theories*.[10]

[10] S-S theories have also been applied to instrumental learning, where it is assumed that the critical elements of the process are the acquisition of the expectancy that, in the presence of Stimulus 1 (the positive stimulus or "cue") the organism learns that Stimulus 2 (a positive reinforcer,

Standing in sharp contrast to theories that emphasize the association of the two sets of stimuli are theories that assume the association to be one of stimuli and responses. The S-R theory developed by Guthrie (1935, 1952, 1959) is an example of such an approach. Guthrie assumed that it is a property of organisms that whenever a response occurs, that response is immediately and completely associated with all stimuli present at that instant. Thus, the analysis of behavior from this point of view requires the description of the response and the specification of all afferent activity occurring at the same time. The response in classical conditioning may at first be the UR, but over a number of trials the form and the temporal characteristics of the response may change markedly. The stimulus may also vary over trials, since the response-produced stimuli generated by reactions of the organism are an important portion of the total afferent state. Yet on every trial, it is assumed that mere temporal contiguity insures the immediate and the complete conditioning of whatever response occurred to whatever sensory pattern existed at that moment. (The evolution of statistical learning theory from these rather imprecise assumptions is described in Chapter 19.)

But if temporal contiguity is the requisite for conditioning, how is it that some interval *other than* simultaneity of CS and US is *always* found to be superior to simultaneity? Guthrie explained the necessity for CS priority by assuming that the stimulus to which the response is really conditioned is not the CS controlled by the experimenter, but an afferent pattern that is a consequence of the CS. For example, if Pavlov used an auditory CS, the dog might turn toward the sound source, prick up his ears, and whimper. Each of these responses would, of course, have sensory consequences, and these response-produced stimuli would be added to the other stimuli to which the response is conditioned. This suggestion seems reasonable enough

as an explanation for conditioning with relatively long CS-US intervals, where such stimulus-producing responses may easily occur between CS and US onsets, and where the latency of the CR may increase until it is occurring just prior to US onset.

Note in Figure 14.2 that the relative efficiency of the various CS-US intervals diminishes sharply as exact simultaneity of stimuli is imposed, and that onset of the US prior to the CS also generates few CRs on test trials. Such results, in which "small amounts of conditioning" seem to be obtained from the simultaneous or the backward orders of presentation, are common when the US is electric shock or some other aversive stimulus, and the amount of "conditioning" obtained typically is no more than is generated by control procedures in which the CS and the US are not paired at all. For this reason, it is rather generally believed that backward conditioning does not occur, that the responses obtained on test trials do not represent "true conditioning, but that they are probably the results of pseudoconditioning or sensitization (see below).[11]

Effects of instructions and attitudes   If the level of responding shown by the backward-order groups is supposed to be indicative of no conditioning at all, how are we to explain the fact (see Figure 14.2) that the longer forward-order groups actually attained even lower levels of responding? One possibility is that these longer CS-US intervals allow time for the subjects to inhibit their hand move-

---

or some aversive stimulus) will follow. See, for example, Tolman (1932) and Humphreys (1939). A variation of this theme is the S-R-S view, which assumes that in the presence of Stimulus 1 the organism learns that if Response 1 is emitted, Stimulus 2 will follow (see MacCorquodale & Meehl, 1953, 1954; Tolman, 1959).

[11] Pavlov later decided that some degree of conditioning could be obtained with the backward order of presentation if but a few trials were given. However, he concluded that, if more CS-US pairings occurred, whatever slight amount of backward conditioning had been established would be masked by the stronger inhibitory effect exerted by the US acting as an "external inhibitor," much as would any strong stimulus if presented before the CS (Pavlov, 1927, pages 391–394; see also Varga & Pressman, 1966). Here again we see another reason for suspecting that classical and instrumental conditioning procedures are operating on fundamentally different processes: pre-trial presentation of a bit of food in classical conditioning inhibits the well-trained response to CS, while in the instrumental situation, such "priming" would usually have no inhibitory effect, and would sometimes increase vigor of the previously trained response.

ments on test trials. This type of "voluntary" control over responses is always a problem when adult human subjects are used, and the instructions they are given must be carefully prepared and pretested. If the experimenter says nothing about the attitude to be taken when serving as a subject, some persons will do their best to resist the effects of the stimuli, inhibiting their reactions to both US and CS as far as possible; others will try to "help" the experimenter by emitting the responses they think are appropriate; some will attempt to relax and avoid exercising any conscious control over responding. In most cases, it is this last attitude that experimenters attempt to engender with their "neutral" instructions, but if they are really neutral, the way is left open for all possible shades of meaning to be read into the instructions.

How much difference can instructions make in classical conditioning? In the first place, they can substitute for the time-consuming training that is necessary when preverbal humans or nonhuman subjects are used. Of course, this is an obvious point, but its importance sometimes is overlooked. If it takes three months or more to train a rhesus monkey to hold his hand on a key and withdraw it as swiftly as possible when a signal is given, we would certainly expect this "pretraining" to have an influence on whatever experiments were to follow. With human subjects, verbal instructions can create in a few moments the same behavior produced by the long pretraining of the monkey, and the instructions are worthy of the same concern by the experimenter as the more lengthy and laborious nonverbal pretraining.

It is perhaps unfortunate from the experimenter's point of view that humans are not just organisms capable of heeding instructions. Instead, they come to the experiment with a rich history of interactions with other situations and people, and as a result will approach the experiment and the experimenter with a very great variety of attitudes. Consider the classically conditioned hand-withdrawal experiment (see, for example,

Wolfle, 1932; Spooner & Kellogg, 1947): If the experimenter tells the subject to withdraw his hand as soon as he hears the CS, it is no longer an experiment in conditioning, but one of reaction time. In contrast, the experimenter dare not tell his subject *not* to allow his hand to move, else the experiment would be doomed to failure. The middle ground—telling the subject to allow the occurrence of whatever responses seem natural—constitutes "neutral" instructions that usually are employed. Miller (1939) covered an even wider range with the instructions given to subjects in a conditioned eyeblink experiment. Each of six groups received instructions ranging from (1) "Be sure you do not wink or start to wink before you have felt the puff" to (6) "In case you feel your eyes closing or starting to close, do nothing to prevent it." The latter set of instructions resulted in conditioned responses on 71 percent of the trials; the former produced only 26 percent responses; and the intermediate instructions produced intermediate results. Other experimenters (for example, Hilgard & Humphreys, 1938; Norris & Grant, 1948) have obtained results consistent with these findings, and Nicholls and Kimble (1964) have shown that the effect of inhibitory instructions is primarily one of reducing the amplitude of the UR.

Interestingly, the same general effects of attitudes are seen when involuntary responses are conditioned. For example, Razran (1935) demonstrated that conditioned salivation could be obtained when subjects were told to associate the CS (for example, a nonsense syllable) with the US (for example, pretzels), and he also demonstrated that conditioning would not occur if subjects were told to avoid associating the two. Salivation is an "involuntary" response in the sense that we cannot directly control the secretion, but at least some of the time we can indirectly initiate it by thinking of certain foods (a dill pickle, for example) or inhibit it by thinking of emotion-provoking situations (for example, a recent embarrassing event).

To observe conditioning processes without such attitudinal influences seems to be an impossibility when adult subjects are employed. Children probably bring fewer preconceived notions to the experiment; at least, this might account for the relatively faster conditioning of young children and subnormal children that has sometimes been reported (see, for example, Osipova, in Razran, 1933). However, even adult attitudes can be more or less neutralized if appropriate procedures are followed. For example, Razran (1939) demonstrated typical Pavlovian conditioning, extinction, spontaneous recovery, and stimulus generalization, among others, by the simple expedient of providing his subjects with a good (but inaccurate) reason for the experiment. Stating that he was studying the effects of eye fatigue on digestion, he presented previously neutral stimuli during periods of eating. For example, he spaced forty flashes of lights during a two-minute session of pretzel eating. Later, the presentation of the lights elicited salivation, but none of the subjects gave evidence of concern with whether they should or should not salivate. This, then, would seem to be one solution to the problem of instructions: Set up a situation which is both believable and which directs attention away from the conditioning problem. (At the conclusion of the experiment, the experimenter has an obligation to explain the proceedings and the results to his subjects.)[12]

Conditioning as the prototype of all learning Pavlov's work seemed to offer a reliable and objective method for analyzing learning processes, and therefore it was seized upon by many psychologists during the 1920s and 1930s as the prototype of all learning. Most notably, Watson (e.g., 1916) frequently wrote as if all experience could be translated into Pavlovian conditioned reflexes. Some other behaviorists of the period followed Watson's lead, and especially after the reports of con-

ditioning of fear responses by Watson and Raynor (1920), "the conditioned reflex" became almost synonymous with "learning." Textbooks of general psychology (for example, Watson, 1919; Smith & Guthrie, 1921) with a systematic conditioning orientation introduced several generations of students to the basic ideas of Pavlov and their application to specific problems in psychology. Furthermore, Watson wrote several books (for example, 1928) aimed at the layman, which were widely read and which introduced the general public to "the conditioned response." So uncritically was this term applied by some authors that behaviors ranging from the simplest to the most complex activities were blithely labeled as "conditioning," with the general implication that their origins or their future courses were thereby better understood.

> For the most part, this adoption of conditioning terminology occurred prior to the time any detailed information concerning conditioning itself had become available. Pavlov's Huxley Lecture (Pawlow, 1906) was published in *Lancet* and in *Science*, where many readers of English had their first introduction to conditioning techniques. A more detailed account was published by Yerkes and Morgulis (1909) and included a summary of the findings from Pavlov's laboratory up to 1909. However, it was not until Anrep translated Pavlov's lectures (Pavlov, 1927) that a full account of the basic methodology and results were available to those who did not read Russian.
>
> Meanwhile, outside Russia considerable experience was being accumulated by experimenters using Pavlov's basic methods, usually without being aware of the range of experimentation conducted by Russian physiologists (and later, by Russian psychologists). Mateer (1918) and Watson and Raynor (1920) applied the methods to the conditioning of feeding responses and emotional reactions in children; Liddell (1926) established a laboratory for the study of conditioning (especially defensive reactions) in sheep and goats; and Cason (1922) and Schlosberg (1928) developed methods appropriate for conditioning adult human subjects.

Two trends are discernible in the conditioning literature of the period before 1940. On the one hand, no indication was given in the earliest Russian reports of the extent to

---

[12] The effects on experimental results of the attitudes, hopes, and expectations of the experimenter have been examined by Rosenthal (1966).

which the methods and concepts could be applied to species other than dog or to behaviors other than those associated with Pavlov's "alimentary reflexes." Thus, it is understandable that there should have been numerous publications in which demonstrations of successful conditioning of other organisms and other responses were reported. The first edition of this book (Woodworth, 1938) concluded from such investigations that, although *any* response of the organism probably could be conditioned—in man as well as in other species—conditioning was in no sense an automatic and inevitable consequence of pairing CS and US, but instead was as sensitive to variations in the procedure and in the conditions of the subject (including the attitudes of human subjects) as other varieties of learning. This conclusion still seems valid.

At the same time that the range of conditioning was being explored, there was a growing appreciation of the fact that conditioning represented not "the" but just one paradigm for behavior modification. Skinner (1935), Schlosberg (1937), and Mowrer (1947) presented three rather different sets of reasons for distinguishing between Pavlov's method and that in which the behavior of the organism influences the immediate outcome of the procedure. In their influential summary and interpretation of the literature, Hilgard and Marquis (1940) distinguished between the "classical" method of Pavlov and those in which the behavior of the subject was "instrumental" in determining the consequences of the procedure. The classical conditioning procedure, of course, presents CS and US according to the temporal order established by the experimenter, without reference to the behavior of the subject. Schlosberg (1934, 1936, 1937), for example, found that classical conditioning procedures seemed to produce "diffuse preparatory responses," whereas more precise and adaptive behaviors seemed to be the product of procedures in which the behavior influenced the stimulation—in his case, reducing or avoiding electric shock. Skinner's primary argument

rested on the operations involved in the two procedures: pairing of conditioned and unconditioned reflexes versus contingency of reinforcement on a response. Skinner also suggested that Pavlovian conditioning was largely concerned with autonomic responses, whereas operant (instrumental) procedures largely influenced skeletal responses. Mowrer drew an even sharper distinction between these latter categories, arguing that all autonomic responses follow Pavlovian laws and that all skeletal ones are acquired through reinforcement by drive reduction.

This distinction along autonomic-skeletal lines has recently been called into question by N. E. Miller and his colleagues (see, for example, Miller, 1969), who have demonstrated that such autonomic reactions as heart rate and intestinal responses can be modified through instrumental procedures.

The other combination—Pavlovian procedures successfully conditioning skeletal responses such as eyelid blinks or the patellar reflex—has long been accepted as a fact (see, for example, Schlosberg, 1928).

Pavlov's original interest in conditioning (that is, the explanation of the "psychic secretions") led him into an investigation of the empirical laws of the phenomenon. At the same time, he constructed a theory of how the nervous system might operate, giving it properties congruent with his behavioral data. For example, he noted that "if a tone of 1000 d.v. is established as a conditioned stimulus, many other tones spontaneously acquire similar properties, such properties diminishing proportionally to the intervals of these tones from the one of 1000 d.v. Similarly, if a tactile stimulation of a definite circumscribed area of the skin is made into a conditioned stimulus, tactile stimulation of other skin areas will also elicit some conditioned reaction, the effect diminishing with increasing distance of these areas from the one for which the conditioned reflex was originally established" (1927, p. 113). From these facts of stimulus generalization (see pp. 758–763), Pavlov concluded that there must be an area in the cerebral hemispheres for the analysis of each of the sensory systems, with the focus of the activity aroused by a stimulus being in these areas, and with the activity irradiating outward from this focal point in ever-decreasing strength.

Similarly, for the other behavioral phenomena he discovered, Pavlov invented neurological-like processes which could conceivably underlie the behavior. Again using stimulus generalization as an example, it has been found that the behavioral data do not conform to the predictions that should be made from a Pavlovian model of a center of activity (the analyzer) and spreading excitation. For example, Grant and Dittmer (1940) used vibrotactical stimulators to produce the CS, placing the stimulators on the hand for one group of subjects, and on the back for another group. One stimulator served as the CS, and after conditioning, the other stimulators were included in generalization tests. Both groups showed about equal generalization, but because the cortical areas representing the hand are far more spread out than those serving the skin areas of the back, Pavlov's theory should have predicted a steeper generalization gradient for the subjects stimulated on the hand.

Such experiments have diminished much of the original interest in Pavlov's model of the nervous system, and it now plays a relatively minor role in contemporary brain-behavior research. (See, however, Asratyan, 1961a, b.) The Pavlovian *methods,* in contrast, continue to be used in much of this research, primarily because they offer excellent control over the stimulation of the organism and because they seem to offer conceptually simple pictures of the learning processes under investigation (see Doty, 1969).

Conditioning as a "model system" Two comments might be made about the assumption that conditioning offers a simple picture of learning. First, it is dangerous to assume that all applications of classical conditioning procedures involve the same type of behavioral modification, and any attempt to construct a theory of the anatomical or physiological mechanisms of conditioning must be alert to these differences.

For example, Grant (1964) suggests that at least four "subclasses" of classical conditioning can be distinguished on operational grounds:

"Pavlovian A conditioning"—the procedure as developed by Pavlov, involving the pairing of CS and US, with the stimulation from the US being, at least in part, influenced by the subject's responses. For example, the stimulation from a food US that is seized and chewed would be

different from that received if, because of partial food satiation, the food was not eaten with equal eagerness.

"Pavlovian B conditioning"—the procedure developed during Pavlov's investigations of conditioned morphine reactions (see, for example, Pavlov, 1927). In such cases, stimulation by the US is not influenced by the behavior of the subject: the nausea and salivation occur essentially independently of instrumental responses of the subject.

"Anticipatory instructed conditioning"—the procedure employed by Ivanov-Smolensky (1927), in which subjects are told to make a specific response to a given signal, and a neutral stimulus is then introduced prior to the signal. Subjects may not be able to report the presence or significance of this "CS" even though they respond to it with great regularity. The feature of the procedure which most clearly distinguishes it from the other Pavlovian procedures is the reliance on instructions and the use of voluntary responses.

"Sensory preconditioning"—the procedure employed by Brogden (1939; see also Hoffeld et al., 1960; Prewitt, 1967; and review by Seidel, 1959) in which two CSs are paired during "preconditioning" sessions. One CS then is paired with a US during the conditioning phase of the experiment, and then the other CS is brought in for testing.

Grant points out that not only are these "types" distinguishable on purely operational grounds, but (1) that they also seem to involve motivational variables to different degrees, and (2) that they may also be different in a functional sense. For example, "Pavlovian A" procedures seem to establish the CS as a signal that US is coming, and the CR is only an abstract of the UR; "Pavlovian B" procedures, on the other hand, seem to come closest to substituting CS for US, with CR being a more faithful replica of UR than in the "A" situation. In the "anticipatory instructed" method, however, the nature of the voluntary response may be quite different from typical URs or CRs, and the CS seems to play the role of "triggering" a reaction that has been preset by the instructions.

The "anticipatory instructed" subclass may include some experiments that are more conveniently analyzed in terms of instrumental learning terminology, with the "US" being a reinforcer of the response on which it is contingent. However, there are other experiments (see, for example, Marquis & Porter, 1939) in which reinforcement in neither the classical nor the instrumental sense seems to be present, and the categorization of such procedures as of one type of learning or another (see Kimble, 1964) seems to depend as much upon faith as upon fact.

A second snare which awaits the unwary investigator is the assumption that the UR and the CR are the same (or essentially the same) response. This misconception is encouraged by summary diagrams of classical conditioning which show the CS becoming "connected" to the UR during the conditioning process. In fact, it is the rare case in which the UR and the CR are identical in form or amplitude. Even when such similarity is found, there usually is a difference in the latency of the two responses. For example, the eyeblink of the human adult in response to an airpuff aimed at the cornea has a latency of 50–100 msec, whereas the latency of the conditioned blink has a latency of 300–400 msec (Hilgard, 1936; Grant & Norris, 1947). In addition to such temporal differences, much more striking differences in the form of the response are usually seen as conditioning progresses. In the majority of cases (with Grant's "Pavlovian B" reactions a possible exception), some components of the original UR drop out, while previously unobserved responses accrue to the conditioned reaction. In the Pavlovian situation, conditioned salivation without chewing, or conditioned chewing without swallowing may be seen. In defensive reactions, leg movements may become mere gestures, and the struggling or barking included in the original UR may disappear (Hilgard & Marquis, 1940). A further complication is introduced into the analysis if the experimenter happens to observe and record a variety of response measures. For example, Zener (1937) repeated the essential portions of Pavlov's procedure, but he also took motion-picture records of the gross behavior of the dog. He found that, in addition to the dropping out of some portions of the UR as conditioning proceeded, new responses came into the sequences of behavior. The general pattern of changes suggested to him that the dog was looking for, and expecting,

the delivery of the US (food) and that his behavior could be described as expectant and preparatory. This behavior is exactly what we should expect if, in parallel with the classical conditioning of some features of the original reaction to the US (for example, salivation), there were a loss of other components (such as chewing), possibly through extinction of some responses and habituation of others, and at the same time reinforcement and subsequent strengthening of new responses was provided through instrumental learning. Pavlov circumvented these complications by concentrating on the salivary response and ignoring most of the other behavior of his dogs. A broader view of the behavior, however, shows that classical conditioning procedures probably always involve some instrumental learning, and vice versa (see, for example, Shapiro, 1961; Shapiro & Miller, 1965).

Instrumental (Operant) Training

We are indebted to Hilgard and Marquis (1940) for suggesting the term "instrumental conditioning" as well as for the term "classical conditioning." The term is an apt one, for, in the experiments utilizing such procedures, the behavior of the organism is indeed instrumental in determining the stimulation of the immediately succeeding moments. Skinner (1935) had earlier suggested the term "operant" in recognition of the same fact—that the behavior of the subject "operates upon" his environment. This characteristic is to be contrasted with the dominant feature of true Pavlovian procedures in which the behavior of the organism in no way determines the sequential presentation of the conditioned and unconditioned stimuli.[13]

The term "conditioning" frequently is applied to both the classical and the instrumental procedures, but for ease of discrimi-

[13] Synonymous terms used to label the two paradigms are: "classical" and "instrumental" conditioning (Hilgard & Marquis, 1940); "Type I" and "Type II" conditioned reflex (Miller & Konorski, 1928); and "respondent" and "operant" conditioning (Skinner, 1935, 1938).

nation we reserve the term "conditioning" for the methods of Pavlov, and say "instrumental" or "operant" *training* or *learning* when referring to the latter procedures. It is unfortunate that "conditioning" has been used to refer to two procedures that are so different, for it suggests that they somehow share properties not shared by other techniques used in behavior modification. Such terminology certainly must be a source of confusion to laymen and may be partially responsible for the misconception held by many biological scientists that these are merely two slightly different forms of the same procedure and that they probably involve the same neuronal process.

Comparison of classical and instrumental procedures The distinction between the classical and the instrumental procedures may be more clearly understood if we compare the manner in which the acquisition of a leg flexion response might be studied using these two methods. For convenience, a non-injurious electrical shock may be used to elicit leg flexion; in the classical procedure the active electrode would be fastened to the leg of the animal so that, regardless of movements which it might make, the onset and duration of the US would remain under the control of the experimenter (see Liddell, 1926; Liddell, James & Anderson, 1934). On the other hand, if the instrumental procedure were to be employed, a switch might be attached to the foreleg so that flexion of the leg would interrupt the shock circuit, thus terminating the shock or preventing a shock from being given (see Culler et al., 1935). In this way, the apparatus insures that the behavior of the organism will be instrumental in determining the outcome of each trial.

The basic paradigm for instrumental (operant) procedures utilizing positive reinforcers may be summarized in this manner:

Response → Reinforcing stimulus

If aversive stimuli are employed, the response terminates or postpones the stimulus. In cases where discriminative stimuli are introduced,

the paradigm is modified slightly:

Positive stimulus : Response →
                            Reinforcing stimulus
Negative stimulus : Response →
                    Omission of reinforcing stimulus

Note that the discriminative stimuli do not stand in the same relation to the reinforcing stimulus as does the conditioned stimulus of Pavlov. In the instrumental paradigm, the positive stimulus and the reinforcing stimulus occur in temporal contiguity only if the response is emitted; in classical conditioning, the temporal relation of the two stimuli is controlled by the experimenter and not by the responses of the subject. Note also that the instrumental response is *emitted* by the subject, whereas the unconditioned response in the classical situation is *elicited* by the US.

In summary, it might be said that the Pavlovian paradigm provides a rule about certain *antecedents* of behavior, whereas the instrumental paradigm provides a rule about some of the *consequences* of behavior.

The role of reinforcing stimuli The key term in the instrumental paradigm is the *reinforcing stimulus*. Reinforcing stimuli are discussed in the next chapter, but here we may note that a reinforcer is defined as any stimulus which increases the probability of the response upon which it is contingent.

As we see in Chapter 15, there is no single property common to all of the stimuli that prove to be reinforcers other than the property by which they are defined. There is thus a similar problem of definition and identification of key terms for the instrumental paradigm as there is for the classical conditioning paradigm, in which the only criterion by which we are able to define an unconditioned stimulus is the regularity with which it elicits the unconditioned response.

To define a reinforcing stimulus as "one which reinforces" may seem patently circular.[14] It has

---

[14] The circularity, Skinner (1953) has argued, is introduced only when we define the stimulus as a reinforcer based on its property of increasing response probability and then close the circle by explaining why the stimulus has this

been suggested (Meehl, 1950) that such circularity might be avoided if we emphasized the general, *trans-situational* properties of reinforcers. For example, if a given stimulus has been shown to increase the probability of a certain response in one situation, it should produce similar effects on other responses in new situations. Although trans-situational reinforcers do exist (for example, food for a food-deprived organism), there are many stimuli which prove to be reinforcers (1) of some but not all possible responses, and (2) in some, but not all situations. We are often made painfully aware of the dependence of reinforcing effects on the context in which they are applied. Saying "Good boy!" may be a potent reinforcer for the well-trained hound, but the sudden appearance of a bitch in heat may nullify the reinforcing effects of his master's voice. It is tempting to explain such changes as due to shifts in dominance within a hierarchy of "drives" or "motives," but similar changes occur as we go from home to schoolroom, from laboratory to playing field, and in these cases we have no independent means of identifying the drives that might be correlated with the reinforcers. Under such conditions, it does not seem that we can deny the existence of situational-specific reinforcers, and so we probably cannot insist on trans-situational properties in defining reinforcing stimuli. We thus are left with our simple behavioral criterion: Reinforcers are those stimuli which increase the probability of the response on which they are contingent. (See the discussion in Chapter 18 of the definition of drives in terms of reinforcers, pp. 796 ff.)

The theoretical role of reinforcing stimuli has been central to the attempts to subsume both classical and instrumental procedures under a single paradigm. For example, Hull (1943), suggested that all instrumental learning was based upon the action of reinforcers which were drive reducers, and raised the possibility that classical conditioning might involve the same processes. Inasmuch as the response in classical conditioning *follows* the *onset* of the unconditioned stimulus during at least the earliest phases of conditioning, the suggestion that drive reduction could account for classical conditioning never

gained wide acceptance. Zeaman and his coworkers have examined classically conditioned changes in heart rate from the point of view of drive reduction, and have concluded that the relative lack of effects of varying the duration or intensity of the US provides strong evidence against the drive-reduction hypothesis. (See the survey in Zeaman and Smith, 1965.)

An alternative suggested by Guthrie (1935, 1952) interpreted both classical and instrumental procedures as variants of the conditioning of responses to stimuli through contiguity. As we have already mentioned, Guthrie[15] postulated the complete and instantaneous conditioning of each response to every stimulus present at the moment and argued that all training methods and conditioning procedures are merely techniques whereby the necessary temporal relations may be produced, and the resulting conditioning may be protected from eradication by subsequent conditioning. For example, given the problem of gaining control over a response R_A, we might passively await its occurrence or try to elicit it through manipulation of stimuli; at the same time that the response is occurring, we would seek to have present some set of stimuli (S_1) which we can control. Once there is an occurrence of R_A in the presence of S_1, the response becomes (according to Guthrie) completely conditioned to S_1. However, because behavior never is abruptly terminated, other responses may follow R_A, and if we have failed to terminate S_1 as soon as R_A occurred, these other responses will, as each occurs, become conditioned to S_1 and each, in turn, will displace its immediate predecessor. Thus, temporal contiguity not only will condition R_A to S_1 but, if we allow S_1 to continue, will condition interfering responses to S_1.

In situations where we cannot exercise adequate control over the stimuli, a some-

property by stating that it is a reinforcer. If we stop with the definition, we are classifying the stimulus but not explaining the property. At present, there is no satisfactory explanation that applies to all instances of reinforcement.

[15] Guthrie did not attempt to provide a set of formal statements summarizing his theoretical position. One set of postulates consistent with his theory has been presented by Voeks (1950). For a concise statement of a contiguity theorist's interpretation of the role of reinforcing stimuli, see Sheffield (1965).

what different problem exists. Suppose we have managed to obtain the contiguous occurrence of S_1 and R_A, but the nature of the response is such that it must occur in bursts; if the stimuli vary during the burst of R_A responses, whatever is the stimulus set present when the last R_A occurs will be its controlling stimulus.

Of course, we know from both practical experience and laboratory investigation that reinforcement and punishment are effective in modifying and maintaining behavior, but Guthrian contiguity theory denies the necessity of these factors, and explains their effectiveness by referring to the manner in which they change the stimulus situation or the response pattern. Why does a single delivery of a food pellet greatly increase the probability that the response that is just being made will reoccur? Because, says Guthrie, the food pellet changes the stimulus situation from what it was just as the response occurred and (by drawing the animal toward it and away from the place where the response was made) insures that the response cannot become conditioned to a different set of stimuli. A similar analysis is offered for the roles of aversive stimuli and their terminations: The burned child withdraws his hand from the flame, thereby insuring that withdrawal is the last response made in the presence of the flame. Hence, the very next presentation of the flame should produce the withdrawal movement.

This interpretation of the role of reinforcers implies that if the subject is promptly removed from the environment in which a response is made the response just conditioned will not suffer any interference from conflicting conditioning. "Removal" from the environment would desirably be accompanied by changing all the stimuli impinging on the organism—a practical impossibility, of course, since many of our stimuli are the products of relatively steady bodily states. However, if effective removal does immediately follow a response, and if the subject is later reintroduced to that environment, that last response should again be made. Whether such effects

have indeed been demonstrated under controlled laboratory conditions is a moot point. Some indirect evidence is provided by a study of one-trial avoidance behavior (Hudson, 1950; see also Tolman, 1948, pp. 200–201). Hudson equipped a chamber with a food cup and a distinctive striped wall panel. Rats were used as subjects and electric shock was delivered to some of them when they touched the food cup; at the same moment, the chamber was completely darkened, and the food cup and the pattern were removed. The lights were then turned on again, and the animal was removed from the apparatus. When the rats were returned to the lighted chamber the next day, many (but not all) repeated the last response they had made in that situation: They approached the striped pattern and touched the food cup. This result is exactly what Guthrie would have predicted—although it is difficult to see how he would have accounted for the many other types of reactions that also occurred. For example, some animals later avoided the cup, while others seemed to be avoiding other areas of the chamber. Because the lights were turned off and the striped pattern and cup were removed at the instant the shock occurred, it is difficult to imagine that any response other than approach could have been the last response made in the presence of the cup and stripe stimuli. This is an intriguing problem which certainly deserves additional investigation.

The results of a study of removing the subject from the situation in which no aversive stimulation was employed also are rather equivocal so far as contiguity theory is concerned. Seward (1942) compared the effects of three treatments, removing each rat from the apparatus as soon as (1) a bar press had been emitted, (2) the animal had seized the food pellet delivered when he pressed the bar, or (3) one minute had passed. Mere removal following the bar press was less effective than food reinforcement, but more effective than noncontingent removal, in terms of the latency of the first response on each training day and the number of responses emitted on extinction tests. Perhaps as interesting as these results was Seward's observation that eight of ten animals removed following the bar press response also learned to "anticipate" removal: "They approached the bar, pressed it with a forefoot, quickly swung around, sometimes looking up at the experimenter, and waited motionless a second or two" (p. 254). Again, this is what Guthrie might have predicted, but that the behavior was conditioned by contiguity and protected by removal from the chamber is impossible to prove, because there is always the possibility that reinforcement of some kind was present (for example, in the procedure of handling the animals, which so frequently in their lives has been paired with feeding).

In summary, Guthrie suggested that the basic unit of learning was the association of response and stimulus, based solely upon their contiguous occurrence, with reinforcing stimuli aiding the process by protecting what had already been accomplished by contiguity. This theory differs from usual interpretations of instrumental learning in that it denies the necessity of reinforcement. It differs from the usual interpretations of classical conditioning by maintaining that the association is between stimulus and response, rather than between two stimuli.

We have reviewed these theories because the basic ideas are still to be found in contemporary theorizing and, in at least some cases, are more easily understood in the simpler forms of an earlier generation. At the present time, many writers feel that some variety of two-factor theory is needed to account for the differences produced by the classical and the instrumental procedures. Representative two-factor theories have already been mentioned (p. 563); for an evaluation of the applicability of this point of view to avoidance learning, see Rescorla and Solomon (1967).

Experimental Extinction

The second of Pavlov's major contributions to the understanding of learning processes was the discovery of experimental extinction.

Perhaps "discovery" is an inappropriate word, for the general idea of extinction—like that of conditioning—was well known in folklore, even if the philosophy of Associationism had never given it formal recognition. But it is a long step from knowing that the villagers eventually will cease to respond if one repeatedly cries "Wolf!", to the specification of the conditions under which the process will occur. Moreover, the facts of experimental extinction seemed to run counter to the Associationists' Law of Frequency, which made the "discovery" of extinction that much more difficult.

Extinction sometimes is treated merely as a technique for the elimination of previously conditioned responses. Such impressions miss the significance of the phenomenon: Extinction does not involve a simple unstacking of the associations built up through conditioning; it is an active process in which something new is learned about the environment.

The paradigms for extinction always assume prior classical conditioning or instrumental training. Given that, the paradigms are:

Following Classical Conditioning	Following Instrumental Training
Present CS; omit US	Omit reinforcing stimulus

In the classical situation, the experimenter controls the spacing of extinction trials, and although the subject sometimes makes responses between trials in the absence of the CS, for the most part the intervals between trials can be manipulated to suit the purposes of the experiment. The same is true of those instrumental situations in which trial-by-trial procedures are employed. However, in many cases, the "free operant" technique is the procedure of choice, and then the rate with which responses are emitted is the primary datum and the experimenter strives to avoid any contamination of this rate by arbitrary divisions of the observation periods. This matter of technique becomes important when the spacing of responses in extinction is considered (see pp. 576–577; and Figure 14.3).

In all important respects, extinction following classical conditioning and following instrumental training appears to be the same general phenomenon, and there has thus far been no need to construct any "two-factor" theories of extinction.[16] Considering the differences between the two situations, it is somewhat surprising that this is so. If, for example, classical conditioning is basically an association of two stimuli, and the instrumental procedure is one which generates an association of a response and a stimulus (that is, the reinforcer), we might expect different effects, different important parameters, different functional relations to obtain in the two cases when we break the correlation between the paired terms. This is not the case. The same kinds of effects seem to be found in extinction following both procedures.

We are indebted to Pavlov for the description of the basic phenomena associated with the omission of the US.

Briefly, the major ones are:

Extinction—Pavlov used the term to refer both to the *procedure* of omitting the US and to the *result* of the procedure, which usually was continued until the first trial on which no CR occurred. At that point, it was said that extinction was "complete."

Spontaneous recovery—after a pause in the extinction procedure, an increase in the CR may be seen.[17]

Disinhibition—if a novel stimulus is introduced

during or immediately following extinction trials, an increase in the CR may be seen.

Reconditioning—if extinction trials are followed by a single presentation of the CS-US combination, much or all of the effects of extinction will be overcome.

Differentiation—if one stimulus is paired with the US and another stimulus is not paired with it, the former will become a CS and the latter will not.

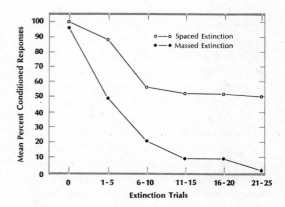

Figure 14.3. Extinction with massed and spaced extinction trials. Subjects were conditioned with an auditory CS and air puff US; the response was the eyelid closure to CS. These results are for subjects conditioned with a 450 msec CS-US interval, with 1–2 min between trials. Spaced extinction trials had 1–2 min intertrial intervals; massed extinction had 10–20 sec between trials. Note that there was a change in intertrial interval for subjects in the massed extinction group, which might (through generalization decrement) produce some difference between the groups. At least, this has been suggested as an explanation for some of the failures to find massed extinction to be more rapid than spaced extinction where instrumental behavior is involved (Teichner, 1952). In Reynolds' experiment, other groups conditioned with massed trials and extinguished either with massed or with spaced trials showed little difference during extinction. This could be taken as partial support for Teichner's hypothesis, if we assume that the spaced groups in this instance had response decrements due to changes in intertrial intervals, thus canceling the "normal" difference between massed and spaced extinction procedures. (After Reynolds, 1945.)

TABLE 14.2 INTERFERENCE THEORY INTERPRETATIONS OF "HABIT BREAKING"

Name	Procedure	Explanation	Examples
1. Exhaustion method	Present CS continually until CR no longer occurs (as a result of fatigue, exhaustion, etc.)	Although CR ceases, CS is still present and whatever other responses now occur are conditioned to CS	Typical experimental extinction procedure; bronco busting
2. Incompatible response method	Present CS while also presenting stimuli which control responses that are incompatible with CR	Since CR is "blocked" by other responses, and these are made in presence of CS, CR is displaced as the reaction to CS	Counterconditioning therapy (e.g., present to male homosexual a picture of a man, and then present electric shock)
3. Toleration method	Present CS in a weakened or disguised form; gradually bring CS back to original condition	By greatly modifying CS, occurrence of CR is avoided; by gradually changing CS, whatever other responses had been occurring to altered CS will continue to occur	Halfway-house techniques (e.g., gradual introduction of some of the cues that in the past have produced aberrant behavior); gentling procedures; seductions

In these phenomena we see some of the reasons why extinction cannot be thought of merely as an undoing of prior conditioning. For example, if that were a sufficient interpretation, then there should be no spontaneous recovery. For the same reason, extinction cannot be considered to be the conditioning of some other response that blocks the original CR, for conditioning is relatively permanent and its effects would not be expected to dissipate spontaneously to allow the recovery of the first CR. Neither should a single reinforcement of the extinguished CS (that is, reconditioning) bring it back to such strength if extinction were a matter of conditioning incompatible responses. Finally, there is the important point that conditioning usually progresses best when trials are broadly spaced (see, for example, Schlosberg, 1934), while extinction effects usually are most readily obtained when trials are massed (Figure 14.3).

Interference theories The observations discussed above seem to offer serious difficulties for theories such as those proposed by Guthrie (1935, 1952) and Wendt (1936),

which hold that extinction and conditioning are really a single process. Guthrie countered such arguments by maintaining that many instances which are labeled "extinction" really should be called "habit breaking" and that they are quite clearly situations in which one response is replaced by another.

Guthrie described three types of situations that he felt would include the bulk of the classical and instrumental procedures that usually are categorized as "extinction." In each, the key to successful replacement of the unwanted response involves a recombination of stimuli and responses, so that new responses become conditioned to the old stimuli, and vice versa. Guthrie's suggestions are summarized in Table 14.2. Whereas everyday examples of these procedures are quite common, few studies have examined the techniques under carefully controlled conditions.

In what must have been one of the first investigations of behavior therapy techniques, Mary Cover Jones (1924) examined the efficacy of procedures designed to eliminate children's fears. In one such test, the child was placed in a high chair and given something to eat. The feared object then was introduced

TABLE 14.3 COMPARISON OF "TOLERATION" AND "EXHAUSTION" METHODS OF ELIMINATING RESPONSES

| Group | Mean number of extinction responses | | | Opportunities for responding | Mean Rs/op |
	In 16 min of toleration procedure	In 30 extinction trials	Total		
Toleration	1.1	5.4	6.5	92	.07
Exhaustion	—	14.4	14.4	30	.48

From Kimble & Kendall, 1953

at a distance. While the child was eating, the object was brought slowly toward him, until finally it could be placed next to him or close enough to be touched, without fear responses having occurred. Note that this procedure involved a combination of gradual introduction of the feared object (Case 3) and simultaneous elicitation of a behavior (eating) that was incompatible with fear (Case 2), and that it was essential to adjust the rate of approach of the feared object so that eating was not completely disrupted, for this might have had the undesirable effect of making food the CS for emotional reactions.

The toleration technique was compared with the more usual extinction procedure (Case 1) by Kimble and Kendall (1953). First, laboratory rats were given 60 trials of avoidance training, using a light as CS and foot shock as US. The CS came on 5.8 seconds before the shock. The compartment contained a wheel which would terminate both CS and US if rotated by the rat. If the wheel were turned during the preshock interval, the CS went off and the shock was cancelled. Thus, the rat could avoid all shocks by turning the wheel within 5.8 seconds after the light was turned on.

Following this avoidance training, one of two types of treatment was used. One group received typical experimental extinction: on each of thirty trials, the CS came on for 15 seconds or until the rat turned the wheel. The second group was exposed to seven "toleration" trials, in which the CS intensity was increased every 15 sec, starting at a brighter value each trial. At the end of each trial, it was as bright as it had been during training (and, of course, as the other group's CS had

been throughout). Once the light was turned up to this level, thirty trials of regular extinction were given. The results are summarized in Table 14.3. Note that the toleration procedure was effective: The rats in the toleration group made very few wheel-turning responses during the extinction phase.

Because spontaneous recovery usually follows typical experimental extinction procedures, we might expect the animals in the exhaustion group to make many responses if they were placed in the apparatus again on the following day. In contrast, Guthrie's theory would predict that the animals in the toleration group would show relatively little spontaneous recovery. There does not seem to be any published data on this problem, but were this to be the case, we could count the toleration procedure superior as a technique for both immediate and for long-term behavior modification.

Why does the typical extinction procedure have the effect of reducing the strength of the CR? Guthrie suggested that the first omission of the US (or of the reinforcing stimulus, in operant situations) creates a major change in the stimulus situation, both directly and indirectly, through feedback from the resultant excited or agitated behavior. If the next trial follows soon afterward, the CS might be expected to be lost in this mass of changed stimuli, and so a lowered probability of the response would be predicted. With time, the excitement or agitation should pass, the stimulus situation should become more similar to the earlier conditioning situation, and therefore spontaneous recovery might be expected.

Applied to extinction problems, contiguity

theory would seem to imply that very widely spaced extinction trials would not result in any decrement in the CR, for if we remove the subject from the experimental situation immediately following the response, we should "protect" the conditioning and make the extinction trial the equivalent of another training trial. However, extinction *does* occur when trials are spaced as much as one a day (Weinstock, 1964). Contiguity theory accounts for this apparent contradiction by assuming that the omission of the reinforcing stimulus on the first extinction trial immediately causes marked changes in behavior, and these new responses are, of course, immediately conditioned to the stimuli present at that moment.

Consider the simple running response of an animal placed in a straight alley. On the first extinction trial, the animal approaches the portion of the goal box where food previously had been placed; there being none, he now emits other responses (standing up, jumping, and so on) which are immediately conditioned to apparatus stimuli and which, on the next trials, interfere with swift running. Such responses become conditioned to greater proportions of the stimuli on succeeding trials, thus generating the familiar extinction curve.

Such new and potentially interfering responses do occur on extinction trials, but the extent to which they are incompatible with the previously reinforced responses is difficult to estimate. Adelman and Maatsch (1955) maximized the differences in such behaviors during extinction by allowing one group of rats to retreat from the goal box into the alleyway, allowing another group to leap out of the goal box onto its upper edge, but giving a third group the "normal" treatment of confining the rat briefly in the empty goal box. The "jump" group showed almost no extinction of the response of running in the alley, whereas the group allowed to "recoil" into the alleyway extinguished more rapidly than the "normal" group. These results are interpreted as support for interference theory because the "recoil" response is thought to be most incompatible with forward locomotion

in the alley, and the "jump" response is said to be compatible with forward locomotion (see also Weisman et al., 1966). Quantifying the degree of incompatibility of responses is an obvious next step for the proponents of such hypotheses.

Inhibition theories Pavlov assumed that activity of the nervous system could be categorized as either excitatory or inhibitory, with the former being associated with the occurrence of reflexes and the latter with their nonoccurrence. He postulated several types of inhibition. On some occasions, the sudden appearance of a novel stimulus may disrupt a CR; Pavlov assumed that the stimulus must have initiated an inhibitory process which, because it was associated with changes in the external environment, he labeled *external inhibition*. Such effects typically are maximal on their first occurrence and diminish with repetition. *Internal inhibition* was assumed to be generated whenever the CS is presented: "The cortical cells under the influence of the conditioned stimulus always tend to pass, though sometimes very slowly, into a state of inhibition. The function performed by the unconditioned reflex after the conditioned reflex has become established is merely to retard the development of inhibition" (Pavlov, 1927, p. 234). If the CS is regularly presented for many seconds (for example, 30) before the US, *inhibition of delay* (another form of internal inhibition) is built up, and the CR occurs later and later after the onset of the CS. If, however, the US is omitted altogether, inhibition develops with greatest rapidity, and extinction is observed. Even when CS and US are paired, if the pairings are closely massed, or if they are continued for weeks or months, gradual diminution of the CR may occur (*inhibition of reinforcement*: see Hovland, 1936; Kantrow, 1937). Inhibition, like excitation, is subject to disruption; introduction of an external inhibiting stimulus during a long CS, or during extinction trials, may result in the immediate reappearance of the CR (interpreted as inhibition of internal inhibition by external inhibition, or *disinhibition*).

From the point of view of theory construction, it is interesting to note that none of these inhibitory processes were directly observed; they were instead inferences from observations of behavior. Many psychologists have found the hypothetical physiological processes attached to the concepts not very helpful and have therefore discarded them, while keeping the functional aspects of these or similar notions. For example, Hull (1943) postulated an inhibitory factor, *reactive inhibition,* which (1) was generated whenever a response occurred, and which (2) dissipated spontaneously with the passage of time. Furthermore, he assumed that (3) the more work that was involved in the execution of the response, the greater the increment of reactive inhibition per response. With reactive inhibition given these properties, it could be used to deduce such phenomena as selection (other things equal) of the shorter path or the response that requires the least effort (the "Law of Less Effort"; see Thompson, 1944; Solomon, 1948); more rapid conditioning with spaced trials and more rapid extinction with massed trials; spontaneous recovery of extinguished responses; and reminiscence following massed practice.

However, because spontaneous recovery rarely is complete, and because a consistent use of closely massed trials leads to poorer conditioning than does the use of more widely spaced trials, Hull postulated a more permanent form of inhibition, *conditioned inhibition.* In essence, this was conceived to be a learned response of not responding; as a learned response, it had (according to Hull's theory of reinforcement) to be reinforced by drive reduction, and so reactive inhibition was given the property of being an aversive drive, thus making its dissipation reinforcing. The occurrence of several effortful responses in close succession would, according to this theory, produce an accumulation of considerable reactive inhibition, which would begin to dissipate when the response was not made (that is, the subject was either "resting" or making some other responses), and this be-

havior of not responding (the conditioned inhibition of the response) would therefore be strengthened. Being a learned response, conditioned inhibition would acquire its habit strength gradually; it would generalize to similar stimulus situations, and otherwise

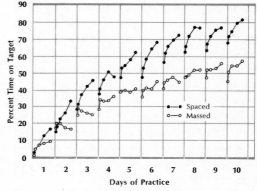

Figure 14.4. Massed and spaced practice on a pursuit rotor. The subject's task was to keep a stylus tip on a small target as it rotated at 78 revolutions per minute. The response was recorded as the amount of time during each trial that the stylus was on the target. Our curves here are smoothed within each day except for the first, second, and last trials of each day; these are shown separately to bring out the following features: (1) the rapid rise in proficiency shown by the jump from Trial 1 to Trial 2 on each day, usually thought to be due to a "warm-up" effect or reinstatement of the appropriate modes of response; (2) the decline in proficiency within daily sessions shown by the massed practice group; (3) the recovery from this decline; and (4) the overnight loss after a day of rising scores. In spite of the complications introduced into the curves by warm-up and work decrement, the general course of learning can be seen. The second trial of each day is least affected by these complications; drawing an imaginary curve through all of the Trial 2 points shows that the massed practice group is already falling behind after two days of practice. As long as conditions remained unchanged, the spaced practice group would probably continue its superiority; if conditions were interchanged for a few days, the groups might reverse their positions. (After Kimble & Shattel, 1952, as modified by Woodworth & Schlosberg, 1954.)

would show the properties of habits in the Hullian system.

This form of inhibition theory has been most thoroughly developed and applied in the interpretation of "massed" versus "spaced" (or "distributed") practice (Ammons, 1947; Irion, 1966). For example, Kimble and Shattel (1952) gave college students the task of learning to keep a stylus on a rotating target ("rotary pursuit"), where the score is the time per trial that the stylus tip is on the target. Two groups of subjects were run, each subject receiving 15 trials a day for 10 days, with each trial lasting 50 seconds. The group that had been given massed practice was allowed a 5 to 10 sec pause or rest between trials, while the group that was given distributed practice had 65 to 70 sec between trials. The average scores for the two groups are shown in Figure 14.4. Note that both groups became increasingly proficient with practice, but that the superiority of the spaced-practice group increased as the experiment continued, a result attributed to the greater amount of conditioned inhibition acquired under the massed practice conditions.

The rapid increase in proficiency following a period of no practice has been attributed to the dissipation of reactive inhibition. Such gains in performance associated with "resting" are called reminiscence effects, and frequently are quite large in situations involving motor skills. They are not merely a result of recovery from fatigue in the limbs used in making the skilled responses. Subjects can be asked to practice using one hand and then shift to the other hand. Those forced to wait a few minutes before beginning the bilateral test perform better than those who are given no such pause in the schedule (Grice & Reynolds, 1952; Irion & Gustafson, 1952; Kimble, 1952). Adams (1955) showed that some of the inferior performance of subjects allowed no rest in such bilateral transfer studies might be associated with the perceptual side of the skilled behavior. He required some subjects to devote the periods during which they were not practicing to close observation of the performance of other individuals. When they resumed practice, such subjects showed less reminiscence than did those who received the standard type of treatment (that is, "rest") during the pause. Such results showed that reminiscence could not be attributed merely to dissipation of an inhibitory factor which was presumed to be localized in effectors.

These experiments were among the last of the several score of studies that were largely prompted by Hullian inhibition theory and which appeared during the decade following the publication of Principles of Behavior (Hull, 1943). On the whole, good progress had been made toward specifying conditions under which temporary and permanent decrements in performance would be found, but it seemed that each new experiment required an additional amendment to the properties ascribed to reactive and conditioned inhibition. Eventually, enthusiasm for such research just seemed to evaporate.

Of course, there are fads and fashions in research just as in other areas of human endeavor, but more than this is needed to explain the very rapid disappearance of experiments directed toward Hullian inhibition theory. Underwood (1966) suggests that one factor might have been the growing recognition that these concepts had relatively little to contribute to some of the key problems in verbal learning. At the same time, the emphasis in much of animal learning was shifting toward the use of free operant techniques, where—by releasing the responses of the subject from direct control and making response rate a dependent variable—the experimental study of Hullian-type inhibitory effects becomes exceedingly difficult. Finally, the newest trends in learning—quantitative models, short-term processes, analysis of behavior changes in the individual organism, and the physiological and anatomical investigations—all took attention away from Hullian inhibition theory.

Inhibition theory may be just temporarily in the doldrums, awaiting some new ideas and experimental techniques. However, the concept of conditioned inhibition has become so encumbered by ad hoc properties that it probably will not again be as widely employed as it once was. (For a critique of these concepts, see Underwood, 1953; Gleitman, Nachmias, and Neisser, 1954. For a survey of experiments on massed versus spaced practice, see Woodworth and Schlosberg, 1954, pp. 786–794.)

In several important respects, Hull's intervening variables of reactive and conditioned inhibition differed from Pavlov's hypothetical inhibitory process. For example, Pavlov concluded that all inhibition, regardless of its origins, was of one type; that it was an inherent protective activity of the cerebral cortex; and that it was associated with the presentation of stimuli, and, in conditioning, especially with the presence of the CS. Hull, as we have seen, postulated two quite different forms of inhibition, the one associated with effector activities and the other with learning to withhold a response. In general terms, it might be said that Pavlov's ideas about inhibition revolved around the hypothetical mechanisms of the cerebral cortex which protect it from repetitive and interruptive stimulation, while Hull's thoughts on inhibition concentrated on the response mechanism and the adaptive habits of resting or of varying responses.

Before leaving the topic of inhibition, we should mention still another way in which it is used. Just as the physiologist finds the terms *excitation* and *inhibition* to be useful ones with which to refer to processes associated with activity, on the one hand, and the lack of activity, on the other, so have behaviorists found these terms convenient to describe parallel changes in responding. Furthermore, just as there are numerous mechanisms which may produce excitatory or inhibitory consequences at the levels of cells, tissues, and organs, so there may be many ways in which behavioral outcomes of an excitatory or inhibitory nature may be effected. For example, both nonreinforcement (that is, extinction) and punishment of a response will decrease its probability of occurrence, and therefore both procedures could be said to generate inhibition of that response.[18] It is in this descriptive sense that inhibition was used by Spence (for example, 1936) and others to describe the consequences of nonreinforcement in discrimination learning (see pp. 764; and 770 ff.).

[18] Punishment (see Chapter 16) generates "passive avoidance" behavior, with mere withholding of responding being sufficient to avoid aversive stimuli. In many other situations, "active avoidance" is required if the aversive stimulus is to be avoided. Typical active avoidance responses used in the laboratory are jumping into a "safe" compartment of a shuttle box, or pressing a lever or panel. McCleary (1961) has demonstrated that passive avoidance behavior in cats is diminished or destroyed when lesions are placed in the subcallosal cortex and adjacent septal region of the brain, while active avoidance remains unimpaired by such damage. For this reason, these areas have been called "inhibitory areas" for avoidance behavior, since the ability of the cat to inhibit the emission of a response which will be punished is much diminished when bilateral lesions are placed in such regions.

Spacing of extinction trials In operational terms, extinction is the omission of reinforcement. If every response has been reinforced, the first omission of reinforcement frequently is followed by recognizable signs of disturbance, often identified with "frustration." One of the attributes of this frustration reaction is an increase in the vigor of whatever responses are occurring at the moment. As a consequence, there may be a period during which the previously reinforced response shows an increase in vigor and/or rate of occurrence when extinction is first introduced. For example, if a rat has found food in the goal box of a straight alley (Figure 15.1, p. 618) on every previous trial, on the first occasion when he does not find it he may show overt agitation, be difficult to handle, jump about in the goal box, and so on. If he then is placed directly into the start box and the next trial is initiated, the excitement caused by the frustration may cause the rat to run even faster than during reinforced trials (see Amsel, 1958; Wagner, 1959).

Now, in such situations, closely massing the extinction trials keeps activity at high levels and increases the number of extinction trials needed to attain an extinction criterion, whereas spacing the extinction trials allows the excitement to diminish, with the consequence that running becomes slower and extinction criteria are met in fewer trials (Sheffield, 1949). Such effects of "frustrative nonreward" are likely to be found wherever the response measure is one which is enhanced by excitement. That it does not represent a contradiction of Pavlov's general rule (that is, extinction is faster with massed than with spaced trials) has been demonstrated most clearly by Stanley (1952), who showed that massing extinction trials slows down the extinction of running responses while it speeds up the extinction of the response of turning into the formerly reinforced side of a T maze. Hence, we must qualify our general rule about extinction and the spacing of extinction trials: For responses that are not augmented by increased overall excitement, the number of trials to extinction is positively correlated with the time between trials; for responses that are augmented by excitement, the number of trials to extinction is negatively correlated with the between-trials interval.

How can we summarize the simple facts about extinction? First, it is not a mere cancellation of the effects of reinforcement, else spontaneous recovery would not occur. Next, it is (like other learned reactions) sensitive to distractions, as shown by Pavlov's "disinhibition." Furthermore, it shares with other learned reactions the phenomenon of stimulus generalization: If a response is extinguished in the presence of one stimulus, varying the stimuli along some dimension will diminish the extinction effects in proportion to the amount of stimulus change between extinction and testing (Kling, 1952; Honig, 1961). Finally, extinction procedures may generate considerable excitement which in some cases may increase the vigor of responding, while in others it may interfere with the emission of previously reinforced responses.

Sensitization

Ordinarily, when we discuss the definition of learning, we mention certain modifications of behavior that are said to be artifacts of the methods of experimentation rather than instances of "real learning." *Sensitization* and *pseudoconditioning* are the two most frequently mentioned "artifacts." They are especially likely to be encountered in conditioning studies involving aversive stimulation; they are said not to be instances of true conditioning because they do not depend upon pairing of the conditioned and the unconditioned stimuli. The implications of this statement will be better appreciated when we examine the phenomena themselves. Let us look first at sensitization.

In a typical classical conditioning experiment, we assume that the experimenter has satisfied himself that the stimulus to be used as the conditioned stimulus is neutral so far as the response to be conditioned is concerned. However, there are some responses which can be elicited by a very broad range of stimuli; with such responses, it is possible that the to-be-conditioned stimulus is, in fact, itself an unconditioned stimulus. But how could an experimenter be unaware that his conditioned stimulus was not neutral? Imagine that the intensity of an unconditioned stimulus be reduced to the point where it does not quite elicit the unconditioned response, and further, that our experimenter is unfortunate enough to have selected this stimulus *at this intensity* for his conditioned stimulus. On testing, the stimulus would appear neutral. Now imagine that circumstances exist which somehow make the organism more sensitive to the stimulus, so that the response to it will occur even though the intensity of the stimulus remains at what previously had been a "subthreshold" level. If this were to happen during the experiment, responses to the "neutral" stimulus would begin to occur and might easily be mistaken for conditioned responses.

An example of this type of effect can be seen in a study by Prosser and Hunter (1936). As part of a series of studies on the conditioning of spinal reflexes, they presented auditory stimuli (clicks) followed by electrical shocks of the hind limbs. After pairing click and shock a number of times, the click alone elicited the hind limb responses. At this point, less astute experimenters might have accepted the behavior as evidence of classical conditioning and gone on to the next problem. Prosser and Hunter, however, were made suspicious by the constancy of the latency of the "CR" across trials, for ordinarily there is a latency difference between CRs and URs (Hunter, 1937; see also Fig. 14.1). Eventually they concluded that the shock raised the excitability of the neural "centers" involved in the reaction to the click, so that the previously ineffective clicks could become—and remain—capable of eliciting the limb movements.

This, then, is the general line of reasoning followed whenever the behavior change is imputed to sensitization: The CS is not neutral, but merely ineffective under present conditions, and the US (or other aspects of the procedure) either heightens excitability or shifts the response bias (see p. 37) of the subject so that responses to the CS now occur.

Similar effects were noted by Sears (1934). He found that in his experimental conditions, presenting a light to goldfish caused them to swim excitedly. Repeated presentations of the light produced a waning of the response, but isolated shocks (that is, shocks not paired with the light) reinstated the response to the light—and to other stimuli (for example, vibration) as well. This same phenomenon may underly some of the "learning" which has been observed in the headless cockroach and other surgically isolated preparations (see, for example, Horridge, 1962; Eisenstein & Cohen, 1965; Pritchatt, 1968; and Kling & Stevenson, in press).

In such experiments, the UR and the response elicited by the supposedly neutral stimulus may be identical, or they may be so similar that they easily can be confused. This is a highly probable state of affairs if the behavior to be measured is gross activity, or startle responses, or components of the orienting reflex. One of the experimenter's best defenses against mistaking sensitization for conditioning lies in the selection of a response to be conditioned that cannot be confused with one of the preconditioning reactions to the CS. Where this is not possible, control groups must be run which do not have CS and US paired in presentation, and comparisons of the level of responsiveness shown by experimental and control groups must be used to estimate the level of unconditioned behavior attributable to sensitization (see, for example, Bitterman, 1964).

In brief, "sensitization" implies that the reactivity of the organism *to the CS* has been increased by presentations of the US, and that the CS never was originally neutral.

Pseudoconditioning The classical study of pseudoconditioning is that of Grether (1938). While studying the acquisition of emotional reactions, Grether developed a technique for restraining his rhesus monkeys in a chair and eliciting the characteristic fear response with a sudden, explosive US. His CS was an electric bell, and in preliminary tests he had found the bell to be quite neutral so far as the fear response was concerned. Two monkeys were "conditioned" by presenting the US, followed 3 seconds later by the CS; after ten of these trials, the CS alone elicited the fear reaction. Grether did not accept this evidence for backward conditioning at face value, but instead adapted two more monkeys to the procedure and trained them with ten presentations of the US alone. When the CS, *or any other sudden noise* was presented, the characteristic fear response was emitted. On the following day, the bell still caused the fear

TABLE 14.4 COMPARISON OF PARADIGMS FOR SENSITIZATION, PSEUDOCONDITIONING, AND CONDITIONING

Phase	Sensitization		Pseudoconditioning		Conditioning	
	present	*observe*	*present*	*observe*	*present*	*observe*
Preliminary tests	"CS" US	? UR	CS US	? UR	CS US	? UR
Experimental procedure	US	UR	US	UR	CS-US	CR & UR
Final test	"CS"	UR	Any novel stimulus	UR	CS	CR

reaction when the monkeys were brought into the experimental room and placed in the chair, but outside this room, the bell was "neutral." Thus, it is reasonable to assume that the cause of the heightened excitability that allowed the bell or any other noise to set off the fear reaction was partly in the experimental room itself (that is, in the "contextual stimuli" provided by apparatus, restraining chair, and so on) and not just in the "CS" alone. In this sense, Grether's description of the behavior as "pseudo-conditioning" was especially apt, for there was no evidence that the bell acquired any new properties as a result of pairing with the US.

The paradigms for sensitization and pseudoconditioning are very similar to those for conditioning (see Table 14.4), and it is not surprising that the earliest studies of conditioning using aversive stimuli did not include appropriate safeguards against these artifacts. The basic difference between the two artifacts is that sensitization occurs because a stimulus is used which is not neutral under all possible conditions of the experiment, whereas pseudoconditioning involves no such special reflex, but does introduce a state of affairs in which any sudden or novel stimulus will elicit a response which cannot be distinguished from the UR. Almost always these are complications that must be suspected to exist when we are using stimuli which cause emotional upset, and almost certainly one or both can account for most or all of the reported instances of backward conditioning (see p. 557). At least, since awareness of these problems and the use of appropriate control groups has become increasingly widespread, there has been a noticeable dearth of claims for backward conditioning!

Examples of the use of such control groups may be found in the experiments of Mowrer and Aiken (1954) and Matsumiya (1960). They were studying the effects of CS-US relations on the acquisition of fear responses (see p. 719) by noting how much suppression of food-reinforced bar pressing occurred when a CS which had been paired with shock was introduced into the bar-pressing session. If the CS had acquired strong fear-producing properties, bar pressing should be markedly suppressed, but the very same effects could be caused by sensitization and pseudoconditioning. Sensitization might be expected because the stimuli used as CSs (flashing lights and buzzers) could conceivably elicit some fear reactions if prior foot shock made the animals more sensitive to these stimuli. Pseudoconditioning might occur because the emotional upset created by the foot shock could be triggered by any sudden change in stimuli, as when the CS is introduced into the test session. Hence, these experiments included control groups in which the CS and US were presented with several minutes between them, to preclude any conditioning. During the test session, animals in such control groups did show some suppression, but the amount of the effect was small and short-lived as compared with the effects seen among those animals who experienced CS-US pairings (see Figure 16.10, p. 718).

Exposure Learning

This phenomenon, which seems to be distinctly different from the effects of either the classical or the operant procedures, has sometimes been called "perceptual learning," although the term "exposure learning" is currently in greater favor because it seems to be less restrictive in its implications. The paradigm for exposure learning may be summarized in this manner:

1. Expose subjects to stimulus.
2. Test, using stimulus as S+ or S− in discrimination problems.

The assumption underlying the use of discrimination tests is that if mere exposure of the stimulus has had any effects at all, it will be more readily discriminated than some stimulus to which the subject has not been exposed.

It is important to note that use of the term "exposure" implies that any means of expos-

ing the organism to stimuli will, on later testing, prove to have caused a "relatively permanent change in behavior" so far as this
stimulus is concerned. Whereas the earlier
investigations (for example, Gibson & Walk,
1956) were interpreted by many readers as
implying such a simple state of affairs, subsequent investigations have shown that mere
exposure may not be sufficient to cause later
behavioral changes. For example, Gibson,
Walk, and Tighe (1959) found that geometric
forms painted on the walls of the living cages
of rats apparently had no effects on later discrimination of those forms, whereas exposure
to geometrical forms cut from sheet metal did
have such effects, thus reproducing their
original results. Gibson, Walk, and Tighe suggest that the three-dimensional characteristic
of the metal cut-outs is an important factor
in establishing the forms as stimuli which will
be more readily discriminated in later training.
It would therefore seem that "exposure" must
imply something more than mere presence in
the environment, and it is possible that some
form of differential response to the stimuli
is needed. However, the exposure procedures
in these experiments in no way allow feeding or handling to be systematically paired
with one stimulus, and the effects that are
obtained are not limited to any special role
played by the stimuli in later discrimination
training. For example, the effect is seen as
readily if an exposed stimulus becomes the
negative stimulus in the two-choice discrimination situation as if it has been made the
positive stimulus (Gibson et al., 1958). For
such reasons, explaining away this phenomenon as due to secondary reinforcement does
not seem reasonable.

It may seem strange that a process which
seems to be so intimately involved with perception should be introduced by referring to
experiments with rats, when perceiving itself is
almost always studied with human subjects who
can add their verbal reports to their nonverbal
responses. In part, this is necessary because the
animal experiments let us manipulate the conditions of prior experience which presumably
influence the perceptual learning. Of course,

most of us would not doubt that perceptual
learning in humans does occur, if by that we
mean that we learn what to perceive in certain
situations. For example, when we are novices, we
see and hear quite different things than are perceived by the master, but with accumulated,
guided experience we begin to detect some of
the features of the situation that formerly
seemed to be just so much noise. After appropriate experiences, not only can we pick out
details that previously had been hopelessly buried in the total flux, but we can also recognize
patterns even when they are presented at lower
intensities or for briefer intervals (change in
recognition thresholds), and our effective reactions to the stimuli also become markedly
altered. We experience these changes each time
we enter some new situation, whether it is the
learning of a new language or the techniques
of wine tasting, or merely the accumulation of
experience from hours of watching football on
television. Usually the changes occur so slowly
that it is difficult for us to remember that once
we could not distinguish between what now
seem to be the most gross differences; perhaps
the skillful tutor is one who remembers better
than the rest of us what some of those early
difficulties were and can guide his pupil in the
direction of detecting salient features of the
stimulus situation. It is interesting to try to
imagine what the infant or child must perceive
in some of the situations which to us seem so
well structured, and we know—from conflicts
between members of different subcultures—
how much the perceptions of the "same" situations depend upon the prior experiences of the
perceivers.

However, if we wish to determine whether
perceptual learning is distinct from the more
familiar varieties of learning, we must eliminate
the possibility that learning to perceive depends
upon such processes. Suppose, for example, that
the infant and child were differentially reinforced
for responding to some aspects of the environment and not to others. Could we then account
for the facts of exposure learning by reference
to what we know about the role of reinforcement
in operant behavior? In the world at large, the
complexities of the situation make it impossible
to discern the relative contributions of reinforcement to changes in the significance of
stimuli, but in the laboratory, an approach to such
problems is possible. Thus, the experimenter
exposes rats (or some other convenient organism)
to stimuli which presumably have no special
significance, under conditions in which the reinforcement of differential responses to these

stimuli is unlikely, and he then tests to see whether mere exposure has changed the ways in which the organism reacts to those stimuli.

At the present time, the conditions that are sufficient for exposure learning to occur are not known, but it does seem fairly clear that the effects cannot be explained as due, in every case, to reinforcement of specific responses to the exposed stimuli during the exposure period. Nor does it seem likely that habituation of orienting responses to novel stimuli could account for the effects, for the change from the conditions under which the stimuli are exposed (living cages, for example) to those in which the effects of the exposure are tested (discrimination apparatus, for example) would certainly be sufficient to cause a reappearance of orienting responses. For the present, it seems that there is considerable reason to accept the exposure learning paradigm as one that produces a relatively permanent change which cannot easily be ascribed to other, more thoroughly studied procedures for modifying behavior. (See the discussion of the more perceptual problems involved in this question, in Chapter 13.)

Imprinting One of the most striking of all behavioral phenomena is that of imprinting. While the origins of this research can be traced back to Spalding (1873), the impetus for the present research on the topic seems to have stemmed from the work of Konrad Lorenz (1937). By now, most people are aware that the young of many species may "imprint" upon whatever conspicuous object is first exposed to them. The phenomenon has been studied primarily in species in which the young are capable of locomotion from the first day of life because locomotor responses are frequently used to evaluate the effects of the imprinting procedure. A typical experiment might expose chicks or ducklings to a flashing light or a moving object as soon as they are brought from the total darkness of the incubator into a lighted room. Later, most of the animals will follow this object and will

emit "distress" calls in its absence and "contentment" calls in its presence. If faced with this object and a new one, they will ordinarily approach the familiar object and avoid the strange one. If presentation of the previously exposed object is contingent upon the emission of some more-or-less arbitrary response, the rate with which that response will be made will increase (Peterson, 1960; Hoffman et al., 1966). Similarly, if one side of a T maze leads to the imprinted stimulus, or to the alley in which imprinting took place, chicks will run to that side of the T maze (Campbell & Pickleman, 1961). In other words, not only is the imprinted object one which controls such behavior as following the object, but it also seems to control emotional responses, and it has demonstrable reinforcing properties. As a result, imprinting may determine both the initial and the adult social responses, and may influence the choice of adult sexual partners.

The favorite subjects for imprinting experiments have been ground-nesting birds because their young ordinarily are capable of walking within a few minutes of hatching and they can be incubated and hatched under nonsocial conditions. However, imprinting has also been claimed for mammals such as sheep, goat, buffalo, and zebra (Collias, 1956; Scott, 1958; Thorpe, 1963; Cairns, 1966). In such precocious animals, the assumption of imprinting is based on the responses of following an object other than the biological mother. For example, lambs reared by hand follow their human foster parents and ignore—and sometimes flee from—members of their own flocks. Continued exposure to flock living may reverse such early preferences (Thorpe, 1963, p. 404; Cairns & Johnson, 1965; Cairns, 1966).

More recently, there has been considerable interest in the possibility that newborn humans may show similar effects, with the infant becoming imprinted upon conspicuous stimuli in his prenatal and immediately postnatal environment. Of course, we cannot demand that the neonate follow a moving object to prove that he has been imprinted, but even his quite limited response capabilities allow him to choose between objects and to maximize contact with certain stimuli. For example, when objects move about he can follow them with his eyes; he can become quiet, thus "following" in "auditory pursuit"; and he can "search" for objects within range of his mouth by twisting and turning his head. Using these responses, some researchers have concluded that imprinting (or something analogous) does occur in the neonate. Salk (1962) tested the hypothesis that infants become imprinted upon their mothers' heartbeats during the latter portion of the prenatal period by presenting a "lub-dub," imitation heartbeat sound to 102 infants during the first four days of life, and compared their weight gains with a control group not exposed to the sound. The rationale for measuring weight gain as an index of imprinting involved the following assumptions: If imprinting occurs, the presence of the imprinted stimulus produces emotional tranquility, while its absence produces fearfulness and anxiety; an emotionally upset or anxious infant should eat less and gain weight less rapidly than a nonanxious infant. It was also assumed that the lub-dub sound presented to half the infants was a reasonable replica of the stimulation that each fetus received through the tissues and fluids surrounding him before birth. The group that was exposed to the lub-dub sound did indeed gain significantly more weight than the controls, thus supporting the hypothesis that imprinting *in utero* had occurred. Ideally, there would have been a control group exposed to auditory signals not like the supposed imprinted stimulus; it was not possible to include that condition in the first experiment, but Salk (1966) did compare lub-dub with other signals in a subsequent study. In this case, toddlers (16 to 37 months old) were assigned to groups, each of which was exposed to a different sound at bed time. One group heard the 72 lub-dubs a minute of the imitation heartbeat, another heard lullabies, and a third group heard 72 single "dubs" per minute. The dependent variable was the time

taken to fall asleep, again assuming that decreased fearfulness or anxiety should result from presentation of an imprinted stimulus, and that the stimulus should thus encourage relaxation and sleeping. The results supported the hypothesis: The experimental group required (on the average) only half the time needed by the others to fall asleep.

One of the most general ways of describing the effects of initial exposure to such stimuli is that the effective range of stimuli for a given response is subsequently narrowed (see Hinde, 1970, p. 509ff.). The chick who is exposed to a flashing orange light when he first emerges from the egg will follow that light (and similar ones; Cofoid & Honig, 1961). By thus promoting an attachment to this stimulus, the early experience has largely eliminated the possibility that other stimuli will be followed. From a variety of observations, it is concluded that there is a "sensitive" period during which such attachments are most readily made, and some investigators have suggested that such phenomena may occur in humans as well as in other species. For example, Gunther (1955) provides evidence that the first few days in the infant's life are the sensitive period for nursing and that if the responses of suckling are to become firmly attached to the stimuli of breast or bottle, the exposure must occur during this period.

The earlier reports of imprinting by Lorenz (for example, in 1937) emphasized the following features of the phenomenon. First, it was said to be a process which could occur only during a very limited period during which the organism was in some critical stage of development, and that if an object were exposed at some time outside this critical period, imprinting would not occur. Second, the effects of imprinting were said to be irreversible. Third, it was said that the process was a sudden and an all-or-none phenomenon.

It now is known that all three of these statements must be modified. The "critical" period has been shown to be a rather broad one, and as a result, most writers now prefer the term "sensitive period." Although there

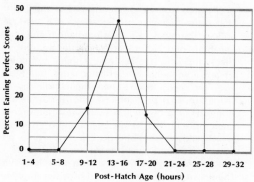

Figure 14.5. Imprinting as a function of age at exposure to imprinting stimulus. Mallard ducklings were kept in isolation from hatching until placed in the imprinting apparatus, where they were exposed to a model of a *male* mallard. The model moved slowly around the circular enclosure, emitting a recorded "gock, gock" sound. Ducklings were removed from the enclosure after they had followed the model 150–200 ft in 10 min. Between imprinting and testing, they were kept in isolation. Tests consisted of releasing the duckling midway between the male model and a female model. In order, each duckling was given the following tests: (1) Both models silent, both stationary; (2) Both calling, both stationary; (3) Female calling, male silent, both stationary; (4) Female calling and moving, male silent and stationary. These tests are thought to represent increasing likelihood of a non-imprinted duckling approaching the female model. The percent of all ducklings earning a perfect male-following score (thus indicating strong degrees of imprinting) increased as age at time of imprinting increased, reaching a maximum at 13–16 hours, and then falling. The decline probably reflects increasing fearfulness of the model when the first exposure to it is delayed until 20 or more hours after hatching, for by then the duckling has already become familiar with the appearance of his environment. Moltz and Stettner (1961) prevented such familiarity by placing light-diffusing hoods on their ducklings; for these animals, the "sensitive period" for imprinting was extended to 48 hours or more, thus supporting their hypothesis that the sensitive period is not completely determined by maturational processes, but at least partially influenced by prior sensory experiences. (Hess, 1959.)

is a period of peak effectiveness in most species in which imprinting occurs, the procedures are effective over a rather broad period. For example, in the domestic varieties of chick, and in many ducklings, the first exposure may be given during any of the first seven or more days of life. Of course, it is essential that no other conspicuous stimuli be presented to the animals before their exposure to the stimulus to which they are to be imprinted. The hatchlings may be left in the dark for two, or possibly three days, for they will survive quite nicely for this period on their remaining yolk sacs; if longer periods are needed, they may be isolated and placed in homogeneous environments, or they may be fitted with visual occluders. Such isolation is necessary to prevent imprinting on the other chicks. Usually the emphasis is on the control of visual stimuli (to which these animals seem to be most sensitive), but it can also be shown that they will imprint upon auditory stimuli (Bateson, 1966, pp. 187–188); hence "isolation" should be acoustic as well as visual.

If separate groups of animals are removed from isolation and exposed to the imprinting stimuli at different ages, the typical result is a nonmonotonic relationship, with a period during which peak effectiveness of the imprinting procedure is attained, and with relatively less effectiveness if the exposure occurs earlier or later (Figure 14.5). This relation between age and the effectiveness of imprinting usually has been interpreted as an interaction of two factors. The initial increase in effectiveness is thought to reflect nothing more than the increasing maturity and perceptual-motor ability of the organism. The decline in effectiveness after a few days has been variously attributed to a decline in an innate tendency to follow moving objects (Lorenz, 1937); or to an inhibition of following caused by incompatible responses, such as fear reactions, which are more readily elicited as age increases (Hinde, Thorpe, & Vince, 1956; Hess, 1959); or to an increasing awareness of what characterizes the normal environment, with increasing likelihood that non-normal (that is, novel) objects will elicit fear responses which inhibit following and elicit withdrawal (Moltz, 1963; Bateson, 1964; Sluckin, 1965). Indeed, this matter of learning what is the normal environment, and becoming "attached" to it, has been suggested as one of the key features of imprinting (Thorpe, 1963, pp. 416–418).

> It had once been thought that all imprinting was much more permanent than other modifications of behavior by experience, but although animals may continue to follow the objects on which they have been imprinted for weeks or even months, in other cases, the effects are found to last for much shorter periods. In the natural situation, the young of most precocial species follow the mother closely for the first few days or weeks, but gradually they widen the area over which they roam. Eventually, of course, they must cease to follow the mother, else adult behavior, such as pairing for mating purposes, could never occur. Furthermore, when the young female becomes sexually mature, she responds appropriately (which in some cases includes following . . .) to a male and not an organism that looks exactly like her mother. These facts of life remind us that imprinting is not necessarily permanent nor all-pervasive; that some of the stimulus dimensions to which imprinting occurs may be quite broad ones (such as general shape of body or head) which may then serve important roles in recognition of one's own kind; and that in some other situations, imprinting may occur to highly specific stimuli (body odors, for example), which allow offspring to identify their mothers—and vice versa (Hersher, Richmond, & Moore, 1963).
>
> In less natural situations, lifelong effects of early exposure have been noted. For example, Lorenz (quoted in Thorpe, 1963, p. 407) exposed some newly hatched budgerigars to himself and one of his colleagues. The birds then were isolated from humans for two years, during which time they bred and reared young. However, after this period, when they were first reexposed to Dr. Lorenz, they immediately courted him and neglected their own kind. Perhaps such rather permanent effects of initial experiences might also be seen in nature, save for the fact that there is continual stimulation from changing situations and reinforcement of variations in responding. Such changes are less likely to occur among caged birds (such as Lorenz' budgerigars) because their keepers maintain rather constant conditions and minimize the opportunities for the reinforcement of new responses.

> Perhaps it is worth mentioning at this point that other behavior modifications may also be so long lasting as to appear permanent and irreversible. Food preferences, attitudes and prejudices, and language skills are familiar examples of acquired behaviors which change but little over the years, even when the conditions of living are such that some of the responses are emitted but rarely and thus but rarely reinforced. Even more impressive are the laboratory studies which show essentially no effects of time on retention even though it is certain that no possibility for further practice had been offered during the retention interval. A well-known example is the perfect retention of a visual pattern discrimination by a pigeon after seven years of "retirement" (Skinner, 1960). No one would claim that such perfect and long-lasting discriminative responding would be irreversible. Instead, they probably would suggest that the errorless retention was attributable to the lack of opportunity for incompatible or interfering responses during the retention interval. The same logic could be applied to Lorenz' budgerigars: by isolating them from humans during the two-year interval, the birds were protected from the interfering responses which otherwise would have occurred, and the perfect retention of their approaches to humans might just as reasonably be attributed to this isolation from interference as to some special characteristics of the attachment to the imprinted object.

The apparent irreversibility of imprinting suggested to Lorenz that this was a phenomenon quite distinct from the usual forms of learning. When Lorenz presented himself to newly hatched goslings, it was the creeping, honking Lorenz that the goslings followed—and they continued to follow him when they became juveniles and adults. However, even though Lorenz' geese failed to form appropriate social attachments to others of their kind, showed distress when Lorenz disappeared, and courted him while ignoring their own species, other observations suggest that early imprinting does not necessarily make later attachments to different objects impossible. In commercial breeding establishments, for example, domestic fowl are frequently used to hatch out gamebird eggs (such as partridge or pheasant). Although the hatchlings follow the foster mother closely and show distress at her absence, they seem to have no difficulty in later mating with their own kind. Such observations suggest that the apparent "permanence" and "irreversibility" of attachments shown by some animals for their foster parents are not inevitable, and such preferences as are shown may be over-ridden by later experiences.

> Relatively permanent social and sexual attachments are not necessarily caused by short exposures to an object during a particular sensitive period. For example, the studies of developing affectional relations in rhesus monkeys (Harlow, 1958, 1959, 1961; Harlow & Harlow, 1962) indicate that the ties between infant and mother (or surrogate mother) are not formed instantly and that they are significantly modified by day-to-day experiences. The infant reared with a soft and warm substitute mother clings to her, as if the sheer tactual stimulation is of itself sufficient reinforcement to create a strong attachment. In the presence of novel stimuli, the infant runs to the figure in the same way that infants reared with their own mothers flee to them when frightened, and he continues to do so long after the nursing function of the mother substitute has ceased. In another context, those young monkeys denied the opportunity for the usual interactions with behaving mothers and the rough-and-tumble experiences of youthful play are later found to be inept in or incapable of mating and mothering. All this sounds like "irreversibility," but although the limits of change have not been thoroughly explored, it is clear that the infant monkeys can adopt a new mother surrogate and develop what seem to be "normal" relations with her as late as the eighth month, as compared with the usual attachment which occurs in the first days of life (Harlow, 1958). Here, then, is the development of a set of filial and affectional relations which seem at least as "permanent" and "irreversible" as any of the adequately documented cases of imprinting, but the relations are developed rather slowly, the sensitive "period" is apparently quite broad and rather flexible, and, given the opportunity, subsequent experiences can modify at least some of the affectional relations and object choices.

The third of the three characteristics of imprinting was said to be the sudden, all-or-none nature of the process. As usually observed in the field or barnyard, imprinting does seem well described by such terms: The chick nestles under the hen, follows her closely if she moves, emits "distress" or "contentment" calls depending on her absence or presence, and seems to do all these things with great proficiency from the very first day. However, systematic study reveals that there are some fairly large individual differences in the behaviors of chicks. The latency to the first act of following, the proportion of opportunities on which following occurs, and the closeness with which the chicks follow all show considerable variation between individuals (Jaynes, 1956; Salzen & Sluckin, 1959), suggesting that imprinting may occur in varying degrees among chicks given the same initial exposures. Such differences are not merely the result of general weakness or the stupidity of the animals which show little or no evidence of imprinting: Fischer (1966) compared chicks that gave strong evidence of imprinting with those that gave no such evidence at all, and found the two groups indistinguishable on a variety of discrimination problems.

The apparently simple question of whether or not the effects of imprinting occur in an all-or-none manner, going from absence to full presence at a single exposure, is really not answerable, since the dependent variables that are employed are not pure measures of degree of imprinting. For example, if the following behavior of birds is observed over the first few days, those that follow at all usually follow more vigorously and dependably on successive "practice" days (for example, Jaynes, 1957; Bateson, 1964a); but this might indicate nothing more than an increased maturity and ability to follow, and the "attachment" underlying the overt behavior indeed might exist only in two stages: zero and full strength. As measured, indices of following behavior, signs of recognition (as inferred from vocalizations or failure to avoid objects), and choice behavior in discrimination situations all increase as the number of exposures to the model increase. (However, these functional relations are distorted, if they are plotted over several days, by the declines that occur as a function of age.) Thus, although it is frequently the case that the effects of the imprinting procedure occur over a relatively short time period, the degree to which the "attachment to the model" is formed probably is a function of the amount of exposure, the opportunity for approach responses, and so on.[19]

Before concluding that imprinting is a unique process, we should consider the possibility that it might be deduced from one of the other means of producing behavioral modifications. For example, might all the phenomena of imprinting be based on classically conditioned responses? To defend such an argument, we would first have to postulate certain unconditioned (but not necessarily species-specific) responses. Suppose, for example, that the members of some (or all) species orient toward and approach (within the limits of their capabilities) whatever is the first conspicuous stimulus to which they are exposed. This might not be too far-fetched an assumption, for orienting and investigatory responses are characteristics of most forms of animal life. Because some of the characteristics of this stimulus object would inevitably be more conspicuous than others, these might become the conditioned stimuli for the approach responses which were initially elicited by the object just because it was the first one exposed to the organism. Thus, on later occasions, approach might be elicited by the CSs even though the unconditioned reactions on which the process originally was based no longer exist.

The hypothesis that an unconditioned reflex might decline with age is not unreasonable: The Babinski and the palmar grasping reflexes are well-known examples of just such changes. Neither should we be greatly troubled by the assumption that some char-

acteristics of an object or situation may serve as the US while other features of the same object become CSs. An everyday example of this situation is the sight of food, which becomes the conditioned stimulus for salivation because it has been paired with the US of food in the mouth. Nor should we find it too difficult to accept (tentatively) the very vague description of the US as "the first conspicuous stimulus to which the organism is exposed," for there are many such imprecise descriptions of unconditioned stimuli which have been found fairly useful. Well-known examples are the "novel" stimuli that elicit orienting reflexes, or "sudden" or "intense" stimuli that elicit startle or fear, or the "strange" and "unusual" objects that evoke emotional upsets (see Hebb, 1946; Melzack, 1952).

The most obvious difficulty faced by any attempt to force all instances of imprinting into a classical conditioning mold is that such an interpretation would require that whatever responses occurred during the first presentations of the conspicuous stimulus should be the ones conditioned to the stimulus and, on subsequent occasions, elicited by it. So, if we present the stimulus but prevent any approach behavior, subsequent presentations should not yield approach. Such experiments have been done (for example, by Moltz, Rosenblum, & Stettner, 1960); the general result has been that *equally strong following* occurs on later tests whether the animals have been exposed to the model under "normal" conditions, where they can approach and follow, or under restricted conditions, where they are held in restraining chambers.

Attempts to explain imprinting by reference to well-known principles of operant behavior have not been any more successful. To fit the model, it would be necessary to demonstrate that (1) the nature of the response during the initial exposure is relatively unimportant, so that almost any one of a large number of responses might be substituted (just as treading on a pedal may be substituted for pecking a key, if convenience is served by such selection), and (2) the pres-

[19] The common indices of imprinting are: approach toward the imprinting stimulus; decrements in emotional upset and/or increments in contentment, as evidenced by vocalizations, food ingestion, nestling, etc.; positive reinforcing effects of the imprinting stimulus; and choice of the imprinting stimulus over other stimuli. The latter test seems to be the least ambiguous.

entations of the conspicuous object increase the probability that the arbitrarily selected response will occur and that subsequent withholding of the stimulus produces typical extinction phenomena.

On the first point, the evidence is unequivocal: The nature of the response is not immaterial; it is what is usually called an *elicited* response rather than an emitted one, for its original occurrence is under the control of the conspicuous stimulus. Thus, we may conclude that the typical "filial" behavior, of which following responses are so conspicuous a part, is not an operant that is reinforced by presentation of the stimuli from mother or model.

This does not mean that such conspicuous stimuli cannot reinforce other responses, or that they cannot reinforce and further strengthen approach and following behavior. Imprinted stimuli may be rather effective reinforcers, allowing an arbitrary response (such as pecking a key) to be strengthened if brief presentations of the stimulus are contingent upon emission of such responses (see, for example, Peterson, 1960; Hoffman et al., 1966). However, stimuli need not be "imprinted" to have reinforcing properties, for at least some such stimuli are quite effective reinforcers in the absence of any prior exposure. For example, Bateson and Reese (1968) imprinted chicks and ducklings on a rotating light and then made presentations of the light contingent upon depression of one of the pedals in a chamber containing two pedals. They demonstrated acquisition, extinction, and reconditioning of this pedal response by the previously imprinted birds. However, they also showed as great—or greater—a reinforcing effect from presentations of the light to birds that had been kept in total darkness during the time the others were being imprinted. We may conclude that the reinforcing effects of such stimuli do not necessarily depend upon prior imprinting and, in some cases, the same stimuli that are effective in imprinting may also be effective reinforcers in operant situations in the absence of prior

imprinting. Such reinforcing effects of "stimulus change" have been demonstrated in many different situations with more mature organisms as well as with very young ones (see p. 673), and although they may not account for all the rich variety of behavior encompassed by the term "imprinting," they certainly complicate the situation, for in the very first presentations of the mother or model, whatever operants occur (approach, for example) must immediately be rendered more likely to occur again by the reinforcing properties of many such stimuli.

Thorpe (1963) has suggested that imprinting and exposure learning have much in common and may be basically similar, and Sluckin (1965) seems to agree. However, we must also take into account the fact that, in imprinting situations, the conspicuous stimuli elicit approach when first presented, and this is not deducible from the facts of exposure learning. To bridge this gap, it is sometimes assumed that the animal will approach any conspicuous object during the "sensitive period" of life; that increasing fearfulness of objects not previously encountered develops during this period, bringing it to an end; and that exposure learning plays a role by establishing which stimuli are familiar and which strange (see Bateson, 1964b; and Hinde, 1966, pp. 368–369). Thus, although the basic paradigms for exposure learning and imprinting are the same (expose stimulus, test for recognition), the overt approach reactions and the emotional attachments of the imprinting situation are not typically observed in exposure learning situations. For the present, it seems that imprinting might profitably be considered as a complex situation involving several unconditioned (and sometimes species-specific) reactions, some of which may determine the reinforcing properties of environmental stimuli, and some of which may also determine the nature and strength of emotional reactions to such stimuli. There does not seem to be any special advantage in assuming, at this time, that imprinting is some special form of learning process, or that it involves principles which are unknown in other contexts. (For valuable reviews and analyses of imprinting, see Moltz, 1963; Thorpe, 1963; Klopfer, 1965; Sluckin, 1965; Bateson, 1966; Hinde, 1970.)

Habituation

In the most general terms, a response may occur at a constant rate, or it may increase or decrease in rate. Reinforcement is one of the major determinants of rate increases and extinction is an important cause of rate decreases, but there are other ways of producing the same effects. For example, motivational changes (such as deprivation and satiation) may cause either increases or decreases in response rates, and inherent (such as circadian) rhythms may do the same. Sensory adaptation (for example, p. 283) is a frequent cause of decrements in response rate, as is simple fatigue. Habituation also causes decrements in responding, but although adaptation and fatigue (and many of the rhythms) can be analyzed without invoking so complicated a process as learning, habituation appears to be very much involved with such problems. Indeed, it is possible that habituation is one of the most rudimentary forms of learning, and thus of central importance to an understanding of how experiences are coded, stored, and retrieved.

Habituation and the orienting reaction

Most frequently, the term "habituation" refers to the waning of orienting (investigatory) responses after repeated presentations of a "neutral" stimulus. These orienting reactions include: "targeting" responses (like turning toward the source of a sound, or sniffing) which increase the probability of receiving further stimulation from the CS; autonomic responses of the type usually mediated by the sympathetic portion of the autonomic nervous system; and desynchronization of the rhythms of the electroencephalogram (Konorski, 1967). During the first tests of a stimulus, the orienting responses would be seen in their full form; with successive presentations, decrements in the magnitudes of all three aspects of the reaction usually occur.

The orienting reaction is, of course, an unconditioned one, and the stimulus which elicits it is an unconditioned stimulus, but because the reaction wanes so readily, such US-UR combinations cannot be made the basis for ordinary classical conditioning. However, it is possible that such relations might underlie "sensory preconditioning" (see p. 564). For example, if a light and a tone are paired, the light might acquire some control over the orienting reactions normally elicited by the tone. Such reactions (pricking up the ears, for example) would also occur in later conditioning sessions, when the tone is paired with a durable US, such as food. If the CS for the salivary CR is not just the tone, but also the stimuli caused by orienting reactions to the tone, it is possible that the light could cause some salivation, inasmuch as the light causes some of the same orienting reactions. Such effects, based upon mediation via shared portions of the orienting reaction, might be expected to be weak and transient, since the orienting reaction itself wanes so readily. Sensory preconditioning typically is such an evanescent phenomenon.

Note that the operations involved in habituation and extinction are exactly the same: repeated (or continuous) presentation of a single stimulus. In extinction, of course, the stimulus previously has been established as a CS, and the response that is waning is the CR; in habituation, the stimulus has not been paired with a US, and the response that is waning is the UR to it (that is, the orienting reaction).

Other response decrements In recent years, "habituation" has been applied to a much wider range of phenomena than just those associated with orienting reactions, so that it now is quite commonly applied to all response decrements (1) associated with repetitious presentations of a stimulus, where (2) the stimulus is not a CS, and (3) where sensory adaptation, fatigue, satiation, and inherent rhythms may be discounted as causal factors. Adaptation and fatigue may sometimes be ruled out if the response *reappears* when the stimulus is altered by *reducing* its intensity, for an adapted or fatigued sensory system should not be expected to react to the first *decrease* in stimulation. Varying the stimulus interval can be used in the same way.

Satiation effects should be relatively slow to disappear, whereas recovery from habituation is essentially instantaneous, thus allowing these effects to be distinguished. Rhythmic changes in activity usually occur over sufficiently long intervals and swing both towards increases and decreases in activity, so that there is rarely any difficulty in distinguishing these from habituation.

Contemporary usage applies "habituation" to decrements in all types of responses, from adjustments to environmental temperatures or elimination of seasickness (Glaser, 1966), to the waning of reactions in isolated neural preparations (see Horn, 1967). The term obviously fills a vacuum that had existed in our technical vocabulary, but there is the possibility that its usefulness will be diluted by even wider applications.

Of course, there are some unconditioned responses which do not show habituation (and these make the best unconditioned stimuli), but even in the most persistent cases, some change in the response pattern usually can be detected. For example, a moderately intense electrical shock will usually elicit vocalizations, withdrawal, or struggling, and increased heart rate, blood pressure, and other signs of autonomic upset. If it is repeatedly presented, the shock may gradually cease to elicit the vocalizations and struggling, suggesting that even with so salient a stimulus there is likely to be at least some degree of decrement for every facet of the elicited behavior.

The time course of habituation The general pattern of changes in responding during habituation is reasonably described by the familiar negatively accelerated curve. That is, the reaction to the stimulus decreases with successive presentations, but the absolute amount of the decrease per stimulation declines as the number of stimulations increases. Because this functional relation also is characteristically found in studies of sensory adaptation, fatigue, and extinction, and because the operations for habituation, adaptation, fatigue, and extinction all involve the successive (or continuous) presentation of stimuli, it is sometimes difficult to decide which label is the appropriate one for a given experiment.

These problems are illustrated in the investigations of the mobbing responses of chaffinches (*Fringilla coelebs*) by Hinde (1954a, b; 1961). "Mobbing" refers to the behavior shown by many species of bird in the presence of a predator, and usually includes a characteristic call as well as the motor behavior of alternating approach and withdrawal. The "chink" call emitted during mobbing by chaffinches (and at other times when the bird is disturbed) occurs once or twice a second when a novel stimulus is introduced. In the wild, when chaffinches discover a predator, they chink loudly.[20] If the predator moves out of range, the chinking dies down; but even when an immobile predator is found in the immediate vicinity, waning of the chink calls eventually occurs. For example, an owl may remain sleepily in place while being mobbed, but even though the owl has not left the area, the chinking may subside.

Considering the survival value of mobbing (that is, alerting others to the potentially dangerous object), it is somewhat surprising that the behavior shows any waning. These field observations have been confirmed and extended by controlled laboratory experiments. In one such experiment, each chaffinch was in turn exposed to an owl placed just outside its aviary. Under these conditions, the behavior appears to be much the same as that seen in the field: There is an initial retreat to a distant perch, and during the first minute or two the rate of chinking increases to a maximum; it then declines over the next half hour or so. Moreover, if the procedure is repeated day after day, a sys-

[20] Calls when a nonflying predator is encountered tend to be abrupt and therefore easily localized; calls when a flying predator is seen are usually more drawn out, with gradual onsets, and therefore difficult to localize. For communication purposes, such calls probably are equally efficient, and they have the advantage of letting others know where a nonflying predator has been located while not giving away the location of the callers to the flying predator (Marler & Hamilton, 1966).

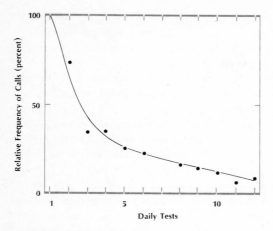

Figure 14.6. Decline in "chink" calls emitted by chaffinches on successive daily tests with a live owl. Each chaffinch was exposed to the owl for 20 min a day. The number of calls emitted by each bird on each day was expressed as a percentage of the number of calls he made on his first day of exposure; the mean of these percentages is plotted in this figure. (After Hinde, 1954b.)

tematic decrement takes place in the amount of daily chinking (Figure 14.6).

Consider first the waning of the response during a single session: How are we to distinguish between the effects of (1) fatigue of the mechanism involved in chinking; (2) sensory adaptation to the novel stimulus (the owl); (3) extinction of a previously conditioned response; or (4) habituation? Fatigue seems an unlikely explanation, since introduction of a new stimulus (for example, a stuffed dog) produces an immediate recovery in chinking. Sensory adaptation seems unlikely to occur when stimulus conditions are constantly varying, as they do in these experiments. Extinction presumes prior conditioning, but it is unlikely that mobbing behavior is a conditioned response, since it also occurs when stuffed figures are shown to birds that have been reared in the laboratory where they have seen no other animals and could not have acquired either the fear of predators or the specific responses of reacting to them. Furthermore, when the day-to-day decrements (Figure 14.6) are consid-

ered, fatigue and sensory adaptation seem even less likely explanations. We are left, therefore with the conclusion that the waning of the mobbing behavior cannot be satisfactorily explained by any one of these other well-known phenomena, and that the use of yet another label ("habituation") is warranted.

It would be dangerous, however, to conclude that there is a single behavioral or physiological process underlying all the decrements in mobbing, for within the overall systematic decrement can be detected a variety of local changes. In the mobbing behavior of chaffinches, for example, Hinde (1954b) has identified both positive and negative effects of the presentation of predators. The waning, for example, shows short-term effects from which there is considerable recovery if the stimulus object is removed for just a few minutes, and it also shows long-term effects which are relatively permanent. Within the short-term effects, there appears to be a warming-up effect, as chink calls increase in frequency during the first minute or two before beginning the overall decrement. Within the long-term effects, there is a *decrease* in the latency to the first response on successive daily sessions, even while the total number of chinks per session decreases.

Similar complexities exist when decrements in responses are studied in newborn humans, where the effects of prior experience may be assumed to be minimal. For example, in studying the reactions of neonates to a combination of odors, Engen and Lipsitt (1965) found a short-term decrement which was essentially complete in ten presentations of the odorants, with each presentation lasting 10 sec, and one trial being given each minute. That this was not sensory adaptation was shown by the recovery to the preexposure level of the response to one of the two odors in the compound when it was presented alone, immediately after the series of ten exposures. Instead, it seems that the change from stimulation with the compound to stimulation with just one of the elements of that compound introduced a degree of novelty into the situation which might account for the "dishabituation." This emphasis on the role of novel stimulation has been characteristic of many recent experiments on habituation, and it seems especially appropriate when the habituating and the dishabituating stimuli differ only in pattern or sequence. For example, Bartoshuk (1962a, b) examined the response decrement shown by infants to repetitive presentations of auditory stimuli and found that the response recovered when the pattern of the stimulus was changed. For example, if a rising tone had been used as a stimulus, successive presentations produced a decrement, but the first change of the tone to one which fell from high to low pitch caused a recovery in the response. Such decrements following repeated stimulation can be demonstrated after a 24-hour interval, indicating that long-term effects as well as the short-term ones exist even for human neonates (Keen, Chase, & Graham, 1965).

Habituation and neuronal models of learning

These complexities are emphasized here because it has sometimes been assumed that the type of waning of responses called "habituation" is a simple (and a single) process. As we have seen, it sometimes is possible to detect several different behavioral changes within overall habituation effects. It therefore is as important to control conditions of stimulation and past experience in habituation experiments as in any other behavioral investigation (see Hinde, in press). Still, because this decremental change seems to represent a *relatively* simple effect of experience, habituation has been receiving increasing attention in recent years. This has been especially true of researchers seeking the physiological and anatomical correlates of learning, for response decrements of the type called "habituation" can be demonstrated in organisms whose nervous systems are relatively simple and hence relatively better understood than those of organisms usually used in studies of learning and retention. For example, the sea slug, *Aplysia,* has an abdominal ganglion of relatively few cells, some of which are very large, which simplifies considerably the stimulation and recording of electrical and neurohumoral changes. Some of these giant cells have been found to change their excitatory postsynaptic potentials to a "test" stimulus ap-

plied to one of its input nerves if that stimulus previously has been paired (in the manner of classical conditioning) with a "priming" stimulus delivered to another of its input nerves. Appropriate controls have shown that this change does not occur when the two stimuli are presented in a nonpaired manner (Kandel & Tauc, 1965). Response decrements to repeated stimuli and recovery under novel stimulation conditions have also been observed, suggesting that the ganglia show "habituation" (Kehoe & Bruner, 1966). The motor cells controlling spontaneous or reflex withdrawal reactions of the siphon have also been identified, so that modifications of gross behavior may now be studied (Kupfermann & Kandel, 1969).

Such observations are obviously relevant to any attempt to construct a neuronal model for learning. Pavlov (1927) concluded that habituation of the investigatory reflex was a reflection of changes in the cerebral cortex, and there is now very good evidence that changes of this type do occur. For example, the arousal pattern in electroencephalograms shows a systematic waning as a stimulus is repeatedly given (see, for example, Knott & Henry, 1941; Sharpless & Jasper, 1956; Sokolov, 1960). However, what seems to be a similar type of waning also occurs at lower levels in the central nervous system (see, for example, Hernández-Peón & Brust-Carmona, 1961). Furthermore, similar decrements also occur in the hind limb reactions of spinal animals (Prosser & Hunter, 1936; Thompson & Spencer, 1966; Spencer, Thompson & Neilson, 1966), where the cortex cannot influence the waning.[21] In addition, there are numerous studies demonstrating habituation, dishabituation, and maintenance of the decrements over time in lower organisms possessing no tissues analogous to the cerebral cortices of higher vertebrates (see, for example, Humphrey, 1933; and the survey in Thorpe, 1963, especially Chapter 10). Finally, we may mention the experiments of the type mentioned above, showing these same effects in individual cells or groups of cells (see, for example, Kehoe & Bruner, 1966; Horn & Fraser Rowell, 1968).

For these and similar reasons, Horn (1967) has suggested that a "low-level" mechanism (or mechanisms) might mediate habituation in many cases. He postulates a self-generated depression

---

[21] In a spinal preparation, the spinal cord is transected, thus preventing impulses resulting from the experimental treatment from reaching the brain. Habituation of hind limb reactions therefore could not be attributed to the action of the cerebral cortex when a spinal preparation is employed.

of sensitivity resulting from repetitive stimulation of neurons, such that responses at these more-or-less local levels would lessen with stimulation while sensitivity to altered stimulation would be maintained. Sensitivity is assumed to recover after an interval of no stimulation. Such changes in sensitivity might result from a progressive reduction in the available supply of transmitter substance in the synaptic terminals of the stimulated system (Bruner & Tauc, 1966), with different "circuits" being excited by different stimuli. This line of thought likens habituation to sensory adaptation but places the mechanism outside (and more central than) the immediate receptor system.

All the models of habituation involve one common assumption: Somewhere there is a "comparison" made between stimuli that have been presented in the immediate past and the stimulus just now arriving. In this sense, habituation might be thought of as involving a form of perception (Konorski, 1967). The distinction drawn between habituation and other decremental processes (such as sensory adaptation or fatigue) is that in habituation, the sensitivity of receptors and effectors is thought to be unaltered. The changes are assumed to be occurring in cells more central than these.

Some writers have also emphasized the duration of habituation in contrasting it with adaptation or fatigue. For example, Thorpe (1963) has observed that ". . . the long-maintained waning of response as a result of a stimulation must be a kind of learning, and we assume that it is correlated with a change in the central nervous system and not merely with one in the sense organ" (p. 62). This, of course, is frequently the criterion used to decide whether a response decrement is a form of learning: Does it persist, showing effects on a later retest or transfer test? If it does, it is assumed that we cannot attribute it to more peripheral—and better understood—factors. This seems to be true of habituation, and, in this and in other respects, it seems to be consistent with our usual usage of "learning" to apply the term to habituation.

Verbal learning The earliest systematic studies of learning processes were those of Ebbinghaus (1850–1909). Working by himself, he tested his acquisition and retention of connected verbal materials (such as poems) and lists of discrete items. For the latter, he used both words and relatively meaningless "nonsense syllables," which he invented in an attempt to minimize associations between items. To conduct his experiments, he devised procedures for controlling practice and measuring retention. The results of his early experiments were reported in a monograph (Ebbinghaus, 1885) which inspired many others to undertake research in the experimental psychology of learning and forgetting. Research in this area was therefore well under way before Pavlov began his studies of "psychic reflexes" and while Thorndike was still a mere schoolboy.

In light of the historical priority of the use of verbal materials in the experimental psychology of learning, and in light of the fact that this interest area is one of the largest in experimental psychology, it may seem strange that this topic is relegated to last place in a survey of basic approaches to the study of learning. There are two reasons for this: (1) "verbal learning" is a description of the *materials* that are used in experiments, and not of the methods employed; and (2) there are now so many specialized techniques for the presentation and control of these materials, and for the regulation of practice conditions, that no brief survey could begin to mention their most salient features. (The concluding three chapters of this book deal almost exclusively with problems related to verbal materials, as well as the basic paradigms employed in such experiments.)

There are, however, a few rather general statements about verbal learning that may help place this topic in perspective. In the first place, verbal learning frequently is studied with exactly the same techniques that are used for the investigation of other forms of operant behavior. However, since verbal materials may be manipulated covertly, additional problems of control are raised. Under the conditions of most experiments, a subject is free to repeat the materials to himself during, between, and after trials; thus, he may engage in periods of practice or rehearsal that are not directly under the control of the experimenter. Where such uncontrolled manipulation of materials is to be minimized, experimenters sometimes introduce a conflicting task, such as mental arithmetic or color naming (see pp. 1028, 1035). This, of course, greatly increases the number of problems the experimenter must deal with, as compared, for example, with the between-trials vigilance needed by the Pavlovian researcher, who can maintain secure control over the occurrence of the stimuli—and thus exercise control over the responses—in his experiments.

Verbal materials frequently are treated in the same manner as nonverbal operants, with the experimenter presenting or withholding reinforcements to manipulate the behavior. In such experiments, the experimenter may say "good" or "um-hum" following certain responses, or he may advance a counter that indicates the number of points earned by the subject. In many other experiments, however, no special event is programmed to follow correct responses, it being assumed that recognition and confirmation are sufficiently potent factors to insure that positive practice effects will occur. This is a second characteristic of many verbal-learning experiments, and one which distinguishes them from most other experiments in learning: The experimenter may decide not to program any special reinforcers, and he may even do his best to eliminate any rehearsal and/or subsequent recognition of the materials previously presented.

The various procedures developed for the study of verbal learning share only one common characteristic: They all use materials that can be verbalized. Although this is a trivial generalization, it nevertheless deserves mention, for it sometimes is overlooked in comparisons of experimental results. For example, every time human subjects are used in an experiment, it is reasonable to assume that some subjects will verbalize materials if it is possible to do so; they will convert the problem into a verbal-learning experiment regardless of the desires of the experimenter. If a finger maze problem is presented, the majority of college students will immediately attack it as a problem to be coded into verbal form: Some will grope their way through the maze, trying to remember the sequence of choice-point turns in terms of patterns of "left" and "right"; others may discover in the earliest moments that they need only code responses as left or right, and so they need discover and memorize only the numbers of the choice points where they must, for example, go to the left. If the maze has, let us say, eleven choice points, a student following the first scheme would have to discover and memorize an eleven-item list made up of the responses "left" and "right"—a task offering many opportunities for within-list interference. The other student has only to discover and remember the numbers (for example, "1, 2, 4, 6, 7, 9") which will serve to identify the ordinal positions of choice points at which the correct response is "turn-left." Not only has this student a shorter list to remember, but there is much less chance that he will be confused by intra-list interference, for each item in his list is a different digit.

Still other techniques for coding the maze in verbal terms may turn up in the course of the experiment, but it is almost certain that the error or time scores of students who use any such verbal procedures will not be comparable with those of students who attempt to learn the finger maze in nonverbal terms (as, by forming a mental picture of the route or gaining a kinesthetic image of it). For example, if we plot the number of errors made at each choice point in the maze during all the trials needed to master it, those subjects who try to discover and memorize the serial list of left-right responses will ordinarily produce the familiar *serial position curve* (see p. 1015). They will have made relatively few errors at the first and second choice points, somewhat more at the next points, and relatively few again at the last choice points, making the greatest number of errors just past the midpoint of the maze. In contrast, subjects who go through the maze discovering which number is, for example, a "left" usually master the task in just a few trials and show no discernable curvilinear error distribution. Still different is the error curve for those who manage to approach the task without verbalizing it, for not only will they need more trials to eliminate their errors, but they also will usually show no peaking of errors near the midpoint of the maze. Such differences between subjects remind us that situations that can be verbalized provide especially rich opportunities for covert manipulations of materials by subjects, and require extra diligence and imagination by experimenters to control and/or analyze the effects of such individual styles of approach.

In at least one more way, studies of verbal learning entail complications not usually found in experiments of a nonverbal nature. Both the stimuli and responses used in most nonverbal experiments are sufficiently different from those encountered in situations outside the experiment that no great amount of interaction ordinarily occurs. Verbal behavior, to the contrary, is always with us, and these continual experiences almost always will influence performance in verbal-learning experiments (see especially, pp. 1122 ff.). Do we ask a subject to memorize a list of disconnected words? Prior experiences with such a list both color his reactions to them as individual items and determine his associations between them; previous use of the words may interfere with subsequent retention of the list; and experiences that intervene between the learning of the list and later retention tests will also distort the retention score. All these are complications that ordinarily can be ignored when we are working with nonhuman subjects or with situations that cannot be verbalized, for the stimuli and the responses involved in such experiments are not likely to be encountered anywhere except in the experimental sessions.

Having surveyed some of the more frequently encountered paradigms, let us now consider some of the concepts used in learning experiments and theory.

SOME GENERAL CONCEPTS

The Basic Units of Behavioral Analysis

With very few exceptions, the psychological analysis of behavior is based on units of stimulus and response. This point of view is a heritage of the physiology of the nineteenth and early twentieth centuries, during which the investigations of reflexes proved especially amenable to such analysis. The same point of view was carried over into the study of conditioning by Pavlov, and into other branches

of behavioral investigation by psychologists in the early part of the twentieth century.

At first glance, it may seem obvious that responses are the outputs of organisms and stimuli are the inputs. The situation, of course, is far more complex than this simple statement would make it seem. For example, behavior is constantly being emitted by living organisms, and from this flux we attempt to dissect the relevant responses for further analysis. Similarly, there is continuous stimulation through multiple sensory channels, and although the experimenter may hold *his* source of stimulation constant, variations in the receptors and in other characteristics of the organism may cause changes in stimulation from one moment to another. Thus, to speak of "the stimulus" and "the response" is merely a convenient oversimplification.

The definition of stimuli Stimuli are sometimes specified in terms of energies presented by the experimenter. Thus, we say that one stimulus is a light with a certain distribution of wavelengths and another is a chemical solution of specified concentration and composition. Although it has been a matter of some importance to philosophers whether sensations may exist in the absence of sensing organisms, psychologists are not really interested in situations in which there are no organisms and thus do not find any great interest in this hypothetical question. On the contrary, a psychologist must be concerned with the question of reception of the energies he presents to the organism, for it is quite obviously possible for organisms to be insensitive to lights we present, or to be looking in another direction, or even to be gazing at a light without paying attention to its relevant dimensions. It *is* necessary to have a more elaborate specification of the stimulus than merely the description of its physical properties.

The position adopted by many psychologists has been clearly stated by Skinner (1935, 1938). Skinner argued that the definition of a stimulus ought not to be independent of a demonstration of its correlation with speci-fied responses. Thus we say the light is a stimulus if the subject says "I see the light," or presses a key which delivers the reinforcing stimulus only in the presence of the light, or in some other way shows by his behavior that the light has been detected. "Behavior" in this case is used in the most general sense to mean any changes in the functioning of the orga-nism, and not just coordinated patterns of movements. For example, changes in neural activity (measured as changes in electro-encephalograms or electroretinograms, for example), or in patterns of breathing or per-spiring, may also be useful indices of detec-tion of stimuli.

The definition of responses There are two basic ways to view the response term. The first of these may be thought of as *responses defined by consequences*. Consider, for ex-ample, the behavior of pressing a bar or a key: When the device is sufficiently depressed to close the switch, the apparatus defines the response as having just occurred, and the topography of the behavior which caused the switch closure is ignored. The value of such a consequence-derived concept of the re-sponse has been shown in countless experi-ments and practical applications. For example, if we wish to increase the probability of cor-rect spelling of a word, we reinforce correct spelling whenever and however it occurs, and we disregard the movement characteristics of the behavior. The fact that orderly changes occur in responses defined in terms of conse-quences is the best evidence that such levels of analysis are psychologically meaningful.

On the other hand, there are situations in which the specific responses are of central concern, and a description and measurement of the pattern or sequences of patterns, and of the strength of the responses, then be-comes the critical portion of the definition. The shape of an evoked potential, the raising of one paw rather than another, or the "clustering" of certain verbal responses are obvious instances in which the response must

be examined in terms of its inherent charac-teristics rather than its consequences (see Hinde, 1966, pp. 9–12).

Levels of Explanation

In the most straightforward form of be-havioral analysis, the experimenter presents or withholds one antecedent condition (see p. 3), observing the effects upon behavior each time the manipulation is made. From such experiments we can derive statements describing the importance of the presence or absence of the condition, but we cannot make statements about the functional relations be-tween various values of the antecedent con-dition and the amount of change in behavior. Before we can make such a statement, it of course is necessary to present more than one value of the antecedent condition and, be-cause organisms frequently are sensitive to the sequential effects of conditions, it usually is necessary to counterbalance the order in which the values of the antecedent condition are presented.

The history of most problems in psychol-ogy usually shows that experimenters first searched for significant variables, and that the functional relations of the variables and their associated behavioral effects were worked out later. For some students of behavior, the dis-covery of these functional relations is an ap-propriate endpoint. Still others aim to make their analysis on a more conceptual level, and attempt to abstract from the data more gen-eral concepts, some of which may make as-sumptions about the nature of processes which are not directly observable. Because we discuss some of these concepts in the following chapters, let us survey a few of those that are most frequently encountered.

Some Behavioral Concepts

Excitation and inhibition We have already encountered the concepts of excitation and inhibition. These terms have been borrowed from physiology, where they have reference to processes which underlie the occurrence or nonoccurrence of reactions. For example, neural excitatory processes are those which excite other neurons, or give rise to muscular contractions or glandular secretions. Neural inhibitory processes, on the other hand, are those which work against the excitatory ones.

In behavioral descriptions, the terms have the same connotations: excitatory "tendencies" are those which lead to the occurrence of responses, except as they are blocked by inhibitory "tendencies." Excitation generally is associated with the effects of reinforcement; inhibition usually is associated with the effects of punishment or of nonreinforcement after prior reinforcement (extinction).

Note that the terms imply more than the mere occurrence or nonoccurrence of behavior: if that were all that were meant, there would be no need to use terms like "inhibition." Instead, these terms refer to hypothetical variables or processes to which theorists give *ad hoc* properties based on prior research, and which they hope will allow them to predict the outcomes of future experiments. Pavlov's (1927) excitatory and inhibitory processes (see p. 573), Hull's (1943) reactive inhibition (see p. 574), and Spence's (1936, 1937) excitatory and inhibitory effects (see p. 776 and Figure 17.11, p. 764) are well known examples of such theorizing.

Response strength The term *response strength* refers to the speed, intensity, or persistence with which responses occur. The term is not just a synonym for one of these dependent variables; it implies something more than is measured by any one of them. For example, Skinner (1938) spoke of the "strength" of an operant as it is reflected in response rate and in the number of responses emitted in extinction. However, because rate and resistance to extinction rarely are perfectly correlated, it is obvious that response strength must refer to something related to both, but identical with neither.

Response strength, then, is a low-level concept which is more general than any of the individual measures of behavior that we

plot on the ordinate of figures. It has not been given formal theoretical status or development, but it is usually assumed that response strength increases with reinforcement and decreases with extinction.

Habit strength William James made "habit" a psychological term when he used it to label those very well practiced behaviors which keep each of us behaving in such highly predictable ways that habit becomes "the enormous fly-wheel of society, its most precious conservative agent" (1890, p. 121). Subsequent usage, however, has made habit the term for *any* learned response, no matter how thoroughly learned it might be.

Hull (1943) made habit strength one of the intervening variables in his theory of behavior, relating it on the antecedent side to the number of reinforcements,[22] and on the consequent side to the behavior measures of response latency, amplitude, probability of response in choice situations, and number of responses during extinction. Habit strength was to be scaled by observing the relations between reinforcements and responding, other factors (such as deprivation) being held constant.

When the term *habit strength* is used today, it usually is employed in a much less formal sense than in the Hullian system, but there still is the implication that the dimension referred to is habit ("learning") itself, and that other factors, as those of drive or incentive, are needed to turn habit into behavior. Here, then, is the primary difference between the concepts of "response strength" and "habit strength": the latter assumes a

---

[22] In *Principles of Behavior*, Hull (1943) had the limit to which habit strength could grow set by the quantity and quality of the reinforcer. In subsequent versions of his system (for example, 1952), he introduced a new *incentive* term which was sensitive to reinforcer characteristics, and let habit strength be determined solely by the number of reinforced occurrences of the response. This modification allowed the system to "predict" sudden shifts in speed or vigor of response when amount or quality of the reinforcer was shifted (see Chapter 15). Spence (1956) adopted a similar approach, but assumed that habit strength was determined by the number of times the response and the stimulus occurred contiguously, whether or not reinforcement occurred.

TABLE 14.5 TYPE OF EXPERIMENTAL DESIGN EMPLOYED WHERE A LEARNING-PERFORMANCE DISTINCTION IS SOUGHT

Drive or incentive condition	Amount of practice		Differences attributed to motivation
	Large	Small	
High	a	b	(a+b) vs.
Low	c	d	(c+d)
Differences attributed to learning	(a + c) vs. (b + d)		

learning-performance distinction while the former does not take any special position on this question.

The learning-performance distinction
Ask a child his name and he ordinarily will respond with alacrity, but if the question is repeated several times, there usually will be marked changes in the manner in which he responds—and after a few such repetitions he is quite likely to cease playing our game. However, we do not assume that his failure to continue saying his name reflects the loss of the ability to do so. This simple situation illustrates the nature of the learning-performance distinction that has played an important role in theories of learning. The distinction is a necessary one if it is assumed that (1) there is a state in which the effects of past experiences are coded and stored, (2) that it is this which is called "learning," and (3) that other factors (such as the child's exasperation when he is repeatedly asked for his name) modify the manner in which the learning is expressed but do not change the learning itself.

Many psychologists find it helpful to think of a model similar to those devised by Hull (1943, 1952) and Spence (1956), in which the effects of practice determine the learning (or habit) factor, whereas the final performance is determined jointly by a multiplicative relation of habit and motivational factors. Following this line of reasoning, it generally has been assumed that any indication of the separate effects of the habit and the motivational

contributions to the final performance can only be estimated by using an experimental design in which at least two levels of amount of practice and two levels of motivational-incentive conditions are combined factorially. For example, imagine an experiment in which subjects are assigned to the four cells a, b, c, and d, each of which represents one of the possible combinations of practice and motivation (see Table 14.5). At the conclusion of the experiment, the differences between the sums of the columns would be taken as the reflection of the effects of the training and testing conditions on the habit factor while the differences in the sums of the rows would be said to reflect the differences in performance attributable to motivational factors.

The learning-performance distinction was introduced into experimental psychology during the 1930s, primarily as a consequence of the studies by Tolman (1932) and his associates, in which the effects on behavior of modifications in deprivation or incentive conditions were studied. The striking and sudden effects on behavior of changing the reinforcer from a less to a more highly preferred food seemed to contradict a view of learning which assumed that whatever responses occurred were direct reflections of "habits" or of "bonds" between the stimulus and response (Thorndike, 1913), for these generally were considered to be "relatively permanent." To explain rapid shifts in responding, the distinction between learning (the "bonds" or "habits") and performance (learning as activated by motivation) was introduced, and it continues to be a distinction accepted by many investigators of learning. There are, however, many experimental and theoretical papers on the topic of learning in which this distinction is never introduced. For example, in much of the literature on verbal learning, in most of that on classical conditioning, and in almost all published papers on the analysis of operant behavior, the learning-performance dichotomy seems to be of little relevance.

THE GENERAL SCHEME OF A LEARNING EXPERIMENT

Once having obtained a fairly clear statement of the question to be investigated, the experimenter's next step is to decide upon the general *tactics* he will adopt in his experiment; the specific *method* he will employ, including the *subjects* to be utilized; and the *measures* of behavior which he will take.

Tactics of Experimentation

The term "tactics" was applied by Murray Sidman (1960) to the ways in which the experimenter behaves toward his experiments. By tactics, Sidman referred to the general orientation of the experimenter toward what he considers the primary problems of his discipline, and also the means by which he thinks those problems should be approached in the laboratory. Sidman was especially concerned with a description and analysis of some of the methods employed by those who study the behavior of individual organisms in depth, as contrasted with the methods typically used in the study of groups of organisms where each group is exposed to a separate treatment or set of conditions. Inasmuch as there is no one set of tactics which always will be superior to its alternatives, questions like those raised in the following sections must be considered each time we start an experiment.

Raw scores or averaged scores? Some of the earliest experimental studies of psychological problems (in sensing, perceiving, and psychophysics) found it necessary to average the results of numerous runs of an individual subject to obtain stable estimates of threshold values, psychophysical functions, and so on, and Ebbinghaus (1885) adopted this approach when developing his methods for studying human learning. Thorndike (1898) and Pavlov (1927), on the other hand, frequently presented the raw scores of individual animals, selecting for publication such sample records as (in their experiences) fairly represented the many experiments they had conducted.

At the same time, however, Galton (1883) was developing methods for describing the characteristics of groups of subjects, and Binet and Henri (1896) were devising techniques for obtaining average mental age values for test items. Thus, from the very beginnings of scientific psychology, all degrees of grouping and averaging of scores have been employed.

It seems that, as each new problem or technique was introduced into psychology, the earliest investigations concentrated on the study in depth of one or two individuals, but subsequent experiments frequently emphasized averaged, group data. The use of the multiple-unit maze is a case in point. Small (1899, 1900) constructed a scaled down replica of the Hampton Court maze, and observed the behavior of two rats in it under a variety of conditions. The data were largely qualitative, but they created an interest in this new technique for the study of learning, and within a few years there were many more published experiments using mazes. Most of these early experiments reported data derived from individuals only, but the variability of the individual animals was sufficiently large to discourage most attempts to see order in the data. Thus, averaged data gradually came to be used more and more to report the results of maze and discrimination experiments, as well as those of most verbal learning studies. Today it is relatively rare to find raw data or individual protocols used as other than illustrative materials. Still, many experimenters find their greatest satisfaction in obtaining sufficient control of their situations to allow the direct recording of publishable records. This has long been an objective of many physiologists and physiological psychologists (see, for example, Figure 4.8, page 96), and also has been a favored tactic of students of operant behavior (see, for example, Figure 15.19, p. 662).

One or several independent variables? An entirely new dimension of complexity was introduced into the study of behavior when the methods devised by R. A. Fisher (1935) and others began to be adopted by psychologists. Basically, these methods (called "analysis of variance") allow the experimenter to compare the effects of several treatments and to estimate the probability that the difference between the means of the various sets of scores is attributable to chance fluctuations. These techniques also allow the experimenter to evaluate *interactions* of variables. For example, suppose we asked children to try to recall a list of words they had seen 1, 10, or 100 minutes earlier. Suppose also that we had some children who had high scores on an intelligence test, some who had average scores, and some who had scored below average. We could, by these techniques, decide whether the effects of the retention interval on recall depend in part upon the intelligence of the child.

The value of designs in which more than one independent variable is included is clear, but the danger in the use of such designs is also clear: In many cases, the experimenter is tempted to include just two values of a variable (presence versus absence, or high amount versus low) and, at the conclusion of the experiment, finds he can say only that a given factor does or does not have a statistically significant influence on the behavioral measure he employed. For the majority of psychological problems, such screening of potential variables may be an important preliminary step, but in many cases it is not so informative as a more thorough study of a single variable, yielding an orderly relation.

Individuals or groups? The argument about appropriate tactics sometimes seems to boil down to this question: Should we concentrate on observing the behavior of a few individuals for a relatively long time or a larger number of individuals for shorter periods? It has sometimes been implied that the control of conditions is better when the experimenter concentrates on a few individuals, but this is not necessarily true. Instead, the decision concerning the procedures to be employed should be based on the problem to be attacked. There are some problems that just cannot be investigated with one or the other of these types of designs, but there are also some problems that may be approached either way, and there are some problems that seem to need a combination of the approaches. An example or two may clarify this question.

If we wish to know the functional relation of an antecedent variable and behavior, we ordinarily are concerned with the behavior of individuals, and thus we would seek the answer by running each individual through all of the conditions. For example, Keesey (1962) investigated the effects on the rate of self-stimulation of the amount of electrical brain stimulation per reinforcement (see p. 646). After implanting chronic electrodes in the brain of each rat he gave all of them sufficient practice in the self-stimulation situation to allow them to attain stable performance levels. On the basis of preliminary experiments, Keesey had decided that six different intensities would be sufficient to cover the working range of intensities. Preliminary experiments had also indicated that the rate at which the subjects would respond under any one of the conditions of stimulus intensity was influenced by the value of the stimulus immediately preceding. Therefore, a sequence of stimulus intensities was constructed which allowed each intensity to be given in every position in the sequence. This form of design (known as a *Latin square order*) allows the effects of the sequence of stimuli to be averaged out across the entire experiment. Note that the results from such a procedure do not eliminate sequence effects, but the averages of the individual observations provide a reasonable estimate of what the behavior might be like if there were no such effects due to the sequence of the stimuli.

The results for each of the ten animals showed the same general trend as the average values for the entire group (see Figure 15.14, p. 645). However, there were some rather marked differences in the response rates and the functional relations within the sample of ten animals, so that no one of the animals duplicated precisely the average results. This experiment illustrates some of the problems facing the experimenter who must decide which tactic to follow in his research. Where both individual and group data can be obtained, it is obviously of interest to do so.

It is also interesting to note the effects of repeating the procedure. In this portion of the experiment (which was also replicated with two other dimensions of stimulation), most of the animals increased their response rates on subsequent occasions, and most of them also revealed some decline in response rates at the higher intensities. Both these trends are faithfully depicted in the average curves.

How else might this experiment have been designed? Two extreme procedures could have been adopted. In one case, the experimenter could have assigned one group of animals to each of the six intensities, giving the animals sufficient exposure to that intensity to allow their behavior to stabilize. The final results then would have been presented as an average curve drawn through the points for each of the groups. The disadvantages of this procedure are obvious. A relatively large number of subjects is needed, multiplying the amount of time needed for surgery and postoperative care; and the variability attributable to individual differences might make the validity of the group curves doubtful. For example, when Keesey's animals were receiving 3.0 mA the individual response rates varied from about five responses per minute to almost twenty-five responses per minute. Such variability in the absence of the evidence of the orderliness of the individual data might leave considerable doubt as to the effect the intensity dimension would have on the behavior of an individual if he were subjected to more than one intensity. (Incidentally, the procedure of exposing each of the separate groups of subjects to only one intensity might have produced an average curve which was flatter than the curves obtained when each subject was exposed to every value of the stimulation. At least, this is an implication of many other studies of reinforcer variables; see, for example, the discussion [pp. 631–641] of separate groups and within-individual designs as applied to the problem of amount of reinforcer; and Guttman, 1953; Grice & Hunter, 1964.)

Stable behavioral baselines An alternative design might have exposed one or two animals to all intensities, perhaps maintaining each set of conditions until some criterion of stable responding had been obtained. One of the inherent problems in this procedure is the difficulty in determining when responding has reached a sufficiently stable point to be considered as stable. Very often, if we run just one more session after some predetermined criterion of stability has been obtained, we will find the behavior straying beyond the limits we have set.

Instead of attempting to achieve stability of behavior at every intensity, it is sometimes more practical to attempt to regain the same "baseline behavior" between the sessions in which other variables are presented. In the experiment discussed above, one of the stimulus intensities might have been adopted as the reference point, a number of sessions at

one of the other intensities might have been given until the variability from session to session seemed to have become acceptably small, and then the reference stimulus might have been reintroduced and maintained until the original (that is, the baseline) level of responding was once more obtained. In this way, sessions with the reference stimulus would have intervened between presentations of all the other values. This would allow the experimenter to be fairly sure that systematic changes in responsiveness were not occurring over the course of the experiment. (See the discussion by Sidman, 1960.) Unfortunately, baselines sometimes drift after subjects have been exposed to other variables, and this complicates the analysis of the data. Without following such a procedure, however, the drift might never be recognized! A far more serious limitation is the fact that, in many situations, there is likely to be a gradual shift in response rates toward an average value determined by the schedule of reinforcement (see below), and that this effect will gradually obliterate the effects of the variables under examination. Thus, the adoption of such a long-term procedure, involving repeated attempts to recover the baseline, may mask the importance of some variables, making this a less desirable tactic.

As we suggested in Chapter 1, there are some problems that can only be attacked by using independent groups, whereas others can only be studied by making extensive observations on an individual. In such cases, we obviously have fewer degrees of freedom available when designing the experiments. For example, there are the problems in which we can, as it is said, only skin the fox once. Familiar examples are those in which a treatment immediately changes the organism so that the baseline behavior could never be recovered and other values of the variable could not be applied. The effects of chronological age at time of imprinting or the influence of electroconvulsive shock at various times after completion of practice are familiar examples requiring separate groups of subjects at each age level or time.

However, we should not be too quick to assume that the procedure involving repetitive treatment cannot be applied to a given problem.

For example, we ordinarily assume that there can be but one uncontaminated test of the retention of previously learned materials, and that subsequent tests are influenced by the facilitating effects of the prior recall sessions. However, if we could devise a sufficient number of equivalent tasks, each could be learned and then tested for retention after varying intervals. This, of course, was the procedure used so successfully by Ebbinghaus (1885).

Similarly, it had been assumed for many years that stimulus generalization gradients could only be plotted from the data points obtained from separate groups of subjects at each of the stimulus values to be tested, since each test of generalization extinguished responding at that test point and thus provided discrimination training which distorted the hypothetical "pure" gradient. Generalization tests in which the same subject was tested at various points on the stimulus dimension (for example, Bass & Hull, 1934) were frequently thought to produce not a "primary generalization gradient" but the compound effects of generalization, extinction, and differential reinforcement. In recent experiments (see pp. 759-762), generalization gradients have been obtained from individuals by giving them prior training which minimizes the effects of extinction during the generalization test. The development of such procedures, which allow us to study gradients in the individual organism, have led to the discovery of valuable new phenomena such as the "peak shift" effect (see p. 778).

Methods of Experimentation

Most learning experiments utilize either the *free operant* or the *discrete trials procedure,* each of which has its own special advantages and liabilities. A few of the more general points about these procedures are discussed, and a description of a hybrid technique given.

In most cases, experimenters may choose their subjects from among several species, age groups, and so on. However, potentially important factors sometimes are overlooked in selecting subjects, and a few are described below.

Finally, some of the more common dependent variables in learning experiments will be considered, and a few of the means of presenting experimental results will be described.

Procedures employing trials The meaning of "trial" varies from one experimental situation to another. For example, in the Ebbinghaus procedure, a trial might consist of one reading through a list of words at a set rate of progress, or it might consist of one attempt to recall previously studied materials. In the first case, the word "trial" refers to a period of exposure to stimuli, while in the second it refers to a testing period. Both meanings also exist in the Pavlovian situation: early in conditioning, the trial consists of the presentation of CS and US; later in conditioning, a trial may be a test where CS alone is presented.

But even more confusion is possible! When training animals on a Lashley jumping stand (see p. 749), many experimenters follow Lashley in designating as *one trial* all jumps up to and including a correct response. Thus, one animal may make many times more *responses* than another, but because both have had an equal number of reinforcements, they are said to be equivalent in trials. For such reasons, comparisons of the efficiency of two procedures or of two types of apparatus should always include scrutiny of the definition of "trial" used in each situation.

When the experimenter arbitrarily breaks his practice sessions into trials, he interrupts the continuity of behavior. In many instances, this is of no consequence because the behavior is itself phasic, and/or it is securely under the control of known stimuli. For example, in the classical conditioning of the patellar reflex (Schlosberg, 1928), there is little probability that the reflex will occur at times other than following stimulation of the patellar tendon, and the experimenter need not fear that his procedure of scheduling separate trials is destroying any essential characteristic of the behavior. On the other hand, where the response in question has some free-running rate greater than zero, the decision about when to begin a trial may affect in significant ways the behavior being measured. For example, if the blink of an eyelid were the response being measured, the probability that a blink might occur just at the instant that a trial is initiated is sufficiently large to have noticeable effects on results. For this reason, subjects usually are told to blink a few times and then get ready for the start of a trial, with the hope that the "spontaneous" blinks will thus be minimized during that trial.

The primary advantage of using a discrete trials procedure is that the experimenter maintains control of the spacing of responses. The primary disadvantage of the discrete trials procedure is that the behavior of the subject may be disrupted arbitrarily. Often special features are included in discrete trials procedures which reduce such disruption of behavior. One of these techniques involves the consistent presentation of some stimulus just before the trial is begun, which allows the subject to orient toward the relevant stimuli, and also alleviates some of the upset which might accompany sudden introduction of the trial stimuli. The opaque, vertically sliding door of the WGTA (see p. 750) comes to serve as a discriminative stimulus for responses of orienting toward the front of the chamber and assuming the posture for responding to the stimulus tray when the second (transparent) screen is raised. A similar function is served by the double doors separating the starting compartment from the alleyway proper in some straight-alley devices (see, for example, Logan, 1960). When the first door is raised, the thoroughly adapted rat investigates that end of the start box, and is in position to leave when the second door opens. In learning experiments involving humans, a "ready" signal serves the same purpose.

Free operant procedures The term *free operant* is used to describe procedures in which arbitrary discontinuities are not imposed on the behavior. Instead, a situation is arranged such that responses may be emitted freely, and the emission of each response leaves the organism free to initiate the next response. Although experimenters have long avoided interruptions during naturalistic observation, it is only relatively recently that they

have tried to do so during the laboratory study of behavior (Skinner, 1932, 1956).

There are some who would say that *"free operant"* is redundant, but inasmuch as "operant" has become a synonym for "instrumental," it frequently is helpful to make an unmistakable distinction between those procedures which use trials and those which do not.

Self-paced trials A variant of the free operant procedure allows the initiation of each trial to be determined by the subject, but utilizes the discrete presentation of stimuli that is characteristic of methods employing trials. For example, we might allow the subject to set up the stimuli for the next trial by pressing a button, but the specific character (for example, the stimulus arrangements, or the duration) of each such trial would still be determined by the experimenter. These procedures provide such information as the percentage of presentations on which the correct response was made, which is difficult to obtain in the typical free operant experiment, and measures of the rate with which the organism initiates trials, which cannot be obtained when discrete-trial procedures are employed. Together with free operant procedures, the self-paced trial method shares the disadvantage of turning the distribution of responses over to the organism. Thus, where specific intervals of time must be maintained between presentations of stimuli, trials must be employed. (For a description of a self-paced procedure, see p. 682.)

The Selection of Subjects

It is not often that the experimenter has complete freedom to choose his subjects purely on scientific grounds. More frequently, his selection is limited by practical considerations of availability, economy, or ethics. Within these limitations, however, the experimenter frequently has a considerable choice open to him. But to the beginning student, it frequently must appear as though psychologists disregard the rich variety of organisms and study only four species: man, monkey, pigeon, and rat. Of course, they occasionally use other species, but the majority of experiments have employed these four.

Actually, there are some instances in which the choice of subject seems to be of relatively little importance. For example, Skinner (1956) pointed to the similarity in the patterns of responding emitted by different species under certain conditions of intermittant reinforcement, and concluded that the choice of the species was not an important variable under these conditions. The data indeed support his contention, but it is more than a truism that we would never have known this interesting fact if different species had never been compared. Thus, one reason for using a variety of species is the discovery of similarities between them.

On the other hand, there are problems in which the choice of the species is crucial. The task of the comparative psychologist, according to Bitterman (1960) is the discovery of problems which do reflect species differences, and he has presented evidence that discrimination reversals and the effects of partial reinforcement on resistance to extinction are two problems of this type.

Why rats? In the psychological laboratory, the rat may seem to be preferred out of all proportion to its place in nature. There are, however, many reasons for utilizing the rat in psychological research. For example, the rat is a mammal, and as such it has many biological similarities to other higher organisms. Thus investigations of structural and functional characteristics of the rat have relevance for an understanding of behavior in a broad range of species. Furthermore, the rat is inexpensive, easily bred in captivity, and has a relatively short generation span. For example, the gestation period is only 21 days; the pups may be weaned after another 20 days, and the animals can safely be bred at the age of 8 or 10 weeks. However, even more important than all these practical matters is the fact that an immense amount of information has been accumulated on the anatomy, physiology, and behavior of the rat. This legacy frequently is not appreciated until the experimenter decides to use a new organism. He must then start more or less from the beginning to discover the conditions under which the animals may be maintained in good health and bred successfully in the laboratory, and the conditions that must be established if they are to survive surgery; he must discover for himself what the ranges and the limitations of the animals' sensory capacities are; and he must discover—by trial and many errors—what are the typical modes in which the animals respond in the situations he wishes to study. For these reasons there is considerable reluctance on the part of most researchers to give up the organisms with which they are familiar.

At the same time, it is now thoroughly established that our concentration on a limited range of organisms produces a correspondingly limited view of behavior. Certainly one of the more significant contributions made by ethologically trained investigators is the introduction into the behavioral literature of material from species previously ignored by psychologists (see Hinde, 1966).

Before leaving the topic of selecting subjects, it might be well to add a cautionary note about the assignment of subjects to experimental conditions. When such assignments are best done "at random" and when it is more efficient to try to construct matched groups of subjects is a complex topic better discussed in a textbook of experimental design than here. In general, however, it is true that there is more to be lost than gained by attempting to match subjects unless there is very good evidence that the basis on which the matching is done is really related to a significant degree to the behavior in which the experimenter is interested. For example, if we were to investigate the effects of presenting a lecture with and without accompanying illustrative slides on the recall of the material at the end of the course of study, it would not be to our advantage to try to construct two groups matched for intelligence because in most cases there would not be sufficient variation in the intelligence of the students participating in this experiment to allow intelligence to have a noticeable bearing on the recall scores. Instead, it probably would be more efficient to construct two groups matched on the basis of a previous recall test because there usually is a strong positive correlation between the standings of students on one test and their standings on a second test in the same course.

It is obvious that if we were to assign (deliberately or by accident) all of the most able writers of examination papers to one of the two groups, the experiment would be seriously contaminated. In this case, common sense tells us to be wary of this kind of biasing, but there are other potentially biasing factors of which we are likely to be quite ignorant. Wherever this is the case, a random assignment of subjects to groups is usually adopted in the hope that the differences among subjects will be distributed more or less equally across the groups.

"Random assignment" in the practical situation means that the probability that a subject will be assigned to one group is equal to the probability that he will be assigned to any other group. To achieve this end, experimenters frequently use published tables of "random" numbers to decide which subject to assign to which group. We cannot substitute for such procedures the scattering of subjects across conditions by whim or by accident. Returning to our simple experiment involving two groups, it would not be sufficient for the experimenter to assign every second subject to the lecture in which no slides are shown, nor would it be "random" if he were to assign subjects by saying "Group A, Group B . . ." and so forth in what he thinks is a random sequence of As and Bs. Both of these methods introduce bias, the one because alternate assignment might not equally distribute characteristics which might influence the experiment, and the other because the experimenter cannot call out a sequence of events which approaches a random sequence. Instead, almost all of us tend to balance up the strings of letters or numbers when we try to behave as a random generator, forgetting that in truly random series there frequently are long runs in which the individual items are grossly out of balance (Solomon, 1949).

Another form of biasing sometimes creeps into the assignment of animals to groups or conditions. Imagine that a shipment of animals has just been received from the supplier and that all the animals now are in one large cage or pen. If the first animals withdrawn from the pen are assigned to one group and the second batch assigned to another group, almost certainly the assignment will be biased, for the easiest animals to withdraw from the enclosure are usually quite different in a number of ways

from those which are the last to be caught. The safest way to avoid such biasing is to number each animal as it is obtained, and then use a random number table to assign these animals to the conditions of the experiment.

Schedules of Reinforcement

After he has decided the broad outlines of his procedure and the selection of his subjects, the experimenter must next decide whether his procedure will involve reinforcement of every response, or whether only a portion of the responses will be reinforced. If the latter option is selected, it is also necessary to decide which rules to follow to determine what responses are to be reinforced. These rules are called *schedules of reinforcement*. Familiarity with a few of the basic schedules and their characteristic effects is essential to an understanding of the behavioral literature. We here mention just some of the more obvious facts about schedules (for greater detail, see Honig, 1966; illustrative data and descriptions of procedures will be found in Ferster and Skinner, 1957).

Continuous reinforcement If every correct response is reinforced, the schedule is said to be one of continuous reinforcement (CRF). This is typically the procedure employed at the start of training; rapid increases in response rate ordinarily are obtained at the very outset, and resistance to extinction is minimal. If the rate of response is to be used to evaluate the effectiveness of treatments or conditions of reinforcement, CRF is not to be recommended. The first disadvantage of CRF is the inordinate proportion of the total time that is spent in consummatory behavior, leaving little time for the operant responding and hence a relatively small range over which response rate may vary. The second disadvantage is the rapidity with which satiation may occur when every response is reinforced. Of course, such difficulties will not arise when a reinforcer is used that does not involve time-consuming consummatory responses, or one with which satiation is no problem. Positively reinforcing electrical brain stimulation or negatively reinforcing foot shock are two common examples of reinforcers that meet these requirements.

Ratio schedules Instead of reinforcing every response, it sometimes is preferable to reinforce some, thus making the ratio of responses to reinforcements something greater than 1 : 1. There are two types of ratio schedule in common use. In the first, a fixed proportion of responses is reinforced. If every tenth response were reinforced, the schedule would be described as a fixed ratio 10 (or FR 10). Responses may also be reinforced after varying numbers of responses have been made. In this case the schedule is described as a variable ratio (or VR) schedule of reinforcement. Unless otherwise specified, it is safe to assume that the numerical value given for a VR schedule is the arithmetic mean.

Ratio schedules characteristically generate high rates of responding in free-operant situations as long as the numerical values of the ratios are relatively small. What constitutes a "relatively small" ratio is dependent upon the organism and the situation. For example, ratios of 100 in a lever pressing situation might be relatively small for man or rhesus monkey, moderately large for a pigeon or a six-year-old child, and very large for a rat or a human of toddling age (see Sidman & Stebbins, 1954; Ferster & Skinner, 1957; Long, Hammock, May & Campbell, 1958; Weisberg & Fink, 1966).

The FR schedule typically produces a pattern of responding which shows a post-reinforcement pause followed by a steady response rate until the next reinforcement is delivered. As long as the conditions of the experiment are held constant, this response pattern remains relatively stable. As the ratio requirement is increased, the post-reinforcement pause is lengthened and the response rate is depressed. If the ratio requirements are held constant and deprivation (or other motivational) conditions are increased, the post-reinforcement pause is decreased (see Sidman & Stebbins, 1954; Ferster & Skinner,

1957). With VR schedules, post-reinforcement pauses and "go—no-go" response rates are also seen, but interruptions of responding frequently occur at unpredictable points (Ferster & Skinner, 1957) making VR a less satisfactory schedule for many purposes than FR. Since ratio schedules characteristically generate high response rates, they are useful tools for the analysis of the effects of various treatments on behavior, where we want to determine whether the treatment might have impaired the coordination or the vitality of the organism.

Interval schedules Parallel to the fixed and variable ratio schedules are fixed and variable interval schedules of reinforcement. When using a fixed interval (FI) schedule, we reinforce the first response that occurs after each predetermined unit of time. If, for example, the first response after every four minutes were to be reinforced, the schedule would be described as FI 4 min. The variable interval schedule reinforces the first response after intervals of time that vary according to a prearranged program. Unless otherwise specified, the numerical value of a VI schedule is the arithmetic mean of all of the intervals. In selecting intervals, ordinarily an attempt is made to include at least a few short intervals so that responses emitted soon after each reinforcement will sometimes be reinforced, thus making long post-reinforcement pauses unlikely. (For a discussion of the selection of intervals, see Ferster and Skinner, 1957.)

The typical behavior pattern generated by VI conditions is a steady response rate. Such steady responding is a useful base against which we can compare the effects of conditions of reinforcement, deprivation, or drug or surgical treatments. However, if a VI schedule is maintained for many sessions, the schedule itself determines the response rate and may override the effects of the variables in which we are primarily interested (see Keesey and Kling, 1961, for an example of this effect; see also a discussion of the "locked rate," by Ferster and Skinner, 1957).

When fixed interval schedules are first applied, there may be a short period during which small extinction curves are seen. This usually is followed by a period during which consistent response rates are emitted; these steady response rates then give way to patterns that show a post-reinforcement pause and then gradual acceleration in rate until the next reinforcement is delivered. These "scallops" or periods of positive acceleration are easily disturbed by changes in the conditions of the experiment and hence are a useful index of the extent to which the variations are detected by the organism.

Reinforcement of interresponse times The analysis of interresponse times (IRTs) provides a more detailed picture of the effects of reinforcement schedules (and other antecedent conditions) than does the mere inspection of the overall response rate (see Figure 15.15, p. 648). IRTs can also be directly reinforced, thus bringing the momentary rate of response under experimental control. For example, we might set an interval timer so that it programs a reinforcement if 30 seconds elapses without the occurrence of a response. IRTs shorter than 30 seconds reset the timer, thus postponing the next reinforcement. In comparison with most schedules, this procedure produces low average rates of responding, and is therefore called "differential reinforcement of low rates," or DRL.

In addition to establishing the rule that any interresponse time exceeding some selected value will prime the reinforcement circuit, we also can establish a "limited hold" contingency which sets an upper bound on the period during which reinforcement is available. If, for example, we were to add a 5-second limited hold to our DRL 30 sec. schedule, only IRTs of more than 30 seconds and less than 35 seconds would result in responses being reinforced.

Organisms can be brought under quite tight control with such schedules, allowing the experimenter to determine not only the average response rate but also to control with

considerable precision the momentary rate of response (see Anger, 1956; Morse, 1966).

More complex schedules The simple schedules may be combined in various ways to produce complex schedules suitable for the direct analysis of behavioral or physiological problems. Although the description of even the more common complex schedules is beyond the scope of this volume, an illustration may convey some impression of the value of these techniques.

Suppose we wish to train our subjects to differentiate two stimuli, perhaps as the initial stage of an experiment to determine the limits of their abilities to discriminate between stimuli. After initially shaping the desired response (for example, lever pressing), and a short period of CRF to establish the response, we then might introduce a VI reinforcement schedule and thus generate relatively consistent response rates with relatively few reinforcements. Now we might add periods of extinction to the schedule, so that extinction and variable interval reinforcement occasionally alternate, pairing one of our stimuli with the VI periods and the other with the periods of nonreinforcement. Such schedules, in which two or more simple schedules are combined, with each unit having a correlated discriminative stimulus, are called *multiple schedules* and are frequently used to study discrimination, generalization, sensory thresholds, and similar problems.

Imagine that we found that the typical effect of this procedure was to produce fairly high and steady response rates in the presence of the stimulus correlated with the VI component and much lower rates when the stimulus correlated with extinction was present: Would we be warranted in concluding that the stimuli were actually discriminated and that they were controlling the different response rates? At least one other possibility would first have to be eliminated, for it is conceivable that our subjects were discriminating the presence and/or absence of *reinforcement,* responding relatively slowly until a response was reinforced and then responding rapidly until a long period of nonreinforcement was encountered. To minimize such differential behavior based on the discrimination of the underlying pattern of reinforcement and extinction, several procedures have been devised. For example, by insuring that relatively variable periods of each schedule (VI and EXT) are interwoven, and that the change from one schedule to the other never is made immediately following reinforcement, the probability of "outguessing" the schedule is greatly reduced. However, even in such cases, animals and children can discriminate at least some of the underlying pattern of reinforcement, and the only way to determine just how successful they have been is to remove the discriminative stimuli altogether, and let them work on the underlying *mixed schedule* until they have achieved their best possible performance. By comparing this with the response rates in each segment of the multiple schedule, the extent to which the discriminative stimuli themselves control the behavior can be estimated. (See Ferster and Skinner [1957] and Sadowsky [1970] for some characteristic results of such experiments; also see Blough [1966] for a discussion of the applications of the results to animal sensory processes.)

Partial reinforcement effects Any schedule of reinforcement other than continuous reinforcement is, by definition, a partial reinforcement schedule. As a general rule, a subject is more likely to continue to respond during periods when it does not receive reinforcement if, during prior training, it received only partial reinforcement rather than continuous reinforcement. This phenomenon is called the "partial reinforcement effect" (see reviews by Jenkins & Stanley, 1950; Lewis, 1965). Resistance to extinction is only one of the ways in which different degrees of response persistence can be observed; persistence in emitting the formerly reinforced response when a discrimination has been "reversed" (that is, when the formerly incorrect response is made the correct one, and vice versa) and the extent to which the subject persists in making a response in the face of aversive stimulation also show the same general relationship: Partially reinforced responses are more persistent than responses that have been continuously reinforced.

The schedule of partial reinforcement determines the *pattern* as well as the overall persistence of the behavior during extinction. Following variable interval reinforcement, behavior during extinction usually continues to be emitted at a regular rate, declining slowly as extinction continues. After fixed-ratio reinforcement, on the other hand, responding usually is emitted in streams having quite constant rates, but the pauses between such bursts of responding increase in length, and the bursts become shorter as extinction continues. These behaviors seem to suggest that the stimulation resulting from the organism's own responding plus that from the presentations of reinforcers serve as discriminative stimuli for the further emission of responses. For example, with variable interval reinforcement, responses are reinforced when they have been made after varying intervals, thus allowing varying numbers of nonreinforced reponses and various periods of nonresponding to preceed the occurrence of the reinforced response. Thus, almost everything that the subject can do (respond, pause, engage in displacement activities) has at some time in his past history been followed by the next response being reinforced. Therefore, almost anything the subject does sets the occasion for (that is, produces the discriminative stimuli for) his making yet another response, and so great persistence is produced.

The patterns of responding characteristically generated by reinforcement schedules are the same for members of many species. For example, the characteristic fixed ratio pattern of a post-reinforcement pause followed by responding at a constant rate until the next reinforcement, is seen in humans of various ages (see, for example, Long,

Hammock, May & Campbell, 1958; Weisberg & Fink, 1966), as well as other mammals (see, for example, Sidman & Stebbins, 1954), and birds (see, for example, Ferster & Skinner, 1957). However, when more primitive organisms are used as subjects, we no longer see this pattern. Indeed, when fish are used as subjects the partial reinforcement effect itself seems to be obtained only if massed trials are employed. This suggests that at this level, organisms may be incapable of responding to cues from presence *vs.* absence of reinforcement except as they are conveyed through immediate sensory carryover from one trial to another (Gonzalez, Behrend & Bitterman, 1965).

Common Response Measures

Response rate One of the most frequently used dependent variables is the rate of emission of a response. This is the basic datum in the free operant situation (discussed above). The advantages of response rate as a datum are several: as it is ordinarily observed, response rate can vary over a wide range; it can change quickly in response to changes in experimental conditions; and if the subjects are properly trained, very stable response rates can be obtained. These are not inconsequential advantages, as anyone will realize who has worried over the sometimes disturbingly large fluctuations in response latencies or running times when discrete trial procedures are used. Moreover, changes in rate are directly observable, while changes in some of our other dependent variables (such as percent correct responses) may only be revealed after much data has been collected and analyzed.

Response rate, of course, is not without its limitations as a datum. There has sometimes been concern because the overall rate is an average of a variety of local rates (Verplanck, 1950). For example, while responding at a more or less steady rate of fifty pecks per minute, a pigeon may emit some pecks which follow the preceding one at a tenth of a second and other pecks which have interresponse times of only a hundredth of a second.

This, however, may also be seen as an advantage for rate as a measure, since there is the immediate averaging of these momentary responses (a process which has been likened to the averaging of movements of particles in a gas which produces the average pressure of that gas; see Honig, 1966). On the other hand, rate itself is conditionable, which sometimes reduces its utility as a dependent variable.

Of course, there are some processes which are just not amenable to study with rate as the dependent variable. Most of the phenomena discussed in Chapters 19, 20, and 21 are concerned with the emission of single responses, and response rate in those circumstances has little relevance.

Amplitude or vigor of response Although this was the primary datum in Pavlov's (1927) experiments, contemporary research makes relatively little use of these measures. In part this may be a consequence of the difficulties encountered when measurement of the amplitude or vigor of responses must be made. However it also reflects the current interest in problems that are more readily approached by observing other aspects of behavior.

Response latency One of the more frequently utilized measures is the latency with which a response occurs after the opportunity for the response is given. Like other time-based measures, latency has the advantage of being measured in units which are universally appreciated and clearly specified.

Response latencies almost always have skewed distributions, since there is some absolute level below which they cannot possibly fall while there is almost no limit to how long it may take for the response to occur. Because the mean is so sensitive to extreme scores, response latencies are either transformed to reduce skew before averaging, or else the median is used as the measure of central tendency. The most commonly used transformations are the reciprocals or the logarithms of the latencies.

Response times (such as running times in

mazes or alleyways) usually produce the same kind of skewed distributions. The reciprocal of the running time is, of course, a speed measure, and in addition to making more intuitive sense than does the logarithm of running time, it also allows us to make some comparison across experiments, as when all scores are converted to feet per second.

The Problem of "Learning Curves"

The general problems of presenting the results of experiments are much the same for all areas of science: the data should be presented as clearly and succinctly as possible and related to other findings so that readers can see the relevance of the results.

On the whole, graphical presentations of results are both economical and forceful ways of summarizing data; they also help the experimenter see trends or relations in his results that he might otherwise miss. In general, if a curve summarizes changes in behavior over successive practice periods, it is called a "learning curve." Almost all the curves we find in the literature on learning are just the results of variations in a few basic procedures. Some of the more frequently used procedures, and the assumptions underlying their use, are summarized below.

Classical learning curves   The standard procedure is to plot the results of each trial against the trial number, placing the units in which the behavior is measured on the ordinate, and trials on the abscissa. As long as the behavior being depicted is obtained from a single subject, no problems of interpretation are raised: The curve merely summarizes for the eye what the data sheets contain.

This type of curve was frequently published in the earliest learning experiments (see, for example, Thorndike, 1898, 1911), depicting the time per trial to complete a task (for example, to escape from a puzzle box or traverse a maze). Such experimental situations offered so little control over conditions that there was almost always considerable variability in the data. To provide an estimate of

what the "real" curve would look like under the hypothesized ideal conditions, various averaging procedures were introduced.

One type of average is obtained by combining scores from adjacent trials. For example, instead of plotting the time per trial, the average for blocks of two or more trials is used. Although this form of averaging loses detail, it does smooth out some of the irregularities and makes the more general trends easier to see.

Another type of average may be obtained by repeating a procedure several times and taking the average of the repetitions. This process introduces a new complexity, for it is based on the assumption that the average curve fairly represents the individual curves that went into it. If the individual curves are obtained from one subject who is run through a procedure several times, it is assumed that the functional relations obtained from the several runs are the same; if the average is based on curves obtained from several different subjects, it assumes that their curves are comparable.

> For many years there was considerable interest in the form of "the learning curve," with the assumption being that the acquisition of behavior would always follow the same course, except for uncontrolled variability. This question has never been settled; the problem proved to be an unfruitful one, and interest in it has waned. However, while it was an active topic, many arguments over the most appropriate way of plotting curves appeared in the literature and eventually generated some "backlash" from writers who argued that nothing definite could be told about the behavior of individual subjects from group learning curves (see, for example, Sidman, 1952). This is not quite true: the average curve can be used to test the hypothesis that the individual functions are of a certain form (Estes, 1956). Of course, it is still necessary to assume that all the individual data going into the averages are comparable.

Cumulative response curves   If the units of behavior are allowed to accumulate over the observation periods, a cumulative curve is produced that has certain advantages over

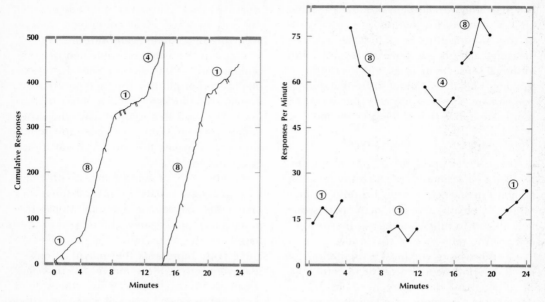

Figure 14.7. Comparison of two procedures for presenting results. The panel on the left contains a segment of a record obtained from a cumulative recorder. The paper is fed through the recorder at a constant speed; each response moves the pen a fixed distance across the paper. Thus, the rate of response is shown by the *slope* of the curve. The pen automatically resets to the baseline at some preselected point (in this case, after 500 responses). The same responses were also indicated on electromechanical counters, and those counts are plotted in the panel on the right. The results show the effects of training a pigeon with different amounts of food per reinforcement. The bird was occasionally reinforced (on the average, once per minute) for pecking an illuminated key. The color of the key indicated which reinforcement condition was in effect. Reinforcements consisted of delivery of either 1, 4, or 8 hemp seeds. The reinforcement condition changed every four minutes. Occurrences of reinforcements are shown by slight oblique marks on the record. Among the advantages of the cumulative record are instant information concerning the progress of the experiment, and an indication of the sequential changes in the behavior. The plot of responses trial-by-trial (or minute-by-minute in this case) allows the dependent variable to be read with greater ease: in the first minute of this experiment, for example, it is clear from the right panel that the average response rate was approximately 14 pecks per minute, but it would be difficult to determine this from the cumulative record. In practice, both cumulative recorders and digital counters are usually used, since each form of recording has its own advantages. (Data from an unpublished experiment of the author.)

the trial-by-trial plots. For example, we can read changes in response rate directly from the curve, and minor fluctuations around the dominant trend are less likely to be distracting. Figure 14.7 shows how the same data appear when plotted in the trial-by-trial manner and as a cumulative curve. Note the effects on these two plots of the same changes in the data: If scores remain the same over several observation periods, the cumulative plot has a constant slope, whereas the trialwise plot proceeds parallel to the base line; where scores decrease, the cumulative curve decreases *in rate of increase,* while the trialwise plot drops; and where scores increase, the cumulative plot shows increasing slope, while the successive trials plot rises. Of course, the cumulative curve can never decrease over time; even if the subject stops responding altogether, the curve only flattens.

In experiments in which response rate is the primary datum, cumulative records of responding usually are recorded "on line," to give immediate information concerning the

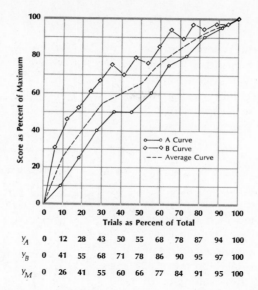

y_A	0	12	28	43	50	55	68	78	87	94	100
y_B	0	41	55	68	71	78	86	90	95	97	100
y_M	0	26	41	55	60	66	77	84	91	95	100

Figure 14.8. One way of constructing a Vincent curve. The rationale of the process is as follows: Along the baseline, the initial trial is numbered zero, and the total number of trials required to attain the performance criterion is called 100 percent, whatever the total may be for any subject. Along the ordinate, the score on the original trial is called zero, and the score on the occasion when criterion was reached is called 100 percent.

In the present example a maze is learned by two suppositious rats, A and B. Rat A makes 20 errors on his first trial; since this is his worst performance, we say he has "20 errors to eliminate," and thus each error eliminated would be 5 percent of his total. Rat A reaches criterion 11 trials beyond the initial (zero) trial, each trial thus being approximately 9 percent of the total trials needed. Rat B starts with 33 errors to be eliminated, each error thus being 3 percent of the total to be eliminated if he is to reach the criterion of an errorless run. Since Rat B reaches criterion in 17 trials, each trial is approximately 6 percent of his total. The x and the y values for each point on the A and B curves are computed as follows:

Subject A						Subject B				
Trial	x	Errors	% errors	y*		Trial	x	Errors	% errors	y*
0	0	20	100	0		0	0	33	100	0
1	9	18	90	10		1	6	23	69	31
2	18	15	75	25		2	12	18	54	46
3	27	12	60	40		3	18	16	48	52
4	36	10	50	50		4	24	13	39	61
5	45	10	50	50		5	29	11	33	67
6	55	8	40	60		6	35	8	24	76
7	64	5	25	75		7	41	10	30	70
8	73	4	20	80		8	47	7	21	79
9	82	2	10	90		9	53	8	24	76
10	91	1	5	95		10	59	5	15	85
11	100	0	0	100		11	65	2	6	94
						12	71	4	12	88
						13	76	1	3	97
						14	82	2	6	94
						15	88	1	3	97
						16	94	1	3	97
						17	100	0	0	100

*y = 100 − % errors

When the A and the B curves have been drawn, the base line is divided into ten equal parts, perpendiculars are erected, the ordinates of A and B are measured on each perpendicular, and a point on the Vincent curve is obtained by averaging the A and B ordinates. The linear interpolation can, of course, be done arithmetically instead of graphically. (Woodworth & Schlosberg, 1954.)

behavior of the subject. The generic term for devices that write out such records is "cumulative recorder." Essentially, they consist of a constant-speed paper-feeding mechanism and a device to move the recording pen a given distance across the paper each time an input is received.

Vincent curves Occasionally it is necessary to construct an average curve to represent the behavior of individuals whose progress through the experiment is grossly dissimilar. For example, one subject may require twice as many trials as another to memorize a list of words, and if we were to take the mean of their scores at each trial, the resulting curve would look like neither of the individual ones. One way of eliminating the effects of such differences in plotting group curves was originally suggested by Vincent (1912) and is still called the Vincent curve although the procedures most likely to be used today have been much modified by later users (see Munn, 1950, pp. 226–230).

The rationale for the Vincent curve is simple: Disregard the actual number of trials needed by each subject to complete the task and plot his results in terms of the percentage of the total number of trials that is represented by each trial; disregard the actual number of errors per trial, and plot his progress in terms of the percentage of his own total errors which are eliminated on each trial. The average curve is then based on these "percentage" curves (see Figure 14.8).

The logic behind Vincent curves is that subjects can be compared when they are at proportionally equivalent points in terms of total practice time needed, total errors to eliminate, and so on. Obviously, the way to tell if this is a warranted assumption for any particular experiment is to examine the data after treating it in this manner.

Traditional Vincent curves are not used very frequently, but "adjustment" of the results for individual organisms along one or the other axis for purposes of plotting results is quite frequently employed. For example, we

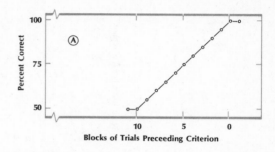

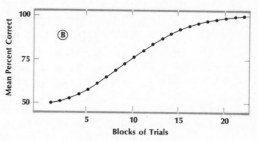

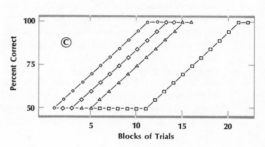

Figure 14.9. Comparison of a learning curve showing average errors with a backward learning curve. Four suppositious subjects are given training in a two-choice discrimination task. Each subject begins to eliminate errors at a different point in practice, but once improvement begins, it is at the same rate for all subjects (Panel C). The mean curve for these subjects (Panel B) is sigmoid rather than linear, suggesting a degree of gradualness of improvement that is absent from the individual data. The backward learning curve (Panel A) is constructed by noting the point where the criterion was met, and then working backward, determining the percent correct for each block of trials. The average percent correct for 1, 2, 3 . . . N blocks of trials preceeding criterion is thus determined. If the curves in Panel C were those of four *groups* of subjects, the backward learning curves would be anchored at the median trial on which members of each group attained criterion.

might disregard the actual number of trials taken during practice and plot the results against the number of reinforcements, on the assumption that the behavior measured is most likely to be modified by reinforcements and to be left essentially unchanged by trials on which no reinforcement occurred. (For an example of such a curve, see Figure 21.36, p. 1124.) Or, we might assume that comparability of performance should be the basis for selecting the points at which our subjects will be matched; the plot of the results from such a procedure has been called a "Melton curve," and ordinarily it is constructed by averaging the number of trials needed by each subject to attain equivalent performance criteria, such as 25, 50, 75, and 95 percent correct (see Melton, 1936; Melton & von Lackum, 1941).

Backward learning curves In the curves just discussed, the anchor point is the start of practice. But imagine a learning task in which every subject begins to make progress at a different time, but that each then progresses at the same rate. A curve of the average of the results from such data will have less slope than any individual curve, and it will show an initial period of positive acceleration which also is lacking in our hypothetical individual curves. Hayes (1953) suggested anchoring the individual curves at (or near) the end of practice, so that the differences in the initial periods could be discounted.

Although there are several variations of the procedure, the general plan followed when constructing such curves is to work backward from the final performance, computing, for example, the percent of correct responses at the last trial, the next-to-last trial, and so forth (see Figure 14.9). Such curves cannot tell us the average accuracy for the group on any specific trial, but they can be used to find the average accuracy on any given number of trials before the performance criterion (or whatever else was used to establish the final level at which all curves were anchored). Backward learning curves have been valuable tools in analyzing the rate of progress, once it has begun, especially when different degrees in the difficulty of discriminations or different complexities of tasks are involved (see, for example, Shepp & Zeaman, 1966).

J. W. Kling and Allan M. Schrier

POSITIVE REINFORCEMENT

15

Before beginning a chapter on the topic of reinforcement, we are obliged to deal with some problems of terminology. Three terms in common use—"reinforcer," "reward," and "incentive"—sometimes are used interchangeably and sometimes are not. Their meaning is changed by each investigator, as well as from one year to the next. Furthermore, the term "reinforcement" is often used in the sense of "reinforcer" and, hence, also confused with "reward."

We define a reinforcer as the thing (such as a piece of food or a sexual partner) that alters the probability of reoccurrence of, or otherwise strengthens, the response that produces it. "Reinforcement," then, will refer to the presentation of a reinforcer. When the terms are used in this manner, it should be kept in mind that reinforcement is not a thing: We do not present a reinforcement—we present a reinforcer.

As generally used, "reinforcer" and "reward" seem to have practically the same meaning, and there do not seem to be any overwhelmingly compelling reasons to choose one of the terms over the other. Some experimenters object to "reward" because it is derived from the language of everyday life and carries with it connotations of something pleasant and good which it seems best to avoid in the laboratory. Others point out that "reward" in other than psychological situations refers merely to that which is bestowed for actions approved by the donor and does not necessarily connote any special influence on the behavior of the recipient. Thus, where we wish to have a term which is neutral in terms of subjective impressions, and which has as one of its defining properties the "strengthening" of a response, "reinforcer" seems the term of choice. Of course, reinforcers may be pleasant when we experience them, or they may consist of the termination of events we would label noxious, or they may be completely outside our realm of experience (such as electrical brain stimulation, which proves to be reinforcing). Sometimes they will even be events which "make no sense" to us, as when the frequency of a response emitted by laboratory rats is increased when each response is followed by the *onset* of mild electrical foot shock (Harrington & Kohler, 1966). Trying to make predictions of the possible reinforcing properties of events from our own experience can be hazardous, even when fairly 'familiar situations are involved: The phrase "generation gap" is a recognition of the differences in the events which are reinforcers for various age groups, and "culturally deprived" often means "his reinforcers are not mine. . . ." On the practical level, determining what constitutes a reinforcer is one of the most important tasks required of the therapist, teacher, or parent; at the present time, the behavioral test for reinforcing properties of events is the only solution to these problems, just as it continues to be the final test for the laboratory worker.

Although some experimenters object to the term "reward," others object to the terms "reinforcer" and "reinforcement" because they feel these terms may have unintended theoretical implications. The definition of reinforcement we have already offered refers strictly to empirically determined relations between events: In the presence of certain stimuli, responses become more likely when they have been followed by certain events (reinforcers) and become less likely when they are no longer followed by these events. However, something underlying the observed empirical relations between events has been implied by these terms in certain theoretical

contexts. Some years ago, for example, the most prominent theory of learning (Hull, 1943) maintained that a reinforcer always was a drive (or drive-stimulus) reducer. Today, however, "reinforcer" and "reinforcement" rarely refer to anything more than the empirical observations. We feel, therefore, that these are the more desirable terms, and use them exclusively in the discussions in this chapter.[1]

This leaves the term "incentive" in need of clarification. "Incentive" sometimes has a meaning that is rarely implied by reward and reinforcer and which certainly deserves a special term. This meaning has recently been stated by Logan (1960):

> "Incentive" is a hypothetical concept referring to what might popularly be described as the subject's expectation of reward. If a rat's performance in an alley is differentially affected by the reward he has previously received in the goal box, then some internal consequent of the reward must be present while he is in the alley before the reward is received. "Incentive" is . . . [the] . . . word for this consequent [p. 3].

For example, even though the experimenter might hold the amount and quality of the reinforcer constant over a series of trials, incentive might be changing. We restrict the term "incentive" to this meaning suggested by Logan (1960). (The concept of "incentive motivation" is discussed in Chapter 18.)

QUANTITATIVE VARIATION IN REINFORCERS: THE "AMOUNT" PROBLEM

Typical Manipulations Defining "Amount" and the Problems Raised by Them

Once it became apparent that the reinforcer was an important determinant of be-

---

[1] For a discussion of some of the theoretical issues which have played a role in shaping the use of "reinforcement" in psychology, see Hilgard and Bower (1966). The term was originated by Pavlov and referred to the pairing of a neutral and an unconditional stimulus in the conditioning situation (and thus, the pairing of the reflexes associated with each stimulus). The "positivistic" concept of the reinforcer now so much a part of psychological literature stems largely from Skinner's writing. A concise summary of this point of view can be found in Skinner (1953, especially Chapter 5).

havior, it was quite natural that researchers should begin manipulating parameters of the reinforcer to determine their effects. In the earliest experimental studies, variations in amount and type of food were investigated (see, for example, Simmons, 1924; Elliott, 1928, 1930; Grindley, 1929). For example, Simmons found that a group of rats fed a bite of bread and milk in the goal box of a maze showed, on the average, better maze performance than rats fed sunflower seeds. Of course, in these studies, many of the parameters of the reinforcer were allowed to vary at once.

Two potentially important dimensions of reinforcers were separated by Wolfe and Kaplon (1941), when they distinguished between the effects of the amount of food and the amount of "consummatory responding" involved in goal box activity.[2] They gave three groups of chicks three behavioral tests (straight runway, detour or "umweg" runway, and black-white discrimination), reinforcing one group with a single, whole piece of popcorn, another with four one-quarter pieces of the corn, and the third group with one of the quarter pieces of corn. The first and the second groups, of course, ingested equal amounts of food, whereas the first and third groups engaged in equal amounts of consummatory activity (a single peck). In all three tests, the group reinforced with the four one-quarter pieces was superior to the others in speed of running and error elimination. Because the variability of the speed and error scores was rather large, and because the same groups were used in all three experiments, it is difficult to decide how reliable an effect was produced by differences in the amount of food per se, or by the amount of consummatory responding. Nevertheless, the study suggested quite strongly that the total

reinforcing effect should be considered in terms of the behavior the organism emits in the presence of the reinforcer, as well as in terms of the sensory and nutritional consequences of the reinforcing event. This fact should be kept in mind when we read the literature on "amount of reinforcement," for the majority of the studies indexed under this heading will have allowed two or more aspects of the situation to co-vary.

Although the term "amount" frequently is used in this loose fashion to refer to any of a number of manipulations of the reinforcer, the results of the many studies in this area seem more easily organized if we distinguish three classes of operations: (1) manipulations of the mass or volume of food, water, or other substance which is ingested by the subject; (2) procedures which cause variations in the amount of consummatory responding (that is, the number of licks, pecks, and so on); and (3) methods which employ differing concentrations of sucrose, saccharin, or other substances.[3] Intensity of positively reinforcing electrical brain stimulation seems to belong with the third category, for it produces functional relations like those found when concentration is varied. In contrast, intensity of aversive stimulation from which escape can occur seems to have behavioral effects analogous to the procedures in category 1 (see pp. 720–721).

Amount of Reinforcer and Amount of Consummatory Responding

Amount of reinforcer The reference experiments in most textbooks are those of Crespi (1942) and Zeaman (1949). Crespi changed the procedure of his experiment as it developed, making it a difficult one to summarize. For that reason, we will describe the method employed by Zeaman. In general, these two studies are prototypes of many that subsequently have been designed to explore specific features of the amount of reinforcement variable.

---

[2] "Consummatory activity" in studies of animal behavior typically refers to the last responses in a behavior sequence (that is, the behavior that consummates or completes that particular activity cycle), rather than to the responses involved in consuming (ingesting) solids or fluids. Frequently these two terms have identical meanings: The consumption of a food pellet consummates the response sequence that started with bar pressing. In other instances, the meanings of the terms are easily distinguished, as when sexual behavior is allowed as the reinforcing operation.

[3] It is not common usage to refer to the number of reinforced trials or reinforced responses as "amount of reinforcement."

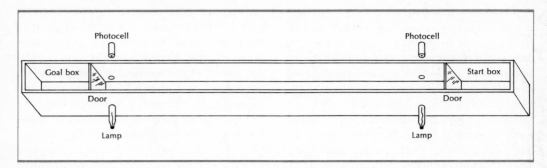

Figure 15.1. Floor plan showing the essential features of a simple alley apparatus. All such devices include at least the following features: a start box in which the animal may be detained until the trial is to begin; a door through which access to the alley itself is gained; the alley, at the end of which is placed the goal box; a second door, to be closed behind the animal to prevent retracing; and devices for timing the performance. Two time indices have been taken in most cases: starting latency, timed from when the start box door opens until the animal leaves the start box; and time to traverse the major portion of the alley. In the earliest alleys, timing was done with stopwatches or by hand closure of switches. Later, depressable floor sections were used to control timing circuits. Today, most alleys use the interruption of a light beam falling on a light-sensitive device to determine when the animal reaches one of the criterion points. In the sketch above, the photocells are placed 5 feet apart, simplifying the conversion of alley time into speed (in feet per second). Speed measures are typically employed, for they can be more readily compared when different lengths of alley are employed, and because they are multiples of the reciprocals of time scores, they are less skewed and more easily adapted to the assumptions of standard statistical techniques than simple time measures. Synonyms that are used commonly are: straight alley, alleyway, or runway. Plastic or metal inserts may be placed in the goal box, start box, or alley to serve as discriminative stimuli. If more than one condition of reinforcement is to be employed, it sometimes is desirable to prevent the subject from seeing the reinforcer from the alley. In such cases, curtains sometimes are hung near the goal area, or the goal box is built in an **L**-shape, requiring the subject to make a 90-degree turn at the end of the run. In spite of the turn, this device continues to be classified as a straight alley.

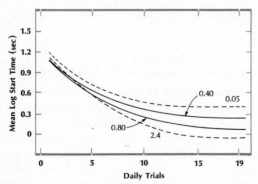

Figure 15.2. Each group of rats was given one run per day in a short alley. The values plotted show the average time the animals needed to leave the start box when the door was raised. The amount of food found in the goal box is indicated by each curve. Two groups (.20 and 1.6) have been omitted for ease of inspection; they fell in their proper places in the distribution. (After Zeaman, 1949.)

Zeaman assigned rats to 7 groups and gave each animal 18 daily acquisition trials in a 3-foot runway. The groups received either 0.05, 0.2, 0.4, 0.6, 0.8, 1.6, or 2.4 g of cheese per trial. Latency of leaving the start box, and time required to run to the goal box were recorded. Both measures indicated that speed was a positive function of amount of food in the goal box.[4] The results for 4 of the 7 groups in this part of the experiment are summarized in Figure 15.2, and the main effect is quite clear: Larger amounts of food produce shorter starting latencies.

The group curves also seem to show relatively similar *rates* of improvement, as if the amount of food might be setting the asymptotic level for

[4] After eighteen days of training, some animals received a different amount of food. These results will be considered in the next section.

each group, with each trial contributing a constant proportion of the improvement needed to attain these "final" levels.[5] Indeed, it seems that almost any experiment in which simple measures of speed are made is likely to produce grossly similar results, whether the data are obtained using tasks that involve measures of reaction time, an alleyway, or simple motor skills (see Woodworth & Schlosberg, 1954, pp. 664–667): speed measures characteristically show less and less absolute improvement per trial as practice increases, with each trial eliminating a constant proportion of the distance remaining to the performance level at which behavior stabilizes. As a descriptive technique, this form of analysis seems to have some value quite apart from the role it was assigned in behavior theory. However, it is only with time-based measures that such treatments of the data are possible, and when we examine indices of performance based on the proportion of correct responses or the elimination of errors, the rate of approach to the final level of proficiency may sometimes show marked discontinuities, with sudden improvements in the scores of individual subjects. It is possible that these discontinuities reflect sudden changes in the way in which the subject perceives the situation (see the discussion of the continuity–noncontinuity problem, Chapter 17). However, it is equally possible that the apparent discontinuity may sometimes result only from an inability to score such responses any more finely than "correct" or "incorrect," whereas speed of response may be measured along a continuously variable dimension. If this is true, we might expect speed measures to be "more sensitive" than choice measures to manipulations of independent variables, in that changes in speed might be detected before changes in choice. This does seem to be the case in at least some tests involving discrimination (Hall, 1960; Terman & Kling, 1968).

Subsequent studies have confirmed the main outcome of the Crespi and the Zeaman experiments: with separate groups of subjects each receiving one condition of reinforcement, and with discrete-trial procedures,[6] large differences in the ratios of the amounts of reinforcers will produce differences in speed of response. However, it is well to note that many experimenters failed to find such effects even though they employed such differences in reinforcers. Such results have led to numerous attempts to separate experimentally the cluster of factors that is involved whenever amount of reinforcer is manipulated, and evaluating such factors as the length of time subjects are exposed to goal box stimuli, the number of responses involved in ingestion, and the amount of the substance itself that is ingested became one of the favorite research topics of the 1950s. Obviously, a complete separation of these factors is impossible in the intact animal, but some partial separations have been accomplished. For example, Fehrer (1956) studied three groups of water-deprived rats in a U maze. She allowed one group 40 seconds to drink in the goal box on each trial and another group 10 seconds to drink. The third group was also allowed to drink for 10 seconds, but then was held in the goal box for an additional 30 seconds. In this way, two durations of goal box time, and two durations of drinking time were compared. Even though there were very marked differences in amount of water drunk per trial using this procedure, there were no differences in speed of running or in choice behavior.

Of course, if the rat is held in an empty goal box, it might have some detrimental effect on the subject's behavior, but other procedures which eliminated this factor have produced results similar to those of Fehrer. For example, Kling (1956) used two sizes of drinking tubes, so that rats would be able to obtain water at high or low rates. Each of four groups was assigned to a different one of the four combinations of conditions produced by large and small drinking tubes, and long (120 seconds) and short (10 seconds) goal-box durations, thus allowing amount of fluid to be separated from the amount of time in the goal box. Despite the large differences in the conditions of reinforcement, equally rapid improvements in running speed, and equally fast terminal rates were found for all groups but the one trained with the short duration and

[5]Data such as these led Hull (1943, Chapter 9) to assume that reinforcers set upper limits to which "habits" might grow. This position soon was modified to give reinforcers "incentive motivation" characteristics (Hull, 1952).

[6]As contrasted with "free-operant" procedures, where the subject's responding is not divided into trial periods. See page 602.

small tube. Again, as in the experiment cited above (Fehrer, 1956), the results indicate that in designs where each group receives but one condition of reinforcement, even quite large differences in amount of reinforcer may have little differential influence on behavior unless several other aspects of the situation are allowed to vary concomitantly. Once this conclusion became apparent, further attempts to break down the influence of the various factors involved in reinforcement began to disappear from the research literature.

One persistent problem encountered in experiments in which alleyways and similar types of apparatus are used is the control of extraneous stimulation: A quiet room and a masking noise can be used to overcome auditory stimulation from outside the experiment, and conditions of illumination and appropriately placed screens can block off unwanted visual stimuli. However, the handling of the animal prior to each of the trials, and the uncontrollable variability in patterns of stimulation from trial to trial and place to place in the apparatus, combined with the fact that we can obtain only a small number of scores from each subject, typically result in relatively large variances in measures of responding. Such variability may conceal reliable differences in behavior attributable to variables such as the amount of reinforcer. Often the only remedy is to use the averaged results from large groups of animals. By comparison, free operant techniques usually are compatible with isolation of the subject, and thus can avoid some of these problems of uncontrolled variation in stimulation. Such controls, plus those afforded by repeated exposure of the organism to the same situation, can produce relatively stable rates of responding in individual organisms. Hence, one might expect that these procedures would be especially valuable in exploring the effects of amount of reinforcer.

Typically, experimenters using free operant techniques prefer to compare the effects of various treatments by applying each treatment to every organism, rather than using separate groups of subjects to evaluate each treatment condition (Sidman, 1960). As we shall see, exposing a subject to more than one condition of reinforcement immediately changes the nature of the problem, but there is still another problem introduced by the use of free operant techniques in this context. The main difficulty can be stated quite simply: The rate of response is very strongly influenced by the reinforcement *schedule,* and it is influenced relatively little by the reinforcing condition itself. It is well known that response rate is conditionable (see, for example, Morse, 1966, especially pp. 73 ff. and 92 ff.), and therefore the more we strive to achieve stability of behavior, the more unlikely it becomes that manipulations of the amount of reinforcer will have significant effects on response rate. This domination of response rate by the schedule of reinforcement seems relatively weak during the early moments of a session or immediately following changes of conditions within a session; comparisons of the effects of providing different amounts of reinforcer on the subject's behavior at these times produce the expected positive correlations of response rate and amount of reinforcer (Keesey & Kling, 1961). In addition, the use of fairly short sessions (such as 15 or 20 min) also allows some of the inflexibility of schedule-determined response rates to be avoided.

Still other possibilities for the independent manipulation of components of the reinforcing situation exist when surgical rearrangement of the organism is employed. For example, if a rat's esophagus is severed, and if the cut end of the upper esophagus is sutured to the skin of the chest, everything he may later drink will emerge from this esophogeal fistula ("sham drinking"). Then, if one end of a tube is passed through the severed end of the lower esophagus and into the stomach while the other end of the tube is brought under the skin to the top of the head and fastened there securely, solutions may be sent into the stomach without making any contact with the mouth or requiring any consummatory responding by the animal (Mook, 1963).[7] For psychologists, one of the most interesting questions to be answered by such techniques is whether or not stimulation of the mouth or changes in the gut can have reinforcing effects when they are divorced from one another. They do, at least in animals that have a past history of normal eating experiences (see, for example, Miller & Kessen, 1952).

How do conditions of reinforcement (such as the amount of food given the subjects) influence behavior? In our own case, we might assume that we recall the reinforcement conditions of past sessions, and then consciously and rationally tune our efforts to the predicted payoffs. Most psychologists have been reluctant to assume that non-human organisms are endowed with similar capacities, at least until simpler hypotheses have been shown to be insufficient. One of the more frequently adopted viewpoints flows logically from the Watsonian brand of behaviorism (Watson, 1930), which conceived of all psychological processes in terms of muscular or glandular responses and their associated stimuli. To extend this reasoning to a nonverbal organism who shows "anticipation of" reinforcement conditions, we might assume that at least some components of the eating responses can occur in the absence of food itself, and that these components can become conditioned to (previously neutral) stimuli that are present in the goal box or are emanating from the feeding device. It is also reasonable to assume that, through stimulus generalization, stimuli similar to those of the goal box can evoke the conditioned components of the eating responses. These conditioned responses have been called "fractional anticipatory goal responses" (Spence, 1956). Of course, eating a larger amount of food allows more opportunities for these responses to become conditioned. Hence, animals re-

inforced with larger amounts of food should show these fractional anticipatory goal responses earlier in training, and with greater reliability, than would animals reinforced with smaller amounts of food.

Although such hypothesized responding was, in the beginning (for example, Hull, 1932), purely a theoretical device, we now know that "anticipatory" responses of this type do indeed occur, and that they do play a role in determining choice behavior and response speed. For example, Miller (1935) found that the use of distinctive goal responses would produce overtly recognizable anticipatory goal responses while the animals were running in a straight alley. Rats were given daily opportunities to eat while in one compartment and drink while in another. The food compartment was so constructed that the food cup could be reached only if the rat climbed up a step and twisted his head to the right; the water compartment was fashioned so that it could be reached only if the rat twisted his head to the left. Half the animals received daily alleyway trials with food in the goal box, and the other half ran to water. In the alley itself, the animals ran holding their heads in the position appropriate to the reinforcer they were to receive, and the "anticipatory" positioning became more noticeable as the animal approached the goal box. Thus, components of the distinctive response patterns previously associated with eating or drinking occurred prior to contact with the reinforcers themselves.

The frequency, and possibly the vigor, with which such anticipatory responses occur increases as the goal area is approached. This phenomenon has been illustrated by use of a preparation of the type developed by Patten (Patten & Rudy, 1967). Under general anesthesia, a few small screws are threaded into the skull of a rat, and a stainless steel tube is anchored to the skull in a small platform of dental cement. Alternatively, the tube can be held in place with a small harness. The tube is curved over the end of the snout, so that the rat can lap from it merely by extend-

---

[7] Other varieties of operation to separate mouth and stomach have been employed for somewhat similar purposes by Miller and Kessen (1952) and by Epstein and Teitelbaum (1962).

ing his tongue a few millimeters beyond his lips. The other end of the metal tube (near the rat's ears) is connected to a piece of flexible tubing, which in turn connects to a source of fluid. Each touch of the tongue against the tube can be sensed and recorded by a "drinkometer" circuit (Stellar & Hill, 1952); the fluid can be held within the tube (in which case the lap is "anticipatory"), or drops can be allowed to escape when the rat laps, thus reinforcing the tongue movements. Even if such reinforcement is given only when the rat reaches the goal area, the anticipatory responses soon develop, and they occur more frequently the closer the animal approaches the goal.

The functional significance ascribed to such anticipatory responses by theorists falls, for the most part, into two classes. For convenience, these may be labeled "motivational" and "associational." As illustrations of the motivational interpretations, we may mention the following assumptions: that the occurrence of anticipatory responses in the absence of the wherewithal to consummate the striving is innately exciting (Sheffield, 1966); that anticipatory responses and non-reinforcement produce frustration responses, which in turn can have a variety of behavioral consequences (Amsel, 1967); or that anticipatory responses and the stimuli they generate are the immediate determinants of incentive motivation (Spence, 1956). The general theme of motivational interpretations is that anticipatory responses in one way or another cause an increase in the vigor or rate of whatever instrumental responses are prepotent in the situation.

An associational interpretation, on the other hand, would ascribe to anticipatory responses a direct involvement in what the organism learns about the situation. In an indirect manner, Hull's (1952) assumption that the stimuli generated by anticipatory responses are secondary reinforcers (because they are similar to the stimuli generated by the consummatory responses themselves) might be considered a peripheral variety of

associational viewpoint, since the secondary reinforcers determine in part what is learned. But a more directly associational viewpoint would emphasize the discriminative stimulus role of the stimuli resulting from anticipatory responses. This was the use made of such hypothetical responses by Hull in his descriptions of the manner in which a stimulus-response psychology could account for anticipation of events (for example, Hull, 1930), and Capaldi (1967) recently has revived interest in this point of view. Seen in this light, any alteration in anticipatory stimuli would have the same effects as all other alterations in discriminative stimuli: errors would increase, speed would decrease, and so forth.

Until fairly recently, "anticipatory responses" ordinarily meant the responses which the theorist assumed to be present. Within the last few years, however, there have been developed several techniques which allow the direct observation of responses which seem to have the properties attributed to fractional anticipatory goal responses by Spence (1956) and others. The measurement of anticipatory lapping has already been mentioned (p. 621). The concurrent observation of classically conditioned salivation and instrumental responses reinforced with food (see, for example, Shapiro & Miller, 1965; Williams, 1965) provides another means of investigating the interactions of reinforcers, instrumental responses, and the anticipatory responses which presumably determine incentive and secondary reinforcement. With such tools, an accelerated program of research involving anticipatory responses may be anticipated in the next few years.

Amount of consummatory responding
Because the amount of behavior involved in obtaining and ingesting foods and fluids ordinarily is perfectly correlated with the amount of the substance, the logical possibility exists that it is the *behavior* of food-getting, rather than the stimulus properties or the metabolic characteristics of the food, that determines reinforcement value. Unfor-

tunately, there seems to be no way to test this hypothesis directly, for even if we employ sham feeding (during which all the food emerges from an esophageal fistula instead of continuing on to the stomach), we still have left the taste and smell of the food which is confounded with the seizing, chewing, and swallowing. Therefore, experimenters have been forced to employ indirect tests of the "consummatory response" hypothesis. Several schemes have been employed, all of which are variations of the basic procedure developed by Wolfe and Kaplon (1941): They gave their chicks a unit of food in one piece or as four quarter pieces; Kling (1956) presented fluids through large or small diameter drinking tubes; Hulse (1960) pumped large or small drops to the end of a drinking tube; and Hall and Kling (1960) distributed a given volume of fluid into two or into six drinking cups. In all cases, a partial separation is obtained of the amount of consummatory behavior and the amount of substance received; and in all cases, the conclusion reached is the same: increasing the amount of consummatory responding will increase slightly the reinforcing properties of the substances. The effect is small, but it is present with such consistency that we dare not ignore the behaviors emitted during reinforcement when evaluating the efficacy of various reinforcers.

A response-probability theory of reinforcement   If consummatory responding contributes to the overall effectiveness of reinforcers, perhaps responding itself has reinforcing properties. Premack (for example, 1965) has proposed just such a theory, making the specific assumption that any response may serve as the reinforcer for any other response that has a lower probability of occurrence. This proposition requires some revision of typical modes of thinking about reinforcers. According to Premack's theory, a reinforcer is not an event but a response. More specifically, *reinforcement* is a relation between a response that is being reinforced and a response that is

reinforcing, with the more-probable response being the reinforcer for the less-probable response. Furthermore, Premack (1965) has suggested that this relational view might also be extended to the problem of why some stimuli function as unconditioned stimuli in the Pavlovian situation, while others do not have this property: Conditioned stimuli usually elicit responses which are weak and, in comparison with the typical unconditioned response, less probable of occurrence, hence the reflex associated with presentation of the unconditioned stimulus can reinforce the reflex associated with the conditioned stimulus, but not vice versa.

How is the probability of responses to be determined? Premack asserts that the probability may be estimated from response durations, and in addition, that the reinforcement relation is independent of the means by which the durations are manipulated: if one can make Response A more probable than Response B, then A will serve as a reinforcer for B. Furthermore, if there is some way to increase the probability of B to where it exceeds A, then the relation can be reversed, and B will become the reinforcer. Several ingenious experiments supporting the theory have been published. For example, monkeys were given the opportunity to manipulate several kinds of gadgets (a lever, a door, and a plunger, among others), and the base level at which each animal manipulated each device was determined. Then, the devices were presented in pairs, but one was locked against movement and the other was left free to be moved. Whenever the unlocked device was operated, the locked device was unlocked and stayed unlocked until the monkey manipulated it, at which time it again was locked. Thus the opportunity to manipulate one device depended on the manipulation of the other. All possible pairs of devices were presented, and in each case where one of the animals had shown a preference for manipulating one of the devices in a pair beforehand, the hypothesis was supported: high-probability responses reinforced low-probability responses, but the reverse was not the case.

Further experiments have shown that drinking and running can be used either as the reinforced or reinforcing activity, depending on their relative probabilities as manipulated by depriving animals of water or activity (Premack, 1962); also playing a game can reinforce candy eating, or vice versa, depending on which activity occurred with the greater probability in a given child (Premack, 1959).

Clearly, a critical problem for adequate evaluation of this theory of reinforcement is the specification of probabilities of responses. In most cases, Premack suggests that comparisons of the duration of each response is likely to be a better index than the rates at which the responses occur. For example, a child may be observed to spend 10 minutes finger painting, but only 10 seconds speaking with others in the room, and yet his rate of emitting words during the time he is speaking might be many times higher than the rate with which he swings his paint-dabbed fingers at the paper. Using the durations to estimate probabilities, the prediction in this case would be that withholding the opportunity to paint until the child has spoken would increase duration of speaking.

Although Premack's theory is a provocative one, it has as yet stimulated but a small amount of research, some of which seems to call into question the generality of the basic hypothesis. For example, Eisenberger, Karpman, and Trattner (1967) used high school and college students in a series of experiments in which the freedom to make one response (such as turning a wheel) was contingent upon their making another response (such as pressing a bar). The results conformed to Premack's predictions only when the response to be reinforced was of low probability to start with; if it was of moderate to high probability, it could not be increased, even though there was considerable room for further improvement. (Indeed, suppression of high frequency responses was observed in

many cases.) Other observations suggested that the key feature of the contingency-reinforcement relation might be the suppression of a response below its free-running rate when it is paired with another response, and that the increase in rate attributed to reinforcement might merely be a recovery from this suppression and a return toward the former, unpaired rate. Premack (1965) had observed such suppression when responses were paired, but Eisenberger et al. suggest that this is not only a result of the paired testing, but the "necessary and sufficient condition for reinforcement in the contingency situation . . ." [p. 350].

Other criticisms of the response-probability theory have been discussed by Leeper (1965), but at the least, Premack's hypothesis has already had the extremely valuable effect of suggesting a fresh way in which to view a broad variety of problems related to reinforcement and motivation.

Effects of Varying the Concentration of Solution Used as a Reinforcer

As we have noted, in the typical animal experiment, amount of reinforcement could not be considered a unitary dimension. When the weight or number of pieces of food are varied, several potentially important variables are confounded. Guttman (1953) suggested that use of liquid food, such as solutions of sucrose (common table sugar) as reinforcers, offered the opportunity for greater control over the reinforcer than did the use of solid food. Amount of reinforcement could be studied by varying the concentration of the solution without concomitantly varying stimulation (visual, olfactory, tactual) prior to ingestion and without introducing possible differences in required consummatory activity.

Guttman proceeded to study the effects of varying the concentration of sucrose solution used as the reinforcer on response rates of rats in a bar-press apparatus. The sugar solutions were delivered to the rats by means of a small (.005 ml) dipper cup which was

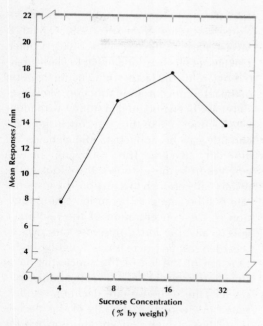

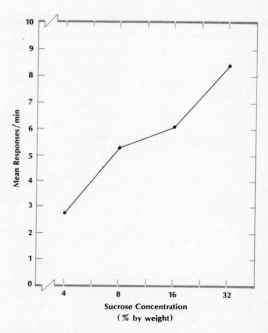

Figure 15.3. Mean rate of bar pressing by rats as a function of the concentration of sucrose solution used as the reinforcer with a continuous reinforcement schedule in effect. The concentrations are plotted on a logarithmic scale. Each point on the curve represents a different group of animals. The data are from the second day of bar-press training during which each animal was given 250 reinforcements. (After Guttman, 1953.)

Figure 15.4. Mean rate of bar pressing by rats as a function of the concentration of sucrose solution used as the reinforcer with a variable-interval 1-minute schedule of reinforcement in effect. The concentrations are plotted on a logarithmic scale. Each point on the curve represents a different group of animals. The data are from 5 successive daily half-hour experimental sessions. These animals had also been used in an earlier phase of the experiment, concerned with continuous reinforcement, the results of which are shown in Figure 15.3. (After Guttman, 1953.)

operated by a motor. The rats were divided into four groups, each group differing in the concentration of sucrose solution. Concentrations were 4, 8, 16, and 32 percent by weight.[8] In the first part of his study, each bar press was reinforced (continuous reinforcement or CRF schedule). The relationship between the rate of bar pressing and concentration of sucrose, which we will refer to as the rate-concentration function, was nonmonotonic (Fig-

ure 15.3). Rate of bar pressing increased with increases in concentration to 16 percent, but then declined with the further increase to 32 percent. In a second phase of the study with the same groups, all conditions were the same, except that a fixed-interval (FI) 1-minute reinforcement schedule replaced the CRF schedule, so that only the first bar press after each one-minute interval was reinforced. The rate-concentration function was no longer nonmonotonic. Bar pressing increased roughly linearly as a function of the log concentration of sucrose solution (Figure 15.4). The concentration of the sucrose solution was clearly

[8]Because confusion might arise from attaching differing meanings to the terms used to describe the concentration of solute in solution, recommendations regarding preparation of solutions were published by Pfaffmann and his colleagues (1954). Percentage concentration by weight refers to the weight of solute divided by weight of solute plus weight of solvent. By this method a 50 percent solution of sucrose would be prepared by adding 10 g of sucrose to 10 g of water, preferably distilled water.

shown to be an important variable, but the exact shape of the rate-concentration function varied with the reinforcement schedule. The reason for this was not entirely clear at the time, although Guttman discussed several hypotheses.

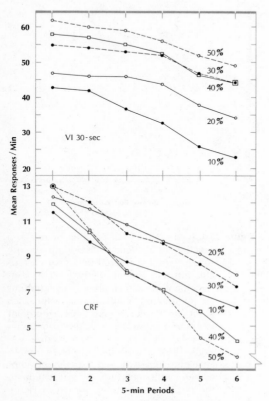

Figure 15.5. Mean rate of bar pressing by rhesus monkeys (*Macaca mulatta*) during successive 5-minute periods within daily experimental sessions. The different curves in each graph are for the different concentrations of sucrose solutions used as reinforcers. The upper graph is for experimental sessions during which the schedule of reinforcement was a variable-interval (VI) 30-seconds and the lower graph is for those during which the schedule was continuous reinforcement (CRF). The VI data are for 6 animals and the CRF for the same 6 plus an additional animal. Note that with the VI schedule the curves are all nearly parallel to one another, whereas with the CRF schedule the curves for the 2 highest concentrations decline considerably more rapidly within sessions than do those for the lower concentrations. (After Schrier, 1965.)

A series of studies by Collier and his co-workers (Collier & Siskel, 1959; Collier & Myers, 1961; Collier & Willis, 1961; Collier, 1962) using rats has done much to clarify matters regarding the factors influencing the form of the rate-concentration function. Similar results have been obtained in studies with monkeys (Schrier, 1965); thus the conclusions apparently can be applied to the behavior of different species. The following picture emerges from these studies: If we look at the results early enough in a session, the response rate will be found to be an increasing function of the concentration of the reinforcer. Specifically, the *initial* response rate may be regarded as an increasing, roughly linear, function of the log of the concentration of the reinforcing solution. Over the course of a session, the response rate declines. As illustrated in Figure 15.5, the rate of this decline is greatest at high concentrations when the volume per reinforcement is large or the density of reinforcement is high (that is, when the time between reinforcements is short, as it is on a CRF schedule, or on a short FI or VI schedule as compared with a long FI or VI schedule). The result of this relatively greater decline at higher concentrations is the nonmonotonic rate–concentration function of the type seen in Figure 15.3. The larger the volume and the higher the density of reinforcement, the lower the concentration at which the peak rate occurs and the earlier in the session the nonmonotonicity is observed.

Results such as those described above suggest that at least two classes of events control the momentary response rate of subjects (McCleary, 1953; Hulse, Snyder, & Bacon, 1960; Collier & Myers, 1961; Schrier, 1965). One of these classes includes the various sensory events (olfactory, gustatory, tactual) accompanying ingestion. The response rate is an increasing function of the intensity of these events. The second class of events is the momentary or immediate post-ingestive load, or what might be called "momentary satiation," with response rate a decreasing function of this load. The adjectives "momentary" and "immediate" distinguish this class of events from variations in the nutritive state of the animal or its metabolic activity, for the changes in response rates within sessions seem to occur well before assimilation of the ingested solutions could be an important factor. The first class of events is most important in control of the initial rate of response, while declines in responding within sessions are primarily attributable to the second class of events—at least when conditions of high density of reinforcement, high concentration, and large volume are combined.

Mook (1963) has recently reached somewhat similar conclusions about the interacting roles of the mouth and postingestive factors on the basis of measures of intake of sucrose and other solutions by rats. By means of surgical procedures, rats were prepared with esophageal fistulas, so that any fluid swallowed emerged from an opening in the throat (sham drinking, p. 620), and with cannulas through which solutions could be injected into the stomach as the animal drank. Thus, Mook was able to compare the intake of different concentrations of solution under conditions of sham drinking and sham drinking combined with a stomach input of the same or different solutions. His results agreed with the conclusions drawn above except for a nonmonotonic intake-concentration function found when sucrose drinking was accompanied by nothing entering the stomach. According to the above-mentioned hypothesis, we would expect under these circumstances to find an increasing, monotonic function. Mook suggests that this nonmonotonic function may reflect sensory adaptation, brought into play as a result of the greater total intake under this condition than when the fluid being drunk was allowed to enter the stomach. Undoubtedly sensory adaptation should be considered as a possible factor influencing responding in operant studies of the type considered in this section, at least when large volumes of highly concentrated solutions are delivered at a high frequency.

One interpretation of the data that have been discussed so far in this section is that the reinforcing effects of a sucrose solution are always directly related to its concentration, or to whatever parameter or parameters determine the intensity of the sensory consequences. The immediate and long term postingestive factors, among others, are superimposed on the sensory factors, concealing the true reinforcement function. As Guttman (1953, p. 222) has put it, ". . . the reinforcing agent . . . can be explicitly treated as a *stimulus* and its properties and functions so described." This in turn suggests that the procedures and results of psychophysics should be directly applicable to the study of reinforcement.

Although a number of sensory modalities are involved during ingestion of a food reinforcer, we would guess, of course, that taste would be one of the most important. Furthermore, at least in the case of the sugars, we might further speculate that the reinforcing effects are directly related to the sweetness of the solution. One bit of evidence which supports this notion was obtained by Guttman (1954), in the same bar-pressing apparatus used in his earlier study. When humans are given equal concentrations of the sugars, sucrose and glucose, sucrose is uniformly judged to be sweeter. Guttman used varying concentrations of glucose and sucrose for reinforcement of bar pressing by rats. He found, throughout the range of concentrations used, that at equal concentrations, sucrose was indeed more reinforcing than glucose, as judged by rate of bar pressing.

Saccharin is a chemical that has interested psychologists for a number of years because it tastes sweet but is non-nutritive. Seventy-five to 90 percent of ingested saccharin is eliminated within the first 24 hours in urine and the remainder in the feces. Rats prefer saccharin solutions to water, as determined by two-bottle tests (Richter, 1939), which tempts us to infer that saccharin solutions taste sweet to these animals also. We would expect, therefore, to find that saccharin is also reinforcing. This has been shown to be the case for rats in a T maze (Hughes, 1957) and in experiments involving bar pressing (Cockrell, 1952; Collier, 1962). In the latter studies, various parameters of the rate-concentration function discussed above were found to operate in the same way for saccharin as for sucrose. Not all species of animals react to saccharin in this way. Squirrel monkeys (*Saimiri sciureus*), for example, show no preference for saccharin solutions when offered a choice of such solutions and water. However, they do prefer another nonnutritive sweetener, dulcin, to water, and dulcin has been found to reinforce bar pressing by these animals (Fisher, Pfaffmann, & Brown, 1965). Although it has not been tried, it would be extremely surprising if saccharin were found to reinforce bar pressing in these animals under circumstances similar to those in which sucrose and dulcin do.

The relationship between preference and reinforcement suggests that the reinforce-

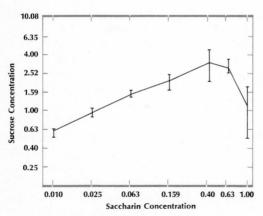

Figure 15.6. Equal-preference function for solutions of sucrose and saccharin. The graph shows the mean concentrations of sucrose (ordinate) that were preferred equally as much as various concentrations of saccharin (abscissa). Concentrations are specified in g/100 ml of solution. Each mean is based on the preference scores of 8 animals, except those for the 2 highest concentrations of saccharin (0.63 and 1.00), which are based on scores of 7 animals. The vertical lines indicate the range of concentrations of sucrose that were equally preferred by individual animals to each concentration of saccharin. The variability was greatest at the highest concentration of saccharin. (Young & Madsen, 1963.)

ment value of a substance is related to its taste and perhaps other sensory qualities. But can it be concluded that a good taste is all that a substance needs to be a reinforcer? This deceptively easy question proves to be impossible to answer with any precision. Suppose we define "tasting good" in terms of preference, so that whichever of two substances is selected is the one which "tastes better" than the other. We could compare, for example, sucrose and saccharin at various concentrations, and then state what concentration of the one is preferred over which concentrations of the other, or which concentrations of each are "equally preferred." Such comparisons have been made for rat (see, for example, Young & Madsen, 1963) and for man (see, for example, Lemberger, 1908, as cited by Pfaffmann, 1951), but for comparisons of the preference data with reinforcement values, we shall have to restrict our attention to the rat.

The average "equal preference" curve obtained by Young and Madsen is shown in Figure 15.6. Note that the most concentrated sucrose solution used was 4 g per 100 ml, or approximately a 4 percent solution; that it was matched by a saccharin solution of approximately 0.4 percent; and that no saccharin solution of any concentration could be found which was preferred to the stronger sucrose solutions. Moreover, as saccharin concentrations were increased beyond 0.4 to 0.6 percent, preference fell, as indicated by the drop in the equal preference curve.

If reinforcement value, as indicated by bar press rates, were determined only by taste preference, we should predict from the "hedonic equivalence function" that the same response rates would be obtained when using either a 3 percent sucrose solution or a 0.4 percent saccharin solution, and that equal response rates would be supported by 0.05 and 1.0 percent saccharin solutions. Unfortunately, no experiment has investigated sucrose and saccharin preferences and reinforcement values under exactly equivalent conditions, so we are forced to compare

TABLE 15.1 SOME EQUIVALENT CONCENTRATION VALUES FOR AQUEOUS SUCROSE SOLUTIONS FREQUENTLY USED IN BEHAVIORAL EXPERIMENTS.[a]

Percent by weight	Molar concentration	Percent by weight	Molar concentration
1	.029	25	.809
2	.059	30	.988
4	.118	30.3	1.0
5	.149	32	1.063
8	.241	40	1.375
10	.303	43.2	1.5
15	.464	50	1.796
16	.497	54.4	2.0
20	.632	64	2.443

[a] Most of these values are from Table 63, pages D 163–164, *Handbook of Chemistry and Physics*, 46th Ed., Cleveland: Chemical Rubber Co., 1965–1966. The other values were determined empirically.

TABLE 15.2 COMPARISON OF RESPONSE RATES WITH DIFFERENT CONCENTRATIONS OF SACCHARIN AND SUCROSE SOLUTIONS USED AS REINFORCERS.[a]

Saccharin		Sucrose	
Approximate percent concentration	Approximate responses per minute	Approximate percent concentration	Approximate responses per minute
0.075	3.2	4.0	4.5
0.45	5.0	8.0	5.25
1.02	5.8	16.0	6.5
1.52	5.4	32.0	7.8

[a] The saccharin data are from Cockrell (1952), Experiment II, Procedure 10b. The sucrose data are from Guttman (1953), PR, each animal as its own control. Response rates have been estimated from published figures.

across experiments and conditions.[9] However, some portions of the experiments of Guttman (1953) and Cockrell (1952) employed quite similar procedures, and we shall therefore hazard a comparison of their findings. Table 15.2 presents the approximate mean response rates obtained by these investigators using a 1-min fixed interval reinforcement schedule, with every animal exposed to every solution on each day. If we interpolate with abandon, we can guess that the response rate that might have been obtained had Cockrell used a saccharin solution of 0.3 percent might have been quite similar to the rate Guttman might have obtained had he used a 3 percent sucrose solution. However, it is only at this

low end of the dynamic range for each solution that any successful predictions of response rates from preference data can be made; all other predictions of rate from preference seem to be wrong. For example, the response rates would suggest that 8 percent sucrose should be about equally preferred to 0.5 percent saccharin, but this is not true: above 4 to 5 percent sucrose, no saccharin solution is ever preferred as much. Similarly, the preference data would suggest that 0.05 and 1.0 percent saccharin solutions would produce approximately equal response rates, but Cockrell's results with the 0.075 percent solution indicate that the response rate would be very low with a 0.05 percent solution, and near its peak with a 1.0 percent solution.

The data compiled by Young and Madsen are based on very brief exposures of the solutions to the rats, which is similar to the exposure to solutions provided by the small

[9] In reading the literature, we frequently are impeded by the need to translate from one mode of specification of concentration to the other. The majority of studies have used either percent concentration by weight or molar concentration. Some typical sets of relations between these are presented in Table 15.1.

amounts of substance carried on the dippers. Preference data based on long-term exposures to saccharin and sucrose (for example, Collier & Novell [1967] and Hammer [1967]), however, seem to lead to similar conclusions: Except in the range below 4 percent sucrose, no saccharin solution will ever be preferred to a sucrose solution.

In summary, we might conclude that the taste quality of substances, as evaluated from equal-preference data, offers only a poor basis for predicting reinforcement values, as reflected in response rates. Of course, we must remind ourselves that, in comparing saccharin and sucrose, we are dealing with solutions that are similar only in that each tastes sweet to man. As do other sweet substances, each has its characteristic flavor, and saccharin also has a marked bitter component (for man) which we begin to detect in concentrations greater than 0.5 percent. Probably only when we compare substances which are almost indistinguishable (as sucrose and glucose, at all but the highest concentrations) will "equal sweetness" or equal preference offer a sound basis for prediction of equal reinforcement values, and even then we should not expect perfect correlations between measures of preference and measures of reinforcing effects.

A Word of Caution

It is difficult to view the studies we describe above with complete objectivity, for we have many preconceptions about the way in which reinforcer variables should influence behavior based on our common-sense notions of how to win friends and influence people and our impressions of the influence that evolutionary pressures should have had on the development of the higher organisms. It therefore comes as something of a shock to some students of behavior when they discover that amount of reinforcer frequently is quite an ineffective variable when manipulated in laboratory studies, and that there is considerable discrepancy between the results of studies which appear to be equally well designed and executed.

At least some of the differences between studies must stem from our tendency to place into a single category some experiments which might better be considered independently. For example, we have discussed as separate problems the manipulation of the amount of food and concentration of sucrose (and other) solutions. Originally (see p. 624), the use of sucrose solutions was thought to provide a superior technique for investigating the amount of reinforcer, but it now seems that manipulation of amount (weight, volume, and so on) may have behavioral effects which are distinct from those resulting from manipulation of taste and other factors correlated with changes in concentration. One reason for thinking that there may be differences between amount and concentration effects stems from the relative potency of these factors in behavioral situations: When both volume and taste factors are manipulated in the same experiment, the total effect attributable to amount always seems to be smaller than that attributable to taste (see Hutt, 1954; Collier, 1962; Schrier, 1965). This effect is seen in striking fashion when experimenters have manipulated volume without a confounding change in ingestion time, as in studies where the size of individual drops coming from the drinking spout can be controlled (Berkley, 1963).

A further source of discrepancies among studies is the failure to take into account the pretraining procedures when we compare the results of experiments. Consider an experimental design in which several reinforcement conditions are to be evaluated, perhaps by using the rate of bar pressing as the dependent variable. One experimenter assigns subjects at random to each experimental condition, gives each of them the necessary magazine and bar training, and then runs the critical sessions (see, for example, Guttman, 1953). Another experimenter gives all his animals magazine and bar training with a single reinforcement condition, and then constructs matched groups of subjects based on the behavior observed during pretraining; each of these matched groups is then exposed to one of the reinforcement conditions in which the experimenter is interested (see, for example, Hutt, 1954). The relative efficiency and power of these two designs may be argued on statistical grounds, but from the point of view of the behavioral effects there can be no doubt that they produce differences: When pretraining and training are carried out using different reinforcement conditions, a "shift" procedure exists, and the effects of differences in the amount and quality of reinforcer are enhanced (see pages 631–640 for a discussion of types of shift procedures and typical results). These and other procedural differences sometimes have been overlooked in attempts to summarize the literature on this area of study and account for at least a portion of the discrepancies among the studies.

SHIFTS IN AMOUNT OF REINFORCER

Constant-Reinforcer versus Variable-Reinforcer Methods

We describe here studies which are concerned with the general question of whether the effects of a particular reinforcer on behavior can be influenced by other reinforcers presented in the same or similar situations. The term that we shall use to indicate that one reinforcer is having an effect on another is "reinforcement-context effect." "Context" is used here in much the same sense as it is used in psychophysics (see pages 58–59) when talking about effects of the stimulus context or series.

Although a variety of methods have been used to study reinforcement context, most of them have involved a comparison of outcomes using two procedures—the "variable-reinforcer" and the "constant-reinforcer." "Variable-reinforcer" refers to any procedure in which the subjects are presented with more than one amount of reinforcer. In practice, this has been accomplished by giving each animal either a *single shift* from one amount to another or *repeated shifts* among amounts of a given set. "Constant-reinforcer" refers to the procedure of training separate groups of animals, each with a different

amount of reinforcer throughout training, so that each animal is presented only one amount. We discuss separately the results of studies which have employed the single-shift type of variable reinforcer procedure and those which have employed the repeated-shift type.

Single Shifts in the Reinforcer

The reference studies on the question of shifts in the reinforcer were the ones carried out on rats by Crespi (1942) and Zeaman (1949), the preshift results of which have been discussed on pages 617–619. Both investigators, it will be recalled, measured performance of rats in a runway apparatus. The animals were given one trial a day. In the Zeaman experiment, after one group of animals was given a large amount of reinforcer (2.4 g of cheese) and another group a small amount (0.05 g) for 18 consecutive days, the amounts were reversed. On Day 19 and for the remaining 8 days of the experiment, the animals that had received the large amount of reinforcer received the small, and the animals that had received the small amount received the large. Zeaman assumed that the animals had

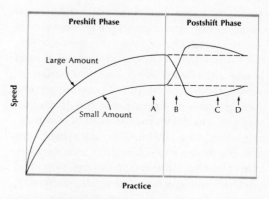

Figure 15.7. Idealized results of shifts in the amount of reinforcer. The curves represent the performance of 2 groups as a function of practice. During the preshift phase, one group was given a relatively large amount of reinforcer on each trial and the other a relatively small amount. During the postshift phase, the amounts given the 2 groups were reversed. The letters refer to regions of the graph that are discussed in the text.

reached the performance asymptote before the shifts were introduced. Though somewhat less straightforward in its experimental design and execution, the Crespi experiment had the same basic plan. Figure 15.7 represents the results as they were conceived by Crespi, Zeaman, and many subsequent writers. The four important regions of the graph are indicated by capital letters. Region A is there to remind us that the performance of the animals was supposed to have been asymptotic prior to the shifts in the amount of reinforcer. Region B shows that, as expected, the average performance level of those animals which were given an upward shift in amount of reinforcer increased, and the average performance level of those given a downward shift decreased. However, Crespi and Zeaman also noted two results that had not been expected. First, as can also be seen in Region B, the changes in performance occurred rapidly, with most of the increase or decrease taking place within the first three days following the shifts in amount. Second, as can be seen in Region C, the performance levels either overshot or undershot the control levels. The performance of the group which received the upward shift in amount of reinforcer increased to a level above that expected of the original large-reinforcer group had the reinforcer shift not occurred. Crespi called this overshooting of the control level by an upward-shifted group an "elation effect", while Zeaman referred to it as a "positive-contrast effect." Similarly, the performance of the group that had gotten a decrease in amount of reinforcer decreased to a level below that expected of the group originally given the small amount had it not received the reinforcer shift. This undershooting was called a "depression effect" by Crespi and a "negative-contrast effect" by Zeaman. Crespi's terminology reflected his belief that the contrast effects were emotional phenomena produced by the "unexpected" rewards. This conception of the nature of the contrast effects led Crespi to predict that they would be temporary in nature (Region D), though there was no clearcut evidence for this in his own data.

Contrast effects, then, represent one type of reinforcement-context effect. Although the discussion to follow deals primarily with contrast effects, other types of reinforcement-context effects are also possible, as we shall see.

On the basis of the Crespi and Zeaman studies the concept of reinforcement-contrast effects was generally accepted and widely quoted by psychologists. Spence (1956), however, questioned whether Crespi and Zeaman had adequately demonstrated a positive-contrast effect. Both Zeaman and Crespi had used the performance of the large-amount group on the few days immediately preceding the shifts as the control level by which to judge the overshooting effect. As we indicate above, these investigators assumed that the performance levels of the animals had reached the asymptote by this time, and thus would not have shown any further change with continued training. Spence claimed that asymptotic performance levels are not reached in straight runway situations until after considerably more training than had been given by Crespi and Zeaman. The preshift "control" levels, then, merely represented a stage of practice at which performance had not reached stable levels. It should be emphasized that Spence's criticism applies only to Crespi and Zeaman's procedures for demonstrating positive contrast; dependence upon extrapolation from nonasymptotic performance for control levels would, in their case, work against a demonstration of negative contrast. Thus, if anything, the magnitude of the negative contrast effect found by Crespi and Zeaman would be expected to be greater if adequate controls were used. (Besides, in one phase concerned with downward shifts, Crespi did run a nonshifted control group during the postshift period.) Spence carried out a study on rats which was of the same general design as the previous ones except that the small-reinforcer and large-reinforcer animals were each given forty-eight daily trials before the amounts were changed. During the preshift training period, the performance of both groups, as measured in terms of running speed, continued to rise well past the point at which Zeaman (but not Crespi[10]) had shifted the amount of reinforcer. As for the postshift period, Spence observed the rapid changes in performance that Crespi and Zeaman had noted and also the negative contrast effect. There was, however, no positive contrast effect. Indeed, the performance of the upward-shifted group remained somewhat below that of the control level.

Spence's critique and experiment, then, raised serious doubts about the existence of a positive contrast effect. This was of considerable importance because it was really the positive contrast effect that created a new problem for behavior theory. The negative effect was relatively easily dealt with in terms of standard concepts used in experimental psychology of learning (such as generalization decrement or frustration[11]), but the positive effect was not so easily dealt with.

Before going further, we might question whether the conditions in Spence's studies were favorable to the appearance of the positive contrast effect. The large reinforcer weighed 1 g (quite a large amount for rats). Also, the animals were deprived of food for 22 hours before each trial and had prolonged training. Thus, by the time the amount of reinforcer was shifted, the group that originally was given the large amount might well have been running at speeds close to the maximum that might be expected under the most favorable conditions of reinforcement, drive, and practice (the so-called "ceiling effect"). If this were true, we would not consider the chances of an upward-shifted group exceeding the speed of the control group to be very great. Also, even after the subjects have been given prolonged training, it does not seem advisable to rely on extrapolation as a means of obtaining control performance under any but the most rigidly controlled and specified conditions, something which is rarely the case

in behavioral studies. In any event, a better way to test for contrast would seem to be to carry out an experiment in much the same way as did Crespi and Zeaman, except that only half the animals in each group should be given the upward or downward shifts in amount of food; the remaining half of each group would continue to receive the original amount of reinforcer and would constitute the control groups. Surprisingly, most of the subsequent studies concerned with demonstrating positive reinforcement contrast in the runway performance of rats have not fulfilled this simple design requirement and, hence, are subject to the same criticisms as the earlier studies. In one case (Di Lollo, 1964), subjects were given prolonged training before the upward shifts in amount of reinforcer, raising the possibility of a ceiling effect; in another (Ehrenfreund & Badia, 1962), no control group was used, and the shifts were introduced before the performance levels had reached the asymptote. However, in a recent study (Schrier, 1967) the design requirements just outlined were adhered to, and again no sign of a positive contrast effect was obtained.

It might be well at this point to describe another approach to the problem of contrast effects which also avoids the difficulties pointed out by Spence (1956). This approach was used in an experiment on rats by Collier and Marx (1959). Three groups of rats were trained in a bar-press apparatus with sucrose solutions used as reinforcers. The groups differed in terms of the concentration of sucrose delivered during magazine training. The concentrations used were 4, 11.3, and 32 percent. When bar-press training was begun following 8 days of this magazine training, the concentration used as the reinforcer was 11.3 percent for animals of all 3 groups. Thus, when going from magazine training to bar-press training the 4 percent group (to designate the groups in terms of the magazine-training concentration) received an upward shift and the 32 percent group a downward shift in concentration. During the 10 days of bar-press training, even though the reinforcer was the same for all animals, the bar-press

---

[10] See Schrier (1967) for details.

[11] For current treatments of these concepts in relation to problems of reinforcement see Capaldi (1967) and Amsel (1967).

rates of the three groups differed significantly with the differences in the direction of contrast effects. The 4 percent group showed a greater frequency of bar pressing than the control group, that is the 11.3 percent group, and the 32 percent group showed a lower frequency of bar pressing than the control group. Although the basic experimental design employed by Collier and Marx is sound, recently completed research by Dunham and Kilps (1969) indicates that, somewhat surprisingly, the results of this widely cited study probably had nothing to do with the shifts in the concentration of the reinforcer following magazine training. Dunham and Kilps present strong evidence, based on 3 separate experiments, that the differences in bar-press rates in the Collier and Marx study might well have been the result of persisting differences in the body weights of the subjects which were produced by the intake of different concentrations of sucrose during magazine training. In one of their experiments, Dunham and Kilps were able to produce "contrast effects" by altering body weight in the absence of shifts in sucrose concentration. When body weight was held constant, in another of their experiments, no contrast effects were observed despite shifts in the concentration of the reinforcer. Body weight has long been recognized as one of the basic variables to be controlled in learning and reinforcement studies, but there was little reason to suspect before this that this variable could operate in as subtle a manner as that demonstrated by Dunham and Kilps. The Collier and Marx design has also been used in experiments with runways (Goodrich & Zaretsky, 1962; Spear, 1965), with pre-feeding in the goal box serving in place of magazine training. Contrast effects were not obtained; rather in each case, the speed of running after all animals were switched to the intermediate concentration, was ordered in accordance with the pre-feeding concentration.

Thus, we would have to conclude that there has as yet been no convincing demonstration of the positive contrast effect using the single-shift procedure. On the other hand,

there have been many runway studies (see, for example, Ehrenfreund & Badia, 1962; Gonzales, Gleitman, & Bitterman, 1962; Di Lollo, 1964; Di Lollo & Beez, 1966; Roberts, 1966) that have been carried out since those by Crespi, Zeaman, and Spence. All of these studies taken together establish beyond a doubt the existence of the negative contrast effect. Indeed, we can go a step further and concern ourselves with the variables influencing negative contrast. The magnitude of the negative contrast effect is directly related to the extent of the downward shift in amount (Gonzales, Gleitman, & Bitterman, 1962; Di Lollo & Beez, 1966); its magnitude may be larger when animals are under high-drive level than when under low (Ehrenfreund & Badia, 1962); if we reduce the amount of the reinforcer by small steps, we seem to prevent its appearance altogether (Gonzales, Gleitman, & Bitterman, 1962); and we might not observe it in animals lower than the mammals (Lowes & Bitterman, 1967).

We mentioned earlier that Crespi (1942, 1944) regarded the postshift effects as emotion-induced and, hence, transitory. We might add at this point that one of the major alternative conceptions of the shift effects is that they are essentially perceptual in nature, involving the same mechanisms as do the context effects in psychophysics (Collier & Marx, 1959; Bevan, 1966; Helson, 1966). This latter approach is consistent with those which assume that the behavioral effects of a reinforcer are related to its stimulus properties (see pp. 627–631). The perceptual explanations, however, assume both positive and negative contrast effects, something which we have already indicated may not be justified.

Whether the contrast effects are viewed as emotional or perceptual in nature, they would be expected to decay as a function of practice following a simple shift in the amount of reinforcer. On the other hand, an associational interpretation would lead us to expect more gradual changes and more lasting effects (Capaldi & Lynch, 1967). In considering this question, we have to limit ourselves to the negative contrast effect for reasons already outlined. Crespi, himself, had no clear-cut evidence of a decay; he merely indicated (1944) that, if contrast effects were emotionally based, they should decay. (Unfortunately, some subsequent writers have failed to distinguish between what has been hypothesized and what actually has been found.) In any event, it has usually been assumed that, at least if they are emotion-induced, the contrast effects should not only decay following a single shift in the amount of the reinforcer, but should be "temporary" or "transient," that is to say, should decay quickly. One problem that arises immediately is that the conclusion we draw depends on our view as to how long a temporary effect should last. In most of the experiments that have been done, there has been no clear-cut sign of a decay within the experimental period. However, in many of these instances (Crespi, 1942; Spence, 1956; Di Lollo, 1964), it could be claimed that the postshift period was too short (8–15 trials) to warrant a conclusion that the effects are long-lasting or permanent.

One study that has often been cited as showing that the shift effects are long-lasting, and, hence, not emotional in origin, is that by Collier and Marx (1959), described a few paragraphs ago, in which bar-press rates of rats were measured following shifts in the concentration of sucrose. There was no sign of a decay in the contrast effects over the 10-day postshift period (during which the animals were given over two hundred reinforcements). However, as we have already mentioned, the outcome does not appear to be related to shifts in the quantity of the reinforcer.

There are also problems connected with studies which purport to have demonstrated a decay in the contrast effect. For example, the conclusion drawn in a study by Gonzalez, Gleitman, and Bitterman (1962) regarding a decay is based on rather limited evidence (the last data point of the experiment). On the basis of the data currently available, we would have to conclude that the assumption that the contrast effects decay rapidly has not yet been adequately tested.

It will be recalled that Crespi and Zeaman concluded that the change in performance level following a shift occurred very rapidly. Indeed, their reports led to a revision of one of the major theoretical systems of the day, that of Hull (1943). As we mention above, Hull had conceived of reinforcer amount as influencing strength of learning (habit strength) directly. Learning, in turn, is usually regarded as something that changes relatively slowly. Thus the change in reinforcer, particularly in the upward direction, should have resulted in a slower change in performance level than turned out to be the case. Have subsequent single-shift studies confirmed this aspect of the findings of Crespi and Zeaman? The situation is somewhat similar to that for the decay problem because the answer seems to depend on what is defined as a "rapid" change. Judging by the conclusions that have been drawn, different people have used different definitions. If we apply the term only to studies in which the changes in performance (relative to the control level) were nearly complete within the first 3 or 4 trials following a shift in amount of reinforcer, we find that at least 3 of the later studies fall in this category (Spence, 1956; Di Lollo, 1964; Schrier, 1967). However, there are a few experiments (Di Lollo & Beez, 1966) in which the rate of change can be reasonably described as being gradual. Such qualitative judgments are rather tenuous and merely emphasize the need for understanding the variables influencing the rate of change in performance and for quantitative analysis of the data. Whatever the case, debate on the role the amount of reinforcer plays in the learning process is still with us to some extent (Pubols, 1960), although the trend today seems to be to view amount as influencing motivation (see pp. 805–807) rather than "learning" per se.

Repeated Shifts in the Reinforcer

There are a variety of ways in which repeated shifts can be accomplished. For example, monkeys can be given (Schrier, 1961) test sessions in which they are trained to displace an object covering a foodwell that is baited with food (such as sugar or banana-flavored pellets or peanuts). The response measure is latency of displacement of the object. During each test session, one of a set of amounts of food is used for a block of several consecutive trials and then the amount is changed for the next block of trials. The order in which the amounts are used is varied from test session to test session. In another procedure, commonly used with rats and somewhat inappropriately called "differential conditioning," training is given each day in two straight alleys, one painted black and the other white. A larger amount of food is placed in the goal box of one alley than in the other. An important common feature of the monkey and rat procedures is that the amount of reinforcer, though varying, is predictable on all or most trials. In the procedure used with rats, different cues (black or white start box), associated with the different amounts are available before the instrumental response occurs. In the procedure used with monkeys, the amount to be used for a given block of trials is predictable once the first reinforcement occurs. Shifts in amount of reinforcer given a subject are referred to as "systematic" whenever they are carried out in such a way that the amount to be used is predictable. Studies have also been done using a "random shift" procedure in which the amount was varied randomly from trial to trial, with no differential cues to indicate which amount was the current one.

Systematic shifts Repeated systematic shifts have almost always been used in amount of reinforcer studies in which the subjects have been monkeys, primarily because the time, effort, and expense involved in handling these animals usually precludes testing them in large enough numbers to use the constant-reinforcer approach. One of the earliest studies of this type was carried out by Meyer (1951). His animals were given a series of object-discrimination-reversal problems in the Wisconsin General Test Apparatus (see Chapter 17). For each problem, a new

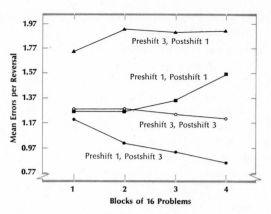

Figure 15.8. Mean number of reversal errors by 8 rhesus monkeys (*Macaca mulatta*) during successive blocks of discrimination-reversal problems. Each curve represents a different combination of prereversal (preshift) and postreversal (postshift) amounts of reinforcer. (After Meyer, 1951.)

pair of junk objects[12] was presented, and depending upon the problem, response to the correct object was reinforced with either one or three pieces of food (raisins or peanuts, depending on the preference of the individual animal). After a number of trials, the discrimination was reversed; the correct object was made the incorrect, and the incorrect one, the correct. On these reversal trials, the amount of reinforcer either remained the same as it was on the prereversal trials or was shifted to the larger or smaller reinforcer. After 3 additional discrimination reversals involving the same pair of objects, a new pair of junk objects was used and the procedure repeated, again with some reversals involving upward or downward shifts in the reinforcer relative to that on the prereversal trials, and some involving no shifts. The frequency of errors was very low throughout the experiment because the animals had had extensive training on object-discrimination-reversal in previous experiments. Despite this, reinforcer level clearly influenced the outcome.

[12]Common, small household and other objects such as a thread spool and a rubber heel. Such objects differ in several attributes (color, form, size, and other characteristics), making possible many different problems.

Performance on the postshift trials (Figure 15.8) was significantly better when the post-shift amount was the large than when it was the small regardless of the preshift amount. This means that the different amounts had significant effects on performance, but it does not tell us anything about reinforcement-context. For information about the latter, we must examine the effects of the postshift amounts in relation to the different preshift amounts. When we do this we find that on the average, fewer postshift errors were made with the large postshift reinforcer when the preshift reinforcer had been the small, rather than a large—a positive contrast effect; similarly, more errors were made with the small reinforcer when the preshift re-inforcer had been the large, rather than the small—a negative contrast effect. The statistical tests that were carried out did not provide a basis for judging the reliability of the contrast effects. Anticipating some recent trends (Collier & Marx, 1959; Helson, 1966), Meyer suggested the possibility of treating reinforcing effects in terms of adaptation level concepts.

Whenever the repeated-shift type of variable reinforcer procedure has been used in studies of effects of amount of reinforcer on discrimination learning, a positive relationship has invariably been reported (see, for example, Meyer, 1951; Schrier & Harlow, 1956; Lawson, 1957). On the other hand, when the constant-reinforcer procedure has been used, relatively few investigators have found such a relationship (Reynolds, 1950; Schrier, 1956), while many have found no relationship at all (Reynolds, 1949; Furchgott & Rubin, 1953; Maher & Wickens, 1954; McKelvey, 1956). Two studies of similar design, one with rats (Lawson, 1957) and one with monkeys (Schrier, 1958), have been carried out in which the constant- and variable-reinforcer procedures were directly compared. In the Lawson study, only a small and non-significant difference was found in the brightness-discrimination performance of a large-reinforcer and a small-reinforcer group. On

the other hand, in the case of a third group which repeatedly received both the large and small amounts, the brightness-discrimination performance was considerably better when the reinforcer was the larger amount of food. In the Schrier study, 2 amount-of-reinforcement functions were compared. One was based on the learning-set performance of 4 groups, each receiving a different amount of reinforcer (1, 2, 4, or 8 food pellets) for correct responses on a series of object-discrimination problems. The other amount-of-reinforcement function was based on the performance of a group of animals for which the amount of reinforcer was varied from problem to problem, so that they re-peatedly received all 4 of the amounts that were used for the 4 constant-reinforcer groups. The upward slope of the amount-of-reinforcement function was significantly

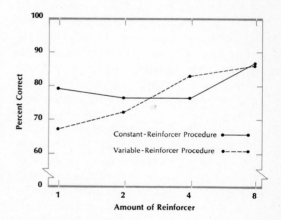

Figure 15.9. Relationship between discrimination performance of rhesus monkeys (*Macaca mulatta*) and the amount of reinforcer, using the constant-reinforcer and the variable-reinforcer procedures. The amounts are plotted on a logarithmic scale. Each point on the curve for the variable-reinforcer procedure represents the performance of the same group of 5 monkeys, whereas each point on the curve for the constant-reinforcer procedure represents a different group of monkeys. There were 4 animals in the group that received 4 food pellets for each correct response and 5 animals in each of the other 3 groups. (Nontransformed version of data from Schrier, 1958.)

greater for the variable-reinforcer group than for the constant-reinforcer groups (Figure 15.9). Thus, both the Lawson and the Schrier experiments clearly suggest that the repeated-shift type of variable-reinforcer procedure is more likely to produce differential amount effects on discrimination performance than is the constant-reinforcer procedure. This has also been shown for speed of rats in a runway (Bower, 1961) and, somewhat less directly, for response latency of monkeys (Schrier, 1961; 1962).

On the question of positive and negative contrast effects, generally speaking the results of both the studies by Lawson (1957) and by Schrier (1958) conformed to expectations based on contrast: In these studies, performance levels were lower for the small amounts when the variable-reinforcer procedure was used than they were for the same amounts when the constant-reinforcer procedure was used. In general, the same was true, but in the opposite direction, in the case of the large amounts. However, neither experiment was designed with the separate positive and negative contrast effects in mind, so tests of significance of these were not conducted. Thus, whereas these studies can be regarded as providing evidence for reinforcement-context effects in the sense that the two procedures produce different results, they must be regarded as only suggestive on the question of such effects as positive and negative contrast. There have, however, been some repeated-shift studies in which tests for contrast effects were carried out. In one, a differential conditioning study (Bower, 1961) in which speed of running of rats was measured, a negative contrast effect was found, but there was no sign of a positive contrast effect. In another study (Leary, 1958) a significant positive contrast effect was reported. That experiment involved serial discrimination learning by monkeys and the method of carrying out the shifts was somewhat similar to that of Meyer (1951) in the experiment described above. All in all, it may be concluded that results of repeated-shift

studies of the type discussed so far are in agreement with those of single-shift experiments in that all have shown trends in the direction of negative contrast. On the other hand, trends in the direction of positive contrast have been seen more often in repeated-shift than in single-shift studies.[13]

In a few instances, the effects of repeated shifts in the reinforcer have been in directions opposite to contrast. Marx and Pieper (1962, 1963) carried out two studies which were like the earlier one by Collier and Marx (1959), which was described on page 633, except that repeated shifts were involved. They regularly alternated sessions of magazine training during which one concentration of sucrose was presented with sessions of bar-press training during which another concentration was given as the reinforcer. In one case (Marx & Pieper, 1963), for example, during the first four days of bar pressing, a group of rats which received a 64 percent concentration periodically during magazine training and an 8 percent concentration (on an FI 1-minute schedule) during bar-press training showed a higher rate of bar pressing than a control group which received an 8 percent concentration during both magazine and bar-press training. It was not until the following 4 bar-press days that the expected result developed, that is performance differences in the direction of negative contrast. The conditions under which these unusual early shift effects occur are not clear as yet.[14] The alternation between

[13] For this reason, it is somewhat surprising that the two recent major reviews of the literature on effects of shifts in the amount of reinforcer (Black, 1968; Dunham, 1968) fail to mention any of these repeated-shift studies. Both reviewers conclude, as we have, that there is very strong evidence for a negative contrast effect. Both also conclude that there is no evidence for a positive contrast effect. Although it is true that, in a majority of the studies on the question, there has not even been a trend in the direction of positive contrast, such a trend has consistently been seen in studies having the following in common: (a) simultaneous two-choice discrimination problems were used; (b) only one choice was reinforced; (c) a repeated-shift procedure was employed.

[14] Because the conditions in the studies by Marx and Pieper were similar to those employed by Collier and Marx (1959), it is quite possible that differences in the animals' weights influenced Marx and Pieper's results also (see the discussion of the findings of Dunham and Kilps [1969] on page 634).

magazine training and bar-press training may not be critical because Anderson (1965) found similar effects in bar-press experiments on monkeys in which the concentration was alternated during successive periods of bar-press training. In none of these cases has the opposite effect persisted, but it should be kept in mind that reinforcement-context effects are not necessarily contrast effects.

It will be recalled that with the single-shift approach both gradual and rapid changes in behavior have been reported following a shift in amount of reinforcer. The appropriate analyses in the case of repeated shifts (that is, analyses of the changes in behavior following each shift in the series of shifts) have not been made, so there is no basis for comparison. However, it can be said that, typically, when repeated shifts are used (Meyer, 1951; Schrier & Harlow, 1956; Schrier, 1958), changes in performance levels under the different amounts of reinforcer are seen which are chiefly in the direction of greater differences in the effects of the different amounts and which seem to take place over the course of many trials. Furthermore, these changes in performance levels seem to reflect, in part at least, a learning process which has to do with the discrimination or the perception of the different reinforcers (Meyer, 1951; Schrier & Harlow, 1956; Hulse, 1960, 1962). This learning seems to be independent of the learning associated with the learning task itself, though it is not easy to separate the two because they are usually taking place simultaneously. Perhaps the typical discrimination learning situation can be conceived of as involving at least 3 partially independent processes: discrimination of the cues, discrimination of the reinforcer, and association of the reinforcer with the appropriate cues.

With the single-shift method, although decay in the contrast effect with practice has been reported, there have also been cases in which it has proved relatively persistent. In none of the repeated-shift studies in which the results have been in the direction of contrast (Meyer, 1951; Lawson, 1957; Leary, 1958;

Schrier, 1958; Bower, 1961) has there been any evidence of a diminishing of the effects of the shifts with practice. However, it cannot by any means be concluded that the effects are permanent, because there is no strong evidence to indicate that the performance levels in question were at the asymptote at the end of the experiments. This is an interesting question because any account of contrast effects which assumes that they are primarily the result of perceptual changes could easily explain the persistence of these effects over the course of a large number of shifts in the amount of reinforcer, but it is doubtful that an account which treats them as strictly emotional phenomena could. So long as the set of stimuli in a series remains constant, there is no reason to believe that, once the initial adjustments are completed, the perception of any of the stimuli would change.

Random shifts How would animals behave when different amounts of reinforcer

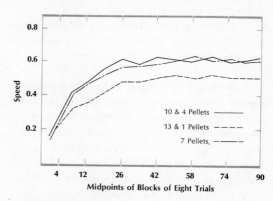

Figure 15.10. Speed of running of rats in a straight-alley apparatus with the average amount of reinforcer held constant over trials, but with different ranges of variation in amount as indicated in the legend. The response measure was the time taken by the animal to traverse a distance for 4 ft, starting at a point several inches beyond the start box and ending at a point a few inches in front of the food cup in the goal box. The ordinate represents the mean of the reciprocals of these running times. (After Beier, 1958, as reported by Logan, 1960.)

are introduced in random order and no cues are available to indicate which amount is present on any particular trial? Would, for example, the animal's performance be influenced more by one amount than another, or would its performance be a simple function of the average amount received? Employing a straight-alley apparatus, Bier (1958, as described by Logan, 1960, pp. 74–77) gave 3 groups of rats an average of 7 pellets per trial. One group was given 10 pellets on a random half of the trials and 4 pellets on the other half. The conditions for a second group were the same, except that the 2 amounts used were 13 pellets and 1 pellet. A third group received 7 pellets on all trials. The mean running speed of the 10- and 4-pellet group was slightly faster than the mean for the 7-pellet group. The running speed of the 13- and 1-pellet group was considerably slower than that of the other two groups (Figure 15.10). Additional data obtained using these procedures (Logan, 1960) suggest that the relationship of the performance of animals receiving random shifts in amount of reinforcer to that of animals receiving a constant amount depends both on the range of amounts and the average amount.

Two-choice situations, either choice reinforced An interesting variation on the repeated-shift procedure involves reinforcement of both alternatives in a two-choice situation. On each trial, the choice of one stimulus is reinforced with one amount of food, whereas the choice of the other stimulus is reinforced with a different amount. This procedure was used by Spear and Hill (1965) in an experiment with rats in a **T** maze. In one instance 3 groups of rats always received 1 pellet of food in 1 goal box of the **T** maze. The treatment of the groups differed in that one of the groups received 1 pellet, the second received 2 pellets, and the third 10 pellets in the other goal box. Forced-choice trials were mixed with free-choice trials to ensure the rats gained experience with both goal boxes. By the end of the experiment, all animals were consistently choosing the side containing the larger amount. This behavior developed more quickly in the group receiving 10 pellets in the large-reinforcer goal box, than in the one receiving 2 pellets. The larger the amount of food they received on the large-reinforcer side, the slower the rats ran to the box containing the small amount of food—a negative contrast effect.

Can positive contrast be demonstrated using the procedures of Spear and Hill? The answer seems to be "No" (Spear & Spitzner, 1966), as it is in the case of the other procedures previously described.

Meyer, Lo Popolo, and Singh (1966) trained monkeys concurrently on four 2-choice visual discrimination problems. Responses to either stimulus of each pair were reinforced using different quantities of food. The ratios of the amounts used for the four pairs were 8:4, 4:2, 2:1, and 8:1, respectively. During the training period, following each choice trial, the stimulus that was not chosen was presented alone and reinforced. The purpose of this procedure was the same as the forced trials in the Spear and Hill study. Following this training, tests were carried out in which the 8 stimuli involved were arranged in new pairs, there being 24 possible new pairs. However, the subjects continued to be trained with the original pairs throughout this period. The results of those tests with new pairs of stimuli in which both members of the pair had been reinforced with equal amounts of food during original training are of most interest here. What, for example, would an animal do when it was faced with two stimuli which had been associated earlier with equal quantities of the reinforcer (one piece of food, for example), but which had at the same time been paired with stimuli associated with different quantities of food (say 2 pieces in one case and 8 pieces in the other)? The stimuli involved will be designated as "1 (2)" and "1 (8)," with the first number in each case indicating the amount that had been associated with the stimulus during original training and the number in parentheses indicating the amount associated with the stimulus with which that stimulus had been paired in original training. A prediction based on contrast would lead us to expect a choice of the 1 (1) stimulus over the 1 (8) stimulus because the negative contrast would be greater in the case of the latter stimulus. In fact, 7 of the 8 animals chose the 1 (8) stimulus more frequently than the other. The eighth animal split its choices evenly. In all other cases, there was either no consistent difference in the frequency of choice—4 (2) as opposed to 4 (8) and 8 (1) as opposed to 8 (4)—or else the difference was in the direction of contrast—2 (1) chosen more frequently than 2 (4). (For a discussion of the possible reasons for these outcomes see Estes, 1966.) Once again, we are reminded that reinforcement-context effects other than contrast are possible.

Behavioral Contrast

Although the topic of behavioral contrast does not really belong in this section of the chapter, we mention it here because behavioral contrast bears at least a superficial resemblance to the kind of contrast phenomena we have been considering up to now and might conceivably involve a similar mechanism.[15] It was first described by Reynolds (1961), who first trained pigeons to peck a key with reinforcement occuring on a VI schedule. After the animals' response rates appeared to stabilize, Reynolds began alternating, within sessions, periods in which key pecking was reinforced on the same VI schedule with periods in which key pecking was not reinforced (extinction). The key color during extinction periods was green or blue and during VI periods it was red or orange. This kind of procedure is called a "multiple schedule of reinforcement," which is one type of operant discrimination training. This term is commonly used to describe repeated shifting among two or more schedules when the schedule changes are accompanied by corresponding changes in external stimuli. Reyn-

[15] For a different perspective on behavioral contrast see Chapter 17.

olds found that response rate was higher on the VI schedule when it was a component of the multiple schedule than when it was the only schedule. This would be positive behavioral contrast (see Figure 17.13, p. 777). Reynolds (1961) introduced control conditions which suggested that the increased rate on the VI component of the multiple schedule was the result of the lowered frequency of reinforcement in the other component of the multiple schedule, rather than the lowered rate of responding. For example, no behavioral contrast was found when the multiple schedule consisted of the VI component and a time-out component, during which neither the response key nor the test chamber was illuminated. Under such conditions, pigeons tend to have a very low response rate or do not respond at all. Similarly, no behavioral contrast was seen when the multiple schedule consisted of the VI component and one involving reinforcement for not responding for either 50 or, in some cases, 75 seconds. One of the components does not have to be extinction in order to produce behavioral contrast, but may simply be a schedule, such as another VI schedule (Findley, 1958), which programs a lower frequency of reinforcement. Negative behavioral contrast can be produced by increasing the frequency of reinforcement in one component of a multiple schedule (Reynolds & Limpo, 1968).

Some interesting parallels between the work on behavioral contrast and that on contrast produced by shifting the amount of reinforcer have developed. Terrace (1966b) has recently reported that the magnitude of behavioral contrast tended to diminish over the course of 60 daily test sessions during which a multiple VI-extinction schedule was in effect. Terrace concluded that behavioral contrast is the result of "frustration, or similar emotional responses." On the other hand, Bloomfield (1967), using procedures that seem to be somewhat more similar to Reynolds' than to Terrace's, found no sign of a decay in behavioral contrast over the course of the same number of daily test sessions. In

Bloomfield's experiment, blocks of daily test sessions (with most blocks consisting of 20 test sessions) during which a VI schedule was used were alternated with blocks of test sessions during which a multiple VI-extinction schedule was used. In addition to the behavioral contrast, Bloomfield reported some upward shifts in the rate of responding during successive blocks of sessions involving only the VI schedule. Because of this, he emphasized the need for final, as well as initial, measures of baseline or control rates of responding. Considering some of the difficulties encountered in interpreting the results of experiments involving shifts in amount of reinforcer, we might also suggest the use of unshifted control groups in experiments on behavioral contrast.

REINFORCING BRAIN STIMULATION

To understand the excitement that was created by the first announcements of positive reinforcing effects from direct electrical stimulation of regions of the mammalian brain, it is necessary to recall the context in which this news was received. Of all the areas of experimental psychology, learning seemed to be the least advanced in terms of the discovery of anatomical and physiological correlates of psychological processes. Almost all psychologists agreed that the effects of experience must somehow be coded, stored, and retrieved from the nervous system; and almost all would also have agreed that some unique physiological event (or events) must occur on those occasions when we say "reinforcement occurred." Yet, after more than fifty years of laboratory research, not a single shred of direct evidence to support either of these beliefs had been found.

It was under these circumstances that the announcement by Olds and Milner (1954) was made. They were investigating the behavioral effects of stimulating various regions of the rat midbrain, a procedure which might be expected to increase the level of activation of the animal (see Chapter 18). They noticed

that when they stimulated one animal, he repeated whatever response he had made just prior to stimulation, and that by the judicious use of the electrical stimulation, they could cause the animal to repeat responses or they could shape him toward entirely new responses (Olds, 1955).[16] In other words, they had found a positive reinforcing stimulus that by-passed the peripheral mechanisms normally activated by reinforcers. Later examination of the animal's brain showed that the stimulating electrodes had been placed in the general region of the septal area, a portion of the forebrain and quite distant from the midbrain. A fortunate error (in the placement of the electrode), plus investigator astuteness (to appreciate the importance of the observations) are the two foremost ingredients of serendipity in science. The third ingredient is, of course, communication of the results. Happily, all three were present on this occasion.

Here then was a technique that promised to uncover the locus of reinforcement. And if the site of the reinforcing stimulation could be specified, what was to prevent the associated neural pathways from being explored, with the eventual discovery of "where" the confluence of sensory and motor activities joined with the reinforcing stimulation to produce the changes that must underlie learning? Such thoughts certainly occurred to many who heard or read about the Olds and Milner experiments during 1953 and 1954: at last the psychology of learning had some solid clues as to where to start the search for the neurological substrates of reinforcement and possibly even of motivation and of "pleasure" (see Olds, 1956).

The next few years saw a rash of investigations of this phenomenon. They fell, for the most part, into two groups: those that sought to specify more precisely the loci in the brain

---

[16] The abbreviations most frequently used when referring to the stimulation are ICS ("intracranial stimulation"), and ESB ("electrical stimulation of the brain"). Both are appropriately neutral regarding anatomical and physiological factors.

that gave reinforcing effects, and those which asked whether the reinforcing effects thus produced were indeed the same as the effects with which psychologists long had been familiar.

Some Problems of Technique

A few facts about techniques are needed to understand the results that have been obtained in the studies. Chronic electrodes for recording or stimulating central nervous system tissues were developed in the 1930s (Hess, 1932) and had been used successfully to stimulate portions of the central nervous system to produce pain-like and fear-like responses, and escape and avoidance learning (Delgado, Roberts, & Miller, 1954).

For stimulation purposes, the electrodes

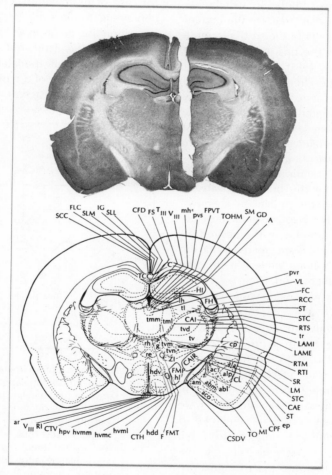

Figure 15.11. A frontal section of rat brain showing an electrode track and a corresponding plate, Figure 34a in the rat brain atlas of König and Klippel (1963). The electrode was lowered through the cortical and subcortical areas of the right hemisphere until the tips of the electrode were thought to be in the region of the lateral hypothalamic nucleus (*hl* in the atlas). In this case, the placement was quite satisfactory. The brain sections usually are cut at an angle to the electrode track, making it easier to keep the sections in one piece. This section was deliberately sectioned in the same plane as the electrode track so that the full course of the track could be shown. The brain was frozen, sectioned at 40μ, and stained with cresyl violet. The triangular gash in the left hemisphere is a mark made in the brain before sectioning as an aid to later orientation.

usually are quite gross: One or more pieces of wire may be used in the assembly, and the diameter of each piece of wire may be .010 in. or more. Thus, in comparison with the size of brain structures, the electrodes may be very large indeed. The electrodes usually are insulated except at the tips, and if a bipolar (two-wire) electrode is employed, the current flows from one tip to another. If these tips are close together, the stimulation will be restricted to a fairly small area, for the current apparently spreads very little to tissue more than 1–2 mm from the tips of the electrode (Valenstein & Beer, 1961; Valenstein, 1966). The early electrodes frequently were made of copper or silver wires, but both of these proved to have deleterious effects on tissue (Rowland, MacIntyre, & Bidder, 1960). At the present time, stainless steel or platinum are the most frequently used materials.

Successful implantation of an electrode requires an atlas of the brain, a means of fixing the head of the animal in a known position, and a device for moving the electrode the proper distance in the desired direction. The brain maps are created by taking serial sections of a brain while it is in some clearly specified orientation. Then, by starting from the same bench marks used in constructing the brain atlas, one can determine the direction in which to move, and how far to move, to bring the tip of an electrode to the desired location. With the animal under general anesthesia, the electrode is lowered through a small hole that has been made in the skull. When the desired coordinates have been reached, the electrode is cemented to the skull leaving only the connector exposed. One or more such electrode sets may be implanted. Usually, the first stimulations are postponed for about a week, on the theory that local trauma in the region of the electrodes will then have subsided. (Techniques for implanting chronic electrodes are described in several chapters in Sheer, 1961.)

Of course, once the experiment is completed, the exact placement of the electrodes must be ascertained. After the animal has

been anesthetized, the tissue is perfused with saline (to flush out blood) and formalin (to kill and preserve the brain tissue). Later, the brain may be prepared for slicing by freezing it or by embedding it in a supporting medium (such as paraffin or celloidin), and then cut into thin sections. Usually the sections are stained to reveal special characteristics, such as nuclei or fiber tracts, and then mounted for ease of examination. Once the sections containing the electrode track are located, the corresponding plates in a brain atlas are consulted, and the estimated position of the stimulating tips of the electrode is determined. An example of a typical section from an animal, and the page of a brain atlas that

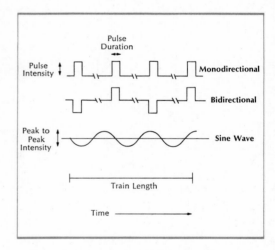

Figure 15.12. The major parameters manipulated during electrical stimulation of the brain. When discrete rectangular pulses are utilized, typical pulse durations are 0.1 or 0.2 msec, and the most common pulse frequency is 100 pulses/sec. Thus, only 1–2 percent of the total train of stimulation is actually made up of stimulating pulses. When sine wave stimulation is employed, practically all of the train duration provides active stimulation. Hence, the currents needed for sine wave stimulation are much lower than for discrete pulse stimulation. When one calculates the total charge per reinforcement, however, sine wave stimuli must have larger charges to produce equivalent behavioral effects of discrete pulse stimulation.

includes the area invaded by the electrode track, are shown in Figure 15.11. Although the amount of tissue damage from such electrodes is rather extensive, it should be borne in mind that behavioral or physiological deficits very rarely result from unilateral tissue

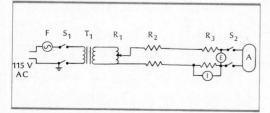

Figure 15.13. A simple circuit for electrical stimulation of brain tissue. F = fuse (1 amp); S_1 = main power switch; S_2 = stimulation switch; T_1 = isolation transformer; R_1 = 10-turn potentiometer, 100K ohms, 2 watt; R_2 = fixed resistors, 1 megohm each; R_3 = fixed resistors, 1K ohm each; E = voltage monitor; I = current monitor; A = animal. S_2 usually is a double pole-double throw relay, with associated timing circuitry to control the duration of the stimulation train. R_3 may be any convenient value; 1 K ohm usually is satisfactory when current is monitored with an oscilloscope. R_2 is large relative to the impedance of the preparation, thus providing moderately good current regulation. With typical bipolar stainless steel electrodes, the preparation will vary between 10,000 and 20,000 ohms in most cases when 60 Hz stimulation is used. Current and voltage monitors should have high internal impedance values, as do oscilloscopes. The leads between S_2 and the animal should be kept as short as possible. Both sides of the circuit should be interrupted by S_2 to avoid accidental production of a difference in potential between the electrode and metal parts of the animal's chamber. When this occurs, an animal will lick or rub his nose on the metal, thus stimulating himself *ad libitum*. An additional degree of protection is offered by eliminating from the chamber all metal parts or all electrical sources other than low voltage direct currents. Retractable bars and drinkometer circuits are especially likely to provide sources of alternating current which the animal will discover, and from which he will obtain stimulation.

loss in the regions through which such electrodes are passed.

It is extremely important that the parameters of the electrical stimulation be described clearly in each experimental report. The major parameters are: frequency, duration of individual pulses or cycles, intensity, and train length. In addition, stimulation may be monodirectional or bidirectional. These dimensions are illustrated in Figure 15.12. In almost all recent work, bidirectional stimulation is employed, for monodirectional stimulation is more destructive of tissue. No special generators need be employed, unless the manipulation of pulse frequency or duration is a major concern. For many behavioral studies, ordinary 60 Hz current from the house line (adequately isolated, of course) is quite satisfactory. A typical circuit for such stimulation is given in Figure 15.13. For experiments in which precise maintenance of current levels

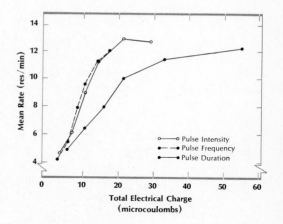

Figure 15.14. Rate of responding as a function of the total electrical charge per stimulation. Average results for 10 rats. Six values for pulse intensity (0.5–4.0 mA) pulse frequency (23–138 pulses/sec), and pulse duration (0.28–2.65 msec) were used. Each animal was exposed to every value on 2 separate occasions. During testing, responses were reinforced with the electrical stimulation on the average of every 16 sec (a variable interval 16-sec reinforcement schedule). Each reinforcement consisted of a 0.5 sec train of bidirectional rectangular stimulus pulses. (After Keesey, 1962.)

is necessary, more elaborate current regulating circuits are needed.[17]

Intensity of stimulation   Rate of self-stimulation increases as the intensity, pulse frequency, and pulse duration are increased (see, for example, Keesey, 1962), but at the higher intensity values, response rates may decline somewhat; the implications of these declines will be discussed later. For the moment, let us consider only the rising portion of the rate-intensity function. Each of the parameters of stimulation represents an independent means of manipulating the total electrical charge per reinforcement: Is it possible that the reinforcing effects of brain stimulation can be simply summarized in terms of the total charge (that is, in coulombs) per reinforcement? If this were true, we would expect the same response curves to be produced regardless of which parameter (that is, intensity, frequency, or duration) is manipulated. Within limits, this does appear to be true. Figure 15.14 summarizes the results of a series of rate-intensity determinations on the same rats, with frequency, intensity, and pulse duration as the parameters. The frequency and intensity curves are quite similar over the range of the values of the charge which they have in common. Note, however, that the pulse duration curve is displaced, so that a greater total charge per reinforcement is required to produce a given rate of self-stimulation, indicating that duration is a less efficient way of delivering a given charge to the tissue. Such relative loss of efficiency is not unexpected, for as pulse durations are increased, direct current conditions are approximated, and these are ineffective as reinforcers.[18]

[17]The intensities of stimulation needed to produce reinforcing effects are far greater than any naturally occurring electrophysiological changes in brain areas, and therefore could be called "nonphysiological" stimulations (see p. 254).

[18]A portion of the loss is probably due to a polarization at the electrodes. Stimulation with direct current also creates lesions, which further reduces the efficiency of the stimulation.

Would extremely brief pulses prove to be especially effective in self-stimulation? Probably not, since it seems likely that the compensatory increases in frequency or intensity that would be needed to maintain responding would soon reach their limits, with high intensities producing trauma and high frequencies (1000 Hz and above) losing reinforcing characteristics (Ward, 1959).

Do animals show any indication of sensitivity to a charge-per-reinforcement dimension? The answer seems to be "yes." For example, if a rat is allowed to control the length of a train of stimulating pulses, he will systematically adjust the train length to counter manipulations of pulse intensity and frequency by the experimenter (Keesey, 1964). We should not conclude from this that all dimensions of the stimulus can be summarized in terms of total charge, for as we have seen, the reinforcing effects of a given charge are in part determined by pulse duration (Keesey, 1962), and possibly also by frequency and wave shape (see Su et al., 1966).

Locus of Stimulation

The regions where positively reinforcing self-stimulation effects can be obtained are scattered quite widely throughout the deeper, subcortical regions of the brain. For the most part, the locations are in the medial forebrain bundle and closely related structures. Positively reinforcing areas are frequently found in phylogenetically old regions of the central nervous system; few positive loci have been found within the cortex or neocortex. No single anatomical system is known which could tie together all these areas, but some common elements among the areas have been discovered. For example, if anterior and posterior electrodes are placed in the medial forebrain bundle of a rat and then bilateral lesions are made at the anterior sites, self-stimulation through the posterior electrodes is diminished, although not eliminated. However, if the lesions are made at the posterior sites, self-stimulation through the anterior electrodes is abolished (Olds & Olds, 1965).

These interactions are thought by some to indicate the existence of a final common pathway for positive reinforcing effects, with the posterior portions of the medial forebrain bundle and the lateral hypothalamic area as the route through which the activity must flow. A somewhat similar conclusion, based on other forms of indirect evidence, was reached by Morgane (1964) and by Stein (1964).

However, there is considerable evidence against this theory of a single positive reinforcement system. For example, Valenstein (1966) reports the results of several experiments in which rats with positive septal placements were then given bilateral lesions in various areas of the brain, including, in some cases, lesions in the medial forebrain bundle and lateral hypothalamus. Destruction of the lateral hypothalamic areas seriously impaired the regulation of body temperature, caused the animals to stop eating and drinking, and produced other signs of the "lateral hypothalamic syndrome" (Teitelbaum & Epstein, 1962). Only by special nursing, sometimes for several weeks, was it possible to bring some of those animals back to health. However, once recovered from the operations, these rats self-stimulated at rates equal to, or higher than, the response levels they had reached during pre-operative tests. On the basis of these, and other studies, Valenstein concludes: " . . . it is unlikely that there is any essential pathway or critical locus for the self-stimulation phenomenon in the limbic system or medial forebrain bundle-lateral hypothalamic area" (p. 180). The failure to eliminate reinforcing effects by surgical destruction of the possible pathways between sites of stimulation and other brain areas suspected of playing a role in self-stimulation "may suggest that some humoral transmission is at work" (p. 182).

Of course, it would be incorrect to assume that such lesion methods leave the electrode tips suspended in limbo; it is impossible in any one animal to isolate the electrode completely from all surrounding tissue, but when the results of many studies with a great many animals are considered, we are left with the impression that there probably is no single positive reinforcement "system," in the sense that there is a single visual or auditory system. Instead, it seems that this work shows another example of the plasticity of the central nervous system, where alternative routes and integrating systems are available for many basic functions.

Evaluations of the behavioral effects of electrical stimulation usually are based on the rate at which the animal self-stimulates when delivery of the stimulation is contingent upon the emission of some simple response, such as pressing a bar. When exploring regions of the brain, some characteristic differences in rates of self-stimulation have been found. For example, in the septal area, rats ordinarily will self-stimulate at fairly high rates, for relatively long periods. In lateral or posterior hypothalamic regions, even higher response rates and greater persistence are typically found. In other areas, higher or lower rates may be found, and more or less steady patterns of responding may emerge. At the present time, only such relatively gross differences in the positive reinforcing effects attributable to locus of stimulation can be mentioned; more precise specification will probably require the use of less massive electrodes, and the development of behavioral techniques capable of detecting finer variations in reinforcing effects. For a summary of some typical results from mapping experiments, see Olds and Olds (1963).

On the whole, the use of self-stimulation rates to examine loci has shown that quite a few portions of the brain are likely to produce positive reinforcing effects; that most are neutral; that some are obviously noxious, and can be used much like other aversive stimuli; and that some are mixed, in that the animal will make one response to turn the stimulus on and another to turn it off (for example, Bower & Miller, 1958). Within the regions that seem to be purely positive, the behavioral effect does not appear until some level of stimulation has been exceeded (in other words, there is an absolute-threshold effect). Then, as further increases in the amount of stimulation are made, the self-stimulation rate may increase, sometimes to be followed by a decline in rate even before there are any behavioral indications that the intensities are producing disruptive motor reactions. Still more intense stimulation may produce obvious signs of distress (such as vocalizing or frantic leaping), disruptive motor reactions, convulsive seizures, or combinations of all three. In most studies, intensities which produce any of these extreme effects are not used, even though the animals may continue to self-stimulate at such intensities if given the opportunity to do so. These upper limits to the usable intensities vary from locus to locus within the same animal, and between animals when all are given what appear to be the same electrode placements.

In light of these reactions to the higher ICS intensities, rate of self-stimulation sometimes may seem to be a misleading index of the reinforcement value of a given locus or set of stimulation parameters. For example, if each stimulation elicits a motor reaction which throws the animal to one side, we might hesitate to conclude that his low rate of self-stimulation reflects the actual reinforcing value of the stimulation. Usually motor involvement is not so gross, but the probability of some degree of interference becomes of considerable concern whenever the higher intensities of stimulation are applied.

Inspection of the temporal distribution of responding in self-stimulation situations reveals an orderly pattern of changes which frequently cannot be detected in the gross response rate. If the interresponse time (IRT) between each pair of responses is recorded, and the probability of each IRT is plotted as a function of the intensity of the stimulation, a systematic decline in both the shorter *and* the longer IRTs is revealed as intensity is increased. Since the suppression of short IRTs outweighs the suppression of long IRTs, the

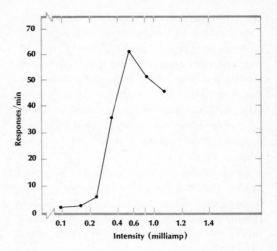

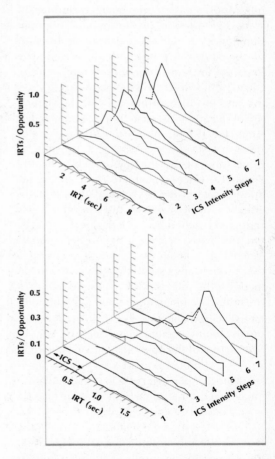

Figure 15.15. Effects of increasing intensity of brain stimulation on rate of self-stimulation. Seven current levels were selected that

overall effect is a decline in response rate. An example of such changes in IRTs as a function of stimulation intensity is given in Figure 15.15. It is important to note that such changes in IRT patterns occur in the absence of grossly discernable motor reactions; the suppression of both the shorter and longer IRTs is not merely a reflection of overtly incompatible behavior elicited by intense stimulation.

Two strategies have been employed to minimize the potential distortion of the rate measure as an index of the value of the stimulation as a reinforcer. The first approach retains response rate as the index, but instead of reinforcing every response, reinforcement schedules are utilized which space the reinforcements so widely that the relative distortion that might possibly result from motor disruptions would have little influence on the average value of the response rates. Such reduction in the density of reinforcements through the use of variable interval reinforcement schedules (Beer, Hodos, & Matthews,

---

covered the effective range of stimulation for the animal. Every response was reinforced with a 0.5-sec train of stimulation; the frequency was 100 bidirectional pulses per second, each pulse lasting 0.2 msec. Electrode placement was in the lateral hypothalamus. *Top curve* shows the response rate as a function of stimulus intensity, showing a "typical" hypothalamic rate-intensity function, with marked positive acceleration once the "reinforcement threshold" is exceeded, and a slight decline at the very highest intensities. *Middle curve:* same results, plotted as IRTs per opportunity for each of the stimulation intensities. Note that the probability of a long IRT (that is, a slow response) is decreased as stimulation intensity is increased. *Lower curve* shows the same results, with the first 2 seconds of the IRTs expanded to show the effects of increasing stimulation intensity on the short IRTs (that is, rapid responses). Note that increasing stimulation intensity first increases, and then "suppresses" the shortest IRTs, especially those emitted while the stimulation from the previous response is still being delivered. (After Terman, Terman, & Kling, 1970.)

1964), or through reinforcement of interresponse times greater than some selected interval (J. Terman, 1968) have been successful in eliminating some of the distortions found in response rates when continuous reinforcement is employed.

A more direct approach is the elimination of rate itself as the primary index of reinforcement value. For example, Hodos (1965) and Keesey and Goldstein (1968) have evaluated ICS reinforcers through use of the progressive ratio method (Hodos, 1961; Hodos & Kalman, 1963). In using this procedure, the experimenter selects the increment to be added to each successive ratio requirement, and reinforces the last response in each of these blocks of work. For example, if the increment is 2, the 2d, 6th, 12th, 20th, 30th . . . responses would be reinforced. In this manner, the ratio of total responses to reinforced responses is progressively increased throughout the experimental session, until a point is reached where the subject no longer will emit responses. Of course, some practical criterion must be adopted to define the end of the session; 5 minutes without responding, or failure to complete a ratio in 15 minutes, is a common criterion for lever-pressing experiments using rats. The value of the largest ratio completed, or the average number of responses per reinforcement, are typical indices of the effectiveness of the conditions of reinforcement.

Still another approach (Valenstein & Meyers, 1964) utilizes a two-compartment chamber, with given stimulation parameters set to be delivered whenever—and for as long as—the animal is in the designated chamber. If the stimulation becomes aversive, he can escape; and if it proves to be of but modest reinforcement value, he may follow it with relatively little vigor as the programming device switches the "hot" side of the chamber from time to time. Typically, the stimulation is available in successive 1-min blocks appearing randomly on one or the other side. Thus, should an animal sit completely still, he would receive 50 percent of the possible

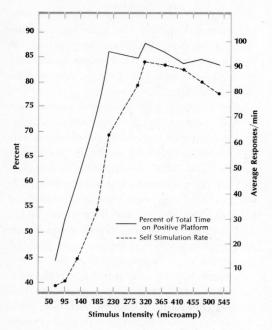

Figure 15.16. Two measures of the influence of intensity on the reinforcing effects of electrical brain stimulation. A rat with a hypothalamic electrode was allowed to stimulate himself (every response was reinforced), and also was allowed to move from side to side in a 2-chamber box, 1 side of which presented repeated bursts of stimulation. The "indifference" levels of stimulation and the points of "peak preference" appear to be highly similar as measured by these two methods. (After Valenstein & Meyers, 1964.)

stimulation, while if he were to respond quickly to the available cues, he could "follow" the stimulation as it is shifted from side to side and obtain almost 100 percent of the programmed stimulation. Comparisons of the shape of the function describing the percentage of stimulation received at various intensities with the shape of the typical rate-intensity function for the same animal (see Figure 15.16) show remarkable similarity.

Because motor skills are of minor importance in the shuttle box, it does not seem reasonable to ascribe the decline in the preference curve at higher stimulation values to "motor side-effects." Instead, it seems that the punishing consequences of the stimulation

might account for a large proportion of this decline. Indeed, by the judicious manipulation of stimulation parameters, it might be possible to determine the relative contribution of various aspects of the stimulation to the positive reinforcing effects, the punishing effects, and the disruptive motor effects.

In such shuttlebox experiments, the stimulation ordinarily is delivered as short trains (such as 0.5 sec) of pulses spaced by brief (such as 1.0 sec) intervals. Thus, the over-all density of stimulation is not unlike that resulting from self-stimulation procedures in which every response is reinforced, and as in the self-stimulation situation, declines in the response curves at higher stimulation intensities are common. Lowering the stimulation density by increasing the interstimulation interval reduces or eliminates the higher-intensity decline. Similarly, enforcing lower stimulation densities in other situations also eliminates this decline. For example, the animal may be required to carry out a series of simple choice responses (Hodos & Valenstein, 1962) or emit a response chain involving 2 levers (Pliskoff & Hawkins, 1967). Or the experimenter may utilize a long variable interval schedule of reinforcement (Beer, Hodos, & Matthews, 1964) or reinforce only those responses separated by some selected minimum interresponse time (J. Terman, 1968). Each of these procedures has the same effect on the average response rate: the immediate post-reinforcement suppression of responding occurs infrequently because reinforcement occurs infrequently, and hence the decline in response indices is largely (or completely) eliminated.

When viewed as a whole, the results of these different procedures suggest that the reinforcing effects of electrical brain stimulation are increased as the stimulating current is increased, that the duration of the post-stimulation response suppression also increases as current is increased, and that if the conditions of the experiment allow the stimulations to be massed, an overall response decline may occur at the upper stimulation values. This decline may occur in the absence of any noticeable conflicting or disruptive responses, and in such cases it seems reasonable to assume that there are aversive sensory consequences of massed stimulations. The similarity of these effects and those found when sucrose or saccharin solutions are presented in high concentration, large volume, and with short inter-reinforcement intervals (see p. 626) may serve to remind us that "aversive" need not always imply that the stimulation is painful.

Comparisons with Other Reinforcers

The very first studies indicated that the reinforcing effects of electrical stimulation could, in some cases, be even more potent than commonly used reinforcers. For example, in an "obstruction box" (Jenkins, Warner, & Warden, 1926), where an electrified floor separates the starting area from the point where the reinforcer is delivered, the intensity of foot shock needed to deter an animal from crossing the grid was higher for brain stimulation than for food (Olds & Sinclair, 1957). In another situation, where animals could press one bar to produce food pellets and another to produce electrical stimulation, some animals so neglected the food bar that eventually they died of starvation (Routtenberg & Lindy, 1965). Similarly, some adrenalectomized animals died when placed in a situation where pressing one bar produced small drinks of life-saving sodium chloride solution and the other bar controlled short bursts of brain stimulation (Eckert & Lewis, 1967). Additional examples of such self-deprivations arising from brain stimulation could be mentioned; there is no doubt that the stimulation is a powerful reinforcer. But why should animals fatally deprive themselves when they could easily survive by devoting just a small portion of their time to working for food or sodium chloride? A clue may be seen in the electrode placements: The electrode tips are aimed at the posterior hypothalamus, just lateral to the midline, from which are obtained very high rates of self-

stimulation that are then further augmented by food deprivation (Olds, 1958a), by adrenalectomy (Eckert & Lewis, 1967), and possibly by other deprivation procedures. In the self-deprivation tests, the animals already have had some exposure to the brain stimulation; there is no satiation phenomenon to "turn off" this self-stimulation; and the increasing food or salt deprivation only causes still greater proportions of the total experimental time to be devoted to self-stimulation. Eckert and Lewis observed that all of their self-depriving animals did show increasing numbers of salt-producing responses during the test period, but some "did not learn fast enough" to survive. The wisdom of the body is considerable, but not infallible.

Extreme self-deprivation frequently is interpreted as an indication of some intimate relation between the site stimulated by the electrodes and the physiological system thrown out of balance. If the rat does not regulate his food intake, and devotes almost all his time to hypothalamic self-stimulation, does this not suggest that the electrical stimulation may (1) serve as a substitute for the food, and/or (2) distort the signals that communicate the need for food to the hypothalamic regulatory "centers"? Such reasoning is made plausible if we consider the relations between food-seeking behaviors and two hypothalamic areas. The ventromedial hypothalamus seems to mediate stop-eating behaviors, for its bilateral ablation produces overeating (see review by Teitelbaum, 1961) and its direct stimulation (Epstein, 1960) produces cessation of eating. In the lateral hypothalamus, a complementary region mediating "hunger" has been hypothesized, inasmuch as chemical (Epstein, 1960) or electrical (see, for example, Margules & Olds, 1962) stimulation of that area produces eating and food-seeking behavior, and its bilateral ablation or its anesthetization causes a reduction in drinking and eating, plus some finickiness in accepting food (see review by Teitelbaum & Epstein, 1962; and Powley & Keesey, 1970).

The type of difficulty faced by such "physiological" interpretations of self-starvation may be mentioned briefly, for this also is pertinent to the more general question of why some electrical brain stimulation is positively reinforcing. Stated in the most simple terms, we might assume that the rat fails to eat when given the opportunity to work for both brain stimulation and for food because the brain stimulation somehow reduces his hunger. This effect might be the result of the brain stimulation providing input which is similar to that ordinarily present in the central nervous system when the animal is satiated, or it might reflect the blocking of the normal signals of deprivation by the brain stimulation. However, direct stimulation of lateral hypothalamic areas produces "stimulus-bound eating" and food-seeking behavior which implies increased (rather than decreased) hunger. Common sense would seem to suggest that stimulation which increases hunger should have punishing, and not positively reinforcing consequences, but the lateral hypothalamus is one of the most effective loci for self-stimulation electrode placements. Of course, it is possible that the brief trains of stimulation used in self-stimulation procedures might decrease hunger, while the much longer trains of stimulation needed for stimulus-bound eating somehow increase hunger. This possibility seems not to have been explored in a systematic manner, although a definite differentiation of self-stimulation with and without stimulus-bound drinking has been reported by Mogenson and Stevenson (1966).

However, there also may be a more behavioral (and "less physiological") factor at work in at least some of the self-deprivation studies. Consider the conditions in which the animals are placed: Two bars protrude from the wall at one end of the chamber, and a food cup is located on the wall at the other end of the box. Responses on one of the bars causes the delivery of brain stimulation, while responses on the other produces food. Why should some animals find it possible to break away from the bar that produces brain stimu-

lation, to make some responses on the bar that produces food, and to leave the bars to gather their food pellets, while others ignore the food bar even though they are severely deprived? One possibility is suggested by the observation of Routtenberg and Lindy (1965), who noted that all their rats with electrodes in the septal area maintained adequate body weights by developing behavior patterns that allowed them to obtain both food and stimulation, while those with electrodes placed in hypothalamic regions were much less successful in breaking away from the ICS bar. At the very least, the behavior of the animals with electrodes in septal areas required a cessation of responses on one bar, and a shift to either the other bar or to the food cup. We know now that the purely behavioral consequences of hypothalamic stimulation make it unlikely that this interruption of self-stimulation will occur, whereas those of septal stimulation make such interruptions highly probable. When viewed closely, the typical immediate consequence of septal stimulation is seen to be a release of the bar and a pause, whereas the typical immediate consequence of hypothalamic stimulation is seen to be a repetition of the response with a very short latency. Indeed, animals with electrodes placed in hypothalamic regions frequently initiate one response while the stimulation from the preceding response is still being received, and only at high stimulation values does a post-stimulation pause appear (see Figure 15.15). This being the case, it is not surprising that some of the animals neglect the food bar. The hypothalamic ICS in these studies of self-starvation thus may simply be functioning as an extremely effective reinforcer, maintaining high rates of response and precluding other forms of activity, and it may actually have relatively little direct physiological effect on feeding "centers."

Further evidence of behavioral causes of self-starvation are found in experiments in which normal feeding is interfered with by prior activities. For example, rats placed in activity wheels sometimes also show self-starvation behaviors, although the typical procedure in such studies provides each animal with a fixed period (such as 30 minutes a day) during which food is available and running in the wheel is prevented. Control animals given equal exposure to food, but no opportunity to run in the activity wheels, show normal maintenance of body weight. One of the possible explanations for the failure of experimental animals to eat as much food as the controls may also be applicable to the brain stimulation experiments: ". . . it may be possible that the reduction in food intake is brought about, in part, by a general heightened excitability, and that when the rat finally does have the opportunity to feed it is unable to eat efficiently because it is too excited" (Routtenberg & Kuznesof, 1967, p. 420). Rarely does one see a more excited laboratory rat than an animal which has had an electrode placed in the lateral hypothalamic areas, and which is stimulating itself under conditions of continuous reinforcement (that is, every response is reinforced with a brief train of stimulus pulses), and with the stimulus parameters adjusted to produce maximal rates. Routtenberg and Kuznesof

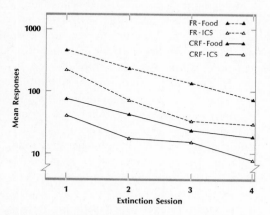

Figure 15.17. Mean number of responses emitted during 4 daily extinction tests. After 1000 reinforced bar presses, each rat was given four 15-minute extinction sessions. All animals were equally deprived. Note that the vertical axis is in log scale. (Culbertson, Kling, & Berkley, 1966.)

suggest that all forms of self-starvation are somehow related through the control of food-seeking behavior by the lateral hypothalamus, but it also seems possible that *any* reinforcer capable of maintaining extremely high response rates might have similar effects.

In contrast to the remarkable persistence subjects show during periods of stimulation is their relatively rapid cessation of responding when stimulation is no longer forthcoming (for example, Olds, 1955), or when the density of reinforcements is markedly reduced (Hodos, 1961). Of course, in most cases the comparisons of resistance to extinction have been between a reinforcer (food) with which the animal has had months or years of experience and brain stimulation with which he may have had only a few hours or days of experience. A typical result from such an experiment is shown in Figure 15.17. In this study, equal numbers of reinforced bar presses were allowed all animals. Some were reinforced for every such response, while others were on a fixed-ratio schedule in which every tenth bar press was reinforced. After 10 sessions of 100 reinforcements each, 4 daily 15-minute extinction periods were introduced. Clearly, the food-reinforced animals were more persistent during the extinction sessions than were those reinforced with electrical brain stimulation. Furthermore, the increased resistance to extinction engendered by utilizing a schedule of partial reinforcement had the same effect on the animals receiving brain stimulation as on those reinforced with food: As is frequently the case, the effect of the type of schedule seems to have a greater behavioral influence than the type of reinforcing stimulus.

Although it certainly is true that typical brain-stimulation procedures will produce low response persistence, there is some evidence that these effects are not inherent characteristics of brain stimulation reinforcement, but are—at least in part—artifacts of the techniques utilized in typical ICS experiments. For example, the onset of brain stimulation usually is administered immediately upon the occurrence of the correct response; food, in contrast, almost always is obtained after a delay during which the animal approaches, seizes, and consumes the food. Following reinforcement, ICS animals are already in position to respond again; those receiving food can obtain reinforcement for their responses only if they leave the food dish and return to the place where responses can be made.

Thus, food-reinforcement procedures usually introduce at least a short delay of primary reinforcement and a short response-chain requirement, both of which are absent from most ICS procedures. That such differences might account for the lesser persistence of ICS-reinforced animals is suggested by the studies of Gibson, Reid, Sakai, and Porter (1965), Owens and Brown (1968), and Pliskoff and his associates (see, for example, Pliskoff & Hawkins, 1967). In these laboratories, brain stimulation has been delivered under conditions which require of the animals behaviors that mimic those commonly emitted by food-reinforced subjects. For example, Gibson and his coworkers reinforced lever pressing by presentation of a dry dipper, the licking of which then triggered the onset of the ICS. Under such conditions, lever pressing was as persistent as that observed when animals were reinforced with sucrose solutions, as measured in tests when only every twentieth response was reinforced, and during subsequent extinction tests. In the procedure used by Pliskoff and Hawkins, a two-unit behavioral chain was established: the animal was reinforced with brain stimulation every time he pressed Bar 2; this bar was withdrawn from his reach, but was presented again when he pressed Bar 1. Thus, responses on Bar 1 were reinforced by presentations of Bar 2, and responses on Bar 2 were reinforced with brain stimulation. In a typical experiment using this procedure, the requirement on Bar 1 might be some fixed ratio (such as, after every 10 responses, Bar 2 appears), or some other schedule of reinforcement might be imposed.

Usually, Bar 2 was allowed to remain in the chamber until the animal had pressed it three times (and thus received three stimulations). Food controls have not been used, so the relative effects of this chained-response procedure and the multiple reinforcements on the persistence with which the subjects responded cannot be evaluated. However, it is clear that animals reinforced with brain stimulation in this manner do show considerable persistence (see Gandleman, Panksepp, & Trowill, 1968).

It also has become clear in recent years that such special treatment of ICS animals is not a prerequisite for persistence of responding, and more and more frequently one encounters research reports in which rats reinforced with brain stimulation are performing with about the same persistence as food-reinforced animals (see, for example, Keesey & Goldstein, 1968; Kling & Berkley, 1968). Why was such persistence not seen in the earlier studies of ICS? In addition to giving the animals relatively limited experience with this type of stimulus, experimenters also were quick to deliver a "free stimulation" whenever the animals paused. Such free stimulations would very rarely be given when food reinforcement is employed, but because satiation is not feared when ICS is utilized, and because the experimenter's hand switch is so easy to squeeze, the delivery of noncontingent stimulation was frequently utilized to keep ICS animals active during initial training and to hasten the emission of responses at the beginning of subsequent training sessions. This procedure probably reinforces such responses as not pressing the bar and thus tends to generate patterns of responding which actually compete with the "correct" one during extinction tests.

Another difference which distinguishes ICS from more typical reinforcers is the relative lack of satiation effects when ICS is employed. In some experiments, rats have been maintained for a day or more under conditions where they could stimulate themselves at any time (Olds, 1958b; Valenstein & Beer, 1964).

If electrodes are placed in hypothalamic regions (where the highest self-stimulation rates are usually found), a rat may self-stimulate more or less continually for the first 24 hours, then fall into exhausted sleep, and then return for bouts of self-stimulation.[19] Nothing akin to typical satiation is seen: The animal seems to stimulate himself until exhausted, and return to self-stimulation as soon as he is sufficiently rested to get back to work.

At one time, Olds (1958c) suggested that some regions might show satiation effects. For example, when the stimulating tips of the electrode were in the septal area, he found that the rate of self-stimulation declined after the first few hours, whereas if the electrode was placed in hypothalamic regions, the animals continued to stimulate themselves for very long periods of time, until it seemed that sheer exhaustion forced the animal to pause. However, recent studies of long-term response patterns in our laboratory suggest that these effects might be due to unintentional variations in the levels of stimulation applied to the septal and the hypothalamic areas. With typical preparations, the impedance of septal tissue is much higher than that of hypothalamic tissue, and thus, if equal voltages are delivered to the two areas, quite different current levels are produced. Animals stimulated in the septal area which show apparent satiation effects at low current levels seem to show more and more persistent responding as the current is increased, and current levels usually can be found where satiation seems not to occur. Further investigation of possible satiation

effects is needed, with a relatively wide range of current levels and loci of stimulation as the independent variables.

In many other respects, it now appears that the reinforcing properties of electrical brain stimulation are no different from those of a typical reinforcer (such as food). For example, the rate with which a simple discrimination is acquired (Kling & Matsumiya, 1962; Sadowsky, 1969), the fineness of discrimination that can be established (Terman & Kling, 1968), and the breadth of stimulus generalization that follows discrimination training (see Figure 15.18 p. 656) all seem to be equivalent whether food or ICS reinforcements are used. In each of these situations, of course, it is the establishment of stimulus control that is observed, and in this domain, any one reinforcer may be the equivalent of any other.[20]

Finally, in some respects, ICS is distinctly superior to other reinforcement procedures, in that it can be delivered with more precise control over its parameters than can most other reinforcing stimuli. Thus, for the study of such problems as delay of reinforcement, ICS yields functional relations like those obtained with other reinforcers (Keesey, 1964a), and its convenience makes it the reinforcer of choice for parametric experiments. Similarly, when a reinforcer is needed which can be delivered at the discretion of the experimenter and without reliance on the responding of the subject, electrical brain stimulation provides the obvious solution. For example, precise temporal pairing of a neutral and a positive reinforcing stimulus in a study of conditioned reinforcement (Stein, 1958), or delivery of a positive reinforcer to a deeply curarized animal whenever a smooth muscle response occurs (Miller & Banuazizi, 1968; Miller, 1969) would be impossible with typical positive reinforcing stimuli, but is simple to engineer with ICS.

[19] The data of Valenstein and Beer suggest that the first orgy of responding and the subsequent exhaustion are followed by rhythmic changes in responding suggestive of a circadian rhythm. Prescott (1967) sampled self-stimulation rates at various points around the clock and also found evidence for such cyclic changes. His chamber contained two bars: Responses on the one were reinforced with brain stimulation, whereas responses on the other were never reinforced. Cyclic effects were seen only in the number of reinforced responses, leading Prescott to suggest that it was the reinforcement value of the brain stimulation, and not merely level of general activity, that was varying in a rhythmical fashion.

[20] Evidence contrary to this conclusion has recently been presented by Keesey and Lindholm (1969), who demonstrated that qualitatively different reinforcers produced consistent group differences in rate of learning a brightness discrimination.

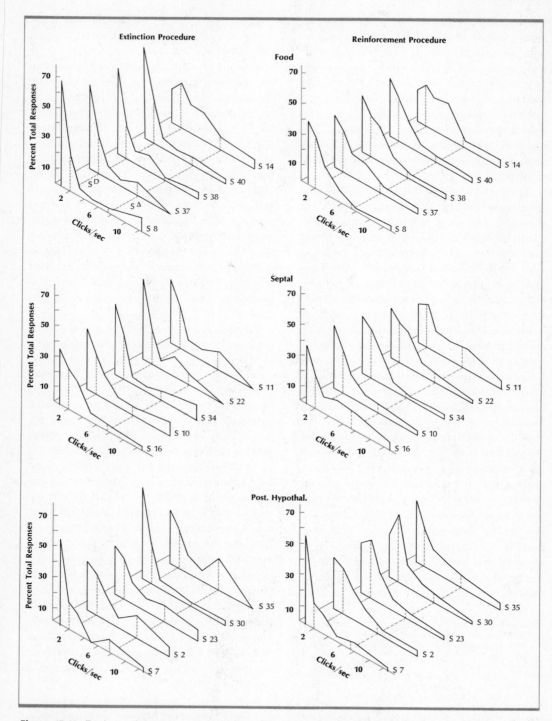

Figure 15.18. During training, responses in the presence of the positive stimulus (S^D) of 2 clicks/sec were occasionally reinforced (variable interval 30 sec reinforcement schedule). Responses in the presence of the negative stimulus (S^Δ) of 7.8 clicks/sec were never reinforced. Training continued until re-

Why does ICS have reinforcing properties? The first attempts to answer this question reveal how little we really know about the phenomenon (phenomena?) called "reinforcement." A brief review of some of the attempts to understand "why ICS works" may help us gain a better perspective about the general problem of reinforcement, as well as a better appreciation of positively reinforcing brain stimulation.

ICS reduces drive level. If reinforcement were always accompanied by drive reduction, we might expect ICS to function through the same mechanism, except (perhaps) with greater rapidity and efficiency. How might such an effect be reflected? Perhaps the momentary level of excitement might be altered; after all, consummation of food-seeking responses eventually reduces activity, and ICS might have a similar quieting effect. However, mere observation of the animal stimulating himself shows that excitement and activity increase during the session, so a decrease in the overall drive level, or in the level of arousal, does not seem to account for the reinforcing effects.

ICS increases drive, excitement, or arousal. One of the chief weaknesses of the drive-reduction theory of reinforcement was its inability to provide a convincing explanation of why responding should be reinforced by conditions which must certainly increase drive level (for example, continued running to inaccessible food, observed by Schlosberg and Pratt, 1956). Perhaps it is drive *induction* that is common to reinforcers (Sheffield, 1966; see also p. 695), and that ICS is

a technique for increasing excitement. How is drive or arousal level to be observed? One suggestion is to use some measure of the level of autonomic nervous system activity, such as heart rate. But stimulation at some electrode placements produces momentary heart rate *decreases*, although in other areas, heart rate *increases* are the immediate consequences of stimulation (Meyers, Valenstein, & Lacey, 1963; Perez-Cruet, Black, & Brady, 1963; Malmo, 1964). To the extent that heart rate reflects drive level, it seems that either an immediate increase *or* decrease in drive may accompany the brain stimulation, and thus such changes do not seem to offer an explanation for why ICS is positively reinforcing.

ICS stimulates a reinforcing network in the central nervous system. In various forms, this hypothesis has been suggested by Olds (see Olds & Olds, 1965). The basic theme that the reinforcing effects of ICS are, in at least some cases, attributable to the activation by the electrical stimulation of a neural system "whose activity serves to facilitate *ongoing* motor mechanisms and possibly to reinforce the firing of *antecedently active* motor systems" (page 381). When electrodes are so placed that they stimulate this system, the strongest possible positive reinforcing effects are found. To allow the hypothesis to account for other reinforcing effects, the reinforcing system is assumed to be spontaneously active and under the inhibitory control of input from "drive" centers. These latter centers are in turn under the control of two types of input: afferent stimulation associated with

---

sponse rates in S^D were at least 8 times the rates in S^Δ. The first generalization test was then given. Clicks were presented during 1-minute periods at a rate of 0.6, 2.0, 3.2, 5.2, 7.8, and 12.3 clicks/sec, each stimulus being given at least 9 times in a randomized order. On the first generalization test (Reinforcement Procedure), the variable interval reinforcement schedule was in effect whenever the S^D was present. In the second test (Extinction Procedure), responses never were reinforced. Between generalization tests, animals were retrained until the discrimination criterion again was attained. Each curve represents the behavior of one animal (identified by S number) on one of the two generalization tests. Results are grouped according to the reinforcing stimulus: food pellets, or electrical stimulation of the septal or of the posterior hypothalamic areas. Note that "peak shifts" (that is, higher response rates during 0.6 than during 2.0 click/sec periods) occur in all reinforcement groups, and that retraining and subsequent testing in extinction sharpen the generalization gradients but also increase response rates during S^Δ periods. (Kling & Berkley, 1968.)

activity of gustatory, olfactory, and visceral receptors, and direct stimulation of the drive centers by the chemical condition of the blood and other body fluids which bathe the cells of the centers. Thus, the smell and taste of food would inhibit drive-center activity, and thus (through inhibition of the inhibitor) increase the activity of the reinforcing system. Continued ingestion of food eventually would cause changes in the drive centers, producing increased inhibition of the reinforcing system and eventual cessation of eating and of food-reinforced responses. (How satiation effects with ICS would occur—if indeed they do—is not spelled out by the theory.)

Direct electrical stimulation of the afferent pathways feeding into the drive centers would have the same positive reinforcing effects that we might obtain through the "normal" presentation of food reinforcers, but the effects of such stimulation would be no more nor less effective than those obtained with food, whereas direct electrical stimulation of the reinforcing system itself would provide the greatest possible positive reinforcing effects.

A single reinforcing system under the inhibitory control of drive centers provides a means of visualizing the relations of normal reinforcers and electrical brain stimulation. By assuming that some positive loci act directly, and that others act indirectly to produce reinforcing effects, the major results of the brain mapping experiments are taken into account. Tentatively, the final reinforcing pathways are identified with systems present in the medial forebrain bundle-lateral hypothalamus complex, while the drive centers are given the suggested locus of the medial hypothalamus.

Whereas Olds and Olds (1965) postulate a single reinforcing system, Glickman and Schiff (1967) suggest the existence of sets of parallel neural pathways, each of which regulates a pattern of consummatory activity. Whatever stimulation activates such pathways, and the approach responses associated with them, would prove to be positive rein-

forcers, and whatever stimuli are present while these motor activities are in progress would become (by mere contiguity) capable of controlling these responses in the future.

ICS stimulates both motivating and reinforcing pathways. One form of this theory (Deutsch & Deutsch, 1966) assumes that every response must have some motivational basis for its first occurrence, and that it must have been reinforced if it recurs. Since ICS obviously can be used to establish and maintain responding in the absence of any of the more familiar procedures for instigating motivational conditions, it is assumed that the stimulation creates drive states directly by tapping into existing motivational pathways and at the same time causes responses to be reinforced by exciting existing reinforcement pathways.

A more elaborate form of this hypothesis has been proposed by Routtenberg (1968), who argues that septal and hypothalamic stimulation must have different substrates since their immediately elicited autonomic reactions (such as heart rate changes) and their interactions with aversive and with fear-provoking stimuli seem to be different. In the latter case, he points out that septal stimulation generally decreases the efficiency of the organism in avoidance or escape situations, while concurrent hypothalamic stimulation seems to increase escape or avoidance responding. He therefore suggests that septal stimulation may have its action through suppression of "Arousal System I," which he associates with the reticular formation, and to which he attributes drive properties. Arousal System I is dynamically related to Arousal System II, which he associates with the limbic system, and for which he postulates positive incentive properties. Thus, septal ICS would cause an immediate decrease in the activity of the drive system, and then compensatory increase in the activity of the positive incentive system. Hypothalamic ICS, on the other hand, is said to stimulate simultaneously both Systems I and II.

In Routtenberg's theory, the reinforcing effects of ICS would be attributed to the suppression of Arousal System I ("drive") by the stimulation. Suppression of drive in turn permits the perseveration of the neural activity reflecting the behavior that led up to the onset of the reinforcer, and this perseveration is said to allow the consolidation of short-term memory. The suppression of Arousal System I is said to be a direct consequence of septal stimulation but only an indirect and delayed consequence of hypothalamic stimulation. Such hypothetical relations would seem to lead to the prediction that as a reinforcer, septal ICS would be superior to hypothalamic stimulation, but the available evidence (see p. 656) seems to suggest that the reinforcing (as distinct from the arousing) characteristics of these stimuli are all more or less the same.

Deutsch suggests that the rate of emission of responses reflects primarily the level of the ICS-produced drive, and he has employed responding during extinction as an index of the rate of decay of this drive (see Deutsch & Howarth, 1963). But as we have seen, the persistence of ICS-reinforced responding during both extinction and periods of low reinforcement density may be interpreted as reflections of the techniques used in training the animals and in delivering the reinforcers. A more direct mode of observing drive effects has been suggested by Quartermain and Webster (1968), who recorded general activity with a stabilimeter device during a one-hour period following reinforcement with water or with electrical brain stimulation. They found the ICS animals to be much more active at first, but to decline in activity over the 60 minutes to the same low level that the water reinforcement group had displayed throughout the entire hour. If general activity is accepted as a reflection of drive (and this is not always a defensible position; see Chapter 18), we might conclude that ICS animals do indeed show a marked drive decay following their last reinforcement. Since the electrode placements were ones which Routtenberg would expect to stimulate both drive and incentive systems, the activity data do not discriminate between the Deutsch and the Routtenberg viewpoints, but a repetition of

the procedure, using septal stimulation, should elicit differential predictions from the theories, with Deutsch predicting no essential difference between the ICS loci, and Routtenberg predicting little or no arousal and subsequent drive decay with septal ICS.

In summary, these theories try to present a schema or a hypothetical organization for the nervous system, suggesting behavior-related functions and interrelations for known anatomical entities, and hypothesizing neurological centers or systems where the behavioral data seem to suggest that they may exist. At the present time, both the neurological and the behavioral data are too fragmentary to permit adequate evaluations of the suggestions that ICS has its effects through stimulation of one or two major systems which subserve such meaningful psychological functions as motivating and reinforcing behavior; indeed, it would be surprising if these rather heterogeneous phenomena proved to have unitary neurological substrates.

ICS stimulates pleasure centers. When one observes self-stimulation behavior for the first time, it is difficult to avoid the conclusion that something akin to stimulation of erogenous zones must be occurring. (Indeed, some wags referred to the self-stimulation procedure as "subcortical masturbation" when knowledge about the phenomenon was still very limited.) But such superficial impressions frequently are misleading: The animal appears to be oblivious to what is going on around him, but actually he can discriminate auditory stimuli even when these are presented only while he is actually receiving the electrical stimulation (Beer & Valenstein, 1960). Furthermore, the designation of this stimulation as "pleasurable" has no more basis than it does for any other event which proves to be a positive reinforcer. Certainly the verbal reports gathered in the studies in which humans (advanced cases of neurological or psychiatric disorders, where nothing else had helped . . .) have had stimulation applied to homologous brain areas have not helped understand the reinforcing effects of the stimulation. The statements are about as helpful as are those obtained when a confirmed cigarette smoker is asked to describe how he feels when he inhales: reports mention that some patients say they like the stimulation or that it feels good (Sem-Jacobsen & Torkildsen, 1960), but no attempt has been made to collect all the statements, or to use the verbal reports otherwise in any systematic manner. This much at least can be said: not all reports refer to any one type of experience. Initially, there were suggestions that loci of positive stimulation might all be in areas subserving sexual behavior, and the occasional placement (for example, Herberg, 1963) that elicits seminal emission gave some support to these notions. However, such reactions are the exception rather than the rule, and clearly are not essential to the positive reinforcing effect.

Summary We are left with the same problem that existed before positively reinforcing electrical brain stimulation became a common tool of the behavioral laboratory: Why do some stimuli have positive reinforcing effects? We can eliminate any theories that hypothesize a single, positive-reinforcement neurological system, although it is more difficult to obtain critical evidence on hypothesized sets of systems that feed into a final common pathway (such as Miller's "go" hypothesis, 1963). We also can eliminate suggestions that any relations with unique endocrine or maintenance conditions are necessary for positive reinforcement, or that reinforcement always involves either arousal or relaxation.

Clearly, there is a need for thoughtful reanalysis of the problem(s) of reinforcement, and for a flexible posture on the part of the theorist.

SECONDARY REINFORCEMENT

Some events are reinforcing when first presented, while others seem to acquire reinforcing properties only after the organism has had certain experiences with them. Events falling into the first category have been called "primary reinforcers," while those of the second type have been called "secondary" or "conditioned" reinforcers. There is an unfortunate ambiguity to the term "secondary," but it has the advantage of neutrality, while "conditioned reinforcement" presumes that the process whereby reinforcing properties are acquired by previously neutral stimuli is that of classical conditioning. As we shall see, there are other interpretations of this phenomenon, and there may indeed be more than one process underlying the variety of acquired reinforcing effects. The term "secondary reinforcement" thus seems to be preferable, and we shall use it to label the phenomena considered in this section.

It is obvious that the reinforcing events which we use in everyday life ordinarily are not primary reinforcers, but rather they are reinforcers which are intimately related to specific past experiences and closely tied to the cultural and intellectual milieu of the individual. Indeed, the understanding and appreciation of the secondary reinforcers that are effective in social groups other than our own represents a major problem for teachers and politicians as well as for social scientists: approval and praise in the classroom may be a powerful reinforcing event for the child reared in a middle-class home, but many a teacher has found to her dismay that such is not always the case for children from markedly different backgrounds.

In psychological theory, secondary reinforcement has carried an unusually heavy burden. We find it involved in explanations of the establishment and maintenance of behaviors in everyday life where primary reinforcers seem to be absent; and we apply it liberally (and occasionally uncritically) when analyzing behavioral sequences observed in the laboratory. It therefore behooves us to examine the conditions under which the use of the concept is warranted, and to consider a few of the alternative interpretations that have been offered for the major phenomena usually explained by appeal to "secondary reinforcement."

How are we to identify the presence of secondary reinforcing effects? Perhaps the earliest procedure was the one used by Pavlov (1927, pp. 33–35) in his studies of higher-order conditioned reflexes. Pavlov described his procedure in these terms: "A dog has two primary alimentary conditioned stimuli firmly established, one to the sound of a metronome and the other to the buzzing of an electric bell. The appearance of a black square in the dog's line of vision is now used as yet a further stimulus, which is to be given the character of a secondary conditioned stimulus. The black square is held in front of the dog for ten seconds, and after an interval of fifteen seconds the metronome is sounded during 30 seconds." After 10 presentations of the square plus one or the other of the conditioned stimuli, salivation in response to the square had reached measurable proportions. However, "it was found impossible in the case of alimentary reflexes to press the secondary conditioned stimulus into our service to help us in the establishment of a new conditioned stimulus of the third order. Conditioned reflexes of the third order can however be obtained . . . in defense reactions such as that against stimulation of the skin by a strong electric current. But even in this case we cannot proceed further than a conditioned reflex of the third order" (pp. 33–34).

Note what had occurred: a previously neutral stimulus (black square) gained control of a response (saliva secretion) through "pairing" with other stimuli which themselves had at one time been neutral so far as control of salivation was concerned. Therefore, these other stimuli (metronome, bell) must have acquired some of the properties of the unconditioned stimulus (food), and thus they must have been not just conditioned stimuli but also "conditioned reinforcers." This, then, represents one way in which the secondary reinforcing properties of a stimulus may be evaluated: see if it can be used to establish a new stimulus as a conditioned stimulus.

A word of caution about the "pairing" of stimuli may be in order. Note that Pavlov specified that the black square was to be presented, withdrawn, and then (after an interval of many seconds) the metronome or bell was to be introduced. He found that if he presented the square and the metronome together, not only did the square never gain any control over saliva flow, but the metronome lost its conditioned stimulus properties.[21] Thus, "pairing" can have at least two effects: if the neutral stimulus is closely paired with a conditioned stimulus, both will become inhibitors of saliva secretion; while if the neutral stimulus precedes the conditioned stimulus by 10 seconds or more, it may acquire some of the properties of the conditioned stimulus.

Why do we refer to these experiments rather than to the more basic examples of Pavlovian conditioning? There seems to be at least one difference between what is conventionally called "secondary reinforcement" and the "mere" establishment of a previously neutral stimulus (such as a metronome) as a conditioned stimulus: the conditioned stimulus has acquired some of the properties of the food, so that the animal salivates, looks toward the food dish, and in other ways indicates that the metronome signals to him that food is about to be delivered. Still, there is nothing in this behavior that shows the metronome to have acquired any properties of a *reinforcer*. Such properties are, however, clearly demonstrated in conditioning of the second (or higher) order, and the distinction suggests one of the criteria we may use in deciding whether secondary reinforcing properties have indeed been acquired by a previously neutral stimulus: can a new stimulus be given control over a response by using the previously neutral stimulus as the reinforcer?

Although the Pavlovian procedure offered some of the earliest examples of secondary reinforcement, and indeed may represent the

[21] Pavlov called this phenomenon "conditioned inhibition," but remarked that it might better have been termed "differential inhibition." It is the former term, however, which has remained in use (see, for example, Maier, Seligman, & Solomon, 1969).

prototype of this phenomenon, the majority of the studies of secondary reinforcement have utilized not the classical, Pavlovian techniques, but instrumental (operant) procedures. Among sitUations employing instrumental behavior techniques, the earliest demonstrations of secondary reinforcement examined the maze learning by rats when the final correct response was followed by entrance into a chamber in which the animal had, on other occasions, been fed repeatedly. In such experiments (see the summaries in Tolman, 1932) it was shown that presentation of food at the end of the maze produced the best performance, in terms of both speed and error elimination, but that performance did improve over trials when the only reinforcement at the end of the maze was entrance into a box that had on previous occasions been used as a place for feeding the animal. Such demonstrations were important in establishing the role of secondary reinforcement in maintaining long, complex chains of behavior in nonverbal organisms, but the very complexity of the maze situation, and the relatively low reliability of many of the early mazes,[22] led experimenters to seek other behavioral situations in which to analyze secondary reinforcing effects.

Indices of Secondary Reinforcement

Extinction tests   A less complex test for the presence of secondary reinforcing effects is derived from the procedures used by Bugelski (1938) and Skinner (1938). In this test, the ability of the supposed secondary reinforcing event to maintain behavior during extinction is evaluated. Skinner trained a rat to press a bar, where each such response produced a loud click from the feeding

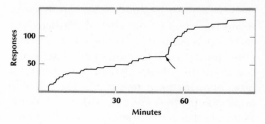

Figure 15.19. Effects of introducing a secondary reinforcing stimulus during extinction. During training, every bar press had produced both a click from the food-pellet dispensing mechanism and a food pellet. During the first portion of the extinction session, neither the food nor a click were presented. The curve shows the effects of this extinction procedure. At the arrow, the click (but not food) was reintroduced. (After Skinner, 1938.)

mechanism as a pellet of food was released into the food cup. After extensive training, the feeding mechanism was disconnected so that depressions of the bar produced neither food nor the noise of the mechanism. When this extinction procedure had lowered the rate of response almost to zero, Skinner reconnected the mechanism, but emptied it of food pellets. Now each press produced the mechanism noise, and the animal emitted a burst of responses. Such reappearance of vigorous and rapid responding (see Figure 15.19) typically is said to demonstrate the secondary reinforcing properties of the mechanism noise.[23]

Bugelski (1938) also observed the effects of feeding-mechanism sounds on responding during extinction, but he utilized separate groups of animals in his experiment. Each rat was trained to eat from the food cup whenever a pellet was delivered, and was then allowed 30 reinforced bar presses. Half the animals were then extinguished with neither pellet nor mechanism noise, while the other half had the characteristic noise occur after each bar press. The mean number of re-

[22] The reliability of a maze refers not to the apparatus itself, but to the behavioral measures resulting from its use. Thus, determining the reliability involves the same problems as determining the reliability of, for example, an intelligence test, with the additional problem that the behavior in which we are interested will be changing in systematic ways during maze "tests" whereas it will be relatively unchanged during intelligence tests. Maze reliability usually is estimated from the correlation of odd and even numbered trials (see Munn, 1950).

[23] These data were presented as evidence of the changes occurring in a behavioral chain when the stimuli for the next unit in the chain were eliminated. For that analysis, see Skinner (1938, pp. 103–104).

sponses emitted by the group extinguished in silence was 54, while the group extinguished with the mechanism noise present emitted, on the average, 78 responses. Again, this difference between the groups in this extinction test frequently is said to demonstrate the secondary reinforcing effects of the mechanism noise.

New response tests In the extinction tests described above, differences (either between groups or within a single organism) in the emission of a previously well-learned response are evaluated, but many factors in addition to secondary reinforcement might influence the rate at which that response occurs. For example, if the overall activity level of the animal were increased by the sound of the feeder, it is possible that many more responses would be emitted when the feeder mechanism noises were present than when they were absent. However, if the supposed secondary reinforcer could be used to train the subject to make a completely new response, one might be able to choose between the "arousal" and the "reinforcing" interpretations of the effects of the mechanism noises. Several variations of this procedure have been developed. For example, Skinner (1938) presented the feeder noise and food pellet 60 times (that is, he "magazine trained" the rats), and then inserted into the chamber a bar which, when depressed, produced only the feeder noise. The emission of responses during this test period was slow and irregular, but it was obvious that some appreciable conditioning of bar pressing occurred. Indeed, Skinner commented (p. 82) that the number of responses emitted was about the same as one might expect after 60 reinforced bar presses. Such potency of secondary reinforcers rarely is observed.

Another form of this test was employed by Clayton and Savin (1960). They trained rats to press a panel, and then introduced the contingencies: white noise-press-food; no noise-press-no food. Following this training, a bar was uncovered, and every depression

of the bar by a rat in the experimental group produced a 5-second noise. Meanwhile, a control group with the same prior discrimination training received noise during the test session more or less at random, since each control animal was paired with an experimental animal and heard only the noises that were produced by the responses of the experimental animal. This "yoked control" design provides one form of control for the nonreinforcing but facilitating effects of a discriminative stimulus. The animals in the experimental group emitted more than twice as many responses as the controls during the test sessions, showing that the noise indeed had acquired secondary reinforcing properties which were over and above the effects due to mere activity arousal.

Choice tests A modified form of new response test utilizes a choice situation in which primary reinforcement is absent and the existence of secondary reinforcing properties is evaluated by observing whether stimuli previously paired with primary reinforcement are approached more frequently than control stimuli. A good example of this procedure is seen in the study by Saltzman (1949). Rats were trained to run from the start box of a straight alley to the goal box where food was placed. To provide distinctive stimulus conditions, half were trained to leap a hurdle into a black goal box, and half were trained to step down from the alley into a white goal box. They then were split into four groups. One group received 5 consecutive food-reinforced runs a day for 5 days, always with the same goal box. An intermittent reinforcement group had nonreinforced runs interspersed among the reinforced trials, but always with the same goal box. A differential reinforcement group received the same treatment as the previous group, but one goal box was always used for reinforced trials and one for nonreinforced trials. The fourth group received the same alley training as the first (consecutive reinforcement) group.

For the first three groups, the test for sec-

TABLE 15.3 MEAN NUMBER OF RESPONSES TO SIDE CONTAINING SECONDARY REINFORCING STIMULI DURING FIFTEEN TEST TRIALS.[a]

Group	Experiment I	Experiment II
Consecutive reinforcement	8.3	11.5
Alternate reinforcement	9.0	10.4
Differential reinforcement	10.7	11.6
Food reinforcement	10.0	—

[a] After Saltzman (1949).

ondary reinforcing effects took place in a U-shaped maze. Each animal had earlier been tested for his "preference" for a right or left turn in a similar apparatus, and now the non-preferred side of the U maze had attached to it the goal box in which food had been received during alley training. The other arm of the U terminated in the other goal box which, of course, had never been paired with food.

The fourth group had both ends of the U equipped with the previously nonreinforced goal box, and was given food for running to the nonpreferred side. In this way, they provided an estimate of U-maze learning with primary reinforcement only. The other groups never received food in the U maze; whatever preferences emerged would be attributable to the secondary reinforcing properties of the previous food-baited box (or possibly to the acquired punishing properties of the previously empty box). On each trial, the animal was detained in the goal box for 30 seconds. Fifteen spaced test trials were given.

The results are summarized in Table 15.3 under Experiment I. Note that the differential reinforcement group actually surpassed the food-control group in number of choices of the "correct" side. The consecutive reinforcement group, in spite of 25 reinforced runs to one of the goal boxes, showed only a small preference (compared to the "chance" value of 7.5 choices) for the goal box in which they had been fed. Saltzman suggested that this was the result of extinction of the secondary reinforcing properties of the goal box during the U-maze test, and that the other groups

showed less extinction because they had been trained with partial reinforcement.

To test this hypothesis, he trained 3 more groups, using the procedures employed in Experiment I. This time, reinforced runs in the straight alley were interpolated among the U-maze tests with the expectation that this procedure would forestall extinction of the secondary reinforcing properties of the goal boxes (see "Maintenance Tests," below). As the results of Experiment II (Table 15.3) indicate, this procedure was an effective means of increasing the number of responses to the side of the U maze where the secondary reinforcing stimuli were located. More important, however, the results suggest that differential reinforcement may be no more effective than consecutive reinforcement in establishing secondary reinforcing properties. This issue will be considered shortly, but usually one would assume that the differential reinforcement procedure would produce discrimination of the goal boxes, and that a discriminative stimulus would be a stronger secondary reinforcer. Indeed, some psychologists assert that only a discriminative stimulus can be a secondary reinforcer—a conclusion quite at odds with Saltzman's results. Certainly these procedures deserve additional study, especially in other behavioral situations, to provide some estimate of their generality.

Maintenance tests As a means of maintaining the secondary reinforcing properties of a stimulus during tests of its efficacy, some experimenters intersperse among the tests occasional pairings of the to-be-tested stimulus and the primary reinforcer. Collectively, these procedures are called "maintenance tests." Such testing and further strengthening of the secondary reinforcer may be carried out within the same situation, or may go on concurrently in two or more situations. A familiar example of the first type may be seen in most operant conditioning situations. If a bird has been magazine trained, the sound made by the operation of the food magazine, and the onset of the light which usually is placed within the magazine, serve as discriminative stimuli for cessation of ongoing responses and for approach to the feeder. When magazine training has become well established, the sounds and the light associated with operation of the food magazine can be shown to have reinforcing properties: if they are presented when some other response (a turn of the head, a peck at some spot on the wall, and so on) has just occurred, the likelihood that the response will be repeated is greatly increased. (At this point we have another example of the "new response" procedure, described above.) In a typical operant conditioning situation, of course, the magazine stimuli are always followed by access to food, so the secondary reinforcing properties of the stimuli presumably are continually renewed by this procedure.

Good examples of the concurrent variety of maintained testing procedures are provided by some of the studies conducted in the context of "token reward" investigations. For example, Wolfe (1936) and Cowles (1937) trained chimpanzees to insert poker chips into a vending machine from which bits of food were discharged. Once the operation of the "chimpomat" was mastered, the poker chips were used as reinforcers for other responses. Either immediately, or after considerable delay, the tokens thus earned could be inserted into the chimpomat and exchanged for food, thus maintaining the secondary reinforcing value of the tokens.

A valuable technique for investigating secondary reinforcement under conditions of maintained responding is provided by the chained reinforcement schedule (Ferster & Skinner, 1957). For example, a pigeon may be trained to peck a red response key, using intermittent food reinforcement to maintain a relatively constant response rate. Now suppose the key is made green, but when it is pecked, it turns red and further responses to the red key are reinforced according to the schedule previously in effect. Under these circumstances, responses to the green key are never directly reinforced with food presentations. Through the imaginative use of different numbers of units in the chain, or by utilizing different schedules of (secondary) reinforcement in various components of the chain, the relative contributions of frequency of primary reinforcement, length of the response chain, and the schedule of reinforcement itself have been investigated. A review of studies utilizing these maintenance procedures has been included in the survey prepared by Kelleher and Gollub (1962).

Yet another form of maintained response procedure utilizes concurrent reinforcement of two or more responses, at least one of which produces both the secondary reinforcing stimulus and a primary reinforcer. For example, J. Zimmerman (1963) equipped a rat chamber with two bars, one of which produced light and food when pressed, while the other produced only the light. The rat was free to operate either bar at any time. Responses on the "light-only" bar occurred with low but consistent rates for many weeks, with no obvious signs that the secondary reinforcing effects of the light were weakening. (For application of this strategy to the study of conditioned punishment, see Hake & Azrin, 1965).

Independent Variables

What are the major independent variables that influence the strength of secondary reinforcing stimuli? Since secondary reinforcing properties probably are established through classical conditioning and/or instrumental learning, we might predict that any factors influencing these learning processes would also have parallel influences on secondary reinforcement. Tentatively, we may conclude that this indeed is the case, although there are many gaps in the available information.

Amount of primary reinforcement The secondary reinforcing strength of a stimulus as a function of the amount of primary reinforcer with which it is paired has been investigated in a number of experiments and the effects are remarkably similar to those obtained when amount of reinforcement is studied in other contexts. For example, if separate groups of animals are given different amounts of food when in the presence of the previously neutral stimulus, later tests of the secondary reinforcing properties of that stimulus may show little (Reynolds, Pavlik, & Goldstein, 1964) or no (Hopkins, 1955) effect of the different amounts of food. On the other hand, if each animal is exposed to more than one amount of food reinforcement (see discussion of shifts in reinforcers, pages 631–642), different degrees of secondary reinforcement correlated with different amounts of food can be demonstrated (for example, D'Amato, 1955b; Reynolds et al., 1964). Thus, differential training that allows each organism to be exposed to more than one condition of reinforcement again proves to be more effective than the absolute (single value) method of presenting the reinforcers.

Number of pairings Since the number of primary reinforcements is almost always a major factor in the initial stages of instrumental or classical conditioning, it is reasonable to assume that the number of times a previously neutral stimulus is paired with a primary reinforcer would determine, in part, the subsequent secondary reinforcing properties acquired by that stimulus. This seems to be the case, but the effect is not as large as one might expect. For example, Bersh (1951) and Miles (1956) used extinction tests to evaluate the secondary reinforcing proper-

ties of a light that had been paired with delivery of a food pellet whenever the rat pressed a bar. Separate groups of animals were allowed different numbers of reinforced responses and thus received different numbers of pairings of light and food.

When such a procedure is used, animals in the various groups will, of course, differ in the extent to which the bar pressing response has been established, and a subsequent extinction test may confound this response strength with the potency of the secondary reinforcing stimulus. Bersh attempted to equalize all groups for response strength prior to the secondary reinforcement test by introducing six 30-minute extinction sessions in which responses to the bar produced neither light nor food. At the end of the sixth session, all groups seemed more or less equal in response rate. Then, 3 test sessions were run, where each bar press produced the light, but no food. Small differences between groups, in the expected direction, were obtained.

Miles (1956) followed his training sessions with a typical extinction test of the secondary

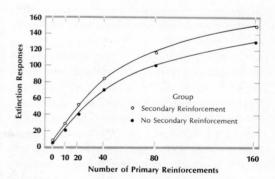

Figure 15.20. Number of responses subjects made during extinction with and without secondary reinforcement. Each point represents the median number of responses emitted by each group during the extinction test. Animals receiving secondary reinforcement were presented both the light and the feeder noise whenever they pressed the bar. The remaining animals received neither stimulus during the test period. (After Miles, 1956.)

reinforcing properties of the light: half of each group was randomly selected and placed in the chamber where depressions of the bar produced the light and the noise of the feeding apparatus, while the other animals were run under identical conditions but with neither light nor noise following their responses. The results are shown in Figure 15.20. Note that the animals extinguished with the light and the click produced, on the average, more responses in extinction than those for whom the stimuli were omitted. These differences support the conclusion that the stimuli indeed did acquire secondary reinforcing properties. Note further that the difference between the two curves increases as the number of pairings in original training increases, suggesting that the strength of the secondary reinforcing stimuli is some positive function of the number of pairings during training. Finally, it should be noticed that, for *both* groups, the overall number of responses emitted during the extinction test is markedly influenced by the number of reinforcements in original training, thus confounding our interpretation of the main effects. It was this "contamination" which Bersh attempted to eliminate by his interpolated extinction sessions, and the results obtained by Miles demonstrate very nicely the type of interpretive problem which Bersh was trying to avoid. Miles recognized this problem, pointing out that his secondary reinforcers merely seemed "to contribute a constant proportion of the total number of extinction responses" (p. 129), with the average of the "no secondary reinforcement" group being approximately 80 percent of the "secondary reinforcement" at each of the values for number of pairings.

Do these results suggest that the number of pairings is a variable of little consequence? Such a conclusion seems to contradict common sense, and yet the studies in which each subject is exposed to but one condition of reinforcement quite consistently show that the number of pairings has a small effect, and even these may be artifacts of the strength at which the response itself was originally

established. On the other hand, where more than one condition of reinforcement is given to each organism, the secondary reinforcing effects of stimuli clearly are influenced by the number of primary reinforcements. For example, Fantino and Herrnstein (1968) gave pigeons training in a 2-key box where responses on each key when they were illuminated with white light led eventually to a change in key color, the left to yellow, the right to red. Pecks during this link in the chain then were reinforced with food. Because the same reinforcement schedule was used when the keys were yellow and red, the rates of response emitted to yellow and red were the same. However, once in force, different numbers of food reinforcements were programmed before the key finally returned to the white condition. In this way, yellow could be given more pairings with food than red, and pecks on the white keys were used as the index of the secondary reinforcing properties acquired by yellow or red. It was found that the rate of response maintained by presentations of the colored keys increased as the number of primary reinforcements increased, up to a limit.

Again, these results remind us that many parameters of reinforcement may have significant behavioral consequences only when each subject is exposed to at least two conditions of reinforcement (see the discussion of amount of reinforcement on page 630).

Investigations of the effects of number of pairings in which the new-response test procedure has been used, support, in general, our previous conclusions. For example, Hall (1951a) gave each rat 25, 50, or 75 food-reinforced runs in a straight alley, and then gave 15 choice trials in a T maze. During this test, one of the goal boxes was that previously employed in the straight alley, and the other was a distinctly different box. Of course, no food was ever placed in the goal boxes during this test. Even the smallest number of pairings gave significantly more choices of the previously reinforced box than would be obtained by chance, and the larger numbers of pairings gave larger proportions of appropriate choices. The differences between the groups, although significant, were relatively small, suggesting that the major effect of number of pairings may occur at some very low number, and that by the time we reach 25 or 50 pairings, the effects are essentially complete.

Effects of deprivation conditions There are several questions concerning relations of deprivation conditions to secondary reinforcement effects that have received fairly extensive study. The investigations of such problems are important because the fundamental nature of secondary reinforcement is not yet understood. One reasonable approach to take toward such problems is to see how manipulation of variables known to be important in other contexts influences the phenomenon in question.

In general, the deprivation conditions existing at the time secondary reinforcing properties are established, or at the time they are tested, appear to be of importance only in determining the basic level of the activity of the organism. For example, Brown (1956) gave half her rats 60 simultaneous pairings of light and buzzer with food pellet, while the other animals received the light and buzzer 28 seconds before a pellet was delivered, and thus presumably had no functional pairing of them. Half of each of these two groups received their training under relatively low food deprivation and half under fairly high deprivation conditions. In a second phase of the experiment, a small brass bar was inserted into the experimental box, and each animal was kept in his chamber until he had pressed the bar twenty times. For every press, the light and the buzzer (but no food) were presented. Half of the animals were tested under the same deprivation conditions used in their initial period of training, and half under the other condition, thus balancing out the effects of change per se in deprivation. Finally, each animal was placed in the box for an hour during which bar presses had no programmed consequences (that is, neither food pellets nor buzzer-light combinations

were delivered at any time). Once again, each previous group was further subdivided into high and low deprivation subgroups. After the one-hour test, further bar presses resulted in the light and buzzer being presented, exactly as had been done in the original testing session.

The results of the experiment (and of a replication which introduced some modifications in the original procedure) were quite clear: pairings of the light and the buzzer with the food pellet did produce secondary reinforcing effects, as shown by the superiority of the experimental group in the 20-response test, and in extinction and retraining tests. However, in all these tests, the only effects of the deprivation conditions were to increase overall levels of responding, such that the relative differences between experimental and control animals remained the same at both high and low deprivation levels.

These results are similar to those of Hall (1951b), where deprivation differences at time of establishment of the secondary reinforcing properties were found to be insignificant, and those of Miles (1956) where differences in deprivation at time of testing were found to have proportionally similar effects on both experimental and control animals. Under such conditions, at least, we may tentatively conclude that deprivation level does not affect secondary reinforcing properties.

A somewhat different problem may be phrased as follows: If qualitative changes in deprivation conditions occur between the original time of pairing of stimuli and testing of the effectiveness of this pairing, will the secondary reinforcing properties of the stimuli diminish? The answer seems to be "yes," in much the same way that most other measures of behavior are detrimentally influenced by changes in the nature of deprivation conditions (D'Amato, 1955a; Wike & Barrientos, 1958). In these and similar studies, the conditions manipulated have been food and water deprivation. Although these indeed are the conditions about which we have the greatest amount of information, they are in a sense unfortunate choices, for they are so intimately related. For example, rats deprived of water reduce their food intake by about one-half, while animals deprived of food similarly reduce their ingestion of water (see, for example, Verplank & Hayes, 1953; Grice & Davis, 1957). Consequently, the results of these experiments might be interpreted as evidence for either of two positions: (1) Secondary reinforcing properties of stimuli are uniquely associated with the deprivation conditions present at the time of the original pairing of the stimuli with the primary reinforcer, but that the rather extensive interactions between food and water deprivations provide the means whereby a partial transfer of secondary reinforcing properties across deprivation conditions might occur; or (2) Any change in the stimulus situation will, through generalization decrement, reduce the secondary reinforcing properties of the previously neutral stimuli. Although the latter hypothesis seems the more reasonable, the former cannot be rejected at this time.

A further relation between deprivation conditions and secondary reinforcing effects is revealed by studies of latent learning, and of the incentive characteristics of inaccessible foods or sham-fed substances. The earlier studies in this group were designed to test the hypothesis that substances which were "irrelevant" to the established deprivation conditions would be ignored by subjects, that they would neither be primary nor secondary reinforcers, and indeed, that subjects would learn nothing about such substances. In a typical experiment, Grice (1948b) trained rats in a T maze under conditions of water deprivation, with pieces of food so scattered around the water cup that the animals had to walk on the food to get to the water. Later, when shifted from water deprivation to food deprivation, the animals showed only chance success in going to the side of the T maze where food had previously been located. Apparently the chunks of food had no reinforcing effects when the animals were not deprived of food.

Similar results were obtained in a study of the reinforcing properties of inaccessible food (Schlosberg & Pratt, 1956). Three groups of rats were run in a T maze, with one arm of the T containing a dish of food that could be seen and smelled, but not reached, while the other arm was empty. One group was always tested when deprived of food for 23 hours; a second group was run under food deprivation conditions for the first half of the experiment, and then switched to the satiation condition; while the third group started under satiated conditions and then was made hungry for the last half of the experiment. Each daily session consisted of one free and one forced trial, to keep the number of responses to each side equal. The results indicate clearly that the conditions of deprivation determine whether the inaccessible food will serve as an effective reinforcer: the animals switched from satiation to food deprivation showed an increase in the proportion of free runs to the food side, while those that changed from deprivation to satiation went in the opposite direction. Surprisingly, the group maintained on food deprivation conditions continued to run to the inaccessible food on the free trials throughout the course of the experiment, showing no significant extinction effects during 24 sessions. The authors conclude that the daily feeding experiences of the animals outside of the experimental situation provided further pairings of the sight and smell of the food with ingestion, thus maintaining the secondary reinforcing properties of the inaccessible food.

Were the hypothesis proposed above correct, we might predict that maintaining animals on an all-liquid diet having a markedly different taste and smell from the laboratory food used in the goal box would result eventually in the loss of such reinforcing properties of the inaccessible food. Or, if male animals previously experienced in mating were never allowed to make contact with otherwise receptive females placed in the goal box, we should predict that the males would run less and less frequently to the side where the females were placed. Results of the latter type have been observed (see, for example, Kagan,

1955), but the former experiment seems not to have been done.

Also in this vein are the studies which suggest that the reinforcing effects of sham feeding may extinguish with time if not occasionally paired with the placement of food into the stomach (see, for example, Hull et al., 1951). An alternative interpretation of these results is that the sham feeding, as conducted in these experiments, has punishing effects, and that if these were eliminated, the species-specific reactions to foods would provide reinforcing effects which would not extinguish. Of course, if this were found to be the case, "secondary" reinforcement would be a distinct misnomer. (See the discussion of sham-feeding, pp. 620, 627.)

Effects of schedules of reinforcement
One of the most potent variables the experimenter has at his disposal is the schedule of reinforcement, for by manipulating the schedule, he can modify the persistence with which a subject will respond and the pattern in which he responds. It is not surprising, therefore, that many investigations of secondary reinforcement should revolve around the schedule of primary reinforcement used during initial establishment of the secondary reinforcer, or around the schedule of presentations of the secondary reinforcer during tests of its efficacy. Wike (1966, pp. 427–428) has summarized a number of possible combinations of training and testing conditions, many of which have now been subjected to experimental analysis.

One of the most puzzling problems concerning secondary reinforcement is its apparent transience as it is studied in the laboratory. Inasmuch as intermittent reinforcement of a response rather consistently increases its resistance to extinction (see review by Lewis, 1960), it seems likely that intermittent pairing of the primary reinforcer with a neutral stimulus might produce a secondary reinforcer of greater persistence. This approach was taken by D. W. Zimmerman (1957), who used a buzzer as a signal preceding presentation of

water to water-deprived rats. Once the animals were making rapid approaches to the water when the buzzer sounded, he reduced the proportion of water presentations until (on the average) only 1 in 10 occurrences of the buzzer were followed by water. This procedure illustrates what is meant by "intermittency" during the training phase; Zimmerman also used intermittent procedures during his test of the utility of the buzzer as a reinforcer for a new response, bar pressing. During this test, the buzzer was presented for each of the first few bar presses, but thereafter only one bar press per minute was reinforced with the buzzer. The animals did show considerable persistence during the test sessions, but whether this was attributable to the intermittent pairing of the buzzer with water, or to the intermittent presentation of the buzzer during bar pressing remained unanswered.

A subsequent experiment by Fox and King (1961) included the control groups needed to answer these questions. They gave their rats initial training which consisted of 100 presentations of a small dipperful of sucrose solution, with each presentation of the dipper preceeded and accompanied by a buzzer sound. Half the animals received continuous reinforcement of the response of approaching the dipper when the buzzer sounded, while the other animals were trained with a gradually decreasing proportion of the buzzer trials on which the dipper was activated. In the end, this intermittent reinforcement group was receiving sucrose only after every tenth buzzer presentation and dipper approach. Overall, this initial training provided every rat with 100 buzzer-sucrose pairings, but in addition the animals in the intermittent group received an extra 100 buzzer presentations, which were not followed by sucrose.

For the test sessions, the animals were divided into 3 groups. A bar was inserted in the rats' box, and those in one group had the buzzer sounded whenever the bar was pressed; those in a second group had only one press per minute followed by the buzzer.

A third group, which never received presentations of the buzzer, provided a baseline against which to evaluate the possible secondary reinforcing effects of the buzzer. Animals in this no-buzzer control group made a significantly smaller number of responses than the others, showing that the training had indeed established the buzzer as a secondary reinforcer. Of the other animals, those trained and tested with intermittent reinforcement made the most responses during the test sessions, while the remaining groups were approximately equal in numbers of responses.

From these results, the investigators concluded that intermittent primary reinforcement produces increased resistance to extinction of secondary reinforcers only if the secondary reinforcer is intermittently presented during the test sessions. Furthermore, they also suggested that intermittent reinforcement during testing does not of itself contribute to increased resistance to extinction of secondary reinforcers.

There are, of course, many other ways to schedule the presentation of the primary and secondary reinforcers, and in light of the variety of behaviors generated by different reinforcement schedules, it would not be surprising if different forms of intermittency produced different results in tests of secondary reinforcement. In part, at least, this seems to be the case. For example, Stevenson and Reese (1962) compared the resistance to extinction of key pecking when half their pigeons had originally been trained with every tenth key peck reinforced with food, while the other animals had every peck reinforced. Each food presentation was accompanied by changes in the chamber light and the key light, and by the sound of the food hopper in operation. During the tests for secondary reinforcing effects of these stimuli, all food was eliminated from the hopper, and each training group was split into 3 groups for testing; one was provided no secondary reinforcement, another was provided secondary reinforcement for every tenth key peck, and the third was given secondary reinforcement for every peck. Their results indicate that intermittency during extinction testing increases the number of responses of birds trained with intermittent or with continuous reinforcement. Furthermore, from comparisons of each experimental group with the relevant control group that received no secondary reinforcement, they conclude that the most effective conditions are those in which the ratio of responses to reinforcements is higher in testing than in training.

Although these experiments lead to somewhat different conclusions concerning the effects of scheduling primary and secondary reinforcers, their results do agree in showing that secondary reinforcement effects are enhanced when intermittent scheduling is introduced. The differences between the studies probably should not be surprising, inasmuch as different reinforcement schedules, species, and test procedures were employed.

Valuable reviews of the effects of scheduling methods have been prepared by Kelleher (1966), by Kelleher and Gollub (1962), and by Wike (1966, especially pp. 427–436). Much of the original interest in scheduling revolved around the search for laboratory methods that might generate durable secondary reinforcers. But just suppose, suggests Wike (1966, p. 477) that it is the nature of all secondary reinforcers *not* to be durable: Would that not suggest a redirection of energies toward a study of conditions for best maintaining the efficacy of secondary reinforcers, possibly through frequent reconditioning and infrequent extinction tests? Of course, it probably never will be possible to conclude that secondary reinforcers are or are not durable, for durability is not an absolute quality. For laboratory study, however, intermittent schedules of primary and secondary reinforcement certainly increase the period over which the secondary reinforcers remain effective and allow us better opportunities to study their complexities.

What is the means through which intermittency increases the durability of secondary reinforcers? One possibility is suggested by the observation of D. W. Zimmerman (1959) that the persistence of the very first responses in the behavior chain controlled by the secondary reinforcing stimulus seemed to be the crucial factor. He had trained rats to run from a start box through a short alley to a goal box where food pellets had been placed. Just before the start box door was opened, a buzzer was sounded. After this training, intermittent reinforcement was introduced, with some of the runs being made to an empty goal box. Next, a bar was inserted in the start box and a press on the bar turned on the buzzer and opened the start box door. From this time onward, no food was ever placed in the goal box, and yet the animals continued to press the bar and scamper out of the start box time after time. Over the course of 10 or more daily sessions, each rat emitted thousands of bar presses. Thus, the stimuli from the buzzer and from the door being opened not only had been shown capable of reinforcing a new response (bar pressing), but also were able to maintain this response with remarkable persistence. During the tests, running in the alley gradually extinguished; eventually, many of the rats ran no more than a few inches into the alley. When picked up and replaced in the start box, however, they repeated the process of pressing the bar and darting through the opening door. Because the rats continued pressing the bar only while their response to the buzzer remained vigorous, Zimmerman concluded that the secondary reinforcing properties of stimuli could be attributed to the ability of the stimuli to cause the next response in the response chain.

One serious limitation to the theory that the secondary reinforcer always elicits (or otherwise controls) a response which previously was instrumental in bringing about the primary reinforcing event is found in free operant studies of secondary reinforcement. In these situations, there rarely is any evidence that a response (for example, an incipient approach to the food tray) consistently is made following the presentation of a secondary reinforcer. For example, in the

"chained schedule of reinforcement" procedure, a certain stimulus (such as a pattern of illumination on a pigeon's key) may always be present when pecks on the key finally are reinforced with food. Now a different pattern is projected on the key, and pecks in the presence of this second pattern eventually result in the reappearance of the first pattern. Observations of the response rates, and especially of the changes in the "local rates" immediately preceeding and following the presentations of the first pattern, are analyzed, and if the presentations of the first pattern have effects on key pecking similar to those to be expected if food had been presented, the first pattern is said to have secondary reinforcing properties.

The same logic as that used above can be applied to other types of reinforcement schedules (Kelleher, 1966). In all such situations it is clear that overt, incipient food-tray responses are not essential for the occurrence of secondary reinforcing effects. Of course, it could always be argued that prior training has extinguished the more gross features of such responses, but until some positive evidence is found that remnants of a response to a food tray are being made, it seems reasonable to conclude that the secondary reinforcing properties of stimuli are not uniquely associated with elicitation of the response which had been next in the original behavior chain.

Some problems of interpretation In almost every experiment in which secondary reinforcement is said to have been demonstrated, one or more alternative explanations for the results might have been offered. Overall, the reaction of most psychologists has been one of interest in these alternative hypotheses, but they persist in relying on the use of the secondary reinforcement concept. The main reasons for this reluctance to substitute other explanations probably lie in the facts that secondary reinforcement is an ubiquitous concept, whereas the alternatives tend to be relatively specific to a few sets of conditions, and that secondary reinforcement has an intuitive appeal, while some of the alternatives seem rather implausible from the point of view of common sense. A brief survey of some of the hypotheses will illustrate their major characteristics.

The "elicitation hypothesis" suggests that a previously neutral stimulus "merely" becomes a stimulus that elicits responses further along in the behavior chain. For example, if more responses are made during extinction when the "click" of the feeding mechanism is present than when extinction is tested in silence, is it possible that the click merely provides the stimuli in the presence of which the rat leaves the bar and approaches the cup? The rat whose pressing is greeted with silence does not receive the stimulus which controls leaving the bar, and so he stays there. In the past, of course, he has pressed only after returning from the food cup, so now he is less likely to make another response to the bar. This hypothesis sometimes has been attributed to Bugelski because he suggested (1956, p. 91 ff.) that secondary reinforcement need not be hypothesized to account for results like those found in his earlier (1938) study. Because Bugelski specifically disavowed any identification of his hypothesis with an interpretation based on a "discriminated stimulus" and leaned instead toward the view that the stimulus caused the subject to approach the cup, this interpretation has been called the "elicitation hypothesis." Yet the context in which he used the phrase "pattern of stimuli" when discussing the function of the feeder click suggests that the click might also be described as a discriminative stimulus for the next response in a previously established behavioral chain (see p. 672; and Zimmerman, 1959).

The "arousal hypothesis" suggests that a previously neutral stimulus arouses activity. There are two versions in which this hypothesis appears. In the first, the assumption is made that the area in which the subject is confined during the experiment is so restrictive of movements that any time his overall activity level increases, the response being measured (bar presses, for example) will of necessity increase. The second variation of the arousal hypothesis assumes that any increase in level of excitement or activity will give a proportional boost to all responses which the subject is likely to make in a given situation, and that if some response has been reinforced sufficiently often to become predominant, the introduction of the arousing stimulus will further increase the prepotency of that response. It is important to note that this hypothesis makes no assumptions about the temporal relations that must exist between the response and the arousing stimulus; hence, adequate controls may be obtained by noncontingent presentation of the stimulus to be tested for secondary reinforcing properties.

The "primary reinforcement" hypothesis argues that many supposedly neutral stimuli really are primary reinforcers, and hence are not really neutral. In many situations, it is possible to demonstrate the reinforcing effects of clicks, lights, snatches of song, momentary brightening of a TV picture tube, and countless other types of stimulation on the responses of birds, rodents, and primates of all varieties and ages. Because these effects cannot be attributed to prior pairing with other, known reinforcers, they must (by definition) be primary reinforcers.

Many of the "previously neutral" stimuli used in studies of secondary reinforcement are very similar to those mentioned above. An adequate control for the primary reinforcing value of the stimulus to be tested is afforded by a treatment that avoids any pairing of the stimulus with a known reinforcer and then presents the stimulus during the test session whenever the response occurs. The level of responding thus produced may be considered to indicate the primary reinforcing value of the supposedly neutral stimulus.

To some it may seem far fetched that the alternative explanations to secondary reinforcement described above can be given serious consideration. Yet we only need remind ourselves of the proven potency of "novel" stimuli as reinforcers to realize the need for incorporating appropriate controls in our experiments. Monkeys will respond with great persistence when the only reinforcer is an occasional chance to peek at the experimenter, an opportunity to manipulate gadgets, or other such "investigative behavior" (see review by Butler, 1965). Rats and mice will emit hundreds of responses when the only contingent event is a brief change in the illumination of their surroundings (see, for example, McCall, 1965). Similarly rats will run faster in an alleyway when the only modification of procedure is the introduction of a change in the patterns on the goal box walls (see, for example, Chapman & Levy, 1957). And humans—three months (Siqueland, 1970) of age, and possibly younger—are readily trained to make selected responses by the judicious use of visual or auditory stimuli. Thus, it is difficult to imagine a situation in which an investigator of secondary reinforcement could afford to ignore the potential primary reinforcing properties of his presumably neutral stimuli. (See reviews by Fowler, 1965, and Berlyne, 1967.)

Necessary and sufficient conditions for secondary reinforcement We have already noted that Pavlov observed the transfer of some of the properties of a conditioned stimulus to what was presumably a neutral stimulus when he presented the neutral stimulus and then, after a pause, introduced the conditioned stimulus. It has frequently been suggested, (for example, by Kimble, 1961), that this "pairing" of stimuli may be the crucial operation in establishing a stimulus as a secondary reinforcer. In what has often been considered a crucial test of the classical conditioning hypothesis, Schoenfeld, Antonitis, and Bersh (1950) demonstrated that merely turning on a light for 1 second after the rat had started to eat his pellet did not generate any more reinforcing effect for the light than was obtained from the control procedure in which the animals saw no light during training. It is well to note that 4 daily 1-hour extinction sessions were given between training and the tests for secondary reinforcing effects, and although it is possible that this interpolated experience had no differential influence on the secondary reinforcing properties of the light, a direct evaluation of the effects of this extinction procedure seems never to have been made.

Nevertheless, the assumption has been that *if* mere pairing of light and food were a sufficient condition for the establishment of secondary reinforcing properties, the study of Schoenfeld, Antonitis, and Bersh should have been able to demonstrate such effects. At about the same time, Dinsmoor (1950) published the results of an experiment in which the discriminative and the secondary reinforcing effects of a light were found to be about equally effective in maintaining responding during an extinction test. These two studies from the Columbia University laboratory did much to sway opinion away from a "mere pairing" hypothesis, and toward the conclusion that, although pairing may be necessary, it is not a sufficient condition for establishing secondary reinforcing properties.

The suggestion that seemed most in harmony with the available data was that discriminative and reinforcing properties of stimuli are indeed distinct, but that a stimulus must acquire discriminative properties for some response before it can be a secondary reinforcer for any response (see, for example,

Keller & Schoenfeld, 1950, pp. 236 ff.). This hypothesis has very specifically been limited to secondary reinforcers as observed in operant situations, and was not meant to be applied to Pavlovian "higher order conditioned stimuli." Yet even within this restriction, the present evidence suggests that, in principle, the hypothesis is wrong.

A crucial argument against the hypothesis is offered by an experiment in which mere pairing of a tone and a positive reinforcing stimulus proved sufficient to endow the tone with secondary reinforcing properties. Stein (1958) implanted chronic, bipolar electrodes in what he hoped would be positively reinforcing brain areas in 18 rats. After recovery from the surgery, each animal was allowed 6 1-hour sessions in a chamber containing 2 bars. Pressing one of the bars produced a 1-second tone; pressing the other bar had no programmed consequences. On the seventh to the tenth days, both bars were removed from the box, and each animal was given 100 pairings of tone and brain stimulation each

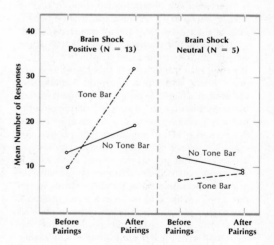

Figure 15.21. Mean number of responses for the 3 sessions before, and the 3 sessions after the tone had been paired with electrical brain stimulation. On the basis of a subsequent test of self-stimulation, the animals were divided into those which showed positive reinforcing effects of the stimulation and those which showed no such effect. (Stein, 1958.)

day. The next 3 days were test days for secondary reinforcing effects. Both bars were again placed in the chamber, and pressing the tone bar again caused delivery of a 1-second tone. Finally, to ascertain the effectiveness of the brain stimulation, each animal was given 1 hour in which he could stimulate his brain by pressing a lever.

The results are summarized in Figure 15.21. Note that the animals were split into two groups, depending on their reactions to the final, self-stimulation test. Thirteen were found to have clearly positive reactions to the electrical stimulation (self-stimulating 9 times a minute or more) whereas 5 made less than 1 response a minute and presumably had neutral or aversive reactions to the stimulation. Of those that were positively reinforced by the stimulation, the procedure of pairing tone and stimulation clearly produced secondary reinforcing effects for the tone, while such effects were absent for the nonpositive animals. Similar results under quite different conditions have been reported by Knott and Clayton (1966).

These are neither exceptionally strong effects, nor are they inevitably obtained (see Seward, Uyeda, & Olds, 1959; Mogenson, 1965). Furthermore, the fact that the experimenter has programmed a neutral and a positively reinforcing stimulus without requiring the subject to make a response before onset of the reinforcer does not insure that some response might not creep in and become established through the accidental contingency of the reinforcer and the response. Such "superstitious" behaviors (Morse & Skinner, 1957) in situations like the one employed by Stein (1958) have been observed (Pliskoff, Hawkins, & Wright, 1964), but they seem to be the exception rather than the rule. So we are left with the general conclusion that mere pairing of a stimulus with a reinforcer probably is a sufficient condition to establish the secondary reinforcing properties, although prior establishment of the stimulus as a discriminative stimulus usually will produce more persisting effects. (For a discussion of

the problems superstitious behavior may present to the experimenter, see Herrnstein, 1966.)

Secondary reinforcing effects interpreted as information processes The hypothesis that a secondary reinforcing stimulus must have acquired discriminative stimulus properties implies that it also conveys information about the forthcoming appearance of the primary reinforcer, inasmuch as a discriminative stimulus gains control over a response through the correlations: discriminative stimulus–response–reinforcement; other stimulus set–response–nonreinforcement. Egger and Miller (1962) gave this supposition a more precise statement, namely, "a necessary condition for establishing any stimulus as a secondary reinforcer is that the stimulus provide information about the occurrence of primary reinforcement" and, if a situation includes more than one stimulus predicting primary

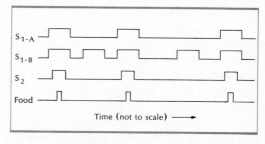

Figure 15.22. Stimulus arrangements used in studying information value and secondary reinforcement. Animals in both Groups A and B always received Stimulus 2 whenever a food pellet was delivered. For Group A, Stimulus 1-A was always given before, during, and after Stimulus 2; because Stimulus 2 never provided any information that was not already provided by Stimulus 1-A, it was said to be redundant and predicted to be low in secondary reinforcement value. For Group B, Stimulus 1-B also enveloped Stimulus 2, but because Stimulus 2 always preceded food pellet delivery while Stimulus 1-B sometimes occurred in the absence of food, Stimulus 2 provided information not carried by Stimulus 1-B and so was predicted to be the better secondary reinforcer. (After Egger & Miller, 1962.)

reinforcement, "the more informative stimulus will be the more effective secondary reinforcer" (p. 97). An "informative stimulus" was assumed to be one which predicted accurately that a response would be followed by a reinforcing stimulus, and which did not have its information value assimilated by some other stimulus. This latter characteristic is difficult to predict: It depends not just on degree of redundancy, but on attentional and perceptual factors. However, for purposes of the experiment, Egger and Miller assumed that a stimulus which always occurred within the temporal bounds of another stimulus (see Figure 15.22) should acquire little or no secondary reinforcing strength because its information value would be assimilated.

Two groups of rats were trained to press a bar under conditions in which every fourth press caused a pellet of food to be dropped into a nearby food cup. The bar was then removed from the chamber, and for the next 5 days, each animal was exposed to presentations of a flashing light, a tone, and food. Animals in Group A always had a 2-second presentation of Stimulus 1 (for example, the light) completely overlapping every 1.5-second presentation of Stimulus 2 (for example, the tone); both of these stimuli overlapped the delivery of the food pellet. The animals in Group B received exactly the same treatment except that they had extra presentations of Stimulus 1 aperiodically interspersed amongst the other stimuli. In other words, Stimulus 1 was not completely reliable as a predictor of food for Group B, while Stimulus 2 was always a dependable indicator that food was coming. For Group A, Stimulus 2 was redundant, carrying no information not already given by Stimulus 1. Over-all, Stimulus 1 was followed by food all of the time for Group A and 55 percent of the time for Group B; Stimulus 2 was always followed by food for both groups.

After the fifth day of presenting stimuli, the bars were reinserted in the chambers; every animal was allowed a short period of food-reinforced responding, and then a 10-minute extinction period (no food, no stim-

TABLE 15.4 MEAN NUMBER OF RESPONSES DURING TWO 25-MINUTE SESSIONS OF SECONDARY REINFORCEMENT TESTING.[a]

| | Reinforcing stimulus | |
Group	Stimulus 1	Stimulus 2
A	115.1	65.8
B	76.1	82.6

[a] After Egger & Miller (1962).

uli) followed. As soon as the 10 minutes had passed, a 25-minute test period was begun, during which the stimulus to be tested for secondary reinforcing effects was delivered for 1 second after every third bar press. The next day, exactly the same procedure was repeated, except the other stimulus was tested. Half the animals were tested first with Stimulus 1, and half with Stimulus 2; half of each group had flashing light for Stimulus 1 and tone for Stimulus 2, and half had the opposite arrangement.

The results (see Table 15.4) indicate that a stimulus which cannot be used as a dependable predictor of food (such as Stimulus 1-B) is a less potent secondary reinforcer than the more dependable predictor (Stimulus 1-A). Furthermore, the results suggest that "enclosing" a stimulus within the temporal bounds of another stimulus (as Stimulus 2 is encompassed by Stimulus 1 for Group A) reduces the secondary reinforcing effects that the enveloped stimulus can acquire.

Such results do not necessarily weaken the discriminative-stimulus hypothesis, for the extent to which a stimulus gains control over bar pressing would supposedly be influenced by the same factors that influence its "information value." Nor do they negate our tentative conclusion that merely pairing stimuli is a sufficient condition for establishing secondary reinforcing effects. Indeed, Egger and Miller (1963) noted in a subsequent experiment that a simple pairing of a stimulus with food produced secondary reinforcing effects as strong as those acquired by a stimulus specifically positioned to gain maximum information value.

Recent studies (Ayres, 1966; Seligman,

1966) in which the Egger-Miller hypothesis has been tested in conditioned suppression situations have found that redundant stimuli do acquire significant new properties. In the conditioned suppression procedure (see pp. 712–717), a steady baseline of behavior is first established, usually by providing intermittent positive reinforcement to the subject. Then a neutral stimulus is paired with an aversive stimulus (such as electric shock), and the extent to which the baseline behavior is suppressed when the previously neutral stimulus is presented is used as an index of acquired aversiveness. Clearly, redundant stimuli do acquire such properties, although "informative" stimuli may be even more effective. Such results would seem to place severe restrictions on the Egger-Miller hypothesis, at least as it currently is formulated.

For some considerations of the applicability of secondary reinforcement to complex problems of human behavior, see Skinner's (1953) discussion of "generalized reinforcers" and Hill's (1968) survey of the uses made of the concept of secondary reinforcement by various theorists.

DELAY OF REINFORCEMENT

"Delay of reinforcement" is a term that refers to the interval of time between the occurrence of a response and the delivery of its reinforcing stimulus. In each situation some criterion must be set which will define the moment of occurrence of the response. Where simple locomotor responses in an alleyway are studied, the moment the subject enters the goal box (as measured by depression of a movable floor or by interruption of a photocell beam) is usually taken as "the" instant that the instrumental response occurs, even though the movements involved are much the same as others which had been emitted earlier. In other cases, specification of the "correct" response may be quite simple: Movement of a bar or key sufficient to close a switch defines the response, and in discrimination situations it is only necessary to add the requirement that such switch

closures occur in the presence of certain stimulus conditions.

All of the experiments which properly belong in this section employ instrumental (Thorndikian, operant) procedures. There is no strictly analogous operation in classical (Pavlovian, respondent) conditioning, although the temporal intervals between the conditioned and the unconditioned stimulus, or between the conditioned stimulus and the occurrence of the response, are sometimes said to be akin to delay of reinforcement. There are two reasons why it does not seem proper to include in the same category the manipulation of temporal factors in the classical and the operant procedures: (1) The hallmark of classical conditioning is the delivery of two stimuli (the conditioned and the unconditioned stimuli) without regard to the behavior of the organism, while the crucial interval in the procedure involving a delay of reinforcement is that which occurs between the execution of the response and the presentation of a reinforcing stimulus. "Reinforcement" in the classical situation means the paired presentation of the conditioned and the unconditioned stimuli, and the onset of the latter usually is timed with respect to the former, and not with regard to any characteristic of the response in the situation. Thus, in the usual sense, there can be no "delay of reinforcement" in the classical conditioning situation. (2) The generally different form of the functional relations obtained in operant and in classical situations, when these temporal factors are varied, increases our suspicions that these are quite different problems. In operant situations, the effect of delay of reinforcement is always to slow acquisition; in classical conditioning situations, there is some temporal interval between the onsets of the conditioned and unconditioned stimuli which is optimal in each situation, and the most rapid acquisition is never obtained if there is no delay between the onsets of these two stimuli. Thus, it is clear that delay of reinforcement is a problem peculiar to operant situations.

There appear to be two major effects of

imposing delays of reinforcement during original training: acquisition is retarded, while subsequent retention *may be* enhanced. The effects on acquisition have received the greater amount of attention from experimenters, and there is rather good agreement among studies that utilized quite diverse procedures. At the empirical level, at least, these effects of delay of reinforcement can be said to be "well understood." In contrast, studies of the effects of delayed reinforcement during retention tests have been less consistent in their findings, although some patterns are beginning to emerge from the many experiments that have been reported in the last decade. Although both types of problem sometimes have been investigated within the same experiment, we shall consider the problems as if they were quite separate.

Acquisition as a Function of Delay of Reinforcement

The roots of this problem reach back to the earliest systematic studies of simple learning in the American laboratories. Thorndike's first experiments (1898, 1911) led him to an appreciation of the role of the reinforcing stimulus in simple learning, which he summarized in his Law of Effect[24] (see also p. 690). Watson (1917) reasoned that a crucial test of the Law of Effect could be obtained by placing a delay interval between the occurrence of the correct response and the occurrence of the "satisfying state of affairs." He conducted an experiment in which laboratory rats were required to dig through sawdust to obtain entry into a compartment from which they could reach a food container. Half of the animals were allowed to eat as soon as they reached the food; the other half found a per-

forated lid on top of the food cup, and were not allowed access to the food until 30 seconds after they had reached the cup.[25] The "correct response" was, in Watson's analysis, the complex act of digging through the sawdust and finding the opening into the enclosure. If Thorndike were correct in his identification of the "satisfying state of affairs" as the crucial factor in "stamping in" the correct response, the occurrence of a great many other acts between the correct response and the attainment of the food by the delay group should impede their acquisition of the task. At least, so reasoned Watson, and when he found the two groups to be similar in their acquisition of the digging response, he concluded that the Law of Effect must be invalid.

Other investigators (Simmons, 1924; Warden & Haas, 1927; Hamilton, 1929; Roberts, 1930) developed less complex behavioral situations in which "the correct response" could be specified more easily than in Watson's problem box. During this time, the T maze gradually replaced the older, multiple-unit maze as the apparatus of choice in many laboratories. When applied to the problem of delay of reinforcement, the T maze allowed the experimenter to obtain both time scores and error scores in a relatively simple situation in which the time interval between the correct turn at the choice point and food reinforcement could be manipulated quite easily. Hamilton (nee Haas) concluded that the relative lack of effect of delay that she and Warden had obtained in their earlier (1927) study might have been a result of delaying the delivery of food by holding the animal in the goal box, where cues associated with prior feedings were no doubt available to him. She therefore introduced into the T maze a set of compartments through which the animal had to pass to reach the goal box. When separate groups of animals were delayed from 0 seconds to 7 minutes in such compartments, de-

---

[24] Thorndike's early statement of the Law of Effect emphasized the "stamping in" of stimulus-response connections when the response was followed by a "satisfying state of affairs," and a "stamping out" when an "annoying state of affairs" followed the response. "Satisfiers" and "annoyers" were defined behaviorally as that which the animal would approach and with which he would maximize contact or that which he would avoid and with which he would minimize contact.

[25] We now know that the inaccessible food probably was immediately effective as a reinforcer. See the discussion of the experiment by Schlosberg and Pratt (1956) on page 669.

creased proficiency was found for all the delay groups. Wolfe (1934) utilized the same technique in studying the acquisition of a black–white discrimination, where the animal had to turn sometimes to the right, and sometimes to the left. Here the effects of delays were even more marked, yet some learning occurred even when delays as long as 20 minutes were imposed.

The fact that delaying the animal briefly in the delay compartments hindered learning was no great surprise, but that the rat could learn *anything* when a delay of several minutes was imposed suggested to some theorists (for example, Tolman, 1932, p. 43) that all animals, regardless of the length of the delay, knew equally well where the food was to be found but that the delayed presentation of food merely decreased the "demand" for the food. Others (Hull, 1932, p. 140) concluded that forms of reinforcement other than those provided by the food itself must have been present in the apparatus, and especially in the delay compartments from which the animal was allowed to escape directly to food. A test of this hypothesis seemed to require the elimination of both the delay compartments and a goal box in which feeding always occurs. Perin (1943) adapted the apparatus devised by Skinner (1938) for the study of this problem. He placed his rat in a cubical enclosure into which a small bar could be inserted. If, in his movements in the vicinity of the bar, the animal happened to depress it sufficiently to close a silent switch, a food pellet was dropped into a cup within reach of the animal. Separate groups of animals were trained, either being given reinforcement immediately or after delays of 2, 5, 10, or 30 seconds between depression of the bar and delivery of the pellet. Immediately after the bar was depressed, Perin withdrew it from the chamber. Thus, for animals receiving delays in the delivery of food, there was no possibility that subsequent bar-pressing responses might possibly be made just as the pellet finally arrived. This procedure precludes the use of error scores or response rates, but is well

suited to the measurement of the time required for the animal to press the bar after it has been presented. All groups showed orderly changes in this latency during training; the most rapid decrease across trials occurred in the immediate reinforcement group, while a less rapid decrease occurred for the groups delayed 2, 5, or 10 seconds. However, the 30-second delay group showed a consistent *increase* in latency across trials, suggesting that they were learning to make some response other than depression of the bar when it was presented.

Based largely on the results obtained by Perin, Hull (1943) suggested that delays longer than 30 seconds would probably result in no learning of "the" reinforced response, and that those improvements in performance that were observed following the longer delays in earlier experiments, probably were a result of immediate secondary reinforcement augmenting the delayed primary reinforcement. Spence (1947) pushed this line of reasoning one step further: he suggested that wherever learning occurs with delay of reinforcement, there must be immediate "secondary reinforcement" present.

It is easy to imagine that stimuli in the delay compartments of a T maze might acquire secondary (or conditioned) reinforcing properties, for they are consistently followed by entry into the goal box and eating. But what might the source of such secondary reinforcement be in Perin's apparatus, in which the animal always was within the same enclosure? Here, all of the stimuli from the apparatus would seem to be associated both with occasional feeding and with more frequent periods of nonreinforcement. Spence (1947) and Grice (1948a) suggested that the stimuli resulting from the animal's own pressing the bar might be one class of stimuli which consistently precede feeding and which thus might acquire reinforcing properties. Were this the case, an experiment in which no one response consistently preceded reinforcement might eliminate even this last set of potential secondary reinforcing stimuli and thus test

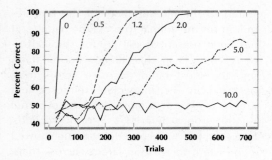

Figure 15.23. Learning curves for each of the 6 groups trained with various delays of reinforcement. The number of trials required to reach 75 percent correct was used to construct the gradient in Figure 15.24. (After Grice, 1948a.)

Spence's hypothesis that no learning at all would occur if even the slightest delay were imposed between the correct response and the delivery of the reinforcing stimulus. To test this hypothesis, Grice (1948a) utilized a black-white discrimination with the correct response requiring a left turn on some trials and a right turn on others. Separate groups of rats were delayed from 0.5 to 10.0 seconds

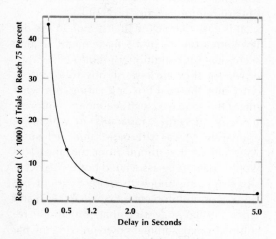

Figure 15.24. Rate of learning as a function of delay of reinforcement. The reciprocal × 1000 of the number of trials to reach the level of 75 percent correct choices is plotted against the time delay. Experimental values are represented by black dots and the smooth curve is fitted to these data. (After Grice, 1948a.)

with the control group receiving immediate reinforcement. The average rate of improvement was inversely related to the length of the interval, and most animals in the 10-second group never reached the performance criterion. The more important finding, however, was the very marked effect of even so short a delay as 0.5 seconds. The average learning curve for each of the groups is shown in Figure 15.23; the number of trials required to reach the 75 percent correct point in training provides the points through which the gradient in Figure 15.24 is drawn.

If all sources of secondary reinforcement had been eliminated, this gradient should have dropped to zero as soon as any delay was introduced. That it did not suggests that some further sources of secondary reinforcement were present. For example, some differential response patterns may have been developed as animals ran through the area where the discriminative stimuli were displayed. Thus, a rat fed shortly after running through a white compartment might come to make eating responses when he later comes to white areas again (see p. 621). These "fractional antedating goal reactions" (Hull, 1952) usually are assumed to have stimulus consequences, and thus these response-produced stimuli could, through their pairing with eating, become the immediate secondary reinforcing stimuli that might be needed to "explain" Grice's results. Fortunately, this cumbersome hypothesis does not seem necessary because Grice's results can be replicated in situations using electrical brain stimulation as the reinforcer (see, for example, Keesey, 1964a; Culbertson, 1970), where the subject makes no overt consummatory responses and the "antedating goal reaction" hypothesis seems superfluous. Furthermore, about the same delay-of-reinforcement gradient is found with delayed brain stimulation as with food reinforcement (Keesey, 1964a). These facts suggest the existence of some finite period during which prior responses can be reinforced without a chain of behavior to bridge the time interval (that is, a "pure" delay of reinforcement process).[26]

For the most part, interpretations of delayed reinforcement effects have clustered around two viewpoints which, for convenience, may be called "motivational" and "associational." As we have noted, Tolman (1932) was an early proponent of the motivational point of view, and in a broad sense, the position to which Spence (1956) came was quite similar, for both assumed that delayed reinforcement reduced the incentive value of the reinforcing stimuli.

"Associational" interpretations are so named because they assume that delayed reinforcement primarily affects what the organism learns to do—and almost all psychologists believe that "learning" is an associational process. Hull's (1943) assumption that the stimulus-response unit received smaller increments in habit strength from delayed than from immediate reinforcement is one example of the associative viewpoint (see also Capaldi, 1967). A quite different variety of associational interpretation is seen in the analysis of delayed reinforcement effects given by Skinner (1938). No spread of reinforcing effects to responses occurring prior to the reinforced response is assumed; whatever response is occurring at the moment the reinforcing stimulus appears is made more likely to reoccur; but prior responses (such as "the correct response" in a delayed reinforcement experiment) can increase in probability of reoccurrence if they are part of a chain of responses of which the reinforced response is the last unit.

This latter interpretation affords a very reasonable explanation for such phenomena as the response patterns which emerge after exposure to a fixed ratio reinforcement schedule (where every nth response is reinforced). Reinforcement is "delayed" in the

sense that the early responses are themselves not reinforced. However, in the initial training sessions individual responses are usually reinforced, and the first imposition of a ratio requirement usually involves so small an increase in the required number of responses between reinforcements that the ratio is emitted without any great pauses between responses, so that one of the responses is soon reinforced. As the ratio requirement is increased, the same process is repeated, so that we might think of the response class being reinforced as "respond after responding." When reinforcement does occur, it is this response unit that is immediately reinforced, and not just the last member of the chain.

The response chains in such scheduled reinforcement procedures usually are homogeneous, and the similarity of the responses early in the chain to the response actually reinforced makes secondary reinforcement a plausible explanation for the persistence of responses far removed in time from the reinforced response. By contrast, if heterogeneous response chains are involved, it usually is necessary to train the subject to make the last (that is, the reinforced) response first, and then build the chain toward the first response.[27] In this process, it is assumed that each response produces stimuli which are both the discriminative stimuli for the next response, and the secondary reinforcing stimuli for the prior response, thus "explaining" how responding can continue to exist in strength when reinforcement is delayed to the end of the chain. This assumption is consistent with widely accepted notions of secondary reinforcement, and the fact that new responses can be added to the distal end of the chain is independent evidence that the response more proximal to the reinforced

---

[26] The results also remind us that even the rat can retain information over a period of a few seconds and suggest that this admirable little creature may be quite comparable to man in holding information about cues and responses in his "short-term memory."

[27] Although this backward order of training organisms to make heterogeneous chains of responses is the only "sensible" procedure from the point of view of contemporary reinforcement theory, it should be realized that systematic comparisons with other procedures (such as starting training with the first response in the chain) seem not to have been published.

response does indeed produce secondary reinforcing effects.

The same reasoning that is applied to the persistence of response chains also is frequently offered as an explanation for the acquisition of responses in delayed reinforcement situations. We mentioned above Spence's (1947) hypothesis that secondary reinforcing stimuli are produced by the responses which occur consistently prior to reinforcement, which is basically the same interpretation as that just discussed for heterogeneous and homogeneous chaining.

To illustrate the problems involved in unraveling behavior in such delayed reinforcement situations, and to see how the hypothesis that proposes that secondary reinforcement is response-produced might be applied, let us trace the sequence of events in a typical delayed reinforcement discrimination experiment (Culbertson, 1970). The major features of the animal's chamber are shown in Figure 15.25.[28] Through a sequence of pretraining procedures the animal has been taught to run to the rear of the chamber whenever the center panel light is turned on. A light beam is located at the rear of the chamber which, when broken by the animal, causes the center panel light to go out and the key lights to be illuminated. If the "correct" (for example, the brighter) key is pressed, the chamber is immediately darkened, and the reinforcement is then delivered after the appropriate delay interval. Pressing the incorrect key produces an immediate blackout, but no reinforcement. Following a fixed period of darkness, the sequence again begins when the center panel light is turned on. In this manner, the start of each trial is under the control of the animal. Therefore, some indication of the incentive value of the reinforcing conditions may be obtained from the rate at which the animal sets up the trials by going to the rear of the chamber, and the speed with which he runs from there to the keys when they are illuminated. The speeds of these

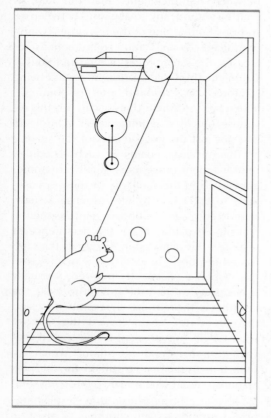

Figure 15.25. A typical animal chamber arranged for 2-choice discrimination problems. On the further wall are 2 response keys and a panel light used to indicate that the next trial may be initiated. Trials begin when the animal breaks the light beam falling on the photocell at the end of the chamber, thus insuring that he always is at least that far from the response keys at the start of each trial. Bars or panels may be substituted for the response keys, and a food cup or liquid dipper may be inserted if those reinforcers are to be used. In this illustration, the animal is connected by chronically implanted electrodes, a flexible lead, and an overhead swivel to a circuit that provides electrical stimulation of the brain.

[28] In this case, reinforcement is provided by electrical stimulation of the brain, delivered to the electrode through the flexible cable from the swivel mounted on the chamber roof. The insertion of a dipper or food cup adapts such chambers for use with liquid or solid foods. Electrical brain stimulation is especially convenient for delay of reinforcement experiments, for the delay interval can be controlled quite precisely, and a true zero-delay condition can be included in the design. However, the same general problems of analysis exist for all types of reinforcing stimuli.

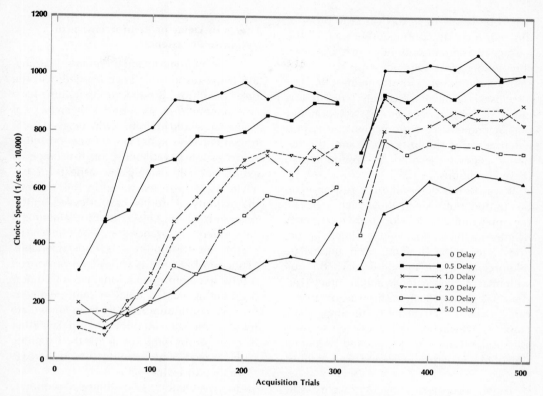

Figure 15.26. The average choice speeds for each of 6 different groups trained with various delays of reinforcement. The break in the curves occurs between Day 1 and Day 2 of the training procedure. Choice speed was measured from the moment the discriminative stimuli appeared on the response keys until the animal displaced one of the keys. (From Culbertson, 1968.)

responses typically are inversely related to the duration of the delay intervals. A set of such data from Culbertson's (1968) experiment is shown in Figure 15.26.

What are the specific responses that are learned by animals in the delayed reinforcement groups? We might imagine a trial on which an animal presses the correct key, turns to his left, and rears up on his hind legs; if, at that moment, reinforcement is delivered, it is this last response (rearing) which the subject will most likely make again, not the pressing of the key in the presence of the positive discriminative stimulus. Of course, reinforcement of such "incorrect" responses as rearing occurs because the delay interval had been initiated by the correct response, and this same sequence of responses might

be (adventitiously) reinforced a few times and thus become more and more frequent. Some animals do indeed show such "superstitious" conditioning (Skinner, 1948), but the majority of animals in delayed reinforcement studies do not show any recognizable, regular pattern of behavior during the delay interval, nor do the most rapid learners show any greater incidence of superstitious behavior than the slower learners. Clearly, bridging the time gap with an overt response chain is not essential to successful performance in discrimination situations utilizing delayed reinforcement. But suppose we deliberately reinforced a chain of responses such as *press the brighter key, turn to the left,* and *stand up.* Would such an animal show the typical delay of reinforcement effects? Almost certainly, the answer would be "no," for in this case the onset of the reinforcer is contingent not upon the passage of a certain amount of time, but upon completion of a specific sequence of responses. Moreover, reinforcement of that last response is given immediately. Thus this is not a delayed reinforcement situation but one of immediate reinforcement of a short heterogeneous response chain, and the behavior generated would be appropriate to these conditions.

If we do not determine the responses to be emitted, but instead allow each organism the opportunity to develop its own sequence by introducing gradually increasing delay periods after initial training with immediate reinforcement, the response may continue with unabated persistence and accuracy (Ferster, 1953; Dews, 1960). In this way, organisms can "adapt to" gradually increasing delays. However, if even brief delays of a few seconds are suddenly introduced, marked deterioration of behavior results (for example, Skinner, 1938).

These observations suggest that it is the absence of a regularly reinforced response or a sequence of responses which is at least in part responsible for the slow acquisition and low response rates characteristically obtained with delayed reinforcement conditions (Grice, 1948a, pp. 10-11). At the same time, it also seems that learning can occur with brief delays in the absence of such "mediating" response chains, and that the presence of overt, easily recognizable "superstitious" response chains in delayed reinforcement situations is no guarantee of superior performance. Indeed, the relatively motionless organism may have developed a pattern of responses that is just as efficient as the sequence which is more easily observed by the experimenter![29]

[29] We do not wish to preclude the possibility that delay intervals may be bridged by "observing behavior" in which the organism attends to sequences of stimuli or by other activities that do not necessarily involve measurable responses. However, at the present there is a distinct lack of evidence for such mechanisms in delayed reinforcement situations.

Effects of Delay of Reinforcement on Response Persistence

Delay of reinforcement retards learning. But if the response is once learned, will the delay conditions present during training have any influence on subsequent behavior? For example, would training with delayed reinforcement have systematic effects on retention, response variability, or resistance to extinction? Surprisingly few aspects of behavior have been examined in this context; the majority of studies have focused on the relation between delayed reinforcement and subsequent resistance to extinction. The reason for this interest is understandable: Extinction behavior is very much prolonged if reinforcement is occasionally omitted during training, and if delayed reinforcements are on a continuum running from immediate reinforcement to infinitely long delays (that is, omission of reinforcement), then training with delayed reinforcement should increase resistance to extinction.

To investigate this possibility, a frequently used experimental design has assigned subjects to separate groups and trained each group with a different delay of reinforcement before introducing the extinction test. However, this design introduces a familiar dilemma: If equal amounts of training have been given all groups, their proficiency at the end of training will be negatively correlated with the durations of delays with which they were trained, and if they do not start extinction with the same proficiency, relative resistance to extinction cannot be evaluated. On the other hand, if a "constant effect" strategy is followed, that is, if every subject is allowed to continue training until all have reached the same proficiency, the unequal amounts of training will produce different degrees of resistance to extinction and thus preclude an unambiguous test of the effects of delayed reinforcement.

Two means of circumventing this dilemma have been devised. In one, the initial training with delayed reinforcement has been followed by a period during which all animals were given immediate reinforcement; then the extinction procedure is introduced (see, for example, Sgro & Weinstock, 1963). Even after this training, the groups may enter the extinction period at different levels of proficiency, making it difficult to evaluate the effects of omission of reinforcement. As an alternative procedure, we might allow sufficient training for all groups to reach the same level of proficiency before extinction is introduced. Where this method has been employed (see Sgro, Dyal, & Anastasio, 1967; Culbertson, 1968) no differences in resistance to extinction appear. Apparently the extra training necessary to allow the groups trained with delayed reinforcement to catch up to those trained with immediate reinforcement eliminates whatever differences might result from the similarity of training and extinction conditions for the subjects trained with delayed reinforcement.

The most obvious way to design a study to investigate the effects of delayed reinforcement on resistance to extinction is to assign each subject to a specific delay and conduct all of his training with this fixed delay interval. As we have seen, this type of experiment does not yield consistent evidence that delay of reinforcement increases resistance to extinction. An alternative design was suggested by the hypothesis that partial reinforcement increases resistance to extinction because the subject cannot discriminate training from extinction conditions. If this hypothesis is correct, and if delayed reinforcement is on a continuum with extinction, then partial delay of reinforcement during training should also make the transition to extinction conditions difficult to discriminate and thus increase persistence of responding during extinction periods. This reasoning was tested by Crum, Brown, and Bitterman (1951) in a study in which one group of rats always received immediate food reinforcement at the end of a short alley, while another group received

immediate reinforcement on half the trials and received the food after a 30-second delay in the goal box on the other trials. The 50-percent delay group ran significantly faster during extinction than the subjects that were immediately reinforced, thus confirming the original prediction. Similar results have been reported for both simple locomotor responses (see, for example, Scott & Wike, 1956) and for discrimination learning (Kintsch & Wike, 1957). However, several other experiments using similar procedures have not shown any significant increase in resistance to extinction that can be attributed to delayed reinforcement during training (see, for example, Wike & Kintsch, 1959; Wike & Remple, 1959). A review of the relevant literature led Renner (1964) to conclude that delays of 30 seconds or more probably were necessary if an increase in resistance to extinction is to be seen. Almost certainly such values would depend upon the situation in which they are applied, and we should not assume that 30 seconds represents a delay of special significance for behavior. Indeed, as we point out below, at least one relevant study (Pubols, 1958) found no further difference in extinction behavior once delays as long as 4 seconds had been introduced. At present, it does not seem possible to give a clear description of the variables which are crucial in producing enhanced resistance to extinction through manipulation of delay of reinforcement.

It is possible, of course, that the enhanced resistance to extinction is a function of the variability introduced into the training conditions by partial delay of reinforcement, for variability per se could also make more difficult the discrimination of a transition from training to extinction. Variable delayed reinforcement (as contrasted with partial delayed reinforcement procedures) has been examined in several experiments, again with inconsistent results. For example, Wike and Kintsch (1959) postponed the presentation of the reinforcer for 10, 20, or 30 seconds, in a random order, thus enhancing the unpredictable nature of the training situation. They found no increased resistance to extinction from this procedure, whereas Logan, Beier, and Kinkaid (1956) found that varying delay of reinforcement between 1 and 30 seconds did increase resistance to extinction. This literature is confounded by the great variety of procedures employed during pretraining, training, and extinction, and no clear picture has yet emerged from the welter of results. Certainly it is not safe to conclude that either delay per se, or the variability introduced by partial or varied delay procedures, will increase resistance to extinction.

Resistance to reversal training has also been used as an index of response persistence. Here the typical design involves training on an initial discrimination, with different groups of animals receiving different reinforcement conditions. The discrimination is then reversed, so that responses to what had been the positive stimulus are now nonreinforced; the animal continues in extinction until the first response is made to the formerly negative stimulus, when reinforcement is delivered. Pubols (1958) trained animals in a simple position discrimination, using delays of 2, 4, 8, or 16 seconds; the same delays were used during reversal training, with some animals from each of the original groups being assigned to each of the reversal groups. The results indicate that the most rapid reversal was made by animals trained with the shortest delay of reinforcement (2 seconds). A greater number of responses to the formerly correct side before the first reversal, and subsequent slower learning of the reversed discrimination problem, was found for all groups trained with the longer delays of reinforcement. There have been some failures to confirm this where slightly different procedures have been used (see Renner, 1965a,b), and it is not clear why delayed reinforcement influences resistance to reversal of discrimination in only some experiments.

Perhaps the requirement by Pubols of a specific response to escape from the delay compartment and gain access to the goal box was a crucial feature of the procedure, for this represents one way in which the procedure could have generated quite different behaviors in the animals delayed for only 2 seconds and those delayed 4 seconds or more. The delay interval was timed from the moment the animals entered the delay chamber, and at the end of the interval the door leading to the goal box was unlocked but not opened. It then was left to the rat to push his way into the goal box. Two seconds probably represents the minimum delay interval that could be handled with reliability in such a situation, and probably did little more than force a break in the locomotion of the rat. Delays of 4 or more seconds might easily provide opportunities for distinctive behaviors to occur and be reinforced, and these might later provide a source of secondary reinforcement during extinction. These speculations are suggested by the fact that neither enhanced resistance to extinction nor increased perseveration of responding to the formerly correct stimulus was found after training with delayed brain stimulation reinforcement (Culbertson, 1968). Use of this reinforcer not only allows the inclusion of a true zero delay baseline group, but it also allows the reinforcer to be delivered at the end of programmed delay intervals without requiring any special response of the animal and without allowing uncontrolled intervals to be added to the end of the delay as a function of the behavior of the animal on that trial. That no enhancement is found when delays of brain stimulation reinforcement are programmed suggests the reasonable conclusion that delay per se may have no effects on resistance to extinction but that the responses which occur during delays may be capable of modifying subsequent response persistence. The importance of the responses which occur immediately after the criterional response (the one on which reinforcement is contingent, and which initiates the delay interval) is emphasized also by the studies which manipulate knowledge of results and other forms of informational feedback.

Delayed Knowledge of Results

At first glance, it might appear self-evident that knowledge of the accuracy of our responses should be reinforcing, and that delays in presentation of this knowledge (or "informational feedback") would have the effects now so well documented in delayed reinforcement experiments. That the situations are not exactly the same was first suggested after a considerable number of experiments failed to reveal any significant effects of delayed knowledge of results on acquisition of such skills as target pursuit, or on verbal rote learning tasks like paired associate learning.

Two general classes of procedure seem to be subsumed under the general heading of "delayed knowledge of results." In the first case, the major (and sometimes, the only) source of information about the accuracy of each response is controlled by the experimenter, with some subjects being given immediate feedback while others receive the information after various delays. For example, a subject may be given lessons on a musical instrument and the auditory feedback delayed for a few tenths of a second. If he has not had extensive experience with this instrument, or if it is one which requires continuous auditory monitoring of the output (such as the violin) the information about the adequacy of each response which can come through nonauditory channels (such as visual, tactual, or kinesthetic) is minimal. Under these conditions, novices show limited or no improvement with practice, and subjects with considerable experience frequently find the situation so disturbing that they refuse to continue the experiment (Smith, 1966). The effects may be even more marked than those produced by delayed feedback of one's own voice, where it is possible for some subjects to speak "without listening" and thus avoid the disruptive influences of the feedback (see Waters, 1968).

In contrast to the very marked effects of delayed informational feedback when the experimenter has control over most or all of the sources of feedback, minimal or no effects of delayed knowledge are found when such skills as lever positioning or target pursuit are studied (see I. McD. Bilodeau, 1966). In these cases, there is some information immediately available about the response just made, and subjects seem to be quite capable of holding such information for several seconds until told how well the response met the requirements.

Holding such information until knowledge of results is given becomes even more efficient when both the stimuli and the responses can be described in words. For example, Brackbill and her colleagues have studied the effects of delayed knowledge of results in several situations, all of which have a definite stimulus display and a response which is clearly defined for the subject. In one such procedure (see, for example, Brackbill, Adams, & Reaney, 1967), children were told that they would be shown pairs of pictures and that they must tell the experimenter which one of each pair they thought was "the correct one." Two major findings emerge from these studies: Delayed knowledge of results, even up to 30 seconds, has relatively little effect on the number of errors made during learning; and subsequent tests of relearning indicate that delayed knowledge facilitates retention.

A major distinction between such procedures and the ones employed in the traditional delayed reinforcement studies seems to lie in the definition given to the situation by the experimenter. Here the child is told that one of each pair of stimuli is correct; he is told how he is to indicate his choice; and the experiment does not proceed until knowledge of results has been given. In delayed reinforcement experiments, on the other hand, everything is done to avoid defining the moment of occurrence of the response, and the question of major interest is the effect of subsequent presentation of the reinforcer when behavior has continued to flow on past the response chosen by the experimenter as the one from which he will begin to time the delay interval (the "correct" response). Such situations seem to be more frequent in everyday life than ones in which we pause after a response and await knowledge of its adequacy. The two types of situations seem to raise some rather different problems for behavioral analysis.

The facilitative effects of delayed knowledge of results on retention has usually been found where subjects are allowed to correct their errors before proceeding to the next trial, and where they are free to make continued responses to the stimuli during the delay interval. In this way, the amount of practice with the stimuli, and the adequacy of the verbal descriptions of them, may vary between immediately informed subjects and those in the delay groups. But whatever prove to be the reasons for the improved retention, the educational consequences seem clear: Programmed instructional devices should allow the interval between response and feedback to be adjusted, for the best interval almost certainly would be different for various types of material and levels of proficiency.

In summary, it would seem that delayed knowledge of results involves qualitatively different processes than those encountered in delayed reinforcement, and that we probably should reserve the latter term for situations in which the subject is not given specific information beforehand as to which of his responses will be the critical one. For those cases, "delayed knowledge of results" or "delayed informational feedback" seem to be equally suitable terms.

Delayed Reinforcement and Mediating Responses

Delays of reinforcement are, of course, of trivial importance if a human subject can verbalize the important characteristics of the situation and later reinstate the essential features through the use of language. Certainly, if adult humans were to be given the simple tasks required of rats or pigeons in some of the studies just reviewed, it would be sur-

prising if they did not perform perfectly even under longer delay conditions. Everyday life presents us with far more subtle discriminations than those used in our experiments, but the principles involved seem to be the same: Where language or other differential responses do not continue through the delay period, acquisition is greatly impaired by even slight delays of reinforcement. As might be expected, young children can tolerate longer delays than completely nonverbal organisms, but children are significantly hindered by delay intervals (such as 30 seconds) which adults would probably find quite inconsequential (Hockman & Lipsitt, 1961).

If verbalizations can extend the duration of the stimulus-response relation until reinforcement arrives, why would delayed reinforcement ever influence adult human behavior? At least three types of situation fall outside our ability to use language in this manner. In the first place, there are countless situations in which we lack the experience to identify and label the significant features of the discriminative stimuli, of our responses, or both. The craftsman sees distinctions and tunes his responses in ways that are beyond the apprentice, but as experience and guidance are provided, these deficiencies may be overcome. In the second, we might not have the necessary talent to apply differential labels to stimuli or responses, often because of sensory deficiencies or low intelligence. Finally, there are failures to apply labels that are usually attributed to the "unconscious" nature of the situation. In general, "unconscious" means that one has no way to speak of or think about a situation or an experience. This inability may represent a lack of a vocabulary to label the experience, or it may be a consequence of the types of motivated forgetting called "repression" by Freud. In either case, the absence of appropriate language removes the major advantage man has over other organisms when coping with delayed reinforcement situations.

While verbal devices allow the most subtle

distinctions to be coded and the most information to be carried across delay intervals, other forms of "mediating responses" (see pp. 779–789) are also employed in similar capacities. We have seen that the opportunity for distinctively different response patterns during the delay interval allows learning to proceed at much more rapid rates than when such response patterns are precluded (see, for example, Grice, 1948a). Postural mediating responses may also be used to "bridge the time gap" in *delayed reaction* experiments, where the interval is placed between the termination of the discriminative stimuli and the earliest instant at which the responses to these stimuli may be emitted (see pp. 786–789). Human adults find little challenge in waiting a minute or so before making a response, *if* the situation can be given appropriate verbal description. Indeed, if told to appear at a certain place in 6 months, most of us could delay our reactions for that period and then respond appropriately. Notes written in appointment books or on calendars are devices used to reinstate the appropriate stimuli when the delay interval has passed. Some appreciation of the value of words as mediating responses can be gained by comparing our success in the face of such lengthy delays with the performance limits shown by organisms which have no such language tools. For example, toddlers who have not yet gained the ability to describe the experimental situation in words may be unable to solve delayed reaction problems which require delays of half a minute. On the other hand, non-human primates such as chimpanzees and macaque monkeys have performed at high levels of accuracy with delays of 5 minutes or more (Tinklepaugh, 1928; Yerkes & Yerkes, 1928). Such observations remind us that language is not essential to solve problems involving temporal delays, but words surely are the most versatile mediating responses and their use frees man of much (but by no means all) of the detrimental influences of delays of reinforcement and delayed reaction situations.

SUMMARY

The Common Properties of Reinforcers

A problem of persisting interest for more than 75 years has been the nature of the physiological and/or structural changes in the nervous system that underlie behavior modifications. In some way, the effects of experience must be coded, stored, and retrieved; and whatever theories are proposed to account for these processes must be in harmony with the facts of behavior as revealed by careful, systematic study in the laboratory. Of course, many of the pioneering theories of the neuronal basis of experience assumed that a single set of processes could account for all the observed behavioral effects of experience, and the apparently rich variety of behavioral changes were seen merely as elaborations of one basic type of "learning." Pavlov (1927, p. 395), for example, asserted that "it is obvious that the different kinds of habits based on training, education and discipline of any sort are nothing but a long chain of conditioned reflexes." He thus felt that the theory of activity of the cerebral hemispheres which was being developed to account for his observations of conditioning would be applicable to the full range of effects of experience. The view that conditioned reflexes were the basis of all experience also was adopted enthusiastically by Watson (for example, 1919), although the difficulties in applying the model based on conditioned reflexes to some of the newly developed experimental techniques (for example, double alternation) led many psychologists to doubt the adequacy of proposing that any single mechanism is responsible for all varieties of learned behavioral changes.

In the last few decades there has been even less confidence in the hypothesis that all the effects of experience are basically of one type. Hull (1943) had remarked that proposing that more than one mechanism was responsible for changes in behavior would seem to be a violation of the principle of parsimony, yet he cautioned his readers that such "seeming improvidence in biological economy . . . is not without parallel in other fields; most organisms possess more than one means of excretion, and some organisms possess more than one independent means of reproduction" (p. 82). Such speculations aside, it is clear that if we restrict our considerations to the operations[30] by which behavior modifications can be effected, we can identify not one but several procedures, which appear to be basically different: classical conditioning, operant training, pseudoconditioning, sensitization, habituation, perceptual (or "exposure") learning, and possibly others. In light of these observations, it would seem wise to adopt a flexible position regarding the number of mechanisms whereby behavior is modified.

If we restrict our attention to modifications of operant behavior, we find that there have been numerous attempts to suggest a single common property for all instances of positive reinforcement. Usually these suggestions have been called "theories of reinforcement"; several representative viewpoints were considered in our discussion of reinforcing brain stimulation (pp. 642–660). In the present context, it may be useful to note that some of these suggestions can be tested directly, whereas others can be evaluated by indirect tests only.

As an example of the hypotheses that can be directly tested, we may cite Thorndike's (1911) well-known conclusion that "satisfiers" (that is, positive reinforcers) all share the property of being stimuli which the organism will approach and with which the organism will maximize contact. A more-recent example of a hypothesis that can be tested directly is Premack's (for example, 1965) suggestion that all reinforced responses share the property of being of lower probability than the reinforcing responses which are contingent upon them.[31] Because the common prop-

erties suggested in connection with the Thorndike and Premack views are behavioral, we need only make the appropriate observations of the behavior of subjects in a variety of situations to evaluate the hypotheses. In the strictest sense, a single clear exception to such generalizations would be sufficient to disprove (or disconfirm) them, but in actual practice the exceptions which we can suggest are themselves subject to a variety of interpretations. For example, Thorndike's definition of "satisfier" can be unambiguously applied to situations in which there is a definite consummatory response (such as eating), the duration of which may be measured; but "approach" and "maintain contact" have no clear referents when reinforcement involves such operations as presenting signs of approval, knowledge of results, or brief sensory changes, for in such cases we are left without overt consummatory responses which might be counted or timed. Indeed, in the case of sensory change, it is the brevity and discontinuity of the presentations which frequently seem to be the most important determinants of the reinforcing effects,[32] and if the subject were to maintain contact with the reinforcers, their effectiveness soon would be lost. Similar problems of interpretation arise in connection with Premack's hypothesis, where the crucial issue becomes the determination of the relative probability of the reinforced and the reinforcing responses.

Perhaps the best known of the theories of reinforcement which required indirect tests was the Hull-Miller drive- (or drive-stimulus) reduction hypothesis (see, for example, Hull, 1943; Miller, 1957; see also Miller, 1963). In the absence of any objective criterion of drive reduction, critics of the theory set out to test it by demonstrating the effectiveness of reinforcers which (from a common sense point of view) would not reduce drive and which might even create an increase in drive. Among the best-known studies of this type were the

---

[30]See pp. 554–594.

[31]See pages 623–624 for a more precise statement and a further consideration of this hypothesis.

[32]A review of stimulus-change reinforcement has been published by Kish (1966).

demonstrations by Sheffield and his students that copulation without ejaculation (Sheffield, Wulff, & Backer, 1951) or ingestion of saccharin, which cannot be metabolized (Sheffield & Roby, 1950), would reinforce instrumental behavior. A review of these and other experiments may be found in Sheffield (1966).

When we consider even the most superficial surveys of reinforcers, the great variety of events which prove to be reinforcers immediately suggests that any property which would be common to all would indeed have to be extremely general. At this time, no such property is known, with the exception of the defining property itself. That is, the only thing which reinforcers have in common is that they have been found to increase the probability of occurrence of the reinforced response. This is not the kind of common property which theorists debated so vigorously a decade or two ago, when "crucial" experiments testing the validity of drive-reduction (and other) theories were frequent features of psychological journals. Furthermore, even this property (as we shall see) requires rather elaborate qualification when we attempt to discuss it apart from the conditions of the specific experiments in which the reinforcers gain their labels.

That "reinforcer" and "reinforcement" are concepts developed by students of behavior to help them think about observed facts of behavior is rather obvious, but we sometimes seem to forget that the emergence of a useful concept does not necessarily prove the existence of a parallel process at the same or at other levels of analysis. For example, there is at this time no evidence for a single physiological process paralleling what we call "reinforcement," nor is there any compelling reason to believe that there is but a single psychological process subsumed under our concept of reinforcement. The limited conceptual status of "reinforcement" may be more readily appreciated if we consider next some of the restrictions which must be observed in utilizing the concept.

Contingency of response and reinforcer

Although we frequently speak of "reinforcing stimulus" or "reinforcing event," such terms are only convenient shorthand expressions for a more adequate description, which always would include a description of (1) the response on which the reinforcer is contingent, (2) the reinforcer and the conditions under which it is applied, and (3) the behavioral measure from which the increase in probability of response was estimated.

Reinforcing properties do not reside in the reinforcer itself; factors related to states of the organism (see below) and to response-reinforcer relationships also determine reinforcing effects. The relationship of response and reinforcer usually is described as being purely a temporal one, for the effects of the reinforcer on behavior do not seem to be dependent upon any foresight or purpose on the part of the subject. In this regard, such neutral words as "conditional" or "contingent" to describe the relation of the reinforcer to the response are especially well chosen. Still, to assume that the nature of the response *in no way* influences the reinforcing effects is to disregard some recent experiments which have rather broad implications for our understanding of reinforcement.

One group of experiments has compared the effects of control of some of the characteristics of the reinforcer by the animal with the effects of control by the experimenter. For example, Keesey (1964b) allowed rats to determine the duration of the positively reinforcing electrical brain stimulation which they received. He then tested response rates when a wide range of durations under his control were presented to the rats. In the subject-controlled portions of the experiments, the animals decreased stimulation durations as the experimenter increased either the current or the pulse frequency of the stimulation; when the experimenter controlled the durations, response rates continued to rise as durations were lengthened, even at high currents. Response rates were determined under variable interval reinforcement to minimize any effects the stimulation itself might have on response rates. It is as if the reinforcing effects associated with dimensions of the stimulation, such as duration, were in part determined by whether the responses of the animals controlled the duration. That the effects were no mere result of a reflexive withdrawal of the rat from the bar after he was stimulated for a certain length of time was shown by a second experiment in which the animals pressed one bar to initiate the stimulation and pressed a second bar, on the other side of the chamber, to terminate the stimulation. Again, the same results were obtained.

A still more striking influence of the response in determining reinforcing properties is seen in an experiment by Kavanau (1963). As one phase of a study of the activity cycles of deer mice (*Peromyscus crinitus*), Kavanau allowed running in an activity wheel to occur under some circumstances only if a bar was pressed (releasing the brake on the wheel), while at other times the wheel was motor driven and pressing one bar could stop the wheel and pressing another bar would start it again. Whether the energy to turn the wheel was provided by motor or mouse, running in the wheel clearly reinforced bar pressing. However, when the experimenter turned on the motor, the mice turned it off; or, if they were running and the experimenter turned off the motor, the mice turned it on again. Hence, to describe the reinforcer as "running" or "presentation of the conditions for running" is obviously incomplete and misleading: it is *running contingent upon bar pressing* which increases the probability of reoccurrence of bar pressing.

Finally, we may mention the technique developed by Steiner, Beer, and Shaffer (1968) to separate reinforcing stimulation from its response contingency. They allowed rats to stimulate themselves, using a variety of reinforcement schedules to manipulate the density of the electrical brain stimulation. A tape recording of the exact pattern of stimulation received by each rat was then played back through the stimulator, but now the bar was

arranged so pressing it would interrupt the stimulation circuit. They found that the animals consistently terminated many of the patterns of stimulation which they had produced themselves when the response-contingent conditions were in effect. In other words, exactly the same stimulation may be positively reinforcing when response contingent, or aversive when not response contingent.

These observations point to one of the gaps in our understanding of the phenomenon of reinforcement: Why is it that such "free" (that is, not response-contingent) stimulations are sometimes not reinforcing, or possibly even aversive, when at other times they reinforce whatever response happens to occur, and generate "superstitious" behavior (Skinner, 1948)? Such adventitious reinforcement may systematically increase the probability of rather restricted (and easily observable) response classes, such as turning clockwise or bobbing and bowing the head, or it may increase the probability of a broad class of responses, which may be detectable only as an increase in general activity. Still, we would always expect to find some reinforcing effects if we present such stimuli without regard for the responses of the organism, and we would be surprised if no systematic effects were observed. However, the implications of the studies just reviewed are that such superstitious behavior may not be an inevitable consequence of noncontingent stimulation, that there may be some as yet unknown additional conditions necessary for its appearance, and that, if given the opportunity, animals in some "superstition" experiments might even make an instrumental response to terminate the free stimulations.[33]

Present and past states of the organism

The term "states of the organism" refers to known (or suspected) physiological condi-

[33] For a summary of some of the effects superstitious behavior may have on behavioral experiments, and a consideration of the applicability of the concept of superstitious conditioning to human behavior, see Herrnstein (1966). For further evidence on the importance of the response-reinforcer contingency, see Neuringer, 1970.

tions, some of which modify behavioral processes and thus come to be called "drives" (see Chapter 18). The range of conditions varies from some rather well known and predictable states (such as estrus, hunger, sleep) to some which are more difficult to define and the behavioral consequences of which are less consistent (such as emotion). Many stimuli have reinforcing properties only when appropriate states of the organism exist. For example, we are all aware that a condition of food or water deficit is necessary when first we attempt to use these substances as reinforcers. Usually it also is necessary to reinstate at least some degree of the deficit when again using these as reinforcers. What we actually observe, of course, is the correlation between depriving the animal and his increased probability of eating, but we know that physiological changes are indeed paralleling (and presumably mediating) the behavioral ones (see Chapter 18).

From such observations we sometimes make the unwarranted assumptions that the existence of a reinforcer indicates the presence of an associated physiological state, or that every known physiological state must have reinforcers associated with it. Reinforcing brain stimulation, many forms of stimulus-change reinforcement, certain "highly palatable" substances, and such effective reinforcers as informational feedback, approval and affection, and stimulation of "erogenous" zones of the body need not be associated with any special prior or current physiological states. Furthermore, although most states which have significant behavioral effects can also be shown to increase the effectiveness of certain stimuli as reinforcers, the relationship is neither necessary nor universal. For example, although estrus in the rat is a state with massive influences on both general activity and acceptance of the male, neither presentation of opportunities for copulation nor the sexual activity itself seems to have reinforcing effects for the female (see, for example, Bolles, Rapp, & White, 1968).

An interesting form of the relation between a reinforcer and the states of the organism is shown in those instances in which some specific prior experiences interact with some specific states of the organism, but where neither factor by itself is sufficient to create the conditions necessary for reinforcement. An everyday example with which many readers will be familiar is the reinforcing effect of attention by an attractive member of the opposite sex: It seems reasonable to assume that without either sexual maturity or appropriate experiences, the full reinforcing effects would not be seen. In the laboratory, the contributions of experience and states may be analyzed separately, as in the studies of the reinforcing effects of bird song by Stevenson (1967, 1969). She has shown that male chaffinches (*Fringilla coelebs*) will increase the relative frequency of emission of an arbitrary response (sitting on one of many perches in a large cage) if each such response is followed by a brief recorded segment of song characteristic of that species, but that the reinforcing effects of the song depend on both the prior experience of hearing the song and on the sexual maturity of the bird. If a juvenile male is trapped in the autumn of his first year, after having heard mature males singing in courtship and in marking their territories (Marler, 1956), and if he is then brought to sexual maturity in the laboratory with injections of testosterone, the recorded song will be an effective reinforcer. If he is not given testosterone, the song is not reinforcing. That the reinforcing effects do not derive from testosterone itself is shown by the lack of a reinforcing effect when hand-reared birds (who never have heard any bird song) are injected and tested. It thus seems that the effects of the prior experiences are latent until sexual maturity; only then does the song have reinforcing effects, and neither familiarity with the song nor sexual maturity by itself is sufficient to produce the reinforcing effects. Whether the autumn-caught male birds bring to the laboratory any relevant experiences other than just having heard the songs (for example, encounters with more mature males) is not yet known.

Other Properties of Reinforcers

In addition to the defining property that is, of course, shared by all reinforcers, there are other properties that are quite commonly found in some but not all instances. For example, stimuli which are reinforcers frequently can be shown to have acquired discriminative properties, in that the presentation (or the withholding) of the reinforcer may serve as the cue that further reinforcements are (or are not) immanent. In the *mixed schedule of reinforcement,* two or more schedules are intermixed without any correlated stimuli to mark off which schedule is in effect at any moment, and to the extent that differential behavior develops, we may assume that the discriminative stimuli must have come from the reinforcers themselves. Suppose the program calls for periods of continuous reinforcement (every response reinforced) to alternate with periods of extinction (no reinforcement): This would constitute about the most simple possible mixed schedule, and most organisms soon would begin to show fairly rapid responding as long as each response is reinforced, but slower rates as soon as one of the responses was not reinforced.

Of course, the mere fact that organisms do come under the control of the discriminative properties of reinforcers presents additional problems for the experimenter to whom this source of differential responding may represent a contamination of his main effects (for example, stimulus detection). Several possible means of avoiding or minimizing such difficulties have been suggested by Blough (1966). One obvious solution, of course, is to run a mixed-schedule control group along with each discrimination experiment. Thus, if one were studying the discrimination of auditory stimuli, and one tone was always present during occasional (variable interval) reinforcement while another tone was always present during extinction, a comparable set of subjects could be run with exactly the same conditions except that the tones would be omitted. The differential responding of this mixed-schedule control group then would indicate how much "discrimination" could be expected if the tones were completely absent (see Sadowsky, 1969), and the extent to which differential responding with tones exceeded that without tones would provide an estimate of the control of behavior exerted by the tones. Furthermore, if one were not interested in transient phenomena (such as acquisition of control), the same subjects could be run sometimes with and sometimes without the tones, thus allowing a direct comparison of within-subjects differences.

Reinforcers also will frequently have demonstrable motivating properties. In this case, by "motivating properties" we refer to the increased vigor or speed of responding when these dimensions of behavior are not themselves reinforced. For example, when stable variable-interval behavior has been established, neither increased force nor increased rate of responding will influence reinforcement because the organism already has settled down to making responses at an intensity and a rate that exceed minimum requirements. If we now increase the amount of food in each reinforcement, we are highly likely to observe both an increase in the rate and the force with which the subject responds, but because neither is specifically differentially reinforced, a gradual return to previous levels is to be expected (see Keesey & Kling, 1961). In this case, motivational and reinforcing properties are congruent, but in some instances, they may change in rather different ways. For example, if some minimal interresponse time is required, so that there is differential reinforcement of low rates (the DRL schedule of reinforcement), rapid responding continually resets the timer which must "time out" (complete its timing cycle) before the next response may be reinforced. After 30 or 40 hours of exposure to a schedule that requires, for example, a minimum interresponse time of 30 seconds, most rats will show a peak in their distributions of the interresponse times in the general region of 30 seconds. If the amount of food per reinforcement is then increased, the animal responds more rapidly, thus reducing the number of reinforcements (Beer & Trumble, 1965). The food is still selectively reinforcing responses which follow pauses of at least 30 seconds, but the increase in amount of food per reinforcement has also wrought a change that seems consistent with the expression "increase in motivation."

If stable behavior is established and then reinforcement is terminated, the subject may respond with greater speed and vigor rather than less. In this case, the change usually is labeled "frustration," and it is thought to reflect yet another variety of motivational effect. Under conditions of complete omission of further reinforcement, this increase is transient and may appear as a "hump" on the extinction curve (Sheffield, 1949; Stanley, 1952; Thompson & Bloom, 1966). However, relatively stable frustration effects can be obtained in certain situations. For example, Amsel (1958) has developed a technique in which the animal is reinforced in a goal box located halfway down an alley, and then immediately thereafter is reinforced in the second goal box for running the rest of the way down the alley. Omission of food in the first goal box characteristically creates an increase in speed in the second segment, an effect which has been labeled the "frustration effect" by Amsel.

This use of the terms "motivation" and "frustration" to describe observed changes in behavior is a convenient form of expression, but we should avoid the all too natural tendency to use such labels to explain the phenomena. We also should draw a clear distinction between "motivation" as used in this context and such more formal, theoretical terms as *incentive motivation* (see Chapter 18). Incentive motivation is one of the central factors in the Hull-Spence-Logan behavior theory (see, for example, Logan, 1960), and it is given the properties of energizing behavior (along with other motivational factors) and of being proportional to the amount

and quality of the reinforcer. The mechanism by which incentive motivation is thought to operate is the "anticipatory" response appropriate to the reinforcer. For example, if the reinforcer be food, such portions of the seizing, chewing, and swallowing complex as can occur in the absence of the food are thought to be conditioned to stimuli present while the animal is eating, and on later occasions these anticipatory responses are assumed to be emitted when the animal is in the presence of similar stimuli. Because there is direct evidence that such anticipatory responses do indeed exist and do serve behavioral functions (see p. 622), the theory seems to offer an interesting and internally consistent view of at least a part of the mechanism whereby ingested reinforcers may influence later behavior. Where other reinforcers are involved (and indeed the bulk of everyday reinforcers would fall in this category), overt consummatory responses are rare. For example, attention and recognition from others and informational feedback from the environment have demonstrable reinforcing properties, but what is the anticipatory response which we make in such situations? The theory could postulate that central nervous system correlates of such responses might serve functions similar to that of anticipatory chewing, but such extensions take us quite beyond currently available techniques for observation and evaluation of neuronal processes.

Motivation and reinforcers also are closely intertwined in the "drive induction" theory developed by Sheffield (for example, 1966; see also p. 657). Sheffield has suggested that Pavlovian conditioning presents a better picture of "the learning process per se" than does behavior in the operant situation (1965, p. 320). The latter, suggests Sheffield, is probably more related to problems of motivation than to learning, for (in his analysis) the crucial fact about what we have been calling "reinforcers" is that they elicit unconditioned responses which consummate (that is, terminate) striving toward them. This motivated striving arises because stimuli associated with the reinforcers become (classically) conditioned stimuli for the appropriate consummatory responses, but until the reinforcer itself is reached, the consummatory responses cannot occur. For example, if food is always given in a white goal box, stimuli from the goal box will become the conditioned stimuli for eating responses, but until the food is actually reached, no eating can occur. The occurrence of such unconsummated responses is said to be "innately exciting," and the excitement is thought to be channelled primarily into skeletal behavior, thus producing a more active organism. If these assumptions are granted, it follows that the organism will be more active when in a white alleyway than when in a dissimilar situation (for example, when in a black alleyway). In this fashion, the organism is led (as it were) toward the reinforcer by his excited activity. When the organism finally makes contact with the reinforcer, the occurrence of consummatory responses brings striving to an end, and at the same time provides one more pairing (in the Pavlovian sense) of stimuli associated with the reinforcer and the reinforcer itself.

Furthermore, the attempt to organize all problems of reinforcement around the idea that each reinforcer has an associated consummatory response, some portions of which occur as conditioned (and excitement-producing) responses, seems apropos for food, water, or sex objects, but (as in the case of incentive motivation, discussed above) the analysis seems strained when we attempt to apply it to the broad spectrum of reinforcers, many of which have no identifiable consummatory responses. Another key assumption is that every reinforcer "inherently carries a component of relaxation" (Sheffield, 1965, p. 318) that brings striving to an end, but (as we have seen) there are some very effective reinforcers (such as electrical brain stimulation) which seem to create more excitement and generate more activity after they are presented than before.[34]

In summary, although problems of motivation certainly overlap those of reinforcement, they are not identical, nor does it seem that any single motivational characteristic is common to all reinforcers.

Increasing the Probability of Response

In defining reinforcement, we specified that the probability of the response must be increased, but we can see that it is not just the probability of the response in general, but of the response in the *presence of certain stimuli* that is increased. These stimuli (or "cues") may come from persons (parents, teachers, traffic policemen . . .) who seek to guide our behavior; from static features of the environment, allowing us to behave differently in the bedroom and the ballroom; from reinforcements themselves, allowing us to discriminate between periods of reinforcement and nonreinforcement. Some of these cues may arise from the properties of the stimuli themselves (such as the color of the traffic light) while others may depend upon temporal organizations within a series of stimuli (as in Morse code) or may be produced by the behavior of the organism itself (for example, kinesthetic stimuli).

In some experimental situations and in most examples from everyday life, our stimuli are so poorly controlled and so difficult to identify that we are forced to give up attempts to manipulate them directly. The rat being shaped to press a bar is a familiar example of this difficulty: We cannot specify the stimuli which come to control the behavior of bar pressing, but we infer their presence from the fact that the well-trained rat emits a smooth pattern of behavior, pressing the bar and seizing food pellets from the food cup each time the feeder mechanism is activated. Because he does not press the food cup nor

---

[34]Such apparent exceptions to the suggestion that reinforcers terminate striving could be multiplied many times.

For example, fighting cocks will peck a key repeatedly if key pecks allow them to see another cock, or a reflection of themselves (Thompson, 1964). Each glimpse creates great excitement in the cock and increases his "striving," yet the operation of presenting the view of another animal clearly is reinforcing, for key pecking is increased and then maintained at high levels.

run to some far corner of the chamber when the feeder mechanism clicks, we conclude that the probability of bar pressing in the presence of stimuli associated with the bar has been increased, and the probability of approaching the food cup has similarly been increased when the rat is in the presence of such stimuli as the click of the feeder.

However, the control exerted by such stimuli is not inflexible in the sense that spinal reflexes are inflexible, and minor modifications in the stimuli do not produce gross disruptions of the behavior. To some of the keenest observers of animal behavior, the fact that the animal can adjust to minor changes in the situation implies that the behavior is purposive and goal directed (see, for example, Tolman, 1932; Thorpe, 1963) or that such behavior might well be called "voluntary" to distinguish it from instinctive or reflexive behavior in which the controlling stimuli, the responses, and the consequences are related in an invariable manner (Teitelbaum, 1966). On the whole, little use has been made of such classifications, and many would agree with Skinner (for example, 1953, 1966) that the labels may even misdirect attention from important research problems.

The control of responses by stimuli correlated with reinforcement is readily demonstrated by systematic manipulation of such stimuli. In some of the earliest studies of this type, the procedures were modeled on the Pavlovian arrangement, using, for example, the method of discrete trials. For example, Grindley (1932) restrained guinea pigs in a holder, sounded a buzzer, and when a head movement of a predetermined direction and angle occurred, he stopped the buzzer and delivered a bit of food to a food cup directly in front of the animal. Although there was an overall increase in the frequency of such head movements, the relatively greater increase in the presence of the buzzer demonstrated the reinforcing effects of food. Presumably, the selective increase in responding in the presence of the buzzer occurred because the complex stimulus of (buzzer plus other stimuli plus head movement feedback) was followed by food while the complex stimulus of (other stimuli plus head movement feedback) was not.

Such discrete-trial procedures introduce a vexing problem for the experimenter: The responses sometimes occur between trials, and the experimenter is left to guess whether, if he starts a trial just now, the behavior might not begin to appear just before he is ready and thus spoil his procedure.[35] Furthermore, the control of the spacing of the trials by the experimenter frequently introduces discontinuities into what seems to be continuous behavior, which may cause additional variability in the data.

For such reasons, many experimenters have adopted procedures which do not involve trials at all, or which allow the subject to determine when each trial is to be initiated (see p. 602). From such situations, the patterning of behavior correlated with reinforcement schedules frequently emerges as one of the most interesting results. For example, if every nth response is reinforced (the *fixed ratio* schedule), a characteristic response pattern emerges, showing a post-reinforcement pause followed by responding at a relatively constant rate. What are the stimuli which govern the emission of such behaviors? Since the pause prior to the start of the response run is relatively insensitive to the size of the ratio requirement, and since an interruption of the procedure immediately after reinforcement (for example, by introducing a blackout which suppresses pigeon responses) will eliminate the pause (Ferster & Skinner, 1957, p. 117), it is concluded that the pause in ratio schedules develops because one reinforced response can never follow immediately after another. Hence, responding in the presence of the stimuli resulting from reinforcement never is reinforced, and thus such responding is extinguished. From this it follows that anything which disrupts such reinforcement after-effects (such as a blackout) will also disrupt these stimuli and thus the start of responding should be hastened. On the other

[35]See Sheffield's comments (1965, p. 314) on this problem in the Pavlovian situation.

hand, reinforcement in ratio schedules would almost never occur after long pauses in responding, but almost always would occur when response follows response in close order. Thus, the stimuli in the presence of which responding is reinforced should be expected to include the after-effects of having just responded, and once a response or two has been emitted, the feedback from such responses should provide the necessary discriminative stimuli for the emission of a run of responses at a rate characteristically emitted under those conditions (see Ferster and Skinner, 1957, for a behavioral analysis of such schedules). Note that even though we have not directly observed either the stimuli produced by responding or the post-reinforcement stimuli, the assumptions that they exist and that they are discriminative stimuli for characteristic response patterns is consistent with what we know about behavior in situations where we can manipulate the stimuli directly; it is also consistent with the indirect evidence just cited (such as inserting blackouts). Again, we conclude that presentation of reinforcers does not increase the probability of the response in an indiscriminate fashion, but instead, that the response shows a selective probability increase in the presence of those stimuli correlated with reinforcement.

Although it seems valuable to assume that the stimulus consequences of each response in ratio runs may in part set the occasion for the next response, we should not assume that each response is necessarily emitted only when stimuli from the immediately preceding response are present. Although such response chains do, of course, play important roles in behavior, there are some response sequences which, as Lashley (1951, p. 123) pointed out, occur with such rapidity that neural impulses from kinesthetic receptors could not possibly reach the central nervous system in time to initiate the activity in motor areas needed to initiate the next response. Instead, it seems that learned responses may become integrated into sequences which then can be run off as units, without requiring response-produced stimuli as the alternate links in a behavioral chain. The movements involved in speaking, typing, or playing musical instruments are everyday examples of sequences of this type.

The problem of analyzing the effects of a reinforcer on behavior is complicated even more if we select a behavioral situation in which the response in which we are interested is not identical with the response we reinforce. Consider a simple position discrimination in a T maze: We select one of the two alternatives as "the response" to be reinforced, but then we actually reinforce the last bit of locomotion into one of the goal boxes. At the choice point in the maze, the animal may show behavior that varies considerably from trial to trial, but if he eventually arrives in the proper goal box, these last few responses are reinforced. Of course, entering that alley from the choice point always precedes (by various intervals) the reinforced response, while other responses which might occur (for example, sniffing, turning around) are less likely to be perfectly correlated with reinforcement, and so eventually the turns toward the "correct" goal box become more and more probable. Although crude, the maze procedure "works," in that species from earthworm (see, for example, Yerkes, 1912; Robinson, 1953) to man (see, for example, Stellwagen & Card, 1965) can be "tested" in this manner, but it is exceedingly difficult to specify and measure with precision the responses which are reinforced or the stimuli in the presence of which that response class is emitted.

A somewhat similar problem exists for reinforcement schedules in which the crucial features of the reinforcement contingencies are not specified in behavioral terms. Interval schedules, or schedules that require some minimal interresponse time, disregard all the emitted behavior except the response that follows the completion of the time interval. In effect, we are leaving to chance the determination of the behavior during the interval, and because we usually are not interested in (nor prepared to measure) idiosyncratic behavior, such procedures may be less useful tools for us to use to analyze reinforcing effects than schedules which allow the experimenter to specify more completely the behavior which will be reinforced.

What we see, then, is that presentation of a reinforcer contingent upon the occurrence of a response increases the probability that the response will occur again and that the stimuli in the presence of which this process is carried out will exert some control over the emission of the response. However, we should not assume that just any and all stimuli impinging on the organism conjointly determine when the subject will make such responses again. Instead, it seems that stimuli present when the response is reinforced, and absent when the response is either not reinforced or cannot be made, are the only stimuli which gain any significant degree of control over that response. For example, in the process of training rats to press a bar, responses of raising the paws and pressing on the food-cup are *not* reinforced, while the same behavior in the presence of stimuli from the bar is followed by delivery of the food pellet. In this sense, stimuli from the bar are discriminative stimuli, but because we cannot systematically vary such stimuli along any dimensions, we have little chance to evaluate the degree of control they exert over responding. When the subject faces away from the bar, the stimuli characteristic of that part of the environment always are paired with the subject's not making the bar pressing response, and so they too probably come to control important aspects of behavior (such as turning toward the bar), much as presenting a key color to a pigeon and withdrawing it rapidly before he can peck the key eventually establishes that color as a discriminative stimulus in the presence of which the pigeon does not peck (Terrace, 1963; see p. 778).

Here, then, we have a further modification of our description of how reinforcers function, for it is not just any and all stimuli present when a response is emitted that later will determine when and where the response will occur, but only those stimuli that are present when the response is made and is reinforced, and absent when the response either is not reinforced, or when the subject cannot make the response. Thus, the "Law of Operant Reinforcement" might be stated in this fashion:

Reinforcement increases the probability that the operant will be emitted in the presence of stimuli differentially associated with reinforcement.

At this time, it certainly is premature to attempt to make any restriction on the term *operant* other than to identify it with responses whose probability can be increased through presentation of reinforcers. All variety of skeletal responses have been shown to be sensitive to such reinforcing operations, and smooth and cardiac muscle responses and even tissue secretions may also be modified through the same procedures (Miller & Banuazizi, 1968). This use of "operant" does not really represent an extension of the original meaning of the term (Skinner, 1937), for in these recent experiments the intestinal movements or changes in heart rate have been given the same basic property as other operants; namely, they control the occurrence of reinforcers and hence operate directly upon the organism's environment.

Role of Reinforcement in Acquisition of Stimulus Control

We have been referring to the fact that after reinforcement, the emission of one class of responses may occur primarily in the presence of one set of stimuli, and that, with changes in stimuli, there may be correlated changes in responses. In recent years, the phrase "stimulus control" has come to be used in contexts where formerly it might have been said that the subject "discriminated the stimuli." Certainly "stimulus control" is a more neutral term, being free of connotations that the subject is always aware of the stimuli that are influencing his behavior. It also avoids the possible confounding of *processes* with observed *functional relations* (Terrace, 1966a). Most users of the term follow Terrace in identifying the degree of control with the change in response probability as a stimulus dimension or continuum is explored. Thus, "stimulus control" refers to control by stimuli that the experimenter can vary in some systematic manner. Of course, this leaves many sources of stimulation which certainly must exert some control over responding, but which we can manipulate only in the most gross sense. One obvious example is the stimulation produced by the animal's behavior: Considering just the intensive aspects, we can make responses somewhat more or less effortful by manipulating the force required to operate the bar (see, for example, Notterman & Mintz, 1962, 1965) or by placing weighted packs on the animal's back (Solomon, 1949), but we have no direct evidence that this produces systematic changes along a single dimension of stimulation. Still, the orderly effects of such manipulations on behavior imply that the procedures produce stimuli which control some aspects of behavior, and it is such (stimulus) control which is left outside current definitions of *stimulus control*.

We then may ask the question: Is reinforcement essential for the acquisition of the control of responses by stimuli? If we restrict our attention to typical operant conditioning paradigms, the answer almost certainly would be "yes" (Terrace, 1966a). However, if we include in our survey such procedures as imprinting (see, for example, Bateson, 1966) or perceptual or exposure learning (see, for example, Gibson, Walk, & Tighe, 1959) we see that significant influences on subsequent responding can be produced merely by presenting stimuli under appropriate conditions, in situations where no demonstrable reinforced responses occur and where no known differential association of the stimuli with reinforcement takes place.[36] In such studies, systematic explorations of possible dimensions of the stimuli usually are not included, but at least one experiment (Cofoid & Honig, 1961) examined wave-length generalization of responses to an imprinted stimulus and obtained gradients suggestive of stimulus con-

[36]See pages 579–581 for a description of such procedures.

trol. Outside operant paradigms, therefore, it would seem that at least some degree of stimulus control can be established without obvious differential reinforcement.

Does the nature of the reinforcer influence the acquisition of stimulus control? If each organism is trained on two or more discrimination problems, each with a different condition of reinforcement (such as different amounts of food per reinforcement), differences in the rate with which the discrimination problems are solved have been consistently reported (for example, Schrier & Harlow, 1956; see p. 639). If each organism is trained with but one condition of reinforcement, the results are less clear, but the evidence suggests that there are at least some conditions under which the amount of reinforcement and the speed with which the discriminations are solved are positively correlated (see, for example, Schrier, 1956; Waller, 1968; Keesey & Lindholm, 1969). Common sense suggests that, other things being equal, the larger or the more preferred the reinforcer, the faster the organism should master the problem we give it. However, as we have seen (p. 617) when we are varying food reinforcers, other things are rarely equal. In Waller's experiment, for example, providing different amounts of food to different groups resulted in different durations of exposure to the stimuli correlated with reinforcement; and adequate adjustment of preliminary training required that every animal be exposed to all the amounts of food used in the experiment. These and similar problems seem inherent in studies in which the amount of food reinforcement is manipulated and seem to require that we use some degree of caution when we conclude that differences in reinforcers produce differences in rate of acquisition of stimulus control when each organism is exposed to but one condition of reinforcement.

Many of these practical problems can be avoided if we use electrical brain stimulation. For example, in studying amount of reinforcement, such dimensions as the intensity or the duration of the stimulation can be manipulated independently. Furthermore, each of these dimensions is continuously variable, allowing us to adjust the reinforcer so that some specific behavioral result (such as a certain response rate) can be obtained from each animal. Using this reinforcer, and food controls for comparison purposes, Sadowsky (1969) found the rate of acquisition of a discrimination between two auditory stimuli to be almost exactly the same for high- and for low-reinforcement groups. After obtaining stable rate-intensity functions (see p. 546) for each animal, he picked out some that responded rapidly at low current and others that responded rapidly at high current. He also found some animals that responded at low rates to high currents, and others that responded at low rates to low currents. He thus created four groups, two of which were made up of rapid responders, and two of slow responders. (Some animals, of course, fell in between the "high" and "low" points, and were therefore consigned to a subsequent experiment.) Then, all the rats were trained in a chamber containing a single bar, where responses in the presence of one auditory stimulus were reinforced (on the average) every 30 seconds, while all responses in the presence of a second auditory stimulus went unreinforced. The rate with which these auditory stimuli came to control the responding was almost exactly the same for all four groups, indicating that rather large differences in the physical characteristics or in the behavioral consequences of reinforcers may have little (or no) effect on the acquisition of stimulus control of behavior.

Of course, this is but one type of discrimination situation, and the results may be peculiar to it, but other recent studies seem to support the generality of these findings. For example, if we ask how fine a discrimination can be obtained using different reinforcers, we find that food and electrical brain stimulation seem to be equally effective when tested in a two-choice brightness discrimination, where the difference between the dis-

criminative stimuli was gradually reduced until differential responding disappeared (Terman & Kling, 1968).

Thus, both rate of acquisition and final level of stimulus control seem remarkably insensitive to rather marked differences in reinforcers. What might be thought of as the obverse effect has also been investigated: Once differential responding has been established, do differences in reinforcers promote differences in generalization? In this experiment (Kling & Berkley, 1968), three groups of rats were trained in a successive discrimination problem using two auditory stimuli and either food pellets or electrical stimulation of the hypothalamic or septal regions of the brain as reinforcers. After attaining a moderately strict criterion of discriminative responding, each animal was tested with the two training stimuli plus four other frequencies. Both the shapes and the relative breadth of the generalization gradients were found to be comparable for all groups (see p. 656 and Figure 15.18).

Although these studies sample but a minute portion of the possible conditions under which stimulus control may be studied, there is already a strong suggestion that differences in reinforcers—even when they produce marked differences in response rates, consummatory behavior, resistance to extinction, and so on—may be relatively unimportant as far as the control of responding by correlated stimuli is concerned. Again, we must urge caution in extending these observations to other situations, for, as we have noted, there seem to be some conditions under which reinforcer differences do influence stimulus control (for example, Keesey & Lindholm, 1969). Unfortunately, we as yet have no insight into the characteristics of situations in which such reinforcer effects will be found.

We are left, therefore, with the tentative conclusions that reinforcers are essential to increasing and maintaining the probabilities of operant behavior; that differential association of stimuli with reinforced responses and with non-reinforcement is essential to the establishment of stimulus control of behavior when operant training methods are employed; that differences in reinforcers have relatively more influence on response rates if each organism is given more than one reinforcement condition than if a single reinforcer is used for each subject; and that while differences in stimulus control certainly are enhanced by exposing each organism to more than one condition of reinforcement, differences in stimulus control obtained when each subject is trained with just one reinforcer are likely to be small and—in at least some cases— may not be seen at all.

Of course, in practical situations (as in the schoolroom), there would rarely be circumstances in which only one condition of reinforcement were used, and thus the last conclusion (above) refers to a problem that has little everyday significance. It is, however, of considerable theoretical importance, for a clear answer to the question of whether all reinforcers make equal contributions to the acquisition of stimulus control would add considerably to our understanding of the phenomenon of reinforcement.

We have organized our survey of positive reinforcement around some of the topics that have been most actively investigated during the last decade. In the process, we have offered a few conclusions where the evidence seems to warrant them, and pointed to gaps in our knowledge or inconsistencies in the published data with the hope that students will see some of these problems as challenges to their ingenuity and skill. Looking into the future, we might hazard the opinion that the next decade will see the fracturing of "reinforcement" into several less global phenomena, each of which would be concerned with a relatively limited set of problems. Paralleling this trend, we would not be at all surprised to see a marked increase in the number of species employed in studies of reinforcement, as the potential contributions of behavioral genetics (for example, McClearn, 1963) and ethology (Hinde, 1966) to the study of reinforcement become more widely recognized. The assault on the neuronal basis of behavior modification can be expected to become even more active than it has been in the last few years, and here we may look for the techniques developed in the study of reinforcement to be especially valuable contributions, for without appropriate behavioral methodology, biochemical or electrophysiological investigations of learning processes will lack the criteria against which they can be evaluated. Finally, it is fairly safe to predict that applications of the laboratory procedures to educational problems, especially those of the nursery and primary schools, will become far more widespread than at present, thus justifying in part the support by society of basic research into problems of reinforcement.

Russell M. Church

AVERSIVE BEHAVIOR

16 Noxious stimuli produce a variety of behavioral effects that will be examined in this chapter. The onset of such stimuli arouses emotional reactions of distress, and their termination induces relief. The onset and termination of a previously neutral stimulus that has preceded a noxious stimulus also arouse emotional reactions. An animal will attempt to escape from a noxious stimulus, and to delay or prevent its occurrence. If a noxious stimulus occurs immediately after a response, or if a response maintains such a stimulus, an animal will reduce its tendency to perform the response.

Unfortunately, none of these behavioral effects is a generally accepted and universally applicable definition of a noxious stimulus. A stimulus that would be classified as "noxious" by one set of criteria might not be so classified by another set of criteria. Perhaps the most satisfactory definition would rely upon a preference measure, that is, a stimulus is noxious if and only if a subject reliably chooses a "neutral" alternative over it. Of course, the noxiousness of a stimulus depends, in part, upon the motivational state of the subject. A cool breeze may serve as a noxious stimulus to a subject in a cold environment but as a positive reinforcing stimulus to a subject in a hot environment. Usually, however, studies of aversive behavior employ a stimulus so noxious that it would not be questioned (for example, intense electric shock), and thus no formal definition is required.

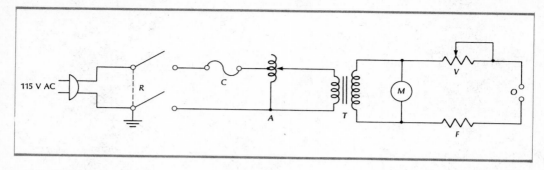

Figure 16.1. General circuit diagram of apparatus to administer electric shock. R = relay switch contacts, C = fuse, A = variable autotransformer, T = transformer, M = voltmeter, V = variable resistance, F = fixed resistance, and O = output.

Many different noxious stimuli have been used in studies of aversive behavior. A loud noise (Watson & Rayner, 1920), a slap from a lever (Skinner, 1938), a bump on the nose and a fall into a net (Maier, 1949), presentation of a toy snake to a monkey (Masserman & Pechtel, 1953), and a swat with a rolled-up piece of newspaper (Stanley & Elliot, 1962) have been used to punish a response. Omission of a usual positive reinforcer may also serve as a punishment (Wagner, 1969). Loud noises, bright lights, pinches, heat, cold water, blasts of air, and a variety of other unpleasant stimuli have been used to produce escape and avoidance behavior. Nonetheless, electric shock has been employed in a large majority of the studies of aversive behavior, for the characteristics of this stimulus are particularly easy to measure and control.

Further research on aversive behavior should make use of noxious stimuli other than electric shock, particularly stimuli that arouse emotional responses other than pain and fear (for example, discomfort, annoyance, anger, nausea). Such work would extend the generality of conclusions about aversive behavior that are now based on the use, primarily, of only one noxious stimulus, electric shock.

METHODS FOR ADMINISTERING ELECTRIC SHOCK

Since the early 1900s electric shock has been used by psychologists to motivate behavior, and many different devices have been used to generate this noxious stimulus. The first experiments used direct current from dry cells (for example, the work of Yerkes, 1903), but these were soon replaced by induction coils (for example, by Yerkes and Dodson, 1908). After alternating current became generally available in psychological laboratories it was widely used as a noxious stimulus. Most research of aversive behavior now makes use of a simple circuit only slightly modified from that used by Jenkins, Warner, and Warden (1926) in their investigation of the obstruction technique.

The Shock Circuit

A general circuit diagram of apparatus used to administer electric shock is shown in Figure 16.1. The autotransformer (A) controls the voltage input to the power transformer (T), up to about 135 V. This transformer increases the voltage to a value that is measured by the voltmeter (M). A fixed resistance (F) and a variable resistance (V) can both be used to control the voltage output (O) applied to the subject. To administer shock the experimenter closes the switch, which normally would be the contacts of a relay (R). For the protection of the subject, experimenter, and equipment, the apparatus to administer electric shock should always contain a fuse (C), a fixed resistor (to limit the maximum current), and a transformer (to isolate the output from the ground).

In such a circuit the experimenter has control over two variables, the source voltage and the resistance in series with the subject, but the subject has control over the third variable, its own impedance. Ideally, one would select a shock circuit in which the experimenter had maximal control over the effective characteristics of the stimulus. Because the subject's impedance is not under the experimenter's control, the experimenter should select a circuit in which variation in the subject's impedance makes little difference in the effect the shock has on responding, that is, the behavior at any particular setting of the source voltage and fixed resistance should be relatively constant. But what is the effective characteristic of the electric shock? Is it the voltage across the subject (volts, E), the current passing through the subject (milliamperes, mA), or the power dissipated in the subject (milliwatts, mW)?

The impedance of a rat receiving a moderately intense foot shock is approximately 150,000 Ω (ohms), and it decreases with increases in the intensity of the shock (Campbell & Teghtsoonian, 1958). If, with respect to the impedance of the subject, the series resistance is small (for example, 10,000 Ω for a rat receiving moderately intense foot shock), then a *constant-voltage* shock circuit is approximated. With this shock circuit a large change in the impedance of the subject makes only a small change in the voltage applied to the subject. This statement follows from Ohm's Law, $I = E \cdot R$, in which E is the voltage at the output of the transformer, I is the current, and R is the total resistance of the circuit.

If, with respect to the impedance of the subject, the series resistance is large (for example, 2,000,000 Ω for a rat receiving moderately intense foot shock), then a *constant-current* circuit is approximated. A large change in the impedance of the subject makes only a small change in the current passing through the subject if this circuit is used. A constant-current circuit usually consists of a transformer with an output of about 500 V, no autotransformer, a fixed resistor of 150,000 Ω, and a variable resistor (potentiometer or decade resistor of 0 to 5,000,000 Ω) for adjustment of intensity.

A series resistance matched to the impedance of the subject (for example, 150,000 Ω for a rat receiving a moderately intense foot shock) is better than any other fixed resistor for holding constant the power ($P = I^2 \cdot R$). A *matched-impedance* shock circuit usually consists of an autotransformer for adjusting intensity, an isolation transformer with an output voltage equal to the input voltage, a fixed resistor of 150,000 Ω, and no variable resistor. If the fixed resistance is no less than 150,000 Ω and the voltage at the output of the transformer is no greater than 500 V, by Ohm's Law and the definition of power, the transformer need not be rated for more than 4 mA, and 2 W resistors should be satisfactory.

Campbell and Masterson (1969) have pro-

vided a thorough treatment of the relative merits of various shock sources. They have come to the conclusion that shock circuits with high source voltages (over 500 V) may cause large variations in current density and even sparks between the subject and the grid. Shock circuits with low resistance (below 150,000 Ω) may result in an increase in effective intensity through time due to a positive feedback mechanism. (A decrease in the impedance of the subject results in an increase in intensity of the shock that leads to a further decrease in the impedance of the subject.) All shock circuits that are adequate to supply a shock of the required intensity and that consist of (1) a series resistance of 150,000 Ω or more, and (2) a source voltage of 500 V or less,

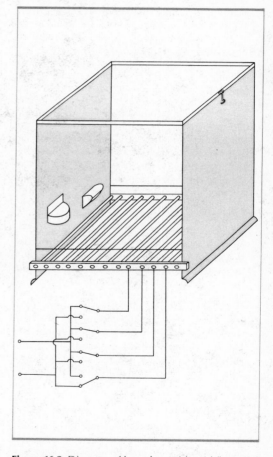

Figure 16.2. Diagram of lever box with grid floor and scrambler. The front wall of the box contains a food cup and a lever; the grid floor is attached to the output of a scrambler and four of these connections are shown in the diagram.

however, are about equally satisfactory. In a preference situation with rats, using shock circuits with 150,000 Ω or 600,000 Ω resistance, and with a constant current circuit of 500 V, Campbell and Masterson (1969) found slightly over 25 jnd's between the aversion and tetanization thresholds.

The Electrodes

If two electrodes are *directly* attached to a subject, the experimenter has control of the current density (because the area of contact is constant). This method is generally employed when the subject is restrained, although it is sometimes used when the subject is permitted to walk around in an experimental enclosure. Electrodes may be attached to the surface (Hoffman, 1960; Azrin, Hopwood, & Powell, 1967; Weiss, 1967), implanted under the skin (Azrin, 1959; Feirstein & Miller, 1963), or located in areas of the brain that presumably produce pain or fear when stimulated (Delgado, Roberts, & Miller, 1954).

There are a number of technical problems related to the administration of electric shock to a freely moving animal by means of attached electrodes, not the least of which is that the animal may dislodge the electrodes unless an excellent swivel arrangement is used to keep the wires out of reach all the time. Therefore, most studies of aversive behavior of freely moving animals use apparatus with a grid floor (for example, a shuttlebox, runway, T-maze, or lever box). The grid usually is constructed of stainless steel bars (about 3/16th in. diameter and 1/2 in. apart) that are inserted into an acrylic insulator that is placed outside the part of the apparatus accessible to the subject (see Figure 16.2). The bars should be cleaned frequently to prevent the accumulation of foreign deposits that can serve to decrease the contact between subject and bars. Also, the insulator supporting the grid should be cleaned to prevent the formation of any conducting film, and feces and other matter should be removed from adjacent grids to prevent current flow through loads other than the subject.

The Scrambler

If shock is administered only for a fraction of a second (as in some punishment studies) it may be feasible to interconnect alternate bars (that is, bars 1, 3, 5, and so on to one side of transformer output, and bars 2, 4, 6, and so on to the other). Some of the bars of the grid are constantly kept at the same polarity as some other bars, however, and the subject may avoid

shock by remaining in contact with only those bars. If the shock is administered for more than a fraction of a second, a subject may find such a position. Because it is obviously undesirable to push the subject, shake the apparatus, or discard a subject that adopts such a position, a variety of units have been devised to shift the relative polarity of the bars. With such a unit (a "scrambler") a subject cannot make contact with two different bars that are always at the same polarity. In terms of components, a scrambler can be made from stepping switches, cam-operated microswitches, motor-driven commutators, and relays, among other devices.

Ideally, any particular bar would be at opposite polarity from any other bar exactly half of the time, but such a device would require $n!/[(n/2)!(n/2)!]$ different patterns. Because this arrangement would become unwieldy if 16 or more bars were attached to the device, most scramblers either do not switch all pairs of bars equally often to opposite polarity (for example, see Skinner & Campbell, 1947) or switch only one bar to opposite polarity from all the others at any given instant (for example, Wyckoff & Page, 1954).[1] A close approximation to a practical scrambler in which each bar is at opposite polarity from each other half the time has been described by Brush (1967).

BASIC PROCEDURES

In any study of aversive behavior there are five classes of stimuli that should be distinguished: (1) experimenter-controlled stimuli, often referred to simply as "stimuli," (2) response-produced stimuli controlled by the subject, often referred to simply as "responses" because they consist of the proprioceptive, visual, auditory, and other consequences of responses, (3) outcomes or events, both rewards and noxious stimuli, (4) temporal stimuli that must be defined as

[1] The diagram of the scrambler in Figure 16.2 has the properties that each pair of bars is equally often at opposite polarity and only one bar is at opposite polarity from all the others at any given instant. One side of the output of the shock source is wired to the normally open contacts of a set of switches, and the other side of the output is wired to the normally closed contacts. The common contact of each switch is wired to a bar of the grid floor. An animal may receive shock if it is standing on bars of opposite polarity (for example, the last bar and any others in the diagram). To change the relative polarity of pairs of grids rapidly, a magnet may be rotated at several revolutions per second to operate, in sequence, the magnetic switches that are mounted in a circle.

beginning from one of the previous kinds of stimuli, and (5) situational stimuli, the relatively fixed aspects of the environment or the apparatus. Each of the basic procedures for the study of aversive behavior can be described in terms of the contingency between a noxious stimulus (its onset or termination) and some other stimulus.

Classical Conditioning

In aversive classical conditioning a noxious stimulus is contingent upon an experimenter-controlled stimulus. For example, in classical eyelid conditioning a puff of air to the eyelid (a noxious stimulus) may follow 1/2 second after each presentation of a light (an experimenter-controlled stimulus); in classical conditioning of the heart rate an electric shock (a noxious stimulus) might be given 10 seconds after each presentation of a tone (an experimenter-controlled stimulus). In all cases of aversive classical conditioning, the task for the subject is to learn the relationship between an experimenter-controlled stimulus or conditioned stimulus (CS) and a noxious stimulus, one kind of unconditioned stimulus (US).

Inferences regarding the learning of the CS-US relationship can be made from various skeletal, autonomic, or visceral responses of the subject to the CS. In the direct procedure, the CS is presented to the subject at an arbitrary time, and some response change is noted. For example, to determine if a subject has learned the relationship between a tone (CS) and a shock (US), the tone may be sounded alone and the change in heart rate recorded. Either an increase or a decrease in rate (relative to appropriate control groups) is evidence that the subject has learned the relationship between the CS and the US.

Alternatively, an indirect procedure may be used to determine if a subject has learned the relationship between the CS and the US. In the conditioned emotional response (CER) procedure, the subject is trained to perform an instrumental response. Either in the same or in separate sessions, it also receives a nox-

TABLE 16.1 CLASSIFICATION OF THE BASIC INSTRUMENTAL TRAINING PROCEDURES WITH NOXIOUS STIMULI

Event	Correlation of event with response	
	Positive	*Negative*
Onset of Noxious Stimulus	Punishment	Avoidance
Termination of Noxious Stimulus	Escape	Preservation

ious stimulus at the termination of an experimenter-controlled stimulus, and then the CS is presented to the subject at an arbitrary time while it is performing the instrumental response. For example, the subject may be trained to obtain food pellets or avoid shock by pressing a lever, and then the change in the rate it presses a lever is noted during presentation of a tone that has had its termination associated with shock. If the subject is pressing the lever for food reinforcement, the tone generally produces a reduction in response rate; if the subject is pressing the lever to avoid shock, the tone generally produces an increase in response rate. Either an increase or a decrease in the response rate (relative to appropriate control groups) is evidence that the subject has learned the relationship between the CS and US.

Instrumental Learning

In aversive instrumental learning the onset or termination of a noxious stimulus is contingent upon a response. There are four clearly distinguishable procedures, and three of them have well-established names (see Table 16.1). In the "punishment" procedure the onset of a noxious event is positively correlated with a response; for example, a lever response by a rat is followed by a brief shock. In the "avoidance" procedure the onset of a noxious stimulus is negatively correlated with a response; for example, a lever response prevents or postpones the occurrence of a shock. In the "escape" procedure the termination of a noxious stimulus is posi-

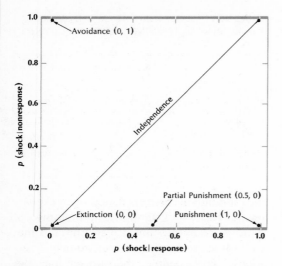

Figure 16.3. Classification of the basic procedures for the study of aversive behavior. See text.

tively correlated with a response; for example, a lever response turns off a shock or reduces its intensity. Logically, there is the alternative of the "preservation" procedure in which the termination of a noxious stimulus is negatively correlated with a response; for example, as long as the rat presses the lever, the shock continues. In all cases of instrumental learning, the task for the subject is to learn the relationship between a response and its consequences. Inferences may be made regarding this learning from (a) the proportion of opportunities on which the subject makes the response, (b) response speed, or (c) choice behavior.

A Classification of the Basic Procedures

Of course, there is an underlying continuum between a perfect positive correlation and a perfect negative correlation, and this is illustrated in Figure 16.3. A point in the lower right-hand corner represents the ideal punishment procedure (the probability of a shock given a response is 1.0, and the probability of a shock given a nonresponse is 0.0). A point in the upper left-hand corner represents an ideal avoidance procedure (the probability of a shock given a response is 0.0 and the probability of a shock given a nonresponse is 1.0). The diagonal between these points would represent a continuum of

procedures between punishment and avoidance. A point in the lower left-hand corner would represent the usual extinction procedure (that is, the probability of getting shock is zero regardless of whether a response is made or not), but the entire diagonal from the lower left-hand corner to the upper right-hand corner represents conditions under which the event (shock onset) is independent of response. The degree of dependence can be represented by the index $(X - Y)/(X + Y)$ where X is the probability of a shock given a response and Y is the probability of a shock given a nonresponse. By this definition, any two points that lie on a straight line whose origin is zero are equivalent in the degree of dependence. For example, the index of dependence is $+1.0$ for all points on the horizontal axis, 0.0 for all points on the drawn diagonal, and -1.0 for all points on the vertical axis.

Of course, two procedures that are equivalent with respect to the dependence of shock upon a response are not necessarily equivalent with respect to the probability of a shock given a response. For example, partial punishment occurs when the index of dependence is 1.0, but the probability of shock given a response is less than 1.0. Most research on the acquisition of aversive behavior has concentrated on the cases in which the dependence was $+1.0$ (punishment) or -1.0 (avoidance); most research on the elimination of aversive behavior has concentrated on a single procedure of nondifferential reinforcement—extinction by omission of the noxious stimulus.

Although Figure 16.3 represents the punishment-avoidance case, if the event were shock termination instead of shock onset, it would represent the escape-preservation case. The lower right-hand corner would represent the usual escape procedure, that is, the probability of shock termination given a response would be 1.0 and the probability of shock termination given a nonresponse would be 0.0. The upper left-hand corner would represent the preservation procedure. All points on the drawn diagonal would represent cases in which shock termination is independent of a response (Overmier & Seligman, 1967).

To represent various cases of classical conditioning, the event could remain shock onset (US), but this event would be conditional upon an experimenter-controlled stimulus (CS) rather than a response. Thus any point below the drawn diagonal would involve explicit association of CS and US, and the lower right-hand corner would represent the usual classical conditioning procedure, that is, the probability of shock onset given a stimulus would be 1.0 and the probability of shock onset given no stimulus would be 0.0. Any point above the drawn diagonal would involve explicit disassociation of the CS and US (Rescorla & LoLordo, 1965). Any point along the diagonal would involve independence of CS and US, and a point in the lower left-hand corner would represent the usual extinction procedure.

Most studies of aversive behavior necessarily involve both classical conditioning and instrumental learning. During a study of classical conditioning the response to the experimenter-controlled stimulus should not affect the nature of the noxious event in any way. Nonetheless, the effect of the puff of air used for classical eyelid conditioning may be different if it hits the open rather than the closed eye; the effect of acid on the tongue used in classical salivary conditioning may be different if the tongue is moist with saliva than if it is dry; the effect of an electric shock used in classical leg-flexion conditioning may be different if the leg is already flexed than if it is extended. Although, in a study of classical conditioning, the behavior of the subject does not influence the experimenter's presentation of the unconditioned noxious stimulus, it may influence the effective intensity of noxious stimulus. Furthermore, in any study of instrumental learning in which a discriminative stimulus is used, there is a relationship between the experimenter-controlled stimulus and the noxious event as well as between a response and an event. For example, if in the presence of a discriminative stimulus a response is followed by a brief electric shock, the subject may decrease its responses in the future either because of the relationship between (1) the stimulus and the noxious event, or (2) the response and the noxious event.

Noxious events may also be presented as a function of time from a stimulus, a response, or another event. All of these procedures will be called "temporal conditioning." Finally, noxious events may be presented in a particular environment randomly with respect to stimuli, responses, and time. Such independent presentation of noxious stimuli will be described as the "noncontingent" procedure, although the events are associated with situational stimuli.

CONDITIONED FEAR

If a noxious event (for example, an electric shock) is contingent upon an experimenter-controlled stimulus (for example, a tone), a subject may become afraid when the tone occurs. In this example, the tone is a conditioned stimulus (CS) or warning signal for the unconditioned stimulus (US) of inevitable shock. This procedure is designed for classical conditioning of fear. Four types of testing procedures have been used to assess the effects of the classical conditioning of fear: (1) direct measurement of elicited autonomic and skeletal responses, (2) conditioned emotional response, (3) acquired drive, and (4) secondary punishment. In the direct procedure the CS is presented at an arbitrary time, and elicited autonomic or skeletal conditioned responses are recorded. In the conditioned emotional response procedure, a subject is trained to perform an instrumental response, and a CS is presented at an arbitrary time. Evidence for a learned association between the CS and the US would be a change of the response rate during the CS greater than that of appropriate control groups. In the acquired drive procedure a specified response terminates the CS; in the secondary punishment procedure a specified response produces the CS. An increase in responding in the acquired drive procedure or a decrease in responding in the secondary punishment procedure is evidence for the acquisition of fear.

The conclusions from these studies of the classical conditioning of fear closely resemble the conclusions of Pavlov that were based on classical salivary conditioning (Pavlov, 1927). In the studies of salivary conditioning the US was food placed in the mouth of a dog (for the alimentary reflex) or acid placed in the mouth of a dog (for the defense reflex). In studies of fear conditioning the US normally is electric shock. Presumably, any stimulus that the animal can perceive may become a conditioned stimulus in either salivary or fear conditioning. Although optimal performance may occur in eyelid and leg flexion conditioning only if the CS precedes the US by a fraction of a second (Woodworth & Schlosberg, 1954), classical fear conditioning and classical salivary conditioning are readily obtained when the interval between CS and US is in the order of minutes. Apparently, the laws of fear conditioning are identical to the laws of salivary conditioning (Maier, Seligman, & Solomon, 1969).

Furthermore, the laws apply not only to a basic principle of acquisition and extinction, but also to the detailed observations of the formation and inhibition of conditioned responses such as the following:

1. *Acquisition of a conditioned response.* If an experimenter-controlled stimulus (S) is repeatedly followed by an unconditioned stimulus (US), it will become a conditioned stimulus (CS+) that will elicit a conditioned response (CR).

2. *Acquisition of a secondary conditioned response.* If an experimenter-controlled stimulus (S) is repeatedly followed by a CS+, it, too, will become a CS+ that will elicit a CR.

3. *Failure of backward conditioning.* If an experimenter-controlled stimulus (S) and a US are in close temporal contiguity, but in the wrong order, that is, the US precedes the S, the S will not become a CS+. On the contrary, it will become an inhibitory stimulus (CS−). (An inhibitory stimulus is one which, when presented in combination with a CS+, reduces the magnitude of the CR more than an equivalent novel stimulus.) (See Fig. 14.2).

4. *Experimental extinction.* If a CS+ is no longer followed by a US the magnitude of the CR will decrease and, eventually, there will be "extinction below zero," that is, the experimenter-controlled stimulus will become an inhibitory stimulus (CS−).

5. *Differential inhibition.* If S_1 is repeatedly followed by a US, and S_2 is not followed by a US, S_1 will become a CS+, and S_2 will become a CS−.

6. *Conditioned inhibition.* If S_1 is repeatedly followed by a US, and a compound stimulus involving S_1 together with another stimulus $(S_1 + S_2)$ is not followed by a US, S_2 will become a CS−.

7. *Inhibition of delay.* If S_1 is followed by a US only after a period of time, the temporal stimuli, shortly after the onset of S_1, will become inhibitory.

8. *External inhibition.* If a novel stimulus is presented during the application of a CS+, the magnitude of the CR will be decreased.

9. *Disinhibition.* If a novel stimulus is presented during the application of a CS−, the magnitude of the CR will be increased.

10. *Induction.* If a CS+ is preceded by a CS−, then the magnitude of the CR will be greater than if the CS+ is preceded by another CS+. The increase in the CR produced by the preceding CS− is called "positive induction." If, on the other hand, a CS− is preceded by a CS+ the CR will be less than if the CS− is preceded by another CS−. The decrease in the CR produced by the CS+ is called "negative induction."

11. *Generalization.* The greater the similarity between an experimenter-controlled stimulus (S) and a CS+, the greater the magnitude of the CR to S (generalization of excitation). The greater the similarity between S and CS−, the greater the inhibitary property of S (generalization of inhibition).

Direct Measurement of Elicited Autonomic and Skeletal Responses

A noxious stimulus elicits a complex set of autonomic and skeletal responses. For example, in the rat, a brief electric shock of sufficient intensity elicits gross motor responses, which may be recorded on a stabilimeter. The responses increase in magnitude as shock intensity is increased (Hoffman, Fleshler, & Abplanalp, 1964). If a relatively weak shock is given, the flinch response predominates, but as the intensity of the shock is increased, jump responses begin to predominate (Kimble, 1955). The probability of vocalization increases as the intensity of the shock increases (Blanchard & Blanchard,

1966). If a dog is given a brief electric shock of sufficient intensity his heart rate increases; also he displays exophthalmic reactions, pupillary dilation, and other autonomic responses (Black, Carlson, & Solomon, 1962).

Predictable reactions are also made following the shock. For example, the termination of an electric shock results in a marked decrease in the heart rate far below the baseline, a phenomenon that has been termed "relief" (Church et al., 1966). Following the termination of shock a subject may remain immobile for long periods of time.

Various emotional states are accompanied by gross cardiovascular changes in heart rate, blood pressure, and so on. Although the association of a previously neutral stimulus (CS) with a noxious stimulus (US) results in the conditioning of all of these responses, typically only the heart rate is monitored. Changes in the heart rate have sometimes been assumed to be an index of "fear," although these changes can also be produced by changes in skeletal movement and breathing.

The presentation of a tone (CS) followed by a shock (US) to a restrained dog rapidly leads to a conditioned increase in the heart rate; presentation of the CS without the US rapidly leads to extinction (Church & Black, 1958). Evidence for inhibition of delay also was reported from the experiment, that is, the latency of the maximum increase in the heart rate was approximately half the interval between CS onset and US onset, under both trace and delayed conditioning situations.

The results of classical conditioning of the heart rate parallel those of salivary conditioning. In the case of heart rate, however, it is possible to get a direct measure both of excitation and inhibition because the heart can beat either faster or slower than a control rate, whereas in the case of salivation, although excitation leads to salivation it is not possible for the amount of secretion to fall below zero (Gantt, 1960).

In the normal subject it is impossible to determine whether the classical conditioning procedure led "directly" to heart rate changes

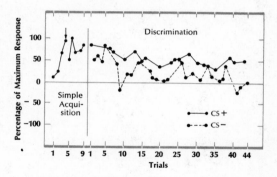

Figure 16.4. Acquisition of a discriminative conditioned heart rate response in a curarized dog. Note that the magnitude of the response to CS+ was greater than to CS−, and that the response to CS− approached 0. (After Black, Carlson, & Solomon, 1962.)

or whether some skeletal mediation was responsible for the results. For example, a CS that is followed by a US could lead to breathing changes or to skeletal movement (for example, struggling) that could be reflected in the measured heart rate change (Smith, 1954). To eliminate such mediating responses, a number of experimenters have conditioned the heart rate response of dogs under curare-like drugs (for example, d-tubocurarine chloride). These muscular relaxants block the junctions between nerves and the striped muscles; with a sufficient dosage, they cause a flaccid paralysis. Despite the lack of all voluntary movement, the subjects apparently suffer no loss of consciousness (Smith et al., 1947) and dogs under curare can still learn.

Figure 16.4 shows the simple acquisition of a conditioned response and a discriminative conditioned response by one curarized dog. (The CS+ was followed by shock; the CS− was not followed by shock.) During the CSs the subject cannot change his breathing pattern because he is paralyzed. (He must, of course, receive artificial respiration.) He does not manifest any overt movement, and even an electromyograph record (EMG) may not indicate change in muscle tension during the CS (Black & Lang, 1964; Black, 1965). Nonetheless, conditioned responses and discriminative conditioned responses do occur.

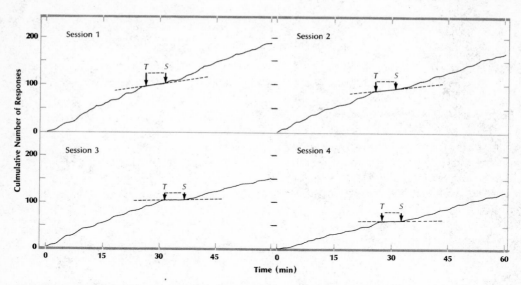

Figure 16.5. The conditioned emotional response of rats. Note the decrease in response rate during the 5-min auditory stimulus during the 4 successive sessions. *T* = tone, *S* = shock. (After Estes & Skinner, 1941.)

Conditioned Emotional Response

One method for the quantitative assessment of anxiety is known as the conditioned emotional response (CER). The reference experiment was performed by Estes and Skinner (1941). Twenty-four rats were trained to press a lever on a 4-minute fixed-interval schedule of reinforcement (a schedule on which the subject received a pellet of food for the first response after each 4-minute interval). After 2 weeks of 1-hour sessions, the subjects were responding at a fairly constant overall rate with local cyclic effects produced by the temporal discrimination of the reinforcement schedule. During each of the next 6 sessions there were 2 presentations of an auditory stimulus, each of which lasted for 3 minutes and terminated with shock. Of course, reduction in the rate of bar pressing did nothing to postpone shock or reduce it. During the first session with the tone-shock pairings the number of responses made during the period of the tone was approximately the same as the average number made during the same fraction of the hour in control experiments, but gradually the subjects began to respond more slowly during the warning signal that was followed by inevitable shock. On subsequent sessions a single 5-minute presentation of the tone was terminated with a shock. Figure 16.5 shows the average cumulative number of responses as a function of time for the 6 subjects with highest response rates during the first 4 sessions with the 5-minute tone. The major result is that subjects markedly decreased their response rates during the presentation of the warning signal. The magnitude of this decrease is frequently regarded as an index of the degree of anxiety. It is thought that the emotional responses elicited by the auditory stimulus somehow interfered with bar pressing. Estes and Skinner (1941) also noted that the magnitude of suppression of bar pressing during the tone (1) increased as a function of sessions, and (2) remained fairly constant throughout the duration of the 5-minute tone. With a substantially greater number of pairings, however, there may be some recovery from the response suppression, and there may be some temporal discrimination (inhibition of delay) during the tone.

Although various autonomic and skeletal

responses may also be made to the CS during a CER experiment, they do not necessarily precede the response suppression (de Toledo & Black, 1966). The CER procedure has provided more complete and reliable information than any of the other methods regarding the determinants of conditioned fear.

The measure of response suppression In the CER experiment of Estes and Skinner (1941) the response rates of the subjects decreased considerably during the tone. The response suppression that takes place during the tone can be readily seen in the cumulative record, but relating the magnitude of the suppression to various independent variables requires a quantitative measure of the suppression. The major consideration in choosing a measure of the effectiveness of a treatment should be its sensitivity to the effects of the treatment. In other words, the measure of the behavior of subjects given any particular treatment should be similar, but the measure of the behavior of subjects given different treatments should be substantially different. An increase in the size of the sample can compensate for any lack of sensitivity in a measure, although, of course, if a more sensitive measure can be used, considerable gains in precision can be made without increase in experimental effort.

Perhaps the simplest measure would be the absolute response rate during the tone. Because there are marked individual differences in the response rate under any particular schedule of reinforcement, however, the rate during the tone does not necessarily reflect the influence of the tone. Whenever there is a substantial correlation between the performance prior to treatment and that during (or following) treatment, as in the case being discussed, some measure of the change will be more sensitive to treatment differences than an absolute measure. Perhaps the simplest combination of the response rate prior to treatment (A) and the response rate during treatment (B) is the difference ($A - B$). In practice, however, most investigators make use of one of the ratio measures. For example, Stein, Sidman, and Brady (1958) used B/A; Hoffman and Fleshler (1961), $(A - B)/A$; and Annau and Kamin (1961) $B/(A + B)$. The range from complete suppression to none at all would be zero to 1 for B/A; 1 to zero for $(A - B)/A$; 0 to .5 for $B/(A + B)$. Measures that are linearly related [for example, B/A and $(A - B)/A$] are necessarily identical in sensitivity. The measure of suppression that is used must be noted carefully before attempting to read a figure based on one of the ratio measures.

The basic procedure for assessing the sensitivity of a measure has been described by Hays (1963), and it has been applied to extensive data from punishment research by Church (1969). The ratio measures for the punishment data were substantially more sensitive to treatment effects than the response rate alone (B) or the difference in response rate ($A - B$).

In many situations a psychologist may choose among various alternative measures of the effectiveness of a treatment. For example, we may use the time taken by a rat to traverse a runway (running time) or its reciprocal (running speed); we may measure the skin resistance (in ohms) or its reciprocal, skin conductance (in mhos). We may use the actual frequency count or the square root or logarithmic transformation of this count. If an arithmetic operation is applied to each of a set of numbers that are recorded by some device, the original numbers are transformed. A measure may be chosen because it can be read directly from standard recording devices, or because it produces scores which may be distributed in a fashion that meets the assumptions of standardized statistical tests. Of course, a measure also may be chosen because it is well established by precedent. The major consideration, however, is the amount of information any measure conveys about a treatment.

Intensity of the unconditioned stimulus The speed of acquisition of the CER and the magnitude of the suppression is a function of the CS, the US, and the relationship between them. A series of studies by Kamin and his colleagues has provided a detailed parametric analysis of these variables. The procedure used in the study of the effect of the intensity of the US (Annau & Kamin, 1961) can serve as the reference for the general procedure. Groups of 8 experimentally naive rats were used as subjects. They were placed on a restricted food schedule that reduced their weight to approximately 75 percent *ad libitum* weight. Then they were trained to press a lever on a 2.5-minute variable-interval schedule of food reinforcement for at least 10 hours. They were then given a series of 2-hour sessions in which the food reinforcement was continued, and, in addition, a CS of white noise was presented for four 3-minute periods. During the pretest session no shock was given, but during the

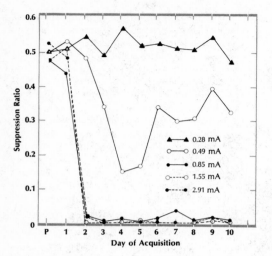

Figure 16.6. The conditioned emotional response as a function of US intensity. The suppression ratio was $B/(A + B)$, where B = response rate during CS, and A = response rate prior to CS. (After Annau & Kamin, 1961.)

next 10 sessions each CS was terminated simultaneously with the delivery of a US of .5 second duration. Each group received a different intensity of the foot shock, the intensities being about .28, .49, .85, 1.55, or 2.91 mA.

Following the 10 sessions of conditioning, 10 sessions of (Pavlovian) extinction were given, during which the treatment was continued, but without foot shock. The dependent measure was a suppression ratio, $B/(A + B)$, where B is the number of responses during the 3-minute interval of the CS and A is the number of responses during the 3-minute interval prior to the CS. The results show that the greater the intensity of the US, the greater the magnitude of response suppression during conditioning (Figure 16.6). At an intense US (.85 mA and above) there was nearly complete suppression by the second conditioning session. At an intermediate level of intensity (.49 mA) there was partial suppression, followed by recovery of the response rate. At the mildest level of intensity used (.28 mA) there was no detectable suppression, although the intensity produced an obvious flinching response.

This intensity, however, was sufficient to suppress a response in the presence of a discriminative stimulus when each response was followed by the noxious stimulus (the punishment procedure).

Disinhibition The presentation of noxious stimuli to a subject while it is responding for food reinforcement may result in a decrement in response rate. At high intensity and at a rapid rate of presentation, particularly if the noxious stimuli are unsignalled, there may be considerable response suppression. When a novel stimulus is presented during response suppression, disinhibition results, in other words, there is an increase rather than a decrease in response rate during the signal (Brimer & Kamin, 1963). This increase in response rate to a novel stimulus was particularly marked in subjects whose response rate was most suppressed by the unsignaled shocks. If subjects were given additional sessions of training without shock, so that their response rate was no longer suppressed, prior exposure to the shock had no residual effect on the response to the novel stimulus. Of course, presentation of a novel stimulus to a subject that has simply been trained to perform an instrumental response will result in a decrement in the response rate (external inhibition). Brimer (1963) has demonstrated, however, that the presentation of a novel stimulus will result in an increase in the response rate if the response previously has been inhibited by a number of different variables (extinction, satiation, free shock, and so on). This procedure provides a method for exploring Pavlovian disinhibition.

Temporal relationship between conditioned stimulus and unconditioned stimulus Most of the research on the CER has employed a delayed conditioning paradigm, that is, the CS remained on during the CS-US interval. A trace conditioning procedure is one in which the CS terminates prior to the onset of the US. Kamin (1961) demonstrated that this procedure is also adequate to produce response suppression. In that study, with the interval between the onset of the CS and the onset of the US constant at 3 min (the CS-US interval), the greater the length of the CS (that is, the shorter the trace interval) the greater the magnitude of response suppression. In the case of subjects with a 2-min CS followed by a 1-min trace, suppression developed during the trace interval and remained specific to that interval.

Although the "association span of the white rat" (Warner, 1932) depends upon the procedure that is used for measurement, it is clear that suppression can occur when an interval in the order of minutes separates CS onset or termination from US onset. Nonetheless, the magnitude of the response suppression is greater if a delayed conditioning procedure is used than it is if a trace conditioning procedure is used, particularly if the interval between CS onset and US onset is long. Even an extremely brief half-second time gap between the termination of the CS and the introduction of the US can greatly reduce the magnitude of response suppression (Kamin, 1965).

As in the case of Pavlovian salivary conditioning, backward conditioning does not occur (see pp. 557; 710). For example, using procedures similar to those of his previous experiments, Kamin (1963) found that rats did not reduce their rate of lever pressing during a 3-min white-noise CS that immediately followed the termination of a 0.5-sec shock US.

Intensity of the conditioned stimulus The rapidity of conditioning is positively related to the intensity of the CS (Kamin & Schaub, 1963). This result implies either that an intense CS is more effective than a weak CS (stimulus intensity dynamism) or that a large stimulus change is more effective than a small stimulus change (discrimination hypothesis). To distinguish between these two hypotheses, comparisons have been made between CSs of various increments in intensity to 80 dB

(70–80, 60–80, 50–80, 45–80 and 0–80) and CSs of various decrements in intensity from 80 dB (80–70, 80–60, 80–50, 80–45 and 80–0). The results indicated that the greater the stimulus change, and the greater the physical intensity contiguous with the US (that could not be separated from the direction of change in this experiment), the greater the magnitude of suppression. Although this function is present when delayed conditioning procedures are used, it is particularly marked when the trace conditioning procedure is used (Kamin, 1965). Similar results for pairs of stimuli differing in intensity have been obtained by Sadowski (1966) under conditions where one stimulus was paired with food reinforcement and the other stimulus was paired with omission of food.

Generalization If a subject is conditioned to one stimulus, the maximum suppression occurs to that stimulus, but suppression also occurs to a range of similar stimuli (generalization). The magnitude of suppression to a stimulus is closely related to the physical similarity between it and the one involved in the original CER conditioning. For example, Ray and Stein (1959) presented a high-frequency tone with shock and a low-frequency tone without shock (discrimination training) and found that intermediate frequencies produced intermediate suppression. Similarly, Hoffman (1965) trained pigeons to peck a key and then adapted them to a 2-minute variable-interval schedule of food reinforcement. The birds then were given pairings of a 1000 Hz tone and shock during food-reinforced sessions. After the degree of suppression had stabilized, they were tested with frequencies above, at, and below the 1000 Hz tone while responding on the schedule of food reinforcement. None of the tones during the tests were followed by shock. Figure 17.8 (p. 759) shows the suppression for one subject to various stimulus frequencies (tones) as a function of trials of testing. Note that the generalization gradient became narrower as extinction proceeded.

The generalization gradient also was narrower for pigeons that had undergone a high degree of deprivation (70 percent *ad libitum* weight) than for pigeons with lower degree of deprivation (80 percent *ad libitum* weight).

Relative duration of the conditioned stimulus In most studies of the CER a CS 3 to 5 minutes in duration is presented no more often than once or twice in an hour. If the CS is on during only a small percentage of the session, for example, less than 10 percent of the time, the absolute duration of the CS does not appear to affect the magnitude of suppression (Kamin, 1965). For example, if a subject with a 2-min or 3-min variable-interval schedule of reward suppresses completely during the CS, it loses relatively few reinforcements. If the CS occurs during a large percentage of the session, the subject would lose many reinforcements if it suppressed completely during the signal. Stein, Sidman, and Brady (1958) varied the duration of the

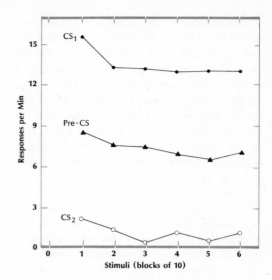

Figure 16.8. The conditioned emotional response and differential inhibition. Response rate prior to the CSs, during CS_1 that had previously been followed by a US, and during CS_2 that had previously (in combination with CS_1) been predictive of a period of safety. (After Rescorla & LoLordo, 1965.)

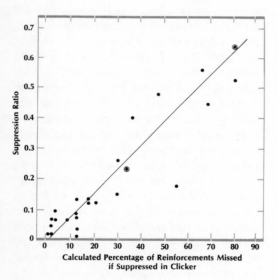

Figure 16.7. The conditioned emotional response as a function of percentage of reinforcements that would be lost if suppression were complete. The suppression ratio was B/A, where B = response rate during CS, and A = response rate prior to CS. (After Stein, Sidman, & Brady, 1958.)

CS and the interval between CS presentations, and they found that the log of the relative duration of the CS (and, therefore, the percentage of reinforcements that would be missed if the subject did not respond during the CS) was linearly related to the magnitude of suppression (Figure 16.7). The implication of this result is that a subject is more likely to suppress during a signal if such suppression does not involve the loss of reinforcements. Alternatively, the results might be interpreted as indicating greater conditioning of the CER if the interval between trials is long relative to the duration of the CS. Such results would be quite consistent with studies of the interval between trials using food reinforcement.

Effect of the conditioned emotional response on avoidance behavior Although the presentation of a CS that has been followed by a noxious stimulus will lead to a decrease in the response rate of a rat pressing a lever for food reward, it will lead to an *increase*

in the rate of a monkey pressing a lever to postpone shock (Sidman, Herrnstein, & Conrad, 1957). This result was replicated and extended by Rescorla and LoLordo (1965) who trained dogs to postpone shock for 30 seconds by jumping from one side of a shuttlebox to the other. In separate sessions, the dogs were confined to one side of the shuttlebox and given presentations of a 5-second CS_1 followed either by a shock or by CS_2. Under these conditions, CS_1 would be expected to elicit fear responses, and CS_2 to inhibit the fear responses (conditioned inhibition). A test session was then run in which CS_1 and CS_2 were presented for 5 seconds each without respect to the dogs' behavior, and without any shocks (an extinction procedure). Figure 16.8 shows that, relative to the pre-CS rate, CS_1 resulted in an increase in response rate and CS_2 resulted in a decrease. As in the experiment by Sidman, Herrnstein, and Conrad (1957), a CS that is followed by shock increased the rate of avoidance responding, presumably because it increased fear. In addition, the conditioned inhibitor (CS_2) decreased the rate of avoidance responding, presumably because it decreased fear. Rescorla and LoLordo (1965) also demonstrated differential inhibition: If CS_1 was followed by shock, a CS_2 that was not followed by shock decreased the rate of avoidance responding. Finally, they demonstrated that in a situation with unsignaled shocks with CS_2 guaranteeing a period of safety, CS_2 also decreased the rate of avoidance. Further research with the same general procedures has demonstrated inhibition of delay, inhibition from backward conditioning, and positive and negative induction (Maier, Seligman, & Solomon, 1969). Such observations demonstrate that Pavlovian inhibitory processes, like Pavlovian excitatory processes, may be investigated by the CER procedure.

This final result is of methodological importance with respect to a pseudoconditioning-control group. If a subject is more responsive to a CS after it has been paired several times with a US, there is still the question of whether the unpaired presentation of the CS and the US would not have led to a similar result (pseudoconditioning). One way to set up a control is to present the same CS and US given to one group of subjects to another group of subjects, but without allowing the US to follow shortly after the CS. The argument for this procedure would be that if the conditioning group (with CS and US paired) were more responsive than the pseudoconditioning control group (with CS and US explicitly unpaired), the conditioning group must have developed an association between the CS and US (an excitatory process) as a result of the pairing. Unfortunately, a difference between the two groups could also result from a disassociation of CS and US (inhibitory conditioning) in the group used as a control for the pseudoconditioning with explicitly unpaired presentations of CS and US. To eliminate the contingency between CS and US the random presentation of CS and US would be the appropriate control for pseudoconditioning (Rescorla, 1967). (This will lead to occasional pairings of CS and US, but the conditional probability of a US given a CS will be equal to the overall probability of a US, that is, the two events will be independent.)

Acquired Drive

If a noxious stimulus is given in one particular location, a subject can learn to perform some response to escape from that location. The reference experiment was reported by Miller (1948). Rats were trained to escape from shock in a white compartment by running through an open door into a black compartment. The animals continued to run from the white compartment into the black compartment during the 5 trials on which no shock was given. The major problem was to determine whether a subject would learn to perform a new response in order to escape from the white compartment. During the next 16 trials the door between the two compartments was closed, but the subject could

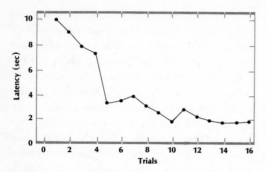

Figure 16.9. Acquired drive. The mean latency of the wheel-rotation response decreased as a function of trials. Rotation of the wheel opened a door that permitted the rat to leave the white compartment (in which it had been shocked) and to enter the black compartment. (After Miller, 1948.)

open the door by rotating a wheel a small fraction of a turn. Thirteen of the 25 animals turned the wheel on 4 or more of the first 8 trials. The response latency of these subjects decreased as a function of trials (Figure 16.9). The situation was changed for the next trials, so that the wheel could not be used to

open the door; rather, using a lever would do so. The median number of turns on the wheel decreased to zero, and the average speed of pressing the lever increased as a function of trials. As a result of the escape training, subjects learned to be afraid in the white compartment and the black compartment acquired secondary reinforcing properties (Lawler, 1965). If the subject makes a response (for example, running, turning a wheel, or pressing a lever) that permits it to terminate the cues for fear, it will learn to make that response, and the reinforcement may be called "fear reduction" or "termination of stimuli associated with noxious stimulus." Some of the early experiments with this procedure are summarized by Miller (1951).

The acquired drive procedure has not been used widely for the evaluation of Pavlovian conditioning because (1) a situational stimulus is used rather than one controlled by the experimenter; (2) if the subject does not "accidentally" perform the arbitrarily selected response rapidly, the repeated or long pres-

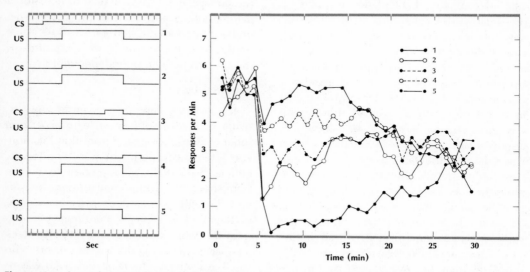

Figure 16.10. Secondary punishment. *Left:* Schematic representation of the five different arrangements of the 3-sec CS and the 10-sec US. In Group 5 the CS occurred 2-min after US termination. *Right:* Mean number of responses per minute of rats in the five groups. Each response produced food reinforcement and a flashing light (secondary punishment) that had previously been followed by electric shock (US). (After Mowrer & Aiken, 1954.)

entation of the CS leads to the extinction of fear; and (3) the duration of the exposure of the subject to the stimuli is not under the experimenter's control.

Secondary Punishment

The secondary punishment procedure has also been used to derive the general principles of acquisition of fear. Mowrer and Aiken (1954), for example, used this procedure to evaluate the role of the temporal relationship between the CS and the US in fear conditioning. Fifty rats were trained in one compartment to press a lever for food reinforcement (20 responses, each followed by a food pellet), and then they were placed in another compartment for fear conditioning. The CS was a 7.5 W light that flickered at the rate of 4 Hz, and the US was an electric shock of 165 VAC (with 175,000 Ω resistance in series). Ten subjects were assigned to each of five groups (Figure 16.10, left panel). The CS occurred either during the 3 seconds preceding the US, the first 3 seconds of the US, the last 3 seconds of the US, 3 seconds following the US, or 2 minutes following the US. On the next 5 days the subjects were allowed to make 5 food-reinforced responses in one compartment, and they later received one fear-conditioning trial in the other compartment. Finally, on the test session each subject was allowed to press the lever for food for 5 minutes and then, for the last 25 minutes of the session, each response was followed not only by food, but also by a 3 second presentation of the CS. The results are shown in Figure 16.10, right panel. In all groups there was a decrease in the response rate followed by some recovery, but the magnitude of the decrease was greater in groups in which the CS preceded or overlapped the beginning of the US than in groups in which the CS followed or overlapped the end of the US. This experiment was replicated by Matsumiya (1960), who extended the study to three shock intensities (.2, .4, and .6 mA). The .2 mA shock produced

no effective secondary punishing effect with any pattern of CS and US, but with the .4 and .6 mA shocks, the results of Mowrer and Aiken (1954) were replicated. These results are consistent with the conclusion that the greater the intensity of the US, the greater the effectiveness of a previously neutral stimulus as a secondary punisher.

It should be noted that studies of this type require careful preliminary investigations to determine appropriate shock levels, amounts of training, levels of deprivation, and so on, to insure that some, but not complete, suppression of the response is produced.

Fear is developed to a CS as a result of the onset of a noxious stimulus, not its termination. Mowrer and Solomon (1954) compared groups with two durations of US (3 and 10 sec) and two conditions of shock termination (abrupt and gradual). The CS for all groups occurred during the 3 sec preceding the onset of the US. The effectiveness of the CS as a secondary punisher was equivalent in all groups, a result that implied that the conditions of onset rather than of termination of the noxious stimulus are critical for the establishment of conditioned fear. Of course, as Mowrer and Solomon pointed out, if the US were very short it would be less effective for producing fear than a shock of longer duration because it would be less severe.

In Mowrer's procedure, the test session introduces no shock, and when a CS is no longer followed by a US, it gradually loses its secondary punishing function. To avoid this extinction effect Hake and Azrin (1965) described a procedure for concurrently maintaining a secondary punishment and a test of its effectiveness. A pigeon was trained to peck a key on a 2-min variable-interval schedule of food reinforcement, and each response produced a 5-sec CS. To develop and maintain the secondary punishment, the pigeon was occasionally given a 15-sec CS followed by a 100-msec shock, the pairings occurring on the average, once every 6 minutes. Under these conditions, there was evidence of a conditioned emotional response (a reduction in response rate during the CS) and secondary punishment (a reduction in response rate in the absence of the CS).

In general, studies of secondary punishment have found that subjects respond more slowly (1) during the warning signal (a conditioned emotional response), (2) prior to the onset of a warning signal because a response may produce a warning signal (anticipation of the CS), and (3) following a warning signal (reaction to the CS). While the experimental literature gives us some clues as to what factors are controlling suppression, at present, knowledge of the basic mechanisms is far from complete.

ESCAPE

Consider the following situation: A rat is placed in the starting compartment of a straight alley that consists of a start box, a 4-ft runway, and a goal box. When the guillotine door is opened a shock begins on the floor of the start box and alley, but not in the goal box. When the rat reaches the goal box a guillotine door is lowered to prevent retracing, and the rat is removed from the apparatus. On the first trial the rat reaches the goal in 5 seconds. Oddly enough, most rats will have a somewhat longer escape latency on the second trial, but in 20 or 30 trials the subject normally reaches or exceeds a speed of 4 ft/sec.

In general terms, the escape training procedure is one that involves the presentation of a noxious stimulus that the subject can reduce or eliminate by an appropriate instrumental response. The escape response may involve moving through an apparatus such as a straight alley or a one-way shuttlebox or, to eliminate intertrial handling, a circular alley or a two-way shuttlebox; it may require manipulating an object in the apparatus such as a lever, a wheel, or a panel, or moving a particular limb.

Because an escape response occurs follow-

ing each presentation of the noxious stimulus, response latency or response speed are the usual dependent variables, and learning is inferred from the reduction of latency or an increase in speed as a function of trials.

Acquisition

Escape learning follows the general laws of learning of instrumental responses for positive reinforcement.[2] Asymptotic performance is a function of the magnitude of reinforcement (relative reduction of shock intensity), the delay of reinforcement (delay of shock termination), and the percentage of responses reinforced.

Magnitude of reinforcement If the response terminates the shock, the asymptotic running speed is positively related to shock intensity, at least through a considerable range of intensity (Trapold & Fowler, 1960). In one experiment 30 rats were trained to escape from shock in an alley consisting of a start box (8 inches long), an alley (48 inches), and a goal box (12 inches). Each subject was given 20 trials of training during a single session. The starting time (to the nearest .01 sec) was measured from the raising of a guillotine door until the subject broke a photobeam 6 inches down the alley. The running time (also to the nearest .01 sec) was measured from the time that the subject broke this photobeam until he broke another photobeam located 2 inches inside the goal

[2] Some reinforcements consist of the onset of a stimulus; others consist of the termination of a stimulus. These have been called "positive reinforcement" and "negative reinforcement," respectively. Food has been called a "positive reinforcer" because its presentation to a hungry animal has been demonstrated to increase the frequency of a preceding response; electric shock has been called a "negative reinforcer" because its termination has been demonstrated to increase the frequency of a preceding response. Thus the "positive" and "negative" refer to the increase or decrease in the magnitude of the reinforcing stimulus. This distinction between positive and negative reinforcement is arbitrary in the case of some reinforcing stimuli. For example, if a change from temperature X to temperature Y is reinforcing, one may equally well say that the onset of Y is a positive reinforcer or the termination of X is a negative reinforcer. The fact of fundamental importance for behavior is whether the stimulus change is reinforcing, neutral, or punishing.

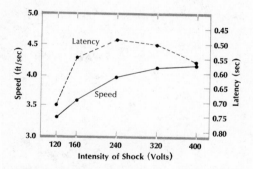

Figure 16.11. Mean escape latency and speed as a function of intensity of the noxious stimulus. (After Trapold & Fowler, 1960.)

box. These times were converted to speed scores (ft/sec) and the results, averaged across the 6 subjects in each group and for the last 8 trials of training, are presented in Figure 16.11. Running speed increased as a function of shock intensity, but starting speed increased with shock intensity up to 240 V (250,000 Ω in series) and then decreased with further increases in intensity. High intensity shock apparently elicits responses that are incompatible with short starting latency, perhaps causing the subject to jump or producing muscle tetany. Throughout most of its

range, however, increasing shock intensity leads to an increase in speed, presumably because the level of drive is higher, or the reduction of the noxious stimulus is greater.

The level to which the shock can be reduced is an important determinant of escape performance, even when the shock intensity from which subjects are escaping is kept constant. Bower, Fowler, and Trapold (1959) trained rats to run from an alley where they were shocked with 250 V to a goal box where they were shocked by 50 V, 150 V, or 200 V. The speed of the subject was related to the voltage of the goal box, and when the intensity of the shock in the goal box was changed there was a rapid change in the speed of the subject appropriate to the new level of shock. A comparison of the speed of rats that were changed to a particular condition with those maintained on that condition provided no suggestion of a contrast effect (Figure 16.12).

It would not be correct, of course, to assume that the reinforcing value of an escape

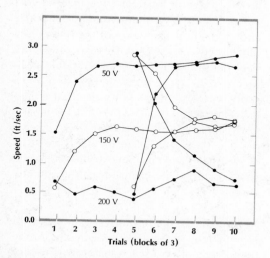

Figure 16.12. Median escape speed as a function of the intensity of the noxious stimulus in the goal box. Shock in the start box and the alley was 250 V. (After Bower, Fowler, & Trapold, 1959.)

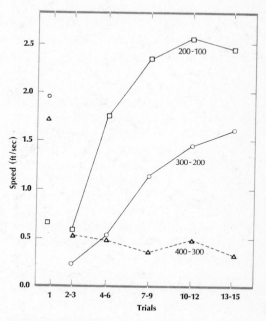

Figure 16.13. Median escape speed as a function of trials for the groups with 100 V reduction in intensity of shock. (After Campbell & Kraeling, 1953.)

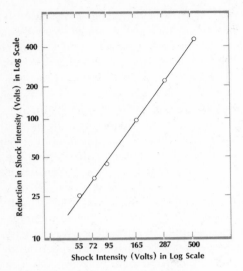

Figure 16.14. The reinforcement difference limen. The reduction in shock intensity necessary for rats to choose the lower shock in a tilt cage 75 percent of the time. (After Campbell, 1956.)

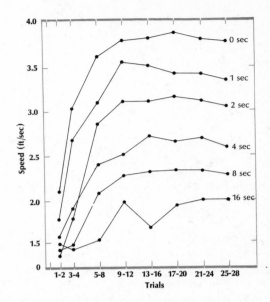

Figure 16.15. Mean escape speed as a function of delay of shock termination. The delay of shock termination is the number of seconds between the rat's entry into the goal box and termination of the shock. (After Fowler & Trapold, 1962.)

response would be accurately measured by the reduction in the absolute number of volts produced by the response. Presumably, the Weber-Fechner relationship, investigated thoroughly in psychophysical studies of stimulus discrimination, would at least be approximated roughly in studies of escape learning. On the basis of this hypothesis, Campbell and Kraeling (1953) compared the reinforcing value of a reduction of 100 V when the initial value was 400, 300, or 200 V. They found that asymptotic running speed was a function of the reduction in shock relative to the initial level and not to the absolute reduction in shock intensity (see Figure 16.13).

In an extension of the research described above Campbell (1956) found the reduction in voltage necessary for a rat to choose the lower voltage in a tilt cage 75 percent of the time. He found that as the intensity of the noxious stimulus is increased, the absolute reduction in intensity necessary to produce a just noticeable difference increases (Figure 16.14).

Delay of reinforcement   If the escape response is reinforced by a reduction in shock intensity when the subject reaches the goal compartment, then the asymptotic performance should be a function of the immediacy of the shock termination. This experiment has been performed by Fowler and Trapold (1962). In six different groups, termination of a shock intensity of 240 volts occurred immediately after a rat reached the goal compartment or 1, 2, 4, 8, or 16 sec after the rat reached the goal compartment. Figure 16.15 shows that the longer the delay before the shock is terminated, the lower the running speed.

Percentage of responses reinforced   If termination of the noxious stimulus is the reinforcement for escape learning, is it conceptually possible for an experimenter not to provide reinforcement on a series of trials? Nonreinforcement would be nontermination

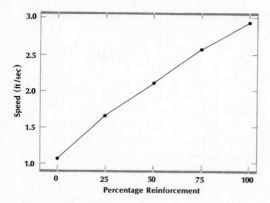

Figure 16.16. Mean escape speed on Trials 13–20 as a function of percentage reinforcement. Reinforcement was immediate termination of the shock; nonreinforcement was a 20-sec delay of shock termination. (After Bower, 1960.)

of the shock, but the subject must sometime be removed. In practice, a relatively long (such as 20 sec) delay of shock termination is considered nonreinforcement. As shown in Figure 16.16, the greater the percentage of responses that are reinforced, the greater the mean speed (Bower, 1960).

In a free-responding situation subjects readily learn to perform instrumental responses for schedules of positive reinforcement far less than 100 percent. If termination of a noxious stimulus is analogous to presentation of a positive reinforcement, then subjects should learn to make an instrumental response under various schedules of shock termination (fixed and variable interval, fixed and variable ratio, differential reinforcement of low response rates, and so on). Some investigators (for example, Winograd, 1965) have obtained evidence that schedules of positive reinforcement and schedules of termination of noxious stimulation lead to similar patterns of behavior. However, the competing responses elicited by electric shock are a major source of interference and preclude investigations of all but relatively short interval and ratio schedules. A noxious stimulus that does not elicit such marked

incompatible responses would be required to demonstrate the essential similarity between the presentation of a reward (positive reinforcement) and the removal of a noxious stimulus (negative reinforcement).

Differential reinforcement of quantitative aspects of the escape response Various qualitative and quantitative aspects of the escape response may be explicitly taught by means of differential (correlated) reinforcement. For example, the speed of the escape response, like other quantitative and qualitative characteristics, can be specifically selected (Logan, 1960). If subjects are given immediate shock termination for reaching the goal slowly (for example, in more than 2.5 seconds) but long-delayed shock termination for reaching the goal quickly, these subjects typically learn to respond just slower than the arbitrarily selected criterion (much slower than otherwise). In one experiment, in which reinforcement was correlated with a slow response, rats learned to reach the goal at a sufficiently slow speed to gain reinforcement in more than 90 percent of the trials (Bower, 1960).

Prior exposure to inescapable shock A number of investigators have found that a series of inescapable shocks profoundly retards the development of subsequent escape behavior. For example, Dinsmoor and Campbell (1956) compared the escape performance of rats that had received a 15-min period in the apparatus, with or without a .2 mA inescapable shock. During a 35-min session of lever-response escape training (with an interval from shock termination to next shock onset of 20 sec) the group with prior exposure to shock made significantly fewer escape responses than the group without such prior exposure. Such interference may be a result of learning incompatible responses, adapting to shock, massive parasympathetic reaction, or learning the independence between a response and shock termination.

Overmier and Seligman (1967) found that prior exposure to inescapable shock markedly interfered with subsequent shuttlebox escape learning, even if the subjects were curarized during the prior exposure to prevent the development of competing skeletal responses. Even if an extremely high (6.5 mA) shock was given during escape training, it did not overcome the interference effect. It is possible that during prior exposure to inescapable shock the subject learns the independence of shock termination and responding, that is, he learns that he is helpless (Maier, Seligman, & Solomon, 1969).

Extinction

Omission of reinforcement What is the procedure for the "extinction" of an escape response? By definition, omission of the reinforcement for a response is the procedure for extinction. If termination of the noxious stimulus is the reinforcement for escape learning, the procedure to bring about the extinction of an escape response would be to continue the shock (or, at least, to provide a long delay of shock termination).

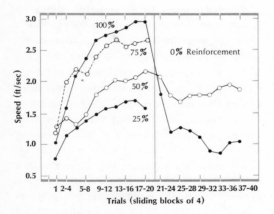

Figure 16.17. Extinction of escape as a function of percentage reinforcement. Reinforcement was immediate termination of the shock; nonreinforcement was a 20-sec delay of shock termination. (After Bower, 1960.)

Although such studies are rare, presumably the same factors that contribute to resistance to extinction of an appetitive response contribute to the resistance to extinction of an escape response. For example, as we see in Figure 16.17, groups of rats that had been trained with immediate shock termination on 50 percent of the trials in a runway (partial reinforcement) had greater resistance to extinction than subjects that had been trained with immediate shock termination on 100 percent of the trials (Bower, 1960).

Omission of noxious stimulus Most studies of "extinction" of an escape response have omitted the noxious stimulus whether the subject made the response or not (for example, Sheffield & Temmer, 1950). Suppose a rat were placed in the starting compartment of a straight alley, the door opened, but no shock presented regardless of the behavior of the subject. This is an extinction procedure from the point of view of classical conditioning, for the unconditioned stimulus (reinforcement) of shock no longer follows the conditioned stimulus of the rising gate. This is an adequate procedure for the elimination of the escape response because (1) the absence of the noxious stimulus results in (a) the classical extinction of fear, (b) a decreased motivational level, and (c) generalization decrement; and (2) there is no differential reinforcement (that is, shock reduction) for performing the instrumental escape response. Omission of a noxious stimulus may also produce extinction of secondary escape, that is, extinction of escape from a stimulus that has been paired with a noxious event.

Punishment extinction The previous two procedures for the elimination of an escape response (omission of reinforcement of the instrumental response and omission of the noxious stimulus) were similar in that they provided nondifferential reinforcement, that is, terminating the shock was independent of the response. Explicit punishment of an escape response, however, may lead to even more rapid elimination of the response than mere omission of the noxious stimulus (Seward & Raskin, 1960). Paradoxically, however, under some conditions punishment of an escape response may lead to an increase in the response speed and an increase in the number of trials necessary to reach a criterion of extinction (Gwinn, 1949; Brown, Martin & Morrow, 1964). This has been called "vicious-circle behavior" because the behavior leads to punishment that leads to an increase in response speed, and so on. It has also been called "masochistic" or "self-punitive" behavior because the rat appears to seek the noxious stimulus. Brown (1969) has reviewed the relevant studies and described the conditions under which punishment of an escape or avoidance response is most likely to increase resistance to extinction. Self-punitive behavior often occurs if the conditions of punishment extinction are similar to the con-

ditions of escape training, and the response elicited by the shock and the response that terminates the shock are similar to the escape response.

AVOIDANCE

Consider the following situation: A dog was placed in one side of a shuttlebox having two similar compartments (see Figure 16.18). Every 3 minutes the gate separating the two compartments was raised and the lights in the compartment in which the subject was confined were turned off (a compound warning signal CS). If the subject failed to jump across the barrier separating the two compartments within 10 seconds a shock was turned on. Both signal and shock terminated when a subject eventually entered the other compartment; such a response is called an *escape*. If, in contrast, the subject moved to the other compartment within 10 seconds after the onset of the signal, the signal terminated and no shock occurred. Such a response is called an *avoidance*. (If no response occurred within 2 minutes, both signal and shock were terminated.)

The behavior of a fairly typical subject during the procedure described above is given by Solomon and Wynne (1953): On the first trial the subject showed a general investigatory response at the onset of the signal, but when the shock went on, the subject began to move about the compartment vigorously and to manifest considerable emotional upset (vocalization, urination, defecation). Eventually, by chance, the subject jumped across the barrier to the other compartment, a response that resulted in escape from the shock and termination of the signal. Within a few trials the subject became motionless at the onset of the signal, perhaps with signs of emotionality. When the shock went on the subject rapidly moved into the other compartment (escape). A few trials later, when the signal occurred, the subject moved into the other compartment (avoidance), the signal termi-

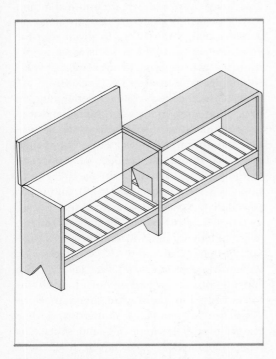

Figure 16.18. Diagram of a shuttle box with swinging door separating the two compartments.

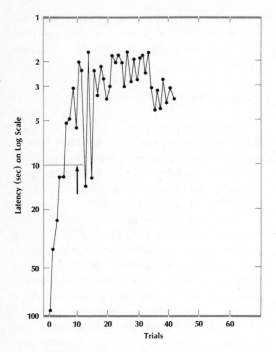

Figure 16.19. Acquisition of an avoidance response as a function of trials. Latency on successive trials for a single dog. (After Solomon & Wynne, 1953.)

nated, and the shock did not go on. During subsequent trials of training the proportion of avoidance responses increased and the latency of the avoidance responses decreased (Figure 16.19). The important determinants of the acquisition and maintenance of such discriminative avoidance behavior have been summarized by Brush and Solomon (1956) and Hoffman (1966).

Acquisition of the Avoidance Response

Conditioned fear Any avoidance learning situation that involves a warning signal (S+) provides the opportunity for the development of conditioned fear.[3] Two-process

[3] The warning signal in an avoidance learning situation is often called a conditioned stimulus (CS+). In this chapter the terminological convention has been adopted to call a signal a conditioned stimulus (CS+) if the noxious stimulus is independent of any instrumental response, and to call the signal a discriminative stimulus (S+) if the noxious stimulus depends, at least in part, upon some instrumental response.

theories of avoidance learning emphasize the distinction between the conditioning of fear to the signal and the consequences of an instrumental avoidance response (for example, Schlosberg, 1937; Mowrer, 1947). The conditioned fear presumably serves a critical role in the development and maintenance of the avoidance response. A systematic review of evidence relevant to two-process theories of avoidance learning has been provided by Rescorla and Solomon (1967).

The development of conditioned fear can be monitored during avoidance learning by measuring heart rate changes in the presence of an S+ (Black, 1959), but the interpretation of such data is complicated by the influence of gross motor movements on the heart rate. During the course of avoidance learning most subjects appear to learn to be afraid of the warning signal within a few trials, but eventually they learn to perform the avoidance response in an automatic and matter-of-fact manner. (A danger signal on a boiler dial is not likely to produce great emotion in a man who has learned a simple instrumental response to prevent an explosion, unless the response is blocked.)

Because the heart rate is dependent, in part, upon gross motor responding, an independent measure of fear is necessary to support the notion that fear increases and then decreases during the course of avoidance learning. One such measure is the conditioned emotional response (CER), and it has provided tests of the course of fear during avoidance learning (Hoffman & Fleshler, 1962; Kamin, Brimer, & Black, 1963). In the experiment by Kamin and his coworkers, rats were trained to press a lever on a 2.5-min variable-interval schedule of food reinforcement, and then were given trials of avoidance learning in a shuttlebox, with a 20-sec interval between S+ and shock. Independent groups were given trials until they reached a criterion of 1, 3, 9, or 27 avoidance responses. They then were returned to the lever box for further training, but now there was a 20-sec S+ presented on the average of once each 4 minutes. The magnitude of the suppression of bar pressing after the subject was exposed to an S+ was a U-shaped function of the number of avoidances in the shuttlebox; that is, the maximum suppression occurred with intermediate criteria. The initial training trials were almost always escape trials, with S+ followed by shock. Therefore, additional trials of avoidance training initially increased the magnitude of conditioned fear because they resulted in an increase in the number of classical conditioned fear acquisition trials.

The magnitude of suppression of subjects that received 1, 3, 9, or 27 classical pairings of CS and US in the shuttlebox was an increasing function of the number of pairings. Eventually, however, additional trials of avoidance training may decrease the magnitude of conditioned fear since each successful avoidance is an extinction trial for conditioned fear; S+ is not followed by the shock. (The magnitude of the suppression of subjects that received extinction of avoidance responding in the shuttlebox to a criterion of 0, 5, or 20 failures to avoid was a decreasing function of the criterion.) The decrease in the magnitude of conditioned fear during avoidance training may also have been a consequence of the formation of conditioned inhibition. The S+ and a response was never followed by the shock, and the S+ without the response was always followed by the US. Therefore, the response (a subject-produced stimulus) could serve as a conditioned inhibitor of fear. If the response were blocked, the latent fear would be manifested (Solomon, Kamin, & Wynne, 1953).

Emergence of the avoidance response In the case of a response that is followed by positive reinforcement, most theories of learning make no attempt to account for the emergence of the first response. When it occurs, however, the principles of classical conditioning and instrumental learning are used to account for the selective strengthening or weakening of specific responses in the presence of specific stimulus configurations. In the case of avoidance learning, however, some attempts have been made to account for the emergence of the first avoidance response. Before they make the first avoidance response, most subjects have developed conditioned fear to the S+, and they have learned to escape rapidly from the shock. A substitution theory, that S+ becomes equivalent to the shock, would imply that the latency of the first avoidance response to an S+ typically would be as short as the escape response to the shock. However, if the first avoidance response had a latency nearly as long as the interval between S+ and shock, the response might be regarded as an escape response that had "moved backward in time." Neither position is strongly supported by the data.

As in the case of a positively reinforced response, any factor that increases the general level of spontaneous activity (for example, deprivation conditions) will increase the rate of most responses that are arbitrarily selected to be the active avoidance response. In addition, the treatment on the escape trials is crucial. A subject will learn an avoidance response more rapidly if (1) it has had prior escape learning (Church & Solomon, 1956), (2) the same response is used for avoidance as for escape (Mowrer & Lamoreaux, 1946), (3) the noxious stimulus terminates at the time of the escape response rather than, say, 5 sec afterwards, and (4) the S+ terminates at the time of the escape response rather than at shock onset or 5 sec after the escape response (Kamin, 1959; Kamin et al., 1959).

Reinforcement of the avoidance response Escape responses are reinforced by termination of the noxious stimulus, but what reinforces avoidance responses? Inasmuch as such responses result in termination of the warning signal, and prevent the occurrence of the noxious stimulus, it is reasonable to ask if one or both of these consequences of the avoidance response might reinforce it. Since, during trials on which the subject escaped (but had failed to avoid), the warning signal had been followed by the noxious stimulus, there should be formation of conditioned fear to the warning signal. Termination of such an experimenter-produced signal could produce relief from fear, and thus it could serve as the reinforcement of the avoidance response. On the other hand, a response during the warning signal guarantees a long interval without a noxious stimulus, so that stimuli produced by that response could become safety signals and thus serve as the reinforcement of the avoidance response. Kamin (1956) compared the effects of response termination of the warning signal and prevention of the noxious stimulus on avoidance learning. Under the "classical" procedure a trial consisted of a 5-sec CS followed by a US, from which the subject could escape. In the "avoid shock" procedure, a response did not affect the S+ but it did prevent the occurrence of the shock. In the "terminate signal" procedure, a response did not affect

the shock but it did terminate the S+. In the "normal" procedure a response both terminated the S+ and prevented the occurrence of the shock. The results are shown in Figure 16.20. Both termination of the warning signal and avoidance of the shock increased the percentage of avoidance responses, and decreased the response latency.

Determinants of Avoidance Learning

The warning stimulus   Not all stimuli that are discriminable are equally effective as a warning signal in avoidance learning. In general, an intense, complex stimulus with a sudden onset is particularly effective for rapid acquisition (Myers, 1960). But with any warning signal termination is one of the sources of reinforcement of avoidance learning, and delay of termination of the S+ decreases the level of performance. In one experiment Kamin (1957) demonstrated that the percentage of avoidance responses of rats, each with 100 trials in a single session, was inversely related to the interval between response and termination of the warning signal (0, 2.5, 5.0, and 10.0 sec). Stimuli that have become CS+ and CS− on the basis of discriminative classical conditioning can control subsequent avoidance responses (Solomon & Turner, 1962).

The noxious stimulus   Although the magnitude of conditioned fear is positively re-

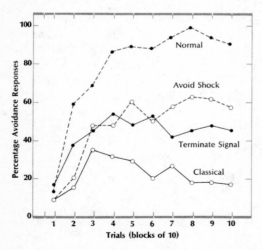

Figure 16.20. Two sources of reinforcement of an avoidance response. Percentage of avoidance responses for groups in which a response during the signal (1) avoided the shock, (2) terminated the signal, (3) both avoided the shock and terminated the signal (normal), or (4) neither avoided the shock nor terminated the signal (classical). (After Kamin, 1956.)

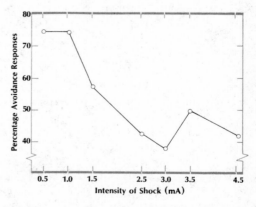

Figure 16.21. Avoidance responses as a function of shock intensity. (After Moyer & Korn, 1964.)

lated to the intensity of the noxious stimulus, high intensities of electric shock interfere with the acquisition of the avoidance. For example, Moyer and Korn (1964) found that the percentage of avoidance responses of rats in a shuttlebox decreased as shock intensity increased (Figure 16.21).

The percentage of avoidance responses made by rats in a lever box is greater if a shock is used that is moderate and pulsating than if a shock is used that is intense and continuous (D'Amato & Fazzaro, 1966), although a higher level shock may be superior for the maintenance of avoidance behavior after it has been acquired (D'Amato, Fazzaro, & Etkin, 1967). Apparently high-intensity shock elicits motor responses (for example, freezing) that are incompatible with instrumental avoidance responding. If an extremely low shock intensity is used, of course, the mean response latency is long (Kimble, 1955) and few subjects learn the avoidance response (Brush, 1957).

Interval between the warning stimulus and the noxious stimulus   Early studies of the interval between warning stimulus and shock in avoidance learning arose from an interest in the "span of association" (Warner, 1932). The studies have shown that rats can successfully learn an avoidance response if the interval between the onset of the S+ and the onset of the shock is 20 seconds or more. (A much longer association span has been demonstrated with the CER technique.) The major finding of these experiments is that the longer the interval between the S+ and the shock the longer the mean avoidance latency, both in the case of delayed and trace conditioning (for example, Church, Brush, & Solomon, 1956). This result is presumably closely related to the "inhibition of delay" in classical conditioning described by Pavlov (1927). An increase in the interval between the warning signal and the shock results in an increase in the latency of classically conditioned responses and avoidance responses in various species, for example, the fish (Bitterman, 1965) and the dog (Church & Black, 1958). Of course, the mean avoidance latency would be related to the interval between the warning stimulus and the noxious stimulus, even if the response were emitted randomly in time (because only the longer intervals could contain long latency responses). Analysis of the conditional probability of responses of various latencies, and of the response latency on the first extinction trial, however, suggest that if the subject has a short interval between signal and shock he is maximally responsive sooner than if he has a long interval between signal and shock. Thus the possibility that the relation of the interval between S+ and shock on the one hand and avoidance latencies on the other is merely an artifact of the procedure can be dismissed: Subjects apparently learn when to respond as well as how to respond in avoidance situations.

The relationship between the rate of avoidance learning and the interval between the S+ and the noxious stimulus is complex. In different studies the mean number of trials to criterion has been found to vary directly with the interval (Kamin, 1954), to be independent of the interval (Brush, Brush, & Solomon, 1955), and to be inversely related to the interval (Behrend & Bitterman, 1962). The problem is that the "mean number of trials to criterion" reflects not only the degree of association between S+ and the noxious stimulus, but also the opportunity to respond (Bitterman, 1965). Thus a subject exposed to a 20-sec interval between S+ and noxious stimulus has a greater opportunity to make an avoidance response than a subject allowed only a 5-sec interval. If subjects are trained at different intervals, and then are tested at the same relatively long intervals, the opportunity for avoidance responses is equalized (although the magnitude of generalization decrement is not). Such a transfer design has led to the conclusion that the rate of acquisition of avoidance response to a delayed S+ is roughly equal across intervals from 1 to 60 seconds.

Pseudoconditioning   If, under the conditions of avoidance training, a subject performs the instrumental response to the conditioned stimulus, does this imply that the subject has learned the association between the S+ and the shock? If the subject had been given the opportunity to escape from the S+ before the beginning of avoidance training, and it had failed to do so, this would be evidence that the S+ was not initially a noxious stimulus. After a number of presentations of the shock, however, the subject may perform the instrumental response to the S+ whether or not it had been followed by the shock. The shock may serve to predispose the subject to react to almost any stimulus, and when a frightened subject is startled by any novel stimulus it may accidentally perform the instrumental response, and thus the termination of the novel stimulus may reinforce this behavior. Many examples of pseudoconditioning have been reported (for example, Smith, McFarland, & Taylor, 1961), and it occurs more readily with buzzers than with physical stimuli that are easier to specify (pure tones, white noise, lighted panels). The random presentation of S+ and shock in a pseudoconditioning control group may lead to a higher state of anxiety than the signaled presentation of the shock in the avoidance conditioning group. At least, subjects prefer a signaled to an unsignaled shock in a choice experiment (Lockard, 1963). (See also p. 578.)

Failures of acquisition Many experimenters have reported difficulty in training rats to perform a discriminative avoidance response in a lever box. Such failures are not rare. Typically, these subjects become alert and hover at the lever when the signal is turned on and then, when the shock is turned on, they press the lever rapidly (escape). Despite the fact that they have demonstrated a clear association of the S+ with the shock, and have learned an instrumental act to the shock, they do not learn to perform the avoidance act (for example, Meyer, Cho, & Wesemann, 1960). The major difficulty is that the warning signal causes the subject to "freeze." Thus, if a drug that increases mobility (for example,

amphetamine) is administered, the rate of avoidance responses is increased.

Subjects can be trained to press a lever to avoid a shock, if the shock is mild and pulsating, but training the subjects to press a lever is more difficult than training them to run away from the stimulus (in a shuttlebox). This observation is not merely a peculiarity of rats, for although the conditions are otherwise the same, the particular response that is chosen for avoidance will be an important determinant of the rate of learning and the asymptotic performance of any species. Turner and Solomon (1962), for example, reported that human subjects in a traumatic avoidance learning situation failed to learn to avoid a shock significantly more often if a short-latency, reflexive movement were required than if a longer-latency, gross motor movement were required.

Even after a subject is performing an avoidance response with a high probability, he may stop doing so in some subsequent trials (Coons, Anderson, & Myers, 1960). This phenomenon has been replicated under a number of conditions, but it has not been adequately explained.

Nondiscriminative Avoidance

Any avoidance learning situation that does not involve a warning signal may be called "nondiscriminative avoidance." That is, a subject can learn to make an instrumental response to postpone a noxious stimulus even if there is no experimenter-controlled stimulus (S+). Furthermore, a subject can learn to make an avoidance response even if there is no possibility of escape from the noxious stimulus. This procedure has been extensively investigated by Sidman (1953, 1966), and it is often called "Sidman avoidance." A representative situation is the following: When a rat makes a lever response it postpones the occurrence of shock for 20 seconds. (This minimum interval between the response and the shock is called the "R-S interval.") If the rat fails to press the lever within 20 seconds a brief (.2-sec) shock is given, and it reoccurs

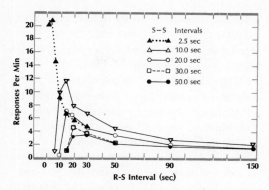

Figure 16.22. Rate of avoidance responding as a function of the response-shock (R-S) and the shock-shock (S-S) intervals. (After Sidman, 1953.)

every 5 seconds. (This interval between the onset of one shock and the next is called the "S-S interval.") A response during the S-S interval returns the subject to the R-S interval. Under this condition, if a subject responds at least once each 20 seconds it will avoid all shocks. The mean response rate of one subject under various S-S and R-S intervals is shown in Figure 16.22. After initial nondiscriminative avoidance training this subject received a series of 3-hour sessions at a particular R-S and S-S interval. The criterion of stability was a difference in rate not greater than 0.1 response per minute between the third hour of 2 out of 3 consecutive sessions. After the criterion was met, another value of the R-S interval was used. After all the R-S values had been used at one S-S value, they were repeated in another order at another S-S value. Under these conditions, as the R-S interval decreased the response rate gradually increased to some maximum value, and then declined abruptly. The R-S interval that resulted in the maximum rate was positively related to the S-S interval.

If the R-S interval were made shorter than half the S-S interval a subject responding randomly in time would actually increase the frequency of shocks received (Sidman, 1966). This may be the primary factor accounting for the decline in the response rate when the R-S interval is made short relative to the S-S in-

terval (the falling of the curves to the left of the maxima). The longer the R-S interval is made, the lower the frequency of shocks received, and because many subjects made a burst of responses following a shock under this condition, the reduction in shock frequency may have been the primary factor accounting for the gradual decrease in the response rate as the R-S interval increased (the falling of the curves to the right of the maxima). On the other hand, this function may reflect a temporal discrimination (that is, if the subject responded shortly before each shock was due, the longer the R-S interval was made, the lower the response rate would be). Although the temporal discrimination may emerge as a function of repeated training, the acquisition of the avoidance response may depend primarily upon a reduction of shock density. Just as a subject may change his response rate when the S-S interval is changed from zero minutes (continuous shock) to 2 minutes between shocks, so may a subject change his response rate when the S-S interval is shifted from an average of 9 shocks per minute to an average of 3 per minute (Herrnstein & Hineline, 1966). This implies that the same principle that was used to account for the acquisition of escape behavior can be extended to account for some cases of avoidance behavior. The reinforcement of an escape response is reduction in the severity of a noxious stimulus. If shock density (frequency per unit time) as well as intensity and duration of a shock is a determinant of severity, then avoidance behavior in the absence of a warning signal, like escape behavior, may be reinforced by reduction of the severity of a noxious stimulus.

In contrast to most subjects used to study the nondiscriminative avoidance procedure in the shuttlebox, those placed in the lever box usually do not show an obvious temporal discrimination. However, examination of the conditional probabilities of interresponse times often reveals some temporal discrimination (Anger, 1963). A subject with a 20-sec

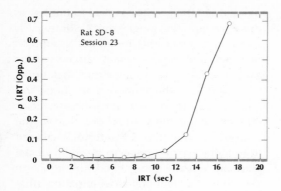

Figure 16.23. Temporal discrimination in Sidman avoidance. The probability of a response given the opportunity for a response increased as the time from the last response increased. (After Anger, 1963.)

R-S interval has the opportunity to make a response between 0 and 1 sec after the last response each time it responds, but it has the opportunity to make a response between 19 and 20 sec after the last response only on those rare occasions that it has waited for 19 sec. Therefore, evidence for a temporal discrimination is provided by the conditional probability of a response (the probability of a response given the opportunity for a response—the IRTs/opp). The distribution of the conditional probability of a response of one subject with an excellent temporal discrimination under conditions of 20-sec R-S interval and a 20-sec S-S interval is shown in Figure 16.23 (Anger, 1963). The conditional probability of a response was an increasing function of the time since the last response.

Extinction of Avoidance Responses

The usual extinction procedure for avoidance is omission of the shock. Thus, for extinction of discriminative avoidance behavior, if the subject responds within the signal-shock interval used in training, the treatment is identical to that used during training (that is, the signal terminates and the shock does not occur). If the subject fails to respond within the signal-shock interval, however, the treatment during extinction differs from that used during training (that is, the signal terminates and the shock does not occur).

If the conditions of avoidance training produce a subject that always performs the avoidance response, by definition, it should continue to respond during extinction indefinitely. Extremely high resistance to extinction has been reported for some cases of avoidance learning. For example, Solomon, Kamin, and Wynne (1953) reported that dogs that had met a criterion of 10 avoidance responses on a session of training failed to extinguish the responses during the next 20 sessions of 10 trials per day. In fact, over 99 percent of the responses were made within 10 seconds of the S+ onset; also during the sessions the mean latency continued to decrease despite the absence of any shock.

However, it would not be correct to say that avoidance responses are more resistant to extinction than responses reinforced by food. A subject may be trained to make an instrumental response during a 10-sec stimulus to receive food reinforcement at the end of the stimulus. Such a subject would have an extremely high resistance to extinction, if the extinction procedure consisted of presenting the food at the end of the stimulus, whether or not the subject made the response. Furthermore, in many cases of avoidance learning, omission of the noxious stimulus without prompt termination of S+ results in fairly rapid extinction (Kamin, 1954; Katzev, 1967).

Resistance to extinction is decreased if a subject is prevented from making the instrumental response during the early trials of extinction. One way to prevent a subject from making a previously learned avoidance response is to administer a massive dose of d-tubocurarine chloride, or a similar drug, to produce a flaccid paralysis. Such a subject can develop conditioned fear to the S+, but it cannot move. Black (1958) demonstrated that the amount of extinction produced by 50 trials of S+ without shock was greater if the subject was prevented from making the instrumental response than if it were not.

PUNISHMENT

Consider the following situation: A rat is placed in a box that contains a retractable lever, a food cup, and a grid floor that can be electrified. On the average of once each 3 minutes a tone begins, and the lever is automatically inserted into the box. If the subject presses the lever within 10 seconds, a small pellet of food is automatically dropped into the food cup, the tone ceases, and the lever is withdrawn; if the subject fails to press the lever within 10 seconds the tone stops and the lever is withdrawn, but no food is delivered. If the animal is hungry, and if it is not frightened, this procedure is sufficient to teach the subject to press the lever.[4]

After the rat learned to press the lever reliably and quickly, a punishment procedure was begun. On the first trial under the changed conditions, the tone began, the lever was inserted into the box, and (in about 2 seconds) the subject depressed the lever. On this occasion the subject received a brief electric shock through the grid floor, and a pellet of food was dropped into the food cup. The subject squeaked and jumped back, and then it approached the food cup and ate the pellet of food. On the next trial the tone again began and the lever was inserted, but this time the response latency was much longer (about 7 seconds). Again the rat received both the punishing and the positive reinforcing events. About 3 minutes later the next trial occurred, and the rat failed to respond within 10 seconds. No response was made on any of the next 20 trials, and the experiment was terminated.

Punishment, in this example, clearly led to a suppression of the instrumental lever-pressing response, but there are numerous alternative explanations regarding the mechanism through which it exerted this effect. First of all, there are the *situational cues* of the box with its grid floor and food cup. Second, there are the *experimenter-controlled* stimuli of the tone and (since a retractable lever was used) of the lever. Third, there are the *response-produced* stimuli of the proprioceptive feedback of the lever-press response, and also of the visual and auditory consequences of the response. Finally, there are the *events* of presenting food to a hungry subject (positive reinforcement) and shock (punishment), both of which have obvious stimulus properties. The observed response suppression could have been a result of the association of the shock with the situational stimuli (generalized anxiety), the experimenter-controlled stimuli (CER), the response-produced stimuli, or any combination of these stimuli.

An explanation of the suppression produced by punishment requires, in addition to the identification of the relevant stimuli, a statement of the manner in which these stimuli affect behavior. According to a *fear hypothesis,* the subject becomes afraid and immobile in the presence of the stimulus and thus fails to make many responses, including the instrumental lever-pressing response. In some cases (for example, Hunt & Brady, 1955) the magnitude of suppression in the presence of a signal is similar whether the shock is inevitable (CER) or dependent upon a response (discriminative punishment). Alternatively, the subject may begin to make skeletal responses similar to those elicited by the onset of the punishment, which may interfere with its response of pressing the lever (the *competing response hypothesis*), or it may make skeletal responses similar to those it typically made at the termination of the punishment, which may also interfere with the lever-pressing response (the *escape hypothesis*). If the skeletal responses to the onset of

---

[4] To establish a stable level of hunger the subject should be maintained for several weeks on a schedule of restricted food intake, and to reduce fear the experimenter should handle the subject daily for several weeks.

punishment or its termination are compatible with the learned instrumental response, then punishment of a response might facilitate that response (Guthrie, 1952; Fowler & Miller, 1963).

According to the *avoidance hypothesis,* response suppression produced by punishment may occur for the same reason as response acquisition during avoidance learning (Dinsmoor, 1954). In the case of avoidance learning (sometimes called "active avoidance") a specified response prevents the noxious stimulus, but all other responses result in the noxious stimulus being given. In the case of punishment learning (sometimes called "passive avoidance") the opposite is true; that is, a specified response results in the presentation of the noxious stimulus, but all other responses prevent it. Similar principles may account for active and passive avoidance.

Thorndike's (1911) original interpretation of the effect of punishment on behavior may be called the *negative law of effect.* He stated that a noxious stimulus weakened a response tendency in a direct manner similar to the direct strengthening of a response tendency by a positive reinforcer (positive law of effect). Although he later abandoned this position (Thorndike, 1932) he apparently did so for insufficient reason, for at the present time the data on punishment are most conveniently organized around the negative law of effect (which is sometimes called the "suppression hypothesis").

Of course, the theories of punishment described above are not mutually exclusive. In fact, there is reasonably strong experimental evidence to indicate that each of them offers a partial explanation for the observed reduction in the tendency to respond (Church, 1963).

Determinants of Magnitude of Suppression

Punishment is a technique for the suppression of a response. In general, the effect of a response-contingent noxious event (a punishment) is opposite of the effect of a re-sponse-contingent reinforcing event (a positive reinforcement), and some of the same variables determine the magnitude of these opposite effects. For example, an intense punishment is more effective in suppressing behavior than a mild one, and a punishment is more effective in suppressing behavior if it is presented immediately after a response than if it is delayed by several seconds. The same variables of magnitude and delay of reinforcement influence the effectiveness of positive reinforcers for strengthening a response and presumably such parallels would exist with regard to other variables as well. Brief summaries of many of the relevant experiments are available (Azrin & Holz, 1966; Church, 1963, 1969).

Intensity   The degree to which a response is suppressed is an increasing function of the intensity of the punishment. In one experiment (Karsh, 1962) groups of rats were trained for 75 trials to run to the end of an 8-ft alley for food reinforcement. Then each subject received 1 trial per day for 40 days during which both food and shock were given at the goal. The intensity of shock for the various groups was 0, 75, 150, 300, and 600 V for .1 sec, administered through 250,000 Ω in series with the subject. At the lowest intensity of punishment used (75V) the rats were indistinguishable from control subjects in their running speed, although the shock level was undoubtedly above a detection threshold so that it could be used as a cue. At intermediate levels of intensity there was partial suppression followed by a considerable recovery in the response rate, with the initial effect of the punishment on the early sessions far more pronounced than that on later sessions. At higher intensity of punishment there was partial suppression, without complete recovery, and at the highest level of intensity virtually total response suppression.

In another experiment (Azrin & Holz, 1961) two pigeons were trained to peck a response key with food delivered on a 5-min fixed-

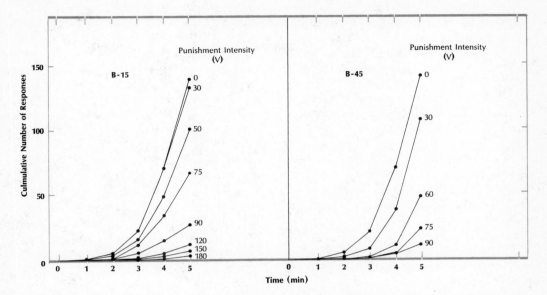

Figure 16.24. Intensity of punishment. The cumulative number of responses of two pigeons receiving punishment of each response during fixed-interval food reinforcement. (After Azrin & Holz, 1961.)

interval schedule of reinforcement; they received a brief (.1 sec) shock following each peck. (The shock was administered through electrodes implanted in the tail region of the bird and the circuit had 10,000 Ω in series with the subject.) Under the fixed-interval schedule of reinforcement the birds developed a temporal patterning of responses such that they responded more rapidly as the end of the fixed interval approached. Although they maintained this temporal pattern under the conditions of punishment, the cumulative number of responses was inversely related to the punishment intensity (Figure 16.24). Thus, both under conditions of one trial per day and under conditions of free responding, the degree of response suppression was a function of the intensity of the punishment. If only a moderate intensity of punishment was administered, however, the magnitude of suppression decreased as a function of the increasing number of sessions of punishment.

Duration   The effect of an increase in the duration of a punishment is similar to an increase in its intensity. If punishment of

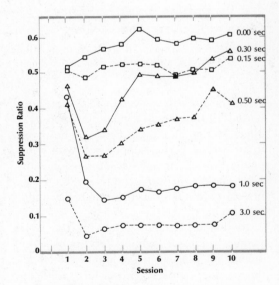

Figure 16.25. Duration of punishment. Response suppression as a function of duration of punishment in seconds. The suppression ratio was $B/(A + B)$, where B = response rate on a session of punishment, and A = response rate on the final session prior to punishment. (After Church, Raymond, & Beauchamp, 1967.)

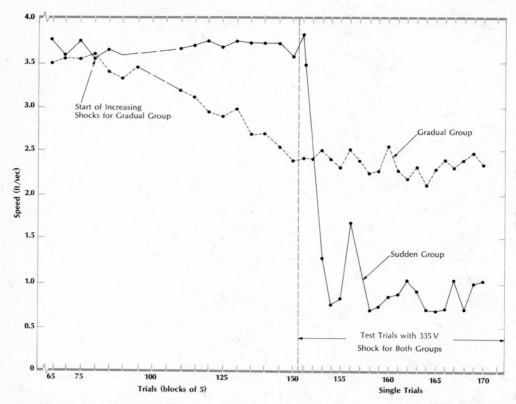

Figure 16.26. Mean speed of approach to food reinforcement of rats with gradual or sudden introduction of electric shock at the goal. (After Miller, 1960.)

moderate intensity is given for extremely brief periods of time, there will be no suppressive effect. As the duration is increased, however, there will be partial suppression with complete recovery, then partial suppression without complete recovery, and finally, total suppression without recovery (Church, Raymond, & Beauchamp, 1967).

In that experiment groups of rats were trained to press a lever for food pellets, delivered on a 1-min variable-interval schedule of reinforcement into which were inserted occasional punishing shocks with durations of 0.15, 0.30, 0.50, 1.00, or 3.00 sec. The mean suppression ratio, $(B/(A + B))$ with B = response rate on a particular session of punishment training and A = response rate on the final session prior to punishment training is shown in Figure 16.25. When the intensity as well as duration of the punishment was varied, the mean suppression ratio was a linear function of the logarithm of the product of the intensity and the duration of the punishment. Presumably, the intensity and duration of punishment jointly determine the severity of the punishment, and the magnitude of response suppression is a function of the severity of the punishment.

Prior exposure to the noxious stimulus The magnitude of response suppression to a punishment is a function of the prior experience of the subject with the punishing stimulus. Miller (1960) demonstrated that rats may learn to resist the effects of pain and fear if the intensity of the punishment is only gradually increased. Figure 16.26 shows the results from one experiment. Rats were trained to run to the goal box of an 8-ft alley for a wet morsel of food, about the size of a pea. When the subject touched the food it completed a circuit of subthreshold current that operated an electronic relay. This relay (a) stopped a clock for the running time, and (b) delivered a shock of .1 sec duration through 250,000 Ω in series with the subject on the punishment trials. After 75 trials of reward training half the subjects received a punishment of gradually increasing intensity (as well as a reward) and the other half received only the reward. After 75 trials of this differential treatment both groups received punishment of 335 V. The average speed of subjects with prior exposure to punishment of increasing intensity was reliably faster than that of subjects that had not had such exposure. Thus prior exposure to punishment of gradually increasing intensity attenuates the suppressive effects of subsequent punishment.

Other studies have shown that prior exposure to a single condition of punishment that is of low intensity, brief duration, low frequency, or long-delayed after a response, attenuates the subsequent response suppression produced by a punishment that is more intense, of longer duration, more frequent, or temporally closer to a response (Feirstein & Miller, 1963; Banks, 1966; Karsh, 1966; Church, 1969).

In contrast to the effects described above, there are some situations in which prior exposure to an intense electric shock can increase the effectiveness of a subsequent shock when it is used as a punishment (Walters & Rogers, 1963; Pearl, Walters, & Anderson, 1964). When prior exposure increases the effectiveness of subsequent punishment, the phenomenon may be labeled "sensitization," and when prior exposure decreases the effectiveness of subsequent punishment, the phenomenon may be labeled "adaptation" or "habituation," but such labels, of course, do not explain the results. In general it appears that prior exposure to a noxious stimulus of low severity minimizes the effects of subse-

quent noxious stimuli of greater severity, whereas prior exposure to a noxious stimulus of high severity increases the effects of subsequent noxious stimuli of less severity (Karsh, 1963). One interpretation is that there is a degree of behavioral inertia such that the suppression produced by punishment may be intermediate between the amount that would occur to that punishment in the absence of previous exposure to shock and the amount produced by the prior exposure.

Temporal relationship between response and punishment The extent that a response is suppressed by punishment is greater if the noxious stimulus follows immediately after the response than if it is delayed by several seconds. In the case of punishment of a shuttlebox avoidance response, Kamin (1959) demonstrated this delay-of-punishment gradient, showing that the shorter the temporal interval between response and punishment, the fewer the number of responses in extinction. Such a result is not a consequence of the temporal interval between the warning signal and the noxious event because it also occurs in the free-responding situation (Camp, Raymond, & Church, 1967).

Contingency between response and punishment A noxious stimulus may suppress the rate of an appetitive response even if it is not contingent upon a response (Estes, 1944; Camp, Raymond, & Church, 1967). However, if there is a positive correlation between the occurrence of the noxious stimulus and the occurrence of the response, the magnitude of response suppression will be greater.[5] For example, Azrin (1956) compared the response rates of pigeons under conditions of response-contingent and response-

[5] The dependence of a noxious stimulus (S) upon a response (R) may be represented as $[p(S|R) - p(S|\bar{R})]/[p(S|R) + p(S|\bar{R})]$. The degree of dependence (contingency) between a response and a noxious stimulus is a determinant of the magnitude of suppression, as well as the probability of the noxious stimulus per unit time $[p(S)]$ or the probability of a noxious stimulus given a response $[p(S|R)]$.

independent presentation of shock. During each session a pigeon received a 3-min variable-interval schedule of positive reinforcement. In the presence of one discriminative stimulus, only this reinforcement schedule was in effect; in the presence of the other discriminative stimulus, both positive reinforcement and an aversive stimulus were presented. The noxious stimulus was either contingent upon a *response* (scheduled to follow the first response after a fixed or variable interval from the onset of the discriminative stimulus) or it was independent of the response (scheduled to occur a fixed or variable *time* after the onset of the discriminative stimulus). The response rate of pigeons in the presence of the discriminative stimulus for noxious stimulation was lower in the case of contingent shock (punishment) than in the case of independent presentation of the noxious stimulus.

Punishment and Resistance to Extinction

Punishment serves to reduce the frequency of occurrence of some unwanted behavior, both during the period that it is being applied and after the punishment period has been completed. If the punishment is severe, the suppression of the behavior may be complete. For example, dogs may develop a profound inhibition of eating if they have been punished only a few times in the act of eating in a particular apparatus (Lichtenstein, 1950). A rat may starve to death rather than respond in a situation that produces food reward on half the trials and punishment on the other half (Klee, 1944).

In contrast, several studies seem to indicate that a brief period of mild punishment early in extinction does not reduce the total number of responses during regular extinction. These studies have employed as the "punisher" an event that was perhaps no more noxious than many other novel stimuli (Skinner, 1938), or a level of shock that did not produce reliable suppression even while it was being applied (Estes, 1944, Experiment

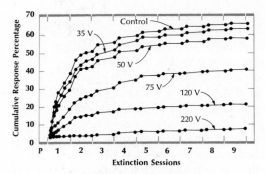

Figure 16.27. Permanent effects of punishment during extinction. The response percentage was $(B/A) \times 100$, where B = response rate on a session of extinction, and A = response rate on the final session prior to punishment. Punishment (P) was contingent upon lever pressing during minutes 5–20 of the first extinction session. (After Boe & Church, 1967.)

A).[6] However, even a short period of moderate punishment early in extinction reduces the total number of responses during extinction (Estes, 1944; Boe, 1964; Boe & Church, 1967; Estes, 1969). Under one procedure rats were trained to press a lever during three 1-hour sessions of acquisition on a 4-min fixed-interval schedule of food reinforcement, and then were given successive daily 1-hour sessions of extinction (Estes, 1944; Boe & Church, 1967). During a 15-min period of the first extinction session (the fifth through the twentieth minute), subjects in the experimental group were given a brief electric shock contingent upon responses on a 30-sec fixed-interval schedule of punishment. (Thus, a subject would receive a maximum of 30 punishments if it responded at least once during each 30 sec of the 15 min punishment-period.) During the remainder of this first extinction session, and during the subsequent 1-hour extinction sessions, responses were neither

---

[6]Such results may have served as the basis for the widespread belief that punishment is an ineffective method for control of behavior. Solomon (1964) has questioned the empirical bases for this statement, as well as for the belief that intense punishment typically leads to neurosis.

reinforced nor punished. Figure 16.27 shows the cumulative response percentage (relative to the number of responses on the final session of acquisition) as a function of the source voltage of the punishment (150,000 Ω in series). Punishment produced both an immediate decrease in responding during the punishment period and a permanent decrease in responding during the nine sessions of extinction. The magnitude of both effects of punishment was related to the intensity of the punishment.

The Role of Punishment in Discrimination Learning

Early research on punishment attempted to compare the relative incentive value of reward and punishment (for example, Warden & Aylesworth, 1927). Thus a rat would be trained to enter the compartment of a discrimination box under one of three conditions: (1) Reward: The subject received food if correct and was removed from the apparatus if incorrect. (2) Punishment: The subject was simply removed from the apparatus if correct but received a punishment if incorrect. (3) Reward and punishment: The subject received food if correct and punishment if incorrect. The direct comparison of performance under conditions of reward alone or punishment alone has not been satisfactory, and probably the question has not yet even been formulated properly, for the punished subjects have no clear reason for entering either compartment. Nonetheless, such research has lead to the unequivocal conclusion that punishment of the incorrect response (in addition to reward of the correct response) leads to faster discrimination learning than merely reward of the correct response.

Although it agrees with common sense that punishment of the incorrect response should increase the rate of discrimination learning, it is not intuitively obvious that punishment of the correct response should sometimes have a similar effect, but this result

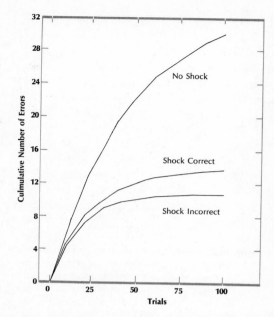

Figure 16.28. Cumulative number of errors as a function of trials for groups that received no shock, shock for the correct (reinforced) response, and for the incorrect (nonreinforced) response. (After Muenzinger, 1934.)

has been obtained. Muenzinger (1934) compared the rate of learning a two-choice visual discrimination task by rats that either were punished for the correct response (the one that was rewarded), were punished for the incorrect response (the one that was not rewarded), or were not punished for either response. The subjects that received the noxious stimulus learned the discrimination task more quickly than subjects that were not punished, and there was no significant difference between the cumulative number of errors of subjects that were punished for the correct response and those punished for the incorrect response (Figure 16.28). However, subsequent research by Muezinger and others (for example, Wischner, 1947) demonstrated, under a variety of conditions, that punishment for making an incorrect response increased the rate of discrimination learning more than punishment for making the correct response. In one experiment (Wischner,

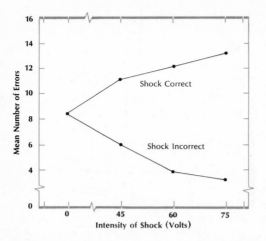

Figure 16.29. Mean number of errors as a function of intensity of punishment for group that received shock for the correct response and group that received punishment for the incorrect response. (After Wischner, Fowler, & Kushnick, 1963.)

Fowler, & Kushnick, 1963), as the intensity of the punishment increased, the number of errors in the group punished for the correct response increased and the number of errors in the group punished for the incorrect response decreased (Figure 16.29). In these studies subjects punished for the correct response did not perform any better than the unpunished control group. Nonetheless, if the punishment is very mild and the task is relatively difficult (the two cues to be discriminated are similar) a group punished for the correct response will make fewer errors than an unpunished control group (Fowler & Wischner, 1965). Although there are a number of plausible explanations for this paradoxical effect of punishment, the major function of the punishment may be to increase the discriminability of the two stimulus alternatives (Fowler & Wischner, 1969), perhaps by slowing responding and thus increasing the time during which the discriminanda are exposed before a choice is made.

These studies demonstrate that punishment is not only a technique that contributes to the elimination of old modes of response but that it also contributes to the rapid ac-

quisition of new modes of response. As a general rule, punishment is particularly effective for the suppression of a previously learned response if an alternative response is concurrently reinforced (Whiting & Mowrer, 1943). For that reason, in many practical situations, the most effective training techniques involve a judicious combination of reward and punishment.

REQUIREMENTS FOR A GENERAL THEORY OF AVERSIVE BEHAVIOR

At the present time there is no general theory of aversive behavior, but such a theory will undoubtedly emerge from the extensive research findings that have been published, particularly in the last 25 years. Such a theory should describe interrelationships among the following concepts:

Classical conditioning and instrumental learning. The principles required to account for the behavior resulting from contingencies between experimenter-controlled stimuli and noxious events (the classical procedures) may be similar to those required to account for the behavior resulting from contingencies between responses and noxious events (the instrumental procedures).

Avoidance, punishment, escape, and preservation. In this chapter the various instrumental procedures involving noxious events have been treated separately, but there are important interrelationships among them. A general theory of aversive behavior should reveal the essential continuity among them, and it should explore the cases that are intermediate between the ideal cases.

Negative and positive events. The principles required to account for the behavior resulting from events from which organisms avert may be similar to those required to account for behavior resulting from events they approach. A relativistic view would be that the behavioral result depends not solely upon the particular event (for example, a mild shock or a small bit of food) but that it is dependent upon the direction of change.

For example, an animal may approach a shock intensity of 0.1 mA if currently stimulated by a higher intensity, but may avoid a shock intensity of 0.1 mA if presently stimulated by a lower intensity. Although most general theories of learning (for example, Tolman, 1932; Skinner, 1938; Hull, 1943; Spence, 1956) have been based primarily upon evidence from instrumental procedures with positive events, presumably a general theory could equally well be made that is based on evidence from procedures with negative events.

A general theory of aversive behavior undoubtedly will evolve in two directions: "formal" and "physiological." A formal theory of aversive behavior involves a precise description of the input to and the output from a subject, but no consideration of events occurring inside its body. It would undoubtedly become increasingly quantitative, rather than verbal, and it might make considerable use of mathematical models and computer simulation. A physiological theory would necessarily make considerable use of the great advances in knowledge regarding the biological basis of behavior (neuroanatomy, neurophysiology, psychopharmacology, and behavioral genetics). It would make use of results of research on the brain (electrophysiological and chemical stimulation, recording, and lesions). Either type of theory could provide important guidance for further research on aversive behavior.

Donald S. Blough and Lewis P. Lipsitt

THE DISCRIMINATIVE CONTROL OF BEHAVIOR

17

THE NATURE OF DISCRIMINATIVE CONTROL

The study of discriminative control is concerned with the covariation of stimuli and responses from moment to moment. A stimulus is said to control some aspect of behavior if a change in the behavior regularly follows a change in the stimulus. We "go" when we see a green light, and "stop" on red; we slap at the stab of a mosquito, which, in its turn, was attracted by the warmth of our body. Clearly, much of our activity and that of other animals is regulated by a never-ending flux of stimuli, yet stimuli cannot be taken for granted. To some physical changes our sense organs are insensitive (for example, radio frequency radiation). To many others, at a particular moment, we are potentially sensitive but actually indifferent, for we live in a sea of stimuli and can react to relatively few. Some stimuli come from external sources, some from within our bodies.

Stimuli have other functions that are not specifically tied to the current direction of activity; for example, they may act as reinforcers or punishers. They may cause satiation or bring about a variety of physiological changes. These important stimulus functions are discussed elsewhere in this volume and so are not the principal focus of this chapter.

743

Our concern here will be mainly with learned control, with the correlations between stimuli and responses that arise from past experience. Although the bulk of research on discriminative control concerns such learned behavior, it is well to recognize the variety of sources from which control may spring. Let us consider for a moment some functional aspects of this problem, in order to provide a background for our concentration upon the learning research.

Sources of Discriminative Control

To survive as individuals—and as species—animals must do the right thing at the right time, just as they must have appropriate bodily structures. According to the "survival of the fittest," the animal with the fittest behavior survives. Thus, behavior has evolved, just as has structure, and the result is a variety of behavioral mechanisms, each appropriate to its function for the organism.

Some stimuli have constant consequences for a species from year to year and generation to generation. If simple reactions to these stimuli suffice, an organism may be equipped to deal with them without benefit of experience. However, as behavior grows more complex, and the environment more demanding, it becomes efficient, even necessary, for the animal to acquire some of its behavioral equipment through experience. If survival depends on adaptation to changing circumstances, so that a response to a stimulus that was effective at one time becomes useless or harmful at another, it becomes vital for the organism to learn. In most higher animals it is clear that the genetic information that controls behavior is supplemented by information arising from the individual's contact with its environment.

It is equally clear that the genetic and environmental are not strict alternatives, as the old "nature-nurture" controversy might suggest. In any given case there seems usually to be a very complex interplay between the two. Nonetheless, it is useful to think of discriminative control as a kind of continuum.

At one end fall genetically controlled, stereotyped responses to simple stimuli; at the other fall complex modifiable responses to complex, changing stimuli. At one end, we find the simplest unconditional reflexes—an eyeblink to a puff of air, salivation to food in the mouth. Even these are complex and labile in higher organisms, when compared to some responses in insects and simple organisms. The adaptive possibilities of even simple reflexes are expanded enormously by the possibility of habituation and, at least in higher forms, of Pavlovian conditioning. These may alter the incidence of a response or put a response under the control of an indefinite number of stimuli; the sight of food elicits salivation, a signal paired with shock elicits various emotional responses, and so on.

Orientation

A type of discriminative control that has long fascinated researchers involves responses to "guiding" environmental stimuli. The moth's attraction to light, the behavior of homing or migrating birds, the swimming patterns of spawning salmon, and the tendency of human infants to maintain eye-to-eye contact with the mother while nursing are examples of such "locked-in" or guided behavior probably under the control, at least initially, of genetically programmed stimuli.

Such behavior has been classified into categories bearing descriptive names, only a few of which we can mention here. In *kinesis,* the stimulus does not point the organism in any particular direction but simply stimulates it to move or turn. Certain insects, for example, congregate in damp places, presumably because dryness generates activity that diminishes or stops when, in moving here and there, the insect comes upon damper conditions. In *taxes,* the position of the body is determined by the source of stimulation. For example, an animal may sample light stimuli arriving at its two sides, either successively, by swinging its head, or simultaneously, if it has lateral eyes. Often the result is a movement that equalizes the stimulation coming from the two sides. The animal would approach a light, for example, if as it moved it turned continually toward the side of its body receiving the most light.

Modern workers have suggested the similarity between the behavior described above and man-made control systems, in which deviations of input from a prescribed balance produce "feedback" adjustments that change the input until the balance is reached. This is the principle behind an aircraft's automatic pilot. Even the malfunctions of such systems have their counterparts in the mechanism of orientation in living things. Thus an organism that turns toward the light may whirl endlessly if one eye is blinded or covered.

Complex problems of animal orientation, such as the interesting work of von Frisch on food-finding in bees, or the still little-understood mechanisms underlying the feats, undoubtedly in part learned, of homing or migrating birds, cannot be considered here in detail. (For more extensive discussion of such behavior, see Fraenkel and Gunn [1940], von Frisch [1950], and Hinde [1970].)

Fixed Action Patterns

At another point on our adaptive continuum are certain stereotyped behavior patterns, often quite complex, that have usually been observed and analysed in relatively natural settings. A defining characteristic of these

Figure 17.1. Greylag goose retrieving an egg, an example of a "fixed action pattern." If the egg is removed while it is being rolled back, the head continues its stereotyped movement toward the nest. (After Tinbergen, 1951.)

fixed action patterns is that once they have been set in motion, they keep going independently of the initiating stimuli, which are said to "release" them. An oft-cited example is the egg-rolling response of the greylag goose, which serves to get misplaced eggs back into the goose's nest (Figure 17.1). The goose, in a manner similar to that of many other ground-nesting birds, stands up and, stretching its head forward, rolls the egg back with the underside of its bill. The presence of the egg in this case releases the retrieving motion, but the stereotyped nature of the response is evident, for if the egg is removed during retrieval, the goose continues to "roll" the now vanished egg until the pattern of motion is complete.

Many such fixed action patterns have been studied, and specific stimuli that trigger them have been identified. The manner in which the effective stimuli are found is essentially the same as that which, as we shall see, is used to identify stimuli in complex learned tasks. One varies the situation in this way and that, and notes which variations leave the response unchanged. For example, Tinbergen (1952) used fish models to determine which stimuli released fighting and courting behavior in the male stickleback, a small fish. When sexually active, the male stickleback often attacks intruding males, but attacks females less often and may court them. Sexually active males have bright red bellies. Males attacked even very crude models that were painted red on the bottom but reacted much less to good likenesses of the fish lacking the red bottom. Similarly, crude models with swollen bellies elicited more courtship behavior than did more realistic but slim models.

Imprinting

Though cues eliciting responses of the kind just discussed are not learned in the sense that neutral stimuli are transformed into effective ones through reinforcement or other experience, it is not correct to conclude that experience is irrelevant to this sort of discriminative control. Our discussion of this matter follows, to a large extent, that of Hinde (1966), where further details may be found. It is most significant that naive animals—newborn, or isolated from stimuli in one way or another—often emit characteristic patterns of response to a very wide range of stimuli. Certain baby birds, when they first open their eyes, will "beg" to a wide range of stimuli (for example, a pair of forceps); very young kittens will suckle from any receptive mother; newly hatched chicks will peck at any small dark or bright spot. In these and similar cases, the range of stimuli that elicit the response becomes drastically narrowed with time. Thus, in the normal course of events, the bird will beg only from the mother (or other object to which it is accustomed); the kitten will suckle only from its own mother; the chick will peck only at food grains or similar stimuli. Hinde attributes much of this narrowing of effective cues to habituation (that is, a diminution in the number of responses made to frequently presented stimuli that lead to no consequence) and to reinforcement. For example, chicks continue to peck at stimuli that release the actions of grasping and swallowing, and stop pecking at those that do not.

The most studied case of such a narrowing of the range of effective stimulation concerns the stimuli that elicit following behavior in birds that leave the nest soon after hatching. A gosling or duckling will follow almost any moving object it first sees—its mother, a slowly walking man, an inflated balloon, and so on. Shortly, new objects will not elicit following; the bird will only follow the objects it has already experienced, or similar ones. This phenomenon is called "imprinting." Controversy still surrounds the nature of the acquisition process here (Sluckin, 1965). Some writers feel that it is a special case of ordinary conditioning, others that it is different enough to be considered as a quite distinct process. A most interesting property of imprinting, in any case, is that it can only occur within a relatively short "sensitive period." Chicks, for example, come to follow an object to which they are exposed from the age of a few hours to a few days, but if their experience comes earlier, or is put off later than this, they will not even learn to follow the mother hen. (See also the discussion of imprinting, pp. 581–588.)

Various forms of discriminative control may be intertwined at every behavioral level. Two examples serve to illustrate this point. Lorenz (1937) found that greylag geese easily became imprinted upon him if they saw him moving near them right after they hatched. The goslings followed him consistently as he walked and swam, yet one specific unlearned releasing stimulus—the wing-pattern of the goose upon taking flight—would supersede the "learned" response to Lorenz and elicit following behavior. Likewise, Breland and Breland (1961) discovered with some surprise and disappointment that species-specific control intruded into the acts of performing animals that they tried to train. For example, pigs trained to deposit large wooden coins in a "piggy bank" developed the habit of rooting and tossing the coins about—behaviors controlled by food stimuli in the ordinary life of a pig.

Discrimination Learning

From an adaptive point of view, it is the consequences of behavior, rather than particular actions themselves, that are important to the animal. Food must reach the stomach of the parent, and also the stomachs of the helpless young. Predators must be avoided, eggs fertilized, and so on. These consequences remain relatively simple, as compared with the complexity and variety of the behaviors that can lead to the consequences. It is not surprising, therefore, that mechanisms have evolved that will lead animals to appropriate consequences, without passing on genetically a relatively large burden of information about the necessary specific actions involved. This is the evolutionary rationale for the principle of "reinforcement," which we have met before (Chapters 15–16). Most of this chapter is concerned with modifications in stimulus control under the influence of reinforcement.

Reinforcement and punishment are applied systematically in experiments to yield discriminative control. The responses controlled may be of any instrumental type, such as running toward, jumping at, or pushing on a stimulus source. The response locus can actually be some distance removed from the cue source or sources. The stimuli for discrimination learning may involve any of the sense modalities or even, as in position discrimination, kinesthetic feedback from the organism's own activity.

This chapter is concerned with both discrete-responding and free-operant (or multiple-responding) learning situations. Differential conditioning (also a form of discrimination learning, perhaps the most rudimentary) has been mentioned elsewhere. In discrete-trial situations, the experimenter controls the stimulus presentations, and the trial ends when a response has been made. The subject is either reinforced or not, depending upon the "correctness" of the behavior and the reinforcement schedule employed. Under discrete-trial procedures, the subject is usually permitted either one response or a predetermined amount of time during which a response may be made. In the free-operant situation (Ferster, 1953) the organism can continue responding in the presence of the discriminative stimuli until a correct response has been made, or until a certain time has passed, or until an arbitrary number of responses has occurred.

Historically, studies of performance in discrimination learning situations often were carried out to assess the sensory and behavioral capacities of various animal species. Animals can be trained to respond differentially to quite different stimuli, and then tested with stimuli that are progressively more similar, until a limit is reached at which no difference can be detected. For example, an animal might be fed for approaching the brighter but not for approaching the dimmer of two lights. One could then determine the smallest brightness difference between two stimuli that still permits the animal to respond differentially.

The techniques described above were originally designed by comparative psychologists to find out what animals hear, see, taste, and smell. However, it became increasingly apparent that discrimination learning depends upon experimental variables the effects of which should be studied in their own right. For example, why are some discriminations learned faster than others? To find out, stimuli and reinforcement conditions may be varied, and the course of acquisition may be followed by plotting some response measure over practice trials. Usually, response strength is expressed as the proportion of responses or the number of trials that are correct. Learning trends may also be assessed in terms of the relative latencies of response to different stimuli, a procedure that is particularly appropriate when there are no "incorrect" responses but, instead, alternatives that yield different reinforcing consequences (Logan, 1952).

It should be apparent that discrimination, or differential responsivity, is the obverse of generalization. When an organism responds in the same way, or similarly, to two or more stimuli it may be said that generalization exists among the stimuli—for *that* organism executing *that* response. Discrimination involves the absence or diminution of generalization and, in discrimination learning, the progressive increase in the probability of making different responses to different stimuli. Between total generalization and perfect discrimination lies a continuum of differential responding, manipulable through reinforcement contingencies. The study of this differential responding, and the variables that affect it, comprises the study of discrimination learning.

Because an organism's discrimination is always assessed through the measurement of some particular response property, discrimination performance can be at the same time both excellent and poor, even with respect to the same set of stimuli. Thus, a subject might choose an incorrect stimulus as often as a correct stimulus, but take longer to choose the incorrect one. "Percent correct" would show no discrimination, but "latency" would. Thus the discriminative capacity of the subject must always be defined in terms of the response measures that are used. Realization of this point helps to avoid the empty questions that sometimes arise as to whether an organism *really* can tell the difference between two stimuli even though it is not currently responding differentially. To say that a rat can tell the difference between a black card and white card means that under some circumstances a differential response will be made.

PROCEDURES

Many methods have been devised since the start of systematic work on discrimination learning about 1900. To some extent, the variety of the methods reflects the variety of the subjects studied, for one cannot present the same stimuli to, nor record the same responses from, a child, a mouse, a worm, a chimpanzee, and an octopus, although all of these, and many other organisms, have been used in discrimination experiments. The great bulk of the work, however, has been done on just a few species, the white rat mostly, but children, monkeys, and pigeons are currently popular subjects also. Methods also vary widely with the purposes of the experimenter, who may proceed quite differently if he is interested in, say, visual acuity of an animal subject than if he is interested in the effects of food deprivation upon learning speed. His apparatus and procedure may also include aspects dictated by his particular theoretical orientation.

Despite the diversity of prevalent methods for the study of discrimination, they all involve certain common problems as well as common principles. Also, the evolution of method has shown consistent trends through time. These trends are in the direction of gaining increasingly precise control of variables (making it possible, for example, to state exactly what stimulus is reaching the subject), eliminating extraneous variables (for example, by isolating the subject), improving

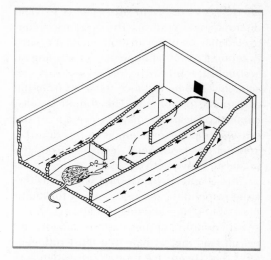

Figure 17.2. Partial floor plan of the Yerkes discrimination box. The small squares represent the positive and negative cues on the wall, and the broken lines are the alternative routes. The route that passes the positive cue leads to food.

efficiency (producing, for example, faster learning, thus allowing more trials per day), and greater simplicity. This last trend is particularly important; it contributes to all the others, and in addition the outcome of a simple experiment (few stimuli, few response possibilities) is usually easier to interpret than the experiment with many complex possibilities.

Discrete Trial Methods

An early apparatus used to teach animals to discriminate between stimuli was designed by Yerkes (1907; Yerkes & Watson, 1911) for the study of visual sensory capacities in mice and rats. A partial floor plan of this so-called "discrimination box" is shown in Figure 17.2. The little squares on the wall at the far end from the starting position represent the positive and negative cues. The animal chooses a cue by walking past it into the outer alley. If it chooses correctly, it finds food at the end of the outer alley; if not, it gets nothing. As can be seen, this apparatus permits correction: If the animal first responds to the negative stimulus, it may go to the other side and receive the reinforcer. Note several things about this method: the subject cannot see one stimulus while responding to the other; it walks near the stimulus, rather than actually touching or responding "to" it; reinforcement is delayed because the animal must go on to the end of the outer alley to get food; there is no punishment for incorrect responses.

The early experimenters often took greater pains to control stimulus variables such as light intensity than they did to facilitate the animal's learning, and all of the factors just listed are now thought to make for slow and variable learning. Later workers sought methods that would yield faster training, less response variability, and a closer approach to

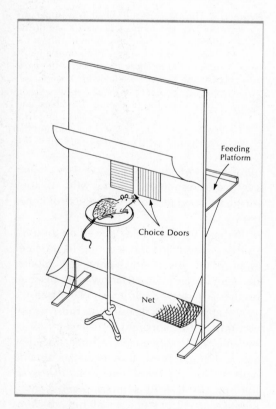

Figure 17.3. The Lashley jumping stand. If the rat jumps against the correct door, it opens and the rat finds food. If the rat jumps against the wrong door, which is locked, it falls into the net.

the subject's discriminative limits. When Lashley (1930), for instance, began an extensive study of pattern vision in the rat, he abandoned older methods because of the enormous number of trials it took an animal to learn to discriminate, for example, between a circle and a square. He devised a "jumping stand" that yielded much quicker learning (Figure 17.3). Improved forms of the Lashley jumping stand have since been reported (Lashley, 1938; Tolman, 1939; Finger, 1941; Ehrenfreund, 1948; Feldman, 1948; Maier, 1949).

Suppose one wanted to teach a rat a black-white discrimination in the Lashley jumping stand, with black as the negative stimulus and white as the positive. In preliminary training, the stand is placed close to an open door, with food behind, and the rat walks in. The stand is moved progressively backward on successive trials until the rat must jump the gap, which may be increased eventually to 10 inches or more. Next the rat is offered an easy choice between a closed black door and an open door with food beyond; then a few trials later a white door is substituted for the open one. Finally, the black door is locked, and if the rat jumps incorrectly it bumps into the door and falls into a net below. If it jumps against the correct door, in contrast, it pushes it open and finds food on the platform behind. When the black and white doors are shifted from side to side in random order, response to the positive stimulus is often established in as few as 4 or 5 trials (see p. 601).

The speed of learning that is achieved with the Lashley jumping stand is probably aided by the fact that the rat can see both stimuli at the time of choice, that it jumps directly at the chosen stimulus, and that it gets food immediately for correct jumps. Also, it is punished by the bump and fall for incorrect responses.

Punishment tends to facilitate learning in many situations, but it can also cause trouble. For example, sometimes rats will not jump, even after a careful, gradual approach to the final conditions. This happens particularly when the stimuli to be discriminated are quite similar or when the discrimination problem is insoluble (for example, both stimuli are correct on a random half of the jumps). Investigators faced with rats that would not jump (Feldman, 1948; Maier, 1949; Maier & Ellen, 1951) have resorted to shocking the animal, or blowing air on it, if its response latency on a trial exceeded an arbitrary limit. Such procedures keep the rat from sitting the whole trial out, but in all likelihood they affect the animal's discrimination performance as well. Animals treated in this way, for example, typically develop perseverative or "fixated" responses (see p. 791).

Other variations of the Yerkes box for small animals have been made that retain its maze-like character in simplified form. In the T-maze and the Y-maze, for example, the animal proceeds from a start box through a single alley to a critical juncture. Here, with both positive and negative stimuli in view, the animal turns either left or right. Correct choices lead to reinforcement at the end of the chosen arm; incorrect choices yield no reinforcement or, in some experiments, punishment by shock.

Variations on the classic techniques just described have been devised to suit many subject species. Subjects that can manipulate objects readily, such as monkeys and humans, have usually been required to grasp or touch choice stimuli rather than to run or jump to different places. Hobhouse (1901) found that monkeys will learn quickly to pull in a food container placed beyond reach but attached to an accessible string. If there are two such containers, one smaller than the other but which always contains the food, the monkey learns to pull in the smaller. Monkeys can learn to rely on brightness and shape as well when they make a choice (Klüver, 1931, 1933). Rats also may be taught, with patience and tact, to pull in food containers by aid of a string (McCulloch, 1934; McCulloch & Pratt, 1934), but this kind of response is not particularly easy for them, whereas it is easy for

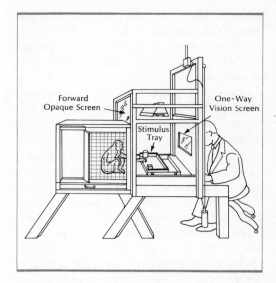

Figure 17.4. The Wisconsin General Test Apparatus (WGTA). The monkey displaces one of the stimulus objects on the stimulus tray. If his choice is correct, the monkey finds a bit of food in a hole under the object. After each trial, the experimenter lowers the forward opaque screen, raises the one-way-vision screen, puts food in one of the holes, and resets the stimulus objects according to a prearranged plan. Then he moves the screens to start a new trial.

monkeys, which naturally use hand-over-hand responses in the wild as they forage for food in the trees or flee from enemies.

Perhaps the most widely used method for studying discrimination learning in primates employs the Wisconsin General Test Apparatus (see Figure 17.4). Harlow and his colleagues (Harlow & Bromer, 1938; Harlow, 1949; Schrier, 1961) devised the most recent versions of this apparatus. The evolution of the apparatus has been interestingly traced by Meyer, Treichler, and Meyer (1965), beginning with the use of the Yerkes-Watson box by Johnson (1914, 1916) adapted to cebus monkeys. Kohts (1923) studied matching in chimpanzees by requiring them to pick an object from a tray after seeing or touching a sample. Gellermann (1933a, b) devised a multipurpose piece of equipment for comparative studies of chimpanzees and children. He mounted a pair of food boxes side by side on a shelf. Initially he had the stimulus patterns placed in an area between the boxes, but this procedure failed; when he placed the cues directly on the box lids the chimpanzees learned to work out the problems. Spence (1937) used an immediate predecessor of the WGTA that Meyer (1965, p. 6) calls the first apparatus ". . . to combine efficiency, convenience, and control of variables . . ." The discriminanda here were sheet-metal forms attached to boxes that the ape could tip up to expose food beneath. Among the reasons that Spence gave for the success of his apparatus were the facts that the relevant cues for learning were set apart distinctly from those that were irrelevant, and that the apes were required to push the stimulus forms directly, so their responses were temporally and spatially contiguous with the presentation of the reinforcement.

In the WGTA, food boxes have given way to food wells cut into a tray, and the stimulus figures cover these wells. The caged animal and the experimenter face one another across a table that supports the test tray. Two screens may be lowered between the subject and the experimenter. An opaque one keeps the subject from seeing the experimenter setting the stimuli on each trial, and a one-way-vision screen allows the experimenter to observe the animal during trials. Several adaptations of the basic WGTA have been developed for the study of visual discrimination learning in infants (Weisberg & Simmons, 1966) and older children (Spiker, 1956; Lipsitt, 1961), and in rats (Shepp & Eimas, 1964).

Automated Methods

One bothersome characteristic of the methods just described is that all require the constant attendance of an experimenter. Apparatus such as the maze or jumping stand also requires the experimenter to pick up the animal after each trial and put it back in the starting location. This is time-consuming and it introduces variability, which sometimes can

be serious, for an inexperienced experimenter may squeeze a rat too hard, while even a trained experimenter has trouble treating each animal the same on all trials every day. To reduce these difficulties, more and more experiments are now controlled by automatic switching equipment and are run with animals completely isolated. Thus, instead of choosing between two doors or two alleys, a rat may be placed in a closed box to press one or two levers or push one or two plastic panels with its nose. The latter arrangement allows visual stimuli to be projected on the panels, so the subject responds directly to the stimuli—a procedure that, as we have seen, was helpful in the older methods. Trials in such experiments are separated by withdrawing the levers or by presenting some obvious inter-trial stimulus during which responses are not reinforced. If pigeons are used as subjects, darkness can often be used to separate trials because the birds are relatively inactive in the dark.

Automation saves time and reduces variability. In addition, more complex stimulus and reinforcement sequences may be scheduled than are possible with manual control, and each event occurs at just the right moment. If switches are attached to response levers or panels, responses may be made to drive counters, chart recorders, tape punches, or computer input systems. Long sessions can be run; sometimes, the animal may even stay in the experimental chamber continuously for days. Automation also means that the animal's behavior can be used to control subsequent events in the experiment. Thus, in discrimination experiments the presentation of the stimuli can be controlled by the subject himself. Such self-presentation of stimuli is often relied upon, for example, in the matching-to-sample experiment. In a typical case, a pigeon subject is confronted by three dark keys. A trial starts when a sample stimulus appears on the center key. This sample remains until the bird pecks at it, an "observing response" that assures the bird's exposure to the stimulus. By making this response, the bird turns off the sample and exposes itself to the choice stimuli, one on each side key, between which it must then choose.

Free-operant Methods

Automatic apparatus is a feature of the methods pioneered by Skinner (1938). However, as is described in Chapter 14, these methods typically measure response rate, rather than recording a series of choices, as in a T-maze, a jumping stand, or a Wisconsin General Test Apparatus. Rate adds a new dimension to the standard variations of the discrete trial methods. Corresponding to the "go–no go" paradigm, where the animal is confronted on any trial with a stimulus to which it may or may not respond, the "multiple schedule" procedure presents a single key or lever to the subject; two or more states of a stimulus indicate periods during which the subject will receive reinforcement on some schedule for responses to this operandum. For example, a red light on the pigeon's key might set the occasion for reinforcement on a variable-interval schedule, while green indicates a period of extinction. In the operant literature, stimuli associated with specific reinforcement contingencies are often called "discriminative stimuli"; if a response is reinforced in the presence of a stimulus, that stimulus is called the "S+" or "S^D." If responses are never reinforced in the presence of a stimulus, the stimulus is called "S–" or "S$^\Delta$." As we have seen in Chapter 14, many schedules of reinforcement may be programmed, with the result that S+ may indicate reinforcement available according to a variety of contingencies; there may be several S+s, each associated with a different schedule.

Corresponding most closely with the typical simultaneous choice procedure (see p. 774) is the so-called "concurrent schedule." Here, two (sometimes more) operanda are available simultaneously. The animal may operate either freely, and may switch from one to the other at will. An analogue of the "successive" procedure in this situation might

be, for example, a bright light in the chamber setting the occasion for reinforcement (on some schedule) of pressing the lever on the right, whereas a dim light indicates reinforcement of pressing the lever on the left. More typical is the "simultaneous" variant. The bright light is always over one lever, the dim over the other. At a given time, the stimulus conditions may reverse, but both levers and both stimuli are always available.

In a given case, many considerations enter into the decision of whether or not to use a discrete-trial single-choice procedure or a free-operant discrimination with a rate measure. For a given stimulus presentation, rate provides more information about the tendency to respond than does a single response; given the simultaneous choice between two stimuli, a subject might always choose a particular one, yet we might find that the subject responds rapidly to its chosen stimulus under certain conditions but slowly under others. In following the course of discrimination learning, the rate of response in the presence of S+ may stay relatively constant, whereas the rate to S– declines; this may imply a process different from that which controls an increasing rate to S+ and a steady rate to S–. However, both of these changes might show up equally in a choice test as a rise in percent correct.

In contrast, the very freedom of the free-operant method often makes it hard to analyse the results of an experiment. For example, when two levers are present, the act of switching from one to the other sometimes appears to be a response quite different from repeated responses to the same lever (Catania, 1966). A further objection to relying on the free-operant method in discrimination studies is the fact that reinforcement itself may enter the experiment as a discriminative stimulus. In a discrete-trial experiment, reinforcement only comes at the end of a trial, and it provides no information about how to respond during that trial. In a multiple schedule, if the S+ remains on after the subject has received one of his scheduled reinforcements, it will not be clear whether subsequent responses are controlled by the S+ or whether they occur, at least in part, because the reinforcement itself has provided a cue that further reinforcement is possible (Blough, 1966; Jenkins, 1968b). Thus, experimenters who have chosen the free-operant method for discriminative work often change stimulus conditions randomly after reinforcement, or examine only data from stimulus presentations that omit reinforcement altogether.

One common application of the free operant method has been to the testing of stimulus generalization, using the technique pioneered by Guttman and Kalish (1956). In this technique, the subject receives prolonged training with intermittent reinforcement in the presence of one stimulus; then reinforcement is omitted entirely, and the stimulus is varied at brief intervals. The rate of response to each test stimulus contributes to a generalization gradient that is not biased by the occurrence of reinforcement, for the test is run in extinction.

Complex variations of operant methods have been applied to specific problems in animal psychophysics, and it is very difficult to describe them briefly in general terms. We shall return to the problems briefly below (see Blough, 1966).

COMPARATIVE PSYCHOPHYSICS

The desire to find out about the sensory capacities of animals has long been an important reason for doing discrimination experiments with animals. This has come about because physiological and anatomical information about animal sensory systems is being collected with increasing rapidity and, with behavioral data from the same subjects, it is possible to put together a much more complete picture of sensory functioning than can be done with physiological data alone. Working with animals also affords the opportunity to carry out sensory research with important but possibly dangerous variables—studies, for

example, of the effect of very intense noise on hearing.

It is in the behavioral study of animal sensory functioning, which could be called "comparative psychophysics," that we see most clearly the overlap between the methods of human psychophysics (Chapters 2 and 3) and those discussed in this chapter. In both kinds of work the experimenter may ask what the subject sees, hears, smells, and so on. Thus psychophysics is set apart from other work on discriminative control by its emphasis on well-learned discriminations rather than upon the learning process itself. It is also set apart by its emphasis upon the effects of simple stimulus changes, rather than complex stimuli or motivational and incentive variables such as level of deprivation or the nature of the reinforcer. In psychophysics, the aim is to find out how dim a light may yet be detected, how similar are two tastes, how loud is a tone, and so on.

Methods

Chapters 2 and 3 discuss in detail the methods employed in human psychophysics. The animal case differs primarily in the way that the subject is instructed and kept responding. The human subject is told what to look for and what to do. The animal must be reinforced for looking and for doing and perhaps punished for inappropriate behavior. These reinforcement conditions must be woven into the psychophysical procedure in such a manner that they generate the desired behavior but do not provide interfering cues. The apparatus and procedure used depend, of course, on the subject species, the sense modality, and the particular problem of interest. Certain common problems are faced in all sorts of research, however, and we can illustrate some of them by describing a single experiment.

Let us ask if pigeons can detect odors. Like other birds they apparently have the necessary physiological apparatus, but there is little evidence that the smell of things affects their behavior. Michelsen (1959) carried out an

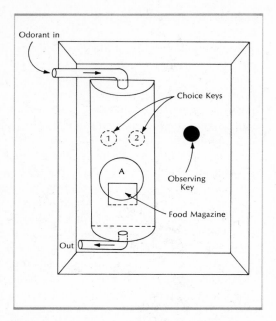

Figure 17.5. Apparatus for pigeons in Michelsen's olfactory experiment. Pecking the observing key started air flowing through the cylinder on the left. Nine seconds later, another peck on the observing key turned off the lights outside the cylinder and turned on a light inside. Then the bird pecked key 1 if an odor was present, key 2 if not. (After Michelsen, 1959.)

experiment to answer this question using a free-operant method. His pigeon subject was isolated in an experimental chamber with one wall built as shown in Figure 17.5. The bird had three keys to peck. Two of these (1 and 2 in Figure 17.5) were choice keys; the left key indicated "odor present," the right "odor absent." Odorous stimuli were introduced on an airstream that flowed down a cylinder covering the choice keys. The bird placed its head in this cylinder through a hole (A) when a choice was to be made.

Let us develop Michelsen's procedure in answer to typical questions about an experiment of this kind. We start with the idea of forming a simple discrimination: reinforce pecks at the left key if an odorous substance is present, reinforce pecks to the right key if it is absent. What dif-

ficulties must the procedure take into account? First, extraneous stimuli must be excluded. The presence or absence of the odorous substance is just one thing that may be correlated with reinforcement. For example, there may be a click when the valve inducing an odorant is operated. The valve should be silent. The air should move at equal speed whether an odorant is there or not. To check such conditions, the odorant is sometimes omitted from the bottle upstream, to see if any discrimination may be maintained without it.

One important extraneous stimulus, unhappily often overlooked, is the occurrence of reinforcement itself. Suppose we decide to present odorous air for 3 minutes and pure air for 3 minutes, alternately, and to reinforce pecking at the left key on an intermittent schedule when the odor is present and at the right key when it is absent. Suppose the schedule of reinforcement is a fixed ratio of 10 (see p. 605). The pigeon can achieve an excellent score without smelling the odor at all, simply by pecking a few times at each key alternately. When reinforcement comes following pecks on the left key, the bird continues to peck on that key until reinforcements stop coming, then switches over and tries the right key.[1] Michelsen solved this problem by dividing his session into trials. A trial ended with reinforcement after 7 correct pecks were made, or without reinforcement if 4 incorrect pecks were made first.

Another difficulty that sometimes arises in two-choice experiments of the kind described above is the appearance of a habit that may mask discriminative control by the stimulus. Let us say that odorous air is present on half of the trials in the experiment, and pure air on the other half. By responding to one key only, on all trials, the pigeon could receive reinforcement on half of the trials. Many subjects are content with this situation; one cannot indicate to them that they would get more food if only they would pay attention

[1] Jenkins (1965a) discusses this general problem in the context of discrimination experiments.

to the stimuli and switch their responses accordingly. For this reason most experiments use a "correction" procedure, as did Michelsen in his odor experiment. If a trial ended with incorrect pecks, the stimulus conditions were repeated on the next trial. Thus, after an error, the pigeon could never get reinforcement, and get on with the experiment, until it switched keys away from the currently incorrect side. Such "correction" trials cannot be counted as part of the measure of the subject's discrimination, of course, because the lack of reinforcement on the previous trial can act as a cue controlling responses on the correction trial.

The correction procedure encourages the subject to abandon position as a cue and to attend to stimuli of interest to the experimenter. Another way to facilitate this attending behavior is to have the subject make some explicit "observing response." We have already seen that the Lashley jumping stand and the WGTA probably work well partly because they make the subject look at the discriminanda. In Michelsen's experiment, the odorous air did not fill the whole chamber, but flowed instead through the cylinder over the choice keys. A key outside this compartment (see Figure 17.5) was used for the observing response. A trial began when a house light was turned on in the outer chamber, with this third key lighted. When the bird pecked this observing key, air began to flow through the cylinder. Nine seconds later, when air bearing the odor had filled the small chamber, another peck on the observing key turned off the house light and turned on lights in the small chamber. This was a signal for the bird to put its head into the small chamber and choose between two keys (key 1 and key 2 in the figure), key 1 if an odor was present, key 2 if not.

Using the method just described, Michelsen found that pigeons did appear to discriminate odors. With two odorous substances the birds did better than 80 percent correct, while on control days, when the stimulus air passed through water without an odorant, performance fell to chance levels. We shall pursue this matter a bit further, since more information has since been gained by a technique that exemplifies a different approach to the problem.

This new method really involves both operant and classical conditioning (Chapter 14), for it uses the "conditioned suppression" (or "conditioned emotional response") effect (pp. 712–717). The main idea is to train an animal to emit a response, using some intermittent schedule of reinforcement such as a variable interval (p. 605). The stimulus that the animal is supposed to detect is then turned on at intervals, and after a brief presentation, which may be considered the CS, a shock (US) is delivered. If this is done, and if the proper values of stimulus and shock are maintained, classical conditioning of emotional responses usually occurs swiftly: the subject slows its responses or stops altogether in the presence of the conditioned stimulus.

Using an apparatus in many ways similar to that of Michelsen described above, and the suppression method, Henton, Smith, and Tucker (1966) studied odor detection in pigeons. However, only a single key was used, and the pigeon was reinforced on a 2-min variable-interval schedule (p. 605) for pecking at this key. This schedule generated a moderate rate of pecking. After this behavior became stable, the birds got 10 suppression trials in each 1-hour session. During these trials, air with an odorous substance added (amyl acetate) passed through the bird's chamber for 18 seconds; then the bird got a brief shock through electrodes implanted below its tail. The experimenters recorded key pecks during the olfactory stimulation, and also key pecks during the 30 sec period just prior to the odorous stimulation. They used the formula for the suppression ratio:

$$\frac{\text{prestimulus responses} - \text{stimulus responses}}{\text{prestimulus responses}}$$

to measure the detection of the odorous substance. If the substance had no effect, this

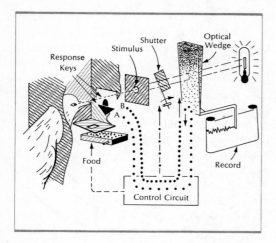

Figure 17.6. Apparatus used to track the pigeon's absolute threshold to light. Pecks on key *A* moved the wedge down (darker); pecks on key *B* moved it up (brighter). See text for details. (After Blough, 1958.)

ratio would be zero, whereas complete suppression would yield a ratio of 1.

The experimenters found that birds gave very few responses in the presence of 5 to 7 percent vapor saturation of amyl acetate. They ran a number of controls, making sure, for example, that changes in the flow of air during stimulation were not being used as a cue. They also showed that response suppression disappeared when the birds' olfactory nerves were cut.

Another method, called "tracking," is very useful for certain kinds of problems. This is again a two-response procedure, but it is distinguished by the fact that the responses not only indicate the subject's choices, but also serve to adjust the stimulus to some value of interest. For example, in a series of experiments, Blough (1958, 1961) reinforced pigeons for pecking one response key (key *A*) when a stimulus patch was visible and another (key *B*) when the patch was not (Figure 17.6). These pecks sent signals to relays that controlled the intensity of the patch. Pecks on key *A* reduced the intensity of the patch whereas pecks on key *B* increased it. Thus, if the bird could see the stimulus, it would peck on key *A*, causing the stimulus to dim and eventually to disappear. Then it would peck on key *B* to brighten the patch until it was visible once again; the cycle could then be repeated. In this fashion the bird kept the stimulus intensity oscillating up and down across its absolute threshold; a continuous record of intensity gave a graphic picture of the bird's threshold through time. Such a continuous record is especially valuable when we are interested in seeing how the threshold changes with time. For example, Blough used the method to study the course of dark adaptation and the course of drug action upon the threshold.

The tracking behavior is maintained by a rather complex set of reinforcement contingencies (for details, see Blough, 1958). Essentially, reinforcement is introduced into the situation at short intervals of random length by allowing responses to key *A* to turn off the stimulus entirely for a brief period. When the stimulus is off, key *B* pecks are reinforced by food, and tracking then resumes. Thus, to anthropomorphize, the pigeon works on key *A* to turn the light out, so that it can switch to key *B* and get food. The basic rationale of the method is that the bird cannot distinguish between the light dimming below threshold and its going out altogether.

Human and Animal Psychophysics: Signal Detectability

A maintained discrimination or a threshold experiment with animals has much in common with corresponding psychophysical experiments run with human subjects. As we have already seen, there are considerable differences in emphasis, for the experimenter using animals must spend much of his time training or "instructing" his subject, and maintaining its performance, whereas the emphasis in human methodology tends to be upon the ways in which stimuli are presented, the nature of responses, and the analysis of their interrelations (Chapters 2 and 3). These are, however, really differences in emphasis rather than in substance. The experimenter working with non-human subjects has to decide upon a stimulus scheme (for example, he may choose the "method of limits," [page 14], or the "method of constant stimuli," [page 23]), and choose appropriate response categories. The human psychophysicist has to instruct his subject, and prepare to deal with motivational factors and response biases analogous to the reinforcement problems the researcher working with animals must face. The basic correspondence between human and animal psychophysics is no better shown than by reference to the theory of signal detectability (which was described with reference to human psychophysics, pp. 34–46).

Basic to the detectability approach is the notion of separating sensitivity from other variables that may affect a response in a discrimination situation. An experimenter can change the criterion of a human subject by such instructions as "Don't say 'yes' unless you are absolutely certain you detect the stimulus." Rewards and punishments may also change the criterion. Here, the experimenter using animals has a freer hand. In a simple case, a rat, for example, may be trained to detect a weak sound. If, during a trial indicated by a light in the rat's box, the sound is presented, the rat presses lever A for reinforcement, and is perhaps punished for pressing lever B. If no sound is presented, the rat can press lever B for reinforcement, and if it presses lever A, it is punished. The rat's sensitivity (as indicated by the quantity, d') is computed just as is a human subject's (p. 41) from the proportion of "hits" (A presses, given a sound) and "false alarms" (A presses, given no sound) that it makes.

The procedure described above has two advantages. If we are interested in the rat's sensitivity (we might be studying mechanisms in the ear, for example), d' gives an estimate that is unbiased by the kinds of lever preferences and motivation changes that plague work with animals. If we are interested in the discriminative mechanisms including motivation and bias, we may change the animal's "payoff matrix" (p. 37) by varying the amount or relative frequency of rewards and punishments for pressing the two levers, while holding constant the influence of signal and sensitivity (see Hack, 1963; Boneau, 1967). Stebbins (1966) obtained additional information by recording the latency of response to an auditory stimulus. His monkeys held down a key until they heard a tone, which varied in intensity from trial to trial and in frequency from session to session. Tones that yielded equal latency were assumed to be equally loud, and Stebbins was able to construct "equal loudness contours" similar to those obtained from human subjects.

THE EFFECTIVE CUES IN DISCRIMINATED BEHAVIOR

What cues actually control the rat's choice between two doors of a jumping stand, a child's decision to press one of two stimulus panels, or, generally, any discriminated response? This is a familiar problem in many areas of psychology. In perception, for example, we may ask what aspects of the environment determine that we shall see objects "in depth" or "at a distance" or enable us to locate sounds at a particular source. These are not easy questions to answer, even in simple learning situations, yet upon the answers depend not only the understanding of any specific situation, but the understanding of discriminative processes generally. In this section we look mainly at the methods that have been devised to find the effective cues; we also look at some of the more important empirical results. In the next section we deal with some of the theoretical issues and debates that have surrounded experiments on discriminative control.

Several basic methods have been used to investigate the nature of effective stimuli. In one group of techniques, stimulus equivalence is directly tested. This group includes studies of "stimulus generalization," and "transposition." These studies start by generating a high degree of stimulus control and then varying aspects of the stimulus situation to see which makes a difference in the response. By definition, "effective cues" are those aspects that, when varied, cause the response to vary.

Other methods do not start with a well-learned discrimination, but instead they measure primarily the subject's performance as he learns some new task. Here the notion is that stimuli that are effective in a given situation may help or hinder new learning; the kinds of tasks that are helped or hindered give us clues about the nature of the stimuli. Among these methods are studies of "reversal learning" and "learning set," for example.

A third group of techniques makes it possible for us to look at the behavior of the subject for indications of selection or attention, while he learns to discriminate between stimuli. Aspects of the learning situation may be changed to make the subject's stimulus selection processes more evident. Studies of "vicarious trial and error," "observing behavior," and "attention" are of this type.

Of course, the distinctions between the methods described above are somewhat arbitrary. Furthermore, many experiments involve the combination of several of these techniques.

Stimulus Generalization

Perhaps the simplest way of determining effective cues is found in the study of stimulus generalization, for here the stimuli are usually drawn from some well-defined physical continuum, and their effectiveness is inferred from a simple measure of response strength, such as rate, force, or latency. Studies of generalization show that the environmental conditions that control behavior are never unique events; one can always find a class of somewhat different events that also will set the occasion for the same response. Such stimulus generalization is necessary for survival, for situations never recur exactly; we must avoid collision with looming objects that come at us from various angles, respond to the same words pronounced with

various tonalities and accents, and so on. The generalization phenomenon appears to be similar for both the conditioned stimuli whose control is established through classical conditioning, and the discriminative stimuli whose control is established through operant training procedures. To study stimulus generalization, experimenters usually train a subject to respond in a given way in the presence of a specific stimulus, and then observe how the response changes as that stimulus is varied.

An early example of the study of stimulus generalization following classical conditioning is an experiment by Hovland (1937a, b) with human subjects. The conditioned stimulus was a tone, and the unconditioned response was the galvanic skin response (GSR) (p. 558) measured in terms of the amount of deflection of a galvanometer. Shock was paired with a tone of 1967 Hz until a good conditioned reflex had been established. Then the subject was presented with other tones (1,000, 468, and 153 Hz) spaced by successive steps of 25 jnds (just noticeable differences, p. 19) from the original conditioned stimulus. The height of the generalized GSR could thus be stated as a function of psychologically meaningful steps along the pitch continuum. The resulting gradient can be seen in the mean GSR (measured as galvanometer deflections) obtained from 20 subjects:

18.3 mm when the original tone was sounded
14.9 mm when the tone 25 jnd away
    was sounded
13.6 mm when the tone 50 jnd away
    was sounded
12.9 mm when the tone 75′jnd away
    was sounded

The gradient is far from steep in view of the wide range of pitch tested.

The experiment described above was actually more complex than it might seem from the description. All four tones were equated for loudness, to avoid any possible influence from this variable. Further, Hovland trained half his subjects on the lowest pitch rather than the highest, and averaged his results in terms of "steps-removed-from-CS," just in case the higher (or lower) tone happened to be the more effective stimulus. (Such measures to isolate the effective stimulus variable are often an important part of generalization experiments.)

Hovland's experiment has the disadvantage that it was necessary to average the data of several subjects in order to show regular generalization gradients. In contrast, techniques more recently developed for use with animals routinely produce gradients from single subjects. An example of this, concerned with respondent generalization, is an experiment of Hoffman (1965), who used the conditioned suppression method that we have met before in this chapter and elsewhere (p. 712). The measure of the strength of the response is indirect; it is the degree of suppression of an on-going operant by a tone (CS) that has been paired with shock. Pigeons were first starved to 80 percent of their origi-

nal weight and adapted to the apparatus, which is shown in Figure 17.7. They were then trained to key peck and placed on a 2 minute variable-interval schedule of intermittent reinforcement. Still without resorting to shock, Hoffman adapted the pigeons to the CS, a tone of 1000 Hz, and the test stimuli, tones of 300, 450, 670, 1000, 1500, 2250, and 4500 Hz. Finally, the CS tone of 1000 Hz was presented on an average of once every 10 minutes, lasting 48 seconds each time. During the last 8 seconds of each CS, shock UCS was presented. Approximately 600 trials over 70 sessions were required to reach a stable suppression of response to the 1000 Hz tone. Suppression was measured by the ratio

$$\frac{\text{pre-tone } Rs - \text{tone } Rs}{\text{pre-tone } Rs}$$

Note that if the bird pecks just as fast during the tone as before, this ratio equals zero, indicating no suppression; if it stops pecking entirely, the ratio is 1, indicating complete suppression.

During generalization testing, the bird was placed in the experimental box with shock

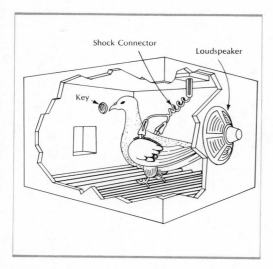

Figure 17.7. A view of the pigeon in the experiment on generalization of conditioned suppression. Shock was delivered through bead chain wrapped around the base of each wing. The pigeon pecked for food, but this pecking was suppressed when the loudspeaker sounded tones that had been paired with shock. (After Hoffman, 1965.)

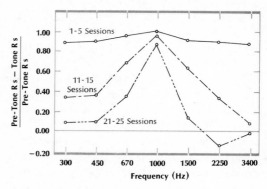

Figure 17.8. Generalization gradients from one bird in the experiment shown in Fig. 7. Prior to these tests, the 1000 Hz tone had been paired with shock. The curves show that in the first few sessions the bird stopped pecking almost entirely whenever any tone came on. By sessions 21–25, its behavior was still suppressed to the 1000 Hz tone, but most of the other tones produced little effect. No shocks occurred during these testing sessions. (After Hoffman, 1965.)

connectors in place, but no shock was ever delivered. Each day, in an hour and a half, the 7 tones (including the CS, 1000 Hz) listed above were presented one every 10 minutes, for 40 seconds each. The sequence of tones was varied from day to day. Figure 17.8 shows the gradients of suppression obtained from one pigeon on successive blocks of 5 sessions. Note that at first the bird stopped pecking almost entirely when it heard any tone, although the 1000 Hz CS caused slightly greater suppression than the others. Gradually, the gradient became steeper and steeper, until only the CS produced substantial suppression. (Remember that no shock accompanied any tone during the testing sessions.) Other experimenters, working in both operant and classical conditioning situations, have also noted a sharpening of the gradient during the course of the testing interval.

Other findings of Hoffman were that increased deprivation narrowed his suppression gradients, and that when testing was resumed after a $2\frac{1}{2}$ year interruption the tones continued to cause suppression in the manner that one might have expected had testing continued without interruption.

The exact shape of the generalization gradient became an issue of considerable interest to some behavior theorists (Spence, 1937; Hull, 1943). However, it is now considered of questionable value to talk of any one particular gradient shape, even in a single experimental setting. The gradients change during testing and vary with things such as deprivation, as the Hoffman experiment illustrates. Also, the measures of response strength (the ordinate of the gradient graph) and of the stimulus dimension (the abscissa) both affect the shape of the curve (Blough, 1965). For example, a different way of measuring suppression (there are several different ratios in use) would change the shape of Hoffman's gradient even if identical data were fed into the suppression formula (see p. 713).

For such reasons as the ones mentioned above, emphasis has shifted from determining "the" shape of "the" generalization gradient,

to attempts to specify the variables that may affect generalization and to interrelate results from differing kinds of experiments. Most of this research has been done using the rate of an operant response as the measure to which stimulus variation is tied. Many experiments have used pigeons as subjects and, as stimuli, different wavelengths of light, projected upon the bird's response key (Guttman & Kalish, 1956). A typical experiment is begun by training the pigeon to peck its translucent response key illuminated from behind by a single narrow wavelength band of light. Often, 550 nanometers (nm) has been used as the training stimulus in these studies. (This stimulus appears yellow-green to human eyes.) For perhaps 10 hour-long sessions the bird is reinforced intermittently on a variable-interval 1-minute schedule. Then, in a testing session, reinforcement is discontinued, and a set of differing wavelengths is given, each for perhaps ten 1-minute presentations mingled in random sequence with the others. The pigeon generally keeps pecking during most of this period, even though no reinforcement is given. Before it quits, it will

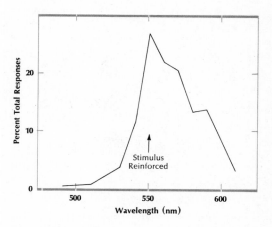

Figure 17.9. A typical generalization gradient from a single pigeon trained to peck a key illuminated by a light at 550 nm. Reinforcement ceased during the test, and lights of different wavelength appeared on the key. The bird pecked most at the wavelength formerly associated with reinforcement, and less at wavelengths differing from this.

have had several opportunities to peck at each of the test wavelengths. To some it responds rapidly, to others not at all. Counters record the total number of pecks emitted to each test stimulus; the gradient drawn from the experiment is made from the totals on these counters, as is illustrated in Figure 17.9.

You should not be led astray by the apparent asymmetry of the gradient in Figure 17.9, for this only illustrates our remarks about the importance of appropriate scales for gradients. Here the scale on the abscissa is a physical measure—wavelength. There is no reason to expect this psychologically arbitrary scale to yield a gradient of any particular shape. Recall that Hovland used for his scale jnds along the stimulus continuum: We might expect that these would have something to do with the degree of generalization between the various test wavelengths. Unfortunately, few data are available on pigeon jnds for hue, but what there is available does not seem to be related to the shape of generalization functions (Guttman & Kalish, 1956). Perhaps it is best to consider the gradient as defining the similarity of the various wavelengths to the training stimulus, as far as the pigeon is concerned. If a test wavelength yields about the same rate of response as the training stimulus, we can say that (by definition) the two wavelengths look similar to the bird; two wavelengths that yield differing response rates look different. Making use of this kind of analysis, it is possible to scale the wavelength continuum for similarity (Shepard, 1965).

Using various measures of response (rate, amplitude, and latency in particular), experimenters have explored stimulus generalization on a number of dimensions (Mednick & Freedman, 1960). Among these are the spatial dimension (that is, the distance between stimuli applied to the skin), frequency of tones, intensity and wavelength of lights, size, and temporal duration of various stimuli. In the last case, the training stimulus might be a tone of a particular duration, the test stimuli tones that are made to last for longer

or shorter periods of time. In all of these cases, more or less regular gradients have been obtained, with response strength falling with decreasing similarity between the test stimulus and the training stimulus. With one or more of these dimensions, several variables have been found to affect the width of the gradient. For example, increased drive generally broadens the gradient, and so (within limits) does the number of training trials and the lapse of time between training and testing.

The conditions for a generalization decrement We have said before, somewhat loosely, that a stimulus is said to control some behavior if a change in the stimulus brings about a change in the behavior. For example, we would not include as "stimuli" those environmental changes, like radio waves, that never control behavior. Furthermore, many events that are potential stimuli never gain such control, because this potentiality is not realized without learning or other experience of some kind. It might seem from the examples of generalization experiments given above that all that is required to make a class of events into a stimulus is to reinforce some response in the presence of members of that class. We shock the subject in the presence of a particular tone, feed the pigeon in the presence of a particular wavelength, and so on. However the situation is not so simple, as is illustrated by an experiment of Jenkins and Harrison (1960). They trained pigeon subjects with intermittent reinforcement on the usual key-pecking task while a single tone (1000 Hz) was presented continuously in the experimental boxes. Following this training, a test sequence of different tone frequencies was presented. However, in this test, the birds responded as much to one frequency as to another. They "generalized perfectly," "failed to discriminate," or "failed to attend" to the frequency changes. Or perhaps we might say that this procedure failed to make tone frequency a stimulus for these birds. Simply exposing a subject to some physical energy

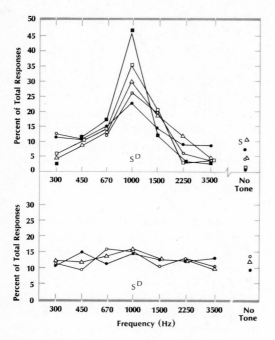

Figure 17.10. Each curve is a generalization gradient from one pigeon. Both groups were reinforced for pecking in the presence of the 1000 Hz tone. For birds shown in the lower graph, this tone was continuously present during training. Birds shown in the upper graph learned a discrimination with the 1000 Hz tone as S+, and no tone as S−. (After Jenkins & Harrison, 1960.)

may be inadequate to make changes in that energy become stimuli.

In contrast we saw above that sometimes simple exposure does seem to yield stimulus control. Do we have to be content to say simply that sometimes it does and sometimes it does not? Fortunately, we are in a somewhat better position than that. In the study mentioned above, Jenkins and Harrison (1960) also gave a group of birds discrimination training, sometimes presenting the 1000 Hz tone with reinforcement and sometimes turning off the tone and withholding reinforcement. When this was done, a gradient much like that found on the wavelength continuum resulted. Figure 17.10 compares the gradients with and without this differential training. Comparable results have been found by ex-

perimenters using other sorts of stimuli and punishment rather than reinforcement (Newman and Baron, 1965; Honig, 1966). So, as it turns out, differential reinforcement with respect to a stimulus is usually sufficient to bring the subject's behavior under the control of changes in that stimulus—provided it is within the capacity of the organism to respond to the given stimulus changes. However, note that the animal does not have to be trained specifically on the dimension that controls its behavior in the test. The birds' response rate changed with tone frequency, yet training was with tone versus no tone.

Is differential reinforcement necessary? In the wavelength generalization study first mentioned, no explicit differential reinforcement was provided—no contrast of occasions during which reinforcement was available with those when it was not. This suggests differential reinforcement is sometimes not necessary, yet there are ways in which such training could have influenced the wavelength experiment nevertheless. For example, perhaps past training with different colors might be influencing the birds' response. Peterson (1962) raised ducklings in yellow sodium arc light (589 nm) so that they never had an opportunity to discriminate one wavelength from another. Given key-peck training and testing as we have described, these ducklings gave flat gradients; their behavior was not affected by wavelength changes. Another group of ducklings reared in normal illumination did give gradients much like the wavelength gradients given by the pigeons. Though the evidence is still mixed, this and a few similar experiments suggest that some kind of differential training may be necessary if a previously neutral stimulus is to control behavior. It should not be forgotten, though, that the unlearned eliciting properties of certain stimuli may control behavior without any history of differential reinforcement.

Generalization among complex stimuli
The old notion of generalization as a "spread

of association" tended to make people think only in terms of tests based on a few simple continua such as intensity or frequency. Stimulus classes, however, may be defined in many ways, and students of generalization have begun to explore some classes defined in more abstract terms. This is really the same thing as studying "concepts," for a concept can also be defined as a class of events occasioning a common response. Because concept learning is considered elsewhere (p. 785), we now look only at an example that relates closely to other generalization research. This is an experiment of Honig (1965), which established "stimulus difference" as a dimension. He trained birds to peck the right one of two keys if both keys were lighted by the same wavelength, but the left key if the wavelengths differed. Each wavelength appeared equally often on both keys, and each was paired equally often with itself and with a different wavelength, so the birds could not learn which key to peck simply by following any particular color or key. They had to learn, as it were, the "color same" and "color different" concepts. Honig collected regular gradients along the dimension of wavelength difference. When the wavelengths on the two keys were physically adjacent on the wavelength continuum, the bird pecked mostly at the "same" key. With larger and larger differences, more and more pecks went to the "different" key. Such experiments suggest that the generalization procedure may be profitably used to find out about animal cognition and perception, as well as to study learning and sensory problems.

Stimulus control is often tested in complex cases where the nature of the stimuli makes the usual kind of generalization experiment impossible. Various aspects of the stimulus may be changed one by one, to see which is effective. For example, Reynolds (1961) reinforced two pigeons for pecking at a white triangle on a red background, and extinguished responses to a white circle on a green background. The birds quickly learned the discrimination, pecking rapidly at the triangle on red and not pecking at the circle on green. What was the controlling stimulus? Reynolds presented the components separately to find out. A triangle on a dark key, a plain red key, a circle on a dark key, and a plain green key were exposed successively. One bird pecked only at the triangle, and not at the red key nor the other stimuli; the other bird pecked only at the red key but not at the triangle nor the other stimuli. Thus, form controlled the response in one case, color in the other, and prior to the tests, it would have been impossible to predict which would be effective.

As we see in more detail shortly, effective stimuli sometimes are not simple, absolute properties of the physical situation. For example, one of the most effective stimuli can only be described as "novelty" or "change"—concepts that certainly go far beyond any specific set of environmental conditions. Many animals "freeze" when a strange event occurs, though if the event becomes common, they may come to ignore it completely. D. O. Hebb (1948) has been one of those who stress the importance of such stimuli and the processes they suggest.

Transposition A fundamental problem of discriminative control has been whether the stimuli are best defined in relational terms ("brighter," "larger") or absolute terms ("brightness X," "size Y"). A complex generalization test called the "transposition experiment" has been used to help clarify this matter. An example will illustrate this method. The subject first learns to discriminate between two stimuli on some continuum, such as intensity or size; for example, the darker or the larger of the two may be correct. Later, new stimuli from the same continuum are presented, but these bear the same relation as did the training stimuli. In this test, the subject often responds on a relational basis. For example, a rat might continue to choose the darker or the larger stimulus in the transfer task, even though it has never seen that particular stimulus before. Even the formerly correct stimulus may be avoided in the new situation if it fails to bear the proper relation to the new display. For example, suppose that a gray stimulus was the darker, and correct, stimulus in original learning. In the transfer test, it becomes the lighter, by virtue of being paired with a still darker stimulus. Subjects show transposition if they choose the new, "darker" stimulus.

At first glance, the behavior described above appears to violate the principle of generalization, which predicts that either the previously reinforced stimulus, or the one most similar to it, would be chosen in the transfer task. The Gestalt psychologist Wolfgang Köhler was perhaps the first, in 1918, to point out that the transposition phenomenon creates difficulties for a simple stimulus-response interpretation of discriminative behavior (Ellis, 1938, pp. 217–227). He found transposition in hens, primates, and children. For example, hens were presented grains of food on the darker of two gray papers. In subsequent tests, if the originally positive dark gray were paired with a still darker paper, the hens chose the new and darker stimulus. Köhler argued that they responded according to the relationship ("darker than") between

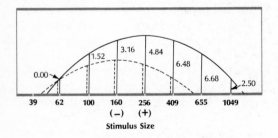

Figure 17.11. A diagram of hypothetical generalization curves following training with size 256 positive and size 160 negative. By subtracting the negative curve (dotted) from the positive (solid), one arrives at the net response strength associated with each size. Size 655 has the greatest net strength, (6.68), and would theoretically be chosen over size 409 (6.48)—an instance of transposition. Transposition would fail in the extreme case, since 655 would also be chosen over 1049 (2.50), though 655 is the smaller of the two.

the papers, rather than to the stimuli in isolation. Klüver (1933) replicated the transposition phenomenon, but he also found that it does not always occur. When he presented new stimuli much different from the original pair, his subjects (monkeys) sometimes chose the stimulus most similar to the original positive stimulus, rather than responding according to "relations." The more distant the test stimuli were from the original pair, the more transposition failed.

Spence (1937) proposed that simple stimulus-response relationships could account for transposition, and the failure of transposition as well, without recourse to new and more complex processes. He did this by reference to two hypothetical generalization gradients as shown in Figure 17.11. The example requires the assumptions that (1) presence of the positive stimulus (in this instance size 256) will produce a certain response strength or excitatory tendency commensurate with the number of reinforcements, while nonreinforced responses will set up inhibitory (or nonresponding) tendencies to the negative stimulus, in this instance size 160, and (2) the organism will respond to that stimulus which has the greater *effective* reaction strength. (The effective strength is the algebraic sum of the excitatory and inhibitory tendencies at each stimulus.) Thus, following simple discrimination training, both stimulus 256 and stimulus 160 will have, by virtue of generalization of both excitatory and inhibitory tendencies, a certain amount of excitation and inhibition associated with them. The *effective* reaction strengths for each will be obtained by subtracting the inhibitory from the excitatory strengths. You can see from the diagram that the organism should choose 256 over 160 when these are presented together (values 4.84 versus 3.16, respectively). More importantly, the simultaneous presentation in a transfer task of stimuli 409 and 256 would predict response to 409 in preference to 256 because the former has the greater net excitatory strength (6.48 versus 4.84). This is the transposition effect. This set of hypothetical gradients also shows that if stimuli 160 and 100 are presented simultaneously the organism should choose 160, even though this was the previously nonreinforced stimulus. Moreover, if the test stimuli are far enough removed from the original training stimuli, failure of transposition, if not an actual reversal, should occur; simultaneous presentation of stimuli 1049 and 655, for instance, should result in choice of the latter.

Since the Gestalt or relational interpretation cannot easily account for failures or reversals of transposition, Spence's ingenious analysis dealt a telling blow to that position. His views are still perhaps the most coherent account of discrimination phenomena, yet subsequent arguments and experiments have made it clear that they are at best an incomplete account of discriminative processes, as we see in detail below. Spence's gradients were, as he admitted, purely hypothetical. Transposition cannot be predicted from gradients of certain other shapes (those proposed by Hull, 1943, for example), and it has proven impossible to predict such phenomena consistently from empirical gradients collected in recent years (Hanson, 1959). Furthermore, more sophisticated types of discrimination and generalization that have been studied, such as Honig's (1965) generalization along a continuum of stimulus difference cannot be handled by Spence's analysis. The possibility of mediational processes further complicates the issues. In Spence's own laboratory, for instance, Kuenne (1946) found that young children, who do not verbalize relationships among stimuli very well, behave rather like infrahuman organisms in that transposition fails with increasing distance from the training stimuli. In older children, however, "relational" responding occurs even on far tests. Other studies with children (Alberts & Ehrenfreund, 1951; Hunter, 1952; Stevenson & Bitterman, 1955; Stevenson, Iscoe, & McConnell, 1955; Reese, 1961) have supported this now well-established phenomenon.

Zeiler (1963, 1967) has proposed a new theory to explain transposition that makes "relational" ideas more explicit than previous discussions. The theory assumes that training stimuli generate a background or "adaptation level" (p. 59). The reinforced stimulus makes a certain ratio with this level, and this ratio dictates the choice made during transposition tests. During these tests, the adaptation level is shifted in the direction of the set of test stimuli, and this in turn produces a shift in choice. This ratio theory predicts the troublesome finding of transposition on near tests but absolute choice on far tests. (For a complete review of the transposition literature on both animal and human subjects, and of the theories invoked to account for transposition, see Reese, 1968.)

Effective Cues During Learning

The presolution period: "hypotheses" Behavior changes systematically over the course of discrimination learning, and these changes may help to reveal what the subject is responding to as learning proceeds. Even before any apparent stimulus control appears, animals usually do not behave randomly. In this "presolution period" subjects may show predispositions that seem genetically determined; rats, for example, will tend to choose dark alleys in preference to brightly lighted ones. In many cases that involve a spatial choice, such as that between two doors or two levers, subjects show "position habits," consistent preferences for one side or the other. Some of the behavioral consistencies prior to solution were catalogued by Krechevsky (1932a, b) and Tolman and Krechevsky (1933). These authors suggested that even inarticulate organisms such as rats develop "hypotheses" concerning the solution of the problem at hand, and that sometimes, one hypothesis after another is tried until the correct one is adopted and controls subsequent choice. For example, Krechevsky (1932a) presented records of individual animals making 40 responses per day in a situation where the positive cue was a hurdle that had to be jumped to enter the alley leading to food.

This hurdle was placed on the right in half of the trials and on the left in the other half. The rats first developed a position habit, taking the right-hand alley almost every time for several days; thus, they responded to the reinforced hurdle alley only about half of the time. Subsequently, the position habit declined and correct choice (hurdle) rose to 100 percent. Once an incorrect hypothesis was abandoned and the consistently reinforced hypothesis was adopted, the animals quickly reached the discrimination criterion.

To explore the nature of presolution behavior over a long period, Krechevsky (1932b) gave his animals an insoluble discrimination problem. Two possible cues were always present, left versus right position, and dark versus light stimulus, but reinforcement was not associated consistently with either cue. Thus, the rats could reach food on only half the trials. (This procedure was also used by Maier and his colleagues to study fixation behavior [p. 791].) Again, the rats developed consistent patterns of behavior with respect to one or another of the cues. You should bear in mind that the use of the term "hypothesis" in these experiments need not imply complex thought processes; it is simply a name for the behavioral consistencies observed. Discrimination training may in many cases be considered partially a process of getting the subject to abandon such persistent behavior patterns when they are nonadaptive (Harlow, 1959).

Reversal learning In many cases, behavioral consistencies ("hypotheses") are inadequate to reveal what aspects of the environment are controlling behavior early in learning. The so-called "cue-reversal technique" was introduced by McCulloch and Pratt (1934) to gain more information on this matter. Rats learned to pull in a food tray to their cage by a string. They were then shown two trays, side by side, each attached to a string, one tray weighing three times as much as the other. Food was put in the lighter tray early in training but in the heavier tray later. For one group, the tray associated with food was reversed as soon as the individual rat began to improve its score (after 84 trials, the median), and for another group after only 28 trials, long before the first signs of learning were observed. For the control group the food was put in the heavier tray from the start. The results showed that the more trials the rat had when the food was in the light tray, the longer it took to reverse and learn to select the heavy tray. For the three groups, the number of trials required during the second period in order to achieve the criterion of correct responses on 75 percent of the trials was 166, 126, and 96, respectively. This result tended to support the Hull-Spence assumption regarding continuity of training effects during the presolution period: The animal appeared to "learn something" even before its score improved (for more on continuity, see page 773).

Spence (1945) and Ehrenfreund (1948) used the technique of first rewarding animals for developing a position habit. Then, when the animals were consistently responding to just one side, nonpositional positive and negative cues were introduced for a number of trials. Finally, these nonpositional cues were reversed until the animals had attained a high criterion of performance. Ehrenfreund used upright and inverted triangles as the nonpositional cues. Following initial training in which a position habit was induced, the triangle in one orientation was consistently reinforced for 40 trials, not enough to cause an improvement in performance. Finally, the triangle cues were reversed. A control group was given an insoluble problem during the presolution training; they received food half the time for responses to one triangle and half the time for responses to the other. It was reasoned that the control group should start its final training with no predisposition in favor of either triangular cue, whereas the experimental group should constitute a "reversal" condition. It turned out that the experimental group took an average of 63 trials to master the reversed cues, whereas the control group required only 37, a significantly lesser number. Ritchie, Ebeling, and Roth (1950) produced essentially the same finding in a similar experiment. These findings support the notion that pre-solution trials do affect subsequent discrimination.

The reversal problem in discrimination learning also has implications for the study of verbal or symbolic processes, as an example will illustrate. The subject views two stimuli, presented simultaneously, that vary both in brightness and in size. A large black square may be presented with a small white square on one trial, and a large white square with a small black square on the next trial. The larger square is reinforced, regardless of brightness. From training in such a task, the subject learns to select the larger stimulus and to "disregard" brightness, which is reinforced only 50 percent of the time.

Subjects so trained now go on to a transfer task with the same stimuli, but with new reinforcement conditions. A "reversal shift" is produced, like that previously discussed: The smaller of the squares is made correct on each trial, rather than the larger. To achieve a "nonreversal shift," reinforcement is shifted to the other stimulus dimension, in this case brightness; either responses to black or responses to white could be selected by the experimenter as the response to be rewarded.

Comparative and developmental psychologists are interested in comparing reversal shift with nonreversal shift performance, because differences appear to be tied to verbal and symbolic processes. Kendler and Kendler (1962) demonstrated that human adults acquire appropriate reversal shift behavior on transfer much more readily than they acquire a nonreversal shift. These authors (1959) also provided data on kindergarten children suggesting that those who are more articulate find the reversal shift relatively easier to make than do those who are less verbal. In contrast, rats characteristically perform somewhat better on nonreversal shift problems than on reversal. The Kendlers suggest that

articulate organisms learn during pretraining more than a simple approach to each of the specific stimuli and that they tend to verbalize either overtly or covertly the dimensional regularity of the stimulus situation. Such a subject might verbalize "the larger one" during pretraining, and this verbal "hypothesis" is quickly refuted upon nonreinforcement in the transfer task. Articulate organisms then merely adopt the obverse hypothesis when presented with the reversal shift problem. Such an organism, however, must attend to a different dimension when confronted with the nonreversal shift problem and switch his behavior accordingly.

The explanation given above has not gone unchallenged by other experimenters interested in such two-process theories of discrimination learning, particularly by those writers (for example, House & Zeaman, 1963) who make somewhat different assumptions concerning the mechanisms underlying discrimination learning and the role of observing responses. A complicating factor is that overtraining in the discrimination prior to transfer seems to have a different effect upon behavior in a reversal task than upon behavior in a nonreversal task. (See Shepp and Turrisi, 1966, for a review of the literature relating to this issue.)

Learning sets We have just seen that transfer tasks may be used to find out what an organism has learned in a previous discrimination. Thus far we have dealt only with transfer tests that involve three successive tasks at most. Also, we have dealt mostly with discrimination tasks that involve a relatively protracted period or large number of trials before the organism achieves some high performance criterion on each task. However it is possible to give the subject many discrimination learning tasks one after the other. When this is done, we find that the number of trials necessary for the subject to learn each new task diminishes gradually, even though the various tasks are of about equal difficulty, until new problems are solved after just one

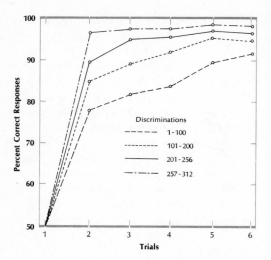

Figure 17.12. Learning set performance of a monkey. These are average learning curves for successive blocks of problems. The more problems the monkey had solved, the faster it learned new problems. (After Harlow, 1949.)

or two trials. Apparently the subject "learns how to learn," a phenomenon that Harlow (1949, 1959) attributes to the formation of so-called "learning sets." Harlow and Harlow (1949) have, in fact, sought to understand the behavioral continuity of species in terms of the rapidity with which they acquire learning sets. These authors argue that apparently insightful behavior, characteristic especially of articulate organisms, is a special case of rapid learning attributable to the previous formation of appropriate learning sets.

In a classic study, Harlow (1949) gave monkeys 312 discrimination problems in the Wisconsin General Test Apparatus. Each problem was presented for 6 trials, the reinforced object being presented randomly at the left and right. Figure 17.12 shows the monkeys' performance over 6 trials plotted separately for blocks of problems. Performance improved remarkably over the series; on problems 1 to 8, the average score rose from the chance level of 50 percent correct to about 75 percent correct during the 6 trials allotted to each problem, whereas, during the final block of problems almost perfect performance was achieved by the second trial.

The trained, now-talented, monkey needed only one nonreinforcement in the two-choice situation to appreciate that the alternative stimulus was the correct one. The learning set phenomenon has been replicated in many studies with primates (Miles & Meyer, 1956; Miles, 1957; Riopelle, 1958), in cats (Warren & Barron, 1956), in rats (Koronakis & Arnold, 1957), and in both normal (Shepard, 1957) and mentally defective (Ellis, 1958; Kaufman & Peterson, 1958) children, in pigeons (Zeiler & Price, 1965), and even in infant monkeys (Harlow, 1960).

An interesting feature of the learning set phenomenon is that it tends to produce a behavioral rank-ordering of primate species that agrees quite well with zoological classifications of phylogenetic standing: the rhesus monkey does better than the squirrel monkey, and the latter better than the marmoset in a series of learning set tasks (Miles, 1957). Similarly, normal children do better than defective children. To examine the relative contributions of intelligence and mental age to learning set formation in children, Harter (1965) used a factorial design involving three levels of IQ (70, 100, 130) and three levels of mental age (5, 7, 9). She gave all subjects ten 4-trial discrimination tasks daily until a performance criterion was reached. Her results demonstrated clearly that both mental age and intelligence were important determinants of learning-set performance, whereas the contribution of chronological age per se was negligible.

Paradoxically, it is not clear what the organism is learning when he is learning to learn. If generalization is involved, it is clear that this is generalization of a special kind, for the phenomenon occurs even under conditions in which the stimuli from task to task are made very dissimilar. In fact, Riopelle (1953) has suggested that the *specific* transfer of response from one cue to another must be *minimized* for a high level of performance to occur. In a sense, the organism must inhibit specific-cue generalization and perhaps adopt a generalization rule of another sort. Another experimenter (Warren, 1954) has suggested that the type of generalization involved may be progressive appreciation that past learning does not count for much in the new settings! Equally plausible is the proposition that the "rules of the game" are the important features learned. For example, there is no reason why an animal should at the outset of a series of learning-set problems respond as if the experimenter will consistently reinforce one of two simultaneously presented stimuli—he must learn this, and it is only after this consistency has been learned that the animal will respond appropriately to its presence. Similarly, the animal must learn the consistency of the experimental arrangements with respect to alternativeness; if the circle is not correct on trial 1, then the triangle will be correct on trials 2 through 6.

We may anticipate here one aspect of Spence's theory of discrimination learning. That theory proposes that the effect of a given nonreinforcement on the future strength of a given response is greater later in training than earlier. The assumption is that a high-probability response accrues greater inhibition after a nonreinforcement than does a low-probability response. Suppose that late in a series of discrimination tasks the strengths of the initial responses to either of the alternative stimuli (even on the first trial) are greater than the strengths were earlier in the learning-set tasks. It would follow that the effect of a given nonreinforcement late in training will be greater than earlier. The learning-set phenomenon may be deduced from these assumptions, which are made more reasonable by the observation of decreased latencies of response with increasing experience in the learning set series.

Attention and Overt Selective Processes

Such phenomena as generalization, transposition, and reversal indicate that, at a given time, behavior is controlled only by certain aspects of the subject's environment. So far, though, we have said little about the selective process itself. When humans "select" per-

ceptually, they may do so covertly—as when they pick out a friend's voice amid the babble at a party. As yet rather little is known about the way such mechanisms work. (For a full discussion, see Deutsch and Deutsch [1963].) However, overt responses are often involved in attending. We move our eyes to fixate an object of interest, sniff perfume, or reach for a fabric the texture of which we wish to examine. Such behavior can also be seen and studied in animal subjects. For example, an animal often hesitates when it confronts a choice. *Vicarious trial and error* behavior is the name given to the observation that the rat peers back and forth between the alternative doors of a jumping stand, or the arms of a maze. Later (p. 784) we shall see in more detail what use theorists have made of such observations.

Instead of simply waiting for observing behavior to occur naturally, some experimenters have attempted to condition and study it directly. For example, in an experiment by Ziegler and Wyckoff (1961), pigeons pressed pedals to expose discriminative stimuli on a pair of response keys. One experiment compared the behavior of birds that could expose the stimuli in this way to that of birds whose pedals did nothing. The birds with the inoperative pedals had discriminative stimuli projected on their response keys throughout each 40-second trial, while the other birds viewed only two identical white keys unless they pressed the treadle. If the keys were white, reinforcement was available for pecks on one key just as if discriminative stimuli were present. The stimuli simply indicated which key was correct.

Ziegler and Wyckoff found that the birds with ineffective pedals spent only about half as much time on the pedals as did the group of observing-response birds. Some birds in the latter group failed to learn the stimulus discrimination well, and these also failed to press the treadle as much as the others. Why did the "observing" birds learn to press the treadle? Wyckoff hypothesized (1952) that the appearance of discriminative stimuli reinforces observing responses to the extent that the subject has learned to respond differently to the discriminative stimuli. Once the observing-discrimination process gets going, it is easy to see that a circular effect could strengthen it. As the discrimination improves, observing is reinforced further, and as observing becomes more probable the subject has more and more chances to make the correct discriminative response. We return to some of these matters when we consider mediational processes below (p. 779).

DISCRIMINATION LEARNING THEORIES

When we considered effective cues in the last section, we mentioned at times what the results might imply about underlying discriminative mechanisms. In this section we consider such mechanisms in more detail. Because a great deal has been written about these matters, we have chosen one relatively formalized and influential theory of discrimination, that of Spence (1936, 1937), to illustrate the role that theorizing has played in this area. We look at the postulates of Spence's theory, controversies into which these postulates led when they conflicted with other theories, and some recent work related to concepts important to the theory.

Spence's theory Spence's discrimination learning theory (1936, 1937) is in the systematic tradition of Clark Hull, who described Spence's contribution in this area as an ". . . extension and formalization of Pavlov's analysis of discrimination" (1952, p. 59). The Spence position capitalizes heavily upon Thorndike's Law of Effect, as the postulates of his system show:

(1) Any response followed by reinforcement in the presence of a stimulating situation will produce an increment in the tendency for that response to occur upon subsequent presentations of the same stimulating condition. That is to say, associative or habit strength is a function of reinforcement trials.

(2) Any response occurring in the presence of a stimulating situation and followed by nonreinforcement leads to a decrement in the associative strength between that stimulus and that response.

(3) The *effective* associative strength between a given stimulus and a given response is a function of the increments and decrements accruing to that S-R relationship resulting from the aforementioned reinforcements and nonreinforcements. Specifically, the excitatory increments and inhibitory decrements summate algebraically to yield the resultant associative strength.

(4) On any given trial, the amount of excitation accrued as a result of reinforcement is determined by a bell-shaped function, whereas the amount of inhibition resulting from nonreinforcement increases linearly with trials. Thus the effect of a given reinforcement or nonreinforcement depends upon the current strength of the response tendency. The least amount of excitatory strength is added at the beginning and end of the learning function. The least amount of inhibition is added at the beginning and the greatest amount of inhibition at the end of the learning function. Because observed performance depends on the sum of excitation and inhibition, these assumptions predict that performance over trials will follow an ogival (S-shaped) function.

(5) Both excitation and inhibition accrued through reinforcement and nonreinforcement will tend to generalize to stimuli similar to the stimulating situation present at the time a given response is either reinforced or not. This generalized excitation and inhibition is greater for stimuli physically closer to the training stimulus than for those farther away on the stimulus continuum.

(6) In situations where more than one associative connection is evoked, that response with the greater effective associative strength will tend to occur. This postulate introduces the assumption necessary for deducing performance in a competing-response situation characteristic of discrimi-

nation learning; all of the other postulates refer to the strength of one response in a given stimulating situation.

(7) Finally, the total effective excitatory strength of a stimulus complex will be the sum of the separate effective excitatory tendencies accruing to the component stimuli as described above.

In order to get from the theoretical postulates to actual behavior, it is necessary to make certain other connecting statements. For example, the effective associative strength relative to a given stimulating situation is revealed in such response parameters as amplitude, probability, latency, and so on. Similarly, there are many problems relating to the definition of the stimulating situation. For example, are we to regard a stimulus as any object or event physically present at the time that the organism makes a response, or must we not be rather more specific and indicate those precise stimulating conditions toward which the behaving organism is attentive or which he is perceiving in some way? However, these matters of definition and method do not constitute assumptions or theoretical imperatives of the same class as those described above.

Absolute vs relational theory Spence's theory, just outlined, is sometimes called an "Absolute Theory" because it assumes that effective cues are identified with specific stimuli present at any given moment. Lashley, on the basis of his extensive research on discrimination learning in rats, particularly in the jumping-stand situation, formulated a rather different set of propositions regarding choice behavior in conflict situations. His view is an example of Relational Theory, for he assumes that effective cues may include relations among, and selections from, available environmental stimuli. The essence of his theory can be distilled from three of his major works (1938, 1942; Lashley & Wade, 1946). Concerning the discrimination of differential visual stimuli, such as geometric figures, he said: "Where the pattern contains many items, the animal solves the problem by disregarding most and reacting to a part-figure" (1938, p. 160). Later (1942, p. 242), the basic postulates were given as follows:

(1) When any complex of stimuli arouses nervous activity, . . . certain elements or components become dominant for reaction while others become ineffective. This constitutes a "set" to react to certain elements.

(2) In any trial of a training series, only those components of the stimulating situation which are dominant . . . are associated. Other stimuli which excite the receptors are not associated because the animal is not set to react to them.

These postulates show that Lashley's theory is of a perceptual kind, for selective attention during learning is important: the effective cues are those to which the organism is "set" to respond. For Spence, all cues impinging on the receptor organs of the learning animal are pertinent. From this difference sprang the so-called "continuity versus noncontinuity" issue. Spence's views imply that the acquisition of discriminative control is continuous, with increments and decrements in response strength accruing, as specified in his postulates, to each stimulus present on each trial of a learning task. In contrast, Lashley's postulates implied that a particular unattended stimulus might acquire no control for many trials, and then suddenly acquire control as a result of a shift in attention.

Lashley and Wade (1946) tested these views in the following way. One group of rats was taught to jump at an 8-cm wide circle and to refrain from jumping at a black square. Another group was taught to jump at a 5-cm wide circle, with the plain black square again the negative stimulus. Next, both groups learned a simultaneous discrimination between the 8-cm and the 5-cm circles, with the 8-cm circle reinforced for both groups. Lashley and Wade reasoned that the original training should have little effect on the second task, for the rats would have had no reason to notice the size of the diameter of the circle when it was paired with the black square. Absolute theory, in contrast, would predict that the rats trained originally to the 8-cm circle should do better in the second task because they had already accrued response strength to the 8-cm stimulus before they started the second task. The opposite occurred, for Lashley and Wade found that the rats originally trained with the 5-cm stimulus learned the second task more rapidly. In other words, the results were contrary to the predictions of both the Absolute and the Relational Theories. However, replications under somewhat altered conditions (for example, after eliminating the punishment characteristic of the Lashley jumping-stand procedure) have for the most part failed to corroborate the Lashley-Wade findings; rather they have supported the Absolute Theory (Grice, 1948b). Although there are now very serious doubts about their generality, the Lashley-Wade findings have at least encouraged caution in applying assumptions derived from situations involving no punishment to procedures where punishment is a significant feature.

The Lashley-Wade experiment illustrates the assumption, implicit in Relational Theory, that subjects will not learn about properties of a stimulus (like circle size) unless given an opportunity to compare stimuli differing in the relevant property. In a further test of this position (Grandine & Harlow, 1948) monkeys first were taught to respond to a single reinforced stimulus; subsequently, they were tested on a simultaneous discrimination with the originally reinforced stimulus presented along with a new stimulus differing in either height or brightness. Contrary to Lashley's prediction, clear evidence of positive transfer resulted. Despite such data, Warren and Brookshire (1959) have asserted that few studies provide the definitive test with experimentally naive primates that was required by the Lashley-Wade formulation. Warren and Brookshire therefore used monkeys that "had no opportunity to develop comparison behavior in formal discrimination learning experiments before participating in this investi-

gation." Experimentally naive animals made reinforced responses to a single stimulus, and then learned a discrimination involving the rewarded stimulus and a new one. For half of the subjects, the previously rewarded stimulus was correct. For the other half, the new stimulus was correct. Again, the evidence weighed against the Lashley-Wade proposition, for fewer errors were made by the animals required to choose the stimulus reinforced in single presentations.

Lashley's requirement that animals must not have had prior experience with making comparisons in discrimination situations is very stringent, and it is unlikely to be truly met by most laboratory animals. It appeared desirable, therefore, to do an experiment in which stimulus comparison was actually encouraged, for that should, according to the Lashley assertion, produce *better* performance than rewarded experience with single stimuli. Accordingly, Lipsitt (1962) provided 4 groups of 20 children with different pretraining experiences, prior to training in a two-stimulus simultaneous task. Group I received 20 single reinforced presentations of the subsequently positive stimulus; Group II received 20 single reinforced presentations of the subsequently negative stimulus. Group III received 20 trials of comparative experience with the discrimination stimuli, and Group IV received 20 single reinforced presentations to each of the subsequent discrimination stimuli. Group I produced the best subsequent discrimination performance, being significantly superior to both Groups III and IV. Group II was significantly superior to IV but not to III. No reliable difference appeared between the performances of Groups I and II, although the tendency was in favor of Group I. Inasmuch as the two groups with prior experience with both of the stimuli that were to be discriminated tended to do more poorly than the groups given single-stimulus pretraining, these data seem to extend the Warren-Brookshire findings to humans, and to contradict the Lashley-Wade proposition that experience with single stimuli does not produce transfer to a subsequent discrimination task.

As has been previously indicated (pp. 766–767) the behavior of animals in reversal learning situations is pertinent to the resolution of the continuity versus noncontinuity controversy. According to the continuity position (Spence, 1951, p. 719):

> . . . discrimination learning is conceived as a cumulative process of building up the excitatory strength (habit, associative strength) of the positive cue as compared with the competing excitatory strength of the negative cue. This process is assumed to continue until the difference between the excitatory strengths of the two cues is sufficiently great to offset any other differences in excitatory strength that may exist between the stimulus complexes of which the cues are members . . . As a critical test of the two opposed theories an experimental design has been employed in which the significance of the stimulus cues during a preliminary period of trials, in which the subject is responding with some irrelevant hypotheses, is the reverse of that used in the subsequent problem (i. e., the positive cue is made negative, and vice versa). According to the non-continuity theory this preliminary training should have no effect on the subsequent learning of the reverse problem. In contrast, the implication of the continuity theory is that the learning of such a reversed group would be retarded as compared with a control group that did not have such initial reversed training but instead was given a 50-percent reinforcement on each of the relevant cues for the same period of trials.

Spence (1951) pointed out that Krechevsky's data (1938) on this issue showed that one group given 40 preliminary trials prior to reversal transfer supported the continuity theory but that another given 20 preliminary trials supported the noncontinuity position. Spence suggested that in the beginning of training on a jumping-stand apparatus, the animal is probably attending most to the bottom of the stimulus cards near the position where it must terminate the jump. This suggests that only later in training does the animal truly receive differential stimulation from the positive and negative stimuli. Says Spence:

> The subject must first learn to make the appropriate receptor-orienting acts that will lead to the reception of retinal stimulus patterns that are discriminable. Krechevsky's subjects presumably failed to do this in the 20 preliminary trials but did so in 40 trials. Hence the former group showed no retardation, whereas the latter did (1951, p. 720).

Corroborative evidence was found by Ehrenfreund (1948) by manipulating the heights at which the stimuli were presented in front of the animal relative to his standing position.

Recent investigators have come increasingly to feel that attention factors play such a fundamental role in discrimination learning that earlier statements implying a continuity-noncontinuity dichotomy may be misleading. After reviewing the mixed evidence, Mackintosh (1965) concludes that both extreme positions were wrong: Subjects do not concentrate entirely on one cue or organization at a time, as Lashley's position implies, nor do they respond equally to every available stimulus, as an extreme reading of Spence's position might suggest. He says: "Animals do not classify their stimulus input with equal effectiveness in all possible ways at once, and it should therefore be possible to influence what an animal attends to by appropriate procedures." In short, one may get either "continuity" or "noncontinuity" results depending on the procedures employed, these procedures affecting the results through their control of attention. Other extended arguments on these issues may be found in Osgood's excellent chapter on controversial issues in learning theory (1953, pp. 413–473) and in Spence (1951, pp. 690–729).

Still another account of the mechanisms underlying discrimination learning performance is provided by Harlow (1950, 1959), and is sometimes called "Uniprocess Learning Theory." This theory is based upon analyses of the errors made by animals in the course of discrimination learning. This theory emphasizes the gradual suppression over learning trials of specific types of incorrect responses that reflect "error factors," such as

TABLE 17.1

Trial	Procedure			
	Simultaneous		Successive	
	+	−	+	−
I	⬜	⬛	⬛	⬛
	−	+	−	+
II	⬛	⬜	⬜	⬜

stimulus perseveration, response shifts, and position preferences. The analysis of errors in the course of learning is, as Kimble (1961) has pointed out, rather similar to the Kreshevsky analysis of behavioral "hypotheses" and their successive testing and elimination in the course of acquiring the "correct hypothesis."

Simultaneous versus successive stimulus presentation We can further understand the interaction of theory with experiment by considering the way in which Spence dealt with a classic methodological issue. Hunter (1914) had labeled two general methods for stimulus presentation the *successive* and *simultaneous* procedures. These are roughly equivalent to the psychophysical procedures called the "Method of Single Stimuli" and the "Method of Paired Comparisons," respectively. Table 17-1 illustrates the two situations. The stimuli in each instance may be visualized as the doors on a Lashley jumping stand. One door is the positive (reinforced) and the other is the negative (nonreinforced) door on each trial. The sides are counterbalanced from trial to trial, as indicated by I and II. In the simultaneous case, the two discriminative stimuli (here, black and white) are both present on every trial. In the successive case, only one stimulus, black or white, occurs on any trial. It would seem that the subject has an advantage in simultaneous discrimination, for he can compare the alternative stimuli within a single trial. To make such a comparison in successive discrimination, he must compare a cur-

rent stimulus with his memory of the alternative stimulus from previous trials.

Spence (1936) described simultaneous discrimination learning as the strengthening of a response to the reinforced stimulus until this response tendency exceeds competing tendencies enough to yield consistently correct choices. Thus, in this instance, reinforcement would cause the response to white gradually to become stronger than response to black. Spence assumed that because the tendencies towards the left or right were reinforced equally often, responses based on positional cues would tend to equalize, and being nondiscriminative, these tendencies would ultimately have little effect upon choice. Bitterman and his colleagues (Weise & Bitterman, 1951; Bitterman & Wodinsky, 1953) challenged this interpretation of discrimination learning, arguing that the mechanisms proposed by Spence predict that no learning should occur under the *successive* stimulation procedure, for white, black, left, and right are all equally reinforced in the long run. They reported data showing, in fact, that not only does successive presentation produce learning but rats under some conditions solve successive problems more rapidly than they do if the simultaneous procedure is used. Spence (1952) extended his discrimination-learning theory to account for the solution of the successive problem as a patterned discrimination. He proposed that the organism approaches certain patterns or combinations of reinforced stimulus components, while response to other patterns is not reinforced.

TABLE 17.2

Trial	Procedure			
	Simultaneous		Successive	
I	$\frac{W}{L} > +$ $\frac{B}{R} > -$		$\frac{B}{L} > +$ $\frac{B}{R} > -$	
II	$\frac{B}{L} > -$ $\frac{W}{R} > +$		$\frac{W}{L} > -$ $\frac{W}{R} > +$	

Under this conception, comparison of simultaneous and successive procedures can be made as shown by Table 17.2, where W is white, B black, L left, and R right. Spence contended that the successive problem may be predicted as solvable without sacrificing the basic propositions of his theory because responses may be learned to the compounds BL, BR, WL, and WR. Moreover, he predicted that, contrary to the findings of Bitterman and his colleagues, under at least some conditions, the successive method should produce slower learning than the comparable simultaneous task because the compounds to be discriminated on each trial are more similar (and thus should generate greater competing generalization) than they are in the simultaneous problem. Under the simultaneous procedure, responses to white in one stimulus setting should generalize to white in the other setting; such generalization would hinder acquisition of differential responding in the successive procedure. Spence presented evidence from T-maze experiments that showed the superiority of the simultaneous over the successive procedure.

Theoretical controversy sometimes serves to highlight the importance of previously disregarded parameters, as it did in the experiment discussed above. Spence called attention to the fact that his original discrimination learning theory applied to instances in which the animal must "orient towards and approach the stimulus complex (path, door, alley, window) containing the positive stimulus cue (white, form, etc.) . . ." (1952, p. 89). Under such circumstances simultaneous presentation should lead to faster learning than successive presentation. In Bitterman's procedures, the stimuli were removed from the locus of response, for the animals were presented with the stimuli in the middle section of the Lashley jumping stand, but they had to jump at windows off to the left and right.

The present state of affairs with respect to the simultaneous-successive issue seems to be as follows. When a response is made to the locus of stimulation, the simultaneous method tends to produce better learning than the successive method, but when the locus of responding is to some point removed from the stimulus source, the successive often produces better performance than the simultaneous method of presentation (Bitterman, Tyler, & Elam, 1955). It would appear, however, that the similarity between stimuli interacts with other parameters to determine the rapidity of learning under the simultaneous and successive procedures. Loess and Duncan (1952) have shown that, with highly similar stimuli (difficult discriminations), simultaneous procedures proved better than successive procedures, but when the stimuli were less difficult to discriminate there was no statistical difference between the procedures, although, in fact, the successive method appeared to produce slightly superior results. MacCaslin (1954), using a Lashley apparatus, also showed a superiority of the simultaneous over the successive method when the stimuli were similar, but found no difference under a distinctive-stimulus condition.

In a series of experiments with children involving comparisons of simultaneous and successive presentation procedures, Lipsitt (1961) found the successive procedure to produce better learning than simultaneous presentation when the response was made to buttons removed several inches from the stimulus sources, but showed the effect to be reversed when the children responded directly to the stimulus source. He showed further that this relationship is affected by the degree of similarity between stimuli, for under conditions of high similarity, simultaneous presentation provided better learning than successive, whereas if highly distinctive stimuli were presented, this difference disappeared or resulted in an inversion, with the successive procedure producing superior results. Thus, a high degree of similarity between stimuli and a response locus close to the stimulus source tends to maximize the superiority of simultaneous over successive procedures, whereas under opposite conditions the successive method tends to become superior. Other experimental manipulations that tend to depress discrimination learning generally, such as increasing the delay of reinforcement or separating the stimuli in space or time, might have similar effects on performance in these two tasks.

The Problem of "Inhibition"

Discriminative control, in Spence's theory, can largely be seen as an interaction of excitatory tendencies, associated with reinforcement, and inhibitory tendencies, associated with nonreinforcement. In this regard Spence follows Pavlovian theory; the basic idea has been quite popular with other theorists as well. Recent work, much of it done with pigeons in free-operant situations, has added substance to the notion of inhibition. This work has also suggested that an inhibitory process need not always be involved in discriminative control in the manner that has often been supposed by theorists.

Errorless discrimination training Let us consider for a moment different ways in which discriminative behavior may be brought about. One might choose among many procedures and still use "differential reinforcement" in the sense that behavior would be reinforced differently in the presence of the two stimuli. In the most common free-operant discrimination procedure, responses to one stimulus (the "S^D," or "S+") bring reinforcement, often on an intermittent schedule. Responses to another stimulus ("S^Δ," or "S−") yield no reinforcement, and sometimes such responses prolong the duration of the S−. For example, a monkey might press a lever whenever a lamp glows above it (S+), such responses producing a food pellet once a minute on the average. When the lamp is out, pressing the lever produces no food. Usually in such a case the monkey responds many times early in the experiment, both when the lamp is on and when it is off. As discrimination develops, responses when the lamp is off gradually cease.

A second method avoids responses in the S−, and thus it has come to be called "errorless" discrimination training. The experimenter starts with a situation in which some discriminative control already exists, a "very easy" discrimination task, and gradually works toward a more exacting task. This general idea has been used for many years, but its importance has only recently been fully recognized, largely as the result of a series of experiments by Terrace (see Terrace, 1966a). One example will illustrate the basic features of the procedure. Pigeons were trained to discriminate a red response key (S+) from a green key (S−) without ever making responses to S−. First, the S+ came on for 30-sec intervals, and in its presence pecks at the key brought food on a variable interval schedule. After the birds were responding regularly, the green S− was introduced in three stages. First, interspersed with S+ presentations, the key went dark briefly (5 sec) and then S+ reappeared. Then, over successive presentations, the dark period was increased gradually to 30 sec. During this time, the pigeon kept pecking when the S+ was on, but withdrew from the darkened key. In the next training stage the S− duration was again reduced to 5 seconds, but a very dim green light was turned on behind the key during this time. The intensity of this light was gradually increased over successive presentations. Finally, with the green S− now up to full intensity, the duration of the S− was increased from 5 to 30 sec. Later S+ and S− were both increased to 3 min.

Terrace found that birds trained in this way responded little or not at all to S−. Birds that did not have the final S− gradually introduced, and birds that first saw the S− only after considerable experience (14 sessions) with the S+ alone all gave many responses to the green S− before finally learning the discrimination. Terrace trained birds that had learned the red-green discrimination without errors on a more difficult discrimination, still without allowing errors. They were trained to peck at a vertical white line but not at a horizontal white line. This was done by first super-imposing the lines on the key colors already learned (vertical line on red S+, horizontal line on green S−), and then gradually fading out the colors.

Our reason for studying the errorless discrimination method is not simply because it is an efficient method for sharpening discriminative control, although such a gradual introduction to a difficult discrimination may be very helpful. More important is the fact that discriminations learned through errorless training seem to differ from those learned through the use of extinction or punishment, and the differences give some hints of the behavioral mechanisms involved. Before getting into these differences, however, let us look at some interesting outcomes produced when ordinary (that is, errorful) discrimination procedures are used.

Behavioral contrast Pavlov noted long ago (1927) that when positive and negative conditioned stimuli were presented one after the other in a discrimination experiment, the conditioned response to the positive stimulus was greater just after the negative stimulus had been presented, and often the response to the negative stimulus (if there was any) was less if the negative stimulus was presented just after the positive (see "induction," p. 710). These observations are strikingly parallel to contrast in sensory systems, which is often attributed to the generation and release of inhibitory effects.

A somewhat similar phenomenon has recently attracted interest in operant experiments. An experiment of Reynolds (1961) provides a good example. Pigeons were trained to peck a key with reinforcement on a variable-interval 3-min schedule. Sometimes the key was red, sometimes green, but at first these colors were of no significance, and the birds pecked equally at the two colors. Then a discrimination was programmed, such that the birds were still reinforced on the same schedule for pecks at the red key, but were extinguished for pecks at green.

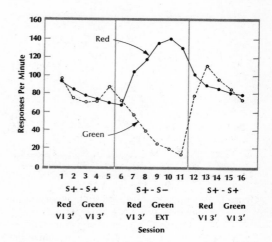

Figure 17.13. Behavioral contrast in one pigeon. At left, pecking yields reinforcement at the same rate (VI 3 min) whether the key light is red or green. In the center, green goes unreinforced and pecking to red speeds up, though red is reinforced no more frequently than before. At right rates to red and green converge again with equal reinforcement. (After Terrace, 1966; data from Reynolds, 1961.)

Now, according to older notions of discriminative mechanisms, we might predict the following: The rate of response to green should decline, certainly, because no food is forthcoming for responses in green. What about the rate of response to red? This might also go down, for the bird is getting less reinforcement overall than before. More important, theory suggested that inhibition now building up in association to the green S− would generalize to the red S+ and cause some reduction of rate to that stimulus (see Spence, 1937). Just the opposite happened. As the discrimination was acquired, the rate to the red S+ rose as the rate to the green S− declined. The rates reversed their trends when both colors again were correlated with reinforcement (Figure 17.13). This contrast effect has appeared in a number of experiments with response rate; response latency also has been shown to change in similar ways (Jenkins, 1961). The similarity of this effect and "reinforcement contrast" has already been noted (p. 641).

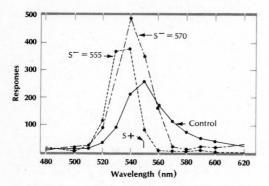

Figure 17.14. Generalization peak shift in two groups of pigeons given discrimination training on a wavelength continuum, compared to a control group with no discrimination training. All birds were reinforced for pecking at the 550 nm stimulus (S+). The group that received no discrimination training (solid curve) gave a curve with a peak at the S+. The group given discrimination training with an S− of 570 nm yielded the curve peaked at 540 nm, while the gradient of birds trained with an S− of 555 is still further displaced. (After Hanson, 1959.)

Generalization gradient peak-shift Related to behavioral contrast is another experimental result of ordinary discrimination training "with errors." As we have seen, the generalization gradient is usually obtained in operant experiments by training the subject to respond in the presence of a particular stimulus and then, during an extinction session, varying some aspect of that stimulus while recording the number of responses emitted in the presence of each test stimulus. The resulting gradient, while not necessarily symmetrical, ordinarily has a peak at the stimulus value to which the subject was exposed during training. However, this is not the case if the subject is originally trained not on a single stimulus but on a discrimination that involves the stimulus dimension later to be tested. When such discrimination training is given, the gradient resulting from a generalization test is displaced away from the S− used in the discrimination. The classical demonstration of this is shown in Figure 17.14. Here, in an experiment by Hanson

(1959), the solid curve shows the generalization gradient on a wavelength continuum from pigeon subjects after ordinary single stimulus training. The other gradients come from other groups of birds that received, before testing, discriminations with the same stimulus as S+ (550 nm), but various other stimuli as S− in a successive discrimination procedure. Note that not only are responses lacking to the S− wavelengths, but that most responses are given not at the wavelength used for training but at other wavelengths displaced to the side opposite the S−. Note also that these post-discrimination gradients are higher than the control gradient; this is another instance of the behavioral contrast phenomenon.

Two kinds of discriminative control? Both behavioral contrast and the peak shift were found to follow ordinary discrimination training done "with errors." However, neither of these effects seems to arise if the discrimination is learned without errors, according to recent experiments (Terrace, 1963a, 1964). That is, if pigeons are trained to respond to green and not to red in such a way that many responses to the red S− occur before the discrimination is learned, they speed up in the green S+ (behavioral contrast) and testing for generalization with various stimulus wavelengths reveals a peak shifted away from the red end of the spectrum. If the birds are trained to discriminate by the errorless method, they do not speed up in S+, and the generalization gradient peak falls at the same green on which the birds were trained.

These observations suggest that two different sorts of discriminative control arise from the two kinds of training. Do any other observations suggest such a difference? Terrace (1966a) lists several. For one thing, pigeons act quite differently during training in the two cases. The bird learning without errors simply settles down quietly when S− appears and waits for S+ to return. The bird learning "with errors," in contrast, often reacts emotionally to the S−, flapping its wings, turning, sometimes jumping or cooing. It looks for all the world as though the bird were getting a mild shock or some other punishment. This suggests that the S— becomes aversive during training with errors, a conclusion supported by the fact that shock in the presence of a stimulus can produce behavioral contrast and peak-shift (Brethower & Reynolds, 1962; Gousec, 1968).

Another notable difference between discriminations with and without errors lies in the later performance of the subject. Even though responding to S— has been near zero for some time, the subject that learned with errors is apt to give occasional bursts of responses to the S—. The errorless-trained subject never does this unless some change occurs in the situation, such as a too-rapid advance to a difficult discrimination or a period of extinction on S+. If, as a result of such changes, the errorless-trained subject is induced to respond to the S—, all is lost. Even earlier, easier discriminations are upset, and discriminative control is only regained by training with errors.

A final test for differences between the two types of training is in the reaction of trained subjects to drugs. It has been found that certain drugs will disrupt even well-learned discriminations, leading to extensive responding in S—. Testing two of these drugs, Terrace (1963b) collected several thousand responses in S— from each error-trained pigeon with heavy doses, and proportionately fewer with lighter doses. Errorless-trained birds did not give a single response to S— at any dose level.

Observations such as those we have reviewed suggest that there are indeed at least two kinds of response rate decrements involved in discriminative control. It is tempting, and perhaps appropriate, to apply the two labels that Pavlov, Spence, and other theorists have used for many years. The ordinary generalization decrement, where responding diminishes as we move away from the S+, and the decrement in response to the S— in errorless training may be thought to involve only "excitatory" control. Such responding follows

the rule: "Respond if S+, otherwise do not respond." The decrement developed by ordinary discrimination training with errors, and presumably by punishment for errors, involves in addition "inhibitory" control. It follows the rule: "Respond if S+, do not respond if S—." Jenkins (1965) states these rules and discusses how we might test to find out if inhibitory control is involved in any given case. It would appear that, with inhibitory control, S— stands out as a "stimulus not to respond to." Where such inhibitory control is absent, an S— is simply one of all the indefinite number of situations that do not prompt the subject to respond. It is a part of the background, as it were. If this is the case, one might expect to be able to measure a generalization gradient around an inhibitory S—; with changes away from a particular value, the "tendency not to respond" ought to diminish. No gradient would be expected for an S— that exerts no inhibitory control for in changing this stimulus we simply move on to another stimulus that is equally "not the S+."

Some gradients of inhibition have indeed been collected around inhibitory S— stimuli. For example, Jenkins and Harrison (1962) set up a discrimination between a pure tone S— and either silence or white noise as S+. Varying the frequency of the tone now *increased* the response rate, which thus made the inhibitory gradient an empirical reality. Terrace (1966b) rounded out the picture by showing that, following errorless training, no increase in responding occurred when the S— was changed. The generality of all these results needs to be established by work with other species and situations, but at the moment the case for separating excitatory from inhibitory control seems rather convincing.

MEDIATION PROCESSES

Thus far we have dealt almost entirely with controlling relations between physical stimuli and responses. We must also appreciate, however, that the choices of both animals and humans are determined in part by responses themselves, for responses may have stimulus counterparts capable of becoming part of the total stimulus to which the organism responds.

Acquired distinctiveness and equivalence of cues Suppose an animal is taught (let us say by the use of positive reinforcement) to lean a little to the left in the presence of a given stimulus such as a triangle. If subsequently that triangle becomes one of two stimuli between which the animal must choose, the lean may be a factor in the acquisition of differential responding to the two stimuli. Picture an animal that leans to the left in response to a triangle and stands upright in response to a circle when it is first placed in a simultaneous discrimination situation. The animal is likely to engage in appropriate swaying responses as it looks at these two stimuli, with the distinctive leaning to the left becoming part of the stimulus complex with the triangle and the upright stance becoming part of the complex with the circle. Such increased distinctiveness of the circle and the triangle, *mediated* by the organism's responses and the proprioceptive counterparts of these responses, is likely to facilitate subsequent discrimination learning of new responses, such as jumping to the circle and not jumping to the triangle. Such facilitation apparently is quite general, even allowing animals to discriminate more accurately among deprivation and reinforcement conditions (Miller, 1935). This kind of facilitation has been attributed to the "acquired distinctiveness of cues" (Dollard & Miller, 1950, p. 101). The opposite of this phenomenon occurs when the same response and its associated proprioceptive stimulation is first attached to both of the stimuli to be discriminated, thus retarding the learning of a discrimination between these stimuli. This is termed "mediated generalization" or "acquired equivalence of cues" (Miller, 1948). Although these concepts of acquired distinctiveness and equivalence have helped to explicate some animal behavior (Riley, 1968,

pp. 58–63) they have been used principally to extend basic stimulus-response theory to encompass the complex discriminative behavior of articulate, symbol-using humans.

A student of Miller, Birge (1941), performed some of the earliest systematic research on mediational phenomena in children. She asked whether a response will transfer from one stimulus to another more readily when those two stimuli have the same name attached to them than when they have different names. She taught third-, fourth-, and fifth-grade children to call two pictures of nonsense animals by one name and two other pictures by another name. Then pairs made up of one picture from each name pair were presented, and the children learned under which of these a piece of candy was consistently hidden. In the third stage of the study, the remaining stimulus picture of each name pair was presented to discover which of the two the subjects would now choose. Most subjects chose the stimulus bearing the same name as that one under which the candy was previously found. This is the result one would expect from the concept of mediated generalization. Birge also showed that when overt verbalization of the names was required during both the candy-finding and test stages, performance was better during the test than when such "overt mediation" was not involved.

Another study demonstrating the phenomenon of mediated generalization, of both a verbal and a motor sort, is that by Jeffrey (1953). He taught preschool-aged children to move a lever in one direction to a white stimulus and in another to a black stimulus. Then some subjects were taught to call a gray stimulus by the name "white" and others to call it "black." After a retraining session in which the subjects again moved the lever appropriately to the white and black stimuli, Jeffrey presented the white, black, and gray stimuli successively and randomly to determine the direction in which the lever would be moved to each of these stimuli. The general finding was that the children who were given the "white" name for the gray stimulus now moved the lever in the direction appropriate for white, while those taught the name "black" for the gray stimulus moved the lever appropriately for black. Thus the subjects behaved toward the gray stimulus as if it were white or black, depending upon their mediational pretraining. Likewise, children who were taught to turn the handle in a special way for white and a different way for black and then had motor mediational training to make one or the other of these motor responses to the gray stimulus, produced data in the test task comparable to that produced by verbal pretraining.

An interesting adaptation of the acquired equivalence paradigm was made by Eisman (1955) to the area of attitude or opinion formation. Eisman first taught children a different name for each of three white geometric blocks. The children were then reinforced for selecting a particular one from among the three blocks. Following this, they were taught to associate the three names respectively with each of three different colored blocks. When the children were next required to find a reward under one of the three colored blocks, they tended to choose the color with the same name as the previously reinforced white block. Several adaptations of the final testing procedure yielded the same finding. For example, Eisman demonstrated that children would verbalize a preference for a fictitious group of children that had been assigned the color name consistent with the rewarded white-block experience. In several ways, then, it was established that children's color preferences (even for playmates) may be engendered through mediational learning mechanisms. Studies that have demonstrated other facets of the acquired equivalence phenomenon include those by Murdock (1952), Bugelski and Scharlock (1952), and Russell and Storms (1955).

The other side of the mediational coin has to do with the enhanced distinctiveness that results when distinctive verbal labels are attached to stimuli. This has also been studied

rather thoroughly in recent years. In a study of both acquired equivalence and distinctiveness, Gerjuoy (1964) used second-, third-, and fourth-grade children to test discrimination following the attachment of either dissimilar-sounding or similar-sounding names to the discriminative stimuli. The expectation was that similar naming would retard, while dissimilar naming would enhance, subsequent learning relative to a control group that was merely required to observe the discriminative stimuli. However, it developed that both of the name-learning groups showed enhanced performance relative to the control.

Such results remind us that if we are to demonstrate that acquired distinctiveness effects in transfer tasks are the result of specific verbal pretraining, it is necessary to rule out the effects of aspects of the pretraining situation other than the simple attachment of discriminative verbal responses to the pertinent stimuli. Sometimes it might be argued that the "real" distinctiveness effect was obtained merely by calling the subject's attention to certain features of the two stimuli. An experiment by Cantor (1955) investigated this possibility. The transfer task was a simultaneous discrimination involving reinforcement for choosing one of two toy cars with different stimuli attached to them. The stimuli were facial drawings of two similar-looking girls. One group of subjects first learned a different name for each of the faces. This was called the "relevant pretraining" group. A second group, called the "attention pretraining" group, learned no names, but received comparable trials in which they were required to look at and point to various facial features, thus committing them to observation of the stimuli to be used in the transfer task. An "irrelevant pretraining" group learned names for an alternate pair of faces. The relevant pretraining group learned the transfer task the fastest, but the other two groups were comparable in performance, indicating that mere perceptual experience with the pretraining stimuli does not produce an effect comparable to that produced by specific distinctiveness pretraining. Kurtz (1955) in fact suggested that acquired distinctiveness effects might result as a kind of artifact attributable to the subject's enhanced "observing behavior." The poorer performance of the attention pretraining group in Cantor's experiment relative to the relevant pretraining group tends to negate the Kurtz interpretation in this case.

A study by Norcross and Spiker (1957) further attempted to rule out the "observing response" interpretation of "acquired distinctiveness" effects. The subjects were preschool children and the stimuli used were the same as those used by Cantor. A relevant pretraining group again learned a different name for each of the faces. A second group received discriminative experience with the relevant stimuli but learned no names. Instead, these subjects were given the stimuli simultaneously and were asked to respond "same" or "different"; on some trials duplicate pictures were presented and on others the two transfer stimuli were presented together. This pretraining necessitated discrimination between the stimuli but did not foster the attachment of differential names. A second discrimination group was presented the two stimuli successively during this period; the subjects were merely asked whether each stimulus was the same as or different from the previously observed one. This group was included to preclude any possible argument that the successive stimulus presentation method tends more than the simultaneous to induce appropriate observing behavior on the part of the subjects. The results of this experiment clearly indicated that the discrimination groups did not differ reliably from one another, but the relevant pretraining group did perform significantly better than those two.

Spiker provides an incisive review of these and other related studies. He says (1963, p. 259):

> The results of these experiments suggest that there is facilitation resulting from prior learning of distinctive names for stimuli that cannot be attributed to warm-up, learning-to-learn, or observing responses. Apparently, there is something

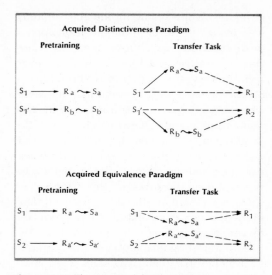

Figure 17.15. The acquired distinctiveness and equivalence processes. See text. (After Spiker, 1963.)

about the learning of names, per se, that results in the subsequent facilitation. To the extent that other implications of the acquired distinctiveness of cues hypothesis can be experimentally confirmed, the hypothesis may be used as a plausible explanation for these and similar findings.

Figure 17.15 symbolizes, in stimulus-response terms, the presumed mechanisms underlying the facilitation of transfer in acquired distinctiveness studies, and the deleterious effect upon transfer of acquired equivalence pretraining. The diagrams suggest that acquired distinctiveness training probably works best with relatively similar stimuli, symbolized as S_1 and S_1', whereas acquired equivalence pretraining likely has its greatest effect with relatively dissimilar stimuli, symbolized as S_1 and S_2. The subscripts associated with R reflect the relative distinctiveness of the responses being associated during the pretraining period. The diagram indicates that the response-produced stimulation, associated with R_a and R_b in the acquired distinctiveness task, enhances the effective distinctiveness of S_1 and S_1' during transfer. Similarly, the response-produced stimulation from R_a and R_a', in the equivalence task, diminishes the effective distinctiveness of S_1 and S_2.

In a study that sought to examine acquired distinctiveness and equivalence simultaneously in the same subjects, Norcross (1958) conducted two experiments that provided control of the variables during the sessions for warm-up and learning to learn that might obscure true mediational effects. In the transfer task, kindergarten children were required to press one of 4 buttons to each of 4 pictorialized faces presented successively, 2 female and 2 male. In pretraining, the subjects learned similar names ("zim" and "zam") for one pair of faces and dissimilar names ("wug" and "kos") for the other pair. During transfer, the subjects overtly verbalized the stimulus names before responding to the buttons. As expected, performance was better when the subjects were presented the faces that were differently named than when they were presented the similarly named ones.

The hypothesis that observing responses underlie the enhanced "acquired distinctiveness" effects (Kurtz, 1955) cannot account for the differences obtained on the similarly named and dissimilarly named stimuli in such an experiment as that of Norcross, for the subjects had equal opportunity to develop appropriate observing behavior for both types of learning pairs. Nevertheless, we cannot infer from the results of such a study whether both acquired distinctiveness and equivalence have occurred or whether just one of these effects was responsible for producing the difference in performance on the two types of pair. In a complex and elaborately counterbalanced experiment, Reese (1960) explored the effects of pretraining with distinctive names, similar names, or no verbalization associated with the stimuli to be used in the transfer task. On the basis of the results obtained, Reese suggested that (1) poorly learned names, regardless of how distinctive or similar they may be, will produce interference in a transfer task, and (2) both distinctive and similar

names, if thoroughly learned during pretraining, will produce transfer facilitation.

Although all of the mediation studies considered thus far have used human subjects, the acquired distinctiveness and equivalence phenomena are not necessarily limited to articulate organisms. On the contrary, an extensive series of experiments by Lawrence (1949, 1950), Bauer and Lawrence (1953), Lawrence and Mason (1955), and Goodwin and Lawrence (1955) suggest that mediating processes of the sort discussed here are evidenced by rats. This is made more plausible by noting that, in humans, motor mediation works essentially the same as verbal mediation (Jeffrey, 1953). Lawrence proposes that the execution of distinctive responses to differential stimuli yields response-produced stimulation, which in turn facilitates subsequent discrimination learning involving the same stimuli. In one experiment, for instance, Lawrence (1949) first trained animals in a simultaneous discrimination procedure to respond to black versus white visual stimuli, or rough versus smooth tactual stimulation underfoot. Following this, the animals were trained to perform a successive discrimination in a T-maze, being reinforced for turning left in the presence of one level of brightness and right in the presence of another. Roughness of the flooring was present (though irrelevant) in the transfer task. The group initially trained to brightness showed positive transfer to the second task, whereas no positive transfer was made by the group trained with differential tactile stimulation. Presumably the first task for the brightness pretraining group provided a set for differential responding to the brightness cues that was still present at the time of learning the second task; the differential responses learned by the tactual pretraining group, however, were irrelevant to the transfer task and may even have been expected to produce negative effects.

Other evidence for mediational processes involved in animal learning comes from a study of Grice (1948), who facilitated discrimination learning under delays of reinforcement by (1) allowing the animal to feed in a goal box of the same color as the reinforced stimulus, or (2) forcing the animal to make characteristically different motor responses while traversing the alley in the presence of the discriminative stimuli. Similarly, Riesen (1940) found that stimulus predifferentiation training facilitated chimpanzees' subsequent discrimination learning under delayed reinforcement. In these experiments, it may be presumed that learning under delay was facilitated when distinctive response-produced stimulation was paired with each of the discriminative stimuli, thus making the stimulus complexes *effectively* more distinctive.

Vicarious trial and error It is interesting to speculate on the possibility that "vicarious trial and error" (VTE, see p. 769) behavior is a visible indicant of mediational processes in operation. As early as 1912, Lashley observed that his rats hesitated and waved their heads back and forth when faced with the choice of one or another discriminative stimulus in a discrimination box. As Lashley again observed (1938), the head waving and alert watchfulness is very apparent in the jumping-stand situation. The behavior is often described as "crouching to jump at one door and then crouching before the other door, before finally jumping"; often such behavior is most marked just before a run of correct responses is noted. This increase in VTE up to the point of solving the discrimination problem was named by Muenzinger (1938), who also noted its decline following attainment of asymptotic performance in animals. White and Plum (1965) have recorded the same trend in children as they oriented their eyes while undergoing visual discrimination learning. A number of experiments with animals (for example, Muenzinger, 1934; Muenzinger & Wood, 1935; Muenzinger & Newcomb, 1936; Muenzinger & Fletcher, 1937; Muenzinger, Bernstone, & Richards, 1938) have shown that shock for incorrect responses increases VTE in a discrimination learning situation, and these writers report that such behavior seems to prolong and improve the animal's reception of the pertinent cues. Contrary to what one might expect, however, Tolman (1939) observed that rats exhibit more VTE in learning a simple white-black discrimination than while learning more difficult grey-black discriminations. This may merely suggest that discrimination problems that afford more "conflict" generate more VTE; an animal in a situation that calls for discrimination between distinctive stimuli should soon learn that reinforcement is differential, whereas an animal in a situation that calls for discrimination between similar stimuli might not learn that reinforcement is differential until much later in training. It is only after that aspect of the learning situation has been appreciated by the subject that head-waving and other eye-orienting skills should appear.

Tolman (1941) pointed out that human subjects in psychophysical experiments tend to evidence VTE from the start, but humans are usually aware at the outset through instructions that there is a solvable problem at hand. Tolman and Minium (1942) conducted an experiment which lends credibility to this interpretation. They started a group of rats on a white-black discrimination that was continued well past the attainment of asymptotic performance. The VTE count was high just prior to solution and then diminished, as is typical. Then the task was made more difficult by substituting light gray for white as the positive stimulus. VTE rose again as the animals made errors in the early stages of the changed problem, then declined. The task was again made more difficult by substituting dark gray as the positive stimulus, and VTE was again in evidence. It would appear that as a solution is approached, less orienting behavior is required and that VTE is most in evidence when conflict is maximal.

Perhaps VTE can be most easily and parsimoniously viewed as an adaptive mechanism designed to enhance proprioceptive and visual feedback in association with the pertinent discriminative stimuli. This feedback is self-administered through VTE and combines with external physical stimuli to enhance the distinctiveness of the cues to which differential responses must be learned. VTE facilitates, then, the development of a type of acquired distinctiveness of cues.

Concept formation A word should be said of the relationship of mediational processes to concept formation. Acquired equivalence of cues has already been described as involving the learning of a common (or similar) response to two or more discriminable stimuli. This common response produces negative transfer when those stimuli are again encountered. Thus, if a subject learns to say "zim" to two physically different stimuli, such behavior will retard the acquisi-

tion of different responses to those stimuli. However, the effect of such pretraining is not always "negative." In fact, this kind of event plays a role in the formation of concepts. In this view, if a child learns that objects as dissimilar as a train, bicycle, and boat are all "vehicles," he is helped to deal with all in terms of their common properties as means of transportation. In such cases, facilitative generalization enables the articulate human to engage in high-level or abstract cognitive processes.

A relatively simple experiment on concept formation was conducted by Long (1940) on children 3 to 6 years old. A box with two small windows was placed before the child. If he pressed on the correct window, he received some candy. Through one window could be seen a rubber ball, through the other a rectangular wooden block. The ball was the

Figure 17.16. Six of the radicals used in Hull's study, with their assigned nonsense names and some characters containing each radical. (Hull, 1920.)

positive stimulus. When the child had learned to choose the ball regularly, he was tested with spherical objects of various sizes, colors, and materials. As expected from a mediational interpretation, which would suppose that the children were taught the concept of sphere or ball, the subjects chose the spherical objects in preference to the angular objects with which they were paired. Moreover, the extended generality of the concept was made manifest when the children tended to pick flat cardboard circles over flat polygons. They also chose the one more nearly circular when two polygons were presented, this effect being most pronounced for the older children in the study.

Other studies of concept learning in adults and children include those of Welch (1938), Welch and Long (1940), Heidbreder (1946), Buss (1950), and Vinacke (1951).

A study by Hull (1920) remains a systematic classic in the area of concept formation. Hull's concepts consisted of Chinese characters; because his subjects were Americans unfamiliar with the Chinese letter system, the use of these stimulus materials assured that the learning of new concepts was truly involved. Nonsense names such as "li," "ta," and "deg" were assigned to various components of larger Chinese characters or compounds, and the subjects tried to discover and to memorize the names of each of these components. Each of the compounds employed by Hull contained one of the 12 selected components, and all of the compounds containing the same component were assigned the same name. The compounds were written on separate cards, and the cards were assembled into packs of 12 so that each pack contained all 12 components (Figure 17.16). Pack No. 1 was exposed serially and, as each character was shown, its name was spoken by the experimenter and repeated by the subject. The subject tried to anticipate (through paired associate learning) the successive items beginning with the second complete presentation of the pack until all the 12 names of the 12 compounds had been

learned. Then Pack No. 2 was shown, and the subject was told that the same names were pertinent and that guessing could begin on the first presentation of Pack No. 2. After each guess, the experimenter spoke the correct response, so the subject always knew whether he was correct, and had the benefits of instant correction of his mistakes. The order in which the components appeared, of course, was different from one pack to another. Six packs were learned in this manner and the percent of first-trial "guesses" was shown to increase with each successive pack. It may be presumed that this positive transfer involved the operation of response-produced stimulation, which served to guide the eyes in their search for the "li," "ta," or "deg." Calling attention to pertinent cues of complex discriminative stimuli is apparently a functional property of mediational or conceptual processes. At the end of the experiment, each subject was asked to sketch each of the components that corresponded to each name. In some cases, components that were correctly identified during the experiment could not be correctly sketched. This is a familiar phenomenon in everyday life: objects (or people) may appear similar without our being able to specify exactly how they are similar.

The delayed-reaction procedure   Often, a choice must be made at some time after the controlling discriminative stimuli have disappeared. How long can information about stimuli be "held" by the organism during such a period of "stimulus black-out"? We know that sometimes humans do very well at such tasks (you may put away a book and return in a week to retrieve it), but the abilities among other animals vary widely. Systematic study of the question has been carried out with the "delayed reaction" method pioneered by Hunter (1913, 1917). In this kind of experiment, discriminative stimuli are observed by the subject, and then the stimuli disappear for an interval before a discriminative response is permitted. Hunter found that

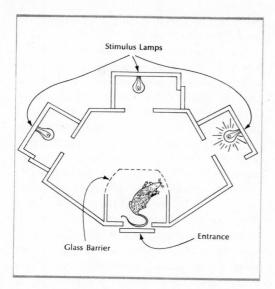

Figure 17.17. Hunter's delayed-reaction box of the size used for rats. One of the three stimulus lamps was lit, but the rat was detained behind the glass barrier after the lamp went out. After an interval, the barrier went up and the rat could go to any one of the doors. If it entered the door where the lamp had been lit, it was free to run around to the entrance and find food. Rats went to the correct door after delays of less than a few seconds, but only if they maintained their orientation toward that door during the delay.

the proficiency of children in this type of task increases with age (and verbal skill) and also found evidence that animals higher on zoological or evolutionary orderings do better at delayed response tasks.

Two kinds of delayed reaction situation were investigated by Hunter, the two-stage (or indirect) and the one-stage (or direct) method. The two-stage method involves first training the organism in the basic discrimination problem, to which the delayed reaction procedure will later be added. In Hunter's procedure (see Figure 17.17), the subject was confronted with a three-choice discrimination problem which required going from a start box to the one of three doors which was lighted with a cue light. On different trials, the cue light appeared over a different door.

Once this discrimination was learned, the delay period was introduced by turning off the cue light while the animal was still in the start box. The start box, however, had a transparent wall facing the doors and cue lights, so the animal could observe the location of the cue light and "note it" prior to his eventual release. The delay was introduced gradually, the light being turned off at first while the animal was on his way to the door, then just as he was released from the start box, then before the release, and with increasing intervals thereafter. The delay was eventually lengthened until the animal could no longer perform correctly on more than one-third of the trials. Most rats in this situation could not "hold" the information provided by the stimulus for more than 4 seconds or so, although occasionally it seemed that an animal could succeed at 10 seconds. (It is difficult to assess the performance of animals from individual trials, for a correct choice would be expected by chance on one-third of the trials.) Hunter noted that animals performed better under the delay situation if they adopted some technique for maintaining their bodily orientation in the direction of the vanished cue, and he noted that dogs run in a comparable chamber could respond correctly after a delay of as long as 5 minutes if they stood, sat, or lay with their bodies or heads pointed in the direction of the cue light.

Raccoons and children were also studied in discrimination chambers adapted to their respective sizes. Children, of course, were able to "hold" the stimulus after-effects the longest of all subjects, responding correctly even in the absence of body-orientation or leg-pointing behavior after 4 minutes or longer. Because older children and adults are capable of verbalizing the location of the correct door ("left," "middle," or "right") and can use these response-produced cues in place of body orientations to guide them at the end of the delay interval, there is almost no limit to the delay intervals such subjects can master.

The one-stage method for testing delayed reactions simply involves the immediate introduction of the delay period without prior discrimination training. In a study with his own 13-month-old daughter, Hunter (1917) seated the child in easy reach of a three-box arc. She watched as a toy was placed in one of the boxes and the lid closed. Her eyes were then closed, or she was picked up and turned around. Finally she was reseated before the boxes and allowed to make her choice. By the end of the study she was able to perform correctly in about 80 percent of the trials after a delay of 15 seconds. By this time she was approximately 16 months of age.

Hunter's commentary in this 1917 report is relevant to our consideration of mediational processes and their effects upon discrimination learning.

> The delayed reaction problem can be solved in at least two ways: (1) by the maintenance of bodily orientation in whole or in part during the interval of delay or by chance recovery of the proper orientation just at the moment of release; and (2) by the use of some intra-organic factor which is *non*observable by the experimenter. . . . The cue used in the second method may or may not be retained in the focus of neural activity during the delay. . . . What one has, then, is a system of processes or cues which "stand for" certain differential responses as a result of association. These cues are susceptible to selective re-arousal and subsequent successful functioning in initiating responses (p. 86).

Following these passages, Hunter goes on to speculate that in articulate organisms the "holding" of the appropriate cues may be through the vocal organs, but he insists that other sites may also be involved, as in kinesthetic stimulation. "Language is ideational in nature. So also are the cues which function in many responses of raccoons, of children, and possibly of dogs. The resulting conception of these cues is that they are kinesthetic sensory ideas" (Hunter, 1917, pp. 86–87). By thus invoking covert vocal and motor mediation, Hunter was one of the earliest learning theorists to elaborate a basic stimulus-

response interpretation of complex discrimination learning processes.

Since Hunter's work, other studies have provided additional evidence of mediation during delayed response in human and animal subjects. Spiker (1956) studied 54 preschool children who were divided into two groups. One group initially learned distinctive names for stimuli, while the other was given discrimination training that did not include name learning. The subjects were then given a delayed-reaction test involving the pretraining stimuli. The subjects who had associated names with the discriminative stimuli made more correct choices following delay than the subjects who had not associated names for the stimuli, and this difference was most pronounced for younger subjects. In accordance with the mediation hypothesis, Spiker suggested that having names for the stimuli permits the subject to produce a representation of the absent stimuli during the delay period.

As we have seen, Hunter and others showed how animals might mediate a delay by orientating themselves toward the correct stimulus. Blough (1959) set up a matching task

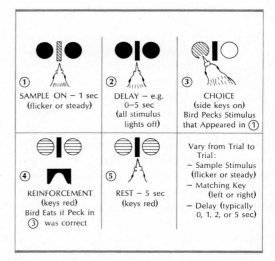

Figure 17.18. Scheme for delayed matching to sample in pigeons. (After Blough, 1959.)

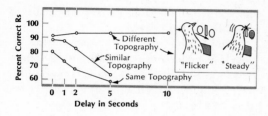

Figure 17.19. Performance of a bird on the delayed matching task shown in Figure 17.18. The bird cannot bridge the delay by maintaining orientation, as in Figure 17.17. In some cases, symbolic behavior appeared to bridge the delay interval. One instance is shown: when the sample flickered, the bird began to wave its head back and forth, and when the sample was steady, the bird began to peck. When these behaviors continued during the delay interval the bird responded correctly after the delay. Other behaviors that were not as different as head waving and pecking were not as successful in bridging the delay. (After Blough, 1959.)

with pigeons where this was impossible since position was not a critical cue (Figure 17.18). The pigeon had to "remember" whether the center rectangle or "sample" was a flickering or steady light and after a delay peck at the circular key, which might be either right or left, that matched the sample. Two out of four subjects developed mediating behavior that helped them bridge the delay. The most marked example of this behavior is shown in Figure 17.19. When the sample flickered, the bird backed quickly away from the keys and waved its head slowly back and forth during the delay. Following a steady sample, the bird spent the delay pecking rapidly at the top of the rectangular sample. Sometimes, the bird did not maintain its head waving following a flickering sample through a long delay but began, instead, to peck at the sample. When this happened, the bird almost always pecked the wrong key (the steady stimulus, in this case) at the end of the delay. These and other observations reported by Blough suggest that the motion of the bird's head served to mediate the matching performance. Of course,

the mediation here was overt, and yet it was "symbolic" in the sense that, like names, but unlike the orientation of animals in Hunter's experiments, the mediating behavior was apparently arbitrary. Blough shows how such mediating behavior might arise from "superstitious" responding (pp. 675, 692) and be maintained because it leads to a high percentage of reinforced trials.

MOTIVATIONAL VARIABLES IN DISCRIMINATION LEARNING

Hunger, anxiety, frustration, and other members of that ill-defined category of variables that we identify as "motivational" can play critical roles in the control of discriminative behavior and in the course of discrimination learning. We have neglected such factors thus far in this chapter, and although they are discussed in detail elsewhere (Chapter 18), we suggest in the present section two examples of research concerning the effects of motivational states on discrimination learning.

Anxiety and stress effects Capitalizing upon the basic Hullian assumption that habit or associative factors (H), on the one hand, and drive or motivational attributes (D) of the organism, on the other, combine multiplicatively to determine response strength, Spence (1956, 1958) and Taylor (1956) deduced that increases in the level of drive should have differential effects depending upon the type of learning task at hand. They reasoned that because drive is presumed to enhance all response tendencies indiscriminately, such enhancement will (1) facilitate discrimination learning when the response to be learned is of higher strength than other competing responses in the habit-hierarchy, and (2) impair learning when the response to be learned is of lower strength than other responses in the hierarchy. In the latter instance, increases in drive will enhance the probabilities of the competing, higher-strength responses, thus retarding acquisition of the response lower in the hierarchy. Spence and Spence (1966) have reviewed in detail the rationale of these deductions, and data bearing on them, particularly in experiments that use measures

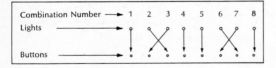

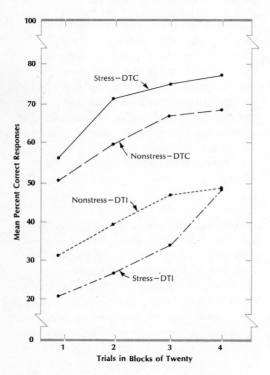

Figure 17.20. Experiment showing the differential effects of stress on different response tendencies. The "dominant tendency" of children is to press the button below the lighted lamp (see diagram above). In some cases, this was the correct thing to do (dominant tendency correct—DTC); in others, a different button had to be selected (dominant tendency incorrect—DTI). The curves show that stress improved performance of the dominant-tendency-correct task, but made performance worse on the dominant-tendency-incorrect task. (After Castaneda & Lipsitt, 1959.)

derived from the Manifest Anxiety Scale to indicate human drive level.

Although many of the studies on the interaction between drive level and task difficulty (or amount of intra-task competition) have employed verbal learning materials, some have used learning tasks involving motor discrimination (Castaneda & Palermo, 1955; Castaneda, 1956, 1961; Castaneda, Palermo, & McCandless, 1956; Palermo, 1957; Castaneda & Lipsitt, 1959). These studies used both anxiety measures and stress manipulations as drive variables, with children as subjects. Castaneda and Lipsitt, for example, used an 8-stimulus, 8-response apparatus (see Figure 17.20) in which fifth-grade children had to learn to press the appropriate button when each of the 8 stimulus lights was successively activated. The buttons were lined up below the lights, and for some of the lights the buttons immediately underneath were correct, but for others, the correct button was displaced by one position. Preliminary observations of children's behavior in this situation indicated that without instructions children would tend to press the button below each light; this, then, was the "dominant tendency." The learning situation was so structured that some of the S-R pairings were of the dominant-tendency-correct kind whereas others were dominant-tendency-incorrect. In line with the Spence deductions, it was presumed that drive increases would facilitate learning of the dominant-tendency-correct S-R pairings but would retard learning on the dominant-tendency-incorrect pairs. The drive condition was manipulated through stress instructions; the high-drive subjects were put under a time pressure to respond as quickly as possible, but the low-drive subjects were not so pressured.

As expected (see lower portion, Figure 17.20), the interaction between the type of pair, on the one hand, and drive level, on the other, was obtained. The subjects performed better on the dominant-tendency-correct pairs when under a high-drive condition, but performed more poorly than their counterparts with low drive on the dominant-tend-ency-incorrect pairs. Thus both facilitation and impairment were produced through this within-subjects design in the same subjects at the same time depending upon the type of S-R pair being considered. A companion experiment by Castaneda (1961) replicated the study with higher and lower Manifest Anxiety Scale scorers, rather than stress instructions, and produced the same findings.

The insoluble discrimination problem In all of the discrimination methods thus far considered, the subject may maximize the number of reinforcements received by adopting a consistent mode of behavior in relation to the stimulating circumstances. There exist, however, situations similar to discrimination tasks in which the subject cannot possibly obtain more than the chance number of reinforcements. In a jumping-stand, for instance, the experimenter may give a rat reinforcement half of the time whether it goes to the left, the right, to black, or to white. Such a procedure presents to the animal an insoluble discrimination problem, and such problems sometimes lead to rather unusual, if not bizarre, reactions, at least in some infrahuman organisms.

In extensive studies with insoluble discrimination situations, N. R. F. Maier and his colleagues found that a "frustration-fixation" phenomenon characteristically resulted from subjecting animals to an essentially random schedule of reinforcement that bears no relation to responding (Maier, Glaser, & Klee, 1940; Maier & Klee, 1941, 1945; Maier, 1949; Feldman & Ellen, 1951; Ellen, 1956). The animal's "fixation" reaction under such conditions usually took the form of so-called "perseverative responding" to a position cue: it might, for example, jump repeatedly to the left. An interesting outcome was that even when the stimulus problem changed such that the animal could now receive reinforcement all of the time by responding to one of the cues (such as black or white), the fixation persisted. The animal did not readjust his

behavior to the now-consistent reinforcement consequences, even if administered hundreds of trials on which he was positively reinforced for going to black and punished for going to white. Not only did the fixation persist, but so did the interesting appearance of the animal that was subjected to the frustration condition. Rats that have been treated in this way may become like a ball of fur in one's hand; these rats behave very oddly even by rat standards, failing to show the usual kinds of righting reflexes during a fall, and showing great flaccidity in general. Their condition, in fact, has been likened to that of the typical catatonic schizophrenic human, and Maier has been tempted (1949) to draw the parallel between the conditions producing this characteristic in animals and the likely conditions producing catatonia in humans. The parallel with human psychopathology is made even more striking, moreover, by the demonstration (Maier & Klee, 1945; Ellen, 1956) that guidance of the fixated animals to the correct stimulus is effective in breaking up the animal's discrimination fixation and restoring muscular tone.

Whereas Maier tends to regard the behavior of animals in these frustration situations as representing the consequences of "behavior without a goal," others (for example, Farber, 1948) have insisted that such behavior is best understood in reinforcement terms as a type of avoidance reaction. According to this latter view, the animal is in effect reinforced for *not* paying attention to the "discriminative" stimuli (which are not discriminative at all); they must jump in this situation because typically an air-blast or an electric current is applied on the jump-stand if a certain latency of response is exceeded. Thus the animals make the "adaptive" response of jumping, even if abortively. For another treatment of the manner in which learning principles may be applied to account for seemingly abnormal behavior in animals and humans, see Lundin (1961).

Although the studies reviewed in this section are fairly representative of the ways in which standard discrimination learning situations can be utilized in the study of motivational states and individual differences, laboratory techniques have not yet been used as extensively as they might be for the study of behavioral abnormalities. Techniques of the learning laboratory—careful specification of stimulating conditions, development of reliable procedures to assess responses, study of the acquisition of new behavior, and search for ways in which many factors interact lawfully to produce behavioral outcomes—will eventually be used more widely to illuminate the genesis of anomalous behavior patterns.

Alexander K. Bartoshuk

MOTIVATION*

18

INTRODUCTION

For approximately the last fifty years of experimental psychology, most motivational formulations may be viewed largely as variations and elaborations on a theme by Woodworth (1918). For the sake of brevity, we will start with this reference point;[1] then we will turn to a consideration of related contemporary motivational theories, with emphasis on their empirical bases and implications. We will not be primarily concerned with representing the great diversity of views on motivation. Instead, we will examine a frequently postulated and emphasized factor: nondirective generalized drive, which energizes behavior without guiding it; and we will discuss some related psychophysiological conceptualizations of activation or arousal as a general energizer without steering properties. We will refer briefly to the hypotheses that instrumental responses are reinforced by drive reduction and punished by drive onset; these are important aspects of drive theory (see Chapters 15 and 16 for more extensive treatments of positive reinforcement, and of negative reinforcement and punishment). In addition, generalized drive theory will provide us with a frame of reference within which we will consider

*Preparation of this chapter was supported in part by a United States Public Health Service Research Scientist Development Award, Type II (5-KO2-MH21837), from the National Institute of Mental Health.

[1] For earlier related formulations of psychological forces or "activators," mostly implicit, see Boring (1950), Woodworth (1958), and Bolles (1967).

several theoretical alternatives to generalized drive theory for interpreting or explaining particular results or problems.

Mechanism (S-R) and Drive

In an important work on the history of experimental psychology, Boring (1950, pp. 722-723) portrays the essentials of Woodworth's (1918) "Dynamic Psychology" as follows:

> Woodworth in 1918 was emphasizing the importance of *mechanism* and *drive,* trying to show that these two concepts can together account for all human activity. The mechanism of an act is the linkage. . . . stimulus-and-response relations (S-R) are mechanisms which can be described. Outside the mechanism, however, lie sources of energy ready to activate this or that mechanism . . . They are drives. If an animal is thirsty, the go-to-water mechanism is activated by the thirst drive; if hungry, the hunger drive activates the get-food mechanism.[2]

How the topic of motivation was delimited by Woodworth and Schlosberg (1954) may be gathered from the following introduction to the 1954 chapter:

> It is recognized in everyday life that a person's performance on a given occasion does not always measure up to his ability. He does not run as fast or shoot as accurately or speak as convincingly as he has on other occasions. He is perhaps not highly motivated, or he may be over-motivated and so eager to succeed as to lose control of his resources of energy and skill. Both ability and motivation are factors in performance,

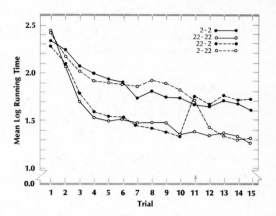

Figure 18.1. Effects of shifts in deprivation time on the mean log time taken to run a 10-unit T-maze for water by water-deprived rats. Group 22-2 (●--●) ran trials 1-10 under 22-hr deprivation and trials 11-15 under 2-hr deprivation; Group 2-22 (O--O) ran trials 1-10 under 2- and 11-15 under 22-hr deprivation. The arrow indicates the initial trial after the deprivation times were shifted. Groups 2-2 (●—●) and 22-22 (O—O) were controls run under the same deprivation times throughout trials 1-15. Note the increase in running time immediately after the 22-2 shift, and that within 2 trials Group 2-22 ran almost as quickly as Group 22-22. (Hillman, Hunter, & Kimble, 1953)

and if either of them is entirely lacking, the performance does not occur. Ability is like a machine which cannot do its work unless power is applied.

These ideas may be viewed as preliminary attempts to identify the broad categories of variables ("mechanism" and "motivation") that together determine performance under conditions that need to be specified.[3]

Illustrations of Motivational Effects

Several effects of an alleged motivational variable (water deprivation) on performance are illustrated in Figure 18.1. With either 2 or

---

[2] Woodworth's (1938) *Experimental Psychology* did not have a chapter on motivation; the index did not include the term "Drive," and only five pages are cited under "Motivation." In his Preface, Woodworth explains the omission of the topic of motivation as follows: "All of these branches are of great interest to me, personally, but the scope of the book is fully broad enough when confined as it is to the usual content of a course in experimental psychology, in which the students and subjects are young human adults. I should have liked to include chapters on work and motivation, but must content myself with a reference to Robinson's comprehensive chapter on the 'Work of the Integrated Organism' in Murchison's *Handbook,* and to such treatments of motivation as are given by Troland, Young and Gordon Allport." *Experimental Psychology* by Woodworth and Schlosberg (1954) does have a chapter on motivation in learning and performance; the index includes thirty-one items under "Motivation" and thirty items under "Drive." Woodworth's (1958) updated version of *Dynamic Psychology* became *Dynamics of Behavior.* It reveals his enduring interest in motivation and drive in relation to contemporary research.

[3] The lack of agreement among psychologists on the definition of a concept of motivation, and the diversity of topics labeled as motivation may be gathered from the articles by Mowrer (1952), Cofer (1959), Irwin (1961), O'Kelly (1963), Brown and Farber (1968), and Campbell and Misanin (1969) in the *Annual Review of Psychology,* and from the annual series of articles in the Nebraska symposium on motivation from 1953 on.

22 hr of water deprivation, we see that on a 10-unit elevated T-maze rats ran faster for water at the higher deprivation. When subgroups were shifted from 2 to 22 or from 22 to 2 hr of water deprivation, performance shifted appropriately: 2–22 subjects ran faster within two trials after the shift, and 22–2 subjects ran more slowly immediately after the shift than they had on the preceding trial. The important assumption is made that this rapid shift in performance, perhaps especially the slowing down, does not appear to be a learning phenomenon (although possible associative explanations, such as generalization decrement, will be considered later). These rapid performance shifts illustrate the type of performance changes which would be predictable if performance was a multiplicative function of learning and drive.[4] More simply, Figure 18.1 illustrates performance changes attributable to a motivational variable (in this case, shifts in hours of water deprivation as a source of drive). We should also emphasize that as is often the case, the number of errors was *not* related to degree of deprivation throughout the 15 trials; this illustrates the important fact that the observed effects of motivational variables on behavior can vary markedly with the particular response measures used.

Shifts in magnitude of both positive and negative reinforcing stimuli may produce changes in performance somewhat similar to those observed with deprivation shifts: in other words, it seems reasonable to think of such shifts having motivational effects. Thus, besides deprivation as a source of drive, additional "energization" or facilitation of performance may arise from the reinforcers as a source of incentive motivation. An early example was provided by Blodgett (1929), who demonstrated that food-deprived rats run in a maze without food showed marked improvement in speed and accuracy immedi-

ately after the introduction of food in the goal box. Rapid shifts in asymptotic starting latencies were found by Zeaman (1949) when large and small amounts of food were interchanged (see p. 631ff.). These aspects of Zearman's data confirm the findings of Crespi (1942, 1944), who emphasized their motivational significance. Such rapid performance shifts with reinforcement shifts illustrates that so-called "motivational effects" may depend in part at least on incentive motivation (based on learned associative mechanisms), and to that extent motivational effects cannot be uniquely attributed to deprivation conditions as sources of drive. Hence "motivation" is frequently used as a generic term which subsumes drive and incentive motivation.

CRITERIA FOR MOTIVATIONAL VARIABLES

Concise, valuable discussions of the criteria for identification of motivators defined as manipulable empirical motivational variables (for example, food deprivation, electric shock) are provided in Brown (1961) and in Brown and Farber (1968). Briefly, three possible criteria appear to be most often invoked: First, a motivational variable should energize many different responses under standard stimulus conditions appropriate for each response tested; second, a motivational variable's offset should reinforce immediately preceding responses; third, its onset should punish immediately preceding responses.

For example, electrical shock functions as an energizer, its onset as a punisher, and its offset as a reinforcer. Because electrical shock appears to meet all three criteria, it qualifies as a motivational variable. However, for other motivational variables, the empirical correlations among these criteria are not known for a wide variety of situations, and therefore Brown and Farber (1968, p. 102) note that ". . . it is uncertain whether more than one criterion must be met." The question of unknown correlations among the three criteria is mentioned here to make explicit the fact that fulfillment

[4] The use of an experiment, such as that described here, to illustrate a particular theoretical formulation does not necessarily mean that all available data are unequivocal with regard to this interpretation. For opposing views see Webb (1955) and Bolles (1958, 1967).

of one criterion does not ensure fulfillment of the others.

This chapter is concerned primarily with the first criterion and the usefulness of the concept of drive as a general energizer. We refer to the other two criteria here only to a limited extent in the context of drive theory because the relevant topics of reinforcement and punishment are discussed in two other chapters.

Energizer

Probably the most widely accepted criterion for identification of a motivational variable is that it should facilitate or energize behavioral response tendencies. Earlier drive theories often implied selective facilitation (for example, food deprivation activates the get-food mechanism). Recently, facilitation of a wide variety of response tendencies has been favored (Brown, 1961, p. 41). Thus for some theories an essential property of drive originating from food deprivation is that it energize or facilitate other mechanisms besides those regulating eating or reinforced with food (Hebb, 1955; Brown, 1961). Although the S–R associative mechanism can result in only one dominant response in a particular situation, the idea of a generalized energizer is still testable because, in principle, any one of a wide variety of responses can be made dominant, provided the stimulus conditions are varied appropriately. To illustrate, R_1 can be made dominant in one situation, R_2 in another, and so on; each of these different responses should be demonstrably energized by any motivator as a source of generalized drive, provided the test response is the dominant response in the test situation.

Some observations on spinal reflexes are at least suggestive of a general energizer such as drive (and/or arousal as discussed in a later section). Sherrington noted that (1900, p. 845, cited by Brobeck, 1960, p. 1203):

> As a broad rule, spinal reflexes are more easily elicited when a well-nourished animal is hungry and expecting food, and less readily when it has just heavily fed.

It is interesting that Sherrington's wording includes reference to factors now considered as drive and incentive motivation. Experimentally produced thirst results in facilitation of evoked responses from spinal ventral horn cells (Wayner, 1964). Both of these observations are at least suggestive that the procedures alleged to produce drive tend to facilitate skeletal responses in general.

This view receives some support from the finding that startle responses to the sound of a pistol shot were reliably greater in rats food-deprived for 46 hr (high drive) than for 1 hr (low drive); but the initial effects of food deprivation on startle were extremely slight relative to the tremendous enhancement of startle by fear (Meryman, 1952; cited by Brown, 1961, pp. 152–154). These quantitative data on the effects of food deprivation on startle suggest that any generalized energizing effect of food deprivation per se is small.

The example with startle as a test response illustrates attempts to translate into experimental terms the proposition that motivational variables act as a general energizer; the assumption is made that startle is not relevant to "get-food" behavioral patterns and consummatory mechanisms, and therefore startle would not be enhanced by food deprivation if the latter only energized specific mechanisms relevant to the deprivation. On the other hand, if startle were enhanced by food deprivation (as indeed seems to be the case), it might be seen as evidence in favor of the general energizing theory of drive.

Reinforcement by Motivational Variable Offset

In escape from electrical shock, escape turns off the alleged motivational variable (electrical shock) and the responses leading to escape are supposedly reinforced by the shock offset. Now, if escape becomes more precise, more rapid, and in other ways shows evidence of learning, we might say that electrical shock is a motivational variable (that is, an empirical one) because it has met one of the criteria. Acceptance of this paragraph so far does not commit one to accept theoretical concepts of generalized drive or multiple drives, nor that drive reduction is essential for reinforcement.

Hours of food deprivation can be considered as a manipulable empirical variable in the sense that duration of the privation can be systematically varied, but in the present context we should note that the precise empirical assessment of this variable's offset poses difficulties. Earlier thinking involved the view that there are primary biological needs which must be met for survival, that these need states are sources of drive, and that reduction of a biological need is accompanied by drive reduction which reinforces the instrumental activity leading up to need and drive reduction. The marked reduction in the efficacy of reinforcers when delayed only a few seconds (see delay of reinforcement section, pp. 677–689) makes it clear that reinforcement must be occurring minutes before the ingested food could be transformed into usable forms and transported to bodily tissues where it could reduce need. Ingestion of water seems to reverse deprivation conditions more rapidly, but this delay is still very long by delay-of-reinforcement standards. Clearly, the reinforcing event precedes need reduction and the offset of this alleged motivational variable apparently occurs at the wrong time to be the immediate cause of reinforcement.

Perhaps food deprivation should be empirically defined as a period of noneating which is terminated by eating food. However, available data show that eating nonnutritive materials can also reinforce responses. For example experiments with nonnutritive saccharin have demonstrated that it is ingested avidly by most animals and that it is an excellent positive reinforcer although it does not reduce caloric needs (see pp. 627–630). Hence, it has been suggested (for example, Sheffield, Roby, & Campbell, 1954) that reinforcement may be primarily due to the occurrence of consummatory activity.

However, even consummatory activity is not essential for food to be a reinforcer for a food-deprived subject. Experimental data have shown convincingly that instrumental activity can be reinforced with food given through a stomach fistula (Miller & Kessen, 1952) or through a nasopharyngeal gastric tube (for example, Epstein & Teitelbaum, 1962; Borer, 1968). However, nonnutritive saccharin (which does not, of course, directly reduce caloric needs) does not reinforce behavior when it is given via a stomach fistula (Miller, 1955).These results seem to indicate that need-reduction can be a sufficient (though not a necessary) condition for reinforcement, even in the absence of consummatory activity.

It should not be concluded that just because saccharin passes through the body without chemical change it is therefore physiologically inert. Ingesting saccharin has sometimes increased and sometimes decreased blood sugar levels, and even rinsing the mouth with saccharin and other substances may produce such changes (Jorgensen, 1950; Nicolaides, 1969). Some of these changes (called "anticipatory reflexes" by Nicolaides) occur within a minute of oral stimulation, but even such intervals are long by delay-of-reinforcement standards. Results such as these provide some support for the hypothesis that saccharin may interact with need-reducing mechanisms in as yet undetermined ways (see also Smith & Capretta, 1956; Valenstein & Weber, 1965).

Still another type of experiment used to support the argument that reinforcement can occur without drive reduction was performed by Sheffield, Wulff, and Backer (1951). Male rats were tested to determine whether running and hurdle-climbing could be reinforced by copulation with a receptive female which was interrupted before ejaculation. (The male rat dismounts after each copulation, and a series of about a dozen mountings occur before ejaculation, so removal of the male after the second copulatory response ensured that copulation occurred without ejaculation). Significant improvement in instru-

mental response speeds supported the conclusion that instrumental responses were reinforced by copulatory activity, even when
copulation had never been followed by an
orgasm, and thus presumably without any
reduction in drive of a sexual origin. Kagan
(1955) reports that sexual behavior allowed
to continue until ejaculation was a better
reinforcer for rats than coital behavior without ejaculation; this differential reinforcing
efficacy was apparently primarily due to
deteriorating performance of males not allowed to ejaculate. Whalen (1961) has shown
that intromission without ejaculation is self-
maintaining and reinforces T-maze learning
when no other type of sexual activity is allowed. He suggests that complex effects resulting from intromission on some trials and
mounting without intromission on other trials
(such as mounting a vaginally closed, non-
receptive female) may be involved in the
failure of intromission without ejaculation to
be self-maintaining in Kagan's study.

Research in this area has been hampered
by lack of techniques for the quantitative
assessment of the current drive level. Interrelated with this problem is the question of
how convincing the evidence is that drive
reduction is essential for reinforcement. Probably the predominant current view is to reject
a "strong" version of the drive-reduction
hypothesis, and accept it in a weak form such
as: drive reduction may be a sufficient condition for reinforcement, but it is not an essential one. Of course, even if this weak form
of the hypothesis is accepted, we can still use
the presence of a reinforcing effect as one
of the criteria of a motivational variable.

Punishment by Motivational Variable Onset

A third criterion for the identification of
a motivational variable is that its onset punishes preceding responses. For example, an
instrumental response followed by onset of
electrical shock then has a lowered probability of recurrence. This criterion works best
when applied to the presentation of external
stimuli such as electrical shock to the feet,
or stimuli which elicit conditioned fear

(Brown & Farber, 1968) or the "alarm reaction"
(Roberts, 1958a, b, 1962). (The topic of pun-
ishment is discussed in greater length in
Chapter 16.)

Application of this criterion to deprivations
has been difficult because until recently it was
not feasible to have an instrumental response
followed immediately by a sufficiently rapid
onset of hunger or thirst. However, the use
of stimulating electrodes chronically implanted in the brain may help to solve some
of these problems. For example, Margules &
Olds (1962) found that electrical stimulation
of the lateral hypothalamus (the so-called
"feeding area") caused stimulus-bound eating
in 28 out of 46 rats tested. That is, eating
began within two seconds of stimulus onset,
continued throughout stimulation, and
ceased with stimulus offset. Such effects are
sometimes interpreted as evidence that the
electrical stimulation of the lateral hypothalamus was suddenly turning on hunger,
which was reflected in the consummatory
activity of eating and the organized searching
for food (see Miller, 1960).

If this were the case, our third criterion
would predict that immediately preceding
instrumental responses would be punished.
Instead, they are positively reinforced. For
example, bar-pressing increases (Hoebel &
Teitelbaum, 1962; Margules & Olds, 1962) and
T-mazes are run with increasing speed and
accuracy (Miller, 1960; Mendelson & Chorover, 1965) when the same electrical stimulation is turned on immediately following the
occurrence of the response.

These results would seem to suggest that
forms of stimulation that do not elicit strong
withdrawal reactions can be positively reinforcing at the same time that they are drive-
inducing (see pp. 657, 695), and that our third
criterion may thus be relevant only to stimuli
that are aversive in nature.

DEFINING CONDITIONS OF SOURCES OF DRIVE (vs DRIVES)

In a discussion of drive as a motivational
concept, the requirements include *both* an
operational definition of an alleged source of

drive that can be manipulated as an independent variable (such as hours of food deprivation) and appropriate tests to assess whether any of the criteria for the identification of a motivational variable have been met (energizing, reinforcing, punishing). Examples may make this clearer. Air deprivation for rats under water acts as a source of drive (Broadhurst, 1957). Speed of underwater swimming was an increasing monotonic function of duration of air deprivation up to about 20 seconds. Following air deprivation, access to air successfully reinforced the acquisition of a brightness discrimination. In this case, seconds of air deprivation while underwater provides an operational definition of a source of drive; and two criteria for identifying a motivational variable were met: swimming speeds increased with increases in deprivation times and termination of air deprivation reinforced a discriminative escape response. However, mere reduction of the oxygen concentration of air without interfering with breathing apparently does not act as a source of drive: responses are not energized, nor are any instrumental responses reinforced. For example, airmen have lost consciousness when flying at high altitudes even though they could increase their oxygen concentration, either by turning on a supply line or by selecting a lower altitude. There apparently is no physiological mechanism to monitor the oxygen supply directly and to instigate adaptive, nonreflexive behavior. Thus although one can operationally define a technique of oxygen deprivation without interfering with breathing, this does not act as a source of drive.

On this point Brown (1961, pp. 44–47) emphasizes an important distinction between merely operational definitions and significant definitions of drive. A significant definition of a source of drive is essentially an operational definition that works (meets at least one of the criteria for identifying a motivational variable). In other words, identifying a significant source of drive requires both a formal operational definition concerning the manipulation of an empirical variable, plus an empirical test to see if at least one criterion is empirically fulfilled. This means that the identification of a significant source of drive is at best probabilistic and not a logical certainty based on a formal definition.

When discussing significant sources of drive, needs and drive must be distinguished. In some cases, such as food deprivation, one might expect the growing need for calories and the increasing drive level to follow parallel functions. However, even here, a growing physiological need for particular vitamins or minerals can fail to act as an energizer. Failure of oxygen deficits to act as energizers was mentioned at the start of this section. Similarly, carbon monoxide is odorless and poisonous; one can say there is a physiological need to avoid it, but the breathing of air containing such carbon monoxide does not energize responses. On the other hand, clearly aversive intensities of electrical shock are very effective in producing what appears to be a heightened drive state, even though these intensities of shock do not cause any gross peripheral tissue damage, and consequently there is no great and immediate physiological need to avoid such shock to prevent tissue damage. In summary, a one-to-one relation between physiological need and drive does not always occur, and it is not required by contemporary drive theory. It follows as well that the detection or measurement of physiological need in itself does not necessarily provide an index of drive level.

We will now discuss sources of drive under the headings of primary (unlearned), secondary (learned), and response-defined level of drive (where either the source is unknown or where drive level is suspected to have changed although the antecedent deprivation has not changed).

Primary (unlearned) Sources of Drive

Whether spoken of as primary drives or primary sources of drive, lists of primary motivators typically include hunger, thirst, sex, aversive stimuli, perhaps maternal drive, and, recently, something variously called boredom, curiosity, or exploratory drive. No general agreement exists about the length of the list, except that the need for parsimony dictates that the list be kept relatively short. Inclusion in the class of primary motivators rests on the assumption that they are present in normally raised animals and do not require the special procedures used to establish alleged secondary or acquired sources of motivation.

Antecedent conditions   It is customary to consider hunger and thirst as being operationally defined in terms of antecedent conditions (for example, hours of food or water deprivation, respectively). Sometimes, however, food or water deprivation is used to produce a body-weight deficit, and the latter is used as the operationally defined motivational variable. Our earlier discussion of significant definitions of motivational variables emphasized that they only included those variables which met at least one of the empirical criteria for identification of motivational variables. In other words, significant motivational variables as a class are defined by their behavioral consequences as well as their antecedent conditions. Sometimes the behavioral consequences are even emphasized, as in Miller's use of behavioral responses to "measure" hunger, and to argue for drive reduction by saccharin in the absence of need reduction (1957). A response definition or measure of hunger is sometimes implied in studies purporting to show that experience with food-deprivation schedules can override the effects of food deficit per se (see section below on deprivation effects on consummatory activity). Sexual and maternal motivational variables are less clearly anchored on the antecedent side, and in their assessment more weight is given to response measures. Presentation of strong electrical shock to external bodily parts meets the criteria for a significant motivational variable, and has provided a basis for suggesting that at least some significant motivational variables are due to intense stimuli. Attempts have been made to relate curiosity and exploratory

behavior to antecedent conditions of stimulation or perceptual deprivation and/or stimulus satiation (boredom); here too, response measures play an important role in current research devoted to identifying significant definitions of antecedent conditions as motivational variables.

Discrimination of deprivation states   It is important to note that rats can discriminate between hunger and thirst, and between different degrees of hunger. First, let us survey some of the data, and then consider four possible theoretical interpretations. Hull (1933) used a maze with two different routes that led to a common goal box in which either food or water was placed. Rats eventually learned after many trials to take the path that provided access to food when food-deprived, and the other path when water-deprived. This

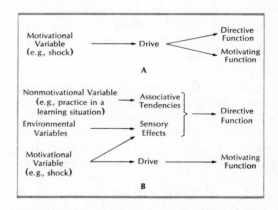

Figure 18.2. Part A illustrates the possibility that an empirical motivational variable instigates a hypothetical drive with both energizing and directive functions. This involves the assumption of multiple drives, such as hunger, thirst, and sex. Other, nonmotivational variables have directive functions, which theoretically could act in conjunction with multiple drives *or* with the general drive illustrated in Part B. Motivational variables, in Part B, are a source of general drive and also have sensory effects with directive functions. The two theoretical formulations of drive depicted in Parts A and B were treated as being mutually exclusive in Brown (1961). (Redrawn from Brown, 1961.)

selection of path in accordance with the current deprivation state was confirmed by Leeper (1935) with fewer acquisition trials by the use of separate goal boxes. More recent experiments (for example, Amsel, 1949; Manning, 1956) support earlier data and strengthen the case for discriminations between hunger and thirst based on some aspect of deprivation and its consequences other than merely generalized drive intensity; some associative mechanisms seem to be required to explain such results. Thus food and water deprivation might each be assumed to have both motivational and directive functions. This is probably true for any motivational variable. We will consider four principal ways to incorporate these two functions into theory.

Figure 18.2, based on Brown (1961, pp. 58–59), illustrates two major alternatives for drive theorists. In Figure 18.2A, the motivational variable instigates a drive with both directive and motivating functions; the directive function presumably would vary according to the motivational variable involved, and in this case it may be meaningful to speak of various drives (such as hunger, thirst, and sex drives). In Figure 18.2B the motivational variable, as a source of drive, contributes to a unitary general drive that is capable of energizing all response tendencies; in addition, the motivational variable (such as electrical shock) has sensory effects that can become associated with response tendencies (be part of the S-R mechanism). These sensory effects of motivational variables have been called drive stimuli by Hull (1943). According to Brown (1961), the terminology "drive stimuli" may have the misleading implication that they have a drive function (they energize response tendencies). Instead, Brown proposes that these sensory effects be called motivation-variable stimuli ($S_{MV}s$); such terminology may serve to indicate more clearly the purely directive function attributed to them. In this formulation, illustrated in Figure 18.2B, drive energizes but does not direct behavior. The assumption that motivational variables have

sensory effects provides a theoretical basis for the experimental data which show rats can discriminate between food and water deprivation. For this formulation, the same procedure (such as food deprivation) can manipulate both drive (D) and motivation-variable stimuli ($S_{MV}s$). In the absence of clear empirical indices of D and $S_{MV}s$, practical problems may arise where it may be difficult to assess empirically how much of a behavioral effect is due to D, the general energizer, and how much is due to the cue properties of $S_{MV}s$ and the associative mechanisms noted next.

A third possibility for dealing with the alleged motivational and directive functions of deprivation procedures is to attempt to account for all of the effects of motivational variables in terms of stimulus elements (Estes, 1958). Drive stimuli are treated as any other stimuli capable of becoming associated with responses. It is assumed that as deprivation time increases, the probabilities of occurrence of deprivation cues increase and those of satiation cues decrease. These two sources of cues provide a basis for discriminating among deprivation states. How successful this approach will be in accounting for motivational phenomena is not yet known.

A fourth possibility for dealing with these problems is to invoke the directive consequences of the stimuli arising from the hypothesized fractional anticipatory goal responses, that is, the r_g–s_g mechanisms (Spence, 1951; Logan & Wagner, 1965; Bolles, 1967). When a subject is water deprived but satiated on food, the fractional anticipatory goal response related to eating (r_e) should be reduced, but not the fractional anticipatory goal response related to drinking (r_d), and hence the directive consequences of r_d would contribute cues leading to the place where water previously has been encountered. If it can be shown that this approach adequately accounts for the data on discrimination of deprivation conditions, then there would be no need to postulate deprivation stimuli with cue properties. In fact, Bolles (1967) has suggested that perhaps it is not essential to postulate either a general energizer called drive *or* deprivation stimuli, and that (p. 367) "Whatever the status of r_g, incentive theories of motivation offer a clear alternative to drive theories."

Drive level as a function of significant motivational-variable parameters   In the consideration of food deprivation as a source of drive, it has sometimes been assumed that drive level increases monotonically as a function of the number of hours of food deprivation (see Hull, 1952, pp. 6–7). It has also appeared reasonable to postulate inanition (general physical weakness), and although there were few empirical studies of inanition per se, such enfeeblement has been assumed to increase monotonically as an exponential function of deprivation time. When D was corrected for inanition, the resulting effective drive ($\bar{D}$) was an inverted-U function of deprivation time (for example, Yamaguchi, 1951). In this context, the dominant response tendency should be energized to the extent of $\bar{D}$, and this should be apparent in one or more performance attributes (such as likelihood of occurrence, speed, number of responses, vigor). Therefore, other things being equal, some characteristics of the dominant response should keep increasing as a function of hours of food deprivation, until under sufficiently extreme conditions inanition significantly reduces $\bar{D}$. Similarly, with water deprivation as a source of drive, $\bar{D}$ should be a rising monotonic function of deprivation time until inanition becomes severe enough at extreme deprivations to lower $\bar{D}$.

Among other so-called primary sources of drive, a major one consists of the presentation of strong external stimulation, such as electrical shock. Here drive is assumed to increase monotonically[5] as a function of shock intensity.

Generalized drive theorists assume that drive from these various defining conditions is additive; the various sources contribute, perhaps by simple summation,[6] to a general drive factor (D). Regardless of the sources involved, D supposedly energizes all response tendencies. Actual behavior, therefore, will depend on the S-R mechanism; what the subject does will depend on which response is the dominant one in that particular situation.

Secondary (Learned) Sources of Drive

The basic question here is whether it is possible to take stimulus conditions that normally do not act as sources of drive and, by appropriate procedures, transfer them into learned sources of drive.

Acquired sources of drive derived from strong aversive stimuli   A representative experimental paradigm is provided by Miller's (1948, 1951) study of neutral stimuli acquiring fear-arousing properties as a result of being associated with electrical shock (see pp. 717–718). Rats were shocked in a white compartment and allowed to escape into a black compartment. Subsequently, 13 of 25 animals acquired new responses when these were necessary in order to leave the white compartment, even though no further shock was given after the initial experience. These data are consistent with the conclusion that the initially neutral white compartment became a source of drive which energized responses, as a result of the stimuli of the white compartment having been paired with shock. It is frequently assumed that the white compartment now is a conditioned stimulus (CS) which causes a conditioned response of fear.

---

[5] Hull (1952) did not explicitly suggest that the subject was generally weakened when electrical shock was used as a source of drive.

[6] Food and water deprivations are not independent; water-deprived rats eat less food and food-deprived rats drink less water (see the section on consummatory activities). Attempts have been made to bypass the difficulty due to interaction between hunger and thirst by depriving subjects of either food or water, and then presenting them with other sources of drive, such as electrical shock. These studies on the summation of drive are reviewed in Bolles (1967). How incentive motivation (K), as an alleged general energizer, combines with generalized drive (D) is considered in our section on incentive motivation as a learned source of drive.

Moreover, this point of view predicts that escape from the white compartment (and the fear-arousing stimuli) into the black compartment should be reinforced by motivational-variable offset (that is, termination of the white-compartment cues); and indeed new instrumental responses were learned, apparently on the basis of this reinforcement.

An extensively held view is shared by Brown and Farber (1968, p. 108) when they conclude that: ". . . there is little doubt that the termination of a fear-arousing CS functions as a reinforcer for a wide variety of responses whose occurrence antedates such reactions . . ." and they cite key experimental studies which seem to support their point.

Recently, however, Allison, Larson, and Jensen (1967) have warned against possible misleading and oversimplified interpretations of Miller's results. First, they found in their own experiment that fear conditioning initially depressed speed of escape from one into another compartment in a shuttlebox, relative to nonshocked controls, thus confounding any reinforcement interpretation of the subsequent improvement in performance for experimental subjects escaping a white CS into a black compartment. Moreover, nonshocked controls showed a reliable preference for black over white compartments, both in terms of initial choice and time spent within compartments, so that experimental subjects with a black CS did not show reliable performance improvement for escaping the black CS into the white compartment.

With regard to Miller's (1948) and other studies on avoidance, Bolles (1967) questions whether a really "new" response has been acquired. He argues that on the basis of available data (p. 408) ". . . there seems to be room for considerable doubt whether the rat can learn any arbitrary response in an avoidance situation." Bolles apparently is not only questioning a current view, expressed for example by Brown and Farber (1968), that "a wide variety of responses" can be acquired as avoidance responses; he also suggests (p. 409) that the fear-arousing CS ". . . may merely elicit species specific defense reactions."

In a frequently cited study, Brown, Kalish, and Farber (1951) demonstrated with rats that after a CS had been paired with electrical shock to the feet, startle responses to a sudden intense auditory stimulus (a pistol shot) were enhanced relative to controls for whom the CS had not been paired with shock. This finding is consistent with the view that conditioned fear elicited by the CS acted as a source of generalized drive which energized the indicant or test response, startle. Recently, however, Kurtz and Siegel (1966) found that the amplitudes of startle responses were enhanced (relative to control groups for pseudoconditioning) only by a compound-stimulus CS paired with electrical shock to the rat's feet, but not by the same compound stimulus when it had been paired as a CS with shock to the rat's back. They suggested that foot shock elicited a postural adjustment (crouching) which reduced the severity of the shock. In the presence of the CS for foot shock, on test trials without shock, the rats maintained a crouching posture which apparently heightened startle responses. The crouching posture was not maintained in the presence of the same compound stimulus when it had been paired with back shock, nor in the presence of the same compound stimulus when it had not been paired with shock in the two control groups for pseudoconditioning.

In seemingly good correspondence with the postural data, startle responses tended to be about equal in the back-shock experimental group and in the back-shock and foot-shock control groups for pseudoconditioning, but about 50 percent larger in the foot-shock experimental group. Kurtz and Siegel granted the possibility that back shock might have produced postural adjustments which tended to reduce the amplitude of startle responses (and presumably that the conditioned postural response might negate the energizing increment due to fear as a source of drive). They noted, however, that acceptance of this possibility serves to underscore the important influence of posture on the magnitude of startle responses, and to question the generality of the "energization" reported by

Brown et al. (1951). However, Kurtz and Siegel were not merely questioning the adequacy of the startle response to test for generalized drive. They tentatively suggested that their findings call into question the view of Hull (1943) and Brown et al. (1951) that drive from any source "energizes any and all behavior for which an adequate stimulus is present" (Kurtz & Siegel, 1966, p. 14).

Another apparent difficulty for generalized drive theory is the highly reliable suppression effect in the CER situation (see pp. 712–717 for discussion of this phenomenon). The CS preceding shock is more likely to elicit freezing than enhance or energize the on-going baseline behavior (for example, bar pressing for food or water). Proponents of generalized drive theory might say that cowering tends to be the dominant response for the rat in fearful situations, and that as fear-produced energization increases, so does freezing, and thus overt general activity of necessity decreases. The expression of "more and more vigorous inactivity" appears to strain normal verbal usage, even if it does not actually strain the loosely stated generalized drive formulation.

On the punishment criterion we can only note here that Brown and Farber (1968) cite studies which lead them to conclude that the onset of a CS previously paired with aversive events is punishing (see the discussion of "secondary punishment," pp. 719–720).

A key point may be emphasized by including these comments from Brown and Farber (1968, p. 110):

". . . the energizing criterion, loosely stated as it is, does not require that every response in an animal's repertoire be augmented by the CS under test. Nor is such an outcome expected, even by those who still hold to a generalized drive theory, simply because substantial weight must always be given to the associative properties of any CS. Whenever the energizing criterion is met one is obliged to consider the possibility that the outcome is due to facilitative responses evoked by the CS. Likewise, when it is not met, a search for interfering tendencies is also mandatory."

Careful analyses of the associative properties of any CS are needed as well in tests of rein-forcement by CS offset. A major general theme of this chapter is the need to assign a very important role to associative analyses of any situation alleged to involve generalized drive.

Acquired sources of drive from deprivation states   In a paradigm somewhat comparable to Miller's (1948) experiment, Myers and Miller (1954) attempted to establish an acquired source of drive based on hunger. Food-deprived rats were placed in a white compartment, and supposedly this CS (white-compartment stimuli) should have become associated with the hunger state. Moreover, the food-deprived subjects learned a door-touching response that opened the door and provided access to food in the black compartment. Four groups were given 0, 10, 30, and 70 "drive-acquisition trials" respectively. Later these subjects were tested when satiated on food. At this time there was no food in the apparatus. Access to the black compartment was now contingent on performing a new instrumental response (bar pressing). It was hypothesized that the white compartment stimuli as a CS would instigate hunger (act as a source of drive), and that CS offset (escape from the hunger-eliciting CS) would reinforce bar pressing. Spaced testing trials were used (one a day). The control group and the three experimental groups performed the required instrumental activity about equally quickly. Thus the effect could not be attributed to an acquired source of drive based on hunger. Myers and Miller (1954) performed a second experiment which revealed that opportunity to explore the new compartment was involved; this was true for both the white-to-black and the black-to-white groups. Moreover, in the second experiment, instrumental responses were performed less often during massed trials (approximately 3-min intertrial intervals) presumably because the second compartment lost its novelty and incentive value. As a consequence, they entitled their experiment, "Failure to find a learned drive based on hunger; evidence for learning motivated by 'exploration.' "

Although negative findings predominate, the issue might be said to be still in doubt, since some suggestive evidence for an acquired source of drive based on hunger was obtained by Calvin, Bicknell, and Sperling (1953). Rats were food-deprived for either 1 hr (WD = weak drive) or 23 hr (SD = strong drive) and then placed in striped boxes for 30 min daily for 24 consecutive days. Food consumption was subsequently tested with all subjects at $11\frac{1}{2}$ hr of food deprivation. On the assumption that the striped boxes would arouse higher acquired drive in SD than WD subjects, one would predict that more food would be eaten by SD than WD subjects when both groups were tested at $11\frac{1}{2}$ hours deprivation. The expected result occurred at a significant level of confidence. Siegel and MacDonnell (1954) repeated the Calvin et al. (1953) study; they found no reliable group differences, and the trend was even in the opposite direction: the WD group had slightly larger mean food intakes than the SD group during test trials. Brown and Farber (1968) cite other negative findings and emphasize that even with the positive results found in the Calvin et al. type of study, unambiguous interpretation is not possible because satiation (that is, at 1-hr food deprivation) in the WD group may have, by association with the striped boxes, depressed food intake on the test trials. We must agree with their conclusion that as yet there is insufficient evidence to support the hypothesis that acquired sources of drive can be based on the association of any CS with the presence of deprivation states such as food or water deprivation.

Incentive motivation (K) as a learned source of drive In the introductory section illustrating motivational effects it was shown that performance speed can be increased or decreased by appropriate shifts in either deprivation time or amount of reinforcer. Such rapid shifts in performance were interpreted

by most theorists as due, not to rapid learning and unlearning of how to run in the runway, but to shifts in the motivational level energizing behavior. Of course, such theorizing required that reinforcer magnitude be conceived as a determinant of motivation during a trial, and that previously neutral stimuli that have been paired with the reinforcer would now be able to energize behavior before the subject was actually exposed to stimulation from the reinforcer on that trial. It is primarily this anticipation of the reinforcer as an alleged source of drive that is our concern here; other aspects of positive reinforcement are discussed in Chapter 15.

We will start with a review statement of several assumptions typically made within the Hull-Spence S-R theory of r_g. It has been assumed that various consummatory (goal) responses (R_Gs) have components which can become classically conditioned to goal box stimuli and perhaps to internal deprivation stimuli. Some of these conditioned fractional goal responses (such as salivation), because of stimulus generalization, may be elicited by runway stimuli and occur as fractional anticipatory goal responses (r_gs) during the trial and before exposure to the food stimuli in the goal box on that trial. An r_g, like any response, is assumed to have some sensory effects. In addition, this r_g–s_g mechanism has been assumed (Spence, 1951, 1956; Hull, 1952) to be a source of incentive motivation (K). The r_g–s_g–K mechanism has been proposed within S-R theory to deal objectively and systematically with "expectancy" or anticipation of a reinforcer. With regard to this r_g–s_g–K formulation, we need to know the strength of r_g, which determines the magnitude of K.

Since it is assumed (Spence, 1956) that r_g is a classically conditioned response, the habit strength of r_g should be assumed to vary with the number of conditioning trials in the goal box. In addition, characteristics of the goal object (such as amount of food) which produce unconditioned consummatory or goal responses (R_Gs) of different vigor may contribute to either the habit strength of r_g or to the conditioning of different responses, each with its characteristic

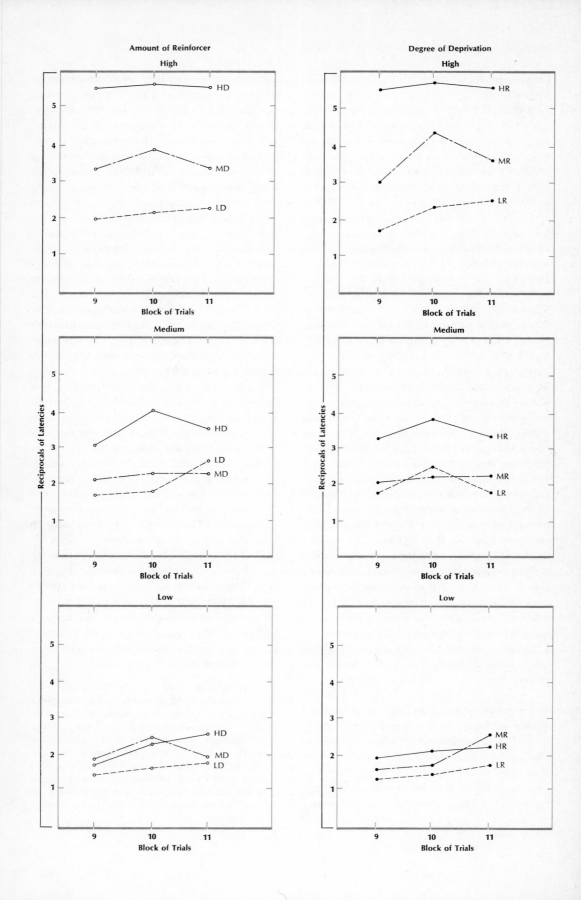

vigor. Moreover, the similarity of cues outside the goal box to those in the goal box will influence the strength of r_g elicited at various distances from the goal box.

K should be expected to vary with changes in deprivation as well as with changes in the reinforcer. Brown and Farber (1968) note that internal consistency within Hull-Spence S-R theory would seem to require that D energize both R_G and r_g. Higher D values should produce stronger R_Gs, which in turn should lead to stronger conditioned r_gs, and these stronger r_gs should be energized still further by D, resulting in higher K values. This logic makes K in part a function of D, which in turn makes K in part a function of deprivation time. If D were zero, according to this view, r_gs would not occur because they were not being energized, and K should be zero. However, it should still be possible to have demonstrable D levels in situations idealized as being completely devoid of incentive motivation, that is, in a situation devoid of any effective external cues to elicit conditioned generalized r_gs, and perhaps with subjects devoid of experience with various deprivation schedules in order to minimize generalized r_gs conditioned to internal deprivation cues.

There are experimental data which are consistent with the view that the r_g-s_g-K mechanism is in part a function of deprivation. For example, Kintsch (1962) used three degrees of water deprivation and three amounts of water as reinforcer. Figure 18.3 shows the obtained asymptotic starting speeds in a runway as a function of the nine combinations. The differences between low, medium, and high amounts of water as reinforcer are minimal at low deprivations and maximal at the highest deprivation used. In this example at least, incentive motivation apparently interacted with degree of deprivation. However, the more typical finding seems to be that an analysis of variance reveals no reliable interaction between the deprivation and reinforcer magnitude variables, except in studies which employed a zero value for at least one of these variables (Black, 1965; Bolles, 1967).

An experimental demonstration that r_g functions as a secondary source of generalized drive, in accordance with the systematic approach we adopted earlier, must fulfill at least one of the three criteria for identification of a motivational variable. It should be possible to show that the onset of an r_g-evoking CS punishes antecedent responses, and/or its presence energizes concurrent responses, and/or its cessation reinforces antecedent responses.

Brown and Farber (1968) concluded that the r_g mechanism probably cannot fulfill the punishment criterion, since eating food is drive-reducing and tranquilizing, and that therefore it is unlikely that conditioned cues for food would not be tranquilizing as well. The experimental paradigm that allegedly conditions a CS to elicit an r_g is the same classical conditioning procedure of pairing a CS with food that allegedly makes the CS a secondary reinforcer. Studies of secondary reinforcement have shown that, after CS-food conditioning, CS onset alone enhances but does not generally weaken instrumental responses (see pp. 660–677).

Figure 18.3. Asymptotic starting speeds (reciprocals of latencies) in a runway for all combinations of 3 levels of water deprivation (drive) and 3 amounts of water as a reinforcer. The lowest set of curves on the left show that, with the smallest reinforcer magnitude, variations in drive level had minimal effects on performance; similarly (lower right) at the lowest drive level, variations in reinforcer magnitude had minimal effects. The top set of curves on the left show that, with the highest reinforcer magnitude, performance varied markedly with drive level: high drive (HD) was best, low drive (LD) was poorest, and medium drive (MD) was intermediate. Similarly (top right) at high drive, performance varied markedly with reinforcer magnitudes: highest reinforcer magnitude (HR) was best, lowest reinforcer magnitude (LR) was poorest, and medium reinforcer magnitude (MR) was intermediate. The left, middle set of curves show that, with a medium reinforcer magnitude, performance was best at high drive and latencies at low and medium drive were interchangeable. Similarly (middle right) at medium drive, performance was best with the highest reinforcer magnitude, and latencies were interchangeable for the medium and lowest reinforcer magnitudes. (Kintsch, 1962.)

The reinforcement criterion requires that an instrumental response should be reinforced when it is followed by the offset of the CS which elicits r_gs. Brown and Farber (1968) commented that it seemed unlikely that the r_g mechanism could fulfill this criterion, although apparently this particular test has not been made.

The third criterion is that the presence of a motivational variable functions as a nonspecific generalized energizer of responses. Several attempts have been made to circumvent associative interpretations of motivational effects attributable to a food-associated CS by the use of a response believed to be, in the history of the subject, entirely independent of both the r_g-eliciting CS, and the reinforcer used to establish incentive motivation. Specifically, amplitude of a startle response was selected to test for generalized drive because presumably startle responses have not been associated with get-food behavioral patterns, nor reinforced with food. The experimental paradigm employed has been a classical conditioning procedure for a large number of trials (CS paired with food as the UCS), and the evocation of startle responses with a cap pistol shot, both in the presence of the CS and in its absence.

In one such study, Trapold (1962) found that the experimental group conditioned with 24 percent sucrose as UCS made reliably more approach responses to the food location between CS and UCS onset than the experimental group conditioned with 6 percent sucrose, and both experimental groups had markedly more "instrumental" responses than the control group. In other words, the relation between instrumental responses and reinforcer magnitude (concentration) usually attributed to r_g as a general energizer was present in this experiment. However, the startle-amplitude measure was *not* reliably different for the three groups. Therefore, there was no evidence that the supposedly r_g-evoking CS enhanced startle responses during the conditioning trials when the CS did enhance instrumental responses. Moreover, Armus,

Carlson, Guinan, and Crowell (1964) and Armus and Sniadowski-Dolinsky (1966) found that a food-associated CS actually lessened the size of the startle response. Thus, these experiments provide no support for the view that an r_g-evoking CS serves as a general energizer; instead, they tend to favor the view that the CS paired with food has become a secondary reinforcer which *reduces* generalized drive.

> It may be premature, however, to discount the possible influence of postural and instrumental responses on the apparent reduced size of startle in the presence of a secondary reinforcer. For example, if one happened to utilize conditions that led rats to maintain a crouching posture during the CS-food conditioning, then a CS-elicited crouching posture might enhance startle responses, as it did in the Kurtz and Siegel (1966) study of fear as a source of generalized drive. The use of startle responses to test for generalized drive requires better control and understanding of the influence of postural and instrumental responses on startle magnitude than we now have.

The conclusion that stimuli which precede positive reinforcers are tranquilizing or drive-reducing appears to be contrary to observations that the general activity of animals increases immediately before their normal feeding time. Presumably such activity is not merely a function of deprivation, but is in part controlled by the presence of cues associated with feeding. Experimentally, Sheffield and Campbell (1954) demonstrated heightened stabilimeter activity in the presence of a five-minute CS when its termination was followed by food, but not for controls when the CS termination was not paired with feeding. Here is a seeming paradox: presentation of food-associated stimuli sometimes increases and sometimes decreases instrumental activity. Perhaps such stimuli "energize" only certain subsets of responses (such as get-food responses). In this case, the concept of generalized drive may itself be at fault and D may need to be replaced by multiple, specialized energizers. For example, Bindra and Palfai (1967) found that, after classical conditioning of restrained rats, a water-linked CS enhanced perambulation whereas a shock-linked CS enhanced "sitting" (crouching), with apparently compensatory changes in the time spent grooming in the presence of either water- or shock-linked CSs. Such data are not readily reconciled with a single general energizer. Bindra and Palfai interpreted their data as supportive evidence for two central drive states: a positive incentive-motivational central state that is related to appetitive functions, and a negative incentive-motivational central state that is related to defensive functions. The case for viewing incentive motivation as classically-conditioned central drive states is developed further by Bindra (1968), and by Rescorla and Solomon (1967). These approaches represent a strong agrument against the continued acceptance of the concept of incentive motivation as a source of generalized drive which energizes all responses. Even one of the major proponents of generalized drive theory (Brown, 1961) has recently proposed a graduated-drive theory that drastically changes the properties of a general energizer.

According to the graduated-drive theory, ". . . all habits are multiplied by the drive arising from any source, but *the numerical value of the multiplier is graduated according to the relevance of the response to the motivational variable*" (Brown, Anderson, & Brown, 1966, p. 400, italics in the original), These recent developments favor replacing the concept of a generalized energizer with some degree of selective energization of responses, but leave the experimenter with the knotty problem of deciding the relative relevancies of responses.

To recapitulate, we can conclude that neither theoretical considerations nor experimental data support the r_g-s_g-K formulation of incentive motivation as a source of generalized drive. The contemporarily very important research area of incentive motivation has provided evidence that considerably extends the range of plausible associative accounts of motivational effects attributed to

reinforcer-linked CSs, and recent developments favor the likelihood that responses are selectively energized by multiple central drive states.

Frustrative nonreinforcement as a source of drive Our discussion of frustration will be limited and guided by a question which initially can be put loosely as follows: Do unfulfilled expectancies of reinforcers serve as primary or secondary sources of drive? An influential experimental demonstration of the basic "Frustration Effect" was provided by Amsel and Roussel (1952).

Their standard two-runway situation has been much used since; alley one (A_1) and its goal box (G_1) are linked in series with alley two (A_2) and goal box two (G_2). The major dependent variable is running time (or speed) in the second alley (A_2). Food-deprived rats were run with food in both goal boxes until running speeds apparently reached a stable maximum. Next, food was absent in G_1 on half of the trials, but food was still always present in G_2. The initial 8 trials of intermittent reinforcement in G_1 revealed that A_2 performance differed very little between the 4 test trials (food absent in G_1) and 4 control trials (food present in G_1). On the remaining 28 trials of 50 percent reinforcement in G_1, 14 paired comparisons revealed that the median A_2 running times were shorter on each test trial than on its control trial. Since A_2 running times were shorter on test trials than on any other trials in the entire experiment, apparently performance in A_2 was energized when the customary food was absent in G_1. The greater vigor of A_2 performance on test than on control trials has been referred to as the Frustration Effect (FE), and the FE is used as an indicant of a primary frustration reaction (R_F) which is evoked in G_1 by the absence of an anticipated reinforcer. To account for the absence of a clear FE on the first four pairs of test and control trials, Amsel and Roussel suggested that several test trials may have been required to reduce the effectiveness of secondary reinforcers in G_1 sufficiently to permit the appearance of the FE. Acceptance of this explanation for the absence of the FE on test trials 1–4 would evidently permit one to maintain that the omission of a customary primary reinforcer immediately gives rise to an unlearned, primary R_F.

The view that anticipation of reinforcement is a prerequisite for frustrative nonreinforcement has been supported by the more gradual development of the FE during intermittent reinforcement from the onset of the experiment than after continuous reinforcement (Roussel, 1952, cited by Amsel, 1958; Amsel & Hancock, 1957; Wagner, 1959). Amsel (1958, 1962, 1967) has retained the basic Hull-Spence r_g formulation of anticipatory goal responses; however, he has used r_R to symbolize conditioned fractional anticipatory responses derived from the responses to the positive reinforcer (such as food) in the goal box, and r_F to symbolize the conditioned anticipatory form of R_F.

This view that r_Rs are prerequisites for the FE would predict that r_R (and therefore the FE) would be stronger when A_1 and G_1 cues are similar than when they are different (because the more A_1 cues resemble G_1 cues, the more effectively A_1 cues can elicit conditioned r_Rs with less stimulus generalization decrement). Amsel and Hancock (1957) did indeed find that the FE was larger when both A_1 and G_1 were white than when a black A_1 was used with a white G_1.

A related prediction is that, because the strength of r_R is a function of reinforcer magnitude in G_1, the size of the FE due to frustrative nonreinforcement should depend in part on reinforcer magnitude in G_1. To test this, Peckham and Amsel (1964) used a within-subjects design wherein two brightnesses (black or white) of A_1 were cues for either 8 or 2 pellets in G_1. With the usual FE measure (A_2 speed after G_1 nonreinforcement minus A_2 speed after G_1 reinforcement), they found reliably greater FEs after omission of 8 than omission of 2 pellets in G_1.

On the other hand, if G_1 food is reduced but not eliminated on test trials, speed in A_2 is inversely related to the amount just eaten in G_1 (Barrett, Peysey, & McHose, 1965; McHose & Ludvigson, 1965). A drive-reduction interpretation of this situation would lead to the prediction that hunger and A_2 speed would be reduced in proportion to the amount of food ingested in G_1. Such a drive-reduction hypothesis could not account for the FE observed with complete reduction of reinforcer magnitude to zero on test trials (Wagner, 1959; Peckham & Amsel, 1964). However, McHose and Ludvigson suggested that the drive-reduction hypothesis most readily fits their data on incomplete reduction of reinforcer magnitude to above zero values. McHose and his colleagues (1965) note that there is room for doubt that Bower's (1962) findings demonstrate

the FE is graded in proportion to the extent of reduction in reinforcer magnitude. Although A_2 response vigor was proportional to the extent that an initially large amount of food in G_1 was subsequently reduced, this may be due in part to depression of A_2 performance in proportion to the amount of food ingested in G_1. Appropriate controls are required to distinguish between the FE genuinely attributable to frustrative reinforcer-magnitude reduction in G_1 and the effects of reinforcer magnitude in G_1 on A_2 performance without reinforcer magnitude shifts, and therefore presumably without any reason for an assumption of an R_F.

Marx (1956) suggested that the FE can be accounted for by a strictly associative interpretation. For example, Marx referred to a pilot study of rats reared in overcrowded social cages in which it may be assumed that competitive behavior was probably differentially reinforced. A later test for frustration seemed to indicate that increased vigor (supposedly as in the FE) was at least in part due to transfer from prior learning to react to frustration with more vigorous responses. Amsel and Penick (1962) extended this investigation to include three experimental variables: litter size, conditioned activity or inactivity, and inaccessible food (shielded by a wire cover). Tests for the FE in the double runway did not support the hypothesis that prior learning to respond vigorously would transfer to this situation in the form of larger FEs. Instead, the inaccessible food initially tended to elicit a variety of responses directed at obtaining the food (such as biting and clawing through the screen), and these responses interfered with the FE. In other words, this study found that the FE could be *reduced* associatively by specific competing responses, but it apparently failed to find any evidence that the FE was increased by the particular associative variables investigated in this experiment.

It seems reasonable to conclude that the FE by itself is not definitive evidence for the view that frustrative nonreinforcement is a primary source of generalized drive, although the use of additional response measures besides runway performance and bar pressing might improve the argument for generalized drive. Particular requirements for the further elucidation of frustrative nonreinforcement might include a more adequate description of the various R_Fs, their sensory and associative effects, and further tests with a variety of responses to assess whether a particular R_F qualifies as a source of generalized drive or as a source of a more restricted energizer which enhances only some subset of responses.

More direct tests have been made of conditioned frustration as a secondary source of drive. For example, Wagner (1963) has shown that a CS paired with frustrative nonreinforcement fulfilled two criteria for the identification of a motivational variable: its presence temporarily enhanced a startle response and its offset reinforced hurdle responses. Replication and extension of this research would be especially valuable because it has apparently provided the most direct test of basic assumptions concerning the properties of a CS linked with frustrative nonreinforcement.

Recently, Wagner (1966) has reviewed evidence for the view that nonreinforcement and punishment often have similar effects, although their over-all effects are not necessarily identical. For example, approach responses have been reduced by punishing electrical shocks and by frustrative nonreinforcement, and alcohol reversed both these effects. In another study, training to approach a goal box in the presence of conditioned fear subsequently transfered when approach was tested in the presence of conditioned frustration, and vice versa. Such evidence supports the view that when a CS has been linked with frustrative nonreinforcement, the CS is reacted to as an aversive stimulus (that is, in some ways the CS has become comparable to electrical shock). Therefore, we might tentatively conclude that a CS linked with frustrative nonreinforcement represents an aversive condition which has fulfilled at least two of the criteria for identification of a motivational variable.

Response-defined Level of Drive

Brown (1961, pp. 35–40) considers four objective ways to define drive which avoid circular "explanations" of behavior. Two of these refer respectively to antecedent conditions (such as deprivation times) and stimulus conditions (such as strength of electrical shock used as UCS), both of which presumably can and should be manipulable independently of the dependent variable they allegedly influence. The third class of objective definitions are organismic and/or physiological measures (such as body weight deficit, blood sugar level, hormonal level, or heart rate); some of the physiological measures in this third category are classifiable as responses. Fourthly, a behavioral response measured in one situation can be used as an index of drive in other situations provided at least one of the criteria for a motivational variable can be fulfilled. Examples of possible response-defined indices of motivational level are amount of food consumed, over-all general activity as seen in a stabilimeter, activity wheel measures, or the score on a standardized paper and pencil test such as Taylor's manifest anxiety scale (Brown, 1961, pp. 253–263). In considering the relative merits of these four ways of "defining" drive within contemporary drive theory, we should recall that needs and drive must be distinguished, that associative explanations of "motivational effects" must always be considered as possible alternatives to alleged motivational ones, and that a significant definition of a source of drive requires satisfying at least one of the criteria for motivational variables. Brown and Farber (1968) note, for example, that muscle tension may be a useful measure in drive research, provided it can meet the motivational criteria, even when the stimuli eliciting muscle tension cannot be precisely specified. Brown (1961, pp. 238–239) defends the principle of response-defined drive levels, including the selection of subjects on the basis of test scores. He concludes (p. 239): "No one can predict, at present, which of the many varieties of each method will ultimately yield the most useful and significant estimate of drive, nor whether one of the methods will ultimately prove to be better than the other."

CONSUMMATORY ACTIVITY AS AN INDEX OF DRIVE

Although deprivation procedures have been used extensively and effectively "to motivate" laboratory animals to some unknown degree ("low" or "high") in a wide range of psychological experiments during past decades, the precise quantification of deprivation-produced generalized drive has continued to be difficult to achieve. On the assumption that generalized drive energizes all responses, we may seek quantitative descriptions of how dependent variables such as consummatory and instrumental responses are related to the independent variable of degree of deprivation. Any consistent pattern in such studies may permit one to infer how the alleged energizer of these responses, generalized drive, increases with degree of deprivation. With this purpose in mind, consummatory measures will be discussed here; the next two sections will be devoted to general activity and instrumental responses.

Definition and Measurement of Degree of Deprivation

Before we examine consummatory activities as a function of degree of deprivation, we must first consider how to define and measure the degree of deprivation. Deprivation time (hours of food or water deprivation) has frequently been used as an operational measure of the degree of deprivation, with the intensity of the deprivation-produced drive level being inferred from deprivation time. The extensive use of deprivation time to produce various drive levels may be largely attributed to its apparent simplicity and ease of use, but in part it is due to the influence of Hull (1943, 1952) and Spence (1956), since many experiments have been performed to

investigate their theoretical formulations. However, there also is good evidence for the view that relative body-weight loss may provide a better index of degree of either caloric or water deprivation (Stolurow, 1951; Ehrenfreund, 1959; see review by Bolles, 1967).

Physiological approaches to the determinants of food intake have tended to emphasize the homeostatic regulation of caloric intake in relation to energy expenditures (Anand, 1961; Grossman, 1967). In support of such an energy balance, Anand (1961) observed that, even when energy outputs vary greatly, most adults maintain a constant weight, and young animals "grow at well-defined rates." The inference was made that food intake varies in accordance with caloric requirements, and "that two types of regulation are at work. The first, and most important, is the short-term regulation, which adjusts from day to day the calories eaten to calories spent. The second, long-term and working slowly, corrects over a period of time whatever error of which the rapid mechanism is guilty" (p. 692). In the study of Adolph (1947), for example, when nonnutritive roughage was mixed with food, rats increased the total bulk eaten, whereas the utilizable nutrients consumed did not exceed the control values.

From this view of the regulation of food intake in terms of energy balance, one might expect that the degree of any imposed caloric deprivation should be reflected in a body-weight deficit. Moreover, many variables which influence metabolic rate, and therefore energy expenditures, would presumably be reflected in the observed body-weight deficit. Hence, differences in body weight, age, sex, and environmental conditions (such as temperature, humidity) which influence energy expenditures (Kleiber, 1961) may confound the interpretation of X hours of food or water deprivation. For example, with the same food-deprivation times, the percentage weight loss of young rats will be much greater than that of more mature animals (Campbell,

Teghtsoonian, & Williams, 1961). Similarly, to produce any given percent weight deficit requires longer deprivation periods for older animals (Bolles, 1965b), and the effects of water-deprivation times on relative weight deficits vary with age (Campbell & Cicala, 1962).

Bolles (1965b) found that the percentage weight loss was a linear function of food-deprivation time when both were plotted in log units. Groups of different ages had power functions with similar slopes but, as noted above, the same deprivation time produced markedly different relative weight losses for the various ages. On the basis of these results one might expect that, under standard conditions, the percentage weight deficits may be estimated from deprivation times. This may often be difficult to do for published studies, however, which vary significantly in species, strains, age of subjects, and in the experimental conditions. In the present context, the essential point is that consummatory responses, general activity, and instrumental responses may be found to be more consistently and precisely related to relative body-weight deficits than to deprivation times. It is in this sense of providing a more concise

and coherent description of the behavioral data that the relative body-weight deficit may be considered as the more useful index of the degree of deprivation and of the magnitude of the deprivation-produced drive.

Consummatory Measures as a Function of Degree of Deprivation

Water deprivation Siegel (1947) found that the water intake of male rats increased monotonically as a function of hours of water deprivation up to 48 hr (Figure 18.4), although the 5-min water intakes were not reliably different for 24 and 48 hr deprivation. Siegel also noted that percentage body-weight deficit was a rising monotonic function of hours of water deprivation, and that water intake increased monotonically with size of percentage weight loss.

A wider range of water deprivations were studied by Stellar and Hill (1952) with an electronic drinkometer that provided cumu-

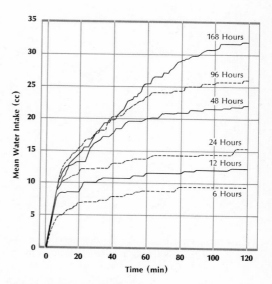

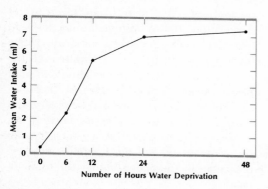

Figure 18.4. Mean 5-min water intake in milliliters as a function of water-deprivation times. Separate subgroups of rats were tested once at 6, 12, 24, or 48 hr of deprivation. Five-minute water intakes after 24 and 48 hr of deprivation were not reliably different. (Siegel, 1947.)

Figure 18.5. Mean cumulative water intake throughout 2 hr of 4 rats tested under each of the water deprivation times. Total water intake for 120 min increased monotonically with hours of water deprivation: 6 (lowest curve), 12, 24, 48, 96, and 168 (highest curve). (Stellar & Hill, 1952.)

lative curves of the temporal course of drinking during the 2-hr test period. Four 5-month-old male rats were habituated for a month to the living situation and then underwent an increasing series of water deprivations, each of which was separated by a period of *ad libitum* feeding and drinking until recovery from any previous weight deficit. The mean water intake during the 2-hr test was an increasing monotonic function of deprivation between 6 and 168 hr of water deprivation (Figure 18.5). Stellar and Hill (1952) also reported that regardless of deprivation times, the rat either does not drink or drinks at a constant rate of 6 or 7 tongue laps per sec (cf. Keehn & Arnold, 1960; Schaeffer & Premack, 1961; Collier, 1964). (The constancy of drinking rate is not seen in Figure 18.5 because the momentary intakes of four rats were averaged before plotting.) For dep-

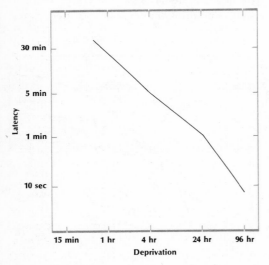

Figure 18.6. Median latency to start drinking water for naively thirsty rats (that is, upon initial deprivation) when tested after water deprivations of 4, 24, and 96 hr. The lowest "deprivation" time is the time to start drinking water in the test situation after removal from the *ad libitum* conditions in the home cage (that is, without an experimentally imposed deprivation). Note that both deprivation times and drinking latencies are on logarithmic scales. (Modified from Bolles, 1962.)

rivation periods of more than 6 hr, fairly constant drinking occurred for at least 5 min; after longer periods of drinking, the frequency and the duration of pauses distinguished the effects of varying degrees of deprivation. Hence, intake during a brief test period is unlikely to reflect differences among longer deprivation periods. On the other hand, readiness to drink in a novel situation does continue to increase over longer deprivation periods. For example, Bolles (1962) found that as deprivation times increased up to 96 hr, latencies to drink decreased proportionately without any evidence of inanition (Figure 18.6).

A somewhat different behavioral index of the severity of water deprivation is based on the observation that a rat's water intake can be reduced or completely suppressed by the addition of quinine hydrochloride, a substance which humans call "bitter." For example, after various hours of water deprivation, Campbell and Cicala (1962) measured the 24-hr consumption of 0.001M quinine solution by experimental subjects and water intake by equally deprived controls. They found that intake of the quinine solution was almost completely suppressed at zero weight loss. As the weight loss increased up to 30 percent, reflecting increasingly severe water deprivation, 0.001M quinine became less and less effective in suppressing drinking. A single inverse function represented quite well the averaged data based on weight deficits of 25-day-old rats water deprived for 0, 24, 48, or 72-hr and 100-day-old rats water deprived for 0, 24, 48, or 192 hr. (The implications for a concept of generalized drive of these studies on water intake will be discussed after the presentation of related studies of food intake.)

Food deprivation In one of the earlier experiments on food intake at different deprivation times, Bousfield and Elliott (1934) maintained rats for at least three weeks on a feeding schedule of daily access to a liberal supply of food between 9:30 A.M. and 10:30

A.M. Subsequently, they introduced delays in the feeding hour and they found that after 24- and 48-hr delays (that is, after 47 and 71 hr of food deprivation) the 1-hr food intake was approximately 86 and 74 percent, respectively, of the amount eaten after the regular 23-hr deprivation. Water was available at all times. After each delayed feeding, animals were returned to the regular 23-hr deprivation schedule for at least a week. Bousfield and Elliott suggested that changes in the stomach's tonicity reduced capacity after the longer deprivations. Measurements of eating rate demonstrated that at the longer deprivations (47 and 71 hr) the rats not only ate fewer pellets, but ate them more slowly, and "more steadily and persistently." In summary, Bousfield and Elliott found that when rats were maintained on a 23-hr food deprivation schedule, longer deprivation times and presumably greater body weight deficits were accompanied by significant reductions in rate of eating and amount consumed. Recently, Dufort (1964b) confirmed that 1-hr food intake is less after 47 or 71 than after 23 hr of food deprivation, even though these 6-month-old rats apparently never had any prior exposure to a 23-hr food-deprivation schedule. Thus, the decreased intake at the longer in-

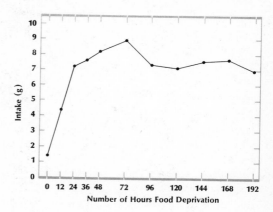

Figure 18.8. Mean 2-hr food intake for a separate group of 4 rats for each food-deprivation time tested. Each rat had no past history of deprivation and it was tested only once. (Dufort & Wright, 1962.)

tervals does not seem attributable to adaptation to a once-per-day feeding regimen.

On the average, food intake during test periods increases as deprivation time increases up to about 24 hr without food, for both highly experienced animals (Figure 18.7) and animals tested with but one deprivation condition (Figure 18.8).

In the later section on instrumental behavior we refer to Miller's (1956) comparison of several behavioral "measures" of hunger. The drinking curve in Figure 18.10 (p. 827) refers to intake of enriched milk until satiation and this measure can be properly considered here under food intake. The nonsignificant decrement from 30 to 54 hours of food deprivation is consistent with the above evidence that food intake (within 120 minutes) does not increase significantly for food deprivations beyond 24 hours. The same figure also shows that, in order to prevent eating, milk had to be adulterated with greater amounts of quinine at higher food-deprivation times.

A modified version of the "quinine measure" described by Miller (1956) was used in a study of food deprivation with 23- and 100-day-old rats (Williams & Campbell, 1961). They found that the quinine suppression of

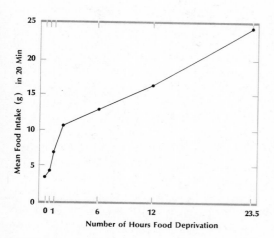

Figure 18.7. Mean 20-min food intake of the same group of rats tested at each of the food deprivation times. (Horenstein, 1951.)

milk intake was inversely proportional to percent weight loss (in other words, a constant concentration of quinine prevented milk intake to a lesser extent at higher deprivations). The functional relation of intake and percent weight loss was the same for both age groups.

The relation between latency to eat and food deprivation appears to be simpler and more orderly than some of the other measures considered. Bolles (1962) assigned separate groups of rats to 0, 4, 24, 72, and 96 hours of food deprivation. When latency to eat was plotted versus the independent variable of deprivation time on a log-log scale, the result was an inverse linear function. A power function was also found when latency to eat was plotted against percentage body-weight loss for male and female rats of different ages (Bolles, 1965b). For the pigeon as well, readiness to eat was found to be directly proportional to body-weight loss (Megibow & Zeigler, 1968).

Interactions of food and water deprivations Although there are important species differences, for man, rat, and some other species, food intake is reduced during water deprivation, and water intake is reduced during food deprivation. The extensive physiological literature and some of the psychological studies are discussed in Wolf's (1958) comprehensive treatment of thirst.

Verplanck and Hayes (1953) emphasized that, for learning experiments involving the summation of drive from food deprivation and from water deprivation or the discrimination between food and water deprivation, it is important to note that food and water deprivations are not independent. Their data supported the conclusion that water-deprived rats eat less food and food-deprived rats drink less water than when both food and water are freely available. As a result, body weight declines when either food or water intake is restricted (Dufort, 1963b), with the major portion of the weight deficit during water deprivation accounted for by the amount of

reduction in the intake of freely available food (Collier, 1964; see also Campbell, 1964).

For behavioral studies under standard laboratory conditions, weight deficits may continue to be one of the more useful indices of the degree of deprivation produced by withholding either food or water. Eventually it may be possible to calibrate weight deficits in terms of more fundamental physiological measures of deprivation severity and correlate these measures with consummatory activity (see, for example, Corbit, 1969).

Implications for generalized drive Do studies of food and water intake provide a satisfactory basis for inferring how the magnitude of drive varies with degree of deprivation? Differences between the various tests of ingestion, and between ingestion measures and latency scores, indicate that, on the basis of consummatory activity, we cannot construct even an ordinal scale of drive that would have general applicability (see Brown, 1961, p. 53, and Bolles, 1967, pp. 160–161). There thus is little evidence here for a concept of a unitary, generalized drive associated with food or with water deprivation.

Associative Influences on Consummatory Activity

Reinforcement of consummatory responses Would a consummatory activity such as eating extinguish in the sham feeding situation (see pp. 620, 627), if eating were not followed by primary reinforcement from need reduction? Such extinction apparently failed to occur in some of Pavlov's experiments (Rosenzweig, 1962). This apparent lack of extinction of sham feeding is in sharp contrast with the observations of Hull, Livingston, Rouse, and Barker (1951) in a pilot study with one dog. They found that the dog "ate" very large quantities of gruel during the first few days (three-quarters of its body weight per session). Consumption diminished to a few licks by the eighth day. This experimental extinction of eating was apparently associated with particular cues in the experimental room because outside the experimental room the dog sham fed again.

> At one point Pavlov had mentioned feeding his dogs meat, so perhaps differences in foods used might partly account for the contrast in results. Eating responses might be reinforced by taste as well as by need reduction. It is not clear that one can rule out the possibility that eating may have been intermittently reinforced for Pavlov's dogs by having sham feeding associated with the absorption of food which had been placed directly into the stomach via the other esophageal fistula (analogous to the effect reported by Smith & Capretta [1956] on saccharin)

The fact that the extinction of sham eating was apparently specific to cues in the experimental room could be interpreted as indicating that either the punishment resulting from occasional clogging of the upper fistula and resultant retching and gagging, or the lack of positive reinforcement from drive reduction, could have become associated with particular experimental cues. If either of these interpretations were confirmed, it would illustrate associative effects modifying eating.

Premack (1965) has demonstrated that the consummatory activities of eating and drinking can be reinforced by other activities. For example, access to a pinball machine was made contingent on the prior consumption of candy by children who preferred playing with a pinball machine to eating candy. Under these conditions Premack (1959) found that the increased intake of candy was significantly greater than in a control group with the reverse contingency. In another experiment (Premack, 1962), rats' water drinking was markedly augmented when limited access to an activity wheel was made contingent on prior drinking responses. It appears reasonable to conclude from such observations that at least some aspects of consummatory activities are modifiable by reinforcement.

Effects of taste on consummatory measures Some degrees of sweetness enhance intake measures, but the effect interacts with caloric deprivation. Food-deprived rats consume much more nonnutritive saccharin solution than nondeprived controls (Sheffield & Roby, 1950), and similarly, the intake of a diet with saccharin added is much greater for food-deprived than for nondeprived dogs (Jacobs & Sharman, 1969). It appears that the degree of enhancement of intake by saccharin interacts with the degree of food deprivation.

Quinine (presumably because of its bitter taste) depresses intake measures, and again there is an interaction with deprivation. For rats, intake of food or water adulterated with quinine is proportional to the degree of deprivation (Williams & Campbell, 1961; Campbell & Cicala, 1962). For dogs, on the other hand, food deprivation seems to increase reactions to quinine (Jacobs & Sharma, 1969).

Taste properties of a high-fat diet can enhance the rat's food intake as well. Rats had a higher caloric intake and gained weight at a greater rate on a high-fat diet than on laboratory chow pellets. When the pellet diet was matched for caloric density with a mineral oil diet which had the taste properties of the high-fat diet, again the caloric intake was greater for mineral oil than pellets. These taste effects were accentuated and quite large in rats with obesity resulting from lesions in the ventromedial hypothalamus (Corbit & Stellar, 1964). In this context, it may be interesting to note that obese humans ate larger amounts of high-quality ice cream and smaller amounts of low-quality ice cream than subjects who were either of normal weight or underweight (Schachter, 1968).

Since the effects of taste on consummatory responses are large under some conditions, and since they interact with other variables (such as deprivation, obesity, or novelty) in a complex manner, a single general statement about the magnitude of the effect of taste on consummatory measures cannot be made: it depends on the test conditions.

Practice effects and "adaptation" to deprivation schedules The main question considered here is whether specific degrees of deprivation produce particular internal deprivation stimuli that selectively form associations with specific consummatory responses.

> Our analysis is made more difficult by the fact that there are at least three types of confounding influences which might produce increased consummatory responding after repeated periodic deprivations without involving more and/or stronger associations between internal deprivation stimuli and the consummatory behavior. Briefly, these factors are: (a) cumulative weight deficits produced by repeated periodic deprivations; (b) waning of "novelty reactions" (Bindra, 1959b, 1961) that interfere with consummatory responding in unfamiliar situations; and (c) conditioning of consummatory responses, instrumental approach responses, or central excitatory states to stimuli in the test situation. In this latter case, it seems plausible that reinforcer-linked CSs might elicit central drive states without the mediation of overt behavioral responses, in the same way that CSs acquire reinforcer-linked properties when animals are physically restrained (Bindra & Palfai, 1967) or immobilized by curare (Solomon & Turner, 1962).

A number of studies of "adaptation" to repeated deprivations were directly or indirectly influenced by Hebb (1949), who demonstrated that rats used only a small fraction of the available eating time when first tested after 24 or 48 hr of deprivation. Hebb argued that, in part, the animals had to learn when to eat and when to cease eating, and that need for food and the stimuli from the food were not sufficient to produce entirely appropriate eating behavior.

These observations have been extended and confirmed in subsequent experiments (for example, Ghent, 1951, 1957; Bolles & Rapp, 1965). If the procedure of depriving and testing is continued, rats typically increase their intakes to the point where, with one feeding a day, they are able to maintain stable body weights. Such adaptation to 23-hr food-deprivation routines requires about 2 weeks (Reid & Finger, 1955; Lawrence & Mason, 1956; Dufort, 1964b); with 47- or 71-hr schedules, however, rats fail to stabilize their weights (Dufort, 1964b). With water deprivation, on the other hand, rats do achieve stable body weights when maintained on 23-, 47-, or 71-hr

deprivation schedules. The usual interpretation of these experiments is that drive is increasing up to the point where body weight stabilizes. Hence, experiments using food or water deprivation usually maintain the animals on the deprivation schedule until weights stabilize before introducing the main treatment.

A direct test of the view that consummatory responses, such as eating and drinking, are partially under control of previously experienced external stimuli is provided by Fink and Patton (1953). Rats were trained to drink in the presence of one intensity level of sound, light, and tactual stimulation respectively, and then various degrees of stimulus change were introduced by changing the intensity level in 1, 2, or 3 modalities. A balanced design was employed wherein some subjects were shifted from a high to a low intensity level and other subjects had the reverse order. A significant decrement in drinking resulted which was proportional to the degree of stimulus change (that is, changes in 1, 2, or 3 modalities). Decrements in drinking were largest for light changes and smallest for tactual changes. The overall results are consistent with the view that particular stimuli in the drinking situation became water- or reinforcer-linked CSs which facilitated drinking, and that subsequent decrements in drinking presumably reflected the loss of some stimuli which were reinforcer-linked CSs. Since there were no changes in the burette used for the tube-drinking response, or in its location, the rats presumably "knew" where the water spout was. (A possibility which does require further analysis is that the changes in stimulation produced so-called novelty reactions which interfered with drinking.)

> Note that associative influences on consummatory measures may mask some of the effects of degree of deprivation. For example, in the experiment of Stellar and Hill (1952), each rat's water intake was measured in the individual home cage under all the deprivations. Moreover, each rat had been housed, fed, and watered there

for a month before the deprivations were initiated. At the end of a month, interference with drinking by novelty reactions should have been negligible, and the acquired effects of water-linked conditioned stimuli in the experiment should have been strong enough to facilitate prompt and persistent drinking, at least during the initial minutes of the 2-hour test; this would tend to reduce any differences in 5-minute water intakes among the various deprivation times, since species such as rats cannot drink enough in 5 minutes to correct their water deficit completely. We should also note Collier's (1964) point that when the 2-hour water intake data of Stellar and Hill are re-plotted on log-log coordinates, the intake is linearly related to the deprivation time. Apparently a 2-hour water intake measure is meaningfully related to the degree of deprivation whereas the 5-minute intakes may be distorted to some extent by associative influences.

Up to this point we have considered evidence for two principal kinds of associative effects on consummatory activities that may be attributed to *external* stimuli in the test situation. First, performance of the consummatory response in the test situation permits external stimuli to become reinforcer-linked CSs. Later, these CSs may tend to elicit the consummatory response or to facilitate or enhance the subsequent occurrence of the consummatory response. Second, even in the absence of the consummatory response, exposure to the test situation may result in a decrement in novelty reactions as the situation becomes more familiar, and subsequently there may be less interference with the consummatory response.

We can now recapitulate the reasons for the view that so-called "adaptation" to periodic deprivations does *not* provide unambiguous evidence that *internal* deprivation stimuli ($S_{MV}s$) have acquired some degree of associative control of behavior. When rats have been maintained on a 22- or 23-hr food-deprivation schedule, it has been found that food intake usually increases across days.

Although it is clearly a digression from our main question, we will cite several studies on "adaptation" to deprivation schedules because they have practical implications for the design of

experiments wherein drive is alleged to be constant when the deprivation times are constant. Certain studies report that it may take about two weeks for the rat's food intake and body weight to stabilize on a 23-hr food-deprivation schedule (Lawrence & Mason, 1955b; Reid & Finger, 1955; Dufort, 1964b). Apparently the rat fails to stabilize its body weight when it is maintained on 47- or 71-hr food-deprivation schedules (Dufort, 1964b).

In the case of water deprivation, rats maintained on 23-, 47-, and 71- hr deprivations have, after initial weight losses of varying severity, reached a point where their weight was relatively constant (Dufort, 1963a, 1964a). Beck (1962) found that when the days of water deprivation were separated by recovery days, increments in drinking across deprivation cycles did not occur. He attributed the absence of the increased water intake across deprivation cycles to the absence of a cumulative water deficit. Reid and Finger (1955) noted that, contrary to the constancy of drive level that has been assumed for 23 hr of food deprivation, the daily variations in body weight deficit before body weight is stabilized presumably reveal daily variations in the strength of drive. Ehrenfreund (1960) described a weight control apparatus whereby the rat's food supply is precisely regulated by the rat's weight. In this way one can maintain constant the percentage weight deficit, and presumably the amount of drive due to food deprivation. Due to shifting cumulative weight deficits and the acquired associative effects of external stimuli, the cited studies of "adaptation" to deprivation schedules cannot be interpreted unequivocally as evidence that the rat is learning to discriminate the presence or degree of deprivation, or that learning is occurring in the form of the internal deprivation stimuli ($S_{MV}s$) becoming associated with eating.

Sometimes increments in food and/or water intake have been interpreted as evidence that the rat learned to associate *internal* deprivation stimuli with consummatory responses which terminate the deprivation ($S_{MV}s$ became CSs for consummatory responses). We have emphasized that the unequivocal interpretation of such studies has been hindered by at least three confounding variables, and we have presented evidence that these three variables influence consummatory responses. These factors are, first, when rats are maintained on a 23-hr food-deprivation schedule for several days, the presence of an increasing cumulative weight deficit can preclude the unequivocal interpretation of any alleged signs of learning to eat promptly, persistently, and larger quantities of food. Other complications are that, with repeated feedings in the test situation, the effects of *external* stimuli can confound tests of the alleged effects of hypothesized *internal* deprivation or satiation stimuli (for example, external stimuli associated with food and eating may become reinforcer-linked CSs which enhance eating, and decrements in novelty reactions to external stimuli may result in more eating).

After adaptation to one feeding a day, rats eat *less* if tested after deprivation periods longer than 24 hr (Bousfield & Elliot, 1934; Lawrence & Mason, 1955a). But they also eat less at 47 and 71 hr of deprivation the first time they are exposed to such treatment (Dufort, 1964b). On the other hand, if the animals are exposed to deprivations that are

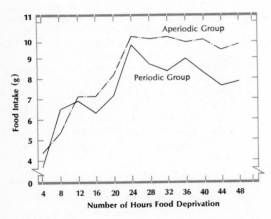

Figure 18.9. Three-hour food intake as a function of hours of food deprivation. Periodic Group (solid curve) had been maintained on a regular 24-hr feeding schedule and its food intake decreased in tests which followed deprivations in excess of 24 hr. Aperiodic Group (dot-dash curve) had been exposed to deprivations of 4 to 48 hr, in random sequences, and its food intake remained essentially constant on test trials after deprivations between 24 and 48 hr. (Modified from Lawrence & Mason, 1955a.)

varied randomly between 4 and 48 hr, a higher food intake at the longer interval will be maintained (Figure 18.9). Apparently it is adaptation to a once-a-day feeding and its relation to the daily rhythms of the organism that makes the intake at 24 hr greater than at other deprivation intervals (see Bolles & deLorge, 1962; Bolles & Stokes, 1965).

Moll's (1964) experiment, with cumulative percentage weight deficits effectively controlled, demonstrated reliable practice effects. Rats of three age groups (33, 63, and 93 days) were maintained at a constant percentage of their satiated weight, derived from estimations of anticipated growth. Half of the subjects were maintained at 80 and the other half at 90 percent normal body weight. Practice over 15 days in a new situation had highly significant over-all effects resulting in shorter latencies to eat, more time spent eating, larger amounts eaten, and faster eating rates in a 5-min test. Since the percentage body weight deficit was held constant, this study appears to provide excellent support for the hypothesis that measures of consummatory activity can show improvement with practice which cannot be attributed to an increasing percentage weight deficit. Again, these data do not prove that *internal* deprivation stimuli became increasingly associated with eating: it is also possible that *external* stimuli developed progressively as reinforcer-linked CSs which elicited or facilitated eating, and decrements in novelty reactions to external stimuli may have permitted increments in measures of eating.

Recently, the study of Williams (1968) provides additional evidence that food intake increases with practice in a new test situation in the absence of a rising cumulative percentage weight deficit. In her first experiment, rats were food-deprived for 21 hours on every fifth day for a series of seven completed cycles. *Ad libitum* food was available the rest of the time and water was always available in the home cage. The subjects were normally fed Purina laboratory pellets in the home cage and they were tested with sweetened milk in a test cage. More milk was consumed during the 3-hour test period on deprived than on nondeprived control days. Moreover, a practice effect was observed: intake of sweetened milk during the 3-hour test period increased across days for both the deprived and nondeprived conditions considered separately. In Williams' (1968) second experiment, the time in the test cage was reduced to two hours, so in this case the deprivation every fifth day was 22 hours. Fourteen deprivation cycles were employed, which extended a little over two months. The 2-hour intakes of sweetened milk increased across days for both the deprived rats and the nondeprived control subjects, but, as expected, the deprived rats had a larger milk intake than controls.

"GENERAL ACTIVITY" AS AN INDEX OF DRIVE

Concept and Measurement of "General Activity"

The effects of deprivation states on "general activity" were studied before the development of formal drive theory. It seemed reasonable, from a common-sense point of view, that increased behavioral activity due to hunger would have survival value and help to perpetuate the species because, in a natural environment, heightened activity would supposedly increase the chances that a hungry animal would find food. Accordingly, mechanisms might have been inherited whereby food deprivation per se would be expected to enhance locomotion and exploratory activities.

Alternatively, one might assume that strong internal and external stimuli have similar drive properties, and that these evoke vigorous activity, so that during starvation strong internal deprivation stimuli would innately evoke vigorous activity (see Miller & Dollard, 1941; Miller, 1959).

All of us have observed that most organisms seem to be engaged in a continuous sequence or stream of behavioral activities.

Many of these activities are species-specific activities, and ethologists have emphasized the desirability of becoming familiar with the complete repertoire of "naturally" or "normally" occurring behavioral activities of a species.

It is obviously important for experimental psychologists to consider the extent to which recording techniques may influence or modify the behavioral activities being studied. One must also consider whether the observational technique accurately represents the behavioral activities or whether, in some incompletely specified way, the recording device emphasizes some behavioral activities at the expense of neglecting others. The design of suitable devices to record a wide assortment of activities, in other words, involves serious methodological problems if one is to avoid a completely arbitrary or capricious assignment of importance to different individual acts.

Several different designs of stabilimeters have permitted automatic recording of behavioral activities of freely moving animals (Reed, 1947; Munn, 1950; Baumeister, Hawkins, & Cromwell, 1964). The total activity recorded in this way might be unchanged at times when important changes in the patterns of activity have occurred, and there may be artifactual changes in apparent activity level because recording devices can more readily detect and record some activities than others. For these reasons, the expression "random activity" appears to be a misnomer in the sense that, if used descriptively, it implies that the behavioral activities are occurring in random sequences, a factual question for which the usual tracings or counts of stabilimeter activity have not provided objective answers. Similarly, if "general activity" is interpreted in a literal descriptive sense, one would expect different "valid" measures of general activity to be positively and significantly intercorrelated; this has not been the case (Reed, 1947; Baumeister et al., 1964). For example, Bolles (1959) tested adult male rats in six different situations (open-field apparatus, feeding-drinking box, elevated runway, alley runway, home cages, and stabilimeter cages) and found that correlations and other analyses revealed a lack of generality across situations (see also Campbell et al., 1966; and review by Reed,

1947). What seem to be needed, at this point, are careful detailed analyses of the specific components of "general activity" (Bindra, 1961; Hinde, 1966).

Associative Influences on Activity Measures

External stimuli "evoke" stabilimeter activity Campbell and Sheffield (1953) tested the effects of food deprivation on stabilimeter activity under conditions designed to minimize variations in environmental stimuli. The cages were in a soundproofed cabinet within a soundproofed room and in the dark except when lights within the cabinet were turned on. A controlled 10-minute stimulus change was introduced at noon which consisted of turning the cabinet lights on and the exhaust fan, with its continual hum, off. Stabilimeter activity was significantly higher during the period of changed stimulation than during the preceding 10 min. This effect was reliably present before food deprivation was initiated; when continuous food deprivation was initiated, the 10-min activity scores during altered stimulation increased across 3 days, while the activity scores during the 10-min period preceding the stimulus change were apparently unaffected by the presence or absence of food deprivation. In other words, experimentally controlled changes in external stimulation produced large and significant changes in stabilimeter activity of food-sated rats, and this effect was markedly enhanced by food deprivation, but there was little evidence that food deprivation per se caused increased activity.

More recent experiments (for example, Teghtsoonian & Campbell, 1960) also seem to indicate that any effect internal deprivation stimuli may have in goading adult rats into activity is at most a minor one and probably not even detectable in a controlled stabilimeter environment until there has been extended and continuous food deprivation.

Campbell, Teghtsoonian, and Williams (1961) studied the effects of continuous food deprivation on rats of four age groups: 23, 38,

54, and 100 days old at the start of the experiment. Stabilimeter activity increased markedly for the younger rats (23, 38, and 54 days old) but scarcely at all for 100-day rats.

In a parallel experiment with continuous water deprivation (Campbell & Cicala, 1962), at no time was there any appreciable increase in stabilimeter activity. On the basis of such observations, we are led to discount any theory which assumes that organismic needs lead directly to increased activity. Furthermore, if the concepts of general drive and drive stimuli are to be applied meaningfully, some explanation is required for the different effects of food and water deprivation on the stabilimeter activity of young rats.

External stimuli: reinforcer-linked CS effects on stabilimeter activity The amount of stabilimeter activity of hungry rats that occurs in response to environmental change depends on whether the environmental change and stabilimeter activity are paired with *food* (Sheffield & Campbell, 1954). For experimental subjects, a 5-min stimulus change was followed by presentation of the daily food ration; their total activity for the 5-min stimulus-change period increased across daily trials (as in the so-called conventional learning curve). For control subjects, the termination of the 5-min stimulus change was not immediately followed by the presentation of food, and their total activity for the 5-min stimulus-change period decreased over the 12 days studied. Thus food deprivation interacted with stimulus conditions and reinforcement contingencies to increase stabilimeter activity markedly for the experimental group and to decrease it for the control group.

In extensions of the Sheffield and Campbell (1954) experiment, Amsel and Work (1961) and Amsel, Work, and Pennick (1962) included additional groups which were fed on only half of the stimulus-change trials in order to permit observation of the development of any effects attributable to frustrative nonfeeding. They confirmed the main findings of Sheffield and Campbell (1954), and also found some activity increments associated with nonfeeding when it was introduced after extensive prior experience with a food-paired stimulus.

Although Bindra and Palfai (1967) did not study stabilimeter activity, their inclusion here may serve to clarify some of the reinforcer-linked CS effects on behavior, including stabilimeter activity measures. They placed water-deprived rats in a restraining cage, and during the conditioning procedure, a 15-min auditory CS+ was paired with water delivery during the terminal 1 second of the CS+; a CS— was paired with electric shock applied through electrodes attached to the hind limbs, and CS_0 was not paired with either shock or water. Subsequent tests revealed that CS+ increased "exploratory perambulation" and the CS— increased "motionless sitting," relative to control conditions. In part because specific responses which compose "exploratory perambulation" could not have been conditioned in the restraining cage, they suggested that the reinforcer-linked conditioned stimuli induce positive and negative drive states which (p. 297) ". . . raise the level of motor readiness, presumably by increasing the excitability of the response system."

Further observations on the "threshold of behavioral arousal" have been provided by Bolles and Younger (1967), who presented a series of ascending intensities of "high frequency white noise" to individually-housed rats, while an observer recorded which subjects responded to it. Startle, disruption of on-going behavior, and orienting or exploratory behavior were all simply scored as a response. In one of their experiments, median thresholds (derived from the decibel level of auditory stimulation required for behavioral arousal) were not reliably different between 8 nondeprived controls and 8 experimental subjects during 7 days of continuous food deprivation which resulted in a weight deficit of 30 percent or more. In another experiment, control and experimental subjects differed only before a regularly scheduled feeding, when food-deprived subjects had reliably lower thresholds for behavioral arousal (that

is, weaker auditory stimuli were effective). These data, therefore, do not support any hypotheses that food deprivation is in itself sufficient to lower sensory or response thresholds. However, 30 min before a regularly scheduled feeding and presumably in the presence of incentive motivation (that is, food-linked CS effects), weaker auditory stimuli were more effective in eliciting behavioral arousal in experimental subjects with a slight weight deficit than in controls fed *ad libitum*. Since the half-second test noise had not been paired with food, it would appear that in the presence of incentive motivation rats were more responsive even to a "neutral" test noise of low intensity.

Running in activity wheels This activity measure has been found to vary with the severity of food deprivation, at least for rats, hamsters, and guinea pigs. Before we attempt to evaluate the significance of such data for the concept of drive as a general energizer, we will first consider several possible sources of reinforcement which apparently influence the running of rats in activity wheels.

Finger, Reid, and Weasner (1960) investigated the effects of food as a reinforcer on running in an activity wheel. Controls were in the activity wheel for an hour, and then were placed in a delay chamber for an hour without food or water; their running did not reveal any systematic trend across 30 test days. Experimental rats were taken from the activity wheel and returned at once to their home cages and food. The experimental group showed an approximately fourfold increase in 1-hr running scores across the 30 test days. Clearly, if running in an activity wheel is followed by food, there is enhancement of running.

It should also be recalled (see pp. 623–624) that running in an activity wheel can serve to reinforce other instrumental and consummatory responses (Premack, 1962, 1965), and vice versa. Such effects may greatly confound experiments using activity wheels, and at the very least, they indicate that running cannot be used as an uncomplicated index of deprivation.

Thermo-regulatory mechanisms have been implicated as a possible source of reinforcement for running in activity wheels during starvation. Stevenson and Rixon (1957) proposed that running in the activity wheel involves vigorous skeletal activity which in food-deprived rats contributes to maintaining body temperature. They found that running in activity wheels was greater in food-deprived than sated rats, and that the extent to which activity scores were enhanced by food deprivation was inversely proportional to the environmental temperature.

Campbell and Lynch (1968) made continuous subdermal temperature recordings while rats were in either stabilimeter or modified activity-wheel cages, under *ad libitum* feeding or food or water deprivation. When observed in the activity-wheel cages, body temperatures decreased sooner during food than during water deprivation. Conversely, in stabilimeters, body temperatures dropped (contrary to Stevenson & Rixon, 1957) sooner and more during water than during food deprivation. Activity in the wheel and in the stabilimeter increased more markedly during hunger than during thirst. In another experiment, running in cool activity wheels increased quite similarly during food or water deprivation, even though an adjacent heated compartment was readily accessible through small swinging doors. In spite of the very similar running scores, time spent in the heated compartment increased markedly throughout terminal food deprivation but it decreased during terminal water deprivation. In agreement with these results is the finding reported by Smith, Satinoff, and Rozin (1967) that, relative to controls, food-deprived rats still ran more in activity wheels even when they were able to obtain warmth easily by pressing a bar. Such results indicate clearly that the rat's increased running in activity wheels as a function of food deprivation cannot be attributed solely to the need to raise body temperatures to a normal level.

Activity Measures as a Function of Deprivation

Most of the data on running in activity wheels as a function of body-weight deficits appear to be consistent with the view that,

for rats at least, running is the dominant response in the activity wheel and that running scores increase as a function of body-weight deficit because the dominant response is being increasingly energized as the drive level rises. Inanition is not a helpful concept in this context, over most of the useful working range of degrees of food and water deprivations for rats as subjects. In stabilimeter-type apparatuses, on the other hand, when variations in external stimuli are minimized, food- or water-deprived rats are performing passive forms of behavior (such as lying) most of the time, and these do not contribute to raising stabilimeter activity levels. More importantly for drive theory, there are few active responses to be increasingly energized as deprivation progresses and drive allegedly rises. Such gross apparatus effects must be kept in mind when deprivation effects are discussed.

Inherited individual and species differences in activity Rundquist (1933) used activity wheel scores to identify active and inactive rats, and by selective breeding successfully separated and maintained active and inactive strains.

Campbell, Smith, Misanin, and Jaynes (1966) studied stabilimeter activity during continuous deprivation (either food or water) of chicks, rabbits, guinea pigs, and hamsters; they also studied the effects of continuous deprivation (either food or water) on running in activity wheels by guinea pigs and hamsters. Their results reveal marked differences attributable to differences in measuring devices (stabilimeter versus activity wheel), type of deprivation (food or water), species, and perhaps age. Such data pose serious difficulties for anyone who still maintains that deprivations produce generalized drive which necessarily increases "general activity" (see also DeVito & Smith, 1959; Glickman & Hartz, 1964).

Estrus and activity cycles If sexual hormones are considered to determine the amount of drive of sexual origin, then the estrus cycles of mature female rats should be accompanied by corresponding cyclical variations in drive. Wang (1923) found that, in the absence of male rats, the amount of running in the activity wheel did vary cyclically in close correspondence with the estrus cycles. Such cycles in amount of running in activity wheels were absent in female rats before sexual maturity and after ovariectomy. Finger (1961) found similar cyclical variations in activity; he measured running in activity wheels and the number of interruptions of a light beam in a stationary cage. Although the periodicities of these activity cycles were of the same magnitude as estrus cycles, apparently tests for consistent phase relations between the estrus and activity cycles were not made. Bolles (1963a) used sexual receptivity to determine cycle phase, and a time-sampling procedure to observe home-cage behavior, which was classified in one of these categories: "sleeping, lying, grooming, sniffing, eating, drinking, locomotion, rearing, or manipulating objects." There was no correlation between these activity scores and sexual receptivity. We are therefore left with the conclusion that estrus does not increase behavior in an indiscriminate manner, as sometimes seems to have been implied by earlier writers.

Over-all Conclusions on "General Activity" as an Index of Drive

Our primary objective has been to see whether studies of so-called "general activity" reveal any consistent relation between activity measures and degree of deprivation, because this could tell us how drive varies with degree of deprivation. Hullian drive theory specifies that, over an extended range of deprivation times, effective drive (that is, drive minus inanition) should be a curvilinear or inverted-U function of deprivation times. Thus a dominant response measure energized by effective drive should tend to be curvilinearly related to deprivation times as well.

An explicit estimate of how inanition varies with deprivation time has been made for rats by Yamaguchi (1951); inanition reportedly increases exponentially with deprivation time so that the resultant effective drive increases during food deprivation up to about 60 hours and thereafter effective drive decreases as food deprivation continues.

Data on running in activity wheels indicate clearly that rats increase the amount of running progressively and monotonically during continued starvation, up to a very severe degree of deprivation. This may be an indication that, for adult rats, there is no appreciable inanition during relatively prolonged continuous food deprivation. It could also mean that rats can respond vigorously in spite of inanition, and this would account for the fact that during starvation rats succumb sooner in activity wheels than in stabilimeter cages. If the latter hypothesis were correct, we would have to know when, and under what conditions, the hypothesized inanition will be reflected in behavior. Obviously inanition should not be invoked in a post hoc manner only to "explain" curvilinear relations between behavioral measures and degree of deprivation, without explaining as well how it is that some responses increase monotonically over the same range of deprivations.

Another problem for a drive interpretation of functional relations between activity measures and degree of deprivation is that the effects of drive may be confounded by the effects of drive stimuli as continuous food or water deprivation progresses. It appears one can safely conclude that for adult rats, in the absence of food and food-linked CSs, internal drive stimuli defined in relation to deprivation time do not readily acquire associative "control" of running in activity wheels, nor of whatever responses are being recorded in stabilimeters.

With regard to the question whether internal drive stimuli instigate activity, the acceptance or rejection of this hypothesis appears to depend on an individual's theoretical bias as to what will be the most fruitful way of viewing and integrating data from various experiments. Nowadays, the more significant problem appears to be one of understanding the different patterns of activity that result from differences in age, species, type of deprivation (food or water), and apparatus (stabilimeter or activity wheel). These differences in results are not easily reconcilable with assigning an important role to internal drive stimuli as instigators of activity in young subjects.

Finally, the available data on "general activity" do not demonstrate unequivocally *the* rate of increase of effective drive as a function of deprivation times or body weight deficits, nor do these data reveal unambiguously over what range of deprivation times or weight deficits effective drive can be assumed to increase.

INSTRUMENTAL ACTIVITY AS A FUNCTION OF DEPRIVATION

Deprivation Effects on Instrumental Responses During Extinction

Analysis of the effect of food deprivation time on an instrumental response during the extinction procedure would appear to be of special interest because food no longer follows the instrumental response. The results obtained are not likely to represent a pure deprivation effect, however, because the associative strength of the incentive motivation (food-linked CS effects) acquired on the previously reinforced trials presumably is present at the start of the extinction procedure and supposedly decreases progressively at some unknown rate during extinction. Moreover, if a response has been reinforced on a continuous reinforcement schedule (for example, with each bar press reinforced with a pellet of food), and if this is followed by the extinction procedure, we may have satisfied the conditions for frustrative nonreinforcement, which some view as a source of a general energizer.

Degree of food deprivation has a significant over-all effect on the persistence of instrumental responding during the extinction procedure. For example, Perin (1942) trained rats to press a bar by reinforcing each of 16 bar presses with one pellet of food. This training took place at 23 hr of food deprivation. After the next daily feeding, extinction tests were conducted. Resistance to extinction was

tested at 1, 3, 16, and 23 hr of food deprivation, with a separate group of 40 subjects for each deprivation state. Number of responses to meet the extinction criterion (no responses within a 5-min period) was an increasing monotonic function of hours of food deprivation. Hull's (1943) formulation, which relates behavior to $_sH_R \times D$, was in part based on these data. It is also true, however, that resistance to extinction was greatest when the hours of deprivation were the same during training and extinction (that is, 23 hr), and progressively less as the deprivation during extinction became increasingly different from that during training. Thus the results might, at least in part, be attributed to the response decrement expected from a generalization gradient.

Saltzman and Koch (1948) explored the range of low intensities of food deprivation and concluded that resistance to extinction dropped off more rapidly than predicted from extrapolation of Perin's (1942) results. Yamaguchi (1951) investigated deprivation times up to 72 hr, and found that increments in food deprivation beyond 24 hr had little if any additional effect on resistance to extinction.

Deprivation Effects on Reinforced Instrumental Responses

Heron and Skinner (1937) observed the number of bar presses in daily 1-hour tests where only the first response after every fourth minute was reinforced with food. This provided a daily food ration of about 0.7 grams of Purina dog chow (water was always available). On the average, rate of bar pressing increased in an approximately linear fashion during the initial 5 days of deprivation, and then decreased slightly on the sixth day. However, the peak rate of bar pressing occurred as late as on the eleventh day of testing for 2 rats and on the thirteenth day for 1 rat.

Stolurow (1951) found that rats kept at 70 percent of their *ad libitum* body weights penetrated a barrier to obtain food faster than a group kept at 80 percent of their *ad libitum* weights. A shift of body weight from 80 to 70

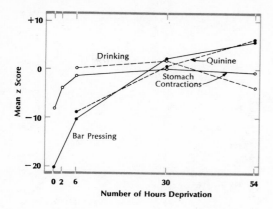

Figure 18.10. These curves illustrate the lack of agreement among 4 potential response indices of hunger as a function of hours of food deprivation. The z or standard scores were "derived from the average within-test-condition variability" for the 6, 30, and 54 hr of deprivation. Maximal mean differences within any response measure between 6 and 54 hr of deprivation were less than 2 standard deviations. Bar pressing (●—●) on a variable-interval reinforcement schedule and amount of quinine (●--●) adulteration required to stop drinking milk increased monotonically up to 54 hr deprivation; stomach contractions (○—○) changed very little between 6 and 54 hr; drinking milk (○---○) increased slightly from 6 to 30 and decreased from 30 to 54 hr deprivation. (Modified from Miller, 1956.)

percent was accompanied by a significant improvement in performance on the barrier penetration test. However, rats tested at 60 percent body weight tended to resemble more closely 80 percent body weight group than the 70 percent group. There is a suggestion, therefore, that performance on the barrier penetration test was optimal at 70 percent of *ad libitum* body weights.

Miller (1956) has compared various consummatory and instrumental activities as measures of so-called hunger (Figure 18.10), and they clearly diverge from each other to some extent. Bar pressing for food on a variable-interval reinforcement schedule apparently increased monotonically up to 54 hr of

food deprivation in an intrasubject comparison.

Data on running in mazes and activity wheels are somewhat similar, for rats at least, in the sense that amount of running per unit time tends to increase with deprivation times (food or water) for the initial 72 hr. King (1959, cited by Kimble, 1961) found that the mean time required to traverse a runway decreased monotonically for food deprivations of 2, 24, 48, and 72 hr respectively (independent groups of rats tested at each deprivation). The results were essentially similar regardless of whether or not competing responses were included for deprivations of 24 to 72 hr (see Figure 13.5 in Kimble, 1961). Granger, Ducharme, and Bélanger (1969) have likewise found that runway speeds increased during water deprivation, without any signs of a decrement in speed for continuous deprivations up to 72 hr.

In marked contrast to the above results, bar pressing has been found to be curvilinearly related to the duration of continuous

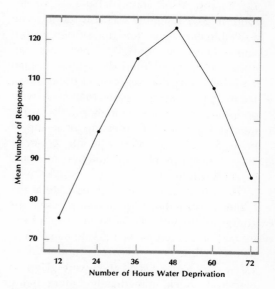

Figure 18.11. Number of bar presses for water on a continuous reinforcement schedule in a 5-min test as a function of the hours of water deprivation. Each rat was tested at each deprivation in an ascending order. (Bélanger & Feldman, 1962).

deprivation when every bar press is reinforced ("continuous reinforcement" or crf schedule).

Bélanger and his colleagues have performed a series of studies designed to investigate systematically the effects of a wide range of deprivation intensities on bar pressing on a crf schedule. In order to ensure a steady rate of responding Bélanger and Feldman (1962) began with a 20-day training period in which 24-hr water-deprived rats bar pressed for water on a crf schedule. Next, prior to the main part of their experiment, they tested the rats under several different durations of a continuous water deprivation so as to provide the rats with exposure to varying degrees of water deprivation, and with the opportunity to adapt to the deprivation and testing procedures. Throughout the experiment, the subjects had free access to water for three or four days after every deprivation condition in order to prevent any cumulative deficits over the series of deprivations. Rate of bar pressing for water was a curvilinear function of hours of water deprivation; the average peak rate of bar pressing occurred at 48 hours of water deprivation (Figure 18.11).

In a similar study with different durations of continuous food deprivation (0, 6, 12, 18, 24, 36, and 48 hr), rate of bar pressing for food on a crf schedule was also found to be a reliable curvilinear function of deprivation times (Dufresne, 1961). The peak rate occurred at 18 hr of food deprivation, which is much sooner than with water deprivation. These data indicate clearly that even with performance of the seemingly simple instrumental response of bar pressing for an appropriate reinforcer on a crf schedule, performance is not a monotonic function of hours of deprivation.

Does the decrease in response rate at the higher deprivation levels indicate inanition? To test this hypothesis, rats were adapted and trained (as in the Bélanger & Feldman experiment) to bar press for water under 23 hr water deprivation. Then they were given an electrical shock immediately before being placed into the Skinner box (Ducharme & Bélanger, 1961). When given in this way, the electrical shock may be expected to raise the drive level without there being any opportunity for the electrical shock itself, as a stimu-

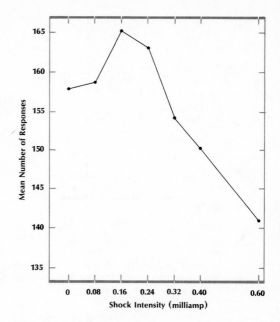

Figure 18.12. Mean number of bar presses for water on a continuous reinforcement schedule in a 6-min test as a function of prior shock intensity in milliamperes. Each rat was water deprived for 23 hr and tested at each shock intensity in an ascending order, given one shock per day on separate days. (Modified from Ducharme & Bélanger, 1961.)

lus, to become associated with stimulus features in the Skinner box. In other words, the use of shock before placement into the Skinner box was intended to prevent any stimuli within the Skinner box from acquiring conditioned aversive properties because of the shock. Intra-individual comparisons were made for several different shock intensities. A single shock was given each day, and the seven intensities of shock were given in an ascending series over seven days. Rate of bar pressing for water on a crf schedule was a curvilinear function of shock intensity, and reliably different from any possible linear fit (Figure 18.12). In this case, the rats were deprived of water for only 23 hr, and inanition appears to be effectively ruled out. These data are also relevant to the question of how an instrumental response is influenced by the alleged summation of generalized drive from multiple sources. A weak shock should elevate the drive level slightly, and on the basis of Figure 18.11 it is reasonable to predict that, at 23-hr water deprivation, a prior weak shock would raise the rate of bar pressing for water, as it did (Figure 18.12). Similarly, on the basis of Figure 18.11, we can see how a strong shock would raise the combined drive level at 23-hr water deprivation in excess of the optimal level, and rate of bar pressing for water would decrease, as it did (Figure 18.12). These effects of shock (that is, the reliable curvilinear function between shock intensity and rate of bar pressing for water) cannot be accounted for by merely assuming that shock as an aversive stimulus tended to elicit responses incompatible with bar pressing for water. Ducharme and Bélanger (1961) predicted their result from the hypothesis that there is an optimal level of drive or arousal for this instrumental response.

In a second experiment, rats did not show the decrement in rate of bar pressing for food be-

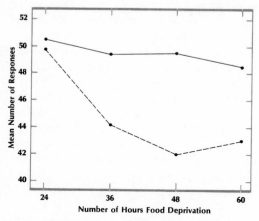

Figure 18.13. Effect of meprobamate on the mean number of bar presses for food on a continuous reinforcement schedule in a 5-min test as a function of hours of food deprivation. A significant response decrement between 24 and 60 hr of food deprivation was present in placebo-treated controls (dashed line) and in untreated controls (not shown here), but not in the meprobamate-treated experimental subjects (solid line). (Modified from Dufresne, 1961.)

tween 24 and 60 hr of food deprivation when they were given meprobamate, a relaxant of the skeletal musculature (Figure 18.13); a control group, given a placebo, essentially replicated the earlier finding of a decrement in rate of bar pressing for food between 24 and 60 hr of food deprivation. The superior performance with meprobamate appears to rule out inanition as the essential cause of a response decrement during 24–60 hr of food deprivation.

Another feature of this series of experiments is especially relevant to an assessment of reinforcer-linked CS effects on instrumental activity. For this reason we will refer briefly, at this point, to some data on heart rate as an indicant of arousal level. It has been found that the function between heart rate and hours of deprivation apparently depends on situational cues (Ducharme, 1966b). In Figure 18.16, we see that for experimental subjects trained to bar press for water, heart rate was linearly related to hours of water deprivation (up to 72 hr) while they were bar pressing for water. An approximately similar monotonic function between heart rate and deprivation time was obtained for these trained subjects in their home cage, but their heart rates were reliably lower (the attachment of recording electrodes in the home cage may have provided some stimuli which in the Skinner box had become water-linked CSs). Controls were not trained to bar press for water and their heart rates were unrelated to hours of water deprivation, up to 72 hr. In other words, heart rate as an indicant of arousal level did not automatically increase with degree of deprivation; instead, the effect of deprivation depended on an interaction between deprivation and appropriate cues. (that is, water-linked CSs).

Some of the relations observed between instrumental responses and degree of deprivation have been curvilinear functions, which would be predicted from the so-called "Yerkes-Dodson Law." Yerkes and Dodson (1908) varied both difficulty of a brightness discrimination and intensity of shock used to punish incorrect responses. Their results are consistent with the view that as the difficulty of the discrimination increased, the optimal shock intensity for acquisition of the discrimination approached a lower limiting value. It has been claimed (for example, Brown, 1965) that other interpretations of these data are possible for a variety of reasons, but especially because a factorial design was not used and there were too few subjects (2 to 4 mice) per group.

Broadhurst (1957) provided further evidence that task difficulty is one of the parameters to consider when studying the relation between discrimination learning and drive level. Rats were deprived of air for varying durations and then forced to swim underwater. Next, rats were trained to make a brightness discrimination in order to obtain access to air. Separate groups were tested at 0, 2, 4, and 8 sec of air deprivation. In the acquisition of the brightness discrimination, there was a reliable interaction between air deprivation time and difficulty of the brightness discrimination for accuracy. Performance on the difficult brightness discrimination showed best acquisition at 2 sec and poorest acquisition at 8 sec air deprivation, whereas the easy and moderately difficult discriminations were poorest at 0 sec and generally equally superior throughout 2 to 8 sec of air deprivation. These data, therefore, provide evidence for an optimal duration of air deprivation during the acquisition of a difficult discrimination, but there is no statistically adequate evidence in these data for an optimal drive level for acquisition of discriminations of easy or moderate difficulty. At present, the "Yerkes-Dodson Law" remains a plausible but relatively unexplored generalization.

Associative Effects of Internal Deprivation Stimuli on Instrumental Responses

To the extent that instrumental responses become associated with specific internal deprivation stimuli, any shift in degree of deprivation should produce at least a slightly different set of internal deprivation stimuli and, therefore, a response decrement due to the generalization gradient. Thus any response decrement produced by a shift from a higher to a lower deprivation level may theoretically be attributable to a lower drive level and/or a shift in drive stimuli. However, a shift from a lower to a higher deprivation level would theoretically have two opposing potential effects: increased drive should

energize the instrumental response to a greater extent and make it stronger, whereas a shift in deprivational stimuli should produce a response decrement. The study of Hillman, Hunter, and Kimble (1953), referred to earlier in our illustrations of motivational effects, provides an example of data which are in accord with an emphasis on the drive concept: a change from 2 to 22 hr of water deprivation resulted in running times within two trials as short as those for rats maintained on 22 hr deprivation throughout the experiment (Figure 18.1).

In one of the most extensive studies of this topic, Yamaguchi (1952) trained rats to move a manipulandum leftward for food. A shutter made the manipulandum accessible only in discrete trials and a response latency was measured. In a factorial design, 5 groups of rats (195 in all) were trained at 3, 12, 24, 48, or 72 hr and tested at 3, 24, 48, or 72 hr of food deprivation. For the most part, the group differences in median latencies were relatively small. However, a shift in deprivation time from training to testing resulted in a response decrement (that is, longer median latency) in 14 out of 15 comparisons of group medians, when comparisons were made among groups tested at the same deprivation time (and therefore the effects of drive stimuli were never obscured by any test effects attributable to increased energization by heightened drive).

These results thus suggest that there may be associative effects attributable to internal deprivation stimuli, but at best the effect appears to be small.

Although Birch, Burnstein, and Clark (1958), with a single group of subjects, observed generalization decrements in food-trough depression responses when continuous food-deprivation extended beyond the hours of deprivation used during training, this result is most likely due to the food-trough responses undergoing extinction. Brown and Belloni (1963) tested separate groups at 5 different deprivation times and they found no evidence of generalization decrements in food-trough responses for continuous deprivation times in excess of the training deprivation time of 22 hr. They were also unable to replicate the finding by Birch et al. (1958) of generalization decrements in running speeds, although both studies employed separate groups at different deprivation times to test for this effect. Bolles (1961) found generalization decrements following maintenance on a 24-hr diurnal feeding schedule, but not for a 29-hr a-diurnal schedule. Significantly fewer bar presses for food were observed in tests at 19 and 29 than at 24 hr of food deprivation for rats trained and maintained on the 24-hr feeding schedule. Another group, trained and maintained on the a-diurnal 29-hr feeding schedule, had the largest number of bar presses at 34 hr, and fewer bar presses at 29 than at 24 hr of food deprivation.

Thus the various studies we have considered on generalization decrements attributable to shifts in hypothetical internal deprivation stimuli have revealed that a shift in duration of deprivation from training to test trials has typically resulted in either no significant generalization decrements, or in decrements of relatively small magnitudes. When other than 24-hr diurnal cycles are used during training and maintenance, it has been especially difficult to identify any experimental situation that can yield replicable evidence for generalization decrements. It therefore would seem that considerable reservations are in order concerning any theory which assigns *major* importance to alleged associative effects of hypothetical internal deprivation and satiation stimuli.

AROUSAL LEVEL = GENERAL DRIVE?

Concept and Measurement of Arousal

For at least three decades several kinds of physiological data appeared to be suggestive of a factor that has been variously called degree of excitation, energy mobilization, activation, and arousal. These terms have at times been used interchangeably; they generally refer to measures that in varying degrees may be indicative of the organism's overall level of physiological activation or excitation. Some of the physiological data that led to arousal-type formulations consisted of recordings of autonomic activity and skeletal

muscle tension (in the form of electromyographic, or EMG, potentials) in experiments with human subjects (see, for example, Lindsley, 1951; Woodworth & Schlosberg, 1954; Malmo, 1958; Duffy, 1962).

Electroencephalograms (EEGs) have provided an important part of the data relevant to arousal theories; these data are recordings of electroencephalic potentials ("brain waves") from the scalp and from the exposed cortex. (In recent years, electrical recordings have been used extensively to study subcortical areas of the brain as well.) A frequently used index of arousal is the amplitude of the alpha rhythm (approximately 10 Hz), which is maximal in the relaxed, awake human adult with eyes closed, but whose amplitude and incidence both decrease if the subject *either* becomes excited (when lower amplitude, faster rhythms predominate) or becomes drowsy (when lower amplitude, slightly slower rhythms may temporarily predominate, to be followed by slower waves of higher amplitude as the subject falls asleep). Since the EEGs from different cortical areas usually can be categorized within the same stage of sleep–wakefulness, this suggests that there is some diffusely acting mechanism which serves to maintain the cortex as a whole at the relatively same over-all level of excitation.

Pivotal importance of general activation In the late 1940s neurophysiological research seemed to reveal brain structures capable of functioning as a general activating mechanism. Lindsley (1951) proposed an activation theory of emotion which was highly influential in suggesting to many psychologists that the then contemporary neurophysiological research on diffusely activating mechanisms in the central nervous system was highly relevant to research and theories on a wide range of behavioral phenomena. His own summary of the theory is as follows (Lindsley, 1951, p. 505):

The theory rests mainly upon the following points, which are supported by experimental evidence:

1. The electroencephalogram in emotion presents an "activation pattern," characterized by reduction or abolition of synchronized (alpha) rhythms and the induction of low-amplitude fast activity.

2. The activation pattern in the EEG can be reproduced by electrical stimulation of the brainstem reticular formation extending forward into the basal diencephalon through which its influence projects to the thalamus and cortex.

3. Destruction of the basal diencephalon, i.e., the rostral end of the brain-stem activating mechanism, abolishes activation of the EEG and permits restoration of synchronized rhythmic discharges in thalamus and cortex.

4. The behavioral picture associated with point 3 is the antithesis of emotional excitement or arousal, namely, apathy, lethargy, somnolence, catalepsy, hypokinesis, etc.

5. The mechanism of the basal diencephalon and lower brain-stem reticular formation, which discharges to motor outflows and causes the objective features of emotional expression, is either identical with or overlaps the EEG activating mechanism, described under point 2, which arouses the cortex.

Lindsley (1952, 1957, 1960) suggested that changes in EEGs and in behavioral efficiency could be related to changes in a continuum which ran from sleep to wakefulness to strong excitement. These speculative formulations posit an inverted-U relation between behavioral efficiency and the behavioral continuum of sleep, wakefulness, and strong excitement. For example, behavioral efficiency is reportedly poor ("lack of control, freezing up, disorganized") at the "strong, excited emotion" end of the behavioral continuum; EEGs consist of desynchronized activity of relatively low voltage and fast frequencies (incidence of alpha is minimal). Behavioral efficiency is relatively good for intermediate segments of the behavioral continuum: during alert attentiveness when EEGs consist mainly of low voltage tracings with less activity above alpha frequencies than occurs during extreme excitement; and during relaxed wakefulness when alpha activity tends to be maximal in incidence and voltage. The next lower level of activation is drowsiness, when EEGs are of lower voltage, with a lower incidence of alpha, and occasional waves slower than alpha may be seen; behavioral efficiency is said to be poor, due to lack of sequential timing and coordination. As we progress to-

wards deep sleep, large slow waves predominate in the EEGs and behavioral efficiency is absent. This seems to say, essentially, that behavioral efficiency is poor or absent at or near both ends of the dimension (sleep and extreme excitement) and behavioral efficiency is good over the not-too-well defined middle segment of the sleep-wakefulness-excitement dimension. Some of the same data and ideas on activating mechanisms are discussed with regard to motivation in Lindsley (1957), and with regard to perception in Lindsley (1958).

Hebb (1955, 1966) pointed out that afferent fibers of the primary sensory pathways apparently have collateral branches which terminate in the reticular formation. He assumed that such collaterals (or an equivalent mechanism) function to provide a general background of tonic excitation without cue properties or steering functions: a general excitation which can facilitate various response tendencies, much as general drive is supposed to do. In fact, Hebb (1955) suggested that arousal level in this sense is the physiological equivalent of the behavioral concept of general drive. In spite of this similarity between the concepts of drive and general arousal level, Hebb's position differs from general drive theory in assuming that there exists an optimal arousal level for performance efficiency. At very high levels of arousal, performance is supposedly impaired, and a decrease in arousal level should result in improved performance; at very low arousal levels, performance is also poor, and improvement of performance should be facilitated by increased arousal. This hypothesis of an optimal arousal level should be distinguished from the general drive view that, provided competing response tendencies do not increase disproportionately, performance of the dominant response tendency simply increases as a function of increasing drive level (up to where inanition allegedly prevents further monotonic increases in effective drive, when food or water deprivation is the source of drive).

Malmo (1957, 1958, 1959, 1962) has argued

for the use of a variety of physiological indicants of a general energizer which may be called general drive or arousal level or activation level. These indices include peripheral physiological response measures, such as skeletal muscle potentials, skin conductance, and heart rate, in addition to more direct measures of activity in the central nervous system. Malmo (1958, p. 250) emphasized that behavioral "general activity" did not appear to be a "promising measure of drive," and proposed that physiological indicants can contribute importantly to the unsolved problem of measuring drive level. Lacey (1967) provides a recent critique of the use of peripheral physiological indices of a single general arousal level in situations where either inter-individual or intra-individual comparisons are made, in studies of prolonged tonic reactions as well as brief or phasic changes in arousal level. Malmo and Bélanger (1967) include an assessment of Lacey's (1967) comments. They acknowledge instances of apparent disassociation or even negative correlations among indices of brief or phasic arousal reactions. They claim, nevertheless, that there is substantial empirical support for the use of physiological indices of general arousal level (that is, tonic rather than phasic arousal).

Theoretical construct of arousal level
Arousal level, as a general energizer, is a theoretical construct and its alleged level at any time is inferred from objective data rather than observed directly. Arousal level in this sense might be viewed as the theoretical net result in the central nervous system of all activity in excitatory and inhibitory neural circuits or systems. Viewed this way, arousal level becomes a statistical conceptual device, and the various physiological measures, such as EEGs, muscle potentials, heart rate, blood pressure, and skin conductance, are seen not as actual measures of arousal level, but only as indicants of the arousal level (see, for example, Stevens, 1951, on the distinction between measures and indicants).

Since physiological indicants of arousal level involve response mechanisms, a distinction between phasic and tonic responses is relevant. A phasic response refers to the situation where a stimulus evokes a physiological response with a more or less characteristically short latency and the response is of relatively short duration (a fraction of a second, up to perhaps a few seconds). On the other hand, a tonic physiological response is one that may persist for several minutes or longer (see, for example, Sharpless & Jasper, 1956). Physiological indicants of arousal level are importantly influenced by tonic arousal reactions and, accordingly, stimulation and associative variables are important considerations in the evaluation of physiological indicants of arousal level.

The physiological indicants of arousal level have the same conceptual status as other response indices of states of the organism. The response status of a physiological indicant of arousal level is especially clear when the indicant is skeletal muscle tension, as represented by electrical recordings of muscle potentials from a group of muscle fibers, or from one or more muscles with electrodes placed on the skin. For example, muscle potentials have been observed to increase progressively during mirror tracing. Such rising gradients occurred reliably not only in muscles of the active arm, but in muscles of the passive arm and elsewhere as well. This might be taken to be suggestive of general activation, but it was noted that muscle loci and individual differences of subjects both contributed significantly to the variance in slope of muscle potential gradients (Bartoshuk, 1955). In addition, although the slopes of gradients in active arm flexors and extensors were significantly intercorrelated, the slopes of active arm gradients were not reliably correlated with the slopes of gradients in the passive arm. This necessarily means that these measures of muscle potentials were importantly influenced by other variables (possibly associative ones) in addition to the possible contribution of a general energizer. Moreover, rising muscle potential gradients have occurred in the absence of any gradients in simultaneously recorded and integrated EEGs (Bartoshuk, 1956; Malmo, 1965). This apparently means that a localized increase in muscle potentials does not necessarily indicate a rise in general arousal level, to the extent that EEGs are acceptable as indicants of general arousal level.

The response status of physiological indicants of arousal level must also be considered when the physiological measures used are autonomic measures (such as skin conductance, blood pressure, or heart rate) and EEG measures. We are not referring here to brief, phasic responses but sustained tonic ones. For example, in an experiment on auditory thresholds, there were both intrasession and interday progressive decreases in skin conductance levels (Duffy & Lacey, 1946). These data are consistent with the view that skin conductance was elevated initially by a tonic response to the general test situation, and that skin conductance decreased as the female undergraduate subjects "adapted" to the general test situation. Systolic blood pressures were significantly higher for psychoneurotics in an experimental situation before the experiment had started than in a familiar ward setting, presumably because of a tonic reaction to the general test situation. Control subjects revealed a progressive decline in systolic blood pressures throughout the experimental session (Malmo, Shagass, & Heslam, 1951). Heart rates have remained significantly elevated in human newborns one minute after a brief, relatively intense auditory stimulus (Bartoshuk, 1962b). Electrical recordings of cortical activity in sleeping cats revealed prolonged, sustained activation patterns after a novel auditory stimulus of intermediate intensity was presented (Sharpless & Jasper, 1956). Similarly, sustained EEG reactions to brief auditory stimulation can be observed in humans (Bartoshuk, 1959), and in some instances the auditory stimulus can change an EEG characteristic of drowsiness (low voltage with occasional waves slower than alpha) into an EEG characteristic of relaxed wakefulness (continuous alpha activity of relatively high amplitude). This series of examples illustrates some of the evidence which reveals the response status of physiological measures used as indicants of arousal level.

To recapitulate, we have referred to some of the evidence and theorizing concerning neural mechanisms that might serve as a general energizer and to their potentially important implications for drive theory. We have also given reasons for our view that any single physiological measure is at best an imperfect indicant of a hypothetical arousal level; such a measure may nevertheless be useful to the extent that it qualifies as a motivational variable.

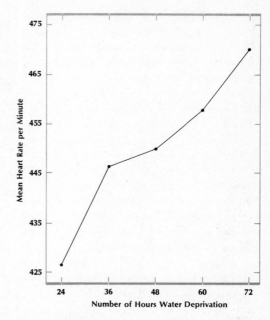

Figure 18.14. Mean heart rate per minute as a function of hours of water deprivation. Heart rates were recorded while rats were bar pressing for water on a continuous reinforcement schedule. (Bélanger & Feldman, 1962.)

Effects of Traditional Motivational Variables on Arousal

To start with, we will review a number of experiments which have varied food or water deprivation or shock intensity parametrically over a wide range and which report the effect that these traditional examples of an empirical motivational variable had on an assumed indicant of arousal level (which allegedly is equivalent to general drive). Then we will look at some effects of thirst on reflex spinal excitability and of deprivation on EEGs.

Thirst, hunger, and electrical shock effects on heart rate   Bélanger and Feldman (1962) found a significant linear relation between heart rate and hours of water deprivation up to the 72 hr tested (Figure 18.14). The rat's heart rate was recorded while it bar pressed for water on a continuous reinforcement (crf) schedule, on which each bar press was reinforced with a drop of water. Since the number of bar presses was a curvilinear function of deprivation time (Figure 18.11), with the peak number of bar presses at 48-hr deprivation, the increase in heart rate beyond 48-hr deprivation occurred in spite of the decreasing number of bar presses. Dufresne (1961) found that the rat's heart rate during bar pressing for food on a crf schedule increased monotonically with food deprivation times up to the maximum tested of 48 hr in her first experiment. Heart rates went up somewhat irregularly between the 24 and 60 hr of food deprivation studied in her second experiment, and the curves were virtually identical for the meprobamate-treated and placebo groups, respectively (her figure is reproduced in Malmo and Bélanger, 1967). Ducharme and Bélanger (1961) recorded the heart rate of rats in a Skinner box during bar pressing for water on a crf schedule at 23-hr water depriva-

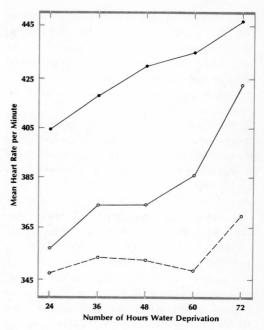

Figure 18.16. Mean heart rate as a function of hours of water deprivation and water-linked conditioned stimuli as incentive-motivational stimuli. Heart rates increased as a function of deprivation times for experimental subjects (solid line) while bar pressing for water (●) in a Skinner box and in the home cage (○). Controls (dashed line) had not been trained to bar press for water and their heart rates in the home cage were not related to the deprivation times shown here. (Modified from Ducharme, 1966b.)

tion, and they found that heart rate increased as an approximately linear function of milliamperes of shock intensity given to the rat immediately before its placement into the Skinner box (Figure 18.15). In all these studies the relation between heart rate and number of bar presses is a curvilinear one, and so the heart rate changes cannot be attributed simply to the physical work required to press a bar. In fact, Ducharme (1966a) found that, with the lever either in or out, heart rate increased linearly as a function of increasing water-deprivation times between 24 and 72 hr for rats trained to bar press for water in the Skinner box. The slopes of the two curves were similar, but heart rates were ac-

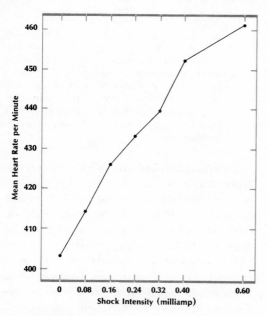

Figure 18.15. Mean heart rate per minute as a function of prior shock intensity in milliamperes. Heart rates were recorded while 23-hr water-deprived rats were bar pressing for water on a continuous reinforcement schedule, after a single shock. (Modified from Ducharme & Bélanger, 1961.)

tually higher when the retractable lever was out than when it was accessible. (Of course, in all these experiments, we are left with the possibility that the animals are active even though not pressing the bar, and that such activity is responsible for at least a part of the heart rate changes.)

Evidence for the importance of incentive-motivational stimuli appears to be provided by Ducharme's (1966b) data. Heart rates were higher in the Skinner box and lower in the home cage, and in both locations heart rates increased as a function of hours of water deprivation when the same rats, trained to bar press for water, were tested under both conditions (Figure 18.16). This shows that bar pressing or ingestion of water are not essential for the increments in heart rate as a function of water-deprivation times. A separate control group, which had not been trained to bar press for water, did not have any significant changes in heart rate associated with water-deprivation times up to 72 hr. In the latter case, presumably the electrodes for recording heart rate had not been associated with water as a reinforcer, and apparently in the absence of reinforcer-linked conditioned stimuli (in this case, water-linked CSs), continued water deprivation up to 72 hr was not in itself sufficient to result in reliable progressive increments in heart rate. In other words, the observations of approximately monotonically rising functions relating heart rates to hours of water deprivation apparently have been dependent on the presence of incentive-motivational stimuli in the form of water-linked CSs.

Research in other laboratories provides at least partial support for the pattern of results noted in the preceding paragraph. Hahn, Stern, and McDonald (1962), and Hahn, Stern, and Fehr (1964) found heart rate to be a linear, and performance a curvilinear, function of increasing hours of water deprivation. With extended practice on a partial reinforcement schedule, rates of bar pressing were stable within sessions and heart rates reflected deprivation levels only after the sessions had been in progress for at least 25 min (Doerr & Hokanson, 1968). Such

stability is probably what we should expect after training of this type.

Moller (1963) reported that heart rate was a significantly decreasing monotonic function of continuous food-deprivation time, when recordings were made in a constant environment while rats were behaviorally inactive (that is, apparently in the absence of food-linked CSs as incentive-motivational stimuli). Similar results from recordings in home cages were found by Doerr and Hokanson (1968).

Eisman (1966) found that 48 hrs of water deprivation ". . . under relatively constant environmental stimulation, in the absence of prior conditioning, has no systematic effect on HR in Ss never previously deprived." He also replicated the finding that heart rates were not related to different deprivation times per se, and he found significant positive increments in heart rates during drinking. Eisman (1966, p. 75) concluded with some additional highly relevant observations in his discussion:

> It has been found that when a signal (CS) precedes drinking (US), it quickly acquires the capacity to elicit a tachycardic response (CR) which is always greater than the simple response elicited directly by US. Furthermore, the magnitude of the CR is positively related to the deprivation conditions under which it is elicited, yielding a function compatible with the linear function under discussion.

Dehydration effects on spinal reflex excitability Observations that intracarotid injections of hypertonic saline increase spinal reflex excitability in rats (Wayner, 1964) are consistent with viewing this method of producing dehydration (and "thirst") as an empirical motivational variable (that is, as a method whereby drive can be increased). Intracarotid injections of hypertonic saline resulted in markedly increased amplitude of the monosynaptic reflex discharge recorded from the fifth lumbar ventral root of the rat's spinal cord. The increased spinal excitability has been observed for as long as 25 min, and was reportedly reversed by the injection of distilled water (Wayner, 1964).

There do not appear to be any observations

on whether spinal reflex excitability would be enhanced or depressed by a food-linked CS in food-deprived animals (recall the quotation from Sherrington, p. 796), or by water-linked CS in water-deprived animals. However, observations that food-linked conditioned stimuli reduce the magnitude of startle responses to probe stimuli (p. 808) suggest that such CSs would have tranquilizing effects, with consequent decrements in spinal excitability. Such observations might provide a useful means of analyzing reinforcer-linked stimuli.

Deprivation and satiation effects on EEGs
Electroencephalograms during food and/or water deprivations are apparently characterized by what has been called an "activation pattern" of low voltage, fast activity, as compared to the higher amplitude, slow waves of at least one phase of sleep. Any such effects of food and/or water deprivation on EEGs, however, should be considered in relation to the behavioral evidence that during food or water deprivation there is an increased responsiveness to external stimuli in general, and especially to food- or water-linked CSs, and that thwarting (frustrative nonreinforcement) may produce arousal reactions. We will consider how food- or water-linked CSs influence the background EEG activity of appropriately deprived animals, and whether food- or water-linked CSs may be considered as activators and/or deactivators.

To explore EEG activity in thirsty rats (dehydrated by either 23.5 hr of water deprivation or by stomach loads of hypertonic saline), cortical and subcortical activity were sampled in each rat (Steiner, 1962). Although electrode placements in the anterior and posterior cortex, septum, and hypothalamus, in general accord with an activation view, revealed relatively less slow wave activity during the water deprivation than the water-sated condition, interpretation of these EEG data is made difficult by interactions among electrode loci, EEG frequencies, and the thirst-satiation conditions. Furthermore, it is difficult to determine the extent to which interactions among the

thirst conditions, external stimulation in general, water-linked conditioned stimuli as incentive-motivational stimuli, and frustrative nonreinforcement influenced the EEG records.

Sadowski and Longo (1962) observed activation EEG patterns in the food-deprived rabbit as soon as it was placed in a sound-proof room where it had been reinforced whenever an instrumental response occurred in the presence of a buzzer. In trained rabbits, presentation of the buzzer to hungry subjects had the effect primarily of altering the hippocampal tracing, wherein the 4–6 waves per second were replaced by slightly faster waves (up to 8–9 per second) of slightly higher voltage. When the subjects became "satiated" in the experimental cage, they did not perform the instrumental response even when the buzzer was sounded, and their EEGs were now characterized by high voltage slow waves of about 2–3 per sec, with intermittent spindle activity in the anterior cortex. During this "satiation" phase the buzzer had no effect on the EEGs. Nevertheless, when a rabbit was returned to its home cage, it typically consumed its daily food ration immediately. Sadowski and Longo (1962) suggested that the cessation of instrumental performance in the experimental situation after 20–30 reinforced responses was due to inhibition produced by the conditioning procedure, and that another environment (the home cage) resulted in disinhibition.

Activation EEG tracings have been observed in food-deprived rats and more slow wave activity was present in the food-sated than in the food-deprived condition (Hockman, 1964). The results were essentially similar for recording electrodes in the mesencephalic reticular formation, and the ventromedial and lateral hypothalamic nuclei, respectively (in the so-called "satiety" and "feeding" areas or systems, respectively, in the hypothalamus). An explicit analysis was not made in this study of the effects of food deprivation per se on the EEGs, nor of the contributions of external stimuli, including food-linked CSs as incentive-motivational stimuli.

In general correspondence with the observations of increased amounts of slow wave activity in the EEGs of food- and water-sated rats, we may note behavioral and EEG evidence of drowsiness and "sleep" in female rabbits following coitus (Sawyer & Kawakami, 1959). The "sleep" phase was followed by a "hippocampal hyperactivity" phase which is characterized by high amplitude 8/sec EEG waves in the hippocampus and its projections, and a further decrease in skeletal muscle tonus and slowing of heart rate and respiration. The postcoital latency of the hippocampal hyperactivity was about 13 min on the average, but it varied between about 4 and 23 min for 11 rabbits, and it apparently failed to occur in 2 rabbits. This hippocampal hyperactivity phase reportedly lasted only a few minutes; it was followed by behavioral arousal and behavioral activity, as well as a transition from the hippocampal hyperactivity to lower voltage, less rhythmic electrical activity.

Clemente, Sterman, and Wyrwicka (1964) investigated explicitly the occurrence of a discrete EEG shift in activity immediately after an instrumental response had been reinforced with food, and they called this phenomenon "postreinforcement EEG synchronization." Cats were food deprived for 23.5 hr and tested daily for about 20 min. They were trained to press a cup for food. Each cup press was reinforced with 0.25 ml of a liquid food. After several days of training, the typically low voltage, fast activity of the EEG was sometimes briefly interrupted by a burst of high voltage (100–150 microvolts) slow waves (4–8 per sec), which occurred after the cat pressed the cup and during the consumption of the liquid food reinforcer.

This postreinforcement cortical synchronization was absent after a novel external stimulus (hand clapping) and after electrical stimulation of the ascending reticular activating system, even though there was no observable behavioral disruption in several cycles of instrumental and consummatory activities. A classical conditioning experiment provided evidence that the postreinforcement EEG synchronization can be made to occur in the form of a conditioned response.

Subsequently, more extensive behavioral and quantitative analyses have revealed that the "postreinforcement EEG synchronization" is not uniquely associated with reinforcement of instrumental activity as it is typically de-

fined, and that there are statistically reliable bases for differentiating between EEG patterns of synchronization associated with "relaxation" and "inhibition" behaviors, respectively (Roth, Sterman, & Clemente, 1967).

In conclusion, it appears to be necessary to view at least some aspects of EEG activity as responses (or the concomitants of responses) that can be influenced by reinforcers, incentive-motivational stimuli, and by discriminative stimuli that are correlated with the subsequent reinforcement of specified behaviors. In other words, the effects of food or water deprivations on EEGs appear to vary with the specific experimental conditions at the time EEGs are recorded. Likewise the effects of stimuli on the EEGs of hungry or thirsty subjects are likely to depend on how specific stimuli are related to instrumental activities and reinforcers.

Conclusions on heart rate, spinal reflex excitability, and EEG data A major conclusion derived from this research is that results obtained with various physiological measures during hunger or thirst depend on environmental stimuli and the way in which these stimuli are related to the actual occurrence of instrumental and consummatory activities. For example, a localized EEG burst of high voltage, slow waves was observed in hungry cats drinking milk, and such a localized burst of large slow waves was also elicited by a food-linked CS (Clemente et al., 1964). Similarly, it looks as if cardiac acceleration occurs in rats during the consumption of water or food, and that appropriate water- or food-linked CSs can elicit cardiac acceleration as a conditioned response (for example, Eisman, 1966). When availability of food was made contingent on the prior occurrence of a particular localized burst of EEG activity (Sterman & Wyrwicka, 1967), the incidence of this EEG activity increased significantly (that is, a localized burst of large slow waves, for example, was reinforced with food). Recent data also show convincingly that changes in heart rate can be differentially reinforced as an instrumental response (DiCara & Miller, 1968; Katkin & Murray, 1968; Miller & Banuazizi, 1968). Thus EEG and cardiac data obtained during hunger and thirst states might be influenced by food or water as elicitors of "unconditioned" responses, by food or water as reinforcers, and by food- or water-linked CSs.

Considering these observations, we may tentatively make these conclusions. Heart-rate data are in agreement with stabilimeter data: food or water deprivations are not sufficient to raise heart rates or stabilimeter activity levels of adult rats. Data on heart rate, spinal reflex excitability, and stabilimeter activity levels are in agreement in revealing greater responsiveness to stimulation in thirsty rats (and this may be true for hungry rats as well). It seems likely that the activation patterns noted in EEG studies of hungry or thirsty rats also reflect a similar enhanced activating effect of stimuli in food- or water-deprived versus satiated states. Finally, the effects of food- or water-linked CSs appear to vary in ways that at present are inadequately understood. Data on heart-rate and stabilimeter activity of adult rats are consistent with water- and food-linked CSs having excitatory effects (higher heart rates and increased behavioral activity). There do not appear to be any recent relevant experimental data on reinforcer-linked CS effects on spinal reflex excitability of appropriately hungry or thirsty subjects. The EEG data seem to indicate that in the presence of food- or water-linked CSs, appropriately deprived subjects are likely to have activation patterns, except perhaps for certain localized EEG effects.

The greatest discrepancy with this current over-all pattern of results is found in studies of startle responses. Whereas food deprivation enhances the magnitude of startle evoked by a probe stimulus (which is consistent with greater spinal reflex excitability in thirsty subjects, and the cardiac and stabilimeter data), food-linked CSs reduce the magnitude of startle, and this appears to be inconsistent with data on stabilimeter activity, heart rate, and some of the EEG data. It is

possible that these data on reduced startle during the presence of a food-linked CS may be due to postural or locomotor effects. In our earlier discussion of fear as an acquired source of drive we noted that a CS linked with shock to a rat's feet was likely to become a CS for crouching, which enhanced startle. Perhaps a food-linked CS reduces crouching by eliciting a raised posture or exploratory perambulation. In comparing these various measures in separate studies we should recall that rats, cats, and rabbits have been subjects, and differences attributable to species may be important. At the same time it appears that at least some distinction is required between a stimulus linked with food which serves as a discriminative stimulus for instrumental activity and a CS which consistently precedes the occurrence of food independently of any behavior. This means that to understand the effects of hunger and thirst on spinal reflexes, autonomic reactions and EEG activity, it will be necessary to undertake detailed analyses of environmental stimuli and their functional relations to instrumental and consummatory activities.

Stimulation Effects on Arousal Level

Our introductory discussion of activation or arousal theories revealed the important role assigned to the arousal function of all stimuli. One can inquire, therefore, whether physiological response measures, as indicants of arousal reactions, vary systematically with stimulus intensities which can be varied over an appreciable range, and for which there are meaningful scales. Secondly, environmental stimuli are likely to elicit exploratory behavior, and one can examine whether the exploration of stimuli is related to arousal level and to the arousal effects of these stimuli. Thirdly, direct electrical stimulation of arousal brain sites can be used to vary arousal level, and the behavioral consequences of arousal mechanisms may be studied in this way.

Intensity of external stimuli Hovland and Riesen (1940), with undergraduate subjects, found that skin potential responses to a 1000-Hz tone increased in magnitude as a positive monotonic function of the decibel level above the psychophysical threshold. When response magnitude and stimulus intensity are both expressed in logarithmic units, the resulting curve has a slight but definite downward curvature. In human newborns, the logarithm of cardiac acceleration increased as a positive monotonic function of the sound level of a 1000-Hz tone (Bartoshuk, 1964). The exponent for the neonatal data was about 0.53, which is surprisingly close to psychophysical estimates of exponents for loudness. These data on galvanic skin responses and cardiac acceleration elicited by auditory stimuli appear to illustrate the diffuse or general activation attributed to all stimuli by activation or arousal theories. Not only does this "activation effect" depend in part on stimulus intensity but, more importantly, these data are suggestive that the "activation effect" of stimulus intensity might vary in accordance with a power function for at least an appreciable range of intensities. Perhaps with appropriately refined techniques one might find that "arousal reactions" and psychophysical magnitude estimations are similar functions of stimulus intensity.

Exploration of external stimuli Harlow (1953a, b) emphasized that food- and water-sated primates spend a great deal of time in manipulatory and exploratory activities, and that these activities are intrinsically reinforcing. Curiosity about external stimuli increases progressively from monkeys to anthropoid apes and man. Hebb (1955) has likewise emphasized the attractions of problem-solving situations for primates. He suggests (1955, 1966) that when the arousal level is below the optimal level, there is a positive attraction to situations involving risk-taking and mild fear, which are likely to raise the arousal level closer to an optimal level.

Butler (1957) maintained rhesus monkeys individually in a test box for periods of 0, 2, 4, or 8 hr during which time they were not exposed to any visual stimuli from outside the test box. Next, a Plexiglas sheet was inserted between a small window opening and an outside door. Pushes on the Plexiglas opened the door on a variable-interval reinforcement schedule. The door remained open for 12 sec and this permitted the experimental subject to see the monkey colony outside the test box. In a 1-hr test monkeys averaged over 400 responses for this visual reinforcer. The number of instrumental responses in a 1-hr test increased monotonically and significantly with the number of hours since the monkeys were last exposed to visual stimuli from outside the test box.

The term "exploration" may be misleading in some instances when the reinforcers are quite simple stimulus changes. For example, Premack, Collier, and Roberts (1957) found, with rats, that rate of bar pressing for weak light onset increased with light deprivations of 12, 24, and 48 hr respectively. When monkeys were submitted to prolonged light deprivation during infancy they subsequently pressed at very high rates for unpatterned light (Wendt et al., 1963). Control data in this study and in Fox (1962) supported the conclusion that light deprivations during infancy are more effective than similar deprivations in older subjects.

College students have been submitted to "information deprivation" by means of isolation in a lightproof room, with earplugs and earmuffs to attenuate sounds (Jones, Wilkinson, & Braden, 1961). Pressing a button produced a pattern of lights in the otherwise featureless room. In one experiment, subjects were allowed to press the button only after either 1 or 5 hr of deprivation. Subjects with 5 hr deprivation emitted more responses during the initial hour of access to the button (see also Jones, Gardner, & Thornton, 1967).

These experiments appear to be consistent with the view that deprivation of light, varied stimuli, and/or information are sources of drive, and that an instrumental response is reinforced by the drive reduction produced by the presentation of appropriately varied stimuli. However, it also may be argued that the stimulus configurations which serve as reinforcers elicit an increase in arousal level which has fallen below optimal values in the isolation-type environments. Berlyne and McDonnell (1965) cite supportive data on galvanic skin responses (GSR) and EEGs, and they present additional EEG evidence on the blocking of rhythmic alpha activity (flattening of EEG traces) by various 3-sec projections of visual patterns. The durations of the periods that synchronous, rhythmic EEGs were replaced by desynchronized, flattened EEG tracings were significantly related to the complexity and incongruity of the test stimuli. Desynchronization of the EEGs persisted longer when more complex or incongruous visual patterns were presented than when simpler patterned stimuli were presented. The authors interpret their results as congruent with the view that (p. 156): "A substantial body of experimentation has shown exploratory responses to occur as part of a comprehensive 'orientation reaction,' which includes all the indices of heightened arousal. . ." The hypothesis that arousal levels are progressively lowered during conditions of prolonged, homogeneous, monotonous stimulation receives some support from evidence of progressive slowing of the dominant EEG rhythms over the occipital areas of human adults during 14 days of perceptual deprivation (Zubek, Welch, & Saunders, 1963).

> It will not be possible to review in detail the various studies on curiosity and exploration, but because of their important implications for any comprehensive theory of motivation we will briefly note here several additional references. Fowler (1965, 1967) has provided systematic analyses of the antecedent conditions of stimulation as sources of drive and of the test stimuli used as reinforcers, together with an emphasis on reinforcer-linked CSs as incentive-motivational stimuli. Arousal approaches to curiosity and exploration are represented in Berlyne (1960, 1966, 1967), Fiske and Maddi (1961), and Hunt (1963).

To recapitulate, we may tentatively conclude that arousal levels are not necessarily

elevated and they may be lowered somewhat during prolonged exposure to homogeneous stimulation and perceptual or information deprivation. The view that information or perceptual deprivation per se does not elevate arousal level is analogous to the view that food or water deprivation per se, in the absence of relevant incentive-motivational stimuli, tends to either lower heart rates slightly or have no effect on heart rates as indicants of arousal level; indeed, in some cases we have even noted EEG and behavioral evidence of sleep in food-deprived animals. Similarly, subjects apparently have gone to sleep in an information-deprivation situation (Jones et al., 1967), perhaps in spite of any residual information deprivation as a source of drive, although this cannot be readily assessed in the absence of instrumental activity.

Electrical stimulation of arousal brain sites To investigate whether behavioral efficiency is a function of arousal level in an awake, behaving subject one can attempt to manipulate the arousal level without introducing associative cues by electrical stimulation of brain sites which allegedly form part of a neural arousal system. Although this approach has yielded some interesting results, there are probably too few studies available to permit unequivocal interpretations.

In a much cited study, Fuster (1958) trained six monkeys to perform a series of difficult discriminations. He found that speed and accuracy of the discriminations were improved during relatively weak stimulation and impaired during stronger stimulation of the brain stem. The deleterious effects of more intense stimulation of the brain stem may be attributable to associative factors (for example, the elicitation of incompatible activities such as eye movements and startle reactions) rather than to heightened arousal (see Fuster & Uyeda, 1962, as well). Similarly, the data of Wilson and Radloff (1967) may in part reflect associative effects of electrically elicited brain activity rather than purely arousal effects.

With regard to the equivalence of arousal

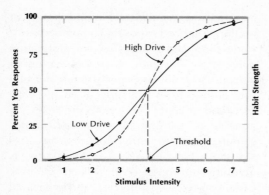

Figure 18.17. The effects of changes in general drive level on the relation between "yes" responses and stimulus intensity in a psychophysical experiment. On the basis of a theoretical analysis referred to in our text, an increase from low drive (solid line) to high drive (dashed line) is expected to increase the steepness of the psychophysical function, but the absolute threshold (stimulus intensity corresponding to 50 percent "yes" responses) should not be altered. (Brown, 1961.)

level and general drive which has been hypothesized by some theorists (Hebb, 1955; Malmo, 1958), it is interesting to note that the data of Fuster (1958) may differ in a very important way from the predictions which logically appear to follow from general drive theory. At absolute threshold levels in a psychophysical experiment, Brown (1961) observed that "yes" and "no" responses are equally likely, and an increase in the drive multiplier should not favor either response. Whenever a difference in the habit strength of the "yes" and "no" responses exists, an increase in the drive multiplier amplifies the absolute difference between the two response tendencies. Therefore, as illustrated in Figure 18.17, if only the drive multiplier is increased and the associative habit strengths are not changed, then the psychophysical curve relating the proportion of "yes" responses to stimulus intensity should become steeper throughout the central intermediate range of those stimulus values which elicit the same response less than 100 percent of the time. Fuster (1958) used exposure times

of 10, 20, 30, and 40 msec for the test stimuli, and on control trials the percentage of correct responses was slightly below 50 at the shortest exposure and increased monotonically to a high of about 85 percent at the longest exposure. On experimental trials, the curve for percent correct appears to have been simply displaced upwards; experimental and control curves are approximately equidistant from each other for the four pairs of data points. Even when control performance was slightly below 50 percent correct, the improvement in accuracy produced by electrical stimulation of the brain stem was as great as for the 20-, 30-, and 40-msec test exposures which had yielded about 70 to 85 percent correct on control trials. The lowest mean percentage correct in Figure 4 of Fuster and Uyeda (1962) is about 57 and it occurs on control trials at a 10-msec test exposure. Here again, the experimental and control curves of percentage correct do not appear to depart systematically or significantly from being equidistant from each other for the four pairs of data points. These results appear to be consistent with the suggestion made by Fuster and Uyeda that electrical stimulation of the mesencephalic reticular formation lowered the tachistoscopic recognition threshold rather than just elevating general drive.

Lindsley (1957, 1958, 1961) has reported that electrical stimulation in the reticular formation can improve the resolving ability of the visual system. When a light flash of 10 μsec duration was presented twice, two evoked responses were recorded on the cat's visual cortex provided the interflash interval was long enough. When the interflash interval was only 50 msec, only one cortical evoked response was discernible. For about 10 sec after electrical stimulation in the reticular formation, two cortical evoked responses were discernible even with an interflash interval of 50 msec.

Mahut (1964) has investigated the effects of low intensity, 10-sec stimulation of subcortical loci on discrimination learning in cats with food as a reinforcer. Stimulation during choice behavior significantly enhanced learning. Improved visual function was considered an unlikely explanation of the facilitatory effects of electrical stimulation because the test objects were large and exposed for 10 sec. To the extent the electrical stimulation during choice behavior increased arousal level, such slight increments in arousal during discrimination learning would have accompanied both correct and incorrect responses. Mahut tentatively attributed an attentional function to any arousal increments responsible for the facilitatory effects of stimulation.

Chemical stimulation of the reticular formation has been explored in behavioral studies of instrumental activities as well. Nakajima (1964) injected electrolytes (sodium, potassium, and calcium chloride) into the mesecephalic reticular formation of rats. He found impairment of lever pressing for food, and both significant increases in activity wheel running (by calcium) and suppression (by potassium). Grossman (1966) has extended his work on the use of selective activation of neural mechanisms by chemical means to a study of the midbrain reticular formation of rats. Avoidance behavior was especially susceptible to impairment by implant treatments which did not interfere with an instrumental escape response.

Although some of the results we have considered are consistent with the view that direct stimulation of "arousal" areas of the brain serves as a general energizer, the results are far from conclusive.

Do Indicants of Arousal Meet the Criteria for Motivational Variables?

In our discussion of objective criteria for the identification of an empirical motivational variable, we concluded that apparently the three most generally accepted criteria are that a motivational variable is a general energizer, its onset punishes, and its offset reinforces.

General energizer Throughout our discussions of energizers we have indicated that it has been extremely difficult to devise meaningful tests to assess whether an empirical variable genuinely functions as a *general* energizer. These difficulties arise from the need to rule out confounding associative effects and possible selectively energizing mechanisms. Incentive-motivational stimuli (such as food- or water-linked CSs) appear to be a major source of selective effects that can be mistakenly attributed to a general energizer.

The most extensive, systematic data discussed here on a physiological indicant of arousal level for different degrees of food and water deprivation are provided by the series of heart-rate studies. The evidence we have reviewed on heart rate as an indicant of arousal level tends to support the following conclusions. Heart rates are not elevated by food or water deprivation per se; heart rates of water-deprived rats are elevated during the drinking of water and even in the absence of water, provided water-linked CSs as incentive-motivational stimuli are present; similarly, heart rates of food-deprived rats are elevated during the consumption of food, and probably in the mere presence of food-linked CSs as incentive-motivational stimuli. Thus the heart-rate data reflect incentive-motivational effects, at least to some extent. We have also noted that EEGs are likely to be influenced by incentive-motivational stimuli, and that both EEG and heart-rate changes can be reinforced.

In our discussion of incentive motivation we noted that a relation between instrumental performance and a reinforcer-linked CS does *not* prove that incentive-motivational stimuli are a source of *general* drive. At least some of the effects of food- or water-linked CSs (as incentive-motivational stimuli) on instrumental performance are undoubtedly associative (Logan, 1960, 1966; Bower, 1961).

In attempts to rule out confounding associative effects, startle has been selected as a criterion response in some behavioral studies because the startle response does not have a past history of reinforcement in the test situation, and there normally would have been no opportunity for the reinforcer-linked CSs, as incentive-motivational stimuli, to form associations with the startle response. Some such criterion response measure which has not formed associations with the incentive-motivational stimuli in the test situation is required. For a definitive assessment of these heart-rate studies we need to know more about the associative and activating and/or deactivating properties of food- and water-linked CSs as incentive-motivational stimuli, and we need to know whether heart rates can be used to predict the magnitude of a criterion response measure which has not been associated with the food- or water-linked CSs as incentive-motivational stimuli.

Reinforcing and punishing criteria Application of the other two criteria for the identification of an empirical motivational variable requires the demonstration, for example, that cardiac acceleration punishes immediately preceding responses and that cardiac deceleration reinforces immediately preceding responses. There apparently have not been any direct tests of these criteria with hungry or thirsty rats. Since cardiac acceleration has been elicited by water-linked CSs, which are likely to reinforce rather than punish, and cardiac acceleration occurs during drinking water by thirsty rats, it seems highly unlikely that these levels of cardiac acceleration in thirsty rats could be shown to punish responses which lead to water-linked CSs and water. The view that increases in arousal are not necessarily punishing is consistent with evidence of sites in the reticular activating system where arousal can be elicited at low thresholds of electrical stimulation without any apparent reinforcing or punishing effects (Olds & Peretz, 1960).

Tenability of Arousal Level as a General Energizer

In our discussion of experiments on arousal we have questioned whether various experiments have provided definitive evidence for the view that arousal level func-

tions as a general energizer, and we have suggested in several instances that alternative intepretations of the data were possible. Although we have tended to emphasize difficulties in finding definitive positive evidence for arousal as a general energizer, this does not mean that we have intended to argue against the tenability of hypothetical arousal mechanisms which could function as a unitary general energizer. We should add that neither do the negative data and criticisms currently available appear to be definitive.

The hypothesis of an arousal system as a general energizer may seem to be highly implausible for several reasons, based especially on neuroanatomical data, and the effects of drugs and lesions. Thompson (1967) provides a useful summary of the "classical view" of the ascending reticular activating system (ARAS) of the mid-1950s and of recent developments. He notes that even in 1954 some 98 histologically distinguishable reticular nuclei were reported, and he cites various studies which have demonstrated that EEG arousal and behavioral arousal can be dissociated by the use of drugs and by certain lesions. At the beginning of his discussion of recent developments, Thompson (1967, p. 435) noted that, "While these anatomical findings contrast with earlier views of the structural organization of the ARAS, they do not necessarily contradict the classical view of the *functional* organization of the ARAS."

On the general question of the relation between structures and functions, perhaps a few illustrative questions about the visual system may be helpful. Cyclopes might argue that men with two spatially separated eyes must normally have double vision; if they found the appropriate patients with neurological lesions or disorders, or under the influence of appropriate drugs, their hypothesis would seemingly be confirmed. The neuroanatomy of the visual system is complex and, perhaps on this basis, the hypothesis of a perceptually unified visual field would be rejected by some one-eyed theorists as a highly implausible one, while others might be inclined to retain it as a useful working hypothesis. Similarly, in spite of the neuroanatomical complexities, and the data obtained from dissociations by drugs and lesions, it seems that a general energizing functional system may still be quite possible. It is noteworthy that it apparently can be difficult, for example, to account for the sparing and recovery of function after lesions (especially when they are done in two stages, or in comparisons of the effects of lesions incurred during infancy versus adulthood); such sparing and recovery of function has been observed not only in the reticular system, but in the visual (Meyer, 1958), somatic sensory (Benjamin & Thompson, 1959), and motor (Travis & Woolsey, 1956) systems as well.

The existence of selective associative effects, and the probable existence of selective energizing effects, does not logically rule out a general energizer. Berlyne (1967), for example, has noted the possible analogy with research on intelligence where models with both a general and various specific factors have been explored. To change analogies once more, if one collected data on velocities attained by feathers, stones, and other objects dropped from the roof of a building, there might be a lack of agreement in results for different objects, and such data would be unlikely to provide good support for Newton's gravitation constant. In this case, however, Newton's conception of gravitation is less at fault than our proposed rooftop experiment. Perhaps the arousal (and general drive theory) formulations of a general energizer can be improved to specify better under what conditions the most relevant experiments can be performed.

OVER-ALL CONCLUSION

Throughout this chapter we have been evaluating the hypothesis that behavioral response measures vary as a function of the degree of deprivation. As we have seen, much of the available data is not easily reconcilable with the hypothesis that behavior is the product of habit strength multiplied by general drive, even when drive is corrected for inanition. Instead, the forms of the functional relations are quite clearly influenced by such factors as the nature of the response measures, specific reinforcement schedules, means of manipulating deprivation, and species differences.

Deprivation operations probably selectively favor the occurrence of relevant consummatory responses, and this bias probably increases as deprivation increases. So, in part at least, some of the decrement in instrumental responding at high levels of deprivation may be attributable to interference from consummatory (and closely related) responses.

This view would suggest that each behavioral situation and each deprivation procedure might combine in a unique fashion, for different consummatory responses would interfere with different instrumental responses to varying degrees at each deprivation level. Were this the case, there would be no general solution to the problem of how behavior is influenced by drive level (as inferred from empirical motivational variables). In essence, this appears to be true for contemporary motivational research, although some may still believe that a more general solution is eventually attainable.

Charles N. Cofer

PROPERTIES OF VERBAL MATERIALS AND VERBAL LEARNING

19

This chapter is concerned with verbal learning and with certain of the variables that are known to help or hinder it. Our major goal is to describe the ways in which verbal materials differ from one another, for such differences have important relations to the efficiency of verbal learning. In discussing such differences, we shall, to a large extent, be dealing with *association,* a term which designates concepts that have a long history and refers to problems and procedures that have figured in psychology since almost the beginning of its history of experimentation.

The term *verbal learning* denotes a field of inquiry of which the focus of interest lies in the phenomena of and the processes by which individuals come, through practice, to link two verbal items together, to learn the sequence in which a set of verbal items occurs, to differentiate between verbal items, or to recall a set of items without regard for the order in which they occurred originally. There are, then, four major methods or procedures that are used, in the experimental laboratory, to study the phenomena and processes of interest: paired-associate learning, serial learning, verbal discrimination, and free recall. These are the names of the major tasks which are employed, although there are, of course, variants of each.

The systematic experimental study of verbal learning began when Hermann Ebbinghaus (1885) initiated his experiments on serial learning. Ebbinghaus' interest lay chiefly in the retention or forgetting over time of material we previously have learned; however, in order to study retention he realized that it was necessary to specify, first, what had been learned, and, second, the conditions prevailing at the time of learning. Many of the problems Ebbinghaus studied are taken up in the succeeding chapters. One particular innovation he introduced, however, has direct concern for us here.

Ebbinghaus invented the nonsense syllable in order to provide units that are unrelated to one another and are equal in size and significance. He wished to avoid the problems of word meanings, the interrelations among words, and their differential significance for the sense of a sentence. The nonsense syllable consists of two consonants with a vowel between them, with the condition that the result be a meaningless unit. Thus, one might write "DAJ," "GEX," "MUB," and so on (in English). Syllables of this kind are often referred to as CVCs (consonant-vowel-consonant) to distinguish them from another kind of trigram, the CCC, which consists entirely of consonants.

A number of writers (Irion, 1959, p. 541; Deese, 1961, p. 14; 1965) have observed that Ebbinghaus' studies represent the development and application of experimental methods for the study of *associations*. They suggest that Ebbinghaus' work was an outgrowth of the tradition in philosophy, especially British philosophy, known as "Associationism." This tradition, some of the notions of which we summarize below, exerted a major influence on the development of psychology, although it was, in the hands of the philosophers, not connected with laboratory experimentation.

Ebbinghaus (1885, p. 33) initiated his formal experiments in 1879–1880. In that same period, Francis Galton (1879–1880) reported studies of association of a rather different kind. Among other procedures, Galton determined what thoughts occurred to him when he looked at words one at a time. His procedure was the forerunner of word-association tests, which, like Ebbinghaus' methods,

continue to be employed. Word-association tests, however, were not often used in conjunction with Ebbinghaus' procedures until about 1950. Thus, since their inception verbal learning and word association have been separate fields of inquiry. Since about 1950, however, these fields have come into major interaction. (Consequently, the chapter on Association, which stood alone in the editions of this book published in 1938 and 1954, has for the present edition been retitled, and its content has been drastically modified.)

We may suppose that word-association tests give evidence of characteristics of words and of their interrelationships that have been built up by a subject from his experiences with his native language. Ebbinghaus' nonsense syllables are not words, but there is now abundant evidence that they are not all nonsensical. Nonsense syllables are constructed from the letters of a language, and the fact that they are not, in many instances, without sense and the fact that they differ from one another in various ways may be attributed to the subject's experience with the letters and with their combinations in his language. In other words, Ebbinghaus was not successful in constructing equal and meaningless units, a fact he recognized when he said of series of syllables that they "exhibit very important and almost incomprehensible variations as to the ease or difficulty with which they are learned" (p. 23). A major field of work has grown up with respect to the ways in which the differences among "nonsense" materials may be described and assessed. There are similarities between the procedures for doing so and those involved in word-association tests, though there are differences, also.

In this chapter we are concerned first with describing the characteristics of verbal materials, sensical and nonsensical, when the concern is with the individual item. However, interest has also been shown in the effects of the grammatical organization of items, as exemplified in poetry and in prose. We are, therefore, also concerned with connected materials, and we shall wish to ascertain the effects of item characteristics and of grammatical organization in verbal learning situations. The major burden of this chapter is to describe these matters, but attention also is devoted, at suitable places in the account, to questions of theory, both with respect to item characteristics (such as association) and grammatical organization and with respect to the nature of the learning tasks in which the effects of the characteristics and the organization are investigated. But first we take a further brief look at history.

HISTORICAL BACKGROUND

Although Plato made some comments (in the *Phaedo*) that seem to refer to association and some of its possible laws, it was Aristotle who, according to Warren (1921), achieved the fullest account of association in antiquity. Aristotle pointed out in the *De Memoria* that in the sequence of ideas in a train of thought the ideas that appear one after another bear relationships to each other, that is, they are similar, they are in contrast, or they have been present together at the same time in the thinker's past experience. Similarity, contrast, and contiguity in space or time were later referred to as *laws of association* or as the *primary laws of association*. A long period of time elapsed between Aristotle's enunciation of these processes of association and their active and affirmative use as major factors in the development and the functioning of the mind. It was Thomas Hobbes (1588–1679) who made the processes of association important features of his philosophy and psychology, and emphasis on association was a hallmark of British philosophy for two centuries thereafter.

According to British Associationism or Empiricism, the nature and the contents of the mind are held to be the results of experience. In general, the source of knowledge, according to this view, is sensation produced by the impact of the outside world. These sensations, and their weaker copies, Images or Ideas, are hooked together or amalgamated

by the automatic processes of association—hence the importance of the laws of association. On this basis, the Associationists offered detailed and often complex accounts of such processes as thinking.

That there are three primary laws of association is a proposition that was not always accepted. For example, some of the Associationists made contiguity the primary law and attempted to derive similarity and contrast from it. To the contrary, other writers, such as Thomas Brown (1778–1820), accepted the three primary laws but added other laws, called *secondary laws*. In his secondary laws, Brown postulated factors in the formation of associations some of which later empirical investigators were to study extensively. The secondary laws are (1) *duration*, (2) *liveliness* (or vividness), and (3) *frequency*, all of which refer to the characteristics of the original experiences brought into association by contiguity and which, therefore, state conditions of learning; (4) *recency*, and (5) *freedom from competing associations*, which seem perhaps to refer to factors involved in the retention or forgetting of associations; (6) *constitutional differences among individuals*, (7) *emotional variations in the same individual* at different points in time, (8) *temporary states*, for example, health, and (9) *prior habits of life and thought*, which represent a recognition of the variability in behavior that occurs between individuals and within an individual in time and suggest factors that may be involved in this variability.

It should be clearly understood that the importance of association and the nature of its laws were problems dealt with by the British Associationists by means of analyses of their own experience. They analyzed their thinking processes and attempted to recall or discover the possible factors, past or present, responsible for the occurrence of ideas together in thought. These men did not conduct experiments, but when experimentation was undertaken, as it was by Ebbinghaus, it was influenced by or was even designed to test the ideas of these philosophers (Irion, 1959).

Deese (1965) has argued that the processes, laws, and other contributions of the Associationists have *misguided* experimentation because the problems they have set for experimentalists grew out of the introspective account of thought, and the nature of thought as revealed by introspection may have little or nothing to do with the ways in which associations are originally acquired. We discuss this later in describing Deese's contributions concerning the analysis of associations. Mandler and Mandler (1964) have brought together selections from the writings of major associationists as well as from their critics and have offered commentaries on many aspects of the history of the study of association and its conceptualization.

This brief historical sketch should indicate why Galton's study of word association and why Ebbinghaus' attempts to study *de novo* the formation and retention of associations were so important; they represent techniques for actually studying associations, as opposed to introspecting about them. Galton and Ebbinghaus attacked the problem of association in very different ways, but their goals were not perhaps dissimilar. Galton's methods tell us what words are related to one another but nothing about how these relations were established originally. Ebbinghaus' procedures tell us how associations can be formed, and it is at least possible that Ebbinghaus' methods show the kind of things that went on when the associations were formed that Galton measured (see Russell, 1961; Deese, 1965).

PROPERTIES OF VERBAL MATERIALS: DISCRETE ITEMS

Although words and nonsense syllables differ from each other in many ways, several of the procedures for describing and measuring their properties have common features. We may classify these procedures into three kinds: *output methods,* which yield production measures and relational measures, *counts,* and *ratings.* Output methods include

the procedures usually referred to in discussions of word association. Many properties of verbal stimuli have been studied by rating methods. In fact, ratings are often used as alternatives to output methods and counts. We shall therefore consider ratings with output methods and counts in the cases where ratings are being used as alternatives to them, reserving, however, to a separate section, the discussion of ratings of properties that are not obtained by means of output methods and counts.

Output Methods

As is suggested above, output methods include the Word Association Test. However, they include other techniques as well, although all of the techniques share a common feature: The subject is asked to respond, one or more times, to each of a set of stimuli, the stimuli usually but not necessarily being verbal. In general, the subjects' responses are used in one of two ways. For one they are used to determine the sheer number of responses the stimulus elicits or that is produced in response to it. This we shall call the *production measure.* The second way they are used is to determine associative relationships between two stimuli or among the members of some set of stimuli. This we call the *relational measure.* The two methods differ, essentially, in what is done with the subject's responses. Because of this fact, we turn first to the description of the actual procedures for obtaining the responses and second to what is done with them and what the measurements have to do with verbal learning.

Procedures in output methods: Obtaining the data Six methods may be distinguished and are named here in accordance with past practice (Woodworth, 1938; Noble, 1952, p. 424, n. 4; Woodworth & Schlosberg, 1954). They involve single or multiple responses, and free or controlled association.

Single-response Free Association. This method involves presenting a stimulus word (or other item) to the subject, and asking him to respond by giving the first word that comes to his mind, other than the stimulus word itself. The stimuli may be presented one by one in an exposure device, they may be spoken by the experimenter, or they may be read silently by the subject from a list. The experimenter may record the response by means of writing it down or by means of a tape recorder. He also may record the latency of the association by measuring the time that lapses between the exposure of the word and the occurrence of the response. Such times may be recorded by the use of a stopwatch, but a preferred procedure is to use voice key mechanisms which actuate a clock when the stimulus word is spoken and which stop the clock at the first sound made by the subject.

The bulk of available normative data, however, has been obtained by having people write their associations alongside each stimulus word. This procedure enables large amounts of data to be collected quickly, for it can be used with groups of subjects. Obviously, details of the responses, such as their latencies, cannot easily be obtained.

Associations obtained in the ways described above are considered to be free, in the sense that any response is satisfactory so long as it is not a repetition of the stimulus. In other words, no restrictions are placed on the responses that may be given.

Single-response Controlled Association. In all ways but one, what we have said about single-response free association applies to the procedure producing single-response controlled association. The difference is that to produce controlled association the subject is required to give responses of some given type. For example, a subject may be asked to give opposites or synonyms in response to the stimulus words. Here, then, restrictions are placed on what responses can be given in carrying out the task. In the procedure producing free association, any response will do, other than the stimulus word; in controlled association a response must match the re-

quirements set by the instructions for each stimulus.

Multiple-response Free Association. Two methods are involved in the procedure to produce a multiple-response free association. One may be called *continuous association,* the other *continued association.* In the former, the subject responds to the stimulus by giving as many responses as he can within a stipulated interval of time. In doing so, the subject may be responding to the original stimulus or he may be responding or may be encouraged to respond to the responses he has already given. To produce continued associations, however, the original stimulus is repeated a number of times, so that each of the subject's responses is more likely to have occurred to the original stimulus than to responses he has already made. In Noble's method (1952), for example, a given stimulus word is printed on each line of the response sheet, and the subject is instructed to write each of his responses beside the printed stimulus word. This method presumably reinstates the original stimulus to an extent not true of the technique of continuous association.[1]

Multiple-response Controlled Association. The procedure to produce multiple-response controlled associations also involves a continuous or a continued procedure, with instructions setting limits on the kinds of responses that are acceptable.

Is Free Association "Free"? The answer to this question is that we do not know, but that

[1]Woodworth (1938, p. 341) seems to have coined the term *continued association,* although his description does not clearly differentiate it from *continuous association,* a term discussed by Woodworth and Schlosberg (1954, p. 47). Noble (1952, p. 424, fn. 4) adopted the term *continued association* from Woodworth and defined continued associations as "those which are successively elicited by the same stimulus. . . ." Woodworth and Schlosberg (1954, pp. 46–47) have spoken of discrete free association and discrete controlled association as contrasted with continuous association. The present writer has chosen to substitute "single-response" for discrete and "multiple response" for continuous (or continued) association, as giving a clearer indication than the other words of what is required in each task. Noble's method has, in general, been used more commonly than continuous association, and the two procedures for multiple response association apparently have not been compared.

it is probable that free associations are free only in the sense that the experimenter imposed no restrictions on acceptable responses. What restrictions the subject may place on himself we cannot say (see Koffka, 1912) in the general case.

Measuring meaning: the production measures The first use of a procedure and a measure of this type was apparently Glaze's (1928) calibration of the association value of nonsense syllables. Glaze used 2,019 CVCs and determined their association values (av) from 15 subjects. Glaze exposed each syllable in a tachistoscope for from 2 to 3 sec, spelling the syllable at the same time. The subject was to indicate what the syllable meant and to indicate that it meant something even if he could not verbalize the meaning. The av for each syllable was simply the proportion of the 15 subjects who indicated that a syllable meant something that could be verbalized or not. None of them could find any meanings for JYC (Y was considered a vowel by Glaze), GAX or KYV, whereas all of them found meanings for FAC, LIM, and WIS. The first three syllables thus have 0 percent av, whereas the last three have a 100 percent av. Of course, many other syllables were found to have values intermediate between these. Hull (1933) and Krueger (1934) used procedures somewhat like the one employed by Glaze in further efforts to measure the av of CVCs. Because Krueger used more subjects than Glaze and many more syllables (2,183) than Hull, his values are probably the best. Witmer (1935) measured the av for 4,524 CCCs (all-consonant trigrams). [Her data are reproduced by Underwood and Schulz (1960) in their Appendix B. Their Appendix A gives Glaze's and Krueger's values for CVCs.]

We refer to the production measure just described as *association value*. Another technique has been employed by Noble (Noble, 1952; Noble & Parker, 1960). Noble obtained continued associations for 96 dissyllables (2-syllable items, some of which were words and others of which were paralogs, for exam-

ple, gojey). He then determined the average number of responses given to each stimulus in 60 sec. This gives, according to Noble, the *meaningfulness* or *m* of each item. Noble obtained a value of .99 for *gojey* and of 9.61 for *kitchen*. (His data are reproduced by Underwood and Schulz, 1960, as their Appendix C.) Mandler (1955) scaled the *m* of 100 nonsense syllables by what is essentially Noble's method.

Rating methods for assessing *av* and *m* also have been used. Noble, Stockwell, and Pryer (1957) obtained ratings for 100 nonsense syllables. They asked their subjects to rate each syllable in terms of "the number of things or ideas" it made them think of and to do so on a 5-point scale ranging from None to Very Many. These ratings permitted Noble and his coworkers to compute measures of association value and scaled meaningfulness (*m'*). Scaled meaningfulness was arrived at by converting weighted frequencies for the 5 rating categories into deviates of the normal curve. Noble (1961), using the same methods, has reported association value and *m'* scores for 2,100 CVC combinations obtained from 200 college students. Archer (1960) used 2,480 CVCs and determined the percentage of the 216 students who for a given trigram answered "yes" to any one (or more) of the following questions: "Is it a word? Does it sound like a word? Does it remind me of a word? Can I use it in a sentence?" These percentages range from 1 for XYH to 100 for real words like ZIP (the values are reported in Archer's monograph). Archer's method does not ask for ratings, but it is not exactly a production procedure, either. In general his questions and his procedure of scaling trigrams in terms of the proportion of subjects answering yes to any of his 4 questions are similar to the technique used by Glaze.

The reliability of both the values obtained from production and rating measures is usually reported to be quite high. In collecting his original data on dissyllables, Noble (1952) used 4 separate groups of subjects, each composed of from 27 to 32 airmen. He computed the *m* values for the items in each of these groups and found intercorrelations between average *m* values for the groups ranging from .96 to .98; the mean intergroup reliability was estimated at .975. Noble and Parker (1960) used the original 96 dissyllables with 100 college students. They produced, on the average, 2.11 more associations per stimulus than the airmen, but the relative scores for the items were highly stable as indicated by an *r* of .97. Other investigations (Noble, 1963, p. 85) have also yielded high reliabilities.

Noble (1961, pp. 505, 510) has reported very high reliabilities for his measures of *av* and rated meaningfulness (*m'*). Archer (1960, p. 22) reports a test-retest reliability over 48 hours for his measure of .882.

Rather high correlations have been reported, also, for *av, m,* and *m'* for sets of items common to different studies. Thus it is of interest to know whether values obtained by Glaze, Hull, Krueger, Mandler, Noble, and Archer are comparable. Summaries of the correlations which have been obtained may be found in Archer, 1960, Table 4; Goss & Nodine, 1965, Table 3, p. 42; Noble, Stockwell, & Pryer, 1957, Table 2; and Underwood & Schulz, 1960, Table 2, p. 16. The majority of these correlations fall between .70 and .90, and in view of variations in procedure, the time at which the studies were done, the unknown comparability of subject samples, and the like, it seems to most writers that these correlations are so high as to indicate that the measures are probably all indicative of much the same basic variable. It should be noted, however, that in some cases correlations are higher when curvilinear relations are taken account of than they are when curvilinearity is ignored. Thus *av* (Noble, 1961, Figure 4.2, p. 88) increases as *m* increases up to a point but does not do so as *m* increases beyond that point. When he plotted Archer's scores for 120 representative CVCs against their *m'* values, Noble (1961, Figure 7, p. 519) found the relation to be linear only for the middle of the *m'* scale.

A number of materials and procedures other than those we have summarized here have been reported in the literature. They have been brought together in a convenient tabular form by Goss and Nodine (1965, Table 2, pp. 21–39). We mention some of them again later.

The production measure and verbal learning A major question of interest with respect to all of the procedures and methods we are considering is whether they in fact have relationships to verbal learning. To answer this question requires first that the methods used in verbal learning research be clearly understood. In what follows, each of the 4 major methods is described, together with information pertinent to the question just raised.

Serial Learning. There are several procedures for studying serial learning. However, perhaps the one most often used is called the *serial anticipation method.* Let us suppose that you are to learn a 10-item list consisting of CVCs by this method. The experimenter will use some device, commonly a memory drum,[2] to expose each item one by one. The first thing you would see is some symbol, such as asterisks; this would be followed by the first CVC, then the next one, and so on until the last CVC is exposed (a symbol indicating the end of the list is sometimes presented following the last CVC). These items would be shown in the same order during subsequent presentations or *trials.* On the second trial, however, you would be asked to anticipate what item will come next and to do so before it appears. Thus, when you see the

[2]Methods for exposing materials for learning experiments have been described in Woodworth and Schlosberg (1954, p. 703) and Runquist (1966, pp. 513–514). The basic requirements for any device are that it must expose only so much of the "lesson" at one time as the procedure calls for; and the duration of each exposure must be controllable. In the memory drum, these requirements are met by printing the words or syllables on a strip of paper or cloth and fastening the strip around the cylindrical "drum." A screen hides the drum from the subject; an aperture is cut into the screen to allow one line of the material to be seen; and the drum is moved by discrete steps from line to line, so new material is exposed in the aperture of the screen. In recent years, slide projectors that allow controlled exposure have become relatively inexpensive and are replacing the memory drum in many laboratories.

asterisks you would try to say aloud the first CVC (for example, GAX); when GAX appears, you would know what it was if you failed to say anything at all or whether what you said was right or wrong. Seeing GAX, you would then respond with the next CVC (for example, BUP); seeing it, you would try to anticipate the next one, and so on to the end of the list. Typically, a number of presentations or trials would be necessary before you could anticipate all the syllables correctly. Practice frequently continues until this criterion of learning or of mastery is attained.

Ebbinghaus (1885) studied serial learning, but he did not use the type of method described above. Rather, he read his CVCs one by one (to himself), but after the presentation he attempted to recall the syllables in the order in which they were presented. In other words, he used the method of *serial recall* to study serial learning. Other procedures are sometimes used. For example, after presentation the subject may be given the items, typed on cards, and be asked to reconstruct their serial order.

There is a good deal of consistent evidence indicating that as the association value (*av*) or the meaningfulness (*m*) of the items in serial lists increases, the lists require fewer trials to learn (see Underwood & Schulz, 1960, pp. 27–31, for a review). For example, McGeoch (1930) used CVCs varying in *av*, according to Glaze, and the method of serial recall. When a 2-min study interval was allowed, the mean number of the 10 items recalled was just under 6 for the 0 percent *av* list; for the 100 percent *av* list, the corresponding value was 9. Noble (1952b) found similar effects for serial anticipation learning of CVCs which varied in Glaze *av*. Postman (1961) employed 2-syllable words varying in *m* and also obtained differences in learning with the serial anticipation procedure.

Verbal Discrimination Learning. In verbal discrimination learning (see McClelland [1942]), a series of pairs of verbal items is presented, usually visually, and the subjects are asked to learn which member of

the pair is "correct," that is, the one arbitrarily selected by the experimenter as the right one. The subject responds to each pair and is told or otherwise informed whether his choice is the correct one. Again, trials are continued until the subject reaches the criterion of mastery established by the experimenter. Commonly, the members of a pair are presented simultaneously, one above the other, and the position of the correct and incorrect pair members is varied from trial to trial, as is the serial position of the pair in the total set of pairs. However, the pair members sometimes may be presented successively.

Little work has been conducted concerning the relation between *m* or *av* and verbal discrimination learning (see Ekstrand, Wallace, & Underwood, 1966, pp. 575–576). What there is has not indicated important relationships. Keppel (1966) found no significant difference in the number of trials subjects required to learn a list of 12 words and a list of 12 CVCs taken from the range of 34 to 37 percent *av* in Archer's scaling. Postman (1962, Experiment III) studied verbal discrimination learning for 3 lists of pairs, the words in the lists differing in the frequency of their occurrence in the English language from high to low. Presumably, these lists differed in *m* or *av*, for the frequency of occurrence shows a positive relation to *m* and *av* (Underwood & Schulz, 1960, pp. 60–62). However, Postman obtained the most rapid verbal discrimination learning for his lists of words that occurred with medium frequency and the slowest learning with his lists of words that occurred with a high frequency. It is likely that this result, which is not an expected one, is due to associations among words in different pairs; there is evidence that words occurring with a high frequency have associations with other such words (Deese, 1960) to an extent greater than is true for words of lesser frequency of usage.

Free Recall. In the method of free recall a list of items is presented orally or visually to subjects, and each is asked to recall as many of them as he can *in any order in which they occur to him.* The distinguishing feature of this method is the freedom it gives to the subject as far as the ordering of items in his recall is concerned. Many studies of free recall involve only a single presentation and a single recall, but multiple presentations, each followed by a recall, have been employed. Tulving (1962) has referred to this multitrial method in the case of free recall by the term *free recall learning.* Many investigators using several trials vary the order in which the items are presented in successive trials, although a constant order of items can also be used.

Free recall has been extensively employed since about 1950 because investigators have been concerned with the sequences in which items are recalled and variables related to the occurrence of these sequences. In free recall learning groups of constant sequences of items develop over trials. We shall have more to say later about the variables which relate to free recall learning. The sheer number of items recalled is the measure that has been studied with respect to m or av.

Postman, Adams, and Phillips (1955) used a list of 20 CVCs, which varied in av (Glaze) from 0 to 100 percent. An immediate retention test indicated that free recall varied with the av of the CVCs, being poorest for those of 0 percent and 33 percent av, being better for those at 66 percent av and best for those at 100 percent av. However, there were no differences as a function of av when a recognition test was used. Postman and Adams (1956) compared the free recall of 30 CVCs (av values of 40 and 46.67 percent from Glaze) and of 30 adjectives. Presumably the words are higher in av and m than the CVCs. Recall was much better for the adjectives than for the CVCs, a result confirmed by Postman and Phillips (1961) with different lists. Although this evidence is not extensive there seems little reason to doubt that av and m relate positively to the amount recalled in free recall. There is a problem of interpretation here in the comparison of words with CVCs, for words may be interassociated to an extent greater than is likely to be true of

CVCs. However, the correlation seems well established.

Paired-associate Learning. Learning by the paired associate method has figured very prominently in research on verbal learning since 1940 or 1950, and it has perhaps been studied more often than all the other methods combined since then. It is popular because many workers regard it as the most analytic of the methods in the sense that it supposedly allows for the study of the development of associations between one term and another one. Other investigators (see Battig, 1965, 1967), however, believe that the method involves complex processes and therefore does not permit the observation of simple associative development.

In the paired-associates method, the subject is asked to learn that when he sees or hears one item he is to respond with another one that is associated with it. For example, when one member of a pair (often called the *stimulus term* or the *left-hand term*) is presented, the subject is asked to produce the item which is the other member of the pair (the *response term* or the *right-hand member*) before this response term appears alongside its stimulus word. A list of pairs is usually employed, the pairs being presented in the sequence: stimulus member$_1$—pair$_1$; stimulus member$_2$—pair$_2$; and so on, and the subject attempts to anticipate the second member of the pair before it appears in view alongside the stimulus member. This is called the *anticipation method in paired associate learning,* and it is differentiated from serial anticipation learning by the facts that the subject never anticipates the stimulus term, that the sequence of the pairs is altered from trial to trial, and that the subject is told that he is not to learn the items in serial order. Trials are continued until the subject successfully anticipates all the response members or fulfills some other criterion.

An alternative to the anticipation method is the *study-test* or *recall* method. In this procedure, each trial consists of two parts. In part 1 the pairs are presented, and the subject responds by pronouncing or spelling them. In part 2, the stimuli are presented alone one by one (usually in a new order), and he is asked to recall the response for each one. The anticipation method has been the more popular in recent years, but there are good arguments for the use of the study-test method (Battig, 1965).

Association value (*av*) and meaningfulness (*m*) have been most extensively investigated in the case of paired-associate learning. The effects of these variables have been examined with respect to the stimulus, the response, and both the stimulus and the response, that is, the pair (Underwood & Schulz, 1960, pp. 31–42; Goss, 1963; Noble, 1963; Goss & Nodine, 1965, pp. 65–110).

From the substantial amount of work that has been carried out on paired-associate learning, the following generalizations seem to hold whether meaningfulness values have been based on production or ratings and hold similarly for *av*: Pairs with an average *m* or *av* that is higher than those of other pairs are learned more rapidly than pairs with lower *m* or *av* values; learning is a function of stimulus *m* or *av*, being more rapid for higher values of these measures; learning is a function of response *m* or *av*, again being more rapid for higher values of these measures; learning seems to be more influenced by response *m* or *av* than by stimulus *m* or *av*. The literature contains occasional exceptions to these generalizations, but the weight of the evidence seems to support the generalizations for CVCs, dissyllables, and words. The experiments that have produced results that vary from these generalizations have been criticized by Underwood and Schulz (1960, p. 41) and by Goss and Nodine (1965, pp. 65–110).

Illustrative data may now be shown. In their Experiment 1, Cieutat, Stockwell, and Noble (1958) used dissyllables, scaled for *m* by Noble (1952). Separate lists of 10 pairs were set up with the patterns of meaningfulness being designated by letters. The first letter stands for the stimulus term, the second for the response term; H means high *m*, L means low *m*. Thus, we have H-H, H-L, L-H, L-L.

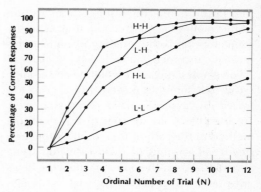

Figure 19.1 Learning curves for paired-associate lists in which the stimulus and response terms were high (H) or low (L) in *m*. The first letter designates the stimulus term, the second the response term. (Cieutat, Stockwell, & Noble, 1958, Fig. 1, p. 195.)

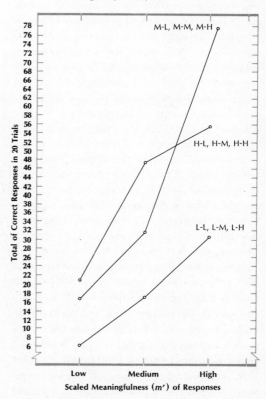

Figure 19.2. Total number of correct responses in 20 trials for paired-associate lists in which the stimulus (first-letter) or response (second-letter) varied in *m'* from High (H), to Medium (M), to Low (L). (Plotted from data reported by Cieutat, Stockwell, & Noble, 1958, Table 3, p. 199.)

Figure 19.1 shows the results for the percentage of correct responses over 12 acquisition trials for each list. The 2 curves for the lists with high-response *m* show better performance throughout than those for lists with low-response *m*, but the difference between the H-L and the L-L curves clearly shows an effect of stimulus *m*. Analysis of the data revealed that response *m* was associated with a larger portion of the variance than stimulus *m*.

In a second experiment, Cieutat, Stockwell, and Noble used CVCs with three levels of scaled meaningfulness (*m'*) for both the stimulus and response terms. The CVCs were taken from the norms for *m'* reported by Noble, Stockwell, and Pryer (1957) and were placed into 10 pair lists with the following patterns: H-H, M-H, L-H, H-M, M-M, L-M, H-L, M-L, and L-L. Figure 19.2 shows the total number of correct responses made over 20 acquisition trials. The curves are plotted for the three levels of stimulus *m'*, with the *X* axis representing response *m'*. Both stimulus *m'* and response *m'* have large effects, but the magnitude of the effects is greater for response *m'* than for stimulus *m'*, both as shown in Figure 19.2 and by statistical analysis.

Postman (1962) made up lists of paired associates composed of pairs of 2-syllable nouns. These nouns varied in the frequency of their usage in the language but also varied in *m* (Postman, 1961, Table 1, p. 100). He set up pairs in which stimulus word frequency and response word frequency varied in each case across three levels—low, medium, and high (so that *m*, which is correlated with frequency, presumably varied in the same way). For the levels of response word frequency or *m* the number of trials to criterion was 11.0, 13.6, and 14.6 as response *m* varied from high through medium to low. Corresponding values as stimulus *m* ranged from high to low were 13.2, 11.3, and 14.7. Postman has therefore found for words an effect of response *m* corresponding to effects we have described already. The irregular findings for stimulus *m* are perhaps explicable

on the basis of associative interference, as is brought out elsewhere.

We can conclude, from what we have said, that *m* and *av* show strong relationships to paired associate learning. The assessments of *m* and *av* are essentially normative, however, based on responses or ratings from groups of subjects. Is it possible to develop *av* or *m* experimentally, that is, by having people learn varying numbers of associations to, say, CVCs, and then determining whether the CVCs differ in the rate at which they can be learned? Some attempts along these lines have been made, but it has not yet been possible to show that experimentally induced *m* has effects on learning that are independent of other, confounded variables such as induced familiarity (see Goss & Nodine, 1965, pp. 185–187, for discussion and references).

Relations of m, m', *and* av *to Other Variables.* There are many ways in which words can be characterized, and there is often reason to anticipate that such characteristics may be related to the ease with which words are learned in verbal learning situations. Examples of such characteristics are emotionality, form class, and the abstract-concrete character of words.

With regard to characteristics of words, however, it is useful to raise the question whether they are correlated with other properties, such as *m, m',* or *av.* To the extent that they are, our understanding of the significance for learning of matters like emotionality may be improved. This is to say that when the emotionality of stimuli influences learning rate it may be because emotionality is, in a sense, an index of *m*. If we know the nature of the relation of *m* to learning, we may require no other interpretative basis to comprehend why emotionality is related to learning.

We will discuss the relationship of emotionality to *m*, among other things, and to relational measures later. Here, however, we may point out that Epstein (1962) constructed pairs of concrete nouns, of abstract nouns, and of prepositions and conjunctions, obtaining also *m* values for the 3 kinds of words. The values were highest for the concrete words, next for the abstract words, and least for the function words. Underwood and Schulz (1960, pp. 264–267) also found for interstitial words, like prepositions, conjunctions, and personal pronouns, lower *m* values than for 3-letter concrete nouns. Epstein's subjects learned the 3 lists in an order of difficulty corresponding to the *m* values. Lambert (1955) found greater "associational fluency" for concrete than for abstract nouns, a finding replicated by Paivio (1965); the latter reported substantial correlations between *m*, ratings of words as to the ease with which words provoke sensory images, and ratings of their auditory familiarity.

Results like those described above imply that many characteristics of words are related to *m*, as well as to *m'* and *av*. In many of these experiments, the effect of *m* is probably on the associative stage of learning, that is, in the "hooking" of the stimulus to the response in the case of paired-associate learning, rather than on the response integration stage. The meaning of these notions is given in the next section.

Interpretation of the Effects of m, av, m'. Underwood and Schulz (1960, pp. 92–94) have followed the lead of other writers in suggesting a two-stage interpretation of verbal learning. The first stage is termed the *response-learning* or *response-integration stage*, in which the subject must identify the response terms with which he is to deal and, further, in the case of unlikely combinations of letters (for example, PXL), that these letters go together in a required order. The idea is that some of the subjects' learning time must be devoted to learning the composition of the responses before these responses can be linked, as in paired-associate learning, to their stimuli. The linking of responses to stimuli is the second stage of learning, referred to as the "hook-up" or "associative" stage. It is conceded, of course, that the two stages will, in fact, overlap, but for various reasons there seems to be value in postulating two stages.

One such reason, in the light of our earlier discussion, is the greater effect of response than of stimulus *m* in paired-associate learning. For this method of learning, stimuli do not have to be produced, whereas responses do. A well-integrated response, then, would be available for association to its stimulus sooner than a poorly integrated response. In verbal discrimination learning, however, neither item must be produced. Meaningfulness (*m*) has little effect in this situation. The greater availability of items with high *m* is probably shown in the influence of *m* in free recall and in serial learning.

Underwood and Schulz have suggested that *m, av, m'*, and other variables (several of which are discussed later, such as frequency of occurrence, familiarity, pronunciability and others) relate to learning scores as they do in part, at least, because they index response integration. It seems likely that the differential integration of items at the time an experiment in verbal learning is started is due to the learner's prior experience with the language. Unfortunately, it is not possible to say at present just what feature of this experience is the critical one so far as response integration is concerned.

It is very likely that *m* has effects on the associative stage of verbal learning, also. Perhaps the effect of stimulus *m* illustrates this: stimuli with many associates can be easily linked to responses (and conversely) since these associates may provide ready mnemonic ways of putting stimulus and response together. This idea, similar to the "associative probability hypothesis" discussed by Underwood & Schulz (1960, pp. 45–46) runs afoul, however, of the "interference paradox," which would arise from the proposition "that the greater number of associates, the greater the amount of interference" there would be in forming a specific S-R association (Underwood & Schulz, 1960, p. 46).

A possible resolution of the interference paradox but one which does not subscribe to the notion of associative probability has been suggested by Howe (1969). Howe has looked at data for words and non-words (trigrams) with varying m or m' values by means of the single response free association method. He finds that m and m' are inversely related to the number of associates obtained over a sample of subjects by the latter method, that is, the high m or m' stimuli produce a relatively small number of different associates in single-response free association. However, this finding is limited to words with quite low frequencies of occurrence in printed English and to non-word low-frequency trigrams. For either multisyllabic or monosyllabic words, the relationship does not hold, if the frequencies of occurrence of the words are one in a million or higher. Thus, for certain low-frequency stimuli where m is high (or response m is high) the associative stage is easier than it is for items of low m, because there are fewer different associates to get in the way in the case of a high m stimulus than in a low m stimulus. This can be visualized if we realize that, according to Howe, the high m stimulus will have a steep slope for the frequency curve for its responses obtained by means of single-response association, whereas the corresponding curve for low m stimuli will have a more gradual slope. In the next section, we will see that the number of different responses a stimulus elicits in free association is an important variable with respect to response faults and response time and these findings, in a general way, support Howe's interpretation.

Relational measures In the production measure, we were concerned almost entirely with the sheer number of verbal responses elicited by a stimulus and it thus was sufficient to compare stimuli in terms of the number of responses they elicited or the number of people who reported an association to them. We were not concerned with what associations occurred or with the characteristics of their distributions.

Relational measures, however, are mainly used to describe the associations obtained to a stimulus or to describe the similarity in associations between two (or among several) stimuli. They represent the traditional work

on the word association test, starting with Galton (1879–1880), whereas the production measures derive from Glaze (1928). In dealing with relational measures, we shall have much more to say than we did about production measures. We must give an account of (1) the distribution of associations to stimuli, (2) the conditions which influence the distribution obtained, (3) the classification of associations, (4) the measures of associative relation be-

TABLE 19.1 RESPONSES OBTAINED IN FREE ASSOCIATION TO THE STIMULUS WORD *NEEDLE* FROM 1000 SUBJECTS[a]

Frequency	Response
160	thread
158	pin(s)
152	sharp
135	sew(s)
107	sewing
53	steel
40	point
26	instrument
17	eye
15	thimble
12	useful
11	prick(s)
9	pointed
7	cotton
6	work
5	implement
5	tool
4	cloth
4	darning
4	knitting
4	sharpness
3	article
3	fine
3	metal
2 each	books, button(s), clothes, coat, dressmaker, hurt, hypodermic, industry, pricking, small, sting, thick, thin,
1 each	blood, broken, camel, crocheting, cut, diligence, embroidery, handy, help, hole, home, housewife, labor, long, magnetic, material, mending, nail, ornament, patching, pincushion, shiny, slippers, stitching, surgeon, tailor, use, using, weapon, wire, woman
1000	

[a]Reproduced from Woodworth and Schlosberg (1954, p. 51).

TABLE 19.2 ASSOCIATION RESPONSE FREQUENCIES FOR 4 ADJECTIVE STIMULI BASED ON RECORDS FROM 350 COLLEGE STUDENTS[a]

Sacred	Little	Hidden	Holy
church 85	small 167	lost 30	church 78
holy 57	big 42	secret 20	sacred 53
religion 19	boy 28	treasure(s) 17	God 40
God 17	girl 17	cave 15	Bible 28
religious 14	tiny 9	behind 12	religious 15
heart 14	baby 8	concealed 12	cross 15
afraid 13	child 8	entrance 12	religion 9
frightened 13	dog 6	covered 10	Christ 8
cow 11	large 4	found 10	grail 6
cross 10	man (e) 4	meaning 8	ghost 5

[a] Unpublished data collected by the author.

tween or among stimuli, (5) the ideas about the character of the structure of associations, and finally, the relations between measured associational relations and performance in verbal learning tasks.

The Distribution of Associations. When many people are asked to give single-response free associations to verbal stimuli, it is commonly found that some of the responses are unique, being made by one subject only. Many responses, in contrast, are given by more than one person; some of these responses are made much more often than others. This kind of observation has been made for over 70 years (see Woodworth & Schlosberg, 1954, p. 50), but it remained for Kent and Rosanoff (1910) to test a large number of people (1,000), each of whom responded to 100 familiar English nouns and adjectives. Kent and Rosanoff listed the responses given to each stimulus word and tallied the number of subjects who gave each response. The result is a distribution of response words and their frequencies of occurrence as associates for every one of the 100 stimuli. An example is shown in Table 19.1, which exhibits the associative distribution for the stimulus word *Needle* as obtained by Kent and Rosanoff. It is noteworthy that a few responses (*thread, pin(s), sharp, sew(s), sewing*) occur in at least 100 records, whereas others, such as *pointed, cotton, work,* occur infrequently, and some (*blood, broken,* and

so on) occur only once in the sample. We can speak of the most frequent response as the *cultural primary* and of the responses occurring only a single time as *idiosyncratic responses.*

Associative distributions vary in several ways. Table 19.2 shows, for 4 adjective stimuli, the response frequencies for the 10 most common responses given by a sample of 350 college students. Each stimulus has a cultural primary, but it is clear that these primaries vary in their dominance in the distributions. Thus, the primary for *Little* is *small,* at a frequency of 167 (about 48 percent of the students), whereas the primary for *Hidden* is *lost* at a frequency of only 30 (8 to 9 percent). The other primaries in the table have frequencies intermediate to these. A second difference in the distributions is their slope from high to low. In the case of *Hidden,* a graph of the frequencies for the 10 most common responses would show a gentle slope from the most frequent response to the least frequent response (from 30 to 8), whereas the slope for *Little* would be sharp (from 167 to 4). Horvath (1963) has suggested that distributions of this kind can be characterized by a parameter a, defined as the ratio of the number of different response words to the total number of response words. This parameter gives a quantitative expression to the slope of the associational distribution. The third difference in distributions is obvious for equal *N:* For distributions with a high-frequency primary there will be fewer idiosyncratic responses than for distributions with a low frequency primary.[3]

Another thing worth noting about the distributions shown in Table 19.2 is that two of the stimuli, *Sacred* and *Holy,* share responses such as *church, God, religion, religious,* whereas neither has any responses in common with the other two stimuli. We shall have more to say about the overlap of associations later, but the fact just summarized can be restated by saying that *Sacred* and *Holy* are associatively similar, whereas *Little* and *Hidden* are not associatively similar to each other or to *Sacred* and *Holy.*

There are available in the published literature several sets of association norms to verbal stimuli. They can be found in Palermo and Jenkins (1964), Bilodeau and Howell (1965), Entwisle (1966), and Postman (in press), as well as in earlier sources to which reference is made below. There are also many collections of norms that are unpublished and available only from the investigator who collected them. Occasional reference to these norms is made in subsequent sections (see Cramer, 1968).

The significance of distributions of associations and of associative overlap will become clear as we proceed further in this chapter. However, we may mention here a relationship that has been obtained between the frequency of responses in association tables and the reaction time for the occurrence of the responses. The importance of this

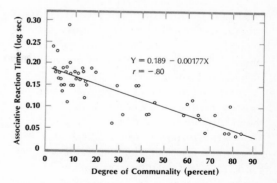

Figure 19.3. The relationship between associative reaction time and degree of communality. Each point represents the median log reaction time of all responses that occurred with a given degree of communality. In the equation, *Y* is in log seconds and *X* is in percent. (Schlosberg & Heineman, 1950, from Woodworth & Schlosberg, 1954, Fig. 3-6, p. 65.)

relationship is that reaction time or latency is usually taken as an indication of the strength of an associative relation between a stimulus and a response. During learning of a new pair of associates the reaction time diminishes as learning progresses, and this fact, together with others, seems to justify the use of latency as a measure of association strength. Many years ago, Thumb and Marbe (1901) found that the responses made more frequently in association tests occurred more rapidly than those made less frequently; this relationship has become known as Marbe's Law. Schlosberg and Heineman (1950) verified it in a systematic study. They obtained associations and associative reaction times from 204 college students for 25 monosyllabic stimulus words from the Kent-Rosanoff set. Figure 19.3 shows the relationship they obtained between the logarithm of the latency and the degree of communality (percent of students) for each response. The correlation between these measures was −.80, meaning that on the average, a response that was given by many subjects was made with a shorter latency than was a response given by fewer subjects. This correlation has led many in-

[3]Another way of characterizing distributions is entropy or the uncertainty statistic (H). This has been used by Laffal (1955, 1965) and by Howe (1965), among others. This statistic is calculated by first obtaining the probability of the occurrence of each response to a stimulus, and entering probability values in the formula, $H = -\Sigma p_i \log_2 p_i$, where p_i is the probability for any given response. A response hierarchy that has a small number of different responses, with, of course, high probabilities for these responses, is one of low entropy. This measure is clearly related, then, to number of different responses and number of idiosyncratic responses given to a stimulus (Howe, 1967, personal communication). Laffal (1955, p. 268, footnote to Table 2) has suggested, on the basis of some data, that the number of different responses may be a more reliable measure of the response hierarchy than H.

vestigators to regard the relative (group) frequencies with which responses occur to word association test stimuli as representing the strength of the association between the stimuli and the responses.

Some experimental work has been reported in which association hierarchies have been established and then properties of association responses studied. Peterson (1966) presented four pairs of 0 percent association value (av) syllables as stimuli and paired them with words as responses. One pair was JID WUB and another JID LAJ; the two pairs were presented with *salt* and *moon,* respectively. An anticipation-paired associate method was used. In the example given, JID is paired with two responses and thus is ambiguous, whereas WUB and LAJ are paired with one response each and are thus unambiguous. (The same arrangement was used for the other two pairs.) In addition, in a block of six trials, two of the response terms were presented twice as often as the others, that is, 2 to 1, and there were seven such blocks of trials. Twenty seconds after the subject met the criterion established for this task, the individual nonsense syllables (not the pairs) were presented, and the subject was instructed to respond to each syllable with one of the words he had learned. For the unambiguous stimuli, the responses associated with them were given, in the association test, 91 percent of the time. For the ambiguous stimuli, the more frequent response was made 59 percent of the time, and the less frequent response about 30 percent of the time. Although these data show that the more frequently made response does not exclude the less frequently made one for the ambiguous stimuli, the differences are consistent with an interpretation of the frequency of occurrence in free association as being related to the prior frequency of experience of the response with the stimulus. Wiggins (1957) manipulated the number of nonsense syllable response alternatives he built into the association hierarchy for a nonsense syllable stimulus from 2 to 8,

and he also varied the frequency with which he presented the pairings. After this training, his subjects responded to the stimulus syllable with the first other syllable that came to mind. His results show that associative reaction time increases as the number of alternatives increases and that reaction time decreases as number of presentations increases. The latter result is consistent with the usual interpretation of the findings of Schlosberg and Heineman, and the former result is consistent with interpretations offered by Laffal (1955) and by Davidson (1965) in other contexts, which we discuss shortly. Osgood and Anderson (1957) have presented evidence that essentially confirms the findings of Peterson.

Another matter concerning the distributions of associations pertains to the relationship between the words found in the distributions and words used generally in the language. Are responses to an association test special in any sense? It is not possible to give a general answer to this question, but Howes (1957) compared the associative frequencies of responses in the Kent-Rosanoff norms with their frequencies of usage in the Lorge magazine count (Thorndike & Lorge, 1944). When he eliminated from consideration certain words that occur with high frequency in English (conjunctions, articles, prepositions, auxiliaries, and pronouns), but which tend not to occur as associations to the nouns and adjectives used as stimuli by Kent and Rosanoff, Howes found for the remaining words a correlation of .94 between the frequency with which they were given as associates and the frequency of usage. This suggests that the associates are not a special class of words, unrelated to those in general linguistic use.

Conditions Affecting the Responses Obtained. There are a number of variables of which the responses that occur in a word-association test are a function (see Jung, 1966). They have not been investigated as extensively as would be desirable, but enough work has been done to suggest that association strength is not the only factor that operates to cause a particular response to occur to a given stimulus.

Time pressure: In the typical association test procedure, the subject is placed under some time pressure, for he is asked to respond quickly. In some experiments, however, subjects have been asked to respond even more quickly than this, or, in contrast, they have been asked to respond without pressure. Siipola, Walker, and Kolb (1955) induced time pressure in one group of subjects and a relaxed, "time does not matter" attitude in another group. Both groups responded to 25 of the Kent-Rosanoff words. The subjects under the pressure of time responded to the stimuli that were adjectives by giving adjective responses 58 percent of the time; this percentage shrank to 35 percent under the relaxed conditions and nouns were given 62 percent of the time. In addition, contrast responses to noun stimuli appeared more often under pressure than under the relaxed conditions. Flavell, Draguns, Feinberg, and Budin (1958) compared groups instructed to respond very rapidly (one such group was rewarded with a nickel for every response made within 5 seconds) with groups given no time pressure. In one experiment they found that the group placed under time pressure produced more reactions classified as *perseverative responses* or as *distant associations* than the relaxed group, and, in another experiment which employed the same subjects under both conditions, they again found that more perseverative responses were made under the pressure of time than under relaxed conditions as well as a few other differences. Horton, Marlowe, and Crowne (1963) found that the responses given were more frequently common ones when the subject is under time pressure than when he is not.

Perhaps the only conclusion that is justified by the three studies just summarized is that pressure does have an effect on the responses obtained in an association test. Direct comparisons of the three studies do not seem warranted, for they employed different stimulus words and different procedures; they also used dependent variables that cannot be compared directly.

Stimulus characteristics: Verbal stimuli differ from one another in a great many ways, some of which might well influence the characteristics of their associative distributions. For example, the original Kent-Rosanoff stimuli were common English words, mainly nouns and adjectives. Immediately the questions arise whether uncommon words and words from other parts of speech (or form classes) will yield similar distributions. In addition, some attention has been paid to the emotionality of the stimulus words. Unfortunately, it has been difficult to ascertain the significance of any one of these factors independent of the others.[4]

The commonness or familiarity of words is usually assessed on the basis of their frequencies of occurrence in the English language according to the count made by Thorndike and Lorge (1944). Emotionality or affectivity is typically based on ratings, whereas the form class of words is identified by dictionary indications of usage, by the use of test frames (see Deese, 1963, p. 80), or by study of the use of words in sentences (West, 1953).

Shortly after 1900, the word-association test was employed as a means of determining what stimuli were emotionally disturbing to subjects. Clinical applications involved the attempt to diagnose "complexes" in terms of the stimuli to which disturbed responses occurred, and there were also attempts to detect "guilty knowledge," again by means of disturbed reactions to stimuli, which were known to represent aspects of a situation a guilty person would know about but an innocent person would not. This work has

[4]In this discussion, the writer has relied on part of the book by Phebe Cramer (1968), to whom grateful acknowledgment is made for the privilege of seeing the manuscript prior to its publication. Dr. Cramer has also provided a bibliography of over 300 titles concerned with word association tests. (See also Skilling, 1962.)

been summarized in the earlier editions of this book (Woodworth, 1938, pp. 363–367; Woodworth & Schlosberg, 1954, pp. 66–71) and because the area has not been an active one for investigation since then it will not be treated here. However, see Cramer (1968), Rapaport (1951), and Rapaport, Gill, and Schafer (1946). Such uses of the word-association test imply that features of the association response distribution are influenced by the affective or emotional character of stimuli.

The criteria of associative disturbance or of response faults made to stimulus words usually include delay in making the response (prolonged reaction time) and failures by a subject, on a second run of the same association test, to reproduce, when he is instructed to do so, the response he gave to the stimulus the first time through. Laffal (1955) employed these criteria, and others, in evaluating the responses of 80 subjects to 100 stimulus words, but he also examined other properties of the response distributions to determine whether variables other than emotionality were correlated with the occurrence of disturbances to the stimuli that produced them. Laffal found that response faults were made mainly to stimuli that have many different responses in their associative distributions and that they occur less frequently to stimuli with fewer responses in the distribution. (A measure of response entropy for the distributions yielded the same result.) He concluded that response faults do not necessarily indicate that the stimuli to which they occur are emotional ones or arouse emotional reactions.

Laffal did not obtain information concerning the emotionality of his stimulus words, and it remains a possibility that emotional stimulus words have the characteristic of producing a greater number of different responses than do neutral words, other things being equal. Cramer (1965) gave a word-association test composed of 20 traumatic and 40 neutral stimulus words to college students and to schizophrenics. She found that both groups gave a greater number of different

responses to the traumatic than to the neutral words but that the Thorndike-Lorge frequency of the words was not significantly related to the number of different response words for either group. Brown (1965) found differences between neutral and emotional words even though the two sets of items did not differ significantly in the number of unique responses (closely related to number of different words) they elicited; the differences Brown found pertain mainly to indicators such as repeating a previous response, repeating stimulus words, forgetting (or remembering incorrectly) the response given to the stimulus on the previous testing, and elongated reaction time. On all of these measures, there were more response faults for emotional than for neutral stimuli.

It appears to be legitimate (see Cramer, 1968) to conclude that the emotionality (mostly negative) of stimulus words is associated with response faults and with a greater variety of responses, at least for single-word association tests. There is evidence, however, that in multiple-response association procedures, neutral stimuli may elicit the same number of responses as emotional stimuli (Koen, 1962). This suggests that somewhat different processes may be involved in the procedures, the single-response measure perhaps getting at the most available responses, the multiple-response method getting at the associative repertoire.

There is some tendency for the responses given to affective stimuli to have affective characteristics similar to those of the stimuli (Cramer, 1968). Pollio (1964) compared the semantic differential ratings (see the section on rating methods) for 52 Kent-Rosanoff stimulus words with the same ratings for their primary associates. The correlations ranged from .52 for the evaluative factor to .36 for activity and .26 for the potency factor; higher correlations than these were obtained for 38 stimuli and their primaries from norms for children (Woodrow & Lowell, 1916). Pollio also computed parallel correlations (for adult norms) for stimulus words with high-frequency primaries (probability of .65) and words with low-frequency primaries (.26). The correlations between the semantic differential ratings for the stimuli and the low-frequency primaries ranged from .41 to .66 for the three factors that the semantic differential analysis yielded but for the cases of the high-frequency primaries the correlations were zero. This suggested to Pollio that meaning, as measured by the semantic differential, is involved in the selection of associates as low-frequency primaries, whereas word-word habits (such as table-chair) are involved in the high-frequency primaries. Pollio also found, in a separate analysis, that strongly negatively evaluated stimulus words elicit association responses that are considerably less negative than the stimuli themselves; positively evaluated stimuli, however, tended to elicit positively evaluated responses (see also Pollio & Lore, 1965, and Staats & Staats, 1959).

Howe (1965) compared features of the associative distributions for 58 words with a composite value (D_4) for their rated deviation from neutrality on the semantic differential (see Jenkins, 1960). The associative measures he used were an uncertainty measure (see footnote 3), the number of different responses in the distribution, the frequency of the primary response, and the frequency of idiosyncratic responses. Twelve of the stimulus words were "bad" words, that is, evaluated negatively on the semantic differential, and the rest were "good" words. Howe found moderately high correlations (.406 to .682) between D_4 and the four associative measures for bad words and similar correlations for the good words, which are highly polarized (high D_4 words), but none for the good words of little polarization. The separate factors of evaluation and activity, however, also correlated with the associative measures, leaving some uncertainty about the importance of the correlation of these variables with D_4.

Pollio (1963) developed evaluative reactions to nonsense syllables by the following procedure. One syllable was paired with nine words (one at a time) such as *music, comfort,* or *beautiful,* all of which are positively evaluated on the semantic differential; a different syllable was paired with nine negatively evaluated words (for example, *sickness, anger, afraid*), and a third with nine neutrally evaluated words (for example, *boulder, glow, run*). Suitable balancing of syllables with word sets was carried out. Following these pairings, each subject was asked to give associations to the nonsense syllables on which he had been trained; the associations thus given were rated by other subjects on the evaluative scale of the semantic differential. Pollio found that the associates, whether they were words that had been paired with the syllables or not, were evaluated as positive if the syllables had been paired with positive words, negative if the syllables had been paired with negative words, and so on. This is an experimental confirmation of the conclusion made earlier: The association responses are affectively similar to their stimuli.

It has sometimes been proposed that the familiarity or the frequency with which a word occurs in the language has an influence on the association response distribution. Hall and Ugelow (1957) obtained single-response free associations to 48 words, half of which had a high frequency according to the Thorndike-Lorge list, while the other half were low frequency words. They determined the number of different words given for each stimulus word by their 40 subjects and divided this number by the total number of words given to it. The ratio so obtained for the high-frequency words was .381, whereas for the low-frequency words it was .642. This result means, of course, that relatively fewer different responses were obtained for high-frequency than for low-frequency words. Cramer (1968) has observed that this same relationship has been obtained by Postman for a sample of 1,000 college subjects and a larger sample of stimulus words. (Postman, 1964, reports briefly some features of these data, not including those mentioned by Cramer.)

There is evidence, however, that runs con-

Stimulus word	Response before practice	Time (sec)	Response after practice	Time (sec)
Bank	building	2.6	England	1.8
Axle	hub	2.2	grease	1.2
Spread	distance	3.4	bed	1.4
Sister	Anna	5.0	brother	1.4
Suffer	weak	2.2	pain	0.8

trary to this inverse relationship between stimulus frequency and the number of different responses (Veness, 1962; Cramer, 1965). Cramer (1968) has suggested that in some studies of this relationship the factor of emotionality has been confounded with that of familiarity or frequency, that is, that high-frequency stimuli tend more often to be neutral than low-frequency stimuli. Because emotional stimuli produce a greater variety of responses than neutral ones, this could produce the inverse relation obtained between frequency and number of different responses. However, Cramer does conclude that there is a slight inverse relation between stimulus frequency or familiarity and number of different responses which occur to verbal stimuli.

Another factor that is involved, however, is the form class of the stimuli. By *form class* is meant, essentially, the part of speech of a word, that is, whether it is typically a noun, verb, adjective, and so on. (Many words, of course, are found in more than one form class.) For adjectives, Deese (1962) found that responses of the same form class as the stimuli are made when the adjective stimulus was high in Thorndike-Lorge frequency, but not otherwise. For stimuli in other form classes there was no relationship between the form class of the response and the frequency of the stimuli.

In two studies, the Thorndike-Lorge frequency of the responses made in continued association was found to be positively related to the frequency value of the stimuli to which the responses were made (Johnson et al., 1965; Schulz & Thysell, 1965).

From the material we have just reviewed,

it appears that characteristics of the word associations obtained are or may be influenced by the emotionality, the familiarity and the form class of the stimuli. A fully adequate assessment of these relationships must await the conduct of further investigation.

Practice and instructional conditions: Wells (1911) investigated the effects of practice on word-association performance. He tested each of his six subjects with 50 words each day, using new words each day, over 20 consecutive days. On the two following days he repeated the lists employed on the first two days. Wells found that the average reaction time declined over the 20 days from about 1.75 sec to 1.2 to 1.3 sec, despite the fact that different stimuli were being used each day. Quite obviously, the reduction in latency could not have been due to practice on specific associations. The minimum reaction times obtained each day remained throughout at 1.2 seconds, but long reaction times tended to drop out with practice. On the repetition of the first two lists after this practice, Wells found results like those shown at the top of the page for five stimulus words.

The changes in responses have been said to show that, with practice, the responses become more superficial; what is meant here is that the response appears, with the stimulus, to complete a phrase (*Bank of England, axle grease*) or to make a common pair (*sister-brother*), or the response has a sound similar to that of the stimulus (*spread-bed*). If these responses are, in some sense, "easier" to make than are those to the same stimuli at initial testing, it may be that this kind of change accounts for the reduction in reaction time with practice. Some parallels may be noted in these results with those obtained under time pressure.

Training of a somewhat different kind has been studied by Maltzman, Bogartz, and Breger (1958) and by Maltzman, Simon, Raskin, and Licht (1960). In many of their experiments, the basic conditions were (1) the administration of a 25-item free association test (training list) and (2) the administration of a second, similar test (test list). Between these two test administrations a variety of training procedures was employed. The interest of these investigators has been concerned with the effect of this training on the originality of responses to the second test. (Originality here is defined as the mean frequency of the responses given by each subject, the frequencies being based on normative data for the lists.)

In one experiment (Maltzman et al., 1960), two control groups were used. One simply took the training and test lists in sequence. The second took the training list and then retook it five times, each time attempting to repeat the response to a given stimulus that each member of the group had made before. Then the test list was administered. Two experimental groups responded associatively to 125 new words between the training list and the test list, one set of new words being of high and the other of low frequency. Finally, a third experimental group took the training test and then retook it five times, each time attempting to give a different response to each stimulus. Then it took the test list.

The scores of the two control groups showed an increase in originality on the test list, relative to the training list.[5] However, the three experimental groups showed much larger increases in originality on the test list. Comparable results have been reported by these investigators for the training condition in which the training list is repeated several times with the subject attempting to give a new response each time, although various

other training procedures were not successful. Gallup (1963, Experiment 3) has not replicated these findings, and the reasons for the failure are not at all clear (Maltzman & Gallup, 1964).

Maltzman and his coworkers (1958, 1960) have also analyzed the changes in the number of idiosyncratic or unique responses given to the stimuli of the training list when it is repeated five times (after the initial testing) under the instructions to give a different response each time to each stimulus. The percentage of unique responses changes from about 10 on the first testing to about 70 on the sixth testing (Maltzman et al., 1960, Figure 1, p. 4), a result confirmed by Caron, Unger, and Parloff (1962–1963).

On the basis of the information available, it is not possible to compare the findings reported by Wells (1911) with those reported by Maltzman, for Wells's characterization of changes in the kinds of responses arising from practice did not include the measurement of originality. Nevertheless, it is clear, from these studies, that successive presentations of the same or different lists alter the characteristics of responses found on a second list and on the same list when it is repeated.

In the study already mentioned, Maltzman and his coworkers (1958) included a condition in which after responding to the training list the first time, and, where appropriate, during the repetitions of this list, students were asked to respond to the test list by being "as original as possible on the new list of words." Again, scoring the responses on the basis of the norms for frequency, Maltzman and his coworkers found a mean of 7.61 for the control subjects given instruction and one of 23.98 for subjects that had not been given instruction (the lower the value the more original the responses); similar differences were found for the two experimental groups that had responded with different responses to each of the five presentations of the training list. Clearly, these instructions had a powerful effect on the originality of associations. The reverse procedure was followed

[5]Maltzman & Simon (1959) found this effect to be a function of time between testings.

by Jenkins (1959), who, after giving the association test once, administered it again later (after 5 min or one month) under the instructions to "make the response that other college students would make." For both time intervals, the number of primary responses increased at the second test, and the frequency of the primary increased for 89 of the 100 items. Jenkins also found that subjects who, on test one, infrequently gave primary responses showed a vastly greater increase in such responses under the "popular instructions" than did those whose records on the first test showed many primaries (see also Horton et al., 1963). Kjeldergaard (1962) also increased the number of primaries on the Kent-Rosanoff test by asking his subjects to give opposites as responses where possible; this result is understandable when it is realized that the primary responses for many of the Kent-Rosanoff stimuli are opposites.

To evaluate the hypothesis that subjects might instruct themselves to respond in given ways, Jung (1966, p. 131) tested them in pairs after instructing them to give their responses aloud. There were five repetitions of a list of 10 stimuli, but each subject was given a different list. The subject in each pair who responded second was given written free association instructions, but half the subjects who responded first were told to give the same response each time the same stimulus appeared and the other half were told to give different responses. Jung found that the number of different responses given by the second subjects reflected the instruction given the first subjects. This kind of finding probably indicates that the second subjects were modifying their behavior (self-instruction) on the basis of what they heard the first member of the pair say. This may be an example of a "set" to respond in a given way. Usually, however, sets are not engendered so directly, that is, a means more indirect than instructions is employed. For example, Jung (1966, p. 128) led subjects to think that an association test either was a measure of creativity or of social adjustment. Subjects responding under the former set gave a greater number of different and less common responses than those functioning under the adjustment set to the same stimulus words. We shall see what is also probably the same thing as set when we examine the effects of context on responses to the stimuli of association tests.

Controlled association: When instructions are used that limit the kind of response a subject may give on the basis that the response must bear some kind of relationship to the stimulus (for example, opposite, synonym), we have controlled association (see p. 851). The characteristics and processes of controlled association have long been of interest to students of thinking (Humphrey, 1951) and other processes involving response selection. Where evidence for response selection exists, the important question concerns the mechanism by which the selectiveness is achieved.

The main emphasis in the study of controlled association has been on association latency because, under the conditions in which latencies are measured (individual testing, with responses given aloud), very few responses occur which are incorrect, that is, inappropriate to the stimulus in relation to the kind of response required by the instructions. It has usually been concluded that responses under controlled association are given quickly, typically somewhat more so than is the case with free association.[6]

Baker and Elliott (1948) investigated the question of the time for the occurrence of free and controlled associations in circumstances which provided that the same response would occur under each set of instructions. They selected stimulus words that had opposites as high-frequency responses. To half of these words subjects gave free associations and then to the other half they responded after being told to give opposites. For another group, the sets of words were reversed, although free associations were

---

[6]See page 56 ff. in the 1954 edition of this book for a summary of this literature.

obtained first. Baker and Elliott found that associations were given more quickly under the instructions to give opposites than under free association instructions, despite the fact that identical responses occurred in both conditions. (They found similar results for part-whole associations.) A possible objection to this conclusion, that the faster controlled association times might have been due to the practice afforded by the prior free association procedure, was overcome in an unpublished experiment by E. H. Davidson and the writer. Independent groups of subjects were used for the two instructional conditions, and the results paralleled those reported by Baker and Elliott.

An extensive study of controlled association has been reported by Davidson (1965), and it is possible to make some interpretations of the process of response selection on the basis of his investigation. Davidson used three lists of 10 words each; one was composed of stimuli the primary free associations of which are opposites, the second contained stimuli that elicit synonyms as primaries, and the third stimuli the primaries of which are words other than synonyms or opposites. Twenty-one groups of 27 subjects each were used, and each stimulus list was presented to independent groups under one of seven instructional conditions. The conditions were as follows: To give (1) opposites, (2) synonyms, (3) opposites *or* synonyms, (4) free associates, (5) any word *except* an opposite, (6) any word *except* a synonym, (7) any word *except* an opposite or a synonym. From normative data, it was known that, for all the stimuli employed, opposite, synonym, or other word responses were possible, although the words differed, as indicated, in terms of their primaries.

Most of the responses Davidson obtained were appropriate to the stimulus under the given instructional condition. His results indicate that controlled association times are not always shorter than free association times. For example, the mean latency of the response to the stimuli with opposites as primaries was 1.09 sec when the free associations obtained were the normative opposite primaries, and was 0.99 sec for the same responses if instructions were given to state opposites. This difference is in the same direction as that reported in the literature but is not significant. The same comparison made of the responses to stimuli whose primaries are synonyms (primary responses only) yielded latencies of 1.35 sec under free and 1.47 sec under controlled association instructions. This difference was not significant, but it is the reverse of that expected from the literature.

However, responses under conditions of controlled association were made more slowly than under conditions of free association when the restriction involved giving a response *other than* or *except* some response. For example, in the case of stimuli whose primaries are opposites and with instructions to make any response except a synonym (which, of course, permits the opposite primary), association latency increased to 1.24 sec, as compared with 1.09 sec, a significant difference. If words with other word primaries are used and the instructions are given to make responses of any word except an opposite, an average latency of 1.50 sec was obtained; if the instructions were given to state any word except a synonym, a latency of 1.49 sec, was obtained; this may be compared with the latency of 1.32 sec if the same responses were requested under conditions of free association. Clearly, certain kinds of response restriction conditions lengthen, rather than shorten, associative latencies. Other findings reported by Davidson are consistent with this finding.

Davidson also examined the free association frequencies of all the appropriate responses and found a correlation, across all association conditions, between the logarithm of association frequency (%) and the latencies of these responses of $-.83$, indicating that the more frequently made responses (in free association) occurred more rapidly, across all of the association conditions of his experiment, than the infrequent responses. A parallel finding emerged in terms of the number of responses in the free association hierarchy which had higher free association frequencies than the one given (and correct) in the conditions of Davidson's experiment. The correlation between this value and the association latencies was .81. (Both measures, frequency in free association and number of more frequent responses, intercorrelate at − .88, so both are measures of the same variable.)

These results suggested to Davidson a model of controlled association of the following kind. Given instructions and a stimulus, a subject scans his free association hierarchy for that stimulus to find a response which matches the instructional restrictions for that stimulus. If the desired response is high in the hierarchy, the subject can find it after a short time; if it is not high, responses that are high must be rejected and the search continued until the appropriate response is found; this takes time. That association frequency or number of competing responses is not the whole process, however, is indicated by the lengthening of the latency that occurs, for example, when an opposite is given to a stimulus with an opposite as its primary even when the instructions were to give any word *except a synonym.* The prolongation of the latency here may be due to the necessity of deciding whether the high-frequency opposite is not a synonym. Baker and Elliott's opposite primaries had a mean frequency of 88.1 percent, whereas Davidson's parallel stimuli had primaries with a mean frequency of 55.5 percent. It may be that the very high frequency of the former primaries permitted them to occur so quickly and to be matched according to the instructional requirements so quickly that their latencies were shorter if the subjects were given instructions to give opposites than they were if they responded under free association conditions. Perhaps free association conditions induce some degree of uncertainty as to the proper response to give, a condition not present

with Baker and Elliott's high frequency opposites when subjects were under instructions to give them.

Under some conditions, controlled associations are not as appropriate as it has been indicated that they are in the experiments involving latency measurements. Cofer (1967) obtained data for four controlled association conditions by administering tests, on printed forms, to one group at one time. Thus the subjects remained anonymous and, of course, were not subject to an evaluation of their responses as they gave them. Responses inappropriate to the stimulus word under the instructions given were made with considerable frequency under these conditions. Furthermore, there was evidence indicating that the more frequent a response was in the free association distribution to a stimulus, the more likely it was to occur inappropriately to that stimulus in controlled association. The matching of responses against instructional requirements under these conditions appears not to be so careful or precise as it is in conditions like those used by Davidson.

Cofer also compared the responses obtained for the same stimuli under free and controlled association conditions and found a marked overlap in the responses occurring under free association and each of his controlled association conditions. This suggests that the restrictive instructions of controlled association lead to a selection from the large pool of responses that are available or are somehow related to verbal stimuli and which appear in free association hierarchies.

Contextual conditions and priming: Stimulus words cannot be presented for free association in isolation from all other words, so that the factor of context, that is, the other items in which a stimulus word is embedded, undoubtedly influences the responses obtained. There is no way to eliminate context entirely, so determinations of the effects of context involve comparisons of one contextual situation with another. Several approaches have been used.

One way to detect the effects of context

is to determine whether responses obtained in a word-association test are determined by the order in which the stimuli are given in the test. Wynne, Gerjuoy, and Schiffman (1965) employed a stimulus list composed of 54 of the Kent-Rosanoff stimuli, for 24 of which (A-items) the primary response is an antonym. They arranged three orders of the 54 stimuli such that in one order (List 1) the first nine items and 12 of the next 30 were A-items. In the other two orders the A-items were dispersed more widely through the set; in List 2 they were fairly evenly distributed but with four of the first nine being A-items, whereas in List 3 no A-items occurred in the first nine but were concentrated in the last 15 items. Lists 1 and 2 produced significantly more antonym responses than List 3, this effect presumably being due to the context of from four to nine A-items among the first nine of the list. Similar differences were also obtained between Lists 1 and 3 under different instructional conditions (see also Carroll, Kjeldergaard, & Carton, 1962). These findings indicate that norms of word associations are affected by the context within the list, and thus it would seem to be advisable to use a variety of orders of items for different subjects in collecting further word-association norms.

Another way of studying the effect of context on the word associations obtained is to present a stimulus in the context of one or more other words, that is, as a component of a compound. When this is done, interest focuses either on the frequencies of specific words made as responses to the compounds or on characteristics of the entire distribution of associations to the compound, as compared with the case for one or the other of the individual components of the compound (see Cofer, 1967).

Howes and Osgood (1954), for example, were interested in the responses *bad, evil, fear, fright, frightening, gloomy, hell, mysterious, scared,* and *scary* as they were made to the stimulus *Dark* presented either in a neutral context or presented in the context *Devil, Fearful, Sinister, Dark.* Their subjects were instructed to listen to the entire compound but to respond to the terminal word (in this case, *Dark*). The frequencies of the occurrence of the responses of interest were augmented by the context just indicated, as compared with the neutral context (numbers or nonsense words). Rouse and Verinis (1965) replicated this finding, augmenting the frequencies of specific primaries by using as context for the stimulus items words which tended to define the response word or tended to go with it in English. For example, *town* is the primary response of the stimulus *City;* the frequency of town was augmented when the stimulus was made *Small City.* When *city* is modified by *small,* the compound is almost definitive of the response, *town.* Further, small often occurs in the language with town, as in the phrase, *small town.*

Cramer (1964) has studied "indirect priming"; the operations she has used are very similar to those employed by Howes and Osgood. In Cramer's experiments, a specific word is chosen, and the contextual arrangements are designed to influence this specific response. For example, the words *Moth, Bird, Eagle,* and *Spider* each elicits the response *fly* when they are used as individual free association stimuli in single-response free association tests. Cramer's procedure was to present the context *Moth, Bird, Eagle,* and then the stimulus word, *Spider.* She found augmentation of the response *fly* under these conditions, as compared to the frequency with which it was made as a response to the stimulus *Spider* alone. Cramer also found other arrangements of context that did not augment the frequency of the target word (see Cofer, 1967, for a discussion of possible factors in the successful and unsuccessful instances in Cramer's work).

Jenkins and Cofer (1957) and Rouse and Verinis (1965) have observed that the distribution of responses made to compound stimuli is often very different from those obtained for either component alone. For example, responses to the compound, *Thirsty Girl,* were more scattered, that is, the response frequency distribution was flatter, than it was to the stimulus, *Thirsty* or *Girl*, alone. It appears likely that the effects of context on specific association responses and on the distribution of associations will vary markedly with the kinds of context used and the relationships among the components and between each of them and target responses. When prediction formulas have been used in attempts to forecast the frequency of a response to a compound on the basis of the frequency of that response as a response to each of the components, predictive accuracy has sometimes been good (Podell, 1963) and sometimes poor (Cofer, 1967).

From what had been said about stimulus compounding and indirect priming, it is clear that context can have a powerful influence on associative behavior. Unfortunately, to date, no clear principles have emerged in terms of which positive and negative effects can be conceptualized.

Another form of contextual influence has been named *direct priming*. This influence can be illustrated by examples studied by Storms (1958; see also Clifton, 1966). The response word, *eagle*, occurs in free association at a frequency of 1 percent as a response to the stimulus *Bird*. Suppose now that *eagle* is embedded in a list of words to be learned prior to the administration of an association test in which the stimulus *Bird* occurs. The frequency of *eagle* as a response to *Bird* under these conditions is 10.2 percent, a significant increase. Direct priming of associations has been studied fairly extensively (see Cofer, 1967), but, again, all the principles that govern whether or not it will occur have yet to be identified. At a gross level, however, direct priming illustrates again the powerful influence of context on association test behavior.

Multiple-response and single-response tests: When multiple responses are made to stimuli, it is of some interest to compare the resulting response distributions with those obtained for the same stimuli by the single-response method. Rosen and Russell (1957) presented each of 100 association test stimuli

twice in succession, asking their subjects to respond to the second presentation with a word different from the response given the first time. The second response, on the average, was one of lower normative frequency than the first one. For 15 stimulus words the median rank-order correlation for the second responses which occurred more than once with their ranks in the cultural norms was 0.75; this suggests that there is some similarity between the hierarchies obtained under single- and multiple-response conditions. A similar conclusion was reached by Cofer (1958), who obtained continued associations for 25 stimulus words, on which there were also single-response norms, from 48 subjects. The primary response for 16 of the 25 words was the same word when either method was used; six other primaries given as responses under the single-response conditions were among the 10 most frequent responses given to the appropriate stimuli under the multiple-response conditions. Cofer computed the median single-response ranks for the words in the top 10 ranks in frequency for the multiple-response data. The median single-response rank for his highest ranking responses (across 25 words) was 1.28, and for his responses with ranks 2, 3, 4, and 5 the single-response ranks were 3.21, 6.00, 6.96, and 9.25, respectively. These relative correspondences led Cofer to conclude that the methods produce roughly comparable hierarchies, expecially considering the possibility that the ranks assigned to responses below the first two to four ranks are probably not very reliable for either method.

Laffal and Feldman (1962; see Laffal, 1965) have analyzed word-association responses in terms of the categories that the responses represent. For example, words like *huge* and *tall* are allocated to the category *Big*, and words like *table, chair, lamp, couch*, and *furniture* are classified in the category *Household* (see Laffal, 1965, Appendix 1, for an extensive description of the categories and their use in scoring association responses). Laffal and Feldman found by means of factor analysis that the structure of word categories for the single- and multiple-response methods is substantially the same. This indicates further support for the conclusion implied above that multiple-response methods yield hierarchies for stimulus words that are much like those generated by single-response methods.

There is interest, of course, in whether the hierarchies of association responses obtained from groups of subjects are also indicative of the relative strengths of responses in an individual's repertoire. The data of Rosen and Russell (1957), limited as they are to the first two responses, support the conclusion of a considerable resemblance. (We shall have a little more to say about this later.) Cofer's and Laffal's data, however, do not bear on this issue (Karen Stark, personal communication).

Subject and cultural variables and cultural change over time: The *word-association test,* almost from its inception, has seemed to afford a way to study personal characteristics and, thus, differences among individuals. Indeed, Galton (1879–1880) stated, referring to his own associations, that "They lay bare the foundations of a man's thoughts with a curious distinctness, and exhibit his mental anatomy with more vividness and truth than he would probably care to publish to the world." We mentioned above the early interest of clinicians in word associations as a means for detecting "complexes," although clinical interest in word-association tests has not been a major impetus to their use for some time. Nevertheless, there are scattered findings of relationships between word-association responses and individual differences, and there is evidence concerning cultural differences and cultural changes in word associations. Furthermore, it is of interest to inquire whether normative word associations adequately reflect the individual's own association hierarchy. The individual differences that have received the most attention are those having to do with sex, age, and personality characteristics and styles.

Mandler and Parnes (1957) found striking individual consistencies in the number of continuous association responses given to both verbal and nonverbal stimuli; the subjects were likewise fairly consistent in the proportion of idiosyncratic responses they gave. Jenkins (1960) has distinguished people on the word-association test on the basis of the number of responses they make that are popular ones (that is, primaries in group norms); there is a wide range of variation in this commonality score over groups of subjects, and it is a consistent trait. Tested with the same stimuli on more than one occasion, the subjects showing a high commonality tend to repeat the same responses and continue to make high commonality scores; subjects showing low commonality tend to vary their responses from occasion to occasion, still giving uncommon responses (Jenkins, 1960, p. 312). Carroll, Kjeldergaard, and Carton (1962–1963), however, have shown that a large portion of this commonality score comes from stimuli that frequently elicit opposite responses. This may account for the failure of the commonality score to relate well to other individual differences, aside from other association tests (Jenkins, 1960).

Girls and women yield somewhat higher commonality scores than men (Palermo, 1963, p. 43; Jenkins & Russell, undated). Also Palermo and Jenkins (1965a) found that female college students made significantly higher frequency primary, secondary, and tertiary responses to 200 word-association stimuli than did males. Another variety of sex difference was studied by Goodenough (1942, 1946), who developed a test using homographs with more than one meaning as stimuli. Thus, *bow* can be a ribbon for the hair or a device with which to shoot an arrow, the former being perhaps a "female response," the latter a "male response." Goodenough was able to differentiate reliably between male and female subjects on the basis of the content of their responses to a set of such homographs.

There is evidence for shifts of associative responses with chronological age. For example, Kent and Rosanoff (1910), for a sample of 1,000 men and women, found the following primaries for the stimuli *Table, Dark, Man, Deep, Soft: chair, light, woman, shallow, hard.*[7] For children, however, Woodrow and Lowell (1916) found these primaries: *eat, night, work, hole, pillow.* One characteristic of the responses of the children is that they would easily follow the stimulus word in ordinary language, for example, *Dark-night, Deep-hole, Soft-pillow; Table-eat,* and *Man-work* would seem to involve a verb as the response to noun stimuli. The responses of the adults, however, to these five stimuli would not ordinarily occur with their stimuli in the language (without an intervening word), for example, *Dark-light, Soft-hard,* and *Table-chair.* The responses in each case belong to the same form class as the stimulus, that is, *Table* and *chair, Man* and *woman* are usually nouns, and *Dark-light, Deep-shallow,* and *Soft-hard* are usually adjectives.

Ervin (1961) obtained free associations from children in kindergarten, the third and sixth grades and classified their responses to 30 stimulus words according to whether they belonged to the same form class as the stimulus and whether they would *not* follow the stimulus in sequence in ordinary continuous speech. (Responses meeting these two criteria are called *paradigmatic associates.*) She found that the proportion of paradigmatic responses tended to become greater over the age range of her subjects. Thus, for eight noun stimuli, the kindergarten subjects gave on the average 50 percent paradigmatic responses, whereas the third grade gave 73 and the sixth grade 76 percent (calculated from Ervin, 1961, Table II, p. 367). Similar changes were observed for responses to verbs, prepositions, adverbs, pronouns, and comparative adjectives (see also Brown & Berko, 1960; Palermo, 1963, Table X, p. 55; Entwisle, Forsyth & Muus, 1964). Paradigmatic responses were made with increasing frequency by the children in the first three grades of the Paris

Municipal Schools (Rosenzweig & Menahem, 1962).

The increase in the proportion of paradigmatic responses with age has been reported (see references above) to be accompanied by a decline in syntagmatic responses, that is, responses which can easily follow the stimulus in ordinary speech (for example, *Deep-hole*). Although the trends we have indicated are well documented, they are subject to two qualifications. For one thing, the sample of stimuli used in most of these studies has been relatively limited. The other is that cultural changes can apparently alter the age and the course of the shift from syntagmatic to paradigmatic responses.

The first of these points has been made by Deese (1962), and the data reported by Fillenbaum and Jones (1965) agree well with his. Deese obtained free association responses from 100 male college students to 600 English words. The words represented a wide range of Thorndike-Lorge G-count frequencies: 253 nouns, 118 adjectives, 101 verbs, and 32 adverbs were used (the remaining 96 words were not analyzed for several reasons). Using this set of stimuli, Deese found the percent of paradigmatic responses to be 78.6 for noun stimuli, 51.9 for verb stimuli, 51.1 for adjective stimuli, and 27.2 for adverbs. (The high-frequency adjective stimuli yielded a high proportion of paradigmatic responses, whereas the low-frequency adjective stimuli produced a predominance of syntagmatic responses.) These results suggest that paradigmatic responding in adults is the rule for noun stimuli and for high-frequency adjective stimuli but that it is barely dominant for verbs and not at all dominant for adverbs and low-frequency adjectives. Deese's values may be compared with those reported for twelfth-graders by Palermo (1963, Table X, p. 55), whose value for nouns is 71.2, for adjectives 42.2, for verbs about 37, and for adverbs 44.2. The large discrepancies for verbs and adverbs may be due to the differing numbers of the stimuli in the sets used by Deese and Palermo.

[7]The same primaries again were obtained by O'Connor (1928).

The other limitation came to light when Jenkins and Russell (1960) compared norms from about 1,000 college students for the 100 Kent-Rosanoff stimuli obtained at the University of Minnesota in 1927 and again in 1952. Finding certain marked changes in these sets of data, they also made comparative studies with other norms collected elsewhere in 1910, 1925, and 1933–1934. The average frequency of the primaries for the two Minnesota samples showed an increase between 1927 and 1952 from 267.5 to 377.5, and there was also an increase in the frequency of the second response, from 111.9 to 137.1. However, 71 percent of the primaries in the 2 sets of norms were identical, and 22 of the remaining primaries in 1927 had shifted to either the second or the third rank by 1952. The response primaries that dropped in frequency between 1927 and 1952 tended to come from superordinate pairs (for example, *Red-color, Sheep-animal*) or from synonym pairs (for example, *Sickness-illness, Comfort*-ease) and to be replaced by more specific and concrete responses or by pairs indicating a sequential relation (for example, *Red-white, Sheep-wool, Sickness-health, Comfort-chair*). Other data from college populations agree with the trend to an augmented frequency of primaries over time, and the identity of primary responses is greatest for norms collected nearest in time to each other. The decline in the occurrence of superordinate responses also was confirmed in the comparisons of other norms. Jenkins and Palermo (1965) have analyzed additional evidence that tends to support the trends described by Jenkins and Russell, and Palermo and Jenkins (1965b), comparing norms for fourth- and fifth-grade Minneapolis school children obtained in 1916 and 1961, found increases, over this time period, for the frequencies of popular responses, of paradigmatic responses, and of contrast responses, among other changes.

Cultural changes, then, must be taken into account with respect to comparisons of groups differing, for example, in age. The prevalence of the syntagmatic response in children, true in 1916, is no longer so prevalent in 1961.

In conjunction with cultural changes, it is worth mentioning that some attention has been paid to occupational and nationality variables in word association. Rosenzweig (1961) has made comparisons of word-association data collected with the Kent-Rosanoff stimuli in several countries—France (Rosenzweig, 1957), Germany (Russell & Meseck, 1959), and Italy (unpublished data made available by Mario Levi); the data for American English were from the Russell-Jenkins (1954) norms. In general, the primaries obtained in the four languages agree fairly well, best agreement across languages being obtained for the highest frequency primaries. The frequencies with which the primary responses are given tend to be substantially higher in the United States than they are in the European countries studied. Foley and MacMillan (1943) studied associative responses of students in medical school and in law school using words that have different meanings in the two professions but which are spelled alike. For example, the word *administer* is used differently in law and medicine; the medical students responded to it with words like *dosage, sick,* and *attend,* the law students with words like *estate, govern,* and *justice* (see also Murphy, 1917). Other differences between occupational groups occur but may be confounded with other characteristics of the groups, such as education (see Rosenzweig, 1964).

A number of studies have been carried out to explore possible relations between characteristics of personality and features of word association (see Nunnally & Flaugher, 1963). Many of these have offered suggestive findings, which have not, however, been followed up. Consequently, we restrict our discussion here to investigations that have stressed the presence of "styles" of response to word-association tests.

Dunn, Bliss, and Siipola (1958) employed instructions which relaxed the pressure of time. As Siipola and her coworkers (1955) had previously shown, however, under these conditions subjects still vary, some subjects setting a fast tempo of response for themselves, others responding in a leisurely manner. Associated with these response tempos are differences in the kinds of responses which occur and in the amount of imagery which each subject can report as having been involved in the generation of the response to the stimulus. Thus, the subjects who responded quickly tended to give contrast responses and report little imagery, whereas the others concentrated on noun associates to adjective stimuli and report complex processes intervening between a stimulus and the response. Dunn and her coworkers were able to show that subjects classified as impulsive by a personality test responded significantly more quickly, gave more contrast responses, and displayed less evidence of imagery than did subjects classified as inhibited; similar differences appeared for extroversion-introversion but were of borderline significance. In a further study with different subjects, Dunn and her coworkers found that subjects with high scores on economic, theoretical, and social values, classified together as objective, impersonal, and practical, gave responses more rapidly and with a higher proportion of contrast responses and with less imagery than did subjects with high scores on aesthetic, religious, and social values, classified together as subjective, personal, and impractical (to name the corresponding adjectives indicated above from among the many adjectives which differentiate the two groups). It would appear from these results that the manner of responding to a word-association test is related to the broad personality trait of impulsivity-inhibition and to broad values. Havron, Nordlie, and Cofer (1957) have also reported that subjects with religious or with political-economic values can be differentiated by their choices of which one of two words goes best with a stimulus word. In addition, the stronger the value the more rapidly the subject finished the test.

Moran (Moran, Meffered, & Kimble, 1964;

Moran, 1966) has identified "idiodynamic sets" in word associations in both normal and schizophrenic subjects. Three of the sets, of which individuals characteristically give responses descriptive of one, are (1) object-reference, that is, responses which name another object often found in daily life with the stimulus object (for example, *Foot-shoe*); (2) concept-reference, that is, responses which are often synonyms (for example, *Small-little*), or superordinates (for example, *Cabbage-vegetable*) of the stimulus; and (3) rapid contrast and coordinate set, illustrated by *Black-white* and *Apple-orange,* which may exemplify a set for speed in response (Moran et al., 1964). These sets were found again in a later study (Moran, 1966), and a fourth set was also uncovered, which involves adjective-noun, noun-adjective associates and is called "perceptual-referent"; it enters into contrast with the rapid contrast and coordinate set. Although the evidence for these response sets appears to be substantial, Moran has apparently not yet studied their relationships to personality measures or behavior in other situations.

As a final topic within this section, we may consider how well group norms represent the associative hierarchy of an individual subject. Considering the evidence we have summarized with respect to age, sex, occupation, nationality, and personality, it would be surprising if group norms were found to give an accurate prediction of individual response hierarches. We have already seen, however, that Rosen and Russell (1957) presented limited evidence for the comparability of individual and group hierarchies. Further evidence has been provided by Jenkins and his associates (unpublished data, cited by Jung, 1966, p. 129); Brody, (1964); and Silverstein, (1967). In the Jenkins study, subjects were asked to give associations to 50 stimuli on 8 consecutive trials. The comparisons of group and individual data, according to Jung, "demonstrated the equivalence of the two measures." Brody (1964) employed 30 stimulus words taken from Laffal's (1955) list and obtained word associations to them on 15 consecutive trials. He obtained a correlation of .82 between the frequency with which a response occurred as an associate on the first presentation of the list (this is a measure between subjects) and the frequency of repetition of that response through the remaining administrations of the list. Thus, the repetition of an associate on subsequent tests is a positive function of its initial or normative frequency. Brody also showed that, where a subject did not repeat his first associate, he tended to give the normative primary, as established on the first test, even though he himself did not give that response on his own first test. This, too, shows the use by the individual of common word associates. Finally, Silverstein used two 20-item lists, each of which was presented three times in succession. The probability of repeating a response on trials 2 and 3 increased directly with the normative frequency of the response given on trial 1, and the inverse relationship was found for failures to repeat the trial 1 response on either of the subsequent trials. This again suggests a correspondence between the group or cultural hierarchy of responses for a stimulus and the relative strength of these responses for an individual.

In attempting to measure the response hierarchy for an individual, an alternative to the repetition of the test may be used, as in the studies just mentioned. The responses may be treated as varying in strength according to their order of occurrence, with the first response being the strongest. Garskof (1965) has computed correlations between the frequency of responses obtained in single-response free association and scores obtained in continued association. The score was based on the average rank in order of emission over 20 subjects, weighted by the frequency of occurrence among these subjects; the single response data were taken from 100 different subjects. The correlations ranged from .52 to .94, with 15 of them being over .70. This suggests that the order-frequency measure, based on a small group of subjects and continued

association, yields results comparable to those obtained using a large number of subjects and the single-response method (see Cofer, 1958, discussed above).

Classification of Associations and Relational Measures. From the time of Galton to Laffal (1965) attempts have been made to classify the associations found for word-association stimuli on a basis other than frequency or other than parts of speech. Wells (1927), for example, suggested dividing associations into 5 types with respect to their stimulus words: (1) egocentric or subjective, which involves an emotional or personal reaction to the stimulus word (for example, *Success-I must*); (2) supraordinate (for example, *Table-furniture*); (3) contrast (for example, *Black-white*); (4) miscellaneous, which is a large class; and (5) speech habit (for example, *Forward-march, Black-board, Deep-depth*). Woodworth (1938, p. 352) suggested a 4-way classification: (1) definitions, including synonyms and supraordinates; (2) completion or predication; (3) coordinates, including contrasts; and (4) valuations and personal associations. Examples of these classes, taken from the associations to the stimulus *Needle,* are (1) *instrument, tool;* (2) *sharp, eye, work;* (3) *thread, thimble, cotton;* (4) *hurt, sting, blood.* Laffal's (1965) method of analysis provides many categories into which the relation between a response and its stimulus may be classified (see page 885). The earlier classification systems have been summarized by Woodworth (1938, pp. 348–354), Woodworth and Schlosberg (1954, pp. 52–56); Osgood (1953, pp. 708–712); and Deese (1965, pp. 21–29).

Such classifications as those described above imply bases for organization or for the structure of associations. This is to say, for example, that if a large proportion of all word associations can be classified as definitions or coordinates of stimulus words, whatever psychological processes lie behind definition or coordination would be the foundation for the way associations are organized and for the occurrence of these kinds of responses in association tests. Further, if people differ in which kind of association is dominant (and this is suggested in Moran's work, mentioned above), then association test behavior may represent different associative, or, even, "mental," organizations the implications of which could be sought in other situations and tasks. Unfortunately, relatively little has been accomplished along these lines. Most of the classifications proposed have been based on logical analyses of the relations between stimuli and their responses but have gone little further. Except for an occasional program, such as Moran's, little has been done to identify individual differences systematically in terms of the classification of associations or to relate such individual differences to other behaviors.

So far as the structure of associations is concerned, the work of Deese (1965) and of Laffal (1965) represents a departure from the classification systems of the past, for they analyze associations in terms of measured overlap in the response distributions obtained for two or more word-association stimuli. Because their work is predicated on relational measures, it is taken up in the next section, after these measures are described.

Measures of Associative Relations. If a stimulus word elicits another word as a response, we can say that they are associatively related. Thus (see Table 19.2), *Sacred* and *Holy* are related because *Sacred* was found to elicit *holy* 57 times from a group of 350 subjects, and *Holy* to elicit *sacred* 53 times. The simplest way of describing an associative relation,

TABLE 19.3 INTERITEM ASSOCIATIVE MATRIX FOR FIFTEEN HIGH-FREQUENCY ASSOCIATES OF BUTTERFLY[a]

	Moth	Insect	Wing	Bird	Fly	Yellow	Net	Pretty	Flowers	Bug	Cocoon	Color	Stomach	Blue	Bees	Average
Moth		2	2		10				2	10						
Insect	4				18					48					2	
Wing				50	24											
Bird			6		30									2		
Fly		10		8						18						
Yellow									3			11		16		
Net	2	2		2												
Pretty																
Flowers						2						2		2	2	
Bug	2	36		2	4										4	
Cocoon	16	6		4						10						
Color														20		
Stomach																
Blue												10				
Bees				15					5							
	24	56	8	81	86	2	0	0	10	86	0	23	0	40	8	28.3

[a] The numbers presented in the table are percentages. Reprinted with permission from Deese (1961, p. 18, Table 2.1).

then, is to indicate the proportion of times one word occurs as an associate to the other. In the case of *Sacred* and *Holy*, however, there is the additional fact that each word, as stimulus, elicits the other as response, and at about the same frequency. The association for these two stimuli, then, is bidirectional. There are cases of unidirectional association, of course, in which a stimulus, such as *Little*, elicits a response, such as *man*, at some frequency, but the reverse association, *little* as a response to *Man*, does not occur (Palermo & Jenkins, 1964). Also there can be bidirectional associates in which the frequencies are not equal. For example, *Little* elicits *boy* from 8 percent of the subjects (Table 19.2), whereas *Boy* elicits *little* in less than 1 percent of college subjects (Palermo & Jenkins, 1964). In order to assess the nature of the associative relation between two words, it is desirable to have available the associative distributions for both of them as stimuli. Otherwise the bidirectional or unidirectional character of the relation is unknown, as well as the relative strengths of the two associations.

The associative relations among more than two words is also of interest, and several measures have been described (see Marshall and Cofer, 1963). One is the *Index of Inter-item Associative Strength* (IIAS), described by Deese (1959a) in the context of studies of the recall for lists of words. Suppose we take 15 words, all of them associates to one word, say *Butterfly*, such as *moth, insect, bug, wing, bird, fly*, and so on. To obtain IIAS for the set, we must first obtain free associations to each of these associates. Having done so, we can then determine how often each of the associates occurs as a response in free association to each of the other associates when used as stimuli. An illustration is provided in Table 19.3 for the first 15 associates to *Butterfly*. The index for this set is 28.3, one of the highest of those used by Deese.

A simple index can also be used for controlled associations. For example, Cohen, Bousfield, and Whitmarsh (1957) asked subjects to give instances appropriate to a stimu-

lus that was a category name. This involved controlled association because the subjects were not free to give just any response. Over a large number of subjects certain responses were found to occur with high frequencies, others with low. For the category "four-legged animal," for example, *dog* and *cat* occur at high frequencies, *zebra* and *giraffe* at intermediate frequencies, *aardvark* and *llama* at very low frequencies.

A somewhat different approach to this kind of associative measure has been taken by Rothkopf and Coke (1961a) and by Pollio (1963). For a set of stimulus words, Rothkopf and Coke's measure (the cue number) is the number of the stimuli which elicit a given response. They (1961b) have given the cue numbers for 99 of the Kent-Rosanoff stimuli.

Pollio (1963, 1964) has analyzed associative relations by means of matrix algebra. He sets up a matrix, to begin with, in which the words in the set are listed across the top and also down the left side. The cell entries are either "0" or "1," with the "1" meaning that a given word occurred as an associate to another word in the set (frequencies of occurrence are ignored). By multiplying out these matrices, Pollio has been able to describe various ways in which the items of the set are interrelated.

Measures of association like those described above, as already indicated, take account only of the occurrence of one stimulus word as a response to another stimulus word and conversely. As is indicated in Table 19.2 for *Sacred* and *Holy*, there are other words besides these that occur as common associative responses to both, for example, *church*, *God*, and the like. For convenience we may refer to the elicitation of one of two stimulus words in a set by another one in the set as *direct associates*; in this example, *sacred* and *holy*, as responses respectively to *Holy* and *Sacred*, would be direct associates; *church* and *God* would be *nondirect associates*. Measures have been developed that take account of both direct and nondirect associates. One such index is the *Mutual Related-*

TABLE 19.4 DATA FOR COMPUTATION OF ASSOCIATIVE OVERLAP (MR) FOR STIMULUS WORDS SACRED AND HOLY

Common response words	Sacred (A)	Holy (B)	Common Frequencies (R_c)
Sacred	(350)	53	53
Holy	57	(350)	57
Church	85	78	78
Cross	10	15	10
God	17	40	17
Religion	19	9	9
Religious	14	15	14
			238

$$\text{Overlap (MR)} = \frac{\Sigma R_c}{N_A + N_B} = \frac{238}{700} = .34 \quad \text{where } N_A = N_B = 350,$$

or

$$\frac{\Sigma R_c}{\sqrt{(N_A \cdot N_B)}} = \frac{238}{700} = .34 \quad \text{where } N_A = N_B = 700.$$

ness (MR) *Index,* developed by Jenkins and Cofer (1957) and by Bousfield, Whitmarsh, and Berkowitz (1960) (see Marshall & Cofer, 1963, pp. 410–413).

Table 19.4 shows the associative responses that are made to *Sacred* and *Holy* (thus several responses to each stimulus alone, listed in Table 19.2, are not present in Table 19.4). The index indicates the common responses for both words as a proportion of all the responses in the distributions for them. Thus, in column R_c for the response word *religion,* the value 9 appears; it is 9 rather than 19 because only 9 responses of *religion* are made in *both* response distributions. These 9 are common, whereas the other 10 responses of *religion* to *Sacred* are not common to the two distributions. In column R_c, the lower of the two values for a given response is entered (in the case of equal response frequencies, say 10 and 10, the value 10 would be entered as R_c). Summing the column R_c and dividing by the total N (350 subjects in each distribution, thus 700) gives an index for this pair of 0.34. Deese has used the same index, calling it an *Index of Commonality of Associative Meaning,* except that he divides R_c by the geometric mean of the number of cases in the distributions and makes the N of each distri-

bution 700, thus taking account of the values in parentheses in Table 19.4. (See Deese, 1965, pp. 51–52.) His IC value for the two words of the table is the same as that shown in Table 19.4. The argument for taking the N for each word as twice the actual number of subjects (350) used is that before giving his association the subject repeats the stimulus word to himself. Thus, *sacred* and *holy* each occurs as a response when *Sacred* and *Holy,* respectively, are presented as stimuli, and this fact is acknowledged by putting 350 in parentheses in Table 19.4 for each. This assumption permits the counting of the 53 occurrences of *sacred* as a response to *Holy* in R_c, for *sacred* always occurs as an implicit response to the stimulus *Sacred* but only 53 times to *holy.* An index closely related to MR, called the *Index of Generalization,* has been proposed by Bousfield, Whitmarsh, and Danick (1958), and another one, *Associative Overlap,* by Rothkopf (1960).

Indices which, like IIAS, can be extended to more than two words, have been developed by Marshall and Cofer (1963). One is the *Index of Total Association,* which includes both direct and nondirect associations common to any two or more words in the set. Another, the *Index of Concept Cohesiveness,* takes account *only* of response words common to *all* the words of a set. An index related to both of these indices is the *Measure of Stimulus Equivalence,* proposed by Bousfield, Steward, and Cowan (1961). All of these indices are based on the assumption that common associations, other than direct associations, should be used to measure the associative relatedness of words. Because they have been fully described elsewhere (Marshall & Cofer, 1963) but have not yet had extensive use in experimental work, they are not treated further here.

It is worth mentioning that Underwood and Richardson (1956) have described a measure which they have used to calibrate verbal materials for use in the study of concept attainment. First, they obtained controlled associations to words like *Brick, Cherry, Tomato,* and *Lips.* Their subjects were restricted by instruction to give only "sensory" associations to each word, for example, *red.* To the word *Cigar,* 40 percent of the subjects gave *smelly,* 26 percent gave *brown,* and 14 percent gave *long* as sensory responses. *Smelly,* in this case, is the dominant response, and the others are less-dominant responses. In using materials like these to study how concepts are formed, we would choose, say, four words, like *brick, cherry, tomato,* and *lips* and ask our subject to indicate how they are alike or what they have in common. The dominance level of the correct sensory impression can be varied for the sets of words employed, and when this is done success on the problem is found to be related to the average dominance of the correct response as a controlled associate to the members of the set.

Garskof and Houston (1963) have developed a measure, the *relatedness coefficient,* or RC, which can be used for individuals to determine the associative relatedness of words. Their procedure involves, first, obtaining continued associations for each stimulus word and ranking the responses in order of occurrence. Then the ranks of the words common to the two stimuli are multiplied and divided by a denominator that represents the maximum possible overlap. For example, suppose that the common responses to the stimuli *Eagle* and *Bird* are *bird, fly,* and *nest.* To *Eagle* these responses occur at ranks 5, 3, and 2 and to *Bird* at ranks 3, 4, and 2. Multiplying these ranks gives 15, 12, and 4, and assuming five response words for each, multiplying them ($5 \times 5, 4 \times 4, 3 \times 3, 2 \times 2, 1 \times 1 = 55$) gives 55. Adding the ranks for the three common words yields 31, subtracting one from 55 gives 54, and dividing 31 by 54 yields an RC for this case of .57. RC can vary from zero to 1.00. Garskof and Houston found this measure to be highly related to judgments of the relatedness of pairs of words, the rank-order correlations for 20 subjects, ranging from around .90 to about .60.

Garskof and Marshall (1965) computed RC and MR for 2 sets of word pairs. In one set, the pair members had direct associations in common but in the other set did not. For the first set of pairs MR and RC correlated (*r*) at .540 and for the other set at .504. These correlations indicate that the 2 measures are related, but not highly. However, the samples of pairs used were not large (34 and 20 words), and so the full extent of the relation between these measures is not known. Little has been done to compare the utility of various other indices mentioned in this section, but all of them differ to some extent from one another and would not, therefore, be expected to be very highly interrelated.

In the two sections that follow, measures of associative overlap figure importantly in considerations of the structure of associations and in studies of the relationship of preexisting association to performance in verbal learning situations.

The Structure of Associations. In the beginning of this chapter, we mentioned the laws of association. These laws, especially the primary ones, imply the bases on which associations are organized and identify the kinds of dimensions which underlie associations between words, that is, contiguity in experience, similarity, and contrast. As was said

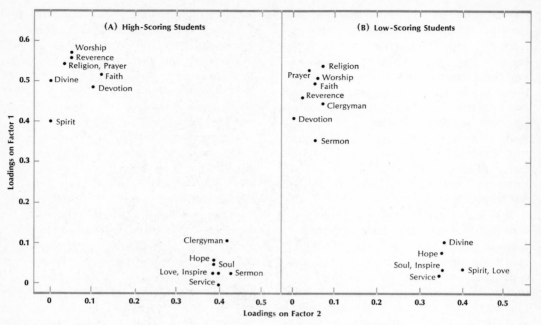

Figure 19.4. First and second factor loadings for 15 religious-value words for (a) subjects scoring high and (b) for subjects scoring low in religious value. (From data presented by Deese, 1965, Table 12, p. 84.)

then, Deese (1965) has argued that the identification of the laws and the structure of associations on the basis of introspective evidence may be faulty. His point is that the temporal sequence of items in thought may not indicate how the items of thought themselves became associated. Thought and language have an intrinsic sequential character, and evidence from introspection, which is like thought and which involves language, may lead to erroneous ideas as to how the items became associated in the first place.

Deese has studied the associative interrelations of words in the following way. First, he has collected single-word free associations from each word in a set of words and has then calculated the index of associative commonality for every pair of words in the set. Following this, he has factor-analyzed the commonality coefficients in order to identify the basic dimensions that underlie the interword associations of the set. The results of these procedures have led him to postulate two new laws of association. The new laws are

as follows: "(1) Elements are associatively related when they may be contrasted in some unique and unambiguous way"; and (2) "Elements are associatively related when they may be grouped because they can be described by two or more characteristics in common" (Deese, 1965, p. 165). The evidence which has led to these laws is our next concern. Comment on the laws will be made later.

Among the sets of words Deese analyzed are 15 words having to do with religion. Associations were obtained for each of these words from a group of subjects for whom religion had a high value and from another group for which religion had a low value. In Figure 19.4 the first two factors for this group of words are plotted for both groups of subjects. It may be seen, for both kinds of subjects, that the words are cleanly divided by the two factors, though the composition of the factors is slightly different for the two kinds of subjects. For the highly religious students, *religion, worship, reverence, prayer, spirit, divine, faith,* and *devotion* are found

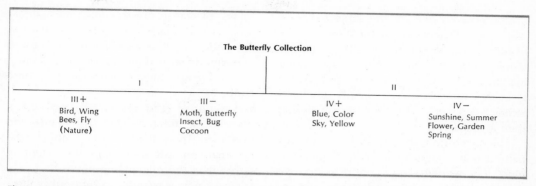

Figure 19.5. Tree diagram for the words in the *Butterfly* collection based on their loadings on the first 4 factors extracted. (Cofer, 1967, Fig. 9, p. 10, from data reported by Deese, 1965, Table 7, p. 76, and Fig. 2, p. 78.)

together on Factor I; *sermon, clergyman, service, soul, inspire, love,* and *hope* are found together on Factor II. Perhaps for them, Factor II words are related to church services, whereas Factor I words have more to do with the nature of their religious involvement. However this may be, it is clear that the factor structure clearly separates out words which go together from other words. For a set of 19 words which, to begin with, were the stimulus word *Butterfly* and its associates, Figure 19.5 displays in a tree diagram the items that appear on the first four factors extracted from the matrix. Again, there are clear separations, the first two factors splitting the words into animate and inanimate sets. Factor III splits the animate words into two groupings, and Factor IV does the same for the inanimate words. Factors III and IV imply contrasts between the sets of words on each factor, for these factors are bipolar. Deese has reported that his analyses of associations yield similar findings for various other word sets. This is true for 17 words related to *Music,* 16 related to *Slow,* 50 aggressive words, 14 verbal auxiliaries, 11 personal pronouns, and 7 conjunctions. Clearly, there appears to be an underlying order among the common associates for sets of words, and for the auxiliaries, pronouns, and conjunctions this order parallels grammatical function. How may this underlying order be characterized? The two laws of association, mentioned earlier, repre-

sent a summary of the characterization of this order. They were reached in the following way (adjectives and nouns will be our main concern). Deese suggests that the structure of verbs (aside from the auxiliaries) will resemble that for nouns. Adverbs yield mainly syntagmatic associations, and this characteristic suggests that their associates come largely from their immediate verbal environments (for example, mainly because . . . , blissfully happy . . . , and so on).

Study of associations to adjectives, as we saw earlier, revealed that high-frequency adjectives tend to elicit paradigmatic associates; infrequently occurring adjectives yield syntagmatic associates. Deese suggests (1965, p. 120) that the members of this latter group take their meaning, typically, from a root which is a noun; this fact, he thinks, would cause them to have syntagmatic associates.

A large proportion of the high-frequency adjectives appear to generate paradigmatic associations by eliciting contrasts as responses (for example, *Hot-cold, Slow-fast, Dark-light,* and so on). To test this proposition and to study it further, Deese obtained free associates to each one of 278 adjectives known from word counts to occur 50 or more times per million words in English. He then calculated by means of a computer the 38, 503 overlap coefficients this set of adjectives provides. He examined first 39 pairs of adjectives in which each member of the pair elicits the other as its primary and subjected their overlap coefficients to factor analysis. The result was that the polar opposite for a given word was the only one that had a substantial loading on the factor for that word. Words from the other pairs were simply unrelated to any given pair by this method of analyzing their associations.

The suggestion, then, is that the contrast pairs define a large number, perhaps 40 or more, independent dimensions of associative meaning. What of other adjectives, not included in this set of contrasting adjectives? Part of the answer is suggested by the use of the word *dimension* just now: Many adjectives are related primarily to other adjectives, which themselves relate to those which form contrasts (and to each other). Thus, if a basic contrast is provided by *big* and *little,* we find that *tiny, slight, small, large, great, grand, vast, huge* are related to *big* and *little* (and to each other) and in a way that describes a scale from one end of the dimension to another. Deese estimates that around 64 percent of the adjectives he used are either found in contrasting pairs or in one or more scalar dimensions anchored by such pairs. Many of the remaining ones, he thinks, would fit into this scheme if more data were available. Other adjectives, which do not enter into this scheme, are the color adjectives. They do not form contrasting pairs and their associative overlap coefficients generate several factors, such as the one we saw for the butterfly collection (Figure 19.5); they, then, tend to resemble nouns in this regard (and they are, of course, color *names* as well as adjectives).

The contrast arrangement, Deese suggests, arises because the contrasting adjectives can occur in common linguistic contexts. Thus, we can say "the tiny bird," "the large bird," "the small bird," and so on, "the big boy," "the little boy," or "the fast train," "the slow train," and the like, given that the choice of the adjective is determined by the actual feature of the bird, boy, or train of which we are speaking. Such common contexts presumably provide a way in which the contrasting adjectives become associated. There are

others, of course. For example, one training drill, used in many language arts classes in the grade school, emphasizes the relation of opposition and, in doing so, provides pairings of the common adjectives representing these contrasts.

For nouns (and presumably for verbs), however, a different kind of organization must exist. This statement is supported by the fact that contrasts are perhaps the exception rather than the rule among nouns. It is also true, as we have seen for the butterfly collection, that the associative structure of nouns is multidimensional. Deese suggests, in consequence of these facts, that another principle must underlie the associative structure of nouns.

This principle, as summarized in the second law of association, is that nouns are organized in terms of common features, that is, they are grouped together conceptually, rather than in terms of their common linguistic environments. In their pattern of common associations, one way in which their common properties is manifested is through their common adjectival associates; a given noun, Deese says, "selects" some adjectives and "rejects" others. Kittens and puppies can be grouped together, he points out, because they are warm, young, furry, helpless, cute, and the like. However, the dominant associations to nouns are other nouns, and this fact must provide the basis for the grouping of nouns into sets, along with commonality of adjectival descriptions. The noun associates are of two kinds: one is the same "type" as the stimulus—for example, *Academician* yields *scholar, student, professor,* and so on. The other "type" consists of nouns "that are merely present with or related to" (Deese, p. 144) the stimulus—for example, for *Academician* instances are *academy, study, school, university, diploma,* and so on. Perhaps the first type may be regarded as synonyms or quasisynonyms; the second type is composed, at least to some extent, of coordinates (the terms "synonym" and "coordinate" are not used by Deese). These 3 kinds of associations—attributive and nominals of the same or different type—together with a fourth category, "Other"—are said by Deese to characterize the associates to nouns. The first 3 kinds, of course, are related. Nouns grouped together share attributes, and those of the same type share conceptual or physical environments with nouns of different type, as *academician, student,* and *professor* can share the environments *school, university,* or *academy.* The organization of the associations in the case of nouns is, then, conceptual.

There is a parallel between these views of association offered by Deese and those expressed by Laffal (1965). Laffal, as we said earlier, has classified associations according to a system of categories. Then he has computed overlap measures for stimuli in terms of the categories (and their frequencies of occurrence) of the associations the stimuli elicit. Subjecting these measures to factor analysis, he finds structures for sets of words that appear generally similar to those obtained by Deese, as exemplified by the Butterfly collection. These findings have led Laffal to say "that there is a basic category structure in vocabulary and that associations reflect this structure."

It remains to discuss a little further Deese's laws of association and his suggestions as to the conditions under which they operate to bring a word into an associative relation with other words. It is obvious that he has retained the principle of contrast, though in doing so he has highlighted common linguistic environments as the reason that contrasting adjectives become associated. It appears to the writer that Deese has retained the principle of similarity, in some sense. The group of conceptual relations among associated nouns (and verbs) seems to involve a common feature (or element), and this notion is certainly one way of describing similarity. His emphasis on the group of associatively related words as a *structure,* whatever that may mean, has not been prominent in classical association theory. However, it is in his rejection of contiguity of experience that Deese is the most rejecting of the association theory of the past. In learning new items, Deese goes on to say,

"we assimilate them to existing groups or establish them with reference to some fundamental attributive contrast" (p. 165). Clearly, this suggests the influence of organizations that are already in existence, but new groups may appear "when there are a sufficient number of objects in experience and memory to establish some new and unique collection of attributes" (p. 166). The rule here is represented by concept formation rather than by associative learning as in the case of paired associates, and one may view associations "as generated from structural types or schemata" (p. 177), after, presumably, a structure has been formed.

Unfortunately, little is known about the conditions under which the associations revealed in association tests are established. Implicit in Deese's discussion of the different "types" of noun associates (the ones referred to by the writer as perhaps being coordinates) is, in the writer's view, the principle of contiguity—spatial, in all likelihood, rather than in the form of temporal succession. Most of us have seen academicians in universities or read that it is in universities that they will be found. It seems too early to the present writer to abandon the principle of contiguity, but the impressive evidence Deese and Laffal have accumulated for the existence of associative structures certainly sets an explanatory problem for the doctrine of association by contiguity.

Relational measures and verbal learning
With relational measures, the greatest amount of work has centered on the Paired Associates and the Free Recall situations, and information with regard to the measures and the serial learning and verbal discrimination tasks is sparse. However, in the discussion that follows, we cannot review the entire literature concerning relational measures and any verbal learning situation and will, therefore, concentrate on studies illustrating major problems.

Serial Learning. Using the serial anticipation procedure, Underwood and Postman (1960) found no differences between a list of

12 high-frequency 3-letter words and one composed of low-frequency 3-letter words in either trials to achieve criterion or in mean errors per trial. If high-frequency words are interassociated to a greater extent than low-frequency words, as there is reason from Deese's (1960) work to expect, we might have expected the high-frequency list to be more difficult to learn than the low-frequency list because the inter-word associations for the high frequency words should have interfered with the learning of the items in the sequence required in the experiment. There was, however, a somewhat larger proportion of intra-list errors for the high-frequency list than for the low-frequency list, in keeping with this expectation. Postman (1961), however, did find more rapid learning of a serial list composed of high-frequency 2-syllable adjectives than of a comparable low-frequency list. Again, however, intra-list errors, presumably reflecting associations between items, differentiated the two lists. Errors made in response to high-frequency words came at positions more remote from the correct item than was the case for low-frequency words. The more rapid learning of the high-frequency list in this case seems to be due to greater item availability, which apparently overcame the *intra-list intrusions* generated by associations between items.

If a serial list were composed such that the items followed one another in congruence with their associative relations, we might expect faster learning for such a list than for one in which the succession of items bears only a chance relation to associative interrelatedness, as was the case with the lists in the experiments just mentioned. Weingartner (1963) ran an experiment in which the arrangement of the serial items was organized to reflect the factor structure found for associations by Deese (see above). He used 16-item lists. In one arrangement (*moth, butterfly, insect, bug, bird, wing, bees, fly, blue, color, sky, yellow, sunshine, summer, garden, spring*), the words were presented in an order which preserved the factor structure shown in Figure 19.5, Factors III and IV. In other

orders, this arrangement was disrupted, including one in which the sequence of the 16 words was random. For the first, most orderly arrangement of the items 9.0 trials were required to learn the list, whereas for the random order (which remained constant over presentations) the mean was 15.2 trials. Clearly, the preservation of the associative relations between items in the first list gave it a marked advantage over the list in which the same items were used but in which their associative structures were disrupted. It is probable that these findings illustrate positive transfer from prior associations between words in the case of the first arrangement and negative transfer in the case of the disrupted arrangement.

Verbal Discrimination Learning. Underwood (1965) has reported that errors can arise in a recognition situation if a given item in the test has a strong associate (see also Schwartz & Rouse, 1961; Cramer, 1965). In his study a list of 200 words was recorded and then presented, one at a time at a 10-sec rate. As he heard each word, each subject judged whether or not the word had been presented earlier in the list. To illustrate what Underwood did and found, let us suppose that *dark* and *heavy* appeared fairly early in the sequence of 200 words and in different ordinal positions. Later on in the list (at least 30 serial positions later) the word *light* appears. Now *light* is an associate of both *Dark* and *Heavy*; if at the time the subject heard these latter two words he made the implicit associative response (IAR) *light* to either or both of them, we might expect that, when *light* is actually presented later on, the subject will judge it as having been presented before. In fact, this happened. In a group of 107 subjects, *light* was judged as having occurred before by 42 subjects, as compared to 13 times for a suitable control word. Underwood describes several other conditions which, apparently capable of arousing an IAR at the time one word is presented, produce false recognitions of this kind.

In verbal discrimination learning, one of

the members of a pair is arbitrarily designated by the experimenter as correct. What happens if the pair members are interassociated? Ullrich (1966) has reported that the more highly associated two words are, the more difficult it is for the subjects to learn to discriminate them in the verbal discrimination task. This is perhaps because, when the subject is told that one pair member is correct, he cannot, in view of the IAR which produces the other one, remember which one was said to be correct. Eckstrand, Wallace, and Underwood (1966) have provided evidence of a somewhat different kind. In one list, for example, two words that are associated were placed in different pairs. In one kind of pair the associated words were both correct (for example, *Queen* (+)— *fast, King* (+)— *pepper*); in another list one word was correct, the other incorrect (for example, *Queen* (+)— *fast, King-pepper* (+)); in still a third list, both associates were wrong in their respective pairs. As compared with a control, fewer errors were made on the pairs where both associates were correct; the items in which the associate was right in one but wrong in the other pair produced the largest number of errors, and there was little difference in errors between the control condition and the case in which the associates were wrong in both pairs. These findings indicate the role of IARs in verbal discrimination learning, although a more complete account of the findings just summarized requires consideration of frequency factors, as is indicated in a later section.

Free Recall. Deese (1959a) set up lists of 15 words each in such a way that the lists varied in the inter-item associative strength (IIAS) over a wide range. He obtained free recalls after a single presentation of each list. The correlation (*r*) between the number of items recalled and the IIAS was 0.88 (see Cofer, 1967, for a successful replication). Deese also reported that *intra-list intrusions* were less frequent for the lists high in IIAS than for those low in IIAS and that the intrusions given in the recall of a list high in IIAS were "agreed" upon by subjects, whereas the intrusions were scattered over many subjects in the lists with low IIAS (see Deese, 1959b). There have been several other reports in which measures of association have been found to be related to the amount of free recall (Bousfield et al., 1960; Rothkopf & Coke, 1961a). Marshall (1963) found modest degrees of correspondence between MR (mutual relatedness; see p. 880) and the number of items in free recall.

In free recall we can study not only the sheer number of items produced but also the sequence in which they occur in a subject's recall. Remembering that in this method each subject is free to order the items in his recall in any way he chooses, we might anticipate that the order the subject adopted will reflect interrelations among the words of the list presented to him. One way in which these interrelations could be manifested in recall is that related words might be placed together in sequences, that is, in recall *clusters* of related words might be produced. One reason for the great interest in free recall over the period since about 1950 is that subjects do cluster related responses in their recalls and that the clusters bear regular relationships to independently determined relationships between words.

Jenkins, Mink, and Russell (1958) set up four lists of 24 words each..In one list the words were taken from highly associated pairs (for example, *man-woman*), and the degree of association between pair members was varied in the other lists, so that it was low in the fourth list (for example, *whistle-stop*). The 24 items were presented one by one; that is, the pair members were separated at the time of the single presentation. Jenkins and his co-workers were interested in whether the pair members would occur together in recall and whether the extent to which this associative clustering occurs would be related to the free association strength known from the norms to vary in the four lists. Both phenomena occurred, that is, associative clustering was ob-. served, and its extent was directly related to the free association strength for the pairs. Thus, an average of 3.57 associative clusters was obtained for the highly associated list and only 0.78 for the list with the least association. A number of other studies have confirmed these findings with several indices of associative strength (see Marshall & Cofer, 1963, for a summary and references).

Amount of recall and clustering are thus related to relational measures of association. We see a little later that there is another kind of clustering (category) and will be concerned with the question of whether it can be differentiated from associative clustering.

Paired-associate Learning. Because in paired-associate learning we ask a subject to learn a given response in conjunction with a particular stimulus, it would appear to be reasonable that learning rate should vary with the frequency with which that response is made to the stimulus in free association.

With adults, however, this expectation has not often been fulfilled. Several investigations (summarized by Jenkins, 1963, p. 215) have failed to obtain differences among pairs in which the free-association strength of the response to its stimulus varied over a range from 70 to 0.2 percent, although pairs with associative strength in this range are learned more quickly than unrelated (control) pairs. The associated pairs are learned very rapidly, so rapidly that measures such as trials to criterion and number of correct responses or of errors are perhaps insensitive to differences occasioned by variations in pre-experimental associative strength. Using latency of response as a measure, Shapiro (1966) found differences of the expected kind.

There are reports, however, in which the speed of learning is found to be associated with free-association strength under certain conditions. For example, Postman (1962; also Martin, 1964) found this relation to hold when the stimuli used were low-frequency words but did not find it when the stimuli were high-frequency words. This may suggest that properties of the associative hierarchy, as well as free-association response strength per se, are significant to the relationship obtained, a factor which Howe (1967, personal communication) has investigated, and which was summarized above when we considered interpretations of the relation of verbal learning to *m*, *m'*, and *av*.

With children, in contrast, relations between free-association strength and paired-associate learning have been obtained, and certain representative studies will be described. Palermo and Jenkins (1964b) used children's association norms (Palermo & Jenkins, 1964a) to establish pairs with high-strength primaries (32 to 44 percent) and with weak primaries (9 to 12 percent). Control pairs contained the same stimuli but unassociated responses. Mixed lists were used with fifth-grade children. Associated pairs at both levels were learned more rapidly than control pairs, and the ease of learning varied directly with the associative strength in the pairs containing stimuli and their primaries. Similar results have been obtained by several investigators at this grade level as well as at higher and lower grades.

The suggestion in these differences between children and adults in the relation of free-association strength to paired-associate learning is that perhaps for adults all the possible associative responses, whatever their strength, are so highly available to their stimuli that little effort is required to "learn" them in the paired-associate situation. With children, however, due to their having had less experience with the language, response availability varies in accordance with associative strength and is therefore reflected in PA learning.

A further finding in the study by Palermo and Jenkins (1964b) appeared with the control pairs. In these pairs, of course, the responses were unassociated with their stimuli. Yet control pairs in which the stimuli were known to have high-strength primaries produced fewer errors than pairs in which the stimuli were known to have low-strength primaries. What this finding appears to mean is that, if stimuli with low-strength primaries are used, there are more responses of moderate strength that can interfere with the learning of the unassociated response term than there are in the case of the stimuli with high-strength primaries. This is to say that the steepness or the shape of the hierarchy, as well as the absolute strengths of the associations themselves, are involved in the results of experiments relating free-association strength to rapidity of PA learning. This is consistent with the interpretation offered by Howe and mentioned above.

Several studies have also investigated PA learning in pairs in which the S-R associative strength varies as indicated by controlled association norms. As we mentioned above, Underwood and Richardson (1965a) used nouns to which they asked their subjects to give "sensory associations," that is, words descriptive of properties of the nouns that can be perceived directly via the senses. As we said above, response words vary in dominance level under these conditions. The question, then, may be asked: Will the learning of pairs vary as a function of their dominance levels? The answer is affirmative. Underwood and Richardson (1956b) found that if four noun stimuli were paired with a single sensory association, the mean dominance level for that association (for its four stimuli) was directly related to ease of learning. Parallel findings were reported by Underwood and Schulz (1960) for mixed and unmixed lists of pairs varying in dominance level.

Coleman (1963) required his subjects to give continued associations to stimuli, restricting the associations to adjectives. He argued that the first response obtained in this way should be stronger for a given subject than later responses. If, for example, the associates to *Doughnut* are *sweet, round,* and *crusty,* in that order, we should expect the sentence, *Doughnut is sweet,* to be learned more rapidly than the sentence, *Doughnut is crusty.* This would be so because there are no stronger adjective associations than *sweet* to interfere with the learning of the first sentence, whereas both *sweet* and *round* can interfere with the learning of the sentence, *Doughnut is crusty.* Using as learning mate-

rials sentences like those just indicated, Coleman obtained results confirming his expectations (see also Coleman, 1964).

Finally, there are also some preexisting "serial structures" that one brings to any learning situation that certainly influence both the ease of learning paired-associate (and other) tasks and the nature of the errors which occur. For example, almost all of us are aware of a dimension running from freshman to senior, with intermediate points (sophomore, junior) having determinate serial positions. DeSoto and Bosley (1962) used these terms as the responses in a paired-associate learning task, with the names of fictitious persons as the stimuli. The entire list contained 16 pairs to be learned, with 4 names associated with each of the responses. Thus, a subject had to learn to say "Junior" when he saw "Fred Brown," and "Freshman" when he saw "Harry Smith." The important point here is that the errors that occurred during this learning were "good" ones far more frequently than might be expected on the basis of chance: If a name should have been called "Freshman," the most frequent error was to call it "Sophomore," and the least frequent error was to say "Senior." Furthermore, the correct application of the labels "Freshman" and "Senior" was made most quickly, suggesting that subjects were using some type of end anchoring system, even though this had no real relevance in this situation. Pollio (1966) and Pollio and Draper (1966) have shown how such serial structures influence word associations and serial learning. Clearly, this is a property of verbal materials that is dependent upon our familiarity with a language and one which can have important influences on verbal learning.

Summary. From this rather brief and selective review of the evidence concerning relational measures and verbal learning situations, it is clear that relations between prior associations and learning are often substantial ones. It is also clear, however, that associative strength is not the only variable, for the presence of other conflicting associations must also be considered in anticipating the outcomes of experiments of these kinds.

So far as paired-associate learning is concerned, there are many other studies in which free association has been investigated. These studies have been concerned with mediated transfer and therefore are outside the scope of the present chapter.

Conceptual relations Words may, of course, be related to one another in many ways aside from those encompassed in measures of associative relation. Actually, measured associative relations are often confounded with other ways in which words are related, and conversely. Words may bear many logical relations to one another—they may be synonyms, antonyms, coordinates, subordinate members of a class, class names for subordinates, members of the same form class, and so on. Dimensions of this kind, especially those of synonymity and antonymity, have sometimes been used in experiments on verbal learning and retention when the similarity between items has been a problem of interest to investigators. One question that can be raised at once is whether these properties are independent of one another and of associative interrelations.

This is not an easy question to answer, aside from the problem of the extent of the intercorrelations. This is to say, given a correlation, it is difficult to determine whether the associative relation is fundamental to the conceptual relation, or conversely. At the present stage of inquiry, we must be content with a statement of such correlative relations as have been established.

Haagen (1949)[8] selected 80 "standard" words, and for each standard word used five other words that appeared to have some degree of synonymity to the standard. He then asked subjects to rate each of the five words against the standard on a scale of syn-

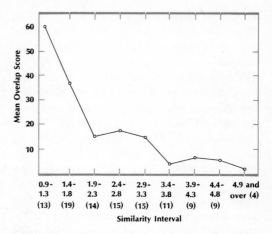

Figure 19.6. Associative overlap in pairs of words as a function of judged synonymity between the members of the pair. (Synonymity ranges from high—0.9–1.3—to low—4.9+.) The numbers in parentheses along the abscissa indicate the number of pairs represented in the mean overlap score for the synonymity interval. (Cofer, 1965, Fig. 1, p. 262.)

onymity. (A rating of 1 indicated high synonymity.) As an example, consider the following set of words: *Royal* is the standard word, and the five synonyms, with the rating of the degree of synonymity to royal, are as follows: *regal* (1.1), *kingly* (1.6), *stately* (2.4), *sceptered* (3.3), *ruling* (3.9). Cofer (1957) obtained free associations to a number of Haagen's words and computed associative overlap between a number of the words and their standard words. Figure 19.6 shows a plot of associative overlap scores against rated synonymity. Clearly, the words rated as highly synonymous also show high associative overlap, and the decline in rated synonymity roughly parallels the decline in associative overlap. For these items, then, synonymity and associative overlap vary together. If we wished to uncover the role of synonymity in some verbal problem, we would be well advised to control for degree of associative overlap.

The only other data known to the author that provide for an analysis of conceptual relations among words in conjunction with

[8]Similarity ratings for pairs of 2-syllable adjectives have been published by Hilgard (1951, Table 11, pp. 548–552). The data came from an unpublished study by Melton and Safier.

association were reported by Cohen, Bousfield, and Whitmarsh (1957). They selected a number of conceptual categories and asked subjects to provide instances of each category. The data, then, were obtained under instructions for controlled association. It is clear from their norms that certain responses are much more likely than others to be given as instances for a given category. For example, the category four-legged animals yields the words *dog, cat,* and *lion* at high frequencies, the words *zebra* and *giraffe* at much lower frequencies.

Only a few attempts have been made to study conceptual relations in conjunction with verbal learning situations, and even fewer have been controlled for associative overlap to allow for an assessment of the independent contribution of the conceptual factor. The writer knows of no studies of conceptual relations in regard to verbal discrimination learning, and such studies as there are of synonymity in serial learning are treated in the next section. This leaves free recall and paired-associate learning, to which we turn now.

Free Recall. Bousfield's (1953) first study of clustering under free recall conditions made use of a list of 60 words, 15 in each of the following four categories: vegetables, animals, professions, and men's first names. The items were presented in a randomized order, and the single recalls were scored for the occurrence of category clustering, that is, the appearance in sequence of items from the same category. Thus, using letters to indicate items from the categories just indicated, the following sequence would show four clusters: AVVVPAAVNPPNNNN. The clusters vary in size, from two to four items. Bousfield developed procedures for comparing the amount of clustering obtained with the amount expected by chance. He has found category clustering over a wide range of materials and has investigated extensively variables which are pertinent to it.

Because of his interest in clustering, Bousfield did not include a control list of unrelated words, but Underwood (1964, pp. 63–65) has reported that word lists that contain categorized items produce more items in recall than comparable lists of unrelated words. Cofer (1967a) obtained similar findings. However, the interpretation of the augmentation of recall is not entirely clear, that is, it is not certain whether it is the categories or perhaps associative interrelations among the items in the categories that are responsible for the augmented recalls of lists of categorized items. It is also possible that the increased recall, on either basis, may represent not so much an increase in the number of items remembered but rather the fact that category and associational relations may permit a subject to generate additional items on the basis of those he does remember. A generative process, accompanied by the ability to recognize which of the items generated were and were not on the list presented, would account for the augmented recall. Cofer (1967a) has summarized evidence for this generative and editing interpretation.

However, categorization has been found to be related to the amount of clustering and to some extent to the number of items produced in recall, when the degree of associative overlap is equated. Marshall (1963) studied lists composed either of pairs or of four-word sets of words (presented in a randomized order). The pair members were either readily categorizable (for example, *Eagle-Crow*) or were not easily categorized (*Soft-Silk*). Marshall arranged to have pairs of both types (and four-word sets) in which associative overlap was equated. As indicated, he found that categorized members clustered more and were somewhat better recalled than noncategorized items, although these differences appeared mainly at low and intermediate mutual relatedness (MR) levels. Where associative overlap was high, it made no difference whether the pair members were categorized or not.

In a study of some of Marshall's pairs, Cofer (1966) asked subjects to write a word or phrase which could link or relate the members of the pair. He tabulated the number of such words or phrases for the two kinds of pairs, finding that about half as many such words or phrases were given for categorized pair members as for uncategorized pair members. This means that there is better agreement on which linking words or phrases are to be assigned to the categorized than to the noncategorized pairs. This suggests that categorization may provide a ready means of coding categorized pair members. Whether this should be interpreted as an associative mechanism of coding is perhaps impossible to say. Incidentally, there was no relation between the number of linking words or phrases and MR level, for either kind of pair.

At the present time, it is not possible to reach a firm conclusion with respect to the role of conceptual relations in free recall, in view of the question of confounding with association. (For a contrasting viewpoint, see Mandler, 1967.)

Paired-associate Learning. The situation is little better in the case of paired-associate learning. In the author's laboratory, evidence for more rapid acquisition over the first five trials of PA learning of categorized than of uncategorized pairs has been obtained (after being equated for associative overlap). It is uncertain how far this finding can be generalized.

Richardson (1958, 1960) has used a kind of paired-associate learning, in which he paired several stimuli with the same response. The stimuli with a common response were similar (for example, *sacred, divine, hallowed, holy*), were members of the same class (for example, *pine, maple, walnut, elm*), had a common property (*barrel, doughnut, knob, balloon,* all of which are round), or were unrelated (*perfect, dirty, removed, rising*). Several sets of stimuli were used in each list. Some advantage was present in paired-associate learning for the lists containing sets of similar stimuli and for sets of stimuli belonging to the same class; it is possible, of course, that these sets of stimuli were associatively interrelated (see also Cohen & Hut,

1963). Hence, it is uncertain at the present time how much credit should be given to the conceptual relations involved and how much to inter-item associations.

Inter-item similarity Similarity between items in a list can take several forms. These same forms of similarity, of course, can be present between lists, and this similarity has been of interest to investigators working with transfer between lists and interference effects. In this chapter, however, we confine our discussion to the similarity between items (or within lists) so far as acquisition is concerned.

Variations in similarity can be accomplished in several ways. With nonsense-syllable and CCC trigrams, similarity is usually defined in terms of letter duplication. Thus, GAX and DUP have no letter duplication, whereas DUP and DAX have 1, and DUP and DUX have 2 letter duplications. In the case of words, high associative overlap between words would indicate associative similarity, as would conceptual relations, such as synonymity and common class membership. We have, of course, already described several of these ways in which words may be similar.

Similarity has a profound effect in the acquisition phase of verbal learning. It is now common (Underwood & Schulz, 1960a, pp. 92–94), however, to divide acquisition itself into two processes or stages (on which inter-item similarity may have different effects). One stage is response learning or response integration. During this stage, the subject learns what the responses are and, in the case in which the responses represent unusual combinations of letters (for example, TPL), he must also learn the combination as a unit. The second stage is the associative or hook-up stage, in which the responses become associated with their stimuli.

The response learning stage is usually regarded as being reflected especially well in free recall. This is because the responses in free recall are not associated with specific stimuli. We have seen that various kinds of similarity between words appear to augment free recall, and we see below that, in general, similarity between items is thought to facilitate free recall. In discriminating items, as in a recognition test, for example (see Bahrick & Bahrick, 1964; Bruce & Cofer, 1967), subjects have difficulties when the items are similar. In the associative stage in serial learning and in paired-associate learning, inter-item similarity is also a factor which makes learning difficult.

An illustration of the different effects of the similarity between items on free recall and on the formation of associations is provided by an experiment reported by Underwood, Runquist, and Schulz (1959). They began with five presentations of two different lists of words, obtaining a free recall after each presentation. One list contained 10 nearly synonymous words (for example, *sunny, carefree, cheerful*), the other 10 unrelated words (for example, *rounded, spicy, hairy*). The number of correct responses over the first three trials of this procedure was greater for the list with similar items than it was for the list of unrelated words. These two lists were also employed in paired-associate learning (with nonsense syllables as stimuli). At certain trials, free recall of the response terms were obtained. In the early trials, free recall was again greater for the similar than for the unrelated items, but, over 15 trials of paired-associate learning the reverse took place, that is, more correct responses were given for the list of unrelated words than for the list of similar words. If the free recall procedure indexes the response learning stage and paired-associate learning the associative stage, we can say that similarity between items facilitates the former and retards the latter stage of learning.

Somewhat similar results were reported by Horowitz (1961) for serial learning of 12 trigrams. One list of trigrams was made up from only four letters (high similarity), the other from 12 different letters (low similarity). Each list was learned by a free recall group and a group which had only to reconstruct the serial order of the trigrams, the trigrams themselves being provided on a set of 12 cards. More similar than dissimilar trigrams were recalled over the first five of 10 trials of the free recall procedure, whereas the dissimilar trigrams resulted in a higher score than the similar trigrams on a measure of success in reconstructing the serial order over the 10 trials. If serial ordering requires learning in the associative stage, the results again show more rapid learning in this stage for dissimilar items, whereas free recall showed better learning for the similar items. Whether this conclusion for trigrams can be generalized, however, beyond Horowitz's particular high-similarity list is doubtful (see Underwood, Eckstrand, & Keppel, 1964, pp. 207–208).

Aside from the influence of similarity between items in relation to the two stages of learning, there is other evidence that it may have profound effects. In paired-associate learning, Underwood and his coworkers (1964) used color names as stimuli and trigrams as responses. In one list, the six trigrams were dissimilar, no letters being duplicated, but the trigrams in the other list were similar, being composed from only five letters. In 15 trials the dissimilar list yielded a mean of 31.50 correct responses per subject, whereas the similar list yielded only 5.77 correct responses. This difference, five- or sixfold, illustrates the profound effect interresponse similarity can have in the PA situation.

In another experiment with this task, Feldman and Underwood (1957) used lists of seven pairs. In one case, the stimuli were similar trigrams and the responses unrelated words. This list required 28.53 trials to learn, whereas with the same responses but with dissimilar trigram stimuli only 15.13 trials were required. Combined similarity between stimuli (trigrams) and between responses (words), in another condition, yielded a list requiring 34.20 trials to learn.

As can be readily guessed, similarity is a factor in serial anticipation learning. Using a list of 14 similar adjectives, Underwood and Goad (1951, Table 1, p. 127) reported that this list required 18.70 trials, whereas a list of dissimilar adjectives required only 13.75 trials for learning. Manipulating trigrams by means of letter duplication into serial lists varying at three levels of similarity, Underwood (1952) also found ease of learning to vary inversely with level of similarity from low to high.

Higa (1963) manipulated associative and conceptual similarity in PA learning in several ways. The stimuli included in all the lists were 12 trigrams. In one list the response words were six pairs of antonyms (for example, *dark, light*), in another, six pairs of associates (*scissors, cut*), in yet another, six pairs of synonyms (*fast, rapid*), and in a fourth six pairs of coordinates (for example, *apple, pear*). Unrelated words were used in a control list. Lists in which the response members involved antonyms, synonyms, or coordinates were more difficult to learn than the control list. This presumably means that subjects had difficulty in determining which antonym, which synonym, or which coordinate of the two available in each list to pair with the appropriate stimulus. This is a case of interference, and in some instances (as with the associates) may have arisen because of implicit associative responses (see above).

Inter-item similarity, then, is a potent characteristic of materials in acquisition in verbal learning tasks. It seems to facilitate response learning but to hinder the learning of associations between particular responses and specific stimuli. This topic will be encountered again in the discussions of retention and transfer, with respect to similarity between lists. (For a more complete review of the literature and for the report of their experiments, see Goss and Nodine, 1965, Chapter 5 and Appendix.)

Counts

As is indicated in the introduction to this chapter, one of the secondary laws of association is frequency; that is, in the formation of associations the frequency with which the items are experienced together is a factor in their becoming associated. Frequency of occurrence is a variable which is easily mani-

pulated in the laboratory, and many investigations, especially those concerned with retention over time, have included this variable as an important element. The whole notion of the incremental growth of habit strength, with each contingency between the stimulus and response adding some strength to the association between them, is a reflection of the law of frequency. One of the theoretical issues in the study of learning is whether frequency is a necessary and sufficient condition for the acquisition of an association. We do not enter into the discussion of this issue here but register the issue as an indication of why frequency has been considered as so important.

A notion closely related to frequency is that of familiarity. Presumably, frequently experienced items are familiar ones. Hence, ratings of familiarity are often employed instead of actual frequency counts to assess, essentially, frequency. The validity of such ratings is, of course, then of interest, and, to the extent that the ratings are valid, indicates that people have and can report information concerning frequency characteristics of their language.

Counts have been made of the frequency with which words, letters, and combinations of letters appear, usually, in printed sources and, occasionally, in records of speech. We discuss them first and some of their properties as well as indicating whether ratings of familiarity relate to frequency counts.

Word counts   Although a number of word counts have been published in part or whole (see Goss and Nodine, 1965, p. 18, for references), the most important count is the one published by Thorndike and Lorge (1944). This count brings together data collected by Thorndike and reported in 1921 and 1931, a count made from magazines by Lorge, one made from books for juveniles, and a semantic count.[9] The collection was made by hav-

---

[9] The semantic count involved the determination of the apparent meaning of a word in context, and the meanings were classified by means of the list of meanings provided by the *Oxford English Dictionary*. A valuable abridgment

ing readers tally words as they read various kinds of texts, aggregating 4.5 million words for all of the counts. (The magazine count included only 1 million words [Thorndike & Lorge, 1944, p. 252].) The kinds of materials used by Thorndike included selections from sources as diverse as *Black Beauty, Little Women,* an issue of *The Youth's Companion, A Garden and Farm Almanac,* newspapers, and a book entitled *Pioneers of Australian Industry.* The sources for Lorge's magazine count were popular magazines, such as the *Saturday Evening Post, True Story,* and the *Reader's Digest,* published between 1927 and 1938. Similar sources were used for the other counts.

In the Thorndike-Lorge book itself, there are listed over 19,000 items which occurred once or more per million words. The frequencies are shown for each word in columns for the Thorndike (T), Lorge (L), juvenile (J), and semantic (S) counts. There is also a column headed "G," for general count. The G count is said to be "a summary from all four counts" (p. x) and is the one most commonly used. In it words that occur more than 100 times per million are simply designated AA and those occurring between 50 and 100 times per million as A; no actual frequencies are indicated for AA and A words. The book also includes lists of words occurring four times per 18,000,000 words. There are 30,000 words, altogether, in this volume, representing, probably, the words in most common use (at the time the tallies were done) of the roughly half-million lexical units in the English vocabulary that may be found in the *Oxford English Dictionary.*

Although quite out of date, the Thorndike-

Lorge word list has been and continues to be useful and widely employed. Aside from its age, however, a further limitation on it is that it is based on printed English. There is some reason to believe that a word count of spoken English might indicate different word frequencies. Howes (1966) has published such a count, based on 250,000 spoken words recorded between 1960 and 1965. To obtain these data, interviews were conducted and recorded from 41 different subjects, 20 of whom were college sophomores and 21 of whom were patients hospitalized mainly because of bone injuries and peripheral nerve disease. The total number of different words he recorded was 9,699 of which 4,097 occurred only a single time each. So far, no use has been made of the Howes word count in studies of verbal learning, due to the fact that it has appeared so recently.

Before going on to indicate the significance of variations in word frequency to verbal learning, it is worth noting that there are a number of statistical relations in language behavior that appear in both spoken and written language and in a variety of languages. Among these are that a relatively small number of words from the total vocabulary occur with great frequency, whereas other words occur infrequently. In general, the frequently occurring words are shorter than the infrequently used words. There is much regularity in these and other statistical properties of language, although the speaker and the writer are probably not ordinarily aware that their verbal outputs obey these laws. (For further discussion and references, see Miller, 1951; Osgood, 1953.)

Word frequency is related to learning in certain verbal learning situations, although the available evidence is not extensive. Hall (1954) used four lists of 20 words each, presenting each list five times before asking for recalls. The lists varied, in Thorndike-Lorge frequency, from occurrences of 50 to 100 times per million words for the highest frequency list to one per million for the lowest frequency list. Recalls for the first of these lists averaged 15.04 words as against 12.04

---

of this work has been provided by West (1953). West's volume contains about 2,000 entries, and the meanings as well as the form classes determined for each word are recorded, together with their relative frequencies. For example, the word *man* (Rosenzweig & McNeill, 1962) is listed as having the following meanings with the percentage of occurrence of each in parentheses: *human* (10), *adult* (14), *male* (9), *soldier* (6), *servant* (1), *person* (54); all of these meanings are most likely nominal uses of the word *man.* However, the verb form also occurs 0.4 percent of the time.

words for the low-frequency list, a small but significant difference. There is a question, however, whether the difference reflects the variation in frequency or in inter-word association. As we know, free recall is greater for words that are associated than it is for words that are not associated. Deese (1960) verified Hall's findings but was also able to show that there were more inter-word associations in the case of high-frequency words than among low-frequency words. The differences in inter-item associations may, then, have been responsible for the relation of word frequency to recall, found by Hall.

In contrast, in serial-anticipation learning and in paired-associate learning it could be argued that associations between words should interfere with acquisition; we have seen evidence of this effect already. However, in serial-anticipation learning, a list composed of high-frequency words is learned more rapidly than one composed of low-frequency words (Underwood & Postman, 1960, Postman, 1961), and acquisition was faster in paired-associate learning when the response terms were high-frequency words than when they were of moderate frequency; the slowest acquisition occurred when low-frequency response words were to be learned. In contrast, when the word frequency was varied on the stimulus side, learning rate was best for words of moderate frequency. It is possible that associations between stimuli (for example, between *country* and *doctor*) may have handicapped paired-associate learning in the case of the high-frequency stimulus list.

It is worth noting that judgments of word frequency, which are like familiarity, correlate fairly well with the actual counted frequencies of the words judged. The judgments are highly reliable and are correlated with actual frequency at about .80 over five sets of words (Howes, 1954).

Letter, bigram, trigram, and other counts
A number of counts have been reported for the frequencies with which single letters, bigrams,

and trigrams occur in printed words (see Goss & Nodine, 1965, pp. 18–20, for references). The techniques employed are simply to select samples of so many words from each of a variety of printed materials such as magazines, newspapers, novels, encyclopedias, and the like. Single-letter counts are made by simply tallying occurrences of each letter as they are encountered in the material. Bigram and trigram counts are made as the following example illustrates: The word *Learning* contains the following bigrams, *Le, ea, ar, rn, ni, in, ng,* and the following trigrams, *Lea, ear, arn, rni, nin, ing.* Similar breakdowns would provide tetragrams such as *Lear, earn, arni, rnin, ning,* and pentagrams such as *Learn, earni, arnin, rning.* As each word is analyzed in this way, the resulting bigrams, trigrams, and so on, are recorded and tallies are made for frequencies of occurrence.

Single-letter frequencies are reported by Underwood and Schulz (1960, p. 69, Table 6), who also include data from other sources, and by Mayzner and Tresselt (1965). Mayzner and Tresselt report that a rank-difference correlation between the rankings for their total frequencies for single letters and the "U" count of Underwood and Schulz is .97. Mayzner and Tresselt report their frequencies not only as totals for a letter but also as number of occurrences in each position for 3-, 4-, 5-, 6-, and 7-letter words. Illustrative of their data is that the letter *A* occurs a total of 7,071 times in their sample of 20,000 words, as compared to 5,417 for Underwood and Schulz's sample of 15,000. It occurs 1,225 times as the first letter of a 3-letter word and only eight times as the third letter. These values may be compared to 129 times as the first letter and five times as the seventh letter in a 7-letter word.

In their Appendix D, Underwood and Schulz (1960, pp. 332–369) report frequency data for bigrams and trigrams. Mayzner and Tresselt (1965) report bigram frequencies (and their results again correspond well to those presented by Underwood and Schulz). Mayzner, Tresselt, and Wolin (1965a, b, c) provide

tables for trigrams, tetragrams, and pentagrams. These counts are also broken down for
word length and position of the combinations
in the words of different lengths.

When single letters are used as responses
in paired-associate learning, and 2-digit numbers are employed as stimuli over 15 trials,
more correct responses are made as letter
frequency increases (Underwood & Schulz,
Experiment 9, pp. 163–167, Figure 22). A similar
but less regular relation is found between
learning and frequency when bigrams are
used as responses (Underwood & Schulz,
1960, pp. 167–169, Figure 23). Korn and Lindley
(1963) studied the serial recall for strings of
consonants, one string being composed of
high-frequency consonants, the other of
low-frequency consonants. Serial recall was
better for the string of frequent consonants
than for the string of less-frequent consonants. Mayzner and Schoenberg (1964) used
the same sets of consonants to construct
bigrams but arranged each set so as to manipulate bigram frequency. With the high-
frequency consonants it was possible to arrange the letters so that bigram frequencies
were high (H-H) and also so that the bigram
frequencies were low (H-L). With the low-
frequency consonants, it was possible to
arrange only bigrams of low frequency (L-L).
Over six strings of each type, the H-H list
yielded 42.25 correct responses, the H-L string
32.50, and the L-L set 21.96 correct responses.
Clearly, then, frequency of single letters and
of bigrams has some relation to learning in
PA learning and serial recall tasks.

With trigrams which vary in frequency,
however, the relation to learning has been
inconsistent and mostly of low or zero magnitude. Underwood and Schulz (1960) report
eight experiments with paired-associate
learning and one with serial-anticipation
learning in which trigram frequency has been
studied. Within the range where meaning (as
estimated from m, av, and related measures)
makes a difference to learning, no systematic
relation between counted frequency (which
Underwood and Schulz suggested was the

variable underlying m and av, and so on) and
learning was found when pronunciability of
the items is taken into account. Although not
all writers are agreed that pronunciability is
a more important variable than frequency or
m (Johnson, 1962; Noble, 1963, pp. 109–110),
the data amassed by Underwood and Schulz
on this score are impressive. We have more
to say on this problem in the section on
ratings. That the frequency of trigrams does
not to relate to learning, independently of
pronunciability, however, does not invalidate
the relations we have seen between learning
and single-letter frequency, bigram frequency, and word frequency. In addition,
there are trigrams for which a kind of frequency is predictive of learning (Underwood
& Schulz, 1960, pp. 279–280). These are consonant syllables or other items with low
association values, which are difficult to
pronounce. For them the summed letter
frequencies predict learning, when alphabetical sequences are eliminated. Although pronunciability ratings also predict learning in
these cases, Underwood and Schulz are able
to argue that pronunciability, for these items,
may depend on summed letter frequency.

Before leaving the question of frequency
counts, it is worth mentioning that ratings or
rankings of items for familiarity or frequency
do reflect the actual frequencies obtained
from counts. For individual letters, Attneave
(1953) asked a large number of Air Force
trainees to think of a newspaper clipping
containing 1,000 letters and then to estimate
for each letter of the alphabet the frequency
with which it would appear. The judgments
of frequency and the actual frequency of
letters in one group correlated at .79 and in
another at .88. Underwood and Schulz (1960,
pp. 52–56) presented their subjects with a pair
either of bigrams or trigrams and asked them
to choose the more frequently occurring one;
they found that the judgments, on the average, were more often correct than incorrect.
In another study of trigrams (pp. 184–187)
judged frequency was correlated with
counted frequency at from .46 to .51. (See

also Mayzner & Tresselt, 1962; Mayzner, 1964.)[10]

A frequency theory of verbal discrimination learning Eckstrand, Wallace, and Underwood (1966) have proposed that frequency differentials are critical to verbal discrimination learning. In this situation, it will be recalled, two items are presented simultaneously or successively, and a subject is asked to indicate which one is correct (C) or incorrect (I). The argument made by Eckstrand and his coworkers is that "the cue for discrimination is the subjective difference in frequency of occurrence between the C and I item" (p. 567) in each pair. When the frequency difference reaches a 2:1 difference between C and I, it serves as a cue for the application of a rule by the subject, that is, the rule of always selecting the more frequent of the members in a pair.

There are several sources by means of which frequency may be established. On the first or guessing trial, for example, a subject reads each pair member, thus giving each member a unit of frequency from these "representational responses." Then, the subject chooses one pair member and pronounces it, adding another unit of frequency by means of this pronouncing response (PR). In order to build up frequencies in favor of the correct response (because learning occurs in this situation), it is also supposed that when the experimenter tells his subject what the correct response is, the subject will rehearse the correct response (RCR), which adds a frequency unit to the correct choice. The com-

bination of frequency increments from these three sources will, ultimately, over trials, favor the C alternative. A fourth factor which may add to the frequency is, for the case in which items in the same or different pairs are associated, the occurrence of implicit associative responses (IARs). We have already discussed the role of IARs in verbal discrimination learning.

The theory described above fits data already in the literature and was, indeed, developed to account for these data. Eckstrand and his coworkers provide further data in support of the formulation. Systematic differences in the difficulty of learning were found when a given element was the correct alternative in two pairs, and when it was incorrect in two other pairs in the list. The difficulty was greatest for the case of an item that was right in one and wrong in another pair, next for the case of an item that was incorrect in two pairs, and least for the case of an item's being correct in two pairs; the last case was superior to a control condition. Because the same items were used in the different arrangements in the experiment by Eckstrand and his coworkers the results are presumably due to the sources of frequency outlined above and cannot be explained on the basis of *m*, pronunciability, and other similar factors.

Ratings

It is possible to rate or to rank verbal units in a great many ways. We have already discussed several kinds of ratings, including those used as alternatives to production measures and frequency counts, for example. In this section other dimensions are mentioned, their relations to learning scores are summarized, and their intercorrelations will be described. Finally, we can raise the question whether these several dimensions are really different or whether in fact they represent alternative ways of assessing the place of verbal units on some more basic or underlying dimensions. Goss and Nodine (1965, pp.

---

[10] Familiarization procedures are a way of studying frequency experimentally. Basically, they provide for experience with the list items or with the stimuli or the responses of the items before the items are arranged in a list for actual learning. The results of experiments involving familiarization have been summarized by Goss and Nodine (1965, Chapter 6). Unfortunately, the effects of familiarization, as carried out in a number of experiments, have been inconsistent. That is, sometimes familiarization facilitates, sometimes inhibits, and sometimes has no effects on learning. Goss and Nodine (p. 178) say of these results, "at the present time . . . factors responsible for inconsistencies cannot be specified. . . ." Despite the interest and the importance of familiarization to verbal learning, the topic will not be discussed here because of the inconsistent findings.

20–59) have provided a comprehensive review of this topic.

In addition to familiarity and scaled meaningfulness, which are discussed above, the following dimensions or attributes have received some study.

Ratings of learning speed Underwood and Schulz (1960, pp. 19–21) obtained ratings of 96 words on a 9-point scale ranging from Difficult to Easy to learn. The ratings were made in the context of 10 words which each subject was asked to inspect first and which covered the range of m values obtained for dissyllables by Noble (1952). The 96 items used were Noble's dissyllables. The correlation of the ratings with the m values was .90. A parallel study on 90 nonsense syllables yielded an r of .86 between ratings for ease of learning and ratings for the number of associations each syllable would evoke. After completing the ratings, Underwood and Schulz asked their subjects to indicate what factors they had used in making their ratings for speed of learning. Three were mentioned most prominently—associations an item suggested, the familiarity of an item, and how easy it was to pronounce.

Ratings of a similar kind to those described above have been obtained for pairs of stimuli. Richardson and Erlebacher (1958) asked one group of subjects to rate the association or connection between the members of each pair, and asked another group of subjects how easy it would be to learn the second member of a pair as a response to the first member as stimulus. For words, nonsense syllables, and CCCs the two sets of ratings were very highly correlated (rho = .96). Battig (1959, 1960) obtained ratings of the ease with which pairs of nonsense syllables could be learned from a restricted range of Glaze av (47–53 percent). Despite the homogeneity of these items for av, the mean ratings for the pairs covered a wide range over a 9-point scale. His values, however, correlated .69 with the average Archer av for the members of each pair.

Occurrence as words When CVCs (consonant-vowel-consonant units), which had been scaled for meaningfulness (m'), are inspected to see how many are actual 3-letter words, it is found that the relative frequency of words increases with m' (Noble, 1963, p. 90, Figure 4-4, p. 91; Noble cites other references on this question). For example, over 90 percent of the items rated at above 4.0 on m' are words as compared to approximately 10 percent of those rated at about 2.75 on m'.

Pronunciability Underwood and Schulz (1960, pp. 23–25) used a 9-point scale for ratings of the pronunciability of trigrams, including words, CVCs, and CCCs. Each subject was asked to attempt to pronounce each trigram to himself before rating it. (Pronunciability ratings for 239 trigrams are given in their Appendix E, pp. 370–372.) There was a correlation of .78 between these ratings and m' values for the CVCs (100 of the 178 items), and, for 86 CVCs, the correlation between m' and judged speed of learning was .92.

Underwood and Schulz (1960, pp. 185–187) obtained the following measures for 36 trigrams: counted frequency, rated frequency, pronunciability ratings, and learning scores, and they computed intercorrelations and partial correlations for these measures. The correlations between rated frequency and counted frequency ranged from .46 to .51, between rated frequency and pronunciability from .73 to .79, between pronunciability and learning from .76 to .82, and between familiarity and learning from .68 to .69. Clearly, pronunciability is the best predictor of learning, and it is more closely related to rated frequency than is counted frequency. As we said in the last section, counted frequency does not relate well to learning scores, independently of pronunciability, and we have seen that, among the predictors used by Underwood and Schulz, pronunciability, for trigrams in the range between words and poorly integrated CCCs, is the best one so far as learning is concerned. Pronunciability does not correlate well with counted frequency.

Johnson (1962) has questioned whether pronunciability is as basic a variable to learning as Underwood and Schulz suggest that it is. He classified response members (trigrams) in paired-associate learning as words, syllables, and nonsyllables and found that the number of correct responses decreased in this order. For each class of item, Johnson split the items at the median for pronunciability. He found no difference in the number of correct responses made for any class between items above and below the median for pronunciability.

Affectivity   We said above that the emotionality of stimulus words is a factor in the properties of word association distributions. In this section, we are concerned with ratings of emotionality over a range of emotionality, rather than simply the comparison of emotional and neutral words, and we are also interested in whether these variations in emotionality are related to other properties of the verbal items.

Noble (1958a, b) had subjects rate his 96 dissyllables by placing each in one of four categories, neutral, pleasant, unpleasant, or mixed, and weighted these categories from 1 to 4 respectively. He found a correlation of .57 between these values and m (see also Strassburger and Wertheimer, 1959), but Underwood and Schulz (1960, pp. 151–152), embedding 27 of the dissyllables among 34 words which had more pronounced affective characteristics, obtained an r of only −.300. Ratings of goodness and badness of words have been obtained by Johnson, Thomson, and Frincke (1960) and Johnson, Frincke, and Martin (1961). Johnson, Weiss, and Zelhart (1964) found higher m for "good" than for "bad" words (see also Howe, 1965). Keppel (1963) found that correlations between ratings of goodness and Noble av are high. However, pronunciability and goodness were also highly correlated and, when the effects of pronunciability were taken out by partial correlation, goodness and av became insignificantly correlated.

Other kinds of emotional ratings of words have been reported—for example, for aggressiveness (Buss, 1961)—but little systematic work on them has been carried out. Furthermore, in most of the investigations in which emotionality of words has been studied, other characteristics such as m or av have not been controlled. Thus, it is difficult to know to what variable to attribute any differences that are found (see Goss & Nodine, 1965, pp. 71–72, fn. 2).

Semantic differential   In the semantic differential, words or other concepts are rated on 7-point scales, the extremes of which are anchored by bipolar adjectives (for example, *good-bad, hot-cold*). Jenkins, Russell, and Suci (1958) have reported mean ratings on each of a number of scales for 360 words. Koen (1962) obtained m values and scores on 12 semantic differential scales for two lists of 15 emotional and 15 neutral words each. He found correlations between the degree of polarization of the semantic differential ratings with both m and counted frequency for neutral words, but the correlations were zero with m and were reduced with frequency for emotional words. Jenkins (1960) has reported a relationship between m and polarization; a small correlation between these variables has also been reported by Wimer (1963). There are also correlations between polarization and frequency (Koen, 1962). Unfortunately, the semantic differential ratings have not, apparently, been studied with respect to acquisition in verbal learning situations.

Pairs of stimuli   We have already mentioned, in discussing similarity between items, that scalings of pairs of items have been reported for synonymity. Haagen (1949) also provides ratings on vividness and strength of association. Haun (1960) used a paired comparison technique to determine the strength of the association between items; he suggests this method as an alternative to obtaining associations. Jenkins, Russell, and Suci (1959) present values for similarity of meaning in terms of semantic differential values for each of 360 words paired with every other word. Flavell (1961) obtained evaluations for the probability of 2 objects, events, and the like occurring together in the real world, as well as estimates of the similarity of meaning of the items in each pair. Their occurring together and their similarity of meaning were highly correlated; adding a measure of similarity from the semantic differential did not raise the relationship further. Flavell and Johnson (1961) studied similarity, further, with associational techniques. Aside from Haagen's ratings, little work has been done with these measures in actual learning situations (see Goss & Nodine, 1965, pp. 102–103).

Comment As may be seen from the findings summarized in this section on ratings, many of the ratings are correlated with others or with *m, f, av,* and the like. Spreen and Schulz (1966) have published ratings for 329 nouns on 7-point scales for specificity and concreteness, as well as *m* values. They also computed intercorrelations among these measures, along with pronunciability. Specificity (*s*) and concreteness (*c*) are highly correlated (.63), and *s* and *c* are correlated with *m* (.56 and .70, respectively). Pronunciability was not highly related to these measures. So far as *s, c,* and *m* are concerned, Spreen and Schulz (pp. 465–466) conclude "that the interrelationships . . . are sufficiently strong that in an attempt to manipulate one of them in a perceptual and/or learning situation all others will have to be controlled, if analytic conclusions regarding the effects of the manipulated variable are to be ascertained."

Unfortunately, it is not possible, despite all the strong, positive correlations that have been found among measures of properties of verbal material, to say which one or ones are basic to the others or whether none of these measures is itself basic but rather that there is some more fundamental dimension which underlies them all.

PROPERTIES OF VERBAL MATERIALS: CONNECTED DISCOURSE

In actual language, whether spoken or written, which we here designate by the term *connected discourse,* any given word no longer appears in the degree of isolation from others that is characteristic of list-learning, association tests, rating procedures, and counts. No word is perhaps ever completely isolated from others even in these situations (Deese, 1961), but in connected discourse there is no question of isolation. This is because ordinary language is structured in ways that are not ordinarily reflected in experiments involving the learning of lists. In this section we attempt to describe some of the ways in which the structure of connected discourse has been described.

In the history of the study of verbal learning, connected discourse entered at the beginning. Ebbinghaus learned poetry, as part of his study on memory, and many other investigators have reported observations on the learning of poetry and prose. However, investigations of the learning of connected discourse have been handicapped by two problems. One is the problem of scoring achievement in learning and retaining connected discourse. Because this problem is essentially the one of finding suitable units in terms of which recall can be scored, it is closely related to the second problem: How may the structure of connected discourse be conceived? Two kinds of answers have been given to this second question, which will be considered after the scoring problem.

The Problem of Scoring

In writing or speaking, one can often say the same thing in several ways. To say, "The ball was hit by the man" is tantamount to saying, "The man hit the ball." The problem of scoring is to evaluate the equivalence of these two expressions and to evaluate the equivalence of other expressions which are less synonymous than these. Such problems

arise when we wish to measure the subjects'
recall in terms of the content, the sense, the
ideas, or the substance of what the passage
contained. There are also problems when
verbatim reproduction of the passage is required. In the example given above, shall
order be considered? The noun phrase, "The
man," occurs in both sentences, but at opposite ends. So also with "The ball." Problems
like these beset anyone who wishes to score
recalls of connected material.

King (1960; King & Schultz, 1960; King &
Yu, 1962) has made some direct studies of the
scoring problem. In doing so, he began by
developing a judgmental criterion for the
adequacy of the recall. He first collected a
number of recalls of a story and then employed judges who were to scale each for
accuracy by comparing it with the original
passage. He found that judges agreed with
one another very well in the judgments they
made. He was then able to study the validity
of other scoring methods, using the judged
accuracy of the recall as a criterion. King
has used several such measures and has
employed factor analyses of correlational
matrices for the measures and the criterion
in order to define the dimensions on which
recalls might vary. He has repeatedly found
that the matrices yield two factor solutions, and the factors tend regularly to be (1)
a quantitative one, indexed by total number
of words recalled or number of identical
content words in the recall and in the passage
and (2) an organizational one, indexed by
sequences of words identical in the recall and
in the original passage. King's work gives
promise that the problem of scoring recalls
can ultimately be solved.

The Structure of Connected Materials

Connected materials have two main
properties that have been studied in the
laboratory: the sequential dependencies in
connected material and their grammatical
organization. The two properties are not
unrelated.

Sequential dependencies or redundancy

When we hear someone speak, we are often
able to anticipate what he will say before he
says it. Thus, if someone says, "The ball," we
are likely to expect that he will go on to say
"and the bat" or that he will follow the initial
phrase with the verb "is" and continue with
"red," "large," "round," among other things.
It appears that there are two kinds of redundancy here. One is that after a noun
phrase like "The ball," we are more likely
to use a verb (*is, rolled*) or a conjunction
(*and*) than we are to use another noun or
an article. In other words, the choice of
the form class of a word to follow another
one is not free but, rather, is partly determined by what has gone before (and what
may come afterward, as in "The ball slowly
rolled . . ."). This is no doubt one basis
for our ability to anticipate what a speaker
will say, if, as speakers usually do, he follows
one form class with another one in an ordinary way. The other kind of redundancy is
semantic. Having said, "The ball and the," the
speaker is unlikely to say "dog," "desk,"
"curtain," "machine" or "spinach," but he is
likely to say "bat" or "glove." This is to say
that the selection from within a form class
(for example, nouns) is limited by what is
said. The sentence, "The card was placed in
the box," contains both sources of redundancy. If we scramble these words, as in "Box
the in card the was placed," we have destroyed the ordinary sequence of the form
classes. However in the following sentence,
"The card was shining in the pencil," we have
lost the redundancy arising from semantic
relations, while preserving an ordinary sequence of form classes.

To study the role of sequential factors in
recall of connected discourse, Miller and
Selfridge (1950) developed passages in the
following way, calling them approximations
to the English language. A second-level approximation was developed as follows. Let us
choose a word, any word, say, *watch*. Then
we ask a subject to give a sentence including

this word. He says, "The watch keeps good time." We then take *keeps* and ask another subject to use it in a sentence. He provides, "The boy keeps water in a bottle." Giving the next subject *water*, we get from him "Water those plants!" Using now just the first words generated by each subject, we have *keeps, water, those*, a sequence in which each word was provided in the context of one other word appropriately used in a sentence. Miller and Selfridge developed strings in this way for several passage lengths and also for several amounts of context, by using, for example, 3, or 4, or 5, or 7 words in the context of which a person was told to add one in a sentence. A first-order approximation was obtained by scrambling words of the other orders, and a zero-order approximation by taking words at random from a dictionary.

Miller and Selfridge obtained recalls for strings of words of varying length and different approximations to English. In general, they found an effect of both variables on recall; that is, the recalls were better for higher orders of approximation, especially with the longer strings (up to 50 words). Deese (1961) has indicated that this increase in recall may, however, be due not to better recall as such but rather to an ability to "reconstruct" what must have been in the string for the high approximations. Thus, in the zero-order list there are hardly any function words (articles, preposition, pronouns), whereas in the higher orders there are. Thus a subject can improve his recall of the latter, but not the former, by inserting a few function words in his "reproduction."

Grammatical organization There are several ways in which grammar enters connected discourse. One is in terms of "tags" that tell us, in some cases, what kind of word a word is. Thus we pluralize nouns, often by adding "s" or "es," make the past tense of many verbs by adding "ed," often make adverbs by adding "ly" to a stem, and make the comparative and superlative forms of some adjectives by

adding "er" and "est." The parts of speech themselves are a part of grammar. Perhaps more important is the fact that sentences are organized in certain ways and never in others and the fact that some words go together whereas they do not go with others.

Epstein (1961, 1962) added certain grammatical features to a string of nonsense syllables. Thus, the string "yig wur vum rix hum jeg mir" in one arrangement was preceded by the article "The" and the preposition "in" was inserted between "hum" and "jeg." In another, the following was used: "The yigs wur vumly rixly hum in jegest mir." Epstein found this last arrangement to be easier to learn than others. He also found that a non-sense sentence, which preserves ordinary grammar, such as "Cruel tables sang falling circles to empty bitter pencils," was easier to learn than a random string of the same words (see also Marks & Miller, 1964).

Glanzer (1962) used paired-associate learning to study the learning of words representing form classes. In one arrangement he used word-CVC pairs and in the other CVC-word pairs. When the words were content words (nouns, verbs, adjectives, adverbs), learning was more rapid than it was when the words were function words; also the CVC-word pairs were easier to learn than the word-CVC pairs, reflecting, probably, the relative roles of response- and stimulus-m.

In the case of the sentence, "The boy read the large book," it is obvious to speakers of English that the sequence "read the" is not a unit in the sense that "The boy" is a unit. Some words are related to one another in a sentence whereas other words are not so related. In linguistic descriptions called "phrase structure grammars" (Chomsky, 1957), we can represent a sentence like the one just given as being composed of a noun phrase and a verb phrase and further decompose these units to show which words are interrelated and which are not. Thus we may write as follows:

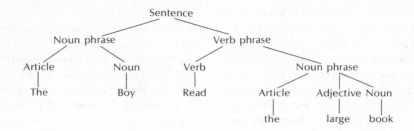

Johnson (1965) has shown that the division of a sentence into its constituents is reflected in learning. He made up eight pairs, each composed of a digit and a sentence. The subject's task was to learn to say a sentence when he saw the digit that had been paired with it. Johnson analyzed the errors made in the recall of the sentences. To do so, he measured the "transitional error probability." Given the correct recollection of one item, say, *boy,* what is the probability that the next element (*read*) will be recalled? The answer to this question is the transitional error probability or TEP. Johnson found, essentially, that more TEPs were given at points of transition between major components of sentences (for example, between the noun phrase and the verb phrase) than within components, thus lending support to the notion that the phrase structure of a sentence is related to the way in which it is learned. Johnson used sentences more complex than our example given above, such as "the house across the street is burning."

The sentences we have used as examples so far are relatively simple, active, affirmative, declarative sentences. There are many other sentences in the language, such as "The large book was read by the boy," "Is the boy read-ing the large book?," "Is not the boy reading the large book?," "Was the large book read by the boy?," and many others. Chomsky (1957)[11] has suggested that these sentences are achieved by transformations of an under-lying structure of such sentences. The sim-plest transformations yield the simple, active, affirmative, declarative sentences, and other transformations alone or in combination pro-duce the more complex sentences (see Miller, 1962). Mehler (1963) has reported evidence suggesting that complexity of transformation may be involved in the learning rate for sen-tences. The major difference he obtained, however, was an advantage for the simple, active, affirmative, declarative sentence as against others.

The topic of grammatical organization has only recently entered the study of verbal learning, and it is perhaps too early to tell whether linguistic descriptions of this orga-nization will have systematic relations to characteristics of the learning of connected discourse.

[11] Later developments in Chomsky's analysis are not entirely consistent with this statement, but it is beyond the scope of this chapter to follow these developments further (see Chomsky, 1966).

Richard B. Millward

THEORETICAL AND EXPERIMENTAL APPROACHES TO HUMAN LEARNING*

20

INTRODUCTION: THE NATURE OF THEORY

In this chapter, four basic human learning procedures will be described, along with some current techniques and theories used for analyzing these procedures.[1] The procedures are probability learning (PL), concept learning (CL), paired-associate learning (PAL), and serial learning (SL). To a certain extent, this chapter also provides an introduction to quantitative theories in experimental psychology, but with the restriction that all examples are of human-learning paradigms. Specific models developed in close conjunction with data are constructed for each experimental routine.

In all the material discussed below there is a mixture of empirical results, procedure, and theory. Unlike some areas of psychology and much of the material in sciences such as physics, chemistry, and biology, the role of theory is often considered to be a controversial rather than an accepted interpretation of the facts. For this reason, some discussion of the role of theory

*Preparation of this chapter was supported in part by Grant No. MH 11255 from the National Institutes of Health to the author, Richard B. Millward. The author wishes to express a special thanks to his wife, Celia, who despite her own professional and family duties has provided editing help throughout the preparation of this chapter.

[1] The coverage of human learning is not intended to be comprehensive but in so far as space permits, a complete coverage of the 4 paradigms is made.

in science seems pertinent at this point. We often find it difficult to think of a theory as a hypothesis about the empirical world; instead, we tend to think of a theory as a factual statement about the empirical world. However, theories are a combination of the obvious, the proved, and the possible. They begin by dealing with the obvious; if they are to be accepted, they cannot contradict what is patently clear to ordinary observation (although what is patently clear is not always independent of theory and sometimes the obvious must be demonstrated). As a theory is elaborated, new principles, new interpretations, and new rules for application are developed. These often require experimental support. But even a very well grounded theory, one with a large number of reliable statements accounting for empirically observed relationships, has implications that are merely possible and thus could be proved wrong. The working scientist sometimes loses sight of this distinction between the empirical world and the theoretical statements made about it.

A theory begins when we posit some givens, the primitive terms. Next, we assume that relations exist between these givens; these relations form the axioms of the theory. From the given primitive terms and axioms, we can derive new relationships by a deductive process. An important requirement at this level is consistency; that is, no two deductions can be contradictory. Because any set of axioms of reasonable complexity has a large number of possible deductions, we cannot always state all the possible deductions. In such cases, we can demonstrate the consistency of the set of axioms by showing that a model exists. A model is a realization of the set of axioms that uses all the axioms. If a model exists, the set of axioms is consistent, for the impossible cannot exist. This is a rather technical definition of a model introduced by philosophers of science (see Suppes, 1957; Nagel, 1961). For our purposes the simpler, less exact distinction suggested by Atkinson, Bower, and Crothers (1965, p. 6) will do just

as well. "A model is viewed as a special case of a theory. Theories are general formulations that are applicable to more than one class of phenomena. Restrictions on the general theory lead to specific models for particular experimental situations." At this point we have a theory, but we still have not determined whether or not it is a theory of any empirical phenomenon or process. To make the theory a working theory, we must make statements relating the primitive terms and axioms to the empirical world. In the original statement of a theory, these relationships are usually implicit.

The first statements of a theory properly handle only a limited set of empirical relationships. However, by deduction, new statements about the empirical world are made. If, by experimentation, these statements are found to be adequate, the theory is strengthened. Often a theory is said to be proved, but such an assertion is too strong, for there are often other statements yet to be tested. If and when additional deductions prove erroneous, modification of the original theoretical structure or of the rules for applying the theory must be made. Gradually, by deductions, tests, re-evaluation, and continual restructuring of the theory, a theoretical statement of broad applicability and high reliability evolves. The important points are as follows.

(1) The primitive terms and axioms of a theory should be as clear and as independent of empirical content as possible.
(2) The rules for applying the theory should be clearly stated.
(3) Deductions should be made by logical or mathematical rules that limit the role of intuition as much as possible.
(4) The deductions of the theory must be experimentally tested.

There have been thousands of experiments run according to the four paradigms of this chapter. In a great many cases, the interest of the experimenter was purely empirical. These are the "let's see what happens" kind of experiments. More often, to varying ex-

tents, the researcher was interested in demonstrating the correctness of some deduction
from a theory or in showing the error in some
tenet of a theory. Because premature theorizing has led many a researcher astray, there
is often strong criticism against theorizing of
any kind. Both the operant approach (see
Skinner, 1950, "Are Theories of Learning Necessary?") and the functionalist approach have
stated this position strongly. Although their
arguments are cogent, the importance to science of a clearly stated theory must not be
overlooked. Whether a scientist cares to
theorize or not, he usually has some implicit
conceptualization of the process. Insofar as
this conceptualization can be made explicit,
critical tests of basic assumptions can be
made. In any case, the literature related to
PL, CL, PAL, and SL is heavily dosed with
theory and because our goal is to understand
this literature, we are forced to deal with
theory.

PROBABILITY LEARNING

During the 1920s, 1930s, and 1940s, maze
learning was the most important experimental
procedure for many theoreticians and experimenters. Indeed, in the revised edition of
Woodworth and Schlosberg (1954) there is a
complete chapter on maze learning. However,
since the 1950s, the interest in complex mazes
has diminished, while probability learning has
played an increasingly larger role in research.
Probability learning has one of its roots in
maze learning—it is analogous to a maze with
a single choice point. More recently there has
arisen an area of study concerned with choice
behavior, which treats only the behavior of
subjects at the point during which a choice
is made. Now, although PL concerns learning,
on any given trial the subject is making a
choice. Thus, there is actually a great deal in
common between work in PL and in choice
behavior. However, because there has been
so much study and literature produced that
is solely concerned with PL, we must of necessity omit dealing directly with the choice

paradigm. The reader is referred to two excellent articles for this area: Bush, Galanter,
and Luce (1963), and Luce and Suppes (1965).

Some authorities on human rote learning
argue that PL is not an instrumental learning
procedure. Underwood (1966), for example,
includes it under classical conditioning. Other
theorists consider it a form of concept learning (see Goodnow, 1955; Galanter & Smith,
1958; Feldman, 1963). However, because
most studies in probability learning have been
with human subjects, there is good reason for
including it under human learning. Further,
this chapter emphasizes theory, and PL has
served as the main experimental procedure
for testing statistical learning theory.

Historical Background

During the 30 years from 1920 to 1950, most
of the theoretical work related to verbal
learning or rote learning was derived from
work done on animals, in the belief that there
was a simple hierarchical structure to learning. It was felt that basic laws and principles
had to be developed first and that these laws
could best be discovered using animals as
subjects. Once established, these laws could
be applied to human learning. Therefore, researchers studying human learning became
either pure functionalists, and did not enter
into the debates and controversies of such
prominent theoreticians as Hull, Guthrie,
Tolman, and Skinner, or else they ran a conditioning type of experiment involving nonsense syllables and humans. McGeoch and
Irion (1952) summarize the state of work up
to the decade of the fifties.

Statistical learning theory (SLT), basically
a quantitative description of many of the
principles worked out during the first half of
the century, bridges the periods before and
after McGeoch and Irion. SLT also represents
the beginning of the quantitative theorizing
that has taken place since 1950. Few people
today believe that SLT adequately describes
all aspects of PL, and even fewer believe that
it can be applied in its early form to paired-
associate learning, concept learning, or serial

learning. Nonetheless, even its shortcomings are important, for they have pointed to new approaches and concepts.

Humphreys (1939) introduced a variant of classical or Pavlovian conditioning for humans that he called *verbal conditioning*. The name of the routine indicates what earlier investigators considered it to be—a form of classical conditioning.[2] In the classical paradigm, a signal (the conditioned stimulus or CS) is given, followed soon afterwards by a strong response-producing stimulus (the unconditioned stimulus or US). The initial response to the signal is usually minimal, but eventually a response resembling the unconditioned response to the US occurs following the CS. For example, in Humphreys' version of verbal conditioning, subjects are instructed to predict whether or not a light will occur on each of a series of trials. Each trial begins with a signal (the CS); then the light either is flashed on or is not. The light is assumed to be the US; presumably, it will evoke a strong expectancy response. After a number of trials, the signal itself will also evoke the expectancy response, and conditioning then is said to have occurred. The simple piece of equipment (now called a Humphreys board) that Humphreys used to run subjects in this basic design consists of a vertical board with two lights and a telegraph key for the subject to press. One light acts as the CS and the other as the US.

Estes and Straughan (1954) noted that, in the conditioning version of Humphreys' design, a failure to respond could mean that (1) the subject did not expect the light to be turned on, (2) the subject delayed too long, or (3) the subject simply did not care. They varied Humphreys' procedure by introducing two lights and two response keys and instructed subjects to predict on each trial which light would go on by pressing the corresponding key. They used a probabilistic reinforcement schedule, that is, on 70 per-

cent of the trials, the left light went on, and on 30 percent of the trials, the right light went on. Estes and Straughan confirmed a result previously noticed by Hake, Grant, and Hornseth (1951). Subjects predicted the left light and the right light with the same frequency as these lights were reinforced, that is, 70 percent and 30 percent, respectively. In other words, they matched probabilities. Today, there are some questions about the exactness with which probabilities are matched, but in any case deviations are not large. However, probability-matching does not maximize correct responses, a fact that has produced some serious theoretical arguments.

The experimental verification of probability-matching was made just after Estes (1950) had developed the preliminary structure for statistical learning theory (SLT). Estes then showed that SLT predicted probability-matching on the basis of some very simple assumptions about the conditioning process (Estes & Straughan, 1954). Probability learning and statistical learning theory were thus wed; since that time, the majority of PL studies has been run in order to test SLT and SLT has most often been tested by a PL experiment.

Prior to the work of Estes, some of the basic tenets of SLT had been expressed in a much less formal manner by Guthrie (1935, 1959; see also pp. 560; 567 ff.). Three important ideas are central to Guthrie's theory. The first is that all learning takes place by a contiguity principle rather than a drive-reduction principle. That is, no need or drive has to be reduced for learning to occur. All that is necessary is that a stimulus and a response occur together, or, more exactly, that the desired response be the last one made in the presence of the stimulus. When this is the case, the stimulus, on its next occurrence, will evoke the same response. Guthrie's second principle is that the strength of such an S-R bond is either zero or at a maximum. There are no intermediate degrees of strength. The third principle is that most observed and measured stimuli and/or responses are not unitary but

---

[2] Today the term *verbal conditioning* is generally reserved for a variant of operant conditioning (see Verplanck, 1955; and Greenspoon, 1955).

are composed of a number of simpler, more elementary components. Thus, a stimulus, such as a tone, is composed of a large number of elementary stimuli, and a response or act, such as pressing a key, is composed of a number of simpler movements. The all-or-none connection of a stimulus and a response by contiguity alone is true at the elementary level for stimulus components and response movements but not for gross stimulus compounds and response acts. Thus, gross stimuli and responses, being composed of a number of elementary units, are connected only by repetition, which gradually connects all the elementary units.

To what extent Estes was influenced by Guthrie is difficult to say, although he does give explicit credit to many of Guthrie's ideas (see Estes, 1959b, p. 399). Certainly the basic ideas of the stimulus as a set of elementary stimuli, the all-or-none connection of each stimulus element to some response (Guthrie did not make it explicit whether or not an element always had to be connected to some response), and the simple requirement of contiguity only are present in both theories. However, to conclude from this similarity that SLT is merely a mathematical formulization of Guthrie's ideas would be erroneous. The crucial added ingredient is the use of probability theory and the commitment to the probability of a response as a dependent variable.

Basic PL Paradigm

In a typical PL experiment, the subject sits facing two outcome lights with two response keys directly below them. Between the two lights, but slightly elevated, there is a signal light. A trial begins when the signal light is turned on for about 2 sec. During this time, the subject is to press the key under the outcome light that he thinks will come on. Following his response, one of the outcome lights comes on for about 1 or 2 sec. Then, about 2 sec later, the signal light is turned on again. In a noncontingent PL ex-

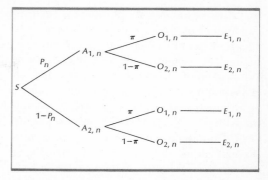

Figure 20.1. Trial paradigm for noncontingent probability learning. S signifies signal. P_n is an abbreviation of the probability of an A_1 response on trial n, $P(A_{1,n})$. The outcome probability, $P(O_{1,n}) = \pi \cdot O_{i,n}$ represents the ith outcome on trial n, and $E_{i,n}$ is the assumed reinforcing event associated with the $O_{i,n}$ th outcome.

periment, the outcome on one trial does not depend on the outcome on any other trial. (In probability theory, such a sequence is known as a Bernoulli sequence.)

Figure 20.1 provides some of the symbolism necessary to discuss the noncontingent experimental routine. The two outcome lights are labeled O_1 and O_2 to indicate outcomes 1 and 2. The subject's corresponding responses are labeled A_1 and A_2. (The values of $E_{i,n}$ will be discussed later.) The basic independent variable in PL is the probability that one or the other of the lights will be turned on. Let $P(O_{1,n}) = \pi_n$, that is, the probability of an O_1 outcome on trial n. In most studies, this probability is the same for all trials and thus the subscript is dropped (that is, $P(O_{1,n}) = \pi$). Further, because we are concerned here with a noncontingent PL experiment, O_1 is determined probabilistically and independently of the subject's response. Finally, P_n refers to the basic dependent variable, the probability of an A_1 response on trial n, $A_{1,n}$. There is no direct measure of P_n, so it must be inferred from the results of the experiment. Such an inference depends on what assumptions we make; for this reason, a theory of PL is necessary.

Before considering the application of SLT

to PL, some details about running such an experiment should be presented. First, the experimenter must generate the outcome sequence. For example, if $\pi = .7$, he could consult a table of random numbers and pick an O_1 outcome when a digit between 1 and 7 is observed and an O_2 outcome when the digits 8, 9, or 0 occur. Or, to insure exactly $.7N$ O_1 outcomes per block, he could randomize within a block of N trials by picking $.7N$ numbers from the numbers 1 through N. Fixed-block randomization, however, is often avoided because it restricts the distributions of outcome runs, thereby raising certain theoretical problems. The experimenter must record each outcome and each subject's corresponding response for the trial. The resulting data protocol consists of a numbered sequence of O_1 and O_2 outcomes, along with a sequence of A_1 and A_2 responses for each

subject. Usually, 10 to 20 subjects are run under exactly the same conditions except for outcome sequences. If each subject cannot be presented with a unique sequence, two or more subjects may be given the same sequence. Normally, over 200 trials are run; in more recent experiments, up to 1,000 trials have been run.

Theoretical Analysis

Axioms   Properly speaking, SLT is not one single theory. Here, we use the term SLT for the early version of the theory as described by Estes (1959b). Estes gave a detailed discussion of the theory in which he also presented his own view of how it was developed. All the many versions or elaborations of this early structure are usually called *stimulus sampling theory* (SST). Much of the theoretical work in PL has been done using a mathematical

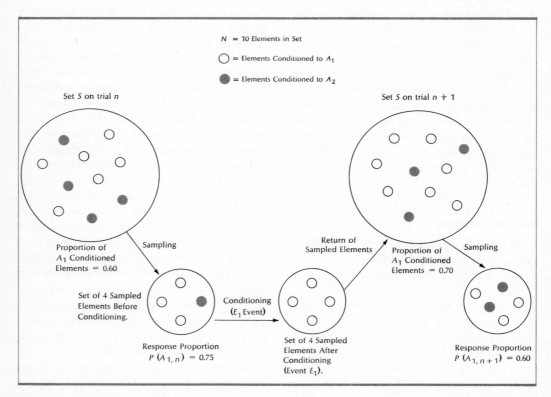

Figure 20.2. Schematic diagram showing the axioms of SLT in operation. One trial with an E_1 reinforcing event is illustrated. (See text.)

approach developed by Bush and Mosteller (1955), which does not require the stimulus-sampling assumptions of SLT. But there has been a great deal of mutually beneficial interaction between the stochastic learning theorists and the stimulus-sampling theorists. SLT as considered here consists of four sets of basic axioms (see, for example, Estes & Suppes, 1959; Atkinson & Estes, 1963; Atkinson, Bower, & Crothers, 1965).

1. *Representation Axioms*
   a. The stimulus environment consists of a set S of N stimulus elements.
   b. There are r mutually exclusive and exhaustive responses, $A_1, A_2, \ldots, A_r$. One and only one response is made on each trial.
   c. Each response A_i has a reinforcing event E_i. A neutral reinforcing event E_0 may also exist. One and only one reinforcing event is given on each trial.

2. *Conditioning Axioms*
   a. Each element of S is conditioned to one and only one response.[3]
   b. An element that is sampled on a trial becomes conditioned automatically to the reinforced response of that trial (to A_i if E_i occurs). Its previous conditioning status is lost.
   c. An element that is not sampled on a trial remains conditioned to its previously conditioned response.
   d. The E_0 event leaves sampled elements conditioned in the same way as before the trial.

3. *Stimulus-Sampling Axioms*
   a. On each trial, each element i has a probability θ_i of being sampled. Sampling produces a subset of S. It is usually assumed that $\theta_i = \theta_j = \theta$ for all i and j.
   b. On each trial, all sampled elements

are returned to the total set of elements.

4. *Response Axiom*
   a. The probability of an A_i response on a trial equals the proportion of sampled elements conditioned to the A_i response.

Figure 20.2 is a simple schematic diagram that illustrates how these axioms function to produce learning in the two-response ($r = 2$) situation. On trial n there is a certain proportion of elements in S conditioned to A_1. We can call this proportion p_n. If we make the simplifying assumption that all θ_i are the same, the average sample size will be θN. (At this point, the student should work out the following example: Assume $N = 3$ and $\theta = .6$. What are all the possible samples? Is the average size 1.8? With a small N, the probability of not sampling any elements remains relatively high and causes trouble with the sampling axiom. In applying this version of the theory, we assume a sufficiently large N so that the probability of no elements being sampled, $(1 - \theta)^N$, is essentially zero.) Because the sampling is random, there should be approximately $\theta N p_n$ conditioned elements in the sample; thus, $P(A_{1,n})$ is approximately equal to p_n, the proportion of conditioned elements in the set S. (It is implicitly assumed that the average of a ratio is the ratio of the averages, an assumption which, for large N, is approximately correct.) After sampling, S contains $(N - \theta N)$ elements. These have not changed their conditioning state, so for them the proportion of elements conditioned to the A_1 response remains p_n. The sample consists of θN elements, all of which return to S conditioned to A_1 if an E_1 event occurs. Thus, on trial $n + 1$, the set S contains $(N - \theta N)p_n + \theta N$ conditioned elements, or a proportion

$$p_{n+1} = (1 - \theta)p_n + \theta \tag{1}$$

obtained by dividing the number of conditioned elements in S by the total number of elements N. If an E_2 event had occurred, the

---

[3]La Berge (1959) has introduced a variant of SLT which does not make the assumption that all elements are conditioned at the beginning of an experiment. Some are neutral and become conditioned as they are sampled and reinforced.

$N - \theta N$ elements not sampled would remain conditioned as they were before the reinforcement, but all the θN elements sampled would return conditioned to A_2; thus

$$p_{n+1} = (1 - \theta)p_n \qquad (2)$$

Derivation of the fundamental learning equation Equations 1 and 2 are called *linear operators* or *linear difference equations*. They are analogous to differential equations, but they are used for discrete trials instead of continuous time. (See Goldberg, 1958, for a good exposition of difference equations.) Following Bush and Mosteller,[4] we can simplify later derivations by rewriting Equations 1 and 2 using operator notation.

$$L_1(p_n) = (1 - \theta)p_n + \theta \qquad (1a)$$
$$L_2(p_n) = (1 - \theta)p_n \qquad (2a)$$

The axioms presented above express the primitive terms and the axiomatic relationships of the theory. "Stimulus element" and "response" are primitive terms of the theory. They are not defined explicitly and, within the theoretical structure, they need not be. The events, E_i, have the same status as responses. The axioms are likewise empirically undefined. Elements are "connected" to responses, elements are "sampled," and the sampled elements determine the probability of a response. To establish a theory of any empirical process, we must state rules of correspondence for the primitive terms and basic axioms. Of course, the words used to describe the primitive terms help to show the kind of correspondences we expect. We can now consider the rules of correspondence for PL.

As we have stated, the signal is considered to be composed of a set of N elements. The key presses are the responses A_1 and A_2. The outcomes O_1 and O_2 seemingly reinforce re-

sponses A_1 and A_2, and thus they are designated E_1 and E_2. Sampling occurs when the signal is turned on. The sample determines the probability of the response that the subject makes. One of the outcomes occurs and acts so as to reinforce the corresponding response. Estes justifies this reinforcement rule with the contiguity assumption. The O_j outcome is assumed to produce the A_j response. Thus, the A_j response is the last response made on the trial and, by the contiguity rule, the last response made in some stimulus context becomes associated with that context. Note that some of Guthrie's (1959) notions about how reinforcement works are brought into the description at this point. They are not formally represented in the axioms, but are used to justify why elements are connected to the response associated with the outcome on the trial.

We must now say something about initial conditions. On the first trial, that is, the first time the signal is presented, we assume that the elements are in some way conditioned in order to evoke a response. Because the experimental situation is symmetrical, we assume an initial probability of .5 for either response. To eliminate any possible bias toward the left or right response, half of the subjects are run with the left response an A_1 and the right response an A_2. For the other half, the left response is an A_2 and the right response an A_1. In practice the probability on the initial trial is always close to .5.

We can now make some simple deductions from the model. Assume that, on trial 1 of a learning experiment, the initial probability is p_1. Now assume that the E_1 reinforcing event is repeated once every trial thereafter. By Equation 1a

$$p_2 = L_1 p_1 = (1 - \theta)p_1 + \theta$$
$$p_3 = L_1 p_2 = (1 - \theta)p_2 + \theta$$
$$= (1 - \theta)^2 p_1 + (1 - \theta)\theta + \theta$$

and

$$p_4 = L_1 p_3 = (1 - \theta)^3 p_1 + (1 - \theta)^2\theta$$
$$+ (1 - \theta)\theta + \theta$$

---

[4]Bush and Mosteller (1955) began by assuming a very general linear operator to represent the change in probability from one trial to the next. Equations 1 and 2 are special cases of the more general approach they took. As we shall see later, it is the stimulus representation of the theory that has been more productive of new ideas and research in human learning and therefore the more general linear operators are not of major concern at this time. For a recent discussion of this approach see Sternberg (1963).

Generalizing, we can make the hypothesis that

$$p_n = (1 - \theta)^{n-1}p_1 + (1 - \theta)^{n-2}\theta$$
$$+ \cdots + (1 - \theta)\theta + \theta$$

The terms to the right of the plus sign comprise a geometric series of the form

$$S_k = \sum_{i=0}^{k} ar^i = a\frac{(1 - r^{k+1})}{(1 - r)} \qquad (3)$$

where $a = \theta$, $k = n - 2$, and $r = (1 - \theta)$. The solution to this series is easily proved by noting that

$$S_k - rS_k = S_k(1 - r)$$
$$= a + ar + ar^2 + ar^3 \ldots ar^k$$
$$- ar - ar^2 - ar^3 \ldots -ar^k - ar^{k+1}$$

which equals $a - ar^{k+1}$. Thus, $S = a(1 - r^{k+1})$ $/(1 - r)$. In terms of θs and $k = n - 2$,

$$p_n = (1 - \theta)^{n-1}p_1 + \frac{\theta[1 - (1 - \theta)^{n-1}]}{1 - (1 - \theta)} \qquad (4)$$

and after algebraic simplification

$$p_n = 1 - (1 - p_1)(1 - \theta)^{n-1} \qquad (5)$$

Equation 5 is correct for $n = 1$. Is it correct for $n + 1$? By Equation 1, $p_{n+1} = (1 - \theta)p_n + \theta$. Applying the basic difference equation to Equation 5 yields

$$p_{n+1} = (1 - \theta) - (1 - p_1)(1 - \theta)^n$$
$$+ \theta = 1 - (1 - p_1)(1 - \theta)^n \qquad (6)$$

which is the same as Equation 5 if n is replaced by $n + 1$. Thus, by proof by induction,[5] we can show that Equation 5 is the general solution to the difference equation. By a general solution, we mean that values for any trial n are expressed in an explicit formula in which only a fixed number of constants are required—in this case, the initial probability value, p_1. A few points about

Equation 6 should be noted. Remember that θ is the probability that an element will be sampled on a given trial. If $\theta = 0$, then no element will ever be sampled, $p_2 = p_1$, and no learning occurs immediately after one reinforcement. Therefore, $p_n = p_{n-1} = \ldots = p_2 = p_1$. For $\theta \neq 0$ or $\theta \neq 1$, $(1 - \theta)^n$ will decrease to zero, so that at asymptote, as $n \rightarrow \infty, p_\infty = 1$. In other words, eventually the probability of an A_1 response will become 1.

Theory applied to probability learning The first deduction from the theory is that if an outcome such as O_1, which has reinforcing event E_1 associated with it, is repeated

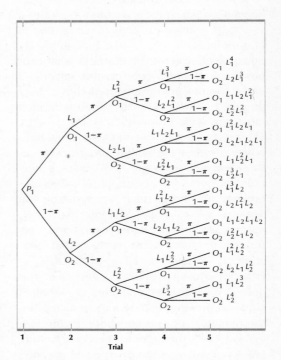

Figure 20.3. Tree diagram representing four trials of probability learning. Each path of the tree presents two probabilities; the probability of transitions between nodes is on the stems between these nodes. The response probability at each node is indicated by the operators at that node. Thus, at the top node on the far right, after 4 O_1 outcomes, the response probability is $L_1^4 p_1$, and the probability of making the transition to that node is π^4.

[5] A proof by mathematical induction is a proof that a given general proposition $G(n)$ is true for all n. There are two steps to an inductive proof. First, $G(n)$ must be shown to be true for $n = 1$. Second, for any n, if $G(n)$ is true, it must be shown that $G(n + 1)$ is also true. Thus, starting with $G(1)$, any value of $G(n)$ can be shown to be true by repeated application of the second step.

indefinitely, the probability of an A_1 response will eventually become 1 on every trial. The rate at which the probability p_n approaches 1 depends directly on the value of θ. Intuitively, this result is not surprising. If the O_1 light comes on repeatedly, subjects will begin to predict it repeatedly. This much, the obvious, is expected of a theory. The not-so-obvious occurs when the theory is developed for the situation in which O_1 and O_2 outcomes are presented randomly with a probability of π for the O_1 event and $1 - \pi$ for the O_2 event. The rules of correspondence are the same in this case, but the derivation becomes somewhat more difficult.

It is important to start correctly, or later deductions will not be possible. Consider a very large number of subjects run under the PL experiment with π as the probability for outcome O_1. Figure 20.3 illustrates what happens to a group of subjects through trial 5 under the procedure described above. After the first reinforcement, the group is divided into two, with proportions π and $(1 - \pi)$. Those subjects who get an O_1 outcome have a new response probability of $L_1 p_1$, whereas those subjects who get an O_2 have a new probability of $L_2 p_1$. The group of subjects is broken into smaller subgroups until, by trial 5, there are 16 subgroups. Note that $L_1 L_2 p_1$ means that first the $L_2 p_1$ operation is performed, and then, on the results of that operation, L_1 is applied. $L_2 L_1 p_1 = (1 - \theta)^2 p_1 + (1 - \theta)\theta$, while $L_1 L_2 p_1 = (1 - \theta)^2 p_1 + \theta$. The order in which the operators are applied makes a difference in the result. In such cases, the operators do not *commute*. In the tree in Figure 20.3, the order of the Ls is carefully preserved, whereas the order of the πs need not be because it is a simple product and does commute; that is, $\pi(1 - \pi) = (1 - \pi)\pi$.

Generally, at least 100 to 200 trials are run in PL experiments. At the end of 100 trials, there would be a possibility of 2^{99} subgroups. Usually, every subject is presented with a unique sequence of outcomes, and theoretically the particular path followed could be used to compute his exact probability for

every trial. However, in addition to the practical problem of computing the probabilities, the θ and p_1 values are not necessarily known. Furthermore, we cannot measure a probability on a single trial: Either an A_1 or an A_2 response is made, giving us no information as to what the underlying probability really is. Therefore, to test the theory, a reasonable estimate of the probability is needed; it can be obtained by averaging across subjects. Assuming that all subjects have about the same p_1 and θ values, what is the probability of an A_1 response on trial 2 $[P(A_{1,2})]$? It is simply the average of the probability value obtained by the subjects who had an O_1 outcome and the probability value of those who had an O_2 outcome. Because there is not an equal number of subjects in both subgroups, the probabilities must be weighted by the proportion of subjects with each probability, namely, π and $(1 - \pi)$.

$$P(A_{1,2}) = \pi L_1 p_1 + (1 - \pi) L_2 p_1$$
$$= (1 - \theta) p_1 + \theta\pi \tag{7}$$

Carrying the process one step further to trial 3:

$$P(A_{1,3}) = \pi^2 L_1^2 p_1 + \pi(1 - \pi) L_2 L_1 p_1$$
$$+ (1 - \pi)\pi L_1 L_2 p_1 + (1 - \pi)^2 L_2^2 p_1$$
$$= \pi L_1 P(A_{1,2}) + (1 - \pi) L_2 P(A_{1,2})$$
$$= \pi((1 - \theta) P(A_{1,2}) + \theta) + (1 - \pi)$$
$$(1 - \theta) P(A_{1,2})$$
$$= (1 - \theta) P(A_{1,2}) + \theta\pi \tag{8}$$

More generally, it can be shown that

$$P(A_{1,n+1}) = (1 - \theta) P(A_{1,n}) + \theta\pi \tag{9}$$

(You should demonstrate this for yourself.) We have shown here that the average response probability on any trial $n + 1$ can be expressed as a linear function of the average response probability on the preceding trial n. According to the theory, the linear operators are applied to individual probabilities, not to the average probability over subjects. However, we have just shown that applying the average operator to the average probability correctly expresses the change in the average probability. It is as if L_1 and L_2 were applied to every branch of the tree and the resulting changes in the individual probabilities averaged. The fact that the average operator correctly computes probability changes is important, for it allows us to make a statement about the average probability for the process. It also permits a statement to be made about observable results or $P(A_{1,n})$, the average probability of a large number of subjects. If only 20 subjects were run, all branches could not be followed out beyond trial 4, but there is still no reason for any one branch to be chosen over any other branch and the expected value of $P(A_{1,n})$ as computed from the average operator is the value we would expect on the average. Of course, with a small number of subjects, deviations from this average can be expected, depending on the branches selected. Predictions are not exact but probabilistic.

The successive application of the recursive Equation 9 in a manner similar to that used in the development of Equation 5 yields a result very similar to that of Equation 5.

$$P(A_{1,n}) = \pi - [\pi - P(A_{1,1})](1 - \theta)^{n-1} \quad (10)$$

with π replacing 1. The π occurs because L_1 and L_2 are applied randomly, and the probability of an A_1 response cannot continue to increase to the value 1. Instead it tends to level off at π as an asymptote. Because π is the probability of reinforcing with the outcome O_1, the probability-matching law results.

Parameter estimation There should be, ideally, an addition to the theory stating how to compute the θ value because, without it, exact predictions cannot be made. The mechanism for such an estimate is present (the average proportion of elements sampled on each trial), but, as was observed earlier, one of the characteristics of the theory is its lack of specificity about the nature of elements. The lack of specificity was considered an advantage because, at this point in theory construction, there is little evidence to guide the experimenter in tying elements to physi-

cal aspects of the environment. (Later, we shall see that such assignments may be very difficult indeed.) The purpose of the theory is to predict the form of the learning curve and to see if the data conform to the prediction. Therefore, a θ value that will give the best fit of data and theory is sufficient at this time. There are two parameters, $P(A_{1,1})$ and θ. The $P(A_{1,1})$ value is usually evaluated a priori on rational grounds; that is, because of symmetry and counterbalancing, $P(A_{1,1}) = .5$. To estimate θ, some statistic of the data is equated with its theoretical expression and the resulting equation solved for θ, a procedure known as an estimation by the method of moments. One straightforward and simple technique is to equate the total number of A_1 responses observed over N trials to the theoretical expression for that number. If the learning curve (Equation 10) were continuous, the total area under it could be determined by integration and a θ value selected that would yield the same area. However, Equation 10 is discrete rather than continuous; therefore, summing, the operation analogous to integration, is used. In this case, the sum of Equation 10 for N trials is

$$P_1^{(N)} = \sum_{n=1}^{N} P(A_{1,n})$$

$$= \sum_{n=1}^{N} [\pi - (\pi - P(A_{1,1}))(1 - \theta)^{n-1}]$$

$$= N\pi - (\pi - P(A_{1,1})) \sum_{n=1}^{N} (1 - \theta)^{n-1} \quad (11)$$

The last summation term is evaluated as before (Equation 3), yielding

$$P_1^{(N)} = N\pi - (\pi - P(A_{1,1})) \frac{(1 - (1 - \theta)^N)}{\theta}$$

$$(11a)$$

If N is sufficiently large and if $(1 - \theta)$ is sufficiently smaller than 1, $(1 - \theta)^N$ will be near enough zero to ignore. In that case, the estimate for θ is found by taking the observed value of $P_1^{(N)}$, call it $\hat{P}_1^{(N)}$, and solving Equation 11 for θ. The solution is

$$\hat{\theta} \approx \frac{[\pi - P(A_{1,1})]}{N\pi - P_1^{(N)}} \quad (12)$$

where θ represents the estimate of θ.

Average learning curve by blocks If an experiment is run for 250 trials, 250 probabilities would have to be predicted and plotted using Equation 10. However, there are two problems with using Equation 10 as it is: One is the tedium of computing and plotting so many points. The second is the lack of stability of each data point if, for example, only 20 subjects were run. Obviously, the way to handle the problem is to average over trials and plot response proportions for a block of K trials. The expected number of A_1 responses in N trials was stated in Equation 11a. By substituting K for N, we obtain the expected number of A_1 responses in the first K trials. Likewise, if in Equation 11, the sum went from $n = K + 1$ to $2K$, we would obtain the expected number of A_1 responses in the second block of K trials. In general, if $n = (m - 1)K + 1$ to mK, we would obtain the expected number of A_1 responses in the mth block. If we divide the number of A_1 responses in a block by the number of trials in the block, we obtain the expected proportion of A_1 responses in the block. Thus, the proportion of A_1 responses in the mth block of K trials is

$$P_m^{(K)} = \pi - \frac{[\pi - P(A_{1,1})]}{K} \frac{[1 - (1 - \theta)^K]}{\theta}$$
$$(1 - \theta)^{K(m-1)}$$
$$= \pi - C(1 - \theta)^{K(m-1)} \quad (13)$$

where

$$C = \frac{[\pi - P(A_{1,1})]}{K} \frac{[1 - (1 - \theta)^K]}{\theta}$$

Averaging of Data

Psychological data, like all biological data, are characterized by a great deal of noise. The experimenter tries to reduce variation between measures of the dependent variable by controlling as many factors as possible.

However, even in the best of situations, the experimenter is often left with a dependent variable that is noisy. When faced with variable response measures, the experimenter can average scores and treat means instead of individual cases.

Two important points about averaging should be made at this time. The first is related to theory construction. Earlier theoretical approaches to learning in psychology, particularly that of Hull, assumed a deterministic process. The fact that deterministically predicted outcomes rarely occurred was handled by assuming that each determined response was influenced by a distortion process of a random nature. Usually, the experimenter superimposed a normal curve upon the response, if not explicitly as Hull did, at least implicitly by assuming that, when an average was taken, the effect of random influencing factors would average out. In SLT a different approach is taken. We assume from the initial axioms of the theory that variation in responses is to be expected. This variation results from the sampling of stimulus conditions, from the fact that the sample determines only the probability of a response (that is, the probability of a response is determined by the ratio of conditioned to unconditioned elements), and from the fact that the response changes due to reinforcement also change probabilistically. In SLT, variation in behavior is axiomatic, not the result of poor control or of factors of no concern to the theorist. However, if the stimulus were completely controlled, so that the particular elements presented could be designated, the response would become more determined, and perhaps even completely determined. In other words, the theorist admits that complete control of the stimulus is impossible because the subject participates in determining what it is by his very attention to it and because any environment is likely to change somewhat from trial to trial and from organism to organism. Thus, SLT is referred to as a stochastic theory as opposed to a deterministic one.

The second point has to do with when it is proper and when it is not proper to average data. The scientist is basically interested in the on-going process. When the dependent variable is noisy, he can usually get some idea of the process by averaging data. Now in PL, almost all experimental results have been based on average data. Nearly every paradigm to be discussed in this chapter depends on average data. The same is true for the bulk of research on problems of learning, even including the operant work in which cumulative curves are presented for individual subjects. However, averaging may conceal or distort the fact that various processes are going on in different subjects. In other words, it is not proper to infer that the average reflects the behavior of the individual subject (see, for example, Skinner, 1938; Sidman, 1952). How then is the psychologist to discover basic learning processes when confronted with noisy data? The solution is analogous to testing a theory. The average curve is derived as a logical consequence of the hypothetical individual curves. Those who argue that it is never appropriate to average do not regard the average curve as a deduction but as an induction. However, the scientific process is somewhat more complicated than empirical laws dictated by overwhelming data. Furthermore, a finite collection of data can usually be accounted for by a number of theories (Kemeny, 1959). The solution is a dynamic process between induction and deduction. The data are used to evaluate a hypothesis. If the data are not compatible with the hypothesis, then another hypothesis is considered that retains all the correct predictions of the previous hypothesis but also predicts the new set of data correctly. (See Platt, 1964.) In a similar way, the average curve does not necessarily give information about the underlying process, but rather it is or is not compatible with hypothesized underlying processes.

Estes (1956) has treated this problem in a very exact and complete manner. He designates three types of function. In the first type,

the average curve is similar in form to the individual curves and has parameter values that are the average of the parameters of the individual curves. An obvious example would be a simple linear equation of the form $y = a + bx$. In this case, of course, no problems arise in averaging over subjects. In the second class of curves, the form remains the same, but the parameters of the average curve are not the average of the parameters of the individual curves. Estes gives the example $y = \log (bx)$. In this case, averaging will not distort the form of the results, but no inference can be made about the individual parameter values. In the third class of curves, both the form and parameters are changed by averaging. An example is the typical growth function illustrated by Equation 10. In Equation 10, notice first that, because π is only an added constant, as is a in the linear equations, it is not affected by averaging. Regardless of parameter values, the asymptote of π is predicted. However, the rest of the equation involves averaging exponentials, a process that distorts the form of the curve to some degree if the parameters are very variable.

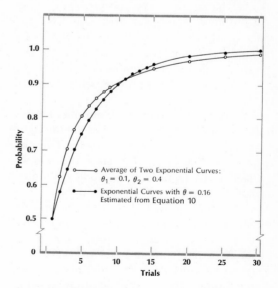

Figure 20.4. Contrast between (1) the average of two exponential curves and (2) the exponential curve fitted with the parameter estimated from the average data.

Two curves are presented in Figure 20.4. The average curve results from averaging the expected curve from two subjects with different learning rates: $\theta = .1$ and $\theta = .4$. The second curve is the best-fitting exponential of the type presented in Equation 10. The effect of variation in the θ parameter value can be seen in the fit obtained. Extreme θ values do not distort the fit a great deal and the distortion is such that the theoretical exponential is too low in the beginning and too high near the end. In general, such a discrepancy in fitting a learning curve results from heterogeneity of learning parameters. If there is not much variability in the θ values, it is not a serious problem. One additional point must be made: If individual parameters are estimated, individual curves should be generated and averaged. This average curve should agree with the average curve of the original data. Individual parameters should not be averaged to obtain the average parameters for the best-fitting group curve.

Basic Facts about PL

Thus far, the discussion of PL has been somewhat abstract. We can now apply some of the ideas to see just what is and what is not known about PL. Investigators have been interested in three important statistics: (1) the learning curves and asymptotic behavior, (2) recency analyses, and (3) sequential statistics.

Learning curves and asymptotic behavior We have already presented the theoretical work for the learning curve. Edwards (1956) and more recently Luce and Suppes (1965) have summarized the studies in simple noncontingent PL with respect to the asymptotes observed. An examination of some 16 experiments by almost as many experimenters, involving a complete range of π values and over 685 subjects, has led Luce and Suppes to conclude that "with the exception of Edwards' (1961) 1000-trial study, the experiments without payoff appear to confirm the probability-matching hypothesis, at least for group averages" (Luce & Suppes, 1965,

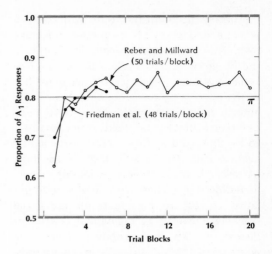

Figure 20.5. Learning curves from two probability learning experiments.

p. 393). Now, of the 39 groups that Luce and Suppes considered, 8 did not seem to be at asymptote, and 19 of the groups were over the π values (or under for πs less than .5). The number of trials seems to be crucial here—longer experiments tend to show overshooting. For example, Myers, Fort, Katz, and Suydam (1963) and Edwards (1961) ran 400 and 1000 trials, respectively, and all their groups showed overshooting.

Figure 20.5 presents two learning curves from two different studies. The six-block curve is from the Friedman et al. study (1964), in which 288 trials were run after a series of 17 48-trial blocks with changing π values. The 288 trials began on the third day of testing after 48 trials with $\pi = .5$. The 80 subjects in the Friedman et al. study had a great deal of heterogeneous previous experience. The Reber and Millward data (1968) consisted of 1000 trials of $\pi = .8$, with four sequences and 15 subjects. Both curves are representative of results of other experiments. When overshooting occurs, it is, for example, around .85 for $\pi = .8$. The Reber and Millward asymptote seems to stabilize at the new level.

Various explanations for the overshooting discussed above have been suggested. Perhaps the most obvious one is that a few subjects tend to "maximize"; that is, they always

TABLE 20.1 RUNS ANALYSIS STATISTICS

Trial	1	2	3	4	5	6	7	8	9	10	11	12	13	14	15	16	17	18	19	20
Event	1	2	1	1	1	2	2	1	2	1	1	2	2	2	2	1	1	2	2	2
Response	1	2	2	2	1	1	1	1	1	2	2	2	2	2	2	1	1	1	1	1

Run Length	Event Run				Number of Runs	Trials	Number of $A_{1,n+k+1}$	$P(A_{1,n+k+1} \mid E_i$ run of length k)
	n	n + 1	n + 2	n + 3				
0	2				10	2, 6, 7, 9, 12, 13, 14, 15, 18, 19	6	.60
1	2	1			4	2–3, 7–8, 9–10, 15–16	2	.50
2	2	1	1		3	2–4, 9–11, 15–17	2	.67
3	2	1	1	1	1	2–5	1	1.00
0	1				9	1, 3, 4, 5, 8, 10, 11, 16, 17	5	.56
1	1	2			5	1–2, 5–6, 8–9, 11–12, 17–18	2	.40
2	1	2	2		3	5–7, 11–13, 17–19	2	.67
3	1	2	2	2	1	11–14	1	1.00

predict the more frequent event. Although such a hypothesis seems straightforward, it is not a simple one to test because we need to know the expected distribution of A_1 proportions within a block of trials. For the linear model, this distribution is not known (Estes & Suppes, 1959). Remember that every subject is not expected to match π exactly; the event sequence and the size of θ tend to cause subjects to spread around the π asymptote. Researchers often look at their protocols and find a subject who seems to be systematically behaving in a way not in accord with the theory. However, in his 1964b study, Estes compared "stat"[6] subjects with real subjects and found that stat subjects, run exactly as the theory requires, also show such aberrant protocols. Although there has been no definitive study, the evidence seems to point to a small shift involving almost all subjects,

rather than a large shift involving only a few subjects. To demonstrate otherwise, statistics would have to be derived showing individual protocols that deviate systematically from the prediction.

In general, there is little question about the adequacy of the negatively accelerated learning curve before asymptote. Deviations, when they occur, can usually be accounted for by the heterogeneity of the learning rate or by the results of subjects systematically "tracking" the varying sequence of events. In most studies, only a few sequences have been used for the 15 to 25 subjects in a group. If a particular sequence happens by chance to fluctuate widely, this produces a similar fluctuation in the response probabilities. Tracking behavior is, of course, predicted by SLT; the neatness of the tracking behavior can be seen in the Friedman et al. study (1964).

Recency analyses Gamblers are believed to be sustained in their gambling behavior by

[6]A stat subject is a subject-protocol generated by numeric means which corresponds exactly to some theory (Bush & Mosteller, 1955).

the fallacious belief that the longer their string of losses, the more likely they are to win on the next gamble. This is a fallacy because each gamble should be considered an independent event with the same constant probability of a win or a loss, regardless of the number of previous wins or losses. Jarvik (1951) observed that, in the PL routine, subjects predicted the O_2 outcome with a very high probability after a long string of O_1 outcomes had taken place. He labeled such behavior the *gambler's fallacy*. More technically, the analysis of the effects of outcome runs on prediction probabilities is called *recency analysis*. Consider a subject on trial n with a response probability $P(A_{1,n})$. Now present the subject with $k\, O_1$ outcomes in a row, starting on trial n. His new probability on trial $n + k$, $P(A_{1,n+k}) = 1 - (1 - P(A_{1,n}))(1 - \theta)^{k-1}$ (see Equation 6). Obviously, this is a monotonically increasing function with an asymptote of 1, yet Jarvik (1951), Nicks (1959), Edwards (1961), and many others have observed a nonmonotonic function. Usually, after from one to three outcomes, the empirical curves begin to decrease. Such a result is called a negative-recency effect, meaning that recent events are acting as negative reinforcers.

Table 20.1 presents 20 trials of events and responses. The probabilities $P(A_{1,n+k+1}|E_{i,n+k}, E_{i,n+k-1}, \ldots, E_{i,n+1}, E_{j,n})$ for $k = 0, 1, 2, \ldots$, stand for the $P(A_{1,n+k+1}|$ a run of E_i events of length k). Although it is not necessary, it is customary to begin the run on trial n with an E_j event (different from E_i). There are two values of both i and j, but because only the cases where $i \neq j$ are of interest, there are only two recency curves: $P(A_{1,n+k+1} \mid E_{1,n+k} \ldots E_{2,n})$ and $P(A_{1,n+k+1}|E_{2,n+k} \ldots E_{1,n})$.

To begin the analysis, let $k = 0$. First count the number of times an E_j event occurs on trials 1 through 19. There are 10 such trials for $j = 2$. Then, for just those trials (2, 6, 7, 9, . . .), count the number of times that an A_1 response is made on the very next trial (3, 7, 8, 10, . . .). There are 6 A_1 responses following E_2 events. The ratio of the A_1 responses to the E_j events determines $P(A_{1,n+1}|E_{j,n})$. In

the example, $P(A_{1,n+1}|E_{2,n}) = 6/10 = .60$. If $k = 1$, count the number of pairs of trials, n and $n + 1$, that contain $E_{j,n}E_{i,n+1}$. Table 20.1 shows four trials for $j = 2$ and $i = 1$: 2 and 3, 7 and 8, 9 and 10, and 15 and 16. Now count the A_1 responses on trials 4, 9, 11, and 17. In our example, there are two A_1 responses and $P(A_{1,n+2}|E_{1,n+1}E_{2,n}) = .50$. Continue the procedure for as many k values as are statistically reasonable. Usually, of course, more than one response and event sequence are involved. In such cases, the total number of A_1 responses summed over subjects and trials is divided by the total number of event patterns meeting the criteria defining the run. Although analyses of runs are tedious to calculate by hand, computers can easily be used to calculate hundreds of trials for large numbers of subjects. Because the sequence begins with the event opposite from the one involved in the run itself, the theoretical equation for these statistics is slightly different from Equation 6. Because each run of an E_1 event begins on trial n with an E_2 event, $P(A_{1,n})$ is first operated on by L_2:

$$L_2 P(A_{1,n}) = (1 - \theta)P(A_{1,n})$$

The L_1 operator is then applied successively for $k\, E_1$ events, yielding

$$(1 - \theta)^{k+1}P(A_{1,n}) + \theta[(1 - \theta)^{k-1} + (1 - \theta)^{k-2} \cdots (1 - \theta) + 1]$$

which leads to the solution

$$P(A_{1,n+k+1}|E_{1,n+k} \ldots E_{2,n}) = 1 - (1 - \theta)^k[1 - (1 - \theta)P(A_{1,n})] \quad (14)$$

Likewise, if E_2 runs are considered,

$$P(A_{1,n+k+1}|E_{2,n+k} \ldots E_{1,n}) = (1 - \theta)^k[P(A_{1,n})(1 - \theta) + \theta] \quad (15)$$

Sequential statistics are usually computed after response proportions have reached an asymptote; in this case, as $n \to \infty$, $P(A_{1,n}) \to \pi$. Notice that both functions are monotonic, one increasing to 1 and the other decreasing to 0. They begin slightly below and above $P(A_{1,n})$, respectively, because of the opposite event that initiates the run.

TABLE 20.2 RECENCY CURVES FROM THE EXPERIMENTS BY FRIEDMAN ET AL. AND REBER AND MILLWARD

$$P(A_{1,n+k+1} \mid E_{i,n+k}, E_{i,n+k-1}, \ldots, E_{i,n+1}, E_{j,n}), \quad i \neq j$$

		k value									
	i	0	1	2	3	4	5	6	7	8	9+
Friedman et al.	1	.67	.78	.84	.85	.89	.92	.89	.91	.87	.90
Reber and Millward	1	.84	.85	.86	.83	.85	.84	.87	.85	.88	.85
Friedman et al.	2	.83	.75	.57	.31	.19					
Reber and Millward	2	.85	.75	.77	.33	—					

The recency prediction by SLT has provoked a great deal of discussion. Jarvik (1951) was the first to report negative recency effects. Since his report was made, most PL experiments have shown a negative recency effect. However, few experiments have run more than 300 to 400 trials, and many of these have randomized in such a way as to insure $N\pi$ O_1 outcomes within each trial block of size N. Selecting events in a trial block of some restricted size, such as 25 or 50, restricts the length of the runs that can be made by chance in the sequence. A study by Jones and Myers (1966) demonstrated that this restriction is crucial in the recency analysis. Jones and Myers randomized the events in blocks of 20 and 300 trials. The distributions of the length of the runs of the events were very different: Runs longer than 4 or 5 were rarely generated in the short blocks, but they were rather frequent in the longer block. Jones and Myers found that the responses that subjects made after being tested with runs of different lengths reflected the relative probabilities of the lengths of the runs themselves. An earlier study by Derks (1963) had reported a very similar result. In another study (1962), Derks plotted recency curves as a function of trials. The curves for the first 250 trials showed large negative recency, but were nearly flat by the trial block 751–1000. The change over trials in the recency function was noted by Edwards (1961). Lindman and Edwards (1961) performed a follow-up study to compare the results reported by Edwards with those of

Nicks (1959), who had observed large negative recency effects. Lindman and Edwards confirmed that on early trials there is negative recency, which begins to diminish after only 100 trials. Witte (1964) built in negative recency effects by presenting event sequences with alternation tendencies much larger than is found in simple Bernoulli trials. The subjects were given 300 trials under these conditions and then 1200 regular Bernoulli trials. By the end of the 1200 trials, the subjects were showing positive recency. Finally, Gambino and Myers (1966) have shown that the degree of negative recency depends on the variance of the runs as well as their average length: More variability leads to less negative recency. They suggest that the function of increased average run length is to increase run-length variability.

An illustration of typical recency curves after a large number of trials is shown in Table 20.2, which presents the recency data from two different experiments. The data from Friedman et al. represent the last 96 trials of a $\pi = .8$ sequence of 288 trials that followed 864 trials with a variety of π values changed every 48 trials. The data of Reber and Millward plot the runs analysis from the second block of 500 trials of a simple probability-learning experiment with $\pi = .8$. The Friedman et al. curve, involving $P(A_1 \mid E_1)$ runs, rises at first, showing good positive recency, but it becomes too flat after $k = 4$. The Reber and Millward curve is remarkably unchanging. However, note that the curves of the

$P(A_1|E_2)$ runs in both experiments show large changes.

Sequential statistics   By a *sequential statistic,* we mean the response probabilities following any pattern of events and/or responses. The runs analysis, a special kind of sequential statistic, is the probability of a given response following a run of events. Other patterns include alternations of events and runs of responses. Derivations of a number of these special statistics can be found in Bush and Mosteller (1955), Estes and Suppes (1959), and Atkinson and Estes (1963). Anderson's article (1959) on the procedures for deriving such statistics is especially good.

We consider only two special statistics at this time. The first is the alternating-event sequence. Anderson (1960, 1964) has calculated a number of special sequential statistics of the form $P(A_{i,n+k+1}|E_{j,n+k}, E_{k,n+k-1}, \ldots, E_{m,n})$. By a judicious choice of pairs of these statistics, he found a set of pairs with the same theoretical value according to statistical learning theory. However, in a study he ran with $\pi = .5$ for 500 trials, the observed values for the set of pairs were not equal. The discrepancies he found suggest that there are response patterns in the data other than negative recency and alternation tendencies. For example, one pattern difference considered was $E_{1,n+3}E_{2,n+2}E_{2,n+1}E_{1,n} - E_{2,n+3}E_{2,n+2}E_{2,n+1}E_{1,n}$, which had an expectation of $\theta(1-\theta)^3$. The expected value was .1, but a value of 0 was observed. This seems to show that the E_1 event on the immediately preceding trial has no effect on the response probability on trial $n + 4$.

The second sequential statistic involves the event and response on the previous trial. This statistic is important because it relates to whether being right is more or less reinforcing than being wrong. In other words, does an E_1 reinforcement increase the A_1 response probability more if it occurs on an A_1 response trial than on an A_2 response trial? Consider the following two expressions:

$$P(A_{1,n+1}|E_{1,n}A_{1,n}) - P(A_{1,n+1}|A_{1,n}) \qquad (16)$$

and

$$P(A_{1,n+1}|E_{1,n}A_{2,n}) - P(A_{1,n+1}|A_{2,n}) \qquad (17)$$

According to SLT, there is no difference between Equations 16 and 17. The $P(A_{1,n+1}|A_{i,n})$ terms are subtracted to adjust for the difference in the expected response probability on trial $n + 1$ because the response on the previous trial is now known. Knowledge of the response on trial n provides information about the probability of the response on trial $n + 1$ because the A_1 response on trial n selects unequally those subjects with a higher A_1 response probability on trial n. Estes' analysis (1964b) shows that most learning seems to occur on correction trials, that is, those on which an error is made and the subject must make a correction response. Estes' analysis is supported by the fact that another model, the pattern model, which allows response-probability changes only on error trials (Atkinson & Estes, 1963), fits a little better than SLT. Estes shows that, with large θ values and large $P(A_1)$ values, SLT predicts that the largest probability changes are on error trials. These conclusions can be interpreted as support for a contiguity theory of learning as opposed to a drive-reduction theory. Such use of sequential statistics to analyze results, so that a clear statement concerning issues can be made, represents an important development in the psychology of learning.

The derivation of sequential statistics is not simple, and a proper development of the probability sample space of the model is needed to make the derivations correctly. The reader is referred to Anderson (1959), Estes and Suppes (1959), and Atkinson, Bower, and Crothers (1965) for detailed treatments of the derivation of sequential statistics.

To illustrate some of the pitfalls in deriving sequential statistics as well as to explicate Equations 16 and 17, these equations will be derived. First, note that $P(A_{1,n+1}|A_{i,n})$ does not equal $P(A_{1,n+1})$. The lack of equality is due to the fact that the subjects have different response probabilities. Those subjects with a high probability of making an A_1 response are more likely to make that response on trial n and on trial $n + 1$. Thus, when considering only those subjects who make an A_1 on trial n, we automatically select those subjects with a higher probability of making an A_1 response. This selection also occurs in the analysis of the sequential statistics $P(A_{1,n+1} | E_{i,n}, A_{k,n})$. Thus, if we look only at $P(A_{1,n+1} | E_{1,n}, A_{1,n})$ and $P(A_{1,n+1} | E_{1,n}, A_{2,n})$, we cannot answer the question of whether presenting an E_1 on trials when a subject makes an A_1 response is more or less reinforcing than presenting an E_1 on trials when a subject makes an A_2 response.

Perhaps the simplest way to illustrate these statistics without extensive formal development is to consider only the first three trials. If all subjects start with p_1 as the initial probability of an A_1 response, by trial 3 they branch into four different probabilities. Figure 20.3 presents the tree of response probabilities and the probabilities of the paths taken by each subject. On trial 2, there are two subsets of subjects. The first has the response probability $L_1 p_1 = (1 - \theta)p_1 + \theta$ and the second $L_2 p_1 = (1 - \theta)p_1$. Let us call these two probabilities $p_{1,2}$ and $p_{2,2}$, respectively. The probabilities of taking the two different paths (or in a real experiment, the proportion of subjects who will follow each path) are π and $1 - \pi$. Now consider $P(A_{1,3} | A_{1,2})$.

$$P(A_{1,3} | A_{1,2}) = P(A_{1,3}, A_{1,2})/P(A_{1,2})$$

where

$$P(A_{1,3}, A_{1,2})$$
$$= \pi p_{1,2}[\pi L_1 p_{1,2} + (1 - \pi)L_2 p_{1,2}]$$
$$+ (1 - \pi)p_{2,2}[\pi L_1 p_{2,2} + (1 - \pi)L_2 p_{2,2}] \quad (18)$$
$$= \pi p_{1,2}[(1 - \theta)p_{1,2} + \theta\pi]$$
$$+ (1 - \pi)p_{2,2}[(1 - \theta)p_{2,2} + \theta\pi]].$$

Now,

$$P(A_{1,2}) = \pi p_{1,2} + (1 - \pi)p_{2,2} \quad (19)$$

is called "the first raw moment of the response distribution." A similar statistic, the second raw moment, is defined as

$$P(A_{1,2}^2) = \pi p_{1,2}^2 + (1 - \pi)p_{2,2}^2 \quad (20)$$

In terms of these quantities,

$$P(A_{1,3}, A_{1,2})$$
$$= (1 - \theta)P(A_{1,2}^2) + \theta\pi P(A_{1,2}) \quad (18a)$$

If we divide Equation 18a by the first moment, $P(A_{1,2})$, we obtain the conditional probability

$$P(A_{1,3} | A_{1,2}) = \frac{(1 - \theta)P(A_{1,2}^2)}{P(A_{1,2})} + \theta\pi \quad (21)$$

Note that $P(A_{1,2}^2) \neq P(A_{1,2}) \cdot P(A_{1,2})$. The second raw moment is the weighted sum of the square of the individual probabilities, not the square of the weighted sum of the individual probabilities. Proceeding in an exactly analogous way, the following statistic is derived.

$$P(A_{1,3} | A_{2,2})$$
$$= (1 - \theta)\frac{P(A_{1,2}) - P(A_{1,2}^2)}{1 - P(A_{1,2})} + \theta\pi \quad (22)$$

Similarly, but restricting the transitions considered to those appropriate to applying an E_i event, the two conditional probabilities involving the event on the preceding trials are derived.

$$P(A_{1,3} | E_{1,2}, A_{1,2})$$
$$= (1 - \theta)\frac{P(A_{1,2}^2)}{P(A_{1,2})} + \theta \quad (23)$$

$$P(A_{1,3} | E_{1,2}, A_{2,2})$$
$$= (1 - \theta)\frac{P(A_{1,2}) - P(A_{1,2}^2)}{1 - P(A_{1,2})} + \theta \quad (24)$$

Now, to correct for the bias due to the response made on trial 2, we subtract Equation 21 from 23, and Equation 22 from 24 and, in both cases, obtain $\theta(1 - \pi)$ as the expected effect of an E_1 event. According to SLT, the response made on the previous trial is irrelevant to the change in response probability. Estes (1964b) reports results for this test and cannot find significant differences between Equation 23 minus Equation 21 on the one hand and Equation 24 minus Equation 22 on the other, indicating that in fact the reinforcing effect of the event is independent of the response made.

Further Developments of SLT: Stimulus Variables

There are various ways to extend theories. One is to try different versions of the basic axioms and determine the implications for the various axioms tried. These implications can then be related to psychological processes to see if they are or are not reasonable. Another way to extend theories is to attempt to apply them to new or modified experimental situations. An experimental routine is a complex procedure involving many arbitrarily determined parameters. The trial times, the stimuli used, the response the subject makes, and so on, are arrived at through trial and error in the laboratory. The experimenter is constantly thinking of variations in his procedure, many of which seem important psychologically because they test a different aspect of the process under investigation. These two methods of extending theories are rarely independent but usually go on simultaneously. In the material that follows, both extension of theory and variation in experimental procedure are discussed.

In the section on theoretical development, the basic concepts of statistical learning theory are presented. In this section we expand the basic idea of representing the stimulus environment by a set of elements (Estes & Burke, 1953; Burke & Estes, 1957). The treatment of discrimination, stimulus-compounding, generalization, stimulus fluctuation, and other experimental procedures that require manipulation of the stimulus conditions are qualitatively handled fairly adequately by the extensions of SLT to be discussed. Experimental facts established since these ideas were formulated have uncovered shortcomings in most of them, but because so much of the later theoretical elaboration depends on these early formulations, they are worth reviewing briefly now.

Discrimination   A discrimination procedure consists of a series of trials containing various stimuli, some of which are to be re-

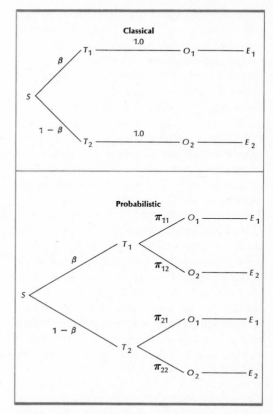

Figure 20.6. Paradigms of classical and probabilistic discrimination procedures. S signifies the beginning of the trial. T_i is the type of trial presented. Trial type T_i is presented with probability β, and π_{ij} is the probability that outcome O_j will follow trial type T_i.

sponded to in one way and others in a different way. Figure 20.6 presents a paradigmatic representation of the simple two-stimulus classical discrimination situation. (The term *classical* denotes a perfect correlation between outcome O_1 and stimulus T_1 and between outcome O_2 and stimulus T_2.) β represents the probability or proportion of the times that stimulus T_1 is presented. Typically, T_1 and T_2 are presented randomly and equally often.

The SLT analysis of classical discrimination learning is quite straightforward. First, we represent each stimulus T_i by a set of stimulus elements S_i. Now if we wish to represent anything other than two simultaneous acquisition processes, the two sets of stimuli must have some elements in common. These common elements constitute a set designated S_C^* and equal to the intersection of the set S_1 and S_2, that is, $S_C^* = S_1 \cap S_2$. The set S_C^* reflects the degree of similarity between the two stimuli. The number of elements in the intersection is designated N_C. With N_C elements common to S_1 and S_2, there are only $N_1^* = N_1 - N_C$ elements in S_1^* that are unique to the T_1 stimulus. Similarly, $N_2^* = N_2 - N_C$ elements in S_2^* are unique to T_2. The presence of common stimulation is critical in determining both the rate of learning the discrimination and the asymptotic performance. Consider the learning function for the elements in S_1^*, which are consistently reinforced on a proportion β of the trials and are not changed on a proportion $1 - \beta$ of the trials. Let $p_{i,n}^*$ represent the proportion of elements in set S_i^* conditioned on trial n. Then $p_{1,n+1}^* = (1 - \theta_1)p_{1,n}^* + \theta_1$ with a probability β and $p_{1,n+1}^* = p_{1,n}^*$ with a probability $1 - \beta$. On the average, the change on each trial will be

$$p_{1,n+1}^* = (1 - \theta_1\beta)p_{1,n}^* + \theta_1\beta \qquad (25)$$

The general solution is

$$p_{1,n}^* = 1 - (1 - p_{1,1}^*)(1 - \theta_1\beta)^{n-1} \qquad (26)$$

This function has an asymptote of 1, so all the elements in S_1^* become conditioned to the A_1 response. Similarly,

$$p_{2,n}^* = p_{2,1}^*[1 - \theta_2(1 - \beta)]^{n-1} \qquad (27)$$

and all the elements in S_2^* are conditioned not to A_1 but to A_2. Note the relationship between Equation 5 and these equations.

In each of these functions, the rate of learning is a function of the β parameter—as intuitively it should be, for, if a stimulus is presented only on a small proportion of the trials, we would expect learning to occur proportionally more slowly. Now consider the elements in S_C^*. They are sampled on every trial, but when they are sampled with S_1^*, they become conditioned to A_1, whereas when they are sampled with S_2^*, they become conditioned to A_2. The derivation for this

situation is exactly the same as that for the probability-learning situation (Equations 9 and 10), but with β replacing π. Thus, the learning curve for these elements becomes

$$p_{C,n}^* = \beta - (\beta - p_{C,1}^*)(1 - \theta_C)^{n-1} \qquad (28)$$

The dependent variables in a discrimination situation are $P(A_{1,n}|T_{1,n})$ and $P(A_{1,n}|T_{2,n})$. These variables reflect the response proportions to the two stimuli. When stimulus T_1 is presented, $N_1\theta_1$ elements are sampled on the average from S_1^*, and $N_C\theta_C$ elements are sampled from S_C^*. Likewise, on T_2 trials, $N_2\theta_2$ elements are sampled from S_2^*, and $N_C\theta_C$ elements are sampled from S_C^*. Of the $N_1\theta_1$ elements sampled from S_1^* on trial n, $P_{1,n}^*$ are conditioned to A_1. Also, $p_{C,n}^*$ of the $N_C\theta_C$ elements sampled from S_C^* are conditioned to A_1. Then,

$$P(A_{1,n}|T_{1,n}) = \frac{p_{1,n}^*N_1\theta_1 + p_{C,n}^*N_C\theta_C}{N_1\theta_1 + N_C\theta_C} \qquad (29)$$

and similarly,

$$P(A_{1,n}|T_{2,n}) = \frac{p_{2,n}^*N_2\theta_2 + p_{C,n}^*N_C\theta_C}{N_2\theta_2 + N_C\theta_C} \qquad (30)$$

Asymptotically, $p_{1,n}^* = 1$, $p_{2,n}^* = 0$, and $p_{C,n}^* = \beta$, so asymptotically,

$$P(A_{1,\infty}|T_{1,\infty}) = \frac{N_1\theta_1 + \beta N_C\theta_C}{N_1\theta_1 + N_C\theta_C} \qquad (31)$$

and

$$P(A_{1,\infty}|T_{2,\infty}) = \frac{\beta N_C\theta_C}{N_2\theta_2 + N_C\theta_C} \qquad (32)$$

If there are no common elements sampled, that is, if $N_C = 0$ and/or $\theta_C = 0$, perfect discrimination occurs.

Let $W_i = N_C\theta_C/(N_i\theta_i + N_C\theta_C)$. Then the functions become

$$P(A_{1,n}|T_{1,n}) = (1 - W_1)p_{1,n}^* + W_1p_{C,n}^* \qquad (33)$$

$$P(A_{1,n}|T_{2,n}) = (1 - W_2)p_{2,n}^* + W_2p_{C,n}^* \qquad (34)$$

and asymptotically,

$$P(A_{1,\infty}|T_{1,\infty}) = 1 - W_1(1 - \beta) \qquad (35)$$

and

$$P(A_{1,\infty} | T_{2,\infty}) = W_2\beta \qquad (36)$$

The learning rate and asymptotes are functions of β and of the relative weights of the sample sizes from the sets S_1^* and S_2^* to S_1 and S_2, respectively. Note that, although there are parameters N_i and θ_i for $i = C$, 1, and 2, only two parameters, W_1 and W_2, are needed to represent these six parameters. In this learning process, the asymptotes are determined by three parameters and the learning functions by five. One parameter of each set, β, is determined by the experimenter. In applications of discrimination problems, certain assumptions usually can be made about the stimuli that can further reduce the number of parameters. For example, an argument of symmetry usually allows $W_1 = W_2$ to be assumed.

From the point of view of the theory, the most important finding of this derivation is that, if the two discriminative stimuli overlap at all, perfect discrimination cannot be obtained. The simple notion that discrimination consists of two simultaneous acquisition functions will not handle the results of most discrimination experiments. Somehow subjects learn to ignore the common stimulation in most discrimination situations.

A natural extension of classical discrimination is probabilistic discrimination. Figure 20.6 presents the paradigm of such a procedure. Instead of always reinforcing T_i with O_i, the reinforcement is probabilistic; that is, $P(O_j | T_i) = \pi_{ij}$. Another way to think about probabilistic discrimination is to assume a single set of elements partitioned into subsets. Each subset has one probability of being sampled on O_1 trials and a different probability on O_2 trials. The derivation for classical discrimination is repeated for probabilistic discrimination with one difference: The $p_{i,n}^*$ functions must include the π_{ij} probabilities of O_j reinforcement (see Equations 9 and 10). They become

$$p_{1,n}^* = \pi_{11} - (\pi_{11} - p_{1,1}^*)(1 - \theta\beta)^{n-1} \qquad (37)$$

and

$$p_{2,n}^* = \pi_{21} - (\pi_{21} - p_{1,1}^*)[1 - \theta(1 - \beta)]^{n-1} \qquad (38)$$

S_C is reinforced with E_1 on a proportion $\beta\pi_{11} + (1 - \beta)\pi_{21} = \pi_C$ of the trials.

$$p_{C,n}^* = \pi_C - (\pi_C - p_{C,1}^*)(1 - \theta)^{n-1} \qquad (39)$$

Popper and Atkinson (1958) made one of the first studies to test the predictions of SLT for probabilistic discrimination. They used nonsense syllables MEF and ZIL as the T_1 and T_2 stimuli with a constant $\beta = .50$ and $\pi_{11} = .85$ with π_{21} varying across groups. The results were inconsistent with predictions of the theory in that, for $\pi_{21} = .85$, .70, and .50, the estimate of $W_1 = W_2 = W$ was 0, but for $\pi_{21} = .30$ and .15, the curves could not be fit by $W = 0$. Groups run on these last two π_{21} values were not at asymptote; perhaps if they had been run longer, W would also have equaled zero. However, such a result is still inconsistent with the theory, which predicts not only that the asymptote will depend on W but that the rate of learning will too. (See Equations 33 and 34.) The five groups were definitely learning at different rates, a phenomenon incompatible with the $W = 0$ value observed. In a follow-up study, Atkinson, Bogartz, and Turner (1959) observed essentially the same results. Although the theory could be used to predict the results as a function of β correctly, even if it failed for various π values, it could not be used in a later study in which Juliet Popper Shaffer (1963) fixed $\pi_{11} = 1.0$ and $\pi_{21} = .5$ but varied β for three groups, $\beta = .33$, .50, and .67. Shaffer noted that $P(A_{1,n} | T_{1,n})$ and $P(A_{1,n} | T_{2,n})$ should be linearly increasing functions of β with equal slopes and that the difference between them should be constant for the three β values. (See Equations 35 and 36.) She found that $P(A_{1,n} | T_{1,n})$ increased linearly as expected, but that $P(A_{1,n} | T_{2,n})$ decreased. Thus, the slopes were not equal nor was the difference a constant. These experiments have raised theoretical questions that have had a wide influence on the development of learning theory. The main fault of the theory is that subjects are only temporarily influenced by the common stimulation. If the model is to be correct, the stimuli T_1 and T_2 must provide a common stimulation that cannot be ignored by the subject (see Uhl, 1964; Halpern & Moore, 1967).

There are obvious problems with the extensions of SLT into discrimination learning by humans. The main difficulty seems to be that human beings have a much better analytical ability than that assumed by the model. Further theoretical ideas derived from SLT have been suggested as alternative solutions to discrimination learning. Among these are the pattern model (Estes, 1959a) and one of its variants, the mixed model (Estes & Hopkins, 1961; Atkinson & Estes, 1963). These are discussed in the section on paired-associate learning.

Stimulus compounding Any learning theory should be able to make predictions about behavior in new situations based on given information about the subject's behavior under similar or more elementary situations. For example, if a subject makes an A_1 response to stimulus S_1 with the probability p_1, and an A_2 response to stimulus S_C with probability p_C, how will he respond if the two stimulus situations are combined, T_1, and presented simultaneously? The solution suggested by SLT is given in Equation 33. In any stimulus-compounding experiment, the weights of the stimuli must be considered. SLT does this through the product of the set size and the sampling probability $N\theta$. Of course, the proportion of conditioned elements in each set influences the response probability also.

One important use of the compound-stimulus analysis is to estimate the weight of a stimulus set. Let us consider an example in which the problem is to estimate N_1 and N_2. Assume that T_1 and T_2 have no common stimulation. If $\theta_1 = \theta_2$, and through training, $P(A_1|T_1) = 1$ and $P(A_1|T_2) = 0$, then, when presented together, $P(A_1|T_1 \text{ and } T_2) = N_1/(N_1 + N_2)$. Thus, their relative sizes can be estimated. Of course, more elaborate procedures can also be used to estimate each value of θ.

Schoeffler (1956) ran a compound-stimulus study involving three sets of lights, two of which were first discriminated in a classical discrimination experiment. The sets were defined by partitioning 24 lights on a panel into three equal subsets of size 8. Then subset T_1 was reinforced with O_1 and T_2 with O_2, where O_1 and O_2 were event lights indicating which of two responses was correct. Subset T_3 was never presented. Discrimination training consisted of presenting all eight lights of each set with $\beta = .5$. After discrimination training (which was described very satisfactorily by the discrimination model discussed earlier) stimulus compounds were formed by combining at random n_i lights from each of the T_i sets. Because the three sets were randomly determined uniquely for each subject, and because of the homogeneity of the lights themselves, the assumption that the theoretical stimulus set, S_i associated with T_i, had an equal number of elements could be made. On test trials, no reinforcement was presented. The stimulus set that was not presented during discrimination training (T_3) was assumed to have its elements conditioned with a probability of .5 to each response. The expectation for an A_1 response, assuming $P(A_1|T_1) = 1$ and $P(A_1 | T_2) = 0$ was simply $(N_1 + .5N_3)/N_1 + N_2 + N_3)$. Only the data for one test pattern out of nine were significantly different from expectation. These results may not seem too surprising, but remember that the behavior exhibited is by no means the most rational. To maximize correct responses, the subjects should respond A_1 if $N_1 > N_2$, A_2 if $N_2 > N_1$, and ignore N_3 elements. However, if each subject had a deterministic response rule for each pattern depending in some way on the elements he attended to, the proportions would then represent the proportion of subjects and not a response probability for each subject. Further work is needed to evaluate this possibility. Once again we have the problem of interpreting average data.

The Estes, Burke, Atkinson, and Frankmann experiment (1957) investigated two aspects of SLT: probabilistic discrimination and compounding of stimuli. The T_i trial was followed by O_i on all trials, but the stimuli selected varied. Twelve stimuli were evenly spaced around a circle, and were designated randomly by the numerals 1 through 12. Then the probability of selecting light i on a T_1 trial was $5i/78$ and the probability for a T_2 trial was $(65 - 5i)/78$. Two groups were run: The β probability was .50 for one group and .25 for the other. After 520 training trials, triads of lights were presented. The proportion of correct responses observed may have been slightly higher than that predicted for the two groups but was not significantly so. For $\beta = .50$, the observed proportion was .67, and the predicted proportion .64, whereas for $\beta = .25$, the observed proportion was .74 and the predicted .72. All these are well below the maximum possible correct proportions. Response proportions to individual lights presented during the test trials were systematically related to the reinforcement probability for each light, indicating probability-matching for the individual components of the stimuli. The slight regression observed toward .50 for the signal lights with high or low π values would be expected if there were some background stimulation that was not taken into account in the matching prediction. All in all, SLT is not perfect in its description of classical and probabilistic discrimination or in its account of stimulus-compounding, but the overall handling of the data is impressively good.

Stimulus generalization According to Estes' early development of SLT, stimulus generalization was to be accounted for by considering the stimulus as a series of overlapping sets. The normal procedure in generalization experiments is to train a subject to respond A_1 to stimulus T_1 until $P(A_1|T_1) = p_i$. Then a similar stimulus T_1^* is presented. There is usually a decrement in the probability of the A_1 response; that is, $P(A_1|T_1^*) < P(A_1|T_1)$. If the stimulus situation associated with T_1 is conceived of as being composed of a set of elements, some of which are also included in T_1^*, then as A_1 is conditioned to T_1, A_1 is also conditioned to part of T_1^*. The degree of conditioning depends on

$T_1 \cap T_1^*$, which in the discrimination experimental situation is the set S_C^*.

Generalization is usually treated along either quantitative dimensions or substitutive dimensions (prothetic or metathetic dimensions, according to S. S. Stevens, 1957). Both of these dimensions have been treated from the point of view of set theory (Restle, 1961; Atkinson & Estes, 1963). We confine our discussion to a sketchy presentation of the metathetic dimension. First, note that a general measure of overlap will produce stimulus generalization but will not specify the form of the generalization gradient. A set of stimuli T_i^* on some physical dimension A, such as wavelength of light or frequency of tone, is presented after the subject has been trained to a specific value T. Because the basic notion here is one of substitution, each set of elements associated with a stimulus different from the one originally conditioned is assumed to have some new and perhaps some common elements. A further assumption is that, as the physical stimulus is systematically increased or decreased, the sets of stimulus elements introduced are correspondingly related in a linear way. These ideas are spelled out in greater detail by Atkinson and Estes (1963).

Three axioms define a linear array of sets (Restle, 1961). If $T_i^* \leq T_j^* \leq T_k^*$ are ordered on some substitutive dimension, then $S_i \cap S_k \subseteq S_j$. In other words, this axiom states that, if an element belongs to any two sets, it also belongs to the sets in between. The second axiom states that, if the intersection of S_i and S_k is not null ($S_i \cap S_k \neq 0$), then $S_j \subseteq (S_i \cup S_k)$. The second axiom requires that all elements of any set between two nondisjoint sets belong to one or the other of the two sets. Finally, the third axiom states that all sets S associated with T stimuli have the same number of elements ($N_i = N_j = N$). The first task in any application of this theory is to establish a set of stimuli T_i that meet the requirements of the above axioms. Then tests of the generalization process in conditioning can be carried out.

Two generalization experiments have been

carried out using human subjects and a probability learning task in which the substitutive dimension of the position of a light stimulus along a line was used. LaBerge (1961) trained subjects on a vertical dimension by reinforcing T_1 with O_1 and T_2 with O_2 on all of the trials. Test stimuli given between these two stimuli showed very orderly response characteristics that were quite linear for individual subjects. When the two stimuli were widely spaced, the generalization function showed a plateau at the centrally located stimuli. As would be expected, the gradients were steeper when T_1 and T_2 were closer. The average generalization gradients were somewhat sigmoid in shape (which unfortunately could be due to averaging of subjects with different slope gradients). LaBerge found that latencies increased monotonically with distance from the training stimulus. No attempt was made to test SLT in this experiment.

The second experiment (Teresa Carterette, 1961) involved summated generalization. The stimuli consisted of a $2\frac{3}{4}$-in. square of light presented on a horizontal line in $\frac{1}{2}$-in. steps. Each block of trials began when the experimenter presented and identified for the subject first stimulus A and then stimulus B. Eight test trials were then given, on which either A or B or some other stimulus might be given. The subject's task was to distinguish between training stimuli A and B and the other presented stimuli. Two predictions from the theory were supported. First, the level of responding to test stimuli between training stimuli decreased as the training stimuli were spread further apart. Second, the slopes of the gradients on either side of the training stimuli were parallel for different groups. In contrast, gradients between the two training stimuli were shallower than predicted, and the range of the generalization was greater than expected. All in all, the theory did not do badly, but further testing is certainly called for because few assumptions of the generalization model have been experimentally tested.

Stimulus fluctuation   This is not the place for an extensive review of stimulus fluctuation, but the student should at least be aware of this development in SLT and probability learning. More detailed discussions may be found in Estes (1955, 1959b). SLT predicts that,

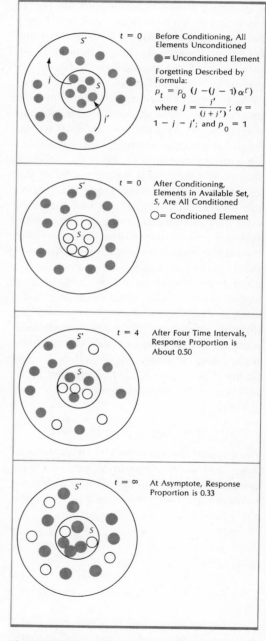

Figure 20.7. Schematic diagram showing the fluctuation model of SLT applied to a simple forgetting experiment. (See text.)

as the stimulus conditions increase in variability, learning will be slower. An early study
by Burke, Estes, and Hellyer (1954) supported
this notion, but the Estes and Burke (1955)
discrimination study, the study by Friedman
et al. (1964), and a replication of the Burke,
Estes, and Hellyer study by Anderson (1966)
have raised serious doubts as to whether this
prediction is generally true. In none of these
experiments did variability function as
consistently as predicted.

By assuming sets of stimulus elements that
change over time, stimulus fluctuation is also
used to account for such processes as forgetting, spontaneous recovery, distribution of
practice effects, trace conditioning, and drive
factors. We shall use a simple model of forgetting as an illustration. Figure 20.7 shows
the theoretical changes in stimulation over
time that can account for a decrease in response proportions over time. We assume that
the total stimulation consists of a set of elements S that are available for sampling and
another set S' that cannot be sampled from
at the moment. Within each time interval Δt,
arbitrarily specified but of a sufficiently long
duration to observe the changes taking place,
each element in S has a probability j of entering S', and each element in S' has a probability j' of entering S. Let $f(t)$ be the probability that any given element is in S at time
t. Then

$$f(t + 1) = f(t)(1 - j) + [1 - f(t)]j' \quad (40)$$

An element remains in S with probability
$1 - j$ and an element in S' enters S with
probability j'. This is a simple linear difference
equation as observed in Equation 10. It has
the solution

$$f(t) = J - [J - f(0)]\alpha^t \quad (41)$$

where

$$J = \frac{j'}{j + j'} \quad \text{and} \quad \alpha = (1 - j - j')$$

The j and j' values are between zero and 1
and thus α is between -1 and $+1$. Eventually,
α^t will decrease to zero and the asymptotic

probability that an element is in S will become J. If there are N^* elements in $S \cup S'$,
then N, the number of elements in S, is determined by the relation $N = JN^*$. The number in S' can be designated N', so $N^* = N + N'$.

The purpose of the fluctuation model is
to determine response probability after a time
interval when we have information about the
initial response probability. Assume that the
N elements in S are conditioned so that a
proportion p_0 is associated with the A_1 response in the $t = 0$ time interval. Of the
original N elements in S,

$$Nf(t) = N(J - (J - 1)\alpha^t) \quad (42)$$

elements will still be in S after t time intervals.
These elements that remain in S will be conditioned with probability p_0, so that $p_0 Nf(t)$
conditioned elements are in S that were in
S at time $t = 0$. Likewise, if a proportion p_0'
elements are conditioned in S' at time $t = 0$,
then, after t intervals of time $p_0' N' f'(t)$ conditioned elements are in S that were in S'.

The probability $f'(t)$ is computed by setting
$f(0) = 0$ in Equation 41 because this is the
probability that elements in S' are in S after
t intervals of time: $f'(t) = J(1 - \alpha^t)$. To compute the probability of a conditioned response at time t, p_t, we must determine the
proportion of conditioned elements in S.
There are N elements in S, so

$$p_t = \frac{1}{N}[p_0 Nf(t) + p'N'f'(t)] =$$
$$p_0(J - (J - 1)\alpha^t) + p_0'(1 - J)(1 - \alpha^t). \quad (43)$$

In the case of simple conditioning, we
might assume that $p_0 = 1$ and $p_0' = 0$. Then
response proportions will decrease to an
asymptotic level, $p_0 J$. Because J depends on
the ratio of the elements available for sampling to those that are not available, the
amount of forgetting is a function of the
amount of stimulus change. In Figure 20.7,
$j = .20$, $j' = .10$, so $J = .33$, $N = 6$ and
$N' = 12$. Before training, all elements are assumed to be unconditioned. After training,
at $t = 0$, all six elements in S are conditioned.

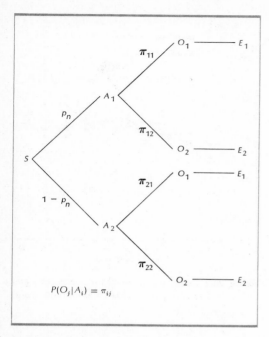

Figure 20.8. Trial paradigm for contingent reinforcement in probability learning. π_{ij} is the probability of an O_j outcome following an A_i response. (See Figure 20.1 for noncontingent paradigm.)

Two steps in the forgetting process are plotted by the formula $p_t = .33 - (.33 - 1.0)$ $(1.0 - .20 - .10)^t$, where $p_0 = 1.0$ and $p'_0 = 0$. The first step, at $t = 4$, leaves a proportion of about .50, the second, at asymptote, leaves a proportion .33.

Further Developments of SLT: Reinforcement Contingencies

Contingent reinforcement   Thus far, we have limited our discussion to the noncontingent reinforcement procedure in which $P(O_1) = \pi$, independently of the subject's response and the trial number. The contingent reinforcement schedule defines a different probability for each of the two responses. Figure 20.8 is a schematic diagram of this procedure, in which the reinforcement of the A_i response is probabilistically determined by $P(O_j|A_i) = \pi_{ij}$. Again, the reinforcing event is directly associated with the experimental

outcome, E_i with O_i. The learning curves for this situation are developed in a manner completely analogous to that for Equation 10.

Operator Applied	Probability on Trial $n + 1$	Probability of Applying Operator
$L_1 p_n$	$(1 - \theta)p_n + \theta$	$p_n \pi_{11}$
$L_2 p_n$	$(1 - \theta)p_n$	$p_n(1 - \pi_{11})$
$L_1 p_n$	$(1 - \theta)p_n + \theta$	$(1 - p_n)\pi_{21}$
$L_2 p_n$	$(1 - \theta)p_n$	$(1 - p_n)(1 - \pi_{21})$

By averaging these changes in probability, the average change in probability over each trial is determined:

$$p_{n+1} = [1 - \theta(\pi_{12} + \pi_{21})]p_n + \theta\pi_{21} \quad (44)$$

which has the solution

$$p_n = \bar{\pi} - (\bar{\pi} - p_1)[1 - \theta(\pi_{12} + \pi_{21})]^{n-1} \quad (45)$$

where

$$\bar{\pi} = \frac{\pi_{21}}{\pi_{12} + \pi_{21}}$$

Because the expected asymptote $\bar{\pi}$ is not particularly intuitive, subjects would not be expected to "compute" it in any ordinary sense. However, the theory implies that $\bar{\pi}$ is the asymptote that will be reached with the contingent procedure. The data from early studies with contingent reinforcement did not always attain this asymptote. However, in some cases, the contingency was set up so that the subject was to select a response that would turn on a single light. It is important in the application of the model to ensure that every trial be followed by O_1 or O_2, and that the two outcomes lead unambiguously to reinforcements E_1 or E_2 (*determinate reinforcement*). If the light did not go on, the subject might or might not have assumed that the other response would have turned on the light. Actually, in this schedule, without two explicit outcomes, it is possible that neither response might turn on the light. Let O_1 represent the instance in which the light is turned on and O_2 that in which the light is not turned on; then $p_n\pi_{12} + (1 - p_n)\pi_{22}$ is the probability the light will not be turned on. If the π_{i2} values are large, subjects may detect the fact that the light comes on very infrequently. Then, covertly, a third reinforcing event may occur, namely, one that occurs when the subject covertly responds to no outcome with the interpretation that neither response would have turned the light on. (Reinforcement situations without clear assignments of outcomes are referred to as *indeterminate reinforcement situations*.) This interpretation of the effects of instructional and procedural changes is supported by the pattern of results observed in experiments by Detambel (1955), Brand, Woods, and Sakoda (1956), Woods (1959), and Koehler (1961).

In a study on noncontingent PL, Reber and Millward (1968) asked two groups of subjects simply to observe outcomes for 500 trials, one group at the rate of one outcome every 4 sec, and the other group at the rate of two outcomes every sec. Following the simple observation trials, subjects were asked to predict for another 500 trials in a manner similar to noncontingent PL. Neither group differed in the asymptote they attained or in runs statistics from a group tested under a regular prediction procedure. (Figure 20.5 presents the data of the control group from which the two observation groups did not differ.) The sequential statistics differed across groups, but the difference is not systematically related to observation versus regular PL. During the 500 prediction trials, both groups remained at a stable asymptote of about .84 for $\pi = .80$. Lambe (1968) used the observation procedure to investigate the contingent reinforcement schedule. The subjects were first brought to asymptote by observation trials at $\overline{\pi}$, and then the contingencies were introduced. The two groups of primary interest had reinforcement values: (1) $\pi_{11} = .6$; $\pi_{21} = .8$, and (2) $\pi_{11} = .8$; $\pi_{21} = .4$. In both cases, $\overline{\pi} = .67$. In Group 1, outcomes tended to reinforce the opposite response from the one predicted, whereas in Group 2, the outcome predicted was very likely to be reinforced. Lambe was interested

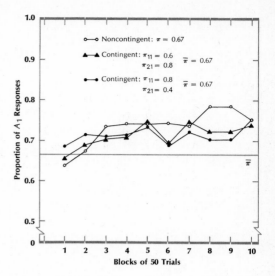

Figure 20.9. Learning curves from contingent and noncontingent probability-learning paradigms.

in whether these different schedules, both of which had the same expected asymptote, would remain at the initial response probability established through the observation of outcomes. Figure 20.9 presents the results for the 500 trials after observation trials for Group 1, Group 2, and Group 3, a noncontingent control group with $\pi = .67$. Note first that the subjects begin at about .67, showing that the observation trials were effective in establishing asymptotic responding. Second, the three groups remain at asymptote after an initial rise over the first 100 prediction trials. The asymptotes from trials 101 to 500 are not significantly different, but the rise from trial 1 to trial 100 is significant. The asymptote is not $\overline{\pi}$ as predicted, but rather a slight overshooting of $\overline{\pi}$ very similar to that observed in the results by Reber and Millward (1968) (see Figure 20.5).

"Blank" trials   Another variation in reinforcements related to the contingent procedure is the effect of so-called "blank" trials. A trial in PL is usually followed by an O_1 or an O_2. On blank trials, neither O_1 nor O_2 occurs (the O_0 outcome). From the subject's point of view, it is an ambiguous outcome and therefore the experimenter cannot a priori associate a reinforcing event with O_0. A number of experiments have been run to determine the effect of O_0 on response probability. An early study by Neimark (1956) led to the formulation of the identity hypothesis, that is, the hypothesis that no change occurred on O_0 trials. Later studies that relied on asymptotic responding to determine whether or not the O_0 outcome had an effect have found that the identity operator L_0 yields the best fits. Atkinson (1956) and Millward (1967), using contingent reinforcement schedules, found that $L_0p_n = p_n$, applied on O_0 trials, adequately described the asymptotes. On the other hand, investigators who looked at sequential statistics have found that the O_0 outcome produces changes in p_n. Anderson and Grant (1957, 1958) suggested from sequential statistics applied to double-outcome trials (that is, trials on which both O_1 and O_2 occurred) that there was a regression to .5 on double-outcome trials. LaBerge, Greeno, and Peterson (1962) and Greeno (1962) equated groups on the total number of O_i, $i = 1, 2$, outcomes received, but gave different groups different numbers of O_0 outcomes. A neutral or identity hypothesis would predict that the groups would all be the same when the response proportions were plotted according to O_1 and O_2 trials received. They were not. In both papers, the conclusion was that there was a regression to .5. Greeno further concluded that the regression was controlled by the outcome frequency and not by the response frequency. By using different payoff schedules, he stabilized groups with the same outcome probabilities at different response probabilities. One interpretation of the identity hypothesis is that it amounts to no change on the average, although each subject may change after an O_0 outcome. If the effect of an O_0 depended on the p_n value, so that $p_{n+1} = (1 - \theta)p_n + \theta$ with probability p_n, and $p_{n+1} = (1 - \theta)p_n$ with a probability $1 - p_n$, then, on the average, $p_{n+1} = p_n$. The probability of

each subject might change, depending on the response he made. Greeno's results provide evidence against this hypothesis and in fact against the identity operator in general. However, the picture is still not completely clear because it is not known whether the O_0 outcome reduces p_n all the way to .5. In the Reber and Millward experiment (1968), 500 trials of only O_0 outcomes reduced asymptotic responding from about .84 to .80. This is certainly not a very large effect and does not agree with the Greeno results.

Amount of reward One topic of wide interest in PL has been the role of the amount of the reward given subjects. The usual simple procedure is to reward the subject with money or points when he is correct and to take away money or points when he is wrong. Under symmetric payoff, all correct responses and all wrong responses are rewarded equally and penalized equally. In general, under symmetric payoff conditions, asymptotes are well beyond the matching values although maximizing still does not take place. Under differential payoff, each response has a specified payoff and loss associated with it. One of the most interesting findings in this area of research is the usefulness of the idea of "regret." Myers and Atkinson (1964) have applied a weak-and-strong conditioning model (a derivative of stimulus-sampling theory) to payoff studies with quite satisfactory results. When various amounts of reward are presented, we might assume that each reward value would have a certain reinforcing effect, positive or negative. However, this does not seem to work. Instead, Myers and Atkinson calculated the difference between what was obtained and what might have been obtained if a different outcome had occurred. This difference, or regret, seems to determine the reward value of the payoff (see Myers, Suydam, & Heuckeroth, 1966).

Other procedures We mention briefly two other procedures simply to illustrate the breadth of the application of ideas originating in SLT. Suppes and Zinnes (1961, 1966), Suppes and Frankmann (1961), and Suppes, Rouanet, Levine, and Frankmann (1964) have extended the linear operator models to a situation in which the subject responds, not from a finite set of responses, but on some continuum. In their book (1960), Suppes and Atkinson have presented a series of experiments on two-person interactions. These involve a situation very much like PL but in which the probability of a reinforcing outcome depends on the responses of both subjects. In this sense, a contingent procedure is involved. Other studies by Burke (1959, 1960, 1962) have further developed the two-person interaction area.

Special Approaches and Studies

The role of event sequences The most salient features of PL not properly accounted for by SLT all involve aspects of the sequence of events. In fact, almost all attempts to account for PL learning (except SLT) have heavily emphasized the role of past events in determining what a subject will predict (see Hake & Hyman, 1953). For example, very early in the history of experimental work in PL, Goodnow (1955) suggested that what subjects recognize on a trial is the run of events. One advantage of an analysis in terms of runs is that the stimulus situation is made relatively more complex but not as unwieldy as it would be if it included all stimulus patterns. Restle (1961) suggested that runs of events were of primary importance and built them into a theoretical structure for PL that predicted negative recency. He assumed that the probability of an A_1 response after a run of m O_1 events $(O_2 O_1 O_1 O_1 \ldots O_1)$ would be equal to the number of times that such a run was followed by an O_1 event in the past history of the experiment weighted by the run length itself. For preasymptotic data, we can compute the function directly from the event sequences involved. The theory thus has the advantage of being able to handle any kind of sequence. However, while Restle was developing his schema theory, Friedman et al.

published their results (1964), showing relatively good positive recency for runs up to length 5. Restle's theory could still handle these results because he took into account the past training sequence, which involved a number of different π values. Nonetheless, the theory was in for difficulty, and the following studies illustrate the problems.

The first study was that by Witte (1964), who was testing two ideas mentioned earlier. One was Anderson's contention (1964) that various reinforcement probabilities have long-term effects. Witte introduced sequences of Markov-chain event probabilities on the first day of training. One group had perseverance of similar events, leading to long runs (where $P(O_{1,n+1}|O_{1,n}) > P(O_{1,n})$ and $P(O_{2,n+1}|O_{2,n}) > P(O_{2,n})$). The other group had alternation of events, leading to short runs (where $P(O_{1,n+1}|O_{1,n}) < P(O_{1,n})$ and $P(O_{2,n+1}|O_{2,n}) < P(O_{2,n})$). A control was also run without outcome contingencies. Witte's first conclusion was that, after a sufficient number of random reinforcement trials, we cannot detect in the response proportions differing earlier histories of reinforcement. Witte's conditional probabilities $P(A_{1,n+1}| O_{i,n})$ were in agreement with the Burke and Estes theory (1957). However, even after 1200 trials, the early difference in runs showed up in the recency analysis; the perseverance group showed strong positive recency and the alternation group only moderate positive recency. Nonetheless, the presence of positive recency and the lack of any difference in alternation responding for the three groups seem to discount Anderson's argument against the Friedman et al. experiment (1964). Although SLT did not accurately describe the runs statistics even after extended trials, the strong negative recency predicted by Restle simply did not take place. Furthermore, the problem with SLT seemed to be one of parameter values. The curve could have been described if the learning parameter had been estimated from the recency data and not from the asymptotic training data.

The second experiment was performed by

Restle (1966) to test his own theory about the effect of runs. It is a neat and ingenious experiment and worth discussion as an example of how exact models can be decisively discarded. His design consisted of presenting subjects with a sequence of events consisting of only two run lengths (for example, 11 22 11 22222 11111 22 11111 22222 11). Another example might be (1 2222 1111 2 1111 2 1 2 1111). The first group has runs of length 2 and 5 (2,5) and the second group has runs of length 1 and 4 (1,4). If the probability of the two kinds of runs is varied, Restle's theory can be made to predict various response probabilities for the response on the trial immediately after two events in a row—the only trial that has to be guessed. If a 1 follows two 1's on 50 percent of the trials, then the subject has a response probability of $\frac{2}{7}$ of predicting a 1. (The run of length 2 has weight 2, and the run of length 5 has weight 5; because each is equally likely, the ratio is determined.) These predictions were compared with those of (1) a stimulus-conditioning hypothesis proposed by Greeno and (2) a 1-trial contingency hypothesis. Greeno's hypothesis looks at each run sequence $O_{2,n}O_{1,n+1}O_{1,n+2} \cdots O_{1,n+k}$ as consisting of $k + 1$ distinct run stimuli: $O_{2,n}$; $O_{2,n}O_{1,n+1}$; $O_{2,n}O_{1,n+1}O_{2,n+2}$; $\cdots$ $O_{2,n}O_{1,n+1}O_{1,n+2} \cdots O_{1,n+k}$. He assumed that when $O_{2,n}$ occurred and was followed by $O_{1,n+1}$, the latter reinforced A_1 as a response to $O_{2,n}$. Also, when $O_{1,n+2}$ occurred, it reinforced the A_1 response to both $O_{2,n}$ and $O_{2,n}O_{1,n+1}$ run stimuli. In the same manner each of the other run stimuli was successively reinforced by later outcomes of the run. The process stopped when the run changed; that is, the last reinforcement for all run stimuli listed would be the $O_{2,n+k+1}$ outcome. This would then start a run of O_2 outcomes which would be similarly reinforced.

The third hypothesis considered by Restle in this experiment assumed that, in ambiguous situations such as those that exist after a run of two events in the 2- and 5-run string mentioned earlier, subjects may simply pay attention to the 1-trial event contingency,

that is, $P(O_{1,n+1}|O_{1,n})$. The three hypotheses differ in the nature of their dependency on run structure: The Restle hypothesis depends on the ratio of the run lengths, the Greeno hypothesis on the difference of run lengths, and the simple 1-trial contingency hypothesis on the average run length, or the sum. Restle ran four groups with equally frequent run lengths (1,4), (2,3), (2,8), and (6,9). The runs for the first and the third groups are in the same ratio, as are those of the second and the fourth. If the ratio hypothesis is correct, these pairs should perform alike. The first and fourth groups have the same difference, the second is smaller, and the third much larger. According to the Greeno hypothesis, the groups should be ordered $(2) < (1) = (4) < (3)$. If the contingency hypothesis is correct, the first and second should be the same, but the third and fourth should show increasing learning difficulty. Restle's results unambiguously supported the contingency hypothesis. Interestingly enough, the subjects did not learn perfectly the contingencies concerning the events on unambiguous trials (that is, within the runs).

In an experimental analysis of sequential learning by Keller (1963), the routine was not exactly that of PL because a given sequence such as 11010001 was repeated successively. However, the routine is of interest to PL, for it involves the manner in which subjects encode the stimulus sequence. Keller had subjects learn sequences of a fixed length repeated over and over without a break. He found that the total number of errors was a simple mutiple of the number of runs and that errors occurred at the junctions between runs.

In an attempt to analyze such learning, Restle (1967) introduced the idea that the subject encodes the runs of the sequences. That is, the subject develops a kind of "generative grammar" for the event runs. For cases where alternative "grammatical" rules are possible, Restle considered the idea that the subject generates second-order rules indicating how to apply the first-order rules. One such set of second-order rules would be in terms of runs of runs. One problem with this analysis is that sequences can be written requiring even higher-order runs of runs; such sequences would necessitate the postulation of third- and higher-order runs of runs—a seemingly rather unlikely phenomenon. Thus, Restle discounts the second-order rule idea for a general subsequence theory that is less exact but intuitively more appealing. It is a second-order rule, not in terms of runs, but rather in terms of easily encoded patterns. Restle makes the point that first-order rules seem to be learned as a 1-stage or all-or-none process, whereas second-order rules are learned by a 2-or-more-stage process.

The importance of runs for subjects' memory of the event structure has received support from a study by Millward and Reber (1967). On each trial n, subjects were required not only to predict the next event E_{n+1} but to try to recall the event on a past trial $n - x$. The variable x ranged from 1 to 9. Different groups were defined by the frequency distribution of x that was used. Three results were observed. The first was that when the probe was limited to only five trials back ($x = 1,2,3,4,5$) or when it occurred more than 50 percent of the time with $x = 1$, 2, or 3, the $P(A_1)$ response was nearer .5 than when x emphasized trials farther back than $5(x > 5)$. This seems to imply that, if subjects attend to long sequences of events, they tend to overshoot more. Second, the recall of events x trials back depended more on the number of runs intervening between $n - x$ and n than on the value of x itself. Adding one more run almost linearly decreased the recall probability for 1 to 4 runs. The third result was that the guessing probability for events on trial $n - x$, when the event presumably was not known, matched the probability of the event. This provides an example of probability matching in reverse and seems to support a type of conditioning model that assumes that the effect of reinforcing events is to develop some simple response strength.

Rose and Vitz (1966) investigated two models for PL. One was the Restle model assuming that subjects encode the runs of events. The other model was the component model in which each pattern of events k trials back is considered a stimulus component. Rose and Vitz ran a standard PL experiment except that specific event patterns were included. For example, no runs of length 3 occurred (that is, 0111 was always followed by 1 and 1000 was always followed by 0). They found that, although the runs model was better than the component model, it failed because more than the previous run was encoded and subjects did utilize information about the run that preceded the run in progress. They also found that the memory for the preceding run is better if the run is long. Confusion of patterns occurred, indicating another factor that must be considered in any theory based on runs.

Feldman and Hanna (1966) ran a study involving discrimination of event sequences in which they generalized the idea that subjects encode event runs to the idea that they encode a number of event pattern types and encode in a way that depends on the sequence itself. The theory is too complicated to discuss here, but it will influence future work because the emphasis in PL at present is on analysis of encoding structures developed by subjects during a PL experiment.

The experiments just discussed indicate that runs are particularly important in learning responses to sequences, although the findings have not yet been incorporated into a theoretical structure with the predictive power of SLT and its variants.

The N-element pattern model The earlier version of SLT regarded the stimulus environment as consisting of N elements, any of which could be sampled on every trial. In the pattern model, N is generally considered to be relatively small and only one element is sampled on each trial. The pattern model also introduces a different reinforcement axiom: Instead of assuming that the E_i reinforcing event changes the conditioned state of the sampled element so that it is conditioned to the A_i response, the E_i event produces such a change with a probability c. Thus, every reinforced trial does not automatically produce a change in the number of conditioned elements. Instead of linear operators, Markov-chain analysis is used in the development of the model (see the section on concept learning). In contrast with the linear model, the pattern model assumes that $P(A_{1,n+1}|E_{1,n}A_{1,n}) = P(A_{1,n})$. The reason for this is that, for the $A_{1,n}$ response to occur, an element conditioned to the A_1 response must be sampled. The E_1 reinforcing event cannot change its conditioning state and therefore no change in response probability can occur.

The predictions of the linear model with respect to the asymptotic variance of A_1 responses have received little empirical support. The linear model always predicts too small a variance. Although all simple statistics derived from the pattern model and the linear model are identical, the pattern model predicts a larger variance in asymptotic response proportions and agrees better with observed results. It therefore appears that the N-element pattern model is a better underlying model for PL than the linear-operator model.

Yellott (1965) attempted to make a more definitive test of the two models discussed above, using a noncontingent-success procedure (NCS). The procedure involves contingent reinforcement in which, instead of determining the probability of an O_i outcome, the experiment specifies the probability of presenting the O_i outcome if the A_i response is made. Let $P(O_i|A_i) = d$, $i = 1,2$. If $d = 1$, then on every trial the subject is presented with the outcome that he predicts. If $d = 0$, he is always presented with the opposite outcome. Under this reinforcement procedure, Yellott found that the N-element pattern model and a variant of the linear-operator model with two parameters made two quite different but easily tested predictions. To consider one rather crucial difference, let us take the predictions of the probability of an alternation after m NCS trials with $d = 1$. An

alternation is defined as $P(A_{i,n+1}|A_{j,n})$, where $i \neq j$; $i,j = 1,2$. The interest here is in the probability of an alternation as a function of the number of trials on which a subject has been correct in his prediction. Of course with $d = 1$, he is always correct. If, before the m success trials, the subjects are at an asymptote of π and there are N elements, the alternation statistic is

P (alternation $|N$-element model) $=$

$$2\pi(1 - \pi)\frac{(N - 1)}{N}$$

In contrast, if we assume that the subjects are at asymptote but are responding according to the linear model, then

P (alternation $|$ linear model) $=$
$$2(1 - \theta)[P(A_{1,\infty}) - P(A_{1,\infty}^2)](1 - \theta^2)^{m-2}$$

Note that the linear model statistic is a function of m, the number of successes in a row, whereas the N-element model is not. The alternation statistic of the linear model decreases as a function of m until it reaches zero while the N-element model statistic remains constant for all m. The NCS schedule makes a very sharp difference in the predictions of these two models. Other statistics usually computed with the standard PL procedure do not differentiate between the models. Yellott found that alternations did not decrease over repeated success trials. Thus, his results support the N-element pattern model over the linear-operator model. Many other statistics tested against the pattern model gave excellent overall results.

This example illustrates that, although subjects seem to be fairly cognitive in their behavior in the PL routine, a generally path-independent conditioning model handles most of the fine structure accurately. Furthermore, SLT and its derivative theories have led to the development of various kinds of routines and have described the results of these new procedures quite adequately. This is not to claim that all aspects of PL are handled perfectly by SLT or SST. It is the task of the theoretician to bring the cognitive aspects into the picture, not so much as an alternative to SLT, but as a supplement to it so that the failures of SLT that are apparently due to cognitive aspects of behavior can be handled.

CONCEPT LEARNING

Definition of a Concept

A concept has been defined as any rule that allows a set of stimulus objects to be classified into two or more mutually exclusive subsets representing exemplars of the concept. Because the definition of a concept is intimately tied to the definition of a stimulus, we must discuss briefly what is meant by the term "stimulus" before we can attempt to refine this definition of a concept. Most stimuli used in learning studies are composed of a number of different elements, cues, and/or dimensions. That is, most stimuli can be responded to on the basis of a number of different characteristics. Now if a theory is to describe behavior, it must state the nature of the stimulus exactly, for the stimulus is one of the fundamental independent variables in learning experiments. Furthermore, not only must the physical stimulus be defined for the theory but also the stimulus as perceived or encoded by the subject. In an attempt to deal with conceptual behavior independently of the way in which the subject perceived or encoded the stimulus, Hovland (1952) introduced a notation system that established an agreement between the experimenter and the subject about what the stimulus characteristics would be. Hunt (1962) has developed a more elaborate and exactly defined version of Hovland's notation system (see Restle, 1961; Banerji, 1962; Iverson, 1962; Hunt, Marin & Stone, 1966). Hunt's definition of a concept is presented here.

1. There is a universe of objects *U* that may be observed by the subject in a concept-learning experiment.

2. An attribute is a dimension along which objects can differ one from the other. Objects with the same attribute can differ according to the different values that they assume on the attribute.

3. A value is an equivalence class defined for an attribute. Some attributes are finite, in which case the value is simply that aspect of the attribute observed. However, if the attribute is infinite or continuous, then some set

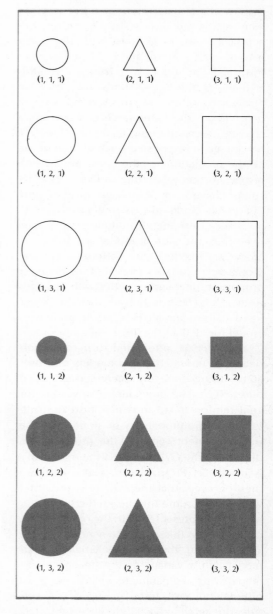

Figure 20.10. Examples and descriptive space for a set of concept-learning stimuli. The three dimensions represented are shape, size, and filled–unfilled objects.

of possible observations must be classed together to denote a value. For example, if size is the attribute or dimension, we might make a classification by calling every object greater than or equal to some number a on the continuum "large," every object greater than or equal to b but less than a "medium," and every object less than b "small." For a given object, only one value may be assigned per attribute.

4. The description of an object is a statement defining the value of every attribute for that object.

5. A descriptive space is the set of all possible descriptions of objects. The universe may contain an object for every description or it may not. Every object has its point in the descriptive space.

Consider the set of stimuli in Figure 20.10. Eighteen objects are presented, constituting the universe U. The attributes of the objects are "shape," "size," and "filled versus unfilled." A verbal description of the first object might be "small unfilled circle," whereas a verbal description of the last might be "large filled square." We can define a vector, the ith element of which specifies the value of the ith dimension. If the dimensions are ordered "shape," "size," and "unfilled-filled," and if circle $= 1$, triangle $= 2$, and square $= 3$; small $= 1$, medium $= 2$, and large $= 3$; and if unfilled $= 1$ and filled $= 2$, the first object is described by (1, 1, 1) and the last by (3, 3, 2). The descriptive space can be represented by a matrix with columns for the attributes or dimensions and rows for values. However, to complete the matrix, null values, 0, have to be added to all dimensions that have values less than the dimension with the maximum number of values.

	Dimension		
Value	Shape	Size	Unfilled-Filled
1	1	1	1
2	2	2	2
3	3	3	0

In general, then, let there be n dimensions and let the maximum number of values on any dimension be m. Then a matrix ($m \times n$) describes the descriptive space in which each row without a null element corresponds to an object. If there are v_i values on the ith dimension, then there are

$$\prod_{i=1}^{n} v_i = N$$

objects in the descriptive space.

If the total set of objects in the universe is the set characterized by the descriptive space, then there are $2^N - 2$ binary concepts possible, corresponding to the $2^N - 2$ partitions of the N objects into two subsets. (A partition is a mutually exclusive and exhaustive division of a set of objects.) In this case, the partition is into two subsets, for one set corresponds to the set of objects that meet the definition of the concept and the other to those that do not—that is, the exemplars and nonexemplars of the concept. The two cases of objects that are all exemplars and objects that are all nonexemplars of the concept have been excluded because they are meaningless as concepts.

Note that, although these $2^N - 2$ partitions exhaust the ways of dividing up the objects into two classes, there can be many ways of defining a given partition. To illustrate these ideas more fully without dealing with astronomically large numbers, let us consider nine of the objects defined in Figure 20.10 (ignoring the unfilled-filled dimension). With only three values on two dimensions, there are still $2^9 - 2 = 510$ partitions. However, for the purposes of defining concepts in general, we are not particularly interested in the difference between the concept "all squares" and "all circles" because they differ only in the particular value and are logically equivalent.

Haygood and Bourne (1965) present a method for discussing concepts that, though limited, is helpful. Assume that the concept is to be defined by specifying some relationship between single values on each of two dimensions. (If there were more than two dimensions, the other dimensions could be ignored or else the scheme could be generalized.) The two values are called the *focal values*. Let us consider a simple example: Let the universe of stimuli U be the stimuli defined by shape (circles, triangles, and squares) and size (small, medium, and large). A simple affirmative concept would be one that selected a single value on a single dimension. Whenever that value occurred, the stimulus would be an example of the concept, and whenever the value did not occur, the stimulus would not be an example of the concept. For instance, if we selected "squareness," the three square stimuli (small square, medium square, and large square) would constitute all examples of the concept, and the remaining six stimuli would not be examples. Now let us consider

the conjunctive concept. Here, two focal stimulus values are chosen, say A and B, where A is a single value on dimension 1, and B a single value on dimension 2. According to the conjunctive rule, the stimulus is an example of the concept only when both values are present. Thus if "squareness" and "largeness" are chosen, only the single stimulus "large square" satisfies the concept and the other eight do not.

To introduce all the concepts that can be formed by this procedure, we must become slightly more abstract. Let us designate dimensions by 1 and 2 and values by a, b, and c. The nine stimuli are then (1) 1a–2a, (2) 1a–2b, (3) 1a–2c, (4) 1b–2a, (5) 1b–2b, (6) 1b–2c, (7) 1c–2a, (8) 1c–2b, and (9) 1c–2c. If the two

TABLE 20.3 CONCEPT RULES BASED ON LOGICAL CONNECTIVES

	Name	Symbolic Description	Verbal Description	Contingency Patterns Indicated				Stimuli
				1 AB	2 $A\overline{B}$	3 $\overline{A}B$	4 $\overline{A}\overline{B}$	
1a	Affirmation[a]	A	All A are $+$	$+$	$+$	$-$	$-$	1, 2, 3
		B	All B are $+$	$+$	$-$	$+$	$-$	1, 4, 7
1b	Negation[a]	$\overline{A}$	All $\overline{A}$ are $+$	$-$	$+$	$-$	$+$	4, 5, 6, 7, 8, 9
		$\overline{B}$	All $\overline{B}$ are $+$	$-$	$-$	$+$	$+$	2, 3, 5, 6, 8, 9
2a	Conjunction[b]	A & B	All A & B are $+$	$+$	$-$	$-$	$-$	1
2b	Alternative Denial[b]	$\overline{A}$ or $\overline{B}$	All $\overline{A}$ or $\overline{B}$ are $+$	$-$	$+$	$+$	$+$	2, 3, 4, 5, 6, 7, 8
3a	Inclusive Disjunction[b]	A or B	All A or B are $+$	$+$	$+$	$+$	$-$	1, 2, 3, 4, 7
3b	Joint Denial[b]	$\overline{A}$ & $\overline{B}$	All $\overline{A}$ & $\overline{B}$ are $+$	$-$	$-$	$-$	$+$	5, 6, 8, 9
4a	Conditional[b]	$A \rightarrow B$	If A then it	$+$	$-$	$+$	$+$	1, 2, 3, 5, 6, 8, 9
		$B \rightarrow A$	must be B	$+$	$+$	$-$	$+$	1, 4, 5, 6, 7, 8, 9
4b	Exclusion[b]	A & $\overline{B}$	All A & $\overline{B}$	$-$	$+$	$-$	$-$	4, 7
		B & $\overline{A}$	are $+$	$-$	$-$	$+$	$-$	2, 3
5a	Biconditional[c]	$A \leftrightarrow B$	A if and only if B	$+$	$-$	$-$	$+$	1, 5, 6, 8, 9
5b	Exclusive Disjunction[c]	A $\overline{\text{or}}$ B	All A or B but not A & B are $+$	$-$	$+$	$+$	$-$	2, 3, 4, 7

[a] Level I.
[b] Level II.
[c] Level III.

values 1a and 2a are the focal values A and B respectively, each stimulus can be characterized as containing A or not ($\overline{A}$), and containing B or not ($\overline{B}$). There are thus four combinations of the focal values: AB, $A\overline{B}$, $\overline{A}B$, and $\overline{A}\overline{B}$. These four combinations include all nine stimuli: AB = stimulus 1; $A\overline{B}$ = stimuli 2 and 3; $\overline{A}B$ = stimuli 4 and 7; and $\overline{A}\overline{B}$ = stimuli 5, 6, 8, and 9. Even if dimensions had more than three values and/or if there were more dimensions not involved in defining the concept, there would still be only four categories to consider. The generalization to concepts involving three or more dimensions is straightforward. With three dimensions, there would be eight basic combinations of focal values, ABC, $AB\overline{C}$, $A\overline{B}C$, and so on.

The purpose of this scheme is systematically to reduce the $2^N - 2$ possible concepts to the definable logically distinct relationships. Table 20.3 presents these patterns for two dimensions with three values each. Of the 510 patterns, five basic concepts are described. These basic concepts are composed of two classes within each of the five concepts by taking advantage of the fact that, for each of the basic five, there is a complementary concept. The five basic concepts are listed in the rows of Table 20.3. The first column provides names for the relationships based on logic; the second column gives the relationship between the two focal values; the third column gives a simple verbal description of the concept; and the fourth column indicates the partition of the combinations used to define the concept. Thus, for example, negation has the pattern $- + - +$, which means that AB and $\overline{A}B$ combinations are not examples and that the $A\overline{B}$ and $\overline{A}\overline{B}$ combinations are examples.

Let us pursue this example further and consider again the set of nine stimuli illustrated in Figure 20.10. Assume that the focal values are A = smallness and B = circle. Then, the four combinations of "circle" and "smallness" are: "small circle," "small $\overline{\text{circle}}$," "$\overline{\text{small}}$ circle," and "$\overline{\text{small}}$ $\overline{\text{circle}}$," where the bar over a word means the absence of that value.

The partition for the negation concept $\overline{A}$ says that all $\overline{A}$ are examples of the concept ($+$). Thus $\overline{\text{small}}$ circles and $\overline{\text{small}}$ $\overline{\text{circles}}$ are examples of the concept. That is to say, medium circles, large circles, medium squares, large squares, medium triangles, and large triangles are examples. These are stimuli 4, 5, 6, 7, 8, and 9 as they were defined earlier and as presented in the last column of Table 20.3. The last column presents all the different possible partitions for the case when A and B are selected as the focal values. Of course, if A and B represented different focal values, other partitions, presumably equivalent to these, would be selected. Notice also that there are two equivalent partitions for each of the affirmative, negative, conditional, and exclusive concepts; this partitioning occurs because each concept involves the two focal values in an asymmetrical way.

We can now define a concept as a partition of the universe of objects. When n dimensions are involved, but only $r = n - i$ are used in defining the concept, the r dimensions are called "relevant" and the i dimensions "irrelevant." In the negative concept $\overline{A}$ above, shape is an irrelevant dimension. Irrelevant dimensions are those the values of which occur in conjunction with both defining and nondefining values of the relevant dimensions with equal probability. Although this scheme can be extended so that focal values are chosen for more than two dimensions, doing so makes the concepts extremely numerous and psychologically very difficult.

An important result of the Haygood and Bourne scheme for representing concepts is that it results in an ordered classification. Definite logical relations are specified, equivalence classes are apparent, and the logical relations can be ordered: Level I, unidimensional concepts; Level II, conjunctions and disjunctions of both relevant attributes; Level III, conditional and biconditional cases. Neisser and Weene (1962) noted earlier that each level can be defined in terms of the lower level. For example, $A \rightarrow B$ can be written $\overline{A}$ or B and $A \leftrightarrow B$ can be written [(A and B)

or ($\overline{A}$ and $\overline{B}$)]. More will be said about this classification scheme when results of experiments are discussed.

Two aspects of the classification scheme described above deserve further discussion. First, the idea of a single focal value limits the concepts to some extent. If there were four values on a dimension, it would be possible to define a concept that involved two values. Although this would require a new table analogous to Table 20.3, it would not be very different logically. We could simply define a new value consisting of the two values together. To consider an affirmative concept again, if there were four values on a dimension, we might define the concept as any stimulus containing either value 1 or value 2. To use shape as an example of the attribute, the values might be circles, squares, triangles, and ellipses, and the presence of circles or triangles might constitute the concept. In such a case, these two values could together be called A and the combinations relisted.

The second point concerns what might be called *multiple concepts*. Instead of a simple dichotomization of the set of objects, there is a multiple partition. For example, the following concepts might be defined: "red square," "not red square," "red not square," "not red not square." For each stimulus (for example, "red square"), the analysis just presented still holds. However, for all other stimuli that do not meet the criterion "red square," a further concept may apply (for example, "red not square"). One way to regard such concepts is as two independent concepts applied simultaneously so that the four-fold table C_1C_2, $\overline{C}_1C_2$, $C_1\overline{C}_2$, and $\overline{C}_1\overline{C}_2$ results, where C_i is concept i and the bar indicates that it is not true. Then in the earlier example, the C_1 concept would be "redness" and the C_2 concept "squareness." Of course, not all cases with more than three values are composed of independent concepts in combination as in this example. For instance, a color dimension could be partitioned into four concepts: "redness," "greenness," "blueness," and "other colors."

Most experiments in concept learning have involved affirmative, conjunctive, or disjunctive logical relationships. Usually no more than three to five dimensions and three to four values on a dimension are presented. Naturally, the size of the universe of objects depends on the experimental procedure. In some relatively easy procedures, more complex stimuli are presented. Also, ever since the earlier studies, most concept-learning studies have used dimensions that the subject could clearly differentiate and name. The exceptions are verbal mediating studies and some studies dealing with generalization across stimuli.

Further Points about the Definition of a Concept

Few attempts have been made to define precisely what a concept is or even how psychologists use the term (see Kendler, 1964; Archer, 1966). Our earlier definition of stimuli suitable for concept-learning experiments provides a good operational beginning, but it does not satisfy all experimental procedures. One difficulty in defining concept learning is that various experimentalists have used various procedures that are not easily organized according to a simple principle; that is, it is hard to induce the criterial attributes used by different experimentalists. Our solution here will be to follow Hunt and Hovland (1961) by first defining what we mean by a concept and concept learning, then, on the basis of our definition, discussing studies that meet the definition and excluding those that do not.

When first asked what a concept is, the layman replies by giving examples such as "infinity," "love," "communism," "force," and so on. When pressed, the individual can usually distinguish between examples of the concept and the concept itself. A name usually implies a set of anything: objects, symbols, descriptions, attributes. The concept that the layman is trying to express when he gives an example is related to the meaning, the defining characteristics, the necessary and sufficient conditions that are usually evoked by the example. Hunt discusses Church's idea (1958) about the distinction between the denotation of a name and the "concept of a name." The concept of a name is a statement or classification rule about the conditions that must be met before an entity can be called by or given a name. The denotation of a name is the class of things that can be given the name. Before classification rules can be applied, the set of dimensions over which all objects denoted by the name can vary must be specified. Let this set of dimensions be called E. Then, the classification rule is a function with its arguments the set E and its range a binary outcome, that is, something is an example of the concept or it is not. The set of dimensions E and the values on each dimension of E determine the descriptive space. The concept determines the partition of the descriptive space into those items that do and do not meet the definition.

Now we can see why there is difficulty in clarifying the "concept" of, say, "love." Who can state the dimensions and the values on the dimensions necessary to define it? At this point, the student may feel that the crucial issue has simply been avoided, but the truth is that the definition of most "verbal concepts" such as "love" is beyond our scope. Nonetheless, there are some advantages to a scheme thus limited. A concept can be defined without reference to the set of objects that it denotes. The set of objects can be null (for example, imaginary concepts) or infinite (for example, points on a line). The set of objects is not the concept; thus, just because two concepts have the same denotation does not imply that they are the same concept. If exactly the same set of dimensions E is involved and all objects are possible, then two concepts with the same denotation are equivalent.

Hunt raises another important question. Does the definition given here allow us to use names as we ordinarily do? Hunt mentions two criteria discussed by Suppes (1957) for the use of symbols in sentences: elimina-

bility and noncreativity. A name is eliminable if, when it occurs, it can be replaced by the concept of the name. A name is noncreative if any object to which the name applies can be substituted for the name. These criteria are met if the classification rule defines exactly the same set of objects in the universe as does the name. Say that the name can be applied to the set A and the classification rule defines a set B. Then, $A \subset B$ (A is contained in B), or $B \subset A$ (B is contained in A), or they simply overlap with unique objects in A and B. Only when A is equivalent to B will the use of the name be correct.

Certain uses of the word "concept" are not met by this definition. For example, scientific concepts (such as the concept of gravity) are not classification rules by which names are associated with sets of objects. Instead they seem to be explanatory principles. Piaget's work consists more of explanatory concepts than of studies of the classification concepts defined here.

Concept Learning

Perceptual and conceptual distinction Although it is true that no situation recurs identically for any human at any time in his life, it is the constancy and order of his existence that allow an individual to make categorizations. Bruner, Goodnow, and Austin (1956) have investigated the response categories of identity and equivalence. Identity categories comprise that class of objects that are responded to as being identical. Equivalence categories comprise the class of objects that are discriminable but to which the same response is made. From the immediately obvious equivalence response "It's an apple" to the highly sophisticated classification behavior of a geologist specifying the composition of a rock sample, there is a continuum of categorization behavior. Perhaps arbitrarily, perhaps on the basis of some intuitive psychological knowledge, this continuum has been divided into *conceptual behavior* and *perceptual behavior*. Although Hunt (1962) does not include perception in his definition of concept learning, Bruner et al. do. Hunt's definition of the difference is about the same as that of Bruner. According to Hunt, (1) perception is immediate, whereas conceptual behavior is more derived; (2) there is no statable rule for perceptual responses, but conceptual responses must have a rule; (3) there is no "set" to categorize perceptually, but conceptual behavior usually requires a "set" to classify; and (4) the perceptual response depends on the stimulus object and also context, whereas the conceptual response must be independent of context. Undoubtedly, there are ambiguous cases. Many conceptual responses become nearly perceptual with practice. For example, many a beginning student of German has difficulty with the Gothic uppercase letters and has to remind himself regularly, for example, that it is "G" that has a vertical stroke coming down from the top. But after a semester's practice, he responds to 𝕲 automatically. Generally, in concept learning, the set of stimuli and the rule determining the concept to be learned are not perceptually determined. However, as the conceptual behavior of young children is studied more thoroughly, this division may have to be revised. Young children do not have the concept of number nor do they categorize in the same manner as older children. Thus, much of the "acquisition or utilization, or both, of a common response to dissimilar stimuli" (Kendler, 1961) performed by young children involves situations that might be classified as perceptual by Hunt.

Attainment and formation distinction
The term "learning" or "acquisition" raises another distinction that must be made in order to define conceptual behavior. In general, concept learning refers to the learning of "identified" concepts (Archer, 1966). It is generally assumed that the subject knows the rules and attributes by which the stimuli can be classified, but he does not know which rule and/or attribute is used. Bruner et al. define concept attainment as the process of "seeking defining attributes that will

distinguish exemplars" of two given classes. In contrast, they define concept formation as the determination of some meaningful set of categories into which a set of objects may be classified. The important distinction between attainment and formation is whether a partition exists as it does in concept attainment or whether the subject is to form the partition himself. Again, however, with young children, these distinctions are not so easily made. Even if one feels that a child knows what a conjunctive concept is, the child may not be able to utilize it in some simple concept-attainment task where it defines the categorization.

There appear to be three aspects to learning concepts: First, when the subject does not know the specification of the dimension upon which the stimuli can vary, he has to experience a number of stimuli before he can be expected to form a hypothesis. Second, the rule of relationship between values that define the partition of the objects must be one that the subject knows or else it must be "formed" as part of the task. Third, if the dimensions and their values are known, and if the possible rules are known, the subject must select the rule(s) and dimension(s) that define the concept (see Haygood & Bourne, 1965).

Deterministic and probabilistic distinction   Not all classification schemes are deterministic. Often a set of stimuli or objects are associated with two different categories on some probabilistic basis. Hunt excludes nondeterministic categorizations, but Bruner et al. deal extensively with them. (The treatment by Bruner et al. overlaps the material on probability learning and is therefore relevant to both probability learning and concept learning. However, because most of the experimental material that has been called "concept learning" has been deterministic, the probabilistic concept-learning cases are omitted here.)

Verbal and behavioral distinction   Hunt (1962) makes one further requirement that may seem restrictive and that eliminates much of the behavioristically oriented research on concept learning. He requires that "the subject must, conceivably, be able to instruct a human to apply the classification rule. The subject is not allowed to use examples during the course of this instruction." This precludes all animal "concept learning" but allows inclusion of machine or computer concept-learning programs. Hunt makes this restriction because he wishes to limit concept learning to situations where the subject has learned a classification rule. This is an important point and introduces another aspect of the definition of concept learning with which most experimental psychologists would concur. Once a subject has learned to classify a set of objects, what has the subject learned? If he has learned specific associations to each of the stimuli, this is generally not considered concept learning. Concept learning requires that a subject learn a rule, a generalizable response habit, a mediated response, or some hypothetical abstract response system so that, on transfer tests with new stimuli, previous learning can be demonstrated to yield positive or negative transfer. The transfer test ordinarily consists of the presentation of a stimulus that has not been presented before but that contains dimensions relevant to the concept.

Let us summarize our definition of concept learning and then apply it to some experimental studies. Concept learning is learning to apply a label to a set of stimuli that vary in a number of ways but that have some common aspect which determines the correct classification of the stimuli. Although the demarcation line between perception and conception cannot be precisely located, perceptual learning is in general to be excluded. Although various distinctions between concept "attainment" and "formation" have been made, it might be better to make a four-way specification: (1) discovering the rules of classification, (2) discovering the dimensions used in classification, (3) learning the rules used in classification, and (4) learning the dimensions used in classification. The latter two are usually assumed or spelled out to the subject except when children are involved; the former two historically have not been clearly separated, but they constitute the problem for the subject. The concept learned must be transferable or statable so that we can be sure that a rule and not just a set of associations has been learned.

Early Concept-Learning Studies

Before we proceed with basic paradigms and theoretical developments in concept learning, we should apply our definition of concept learning to some early studies. Hull (1920) presented subjects with 12 sets of pseudo-Chinese ideograms to be classified on the basis of unique radicals (see Chapter 17, p. 785). A set consisted of 12 ideograms, each with its own radical. After a subject had learned one set to a criterion, he was presented with the next set, which contained the same 12 radicals, but embedded in different ideograms. Certainly, learning the first set was not concept learning because the subject could not determine the criteria to classify each stimulus. In fact he might have learned the ideogram on the basis of the wrong cues, for each ideogram was·a compound of cues. When the second set was presented, the percentage correct on the first trial jumped from chance to 27 percent, then to 38, 47, 55, and 56 percent on sets 3, 4, 5, and 6, respectively. (See Woodworth and Schlosberg [1954] for a more complete presentation.) Thus, Hull's experiment is primarily a discrimination task with common and changing cues, and it only partially meets the criteria of concept learning. It is not really perceptual, though more so than is common in current concept-learning studies. Transfer occurs, but, what is more important, the subject is not trying to discover the rule of classification in the situation: The ideograms lack easily specified dimensions and values. Thus, relationships between values are impossible. Although the task does not conform to our ideal experimental definition, the experiment is important because it illustrates that discrimination learning and concept learning are on a continuum. Forcing polarization is experimentally and analytically useful, but the area in between the extremes must also be handled. Even when only common elements are involved, many researchers feel that the subject is using a rule. If the criterion was always invoked that the concept-learning experiment be more than association of common elements, many of the experiments intended to investigate concept learning would have to be called "discrimination experiments." Certainly, in particular, the simple affirmative concept experiment differs little from a classical discrimination experiment (see p. 924).

Smoke (1932) dealt with stimuli that had to be sorted on the basis of common perceptual structures or patterns. Instead of always presenting the same physical stimulus, he always presented the same relationship. For example, this relationship might be based on whether there were two dots in a figure or only one dot—but the position of the dots could be varied. The stimuli were identical only in that the subject already had an equivalence class for the various physical examples presented. Such an equivalence class might be a perceptual response, a categorizing response, or a mediational response (that is, an association common to all examples). Smoke introduced the rule explicitly for his subjects. "Let us suppose the concept is 'zum' and may be defined thus: 'three straight red lines, two of which intersect the third, thereby trisecting it.'" In line with later concept-learning research, the subjects were told explicitly to look for the rule defining, say, a *tov*. However, Smoke noted that many subjects performed correctly but could not verbalize the hypothesis correctly. Thus, Hunt's criterion of verbalization was not fulfilled.

On each of a series of trials, Reed (1946a, b, c) presented the subjects with a different set of four words. Each set had to be classified with a nonsense syllable. In each set of four words, one word defined the category to which the set belonged. For example, one set

for KUN was (*horn-leaf-monkey-debt*), and a second set for KUN was (*fame-ought-tiger-saucer*). The common concept is presumably "animal." Initially, the subject had to make the correct associative response, but once a few examples had been presented and associated with the same response, the list could easily be searched and classified. Reed found that increasing the length of the list did not increase the learning difficulty. He informed some of his subjects that each nonsense syllable defined a class of similar things; these subjects learned faster than others. In contrast, subjects who looked for association rules based on the first letters of the words were slower to learn. There was very little forgetting over days, and in all ways the learning in this task was superior to paired-associate learning of a list of equivalent length. Our definition of a stimulus may seem to have left out the crucial element in Reed's experiments, namely, the classification by the association made to a set of words. However, for such stimuli as Reed's, the dimensions must be defined in terms of the subject's associations to the words and not in terms of the physical characteristics or even the defining characteristics of the word. Certainly, there would have been many individual differences, and many dimensions considered by the subject would have been irrelevant. Also, of course, there is the likelihood that different examples might have elicited the same classification word. The important point is that the dimensions according to which the concepts were defined were not presented in the stimulus itself but consisted of fairly well learned associations that subjects had to the words. The fact that the dimensions need not be physically present in the stimulus adds a new level of complexity to concept learning. See the discussion of Greeno and Scandura (1966) on page 1007 for a recent analysis of this experimental procedure.

Heidbreder's thesis (1947), derived from Gestalt psychology, was that cognitive reactions could be ordered. For example, the perception of concrete objects should be the easiest and most dominant, whereas spatial forms should be less likely to be noticed, but still easier than abstract ideas such as number. She presented a list of pictures to subjects in a paired-associate procedure. After the list was learned, a new list was introduced containing objects that could be classified in exactly the same way as the items on the previous list. Examples of the pictures are: 5 glasses, 5 spoons, 5 letters, and so on; a Greek building, a cabin, a church, a simple house, and so on. Eventually, the subjects would respond correctly to an item the first time it was presented, illustrating that some mediating response was taking place.

Heidbreder's experiments were similar to Reed's in that the dimension of categorization was provided by the subject's response to the stimuli. Such responses provided by the subject are usually called *mediating responses*.

The early experiments in concept learning just discussed were not sufficiently well controlled to allow definitive analysis. One problem was the complexity of the stimulus material and the subjects' idiosyncratic reaction to it. A second problem was inexact instructions, which resulted in a poor definition of the task for the subjects. From the late 1940s to the present day, the trend has been toward giving clearer instructions, more carefully structured stimuli, and maintaining more control over the presentation procedure. With these changes have come more precise theories and a refinement of what is meant by concept learning.

Procedures in Concept Learning

The most common procedure for testing concept learning is derived from discrimination experiments. In the usual discrimination experiment, two stimuli are presented successively or simultaneously with position randomized. However, in concept-learning experiments, more than two different stimuli must be presented, so these are randomized and presented one after the other until the list is exhausted. Then the stimuli are randomized once more and presented again. If the set of stimuli is large (for example, five 4-valued dimensions yield 1024 stimuli), then usually only a sample is selected and presented. On each trial, the subject makes a classification response such as "yes" (it is an exemplar of the concept) or "no" (it is not an exemplar of the concept). Although it is not necessary, and indeed is sometimes impossible, the stimuli are ordinarily divided into two classes. When more categories are defined, the problem can be regarded as a multiple concept-learning problem, or a problem with multiple categories related to the concept. Still following the discrimination paradigm, many studies present two stimuli simultaneously. In such cases, the two stimuli usually differ on all dimensions; that is, they are complementary. If this were not the case, the subject could eliminate dimensions with the same value on both stimuli if one of the stimuli were always correct and the other always wrong.

Of course, the experimenter can present more than two stimuli at a time. Bruner et al. (1956) presented the total set of stimuli but at the same time varied the standard procedure. First, the experimenter presented a stimulus and stated that it was or was not an example of the concept. Then, instead of asking the subject to decide whether or not another stimulus was an example of the concept, the subject himself picked the next stimulus and was informed by the experimenter whether or not it was an example of the concept. At each choice point, the subject could state the rule he thought was operating. Subjects were told to make as few choices as possible in determining the conjunctive concept. When more stimuli are presented, the questions arise as to how much information the subject gets before he must make a choice, and, if the choices are serial, whether the procedure differs from ordinary successive procedure. Possible variations of this procedure include ordering or scrambling the stimulus cards and replacing or separating selected cards according to their classification. Such variations have not been thoroughly investigated.

Another procedure frequently employed is the card-sorting task, usually used with the Wisconsin Card Sorting Stimuli. The stimulus deck consists of four values on each of three dimensions: color, form, and number. The subject is first given four cards to start the piles—single red triangle, two green stars, three yellow crosses, and four blue circles. Then the subject is instructed to sort the remaining cards into four categories. The procedure normally involves changing the correct sorting rule after one rule has been learned.

Theoretical Analysis

Early theoretical work treated concept learning as an extension of discrimination learning. The minimum condition for concept learning is the ability to distinguish between a set of common cues or attributes that define the concept and all other cues with which the common cues might occur. However, the simple treatment of discriminative processes by SLT is inadequate for describing the perfect discrimination that usually occurs: Attainment of a concept is certainly evidence for perfect discrimination. Hence to handle even the minimum requirements of concept learning, a better model of discrimination learning is needed. During the late 1950s, a number of approaches were developed in attempts to solve the problem of overlapping cues in discrimination. Some of these approaches have been extended to concept learning.

Observing responses A fairly natural extension is simply to note that animals and humans do not take in all the cues of a situation at once. Although SLT handled separate manipulable cues by assuming different sets of elements for each cue, these cues were controlled by the experimenter. When they were presented, the subject was assumed to observe or sample them. But a subject can either orient toward specific cues or attend to them differently, according to their utility

in a situation. Atkinson (1960) and Wyckoff (1952) developed models that assumed that subjects learned orienting responses. If a subject oriented toward relevant cues, he would ignore the irrelevant ones. An observing response is usually considered a physical response, probably measurable in principle. An extension of this idea is the attentional response, which is usually considered more "abstract" or "perceptual" than the observing response. Many have argued that there is a definite difference between an observing response and an attentional response, but sharp theoretical distinctions have not been established. Perhaps the clearest statement would be that an observing response involves muscular changes which orient the subject's senses so that they respond to specific cues, whereas an attentional response involves some central mechanism, presumably not muscular, which selects specific cues after they are received. Operationally, the distinction seems to be that an observing response is directly measurable but an attentional response is only inferred.

Adaptation of cues A second approach, equivalent in many ways to that of the observing response, is to assume that irrelevant or common cues become inhibited or adapted; that is, they diminish in their probability of being sampled over trials. Bush and Mosteller (1951) and Restle (1957) introduced this idea into their formal models. However, neither the idea of the observing response nor that of adaptation of cues can handle discriminative situations involving patterns or concept-learning situations involving disjunctive concepts. Another problem with the idea of adaptation of cues is that of "unadapting" them. In successive reversals of concepts, subjects get better and better, a phenomenon difficult to predict if it is assumed that cues are alternately being adapted and unadapted (Gormezano & Abraham, 1961).

Mediational responses Another suggested solution to the problem of overlapping stimuli is Goss's *mediational response anal-*

ysis (1961), which assumes that a second response is associated with each component or cue of the stimulus. This association is either one previously conditioned or a generalization from some previously conditioned association. Mediational analysis has been particularly useful with verbal hypotheses such as those represented by the Reed and Heidbreder studies. Reversal-shift studies have also relied heavily on mediational analysis of their results. Although a mediational response, or some equivalent abstraction from the stimulus, is required to handle concept learning, there is still a question as to whether it is sufficient. Hunt (1962) feels that it is not, arguing that mediational theory is not stated rigorously enough. However, with a rigorous statement of the axioms, the predictive power of the mediational extension of S-R formulations is weakened. Another problem with mediational theory is that there are various views as to what constitutes a mediational response. These alternative views must be better defined and put to a systematic test before further quantitative work can be done. Conceivably, all variations could be correct, but if so, the theory must be made to state when each is appropriate. Most tests of mediational theory have been qualitative. The only quantitative theoretical development has not always been correct (Popper, 1959). (For further discussion, see Jenkins, 1963; Mandler, 1961, 1963, 1967.)

Quantitative theories Another class of theories must be mentioned, although it includes primarily theories of discrimination. Zeaman and House (1963) and House and Zeaman (1963) have developed theories of attentional processes in retardates. Although their work has dealt mostly with the discriminative reversal situation, many of their ideas have supported and inspired the trend toward quantitative work in discrimination learning and concept learning.

The first quantitative theory of concept learning was developed by Bourne and Restle, following an earlier theory of discrimination learning developed by Restle (1955a, b, 1957).

The Bourne and Restle theory (1959) was one of cue conditioning in which overlapping cues adapt out. Five processes within concept learning were very successfully handled: (1) the role of redundant relevant cues, (2) the analysis of two-choice problems and the extension to four-choice problems in which two dimensions were simultaneously relevant, (3) the additivity of irrelevant cues, (4) the effects of delaying reinforcement, and (5) the effects of omitting feedback on some trials. We consider here a later theory by Restle (1962) and a modified version of it by Bower and Trabasso (1964) that do not have the drawback of a model with adaptation of irrelevant cues. These two theories also incorporate some of the newer ideas concerning concept learning by assuming that subjects test hypotheses.

Hypothesis- or Cue-Selection Models

In his original development of the all-or-none concept-learning model, Restle (1962) emphasized that in cue-learning studies (discrimination learning and concept learning), the subject's task is not to form associations between stimuli and responses, but to select the association intended by the experimenter. The response itself and the discrimination of the stimuli along various dimensions are all within the capacity of the subject when the problem starts. The suggestion is made that concept learning is not so much an association process as a selection process. But what is selected? Restle assumes that the subject selects strategies or hypotheses that are particular patterns of responding to stimuli. Examples are "win-stay lose-shift" or "alternate" or "respond to the red stimulus." In Bower and Trabasso's cue-selection model (1964), in contrast, the main behavioral process is the selection of relevant stimulus attributes rather than the selection of strategies. They assume that the subject first encodes the stimulus. Encoding is a process of answering questions about stimuli; for example, How many objects? What color? What shape? These attending responses are like observing responses or attentional responses but are usually not observable. Certain qualities of the coding response assumed by Bower and Tra-basso are important: It can be influenced by learning, as is illustrated in the reversal and dimensional-shift experiments that show negative transfer effects presumably due to attention to one stimulus aspect. It can be rapidly changed by instructions and set. In contrast to Restle's hypothesis model, the cue-selection model has two sets of habits to be learned. One is the attentional response, the other the association of the response to the attributes on the dimension attended to. Such a breakdown has one advantage. In concept-learning problems or discrimination problems in which multiple responses are associated with multiple values on a single dimension, solving the problem also requires paired-associate learning. When the problem involves only two values (say, red is a 1; green is a 2), the paired-associate learning is almost immediate, but if, say, five colors and five responses are involved, the process will take at least a few trials. Restle puts such associations into the strategy itself. Aside from this difference in the qualitative abstract way of looking at the problem, the theories of Restle and of Bower and Trabasso are nearly identical. (See the discussion of Restle's theory for paired-associate learning on page 1005.

Hypotheses   Restle assumes that a subject has a population of hypotheses that includes three types of hypotheses: (1) relevant or correct hypotheses, (2) irrelevant hypotheses that are correct with a probability of .5, and (3) wrong hypotheses that are never correct. He labels these C, I, and W; $C + I + W = H$, the total set of hypotheses. The theory has three possible sampling rules: (a) A subject can select one hypothesis on each trial, (b) the subject can select more than one hypothesis but less than H, or (c) the subject can select all H hypotheses. When the subject considers all strategies at once, it is assumed that, on each trial, he decides on a response and eliminates hypotheses not in agreement with it. Restle postulates that the subject eliminates hypotheses because he has only a

finite memory. A similar process is assumed when the subject considers only a few hypotheses at once. Once the subject has selected the correct hypothesis, he will make no more mistakes. Until he does discover the correct hypothesis, however, he is selecting mostly from the I hypotheses, which produce correct responses with a .5 probability. The W hypothesis produces an error immediately, but W hypotheses are assumed to be infrequent because they must be complementary to the correct hypothesis. Also, they produce an error and thus are not maintained for more than one trial. Subjects respond at approximately a chance level until the correct hypothesis is selected. From that trial on, they respond correctly. The trial on which they select the correct hypothesis is a random variable depending on the proportion of correct hypotheses in the population of hypotheses. Note that this differs from SLT in that, besides hypotheses in the place of elements, the learning rate here depends on the initial proportion of correct hypotheses and not on the sampling probability. An important result of Restle's analysis is that the sample size does not change the learning rate at all.

Cues   Let us now introduce the theory as developed by Bower and Trabasso (1964), who have given it the structure of a Markov chain. The axioms of the theory follow.

1. *Psychological States.* There are three states: S is the correct state when the subject has selected the correct dimension and his responses are conditioned correctly to the various values on the dimension. E is the error state when the subject has not selected the correct dimension and his response is wrong. C is the correct state when the subject has not selected the correct dimension, but when his response is correct.

2. *Initial State Probabilities.* On trial 1, subjects enter states S, E, and C with probabilities 0, q, and p, respectively, $p + q = 1$. Probability p is the probability of guessing correctly; it is determined by the stimulus conditions and response conditions of the

experiment. With simple binary-valued dimensions and affirmative concept rules, $p = q = .5$ can be assumed. However, as values increase and categories of classification increase, p should decrease. Also, specific presentation schedules may change the p values.

3. *Transition Probabilities.* The probabilities that the subject will make a transition from any state to another state on a given trial are determined by the effect of information feedback on every trial, by the stimulus dimension to which the subject is attending, and by the stimulus presented by the experimenter. These transitions are represented in the matrix **T**:

Markov chain The three axioms just presented define a Markov-chain process. A Markov chain is a special kind of stochastic process in which the transitions between states depend only on the state that the process is in on the trial immediately before the transition, and not on any earlier states that may have been entered. Thus, if a subject passed through states *CCCCCCCCCCE* on trials 1 through 11 and another subject passed through states *EEEEEEEEEEE* on trials 1 through 11, according to the theory they would both have the same probabilities of a transition to *S*, *E*, or *C*: e, $q(1 - e)$, and $p(1 - e)$, respectively. In other words, a transition from *E* to

$$
\mathbf{T} = \begin{array}{c} \\ \text{Trial} \\ n \end{array} \begin{array}{c} \\ S \\ E \\ C \end{array} \begin{array}{|ccc|c} \multicolumn{4}{c}{\text{Trial } n + 1} \\ S & E & C & P(\text{Correct Response}) \\ \hline 1.0 & 0 & 0 & 1.0 \\ e & q(1 - e) & p(1 - e) & 0.0 \\ 0 & q & p & 1.0 \end{array} \qquad (46)
$$

The parameter e is the probability that the subject will select the correct dimension and that the appropriate response will be conditioned. This parameter is assumed to remain constant throughout the experiment. Because 2-valued dimensions are assumed in this model, there is no state to represent correct selection without all responses being correctly conditioned. With only two values, conditioning of either response implies conditioning of the other. Note that, once the correct dimension has been selected and the response conditioned, no transitions take place. A state such as *S* is known as an *absorbing state*. Also note that learning occurs only on error trials, that is, from state *E*. Whereas justification for this assumption is originally empirical (Bower & Trabasso, 1964), the psychological interpretation is that only on error trials do subjects consider trying a new dimension. On correct trials, they stay with the dimension or hypothesis that led to the correct response. The same argument justifies making state *S* an absorbing state.

S, when learning occurs, is independent of the number of trials preceding the entry into state *E*, the number of correct responses, and the number of error responses. This important implication of the theory leads to a number of statistical tests designed to test the implication directly (Suppes & Ginsberg, 1963).

Stationarity The subject selects the correct dimension on an error trial—the trial of the last error *L*. (The trials before *L* are called the *presolution trials*.) Before this last error, he responds at chance with $p = $ probability of a correct response and $q = $ probability of an error. These probabilities do not change over trials and are independent from trial to trial. A process known as *Bernoulli trials* is defined in exactly this way. It is analogous to flipping a biased coin with $p = $ probability of heads for *L* trials. A chi-square test to see if the response proportions are stationary before the last trial can be set up. For each trial or block of trials before the last error, we can determine the frequency of correct responses and error responses. On each successive trial or trial block, the number of cases will decrease because subjects are excluded on their last error. The overall proportion of correct responses over all trials and subjects yields an estimate of p from which the theoretical expectations can be computed. A chi-square goodness-of-fit test is then appropriate.

Independence Another implication of the model concerning presolution trials is that errors are independent from trial n to trial $n + 1$; that is, $P(\text{Err} | \text{Cor}) = P(\text{Err})$ and $P(\text{Cor} | \text{Err}) = P(\text{Cor})$, where "Err" and "Cor" stand for "error" and "correct," respectively. A chi-square test is again appropriate. Let $f_{i,j}$ = frequency of trials on which an i response occurs on trial n and a j response on trial $n + 1$, where i and j = Err or Cor. These four frequencies form a 2×2 contingency table, which is appropriately tested by a chi-square test.

The previous stationarity test could be erroneously nonsignificant if individual subjects' proportions changed over trials (see the discussion of averaging in the section on probability learning). However, other tests to see if the presolution trials are Bernoulli trials can easily be devised. Suppes and Ginsberg (1963) mention a test based on expected binomial distribution. Another reasonable procedure is to form a Vincent curve on the response sequences made before trial L. Say that a blocking factor of four is chosen. Then each sequence of error and correct responses before L is divided into four equal parts. The errors in each of these four parts are added across subjects. The first block represents the first fourth of the presolution responses for each subject; the second block the second fourth of each subject's presolution responses, and so on. These various blocks should have equal proportions of error responses. Without knowledge of the underlying function, the Vincent technique can lead to unknown functions, but in this case the simplicity of the assumed function makes the test quite legitimate. A simple variation of this technique is to take for each subject the proportion of errors in the first half and second half of the presolution trials and run a t-test on the difference between these two proportions to test whether or not individual subjects change over trials.

Statistics of the model We derive two statistics of the model: the distribution of the total number of errors and the distribution of the trial of the last error. Most other statistics are simple tests of the Bernoulli assumption for presolution trials.

Total number of errors. Because the subject can learn only on error trials, one simple observation makes this derivation quite easy. The correct trials can occur with any frequency or density across trials without changing the expected number of errors. Consider a subject who makes an error on any trial. The subject then selects the correct dimension with probability e or he does not with probability $(1 - e)$. If he does select the correct dimension, he makes a transition to state S where no more errors are made. Thus, the probability of one error is e because at least one more error must occur if a transition to S did not occur. The probability of making two errors is $(1 - e)e$; the first error does not lead to a transition to S, but the next error does. The probability of making three errors is $(1 - e)(1 - e)e$. The pattern is now clear: Let T be the total number of errors; then,

$$P(T = k) = e(1 - e)^{k-1} \qquad (47)$$

This is a simple exponential function with asymptote zero. The expectation of T, $E(T)$, is defined as the first moment and is computed by weighting each value of T by its probability.

$$E(T) = \sum_{k=1}^{\infty} ke(1 - e)^{k-1}$$

The solution to this sum is

$$E(T) = \frac{1}{e} \qquad (48a)$$

The variance of the distribution is defined as $E[T - E(T)]^2$. By simple algebraic manipulations it can be written $E(T^2) - [E(T)]^2$. The $E(T^2)$ is

$$E(T^2) = \frac{1}{e^2}$$

and the variance becomes

$$\text{Var } (T) = \frac{(1 - e)}{e^2} \qquad (48b)$$

Trial of the last error. Let L designate the trial of the last error. In order for any trial k to be the trial of the last error, an error must occur on that trial and selection of the correct dimensions must also occur. Given that the subject is not in state S, the probability of both an error and conditioning is qe. But what is the probability that a transition to S has not occurred before trial k? The probability that a transition to S does not occur is $p + q$ $(1 - e) = 1 - qe$. The probability that a transition to S does not occur for $k - 1$ trials is $(1 - qe)^{k-1}$. Thus the probability that k is the trial of the last error is

$$P(L = k) = qe(1 - qe)^{k-1} \qquad (49)$$

The expectation and variance are easily derived. Note, for instance, that if e is substituted for qe, exactly the same function occurs for L as for T.

$$E(L) = \frac{1}{qe} \qquad (50a)$$

and

$$\text{Var } (L) = \frac{(1 - qe)}{(qe)^2} \qquad (50b)$$

A simple relationship exists between $E(T)$ and $E(L)$:

$$E(T) = qE(L) \qquad (51)$$

If q, the probability of an error, $= .5$, as in binary-valued dimensions classified into two categories, then there should be one-half as many errors as trials before the last error.

The value $E(T)$ can be used to estimate the parameter e, and the presolution proportion of correct responses can be used to estimate p. When these parameters are known,

the model can predict the distributions just presented and their variances, as well as other statistics such as runs of errors, trials until the first success, and autocorrelation of errors with different lags. If the experiment is large enough and is carefully run, such a wealth of statistics will almost certainly ensure finding any lack of correspondence between the model and the data. Bower and Trabasso (1964) present the derivation of these other statistics; an elementary but complete treatment of the model itself can be found in Atkinson, Bower, and Crothers (1965).

The correspondence between e and the stimulus set When we introduced Restle's idea of a pool of three different types of hypotheses, C, I, and W, we implied that the learning rate is a function of the ratio of relevant cues to the total number of cues. Further, p is determined by $(C + .5I)/(C + W + I)$. Bower and Trabasso also assume that e and p are functions of the stimuli and associate with each stimulus dimension a weight reflecting the attentional value of the attribute. Let w_i be the combined weight of all irrelevant cues, and w_r the combined weight of all relevant cues. Then the probability that the subject selects a relevant dimension is

$$r = \frac{w_r}{w_r + w_i} \qquad (52)$$

Given that the dimension is selected, the cue is conditioned with probability θ, and the effective learning rate e is $e = r\theta$. Bower and Trabasso assume that the conditioning process goes on even for irrelevant dimensions, an assumption that allows a prediction apparently not allowed by Restle's version of the model. The prediction is that if an irrelevant cue is partially redundant (that is, if it correlates with the relevant cue above a chance level), the subjects will sometimes select this redundant cue and condition it before making a transition to the S state. Such conditioning will reflect the level of redundancy, and on future tests subjects should show a kind of probability learning. For example, if the relevant dimension were color and a red triangle occurred on 75 percent of the "red" trials, then the subjects' responses to a triangle alone (color being omitted) should be biased toward the response associated with the color red. Results supporting this assumption have been reported by Binder and Feldman (1960).

The assumption that the learning rate or selection probability depends on the weights of the cues leads to some very important tests of the theory. By evaluating the various weights of dimensions with independent groups of subjects, a priori predictions can be made about the learning rate of new groups and groups with combined cues. An example will show how the theory allows such predictions. Assume that three different groups are tested. One group learns on dimension 1, the second on dimension 2, and the third can learn on either dimension. The third group has redundant cues, which means that the values on dimension 1 and dimension 2 are perfectly correlated; that is, for example, value 1 on dimension 1 is always combined with value 1 on dimension 2. Let the weights of the two dimensions be w_1 and w_2. Then the learning rates for the three groups are

$$(1) \quad e_1 = \frac{\theta w_1}{w_1 + w_2 + w_i}$$

$$(2) \quad e_2 = \frac{\theta w_2}{w_1 + w_2 + w_i}$$

$$(3) \quad e_3 = \frac{\theta(w_1 + w_2)}{w_1 + w_2 + w_i} = e_1 + e_2$$

Note that the third group should have a learning rate equal to the sum of the learning rates for the two other groups, and thus the number of errors for the third group, T_3, can be derived from Equation 47.

$$T_3 = \frac{T_1 T_2}{T_1 + T_2}$$

Evaluation of the Cue-Selection Model

Three assumptions of the cue-selection model require verification. One is the sudden, all-or-none learning assumed to occur when

the correct dimension or attribute is selected. A corollary to this axiom is that, prior to the trial on which learning occurs, there is no change in the probability of a correct response. On the other hand, subjects might learn a few stimuli by rote association. The responses to these stimuli would then be correct and would change the probability of a correct response before the trial of the last error. A second assumption is that the learning rate remains constant over trials. However, it is possible that subjects might continue to guess at a chance level (that is, at the p level) even though they are learning about relevant and irrelevant hypotheses. By eliminating dimensions when they find them wrong, subjects could eventually learn the correct hypothesis and begin to select from a smaller set of dimensions. This would make the learning parameter e change over trials. The third assumption is that cues are additive. However, if subjects selected cues systematically rather than at random according to their weights, w_i, the cues would not be additive.

Concept reversals Bower and Trabasso (1963) have run a study to test the constancy of the parameter e. The crucial aspect of the design was borrowed from the earlier continuity-noncontinuity studies in discrimination learning (Krechevsky, 1932; McCulloch & Pratt, 1934). Subjects are trained on the wrong hypothesis for a number of trials and then are switched to the correct response assignments. Whatever was learned during the presolution trials should retard later learning. Bower and Trabasso found no evidence in support of these assumptions for partial learning of relevant cues or for elimination of irrelevant cues for two different problems varying in difficulty. Other aspects of the data were extremely well described by the cue-selection model. In another experiment, Bower and Trabasso switched the response assignments of one group between two dimensions (successive dimensional shifts, SDS) after every second error. The subjects were informed of the first error, but if and when they made another error, the experimenter told them they were correct and immediately switched to the other response assignment. The SDS group was compared with the average of two other groups that learned the two relevant dimensions without switches. Bower and Trabasso found no difference between the averages, presumably because, on the average, subjects learned with one or the other dimension. They concluded that, after an error, subjects select dimensions randomly, including the dimension just rejected.

Of course these results supporting the theory are not independent of procedural variables. We may conclude that, while the simple all-or-none cue-selection model cannot handle all concept learning, it does quite well with concept learning in which the stimuli are complex and presented rapidly, and in which subjects are given a "set" to look for the relevant dimensions in simple affirmative concepts.

Extended training In those studies of concept learning that have been well described by the cue-selection model, subjects have generally been given only a simple preliminary practice problem and explicit instructions. However, Millward (1968) ran an experiment in which each subject learned 120 affirmative concept-learning problems. The four stimuli for each problem consisted of combinations of two shapes and two colors selected from eight shapes and colors for each problem. The cue-selection model quite adequately handled the results of the first problem; for example, the trial of the last error was almost exactly twice the total number of errors. However, if repeated problems are given subjects, the model, as defined earlier, becomes inadequate. Two assumptions made in the cue-selection model seem particularly inappropriate with practiced subjects. The first assumption is that subjects always start in either state E or state C. Bower and Trabasso made this assumption primarily because it was empirically called for—subjects rarely learn

without making at least one error. However, we would expect that subjects with a great deal of practice on problems in which one of two dimensions was always relevant would begin to select one of these two dimensions on the very first trial. The second questionable assumption is that subjects select dimensions with replacement of the dimension that led to the error. Millward modified the cue-selection model so that subjects could initially select the correct dimension and make no errors at all. After many problems, the parameter measuring the probability of initially selecting the correct dimension was about .45, indicating that subjects selected one of the two dimensions most of the time.

In the cue-selection model, the parameter e is supposedly related to the probability that a subject will select the correct dimension and condition the appropriate response after correct selection. We might assume that, when only two dimensions were ever relevant, subjects would learn to select between these two and, indeed, the initial selection probability indicated that they did. However, e was estimated well above .5: After an error, subjects were not sampling with replacement, but without replacement. After an error they switched to the other dimension with a probability of about .9. With appropriate parameter values, the model can predict optimum performance, and after 100 problems, nearly optimum performance was observed.

Random reinforcements Levine (1962) ran a study in which he showed that only six random reinforcements (RR) produced a decrease in the rate of learning a concept. These results contradicted the predictions of the cue-selection model, but Bower and Trabasso explained the contradictions by the fact that only two dimensions had been used and that subjects probably did learn to eliminate hypotheses. However, Holstein and Premack (1965) ran another random reinforcement study in which six dimensions were employed. Their results supported those of Levine, and they suggested that RR may in fact increase the pool of hypotheses considered by a subject. Hence, after a certain number of RR trials, learning would tend to be retarded.

Memory factors in cue-selection models

Trabasso and Bower (1966) noted that their analysis of the successive dimensional-shift (SDS) procedure was theoretically incorrect. Assume that Group 1 had learned with cue 1 relevant, Group 2 with cue 2 relevant, Group 1-2 with both cue 1 and cue 2 relevant and redundant, and Group SDS with the switching procedure. Trabasso and Bower had assumed earlier that the total number of errors for the SDS group would be equal to $(T_1 + T_2)/2$, where T_i is the total number of errors for Group i. However, the correct analysis indicates that the SDS group would learn exactly like a group for which both cue 1 and cue 2 are relevant and redundant (that is, Group 1-2). If $e_1 = w_1/(w_1 + w_2 + w_i)$ and if $e_2 = w_2/(w_1 + w_2 + w_i)$, then $e_{1-2} = (w_1 + w_2)/(w_1 + w_2 + w_i)$ and

$$T_{1-2} = \frac{T_1 T_2}{T_1 + T_2} < \frac{T_1 + T_2}{2}$$

In the SDS procedure, either cue will solve the problem because, if a subject is working with cue 2 and the experimenter is giving reinforcements according to cue 1, the subject will make an error. Then the subject can select cue 1 and make no more errors. Or he can select cue 2 and make a second error. However, after the subject has made the second error, the experimenter does not tell the subject it is an error; the subject does not resample, and the experimenter switches to cue 2, which is now in agreement with the subject's hypothesis. One fact is important here: The experimenter assigns the values of dimension 2 in a way consistent with the subject's responses. Thus, the correct analysis indicates that the SDS procedure should be identical to the Group 1-2 condition with both cues relevant and redundant. Previous results had not indicated that SDS was easier to learn than $(T_1 + T_2)/2$, and another, more

reliable, experiment that Trabasso and Bower ran (1966) also failed to show the additivity of cues that the re-analysis had predicted. The SDS group made a mean number of errors less than the average mean number of errors made by Groups 1 and 2, but it still was not equal to $T_1 T_2/(T_1 + T_2)$ as predicted.

To handle this empirical discrepancy from the theory, Trabasso and Bower modified the theory by adding a simple memory process, the *memory-cue-selection assumption*. On an error trial, the subject was assumed to (1) remember the stimulus pattern and correct response assignment from the previous trial, (2) compare the stimuli occurring on each trial and eliminate any dimension that was inconsistent, and (3) remember the eliminated dimensions for k trials. Memory of inconsistent hypotheses implies that they will not be used for k trials. The comparison is made between the stimuli on trial $n - 1$ and the stimuli on the error trial n. Any dimension that keeps the same values when different responses are assigned to the two stimuli or any dimension on which the values change when the stimuli are assigned the same response is eliminated. With this assumption added to the cue-selection model, the results of the SDS group were fairly adequately described when stat-subjects were run to test it. (Stat-subjects are simulated subjects that perform as the model specifies; because explicit derivations are difficult to make with this model, Trabasso and Bower had to simulate the model.)

Of perhaps greater interest is the fact that this revision of the model explains Levine's and Holstein and Premack's random-reinforcement results. The effect of random reinforcement is to reinforce the subject inconsistently so that he sets aside a number of dimensions. After about 6 trials, the subject would have had ample opportunity to set aside the relevant dimension. Once this dimension had been set aside and when the experimenter switched to consistent reinforcement, it would take a constant k number of trials before the subject would reconsider the hypothesis previously set aside. These predictions conform exactly to Holstein and Premack's results. Learning was increasingly retarded up to 6 trials of RR, but thereafter the retardation effect of more RR trials was constant. Apparently the simple idea that cues are resampled with replacement is not correct.

The memory version of the Trabasso and Bower cue-selection model (1966) has been questioned by Dodd and Bourne (1967). Three assumptions crucial to the memory-cue-selection model are: (1) hypotheses are changed only on error trials, (2) a new hypothesis is always consistent with the information given on error trials, and (3) a new hypothesis is consistent with information given on the previous trial. Three deductions that can be made from these assumptions were tested by Dodd and Bourne. Consider all the subjects in an SDS procedure who make an informed error, later make an error that is called "correct," and then make no more errors. (1) Between the informed error and the uninformed error, the subjects should respond in a manner consistent with the final correct response assignment—call it the "solution hypothesis." (2) The solution hypothesis should be consistent with the information provided by the last error trial. (3) The solution hypothesis should be consistent with the information provided by the trial immediately preceding the trial of the last error. Dodd and Bourne found instances that violated all three of these deductions. A violation of the first deduction occurs when subjects switch hypotheses on correct trials. Violations of the other two occur when subjects do not efficiently use the information from the error trial and from the trial before the error trial.

Other results Many experiments have yielded generally satisfactory results for the additivity-of-cues assumption made in this theory. Papers by Restle (1955a, b, 1957, 1958, 1959), Bourne and Restle (1959), and Trabasso (1960, 1963) review the literature on additivity of cues very thoroughly.

When the underlying theory is a Markov chain, one way to relate latency as a dependent variable to response proportions is to associate with each state of the Markov chain a latency distribution. Presumably, each state has a latency distribution with its own mean. In the all-or-none model there would be two latency distributions. Millward (1964b) and Suppes, Groen, and Schlag-Rey (1966) provided support for the all-or-none model in studies applying all-or-none Markov chains to paired-associate learning. Latencies seemed to remain stable for trials before the last error and decrease rapidly after the last error. Kintsch (1965) observed similar results for latencies and GSR responses in paired-associate learning. In a similar analysis for concept identification, Erickson, Zajkowski, and Ehmann (1966) found that latencies on correct trials and error trials were not different, that latencies on trials following error trials were longer than latencies on trials following correct trials, and that latencies showed a rapid decrease on trials following the last error. The results of Erickson et al. are consistent with the cue-selection model in that we would not expect latency differences between error and correct trials; rather we would expect longer latencies on a trial after an error when a new hypothesis was selected. In contrast, the decline in latency after the trial of the last error is not exactly in support of the all-or-none theory. We would expect either a sudden decrease in the subject's latency or a change to the latency level for correct responses after a correct response.

In the cue-conditioning model developed by Bourne and Restle (1959), an analysis of four-choice concept-learning problems was made. (A four-choice concept-learning problem is one on which the subject must classify a concept into four categories.) The classification is based on two affirmative rules defined for two independent binary dimensions. For example, if shape and color were the relevant dimensions, the following classifications might be set up: red square = 1, green square = 2, red circle = 3, and green cir-

TABLE 20.4   ORTHOGONAL STIMULI

| | Stimulus pairs | | | | | | | | Response pattern for various hypotheses | | | | | | | |
| | Left | | | | Right | | | | H_1 | | H_2 | | H_3 | | H_4 | |
Trial	D_1	D_2	D_3	D_4	D_1	D_2	D_3	D_4								
1	1	1	1	1	2	2	2	2	L	R	L	R	R	L	L	R
2	1	2	1	2	2	1	2	1	L	R	R	L	R	L	R	L
3	2	2	1	1	1	1	2	2	R	L	R	L	R	L	L	R
4	2	1	1	2	1	2	2	1	R	L	L	R	R	L	R	L

cle = 4. Bourne and Restle's suggestion that subjects learn two independent problems was confirmed by their results in terms of the mean total number of errors. Trabasso and Bower (1964a) ran a four-choice experiment and analyzed it in detail according to the all-or-none, cue-selection model. Their analysis indicated strongly that the two dimensions were learned independently and that each was learned as an all-or-none process.

Trabasso and Bower's model for the four-choice problem is a three-state Markov chain. State S_0 is assumed to occur when neither subproblem is learned; S_1 occurs when one or the other subproblem is learned; and S_2 occurs when both are learned. This model gave excellent predictions; only the predictions for the standard deviations of the total number of errors and the trial of the last error failed to describe the results obtained. Trabasso and Bower suggest that this latter failure might be due to interference from the first-learned subproblem while the second subproblem was being learned. Although this experiment shows that the original cue-selection model bears up well when it is extended to more complex situations, a study by Crawford, Hunt, and Peak (1967) on disjunctive problems indicates that the model as stated cannot be automatically applied to all concept-learning problems. Crawford et al. did not obtain stationarity—in fact, there was an increase in the probability of an error before the last error, a result contrary to the predictions of almost all present-day learning theories. In another experimental procedure, Mandler, Cowan, and Gold (1964) and Grier

and Bornstein (1966) also failed to observe stationarity. In their experiments, they varied the relative frequency of stimuli so that one of the category responses occurred more than half the time. Subjects increased the frequency with which they made the higher-frequency category response, thus showing a kind of probability learning.

Direct search for hypotheses   A basic assumption of the cue-selection model is that reinforcement affects hypotheses and not responses themselves; responses are determined by the current hypothesis that the subject holds.

Levine (1963) has extended his theoretical analysis of human discrimination learning to human concept learning. He modified the successive procedure by taking a four-dimensional binary-valued problem and, instead of presenting a single stimulus on each trial, he presented pairs of orthogonal stimuli. Such pairs have a different value for each dimension on the two stimuli. The innovation in his experimental design was the introduction of blank trials. On such trials, the subject was not informed whether or not his response was correct. By presenting four stimulus pairs ordered as in Table 20.4, he could analyze the subject's guessing behavior on blank trials, thus determining which hypothesis the subject was using. In Table 20.4, the left stimulus of the pair is specified by the values on each of its four dimensions—the same is true for the right stimulus. Each of the four hypotheses corresponds to selecting one of the dimensions and responding consistently to it. There are two versions for each hypothesis, depending on the particular stimulus that the experimenter calls correct. In most of Levine's work, the subjects are sufficiently familiar with the problem so that it can be assumed that they will pair the correct response with the correct value.

Levine showed that subjects have what he calls "prediction hypotheses." These are hypotheses that change as a function of reinforcement. Subjects do not have response hypotheses independent of reinforcements. By instructions and simple experimental demonstrations, the subject can be "set" to use one of the four hypotheses listed in Table 20.4. The proportion of each hypothesis used can be determined by fairly simple arithmetic operations. From his experimental analyses, Levine concludes that (1) the hypothesis and not the response per se is the unit of behavior affected by reinforcements; (2) a hypothesis is not a response pattern but a mediational response that can reasonably be considered to exist even on nonoutcome trials; (3) human subjects, in contrast to animals, use prediction hypotheses depending on outcomes and not response hypotheses independent of outcomes.

Another set of experiments by Levine, Leitenberg, and Richter (1964) established the "blank trial law." Four experiments were run: a 2-trial discrimination experiment, a modified double-alternation experiment, a contingent discrimination experiment, and a probability-learning experiment. In each of these four experiments, four specific trials were set apart, and a contrast was made between (1) reinforcing the subject on each of these trials by telling him that he was right and (2) telling him nothing, that is, the blank-trials procedure. In none of the four experiments was there a difference in the pattern of responses over these four contrasted trials. From the results of these studies, Levine et al. conclude that telling the subject that he is correct serves to maintain the mediational response, but that giving the subject no information about whether he was correct or not also serves to

maintain the same mediational response. The reinforcing effect of "right" is not to fix a response or make it more likely. The law then states that the effect of no information is the same as the effect of saying "right."

Two more experiments involving the use of blank trials provide some pertinent facts about concept learning. In 1966, Levine reported an experiment in which 16 trials were given with stimuli as presented in Table 20.4. On trials 1, 6, and 11, the subjects were given outcomes, but all other trials were blank. All eight possible patterns of outcomes over these three trials were given (that is, right-right-right; right-right-wrong; right-wrong-wrong, and so on). The patterns of responses on the blank trials were of primary interest. First, 92 percent of the hypotheses were of the four types listed in Table 20.4. Furthermore, if a hypothesis was confirmed (on trials 6 or 11), then it was retained with probability .95. If it was not confirmed on trials 1, 6, or 11, it was retained with probability .02. This finding contradicts the assumption of the cue-selection and hypothesis-selection models, which assume sampling with replacement. If the hypothesis were replaced, it would be resampled with probability .125. Further refined analyses are possible. On the first trial, if the experimenter says "wrong" the subject can eliminate four of the eight hypotheses. His probability of selecting from the remaining four should then be 1.0; it was found to be .87. Presumably, on the average, subjects nearly eliminate—but not completely—the four erroneous hypotheses. This analysis can be carried out over the three outcome trials. If, on each outcome trial, the experimenter said "wrong," the number of hypotheses would be reduced by one-half, so that theoretically the subject could be correct on trials 12, 13, 14, and 15. On the other hand, if subjects replaced erroneous hypotheses and did not learn from the feedback, they would remain at chance and still be selecting from the original eight hypotheses on trials 12 to 15. Levine found that subjects did eliminate hypotheses, but not by one-half, each time they were told that they were wrong. Finally, an unexpected result was that, even on successive "right" feedback outcome trials, the subjects continued to learn about the correct hypothesis. Levine found that the probability of selecting the correct hypothesis on the last four blank trials after three "wrong" outcomes was less than after two "wrong" outcomes, which in turn was less than after only one "wrong" outcome. Levine suggests that the subject encodes the stimulus chosen on each outcome trial. When another outcome trial occurs, he encodes the intersection of the previously encoded stimulus and the correct stimulus on the current trial. That is, the subject uses a focusing strategy. In contrast, if an outcome trial is "wrong," the subject must forget the old dimensions and encode the new dimensions—hence the increased efficiency of "right" in this experiment. Levine's experiment, of course, differs from the usual procedure on which outcomes are produced on every trial; the four intervening trials may aid the subject in forming his hypotheses.

Levine, Miller, and Steinmeyer ran another experiment (1967) in which the blank-trial procedure was used to probe the hypotheses used by subjects. The procedure was similar to that of Levine (1966) except that trials were presented until learning occurred. Again, every fifth trial was an outcome trial and the four intervening trials were blank trials. The error stationarity curve, defined by outcome trials before the last error, was stationary, but it was above the expected chance level of .5. The hypotheses inferred from the blank trials were limited to the reasonable ones indicated in Table 20.4 except that, prior to the trial of the last error, the correct hypothesis did not occur. The hypothesis which is the complement to the correct one also did not occur, suggesting that subjects determine their responses by dimensions and not by values. Immediately after the trial of the last error, the four blank trials indicated that subjects had attained the correct hypothesis with a probability of only about .95. The low proba-

bility (.95 instead of 1.0) of the correct hypothesis after the trial of the last error is unexplained. Perhaps the most interesting result is the fact that, prior to solution, the subjects made more errors than we would expect by chance. The analysis by Levine et al. depends on the fact that the four blank trials are orthogonal, as is indicated in Table 20.4. These blank trials have two important features: (1) no attribute is paired with the correct attribute for more than two trials, and (2) for any two trials only one attribute is so paired. These restrictions, along with the assumptions that subjects tested only the hypotheses listed in Table 20.4, maintained their hypotheses when right, and switched when wrong, lead to two predictions. First, if the subject was maximally efficient in eliminating hypotheses, his correct performance would be about .33 by chance. Second, if the subject eliminated no hypotheses when wrong, his chance performance would be .415. Interestingly, the more efficient strategy leads to poorer presolution behavior. Levine et al. observed a presolution level of about .38, which is somewhere in between these two predictions.

There seems little doubt that subjects select cues or test hypotheses in the simpler concept-learning tasks where instructions are explicit and the dimensions clearly labeled. The cue-selection model is weakest in its assumption of no memory. A number of experiments reported here have shown that memory for previously tested hypotheses as well as memory for past stimuli and their assignments (at least on the immediately preceding trial) enter into the behavior of subjects when they are selecting a hypothesis (see Hunt, 1961; Trabasso and Bower, 1964b). Further studies must investigate more complex learning problems.

Concept-Learning Variables

The learning of concepts is a complex process. By restricting the class of stimuli and instructing subjects carefully, a reasonably reliable set of results can be obtained. As we have seen, such results have been adequately described by the simple cue-selection model. However, as stimuli are made more complex, as rules are expanded, and as procedures are modified to conform more with concept learning in real-world situations, a number of new variables will have to be investigated and accounted for by modifications of the model. We discuss here some of the results obtained so far by various investigators using different stimuli, rules, and procedures.

Perceptual processes Heidbreder's basic idea (1947) was that different concepts could be ordered according to their perceptual bases. She concluded that objects were easiest to classify, followed by shapes, and that abstract or analytical concepts such as number were most difficult. In a series of experiments using the Wisconsin Card Sorting Test or Weigl-type card sorting test (Grant, Jones, & Tallantis, 1949; Grant, 1951; Grant & Curran, 1953), Grant and his coworkers found that in some cases number was the easiest of the three dimensions used (color, form, and number). In later experiments, when the number involved was not clearly laid out perceptually, number was about as difficult to classify as form but still easier than color. This change in the difficulty of classifying the concept "number" came about when the number was arranged in unsystematic configurations instead of symmetric patterns. Grant's results relate to the weight of the dimensions as discussed in the cue-selection model; from such results, we must conclude that weight is a function of configural arrangements.

Another study that manipulated the weight of cues was that of Trabasso (1963), who varied the saliency by what he called "emphasizers"— adding color to cues or making the values more discriminable, for example. In studies of concept learning, the values themselves on any dimension must be discriminable or else a discrimination problem will be mixed with the concept problem. If two stimuli differ in size, but are not easily discriminable because of successively presented stimuli, the subject may simply confuse the value observed. Certainly, this variable will determine the weight of the dimension. Unfortunately, there is at present no theory to determine the saliency of cues.

Problem type In their very complete discussion of concept learning, Bruner, Goodnow, and Austin (1956) note that subjects use a variety of strategies to solve concept problems. These strategies are related to the procedures used to present the stimuli and to the type of concept (conjunctive and disjunctive). One of the first universally observed facts in concept-learning literature was that subjects find conjunctive problems much easier than disjunctive problems. Related to this finding is the finding that subjects seem to prefer positive instances (objects that are exemplars) to negative instances (objects that are not exemplars) and utilize the information contained in positive instances more thoroughly.

We shall first discuss conjunctive rules, that is, rules in which the intersection of two values from each of two dimensions defines the concept. One presentation procedure is to lay all the stimuli in the universe before the subject and present him with one stimulus that is either positive or negative. The subject's task is to select stimuli that are exemplars and to state the rule when he thinks he knows what it is. This procedure resembles the experimental approach in that a hypothesis is stated and stimuli are chosen to test it. The *simultaneous scanning strategy* assumes that the subject considers all possible hypotheses that remain after the first stimulus has been presented and selects another stimulus that will reduce this set of hypotheses by the greatest amount. No subject can use this strategy efficiently because it requires a very large memory and a great deal of analysis to determine the implication of each selection. A strategy requiring little memory and giving the subject a direct test of his hypothesis, rather than the negative test provided by the simultaneous scanning procedure, is the *successive scanning strategy*. Here, the subject chooses one hypothesis and selects a stimulus to test it. If the stimulus is positive, the hypothesis is retained, whereas if the stimulus is negative, another hypothesis is selected. Of course, the subject should also remember all the rejected hypotheses in order not to use them again.

In contrast to the scanning strategies are the focusing strategies. In *conservative focusing*, the subject selects a positive instance and systematically varies one dimension at a time. If the dimension is relevant, it is retained in the hypothesis; if irrelevant, it is dropped. The first positive instance contains all relevant dimensions and a number of irrelevant ones. The procedure is quite efficient, for no test is redundant with previously tested stimuli. The subject has to remember only a list of the values on each dimension, but he may test more than one dimension when he chooses the next stimulus; such a strategy is called *gambling focusing*. The problem with "gambling" is that, if the selected stimulus is negative, either the subject ignores it or he reverts to simultaneous scanning and analyzes which hypotheses were eliminated by the negative instance. Bruner et al. found that the learning rate was a direct function of whether subjects used successive scanning or conservative focusing. They also found that some subjects used a kind of successive scanning in which they tested more than one hypothesis at a time.

When the procedure is changed so that the experimenter determines the order in which the stimuli are presented, the subject must change his strategies because instances come his way without his being able to control their order. The subject must emphasize the hypotheses to be tested rather than the stimuli to be selected. These are called *reception strategies*. Bruner terms the strategy analogous to the focusing strategy under this procedure the *wholist strategy*. The subject uses the first positive instance to compile a list of values and then classifies stimuli ac-

cording to the list held in his memory. Any stimulus with a different value from the value held in the list is classified as negative. For example, the first positive instance might be a large red circle on the left. The next stimulus might be a large red square on the left and would be classified by the subject as not being an example of the concept. If indeed it were not an example, the subject would not change his list. However, if it were an example, the subject would eliminate shape from his list because it has been found irrelevant. His list then consists of a large red object on the left. If the subject makes no errors in using the wholist strategy, a stimulus with all different values (for example, a small green object on the right) must be negative. Here, no information is gained. Eventually, all irrelevant dimensions are eliminated and the subject is left with the pair of values that defines the conjunctive concept.

Scanning strategies also may be used with the procedure under which the experimenter presents the stimuli. Again, the simultaneous scanning strategy is so taxing in terms of analysis and memory that no subject could use it. It requires, at each stimulus presentation, that the subject consider all hypotheses and eliminate all those that are disconfirmed by the examples presented so far. The successive scanning strategy, the strategy assumed in the cue-selection or hypothesis-selection model previously discussed, is reasonable but not especially efficient. Bruner et al. state that subjects use a more elaborate strategy—the *partist strategy*—in which more than one hypothesis is considered at a time. If, according to the subjects' current hypothesis or hypotheses, a stimulus is positive and should be, or if it is negative and should be, then no change is made in the hypotheses considered. However, when a subject incorrectly assigns a stimulus, he must form a new hypothesis consistent with the old and the new information. As with the selection strategies, the reception strategies vary in efficiency, and subjects using the different strategies accordingly vary in the number of trials they take to solve problems. Further details of how and when subjects use these strategies can be found in Bruner et al. (1956).

With disjunctive concepts, the strategies thus far discussed present immediate problems. For example, consider the disjunctive concept of all red and/or square stimuli. The strategies discussed above would eliminate red when a green square occurred and would eliminate squares when a red circle occurred. The appropriate strategy is *negative focusing*, in which a negative instance is selected and dimensions are varied one at a time. The set of dimensions that remains defines what the concept is not—a conjunctive definition that is the complement of the correct disjunctive concept. Most subjects attempt common-element solutions, hypotheses that contain only the values that have always been correct. Two factors seem to make disjunctive concepts more difficult to learn than conjunctive concepts: One is that subjects tend to use strategies appropriate for conjunctive concepts but not for disjunctive. The second is that subjects tend to avoid negative formulations, even though negative formulations make disjunctive concepts relatively simple.

Hunt and Hovland (1960) presented subjects with sets of positive and negative stimuli for which one conjunctive, one relational, and one disjunctive concept were all compatible. Following this pretraining, the subjects were asked to select exemplars of the concept from a set of unlabeled stimuli. The subjects selected conjunctive and relational stimuli significantly more often than disjunctive stimuli, indicating that, given an ambiguous situation, subjects would conclude that a concept was conjunctive or relational more readily than they would conclude that it was disjunctive.

Wells (1963) found that subjects who had previously learned a disjunctive concept increased the proportion of disjunctive concepts selected when a given set of stimuli was compatible with either a conjunctive or disjunctive concept. In a second experiment, Wells found that an exclusive disjunctive

concept (*A* or *B* but not both) was harder to learn than an inclusive disjunctive concept (*A* or *B* or both). This tends to support the explanation given by Bruner et al. that conjunctive concepts are easier to learn because subjects look for common positive values. The stimulus containing both values would appear crucial in this respect and could account for the difference observed in these two disjunctive concepts.

Conant and Trabasso (1964) set up an experiment in which the conjunctive and disjunctive problems were structurally, perceptually, and informationally equivalent. The 16 stimuli consisted of a triangle on the left and a circle on the right. Each shape varied in size (large or small) and color (red or green). The subjects were clearly instructed about the two types of concepts possible and were first given a card identified as positive or negative. The subjects then selected stimuli until they had decided on the correct concept. Conant and Trabasso found that the conjunctive concept was easier to learn than the disjunctive; the subjects tended to select positive instances sooner than negative instances. However, their subjects eventually did show positive focusing strategies for conjunctive problems and negative focusing strategies for disjunctive problems. The responses on the disjunctive concepts were more redundant, accounting for most of the difference between the learning rates. Conant and Trabasso noted the problem of verbalizing a disjunctive concept. They analyzed the trial of the first concept that was verbalized and found no difference in trials until the first stated hypothesis, but the conjunctive concepts were right 75 percent of the time while the disjunctive concepts were right only 56 percent of the time.

Crawford, Hunt, and Peak (1967) unsuccessfully attempted to apply the cue-selection model to disjunctive concepts. Stationarity was not obtained because, interestingly enough, the proportion of errors made increased over trials. Thus, disjunctive concepts are not learned in an all-or-none fashion. The authors suggest that the Trabasso and Bower (1964a) four-category model (developed earlier for the two independent affirmative concepts) might be more appropriate.

In evaluating the use subjects make of positive and negative instances in concept learning (CL) it is necessary to determine the amount of information that each instance provides. An early study by Smoke (1933) concluded that subjects made no use of negative instances, but Smoke failed to take into account the amount of information that the negative instances provided. If, for example, the concept is a simple affirmative one and there are more than two values on a dimension, then a negative stimulus yields less information than a positive one. Hovland and Weiss (1953) ran an experiment with three dimensions (color, form, and number) with two values each in which the solution was a simple conjunctive one. Such a problem requires a minimum of two positive instances and five negative instances. For example, if "red-square" is the concept, and the first and second positive stimuli are 1-red-square and 2-red-squares, the subject can select the correct concept. However, the five negative examples, 2-red-circles, 1-black-square, 1-red-circle, 2-black-circles, and 2-black-squares are required to convey the concept by negative instances. The subject was instructed to look for a conjunctive concept and was shown each of these instances successively for 5 sec each and afterwards was asked to state the concept. All stated the correct concept when positive instances were given but only 16 percent stated the correct concept when all negative instances were given. Because it took 5 negative instances to provide information for solution but only 2 positive instances, a memory difference is obviously a possible factor here even though the information transmitted has been controlled. In a second experiment, Hovland and Weiss eliminated the memory factor by presenting all instances at once. Again, significant differences occurred in favor of the positive instances. In a third experiment, they equated the number

of instances as well as the information content of the simultaneously presented stimuli. Once again, the results clearly indicated the superiority of positive instances, but also clearly showed that subjects do learn from all negative instances.

A distinction which must be made in all studies concerning the difficulty of problem types is whether the observed differences reflect past training and/or a bias in the way most concepts are defined in our culture, or whether an innate processing difficulty is involved. Freibergs and Tulving (1961) raised this question with respect to the Hovland and Weiss results in which subjects were not given practice. Freibergs and Tulving presented one group of subjects with a successive series of all positive stimuli and another group with a successive series of all negative instances. There was a substantial difference between the responses made by the two groups during the early problems; negative instances were not used at all efficiently. However, by the end of 20 problems, there was almost no difference and subjects showed great improvement in the speed with which they could name the concept after the presentation of the 4 positive or negative instances.

There are still gaps in our knowledge about the use of positive and negative instances. Freibergs and Tulving's results may not hold up for problems more complex than conjunctive ones. Further studies with concepts other than conjunctive and affirmative are needed. The best explanation for the results obtained thus far seems to be that subjects have a learned bias to use positive focusing or wholist strategy and these strategies utilize positive instances only. This bias can be modified when it is not useful, but such modification takes practice or a thorough knowledge of the nature of the problem. Studies by Wason (1959, 1960, 1961) indicate that this bias for positive instances extends to forms of problem-solving tasks other than those specifically discussed here.

We can now turn to other concepts, such

as those called the *biconditional* and the *conditional concepts*. The first study to investigate a broad class of concepts was that of Neisser and Weene (1962). They noted that the concepts in Table 20.3 could be ordered on three levels. The concepts on the second level are defined in terms of those on the first, and those on the third in terms of those on the second. This ordering depends on assuming that negation, conjunction, and disjunction are the basic operations as opposed to other logical operations. All second-level concepts are defined from a conjunctive or disjunctive combination of affirmative or negative instances, whereas all third-level concepts require a combination of second-level concepts. For example, exclusive disjunction, $A \overline{\text{ or }} B$, can be $(A \text{ or } B)$ and $(\overline{A \& B})$. Their stimuli were strings of four consonants (for example, *JQVZ, JJQZ, QJZZ, . . .*) where order was unimportant. The concepts were defined on the basis of the presence or absence of a pair of letters. Neisser and Weene concluded that problems were ordered in terms of difficulty according to the three levels, and argued that the ordering has some relationship to the definitions of the levels, that is, the basic operators required.

Haygood and Bourne (1965) provided a more complete analysis of concept learning. They first noted that the usual concept-learning (CL) problem is ambiguous in two respects: First, the subject does not know the dimensions used in defining the concept, and, second, the subject often is not clearly told what the rule is (that is, he is not always told that it is a conjunctive or disjunctive concept, for example). However, even when told the rule, the subject's past learning may have been appropriate for conjunctive rules but not for disjunctive rules. Haygood and Bourne therefore suggest that three types of problems be considered. One is called *attribute identification* (AI), under which the subject is clearly informed and practiced in using the appropriate rule but is not told what the necessary dimensions for solution are. The dimensions are still assumed to be readily namable and codable. The second type of problem is *rule learning* (RL). Here the dimensions and the rule are given to the subject, but presumably before he knows how to use them. Through practice problems, the subject learns to use the rule appropriately. The third type of problem is that of *rule identification* (RI). Here the rules have been learned according to the rule-learning paradigm, the dimensions are given, but the particular rule in force is not known. The subject must determine whether a conjunctive, disjunctive, or biconditional rule defines the concept, for example.

This analysis by Haygood and Bourne clarifies the task and what is involved in it. By presenting subjects who know the rules with rule-identification problems, the intrinsic difficulty of utilizing rules can be judged. By presenting rule-learning problems, the difficulty of learning the rules can be evaluated. Also, in the AI problems, the selection process assumed for earlier studies becomes less likely to be mixed with rule learning or rule identification. In a factorial experiment with four rules and three procedures (AI, RL, and CL), Haygood and Bourne found that CL in which both the rule and the relevant dimension were unknown was more difficult than AI, which in turn was more difficult than RL. There was steady improvement over the five problems (all with the·same rule) that each subject received. Listed in order of increasing difficulty, the rules used were conjunction, joint denial, inclusive disjunction, and conditional. The difficulty of the conditional is due to the high number of positive focus instances (AB, $\overline{A}B$, and $\overline{AB}$) and to the fact that both AB and $\overline{AB}$ are positive instances. Haygood and Bourne suggested that another reason the subjects had difficulty with the conditional rule is its asymmetry; that is, $\overline{A}B$ is positive but $A\overline{B}$ is negative. This asymmetry means that the subject must maintain the correct order of the rule; "red and not square" is an example of the concept but "not red and square" is not. All rules except the conditional were learned well enough so that by the fifth problem subjects were performing perfectly. Although the AI learning was poorer in terms of number of errors than RL, the comparison is not justified without further analysis. In AI problems, some errors are necessary, while in RL the subject can learn without errors. The most efficient learning possible for AI problems would give 4.7, 10.8, 9.7, and 8.0 as the minimum expected trial of the last error for the conjunctive, inclusive disjunctive, joint denial, and conditional problems, respectively. Haygood and Bourne observed 7.4, 16.0, 16.6, and 34.0, respectively, indicating that subjects were not using a simultaneous scanning strategy since performance would have been optimal if they had been.

In their second experiment, Haygood and Bourne investigated rule identification (RI) after prior RL training on four different rules from Levels II and III (Table 20.3). The subjects received three training problems—a disjunctive, a conditional, and a biconditional. Following these training problems, subjects were presented with two RI problems. They did not solve the problems with maximum efficiency, but they did show transfer from RL problems, indicating transfer across problem types. In RI, the biconditional and conditional rules were more difficult than the conjunctive and disjunctive. An analysis of the learning of each combination of patterns (AB, $\overline{A}B$, $A\overline{B}$, and $\overline{AB}$) showed that, before the last error was made on each combination, the subjects performed at about chance for that combination, that is, .56 in RL and .53 in RI. The difficulty of the pattern combinations helped in the analysis of why conditional and biconditional problems are more difficult. In the biconditional problem, for example, where AB and $\overline{AB}$ are both positive, the strategy of looking for common elements would fail completely. Similarly, under the conditional rule, the combination $\overline{A}B$ and $A\overline{B}$ is particularly difficult. According to Haygood and Bourne, subjects did not attain perfect performance in RI because they did not learn well enough the mapping of responses to the

combination of values. Haygood and Bourne conclude that rule learning (RL) is a 2-stage process: The first stage is learning to recode the stimuli in the four combinations AB, $\overline{A}B$, $A\overline{B}$, and $\overline{AB}$, and the second stage is learning the response assignment that goes with each combination for each rule.

In a follow-up report of research on RL and AI, Bourne (1967) discussed various attempts to show that subjects do in fact recode the stimuli into four relevant classes. He reported that with extended problems and "sample patterns illustrating the proper response assignment of each of the four stimulus classes," subjects could learn conjunctive, disjunctive, conditional, and biconditional problems without errors, although subjects took longer to reach perfect performance on conditional and biconditional problems. The difference in the difficulty the subjects experienced with different problem types was accounted for by the response assignments: "Particularly noteworthy are class FF for the conditional and biconditional problems and classes TF and FT for the conditional. . . . The asymmetry of the conditional rule produces a unique difficulty in handling TF and FT instances." (FF, TF, and FT instances are our $\overline{AB}$, $A\overline{B}$, and $\overline{A}B$ classes, respectively.) When subjects were given a number of different types of problems they performed better. The reason seemed to be that, when mixed problem types were presented, the nature of the conditional and biconditional problems was highlighted. It must be emphasized that, in all the experiments reported by Bourne, the first presentations of problem types varied in the ease with which they could be learned. Only by providing practice and clear separation of rule learning from attribute identification was Bourne able to obtain perfect performance on all problems. He emphasized that the change in the subjects' performance is a change in the way they encode the set of stimuli; that is, they eventually reduce the problem to one of learning four paired-associate assignments.

In an extensive study of simulation of concept identification and artificial intelligence,

Hunt, Marin, and Stone (1966) ran three experiments involving the following problem types: (1) conjunction, (2) inclusive disjunction, (3) conditional, (4) exclusive disjunction, and (5) biconditional. (These problem types were run to be compared with a variety of concept-learning systems (CLS) which will be discussed later under information-processing models.) Their experiments used a successive reception presentation procedure, but, unlike the usual procedure as used by Bourne, for example, the stimuli were left in view of the subjects (experiment X) or were presented in sets (experiments XI and XII). The results of the first experiment are consistent with previous results: According to ease of learning, the groups above were ordered 1, 3, 2, 4, and 5. Hunt et al. were concerned that subjects might not have attended to all the stimuli because, at times, up to 40 stimuli were present for the subject to look at. Therefore, in experiment XI, a set of 16 stimuli, 8 positive and 8 negative, were presented, and the time it took for the subject to announce the solution was recorded. The order of learning based on the time it took the subject to reach a solution with this procedure was only slightly different: 1, 2, 3, 4, and 5. In experiment XII, a slightly different procedure was used, but again with similar results. Hunt et al. conclude, along with Neisser and Weene (1962), that these differences in the difficulty of problem type reflect differences in subjects' hierarchical organization of conceptual processes and not a difference in the amount of information being conveyed or needed to solve the various problems. To show that amount of information was not the relevant variable, Neisser and Weene (1962) used a maximally efficient artificial concept-learning system, under which a simple conjunction took longer to learn than the more complex problems. In other words, there was actually more information provided to real subjects in the complex problems but they were still solved more slowly. Hunt et al. were comparing their subjects' results to the prediction of concept-learning theory based on an infor-

mation-processing model. One model they considered had no memory limitations and thus the experiments they ran were such as to require no memory on the part of the subjects—all stimuli were continuously present for analysis by the subjects. Their CLS model is based on the following set of information-processing rules:

(1) A search is made of the available set of stimuli for some characteristic (value or dimension) or set of characteristics associated with only the positive instances of the concept.

(2) If no such characteristic(s) is found in (1), then a set of characteristics common to all negative stimuli is the object of the search.

(3) Given that both steps (1) and (2) fail, the CLS determines which value occurs most frequently in the positive instances only. The set of stimuli are divided into two subsets on the basis of this value (present or not present) and steps (1) and (2) are repeated separately for the two subsets. After (3), when the CLS tries to find common values for subsets, the process may again fail, and step (3) may be repeated on a subset. The process is thus recursive in its application.

The results of the CLS can be represented in tree notation. For example, an efficient solution to a biconditional problem is illus-

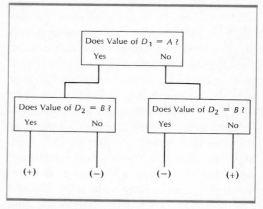

Figure 20.11. Decision process necessary to solve a biconditional problem with focal values A for dimension D_1 and B for dimension D_2. (See Table 20.3 for details; adapted from Hunt et al., 1966).

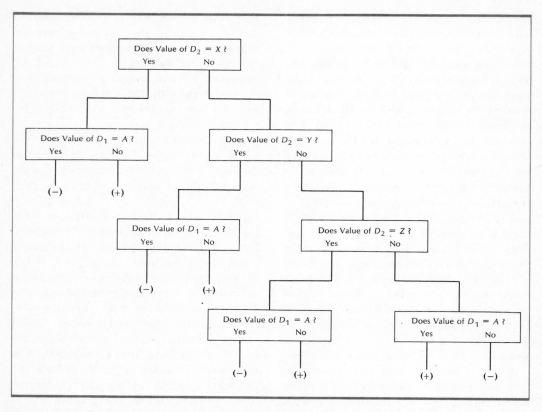

Figure 20.12. Decision tree formed by CLS-1 for a biconditional concept after presentation of 31 items. Items remain available until a solution is reached. Focal values are $D_1 = A$ and $D_2 = B$. Other values of D_2 are X, Y, and Z.

trated in Figure 20.11. Note that the CLS system would not necessarily develop the tree indicated in Figure 20.11, for the items would be presented in random order and a more elaborate tree might result. In Figure 20.12, an example of the results obtained by Hunt et al. is presented. The important point to note here is that the difficulty of the problem is supposedly related to the kind of tree that must be developed in order to solve the problem. Hunt et al. show by their simulation work that, in a general way, the rank order of the problem difficulty is reproduced by the CLS model described above. The model just presented has no memory limitations, but in a second version, Hunt et al. limited memory so that only a small number of stimuli were worked on at one time. There is little differ-ence in the performance of the two models. We shall say more about simulation models later; our main purpose here is to present the results for various concepts where memory is not a limitation and to show that the difficulty of the various problems lies in the nature of the information that must be processed.

A paper of great theoretical importance (Shepard, Hovland, & Jenkins, 1961) provides some further information about the difficulty of learning various concepts. The stimuli for the experiments consisted of three binary dimensions. A number of different sets of stimuli were used. For example, in one set of eight stimuli the dimensions consisted of pictures: (1) a candle or light bulb, (2) a screw or nut, and (3) a violin or trumpet. Other sets were similarly made up. Another type of

TABLE 20.5 THE SIX CONCEPT TYPES USED BY SHEPARD, HOVLAND, AND JENKINS

Stimulus	D_1	D_2	D_3	Type					
				I*	II*	III†	IV†	V†	VI†
1	1	1	1	+	+	+	+	+	+
2	1	1	2	+	−	+	+	+	−
3	1	2	1	+	+	+	+	+	−
4	1	2	2	+	−	−	−	−	+
5	2	1	1	−	−	−	+	−	−
6	2	1	2	−	+	−	−	−	+
7	2	2	1	−	−	+	−	−	+
8	2	2	2	−	+	−	−	+	−
Number of each type				6	6	24	8	24	2

*Type I is affirmative or equivalently negative; Type II is biconditional or equivalently exclusive disjunctive (see Table 20.3).
†Types III through VI depend on all 3 dimensions.

Adapted from Shepard, Hovland, & Jenkins, 1961.

stimulus was called "compact" because all values were represented in a single stimulus, for example, a small, black circle or a large, white triangle. The compact stimuli were contrasted with "distributed" stimuli, which consisted of three figures (triangle, circle, and square) each of which was used to represent one of the three dimensions. In one distributed representation each figure could be either small or large, thus providing the eight stimuli. In another representation, the triangle could be large or small, the circle black or white, and the square grey or white.

In contrast to most of the experiments discussed so far, all three dimensions were required to define most of the concepts used by Shepard et al. In all cases, the set of eight stimuli was partitioned into two equal subsets of four each. There were 70 such partitions, but only six different ones. These are presented in Table 20.5. The Type I concept consists of the simple affirmative and negative concepts, and the Type II is the biconditional and exclusive-disjunctive concepts as illustrated in Table 20.3. These pairs are combined here because only binary-valued dimensions are involved, and, of course, the affirmative and negative pair depends on only one dimension while the biconditional and exclusive-disjunctive pair depends on only two dimensions. Types III through VI depend on all three dimensions. The number under

each concept type indicates the number of stimulus configurations of the 70 associated with each of the six basic types.

In the first experiment, subjects learned all six concept types in different orders. Five problems of each type were learned before another type was presented. The total time to learn each response assignment, the trial of the last error, the total number of errors, and the errors in the first 32 trials were all measured and were highly correlated with each other. The ranking of difficulty of the problems was I < II < (III = IV = V) < VI. With extended training, Type VI moved in between Type II and (III = IV = V); the others remained as ranked above. In an attempt to determine why these classification types were ordered in the way they were, the authors classified the verbal statements of the subjects concerning the rules used to solve the problems. The classification was made in terms of the complexity of the stated rule. The number of errors and mean rating of complexity were as follows for the 6 ordered types: (errors, rated complexity) = (8.3, 1.6), (13.2, 1.7), (32.0, 2.9), (16.7, 1.8), (23.6, 3.2), and (28.0, 2.3). These have a correlation of $r = .80$, which is significant. Thus, the difficulty in stating a rule was highly correlated with the errors produced.

In their second experiment, Shepard et al. tested rule formulation and memorization by presenting subjects with the eight stimuli appropriately divided. For the rule-formulation task, they asked subjects to state the rule that defined the partition; for the memorization task, they asked subjects to re-sort the stimuli. Again, the rank order of ability to state rules and/or memorize the classification was I $<$ II $<$ (III $=$ IV $=$ V) $<$ VI. In experiment II (and experiment III, which was a replication of experiment II), the compact and distributed stimulus sets were used. These different sets did not substantially change the results. The classification types II through VI became more difficult with the distributed stimuli. Type I was unaffected. Only some main points of their extensive analysis can be mentioned now. The first is that subjects abstract relevant dimensions from stimuli in any learning problem. The second point that the authors make is that subjects use Type I classifications to formulate rules for building up higher-order classifications. Shepard et al. feel that the rank order observed can best be understood with this kind of explanation, essentially the explanation that Hunt et al. have more recently offered.

Memory Factors

The role of memory was mentioned briefly during the discussion of the all-or-none hypothesis or cue-selection model. Trabasso and Bower (1966) questioned the assumption that a hypothesis was selected on error trials with replacement; they introduced a modified version of the model which assumed that selection was limited to agree with the information received from the error trial and from the preceding trial. As was mentioned earlier, the Dodd and Bourne (1967) experiment raised questions about that interpretation.

The rather limited literature on the role of memory in concept learning indicates that memory is not independent of the strategy used by the subject. Concerning the selection-strategy procedure where the subject himself selects the stimuli to test, Bruner et al. (1956) discussed two main strategies that

subjects can use: successive scanning in which a single hypothesis is tested and conservative focusing (or positive focusing) in which a positive stimulus is used as a focus and successive stimuli are chosen to eliminate one attribute value at each choice point. The two strategies related to successive scanning and conservative focusing—simultaneous scanning and focus gambling—are not of importance here. The simultaneous-scanning strategy in which each stimulus is chosen to eliminate the maximum number of hypotheses requires an extremely large memory as well as many calculations on the part of the subject; it is never used perfectly by subjects when the stimuli are complex. Similarly, the focus-gambling strategy is used infrequently, not so much because it requires such a large memory as because it leads to errors and backtracking.

What are the memory requirements for the successive-scanning and conservative-focusing strategies? The successive-scanning strategy, the basic assumption of the cue-selection model, is analogous to the wholist strategy in reception procedure. No memory is required at first, but, as stimuli are chosen and hypotheses are rejected, the amount of information that must be remembered increases rapidly if optimum performance is to occur. Of course, as is the case with the cue-selection model, a solution can eventually be obtained without using any memory, but performance will not be very efficient. The conservative-focusing strategy requires the subject to remember all values of all attributes on the focus card (the first positive stimulus selected). As each dimension is tested and found irrelevant, that value can be dropped from memory. The rule for the choice of the next test stimulus is simple: Pick a stimulus which differs from the focus card in only one dimension. Thus, although early trials require a fairly large memory, memory requirements decrease over trials.

Bruner et al. ran a study to see if the performance of subjects using successive scanning and conservative focusing was affected when the memory requirements in the task were increased. Twelve subjects were given three conjunctive problems consecutively. The first two problems had all stimuli ordered according to dimensions and values and all stimuli were clearly in view of the subjects. Five subjects solved these problems by successive scanning and seven by conservative focusing. The third problem was then presented, but the subjects were not allowed to see the stimuli. Because they had just worked with the stimuli, the nature of the problem was clear to them, but in the third problem all their tests had to be remembered. Subjects who continued to use conservative focusing performed just as well as before; two did not and showed a performance decrement. In contrast, the subjects using successive scanning required significantly more choices to solve the problem and their performance was less regular. If these results are generalized to the reception procedure used in all concept-learning studies tested by the cue-selection model, we see that because the stimuli are not in view the task involves the subjects' remembering all stimuli presented. Subjects who used the conservative-focusing strategy could still perform accurately and make use of their memory of previously presented stimuli. If there were a significant number of these focusers in problems used to test the cue-selection model, they could be detected only by the distribution of the trial of the last error, since their presolution behavior would remain at chance and the total number of errors statistic $E(T)$ would still be expected to be $gE(L)$. (See the section on Theoretical Analysis.) We do not know whether the statistical tests based on the distribution of the trial of the last error are sensitive enough to detect a small proportion of focusers in a sample of subjects. Procedures such as the one in which the relevant dimension is successively reversed on every other error (see p. 956) would render any attempt to use conservative focusing fruitless because the dimension switched to after an error might have been

eliminated on an earlier error trial. The results of the SDS (successive dimensional shift) procedure suggest that, in experiments run to test the cue-selection model, few subjects consistently use a focusing strategy.

It seems intuitive that, in the successive-reception procedure, one difficulty for the subject is remembering past instances. Cahill and Hovland (1960) directly tested this supposition by comparing the performance of two groups of subjects. The successive group received stimuli one at a time with each stimulus being removed after the subject's response. The simultaneous group received the stimuli one at a time but stimuli remained in sight after being presented. The latter group performed much better than the former. Perhaps even more interesting was the fact that the hypotheses selected were consistent with the stimulus (or stimuli for the simultaneous group) within the subject's view. Most of the errors for the successive group were made when the subject selected a hypothesis inconsistent with a previously presented stimulus. Subjects who made more memory errors performed more poorly. Hunt (1961) took a slightly more refined look at the role of memory for previous stimulus instances. He presented subjects with three sets of stimuli. First, the key set was presented. It contained a varying number of stimuli before and after a critical stimulus. Then the second set was presented, which, along with the information from the key set, eliminated all but two hypotheses. The critical stimulus was relevant to a choice between these two hypotheses. The third set tested the hypothesis held by the subject. By this design, the ability of subjects to remember information from previous stimuli in the key set could be measured. The number of instances preceding the critical stimulus in the key set was not influential in determining the proportion of correct responses in the third set, but the number of instances following the critical stimulus was. These results are comparable to those of Cahill and Hovland but differ in that the latter noticed a primacy effect, whereas Hunt did not; that is, Cahill and Hovland noticed a change in the effect of recent items as a function of the number of preceding items.

A third study on memory for previous instances was carried out by Bourne, Goldstein, and Link (1964). They extended the dichotomy of successive versus simultaneous presentation to a continuum by varying from zero to 10 the number of stimuli which remained in the subject's view. They found that a group with 10 stimuli in view showed poorer performance than a group with five stimuli in view! An explanation for the lack of continued improvement when more stimuli were exposed was offered by another experiment in which the subject was given no limit on the time to respond. The previous experiment had required the subject to respond within 15 sec; apparently, this limit pressed the subject so that he could not use the information from more than five stimuli, and the time limit actually produced a slight deterioration with more than five stimuli. Bourne et al. observed some other aspects of the role of memory with simultaneous presentation. Simultaneous presentation is more effective with complex stimuli than with simple stimuli. This seems to be due in part to the fact that simple problems are solved in a few trials and simultaneous presentation does not have a chance to become effective. Bourne et al. observed, in agreement with Cahill and Hovland, that simultaneous presentation reduced memory errors but not perceptual or logical errors.

The studies just discussed had easier memory requirements than the typical successive presentation procedure, that is, subjects had more stimuli in view. Restle and Emmerich (1966) introduced a procedure that increased the memory load over that of the typical successive-presentation procedure. Instead of learning one concept problem at a time, subjects had to learn two, three, or six at a time. This was done by presenting stimulus 1 of problem 1, then stimulus 1 of problem 2, then stimulus 2 of problem 1, then stimulus 2 of problem 2, and so on. Thus, for problem 1,

there was an increased time between presentations of the stimuli and, probably more important, this time was occupied by the subject's attending to the stimulus of the next problem. Studies in short-term memory indicate that filled intervals produce a great deal of forgetting (Peterson & Peterson, 1959). Restle and Emmerich note that, according to the cue-selection model, as long as the memory for the single hypothesis being tested for each problem is not disrupted, the multiple-problem task should be no more difficult than the single-problem task. On the other hand, if the subject is remembering previous stimuli and selecting hypotheses on the basis of these stimuli, then reducing memory for previous stimuli by introducing multiple problems should make the multiple-problem task more difficult. Restle and Emmerich found that 1- and 2-problem tasks were not significantly different in difficulty, nor were 3- and 6-problem tasks, but the latter pairs were significantly more difficult than the former pairs. Apparently subjects begin to lose information at the point when three problems are being presented at a time. In their second experiment, Restle and Emmerich found that leaving the stimulus on for a longer period of time after feedback was given was beneficial for the 1-at-a-time problem but not for the 6-at-a-time problem. These results do not agree with those of a series of studies by Bourne and his coworkers (to be discussed later). In Restle and Emmerich's third experiment, the same stimulus was presented twice, separated only by the other problems in the multiple-problem condition. If a subject following the predictions of a cue-selection model does not remember the previous stimulus, then, (1) if he was correct on the previous stimulus, he will keep the same hypothesis and will be correct, but, (2) if he was wrong on the previous stimulus, he will select a new hypothesis and will be right or wrong at a chance level, provided that he does not select the correct hypothesis (that is, provided that there is a later error). However, if the subject remembers both the stimulus and the feedback, he will not make an error in either case (1) or case (2) above. Restle and Emmerich presented the repeated stimulus on an early trial (trial 3 or 4) and on a late trial (trial 24 or 25). When six concurrent problems were being learned, there was a significant difference, for the early-trial test, in the number of errors following correct responses and the number of errors following incorrect responses. Problems presented one at a time produced no such difference; the subjects showed excellent memory for the previous stimulus. The group that was given six concurrent problems did not do as well but still showed some ability to remember stimuli. On the later-trial test, the group given one problem at a time had all learned by trial 24, but the group given six problems at a time performed at chance.

Taking into consideration early theoretical ideas that concept learning is a variety of discrimination learning, Bourne (1957) wished to see the effects of delaying the reward in concept learning. He combined task difficulty, defined by the number of irrelevant dimensions (1, 3, or 5), with delay of reward (.0, .5, 1.0, 2.0, 4.0, and 8.0 sec between the subject's response and the reinforcing feedback). Both variables were significant in their effect. Learning became slower with greater delay of reward. The delay condition was handled theoretically by a trace model by Bourne and Restle (1959). An important aspect of this task was that the interval between trials was kept constant. Thus, as the reinforcing feedback was delayed, the time between the feedback and the presentation of the next stimulus was decreased.

Bourne and Bunderson (1963) then examined the effects of (1) delays of 0, 4, and 8 sec between the subject's response and the information feedback, and (2) delays of 1, 5, and 9 sec between the information feedback and the next stimulus (that is, with changing intervals between trials). They found no significant effect due to delays of type (1) but highly significant effects due to delays of type (2). The apparently contradictory results of the

earlier Bourne study (1957) could easily be explained by the confounding of type (1) and type (2) delays in that study. The Bourne and Bunderson study raises serious questions about Bourne and Restle's theoretical analysis (1959) of the earlier Bourne study (1957), adds one more reason to reject the adaptation-of-cues model which Bourne and Restle introduced, and provides some further support to the cue-selection model. In a later study by Bourne, Guy, Dodd, and Justesen (1965), the intertrial interval was extended to 1, 15, and 29 sec. The stimulus was either present or not present throughout the interval, and the information feedback indicating the classification of the stimulus did or did not remain in the subject's view throughout the interval. The length of the interval and the presence of the stimulus throughout the interval were significant factors, but the continuous presence of the feedback signal was not. If the stimulus was absent, subjects with the 29-sec interval did more poorly than those for whom the stimulus was present, although with a 15-sec interval there was no difference due to this factor. The superior performance of the group with the 29-sec interval when the stimulus remained in view suggests that the subjects used this time to search the stimulus attributes and select another hypothesis. The poorer performance of the group working at the same 29-sec interval but without the stimulus left in view may reflect some forgetting of aspects of the stimulus or simple loss of attention and motivation. If the subjects did attend to other things during this time, the 29 sec is certainly a long enough period to produce large memory decrements. One interpretation of these results is that the subjects need the time after feedback to search the stimulus and choose another hypothesis to test.

All of the experiments discussed thus far have introduced variables that presumably change the memory for past stimuli in concept learning. Trabasso and Bower (1964b) made a direct test of how well subjects remember past stimuli. Subjects were presented with six stimuli in an affirmative problem with four binary-valued dimensions. The subjects were told not only to solve the problem but to remember the stimuli. After the six stimuli had been presented, the subjects were asked to write their solution and then were tested for their memory of the six stimuli presented. On the test, the subjects were asked to describe the stimulus presented on trial x, where $x = 1 - 6$ in some random order different from the presentation order. The subjects circled one of two values for each dimension on prearranged data sheets. Trabasso and Bower found a small serial-position effect (stimuli presented on early or late trials were remembered slightly better than those presented on intermediate trials), whereas the order of recall did not produce an effect. The amount of recall above chance was less than one dimension per stimulus. Solved and unsolved problems were different, with the former showing better performance, particularly on the relevant dimension, and the latter showing better performance on the dimension stated in the hypothesis. All in all, there was little evidence for any substantial memory for the stimuli on past trials.

Although these findings may seem inconsistent with previously reported results, it must be remembered that the previous experiments mostly varied the demands made on memory, either by leaving the stimuli in the subject's view or by modifying the time the subject was allowed to look at a given stimulus. Performance of subjects in the Restle and Emmerich (1966) study in which the time between stimuli was increased would seem to imply that learning is a function of memory for past stimuli. However, a different explanation is possible. If concurrent problems are presented to a subject, not only may his memory for past stimuli be impaired (if indeed there is much memory for past stimuli), but his memory for the hypotheses tested on each problem may be impaired. There is here an important point about memory in concept learning, namely, that there are two kinds of memory. One is memory for stimuli and the other is memory for hypotheses tested and

eliminated. Two experiments concern this very point. Erickson, Zajkowski, and Ehmann (1966) ran a successive-presentation concept-learning problem which was extremely well described by the all-or-none cue-selection model. They analyzed the latency of the subjects' responses, finding that latencies were longer on trials following an error than on trials following a correct response, but that latencies on the correct and error trials themselves did not differ. Erickson et al. used the Bower and Trabasso procedure (1963) of reversing the response assignments after every second error and substantiated their own expectation that latencies following uninformed errors would be equal to latencies following correct responses. Two of their predictions were not confirmed: One was that latencies after the last error would be constant and equal to latencies following correct responses; instead, they declined in a negatively accelerated function. The second prediction was that latencies before the last error would be constant; instead, latencies declined significantly. Erickson et al. explained the failure of the latter prediction by assuming that the pool of hypotheses from which the subject was sampling after an error was decreasing in size. They explained the difference in latencies following correct and error trials as being due to the time it took to sample another hypothesis—presumably no sampling occurred after a correct trial. Note that they assume that the sampling occurs on the trial following an error. This would probably not be true if the stimulus were left in view for a long time after the feedback (see Bourne et al., 1965). However, Erickson et al. presented the information feedback 2 sec after the response and only for 1 sec. Under such conditions, it is reasonable to assume that sampling occurs on the next trial.

The second experiment (Erickson & Zajkowski, 1967) was a follow-up to the previous one and consisted of simultaneous problems as in the Restle and Emmerich study. Erickson et al. introduced a reversal or a dimensional shift on every second error for two of the problems; the third problem was a straight concept-learning routine. Thus they combined the Restle and Emmerich and the Trabasso and Bower (1964a) SDS procedures with good replication of both experiments. There was a large increase in the latency of response for these problems over that of their earlier study, but, more importantly, the latency for trials following an error did not decrease across trials. Their earlier explanation for the decrease in function across trials for these latencies was that the pool of hypotheses decreased. A consistent interpretation would hold that the pool was not diminishing in size in the multiple-problem concept-learning procedure. Thus, by introducing multiple problems, Restle and Emmerich may not be affecting memory for past stimuli, but rather they may be affecting memory for eliminated hypotheses. (A further discussion of this idea is presented in the section on information-processing models.)

In an early paper on the role of memory in concept learning (1952), Underwood discussed two ideas: *instance contiguity* and *spaced practice*. By instance contiguity he meant the degree to which instances associated with other concepts were interspersed among instances of the concept being learned. The standard successive concept-learning procedure has perfect instance contiguity whereas the Restle and Emmerich procedure introduces a great deal of irrelevant material between instances of the same concept. The spaced-trial problem is really the problem dealt with by Bourne (1957), and Bourne and Bunderson (1963). Dominowski (1965) has given a very good review of studies related to Underwood's hypothesis.

Information-Processing Theories

Definition and general discussion Psychological theory, like all theory, often proceeds by analogy. Descartes described man as being mechanically driven by fluids in tubes—a picture in line with the automata of his day. The associationists considered models of the association of ideas which followed the chemistry of their day. More recently, behaviorists developed models along the line of electrical switchboards. Today, we have the computer with which to form an analogy, and there is no denying the strong influence of computer technology on models of learning and thinking. Let us consider the analogy somewhat more closely. A computer consists of a number of special input and output devices. These can be considered as analogous to sensory systems or motor systems. The computer has a number of storage systems (core memory, disks, tapes, and so on) that can be considered analogous to memory systems. We do not yet know whether one or many types of memory should be posited for humans, but the distinction between a short-term memory system and a long-term memory system has natural parallels in the accumulator and the permanent core storage of computers. (This idea of short-term memory has received a great deal of emphasis in recent theoretical work, and will be discussed in more detail later; see page 997.) Another point about both human and computer memory systems worth mentioning is that the input signals stored are encoded versions of the original input. Computers do not store holes in punched cards or electrical impulses from switch closures. We do not store sound waves or light energy but patterns of nerve responses. Finally, at the level of physical hardware, the computer is a serial processor. This means that it considers one piece of encoded information at a time. The human system probably does not process input information serially, especially sensory input. However, with higher mental processes, we can assume with good reason that some mechanism limits the organism to thinking about one thing at a time. Perhaps a more important analogy between the computer and the human is to be made at the programming level. Obviously, at the hardware level, there are gross differences. However, we can make a convincing case (see Miller, Galanter, & Pribram, 1960) for picturing thinking as a complex computer program.

Learning consists of building appropriate subroutines to handle special tasks. These subroutines are combined appropriately by some central processing program which (1) monitors input, (2) stores tasks to perform and data to act upon, (3) sets priorities, and (4) controls output.

An exact definition of information-processing theories (IPT) is difficult to formulate. The fundamental premise is that learning consists of establishing elementary processes for manipulating symbols. In general, an encoded stimulus is treated as a set of information-carrying components. The subject is presumed to analyze, compare, and organize these components. Then decision rules that compare past information input and outcome contingencies with the state of current input components are used to determine the next response. In contrast to mathematically stated theories or verbally stated theories, most information-processing theories are stated in the language of a computer program. This does not necessarily mean that the theory in any way resembles a computer or a computer program. In fact, as we shall see, it can be simply a way of realizing a verbally or mathematically stated theory.

Another feature of IPT is the tendency to incorporate into them heuristics or rules of thumb that are helpful in learning or problem-solving. Heuristics do not guarantee a solution to a problem but often help in finding the solution. An example of a heuristic, used by Hunt et al. (1966) in their concept-learning system (CLS), is the division of the set of presented stimuli according to the value that occurs most frequently in the set of correct stimuli (see step 3 of Hunt et al. p. 967).

Reasons for using information-processing theories Most advocates of IPT would argue that they have turned to IPT because IPT more closely resemble the "true" state of affairs. (But IPT are of course by no means in any unique position with respect to truth or correctness of interpretation.) IPT are usually relatively complex and dynamic. Certainly all of human learning has not been satisfactorily described or explained by any existing model, mathematical or verbal. Thus, it is argued, because IPT represent more facets of the total behavior, they are more realistic. Another reason for introducing IPT is that mathematical and verbal analyses have not been powerful enough as tools and, presumably, the language of the computer is more powerful. This is probably true in the sense that complex interactions and nonlinear relationships can be stated in computer programs, and, by simulation, some indication of the results of these interactions can be obtained. Another advantage of the IPT is that one may compute some statistic on the data and wish to know what a particular theory would predict for that statistic. It may be impossible to derive the statistic formally but a rough idea of its value can be obtained from simulation of the IPT. Furthermore, IPT are often broad and general in scope and not procedure-specific. For example, the General Problem Solver (GPS) makes no specific reference to the subject matter of the problem to be solved. The approach taken is to (1) set up goals, (2) transform goals so that operators can be applied, (3) apply operators, and (4) look for differences to reduce by some operator. Newell, Shaw, and Simon (1958) and Newell and Simon (1961, 1963) have presented the details of this program. IPT are superior to verbally stated theories because they must be stated exactly and consistently. Although inconsistent statements may survive in verbally stated theories because a proof of their inconsistency may be difficult to derive, this is not possible in an IPT stated as a computer program. If indeed an inconsistent theory can be programmed at all, it will always fail to operate at some point. Thus, stating a theory as a computer program can be worthwhile for this reason alone.

Problems with using information-processing theories Programming a computer is costly and difficult. Further, stating a theory as a computer program limits the accessibility of the theory, and thus the number of researchers working with it, because not all researchers have easy access to computers. (These points are certainly becoming less valid with modern computers.) Another problem with IPT is that they are usually complex and have built into them a number of hidden assumptions. This, of course, is related to their ability to deal with more complex processes. However, it means that, in testing the theory, we are testing a total complex structure. If it proves to be inadequate, it is difficult to say exactly how or where it is inadequate. Perhaps the most serious problem with computer-stated theories is that of testing them. Because we do not have exact mathematical statements, parameters are difficult to estimate. We do not obtain theoretical expressions but only the results of simulation. Thus, we generally do not try to test the theories exactly (as with a chi-square goodness-of-fit test, for example), but rather qualitatively: Do the results correspond in general with the observed results? These difficulties are mentioned in order to insure that a fairly realistic appraisal of IPT be made by the reader.

Concept-learning information-processing models To date, there have not been many IPT for concept learning, nor have they been responsible for generating many experiments. However, they are rapidly becoming more numerous and more sophisticated. Therefore, it is necessary for us to review, albeit briefly, the current approaches using IPT.

The first IPT, discussed by Hunt and Hovland (1961), contains five basic subsystems for data processing. The first subsystem determines what aspect of the stimulus is encoded and put into memory. The second is the memory storage system.

Two versions of memory storage are considered: finite memory with serial input and infinite memory; these correspond to the reception and selection presentation procedures. The core of this IPT lies in the "answering developing routine," which in many ways is similar to the CLS system discussed earlier (CLS-1). There is an executive routine which orders the calls of four basic routines. One of these basic routines is the ordering routine, which separates items into mutually exclusive and exhaustive subsets, thus accomplishing essentially what steps 1, 2, and 3 of the CLS-1 system do. The second basic routine, the solution routine, looks for particular logical relationships that account for the order determined by the ordering routine. The usual procedure is to consider conjunctive routines first and then disjunctive routines. The third basic routine, the descriptive routine, looks for alternative descriptions on which to make comparisons. In its simplest form, this routine amounts to finding a new set of dimensions to consider in the ordering and solution routines. However, it can also mean finding relational characteristics of the stimuli (for example, "larger," "smaller"). Finally, there is a time-checking routine to limit the time spent on each of these processes. Because subjects cannot do all this processing without taking time, and because, in many cases, stimuli are presented too fast for a complete check to be made, the time-checking routine halts processing and makes the subject return to the executive routine to initiate the processing of a new stimulus.

The final two major routines in the information-processing routine discussed by Hunt and Hovland are the answer-checking routine, which simply checks the simulated subject's answer with the answer determined by the experimenter, and the transfer routine, which considers what sort of transfer one problem should have on another. Little is known or even speculated about the details of this latter routine except that certain transfer functions, such as carrying over the same solution system to the next problem, seem obvious.

This brief description should indicate some of the problems with specifying *in toto* a theory of concept learning. For example: How does one specify the order in the ordering routine? The times for each part of the processing unit? The particular solutions in the solution routines? What variables influence the kind and order of descriptions subjects will attempt to use?

Hunt, Marin, and Stone (1966) have introduced a more systematic investigation of concept learning. Instead of beginning with a very complex structure as Hunt and Hovland did, they begin with some simple models and gradually change them to see what effect each change brings about. They are interested not only in developing a theory of human concept learning but also in developing an artificial intelligence system, that is, a program to solve concept problems not already solved by humans. Examples of the latter include content analysis, in which verbal documents are coded according to a set of variables (dimensions and values as usual); the variables are then read into the program in order to see if a structure can be developed that will "solve" the problem. Hunt et al. apply their programs to such diverse topics as suicide notes, the California Money Bill, biographies, and medical statistics. The second general area of application of the general CLS program is *pattern recognition*. Although pattern recognition seems rather far afield from concept learning, Hunt and his associates show how closely the concepts and problems in these two areas are related. (See also Uhr, 1966.)[7] Hunt et al. have studied 10

versions of the concept-learning system (CLS); we have already introduced the simplest version. CLS-2 and CLS-3 add a limited memory to the system. The general conclusion is not necessarily intuitive: With limited memory systems, the number of items needed to solve concept problems increases but the amount of computing decreases, and the latter effect offsets the former. The CLS-4 and CLS-5 models were developed for the selective-sampling procedure as opposed to the receptive-presentation scheme. The basic heuristic used was to select stimuli at random until an error was made, at which point stimuli "close to the error stimulus" were selected. CLS-6 introduced a substitute for step 3 discussed earlier (see p. 967). Instead of counting the most frequent value on positive instances, CLS-6 computed the value with the largest difference between positive and negative instances. Thus, if red objects occurred with positive stimuli 10 times and with negative stimuli 2 times, the difference $10 - 2 = 8$ was computed. The stimulus value with the largest difference was used to sort the items. These examples should be sufficient to illustrate the nature and ideas behind this approach. For further information about work in this area see Hunt (1967) in which CLS-10 is developed and discussed.

We noted above that Trabasso and Bower (1966) could not solve explicit equations for the various statistics of their extended model; thus, they simulated the model. The extended model can be considered an information-processing model. A similar approach was used by Gregg and Simon (1967), who began with the basic ideas of the cue-selection model and extended it by introducing assumptions about the nature of hypothesis sampling. Their point is that their IPT is more general and encompasses the cue-selection model as a special case. Essentially they have taken general ideas that have appeared in the literature mostly in verbal form and have developed a model for them. Gregg and Simon suggest three alternative sampling schemes: (1) *local nonreplacement,* in which

---

[7] The point to be made here about artificial intelligence is that it is important to our conceptualization of concept learning. Too often perhaps, the solution to a problem is attempted in the most direct manner possible. An experimental psychologist wishes to know how concepts are learned and immediately starts to run experiments. The approach of artificial intelligence is to put aside the direct behavioral question of how humans solve problems and consider first the broader question of how problems can be solved in general. If a sufficiently general theory is formulated, the question of how humans solve problems might possibly be answered simply by picking the approach that best describes their behavior. Of course, artificial intelligence provides no philosopher's stone for understanding human behavior. Indeed, in certain fields, for example, pattern recognition (Uhr, 1966), the most powerful computer programming techniques developed so far perform more poorly than humans. Probably when human behavior is better understood more powerful techniques will be available.

the hypothesis rejected on trial *n* is not returned to the pool of hypotheses from which the subject samples, (2) *local consistency,* in which the pool of hypotheses from which a subject samples after an error is limited to those hypotheses consistent with the last presented stimulus, and (3) *global consistency,* in which the pool of hypotheses from which a subject samples after an error is limited to those hypotheses consistent with all stimuli presented previously. In line with the cue-selection theory of weighting the various dimensions according to their saliency, Gregg and Simon note that all the alternatives above can have unequal hypothesis-selection schemes.

As Gregg and Simon point out, one advantage of the IPT approach over the mathematical approach is a more complete statement of the theory. Many qualifications about the applicability of the cue-selection model were made by Bower and Trabasso because the mathematical version they developed incorporated a fixed set of assumptions appropriate only to the situation they studied.

Other IPT for concept learning have been introduced. A particularly interesting one is by Simon and Kotovsky (1963). The concept-learning task does not fit into the scheme we have described here, but, because that scheme is not appropriate to all concepts, perhaps a slight shift at this point will indicate some of the possibilities not touched on in this section. If you were presented with a sequence *abababab* . . . and asked to continue it, most people would continue the pattern and write *abab.* . . . Although, mathematically, any sequence of finite length can be extended in any manner whatsoever, a given pattern usually restricts the type of continuation patterns that most subjects will give. There seems to be a set of rules that almost all subjects follow to determine the pattern which is presented. The universality of these rules allowed Simon and Kotovsky to study the ease of finding consistent patterns in sequences such as the example above. Simon and Kotovsky attempt to include in a

process model the rules that subjects use and to see if the model will simulate the performance of human subjects. They assume that subjects come into the task with the following generative rules and processing abilities: (1) the English alphabet and its sequential order, (2) the English alphabet in its backward order, (3) the concept of "same" or "equal," (4) the concept "next" on a list, (5) the concept of a "cycle," a repetition of a fixed sequence, (6) a small memory for symbols. They then derive a model for searching for patterns in sequences such as *abmcdmefmghm* . . . , stating the patterns discovered as generative rules, and extrapolating the pattern. The theory rank-orders the difficulty of sequences and is in good agreement with the rank order determined by subjects.

PAIRED-ASSOCIATE AND SERIAL LEARNING

Paired-associate learning (PAL) and serial learning (SL) are the two most widely used experimental procedures in human learning. They appear to tap directly fundamental processes and provide a natural and convenient vehicle for the study of verbal behavior. They are rivaled in these respects only by free-verbal learning (see Chapter 19). Underwood (1964) characterizes rote verbal learning as consisting of four tasks: free-verbal learning, serial learning with or without syntactical ordering of units, verbal discrimination, and paired-associate learning. He argues that these tasks are central to all human learning. However, other aspects of human learning seem to be neglected in Underwood's analysis. For example, Underwood is reminded by Wickens (1964) that motivation is conspicuously absent in the field of rote learning. Also, there seem to be some differences between verbal learning and traditional motor learning, although a good case can be made that very similar processes are involved in both (see, for example, Fitts, 1964). Because of space limitations, we shall not discuss motivation, motor learning, or all of the four tasks of verbal learning. Instead we shall limit the discussion to the two specific verbal-learning procedures of PAL and SL.

A great many of the studies in verbal learning have been concerned with the measurement of relationships between verbal items. Although we shall be interested in how subjects encode stimuli in order to respond correctly in PAL and SL, we shall not discuss the many experiments that have investigated various similarity measures of verbal stimuli such as meaningfulness, associative strength, or relative frequency.[8]

Another class of studies has been concerned primarily with transfer of training, distribution of practice, incidental learning, and interference effects. This class is covered in Chapter 21.

Historical Background

In current terminology, studies in PAL and SL deal with connections between stimuli and responses. However, such connections were formerly referred to as "associations." The notion of associationism goes back to Aristotle, who emphasized the importance of three factors in the formation of associations: contiguity, similarity, and contrast. In the past 60 to 80 years, every major psychological theory has in some way modified and shifted the work in verbal learning. We shall not trace this development, but recommend earlier works (Robinson, 1932; Woodworth, 1938; Woodworth & Schlosberg, 1954; and McGeoch & Irion, 1952).

Prior to 1940, most studies concentrated on serial learning, although in the last 15 years there have been many more PAL studies than SL studies, and the general consensus is that SL is more complex and less useful as a basic paradigm for the study of how associations are learned. Ebbinghaus (1885) studied SL extensively and many of the basic phenomena of serial learning were discussed by him, whereas PAL was first recognized clearly in

[8] Chapter 19 describes and analyzes such measures.

an article by Gibson (1940). A psychologist in 1940 may have felt that serious quantitative theorizing was about to begin in serial learning with the publication of *The Mathematico-Deductive Theory of Rote Learning* (Hull, Hovland, Ross, Hall, Perkins, & Fitch, 1940). However, the lack of parsimony in the Hull et al. theory has negated its precision. In any case, these two publications provided the fundamental analysis of PAL and SL that has dominated theoretical research since 1940. The last 10 years has seen a flood of experiments that have illustrated many shortcomings in the earlier theoretical approaches, but, as yet, no comprehensive theory has been substituted for them. Our discussion here describes the traditional approach, samples a number of research studies which are detrimental to it, and presents some recent alternative theoretical approaches.

Basic Paradigms

There are two basically different procedures for both PAL and SL. One is the *anticipation method* of presentation and the other is the *reinforce-test* or *study-recall method* of presentation. In the paired-associate paradigm, a list of *N* stimulus-response pairs is presented to the subject, who is explicitly instructed to learn to recite the response when presented with the stimulus. In the anticipation method, the stimulus of the first pair is presented and the subject is expected to make the appropriate response. Many recent studies have violated the condition that the time to respond be fixed. Traditionally, the stimulus item was presented for a fixed time (usually a few seconds) during which the associated response was to be made. Naturally, with short intervals, there are many more trials without responses than when more flexible time limits are employed. Whether fixed or flexible periods for responding are provided, almost always the response item is exposed for a fixed period following the subject's response. Then, after an interitem interval, the next stimulus item is presented. The stimuli are all presented and, except when the effects of serial presentation are of explicit interest, the items are randomized before the next trial. In the reinforce-test procedure, all S-R pairs are presented randomly, one pair at a time. The next trial is then a test trial on which only the stimuli of the S-R pair are presented one at a time in a new random order. Of course, there are many possible variations on this procedure, some of which will be mentioned later.

The PAL task may be thought of as consisting of three psychological processes. The first process is that of discriminating the various stimuli one from the other (Gibson, 1940). The second process is that of learning the responses themselves, which is basically a free-verbal recall task. In order for the subject to give the response, he must know it. The typical PAL experiment often uses a list of nonsense syllables for responses and such a list may require quite a few trials to be learned. Finally, the third process is that of associating each stimulus with its appropriate response.

In serial learning, the subject learns a list of stimulus terms in the order in which they are presented. Under the anticipation procedure, one item is presented and provides the stimulus for the next, which in turn becomes the stimulus for the third item. Although this description seems to emphasize the similarity between paired-associate learning and serial learning, many investigators doubt that we can look at SL as a chain of S-R paired associates. In the reinforce-test procedure, the list is presented and then the subject is asked to repeat it exactly as presented.

It should be emphasized that there is no right or wrong procedure per se. One reason for many of the variations in procedure is that each different procedure allows us to investigate a different aspect of the problem. Of course, procedures differ due to the different underlying psychological processes involved and in the different strategies that subjects will use in trying to learn what is asked of them. At the present time, there is no theory sufficiently general to describe all the processes involved or the strategies that will be

used, although such a general theory is a central goal of studies in PAL and SL.

No discussion of PAL and SL, or any other rote-learning procedure for that matter, would be complete without mention of the memory drum (see p. 853). In most PAL and SL experiments, the list is presented on a memory drum, which has the advantage that the presentation of stimuli can be timed precisely. (Early emphasis on the idea that rote learning was an extension of conditioning theory made such strict control of time important in learning studies. Recent experimental results have raised questions about strict pacing since such pacing may produce fluctuations in stimulus selection.) In an alternative procedure the subject is allowed to determine when the next stimulus is to be presented; that is, he is allowed as much time as he wants in which to respond. In either case, the subject himself has a certain amount of control over the actual learning procedure. With the memory drum, the subject may pick a few stimuli to rehearse and let others go by. With the self-paced procedure, the subject can repeatedly rehearse an item, so that there is no control over what constitutes a trial. In any case, timing factors are crucial in both PAL and SL. Obvious independent variables to be determined include the time the stimulus is left on, the time allowed for a response to be made, the time between the response (or stimulus) and the next stimulus presentation, and the time between trials (complete repetitions of the list). Some of these can be fixed by the experimenter, some by the subject only, and some by both the experimenter and subject.

Perhaps the other general variable of most interest is the nature of the stimulus and response material. Traditionally, studies have usually used nonsense syllables (CVC) or consonant clusters (CCC) as stimuli and responses. But words and visual nonverbal stimuli have also been used. If CVCs or CCCs are used, the appropriate response is usually a spelling out of the letters. If words are used, a simple oral response is most common. Some studies have required the subject to make a motor response such as pushing one or more buttons. If visual forms or motor responses are used, Underwood (1963) questions whether the learning should be called verbal. Nevertheless, the predominant response to any stimulus is verbal, for most subjects number or name their responses.

There is a large literature concerned with how to organize stimuli to account for their role in determining the difficulty of learning. That is, a variety of scales have been devised that correlate with the difficulty of learning. Perhaps the first consideration of the correlation between learning and the stimulus material was made by Ebbinghaus (1885). He theorized that, because words are meaningful, they are highly associated with each other, and learning involving words is therefore partially a function of past learning. Ebbinghaus' idea was to begin with new material, the nonsense syllable. At this level of analysis, there is no doubt about the results: CVCs and CCCs are more difficult than words. But nonsense syllables also differ one from another. Thus, Glaze (1928) scaled nonsense syllables according to the percentage of 15 subjects who had an association to each nonsense syllable within 3 seconds. Archer (1960) redid Glaze's list for CVCs and Witmer (1935) applied Glaze's method to CCCs.

Of course there are other ways to scale such materials, many of which are described in Chapter 19. Noble (1952) asked his subjects to write all the associations they could think of. More recently, Noble, Stockwell, and Pryer (1957) had subjects simply rate the association values. Underwood and Schulz (1960) considered pronounceability, and Noble (1953) had subjects rate familiarity. Finally, the frequency with which subjects have experienced the stimuli may be determined by such measures as the relative frequency of the clusters or letter pairs in the language. All these scaling procedures have correlated positively with learning rate. However, Underwood and Schulz (1960, p. 86) feel that this is because all such scales are actually measuring the past

frequency of use or experience with the item. They posit a basic hypothesis, the *spew hypothesis,* which states that "the order of emission of verbal units is directly related to frequency of experience with those units."

Relationships between Procedures

Whether or not there are fundamental psychological relationships between the PAL and SL procedures and the PL and CL procedures is still very much a matter of debate. For the most part, psychologists try to stay with a single theoretical structure and apply it differently for different procedures. Thus, in the discussion of PL presented here, statistical learning theory is emphasized, but recent studies that have raised serious doubts about its applicability are mentioned. In the discussion of CL, a cue-selection theory was emphasized, but much of the early work treated CL as a form of discrimination learning. Similarly, in PAL and SL, the predominant theoretical position has been to consider these procedures from a conditioning and/or mediation point of view. However, as we see below, there are other views and we cannot choose one theoretical explanation to the complete exclusion of others.

There are some close relationships between the four tasks in terms of procedure. For example, if a list of length N in PAL is composed of r responses, where $r < N$, then, in terms of the procedure, we potentially have a CL experiment. The difference depends on the existence of a rule assigning the stimuli to the response classes. But if the subject does not yet know the rule, he may learn the associations as in a PAL procedure. On the other hand, if there is only one stimulus and two responses, or if each response is probabilistically associated with each of the stimuli, then, for a single trial or more when a single stimulus and response are consistently paired, a PAL procedure is in effect. One much-discussed procedure in PAL is the "S-R_1 followed by S-R_2" paradigm, in which first the R_1 response is learned to the S stimulus and then the R_2 response is learned to the same stimulus. Except for the extent of learning, this procedure looks a great deal like the learning that occurs in PL. Finally, in SL, there is the problem of integrating responses over time. Although the traditional SL procedure has involved a different stimulus for each unit in the series, if only two or three units were used, we would have the procedure investigated by Keller (1963) and Restle (1966) in which a fixed binary sequence was repeated over and over. As yet not enough work has been done on such relationships, for different theoretical questions and techniques of analysis are used for the different designs. Probably the most common manner of relating the designs is to begin with a theoretical structure and to consider how it applies to each procedure.

Traditional Theoretical View of Rote Learning

Many researchers in human learning have avoided theoretical speculation and have considered themselves functionalists. Nonetheless, there is an underlying theoretical view which stems from Pavlovian and Hullian theory and from extensions made by theoreticians during the late 1930s, 1940s, and 1950s. A number of surveys of this system are available (see, for example, Koch, 1954; Kimble, 1961; Hilgard & Bower, 1966), so we merely summarize at this time.

The central idea in Hullian theory is habit strength, which is the strength of a bond between a stimulus and a response. This bond is assumed to be strengthened each time the stimulus and the response are paired and the response is followed by a reinforcer. The functional relationship is a familiar one, a negatively accelerated growth function with asymptote H_∞, initial value H_1, and learning rate α (see Equation 10).

$$H_n = H_\infty - (H_\infty - H_1)\alpha^{n-1} \qquad (53)$$

We shall not discuss here all the variables which control H_∞ and α because these represent applications of the theory. However, it is important to emphasize that the probability of a response is not directly related to H_n. H_n represents learning; however, performance, as measured by the probability of a response, the latency of a response, the magnitude of a response, and so on, is derived from H_n and a number of other variables. The variable which is important in determining these performance measures is called *excitatory potential, E*. Excitatory potential is a function of H_n and other factors; that is,

$$E = F(H_n, L, O_t, I_n, D, \ldots)$$

In turn, response measures such as the probability of a correct response are related to E by other functions specific to the measures themselves,

$$G_p(E) = G[F(H_n, L, \ldots)]$$

We shall discuss only some of the major variables.

In animal learning, drive (D) is a central concept of Hullian theory; in human learning, a more important concept is threshold L. Although learning may be going on, no measure of it can be made until it has reached and exceeded threshold. Further, various dependent variables, such as recognition and recall, may have different thresholds. But for any one measure, until H_n exceeds the threshold for that measure, there is no change in performance.

Another important Hullian concept is oscillation O_t. The discussion above might lead one to believe that once H_n exceeded threshold, the subject would always perform correctly. However, the theory also assumes that many factors tend to inhibit and reduce performance below optimum levels. These factors, which vary from trial to trial in a nonsystematic way, are referred to as the oscillation of inhibition. Hull assumed that these inhibiting factors subtracted from the H_n factor and that they were normally distributed.

Finally, there is the concept of conditioned inhibition I_n. Each time a stimulus-response bond is not reinforced, a negative factor tends to prevent the stimulus from eliciting the response which has been built up (Spence, 1956, p. 120). In general, $I_{n'}$ is assumed to accumulate in a manner very similar to H_n, except that it changes only on nonreinforced pairings:

$$I_{n'} = I_\infty - (I_\infty - I_1)\beta^{n'-1} \qquad (54)$$

when n' is the number of nonreinforced trials. The terms described above can be combined to describe various aspects of learning.

One difficulty in dealing with the normal-curve assumption for oscillation is that the normal curve is a continuous distribution from $-\infty$ to $+\infty$, but because the oscillation of inhibition always subtracts from H_n, it is necessary to assume some arbitrary point on the normal curve to call the point of zero subtraction. Hull usually assumed a point at 3 or 4 standard deviations. A second difficulty in dealing with a normal curve is that, to compute the probability of a response, the normal curve must be integrated. Tables are used for such evaluations. We assume that we can roughly approximate the normal distribution of the oscillation function with a uniform distribution $y = x/\delta$, where δ is the range of the oscillation function ($0 \leq x \leq \delta$). First, until H_n exceeds the threshold value γ, no response can be made. After H_n exceeds

γ, the probability depends upon the portion of the uniform curve which exceeds γ; that is, $H_n - \gamma$. If $H_n - \gamma$ is greater than δ, the probability of a response is 1.0. From the point where $H_n = \gamma$ until $H_n > \gamma + \delta$ the curve rises directly with H_n. Figure 20.13 illustrates such a function. If we used the normal curve for oscillation, the probability curve would rise slowly at first, then rapidly, and then slow down again—an ogival-shaped function. It is important to note that, in addition to the initial habit strength H_1 and the asymptote of habit strength H_∞, δ, γ, and α must be estimated as well. If conditioned inhibition is important, I_1, I_∞, and β must be added to the list of parameters to be estimated. The function also depends upon the form of the oscillation function, which has historically been chosen arbitrarily. However, the drawbacks to postulating so complex a function are perhaps outweighed by the versatility of the function. The "silent period" when habit strength is changing but no responses occur can be used to explain why one reinforcement does not always lead to some performance change. During the so-called "overlearning period" after perfect performance is reached, reinforcements can be used to increase the strength of a habit, an increase that might be measured by noting the number of trials needed to produce extinction or counterconditioning.

When Gibson introduced the notions of Hullian theory to paired-associate learning in 1940, the above-mentioned tripartite conception of paired-associate learning had not been formulated; simple classical conditioning ideas predominated. Gibson's main contribution was to emphasize that a principal source of difficulty in PAL was that of differentiating the stimuli. Thus, each stimulus and response should develop some habit strength connecting them, but if two stimuli were similar, the habits would interact to produce error responses. Consider, for example, stimulus-response pairs, $S_1 - R_1$ and $S_2 - R_2$. To each is associated a habit strength, H_{11} and H_{22}, respectively. But if S_1 and S_2 were similar,

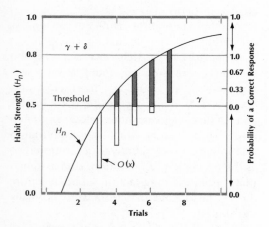

Figure 20.13. Schematic representation of a Hullian-type model. To make calculations easier, the oscillation $O(x)$ is assumed to be uniformly distributed rather than normally distributed.

there would also be an $S_1 - R_2$ (H_{12}) habit strength built up and an $S_2 - R_1$ (H_{21}) habit strength built up. This would be due to primary generalization between S_1 and S_2; that is, the degree to which H_{12} and H_{21} developed would depend upon the similarity between S_1 and S_2. The analysis proceeded as follows. At first, all Hs were below threshold, so that when S_1 or S_2 was presented, the subject could not respond. Thus, early in learning the subject did not respond (omissions occurred). Later, Hs were above threshold and responses occurred. When S_1 was presented, because of H_{11} and H_{12} habit strengths, both responses R_1 and R_2 tended to occur in a ratio depending upon their relative strengths. This competition among responses produced random-like sequences of R_1 and R_2 responses. However, whenever R_2 occurred to S_1, it was not reinforced, and the lack of reinforcement led to the development of conditioned inhibition. Conditioned inhibition, like the inhibition of oscillation, subtracted from the H_{12} habit strength, so the excitatory potential for R_2 diminished. The R_2 response weakened while the R_1 response increased in strength. This was the discrimination process. Finally, only H_{11} and H_{22} remained strong and uninhibited. An intertrial interval allowed spontaneous recovery of the inhibited H_{12} and H_{21} habits. So after a rest interval, confusion errors reoccurred. Continued discrimination training finally built up permanent inhibition of the H_{12} and H_{21} habits.

Gibson's discussion of the similarity between stimuli was for the most part tied to the physical characteristics of the stimuli, although she did not state any rules for the measurement of similarity. In his review of Gibson's thesis, Underwood (1961) notes that the notion of similarity allows generalization along a semantic or meaningfulness scale to be easily included in the scheme. In fact, most tests of her theory have used this dimension of similarity. Gibson stated many more implications of this way of looking at PAL, but since most of them are concerned with

transfer phenomena, they will be covered in Chapter 21.

When applied to serial learning, the Hullian formulation of conditioning processes was more rigorous (see McGeoch & Irion, 1952). A serial-learning experiment yields one result, the serial-position curve, which is unique to the procedure. If the number of errors made in learning each item is plotted against the position of the item in the list, a bow-shaped curve results. For example, a list of six items might yield 1, 3, 10, 25, 10, and 3 errors for items in positions 1 through 6, respectively. Note that the maximum number of errors is just beyond the middle of the list (at position 4). The ability of a theory to explain and predict this function was considered of primary importance in evaluating the theory. The Lepley-Hull theory, developed specifically to handle the serial-position effect, made the following assumptions. First, SL consists of a series of stimuli, S_i, $i = 1, 2, \ldots n$, presented repeatedly in the same order. Each stimulus leaves a trace that persists over time; thus, when S_i is presented, the stimulus consists of not only S_i but also $S_{i-1}, S_{i-2}, \ldots S_1$ to varying degrees. Furthermore, because of the facts of trace conditioning, when S_j occurs, it is connected as a response (that is, some habit strength develops) to S_i, $i < j$. The larger the distance between i and j ($j - i$ distance), the smaller the habit strength. In order for the stimulus S_i to evoke S_{i+1} and only S_{i+1}, the associations to S_{i+j}, $j = 2, 3, \ldots$ have to be suppressed by the conditioned inhibition process. With a list of length n, S_1 has $n - 2$ inhibitions to establish so that only S_2 occurs to S_1. When S_2 occurs, the stimulus consists of the trace of S_1 and S_2. There are $n - 3$ inhibitions for S_2 and $n - 3$ for S_1; that is, $2(n - 3)$. In general, the sources of inhibition for making the ith response to stimulus $i - 1$ are $(i - 1)(n - i)$. The resulting number of inhibitions for a 6-item list are: 0, 4, 6, 6, 4, 0. The displacement beyond the center point in the error curve is produced by other factors in the Hullian model. A virtue of the Lepley-

Hull theoretical scheme was the close contact it made with the basic theoretical processes assumed to be occurring in classical conditioning. Hence, a complex human-learning situation was analyzed and explained by these basic psychological mechanisms.

The description just presented is by no means complete, and is therefore to some extent unavoidably misleading, but it should give the reader some idea of the predominant interpretation of learning in PAL and SL up to 1950. Later in this chapter we emphasize some opposing views and how they contrast with the Gibson and Lepley-Hull descriptions. We begin by considering some alternative theoretical views of the acquisition process itself. Later we return to questions about stimulus confusions and response learning.

The All-or-None Theoretical View

Empirical basis The standard statistical way of indicating that learning has taken place or is taking place is to present a learning curve. In general, any average measure of performance (percentage correct, average number of correct responses, decreasing number of errors, and so on) shows a gradual change over trials. This result is so common that it has been accepted as fundamental and has provided the rationale for the linear operators discussed earlier and the change in H_n we have just derived. However, in going from the observed performance curve to statements of fundamental process, an important caveat mentioned earlier has been ignored. The performance curve is an average curve. Many functions can yield an average curve, although they themselves are not of the same form as the average. We can easily make the mistake of inferring a fundamental process from an average curve instead of considering some process for the individual and deducing what the average curve would be according to that process. If the theoretical average agrees with the observed average, we have support for the assumption about the individual function—but have not proved it. Of

course, the inference that learning is a gradual process is not based solely on the learning curve. Many other facts about learning seem to lead to the conclusion that each reinforcement produces a small increase in the S-R bond. Nonetheless, a number of situations suggest a different function. In the animal literature, the Krechevsky-Spence controversy over whether animals test hypotheses has raised the issue of the learning function. In operant conditioning, an animal will often suddenly start responding at what seems to be a terminal rate. In avoidance situations, an animal may make his first avoidance and then never again fail to avoid. In the human learning situation, elementary laboratory instructors often find subjects who learn a serial or paired-associate list in one trial. Do these instances represent cases of fast learning rates, chance occurrences, or do they suggest that the assumption of gradual change in learning is not always correct?

Rock (1957) and Rock and Heimer (1959) ran a series of experiments that raised serious questions about the incremental learning process. A list of stimulus-response pairs (double letters or nonsense syllables paired with 2-digit numbers) was presented for 3 sec with a 5-sec interval between pairs. After the presentation of the complete list, a test trial was given on which only the stimuli were shown, again one at a time. All items for which a subject gave an incorrect response were removed from the list and new items were added for later trials. Rock argued that if there was a gradual increase in associative strength, then, by removing items, the learning process would be slowed down because all missed items would have to start again at the H_1 strength of association. The necessary control group did not have error items removed. Rock found no difference in the learning rate of the control and experimental groups. If items were learned all at once, or on a single trial, then these results would be easily explained.

Although the experiment is provocative, there are several problems associated with it.

Clark, Lansford, and Dallenbach (1960), Underwood, Rehula, and Keppel (1962), and Postman (1962, 1963) raised a number of questions about the Rock procedure of eliminating error items. The first objection concerns the slow rate at which the stimuli were presented. If the stimuli are presented slowly, subjects can rehearse a given pair of items many times. This criticism raises the question of what constitutes a trial. The usual procedure is to present items for about 2 sec with 2 sec between items. In replicating Rock's experiment, Clark et al. found that if stimuli were presented for 1 sec each with no interval between items, the control group was poorer than the experimental groups. However, because others have found the reverse, rate factors as such are not clearly related to the Rock effect.

A second objection, and one with substantial support, is that, under Rock's procedure, the list of items learned by the experimental group is an easier list. The items thrown out, on which errors were made, are prima facie more difficult than those left in the list. There are a number of arguments supporting the contention that the lists are not of equal difficulty. One argument concerns individual or idiosyncratic factors that make items easier or more difficult for different subjects. It seems nearly impossible to isolate such factors, and insofar as they exist, they make the Rock procedure difficult to control. Also related to the difference in difficulty of the items remaining in the experimental list and in the control list is the role of interference. Certain items might interfere with each other; this would lead to errors and the elimination of the confusing items. Eventually a less confusing list for the experimental subjects would result. Intralist interference is certainly known to play an important role in paired-associate learning (see Chapter 21 for additional material). Third, as Postman points out (1962), in some of Rock's experiments, the subjects had to learn responses as well as stimulus-response bonds. Postman argues that two learning processes would not, in general,

yield all-or-none learning. Interestingly enough, Kintsch (1963) has used the argument that two learning processes exist in the Rock experimental design to support all-or-none learning. By using a 2-step model, Kintsch explains the differences that he observed between control and experimental groups in this design. He assumes that response learning and an association process are involved. These arguments certainly leave the all-or-none vs. incremental learning question unanswered. It appears that the particular experimental design used by Rock is not ideally suited to provide unambiguous results.

The RTT design In a series of papers and associated experiments, Estes (1960, 1961, 1964a), Estes, Hopkins, and Crothers (1960), and Izawa (1966, 1967) probed the all-or-none learning question more deeply. Let us assume for the purpose of derivation and simplification that we have a set of homogeneous subject-items.[9] The reinforce-test trial procedure is used in the RTT design, and it is assumed that test trials are neutral; that is, no change is made in the stimulus-response bond on trials when a subject has to respond to a stimulus with no feedback concerning whether or not he was correct. Now, if learning is incremental, then, when each item is reinforced, the S-R bond increases in strength. Assuming homogeneous learning rates, and all S-R bonds at zero before reinforcement, then after one reinforcement, all items will have the same probability α of a correct response. If we give a test trial with N subject items, then, on the average, αN of them will be correct. Estes (1961) asked the simple question: What proportion of the items correct on the first test trial will be correct on a second test trial? Thus the design was RT_1T_2, with R being one reinforced trial, and T_1T_2 being two test trials. Let us designate the correct and error items by C = correct and E = error, with a sub-

---

[9] If there are M subjects, each of whom receives N stimulus-response items, then there are $M \cdot N$ subject items. A subject item is any stimulus-response pair from any subject.

TABLE 20.6 ALL-OR-NONE AND INCREMENTAL PREDICTIONS FOR THE RT_1T_2 DESIGN

Outcome for test trials	Observed results	All-or-none model		Incremental model			
		Simple	Forgetting	Simple	Individual difference	Retention differences	Test-trial learning
C_1C_2	.238	α	$\alpha\beta$	α^2	$\dfrac{\Sigma\alpha_i^2}{N}$	$\dfrac{\alpha\Sigma\beta_i}{N}$	$\alpha[(1-\beta)\alpha+\beta]$
C_1E_2	.147	0	$\alpha(1-\beta)$	$\alpha(1-\alpha)$	$\dfrac{\Sigma\alpha_i(1-\alpha_i)}{N}$	$\dfrac{\alpha\Sigma(1-\beta_i)}{N}$	$\alpha[(1-\beta)(1-\alpha)]$
E_1C_2	.017	0	0	$(1-\alpha)\alpha$	$\dfrac{\Sigma(1-\alpha_i)\alpha_i}{N}$	$\dfrac{(1-\alpha)\Sigma\beta_i}{N}$	$(1-\alpha)(1-\beta)\alpha$
E_1E_2	.598	$(1-\alpha)$	$1-\alpha$	$(1-\alpha)^2$	$\dfrac{\Sigma(1-\alpha_i)^2}{N}$	$\dfrac{(1-\alpha)\Sigma(1-\beta_i)}{N}$	$(1-\alpha)[1-(1-\beta)\alpha]$

script 1 or 2 for the test trial of interest. Each item must fall into one of the four classes: $C_1C_2, C_1E_2, E_1C_2,$ and E_1E_2. According to an incremental model, α^2 should be in the C_1C_2 class, $\alpha(1-\alpha)$ in the C_1E_2 class, $(1-\alpha)\alpha$ in the E_1C_2 class, and $(1-\alpha)^2$ in the E_1E_2 class. In a number of experiments, to be discussed more thoroughly below, Estes found this not to be the case. Items correct on the first test trial tended to be correct on the second, and items wrong on the first test trial tended to be wrong on the second. One possible explanation is that items are learned in an all-or-none fashion. The all-or-none theory would say that a proportion α of the items were learned, and a proportion $1-\alpha$ were not learned. Then the four outcome classes would have probabilities α, 0, 0, and $1-\alpha$. Although this pattern of results was not obtained exactly, the pattern of results was closer to the all-or-none version than to the incremental version. The logical next step is to see what restrictions or assumptions are most likely to be responsible for the deviations from the theories.

To account for the observed results, Estes (1961) considered three possible variations in incremental conditioning. Estes used consonant trigrams as stimuli and English words as responses. Because the subjects did not know the words beforehand, the initial probability of a correct response was zero. The RT_1T_2 design was used, yielding the values .238, .147, .017, and .598 for the joint events $C_1C_2, C_1E_2, E_1C_2,$ and E_1E_2 (see Table 20.6). If, instead of a simple α for all subject items,

there was a different α_i for all subject items, then the expected results for the four joint probabilities would be as indicated for the incremental model with individual differences in Table 20.6. The assumption of different learning rates for each subject item requires that the second and third joint events be identical, an assumption contrary to the observed results. Thus, individual differences in learning rate will not explain the results. If a retention factor assumed to vary across subject items is included, the four probabilities listed in the next-to-last column of Table 20.6 result. The parameter β_i is the probability of remembering the ith subject item from T_1 to T_2. Here, as the data require, there is a difference between the second and third probabilities. But can the parameters be estimated to make a good fit? The problem is clear: Either a small α or a small $\Sigma(1-\beta_i)/N$ is needed to make E_1C_2 near the zero observed. However, if α is small, then C_1C_2 cannot be adequately fit, and if $\Sigma(1-\beta_i)/N$ is small, C_1E_2 cannot be adequately described.

Estes goes on to consider the possibility that there is some learning on test trials. Assume α is the probability of a correct response after R. Assume that the incremental linear operator

$$P(T_2) = (1-\beta)P(T_1) + \beta$$

is applied when the correct response is made on T_1 and the decremental operator

$$P(T_2) = (1-\beta)P(T_1)$$

is applied when an error occurs on T_1. The idea here is that the only reasonable response to learn on test trial T_1 is the response made, for no feedback informs the subject about the correct response. The theoretical results in the last column of Table 20.6 again show that C_1E_2 and E_1C_2 should be equal. Thus, reasonably simple assumptions do not bring an incremental model into agreement with the data.

As was mentioned above, the prediction of $\alpha, 0, 0, 1 - \alpha$ for the four probabilities does not do very well either. However, a simple suggestion that forgetting occurs between T_1 and T_2 does account for the data quite well. The prediction is then $\alpha\beta, \alpha(1 - \beta), 0, 1 - \alpha$ with probabilities .241, .151, .000, and .608. (See Column 4 of Table 20.6.) The only flaw seems to be the .017 value for E_1C_2, and if there was any small probability of correct guessing this discrepancy could easily be accounted for. Estes' work thus implies that learning is all-or-none but that forgetting occurs.

Before discussing further the explanations for the forgetting factor, we should note the arguments against the position Estes takes and alternative theoretical approaches. The strongest attack came from Underwood and Keppel (1962) who criticized the results of the R T_1T_2 experiment on both theoretical and empirical grounds. Their theoretical argument was essentially that an incremental model of the Hullian type could account for his results. (Note that the incremental model discussed above is not a Hullian model but one related to statistical learning theory.) Underwood and Keppel make the point that the very concept of a threshold implies that items well below it will be wrong twice in a row and items well above the threshold will be correct twice in a row. Items which are correct and then wrong, or vice versa, can be accounted for by assuming they are close to the threshold and then invoking the oscillation principle. However, there seems to be a flaw in this line of reasoning. If oscillation is introduced, then a probability of being above threshold is associated with every item. The analysis made above holds exactly as Estes developed it. The

only solution is to assume that the oscillation value or inhibition is not truly random but is correlated from trial to trial, an assumption that is possible but that is extremely unparsimonious and mathematically intractable. The second point made by Underwood and Keppel is that items are not learned at the same rate. In the context of the Hullian model, this would mean that some items may be above threshold while others are not. Assume that a proportion β are below threshold. These will give two errors in succession on the T_1 and T_2 test trials. The $1 - \beta$ remaining items will be above threshold and the subject will have some probability θ of being correct. Thus, two correct responses will have probability $(1 - \beta)\theta^2$; a correct and an error response, in either order, will have probability $(1 - \beta)\theta(1 - \theta)$; and two error responses will have probability $\beta + (1 - \beta)(1 - \theta)^2$. Thus, a higher proportion of pairs of errors, E_1E_2, are allowed by this assumption, but the E_1C_2 and C_1E_2 outcomes still have the same probability. Again individual differences in θ will not help. However, these arguments are against only one interpretation of Hullian theory and other interpretations could be made. In fact Restle (1965) has illustrated how a number of different incremental models could still lead to all-or-none learning.

Underwood and Keppel's empirical arguments against Estes' experimental procedure are much harder to evaluate. However, in light of all the research related to the all-or-none issue, the particular arguments against one experiment should not be overweighted.

Other extensions of the RT_1T_2 design have been made. For example, Estes, Hopkins, and Crothers (1960) discussed the effect of inserting multiple reinforcements between test trials. The experiment raised a number of questions about the simple design. For example, do multiple reinforcements increase retention? Estes et al. concluded that they did not, but they found that multiple test trials followed by reinforcements did increase retention. There was a sign of increased stereotypy in responding over repeated test trials, seemingly implying a learning process on the test trial—but learning of the response made rather than of the correct response. They also observed a retention loss between T_1 and T_2. Their explanation of the retention loss was that the stimulus conditions on the second test trial were different from those on the first test trial, and this produced a decrement in performance. It could also account for the observed better retention with test trials interspersed between reinforced trials as opposed to reinforced trials alone, that is, $RTRT_1T_2$ shows better retention than RRT_1T_2. In the mixed test and reinforced trials condition, there is more change in the stimulus from one reinforcement to another. This would presumably produce better retention. Izawa (1966, 1967) has followed up this last idea in a series of experiments. She applies the stimulus fluctuation model of stimulus sampling theory with a great deal of success (see p. 929). Although other researchers such as Seidel (1963) and Jones (1962) have raised questions about the miniature procedure and the interpretation given to the results, the weight of the evidence seems to favor an all-or-none learning process with a forgetting process due to stimulus change. Other factors are no doubt involved in many experiments, but their effects are small in comparison to all-or-none learning and forgetting over repeated test trials.

The all-or-none model for the traditional PAL procedure Bower (1961) introduced the one-element Markov chain model to describe paired-associate learning. (Although Estes [1959a], and Suppes and Atkinson [1960] had used a one-element model for analysis of probability-learning experiments, it was inadequate for that experimental routine.) The simplicity of the one-element model made it very tractable and Bower derived many statistics for the learning process. Some of these will be derived here. Much of the material is similar to that derived for the concept-identification model and the reader may wish to refer back to it for a review (see page 950).

Axioms: The main assumptions can easily be stated.

(1) *Each item is to be represented by a single stimulus element which is sampled whenever the stimulus item is presented.*

(2) *The element is in one of two conditioning states; C_0 or C_1, where C_0 means that the element is not conditioned and C_1 means that it is conditioned.*

(3) *On each trial when the item is reinforced, the element changes states according to the following transition matrix* **T**, *where c is the probability of a transition from state C_0 to state C_1 on each reinforced trial.*

$$\mathbf{T} = \begin{array}{c} C_1 \\ C_0 \end{array} \begin{array}{|cc} C_1 & C_0 \\ \hline 1 & 0 \\ c & 1-c \end{array} \quad \begin{array}{c} P\ (correct) \\ \\ 1.0 \\ g \end{array} \tag{55}$$

(4) *The parameter c is assumed to be a constant for each and every trial.*

(5) *In state C_1, the probability of a correct response is 1.0 and in state C_0 the probability of a correct response is g.*

Usually, g will be $1/r$, where there are r responses from which the subject may choose. Of central interest in the mathematical development are the probabilities of being in the two states on any trial. Let $p_{i,n}$ be the probability of being in state C_i on trial n. Then, $\mathbf{P}_n = (p_{1,n}, p_{0,n})$ is the vector of state probabilities on trial n. Because, at the beginning of the experiment, the subject does not know the correct response for a stimulus item, it is natural to assume that all subject items start in state C_0 on trial 1, that is, $p_{0,1} = 1$.

Notice that this is a model for the acquisition of a single item in a list of paired-associate items. Any interaction between the learning of various items is avoided. The theory thus directly denies the principle of stimulus interaction and confusion, which was emphasized by Gibson (1940). The rationale for this seemingly unreasonable assumption lies in the rules of application for the theory. (It is not claimed that this model is appropriate for all paired-associate learning situations; in particular, it is probably not appropriate for lists composed of pairs of nonsense syllables.) The axioms state that the stimulus may be represented by a single element. The model also assumes that the subject knows the responses which are to be associated to the stimuli since when he does not know he is to guess.

Learning curve. To derive the learning curve, we must know the probability of being in states C_0 and C_1 on each trial. It is clear from the transition matrix that there is no transition from C_1 to C_0. Thus, because $p_{1,n} + p_{0,n} = 1$, $p_{1,n} = 1 - p_{0,n}$. If we can derive $p_{0,n}$, then both the state probabilities will be known. The value $p_{0,n+1} = p_{0,n}(1 - c)$ is the recursion relating the state probabilities and has a solution

$$p_{0,n} = (1 - c)^{n-1} \qquad (56)$$

Note that, in general, all state probabilities can be solved by direct matrix equations. Of course, a matrix solution would be required only when the above simple calculations did not work. In general,

$$\mathbf{P}_{n+1} = \mathbf{P}_n \mathbf{T}$$

which has the solution

$$\mathbf{P}_n = \mathbf{P}_1 \mathbf{T}^{n-1} \qquad (57)$$

Of course, in this equation we must find the powers of $\mathbf{T}$. For the transition matrix above (Equation 55)

$$\mathbf{T}^{n-1} = \begin{array}{c} \\ C_1 \\ C_0 \end{array} \begin{array}{|cc} \multicolumn{1}{c}{C_1} & \multicolumn{1}{c}{C_0} \\ \hline 1 & 0 \\ 1 - (1 - c)^{n-1} & (1 - c)^{n-1} \end{array} \qquad (58)$$

For the learning curve in this case we shall derive the proportion of errors on each trial. Because the probability of an error is $1 - g$ when the element is in state C_0, and zero in state C_1, the

$$\begin{aligned} P \text{ (error on trial } n) = q_n &= p_{0,n}(1 - g) \\ &= (1 - g)(1 - c)^{n-1} \quad (59) \end{aligned}$$

This is a geometric distribution function and does not differ from the learning curve predicted by the application of simple linear operators (Equation 59 is 1 minus Equation 5 with c replacing θ and g replacing p_1).

The distribution of the total number of errors. Let T be the statistic representing the total number of errors that a subject makes on a particular item before the item is learned. (For all statistics to be derived, we assume that all items are repeatedly presented until learned, that is, until they are absorbed into the absorbing state C_1.) First, what is the probability of no errors? Because we assume that each subject-item starts in state C_0 on trial 1, the subject must guess correctly until the item is conditioned. We write a sequence with zero for correct and 1 for error and indicate the terminal string of zeros generated in state C_1 by a $-$. Thus, $T = 0$ for all of the following sequences: $0-$, $00-$, $000-$, $0000-$, ... with probabilities gc, $g(1 - c)gc$, $g^2(1 - c)^2 gc$, $g^3(1 - c)^3 gc$, ..., respectively. The $0-$ string occurs if the subject guesses on the first trial and then moves to state C_1 (gc) with probability c. The $00-$ sequence occurs if the subject guesses on trial 1 (g), does not condition $(1 - c)$, guesses correctly again (g), and conditions on trial 2 (c), yielding the $g(1 - c)gc$ probability. In each case the subject guesses correctly as long as he does not condition, then guesses correctly and conditions. In general we have the probability $g^j(1 - c)^j gc$ for the sequence with j correct responses before conditioning. We wish to sum these probabilities for all $j = 0, 1, 2, \ldots$ to get the $P(T = 0)$:

$$gc \sum_{j=0}^{\infty} [g(1 - c)]^j = \frac{gc}{1 - g(1 - c)} = gb \quad (60)$$

where b represents the probability that no more errors will be made after the response in state C_0. Now, the following argument yields $P(T = 1)$. If b is the probability that no further errors will be made after an error (or after a correct response in state C_0), then $1 - b$ is the probability that at least one further error will be made. First, there must be at least one error $(1 - gb)$; second, one error

TABLE 20.7 COMPARISON OF TWO METHODS OF COMPUTING THE STATIONARITY STATISTIC FOR THE HYPOTHESIS AND ONE-ELEMENT MODELS

		All-or-None Model	
		One-element	Hypothesis
Statistic	P (error on trial $n \mid n <$ trial of last error)	$1 - g*$	$\dfrac{(1 - c)q\dagger}{(1 - cq)}$
	P (error on trial $n \mid n \leq$ trial of last error)	$1 - g + gc$	q

*$g = P$ (correct response) in the PAL model.
†$q = P$ (error response) in the CL model.

must occur $(1 - b)$; and third, no further errors can occur (b). The error response ensures that the subject is in state C_0, allowing us to use b for the probability that no further errors will be made after a response in state C_0. Thus, $P(T = 1) = (1 - gb)(1 - b)b$. For two errors, again $T \neq 0$, which has probability $1 - gb$; two errors must be made, which has probability $(1 - b)^2$, and no further errors can occur, which has probability b. So, $P(T = 2) = (1 - gb)(1 - b)^2 b$. In general,

$$P(T = k) = \begin{cases} gb & k = 0 \\ (1 - gb)b(1 - b)^k & k \geq 1 \end{cases} \quad (61)$$

The trial of the last error. Let L represent the trial of the last error and let $L = 0$ indicate no errors, which has probability gb. For $L = k$, we must have an error on trial k, then no more errors. To have an error on trial k, the item must be in state C_0 on trial k $((1 - c)^{n-1})$; the subject must guess incorrectly $(1 - g)$; and no more errors can be made after the error response in C_0 (b). This leads to

$$P(T = k) = \begin{cases} gb & k = 0 \\ b(1 - g)(1 - c)^{k-1} & k \geq 1 \end{cases} \quad (62)$$

Bower derived many other statistics, including run probabilities for error and correct responses, autocorrelation of errors with lag m, distribution of the number of errors between the kth and $(k + 1)$st successes, and the distribution of the number of correct responses between the kth and $(k + 1)$st error. One statistic of interest, because it seems so counterintuitive, is the expected number of errors after the kth error. Let us first compute the expected number of errors for an item starting in state C_0 on trial 1, that is,

the expected number of errors per item in the entire experiment. Using Equation 61,

$$E(T) = (1 - gb)b \sum_{k=1}^{\infty} k(1 - b)^k = \frac{1 - g}{c} \quad (63)$$

Now assume the kth error has been made; then with probability $(1 - c)$ the item does not condition on the error trial and remains in state C_0. However, starting in state C_0 was exactly the initial condition used to compute $E(T)$ in Equation 63. Thus, the process is a renewal process, and the expected number of errors after any error is $(1 - c)E(T)$, a constant. One further point should be made about this model. Like the all-or-none model used for concept identification discussed earlier, it predicts stationarity. Until the item enters the absorbing state C_1, the subject should be performing at a chance level. All the statistics used for the hypothesis model to test for stationarity can be applied here also. However, we must again emphasize the importance of careful calculations and derivations. In this model, the stationarity statistics should be computed only on the trials before the last error. That is, in the one-element model for PAL, the last error is not included, whereas in the hypothesis model for CL, the last error should be included.[10] Table 20.7 indicates the basic results. Thus, although a constant probability is expected regardless of how the statistic is computed, the value will not be the guessing rate $(1 - g)$ in PAL or q in CL unless the last error is excluded in the computations for PAL and included for CL.

[10] For the interested reader, these stationarity curves are worked out by Batchelder, Bjork, and Yellott (1966).

Evaluation of the One-element model
Early applications of the one-element model were exceptionally successful (Bower, 1961). However, these studies made severe restrictions on the stimuli and the responses. In particular, most of them were studies involving two responses or verbal discrimination. Restle (1965) noted a fact about such studies which has been obvious to many researchers. With only two responses, the subject might use a strategy of list learning, attending to items associated with one of the responses and ignoring items associated with the other response. When an item is presented, the subject simply asks if it is included in the list of items he is using. If it is, the response is known; if not, the item requires the other response. Although most of the studies successfully described by the one-element model probably did not involve learning of this type, some may have. In any case, the success of the all-or-none model was soon to be questioned.[11]

Multistage Models for PAL

At the beginning of our discussion of PAL, we noted that there were three components to the learning: response learning, association, and stimulus discrimination. Can the failures of the one-element model be attributed to one of these? Actually, all three have been suggested, and in the following pages we shall discuss some of the suggested revisions.

Response factors Mandler (1954) discussed the need for segmented response units to be integrated into a whole response before they could become connected to the stimulus in the situation. Underwood, Runquist, and

Schulz (1959) showed experimentally that variables that retard response integration would also affect PAL in a way consonant with the theory that the responses had to be learned before the stimulus-response association occurred. Using PAL lists which varied in the meaningfulness of the responses, they assumed that highly similar responses would be learned more easily, and thus the total PAL problem would be easier since the responses would not have to be learned. Furthermore, if the responses were known, then the lists should not differ significantly. The results of their experiments tended to confirm the hypothesis that response learning is one of the component processes in PAL learning.

One explanation for some of the failure to find all-or-none learning can be made in terms of response-learning factors. In the successful applications of the all-or-none model, the number of response classes has usually been small (normally two), and subjects simply have not had to learn responses. This has not been the case for PAL experiments in general, which have, in fact, involved response learning. Crothers (1964) attempted to show directly that the one-element model would not work with response learning. He used the RTT design with some variations and a response set consisting of the six responses: red circle, red square, green circle, green square, blue circle, and blue square. The subject could guess the color (red, green, or blue) and he could guess the shape (circle or square). However, in order to learn which response went with which three-letter trigram stimulus, two responses had to be hooked up. Crothers assumed that each response would be independently hooked up in an all-or-none fashion. The same learning rate was not assumed for each response component. We see here that the final learning will not be all-or-none but rather will involve a two-stage process. However, the underlying processes are assumed to be all-or-none. The fit of the model was only moderately successful. The assumption of independent learning of the two-response components was perhaps the weakest assumption.

---

[11]It is scarcely surprising that so simple a theory was questioned, particularly when the exactness of its various predictions is considered. By a simple increase in the number of subjects, any slight deviation from the theory could be made significant. In fact, in terms of scientific strategy, the ability to test theories with extremely powerful statistical tests has raised some serious second thoughts about the adequacy of simple goodness-of-fit tests. The strategy now suggested as more appropriate is that of choosing the better of a number of theories rather than trying to establish that the theory cannot describe the data. (For a detailed statistical treatment of this question, see Kraemer, 1965.)

We mentioned earlier that the all-or-none model was most successful when only two responses were involved. One explanation for the failure of the model with more than two responses is that subjects eliminate the learned responses and guess more efficiently. Thus, given eight stimulus items and eight response items, when three of the stimulus-response pairs have been learned, the subjects may begin guessing on unlearned items from the set of responses they have not yet used. This would change the guessing rate and distort the fit of the model. A related explanation is that, for each item, the subject learns not only the correct response, but also learns which responses are not correct. With the correction procedure this assumption is not too reasonable since the correct answer is seen on every trial and it is rehearsed instead of the error response. But with the noncorrection procedure, the assumption becomes plausible. For example, assume that there are r responses in a noncorrection procedure. When a subject makes a wrong response, he is not told the correct answer but is told simply that he is wrong. A rational strategy for the subject would be to learn which responses are wrong; then, the next time the item is presented, he could choose his response from the remaining possible responses. Millward (1964a) developed a Markov-chain model for such a learning process. A related model was introduced by Nahinsky (1964, 1967).

Bower (1962) considered the general relationship between the correction and noncorrection routine. In the latter routine, when a subject makes a wrong response, the experimenter simply says "wrong." If there are only two responses, the obvious assumption is that the other response is correct. However, if multiple responses are involved, the subject must act in some other, more complicated way. In a preliminary experiment, Bower found that nothing was learned during error trials in two groups given three and eight response alternatives. His explanation was that the subjects responded emotionally to being told that they were wrong and thus did not

act rationally. He then considered a more general routine that allowed for a partial correction along with correction and noncorrection. In partial correction, the subject is not told that he is wrong; instead he is given a subset of the alternative responses which includes the correct response. Given instructions about the procedure, the subjects might not be so likely to act emotionally and more rational behavior might result. Bower assumed that the subjects would select an item from the subset and rehearse it. If the selected item was correct, then it was learned. If it was wrong, then, on the next trial, the subjects would again choose from the presented subset. After the first correct response was made for a given item, the item would either be learned or it would not be learned. If it was not learned, Bower assumed that the subjects would recognize the correct response in the subset and would select it. Thus, after the first correct response, all trials for an item would be essentially correction trials. Bower ran an experiment to test these ideas using three- or eight-response alternatives and a subset of size 2. Correction, noncorrection, and partial correction groups were run. The learning parameter c of the one-element model was estimated from the correction group and was "dragged" to the partial and noncorrection groups. The theory was modified according to the set of assumptions made above for these groups. The modified theory involved only the parameter c. The all-or-none theory described the data very satisfactorily.

The discussion just presented illustrates how various aspects of the PAL procedure related to the response phase of learning can be analyzed and integrated with the all-or-none model of learning. In the general PAL experiment with paired associates using nonsense syllables for responses, the subject would presumably have to learn each of the nonsense syllables—and learn to differentiate them also—before he could respond correctly. Further work on the integration of models for response learning and association learning is needed. The fact that all PAL experiments do not show all-or-none learning is not conclusive evidence against this hypothesis unless we can be sure that the response-learning phase is not contributing to the process. This is the main point made by the all-or-none theorists at this time.

Association processes If the response-learning process is effectively eliminated, will the basic association process of learning always be all-or-none? If not, what might it be? Earlier in this section we reviewed the Hullian theory involving habit strength, threshold, and oscillation and saw that it proposed a complicated process of the incremental type, similar in some respects to the linear operator model. Between the linear processes and the all-or-none processes, there are multiple-step processes. We now review three classes of multiple-step models: the *N-element model,* the *random-trial-increments (RTI) model,* and the *short-term memory (STM) model.*

Consider first the *N*-element pattern model (Estes, 1959a; Atkinson & Estes, 1963). The *N*-element model is a natural generalization of the one-element model.[12] On each trial, one of the *N* elements is randomly sampled. Each element is either conditioned to the correct response or it is not conditioned. Generally, if it is not conditioned, the subject is assumed to guess. The reinforcement conditions the sampled element to the correct response with a probability c; fails to condition the sampled element with a probability $1 - c$. After the reinforcement, the element is returned to the pool of elements. The states of the process are simply the number of elements conditioned to the correct response. Thus there are $N + 1$ states representing the number of elements conditioned, $0, 1, \ldots, N$. A transition from state i to state $i + 1$ occurs with probability $c(N - i)/N$, for with probability $(N - i)/N$ an unconditioned element is sampled, and with probability c the sampled element is conditioned. If the process is in state i, then the probability of a correct response is $1(i/N)$ when a conditioned element is sampled, and $(1 - i/N)g$ when an unconditioned element is sampled, or, on the average, $i/N + (1 - i/N)g$, where g is the probability of guessing correctly when an unconditioned element is sampled. The subject starts with a probability g of a correct response and moves by steps of $(1 - g)i/N$, $i = 1,2,3 \ldots N$ until perfect learning has occurred. Of course the increments do not occur on every trial, but depend upon the state i and the learning parameter c. Let us consider the case where $N = 2$ and derive the learning curve for the process.

The states are defined by the number of elements conditioned, that is, S_0, S_1, and S_2 for 0, 1, and 2 conditioned elements, respectively. The transitions between states define the transition matrix of the Markov chain, **T**.

$$\mathbf{T} = \begin{array}{c} \\ S_2 \\ S_1 \\ \\ S_0 \end{array} \begin{array}{c} \begin{array}{cccc} S_2 & S_1 & S_0 & P(\text{correct}) \end{array} \\ \left[\begin{array}{ccc} 1 & 0 & 0 \\ \frac{c}{2} & 1 - \frac{c}{2} & 0 \\ \\ 0 & c & 1 - c \end{array} \right] \begin{array}{c} 1 \\ \frac{1}{2} + \frac{1}{2}g \\ \\ g \end{array} \end{array} \quad (64)$$

Because there is no transition from state S_1 to S_0, the state probabilities are fairly easy to compute (see p. 991). (The computation is instructive because it introduces a new mathematical concept, the convolution of two sequences; see Feller, 1957, p. 250.) First, the probability of remaining in state S_0 is $1 - c$. The recursion is exactly the same as that presented in Equation 56; $P(S_{0,n}) = (1 - c)^{n-1}$. We have assumed that the process starts in state S_0, so $P(S_{1,1}) = 0$. A step-by-step calculation of the probability of being in state S_1 on successive trials will lead to the probability of being in state S_1 on trial n, $P(S_{1,n})$. The basic recursion is easily stated: $P(S_{1,n+1}) = (1 - \frac{1}{2}c)P(S_{1,n}) + cP(S_{0,n})$. Hence,

$$P(S_{1,2}) = (1 - \tfrac{1}{2}c) \cdot 0 + c \cdot 1 = c$$
$$P(S_{1,3}) = (1 - \tfrac{1}{2}c) \cdot c + c(1 - c)$$
$$P(S_{1,4}) = (1 - \tfrac{1}{2}c)^2 \cdot c + (1 - \tfrac{1}{2}c)\,(1 - c)c$$
$$\qquad\quad + (1 - c)^2 c$$

---

[12] Historically, the *N*-element model is derived from statistical learning theory (see p. 936 and Estes, 1959a).

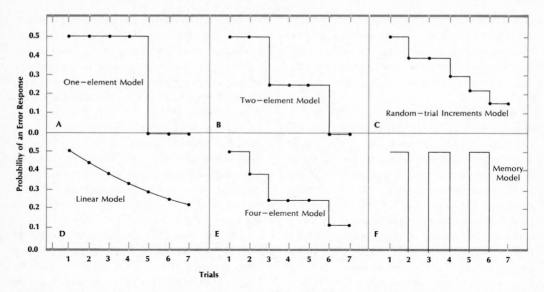

Figure 20.14. Examples of individual learning curves for six models. The models differ in the manner in which the probability of an error response decreases toward zero.

To derive the three terms of $P(S_{1,4})$, first, a transition is made immediately to state S_1 on trial 1 with probability c, and the process remains in state S_2 for two trials with probability $(1 - \frac{1}{2}c)^2$. The second term occurs when the process stays in state S_0 for one trial, then moves to state S_1 and remains there for one trial. Finally, the last term occurs when the conditioning of the sampled element does not occur for two trials and then the element sampled on the third trial is conditioned. The pattern should be clear:

$$P(S_{1,k}) = c[(1 - \tfrac{1}{2}c)^{k-2} + (1 - \tfrac{1}{2}c)^{k-3}(1 - c) + (1 - \tfrac{1}{2}c)^{k-4}(1 - c)^2 + \cdots + (1 - \tfrac{1}{2}c)(1 - c)^{k-3} + (1 - c)^{k-2}] \quad (65)$$

A convolution is defined as a sequence c_k, $k = 1, 2, \ldots$, which results from the sum of the products of two other sequences: let a_i and b_j be the two sequences; then $c_k = \displaystyle\sum_{i=0}^{k} a_i b_{k-i}$. If we think of the two sequences as $(1 - \frac{1}{2}c)^i$ and $(1 - c)^j$, the terms in the bracket in Equation 65 form the kth term of the convolution for $k > 2$. The first and second terms of the convolution are $P(S_{1,1}) = 0$ and $P(S_{1,2}) = c$.

Equation 65 can be written more concisely:

$$P(S_{1,k}) = c \sum_{i=0}^{k-2} (1 - \tfrac{1}{2}c)^i (1 - c)^{k-2-i}$$

$$= c(1 - c)^{k-2} \sum_{i=0}^{k-2} \left(\frac{(1 - \tfrac{1}{2}c)}{(1 - c)} \right)^i \quad (66)$$

Equation 66 is a sum of a geometric series with the solution

$$P(S_{1,k}) = 2[(1 - \tfrac{1}{2}c)^{k-1} - (1 - c)^{k-1}] \quad (67)$$

The learning curve is then simply

$$P(\text{error on trial } k)$$
$$= P(S_{0,k})(1 - g) + P(S_{1,k})\tfrac{1}{2}(1 - g) \quad (68)$$
$$= (1 - \tfrac{1}{2}c)^{k-1}(1 - g)$$

The idea of two states is important, and various models similar to the one sketchily presented here have been developed for a number of learning situations (Kintsch, 1963; Suppes & Ginsberg, 1963; Bower & Theios, 1964; Theios & Brelsford, 1966).

The linear model and the one-element model represent two extremes, which are illustrated in Figure 20.14 where the change in response probability for an individual subject is plotted. For the linear model, Figure

20.14D, all subjects would be identical to the curve presented. For the one-element model, the subjects would make the jump to zero probability on different trials, depending on the statistic for the trial of the last error. The curve for the one-element model (Figure 20.14A) shows a subject who responds at chance on trials 1,2,3, and 4 but who becomes conditioned to make the correct response on trial 4 so that he is correct on trial 5 and all later trials. Figure 20.14B illustrates the effects on the learning process produced by assuming more than one element; it presents the curve of an individual subject as interpreted by the two-element model. Figure 20.14E presents the curve of an individual subject as interpreted by the four-element model. Note that, in a multiple-element model, each subject passes through the same states but not necessarily on the same trials. Figure 20.14C represents graphically the assumptions of the random-trial-increments (RTI) model, which combines the linear model and the one-element model. Let q_n be the probability of an error on trial n. Let c be the probability that a reinforcement is effective on any trial. Then, the model can be stated as

$$q_{n+1} = \alpha q_n \quad \text{with probability} \quad c \quad (69)$$
$$q_{n+1} = \quad q_n \quad \text{with probability} \quad 1 - c$$

The first equation is simply the linear-operator model. But the RTI model, unlike the linear-operator model, does not allow a change on every trial. The effective trials are determined by a random Bernoulli process with probability c. Figure 20.14C shows one possible sequence which follows an RTI model. In the example, $\alpha = 3/4$ and $c = 1/2$. The subject starts at chance (1/2) on trial 1, on which reinforcement is effective, and the new probability of an error is $\alpha q_1 = 3/8$. He stays at 3/8 on trials 2 and 3. On trial 3, reinforcement is again effective, yielding the new probability $\alpha^2 q_1 = 9/32$ for trial 4. Trial 4 is also effectively reinforced and the subject's error-response probability changes to $\alpha^3 q_1 = 27/128$ for trial 5. This learning curve for an individual subject illustrates two

crucial points about the RTI model. First, unlike the case with the linear model, every trial is not effectively reinforced. Second, the response probability changes in accordance with the linear-operator model, $q_{n+1} = \alpha q_n$. In other words, this model assumes that an effective reinforcement changes the subject's response probability in accordance with a negatively accelerated growth function. By setting the parameters c or α to a particular value, either the linear model or the one-element model results. To illustrate, let $c = 1$. Then, every trial is effectively reinforced and the linear model results: $q_{n+1} = \alpha^{n-1} q_1$. However, by setting $\alpha = 0$, the one-element model results. One advantageous feature of the RTI model is that, when it is applied, the estimated values of the parameters will determine whether a pure linear model or a pure all-or-none model best describes the data. If $c \neq 1$ or $\alpha \neq 0$, then neither model is satisfactory. For a number of experiments, Norman (1964) and Atkinson and Crothers (1964) found the RTI model to be better than either the one-element or the linear model. Of course, any deviation in the data from the predictions of either of these "extreme" models means that the RTI model has to be superior, so the results of their experiments imply that neither extreme model is generally adequate.

A third way of relaxing the all-or-none process is to introduce a short-term memory factor. Broadbent (1958), Peterson and Peterson (1959), Murdock (1961), Melton (1963), and others have investigated the role of STM. As we saw earlier, subjects in probability-learning experiments remember the five or so most recent events, and in concept-learning experiments, subjects remember the previous hypotheses tested as well as specific stimuli presented on past trials. Similarly, in PAL and SL, subjects remember almost perfectly the last few items presented. This facet of memory has not yet been incorporated in any way in the conditioning models discussed above, but there are some historical precedents for introducing memory processes. Pavlov introduced the notion of a stimulus trace to account for trace conditioning. Hull used the same notion to bring together in time the stimulus, response, and reinforcement, which usually were separated temporally. A more recent and dynamic view of the "trace" of a stimulus was introduced by Broadbent (1958).

The main point of interest to us here is the postulation of two types of memory, short-term memory (STM) and long-term memory (LTM). Long-term memory may be defined as the ability to recite a list, respond to a stimulus, remember an association, and so on, following some long interval of time after the material was practiced or presented. It is obviously very much related to what is meant by learning itself. Short-term memory, in contrast, is the appropriate performance immediately or very shortly after the material was presented. It is usually conceived of as different from LTM because it has different characteristics, such as a rapid rate of decay, and a limit to the amount of material which can be remembered. Since any performance measure of STM usually mixes both of these two memory types, it is not easy to prove that the two types of memory exist. The arguments for a single type of memory derive mostly from the experiments demonstrating similar processes in STM and LTM experiments (Hebb, 1961; Melton, 1963; Postman, 1964). Arguments for two types of memory stem from experiments that show rapid forgetting due to interruption of rehearsal (Broadbent, 1958, 1963; Peterson & Peterson, 1959; Murdock, 1961). However, simply positing two types of memory does not help a great deal; in fact, it requires giving detailed specifications for two systems instead of one. The evidence supporting two types of memory, though not conclusive, seems sufficiently compelling to justify the development of theories assuming a STM process. A brief description of the STM process will help to explain the models to be presented.

Items in STM appear to become less available, either as a function of time or as a function of other items' having been placed into the short-term memory. The difficulty of

determining which variable—time or interference of new items—causes the loss of memory for items in STM arises because, if no items are presented during the time interval of interest, a subject can rehearse the items in the short-term memory. Hence memory for the items does not decay. If other items are presented, preventing rehearsal, memory loss can be due to either interference or decay (Melton, 1963; Wickelgren & Norman, 1966). If one assumes a STM, one generally (though not invariably) assumes that there are a fixed number of "slots" that hold encoded items. After each item is encoded, it is placed in a slot. Support for this idea comes from experiments showing that a single word and a single letter are forgotten at the same rate and also that three words and a three-letter nonsense syllable are forgotten at the same rate, but at a rate faster than that for single words or letters (Melton, 1963). Thus, the number of letters comprising the unit is not important, but the number of encoded units is. Another assumption often incorporated into STM models is that there are about seven slots in all. This assumption is related to the ubiquitous role of the number 7 in many information-processing tasks (Miller, 1956). Finally, if we assume a STM system, then the manner in which items go from STM to long-term memory (LTM) must be specified. At this stage in studies on memory, few conclusive answers are available. Nonetheless, theories of PAL and SL must take into account some version of stimulus-trace theory. The assumption of simple single-link associations is inadequate if only because, immediately after a single stimulus-response presentation, a subject has a very high probability of knowing the response to the stimulus. In contrast, after a short time interval, or after a few additional items have been presented, the probability of perfect recall decreases a great deal.

Atkinson and Crothers (1964) have incorporated the idea of a short-term memory into an all-or-none model of learning which assumes that an item can be in one of four states. The first is a state, *U,* in which items are not encoded well enough to be placed into STM, and even rehearsal will not affect learning for them. However, after an item has been encoded, it can be in either the STM state, *S,* or in the forgetting state, *F,* depending upon some forgetting factor. Learned items are in the learned state, *L.* The following transition matrix summarizes the transitions between the states of the model.

from the number of intervening items and thus time and number of items are confounded. They found that learning, that is, entering the long-term memory state, had a higher probability when the transition was from state *S* than it did when the transition was from state *F.* However, these results were contradicted by those of an experiment by Greeno (1964, 1967), which showed that if an item was presented twice in

$$
\mathbf{T} = \begin{array}{c} L \\ S \\ F \\ U \end{array} \begin{array}{|cccc} L & S & F & U & P(\text{correct}) \\ \hline 1 & 0 & 0 & 0 & 1.0 \\ a & (1-a)(1-f) & (1-a)f & 0 & 1.0 \\ a & (1-a)(1-f) & (1-a)f & 0 & g \\ ca & c(1-a)(1-f) & c(1-a)f & 1-c & g \end{array} \tag{70}
$$

We see from this matrix that the probability of encoding an item is *c.* After an item has been encoded, it remains encoded. It is placed in the permanent learning state *L* with probability *a.* If it is encoded, then, depending on the forgetting parameter *f,* the subject either responds correctly or he makes a guess. Figure 20.14F shows the response probabilities for a sample subject. Notice the subject jumps between knowing the answer and guessing. This model does not predict stationarity. It was applied to the results of eight experiments and found to be better than six other models, including the linear model, the one-element model, the RTI model, and the two-element model. However, this STM model has three parameters, whereas the others have one or two parameters. When *c* is a priori set equal to 1, a two-parameter version of the above model results. The two-parameter version of the model is still better than all the other models tested.

To account for the effect of list length in PAL, Calfee and Atkinson (1965) made the parameter *f* a function of the number of items that intervened between two presentations of the same item. The choice of the parameter *f* was based on results that show STM to be more a function of intervening items than of time. Unfortunately, Calfee and Atkinson's experiment does not separate time for decay

a row, it was not learned any faster than those presented only once. Yet an item recently presented certainly should be in the short-term memory. Items repeated twice, but *not* in succession, were learned more rapidly.

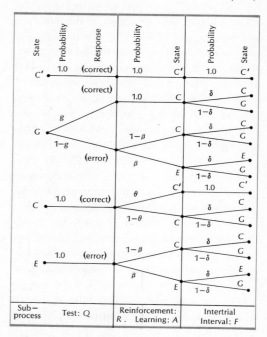

Figure 20.15. Schematic representation of Bernbach's short-term memory model. The four subprocesses are those associated with (1) the tests, (2) reinforcement, (3) learning, and (4) the intertrial interval.

Bernbach (1965) based his STM model for paired-associate learning on results obtained by Peterson and Peterson (1962), which showed that with repetition the forgetting curve for STM decreased less rapidly. Bernbach assumed that an item started in a guessing state, G on trial 1 (Figure 20.15). Then, if it was guessed correctly, the item went into a STM state C, in which the response was remembered but not learned. From state C, the item was either forgotten during the interval between trials, with probability δ, or else it was held in C with probability $(1 - \delta)$. When an item was in C and was reinforced, it went into C' with probability θ. In C' it was permanently remembered. If an item in G was guessed incorrectly, one of two transitions could take place. Either the error response could be placed in STM (this was introduced to account for *proactive inhibition*), with probability β, or the correct response could be placed in STM with probability $1 - \beta$. Presumably, the correct response was placed in STM when reinforcement was effective. If the error response was placed in STM, it was forgotten with probability δ, or remembered with probability $1 - \delta$. The important point about this model is that some of the subprocesses which have been postulated for PAL are built into the general model. Bernbach has shown how several subprocesses can be isolated for recombination in a miniature experiment (Jones, 1962) of the form $R_1R_2T_1T_2T_3T_4$. One subprocess is the effect of a test trial, a second is the effect of a reinforcement, a third is the effect of the intertrial interval, and a fourth is the transition from the STM state to the learned state. By estimating parameters involved in the various subprocesses, we can obtain some indication of what happens at each stage of a PAL experiment. Note that we have here the idea of building a general model from associative subprocesses, each of which can be analyzed by special experimental procedures.

We have examined a number of attempts to relax the strong all-or-none learning process. The rationale for the STM model seems

clear enough—there are two memory processes and both must be included in any model of learning. The rationale for the RTI model is that, although learning is incremental, an item does not always receive an effective reinforcement. This could be due to a number of psychological factors. One might be attention, that is, a subject might be rehearsing one item while the next item is being presented. The second item would, essentially, not be reinforced. Another factor might be STM. Unless an item is in STM it may not be effectively reinforced. It is in STM with a probability c and not in STM with a probability $1 - c$.

An argument for an N-element model might be based on the assumption of more molecular events such as the number of neural connections required to establish a reliable S-R bond or the number of stimulus components that must be connected.

The adequacy of these multistage models and the inadequacies of both the one-element model and the linear model imply that many situations involve a number of subprocesses that can be described by assuming that a stimulus-response bond is in one of a few states. At present, the STM process seems to be a promising one for accounting for these various states. However, an idea such as proactive interference may also be required; that is, if a subject makes a wrong response, the wrong response may be remembered instead of the correct response (see Bernbach's model). These various models for the association process are certainly not exhaustive. However, presenting them should help to make clear that a large number of ideas are possible and premature fixation on any one model is uncalled for at this time.

Stimulus variables   We turn now to what is perhaps the most important process increasing the complexity of PAL learning, namely *stimulus confusion*. Perhaps the most important fact relevant to a treatment of stimulus variables in learning is the distinction between the physical stimulus as presented and the functional stimulus used by the subject. Lawrence (1963) referred to this functional stimulus as the "stimulus-as-coded" or "sac." Thus, a subject does not respond to a nonsense syllable TUZ as if it were composed of wiggly lines, but as the letters T, U, and Z or the sound /təz/. The way in which he responds determines what aspects of the set of stimuli may be confused. When the stimuli are composed of a number of dimensions, the subject may attend to only a few dimensions, or only a few values on each dimension. This idea of selective attention makes it even more difficult to postulate a one-to-one relationship between the stimulus presented and the functional stimulus (see Shepard, 1963; Shepard & Chang, 1963).

Still another manner of responding can influence the nature of the active stimulus. This is the notion of a mediated response whereby the stimulus itself may produce some encoded form which then elicits another response. The elicited response serves to differentiate this stimulus from all others and thus produces a unique stimulus. Mediated responses or mnemonic devices have a long history in the work on memory. The memory aids of so-called "memory wizards" involve making some unique association with each name or face. To this association, often bizarre in some respects, they can easily associate further material. Similarly, if subjects in PAL and SL experiments are trained to use mnemonic schemes, they perform much better. However, if the items are presented rapidly, there may not be time enough to evoke a mediated response, and the learning may still be relatively slow.[13]

In our discussion of PL, we observed that SLT could not handle discrimination problems in which certain stimulus components were

shared by the two discriminative stimuli. We noted that, by assuming adaptation of these common elements, Bush and Mosteller (1951) and Bourne and Restle (1959) were able to account for the perfect learning which usually occurs in such situations. The Hullian notion of inhibition for the randomly reinforced components shared by the two discriminative stimuli is essentially the same form of solution as adaptation of cues.

In the preceding paragraphs, we mentioned three mechanisms which can be used to explain the same phenomenon. Any theoretical treatment of learning which emphasizes encoding, selective attention, or some kind of mediated response must incorporate these mechanisms into a complete model that explains how the stimulus (or the sac) gets connected to the response. There are a variety of possible association schemes. Those approaches that assume a continuous change in the strength of associations and those approaches based on attentional responses to crucial cues in the stimulus have been applied primarily to discrimination learning in animals and children (Sutherland, 1959; Atkinson, 1961; Zeaman & House, 1963; Lovejoy, 1966). The models we shall discuss here assume discrete changes in stimulus-response connections and have been developed more for human-learning paradigms.

The one-element model assumes that each stimulus can be treated as a whole; that the stimulus as coded is unitary and will be associated in an all-or-none manner with the response. Some stimuli might be composed of three (or, if they are words, more than three) letters, and, if the subject can produce a single sac functional stimulus, all-or-none learning can occur. One obvious way to relax the one-element model and allow for nonunitary stimuli would be to go to a two-element or N-element model and assume that subjects will make a random sampling of the component cues. However, such an assumption might be too restrictive. For example, there is a great deal of evidence (Underwood, 1963) that, while forming an association in PAL

---

[13]There has been a great deal of theoretical discussion concerning stimulus encoding, attention, and mediational responding. Although certainly related to paired-associate and serial learning, these topics are too general for discussion in this chapter. They are discussed in Chapter 17 on discrimination learning. Note also Shepard, Hovland, & Jenkins, 1961; Underwood, 1963; Shepard, 1964; Blough & Millward, 1965; and Wickelgren, 1965, 1966.

experiments, subjects predominantly attend to the first letter of a nonsense syllable. The N-element solution also has the difficulty, mentioned earlier, that perfect learning would not result if there were any common stimulus cues. Thus, if TUZ-3 and TOX-5 are two items in a PAL experiment, and if TUZ and TOX are each considered to be unitary stimuli, they can be learned perfectly in an all-or-none fashion according to the one-element pattern model. However, if they are not learned in an all-or-none fashion, a simple change to the N-element model is inadequate since perfect discrimination between the items could not occur. (We are assuming here that the sac would include common cues.)

Estes (1959a), Estes and Hopkins (1961), and Atkinson and Estes (1963) developed the mixed model to handle situations in which cues overlapped but in which perfect performance eventually resulted. The assumptions of the one-element model are made (see p. 990), but a new axiom is introduced: Before an item is conditioned, the response a subject makes to it is determined by the components which that item has in common with other stimulus patterns which are conditioned. The stimulus description axiom (see Axiom 1, p. 990) is changed slightly as follows:

"The effective stimulus S on any trial is partitioned into subsets $s_i (i = 1, 2, \ldots r)$, where r is the number of response alternatives, and the ith subset contains the elements conditioned to response A_i." This new axiom permits each stimulus to be composed of subsets of elements conditioned to different responses. But how do component cues get conditioned to responses other than the correct response to the item? The basic assumption of the one-element model is that when the stimulus S is conditioned to the correct response, the subject always responds to the pattern as a whole. The components remain conditioned as they were before conditioning of the pattern. The mixed model does not modify this basic assumption. How-

ever, according to the mixed model, before this pattern-conditioning occurs, the various subsets can be conditioned to other responses. If the subset s_i occurs in both stimulus S_1 and S_2, and if S_2 is conditioned as a pattern to response R_1, then s_i in S_1 is conditioned to response R_1 also. If s_i also occurs in S_3, which is also conditioned before S_1, then S_2 or S_3, whichever occurred last, determines to which response s_i is conditioned. Not all subsets of each stimulus are necessarily conditioned. When a component is not conditioned, its contribution to the overall response probability is $1/r$ or a chance probability.

The response rule can now be stated. Assume that stimulus S is not conditioned as a pattern and that there are i cues conditioned to A_i, j cues conditioned to A_j, $j \neq i$, and k cues not conditioned, then

$$P(A_i) = \frac{i + (k/r)}{i + j + k} \qquad (71)$$

$P(A_i | S \text{ conditioned to } A_j \text{ as a pattern}) = 0$
$P(A_i | S \text{ conditioned to } A_i \text{ as a pattern}) = 1.0$

The one-element model developed earlier is consonant with this formula if we assume that there are no overlapping cues. In such a case, conditioning S_j will not condition any of the subsets of S_i, and all subsets of S_i will remain unconditioned. Then, responding is $P(A_i) = 1/r$, where there are r responses.

Let us consider an example introduced by Atkinson and Estes (1963), paralleling closely the two-element model developed earlier. However, in this case, the two elements of each stimulus are not unique to each stimulus. The two stimuli can be represented by the elements a, b, and c: $S_1 = (a,b)$ and $S_2 = (a,c)$. We represent these as ab and ac. The responses are A_1 and A_2; that is, $ab - A_1$ and $ac - A_2$ represent the PAL list. The subsets consist of the individual letters, a, b, c. Before any reinforcements, all subsets are unconditioned. If S_1 is conditioned as a pattern and S_2 is not conditioned, then the components in S_2 are conditioned as follows: $a - A_1$, $c - A_0$; where the A_0 indicates unconditioned. Likewise, if S_2 is conditioned as a pattern and S_1 is not conditioned, $a - A_2$ and $b - A_0$. Finally, when both S_1 and S_2 are conditioned, each pair of components is treated as a single stimulus, $S_1 - A_1$ and $S_2 - A_2$. Hence the subject can be in one of four states of conditioning: (S_1,S_2), $(S_1, \overline{S}_2)$, $(\overline{S}_1,S_2)$, $(\overline{S}_1,\overline{S}_2)$, where the bar indicates an unconditioned stimulus pattern.

Let the vector of state probabilities on trial n be $\mathbf{P}_n = (p_{1,n}, p_{2,n}, p_{3,n}, p_{4,n})$ where $p_{i,n}$ is the probability of being in state i on trial n, $i = 1$, 2, 3, 4, corresponding to the list of states above. To see how response probabilities change, consider a PAL experiment in which there are reinforced trials followed by test trials, RTRTRT. . . . On each reinforced trial R both items are presented. The initial state probabilities are assumed to be (0,0,0,1), for there would be no way for the subject to know the correct response to either stimulus ab or stimulus ac. During the R trial, S_1, S_2, both, or neither of the stimulus patterns might be conditioned. Thus, for the first test trial, the state probabilities would be $[c^2, c(1 - c), (1 - c)c, (1 - c)^2]$. Now the average probability that an A_1 response would be made to the stimulus ab would be $[c^2 + c(1 - c)] \cdot 1 + \frac{1}{4}c(1 - c) + \frac{1}{2}(1 - c)^2$, where we have assumed a guessing probability of $\frac{1}{2}$. The probability that an A_2 response would be made to the stimulus ac would be the same. Note that a subject who learned S_2-A_2 and not S_1-A_1 would show a probability of responding to ab with A_1 of only $\frac{1}{4}$, less than his guessing probability of $\frac{1}{2}$. This reflects the negative transfer incorporated into the design. Yet perfect learning would eventually be accomplished.

The mixed model represents a first attempt to incorporate into an all-or-none model the effects of stimulus overlap. A number of experiments have been run to test the assumptions of the mixed model as well as variations in it. These experiments raise as many questions as they answer and for that reason they are worth reviewing at this time. Estes and Hopkins (1961) ran an experiment investigat-

ing the transfer during learning of stimuli with overlapping components. There were six stimuli and two responses. The PAL list consisted of Russian letters (designated here by a, b, c, and d) paired with a response that consisted of moving a lever switch up or down (designated here as 1 and 2). A cycle consisted of a single random presentation of a-1, b-2, c-1, d-2, and a double presentation of ab-1 and cd-2. After eight cycles and after 16 cycles of these stimuli, test trials were introduced. On the test trials, all single-, double-, and triple-letter combinations of a, b, c, and d were presented. The training items were repeated on the test trials to see if there was any decrease in performance during the test trials. Estes and Hopkins found that, although all six patterns were not completely correct, the subjects learned sufficiently well that further training could be expected to produce perfect learning. The double-letter stimuli were not learned more slowly than the single-letter stimuli. The subjects made more mistakes with components b and c than with components a and d, indicating transfer from the ab and cd patterns. A final result of some interest can be illustrated with the test pattern abd. The elements a, b, and d are the components of the stimulus pattern abd. The pair of letters, ab, in contrast, is referred to as a subpattern of abd because ab constituted a pattern in the original list. The letter pair cb, for example, was not a pattern in the original list and thus is not a subpattern here. The question of interest is whether a subject treats abd as a mixture of three simple components, a, b, and d, or whether a subject treats the stimulus pattern abd as composed of the subpattern ab and the component d. The former is referred to as the "molecular version" of the mixed model whereas the latter is called the "molar-mixed model." Estes and Hopkins found that early in learning, after eight cycles, the subjects seemed to use a mixture of both the molar and molecular models, but after 16 cycles they used the molar model for the most part. This finding complicates the mixed model because transfer from conditioned patterns to components of unconditioned patterns might be in terms of components or subpatterns, and might even be a changing process with trials.

Another experiment by Friedman (1966) confirmed the result noted by Estes and Hopkins in which subjects demonstrated transfer from a pattern such as ab to a simple pattern such as a. He also found transfer from a to ab. However, the results became complicated when the transfer to novel compounds was considered. There were two groups defined by the response assignments. Group 1 had the list a-1, b-2, ab-3, and ba-3, and Group 2 had the list a-1, b-2, ab-2, and ba-2. These lists were expanded so that a total of 12 items occurred in which each of the three responses occurred equally frequently and all were associated with both single- and double-letter patterns. There was strong evidence that Group 2 subjects responded on the basis of subpatterns while Group 1 subjects did not. Friedman interprets the difference on the basis of the list itself. In Group 1, the components, a and b, were always assigned different responses than the double-letter patterns that contained them. In contrast, in Group 2, half of the components were consistent with the double-letter patterns. Thus, subpatterns produced by Group 2 were important; they appeared to be used by the subjects in the transfer tests. A further result of this study was that the frequency with which a given response was reinforced in the presence of a single cue did not determine response probability. This contradicted earlier work by Binder and Feldman (1960).

A more extensive test of the mixed model was made by Friedman and Gelfand (1964). They investigated seven transfer conditions, including double reinforcements, retroactive interference, proactive interference, retroactive facilitation, proactive facilitation and two control groups. The design was essentially a miniature experiment, $R_1 R_2 T$, in which various compound stimuli were reinforced on R_1 and R_2 and tested on T. For example, retro-

active interference consisted of reinforcing ab-1 on R_1, reinforcing ac-2 on R_2, and testing ab on T. The proactive facilitation condition consisted of reinforcing ac-1 on R_1, ab-1 on R_2, and testing ab on T. They modified the mixed model presented earlier by assuming that a STM process was also involved. Thus, in the time from the reinforcement until the test, the pattern can be maintained in STM or lost. If it is maintained, the correct response is made. If lost, then patterns retained in STM with overlapping cues determine the response according to the mixed model. If no patterns with overlapping cues are in STM, then the subject guesses. All in all, the mixed model predicted the results fairly well. Two problems were noted: The proactive interference condition showed a greater loss than predicted and there was a greater number of intrusions in the retroactive interference condition than predicted.

A more elaborate experimental test of the mixed model was reported by Friedman, Trabasso, and Mosberg (1967), who were concerned with a question similar to that raised by Estes and Hopkins when they discussed the molar versus the molecular transfer of components. Here, Friedman et al. assume that a component can be conditioned to more than one response if it is part of more than one conditioned pattern. They also assume that the subject responds to an unconditioned stimulus by choosing only one component from the conditioned components. If no components are conditioned, the subject simply guesses. (This differs from the response rule of the earlier mixed model, which assumed weighted probabilities involving all components simultaneously.) Consider a stimulus with components a and b, both of which have been conditioned to one or more responses because both belong to one or more stimulus patterns which are conditioned. The important question is what determines which of the two conditioned components is chosen. One possible variable here is the overall frequency with which the component cue is presented, the assumption being that frequency makes a cue salient. An earlier study by Binder and Feldman (1960) seems to support such a notion. A second possible variable is relevancy. A *relevant cue* is one that has consistently been paired with the same response; a *partially relevant cue* is one that is paired with more than one response but with unequal probabilities; an *irrelevant cue* is one which is paired with two or more responses with equal frequency. In the selection of a component cue for determining a response, the probability of selecting component *a* or *b* might depend upon the relevancy of the cues, that is, the more relevant cue would be more likely to be selected. In this experiment, Friedman et al. found that relevancy was important and frequency was not.

In an extensive series of studies on the same problem, Binder and Estes (1966) considered only cases of component transfer. Compound stimuli were composed only of components of previously reinforced patterns. Thus, the molar-mixed model is not of interest here. They found that the two main assumptions of the mixed model were supported. These assumptions are (1) the response rule of the mixed model, which assumes a weighted average of the components from other conditioned patterns, and (2) the matching rule, which assumes that if a component has been reinforced with probability π and $1 - \pi$ for two responses, the subject will respond to that component with probability π and $1 - \pi$. One new principle emerged from their work: It was the effects of novelty. Although the mixed model was fairly accurate, deviations that did occur were attributed to this so-called "novelty effect," which amounts to responding to a component that has occurred with less frequency in the set of stimuli. Because such low-frequency cues were often negatively correlated with relevancy, there was some indication that relevancy (or validity, as Binder and Estes call it) was the important variable. However, when relevancy was controlled, the results suggested that low frequency or novelty was

the important factor. It is clear from these studies that further work is needed to untangle the critical variables controlling the subject's selection of components from stimulus compounds. The fact that novelty plays a role in the subject's responses to compound stimuli suggests that more than a simple learning process determines these responses. It may be that a number of different response strategies, as yet unspecified, determine much of the behavior.

Restle (1964) has developed a theoretical point of view compatible either with all-or-none learning or with learning involving a number of successive steps. However, according to Restle, the steps occur, not because the subject learns a number of molecular components, but rather because he uses a number of different learning strategies. Restle's theory often leads to specific models of a given situation, which are similar to those discussed above, but he derives his models from a different fundamental concept of the learning process. First, he assumes that every experience leaves a memory trace. This means that on every trial another trace enters memory (Restle, 1961). The learning problem for the subject is that of finding the relevant trace when it is needed. Traces are not assumed to decay. They become difficult to find because there are many of them to search and search rules fail. Relevant traces are retrieved from memory by "search strategies," which in PAL learning are mnemonic devices. In every learning situation a subject has a set of possible mnemonic devices. When a stimulus item is presented, the subject is assumed to select one of the possible mnemonic devices as an aid to remembering the item when it is next presented. Good mnemonic devices will allow retrieval of the correct answer; poor ones will not. Under some conditions, such as an experiment with practiced subjects who deliberately use mnemonic devices, learning may be all-or-none. Under other conditions, however, such as an experiment with highly confusing stimuli, more than one mnemonic device may have to be relied upon. For example, one mnemonic device may have to be selected to separate stimuli that are very similar and, in addition, another may have to be selected to connect the stimulus and the response together in some idiosyncratic way, simultaneously solving both the discrimination and the learning problems for a set of stimuli. Each item on the list may require a discrimination and an association mnemonic device.

Restle makes two specific assumptions about PAL learning which lead to his model for the PAL paradigm. The first is that the association process is an all-or-none process exactly like that of the one-element model discussed above. The constant probability of a correct response before the last error depends upon the assumption that strategies are either successful or unsuccessful, that there are no partially successful strategies. However, Restle does not believe that this assumption will always be true. The second assumption is that, in the association process, an unsuccessful strategy leads to a failure to recall. Such a failure requires the subject to guess and also to resample a mnemonic device. In contrast, if an unsuccessful strategy is selected in the discrimination process, one item will be confused with another item. Such confusion may not immediately lead to an error, and if it does not, resampling will not occur. However, eventually an error will be made, and the subject will select again from the pool of strategies. Thus, the discrimination process assumes the same model as the hypothesis-selection model discussed under the CL section, whereas the association process assumes the one-element model. These two processes are placed in succession and lead to a Markov chain with the following transition matrix.

The parameter θ is the probability that a subject will select a successful association strategy, which takes the subject out of the guessing state S_0. The parameter d is the probability that the subject will select a successful discrimination strategy. The parameter p is the probability that he will make a correct response in the discrimination states S_1 and S_2. As long as the subject is correct, he will not select a new discrimination mnemonic. When he is wrong, with probability q, he will select another discrimination mnemonic and move to state S_3 where he will make no more errors. Note that if $d = 1$, the one-element model results, and if $\theta = 1$, then, after the subject has guessed on the first trial, the hypothesis-selection model results.

In a further development of these ideas, Restle (1964) has introduced another step to account for response generalization. In this same paper, Restle shows how the theory can be applied to analyze learning situations and to extract the different processes involved in the learning of a reasonably complex PAL experiment. In a later experiment by Polson, Restle, and Polson (1965), a list of 16 stimuli was presented in a standard unpaced anticipation PAL procedure. Eight of the stimuli were so constructed that four pairs of similar stimuli resulted. The other eight stimuli were very dissimilar. There were five responses, all of which were known to the subject. The purpose of the experiment was to show all-or-none learning for the unique stimuli and two-step learning for the confusing stimuli. The results support a two-process model for stimuli which require discrimination, but some discrepancies were found. In particular, it appears that the idea that each S-R association is made before the discrimination phase is not correct. For example, assume that the

$$\mathbf{T} = \begin{array}{c} \\ S_3 \\ S_2 \\ S_1 \\ S_0 \end{array} \begin{array}{|cccc|c} S_3 & S_2 & S_1 & S_0 & P(\text{correct}) \\ \hline 1 & 0 & 0 & 0 & 1 \\ d & q(1-d) & p(1-d) & 0 & 0 \\ 0 & q & p & 0 & 1 \\ \theta d & q\theta(1-d) & p\theta(1-d) & 1-\theta & g \end{array} \qquad (72)$$

two confusing pairs are *ab*-1 and *ac*-2. The model assumes that both *ab* and *ac* must be in either state S_1 or S_2 before confusions can occur. The subject only guesses at items in S_0. However, Polson et al. found that one of the pair of items could be in S_1 or S_2 while the other was in S_0. In the raw scores, one of the items of the pair of confusing items has a string of correct responses, while the other item shows confusion responses followed by a string of random errors.

Restle's approach is an attempt to integrate the theoretical positions of Gibson (1940), who emphasized the role of stimulus generalization and discrimination in PAL, and that of Underwood, Runquist, and Schulz (1959) and Underwood and Schulz (1960), all of whom emphasized response learning. A paper by McGuire (1961) also clearly pointed out the discrimination, association, and response learning factors and analyzed them from a Hullian point of view. Although McGuire's ideas (1961) are very similar to Restle's, the increased mathematical tractability of successive all-or-none processes over mixing habit strengths makes the Markov-chain model potentially more useful. It should be obvious by now that the strategy-selection theory, or variants of it, applies to both the CL experimental situation and the PAL situation.

Greeno and Scandura (1966) have used a verbal concept-learning situation to approach certain issues raised by the mixed model and the strategy-selection model. The mixed model assumes that the total pattern is associated to the correct response, but that transfer to similar stimuli is by components. Thus, any stimulus that contains components of a conditioned stimulus will show either a facilitative or an interference effect, depending on whether it has the same or a different response assignment. The strategy-selection model assumes that any subset of components of the stimulus may be used as the coded stimulus for conditioning. Transfer is limited to stimuli with the same encoded

subset. The more general theory described by Greeno and Scandura (1966) allows for conditioning to any coded subset of components and transfer to any stimulus that contains components that are in the coded subset used in learning. Their analysis shows clearly the interweaving of ideas developed from stimulus-sampling theory and hypothesis-selection theory.

From our discussion of the past few pages, we can glean the major points of a complete theory of PAL. The theory allows for variation in the stimulus-encoding conditions, either by stimulus selection or mnemonics. It considers stimulus interaction factors at the level of the encoded stimulus. The association process is assumed to be all-or-none, either because basic conditioning is all-or-none or because strategy-selection is all-or-none. Short-term memory processes are incorporated when they are necessary. Response learning and differentiation are all taken into account. As yet the theory is somewhat vague in its statement of rules of correspondence; it is used mainly as an analytical device and its application depends to a great extent on the intuition of the experimenter. Although further work on the rules of correspondence is certainly needed, it may turn out to be impossible to state such rules in any single final form, for they no doubt will depend very heavily upon instruction, past learning, and developmental factors. To mention only one possible factor, consider the encoding of stimuli. For college students given the task of learning nonsense syllables, the first letter of the nonsense syllable is very salient. While this is a fact to be explored further, it is not necessarily the kind of information that should accompany a general theory of PAL. Each situation to which the theory is applied will no doubt require boundary conditions and specific rules for its application.

We conclude our discussion of PAL with the description of a theoretical approach that differs greatly in underlying concepts from the theories just described.

An Information-Processing Theory

The Elementary Perceiver and Memorizer (EPAM) was introduced and developed by Feigenbaum (1959, 1963), Feigenbaum and Simon (1961, 1962, 1963) and Simon and Feigenbaum (1964); it consists of two levels of analysis: a *microprocessing level* and a *macroprocessing level*. Hintzman (1968) has developed a one-level information-processing theory which closely parallels the microprocessing level of EPAM. We shall consider Hintzman's version of the microprocessor now and later treat the macroprocessing level with reference to the serial position curve. Hintzman called his information-processing theory the Stimulus and Association Learner (SAL). There are three versions of the theory:

SAL-I is the basic theory, SAL-II allows learning on correct response trials, and SAL-III provides for storage of more than one response for each stimulus by using a push-down store system. The basic assumption about memory is that a discrimination net exists, a sorting tree in which each node of the tree is a test of certain aspects of the stimulus input and in which the terminal nodes contain the response or some encoded form of the response called the *image*. The tests at the nodes are based on the letters of the stimulus although other attributes of the stimulus could also be tested.

Let us follow through the growth of a tree for a PAL list: TUZ-3, MEF-1, TOK-2, TUQ-4, PUZ-5. Assume that TUZ-3 is the input stimulus to the subject. The subject is assumed first

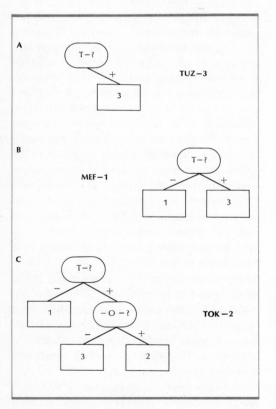

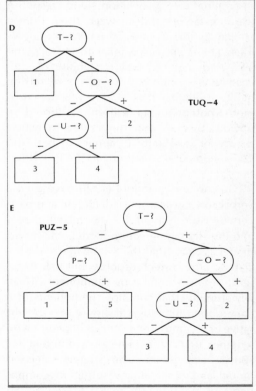

Figure 20.16. Example of PAL learning according to Hintzman's Stimulus and Association Learner (SAL). As each item in the PAL list is presented, new decision nodes are added to the discrimination net.

to grow a discrimination net on the basis of the first letter. Figure 20.16A shows the net after TUZ-3 is presented. If MEF-1 is presented next, the sorting process leads to a negative branch when the stimulus item is checked for T in the first position, and the response 1 is placed on the negative node (Figure 20.16B). When TOK-2 is presented, a positive branch is followed and leads to the response 3, which is wrong. This sets the process to look at the second letter and test if it is an "O." If it is, then TOK-2 is sorted and the previous response is placed on the negative branch (Figure 20.16C). When item TUQ-4 is presented and is sorted incorrectly on the second letter yielding response 3, another negative branch is inserted so that it can be sorted correctly. Note that when TUZ is next presented it will be sorted to the response 3. Another sort on the third letter will be needed to separate TUZ and TUQ. Figures 20.16D and 20.16E illustrate the tree for the items TUQ-4 and PUZ-5. In the original version of the theory (EPAM), the tree determines the response exactly, but Hintzman has added a probabilistic function in SAL. In particular, he assumes that, after an error, a new node is developed with probability *a*. When, with probability $1 - a$, the new node is not developed, then, with probability *b*, the new response replaces the old; with probability $1 - b$, the old response remains.

SAL is not stated as a mathematical theory but rather as a computer program. Thus, fits to data cannot easily be made because methods of estimating parameters are not available. Instead, a reasonable set of parameters (*a* and *b* in this case) is assumed, and the gross characteristics of the data resulting from simulation of a group of subjects are compared with the data resulting from a real experiment. The comparison emphasizes comparable phenomena such as negatively accelerated learning curves, distinct changes in the distribution of the trial of the last error, and so forth. The emphasis is on relating the parameters to the experimental conditions and

procedures. Hintzman has investigated the ability of the model to simulate a large number of experiments in PAL and other human learning procedures and has provided a summary list of results of the tests of his theory. He has found that, as predicted by SAL-I, if the list of stimuli is made more similar, the learning is usually made more difficult. With an increased number of alternatives, SAL-I predicts a stationarity type of curve which rises from $1/r$ to a maximum of .5, where *r* is the number of response alternatives. This prediction has been borne out in experiments run by Hintzman (1967). It has been observed that if items are repeated with a varying number of different items presented between the repetitions, massed repetition becomes ineffective (Greeno, 1964). This is predicted by SAL-I because no learning occurs independently of other pairs in the list. The model also correctly predicted faster relearning and transfer effects arising from the similarity between lists. Three predictions failed. One was the effect of "whole," "part," and "repeated-parts" learning methods. The "whole" method exists when the list or set of items is learned all at once. The "part" method exists when the material to be learned is divided into parts and each is learned separately and then recombined. The "repeated-parts" method is present when the first part is learned, combined with the second, and these learned together, then the third part is combined with the first two, and these learned, and so on. Although Postman and Goggin (1966) found the "repeated-parts" method to be more effective, SAL-I did not produce any differences in the three methods. The second failure was the fact that the length of the list proved to have no effect on the learning rate. Calfee and Atkinson (1965) showed that a short-term memory process helped to account for this effect, and Hintzman suggests that a STM process might have to be added to SAL to account for the list-length effect (see below). Finally, SAL-I failed to predict positive transfer in an A-B, A-C paradigm (see Chapter 21). Hintzman does not know exactly what aspects of SAL-I cause these failures. Certain weaknesses of SAL-I have been corrected by more elaborate versions which we shall review below.

As we have seen, a wide variety of learning experiments have been tested with the SAL model. Although the tests are not quantitative, the fact that certain main effects due to gross variables such as stimulus similarity, number of response alternatives, and massed versus spaced repetition of items are qualitatively handled is impressive. One point that should be emphasized is the similarity between this model and the ideas developed in the general model by Greeno and Scandura (1966). Where Greeno and Scandura talk about encoding, SAL-I relies on the order in which the letters of the stimuli are noticed by the subjects. SAL-I makes a specific assumption about the type of encoding response, whereas Greeno and Scandura leave this less well specified. However, because SAL might require a different encoding rule for a different kind of stimulus, the two theories are really not so different in this respect. A second point of similarity is the fact that errors require a new encoding scheme in both. In SAL-I, another aspect of the stimulus is added, whereas in the general model a new sample of cues is selected. Of course, differences in the combinations of these common ideas make the theories different. The exact differences have not yet been clearly stated; these differences and the useful constructs in each will have to be sorted out in the future.

Hintzman has developed two other models that increase the flexibility of SAL-I. SAL-II was developed to allow overlearning to occur. According to SAL-I, once a verbal list is learned perfectly, no further learning occurs. The perfect learning may involve only the first letter of each stimulus item. In SAL-II, learning can continue to occur on correct trials. After a correct response, the next letter in line in the noticing order is added to the discrimination net with a probability c. This allows the creation of empty terminal nodes. When these empty nodes are encountered later, the model assumes that the subject guesses. SAL-II has been successful in handling results from proactive and retroactive transfer paradigms.

The third version of SAL, SAL-III, introduced a new idea to all-or-none models. The Hullian models had assumed that two responses could be associated with the same stimulus, thus leading to the concept of the habit hierarchy in which various responses would compete with each other. All-or-none models have to assume that either one response or the other is associated to a given stimulus. The SAL-III model assumes a so-called "push-down store" (PDS). At each response node, when a response is stored, the previous response is not erased but is "pushed down." With the passage of time, or with interfering factors, the more recently stored responses are pushed off the stack and lost forever. This process, added in SAL-III, allows better predictions to be made of proactive and retroactive effects with time. In particular, with the passage of time, proactive interference increases and retroactive interference decreases. The assumption of a push-down store also accounts for the effect of distributed practice. The interaction of the PDS and the discrimination net leads to four additional predictions, which further extend the generality of the model: (1) If a subject is simply required to recognize a response among a set of responses, he has a higher probability of being correct than if he has to recall the correct response from memory. SAL-III accounts for this. In recognition, the list at each node is examined and if the item is anywhere on the list, recognition occurs. In recall, the subject does not examine the entire list; only the top item is retrieved. (2) Studies in which second and third guesses are allowed show that the second guesses made by subjects are better than chance; this result can be accounted for by the PDS and the discrimination net (see Binsford & Gettys, 1965). (3) The SAL-III model yields results in good agreement with those reported by Barnes and Underwood (1959) for the modified-modified free-recall procedure. This is a paradigm in which the first-learned list and the second-learned list consist of the same stimulus items, designated A, but with different responses, designated B and C, respectively. This procedure is usually called the A-B, A-C paradigm. When learning the second list, the subjects are asked to give both the B and the C response to the stimulus A. The experimenter can observe the learning of the C responses and the forgetting of the B responses from trial to trial. (4) Finally, Hintzman assumes that the depth of the responses in the PDS determines the latency of a response.

Our summary of the SAL models has been rather cursory, but perhaps we have been able to illustrate the wide range of phenomena that are at least qualitatively predictable by them. Certainly, the results of this approach justify further serious consideration of the information-processing models.

Serial Learning: Specific Issues

Our discussion of PAL involved general questions of response learning, association processes, and stimulus discrimination. The same questions arise in SL, but the analysis of SL has not reached the same level of precision as that of PAL. The major difficulty seems to be defining the functional stimulus in SL. When we do not know what the stimulus is or how to characterize it, the nature of the association process remains very unclear. Furthermore, the fact that the stimuli and the responses are physically the same leads to further problems. If the functional stimulus is determined, is it identical with the functional response? In general, it appears that it is not identical, for the subject must respond in a way isomorphic to the actual physical stimulus in order to demonstrate learning. Finally, there are many facts about SL that suggest that the fundamental notion of forming a S-R bond simply does not work for SL learning.

Earlier we presented a brief view of the Lepley-Hull analysis of SL. Its main features included the idea that the stimulus for item i was the preceding series of items, $i-1$, $i-2$, . . . and that this stimulus was associated by trace conditioning with items $i+1$, $i+2$, ... Nonreinforcement of the remote associations eventually eliminated error responses due to remote associations. These basic assumptions were interdependent and provided a neat explanation of the serial-position effect. This theoretical view went without serious challenge until the late 1950s. Since that time, however, both the definition of the stimulus and the idea of remote associations have been strongly attacked on empirical grounds.

The functional stimulus in SL The experimental studies conducted to determine the functional stimulus in a list of items learned serially assume a basic similarity between the paired-associate procedure and the serial procedure. A stimulus is presented to which the subject is to make an appropriate response. In serial learning, the response itself becomes the next stimulus. The basic assumption of the Lepley-Hull theory is that an association is formed between adjacent items on a serial list. If serial learning is indeed the formation of a succession of associations, then there should be a large amount of transfer from a list of paired associates A–B, C–D, E–F, . . . when it is relearned as a serial list A–B–C–D–E–F. . . . Likewise, after learning a serial list, transfer to a PAL situation with pairs composed of adjacent items of the serial list should produce positive transfer. Underwood (1963) reviewed a number of studies and raised the question of whether SL is learned as a chain of associations. One of the studies reviewed by Underwood which bears on this issue is an early one by Primoff (1938), who found that a paired-associate list which involved items used as both stimuli and responses, the so-called "double-function list," was extremely difficult to learn. An example of a double-function list is one composed of pairs A–B, B–C, C–D, D–E. A single-function list of the same items would be A–B, C–D, ... Both could be made into the serial list A–B–C–D–E. A serial list is, according to the chaining assumption, a double-function list of paired associates. Yet, as Underwood points out, a serial list is much easier to learn than a comparable single-function list of paired associates. However, in the paired-associate double-function list, a response item does not occur as a stimulus immediately after it has occurred as a response. Underwood suggests that the difficulty with the double-function PAL procedure may be due to the fact that subjects in the standard PAL procedure tag the stimulus items and the response items differently, whereas the double-function list mixes these tags, thereby causing a large amount of interference. In the serial list, on the other hand, the systematic repetition eliminates the need for tagging.

In a number of experiments (Young, 1959; Jensen, 1962c) designed to study transfer from a paired-associate list to a serial list, some positive transfer has been found. Negative transfer also occurs to an even greater extent (Young, Milauckas, & Bryan, 1963). Thus, subjects can use the associations learned in a PAL task to aid their learning of a related SL task. It should be emphasized that the amount of transfer is not very great.

The second class of studies run to investigate the functional stimulus in serial learning reverses the transfer procedure. First a serial list is learned, and then either a list of single- or double-function paired associates is made from the items of the serial list. One would expect a large amount of transfer if successive items on a serial list were associated. However, Young (1961), Young and Casey (1964), and Jensen and Rohwer (1965) found even less transfer. Nonetheless, in two more recent experiments, Postman and Stark (1967) and Shuell and Keppel (1967) conclude that, although serial learning involves more than a single process, preceding items *are* among the effective functional stimuli. However, in Postman and Stark's experiment, the maximum transfer occurred for a group of subjects who were explicitly instructed about the na-

ture of the transfer task, and they showed only a 61 percent transfer. Another equivalent group of subjects who were not instructed about the transfer procedure showed only 24 percent transfer. It is possible that some of those subjects not instructed saw the nature of the transfer and provided the transfer which did occur. If this was the case, we could argue that a basic association process was not involved, but rather that rule-following behavior might be responsible.

Within the context of stimulus-response theories, there are two major hypotheses concerning the nature of the effective stimulus in SL. The first is that the effective stimulus is composed of some sequence of preceding stimulus items. Exactly how many preceding items are involved and how they enter into the association has not been spelled out. Although Young (1962) did not find support for this hypothesis, Horowitz and Izawa (1963) found that clusters of items could serve as stimuli when the items in the list were not strong associates of each other. The second hypothesis is that the effective stimulus is the position of the item in the list. According to this hypothesis, the subject learns a response to each position. Among the problems with this hypothesis is the fact that subjects have difficulty stating exactly where they are in a serial list at a given point. Further, a serial list can be learned even if each item is presented one position earlier on each successive trial; that is, if trial 1 is A–B–C–D–E, trial 2 is B–C–D–E–A, and so on. In tests of transfer using position as the stimulus cue, there is the possibility that the subject quickly recites the serial list until he finds the stimulus associated with the position, and then relies on this stimulus to respond correctly. However, Ebenholtz (1963a, b) and Young (1962) have produced evidence supporting the interpretation that position is used as a stimulus cue. Two other hypotheses, combining these major hypotheses, have been suggested. One assumes a sequential stimulus for the ends of the list and a positional stimulus for the middle part of the list (Young, Patterson, & Benson, 1963). The other assumes a positional stimulus for the ends of the list and a sequential stimulus for the middle positions (Ebenholtz, 1963b). Actually, both investigators would allow both types of cues throughout the list but assume that the relative weights of the positional cue and sequential cue change from the ends to the middle of the list.

The difficulty in identifying the stimulus in a serial list is perhaps symptomatic of a serious theoretical flaw. Historically, a number of researchers have raised questions about the explanation that serial learning is based on the associative chain or trace conditioning. Primoff (1938) stated flatly that PAL and SL are different. Lashley (1951), in a brilliant paper which approached serial behavior from a very broad point of view, dismissed the simple chaining interpretation of serial learning. His argument ranged from an analysis of language behavior, through motor responses, to physiological aspects of serial responses. Jensen (1962a, b, c, d) and Jensen and Rohwer (1965) take the view that serial learning is not an associative chain. Jensen's theoretical view is compatible with Lashley's in that both assume that there is a difference between stimulus-response associations and response integration. Instead, they propose that an integrated response is encoded as a single unit and not as a string of stimuli and responses. Furthermore, they suggest that the series of responses is manipulated as a single unit, and an impulse to make a given integrated response is sufficient to evoke the whole serial chain. Presumably, such an integrated response would be learned in a different way than a list of discrete, independent stimulus-response associates. To account for the results of the transfer experiments described above, Jensen relies heavily on the idea of set. If the subject keeps his set of the original learning (PAL or SL), some transfer may occur to the new situation (SL or PAL). However, maintaining a paired-associate set when the task involves serial learning (or vice versa) may, in the long run, cause more learning difficulty. The sets are different, and trying to learn while using the inappropriate set can be

very difficult. Jensen feels that the failure to control set in most experiments accounts for the wide range of inconsistent results. One strong piece of evidence in favor of two types of learning is the magnitude of the difference in the difficulty of SL and PAL. A 9-item serial list should have eight associations; yet it is learned as fast as a 4-pair list of paired associates, even when the latter is unpaced and the serial list is presented at 3 sec per item (Jensen, 1962c).

Remote associations Ebbinghaus (1885) first introduced the idea of remote associations. He asserted that every item was associated with every other item in the list and that the strength of the association was inversely proportional to the distance between the items. This basic idea was incorporated into the Lepley-Hull hypothesis and was given a rationale in terms of trace conditioning. Thus, the idea of remote associations is basic to studies of SL, not only because it has existed since the first investigations, but also because it plays a central role in accounting for the serial-position effect. Despite its well-entrenched position in the SL literature, Slamecka (1964) has challenged the basic idea itself. We review his arguments against the experiments supporting remote associations because his arguments lead to a conclusion in accord with the position taken by Lashley (1951), Jensen (1962b), and Feigenbaum and Simon (1962). The three experimental procedures that have been used to support the assumption of remote association are the method of derived lists, the association method, and the method of anticipatory errors (McGeoch & Irion, 1952).

Ebbinghaus' belief in remote associations was based on the procedure of derived lists. A derived list is a new serial list derived from an original serial list by some simple scheme such as taking every other item to form the new list (second order), or taking every third item (third order), and so on. For example, ACEBD is a second-order list derived from ABCDE. If remote associations are formed,

Ebbinghaus argued, then a second-order list would be easier to learn than a third-order list, which in turn would be easier than a fourth-order list. This is the case because, the further that item i is from item j, the weaker the association between items i and j. The remoteness of items in an ith-order list is i. Slamecka makes two crucial points. The first is that Ebbinghaus was his own subject and knew how the lists were constructed. The second point is that many later experiments have failed to show a difference among lists of different orders. Slamecka concludes that the lists are ordered in ease of learning according to remoteness only because the order or rule for making up the list is less likely to be perceived by the subjects if it is more remote. He ran two experiments demonstrating this interpretation very clearly. Thus, the method of derived lists gives the expected results because subjects use a rule to control their performance.

The association method for testing remote associations is quite direct. After a serial list has been learned, each item on the list is presented to the subject, who is to respond with the first item that comes to mind. The response given is coded for its degree of remoteness in the original list from the presented stimulus. Even before Slamecka's analysis, two problems had arisen with this method. One was that the latency of the responses did not correspond with the remoteness analysis, that is, low-order remoteness was not accompanied by short latencies. On the contrary, low-order remoteness was accompanied by longer latencies (McGeoch & Irion, 1952, p. 95). The other problem was the fact that early researchers had used the absolute number of associations to indicate the relationship between remoteness and frequency of response; that is, more remote items occur less frequently (Raskin & Cook, 1937). However, there is an inverse relationship between the degree of remoteness and the number of items at that degree of remoteness. For example, in a list of length N, the maximum degree of remoteness is $N - 1$,

and there is only one item at that degree. At the $N - 2$ degree of remoteness, there are two remote associations, response $N - 1$ to item 1 and response N to item 2. According to Slamecka, correcting for the different absolute number of items at each degree of remoteness yielded a **U**-shaped function instead of the traditional monotonic function. He postulated that these results were due to the relative frequency with which responses had been given in the learning of the serial list. Because of the serial-position function, the items in the middle of the list were not given as responses until near the end of learning. Thus, these items were given as responses only a few times, whereas the items near the ends of the list were given from the very first trial on. Slamecka made up a list in which the items were duplicated in such a way that each item corresponded in frequency to an item from a serial list of the same length. The six items were duplicated 25, 10, 3, 1, 3, and 10 times. Subjects were shown the list of 52 items in a random order and told to look carefully at each. When they were later presented with the items and told to respond with the first item that came to mind, a **U**-shaped function similar to that he had observed in the association method was obtained. Thus Slamecka contended that the method of association does not support the idea of remote associations because the associations can be explained on the basis of past frequency or experience. Although his experiment does not rule out the presence of remote associations, the fact that they can be explained on the basis of a potent variable such as frequency certainly puts the burden of proof on the proponents of remote association.

The method of anticipatory errors considers all error responses made during the learning of a serial list. These error responses can be classified according to whether they are anticipatory or perseverative. Anticipatory errors are those responses to item i, but appropriate for a later item, whereas perseverative errors are those made to item i but appropriate for an earlier item. In general, very few perseverative errors are made compared to anticipatory errors; the errors follow the inverse function with respect to remoteness, and they decline with learning. Also, errors made early in learning are likely to be more remote than errors made later on in learning.

Slamecka did not accept the findings described above (which were confirmed in his own experiments) as support for the idea of remote associations. Instead, he argued that the findings reflect the fact that the subject must learn the items themselves. In the beginning, only the first few and last few items are known. Because the subject has just seen the most recent items, he does not guess these when he is asked to guess what items will occur next; instead, he guesses from the other items he knows, which are likely to be those at the end of the list. Thus, early in learning, many high-order remote associations relative to the total number of remote associations are produced. As learning increases, the subject's uncertainty decreases, and the middle items are the only ones he remains uncertain about. Responses from the middle of the list to stimuli from the middle of the list must be of a relatively low order of remoteness. This is a plausible explanation for the change in the relative frequency of high- and low-order remote associations which does not require the assumption of remote associations.

Needless to say, such an uncompromising attack on so fundamental a principle has not gone without a counterattack. Dallett (1965) and Bugelski (1965) contend that there are flaws in Slamecka's arguments and that he has gone too far in his conclusions. Nonetheless, when we consider Slamecka's arguments along with the difficulties encountered in identifying the stimulus in serial learning, doubts about the traditional view must inevitably arise. We can conclude by presenting an information-processing model which seems to be in accord with the newer approach to serial learning.

The serial-position curve—an information-processing explanation The serial-position function plots some measure of the number of errors against the items according to the position of the items in the list. It has been found that the curve rises to a maximum point just past the middle item of the list and then declines again. Usually the last item causes more errors than the first—about the same number of errors as for the second item. Historically, the practice had been to plot the

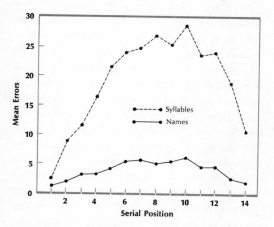
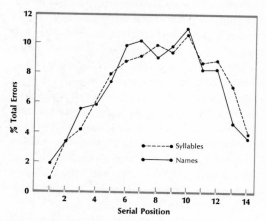

Figure 20.17. Serial-position effects in lists of 14 nonsense syllables and in (easier) lists of 14 familiar names. The left figure, plotted in terms of the absolute numbers of errors, seems to show a much more marked piling up of errors in the middle of the more difficult list (quite in accordance with the inhibition theory). But when the errors in each serial position are expressed as percentages of the total number of errors for the whole list, the two curves appear identical. (McCrary & Hunter, 1953.)

absolute number of errors, but McCrary and Hunter (1953) found that if they plotted the percentage of the errors at each position relative to the total number of errors (as in Fig. 20.17), absolute error curves of very different levels and shapes became identical (with the same length list, of course). Thus, over a wide range of variables, relative errors at each position remain constant. However, as Feigenbaum and Simon (1962) have pointed out, there are ways of distorting the shape of the serial-position curve. If one item is made clearly distinct from other items (Von Restorff effect), it will be learned much faster. Or, for example, if half the list is colored red and the other half black, the curve shows a large decrease in errors on the last item of the red half of the list and the first item of the black half. This occurs right at the point where the maximum number of errors is usually observed (Wishner, Shipley, & Hurvich, 1957).

On the basis of these and a few other facts about the serial-position curve, Feigenbaum and Simon have developed their information-processing theory of serial learning. Earlier we presented Hintzman's information-processing theory for rote learning, which is a modified version of the microprocessing system of the Elementary Perceiver and Memorizer (EPAM) first introduced by Feigenbaum (1959). The original theory also contained a macroprocessing system which worked in conjunction with the microprocessing system. The serial-position effect is primarily accounted for by the macroprocessing system. We discuss the macroprocessing system here and the reader can see how the microprocessing and macroprocessing systems interact. We follow the Feigenbaum and Simon paper (1962). (The reader should refer to page 975 for a review of information-processing models.)

Postulate 1. Serial mechanism. The central processing (CP) mechanism is assumed to be serial, that is, it processes one item at a time. When, as in SL or PAL, many items require processing, the CP takes them in some order.

Postulate 2. Fixed processing time. Each item requires a fixed amount of time to be processed. (At this point, the microprocessing aspect of the general theory comes in. Each item selected by the CP must be sent through a discrimination net such as that described in the Hintzman model. The time required for this process may vary but has some fixed minimum. The CP must allow enough time for the item to be sorted through the discrimination net.)

Postulate 3. Immediate memory. An immediate memory or short-term memory system holding about seven basic "chunks" is assumed. To apply the theory here, we have to postulate what the basic unit of analysis is for the subject. For most nonsense-syllable work, Feigenbaum and Simon consider the letters of the syllables as basic units; about six letters or two CVC nonsense syllables can be contained in the memory buffer. They are not very explicit about the duration of items in the STM, but presumably if they decay in time, CP can restore or rehearse them so that, if no new items are presented, the six items remain permanently in STM.

Postulate 4. Anchor points. This very basic postulate of the system has been added primarily to handle SL and the serial-position curve. An anchor point is related to the idea of attention. It is assumed that certain stimulus items are selected by the subject in order to provide a point of reference for other items. For serial learning, the attention is assumed to be focussed on specific items or positions of the list, items at the so-called "anchor points." In the ordinary SL task, before any learning, these anchor points are at the first and last items. Feigenbaum and Simon assume that the items are learned in a systematic way. Once the first and last items have been learned, they in turn define anchor points for items adjacent to them. For the serial-learning task, another, more specific assumption is made. It states that the first and second items are learned first. Then either the third or the last item is learned, each with probability $\frac{1}{2}$. If the third is learned, then the fourth or last is picked for learning, again each with probability $\frac{1}{2}$. This particular mechanistic ordering of how items are learned produces a very reasonable serial-position curve (Feigenbaum & Simon, 1961).

Although response-learning and guessing factors must be brought into the picture (Slamecka's ideas are relevant here), the basic processing of the system gives a good account of most facts known about the serial-learning curve. The effects of coloring different parts of the list, or of introducing some salient cue to a single item, are incorporated into the scheme by assuming that they change the anchor points. Feigenbaum and Simon note that their theory is an all-or-none theory and treat Rock's and Estes' results as consistent with theirs. Feigenbaum and Simon feel that their theory, in both its microprocessing and macroprocessing versions, represents a new approach to verbal learning.

The successes of information-processing theories do not invalidate all earlier conditioning-type theories. Rather, they indicate that learning processes can be analyzed at a number of levels. Different theories may be needed at different levels. Perhaps for higher-level analyses, we need theories such as the information-processing theories with their memory, attentional, and organizational processes. The role of variables such as frequency may be handled by the conditioning theories. Ultimately, we may hope for an integration of the findings from all levels.

Leo Postman

TRANSFER, INTERFERENCE AND FORGETTING*

21

Learning is a cumulative process. The more knowledge and skills an individual acquires, the more likely it becomes that his new learning will be shaped by his past experiences and activities. An adult rarely, if ever, learns anything completely new; however unfamiliar the task that confronts him, the information and habits he has built up in the past will be his point of departure. Thus transfer of training from old to new situations is part and parcel of most, if not all, learning. In this sense the study of transfer is coextensive with the investigation of learning. However, it is only when the conditions of prior training are brought under experimental control that the contributions of transfer can be precisely evaluated. Experimental studies of transfer are, therefore, concerned with the influence of circumscribed learning experiences on subsequent performance in specific test tasks. It is clear that experimentally produced effects represent at best only a small fraction of the total transfer from past training which the individual brings to the test situation. Manipulation of the subject's learning history on a limited scale may nevertheless permit the identification of some of the dimensions and mechanisms of transfer.

*The material considered in this chapter is restricted to studies of verbal learning and memory.

Nature of Transfer Effects

A study of transfer is by definition a two-stage experiment comprising a training phase and a test phase. The basic question is how the training provided during the first stage influences performance during the second stage. The observed effects may be zero, positive, or negative: The prior activity may fail to influence performance in the test situation, facilitate it, or interfere with it. The presence of significant transfer effects, whether positive or negative, implies that at least some of the responses established during the training phase are carried over to the test task. The effects are positive or negative depending on whether these responses are appropriate or inappropriate in the new situation. The emphasis in the formulation and interpretation of experiments on transfer is, therefore, on the similarities and differences in the requirements of the successive tasks.

What tasks are functionally similar depends on the nature of the dispositions that the individual carries over from one situation to the next. Historically, theoretical controversy centered on the question of the breadth of the changes produced by practice. At one extreme was the doctrine of formal discipline, which held that such "faculties" as memory, judgment, and reasoning could be strengthened by exercise on the appropriate materials. Learning tasks were considered to be similar to the extent that they called for use of the same faculty. Mathematics and law both engage the individual's power of reasoning, so that training in one of these subjects should be a preparation for success in the other. This view had, of course, a profound influence on the development of school curricula. Diametrically opposed was the theory of "identical elements," espoused by Thorndike (1903), according to which the amount of transfer is determined by the degree to which performance in successive situations depends on the same associative connections.

Early experimental studies designed to decide between the opposed conceptions of transfer appeared to give clear support to the theory of identical elements. A few relevant studies are summarized below. Today the controversy in its original form is largely of historical interest. In the context of empirical investigations of transfer the concept of mental faculty was intractable to manipulation and measurement. The theory of identical elements insisted that transfer effects reflect concrete and circumscribed changes in behavioral tendencies; in that sense the theory gained wide acceptance, even though Thorndike's description of the elements lost its currency. From a historical point of view it is interesting to note than Thorndike's position was not as "atomistic" as the notion of identical elements implies. He suggested that among the major components of transfer are "ideas about aims and ideas of method and general principle" as well as "associations involving elementary facts of experience" (1903, p. 81). In modern studies of transfer it has remained useful to maintain a distinction between the transfer of general principles or strategies of learning on the one hand, and of specific associations on the other.

Transfer as a Measure of What Is Learned

Instead of focusing on the cumulative effects of practice one may use the transfer test as an analytic device for determining what has been learned in the training phase. When a task is mastered under controlled conditions of practice, interpretative questions often arise about the nature of the habits or dispositions that the subject acquires and that allow him to satisfy the experimental requirements. To answer such questions we construct transfer tasks that distinguish between alternative hypotheses about what has in fact been learned. The procedures used to determine the functional stimulus in paired-associate learning will serve to illustrate this use of transfer tests and at the same time exhibit the limitations on the conclusions that can be based on the results of such tests.

Suppose a subject learns a paired-associate list in which the stimuli are compounds composed of distinctive elements, such as nonsense syllables presented against colored backgrounds; the responses are words or digits. When the subject has mastered the list, the question remains open as to how many responses were associated with single elements (syllables or colors) rather than with the total compounds. As long as the elements are consistently paired, the subject can use one of the components as the cue to the correct response and disregard the other component. The compound is the nominal stimulus defined by the experimenter, but one of the elements may be selected as the functional stimulus by the subject (see Underwood, 1963). The extent to which such stimulus selection has occurred is determined by means of transfer tests in which the subject is required to give the prescribed responses to one or the other of the elements, such as syllables alone or colors alone, or to the total compound. The available evidence shows clearly that the more meaningful element will, in fact, be selected in the majority of cases. In the transfer phase the colors alone are as effective as the total compound in eliciting the correct responses, whereas performance drops to an extremely low level when the syllables alone are presented (Underwood, Ham, & Ekstrand, 1962). It must be recognized, however, that transfer tests for cue selection provide information only about the stimuli which are functional at the end of practice. Stimulus selection that occurs early in learning but is abandoned in the later stages of acquisition will not be detected by such tests. It has, in fact, been found that subjects who practice cue selection up to the point of the initial mastery of a list begin to develop associations to the nonpreferred, redundant elements of the stimulus during a period of overlearning (James & Greeno, 1967). To obtain information about the course of selection, transfer tests would have to be administered after varying amounts of practice. The basic point here is that tests of transfer can be used to determine what has been learned after a given amount of training but usually

yield far from conclusive information about how the terminal stage of mastery was achieved.

We have identified two general objectives of experimental studies of transfer: the assessment of the effects of prior training on the mastery of new tasks and the determination of what has been learned as a result of a given learning experience. The two problems are, of course, closely interrelated. There is, however, an important difference in emphasis between the two types of experiments. In one case the focus is on the conditions of improvement in the test stage. In the other case the characteristics of the first task are under investigation. The characteristics of interest, such as stimulus selection, may or may not be related to efficiency of performance.

Relation of Transfer to Interference and Forgetting

In the history of research on verbal learning the study of transfer and the analysis of the process of forgetting have been closely linked in terms of both experimental operations and theoretical interpretations. This continuity becomes readily apparent when we consider the classical paradigm of negative transfer in which different, unrelated responses are successively learned to the same stimuli (A–B, A–D). Under these conditions the prior acquisition of A–B usually retards the formation of the association A–D. In addition, the association of different responses to the same stimulus serves to impair the retention of both the first and second task, as compared to appropriate control treatments in which a single list is learned and recalled. Thus, there are negative transfer effects attributable to associative interference in the learning of A–D, retroactive inhibition of A–B, and proactive inhibition of A–D. Because they are produced by the same experimental operations, negative transfer and interference in recall came to be viewed as complementary manifestations of the same underlying process (McGeoch, 1942). Moreover, since it was possible to control the amount of forgetting in the laboratory by manipulating the conditions of prior and interpolated learning, it was parsimonious to infer that all forgetting is the result of habit interference (McGeoch, 1932a; Underwood & Postman, 1960). That is, whether forgetting occurs inside or outside the laboratory, interference between successive learning activities may be responsible for the retention losses. The interference hypothesis has not only been highly productive of empirical research but has also occupied a focal position in theoretical discussions of forgetting. Thus interference theory provides a convenient point of departure for a discussion of the phenomena of forgetting. It is because of these theoretical and empirical continuities that the problems of transfer, interference, and forgetting are considered together in this chapter.

DESIGN OF TRANSFER EXPERIMENTS

The basic question that an experimental study of transfer is designed to answer is whether and in what ways the manipulated conditions of prior training influence performance in a test task. Let A represent the training phase and B the test phase. The desired information is provided by the comparison of an experimental and a control group:

	Training	Test
Experimental	A	B
Control	—	B

The test task is the same for the two groups; the difference between the two treatments lies entirely in the presence or absence of prior training. As in any other experiment, the validity of the conclusions about the effects of the independent variable depends on the comparability of the groups subjected to different treatments. To obtain groups of equal ability the investigator must rely on appropriate sampling procedures and random assignment of subjects to conditions. It is also possible to equate subjects on characteristics known or presumed to be related to performance in the critical task.

The control group is represented as receiving no prior training. A more precise statement is that the activity of the control group is not manipulated before the test on B. Actually these subjects engage in a variety of activities during the period preceding the test that are assumed to be irrelevant to their subsequent performance (see Murdock, 1957, p. 314). (The same is true for the activities of the experimental subjects prior to the start of training, but our present concern is only with the period immediately preceding the transfer test.) A more complete description of the design is, therefore, as follows, where X stands for unknown and presumably irrelevant prior activities:

	Training	Test
Experimental	A	B
Control	X	B

A difference between the experimental and the control group in the performance of B permits the inference that A is a source of transfer. The exact nature of the transfer effect cannot, however, be specified. Training on A may not only establish specific habits that are carried over to B but may also serve to adapt the subject to the experimental situation and the requirements of the learning task. The observed transfer is, therefore, likely to reflect a combination of nonspecific and specific habits and skills acquired during the training phase. When interest centers on the specific transfer effects attributable to the similarity relations between successive tasks, nonspecific practice must be given to the control group. If N is a task assumed to provide such practice, the design takes the form:

	Training	Test
Experimental	A	B
Control	N	B

If both control conditions (X and N) are included, the difference between them provides an estimate of the nonspecific or general transfer effects. The choice of task N will depend on the investigator's assumptions about the potential sources of nonspecific transfer from task A. Whenever possible, tasks A and N should be equivalent in all respects except for the specific similarity relations to B. Thus, in studies of transfer between lists of paired associates both the stimulus and the response terms of the training list (N) in the control condition are unrelated to those in the test list (B), whereas there is a specified degree of similarity between the units in the two tasks (A and B) in the experimental condition.

The similarity relations between successive tasks may be such as to make it an arbitrary matter in which order the two activities are carried out. That is, with respect to the variables under study the experimental sequences AB and BA are equivalent. A typical example is provided by two lists of paired associates in which the stimuli are the same but the responses are unrelated. The variable defining the condition of transfer is the relation between the successive responses. If the same rules are used in the construction of the two lists, there is no basis for distinguishing between the alternative sequences. For purposes of increasing the generality of the findings, it is advisable to use both sequences equally often in a balanced design. It is possible, of course, that for unknown reasons the observed transfer effects may not be strictly symmetrical; whatever differences between the two sequences are found would have to be attributed to uncontrolled sources of error. Under these circumstances it is possible to dispense with the control group if the investigator's interest is limited to the question of whether or not there is a net transfer effect. With half the group learning the tasks in the order AB and the other half in the order BA, each subject serves under both a control and an experimental treatment, and the two acquisition functions can be compared directly.

The situation changes when the successive tasks are known not to be equivalent, as, for example, when they differ in difficulty or in response requirements. Contrary to what has been implied in the literature, it is not appropriate to balance the order of tasks and pool the results for the two sequences under these circumstances. The design in question is usually presented in the following form:

	Training	Test
Group I	A	B
Group II	B	A

The difference between the training phase and the test phase for the combined groups is then used as a measure of the net change attributable to prior practice. The basic objection to this design is that transfer effects cannot be assumed to be symmetrical when there are systematic differences between tasks. Pooling the results for the two groups may, therefore, mask significant effects associated with order. For example, transfer is not symmetrical between serial and paired-associate learning when the sequential order of items is preserved in the successive lists (Young, 1959). Whenever the task requirements in the training and in the test phase are not equivalent, the transfer effects in each direction—from A to B and from B to A—must be evaluated separately.

In light of the preceding discussion it will be useful to distinguish explicitly between two cases of counterbalancing of tasks in a transfer design. When the tasks are equivalent, counterbalancing represents a sampling of conditions and increases the generality of the conclusions. Failure to obtain symmetry of transfer contributes to the unexplained error variance. When the tasks are not equivalent, counterbalancing has the effect of averaging out differences associated with the order of practice, that is, it serves to eliminate systematic sources of variance from consideration.

The designs discussed so far apply to situations in which new tasks, presumably encountered by the subject for the first time, are practiced in both stages of the experiment, such as successive lists of paired associates in studies of verbal transfer. Such studies are categorized as employing the method of successive practice; the dependent variables are measures of acquisition of the test task. Historically, experiments on transfer have also been concerned with the effects of practice on abilities which the subject brings to the experimental situation but which are capable of improvement. In order to evaluate the effects of practice on such abilities, both the initial and the terminal level of performance must be assessed. When the degree of change in an existing ability is the dependent variable, the experimental design characteristically has the following form:

	Pretest	Training	Posttest
Experimental	A	B	A (A')
Control	A	X	A (A')

The tasks used in the pretest and the posttest must be either identical (A) or strictly equivalent (A and A'). The experimental group is given practice on B, whereas the control group is not; the latter engages in irrelevant activities (X), which may or may not be prescribed by the investigator. The administration of the pretest makes it possible to determine the initial comparability of the groups; in many investigations the experimental and the control subjects are matched on the basis of the pretest. If the match is perfect, the difference on the posttest provides a direct measure of transfer; if there are initial differences, the amounts of change are compared.

A widely recognized shortcoming of this design is the practice afforded by the pretest, which by itself is likely to result in improved performance on the posttest. It is true that the gains attributable to the pretest should be equal under the experimental and the control treatment, so that there is no bias in the evaluation of the transfer effect. However, if the practice curve for the ability under study is negatively accelerated, the pretest may

account for a substantial proportion of the total possible improvement, and the measure of transfer becomes relatively insensitive to the effects of additional practice. Another difficulty was pointed out by Solomon (1949): The pretest may not only permit practice on the test task but may also have a direct influence on the effectiveness of training under the experimental condition. Taking the pretest may affect the subject's set and may serve to activate either correct or incorrect response tendencies, which are carried over into the training phase. The net effect of the pretest on training may thus be either beneficial or detrimental. The influence of training per se cannot, therefore, be assessed unequivocally by the difference between the experimental and the control group on the posttest. In order to take account of this possible source of bias, Solomon suggested the addition of a second control group to the conventional design:

	Pretest	Training	Posttest
Experimental	A	B	A
Control I	A	X	A
Control II	X	B	A

The second control group goes through the training phase and receives a posttest but is not given a pretest. For purposes of analysis the best estimate of the pretest performance of control group II is the grand mean of the scores of the other two groups. The change between the observed posttest score and the inferred pretest score represents the effects of practice per se, whereas the change for control group I measures the influence of the pretest. If the change score of the experimental group fails to equal the sum of the change scores for the two control groups, a systematic effect of the pretest on the effectiveness of the training procedure is indicated. Solomon reports the results of a demonstration experiment in which the three-group design was used. The noteworthy finding was that the pretest appeared to have an adverse influence on the results produced by practice, that is, the conventional two-group design would have led to an underestimation of the amount of improvement attributable to training.

It has been customary to describe a number of alternative experimental plans for the investigation of transfer. The present discussion suggests that the options with respect to design are quite limited. When the effects of prior training on new learning are under study, the *same test task* must be used under the experimental and the control treatment. There may, of course, be a number of different experimental treatments; the requirement of a common test task obtains with equal force in such cases. There are circumstances in which the characteristics of the materials, for example, the associative relations between items in successive lists, make it expedient to use different test tasks. If that is done, the tasks must be shown to be strictly equivalent in difficulty, so that the test-stage requirements may be assumed to be the same under all conditions. Thus, most acceptable designs reduce to the basic format illustrated by the comparisons of *AB* with *XB*, and *AB* with *NB*. When interest centers on improvement in an existing ability, the use of pretests is necessitated. These tests must, of course, be equivalent and the same under all treatments.

MEASUREMENT OF TRANSFER

Let us return to the basic design in which the sequence of events is *AB* under the experimental treatment and *XB* under the control treatment. The direction and amount of transfer are measured by the difference in performance between the two groups on the common test task *B*. Transfer can be measured at any or all points in test-task learning for which data are available. As a practical matter it is advisable to carry practice on the test task to a high performance criterion or for a substantial number of trials. It is then possible to determine both the initial level of facilitation or interference and the changes in transfer

effects that develop in the course of acquisition.

There are a priori reasons for expecting measures taken early in test-task learning to be maximally sensitive to transfer effects. The difference in prior experience between the experimental and the control group is greatest at the beginning of the second stage. The two groups are treated alike during the acquisition of the test task, and the relative weight of the earlier training will diminish as test learning continues. It must be recognized, however, that much will depend on the components of performance that are carried over from the training to the test phase. If the previously acquired habits first come into play relatively late in the acquisition of the test task, the manifestation of significant transfer effects will be correspondingly delayed. In some cases prior training is a source of both facilitation and interference, and the opposing influences may come to the fore at different points in the acquisition process, so that the sign of the transfer effects changes in the course of test-task learning. It is clear that there can be no general rules specifying the points in test-task learning that should be considered in the determination of transfer effects. Nevertheless the likely importance of measures obtained early in acquisition is worth emphasizing, especially in view of the fact that there is sometimes an undue reliance on criterial measures. For example, in verbal learning a criterion of mastery not only represents a chance peak in a fluctuating curve of performance (Melton, 1936), but the time required to attain it also depends heavily on the speed of acquisition of the most difficult item in the list. Thus criterial measures are peculiarly insensitive to transfer effects and in fact often yield null results when there are significant differences between treatments early in learning (see Postman, 1968a, p. 565).

For any given performance measure, for example, the number of correct responses in a fixed number of trials on the test task, the difference between the experimental and the control group expresses the amount of transfer in terms of raw scores. One limitation of such a score is that it is not comparable from one study to the next if there are variations in the scale of measurement or the level of attainment. It is common practice to translate the absolute difference scores into measures of relative transfer. A widely used index of relative transfer is the percentage of improvement shown by the experimental group over the control group:

$$\text{percent transfer} = \frac{E - C}{C} \times 100$$

where E and C are the scores of the experimental and the control group, respectively. If the scores vary inversely with level of performance, for example, when the dependent variable is the number of trials to criterion or a count of errors, the difference $C - E$ is used in the numerator. The same formula can be applied to measures of change between a pretest and a posttest.

Unfortunately, such percentage measures are no more comparable than the raw difference scores if they are based on different units of measurement. If the control group makes 10 errors in one task and 100 errors in another, 50 percent transfer—a reduction to 5 errors in one case and to 50 errors in the other—does not necessarily signify equivalence of practice effects. If the learning curves for the two tasks have different shapes, the percentages obviously do not have the same meaning. In light of these considerations Gagné, Foster, and Crowley (1948) proposed a relative measure that expresses the difference between the experimental and the control treatment as a percentage of the maximum score that can be achieved in the test stage. The maximum score can often be specified in advance, for example, zero errors in the recitation of a list or attainment of the criterion of mastery on the first test trial. In other cases the maximum has to be determined empirically; for example, the highest score achieved by any of the groups in the experiment over the specified period

of practice is used (Gagné & Foster, 1949). The proposed formula is

$$\frac{E - C}{T - C} \times 100$$

where T is the maximum possible score in the test stage. The advantage claimed for this formula is that it "makes use of a scale of improvement the limits of which are determined," that is, the zero point is defined by the initial score of the control group, which received no prior training, and the 100 percent point by the maximal value attainable in the test. It should be apparent, however, that the problem of comparability is no more solved by this means than it is by the use of the earlier formula. As Gagné et al. recognized, the units of the scale cannot be assumed to be equal because the curve of acquisition is likely not to be linear but rather negatively accelerated. When the C scores are at different distances from the maximum, a direct comparison of percentages may be misleading. The authors also acknowledge the fact that the index becomes ambiguous when transfer is negative because there is no way of defining maximal possible interference analogously to total possible improvement. The shortcomings of this measure of relative transfer have been discussed in some detail by Murdock (1957), who emphasizes the point that the determination of the limits of improvement is often difficult or of questionable validity. Murdock himself suggested a modified formula which yields symmetrical values of positive and negative transfer, with the upper limit at each end of the scale equal to 100 percent:

$$\text{percent transfer} = \frac{E - C}{E + C} \times 100$$

This formula, like the others, does not resolve the problem of comparability of units if the results of different studies are to be compared.

A final example may serve to illustrate this difficulty. Suppose a 10-item list is used as the test in one study, and a 20-item list in another study. The scores obtained on the initial test trial are as follows:

	10-item list	20-item list
E	5	7
C	2	4

The absolute amount of transfer is the same for the two tasks. By the conventional transformation the percentages of transfer are 150 for the 10-item list and 75 for the 20-item list. The formula of Gagné et al. yields 37.5 and 18.8 percent, respectively, and Murdock's formula 43 and 27.3 percent. The three indices are of strikingly different magnitudes but agree in showing about twice as much transfer for the short as for the long list. However, the psychological implications of this finding are far from clear. It cannot be inferred that the reduction in effort is twice as great for the 10-item as for the 20-item task because the amount of study time per item required for a given probability of recall increases with length of list. There is obviously no implication that the training and test task are twice as similar in one condition as in the other. In fact, the difference in percentages does not appear to entail any determinate conclusions about the transfer process in the two situations. Complementary ambiguities develop when trials or time to mastery is the dependent variable. When control groups differ in ability or in level of attainment, the uncertainties of interpretation parallel those created by variations in task difficulty.

The difficulties inherent in the use of relative measures have been recognized but apparently have not been viewed as decisive. A re-examination of these problems has led us to the conclusion that inferences from percentage measures must remain ambiguous when there are substantial differences in task difficulty or ability level among the studies to be compared. There is, indeed, a risk that the use of transformations into relative terms may draw attention away from the systematic effects of such variables as task difficulty or ability level or lead to incorrect conclusions about the influence of such variables. It is not apparent that the use of percentage measures has promoted the discovery of important functional relations in transfer. In fact, the frequency of use of such measures has declined in recent years, certainly in the field of verbal learning. Relative measures may have practical value in certain situations in which interest centers on the most efficient utilization of available training time; they should be used with extreme caution, if at all, in the examination of theoretical issues in transfer. Absolute measures reflect directly the outcome of experimental observations and convey unequivocal information. For these reasons they are to be preferred in principle to derived measures. Conclusive comparisons among experiments can rarely be achieved by the projection of scores onto a common scale; rather such comparisons are a primary task of systematic theoretical analysis.

INTERFERENCE DESIGNS

We turn now to a consideration of the designs used in the study of interference at recall. There are two basic designs representing the experimental arrangements for the measurement of retroactive and proactive inhibition, respectively.

Retroactive Inhibition

Retroactive inhibition refers to the detrimental effects on retention of a learning activity interpolated between the end of acquisition and the test of recall. The standard design has the following form:

	Original learning	Interpolated learning	Recall
Experimental	Yes	Yes	Yes
Control	Yes	No	Yes

In the application of this design it is essential that the experimental and control groups be strictly comparable and treated in the same way except for the nature of the activity filling the interval between learning and recall. In particular, degree of original learning and length of the retention interval must be strictly equivalent. With respect to the critical manipulated variable, the control condition is defined in a negative way: It does not engage in interpolated learning. For this reason the control treatment is often designated as the rest condition. In practice, rest means some activity that is judged to be entirely irrelevant to the experimental task. A variety of filler activities has been used: working puzzles, solving arithmetic problems (when the learning materials are verbal), rating cartoons, and so on. It is clear that the designation of such tasks as irrelevant is based on the assumption that interference will develop only if there is some determinate degree of similarity between the original and the interpolated activity. To the extent that this assumption is false, the control treatment fails in its purpose.

A further caution that must be borne in mind concerns the possibilities of uncontrolled rehearsal. If the control subject is not fully and continuously occupied by the filler activity, he may engage in rehearsal of the original task. Such uncontrolled rehearsal introduces a bias in favor of the control group in the assessment of the recall results. There has been little evaluation of the effectiveness of different rest activities, although this problem has begun to receive some systematic attention in recent studies of short-term memory. It is likely that differences between rest activities contribute to the variation in findings from one experiment to the next.

It will undoubtedly have been noted that the formal structure of the experimental design for retroactive inhibition is identical with the transfer design in which pre- and posttests are used. The first stage, however, is no longer defined as a test of pre-experimental proficiency which may incidentally function as a practice period; rather it is the phase during which the critical habits are established under controlled conditions. (This does not rule out the possibility, of course, that the acquisition of the experimental tasks is influenced by pre-experimental habits.) The interaction between the first and the second stage, to which Solomon called attention, now is not an uncontrolled source of variation but rather one of the very processes the experimental operations are designed to assess.

If recall is higher for the control than for the experimental group, the difference defines the amount of retroactive inhibition (RI), that is,

$$RI = C - E$$

On the other hand, if the experimental group surpasses the control group, that difference defines retroactive facilitation; in this case $C - E$ is a negative rather than a positive quantity. As in the case of transfer, percentage measures have frequently been used, again with a view to permitting comparisons among the results of different studies. The usual formula is

$$\%RI = \frac{C - E}{C} \times 100$$

The difficulties of interpretation posed by such relative measures are the same as before. Thus, when the C and E scores are 2 and 1 in one case, and 10 and 5 in another, we obtain 50 percent RI for both, but the psychological implications may be quite different. If the maximum possible is taken to be 10 in both cases, the degree of learning of the items which failed to resist interference is clearly not comparable. That fact is, of course, of critical importance in the interpretation of the results. It is also obvious that the percentages become increasingly unstable as the control baseline becomes smaller. In the rather extreme case we have chosen for illustrative purposes, the loss of a single item, which may not be a reliable observation, represents 50 percent RI. The example is not, however, as far-fetched as it may seem, since

TABLE 21.1

	Prior learning	Test-task learning	Retention interval	Recall
Experimental	Yes	Yes	Yes	Yes
Control	No	Yes	Yes	Yes

bases of this order of magnitude have, in fact, been frequently used in the calculation of percentages of *RI*. Again the absolute measure is to be preferred because it remains close to the experimental observations and because it does not permit the investigator to ignore systematic differences among experiments.

Proactive Inhibition

Proactive inhibition refers to the detrimental effects of prior learning on the retention of subsequently learned materials. As such it should be distinguished sharply from negative transfer effects in acquisition. The standard design is shown in Table 21.1. Note that there is a retention interval between the end of test-task learning and recall. To satisfy the requirements of the design, this interval must be longer than that between successive trials in acquisition. Given this definition, proactive inhibition, if it occurs, must necessarily be some increasing function of the time since the end of learning. As long as that time is equal to or shorter than the intertrial interval, acquisition will presumably continue to a maximum. When the interval exceeds that critical length, there is an opportunity for forgetting to set in and for the interfering effects of prior learning on retention to manifest themselves.

As in the case of retroactive inhibition, the logic of the design calls for equal treatment of the experimental and the control groups except for the manipulated condition of prior learning. However, reference to the temporal arrangements of this design reveals a difficulty that was not present in the earlier case. For the experimental group, the test task is the second phase of practice; for the control group, it is the first. Consequently, the experimental subjects acquire the test task under more favorable conditions than do the control subjects; the former, but not the latter, have had an opportunity to become habituated to the situation and to develop general learning skills.

Carrying the two groups to the same criterion of performance does not necessarily resolve the difficulty because associative strength at criterion is likely to be greater for the group that learns faster. It is possible to equate the amount of prior experience for the two conditions by having the control group learn an unrelated task; as we have already seen in discussing the problem of a rest interval, the designation of an activity as irrelevant or unrelated depends on assumptions about the range of similarity relations between successive tasks that are capable of producing interference; but that is precisely one of the questions studies of proactive inhibition are designed to answer. While these sources of uncertainty are inherent in the design, they usually do not constitute insuperable difficulties. The magnitude of the bias favoring the experimental group in acquisition can often be assessed and taken into account. If prior practice is equated, proactive interference under various experimental treatments can be evaluated relative to a stable control baseline.

The considerations which bear on the measurement of proactive inhibition parallel those already discussed for retroaction. The amount by which the recall of the control group exceeds that of the experimental group provides a measure of proactive inhibition (*PI*):

$$PI = C - E$$

If the difference favors the experimental group, we speak of proactive facilitation. The difficulties posed by the use of percentage measures are the same as before. Finally, it should be noted that in the interest of simplicity of exposition only a single experimental condition was included in both the interference designs. The problems of control and inference remain the same when there are multiple experimental treatments.

NONSPECIFIC TRANSFER: ABILITY TRAINING

As was noted above, early experimental studies of transfer were stimulated by the growing skepticism with which psychologists came to view the doctrine of formal discipline. Interest centered on the question of whether there was transfer of training between tasks that presumably engaged the same mental function, for example, the ability to memorize or to make sense discriminations. We shall review a few of the classical experiments bearing on this problem, with special emphasis on the work concerned with memory training. These studies are not only of historical interest, but they can also be seen as being in a direct line of continuity with contemporary investigations of nonspecific transfer.

The first phenomenon of transfer to be investigated experimentally was cross-education, that is, the spread of the effects of training from one part of the body to its symmetrical counterpart. Changes between a pretest and a posttest were used by Volkmann (1858) to measure the bilateral transfer of practice in tactual discrimination. It remained for William James to extend this procedure to the study of higher mental processes. James had come to doubt the popular belief that the faculty of remembering can be strengthened by exercise and decided to put his view to an experimental test (1890, I, pp. 666f.). He set out to determine whether prolonged practice in memorizing the poetry of one author would lead to increased efficiency in memorizing the poetry of another author. Equivalent selections from one poet were used in the pretest and the posttest, and

verses of another poet were used during the intervening period of training. There was no evidence of transfer. The absence of transfer effects appeared to confirm James's view that the capacity for remembering—what he called general retentiveness—is a physiological trait not susceptible to training. Whatever increases in the proficiency of memory do occur must be attributed to "the improvement of one's habitual modes of recording facts" (p. 667).

James's experiment presaged the approach to the problem of ability training that was soon to come into general use. The training and the test tasks were assumed to sample the same general ability—if such an ability did, indeed, exist—but they differed in content, so that the specific habits which had to be mastered were not identical. Some of the methodological problems that had to be resolved in subsequent work are also apparent. Only differences between pretest and posttest were considered; changes in performance during the daily practice sessions were not measured. A failure to observe transfer to a new task is inconclusive as long as it is not known whether the training procedure had a direct effect. The equivalence of the pretest and the posttest was not established, and the need for a control treatment also remained to be recognized. The necessary changes in design and analysis were introduced gradually in the studies which followed.

Even when the training produces no apparent improvement, as in James's experiment, the lack of a control baseline may lead to incorrect conclusions. It is possible that the transfer effect from pretest to posttest is negative, in which case a zero difference indicates a positive influence of training. A much more probable source of error is, however, a failure to take account of the improvement attributable to the pretest when the experimental treatment is apparently effective. The well-known experiment by Ebert and Meumann (1905) is a case in point. In this study the training phase consisted of daily practice in the memorization of nonsense syllables. The pretests and posttests comprised a variety of memory tasks; the materials to be recalled included letters, numbers, nonsense syllables, nonsense figures, words, German-Italian vocabulary, verses, and prose passages. After the pretest there were two eight-day periods of training, each followed by a posttest. The subjects showed considerable improvement in their ability to memorize nonsense syllables; in addition there were successive increases in performance on the posttests. Thus, the training activity appeared to have produced broad transfer effects. However, the lack of a control treatment proved to be a fatal shortcoming and subsequent work showed the conclusions to be invalid. Gains comparable to those in the original experiment were observed when the training was omitted and only the tests were administered at the appropriate intervals (Dearborn, 1909). In a repetition of the original experiment with a control group added, Reed (1917) again observed a striking improvement in the performance of the training task but found no consistent differences between the test scores of the experimental and the control group.

The inclusion of a control group became standard practice in studies of memory training, but the findings remained inconclusive at best. Winch (1908) reported an improvement in the memorization of prose after a period of training on poetry; in a subsequent study (1910) he also observed substantial gains from practice on letter series to the memorization of prose. It is not known, however, whether the pretest and posttest in these experiments were of equal difficulty. In a more extensive investigation Sleight (1911) for the first time introduced the precaution of counterbalancing pretests and posttests. In Sleight's main experiment the subjects were girl pupils whose average age was 12 years 8 months. On the basis of ten different pretests, which provided measures of both immediate memory and rote learning, the subjects were divided into four matched groups. Three groups were assigned to experimental treatments and were given practice in memorizing

either poetry, tables of measures and other quantitative facts, or the substance of prose passages. There were two three-week cycles of practice (four 30-minute sessions per week), each followed by a posttest. The control activity consisted of work on arithmetic problems. There were gains on the posttests under all conditions. However, the net transfer effects on the final tests, as measured by the differences between the control and the experimental groups, were for the most part small and not significant; 14 of the 30 differences were negative. A further study with adults yielded similar results.

Sleight's study is free from the major methodological flaws that vitiated some of the earlier work: An appropriate control condition was included, the groups were well matched, and the pretest and posttest tasks were counterbalanced. One important shortcoming was the failure to obtain measures of performance during the training phase; it is probable, however, that the practice was effective. The results could reasonably be viewed as damaging to the hypothesis that any training in memorization produces broad transfer effects that facilitate the performance of any new and different memory task.

There are two inherent limitations in the formulation of the experiments designed to measure the spread of ability from a given amount of special memory practice. First, there was no systematic manipulation of the similarities and differences between the training and the test tasks; this is true for both the specific content of the material and the performance requirements at each of the stages of the experiment. The question at issue was, after all, how specific the effects of training are. There could be no answer to this question as long as dimensions of intertask similarity were not specified with sufficient precision to permit of experimental manipulation. In that respect the findings of Thorndike and Woodworth (1901) on transfer of training in observation and judgment were far more illuminating and theoretically significant. In some of their experiments the subjects were trained in perceptual skills such as the estimation of rectangular areas. In the transfer tests the stimuli to be judged were varied systematically with respect to such characteristics as shape and size; in other experiments subjects had practice in canceling particular letters and then were tested with other letters or words. Transfer effects were typically small and irregular; that is, the benefits derived from practice were sharply reduced when the training and test stimuli were not identical even though they were drawn from the same general class.

A second pervasive shortcoming of the experiments on memory training was the failure to determine the limits of possible improvement in the performance of the transfer tasks even if training were successful. The test tasks were frequently activities with which the subjects undoubtedly had had considerable experience prior to the experiment, such as memorizing poetry or the substance of prose passages. If they had already reached a reasonable level of proficiency before embarking on their special training, there would be little opportunity for detecting an improvement. On the other hand, if the test task is novel and difficult, for example, the memorization of a list of nonsense syllables, the limited experience afforded by the pretest is likely to produce substantial improvement under both the experimental and the control treatment; consequently, the sensitivity of the posttest to the transfer effects of the intervening training is reduced.

The evidence remained consistent with James's dictum that "all improvement in memory consists . . . in the improvement of one's habitual methods of recording facts." The repeated failures to find broad transfer effects implied that the habits permitting the efficient performance of a given task were highly specific and unlikely to generalize to new situations. Such specificity may be entailed by differences in the requirements of successive tasks, but it may also be a consequence of the learner's failure to develop methods of practice that can be carried over from one assignment to the next. Both these factors may, of course, be responsible for the lack of transfer in any given case. However, as long as the subject is left to his own devices during the training phase, the potentialities for transfer through the development of widely applicable methods of practice remain unexplored. Thus, even when there are no gains under standard conditions of practice, appropriate guidance during the training phase may substantially increase the breadth and amount of transfer.

This possibility was examined in an experiment by Woodrow (1927). All subjects received pretests and posttests on six different memory tasks. The materials to be memorized included poetry, prose, factual information, Turkish-English vocabulary, and historical dates. The span of immediate memory for strings of consonants was also measured. During the four-week period intervening between the two tests the subjects were divided into three groups. A control group received no memory training. A "practice group" devoted two sessions per week to the memorization of poetry and of lists of nonsense syllables. The total amount of time spent on these exercises was approximately three hours. A "training group" followed the same schedule but divided its time between the memory tasks and instruction in efficient methods of memorizing. About 40 percent of the training time was given over to instruction. The techniques in which the subjects were trained included the following: "learning by wholes; use of active self-testing; use of grouping and rhythm; attention to meaning and use of images and symbols to embody meaning; mental alertness and concentration; confidence in one's ability to memorize; in certain cases, as in learning nonsense syllables, the use of secondary associations." On the posttest the difference in improvement between the practice and the control group was small and unreliable; the training group, however, showed considerable gains and surpassed the other two groups by a substantial amount. It should be noted that under the control condition the intercorrelations among the various tests tended to be low, averaging .38, so that a rather broad transfer effect was demonstrated. The results leave open the question, however, whether it was the instruction alone, or the instruction in combination with the memory exercises, that was responsible for the superior performance of the training group. To answer this question, an additional group given the instruction but not the exercises would have been needed. In any event, Woodrow's findings call attention to the fact that in the classical studies of memory training the composition of successive tasks was emphasized at the expense of the methods which make for efficient performance.

While the early results concerning intertask transfer were variable and inconclusive, all the available evidence indicated that as long as the nature of the task remained the same, subjects would show progressive improvements in performance. The more unfamiliar and difficult the learning task, the more likely such practice effects were to be observed. Most of the subsequent studies of nonspecific transfer concentrated on the conditions and characteristics of the improvement in the performance of one particular type of task. Such progressive increases in speed of learning will obviously influence test-task performance in any transfer experiment in which the nature of the task remains unchanged. It is a curious fact, however, that the methodological implications of this state of affairs for the measurement of specific transfer effects were very slow to be recognized. As we pointed out in our discussion of experimental designs, specific transfer effects must be measured from a control baseline which permits an assessment of the nonspecific effects of prior training. Such control treatments have become a standard feature of transfer designs only in the relatively recent

past; in the many experiments which failed to include these essential controls there was a systematic bias toward overestimating specific positive transfer effects and underestimating specific negative transfer effects.

NONSPECIFIC TRANSFER: WARM-UP AND LEARNING TO LEARN

Warm-up

A failure to observe associative interference where it would be expected on theoretical grounds first led to an explicit discussion of the need for separating net transfer effects into nonspecific and specific components. In 1928 Heron reported the results of an experiment in which he had intended to investigate the interference produced by the attachment of a new response to an old stimulus (A–B, A–D). In a given experimental session two lists of six pairs of nonsense syllables were learned in immediate succession. The second list had either zero, two, or four pairs in which the stimulus terms were the same as in the first list. In addition, there was a preliminary practice session. A counterbalanced design was used, and subjects served under all four treatments in sessions four weeks apart. The somewhat unexpected finding was that in each session the second list was learned faster than the first; that is, no absolute negative transfer effects were observed. There was, however, no improvement between sessions. Heron attributed the transitory within-session improvement to a process of "warming-up" akin to the "limbering up" in the performance of a motor skill. He viewed this process as distinct from the transfer of habits. Thus, the positive effects of warm-up served to counteract the associative interference during the acquisition of the second list but did not influence speed of learning in the session which followed four weeks later.

Definition of warm-up The assumption that warm-up is a source of improvement in verbal learning eventually gained wide acceptance. It is interesting to note, however, that 20 years elapsed between the appearance of Heron's article and the initiation of studies of the characteristics of warm-up in rote learning. Interest in the problem was reactivated by Ammons' (1947) systematic analysis of warm-up effects in motor learning. In this analysis warm-up was identified with the establishment of the postural set required for the efficient performance of a motor task such as rotor pursuit. The set is assumed to dissipate gradually during rest intervals. The loss of set results in reduced efficiency of performance, designated as warm-up decrement. This conception of warm-up in terms of task set was found to be readily applicable to the rote-learning situation (Irion, 1948). The set comprises the postural and attentive adjustments that make for optimal reception of the verbal stimuli and modes of responding appropriate to the experimental arrangements, for example, the rhythm of the memory drum. The subject's adjustments also provide a feedback of response-produced stimulation which serves to maintain a distinctive situational context. In agreement with the principles established in the area of motor learning, the beneficial effects of warm-up on the performance of a subsequent task should be an increasing function of the amount of set-inducing practice and inversely related to the time interval between the two activities (McGeoch & Irion, 1952, p. 334).

Certain features and implications of this interpretation of warm-up deserve emphasis. First, warm-up is viewed as the establishment of a transitory set that prepares the subject for the perceptual and motor requirements of the experiment. The set is built up and maintained as long as the warm-up activity is continued but begins to dissipate as soon as that activity is terminated. Thus, transitoriness is a defining characteristic of warm-up effects. Second, to facilitate the subsequent performance of a learning task, the warm-up activity need not involve any learning; any activity that induces the appropriate postural and attentive adjustments should be effective. However, prior learning

is obviously one such activity. When non-specific transfer is observed from one learning task to the next, the question arises at once whether all of the facilitation is attributable to warm-up, or whether in addition efficient methods of learning were acquired as a result of the prior training. The latter would constitute learning to learn as distinct from warm-up. To distinguish between these two components of nonspecific transfer, the criterion of temporal persistence has been invoked. The logic of inference is as follows. By definition, there is a rapid dissipation of warm-up effects after the cessation of practice. On the other hand, the habits that constitute learning to learn are assumed to represent relatively permanent changes in behavior. Thus, nonspecific transfer effects that dissipate rapidly are attributable to warm-up, and those which persist over protracted intervals of time are evidence of learning to learn (Thune, 1951).

To validate these assumptions, it was necessary first of all to demonstrate that warm-up effects in rote learning have the characteristics attributed to them, namely, a cumulative build-up during the set-inducing activity and a progressive and rapid dissipation after the end of the activity. Two closely related experiments by Thune (1950) and Hamilton (1950) were directed at this objective.

The influence of warm-up on learning
Thune's study comprised two experiments. The first of these was designed to test the hypothesis that the magnitude of the warm-up effect is an increasing function of the amount of prior set-inducing activity. Since interest centered on the determination of warm-up effects, an attempt was made to hold the opportunities for learning to learn constant and to minimize specific transfer by the use of unrelated lists. The experiment was carried out on two successive days. On Day 1 all subjects first received six trials on a practice list of 15 paired associates composed of one-syllable nouns. The second stage consisted of 10 trials on a list of 15 pairs of

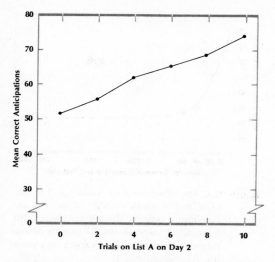

Figure 21.1. Nonspecific transfer effects in acquisition. Performance on a paired-associate test list as a function of the number of immediately preceding trials on an unrelated practice list. (Thune, 1950.)

two-syllable adjectives (List A). The various groups in the experiment differed with respect to the distribution of these trials between Day 1 and Day 2. For one of the groups the distribution was 10-0; that is, all 10 trials were given on Day 1; other combinations were 8-2, 6-4, 4-6, 2-8, and 0-10. The final test task was administered on Day 2 and consisted of 10 trials on a list of 15 pairs of one-syllable nouns (List B). Practice on List B was preceded by a 10-minute rest interval during which the subjects sorted cartoons. Thus, all subjects had the same amount of experience with paired-associate learning but had varying numbers of trials on List A immediately before the beginning of the test trials on List B. Figure 21.1 shows the mean numbers of correct responses during the acquisition of List B as a function of the number of trials on List A completed just previously. Performance on the test task is related directly to the number of preceding practice trials. Thune attributed this relation to the progressive build-up of a warm-up effect during the trials on List A.

The second experiment in Thune's study evaluated the effectiveness of a nonlearning

activity as a condition of warm-up. The activity chosen was color guessing which was carried out in a manner designed to simulate the experimental arrangements in paired-associate learning. Specifically, when a large capital X appeared in the window of the memory drum, the subject was required to guess which one of five colors would appear when the shutter lifted. The colors were presented in different random orders on successive trials. Two groups were compared. On Day 1 both groups received six practice trials of paired-associate learning and 10 trials on List A. The second stage consisted of 10 trials of color guessing, and as before the critical variable was the temporal locus of the warm-up activity: for one group these trials occurred on Day 1, and for the other on Day 2 just prior to the acquisition of list B. Performance on the test task was substantially better in the latter case. Perhaps even more important, comparison of corresponding groups in the two experiments showed that 10 trials of color guessing and 10 trials on List A immediately preceding the test task

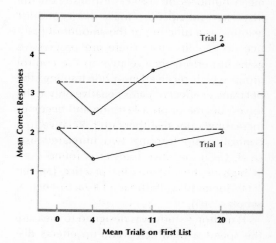

Figure 21.2. Mean number of correct responses on the first 2 anticipation trials in the acquisition of a transfer list as a function of the degree of first-list learning. The successive lists conformed to the A-B, A-D paradigm. The dashed lines represent the performance of the control group which had no prior learning. (Underwood, 1949.)

produced equal amounts of improvement. This finding led Thune to conclude that regardless of whether or not the prior activity involved learning, the source of facilitation was the reinstatement of an appropriate perceptual-motor set. We shall return to this conclusion below.

The implication of Figure 21.1, that the amount of nonspecific transfer is a direct function of the number of prior practice trials, is confirmed by the results of other studies. As was suggested by Heron's results, the gains in performance may be sufficiently great to mask the presence of associative interference. A clear example appears in Figure 21.2. The data are from an experiment by Underwood (1949) in which the relation between degree of prior learning and proactive inhibition was investigated. The learning materials were lists of 10 paired adjectives which conformed to the A–B, A–D paradigm. First-list learning was carried to one of three criteria: 3/10, 8/10 or 10/10 plus 5 overlearning trials. The average numbers of trials to these criteria were 4, 11, and 20, respectively. The figure shows the mean numbers of correct responses on the first two anticipation trials of second-list learning as a function of the amount of practice on the first list. There are progressive gains in performance relative to the control group which received no prior training; the net transfer effect remains negative only at the lowest degree of prior learning and becomes increasingly positive thereafter. Relative to a control group learning two unrelated lists (A–B, C–D), negative transfer is found even at high degrees of first-list practice (Spiker, 1960; Jung, 1962; Postman, 1962a; Spence & Schulz, 1965).

Hamilton's study was designed to measure the speed with which warm-up effects dissipate. The general procedure and learning materials (Lists A and B) were the same as in Thune's experiment described earlier. All subjects received preliminary practice on Day 1, and on Day 2 learned Lists A and B. The time interval between the first and the second list was varied over a range from 8 seconds

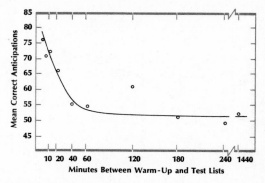

Figure 21.3. The dissipation of warm-up. The decline in the mean number of correct anticipations reflects the effect on test-list learning of increases in the length of the interval since the end of practice on a prior list. (Hamilton, 1950.)

to 240 minutes. Figure 21.3 shows the relation between the length of the rest interval and the mean numbers of correct responses in test-list learning. As the interval is lengthened, performance declines rapidly at first and more slowly thereafter. Thus, the relation is adequately described by a negatively accelerated function.

Warm-up vs. learning to learn   Taken together, the results of Thune and Hamilton indicate that both the build-up and the dissi-

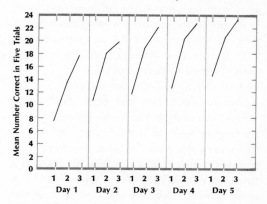

Figure 21.4. Temporal trends in nonspecific transfer effects during continued practice. Three successive lists of paired associates were learned on each of 5 days. The large gains within sessions are to be contrasted with the relatively small gains between sessions. (Thune, 1951.)

pation of warm-up effects occur rapidly. In a subsequent study Thune (1951) presented further evidence for the apparent transitoriness of warm-up effects and attempted to assess the relative contribution of warm-up and learning to learn to cumulative gains in performance. The subjects in this experiment learned three lists of 10 paired adjectives each day for five days. Practice on each list was for 10 trials or to a criterion of one perfect recitation. Meaningful relations among the words in the successive lists were minimized as far as possible; that is, the paradigm of transfer was A–B, C–D, E–F, and so on. The mean numbers of correct responses on the first five anticipation trials for each of the three lists learned in the five successive sessions are shown in Figure 21.4. Two trends are at once apparent: the presence of very large gains within sessions and much smaller ones between sessions. The difference between the two improvement functions is well brought out by the fact that the first list on the fifth day was learned to criterion less rapidly than the second list on the first day. In principle, both warm-up and learning to learn may contribute to the gains observed on a given day. However, since warm-up effects are known to dissipate rapidly, Thune considered it likely that most of the within-session improvement was a matter of warm-up. The cumulative changes between sessions, on the other hand, provide an estimate of the temporal course of learning to learn. It appears that the gains attributed to learning to learn describe a negatively accelerated increasing function, and the magnitude of the warm-up effects appears to be largely independent of the level of practice. The fact that the within-session gains are greatest on the first day is attributed by Thune to the greater initial weight of the learning-to-learn component.

These conclusions are predicated on the assumption that the effects of learning to learn persist between successive days, whereas those of warm-up dissipate. There is empirical support for the latter supposition,

although it is by no means certain that some of the adjustments subsumed under warm-up are not conditioned to the situation and hence carried over from one session to the next. The assumption that the habits that constitute learning to learn are not forgotten is ad hoc and open to question. In support of this assumption McGeoch and Irion (1952, p. 308) cite the finding of Bunch (1936) that transfer is highly resistant to forgetting, but the "rational learning problem" used in this study may well represent a special case. Consider on the other hand the results found in an experiment by Newton and Wickens (1956, Exp. II) in which two lists of paired adjectives (A–B, C–D) were learned either 0, 24, or 48 hours apart. The average number of trials to criterion on the first list was about 20. The mean numbers of trials required to master the second list to the same criterion were 10, 16, and 21 at the successively longer intervals. On the assumption that warm-up effects had fully dissipated, the trend indicates a progressive forgetting of learning to learn, which was complete after 48 hours. If the intervals between sessions in Thune's experiment had been 48 hours (or perhaps longer in view of the higher levels of practice), the estimates of learning to learn would most likely have been substantially smaller. In short, the identification of learning to learn with between-session improvement is questionable; consequently assessments of the differential effectiveness of warm-up and learning to learn on the basis of comparisons of within-session and between-session gains are of very uncertain validity.

The finding in Thune's earlier study that color guessing and list learning produced equal amounts of facilitation suggested that the rapid gains observed early in practice were largely a matter of warm-up. However, all of the subjects in that experiment had had prior experience with the learning procedure used in the terminal test task. It is possible, therefore, that the effects of the warm-up treatment were not independent of the prior learning experience. The color-guessing trials

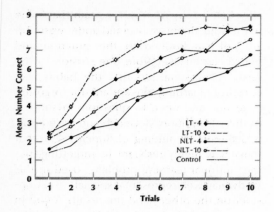

Figure 21.5. The development of nonspecific transfer effects in naive subjects. Performance on a paired-associate test task after practice on either another learning task (*LT*) or a non-learning task (*NLT*). Under each condition there were either 4 or 10 training trials. The control group had no prior practice. (Schwenn & Postman, 1967.)

may have been effective in producing facilitation not so much because they reinstated the subject's perceptual-motor set but because they served to reactivate habits acquired during the previous verbal practice. To compare the effectiveness of a learning and a nonlearning activity in the initial stage of practice it is necessary to use naive subjects.

Such a comparison was made in a study by Schwenn and Postman (1967). The test task was the acquisition of a list of paired adjectives. The prior activity consisted either of learning a list of unrelated pairs of adjectives (*A–B, C–D*) or of number guessing under conditions simulating as closely as possible the experimental arrangements in the learning situation. There were either four or ten trials of prior practice. A control group was not given any preliminary training. Performance on the common test task is shown in Figure 21.5. At both levels of practice there is a substantially greater gain after a learning than after a nonlearning activity. Four trials of number guessing had no effect whatever, whereas the same number of learning trials was sufficient to produce a significant amount of improvement. There is a small but consist-

ent gain after 10 guessing trials, but the differential effectiveness of the two treatments remains clearly in evidence at the higher level of practice. Since both activities would presumably be conducive to the development of an appropriate perceptual-motor set, it follows that the rapid improvement in performance typically shown by naive subjects reflects primarily the acquisition of skills relevant to the requirements of a learning task per se.

These results do not necessarily call into question the importance of perceptual and motor adjustments, especially under the conditions of rapid pacing, which are characteristic of rote-learning situations. However, there may be important differences between the adjustments required by a learning and a nonlearning task. In learning a list, the subject must spend some of the available time in rehearsal, in searching for mnemonic devices, and in editing his responses. The demands on the subject's time are not the same during the performance of, say, a guessing task. Consequently, the optimal distribution of attention and most efficient rhythm of responding are probably far from identical in the two situations. In fact, modes of responding appropriate in a "pure" warm-up task may make for errors in a subsequent learning situation. For example, the color-naming procedure often used in studies of distributed practice to fill the intertrial intervals has been shown to increase the probability of overt errors because the set to respond to every stimulus is carried over into the learning trials (Underwood, 1952). Along similar lines, it was observed in the study of Schwenn and Postman that relative to the control condition the rate of overt errors was higher after number-guessing but lower after list-learning. It is true that error rate and speed of learning are not necessarily correlated (Scheible & Underwood, 1954). Nevertheless the possibility cannot be ruled out that a warm-up activity may, under certain circumstances, become a source of interference as well as of facilitation. Thus, a sharp separation between perceptual-motor adjustments and the development of efficient methods of learning may not be psychologically valid. In any event, the studies of Thune and of Schwenn and Postman taken together point to an interaction between stage of practice and warm-up effects. In a naive subject preliminary training on a set-inducing task produces little facilitation; when the subject is experienced, a few trials on such a task may reinstate the complex of adjustments and habits that make for efficient learning.

Warm-up and retention   Interest centers explicitly on the effects of the reinstatement of an appropriate performance set when the influence of warm-up on retention is considered. One basic approach to this problem was developed in the analysis of motor-skill performance (Ammons, 1947). In skill learning the concept of warm-up decrement refers to a loss of set during a rest interval which produces a transitory decline in performance. The presence of a warm-up decrement is indicated by the fact that the initial segment of the relearning curve after rest has a steeper slope than the original acquisition curve at a comparable level of initial proficiency (Irion, 1948). The relearning curve is steeper because of the rapid reinstatement of set when practice is resumed. If the entire decline in performance represented "true" forgetting, the learning and relearning curves at comparable levels should have the same slope. When the amount retained is measured on a recall trial, the role of warm-up decrement in forgetting can be assessed by the introduction of a set-reinstating activity immediately prior to the retention test proper. The gain in recall produced by the warm-up activity provides an estimate of the extent to which a loss of set contributes to the total amount of forgetting. The amount of gain should be related directly to the degree of continuity between the warm-up and learning tasks.

A study by Irion (1949) provided impressive support for the hypothesis that warm-up decrement is a major determinant of retention loss. In a first experiment a list of 15 paired adjectives was learned for 10 trials and then relearned for 10 trials after varying intervals ranging from 1 minute to 24 hours. A no-rest control group received 20 successive acquisition trials. The amount recalled on the first relearning trial was a negatively accelerated decreasing function of the length of the retention interval. As predicted, the slope of the relearning curve, at least after a 24-hour interval, was steeper than that of the original learning curve at the same level of initial proficiency. In Irion's second experiment it was found that a warm-up trial of color naming just prior to the start of relearning eliminated most of the forgetting after a 24-hour interval. In fact, the subjects given a delayed test after warm-up did not differ significantly from the no-rest control. In a subsequent study (Irion & Wham, 1951), in which serial lists of nonsense syllables were the learning materials, a rest interval of 35 minutes was used and the amount of warm-up was varied systematically. The recall scores showed an upward trend as a function of increasing amounts of warm-up, although the relation was rather irregular. It is noteworthy that after four trials of warm-up, recall was significantly higher than under the no-rest control condition.

Irion's results suggested that a loss of set may account for much of the forgetting normally observed on delayed tests of retention. This conclusion would, of course, have important implications for forgetting theory. Unfortunately, however, it has proved impossible to replicate the original finding reported in Irion's (1949) study, namely, that retention losses after 24 hours are drastically reduced by having subjects engage in a warm-up activity before the test of recall. Complete failure of an attempt at replication was reported by Rockway and Duncan (1952) in spite of concerted efforts to duplicate the conditions of the original experiment as closely as possible. These investigators also failed to find an effect on retention of the amount of warm-up activity; the similarity between the warm-up and the learning task with respect to length and rate of responding likewise had no reliable influence on performance. Later Dinner and Duncan (1959) found a significant increase in recall after warm-up, but only when the degree of original learning was substantially higher than in the earlier experiments. Recently Lazar (1967) carried out a series of experiments in which the conditions of warm-up prior to recall were varied in a number of different ways but with almost entirely negative results. The reasons for the striking discrepancy between the results of Irion and those of subsequent investigators are unclear. It is apparent by now, however, that the reduction in retention loss by a set-reinstating activity is not a dependable phenomenon.

The concept of warm-up and the phenomena presumably associated with it pose some serious interpretative difficulties, at least as far as verbal learning and memory are concerned. One major problem, to which reference was made earlier, is the definition of an appropriate perceptual-motor set which is independent of the element of learning. The assumption that an activity such as color naming or number guessing establishes such a set may in some cases be wholly or partially erroneous, and there is a risk that sources of negative as well as positive transfer may be disregarded. A second problem concerns the interaction of warm-up effects with stage of practice. As we have seen, there are reasons to believe that a warm-up activity influences the behavior of naive and experienced subjects differentially, perhaps because there is a change in the function which it serves. Finally, the problem of separating out the relative contribution of warm-up and learning to learn to the improvement observed within a given learning session has not been fully solved.

Conditions and Characteristics of Learning to Learn

We now turn to a consideration of experiments concerned primarily with learning to learn, that is, the acquisition of learning skills

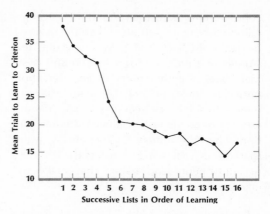

Figure 21.6. Progressive improvement in the acquisition of serial lists of nonsense syllables. Each list consisted of 12 items. The mean numbers of trials to a criterion of one perfect recitation are plotted for the successive lists. (Ward, 1937.)

as a result of practice. The conditions of these experiments make it possible in most cases to set aside the problem of the relative weight of warm-up and learning to learn. In many cases the successive practice sessions were spaced sufficiently far apart to justify the assumption that strictly transitory warm-up effects had fully dissipated between one task and the next; improvements in performance may then be seen as the retention of learned skills. In other cases the primary interest is in comparisons of different conditions of practice, with warm-up effects assumed to be held constant.

Serial and paired-associate learning There are typically substantial increases in speed of acquisition when lists of the same type are learned in succession. Figure 21.6 shows the progressive changes in rate of learning observed in an experiment by Ward (1937) in which subjects learned 16 successive serial lists of nonsense syllables. The sixteenth list required less than half as many trials to criterion as the first list. The magnitude of the practice effects is especially noteworthy in view of the fact that there inevitably is considerable duplication of letters among lists of nonsense syllables. Consequently there is a build-up of formal interlist similarity and

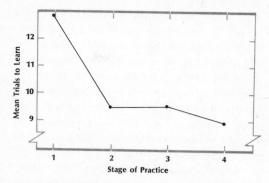

Figure 21.7. Speed of paired-associate learning as a function of stage of practice. Each list was carried to a criterion of 8 out of 10 responses correct. (Greenberg & Underwood, 1950.)

hence of sources of associative interference. Nevertheless the numbers of trials to criterion decline steadily. The function has the characteristic negatively accelerated form, but the limits of improvement for this type of task were probably not reached. For example, Melton and von Lackum (1941) reported that subjects who had had 28 days of previous practice in learning nonsense syllables, words, and numbers still showed improvement in an experiment in which the materials were lists of consonant syllables. It is likely that the period of continued improvement varies directly with the difficulty of the materials; thus, practice effects appear to level off quite rapidly in serial learning when the lists are composed of English words (Postman, 1962c).

Figure 21.7 shows changes in the speed of acquisition of lists of paired adjectives (Greenberg & Underwood, 1950). Successive sessions were spaced either 24 or 72 hours apart; learning on each list was carried to a criterion of 8/10. There was a substantial amount of improvement, but virtually all of it occurred in a single session. When a higher criterion is used, such as one perfect recitation, improvement in this type of task is more gradual and extends over a large number of sessions (Warr, 1964; Keppel, Postman, & Zavortink, 1968). Nevertheless the contrast between Figures 21.6 and 21.7 supports the conclusion that the speed with which the

practice curve reaches asymptote is inversely related to the difficulty of the task. The magnitudes of the gains are difficult to compare in view of the differential opportunities for improvement.

A detailed description of the changes in performance that reflect learning to learn has been given by Duncan (1960). A nonverbal paired-associate task was used, with visual forms as stimuli and lever movements as responses; it is likely that the major quantitative trends apply to verbal lists as well. There were 10 sessions distributed over two five-day weeks. A different task was practiced for 20 trials on each day. The basic conclusions regarding the progressive changes in performance may be summarized as a series of points. (1) As usual, overall performance increased as a negatively accelerated increasing function of the number of preceding sessions. (2) Learning to learn had its greatest effect fairly early during the practice on a given task, namely, during the second fifth of the learning period. The ceiling of performance limits the possibilities of improvement. (3) Consequently the learning curves will show progressively steeper slopes even when the asymptote is not affected. (4) As learning to learn continues, the stability of correct responses increases; that is, it becomes less and less likely that the first occurrence of a correct response will be followed by an error. (5) Initially slow learners register considerably greater gains than do initially fast learners. Such a difference is to be expected whenever the opportunities for detecting improvements are limited by an asymptote. It cannot, therefore, be inferred that the benefits of practice are greater for slow than for fast learners in an absolute sense. The analysis brings into focus the sensitivity of indices of learning to learn to the opportunities for improvement at a given point in practice.

Conditions of learning to learn Once learning to learn has been demonstrated, the question arises of what the habits and skills are that are responsible for the progressive improvements in performance. The designation of transfer as nonspecific clearly does not answer this question and conceptually does not advance very far beyond the historical assumption that some kind of ability has been strengthened. While the changes in performance cannot be attributed to the carrying over of specific discriminations or responses from one task to the next, they must nevertheless be assumed to reflect circumscribed habits and skills that depend on the conditions of prior practice and are applicable to a limited range of new situations. One approach to the identification of the components of nonspecific transfer is the comparison of conditions of practice which may be assumed to foster different kinds of skills. A few studies bearing on the analysis of improvement in paired-associate and serial learning will illustrate this line of investigation.

It is known that the efficiency of performance on a given task is an increasing function of the amount of prior practice on similar tasks. Is the progressive improvement attributable to the amount of practice per se or to the experience with a variety of tasks afforded by continuing practice? To the extent that the latter factor can be shown to be significant, it follows that one of the skills which is developed is the application of effective methods of practice to different tasks of the same type. In an experiment directed at this question Duncan (1958) used the nonverbal paired-associate task described earlier. The number of training tasks and the amount of practice were manipulated in an orthogonal design. Different groups received training on either 1, 2, 5, or 10 tasks. The amount of training was manipulated by giving 2, 5, or 10 days of practice at the rate of 20 trials per day. All groups were tested on two common final tasks. Improvement was found to be a direct function of both the total amount of practice and the degree of variation in training, with no interaction between these variables. Thus, varied training produced greater effects than constant training when the amount of practice was held constant; with degree of variation held constant, transfer increased with the amount of practice. Duncan suggests that experience with a variety of tasks renders the subject increasingly sensitive to the relevant dimensions of the stimulus terms. He may learn "as a general, transferable principle, that it is of value to look carefully at each stimulus presented, not only to its obvious characteristics, but also to any minor details" (1958, p. 71).

An analysis of the conditions and characteristics of learning to learn must inevitably return to the question which was at issue in the early studies of memory training: How specific is nonspecific transfer, that is, how wide is the spread of improvement from training on a particular task? To answer this question it is necessary to vary systematically the similarity relations between training and test tasks. In this context similarity refers, of course, not to particular stimulus or response elements but rather to the nature of the requirements that must be met by the learner. Thus, one may inquire to what extent the habits and skills that constitute learning to learn are peculiar to the method of practice and the class of materials used in the training phase. The specificity of learning to learn with respect to these task characteristics was investigated in an experiment by Postman and Schwartz (1964). There were four conditions of training that represented the factorial combination of two methods of practice and two classes of materials. The method used in the training phase was either serial or paired-associate learning, and the materials were either trigrams or familiar adjectives. There were two test tasks: a serial list of adjectives or a paired-associate list of adjectives. For each test task there were two groups, therefore, for which the method of practice in training and test remained the same and two groups for which it changed. Similarly, there were two groups for which the class of materials was kept constant and two groups for which it changed. There was no prior training under the control treatment. The acquisition curves for the paired-associate

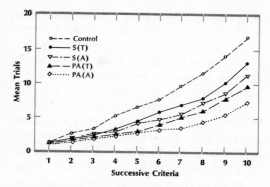

Figure 21.8. Mean numbers of trials to successive criteria on a list of paired adjectives after different conditions of prior training. The preceding list was learned by either the paired-associate (PA) or the serial (S) method and consisted of either adjectives (A) or trigrams (T). The control group had no prior training. (Postman & Schwartz, 1964.)

test list are shown in Figure 21.8. While all conditions of training produced increases in speed of learning, the gains were significantly greater when the method of practice remained the same than when it changed; that is, subjects with prior experience in paired-associate learning were superior to those shifted from a serial to a paired-associate task. The findings are parallel for class of materials but the effects are less pronounced. Differences among the conditions of training were less important when the test task was serial. The nature of the prior training did appear to influence the subjects' mode of attack on the serial task; for example, there was evidence that experience with paired-associate learning disposed the subjects to subdivide the series into a sequence of pairs. However, variations in speed of learning were minor, apparently because the different modes of attack fostered by the prior training proved to be equally effective. The results of the experiment support three general conclusions: (1) There is sufficient communality between the habits established by serial and by paired-associate training for substantial improvement to occur under all conditions; the same holds for the acquisition of meaningful and of nonsense material. (2) The differences among treatments reflect components of learning to learn specific to method of practice and class of materials (see Postman, Keppel, & Zacks, 1968). The differential transfer effects evident in Figure 21.8 appear relatively late in practice and may be attributed to increases in relevant associative skills. (3) When a task such as serial learning can be approached in alternative, and equally effective ways, more than one appropriate condition of prior training may produce equivalent amounts of gain but for different reasons. Thus, there may be systematic transfer effects that are not revealed by measures of speed of learning.

Free-recall learning The distinguishing characteristic of free-recall learning is that the subject is permitted to reproduce the items in the list in any order he wishes, that is, without regard to the order of input. The score on a test of free recall is, therefore, determined by the sheer number of items reproduced. When multiple trials are given on the same list, progressive improvements in performance have been shown to be related to the subjects' tendency to group individual items into higher-order units (Tulving, 1962, 1968). Hence, increased skill in the formation of higher-order units is a potentially important source of nonspecific transfer.

Evidence concerning nonspecific transfer in free-recall learning has been accumulating slowly, and there are still some apparent inconsistencies in the existing data. Progressive improvements are in general not as great as in the classical rote-learning situations, and the amount of nonspecific transfer is more sensitive to variations in the conditions of practice. An early study showing very substantial practice effects in free-recall learning was reported by Meyer and Miles (1953). The materials were lists of 12 nonsense syllables which were presented for five study-recall cycles. For a given list the order of presentation was fixed but recall was free.

The "method of retained members" was used, that is, subjects were given 30 seconds on each trial to study the entire list and then 30 seconds for free recall. One list was learned under these conditions in each of 20 successive sessions. The amount recalled increased as a negatively accelerated function of the number of prior sessions. The overall mean score rose from 24 to 34 between the first and the twentieth session. While these are impressive transfer effects, it must be recognized that the conditions of this study differ in important respects from those characteristic of most experiments on free-recall learning. First of all, the learning materials were nonsense syllables. A major part of the subjects' effort had, therefore, to be devoted to the integration of the items per se. Thus, much of the improvement may have been due to increases in response-learning skills. Unless there is an explicit concern with response learning, words are typically used in studies of free recall because of the emphasis on such factors as the subjective organization of items and the relation between input and output order. Thus, the use of the method of retained members, with presentation of nonsense syllables in a fixed serial order, represents an experimental arrangement that is not readily generalized to other studies of free recall.

A well-known study by Murdock (1960) also used rather special conditions, in this case with respect to test-trial procedures. The materials were lists of 30 common English words which were presented for four study-test cycles. On the test trials subjects were presented with a list of the initial letters of the items and were required to complete the words. In one experiment there were five sessions spaced at one-week intervals during each of which a single list was learned; in another experiment six successive lists were learned in one session. In neither case was there any evidence for nonspecific transfer. There are reasons to believe that the conditions of testing served to minimize the opportunities for improvement. The use of alphabetized blanks may have discouraged

subjective organization of items according to their meaning (see Tulving, McNulty, & Ozier, 1965, p. 251). As will be shown shortly, improved effectiveness of subjective organization is one of the factors making for improvement in free recall. Moreover, because of the inevitable overlap in initial letters an A–B, A–D relation obtained for at least some of the cues and responses in the successive lists, which is known to be conducive to interference (Zavortink & Keppel, 1968).

More recent studies have produced clear evidence for nonspecific transfer in free-recall learning but have also served to delimit the conditions under which it may be expected to occur. In an experiment by Dallett (1963) practice effects within a single session extending over 10–15 lists were investigated for ordered as well as for free recall. (Under conditions of ordered recall the sequence of items in presentation is kept constant, and subjects are required to reproduce the list in the correct serial order.) An important variable manipulated in this study was the frequency of test trials. In Dallett's first experiment 10-item lists were presented one, three, or five times before the first and only test of recall; in the second experiment there were 10 cycles consisting of a study and a test trial for each list. There was evidence for learning to learn for ordered recall in both experiments, but for free recall only when multiple test trials were given. Analysis of serial-position curves indicated that one source of improvement in ordered recall is a shift in the distribution of effort from the beginning of the series to the list as a whole, and particularly to the terminal items that have the benefit of recency in recall. These changes in learning strategy appear to develop in the absence of interspersed test trials. Where recall is free, it is likely that the subjects' ability to organize the list into higher-order units is significantly aided by interspersed tests. The fact that speed of free-recall learning and degree of subjective organization increase concurrently as a function of practice was demonstrated in a study by Tulving, McNulty, and Ozier (1965) in which three successive lists were presented for eight study-recall cycles each within a single session. This conclusion also receives support from a recent experiment by Mayhew (1967) in which the design paralleled that of Thune's (1951) study of within-session and between-session changes.

In Mayhew's experiment each subject learned six 30-word lists, two per day for three consecutive days. Each list was presented for 10 study-recall cycles. Half the subjects were given standard free-recall instructions, whereas the other half were given information about potentially useful ways of organizing the words in a list. The learning scores and the indices of subjective organization (Tulving, 1962) showed parallel trends, which were not unlike those reported by Thune: substantial increases within sessions but much smaller gains between sessions. The indices of subjective organization were higher and increased at a faster rate for the instructed than for the standard group, and the differences in recall were in the same direction. It is interesting to note that the indices of subjective organization as well as the recall scores show rapid rises within sessions followed by a decline from one day to the next. It would not be reasonable to consider degree of subjective organization a matter of warm-up; nevertheless the temporal trends are those conventionally identified with warm-up effects. Thus, these findings help to reinforce the question raised earlier about the criterion of temporal persistence used to differentiate between warm-up and learning to learn.

SPECIFIC TRANSFER: SIMILARITY RELATIONS

Stimulus-Response Analysis

Transfer effects are designated as specific when they are attributable to known similarity relations between the components of successive tasks. The similarity relations are critical because they determine what responses and dispositions are carried over from one situation to the next. If the laws of specific transfer are to be determined experimentally, it is necessary to identify the relevant components of the successive tasks and to vary them systematically. The usefulness of a stimulus-response analysis for this purpose was demonstrated in an early study by Poffenberger (1915), whose procedures represented a transition between the conventional design used in studies of ability training and the method of successive practice. In one investigation the experimental group was given protracted training in naming the opposite of each of 50 adjectives, for example, *broad-narrow*. In the pretest and the posttest both the experimental and the control group were instructed to give an appropriate noun to each of the same adjectives, for example, *street* or *shoe* to *narrow*. The expected negative transfer effect was observed. In another phase of the study the experimental subjects were practiced in canceling particular numbers and were tested on either the same or different numbers. A positive transfer effect was found when the numbers remained the same but none when they changed. On the basis of his findings Poffenberger proposed three generalizations: transfer effects are (1) positive when both the stimulus and the response remain the same, (2) negative when the stimulus remains the same and the response changes, and (3) zero when both the stimulus and the response change. In terms of current notation, the three paradigms are: $A-B, A-B$—positive; $A-B, A-D$—negative; $A-B, C-D$—zero. A short time later Wylie (1919) added a fourth principle, namely that the transfer effects are positive when the stimulus changes and the response remains the same ($A-B, C-B$). Evidence for the latter principle was obtained in a study of maze learning with rats in which the animals were successively trained to make the same response to different signals such as lights and sounds.

These principles were subjected to a comprehensive test in a study of paired-associate transfer by Bruce (1933). He used lists of

TABLE 21.2

Paradigm	Trials of List-1 Learning			
	0	2	6	12
A–B, C–D (IX)[a]	9.9	9.9	10.7	8.3
A–B, A'–B (VIII)	13.5	11.4	8.7	5.9
A–B, C–B (V)	14.4	16.6	12.0	9.0
A–B, A–B' (IV)	9.6	9.8	9.7	7.7
A–B, A–D (I)	10.3	12.1	11.9	11.2

[a]The number of the condition in the original article is given in parentheses.

paired nonsense syllables as learning materials. The number of trials on the first list was either 0, 2, 6, or 12; the second list was learned to a criterion of one perfect recitation. There were nine paradigms of transfer defined by the similarity relations among the stimulus and the response terms in the two lists. The lists were not balanced; thus a different test list was used under each condition of transfer. The subjects assigned to a given paradigm were tested at all four degrees of first-list learning. This was repeated for four cycles, with one list learned per day. Of the nine paradigms of transfer we will consider only five, which represent the basic conditions of interlist similarity; in the remaining cases intrapair and interlist similarity were varied concomitantly, and it is difficult to separate the relative contributions of these two factors. Table 21.2 lists the five paradigms of interest in current alphabetical notation. Similar stimuli are designated as A and A', similar responses as B and B'. In this experiment, such items have the first two letters in common but different third letters. The entries in the table are the mean numbers of trials to criterion on the second list.

The scores obtained without prior learning suggest that not all transfer lists were of equal difficulty. Ability differences among the groups ($N = 9$) may have been a contributing factor. (In previous discussions of this experiment the transfer results have usually been presented in terms of percentages to the base of trials to mastery without prior learning. However, in view of the apparent differences among test lists the percentages may be somewhat misleading.) Precise evaluation of at least some of the differences among paradigms is, therefore, difficult. A reasonably unbiased comparison can be made only between the C–D condition on the one hand, and the A–B' and A–D paradigms on the other. In general, the results appear to show the expected pattern: There is evidence of negative transfer for A–D, and of positive effects increasing with the degree of List-1 learning when the responses are the same or similar. To the extent that the proposed principles were confirmed, they were shown to hold for degrees of similarity other than identity. Attention was also focused on the importance of the level of first-list learning as a determinant of transfer. The study is certainly of historical importance as an early systematic investigation of the paradigms of transfer. From the vantage point of present-day methodology it is not a satisfactory experiment because different test lists were used under the various treatments. The resulting problems of interpretation have already become obvious. This difficulty applies to many studies of transfer in the literature, since the use of a common test list has become standard practice only in the fairly recent past.

Generalization and Transfer

Gradients of transfer When degrees of stimulus similarity short of identity are considered, the continuity between the operations used to measure transfer and the generalization of conditioned responses becomes apparent. In both cases the question is asked whether and to what extent a response associated with a training stimulus is elicited by more or less similar test stimuli. Stimulus generalization is typically measured by means of tests of performance (somewhat analogous to posttests), whereas the method of successive practice is the characteristic procedure for assessing transfer. Recognition of the continuity between these two classes of operations was important because the principles of stimulus generalization proved to be a significant tool in the theoretical analysis of transfer. For this reason some historical importance attaches to the early transition experiments, which were designed to demonstrate stimulus generalization in associative learning. A classical study by Yum (1931) is a case in point.

In Yum's first experiment the learning materials were lists of 14 paired associates, with two hyphenated nonsense syllables as the stimulus terms and English words as responses. The list was learned to a criterion of one perfect recitation, and a test of generalization was given 24 hours later. There were seven types of test stimuli represented by two items each. One condition of testing consisted of the presentation of the original syllables; in the other cases either the first letter, the second letter, or both were changed in one of the syllables. With three types of alterations for each of the two syllables, there were six kinds of generalization stimuli. Significantly fewer correct responses were given to all the altered stimuli than to the original ones. A change in the first letter of either syllable was more damaging than a change in the second letter; in fact the alteration of two letters produced only slightly poorer performance than alteration of only the first. The results show a generalization decrement at recall and at the same time indicate that the effective similarity between the training and the test stimulus depends critically on the locus of the change. The latter finding is consistent with the evidence subsequently obtained in studies of stimulus selection; that is, the first letter of a trigram is more

likely to become a functional stimulus than the middle one (Jenkins, 1963a; Postman & Greenbloom, 1967).

In the second experiment lists of 12 paired words were learned. The stimuli used on the delayed test were either the original words or words rated as having one of two degrees of meaningful similarity to the items in the list. Pronounced generalization decrements were again observed. In the third experiment the learning materials were lists of 15 pairs, in which visual nonsense forms were the stimuli and English words the responses. There were five types of test stimuli: original figures and figures having four rated degrees of similarity to the original ones. The percentage recalled was a negatively accelerated decreasing function of the degree of similarity between the training and the test stimulus. Comparable findings were reported by Gulliksen (1932) and McKinney (1933).

Studies such as Yum's served to exhibit the continuity between the measurement of stimulus generalization and of associative transfer. As will become apparent shortly, subsequent theoretical analysis of verbal transfer leaned heavily on the assumption that verbal stimuli generalize along dimensions of both meaningful and formal similarity. It is useful to note at this point that there has been substantial independent confirmation of this assumption. One important line of evidence comes from experiments showing semantic generalization of conditioned responses. When the conditioned stimulus is a word, the level of generalization of the conditioned response varies with the degree of similarity or of associative connection between the conditioned and the test stimulus (for example, Razran, 1939, 1949; Mednick, 1957). Conditioned responses have also been shown to generalize along a dimension of formal similarity defined, much as it was by Yum, in terms of the number of altered letters (Abbott & Price, 1964). Mention should also be made here of studies investigating mediated generalization of instrumental responses, such as a lever press. In these experiments the relation between the training and the test stimuli is one of associative linkage (Mink, 1963) or similarity of connotative meaning (Dicken, 1961). It is by no means certain that the mechanisms responsible for the generalization of conditioned or instrumental responses to verbal stimuli and for similarity effects in verbal transfer are the same (for a review of theoretical interpretations of semantic conditioning see Maltzman, 1968). The results of the conditioning experiments do, however, constitute independent empirical evidence of generalization among verbal stimuli.

Tests of generalization are usually administered after the end of practice. A variation on this procedure was recently introduced by Jenkins and his collaborators (Jenkins & Brown, 1965; Brown, Jenkins, & Lavik, 1966). The basic feature of the technique is the use of interspersed tests of generalization during the later stages of practice on a learning task. In one experiment (Brown et al., 1966), a list of nine paired associates composed of English words as stimuli and nonsense syllables as responses was learned for 10 trials. On trials 11 through 19, four of the nine stimuli presented to the subject were new, whereas the remaining five were from the original list. The subject was instructed to guess what the responses to the new stimuli might be; there was no feedback after the guesses. The new test stimuli had either a zero, low, intermediate, or high normative probability of being given as a response to the original stimulus in free association. The number of transfer responses increased progressively as a function of the degree of associative connection between the original and the test stimulus. In another experiment (Jenkins & Brown, 1965) the same test procedure showed that generalization is greater when the original and the test stimuli are associatively rather than semantically related (see Ryan, 1960). This finding was confirmed by Kasschau and Pollio (1967) who used separate lists for each type of response relation.

A gradient of generalization has also been reported for the recognition of verbal items, with degree of similarity again defined in terms of the number of changed letters (Postman, 1951). The experimental arrangements for the measurement of recognition and of associative learning are, of course, quite different, so that extrapolations from one process to the other must be made with considerable caution. Recent evidence suggests, however, that recognition of the stimulus term may be an essential condition for the elicitation of associative responses (Bernbach, 1967; Martin, 1967a, b). It is possible, therefore, that generalization of recognition plays a part in associative transfer.

Gibson's hypothesis A systematic application of the complementary concepts of generalization and differentiation to verbal learning, and to transfer and interference in particular, was formulated by Gibson (1940) in an influential paper. Gibson's analysis takes its point of departure from the proposition that generalization occurs among verbal stimuli and that the reduction of generalization (differentiation) is an essential condition of learning. Generalization is exemplified in the paired-associate situation when a response learned to one stimulus is elicited by other stimuli as well. If the list is to be mastered, generalization must be reduced by differential reinforcement. That is, the correct responses must be reinforced and the generalized responses not reinforced. (In the verbal-learning situation presentations of the correct responses presumably create the necessary conditions of reinforcement.) The greater the initial degree of generalization the more reinforced practice is required for differentiation to be established and the more difficult the learning task becomes. After the end of practice differentiation dissipates over time, that is, generalization tendencies show spontaneous recovery, just as do extinguished conditioned responses. The more differential reinforcement has been given during acquisition the more slowly spontaneous recovery will occur.

Before the extension of this analysis to transfer and interference is considered, it will be useful to make explicit certain inherent limitations of the theory and to examine the experimental operations that were used to test it. Most of the points to which attention will be called were considered in detail in an evaluation of Gibson's theory by Underwood (1961).

1. The degree of generalization that obtains among a particular group of stimuli is specified on an entirely empirical basis. "A *generalization gradient* is said to be formed when a number of stimulus items show decreasing degrees of generalization with a standard stimulus. The hypothesis need make no assumption as to the type of stimulus continuum which will yield a generalization gradient" (p. 204). Gibson adds, however, that it is consistent with the hypothesis to suppose that stimuli arranged along a scale of similarity will yield such a gradient; hence the degrees of interitem similarity and of generalization would normally be expected to be correlated. The decision to specify gradients of generalization in purely empirical terms led to experimental operations that tended to blur somewhat the distinction between independent and dependent variables in tests of the theory.

The stimuli used by Gibson were nonsense forms (Figure 21.9). To obtain sets of stimuli that could be ordered with respect to degree of generalization Gibson (1941) used the following procedure. Each of a series of standard forms was given a nonsense name, and the subjects had five study-test cycles on these paired associates. On the following day a test list was presented that contained some of the standard forms, variants judged to represent two different degrees of similarity to the standards, and some entirely unrelated forms. The subjects were instructed to write down the appropriate name of the form whenever they could. The percentages of recall were 85, 41, and 10 for standard, similar and less-similar forms, respectively. There were less than 3 percent attempts to respond to the unrelated forms. The results of this normative procedure were then used to define three degrees of interstimulus generalization for subsequent experiments. This method of specifying a theoretically anchored independent variable is relatively weak because essentially the same effects are measured in the normative situation and in the experiments in which the norms are applied: the probability that a variant will elicit a response associated with the standard. Thus Gibson (1942) found that high-generalization lists, in which both standards and their variants appeared as stimuli, were learned more slowly and yielded higher error frequencies than low-generalization lists composed of standards only. The learning experiment can be seen as a validation of the results of the normative test, and the same holds true for some of the findings on transfer to be discussed later. That is not the same, however, as a prediction of differences in learning and transfer on the basis of independently scaled stimulus characteristics. To be sure, judgments of similarity were

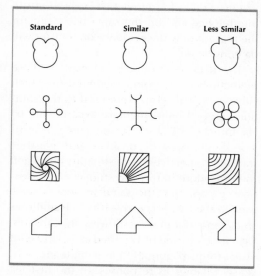

Figure 21.9. Examples of nonsense figures used by Gibson as stimulus terms in paired-associate lists. The similar and the less similar figures define two different degrees of generalization with respect to the standard. (Gibson, 1941.)

obtained by Gibson in the development of her figures, but the point at issue concerns the method used to *scale* the degree of generalization for the purpose of predicting learning and retention. A predictor variable determined by operations quite independent of behavior in a learning situation is much to be preferred.

2. As Underwood points out, the emphasis in the development of the hypothesis is on sensory generalization, just as it was in Pavlovian conditioning. Within this framework there is a disposition to view generalization as the mechanism responsible for the effects of nonsensory as well as of sensory characteristics of stimuli. Thus meaningfulness is conceptualized by Gibson in terms of interitem discriminability. Specifically, it is assumed that the degree of interitem generalization is inversely related to meaningfulness. It is on this basis that speed of learning is predicted to increase with stimulus meaningfulness. As it turned out, the influence of meaningfulness on speed of acquisition is at best moderate when this factor is varied on the stimulus side in a paired-associate list, as compared with the powerful effects on the response side (Underwood & Schulz, 1960). There is little in the available evidence that points to degree of interitem generalization as the variable underlying the relation between meaningfulness and learning. In short, discriminability is stressed at the expense of other potentially critical properties of verbal items.

3. The theory fails to consider the effects of response generalization. There was no strong evidence for the importance of this mechanism at the time when Gibson's position was formulated. As will be seen shortly, the significant role of response similarity, notably in transfer and interference, was not long in being established.

These limitations have to be borne in mind when the applications of the theory to the problems of transfer and interference are considered. (It must be recognized, of course, that the criticisms are made largely from the vantage point of information based on more recent developments. There is little question but that Gibson's theory made an important contribution in opening up new avenues of analytic experimentation.)

Stimulus generalization and transfer
Gibson's point of departure in the analysis of transfer and interference is the assumption that stimulus generalization occurs not only within lists but also between lists. When there is generalization between the stimulus terms in two successive lists, the first-list responses will be elicited during second-list learning. The higher the degree of generalization, the greater will be the magnitude of the resulting transfer effects. The direction of transfer will depend on whether the responses in the two lists are the same or different. If the responses remain the same, the effects will be positive because the generalizing and the correct responses coincide. If the responses change, the effects will be negative because the generalizing and the correct responses are in conflict. Parallel predictions are made for recall of the first list, that is, for retroactive facilitation and interference and on the same basis, but for the present only the evidence on transfer will be considered.

The data most directly relevant to these predictions come from experiments in which Gibson's visual forms were used as the stimulus terms. Complementary experiments by Hamilton (1943) and Gibson (1941) investigated the cases of positive and negative transfer, respectively. The stimulus items and the procedure in the two studies were identical, except that the same responses were used in the two successive lists in Hamilton's study and different responses in Gibson's. Each list consisted of 12 paired associates with visual forms (Figure 21.9) as stimuli and nonsense syllables as responses. In the first list the standard forms were the stimuli. There were four conditions of second-list learning distinguished by the characteristics of the stimuli: the forms in the second list were either the same as those in the first or rep-

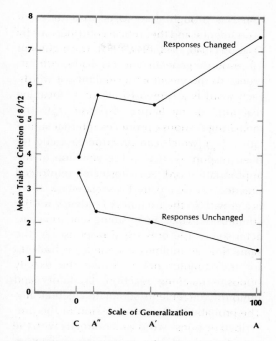

Figure 21.10. Transfer as a function of degree of interlist stimulus generalization. Mean trials to a criterion of 8/12 on the transfer list are plotted. In Gibson's experiment the response syllables in the first and in the second list were different; in Hamilton's experiment they were the same. (Data from Gibson, 1941; and Hamilton, 1943.)

resented first-degree, second-degree, or zero-degree generalization between the successive stimuli. Both lists were learned to a criterion of 8/12. The conditions in Hamilton's experiment may be denoted as A–B, A–B; A–B, A'–B; A–B, A''–B; and A–B, C–B. The corresponding groups in Gibson's experiment are: A–B, A–D; A–B, A'–D; A–B, A''–D; A–B, C–D. Speed of List-1 learning was quite similar in the two experiments, so that a direct comparison of the transfer results is in order. The mean numbers of trials to criterion on the second list are shown in Figure 21.10. It will be noted, first of all, that second-list learning is much faster when the responses remain the same than when they change. This difference is undoubtedly attributable to the transfer of response learning (availability of the nonsense-syllable responses) in the former case.

There is only limited evidence for the predicted relation between degree of stimulus generalization and amount of transfer. Moreover, the shape of the gradient is quite different in the two experiments. All that can be said is that the amount of transfer diminishes as one moves from identical to similar and then to unrelated stimuli. This relation is less pronounced when the effects are positive than when they are negative. The two degrees of generalization (A' and A'') differ but little from each other. Since the case of stimulus identity does not appear to be admitted by Gibson as a case of maximal generalization (see Underwood, 1961, p. 201), the prediction is only weakly supported. If the C–D condition in Gibson's experiment is considered as the control baseline, there is negative transfer for all groups with changed responses and positive transfer for all groups with identical responses. The results for the corresponding conditions obtained in a subsequent study by Bugelski and Cadwallader (1956) show a gradient for the positive, but not for the negative, paradigms.

All three studies share the limitation that a different second list was used under each of the conditions, so that precise comparisons of the amounts of transfer are not possible. A more recent experiment by Dallett (1962a), in which Gibson's forms were again used as stimuli and English words as responses, did use a common second list. The two 12-pair lists were learned for 7 trials each. The mean numbers of correct responses in second-list learning were as follows:

A–B	—[a]	A–D	47.4
A'–B	61.2	A'–D	45.6
A''–B	62.7	A''–D	51.5
C–B	48.7	C–D	52.0

[a]Not included in this study.

There is positive transfer relative to the C–D control baseline when the stimuli are similar and the responses remain the same (but note that the effect is negative when the stimuli are unrelated). However, there is no difference between the two degrees of stimulus similarity. When the responses are new, the transfer effects are negative, and the expected difference between the two degrees of similarity is found. However, A''–D and C–D are equal. The predicted regular transfer gradients once more failed to materialize. Again all that can be concluded is that the amount of transfer is some increasing function of stimulus similarity.

Changes in transfer as a function of similarity have also been investigated with English words as the stimulus terms. One common definition of similarity is in terms of synonymity (Haagen, 1949). Using lists of eight paired adjectives as the learning materials, Staner (1956) compared the amounts of transfer obtained under conditions of high, medium, and low stimulus similarity when the responses in the successive lists remained identical. As expected, the amount of transfer increased directly with stimulus similarity. A pattern consistent with Staner's results may be found in a study by Wimer (1964), but the latter failed to find corresponding effects when responses were unrelated, that is, for negative transfer.

The degree of relation between stimulus (or response) words has also been scaled in terms of the strength of the associative connection between them. When the stimulus words in successive lists are associatively related, transfer is greater than when they are unrelated. Thus, Ryan (1960) found that after the acquisition of A–B, positive transfer effects were greater for the A'–B than C–B paradigm. In general, then, the amount of transfer is an increasing function of the degree of meaningful similarity or associative connection between the stimulus words in successive lists.

Response generalization in transfer
Gibson's theory was basically incomplete because it failed to consider the role of response generalization along with that of stimulus generalization. The importance of relating transfer to both types of generaliza-

tion was brought into focus in a series of experimental and theoretical contributions by Osgood (1946, 1948, 1949, 1953). The argument for response generalization is made with reference to the meaningful similarity of words. Each word is assumed to evoke a "meaning reaction" or mediating response (r_m). The mediating response produces internal stimulation (s_m), which can function as a cue for overt responses such as the emission of the appropriate word. As a result of reinforced practice, say on a paired-associate task, there is a growth in the excitatory tendency for the stimulus to evoke the meaning reaction characteristic of the prescribed response. At the same time an inhibitory tendency is built up for the stimulus not to evoke the exactly opposite meaning reaction. Excitatory and inhibitory increments summate algebraically. The probability of overt emission of the prescribed response word varies directly with the net strength of the appropriate excitatory tendency. Both the excitatory and inhibitory tendencies are assumed to generalize, with generalization occurring among r_ms and s_ms. The assumption of complementary tendencies of excitation and inhibition, which are built up concurrently by reinforced practice, introduces a feature not found in conven-

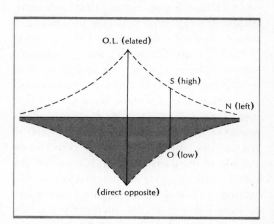

Figure 21.11. Hypothetical gradients of response generalization in paired-associate learning, showing spread of excitatory and inhibitory tendencies. For a full explanation see text. (Osgood, 1946.)

tional analysis of mediated generalization (Hull, 1943).

The implications for transfer become apparent when we consider the gradients of excitation and inhibition that are assumed to exist at the end of first-list learning. A picture of the theoretical situation is shown in Figure 21.11. Consider a list in which the stimuli are bigrams and the responses are adjectives. One of the pairs is *cm-elated*. This association has been built up during the learning trials. The excitatory tendency will generalize to similar meaning reactions, for example, *high,* but not dissimilar ones, for example, *left.* In addition, there is an inhibitory tendency for the stimulus not to evoke the directly opposite reaction, in this case *dejected.* This tendency will in turn generalize to responses which lie on the gradient for *dejected,* such as *low.* The latter is described by Osgood as an "opposed," as distinguished from an opposite or "antagonistic," reaction. The transfer effects in second-list learning will vary with the position the new response occupies on one or the other of the generalization gradients. The analysis can be extended readily to predict variations in retroactive inhibition since the generalization of excitatory tendencies developed during interpolated learning will add to the strength of the original association, and generalization of inhibitory tendencies will subtract from it.

The predictions derived from this analysis were tested by Osgood in two experiments. Both were studies of retroactive interference, but for the present only the transfer data will be considered in detail. In the first experiment (1946) the learning materials were lists of 15 paired associates, with bigrams as stimuli and adjectives as responses. The responses in the second list were either similar, unrelated, or opposed in meaning to those in the first list. Each similarity relation was represented by five responses in the second list. (The use of a mixed list is favored by Osgood because it prevents the establishment of a systematic response set.) Each pair in the first list was learned to a criterion of one correct anticipa-

tion, whereas the pairs in the second list were carried to two correct repetitions. The lists were so balanced that each pair represented the three similarity relations equally often. A measure weighted for speed of responding was used to assess performance on the transfer list. Similar pairs were learned better than either unrelated or opposed ones; the latter did not differ. In the second experiment (1948) the lists consisted of 14 paired associates constructed as before. The responses of half the pairs were similar in the two lists; the other half were opposed (but not antonyms). The pairs in the first list were learned to a criterion of one perfect anticipation; the second list was learned for either 1, 2, 4, or 8 trials. The transfer performance of all the groups was evaluated on the first trial. There was no reliable difference in the number of correct responses between the two types of pairs, but response latencies were shorter when the responses were similar than when they were opposed. In both experiments the variations in amount of retroactive interference parallel the findings for transfer. In general, the support for the hypothesis is not impressive. The observed effects of response similarity are not large and are limited to latency measures or indices of performance weighted for speed of responding. There is no evidence of a regular gradient of response generalization.

Osgood's transfer surface Leaning heavily on the data obtained by Gibson and Hamilton, and in his own studies, Osgood (1949) formulated the following empirical laws of transfer and retroaction:

1. Where stimuli are varied and responses are functionally identical, positive transfer and retroactive facilitation are obtained, the magnitude of both increasing as the similarity between the stimulus members increases. This law is supported by Hamilton's (1943) results.

2. Where stimuli are functionally identical and responses are varied, negative transfer and retroactive interference are obtained, the magnitude of both decreasing as similarity

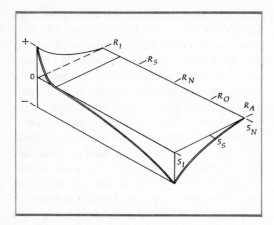

Figure 21.12. Osgood's transfer and retroaction surface. (Osgood, 1949.)

between the responses increases. The paradigms ranging from A–B, A–B' to A–B, A–D are encompassed here; the relevant evidence is a composite of the findings of Gibson (1941) and Osgood (1946, 1948). Note that negative transfer is expected to decrease as responses become more similar but that the law stops short of predicting positive transfer.

A third law is added which is designed to account for the fact that in studies of serial learning negative transfer and interference increase with the degree of similarity between successive lists (McGeoch & McDonald, 1931; Johnson, 1933; McGeoch & McGeoch, 1936; Melton & Von Lackum, 1941). The formulation of this law is based on the assumption that in a serial list each item serves as both a stimulus and a response.

3. When both stimulus and response members are simultaneously varied, negative transfer and retroactive interference are obtained, the magnitude of both increasing as stimulus similarity increases.

The three laws are integrated in the well-known transfer and retroaction surface (Osgood, 1949) which is reproduced in Figure 21.12. The vertical dimension represents the direction and amount of transfer or retroaction. Degrees of stimulus similarity ranging from neutrality (unrelated items) to identity are spaced along the width of the solid.

Degrees of response similarity, which vary from identity to antagonism, are distributed along the length of the solid. The median horizontal plane represents zero transfer or retroaction. When the stimuli in successive tasks are unrelated, all points fall on the median plane of the surface. For other degrees of stimulus similarity zero effects are expected at some point between response identity and response similarity. Thus, the occurrence of greater than zero transfer is shown to depend on the presence of some degree of stimulus similarity; the direction of transfer depends on response similarity. However, as the sharply inflected function on the front edge of the surface indicates, positive effects are predicted only for identical or nearly identical responses.

The surface represented an important systematic attempt at an integration of the total range of transfer and interference phenomena. However, it is fair to say that the surface was erected on a rather shaky empirical foundation even when the data available at that time are considered.

The most important empirical weakness was the lack of clear evidence for the orderly transfer gradients which are a central feature of the model. For stimulus similarity the data of Gibson and Hamilton, on which Osgood placed heavy reliance, give only limited support to theoretical expectations. As for response similarity, Osgood's own data contain some evidence for the positive influence of this variable but in no way confirm the extension of the gradient to opposed and antagonistic responses. No difference between unrelated and opposed responses was found; antonyms were not included in the lists. The transfer effects for opposed and antonymous responses are likely to be complexly determined because differences in meaning may be offset by associative connections.

Two other uncertain assumptions incorporated in the surface should be noted. The first of these is that as long as the stimuli are unrelated, transfer effects will remain at zero, regardless of the similarity relation between responses (back edge of surface). The empirical basis for this principle was provided by the combined data of Gibson and Hamilton (see Figure 21.10). However, there were indications in Bruce's (1933) results that a difference in favor of the paradigm of response identity (A–B, C–B) may emerge at higher degrees of first-list learning. Subsequent work has supported the conclusion that significant transfer effects occur for this paradigm, with the amount and direction of transfer determined by both the meaningfulness of the responses and the degree of first-list learning. The second assumption which proved questionable concerns the one-to-one correspondence between variations in transfer and retroaction. Such congruence was to be expected on theoretical grounds and in general was found in the available data. There was, however, an important exception in the results of one of Gibson's studies which gave an early indication that the functions for transfer and retroaction are not necessarily identical. The conditions in that experiment were the same as those depicted in Figure 21.10 except that there was also a control group which learned and recalled a single list (Gibson, 1941, Exp. I). Relative to the control group the A–B, C–D paradigm (unrelated stimuli and unrelated responses), which defines the condition of zero transfer, yielded a substantial amount of retroactive inhibition. We shall encounter other cases in which the correlation between transfer and retroaction does not hold.

Other surfaces The similarity relations depicted in Osgood's surface apply to individual pairs in the successive lists. The influence of list structure cannot be taken into account. Consequently, the surface cannot generate accurate predictions for what later turned out to be a powerful paradigm of negative transfer, namely, the re-pairing of the first-list stimuli and responses in the second list (A–B, A–Br). Within the framework of the surface, this paradigm reduces to A–B, A–D since the stimuli remain identical and the second-list response to each individual stimulus is new. However, as originally predicted by Gagné, Baker, and Foster (1950), re-pairing maximizes negative transfer and produces greater effects than the attachment of new responses to old stimuli. For paired-associate verbal learning the differential effectiveness of the A–Br and A–D paradigms in producing negative transfer effects was demonstrated by Porter and Duncan (1953), Besch and Reynolds (1958), and numerous other investigators thereafter. The stimuli and responses in the successive lists that are re-paired need not be identical but may be more or less similar to each other, for example, A–B, A'–B'r; A–B, A"–B"r; and so on. A surface representing the effects of stimulus and of response similarity for such noncorresponding pairings has been constructed by Dallett (1965). The surface complements Osgood's for corresponding pairings. However, for the points from the two surfaces sampled in Dallett's experiment the results are not complementary: variations in both stimulus and response similarity influenced the transfer effects for Osgood's paradigms, whereas only stimulus similarity had an effect in the re-paired conditions.

Even when only individual pairs are considered, Osgood's surface does not exhaust all the similarity relations between the members of the pairs in the successive lists. The stimuli in the first list (S_1) may be more or less similar to the responses in the second list (R_2), and so also for first-list responses (R_1) and second-list stimuli (S_2). To represent the effects of these similarity relations on transfer, Houston (1964a) relabeled Osgood's surface, substituting S_2–R_1 for stimulus similarity, and S_1–R_2 for response similarity. It follows from the geometry of the surface that the amount of transfer is predicted to be zero as long as S_2 and R_1 are unrelated. As these two terms become more similar, the amount of transfer increases, reaching its maximum when S_2 and R_1 are identical. The direction of transfer is determined by the relation between S_1 and R_2, being maximally negative when they are unrelated and maximally positive when they are identical (A–B, B–D and A–B, B–A, respectively). Differences in transfer effects in accord with the predictions were later reported by Houston (1966a, 1966b). However, as Thompson (1966) has pointed out, the Osgood and Houston surfaces are incompatible and make divergent predictions for numerous paradigms. Perhaps the most telling objection to Houston's surface mentioned by Thompson is that it entails the prediction that learning will not take place. The paradigm for continued practice is $A-B$, $A-B$, in which S_2 and R_1 are unrelated, which according to the model means zero transfer effects from one trial to the next. On the other hand, Osgood's surface implies zero transfer for $A-B$, $B-A$, which is known to produce substantial positive effects (Murdock, 1956) as predicted by the other model.

One surface appears to lead to another. After the appearance of Dallett's (1965) surface for conditions of re-pairing, Houston (1965) developed one representing the re-paired versions of his own paradigms. It was predicted that negative transfer would increase as S_2 and R_1 become more similar; this increase should be greater when S_1-R_2 similarity is high than when it is low. The re-paired version encounters the same difficulties as the original one; for example, it appears to predict minimal negative transfer for the basic $A-B$, $A-Br$ paradigm itself, since S_2 and R_1 are unrelated! A subsequent experimental test failed to yield the expected differences among re-paired paradigms (Houston & Morony, 1966).

The fact that a surface such as Houston's (1964a) has some apparent empirical validity but at the same time entails the absurd implication that learning cannot occur points up a basic weakness of such models. The source of the difficulty is that total transfer is related to two single dimensions of variation such as stimulus or response similarity. Both of the dimensions may well represent significant independent variables, but between them they determine only some of the component processes on which transfer depends. As a consequence some of the predictions fail, and important paradigms reflecting the contribu-

tions of other components cannot be accommodated. Thus, Osgood's surface applies to the transfer of forward associations, such as $A-B$, $A-D$. The $A-Br$ paradigm cannot be handled because additional sources of transfer become critical—certainly backward associations and probably list differentiation. An examination of the paradigms on Houston's surface indicates that the operative factor is the relation between the forward associations in one list and the backward associations in the other, as illustrated by the contrast between $A-B$, $B-A$ (maximally positive) and $A-B$, $B-D$ (maximally negative). Surfaces are convenient representational devices, but any given model will be descriptive of some but not all of the *components* of transfer. The analytic usefulness of component surfaces will be illustrated shortly.

Response similarity: parasitic reinforcement or mediation? Regardless of the ultimate validity of the surface, Osgood's analysis made a major contribution in focusing attention on response similarity as a determinant of transfer. The particular scale of response similarity represented in the surface has not received much empirical confirmation. Tests of the total surface were carried out in the studies of Bugelski and Cadwallader (1956) and Wimer (1964) mentioned earlier. The former used identical, similar, neutral, and opposed responses; the latter included antonymous responses as well. In neither case was the predicted gradient of increasingly negative transfer effects obtained. In Dallett's (1962a) study, in which only identical, similar, and unrelated responses were used, the results conformed reasonably well to the predictions of the Osgood surface.

When only the range from response identity to neutrality is considered, there is substantial other evidence that as responses become more similar, the acquisition of the transfer list is increasingly facilitated (Morgan & Underwood, 1950; Underwood, 1951; Young, 1955; Staner, 1956). The assumption that response generalization is the mechanism responsible for the gradient of facilitation (Osgood, 1946) was also formulated as the hypothesis of parasitic reinforcement (Morgan & Underwood, 1950). According to this interpretation reinforced practice on A–B during first-list learning not only strengthens the connection between A and B, but also between A and a range of responses similar to B. These generalized associations—A–B', A–B", and so on—receive parasitic reinforcement during the acquisition of A–B. The gradient of response generalization indexes the effects of parasitic reinforcement. To the extent that parasitic reinforcement has occurred, the List-2 associations are prelearned and require correspondingly less new learning.

One important implication of this hypothesis is that at a given level of response similarity the amount of positive transfer should be an increasing function of degree of first-list learning. This prediction follows from the assumption that direct and generalized associative strength vary together. Moreover, the higher the response similarity, the greater should be the gains in transfer produced by increases in degree of first-list learning. These expectations were fully confirmed in an experiment by Underwood (1951). The learning materials were lists of 12 paired adjectives. The degree of synonymity between the responses in the two lists was either high, medium, or low (zero). There were three criteria of first-list learning—4/12 correct responses, 7/12, or two successive errorless trials. The mean numbers of trials required to learn the second list to a criterion of 7/12 are shown in Figure 21.13. When the responses are unrelated, degree of first-list learning does not influence transfer. As degree of response similarity increases, the effects become substantial. This conclusion was strongly supported by the results of an item analysis. The relation was determined between the number of times the response to a given stimulus was reinforced during List-1 learning and the probability of a correct response to the same stimulus on the first transfer trial. The greater the response similarity, the more marked the positive relation was found to be. A further finding, which has been confirmed repeatedly, was that the frequency of intrusions from the first list during the acquisition of the transfer list increased with the degree of response similarity. Intrusions may be expected to occur when the responses from the two lists are of approximately equal strength, and this condition is most likely to develop when the level of generalization is high.

While many of the observed effects of response similarity are consistent with the hypothesis of parasitic reinforcement, there is strong support for an alternative interpretation, namely, that these effects are the result of mediation. Consider the A–B, A–B' paradigm, where there is a high degree of similarity between B and B'. Meaningful similarity and associative relation tend to be highly correlated (Haagen, 1949). It is possible, therefore, that after acquisition of A–B, activation of the associative chain A–B–B' will permit the subject to make the correct response in the transfer stage. There are several lines of evidence that suggest that such mediational chaining is in fact the effective mechanism of facilitation. (1) When the responses are synonymous, the amount of facilitation observed under optimal conditions of testing has been found to be extremely high. For

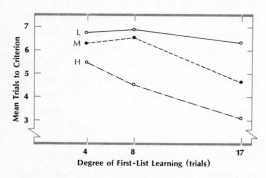

Figure 21.13. Mean numbers of trials to a criterion of 7/12 on the transfer list as a function of interlist response similarity and degree of first-list learning. L, M, and H refer to low, medium, and high response similarity, respectively. (Underwood, 1951.)

example, in a study by Barnes and Underwood (1959) an unpaced test of recall showed that list A–B' was learned almost perfectly in a single trial. As the investigators point out, one-trial transfer would indicate that there is essentially no gradient between B and B'. Thus, it becomes difficult to attribute the positive transfer effects to response generalization. On the other hand, an unpaced test would presumably maximize the opportunity for mediation and thus permit a very high level of performance. (2) In the same study nearly all the subjects reported that they had, indeed, used the first-list responses as mediators in learning the second list. (3) When the manipulated relation between B and B' is defined in terms of the degree of associative connection, for example, when the responses in the second list are normative primaries of those in the first although not necessarily synonymous, very substantial amounts of positive transfer are obtained (Bastian, 1961; Postman & Stark, 1964). In the latter study the characteristics of transfer performance were shown to parallel those observed with synonymous responses (Underwood, 1951).

Recently the mediation hypothesis has encountered a potentially serious difficulty. On the reasonable assumption that mediation takes time, mediational effects should increase as the response interval is lengthened. That is, the more time the subject has to give the required response in the transfer stage, the greater should be the likelihood of the mediational chain being successfully completed. The expected relation between the length of the response interval and amount of mediated transfer has, however, failed to materialize in several experiments. When the C–D, A–D, and A–B' paradigms were compared, there were no differential effects of changes in the duration of the response interval. The durations used in a study by Spear, Mikulka, and Podd (1966) were 1, 2, and 4 seconds; in an experiment by Richardson (1967c) they were .75, 1.5, and 3 seconds. Increases in the length of the interval serve

to improve performance but do so about equally for all paradigms. Response time (1, 2, or 4 seconds) also failed to influence the amount of transfer in a study by Schwenn and Underwood (1965) in which the associative connection between the responses in the two lists was built in experimentally through prior paired-associate training. It is possible to ask whether the reductions in response time were perhaps not great enough to preclude mediation. Independent determinations of the latencies of implicit verbal responses (Richardson, 1967b, 1968b) indicate, however, that such is probably not the case.

An alternative explanation was recently proposed by Richardson (1968b) who did obtain the expected relation between the length of the response interval and amount of positive transfer when the study interval was shorter than in the other studies, that is, 1 second rather than 2 seconds. Given a sufficiently long study interval, the control as well as the experimental subjects have an opportunity to develop mediational links between the stimulus and the response; consequently both benefit from increases in the length of the response interval. However, when the study interval is very short, mediators are much more available to the experimental subjects who therefore derive a greater advantage from increases in the response interval. Implicit in the analysis is the recognition of the fact that mediated transfer depends on both the discovery and the utilization of the appropriate associative links (Schulz & Lovelace, 1964). Discovery is most likely to take place during the study intervals; utilization must occur during the response intervals. The amount of time available for both processes, under the control as well as the experimental treatment, must be taken into account. Richardson's hypothesis does not, however, explain positive transfer effects obtained with response intervals that are presumably too short to allow any mediation to occur. In accounting for such findings, the hypothesis of response generalization appears to have an advantage.

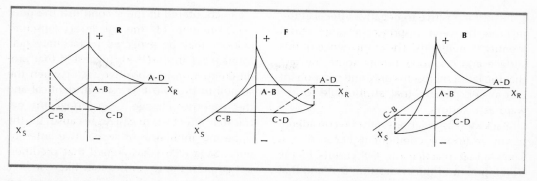

Figure 21.14. Component surfaces for response availability (*R*), forward associations (*F*), and backward associations (*B*). Degree of stimulus similarity is spaced along the X_S axis, and degree of response similarity along the X_R axis. The point of origin represents identity of both the stimulus and the response. Direction and degree of transfer are indicated along the vertical axis. (Martin, 1965.)

Components of Transfer

As became apparent in our discussion of surfaces, it is not possible to conceive of transfer effects as unitary because multiple processes come into play during the acquisition of both the training and the test list. Depending on the similarity relations between successive tasks, different sources of transfer become effective and influence the component processes of learning in the test stage to varying degrees. When there is more than one source of transfer, the magnitude and direction of their effects on performance may not only be different but may indeed be in opposition to each other. In the analysis of the components of transfer it has proved useful to specify what is carried over from the training to the test phase with reference to the distinction between response learning and associative learning.

According to this two-stage conception of acquisition (Underwood & Schulz, 1960, p. 92), the prescribed responses must become available before they enter into new associations. Thus, the subject who has mastered the first list carries over to the transfer task the results of both response learning and associative learning. The next step is to determine how these component habits influence second-list learning, again within the framework of a two-stage analysis (Postman, 1962a; Martin,

1965). Nonspecific transfer effects may influence both stages of acquisition and are assumed to be present for all paradigms. The locus, magnitude, and direction of the specific effects, on the other hand, depend on the conditions of intertask similarity. These have been conceptualized by Martin (1965) in the form of three component surfaces, which are reproduced in Figure 21.14.

The first of these represents the influence of response learning (*R*). The positive transfer effects decline progressively from a maximum to zero as the relation between the successive responses changes from identity to dissimilarity. The weight carried by this component of transfer is independent of the degree of stimulus similarity. The other two surfaces depict the conditions of associative transfer. The influence of forward and of backward associations is considered separately. Except for a change in the scale of response similarity, the surface for forward associations (*F*) is the same as Osgood's. Martin suggests that the scale position of opposite responses should reflect the degree of associative connection between them, and on this basis they would be located above, rather than below, entirely unrelated responses. For forward associations we find, as before, that the amount of transfer is an increasing function of the degree of stimulus similarity and that there is a shift from positive to negative effects as the relation between responses changes from identity to neutrality. The coincidence of this surface and Osgood's brings home the fact that the latter represents only one component of transfer, namely, that attributable to forward associations.

Backward associations must be considered as an additional component because it is known that practice on A-B results in the development of the association B-A and that the latter can be a significant source of transfer. (For a review of the literature on backward associations see Ekstrand, 1966.) The B surface in Figure 21.14 shows the expected variation in transfer effects as determined by the relation between first-list and second-list backward associations under the various paradigms. The B surface is symmetrical in form to the F surface, so that the amount of transfer increases as a function of the degree of similarity between the response terms, ranging from maximally positive for A-B, A-B (backward associations B-A, B-A) to maximally negative for A-B, C-B (B-A, B-C). It should be noted that only relations between congruent associations are represented, that is, successive forward ones and successive backward ones.

These three components do not, of course, exhaust all the sources of specific transfer that can be postulated on theoretical grounds. In particular, the transfer of stimulus and of response differentiation from one list to the next (predifferentiation) may be added. Mastery of the first list requires discrimination among the stimulus terms and among the response terms. If the same or similar items are encountered in the second list, the prior establishment of the necessary discriminations may be expected to facilitate performance. Gibson (1940) suggested that predifferentiation is a positive factor when the stimuli in the two lists remain identical and the responses change, even though the net transfer effect is negative because of the opposing influence of associative interference. Saltz (1961) has argued that predifferentiation of the responses may likewise be a source of facilitation. It is his contention, for example, that the positive effects of prior response familiarization on paired-associate learning (for example, Underwood, Runquist, & Schulz, 1959) are to be attributed to the predifferentiation rather than the increased availability of the response terms. Thus, both types of differentiation deserve consideration in principle as potential components of transfer. To these a third type should be added, namely, list differentiation.

One possible source of error during the acquisition of a transfer list is the failure to identify the list membership of a pair correctly. For example, in learning A-D after A-B, the subject may know both the responses but give B instead of D because of a confusion between the two lists; such an error would be classified as an interlist intrusion. Alternatively, he may withhold D because he incorrectly identified it as a first-list response. It is reasonable to suppose that accuracy of list differentiation will vary inversely with the similarity of both stimulus and response terms; changes in either class of items provide the learner with distinctive cues to list membership. As the name implies, the differentia-

TABLE 21.3

Component	Paradigm				
	C-D	A-B'	A-D	C-B	A-Br
Response learning	0	(+)	0	+	+
Response differentiation	0	(+)	0	+	+
Stimulus differentiation	0	(+)	+	0	+
Forward associations	0	(+)	−	0	−
Backward associations	0	(+)	0	−	−
List differentiation	+ +	−(−)	− +	+ −	− −

tion here is between the lists as a whole rather than between the members of individual pairs. However, since the similarity relations between stimuli and between responses are assumed to be critical, list differentiation may be appropriately included among the components of specific transfer.

The Standard Paradigms of Specific Transfer

Recent experimental analyses of transfer have been largely limited to five basic paradigms: A–B, C–D; A–B, A–B'; A–B, A–D; A–B, C–B; A–B, A–Br. The reasons for the choice of these paradigms should by now be apparent; they represent conditions that may be expected to maximize the operation of various components and mechanisms of transfer, with C–D providing the control baseline for the effects of warm-up and learning to learn.

Table 21.3 identifies for each of the standard paradigms the component processes that are assumed to come into operation during the acquisition of the transfer task (for other such summaries see Martin, 1965, p. 339; Underwood, 1966, p. 525). A plus sign indicates a positive, and a minus sign a negative, effect. There are two entries for list differentiation: the first refers to the expected consequences of stimulus relations and the second to those of response relations. A zero entry means that the given component does not apply. For purposes of this tabulation it is assumed that the A–B, A–B' paradigm represents a high degree of synonymity or associative connection between responses. However, the effects of various components are taken not to be as great as they are in the case of response identity and they are therefore listed in parentheses.

A–B, C–D Table 21.3 makes it apparent why the C–D paradigm has become the standard control condition for the evaluation of specific transfer effects. The amount of warm-up and learning to learn may be reasonably supposed to be the same as for the other paradigms. The specific components are not applicable because both stimuli and respon-

ses are new, but the present table points to the possibility of an important exception: Precisely because all items in the first task are entirely dissimilar from those in the second, list differentiation is maximal. To the extent that failures of list differentiation can influence transfer performance, the control condition has a distinct advantage. Two other reservations regarding the validity of the C–D control baseline must be expressed. First, complete dissimilarity of both the stimulus and the response terms in the two lists is an essential defining property of this condition, but it may be difficult to meet this requirement in practice. In fact, when nonsense syllables are used as stimuli or responses, the requirement is bound to be violated because of the limited pool of letter elements. Nevertheless such materials continue to be used in experiments in which the appropriate implementation of the C–D paradigm is of critical importance for the interpretation of the results (e.g., Dean & Kausler, 1964; Houston, 1967b; Slamecka, 1967). In such cases severe biases in the interpretation of transfer and interference effects are likely to result. Second, it is in the nature of the C–D condition that during the acquisition of the successive lists the subject is exposed to a larger number of items than under any of the other standard paradigms. Thus, there is an inevitable bias against the control condition with respect to the amount of material learned; moreover, as the total pool of different verbal units is increased, it becomes more and more difficult to avoid uncontrolled interitem similarities both within and between lists. It must be concluded that the C–D paradigm represents at best an approximation to a control condition that is free of specific transfer effects. Absolute measures of specific transfer taken with respect to this baseline are, therefore, of uncertain validity for all types of materials, and certainly highly suspect when nonsense items are used. The use of this control remains nevertheless essential because of the need to take account of nonspecific transfer effects; clearly, however, it must be evaluated with considerable caution.

A–B, A–B′ Given a high degree of similarity or associative connection between the responses, all the entries in Table 21.3 are positive, with the exception of list differentiation. The latter is seen as difficult because of the identity of the stimuli and near identity of the responses. The characteristic course of transfer under this paradigm appears to bear out this assessment of the component processes. Transfer effects in the early stages of second-list learning are typically positive, especially when responses are associatively related but tend to become negative as practice on the test list continues (Postman, 1964a; Keppel & Postman, 1966; Postman & Stark, 1969). As was noted earlier, the frequency of interlist intrusions is relatively high; moreover, the intrusions are often persistent and their number is likely to increase during the early learning trials. These trends are consistent with the assumption that the positive effects are counteracted by failures of list differentiation which manifest themselves in generalization errors or confusions between mediators and mediated terms.

Within the framework of a mediational interpretation, the designation of the various components as positive rests on the assumption that the process of mediational chaining continues to operate throughout the course of transfer learning. To the extent that mediators are not used or drop out, *A–B′* reduces to *A–D*. The fact that the *A–B′* paradigm typically yields some retroactive inhibition, even under unpaced conditions (Barnes & Underwood, 1959; Postman, 1962b; Zavortink & Keppel, 1968), indicates that the *A–B′* and *A–D* paradigms may, indeed, shade into each other.

A–B, A–D This is the classical paradigm of negative transfer, with forward associations as the source of interference. Some of the early evidence for negative transfer in this condition has already been discussed. Recent studies have in general yielded the same result (for example, Twedt & Underwood, 1959; Postman, 1962a). There are growing indications, however, that the amount of negative transfer may

be a function of meaningfulness. Using adjectives as stimuli and trigrams as responses, Jung (1963) found a relatively small amount of negative transfer when the meaningfulness of the response terms was low but a substantial effect when it was high (see Merikle, 1968). In an experiment by Goulet (1965), in which the learning materials likewise were adjective-syllable pairs, the meaningfulness of the first-list and second-list response terms was varied factorially. Negative transfer effects were greater when the meaningfulness of the first-list responses was high than when it was low. The results also indicated that a change in the meaningfulness of the responses served to reduce negative transfer, presumably by facilitating list differentiation. Other things being equal, high meaningfulness of the first-list responses favors the development of associations that can interfere effectively with second-list learning. A study by Richardson and Brown (1966), in which trigrams were used as stimuli and words as responses, shows that negative transfer also increases with the degree of stimulus meaningfulness.

Stimulus differentiation is a potential source of positive transfer whenever the stimuli in the successive lists remain identical. We shall not consider the investigations of pre-differentiation in which attempts were made to enhance the discriminability of perceptual stimuli through the attachment of distinctive labeling responses (for a review see Arnoult, 1957). Suffice it to say that such pre-differentiation procedures have met with rather limited success. At this point we shall confine ourselves to the description of a recent study by Underwood and Ekstrand (1968b) that focused on the question of whether a positive component of stimulus differentiation can appreciably reduce the amount of negative transfer in the *A–B, A–D* paradigm. The study took its point of departure from the assumption that the weight of this positive component should depend on the degree of intralist stimulus similarity. When the similarity is high, stimulus differentiation is difficult; hence transfer of the differentiation accomplished during first-list

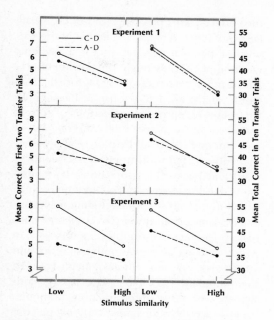

Figure 21.15. The role of stimulus differentiation in transfer. Measures of transfer performance under conditions of low and high intralist stimulus similarity. To the extent that there is transfer of stimulus differentiation, performance under the *A–D* paradigm should become increasingly superior to that under the *C–D* paradigm as similarity changes from low to high. (Underwood &Ekstrand, 1968b.)

learning should be a source of considerable facilitation under the *A–D* as compared to the *C–D* paradigm. This advantage should be greatly reduced when interstimulus similarity is low and differentiation is easy. Three related experiments were carried out in which the learning materials were lists of six paired associates, with consonant trigrams as stimuli and common words as responses. The interstimulus similarity was either high or low. At each level of similarity a comparison was made between the *A–D* and *C–D* paradigms. The individual experiments differed only with respect to the criterion of first-list learning— one perfect recitation in the first experiment and three perfect recitations in the second and the third. Performance on the common transfer list is shown in Figure 21.15. As expected, the amount of negative transfer is less when interstimulus similarity is high than

when it is low, but the effects are in general small and of borderline statistical significance. The investigators conclude that the transfer of stimulus differentiation is so slight that the subjects in the *A–D* condition apparently must start this process almost afresh in learning the transfer list. Thus, theoretical expectations regarding the role of this component are only weakly supported. It appears that it is difficult to separate stimulus differentiation per se from the acquisition of specific associations.

A–B, C–B Consideration of the *A–B, C–B* paradigm brings into sharp focus the role of response meaningfulness as a determinant of transfer. Response learning is a source of facilitation whereas interference between backward associations is a negative component in this paradigm. The relative weight of these two factors in determining the net transfer effect should depend on the meaningfulness of the responses: the lower the meaningfulness the greater should be the influence of the response learning relative to the associative component. Since the integration of responses from outside the subject's repertoire occupies a large proportion of the total learning time, the direction of the net transfer effect may be expected to shift from positive to negative as the meaningfulness of the responses varies from low to high. Precisely such a result was found in Jung's (1963) experiment when the meaningfulness of trigram responses to adjective stimuli was changed from low to high. The shift in transfer was from a large positive effect to a slight negative one. In general, experiments in which the responses were nonsense items have yielded some evidence of positive transfer (Bruce, 1933; Mandler & Heinemann, 1956; Dean & Kausler, 1964; Merikle, 1968), but there are exceptions (Harcum, 1953), and as will be seen shortly, the observed net effects may depend on the degree of first-list learning. With words as responses, there is usually a small negative effect (Twedt & Underwood, 1959; Dallett, 1962a; Postman, 1962a; Kausler & Kanoti, 1963; Goulet & Behar, 1966).

When negative effects are observed, the

question arises as to the mechanism by which a conflict between backward associations interferes with transfer learning. Any explanation must take account of the fact that the subject is not required to reproduce the stimulus terms while learning the second list; that is, the first-list backward associations do not constitute competing responses in the usual sense. Twedt and Underwood (1959) have suggested that during the acquisition of the transfer list the elicitation of first-list backward associations may cause the subject to withhold correct responses. The hypothetical mechanism is as follows: During transfer learning the subject may be about to give the correct *B* to a given *C,* but the activation of the old backward association *B–A* leads to the inference that *B* "belongs with" *A* rather than *C.* Consequently the response is erroneously rejected and withheld. In short, the backward association serves a "checking" function (see McGovern, 1964) and is used by the subject for purposes of editing his responses. One implication of this account is that the negative effects should be reduced if the stimulus terms in the successive lists are made highly distinctive, for example, are drawn from different classes such as letters and adjectives. This expectation was not confirmed in a study by Schwartz (1968); however, the absolute levels of transfer were too small to permit a sensitive test of the hypothesis. The prediction appeared to receive confirmation in an experiment by Olivier and Kausler (1966); but since stimulus dissimilarity and meaningfulness were confounded, the results cannot be regarded as conclusive. To the extent that the interpretation of Twedt and Underwood proves valid, the effectiveness of the interference from backward associations would have to be considered as dependent on the degree of list differentiation.

It should be recalled at this point that transfer effects have also been shown to be influenced by the relation between the backward association in the first list and the forward association in the second list, for example, *A–B, C–A* and *A–B, B–C.* When the two associations are symmetrical, that is, *A–B, B–A,*

the effects are positive (Murdock, 1956; Palermo, 1961). When one member of the second-list pairs is new, as in the paradigms mentioned just previously, the transfer effects are negative (Harcum, 1953; Murdock, 1958; Goulet & Barclay, 1965; Houston, 1966a, b). In such cases inappropriate rejections of correct responses in the manner described by Twedt and Underwood would occur to the extent that subjects fail to distinguish between forward and backward associations. It is more likely that the change in the function of individual items, old stimuli becoming responses or vice versa, is an important source of confusion. The fact that double-function lists, in which each item serves as both a stimulus and a response, are much more difficult to learn than standard paired-associate lists is consistent with this interpretation, although backward associations must certainly be considered a major source of interference in this task (Primoff, 1938; Young, 1959; Young & Jennings, 1964).

A–B, A–Br   Reference to Table 21.3 makes clear the presence of multiple negative components in the *A–Br* paradigm: forward and backward associations, and list differentiation. However, response learning is a source of facilitation. As in the case of *C–B,* we would, therefore, expect the net observed effects to vary with the level of meaningfulness of the responses, that is, to become increasingly negative as one moves from nonsense items to words. Such is, indeed, the case. With trigrams as responses, facilitation relative to the *C–D* baseline has been reported (Mandler & Heinemann, 1956) or relatively moderate negative effects which are not appreciably greater than for *A–D* (Jung, 1962). When the meaningfulness of trigram responses is changed from low to high, transfer effects shift from positive to negative (Merikle, 1968). When the responses are words, the amounts of negative transfer are typically very heavy and exceed those for *A–D* (Porter & Duncan, 1953; Besch & Reynolds, 1958; Twedt & Underwood, 1959; Postman, 1962a, 1964a; Kausler & Kanoti, 1963).

With respect to the interference falling on individual associations, *A–Br* may be seen as a combination of *A–D* and *C–B*. However, such an analysis is incomplete because neither the *C*s nor the *D*s are in fact new but rather are old stimuli and old responses, and the items which they replace are still present in the list. Besch, Thompson, and Wetzel (1962) have suggested that during the acquisition of a re-paired list the associations of the stimuli with their former responses continue to receive some generalized reinforcement and consequently are resistant to extinction. As expected, they found that the re-paired items became less difficult to learn when the old responses to the stimuli were removed from the list. It is clear that for *A–Br*, more than for the other paradigms, it is not possible to specify the conditions of transfer without reference to the relations between lists rather than those which obtain for single pairs. As Table 21.3 brings out, the possibilities of list differentiation are minimized when old stimuli and responses are re-paired; this factor probably contributes to the persistence of the negative transfer effects.

Rank order of paradigms When the standard paradigms are compared within the same experimental situation, there are usually reliable differences in the direction and amount of transfer relative to the *C–D* control baseline. The differences are orderly in so far as they can be related to the number and assumed effectiveness of the component processes contributing to the net transfer effects. When the response terms are familiar units that do not require integration, the typical alignment of paradigms is as follows: *A–B'* is positive (at least early in transfer learning) and is followed, in order of increasing negative effects, by *C–B*, *A–D*, and *A–Br*. This order can be seen as consistent with the specification of component processes in the table above.

When English words are the responses, it may appear reasonable to suppose that the rank order of paradigms reflects primarily the operation of associative components. However, even in such cases response learning may be an important factor, in the limited sense of establishing the pool of responses to be used in the list. That is,

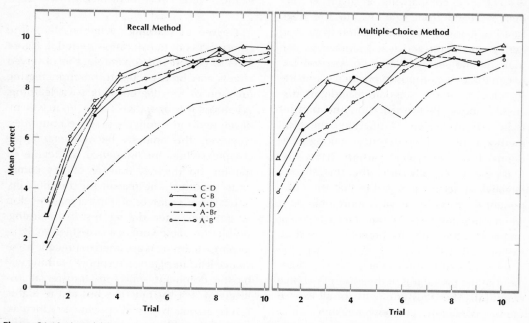

Figure 21.16. Acquisition of the transfer list under various paradigms when performance is tested by the recall method (left) and by the multiple-choice method (right). (Postman & Stark, 1969.)

response learning encompasses both item integration and item recall. Both subcomponents are relevant when the responses are from outside the subject's vocabulary, only the latter when they are familiar words. To assess the contributions to transfer of strictly associative components and of response recall, Postman and Stark (1969) compared two conditions of practice—one in which both associative learning and response recall were required and one in which the latter was minimized if not eliminated.

Two successive lists of 10 paired associates, with single letters as stimuli and adjectives as responses, were learned either by the recall method or the multiple-choice method. Under both procedures study trials were alternated with test trials. The difference between the two treatments was in the nature of the test trials. In the recall method the subject was required to reproduce the responses to each of the stimuli; in the multiple-choice method he had to choose the correct response to a given stimulus from among four alternatives, all of which were response terms from within the list. The three distractors accompanying a given correct item changed from one test to the next. First-list learning was to a criterion of one perfect recitation and was followed by ten trials on the second list. A comparison between the two methods of practice was made for all five of the standard paradigms discussed above. Performance on the transfer trials is shown in Figure 21.16. When the recall method is used, the differences among paradigms show the typical pattern. (However, $C-B$ yields essentially zero rather than slightly negative effects; it is possible that the component of response recall is more important when study and test trials are alternated than under the anticipation procedure used in earlier studies.)

There are substantial changes in the alignment of the paradigms in the multiple-choice condition. The transfer effects for all experimental paradigms are now negative. Thus, there are shifts from zero to negative transfer for $C-B$, and from positive to negative effects for $A-B'$. The separation between $A-D$ and $A-Br$ occurs earlier than in the recall condition. The differences between the patterns of transfer effects under the two methods indicate that the positive factor of response recall serves to mask or to delay the manifestations of associative interference. This is true not only for the paradigms of response identity ($C-B$ and $A-Br$) but also for $A-B'$ where the responses are synonymous. The relation of synonymity (or associative connection) restricts the range of alternative responses in the recall method; once this positive factor is eliminated, the negative effects attributable to the confusion between words with similar meanings (or between mediators and mediated terms) become fully apparent and outweigh whatever positive components are present. The same negative effects are evident late in practice under the recall condition where $A-B'$ falls below $C-D$. In general, the findings call attention to the fact that a precise analysis of transfer into its components depends on the development of methods of measurement that are differentially sensitive to the several constituent processes.

Degree of learning When each of the components of transfer represented in Figure 21.14 is considered separately, the observed effects may be expected to be an increasing function of the degree of first-list learning. Whatever the operative factor is, it will be developed more fully as practice continues. However, the analysis becomes far more complex when the influence of degree of training on the net transfer effects comes under scrutiny. The reason for the difficulty is that various sources of transfer may develop at different rates during first-list learning. Within the framework of a two-stage analysis, response learning is assumed to precede associative learning. Hence, response learning will be the dominant source of transfer at low levels of first-list practice, but at the higher levels, associative learning will carry increasing weight with the relative durations of the two stages depending on the meaningfulness of the responses (see Martin, 1965). Add the fact that the components may influence transfer performance in opposing directions, as in the *C–B* paradigm, and it becomes apparent that a monotonic relation between degree of first-list learning and transfer effects is not necessarily to be expected.

The empirical evidence on this question is not extensive. We shall consider only studies of verbal transfer that include a control for warm-up and learning to learn (*C–D*), which is essential since nonspecific effects are known to increase with the amount of prior training. (It may be noted in passing that the omission of the necessary control condition is not entirely a thing of the past as witness a recent study of the relation between over-learning and transfer by Holborn and Boe, 1965). Since the relative contribution of response learning and of associative factors may be expected to vary with degree of first-list learning, the functional relations observed with materials of high and of low meaning-

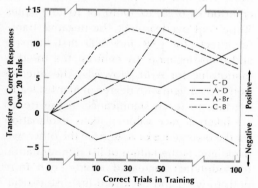

Figure 21.17. Transfer performance as a function of the degree of first-list learning. The stimuli were single digits, and the responses were consonant syllables. To take account of differences in item difficulty, the data were corrected to permit plots from a common origin. Note that the curve for the control condition (*C–D*) represents actual changes in performance, whereas transfer measures (differences between scores on experimental and control pairs) are shown for the other paradigms. (Mandler & Heinemann, 1956.)

fulness must be carefully distinguished. A study by Mandler and Heinemann (1956) will serve as a convenient point of departure for consideration of the latter. The learning materials in this experiment were paired associates with digits as stimuli and consonant syllables as responses. The first list consisted of four pairs and the second list of eight pairs. The transfer list was mixed and was so constructed that the following four paradigms were represented by two pairs each: *C–D, C–B, A–D, A–Br.* There were five levels of first-list learning: one group received no training and the others were carried to a criterion of either 10, 30, 50, or 100 errorless trials. Thus, the effects of varying degrees of over-learning on transfer were examined. These effects are summarized in Figure 21.17. The upward trend for *C–D* reflects progressive increases in nonspecific transfer. Both conditions of response identity (*C–B* and *A–Br*) show increasing amounts of positive transfer, indicating that the response-learning component outweighs associative interference. A rather unusual feature is the finding of greater positive transfer effects for *A–Br* than for *C–B*. The explanation probably lies in the fact that only two pairs were used per paradigm. If the subjects could identify the two stimuli whose responses had been re-paired, the presentation of the first pair conveyed full information about the correct response in the second. As for the *A–D* paradigm, the function is somewhat erratic and yields no statistically reliable differences; note, however, the reversal in the initial trend toward increasingly negative transfer. The authors suggest that this apparent reduction in negative transfer reflects the development of "symbolic analogues" of the first-list associations at the higher levels of overlearning which facilitate implicit trial-and-error. Such an intervening process presumably permits the rejection of incipient errors and thereby reduces interference. A further discussion of this interpretation of the effects of overlearning on transfer may be found in a theoretical paper by Mandler (1962) and in a subsequent interchange between Jung (1965) and Mandler (1965).

The fact that the results of Mandler and Heinemann yield no evidence of a gradual build-up of associative interference in the C–B condition is of theoretical interest. The evidence for such a build-up is also minimal in the study of Jung (1962), which compared the same four paradigms but used lower degrees of first-list learning. With adjectives as stimuli and trigrams as responses there was no reliable transfer for the C–B condition (the effects for A–Br as well as A–D were negative, but the level of meaningfulness was probably higher than in the earlier study). Under the conditions of response identity there is a slight trend in the direction of greater negative effects as the degree of first-list learning increases, but the trend is far from significant. Other findings for the C–B paradigm, which bear on the question of the development of associative interference, are inconsistent. As noted earlier, there was some apparent increase in positive transfer as a function of degree of first-list learning in Bruce's (1933) data. On the other hand, Dean and Kausler (1964) reported a shift from positive to negative transfer effects as the level of practice on the first list was increased. The fact that Harcum (1953) found negative transfer for the C–B paradigm after a high degree of first-list learning is also relevant here. It should be noted that the three studies mentioned last all used paired nonsense syllables in the successive lists. Because of the inevitable overlap of elements both within and between lists, the similarity relations under these conditions are likely to be very complex and also variable from one experiment to the next. The use of such materials for purposes of isolating particular components of specific transfer is, therefore, inadvisable. Taken together, the experiments considered in this section confirm the importance of response learning as a source of transfer but do not shed much light on the development of associative effects.

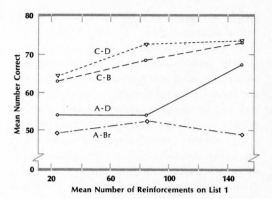

Figure 21.18. The effect of degree of first-list learning on transfer, with paired adjectives as the learning materials. The degree of first-list learning is scaled in terms of the number of reinforcements (correct anticipations) during acquisition. (Postman, 1962a.)

Figure 21.18 shows the result of an experiment (Postman, 1962a) that investigated the relation between degree of first-list learning and transfer with materials of high meaningfulness, namely, lists of paired adjectives. The first list was learned either to a criterion of 6/10, to 10/10, or to 10/10 plus 50 percent overlearning. The negative transfer effects for C–B and A–D first increase and then decrease; by contrast the trend is monotonic for A–Br. However, the interaction of paradigm with degree of first-list learning fails to reach significance. If the trends are taken at face value, a likely explanation for the divergence of A–Br from the other two paradigms is the failure of list differentiation to counteract increased interference from both forward and backward first-list associations. List differentiation may be expected to increase with degree of first-list learning (see Underwood, 1945) but would develop most slowly when both the stimulus and the response terms remain the same.

Mandler's (1962) hypothesis that overlearned first-list associations form analogic structures that function to reduce interference was tested in an experiment by Spence and Schulz (1965). The first list, which was composed of strongly associated pairs (normative primaries), was presented for either 1, 5, 20, or 40 trials. The pairs in the second list (A–D) had a minimal degree of pre-experimental associative connection. Negative transfer relative to a control condition increased as the number of first-list trials went from one to five and remained relatively constant thereafter. Neither high associative strength nor protracted practice was sufficient to produce the reduction in interference predicted by Mandler. List differentiation was probably maximal at all levels of practice in view of the very large differences in associative strength. Other experiments in which the V-shaped function for A–D transfer implied by Mandler failed to materialize do not bear critically on the hypothesis because low degrees of first-list learning were compared (Schulman, 1967), different methods of practice were used in the successive lists (Goulet, Meltzer, & O'Shaunessy, 1967), or both (Goulet, 1967).

The most important conclusion to be drawn from these studies is that increases in negative transfer effects are not proportional to the degree of first-list learning. It appears that the amount of interference is a negatively accelerated increasing function of the strength of the competing associations. Hence increments in first-list strength yield diminishing returns. In addition, positive factors may come into play to counteract the growth of interference. There is little support for Mandler's hypothesis inasmuch as the development of the postulated structures is seen as critically dependent on degree of associative strength per se. Whether such factors as list differentiation do in fact mitigate associative interference is still an open question.

Unmixed versus mixed transfer designs
When we speak of a paradigm of transfer, we refer to the rule governing the relation between pairs in the successive lists. It is reasonable to suppose that a subject who can identify this rule and attempts to conform to it would be aided in his performance of the

transfer task. For example, in learning a C–B list he would limit himself to the repertoire of B's already available to him, whereas he would withhold old responses in an A–D condition. Such strategies can be carried out effectively as long as the transfer list is unmixed, that is, all the pairs represent the same paradigm. When the transfer list is mixed, so that subgroups of pairs conform to different paradigms, the implementation of paradigmatic rules clearly becomes more difficult because it depends on the subject's ability to classify the individual pairs according to the relation which they bear to the first list. On the basis of these considerations, transfer performance would be expected to be superior when unmixed rather than mixed lists are used. The experimental facts have, however, given only limited support to this expectation. A systematic comparison between the results obtained with unmixed and mixed lists was made by Twedt and Underwood (1959) for the C–D, C–B, A–D, and A–Br paradigms. The transfer effects obtained under the two conditions of testing were essentially identical. Thus, the differential opportunity for applying a consistent rule to all the pairs in the list was not reflected in performance. Either the subjects learning the unmixed lists did not attempt to apply the appropriate rule, or if they did, this strategy had no discernible influence on learning.

The possibility remained open, however, that the picture would change if a different grouping of paradigms were used in the mixed list. All the paradigms used by Twedt and Underwood yielded negative transfer effects, and none of the implied rules specified the correct responses to individual stimuli; rule-governed behavior may not have provided an effective guide to performance. To explore this possibility, Postman (1966) included a condition of positive transfer among those used in a comparison of unmixed and mixed designs. There were again four paradigms: C–D, C–B, A–D, and A–B', the last of these representing the condition in which a mediational rule was available. The unmixed condition resulted in better transfer performance for all paradigms except C–D. However, the differences, while consistent, were small. It appears, then, that the differences in the amount of transfer obtained with mixed and unmixed lists depend on the range of paradigms included in the design.

This conclusion receives strong confirmation from the results of a recent study by Wickens and Cermak (1967) in which the effects of different similarity relations between responses were evaluated in unmixed and mixed transfer designs. Successive responses to identical stimuli were either synonyms, antonyms, or unrelated. The most noteworthy finding was that when the responses in the two lists were antonyms, the transfer effects were clearly positive for unmixed lists but shifted to negative in the mixed condition. As the authors point out, antonymity implies a mediational rule that can be applied during the acquisition of an unmixed transfer list. In a mixed list the rule cannot be applied effectively, and antonymous responses behave like unrelated ones (A–D). By contrast, the transfer effects remained positive for synonyms under both unmixed and mixed test conditions; the authors view this fact as consistent with the hypothesis of response generalization. A report by Slamecka (1967) is in sharp disagreement with these findings. In the experimental paradigms the stimuli remained the same and the response words were either identical, synonyms, antonyms, or re-paired (A–Br). The transfer effects remained positive for antonyms as well as synonyms in both mixed and unmixed lists. However, these data are difficult to interpret for a number of reasons. Trigrams were used as stimuli in successive 20-pair lists, so that there probably was considerable interference under the control (C–D) condition. The atypical absence of negative transfer in the A–Br paradigm in the case of the unmixed list indicates that the control baseline may, indeed, have been seriously biased, and perhaps differentially so under the mixed and unmixed treatments.

Moreover, the testing rate was subject-paced, and the possibility of differential rehearsal on test trials cannot be excluded. Hence Slamecka's conclusion, based on the lack of differences between transfer effects under the unmixed and mixed conditions, that subjects do not in fact use mediational rules, may be regarded as premature.

Acquisition of transfer skills Higher-order habits in the performance of transfer tasks, such as the systematic application of paradigmatic rules, have also received attention in studies of learning to learn. It has been found that repeated experience with a given paradigm enhances the efficiency of performance in the transfer stage. The magnitude of the gains in performance varies with the nature of the paradigm: there are greater increases in positive transfer (A–B') than there are decreases in negative transfer (A–D and A–Br). The very substantial improvements in the A–B' condition point to increased efficiency in the utilization of the appropriate mediational rule (Postman, 1964a). The effects of experience in the performance of transfer tasks appear to be highly generalizable since the amount of improvement is equal when the paradigms used in the training and the test phase remain the same and when they change (Keppel & Postman, 1966; Martin, Simon, & Ditrichs, 1966). This conclusion must, however, be limited to standard paradigms such as A–B' and A–D in which the appropriate response rules are readily identified. When the intertask relations are more complex, as in the three-stage chaining paradigms to be discussed shortly, the effects of training are specific to the particular paradigm with which the subject has had prior experience (Postman, 1968b).

HIGHER-ORDER MEDIATION

For purposes of introducing the topic of higher-order mediation it is useful to refer back to the standard A–B, A–B' condition. As far as the experimental arrangements are con-

TABLE 21.4

	Paradigm							
	I	*II*	*III*	*IV*	*V*	*VI*	*VII*	*VIII*
Stage 1	A–B	B–D	B–A	D–B	A–B	D–B	B–A	B–D
Stage 2	B–D	A–B	D–B	B–A	D–B	A–B	B–D	B–A
Stage 3	A–D	A–D	A–D	A–D	A–D	A–D	A–D	A–D

cerned, this is a two-stage paradigm since the procedure is confined to the acquisition of two successive lists. However, to the extent that mediational chaining is invoked as an explanation of the observed transfer effects, a third stage of learning is implied, which has occurred prior to the experiment: the development of an associative connection between *B* and *B'*. When the implied conditions of prior learning are taken into account, *A–B*, *A–B'* is seen to represent a three-stage paradigm of transfer:

Stage 1	*B–B'*
Stage 2	*A–B*
Stage 3	*A–B'*

This schema exhibits the defining property of a mediate association: When two terms (*A* and *B'*) are each independently associated with a third (*B*), an associative connection develops between these two terms. Thus, the association *B'* to *A* may be available at the beginning of Stage 3 even though this pairing has not occurred previously. The association between *A* and *B'* is indirect and depends on a common third term (*B*), which is linked separately to each of them.

The concept of mediate association arose early in the history of association theory (see Peters, 1935, pp. 20–25); in contemporary psychology it has been endowed with considerable theoretical significance by its systematic application in the analysis of secondary generalization and problem solving by behavior theorists (see Cofer & Foley, 1942; Goss, 1961). An early attempt by Peters (1935) to demonstrate verbal mediation was largely

unsuccessful, but the problem was reopened by Bugelski and Scharlock (1952), who obtained positive results of borderline significance and also found that mediational processes may occur without apparent awareness on the part of the subject. Largely under the influence of Jenkins and his associates, the last decade has produced a large volume of experimental work on multiple-stage mediation in transfer. There have been several extensive reviews of this research (Jenkins, 1963b; Earhard & Mandler, 1965a; Horton, 1967; Kjeldergaard, 1968). We shall now consider some of the major experimental findings and theoretical issues.

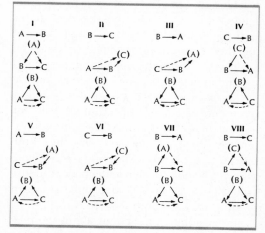

Figure 21.19. Analysis of the associative links assumed to be established under each of 8 paradigms of mediation. ⟶ and ⟵ indicate explicit forward and backward associations, respectively. ( ) denotes an hypothesized implicit response, ‑ ‑ ‑→ a presumed implicit forward association, and ←‑ ‑ ‑ a presumed implicit backward association. (Horton & Kjeldergaard, 1961.)

Paradigms of Three-stage Mediation

When three lists of paired associates are learned in succession, and three of the terms occur in two lists each, a possibility of mediated transfer exists. The associative relations that have to come into play in order to permit mediation depend on the arrangement of the individual terms. Eight paradigms of three-stage mediation (Horton & Kjeldergaard, 1961) are reproduced in Table 21.4. The table should be considered along with Figure 21.19 which depicts the implicit responses and mediating links assumed to function in each of the eight situations.

These eight paradigms form three distinct groups. Conditions I, II, III, and IV are chaining paradigms; in such paradigms the term common to the first two stages occupies the stimulus position in one of the lists and the response position in the other. For example, in condition I a mediational chain is assumed to function because after acquisition of A–B in the first stage the backward association B–A is elicited during the second stage, allowing A and D to become associated. Alternatively, or in addition, the associations learned during the first two stages are put together during the test stage to yield the chain A–B–D. In the remaining paradigms the common term occupies the same position in the first two stages. Conditions V and VI represent paradigms of acquired stimulus equivalence. That is, A and D become equivalent by virtue of the fact that they both elicit B as a forward association. Finally, conditions VII and VIII are paradigms of response equivalence: A and D become equivalent because they are both responses to B.

In developing predictions about the relative efficacy of the various paradigms, Horton and Kjeldergaard focused on two characteristics of the mediational links, namely, directionality and contiguity. Greater transfer effects are predicted when the mediated links between A and D established in the second stage are in the forward rather than the backward direction. On this basis para-

digms I, II, VI, and VII should be superior to III, IV, V, and VIII. For example, in paradigm I the assumed sequence of events in the second stage is B–(A)–D; in paradigm III it is D–B–(A). More transfer is also expected when the inferred associative sequence in stage 2 places A and D in direct juxtaposition than when they are separated by another term. This factor of contiguity favors paradigms I, IV, VII, and VIII over II, III, V, and VI. The sequences for paradigms I and III again provide relevant examples. Directionality is assumed to have greater weight than contiguity in determining performance. The final predicted rank order, which takes account of both characteristics, comprises four groups. In descending order these are: I and VII; II and VI; IV and VIII; III and V.

It should be noted that the predictions are based on the assumed properties of the mediational links established in the second stage. However, the implicit associations may not develop in the second stage but may be entirely a test-stage phenomenon, that is, during the acquisition of the test list the subject may use what he has learned previously to generate a link between A and D. The functional links in the second and the terminal stage may have different properties; to the extent that they do, the predictions above do not apply to test-stage mediation. For example, in paradigm I the establishment of an A–D link depends on the elicitation of the backward association B–A. In test-stage mediation only forward links are required to complete the chain from A to B to D. The lack of critical operations for resolving the uncertainty about the locus of mediation remains a persistent source of interpretative difficulties.

Inspection of the table of paradigms at once calls attention to another basic problem of interpretation. When we consider the stages of the various paradigms in pairs, we encounter in many cases the familiar two-stage paradigms of negative transfer. For example, associative interference is indicated for all three of the possible pairings of the stages in paradigm I: *A–B, B–D; A–B, A–D; B–D, A–D*. Thus, mediational and interference effects must be expected to develop in opposition to each other, and whatever facilitation is observed in the test stage represents a residual effect. In studies of mediation an attempt is made to take account of other sources of transfer by comparing the experimental treatment with an appropriate control condition. In the latter the common term assumed to provide the critical associative link is removed. The sequence of lists in the control treatment for paradigm I is either *A–X, B–D, A–D* or *A–B, X–D, A–D*. The experimental-control difference in the test stage provides a measure of mediation. It should be clear from our previous discussion, however, that the amount of negative transfer in second-stage learning will be greater for the experimental than for the control treatment. The two conditions are, therefore, not in fact equal in all respects except for the possibility of mediation. We shall return to some important implications of this state of affairs shortly. At this point it is useful to emphasize that performance in the successive stages of all the paradigms is complexly determined and that the isolation of mediational effects poses difficult analytic problems.

In typical studies of mediation three successive lists of paired associates are learned which conform to the appropriate experimental or control paradigm. While the degrees of first-list and second-list learning are variables manipulated in some experiments, these lists are normally carried to a high criterion in order to ensure the stability of the mediating associations. An alternative procedure has been used in a series of studies by M. J. Peterson and her associates (for example, Peterson & Blattner, 1963; Peterson, Colavita, Sheehan, & Blattner, 1964; M. J. Peterson, 1964, 1965; Peterson & Jamison, 1965). The pairs representing the first two stages are given a limited number of exposures (sometimes only one), and the test stage consists of a multiple-choice procedure in

which the stimulus term (*A*) is presented with three alternatives including two distractors (new terms) and the mediated response (*D*). The subject is instructed to pick the alternative which seems to him to "go best" with the stimulus term. The method has the advantage of eliminating test-stage learning and thus provides a relatively pure test of mediational effects. Apparent disadvantages are the inevitable ambiguity of the instructions and the fact that subjects are likely to choose a familiar term under both the control and the experimental condition. Consequently, the test procedure may have rather limited sensitivity, which may account for occasional unexpected failures to observe reliable mediational effects, for example, for the chaining paradigms (Peterson et al., 1964).

Four-stage Paradigms

The length of the mediational sequence can be extended to generate four-stage paradigms. Such paradigms are of theoretical interest because they constitute possible models of higher-order transfer effects related to stimulus equivalence and to response equivalence. A sequence illustrating transfer that is contingent upon acquired stimulus equivalence is as follows: *A–B, C–B, A–D, C–D* As stated earlier, *A* and *C* are assumed to become equivalent stimuli during the first two stages because they both elicit the same response (*B*). By virtue of this equivalence a new response (*D*) associated with *A* is expected to be evoked by *C*. Presumably elicitation of the common implicit response *B* during the last two stages provides the mechanism of transfer. This paradigm was used earlier by Shipley (1935) in a well-known experiment in which mediated generalization of a conditioned eye-blink response was demonstrated.

The following four stages exemplify the development of response equivalence as a result of the prior establishment of a mediational chain: *A–B, B–C, D–A, D–C*. A chain leading from *A* to *C* is established during the first two stages. In the third stage *A* is attached as a response to a new stimulus (*D*). In the final stage *C* is attached to the same stimulus. Given the association *D–A*, the completion of the chain *A–B–C* should facilitate the acquisition of *D–C*. As will be seen later, this paradigm has been used extensively in the evaluation of transfer effects attributable to pre-experimental linguistic associations. These examples should be sufficient to indicate the characteristics of four-stage paradigms. Extensive tables of possible arrangements have been presented by Jenkins (1963b, pp. 218f).

Experimental studies of mediation may be conveniently divided into two major classes: those in which all stages are acquired in the laboratory and those in which one or two of the stages are assumed on the basis of normative information about pre-experimental associations. We consider the former first.

Studies of Three-stage Mediation: All Associations Acquired in the Laboratory

A major experimental investigation under this heading was carried out by Horton and Kjeldergaard (1961). All eight of the paradigms listed in the table above were included in the design. The learning materials were lists of eight paired associates; both stimuli and responses were words of very low frequency of usage. A mixed-list design was used, with half of the pairs in the final test lists being experimental pairs and half control pairs. The purpose of the study was to demonstrate the occurrence of mediational effects and also to test the predictions, mentioned earlier, about the relative effectiveness of the various paradigms in producing mediation. Significant amounts of mediated facilitation were obtained for all but one paradigm (the exception was condition III). There was only limited support for the predictions regarding the rank order of paradigms. While the differences generally were in the expected direction, primarily with respect to directionality, the interaction of treatment (experimental versus control) and paradigm was not significant. Post-experimental inquiries failed to

yield any evidence of awareness on the part of the subjects of the interlist relations permitting mediation. Analysis of individual differences indicated that the amount of mediation was greatest for subjects of intermediate, but above average, learning ability as measured by performance in the first stage.

In subsequent studies reports of reliable differences among paradigms have been few and far between, but there are indications that paradigm I (forward chaining) is superior to the other conditions (Seidel, 1962; Horton & Hartman, 1963; Shanmugam & Miron, 1966). However, the multiple-choice procedure appears to favor the stimulus-equivalence and response-equivalence paradigms (Peterson et al., 1964). In general, the original predictions regarding the rank order of paradigms have received little empirical verification. While the available data do not rule out the possibility that directionality is a significant factor, the effectiveness of backward associations in producing mediation has been repeatedly demonstrated (for example, McCormack, 1961; Palermo, 1966).

Since mediation is a special case of transfer, the variables of meaningfulness and degree of learning deserve special attention. There are reasons to expect a mediator of high meaningfulness to be more effective than one of low meaningfulness; the former has the advantage of greater availability and distinctiveness. This prediction has been confirmed (Horton, 1964). Closely related is the finding of Shanmugam and Miron (1966) that the degree of semantic polarization of the mediator has a positive influence on mediated transfer. In the experiments of Peterson and her coworkers using the multiple-choice technique greater effects were obtained when the total pool of materials, that is, all the terms in the successive lists, were of high rather than low meaningfulness. A general methodological point is in order here. There has been a disposition on the part of many investigators to use nonsense items or words of very low frequency as the terms to be linked by the mediator; such items have also been used as the critical common terms. An apparent reason for the choice of such materials is the desire to minimize pre-experimental associations. It is uncertain to what extent this objective is achieved since nonsense items are certainly not free of such associations. An apparent disadvantage is that speed of acquisition is heavily influenced by response learning, so that the experiment becomes relatively insensitive to mediational effects that are entirely associative. If the mediator itself is a nonsense item, it may fail to function because of low availability or discriminability. Some failures to observe mediated transfer may reasonably be attributed to this state of affairs. For example, Crawford and Vanderplas (1959) used difficult lists of paired nonsense syllables in all stages of their experiment and found no evidence at all of mediational chaining (paradigm II). The result is perhaps not surprising when it is noted that a naive control group took nearly 42 trials to learn the test list to a criterion of three perfect recitations. To minimize the influence of the factor of response learning, Schulz and his associates (for example, Schulz & Weaver, 1968) have used a multiple-choice learning procedure in the second and third stages.

The available evidence on the relation between degree of learning in the first two stages and effectiveness of mediation is not impressive. Horton and Hartman (1963) varied the number of trials in both stages concomitantly and reported a positive effect; in the absence of appropriate control groups, however, the findings cannot be evaluated. Shanmugam and Miron (1966) observed increases in transfer as a function of degree of second-stage learning. Schulz and Weaver (1968) manipulated frequency of exposure to first- and second-list pairs independently but did not detect any changes in mediation. Finally, in the multiple-choice situation variations in the frequency of exposure of the pairs appears to have no reliable effect on mediation (Peterson & Blattner, 1963; M. J. Peterson, 1963, 1964). Since the first-list pairs

are subject to interference during second-stage learning, it appears likely that in a given situation there is a ratio of first-list to second-list strength which is optimal for mediation. Some data reported by Kjeldergaard (1968) are consistent with this assumption.

Interference paradigms A sensitive test of the effectiveness of mediators is provided by the use of paradigms in which the assumed associative links should retard, rather than facilitate, test-list learning. Such an interference paradigm is created when the stimulus and response terms in the second stage are paired inappropriately, for example, in the case of the forward-chaining condition, *A–B, B–Dr, A–D*. To the extent that mediation occurs in the test stage, it must lead to misplacement of responses. If we limit our consideration to three-stage paradigms for which all stages are established in the laboratory, the findings are contradictory. Some investigators found no difference between the interference and the control treatment (Jeffrey & Kaplan, 1957); some reported the expected negative effects (Morning & Voss, 1964; Horton & Wiley, 1967b), while still others observed differences in the opposite direction (Earhard & Mandler, 1965b; Earhard & Earhard, 1967). The importance of the interference paradigm for the theoretical interpretation of mediation effects will receive further consideration below.

Studies of Four-stage Mediation: All Associations Acquired in the Laboratory

Jenkins (1963b) reports a major experiment in which the effectiveness of 16 four-stage paradigms was examined. Eight paradigms each were used to test the predicted effects of acquired stimulus equivalence and of acquired response equivalence; the materials and procedure of Horton and Kjeldergaard (1961) were duplicated in most respects. Not a single paradigm yielded a significant amount of mediation. The results suggested that by the time the test stage is reached, the critical implicit response is weak and not likely to be elicited; but even if it does occur, it has little functional utility. Consequently mediation is not reinforced and may indeed be inhibited. It is reasonable to suppose that in most cases the test list can be learned more efficiently with the aid of new and shorter mediational links developed from pre-experimental linguistic associations.

Subsequently some successful demonstrations of four-stage mediation have been reported under conditions designed to counteract the difficulties inherent in the situation, notably the probable weakness of the mediator at the time of the test. In the study of James and Hakes (1965) a paradigm of acquired stimulus equivalence (A–B, C–B, A–D, C–D) was used. The subjects relearned the earlier lists before the final test stage which consisted of a matching task. A substantial amount of facilitation was found which appeared to be limited to subjects who reported the deliberate use of a mediational strategy. The same paradigm was used by Grover, Horton, and Cunningham (1967) whose procedure also included relearning of earlier lists in the course of practice. Both facilitation and interference were observed, each with the appropriate version of the paradigm, in this case without evidence of awareness on the part of the subjects. It appears that four-stage paradigms are effective only when special care is taken to maximize the opportunities for mediation.

Pseudomediation?

Attention has already been called to the fact that conditions of negative transfer obtain between successive lists in the various paradigms. Using this fact as a point of departure, Mandler and Earhard (1964) advanced the hypothesis that apparent mediated transfer may be an artifact attributable to differences in test-stage interference between the experimental and the control conditions. The argument may be exhibited with reference to the three-stage paradigm of forward chaining. The sequence of lists is A–B, B–D, A–D for the experimental group, and A–B, X–D, A–D

for the control group. A–B, B–D is a condition of negative transfer in which there is interference between the first-list backward and second-list forward associations. Mandler and Earhard assume that as a result of interlist interference the first-list associations (forward as well as backward) are unlearned during the acquisition of the second list in the experimental condition. No such unlearning occurs under the control condition. Consequently, the acquisition of A–D during the test stage is subject to less interference from A–B under the experimental than under the control treatment. Hence the difference between the two groups may represent nothing more than differential interlist interference. If such is, indeed, the case, it also follows that the interference paradigm should yield superior rather than inferior performance by the experimental as compared to the control group. The hypothesis is developed and applied to existing experimental findings in a theoretical paper by Earhard and Mandler (1965a).

To test the implications of this argument, Mandler and Earhard (1964) used a design in which the first two stages were the same as in the conventional paradigm, but mediation in the third stage was made impossible by the introduction of a new response term. Thus, the sequence of lists is A–B, B–D, A–E under the experimental treatment, and A–B, X–D, A–E under the control treatment. A significant difference in favor of the experimental group was obtained in the test stage. This effect was designated as pseudomediation. In a subsequent study Earhard and Mandler (1965b) also observed the expected superiority of the experimental group when the conventional interference paradigm was used. In their general review of the literature Earhard and Mandler (1965a) suggest that pseudomediation is responsible for the mediational effects obtained on the basis of successive associations established in the laboratory. When the associations are highly overlearned, notably if they represent pre-experimental language habits, or when the memory requirements of the task are reduced, genuine mediation may occur. In such cases, however, the observed effects are attributed to the utilization by the subject of conceptual rules entailed by the experimental paradigms.

The pseudomediation hypothesis gave rise to a spirited controversy. The relevant evidence is summarized by Horton (1967) in a refutation of the analysis of Mandler and Earhard. We shall outline briefly the main empirical and theoretical objections to the pseudomediation hypothesis. (1) The assumption that first-list associations are unlearned under the experimental arrangements of the mediation paradigms has minimal empirical support. Direct tests of this assumption have yielded largely negative results (Jenkins & Foss, 1965; Carlson, 1966; Goulet, 1966); the one exception is an experiment by Earhard and Mandler (1965b) in which a test of associative matching was used. The latter is not representative of the usual conditions under which mediated transfer is measured. (2) The phenomenon of pseudomediation itself is difficult to replicate. There have been both unsuccessful (Schulz, Weaver, & Ginsberg, 1965; Goulet & Postman, 1966) and successful (Carlson, 1966; Earhard & Earhard, 1967) attempts at replication of the original finding of Mandler and Earhard. The indications are that the occurrence of the effect is contingent on the absence of intertrial intervals during learning. The matter is further complicated by the fact that pseudomediation effects may appear only in the later stages of test-list learning. By contrast, early test trials are typically most sensitive to mediational effects. (3) Comparisons of mediation and pseudomediation within the same design have yielded inconsistent results. Two studies obtained evidence only for the former (Schulz, Weaver, & Ginsberg, 1965; Goulet & Postman, 1966); Carlson (1966) found both effects to be of the same order of magnitude; Earhard and Earhard (1967) also observed both effects, with mediation superior. (4) As was indicated earlier, the evidence

obtained in investigations of mediated interference is contradictory. The outcome of such studies is critical because the alternative theoretical positions generate diametrically opposed predictions. The available data give unequivocal support to neither position. (5) There is growing evidence that after test-list learning first-stage pairs are recalled better under the experimental than the control condition (Horton & Wiley, 1967a, b; Schulz, Liston, & Weaver, 1968). Apparently such pairs acquire strength through mediation. This finding is clearly consistent with the mediation but not the pseudomediation position. (6) The boundary conditions between pseudomediation on the one hand and mediation based on conceptual strategies on the other remain uncertain and difficult to apply. It is fair to conclude that some pseudomediation effects may occur under highly circumscribed experimental arrangements. The attempt to account for mediated transfer in its entirety in terms of pseudomediation appears to be without merit.

Three-Stage Mediation: One Stage Assumed

We now turn from experiments in which all stages of the mediation paradigm are established in the laboratory to those in which at least one stage is assumed to be given on the basis of associative norms. It should be noted first, however, that there are some studies which represent a transition between these two classes of operations; in such cases one or two of the stages consist of pre-experimental associations that are presented to the subjects in the form of learning tasks. This procedure has been favored in studies of mediation with children as subjects (Norcross & Spiker, 1958; Wismer & Lipsitt, 1964; Palermo, 1966) and has provided successful demonstrations of both mediated facilitation and interference. One advantage of the method is that it ensures the activation in the experimental context of the relevant pre-experimental associations; if the latter are strong, the attainment of the learning criterion is, of course, quite rapid.

Presentation of pre-experimentally related terms may also serve to activate and render functional associations which are relatively low in the subject's hierarchy. For example, groups of nouns can be categorized reliably on the basis of certain sensory categories shared by them (Underwood & Richardson, 1956); however, the names of the categories have a low probability of being elicited as associates by individual nouns. In a series of experiments by Richardson (1962; 1966a, b; 1967a) the conditions were explored under which such concept names could serve as effective mediators in a forward chaining paradigm. Specifically, a syllable (A) would be paired with one or more examples of the category (B), and in the test stage the syllable was paired with the category name (D). Presentation of the examples paired with the category names (B–D) proved to be an essential condition of mediated facilitation.

The first stage remains entirely implicit when the A–B, A–B' paradigm is used. As already noted, when the relation between B and B' is defined in terms of the degree of associative connection, substantial amounts of positive transfer are obtained. When the response terms are paired inappropriately, heavy associative interference is observed (Jenkins, Foss, & Odom, 1965). In fact, in the study just cited, the amount of negative transfer was comparable to that for the A–Br paradigm and greater than for A–D. Thus, the effectiveness of forward chaining in producing mediated transfer is substantiated when one of the stages is established pre-experimentally. All eight conditions used by Horton and Kjeldergaard (1961) were investigated by Cramer (1967) in an experiment in which the first stage of each paradigm was assumed on the basis of associative norms, and the appropriate second and third lists were learned in the laboratory. In general, there was good correspondence between her results and those of the earlier study. The rank order of the various paradigms confirmed the importance of the factor of directionality: Mediated transfer was greater when the experimentally acquired associations functioned in the same direction in the test stage as in the training phase than when the direction was reversed.

Four-Stage Mediation: Two Stages Assumed

A well-known experiment by Russell and Storms (1955) offered evidence for four-stage mediation, with the first two stages established pre-experimentally. The two lists learned in the laboratory had identical nonsense-syllable stimuli but different English words as responses. For the experimental pairs the responses in the first and the second list were the initial and the final terms, respectively, of a three-link associative chain. Thus, *cef–stem* was followed by *cef–smell*. According to free-association norms *flower* is the primary response to *stem*, and *smell* is in turn the primary response to *flower*; however, *smell* is not a likely direct associate to *stem*. Second-list learning should be facilitated to the extent that the pre-existing associative chain mediates the correct response during second-list learning: *cef–stem–(flower)–smell*. The paradigm is A–B, B–C, D–A, D–C, where A–B–C is the normative chain, and D–A, D–C are the associations learned in the laboratory. For the control pairs there was no known associative relation between the successive responses. Using a mixed-list design, Russell and Storms found that the experimental test pairs were learned faster than the control pairs (the two sets of pairs were shown independently to be of equal difficulty when there was no opportunity for chaining). The interpretation of the observed difference proved, however, to be far from simple. It was not certain whether associative chaining or enhanced availability of the responses was responsible for the superiority of the experimental pairs; nor to what extent there was absolute facilitation under the experimental treatment or merely reduced interference.

These questions were considered in a subsequent experimental analysis of the Russell-Storms effect by McGehee and Schulz (1961).

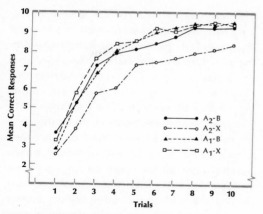

Figure 21.20. Test-list performance in the study of mediation by McGehee and Schulz (1961). For a description of the various experimental treatments see text.

The following four conditions were compared in an unmixed-list design: (1) A_2–B, A_2–D; (2) A_2–X, A_2–D; (3) A_1–B, A_2–D; (4) A_1–X, A_2–D. Condition 1 represents the experimental pairs used by Russell and Storms (B–C–D assumed), and condition 2 the control pairs. Note that a common test list is now used. In condition 3 different stimuli (A_1 and A_2) are used in the two lists in order to assess the possible effects of response availability per se. That is, this condition makes it possible to determine whether the prior practice with B terms facilitates the subsequent use of the D terms as responses. Condition 4, in which both stimuli and responses change, provides the standard control baseline. The results of the experiment are shown in Figure 21.20. Relative to the baseline condition (4), there is substantial associative interference in the acquisition of the Russell-Storms control pairs (2); the mediational effect for the experimental pairs (1) was apparently sufficient to counteract the interference but did not yield absolute facilitation. The advantage of the experimental pairs cannot be attributed to enhanced response availability since conditions 3 and 4 did not differ. In a second experiment evidence for mediated interference was obtained when the experimental pairs were paired inappropriately in the first list (A_2–Br).

Further experimental studies leave some doubt as to whether implicit mediation is the mechanism responsible for the differential transfer effects originally observed by Russell and Storms. Results reported by Martin and Dean (1964) indicate that experimental pairs have an advantage only to the extent that they elicit more explicit mediators (that is, mediators the subject can verbalize) than do the control pairs; however, the reported mediators often do not correspond to the normative ones. In the absence of explicit mediators experimental and control pairs do not differ. The results of a recent study by Richardson (1968a) likewise point to the conclusion that the assumed mediational chains frequently fail to be used. Judgments of congruence between the first-list and second-list responses were obtained; the most frequent matches did not correspond to the normative pairings. These judgments yielded better predictions of transfer than did the association norms, but the differences between experimental and control pairs were found to be small throughout. In light of the recent evidence the Russell-Storms effect can no longer be regarded as a clear demonstration of four-stage mediation.

Mediation Time

The problem of mediation time, discussed earlier in relation to the A–B, A–B' paradigm, is equally pertinent to the experiments we have considered under the heading of higher-order mediation. Do mediated transfer effects increase as the response interval is lengthened? This question has been considered primarily in studies of three-stage mediation, with all stages either established or reactivated in the laboratory. The findings have been inconsistent. The length of the response interval failed to influence the amount of transfer in a number of studies (Schwenn & Underwood, 1965; Richardson, 1966b, 1967a; Richardson & Brown, 1966); the expected relation was obtained in others (Schulz & Lovelace, 1964; Richardson, 1967b, 1968b; Schulz &

Weaver, 1968). The explanation proposed by Richardson, that the response interval significantly influences the amount of mediation only when the study time is very short, does not accommodate all the findings. The results reported by Schulz and Weaver bear directly on this hypothesis. In this experiment study time (1.0 versus 2.5 seconds) and response interval (1.5 versus 3.0 seconds) were varied in a factorial design. The amount of mediation, as measured by the difference between an experimental and a control condition, increased significantly with the length of the response interval. Under both conditions an increase in the study interval was more effective when the response interval was long than when it was short; however, the second-order interaction implied by Richardson's hypothesis was not obtained. It is apparent that the time available for mediation can have an important influence on transfer; the exact conditions under which this factor becomes critical remain to be determined.

RETROACTIVE INHIBITION

The first systematic investigation of retroactive inhibition was carried out by Müller and Pilzecker (1900) who are also responsible for naming the phenomenon. They demonstrated poorer retention of a series of nonsense syllables after interpolation of a second series than after a period of rest. Similarity of the successive tasks did not appear to be essential for the occurrence of the effect: The losses were equally great when the subject engaged in describing landscape pictures during the interpolated interval as after the learning of a second list of syllables. The point in the retention interval at which the interpolated activity was introduced was found to be important, the losses being greater when the second task followed 17 seconds after the first rather than 6 minutes later. To account for these findings, Müller and Pilzecker advanced what became known as the perseveration theory of retroactive inhibition.

The basic assumption of this theory is that after the end of practice on a given task there is a period of continuing neural activity during which the memory pattern that represents the product of learning is consolidated. The performance of any strenuous task during the period of perseveration interferes with the process of consolidation. Since the level of neural activity diminishes progressively after the end of practice, an immediate interpolated task will be more damaging than a delayed one. The theory also implies that it is the intensity of the interpolated activity that is critical rather than the degree of similarity between the successive tasks. It should be clear that this hypothesis does not view retroactive inhibition as a determinant of long-term forgetting; rather the interfering activity is assumed to increase the susceptibility of the products of learning to forgetting.

Similarity Relations

The finding that dissimilar interpolated activities can produce retroactive inhibition was corroborated in an extensive series of investigations by Heine (1914) in which the study of pictures, lists of numbers, or consonants filled the interval between the acquisition and recall of a series of nonsense syllables. (It may be noted in passing that Heine failed to observe any retroactive effects when retention was measured by recognition rather than recall.) However, the degree of similarity between the original and the interpolated activity remained to be manipulated systematically. This variable soon became a major focus of research on retroactive inhibition (for a review of the early work see Britt, 1936). The factor of similarity assumed theoretical importance because the perseveration hypothesis gradually came to be overshadowed by the conception of retroactive inhibition as a special case of transfer between successive activities. Since transfer is known to depend critically on the similarity relations between tasks, this point of view implied that the same should hold true for retroactive inhibition.

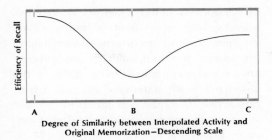

Figure 21.21. The Skaggs-Robinson hypothesis. The theoretical curve shows expected changes in recall as a function of the degree of similarity between the original and the interpolated activity. (Robinson, 1927.)

The Skaggs-Robinson hypothesis A historical landmark in the experimental investigation of the effects of intertask similarity on retroactive inhibition was the Skaggs-Robinson hypothesis. Experiments by Robinson (1920) and Skaggs (1925), in which a wide variety of materials including chess problems, digit series, and paired associates were used, had yielded evidence of greater interference between similar than between dissimilar tasks. Extrapolating from these findings, Robinson formulated the following general law: "As similarity between interpolation and original memorization is reduced from near identity, retention falls away to a minimum and then rises again, but with decreasing similarity it never reaches the level obtaining with maximum similarity" (Robinson, 1927, p. 299). The theoretical function is shown in Figure 21.21. Note that the baseline represents the degree of similarity between activities or tasks rather than between particular components. It soon became apparent that the failure to specify similarity in analytic terms would prove an insuperable obstacle to empirical verification of the hypothesis.

For purposes of testing the law, Robinson (1927) defined similarity in terms of the number of elements common to two series of letters. Instead of using two successive lists, however, he presented to his subject a single series of eight consonants. The first four

letters were considered as the original learning task, and the second four letters as the interpolated material. The two halves had either 0, 1, 2, 3, or 4 letters in common; that is, the entire range from complete dissimilarity to identity was represented. Contrary to theoretical expectations, recall dropped steadily as the number of common elements decreased. Harden (1929) speculated that the results obtained by Robinson might represent only the *AB* section of the theoretical

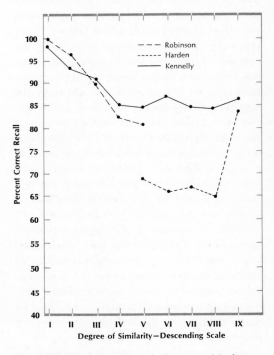

Figure 21.22. The results of three empirical tests of the Skaggs-Robinson hypothesis. Recall is shown for four consonants that appeared in the first half of an eight-item list. In Robinson's experiment the second half of the list also consisted of consonants, with the number of elements in common with the first half varying from four to zero (Positions I through V on the similarity scale). In Harden's experiment the number of digits substituted for consonants in the second half was varied from zero to 4 (Positions V through IX on the similarity scale). Kennelly used the entire range of conditions. (Kennelly, 1941.)

function; in an attempt to extend the range of conditions to the *BC* section, she defined similarity in terms of the number of elements from the same class rather than in terms of identical units. In her experiment the first part of the list consisted of four consonants; in the second part no letter was repeated but either 0, 1, 2, or 3 digits were substituted for consonants. No gradient of recall was obtained, but the most dissimilar condition (four interpolated digits) was superior to the others. Consequently Robinson's and Harden's results together show some agreement with the hypothetical function (Figure 21.22). However, the procedure of combining the functions is questionable in view of the obvious difference in the levels of performance indicated by the discrepancy between the results obtained for the treatment which was common to the two experiments. In a later study by Kennelly (1941) the conditions of both the earlier experiments were included in a single design, As Figure 21.22 shows, Kennelly replicated Robinson's findings but not Harden's, and the theoretical function is clearly not supported. The results are not peculiar to Robinson's method; Kennelly's conclusions remained essentially unchanged when the more conventional procedure of exposing subjects to successive lists was used. Taken together, these studies show little more than the beneficial effects of additional practice when individual elements are repeated.

Another body of data which was viewed as relevant to the Skaggs-Robinson hypothesis came from studies of retroaction in which the successive lists were learned by the method of serial anticipation. In such experiments the similarity between items in the two lists was manipulated in a number of different ways, but no distinction could be made, of course, between the relations existing for stimulus and for response elements. For nonsense materials the degree of similarity was defined in terms of the amount of duplication of letters. This particular manipulation of similarity is complicated, however,

by the opportunities for transfer of response learning. Thus, when identical letters occupy the same positions in corresponding syllables, the relation between similarity and interference is quite complex (Cheng, 1929). In the absence of such systematic sources of bias, retroactive inhibition was found to increase substantially with the degree of interlist similarity (Melton & von Lackum, 1941).

In other experiments the similarity between lists was varied with respect to the class of materials as well as to the degree of meaningful relationship between items from the same class. The results showed that retroactive inhibition increased with both types of similarity. Clear support for this conclusion came from a well-known study by McGeoch and McDonald (1931) which encompassed a wide range of similarity relations. The study comprised two experiments. The original list consisted of two-syllable adjectives. In the first experiment five types of interpolated materials were used: either synonyms or antonyms of the original items presented in corresponding serial positions, unrelated adjectives, nonsense syllables of zero percent association value, three-place numbers. These conditions of interpolation represented decreasing degrees of similarity between the classes of materials in the two lists as determined by independent ratings. There were 5 trials of original learning and 10 trials of interpolation. Only the original list was learned in the control condition. The mean numbers of items recalled out of 10 were as follows:

Interpolated learning	Mean
None	4.50
Synonyms	1.25
Antonyms	1.83
Unrelated adjectives	2.17
Nonsense syllables	2.58
Numbers	3.68

Retroactive inhibition increases as the classes of materials become more similar. Similarity was, of course, confounded with degree of interpolated learning since adjectives were learned faster than syllables or numbers. The results cannot, however, be explained on this basis alone since unrelated adjectives were learned better than either synonyms or antonyms but were less interfering than the latter. In McGeoch and McDonald's second experiment adjectives representing three degrees of synonymity to the first-list items were used in interpolated learning. In this case degree of second-list learning did not vary appreciably, but retroactive inhibition again increased with the degree of interlist similarity (see also McGeoch & McGeoch, 1936). The same trend was observed in an experiment by Johnson (1933) in which the learning materials were series of abstract nouns and the conditions of interpolation represented three degrees of synonymity between first-list and second-list items. A later finding reported by Slamecka (1960b) extends the generality of these results. This investigation found that when subjects learn connected discourse (20-word sentences) by the method of serial anticipation, the amount of retroactive inhibition increases with the topical similarity between the original and the interpolated materials.

The studies in which the meaningful similarity of serial lists was varied supported the Skaggs-Robinson hypothesis no more than did those in which the proportion of identical elements was manipulated. In the former interference increased with the degree of similarity, whereas in the latter the trend was in the opposite direction. McGeoch (1942) considered the possibility that the findings for meaningful similarity might represent the *BC* section of the theoretical function; presumably Robinson's results conform to the *AB* section. Clearly, however, the two implied scales of similarity cannot be joined together to yield a single continuum. The mechanisms responsible for the apparently opposite effects of similarity in the two types of experiments are likely to be quite different. In retrospect it becomes apparent that the Skaggs-Robinson hypothesis failed because it was

essentially a nonanalytic formulation, which did not specify the locus of intertask similarity. The hypothesis lapsed into disuse as the analysis of similarity relations in retroaction, as in transfer, shifted to the investigation of stimulus and response functions.

Generalization and retroaction The application of principles of generalization to the analysis of interlist similarity generates parallel predictions for transfer and retroactive effects. This fact has already become apparent in our discussion of Gibson's hypothesis and of the Osgood surface. The early experimental tests of both these positions were actually carried out in studies of retroaction. As mentioned previously, the results for transfer and interference were entirely congruent. For paradigms of response identity Hamilton (1943) found increases in retroactive facilitation as stimuli became more similar; with unrelated responses Gibson (1941) obtained complementary increases in retroactive inhibition. In neither study, however, did the gradient of retroaction clearly support theoretical expectations. In Osgood's experiments (1946, 1948) there was evidence for reduction in interference as a function of increasing response similarity, particularly when the measures of performance reflected speed of responding. Again the results fell short of verifying the proposed theoretical gradient. In the test of the entire surface by Bugelski and Cadwallader (1956) the expected direct relation between degree of stimulus similarity and retroaction was found. The variations along the response continuum did not agree with the predictions from Osgood's surface; interference was greater when the responses in the successive lists were similar than when they were unrelated or opposed. However, this finding has proved to be quite atypical; the usual finding is that retroactive inhibition increases as the relation between responses changes from a positive degree of meaningful similarity to neutrality (Young, 1955; Kanungo, 1967). In summary, then, although the theoretically derived gradients were not supported in detail, retroaction, like transfer, is an increasing function of the degree of stimulus similarity; for the range from identity to neutrality the amount of interference decreases as a function of response similarity. However, when response similarity is short of identity, there is little evidence for retroactive facilitation (Haagen, 1943). Further evidence bearing on these conclusions will be presented later when the components of interference for the standard paradigms are considered.

In the experiments mentioned above, response similarity was defined in terms of scaled degrees of synonymity. According to a mediational interpretation it is the degree of associative connection between the items that represents the fundamental underlying variable. This variable has been manipulated directly in some experiments in which measures of retroaction were obtained. McClelland and Heath (1943) compared the A–B, C–D and A–B and A'–D paradigms. In the latter A' was the primary normative associate of A, whereas A and C were unrelated words. The amount of retroactive inhibition was greater in the A'–D than the C–D condition. The fact that interlist intrusions were rare during interpolated learning but frequent in relearning suggests that the effect was unidirectional. However, as Slamecka and Ceraso (1960, p. 458) point out, the original and interpolated stimuli would have to be interchanged before unidirectionality of the interference could be inferred with confidence. The demonstration of unidirectional effects would provide important information about the locus of interference. When the stimuli remain the same, first-list recall is higher when there is a strong associative connection between successive responses than when they are unrelated (Bastian, 1961).

Similarity of environmental context It has long been recognized that the degree of functional similarity between successive tasks depends not only on the manipulated relations between the verbal items but also on the environmental contexts in which the tasks are learned. The standard experimental procedure is for original and interpolated learning to take place in exactly the same laboratory situation. Thus, identity of environmental context constitutes a condition of functional stimulus similarity. To the extent that reponses are associated to the environmental context as well as to the nominal stimulus, an A–B, A–D relation obtains between the original and the interpolated habits regardless of the characteristics of the nominal stimuli. It follows that retroactive inhibition should be reduced when original and interpolated learning take place in different environments. While an early test of this prediction by Nagge (1935) was not successful, the expected difference was obtained in an experiment by Bilodeau and Schlosberg (1951). The learning materials were paired adjectives, with half the stimulus terms synonymous in the two lists. The control group learned the original and the interpolated list on the same apparatus and in the same room. Under the experimental treatment the two tasks were presented on different exposure devices and in different rooms; in addition the subject sat while learning one of the lists and stood while learning the other. The test of first-list retention always took place in the same room as the original learning. The amount of retroactive inhibition was found to be substantially smaller in the experimental condition, presumably owing to the discriminative cues provided by the different contexts. These results were confirmed and extended in a subsequent study by Greenspoon and Ranyard (1957). The learning materials were lists of nonsense syllables, with high formal similarity between the first and the second list. The treatments that were compared may be represented as follows, where A and B refer to different environments and the three successive positions designate the condition of original learning, interpolated learning, and recall, respectively: AAA, AAB, ABB, ABA. Retention was highest for ABA and poorest for *AAB,* with *AAA* and *ABB* showing intermediate amounts of loss. This rank order indicates not only a reduction in interference when the successive tasks are practiced in different contexts but also a detrimental effect when recall does not occur in the same context as acquisition.

A recent experiment by Zavortink (1968) suggests that the reductions in interference observed in the earlier studies probably should not be attributed entirely to the effectiveness of differential environmental cues. In this experiment the method of free-recall learning was used. Subjects learned successive lists either in the same situation or in distinctively different ones, with recall tested in the same context as original learning. An additional treatment was, however, added to assess the effect of the disruption produced by the shift from one room to another. After the completion of interpolated learning the subjects in this control condition were sent out of the experimental room on a brief errand; they then returned to the same room to begin the interpolated task. In agreement with the previous findings, the change in environmental context reduced the amount of retroactive inhibition; however, the improvement was equally great for the control group which was disrupted briefly but learned both lists in the same room. A plausible interpretation is that interference is lessened when the successive tasks acquire distinctive "temporal tags" on the basis of which they can be differentiated. A passing disruption as well as a shift in environment can provide the anchor points with respect to which the events can be tagged in temporal order. The possibility remains open, however, that temporal and environmental cues both may be effective.

Degree of Learning

Since retroaction is a consequence of successive practice on different tasks, the magnitude of the effects on retention may be expected to depend on the degree of learning of both the original and the inter-

polated activity. The basic importance of these variables becomes clearly apparent when intertask interference is considered as a special case of transfer.

Degree of original learning   The relation between the degree of original learning and retroactive inhibition has been investigated for lists of numbers (Robinson, 1920), nonsense syllables (McGeoch, 1929; Postman & Riley, 1959), lists of paired adjectives conforming to the *A–B, A–D* paradigm (Briggs, 1957), and connected discourse (Slamecka, 1960a). The common conclusion is that retroactive inhibition is a decreasing function of the degree of original learning. This conclusion holds, however, only for measures of relative interference, that is, the percentages of loss to the base of the control scores. When the trends in absolute differences

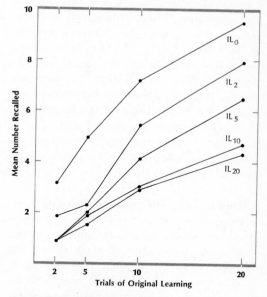

Figure 21.23. Retroactive inhibition as a joint function of the degree of original and of interpolated learning. The learning materials were lists of ten paired adjectives. First-list recall is plotted as a function of the number of trials of original learning, with the number of trials of interpolated learning (IL) as the parameter. IL_0 is the control condition. (Data from Briggs, 1957.)

between the experimental and the control groups are considered, the picture is usually quite different. The absolute amounts of interference fail to decline consistently as the degree of original learning increases; in fact, they often rise, especially at high levels of interpolated learning. The results obtained by Briggs (1957) provide a clear illustration of this trend (Figure 21.23); thus, the apparent decline in relative retroactive inhibition is entirely a function of the progressively higher level of performance under the control condition. In that sense the trend in relative measures is an artifact produced by the calculation of percentages to a changing base. The results are clearly contrary to what would be expected if the amount of interference reflected directly the relative strength of the associations in the two lists. The facts indicate that at a given level of interpolated learning there is a certain proportion of first-list items, presumably the *relatively* difficult and weak ones, which is susceptible to interference. This proportion does not decline as the degree of original learning is increased; rather it is likely to become larger because more and more difficult items are mastered during original learning (and hence are recalled by the control group). The assumption that it is the relatively weak items within a list that are most susceptible to retroactive inhibition is supported by the results of an analysis by Runquist (1957).

Degree of interpolated learning The amount of retroactive inhibition is a negatively accelerated increasing function of the degree of interpolated learning. (Since the retention interval in such experiments is usually held constant and the groups to be compared are evaluated against a common control condition, the trends observed for absolute and relative measures have necessarily been congruent.) This function has been obtained for serial lists of nonsense syllables (McGeoch, 1932b; Melton & Irwin, 1940; Postman & Riley, 1959), for lists of paired associates conforming to the A–B, A–D paradigm (Thune & Underwood, 1943; Briggs,

1957; Barnes & Underwood, 1959), and for connected discourse (Slamecka, 1960a). The slope of the function is extended, that is, the differential effects of the degree of interpolated learning on retroaction become more pronounced, as the degree of original learning increases. This fact becomes clearly apparent in Figure 21.23. The negative acceleration of the increases in retroactive inhibition deserves special emphasis. There is a substantial amount of interference even when the degree of interpolated learning is clearly lower than that of original learning; and continuing practice on the interpolated task yields diminishing returns.

It was noted earlier that the absolute amount of retroactive inhibition is inversely related to degree of original learning for individual items within a list but that this relation does not hold for a list as a whole. The picture is reversed, as it were, when variations in the degree of interpolated learning are considered. For the total list interference increases with the degree of interpolated learning. Such is not the case, however, for individual items: Under the paradigm of associative interference (A–B, A–D) the susceptibility of a first-list association to retroactive interference is independent of the relative strength attained by the corresponding second-list pair (Runquist, 1957). That is, the probability that A–B will be lost is not influenced by the degree to which A–D is reinforced during a fixed number of interpolated trials. As Runquist points out on the basis of this finding, the laws relating retention to associative strength are not the same when strength is measured within a list and when it is manipulated by varying the number of learning trials.

Amount of interpolation A clear distinction has to be made between the degree and the amount of interpolated learning. The latter refers to the number of different learning units, for example, lists, which are introduced during the retention interval. Retroactive inhibition may be expected to increase directly with the number of interpolated lists. As lists are added, the amount of time spent on the interpolated activity increases (just as it does with the number of trials on a single interpolated list); moreover, the pool of potentially interfering associations grows larger. The expected progressive increases in retroactive inhibition were obtained in an early study by Twining (1940), in which the learning materials were serial lists of nonsense syllables and the interpolated materials consisted of either 1, 2, 3, 4, or 5 lists. A control experiment showed that the detrimental effects of additional lists could not be attributed to correlated changes in the length of the interval between the end of interpolated learning and the test of recall.

Subsequent experiments were addressed to the question of whether the number of lists per se is an effective variable when the total time devoted to interpolated learning is taken into account. This question was investigated systematically in a study by Underwood (1945). The learning materials were lists of paired adjectives, with the first list (A–B) learned to a criterion of 6/10. There were two parallel sets of experimental treatments representing conditions of single-list and multiple-list interpolation, respectively. The single interpolated list (A–D) was practiced for either 8, 16, or 24 trials. The corresponding multiple-interpolation groups learned either 2, 4, or 6 lists (A–D, A–E, and so on) for 4 trials each. The amount of retroactive inhibition increased progressively with the number of interpolated lists; at the higher levels of practice, multiple lists produced more interference than a single list. Since the critical comparisons were between groups that had received exactly the same numbers of learning trials, the sheer amount of time spent on the interpolated activity cannot be responsible for the differences.

This conclusion was supported by the results of a later study by Postman (1965) in which all groups received exactly the same number of interpolated trials but the number of lists over which these trials were distributed was varied. Thus, interpolated practice was either for 16 trials on a single list, for 8 trials each on two lists, or for 4 trials each on four lists. The A–D paradigm of transfer was again used, with trigrams as stimuli and adjectives as responses. An unpaced test of recall showed steady increases in retroactive inhibition as a function of the number of interpolated lists (see also Howe, 1967; Birnbaum, 1968).

While it is possible to rule out the sheer duration of interpolated learning as an explanatory factor, the observed differences between single and multiple interpolation continue to pose complex problems of interpretation. When duration of interpolated practice is held constant, changes in the number of lists inevitably entail variations in the degree of learning for individual units. The associations in a single list learned for 16 trials reach a high level of strength; those in the four successive lists learned for four trials each remain relatively weak. Thus, two potentially important determinants of interference vary together: the number and the strength of the interfering associations. Since retroactive inhibition in general increases with the degree of interpolated learning, and yet multiple sets of weak associations produce more interference than a single set of strong ones, one may be led to the conclusion that the number of interfering associations is the overriding factor. It must be borne in mind, however, that the function relating retroactive inhibition to the degree of interpolated learning shows pronounced negative acceleration. Thus, there is little or no buildup of interference once practice on a single list reaches the stage of overlearning. On the other hand, the processes responsible for retroaction may be reactivated each time the acquisition of a new list is begun. We shall return to this problem in our discussion of unlearning.

Theories of Retroactive Inhibition

McGeoch's theory of reproductive inhibition Modern accounts of interference processes in retention represent a line of development that has its origin in McGeoch's theoretical analysis of retroactive inhibition

(1942, pp. 484–500). On the basis of the experimental evidence McGeoch was led to question the general validity of the perseveration hypothesis and to favor a transfer theory of retroactive inhibition.

The main arguments advanced against the perseveration hypothesis were the following: (1) While perseveration of the neural activity after the end of learning is generally assumed to be limited to a period not exceeding a few minutes, interpolated activities introduced after hours or days are known to produce significant interference effects (for a review of the early evidence on this question see Britt, 1936, and Swenson, 1941). (2) There is no apparent support for the prediction implied by the perseveration hypothesis that the amount of interference should vary directly with the intensity of the interpolated activity (McGeoch, 1931). (3) The fact that intertask similarity is a major determinant of retroactive inhibition is at variance with the hypothesis and is clearly seen as constituting the most damaging objection to it. (4) Finally, the hypothesis cannot be reasonably extended to provide an explanation of the phenomenon of proactive inhibition. In light of these considerations the disruption of perseveration could not be accepted as the basic mechanism of interference; McGeoch left open the possibility, however, that such a mechanism may play some role in forgetting, for example, in producing retention losses in the absence of an interfering activity.

McGeoch viewed the demonstrated dependence of retroactive inhibition on intertask similarity as supporting the interpretation of interference at recall as a special case of negative transfer. As a matter of definition, since retroactive inhibition reflects an interaction between the effects of successive learning activities, it must be classified as a phenomenon of transfer. The operative conditions of retroaction can be subsumed under a general principle of negative transfer, namely, that the attachment of different responses to identical or similar stimuli creates conditions of interference. The

reference paradigm is therefore A–B, A–D, A–B. During the second stage elicitation of the competing response B retards the establishment of the association A–D (associative inhibition). In the third stage, when the first association is to be recalled, elicitation of the recently acquired competing response D inhibits the reproduction of B. The interpretation of retroactive inhibition as a special case of negative transfer thus takes the form of a theory of *reproductive inhibition*. That is, retroactive inhibition is interpreted as reflecting the competition of responses at the time of recall: the reproduction of B is inhibited by the recall of D. "Responses thus inhibited are not necessarily lost from the subject's repertoire, but are kept by other responses from appearing" (McGeoch, 1942, p. 495). Thus, the *test of recall* is identified as the temporal locus of the retroactive effects. (For earlier statements of the theory in the context of experimental studies see McGeoch, 1936; McGeoch, McKinney, & Peters, 1937.) The implications of Gibson's generalization hypothesis for retroactive inhibition are equivalent to this position in all essential respects.

In developing his account of retroaction, McGeoch cited the occurrence of interlist intrusions at recall (substitution of D for B) as direct evidence of response competition. He acknowledged that overt intrusions account for only a fraction of the decrement in recall but considered it likely that many such errors remain implicit. That is, subjects recognize the intrusions as inappropriate and withhold them. Moreover, competing implicit tendencies may block each other so that there may be reproductive inhibition in the absence of either overt or reportable intrusions (see McKinney & McGeoch, 1935).

The theory of reproductive inhibition comprises two major hypotheses that should be clearly distinguished from each other even though they are closely linked in McGeoch's formulation. First, it is asserted that the availability of the original associations is not reduced by interpolated learning; the old system of responses remains intact while the new one is being acquired. This assumption has been designated the independence hypothesis (Barnes & Underwood, 1959). Second, competition between alternative responses inhibits recall. One response may be displaced by another that is momentarily dominant, or implicit responses may block each other. This is the hypothesis of response competition, or reproductive inhibition proper, which specified the mechanism of interference *at the time of recall*. The two hypotheses need not necessarily be linked together, and it is possible to reject one and to retain the other (see Postman, 1961a). In particular, even if the independence hypothesis is shown to be false, competition at recall may still be responsible for

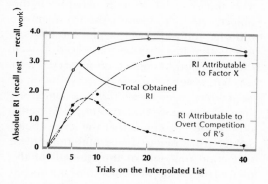

Figure 21.24. Two-factor theory of retroactive inhibition. The empirical function (solid line) shows the amount of retroactive inhibition as a function of the degree of interpolated learning. The two theoretical curves (dashed lines) represent estimates of the relative weights of two factors in determining the observed retention losses. The interference attributable to competition of responses is taken as two times the average frequency of interlist intrusions on the recall trial. The obtained frequency is multiplied by two to take account of intrusions of parts of syllables that could not be included in the count. The curve for factor *X* represents losses not attributable to response competition. Factor *X* was tentatively identified as the unlearning or extinction of the original responses during interpolated learning. (Melton & Irwin, 1940.)

the loss of responses that have remained available. That is precisely the position which gained wide acceptance as a result of subsequent developments.

Two-factor theory   The independence hypothesis was called into question in a classical paper by Melton and Irwin (1940) who proposed a two-factor theory in place of McGeoch's single-factor interpretation. The two-factor theory was formulated on the basis of the results of an experiment which investigated retroactive inhibition as a function of the degree of interpolated learning. Serial lists of 18 nonsense syllables were used as the learning materials. There were five trials of original learning followed by either 0, 5, 10, 20 or 40 trials of interpolated learning. The original list was relearned to a criterion of two perfect recitations at the end of the 30-minute retention interval. The absolute amount of retroactive inhibition at recall was a negatively accelerated increasing function of the degree of interpolated learning (Figure 21.24). Note that there is actually a slight inversion in the function after 40 interpolated trials; dissipation of the interference during relearning was also found to be most rapid for that condition. Interlist intrusions, which could be attributed to either the similarity of the serial positions or the formal similarity of the intruding and the displaced syllables, accounted for only a small percentage of the observed retention losses. More important, the functions relating the amount of retroactive inhibition and the frequency of intrusions to the degree of interpolated learning did not coincide. As Figure 21.24 shows, the number of intrusions rose to a maximum after 10 trials of interpolation and declined thereafter, even though retroactive losses continued to increase.

If the frequency of interlist intrusions is taken as an index of reproductive inhibition, it appears that there is some other determinant of interference that carries progressively greater weight as the degree of interpolated learning increases. Melton and Irwin labeled this factor "X" and tentatively identified it as the unlearning of the first-list associations during interpolated practice. Responses from the original list that occur as overt or implicit intrusions during interpolated learning fail to be reinforced and are weakened. Thus unlearning is conceived to be a process akin to extinction. Responses that have been unlearned are not available at the time of recall. The function for factor X indicates that the amount of unlearning increases with the number of interpolated trials. The rapid dissipation of interference at the highest level of interpolation suggests that unlearned responses can be relearned with considerable saving.

The major innovation introduced by the two-factor theory is the assumption that the processes responsible for retroactive inhibition have a dual locus: as interpolated learning proceeds, an increasing number of the original responses are unlearned and thus become unavailable; those which remain available are subject to competition from interpolated responses at the time of recall. The relative amount of retention loss attributable to reproductive inhibition is maximal when the competing response systems are at or near equal strength.

List differentiation The two-factor theory represented an important alternative to the view that all of the retention losses produced by interpolated learning are the result of reproductive inhibition. The lack of correlation between the frequency of overt intrusions and the absolute amount of retroactive inhibition does not, however, necessarily imply the operation of a factor other than reproductive inhibition. This argument was developed by Thune and Underwood (1943) who carried out an experiment paralleling that of Melton and Irwin but with paired adjectives as the learning materials. In their study, five trials of original learning were followed by either 0, 2, 5, 10, or 20 trials of interpolation. Whereas the amount of retroactive inhibition described the usual nega-

tively accelerated increasing function, the frequency of overt intrusions reached a maximum after 10 trials and declined sharply after 20 trials. Thus the lack of a one-to-one relation between the frequency of intrusions and total retention losses was confirmed. As the investigators pointed out, however, the discrepancy between the two indices of interference may be attributed to systematic changes in the ratio of overt to covert intrusions. This ratio is highest when the strength of the interpolated responses just exceeds that of the original ones. As the difference in favor of the interpolated responses increases further, subjects are more and more likely to recognize intrusion errors as inappropriate and to reject them.

The extent to which competition becomes overt thus can be seen to depend on the subject's ability to identify the list membership of responses; in principle, the amount of retention loss may be influenced as well if the rejection of implicit errors occurs with sufficient speed to permit the substitution of the correct responses. These assumptions were expressed by Underwood (1945) in the form of the hypothesis that the amount and characteristics of retroactive inhibition will be a function not only of the strength of the interpolated responses but also of the degree of list differentiation. At a given level of original learning, list differentiation is an increasing function of the degree of interpolated learning; that is, it reflects the relative strength of the latter. Subsequently Underwood (1949) added the assumption that differentiation also increases with the absolute strengths of the competing response systems. The degree of differentiation will also vary inversely with the length of the time interval between the end of interpolated learning and the test of recall.

The concept of differentiation has been used widely in the interpretation of the characteristics of performance under conditions of interference, and in particular has been invoked to account for variations in the frequency of overt intrusions. For a long time it remained entirely a theoretical construct. Recently, however, Winograd (1968) carried out a series of experiments in which the effects of variables assumed to influence list differentiation were evaluated directly. The basic procedure consisted of the presentation of two successive lists of words followed by a test of differentiation. During the test the two sets of items were shown in a mixed order and the subjects were required to identify the list membership of each. The expected functional relations were observed. Accuracy of list identification was found to be (1) poorer when the frequency of presentations for the two lists was the same than when it differed, (2) more accurate as the absolute frequency of presentations of the two lists was increased, and (3) a decreasing function of the length of the retention interval. It should be noted that the subjects were required to identify the list membership of all items. Recall was not measured, but presumably some items would not have been available, especially on the delayed test. As the author points out, in the application of these findings to phenomena of interference the question remains open of whether loss of differentiation leads to forgetting by increasing response competition or forgetting results in a loss of differentiation. It is also possible that the two processes develop at somewhat independent rates. Thus, Deese and Marder (1957) found that after the acquisition of two serial lists of synonymous adjectives the amount of first-list retention remained essentially constant over a 24-hour period, whereas the frequency of interlist intrusions increased progressively. List differentiation declined more rapidly, therefore, than did recall of the original material.

While the relation between list differentiation and recall remains to be clarified, the available evidence is consistent with the assumption that the overt manifestation of competition, that is, the occurrence of interlist intrusions, is significantly influenced by the subject's ability to identify the list membership of responses. The lack of a consistent relation between intrusions and amount of retroactive inhibition does not, therefore, in itself support the inference that first-list associations are unlearned.

Specific versus generalized response competition Before we turn to a detailed consideration of the hypothesis of unlearning, the factor of competition requires some further discussion. The competition to which McGeoch referred, and which is one of the two sources of interference in the formulation of Melton and Irwin, is a consequence of the successive attachment of different responses to the same stimulus. At the time of recall both responses may be aroused and block each other; or one of the responses may be momentarily dominant and displace the other. With the strength of individual associations fluctuating from moment to moment, the effects of competition are likely to be transitory; given sufficient time, the subject should be able to produce both responses. Since the interference is between the responses to an individual stimulus, the competition may be designated as specific. The extent to which specific competition results in overt intrusions will presumably depend on the degree of list differentiation.

There is evidence pointing to another form of competition that results from the subject's tendency to continue giving responses from the list he practiced last. Thus, when a test of recall is administered immediately after the end of interpolated learning, the persisting dominance of the second-list repertoire will interfere with the recall of responses from the first list. This mechanism of interference has been designated generalized competition by Newton and Wickens (1956). While generalized and specific competition may shade into each other, the conceptual distinction between them is important; the former refers to the dominance of a response repertoire, the latter to the arousal of an interfering response to an individual stimulus. Generalized competition is not likely to result in many overt interlist intrusions. The dominant list was practiced just prior to the test of recall and hence should be readily differentiated from one learned earlier. The primary consequence of generalized competition should, therefore, be an increase in failures to respond.

It should now be fully apparent that in principle reproductive inhibition may be reflected in both overt intrusions and response omissions, with the relative frequency of these classes of occurrences complexly determined by the operative forms of competition and the degree of list differentiation. Validation of the hypothesis of unlearning therefore could not rest on an analysis of error distributions but rather required the direct measurement of the availability of first-list responses after the end of interpolated learning.

Measurement of response availability A first step toward the direct assessment of changes in the availability of first-list responses following interpolation was the introduction of the method of modified free recall (MFR) (Underwood, 1948b; Briggs, 1954; Briggs, Thompson, & Brogden, 1954). An MFR test administered after the acquisition of two lists conforming to the A–B, A–D paradigm consists of the presentation of the common stimulus terms (A) with instructions to the subject to give the first response that comes to mind, if possible either B or D. Under these conditions identification of list membership is not required and the relative strength of first-list and second-list responses can be determined. When MFR tests are administered at successively higher levels of interpolated learning, the proportion of first-list responses decreases progressively and that of second-list responses shows complementary increases (Briggs, 1954). These findings are consistent with the unlearning hypothesis but fail to provide conclusive evidence for it because the MFR procedure limits the subject to one response. Thus, the changes in the distribution of responses may represent increasing dominance of the sec-

ond list rather than unlearning of the first. Briggs' (1954) finding that MFR tests yielded more retroactive inhibition than the conventional recall procedure is consistent with this possibility.

It remained for Barnes and Underwood (1959) to develop a procedure which gained wide acceptance as providing a valid measure of unlearning. The method is a modification of the MFR procedure, and in accord with Melton's (1961) suggestion is usually designated the MMFR test. After the end of interpolated learning each of the common stimulus terms (A) is presented as in the earlier version, but the subject is instructed to give *both* the responses (B and D) in the order in which they occur to him. The test is unpaced, and list identification is not required, although subjects are usually asked at the end of the test to indicate the list membership of the responses they have recalled. The influence of competition is assumed to be minimized if not eliminated because the test is unpaced, so that a temporary blockage can be overcome and a momentarily dominant response need not displace the weaker one; if both responses are available, the subject has an opportunity to give them both. Failures of list differentiation cannot influence performance since both responses are called for without regard to order.

It is important to recognize that the MMFR test is considered to be free of the effects of competition on a priori grounds. There should be no reproductive inhibition owing to the momentary dominance of one response over another, or to the equally transitory mutual blocking of two responses of approximately equal strength. If competition is persistent, the distinction between reproductive inhibition and loss of availability becomes blurred. Thus, it is transitory specific competition that is assumed to be eliminated. There are no equally compelling reasons to suppose that the MMFR test eliminates generalized competition. It will be useful to bear in mind, therefore, that the MMFR test may not in fact provide pure estimates of unlearning as de-

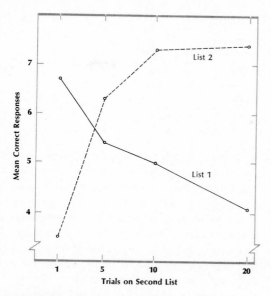

Figure 21.25. Unlearning of first-list associations during second-list learning. The successive lists conformed to the *A–B, A–D* paradigm. Retention was tested by the MMFR method; that is, subjects recalled both the first-list and the second-list responses. Changes in performance as a function of the number of trials on the second list are shown. Scores are based on the numbers of responses given to the appropriate stimulus and identified correctly as to list membership. (Barnes & Underwood, 1959.)

fined in the original statement of the two-factor theory.

In the experiment by Barnes and Underwood the learning materials were lists of eight paired associates, with trigrams as stimuli and adjectives as responses. Two paradigms of transfer were compared, namely, *A–B, A–D* and *A–B, A–B'* (synonymous responses). Original learning was to a criterion of one perfect recitation, followed by either 1, 5, 10, or 20 trials of interpolated learning. The results of the MMFR tests for the *A–B, A–D* paradigm are shown in Figure 21.25. The number of first-list responses recalled declines steadily as the number of interpolated trials is increased. Second-list recall becomes, of course, progressively higher. When both responses were recalled, items from the sec-

ond list tended to be given first. The large majority of the available responses were given to the correct stimuli. At the end of recall the list membership of the responses was identified with a high degree of accuracy; that is, there was little loss of differentiation on the test immediately after the end of interpolated learning. The results support the conclusion that first-list associations are unlearned or extinguished during the acquisition of the second list. Unlearning appears to account for virtually all of the observed retroactive inhibition.

The picture is quite different for the *A–B, A–B'* paradigm. Acquisition of the second list was extremely rapid, recall being nearly perfect after one learning trial. Increases in retroactive inhibition were extremely slow, with a loss of less than one item at the highest level of interpolated learning. As was indicated earlier, these findings strongly point to mediational chaining (*A–B–B'*) during second-list learning. As a consequence, the first-list associations continue to be reinforced during the interpolated trials. The fact that *B* tends to be recalled before *B'* and the subjects' reports are in agreement with this interpretation. The retroactive effects that were observed may be attributed to occasional failures on the part of the subjects to recognize the similarity relation between successive responses, in which case the paradigm reduced to *A–B, A–D*. In addition, it is possible that the mediator ceases to be functionally useful late in interpolated learning when a strong direct association between the stimulus and the response has been established; at this stage the mediator may begin to be unlearned. The difference between the *A–D* and *A–B'* paradigms is obtained with mixed as well as unmixed lists (Postman, 1962b).

The finding of Barnes and Underwood that under conditions of negative transfer there is a substantial reduction in the availability of first-list associations after interpolated learning has been confirmed in many subsequent investigations. The phenomenon of

TABLE 21.5

	Forward associations	Backward associations	Contextual associations
A–B, C–D	no	no	yes
A–B, C–B	no	yes	no
A–B, A–D	yes	no	yes
A–B, A–Br	yes	yes	no

unlearning is, therefore, firmly established, at least to the extent that the retention losses observed on the MMFR test reflect the operation of this process. The major questions of interpretation on which subsequent analyses have centered are (1) what is unlearned, and (2) what is the exact mechanism responsible for unlearning.

Conditions and Characteristics of Unlearning

A component analysis of unlearning A widely accepted answer to the question of what is unlearned is provided in an analysis by McGovern (1964) who identified three classes of associations which are subject to unlearning: (1) forward associations, (2) backward associations, and (3) contextual associations. We shall refer to the first two, which link individual stimuli and responses, as specific associations. Contextual associations refer to connections between the responses and the environmental situation, for example, the cues provided by the room, the experimental equipment, and so on. Response recall, as distinct from associative learning, depends on the development of contextual associations. It is McGovern's thesis that each of these component associations is subject to unlearning whenever the A–B, A–D paradigm obtains for these associations in the successive lists. On the basis of this assumption it is possible to specify exactly which associative components will be unlearned under various paradigms of transfer. Table 21.5 summarizes the application of this analysis to the conditions considered by McGovern in her experiment. Two major predictions are implied. First, unlearning should be greater for

A–D and A–Br than for C–D and C–B because the former paradigms entail an extinctive relation for two components, and the latter for only one. Second, if the requirement of response recall is removed on the retention test by making the responses available and instructing the subject to match them with the appropriate stimuli, there should be a substantial amount of improvement only for those cases in which contextual associations are assumed to be lost (C–D and A–D).

The learning materials in McGovern's experiment were lists of eight paired associates, with nonsense syllables as stimuli and adjectives as responses. (Because of the use of nonsense syllables as stimuli the results for the C–D and C–B paradigms must be interpreted with caution; see page 1061.) The first list was learned to a criterion of one perfect recitation; there were 15 trials on the second list. Retention of the first list was tested either by an unpaced test of recall or by associative matching. Only the former test was administered under the rest condition. The mean numbers of correct responses were as follows:

	C–D	C–B	A–D	A–Br	*Rest*
Recall	6.54	6.42	4.79	4.75	7.71
Matching	7.83	6.87	6.54	5.58	—

It can be seen that the major predictions are confirmed. On the test of recall the losses are greater for A–D and A–Br than for C–D and C–B. The differences between recall and matching are greatest for C–D and A–D. The decline for C–D is taken to reflect directly the extinction of contextual associations.

Note that, with the exception of *A–Br,* the decrements on the matching test are relatively small, that is, of the order of one item. It appears that the unlearning of contextual associations proceeds more rapidly than that of specific ones.

A complementary experiment demonstrating the extinction of backward associations was reported by Keppel and Underwood (1962a). The materials and procedure were the same as in McGovern's experiment, except that recall of backward associations was required on the test of retention. That is, the response terms were provided, and the subjects had to recall the stimuli with which they had been paired. The mean numbers of correct responses were:

C–D	C–B	A–D	A–Br	*Rest*
4.60	1.85	5.05	3.40	5.80

As the authors recognize, the results for the *A–D* and *A–Br* paradigms cannot be interpreted unequivocally since under these conditions the stimulus terms to be recalled on the test received continued exposure during interpolated learning. Nevertheless the pattern of results clearly indicates extinction of backward associations. In agreement with McGovern's analysis, the paradigms for which extinction of backward associations is expected show the greatest losses. The critical comparisons that isolate this factor are between *C–D* and *C–B,* and between *A–D* and *A–Br.* Subsequent studies, in which both nonsense syllables and meaningful words were used as stimulus (*A* and *C*) terms, have consistently yielded evidence for the unlearning of backward associations under the *C–B* paradigm (Ellington & Kausler, 1965; Greenbloom & Kimble, 1965; Houston, 1966c).

When successive lists conform to the *A–B, C–B* paradigm, unlearning of both forward and backward associations has been observed. Greenbloom and Kimble (1965) carried out tests in both directions within the same design and confirmed this conclusion,

with the backward losses considerably larger. The backward associations are in conflict with each other, and to the extent that *B–A* is activated during second-list learning it may be expected to be unlearned. It is less clear, however, why there should also be a reduction in forward recall. McGovern considers two ways in which backward associations may aid forward recall: they may serve a checking function (we considered earlier the description of such a process by Twedt and Underwood, 1959), or they may serve to mediate forward associations when the latter have been weakened. Elimination of these sources of facilitation would lead to decrements in *A–B* recall. An alternative interpretation is that unlearning is in principle bidirectional: backward strength is lost whenever the forward association is weakened, and vice versa. Such an assumption would follow from the principle of associative symmetry (Asch & Ebenholtz, 1962) according to which the forward and the backward strengths of an association are always strictly equivalent; apparent differences in performance are attributed to the differential availability of the terms to be recalled, the items used as responses during training being more available.

There is other evidence that after unlearning has presumably occurred in one direction, there is interference with recall in the other direction as well. Using highly familiar stimulus terms (numbers) in an attempt to minimize the problem of continued exposure to the stimuli during interpolation, Houston (1964b) found significant unlearning of backward associations for the *A–B, A–D* paradigm. In an experiment by Birnbaum (1966) the acquisition of the original list was bidirectional; that is, subjects were given equal amounts of practice on *A–B* and *B–A.* Interpolated learning was in one direction only; however, the losses observed on the test of recall were essentially symmetrical. She concluded that associations are unlearned equally in both directions. The conclusion is probably premature, however, since it is quite

TABLE 21.6

	Rest	C–D	C–B	A–D	A–Br	A–B′
Recall	9.7	9.0	8.5	4.7	6.2	7.1
Multiple choice	9.6	9.6	8.4	8.9	6.5	8.4

possible that the habit of bidirectional practice was carried over from original to interpolated learning. In any event, it is hazardous to generalize from her results to those obtained under standard conditions (Keppel, 1968, pp. 178f.). Somewhat more convincing is the finding of Cheung and Goulet (1968) that the amount of backward unlearning is essentially equal for the A–B, C–B and A–B, B–C paradigms. In the former case the extinctive relation obtains between successive backward associations, in the latter between first-list backward and second-list forward associations.

Differential unlearning of contextual and specific associations In the discussion of McGovern's results it was noted that the amount of unlearning attributable to the loss of specific associations, as indexed by the matching test, was in general relatively low. Subsequent studies in which the same or a closely similar testing procedure and comparable degrees of original learning were used have yielded comparable results (Garskof & Sandak, 1964; Postman, 1965; Sandak & Garskof, 1967; Garskof, 1968). In the case of the A–B, A–D paradigm the associative losses appear to be of a considerably smaller order of magnitude than those attributable to the unlearning of contextual associations. In these studies, however, as well as in McGovern's, response recall was required during the acquisition of the lists. Comparisons (either within or between experiments) of the results obtained on recall and on matching tests are, therefore, not conclusive, for two main reasons. First, with respect to the requirements of the retention task, degree of learning may well be appreciably higher when a test of associative matching rather than of recall is used. On this basis a difference in

favor of the former would be expected. Second, the methods of acquisition and of testing are more nearly continuous for recall than for matching; for the latter the shift in the mode of responding may have an adverse effect on performance. The resulting decrement is likely to be greater for an experimental group which has had more acquisition trials than the control group; the interval between the end of practice and the retention test is also shorter for the experimental group. These difficulties are largely avoided when the same method is used in the acquisition and in the test stage, recall or matching as the case may be, with degree of learning equated as closely as possible. An attempt to meet these requirements was made in the study by Postman and Stark (1969) mentioned earlier (p. 1066) in which the recall and multiple-choice methods were compared under various paradigms of transfer. An unpaced test of first-list retention was given at the end of interpolated learning which permitted an evaluation of the amounts of retroactive inhibition relative to appropriate rest groups. The test scores are shown in Table 21.6 (with the multiple-choice measures corrected for guessing).

On the test of recall the amount of retroactive inhibition varies widely, with the differences among paradigms showing a characteristic pattern. The retention loss is greatest for A–D. By contrast, the decrements on the multiple-choice test are quite small, and there is significant retroactive inhibition only for A–Br. The loss for A–D is now negligible. Two additional test trials were given to all groups. In spite of the absence of feedback there was an upward trend in the scores (see Richardson & Gropper, 1964). On the final multiple-choice trial retroactive inhibition was entirely eliminated for all paradigms except *A–Br*. While the recall scores also increased, the level of retroaction remained substantial.

Taken together, the available evidence indicates that specific associations are highly resistant to interference. The results of the study considered last indicate that there is an appreciable amount of associative unlearning only under conditions of heavy and persistent negative transfer, that is, *A–Br*. Thus, it appears that unlearning is in large measure a matter of reduced response availability. These findings bear directly on the question of the mechanism of unlearning to which we turn next.

The mechanism of unlearning: the elicitation hypothesis In the formulation of the two-factor theory an analogy was suggested between unlearning and the extinction of conditioned responses. First-list responses elicited during interpolated learning fail to be reinforced or are "punished" and thus are extinguished. The more precise analogy is to counterconditioning since a new response to the old stimulus is reinforced. In any event, according to this interpretation, elicitation of old responses as errors is an essential condition of extinction. A correlation would have to be expected between the frequency with which first-list responses occur as errors and the likelihood of their being unlearned (Melton, 1961). When overt intrusions are used to gauge the frequency of errors, such a correlation is not obtained. For example, Keppel and Rauch (1966) produced substantial variations in the number of interlist intrusions without influencing the amount of unlearning. However, such findings do not necessarily entail the rejection of the elicitation hypothesis because it has always been recognized that the large majority of intrusions are likely to remain covert. Conditions that encourage a high error rate may merely raise the ratio of overt to covert intrusions. This point continues to be missed by investigators who attempt to use the frequency of overt interlist intrusions as

an index of the opportunities for extinction (for example, Paul & Silverstein, 1968).

An alternative approach is to compare conditions of unlearning in which the total frequency of unreinforced elicitations, both overt and covert, may be assumed to vary, essentially on a priori grounds. Unreinforced elicitation is treated as an intervening construct, and the results of any one experiment do not provide conclusive evidence for the efficacy of this mechanism. The cumulative findings may, however, permit an evaluation of the heuristic value of the hypothesis. A study by Postman, Keppel, and Stark (1965) took its point of departure from the assumption that the frequency of unreinforced elicitations of first-list responses during interpolated learning should be greater when the class of responses (letters or adjectives) in the *A–B* and the *A–D* list remains the same than when it changes. As expected, significantly more unlearning was found under the former than under the latter condition (see also Friedman & Reynolds, 1967).

Entirely different operations were used by Goggin (1967) in an attempt to influence the frequency of unreinforced elicitations. In her experiment the first list (*A–B*) was learned by the prompting method; that is, the appropriate pair was always exposed just before the subject had to recall the response to a given stimulus. Under these circumstances errors on acquisition trials are extremely unlikely. The second list was learned either by the prompting method or by the anticipation method; the latter is, of course, conducive to interlist as well as intralist errors. It was assumed that interpolated learning under the prompting procedure would minimize the unreinforced elicitation of first-list responses. In accord with prediction, there was significantly less unlearning when the second list was learned by the prompting rather than the anticipation method. This result was obtained in spite of the fact that the similarity of context during original and during interpolated learning must have been greater when the method remained the same (prompting in both stages) than when it changed (prompting followed by anticipation).

Finally, the elicitation hypothesis provides one possible explanation of the increase in retroactive inhibition with the number of interpolated lists (Postman, 1965). When there is a fixed period of interpolated learning, the level of dominance of the new responses over the old responses should vary inversely with the number of different lists practiced during this period. That is, the larger the number of lists, the weaker the several interpolated associations will remain relative to the original ones and the longer should the latter continue to be elicited as intruding errors. Moreover, as Birnbaum (1968) has suggested, quite apart from the developing differences in strength between original and interpolated habits, the introduction of each new list may serve as a "disinhibitor" conducive to the reactivation of the original associations.

It is clear that the evidence in support of the elicitation hypothesis remains highly circumstantial. Even if the available data are viewed as consistent with the hypothesis, the question remains of whether unreinforced elicitations constitute the mechanism of unlearning or are only a link in a chain of events that results in the observed retention losses. We shall return to this question shortly.

Temporal changes in retroactive inhibition: Spontaneous recovery If unlearning has the functional properties of extinction, it should be a partially reversible process. That is, unlearned associations should show spontaneous recovery over time just as do extinguished conditioned responses. This implication was recognized early, and there has been a long history of attempts to find evidence for the recovery of verbal associations.

Absolute increases over time in the recall of first-list associations would constitute direct evidence for recovery if comparable increases do not occur under the control condition. However, since materials acquired in the laboratory are subject to extra-

experimental interferences, a decline in the amount of retroactive inhibition, that is, a reduction of the difference between the experimental and control treatment, has been considered as evidence for relative recovery. It should be noted at the outset that it is hazardous to infer the occurrence of recovery in the absence of absolute rises in first-list recall. When relative recovery is found, it is usually because the rate of forgetting is greater for the control than the experimental group. The reason for the convergence of the amounts recalled may lie in the difference between the distributions of associative strengths under the two conditions. On an immediate test of retention the control group is likely to show little forgetting; that is, weak as well as strong items will be recalled. As the retention interval is lengthened, more and more of the relatively weak items may be expected to be lost. The situation is quite different under the experimental treatment, that is, when the immediate test is given after the end of interpolated learning. Only items sufficiently strong to resist retroactive inhibition will be available on the immediate test; subsequent forgetting of such items is likely to be slow. Consequently the changes between an immediate and a delayed test will be smaller for the experimental than the control group (Birnbaum, 1965).

On the basis of the method used to measure retention the relevant experimental studies may be divided into three groups: those using tests of paced anticipation, MFR, and MMFR, respectively. Under conditions of paced anticipation increases in the availability of first-list responses may be offset to an unknown degree by declines in list differentiation and increases in competition effects over time. The MFR procedure eliminates failures of list differentiation as a source of error, but since performance reflects the relative dominance of original and interpolated responses, changes in availability per se cannot be determined. Such changes are presumably measured directly on MMFR tests.

On paced tests of anticipation only small and unreliable increases in first-list recall have been observed (Underwood, 1948a; Briggs, 1954). Absolute rises in the frequency of first-list responses have been obtained on MFR tests; these rises were substantial and significant in one study (Briggs, 1954) but relatively minor and not significant in others (Underwood, 1948b; Briggs, Thompson, & Brogden, 1954). In each case, however, there was a clear convergence in the frequency of first-list and second-list responses as the retention interval was lengthened, indicating decreasing dominance of the latter.

The results of experiments using the MMFR procedure to assess temporal changes in the availability of unlearned associations have been inconsistent. In the bulk of the studies changes in interference were measured after intervals of hours or days. Significant amounts of recovery were reported in two studies (Ceraso & Henderson, 1965; Silverstein, 1967); in both of these the measure of performance was the number of responses recalled regardless of whether or not they were given to the appropriate stimuli. Trends toward absolute recovery which failed to reach statistical significance were obtained in other experiments (Koppenaal, 1963; Ceraso & Henderson, 1966; Slamecka, 1966). In still other cases there was evidence only for relative recovery owing to greater forgetting under the control than the experimental condition (Birnbaum, 1965; Howe, 1967); Houston (1966d) found neither absolute nor relative recovery. In all the studies mentioned so far the A–B, A–D paradigm was used. To complete the picture, the results of a study by Saltz and Hamilton (1967) should be mentioned in which a significant amount of recovery was observed for the A–B, A'–D paradigm relative to an A–B, C–D control condition.

One possible reason for the discrepant findings may be the variation among experiments in the level of retention at the time of the test for spontaneous recovery. Absolute rises in the recall of unlearned associations appear to be associated with high levels

of retention under the control condition (see Postman, Stark, & Fraser, 1968, Table 1). The losses of the control groups may be taken to reflect the amounts of extraexperimental forgetting for the materials, degrees of learning, and retention intervals under consideration. The less extraexperimental forgetting there is, the more likely it becomes that absolute rises in recall will be detected, if spontaneous recovery does, indeed, occur. The table referred to above shows that in all cases in which there was at least some evidence of spontaneous recovery the recall scores of the control groups exceeded 90 percent; it is hardly surprising not to find any signs of recovery when the control scores are of the order of 50 or 40 percent (Birnbaum, 1965; Howe, 1967). One method of reducing the amount of extraexperimental forgetting is overlearning of the critical list (Silverstein, 1967). An alternative approach is

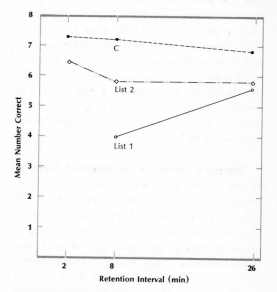

Figure 21.26. Temporal changes in interference: mean numbers of first-list and second-list responses (A–B, A–D) recalled on an unpaced test as a function of the length of the retention interval. The curve labeled C shows the scores of a control group which learned and recalled a single list. Each point represents an independent group of subjects. (Postman, Stark, & Fraser, 1968.)

the measurement of recovery over relatively short retention intervals during which there will be little or no loss under the control condition even after moderate degrees of original learning. A theoretical consideration which favors the use of the latter procedure is that most of the evidence for spontaneous recovery of classically conditioned responses is for intervals measured in minutes rather than days (Kimble, 1961, pp. 284f).

Using retention intervals of the order of 20 minutes, Postman, Stark, and Fraser (1968) obtained reliable evidence for absolute rises in first-list recall. Such recovery was observed when recall of the responses was required. The results of one of these experiments are shown in Figure 21.26. In this series of investigations evidence was also found for systematic temporal changes in performance under conditions of interference. When recall of both the original and the interpolated lists was required, the responses from the most recently learned list were likely to be given first on an immediate test; after a period of delay, however, there was a pronounced shift in the order of recall in favor of the first list. Little evidence of recovery on tests of associative matching was obtained, but since the amount of retroactive inhibition is small to begin with, there is little opportunity for improvement.

Temporal point of interpolated learning

To the extent that there is first-list recovery, the amount of retroactive inhibition should vary systematically with the temporal position of the interpolated activity during a given retention interval. The shorter the period between the end of interpolation and test, the less opportunity there should be for recovery to occur. Investigations of the effects on retention of the temporal position of the interpolated activity go back to the beginning of research on retroactive inhibition. The problem derived its initial theoretical significance from the implication of the perseveration hypothesis that retroactive inhibition should decline as the inter-val between original and interpolated learning is lengthened. Early experiments in which serial lists were used (McGeoch, 1933) did not support this prediction; in fact, relative interference was found to be greater when the interpolated activity occurred immediately before the test of recall rather than directly after the end of original learning. More recent studies in which paired-associate lists were used in an A–B, A–D arrangement failed to find an effect of the temporal point of interpolation (Archer & Underwood, 1951; Newton & Wickens, 1956; Houston, 1967c). In the latter study, however, retroactive inhibition did increase with the length of the interval between original and interpolated learning for the A–B, C–D paradigm. Newton and Wickens attributed this particular result to the factor of generalized response competition which should be maximal when the interpolated list is learned just before the test of recall.

In the studies considered last, the retention interval was 48 hours or longer. Quite apart from the effects of the interpolation, the retention interval was sufficiently long to produce a substantial amount of extraexperimental forgetting: the recall score of the rest group in the experiment of Newton and Wickens was 64 percent. Thus, it is possible that, as in the studies of recovery discussed above, the effect of the temporal variable is masked by extraexperimental forgetting. The demonstration of a recovery effect should again become more likely when the retention interval is short. In recent experiments by the writer a 20-minute retention interval was used, and interpolated learning took place either immediately after the end of original learning or just prior to the MMFR test. First-list recall was, as expected, found to be higher under the former than under the latter condition.

Extinction versus response suppression

What can be said about the success of the extinction analogy in permitting an orderly account of the facts of unlearning? There is some support, by no means conclusive, for the assumption that the unreinforced elicitation of first-list responses during interpolated practice is a condition of unlearning. However, the apparent high resistance of specific associations to unlearning is damaging to the analogy. It is the responses to individual stimuli that are assumed to be elicited as errors and to undergo extinction, but such specific associations appear to remain largely intact while the responses become less available. It is possible to argue, of course, that contextual associations are extinguished far more rapidly than are specific ones, but there is no clear theoretical reason for such an ad hoc assumption. On the face of it, whatever evidence there is for spontaneous recovery points to a functional similarity of unlearning and extinction. However, when rises in first-list recall do occur, they appear to reflect primarily increases in response availability, and the latter have in turn been found to be correlated with shifts in the order of recall. Taken together, these findings carry a strong suggestion that the mechanism of unlearning operates primarily on the entire repertoire of first-list responses rather than on individual stimulus-response associations.

One possible conclusion is that during interpolated learning a mechanism comes into play which serves to suppress the repertoire of first-list responses and allows the subject to limit himself to the currently prescribed responses. The greater the associative interference entailed by the conditions of transfer the more thorough the suppression of the interfering repertoire will become. From this point of view the elicitation of first-list responses as overt or covert errors does not in itself result in unlearning through a process of extinction but triggers the suppressor mechanism which results in reduced availability of the original responses at the end of interpolated learning. Since it is the response repertoire that is suppressed, specific stimulus-response associations remain for the most part intact; it is only under conditions of heavy and persistent negative

transfer, such as under the A–B, A–Br paradigm, that individual associations become subject to suppression or perhaps to a process with the characteristics of extinction. On the basis of these assumptions it becomes understandable that unlearning is largely a matter of reduced response availability. Finally, on the reasonable supposition that response suppression is a reversible mechanism the effectiveness of which diminishes over time, increases in response availability on delayed tests of retention may be expected. For a more complete statement of this position see Postman, Stark, and Fraser (1968). It should be apparent that there is a close relation between the conceptions of response suppression and generalized response competition: Suppression of the response repertoire of the first list implies dominance of that of the second list at the time of recall. In that sense the MMFR test may not be free of all effects of competition.

The generality of unlearning The fact that the availability of a repertoire of responses is reduced rapidly during interpolated learning is demonstrated clearly in studies of retroactive inhibition in free recall. When a procedure equivalent to MMFR is used, that is, recall of both the original and the interpolated material is required, substantial decrements in first-list retention are observed. This result has been obtained with lists of nonsense syllables (Asch & Ebenholtz, 1962) as well as in several experiments in which English words were used as the learning materials. In the latter studies retroactive inhibition exhibits functional characteristics that parallel those obtained with paired-associate lists. Thus, the amount of interference is an increasing function of the degree of interpolated practice on a single list (Postman & Keppel, 1967) and of the number of interpolated lists (Tulving & Thornton, 1959). In view of the evidence for the development of higher-order units in free-recall learning (Tulving, 1968), it would not be plausible to attribute the reduced availability of the first list entirely to the extinction of contextual associations. To the extent that the same conceptual or categorial groupings are used in original and in interpolated learning, the successive lists share common mediating stimuli; with respect to such stimuli the A–B, A–D paradigm obtains for individual words (see Shuell & Keppel, 1967; Shuell, 1968). Thus, the conditions believed to be conducive to the suppression of first-list responses are present. As is true in the recall of paired associates, the responses from the second list are likely to be given before those from the first (Asch & Ebenholtz, 1962; Postman & Keppel, 1967).

Significant reduction in the availability of first-list responses has also been observed in the serial-learning situation (Keppel, 1966). Since there is uncertainty about the functional stimulus in serial learning, the nature of the extinctive relation between successive lists cannot be specified with precision. Nevertheless there is an important parallel to the results obtained with paired associates in the fact that losses in response recall are of a substantially larger order of magnitude than in the reconstruction of the serial order of the items. If serial order is a matter of associative chaining, interitem associations again appear to be relatively resistant to unlearning.

PROACTIVE INHIBITION

It is an interesting historical fact that for many years retroactive inhibition was the only condition of interference that received theoretical consideration. Systematic research on proactive inhibition is of relatively recent origin and has developed within a theoretical framework that grew out of the analysis of retroaction. It has become clear, however, that in forgetting outside the laboratory proactive sources of interference probably carry greater weight than do retroactive sources (Underwood, 1957a). Thus, there has been increasing emphasis on the integration of

both forms of interference within a common conceptual scheme.

A study by Whitely (1927) provided an early indication that the recall of a test list may be adversely influenced by the activities preceding its acquisition. The phenomenon of proactive inhibition was explicitly identified and demonstrated in a subsequent investigation by Whitely and Blankenship (1936). In their experiment the test task consisted of a list of monosyllabic words. The material used in prior learning was either another list of words or a series of nonsense syllables. A control group learned only the test list. Recall after 48 hours was significantly poorer under both experimental conditions than under the control condition. There was only slightly less interference when different classes of materials were used in the two lists. It should be noted, however, that subjects served under all conditions in a counterbalanced design and that the retention losses were extremely heavy, so that the experiment was probably not sensitive to the effects of similarity. A second experiment in which stanzas of poetry were used as the learning materials gave comparable results. Whitely and Blankenship interpreted these results as consistent with a transfer theory of interference.

Implications of Transfer Theories of Interference

At this point it will be useful to consider the implications for proactive inhibition of the theoretical analyses of retroactive inhibition. If reproductive inhibition is the only mechanism of interference, retroactive and proactive losses should be equivalent under otherwise comparable conditions, that is, if the retention interval is held constant and the degrees of learning are the same both for the interfering list and the test list. There is no implication in the hypothesis of reproductive inhibition that the effects of specific competition should be asymmetrical, for example, more damaging to the recall of the first than of the second list. If generalized competition is taken into account, however, there should be less proactive than retroactive inhibition, at least for tests given soon after the end of second-list learning, since the most recently practiced responses are likely to remain dominant at that time. As the degree of dominance diminishes, this difference should become smaller.

The two-factor theory entails the prediction that the retroactive effects will exceed the proactive effects because the first list is subject to both unlearning and competition, whereas the second list is subject only to competition (Melton & von Lackum, 1941). To the extent, however, that unlearned associations recover over time, the advantage of the first list will decline. It must be added that the manifestations of competition may be expected to be influenced by the level of list differentiation at the time of the retention test. Again it is reasonable to suppose that this factor has equivalent effects on the recall of the first and of the second list. This supposition is in general supported by the results of Winograd's (1968) experiments in which differentiation was assessed directly. On the assumption that proactive inhibition is entirely a matter of competition, degree of differentiation may, indeed, become a decisive factor.

These theoretical considerations should be borne in mind as the variables influencing the amount of proactive inhibition are considered.

Degree of Learning

In this section we shall consider the influence on proactive inhibition of variations in the degree of test-list learning and of prior learning. The evaluation of these relations is complicated by the fact that in studies of proaction the test list is the first task for the control subjects, and the second task for the experimental subjects. Thus, there are differences between the experimental and control group in speed of test-list acquisition

which depend on the degree of prior learning; moreover, the magnitude of the transfer effects will also vary with the stage of test-list learning. There is some uncertainty, therefore, about the comparability of proactive effects observed under different combinations of prior and test-list learning.

There is little experimental evidence on the relation between the degree of original learning and proactive inhibition. (To make the discussion comparable with that in the section on retroaction, acquisition of the test list will be referred to as original learning.) In one study in which a serial list of nonsense syllables was used as the learning task (Postman & Riley, 1959) the relation was found to be complex, although there was some evidence for increases in absolute interference when very low and very high degrees of original learning were compared.

If competition is the effective source of interference, the amount of proactive inhibition should be some increasing function of the degree of prior learning. The expected relation was found in some studies in which lists of paired adjectives were the learning materials (Underwood, 1949; Atwater, 1953) but in other cases has failed to materialize. (Dallett, 1964; Underwood & Ekstrand, 1966). A somewhat irregular trend in the expected direction has been obtained with serial lists of nonsense syllables (Postman & Riley, 1959). The amount of proactive inhibition has been consistently found to increase with the number of prior lists, both for paired associates (Underwood, 1945) and connected discourse (Slamecka, 1961). In general, the results are in agreement with those for retroactive inhibition, but not nearly as dependable. That is perhaps not surprising, since the effects of competition alone should not be as stable as those of unlearning and competition combined.

Again in agreement with the findings for retroactive inhibition, list differentiation influences the manifestations of competition. Intrusions are most frequent when the degrees of original and prior learning are comparable; they decline sharply when the level of practice is substantially higher for the first than the second list (Underwood, 1949). At high degrees of prior learning, therefore, differentiation serves to counteract the effects of competition. It is not certain, however, whether only the ratio of overt to covert intrusions is influenced, or the amount of recall as well.

Similarity Relations

A competition theory of proaction must, of course, predict intertask similarity to be a critical variable. The importance of formal similarity was clearly demonstrated in the study of Melton and von Lackum (1941) in which the materials were serial lists of nonsense syllables. Proactive losses, as measured by recall and relearning, as well as the frequency of interlist intrusions, were substantially greater under conditions of high than of low interlist similarity.

Experiments that permit a separation of the interlist relations between stimuli and between responses have focused primarily on the meaningful similarity of the latter. There are theoretical reasons for expecting proactive inhibition to be an increasing function of response similarity. As we have seen, the hypothesis of parasitic reinforcement assumes that the greater the response similarity the more strength accrues to the first-list associations during the acquisition of the second list. The same is implied by a mediational interpretation. When the second list is learned to a fixed level, therefore, the effective strength of the first list should increase directly with response similarity. However, the expected relation between response similarity and proaction has not been found (Morgan & Underwood, 1950; Young, 1955; Dallett, 1962b, 1964; Postman & Stark, 1964). On the contrary, proactive inhibition at recall typically is greatest when the responses are unrelated (A–B, A–D). In some cases at least, the positive transfer effects in the acquisition of the second list are sufficiently great to lead

to the overlearning of test-list items which thus become relatively immune to interference (Postman & Stark, 1964). In general, the results of these studies fail to shed light on the mechanisms of proactive interference. The predictions derived from the hypothesis of parasitic reinforcement are not supported. Moreover, response similarity should be conducive to competition and failures of differentiation at recall, but neither retention losses nor intrusion rates bear out this expectation consistently. The possibility remains that on delayed tests of retention interlist response similarity ensures a high level of response recall which serves to offset associative interferences.

Temporal Changes in Interference

Proactive inhibition is by definition some increasing function of time: The difference between the experimental and the control condition is reliably greater on a delayed test than at the end of acquisition. If the processes responsible for the interference are continuous, proactive inhibition should increase progressively as the retention interval is lengthened. This expectation has in general been confirmed (Underwood, 1948a; Greenberg & Underwood, 1950; Slamecka, 1961; Postman, 1962c).

As predicted by the two-factor theory, there is typically less proactive than retroactive inhibition when the retention interval is relatively short. The first confirmation of this prediction was obtained in the experiment by Melton and von Lackum (1941) mentioned earlier, in which serial lists of nonsense syllables were used and the retention interval was 20 minutes. Essentially parallel results were found with lists of paired adjectives by McGeoch and Underwood (1943), but the difference between the two types of interference failed to reach significance. It appears that a clear-cut difference is most likely to be found when negative transfer is relatively heavy (Young, 1955).

Spontaneous recovery of first-list associations should serve to reduce the difference between the two types of interference. As first-list responses gain in strength, they can compete more and more effectively with those from the second list. Hence there should be not only progressive decreases in retroactive inhibition but also concomitant increases in proactive inhibition. This prediction applies to tests of recall assumed to be subject to specific competition, such as paced anticipation. Convergence over time of the amounts of retroactive and of proactive inhibition has, in fact, been observed under conditions of paced testing (Underwood, 1948a). This convergence occurs, however, primarily because of decreases in second-list recall rather than absolute increases in first-list recall. Thus, a shift in the relative strength of the two response systems is indicated, which is not, however, safely attributable to spontaneous recovery.

On the assumption that MMFR tests are immune to specific competition, the two-factor theory must predict an absence of proactive inhibition on such tests. It is a fact, however, that substantial amounts of proactive inhibition have been observed on MMFR tests in several investigations (Koppenaal, 1963; Ceraso & Henderson, 1965, 1966; Houston, 1967a; Postman, Stark, & Fraser, 1968). In one study (Houston, 1967a), a direct comparison of MMFR and paced anticipation showed the amounts of interference to be equivalent under the two procedures. The retroactive and proactive effects obtained in MMFR converge to the extent that there is less decline for the first than for the second list, or, of course, absolute recovery (see Figure 21.26). Since at least some relative recovery has been usually obtained, convergence is the rule.

The finding that performance on MMFR tests is subject to proactive inhibition poses serious problems of interpretation. On the assumption that specific competition is not operative, the effects of interference between successive response repertoires must be considered. It has already been suggested that the most recently acquired list is domi-

nant on an immediate test of recall but that the degree of dominance diminishes over time. Consequently, the second list loses its initial advantage as the retention interval is lengthened. Moreover, the simultaneous activation of two response systems should have an adverse effect on the recall of both lists as compared to a single-list control condition. Once one of these systems has been aroused at a given point in time, the shift to the alternative system may be impeded sufficiently to depress recall. Such shifts should be facilitated, and the amount of interference be reduced, if the distinctiveness of the alternative response systems can be maintained over time. Thus, if the interference is between response systems rather than specific associations, list differentiation can be seen to remain a critical factor. Such speculations fall short, of course, of specifying the exact conditions responsible for proactive effects observed on MMFR tests. It is important to recognize that this finding cannot be predicted on the basis of current extensions of two-factor theory and that the operative mechanisms are far from being clearly understood.

Cumulative proactive inhibition An important objective of experiments on interference is to examine under controlled conditions some of the variables that are believed to influence forgetting outside the laboratory. Experiments on proactive inhibition are designed to evaluate the influence of prior learning on the retention of recently acquired materials. Prior learning can, of course, be seen as a potential major source of interference outside the laboratory. We turn now to investigations that provide a useful transition between the measurement of proactive inhibition in standard transfer designs and the consideration of extraexperimental sources of forgetting. The findings to be considered concern the effects of prior learning experiences in the laboratory on the retention of newly learned materials. The empirical question here complements that to

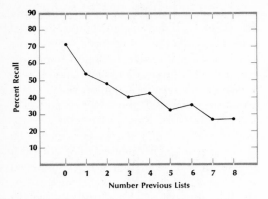

Figure 21.27. Recall of serial lists of adjectives as a function of the number of previous lists. Each 12-item list was learned to a criterion of one perfect recitation and recalled 24 hours later. (Data by E. J. Archer, from Underwood, 1957a.)

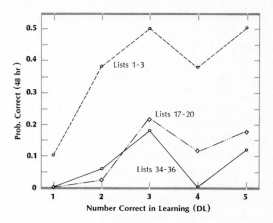

Figure 21.28. Progressive decreases in recall as a function of stage of practice. Subjects learned lists of 10 paired associates to criterion and recalled them 48 hours later. There were 36 learning-recall cycles. For items of a given degree of learning (*DL*) recall dropped sharply as the number of previous lists increased. (Keppel, Postman, & Zavortink, 1968.)

which studies of learning to learn are directed: Are there systematic changes in recall as a function of the number of prior lists learned and recalled in the laboratory? One might expect on a priori grounds that subjects would learn how to recall just as they learn how to learn. Exactly the opposite turns out to be true: The larger the number of previous lists the subject has learned and recalled in the laboratory, the more rapid is the forgetting of the list learned last. The increases in forgetting become more pronounced as the retention interval is lengthened (Greenberg & Underwood, 1950). These trends develop even though the successive lists are unrelated (*A–B, C–D, E–F,* and so on). The basic finding that retention losses become progressively greater as a function of the stage of practice has been confirmed in a number of investigations, both for paired-associate learning (Warr, 1964; Keppel, Postman, & Zavortink, 1968) and free-recall learning (Wipf & Webb, 1962). The results of still another experiment showing the trends obtained with serial lists of adjectives are shown in Figure 21.27. It is clear that massive amounts of proactive interference are built up even in the absence of formal similarity relations among the lists learned in the labo-

ratory. The conditions of proaction must, therefore, be sought in the interference among the successive response systems acquired within the same experimental situation.

It has been suggested (Warr, 1964) that the progressive declines in retention may reflect not proactive interference but rather the reduction in the number of trials to a fixed criterion that is a consequence of learning to learn. This explanation is, however, untenable in light of the experimental evidence. It is a fact, first of all, that the data fail to show the expected inverse relation between the number of trials to criterion and the amount of retention loss; for example, progressive increases in forgetting are observed even when there is no learning to learn (Underwood & Ekstrand, 1967a). The alternative interpretation is again negated when the probability of recall is compared for items which were given correctly with equal frequency during acquisition but which were learned at different stages of practice. As Figure 21.28 shows, there are drastic decreases in the probability

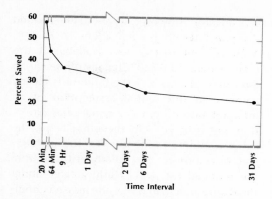

Figure 21.29. Ebbinghaus' forgetting curve. To obtain the data for this function, Ebbinghaus learned eight lists of 13 nonsense syllables each to a criterion of two perfect recitations during a single session and then relearned these lists to the same criterion after a given interval of time. Retention was measured in terms of the percentage of time saved in relearning as compared with the original learning. (Data from Ebbinghaus, 1885.)

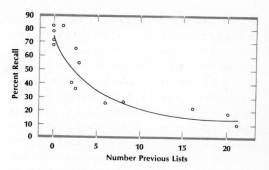

Figure 21.30. The development of cumulative proactive inhibition in the laboratory. The function shows the relation between recall and the number of previous lists learned in the laboratory. Each of the points represents the results of a study in which the subjects served in a number of different conditions, and the critical list was learned to a criterion of one perfect recitation and recalled after 24 hours. (From Underwood, 1957a.)

of delayed recall as a function of stage of practice even when the number of correct responses in learning is held constant.

The fact that proactive inhibition accumulates steadily as a result of prior learning in the laboratory proved to have important implications for much of the experimental literature on forgetting. Until fairly recently it was a standard procedure in studies of learning and retention to use practiced subjects who served under a number of different conditions in a counterbalanced design, often in repeated cycles of the experiment. It was by no means unusual for a subject to learn as many as 20 different lists. (The most famous practiced subject in the history of research on verbal learning is undoubtedly Hermann Ebbinghaus; the number of lists he learned in years of experimentation with himself as the only subject defies a precise count.) The classical experiments agreed in showing massive amounts of forgetting after relatively short intervals. Ebbinghaus' famous curve (Figure 21.29) shows a loss of about 65 percent after 24 hours, and in some subsequent stud-

ies forgetting over the same period exceeded 80 percent. It is now clear that proactive inhibition built up as a result of many laboratory sessions is largely responsible for the magnitude of these losses. In an incisive analysis of the experimental literature on retention Underwood (1957a) showed that the amount of forgetting after 24 hours for a list learned in the laboratory declined in an orderly fashion as a function of the number of prior lists learned in the same experiment (Figure 21.30). For the naive subject who learns only one list in the laboratory the retention loss over 24 hours drops to about 20 percent. This analysis provides impressive confirmation for the phenomenon of cumulative proactive inhibition. From a theoretical point of view an important consequence is that the amount of extraexperimental forgetting for which interference theory (or, for that matter, any theory of memory) must account is far less than had been assumed on the basis of the classical studies.

Proactive inhibition and distributed practice Some recent studies of the relation between distribution of practice and proactive inhibition have led to a shift in theoretical interpretation away from the extinction-recovery hypothesis to increasing emphasis on the role of the process of differentiation.

For purposes of exhibiting the theoretical considerations that link distribution of practice and proactive inhibition let us consider the acquisition of a list of paired associates under conditions of heavy negative transfer, such as, list A–E which was preceded by A–B, A–C, and A–D. During the learning trials on A–E the previous associations to A are presumably subject to extinction. If A–E is learned under conditions of distributed practice, the extinguished prior associations have an opportunity to recover during the intertrial intervals, and each time they do so they must be re-extinguished. Such successive recoveries will be minimal during the short intertrial intervals under massed practice of the terminal list. The assumption is now introduced that the more frequently the cycles of recovery and re-extinction are repeated, the more complete will be the unlearning of the interfering associations; and the more complete the unlearning the lower will be the level of recovery for the extinguished associations during a subsequent retention interval. It then follows that the delayed recall of A–E should be greater when that list is acquired under distributed rather than massed practice because there will be less recovery of prior associations which can become effective sources of competition at recall. Results consistent with this prediction were obtained by Underwood, Keppel, and Schulz (1962), who also concluded that it is the extinction and recovery of contextual associations that are critical for the differences in recall.

That the differences in recall can be impressive indeed was demonstrated by Keppel (1964) in an experiment in which intertrial intervals of 24 hours were used during the acquisition of the terminal list (A–E). Eight days after the end of original learning recall of A–E was 72 percent when acquisition was under distributed practice, and only 7 percent when it was under massed practice. In a later

investigation, however, Keppel (1967) found that the interfering associations (A–B, A–C, A–D) are not in fact less available at the time of delayed recall after distributed than after massed practice. This finding is clearly contrary to the central assumption of an interpretation in terms of differential extinction and recovery. On the other hand, the subjects' ability to identify the list membership of responses, particularly of those from the terminal list, was clearly greater under the distributed than under the massed condition. List differentiation is superior because the terminal list is acquired under a temporal schedule different from that for the prior lists. However, while list differentiation may contribute to the facilitation of recall after distributed learning, it probably does not provide the entire explanation because long intertrial intervals continue to have a beneficial effect on retention when only a single list is learned and recalled. Keppel suggests that under conditions of wide distribution the subject has an opportunity to discard associative links that prove ineffective and to select new ones that are more resistant to forgetting.

The evidence points more clearly to a decisive effect of list differentiation when the contrast between massed and distributed practice is introduced in the stage of prior learning. In an experiment by Underwood and Ekstrand (1966) this variable as well as the degree of prior learning was manipulated. The materials were lists of paired adjectives conforming to the A–B, A–D paradigm, with A–D learning carried to a criterion of one perfect recitation followed by a retention test 24 hours later. There were four degrees of first-list learning, namely, 12, 32, 48, or 80 trials. At each level of prior learning acquisition was either by massed or widely distributed practice. Under the massed condition all trials were given in a single session and were followed immediately by acquisition of the second list. Under the distributed treatment the learning trials were equally spaced over 4 days (3 per day, 8 per day, and so on), and the A–D list was learned on the final day. The degree of prior learning had no significant effect on the retention of the second list. By contrast, the conditions of distribution during prior learning were found to be of major importance. While there was substantial forgetting of the test list when prior learning was massed, the amount of proactive inhibition was minimal when it was distributed. Moreover, an MMFR test showed almost perfect recall of the prior list under the latter condition. It appears, then, that the difference between practice schedules provides a basis for highly accurate list differentiation which serves to reduce drastically the amount of proactive interference. This conclusion is supported by the results of a subsequent study (Underwood & Ekstrand, 1967b) which showed that the beneficial effects of distribution are substantially less when some of the first-list pairs are carried over into the second list. The presence of pairs common to both tasks makes it impossible to differentiate consistently between lists on the basis of the schedule of practice.

The studies discussed last bring to the fore the temporal schedule of practice as a characteristic of verbal tasks on which list differentiation can be based. In earlier analyses of differentiation major emphasis was placed on the relative degrees of learning of the successive lists as a determining factor. It is clear, however, that any feature that permits a valid separation of alternative response systems can serve as an effective basis of differentiation. While the nature of the cues associated with differences in practice schedules has not been specified as yet, it is likely that the "time tags" attached to various tasks do, indeed, play a functional role in differentiation.

INTERFERENCE IN SHORT-TERM MEMORY

In recent discussions of the mechanisms of forgetting interest has centered increasingly on the distinction between short-term and long-term memory. Theoretically, this distinction refers to functionally different processes each of which in turn reflects a different order of events in the nervous system. While there has been a variety of formulations of the dual-process hypothesis (see Melton, 1963a, b; Peterson, 1963), the short-term system is generally viewed as representing the immediate storage of informational input whereas the long-term system provides for relatively permanent storage. The usual assumption is that the short-term store has a limited capacity and that the material in it (the memory trace) is subject to rapid decay. That is, in the absence of rehearsal the trace is assumed to become progressively weaker or less distinct as a function of time. The structural changes that constitute permanent storage are not reversible, and there are no determinate limitations on the capacity of the long-term system.

It is apparent that investigations of these two hypothetical systems call for different experimental operations. The basic concern of studies of short-term memory is with the initial storage of an input or with the fate of the trace representing that input. Hence the procedures in such investigations typically involve a single presentation of stimulus units falling within the subject's span of immediate memory and a test of retention after a brief interval. The memory span is defined by the length of the series (for example, of letters or digits) that can be reproduced without error immediately after presentation; the use of materials falling within the span ensures a sufficiently high level of immediate recall to permit the observation of progressive losses during the period following the presentation. The use of a single presentation reflects the focus on initial storage and on the conditions of retrieval from the short-term store. There is usually no a priori specification of the range of retention intervals that qualifies as "short." There are, however, attempts to infer from empirical data the conditions that limit the operation of short-term memory, such as the number of items that will put an overload on the limited capacity of the system (for example, Atkinson & Shiffrin, 1965; Waugh & Norman, 1965).

In experimental practice, the retention intervals in studies of short-term memory are measured in seconds rather than minutes.

Tests of retention administered after multiple trials of acquisition, or after intervals of minutes rather than seconds, would be normally classified as yielding measures of long-term memory. There are, however, many transitional situations, especially in studies concerned with the relation between the two types of memory processes; in such situations the amount of material may exceed the immediate span, multiple presentations of the materials may be given, and "short" as well as "long" retention intervals may be explored. It is important to note that there are no sharply circumscribed experimental operations that are coordinated with the distinction between short-term and long-term memory, although the practical separation of the procedures is usually not too difficult.

Given the pragmatic usefulness of the distinction between the phenomena of short-term and of long-term memory, there arises the basic theoretical question of whether the evidence does, indeed, support the postulation of separate memory systems or points to a continuity of processes. One approach to this problem has been to test in the context of experiments on short-term memory the principles of interference established in studies of long-term memory.

Methods of Measuring Short-term Retention

Before the question of the continuity of interference processes is considered further, it will be useful to examine in some detail the methods used to measure short-term retention. The most commonly used procedures can be subsumed under two headings, namely, distractor techniques and probe techniques (Murdock, 1967a). We shall discuss each of them in turn.

The distractor technique is characterized by the interpolation of an activity designed to prevent rehearsal between the presentation of the to-be-remembered units and the test of recall. Since the interpolated activity

does not involve new learning, the treatment corresponds to the rest condition in experiments on retroaction. When the activity during the retention interval does involve new learning, the treatment becomes equivalent to the experimental condition of the retroaction experiment. Reference experiments illustrating the use of the distractor technique are those of Brown (1958) and of Peterson and Peterson (1959). Some of Brown's results will be considered below; at this point we will summarize the findings of Peterson and Peterson, which have served as a point of departure for many subsequent investigations of short-term memory.

In what must have been, in Melton's words (1963b, p. 8), "a moment of supreme skepticism of laboratory dogma," Peterson and Peterson set out to investigate the course of retention for a single trigram over intervals measured in seconds. The procedure consisted of three stages: first, a trigram was presented auditorily for 1 second; in the next second a three-digit number was announced to the subject who was instructed to count

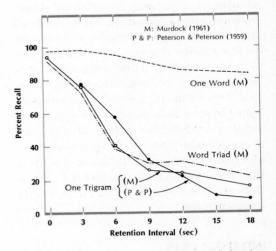

Figure 21.31. Short-term retention of verbal units. Forgetting curves for a single consonant trigram, a single word, and a triad of words. The retention intervals were filled with a counting task to prevent rehearsal. (Data from Peterson & Peterson, 1959; and Murdock, 1961a.)

backwards from that number by threes or fours; finally after the appropriate interval the signal to recall the trigram was given. Six different retention intervals ranging from 3 to 18 seconds were used.

The results obtained by Peterson and Peterson are shown in Figure 21.31. Retention of the single three-consonant unit declined sharply during the period immediately following presentation and was less than 10 percent after 18 seconds. The figure also displays the findings of a subsequent study by Murdock (1961a) in which the same procedure was used. With a view to determining the effect of response integration on short-term memory, Murdock compared the retention functions for a single trigram, a single monosyllabic word, and a cluster of three monosyllabic words. He replicated the Petersons' findings for a single trigram but found only a small amount of forgetting for a single word; the curves for the trigram and the three-word cluster overlapped closely. These results must be interpreted with caution, however, since it is not certain that the degree of learning for the three types of items was the same, that is, near perfect immediate recall may represent different degrees of overlearning (see Underwood, 1964). It appears that the rate of forgetting may remain the same as long as the number of functional units or "chunks" is held constant. That is, in an unfamiliar trigram each of the three letters is a discrete element, whereas a familiar monosyllabic word functions as one unit. Consequently, a cluster of three words contains as many discrete elements which require integration as does the trigram. The basic findings of the Petersons have been replicated in numerous other experiments, although the forgetting curve often fails to drop as precipitously as that in the original investigation (for example, Melton, 1963b).

When the probe technique is used, a series of items is presented to the subject but recall is tested for only one of these items. At the time of the presentation of the material the subject does not know which item will be called for. The nature of the probe depends, of course, on the composition of the series. When each item in the series is a single unit, such as a digit, the cue at recall is the immediately preceding item: The unit which occupied position $n - 1$ is presented and the subject is required to recall the unit in position n (for example, Waugh & Norman, 1965). When the learning materials are paired associates, one of the pairs is singled out on the test trial; the stimulus term is presented, and the subject has to reproduce the response (for example, Murdock, 1961b; 1963a, b; 1964). A complex variant of the probe technique has been used by Peterson and his associates (for example, Peterson, Saltzman, Hillner, & Land, 1962; Peterson, Wampler, Kirkpatrick, & Saltzman, 1963). Under this procedure several experimental conditions are run concurrently, such that the presentation and test trials of one treatment overlap the retention cycles of other treatments.

The distinguishing characteristics of the probe technique are that the retention interval is filled with the presentation (and sometimes the recall as well) of learning materials but that the subject is uncertain about the item to be recalled next. It is clear that the treatment during the retention interval corresponds to the experimental condition in the design for the measurement of retroactive inhibition. There is every reason to believe, therefore, that the retention scores obtained by the probe technique are influenced by the interpolated activity filling the retention interval, that is, that they reflect varying degrees of retroactive interference. While this fact has been recognized (Murdock, 1961b; Waugh & Norman, 1965), there has also been a persistent tendency to ignore or to minimize the essential equivalence of the operations of the probe technique and of the retroaction experiment. As Keppel (1965) has pointed out, it is clearly not appropriate to treat the distractor and the probe techniques as alternative and interchangeable methods for charting the temporal course of short-term retention. This argument is strongly supported by

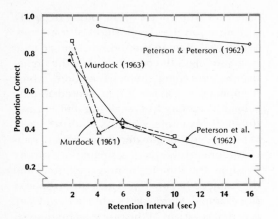

Figure 21.32. Comparison of the amounts of forgetting for a single paired associate under the distractor technique (upper curve) and the probe technique (three lower curves). (Keppel, 1965; data from Murdock, 1961b and 1963a; Peterson & Peterson, 1962; Peterson et al., 1962.)

comparisons of the results obtained by the two techniques for comparable materials and retention intervals (Figure 21.32). As would be expected, the retention losses over a given period of time are considerably greater when the interval is filled with the presentation of learning materials rather than a distractor task. It should be noted that in a recent analysis Murdock (1967a) has argued for the essential equivalence of the distractor and probe techniques. In support of his position he leans heavily on the fact that at least for some materials the *shapes* of the retention functions are the same under the two procedures; it would seem, however, that the similarity in the shape of forgetting curves is not a relevant consideration so long as there are significant differences in the amounts retained. It is true that, as he points out, the nature of the interpolated task is not the only variable that determines the retention function; for example, the number of items to be remembered has a significant effect. Recognition of this state of affairs in no way weakens the basic point exhibited in Figure 21.32, namely, that the interpolation of new learning materials during the retention interval can and typi-

cally does serve drastically to reduce the level of recall.

The conclusion appears to be inescapable that general inferences about the temporal course of short-term memory, and in particular about the decay of the memory trace, based on data obtained by the probe technique are open to serious question. This is not to imply that the distractor technique necessarily permits a valid assessment of the rate of trace decay. Activities such as backward counting cannot be ruled out on a priori grounds as conditions of retroactive inhibition; the fact that potential sources of interference can never be entirely eliminated has posed an intractable methodological obstacle to tests of the decay hypothesis (see Postman, 1964b). The difference between the distractor and the probe procedures is one of degree and must be considered in light of the known dependence of the amount of retroactive interference on the similarity between the original and the interpolated activity. The important point here is that in many experiments on short-term memory interest has centered on the temporal course of retention under highly complex conditions of interpolation and that the conditions of interference have often neither been systematically manipulated nor adequately analyzed.

Proactive Inhibition

Intraexperimental interference The potential importance of uncontrolled sources of interference in studies of short-term memory is well documented by the evidence for the build-up of proactive inhibition in the course of an experimental session. It is customary in such a session to test each subject repeatedly and under a number of different conditions. Since each test requires only a brief period, the number of successive observations is often quite high. For example, in the study of Peterson and Peterson (1959) subjects were tested eight times at each of six retention intervals. As many as 80 tests per session are by no means atypical. The consequent economy of experimentation is often cited as an important advantage. In light of the known relation between stage of practice and rate of forgetting in long-term memory (see p. 1107), the question soon arose of whether there was a comparable build-up of proactive inhibition in the short-term situation which might be responsible, wholly or in part, for the observed rapid drops in retention. This possibility was at first discounted because there were no apparent decreases in performance over successive blocks of trials (see Peterson, 1963). Such comparisons do not, however, answer the question since the degree of learning for the test items may increase as a result of practice, so that the positive effects of nonspecific transfer may mask the build-up of interference.

In a study designed explicitly to permit the evaluation of changes in the rate of forgetting as a function of stage of practice Keppel and Underwood (1962b) demonstrated that proactive inhibition does, indeed, develop progressively under the procedures used by Peterson and Peterson. In one of the experiments the to-be-remembered units were again consonant trigrams, and each subject went through six successive test cycles. Retention intervals of 3 seconds and 18 seconds were alternated (3–18–3–18–3–18 or in the

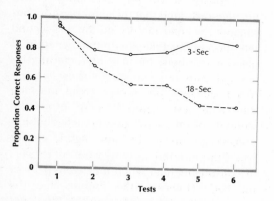

Figure 21.33. Proactive inhibition in the retention of a single verbal unit: proportion of correct recalls as a function of the number of previous items and length of the retention interval. Keppel & Underwood, 1962b.)

reverse order) so that recall could be measured at each stage of practice after both retention intervals. The results (Figure 21.33) show the characteristic interaction of the amount of prior learning with the length of the retention interval. Thus, there are only slight changes in the level of recall on the 3-second tests, whereas the 18-second tests give evidence of a build-up of heavy proactive interference. Note that on the first test retention is perfect after both intervals; this result is in sharp contrast to the 90 percent loss observed after 18 seconds in the Petersons' experiment. It is clear that cumulative proactive inhibition can have a major influence on the level of retention in experiments on short-term memory under conditions of repeated testing (see also Loess, 1964); moreover, as Keppel (1965) has pointed out, the build-up of such interferences may render the experimental observations relatively insensitive to the influence of other variables.

A source of bias that may have contributed to the interaction of stage of practice and retention interval in the experiment of Keppel and Underwood was later pointed out by Peterson and Gentile (1965). Since the two retention intervals were alternated, an 18-second test always followed a 3-second test, so that the immediately preceding trigram was retained better and could function more effectively as a source of interference when the test occurred after the longer of the two intervals. In their own experiment Peterson and Gentile were able to demonstrate that the amount of proactive inhibition increases as the interval between successive tests becomes shorter; however, while the magnitude of the retention losses was affected, evidence for the development of proactive effects within a block of test trials was still found when the source of bias was eliminated (see also Peterson & James, 1967). The conclusion that the amount of proactive inhibition which accumulates within a block of trials varies inversely with the intertrial interval was confirmed in an experiment by Loess and Waugh (1967) in which triads of words rather than trigrams were used as the learning materials. It is possible that differentiation between successive test items is facilitated as the intertrial interval is lengthened.

In all the studies of proactive inhibition discussed so far the distractor technique was used. The evidence concerning the development of intraexperimental interference under the probe technique is less clear. Relevant data were obtained by Murdock (1963a, 1964) whose procedure consisted of a single presentation of a list of paired associates followed by a test of recall for one of the pairs. All positions were tested in the course of a block of trials; under these conditions the length of the retention interval and the number of interpolated pairs are, of course, confounded. The basic data are the functions relating probability of recall to the serial position of the test item. In one experiment (1963a) the results obtained with naive and with experienced subjects were compared, in another (1964) the changes in the retention function over successive stages of practice were investigated. These analyses agree in showing that practice produces a pronounced change in the shape of the retention function. For naive subjects there is both a primacy and a recency effect (that is, the first as well as the last pair in the list has a clear advantage in recall); for practiced subjects there is only a recency effect. Along with the loss in primacy, practice produces an increase in recall for the item occupying the penultimate position in the list; consequently the average probability of recall does not change appreciably. Murdock is inclined to interpret these findings as pointing to a system with a limited capacity for processing information. As practice continues, there is a shift in emphasis away from the initial item to the later ones in the list; however, the amount retained after a constant input remains essentially invariant. It is, of course, possible that changes in the mode of processing information occur as a result of experience. However, a firm conclusion concerning either the development of such changes or the operation of proactive interferences are difficult because the potential determinants of recall under the probe procedure are numerous and complex. There may be changes in degree of learning as a function of practice that are differential for the several positions in the list; for example, recall for the last item is near ceiling from the outset and cannot show improvement, but that is clearly not true for items in the middle positions. The pattern of prior and interpolated items varies for each pair in the list and so does, of course, the retention interval. How the conditions of intralist interference interact with the possible proactive effects of prior lists is not known. It seems necessary to conclude that results obtained by the probe procedure under conditions of multiple testing do not permit a precise assessment of the components of interference.

Formal similarity The question of whether or not interference in short-term memory is influenced by interitem similarity has acquired considerable theoretical significance because of an early assertion that immunity to similarity effects is one of the characteristics distinguishing short-term from long-term processes (Broadbent, 1963). The results of a study by Brown (1958) were consistent with this assumption. Brown first demonstrated that recall for pairs of consonants declined rapidly during a 5-second retention interval filled with the recitation of pairs of numbers; the rate of forgetting increased with the number of to-be-remembered pairs. In a further experiment, in which the same test materials were used, the amounts of retroactive and proactive inhibition were found to be only slightly greater when the interfering items were other pairs of consonants than when they were pairs of numbers. However, the finding that the nature of the interfering material does not influence short-term retention proved atypical.

Using the Petersons' technique, Wickens, Born, and Allen (1963) provided a convincing demonstration of the fact that short-term recall is subject to proactive inhibition only when the successive test items are drawn from the same class of materials. Two types of materials were used: consonant trigrams and three-place numbers. Proactive interference continued to accumulate, that is, recall declined as a function of the stage of practice, as long as the successive to-be-remembered items came from the same class. However, there was a dramatic "release from proactive inhibition" when an item from the other class was introduced. Thus, there was no evidence of proactive interference with the recall of a trigram on the tenth test trial if the preceding nine items had been numbers; by contrast the interference was extremely heavy when the prior items had been trigrams as well. The trends were parallel when there was a shift from trigrams to numbers.

The results are more complex when the formal similarity of items from the same class is manipulated, for example, when the number of duplicated letters in trigrams is varied. In the experiment of Wickens, Born, and Allen this variable failed to influence the amount of proactive inhibition; the same result was reported by Wright (1967). A detailed analysis of the findings in the latter study showed, however, that letter duplication had dual and opposed effects: the recall of the letters themselves was facilitated but there was interference with the reproduction of the letters in their appropriate positions within the trigrams. Consequently the overall amount of proactive inhibition failed to be influenced significantly by the degree of letter duplication.

Letter duplication represents, of course, only one condition of formal similarity and applies only to units such as trigrams which are composed of multiple elements. There is increasing evidence that in short-term memory a major determinant of interference is the acoustic similarity of the to-be-remembered units and that such interference effectively influences the recall of single letters. The variable of acoustic similarity will, therefore, be considered next.

Acoustic similarity Before proactive effects proper are considered, it is necessary to review briefly some of the findings that have served to establish the significance of the factor of acoustic similarity in short-term memory. The basic reference experiments were carried out by Conrad and his associates. A first step was the demonstration of the fact that letters which are confused in a listening test also tend to be substituted for each other in recall following visual presentation. For purposes of determining the correlation between the two types of errors, Conrad (1964) used a vocabulary of 10 letters comprising two groups of five letters each which had high within-group confusability and low between-group confusability: BCPTV and FMNSX. It will be noted that the vowel sound in the names of the letters is ē in the first group, and ĕ in the second group. Sequences of six letters drawn from this alphabet were presented visually, at a rate of 0.75 second per letter. Each presentation was followed immediately by a written test of ordered recall. A matrix showing the frequency with which these letters were substituted for each other in recall was then constructed. A corresponding matrix of perceptual confusion errors was obtained in a listening test in which the letters were presented for identification against a background of white noise. The two error distributions were found to be highly correlated. Thus, acoustic confusions permit an accurate prediction of the errors in recall after visual presentation. It follows that recall for a sequence of letters should vary inversely with the acoustic similarity of the elements. This prediction was confirmed in an experiment by Conrad and Hull (1964). Two three-letter vocabularies and two nine-letter vocabularies were used, one of high and one of low confusability at each length. Six-letter sequences (including repeated letters) were presented visually for immediate ordered recall. The frequency of errors was a negatively accelerated increasing function of the probability of acoustic confusion among the letters but essentially independent of the size of the vocabulary, that is, of the information per item.

The conclusion that recall varies inversely with the acoustic similarity of the elements has received repeated confirmation (for example, Wickelgren, 1965a). The errors in recall have been found to be predictable on the basis of an analysis of the distinctive phonemic features of consonants and vowels (Wickelgren, 1965b, 1966a). In his review of recent developments in research on short-term memory Murdock (1967b) points out three significant implications of the studies of acoustic similarity: (1) It has now been established that interitem similarity is an effective variable in short-term memory; (2) the findings support the hypothesis that the representation of items in short-term memory is through a speech or speech-motor code; (3) in view of the systematic relations between distinctive phonemic features and errors in recall it is possible that "forgetting goes on at a more molecular level even than the single item" (p. 428).

There is some evidence that proactive inhibition in short-term recall increases with the degree of acoustic similarity between the interfering and the test items (Wickelgren, 1966b). At this point it is of interest to note that the systematic effects of acoustic similarity on the temporal course of retention have been interpreted as casting doubt on the assumption that short-term memory is subject to proactive inhibition. This argument was developed by Conrad (1967) on the basis of the results of a study in which recall for four-letter sequences was tested after 2.4 and 7.2 seconds. The vocabulary from which the sequences were drawn contained three groups of letters; the elements within groups were acoustically similar, but the confusability between groups was low. The distractor technique was used, the retention intervals being filled with the reading of digits. Recall decreased as the interval was

lengthened, and in addition there was a significant shift in the distribution of errors. At the shorter interval there was a significant tendency for errors to be acoustically similar to the correct response, whereas at the longer interval the distribution of letters was more nearly random. Conrad views the findings as supporting a modified hypothesis of trace decay: The pattern of confusions reflects the decreasing discriminability of memory traces as a function of time. Thus, at the shorter interval the traces are distinctive and confusable only with highly similar ones; at the longer interval discriminability has declined sufficiently to permit confusion among the traces of widely dissimilar inputs. Conrad also suggests that in light of the shift in the distribution of errors the retention losses cannot be attributed to proactive inhibition. Similar errors are more frequent after a short than after a long interval, whereas such errors would be expected to be extinguished more thoroughly and to recover more slowly than dissimilar ones. However, as we have seen, it is hazardous to draw firm conclusions about the operation of interference processes on the basis of trends in overt errors.

Semantic similarity   The technique used by Wickens, Born, and Allen (1963), namely, a shift in the class of test items, has produced evidence for the effectiveness of semantic similarity as a determinant of proactive interference in short-term memory. Thus, when successive items are drawn from the same conceptual class, there is a build-up of proactive effects; but there is a release from interference when an item from a different conceptual class is introduced (Loess, 1967). The release from interference appears to be contingent upon a shift from a conceptually homogeneous sequence to an item drawn from an entirely new class; when each successive item is drawn from a difficult conceptual class, proactive interference continues to accumulate. It is possible, therefore, that the surprise or arousal produced by the introduction of an unexpected stimulus may play an essential part in bringing about the differentiation between the prior homogeneous sequence and the new disparate item (Turvey, 1968). In any event, these findings make it clear that semantic similarity can play a significant role in producing proactive inhibition in the short-term situation. This conclusion is also supported by the results of a study by Goggin (1966) who compared short-term retention under the A–B, A–D and A–B, A–B' paradigms and found proactive inhibition to be less for the latter.

The point that semantic similarity has been shown to be an effective variable in short-term retention deserves emphasis in view of claims to the contrary. Specifically, Baddeley (1964, 1966b) has advanced the hypothesis that semantic similarity is a significant variable only in long-term memory; short-term memory is influenced primarily by acoustic similarity. To test this hypothesis, Baddeley compared the effects of the two types of similarity on short-term recall. Lists of high and of low acoustic similarity (*mad, man, map,* and so on, versus *bar, cow, day,* and so on) were compared, and also lists of high and of low semantic similarity (*broad, great, large,* and so on versus *hot, old, strong,* and so on). As predicted, acoustic similarity had a far greater adverse effect on recall than did semantic similarity; in fact, the influence of the latter was found to be minor. The experimental procedure suffers, however, from a serious flaw that makes it impossible to draw any firm conclusions from the findings, namely, the failure to ensure that the differences in acoustic and in semantic similarity were equivalent in degree. It is far from obvious that the differences in degree of similarity were in fact equivalent, nor is it clear how these differences can be evaluated. Moreover, acoustic similarity is confounded with formal similarity (letter overlap); attempts to untie these two variables (1966b) were only partially successful but nevertheless served substantially to reduce the apparent effect of the acoustic variable. It should

be noted that in a long-term situation, in which multiple learning trials were used, these particular manipulations had rather complex and not entirely consistent effects, although it could probably be concluded that both types of similarity were effective (1966a). What remains, then, is some form of interaction between two types of similarity, varied to uncertain degrees, and the number of learning trials. Such evidence does not provide convincing support for inferences about fundamental differences between long-term and short-term memory. We shall return to this problem in the next section.

Retroactive Inhibition

All experiments on short-term memory in which either the distractor or the probe technique is used can be said to be concerned with retroactive inhibition. In order to prevent the memory trace from being maintained or strengthened, it is necessary to interpolate some activity between input and recall. In that sense the experimental operations parallel those in studies of retroactive inhibition. Whether and to what extent the retention losses over brief intervals of time are in fact attributable to retroactive interference is, of course, a basic theoretical issue which cannot be settled on a priori grounds. It is useful, however, to evaluate the effects of the various activities used to fill the retention intervals with reference to the principles of retroactive inhibition in order to determine whether these principles continue to apply in the short-term situation. In many cases a precise evaluation is, however, difficult because the formal design of the retroaction experiment is used relatively rarely by investigators of short-term memory.

Nature of interpolated activity   In spite of the complexities of the various probe procedures used, it is clear that interpolated learning produces retroactive inhibition in the short-term situation, and that A–B, A–D, A–B still constitutes an appropriate reference paradigm. Results reported by Peterson et al.

(1962, Exp. III) are a case in point. The learning materials were paired associates, with words as stimuli and numbers as responses. For a given pair, the 10-second retention interval was filled with presentations and tests for other pairs. Two conditions are of interest for present purposes, one in which the stimulus of the test item was paired with a new response halfway through the interval (A–D) and one in which only new items were interpolated (C–D). The probability of recall was substantially lower under the A–D than under the C–D treatment (.14 versus .27). The same study (Experiment II) also contains evidence for competition effects which undergo systematic changes over time. When the same item was tested twice, with a filled interval intervening between the two tests, there was a tendency for errors on the first test to be replaced by correct responses on the second test. This tendency increased with the length of interval between the tests. As the erroneous response which competed successfully on the first test is forgotten, the correct response can recover (Peterson, 1966b, pp. 195f.). The basic pattern of results, including the changes in the relative strength of competing responses, agrees well with the

findings in conventional experiments on retroactive inhibition.

An essential agreement between the results of short-term and long-term experiments is also indicated when the effects of the amount of interpolated material are considered. In the series of experiments by Murdock (1961b, 1963a, b, 1964), in which recall for a single item was tested after presentation of a list of paired associates, forgetting increased at a negatively accelerated rate as a function of the number of intervening pairs. The asymptote of the retention function decreases with list length (Figure 21.34). While there is little question about the interference produced by the interpolated pairs, the procedure yields inherently ambiguous results since there is a perfect inverse correlation between the numbers of prior and of interpolated pairs; in addition, of course, the retention interval covaries with the number of pairs intervening between presentation and recall. The same interpretative difficulties arise in other studies in which conditions of retroaction and proaction are manipulated concurrently (for example, Wickelgren, 1966b). These limitations on the analytic usefulness of the data obtained by the probe technique have been considered earlier.

Not only the input of new items for learning but also the interpolation of recall trials can serve as an effective condition of interference (Murdock, 1963c; Tulving & Arbuckle, 1963, 1966). The study cited last shows that with the serial position of the to-be-remembered unit held constant, interpolated inputs produce a greater reduction in recall than do interpolated outputs. Both sources of interference come into play in a continuous memory task such as that used by Shepard and Teghtsoonian (1961) to measure temporal changes in recognition. A series of three-digit numbers was presented, with each item occurring twice in the course of the series. New and old numbers followed each other in random order, and the delay between the repetitions of an item was varied. The probability of a correct identification declined

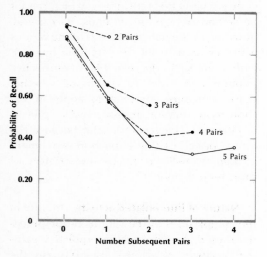

Figure 21.34. Probability of recall of a paired associate after a single presentation as a function of the number of subsequent pairs and length of list. (Murdock, 1963b.)

as a function of the number of intervening items. The retention function brings out the extremely great sensitivity of the recognition measure: better than chance identification remained possible after as many as 60 intervening items (see also Shepard & Chang, 1963).

Similarity relations between the original and the interpolated items influence the amount of retroactive inhibition in short-term as well as in long-term retention. The effects are large and dependable when the degree of acoustic similarity between the units in the successive tasks is manipulated. In an experiment by Wickelgren (1965c) the letters in the interpolated sequence were either similar or different in pronunciation to those in the original list; an interfering list comprising the original letters in a new order was also used. Retention of the first list was scored for both the number of items recalled and accuracy of serial position. In item recall the losses were smallest after interpolation of identical items, greatest when the interfering items were similar, and intermediate when they were different. Both identical and similar items interfered more with position recall than did the dissimilar ones. Intrusion errors were predominantly acoustically similar letters. The pattern of findings is consistent with those obtained in long-term retention when other dimensions of similarity are manipulated. Subsequent findings have confirmed the effectiveness of the variable of acoustic similarity in determining the amount of retroactive inhibition in both recall (Posner & Konick, 1966; Wickelgren, 1966b) and recognition (Wickelgren, 1966c).

There is evidence that, over and above formal or acoustic similarity, the difficulty of the interpolated task is a significant factor in short-term retroactive interference. When the interpolated activity consists of the performance of certain prescribed operations, such as adding numbers, classifying numbers as high and low, and so on, the difficulty of the task can be scaled in terms of the amount of information reduced as a result of the operation. Retention is then found to be a steadily decreasing function of the difficulty of the interpolated operation (Posner & Rossman, 1965; Posner & Konick, 1966). A suggested interpretation of these findings is that the interpolated activity interferes with the continued processing (rehearsal) of the original material. Since the subject's capacity is limited, the degree of forgetting will be related directly to the amount of processing time required for the interpolated activity (Posner & Rossman, 1965). In some situations the factors of similarity and difficulty are not readily differentiated. The findings reported by Neimark, Greenhouse, Law, and Weinheimer (1965) are a case in point. When nonsense syllables of low association value were the to-be-remembered units, greater retention losses were produced by the interpolation of other syllables of low association value than of syllables of high or medium association value, or of numbers. These tasks cannot be ordered along a single similarity dimension, and it is possible that the relative difficulty of the materials is a critical factor determining the effectiveness of the interpolated activity.

We return now to the factor of semantic similarity and Baddeley's hypothesis that this variable is effective in long-term but not in short-term memory. Direct support for this hypothesis was claimed in a study by Baddeley and Dale (1966) in which the effect of the semantic similarity of stimulus terms on retroactive inhibition was investigated. The A–B, A'–D and A–B, C–D paradigms were compared. Stimulus similarity was found to have a significant influence on retroactive inhibition under conditions of conventional list learning but not in a short-term situation in which one presentation of the list of paired associates was followed by a test of recall. The results obtained by the latter procedure were in the expected direction but failed to reach statistical significance. It is fair to say that these results show little more than the limited sensitivity of the short-term technique. While the evaluation of the results is made difficult by the investigators' failure to hold list length constant in the two situations, a rough comparison can be made between the recall scores for an eight-pair list on the conventional test and a six-pair list on the short-term test. The percentage of items correctly recalled by the control (C–D) group was 57 in the conventional situation and 19 in the short-term situation. The corresponding percentages for the experimental (A'–D) groups were 38 and 13. Clearly, there are massive differences in the overall level of retention, and the short-term measures lack sensitivity because they are close to the floor of performance. No conclusions about differences between long-term and short-term memory can be drawn from such data. There is an obvious but important methodological point here: A shift from a statistically significant to a nonsignificant effect should not be attributed to a difference in process unless it is reasonably certain that the opportunity to detect a reliable effect has not changed.

The Role of Interference Processes in Short-term Memory

There is substantial evidence that short-term retention is subject to proactive and retroactive inhibition. While there is a dearth of strictly comparable findings, the available results do not point to a basic discontinuity of the principles governing interference in short-term and long-term memory. That is not to say, however, that all short-term forgetting is necessarily the result of interference. Clearly the facts leave open the possibility that there are determinants of retention that come into play only during the period immediately following input. Such a view is espoused in a theoretical analysis by Peterson (1966b) which holds that short-term retention reflects the interaction of a learning mechanism and a recency mechanism. The former is subject to interference, whereas the latter represents the operation of a transitory postperceptual storage process. The relative

contribution of the two mechanisms is assumed to vary with the length of the retention interval and the nature of the events filling the interval. The recency mechanism is seen as dominant during the period immediately after presentation but to carry progressively less weight as the retention interval is lengthened.

The assumption of a dual mechanism appears to be supported by the nature of the interaction observed in experiments on short-term memory between the effects of distribution of practice and the length of the retention interval. Specifically, when an item is presented twice, recall is an increasing function of the degree of spacing between the repetitions when the retention interval is relatively long, for example, 8 or 16 seconds; there is a trend in the opposite direction when the interval is very short, for example, 2 or 4 seconds (Peterson, Hillner, & Saltzman, 1962; Peterson et al., 1963). This interaction can be understood on the assumption that the relative weight carried by the postulated component mechanisms changes with the length of the retention interval. As long as the recency mechanism is dominant, spacing will be detrimental; as the learning mechanism assumes increasing importance, the beneficial effects of distribution, which Peterson is inclined to attribute to a consolidation process, can become apparent. As we have seen, there are other possible interpretations of a positive relation between distribution of practice and retention. However that may be, it would be an error to claim that all the empirical facts of short-term memory can be readily subsumed under existing principles of interference. On the other hand, there is little question about the effectiveness of interference processes in the short as well as the long term.

Reminiscence   The fine-grain analysis of short-term retention functions has served to revive interest in the phenomenon of reminiscence which has had a long and checkered experimental history. Reminiscence refers to an increase in retention with time which occurs in the absence of formal practice. That is, reminiscence represents a reversal of the usual declining trend of the retention curve over time. Before the recent findings in experiments on short-term memory are mentioned, a few words should be said about earlier results in studies of long-term memory.

The occurrence of reminiscence was first reported in the recall of poetry by children after a period of days (Ballard, 1913; Williams, 1926). In these investigations the same subjects were tested both immediately after the end of learning and after a period of delay. Later work (Ammons & Irion, 1954) has shown that under these conditions the apparent rise in the retention curve is an artifact attributable to the practice effects of the immediate test. In studies of verbal rote learning, in which this difficulty was avoided by the use of single retention tests, reminiscence was found after intervals of the order of 1–2 minutes, typically after massed practice on a serial list (Ward, 1937; Hovland, 1938). The increase in performance was most commonly ascribed to the decline of inhibitory influences during the retention interval, such as the dissipation of reactive inhibition or the forgetting of relatively weak interfering associations. However, attempts to reproduce the phenomenon have in many cases proved unsuccessful (for example, Underwood, 1957b), and the exact combination of conditions required for the occurrence of reminiscence have resisted identification.

It should be noted that in some recent studies (for example, Kleinsmith & Kaplan, 1963, 1964) substantial reminiscence over a one-week interval was reported for materials which produce a state of high emotional arousal at the time of learning. The investigators suggested that the traces of such stimuli are initially characterized by a high level of neural activity which renders them relatively inaccessible but which favors consolidation. Consequently, immediate recall is

low but is followed by reminiscence after an interval of delay. By contrast, materials that produce a low degree of arousal have an advantage in immediate recall, but on the delayed tests forgetting rather than reminiscence is found. Presumably a low level of neural activity is conducive to early accessibility of the traces but is unfavorable to consolidation, and hence to long-term retention. If these speculations prove tenable, the conditions of reminiscence in these experiments are clearly quite different from those in the classical studies of rote learning.

What appears to be reliable evidence for reminiscence has been obtained in two recent experiments on short-term memory in which the distractor technique was used. In a study by Peterson (1966a) lists of five paired associates were presented once and recalled after intervals ranging from 0 to 24 seconds. While the form of the retention functions varied with the serial position of the item during presentation, the characteristic trend was for recall to decrease at first and then to increase. Short-term reminiscence after a single presentation of a list of five paired associates was also observed by Keppel and Underwood (1967) who measured recall after intervals ranging from 4 to 304 seconds. The peak of the retention function occurred at 19 seconds after presentation. In a theoretical discussion Peterson (1966b) attributes the initial retention losses to failures of the short-term mechanism, and the subsequent gains to increases in the effectiveness of an associative mechanism. One possibility is that interference from relatively weak competitors diminishes with time, so that recall of the correct association becomes more probable. The assumption that there is rapid forgetting of interfering associations, which is also discussed by Keppel and Underwood, represents a return to one of the classical theories of reminiscence. It now appears that short-term tests after a single exposure are more sensitive than earlier procedures to temporal changes in the relative strength of correct and incorrect associations. In any event, reminiscence, which was once aptly described as a "now-you-see-it-now-you-don't phenomenon" (Buxton, 1943, p. 337), is again becoming visible in the context of short-term memory.

SINGLE-LIST RETENTION

In this final section we shall consider some of the conditions that determine the forgetting of a single list learned in the laboratory. The losses which are observed after a retention interval must be attributed to extraexperimental influences because they occur in the absence of formal manipulations of either prior or intervening activities. Whether or not such losses reflect retroactive and proactive *interference* from sources outside the laboratory is, of course, a central issue in the theoretical analysis of forgetting. An interference theory of forgetting answers this question in the affirmative: It holds that the principles of retroaction and proaction established in controlled experiments specify the necessary and sufficient conditions of forgetting outside the laboratory as well. Such an assertion may be designated a Strong Law of Interference. A Weak Law of Interference would recognize retroactive and proactive inhibition as sufficient but not as necessary conditions of forgetting.

The strong form of the interference hypothesis was formulated in a classical paper by McGeoch (1932a) in the context of a refutation of the law of disuse (Thorndike, 1914) according to which an association that fails to be exercised grows progressively weaker over time. McGeoch based his rejection of the law of disuse largely on the evidence that the amount forgotten during a fixed interval of time is significantly influenced by the nature of the activities intervening between learning and recall. (At that time retroactive inhibition was the only condition of interference that had been studied intensively; the phenomenon of proactive inhibition remained to be pursued.) Among the results he cited were comparisons of retention

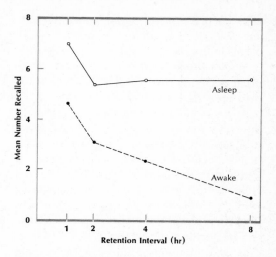

Figure 21.35. Recall after intervals of sleep and of waking. The values shown are the average scores of two subjects who served under all conditions of the experiment. (Data from Jenkins & Dallenbach, 1924.)

after equal intervals of sleep and waking. Such comparisons provide a useful transition from the formal experiment on retroaction to the assessment of extraexperimental sources of interference. A period of sleep is essentially free of activity and hence should produce less interference with the retention of previously learned materials than an equivalent period of normal waking activity.

The Effect of Sleep on Retention

A classical reference experiment on the effect of sleep on retention was that by Jenkins and Dallenbach (1924). The two students who served as subjects in this extended investigation learned lists of 10 nonsense syllables to a criterion of one perfect recitation and were tested for recall either 1, 2, 4, or 8 hours later. The retention interval was spent either in sleep or in normal daytime activity. The results are shown in Figure 21.35. While there was forgetting under both conditions, recall was consistently higher after an interpolated period of sleep than of waking, and this difference increased with the length of the retention interval. Sleep does not, of course, set in all at once, so that an increasing separation between the two treatments would have to be expected. Note that under the sleep condition there are no losses between 2 and 8 hours. The basic finding that sleep reduces forgetting was confirmed in a similar study by van Ormer (1932), who attempted to take account of the effects of diurnal variation on performance and measured retention by the method of relearning. The two retention functions diverged more gradually than in the earlier study, which may in part be a function of the difference between the methods of measurement used. The results were seen as clearly contrary to the law of disuse and consistent with an explanation of forgetting in terms of interference. However, the possibility that sleep favors the process of consolidation could not be ruled out.

In both these early studies each subject served repeatedly under all treatment combinations and hence learned a large number of lists (486 lists in van Ormer's study). Consequently, there is no doubt but that massive amounts of proactive inhibition accumulated in the course of the experiment. The question was, therefore, raised by Ekstrand (1967) of whether a period of sleep facilitated retention in the classical studies by reducing proactive rather than retroactive inhibition. Using naive subjects, and paired words as the learning materials, Ekstrand measured retention after an 8-hour interval. Recall was again significantly higher when the interval was spent in sleep rather than waking (84.6 vs. 73.3 percent). Thus, the positive effect of sleep is not contingent upon interference from prior lists learned in the laboratory. In a further experiment Ekstrand evaluated the effect of sleep on retention under manipulated conditions of interference (A–B, A–D). Performance on an MMFR test after an 8-hour interval showed that sleep facilitated recall of both the first and the second list. This effect was substantially greater in first-list recall; in fact, there was absolute recovery of the first list after a period of sleep but not after a period of wakefulness. The occur-

rence of absolute recovery argues against the hypothesis that sleep favors consolidation, since the trace of A–B must be assumed to have been disrupted during the acquisition of A–D. As was noted earlier, (p. 1099), recovery is most likely to be observed when the overall level of retention remains high, as after a period of sleep.

There is clear evidence, then, that sleep during the period following acquisition facilitates retention. This fact is contrary to the principle of disuse and points to retroactive interference produced by the subject's normal waking activities as a condition of forgetting. The specific sources of interference that result in forgetting, and their mode of action, are left open. As it turned out, the systematic analysis of the latter problem focused on proactive rather than on retroactive effects. Interest came to center on proactive sources of interference for two major reasons. First, since the individual's language habits are the most likely source of interference in the forgetting of verbal materials, proactive effects should carry far greater weight than retroactive ones. That is, the language habits acquired and practiced throughout an individual's lifetime should exert a more potent influence than his particular verbal activities during a limited retention interval. The second reason is closely related to the first. The individual's language habits, which are assumed to constitute the sources of proactive interference, can be specified more fully and more precisely than his uncontrolled verbal activities between the end of learning and the delayed test of recall.

Degree of Learning and Retention

Problems of measurement   Before we consider the evidence bearing on the mechanisms of interference in single-list retention, a methodological digression is required, namely, a discussion of some interpretative problems that arise in the measurement of long-term retention. Our point of departure is the fact that amount of retention is an increasing function of the degree of original learning. The relation is a strong and dependable one, and it applies not only to the levels of acquisition up to the attainment of a criterion of perfect recitation but to degrees of overlearning as well (Kruger, 1929; Postman, 1962d, Underwood & Keppel, 1963). As a consequence of this fact, complex problems of measurement and interpretation develop whenever one wishes to evaluate the effects on retention per se of a variable that influences the speed of original learning. Examples are provided by investigations that are designed to determine whether slow learners forget more than fast learners, or whether materials of high meaningfulness are retained better than materials of low meaningfulness. If a constant number of learning trials is given, the terminal levels of acquisition will differ substantially for fast and slow learners and for easy and hard materials; thus, the amounts of retention cannot be compared directly. The apparent solution of carrying acquisition to a fixed criterion of performance unfortunately leaves the measures of retention subject to systematic biases.

The source of the difficulty is that the level

of performance to be expected following the attainment of a fixed criterion actually depends on the speed of acquisition. Consequently, the predicted levels of immediate retention will likewise depend on the speed with which the criterion is approached. Two factors are responsible for this relation. First, as noted earlier, the attainment of a criterion represents a chance peak in performance and is likely to be followed by a drop on the next trial (the criterion fall); the slower the rate of acquisition, the larger the criterion fall will be. Second, the final acquisition trial on which the criterion is attained provides an opportunity for additional learning; the faster the learning rate, the greater is the resulting increment in associative strength. This fact is apparent in Figure 21.36, which shows growth curves of associative strength for fast and for slow learners. It is clear that each correct response (reinforcement) produces a greater increment in associative strength for the former than for the latter. That will be true on the trial on which the criterion is reached and on overlearning trials as well if practice is continued beyond the point of perfect performance. In sum, the criterion fall will be smaller, and the amount learned on the criterion trial will be greater, for fast than for slow learners; the predicted retention scores differ correspondingly. If the observed scores are compared directly without reference to expected values, there will be a relative underestimation of the amount forgotten by fast learners, or conversely, a relative overestimation of the losses of the slow learners. Exactly the same considerations apply, of course, when retention is compared for materials which are acquired at different rates, such as lists of high and of low meaningfulness.

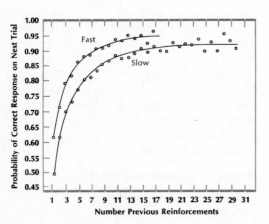

Figure 21.36. Curves of associative growth. The probability of a correct response on a succeeding trial increases as a function of the number of correct anticipations (reinforcements) on the preceding trials. The curve rises more rapidly with the number of reinforcements for fast than for slow learners. (Underwood, 1954.)

The analysis of the logic of measurement in studies of retention is due largely to Underwood who has also taken the lead in developing and evaluating solutions to the difficulties outlined above (Underwood, 1954a, 1964, 1966; Underwood & Keppel, 1962). There are three methods which have been used to reduce biases in measures of retention which result from differences in degree of original learning. First, tests given immediately after the end of acquisition to independent control groups will provide empirical estimates of the expected retention scores for the groups differing in speed of learning. Subjects tested after a period of delay are then compared with the control subjects to determine the amount of retention loss. Second, the expected retention scores are estimated by extrapolation from the curves of associative growth, by a technique known as successive probability analysis. Specifically, the function is determined relating the probability of a correct response to the number of reinforcements (prior correct responses) during acquisition. On the basis of this function a recall probability can be assigned to each item learned by a given subject; the sum of the probabilities constitutes the subject's predicted retention score. The difference between the predicted and the obtained score provides a measure of forgetting. The interpretation of the measures obtained by both the techniques described so far is, however, subject to an important limitation. If the predicted levels of retention are not the same, and the group with the lower expected score shows a greater amount of forgetting, it remains uncertain whether this result is attributable to the difference in degree of original learning or to the operation of the independent variable under investigation (for example, meaningfulness). That is, quite apart from a possible effect of the independent variable, the rate of forgetting may vary inversely with the degree of original learning. This interpretative problem is avoided if one makes sure that the expected retention scores are in fact approximately equal for the groups to be compared. The third available procedure, designed to meet this objective, consists of adjusting the numbers of learning trials given to the experimental groups so as to equalize as closely as possible the expected retention scores. The appropriate adjustment must,

of course, be first determined in a pilot investigation. Thus, one may find that 5 trials on a list of high meaningfulness and 10 trials on a list of low meaningfulness will yield about the same predicted retention scores. In addition, probability analysis can be used to check on the accuracy of the adjustment and to take account of remaining minor differences in degree of learning. It should be noted in conclusion, however, that all three procedures cease to be applicable if original learning is carried beyond the point at which the associations to be recalled have reached asymptotic strength. There is no known technique for predicting in advance the effects of overlearning on the retention of a given type of material.

Retention as a Function of Degree of Learning and Intralist Similarity

The importance of the problems of measurement we have been considering may be illustrated with reference to the relation between intralist similarity and retention. This topic is directly relevant to this section because the theoretical interest in investigations of this relation centers on a possible mechanism of interference in long-term retention. Let us refer back at this point to Gibson's application of the principles of generalization and differentiation to the phenomena of verbal learning (pp. 1048–1052). The point of departure of the hypothesis is that the acquisition of a verbal list requires the reduction of generalization tendencies among the stimulus terms, that is, that learning requires stimulus differentiation. It is assumed further that differentiation decreases over time, leading to spontaneous recovery of the generalization tendencies. The higher the degree of intralist generalization during acquisition the greater will be the recovery and hence the retention loss. It follows that the amount of forgetting should increase as a function of intralist similarity.

Gibson (1942) reported the results of an experiment that appeared to give some support to this deduction from the theory. The learning materials were lists of paired associates composed of geometric forms as stimuli and nonsense syllables as responses; the degree of generalization among stimulus forms was either high or low. The speed of learning to a criterion of one perfect recitation was far greater for the low-generalization than for the high-generalization lists. However, after 24 hours recall was somewhat higher for the low-generalization list. Although the difference was not statistically reliable, Gibson attached importance to it and considered it as consistent with theoretical expectations in view of the greater opportunities for overlearning in the acquisition of the high-generalization lists. It is now clear that such an interpretation is not tenable. As was indicated above, the more gradual the approach to criterion the lower the expected retention score is likely to be. It cannot be assumed, as was suggested by the investigator, that the overlearning of some items in the more difficult list outweighs this relation. Given large differences in speed of acquisition, raw differences in recall scores simply cannot be interpreted. This study was considered in some detail because it exemplifies a fairly common situation: the observation of a difference in recall that is theoretically important but of an order of magnitude which could be produced by inequalities in the degree of original learning.

Subsequent studies in which both the formal and the meaningful similarity of the stimulus terms in paired-associate lists were varied (for example, Underwood, 1953a, b; Beecroft, 1956) have failed to support the theory. When degree of learning is constant, the expected inverse relation between stimulus similarity and retention does not materialize. In fact, trends in the opposite direction have been observed (Joinson & Runquist, 1968). The reasons for the failure of the prediction, which is plausible on both theoretical and common-sense grounds, are not clear.

It is possible that a high degree of intralist similarity reduces the susceptibility of the materials to extraexperimental interference. In a high-similarity list the stimuli are drawn from a limited repertoire: a small number of letters is used when the items are nonsense units, or a circumscribed domain of meanings is represented when they are words. Consequently, as intralist similarity increases, there is a reciprocal restriction in the range of extraexperimental experiences which are closely enough related to become effective sources of interference. This reciprocal relation between intralist and extralist interference becomes clearly apparent when successive lists, all at a constant level of similarity, are learned in the laboratory (Underwood, 1954b). Another factor, which may be important but which is difficult to evaluate, is that the subject learning a high-similarity list is forced to develop especially effective ways of differentiating among the stimuli; as a result, the associations that are established may be very resistant to interference from extralist sources (see Dallett, 1966; Battig, 1968, pp. 165f.). Put another way, at the end of acquisition the level of similarity among the stimulus terms may be functionally less than it was initially, and it is the terminal level which may be critical for the subsequent course of retention.

Extraexperimental Sources of Interference

We now turn to recent systematic applications of principles of interference to extraexperimental forgetting. The basic fact that requires explanation first of all is the retention loss shown by a naive subject for a single list learned in the laboratory—of the order of 20 percent after 24 hours. This loss occurs in the absence of formal manipulations of either prior or intervening activities, and according to the Strong Law of Interference it must be attributed to retroactive and proactive inhibition from extraexperimental sources.

Sources and mechanisms of extraexperimental interference In the forgetting of verbal materials the extraexperimental sources of interference must be sought in the subject's language habits and in his verbal activities prior to and following the acquisition of the experimental task. An attempt to specify some of these sources and their possible mode of operation was made in a theoretical analysis by Underwood and Postman (1960). The major points were as follows:

1. It is assumed that the mechanisms of retroactive and proactive inhibition, as established in the laboratory, are operative in extraexperimental forgetting as well. Greater weight is assigned to proactive than to retroactive effects (see p. 1123).

2. The conditions of interference from extraexperimental language habits conform to the A–B, A–D paradigm, where A–B is a pre-existing linguistic association and A–D is the association prescribed in the experimental situation. The acquisition of the new sequence A–D requires the unlearning or inhibition of the prior habit A–B. However, A–B, which is assumed to represent a strong and stable language habit, will recover over time and interfere with the subsequent recall of A–D. Moreover, if A–B is practiced after the end of the experiment, the retroactive effects of such practice will summate with the proactive ones to enhance the amount of interference at recall.

3. Two classes of language habits (A–B) which are likely to become effective sources of interference are identified: (a) letter-sequence habits and (b) unit-sequence habits. Letter-sequence habits reflect the sequential probabilities of letters in the language. For example, TH and QU are highly probable sequences, whereas TJ and QZ are highly improbable ones. Interference increases as the linguistic probability of the letter sequences in the learning task diminishes. Thus, the degree of letter-sequence interference describes a gradient, declining progressively as the prescribed sequences approximate more and more those occurring most frequently in the language. An alternative statement of this principle is that the more thoroughly integrated a verbal unit is, the less susceptible it is to letter-sequence interference.

Unit-sequence habits represent associations established through linguistic usage between integrated units such as words. They become a source of interference to the extent that these pre-existing associations are of higher strength than those prescribed in the learning task. The more frequently a word occurs in the language, the larger should be the number of other words associatively connected with it (see Noble, 1952 and Chapter 19); hence the number of potentially interfering associations elicited by a word should be an increasing function of the frequency with which it occurs in the language. These considerations lead to the postulation of a gradient of unit-sequence interference. This gradient reflects the assumed inverse relation between word frequency and degree of interference. It should also be noted that the amount of unit-sequence interference is expected to be maximized when pre-experimentally associated words occur within the same list but occupy non-adjacent positions in the sequence to be learned. In such a case the situation is analogous to that in the A–B, A–Br paradigm: interfering responses cannot be inhibited because they are correct elsewhere in the list.

Empirical tests The above analysis can be seen to entail two predictions: (1) the more probable a sequence of letters is in the language the better it should be retained, and (2) the retention of a sequence of words should be related inversely to the frequency of usage of the units of which it is composed. A substantial number of studies designed to test these predictions has been carried out. In general the results have failed to support the theory. When the degree of learning is controlled, the most likely finding is that the amount of retention loss is the same for various types of materials. There have been some exceptions, but only a few of these are in accord with theoretical expectations; others add to the evidence calling for modification of the original analysis.

In most of the studies designed to evaluate the effects of letter-sequence and unit-

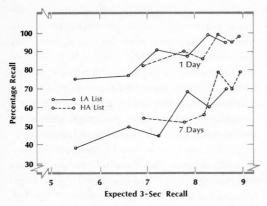

Figure 21.37. An experimental test of the hypothesis of letter-sequence interference. Retention after 1 and 7 days of lists of letter pairs when the associative connection between the stimulus and the response letter was high (*HA*) and when it was low (*LA*). Comparisons are made after amounts of practice on each list which yielded the same expected retention score on an immediate (3-sec) test. (Underwood & Keppel, 1963.)

sequence interference on retention there were multiple acquisition trials, and recall was tested after intervals of days. A few representative studies will serve to illustrate the largely negative findings. To assess the influence of letter-sequence interference, Underwood and Keppel (1963) used lists of

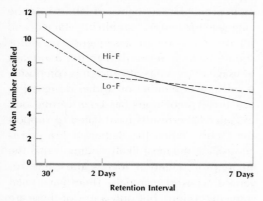

Figure 21.38. An experimental test of the hypothesis of unit-sequence interference: retention curves for lists of words of high and of low frequency of usage. (Postman, 1961b.)

paired associates composed of single-letter stimuli and single-letter responses. The initial associative strength between the paired letters, as determined from normative tables, was either low or high. There were six different degrees of learning, ranging from 2 to 25 anticipation trials; retention was tested after either 1 day or 7 days. As expected, the speed of acquisition was considerably greater when the degree of associative connection between the letters was high than when it was low. However, when the retention losses for the two lists were evaluated after equivalent degrees of original learning, no consistent differences were found (Figure 21.37). This finding is clearly contrary to the hypothesis of letter-sequence interference.

Figure 21.38 presents the results of an experiment (Postman, 1961b) in which unit-sequence interference in the retention of serial lists of words was investigated. Lists composed of nouns of either high or low frequency of usage were compared. In the retention of serial lists there should be interference not only from extralist habits but also from associations among nonadjacent items. Interference from both these sources should be greater for the high-frequency than the low-frequency lists. Original learning was to a criterion of one perfect recitation; retention was tested after intervals of 30 seconds (control), 2 days, and 7 days. The high-frequency lists were learned significantly faster than the low-frequency lists, and this difference in rate of acquisition is reflected on the immediate test. The amounts retained are, however, essentially the same. The curves do cross after seven days, but the difference in the rate of forgetting is far from significant. The expected inverse relation between word frequency and retention also failed to materialize in studies of paired-associate learning (Postman, 1962e) and free-recall learning (Ekstrand & Underwood, 1965).

It is interesting to note that more rapid forgetting for high-frequency than for low-frequency words was observed by Turnage (1967) in a short-term memory experiment in which the Petersons' technique (see p. 1110) was used and the retention intervals ranged from 2 to 30 seconds. It is possible that unit-sequence interference is effective only after very low degrees of practice (see also Turnage & Anderson, 1965). The fact that the predicted differences are typically observed early in list acquisition is consistent with this possibility. If so, the trends observed in the short-term situation cannot be used to explain long-term losses after multiple-trial learning.

When the conditions of prior learning are manipulated in the laboratory, the results again fail to show the expected effects of unit-sequence interference. The theoretical expectation is that proactive inhibition will be greater when the successive lists learned in the laboratory are composed of high-frequency rather than low-frequency words. This prediction follows from the fact that there are more interitem associations among high-frequency than among low-frequency words; hence, there should be more inter-list interference at recall for materials of high than of low frequency. However, the predicted difference in the amount of proactive inhibition has not been found, for either serial lists (Postman, 1962c) or paired-associate lists (Underwood & Ekstrand, 1967a). Thus, formal experiments on proactive inhibition confirm the negative results obtained in studies of single-list retention.

The virtually uniform lack of evidence for the predicted effects of extraexperimental sources of interference poses a troublesome puzzle because it appears to imply a basic discontinuity between the conditions of forgetting manipulated in the laboratory and those which come into play during a retention interval outside the laboratory. For this reason there has been a continuing effort to identify possible shortcomings in theoretical formulations and experimental procedures that may be responsible for the empirical failures. These analyses have been concerned primarily with the role of unit-sequence habits in retention. One approach has been to re-examine the potential role of such habits in long-term retention, and in particular to give consideration to sources of facilitation. Another approach has been to develop empirical tests of the basic assumption that the procedures used to study retroactive and proactive inhibition in the laboratory are representative of the conditions of extra-experimental interference. Some illustrative examples of these lines of attack on the shortcomings of current conceptions of extraexperimental interference will now be given.

It has been suggested (Postman, 1963) that interference theory is apt to predict too much forgetting because it fails to take adequate account of the sources of facilitation that serve to reduce the amount of forgetting produced by such mechanisms as unlearning and competition at recall. The prediction of an inverse relation between word frequency and recall is a case in point. This prediction was based on the fact that high-frequency words have more associative connections than do low-frequency words. The higher the word frequency, therefore, the greater is the number of potentially interfering associations which must be inhibited during acquisition and which may recover or be relearned during the retention interval. These considerations focus on the conditions determining the amount of associative loss; performance on a test of recall will, however, also depend on the availability of the responses. Now it is a fact that the existence of multiple interitem associations, which is characteristic of a sample of high-frequency words, facilitates free recall (Deese, 1959, 1960), that is, has a pronounced positive effect on the availability of the items when the list can be reproduced without regard to serial order. The interitem associations impose what Deese (1962) has called external associative structure on the list and reduce the range of alternative responses. The situation here parallels that discussed earlier with respect to the reciprocal relation between intralist and interlist similarity. It follows that a high degree of interitem association may be expected to have dual and opposed effects on retention: It will enhance not only unit-sequence interference but also the availability of responses. The relative weight of these components will depend not only on the requirements of the retention test, that is, whether or not items must be reproduced in serial order, but also on the length of the retention interval. Conditions determining response availability should become increasingly important as the interval is lengthened.

The following experiment (Postman, 1967) provides evidence for systematic changes over time in the balance of positive and negative effects of pre-experimental interitem associations. The learning materials were serial lists

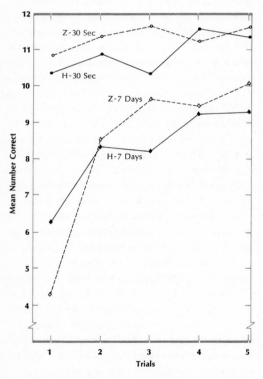

Figure 21.39. Recall and relearning of serial lists of high (*H*) and zero (*Z*) interitem associative strength 30 sec and 48 hr after the end of learning. The score on the first relearning trial provides a measure of recall. (Postman, 1967.)

of familiar English words. There were two types of lists distinguished by the degree of interitem associative strength. The high-strength lists consisted of items that were closely interrelated: The words in a list were all normative associates of a common stimulus and also tended to elicit each other as free associates. There were no known associative relations among the words in the zero-strength lists. Learning to criterion was by the method of serial anticipation, and retention was tested by recall and relearning either 30 seconds or 7 days later. Contrary to the results in free recall, the high-strength lists were learned somewhat more slowly than the zero-strength lists. As Figure 21.39 shows, the latter have an advantage on the immediate test of recall, as would be expected on the basis of their more rapid acquisition. However, on the delayed test there is a substantial difference in favor of the high-strength lists. This difference is not maintained as relearning progresses; rather the curves cross and the zero-strength lists regain the superiority found in acquisition and on the immediate test. Re-exposure to the list restores response recall under both conditions, and the differences in unit-sequence interference once more become apparent. The large difference in recall and the rapid reversal in relearning may be regarded as rather direct evidence for the dual and opposed effects of interitem associations. For other evidence regarding the role of response availability in delayed recall see Postman, Fraser, and Burns (1968), and Underwood and Ekstrand (1968a). It would be inappropriate to conclude, of course, that previous failures to observe differences in retention expected on the basis of the unit-sequence hypothesis can be attributed to a near balance of positive and negative effects. The point is rather that the experimental analysis of long-term retention must seek to specify extraexperimental sources of facilitation as well as of interference.

We now turn to the question of whether the experimental manipulations in conventional laboratory studies of retroactive and proactive inhibition are in principle representative of the conditions of extraexperimental interference. In considering this question, Underwood and Ekstrand (1966) pointed to two potentially important differences between the conditions of interference which are created experimentally and those which may be presumed to come into play outside the laboratory. First, extraexperimental associations are likely to be of much higher strength than interfering associations established in the laboratory. Second, linguistic associations are acquired and used under conditions of distributed practice, that is, varying intervals of time intervene between one occasion of use and the next. By contrast, the acquisition of interfering associations in the laboratory is typically massed, being carried out entirely within a relatively brief experimental period. In an experiment on proactive inhibition described earlier (p. 1108), Underwood and Ekstrand (1966) attempted to assess the probable effects on retention of these quantitative differences between linguistic and experimentally established associations. The major findings were that degree of prior learning had relatively minor effects on retention but that there was a drastic reduction in the amount of proactive inhibition when the interfering lists were learned under distributed rather than massed practice. As was pointed out, the temporal schedule of practice may have provided an effective basis of differentiation between the test task and the prior lists. Accurate differentiation between prior language habits and experimental associations should be possible on the same basis since acquisition is widely distributed for the former and massed for the latter. Again interference theory would appear to predict too much forgetting, in this case because of a critical quantitative difference, namely, with respect to the degree of distribution of practice, between experimentally established and extraexperimental associations.

While some of the shortcomings of existing theoretical formulations and experimental procedures are beginning to be understood, they do not offer a satisfactory explanation of the stubborn empirical fact that with only rare exceptions the amount retained is independent of the nature of the material, as long as the degree of learning is held constant. It is possible that in some cases positive and negative effects counteract each other, but it would be a weak theory indeed which would account for a basic invariance in retention in terms of a precise balance between facilitation and interference. As Underwood and Ekstrand put it, "Until we are able to identify the source or sources of interference producing the constant forgetting in the naive subject the decay theorist has some grounds for glee" (1966, p. 548). The glee should, however, be only moderate since the decay theorist finds himself in the same boat as the interference theorist: the one must aver that the rate of decay remains the same for all kinds of traces as long as the degree of learning is constant, the other that the amount of interference remains the same.

It is important to recognize the difficulties which the apparent invariance in the amount of retention for different types of materials poses for theories of forgetting and to avoid question-begging solutions. Consider, for example, the explanation proposed by Adams (1967) for the empirical failures of the hypothesis of extraexperimental interference. He suggests that the expected differences fail to materialize because the subjects' use of "natural language mediators" renders various types of materials equally resistant to interference. Such mediators are described as "self-imposed" (p. 87) and appear to include any kind of mnemonic or coding device developed during acquisition. In discussing the study of letter-sequence interference by Underwood and Keppel (see p. 1128 above), Adams suggests that natural language mediators may have been formed with equal frequency for the probable and for the improbable letter pairs and that as a consequence there was no difference in retention (p. 195). But how plausible is such an explanation in view of the fact that the learning of the probable pairs was far more rapid than that of the improbable ones? Surely the drastic difference in speed of learning has some implications for the availability and stability of "natural language mediators." It is precisely the fact that the difficulty of acquisition appears to be largely unrelated to the amount of subsequent retention which poses the critical theoretical problem. Whether or not one is inclined to place emphasis on the usefulness of mediators and mnemonics, the finding which requires explanation is that a roughly constant proportion of the originally acquired associations is likely to be lost over a given period of time. So far the factors responsible for these losses have not been adequately specified. The application of experimentally based laws to forgetting outside the laboratory promises to be an arduous task.

BIBLIOGRAPHIC INDEX

Aarons, L., see Riesen, A. H., 1959.

Abbey, D. S. Cross-modality matching of numerosity and pitch. *Canadian Journal of Psychology*, 1962, *16*, 283–290. **86**

Abbott, D. W., & Price, L. E. Stimulus generalization of the conditioned eyelid response to structurally similar nonsense syllables. *Journal of Experimental Psychology*, 1964, *68*, 368–371. **1047**

Abelson, R. P., & Sermat, V. Multidimensional scaling of facial expression. *Journal of Experimental Psychology*, 1962, *63*, 546–554. **57**

Abney, W. de W. The sensitiveness of the retina to light and colour. *Philosophical Transactions of the Royal Society* (London), Ser. A, 1897, *190A*, 155–193. **290**

Abplanalp, P. L., see Hoffman, H. S., 1964.

Abraham, F., see Gormezano, I., 1961.

Abrahams, H., Krakauer, D., & Dallenbach, K. M. Gustatory adaptation to salt. *American Journal of Psychology*, 1937, *49*, 462–469. **184**

Abramov, I., see DeValois, R. L., 1964.

Abrevay, E. L., see Mayzner, M. S., 1964.

Adachi, A. Neurophysiological study on taste effectiveness of seasoning. *Journal of the Physiological Society of Japan*, 1964, *26*, 347–355. **188**

Adachi, A., Funakoshi, M., & Kawamura, Y. Neurophysiological studies on taste effectiveness of chemical taste enhancers. In T. Hayashi (Ed.), *Olfaction and taste*. Vol. II. New York: Pergamon Press, 1967. Pp. 411–413. **188**

Adam, J., see Gibb, M., 1966.

Adams, G., see Brackbill, Y., 1967.

Adams, H. F. The autokinetic sensations. *Psychological Review Monograph Supplement*, 1912, *14*, 1–45. **530**

Adams, J. A. A source of decrement in psychomotor performance. *Journal of Experimental Psychology*, 1955, *49*, 390–394. **575**

Adams, J. A. *Human memory*. New York: McGraw-Hill, 1967. **1131**

Adams, L., see Rock, I., 1965.

Adams, O. S. Stereogram decentration and stereobase as factors influencing the apparent size of stereoscopic pictures. *American Journal of Psychology*, 1955, *68*, 54–68. **480**

Adams, P. A., & Haire, M. The effect of orientation on the reversal of one cube inscribed in another. *American Journal of Psychology*, 1959, *72*, 296–299. **519**

Adams, P. A., see also Postman, L., 1955, 1956; Wallach, H., 1956.

Adams, R. An account of a peculiar optical phenomenon seen after having looked at a moving body. *Philosophical Magazine*, 1834, *5*, 373f. Cited in E. G. Boring. *Sensation and perception in the history of experimental psychology*. New York: Appleton, 1942. **521**

Adelman, H. M., & Maatsch, J. L. Resistance to extinction as a function of the type of response elicited by frustration. *Journal of Experimental Psychology*, 1955, *50*, 61–65. **573**

Adey, W. R., see Wendt, R. H., 1963.

Adler, F. H. *Physiology of the eye: Clinical application*. (3rd ed.) St. Louis: Mosby, 1959. **282**

Adler, S., see Mayzner, M. S., 1964.

Adolph, E. F. Urges to eat and drink in rats. *American Journal of Physiology*, 1947, *151*, 110–125. **812**

Adrian, E. D. Olfactory reactions in the brain of the hedgehog. *Journal of Physiology*, 1942, *100*, 459–473. **201**

Adrian, E. D. Electric responses of the human eye. *Journal of Physiology*, 1945, *104*, 84–104. **308**

Adrian, E. D. Rod and cone components in the electric response of the eye. *Journal of Physiology*, 1946, *105*, 24–37. **308**

Adrian, E. D. Sensory discrimination with some recent

evidence from the olfactory organ. *British Medical Bulletin*, 1950, 6, 330-333. **218**

Adrian, E. D. The mechanism of olfactory stimulation in the mammal. *Advances in Science*, 1953, 9, 417-420. **202, 216, 218**

Adrian, E. D. Basis of sensation: Some recent studies of olfaction (Banting memorial lecture). *British Medical Journal*, 1954, 1, 287-290. **216**

Adrian, E. D. & Matthews, R. The action of light on the eye: III. The interaction of retinal neurones. *Journal of Physiology*, 1928, 65, 273-298. **291**

Adrignolo, A. J., *see* Mayzner, M. S., 1967.

Aiken, E. G., *see* Mowrer, O. H., 1954.

Ajmone-Marsan, C., *see* Jasper, H. H., 1955.

Akesson, C., *see* Ekman, G., 1964.

Akishige, Y. Experimental researches on the structure of the perceptual space. *Bulletin of the Faculty of Literature, Kyushu Univ.*, 1951, 281, 288. **534**

Albee, G. W., *see* Bruell, J. H., 1955.

Alberts, E., & Ehrenfreund, D. Transposition in children as a function of age. *Journal of Experimental Psychology*, 1951, 41, 30-38. **765**

Albrecht, J. J., *see* Inglett, G. E., 1965.

Allen, C., *see* Wickens, D. D., 1963.

Allen, F., & Weinberg, M. The gustatory sensory reflex. *Quarterly Journal of Experimental Psychology*, 1925, 15, 385-420. **178**

Allison, A. C. The structure of the olfactory bulb and its relation to the olfactory pathways in the rabbit and the rat. *Journal of Comparative Neurology*, 1953, 98, 309-348.(a) **197**

Allison, A. C. The morphology of the olfactory system in vertebrates. *Biological Review*, 1953, 28, 195-244. (b) **196**

Allison, J., Larson, D., & Jensen, D. D. Acquired fear, brightness preference, and one-way shuttlebox performance. *Psychonomic Science*, 1967, 8, 269-270. **803**

Allison, V. C., & Katz, S. H. An investigation of stenches and odors for industrial purposes. *Journal of Industrial Engineering and Chemistry*, 1919, 11, 336-338. **199, 201, 203, 204**

Allport, G. W., & Pettigrew, T. G. Cultural influence on the perception of movement: The trapezoidal illusion among Zulus. *Journal of Abnormal and Social Psychology*, 1957, 55, 104-113. **518**

Allyn, M. R., *see* Festinger, L., 1968.

Alpern, M. Metacontrast: Historical introduction. *American Journal of Optometry*, 1952, 29, 631-646. **429, 430**

Alpern, M. Metacontrast. *Journal of the Optical Society of America*, 1953, 43, 648-657. **310, 429**

Alpern, M. The eye. In H. Davson (Ed.), *Muscular mechanisms*, New York: Academic Press, 1962. Vol. 3, pp. 3-229. **371, 383**

Alpern, M., & Campbell, F. W. The spectral sensitivity of the consensual light reflex. *Journal of Physiology*, 1962, 164, 478-507. **393**

Alpern, M., & Dudley, D. The blue arcs of the retina. *Journal of General Physiology*, 1966, 49, 405-421. **286**

Alpern, M., & Ellen, P. A quantitative analysis of the horizontal movements of the eyes in the experiment of Johannes Mueller. *American Journal of Ophthalmology*, 1956, 42, 289-303. **382**

Alpern, M., McCready, D. W. J., & Barr, L. M. The dependence of the photopupil response on flash duration and intensity. *Journal of General Physiology*, 1963, 47, 265-278. **392**

Alpern, M., Mason, G. L., & Jardinico, R. E. Vergence and accommodation: V. *American Journal of Ophthalmology*, 1961, 52, 762-767. **393**

Alpern, M., *see also* Fry, G. A., 1952; ten Doesschate, J., 1967.

Alrutz, S. Untersuchungen über die Temperatursinne. *Zeitschrift für Psychologie*, 1908, 47, 161. **148**

Alston, J. H. The spatial condition of the fusion of warmth and cold in heat. *American Journal of Psychology*, 1920, 31, 303-312. **148**

Amatsu, M., *see* Ishiko, N., 1967.

Amerine, M. A., Pangborn, R. M., & Roessler, E. B. *Principles of sensory evaluation of food*, New York: Academic Press, 1965. **171, 187**

Ames, A. Visual perception and the rotating trapezoidal window. *Psychological Monographs*, 1951, No. 324. **518**

Ammons, C. H., Worchel, P., & Dallenbach, K. M. "Facial vision": Perception of obstacles out of doors by blindfolded and blindfolded-deafened subjects. *American Journal of Psychology*, 1953, 66, 519-53. **270**

Ammons, C. H., *see also* Ammons, R. B., 1959.

Ammons, H., & Irion, A. L. A note on the Ballard reminiscence phenomenon. *Journal of Experimental Psychology*, 1954, 48, 184-186. **1121**

Ammons, R. B. Acquisition of motor skill: I. Quantitative analysis and theoretical formulation. *Psychological Review*, 1948, 54, 263-281. **575, 1034, 1039**

Ammons, R. B. Experimental factors in visual form perception: I. Review and formulation of problems. *Journal of Genetic Psychology*, 1954, 84, 3-25. **519**

Ammons, R. B., Ulrich, P., & Ammons, C. H. Voluntary control of depth in a two-dimensional drawing. *Proceedings of the Montana Academy of Science*, 1959, 19, 160-168. **519**

Amoore, J. E. The stereochemical theory of olfaction: 1. Identification of the seven primary odours. *Proceedings of the Scientific Section of the Toilet Goods Association*, 1962, 37 (suppl.), 1-12. (a) **213**

Amoore, J. E. The stereochemical theory of olfaction: 2. Elucidation of the stereochemical properties of the olfactory receptor sites. *Proceedings of the Scientific Section of the Toilet Goods Association*, 1962, 37 (suppl.), 13-23. (b) **213**

Amoore, J. E. Psychophysics of odor. *Cold Spring Harbor Symposia in Quantitative Biology*, 1965, 30, 623-637. **214**

Amoore, J. E., Johnston, J. W. Jr., & Rubin, M. The stereochemical theory of odor. *Scientific American*, 1964, 210, 42-49. **214**

Amsel, A. Selective association and the anticipatory goal response mechanism as explanatory concepts in learning theory. *Journal of Experimental Psychology*, 1949, 39, 785-799. **801**

Amsel, A. The role of frustrative nonreward in noncontinuous reward situations. *Psychological Bulletin*, 1958, 55, 102-119. **576, 695, 810**

Amsel, A. Frustrative nonreward in partial reinforcement and discrimination learning: Some recent history and a theoretical extension. *Psychological Review*, 1962, 69, 306-328. **810**

Amsel, A. Partial reinforcement effects on vigor and persistence: Advances in frustration theory derived from a variety of within-subjects experiments. In K. W. Spence & J. T. Spence (Eds.), *The psychology of learning and motivation*. New York: Academic Press, 1967. Vol. 1, pp. 1-65. **622, 810**

Amsel, A., & Hancock, W. Motivational properties of frustration: III. Relation of frustration effect to antedating goal factors. *Journal of Experimental Psychology*, 1957, 53, 126-131. **810**

Amsel, A., & Penick, E. C. The influence of early experience on the frustration effect. *Journal of Experimental Psychology*, 1962, 63, 167-176. **810**

Amsel, A., & Roussel, J. Motivational properties of frustration: I. Effect on a running response of the addition of frustration to the motivational complex. *Journal of Experimental Psychology*, 1952, 43, 363-368. **809**

Amsel, A., & Work, M. S. The role of learned factors in "spontaneous" activity. *Journal of Comparative and Physiological Psychology*, 1961, 54, 527-532. **822**

Amsel, A., Work, M. S., & Penick, E. C. Activity during and between periods of stimulus change related to feeding. *Journal of Comparative and Physiological Psychology,* 1962, *55,* 1114-1117. **822**

Amsel, A., *see also* Peckham, R. H., Jr., 1964.

Anand, B. K. Nervous regulation of food intake. *Physiological Reviews,* 1961, *41,* 677-708. **812**

Anastasio, E. J., *see* Sgro, J. A., 1967.

Andersen, E. E., and Weymouth, F. W. Visual perception and the retinal mosaic: I. Retinal mean local sign—an explanation of the fineness of binocular perception of distance. *American Journal of Physiology,* 1923, *64,* 561-594. **301, 305**

Andersen, H. T., Funakoshi, M., & Zotterman, Y. Electrophysiological responses to sugars and their depression by salt. In Y. Zotterman (Ed.), *Olfaction and taste.* Vol. 1. New York: Pergamon, 1963, 177-192. **186**

Anderson, D. C., *see* Brown, J. S., 1966; Pearl, J., 1964.

Anderson, I., & Grosland, H. A method of measuring the effect of primacy of report in the range of attention. *American Journal of Psychology,* 1933, *45,* 701-712. **444**

Anderson, I. H. Studies in the eye-movements of good and poor readers. *Psychological Monographs,* No. 215, 1937. **390**

Anderson, J. F., *see* Rose, J. E., 1967.

Anderson, K. The effects of shifts in sucrose concentration on bar press rates of monkeys. Unpublished doctoral dissertation, Brown University, 1965. **639**

Anderson, L., *see* Osgood, C. E., 1957.

Anderson, N., *see* Turnage, T., 1965.

Anderson, N. H. An analysis of sequential dependencies. In R. R. Bush & W. K. Estes (Eds.), *Studies in mathematical learning theory.* Stanford: Stanford University Press, 1959. Pp. 248-264. **922**

Anderson, N. H. Effect of first-order conditional probability in a two-choice learning situation. *Journal of Experimental Psychology,* 1960, *59,* 73-93. **922**

Anderson, N. H. An evaluation of stimulus sampling theory: Comments on Professor Estes' paper. In A. W. Melton (Ed.). *Categories of human learning.* New York: Academic Press, 1964. Pp. 129-144. **922, 934**

Anderson, N. H. Test of a prediction of stimulus sampling theory in probability learning. *Journal of Experimental Psychology,* 1966, *71,* 499-510. **930**

Anderson, N. H., & Grant, D. A. A test of a statistical learning theory model for two-choice behavior with double stimulus events. *Journal of Experimental Psychology,* 1957, *54,* 305-317. **933**

Anderson, N. H., & Grant, D. A. Correction and reanalysis. *Journal of Experimental Psychology,* 1958, *56,* 453-454. **933**

Anderson, N. H., *see also* Coons, E. E., 1960.

Anderson, N. S., *see* Fitts, P. M., 1956.

Anderson, O. D. *see* Liddell, H. S., 1934.

Anderson, R. E., *see* McLaughlin, S. C., 1968.

Anger, D. The dependence of interresponse times upon the relative reinforcement of different interresponse times. *Journal of Experimental Psychology,* 1956, *52,* 145-161. **606**

Anger, D. The role of temporal discriminations in the reinforcement of Sidman avoidance behavior. *Journal of the Experimental Analysis of Behavior,* 1963, 6 (suppl.), 447-506. **731, 732**

Angrist, B., *see* Leibowitz, H., 1954.

Annau, Z., & Kamin, L. J. The conditioned emotional response as a function of intensity of the US. *Journal of Comparative and Physiological Psychology,* 1961, *54,* 428-432. **713, 714**

Anstis, S. M., & Atkinson, J. Distortions in moving figures viewed through a stationary slit. *American Journal of Psychology,* 1967, *80,* 572-585. **455**

Anstis, S. M., & Gregory, R. K. The after-effect of seen motion: The role of retinal stimulation and of eye movements. *Quarterly Journal of Experimental Psychology,* 1964, *17,* 173-174. **522**

Antonitis, J. J., *see* Kish, G. B., 1956.

Arbuckle, T., *see* Tulving, E., 1963, 1966.

Archer, E. J. A re-evaluation of the meaningfulness of all possible CVC trigrams. *Psychological Monographs,* 1960, *74.* **852, 853, 982**

Archer, E. J. The psychological nature of concepts. In H. J. Klausmeier & C. W. Harris (Eds.), *Analysis of concept learning.* New York: Academic Press, 1966. Pp. 37-50. **942, 944**

Archer, E. J., & Underwood, B. J. Retroactive inhibition of verbal associations as a multiple function of temporal point of interpolation and degree of interpolated learning. *Journal of Experimental Psychology,* 1951, *42,* 283-290. **1100**

Arena, A. J., *see* Wertheimer, M., 1959.

Armington, J. C., & Biersdorf, W. R. Flicker and color adaptation in the human electroretinogram. *Journal of the Optical Society of America,* 1956, *46,* 393-400. **334**

Armington, J. C., Johnson, E. P., & Riggs, L. A. The scotopic A-wave in the electrical response of the human retina. *Journal of Physiology,* 1952, *118,* 289-298. **307**

Armington, J. C., *see also* Riggs, L. A., 1954.

Armstrong, D., Dry, R. M. L., Keele, C. A., & Markham, J. W. Method for studying chemical excitants of cutaneous pain in man. *Journal of Physiology,* 1951, 115, 59-61. **156**

Armus, H. L., Carlson, K. R., Guinan, J. F., & Crowell, R. A. Effect of a secondary reinforcement stimulus on the auditory startle response. *Psychological Reports,* 1964, *14,* 535-540. **808**

Armus, H. L., & Sniadowski-Dolinsky, D. Startle decrement and secondary reinforcement stimulation. *Psychonomic Science,* 1966, *4,* 175-176. **808**

Arnold, E. M. M., *see* Keehn, J. D., 1960.

Arnold, W. J., *see* Koronakis, C., 1957.

Arnoult, M. D. Stimulus predifferentiation: Some generalizations and hypotheses. *Psychological Bulletin,* 1957, *54,* 339-350. **1062**

Arnoult, M. D., *see also* Attneave, F., 1956; Vincent, R. J., 1969.

Arthur, R. P., & Shelley, W. B. The peripheral mechanism of itch in man. In G. E. W. Wolsteinholme & M. O'Connor (Eds.), *Pain and itch, nervous mechanisms.* Boston, Mass.: Little Brown, 1959. Pp. 84-97. **166**

Asch, S. E., & Ebenholtz, S. M. The process of free recall: Evidence for non-associative factors in acquisition and retention. *Journal of Psychology,* 1962, *54,* 3-31. **1095, 1101, 1102**

Asch, S. E., & Witkin, H. A. Studies in space orientation: I. Perception of the upright with displaced visual fields; II. Perception of the upright with displaced visual fields and with body tilted. *Journal of Experimental Psychology,* 1948, *38,* 325-337, 455-477. **539**

Asch, S. E., *see also* Witkin, H. A., 1948.

Asher, H. Suppression theory of binocular vision. *British Journal of Opthalmology,* 1953, *37,* 37-49. **488, 492**

Ashton, E. H., *see* Moulton, D., 1960.

Asratyan, E. A. Some aspects of the elaboration of conditioned connections and formation of their properties. In J. F. Delafresnaye (Ed.), *Brain mechanisms and learning: A symposium.* Oxford: Blackwell, 1961. **564**

Atkinson, J., *see* Anstis, S. M., 1967.

Atkinson, R. C. An analysis of the effect of non-reinforced trials in terms of statistical learning theory. *Journal of Experimental Psychology,* 1956, *52,* 28-32. **933**

Atkinson, R. C. A theory of stimulus discrimination learning. In K. J. Arrow, S. Karlin, & P. Suppes (Eds.), *Mathematical methods in the social sciences,* Stanford: Stanford University Press, 1960. Pp. 221-241. **948**

Atkinson, R. C. The observing response in discrimination learning. *Journal of Experimental Psychology*, 1961, *62*, 253–262. **1001**

Atkinson, R. C. A variable sensitivity theory of signal detection. *Psychological Review*, 1961, *68*, 301–304. **41, 44**

Atkinson, R. C., Bogartz, W. H., & Turner, R. N. Discrimination learning with probabilistic reinforcement schedules. *Journal of Experimental Psychology*, 1959, *57*, 349–350. **926**

Atkinson, R. C., Bower, G. H., & Crothers, E. J. *An introduction to mathematical learning theory*. New York: Wiley, 1965. **906, 911, 922, 953**

Atkinson, R. C., & Crothers, E. J. A comparison of paired-associate learning models having different acquisition and retention axioms. *Journal of Mathematical Psychology*, 1964, *1*, 285–315. **997, 998**

Atkinson, R. C., & Estes, W. K. Stimulus sampling theory. In R. D. Luce, R. R. Bush, & E. Galanter (Eds.), *Handbook of mathematical psychology*, Vol. II. New York: Wiley, 1963. Pp. 121–268. **911, 922, 927, 928, 995, 1002**

Atkinson, R. C., & Shiffrin, R. M. *Mathematical models for memory and learning*. Technical Report No. 79, Institute for Mathematical Studies in the Social Sciences, Stanford University, 1965. **1109**

Atkinson, R. C., see also Calfee, R. C., 1965; Estes, W. K., 1957; Myers, J. L., 1964; Popper, J., 1958; Suppes, P., 1960.

Attneave, F. A method of graded dichotomies for scaling of judgments. *Psychological Review*, 1949, *56*, 334–340. **58**

Attneave, F. Psychological probability as a function of experienced frequency. *Journal of Experimental Psychology*, 1953, *46*, 81–86. **897**

Attneave, F. Some informational aspects of visual perception. *Psychological Review*, 1954, *61*, 183–193. **437, 445**

Attneave, F. Symmetry, information and memory for patterns. *American Journal of Psychology*, 1955, *68*, 209–22. **445, 447**

Attneave, F. Physical determinants of the judged complexity of shapes. *Journal of Experimental Psychology*, 1957, *53*, 221–227. **448, 449**

Attneave, F. Transfer of experience with a class-schema to identification-learning of patterns and shapes. *Journal of Experimental Psychology*, 1957, *54*, 81–88. **449**

Attneave, F. *Applications of information theory to psychology*. New York: Holt, Rinehart and Winston, 1959. **445**

Attneave, F. Perception and related areas. In S. Koch (Ed.), *Psychology: A study of a science*. Vol. 4. New York: McGraw-Hill, 1962. **247, 448**

Attneave, F. Triangles as ambiguous figures. *American Journal of Psychology*, 1968, *81*, 447–453. **451**

Attneave, F., & Arnoult, M. D. The quantitative study of shape and pattern perception. *Psychological Bulletin*, 1956, *53*, 452–471. **446, 449**

Attneave, F., & Frost, R. The discrimination of perceived tridimensional orientation by minimum criteria. *Perception and Psychophysics*, 1969, *6*, 391–396. **499**

Attneave, F., & Olson, R. K. Inferences about visual mechanisms from monocular depth effects. *Psychonomic Science*, 1966, *4*, 133–134. **434n**

Atwater, S. K. Proactive inhibition and associative facilitation as affected by degree of prior learning. *Journal of Experimental Psychology*, 1953, *46*, 400–404. **1103**

Aubert, H. Eine scheinbare bedeutende Drehung von Objekten bei Neigung des Kopfesnach rechts oder links. *Virchow's Archiv*, 1861, *20*, 381–393. As described in Howard & Templeton, 1966. **538**

Aubert, H. Die Bewegungsempfindung. *Archiv für die Gesamte Physiologie*, 1886, *39*, 347–370. **520**

Austin, G. A., see Bruner, J. S., 1956.

Austin, P., see Wallach, H., 1954.

Autrum, H. Electrophysiological analysis of the visual systems in insects. *Experimental Cell Research*, 1958, Suppl. 5, 426–439. **311**

Avant, L. L. Vision in the Ganzfeld. *Psychological Bulletin*, 1965, *64*, 246–258. **426**

Averbach, E., & Coriell, A. S. Short-term memory in vision. *Bell System Technical Journal*, 1961, *40*, 309–328. **430, 444**

Aylesworth, M., see Warden, C. J., 1927.

Ayllon, T., & Sommer, R. Autism, emphasis and figure ground perception. *Journal of Psychology*, 1956, *41*, 163–176. **440**

Ayres, J. J. B. Conditioned suppression and the information hypothesis. *Journal of Comparative and Physiological Psychology*, 1966, *62*, 21–25. **676**

Azrin, N. H. Some effects of two intermittent schedules of immediate and non-immediate punishment. *Journal of Psychology*, 1956, *42*, 3–21. **737**

Azrin, N. H. A technique for delivering shock to pigeons. *Journal of the Experimental Analysis of Behavior*, 1959, *2*, 161–163. **706**

Azrin, N. H., & Holz, W. C. Punishment during fixed-interval reinforcement. *Journal of the Experimental Analysis of Behavior*, 1961, *4*, 343–347. **734, 735**

Azrin, N. H., & Holz, W. C. Punishment. In W. K. Honig (Ed.), *Operant behavior: Areas of research and application*. New York: Appleton, 1966. Pp. 380–447. **734**

Azrin, N. H., Hopwood, J., & Powell, J. A rat chamber and electrode procedure for avoidance conditioning. *Journal of the Experimental Analysis of Behavior*, 1967, *10*, 291–298. **706**

Azrin, N. H., see also Hake, D. R., 1965.

Bach, H. Determination of threshold values of olfaction. *Gesundheits-Ingenieur*, 1937, *60*, 222–225. Cited by R. W. Moncrieff, *The chemical senses*, New York: Wiley, 1944. **201**

Backer, R., see Sheffield, F. D., 1951.

Bacon, W. E., see Hulse, S. H., 1960.

Baddeley, A. D. Semantic and acoustic similarity in short-term memory. *Nature*, 1964, *204*, 1116–1117. **1117**

Baddeley, A. D. The influence of acoustic and semantic similarity on long-term memory for word sequences. *Quarterly Journal of Experimental Psychology*, 1966, *18*, 302–309. (a) **1117**

Baddeley, A. D. Short-term memory for word sequences as a function of acoustic, semantic and formal similarity. *Quarterly Journal of Experimental Psychology*, 1966, *18*, 362–368. (b) **1117**

Baddeley, A. D., & Dale, H. C. A. The effect of semantic similarity on retroactive interference in long- and short-term memory. *Journal of Verbal Learning and Verbal Behavior*, 1966, *5*, 417–420. **1119**

Badia, P. R., see Ehrenfreund, D., 1962.

Bahnson, P. Eine Untersuchung uber Symmetrie und Asymmetrie bei visuellen Wahrnehmungen. *Zeitschrift für Psychologie*, 1928, *108*, 129–154. **433**

Bahrick, H. P., & Bahrick, P. O. A re-examination of the interrelations among measures of retention. *Quarterly Journal of Experimental Psychology*, 1964, *16*, 318–324. **893**

Bahrick, P. O., see Bahrick, H. P., 1964.

Bailey, D. E., see Bolles, R. C., 1956.

Baird, J. C. Retinal and assumed size cues as determinants of size and distance perception. *Journal of Experimental Psychology*, 1963, *66*, 155–162. **496**

Baker, H. D. The course of foveal light adaptation measured by the threshold intensity increment. *Journal of the Optical Society of America*, 1949, *39*, 172–179. **310**

Baker, H. D. The instantaneous threshold and early dark

adaptation. *Journal of the Optical Society of America,* 1953, *43,* 798-803. **287**

Baker, H. D. Initial stages of light and dark adaptation. *Journal of the Optical Society of America,* 1963, *53,* 98-103. **310**

Baker, K. E., see Gagné, R. M., 1950; Graham, C. H., 1948.

Baker, L. M., & Elliott, D. N. Controlled and free association-times with identical stimulus- and response-words. *American Journal of Psychology,* 1948, *61,* 535-539. **868**

Bales, J. F., & Follansbee, G. L. The after-effect of the perception of curved lines. *Journal of Experimental Psychology,* 1935, *18,* 499-503. **469**

Ballard, P. B. Oblivescence and reminiscence. *British Journal of Psychology Monograph Supplements,* 1913, No. 2. **1121**

Bamber, D., see Festinger, L., 1967.

Banerji, R. B. The description list of concepts. *Communications of the ACM,* 1962, *5,* 426-432. **938**

Banister, H. Three experiments on the localization of tones. *British Journal of Psychology,* 1926, *16,* 265-292. **266**

Banks, R. K. Persistence to continuous punishment following intermittent punishment training. *Journal of Experimental Psychology,* 1966, *71,* 373-377. **737**

Banuazizi, A., see Miller, N. E., 1968.

Bappert, J. Neue untersuchungen zum Problem des Verhältnisses von Akkomodation und Konvergenz zur Wahrnehmung der Tiefe. *Zeitschrift für Psychologie,* 1923, *90,* 167-203. **479**

Baradi, A. F., & Bourne, G. H. Localization of gustatory and olfactory enzymes in the rabbit, and the problems of taste and smell. *Nature,* 1951, *168,* 977-979. **189, 220**

Baratz, S. S., see Epstein, W., 1964.

Barclay, A., see Goulet, L. R., 1965.

Bare, J. K., see Pfaffmann, C., 1950.

Barker, A. N., see Hull, C. L., 1951.

Barlow, H. B. Slippage of contact lenses and other artifacts in relation to fading and regeneration of supposedly stable retinal images. *Quarterly Journal of Experimental Psychology,* 1963, *15,* 36-51. **374, 375**

Barlow, H. B., FitzHugh, R., & Kuffler, S. W. Change of organization in the receptive fields of the cat's retina during dark adaptation. *Journal of Physiology,* 1957, *137,* 327-337. **291**

Barlow, H. B., & Sparrock, J. M. B. The role of afterimages in dark adaptation. *Science,* 1964, *144,* 1309-1314. **288**

Barnes, J. M., & Underwood, B. J. "Fate" of first-list associations in transfer theory. *Journal of Experimental Psychology,* 1959, *58,* 97-105. **1011, 1058, 1062, 1086, 1089, 1092, 1093**

Barney, H. L., & Dunn, H. K. Speech analysis: Speech synthesis. In L. Kaiser (Ed.), *Manual of phonetics.* Amsterdam: North-Holland Publ. Co., 1957. **252**

Barney, H. L., see also Peterson, G. E., 1952.

Baron, A., see Warren, J. M., 1956.

Baron, M. R., see Newman, F. L., 1965.

Barr, J., see Warden, C. J., 1929.

Barr, L. M., see Alpern, M., 1963.

Barrett, R. J., Peyser, C. S., & McHose, J. H. Effects of complete and incomplete reward reduction on a subsequent response. *Psychonomic Science,* 1965, *3,* 277-278. **810**

Barrientos, G., see Wike, E. L., 1958.

Bartleson, C. J. Memory colors of familiar objects. *Journal of the Optical Society of America,* 1960, *50,* 73-77. **424**

Bartleson, C. J., see also Burnham, R. W., 1963.

Bartlett, F. C. *Remembering.* Cambridge: Cambridge University Press, 1932. **552**

Bartlett, N. R., see Graham, C. H., 1940.

Bartley, S. H. Subjective brightness in relation to flash rate and the light–dark ratio. *Journal of Experimental Psychology,* 1938, *23,* 313-319. **314**

Bartley, S. H. Some factors in brightness discrimination. *Psychological Review,* 1939, *46,* 337-358. **314**

Bartley, S. H., & Bishop, G. H. The cortical response to stimulation of the optic nerve in the rabbit. *American Journal of Physiology,* 1933, *103,* 159-172. **309**

Bartley, S. H., Paczewitz, G., & Valsi, E. Brightness enhancement and the stimulus cycle. *Journal of Psychology,* 1957, *43,* 187-192. **307**

Bartley, S. H., see also Fry, G. A., 1953; Nelson, T. M., 1956.

Bartolovic, B. Internal regulation of gustatory sensitivity. *Acta Instituti Psychologici Universitatis Zagrebensis,* 1964, *45,* 73-80. **189**

Bartoshuk, A. K. Electromyographic gradients as indicants of motivation. *Canadian Journal of Psychology,* 1955, *9,* 215-230. **833**

Bartoshuk, A. K. EMG gradients and EEG amplitude during motivated listening. *Canadian Journal of Psychology,* 1956, *10,* 156-164. **833**

Bartoshuk, A. K. Electromyographic reactions to strong auditory stimulation as a function of alpha amplitude. *Journal of Comparative and Physiological Psychology,* 1959, *52,* 540-545. **834**

Bartoshuk, A. K. Human neonatal cardiac acceleration to sound: Habituation and dishabituation. *Perceptual and Motor Skills,* 1962, *15,* 15-27. (a) **591**

Bartoshuk, A. K. Response decrement with repeated elicitation of human neonatal cardiac acceleration to sound. *Journal of Comparative and Physiological Psychology,* 1962, *55,* 9-13. (b) **591, 834**

Bartoshuk, A. K. Human neonatal cardiac responses to sound: A power function. *Psychonomic Science,* 1964, *1,* 151-152. **840**

Bartoshuk, L. M. Water taste in man. *Perception and Psychophysics,* 1968. **184, 186**

Bartoshuk, L. M., Dateo, G. P., Vandenbelt, D. J., Buttrick, R. D., & Long, L. Effects of *Gymnema sylvestre* and *Synsepalum dulcificum* on taste in man. In C. Pfaffmann (Ed.), *Olfaction and taste.* Vol. III. New York: Rockefeller University Press, 1969. **177**

Bartoshuk, L. M., McBurney, D. H., & Pfaffmann, C. Taste of sodium chloride solutions after adaptation to sodium chloride: Implications for the "water taste." *Science,* 1964, *143,* 967-968. **81, 184**

Bartoshuk, L. M., & Pfaffmann, C. Effects of pre-treatment on the water taste response in cat and rat. *Federation Proceedings,* 1965, 24 (abstract). **186**

Bartoshuk, L. M., see also Pfaffman, C., 1969.

Bass, M. J., & Hull, C. L. Irradiation of a tactile conditioned reflex in man. *Journal of Comparative Psychology,* 1934, *17,* 47-65. **601**

Bassett, I. G., & Eastmond, E. J. Echo location: Measurement of pitch versus distance for sounds reflected from a flat surface. *Journal of the Acoustical Society of America,* 1964, *36,* 911-916. **271**

Bastian, J. Associative factors in verbal transfer. *Journal of Experimental Psychology,* 1961, *62,* 70-79. **1058, 1084**

Bateson, P. P. G. Changes in chicks' responses to novel moving objects over the sensitive period for imprinting. *Animal Behaviour,* 1964, *12,* 479-489. (a) **584**

Bateson, P. P. G. Effect of similarity between rearing and testing conditions on chicks' following and avoidance responses. *Journal of Comparative and Physiological Psychology,* 1964, *57,* 100-103. (b) **587**

Bateson, P. P. G. The characteristics and context of imprinting. *Biological Reviews,* 1966, *41,* 177-220. **583, 588, 700**

Bateson, P. P. G., & Reese, E. Reinforcing properties of conspicuous objects before imprinting has occurred. *Psychonomic Science,* 1968, *10,* 379-380. **587**

Battersby, W. S., Kahn, R. L., Pollack, M., & Bender, M. B.,

Effects of visual, vestibular, and somatosensori-motor deficit on autokinetic perception. *Journal of Experimental Psychology,* 1956, *52,* 398–410. **530**

Battig, W. F. Scaled difficulty of nonsense-syllable pairs consisting of syllables of equal association value. *Psychological Reports,* 1959, *5,* 126. **899**

Battig, W. F. Comparison of two methods of scaling nonsense-syllable pairs for ease of learning. *Psychological Reports,* 1960, *6,* 363–366. **899**

Battig, W. F. Procedural problems in paired-associate learning research. *Psychonomic Monograph Supplements,* 1965, *1,* 12. **855, 856**

Battig, W. F. Paired-associate learning. In T. R. Dixon & D. L. Horton (Eds.), *Verbal behavior and general behavior theory.* Englewood Cliffs, N.J.: Prentice-Hall, 1968. **855, 1126**

Bauer, F. J., & Lawrence, D. H. Influence of similarity of choice-point and goal cues on discrimination learning. *Journal of Comparative and Physiological Psychology,* 1953, *46,* 241–252. **783**

Bauer, J., *see* Efstathiou, A., 1967.

Bauer, J. A., *see* Held, R., 1967.

Baumeister, A., Hawkins, W. F., & Cromwell, R. L. Need state and activity level. *Psychological Bulletin,* 1964, *61,* 438–453. **821**

Baumgardt, E., & Ségal, J. Facilitation et inhibition, paramètres de la fonction visuelle. *Année psychologique,* 1947, *43–44,* 54–102. **307**

Bayle, E. The nature and causes of regressive movements in reading. *Journal of Experimental Education,* 1942, *11,* 16–36. **390**

Bazett, H. C. Temperature sense in man. In *Temperature, its measurement, and control in science and industry.* New York: Reinhold, 1941. Pp. 489–501. **153**

Beatty, J., *see* Kahneman, D., 1966.

Beauchamp, R. D., *see* Church, R. M., 1967.

Beck, E. C., *see* Brown, H. M., 1966.

Beck, J. Stimulus correlates for the judged illumination of a surface. *Journal of Experimental Psychology,* 1959, *58,* 267–274. **405**

Beck, J. Texture-gradients and judgments of slant and recession. *American Journal of Psychology,* 1960, *73,* 411–416. **502**

Beck, J. Judgments of surface illumination and lightness. *Journal of Experimental Psychology,* 1961, *61,* 368–375. **405, 406, 423**

Beck, J. Supplementary report: An examination of an aspect of the Gelb effect. *Journal of Experimental Psychology,* 1962, *64,* 199–200. **423**

Beck, J. The effect of gloss on perceived lightness. *American Journal of Psychology,* 1964, *77,* 54–63. **422**

Beck, J. Apparent spatial position and the perception of lightness. *Journal of Experimental Psychology,* 1965, *69,* 170–179. **421**

Beck, J. Age differences in lightness perception. *Psychonomic Science,* 1966, *4,* 201–202. (a) **406**

Beck, J. Effect of orientation and of shape similarity on perceptual grouping. *Perception and Psychophysics,* 1966, *1,* 300–302. (b) **434**

Beck, J., & Gibson, J. J. The relation of apparent shape to apparent slant in the perception of objects. *Journal of Experimental Psychology,* 1955, *50,* 125–133. **516**

Beck, J., & Shaw, W. A. The scaling of pitch by the method of magnitude estimation. *American Journal of Psychology,* 1961, *74,* 242–251. **244**

Beck, J., & Shaw, W. A. Single estimates of pitch magnitude. *Journal of the Acoustical Society of America,* 1963, *35,* 1722–1724. **244**

Beck, J., *see also* Hochberg, J., 1954.

Beck, L. H., Kruger, L., & Calabresi, P. The observations on olfactory intensity: I. Training procedure, methods, and data for two aliphatic homologous series. *Annals of the New York Academy of Science,* 1954, *58,* 225–238. **197, 200**

Beck, L. H., & Miles, W. R. Some theoretical and experimental relationships between infrared absorption and olfaction. *Science,* 1947, *106,* 511. **220**

Beck, R. C. The rat's adaptation to a 23.5-hour water-deprivation schedule. *Journal of Comparative and Physiological Psychology,* 1962, *55,* 646–648. **819**

Becker, L. A., *see* Schuck, J. R., 1964.

Becker, R. F., King, J. E., & Markee, J. E. Studies on olfactory discrimination in dogs: II. Discriminatory behavior in a free environment. *Journal of Comparative and Physiological Psychology,* 1962, *55,* 773–780. **202**

Beebe-Center, J. G. The variability of affective judgments upon odors. *Journal of Experimental Psychology,* 1931, *14,* 91–93. **215**

Beebe-Center, J. G., & Waddell, D. A general psychological scale of taste. *Journal of Psychology,* 1948, *26,* 517–524. **175**

Beecher, H. K. Relationship of significance of wound to the pain experienced. *Journal of the American Medical Association,* 1956, *161,* 1609–1613. **155**

Beecher, H. K. *Measurement of subjective responses.* New York: Oxford University Press, 1959. **155, 163, 164**

Beecher, H. K. Pain: One mystery solved. *Science,* 1966, *151,* 840–841. **155**

Beecher, H. K., *see also* Smith, G. M., 1966.

Beecroft, R. S. Verbal learning and retention as a function of the number of competing associations. *Journal of Experimental Psychology,* 1956, *51,* 216–220. **1126**

Beer, B., Hodos, W., & Matthews, T. J. Rate of intracranial self-stimulation as a function of reinforcement magnitude and density. *Psychonomic Science,* 1964, *1,* 321–322. **649, 650**

Beer, B., & Trumble, G. Timing behavior as a function of amount of reinforcement. *Psychonomic Science,* 1965, *2,* 71–72. **695**

Beer, B., & Valenstein, E. S. Discrimination of tones during reinforcing brain stimulation. *Science,* 1960, *132,* 297–298. **659**

Beer B., *see also* Steiner, S. S., 1968; Valenstein, E. S., 1961, 1964.

Beets, M. G. J. A molecular approach to olfaction. In E. J. Ariens (Ed.), *Molecular pharmacology.* Vol. II. New York: Academic Press, 1964, 3–51. **220**

Beez, V., *see* Di Lollo, V., 1966.

Behar, V., *see* Goulet, L. R., 1966.

Behrend, E. R., & Bitterman, M. E. Avoidance-conditioning in the goldfish: Exploratory studies of the CS–US interval. *American Journal of Psychology,* 1962, *75,* 18–34. **729**

Behrend, E. R., *see also* Gonzalez, R. C., 1965.

Beidler, L. M. Properties of chemoreceptors of tongue of rat. *Journal of Neurophysiology,* 1953, *16,* 595–607. **187**

Beidler, L. M. A theory of taste stimulation. *Journal of General Physiology,* 1954, *38,* 133–139. **189**

Beidler, L. M. Facts and theory on the mechanism of taste and odor perception. In J. H. Mitchell, Jr. (Ed.), *Chemistry of natural food flavors.* Chicago: Quartermaster Food Container Institute for the Armed Forces, 1957. Pp. 7–47. **211, 218**

Beidler, L. M. Effect of odor flow rate on olfactory response. *Federation Proceedings,* 1958, *17,* 13. **207**

Beidler, L. M. Physiology of olfaction and gustation. *Annals of Otolaryngology, Rhinology, and Laryngology,* 1960, *69,* 398–409. **205**

Beidler, L. M. Taste receptor stimulation. In J. A. V. Butler, H. E. Huxley, & R. E. Zirkle (Eds.), *Progress in biophysics and biophysical chemistry.* Vol. 12. New York: Pergamon Press, 1961. Pp. 107–151. **186, 189**

Beidler, L. M. Dynamics of taste cells. In Y. Zotterman (Ed.),

Olfaction and taste. Vol. 1. New York: Pergamon Press, 1963. Pp. 133–145. **172**

Beidler, L. M. Comparison of gustatory receptors, olfactory receptors, and free nerve endings. In *Cold Spring Harbor Symposia on Quantitative Biology,* 1965, *30,* 191–200. **171**

Beidler, L. M., & Smallman, R. L. Renewal of cells within taste buds. *Journal of Cell Biology,* 1965, *27,* 263–272. **172**

Beidler, L. M., & Tucker, D. Olfactory and trigeminal nerve responses to odors. *Federation Proceedings,* 1956, *15,* 14. **205, 211**

Beidler, L. M., see also Kimura, K., 1961; Moulton, D. G., 1967; Tateda, H., 1964.

Beier, E. M., see Logan, F. A., 1956.

Békésy, G. von, see von Békésy, G.

Bélanger, D., & Feldman, S. M. Effects of water deprivation upon heart rate and instrumental activity in the rat. *Journal of Comparative and Physiological Psychology,* 1962, *55,* 220–225. **827, 828, 834**

Bélanger, D., see also Ducharme, R., 1961; Malmo, R. B., 1967.

Belcher, S. J., see Clarke, F. J., 1962.

Bell, R. A., & Bevan, W. The influence of anchors upon the operation of certain Gestalt organizing principles. *Journal of Experimental Psychology,* 1968, *78,* 67–678. **434n**

Beller, H. K., see Morant, R. B., 1965.

Belloni, M., see Brown, J. S., 1963.

Benary, W. Beobachtungen zu einein Experiment uber Helligkeitskontrast. *Psychologische Forschung,* 1924, *5,* 131–142. **410, 423n**

Bender, M. B., see Battersby, W. S., 1956.

Benjamin, F. B. Release of intracellular potassium as a factor in pain production. In D. R. Kenshalo (Ed.), *The skin senses,* Springfield, Ill.: Charles C Thomas, 1968, pp. 466–479. **160, 162**

Benjamin, R. M., & Burton, H. Projection of taste nerve afferents to anterior opercular–insular cortex in squirrel monkey (*Saimiri sciureus*). *Brain Research,* 1968, *7,* 221–231. **172**

Benjamin, R. M., Halpern, B. P., Moulton, D. G., & Mozell, M. M. The chemical senses. *Annals of the New York Academy of Sciences,* 1965, *16,* 381–416. **190, 220**

Benjamin, R. M., & Thompson, R. F. Differential effects of cortical lesions in infant and adult cats on roughness discrimination. *Experimental Neurology,* 1959, *1,* 305–321. **845**

Benjamin, R. M., see also Oakley, B., 1966.

Benson, R. W., see Hirsh, I. J., 1952.

Benson, W. M., see Young, R. K., 1963.

Bentley, M., see Mikesell, W. H., 1930.

Benton, A. L., see Swanson, R., 1955.

Benussi, V. Stroboskopische Scheinbewegungen und geometrischoptische Gestaltausscheinungen. *Archiv für die Gesamte Psychologie,* 1912, *24,* 31–62. **464**

Benussi, V. Versuche zur Analyse taktil erweckter Scheinbewegungen. *Archiv für die Gesamte Psychologie,* 1916, *36,* 59–135. Cited in Boring, E. C. *Sensation and perception in the history of experimental psychology.* New York: Appleton, 1942. **408, 526**

Benussi, V. Zur Psychologie der Gestalterfassens. In A. Meinong (Ed.), *Untersuch Gegenstands theorie,* 1904. Pp. 303–448. **464**

Beranek, L. L. Criteria for office quieting based on questionnaire rating studies. *Journal of the Acoustical Society of America,* 1956, *28,* 833–852. **258**

Beranek, L. L. Revised criteria for noise in buildings. *Noise Control,* 1957, *3,* 19–27. **258**

Berg, H. W., Pangborn, R. M., Roessler, E. B., & Webb, A. D. Influence of hunger on olfactory acuity. *Nature,* 1963, *197,* 108. **208**

Bergeijk, W. A. van, see van Bergeijk, W. A.

Bergman, G., & Spence, K. W. The logic of psychophysical measurements. *Psychological Review,* 1944, *51,* 1–24. **246**

Bergman, R., & Gibson, J. J. The negative aftereffect of a surface slanted in the third dimension. *American Journal of Psychology,* 1959, *72,* 364–374. **470n**

Berkeley, G. *An essay towards a new theory of vision.* Dublin: Jeremy Pepyat, 1709. Reprinted New York: Dutton, 1922. **477**

Berkley, M. A. Discrimination of rewards as a function of contrast in rewarded stimuli. *Journal of Experimental Psychology,* 1963, *66,* 371–376. **630**

Berkley, M. A., see also Kling, J. W., 1968; Su, Jiuan, 1966.

Berko, J., see Brown, R. W., 1960.

Berkowitz, H., see Bousfield, W. A., 1960.

Berkun, M., see Kagan, J., 1954.

Berliner, A. *Lectures on visual psychology.* Chicago: Professional Press, 1948. **461**

Berliner, A., & Berliner, S. The distortion of straight and curved lines in geometrical fields. *American Journal of Psychology,* 1948, *61,* 153–166. **459**

Berliner, S., see Berliner, A., 1948.

Berlyne, D. E. *Conflict, arousal and curiosity.* New York: McGraw-Hill, 1960. **841**

Berlyne, D. E. Curiosity and exploration. *Science,* 1966, *153,* 25–33. **841**

Berlyne, D. E. Arousal and reinforcement. In D. Levine (Ed.), *Nebraska symposium on motivation.* Lincoln: University of Nebraska Press, 1967. Pp. 1–110. **673, 841, 845**

Berlyne, D. E., & McDonnell, P. Effects of stimulus complexity and incongruity on duration of EEG desynchronization. *Electroencephalography and Clinical Neurophysiology,* 1965, *18,* 156–161. **841**

Berman, A. J., see Taub, E., in press.

Berman, P. W., & Liebowitz, H. W. Some effects of contour on simultaneous brightness contrast. *Journal of Experimental Psychology,* 1965, *69,* 251–256. **408, 410**

Bernbach, H. A. A forgetting model for paired-associate learning. *Journal of Mathematical Psychology,* 1965, *2,* 128–144. **1000**

Bernbach, H. A. Stimulus learning and recognition in paired-associate learning. *Journal of Experimental Psychology,* 1967, *75,* 513–519. **1048**

Bernstein, S., see Thurlow, W. R., 1957.

Berry, J. H., see Worchel, P., 1952.

Berry, R. N. Quantitative relations among vernier, real depth, and stereoscopic depth acuities. *Journal of Experimental Psychology,* 1948, *38,* 708–721. **300, 486**

Berry, R. N., Riggs, L. A., & Duncan, C. P. The relation of vernier and depth discrimination to field brightness. *Journal of Experimental Psychology,* 1950, *40,* 349–354. **486**

Bersh, P. J. The influence of two variables upon the establishment of a secondary reinforcer for operant responses. *Journal of Experimental Psychology,* 1951, *41,* 62–73. **666**

Bershansky, I. The areal and punctiform integration of warmth and pressure. *American Journal of Psychology,* 1922, *33,* 584–587. **166**

Besch, N. F., & Reynolds, W. F. Associative interference in verbal paired-associate learning. *Journal of Experimental Psychology,* 1958, *55,* 554–558. **1055, 1064**

Besch, N. F., Thompson, W. E., & Wetzel, A. B. Studies in associative interference. *Journal of Experimental Psychology,* 1962, *63,* 342–352. **1065**

Bevan, W. An adaptation-level interpretation of reinforcement. *Perceptual and Motor Skills,* 1966, *23,* 511–531. **634**

Bevan, W., see also Bell, R. A., 1968.

Beyrl, R. Ueber die Grossenauffassung bei Kindern. *Zeitschrift für Psychologie,* 1926, *100,* 344–371. **550**

Bhatt, B. J., see Thurlow, W. R., 1965.

Bicknell, E., see Calvin, J. S., 1953.

Bidder, T. G., see Rowland, V., 1960.

Biddulph, R., see Shower, E. G., 1931.

Biederman, I., see Fehrer, E., 1962.

Bielschowsky, A., see Hoffman, F. B., 1909.

Biersdorf, W. R., see Armington, J. C., 1956.

Bigelow, N. H., see Harrison, I. B., 1943.

Bilger, R. C. Intensive determinants of remote masking. *Journal of the Acoustical Society of America*, 1958, *30*, 817–824. **239**

Bilger, R. C. Remote masking in the absence of intra-aural muscles. *Journal of the Acoustical Society of America*, 1966, *39*, 103–108. **240**

Bilger, R. C., & Hirsh, I. J. Masking of tones by bands of noise. *Journal of the Acoustical Society of America*, 1956, *28*, 623–630. **239**

Bilger, R. C., see also Deatherage, B. H., 1957.

Bilodeau, E. A., & Howell, D. C. Free association norms by discrete and continued methods. Technical Report No. 1 for Contract Nonr-475(10) between Tulane University and the Office of Naval Research, 1965. **861**

Bilodeau, I. McD. Information feedback. In E. A. Bilodeau (Ed.), *Acquisition of skill.* New York: Academic Press, 1966. **687**

Bilodeau, I. McD., & Schlosberg, H. Similarity in stimulating conditions as a variable in retroactive inhibition. *Journal of Experimental Psychology*, 1951, *41*, 199–204. **1084**

Binder, A., & Estes, W. K. Transfer of response in visual recognition situations as a function of frequency variables. *Psychological Monographs*, 1966, *80*. **1005**

Binder, A., & Feldman, S. E. The effects of experimentally controlled experience upon recognition responses. *Psychological Monographs*, 1960, *74*. **954, 1004, 1005**

Bindra, D. Stimulus change, reactions to novelty, and response decrement. *Psychological Review*, 1959, *66*, 96–103. **818**

Bindra, D. Components of general activity and the analysis of behavior. *Psychological Review*, 1961, *68*, 205–215. **818, 822**

Bindra, D. Neuropsychological interpretation of the effects of drive and incentive-motivation on general activity and instrumental behavior. *Psychological Review*, 1968, *75*, 1–22. **809**

Bindra, D., & Palfai, T. The nature of positive and negative incentive-motivational effects on general activity. *Journal of Comparative and Physiological Psychology*, 1967, *63*, 288–297. **808, 818, 823**

Bindra, D., see also Baum, M., 1968.

Binet, A., & Henri, V. La psychologie individuelle. *L'Année Psychologique*, 1896, *2*, 411–465. **598**

Binford, J. R., & Gettys, C. Nonstationarity in paired-associate learning as indicated by a second guess procedure. *Journal of Mathematical Psychology*, 1965, *2*, 190–195. **1010**

Birch, D., Burnstein, E., & Clarke, R. A. Response strength as a function of hours of food deprivation under a controlled maintenance schedule. *Journal of Comparative and Physiological Psychology*, 1958, *51*, 350–354. **830, 831**

Birdsall, T. G., see Swets, J. A., 1961.

Birge, Jane S. Verbal responses in transfer. Doctoral dissertation. New Haven: Yale University Press, 1941. **780**

Birnbaum, I. M. Long-term retention of first-list associations in the A–B, A–C paradigm. *Journal of Verbal Learning and Verbal Behavior*, 1965, *4*, 515–520. **1098, 1099**

Birnbaum, I. M. Unlearning in two directions. *Journal of Experimental Psychology*, 1966, *72*, 61–67. **1095**

Birnbaum, I. M. Unlearning as a function of second-list dominance. *Journal of Verbal Learning and Verbal Behavior*, 1968, *7*, 257–259. **1087, 1098**

Bishop, G. H. Relation of pain sensory threshold to form of mechanical stimulator. *Journal of Neurophysiology*, 1949, *12*, 51–57. **160**

Bishop, G. H. The relation of nerve fiber size to modality of sensation. In W. Montagna (Ed.), *Advances in biology of skin:* Vol. 1, *Cutaneous innervation.* New York: Pergamon, 1960. Pp. 99–111. **162**

Bishop, G. H., see also Bartley, S. H., 1933; Heinbecker, P., 1933.

Bishop, H. P. Separation thresholds for colored bars with and without luminance contrast. *Psychonomic Science*, 1966, *4*, 223–224. **428n**

Bishop, H. P. Separation thresholds for bar targets presented with color contrast only. *Psychonomic Science*, 1966, *6*, 293–294. **428n**

Bitterman, M. E. Toward a comparative psychology of learning. *American Psychologist*, 1960, *15*, 704–712. **603**

Bitterman, M. E. Classical conditioning in the goldfish as a function of the CS–US interval. *Journal of Comparative and Physiological Psychology*, 1964, *58*, 359–366. **559, 578**

Bitterman, M. E. The CS–US interval in classical and avoidance conditioning. In W. F. Prokasy (Ed.), *Classical conditioning.* New York: Appleton, 1965. **559, 729**

Bitterman, M. E., Krauskopf, J., & Hochberg, J. E. Threshold for visual form: A diffusion model. *American Journal of Psychology*, 1954, *67*, 205–219. **443**

Bitterman, M. E., Tyler, D. W., & Elam, C. B. Simultaneous and successive discrimination under identical stimulation conditions. *American Journal of Psychology*, 1955, *68*, 237–248. **775**

Bitterman, M. E., & Wodinsky, J. Simultaneous and successive discrimination. *Psychological Review*, 1953, *60*, 371–376. **774**

Bitterman, M. E., see also Behrend, E. R., 1962; Bridges, C. C., 1954; Crum, J., 1951; Deatherage, B. H., 1952; Gonzalez, R. C., 1962, 1965; Hochberg, J., 1951; Krauskopf, J., 1954; Lowes, G., 1967; Stevenson, H. W., 1955; Weise, P., 1951.

Bixby, F. L. A phenomenological study of luster. *Journal of General Psychology*, 1926, *1*, 136. **427**

Björkman, M., & Ekman, G. *Experimental psykologiska metoder.* Stockholm: Almqvist & Wiksell, 1962. **79**

Black, A. H. The extinction of avoidance responses under curare. *Journal of Comparative and Physiological Psychology*, 1958, *51*, 519–524. **732**

Black, A. H. Heart rate changes during avoidance learning in dogs. *Canadian Journal of Psychology*, 1959, *13*, 229–242. **726**

Black, A. H. Cardiac conditioning in curarized dogs: The relationship between heart rate and skeletal behaviour. In W. F. Prokasy (Ed.), *Classical conditioning.* New York: Appleton, 1965. Pp. 20–47. **711**

Black, A. H., Carlson, N. J., & Solomon, R. L. Exploratory studies of the conditioning of autonomic responses in curarized dogs. *Psychological Monographs*, 1962, *76*. **711**

Black, A. H. & Lang, W. M. Cardiac conditioning and skeletal responding in curarized dogs. *Psychological Review*, 1964, *71*, 80–85. **711**

Black, A. H., see also Church, R. M., 1958; deToledo, L., 1966; Kamin, L. J., 1963.

Black, J. W. Multiple-choice intelligibility tests. *Journal of Speech and Hearing Disorders*, 1957, *22*, 213–235. **255**

Black, R. W. On the combination of drive and incentive motivation. *Psychological Review*, 1965, *72*, 310–317. **807**

Black, R. W. Shifts in magnitude of reward and contrast effects in instrumental and selective learning: A reinterpretation. *Psychological Review*, 1968, *75*, 114–126. **638n**

Black, W. C., see Perez-Cruet, J., 1963.

Blackwell, H. R. Contrast thresholds of the human eye. *Journal of the Optical Society of America*, 1946, *36*, 624-643. **304**

Blackwell, H. R. Psychophysical thresholds: Experimental studies of methods of measurements. *Bulletin of the Engineering Research Institute, University of Michigan*, No. 36, 1953. **19, 20**

Blanchard, D. C., see Blanchard, R. J., 1966.

Blanchard, R. J., & Blanchard, D. C. Food deprivation and reactivity to shock. *Psychonomic Science*, 1966, *4*, 317-318. **710**

Blank, A. A. The Luneburg theory of binocular visual space. *Journal of the Optical Society of America*, 1953, *43*, 717-727. **493**

Blank, A. A. The geometry of vision. *British Journal of Physiological Optics* (3), 1957, *14*, 154-169, 222-235. **493**

Blank, A. A. The Luneburg theory of binocular space perception. In S. Koch (Ed.), *Psychology: A study of a science*. Study I. Vol. 1. New York: McGraw-Hill, 1959. **493**

Blank, A. A., see also Hardy, L. H., 1953.

Blankenship, A. B., see Whitely, P. L., 1936.

Blatt, M. H., see Mayzner, M. S., 1965.

Blattner, K. C., see Peterson, M. J., 1963, 1964.

Blessing, W. W., Landauer, A. A., & Coltheart, M. The effect of false perspective cues on distance- and size-judgments: An examination of the invariance hypothesis. *American Journal of Psychology*, 1967, *60*, 250-256. **514**

Bleything, W. B. Factors influencing stereoscopic localization. *American Journal of Optometry*, 1957, *34*, 416-429. **513**

Bliss, J. see Dunn, S., 1958.

Blodgett, H. C. The effect of the introduction of reward upon the maze performance of rats. *University of California Publications in Psychology*, 1929, *4*, 113-134. **795**

Blodgett, H. C., see also Jeffress, L., 1956, 1962.

Blomquist, A. J., see Benjamin, R. M., 1968.

Bloom, G. Studies on the olfactory epithelium of the frog and the toad with the aid of light and electron microscopy. *Zeitschrift für Zellforschung der Mikroskopische Anatomie: Abtung Histochemie*, 1954, *41*, 89-100. **195**

Bloom, W., see Thompson, T. I., 1966.

Bloomfield, T. M. Some temporal properties of behavioral contrast. *Journal of the Experimental Analysis of Behavior*, 1967, *10*, 159-164. **641**

Blough, D. S. A method for obtaining psychophysical thresholds from the pigeon. *Journal of the Experimental Analysis of Behavior*, 1958, *1*, 31-43. **20, 756**

Blough, D. S. Animal psychophysics. *Scientific American*, 1961, *205*, 113-122. **756**

Blough, D. S. Delayed matching in the pigeon. *Journal of the Experimental Analysis of Behavior*, 1959, *2*, 151-160. **788, 789**

Blough, D. S. Definition and measurement in generalization research. In D. I. Mostofsky (Ed.), *Stimulus generalization*. Stanford: Stanford University Press, 1965. Pp. 30-37. **760**

Blough, D. S. The study of animal sensory processes by operant methods. In W. K. Honig (Ed.), *Operant behavior: Areas of research and application*. New York: Appleton, 1966. **607, 694, 753**

Blough, D., & Millward, R. Operant conditioning and verbal learning. *Annual Review of Psychology*, 1965, *16*, 63-94. **1001n**

Blum, H. B., see Fabian, F. W., 1943.

Blumenfeld, W. Untersuchungen über die scheinbare Grösse im Schraume. *Zeitschrift für Psychologie*, 1913, *65*, 241-404. **493**

Bocca, E., & Calearo, C. Central hearing processes. In J. Jerger (Ed.), *Modern developments in audiology*, New York: Academic Press, 1963. **235**

Boch, R. D., and Jones, L. V. *The measurement and prediction of judgment and choice*. San Francisco: Holden-Day, 1968. **54**

Boe, E., see Holborn, S., 1965.

Boe, E. E. Extinction as a function of intensity of punishment, amount of training, and reinforcement of a competing response. *Canadian Journal of Psychology*, 1964, *18*, 328-342. **738**

Boe, E. E., & Church, R. M. Permanent effects of punishment during extinction. *Journal of Comparative and Physiological Psychology*, 1967, *63*, 486-492. **738**

Boeder, P., see Hardy, L. H., 1953.

Bogart, L. M., see McBurney, D. H., 1962, 1967.

Bogartz, W. H., see Atkinson, R. C., 1959; Maltzman, I., 1958.

Bolles, R. C. The usefulness of the drive concept. In M. R. Jones (Ed.), *Nebraska symposium on motivation*. Lincoln, Nebraska: University of Nebraska Press, 1958. Pp. 1-33. **795n**

Bolles, R. C. Group and individual performance as a function of intensity and kind of deprivation. *Journal of Comparative and Physiological Psychology*, 1959, *52*, 579-585. **821**

Bolles, R. C. Generalization of deprivation-produced stimuli. *Psychological Reports*, 1961, *9*, 623-626. **831**

Bolles, R. C. The readiness to eat and drink: The effect of deprivation conditions. *Journal of Comparative and Physiological Psychology*, 1962, *55*, 230-234. **814, 816**

Bolles, R. C. A failure to find evidence of the estrus cycle in the rat's activity level. *Psychological Reports*, 1963, *12*, 530. **825**

Bolles, R. C. Readiness to eat: Effects of age, sex, and weight loss. *Journal of Comparative and Physiological Psychology*, 1965, *60*, 88-92. **813, 816**

Bolles, R. C. *Theory of motivation*. New York: Harper & Row, 1967. **793n, 795n, 801, 802n, 803, 807, 812, 816**

Bolles, R. C. The role of eye movements in the Müller-Lyer illusion. *Perception and Psychophysics*, 1969, *6*, 175-176. **476n**

Bolles, R. C., & de Lorge, J. The rat's adjustment to a-diurnal feeding cycles. *Journal of Comparative and Physiological Psychology*, 1962, *55*, 760-762. **820**

Bolles, R. C., Hulicka, I. M., & Hanly, B. Color judgment as a function of stimulus conditions and memory color. *Canadian Journal of Psychology*, 1959, *13*, 175-185. **424**

Bolles, R. C., & Rapp, H. M. Readiness to eat and drink: Effect of stimulus conditions. *Journal of Comparative and Physiological Psychology*, 1965, *60*, 93-97. **818**

Bolles, R. C., Rapp, H. M., & White, G. C. Failure of sexual activity to reinforce female rats. *Journal of Comparative and Physiological Psychology*, 1968, *65*, 311-313. **693**

Bolles, R. C., & Stokes, L. W. Rat's anticipation of diurnal and a-diurnal feeding. *Journal of Comparative and Physiological Psychology*, 1965, *60*, 290-294. **820**

Bolles, R. C., & Younger, M. S. The effect of hunger on the threshold of behavioral arousal. *Psychonomic Science*, 1967, *7*, 243-244. **823**

Boneau, C. A., & Cole, J. L. Decision theory, the pigeon, and the psychophysical function. *Psychological Review*, 1967, *74*, 123-135. **757**

Bontrager, H., see Epstein, W., 1962.

Borer, K. T. Disappearance of preferences and aversions for sapid solutions in rats ingesting untasted fluids. *Journal of Comparative and Physiological Psychology*, 1968, *65*, 213-221. **797**

Borg, G., Diamant, H., Oakley, B., Ström, L., & Zotterman, Y. A comparative study of neural and psychophysical responses to gustatory stimuli. In T. Hayashi (Ed.), *Olfaction and taste.* Vol. II. New York: Pergamon, 1967. Pp. 253–264. **175, 185**

Boring, E. G. Urban's tables and the method of constant stimuli. *American Journal of Psychology,* 1917, *28,* 280–293. **33**

Boring, E. G. A new ambiguous figure. *American Journal of Psychology,* 1930, *42,* 444–445. **439**

Boring, E. G. *The physical dimension of consciousness.* New York: Century, 1933. **490**

Boring, E. G. Size-constancy and Emmert's law. *American Journal of Psychology,* 1940, *53,* 293–295. **511**

Boring, E. G. *Sensation and perception in the history of experimental psychology.* New York: Appleton, 1942. **65, 118, 250, 427, 482, 511, 521, 522, 525, 527**

Boring, E. G. The moon illusion. *American Journal of Physics,* 1943, *11,* 55–60. **511**

Boring, E. G. *A history of experimental psychology.* (2nd ed.) New York: Appleton, 1950. **793n, 794**

Boring, E. C., & Edwards, W. What is Emmert's law? *American Journal of Psychology,* 1951, *64,* 416–422. **511**

Boring, E. G. Visual perception and invariance. *Psychological Review,* 1952, *59,* 141–148. (a) **510, 539**

Boring, E. G. The Gibsonian visual field. *Psychological Review,* 1952, *59,* 246–247. (b) **510**

Boring, E. G., Langfeld, H. S., & Weld, H. P. *Foundations of psychology.* New York: Wiley, 1948. **243**

Boring, E. G., *see also* Holway, A. H., 1941.

Born, D., *see* Wickens, D. D., 1963.

Bornstein, R., *see* Grier, J. B., 1966.

Borresen, C. R., & Lichte, W. H. Shape constancy: Dependence upon stimulus familiarity. *Journal of Experimental Psychology,* 1962, *63,* 91–97. **515**

Borresen, C. R., *see also* Lichte, W. H., 1967.

Borst, J. M., *see* Cooper, F. S., 1952.

Bosley, J., *see* Stone, H., 1965.

Bosley, J. J., *see* De Soto, C. B., 1962.

Bossom, J., & Held, R. Shifts in egocentric localization following prolonged displacement of the retinal image. *American Psychologist,* 1957, *12,* 454 (abstract). **537n**

Bossom, J., *see also* Held, R., 1961.

Bouman, M. A. Visual thresholds for line-shaped targets. *Journal of the Optical Society of America,* 1953, *43,* 209–211. **303**

Bourdon, B. *La perception visuelle de l'espace.* Paris: Schleicher, 1902. **520**

Bourne, G. H. (Ed.), *The structure and function in muscle.* Vol. 1, *Structure.* New York: Academic Press, 1960. **91**

Bourne, G. H., *see also* Baradi, A. F., 1951.

Bourne, L. E., Jr. Effects of delay of information feedback and task complexity on the identification of concepts. *Journal of Experimental Psychology,* 1957, *54,* 201–207. **973, 975**

Bourne, L. E., Jr. Learning and utilization of conceptual rules. In B. Kleinmuntz (Ed.), *Concepts and the structure of memory.* New York: Wiley, 1967. Pp. 1–32. **966**

Bourne, L. E., Jr., & Bunderson, T. V. Effects of delay of informative feedback and length of postfeedback interval on concept identification. *Journal of Experimental Psychology,* 1963, *65,* 1–5. **973, 975**

Bourne, L. E., Jr., Goldstein, S., & Link, W. E. Concept learning as a function of availability of previously presented information. *Journal of Experimental Psychology,* 1964, *67,* 439–448. **972**

Bourne, L. E., Jr., Guy, D. E., Dodd, D. H., & Justesen, D. R. Concept identification: The effects of varying length in informational components of the intertrial interval. *Journal of Experimental Psychology,* 1965, *69,* 624–629. **973, 974**

Bourne, L. E., & Restle, F. Mathematical theory of concept

identification. *Psychological Review,* 1959, *66,* 278–296. **949, 957, 973, 1001**

Bourne, L. E. Jr., *see also* Dodd, D. H., 1967; Haygood, R., 1965; Leibowitz, H., 1956.

Bousfield, W. A. The occurrence of clustering in the recall of randomly arranged associates. *Journal of General Psychology,* 1953, *49,* 229–240. **891**

Bousfield, W. A., & Elliott, M. H. The effect of fasting on the eating behavior of rats. *Journal of Genetic Psychology,* 1934, *45,* 227–237. **814, 820**

Bousfield, W. A., Steward, J. R., & Cowan, T. R. The use of free associational norms for the prediction of clustering. Tech. Rep. No. 36, Contract Nonr-631(00), Office of Naval Research and University of Connecticut, 1961. **881**

Bousfield, W. A., Whitmarsh, G. A., & Berkowitz, H. Partial response identities in associative clustering. *Journal of General Psychology,* 1960, *63,* 233–238. **880**

Bousfield, W. A., Whitmarsh, G. A., & Danick, J. J. Partial response identity in verbal generalization. *Psychological Reports,* 1958, *4,* 703–713. **880**

Bousfield, W. A. *see also* Cohen, B. H., 1957.

Bower, G. H. Partial and correlated reward in escape learning. *Journal of Experimental Psychology,* 1960, *59,* 126–130. **723, 724**

Bower, G. H. Application of a model to paired-associate learning. *Psychometrika,* 1961, *26,* 255–281. **990**

Bower, G. H. A contrast effect in differential conditioning. *Journal of Experimental Psychology,* 1961, *62,* 196–199. **638, 639**

Bower, G. H. Correlated delay of reinforcement. *Journal of Comparative and Physiological Psychology,* 1961, *54,* 196–203. **843**

Bower, G. H. An association model for response and training variables in paired-associate learning. *Psychological Review,* 1962, *69,* 34–53. **994**

Bower, G. H. The influence of graded reductions in reward and prior frustrating events upon the magnitude of the frustration effect. *Journal of Comparative and Physiological Psychology,* 1962, *55,* 582–587. **810**

Bower, G. H., Fowler, H., & Trapold, M. A. Escape learning as a function of amount of shock reduction. *Journal of Experimental Psychology,* 1959, *58,* 482–484. **721**

Bower, G. H., & Miller, N. E. Rewarding and punishing effects from stimulating the same place in the rat's brain. *Journal of Comparative and Physiological Psychology,* 1958, *51,* 669–674. **647**

Bower, G. H., & Theios, J. A learning model for discrete performance levels. In R. C. Atkinson (Ed.), *Studies in mathematical psychology.* Stanford: Stanford University Press, 1964. Pp. 1–31. **996**

Bower, G. H., & Trabasso, D. Reversals prior to solutions in concept identification. *Journal of Experimental Psychology,* 1963, *66,* 409–418. **954, 974**

Bower, G. H., & Trabasso, T. R. Concept identification. In R. C. Atkinson (Ed.), *Studies in mathematical psychology.* Stanford: Stanford University Press, 1964. Pp. 32–94. **949, 950, 951, 953**

Bower, G. H., *see also* Atkinson, R. C., 1965; Hilgard, E. R., 1966; Trabasso, T., 1964, 1966.

Bower, T. G. R. Discrimination of depth in premotor infants. *Psychonomic Science.,* 1964, *1,* 368. **547**

Bowers, C., *see* Davis, H., 1967.

Boycott, B. B., *see* Dowling, J. E., 1966.

Boynton, R. M. Theory of color vision. *Journal of the Optical Society of America,* 1960, *50,* 929–944. **328**

Boynton, R. M. Some temporal factors in vision. In W. A. Rosenblith (Ed.), *Sensory communication.* New York: Wiley, 1961. Pp. 739–756. **307**

Boynton, R. M. Vision. In J. Sidowski (Ed.), *Experimental methods and instrumentation in psychology.* New York: McGraw-Hill, 1966. **357**

Boynton, R. M., Bush, W. R., & Enoch, J. M. Rapid changes in foveal sensitivity resulting from direct and indirect adapting stimuli. *Journal of the Optical Society of America,* 1954, *44,* 56–60. **310**

Boynton, R. M., & Das, S. R. Visual adaptation: Increased efficiency resulting from spectrally-distributed mixtures of stimuli. *Science,* 1966, *154,* 1581–1583. **336**

Boynton, R. M., & Gordon, J. Bezold-Brucke hue shift measured by color-naming technique. *Journal of the Optical Society of America,* 1965, *55,* 78–86. **347**

Boynton, R. M., & Kaiser, P. Vision: The additivity law made to work for heterochromatic photometry with bipartite fields. *Science,* 1968, *161,* 366–368. **327**

Boynton, R. M., Kandel, G., & Onley, J. W. Rapid chromatic adaptation of normal and dichromatic observers. *Journal of the Optical Society of America,* 1959, *49,* 654–666. **337**

Boynton, R. M., Schafer, W., & Neun, M. E. Hue-wavelength relation measured by color-naming method for three retinal locations. *Science,* 1964, *146,* 666–668. **348**

Boynton, R. M., Scheibner, H., Yates, T., & Rinalducci, E. Theory and experiments concerning the heterochromatic threshold-reduction factor (HTRF). *Journal of the Optical Society of America,* 1965, *55,* 1672–1685. **343**

Boynton, R. M., & Triedman, M. H. A psychophysical and electrophysiological study of light adaptation. *Journal of Experimental Psychology,* 1953, *46,* 125–134. **310**

Boynton, R. M., & Wagner, M. Two-color threshold as test of color vision. *Journal of the Optical Society of America,* 1961, *51,* 429–440. **343**

Boynton, R. M., see also Scheibner, H., 1968; Wheeless, L. L., Jr., 1966.

Brackbill, Y., Adams, G., & Reaney, T. P. A parametric study of the delay-retention effect. *Psychological Reports,* 1967, *20,* 433–434. **687**

Braden, I., see Jones, A., 1961.

Brady, J. V., see Hunt, H. F., 1955; Perez-Cruet, J., 1963; Stein, L., 1958.

Braine, L. G. Disorientation of forms: An examination of Rock's theory. *Psychonomic Science,* 1965, *3,* 541–542. **451**

Braly, K. W. The influence of past experience on visual perception. *Journal of Experimental Psychology,* 1933, *16,* 613–643. **440**

Brand, H., Woods, P. J., & Sakoda, J. N. Anticipation of reward as a function of partial reinforcement. *Journal of Experimental Psychology.* 1956, *52,* 18–22. **932**

Braunstein, M. L. The perception of depth through motion. *Psychological Bulletin,* 1962, *59,* 422–433. **505**

Braunstein, M. L. Motion and texture as sources of slant information. *Journal of Experimental Psychology,* 1968, *78,* 247–253. **505**

Braunstein, M. L., & Payne, J. W. Perspective and the rotating trapezoid. *Journal of the Optical Society of America,* 1968, *58,* 399–403. **518**

Bray, C. W., see Wever, E. G., 1930.

Brearley, E. A., & Kenshalo, D. R. Behavioral measurements of the sensitivity of cat's upper lip to warm and cool stimuli. *Journal of Comparative and Physiological Psychology,* 1970, *70,* 1–4. **150**

Brefer, L. see Maltzman, I., 1958.

Breland, K., & Breland, M. The misbehavior of organisms. *American Psychologist,* 1961, *16,* 681–684. **746**

Breland, M., see Breland, K., 1961.

Brelsford, J. Jr., see Theios, H. J., 1966.

Bremer, F. Neurogenic factors influencing the evoked potentials of the cerebral cortex. In W. A. Rosenblith (Ed.), *Sensory communication.* New York: Wiley, 1961. **233**

Breneman, E. J., see Bartleson, C. J., 1967.

Bressler, J. Judgments in absolute units as a psychophysical method. *Archives of Psychology* (New York), 1933, *152.* **30**

Brethower, D. R., & Reynolds, G. S. A facilitative effect of punishment on unpunished behavior. *Journal of the Experimental Analysis of Behavior,* 1962, *5,* 191–199. **779**

Brewster, D. Ueber Schwingungen in der Netzhaut, erregt durch die Wirkung leuchtender Punkte und Linien. *Poggendorff, Annalen der Physiologie und Chemie,* 1833, *27,* 490–497. **411**

Bridges, C. C., & Bitterman, M. E. The measurement of autokinetic movement. *American Journal of Psychology,* 1954, *67,* 525–529. **529**

Bridgman, C. S. Analysis of a recently discovered stereoscopic effect. *American Journal of Psychology,* 1964, *77,* 138–143. **483**

Briggs, G. E. Acquisition, extinction and recovery functions in retroactive inhibition. *Journal of Experimental Psychology,* 1954, *47,* 285–293. **1092, 1099**

Briggs, G. E. Retroactive inhibition as a function of degree of original and interpolated learning. *Journal of Experimental Psychology,* 1957, *53,* 60–67. **1085, 1086**

Briggs, G. E., Thompson, R. F., & Brogden, W. J. Retention functions in reproductive inhibition. *Journal of Experimental Psychology,* 1954, *48,* 419–423. **1092, 1099**

Brimer, C. J. Inhibition and disinhibition of an operant response. *Bulletin of the Maritime Psychological Association,* 1964, *13,* 40–45. **714**

Brimer, C. J., & Kamin, L. J. Disinhibition, habituation, sensitization, and the conditioned emotional response. *Journal of Comparative and Physiological Psychology,* 1963, *56,* 508–516. **714**

Brimer, C. J., see also Kamin, L. J., 1963.

Brindley, G. S. The effects on colour vision of adaptation to very bright lights. *Journal of Physiology,* 1953, *122,* 332–350. **368**

Brindley, G. [S.] *Physiology of the retina and the visual pathway.* London: Edward Arnold, 1960. **323**

Brindley, G. S., & Merton, P. A. The absence of position sense in the human eye. *Journal of Physiology,* 1960, *153,* 127–130. **531**

Britt, S. H. Retroactive inhibition: A review of the literature. *Psychological Bulletin,* 1936, *32,* 381–440. **1080, 1088**

Broadbent, D. E. Failures of attention in selective listening. *Journal of Experimental Psychology,* 1952, *44,* 428–433. **259**

Broadbent, D. E. *Perception and communication.* New York: Pergamon, 1958. **236, 258, 259, 997, 998**

Broadbent, D. E. Flow of information within the organism. *Journal of Verbal Learning and Verbal Behavior,* 1963, *2,* 34–39. **998, 1114**

Broadhurst, P. L. Emotionality and the Yerkes–Dodson Law. *Journal of Experimental Psychology,* 1957, *54,* 345–352. **799, 830**

Brobeck, J. R. Regulation of feeding and drinking. In J. Field, H. W. Magoun, and V. E. Hall (Eds.), *Handbook of physiology.* Vol. II. Washington, D.C.: American Physiological Society, 1960. Pp. 1197–1206. **796**

Broca, A., & Sulzer, D. La sensation lumineuse en fonction du temps. *Comptes Rendus de Séances de l'Académie des Sciences,* Paris, 1902, *134,* 831–834; 1903, *137,* 944–946. **307**

Brock, T. C., see Schuck, J. R., 1964.

Brodhun, E., see König, A., 1889.

Brody, N. Anxiety and the variability of word associates. *Journal of Abnormal and Social Psychology,* 1964, *68,* 331–334. **876**

Brogden, W. J. Sensory preconditioning. *Journal of Experimental Psychology,* 1939, *25,* 323–332. **564**

Brogden, W. J., see also Briggs, G. E., 1954; Culler, E., 1935; Hoffeld, D. R., 1960.

Bromer, J. A., see Harlow, H. F., 1938.

Brooks, V., see Hochberg, J., 1958, 1960, 1962.

Brookshire, K., see Parducci, A., 1956.

Brookshire, K. H., see Moran, J. M., 1959.

Brosgole, L., & Whalen, P. M. The effect of meaning on the allocation of visually induced movement. *Perception and Psychophysics*, 1967, *2*, 275–277. **522**

Brosgole, L., see also Rock, I., 1964.

Brown, B. L., see Richardson, J., 1966.

Brown, B. R., see Vincent, R. J., 1969.

Brown, C. S., see Brown, J. S., 1966.

Brown, D. L., see Owens, J. A., 1968.

Brown, D. R., & Owen, D. H. The metrics of visual form: Methodological dyspepsia. *Psychological Bulletin*, 1967, *68*, 243–259. **449**

Brown, D. R., see also Forsyth, G. A., 1967.

Brown, E., see Fisher, G. L., 1965.

Brown, H. M., Dustman, R. E., & Beck, E. C. Sensitization in planaria. *Physiology and Behavior*, 1966, *1*, 305–308. **556**

Brown, H. O., see Smith, S. M., 1947.

Brown, J. Some tests of the decay theory of immediate memory. *Quarterly Journal of Experimental Psychology.* 1958, *10*, 12–21. **1110, 1114**

Brown, J. F. The visual perception of velocity. *Psychologische Forschung* 1931, *14*, 199–232. **508**

Brown, J. F. The thresholds for visual movement. *Psychologische Forschung.*, 1931, *14*, 249–269. **520**

Brown, J. F., & Voth, A. C. The path of seen movement as a function of the vector field. *American Journal of Psychology*, 1937, *49*, 543–563. **459, 527n**

Brown, J. L. The effect of drive on learning with secondary reinforcement. *Journal of Comparative and Physiological Psychology*, 1956, *49*, 254–260. **668**

Brown, J. L. Flicker and intermittent stimulation. In C. H. Graham (Ed.). *Vision and visual perception*. New York: Wiley, 1965. Pp. 251–320. **311**

Brown, J. L., see also Graham, C. H., 1965; Sechzer, J. A., 1964.

Brown, J. S. *The motivation of behavior*. New York: McGraw-Hill, 1961. **795, 796, 799, 800, 801, 809, 811, 816, 842**

Brown, J. S. Factors affecting self-punitive locomotor behavior. In B. A. Campbell & R. M. Church (Eds.), *Punishment*. New York: Appleton, 1969. **725**

Brown, J. S., Anderson, D. C., & Brown, C. S. Conflict as a function of food-deprivation time during approach training, avoidance training, and conflict tests. *Journal of Experimental Psychology*, 1966, *72*, 390–400. **809**

Brown, J. S., & Belloni, M. Performance as a function of deprivation time following periodic feeding in an isolated environment. *Journal of Comparative and Physiological Psychology*, 1963, *56*, 105–110. **830**

Brown, J. S., & Farber, I. E. Secondary motivational systems. *Annual Review of Psychology*, 1968, *19*, 99–134. **794n, 795, 798, 803, 804, 805, 807, 808, 811**

Brown, J. S., Kalish, H. I., & Farber, I. E. Conditioned fear as revealed by magnitude of startle response to an auditory stimulus. *Journal of Experimental Psychology*, 1951, *41*, 317–328. **803, 804**

Brown, J. S., Martin, R. C., & Morrow, M. W. Self-punitive behavior in the rat: Facilitative effects of punishment on resistance to extinction. *Journal of Comparative and Physiological Psychology*, 1964, *57*, 127–133. **725**

Brown, K. T. An optical illusion of spontaneous fluctuations in apparent size. *American Journal of Psychology*, 1954, *67*, 533–538. **480**

Brown, K. T., & Murakami, M. A new receptor potential

of the monkey retina with no detectable latency. *Nature*, 1964, *201*, 626–628. **307**

Brown, K. T., Watanabe, K., and Murakami, M. Early and late receptors potentials of monkey cones and rods. *Cold Spring Harbor Symposia on Quantitative Biology*, 1965, *30*, 457–482. **330**

Brown, L., see Hayes, W. J., 1961; Jenkins, J. J., 1965.

Brown, L. K., Jenkins, J. J., & Lavik, J. Response transfer as a function of verbal associative strength. *Journal of Experimental Psychology*, 1966, *71*, 138–142. **1048**

Brown, L. T., see Robinson, J. S., 1964.

Brown, P. K., see Wald, G., 1965.

Brown, R. H. Velocity discrimination and the intensity–time relation. *Journal of the Optical Society of America*, 1955, *45*, 189–192. **520**

Brown, R. H., & Conklin, J. E. The lower threshold of visible movement as a function of exposure time. *American Journal of Psychology*, 1954, *67*, 104–110. **520**

Brown, R. H., see also Graham, C. H., 1939; Niven, J. I., 1944.

Brown, R. W., & Berko, J. Word-association and the acquisition of grammar. *Child Development*, 1960, *31*, 8–14. **874**

Brown, R. W., & Lenneberg, E. H. A study in language and cognition. *Journal of Abnormal and Social Psychology*, 1954, *49*, 454–462. **423**

Brown, W. To what extent is memory measured by a single recall? *Journal of Experimental Psychology*, 1923, *6*, 377–385. **5n**

Brown, W. L., see Crum, J., 1951.

Brown, W. P. Emotional indicators in word association. *British Journal of Psychology*, 1965, *56*, 401–412. **864**

Brown, W. P. The Yerkes–Dodson law repealed. *Psychological Reports*, 1965, *17*, 663–666. **830**

Brown, W. R. J. Color discrimination of twelve observers. *Journal of the Optical Society of America*, 1957, *47*, 137. **361**

Brown, W. R. J., & MacAdam, D. L. Visual sensitivities to combined chromaticity and luminance differences. *Journal of the Optical Society of America*, 1949, *39*, 808. **361**

Bruce, D., & Cofer, C. N. 1967. An examination of recognition and free recall as measures of acquisition and long-term retention. *Journal of Experimental Psychology*, 1967, *75*, 283–289. **893**

Bruce, H. M., see Parkes, A. S., 1961.

Bruce, R. W. Conditions of transfer of training. *Journal of Experimental Psychology*, 1933, *16*, 343–361. **1045, 1055, 1063, 1068**

Brücke, E. Über den Nutzeffect intermittierender Netzhautreizungen. *S.-B. K Akad. Wiss., Wien, math.-nat. Kl.*, 1864, *49*, II, 128–153. **314**

Bruell, J. H., & Albee, G. W. Notes towards a motor theory of visual egocentric localization. *Psychological Review*, 1955, *62*, 391–399. **530, 534**

Bruell, J. H., see also Werner, H., 1953.

Brugge, J. F., Dubrovsky, N., & Rose, J. E. Some discharge characteristics of single neurons in cat's auditory cortex. *Science*, 1964, *146*, 433–434. **265**

Brugge, J. F., see also Rose, J. E., 1967.

Bruner, J. S., Goodnow, J. J., & Austin, G. A. *A study of thinking*. New York: Wiley, 1956. **943, 947, 961, 963, 970**

Bruner, J. S., Miller, G. A., & Zimmerman, C. Discriminative skill and discriminative matching in perceptual recognition. *Journal of Experimental Psychology*, 1955, *49*, 187–192. **256**

Bruner, J., Postman, L., & Mosteller, F. A note on the measurement of reversals of perspective. *Psychometrika*, 1950, *15*, 63–72. **519**

Bruner, J. S., Postman, L., & Rodrigues, J. Expectations and the perception of color. *American Journal of Psychology*, 1951, *64*, 216–227. **424**

Bruner, J., & Tauc, L. Habituation at the synaptic level in *Aplysia. Nature*, 1966, *210*, 37–39. **592**

Bruner, J., *see also* Kehoe, J. S., 1966.

Brunswik, E. Zur Entwicklung der Albedowahrnehmung. *Zeitschrift für Psychologie*, 1929, *109*, 40–115. **399, 406**

Brunswik, E. *Wahrnehmung und Gegenstandswelt: Grundlegung einer Psychologie vom Gegenstand her.* Leipzig: Deuticke, 1934. **437**

Brunswik, E. The conceptual framework of psychology. In *International Encyclopedia of Unified Science.* Vol. 1, No. 10. Chicago: University of Chicago Press, 1952. **401, 437, 502**

Brunswik, E. *Perception and the representative design of psychological experiments.* (2nd ed.) Berkeley: University of California Press, 1956. **437, 463, 464, 502**

Brunswik, E., & Kamiya, J. Ecological cue-validity of "proximity" and other Gestalt factors. *American Journal of Psychology*, 1953, *66*, 20–32. **442**

Brunswik, E., *see also* Tolman, E. C., 1935.

Brush, E. S., *see* Brush, F. R., 1955; Solomon, R. L., 1956.

Brush, F. R. The effects of shock intensity on the acquisition and extinction of an avoidance response in dogs. *Journal of Comparative and Physiological Psychology*, 1957, *50*, 547–552. **729**

Brush, F. R. An efficient, inexpensive relay grid scrambler for multiple boxes. *Journal of the Experimental Analysis of Behavior*, 1967, *10*, 393–394. **706**

Brush, F. R., Brush, E. S., & Solomon, R. L. Traumatic avoidance learning: The effects of CS–US interval with a delayed-conditioning procedure. *Journal of Comparative and Physiological Psychology*, 1955, *48*, 285–293. **729**

Brush, F. R., *see also* Church, R. M., 1956.

Brust-Carmona, H., *see* Hernandez-Peon, R., 1961.

Bryan, J. D., *see* Young, R. K., 1963.

Bryan, J. S., *see* Nelson, P. G., 1966.

Bryden, M., & Rainey, C. Left-right differences in tachistocopic recognition. *Journal of Experimental Psychology*, 1963, *66*, 568–571. **444**

Buchsbaum, W. H., *see* Mayzner, M. S., 1965.

Buddulph, R., *see* Shower, E. G., 1931.

Budin, W., *see* Flavell, J. H., 1958.

Bugelski, B. R. Extinction with and without sub-goal reinforcement. *Journal of Comparative Psychology*, 1938, *26*, 121–133. **662, 673**

Bugelski, B. R. *The psychology of learning.* New York: Holt, Rinehart and Winston, 1956. **673**

Bugelski, B. R. In defense of remote associations. *Psychological Review*, 1965, *72*, 169–174. **1015**

Bugelski, B. R., & Cadwallader, T. C. A reappraisal of the transfer and retro-action surface. *Journal of Experimental Psychology*, 1956, *52*, 360–366. **1051, 1056, 1083**

Bugelski, B. R., & Scharlock, D. P. An experimental demonstration of unconscious mediated association. *Journal of Experimental Psychology*, 1952, *44*, 334–338. **781, 1071**

Buining, E., *see* Zwislocki, J., 1967.

Bujas, Z. Kontrast- und Hemmungserscheinungen bei disparaten simultanen Geschmacksreizen. *Acta Instituti Psychologica Universitatis Zagrebensis*, 1937, *2*, 3–12. **183**

Bujas, Z. Beobachtungen über den Restitutions Vorgang beim Geschmackssinn. *Acta Instituti Psychologici Universitatis Zagrebensis*, 1939, *3*, 3–14. **185**

Bujas, Z. L'adaptation gustative et son mécanisme. *Acta Instituti Psychologici Universitatis Zagrebensis*, 1953, *17*, 1–11. **184**

Bujas, Z., & Ostojčić, A. La sensibilité gustative en fonction dè la surface excitée. *Acta Instituti Psychologici Universitatis Zagrebensis*, 1941, *13*, 1–20. **175**

Bunch, M. E. The amount of transfer in rational learning as a function of time. *Journal of Comparative Psychology*, 1936, *22*, 325–337. **1037**

Bunderson, T. V., *see* Bourne, L. E., Jr., 1963.

Burgeat, M., *see* Hirsh, I. J., 1958.

Burger, J. F. Front–back discrimination of the hearing system. *Acustica*, 1958, *8*, 301–302. **266, 267**

Burger, J. F., *see also* Lochner, J. P. A., 1961.

Burgess, P. R., & Perl, E. R. Myelinated afferent fibers responding specifically to noxious stimulation of the skin. *Journal of Physiology*, 1967, *190*, 541–562. **162, 165**

Burkamp, W. Versuche über das Farbenwiedererkennen der Fische. *Zeitschrift für Sinnesphysik*, 1923, *55*, 133–170. **407**

Burke, C. J. Application of a linear model to two-person interactions. In R. R. Bush & W. K. Estes (Eds.), *Studies in mathematical learning theory.* Stanford: Stanford University Press, 1959. Pp. 180–203. **934**

Burke, C. J. Some two-person interactions. In K. J. Arrow, S. Karlin, & P. Suppes (Eds.), *Mathematical methods in the social sciences, 1959.* Stanford: Stanford University Press, 1960, 242–253. **934**

Burke, C. J. Two-person interactive learning: A progress report. In J. H. Criswell, H. Solomon, & P. Suppes (Eds.), *Mathematical methods in small group processes.* Stanford: Stanford University Press, 1962. Pp. 49–68. **934**

Burke, C. J., & Estes, W. K. A component model for stimulus variables in discrimination learning. *Psychometrika*, 1957, *22*, 133–145. **924, 934**

Burke, C. J., Estes, W. K., & Hellyer, S. Rate of verbal conditioning in relation to stimulus variability. *Journal of Experimental Psychology*, 1954, *48*, 153–161. **930**

Burke, C. J., *see also* Estes, W. K., 1953, 1955, 1957; Friedman, M. P., 1964.

Burmeister, E. Beitrag zur experimentellen Bestimmung geometrisch-optischer Taeuschungen. *Zeitschrift für Psychologie und Physiologie de Sinnes*, 1896, *12*, 355–394. **458**

Burnett, N. G., & Dallenbach, K. M. The experience of heat. *American Journal of Psychology*, 1927, *38*, 418–431. **148**

Burnham, C. A. Adaptation to prismatically induced curvature with invisible arm movements. *Psychonomic Science*, 1968, *10*, 273–274. **542**

Burnham, C. A., *see also* Festinger, L., 1967.

Burnham, R. W. Bezold's color-mixture effect. *American Journal of Psychology*, 1953, *66*, 377–385. **408**

Burnham, R. W., Hanes, R. M., & Bartleson, C. J. *Color: A guide to basic facts and concepts.* New York: Wiley, 1963. **348**

Burnham, R. W., *see also* Newhall, S. M., 1957.

Burns, S., *see* Postman, L., 1968.

Burnstein, E., *see* Birch, D., 1958.

Burrill, D. Y., *see* Goetzl, F. R., 1943.

Burton, H., *see* Benjamin, R. M., 1968.

Burzlaff, W. Methodologische Beitrage zum Problem der Farbenkonstanz. *Zeitschrift für Psychologie*, 1931, *119*, 177–235. **399, 406**

Bush, R. R., Galanter, E., & Luce, R. D. Characterization and classification of choice experiments. In R. D. Luce, R. R. Bush, & E. Galanter (Eds.), *Handbook of mathematical psychology.* Vol. I. New York: Wiley, 1963. Pp. 77–102. **907**

Bush, R. R., & Mosteller, F. A model for stimulus generalization and discrimination. *Psychological Review*, 1951, *58*, 413–423. **948, 1001**

Bush, R. R., & Mosteller, F. *Stochastic models for learning.* New York: Wiley, 1955. **911, 912n, 919n, 922**

Bush, R. R., *see also* Luce, R. D., 1963.

Bush, W. R., *see* Boynton, R. M., 1954.

Buss, A. *The psychology of aggression.* New York: Wiley, 1961. **900**

Buss, A. H. A study of concept formation as a function of reinforcement and stimulus generalization. *Journal of Experimental Psychology*, 1950, *40*, 494–503. **786**

Bussey, T., *see* Leibowitz, H., 1957.

Buswell, G. T. Fundamental reading habits: A study of their development. *Education Monographs* (Supplement), 1922, *21*. **389, 390**

Buswell, G. T. How adults read. *Education Monographs* (Supplement), 1937, *45*. **390**

Butler, B., *see* Seward, J. P., 1957.

Butler, R. A. The effect of deprivation of visual incentives on visual exploration motivation in monkeys. *Journal of Comparative and Physiological Psychology*, 1957, *50*, 177–179. **840**

Butler, R. A. Some effects of unilateral auditory masking upon the localization of sound in space. *Journal of the Acoustical Society of America*, 1962, *34*, 1100–1107. **263**

Butler, R. A. Investigative behavior. In A. M. Schrier, H. F. Harlow, & F. Stollnitz (Eds.), *Behavior of nonhuman primates.* Vol. II. New York: Academic Press, 1965. **673**

Butler, R. A., & Naunton, R. F. Role of stimulus frequency and duration in the phenomenon of localization shifts. *Journal of the Acoustical Society of America*, 1964, *36*, 917–922. **263, 266**

Butler, R. A., *see also* Roffler, S. K., 1968.

Buttrick, R. D., *see* Bartoshuk, L. M., 1969.

Buxton, C. E. The status of research on reminiscence. *Psychological Bulletin*, 1943, *40*, 313–340. **1122**

Byford, G. H. Non-linear relations between the corneal-retinal potential and horizontal eye movements. *Journal of Physiology*, 1963, *168*, 14P. **372**

Byram, G. M. The physical and photochemical basis of visual resolving power: I. The distribution of illumination in retinal images. *Journal of the Optical Society of America*, 1944, *34*, 571–591. **299**

Cadwallader, T. C., *see* Bugelski, B. R., 1956.

Cahill, H., & Hovland, C. I. The role of memory in the acquisition of concepts. *Journal of Experimental Psychology*, 1960, *59*, 137–144. **971**

Cain, W. S. An analysis of the odor properties of the linear aliphatic alcohols by direct psychophysical scaling. Unpublished M.S. thesis, Brown University, 1966. **85**

Cain, W. S. Olfactory adaptation and direct scaling of odor intensity, Unpublished doctoral dissertation, Brown University, 1968. **75, 210n**

Cairns, R. B. Development, maintenance, and extinction of social attachment behavior in sheep. *Journal of Comparative and Physiological Psychology*, 1966, *62*, 298–306. **581**

Cairns, R. B., & Johnson, D. L. The development of interspecies social attachments. *Psychonomic Science*, 1965, *2*, 337–338. **581**

Calabresi, P., *see* Beck, L. H., 1954.

Calavrezo, C. Über den Einfluss von Grössenanderungen auf die scheinbare Tiefe. *Psychologische Forschung*, 1934, *19*, 311–365. **495**

Calearo, C., *see* Bocca, E., 1963.

Calfee, R. C., & Atkinson, R. C. Paired-associate models and the effects of list length. *Journal of Mathematical Psychology*, 1965, *2*, 254–265. **999, 1009**

Calvin, J. S., Bicknell, E., & Sperling, D. S. Establishment

of a conditioned drive based upon the hunger drive. *Journal of Comparative and Physiological Psychology*, 1953, *46*, 173–175. **805**

Camerer, W. Ueber die Abhängigkeit des Geschmackssinns von der gereizten Stelle der Mundhöhle. *Zeitschrift für Biologie*, 1870, *6*, 440–452. **175**

Cameron, E. H., & Steele, W. M. The Poggendorf illusion. *Psychological Review, Monograph Supplement*, 1905, *7*, 83–111. **465**

Camp, D. S., Raymond, G. A., & Church, R. M. Temporal relationship between response and punishment. *Journal of Experimental Psychology*, 1967, *74*, 114–123. **737**

Campbell, B. A. The reinforcement difference limen (RDL) function for shock reduction. *Journal of Experimental Psychology*, 1956, *52*, 258–262. **722**

Campbell, B. A. Theory and research on the effects of water deprivation on random activity in the rat. In M. J. Wayner (Ed.), *Thirst*. Oxford: Pergamon, 1964. Pp. 317–334. **816**

Campbell, B. A., & Cicala, G. A. Studies of water deprivation in rats as a function of age. *Journal of Comparative and Physiological Psychology*, 1962, *55*, 763–768. **813, 814, 817, 822**

Campbell, B. A., & Kraeling, D. Response strength as a function of drive level and amount of drive reduction. *Journal of Experimental Psychology*. 1953, *45*, 97–101. **721, 722**

Campbell, B. A., & Lynch, G. S. Influence of hunger and thirst on the relationship between spontaneous activity and body temperature. *Journal of Comparative and Physiological Psychology*, 1968, *65*, 492–498. **824**

Campbell, B. A., & Masterson, F. A. Psychophysics of punishment. In B. A. Campbell, & R. M. Church (Eds.), *Punishment*. New York: Appleton, 1969. **705, 706**

Campbell, B. A., & Misanin, J. R. Basic drives. *Annual Review of Psychology*, 1969, *20*, 57–84. **794n**

Campbell, B. A., & Pickleman, J. R. The imprinting object as a reinforcing stimulus. *Journal of Comparative and Physiological Psychology*, 1961, *54*, 592–596. **581**

Campbell, B. A., & Sheffield, F. D. Relation of random activity to food deprivation. *Journal of Comparative and Physiological Psychology*, 1953, *46*, 320–322. **822**

Campbell, B. A., Smith, N. F., Misanin, J. R., & Jaynes, J. Species differences in activity during hunger and thirst. *Journal of Comparative and Physiological Psychology*, 1966, *61*, 123–127. **821, 824**

Campbell, B. A., & Teghtsoonian, R. Electrical and behavioral effects of different types of shock stimuli on the rat. *Journal of Comparative and Physiological Psychology*, 1958, *51*, 185–192. **705**

Campbell, B. A., Teghtsoonian, R., & Williams, R. A. Activity, weight loss, and survival time of food-deprived rats as a function of age. *Journal of Comparative and Physiological Psychology*, 1961, *54*, 216–219. **813, 822**

Campbell, B. A., *see also* Sheffield, F. D., 1954; Teghtsoonian, R., 1960; Williams, R. A., 1961.

Campbell, B. J., *see* Cong, E. R., 1958.

Campbell, D., *see* Kamin, L., 1959.

Campbell, D. T., *see* Segall, M. H., 1963, 1966.

Campbell, F. W., & Robson, J. G. High-speed infrared optometer. *Journal of the Optical Society of America*, 1959, *49*, 268–272. **394**

Campbell, F. W., & Robson, J. G. Application of Fourier analysis to the visibility of gratings. *Journal of Physiology*, 1968, *197*, 553–568. **300**

Campbell, F. W., & Rushton, W. A. H. Measurement of the scotopic pigment in the living human eye. *Journal of Physiology*, 1955, *130*, 131–147. **322**

Campbell, F. W., & Westheimer, G. Dynamics of accommodation responses of the human eye. *Journal of Physiology*, 1960, *151*, 285–295. **391**

Campbell, F. W., *see also* Alpern, M., 1962.

Campbell, R. A., & Small, A. M., Jr. Effect of practice and feedback on frequency discrimination. *Journal of the Acoustical Society of America,* 1963, *35,* 1511–1514. **249**

Campbell, R. A., *see also* Small, A. M. Jr., 1961.

Campbell, S. L., *see* Dinsmoor, J. A., 1956; Skinner, B. F., 1947.

Campbell, T. C., Lewis, N. A., & Hunt, W. A. Context effects with judgmental language that is absolute, extensive, and extra-experimentally anchored. *Journal of Experimental Psychology,* 1958, *55,* 220–228. **60**

Canestrari, R., & Farné, M. Depth cues and apparent oscillatory motion. *Perceptual and Motor Skills,* 1969, *29,* 508–510. **518**

Cantor, G. N. The effects of three types of pretraining on discrimination learning in children. *Journal of Experimental Psychology,* 1955, *49,* 339–342. **781**

Capaldi, E. J. A sequential hypothesis of instrumental learning. In K. W. Spence & J. T. Spence (Eds.), *The psychology of learning and motivation.* Vol. 1. New York: Academic Press, 1967. Pp. 67–156. **622, 633n, 681**

Capaldi, E. J., & Lynch, D. Repeated shifts in reward magnitude: Evidence in favor of an associational and absolute (noncontextual) interpretation. *Journal of Experimental Psychology,* 1967, *75,* 226–235. **634**

Capretta, P. J., *see* Smith, M. P., 1956.

Card, G. W., *see* Stellwagen, W. T., 1965.

Carel, W., *see* Gibson, J. J., 1952.

Carhart, K., *see* Olsen, W. O., 1966.

Carhart, R., Tilman, T. W., & Johnson, K. R. Release of masking for speech through interaural time delay. *Journal of the Acoustical Society of America,* 1967, *42,* 124–138. **258**

Carlin, S., Ward, W. D., Gershon, A., & Ingraham, R. Sound stimulation and its effect on dental sensation threshold. *Science,* 1962, *138,* 1258–1259. **164**

Carlson, J. Pseudomediation effects with no intertrial intervals. *Psychonomic Science,* 1966, *5,* 77–78. **1077**

Carlson, K. R., *see* Armus, H. L., 1964.

Carlson, N. J., *see* Black, A. H., 1962.

Carlson, V. R. Satiation in reversible perspective figure. *Journal of Experimental Psychology,* 1953, *45,* 442–448. **471**

Carlson, V. R. Overestimation in size constancy judgments. *American Journal of Psychology,* 1960, *73,* 199–213. **509, 514**

Carlson, V. R. Size constancy judgments and perceptual compromise. *Journal of Experimental Psychology,* 1962, *63,* 68–73. **509**

Carlson, W., *see* Eriksen, C. W., 1966.

Carmichael, L., & Dearborn, W. F. *Reading and visual fatigue.* Boston: Houghton Mifflin, 1947. **371**

Carmichael, L., *see also* Warren, H. C., 1930.

Caron, A. J., Unger, S. M., & Parloff, M. B. A test of Moltzman's theory of originality training. *Journal of Verbal Learning and Verbal Behavior,* 1963, *1,* 436–442. **867**

Carpenter, J. A. Species differences in taste preferences. *Journal of Comparative and Physiological Psychology,* 1956, *49,* 139–144. **190**

Carr, H. A. The autokinetic sensation. *Psychological Reviews,* 1910, *17,* 42–75. **530**

Carr, H. A. *Psychology: A study of mental activity.* New York: Longmans, Green, 1925. **533**

Carr, W. J. The effect of adrenalectomy upon the NaCl taste threshold in rat. *Journal of Comparative and Physiological Psychology,* 1952, *45,* 377–380. **176**

Carr, W. J., & Caul, W. F. The effect of castration in rats upon the discrimination of sex odours. *Animal Behaviour,* 1962, *10,* 20–27. **210**

Carr, W. J., & McGuigan, D. I. The stimulus basis and modification of visual cliff performance in the rat. *Animal Behaviour,* 1965, *13,* 25–29. **549**

Carroll, J. B., Kjeldergaard, P. M., & Carton, A. S. Number of opposites versus number of primaries as a response measure in free-association tests. *Journal of Verbal Learning and Verbal Behavior,* 1962, *1,* 22–30. **871, 873**

Carter, E. A., *see* Seashore, E. C., 1908.

Carter, S., *see* Gelfan, S., 1967.

Carterette, E. C., *see* Egan, J. P., 1954.

Carterette, T. S. An application of stimulus sampling theory to summated generalization. *Journal of Experimental Psychology,* 1961, *62,* 448–455. **929**

Carton, A. S., *see* Carroll, J. B., 1962.

Casella, C., *see* Rapuzzi, G., 1965.

Casey, A., *see* Epstein, W., 1961.

Casey, K. L., *see* Melzack, R., 1968.

Casey, M., *see* Young, R. J., 1964.

Cason, H. The conditioned eyelid reaction. *Journal of Experimental Psychology,* 1922, *5,* 153–196. **562**

Casperson, R. C. The visual discrimination of geometric forms. *Journal of Experimental Psychology,* 1950, *40,* 668–681. **443**

Castaneda, A. Effects of stress on complex learning and performance. *Journal of Experimental Psychology,* 1956, *52,* 9–12. **790**

Castaneda, A. Supplementary report: Differential position habits and anxiety in children as determinants of performance in learning. *Journal of Experimental Psychology,* 1961, *61,* 257–258. **790, 791**

Castaneda, A., & Lipsitt, L. P. Relation of stress and differential position habits to performance in motor learning. *Journal of Experimental Psychology,* 1959, *57,* 25–30. **790**

Castaneda, A., & Palermo, D. S. Psychomotor performance as a function of amount of training and stress. *Journal of Experimental Psychology,* 1955, *50,* 175–179. **790**

Castaneda, A., Palermo, D. S., & McCandless, B. R. Complex learning and performance as a function of anxiety in children and task difficulty. *Child Development,* 1956, *27,* 327–332. **790**

Castaneda, A., *see also* Lipsitt, L. P., 1959.

Catania, A. C. Concurrent operants. In Honig, W. K. (Ed.), *Operant behavior: Areas of research and application.* New York: Appleton, 1966. **752**

Catania, A. C., *see also* Lane, H. L., 1961.

Cattell, J. McK. A statistical study of American men of science. *Science,* 1906, *24,* 658–665, 699–707, 732–742. Reprinted in *James McKeen Cattell: Man of science: 1860–1944.* Vol. 1. Lancaster, Pa.: Science Press, 1947. **62**

Cattell, J. McK. Statistics of American psychologists. *American Journal of Psychology,* 1903, *14,* 310–328. Reprinted in *James McKeen Cattell: Man of Science: 1860–1944.* Vol. 1. Lancaster, Pa.: Science Press, 1947. **61**

Cattell, J. McK., & Hoagland, H. Response of tactile receptors to intermittent stimulation. *Journal of Physiology,* 1931, *72,* 392–404. **165**

Cattell, J. McK., *see also* Fullerton, G. S., 1892.

Caul, W. F., *see* Carr, W. J., 1962.

Cauna, N. Light and electron microscopal structure of sensory end-organs of human skins. In D. R. Kenshalo (Ed.), *The skin senses.* Springfield, Ill.: Charles C Thomas, 1968. Pp. 15–37. **129**

Caviness, J., *see* Schiff, W., 1962.

Ceraso, J., & Henderson, A. Unavailability and associative loss in RI and PI. *Journal of Experimental Psychology,* 1965, *70,* 300–303. **1099, 1105**

Ceraso, J., & Henderson, A. Unavailability and associative loss in RI and PI: Second try. *Journal of Experimental Psychology,* 1966, *72,* 314–316. **1099, 1105**

Ceraso, J., *see also* Slamecka, N. J., 1960.

Cermak, L. S., *see* Wickens, D. D., 1967.

Chalmers, E. L. Monocular and binocular cues in the perception of size and distance. *American Journal of Psychology*, 1952, 65, 415-423. **513, 514**

Chang, J. J., see Shepard, R. N., 1963.

Chapanis, A., & McCleary, R. A. Interposition as a cue for the perception of relative distance. *Journal of General Psychology*, 1953, 48, 113-132. **498**

Chapanis, A., & Mankin, D. A. The vertical-horizontal illusion in a visually-rich environment. *Perception and Psychophysics*, 1967, 2, 249-255. **456**

Chaplin, M. R., see Pollack, R. H., 1963.

Chapman, R. M., & Levy, N. Hunger drive and reinforcing effects of novel stimuli. *Journal of Comparative and Physiological Psychology*, 1957, 50, 233-238. **673**

Chapman, W. P., & Jones, C. M. Variations in cutaneous and visceral pain sensitivity in normal subjects. *Journal of Clinical Investigation*, 1944, 23, 81-91. **156**

Charnwood, J. R. B. *Essay on binocular vision*. London: Hatton, 1951. Pp. 106-108. **490**

Chase, H. H., see Keen, R. E., 1965.

Chase, W. G., see Keele, S. W., 1967.

Check, R., see Fox, R., 1966a, b.

Cheng, N. Y. Retroactive effect and degree of similarity. *Journal of Experimental Psychology*, 1929, 12, 444-449. **1082**

Cherry, C., see Leakey, D. M., 1958.

Cherry, E. C. Some experiments on the recognition of speech, with one and two ears. *Journal of the Acoustical Society of America*, 1953, 25, 975-979. **259**

Cherry, E. C., & Sayers, B. McA. On the mechanism of binaural fusion. *Journal of the Acoustical Society of America*, 1959, 31, 535. **263**

Cheung, C. C., & Goulet, L. R. Retroactive inhibition of R-S associations in the A-B, B-C, C-B paradigms. *Journal of Experimental Psychology*, 1968, 76, 321-322. **1096**

Chinetti, P., see Leibowitz, H., 1955, 1956, 1957.

Chinn, R. McC., see Riopelle, A. J.

Chistovitch, L. A., & Ivanova, V. A. Mutual masking of short sound pulses. *Biophysics*, 1959, 4, 46-56. **241**

Cho, C., see Meyer, D. R., 1960.

Chomsky, N., *Syntactic structure*. The Hague: Mouton, 1957. **904**

Chomsky, N. *Aspects of the theory of syntax*. Cambridge, Mass.: The MIT Press, 1966. **904***n*

Chorover, S. L., see Mendelson, J., 1965.

Chow, K. L., & Nissen, H. W. Interocular transfer of learning in visually naive and experienced infant chimpanzees. *Journal of Comparative and Physiological Psychology*, 1955, 48, 229-237. **548**

Chow, K. L., see also Lashley, K. S., 1951.

Church, A. A. *Introduction to mathematical logic*. Princeton: Princeton University Press, 1958. **943**

Church, R. M. The varied effects of punishment on behavior. *Psychological Review*, 1963, 70, 369-402. **734**

Church, R. M. Response suppression. In B. A. Campbell, & R. M. Church (Eds.). *Punishment*. New York: Appleton, 1969. **713, 734, 737**

Church, R. M., & Black, A. H. Latency of the conditioned heart rate as a function of the CS-US interval. *Journal of Comparative and Physiological Psychology*, 1958, 51, 478-482. **711, 729**

Church, R. M., Brush, F. R., & Solomon, R. L. Traumatic avoidance learning: The effects of CS-US interval with a delayed-conditioning prodecure in a free-responding situation. *Journal of Comparative and Physiological Psychology*, 1956, 49, 301-308. **729**

Church, R. M., LoLordo, V., Overmier, J. B., Solomon, R. L., & Turner, H. Cardiac responses to shock in curarized dogs: Effects of shock intensity and duration, warning signal, and prior experience with shock. *Journal of Comparative and Physiological Psychology*, 1966, 62, 1-7. **711**

Church, R. M., Raymond, G. A., & Beauchamp, R. D. Response suppression as a function of intensity and duration of a punishment. *Journal of Comparative and Physiological Psychology*, 1967, 63, 39-44. **735, 736**

Church, R. M., & Solomon, R. L. Traumatic avoidance learning: The effects of delay of shock termination. *Psychological Reports*, 1956, 2, 357-368. **727**

Church, R. M., see also Camp, D. S., 1967.

Cicala, G. A., see also Campbell, B. A., 1962.

Cieutat, V. J., Stockwell, F. E., & Noble, C. E., The interaction of ability and amount of practice with stimulus and response meaningfulness (m, m') in paired-associate learning. *Journal of Experimental Psychology*, 1958, 56, 193-202. **856**

Cisek, J. G., see Harvey, F. K., 1963.

Clack, T. D. Aural harmonics: Preliminary time-intensity relationships using the tone-on-tone masking technique. *Journal of the Acoustical Society of America*, 1968, 43, 283-288. **238**

Clark, J. R., see Newhall, S. M., 1957.

Clark, L. L., Lansford, T. G., & Dallenbach, K. M. Repetition and associative learning. *American Journal of Psychology*, 1960, 73, 22-40. **987**

Clark, R. A., see Birch, D., 1958.

Clark, W. C., Smith, A. H., & Rabe, A. Retinal gradient of outline as a stimulus for slant. *Canadian Journal of Psychology*, 1955, 9, 247-253. **501**

Clark, W. C., Smith, A. H., & Rabe, A. The interaction of surface texture, outline gradient, and ground in the perception of slant. *Canadian Journal of Psychology*, 1956, 10, 1-8. **501**

Clark, W. C., see also Gruber, H. E., 1956.

Clark, W. H., see Glanzer, M., 1963, 1964.

Clarke, F. J., & Belcher, S. J. On the localization of Troxler's effect in the visual pathway. *Vision Research*, 1962, 2, 53-68. **453**

Clarke, R. H., see Horsley, V., 1908.

Clayton, F. L., & Savin, H. B. Strength of a secondary reinforcer following continuous or variable ratio primary reinforcement. *Psychological Reports*, 1960, 6, 99-106. **663**

Clayton, K. N., see Knott, P. D., 1966.

Clement, D. E., & Varnadoe, K. W. Pattern uncertainty and the discrimination of visual patterns. *Perception and Psychophysics*, 1967, 2, 427-431. **448**

Clement, D. E., see also Garner, W. R., 1963.

Clemente, C. D., Sterman, M. B., & Wyrwicka, W. Postreinforcement EEG synchronization during alimentary behavior. *Electroencephalography and Clinical Neurophysiology*, 1964, 16, 355-365. **838**

Clemente, C. D., see also Roth, S. R., 1967; Wyrwicka, W., 1962.

Clifton, C., Jr. Some determinants of the effectiveness of priming word associations. *Journal of Verbal Learning and Verbal Behavior*, 1966, 6, 161-171. **872**

Clowes, M. B., & Ditchburn, R. W. An improved apparatus for producing a stabilized retinal image. *Optica Acta*, 1959, 6, 252-265. **375**

Clynes, M. The non-linear biological dynamics of unidirectional rate sensitivity illustrated by analog computer analysis, pupillary reflex to light and sound, and heart rate behavior. *Annals of the New York Academy of Science*, 1962, 98, 806-845. **392**

Cockrell, J. T. Operant behavior in relation to the concentration of a nonnutritive sweet substance used as a reinforcement. Unpublished doctoral dissertation, Indiana University, 1952. **627, 629**

Cofer, C. N. Associative commonality and rated similarity of certain words from Haagen's list. *Psychological Reports*, 1957, 3, 603-606. **890**

Cofer, C. N. Comparison of word associations obtained by the methods of discrete single word and continued association. *Psychological Reports*, 1958, *4*, 507–510. **872, 877**

Cofer, C. N. Motivation. *Annual Review of Psychology*, 1959, *10*, 173–202. **794n**

Cofer, C. N. On some factors in the organizational characteristics of free recall. *American Psychologist*, 1965, *20*, 261–272. **890**

Cofer, C. N. Some evidence for coding processes derived from clustering in free recall. *Journal of Verbal Learning and Verbal Behavior*, 1966, *5*, 188–192. **891**

Cofer, C. N. Does conceptual organization influence the amount retained in immediate free recall? In B. Kleinmuntz (Ed.), *Concepts and the structure of memory*. New York: Wiley, 1967. (a) **883, 887, 891**

Cofer, C. N. Conditions for the use of verbal associations. *Psychological Bulletin*, 1967, *68*, 1–12. (b) **871, 872**

Cofer, C. N. Some data on controlled association. *Journal of Verbal Learning and Verbal Behavior*, 1967, *6*, 601–608. (c) **870**

Cofer, C. N., & Foley, J. P., Jr. Mediated generalization and the interpretation of verbal behavior: I. Prolegomena. *Psychological Review*, 1942, *49*, 513–540. **1071**

Cofer, C. N., see also Bruce, D., 1967; Havron, M. D., 1957; Jenkins, P. M., 1957; Marshall, G. R., 1963.

Cofoid, D. A., & Honig, W. K. Stimulus generalization of imprinting. *Science*, 1961, *134*, 1692–1694. **582, 700**

Cohen, A. Further investigation of the effects of intensity upon the pitch of pure tones. *Journal of the Acoustical Society of America*, 1961, *33*, 1363–1375. **244**

Cohen, A., see also Mayzner, M. S., 1967.

Cohen, B. H., Bousfield, W. A., & Whitmarsh, G. A. Cultural norms for verbal items in 43 categories. Technical Report No. 22, Contract Nonr 631(00), Office of Naval Research and University of Connecticut, 1957. **879, 891**

Cohen, B. H., & Hut, P. A. Learning of responses to stimulus classes and to specific stimuli. *Journal of Experimental Psychology*, 1963, *66*, 274–280. **892**

Cohen, G. H., see Wheeless, L. L., Jr., 1966.

Cohen, W. Color perception in the chromatic Ganzfeld. *American Journal of Psychology*, 1958, *71*, 390–394. **416**

Cohn, J. Experimentelle Untersuchungen über die Gefühlsbetonung der Farben, Helligkeiten, und ihrer Combinationen. *Philosophische Studien*, 1894, *10*, 562–603. **51**

Coke, E. U., see Rothkopf, E. Z. 1961a, b.

Colavita, F., see Peterson, M. J., 1964.

Colburn, H. S., & Durlach, N. I. Time-intensity relations in binaural unmasking. *Journal of the Acoustical Society of America*, 1965, *38*, 93–103. **243**

Cole, J. L., see Boneau, C. A., 1967.

Cole, N., see Friedman, M. P., 1964.

Coleman, E. B. The association hierarchy as an indicator of extraexperimental interference. *Journal of Verbal Learning and Verbal Behavior*, 1963, *2*, 417–421. **889**

Coleman, E. B. The association hierarchy as a measure of extra-experimental transfer. *Journal of Psychology*, 1964, *57*, 403–417. **889**

Coleman, P. Failure to localize the source distance of an unfamiliar sound. *Journal of the Acoustical Society of America*, 1962, *34*, 345–346. **269**

Coleman, P. An analysis of cues to auditory depth perception in free space. *Psychological Bulletin*, 1963, *60*, 302–315. **269**

Collias, N. E. The analysis of socialization in sheep and goats. *Ecology*, 1956, *37*, 228–239. **581**

Collier, G. Some properties of saccharin as a reinforcer. *Journal of Experimental Psychology*, 1962, *64*, 184–191. **626, 627, 630**

Collier, G. Thirst as a determinant of reinforcement. In M. I. Wayner (Ed.), *Thirst*. Oxford: Pergamon, 1964. Pp. 287–303. **814, 816, 819**

Collier, G., & Marx, M. H. Changes in performance as a function of shifts in the magnitude of reinforcement. *Journal of Experimental Psychology*, 1959, *57*, 305–309. **633, 634, 635, 637, 638**

Collier, G., & Myers, L. The loci of reinforcement. *Journal of Experimental Psychology*, 1961, *61*, 57–66. **626**

Collier, G., & Novell, K. Saccharin as a sugar surrogate. *Journal of Comparative and Physiological Psychology*, 1967, *64*, 404–408. **630**

Collier, G., & Siskel, M., Jr. Performance as a joint function of amount of reinforcement and inter-reinforcement interval. *Journal of Experimental Psychology*, 1959, *57*, 115–120. **626**

Collier, G., & Willis, F. N. Deprivation and reinforcement. *Journal of Experimental Psychology*, 1961, *62*, 377–384. **626**

Collier, G., see also Premack, D., 1957.

Collins, J. F., see Eriksen, C. W., 1964, 1965.

Collins, W. F., Nulsen, F. E., & Randt, C. T. Relation of peripheral nerve fiber size and sensation in man. *Archives of Neurology*, 1960, *3*, 381–385. **156, 162**

Coltheart, M. The influence of haptic size information upon visual judgments of absolute distance. *Perception and Psychophysics*, 1969, *5*, 143–144. **514**

Coltheart, M., see also Blessing, W. W., 1967.

Comrey, A. L. A proposed method for absolute scaling. *Psychmetrika*, 1950, *15*, 317–325. **71**

Conant, M. V., & Trabasso, T. Conjunctive and disjunctive concept formation under equal-information conditions. *Journal of Experimental Psychology*, 1964, *67*, 250–255. **963**

Cone, R. A. Early receptor potential of the vertebrate retina. *Nature*, 1964, *204*, 736–739. **307**

Cone, R. A. Early receptor potential of the vertebrate eye. *Cold Spring Harbor Symposia on Quantitative Biology*, 1965, *30*, 483–493. **330**

Conklin, J. E., see Brown, R. H., 1954.

Conrad, D. G., see Sidman, M., 1957.

Conrad, R. Acoustic confusions in immediate memory. *British Journal of Psychology*, 1964, *55*, 75–84. **1115**

Conrad, R. Interference or decay over short retention intervals? *Journal of Verbal Learning and Verbal Behavior*, 1967, *6*, 49–54. **1116**

Conrad, R., & Hull, A. Information, acoustic confusion and memory span. *British Journal of Psychology*, 1964, *55*, 429–432. **1115**

Cook, B., see Zigler, M. J., 1930.

Cook, C., see Graham, C. H., 1937.

Cook, S. W., see Raskin, E., 1937.

Cook, T. H., Mefferd, R. B., Jr., & Wieland, B. A. Apparent reversals of orientation (perspective reversals) in depth as determinants of apparent reversals of rotary motion. *Perceptual and Motor Skills*, 1967, *24*, 691–702. **518, 519**

Coombs, C. H. *A theory of data*. New York: Wiley, 1964. **63**

Coons, E. E., Anderson, N. H., & Myers, A. K. Disappearance of avoidance responding during continued training. *Journal of Comparative and Physiological Psychology*, 1960, *53*, 290–292. **730**

Cooper, F. S., DeLattre, P. C., Liberman, A. M., Boret, J. M., & Gerstman, L. J. Some experiments on speech perception. *Journal of the Acoustical Society of America*, 1952, *24*, 597–606. **253**

Cooper, F. S., see also Harris, E. S., 1958; Liberman, A. M., 1954, 1958, 1962, 1967.

Copelan, E., see Riopelle, A. J., 1954.

Corbin, H. H. The perception of grouping and apparent movement in visual depth. *Archives of Psychology* (New York), 1942, *273*. **527, 528**

Corbit, J. D. Osmotic thirst: Theoretical and experimental

analysis. *Journal of Comparative and Physiological Psychology*, 1969, *67*, 3–14. **816**

Corbit, J. D., & Stellar, E. Palatability, food intake, and obesity in normal and hyperphagic rats. *Journal of Comparative and Physiological Psychology*, 1964, *58*, 63–67. **817**

Coren, S. Brightness contrast as function of figure-ground relations. *Journal of Experimental Psychology*, 1969, *80*, 517–524. **423n**

Coren, S., & Festinger, L. An alternative view of the "Gibson normalization effect." *Perception and Psychophysics*, 1967, *2*, 621–626. **459, 465, 467**

Coriell, A. S., *see* Averbach, E., 1961.

Corliss, E. L. R., & Winzer, G. E. Study of methods for estimating loudness. *Journal of the Acoustical Society of America*, 1965, *38*, 424–428. **249**

Cormack, R. H., & Upchurch, R. L. Necker cube reversibility and perspective duration as a function of rotation and retinal disparity. *Psychonomic Science*, 1969, *15*, 305–307. **519**

Cornsweet, J. C., *see* Riggs, L. A., 1953.

Cornsweet, T. N. Determination of the stimuli for involuntary drifts and saccadic eye movements. *Journal of the Optical Society of America*, 1956, *46*, 987–993. **375, 376, 380, 387**

Cornsweet, T. N. A new technique for the measurement of small eye movements. *Journal of the Optical Society of America*, 1958. *48*, 808–811. **373**

Cornsweet, T. N. The staircase-method in psychophysics. *American Journal of Psychology*, 1962, *75*, 485–491. **20**

Cornsweet, T. N., *see also* Krauskopf, J., 1960; Riggs, L. A., 1953.

Corso, J. F. The neural quantum theory of sensory discrimination. *Psychological Bulletin*, 1956, *53*, 371–393. **34**

Corso, J. F. Absolute thresholds for tones of low frequency. *American Journal of Psychology*, 1958, *71*, 367–374. **233**

Corso, J. F. Bone conduction thresholds for sonic and ultrasonic frequencies. *Journal of the Acoustical Society of America*, 1963, *35*, 1738–1743. **233**

Corso, J. F. *The experimental psychology of sensory behavior.* New York: Holt, Rinehart and Winston, 1967. **233**

Cortesina, G., *see* Rossi, G., 1965.

Costiloe, J. P., *see* Schneider, R. A., 1958.

Cotzin, M., & Dallenbach, K. M. "Facial vision": The role of pitch and loudness in the perception of obstacles by the blind. *American Journal of Psychology*, 1950, *63*, 483–515. **271**

Cotzin, M., *see also* Supa, M., 1944.

Courten, H. C., *see* Judd, C. H., 1905.

Cowan, A. Test cards for determination of visual acuity. *Archives of Ophthalmology*, 1928, *57*, 283–295. **299**

Cowan, P. A., *see* Mandler, G., 1964.

Cowan, T. R., *see* Bousfield, W. A., 1961.

Cowles, J. T. Food-tokens as incentives for learning by chimpanzees. *Comparative Psychology Monographs*, 1937, *14*, No. 71. **665**

Craig, E. A., & Lichtenstein, M. Visibility–invisibility cycles as a function of stimulus orientation. *American Journal of Psychology*, 1953, *66*, 554–563. **453**

Cramer, P. Successful mediated priming via associative bonds. *Psychological Reports*, 1964, *15*, 235–238. **871**

Cramer, P. Recovery of a discrete memory. *Journal of Personal and Social Psychology*, 1965, *1*, 326–332. (a) **886**

Cramer, P. Response entropy as a function of the affective quality of the stimulus. *Psychonomic Science*, 1965, *3*, 347–348. (b) **864, 866**

Cramer, P. Mediated transfer via natural language association. *Journal of Verbal Learning and Verbal Behavior*, 1967, *6*, 512–519. **1078**

Cramer, P. *Word association.* New York: Academic Press. 1968. **861, 863n, 864, 865, 866**

Craske, B., *see* Howard, I. P., 1965.

Crawford, B. H. Visual adaptation in relation to brief conditioning stimuli. *Proceedings of the Royal Society* (London), Ser. B, 1947, *134B*, 283–300. **287, 288, 310**

Crawford, B. H., *see also* Stiles, W. S., 1933, 1934.

Crawford, J., Hunt, E., & Peak, G. One-trial learning of disjunctive concepts. *Journal of Verbal Learning and Verbal Behavior*, 1967, *6*, 207–212. **958, 963**

Crawford, J. L., & Vanderplas, J. M. An experiment on the mediation of transfer in paired-associate learning. *Journal of Psychology*, 1959, *47*, 87–98. **1075**

Creelman, C. D., *see* Garner, W. R., 1967.

Crespi, L. Quantitative variation of incentive and performance in the white rat. *American Journal of Psychology*, 1942, *15*, 467–517. **617, 631, 634, 635, 795**

Crespi, L. Amount of reinforcement and level of performance. *Psychological Review*, 1944, *51*, 341–357. **634, 635, 795**

Creutzfeldt, O., *see* Grüsser, O.-J., 1957.

Crisler, G., *see* Kleitman, N., 1927.

Crocker, E. C. Odor in flavor. *American Perfumer*, 1947, *50*, 164–165. **213**

Cromwell, R. L., *see* Baumeister, A., 1964.

Cronly-Dillon, J. R. Units sensitive to direction of movement in goldfish optic tectum. *Nature*, 1964, *203*, 214–215. **295**

Cronly-Dillon, J. R., *see also* Wall, P. D., 1960.

Crookes, T. G. The apparent size of after-images. *American Journal of Psychology*, 1959, *72*, 547–553. **511**

Crookes, T. G., *see also* Hall, K. R. L., 1952.

Crosby, E. C., Humphrey, T., & Lauer, E. W. *Correlative anatomy of the nervous system.* New York: Macmillan, 1962. **90**

Cross, H. A., *see* Rosenblum, L. A., 1963.

Cross, J., & Cross, J. The misperception of rotary motion. *Perception and Psychophysics*, 1969, *5*, 94–96. **519**

Crothers, E. J., *see also* Atkinson, R. C., 1964, 1965; Estes, W. K., 1960.

Crovitz, H. F. Köllner effect and suppression of the view of an eye. *Science*, 1964, *146*, 1329–1330. **488**

Crovitz, H. F., & Lipscomb, D. B. Dominance of the temporal visual fields at a short duration of stimulation. *American Journal of Psychology*, 1963, *76*, 631–637. **488**

Crowell, R. A., *see* Armus, H. L., 1964.

Crowley, M. E., *see* Gagné, R. M., 1948.

Crowne, D. P., *see* Horton, D. L.

Crum, J., Brown, W. L., & Bitterman, M. E. The effect of partial and delayed reinforcement on resistance to extinction. *American Journal of Psychology*, 1951, *64*, 228–237. **685**

Culbertson, J. L. The effects of brief delays of reinforcement on the acquisition and extinction of brightness discriminations using brain stimulation as a reinforcer. Doctoral dissertation, Brown University, 1968. Dis. Abstracts No. 69-9950, *30*, Issue 1. **683, 685, 686**

Culbertson, J. L. Effects of brief reinforcement delays on acquisition and extinction of brightness discriminations in rats. *Journal of Comparative and Physiological Psychology*, 1970, *70*, 317–325. **680, 682**

Culbertson, J. L., Kling, J. W., & Berkley, M. A. Extinction responding following ICS and food reinforcement, *Psychonomic Science*, 1966, *5*, 127–128. **653**

Culler, E., Finch, G., Girden, E., & Brogden, W. Measurements of acuity by the conditioned-response technique. *Journal of General Psychology*, 1935, *12*, 223–227. **566**

Cunningham, M., Jr., *see* Grover, D. E., 1967.

Curran, C. R., & Lane, H. L. On the relations among some factors that contribute to estimates of verticality. *Journal of Experimental Psychology*, 1962, *64*, 295–299. **539**

Curran, J. F., *see* Grant, D. A., 1953.

Dadson, R. S., *see* Robinson, D. W., 1956.

Dainoff, M., & Haber, R. N. How much help do repeated

presentations give to recognition processes? *Perception and Psychophysics*, 1967, *2*, 131–136. **445n**

Dale, H. C. A., *see* Baddeley, A. D., 1966.

Dallenbach, J. W., & Dallenbach, K. M. The effects of bitter-adaptation on sensitivity to the other taste qualities. *American Journal of Psychology*, 1943, *56*, 21–31. **182, 186**

Dallenbach, K. The temperature spots and end-organs. *American Journal of Psychology*, 1927, *39*, 402–427. **120**

Dallenbach, K. M. Pain: History and present status. *American Journal of Psychology*, 1939, *52*, 331–347. **157**

Dallenbach, K. M. The staircase-method critically examined. *American Journal of Psychology*, 1966, *79*, 654–656. **20**

Dallenbach, K. M., *see also* Abrahams, H., 1937; Ammons, C. H., 1953; Burnett, N. G., 1927; Clark, L. L., 1960; Cotzin, M., 1950; Dallenbach, J. W., 1943; Edes, B., 1936; Ferrall, S. C., 1930; Foster, D., 1950; Guilford, J. P., 1928; Jenkins, J. G., 1924; Krakauer, D., 1937; Lowenstein, E., 1930; Stone, L. J., 1934; Supa, M., 1944; Worchel, P., 1947.

Dallett, J. M. In defense of remote associations. *Psychological Review*, 1965, *72*, 164–168. **1015**

Dallett, K. M. The transfer surface re-examined. *Journal of Verbal Learning and Verbal Behavior*, 1962, *1*, 91–94. (a) **1051, 1056, 1063**

Dallett, K. M. The role of response similarity in proactive inhibition. *Journal of Experimental Psychology*, 1962, *64*, 364–372. (b) **1104**

Dallett, K. M. Practice effects in free and ordered recall. *Journal of Experimental Psychology*, 1963, *66*, 65–71. **1044**

Dallett, K. M. Proactive and retroactive inhibition in the *A–B, A–B'* paradigm. *Journal of Experimental Psychology*, 1964, *68*, 190–200. **1103, 1104**

Dallett, K. M. A transfer surface for paradigms in which second-list *S–R* pairings do not correspond to first-list pairings. *Journal of Verbal Learning and Verbal Behavior*, 1965, *4*, 528–534. **1055, 1056**

Dallett, K. M. Effects of within-list and between-list acoustic similarity on the learning and retention of paired associates. *Journal of Experimental Psychology*, 1966, *72*, 667–677. **1126**

D'Amato, M. R. Transfer of secondary reinforcement across the hunger and thirst drives. *Journal of Experimental Psychology*, 1955, *49*, 352–356. (a) **668**

D'Amato, M. R. Secondary reinforcement and magnitude of primary reinforcement. *Journal of Comparative and Physiological Psychology*, 1955, *48*, 378–380. (b) **666**

D'Amato, M. R., & Fazzaro, J. Discriminated lever-press avoidance learning as a function of type and intensity of shock. *Journal of Comparative and Physiological Psychology*, 1966, *61*, 313–315. **729**

D'Amato, M. R., Fazzaro, J., & Etkin, M. Discriminated bar-press avoidance maintenance and extinction in rats as a function of shock intensity. *Journal of Comparative and Physiological Psychology*, 1967, *63*, 351–354. **729**

Damianopoulos, E. N., *see* Sqislocki, J., 1967.

Danick, J. J., *see* Bousfield, W. A., 1958.

Darian-Smith, I., *see* Mountcastle, V. B., 1967.

Darwin, C. *Expression of the emotions in man and animal.* London: Murray, 1872. Reprinted by The University of Chicago Press, 1965, with an introduction by Konrad Lorenz. **55**

Das, S. R., *see* Boynton, R. M., 1966.

Dastoli, F. R., & Price, S. Sweet-sensitive protein from bovine taste buds: Isolation and assay. *Science*, 1966, *154*, 905–907. **189**

Dateo, G. P., *see* Bartoshuk, L. M., 1969.

David, E. E., Guttman, N., & van Bergeijk, W. A. On the mechanism of binaural fusion. *Journal of the Acoustical Society of America*, 1958, *30*, 801–802. **263, 266**

David, E. E., Guttman, N., & van Bergeijk, W. A. Binaural interaction of high-frequency complex stimuli. *Journal of the Acoustical Society of America*, 1959, *31*, 774. **263**

David, E. E., *see also* Guttman, N., 1960; van Bergeijk, W. A., 1960.

Davidson, E. H. Some determinants of verbal association times. Doctoral dissertation, Pennsylvania State University, 1965. **862, 869**

Davidson, L., *see* Wallach, H., 1963.

Davies, J. T. A theory of the quality of odours. *Journal of Theoretical Biology*, 1965, *8*, 1–7. **222**

Davis, C. J., & Jobe, F. W. Further studies on the A.C.A. ratio as measured on the ortho-rater. *American Journal of Optometry*, 1957, *34*, 16–25. **384**

Davis, H. Chapter 4 in C. M. Harris (Ed.), *Handbook of noise control.* New York: McGraw-Hill, 1957. **229**

Davis, H. Mechanisms of excitation of auditory nerve impulses. In G. L. Rasmussen & W. F. Windle (Eds.), *Neural mechanisms of the auditory and vestibular systems.* Springfield, Ill.: Charles C Thomas, 1960. **230**

Davis, H., Hirsh, S. K., Shelnutt, J., & Bowers, C. Further validation of evoked response audiometry. *Journal of Speech and Hearing Research*, 1967, *10*, 717–732. **235**

Davis, H., & Krantz, F. W. International audiometric zero. *Journal of the Acoustical Society of America*, 1964, *36*, 1450–1454. **233, 235**

Davis, H., & Silverman, S. R. *Hearing and deafness.* New York: Holt, Rinehart and Winston, 1960. **226, 228, 235, 254, 255, 256**

Davis, H., & Zerlin, S. Acoustic relations of the human vertex potential. *Journal of the Acoustical Society of America*, 1966, *39*, 109–116. **235**

Davis, H., *see also* Deatherage, B. H., 1957; Galambos, R., 1943, 1944; Hirsh, I. J., 1952; Stevens, S. S., 1938; Tasaki, I., 1952, 1954; Teas, D. C., 1962.

Davis, J. D., *see* Grice, G. R., 1957.

Davy, E. Intensity–time relation for multiple flashes of light in the peripheral retina. *Journal of the Optical Society of America*, 1952, *42*, 937–941. **304**

Daw, N. W. Goldfish retina: Organization for simultaneous color contrast, *Science*, 1967, *158*, 942–944. **295**

Day, D. J., *see* Martin, L. C., 1950.

Day, R. H. Application of the statistical theory to form perception. *Psychological Review*, 1956, *63*, 139–148.

Day, R. H. On interocular transfer and the central origin of visual after-effects. *American Journal of Psychology*, 1958, *71*, 784–789. **473**

Day, R. H. Excitatory and inhibitory processes as the basis of contour shift and negative aftereffect. *Psychologia*, 1962, *5*, 185–193. **470, 473**

Day, R. H. Effects of repeated trials and prolonged fixations on error in the Müller-Lyer. *Psychological Monographs*, 1962, *76*. **465**

Day, R. H., Pollack, R. H., & Seagrim, G. N. Figural aftereffects: A critical review. *Austalian Journal of Psychology*, 1959, *11*, 15–45. **469**

Day, R. H., & Power, R. P. Frequency of apparent reversal of rotary motion in depth as a function of shape and pattern. *Australian Journal of Psychology*, 1963, *15*, 162–174. **518**

Day, R. H., & Power, R. P. Apparent reversal (oscillation) of rotary motion in depth: An investigation and a general theory. *Psychological Review*, 1965, *72*, 117–127. **518**

Day, R. H., *see also* Ganz, L., 1965; Singer, G., 1966.

Dean, M. G., & Kausler, D. H. Degree of first-list learning and stimulus meaningfulness as related to transfer in the *A–B, C–B* paradigm. *Journal of Verbal Learning and Verbal Behavior*, 1964, *3*, 330–334. **1061, 1063, 1068**

Dean, S. J., *see* Martin, R. B., 1964.

Dearborn, W. F. The psychology of reading. *Archives of Philosophy, Psychology and Scientific Methods*, 1906, *4*. **388, 390**

Dearborn, W. F. The general effects of special practice in memory. *Psychological Bulletin*, 1909, *6*, 44. **1031**

Dearborn, W. F., *see also* Carmichael, L., 1947.

Deatherage, B. H., Bilger, R. C., & Eldredge, D. H. Remote masking in selected frequency regions. *Journal of the Acoustical Society of America,* 1957, *29,* 512-514. **239**

Deatherage, B. H., Davis, H., & Eldredge, D. H. Physiological evidence for masking of low frequencies by high. *Journal of the Acoustical Society of America,* 1957, *29,* 132-137. **239**

Deatherage, B. H., & Hirsh, I. J. Auditory localization of clicks. *Journal of the Acoustical Society of America,* 1959, *31,* 486-492. **262, 266**

Deatherage, B. H., see also Jeffress, L., 1962.

Deaux, E. B., see Patten, R. L., 1966.

de Boer, E. *On the "residue" in hearing.* 'S-Gravenhage, The Netherlands: Excelsior, 1956. **245**

Decker, L., see Pollack, I., 1959.

Decker, T., see Kenshalo, D. R., 1967.

Deese, J. Influence of inter-item associative strength upon immediate free recall. *Psychological Reports,* 1959, *5,* 305-312. (a) **879, 887, 1129**

Deese, J. On the prediction of occurrence of particular verbal intrusions in immediate recall. *Journal of Experimental Psychology,* 1959, *58,* 17-22. (b) **887**

Deese, J. Frequency of usage and number of words in free recall: The role of association. *Psychological Reports,* 1960, *7,* 337-344. **854, 886, 896, 1129**

Deese, J. From the isolated verbal unit to connected discourse. In C. N. Cofer (Ed.), *Verbal learning and verbal behavior.* New York: McGraw-Hill, 1961. Pp. 11-31. **848, 878, 901, 903**

Deese, J. Form class and the determinants of association. *Journal of Verbal Learning and Verbal Behavior,* 1962, *1,* 79-84. **863, 866, 874**

Deese, J. On the structure of associative meaning. *Psychological Review,* 1962, *69,* 161-175. **1129**

Deese, J. *The structure of associations in language and thought.* Baltimore: The Johns Hopkins University Press, 1965. **848, 850, 877, 878, 880, 882, 883, 885**

Deese, J., & Marder, V. J. The pattern of errors in delayed recall of serial learning after interpolation. *American Journal of Psychology,* 1957, *70,* 594-599. **1091**

de Lange, H. Relationship between critical flicker frequency and a set of low-frequency characteristics of the eye. *Journal of the Optical Society of America,* 1954, *44,* 380-389. **311**

de Lange, H. Research into the dynamic nature of the human fovea-cortex systems with intermittent and modulated light: I. Attenuation characteristics with white and colored light. *Journal of the Optical Society of America,* 1958, *48,* 777-784. **313**

DeLattre, P. C., see Cooper, F. S., 1952; Harris, E. S., 1958; Liberman, A. M., 1954, 1958.

Delgado, J. M. R., Roberts, W. W., & Miller, N. E. Learning motivated by electrical stimulation of the brain. *American Journal of Physiology,* 1954, *179,* 587-593. **643, 706**

Delk, J. L., & Fillenbaum, S. Differences in perceived color as a function of characteristic color. *American Journal of Psychology,* 1965, *78,* 290-293. **425**

De Lorenzo, A. J. Electron microscopic observations of the olfactory mucosa and olfactory nerve. *Journal of Biophysics, Biochemistry and Cytology,* 1957, *3,* 839-850. **195, 196, 197**

de Lorge, J., see Bolles, R. C., 1962.

Dember, W. N., & Purcell, D. G. Recovery of masked visual targets by inhibition of the masking stimulus. *Science,* 1967, *157,* 1335-1336. **431**

Dember, W. N., see also Heckernmueller, E., 1965.

Dement, W., & Kleitman, N. Cyclic variations in EEG during sleep and their relation to eye movements, body motility and dreaming. *Electroencephalography and Clinical Neurophysiology,* 1957, *9,* 673-690. **372**

Dennis, W. Congenital cataract and unlearned behavior. *Journal of Genetic Psychology,* 1934, *44,* 340-351. **548**

Dennis, W. *Readings in the history of psychology.* New York: Appleton, 1948. **118**

Denny, M. R., see Weisman, R. G., 1966.

Derks, P. L. The generality of the "conditioning axiom" in human binary prediction. *Journal of Experimental Psychology,* 1962, *63,* 538-545. **921**

Derks, P. L. Effect of run length on the "gambler's fallacy." *Journal of Experimental Psychology,* 1963, *65,* 213-214. **921**

De Shazo, D., see Epstein, W., 1961.

De Silva, H. R. An analysis of the visual perception of movement. *British Journal of Psychology,* 1929, *19,* 268-305. **527, 528**

De Silva, H. R. The perception of movement. In E. G. Boring, H. S. Langfeld, & H. P. Weld (Eds.), *Psychology.* New York: Wiley, 1935. **528**

De Sisto, M. J., & McLaughlin, S. C. Change in judgment of direction of gaze after autokinetic perception. *Psychonomic Science,* 1968, *10,* 221-222. **530**

De Sisto, M. J., see also McLaughlin, S. C., 1969.

Desmedt, J. E. Neurophysiological mechanisms controlling acoustic output. In G. Rasmussen & W. A. Windle (Eds.), *Neural mechanisms of the auditory and vestibular systems.* Springfield, Ill.: Charles C Thomas, 1960. **233**

Desmedt, J. E. Auditory-evoked potentials from cochlea to cortex as influenced by activation of the efferent olivocochlear bundle. *Journal of the Acoustical Society of America,* 1962, *34,* 1478-1496. **233**

De Soto, C. B., & Bosley, J. J. The cognitive structure of a social structure. *Journal of Abnormal and Social Psychology,* 1962, *64,* 303-307. **889**

Detambel, M. H. A test of a model for multiple-choice behavior. *Journal of Experimental Psychology,* 1955, *49,* 97-104. **932**

Dethier, V. G., see Pfaffmann, C., 1954.

de Toledo, L. & Black, A. H. Heart rate: Changes during conditioned suppression in rats. *Science,* 1966, *152,* 1404-1406. **713**

Deutsch, D., see Deutsch, J. A., 1966.

Deutsch, J. A. A theory of shape recognition. *British Journal of Psychology,* 1955, *46,* 30-37. **450**

Deutsch, J. A. The statistical theory of figural aftereffects and acuity. *British Journal of Psychology,* 1956, *57,* 208-215. **472**

Deutsch, J. A. Neurophysiological contrast phenomena and figural aftereffects. *Psychological Review,* 1964, *71,* 19-26. **473**

Deutsch, J. A., & Deutsch, D. Attention: Some theoretical considerations. *Psychological Review,* 1963, *70,* 80-90. **769**

Deutsch, J. A., & Deutsch, D. *Physiological psychology.* Homewood, Ill.: Dorsey Press, 1966. **658**

Deutsch, J. A., & Howarth, C. I. Some tests of a theory of intracranial self-stimulation. *Psychological Review,* 1963, *70,* 444-460. **659**

Deutsch, J. A., & Jones, A. D. Diluted water: An explanation of the rat's preference for saline. *Journal of Comparative and Physiological Psychology,* 1960, *53,* 122-127. **190**

DeValois, R. Behavioral and electrophysiological studies of primate vision. In *Contributions to sensory psychology.* New York: Academic Press, 1965. **325, 327**

DeValois, R. L., Jacobs, G. H., & Abramov, I. Responses of single cells in visual system to shifts in the wavelength of light. *Science,* 1964, *146,* 1184-1186. **334**

DeValois, R. L., Jacobs, G. H., & Jones, A. E. Responses of single cells in primate red–green color vision system. *Optik*, 1963, *20*, 87. **334**

DeValois, R. L., & Walraven, J. Monocular and binocular aftereffects of chromatic adaptation. *Science,* 1967, *155*, 463. **336**

DeVito, J. L., & Smith, O. A., Jr. Effects of temperature and food deprivation on the random activity of *Macaca Mulatta*. *Journal of Comparative and Physiological Psychology*, 1959, *52*, 29–32. **824**

DeVoe, R. D. Linear superposition of retinal action potentials to predict electrical flicker responses from the eye of the wolf spider, *Lycosa baltimoriana* (Keyserling). *Journal of General Physiology*, 1962, *46*, 75–96. **311**

DeWardener, H. E., & Herxheimer, A. The effect of a high water intake on salt consumption, taste thresholds and salivary secretion in man. *Journal of Physiology*, 1957, *139*, 53–63. **189**

Dews, P. B. Free-operant behavior under conditions of delayed reinforcement: I. CRF-type schedules. *Journal of the Experimental Analysis of Behavior*, 1960, *3*, 221–234. **684**

Diamant, H., Funakoshi, M. Ström, L., & Zotterman, Y. Electrophysiological studies on human taste nerves. In Y. Zotterman (Ed.), *Olfaction and taste*. Vol. 1. New York: Pergamon, 1963. Pp. 193–203. **174, 175**

Diamant, H., *see also* Borg, G., 1967.

Diamond, A. L. Foveal simultaneous brightness contrast as a function of inducing and test-field luminances. *Journal of Experimental Psychology*, 1953, *45*, 304–315. **411**

Diamond, A. L. Foveal simultaneous contrast as a function of inducing-field area. *Journal of Experimental Psychology*, 1955, *50*, 144–152. **410**

Diamond, A. L. A Theory of depression and enhancement in the brightness response. *Psychological Review*, 1960, *67*, 168–199. **412**

Diamond, I. T., *see* Masterton, R. B., 1968.

Di Cara, L. V., & Miller, N. E. Changes in heart rate instrumentally learned by curarized rats as avoidance responses. *Journal of Comparative and Physiological Psychology*, 1968, *65*, 8–12. **839**

Dicken, C. F. Connotative meaning as a determinant of stimulus generalization. *Psychological Monographs*, 1961, *75*, No. 505. **1048**

Dietzel, H. Untersuchungen uber die optische Lokalisation der Mediane. *Zeitschrift für Biologie*, 1924, *80*, 289–316. **534**

Di Lollo, V. Runway performance in relation to runway-goal-box similarity and changes in incentive amount. *Journal of Comparative and Physiological Psychology*, 1964, *58*, 327–329. **633, 634, 635**

Di Lollo, V., & Beez, V. Negative contrast effect as a function of magnitude of reward decrement. *Psychonomic Science*, 1966, *5*, 99–100. **634, 635**

Dingman, H. F., *see* Guilford, J. P., 1954, 1955.

Dinner, J. E., & Duncan, C. P. Warm-up in retention as a function of degree of verbal learning. *Journal of Experimental Psychology*, 1959, *57*, 257–261. **1040**

Dinnerstein, A. J. Image size and instructions in the perception of depth. *Journal of Experimental Psychology*, 1967, *75*, 525–528. **496, 497**

Dinnerstein, A. J., *see also* Gruber, H. E., 1965.

Dinnerstein, D. & Wertheimer, M. Some determinants of phenomenal overlapping. *American Journal of Psychology*, 1957, *70*, 21–37. **498**

Dinsmoor, J. A. A quantitative comparison of the discriminative and reinforcing functions of a stimulus. *Journal of Experimental Psychology*, 1950, *40*, 458–472. **674**

Dinsmoor, J. A. Punishment: I. The avoidance hypothesis. *Psychological Review*, 1954, *61*, 34–46. **734**

Dinsmoor, J. A., & Campbell, S. L. Escape-from-shock training following exposure to inescapable shock. *Psychological Reports*, 1956, *2*, 43–49. **723**

Ditchburn, R. W. Eye movements in relation to retinal action. *Optica Acta*, 1955, *1*, 171–176. **387**

Ditchburn, R. W., & Fender, D. H. The stabilized retinal image. *Optica Acta*, 1955, *2*, 128–133. **386**

Ditchburn, R. W., & Ginsborg, B. L. Vision with a stabilized retinal image. *Nature*, 1952, *170*, 36–37. **305, 306, 374, 375**

Ditchburn, R. W., *see also* Clowes, M. B., 1959.

Ditrichs, R., *see* Martin, R. B., 1966.

Dittmar, D. G., *see* Grant, D. A., 1940.

Dixon, W. F., & Massey, F. J. *Introduction to statistical analysis*. New York: McGraw-Hill, 1956. Pp. 279–286. **20**

Djang, S. S. The role of past experience in the visual apprehension of masked forms. *Journal of Experimental Psychology*, 1937, *20*, 25–59. **440**

Dobelle, W. H., *see* Marks, W. B., 1964.

Dodd, D. H., and Bourne, L. E., Jr. *A direct test of some assumptions of a hypothesis-testing model of concept identification*. Program on Cognitive Processes Report No. 101. Institute of Behavioral Science, University of Colorado, 1967. **957, 970**

Dodd, D. H., *see also* Bourne, L. E. Jr., 1965.

Dodge, R. An experimental study of visual fixation. *Psychological Review*, Monograph Supplement, 1907, *8*, 4, 1–95. **372**

Dodge, S. H., *see* Walk, R. D., 1962.

Dodson, J. D., *see* Yerkes, R. M., 1908.

Dodt, E., & Wirth, A. Differentiation between rods and cones by flicker electroretinography in pigeon and guinea pig. *Acta physiologica Scandinavica*, 1953, *30*, 80–89. **311**

Dodwell, P. C. Coding and learning in shape discrimination. *Psychological Review*, 1961, *68*, 373–382. **450**

Dodwell, P. C. A coupling system for coding and learning shape discrimination. *Psychological Review*, 1964, *71*, 148–159. **450**

Dodwell, P. C., & Engel, G. R. A theory of binocular fusion. *Nature*, 1963, *198*, 39–40. **490**

Dodwell, P. C., & Gaze, L. The role of experience without set in figural after-effects. *Psychonomic Science*, 1965, *2*, 277–278. **470**

Dodwell, P. C., *see also* Gaze, L., 1965.

Doerr, H. O., & Hokanson, J. E. Food deprivation, performance, and heart rate in the rat. *Journal of Comparative and Physiological Psychology*, 1968, *65*, 227–231. **836**

Doetsch, G. S., *see* Erickson, R. P., 1965.

Dolan, T. R., & Robinson, D. E. Explanation of masking-level differences that result from interaural intensive disparities of noise. *Journal of the Acoustical Society of America*, 1967, *42*, 977–981. **243**

Dollard, J., & Miller, N. E. *Personality and psychotherapy*. New York: McGraw-Hill, 1950. **780**

Dollard, J., *see also* Miller, N. E., 1941.

Dominowski, R. L. Role of memory in concept learning. *Psychological Bulletin*, 1965, *63*, 271–280. **975**

Donderi, D. C., & Kane, E. Perceptual learning produced by common responses to different stimuli. *Canadian Journal of Psychology*, 1965, *19*, 15–30. **454**

Doty, R. W. Electrical stimulation of the brain in behavioral context. *Annual Review of Psychology*, 1969, *20*, 289–320. **564**

Douglas, W. W., & Ritchie, J. M. Mammalian nonmyelinated nerve fibers. *Physiological Review*, 1962, *42*, 297–334. **162**

Dove, H. W. Die Combination der Eindrücke beider Ohren

und beider Augen zu einem Eindruck. *Berliner preussische Akademie Wissenschaften,* 1841, 251–252. Cited in C. Osgood, *Method and theory in experimental psychology,* New York: Oxford University Press, 1953, 270. **491***n*

Döving, K. B. Studies on the responses of bulbar neurons of frog to different odour stimuli. *Revue de Laryngologie* (Bordeaux), 1965, *86,* 845–854. **216**

Döving, K. B. An electrophysiological study of odour similarities of homologous substances. *Journal of Physiology,* 1966, *186,* 97–109. (a) **216**

Döving, K. B. Analysis of odour similarities from electrophysiological data. *Acta Physiologica Scandinavica,* 1966, *68,* 404–418. (b) **216**

Dowling, B., see Inglett, G. E., 1965.

Dowling, J. E. The site of visual adaptation. *Science,* 1967, *155,* 273–279. **287, 288, 289**

Dowling, J. E., & Boycott, B. B. Organization of the primate retina: Electron microscopy. *Proceedings of the Royal Society* (London), Ser. B, 1966, *166,* 80–111. **279**

Draguns, J., see Flavell, J. H., 1958.

Draper, D. O., see Pollio, H. R., 1966.

Dravnieks, A. Physicochemical basis of olfaction. *Annals of the New York Academy of Science,* 1964, *116,* 429–439. **220**

Dreher, J. J., see Moser, H. M., 1955.

Drury, M. B. Progressive changes in non-foveal perception of line patterns. *American Journal of Psychology,* 1933, *45,* 628–646. **443**

Dry, R. M. L., see Armstrong, D., 1951.

Dubrovsky, N., see Brugge, J. F., 1964.

Ducharme, R. Activité physique et déactivation: Baisse du rhythme cardiaquè au cours de l'activité instrumentale. *Canadian Journal of Psychology,* 1966, *20,* 445–454. (a) **835**

Ducharme, R. Effect of internal and external cues on the heart rate of the rat. *Canadian Journal of Psychology,* 1966, *20,* 97–104. (b) **829, 835, 836**

Ducharme, R., & Bélanger, D. Influence d'une stimulation électrique sur le niveau d'activation et la performance. *Canadian Journal of Psychology,* 1961, *15,* 61–68. **828, 829, 835**

Duda, W. L., see Rochester, H., 1956.

Dudley, D., see Alpern, M., 1966.

Duffy, E. *Activation and behavior.* New York: Wiley, 1962. **831**

Duffy, E., & Lacey, O. L. Adaptation in energy mobilization: Changes in general level of palmar conductance. *Journal of Experimental Psychology,* 1946, *36,* 437–452. **834**

Dufort, R. H. Adjustment of the rat to 23-, 47-, and 71-hour water-deprivation schedules. *Psychological Reports,* 1963, *13,* 243–250. (a) **819**

Dufort, R. H. Weight loss in rats continuously deprived of food, water, and both food and water. *Psychological Reports,* 1963, *12,* 307–312. (b) **816**

Dufort, R. H. Additional evidence on the rat's adjustment to the 71-hour water-deprivation schedule. *Psychological Reports,* 1964, *15,* 518. (a) **819**

Dufort, R. H. The rat's adjustment to 23-, 47-, and 71-hour food-deprivation schedules. *Psychological Reports,* 1964, *14,* 663–669. (b) **815, 818, 819, 820**

Dufort, R. H., & Wright, J. H. Food intake as a function of duration of food deprivation. *Journal of Psychology,* 1962, *53,* 465–468. **815**

Dufort, R. H., see also Kimble, G. A., 1955.

Dufresne, C. Influence de la privation de nourriture sur le rhythme cardiaque et l'activité instrumentale. Unpublished master's thesis, Université de Montréal, 1961. **828, 829, 835**

Duncan, C. P. Transfer after training with single versus multiple tasks. *Journal of Experimental Psychology,* 1958, *55,* 63–72. **1042**

Duncan, C. P. Descriptions of learning to learn in human subjects. *American Journal of Psychology,* 1960, *73,* 108–114. **1041**

Duncan, C. P., see also Berry, R. N., 1950; Dinner, J. E., 1959; Loess, H. B., 1952; Porter, L. W., 1953; Rockway, M. R., 1952.

Duncan, D. G., see Kenshalo, D. R., 1967.

Duncker, K. Uber induzierte Bewegung. *Psychologische Forschung,* 1929, *12,* 180–259. **522, 528, 531**

Duncker, K. Induced motion. In W. D. Ellis (Ed.), *A source book of Gestalt psychology.* New York: Harcourt, Brace, 1938, Pp. 161–172. **522**

Duncker, K. The influence of past experience upon perceptual properties. *American Journal of Psychology,* 1939, *52,* 255–265. **424**

Dunham, P. J. Contrasted conditions of reinforcement: A selective critique. *Psychological Bulletin,* 1968, *69,* 295–315. **638***n*

Dunham, P. J., & Kilps, B. Shifts in magnitude of reinforcement: Confounded factors or contrast effects? *Journal of Experimental Psychology,* 1969, *79,* 373–374. **634, 638***n*

Dunn, H. K., see Barney, H. L., 1957.

Dunn, S., Bliss, J., & Siipola, E. Effects of impulsivity, introversion, and individual values upon association under free conditions. *Journal of Personality,* 1958, *26,* 61–76. **875**

Durlach, N. I. Equalization and cancellation theory of binaural masking-level difference. *Journal of the Acoustical Society of America,* 1963, *35,* 1206–1218. **242**

Durlach, N. I., see also Colburn, H. S., 1965.

Duryea, R. A., see Krauskopf, J., 1954.

Dustman, R. E., see Brown, H. M., 1966.

Dyal, J. A., see Sgro, J. A., 1967.

Dyson, G. M. The scientific basis of odour. *Chemistry and Industry,* 1938, *57,* 647–651. **220**

Dzendolet, E. A structure common to sweet-evoking compounds. *Perception and Psychophysics,* 1968, *3,* 65–68. **179**

Dzendolet, E., & Meiselman, H. L. Cation and anion contributions to gustatory quality of simple salts. *Perception and Psychophysics,* 1967, *2,* 601–604. (a) **178**

Dzendolet, E., & Meiselman, L. Gustatory quality changes as a function of solution concentration. *Perception and Psychophysics,* 1967, *2,* 29–33. (b) **179**

Eady, H., see Klumpp, R. G., 1956.

Earhard, B., & Earhard, M. Role of interference factors in three-stage mediation paradigms. *Journal of Experimental Psychology,* 1967, *73,* 526–531. **1075, 1077**

Earhard, B., & Mandler, G. Mediated associations, paradigms, controls, and mechanisms. *Canadian Journal of Psychology,* 1965, *19,* 346–378. (a) **1071, 1076**

Earhard, B., & Mandler, G. Pseudomediation: A reply and more data. *Psychonomic Science,* 1965, *3,* 137–138. (b) **1075, 1076, 1077**

Earhard, B., see also Mandler, G., 1964.

Earhard, M., see Earhard, B., 1967.

Earle, A. E., see Hall, K. R. L., 1952.

Eastmond, E. J., see Bassett, I. G., 1964.

Eayrs, J. T., see Moulton, D., 1960.

Ebbecke, U. Über das Sehen im Flimmerlicht. *Pflüger's Archiv für die Gesamte Physiologie des Menschen und der Tiere,* 1920, *185,* 196–223. **314**

Ebbecke, U. Über die Temperaturempfindungen in ihrer Abhängigkeit von der Hautdurchblutung und von den Reflexzentren. *Pflüger's Archiv fur die Gesamte Physiologie des Menschen und der Tiere,* 1917, *169,* 395–462. **153**

Ebbinghaus, H. *Memory: A contribution to experimental psychology:* 1885. (H. A. Ruger & C. E. Bussenius, Tr.) New York: Teachers College, Columbia University, 1913. **980, 982, 1013**

Ebbinghaus, H. *Über das Gedächtnis.* Leipzig: Duncker & Humbolt, 1885. (H. A. Ruger & C. E. Bussenius, Tr.) New York: Teachers College, 1913. Reissued, New York: Dover, 1964. **592, 598, 601, 847, 848, 854, 1107**

Ebbinghaus, H. *Grundzüge der Psychologie,* Vol. II. Leipzig: Dürr, E., Fortges, 1913. **463**

Ebeling, E., *see* Ritchie, B. F., 1950.

Ebenholtz, S., *see* Rock, I., 1959, 1962.

Ebenholtz, S. M. Position mediated transfer between serial learning and a spatial discrimination task. *Journal of Experimental Psychology,* 1963, 65, 603-608. (a) **1012**

Ebenholtz, S. M. Serial learning: Position learning and sequential associations. *Journal of Experimental Psychology,* 1963, 66, 353-362. (b) **1012, 1013**

Ebenholtz, S. M. Adaptation to a rotated visual field as a function of degree of optical tilt and exposure time. *Journal of Experimental Psychology,* 1966, 72, 629-634. **539**

Ebenholtz, S. M., *see also* Asch, S. E., 1962.

Ebert, E., & Meumann, E. Über einige Grundfragen der Psychologie der Übungsphenomene im Bereiche des Gedächtnisses. *Archiv für die Gesamte Psychologie,* 1905, 4, 1-232. **1030**

Ebrey, T. G. Fast light-evoked potential from leaves. *Science,* 1967, 155, 1556-1557. **307**

Eckert, B., & Lewis, M. Competition between drives for intracranial stimulation and sodium chloride by adrenalectomized NaCl deprived rats. *Journal of Comparative and Physiological Psychology,* 1967, 64, 349-352. **651**

Edes, B., & Dallenbach, K. M. The adaptation of pain aroused by cold. *American Journal of Psychology,* 1936, 48, 307-315. **159**

Edwards, B. J., *see* Nealey, S. M., 1960.

Edwards, W. Emmert's law and Euclid's optics. *American Journal of Psychology,* 1950, 63, 607-612. **511**

Edwards, W. Apparent size of after-images under conditions of reduction. *American Journal of Psychology,* 1953, 66, 449-455. **511**

Edwards, W. Reward probability, amount, and information as determiners of sequential two-alternative decisions. *Journal of Experimental Psychology,* 1956, 52, 177-188. **918**

Edwards, W. Probability learning in 1000 trials. *Journal of Experimental Psychology,* 1961, 962, 385-394. **918, 920, 921**

Edwards, W., *see also* Boring, E. G., 1951; Lindman, H., 1961.

Efstathiou, A., Bauer, J., Greene, M., & Held, R. Altered reaching following adaptation to optical displacement of the hand. *Journal of Experimental Psychology,* 1967, 73, 113-120. **538**

Efstathiou, A., *see also* Held, R., 1966.

Egan, J. P. Articulation testing methods. *The Laryngoscope,* 1948, 58, 955-991. **254, 255**

Egan, J. P. Hearing. In C. P. Stone (Ed.), *Annual review of psychology.* Vol. 5. Stanford: Annual Reviews, Inc., 1954. **240**

Egan, J. P. Masking-level differences as a function of interaural disparities in intensity of signal and noise. *Journal of the Acoustical Society of America,* 1965, 38, 1043-1049. **243**

Egan, J. P., Carterette, E. C., & Thwing, E. J. Some factors affecting multichannel listening. *Journal of the Acoustical Society of America,* 1954, 26, 774-782. **259**

Egan, J. P., & Hake, H. W. On the masking pattern of a simple auditory stimulus. *Journal of the Acoustical Society of America,* 1950, 22, 622-630. **238, 239**

Egan, J. P., & Wiener, F. M. On the intelligibility of bands of speech in noise. *Journal of the Acoustical Society of America,* 1946, 18, 435-441. **257**

Egbert, L. D., *see* Smith, G. M., 1966.

Egger, M. D., & Miller, N. E. Secondary reinforcement in rats as a function of information value and reliability of the stimulus. *Journal of Experimental Psychology,* 1962, 64, 97-104. **556, 675, 676**

Egger, M. D., & Miller, N. E. When is a reward reinforcing?: An experimental study of the information hypothesis. *Journal of Comparative and Physiological Psychology,* 1963, 56, 132-137. **556, 676**

Ehmann, E. D., *see* Erickson, J. R., 1966.

Ehmer, R. H. Masking by tones vs. noise bands. *Journal of the Acoustical Society of America,* 1959, 31, 1253-1256. **239**

Ehrenfreund, D. An experimental test of the continuity theory of discrimination with pattern vision. *Journal of Comparative Psychology,* 1948, 41, 408-422. **749, 766**

Ehrenfreund, D. The relationship between weight loss during deprivation and food consumption. *Journal of Comparative and Physiological Psychology,* 1959, 52, 123-125. **812**

Ehrenfreund, D. The motivational effect of a continuous weight loss schedule. *Psychological Reports,* 1960, 6, 339-345. **819**

Ehrenfreund, D., & Badia, P. R. Response strength as a function of drive level and pre- and post-shift incentive magnitude. *Journal of Experimental Psychology,* 1962, 63, 468-471. **633, 634**

Ehrenfreund, D., *see also* Alberts, E., 1951.

Ehrlich, D., *see* Orbach, J., 1963.

Eijkman, E. G., *see* Vendrik, A. J. H., 1968.

Eimas, P. D., *see* Shepp, B. E., 1964.

Eisenberger, R., Karpman, M., & Trattner, J. What is the necessary and sufficient condition for reinforcement in the contingency situation? *Journal of Experimental Psychology,* 1967, 74, 342-350. **624**

Eisenstein, E. M., and Cohen, M. J. Learning in an isolated prothoracic insect ganglion. *Animal Behaviour,* 1965, 13, 104-108. **578**

Eisler, H. On the problem of category scales in psychophysics. *Scandinavian Journal of Psychology,* 1962, 3, 81-87. (a) **83**

Eisler, H. Empirical test of a model relating magnitude and category scales. *Scandinavian Journal of Psychology,* 1962, 3, 88-96. (b) **83**

Eisler, H., *see also* Ekman, G., 1960.

Eisman, B. S. Attitude formation: The development of a color-preference response through mediated generalization. *Journal of Abnormal and Social Psychology,* 1955, 50, 321-326. **781**

Eisman, E., Effects of deprivation and consummatory activity on heart rate. *Journal of Comparative and Physiological Psychology,* 1966, 62, 71-75. **836, 838**

Eissler, K. Die Gestaltkonstanz der Sehdinge bei Variation der Objekte und ihrer Einwirkungsweise auf den Wahrnehmenden. *Archiv für die Gesamte Psychologie,* 1933, 88, 487-550. **515**

Ekman, G. Discriminal sensitivity on the subjective continuum. *Acta psychologica,* 1956, 12, 15-18. **83**

Ekman, G. Two generalized ratio scaling methods. *Journal of Psychology,* 1958, 45, 287-295. **68, 71, 72**

Ekman, G. Weber's law and related functions. *Journal of Psychology,* 1959, 47, 343-352. **18, 80, 81, 83**

Ekman, G. A methodological note on scales of gustatory intensity. *Scandinavian Journal of Psychology,* 1961, 2, 185-190. **80, 81, 175**

Ekman, G. A simple method for fitting psychophysical power functions. *Journal of Psychology,* 1961, 51, 343-350. **68**

Ekman, G. Measurement of moral judgment. *Perceptual and Motor Skills,* 1962, 15, 3-9. **82**

Ekman, G. Is the power law a special case of Fechner's law? *Perceptual and Motor Skills,* 1964, 19, 730. **85, 86n**

Ekman, G., & Akesson, C. Saltiness, sweetness and preference: A study of quantitative relations in individual subjects. *Reports from the Psychological Laboratories, The University of Stockholm,* 1964, *177,* 1-13. **175**

Ekman, G., Eisler, H., & Künnapas, T. Brightness of monocular light as measured by the method of magnitude production. *Acta Psychologica,* 1960, *17,* 392-397. **67**

Ekman, G., & Künnapas, T. Scales of aesthetic value. *Perceptual and Motor Skills,* 1962, *14,* 19-26. (a) **82**

Ekman, G., & Künnapas, T. Scales of aesthetic value by "direct" and "indirect" methods. *Scandinavian Journal of Psychology,* 1962, *3,* 33-39. (b) **82**

Ekman, G., & Künnapas, T. A further study of direct and indirect scaling methods. *Scandinavian Journal of Psychology,* 1963, *4,* 77-88. (a) **82**

Ekman, G., & Künnapas, T. Scales of conservatism. *Perceptual and Motor Skills,* 1963, *16,* 329-334. (b) **82**

Ekman, G., & Sjöberg, L. Scaling. *Annual Review of Psychology,* 1965, *16,* 451-474.

Ekman, G., see also Björkman, M., 1962.

Ekstrand, B. R. Backward associations. *Psychological Bulletin,* 1966, *65,* 60-64. **1060**

Ekstrand, B. R. Effect of sleep on memory. *Journal of Experimental Psychology,* 1967, *75,* 64-72. **1123**

Ekstrand, B. R., & Underwood, B. J. Free learning and recall as a function of unit-sequence and letter-sequence interference. *Journal of Verbal Learning and Verbal Behavior,* 1965, *4,* 390-396. **1128**

Ekstrand, B. R., Wallace, W. P., & Underwood, B. J. A frequency theory of verbal-discrimination learning. *Psychological Review,* 1966, *13,* 566-578. **854, 887, 898**

Ekstrand, B. R., see also Underwood, B. J., 1964, 1966, 1967a, b, 1968a, b.

Elam, C. B., see Bitterman, M. E., 1955.

Eldert, K., see Kirsh, I. J., 1952.

Eldredge, D. H., see Deatherage, B. H., 1957; Kryter, K. D., 1966; Tasaki, I., 1954; Teas, D. C., 1962.

Eldridge, R. G., & Johnson, J. C. Diffuse transmission through real atmospheres. *Journal of the Optical Society of America,* 1958, *48,* 463-468. **498**

Elfner, L. F., see Thurlow, W. R., 1959, 1961.

Elfner, L. L. Systematic shifts in the judgments of octaves of high frequencies. *Journal of the Acoustical Society of America,* 1964, *36,* 270-276. **243**

Ellen, P. The compulsive nature of abnormal fixations. *Journal of Comparative and Physiological Psychology,* 1956, *49,* 309-317. **791**

Ellen, P., see also Alpern, M., 1956; Feldman, R. S., 1951; Maier, N. R. F., 1951.

Ellington, N. R., & Kausler, D. H. "Fate" of List 1 associations in transfer theory. *Journal of Experimental Psychology,* 1965, *69,* 207-208. **1095**

Elliot, O., see Stanley, W. C., 1962.

Elliot, P. B. Tables of d'. In J. A. Swets (Ed.), *Signal detection and recognition by human observers.* New York: Wiley, 1964, 651-658. **42**

Elliott, D. N., see Baker, L. M., 1948.

Elliott, L. L. Backward masking: Monotic and dichotic conditions. *Journal of the Acoustical Society of America,* 1962, *34,* 1108-1115. (a) **241**

Elliott, L. L. Backward and forward masking of probe tones of different frequencies. *Journal of the Acoustical Society of America,* 1962, *34,* 1116-1117. (b) **241**

Elliott, M. H. The effect of change of reward on the maze performance of rats. *University of California Publications in Psychology,* 1928, *4,* 19-30. **617**

Elliott, M. H. Some determining factors in maze performance. *American Journal of Psychology,* 1930, *42,* 315-317. **617**

Elliott, M. H., see also Bousfield, W. A., 1934.

Ellis, N. R. Object-quality discrimination learning sets in mental defectives. *Journal of Comparative and Physiological Psychology,* 1958, *51,* 79-81. **768**

Ellis, W. D. (Ed.) *A source book of Gestalt psychology.* London: Routledge, 1938. **764**

Emmerich, D., see Restle, F., 1966.

Emmers, R., see also Benjamin, R. M., 1968; Wayner, M. J. Jr., 1959.

Emery, D. A., see Köhler, W., 1947.

Engel, G. R., see Dodwell, P. C., 1963.

Engen, T. Effect of practice and instruction on olfactory threshold. *Perceptual and Motor Skills,* 1960, *10,* 195-198. **18, 207**

Engen, T. Direct scaling of odor intensity. *Reports from the Psychological Laboratories, The University of Stockholm,* 1961, *106.* **70, 204, 205**

Engen, T. The psychological similarity of the odors of the aliphatic alcohols. *Reports from the Psychological Laboratories, The University of Stockholm,* 1962, *127.* **215, 216**

Engen, T. Cross adaptation to aliphatic alcohols. *American Journal of Psychology,* 1963, *76,* 96-102. **215**

Engen, T. Psychophysical scaling of odor intensity and quality. *Annals of the New York Academy of Science,* 1964, *116,* 504-516. **200, 205**

Engen, T., Bartoshuk, L., & McBurney, D. H. The effect of food deprivation on the detection of sucrose in distilled water. Unpublished experiment, Brown University, 1964. **36, 43**

Engen, T. & Levy, N. The influence of context on constant-sum loudness-judgments. *American Journal of Psychology,* 1958, *71,* 731-736. **73**

Engen, T., Levy, N., and Schlosberg, H. The dimensional analysis of a new series of facial expressions. *Journal of Experimental Psychology,* 1958, *55,* 454-458. **56, 57**

Engen, T., & Lindström, C. O. Psychophysical scales of the odor intensity of amyl acetate. *Scandinavian Journal of Psychology,* 1963, *4,* 23-28. **75**

Engen, T., & Lipsitt, L. P. Decrement and recovery of responses to olfactory stimuli in the human neonate. *Journal of Comparative and Physiological Psychology,* 1965, *59,* 312-316. **590**

Engen, T., & McBurney, D. H. Magnitude and category scales of the pleasantness of odors. *Journal of Experimental Psychology,* 1964, *68,* 435-440. **64, 216**

Engen, T., & Pfaffmann, C. Absolute judgments of odor intensity. *Journal of Experimental Psychology,* 1959, *58,* 23-26. **199, 205**

Engen, T., & Tulunay, Ü. Some sources of error in half-heaviness judgments. *Journal of Experimental Psychology,* 1956, *54,* 208-212. **67, 70**

Enoch, J. M., see Boynton, R. M., 1954.

Enroth, C. The mechanism of flicker and fusion studied on single retinal elements in the dark-adapted eye of the cat. *Acta Physiologica Scandinavica,* 1952, *27,* Suppl. 100, 1-67. **314**

Entwisle, D. R. *Word associations of young children.* Baltimore: Johns Hopkins University Press, 1966. **861**

Entwisle, D. R., Forsyth, D. F., & Muus, R. The syntactic-paradigmatic shift in children's word associations. *Journal of Verbal Learning and Verbal Behavior,* 1964, *3,* 19-29. **874**

Epley, J. M., see Simmons, F. B., 1965.

Epstein, A. N. Reciprocal changes in feeding behavior produced by intra-hypothalamus chemical injections. *American Journal of Physiology,* 1960, *199,* 969-974. **651**

Epstein, A. N., & Teitelbaum, P. Regulation of food intake in the absence of taste, smell, and other oropharyngeal sensations. *Journal of Comparative and Physiological Psychology,* 1962, 753-759. **621n, 797**

Epstein, A. N., see also Teitelbaum, P., 1962, 1963.

Epstein, W. The influence of syntactical structure on learning. *American Journal of Psychology,* 1961, *74,* 80-85. **903**

Epstein, W. The known-size-apparent-distance hypothesis. *American Journal of Psychology*, 1961, *74*, 333–346. **495, 506**

Epstein, W. Phenomenal orientation and perceived achromatic color. *Journal of Psychology*, 1961, *52*, 51–53. **421**

Epstein, W. Backward association as a function of meaningfulness. *Journal of General Psychology*, 1962, *67*, 11–20. (a) **857**

Epstein, W. A further study of the influence of syntactic structure on learning. *American Journal of Psychology*, 1962, *75*, 121–126. (b) **903**

Epstein, W. The influence of assumed size on apparent distance. *American Journal of Psychology*, 1963, *76*, 257–265. **495**

Epstein, W. Nonrelational judgment of size and distance. *American Journal of Psychology*, 1965, *78*, 120–123. **495**

Epstein, W. *Varieties of perceptual learning.* New York: McGraw-Hill, 1967. **439, 440**

Epstein, W., & Baratz, S. S. Relative size in isolation as a stimulus for relative perceived distance. *Journal of Experimental Psychology*, 1964, *67*, 507–513. **496**

Epstein, W., Bontrager, H., & Park, J. The induction of nonveridical slant and the perception of shape. *Journal of Experimental Psychology*, 1962, *63*, 472–479. **509, 516**

Epstein, W., & DeShazo, D. Recency as a function of perceptual oscillation. *American Journal of Psychology*, 1961, *74*, 215–223. **439**

Epstein, W., & Park, J. N. Shape constancy: Functional relationships and theoretical formulations. *Psychological Bulletin*, 1963, *60*, 265–288. **507, 515**

Epstein, W., & Park, J. Examination of Gibson's psychophysical hypothesis. *Psychological Bulletin*, 1964, *62*, 180–196. **505**

Epstein, W., Park, J., & Casey, A. The current status of the size–distance hypothesis. *Psychological Bulletin*, 1961, *58*, 491–514. **507, 508, 510, 511**

Epstein, W., & Rock, I. Set as an artifact of recency. *American Journal of Psychology*, 1960, *73*, 214–228. **439**

Erickson, J. R., & Zajkowski, M. M. Learning several concept-identification problems concurrently: A test of the sampling-with-replacement assumption. *Journal of Experimental Psychology*, 1967, *74*, 212–218. **974**

Erickson, J. R., Zajkowski, M. M., & Ehmann, E. D. All-or-none assumptions in concept identification. *Journal of Experimental Psychology*, 1966, *72*, 690–697. **957, 974**

Erickson, R. P. Sensory neural patterns and gustation. In Y. Zotterman (Ed.), *Olfaction and taste*. Vol. 1. New York: Pergamon Press, 1963. Pp. 205–213. **180**

Erickson, R. P., Doetsch, G. S., & Marshall, D. A. The gustatory neural response function. *Journal of General Physiology*, 1965, *49*, 247–263. **180**

Erickson, R. P., *see also* Harper, H. W., 1966; Pfaffmann, C., 1961.

Erickson, T., *see* Penfield, W., 1941.

Eriksen, C. W. Unconscious processes. In M. R. Jones (Ed.), *Nebraska symposium on motivation: 1958*. Lincoln, Nebraska: University of Nebraska Press, 1958. **445n**

Eriksen, C. W., & Collins, J. F. Backward masking in vision. *Psychonomic Science*, 1964, *1*, 101–102. **430**

Eriksen, C. W., Collins, J. F., Greenspoon, T. S. An analysis of certain factors responsible for nonmonotonic backward masking functions. *Journal of Experimental Psychology*, 1967, *75*, 500–507. **430**

Eriksen, C. W., & Collins, J. F. Reinterpretation of one form of backward and forward masking in visual perception. *Journal of Experimental Psychology*, 1965, *70*, 343–351. **430**

Eriksen, C. W., Greenspoon, T. S., Lappin, J., & Carlson, W. A. Binocular summation in the perception of form at brief durations. *Perception & Psychophysics*, 1966, *1*, 415–419. **488**

Eriksen, C. W., & Hoffman, M. Form recognition at brief durations as a function of adapting field and interval between stimulations. *Journal of Experimental Psychology*, 1963, *66*, 485–499. **430**

Eriksen, C. W., & Lappin, J. Luminance summation–contrast reduction as a basis for certain forward and backward masking effect. *Psychonomic Science*, 1964, *1*, 313–314. **430**

Eriksen, C. W., & Lappin, J. S. Selective attention and very short-term recognition memory for nonsense forms. *Journal of Experimental Psychology*, 1967, *73*, 358–364. **444**

Eriksen, C. W., & Steffy, R. A. Short-term memory and retroactive interference in visual perception. *Journal of Experimental Psychology*, 1964, *68*, 423–434. **430**

Eriksen, C. W., *see also* Garner, W. R., 1956.

Erlebacher, A., & Sekuler, R. Explanation of the Müller-Lyer illusion: Confusion theory examined. *Journal of Experimental Psychology*, 1969, *80*, 462–467. **463**

Erlebacher, A., *see also* Richardson, J., 1958.

Erulkar, S. A., *see* Nelson, P. G., 1966.

Ervin, S. M. Changes with age in the verbal determinants of word-association. *American Journal of Psychology*, 1961, *74*, 361–372. **874**

Estes, W. K. An experimental study of punishment. *Psychological Monographs*, 1944, *57*, Whole No. 263. **737, 738**

Estes, W. K. Toward a statistical theory of learning. *Psychological Review*, 1950, *57*, 94–107. **908**

Estes, W. K. Statistical theory of distributional phenomena in learning. *Psychological Review*, 1955, *62*, 369–377. **929**

Estes, W. K. The problem of inference from curves based on group data. *Psychological Bulletin*, 1956, *53*, 134–140. **609, 917**

Estes, W. K. Stimulus-response theory of drive. In M. R. Jones (Ed.), *Nebraska symposium on motivation*. Lincoln, Nebraska: University of Nebraska Press, 1958. **801**

Estes, W. K. Component and pattern models with Markovian interpretations. In R. R. Bush & W. K. Estes (Eds.), *Studies in mathematical learning theory*. Stanford: Stanford University Press, 1959. Pp. 9–52. (a) **927, 990, 995, 1002**

Estes, W. K. The statistical approach to learning theory. In S. Koch (Ed.), *Psychology: A study of a science*. Vol. 2. New York: McGraw-Hill, 1959. Pp. 380–491. (b) **909, 910, 929**

Estes, W. K. Learning theory and the new "mental chemistry." *Psychological Review*, 1960, *67*, 207–233. **987**

Estes, W. K. New developments in statistical behavior theory: Differential tests of axioms for associative learning. *Psychometrika*, 1961, *26*, 73–84. **987, 988**

Estes, W. K. All-or-none processes in learning and retention. *American Psychologist*, 1964, *19*, 16–25. (a) **987**

Estes, W. K. Probability learning. In A. W. Melton (Ed.), *Categories of human learning*. New York: Academic Press, 1964. Pp. 89–128. (b) **919, 922**

Estes, W. K. Transfer of verbal discriminations based on differential reward magnitudes. *Journal of Experimental Psychology*, 1966, *72*, 276–283. **641**

Estes, W. K. Outline of a theory of punishment. In B. A. Campbell & R. M. Church (Eds.), *Punishment*. New York: Appleton, 1969. **738**

Estes, W. K., & Burke, C. J. A theory of stimulus variability in learning *Psychological Review*, 1953, *60*, 276–286. **924**

Estes, W. K., & Burke, C. J. Application of a statistical model to simple discrimination learning in human subjects. *Journal of Experimental Psychology*, 1955, *50*, 81–88. **930**

Estes, W. K., Burke, C. J., Atkinson, R. C., & Frankmann, J. B. Probabilistic discrimination learning. *Journal of Experimental Psychology*, 1957, *54*, 233–239. **927**

Estes, W. K., & Hopkins, B. L. Acquisition and transfer in pattern-vs.-component discrimination learning. *Journal of Experimental Psychology,* 1961, *61,* 322–328. **927, 1002, 1003**

Estes, W. K., Hopkins, B. L., & Crothers, E. J. All-or-none and conservation effects in the learning and retention of paired-associates. *Journal of Experimental Psychology,* 1960, *60,* 329–339. **987, 989**

Estes, W. K., & Skinner, B. F. Some quantitative properties of anxiety. *Journal of Experimental Psychology,* 1941, *29,* 390–400. **712, 713**

Estes, W. K., & Straughan, J. H. Analysis of a verbal conditioning situation in terms of statistical learning theory. *Journal of Experimental Psychology,* 1954, *47,* 225–234. **908**

Estes, W. K., & Suppes, P. Foundations of linear models. In R. R. Bush & W. K. Estes (Eds.), *Studies in mathematical learning theory.* Stanford: Stanford University Press, 1959. Pp. 137–179. **911, 919, 922**

Estes, W. K., *see also* Atkinson, R. C., 1963; Binder, A., 1966; Burke, C. J., 1954, 1957; Friedman, M. P., 1964.

Etkin, M., *see* D'Amato, M. R., 1967.

Evans, C. R., & Piggins, D. J. A comparison of the behavior of geometrical shapes when viewed under conditions of steady fixation and with apparatus for producing a stabilized retinal image. *British Journal of Physiological Optics,* 1963, *20,* 1–13. **453**

Evans, D. R. Chemical structure and stimulation by carbohydrates. In Y. Zotterman (Ed.), *Olfaction and taste.* Vol. I. New York: Pergamon, 1963, Pp. 165–176. **190**

Evans, D. R., & Mellon, D. Stimulation of a primary taste receptor by salts. *Journal of General Physiology,* 1962, *45,* 651–661. **189**

Evans, E. F., *see* Whitefield, I. C., 1965.

Evans, R. M. *An introduction to color.* New York: Wiley, 1948. **319, 420**

Evans, R. M. Psychological aspects of color and illumination. *Illuminating Engineering* (New York) 1951, *46,* 176–184. **426, 427**

Evans, R. M. Variables of perceived color. *Journal of the Optical Society of America,* 1964, *54,* 1467–1473. **368**

Evarts, E. V. Relation of pyramidal tract activity to force exerted during voluntary movement. *Journal of Neurophysiology,* 1968, *31,* 14–27. **113**

Everett, N. B. *Functional neuroanatomy.* (5th ed.) Philadelphia: Lea & Febiger, 1965. **128**

Ewert, P. H. A study of the effect of inverted retinal stimulation upon spatially coordinated behavior. *Genetic Psychology Monographs,* 1930, *7,* 177–363. **533**

Exner, J. E., *see also* Smith, O. W., 1968.

Eysenck, M. D. An experimental and statistical study of olfactory preferences. *Journal of Experimental Psychology,* 1944, *34,* 246–252. **216**

Eyzaguirre, C., *see* Kuffler, S. W., 1955–56.

Fabian, F. W., & Blum, H. B. Relative taste potency of some basic food constituents and their competitive and compensatory action. *Food Research,* 1943, *8,* 179–193. **187**

Fagot, R. F., & Stewart, M. R. An experimental comparison of stimulus and response translated power functions for brightness. *Perception and Psychophysics,* 1968, *3,* 297–305. **81**

Fairbanks, G. Test for phonemic differentiation: The rhyme test. *Journal of the Acoustical Society of America,* 1958, *30,* 596–600. **255**

Fairbanks, G., & Kodman, F., Jr. Word intelligibility as a function of time compression. *Journal of the Acoustical Society of America,* 1957, *29,* 636–641. **257**

Fantino, E., & Herrnstein, R. J. Secondary reinforcement and number of primary reinforcements. *Journal of the Experimental Analysis of Behavior,* 1968, *11,* 9–14. **667**

Fantz, R. L. A method for studying depth perception in infants under six months of age. *Psychological Record,* 1961, *11,* 27–32. **547, 549**

Fantz, R. L. The origin of form perception. *Scientific American,* 1961, *204,* 66–72. **549**

Fantz, R. L. Ontogeny of perception. In A. M. Schrier, H. F. Harlow, & F. Stollnitz (Eds.), *Behavior of nonhuman primates: Modern research trends.* Vol. 2. New York: Academic Press, 1965. **549**

Farber, I. E. Response fixation under anxiety and non-anxiety conditions. *Journal of Experimental Psychology,* 1948, *38,* 111–131. **791**

Farber, I. E., *see also* Brown, J. S., 1951, 1968.

Farné, M. Ulteriore contributo allo studio degli stimoli marginali. (Another contribution to the study of marginal stimuli.) *Archivo di Psicologia, Neurologia e Psichiatria,* 1964, *25,* 444–463. **472**

Farné, M. Grado do discernibilita dello stimulo e comportamento percettivo. (Degree of stimulus discriminability and perceptual behavior.) *Archivo di Psicologica, Neurologia e Psichiatria,* 1965, *26,* 566–576. **469, 470n**

Farné, M., *see also* Canestrari, R., 1969.

Farnsworth, D. A temporal factor in colour discrimination. In *Visual problems of colour.* London: HM Stationery Office, 1958. **361**

Farnum, E. C., *see* Seashore, E. C., 1908.

Farrell, W. M., *see* Tallarico, R. B., 1964.

Frazzaro, J., *see* D'Amato, M. R., 1966, 1967.

Fechner, G. T. *Elemente der Psychophysik.* Leipzig: Breitkopf and Härterl, 1860. English translation of Vol. 1 by H. E. Adler (D. H. Howes and E. G. Boring, Eds.). New York: Holt, Rinehart and Winston, 1966. **11, 49, 82**

Feddersen, W. E., Sandel, T. T., Teas, D. C., & Jeffress, L. A. Localization of high frequency tones. *Journal of the Acoustical Society of America,* 1957, *29,* 989–991. **260**

Fedderson, W. E., *see also* Sandel, T. T., 1955.

Fehr, F. S., *see* Hahn, W. W., 1964.

Fehrer, E. Effects of amount of reinforcement and of pre- and post-reinforcement delays on learning and extinction. *Journal of Experimental Psychology,* 1956, *52,* 167–176. **619, 620**

Fehrer, E. Contribution of perceptual segregation to the relationship between stimulus similarity and backward masking. *Perceptual and Motor Skills,* 1965, *21,* 27–33. **430**

Fehrer, E. Effect of stimulus similarity on retroactive masking. *Journal of Experimental Psychology,* 1966, *71,* 612–615. **430**

Fehrer, E., & Biederman, I. A comparison of reaction and verbal report in the detection of masked stimuli. *Journal of Experimental Psychology,* 1962, *64,* 126–130. **430**

Fehrer, E., & Ganchrow, D. Effects of exposure variables on figural after-effects under tachistoscopic presentation. *Journal of Experimental Psychology,* 1963, *66,* 506–513. **469**

Fehrer, E., & Raab, D. Reaction time to stimuli masked by metacontrast. *Journal of Experimental Psychology,* 1962, *63,* 143–147. **430**

Fehrer, E. & Smith, E. Effect of luminance ratio on masking. *Perceptual and Motor Skills,* 1962, *14,* 243–253. **430**

Fehrer. E. V., *see also* Helson, H., 1932.

Feigenbaum, E. A. *An information processing theory of verbal learning.* Report P-1817. Santa Monica. The RAND Corporation, 1959. **1008, 1016**

Feigenbaum, E. A. The simulation of verbal learning. In E. A. Feigenbaum & J. Feldman (Eds.), *Computers and thought.* New York: McGraw-Hill, 1963. Pp. 297–309. **1008**

Feigenbaum, E. A., & Simon, H. A. Comment: The distinctiveness of stimuli. *Psychological Review,* 1961, *68,* 285–288. **1008, 1017**

Feigenbaum, E. A., & Simon, H. A. A theory of the serial

position effect. *British Journal of Psychology*, 1962, *53*, 307–320. **1008, 1013, 1016**

Feigenbaum, E. A., & Simon, H. A. Brief notes on the EPAM theory of verbal learning. In C. N. Cofer & B. S. Musgrave (Eds.), *Verbal behavior and learning: Problems and processes*. New York: McGraw-Hill, 1963. Pp. 333–335. **1008**

Feigenbaum, E. A., *see also* Simon, H. A., 1964.

Feinberg, L. D., *see* Flavell, J. H., 1958.

Feirstein, A. R., & Miller, N. E. Learning to resist pain and fear: Effects of electric shock before versus after reaching goal. *Journal of Comparative and Physiological Psychology*, 1963, *56*, 797–800. **706, 737**

Feldman, J. An analysis of prediction behavior in a two-choice situation. In E. A. Feigenbaum & J. Feldman (Eds.), *Computers and thought*. New York: McGraw-Hill, 1963. **907**

Feldman, J., & Hanna, J. F. The structure of responses to a sequence of binary events. *Journal of Mathematical Psychology*, 1966, *3*, 371–387. **936**

Feldman, R. S. An automatically controlled Lashley discrimination mechanism. *American Journal of Psychology*, 1948, *61*, 414–419. **749, 750**

Feldman, R. S., & Ellen, P. Frustration and fixation. (Film.) Pennsylvania State College: Psychological Cinema Register, 16 mm sound, 1951. **791**

Feldman, R. S., *see also* Zwislocki, J., 1956.

Feldman, S., *see* Laffal, J., 1962–63.

Feldman, S. E., *see* Binder, A., 1960.

Feldman, S. M., & Underwood, B. J. Stimulus recall following paired-associate learning. *Journal of Experimental Psychology*, 1957, *53*, 11–15. **893**

Feldman, S. M., *see also* Belanger, D., 1962.

Feller, W. *An introduction to probability theory and its applications*. (2nd ed.) New York: Wiley, 1957. **995**

Fender, D. H. Torsional motions of the eyeball. *British Journal of Ophthalmology*, 1955, *39*, 65–72. **374**

Fender, D. H., & Nye, P. W. An investigation of the mechanisms of eye movement control. *Kybernetik*, 1961, *1*, 81–88. **379**

Fender, D. H., *see also* Ditchburn, R. W., 1955.

Ferguson, C. V., *see* Langmuir, I., 1944.

Fernberger, S. W. New phenomena of apparent visual movement. *American Journal of Psychology*, 1934, *46*, 309–314. **527**

Fernberger, S. W. The figural after-effect in the third dimension of visual space. *American Journal of Psychology*, 1948, *61*, 291–293. **470**

Ferrall, S. C., & Dallenbach, K. M. The analysis and synthesis of burning heat. *American Journal of Psychology*, 1930, *42*, 72–82. **148**

Ferster, C. B. Sustained behavior under delayed reinforcement. *Journal of Experimental Psychology*, 1953, *48*, 218–224. **684**

Ferster, C. B. The use of the free operant in the analysis of behavior. *Psychological Bulletin*, 1953, *50*, 263–274. **747**

Ferster, C. B., & Skinner, B. F. *Schedules of reinforcement*. New York: Appleton, 1957. **604, 605, 607, 608, 665, 697, 698**

Festinger, L., Ono, H., Burnham, C. A., & Bamber, D. Efference and the conscious experience of perception. *Journal of Experimental Psychology Monograph*, 1967. Whole No. 637. **453, 542**

Festinger, L., White, C. W., & Allyn, M. R. Eye movements and decrement in the Müller-Lyer illusion. *Perception and Psychophysics*, 1968, *3*, 376–382. **467n**

Festinger, L., *see also* Coren, S., 1967.

Fex, J. Auditory activity in centrifugal and centripetal cochlear fibers in cat. *Acta Physiologica Scandinavia*, Suppl. 189, 1962, *55*, 1–68. **233**

Ficks, L., *see* Pollack, I., 1954.

Filion, R. D. C., *see* Harcum, E. R., 1963.

Fillenbaum, S., & Jones, L. V. Grammatical contingencies in word association. *Journal of Verbal Learning and Verbal Behavior*, 1965, *4*, 248–255. **874**

Fillenbaum, S., *see also* Delk, J. L., 1965.

Finch, G., *see also* Culler, E., 1935.

Findley, J. D. Preference and switching under concurrent scheduling. *Journal of the Experimental Analysis of Behavior*, 1958, *1*, 123–145. **641**

Finger, F. W. Quantitative studies of "conflict:" I. Variations in latency and strength of the rat's response in a discrimination-jumping situation. *Journal of Comparative Psychology*, 1941, *31*, 97–127. **749**

Finger, F. W. Estrous activity as a function of measuring device. *Journal of Comparative and Physiological Psychology*, 1961, *54*, 524–526. **825**

Finger, F. W., Reid, L. S., & Weasner, M. H. Activity changes as a function of reinforcement under low drive. *Journal of Comparative and Physiological Psychology*, 1960, *53*, 385–387. **823**

Finger, F. W., & Spelt, D. K. The illustration of the horizontal-vertical illusion. *Journal of Experimental Psychology*, 1947, *37*, 243–250. **458**

Finger, F. W., *see also* Reid, L. S., 1955.

Fink, E., *see* Weisberg, P., 1966.

Fink, J. B., & Patton, R. M. Decrement of a learned drinking response accompanying changes in several stimulus characteristics. *Journal of Comparative and Physiological Psychology*, 1953, *46*, 23–27. **818**

Finn, J., *see* Johnson, T. J., 1965.

Fischer, B. Der Einfluss der Blickrichtung und Änderung der Kopfstellung (Halsreflex) auf die Bárányshen Zeigversuch. *Jahrbach der Psychiatrie und Neurologie*, 1915, *35*, 155–158. **534**

Fischer, G. J. Discrimination and successive spatial reversal learning in chicks that fail to imprint vs. ones that imprint strongly. *Perceptual and Motor Skills*, 1966, *23*, 579–584. **585**

Fischer, R. Genetics and gustatory chemoreception in man and other primates. In M. R. Kare & O. Maller (Eds.), *The chemical senses and nutrition*. Baltimore: Johns Hopkins Press, 1967. Pp. 61–81. **182**

Fischer, R., & Griffin, F. Pharmacogenetic aspects of gustation. *Arzneimittel-Forschung (Drug Research)*, 1964, *14*, 673–686. **182, 190**

Fishback, J., *see* Köhler, W., 1950.

Fisher, G. L. Saline preference in rats determined by contingent licking. *Journal of the Experimental Analysis of Behavior*, 1965, *8*, 295–303. **190**

Fisher, G. L., Pfaffmann, C., & Brown, E. Dulcin and saccharin taste in squirrel monkeys, rats, and man. *Science*, 1965, *150*, 506–507. **628**

Fisher, G. L., *see also* Pfaffmann, C., 1967.

Fisher, L., *see* Weinstein, S., 1964.

Fisher, R. A. *The design of experiments*. Edinburgh: Oliver & Boyd, 1935. **599**

Fisher, S. C., Hull, C., & Holtz, P. Past experience and perception: Memory color. *Amer. J. Psychol.*, 1956, *69*, 546–560. **425**

Fiske, D. W., & Maddi, S. R. (Eds.), *Functions of varied experience*. Homewood, Ill.: Dorsey Press, 1961. **841**

Fitch, F. B., *see* Hull, C. L., 1940.

Fitts, P. M. Perceptual-motor skill learning. In A. W. Melton (Ed.), *Categories of human learning*. New York: Academic Press, 1964. Pp. 243–285. **979**

Fitts, P. M., & Leonard, J. A. *Stimulus correlates of visual pattern recognition: A probability approach*. Columbus: Ohio State University Press, 1957.

Fitts, P. M., Meyer, W., Rappoport, M., Anderson, N. S., & Leonard, J. A. Stimulus correlates of visual pattern recognition: A probability approach. *Journal of Experimental Psychology*, 1956, *51*, 1–11. **447n**

FitzHugh, R., *see* Barlow, H. B., 1957.

Flanagan, J. L. *Speech analysis, synthesis, and perception.* New York: Academic Press, 1956. **229, 231, 251, 252, 253**

Flaugher, R. L., *see* Nunnally, J. C., 1963.

Flavell, J. H. Meaning and meaning similarity: II. The semantic differential and co-occurrence as predictors of judged similarity in meaning. *Journal of General Psychology,* 1961, *54,* 321–335. **901**

Flavell, J. H., Draguns, J., Feinberg, L. D., & Budin, W. A microgenetic approach to word association. *Journal of Abnormal and Social Psychology,* 1958, *57,* 1–7. **863**

Flavell, J. H., & Johnson, B. A. Meaning and meaning similarity: III. Latency and number of similarities as predictors of judged similarity in meaning. *Journal of General Psychology,* 1961, *64,* 337–348. **901**

Fleck F., *see* Rock, I., 1950.

Fleshler, M., *see* Hoffman, H. S., 1961, 1962, 1964.

Fletcher, H. *Speech and hearing.* Princeton, N.J.: Van Nostrand, 1929. **257**

Fletcher, H. Loudness, pitch and timbre of musical tones and their relation to the intensity, the frequency, and the overtone structure. *Journal of the Acoustical Society of America,* 1934, 6, 59–69. **244, 245**

Fletcher, H. Auditory patterns. *Review of Modern Physics,* 1940, *12,* 47–65. **240**

Fletcher, H. The pitch, loudness, and quality of musical tones. *American Journal of Physics,* 1946, *14,* 215–225. **226**

Fletcher, H. *Speech and hearing in communication.* Princeton, N.J.: Van Nostrand, 1953. **250, 254, 256, 257**

Fletcher, J. L., & Riopelle, A. Protective effect of the acoustic reflex for impulsive noises. *Journal of the Acoustical Society of America,* 1960, *32,* 401. **236**

Flock, H. R. A possible optical basis for monocular slant perception. *Psychological Review,* 1964, *71,* 380–391. (a) **501, 502, 505, 516**

Flock, H. R. Three theoretical views of slant perception. *Psychological Bulletin,* 1964, *62,* 110–121. (b) **501, 502, 505, 516**

Flock, H. R. Optical texture and linear perspective as stimuli for slant perception. *Psychological Review,* 1965, *72,* 505–514. **502, 505**

Flock, H. R., Wilson, A., & Poizner, S. Lightness matching for different visual routes through a compound scene. *Perception and Psychophysics,* 1966, *1,* 382–384. **421**

Flom, M. C., Weymouth, F. W., & Kahneman, D. Visual resolution and contour interaction. *Journal of the Optical Society of America,* 1963, *53,* 1026–1032.

Foley, J. M. Desarguesian property in visual space. *Journal of the Optical Society of America,* 1964, *54,* 684–692. **493**

Foley, J. M. Binocular disparity and perceived relative distance: An examination of two hypotheses. *Vision Research,* 1967, *7,* 655–670. **493**

Foley, J. P., Jr., & MacMillian, Z. L. Mediated generalization and the interpretation of verbal behavior: V. "Free association" as related to differences in professional training. *Journal of Experimental Psychology,* 1943, *33,* 299–310. **875**

Foley, J. P., Jr., *see also* Cofer, C. N., 1942.

Folgmann, E. E. E. An experimental study of composer-preferences of four outstanding orchestras. *Journal of Experimental Psychology,* 1933, *16,* 709–724. **53**

Follansbee, G. L., *see* Bales, J. F., 1935.

Forgays, D. Retinal locus as a factor in recognition of visually perceived words. *American Journal of Psychology,* 1953, *65,* 555–562. **444**

Forgays, D. G., *see* Mishkin, M., 1952.

Forsyth, D. F., *see* Entwisle, D. R., 1964.

Forsyth, G. A., & Brown, D. R. Stimulus correlates of tachisto-scopic discrimination–recognition performance: Compactness, jaggedness and areal asymmetry. *Perception & Psychophysics,* 1967, *2,* 597–600. **449**

Fort, J. G., *see* Myers, J. L., 1963.

Foss, D. J., *see* Jenkins, J. J., 1965.

Foster, D., Scofield, E. H., & Dallenbach, K. M. An olfactorium. *American Journal of Psychology,* 1950, *63,* 431–440. **201**

Foster, H., *see* Gagné, R. M., 1948, 1949, 1950.

Fowler, H. *Curiosity and exploratory behavior,* New York: Macmillan, 1965. **673, 841**

Fowler, H. Satiation and curiosity: Constructs for a drive and incentive-motivational theory of exploration. In K. W. Spence & J. T. Spence (Eds.), *The psychology of learning and motivation.* Vol. 1. New York: Academic Press, 1967. Pp. 157–227. **841**

Fowler, H., & Miller, N. E. Facilitation and inhibition of runway performance by hind- and forepaw shock of various intensities. *Journal of Comparative and Physiological Psychology,* 1963, *56,* 801–805. **734**

Fowler, H., & Trapold, M. A. Escape performance as a function of delay of reinforcement. *Journal of Experimental Psychology,* 1962, *63,* 464–467. **722**

Fowler, H., & Wischner, G. J. Discrimination performance as affected by problem difficulty and shock for either the correct or incorrect response. *Journal of Experimental Psychology,* 1965, *69,* 413–418. **740**

Fowler, H., & Wischner, G. J. The varied functions of punishment in discrimination learning. In B. A. Campbell & R. M. Church (Eds.), *Punishment.* New York: Appleton, 1969. **740**

Fowler, H., *see also* Bower, G. H., 1959; Trapold, M. A., 1960; Wischner, G. J., 1963.

Fox, R., & Check, R. Binocular fusion: A test of the suppression theory. *Perception and Psychophysics,* 1966, *1,* 331–334. (a) **489**

Fox, R., & Check, R. Forced-choice form recognition during binocular rivalry. *Psychonomic Science,* 1966, 6, 471–472. (b) **489**

Fox, R., & McIntyre, C. Suppression during binocular fusion of complex targets. *Psychonomic Science,* 1967, *8,* 143–144. **489**

Fox, R., *see also* Harrison, K., 1966.

Fox, R. E., & King, R. A. The effects of reinforcement scheduling on the strength of a secondary reinforcer. *Journal of Comparative and Physiological Psychology,* 1961, *54,* 266–269. **670**

Fox, S. S. Self-maintained sensory input and sensory deprivation in monkeys: A behavioral and neuropharmacological study. *Journal of Comparative and Physiological Psychology,* 1962, *55,* 438–444. **840**

Fox, S. S., *see also* Wendt, R. H., 1963.

Fraenkel, G. S., & Gunn, D. L. *The orientation of animals.* Oxford: Clarendon, 1940. **745**

Frank, H. Ueber den Einfluss inadaquäter Konvergenz und Akkommodation auf die Sehgrosse. *Psychologische Forschung,* 1930, *13,* 135–144. **480**

Frank, M. K., *see* Pfaffmann, C., 1967.

Frankmann, J. B., *see* Estes, W. K., 1957.

Frankmann, R. W., *see* Suppes, P., 1961, 1964.

Fraser, J., *see* Postman, L., 1968.

Fraser-Rowell, C. H., *see* Horn, G., 1968.

Freeburne, C. M., & Goldman, R. D. Left–right differences in tachistoscopic recognition as a function of order of report, expectancy and training. *Journal of Experimental Psychology,* 1969, *79,* 570–572. **444**

Freedman, J. L., *see* Mednick, S. A., 1960.

Freedman, S., *see* Held, R., 1963.

Freedman, S. J., *see* Kalil, R. E., 1966.

Freeman, I., *see* Bigg, M., 1966.

Freeman, R. B. Figural after-effects: Displacement or contrast? *American Journal of Psychology*, 1964, *77*, 607–613. **473**

Freeman, R. B., Jr. Absolute threshold for visual slant: The effect of stimulus size and retinal perspective. *Journal of Experimental Psychology*, 1966, *71*, 170–176. **501**

Freeman, R. B., Jr. Effect of size on visual slant. *Journal of Experimental Psychology*, 1966, *71*, 96–103. (a) **499**

Freeman, R. B., Jr. Function of cues in the perceptual learning of visual slant: An experimental and theoretical analysis. *Psychological Monographs*, 1966, *80*. (Whole No. 610). (b) **499**

Freeman, R. B., Jr. Optical texture versus retinal perspective: A reply to Flock. *Psychological Review*, 1966, *73*, 365–371. (c) **502, 505**

Freeman, R. B., Jr. Contrast interpretation of brightness constancy. *Psychological Bulletin*, 1967, *67*, 165–187. **413**

Freibergs, V., & Tulving, E. The effect of practice on utilization of information from positive and negative instances in concept formation. *Canadian Journal of Psychology*, 1961, *15*, 101–106. **964**

Frenk, S., see Maturana, H. R., 1963.

Frey, M. von, see von Frey, M.

Frey, R. E., see Mayzner, M. S., 1964.

Friedel, R. T., see Mayzner, M. S., 1965.

Friedman, M. Transfer effects and response strategies in pattern-vs-component discrimination learning. *Journal of Experimental Psychology*, 1966, *71*, 420–428. **1004**

Friedman, M., Trabasso, T., & Mosberg, L. Tests of a mixed model for paired-associate learning with overlapping stimuli. *Journal of Mathematical Psychology*, 1967, *4*, 316–334. **1004**

Friedman, M. J., & Reynolds, J. H. Retroactive inhibition as a function of response-class similarity. *Journal of Experimental Psychology*, 1967, *74*, 351–355. **1097**

Friedman, M. P., Burke, C. J., Cole, N., Keller, L., Millward, R. B., & Estes, W. K. Two-choice behavior under extended training with shifting probabilities of reinforcement. In R. C. Atkinson (Ed.), *Studies in mathematical psychology.* Stanford: Stanford University Press, 1964. Pp. 250–316. **918, 919, 930, 934**

Friedman, M. P., & Gelfand, H. Transfer effects in discrimination learning. *Journal of Mathematical Psychology*, 1964, *1*, 204–214. **1004**

Friedman, M. P., see also Furchtgott, E., 1960.

Frincke, G., see Johnson, R. C., 1960, 1961.

Frings, H. Sweet taste in the cat and the taste-spectrum. *Experientia*, 1951, *7*, 424–426. **190**

Frishkopf, L. S., see Simmons, F. B., 1965.

Frommer, G. P. Gustatory afferent responses in the thalamus. In M. R. Kare & B. P. Halpern (Eds.), *Physiological and behavioral aspects of taste.* Chicago: University of Chicago Press, 1961. Pp. 50–65. **182**

Frommer, G. P., see also Pfaffmann, C., 1961.

Frost, R., see Attneave, F., 1969.

Fry, G. A. The stimulus correlate of bulky color. *American Journal of Psychology*, 1931, *43*, 618. **426, 427**

Fry, G. A. Visual perception of space. *American Journal of Optometry*, 1950, *27*, 531–553. **493**

Fuchs, W. Experimentelle Untersuchungen über die Änderung von Farben unter dem Einfluss von Gestalten. *Zeitschrift für Psychologie*, 1923, *92*, 249–325. **427**

Fuchs, W. Experimentelle Untersuchungen über das simultane Hintereinander auf derselben Sehrichtung. *Zeitschrift für Psychologie*, 1923, *91*, 145–235. **435**

Fullerton, G. S., & Cattell, J. McK., On the perception of small differences. *Philosophy Series* #2. Philadelphia: University of Pennsylvania Press, 1892. **30, 33**

Funakoshi, M., see Adachi, A., 1967; Andersen, H. T., 1963; Diamant, H., 1963.

Furchtgott, E., & Friedman, M. P. The effects of hunger on taste and odor RLs. *Journal of Comparative and Physiological Psychology*, 1960, *53*, 576–581. **208**

Furchtgott, E., & Rubin, R. The effect of magnitude of reward on maze learning in the white rat. *Journal of Comparative and Physiological Psychology*, 1953, *46*, 9–12. **637**

Furukawa, H., see Ikeda, S., 1962.

Fuster, J. M. Effects of stimulation of brain stem on tachistoscopic perception. *Science*, 1958, *127*, 150. **841, 842**

Fuster, J. M., & Uyeda, A. A. Facilitation of tachistoscopic performance by stimulation of midbrain tegmental points in the monkey. *Experimental Neurology*, 1962, *6*, 384–406. **841, 842**

Gaensler, E. A. Quantitative determination of the visceral pain threshold in man: Characteristics of visceral pain, effect of inflammation and analgesics on the threshold, and relationship of analgesia to visceral spasm. *Journal of Clinical Investigation*, 1951, *30*, 406–420. **156**

Gage, F. H., see Shaxby, J. H., 1932.

Gagné, R. M., Baker, K. E., & Foster, H. On the relation between similarity and transfer of training in the learning of discriminative motor tasks. *Psychological Review*, 1950, *57*, 67–79. **1055**

Gagné, R. M., & Foster, H. Transfer of training from practice on components in a motor skill. *Journal of Experimental Psychology*, 1949, *39*, 47–68. **1026**

Gagné, R. M., Foster, H., & Crowley, M. E. The measurement of transfer of training. *Psychological Bulletin*, 1948, *45*, 97–130. **1026**

Galambos, R. Studies of the auditory system with implanted electrodes. In G. Rasmussen & W. F. Windle (Eds.), *Neural mechanisms of the auditory and vestibular systems.* Springfield, Ill.: Charles C Thomas, 1960. **232**

Galambos, R., & Davis, H. The response of single auditory-nerve fibers to acoustic stimulation. *Journal of Neurophysiology*, 1943, *6*, 39–57. **230, 231**

Galambos, R., & Davis, H. Inhibition in activity of single auditory nerve fibers by acoustic stimulation. *Journal of Neurophysiology*, 1944, *7*, 287–303. **239**

Galambos, R., Schwartzkopff, J., & Rupert, A. Microelectrode study of superior olivary nuclei. *American Journal of Physiology*, 1959, *197*, 527–536. **264**

Galambos, R., see also Griffin, D. R., 1941; Hubel, D. H., 1959; Morgan, C. T., 1951; Weitzman, E. D., 1961.

Galanter, E. H. Contemporary psychophysics. In *New directions in psychology.* New York: Holt, Rinehart, and Winston, 1962. **84**

Galanter, E., & Holman, G. L. Some invariances of the isosensitivity function and their implication for the utility function of money. *Journal of Experimental Psychology*, 1967, *73*, 333–339. **38**

Galanter, E., & Smith, W. A. S. Some experiments on a simple thought problem. *American Journal of Psychology*, 1958, *71*, 359–366. **907**

Galanter, E., see also Bish, R. R., 1963; Linker, E., 1964; Luce, R. D., 1963; Miller, G. A., 1960; Stevens, S. S., 1957.

Gales, R. S., see Thompson, P. O., 1961.

Gallegos, E. S., see Kenshalo, D. R., 1967.

Galloway, A., see Wallach, H., 1946.

Gallup, H. F. Originality in free and controlled association responses. *Psychological Reports*, 1963, *13*, 923–929. **867**

Gallup, H. F., see also Maltzman, I., 1964.

Galper, R. E., see Hochberg, J., 1967.

Galton, F. Psychometric experiments. *Brain*, 1879–1880, *2*, 149–162. **848, 859, 873**

Galton, F. *Inquiries into human faculty and its development.* London: Macmillan, 1883. **55, 598**

Gambino, B., & Myers, J. L. Effect of mean and variability

of event run length on two-choice learning. *Journal of Experimental Psychology,* 1966, *72,* 904–908. **921**

Ganchrow, D., *see* Fehrer, E., 1963.

Gandelman, R., Panksepp, J., & Trowill, J. The effect of lever retraction on resistance to extinction of a response rewarded with electrical stimulation of the brain. *Psychonomic Science,* 1968, *10,* 5–6. **654**

Ganong, W. F., *see* Martini, L., 1966.

Gantt, W. H. Cardiovascular component of the conditional reflex to pain, food, and other stimuli. *Physiological Reviews,* 1960, *40,* Supplement No. 4, 266–291. **711**

Gantt, W. H. Pavlov's systems. In B. B. Wolman (Ed.), *Scientific psychology.* New York: Basic Books, 1965. **554**

Gantt, W. H. Conditioned or conditional, reflex or response? *Conditional Reflex,* 1966, *1,* 69–73. **555n**

Ganz, L. Is the figural aftereffect an *aftereffect? Psychological Bulletin,* 1966, *66,* 151–165. (a) **473, 474**

Ganz, L. The mechanism of figural aftereffect. *Psychological Review,* 1966, *73,* 128–150. (b) **473, 474**

Ganz, L. Lateral inhibition and the location of visual contours: An analysis of figural aftereffects. *Vision Research,* 1965, *4,* 465–481. **472, 473**

Ganz, L., & Day, R. H. An analysis of the satiation-fatigue mechanism of figural aftereffects. *American Journal of Psychology,* 1965, *78,* 345–361. **472, 473**

Ganz, L., *see also* Sekuler, R. W., 1963.

Gardner, E. Spinal cord and brain stem pathways for afferents from joints. In A. V. S. de Reuch & J. Knight (Eds.), *Myotatic, kinesthetic and vestibular mechanisms.* London: J. & A. Churchill, 1967. Pp. 56–76. **129**

Gardner, J., *see* Jones, A., 1967.

Gardner, M. B. Historical background of the Haas and/or precedence effect. *Journal of the Acoustical Society of America,* 1968, *43,* 1243–1248. **268**

Gardner, M. B., *see also* Steinberg, J. C., 1937.

Gardner, W. J., Licklider, J. C. R., & Weisz, A. Z. Suppression of pain by sound. *Science,* 1960, *132,* 32–33. **164**

Garmezano, I. Yoked comparisons of classical and instrumental conditioning of the eyelid response; and an addendum on "voluntary responders." In W. F. Prokasy (Ed.), *Classical conditioning.* New York: Appleton, 1965. **557**

Garner, W. R. Auditory thresholds of short tones as a function of repetition rates. *Journal of the Acoustical Society of America,* 1947, *19,* 600–608. (a) **234**

Garner, W. R. The effect of frequency spectrum on temporal integration of energy in the ear. *Journal of the Acoustical Society of America,* 1947, *19,* 808–815. (b) **234**

Garner, W. R. Hearing. In C. P. Stone (Ed.), *Annual review of psychology,* Vol. 3, Palo Alto, Calif.: Annual Reviews, 1952. **246**

Garner, W. R. A technique and a scale of loudness measurement. *Journal of the Acoustical Society of America,* 1954, *26,* 73–88. (a) **84, 247, 248**

Garner, W. R. Context effects and the validity of loudness scales. *Journal of Experimental Psychology,* 1954, *48,* 218–224. (b) **84**

Garner, W. R. *Uncertainty and structure as psychological concepts.* New York: Wiley, 1962. **256, 446**

Garner, W. R. To perceive is to know. *American Psychologist,* 1966, *21,* 11–19. **446**

Garner, W. R., & Clement, D. E. Goodness of pattern and pattern uncertainty. *Journal of Verbal Learning and Verbal Behavior,* 1963, *2,* 446–452. **446, 447**

Garner, W. R., & Creelman, C. D. Problems and methods of psychological scaling. In H. Helson & W. Bevan (Eds.), *Contemporary approaches to psychology.* Princeton, N.J.: Van Nostrand, 1967. **49**

Garner, W. R., & Hake, H. W. The amount of information in absolute judgments. *Psychological Review,* 1951, *58,* 446–459. **58**

Garner, W. R., Hake, H. W. & Eriksen, C. W. Operationism and the concept of perception. *Psychological Review,* 1956, *63,* 149–159. **506**

Garner, W. R., & Miller, G. A. The masked threshold of pure tones as a function of duration. *Journal of Experimental Psychology,* 1947, *37,* 293–303. **234**

Garner, W. R., *see also* Handel, S., 1965; Imai, S., 1965; Morgan, C. T., 1951.

Garskof, B. E. Relation between single word association and continued association response hierarchies. *Psychological Reports,* 1965, *16,* 307–309. **877**

Garskof, B. E. Unlearning as a function of degree of interpolated learning and method of testing in the A-B, A-C and A-B, C-D paradigms. *Journal of Experimental Psychology,* 1968, *76,* 579–583. **1096**

Garskof, B. E., & Houston, J. P. Measurement of verbal relatedness: An idiographic approach. *Psychological Review,* 1963, *70,* 277–278. **881**

Garskof, B. E., & Marshall, G. R. Relationship between two measures of verbal relatedness: Preliminary report. *Psychological Reports,* 1965, *16,* 17–18. **881**

Garskof, B. E., & Sandak, J. M. Unlearning in recognition memory. *Psychonomic Science.* 1964, *1,* 197–198. **1096**

Garskof, B. E., *see also* Sandak, J. M., 1967.

Garvey, W. D. The intelligibility of speeded speech. *Journal of Experimental Psychology,* 1953, *45,* 102–108. **257**

Gasser, H. S. Pain producing impulses in peripheral nerves. *Proceedings of the Association for Research in Nervous and Mental Disease,* 1943, *23,* 154–165. **160**

Gasser, H. S. Olfactory nerve fibers. *Journal of General Physiology,* 1956, *39,* 473–496. **197**

Gaze, L., & Dodwell, P. C. The role of induced set in figural after-effects. *Psychonomic Science,* 1965, *2,* 275–276. **470**

Gaze, L., *see also* Dodwell, P. C., 1965.

Geisler, C. D., *see* Rose, J. E., 1966.

Gelb, A. Die "Farbenkonstanz" der Sehdinge. *Handb. norm. path. Phys.,* 1929, *12,* 594–678. **398, 404**

Gelb, A. Die Erscheimungen des simultanen Kontrastes und der Eindruck der Feldbeleuchtung. *Zeitschrift für Psychologie,* 1932, *127,* 42–59. **412**

Geldard, F. A. The perception of mechanical vibration: I. History of a controversy. *Journal of General Psychology,* 1940, *22,* 243–269. (a) **134**

Geldard, F. A. The perception of mechanical vibration: II. The response of pressure receptors. *Journal of General Psychology,* 1940, *22,* 271–280. (b) **134**

Geldard, F. A. The perception of mechanical vibration: III. The frequency function. *Journal of General Psychology,* 1940, *22,* 281–289. (c) **134**

Geldard, F. A. The perception of mechanical vibration: IV. Is there a separate "vibratory sense"? *Journal of General Psychology,* 1940, *22,* 291–308. (d) **134**

Geldard, F. A. *The human senses.* New York: Wiley, 1953. **134, 165**

Gelfan, S., & Carter, S. Muscle sense in man. *Experimental Neurology,* 1967, *18,* 469–473. **129**

Gelfand, H., *see* Friedman, M. P., 1964.

Gellerman, L. W. Form discrimination in chimpanzees and two-year-old children: I. Form (triangularity) *per se. Journal of Genetic Psychology,* 1933, *42,* 3. (a) **750**

Gellerman, L. W. Form discrimination in chimpanzees and two-year-old children: II. Form versus background. *Journal of Genetic Psychology,* 1933, *42,* 28. (b) **750**

Gengerelli, A. Apparent movement in relation to homonymous and heteronymous stimulation of the cerebral hemispheres. *Journal of Experimental Psychology,* 1948, *38,* 592–599. **528**

Gentile, A., *see* Peterson, L. R., 1965.

George, F. H. Acuity and the statistical theory of figural after-effect. *Journal of Experimental Psychology,* 1962, *63,* 423–425. **473**

Glanz, J., see Zwislocki, J., 1967.

Glanzer, M. Grammatical category: A rote learning and word association analysis. *Journal of Verbal Learning and Verbal Behavior,* 1962, *1,* 31–41. **903**

Glanzer, M., & Clark, W. H. Accuracy of perceptual recall: An analysis of organization. *Journal of Verbal Learning and Verbal Behavior,* 1963, *1,* 289–299. (a) **448**

Glanzer, M., & Clark, W. H. The verbal loop hypothesis: Binary numbers. *Journal of Verbal Learning and Verbal Behavior,* 1963, *2,* 301–309. (b) **448**

Glanzer, M., & Clark, W. The verbal loop hypothesis: Conventional figures. *American Journal of Psychology,* 1964, *77,* 621–626. **448**

Glanzer, M., Taub, T., & Murphy, R. An evaluation of three theories of figural organization. In press, 1968. **448**

Glaser, E. M. *The physiological basis of habituation.* London: Oxford University Press, 1966. **589**

Glaser, N. M., see Maier, N. R. F., 1940.

Glaze, J. A. The association value of nonsense syllables. *Journal of Genetic Psychology,* 1928, *35,* 255–267. **852, 859, 982**

Gleitman, H., Nachmias, J., & Neisser, U. The S–R reinforcement theory of extinction. *Psychological Review,* 1954, *61,* 23–33. **575**

Gleitman, H., see also Gonzalez, R. C., 1962; Hochberg, J. E., 1948.

Glickman, S. E., & Hartz, K. E. Exploratory behavior in several species of rodents. *Journal of Comparative and Physiological Psychology,* 1964, *58,* 101–104. **824**

Glickman, S. E., & Schiff, B. B. A biological theory of reinforcement. *Psychological Review,* 1967, *74,* 81–109. **658**

Glorig, A., see Nixon, J. C., 1961; Ward, W. D., 1959.

Goad, D., see Underwood, B. J., 1951.

Goetzl, F. R., Burrill, D. Y., & Ivy, A. C. A critical analysis of algesimetric methods with suggestions for a useful procedure. *Quarterly Bulletin, Northwestern University Medical School,* 1943, *17,* 280–291. **156**

Goff, G. D. Differential discrimination of frequency of cutaneous mechanical vibration. *Journal of Experimental Psychology,* 1967, *74,* 294–299. **136**

Goff, W. R. Measurement of absolute olfactory sensitivity in rats. *American Journal of Psychology,* 1961, *74,* 384–393. **200, 203, 204**

Goff, W. R., see also Rosner, B. S., 1967.

Gogel, W. C. Perceived frontal size as a determiner of perceived binocular depth. *Journal of Psychology,* 1960, *50,* 119–131. (a) **493**

Gogel, W. C. The perception of shape from binocular disparity cues. *Journal of Psychology,* 1960, *50,* 179–192. (b) **493**

Gogel, W. C. The perception of a depth interval with binocular disparity cues. *Journal of Psychology,* 1960, *50,* 257–269. (c) **493, 494**

Gogel, W. C. Size cues to visually perceived distance. *Psychological Bulletin,* 1964, *62,* 217–235. **495**

Gogel, W. C. Equidistance tendency and its consequences. *Psychological Bulletin,* 1965, *64,* 153–163. **512**

Gogel, W. C. The effect of set on perceived egocentric distance. *Acta Psychologica,* 1968, *28,* 283–292. **496**

Gogel, W. C., Gregg, J. M., & Wainwright, A. *Convergence as a cue to absolute distance.* U.S. Army Medical Research Laboratory (Fort Knox, Kentucky), Report No. 467, 1961, 1–16. **480**

Gogel, W. C., Hartman, B. O., & Harker, G. S. The retinal size of a familiar object as a determiner of apparent distance. *Psychological Monographs,* 1957, *71,* 1–16. **495**

Gogel, W. C., & Hess, E. H. A study of color constancy in the newly hatched chick by means of an innate color preference (Abst.). *American Journal of Psychology,* 1951, *6,* 282. **407**

Gogel, W. C., & Mershon, D. H. Depth adjacency in simul-

taneous contrast. *Perception and Psychophysics,* 1969, *5,* 13–17. **423n**

Gogel, W. C., & Mertens, H. W. Perceived size and distance of familiar objects. *Perceptual and Motor Skills,* 1967, *25,* 213–225. **496, 497**

Gogel, W. C., & Newton, R. E. Perception of off-sized objects. *Perception and Psychophysics,* 1969, *5,* 7–9. **508**

Goggin, J. Retroactive and proactive inhibition in the short-term retention of paired associates. *Journal of Verbal Learning and Verbal Behavior,* 1966, *5,* 526–535. **1117**

Goggin, J. First-list recall as a function of second-list learning method. *Journal of Verbal Learning and Verbal Behavior,* 1967, *6,* 423–427. **1097**

Goggin, J., see also Postman, L., 1966.

Gold, C., see Mandler, G., 1964.

Goldberg, J., see Rock, I., 1966.

Goldberg, J. M., see Rose, J. E., 1963.

Goldberg, S. *Introduction to difference equations.* New York: Wiley, 1958. **912**

Gol'dburt, S. N. Persistence of auditory processes within micro-intervals of time (new data on retroactive masking). *Biophysics,* 1961, *6,* 76–81. **241**

Goldhamer, H. The influence of area, position and brightness in the visual perception of a reversible configuration. *American Journal of Psychology,* 1934, *46,* 189–206. **433**

Goldiamond, I. Indicators of perception: I. Subliminal perception, subception, unconscious perception; an analysis in terms of psychophysical indicator methodology. *Psychological Bulletin,* 1958, *55,* 373–411.

Goldiamond, I., & Hawkins, W. T. Vexierversuch: The log relationship between word-frequency and recognition obtained in the absence of stimulus words. *Journal of Experimental Psychology,* 1958, *56,* 457–463. **444**

Goldman, R. D., see Freeburne, C. M., 1969.

Goldstein, E. see Reynolds, W. F., 1964.

Goldstein, E. B. Early receptor potential of the isolated frog (*Rana pipiens*) retina. *Vision Research,* 1967, *7,* 837–845. **307**

Goldstein, J. L. Auditory nonlinearity. *Journal of the Acoustical Society of America,* 1967, *41,* 676–689. **237, 239**

Goldstein, K., & Riese, W. Über induzierte Veränderungen des Tonus (Halsreflexe, Labyrinthreflexe und ähnliche Erscheinungen): III. Blickrichtung und Zeigeversuch. *Klinische Wissenschraft,* 1923, *2,* 2338–2340. **534**

Goldstein, M. D., see Keesey, R. E., 1968.

Goldstein, S., see Bourne, L. E. Jr., 1964.

Gollub, L. R., see Kelleher, R. T., 1962.

Gombrich, E. H. *Art and illusion: A study in the psychology of pictorial representation.* New York: Pantheon, 1960. **442**

Gonzalez, R. C., Behrend, E. R., & Bitterman, M. E. Partial reinforcement in the fish: Experiments with spaced trials and partial delay. *American Journal of Psychology,* 1965, *78,* 198–207. **608**

Gonzalez, R. C., Gleitman, H., & Bitterman, M. E. Some observations on the depression effect. *Journal of Comparative and Physiological Psychology,* 1962, *55,* 578–581. **634, 635**

Goodell, H., see Hardy, J. D., 1940, 1947, 1951; Schumacher, G. A., 1940.

Goodenough, F. The use of free association in the objective measurement of personality. In Q. McNemar & M. A. Merrill (Eds.), *Studies in personality.* New York: McGraw-Hill, 1942. Pp. 87–103. **873**

Goodenough, F. Semantic choice and personality structure. *Science,* 1946, *104,* 451–456. **873**

Goodman, L. S., see Smith, S. M., 1947.

Goodnow, J. J. Determinance of choice-distribution in two-choice situations. *American Journal of Psychology,* 1955, *68,* 106–116. **907, 934**

Goodnow, J. J., see also Bruner, J. S., 1956.

Goodrich, K. P., & Zaretsky, H. Running speed as a function of concentration of sucrose incentive during pretraining. *Psychological Reports*, 1962, *11*, 463-468. **634**

Goodwin, P. E., *see* Mayzner, M. S., 1965.

Goodwin, W. R., & Lawrence, D. H. The functional independence of two discrimination habits associated with a constant stimulus situation. *Journal of Comparative and Physiological Psychology*, 1955, *48*, 437-443. **783**

Gordon, J., *see* Boynton, R. M., 1965.

Gordon, K. Meaning in memory and attention. *Psychological Review*, 1903, *10*, 280-283. **519**

Gormezano, I., & Abraham, F. Intermittent reinforcement, non-reversal shifts, and neutralization in concept formation. *Journal of Experimental Psychology*, 1961, *61*, 1-6. **948**

Goss, A. Verbal mediating responses in concept formation. *Psychological Review*, 1961, *68*, 248-274. **948**

Goss, A. E. Early behaviorism and verbal mediating responses. *American Psychologist*, 1961, *16*, 285-298. **1071**

Goss, A. E. Comments on Professor Noble's paper. In C. N. Cofer & B. S. Musgrave (Eds.), *Verbal behavior and learning: Problems and processes.* New York: McGraw-Hill, 1963. Pp. 119-155. **856**

Goss, A. E., & Nodine, C. F. *Paired-associates learning: The role of meaningfulness, similarity and familiarization.* New York: Academic Press, 1965. **853, 856, 857, 894, 896, 898, 900, 901**

Gottheil, E., & Bitterman, M. E. The measurement of shape-constancy. *American Journal of Psychology*, 1951, *64*, 406-408. **509, 516**

Gottlieb, N., *see* Held, R., 1958.

Gottschaldt, K. Über den Einfluss der Erfahrung auf die Wahrnehmung von Figuren: 1. *Psychologische Forschung*, 1926, *8*, 261-317. **440**

Gottschaldt, K. Über den Einfluss der Erfahrung auf die Wahrnehmung von Figuren: 11. *Psychologische Forschung*, 1929, *12*, 1-87. **440**

Goulet, L. R. Interlist response meaningfulness and transfer effects under the *A-B, A-C* paradigm. *Journal of Experimental Psychology*, 1965, *70*, 264-269. **1062**

Goulet, L. R. Retroaction and the "fate" of the mediator in three stage mediation paradigms. *Journal of Verbal Learning and Verbal Behavior*, 1966, *5*, 172-176. **1077**

Goulet, L. R. Degree of learning and transfer of training. *Psychonomic Science*, 1967, *8*, 245-246. **1069**

Goulet, L. R., & Barclay, A. Comparison of paired-associate transfer effects between the *A-B, C-A* and *A-B, B-C* transfer paradigms. *Journal of Experimental Psychology*, 1965, *70*, 537-539. **1064**

Goulet, L. R., & Behar, V. Bidirectional paired-associate learning and transfer effects in the *A-B, C-B* and *A-B, A-C* paradigms. *Psychonomic Science*, 1966, *6*, 299-300. **1063**

Goulet, L. R., Meltzer, R., & O'Shaunessy, K. Further data on degree of learning and transfer of training. *Psychonomic Science*, 1967, *9*, 469-470. **1069**

Goulet, L. R., & Postman, L. An experimental evaluation of the pseudomediation hypothesis. *Psychonomic Science*, 1966, *4*, 163-164. **1077**

Goulet, L. R., *see also* Cheung, C. C., 1968.

Gourevitch, G. Auditory masking in the rat. *Journal of the Acoustical Society of America*, 1965, *37*, 439-443. **555n**

Gourevitch, G., & Hack, M. H. Audibility in the rat. *Journal of Comparative and Physiological Psychology*, 1966, *62*, 289-291. **555n**

Gousec, T. The peak shift in stimulus generalization: Equivalent effects of errors and non-contingent shock. *Journal of the Experimental Analysis of Behavior*, 1968, *11*, 239-249. **779**

Graham, C. A. Area, color and brightness difference in a reversible configuration. *Journal of General Psychology*, 1929, *2*, 470-481. **433**

Graham, C. H. Vision: III. Some neural correlations. In C. Murchison (Ed.), *Handbook of general experimental psychology.* Worcester, Mass.: Clark University Press, 1934. Pp. 829-879. **290**

Graham, C. H. On some aspects of real and apparent visual movement. *Journal of the Optical Society of America*, 1963, *53*, 1019-1025. **518**

Graham, C. H. (Ed.) *Vision and visual perception.* New York: Wiley, 1965. **84, 296, 358, 520, 526**

Graham, C. H., Baker, K. E., Hecht, M., & Lloyd, V. V. Factors influencing thresholds for monocular movement parallax. *Journal of Experimental Psychology*, 1948, *38*, 205-223. **486, 520**

Graham, C. H., & Bartlett, N. R. The relation of size of stimulus and intensity in the human eye: III. The influence of area on foveal intensity discrimination. *Journal of Experimental Psychology*, 1940, *27*, 149-159. **303**

Graham, C. H., & Brown, J. L. Color contrast and color appearances: Brightness constancy and color constancy. In C. H. Graham (Ed.), *Vision and visual perception.* New York: Wiley, 1965. **410**

Graham, C. H., Brown, R. H., & Mote, F. A. The relative size of stimulus and intensity in the human eye: I. *Journal of Experimental Psychology*, 1939, *24*, 555-573. **290**

Graham, C. H., & Cook, C. Visual acuity as a function of intensity and exposure time. *American Journal of Psychology*, 1937, *49*, 654-691. **304**

Graham, C. H., & Kemp, E. H. Brightness discrimination as a function of the duration of the increment in intensity. *Journal of General Physiology*, 1938, *21*, 635-650. **297**

Graham, C. H., Riggs, L. A., Mueller, C. G., & Solomon, R. L. Precision of stereoscopic settings as influenced by distance of target from a fiducial line. *Journal of Psychology*, 1949, *27*, 203-207. **486**

Graham, C. H., *see also* Hartline, H. K., 1932; Hsia, Y., 1957; Riggs, L. A., 1940, 1947.

Graham, E. H. Figural after-effects as functions of contrast, area, and luminance of the inspection figure. *Psychologia*, 1961, *4*, 201-208. **470**

Graham, F. K. *see* Keen, R. E., 1965.

Granath, L. P., *see* Herget, C. M., 1941.

Grandine, L., & Harlow, H. F. Generalization of the characteristics of a single learned stimulus by monkeys. *Journal of Comparative and Physiological Psychology*, 1948, *41*, 327-338. **772**

Granger, L., Ducharme, R., & Bélanger, D. Effects of water deprivation upon heart rate and running speed of the white rat in a straight alley. *Psychophysiology*, 1969, *5*, 638-643. **827**

Granit, R. Comparative studies on the peripheral and central retina: I. On interaction between distant areas in the human eye. *American Journal of Physiology*, 1930, *94*, 41-50. **290**

Granit, R. *Sensory mechanisms of the retina.* New York: Oxford University Press, 1947. **291, 294, 308**

Granit, R. *Receptors and sensory perception.* New Haven: Yale University Press, 1955. **81, 108, 308**

Granit, R. The visual pathway. In H. Davson (Ed.), *The eye.* Vol. 2. New York: Academic Press, 1962. Pp. 537-763. **282, 308**

Granit, R., Holmberg, T., & Zewi, M. On the mode of action of visual purple on the rod cell. *Journal of Physiology*, 1938, *94*, 430-440. **287**

Grant, D. A. Perceptual vs. analytical responses to the number concept of a Weigl-type card sorting task. *Journal of Experimental Psychology*, 1951, *41*, 23-29. **961**

Grant, D. A. Classical and operant conditioning. In A. W. Melton (Ed.), *Categories of human learning.* New York: Academic Press, 1964. **564**

Grant, D. A., & Curran, J. F. Relative difficulty of number, form, and color concepts of a Weigl-type problem using unsystematic number cards. *Journal of Experimental Psychology*, 1953, *43*, 408–413. **961**

Grant, D. A., & Dittmer, D. G. An experimental investigation of Pavlov's cortical irradiation hypothesis. *Journal of Experimental Psychology*, 1940, *26*, 299–310. **564**

Grant, D. A., Jones, O. R., & Tallantis, B. The relative difficulty of number, form, and color concepts of a Weigl-type problem. *Journal of Experimental Psychology*, 1949, *39*, 552–557. **961**

Grant, D. A., & Norris, E. B. Eyelid conditioning as influenced by the presence of sensitized beta-responses. *Journal of Experimental Psychology*, 1947, *37*, 423–433. **556, 557, 565**

Grant, D. A., *see also* Anderson, N. H., 1957, 1958; Hake, H. W., 1951; Hartman, T. F., 1962; Norris, E. B., 1948.

Grant, V. W. Accommodation and convergence in visual space perception. *Journal of Experimental Psychology*, 1942, *31*, 89–104. **480**

Green, B. F. Kinetic depth-effect. In *Psychology Group 58: Quarterly Progress Report*. Cambridge, Mass.: Massachusetts Institute of Technology, Lincoln Laboratory, March 1959. **505**

Green, D. M. Detection of auditory sinusoids of uncertain frequency. *Journal of the Acoustical Society of America*, 1961, *33*, 897–903. **250**

Green, D. M., Henning, G. B. Audition. In P. H. Mussen & M. R. Rosenzweig (Eds.), *Annual Review of Psychology*, Vol. 20. Palo Alto, Calif.: Annual Reviews, 1969. **243**

Green, D. M., & Swets, J. A. *Signal detection theory and psychophysics*. New York: Wiley, 1966. **42, 240**

Green, H. C., *see* Potter, R. K., 1947.

Green, R. T., & Hoyle, E. M. The Poggendorf illusion as a constancy phenomenon. *Nature*, 1963, *200*, 611–612. **460, 463**

Greenbaum, H. B., *see* Stevens, S. S., 1966.

Greenberg, R., & Underwood, B. J. Retention as a function of stage of practice. *Journal of Experimental Psychology*, 1950, *40*, 452–457. **1041, 1104, 1106**

Greenbloom, R., & Kimble, G. A. Extinction of R-S associations and performance on recall trials without immediate feedback. *Journal of Verbal Learning and Verbal Behavior*, 1965, *4*, 341–347. **1095**

Greenbloom, R., *see also* Postman, L., 1967.

Greene, L. C., & Hardy, J. D. Spatial summation of pain. *Journal of Applied Physiology*, 1958, *13*, 457–464. **160**

Greene, L. C., & Hardy, J. D. Adaptation to thermal pain in the skin. *Journal of Applied Physiology*, 1962, *17*, 693–696. **159**

Greene, M., *see* Efstathiou, A., 1967; Held, R., 1966.

Greenhouse, P., *see* Neimark, E., 1965.

Greeno, J. G. Effects of nonreinforced trials in two-choice learning with noncontingent reinforcement. *Journal of Experimental Psychology*, 1962, *64*, 373–379. **933**

Greeno, J. G. Paired-associate learning with massed and distributed repetition of items. *Journal of Experimental Psychology*, 1964, *67*, 286–295. **999, 1009**

Greeno, J. G. Paired-associate learning with short-term retention: Mathematical analysis and data regarding identification of parameters. *Journal of Mathematical Psychology*, 1967, *7*, 430–472. **999**

Greeno, J. G., & Scandura, J. M. All-or-none transfer based on verbally mediated concepts. *Journal of Mathematical Psychology*, 1966, *3*, 388–411. **946, 1007, 1010**

Greeno, J. G., *see also* James, C. T., 1967; La Berge, D. L., 1962.

Greenspoon, J. The reinforcing effect of two spoken sounds on the frequency of two responses. *American Journal of Psychology*, 1955, *68*, 409–416. **908n**

Greenspoon, J., & Ranyard, R. Stimulus conditions and retroactive inhibition. *Journal of Experimental Psychology*, 1957, *53*, 55–59. **1084**

Greenspoon, T. S., *see* Eriksen, C. W., et al., 1967.

Greenwood, D. Critical band width and the frequency coordinates of the basilar membrane. *Journal of the Acoustical Society of America*, 1961, *33*, 1344–1356. **240**

Greenwood, D. D., *see* Rose, J. E., 1963.

Gregg, J. M., *see* Gogel, W. C., 1961.

Gregg, L. W., & Simon, H. A. Process models and stochastic theories of simple concept formation. *Journal of Mathematical Psychology*, 1967, *4*, 246–276. **978**

Gregory, R. L. Distortion of visual space as inappropriate constancy scaling. *Nature*, 1963, *199*, 678–680. **460, 462**

Gregory, R. L. Eye movements and the stability of the visual world. *Bulletin of the British Psychological Society*, 1959, *38*, 23A. See also *Nature*, 1958, *182*, 1214–1216. **530**

Gregory, R. L. Human perception. *British Medical Bulletin*, 1964, *20*, 21–26. **521**

Gregory, R. L. Visual illusions. In B. M. Foss (Ed.), *New horizons in psychology*. Harmondsworth, England: Penguin Books, 1966. **462**

Gregory, R. L. Comments on the inappropriate constancy scaling theory of the illusions and its implications. *Quarterly Journal of Experimental Psychology*, 1967, *19*, 291–223. **462**

Gregory, R. L., & Wallace, J. G., *Recovery from early blindness. Experimental Psychology Society Monograph 2*, Cambridge: Heffer, 1963. **548**

Gregory, R. L., & Zangwill, O. L. The origin of the autokinetic effect. *Quarterly Journal of Experimental Psychology*, 1963, *15*, 252–261. **530**

Gregory, R. L., *see also* Anstis, S. M., 1964.

Grether, W. F. Pseudo-conditioning without paired stimulation encountered in attempted backward conditioning. *Journal of Comparative Psychology*, 1938, *25*, 91–96. **578**

Grice, G. R. The relation of secondary reinforcement to delayed reward in visual discrimination learning. *Journal of Experimental Psychology*, 1948, *38*, 1–16. (a) **679, 680, 684, 689, 783**

Grice, G. R. An experimental test of the expectation theory of learning. *Journal of Comparative and Physiological Psychology*, 1948, *41*, 137–143. (b) **669, 772**

Grice, G. R., & Davis, J. D. Effect of irrelevant thirst motivation on a response learned with food reward. *Journal of Experimental Psychology*, 1957, *53*, 347–352. **669**

Grice, G. R., & Hunter, J. J. Stimulus intensity effects depend upon the type of experimental design. *Psychological Review*, 1964, *71*, 247–256. **600**

Grice, G. R., & Reynolds, B. Effect of varying amount of rest on conventional and bilateral transfer "reminiscence." *Journal of Experimental Psychology*, 1952, *44*, 247–252. **575**

Grier, J. B., & Bornstein, R. Probability matching in concept identification. *Journal of Experimental Psychology*, 1966, *71*, 339–342. **958**

Griffin, D. R. *Echoes of bats and man*. Garden City, N.Y.: Doubleday, 1959. **270**

Griffin, D. R., & Galambos, R. The sensory basis of obstacle avoidance by flying bats. *Journal of Experimental Zoology*, 1941, *86*, 481–506. **269**

Griffin, F., *see* Fisher, R., 1964.

Grim, K. Über die Genauigkeit der Wahrnehmung und Ausführung von Augenbewegungen. *Zeitschrift für Sinnesphysiologie*, 1911, *45*, 9–26. **520**

Grindley, G. C. Experiments on the influence of amount of reward on learning in young chickens. *British Journal of Psychology*, 1929, *20*, 173–180. **617**

Grindley, G. C. The formation of a simple habit in guinea pigs. *British Journal of Psychology*, 1932, *23*, 127–147. **697**

Grinnell, A. D. The neurophysiology of audition in bats: Intensity and frequency parameters. *Journal of Physiology*, 1963, *167*, 38–66. **270**

Grinnell, A. D., & McCue, J. J. G. Neurophysiological investigations of the bat *Myotis lucifugus*, stimulated by frequency-modulated acoustical pulses. *Nature*, 1963, *198*, 453–455. **232**

Groen, G., *see* Suppes, P., 1966.

Gropper, M. S., *see* Richardson, J., 1964.

Grosland, H., *see* Anderson, I., 1933.

Gross, K., & Stern, J. A. Habituation of orienting responses as a function of "instructional set." *Conditional Reflex*, 1967, *2*, 23–36. **555n**

Gross, N. B., *see* Rose, J. E., 1966; Thurlow, W. R., 1951.

Grossman, S. P. Acquisition and performance of avoidance responses during chemical stimulation of the midbrain reticular formation. *Journal of Comparative and Physiological Psychology*, 1966, *61*, 42–49. **843**

Grossman, S. P. *A textbook of physiological psychology.* New York: Wiley, 1967. **812**

Grover, D. E., Horton, D. L., & Cunningham, M., Jr. Mediated facilitation and interference in a four-stage paradigm. *Journal of Verbal Learning and Verbal Behavior*, 1967, *6*, 42–46. **1076**

Gruber, H., *see* King, W., 1962.

Gruber, H. E. The relation of perceived size to perceived distance. *American Journal of Psychology*, 1954, *67*, 411–426. **506, 513**

Gruber, H. E., & Clark, W. C. Perception of slanted surfaces. *Perceptual and Motor Skills*, 1956, *6*, 97–106. **501**

Gruber, H. E., & Dinnerstein, A. J. The role of knowledge in distance perception. *American Journal of Psychology*, 1965, *78*, 575–581. **496**

Grüsser, O.-J., and Creutzfeldt, O. Eine neurophysiologische Grundlage des Brücke-Bartley-Effektes: Maxima der Impulsfrequenz retinaler und corticaler Neurone bei Flimmerlicht mittlerer Frequenzen. *Pflüger's Archiv der Gesamte Physiologie*, 1957, *263*, 668–681. **314**

Guastella, M. J. New theory of apparent movement. *Journal of the Optical Society of America*, 1966, *56*, 960–966. **518**

Guilford, J. P. Autokinesis and the streaming phenomenon. *American Journal of Psychology*, 1928, *40*, 401–417. **529**

Guilford, J. P. The computation of psychological values from judgments in absolute categories. *Journal of Experimental Psychology*, 1938, *22*, 32–42. **58**

Guilford, J. P. *Psychometric methods.* (ed. 2) New York: McGraw-Hill, 1954. **16, 24, 32, 33, 34, 53, 57, 58, 62**

Guilford, J. P., & Dallenbach, K. M. A study of the autokinetic sensation. *American Journal of Psychology*, 1928, *40*, 83–91. **529**

Guilford, J. P., & Dingman, H. F. A validation study of ratio-judgment methods. *American Journal of Psychology*, 1954, *67*, 395–410. **72**

Guilford, J. P., & Dingman, H. F. A modification of the method of equal-appearing intervals. *American Journal of Psychology*, 1955, *68*, 450–454. **65**

Guilford, J. P., & Helson, H. Eye-movements and the phi-phenomenon. *American Journal of Psychology*, 1929, *41*, 595–606. **527**

Guinan, J. F., *see* Armus, H. L., 1964.

Guirao, N., *see* Stevens, S. S., 1962; Stevens, J. C., 1964.

Gulick, W. L., *see* Lawson, R. B., 1967; Smith, W. M., 1956, 1957, 1962.

Gulliksen, H. Transfer of response in human subjects. *Journal of Experimental Psychology*, 1932, *15*, 496–516. **1047**

Gunn, D. L., *see* Fraenkel, G. S., 1940.

Gunther, M. Instinct and the nursing couple. *Lancet*, 1955, 575–578. **582**

Gustafson, L. M., *see* Irion, A. L., 1952.

Guthrie, E. R. *The psychology of learning.* New York: Harper, 1935. **560, 567, 571, 908**

Guthrie, E. R. *The psychology of learning.* (Rev. ed.) New York: Harper, 1952. **560, 567, 571, 734**

Guthrie, E. R. Association by contiguity. In S. Koch (Ed.), *Psychology: A study of a science.* Vol. 2. New York: McGraw-Hill, 1959. **560, 908, 912**

Guthrie, E. R., *see also* Smith, S., 1921.

Guttman, L. Chapters 2, 3, 6, 8, and 9 in S. A. Stouffer et al. (Eds.), *Measurement and prediction.* Princeton: Princeton University Press, 1950. **63**

Guttman, N. Operant conditioning, extinction, and periodic reinforcement in relation to concentration of sucrose as a reinforcing agent. *Journal of Experimental Psychology*, 1953, *46*, 213–224. **600, 624, 625, 627, 629, 630**

Guttman, N. Equal-reinforcement values for sucrose and glucose solutions as compared with equal-sweetness values. *Journal of Experimental Psychology*, 1954, *47*, 358–361. **627**

Guttman, N., van Bergeijk, W. A., & David, E. E. Monaural temporal masking investigated by binaural interaction. *Journal of the Acoustical Society of America*, 1960, *32*, 1329–1336. **268**

Guttman, N., & Kalish, H. I. Discriminability and stimulus generalization. *Journal of Experimental Psychology*, 1956, *51*, 79–88. **753, 760, 761**

Guttman, N., *see also* David, E. E., 1958, 1959; Simmons, F. B., 1965.

Guy, D. E., *see* Bourne, L. E. Jr., 1965.

Gwinn, G. T. The effects of punishment on acts motivated by fear. *Journal of Experimental Psychology*, 1949, *39*, 260–269. **725**

Haagen, C. H. *Learning and retention as a function of the synonymity of original and interpolated tasks.* Doctoral dissertation, University of Iowa, 1943. **1084**

Haagen, C. H. Synonymity, vividness, familiarity, and association value ratings of 400 pairs of common adjectives. *Journal of Psychology*, 1949, *27*, 453–463. **890, 900, 1052, 1057**

Haas, E. L., *see* Warden, C. J., 1927.

Haas, von H. Über den Einfluss eines Einfachechos auf die Horsamkeit von Sprache. *Acustica*, 1951, *1*, 49–58. **268**

Haber, R. N., & Hershensen, M. The effects of repeated brief exposures on the growth of a percept. *Journal of Experimental Psychology*, 1965, *69*, 40–46. **445n**

Haber, R. N., & Nathanson, L. Post-retinal storage? Some further observations on Parks' camel as seen through the eye of a needle. *Perception and Psychophysics*, 1968, *3*, 349–355. **455**

Haber, R. N., *see also* Dainoff, M., 1967; Harris, C. S., 1963; Weisstein, N., 1965.

Haber, S., *see* Hochberg, J., 1955.

Hack, M. H. Signal detection in the rat. *Science*, 1963, 758–759. **757**

Hack, M. H., *see also* Gourevitch, G., 1966.

Hagen, E., Knoche, H., Sinclair, D., & Weddell, G. The role of specialized nerve terminals in cutaneous sensibility. *Proceedings of the Royal Society; Series B: Biological Sciences*, 1953, *141*, 279–287. **122, 125, 154**

Hagstrom, E. C., *see* Pfaffmann, C., 1955.

Hahn, H. Die Adaptation des Geschmackssinnes. *Zeitschrift für Sinnesphysiologie*, 1934, *65*, 105–145. **183, 184, 552**

Hahn, H. *Beiträge zur Reizphysiologie.* Heidelberg: Scherer Verlag, 1949. **186**

Hahn, J. F. Cutaneous vibratory thresholds for square wave electrical pulses. *Science*, 1958, *127*, 879–880. **136, 137**

Hahn, J. F. Vibrotactile adaptation and recovery measured by two methods. *Journal of Experimental Psychology*, 1966, *71*, 655–658. **136**

Hahn, W. W., Stern, J. A., & Fehr, F. S. Generalizability of heart rate as a measure of drive state. *Journal of Compar-*

ative and Physiological Psychology, 1964, *58*, 305–309. **836**

Hahn, W. W., Stern, J. A., & McDonald, D. G. Effects of water deprivation and bar pressing activity on heart rate of the male albino rat. *Journal of Comparative and Physiological Psychology*, 1962, *55*, 786–790. **836**

Haibt, L. H., *see* Rochester, H., 1956.

Haider, M., *see* Spong, P., 1965.

Haire, M., *see* Adams, P. A., 1959.

Hake, D. R., & Azrin, N. H. Conditioned punishment. *Journal of the Experimental Analysis of Behavior*, 1965, *8*, 279–293. **665, 719**

Hake, H. W. *Contributions of psychology to the study of pattern vision*. WADC Technical Report 57-621. Wright Air Development Center, Aero Medical Laboratory. Project No. 7192-71598, 1957. Pp. 1–118. **428**

Hake, H. W., Grant, D. A. & Hornseth, J. P. Resistance to extinction and the pattern of reinforcement: III. The effect of trial patterning in verbal "conditioning." *Journal of Experimental Psychology*, 1951, *41*, 221–225. **908**

Hake, H. W., & Hyman, R. Perception of the statistical structure of a random series of binary symbols. *Journal of Experimental Psychology*, 1953, *45*, 64–74. **934**

Hake, H. W., & Myers, A. E. Familiarity and shape constancy. *Journal of Experimental Psychology*, 1969, *80*, 205–214. **515**

Hake, H. W., Rodwan, A. & Weintraub, D. Noise reduction in perception. In Kenneth R. Hammond (Ed.), *The psychology of Egon Brunswik*, New York: Holt, Rinehart and Winston, 1966. **449**

Hake, H. W., *see also* Egan, J. P., 1950; Garner, W. R., 1951, 1956.

Hakes, D., *see* James, C. T., 1965.

Hall, J. F. Studies in secondary reinforcement: I. Secondary reinforcement as a function of the frequency of primary reinforcement. *Journal of Comparative and Physiological Psychology*, 1951, *44*, 246–251. (a) **667**

Hall, J. F. Studies in secondary reinforcement: II. Secondary reinforcement as a function of the strength of drive during primary reinforcement. *Journal of Comparative and Physiological Psychology*, 1951, *44*, 462–466. (b) **668**

Hall, J. F. Learning as a function of word-frequency. *American Journal of Psychology*, 1954, *67*, 138–140. **895**

Hall, J. F. Activity as a function of a restricted drinking schedule. *Journal of Comparative and Physiological Psychology*, 1955, *48*, 265–266.

Hall, J. F., & Ugelow, A. Free association time as a function of word frequency. *Canadian Journal of Psychology*, 1957, *11*, 29–32. **865**

Hall, J. F., *see also* Treichler, F. R., 1962.

Hall, J. L., II. Binaural interaction in the accessory superior-olivary nucleus of the cat. *Journal of the Acoustical Society of America*, 1965, *37*, 814–823. **265**

Hall, K. R. L., Earle, A. E., & Crookes, T. G. A pendulum phenomenon in the visual perception of apparent movement. *Quarterly Journal of Experimental Psychology*, 1952, *4*, 109–120. **527**

Hall, M., *see* Hull, C. L., 1940.

Hall, R. D. An integration of discrete-trial and free-operant conditioning techniques. Doctoral dissertation, Brown University, 1960. Ann Arbor, Mich.: University Microfilms No. 62-5747. **619**

Hall, R. D., & Kling, J. W. Amount of consummatory activity and performance in a modified T maze. *Journal of Comparative and Physiological Psychology*, 1960, *53*, 165–168. **623**

Halpern, B. P. Chemical coding in taste-temporal patterns. In Y. Zotterman (Ed.), *Olfaction and taste*. Vol. I. New York: Pergamon, 1963. Pp. 275–284. **182**

Halpern, B. P. Chemotopic coding for sucrose and quinine hydrochloride in the nucleus of the fasciculus solitarius.

In T. Hayashi (Ed.), *Olfaction and taste*. Vol. 2. New York: Pergamon, 1967. Pp. 549–562. (a) **182**

Halpern, B. P. Some relationships between electrophysiology and behavior in taste. In M. R. Kare & O. Maller (Eds.), *The chemical senses and nutrition*. Baltimore: Johns Hopkins Press, 1967. Pp. 213–241. (b) **186, 187**

Halpern, B. P., & Nelson, L. M. Bulbar gustatory responses to anterior and to posterior tongue stimulation in the rat. *American Journal of Physiology*, 1965, *209*, 105–110. **182**

Halpern, B. P., *see also* Benjamin, R. M., 1965; Pfaffmann, C., 1961.

Halverson, H. M. Binaural localization of tones as dependent upon differences of phase and intensity. *American Journal of Psychology*, 1922, *33*, 178–212. **266**

Ham, M., *see* Underwood, B. J., 1962.

Hamilton, A., *see* Kenshalo, D. R., 1967.

Hamilton, C. E. The relationship between length of interval separating two learning tasks and performance on the second task. *Journal of Experimental Psychology*, 1950, *40*, 613–621. **1034, 1036**

Hamilton, C. R. Intermanual transfer of adaptation to prisms. *American Journal of Psychology*, 1964, *77*, 457–462. **537**

Hamilton, E. L. The effect of delayed incentive on the hunger drive in the white rat. *Genetic Psychology Monographs*, 1929, *5*, 133–207. **678**

Hamilton, H., *see* Saltz, E., 1967.

Hamilton, R. J. Retroactive facilitation as a function of degree of generalization between tasks. *Journal of Experimental Psychology*, 1943, *32*, 363–376. **1050, 1051, 1053, 1083**

Hamilton, W. J., III, *see* Marler, P. R., 1966.

Hammer, E. R. Temporal factor in figural after-effects. *American Journal of Psychology*, 1949, *62*, 337–354. **469**

Hammer, L. R. Saccharin and sucrose intake in rats: Long- and short-term tests. *Psychonomic Science*, 1967, *8*, 367–368. **630**

Hammock, J. T., *see* Long, E. R., 1958.

Hanawalt, N. G. The effect of practice upon the perception of simple designs masked by more complex figures. *Journal of Experimental Psychology*, 1942, *31*, 134–148. **440**

Hancock, W., *see* Amsel, A., 1957.

Handel, S., & Garner, W. R. The structure of visual pattern associates and pattern goodness. *Perception and Psychophysics*, 1965, *1*, 33–38. **446, 447**

Hanes, R. M. A scale of subjective brightness. *Journal of Experimental Psychology*, 1949, *39*, 438–452. **67, 70**

Hanes, R. M., *see also* Burnham, R. W., 1963.

Hanly, B., *see* Bolles, R. C., 1959.

Hanna, J. F., *see* Feldman, J., 1966.

Hansen, A. K. "After-image transfer test" in anomalous retinal correspondence. *Archives of Opthalmology*. 1954, *52*, 369–374. **473**

Hanson, H. M. Effects of discrimination training on stimulus generalization. *Journal of Experimental Psychology*, 1959, *58*, 321–334. **765, 778**

Hara, S. Interrelationship among stimulus intensity, stimulated area and reaction time in the human gustatory sensation. *Bulletin of the Tokyo Medical and Dental University*, 1955, *2*, 147–158. **175**

Harcum, E. R. Verbal transfer of overlearned forward and backward associations. *American Journal of Psychology*, 1953, *66*, 622–625. **1063, 1064, 1068**

Harcum, E. R., & Filion, R. D. C. Effects of stimulus reversals on lateral dominance in word recognition. *Perceptual and Motor Skills*, 1963, *17*, 779–794. **444**

Harden, L. M. A quantitative study of the similarity factor in retroactive inhibition. *Journal of General Psychology*, 1929, *2*, 421–432. **1081**

Hardy, D., *see* Hochberg, J., 1960.

Hardy, J. D., Goodell, H., & Wolff, H. G. Influence of skin

temperature on pain threshold. *Science,* 1951, *114,* 149–150. **150, 158**

Hardy, J. D., & Oppel, T. W. Studies in temperature sensation: III. The sensitivity of the body to heat and spatial summation of the end-organ responses. *Journal of Clinical Investigation,* 1937, *16,* 533–540. **143, 146, 147**

Hardy, J. D., & Oppel, T. W. Studies in temperature sensation: IV. The stimulation of cold by radiation. *Journal of Clinical Investigation,* 1938, *17,* 771–777. **143, 146**

Hardy, J. D., Stolwijk, J. A. J., & Hoffman, D. Pain following step increase in skin temperature. In D. R. Kenshalo (Ed.), *The skin senses.* Springfield, Ill.: Charles C Thomas, 1968. Pp. 444–457. **159, 162**

Hardy, J. D., Wolff, H. G., & Goodell, H. Studies on pain: A new method for measuring pain threshold: Observations on spatial summation of pain. *Journal of Clinical Investigation,* 1940, *19,* 649–657. **156, 157**

Hardy, J. D., Wolff, H. G., & Goodell, H. Studies on pain: Discrimination of differences in intensity of a pain stimulus as a basis for a scale of pain intensity. *Journal of Clinical Investigation,* 1947, *26,* 1152–1158. **158**

Hardy, J. D., *see also* Greene, L. C., 1958, 1962; Hendler, E., 1960; Herget, C. M., 1941, 1942; Lipkin, M., 1954; Schumacher, G. A., 1940; Wolf, S., 1941.

Hardy, L. H., Rand, G., Rittler, M. C., Blank, A. A. & Boeder, P. *The geometry of binocular space perception.* New York: Knapp Memorial Laboratories, Institute of Ophthalmology, Columbia University College of Physicians and Surgeons, 1953. **493**

Harford, R. A., *see* Hefferline, R. F., 1959.

Harker, G. S., *see* Gogel, W. C., 1957.

Harlow, H. F. The formation of learning sets. *Psychological Review,* 1949, *56,* 51–65. **750, 768**

Harlow, H. F. Analysis of discrimination learning by monkeys. *Journal of Experimental Psychology,* 1950, *40,* 26–39. **773**

Harlow, H. F. Mice, monkeys, men, and motives. *Psychological Review,* 1953, *60,* 23–32. (a) **840**

Harlow, H. F. Motivation as a factor in the acquisition of new responses. In *Current theory and research in motivation: A symposium.* Lincoln, Nebraska: University of Nebraska Press, 1953. Pp. 24–49. (b) **840**

Harlow, H. F. The nature of love. *American Psychologist,* 1958, *13,* 673–685. **585**

Harlow, H. F. Learning set and error factor theory. In S. Koch (Ed.), *Psychology: A study of a science.* New York: McGraw-Hill, 1959. Vol. 2. Pp. 492–537. **766, 768, 773**

Harlow, H. F. Love in infant monkeys. *Scientific American,* 1959, *200,* 68–74. **585**

Harlow, H. F. The development of affectional patterns in infant monkeys. In B. M. Foss (Ed.), *Determinants of infant behavior.* Vol. I., London: Methuen, 1961. **585**

Harlow, H. F., & Bromer, J. A. A test-apparatus for monkeys. *Psychological Record,* 1938, *19,* 434. **750**

Harlow, H. F., & Harlow, M. K. Learning to think. *Scientific American,* 1949. **768**

Harlow, H. F., & Harlow, M. K. Social deprivation in monkeys. *Scientific American,* 1962, *207,* 137–146. **585**

Harlow, H. F., & Harlow, M. K. The affectional systems. In A. M. Schrier, H. F. Harlow, & F. Stollnitz (Eds.), *Behavior of non-human primates.* New York: Academic Press, 1965. Pp. 287–333. **122**

Harlow, H. F., Harlow, M. K., Rueping, R., & Mason, W. A. Performance of infant rhesus monkeys on discrimination learning, delayed response, and discrimination learning set. *Journal of Comparative and Physiological Psychology,* 1960, *53,* 113–121. **768**

Harlow, H. F., *see also* Grandine, L., 1948; Schrier, A. M., 1956.

Harlow, M. K., *see* Harlow, H. F., 1949.

Harmon, L. D., *see* Simmons, F. B., 1965.

Harper, H. W., Jay, J. R., & Erickson, R. P. Chemically evoked sensations from single human taste papillae. *Physiology and Behavior,* 1966, *1,* 319–325. **175, 178**

Harper, R. On odour classification. *Journal of Food Technology,* 1966, *1,* 167–176. **213**

Harper, R. S. The perceptual modifications of colored figures. *American Journal of Psychology,* 1953, *66,* 86–89. **425**

Harper, R. S., & Stevens, S. S. A psychological scale of weight and a formula for its derivation. *American Journal of Psychology,* 1948, *61,* 343–351. **67, 68**

Harriman, A. E., & MacLeod, R. B. Discriminative thresholds of salt for normal and adrenalectomized rats. *American Journal of Psychology,* 1953, *66,* 465–471. **176**

Harrington, G. M., & Kohler, G. R. Sensory deprivation and sensory reinforcement with shock. *Psychological Reports,* 1966, *18,* 803–808. **616**

Harris, C., *see* Rock, I., 1967.

Harris, C. S. Adaptation to displaced vision: Visual, motor or proprioceptive change? *Science,* 1963, *140,* 812–813. **537**

Harris, C. S. Perceptual adaptation to inverted, reversed and displaced vision. *Psychological Review,* 1965, *72,* 419–444. **533, 537, 540, 541, 543**

Harris, C. S., & Haber, R. N. Selective attention and coding in visual perception. *Journal of Experimental Psychology,* 1963, *65,* 328–333. **444**

Harris, E. S., Hoffman, H. S., Liberman, A. M., Delattre, P. C., & Cooper, F. S. Effect of third formant transitions on the perception of the voiced stop consonants. *Journal of the Acoustical Society of America,* 1958, *30,* 122–126. **253**

Harris, G. Binaural interactions of impulsive stimuli and pure tones. *Journal of the Acoustical Society of America,* 1960, *32,* 685–692. **263, 266**

Harris, G. Periodicity perception using gated noise. *Journal of the Acoustical Society of America,* 1963, *35,* 1225–1233. **245**

Harris, J. D. Pitch discrimination. *Journal of the Acoustical Society of America,* 1952, *24,* 750–755. **29, 249**

Harris, J. D. A brief critical review of loudness recruitment. *Psychological Bulletin,* 1953, *50,* 190–203. **240**

Harris, J. D. Hearing. In P. R. Farnsworth (Ed.), *Annual review of psychology,* Vol. 9. Palo Alto, Calif.: Annual Reviews, 1958. **234**

Harris, J. D. The scaling of pitch intervals. *Journal of the Acoustical Society of America,* 1960, *32,* 1575–1581. **244**

Harris, J. D. Loudness discrimination. *Journal of Speech and Hearing Research,* (Monograph Supplement), 1963, *11.* **249**

Harris, K. S., *see* Liberman, A. M., 1962.

Harrison, I. B., & Bigelow, N. H. Quantitative studies of visceral pain produced by the contraction of ischemic muscle. *Proceedings of the Association for Research in Nervous and Mental Disease,* 1943, *23,* 154–165. **156**

Harrison, R. H., *see* Jenkins, H. M., 1960, 1962.

Hart, G., *see* Miller, N. E., 1948.

Harter, S. Discrimination learning set in children as a function of IQ and MA. *Journal of Experimental Child Psychology,* 1965, *2,* 31–43. **768**

Hartline, H. K. The response of single optic nerve fibers of the vertebrate eye to illumination of the retina. *American Journal of Physiology,* 1938, *121,* 400–415. **203, 309**

Hartline, H. K. The effects of spatial summation in the retina on the excitation of the fibers in the optic nerve. *American Journal of Physiology,* 1940, *130,* 700–711. (a) **291**

Hartline, H. K. The receptive fields of optic nerve fibers. *American Journal of Physiology,* 1940, *130,* 690–699. (b) **291**

Hartline, H. K., & Graham, C. H. Nerve impulses from single receptors in the eye. *Journal of Cellular and Comparative Physiology,* 1932, *1,* 277–295. **293**

Hartline, H. K., Ratliff, F., & Miller, W. H. Inhibitory interaction in the retina and its significance in vision. In E. Florey (Ed.), *Nervous inhibition.* New York: Pergamon, 1961. Pp. 241–284. **293**

Hartline, H. K., Wagner, H. G., & Ratliff, F. Inhibition in the eye of *Limulus. Journal of General Physiology,* 1956, *39,* 651–673. **292**

Hartman, B. O., *see* Gogel, W. C., 1957.

Hartman, R., *see* Horton, D. L., 1963.

Hartman, T. F. Dynamic transmission, elective generalization, and semantic conditioning. In W. F. Prokasy (Ed.), *Classical conditioning.* New York: Appleton, 1965. **555**

Hartman, T. F., & Grant, D. A. Differential eyelid conditioning as a function of the CS–UCS interval. *Journal of Experimental Psychology,* 1962, *64,* 131–136. **558**

Hartman, T. F., *see also* Thurlow, W. R., 1959.

Hartson, L. D. Contrasting approaches to the analysis of skilled movements. *Journal of General Psychology,* 1939, *20,* 276–293. **379**

Hartz, K. E., *see* Glickman, S. E., 1964.

Harvey, F. K., Cisek, J. G., MacLean, D. J., & Schroeder, M. R. Some aspects of stereophony applicable to conference use. *Journal of the Audio English Society,* 1963, *11,* 212–217. **258**

Harvey, L. O. Jr., *see* Leibowitz, H. W., 1967.

Harway, N. I. Judgment of distance in children and adults. *Journal of Experimental Psychology,* 1963, *65,* 385–390. **514**

Hashimoto, H., *see* Kaneko, A., 1969.

Hásler, A. D., *see* Wisby, W. J., 1954.

Hastorf, A. H. The influence of suggestion on the relation between stimulus size and perceived distance. *Journal of Psychology,* 1950, *29,* 195–217. **496**

Hastorf, A. H., & Kennedy, J. L. Emmert's law and size-constancy. *American Journal of Psychology,* 1957, *70,* 114–116. **511**

Hastorf, A. H., & Way, K. S. Apparent size with and without distance cues. *Journal of General Psychology,* 1952, *47,* 181–188. **513**

Hatton, G. I., *see* O'Kelly, L. I., 1965.

Haun, K. W. Measures of association and verbal learning. *Psychological Reports,* 1960, *7,* 451–460. **900**

Havron, M. D., Nordlie, P. G., & Cofer, C. N. Measurement of attitude by a simple word association technique. *Journal of Social Psychology,* 1957, *46,* 81–89. **876**

Hawkins, J. E., Jr., & Stevens, S. S. The masking of pure tones and of speech by white noise. *Journal of the Acoustical Society of America,* 1950, *22,* 6–13. **240, 257**

Hawkins, J. E., *see also* Hudgins, C. V., 1947.

Hawkins, T. D., *see* Pliskoff, S. S., 1964, 1967.

Hawkins, W. F., *see* Baumeister, A., 1964.

Hawkins, W. T., *see* Goldiamond, I., 1958.

Hawley, M., *see* Kryter, K. D., 1963.

Hay, J., *see* Hochberg, J. E., 1956.

Hay, J. C. Optical motions and space perception: An extension of Gibson's analysis. *Psychological Review,* 1966, *73,* 550–565. **505**

Hay, J. C. Visual adaptation to an altered correlation between eye movement and head movement. *Science,* 1968, *160,* 429–430. **545**

Hay, J. C., & Pick, H. L., Jr. Visual and proprioceptive adaptation to optical displacement of the visual stimulus. *Journal of Experimental Psychology,* 1966, *71,* 150–158. **538**

Hay, J. C., Pick, H. L., Jr., & Ikeda, K. Visual capture produced by prism spectacles. *Psychonomic Science,* 1965, *2,* 215–216. **536**

Hay, J. C., *see also* Pick, H. L. Jr., 1964, 1965, 1966.

Hayes, J. R., *see* Verplanck, W. S., 1953.

Hayes, K. J. The backward learning curve: A method for the study of learning. *Psychological Review,* 1953, *60,* 269–275. **613**

Hayes, S. P. Facial vision or the sense of obstacles. *Perkins Publications,* 1935, *12,* 1–45. **270**

Hayes, S. P. *Contributions to a psychology of blindness.* New York: American Foundation for the Blind, 1941. **270**

Hayes, W. H., *see* Robinson, J. S., 1964.

Hayes, W. J., Robinson, J., & Brown, L. An effect of past experiences on perception: An artifact. *American Psychology,* 1961, *16,* 420 (Abstr.). **444**

Haygood, R., & Bourne, L. E. Attribute and rule learning aspects of conceptual behavior. *Psychological Review,* 1965, *72,* 175–195. **939, 965**

Haynes, H., White, B. L., & Held, R. Visual accommodation in human infants. *Science,* 1965, *148,* 528–530. **547**

Hays, W. L. *Statistics for psychologists.* New York: Holt, Rinehart and Winston, 1963. **61, 713**

Heath, H. A., *see* Orbach, J., 1963.

Heath, R. M., *see* McClelland, D. C., 1943.

Hebb, D. L. Distinctive features of learning in the higher animal. In J. F. Delafresnaye (Ed.), *Brain mechanisms and learning.* Oxford: Blackwell, 1961. **998**

Hebb, D. O. On the nature of fear. *Psychological Review,* 1946, *53,* 250–275. **586**

Hebb, D. O. *The organization of behavior,* New York: Wiley, 1949. **451, 452, 470, 763, 818**

Hebb, D. O. Drives and the C.N.S. (conceptual nervous system). *Psychological Review,* 1955, *62,* 243–254. **796, 832, 840, 842**

Hebb, D. O. *A textbook of psychology.* (2nd ed.) Philadelphia: Saunders, 1966. **832, 840**

Hebb, D. O., *see also* Pritchard, R. M., 1960.

Hecht, H. Die simultane Erfassung der Figuren, *Zeitschrift für Psychologie,* 1924, *94,* 153–194. **455**

Hecht, M., *see* Graham, C. H., 1948.

Hecht, S. Vision: II. The nature of the photoreceptor process. In C. Murchison (Ed.), *A handbook of general experimental psychology.* Worchester, Mass.: Clark University Press, 1934. Pp. 704–828. **284, 297, 303**

Hecht, S. Rods, cones, and the chemical basis of vision. *Physiological Review,* 1937, *17,* 239–290. **287**

Hecht, S., & Mintz, E. U. The visibility of single lines at various illuminations and the retinal basis of visual resolution. *Journal of General Physiology,* 1939, *22,* 593–612. **298, 299**

Hecht, S., Peskin, J. C., & Patt, M. Intensity discrimination in the human eye: II. Relationship between ∆I/I and intensity for different parts of the spectrum. *Journal of General Physiology,* 1938, *22,* 7–19. **297**

Hecht, S., & Shlaer, S. Intermittent stimulation by light: V. The relation between intensity and critical frequency for different parts of the spectrum. *Journal of General Physiology,* 1936, *19,* 965–979. **312**

Hecht, S., Shlaer, S., & Pirenne, M. H. Energy, quanta, and vision. *Journal of General Physiology,* 1942, *25,* 819–840. **284**

Hecht, S., & Smith, E. L. Intermittent stimulation by light: VI. Area and the relation between critical frequency and intensity. *Journal of General Physiology,* 1936, *19,* 979–989. **311**

Heckenmueller, E., & Dember, W. N. A forced choice indicator for use with Werner's disc-ring pattern in studies of backward masking. *Psychonomic Science,* 1965, *3,* 167–168. **430**

Hecker, M. H. L., *see* House, A. S., 1965.

Hefferline, R. F., Keenan, B., & Harford, R. A. Escape and avoidance conditioning in human subjects without their observation of the response. *Science,* 1959, *130,* 1338–1339. **87, 115**

Heidbreder, E. The attainment of concepts: II. The problem. *Journal of General Psychology,* 1946, *35,* 191–223. **786**

Heidbreder, E. The attainment of concepts: III. The process. *Journal of Psychology,* 1947, *24,* 93–138. **946, 961**

Heider, F., & Simmel, M. An experimental study of apparent

behavior. *American Journal of Psychology,* 1944, *57,* 243-259. **525**

Heimer, W., see Rock, I., 1957, 1959.

Hein, A. V., see Held, R., 1958, 1963.

Heinbecker, P., Bishop, G. H., & O'Leary, J. Pain and touch fibers in peripheral nerves. *Archives of Neurology and Psychiatry,* 1933, *29,* 771-789. **156, 162**

Heine, R. Uber Wiedererkennen und rückwirkende Hemmung. *Zeitschrift für Psychologie,* 1914, *68,* 161-236. **1080**

Heineman, C., see Schlosberg, H., 1950.

Heinemann, E. G. Simultaneous brightness induction as a function of inducing- and test-field luminances. *Journal of Experimental Psychology,* 1955, *50,* 89-96. **411, 413**

Heinemann, E. G. The relation of apparent brightness to the threshold for differences in luminance. *Journal of Experimental Psychology,* 1961, *61,* 389-399. **411**

Heinemann, E. G., & Marill, T. Tilt adaptation and figural after-effects. *Journal of Experimental Psychology,* 1954, *48,* 468-472. **473**

Heinemann, E. G., Tulving, E., & Nachmias, J. The effect of oculomotor adjustments on apparent size. *American Journal of Psychology,* 1959, *72,* 32-45. **479, 480, 513**

Heinemann, S. H., see Mandler, G., 1956.

Heise, G. A., see Miller, G. A., 1951.

Held, R. Exposure-history as a factor in maintaining stability of perception and coordination. *Journal of Nervous and Mental Disorders,* 1961, *132,* 26-32. **535**

Held, R., & Bauer, J. A. Visually guided reaching in infant monkeys after restricted rearing. *Science,* 1967, *155,* 718-720. **535**

Held, R., & Bossom, J. Neonatal deprivation and adult rearrangement: Complementary techniques for analyzing plastic sensory-motor coordinations. *Journal of Comparative and Physiological Psychology,* 1961, *54,* 33-37. **535, 536, 537n, 540**

Held, R., Efstathiou, A., & Greene, M. Adaptation to displaced and delayed visual feedback from the hand. *Journal of Experimental Psychology,* 1966, *72,* 887-891. **536**

Held, R., & Freedman, S. Plasticity in human sensorimotor control. *Science,* 1963, *142,* 455-462. **535**

Held, R., & Gottlieb, N. A technique for studying adaptation to disarranged hand-eye coordination. *Perceptual and Motor Skills,* 1958, *8,* 83-86. **535**

Held, R., & Hein, A. V. Adaptation of disarranged hand-eye coordination contingent upon re-afferent stimulation. *Perceptual and Motor Skills,* 1958, *8,* 87-90. **535**

Held, R., & Hein, A. Movement produced stimulation in the development of visually-guided behavior. *Journal of Comparative and Physiological Psychology,* 1963, *56,* 872-876. **535, 548**

Held, R., & Rekosh, J. Motor-sensory feedback and the geometry of visual space. *Science,* 1963, *141,* 722-723. **467, 542**

Held, R., see also Bossom, J., 1957; Efstathiou, A., 1967; Haynes, H., 1965; Mikaelian, H., 1964.

Hellman, R. P., & Zwislocki, J. Some factors affecting the estimation of loudness. *Journal of the Acoustical Society of America,* 1961, *33,* 687-694. **247**

Hellyer, S., see Burke, C. J., 1954.

Helmholtz, H. von. *Treatise on physiological optics.* Vol. III (trans. from the 3rd German ed., J. P. C. Southall, Ed.) New York: Dover, 1962. **397**

Helmholtz, H. von. *Handbuch der physiologischen Optik.* (3rd ed.) Hamburg & Leipzig: Voss, 1909-1911. First pub. 1856-1866, 2nd ed., 1896. **403, 455, 466n, 484, 488, 506, 510, 521, 527, 529, 530, 531, 534, 543, 546**

Helmholtz, H. von. *Helmholtz's Physiological optics.* Trans. from the 3rd German ed. (1909-1911) by J. P. C. Southall, Ed. Rochester, N.Y.; Optical Society of America, 1924-25. **288, 301, 397**

Helson, H. Size constancy of the projected afterimage.

American Journal of Psychology, 1936, *48,* 638-642. **511**

Helson, H., Fundamental problems in color vision: The principle governing changes in hue, saturation, and lightness of non-selective samples in chromatic illumination. *Journal of Experimental Psychology,* 1938, *23,* 439-476. **415**

Helson, H. Some factors and implications of color constancy. *Journal of the Optical Society of America,* 1943, *33,* 555-567. **412, 416**

Helson, H. Adaptation-level as a basis for a quantitative theory of frames of reference. *Psychological Review,* 1948, *55,* 297-313. **416**

Helson, H. Studies of anomalous contrast and assimilation. *Journal of the Optical Society of America,* 1963, *53,* 179-184. **408**

Helson, H. *Adaptation-level theory: An experimental and systematic approach to behavior.* New York: Harper, 1964. **59, 60, 412, 416**

Helson, H. Some problems in motivation from the point of view of the theory of adaptation level. In D. Levine (Ed.), *Nebraska symposium on motivation,* 1966. Lincoln: University of Nebraska Press, 1966. **434n, 634, 637**

Helson, H., & Fehrer, E. V. The role of form in perception. *American Journal of Psychology,* 1932, *44,* 79-102. **443**

Helson, H., & Jeffers, V. B. Fundamental problems in color vision: II. Hue, lightness, and saturation of selective samples in chromatic illumination. *Journal of Experimental Psychology,* 1940, *26,* 1-27. **416, 417**

Helson, H., & Lansford, T. The role of spectral energy of source and background color in pleasantness of object colors. *Applied Optics,* 1970, *9,* 1513-1562. **315**

Helson, H., see also Guilford, J. P., 1929; Michels, W. C., 1949.

Henderson, A., see Ceraso, J., 1965, 1966.

Hendler, E. & Hardy, J. D. Infrared and microwave effects on skin heating and temperature sensation. *IRE Transactions on Medical Electronics,* 1960, ME-7, 114-152. **140, 154, 158**

Henkin, R. I. The definition of primary and accessory areas of olfaction as the basis for a classification of decreased olfactory acuity. In T. Hayashi (Ed.), *Olfaction and taste.* Vol. II, New York: Pergamon, 1967. Pp. 235-252. **197, 207**

Henkin, R. I., & Powell, G. F. Increased sensitivity of taste and smell in cystic fibrosis. *Science,* 1962, *138,* 1107-1108. **210**

Henkin, R. I., & Solomon, D. H. Salt-taste threshold in adrenal insufficiency in man. *Journal of Clinical Endocrinology and Metabolism,* 1962, *22,* 856-858. **189**

Henle, M. An experimental investigation of past experience as a determinant of form perception. *Journal of Experimental Psychology,* 1942, *30,* 1-22. **444**

Hennelly, E. F., see Langmuir, I., 1944.

Henneman, R. H. A photometric study of the perception of object color. *Archives of Psychology* (New York), 1935, *179.* **404, 423**

Henning, G. B., see Green, D. M., 1969.

Henri, V., see Binet, A., 1896.

Henry, C. E., see Knott, J. R., 1941.

Hensel, H. Temperaturempfindung und intracutane Warmebewegung. *Pflüger's Archiv fur die Gesamte Physiologie des Menschen und der Tiere,* 1950, *252,* 165-215. **142, 144, 145**

Hensel, H. Physiologie der Thermoreception. *Ergebnisse der Physiologie,* 1952, *47,* 166-368. **141**

Hensel, H., & Kenshalo, D. R. Warm receptors in the nasal region of cats. *Journal of Physiology,* 1969, *204,* 99-112. **151**

Hensel, H., Ström, L., & Zotterman, Y. Electrophysiological measurements of depth of thermoreceptors. *Journal of Neurophysiology,* 1951, *14,* 423-439. **140**

Hensel, H. & Witt, I. Spatial temperature gradient and thermoreceptor stimulation. *Journal of Physiology,* 1959, *148,* 180-187. **153**

Hensel, H., & Zotterman, Y. Quantitative Beziehungen zwischen der Entladung einzelner Kaltfasern der Temperatur. *Acta Physiologica Scandinavica,* 1951, *23,* 291–319. **151**

Henson, C. D., see Hubel, D. H., 1959.

Henton, W. W., Smith, J. C. & Tucker, D. Odor discrimination in the pigeon. *Science,* 1966, *153,* 1138–1139. **755**

Herberg, L. J. Seminal ejaculation following positively reinforcing electrical stimulation of the rat hypothalamus. *Journal of Comparative and Physiological Psychology,* 1963, *56,* 679–685. **660**

Herget, C. M., Granath, L. P., & Hardy, J. D. Warmth sense in relation to skin area stimulated. *American Journal of Physiology,* 1941, *135,* 20–26. **147**

Herget, C. M., & Hardy, J. D. Spatial summation of heat. *American Journal of Physiology,* 1942, *135,* 426–429. **148, 149**

Hering, E. *Beitrage zur Physiologie.* Heft 1. Leipzig: Englemann, 1861. Pp. 305f. **481, 489, 491**

Hering, E. Zur Lehre vom Lichtsinn. *Wien Akademie der Wissenschaften. Mathematische-Naturwissenschaftlichte Klasse Sitzungsberichte,* 1874, *69,* 85–104. **397, 411**

Hering, E. Zur Lehre von der Beziehung zwischen Leib und Seele: 1. Uber Fechner's psychophysisches Gesetz. *Wien Akademie der Wissenschaften. Mathematisch-Naturwissenschaftliche. Klasse Sitzungsberichte,* 1876, *72,* 310–348. **377, 411**

Hering, E. Grundzuge einer Theorie des Temperatursinnes. *Wien Akademie der Wissenschaften. Mathematische-Naturwissenschaftliche. Klasse Sitzungsberichte,* 1877, *75,* 101–135. **154**

Hering, E. Der Raumsinn und die Bewegungen des Auges. In L. Hermann (Ed.), *Handbuch der Physiologie.* Vol. 3, Leipzig; Vogel, 1879. Pp. 343–601. **396**

Hering, E. Über die Grenzen der Sehschärfe. *Ber. math.-phys. Kl. Königl. Sächs. ges. Wiss. zu Leipzig,* 1899, 16–24. **301**

Hering, E. Grundzuge der Lehre vom Lichtsinn. In Graefe & Saemisch (Eds.), *Handbuch der gesammten Augenheilkunde,* Vol. III, ch. 13; 1905. 2nd ed.; W. Englemann, Ed. Leipzig: J. Springer, 1920. **323**

Hering, E. *Outlines of a theory of the light sense.* Cambridge, Mass.: Harvard University Press, 1964. **323, 397, 410, 421**

Hermans, T. G. The relationship of convergence and elevation changes to judgments of size. *Journal of Experimental Psychology,* 1954, *48,* 204–208. **480, 513**

Heron, W. T. The warming-up effect in learning nonsense syllables. *Journal of Genetic Psychology,* 1928, *35,* 219–228. **1033**

Heron, W. Perception as a function of retinal locus and attention. *American Journal of Psychology,* 1957, *70,* 38–48. **444**

Heron, W. T., & Skinner, B. F. Changes in hunger during starvation. *Psychological Record,* 1937, *1,* 51–60. **826**

Heron, W. see also Pritchard, R. M., 1960.

Herrnstein, R. J. Superstition: A corollary of the principles of operant conditioning. In W. K. Honig (Ed.), *Operant behavior: Areas of research and application.* New York: Appleton, 1966. **675, 692n**

Herrnstein, R. J. & Hineline, P. N. Negative reinforcement as shock-frequency reduction. *Journal of the Experimental Analysis of Behavior,* 1966, *9,* 421–430. **731**

Herrnstein, R. J., see also Fantino, E., 1968; Sidman, M., 1957.

Herron, W., see Pritchard, R. M., 1960.

Hershberger, W. A. Comment on "Apparent reversal (oscillation) of rotary motion in depth." *Psychological Review,* 1967, *74,* 235–238. **518**

Hershenson, M. Visual discrimination in the human newborn. *Journal of Comparative and Physiological Psychology,* 1964, *58,* 270–276. **547**

Hershenson, M. Development of the perception of form. *Psychological Bulletin,* 1967, *67,* 326–336. **547**

Hershenson, M., Munsinger, & Kessen, W. Preference for shapes of intermediate variability in the newborn human. *Science,* 1965, *147,* 630–631. **547**

Hershensen, M., see also Haber, R. N., 1965.

Hersher, L., Richmond, J. B., & Moore, A. U. Modifiability of the critical period for the development of maternal behavior in sheep and goats. *Behaviour,* 1963, *20,* 311–320. **584**

Herskovits, M. J., see Segall, M. H., 1963, 1966.

Hertzman, M., see Witkin, H. A., 1954.

Herxheimer, A. see DeWardener, H. E., 1957.

Heslam, R. M., see Malmo, R. B., 1951.

Hess, C., & Pretori, H. Messende Untersuchungen über die Gesetzmässigkeit des simultanen Helligkeits-Contrastes. *Archiv für Ophthalmologie,* 1894, *40,* 1–24. As described in E. Hering, *Outlines of a theory of the light sense* (trans. L. M. Hurvich & D. Jameson). Cambridge, Mass.: Harvard University Press, 1964. **408, 410, 411, 413**

Hess, E. H. Development of the chick's response to light and shade cues of depth. *Journal of Comparative and Physiological Psychology,* 1950, *43,* 112–122. **497**

Hess, E. H. Space perception in the chick. *Scientific American,* 1956, *195,* 71–80. **549**

Hess, E. H. The conditions limiting critical age of imprinting. *Journal of Comparative and Physiological Psychology,* 1959, *52,* 515–518. **583**

Hess, E. H. Attitude and pupil size. *Scientific American,* 1965, *212,* 46–54. **393**

Hess, E. H., see also Gogel, W. C., 1951.

Hess, W. R. Beiträge zur Physiologie des Hirnstammes. I: *Die Methodik der lokalisierten Reizung und Ausschaltung subkortikaler Hirnabschnitte.* Leipzig: Thieme, 1932. **643**

Heuckeroth, O., see Myers, J. L., 1966.

Heyer, A. W., see Osgood, C. E., 1952.

Heymans, G. Quantitative Untersuchungen über das "optische Paradoxon." *Zeitschrift für Psychologie,* 1896, *9,* 221–255. **458, 464**

Higa, M. Interference effects of intralist word relationships in verbal learning. *Journal of Verbal Learning and Verbal Behavior,* 1963, *2,* 170–175. **894**

Higgins, K. E., see Robinson, J. S., 1967.

Hilgard, E. R. The nature of the conditioned response: I. The case for and against stimulus substitution. *Psychological Review,* 1936, *43,* 366–385. **565**

Hilgard, E. R. Methods and procedures in the study of learning. In S. S. Stevens (Ed.), *Handbook of experimental psychology.* New York: Wiley, 1951. Pp. 517–567. **890n**

Hilgard, E. R., & Bower, G. H. *Theories of learning.* (3d Ed.) New York: Appleton, 1966. **554n, 616n, 983**

Hilgard, E. R., & Humphreys, L. G. The effect of supporting and antagonistic voluntary instructions on conditioned discrimination. *Journal of Experimental Psychology,* 1938, *22,* 291–304. **561**

Hilgard, E. R., & Marquis, D. G. *Conditioning and learning.* New York: Appleton, 1940. **563, 565**

Hill, A. L., see Rock, I., 1965.

Hill, J. H., see Stellar, E., 1952.

Hill, W. F. Sources of evaluative reinforcement. *Psychological Bulletin,* 1968, *69,* 132–146. **677**

Hill, W. F., see also Spear, N. E., 1965.

Hillebrand, F. Das Verhältnis von Accommodation und Konvergenz zur Tiefenlokalisation. *Zeitschrift für Psychologie,* 1894, *7,* 97–151. **479, 495**

Hillebrand, F. Theorie der scheinbaren Grösse bei binocularem Sehen. *Denkschr. Acad. Wiss. Wien.,* 1902, *72,* 255–307. **493**

Hillman, B., Hunter, W. S., & Kimble, G. A. The effect of drive level on the maze performance of the white rat.

Journal of Comparative and Physiological Psychology, 1953, *46,* 87–89. **794, 830**

Hillner, K., see Peterson, L. R., 1962.

Hilz, R., see Schober, H. A. W., 1965.

Hind, J. E. Unit activity in the auditory cortex. In G. Rasmussen & W. F. Windle (Eds.), *Neural mechanisms of the auditory and vestibular systems.* Springfield, Ill.: Charles C Thomas, 1960. **232**

Hind, J. E., see also Rose, J. E., 1963, 1966, 1967.

Hinde, R. A. Factors governing the change in strength of a partially inborn response, as shown by the mobbing behaviour of the chaffinch (*Fringilla coelebs*): I. The nature of the response, and an examination of its course. *Proceedings of the Royal Society,* Ser. B, 1954, *142,* 306–331. (a) **589**

Hinde, R. A. Factors governing the change in strength of a partially inborn response, as shown by the mobbing behaviour of the chaffinch (*Fringilla coelebs*): II. The waning of the response. *Proceedings of the Royal Society,* Ser. B, 1954, *142,* 331–358. (b) **589, 590**

Hinde, R. A. Factors governing the change in strength of a partially inborn response, as shown by the mobbing behaviour of the chaffinch (*Fringilla coelebs*): III. Interaction of short-term and long-term incremental and decremental effects. *Proceedings of the Royal Society,* Ser. B, 1961, *153,* 398–420. **589**

Hinde, R. A. *Animal behaviour: A synthesis of ethology and comparative psychology.* New York: McGraw-Hill, 1966. **587, 595, 603, 702, 746, 822**

Hinde, R. A. *Animal behaviour: A synthesis of ethology and comparative psychology.* (ed.2) New York: McGraw-Hill, 1970. **582, 588**

Hinde, R. A. Behavioural habituation. In G. Horn & R. A. Hinde (Eds.), *Short term changes in neural activity and behaviour.* Cambridge: Cambridge University Press, 1970. **591, 745**

Hinde, R. A. Incremental and decremental changes in behaviour. In G. Horn & R. A. Hinde (Eds.), *Short-term changes in neural activity and behaviour.* London: Cambridge University Press, 1970. **591**

Hinde, R. A., Thorpe, W. H., & Vince, M. A. The following responses of young coots and moorhens. *Behaviour,* 1956, *11,* 214–242. **583**

Hineline, P. N., see Harrnstein, R. J., 1966.

Hinshaw, J. R., see Sinclair, D. C., 1951.

Hintzman, D. L. Some tests of a discrimination net theory: Paired-associate learning as a function of stimulus similarity and number of responses. *Journal of Verbal Learning and Verbal Behavior,* 1967, *6,* 809–816. **1009**

Hintzman, D. L. Explorations with a discrimination model for paired-associate learning. *Journal of Mathematical Psychology,* 1968, *5,* 123–162. **1008**

Hirsch, M. J., Horowitz, M., & Weymouth, F. W. Distance discrimination: III. Effect of rod width on threshold. *Archives of Ophthalmology,* 1948, *39,* 325–332. **486**

Hirsh, I. J. The influence of interaural phase on interaural summation and inhibition. *Journal of the Acoustical Society of America,* 1948, *20,* 536–554. **242**

Hirsh, I. J. The relation between localization and intelligibility. *Journal of the Acoustical Society of America,* 1950, *22,* 196–200. **258**

Hirsh, I. J. Hearing. In C. P. Stone (Ed.), *Annual review of psychology,* Vol. 6. Palo Alto, Calif.: Annual Reviews, 1955. **235**

Hirsh, I. J., & Burgeat, M. Binaural effects in remote masking. *Journal of the Acoustical Society of America,* 1958, *30,* 827–832. **239**

Hirsh, I. J., Davis, H., Silverman, S. R., Reynolds, E. G., Eldert, E., & Benson, R. W. Development of materials for speech audiometry. *Journal of Speech and Hearing Disabilities,* 1952, *17,* 321–337. **254, 255**

Hirsh, I. J., Reynolds, E. G., & Joseph, M. Intelligibility of different speech materials. *Journal of the Acoustical Society of America,* 1954, *26,* 530–538. **256, 257**

Hirsh, I. J., see also Bilger, R. C., 1956; Deatherage, B. H., 1959.

Hirsh, S. K., see Davis, H., 1967.

Hoagland, H., see Cattell, McK., 1931.

Hobhouse, L. T. *Mind in evolution.* New York: Macmillan, 1901. **750**

Hochberg, C. B., & Hochberg, J. E. Familiar size and the perception of depth. *Journal of Psychology,* 1952, *34,* 107–114. **495, 496**

Hochberg, J. Figure-ground reversal as a function of visual satiation. *Journal of Experimental Psychology,* 1950, *40,* 682–686. **471**

Hochberg, J. Perception: Toward a recovery of a definition. *Psychological Review,* 1956, *63,* 400–405. **424, 506**

Hochberg, J. Effects of the *Gestalt* revolution: The Cornell symposium on perception. *Psychological Review,* 1957, *64,* 78–84. **437**

Hochberg, J. Naturism and empiricism in perception. In Leo Postman (Ed.), *Psychology in the making,* New York: Knopf, 1962. **427, 441, 546**

Hochberg, J. The psychophysics of pictorial perception. *A–V Communication Review,* 1962, *10,* 22–54. **441**

Hochberg, J. On the importance of movement-produced stimulation in prism-induced after-effects. *Perceptual and Motor Skills,* 1963, *16,* 544. **537, 540, 542**

Hochberg, J. A theory of the binocular cyclopean field: On the possibility of simulated stereopsis. *Perceptual and Motor Skills,* 1964, *19,* 685. (a) **488, 489**

Hochberg, J. Contralateral suppressive fields of binocular combination. *Psychonomic Science,* 1964, *1,* 157–158. (b) **488, 489, 491**n

Hochberg, J. Representative sampling and the purposes of perceptual research: Pictures of the world and the world of pictures. In Kenneth R. Hammond (Ed.), *The Psychology of Egon Brunswick.* New York: Holt, Rinehart and Winston, 1966. **471**n

Hochberg, J. In the mind's eye. In R. N. Haber (Ed.), *Contemporary theory and research in visual perception.* New York: Holt, Rinehart and Winston, 1968. **432, 454, 455, 456, 462, 506, 524**

Hochberg, J. Units of perceptual analysis. In J. Mehler (Ed.), *Handbook of cognitive psychology.* Englewood Cliffs, N. J.: Prentice-Hall, in press. **442, 453**

Hochberg, J. Attention, organization and consciousness. In D. Mostofsky (Ed.), *Attention: Contemporary theory and analysis,* New York: Appleton, in press. **442, 453**

Hochberg, J., & Beck, J. Apparent spatial arrangement and perceived brightness. *Journal of Experimental Psychology,* 1954, *47,* 263–266. **420**

Hochberg, J., & Bitterman, M. E. Figural after-effects as a function of the retinal size of the inspection figure. *American Journal of Psychology,* 1951, *64,* 99–102. **471**n

Hochberg, J., & Brooks, V. Effects of previously associated annoying stimuli (auditory) on visual recognition thresholds. *Journal of Experimental Psychology,* 1958, *55,* 490–491. **440**

Hochberg, J., & Brooks, V. The psychophysics of form: Reversible-perspective drawings of spatial objects. *American Journal of Psychology,* 1960, *73,* 337–354. **435, 436**

Hochberg, J., & Brooks, V. Pictorial recognition as an unlearned ability: A study of one child's performance. *American Journal of Psychology,* 1962, *75,* 624–628. **442, 501**

Hochberg, J., & Galper, R. E. Recognition of faces: I. An explanatory study. *Psychonomic Science,* 1967, *9,* 12. **450**

Hochberg, J. E., Gleitman, H., & MacBride, P. D. Visual thresholds as a function of simplicity of form. *Proc. of* the 28th Annual Meeting of the Western Psychological Association. *American Psychologist,* 1948, *3,* 341–342. **443**

Hochberg, J., Haber, S., & Ryan, T. A. "Perceptual defense" as an interference phenomenon. *Perceptual and Motor Skills,* 1955, *5,* 15–17. **440**

Hochberg, J., Hardy, D. Brightness and proximity factors in grouping. *Perceptual and Motor Skills,* 1960, *10,* 22. **434**

Hochberg, J. E., & Hay, J. Figural after-effect, after-image, and physiological nystagmus. *American Journal of Psychology,* 1956, *69,* 480–482. **472**

Hochberg, J., & McAlister, E. A quantitative approach to figural "goodness." *Journal of Experimental Psychology,* 1953, *46,* 361–364. **437**

Hochberg, J., & Silverstein, A. A quantitative index of stimulus similarity: Proximity vs. differences in brightness. *American Journal of Psychology,* 1956, *69,* 456–459. **434**

Hochberg, J., & Smith, O. W. Landing strip markings and the "expansion pattern": I. Program, preliminary analysis and apparatus. *Perceptual and Motor Skills,* 1955, *5,* 81–92. **504n**

Hochberg, J., & Triebel, W. Figural after-effects with colored stimuli. *American Journal of Psychology,* 1955, *68,* 133–135. **470, 471n**

Hochberg, J. E., Triebel, W., & Seaman, G. Color adaptation under conditions of homogeneous stimulation (*Ganzfeld*). *Journal of Experimental Psychology,* 1951, *41,* 153–159. **416**

Hochberg, J. E., *see also* Bitterman, M. E., 1954; Hochberg, C. B., 1952; Smith, D., 1954.

Hockman, C. H. EEG and behavioral effects of food deprivation in the albino rat. *Electroencephalography and Clinical Neurophysiology,* 1964, *17,* 420–427. **837**

Hockman, C. H., & Lipsitt, L. P. Delay-of-reward gradients in discrimination learning with children for two levels of difficulty. *Journal of Comparative and Physiological Psychology,* 1961, *54,* 24–27. **688**

Hodgson, E. S. Chemical senses in the invertebrates. In M. R. Kare & O. Maller (Eds.). *The chemical senses and nutrition.* Baltimore: The Johns Hopkins Press, 1967. Pp. 7–18. **181**

Hodgson, W. R. Audiological report of a patient with left hemispherectomy. *Journal of Speech and Hearing Disabilities,* 1967, *32,* 39–45. **264**

Hodos, W. Progressive ratio as a measure of reward strength. *Science,* 1961, *134,* 943–944. **649, 653**

Hodos, W. Motivational properties of long durations of rewarding brain stimulation. *Journal of Comparative and Physiological Psychology,* 1965, *59,* 219–224. **649**

Hodos, W., & Kalman, G. Effects of increment size and reinforcer volume on progressive ratio performance. *Journal of the Experimental Analysis of Behavior,* 1963, *6,* 387–392. **649**

Hodos, W., & Valenstein, E. S. An evaluation of response rate as a measure of rewarding intracranial stimulation. *Journal of Comparative and Physiological Psychology,* 1962, *55,* 80–84. **650**

Hoffeld, D. R., Kendall, S. B., Thompson, R. F., & Brogden, W. J. Effect of amount of preconditioning training upon magnitude of sensory preconditioning. *Journal of Comparative and Physiological Psychology,* 1960, *59,* 198–204. **564**

Hodos, W., *see also* Beer, B., 1964; Weitzman, E. D., 1961.

Hoebel, B. G., & Teitelbaum, P. Hypothalamic control of feeding and self-stimulation. *Science,* 1962, *135,* 375–377. **798**

Hoffman, D., *see* Hardy, J. D., 1968.

Hofman, F. B., & A. Bielschowsky. Über die Einstellung der scheinbaren Horizontalen und Vertikalen bei Betrachtung eines von schrägen Konturen erfullten Gesichtsfeldes. *Pflüger's Archiv der gesamte Physiologie,* 1909, *126,* 453–475. **458**

Hoffman, H. S. The stimulus generalization of conditioned suppression. In D. I. Mostofsky (Ed.), *Stimulus generalization.* Stanford: Stanford University Press, 1965. Pp. 715, 356–372. **759**

Hoffman, H. S. A flexible connector for delivering shock to pigeons. *Journal of the Experimental Analysis of Behavior,* 1960, *3,* 330. **706**

Hoffman, H. S. The analysis of discriminated avoidance. In W. K. Honig (Ed.), *Operant behavior: Areas of research and application.* New York: Appleton, 1966. **726**

Hoffman, H. S., & Fleshler, M. Stimulus factors in aversive controls: The generalization of conditioned suppression. *Journal of the Experimental Analysis of Behavior,* 1961, *4,* 371–378. **713**

Hoffman H. S., & Fleshler, M. The course of emotionality in the development of avoidance. *Journal of Experimental Psychology,* 1962, *64,* 288–294. **726**

Hoffman, H. S., Fleshler, M., & Abplanalp, P. L. Startle reaction to electrical shock in the rat. *Journal of Comparative and Physiological Psychology,* 1964, *58,* 132–139. **710**

Hoffman, H. S., Searle, J. L., Toffey, S., & Kuzma, F., Jr. Behavioral control by an imprinted stimulus. *Journal of the Experimental Analysis of Behavior,* 1966, *9,* 177–189. **581, 587**

Hoffman, H. S., *see also* Harris, E. S., 1958.

Hoffman, M., *see* Eriksen, C. W., 1963.

Hogan, F. A., *see* Inglett, G. E., 1965.

Hokanson, J. E., *see* Doerr, H. O., 1968.

Holaday, B. E. Die Grössenkonstanz der Sehdinge bei Variation der inneren und äusseren Wahrnehmungsbedingungen. *Archiv der gesamte Psychologie,* 1933, *88,* 419–486. **509**

Holborn, S., & Boe, E. The effect of overlearning on transfer of training. *Quarterly Journal of Experimental Psychology,* 1965, *17,* 178–180. **1067**

Holland, J. H., *see* Rochester, H., 1956.

Hollingworth, H. L., & Poffenberger, A. T. *The sense of taste.* New York: Moffat, Yard, 1917. **177**

Holm, K. G. Die Dauer der Temperaturempfindungen bei konstanter. Reiztemperatur. *Archiv Physiologica Scandinavica,* 1903, *14,* 242–258. **142**

Holman, G. L., *see* Galanter, E., 1967.

Holmberg, T. *see* Granit, R., 1938.

Holmes, C. E., *see* Kenshalo, D. R., 1968.

Holmes, D. S. Search for "closure" in a visually perceived pattern. *Psychological Bulletin,* 1968, *70,* 296–312. **445**

Holst, E. von, *see* von Holst, E.

Holstein, S. B., & Premack, D. On the different effects of random reinforcement and presolution reversal on human concept identification. *Journal of Experimental Psychology,* 1965, *70,* 335–337. **955**

Holtz, P., *see* Fischer, S. C., 1956.

Holway, A. H., & Boring, E. G. Determinants of apparent visual size with distance variant. *American Journal of Psychology,* 1941, *54,* 21–37. **512, 514**

Holz, W. C., *see* Azrin, N. H., 1961, 1966

Homme, L. E. Spontaneous recovery and statistical learning theory. *Journal of Experimental Psychology,* 1956, *51,* 205–212. **570n**

Honig, W. K. Generalization of extinction on the spectral continuum. *Psychological Record,* 1961, *11,* 269–278. **577**

Honig, W. K. Discrimination, generalization, and transfer on the basis of stimulus differences. In D. I. Mostofsky (Ed.), *Stimulus generalization.* Stanford: Stanford University Press, 1965. Pp. 218–254. **763, 765**

Honig, W. K. (Ed.) *Operant behavior: Areas of application and research.* New York: Appleton, 1966. **604, 608**

Honig, W. K. The role of discrimination training in the generalization of punishment. *Journal of the Experimental Analysis of Behavior,* 1966, *9,* 377–384. **762**

Quarterly Journal of Experimental Psychology, 1961, *13*, 19–33. **471, 519**

Howard, I. P., Craske, B., & Templeton, W. B. Visuo-motor adaptation to discordant exafferent stimulation. *Journal of Experimental Psychology*, 1965, *70*, 189–191. **536**

Howard, I. P., & Templeton, W. B. Visually-induced eye torsion and tilt adaptation. *Vision Research*, 1964, *4*, 433–437. **539n**

Howard, I. P., & Templeton, W. B. *Human spatial orientation.* New York: Wiley, 1966. **473, 529, 533, 538, 540**

Howard, R. P., see Schneider, R. A.

Howarth, C. I., see Deutsch, J. A., 1963.

Howe, E. S. Uncertainty and other associative correlates of Osgood's D₄. *Journal of Verbal Learning and Verbal Behavior*, 1965, *4*, 498–509. **861n, 865, 900**

Howe, E. S. Some quantitative free associative correlates of Noble's m. *Journal of Verbal Learning and Verbal Behavior*, 1969. **858**

Howe, T. S. Unlearning and competition in List-1 recall. *Journal of Experimental Psychology*, 1967, *75*, 559–565. **1087, 1099**

Howell, D. C., see Bilodeau, E. A., 1965.

Howes, D. On the interpretation of word frequency as a variable affecting speed of recognition. *Journal of Experimental Psychology*, 1954, *48*, 106–112. **896**

Howes, D. On the relation between the intelligibility and frequency of occurrence of English words. *Journal of the Acoustical Society of America*, 1957, *29*, 296–305. **255**

Howes, D. On the relation between the probability of a word as an association and in general linguistic usage. *Journal of Abnormal and Social Psychology*, 1957, *54*, 75–85. **862**

Howes, D. A word count of spoken English. *Journal of Verbal Learning and Verbal Behavior*, 1966, *5*, 572–604. **895**

Howes, D., & Osgood, C. E. On the combination of associative probabilities in linguistic contexts. *American Journal of Psychology*, 1954, *67*, 241–258. **871**

Howes, D., & Solomon, R. L. Visual duration thresholds as a function of word probability. *Journal of Experimental Psychology*, 1951, *41*, 401–410. **255**

Howes, D. H., see also Solomon, R. L., 1951.

Hoyle, E. M., see Green, R. T., 1963.

Hsia, Y. Whiteness constancy as a function of difference in illumination. *Archives of Psychology* (New York), 1943, *284*. **409, 414**

Hsia, Y., & Graham, C. H. Spectral luminosity curves of protanopic, deuteranopic, and normal subjects. *Proceedings of the National Academy of Science*, 1957, *43*, 1011–1019. **364**

Hsü, E. H. A factorial analysis of olfaction. *Psychometrika*, 1946, *11*, 31–42. **216**

Hubbard, D., see Smith, O. W., 1958.

Hubel, D. H., Henson, C. D., Rupert, A., & Galambos, R. "Attention" units in the auditory cortex. *Science*, 1959, *129*, 1279–1280. **232**

Hubel, D. H., & Wiesel, T. N. Receptive fields, binocular interaction and functional architecture in the cat's visual cortex. *Journal of Physiology*, 1962, *160*, 106–154. **294, 295**

Hubel, D. H., see also Wiesel, T. N., 1963.

Hudgins, C. V., Hawkins, J. E., Karlin, J. E., & Stevens, S. S. The development of recorded auditory tests for measuring loss for speech. *Laryngoscope*, 1947, *57*, 57–89. **254**

Hudson, B. B. One-trial learning in the domestic rat. *Genetic Psychology Monographs*, 1950, *41*, 99–145. **568**

Hudson, W. Pictorial depth perception in subcultural groups in Africa. *Journal of Social Psychology*, 1960, *52*, 183–208. **500**

Huggins, W. H., & Licklider, J. G. R. Place mechanisms in auditory frequency analysis. *Journal of the Acoustical Society of America*, 1951, *23*, 290–299. **231**

Hughes, J. W. The upper frequency limit for the binaural

localization of a pure tone by a phase difference. *Proceedings of the Royal Society* (*London*), Series B, 1940, *128*, 293–305. **262**

Hughes, L. H. Saccharin reinforcement in a T-maze. *Journal of Comparative and Physiological Psychology*, 1957, *50*, 431–435. **627**

Hulicka, I. M., see Bolles, R. C., 1959.

Hull, A., see Conrad, R., 1964.

Hull, C., see Fischer, S. C., 1956.

Hull, C. L. Quantitative aspects of the evolution of concepts. *Psychological Monographs*, 1920, *28*. (Whole No. 123) **785, 786, 945**

Hull, C. L. Knowledge and purpose as habit mechanisms. *Psychological Review*, 1930, *37*, 511–525. **622**

Hull, C. L. The goal gradient hypothesis and maze learning. *Psychological Review*, 1932, *39*, 25–43. **621, 679**

Hull, C. L. Differential habituation to internal stimuli in the albino rat. *Journal of Comparative Psychology*, 1933, *16*, 255–273. **800**

Hull, C. L. The meaningfulness of 320 selected nonsense syllables. *American Journal of Psychology*, 1933, *45*, 730–734. **852**

Hull, C. L. *Principles of behavior: An introduction to behavior theory.* New York: Appleton, 1943. **567, 574, 575, 596, 597, 616, 619n, 635, 679, 681, 689, 690, 741, 760, 765, 801, 804, 812, 826, 1053**

Hull, C. L. *A behavior system.* New Haven: Yale University Press, 1952. **596n, 597, 619n, 622, 680, 770, 802, 805, 812**

Hull, C. L., Hovland, C. I., Ross, R. T., Hall, M., Perkins, B. T., & Fitch, F. B. *Mathematico-deductive theory of rote learning.* New Haven: Yale University Press, 1940. **980**

Hull, C. L., Livingston, J. R., Rouse, R. O., & Barker, A. N. True, sham, and esophageal feeding as reinforcements. *Journal of Comparative and Physiological Psychology*, 1951, *44*, 236–245. **670, 816**

Hull, C. L., see also Bass, M. J., 1934; Koch, S., 1954.

Hulse, S. H., Jr. A precision liquid feeding system controlled by licking behavior. *Journal of the Experimental Analysis of Behavior*, 1960, *3*, 1. **623, 639**

Hulse, S. H., Jr. Discrimination of the reward in learning with partial and continuous reinforcement. *Journal of Experimental Psychology*, 1962, *64*, 277–233. **639**

Hulse, S. H., Snyder, H. L., & Bacon, W. E. Instrumental licking behavior as a function of schedule, volume, and concentration of a saccharine reinforcer. *Journal of Experimental Psychology*, 1960, *60*, 359–364. **626**

Humphrey, G. *The nature of learning in its relation to the living system.* London: Kegan Paul, 1933. **591**

Humphrey, G. *Thinking: An introduction to its experimental psychology.* New York: Wiley, 1951. **868**

Humphreys, L. G. Acquisition and extinction of verbal expectations in a situation analogous to conditioning. *Journal of Experimental Psychology*, 1939, *25*, 294–301. **560n**

Humphreys, L. G., see also Hilgard, E. R., 1938.

Hunt, C. C., & McIntyre, A. K. Properties of cutaneous touch receptors in cat. *Journal of Physiology*, 1960, *153*, 88–98. (a) **165**

Hunt, C. C., & McIntyre, A. K. An analysis of fibre diameter and receptor characteristics of myelinated cutaneous afferent fibres in cat. *Journal of Physiology*, 1960, *153*, 99–112. (b) **165**

Hunt, E., see Crawford, J., 1967.

Hunt, E. B. Memory effects in concept learning. *Journal of Experimental Psychology*, 1961, *62*, 598–604. **960, 971**

Hunt, E. B. *Concept learning: An information processing problem.* New York: Wiley, 1962. **938, 943, 944, 949**

Hunt, E. B. Utilization of memory in concept-learning systems. In B. Kleinmuntz (Ed.), *Concepts in memory.* New York: Wiley, 1967. Pp. 77–106. **978**

Hunt, E. B., & Hovland, C. I. Order of consideration of logical types of concepts. *Journal of Experimental Psychology,* 1960, *59,* 220–225. **963**

Hunt, E. B., & Hovland, C. I. Programming a model of human concept formulation. *Proceedings of the Western Joint Computer Conference,* 1961, 145–155. **942, 977**

Hunt, E. B., Marin, J., & Stone, P. J. *Experiments in induction.* New York: Academic Press, 1966. **938, 967, 976, 978**

Hunt, H. F., & Brady, J. V. Some effects of punishment and intercurrent "anxiety" on a simple operant. *Journal of Comparative and Physiological Psychology,* 1955, *48,* 305–310. **733**

Hunt, J. McV. Motivation inherent in information processing and action. In O. J. Harvey (Ed.), *Motivation and social interaction: Cognitive determinants.* New York: Ronald, 1963. Pp. 35–94. **841**

Hunt, W. A., *see* Campbell, T. C., 1958.

Hunter, I. M. L. An experimental investigation of absolute and relative theories of transpositional behaviour in children. *British Journal of Psychology,* 1952, *43,* 113–128. **765**

Hunter, J. J., *see* Grice, G. R., 1964.

Hunter, R. S. Methods of determining gloss. *Journal of Research of the National Bureau of Standards,* 1937, *18,* 19–39. **427**

Hunter, W. S. The delayed reaction in animals and children. *Behavior Monographs,* 1913, No. 6. **786**

Hunter, W. S. The auditory sensitivity of the white rat. *Journal of Animal Behavior,* 1914, *4,* 215–222. **774**

Hunter, W. S. Delayed reaction in a child. *Psychological Review,* 1917, *24,* 74–87. **786, 788**

Hunter, W. S. Muscle potentials and conditioning in the rat. *Journal of Experimental Psychology,* 1937, *21,* 611–624. **577**

Hunter, W. S., & Bartlett, S. C. Double alternation in young children. *Journal of Experimental Psychology,* 1948, *38,* 558–567. **5n**

Hunter, W. S., *see also* Hillman, B., 1953; McCrary, J. W., 1953; Prosser, C. L., 1936.

Huntington, D. A., *see* Simmons, F. B., 1964.

Hunton, D. The recognition of inverted pictures by children. *Journal of Genetic Psychology,* 1955, *86,* 281–288. **450**

Hurvich, L. M., & Jameson, D. Some quantitative aspects of an opponent-colors theory: II. Brightness, saturation and hue in normal and dichromatic vision. *Journal of the Optical Society of America,* 1955, *45,* 602. **324, 328, 348**

Hurvich, L. M., & Jameson, D. Perceived color, induction effects, and opponent response mechanisms. *Journal of General Physiology,* 1960, *43,* Suppl. No. 2, 63–80. **337, 417**

Hurvich, L. M., & Jameson, D. *The perception of brightness and darkness.* Boston: Allyn and Bacon, 1966. **307, 408**

Hurvich, L. M., *see also* Jameson, D., 1959, 1961, 1964.

Hurvich, M. S., *see* Wishner, J., 1957.

Hut, P. A., *see* Cohen, B. H., 1963.

Hutt, P. J. Rate of bar pressing as a function of quality and quantity of food reward. *Journal of Comparative and Physiological Psychology,* 1954, *47,* 235–239. **630, 631**

Hyman, R., *see* Hake, H. W., 1953; Jenkins, N., 1959.

Iggo, A. An electrophysiological analysis of afferent fibres in primate skin. *Acta Neurovegetativa,* 1963, *Band 24:* 225–240. **133, 153**

Iggo, A. Cutaneous thermoreceptors in primates and subprimates. *Journal of Physiology,* 1969, *200,* 403–430. **151**

Ikeda, S., Furukawa, H., & Yamaguchi, S. An attempt to establish scales of taste: Measurement of delicious taste intensity by Thurstone-Mosteller's method. *Statistical Quality Control* (in Japanese, English summary), 1962, *13,* 76–79.

Ikeda, H. & Obonai, T. The quantitative analysis of figural aftereffects: I. The process of growth and decay of figural after-effects. *Japanese Journal of Psychology,* 1953, *24,* 179–192. **469**

Ikeda, K., *see also* Hay, J. C., 1965.

Imai, S., & Garner, W. R. Discriminability and preference for attributes in free and constrained classification. *Journal of Experimental Psychology,* 1965, *69,* 596–608. **449**

Immergluck, L. Resistance to an optical illusion: Figural after-effects, and field dependence. *Psychonomic Science,* 1966, *6,* 281–282. **470**

Immergluck, L. Visual figural after-effects and field dependence. *Psychonomic Science,* 1966, *4,* 219–220. **470**

Imparato, N., *see* Smith, O. W., 1968.

Ingham, J. G. Variations in cross-masking with frequency. *Journal of Experimental Psychology,* 1959, *58,* 199–205. **242**

Inglett, G. E., Dowling, B., Albrecht, J. J., & Hoglan, F. A. Taste-modifying properties of miracle fruit (*Synsepalum dulcificum*). *Journal of Agricultural and Food Chemistry,* 1965, *13,* 284–287. **177**

Ingling, C. R. *The spectral sensitivities of receptor systems in human color vision.* Doctoral dissertation, University of Rochester, 1967. **367, 368**

Ingling, C. R. A tetrachromatic hypothesis for human color vision. *Vision Research,* 1969, *9,* 1131–1148. **349**

Ingraham, R., *see* Carlin, S., 1962.

Ipsen, G. Über Gestaltauffassung. Erörterung des Sanderschen Parallelogramms. *Neue Psychologische Studien,* 1926, *1,* 167–278. **458**

Irion, A. L. The relation of "set" to retention. *Psychological Review,* 1948, *55,* 336–341. **1034, 1039**

Irion, A. L. Retention and warming-up effects in paired-associate learning. *Journal of Experimental Psychology,* 1949, *39,* 669–675. **1039**

Irion, A. L. Rote learning. In S. Koch, (Ed.), *Psychology: A study of a science.* Vol. 2. New York: McGraw-Hill. Pp. 538–560. **848, 849**

Irion, A. L. A brief history of research on the acquisition of skill. In E. A. Bilodeau (Ed.), *Acquisition of skill.* New York: Academic Press, 1966. **575**

Irion, A. L., & Gustafson, L. M. "Reminiscence" in bilateral transfer. *Journal of Experimental Psychology,* 1952, *43,* 321–323. **575**

Irion, A. L., & Wham, D. S. Recovery from retention loss as a function of amount of pre-recall warming up. *Journal of Experimental Psychology,* 1951, *41,* 242–246. **1039**

Irion, A. L., *see also* Ammons, H., 1954; McGeoch, J. A., 1952.

Irwin, F. W. Motivation and performance. *Annual Review of Psychology,* 1961, *12,* 217–242. **794n**

Irwin, J. M., *see* Melton, A. W., 1940.

Iscoe, I., *see* Stevenson, H. W., 1955.

Ishak, I. G. H. The spectral chromaticity coordinates for one British and eight Egyptian trichromats. *Journal of the Optical Society of America,* 1952, *42,* 534–539. **461**

Ishiko, N., Amatsu, M., & Sato, Y. Thalamic representation of taste qualities and temperature change in the cat. In T. Hayashi (Ed.), *Olfaction and taste.* Vol. 2. New York: Pergamon, 1967. Pp. 563–572. **182**

Ison, J. R., *see* Rosen, A. J., 1965.

Ittelson, W. H. Size as a cue to distance: Static localization. *American Journal of Psychology,* 1951, *64,* 54–67. **495**

Ittelson, W. H. Size as a cue to distance: Radial motion. *American Journal of Psychology,* 1951, *64,* 188–202. **495**

Ittelson, W. H. *The Ames demonstrations in perception.* Princeton, N. J.: Princeton University Press, 1952. **518**

Ittelson, W. H., *see also* Kilpatrick, F. P., 1953.

Ivanova, V. A., *see* Chistovitch, L. A., 1959.

Ivanov-Smolensky, A. G. On the methods of examining the conditioned food reflexes in children and in mental disorders. *Brain,* 1927, *50,* 138–141. **564**

Iverson, K. E. *A programming language.* New York: Wiley, 1962. **938**

Ives, H. E. Critical frequency relations in scotopic vision. *Journal of the Optical Society of America,* 1922, *6,* 254-268. **313**

Ivy, A. C., see Goetzl, F. R., 1943.

Izawa, C. Reinforcement-test sequences in paired-associate learning. *Psychological Reports,* 1966, *18,* 879-919. **987, 990**

Izawa, C. Function of test trial in paired-associate learning. *Journal of Experimental Psychology,* 1967, *75,* 194-209. **987, 990**

Izawa, C., see also Horowitz, L., 1963.

Jackson, D. N. A further examination of the role of autism in a visual figure-ground relationship. *Journal of Psychology,* 1954, *38,* 339-357. **440**

Jacobs, G. H., see DeValois, R. L., 1963, 1964.

Jacobs, H. L. Observations on the ontogeny of saccharine preference in the neonate rat. *Psychonomic Science,* 1964, *1,* 105-106. **190**

Jacobs, H. L., & K. N. Sharma. Taste versus calories: Sensory and metabolic signals in the regulation of food intake. *Annals of the New York Academy of Sciences,* 1969, *157,* 1084-1125. **190, 817**

Jahoda, G. Geometric illusions and environment: A study in Ghana. *British Journal of Psychology,* 1966, *57,* 193-199. **460**

James, C. T., & Greeno, J. G. Stimulus selection at different stages of paired-associate learning. *Journal of Experimental Psychology,* 1967, *74,* 75-83. **1021**

James, C. T., & Hakes, D. Mediated transfer in a four-stage, stimulus-equivalence paradigm. *Journal of Verbal Learning and Verbal Behavior,* 1965, *4,* 89-93. **1076**

James, L., see Peterson, L. R., 1967.

James, W. *Principles of psychology.* New York: Holt, 1890. **437, 596, 1030**

James, W. T., see Liddell, H. S., 1934.

Jameson, D., & Hurvich, L. M. Note on factors influencing the relation between stereoscopic acuity and observation distance. *Journal of the Optical Society of America,* 1959, *49,* 639. **494, 502**

Jameson, D., & Hurvich, L. M. Complexities of perceived brightness. *Science,* 1961, *133,* 174-179. **409, 411, 412**

Jameson, D., & Hurvich, L. M. Theory of brightness and color contrast in human vision. *Vision Research,* 1964, *4,* 135-154. **412, 417**

Jameson, D., see also Hurvich, L. M., 1955, 1960, 1966.

Jamison, S. M., see Peterson, M. J., 1965.

Jane, J. A., see Masterton, R. B., 1968.

Jardinico, R. E., see Alpern, M., 1961.

Jarvik, M. E. Probability learning and a negative recency effect in the serial anticipation of alternative symbols. *Journal of Experimental Psychology,* 1951, *41,* 291-297. **920, 921**

Jasper, H. H., & Ajmone-Marsan, C. *A stereotaxic atlas of the diencephalon of the cat.* Ottawa: National Research Council of Canada, 1955. **114**

Jasper, H. H., see also Penfield, W., 1954; Sharpless, S., 1956.

Javal, L. E. Essai sur la physiologie de la lecture. *Annales D'Oculistique,* 1879, *82,* 242-253. **389**

Jay, J. R., see Harper, H. W., 1966.

Jaynes, J. Imprinting: The interaction of learned and innate behavior: I. Development and generalization. *Journal of Comparative and Physiological Psychology,* 1956, *49,* 201-206. **585**

Jaynes, J. Imprinting: The interaction of learned and innate behavior: II. The critical period. *Journal of Comparative and Physiological Psychology,* 1957, *50,* 6-10. **585**

Jaynes, J., see also Campbell, B. A., 1966.

Jeffers, V. B., see Helson, H., 1940.

Jeffress, L. A. A place theory of sound localization. *Journal of Comparative and Physiological Psychology,* 1948, *41,* 35-39. **265**

Jeffress, L., Blodgett, H. C., Sandel, T. T., & Wood, C. L.: III. Masking of tonal signals. *Journal of the Acoustical Society of America,* 1956, *28,* 416-426. **242**

Jeffress, L., Blodgett, H. C., & Deatherage, B. H. Masking and interaural phase: II. 167 cycles. *Journal of the Acoustical Society of America,* 1962, *34,* 1124-1126. **242, 243**

Jeffress, L. A., & Taylor, R. W. Lateralization vs. localization. *Journal of the Acoustical Society of America,* 1961, *33,* 482-483. **261**

Jeffress, L. A., see also Feddersen, W. E., 1957; Robinson, D. E., 1963; Sandel, T. T., 1955.

Jeffrey, W. E. The effects of verbal and non-verbal responses in mediating an instrumental act. *Journal of Experimental Psychology,* 1953, *45,* 327-333. **780, 783**

Jeffrey, W. E., & Kaplan, R. J. Semantic generalization with experimentally induced association. *Journal of Experimental Psychology,* 1957, *54,* 336-338. **1075**

Jenkin, N. Effects of varied distance on short-range size judgments. *Journal of Experimental Psychology,* 1957, *54,* 327-331. **514**

Jenkin, N. A relationship between increments of distance and estimates of objective size. *American Journal of Psychology,* 1959, *72,* 345-363. **514**

Jenkin, N., & Hyman, R. Attitude and distance-estimation as variables in size-matching. *American Journal of Psychology,* 1959, *72,* 68-76. **509, 514**

Jenkins, H. M. The effect of discrimination training on extinction. *Journal of Experimental Psychology,* 1961, *61,* 111-121. **777**

Jenkins, H. M. Measurement of stimulus control during discriminative operant conditioning. *Psychological Bulletin,* 1965, *64,* 365-376. (a) **754n, 779**

Jenkins, H. M., Generalization gradients and the concept of inhibition. In D. I. Mostofsky (Ed.), *Stimulus generalization.* Stanford: Stanford University Press, 1965, Pp. 55-61. (b) **753**

Jenkins, H. M., & Harrison, R. H. Effect of discrimination training on auditory generalization. *Journal of Experimental Psychology,* 1960, *59,* 246-253. **761, 762**

Jenkins, H. M., & Harrison, R. H. Generalization gradients of inhibition following auditory discrimination learning. *Journal of the Experimental Analysis of Behavior,* 1962, *5,* 435-441. **779**

Jenkins, H. M., see also Shepard, R. N., 1961.

Jenkins, J. G., & Dallenbach, K. M. Oblivescence during sleep and waking. *American Journal of Psychology,* 1924, *35,* 605-612. **1122**

Jenkins, J. J. Effects on word-association of the set to give popular responses. *Psychological Reports,* 1959, *5,* 94. **868**

Jenkins, J. J. Commonality of association as an indicator of more general patterns of verbal behavior. In T. M. Sebeok (Ed.), *Style in language.* New York: Wiley, 1960. (a) **873**

Jenkins, J. J. Degree of polarization and scores on the principal factors for concepts in the semantic atlas study. *American Journal of Psychology,* 1960, *73,* 274-279. (b) **865, 900**

Jenkins, J. J. Stimulus "fractionation" in paired-associate learning. *Psychological Reports,* 1963, *13,* 409-410. (a) **1047**

Jenkins, J. J. Mediated associations: Paradigms and situations. In C. N. Cofer & B. S. Musgrave (Eds.), *Verbal behavior and learning: Problems and processes.* New York: McGraw-Hill, 1963. Pp. 210-245. (b) **888, 949, 1071, 1074, 1075**

Jenkins, J. J., & Brown, L. The use of interspersed test items in measuring mediated response transfer. *Journal of Verbal Learning and Verbal Behavior,* 1965, *4,* 425-429. **1048**

Jenkins, J. J., & Foss, D. J. An experimental analysis of

pseudomediation. *Psychonomic Science*, 1965, *2*, 99–100. **1077**

Jenkins, J. J., Foss, D., & Odom, P. Associative mediation in paired-associate learning with multiple controls. *Journal of Verbal Learning and Verbal Behavior*, 1965, *4*, 141–147. **1078**

Jenkins, J. J., Mink, W. D., & Russell, W. A. Associative clustering as a function of verbal association strength. *Psychological Reports*, 1958, *4*, 127–136. **887**

Jenkins, J. J., & Palermo, D. S. Further data on changes in word-association norms. *Journal of Personality and Social Psychology*, 1965, *1*, 303–309. **875**

Jenkins, J. J., & Russell, W. A. Systematic changes in word association norms: 1910–1952. *Journal of Abnormal and Social Psychology*, 1960, *60*, 293–304. **875**

Jenkins, J. J., & Russell, W. A. Miscellaneous studies in word association. Technical Report #24, Contract N8ONR-66216, between the Office of Naval Research and the University of Minnesota, undated. **873**

Jenkins, J. J., Russell, W. A., & Suci, G. J. An atlas of semantic profiles for 360 words. *American Journal of Psychology*, 1958, *71*, 688–699. **900**

Jenkins, J. J., Russell, W. A., & Suci, G. J. A table of distances for the semantic atlas. *American Journal of Psychology*, 1959, *72*, 623–625. **901**

Jenkins, J. J., *see also* Brown, L. K., 1966; Palermo, D. S., 1964a, b, 1965a, b; Russell, W. A., 1954.

Jenkins, P. M., & Cofer, C. N. An exploratory study of discrete free association to compound verbal stimuli. *Psychological Reports*, 1957, *3*, 599–602. **871, 880**

Jenkins, T. N., Warner, L. H., & Warden, C. J. Standard apparatus for the study of animal motivation. *Journal of Comparative Psychology*, 1926, *6*, 361–382. **651, 704**

Jenkins, W. L. Studies in thermal sensitivity: VIII. Analytic evidence against the Alrutz theory. *Journal of Experimental Psychology*, 1938, *23*, 417. **148**

Jenkins, W. L., & Karr, A. C. Paradoxical warmth: A sufficient condition for its arousal. *American Journal of Psychology*, 1957, *70*, 640–641. **148**

Jenkins, W. O., & Stanley, J. C., Jr. Partial reinforcement: A review and critique. *Psychological Bulletin*, 1950, *47*, 193–234. **607**

Jennings, P. C., *see* Young, R. K., 1964.

Jensen, A. R. An empirical theory of the serial-position effect. *Journal of Psychology*, 1962, *53*, 127–142. (a) **1013**

Jensen, A. R. Temporal and spatial effects of serial position. *American Journal of Psychology*, 1962, *75*, 390–400. (b) **1013**

Jensen, A. R. Transfer between paired-associate and serial learning. *Journal of Verbal Learning and Verbal Behavior*, 1962, *1*, 269–280. (c) **1012, 1013**

Jensen, A. R. The Von Restorff isolation effect with minimal response learning. *Journal of Experimental Psychology*, 1962, *64*, 123–125. (d) **1013**

Jensen, A. R., & Rohwer, W. D., Jr. What is learned in serial learning? *Journal of Verbal Learning and Verbal Behavior*, 1965, *4*, 62–72. **1012, 1013**

Jensen, D. D. Paramecia, planaria, and pseudo-learning. In *Learning and associated phenomena in invertebrates: Animal Behaviour, Supplement Number 1*, 1965, 9–20. **556**

Jensen, D. D., *see also* Allison, J., 1967.

Jensen, G. D. Effect of past experience upon induced movement. *Perceptual and Motor Skills*, 1960, *11*, 281–288. **522**

Jepson, O. Middle-ear muscle reflexes in man. In J. Jerger (Ed.), *Modern developments in audiology*. New York: Academic Press, 1963. **236**

Jerger, J. *Modern developments in audiology*. New York: Academic Press, 1963. **235**

Jobe, F. W., *see* Davis, C. J., 1957.

Johansson, G. *Configurations in event perception*. Uppsala: Almquist and Wiksells Boktryschkeri AB. 1950. **523**

Johnson, B. A., *see* Flavell, J. H., 1961.

Johnson, D. L., *see* Cairns, R. B., 1965.

Johnson, D. M. Generalization of a scale of values by the averaging of practice effects. *Journal of Experimental Psychology*, 1944, *34*, 425–436. **65**

Johnson, E. P., & Riggs, L. A. Electroretinal and psycho-physical dark adaptation curves. *Journal of Experimental Psychology*, 1951, *41*, 139–147. **288**

Johnson, E. P., Riggs, L. A., & Schick, A. M. L. Photopic retinal potentials evoked by phase alternation of a barred pattern. In *Clinical electroretinography* (Supplement to *Vision Research*), 1966, 75–91. **308**

Johnson, E. P., *see also* Armington, J. C., 1952; Riggs, L. A., 1964, 1966.

Johnson, H. M. Visual pattern-discrimination in the vertebrates: I. Problems and methods. *Journal of Animal Behavior*, 1914, *4*, 319. **750**

Johnson, H. M. Visual pattern-discrimination in the vertebrates: III. Effective differences in width of visible striae for the monkey and the chick. *Journal of Animal Behavior*, 1916, *6*, 169. **750**

Johnson, J. C., *see* Eldridge, R. G., 1958.

Johnson, K. R., *see* Carhart, R., 1967.

Johnson, L. M. Similarity of meaning as a factor in retroactive inhibition. *Journal of General Psychology*, 1933, *9*, 377–389. **1054, 1083**

Johnson, N. F. Linguistic models and functional units of language behavior. In S. Rosenberg (Ed.), *Directions in psycholinguistics*. New York: Macmillan, 1965. Pp. 29–65. **904**

Johnson, R. C. Reanalysis of "meaningfulness and verbal learning." *Psychological Review*, 1962, *69*, 233–238. **897, 900**

Johnson, R. C., Frincke, G., & Martin, L. Meaningfulness, frequency, and affective character of words as related to visual duration threshold. *Canadian Journal of Psychology*, 1961, *15*, 199–204. **900**

Johnson, R. C., Thomson, C. W., & Frincke, G. Word values, word frequency, and visual duration thresholds. *Psychological Review*, 1960, *67*, 332–342. **900**

Johnson, R. C., Weiss, R. L., & Zelhart, P. F. Similarities and differences between normal and psychotic subjects in responses to verbal stimuli. *Journal of Abnormal and Social Psychology*, 1964, *68*, 221–226. **900**

Johnson, T. J., Meinke, D. L., Van Mondfrans, A. P., & Finn, J. Word frequency of synonym responses as a function of word frequency of the stimulus and list position of the response. *Psychonomic Science*, 1965, *2*, 235–236. **866**

Johnston, J. W. Jr. An application of the steric odor theory. *Georgetown Medical Bulletin*, 1963, *17*, 40–42. **212**

Johnston, J. W. Jr., *see also* Amoore, J. E., 1964.

Joinson, P. A., & Runquist, W. N. Effects of intralist stimulus similarity and degree of learning on forgetting. *Journal of Verbal Learning and Verbal Behavior*, 1968, *7*, 554–559. **1126**

Jolliffe, C. L., *see* Sperling, H. G., 1965.

Jones, A., Gardner, J., & Thornton, D. W. The persistence of information motivational phenomena over 48- and 96-hour periods of visual deprivation. *Journal of Experimental Research in Personality*, 1967, *2*, 252–259. **840, 841**

Jones, A., Wilkinson, H. J., & Braden, I. Information deprivation as a motivational variable. *Journal of Experimental Psychology*, 1961, *62*, 126–137. **840**

Jones, A. D., *see* Deutsch, J. A., 1960.

Jones, A. E., *see* DeValois, R. L., 1963.

Jones, C. M., *see* Chapman, W. P., 1944.

Jones, F. N. A test of the validity of the Elsberg method of olfactometry. *American Journal of Psychology*, 1953, *66*, 81–85. **199**

Jones, F. N. A comparison of methods of olfactory stimulation: Blasting vs. sniffing. *American Journal of Psychology*, 1955, *68*, 486–488. **199, 200, 201**

Jones, F. N. A forced-choice method of limits. *American Journal of Psychology*, 1956, *69*, 672–673. **19**

Jones, F. N. Scales of subjective intensity for odors of diverse chemical nature. *American Journal of Psychology*, 1958, *71*, 305–310. **205**

Jones, F. N., & Jones, M. H. Modern theories of olfaction: A critical review. *Journal of Psychology*, 1953, *36*, 207–241. **220**

Jones, F. N., Singer, D., & Twelker, P. A. Interactions among the somesthetic senses in judgments of subjective magnitude. *Journal of Experimental Psychology*, 1962, *64*, 105–109. **147**

Jones, F. N., & M. H. Woskow. On the intensity of odor mixtures. *Annals of the New York Academy of Science*, 1964, *116*, 484–494. **212**

Jones, F. N., see also Jones, M. H., 1952.

Jones, J. E. All-or-none vs. incremental learning. *Psychological Review*, 1962, *69*, 156–160. **990, 1000**

Jones, L. V., see Boch, R. D., 1968; Fillenbaum, S., 1965.

Jones, M. C. The elimination of children's fears. *Journal of Experimental Psychology*, 1924, *7*, 382–390. **571**

Jones, M. H. Second pain: Fact or artifact? *Science*, 1956, *124*, 442–443. **156, 160**

Jones, M. H., & Jones, F. N. The critical frequency of taste. *Science*, 1952, *115*, 355–356. **178**

Jones, M. H., see also Jones, F. N., 1953.

Jones, M. R., & Myers, J. L. A comparison of two methods of event randomization in probability learning. *Journal of Experimental Psychology*, 1966, *72*, 909–911. **921**

Jones, O. R., see Grant, D. A., 1949.

Jones, R. B., see Seward, J. P., 1957.

Jonkhees, L. B. W., & Veer, R. A. On directional sound localization in unilateral deafness and its explanation. *Acta Oto-Laryngologica*, 1958, *49*, 119–131. **267**

Jordan, A. E., see Scott, T. R., 1963.

Jørgensen, H. The influence of saccharin on the blood sugar. *Acta Physiologica Scandinavica*, 1950, *20*, 33–37. **797**

Joseph, M., see Hirsh, I. J., 1954.

Judd, C. H. Some facts of binocular vision. *Psychological Review*, 1897, *4*, 374–389. **479, 513**

Judd, C. H. A study of geometrical illusions. *Psychological Review*, 1899, *6*, 241–261. **458**

Judd, C. H. Practice and its effects on the perception of illusions. *Psychological Review*, 1902, *9*, 27–39. **465**

Judd, C. H. The Müller-Lyer Illusion. *Psychological Review Monograph Supplement*, 1905, *7*, 55–81. **458, 459, 465**

Judd, C. H., & Courten, H. C. The Zöllner Illusion. *Psychological Review Monograph Supplement*, 1905, *7*, 112–139. **458, 465**

Judd, D. B. Hue saturation and lightness of surface colors with chromatic illumination. *Journal of the Optical Society of America*, 1940, *30*, 2–32. **416**

Judd, D. B. Color systems and their interrelation. *Illuminating Engineering* (New York), 1941, *36*, 336. **412, 420**

Judd, D. B. Basic correlates of the visual stimulus. In Stevens, S. S. (Ed.), *Handbook of experimental psychology*. New York: Wiley, 1951. **324, 328, 362, 427**

Judd, D. B. *Color in business, science and industry*. New York: Wiley, 1952. **422**

Judd, D. B. Appraisal of Land's work on two-primary color projections. *Journal of the Optical Society of America*, 1960, *50*, 254–268. **368, 417**

Judd, D. B., & Wyszecki, G. W. *Color in business, science, and industry*. (2nd ed.) New York: Wiley, 1963. **358, 360**

Judd, D. B., see also Newhall, S. M., 1943.

Judd, R., see Kamin, L., 1959.

Julesz, B. Binocular depth perception without familiarity cues. *Science*, 1964, *145*, 356–362. **483**

Julesz, B. Binocular depth perception of computer-generated patterns. *Bell System Technical Journal*, 1960, *39*, 1125–1161. **432, 483**

Jung, J. Transfer of training as a function of degree of first-list learning. *Journal of Verbal Learning and Verbal Behavior*, 1962, *1*, 197–199. **1036, 1064, 1068**

Jung, J. Effects of response meaningfulness (m) on transfer of training under two different paradigms. *Journal of Experimental Psychology*, 1963, *65*, 377–384. **1062, 1063**

Jung, J. Comments on Mandler's "From association to structure." *Psychological Review*, 1965, *72*, 318–322. **1068**

Jung, J. Experimental studies of factors affecting word associations. *Psychological Bulletin*, 1966, *66*, 125–133. **862, 868, 876**

Jung, R. Neuronal integration in the visual cortex and its significance for visual information. In W. A. Rosenblith (Ed.), *Sensory communication*. New York: Wiley, 1961. Pp. 627–674. **288**

Justesen, D. R., see Bourne, L. E., Jr., 1965.

Kaess, D. W., & Wilson, J. P. Modification of the rat's avoidance of visual depth. *Journal of Comparative and Physiological Psychology*, 1964, *58*, 151–152. **549**

Kagan, J. Differential reward value of incomplete and complete sexual behavior. *Journal of Comparative and Physiological Psychology*, 1955, *48*, 59–64. **669, 798**

Kahn, R. L., see Battersby, W. S., 1956.

Kahneman, D. An onset-onset law for one case of apparent motion and metacontrast. *Perceptual and Motor Skills*, 1967, *2*, 577–584. **430**

Kahneman, D. Method, findings and theory in studies of visual masking. *Psychological Bulletin*, 1968, *70*, 404–425. **429, 430, 431*n***

Kahneman, D., & Beatty, J. Pupil diameter: A linear relationship with memory load. *Science*, 1966, *154*, 1583–1585. **393**

Kahneman, D., see also Flom, M. C., 1963.

Kaiser, P. K. Perceived shape and its dependency on perceived slant. *Journal of Experimental Psychology*, 1967, *75*, 345–353. **516**

Kaiser, P. K. Color names of very small fields varying in duration. *Journal of the Optical Society of America*, 1968, *58*, 690–696. **348**

Kaiser, P. K., see also Boynton, R. M.

Kalikow, D. N. Psychofit. Unpublished computer program (Fortran) for the analysis of magnitude estimates, Brown University, 1967. (Expansion of a program by D. W. Panek and J. C. Stevens.) **77**

Kalil, R. E., & Freedman, S. J. Persistence of ocular rotation following compensation for displaced vision. *Perceptual and Motor Skills*, 1966, *22*, 135–139. **537**

Kalish, H. I., see Brown, J. S., 1951; Guttman, N., 1956; Haber, A., 1963.

Kalman, G., see Hodos, W., 1963.

Kalmus, H. The discrimination by the nose of the dog of individual human odours and in particular of the odours of twins. *British Journal of Animal Behaviour*, 1955, *3*, 25–31. **202**

Kamin, L. J. Traumatic avoidance learning: The effects of CS-US interval with a trace-conditioning procedure. *Journal of Comparative and Physiological Psychology*, 1954, *47*, 65–72. **729, 732**

Kamin, L. J. The effects of termination of the CS and avoidance of the US on avoidance learning. *Journal of Comparative and Physiological Psychology*, 1956, *49*, 420–424. **728**

Kamin, L. J. The gradient of delay of secondary reward in avoidance learning tested on avoidance trials only. *Journal of Comparative and Physiological Psychology*, 1957, *50*, 450-456. **728**

Kamin, L. J. CS-termination as a factor in the emergence of anticipatory avoidance. *Psychological Reports*, 1959, *5*, 455-456. (a) **727**

Kamin, L. J. The delay-of-punishment gradient. *Journal of Comparative and Physiological Psychology*, 1959, *52*, 434-437. (b) **737**

Kamin, L. J. Trace conditioning of the conditioned emotional response. *Journal of Comparative and Physiological Psychology*, 1961, *54*, 149-153. **714**

Kamin, L. J. Backward conditioning and the conditioned emotional response. *Journal of Comparative and Physiological Psychology*, 1963, *56*, 517-519. **715**

Kamin, L. J. Temporal and intensity characteristics of the conditioned stimulus. In W. F. Prokasy (Ed.), *Classical conditioning*. New York: Appleton, 1965. Pp. 118-147. **715, 716**

Kamin, L. Predictability, surprise, attention, and conditioning. In B. A. Campbell & R. M. Church (Eds.), *Punishment and aversive behavior*. New York: Appleton, 1969. **556**

Kamin, L. J., Brimer, C. J., & Black, A. H. Conditioned suppression as a monitor of fear of the CS in the course of avoidance training. *Journal of Comparative and Physiological Psychology*, 1963, *56*, 497-501. **726**

Kamin, L., Campbell, D., Judd, R., Ryan, T., & Walker, J. Two determinants of the emergence of anticipatory avoidance. *Journal of Comparative and Physiological Psychology*, 1959, *52*, 202-205. **727**

Kamin, L. J., & Schaub, R. E. Effects of conditioned stimulus intensity on the conditioned emotional response. *Journal of Comparative and Physiological Psychology*, 1963, *56*, 502-507. **715**

Kamin, L. J., see also Annau, Z., 1961; Brimer, C. J., 1963; Solomon, R. L., 1953.

Kamiya, J., see Brunswik, E., 1953.

Kandel, E. R., & Tauc, L. Heterosynaptic facilitation in neurones of the abdominal ganglion of *Aplesia depilans*. *Journal of Physiology*, 1965, *181*, 1-27. **591**

Kane, E., see Donderi, D. C., 1965.

Kaneko, A., & Hashimoto, H. Electrophysiological study of single neurons in the inner nuclear layer of the carp retina. *Vision Research*, 1969, *9*, 37-55. **308**

Kaniowski, W., see Martin, L. C., 1950.

Kanon, D., see Mayzner, M. S., 1965.

Kanoti, G. A., see Kausler, D. H., 1963.

Kantrow, R. W. An investigation of conditioned feeding responses and concomitant adaptive behavior in young infants. *University of Iowa Studies in Child Welfare*, 1937, *13*, No. 3. **573**

Kanungo, R. Meaning mediation in verbal transfer. *British Journal of Psychology*, 1967, *58*, 205-212. **1083**

Kaplan, G. A. Kinetic disruption of optical texture: The perception of depth at an edge. *Perception and Psychophysics*, 1969, *6*, 193-198. **442**

Kaplan, G. A., see also Gibson, J. J., 1969.

Kaplan, R. J., see Jeffrey, W. E., 1957.

Kaplan, S., see Kleinsmith, L. J., 1964, 1964.

Kaplon, M. D., see Wolfe, J. B., 1941.

Kardos, L. Die "Konstanz" phänomenaler Dingmomente. *Beiträge zur Problemgeschichte Psychologie*, 1929, Buhler Festschrift, 1-77. **403**

Kardos, L. Ding und Schatten. *Zeitschrift für Psychologische Ergebnisse*, 1934, No. 23. **405**

Kare, M. R., see Maller, O., 1967.

Karlin, J. E., see Hudgins, C. V., 1947.

Karmel, B. Z., see Walk, R. D., 1965.

Karpinska, L. von, see von Karpinska, L.

Karpman, B., see Woodrow, H., 1917.

Karpman, M., see Eisenberger, R., 1967.

Karr, A. C., see Jenkins, W. L., 1957.

Karsh, E. B. Effects of number of rewarded trials and intensity of punishment on running speed. *Journal of Comparative and Physiological Psychology*, 1962, *55*, 44-51. **734**

Karsh, E. B. Changes in intensity of punishment: Effect on running behavior of rats. *Science*, 1963, *140*, 1084-1085. **737**

Karsh, E. B. Resistance to punishment resulting from training with delayed, partial, and increasing shock. *Proceedings of the 74th Annual Convention of the American Psychological Association*, 1966, 51-52. **737**

Karsh, E. B., see also Wallach, H., 1963.

Kasschau, R. A., & Pollio, H. R. Response transfer mediated by meaningfully similar and associated stimuli using a separate-list design. *Journal of Experimental Psychology*, 1967, *74*, 146-148. **1048**

Kasschau, R. A., see also McBurney, D. H., 1962, 1967.

Katkin, E. S., & Murray, E. N. Instrumental conditioning of autonomically mediated behavior: Theoretical and methodological issues. *Psychological Bulletin*, 1968, *70*, 52-68. **839**

Katona, G. Color contrast and color constancy. *Journal of Experimental Psychology*, 1935, *18*, 48-63. **420**

Katsuki, Y. Neural mechanism of auditory sensation in cats. In W. A. Rosenblith (Ed.), *Sensory communication*. New York: Wiley, 1961. **231**

Katz, D. Die Erscheinungsweisen der Farben und ihre Beeinflussung durch die individuelle Erfahrung. *Zeitschrift für Psychologische Ergebnisse*, 1911, *7*. **396, 398, 426**

Katz, D. *Der Aufbau der Farbwelt*. (2nd ed.) Leipzig: Barth. *The World of Color*. R. B. MacLeod & C. W. Fox, trans. London: Kegan Paul, 1935. **396, 402, 403, 405, 421, 422, 423, 426**

Katz, L., see Myers, J. L., 1963.

Katz, S. H., see Allison, V. C., 1919.

Katzev, R. Extinguishing avoidance responses as a function of delayed warning signal termination. *Journal of Experimental Psychology*, 1967, *75*, 339-344. **732**

Kaufman, H. G., see Mayzner, M. S., 1964.

Kaufman, L. On the spread of suppression and binocular rivalry. *Vision Research*, 1963, *3*, 401-415. **488**

Kaufman, L. Suppression and fusion in viewing complex stereograms. *American Journal of Psychology*, 1964, *77*, 193-205. **492**

Kaufman, L. Some new stereoscopic phenomena and their implications for the theory of stereopsis. *American Journal of Psychology*, 1965, *78*, 1-20. **490, 491, 492**

Kaufman, L. *Research in visual perception for carrier landing: Suppl. 2. Studies on the perception of impact point based on shadowgraph techniques*. Report SGD-5265-0031. Prepared by Sperry Rand Corp., Great Neck, New York, for Physiol. Psychol. Branch -ONR for Contract #Nonr 4081 (00). 1968. **505**

Kaufman, L., & Pitblado, C. Further observations on the nature of effective binocular disparities. *American Journal of Psychology*, 1965, *78*, 379-391. **491, 492**

Kaufman, L., & Rock, I. The moon illusion: I. *Science*, 1962, *136*, 953-961. **511, 512**

Kaufman, L., & Rock, I. The moon illusion. *Scientific American*, 1962, *207*, 120-132. **511, 512**

Kaufman, L., see also Rock, I., 1962.

Kaufman, M. E., & Peterson, W. M. Acquisition of a learning set by normal and mentally retarded children. *Journal of Comparative and Physiological Psychology*, 1958, *51*, 619-621. **768**

Kausler, D. H., & Kanoti, G. A. R-S learning and negative transfer effects with a mixed list. *Journal of Experimental Psychology*, 1963, *65*, 201-205. **1063, 1064**

Kausler, D. H., see also Dean, M. G., 1964; Ellington, N. R., 1965; Oliver, K., 1966.

Kavanau, J. L. Compulsory regime and control of environment in animal behaviour: I. Wheel running. *Behaviour*, 1963, *20*, 251–281. **692**

Kawakami, M., *see* Sawyer, C. H., 1959.

Kawamura, Y., *see* Adachi, A., 1967.

Keehn, J. D., & Arnold, E. M. M. Licking rates of albino rats. *Science*, 1960, *132*, 739–741. **814**

Keele, C. A., *see* Armstrong, D., 1951.

Keele, S. W., & Chase, W. G. Short-term visual storage. *Perception and Psychophysics*, 1967, *2*, 383–386. **444**

Keen, R. E., Chase, H. H., & Graham, F. K. Twenty-four hour retention by neonates of an habituated heart rate response. *Psychonomic Science*, 1965, *2*, 265–266. **591**

Keenan, B., *see* Hefferline, R. F., 1959.

Keesey, R. E. The relation between pulse frequency, intensity, and duration and the rate of responding for intracranial stimulation. *Journal of Comparative and Physiological Psychology*, 1962, *55*, 671–678. **599, 645, 646**

Keesey, R. E. Intracranial reward delay and the acquisition rate of a brightness discrimination. *Science*, 1964, *143*, 700–701. (a) **655, 680**

Keesey, R. E. Duration of stimulation and the reward properties of hypothalamic stimulation. *Journal of Comparative and Physiological Psychology*, 1964, *58*, 201–207. (b) **691**

Keesey, R. E., & Goldstein, M. D. Use of progressive fixed-ratio procedures in the assessment of intracranial reinforcement. *Journal of the Experimental Analysis of Behavior*, 1968, *11*, 293–301. **649, 654**

Keesey, R. E., & Kling, J. W. Amount of reinforcement and free operant responding. *Journal of the Experimental Analysis of Behavior*, 1961, *4*, 125–132. **605, 620, 694**

Keesey, R. E., & Lindholm, E. P., Differential rates of discrimination learning reinforced by medial versus lateral hypothalamic stimulation. *Journal of Comparative and Physiological Psychology*, 1969, *68*, 544–551. **700, 701**

Keesey, U. T. Effects of involuntary eye movements on visual acuity. *Journal of the Optical Society of America*, 1960, *50*, 769–774. **303, 306, 375, 387**

Kehoe, J. S., & Bruner, J. Specificité de l'habituation de la voie activitée etudiée au niveau des neurones centraux de l'Aplysie. *Journale de Physiologie* (Paris), 1966, *58*, 542–543. **591**

Keidel, U. O., *see* Keidel, W. D., 1961.

Keidel, W. D., Keidel, U. O., & Wigand, M. E. Adaptation: Loss or gain of sensory information? In W. A. Rosenblith (Ed.), *Sensory communication*. New York: Wiley, 1961. Pp. 319–338. **184**

Keleman, A., *see* Mayzner, M. S., 1965.

Kelleher, R. T. Chaining and conditioned reinforcement. In W. K. Honig (Ed.), *Operant behavior: Areas of research and application*. New York: Appleton, 1966. **671, 672**

Kelleher, R. T., & Gollub, L. R. A review of positive conditioned reinforcement. *Journal of the Experimental Analysis of Behavior*, 1962, *5*, 543–597. **665, 671**

Keller, F. S., & Schoenfeld, W. N. *Principles of psychology*. New York: Appleton, 1950. **674**

Keller, L. Run structure and the learning of periodic sequences. Unpublished doctoral dissertation, Indiana University, 1963. **935, 983**

Keller, L., *see also* Friedman, M. P., 1964.

Kellogg, W. N. An experimental comparison of psychophysical methods. *Archives of Psychology* (New York), 1929, No. 106. **23**

Kellogg, W. N. *Porpoises and sonar*. Chicago: University of Chicago Press, 1961. **270**

Kellogg, W. N. Sonar system of the blind. *Science*, 1962, *137*, 399–404. **271**

Kellogg, W. N., *See also* Spooner, A., 1947.

Kelly, D. H. Visual responses to time-dependent stimuli: I. Amplitude sensitivity measurements. *Journal of the Optical Society of America*, 1961, *51*, 422–429. **311**

Kelly, M. J., *see* McLaughlin, S. C., 1968, 1969.

Kemble, J. D., *see* Lipsitt, L. P., 1959.

Kemeny, J. G. *A philosopher looks at science*. Princeton, N.J.: Van Nostrand, 1959. **917**

Kemp, E. H., *see* Graham, C. H., 1938; Thurlow, W. R., 1951.

Kendall, J. W., Jr., *see* Kimble, G. A., 1953.

Kendall, S. B., *see* Hoffeld, D. R., 1960.

Kendler, H. H. The concept of the concept. In A. W. Melton (Ed.), *Categories of human learning*. New York: Academic Press, 1964. Pp. 212–236. **942**

Kendler, H. H., & Kendler, T. S. Vertical and horizontal processes in problem solving. *Psychological Review*, 1962, *69*, 1–16. **767**

Kendler, H. H., *see also* Kendler, T. S., 1959.

Kendler, T. S. Concept formation. *Annual Review of Psychology*, 1961, *12*, 447–472. **944**

Kendler, T. S., & Kendler, H. H. Reversal and non-reversal shifts in kindergarten children. *Journal of Experimental Psychology*, 1959, *58*, 56–60. **767**

Kendler, T. S., *see also* Kendler, H. H., 1962.

Kenkel, F. Untersuchungen über den Zusammenhang zwischen Erscheinungsgrösse und Erscheinungsbewegung bei einigen sogenannten optischen Täuschungen. *Zeitschrift für Psychologie*, 1913, *67*, 358–447. **526**

Kennedy, J. L., *see* Hastorf, A. H., 1957.

Kennelly, T. W. The role of similarity in retroactive inhibition. *Archives of Psychology*, 1941, *37*. **1081, 1082**

Kenshalo, D. S. Comparison of the thermal sensitivity of the forehead, lip, conjunctiva and cornea. *Journal of Applied Physiology*, 1960, *15*, 987–991. **129, 154, 162**

Kenshalo, D. R. Improved method for the psychophysical study of the temperature sense. *Review of Scientific Instruments*, 1963, *34*, 883–886. **141, 149**

Kenshalo, D. R. The temperature sensitivity of furred skin of cats. *Journal of Physiology*, 1964, *172*, 439–448. **150**

Kenshalo, D. R. Psychophysical studies of temperature sensitivity. In W. D. Neff (Ed.), *Contributions to sensory physiology*. New York: Academic Press, 1970. (a) **142, 144, 147**

Kenshalo, D. R. Cutaneous temperature receptors: Some operating characteristics for a model. In J. D. Hardy (Ed.), *Physiological and behavioral temperature regulation*. Springfield, Ill.: Charles C Thomas, 1970. (b) **154**

Kenshalo, D. R., & Brearley, Elizabeth A. Electrophysiological measurements of the sensitivity of cat's upper lip to warm and cool stimuli. *Journal of Comparative and Physiological Psychology*, 1970, *70*, 5–14. **152**

Kenshalo, D. R., Decker, T., & Hamilton, A. Spatial summation on the forehead, forearm, and back produced by radiant and conducted heat. *Journal of Comparative and Physiological Psychology*, 1967, *63*, 510–515. **146**

Kenshalo, D. R., Duncan, D. G., & Weymark, C. Thresholds for thermal stimulation of the inner thigh, foot pad, and face of cats. *Journal of Comparative and Physiological Psychology*, 1967, *63*, 133–138. **150**

Kenshalo, D. R., & Gallegos, E. S. Multiple temperature-sensitive spots innervated by single nerve fibers. *Science*, 1967, *158*, 1064–1065. **147**

Kenshalo, D. R., Holmes, C. E., & Wood, P. B. Warm and cool thresholds as a function of rate of stimulus temperature change. *Perception and Psychophysics*, 1968, *3*, 81–84. **145**

Kenshalo, D. R., & Nafe, J. P. A quantitative theory of feeling—1960. *Psychological Review*, 1962, *69*, 17–33. **121**

Kenshalo, D. R., & Scott, H. H., Jr. Temporal course of thermal adaptation. *Science*, 1966, *151*, 1095–1096. **142**

Kenshalo, D. R., *see also* Nafe, J. P., 1958; Rice, C. E., 1962.

Kent, G. H., & Rosanoff, A. J. A study of association in insanity. *American Journal of Insanity*, 1910, *67*, 37–96, 317–390. **860, 874**

Keppel, G. Word value and verbal learning. *Journal of Verbal Learning and Verbal Behavior*, 1963, *1*, 353–356. **900**

Keppel, G. Facilitation in short- and long-term retention of paired associates following distributed practice in learning. *Journal of Verbal Learning and Verbal Behavior,* 1964, *3,* 91-111. **1108**

Keppel, G. Problems of method in the study of short-term memory. *Psychological Bulletin,* 1965, *63,* 1-13. **1111, 1112, 1113**

Keppel, G. Association by contiguity: Role of response availability. *Journal of Experimental Psychology,* 1966, *71,* 624-628. **854**

Keppel, G. Unlearning in serial learning. *Journal of Experimental Psychology,* 1966, *71,* 143-149. **1102**

Keppel, G. A reconsideration of the extinction-recovery theory. *Journal of Verbal Learning and Verbal Behavior,* 1967, *6,* 476-486. **1108**

Keppel, G. Retroactive and proactive inhibition. In T. R. Dixon & D. L. Horton (Eds.), *Verbal behavior and general behavior theory.* Englewood Cliffs, N.J.: Prentice-Hall, 1968. **1096**

Keppel, G., & Postman, L. Studies of learning to learn: III. Conditions of improvement in the performance of successive transfer tasks. *Journal of Verbal Learning and Verbal Behavior,* 1966, *5,* 260-267. **1062, 1070**

Keppel, G., Postman, L., & Zavortink, B. Studies of learning to learn: VIII. The influence of massive amounts of training upon the learning and retention of paired-associate lists. *Journal of Verbal Learning and Verbal Behavior,* 1968, *7,* 790-796. **1041, 1106**

Keppel, G., & Rauch, D. S. Unlearning as a function of second-list error instructions. *Journal of Verbal Learning and Verbal Behavior,* 1966, *5,* 50-58. **1097**

Keppel, G., & Underwood, B. J. Retroactive inhibition of R-S associations. *Journal of Experimental Psychology,* 1962, *64,* 400-404. (a) **1095**

Keppel, G., & Underwood, B. J. Proactive inhibition in short-term retention of single items. *Journal of Verbal Learning and Verbal Behavior,* 1962, *1,* 153-161. (b) **1113**

Keppel, G., & Underwood, B. J. Reminiscence in short-term retention of paired-associate lists. *Journal of Verbal Learning and Verbal Behavior,* 1967, *6,* 375-382. **1121**

Keppel, G., *see also* Postman, L., 1965, 1967, 1968; Shuell, T. J., 1967; Underwood, B. J., 1962, 1962, 1962, 1963, 1964; Zavortinck, B., 1968.

Keppel, J., *see* Shuell, P. J., 1967.

Kessen, M. L., *see* Miller, N. E., 1952.

Kessen, W. *see* Hershenson, M., 1965; Salapatek, P., 1966.

Kiang, N. Y. S., *see* Sachs, M. B., 1967.

Kibler, G., *see* Martin, L., 1966.

Kiesow, F. Beiträge zur physiologischen Psychologie des Geschmackssinnes. *Philosophische Studien,* 1894, *10,* 523-561. **183, 186, 187**

Kiesow, F. Beiträge zur physiologischen Psychologie des Geschmackssinnes. *Philosophische Studien,* 1896, *12,* 255-278. **187**

Kiesow, F. Schmeckversuche an einzelnen Papillen. *Philosophische Studien,* 1898, *14,* 591-615. **175, 178, 183**

Kiesow, F., *see also* von Frey, M., 1899.

Kietz, H. Das raumliche Horen. *Acustica,* 1953, *3,* 73-86. **266**

Killbride, P. L., & Robbins, M. C. Linear perspective, pictorial depth perception and education among the Baganda. *Perceptual and Motor Skills,* 1968, *27,* 601-602. **500**

Kilpatrick, F. P., & Ittleson, W. H. The size-distance invariance hypothesis. *Psychological Review,* 1953, *60,* 223-231. **506**

Kilps, B., *see* Dunham, P. J., 1969.

Kimble, G. A. Transfer of work inhibition in motor learning. *Journal of Experimental Psychology,* 1952, *43,* 391-392. **575**

Kimble, G. A. Shock intensity and avoidance learning. *Journal of Comparative and Physiological Psychology,* 1955, *48,* 281-284. **710, 729**

Kimble, G. A. *Hilgard and Marquis' conditioning and learning.* (2nd ed.) New York: Appleton, 1961. **554n, 557, 674, 774, 827, 983, 1100**

Kimble, G. A. Categories of learning and the problem of definition: Comments on Professor Grant's paper. In A. W. Melton (Ed.), *Categories of human learning.* New York: Academic Press, 1964. **565**

Kimble, G. A., & Kendall, J. W., Jr. A comparison of two methods of producing experimental extinction. *Journal of Experimental Psychology,* 1953, *45,* 87-90. **572**

Kimble, G. A., Mann, L. I., & Dufort, R. H. Classical and instrumental eyelid conditioning. *Journal of Experimental Psychology,* 1955, *219,* 407-417. **558**

Kimble, G. A., & Shattel, R. B. The relationship between two kinds of inhibition and the amount of practice. *Journal of Experimental Psychology,* 1952, *44,* 355-359. **574, 575**

Kimble, G. A., *see also* Greenbloom, R., 1965; Hillman, B., 1953; Nicholls, M. F., 1964.

Kimble, J. P., Jr., *see* Moran, L. J., 1964.

Kimura, K., & Beidler, L. M. Microelectrode study of taste receptors of rat and hamster. *Journal of Cellular and Comparative Physiology,* 1961, *58,* 131-139. **173, 180**

Kincaid, W. D., *see* Logan, F. A., 1956.

King, D. J. On the accuracy of written recall: A scaling and factor analytic study. *Psychological Record,* 1960, *10,* 113-122. **902**

King, D. J., & Schultz, D. P. Additional observations on scoring the accuracy of written recall. *Psychological Record,* 1960, *10,* 203-204. **902**

King, D. J., & Yu, K. C. The effect of reducing the variability of length of written recalls on the rank order scale values of the recalls. *Psychological Record,* 1962, *12,* 39-44. **902**

King, J. E., *see* Becker, R. F., 1962.

King, R. A. The effects of training and motivation on the components of a learned instrumental response. Unpublished doctoral dissertation, Duke University, 1959. Cited by Kimble, G. A., 1961. **827**

King, R. A., *see also* Fox, R. E., 1961.

King, W., & Gruber, H. Moon illusion and Emmert's law. *Science,* 1962, *135,* 1125-1126. **512**

King, W. A., *see* Welker, W. I., 1962.

Kinney, J. A. S. Factors affecting induced color. *Vision Research,* 1962, *2,* 503-525. **410**

Kinsbourne, M., & Warrington, E. K. The effect of an aftercoming random pattern on the perception of brief visual stimuli. *Quarterly Journal of Experimental Psychology,* 1962, *14,* 223-234. (a) **463**

Kinsbourne, M., & Warrington, E. K. Further studies on the masking of brief visual stimuli by a random pattern. *Quarterly Journal of Experimental Psychology,* 1962, *14,* 235-245. (b) **463**

Kintsch, W. Runway performance as a function of drive strength and magnitude of reinforcement. *Journal of Comparative and Physiological Psychology,* 1962, *55,* 882-887. **807**

Kintsch, W. All-or-none learning and the role of repetition in paired-associate learning. *Science,* 1963, *140,* 310-312. **987, 996**

Kintsch, W. Habituation of the GSR component of the orienting reflex during paired-associate learning. *Journal of Mathematical Psychology,* 1965, *2,* 330-341. **957**

Kintsch, W., & Wike, E. L. Habit reversal as a function of length of partial delay of reinforcement. *Psychological Reports,* 1957, *3,* 11-14. **685**

Kintsch, W., *see also* Wike, E. L., 1959.

Kirkpatrick, M., *see* Peterson, L. R., 1963.

Kish, G. B. Studies of sensory reinforcement. In W. K. Honig (Ed.), *Operant behavior: Areas of research and application.* New York: Appleton, 1966. **690n**

Kistiakowsky, G. B. On the theory of odors. *Science,* 1950, *112,* 154-155. **220**

Kjeldergaard, P. M. Commonality scores under instructions

Kolb, D., see Siipola, E., 1955.

Kolers, P. A. Intensity and contour effects in visual masking. *Vision Research*, 1962, 2, 277–294. **430**

Kolers, P. A. Some differences between real and apparent visual movement. *Vision Research*, 1963, 3, 191–206. **520, 528**

Kolers, P. A. Apparent movement of a Necker cube. *American Journal of Psychology*, 1964, 77, 220–230. **471**

Kolers, P. A., & Rosner, B. On visual masking (metacontrast): Dichoptic observation. *American Journal of Psychology*, 1960, 73, 2–21. **429, 430**

Konick, A., see Posner, M. J., 1966.

König, A., & Brodhun, E. Experimentelle Untersuchungen ueber die psychophysische Fundamentalformel in Bezug auf den Gesichtssinn. *Sitzungsberichte Preussische Akademie Wissenschaften*, Berlin, 1889, 27, 641–644. **297**

König, J. F. R., & Klippel, R. A. *The rat brain*. Baltimore: Williams and Wilkins, 1963. **643**

Konorski, J. *Integrative activity of the brain*. Chicago: University of Chicago Press, 1967. **559, 588, 592**

Konorski, J., see also Miller, S., 1928.

Kopfermann, H. Psychologische Untersuchungen über die Wirkung Zweidimensionälar Darstellungen körperlicher Gebilde. *Psychologische Forschung*, 1930, 13, 293–364. Cited in K. Koffka. *Principles of gestalt psychology*. New York: Harcourt, Brace, 1935. Pp. 184ff. **435, 451**

Kopp, G. A., see Potter, R. K., 1947.

Koppenaal, R. J. Time changes in strengths of A–B, A–C lists: Spontaneous recovery? *Journal of Verbal Learning and Verbal Behavior*, 1963, 2, 310–319. **1099, 1105**

Korn, J. H., & Lindley, R. H. Immediate memory for consonants as a function of frequency of occurrence and frequency of appearance. *Journal of Experimental Psychology*, 1963, 66, 149–154. **897**

Korn, J. H., see also Moyer, K. E., 1964.

Kornhuber, H. H., see Mountcastle, V. B., 1967.

Koronakis, C., & Arnold, W. J. The formation of learning sets in rats. *Journal of Comparative and Physiological Psychology*, 1957, 50, 11–14. **768**

Korte, A. Kinematoskopische Untersuchungen. *Zeitschrift für Psychologie*, 1915, 72, 193–296. **526**

Kotovsky, K., see Simon, H. A., 1963.

Kozaki, A. A. A further study in the relationship between brightness constancy and contrast. *Japanese Psychological Research*, 1963, 5, 129–136. **414**

Kozaki, A. A. The effect of co-existent stimuli on brightness constancy. *Japanese Psychological Research*, 1965, 7, 138–147. **414**

Kraeling, D., see Campbell, B. A., 1953.

Kraemer, H. C. The average error of a learning model: Estimation and use in testing the fit of models. *Psychometrika*, 1965, 30, 343–352. **993**

Krakauer, D., & Dallenbach, K. M. Gustatory adaptation to sweet, sour and bitter. *American Journal of Psychology*, 1937, 49, 469–475. **184**

Krakauer, D., see also Abrahams, H., 1937.

Krantz, F. W., see Davis, H., 1964.

Krauskopf, J. The magnitude of figural after-effects as a function of the duration of the test-period. *American Journal of Psychology*, 1954, 67, 684–690. **472, 473**

Krauskopf, J. Figural after-effects with a stabilized retinal image. *American Journal of Psychology*, 1960, 73, 294–297. **472**

Krauskopf, J., Cornsweet, T. N., & Riggs, L. A. Analysis of eye movements during monocular and binocular fixation. *Journal of the Optical Society of America*, 1960, 50, 572–578. **305**

Krauskopf, J., Duryea, R. A., & Bitterman, M. E. Threshold for visual form: Further experiments. *American Journal of Psychology*, 1954, 67, 427–440. **443, 445**

Krauskopf, J., see also Bitterman, M. E., 1954; Shortess, G. K., 1961.

Kravitz, J. H., see Wallach, H., 1963, 1965.

Krechevsky, I. "Hypotheses" in rats. *Psychological Review*, 1932, 39, 516–532. (a) **765, 954**

Krechevsky, I. "Hypotheses" versus "chance" in the pre-solution period in sensory discrimination-learning. *University of California Publications in Psychology*, 1932, 6, 27–44. (b) **765, 766**

Krechevsky, I. A study of the continuity of the problem-solving process. *Psychological Review*, 1938, 45, 107–133. **773**

Krechevsky, I., see also Tolman, E. C., 1933.

Kries, J. von, see von Kries, J.

Krueger, W. C. F. The effect of overlearning on retention. *Journal of Experimental Psychology*, 1929, 12, 71–78. **1124**

Krueger, W. C. F. The relative difficulty of nonsense syllables. *Journal of Experimental Psychology*, 1934, 17, 145–153. **852**

Kruger, L., see Beck, L. H., 1954; Malis, L. C., 1956.

Kryter, K. D. Effects of ear protective devices on the intelligibility of speech in noise. *Journal of the Acoustical Society of America*, 1946, 18, 413–417. **254**

Kryter, K. D. The effects of noise on man. *Journal of Speech Disabilities* (Monograph Supplement), 1950, 1. **236**

Kryter, K. D. Exposure to steady-state noise and impairment of hearing. *Journal of the Acoustical Society of America*, 1963, 35, 1515–1525. **236**

Kryter, K. D. Psychological reactions to aircraft noise. *Science*, 1966, 151, 1346–1355. **236**

Kryter, K. D. Concepts of perceived noisiness, their implementation and application. *Journal of the Acoustical Society of America*, 1968, 43, 344–361. **236**

Kryter, K. D., Licklider, J. C. R., Webster, J. C., & Hawley, M. Speech communication. In C. T. Morgan et al. (Eds.), *Human engineering guide to equipment design*, New York: McGraw-Hill, 1963. **258**

Kryter, K. D., & Pearsons, K. S. Some effects of spectral content and duration on perceived noise level. *Journal of the Acoustical Society of America*, 1963, 35, 866–883. **236**

Kryter, K. D., Ward, W. D., Miller, J. D., & Eldredge, D. H. Hazardous exposure to intermittent and steady-state noise. *Journal of the Acoustical Society of America*, 1966, 39, 451–464. **236**

Kryter, K. D., see also House, A. S., 1965.

Kuenne, M. R. Experimental investigation of the relation of language to transposition behavior in young children. *Journal of Experimental Psychology*, 1946, 36, 471–490. **419**

Kuffler, S. W. Neurons in the retina: Organization, inhibition and excitation problems. *Cold Spring Harbor Symposia on Quantitative Biology*, 1952, 17, 281–292. **291**

Kuffler, S. W. Discharge patterns and functional organization of mammalian retina. *Journal of Neurophysiology*, 1953, 16, 37–68. **293**

Kuffler, S. W., & Eyzaguirre, C. Synaptic inhibition in an isolated nerve cell. *Journal of General Physiology*, 1955–56, 39, 155–184. **222**

Kuffler, S. W., see also Barlow, H. B., 1957.

Kuiper, J. W., & Leutscher-Hazelhoff, J. T. Linear and non-linear responses from the compound eye of *Calliphora erythrocephala*. *Cold Spring Harbor Symposia on Quantitative Biology*, 1965, 30, 419–427. **311**

Kulka, K. Odor control by modification. *Annals of the New York Academy of Science*, 1964, 116, 676–681. **213**

Künnapas, T. M. Influence of frame size on apparent length of a line. *Journal of Experimental Psychology*, 1955, 50, 168–170. **508n**

Künnapas, T. Experiments on figural dominance. *Journal of Experimental Psychology*, 1957, 53, 31–39. **433**

Künnapas, T. M. The vertical-horizontal illusion and the visual field. *Journal of Experimental Psychology*, 1957, 53, 405–407. **461**

Künnapas, T. Scales for subjective distance. *Scandinavian Journal of Psychology,* 1960, *1,* 187–192. **514**

Künnapas, T. Distance perception as a function of available visual cues. *Journal of Experimental Psychology,* 1968, *77,* 523–579. **479, 514**

Künnapas, T., *see also* Ekman, G., 1960, 1962, 1963.

Kupfermann, I., & Kandel, E. R. Neuronal controls of a behavioral response mediated by the abdominal ganglion of *Aplysia. Science,* 1969, *164,* 847–850. **591**

Kurke, M. I. The role of motor experience in the visual discrimination of depth in the chick. *Journal of Genetic Psychology,* 1955, *86,* 191–196. **548**

Kurtz, K. H. Discrimination of complex stimuli: The relationships of training and test stimuli in transfer of discrimination. *Journal of Experimental Psychology,* 1955, *50,* 283–292. **782, 783**

Kurtz, K. H., & Siegel, A. Conditioned fear and magnitude of startle response: A replication and extension. *Journal of Comparative and Physiological Psychology,* 1966, *62,* 8–14. **803, 804, 808**

Kushnick, S. A., *see* Wischner, G. J., 1963.

Kuzma, F., Jr., *see* Hoffman, H. S., 1966.

Kuznesof, A. W., *see* Routtenberg, A., 1967.

La Berge, D. L. A model with neutral elements. In R. R. Bush & W. K. Estes (Eds.), *Studies in mathematical learning theory.* Stanford: Stanford University Press, 1959. Pp. 53–64. **911n**

La Berge, D. L. Generalization gradients in a discrimination situation. *Journal of Experimental Psychology,* 1961, *62,* 88–94. **929**

La Berge, D. L., Greeno, J. G., & Peterson, O. F. Nonreinforcement and neutralization of stimuli. *Journal of Experimental Psychology,* 1962, *63,* 207–213. **933**

Lacey, J. I. Somatic response patterning and stress: Some revisions of activation theory. In M. H. Appley & R. Trumbull (Eds.), *Psychological stress: Issues in research.* New York: Appleton, 1967. Pp. 14–37. **833**

Lacey, J. I., *see also* Meyers, W. J., 1963.

Lacey, O. L., *see* Duffy, E., 1946.

Laffal, J. Response faults in word association as a function of response entropy. *Journal of Abnormal and Social Psychology,* 1955, *50,* 265–270. **861n, 862, 864, 876**

Laffal, J. *Pathological and normal language.* New York: Atherton, 1965. **861n, 872, 877, 878, 885**

Laffal, J., & Feldman, S. The structure of single word and continuous word associations. *Journal of Verbal Learning and Verbal Behavior,* 1962–63, *1,* 54–61. **872**

Lambe, R. *Human binary prediction under two schedules of response-contingent reinforcement.* Doctoral dissertation, Brown University, 1968. **932**

Lambercier, M., *see* Piaget, J., 1943.

Lambert, W. E. Associational fluency as a function of stimulus abstractness. *Canadian Journal of Psychology,* 1955, *9,* 103–106. **858**

Lamoreaux, R. R., *see* Mowrer, O. H., 1946.

Land, V., *see* Peterson, L. R., 1962.

Landauer, A. A., & Rodgers, R. S. Effect of "apparent" instructions on brightness judgments. *Journal of Experimental Psychology,* 1964, *68,* 80–84. **423**

Landauer, A. A., *see also* Blessing, W. W., 1967.

Landgren, S. The response of thalamic and cortical neurons to electrical and physiological stimulation of the cat's tongue. In W. A. Rosenblith (Ed.), *Sensory communication.* New York: Wiley, 1961. Pp. 437–453. **172**

Landis, C. *An annotated bibliography of flicker fusion phenomena, covering the period of 1740–1952.* Armed Forces–National Research Council: June, 1953. **311**

Landis, E. M. Micro-injection studies of capillary blood pressure in human skin. *Heart,* 1930, *15,* 209–228. **162**

Landolt, E. Tableau d'optotypes pour la détermination de l'acuité visuelle. *Societé Français d'Ophthalmologie,* 1889, p. 157. Cited in Cowan, A., 1928. **299**

Lane, C. E., *see* Wegel, R. L., 1924.

Lane, H. The motor theory of speech perception: A critical review. *Psychological Review,* 1965, *72,* 275–309. **254**

Lane, H., *see also* Schneider, B., 1963.

Lane, H. L., Catania, A. C., & Stevens, S. S. Voice level: Autophonic scale, perceived loudness, and effects of sidetone. *Journal of the Acoustical Society of America,* 1961, *33,* 160–167. **77**

Lane, H. L., *see also* Curran, C. R., 1962.

Lang, W. M., *see* Black, A. H., 1964.

Langdon, J. The perception of a changing shape. *Quarterly Journal of Experimental Psychology,* 1951, *3,* 157–165. **515, 517**

Langdon, J. Further studies in the perception of changing shape. *Quarterly Journal of Experimental Psychology,* 1953, *5,* 89–107. **515, 517**

Langdon, J. The perception of three-dimensional solids. *Quarterly Journal of Experimental Psychology,* 1955, *7,* 133–146. (a) **517**

Langdon, J. The role of spatial stimuli in the perception of shape: *Quarterly Journal of Experimental Psychology,* 1955, *7,* 19–27. (b) **517**

Langfeld, H. S., *see* Boring, E. G., 1948.

Langmuir, I., Schaefer, V. J., Ferguson, C. V., & Hennelly, E. F. *A study of binaural perception of the direction of a sound source.* OSRD. Rept. 4079, Publ. 31014 (30 June, 1944). **242**

Lansford, T. G., *see* Clark, L. L., 1960.

Lappin, J., *see* Eriksen, C. W., 1964, 1966, 1967.

Larson, D., *see* Allison, J., 1967.

Lashley, K. S. Visual discrimination of size and form in the albino rat. *Journal of Animal Behavior,* 1912, *2,* 310–331. **784**

Lashley, K. S. The mechanism of vision: I. A method for rapid analysis of pattern vision in the rat. *Journal of Genetic Psychology,* 1930, *37,* 453–460. **749**

Lashley, K. S. The mechanism of vision: XV. Preliminary studies of the rat's capacity for detail vision. *Journal of General Psychology,* 1938, *18,* 123–193. **749, 771, 784**

Lashley, K. S. An examination of the "continuity theory" as applied to discriminative learning. *Journal of General Psychology,* 1942, *26,* 241–265. **771**

Lashley, K. S. The problem of cerebral organization in vision. In H. Klüver (Ed.), *Visual mechanisms and biological symposium,* 7, 1942. **450**

Lashley, K. S. The problem of serial order in behavior. In L. A. Jeffries (Ed.), *Cerebral mechanisms in behavior.* New York: Wiley, 1951. Pp. 112–136. **698, 1013**

Lashley, K. S., Chow, K. L., & Semmes, J. An examination of the electrical field theory of cerebral integration. *Psychological Review,* 1951, *58,* 123–136. **470**

Lashley, K. S., & Wade, M. The Pavlovian theory of generalization. *Psychological Review,* 1946, *53,* 72–87. **771**

Latour, P. L. Visual threshold during eye movement. *Vision Research,* 1962, *2,* 261–262. **377**

Lavik, J., *see* Brown, L. K., 1966.

Law, S., *see* Neimark, E., 1965.

Lawler, E. E., III. Secondary reinforcement value of stimuli associated with shock reduction. *Quarterly Journal of Experimental Psychology,* 1965, *17,* 57–62. **718**

Lawrence, D. H. Acquired distinctiveness of cues: I. Transfer between discriminations on the basis of familiarity with the stimulus. *Journal of Experimental Psychology,* 1949, *39,* 770–784. **783**

Lawrence, D. H. Acquired distinctiveness of cues: II. Selective association in a constant stimulus situation. *Journal of Experimental Psychology,* 1949, *40,* 175–188. **783**

Lawrence, D. H. The nature of a stimulus: Some relationships between learning and perception. In S. Koch

(Ed.), *Psychology: A study of a science*. Vol. V. New York: McGraw-Hill, 1963. Pp. 179-212. **1001**

Lawrence, D. H., & Mason, W. A. Food intake in the rat as a function of deprivation intervals and feeding rhythms. *Journal of Comparative and Physiological Psychology*, 1955, 48, 267-271. (a) **820**

Lawrence, D. H., & Mason, W. A. Intake and weight adjustment in rats to changes in feeding schedule. *Journal of Comparative and Physiological Psychology*, 1955, 48, 43-46. (b) **818, 819**

Lawrence, D. H., & Mason, W. A. Systematic behavior during discrimination reversal and change of dimensions. *Journal of Comparative and Physiological Psychology*, 1955, 48, 1-7. **783**

Lawrence, D. H., *see also* Bauer, F. J., 1953.

Lawrence, L., *see* Gibson, J. J., 1955.

Lawrence, M. Dynamic range of the cochlear transducer. In *Cold Spring Harbor Symposia on Quantitative Biology*. New York: Cold Spring Harbor Laboratory of Quantitative Biology, 1965. **230**

Lawrence, M., *see also* Wever, E. G., 1954.

Lawson, R. Brightness discrimination performance and secondary reward strength as a function of primary reward amount. *Journal of Comparative and Physiological Psychology*, 1957, 50, 35-39. **637, 638, 639**

Lawson, R. B., & Gulick, W. L. Stereopsis and anomalous contour. *Vision Research*, 1967, 7, 271-297. **432**

Lazar, G. Warm-up before recall of paired adjectives. *Journal of Verbal Learning and Verbal Behavior*, 1967, 6, 321-327. **1040**

Leahy, W. R., *see* Schuck, J., 1966.

Leakey, D. M., Sayers, B. McA., & Cherry, C. Binaural fusion of low- and high-frequency sounds. *Journal of the Acoustical Society of America*, 1958, 30, 222. **263**

Leary, R. W. Homogeneous and heterogeneous reward of monkeys. *Journal of Comparative and Physiological Psychology*, 1958, 51, 706-710. **638, 639**

Leeper, R. The role of motivation in learning: A study of the phenomenon of differential motivational control of the utilization of habits. *Journal of Genetic Psychology*, 1935, 46, 3-40. **801**

Leeper, R. W. A study of a neglected portion of the field of learning. *Pediatric Seminar and Journal of General Psychology*, 1935, 46, 41-75. **439**

Leeper, R. Cognitive processes. In S. S. Stevens (Ed.), *Handbook of experimental psychology*. New York: Wiley, 1951, 730-757.

Leeper, R. W. Comments on Dr. Premack's paper. In D. Levine (Ed.) *Nebraska symposium on motivation* Lincoln: University of Nebraska Press, 1965. Pp. 180-188. **624**

LeGouix, J. P., *see* Tasaki, I., 1952.

LeGrand, Y. *Light, colour and vision*. New York: Dover, 1957. **327, 354, 358**

Le Gros Clark, W. E. The projection of the olfactory epithelium on the olfactory bulb in the rabbit. *Journal of Neurology and Psychiatry*, 1951, 14, 1-10. **197**

Le Gros Clark, W. E. Inquiries into the anatomical basis of olfactory discrimination. *Proceedings of the Royal Society (London)*, Ser. B, 1957, 146, 299-319. **197**

Le Gros Clark, W. E., & Warwick, R. T. The pattern of olfactory innervation. *Journal of Neurology and Psychiatry*, 1946, 9, 101-112. **195**

Leibowitz, H. W. Effect of reference lines on the discrimination of movement. *Journal of the Optical Society of America*, 1955, 45, 829-830. (a) **528**

Leibowitz, H. W. The relation between the rate threshold for the perception of movement and luminance for various durations of exposure. *Journal of Experimental Psychology*, 1955, 49, 209-214. (b) **520, 521**

Leibowitz, H. W. Relation between the Brunswik and Thouless ratios and functional relations in experimental investigations of perceived shape, size and brightness. *Perceptual and Motor Skills*, 1956, 6, 65-68. **399**

Leibowitz, H. W., & Bourne, L. E., Jr. Time and intensity as determiners of perceived shape. *Journal of Experimental Psychology*, 1956, 51, 227-281. **515**

Leibowitz, H. W., Bussey, T., & McGuire, P. Shape and size constancy in photographic reproductions. *Journal of the Optical Society of America*, 1957, 47, 658-661. **515**

Leibowitz, H. W., & Chinetti, P. Effect of reduced exposure duration on brightness constancy. *Journal of Experimental Psychology*, 1957, 54, 49-53. **410, 414**

Leibowitz, H. W., & Harvey, L. O., Jr. Size matching as a function of instructions in a naturalistic environment. *Journal of Experimental Psychology*, 1967, 74, 378-382. **509, 514**

Leibowitz, H. W., Mitchell, E., & Angrist, B. Exposure duration in the perception of shape. *Science*, 1954, 120, 400. **515**

Leibowitz, H. W., Myers, N. A., & Chinetti, P. The role of simultaneous contrast in brightness constancy. *Journal of Experimental Psychology*, 1955, 50, 15-18. **410, 414**

Leibowitz, H. W., *see also* Berman, P. W., 1965; Parrish, M., 1968; Zeigler, H. P., 1957.

Leitenberg, H., *see* Levine, M., 1964.

Lele, P. P. Relationship between cutaneous thermal thresholds, skin temperature and cross-sectional area of the stimulus. *Journal of Physiology*, 1954, 126, 191-205. **144**

Lele, P. P., & Weddell, G. Relationship between neurohistology and corneal sensibility. *Brain*, 1956, 79, 119-154. **154, 162**

Lele, P. P., Weddell, G., & Williams, C. M. The relationship between heat transfer, skin temperature, and cutaneous sensibility. *Journal of Physiology*, 1954, 126, 206-234. **153, 158**

Le Magnen, J. Étude d'une méthode d'analyse qualitative de l'olfaction. *L'année Psychologique*, 1942-43, 43-44, 249-264. **200**

Le Magnen, J. Étude des facteurs dynamiques de l'excitation olfactive. *L'année Psychologique*, 1944-45, 45-46, 77-89. **206, 207**

Le Magnen, J. Étude des phénomènes olfacto-sexuels chez le rat blanc: Variations de l'odeur biologique de la femelle avec son état sexuel et la discrimination de ces odeurs par le mâle adulte. *Comptes Rendus de la Sociétié de Biologie*, 1951, 145, 854-857. **210**

Le Magnen, J. L'olfaction: Le fonctionnement olfactif et son intervention dans les régulations psychophysiologiques. *Journal de Physiologie* (Paris), 1953, 45, 285-326. **209, 210**

Lemmon, W. B., & Patterson, G. H., Depth perception in sheep: Effects of interupting the mother–neonate bond. *Science*, 1964, 145, 835-837. **549**

Lenneberg, E. Understanding language without ability to speak: A case report. *Journal of Abnormal and Social Psychology*, 1962, 65, 419-425. **254**

Lenneberg, E. H., *see also* Brown, R. W., 1954.

Leonard, J. A., *see* Fitts, P. M., 1956, 1957.

Lettvin, J., & Gesteland, R. Speculations on smell. *Cold Spring Harbor Symposia on Quantitative Biology*, 1965, 30, 217-225. **217, 218**

Lettvin, J. Y., Maturana, H. R., McCulloch, W. S., & Pitts, W. H. What the frog's eye tells the frog's brain. *Proceedings of the Institute of Radio Engineering*, 1959, 47, 1940-1951. **295**

Lettvin, J. Y., *see also* Gesteland, R. C., 1965.

Leutscher-Hazelhoff, J. T., *see* Kuiper, J. W., 1965.

Levelt, W. J. M. *On binocular rivalry*. RVO-TNO edition. Soesterberg, The Netherlands: Institute for Perception, 1965. **488**

Leventhal, T., *see* Witkin, H. A., 1952.

Levine, M. Cue neutralization: The effects of random reinforcement upon discrimination learning. *Journal of Experimental Psychology*, 1962, *63*, 438–443. **955**

Levine, M. Mediating processes in humans at the outset of discrimination learning. *Psychological Review*, 1963, *70*, 254–276. **958**

Levine, M. Hypothesis behavior by humans during discrimination learning. *Journal of Experimental Psychology*, 1966, *71*, 331–338. **959, 960**

Levine, M., Leitenberg, H., & Richter, M. Blank trials law: Equivalence of positive reinforcement and non-reinforcement. *Psychological Review*, 1964, *71*, 94–103. **959**

Levine, M., Miller, P., & Steinmeyer, C. H. The none-to-all theorem of human discrimination learning. *Journal of Experimental Psychology*, 1967, *73*, 568–573. **960**

Levine, M., *see also* Suppes, P., 1964.

Levine, S., *see* Brush, F. R., 1965, 1966.

Levitt, H., & Rabiner, L. R. Binaural release from masking for speech and gain in intelligibility. *Journal of the Acoustical Society of America*, 1967, *42*, 601–608. **258**

Levy, N., *see* Chapman, R. M., 1957; Engen, T., 1958.

Lewis, C., *see* Wallace, H., 1966.

Lewis, D. *Quantitative methods in psychology*. New York: McGraw-Hill, 1960. **28, 78**

Lewis, D. J. Partial reinforcement: A selective review of the literature since 1950. *Psychological Bulletin*, 1960, *57*, 1–28. **607, 670**

Lewis, D. R. Psychological scales of taste. *Journal of Psychology*, 1948, *26*, 437–446. **174**

Lewis, E. O. The effect of practice on the perception of the Müller-Lyer Illusion. *British Journal of Psychology*, 1908, *2*, 294–306. **465**

Lewis, E. O. The illusion of filled and unfilled space. *British Journal of Psychology*, 1912–1913, *5*, 36–50. **458**

Lewis, H. B., *see* Witkin, H. A., 1954.

Lewis, M., *see* Eckert, B., 1967.

Lewis, N. A., *see* Campbell, T. C., 1958.

Lewis, T., & Pochin, E. E. The double pain response of the human skin to a single stimulus. *Clinical Science*, 1937, *3*, 67–76. **160**

Lewis, W. R., *see* Simmons, F. B., 1964.

Liberman, A. M. Some results of research on speech perception. *Journal of the Acoustical Society of America*, 1957, *29*, 117–123. **253**

Liberman, A. M., Cooper, F. S., Shankweiler, D. P., & Studdert-Kennedy, M. Perception of the speech code. *Psychological Review*, 1967, *74*, 431–461. **253, 254**

Liberman, A. M., Cooper, F. S., Harris, K. S., & MacNeilage, P. F. A motor theory of speech perception. *Proceedings of the Speech Communication Seminar*. Stockholm: Royal Institute of Technology, September 1962. **254**

Liberman, A. M., DeLattre, P. C., & Cooper, F. S. Some cues for the distinction between voiced and voiceless stops in initial position. *Language and Speech*, 1958, *1*, 153–167. **253**

Liberman, A. M., DeLattre, P. C., Cooper, F. S., & Gerstman, L. J. The role of consonant-vowel transitions in the perception of stop and nasal consonants. *Psychological Monographs*, 1954, *68*. **253**

Liberman, A. M., *see also* Cooper, F. S., 1952; Harris, E. S., 1958.

Libet, B. Delayed pain as a peripheral sensory pathway. *Science*, 1957, *126*, 256–257. **161**

Libman, E. Observations on individual sensitiveness to pain with special reference to abdominal disorders. *Journal of the American Medical Association*, 1934, *102*, 335–341. **156**

Licht, L., *see* Maltzman, I., 1960.

Lichte, W. H., & Borreson, C. R. Influence of instructions on degree of shape constancy. *Journal of Experimental Psychology*, 1967, *74*, 538–542. **509, 516**

Lichte, W. H., *see also* Borresen, C. R., 1962.

Lichten, W., & Lurie, S. A new technique for the study of perceived size. *American Journal of Psychology*, 1950, *63*, 280–282. **513**

Lichten, W., *see also* Miller, G. A., 1951.

Lichtenstein, M. Phenomenal simultaneity with irregular timing of components of the visual stimulus. *Perceptual and Motor Skills*, 1961, *12*, 47–60. **454**

Lichtenstein, M., *see also* Craig, E. A., 1953.

Lichtenstein, P. E. Studies of anxiety: I. The production of a feeding inhibition in dogs. *Journal of Comparative and Physiological Psychology*, 1950, *43*, 16–29. **738**

Licklider, J. C. R. The influence of interaural phase relations upon the masking of speech by white noise. *Journal of the Acoustical Society of America*, 1948, *20*, 150–159. **258**

Licklider, J. C. R. Basic correlates of the auditory stimulus. In S. S. Stevens (Ed.), *Handbook of experimental psychology*. New York: Wiley, 1951. **233, 245, 257**

Licklider, J. C. R. Three auditory theories. In S. Koch (Ed.), *Psychology: A study of a science*. Vol. I. New York: McGraw-Hill, 1952. **245, 265**

Licklider, J. C. R., & Miller, G. A. The perception of speech. In S. S. Stevens (Ed.), *Handbook of experimental psychology*. New York: Wiley, 1951. **254, 256, 257**

Licklider, J. C. R., *see also* Gardner, W. J., 1960; Huggins, W. H., 1951; Kryter, K. D., 1963.

Liddell, H. S. A laboratory for the study of conditioned motor reflexes. *American Journal of Psychology*, 1926, *37*, 418–419. **562, 566**

Liddell, H. S., James, W. T., & Anderson, O. D. The comparative physiology of the conditioned motor reflex, based on experiments with the pig, dog, sheep, goat, and rabbit. *Comparative Psychology Monographs*, 1934, No. 51. **566**

Liebman, P. A. *In situ* microspectrophotometric studies on the pigments of single retinal rods. *Biophysics Journal*, 1962, *2*, 161–178. **323**

Liebman, S. Über das Verhalten farbiger Formen bei Helligkeitsgleichheit von Figur und Grund. *Psychologische Forschung*, 1927, *9*, 300–353. **428**

Liljestrand, G., & Zotterman, Y. The water taste in mammals. *Acta Physiologica Scandinavica*, 1954, *32*, 291–303. **186**

Lim, K. S. Cutaneous and visceral pain: Somesthetic chemoreceptors. In D. R. Kenshalo (Ed.), *The skin senses*. Springfield, Ill.: Charles C Thomas, 1968, 458–464. **162**

Limpo, A. J., *see* Reynolds, G. S., 1968.

Lindauer, J., *see* Wallach, H., 1962, 1963.

Lindley, R. H., *see* Korn, J. H., 1963.

Lindman, H., & Edwards, W. Unlearning the Gambler's Fallacy. *Journal of Experimental Psychology*, 1961, *62*, 630–631. **921**

Lindsley, D. B. Emotion. In S. S. Stevens (Ed.), *Handbook of experimental psychology*. New York: Wiley, 1951. Pp. 473–516. **831**

Lindsley, D. B. Psychological phenomena and the electroencephalogram. *Electroencephalography and Clinical Neurophysiology*, 1952, *4*, 443–456. **832**

Lindsley, D. B. Psychophysiology and motivation, In M. R. Jones (Ed.), *Nebraska symposium on motivation*. Lincoln: University of Nebraska Press, 1957. Pp. 44–105. **832, 842**

Lindsley, D. B. The reticular system and perceptual discrimination. In H. H. Jasper, L. D. Proctor, R. S. Knighton, W. C. Noshay, & R. T. Costello (Eds.), *Reticular formation of the brain*. Boston: Little, Brown, 1958, 513–534. **832, 842**

Lindsley, D. B. Attention, consciousness, sleep and wakefulness. In J. Field & H. W. Magoun (Eds.), *Handbook of physiology*. Vol. III. Washington, D. C.: American Physiology Society, 1960, 1553–1593. **832**

Lindsley, D. B. The reticular activating system and perceptual integration. In D. E. Sheer (Ed.), *Electrical stimulation of the brain*. Austin: University of Texas Press, 1961. Pp. 331–349. **842**

Lindsley, D. B., *see also* Spong, P., 1965.

Lindsley, D. F., *see* Wendt, R. H., 1963.

Lindy, J., *see* Routtenberg, A., 1965.

Link, W. E., *see* Bourne, L. E. Jr., 1964.

Linker, E., Moore, M. E., & Galanter, E. Taste thresholds, detection models, and disparate results. *Journal of Experimental Psychology*, 1964, *67*, 59–66. **36, 37, 43**

Linker, E., *see also* Moore, M. E., 1965.

Linksz, A. Physiology of the eye. *Vision*, 1952, *2*, 380. **490**

Linksz, A. *An essay in color vision and clinical color vision tests.* New York: Grune & Stratton, 1964. **363, 367**

Linschoaten, J. *Strukturanalyse der binokularen Teifenwahrenehmung.* New York: Gregory Lounz, 1956. **492**

Lipetz, L. E. Mechanism of light adaptation. *Science*, 1961, *133*, 639–640. **289**

Lipkin, M., & Hardy, J. D. Measurement of some thermal properties of human tissues. *Journal of Applied Physiology*, 1954, *7*, 212–217. **141, 146**

Lipps, T. *Raumaesthetik und geometrischeoptische Täuschungen.* Leipzig: Barth, 1897. **459**

Lipscomb, D. B., *see* Crovitz, H. F., 1963.

Lipsitt, L. P. Simultaneous and successive discrimination learning in children. *Child Development*, 1961, *32*, 337–347. **751, 775**

Lipsitt, L. P. Stimulus generalization and discrimination learning by children. *Perceptual and Motor Skills*, 1962, *14*, 11–17. **772**

Lipsitt, L. P. Learning in the first year of life. In L. P. Lipsitt, & C. C. Spiker (Eds.), *Advances in child development and behavior.* New York: Academic Press, 1963. **556**

Lipsitt, L. P., Castaneda, A., & Kemble, J. D. Effects of delayed reward pretraining on discrimination learning. *Child Development*, 1959, *30*, 273–278. **556**

Lipsitt, L. P., *see also* Castaneda, A., 1959; Engen, T., 1965; Hockman, C. H., 1961; Wismer, B., 1964.

Liston, J. R., *see* Schulz, R. W., 1968.

Lit, A. The magnitude of the Pulfrich stereo-phenomenon as a function of binocular differences of intensity at various levels of illumination. *American Journal of Psychology*, 1949, *62*, 159–181. **309**

Livingston, J. R., *see* Hull, C. L., 1951.

Lloyd, V. V., *see* Graham, C. H., 1948; Mueller, C. G., 1948.

Lochner, J. P. A., & Burger, J. F. The intelligibility of speech under reverberant conditions. *Acustica*, 1961, *11*, 195–200. **257**

Lockard, J. S. Choice of a warning signal or no warning signal in an unavoidable shock situation. *Journal of Comparative and Physiological Psychology*, 1963, *56*, 526–530. **730**

Locke, N. M. Color constancy in the rhesus monkey and in man. *Archives of Psychology* (New York), 1935, No. 193. **407**

Loeffel, R., *see* Mueller, E. E., 1953.

Loess, H. Proactive inhibition in short-term memory. *Journal of Verbal Learning and Verbal Behavior*, 1964, *3*, 362–368. **1113**

Loess, H. Short-term memory, word class and sequence of items. *Journal of Experimental Psychology*, 1967, *74*, 556–561. **1116**

Loess, H., & Waugh, N. C. Short-term memory and intertrial interval. *Journal of Verbal Learning and Verbal Behavior*, 1967, *6*, 455–460. **1113**

Loess, H. B., & Duncan, C. P. Human discrimination learning with simultaneous and successive presentation of stimuli. *Journal of Experimental Psychology*, 1952, *44*, 215–221. **775**

Loewenstein, W. R. The generation of electric activity in a nerve ending. *Annals of the New York Academy of Science*, 1959, *81*, 367–387. **129**

Logan, F. A. The role of delay of reinforcement in determining reaction potential. *Journal of Experimental Psychology*, 1952, *43*, 393–399. **747**

Logan, F. A. *Incentive: How the conditions of reinforcement affect the performance of rats.* New Haven: Yale University Press, 1960. **602, 616, 639, 640, 695, 723, 843**

Logan, F. A. Continuously negatively correlated amount of reinforcement. *Journal of Comparative and Physiological Psychology*, 1966, *62*, 31–34. **843**

Logan, F. A., Beier, E. M., & Kincaid, W. D. Extinction following partial and varied reinforcement. *Journal of Experimental Psychology*, 1956, *52*, 65–70. **686**

Logan, F. A., & Wagner, A. R. *Reward and punishment.* Boston: Allyn & Bacon, 1965. **801**

LoLordo, V., *see* Church, R. M., 1966; Rescorla, R. A., 1965.

London, I. D. A Russian report on the postoperative newly seeing. *American Journal of Psychology*, 1960, *73*, 478–482. **548**

Long, E. R., Hammock, J. T., May, F., & Campbell, B. J. Intermittent reinforcement of operant behavior in children. *Journal of the Experimental Analysis of Behavior*, 1958, *1*, 315–339. **605, 608**

Long, G. E. The effect of duration of onset and cessation of light flash on the intensity–time relation in the peripheral retina. *Journal of the Optical Society of America*, 1951, *41*, 743–747. **304**

Long, J., *see* Solley, C. M., 1958.

Long, L. Conceptual relationships in children: The concept of roundness. *Journal of General Psychology*, 1940, *57*, 289–315. **785**

Long, L., *see also* Bartoshuk, L. M., 1969.

Longo, V. G., *see* Sadowski, B., 1962.

Lopez, L. J., *see* Thomas, D. R.

LoPopolo, M. H., *see* Mayer, D. R., 1966.

Lore, R. K., *see* Pollio, H. R., 1965.

Lorenz, K. The companion in the bird's world. *Auk*, 1937, *54*, 245–273. **581, 582, 583**

Lorge, I., *see* Thorndike, E. L., 1944.

Lovejoy, E. Analysis of the overlearning reversal effect. *Psychological Review*, 1966, *73*, 87–103. **1001**

Lovelace, E., *see* Schulz, R., 1964.

Lowell, F., *see* Woodrow, H., 1916a, b.

Lowenstein, E., & Dallenbach, K. M. The critical temperature for heat and for burning heat. *American Journal of Psychology*, 1930, *42*, 423–429. **148**

Lowes, G., & Bitterman, M. E. Reward and learning in the goldfish. *Science*, 1967, *157*, 455–457. **634**

Lowy, K., *see* Thurlow, W. R., 1951.

Luce, R. D. A threshold theory for simple detection experiments. *Psychological Review*, 1963, *70*, 61–79. **45**

Luce, R. D., Bush, R. R., & Galanter, E. *Handbook of mathematical psychology.* New York: Wiley, 1963. **14, 24**

Luce, R. D., & Galanter, E. Psychophysical scaling. In R. D. Luce, R. R. Bush, & E. Galanter (Eds.), *Handbook of mathematical psychology.* New York: Wiley, 1963. **86**

Luce, R. D. & Suppes, P. Preference, utility, & subjective probability. In R. D. Luce, R. R. Bush, & E. Galanter (Eds.), *Handbook of mathematical psychology.* Vol. III. New York: Wiley, 1965. Pp. 249–410. **907, 918**

Luce, R. D., *see also* Bush, R. R., 1963.

Luchins, A. S. The autokinetic effect in central and peripheral vision. *Journal of General Psychology*, 1954, *50*, 39–44. **530**

Luciani, L. *Human physiology.* Vol. 4. (F. A. Welby, trans.) London: Macmillan, 1917. **187**

Ludvigh, E. The visibility of moving objects. *Science*, 1948, *108*, 63–64. **520**

Ludvigh, E. Visual acuity while one is viewing a moving object. *Archives of Ophthalmology* (Chicago), 1949, *42*, 14–22. **520**

Ludvigh, E. Possible role of proprioception in the extraocular muscles. *Archives of Ophthalmology*, (New York), 1952, *48*, 436–441. **530**

Ludvigh, E. J. Visual and stereoscopic acuity for moving

objects. *Symposium on Physiological Psychology,* School of Aviation Medicine, Pensacola, Florida; Office of Naval Research, Department of the Navy, 1955. Reprinted in I. M. Spigel, 1965. **520**

Ludvigson, H. W., *see* McHose, J. H., 1965.

Lummis, R. C., *see* Simmons, F. B., 1965.

Lundin, R. W. *Personality: An experimental approach.* New York: Macmillan, 1961. **791**

Lundström, C. O., *see* Engen, T., 1963.

Lundy, R. M., *see* Parrish, M., 1968.

Luneburg, R. K. *Mathematical analysis of binocular vision.* Princeton, N.J.: Princeton University Press, 1947. **493**

Luneburg, R. K. The metric of binocular visual space. *Journal of the Optical Society of America,* 1950, *40,* 627–642. **493**

Lurie, S., *see* Lichten, W., 1950.

Lynch, D., *see* Capaldi, E. J., 1967.

Lynch, G. S., *see* Campbell, B. A., 1968.

Maatsch, J. L., *see* Adelman, H. M., 1955.

MacAdam, D. L. On the geometry of color space. *Journal of the Franklin Institute,* 1944, *238,* 195. **361**

MacAdam, D. L., *see also* Brown, W. R. J., 1949.

McAlister, E., *see* Hochberg, J., 1953.

McAllister, W. R. Eyelid conditioning as a function of the CS–UCS interval. *Journal of Experimental Psychology,* 1953, *45,* 417–422. **558**

MacBride, P. D., *see* Hochberg, J. E., 1948.

McBurney, D. H. Magnitude estimation of the taste of sodium chloride after adaptation to sodium chloride. *Journal of Experimental Psychology,* 1966, *72,* 869–873. **175, 184**

McBurney, D. H. A note on the relation between area and intensity in taste. *Perception and Psychophysics,* 1969, *6,* 250. **175**

McBurney, D. H., Kasschau, R. A., & Bogart, L. M. The effect of adaptation on taste jnds. *Perception and Psychophysics,* 1967, *2,* 175–178. **184**

McBurney, D. H., & Pfaffmann, C. Gustatory adaptation to saliva and sodium chloride. *Journal of Experimental Psychology,* 1963, *65,* 523–529. **184**

McBurney, D. H., *see also* Bartoshuk, L. M., 1964; Engen, T., 1964; Pfaffman, C., 1969; Smith, D. V., 1969.

McCall, R. B. Stimulus change in light-contingent bar pressing. *Journal of Comparative and Physiological Psychology,* 1965, *59,* 258–262. **673**

McCandless, B. R., *see* Castaneda, A., 1956.

MacCaslin, E. F. Successive and simultaneous discrimination as a function of stimulus similarity. *American Journal of Psychology,* 1954, *67,* 308–314. **775**

McClearn, G. E. The inheritance of behavior. In L. Postman (Ed.), *Psychology in the making.* New York: Knopf, 1963. **702**

McCleary, R. A. Taste and post-ingestive factors in specific-hunger behavior. *Journal of Comparative and Physiological Psychology,* 1953, *46,* 411–421. **626**

McCleary, R. A. Response specificity in the behavioral effects of limbic system lesions in the cat. *Journal of Comparative and Physiological Psychology,* 1961, *54,* 605–613. **576n**

McCleary, R. A., *see also* Chapanis, A., 1953.

McClelland, D. C. Studies in serial verbal discrimination learning: I. Reminiscence with two speeds of pair presentation. *Journal of Experimental Psychology,* 1942, *31,* 44–56. **854**

McClelland, D. C., & Heath, R. M. Retroactive inhibition as a function of degree of association of original and interpolated activities. *Journal of Experimental Psychology,* 1943, *33,* 420–430. **1084**

McCollough, C. Color adaptation of edge-detectors in the human visual system. *Science,* 1965, *149,* 1115–1116. **543**

McConnell, C., *see* Stevenson, H. W., 1955.

McConnell, J. V., *see* Thompson, R., 1955.

McCormack, P. D. Backward mediated positive transfer in a paired-associate task. *Journal of Experimental Psychology,* 1961, *61,* 138–141. **1074**

MacCorquodale, K., & Meehl, P. E. Preliminary suggestions as to a formalization of expectancy theory. *Psychological Review,* 1953, *60,* 55–63. **560n**

MacCorquodale, K., & Meehl, P. E. Edward C. Tolman. In Estes, W. K., et al. (Eds.), *Modern learning theory.* New York: Appleton, 1954. **560n**

McCrary, J. W., & Hunter, W. S. Serial position curves in verbal learning. *Science,* 1953, *117,* 131–134. **1015, 1016**

McCrary, J. W., *see also* Smith, W. M., 1960.

McCready, D. W., Jr., *see* Alpern, M., 1963.

McCue, J. J. G., *see* Grinnell, A. D., 1963.

McCulloch, T. L. Performance preferentials of the white rat in force-resisting and spatial dimensions. *Journal of Comparative Psychology,* 1934, *18,* 85–111. **750**

McCulloch, T. L., & Pratt, J. G. A study in the pre-solution period in weight discrimination by white rats. *Journal of Comparative Psychology,* 1934, *18,* 271–290. **750, 766, 954**

McCulloch, W. S., *see* Lettvin, J. Y., 1959.

McDermott, W., *see* Rock, I., 1964.

McDill, J. A., *see* Stetson, R. H., 1923.

McDonald, D. G., *see* Hahn, W. W., 1962.

McDonald, W. T., *see* McGeoch, J. A., 1931.

MacDonnell, M. F., *see* Siegel, P. S., 1954.

McDonnell, P., *see* Berlyne, D. E., 1965.

McEwen, P. Figural after-effects. *British Journal of Psychology* (Monograph supplement), 1958, No. 31. **469**

McFarland, J. H. Visual and proprioceptive changes during visual exposure to a tilted line. *Perceptual and Motor Skills,* 1962, *15,* 322. **537, 540**

McFarland, J. H. Sequential part presentation: A method of studying visual form perception. *British Journal of Psychology,* 1965, *56,* 439–446. **454**

McFarland, W. L., *see* Smith, O. A. Jr., 1961.

McGehee, N. E., & Schulz, R. W. Mediation in paired-associate learning. *Journal of Experimental Psychology,* 1961, *62,* 565–570. **1078, 1079**

McGeoch, G. O., *see* McGeoch, J. A., 1936.

McGeoch, J. A. The influence of degree of learning upon retroactive inhibition. *American Journal of Psychology,* 1929, *41,* 252–262. **1085**

McGeoch, J. A. The influence of associative value upon the difficulty of nonsense-syllable lists. *Journal of Genetic Psychology,* 1930, *37,* 421–426. **854**

McGeoch, J. A. The influence of four different interpolations upon retention. *Journal of Experimental Psychology,* 1931, *14,* 400–413. **1088**

McGeoch, J. A. Forgetting and the law of disuse. *Psychological Review,* 1932, *39,* 352–370. (a) **1022, 1122**

McGeoch, J. A. The influence of degree of interpolated learning upon retroactive inhibition. *American Journal of Psychology,* 1932, *44,* 695–708. (b) **1086**

McGeoch, J. A. Studies in retroactive inhibition: II. Relationships between temporal point of interpolation, length of interval and amount of retroactive inhibition. *Journal of General Psychology,* 1933, *9,* 44–57. **1100**

McGeoch, J. A. Studies in retroactive inhibition: VII. Retroactive inhibition as a function of the length and frequency of presentation of the interpolated lists. *Journal of Experimental Psychology,* 1936, *19,* 674–693. **1088**

McGeoch, J. A. *The psychology of human learning.* New York: Longmans, Green, 1942. **1021, 1083, 1087, 1088**

McGeoch, J. A. *The psychology of human learning.* New York: Longmans, Green, 1952. **907, 980, 985, 1013, 1014, 1034, 1037**

McGeoch, J. A., & McDonald, W. T. Meaningful relation and retroactive inhibition. *American Journal of Psychology,* 1931, *43,* 579–588. **1054, 1082**

McGeoch, J. A., & McGeoch, G. O. Studies in retroactive inhibition: VI. The influence of the relative serial positions of interpolated synonyms. *Journal of Experimental Psychology*, 1936, *18*, 1–23. **1054, 1083**

McGeoch, J. A., McKinney, F., & Peters, H. N. Studies in retroactive inhibition: IX. Retroactive inhibition, reproductive inhibition and reminiscence. *Journal of Experimental Psychology*, 1937, *20*, 131–143. **1088**

McGeoch, J. A., & Underwood, B. J. Tests of the two-factor theory of retroactive inhibition. *Journal of Experimental Psychology*, 1943, *32*, 1–16. **1104**

McGeoch, J. A., see also McKinney, F., 1935.

McGovern, J. B. Extinction of associations in four transfer paradigms. *Psychological Monographs*, 1964, *78*, Whole No. 593. **1064, 1094**

McGuigan, D. I., see Carr, W. J., 1965.

McGuire, P., see Leibowitz, H., 1957.

McGuire, W. J. A multiprocess model for paired-associate learning. *Journal of Experimental Psychology*, 1961, *62*, 335–347. **1007**

McHose, J. H., & Ludvigson, H. W. Role of reward magnitude and incomplete reduction of reward magnitude in the frustration effect. *Journal of Experimental Psychology*, 1965, *70*, 490–495. **810**

McHose, J. H., see also Barrett, R. J., 1965.

Machover, K., see Witkin, H. A., 1954.

McIntyre, A. K., see Hunt, C. C., 1960a, b.

McIntyre, C., see Fox, R., 1967.

MacIntyre, W. J., see Rowland, V., 1960.

Mack, A. The role of movement in perceptual adaptation to a tilted retinal image. *Perception and Psychophysics*, 1967, *2*, 65–68. **540**

McKelvey, R. K. The relationship between training methods and reward variables in brightness discrimination learning. *Journal of Comparative and Physiological Psychology*, 1956, *49*, 485–491. **637**

McKenna, A. E. The experimental approach to pain. *Journal of Applied Physiology*, 1958, *13*, 449–456. **158**

McKenna, V. V., see Wallach, H., 1960.

McKinney, F. Quantitative and qualitative essential elements of transfer. *Journal of Experimental Psychology*, 1933, *16*, 854–864. **1047**

McKinney, F., & McGeoch, J. A. The character and extent of transfer in retroactive inhibition: Disparate serial lists. *American Journal of Psychology*, 1935, *47*, 409–423. **1088**

McKinney, F., see also McGeoch, J. A., 1937.

McKinney, J. P. Disappearance of luminous designs. *Science*, 1963, *140*, 403–404. **453**

MacKinnon, G. E., see Matin, L., 1964.

Mackintosh, N. J. Selective attention in animal discrimination learning. *Psychological Bulletin*, 1965, *64*, 124–150. **773**

Mackworth, J. F., & Mackworth, N. H. Eye fixations recorded on changing visual scenes by the television eye-marker. *Journal of the Optical Society of America*, 1958, *48*, 439–445. **373**

Mackworth, N. H., see Mackworth, J. F., 1958.

McLaughlin, S. C., DeSisto, M. J., & Kelly, M. J. Comment on eye movements and decrement in the Müller-Lyer illusion. *Perception and Psychophysics*, 1969, *5*, 288. **467***n*

McLaughlin, S. C., Kelly, M. J., Anderson, R. E., & Wenz, T. G. Localization of a peripheral target during parametric adjustment of saccadic eye movements. *Perception and Psychophysics*, 1968, *4*, 45–48. **467***n*

McLaughlin, S. C., & Rifkin, K. I. Change in straight ahead during adaptation to prism. *Psychonomic Science*, 1965, *2*, 107–108. **537**

McLaughlin, S. C., & Webster, R. G. Changes in straight-ahead eye position during adaptation to wedge prisms. *Perception and Psychophysics*, 1967, *2*, 37–44. **537**

McLaughlin, S. C., see also DeSisto, M. J., 1968.

MacLean, D. J., see Harvey, F. K., 1963.

MacLeod, R. B. An experimental investigation of brightness constancy. *Archives of Psychology* (New York), 1932, No. 135. **405, 423**

MacLeod, R. B., see also Harriman, A. E., 1953.

MacMillan, Z. L., see Foley, J. P., Jr., 1943.

MacNeilage, P. F., see Liberman, A. M., 1962.

McNeill, D., see Rosenzweig, M. R., 1962.

MacNichol, E. F., Jr., & Svaetichin, G. Electric responses from the isolated retinas of fishes. *American Journal of Ophthalmology*, 1958, *46*, 26–40. **308, 325**

MacNichol, E. F. Jr., see Hartline, H. K., 1952; Marks, W. B., 1964; Svaetichin, G., 1958; Wagner, H. G., 1960.

McNulty, J. A., see Tulving, E., 1965.

Maddi, S. R., see Fiske, D. W., 1961.

Madsen, C. H. Jr., see Young, P. T., 1963.

Magnus, R. *Körperstellung*. Berlin: J. Springer, 1924. **385**

Maher, W. B., & Wickens, D. D. Effect of differential quantity of reward on acquisition and performance of a maze habit. *Journal of Comparative and Physiological Psychology*, 1954, *47*, 44–46. **637**

Mahut, H. Effects of subcortical electrical stimulation on discrimination learning in cats. *Journal of Comparative and Physiological Psychology*, 1964, *58*, 390–395. **842**

Maier, N. R. F. *Frustration: The study of behavior without a goal*. New York: McGraw-Hill, 1949. **704, 749, 750, 791**

Maier, N. R. F., & Ellen, P. The effects of lactose in the diet on frustration-susceptibility in rats. *Journal of Comparative and Physiological Psychology*, 1951, *44*, 551–556. **750**

Maier, N. R. F., Glaser, N. M., & Klee, J. B. Studies of abnormal behavior in the rat: III. The development of behavior fixations through frustration. *Journal of Experimental Psychology*, 1940, *26*, 521–546. **791**

Maier, N. R. F., & Klee, J. B. Studies of abnormal behavior in the rat: XVII. Guidance versus trial and error in the and their relation to convulsive tendencies. *Journal of Experimental Psychology*, 1941, *29*, 380–389. **791**

Maier, N. R. F., & Klee, J. B. Studies of abnormal behavior in the rat: XVII. Guidance versus trial and error in the alteration of habits and fixations. *Journal of Psychology*, 1945, *19*, 133–163. **791**

Maier, S. F., Seligman, M. E. P., & Solomon, R. L. Pavlovian fear conditioning and learned helplessness: Effects on escape and avoidance behavior of (a) the CS-US contingency and (b) the independence of the US and voluntary responding. In B. A. Campbell & R. M. Church (Eds.), *Punishment and aversive behavior*. New York: Appleton, 1969. **570***n*, **661***n*, **710, 717, 724**

Makous, W., Nord, S., Oakley, B., & Pfaffmann, C. The gustatory relay in the medulla. In Y. Zotterman (Ed.), *Olfaction and taste*. Vol. 1. New York: Pergamon, 1963. Pp. 381–393. **182**

Malis, L. C., & Kruger, L. Multiple response and excitability of cat's visual cortex. *Journal of Neurophysiology*, 1956, *19*, 172–186. **309**

Mallay, H., see Washburn, M. F., 1931.

Maller, O., & Kare, M. R. Observations on the sense of taste in the armadillo (*Dasypus novemcinctus*). *Animal Behaviour*, 1967, *15*, 8–10. **190**

Malmo, R. B. Anxiety and behavioral arousal. *Psychological Review*, 1957, *64*, 276–287. **832**

Malmo, R. B. Measurement of drive: An unsolved problem in psychology. In M. R. Jones (Ed.), *Nebraska symposium on motivation*. Lincoln: University of Nebraska Press, 1958. Pp. 229–265. **831, 832, 833, 842**

Malmo, R. B. Activation: A neuropsychological dimension. *Psychological Review*, 1959, *66*, 367–386. **832**

Malmo, R. B. Activation. In A. J. Bachrach (Ed.), *Experimental foundations of clinical psychology*. New York: Basic Books, 1962. Pp. 386–422. **832**

Malmo, R. B. Heart rate reactions and locus of stimulation

within the septal area of the rat. *Science*, 1964, *144*, 1029–1030. **657**

Malmo, R. B. Physiological gradients and behavior. *Psychological Bulletin*, 1965, *64*, 225–234. **833**

Malmo, R. B., & Bélanger, D. Related physiological and behavioral changes: What are their determinants? In S. S. Kety, E. V. Evarts, & H. L. Williams (Eds.), *Sleep and altered states of consciousness*. Baltimore: Williams & Wilkins, 1967. Pp. 288–318. **833, 835**

Malmo, R. B., Shagass, C., & Heslam, R. M. Blood pressure response to repeated brief stress in psychoneurosis: A study of adaptation. *Canadian Journal of Psychology*, 1951, *5*, 167–179. **834**

Maltzman, I. Theoretical conceptions of semantic conditioning and generalization. In T. R. Dixon & D. L. Horton (Eds.), *Verbal behavior and general behavior theory*. Englewood Cliffs, N. J.: Prentice-Hall, 1968. **1048**

Maltzman, I., Bogartz, W., & Breger, L. A procedure for increasing word association originality and its transfer effects. *Journal of Experimental Psychology*, 1958, *56*, 392–398. **867**

Maltzman, I., & Gallup, H. F. Comments on "originality" in free and controlled association responses. *Psychological Reports*, 1964, *14*, 573–574. **867**

Maltzman, I., & Simon, S. A recency effect between word-association lists. *Psychological Reports*, 1959, *5*, 632. **867n**

Maltzman, I., Simon, S., Raskin, D., & Licht, L. Experimental studies in the training of originality. *Psychological Monographs*, 1960, *74*, Whole No. 493. **867**

Mandler, G. Response factors in human learning. *Psychological Review*, 1954, *61*, 235–244. **993**

Mandler, G. Associative frequency and associative prepotency as measures of response to nonsense syllables. *American Journal of Psychology*, 1955, *68*, 662–665. **852**

Mandler, G. Comments on Professor Russell's paper. In C. N. Cofer (Ed.), *Verbal learning and verbal behavior*. New York: McGraw-Hill, 1961. Pp. 123–128. **949**

Mandler, G. From association to structure. *Psychological Review*, 1962, *69*, 415–427. **1067, 1068**

Mandler, G. Comments on Professor Jenkin's paper. In C. N. Cofer & B. S. Musgrave (Eds.), *Verbal behavior and learning: Problems and processes*. New York: McGraw-Hill, 1963. Pp. 245–252. **949**

Mandler, G. Subjects do think. *Psychological Review*, 1965, *72*, 323–326. **1068**

Mandler, G. Organization and memory. In K. W. Spence, & J. T. Spence (Eds.), *The psychology of learning and motivation*. Vol. I. New York: Academic Press, 1967. **892**

Mandler, G. Verbal learning. In G. Mandler, P. Mussen, N. Kogan, & M. A. Wallach (Eds.), *New directions in psychology*. Vol. III. New York: Holt, Rinehart and Winston, 1967. **949**

Mandler, G., Cowan, P. A., & Gold, C. Concept learning and probability matching. *Journal of Experimental Psychology*, 1964, *67*, 514–522. **958**

Mandler, G., & Earhard, B. Pseudomediation: Is chaining an artifact? *Psychonomic Science*, 1964, *1*, 247–248. **1076**

Mandler, G., & Heinemann, S. H. Effect of overlearning of a verbal response on transfer of training. *Journal of Experimental Psychology*, 1956, *57*, 39–46. **1063, 1064, 1067**

Mandler, G., & Parnes, E. W. Frequency and idiosyncracy of associative responses. *Journal of Abnormal and Social Psychology*, 1957, *55*, 58–65. **873**

Mandler, G., *see also* Earhard, B., 1965a, b; Mandler, J. M., 1964.

Mandler, J. M., & Mandler, G. *Thinking: From association to gestalt*. New York: Wiley, 1964. **850**

Mangabeira-Albernaz, P. L., *see* Sherrik, C., 1961.

Mangels, J. W., *see* Thurlow, W. R., 1967.

Mankin, D. A., *see* Chapanis, A., 1967.

Mann, C. W. Visual factors in the perception of verticality.

Journal of Experimental Psychology, 1952, *44*, 460–464. **539**

Mann, L. I., *see* Kimble, G. A., 1955.

Manning, H. M. The effect of varying conditions of hunger and thirst on two responses learned to hunger or thirst alone. *Journal of Comparative and Physiological Psychology*, 1956, *49*, 249–253. **801**

Manning, P., *see* Washburn, M. F., 1934.

Marbe, K., *see* Thumb, A., 1901.

Marder, V. J., *see* Deese, J., 1957.

Margules, D. L., & Olds, J. Identical "feeding" and "rewarding" systems in the lateral hypothalamus of rats. *Science*, 1962, *135*, 374–375. **651, 798**

Marill, T., *see* Heinemann, E. G., 1954.

Marin, J., *see* Hunt, E. B., 1966.

Markee, J. E., *see* Becker, R. F., 1962.

Markham, J. W., *see* Armstrong, D., 1951.

Markley, R. P., *see* Vincent, R. J., 1969.

Markowitz, R. A., *see* Smith, G. M., 1966.

Marks, L. E., & Miller, G. A. The role of semantic and syntactic constraints in the memorization of English sentences. *Journal of Verbal Learning and Verbal Behavior*, 1964, *3*, 1–5. **903**

Marks, L. E., & Stevens, J. C. Individual brightness functions. *Perception and Psychophysics*, 1966, *2*, 7–24. **79**

Marks, W. B., Dobelle, W. H., & MacNichol, E. F., Jr. Visual pigments of single primate cones. *Science*, 1964, *143*, 1181–1183. **323**

Marler, P. Territory and individual distance in the chaffinch *Fringilla coelebs*. *Ibis*, 1956, *98*, 496–501. **693**

Marler, P. R., & Hamilton, W. J., III., *Mechanisms of animal behavior*. New York: Wiley, 1966. **589n**

Marlowe, D., *see* Horton, D. L., 1963.

Marquis, D. G., & Porter, J. M., Jr. Differential characteristics of conditioned eyelid responses established by reflex and voluntary reinforcement. *Journal of Experimental Psychology*, 1939, *24*, 347–365. **564**

Marquis, D. G., *see also* Hilgard, E. R., 1940.

Marshall, D. A. A comparative study of neural coding in gustation. *Physiology and Behavior*, 1967. **181**

Marshall, D. A., *see also* Erickson, R. P., 1965.

Marshall, G. R. The organization of verbal material in free recall: The effects of patterns of associative overlap on clustering. Doctoral dissertation. New York University, 1963. **887, 891**

Marshall, G. R., & Cofer, C. N. Associative indices as measures of word relatedness: A summary and comparison of ten methods. *Journal of Verbal Learning and Verbal Behavior*, 1963, *1*, 408–421. **879, 880, 881, 888**

Marshall, G. R., *see also* Garskoff, B. E., 1965.

Marshall, W. H., & Talbot, S. A. Recent evidence for neural mechanisms in vision leading to a general theory of sensory acuity. In H. Klüver (Ed.), *Biological symposia*. Vol. 7: *Visual mechanisms*. Lancaster, Pa.: Jacques Cattell, 1942. **305**

Marten, A. E., *see* Thurlow, W. R., 1963, 1965.

Martin, E. Transfer of verbal paired associates. *Psychological Review*, 1965, *72*, 327–343. **1059, 1061, 1067**

Martin, E. Stimulus recognition in aural paired-associate learning. *Journal of Verbal Learning and Verbal Behavior*, 1967, *6*, 272–276. (a) **1048**

Martin, E. Relation between stimulus recognition and paired-associate learning. *Journal of Experimental Psychology*, 1967, *74*, 500–505. (b) **1048**

Martin, J. G. Associative strength and word frequency in paired-associate learning. *Journal of Verbal Learning and Verbal Behavior*, 1964, *3*, 317–320. **888**

Martin, L., *see* Johnson, R. C., 1961.

Martin, L. C. The photometric matching field. *Proceedings of the Royal Society*, (London), Ser. A, 1923, *104*, 302–315. **426**

Martin, L. C., Day, D. J., & Kaniowski, W. Visual acuity with brief stimuli. *British Journal of Ophthalmology, 1950, 34,* 89–104. **304**

Martin, R. B., & Dean, S. J. Implicit and explicit mediation in paired-associate learning. *Journal of Experimental Psychology, 1964, 68,* 21–27. **1079**

Martin, R. B., Simon, S., & Ditrichs, R. Verbal paired-associate transfer as a function of practice and paradigm shift. *Psychonomic Science, 1966, 4,* 419–420. **1070**

Martin, R. C., see Brown, J. S., 1964.

Martini, L., & Ganong, W. F. (Eds.), *Neuroendocrinology.* New York: Academic Press, 1966. **91**

Maruhashi, J., Mizuguchi, J., & Tasaki, I. Action current in single afferent nerve fibers elicited by stimulation of the skin of the toad and the cat. *Journal of Physiology, 1952, 117,* 129–151. **165**

Maruyama, N., see Katsuki, Y., 1959.

Marx, M. H. Some relations between frustration and drive. In M. R. Jones (Ed.), *Nebraska symposium on motivation.* Lincoln: University of Nebraska Press, 1956. Pp. 92–130. **810**

Marx, M. H., & Pieper, W. A. Acquisition of instrumental response as a function of incentive contrast. *Psychological Reports, 1962, 10,* 635–638. **638**

Marx, M. H., & Pieper, W. A. Instrumental acquisition and performance on fixed-interval reinforcement as a function of incentive contrast. *Psychological Reports, 1963, 12,* 255–258. **638**

Marx, M. H., see also Collier, G., 1959.

Mason, G. L., see Alpern, M., 1961.

Mason, W. A., see Lawrence, D. H., 1955.

Masserman, J. H., & Pechtel, C. Neuroses in monkeys: A preliminary report of experimental observations. *Annals of The New York Academy of Science, 1953, 56,* 253–265. **704**

Massey, F. J., see Dixon, W. F., 1956.

Masterson, F. A., see Campbell, B. A., 1968.

Masterton, R. B., Jane, J. A., & Diamond, I. T. Role of brain-stem auditory structures in sound localization. *Journal of Neurophysiology, 1968, 31,* 96–108. **264**

Mateer, F. *Child behavior.* Boston: Badger, 1918. **562**

Mathews, R. W., see Walls, G. L., 1952.

Matin, E., see Matin, L., 1966, 1969.

Matin, L. Binocular summation at the absolute threshold of peripheral vision. *Journal of the Optical Society of America, 1962, 52,* 1276–1286. **296**

Matin, L. Binocular summation at the absolute threshold of peripheral vision. *Journal of the Optical Society of America, 1963, 53,* 1199–1205. **488**

Matin, L., & Kibler, G. Acuity of visual perception of direction in the dark for various positions of the eye in orbit. *Perceptual and Motor Skills, 1966, 22,* 407–420. **530**

Matin, L., & MacKinnon, G. E. Autokinetic movement: Selective manipulation of directional components by image stabilization. *Science, 1964, 143,* 147–148. **529**

Matin, L., Matin, E., & Pearce, D. G. Visual perception of direction when voluntary saccades occur: I. Relation of visual direction of a fixation target extinguished before a saccade to a flash presented during the saccade. *Perception and Psychophysics, 1969, 5,* 65–80. **531**

Matin, L., Pearce, D., Matin, E., & Kibler, G. Visual perception of direction in the dark: Roles of local sign, eye movements, and ocular proprioception. *Vision Research, 1966, 6,* 453–469. **530**

Matsubayashi, A. Forschung über die Tiefenwahrnehmung: II. *Acta Societatis Ophthalmologica Japonica, 1937, 41,* 2055–2074. Cited in Graham, C. H., 1965. **486**

Matsumiya, Y. The effects of US intensity and CS-US pattern on conditioned emotional response. *Japanese Psychological Research, 1960, 2,* 35–42. **579, 719**

Matsumiya, Y., see also Kling, J. W., 1962.

Matthews, R., see Adrian, E. D., 1928.

Matthews, T. J., see Beer, B., 1964.

Maturana, H. R., & Frenk, S. Directional movement and horizontal edge detectors in the pigeon retina. *Science, 1963, 142,* 977–979. **296**

Maturana, H. R., see also Lettvin, J. Y., 1959.

May, F., see Long, E. R., 1958.

Mayer, B. Messende Untersuchungen über die Umstimmung des Geschmackswerkzeugs. *Zeitschrift für Sinnesphysiologie, 1927, 58,* 133–152. **186, 187**

Mayhew, A. J. Interlist changes in subjective organization during free-recall learning. *Journal of Experimental Psychology, 1967, 74,* 425–430. **1045**

Mayzner, M. S., Abrevay, E. L., Frey, R. E., Kaufman, H. G., & Schoenberg, K. M. Short-term memory in vision: A partial replication of the Averbach and Coriell study. *Psychonomic Science, 1964, 1,* 225–226. **430**

Mayzner, M. S., Blatt, M. H., Buchsbaum, W. H., Friedel, R. T., Goodwin, P. E., Kanon, D., Keleman, A., & Nilsson, W. D. A U-shaped backward masking function in vision: A partial replication of the Weisstein and Haber study with two ring sizes. *Psychonomic Science, 1965, 3,* 79–80. **430**

Mayzner, M. S., & Schoenberg, K. M. Single-letter and digram frequency effects in immediate serial recall. *Journal of Verbal Learning and Verbal Behavior, 1964, 3,* 397–400. **897**

Mayzner, M. S., & Tresselt, M. E. The ranking of letter pairs and single letters to match digram and single-letter frequency counts. *Journal of Verbal Learning and Verbal Behavior, 1962, 1,* 203–207. **898**

Mayzner, M. S., & Tresselt, M. E. Tables of single-letter and digram frequency counts for various word-length and letter-position combinations. *Psychonomic Science (Monograph Supplement), 1965, 1,* No. 2. **896**

Mayzner, M. S., Tresselt, M. E., Adler, S., & Schoenberg, K. M. Correlations between subject generated letter frequencies and observed frequencies in English. *Psychonomic Science, 1964, 1,* 295–296. **898**

Mayzner, M. S., Tresselt, M. E., & Wolin, B. R. Tables of trigram frequency counts for various word-length and letter-position combinations. *Psychonomic Science (Monograph Supplement), 1965, 1,* No. 3. (a) **896**

Mayzner, M. S., Tresselt, M. E., & Wolin, B. R. Tables of tetragram frequency counts for various word-length and letter-position combinations. *Psychonomic Science (Monograph Supplement), 1965, 1,* No. 4. (b) **896**

Mayzner, M. S., Tresselt, M. E., & Wolin, B. R. Tables of pentagram frequency counts for various word-length and letter-position combinations. *Psychonomic Science (Monograph Supplement), 1965, 1,* No. 5. (c) **896**

Mead, S., see Mueller, E. E., 1953.

Mednick, M. T. Mediated generalization and the incubation effect as a function of manifest anxiety. *Journal of Abnormal and Social Psychology, 1957, 55,* 315–321. **1047**

Mednick, S. A., & Freedman, J. L. Stimulus generalization. *Psychological Bulletin, 1960, 57,* 170–200. **761**

Meehl, P. E. On the circularity of the law of effect. *Psychological Bulletin, 1950, 47,* 52–75. **567**

Meehl, P. E., see also MacCorquodale, K., 1953, 1954.

Mefferd, R. B. Endogenously-supplied visual attributes of depth. *Perceptual and Motor Skills, 1968, 27,* 1115–1122. **519**

Mefferd, R. B. Perceptual fluctuations involving orientation and organization. *Perceptual and Motor Skills, 1968, 27,* 827–834. **519**

Mefferd, R. B., Jr., & Wieland, B. A. Perception of depth in rotating objects: 2. Perspective as a determinant of stereokinesis. *Perceptual and Motor Skills, 1967, 25,* 621–628. **524**

Mefferd, R. B., & Wieland, B. A. Apparent size-apparent

distance relationship in flat stimuli. *Perceptual and Motor Skills*, 1968, *26*, 959–966. **462**

Mefferd, R. B., Jr., *see also* Cook, T. H., 1967; Moran, L. J., 1964.

Megibow, M., & Zeigler, H. P. Readiness to eat in the pigeon. *Psychonomic Science*, 1968, *12*, 17–18. **816**

Mehler, J. Some effects of grammatical transformations on the recall of English sentences. *Journal of Verbal Learning and Verbal Behavior*, 1963, *3*, 346–351. **904**

Meinke, D. L., *see* Johnson, T. J., 1965.

Meiselman, H. L. Adaptation and cross-adaptation of the four gustatory qualities. *Perception and Psychophysics*, 1968, *4*, 368–372. **186**

Meiselman, L., *see* Dzendolet, E., 1967a, b.

Meissner, G. Untersuchungen über den Tastsinn. *Zeitschrift für Rationelle Medicin*, 1859, *7*, 92–118. **129**

Meissner, P. B., *see* Witkin, H. A., 1954.

Melamed, L. E., *see* Thurlow, W. R., 1967.

Mellon, D., *see* Evans, D. R., 1962.

Melton, A. W. The end-spurt in memorization curves as an artifact of the averaging of individual curves. *Psychological Monographs*, 1936, *47*, 119–134. **613, 1025**

Melton, A. W. Comments on Professor Postman's paper. In C. N. Cofer (Ed.), *Verbal learning and verbal behavior*. New York: McGraw-Hill, 1961. **1092, 1097**

Melton, A. W. Comments on Professor Peterson's paper. In C. N. Cofer & B. S. Musgrave (Eds.), *Verbal behavior and learning*. New York: McGraw-Hill, 1963. (a) **1109**

Melton, A. W. Implications of short-term memory for a general theory of memory. *Journal of Verbal Learning and Verbal Behavior*, 1963, *2*, 1–21. (b) **997, 998, 1109, 1110, 1111**

Melton, A. W., & Irwin, J. M. The influence of degree of interpolated learning on retroactive inhibition and the overt transfer of specific responses. *American Journal of Psychology*, 1940, *53*, 173–203. **1086, 1089**

Melton, A. W., & Von Lackum, W. J. Retroactive and proactive inhibition in retention: Evidence for a two-factor theory of retroactive inhibition. *American Journal of Psychology*, 1941, *54*, 157–173. **613, 1041, 1054, 1082, 1103, 1104**

Meltzer, R., *see* Goulet, L. R., 1967.

Melzack, R. Irrational fears in the dog. *Canadian Journal of Psychology*, 1952, *6*, 141–147. **586**

Melzack, R., & Casey, K. L. Sensory, motivational, and central control determinants of pain. In D. R. Kenshalo (Ed.), *The skin senses*. Springfield, Ill.: Charles C Thomas, 1968. Pp. 423–443. **155**

Melzack, R., & Wall, P. D. On the nature of cutaneous sensory mechanisms. *Brain*, 1962, *85* (II), 331–356. **119, 121, 167**

Melzack, R., & Wall, P. D. Pain mechanisms: A new theory. *Science*, 1965, *150*, 971–979. **165, 167**

Menahem, R., *see* Rosenzweig, M. R., 1962.

Mendelson, J., & Chorover, S. L. Lateral hypothalamic stimulation in satiated rats: T-maze learning for food. *Science*, 1965, *149*, 559–561. **798**

Merikle, P. M. Paired-associate transfer as a function of stimulus and response meaningfulness. *Psychological Reports*, 1968, *22*, 131–138. **1062, 1063, 1064**

Mershon, D. H., *see* Gogel, W. C., 1969.

Mertens, H. W., *see* Gogel, W. C., 1967.

Merton, P. A. The accuracy of directing the eyes and the hand in the dark. *Journal of Physiology*, 1961, *156*, 555–577. **530**

Merton, P. A., *see also* Brindley, G. S., 1960.

Meryman, J. J. Magnitude of startle response as a function of hunger and fear. Unpublished master's thesis, State University of Iowa, 1952. Cited by Brown, 1961. **796**

Meseck, O. R., *see* Russell, W. A., 1959.

Metelli, F. Zur Analyse der phänomenalen Durchtigkeitser-

scheinungen. In *Gestalt und Witklichkeit: Festgabe für Ferdinand Weinhandl*. Berlin: Duncker und Humboldt, 1967. **427**

Metfessel, M. A proposal for quantitative reporting of comparative judgments. *Journal of Psychology*, 1947, *24*, 229–235. **71**

Metzger, W. Optische Unterschungengen am Ganzfelds: II. Zur Phänomenologic des homogenen Ganzfelds. *Psychologische Forschung*, 1930, *13*, 6–29. **426**

Metzger, W. *Gesetze des Sehens*. Frankfurt am Main: Kramer, 1953. **428, 442**

Meumann, E., *see* Ebert, E., 1905.

Meyer, D. R. The effects of differential rewards on discrimination reversal learning by monkeys. *Journal of Experimental Psychology*, 1951, *41*, 268–274. **636, 637, 638, 639**

Meyer, D. R. Some psychological determinants of sparing and loss following damage to the brain. In H. H. Harlow & C. N. Woolsey (Eds.), *Biological and biochemical bases of behavior*. Madison: University of Wisconsin Press, 1958. Pp. 173–192. **845**

Meyer, D. R., Cho, C., & Wesemann, A. F. On problems of conditioning discriminated lever-press avoidance responses. *Psychological Review*, 1960, *67*, 224–228. **730**

Meyer, D. R., LoPopolo, M. H., & Singh, D. Learning and transfer in the monkey as a function of differential levels of incentive. *Journal of Experimental Psychology*, 1966, *72*, 284–286. **640**

Meyer, D. R., & Miles, R. C. Intralist-interlist relations in verbal learning. *Journal of Experimental Psychology*, 1953, *45*, 109–115. **1043**

Meyer, D. R., Treichler, F. R., & Meyer, P. M. Discrete-trial training techniques and stimulus variables. In A. M. Schrier, H. F. Harlow, & F. Stollnitz (Eds.), *Behavior of nonhuman primates*. Vol. 1. New York: Academic Press, 1965. **750, 751**

Meyer, D. R., *see also* Miles, R. C., 1956.

Meyer, P. M., *see* Meyer, D. R., 1965.

Meyer, W., *see* Fitts, P. M., 1956.

Meyers, R. E., *see* Sperry, R. W., 1955.

Meyers, W. J., Valenstein, E. S., & Lacey, J. I. Heart rate changes after reinforcing brain stimulation in rats. *Science*, 1963, *140*, 1233–1235. **657**

Meyers, W. J., *see also* Valenstein, E. S., 1964.

Michael, C. R. Receptive fields of directionally selective units in the optic nerve of the ground squirrel. *Science*, 1966, *152*, 1092–1097. **296**

Michels, K. M., & Zusne, L. Metrics of visual form. *Psychological Bulletin*, 1965, *63*, 74–86. **449**

Michels, K. M., *see also* Wright, R. H., 1964.

Michels, W. C., & Helson, H. A reformulation of the Fechner law in terms of adaptation-level applied to rating-scale data. *American Journal of Psychology*, 1949, *62*, 355–368. **60**

Michelsen, W. J. Procedure for studying olfactory discrimination in pigeons. *Science*, 1959, *130*, 630–631. **753, 754**

Michotte, A. *La perception de la causalité*. Louvain: Institut Supérieur de Philosophie, 1946. **524, 525**

Mikaelian, H., & Held, R. Two types of adaptation to an optically rotated visual field. *American Journal of Psychology*, 1964, *77*, 257–263. **539, 540, 542**

Mikaelian, H., *see also* Held, R., 1964; Morant, R. B., 1960.

Mikesell, W. H., & Bentley, M. Configuration and brightness contrast. *Journal of Experimental Psychology*, 1930, *13*, 1–23. **410, 423n**

Mikulka, P. J., *see* Spear, N. E., 1966.

Milauckas, E. W., *see* Young, R. K., 1963.

Miles, R. C. The relative effectiveness of secondary reinforcers throughout deprivation and habit-strength parameters. *Journal of Comparative and Physiological Psychology*, 1956, *49*, 126–130. **666, 668**

Miles, R. C. Learning-set formation in the squirrel monkey. *Journal of Comparative and Physiological Psychology,* 1957, *50,* 356-357. **768**

Miles, R. C., & Meyer, D. R. Learning sets in marmosets. *Journal of Comparative and Physiological Psychology,* 1956, *49,* 219-222. **768**

Miles, R. C., *see also* Meyer, D. R., 1953.

Miles, W. R. Effectiveness of red light on dark adaptation. *Journal of the Optical Society of America,* 1953, *43,* 435-441. **284**

Miles, W. R., *see also* Beck, L. H., 1947.

Miller, D., *see* Zigler, M. J., 1930.

Miller, F. Context in the perception of sentences. *American Journal of Psychology,* 1956, *69,* 653-654. **448**

Miller, G. A. *Language and communication.* New York: McGraw-Hill, 1951. **895**

Miller, G. A. The magical number seven, plus or minus two: Some limits on our capacity for processing information. *Psychological Review,* 1956, *63,* 81-97. **205, 250, 998**

Miller, G. A. Some psychological studies of grammar. *American Psychologist,* 1962, *17,* 748-762. **904**

Miller, G. A., Galanter, E., & Pribram, K. *Plans and the structure of behavior.* New York: Holt, Rinehart and Winston, 1960. **975**

Miller, G. A., Heise, G. A., & Lichten, W. The intelligibility of speech as a function of the context of the test materials. *Journal of Experimental Psychology,* 1951, *41,* 329-335. **254, 256**

Miller, G. A., & Selfridge, J. Verbal context and the recall of meaningful material. *American Journal of Psychology,* 1950, *63,* 176-185. **902**

Miller, G. A., & Taylor, W. G. The perception of repeated bursts of noise. *Journal of the Acoustical Society of America,* 1948, *20,* 171-182. **245**

Miller, G. A., *see also* Bruner, J. S., 1955; Garner, W. R., 1947; Licklider, J. C. R., 1951; Marks, L. E., 1964.

Miller, J. The effect of facilitating and inhibitory attitudes on eyelid conditioning. Doctoral dissertation, Yale University, 1939. **561**

Miller, J. D., *see* Kryter, K. D., 1966.

Miller, N. E. A reply to "sign-gestalt or conditioned reflex?" *Psychological Review,* 1935, *42,* 280-292. **621, 780**

Miller, N. E. Studies of fear as an acquirable drive: I. Fear as motivation and fear-reduction as reinforcement in the learning of new responses. *Journal of Experimental Psychology,* 1948, *38,* 89-101. **717, 718, 802, 803, 804**

Miller, N. E. Theory and experiment relating psychoanalytic displacement to stimulus response generalization. *Journal of Abnormal and Social Psychology,* 1948, *43,* 155-178. **780**

Miller, N. E. Learnable drives and rewards. In S. S. Stevens (Ed.), *Handbook of experimental psychology.* New York: Wiley, 1951. Pp. 435-472. **718, 804**

Miller, N. E. Shortcomings of food consumption as a measure of hunger: Results from other behavioral techniques. *Annals of the New York Academy of Sciences,* 1955, *63,* 141-143. **797**

Miller, N. E. Effects of drugs on motivation: The value of using a variety of measures. *Annals of the New York Academy of Sciences,* 1956, *65,* 318-333. **815, 827**

Miller, N. E. Experiments on motivation. *Science,* 1957, *126,* 1271-1278. **690, 800**

Miller, N. E. Liberalization of basic S-R concepts: Extensions to conflict behavior, motivation, and social learning. In S. Koch (Ed.), *Psychology: A study of a science.* Vol. II. New York: McGraw-Hill, 1959. Pp. 196-292. **821**

Miller, N. E. Learning resistance to pain and fear: Effects of overlearning, exposure, and rewarded exposure in context. *Journal of Experimental Psychology,* 1960, *60,* 137-145. **736**

Miller, N. E. Motivational effects of brain stimulation and drugs. *Federation Proceedings,* 1960, *19,* 846-854. **798**

Miller, N. E. Some reflections on the law of effect produce a new alternative to drive reduction. In M. R. Jones (Ed.), *Nebraska symposium on motivation.* Lincoln: University of Nebraska Press, 1963, *11,* 65-112. **660, 690**

Miller, N. E. Learning of visceral and glandular responses. *Science,* 1969, *163,* 434-446. **563, 655**

Miller, N. E., & Banuazizi, A. Instrumental learning by curarized rats of a specific visceral response, intestinal or cardiac. *Journal of Comparative and Physiological Psychology,* 1968, *65,* 1-7. **655, 699, 839**

Miller, N. E., & Dollard, J. *Social learning and imitation.* New Haven: Yale University Press, 1941. **821**

Miller, N. E., & Kessen, M. L. Reward effects of food via stomach fistula compared with those of food via mouth. *Journal of Comparative and Physiological Psychology,* 1952, *45,* 555-564. **621, 797**

Miller, N. E., *see also* Bower, G. H., 1958; Delgado, J. M. R., 1954, 1954b; DiCara, L. V., 1968; Dollard, J., 1950; Egger, M. D., 1963; Feirstein, A. R., 1963; Fowler, H., 1963; Mowrer, O. H., 1936; Myers, A. K., 1954.

Miller, P., *see* Levine, M., 1967.

Miller, R. L. Masking effect of periodically pulsed tones as a function of time and frequency. *Journal of the Acoustical Society of America,* 1947, *19,* 798-807. **241**

Miller, S., & Konorski, J. Sur une forme particulière des réflexes conditionels. *Comptes Rendus des Séances de la Société Polonaise de Biologie,* 1928, *49,* 1155-1158. **565***n*

Miller, S., *see also* Weddell, G., 1962.

Miller, T. M., *see* Shapiro, M. M., 1965.

Miller, W. H., *see* Hartline, H. K., 1961.

Mills, A. W. On the minimum audible angle. *Journal of the Acoustical Society of America,* 1958, *30,* 237-246. **266, 267**

Mills, A. W. Lateralization of high-frequency tones. *Journal of the Acoustical Society of America,* 1960, *32,* 132-134. **266**

Millward, R. An all-or-none model for noncorrection routines with elimination of incorrect responses. *Journal of Mathematical Psychology,* 1964, *1,* 392-404. (a) **994**

Millward, R. B. Latency in a modified paired-associate learning experiment. *Journal of Verbal Learning and Verbal Behavior,* 1964, *3,* 309-316. (b) **957**

Millward, R. Two learning models for two-choice conditioning experiments involving nonreinforced trials. *Psychological Reports,* 1967, *20,* 1211-1229. **933**

Millward, R. B. Probabilistic reinforcement of reversal and dimensional shifts. *Journal of Mathematical Psychology,* 1968, *5,* 196-223. **955**

Millward, R. B., & Reber, A. S. Event recall in probability learning. Technical Report, No. 2; 1967, Brown University. **936**

Millward, R. B., *see also* Blough, D., 1965; Friedman, M. P., 1964; Reber, A. S., 1968.

Milner, P. M., *see* Olds, J., 1954.

Miner, N., *see* Sperry, R. W., 1955.

Mink, W. D. Semantic generalization as related to word association. *Psychological Reports,* 1963, *12,* 59-67. **1048**

Mink, W. D., *see also* Jenkins, J. J., 1958.

Minnaert, M. *Light and colour in the open air.* (Tr. H. M. Kremer-Priest; rev. K. E. Brian-Jay.) London: G. Bell, 1940. **498**

Mintz, D. E., *see* Notterman, J. M., 1962, 1965.

Mintz, E. U., *see* Hecht, S., 1939.

Miron, M. S., *see* Shanmugam, A. V., 1966.

Misanin, J. R., *see* Campbell, B. A., 1966, 1969.

Mishkin, M., & Forgays, D. G. Word recognition as a function of retinal locus. *Journal of Experimental Psychology,* 1952, *43,* 43-48. **444**

Mitchell, A. M., *see* Westheimer, G. H., 1956.

Mitchell, E., *see* Leibowitz, H., 1954.

Mittelstaedt, H., *see* Holst, E. von, 1950.

Mitzuguchi, J., *see* Maruhash:, J., 1952.

Mogenson, G. J. An attempt to establish secondary reinforcement with rewarding brain stimulation. *Psychological Reports,* 1965, *16,* 163–167. **675**

Mogenson, G. J., & Stevenson, J. A. F. Drinking and self-stimulation with electrical stimulation of the lateral hypothalamus. *Physiology and Behavior,* 1966, *1,* 251–254. **652**

Moll, R. R. Drive and maturation effects in the development of consummatory behavior. *Psychological Reports,* 1964, *15,* 295–302. **820**

Moller, J. A. The effect of food deprivation on heart rate under low environmental stimulation. Canadian Psychological Association, 22nd. annual meeting, Quebec, June, 1963. **836**

Moltz, H. Imprinting: An epigenetic view. *Psychological Review,* 1963, *70,* 123–138. **584, 588**

Moltz, H., Rosenblum, L. A., & Stettner, L. J. Some parameters of imprinting effectiveness. *Journal of Comparative and Physiological Psychology,* 1960, *53,* 297–301. **586**

Moltz, H., & Stettner, L. J. The influence of patterned light deprivation on the critical period for imprinting. *Journal of Comparative and Physiological Psychology,* 1961, *54,* 297–283. **583**

Moncrieff, R. W. Olfactory adaptation and odor-intensity. *American Journal of Psychology,* 1957, *70,* 1–20. **203, 204**

Moncrieff, R. W. *The chemical senses.* Cleveland: CRC Press, 1967. **194, 220**

Moncrieff, R. W. *The chemical senses.* (3rd ed.) London: Leonard Hill, 1967. **177, 178**

Mongeon, C. J., *see* Simmons, F. B., 1964.

Monjan, A. *Chromatic adaption and the HTRF in the macaque.* Doctoral dissertation, University of Rochester, 1964. **343**

Montagna, W. *The structure and function of skin.* New York: Academic Press, 1962. **122, 125**

Mook, D. G. Oral and postingestional determinants of the intake of various solutions in rats with esophageal fistulas. *Journal of Comparative and Physiological Psychology,* 1963, *56,* 645–659. **621, 627**

Moon, P. *The scientific basis of illuminating engineering.* New York: McGraw-Hill, 1936. **274**

Moore, J. W., *see* Halpern, J., 1967.

Moore, M. E., Linker, E., & Purcell, M. Taste-sensitivity after eating: A signal detection approach. *American Journal of Psychology,* 1965, *78,* 107–111. **188**

Moore, M. E., *see also* Linker, E., 1964; Wallach, H., 1963.

Moore, M. G. Gestalt vs. experience. *American Journal of Psychology,* 1930, *42,* 453–455. **440**

Moran, L. J. Generality of word-association response sets. *Psychological Monographs,* 1966, *80,* Whole No. 612. **876**

Moran, L. J., Mefferd, R. B., Jr., & Kimble, J. P., Jr. Idiodynamic sets in word association. *Psychological Monographs,* 1964, *78,* Whole No. 579. **876**

Morant, R. B. & Beller, H. K. Adaptation to prismatically rotated visual fields. *Science,* 1965, *148,* 530–531. **539**

Morant, R. B., & Mikaelian, H. H. Interfield tilt after-effects. *Perceptual and Motor Skills,* 1960, *10,* 95–98. **466**

Moray, N. Attention in dichotic listening: Affective cues and the influence of instruction. *Quarterly Journal of Experimental Psychology,* 1959, *11,* 56–60. **259**

More, L. K., *see* Tees, R. C., 1967.

Morgan, C. T., Galambos, R., & Garner, W. R. Pitch and intensity. *Journal of the Acoustical Society of America,* 1951, *23,* 658–663. **244**

Morgan, C. T., *see also* Stevens, S. S., 1941.

Morgan, R. I., & Underwood, B. J. Proactive inhibition as a function of response similarity. *Journal of Experimental Psychology,* 1950, *40,* 592–603. **1056, 1057, 1104**

Morgan, W. L., *see* Kniep, E. H., 1931.

Morgane, P. J. Limbic-hypothalamic-midbrain interaction in thirst and thirst motivated behavior. In M. J. Wayner (Ed.), *Thirst: First international symposium on thirst in the regulation of body water.* New York: Macmillan, 1964. Pp. 429–453. **647**

Morgulis, S., *see* Yerkes, R. M., 1909.

Morning, N., & Voss, J. F. Mediation of R_1–R_2 in the acquisition of S–R_1, S–R_2 associations. *Journal of Experimental Psychology,* 1964, *67,* 51–71. **1075**

Morony, L., *see* Houston, J., 1966.

Morrison, G. R. Behavioural response patterns to salt stimuli in the rat. *Canadian Journal of Psychology,* 1967, *21,* 141–152. **180**

Morrison, G. R., & Norrison W. Taste detection in the rat. *Canadian Journal of Psychology,* 1966, *20,* 208–217. **177**

Morrow, M. W., *see* Brown, J. S., 1964.

Morse, W. H. Intermittent reinforcement. In W. K. Honig (Ed.), *Operant behavior.* New York: Appleton, 1966. **606, 620**

Morse, W. H., & Skinner, B. F. A second type of superstition in the pigeon. *American Journal of Psychology,* 1957, *70,* 308–311. **675**

Mosberg, L., *see* Friedman, M., 1967.

Moser, H. M., & Dreher, J. J. Effects of training on listeners in intelligibility studies. *Journal of the Acoustical Society of America,* 1955, *27,* 1213–1219. **255**

Mosteller, F., *see* Bruner, J., 1950; Bush, R. R., 1951, 1955; Smith, G. M., 1966.

Mote, F. A., *see* Graham, C. H., 1939; Riggs, L. A., 1947.

Moulton, D. G. Studies in olfactory acuity: III. Relative detectability of *n*-aliphatic acetates by the rat. *Quarterly Journal of Experimental Psychology,* 1960, *12,* 203–213. **203, 204**

Moulton, D. G., Ashton, E. H., & Eayrs, J. T. Studies in olfactory acuity: IV. Relative detectability of *n*-aliphatic acids by the dog. *Animal Behaviour,* 1960, *8,* 117–128. **202**

Moulton, D. G., & Beidler, L. M. Structure and function in the peripheral olfactory system. *Physiological Review,* 1967, *47,* 1–52. **195, 220**

Moulton, D. G., & Eayrs, J. T. Studies in olfactory acuity: II. Relative detectability of *n*-aliphatic alcohols by the rat. *Quarterly Journal of Experimental Psychology,* 1960, *12,* 99–109. **199**

Moulton, D. G., *see also* Benjamin, R. M., 1965.

Mountcastle, V. B., Talbot, W. H., Darian-Smith, I., & Kornhuber, H. H. Neural basis of the sense of flutter-vibration. *Science,* 1967, *155,* 597–600. **138**

Mountcastle, V. B., *see also* Poggio, G. F., 1960; Rose, J. E., 1959.

Mowrer, O. H. On the dual nature of learning: A re-interpretation of "conditioning" and "problem-solving." *Harvard Educational Review,* 1947, *17,* 102–148. **563, 726**

Mowrer, O. H. Motivation. *Annual Review of Psychology,* 1952, *3,* 419–438. **794n**

Mowrer, O. H., & Aiken, E. G. Contiguity vs. drive-reduction in conditioned fear: Temporal variations in conditioned and unconditioned stimulus. *American Journal of Psychology,* 1954, *67,* 26–38. **579, 718, 719**

Mowrer, O. H., & Lamoreaux, R. R. Fear as an intervening variable in avoidance conditioning. *Journal of Comparative Psychology,* 1946, *39,* 29–50. **727**

Mowrer, O. H., Ruch, T. C., & Miller, N. E. The corneo-retinal potential difference as the basis of the galvanometric record of recording eye movements. *American Journal of Physiology,* 1936, *114,* 423–428. **372**

Mowrer, O. H., & Solomon, L. N. Contiguity vs. drive-reduction in conditioned fear: The proximity and abruptness of drive-reduction. *American Journal of Psychology,* 1954, *67,* 15–25. **719**

Mowrer, O. H., *see also* Gibson, J. J., 1938; Whiting, J. W. M., 1943.

Moyer, K. E., & Korn, J. H. Effect of UCS intensity on the acquisition and extinction of an avoidance response. *Journal of Experimental Psychology,* 1964, *67,* 352–359. **728, 729**

Mozell, M. M. Electrophysiology of the olfactory bulb. *Journal of Neurophysiology,* 1958, *21,* 183–196. **200, 203, 204**

Mozell, M. M. The spatiotemporal analysis of odorants at the level of the olfactory receptor sheet. *Journal of General Physiology,* 1966, *50,* 25–41. **200, 218, 219**

Mozell, M. M., & Pfaffmann, C. The afferent neural process in odor perception. *Annals of the New York Academy of Science,* 1954, *58,* 96–108. **218**

Mozell, M. M., *see also* Benjamin, R. M., 1965; O'Connell, R. J., 1969.

Mueller, C. G. Frequency of seeing functions for intensity discrimination at various levels of adapting intensity. *Journal of General Psychology,* 1951, *34,* 463–474. **29**

Mueller, C. G., & Lloyd, V. V. Stereoscopic acuity for various levels of illumination. *Proceedings of the National Academy of Science,* 1948, *34,* 223–227. **486**

Graham, C. H., 1949; Riggs, L. A., 1947.

Mueller, E. E., Loeffel, R., & Mead, S. Skin impedance in relation to pain threshold testing by electrical means. *Journal of Applied Physiology,* 1953, *5,* 746–752. **156**

Mueller-Lyer, F. C. Optische Urteilstaeuschungen. *Archiv für Psychologie,* 1889, *Suppl. Bd.,* 263–270. **461**

Muenzinger, K. F. Motivation in learning: I. Electric shock for correct response in the visual discrimination habit. *Journal of Comparative Psychology,* 1934, *17,* 267–277. **739, 784**

Muenzinger, K. F. Vicarious trial and error at a point of choice: I. A general survey of its relation to learning efficiency. *Journal of General Psychology,* 1938, *53,* 75–86. **784**

Muenzinger, K. F., Bernstone, A. H., & Richards, L. Motivation in learning: VIII. Equivalent amounts of electric shock for right and wrong responses in a visual discrimination habit. *Journal of Comparative Psychology,* 1938, *26,* 177–186. **784**

Muenzinger, K. F., & Fletcher, F. M. Motivation in learning: VII. The effect of an enforced delay at the point of choice in the visual discrimination habit. *Journal of Comparative Psychology,* 1937, *23,* 383–392. **784**

Muenzinger, K. F., & Newcomb, H. Motivation in learning: V. The relative effectiveness of jumping a gap and crossing an electric grid in a visual discrimination habit. *Journal of Comparative Psychology,* 1936, *21,* 95–104. **784**

Muenzinger, K. F., & Wood, A. Motivation in learning: IV. The function of punishment as determined by its temporal relation to the act of choice in the visual discrimination habit. *Journal of Comparative Psychology,* 1935, *20,* 95–106. **784**

Mueser, G. E., *see* White, B. H., 1960.

Mulholland, T. B. Motion perceived while viewing rotating stimulus objects. *American Journal of Psychology,* 1956, *69,* 96–99. **519**

Müller, G. E., & Pilzecker, A. Experimentelle Beiträge zur Lehre vom Gedächtniss. *Zeitschrift für Psychologie, Ergbd. #1,* 1900. **1080**

Müller, J. *Beiträge zur vergleichenden Physiologie des Gesichtsinnes.* Leipzig: Knobloch, 1826. P. 46. **481**

Müller, J. H. *Handbuch der Physiologie des Menschen fur Vorlesungen.* Coblenz: Holscher, 1834–1840. Trans. from the German by W. Baly under the title, *Elements of physiology.* Philadelphia: Lea & Blanchard, 1843. Vol. II, Pp. 276–393. **411**

Mundy-Castle, A. C. Pictorial depth perception in Ghanaian children. *International Journal of Psychology,* 1966, *1,* 289–301. **500**

Munn, N. L. *Handbook of psychological research on the rat.* Boston: Houghton Mifflin, 1950. **612, 662n, 821**

Munsinger, *see* Hershenson, M., 1965.

Murakami, M., *see* Brown, K. T., 1964, 1965; Tomita, T., 1967.

Murdock, B. B., Jr. Effects of failure and retroactive inhibition in mediating an instrumental act. *Journal of Experimental Psychology,* 1952, *44,* 156–164. **781**

Murdock, B. B., Jr. "Backward" learning in paired associates. *Journal of Experimental Psychology,* 1956, *51,* 213–215. **1056, 1064**

Murdock, B. B., Jr. Transfer designs and formulas, *Psychological Bulletin,* 1957, *54,* 313–326. **1022, 1026**

Murdock, B. B., Jr. "Backward" associations in transfer and learning. *Journal of Experimental Psychology,* 1958, *55,* 111–114. **1064**

Murdock, B. B., Jr. The immediate retention of unrelated words. *Journal of Experimental Psychology,* 1960, *60,* 222–234. **1044**

Murdock, B. B., Jr. The retention of individual items. *Journal of Experimental Psychology,* 1961, *62.* 618–625. (a) **1110, 1111**

Murdock, B. B., Jr. Short-term retention of single paired associates. *Psychological Reports,* 1961, *8,* 280. (b) **997, 998, 1111, 1112, 1118**

Murdock, B. B., Jr. Short-term retention of single paired associates. *Journal of Experimental Psychology,* 1963, *65,* 433–443. (a) **1111, 1112, 1114, 1118**

Murdock, B. B., Jr. Short-term memory and paired-associate learning. *Journal of Verbal Learning and Verbal Behavior,* 1963, *2,* 320–328. (b) **1111, 1118**

Murdock, B. B., Jr. Interpolated recall in short-term memory. *Journal of Experimental Psychology,* 1963, *66,* 525–532. (c) **1118**

Murdock, B. B., Jr. Proactive inhibition in short-term memory. *Journal of Experimental Psychology,* 1964, *68,* 184–189. **1111, 1114, 1118**

Murdock, B. B., Jr. Distractor and probe techniques in short-term memory. *Canadian Journal of Psychology,* 1967, *21,* 25–36. (a) **1110, 1112**

Murdock, B. B., Jr. Recent developments in short-term memory. *British Journal of Psychology,* 1967, *58,* 421–433. (b) **1116**

Murphy, G. An experimental study of literary *vs.* scientific types. *American Journal of Psychology,* 1917, *28,* 238–262. **875**

Murphy, G., *see also* Schafer, R., 1943; Solley, C. M., 1960.

Murphy, R., *see* Glanzer, M., in press.

Murray, E. N., *see* Katkin, E. S., 1968.

Musatti, C. L. Sui fenomeni stereocinatici. *Archivio Italiano di Psicologia,* 1924, *3,* 105–120. **523**

Mussatti, C. L. Forma e assimilazione. *Archivio Italiano di Psicologia,* 1931, *9,* 61–156. **437**

Muus, R., *see* Entwisle, D. R., 1964.

Myers, A. E., *see* Hake, H. W., 1969.

Myers, A. K. Onset vs. termination of stimulus energy as the CS in avoidance conditioning and pseudoconditioning. *Journal of Comparative and Physiological Psychology,* 1960, *53,* 72–78. **728**

Myers, A. K., & Miller, N. E. Failure to find a learned drive based on hunger: Evidence for learning motivated by "exploration." *Journal of Comparative and Physiological Psychology,* 1954, *47,* 428–436. **804**

Myers, A. K., *see also* Coons, E. E., 1960.

Myers, J. L., & Atkinson, R. C. Choice behavior and reward structure. *Journal of Mathematical Psychology,* 1964, *1,* 170–203. **933**

Myers, J. L., Fort, J. G., Katz, L., & Suydam, M. M. Differential monetary gains and losses and event probabilities in a two-choice situation. *Journal of Experimental Psychology,* 1963, *66,* 521–522. **918**

Myers, J. L., Suydam, M. N., & Heuckeroth, O. Choice

behavior and reward structure: Differential payoff. *Journal of Mathematical Psychology,* 1966, *3,* 458–469. **933**

Myers, J. L., *see also* Gambino, B., 1966; Jones, M. R., 1966.

Myers, L., *see* Collier, G., 1961.

Myers, N. A., *see* Leibowitz, H., 1955.

Nachman, M. Learned aversion to the taste of lithium chloride and generalization to other salts. *Journal of Comparative and Physiological Psychology,* 1963, *56,* 343–349. **180**

Nachman, M., & Pfaffmann, C. Gustatory nerve discharge in normal and sodium-deficient rats. *Journal of Comparative and Physiological Psychology,* 1963, *56,* 1007–1011. **189**

Nachmias, J. Two-dimensional motion of the retinal image during monocular fixation. *Journal of the Optical Society of America,* 1959, *49,* 901–908. **374, 386, 387**

Nachmias, J. Effect of exposure duration on visual contrast sensitivity with square-wave gratings. *Journal of the Optical Society of America,* 1967, *57,* 421–427. **304**

Nachmias, J., *see also* Gleitman, H., 1964; Heinemann, E. G., 1959.

Nafe, J. P. Dermal sensitivity with special reference to the qualities of tickle and itch. *Journal of Genetic Psychology,* 1927, *34,* 14–27. **134**

Nafe, J. P. Pressure, pain, and temperature senses. In C. A. Murchison (Ed.), *A handbook of general experimental psychology.* Worcester, Mass.: Clark University Press, 1934. Pp. 1037–1087. **154**

Nafe, J. P., & Kenshalo, D. R. Stimulation and neural response. *American Journal of Psychology,* 1958, *71,* 199–208. **132**

Nafe, J. P., & Wagoner, K. S. The nature of sensory adaptation. *Journal of General Psychology,* 1941, *25,* 295–321. (a) **130, 131**

Nafe, J. P., & Wagoner, K. S. The nature of pressure adaptation. *Journal of General Psychology,* 1941, *25,* 323–351. (b) **130, 131**

Nafe, J. P., *see also* Kenshalo, D. R., 1962.

Nagel, E. *The structure of science.* New York: Harcourt, Brace, 1961. **906**

Nagge, J. W. An experimental test of the theory of associative interference. *Journal of Experimental Psychology,* 1935, *18,* 663–682. **1084**

Nahinsky, I. D. A duoprocess model for paired-associate learning. *Psychological Reports,* 1964, *14,* 467–471. **994**

Nahinsky, I. D. Statistics and moments-parameter estimates for a duoprocess paired-associate model. *Journal of Mathematical Psychology,* 1967, *4,* 140–150. **994**

Nakajima, S. Effects of chemical injection into the reticular formation of rats. *Journal of Comparative and Physiological Psychology,* 1964, *58,* 10–15. **843**

Nastuk, W. L. (Ed.) *Physical techniques in biological research.* Vol. V, *Electrophysiological methods,* Part A. New York, Academic Press, 1964. **92, 93**

Natsoulas, T. Converging operations for perceptual defense. *Psychological Bulletin,* 1965, *64,* 393–401. **444**

Natsoulas, T., What are perceptual reports about? *Psychological Bulletin,* 1967, *67,* 4, 249–272. **506**

Naunton, R. F., *see* Butler, R. A., 1964.

Naylor, A., *see* Washburn, M. F., 1931.

Neal, E. Visual localization of the vertical. *American Journal of Psychology,* 1926, *37,* 287–291. **539**

Nealey, S. M., & Edwards, B. J. "Depth perception" in rats without pattern vision experience. *Journal of Comparative and Physiological Psychology,* 1960, *53,* 468–469. **549**

Nealey, S. M., & Riley, D. A. Loss and recovery of discrimination of visual depth in dark-reared rats. *American Journal of Psychology,* 1963, *76,* 329–332. **549**

Neff, W. D. Sensory discrimination. In John Field, H. W. Magoun, & V. E. Hall (Eds.) *Handbook of physiology.* Vol III, Sec. I. *Neurophysiology.* Washington, D. C.: American Physiological Society, 1960. Pp. 1447–1470. **118**

Neff, W. D. Neural mechanisms in auditory discrimination. In W. A. Rosenblith (Ed.), *Sensory communication.* New York: Wiley, 1961. **264**

Neff, W. S. A critical investigation of the visual apprehension of movement. *American Journal of Psychology,* 1936, *48,* 1–42. **526**

Neilson, D. R., Jr., *see* Spencer, W. A., 1966.

Neilsen, T. I. Volition: A new experimental approach. *Scandinavian Journal of Psychology,* 1963, *4,* 225–230. **536**

Neimark, E. D. Effects of type of non-reinforcement and number of alternative responses in two verbal conditioning situations. *Journal of Experimental Psychology,* 1956, *52,* 209–220. **933**

Neimark, E., Greenhouse, P., Law, S., & Weinheimer, S. The effect of rehearsal-preventing task upon retention of CVC syllables. *Journal of Verbal Learning and Verbal Behavior,* 1965, *4,* 280–285. **1119**

Neisser, U. An experimental distinction between perceptual process and verbal response. *Journal of Experimental Psychology,* 1954, *47,* 399–402. **445n**

Neisser, U. *Cognitive psychology.* New York: Appleton, 1967. **255, 444, 456**

Neisser, U., & Weene, B. Hierarchies in concept attainment. *Journal of Experimental Psychology,* 1962, *64,* 640–645. **941, 965, 967**

Neisser, U., *see also* Gleitman, H., 1954; Wallach, H., 1953.

Nelson, L. M., *see* Halpern, B. P., 1965.

Nelson, P. G., Erulkar, S. D., & Bryan, J. S. Responses of units of the inferior colliculus to time-varying acoustic stimuli. *Journal of Neurophysiology,* 1966, *24,* 834–860. **232**

Nelson, T. M., & Bartley, S. H. The perception of form in an unstructured field. *Journal of General Psychology,* 1956, *54,* 57–63. **515**

Neuhaus, W. Experimentelle Untersuchung der Scheinbewegung. *Archiv für gesamte Psychologie,* 1930, *75,* 315–458. **526**

Neun, M. E., *see* Boynton, R. M., 1964.

Neuringer, A. J. Many responses per food reward with free food present. *Science,* 1970, *169,* 503–504. **692n**

Newell, A., Shaw, J. G., & Simon, H. A. Elements of a theory of human problem solving. *Psychological Review,* 1958, *65,* 151–166. **976**

Newell, A., & Simon, H. A. The simulation of human thought. In *Current trends in psychological theory.* Pittsburgh: University of Pittsburgh, 1961. Pp. 152–179. **976**

Newell, A., & Simon, H. A. GPS, a program that simulates human thought. In E. A. Feigenbaum & J. Feldman (Eds.), *Computers and thought.* New York: McGraw-Hill, 1963. Pp. 279–293. **976**

Newhall, S. M. The reversal of simultaneous brightness contrast. *Journal of Experimental Psychology,* 1942, *31,* 393–409. **408**

Newhall, S. M., Burnham, R. W., & Clark, J. R. Comparison of successive with simultaneous color matching. *Journal of the Optical Society of America,* 1957, *47,* 43–56. **424**

Newhall, S. M., Nickerson, D., & Judd, D. B. Final report of the O.S.A. subcommittee on spacing of the Munsell colors. *Journal of the Optical Society of America,* 1943, *33,* 385. **360**

Newman, E. B., *see* Stevens, S. S., 1936; Wallach, H., 1949.

Newman, F. L., & Baron, M. R. Stimulus generalization along the dimension of angularity: A comparison of training procedures. *Journal of Comparative and Physiological Psychology,* 1965, *60,* 59–63. **762**

Newton, J. M., & Wickens, D. D. Retroactive inhibition as a function of the temporal position of interpolated learning. *Journal of Experimental Psychology,* 1956, *51,* 149–154. **1037, 1091, 1100**

Nicholls, M. F., & Kimble, G. A. Effect of instructions upon eyelid conditioning. *Journal of Experimental Psychology,* 1964, *67,* 400–402. **561**

Nickerson, D., *see* Newhall, S. M., 1943.

Nicks, D. C. Prediction of sequential two-choice decisions from event runs. *Journal of Experimental Psychology,* 1959, *57,* 105–114. **920, 921**

Nicolaides, S. Early systemic responses to orogastric stimulation in the regulation of food and water balance: Functional and electrophysiological data. *Annals of the New York Academy of Sciences,* 1969, *157,* 1176–1203. **797**

Niehl, E. W., *see* Riggs, L. A., 1960.

Nilsson, W. D., *see* Mayzner, M. S., 1965.

Nissen, H. W., *see* Chow, K. L., 1955.

Niven, J. I., & Brown, R. H. Visual resolution as a function of intensity and exposure time in the human fovea. *Journal of the Optical Society of America,* 1944, *34,* 738–743. **303**

Nixon, J. C., & Glorig, A. Noise-induced permanent threshold shift at 2000 cps and 4000 cps. *Journal of the Acoustical Society of America,* 1961, *33,* 904–908. **236**

Noble, C. E. An analysis of meaning. *Psychological Review,* 1952, *59,* 421–430. (a) **850, 851, 852, 856, 982, 1127**

Noble, C. E. The role of stimulus meaning (*m*) in serial verbal learning. *Journal of Experimental Psychology,* 1952, *43,* 437–446. (b) **854, 899**

Noble, C. E. The meaning-familiarity relationship. *Psychological Review,* 1953, *60,* 89–98. **982**

Noble, C. E. Emotionality (*e*) and meaningfulness. *Psychological Reports,* 1958, *4,* 16. (a) **900**

Noble, C. E. Tables of the *e* and *m* scales. *Psychological Reports,* 1958, *4,* 590. (b) **900**

Noble, C. E. Measurements of association value (a), rated associations (a'), and scaled meaningfulness (*m'*) for the 2100 CVC combinations of the English alphabet. *Psychological Reports,* 1961, *8,* 487–521. **853**

Noble, C. E. Meaningfulness and familiarity. In C. N. Cofer & B. S. Musgrave (Eds.), *Verbal behavior and learning: Problems and processes,* New York: McGraw-Hill, 1963. Pp. 76–119. **853, 856, 897, 899**

Noble, C. E., & Parker, G. V. C. The Montana scale of meaningfulness. *Psychological Reports,* 1960, *7,* 325–331. **852, 853**

Noble, C. E., Stockwell, F. E., & Pryer, M. W. Meaningfulness (*m'*) and association value in paired-associate syllable learning. *Psychological Reports,* 1957, *3,* 441–452. **852, 853, 857, 982**

Noble, C. E., *see also* Cieutat, V. J., 1958.

Nodine, C. F., *see* Goss, A. E., 1965.

Norcross, K. J. Effects on discrimination performance of similarity of previously acquired stimulus names. *Journal of Experimental Psychology,* 1958, *56,* 305–309. **783**

Norcross, K. J., & Spiker, C. C. The effects of type of stimulus pretraining on discrimination performance in preschool children. *Child Development,* 1957, *28,* 79–84. **782**

Norcross, K. J., & Spiker, C. C. Effects of mediated associations on transfer in paired-associate learning. *Journal of Experimental Psychology,* 1958, *55,* 129–134. **1077**

Nord, S., *see* Makous, W., 1963.

Nordlie, P. G., *see* Havron, M. D., 1957.

Norman, D., *see* Waugh, N. C., 1965.

Norman, D. A., *see* Wickelgren, W. A., 1966.

Norman, M. F. Incremental learning on random trials. *Journal of Mathematical Psychology,* 1964, *1,* 336–350. **997**

Norris, E. B., & Grant, D. A. Eyelid conditioning as affected by verbally induced inhibitory set and counter reinforcement. *American Journal of Psychology,* 1948, *61,* 37–49. **561**

Norris, E. B., *see also* Grant, S. A., 1947.

Norrison, W., *see* Morrison, G. R., 1966.

Notterman, J. M., & Mintz, D. E. Exteroceptive cueing of response force. *Science,* 1962, *135,* 1070–1071. **700**

Notterman, J. M., & Mintz, D. E. *Dynamics of behavior.* New York: Wiley, 1965. **700**

Novell, K., *see* Collier, G., 1967.

Nozawa, S. Zukel no lizokushi to sono zonko. 1. Gibson koka no likkrnyekl Kenkyer (Prolonged inspection of a figure and its after-effects. 1. Experimental study of the Gibson effect.) *Japanese Journal of Psychology,* 1953, *24,* 47–58. **470**

Nulsen, F. E., *see* Collins, W. F., 1960.

Nunnally, J. C., & Flaugher, R. L. Psychological implications of word usage. *Science,* 1963, *140,* 775–781. **875**

Nye, P. W., *see* Fender, D. H., 1961

Oakley, B. Altered temperature and taste responses from cross-regenerated sensory nerves in the rat's tongue. *Journal of Physiology,* 1967, *188,* 353–371. **173**

Oakley, B., & Benjamin, R. M. Neural mechanisms of taste. *Physiological Reviews,* 1966, *46,* 173–211. **180**

Oakley, B., *see also* Borg, G., 1967; Makous, W., 1963.

Obonai, T. Induction effects in estimates of extent. *Journal of Experimental Psychology,* 1954, *47,* 57–60. **508n**

Obonai, T., *see also* Ikeda, H., 1953.

Ochs, S. *Elements of neurophysiology.* New York: Wiley, 1965. **95**

O'Connell, D. N., *see* Wallach, H., 1953.

O'Connell, R. Quantitative stimulation of single olfactory receptors. Doctoral dissertation, Department of Physiology, Upstate Medical Center, State University of New York, 1967. **200**

O'Connell, R. J., & Mozell, M. M. Quantitative stimulation of frog olfactory receptors. *Journal of Neurophysiology,* 1969, *32,* 51–63. **200, 217, 218**

O'Connor, J. *Born that way.* Baltimore: Williams & Wilkins, 1928. **874n**

Odom, P., *see* Jenkins, J. J., 1965.

Ogawa, H., *see* Yamashita, S., 1967.

Ogle, K. N. *Researches in binocular vision.* Philadelphia: Saunders, 1950. **480, 481, 539n**

Ogle, K. N. Precision and validity of stereoscopic depth perception from double images. *Journal of the Optical Society of America,* 1953, *43,* 906–913. **491, 493**

Ogle, K., & Reiher, L. Stereoscopic depth perception from after-images. *Vision Research,* 1962, *2,* 439–447. **491n**

Öhrwall, H. Untersuchungen über den Geschmackssinn. *Skandinavisches Archiv für Physiologie,* 1891, *2,* 1–69. **175, 178**

O'Kelly, L. I. The psychophysiology of motivation. *Annual Review of Psychology,* 1963, *14,* 57–92. **794n**

Oldfield, R. C. Continuous recording of sensory thresholds and other psychophysical variables. *Nature,* 1949, *164,* 581. **20**

Olds, J. Physiological mechanisms in reward. In M. R. Jones (Ed.), *Nebraska symposium on motivation.* Lincoln: University of Nebraska Press, 1955. **642, 653**

Olds, J. Pleasure centers in the brain. *Scientific American,* 1956, *193,* 105–116. **642**

Olds, J. Self-stimulation of the brain. *Science,* 1958, *127,* 315–324. (a) **651**

Olds, J. Effects of hunger and male sex hormone on self-stimulation of the brain. *Journal of Comparative and Physiological Psychology,* 1958, *51,* 320–324. (b) **654**

Olds, J. Satiation effects in self-stimulation of the brain. *Journal of Comparative and Physiological Psychology,* 1958, *51,* 675–678. (c) **655**

Olds, J., & Milner, P. M. Positive reinforcement produced by electrical stimulation of septal area and other regions of rat brain. *Journal of Comparative and Physiological Psychology,* 1954, *47,* 419–427. **642**

Olds, J., & Peretz, B. A motivational analysis of the reticular activating system. *Electroencephalography and Clinical Neurophysiology,* 1960, *12,* 445–454. **844**

Olds, J., & Sinclair, J. C. Self-stimulation in the obstruction box. *American Psychologist,* 1957, *12,* 464. **651**

Olds, J., *see also* Margules, D. L., 1962; Olds, M. E., 1963, 1965; Seward, J. P., 1959.

Olds, M. E., & Olds, J. Approach-avoidance analysis of rat

diencephalon. *Journal of Comparative Neurology,* 1963, *120,* 259–295. **647**

Olds, M., & Olds, J. Drives, rewards and the brain. In T. M. Newcomb (Ed.), *New directions in psychology II.* New York: Holt, Rinehart and Winston, 1965. **646, 657, 658**

O'Leary, J., *see* Heinbecker, P., 1933.

Olivier, K., & Kausler, D. H. Transfer in the *A–B, C–B* paradigm as a function of stimulus class. *Psychonomic Science,* 1966, *5,* 47–48. **1064**

Olsen, W. O., & Carhart, K. Integration of acoustic power at threshold by normal hearers. *Journal of the Acoustical Society of America,* 1966, *40,* 591–599. **234**

Olson, R. K., *see* Attneave, F., 1966.

Olum, V., *see* Gibson, E. J., 1960; Gibson, J. J., 1955.

O'Neill, J. J. Recognition of intelligibility text materials in context and isolation. *Journal of Speech and Hearing Disabilities* 1957, *22,* 87–90. **256**

Onizawa, T. Research on the size of the projected afterimage: I. On the method of measurement. *Tohuku Psychologica Folia,* 1954, *14,* 75–78. **511**

Ono, H. Apparent distance as a function of familiar size, *Journal of Experimental Psychology,* 1969, *79,* 109–115. **496, 497**

Ono, H., *see also* Festinger, L., 1967.

Oppel, T. W., *see* Hardy, J. D., 1937, 1938.

Orbach, J. Retinal locus as a factor in recognition of visually perceived words. *American Journal of Psychology,* 1953, *65,* 555–562. **444**

Orbach, J., Ehrlich, D., & Heath, H. A. Reversibility of the Necker cube: I. An examination of the concept of "satiation of orientation." *Perceptual and Motor Skills,* 1963, *17,* 439–458. **471**

Orbach, J., Ehrlich, D., & Vainstein, E. Reversibility of the Necker Cube: III. Effects of interpolation on reversal rate of the cube presented repetitively. *Perceptual and Motor Skills,* 1963, *17,* 459–464. **471**

Orbison, W. D. Shape as a function of the vector field. *American Journal of Psychology,* 1939, *52,* 31–45. **459**

Orlansky, J. The effect of similarity and difference in form on apparent visual movement. *Archives of Psychology* (New York), 1940, No. *246.* **527**

Osgood, C. E. Meaningful similarity and interference in learning. *Journal of Experimental Psychology,* 1946, *36,* 277–301. **1052, 1053, 1054, 1057, 1083**

Osgood, C. E. An investigation into the causes of retroactive inhibition. *Journal of Experimental Psychology,* 1948, *38,* 132–154. **1052, 1053, 1054, 1083**

Osgood, C. E. The similarity paradox in human learning: A resolution. *Psychological Review,* 1949, *56,* 132–143. **1052, 1053, 1054**

Osgood, C. E. *Method and theory in experimental psychology.* New York: Oxford, 1953. **408, 419, 773, 877, 895, 1052**

Osgood, C. E., & Anderson, L. Certain relations among experienced contingencies, associative structure, and contingencies in coded messages. *American Journal of Psychology,* 1957, *70,* 411–420. **862**

Osgood, C. E., & Heyer, A. W. A new interpretation of the figural after-effect. *Psychological Review,* 1952, *59,* 98–118. **470n, 472**

Osgood, C. E., *see also* Howes, D., 1954.

O'Shaunessy, K., *see* Goulet, L. R., 1967.

Osman, E., & Raab, D. Temporal masking of clicks by noise bursts. *Journal of the Acoustical Society of America,* 1963, *35,* 1939–1941. **241**

Ostojčić, A., *see* Bujas, Z., 1941.

Ottoson, D. Analysis of the electrical activity of the olfactory epithelium. *Acta Physiologica Scandinavia,* 1956, *35* (suppl. 122), 1–83. **211, 221**

Ottoson, D. Some aspects of the function of the olfactory system. *Pharmacological Review,* 1963, *15,* 1–42. **220**

Ough, C. S., & Stone, H. An olfactometer for rapid and critical odor measurement. *Journal of Food Science,* 1961, *26,* 452–456. **200**

Ough, C. S., *see also* Stone, H., 1962.

Over, R. An experimentally induced conflict between vision and proprioception. *British Journal of Psychology,* 1966, *57,* 335–341. **536**

Overmier, J. B., & Seligman, M. E. P. Effects of inescapable shock upon subsequent escape and avoidance responding. *Journal of Comparative and Physiological Psychology,* 1967, *63,* 28–33. **708, 724**

Overmier, J. B., *see also* Church, R. M., 1966.

Owen, D. H., *see* Brown, D. R., 1967.

Owens, J. A., & Brown, D. L. ICS reinforcement of DRL behavior in the rat. *Psychonomic Science,* 1968, *10,* 309–310. **654**

Oyama, T. Figure-ground dominance as a function of sector angle, brightness, hue, and orientation. *Journal of Experimental Psychology,* 1960, *60,* 299–305. **433**

Oyama, T., & Torii, S. Experimental studies of figure-ground reversal: I. The effects of area, voluntary control and prolonged observation in the continuous presentation. *Japanese Journal of Psychology,* 1955, *26* (Japanese text, 178–188; English summary, 217–218). **433**

Oyama, T., *see also* Sagara, M., 1957.

Ozier, M., *see* Tulving, E., 1965.

Paczewitz, G., *see* Bartley, S. H., 1957.

Page, H. A., *see* Wyckoff, L. B., 1954.

Paivio, A. Abstractness, imagery, and meaningfulness in paired-associate learning. *Journal of Verbal Learning and Verbal Behavior,* 1965, *4,* 32–38. **858**

Palermo, D. S. Proactive interference and facilitation as a function of amount of training and stress. *Journal of Experimental Psychology,* 1957, *53,* 293–296. **790**

Palermo, D. S. Backward associations in the paired-associate learning of fourth and sixth grade children. *Psychological Reports.* 1961, *9,* 227–233. **1064**

Palermo, D. S. Word associations and children's verbal behavior. In L. P. Lipsitt & C. C. Spiker (Eds.), *Advances in child development and behavior.* Vol. 1. New York: Academic Press, 1963. **873, 874**

Palermo, D. S. Mediated association in the paired-associate learning of children using heterogeneous and homogeneous lists. *Journal of Experimental Psychology,* 1966, *71,* 711–717. **1074, 1077**

Palermo, D. S., & Jenkins, J. J. Word association norms: Grade school through college. Minneapolis: University of Minnesota Press, 1964. (a) **861, 879, 888**

Palermo, D. S., & Jenkins, J. J. Paired-associate learning as a function of the strength of links in the associative chain. *Journal of Verbal Learning and Verbal Behavior,* 1964, *3,* 406–412. (b) **888**

Palermo, D. S., & Jenkins, J. J. Sex differences in word associations. *Journal of General Psychology,* 1965, *72,* 77–84. (a) **873**

Palermo, D. S., & Jenkins, J. J. Changes in the word associations of fourth- and fifth-grade children from 1916 to 1961. *Journal of Verbal Learning and Verbal Behavior,* 1965, *4,* 180–187. (b) **875**

Palermo, D. S., *see also* Castaneda, A., 1955, 1956; Jenkins, J. J., 1965.

Palfai, T., *see* Bindra, D., 1967.

Pallie, W., *see* Weddell, G., 1954, 1955.

Palmer, E., *see* Weddell, G., 1955.

Pangborn, R. M., *see* Amerine, M., 1965; Berg, H. W., 1963; Stone, H., 1962.

Panksepp, J., *see* Gandelman, R., 1968.

Panum, P. L. *Physiologische Untersuchungen über das Sehen mit zwei Augen.* Kiel: Schwers, 1858. **487, 488**

Pappert, S., Centrally produced geometrical illusion. *Nature,* 1961, *191,* 733. **471n**

Pappert, S., *see also* Taylor, J. G., 1956.

Parducci, A., & Brookshire, K. Figural after-effects with tachistoscopic presentation. *American Journal of Psychology*, 1956, *69*, 635-639. **469**

Park, J., *see* Epstein, W., 1961, 1962, 1963, 1964.

Parker, G. V. C., *see* Noble, C. E., 1960.

Parkes, A. S. An olfactory block to pregnancy in mice. Part 2: Hormonal factors involved. *Proceedings of the 4th International Congress on Animal Reproduction* (The Hague), 1961, 163-165. **209**

Parkes, A. S., & Bruce, H. M. Olfactory stimuli in mammalian reproduction. *Science*, 1961, *134*, 1049-1054. **209**

Parks, T. E. Post-retinal visual storage. *American Journal of Psychology*, 1965, *78*, 145-147. **455**

Parks, T. E., *see also* Thurlow, W. R., 1961.

Parloff, M. B., *see* Caron, A. J., 1963.

Parnes, E. W., *see* Mandler, G., 1957.

Parrish, M., Lundy, R. M., & Leibowitz, H. W. Hypnotic age-regression and magnitudes of the Ponzo and Poggendorff illusions. *Science*, 1968, *159*, 1375-1376. **550**

Pastore, N. Some remarks on the Ames oscillatory effect. *Psychological Review*, 1952, *59*, 319-323. **518**

Patt, M., *see* Hecht, S., 1938.

Patten, R. L., & Rudy, J. W. Orienting driving classical conditioning: Acquired vs. unconditioned responding. *Psychonomic Science*, 1967, *7*, 27-28. **621**

Patterson, G. H., *see* Lemmon, W. B., 1964.

Patterson, J., *see* Young, R. K., 1963.

Pattle, R. E., & Weddell, G. Observations on electrical stimulation of pain fibers in an exposed human sensory nerve. *Journal of Neurophysiology*, 1948, *11*, 93-98. **156**

Patton, H. D., *see* Ruch, T. C., 1965.

Patton, R. M., *see* Fink, J. B., 1953.

Paul, C., & Silverstein, A. Relation of experimentally produced interlist intrusions to unlearning and retroactive inhibition. *Journal of Experimental Psychology*, 1968, *76*, 480-485. **1097**

Pautler, E. L., *see* Tomita, T., 1967.

Pavlik, W. B., *see* Reynolds, W. F., 1964.

Pavlov, I. P. *Conditioned reflexes*. (Translated by G. V. Anrep.) London: Oxford, 1927. (Reprinted, New York: Dover, 1960.) **554, 555, 556, 557, 559, 560n, 562, 563, 564, 570n, 573, 591, 596, 598, 608, 661, 689, 709, 729, 777**

Pavlov, I. P. *Lectures on conditioned reflexes*. (Tr. W. H. Gantt.) New York: International, 1928. **554n**

Pavlov, I. P. *Selected works*. Moscow: Foreign Languages Publishing House, 1955. **554n**

Pavlov, I. P. *Experimental psychology and other essays*. New York: Philosophical Library, 1957. **554n**

Pawlow, J. P. The scientific investigation of the psychical faculties or processes in the higher animals. *Lancet*, 1906, 911-915. *Science*, 1906, N.S. *24*, 613-619. **562**

Payne, J. W., *see* Braunstein, M. L., 1968.

Peak, G., *see* Crawford, J., 1967.

Pearce, D. G., *see* Martin, L., 1966, 1969.

Pearl, J., Walters, G. C., & Anderson, D. C. Suppressing effects of aversive stimulation on subsequently punished behavior. *Canadian Journal of Psychology*, 1964, *18*, 343-355. **737**

Pearsons, K. S., *see* Kryter, K. D., 1963.

Pechtel, C., *see* Masserman, J. H., 1953.

Peckham, R. H., Jr., & Amsel, A. Magnitude of reward and the frustration effect in a within-subjects design. *Psychonomic Science*, 1964, *1*, 285-286. **810**

Peiper, W. A., *see* Marx, M. H., 1962.

Penfield, W., & Rasmussen, T. *The cerebral cortex: A clinical study of localization of function*. New York: Macmillan, 1950. **126**

Penick, E. C., *see* Amsel, A., 1962.

Peretz, B., *see* Olds, J., 1960.

Perez-Cruet, J., Black, W. C., & Brady, J. V. Heart rate: Differential effects of hypothalamic and septal self-stimulation. *Science*, 1963, *140*, 1235-1236. **657**

Perin, C. J. A quantitative investigation of the delay-of-reinforcement gradient. *Journal of Experimental Psychology*, 1943, *32*, 37-51. **679**

Perin, C. T. Behavioral potentiality as a joint function of the amount of training and the degree of hunger at the time of extinction. *Journal of Experimental Psychology*, 1942, *30*, 93-113. **826**

Perkins, B. T., *see* Hull, C. L., 1940.

Perl, E. R., *see* Burgess, P. R., 1967.

Peskin, J. C., *see* Hecht, S., 1938.

Peter, R. Untersuchungen über die Beziehungen zwische primaren und sekundaren Faktoran der Tiefenwahrnehmung. *Archiv fur die Gesamte Psychologie*, 1915, *34*, 515-564. **479**

Peters, H. N. Mediate associations. *Journal of Experimental Psychology*, 1935, *18*, 20-48. **1071**

Peters, H. N., *see also* McGeoch, J. A., 1937.

Peterson, G. E., & Barney, H. L. Control methods used in a study of the vowels. *Journal of the Acoustical Society of America*, 1952, *24*, 175-184. **251**

Peterson, J., & Peterson, J. K. Does practice with inverting lenses make vision normal? *Psychological Monographs*, 1938, *50*, 12-37. **533**

Peterson, J. K., *see* Peterson, J., 1938.

Peterson, L. R. Prediction of response in verbal habit hierarchies. *Journal of Experimental Psychology*, 1956, *51*, 249-252. **862**

Peterson, L. R. Immediate memory: Data and theory. In C. N. Cofer & B. S. Musgrave (Eds.), *Verbal behavior and learning*. New York: McGraw-Hill, 1963. **1109, 1113**

Peterson, L. R. Reminiscence in short-term retention. *Journal of Experimental Psychology*, 1966, *71*, 115-118. (a) **1121**

Peterson, L. R. Short-term verbal memory and learning. *Psychological Review*, 1966, *73*, 193-207. (b) **1118, 1120, 1121**

Peterson, L. R., & Gentile, A. Proactive interference as a function of time between tests. *Journal of Experimental Psychology*, 1965, *70*, 473-478. **1113**

Peterson, L. R., Hillner, K., & Saltzman, D. Time between pairings and short-term memory. *Journal of Experimental Psychology*, 1962, *64*, 550-551. **1120**

Peterson, L. R., & James, L. Successive tests of short-term retention. *Psychonomic Science*, 1967, *8*, 423-424. **1113**

Peterson, L. R., & Peterson, M. J. Short-term retention of individual verbal items. *Journal of Experimental Psychology*, 1959, *58*, 193-198. **552, 972, 997, 998, 1110, 1112**

Peterson, L. R., & Peterson, M. J. Minimal paired-associate learning. *Journal of Experimental Psychology*, 1962, *63*, 521-527. **1000, 1112**

Peterson, L. R., Saltzman, D., Hillner, K., & Land, V. Recency and frequency in paired-associate learning. *Journal of Experimental Psychology*, 1962, *63*, 396-403. **1111, 1112, 1118**

Peterson, L. R., Wampler, R., Kirkpatrick, M., & Saltzman, D. Effect of spacing presentation on retention of a paired associate over short intervals. *Journal of Experimental Psychology*, 1963, *66*, 206-209. **1111, 1120**

Peterson, M. J. Effects of knowledge of results on a verbal mediating response. *Journal of Experimental Psychology*, 1963, *66*, 394-398. **1075**

Peterson, M. J. Cue trials, frequency of presentation, and mediating responses. *Journal of Experimental Psychology*, 1964, *67*, 432-438. **1073, 1075**

Peterson, M. J. Effects of delay intervals and meaningfulness on verbal mediating responses. *Journal of Experimental Psychology*, 1965, *69*, 60-66. **1073**

Peterson, M. J., & Blattner, K. C. Development of a verbal mediator. *Journal of Experimental Psychology*, 1963, *66*, 72-77. **1073, 1075**

Peterson, M. J., Colavita, F., Sheahan, D., & Blattner, K. C. Verbal mediating chains and response availability as a function of the acquisition paradigm. *Journal of Verbal Learning and Verbal Behavior,* 1964, *3,* 11-18. **1073, 1074**

Peterson, M. J., & Jamison, S. M. Effects of distribution of practice of the acquisition pairs upon mediating responses and response availability. *Journal of Experimental Psychology,* 1965, *70,* 549-558. **1073**

Peterson, M. J., *see also* Peterson, L. R., 1959, 1962.

Peterson, N. Control of behavior by presentation of an imprinted stimulus. *Science,* 1960, *132,* 1395-1396. **581, 587**

Peterson, N. Effect of monochromatic rearing on control of responding by wavelength. *Science,* 1962, *136,* 774-776. **762**

Peterson, O. F., *see* La Berge, D. L., 1962.

Peterson, W. M., *see* Kaufman, M. E., 1958.

Petraitis, J., *see* Wayner, M. J., 1967.

Pettigrew, T. F., *see* Allport, G. W., 1957.

Peyser, C. S., *see* Barrett, R. J., 1965.

Pfaffmann, C. Gustatory afferent impulses. *Journal of Cellular and Comparative Physiology,* 1941, *17,* 243-258. **180**

Pfaffmann, C. Taste and smell. In S. S. Stevens (Ed.), *Handbook of experimental psychology.* New York: Wiley, 1951. Pp. 1143-1171. **212, 628**

Pfaffmann, C. Gustatory nerve impulses in rat, cat and rabbit. *Journal of Neurophysiology,* 1955, *18,* 429-440. **173, 179, 180**

Pfaffmann, C. The sense of taste. In J. Field, H. W. Magoun, & V. E. Hall (Eds.), *Handbook of physiology.* Vol. I. Washington, D. C.: American Physiological Society, 1959. Pp. 507-533. **174, 179**

Pfaffmann, C. The pleasures of sensation. *Psychological Review,* 1960, *67,* 253-268. **171, 176**

Pfaffmann, C. Taste, its sensory and motivating properties. *American Scientist,* 1964, *52,* 187-206. **189**

Pfaffmann, C., & Bare, J. K. Gustatory nerve discharges in normal and adrenalectomized rats. *Journal of Comparative and Physiological Psychology,* 1950, *43,* 320-324. **189**

Pfaffmann, C., Bartoshuk, L. M., & McBurney, D. H. Taste psychophysics. In L. M. Beidler (Ed.), *Handbook of taste physiology.* New York: Springer-Verlag, 1969. **183**

Pfaffmann, C., Erickson, R. P., Frommer, G. P., & Halpern, B. F. Gustatory discharges in the rat medulla and thalamus. In W. A. Rosenblith (Ed.), *Sensory communication.* New York: Wiley, 1961. Pp. 455-473. **172, 182**

Pfaffmann, C., Fisher, G. L., & Frank, M. K. The sensory and behavioral factors in taste preferences. In T. Hayashi (Ed.), *Olfaction and taste.* Vol. 2. New York: Pergamon, 1967. Pp. 361-381. **176**

Pfaffmann, C., & Hagstrom, E. C. Factors influencing taste sensitivity to sugar. *American Journal of Physiology,* 1955, 183. (Abstract) **189**

Pfaffmann, C., & Powers, J. B. Partial adaptation of taste. *Psychonomic Science,* 1964, *1,* 41-42. **174**

Pfaffmann, C., Young, P. T., Dethier, V. G., Richter, C. P., & Stellar, E. The preparation of solutions for research in chemoreception and food acceptance. *Journal of Comparative and Physiological Psychology,* 1954, *49,* 93-96. **625n**

Pfaffmann, C., *see also* Bartoshuk, L. M., 1964, 1965; Engen, T., 1959; Fisher, G. L., 1965; Makous, W., 1963; McBurney, D. H., 1963; Mozell, M. M., 1954; Nachman, M., 1963; Warren, R. M., 1959; Warren, R. P., 1958.

Pheiffer, C. H. Book retinoscopy. *American Journal of Optometry,* 1955, *32,* 540-545. **393**

Phillips, L. W., *see* Postman, L., 1955, 1961.

Piaget, J. *Judgment and reasoning in the child.* New York: Harcourt, 1926. **540**

Piaget, J., & Lambercier, M. Recherches sur le developpement des perceptions: III. Le problème de la comparaison visuelle en profondeur (constance de la grandeur) et l'erreur systématique de l'étalon. *Archives de Psychologie* (Genève), 1943, *29,* 253-308. **550**

Pick, H. L., Jr., & Hay, J. C. Adaptation to prismatic distortion. *Psychonomic Science,* 1964, *1,* 199-200. **542**

Pick, H. L., Jr., & Hay, J. C. A passive test of the Held re-afference hypothesis. *Perceptual and Motor Skills,* 1965, *20,* 1070-1072. **536**

Pick, H. L., *see also* Gibson, E. J., 1958; Hay, J. C., 1965, 1966.

Pickersgill, M. On knowing with which eye one is seeing. *Quarterly Journal of Experimental Psychology,* 1961, *13,* 168-172. **489**

Pickleman, J. R., *see* Campbell, B. A., 1961.

Pieper, W. A., *see* Marx, M. H., 1963.

Pierce, A. H. *Studies in auditory and visual space perception.* New York: Longmans, Green, 1901. **259**

Pierce, J. Determinants of threshold for form. *Psychological Bulletin,* 1963, *60,* 391-407. **444, 445**

Pierce, J. R., *see* Bergeijk, W. A. van, 1960.

Pieron, H. Nervous pathways of cutaneous pains. *Science,* 1959, *129,* 1547-1548. **161**

Pierrel, R. Taste effects resulting from intermittent electrical stimulation of the tongue. *Journal of Experimental Psychology,* 1955, *49,* 374-380. **178**

Piggins, D. J., *see* Evans, C. R., 1963.

Pilzecker, A., *see* Müller, G. E., 1900.

Pirenne, M. H. *Vision and the eye.* London: Chapman and Hall, 1948. **296, 319**

Pirenne, M. H., *see also* Hecht, S., 1942.

Pitblado, C., *see* Kaufman, L., 1965.

Pitts, W. H., *see* Gesteland, R. C., 1965; Lettvin, J. Y., 1959.

Plateau, J. Ueber das Phänomen der zufälligen Farben. *Poggendorff's Annalen der Physiologie und Chemie,* 1834, *32,* 543-554. **411**

Platt, J. R. Strong inference. *Science,* 1964, *146,* 347. **917**

Platt, S. A., *see* Weisman, R. G., 1966.

Pliskoff, S. S., & Hawkins, T. D. A method for increasing the reinforcement magnitude of intracranial stimulation. *Journal of the Experimental Analysis of Behavior,* 1967, *10,* 281-289. **650, 654**

Pliskoff, S. S., Hawkins, T. D. & Wright, J. E. Some observations on the discriminative stimulus hypothesis and rewarding electrical stimulation of the brain. *Psychological Record,* 1964, *14,* 179-184. **675**

Plomp, R. The ear as a frequency analyzer. *Journal of the Acoustical Society of America,* 1964, *36,* 1628-1636. **250**

Plomp, R. Detectability threshold for combination tones. *Journal of the Acoustical Society of America,* 1965, *37,* 1110-1123. **238**

Pochin, E. E., *see* Lewis, T., 1937.

Podd, M., *see* Spear, N. E., 1966.

Podell, H. A. A quantitative study of convergent association. *Journal of Verbal Learning and Verbal Behavior,* 1963, *2,* 234-241. **872**

Poffenberger, A. T. The influence of improvement in one simple mental process upon other related processes. *Journal of Educational Psychology,* 1915, *6,* 459-474. **1045**

Poffenberger, A. T., *see also* Hollingsworth, H. L., 1917.

Poggio, G. F., & Mountcastle, V. B. A study of the functional contributions of the lemniscal and spinothalamic systems to somatic sensibility: Central nervous mechanisms in pain. *Johns Hopkins Hospital Bulletin,* 1960, *106,* 266-316. **163**

Poizner, S., *see* Flock, H. R., 1966.

Pollack, I. Specification of sound pressure levels. *American Journal of Psychology,* 1949, *62,* 412-417. **226**

Pollack, I. Message uncertainty and message reception. *Journal of the Acoustical Society of America,* 1959, *31,* 1500-1508. **256**

Pollack, I. Ohm's acoustical law and short-term auditory

memory. *Journal of the Acoustical Society of America,* 1964, *36,* 2340–2345. **250**

Pollack, I., & Ficks, L. Information of elementary multi-dimensional auditory displays. *Journal of the Acoustical Society of America,* 1954, *26,* 155–158. **250**

Pollack, I., Rubenstein, H., & Decker, L. Intelligibility of known and unknown message sets. *Journal of the Acoustical Society of America,* 1959, *31,* 273–279. **255, 256**

Pollack, I., *see also* Sumby, W. H., 1954.

Pollack, M., *see* Battersby, W. S., 1956.

Pollack, R. H. Figural after-effects: Quantitative studies of displacement. *Australian Journal of Psychology,* 1958, *10,* 269–277. **470**

Pollack, R. H. Changes in the effects of fixation upon apparent distance in the third dimension. *Psychonomic Science,* 1967, *8,* 141–142. **474**

Pollack, R. H., & Chaplin, M. R. Perceptual behavior: The necessity for a developmental approach to its study. *Acta Psychologica,* 1963, *21,* 371–376. **550**

Pollack, R. H., & Silvar, S. D. Magnitude of the Müller-Lyer illusion in children as a function of pigmentation of the fundus oculi. *Psychonomic Science,* 1967, *8,* 83–84. **461**

Pollack, R. H., *see also* Day, R. H., 1959; Silvar, S. D., 1967.

Pollio, H. R. A simple matrix analysis of associative structure. *Journal of Verbal Learning and Verbal Behavior,* 1963, *2,* 166–169. (a) **879**

Pollio, H. R. Word association as a function of conditioned meaning. *Journal of Experimental Psychology,* 1963, *66,* 454–460. (b) **865**

Pollio, H. R. Composition of associative structures. *Journal of Experimental Psychology,* 1964, *67,* 199–208. (a) **879**

Pollio, H. R. Some semantic relations among word-associates. *American Journal of Psychology,* 1964, *77,* 249–256. (b) **864**

Pollio, H. R. Oppositional serial structures and paired-associate learning. *Psychological Reports,* 1966, *19,* 643–647. **889**

Pollio, H. R., & Draper, D. O. The effect of a serial structure on paired-associate learning. *Journal of Verbal Learning and Verbal Behavior,* 1966, *5,* 301–308. **889**

Pollio, H. R., & Lore, R. K. The effect of a semantically congruent context on word-association behavior. *Journal of Psychology,* 1965, *61,* 17–26. **865**

Pollio, H. R., *see also* Kasschau, R. A., 1967.

Polson, M., Restle, F., & Polson, P. Association and discrimination in paired-associate learning. *Journal of Experimental Psychology,* 1965, *69,* 47–55. **1006**

Polson, P., *see* Polson, M., 1965.

Polyak, S. L. *The retina.* Chicago: University of Chicago Press, 1941. **303**

Polyak, S. In H. L. Klüver (Ed.), *The vertebrate visual system.* Chicago: University of Chicago Press, 1957. **280, 281, 282**

Popper, J. Mediated generalization. In R. R. Bush & W. K. Estes (Eds.), *Studies in mathematical learning theory.* Stanford: Stanford University Press, 1959. Pp. 94–108. **949**

Popper, J., & Atkinson, R. C. Discrimination learning in a verbal conditioning situation. *Journal of Experimental Psychology,* 1958, *56,* 21–25. **926**

Pores, E. B., *see* Warren, R. M., 1958.

Porter, E. K. H. Factors in the fluctuations of fifteen ambiguous phenomena. *Psychological Record,* 1938, *2,* 231–253. **519**

Porter, J. M., Jr., *see* Marquis, D. G., 1939.

Porter, L. W., & Duncan, C. P. Negative transfer in verbal learning. *Journal of Experimental Psychology,* 1953, *46,* 61–64. **1055, 1064**

Porter, P. B., *see* Gibson, W. E., 1965.

Posner, M. I., & Konick, A. On the role of interference in short-term retention. *Journal of Experimental Psychology.* 1966, *72,* 221–231. **119**

Posner, M. I., & Rossman, E. Effect of size and location of

informational transforms upon short-term retention. *Journal of Experimental Psychology,* 1965, *70,* 496–505. **1119**

Postman, L. The generalization gradient in recognition memory. *Journal of Experimental Psychology,* 1951, *42,* 231–235. **1048**

Postman, L. The present status of interference theory. In C. N. Cofer (Ed.), *Verbal learning and verbal behavior.* New York: McGraw-Hill, 1961. (a) **1089**

Postman, L. Extra-experimental interference and the retention of words. *Journal of Experimental Psychology,* 1961, *61,* 97–110. (b) **854, 857, 886, 896, 1128**

Postman, L. Repetition and paired-associate learning. *American Journal of Psychology,* 1962, *75,* 372–389. **987**

Postman, L. Transfer of training as a function of experimental paradigm and degree of first-list learning. *Journal of Verbal Learning and Verbal Behavior,* 1962, *1,* 109–118. (a) **1036, 1059, 1062, 1063, 1064, 1068**

Postman, L. Retention of first-list associations as a function of the conditions of transfer. *Journal of Experimental Psychology,* 1962, *64,* 380–387. (b) **1062, 1093**

Postman, L. The temporal course of proactive inhibition for serial lists. *Journal of Experimental Psychology,* 1962, *63,* 361–369. (c) **1041, 1104, 1129**

Postman, L. Retention as a function of degree of overlearning. *Science,* 1962, *135,* 666–667. (d) **1124**

Postman, L. The effects of language habits on the acquisition and retention of verbal associations. *Journal of Experimental Psychology,* 1962, *64,* 7–19. (e) **854, 857, 888, 1128**

Postman, L. Does interference theory predict too much forgetting? *Journal of Verbal Learning and Verbal Behavior,* 1963, *2,* 40–48. **1129**

Postman, L. One-trial learning. In C. N. Cofer & B. S. Musgrave (Eds.), *Verbal behavior and learning.* New York: McGraw-Hill, 1963. Pp. 295–321. **987**

Postman, L. Acquisition and retention of consistent associative responses. *Journal of Experimental Psychology,* 1964, *67,* 183–190. **865**

Postman, L. Studies of learning to learn: II. Changes in transfer as a function of practice. *Journal of Verbal Learning and Verbal Behavior,* 1964, *3,* 437–447. (a) **1062, 1064, 1070**

Postman, L. Short-term memory and incidental learning. In A. W. Melton (Ed.), *Categories of human learning.* New York: Academic Press, 1964. (b) **998, 1112**

Postman, L. Unlearning under conditions of successive interpolation. *Journal of Experimental Psychology,* 1965, *70,* 237–245. **1087, 1096, 1098**

Postman, L. Differences between unmixed and mixed transfer designs as a function of paradigm. *Journal of Verbal Learning and Verbal Behavior,* 1966, *5,* 240–248. **1069**

Postman, L. The effect of interitem associative strength on the acquisition and retention of serial lists. *Journal of Verbal Learning and Verbal Behavior,* 1967, *6,* 721–728. **1130**

Postman, L. Association and performance in the analysis of verbal learning. In T. R. Dixon & D. L. Horton (Eds.), *Verbal behavior and general behavior theory.* Englewood Cliffs, N. J.: Prentice-Hall, 1968. (a) **1025**

Postman, L. Studies of learning to learn: VI. General transfer effects in three-stage mediation. *Journal of Verbal Learning and Verbal Behavior,* 1968, *7,* 659–664. (b) **1070**

Postman, L. *Norms of word association.* New York: Academic Press, (in press). **861**

Postman, L., & Adams, P. A. Studies in incidental learning: IV. The interaction of orienting tasks and stimulus materials. *Journal of Experimental Psychology,* 1956, *51,* 329–332. **855**

Postman, L., Adams, P. A., & Phillips, L. W. Studies in incidental learning: II The effects of association value and of the method of testing. *Journal of Experimental Psychology*, 1955, *49*, 1-10. **855**

Postman, L., Fraser, J., & Burns, S. Unit-sequence facilitation in recall. *Journal of Verbal Learning and Verbal Behavior*, 1968, *7*, 217-224. **1130**

Postman, L., & Goggin, J. Whole vs. part learning of paired-associate lists. *Journal of Experimental Psychology*, 1966, *71*, 867-877. **1009**

Postman, L., & Greenbloom, R. Conditions of cue selection in the acquisition of paired-associate lists. *Journal of Experimental Psychology*, 1967, *73*, 91-100. **1047**

Postman, L., & Keppel, G. Retroactive inhibition in free recall. *Journal of Experimental Psychology*, 1967, *74*, 203-211. **1101, 1102**

Postman, L., Keppel, G., & Stark, K. Unlearning as a function of the relationship between successive response classes. *Journal of Experimental Psychology*, 1965, *69*, 111-118. **1097**

Postman, L., Keppel, G., & Zacks, R. Studies of learning to learn: VII. The effects of practice on response integration. *Journal of Verbal Learning and Verbal Behavior*, 1968, *7*, 776-784. **1043**

Postman, L., & Phillips, L. W. Studies in incidental learning: IX. A comparison of the methods of successive and single recalls. *Journal of Experimental Psychology*, 1961, *61*, 236-241. **855**

Postman, L., & Riley, D. A. Degree of learning and interserial interference in retention. *University of California Publications in Psychology*, 1959, *8*, 271-396. **1085, 1086, 1103**

Postman, L., & Schwartz, M. Studies of learning to learn: I. Transfer as a function of method of practice and class of verbal materials. *Journal of Verbal Learning and Verbal Behavior*, 1964, *3*, 37-49. **1042, 1043**

Postman, L., & Stark, K. Proactive inhibition as a function of the conditions of transfer. *Journal of Verbal Learning and Verbal Behavior*, 1964, *3*, 437-447. **1058, 1104**

Postman, L., & Stark, K. Studies of learning to learn: IV. Transfer from serial to paired-associate learning. *Journal of Verbal Learning and Verbal Behavior*, 1967, *6*, 339-353. **1012**

Postman, L., & Stark, K. The role of response availability in transfer and interference. *Journal of Experimental Psychology*, 1969 (in press). **1062, 1065, 1066, 1096**

Postman, L., Stark, K., & Fraser, J. Temporal changes in interference. *Journal of Verbal Learning and Verbal Behavior*, 1968, *7*, 672-694. **1099, 1100, 1101, 1105**

Postman, L., *see also* Bruner, J. S., 1950, 1951; Postman, L., *see* Goulet, L. R., 1966; Keppel, G., 1966, 1968; Rosenzweig, M. R., 1957; Schwinn, E., 1967; Solomon, R. L., 1952; Underwood, B. J., 1960.

Potter, R. K., Kopp, G. A., & Green, H. C. *Visible speech.* Princeton, N.J.: Van Nostrand, 1947. **251**

Poulton, E. C. Listening to overlapping calls. *Journal of Experimental Psychology*, 1956, *52*, 334-339. **258**

Poulton, E. C., *see also* Stevens, S. S., 1956; Warren, R. M., 1966.

Powell, G. F., *see* Henkin, R. I., 1962.

Powell, J., *see* Azrin, N. H., 1967.

Power, R. P., *see* Day, R. H., 1963, 1965.

Powers, J. B., *see* Pfaffmann, C., 1964.

Powley, T. L., & Keesey, R. E. Relationship of body weight to the lateral hypothalamic-feeding syndrome. *Journal of Comparative and Physiological Psychology*, 1970, *70*, 25-36. **651**

Pratt, C. H., *see* Schlosberg, H., 1956.

Pratt, J. G., *see* McCulloch, T. L., 1934.

Premack, D. Toward empirical behavioral laws: I. Positive reinforcement. *Psychological Review*, 1959, *66*, 219-233. **624, 817**

Premack, D. Reversibility of the reinforcement relation. *Science*, 1962, *136*, 255-257. **624, 817, 823**

Premack, D. Reinforcement theory. In D. Levine (Ed.), *Nebraska symposium on motivation.* Lincoln: University of Nebraska Press, 1965. Pp. 123-180. **623, 624, 690, 817, 823**

Premack, D., Collier, G., & Roberts, C. L. Frequency of light-contingent bar pressing as a function of the amount of deprivation of light. *American Psychologist*, 1957, *12*, 411 (abstract). **840**

Premack, D., *see also* Holstein, S. B., 1965; Schaeffer, R. W., 1961.

Prentice, W. C. H. The relation of distance to the apparent size of figural after-effects. *American Journal of Psychology*, 1950, *63*, 589-593. **471n**

Prescott, J. W. Neural timing mechanisms, conditioning and the CS-UCS interval. *Psychophysiology*, 1965, *2*, 125-131. **558n**

Prescott, R. G. W. Diurnal activity cycles and intracranial self-stimulation in the rat. *Journal of Comparative and Physiological Psychology*, 1967, *64*, 346-349. **655n**

Pressman, Y. M., *see* Varga, M. E., 1967.

Pretori, H., *see* Hess, C., 1894.

Prewitt, E. P. Number of preconditioning trials in sensory preconditioning using CER training. *Journal of Comparative and Physiological Psychology*, 1967, *64*, 360-362. **564**

Pribram, K., *see* Miller, G. A., 1960.

Price, A. E., *see* Zeiler, M. D., 1965.

Price, L. E. *see* Abbott, D. W., 1964.

Price, S., *see* Dastoli, F. R., 1966.

Primoff, E. Backward and forward association as an organizing act in serial and in paired-associate learning. *Journal of Psychology*, 1938, *5*, 375-395. **1011, 1013, 1064**

Pritchard, R. M. Stabilized images on the retina. *Scientific American*, 1961, *204*, 72-78. **453**

Pritchard, R. M., Heron, W., & Hebb, D. O. Visual perception approached by the method of stabilized images. *Canadian Journal of Psychology*, 1960, *14*, 67-77. **375, 453**

Pritchatt, D., Avoidance of electric shock by the cockroach. *Animal Behaviour*, 1968, *16*, 178-185. **578**

Pronko, N. H., *see* Snyder, F. W., 1952.

Prosser, C. L., & Hunter, W. S. The extinction of startle responses and spinal reflexes in the white rat. *American Journal of Physiology*, 1936, *117*, 609-618. **577, 591**

Pryer, M. W., *see* Noble, C. E., 1957.

Pubols, B. H., Jr. Delay of reinforcement, response perseveration, and discrimination reversal. *Journal of Experimental Psychology*, 1958, *56*, 32-40. **685, 686**

Pubols, B. H., Jr. Incentive magnitude, learning, and performance in animals. *Psychological Bulletin*, 1960, *57*, 89-115. **635**

Pulfrich, C. Die Stereoskopie im Dienste der isochromen und heterochromen Photometrie. *Naturwissenschaften*, 1922, *10*, 533-564; 569-601; 714-722; 735-743; 751-761. **309**

Purcell, D. G., *see* Dember, W. N., 1967.

Purcell, M., *see* Moore, M. E., 1965.

Purdy, J., & Gibson, E. J. Distance judgment by the method of fractionation. *Journal of Experimental Psychology*, 1955, *50*, 374-380. **514**

Purdy, J., *see also* Gibson, J. J., 1955.

Purdy, W. C. The hypothesis of psychophysical correspondence in space perception. Doctoral dissertation, Cornell University. Ann Arbor: University Microfilms, 1958, No. 58-5594. **505**

Quartermain, D., & Webster, D. Extinction following intracranial reward: The effect of delay between acquisition and extinction. *Science*, 1968, *159*, 1259-1260. **659**

Raab, D. Backward masking. *Psychological Bulletin*, 1963, *60*, 118-129. **241, 429**

Raab, D., *see also* Fehrer, E., 1962; Osman, E., 1963.

Rabe, A., see Clark, W. C., 1955, 1956.

Rabiner, L. R., see Levitt, H., 1967.

Radloff, W. P., see Wilson, G. T. 1967.

Radner, M., see Gibson, J. J., 1937.

Rainey, C., see Bryden, M., 1963.

Rand, G., see Hardy, L. H., 1953.

Randt, C. T., see Collins, W. F., 1960.

Rapaport, D. (Ed.). Organization and pathology of thought. New York: Columbia University Press, 1951. **864**

Rapaport, D., Gill, M., & Schafer, R. Diagnostic psychological testing. Vol. 2. Chicago: Year Book Publishers, 1946. **864**

Rapp, H. M., see Bolles, R. C., 1965, 1968.

Rappoport, M., see Fitts, P. M., 1956.

Rapuzzi, G., & Casella, C. Innervation of the fungiform papillae in the frog tongue. Journal of Neurophysiology, 1965, 28, 154-165. **183**

Rashbass, C. New method for recording eye movements. Journal of the Optical Society of America, 1960, 50, 642-644. **373**

Rashbass, C. The relationship between saccadic and smooth tracking eye movements. Journal of Physiology, 1961, 159, 326-338. **376, 378, 380**

Rashbass, C., & Westheimer, G. H. Disjunctive eye movements. Journal of Physiology, 1961, 159, 149-170. (a) **305, 373, 383**

Rashbass, C., & Westheimer, G. H. Independence of conjugate and disjunctive eye movements. Journal of Physiology, 1961, 159, 361-364. (b) **388**

Raskin, D., see Maltzman, I., 1960.

Raskin, D. C., see Seward, J. P., 1960.

Raskin, E., & Cook, S. W. The strength and direction of associations formed in the learning of nonsense syllables. Journal of Experimental Psychology, 1937, 20, 381-395. **1014**

Rasmussen, A. T. The principal nervous pathways. New York: Macmillan, 1947. **126**

Rasmussen, A. T. see also Penfield, W., 1950.

Rasmussen, G. L. Efferent fibers of the cochlear nerve and cochlear nucleus. In G. L. Rasmussen & W. A. Windle (Eds.), Neural mechanisms of the auditory and vestibular systems. Springfield, Ill.: Charles C Thomas, 1960. **233**

Rasmussen, G. L., & Windle, W. A. Neural mechanisms of the auditory and vestibular systems. Springfield, Ill.: Charles C Thomas, 1960. **231**

Ratliff, F. The role of physiological nystagmus in monocular acuity. Journal of Experimental Psychology, 1952, 43, 163-172. **387**

Ratliff, F. Some interrelations among physics, physiology, and psychology in the study of vision. In S. Koch (Ed.), Psychology: A study of a science. Vol. 4: Biologically oriented fields: Their place in psychology and in biological science. New York: McGraw-Hill, 1962. Pp. 417-482. **293**

Ratliff, F. Mach bands: Quantitative studies on neural networks in the retina. New York: Holden-Day, 1965. **292, 293, 428**

Ratliff, F., & Riggs, L. A. Involuntary motions of the eye during monocular fixation. Journal of Experimental Psychology, 1950, 40, 687-701. **305, 374, 386**

Ratliff, F., see also Hartline, H. K., 1956, 1961; Riggs, L. A., 1951, 1952, 1953, 1954.

Ratoosh, P. On interposition as a cue for the perception of distance. Proceedings of the National Academy of Science, 1949, 35, 257-259. **498**

Rauch, D. S., see Keppel, G., 1966.

Rawlings, I. L., see Thurlow, W. R., 1959.

Ray, O. S., & Stein, L. Generalization of conditioned suppression. Journal of the Experimental Analysis of Behavior, 1959, 2, 357-361. **715**

Raymond, G. A., see Camp, D. S., 1967; Church, R. M., 1967.

Rayner, R., see Watson, J. B., 1920.

Razran, G. H. S. Conditioned responses in animals other than dogs. Psychological Bulletin, 1933, 30, 261-324. **562**

Razran, G. H. S. Conditioned responses: An experimental study and a theoretical analysis. Archives of Psychology, 1935, 191. **561**

Razran, G. A quantitative study of meaning by a conditioned salivary technique (semantic conditioning). Science, 1939, 90, 89-91. **1047**

Razran, G. H. Studies in configural conditioning: II. The effects of subjects' attitudes and task-sets upon configural conditioning. Journal of Experimental Psychology, 1939, 24, 95-105. **562**

Razran, G. Semantic and phonetographic generalization of salivary conditioning to verbal stimuli. Journal of Experimental Psychology, 1949, 39, 642-652. **1047**

Reagan, C., see Washburn, M. F., 1934.

Reaney, T. P., see Brackbill, Y., 1967.

Reber, A. S., & Millward, R. B. Event observation in probability learning. Journal of Experimental Psychology, 1968, 77, 317-327. **918, 932, 933**

Reber, A. S., see also Millward, R. B., 1967.

Reed, H. B. A repetition of Ebert and Meumann's practice experiment in memory. Journal of Experimental Psychology, 1917, 2, 315-346. **1031**

Reed, H. B. Factors influencing learning and retention of concepts: I. Influence of set. Journal of Experimental Psychology, 1946, 36, 71-87. (a) **946**

Reed, H. B. The influence of length of series: III. The origin of concepts. Journal of Experimental Psychology, 1946, 36, 166-181. (b) **946**

Reed, H. B. The influence of complexity of the stimuli: IV. Journal of Experimental Psychology, 1946, 36, 252-261. (c) **946**

Reed, J. D. Spontaneous activity of animals: A review of the literature since 1929. Psychological Bulletin, 1947, 44, 393-412. **821**

Reese, E., see Bateson, P. P. G., 1968.

Reese, H. W. Motor paired associate learning and stimulus pretraining. Child Development, 1960, 31, 505-513. **783**

Reese, H. W. Transposition in the intermediate-size problem by preschool children. Child Development, 1961, 32, 311-315. **765**

Reese, H. W. The perception of stimulus relations. New York: Academic Press, 1968. **765**

Reese, T. S. Olfactory cilia in the frog. Journal of Cellular Biology, 1965, 25, 209-230. **195, 196**

Reese, T. S., & Stevens, S. S. Subjective intensity of coffee odor. American Journal of Psychology, 1960, 73, 424-428. **205**

Reese, T. W. et al. Psychophysical research: Summary report, 1946-1952. Psychophysical Research Unit, Mount Holyoke College, 1953. **73**

Reese, T. W., see also Stevenson, J. G., 1962.

Rehula, R., see Underwood, B. J., 1962.

Reid, L. D., see Gibson, W. E., 1965.

Reid, L. S., & Finger, F. W. The rat's adjustment to 23-hour food deprivation cycles. Journal of Comparative and Physiological Psychology, 1955, 48, 110-113. **818, 819**

Reid, L. A., see Finger, F. W., 1960.

Reiher, L., see Ogle, K., 1962.

Reimann, E. Die scheinbare Vergrösserung der Sonne und des Mondes am Horizont. Zeitschrift für Psychologie, 1902, 30, 1-38, 161-195. **511**

Rekosh, J., see Held, R., 1963.

Remple, R., see Wike, E. L., 1959.

Renner, K. E. Delay of reinforcement: A historical review. Psychological Bulletin, 1964, 61, 341-361. **685**

Renner, K. E. Delay of reinforcement and resistance to extinction: A supplementary report. Psychological Reports, 1965, 16, 197-198. (a) **686**

Renner, K. E. Influence of delay of reinforcement and overlearning on position reversal. *Psychological Reports,* 1965, *16,* 1101–1106. (b) **686**

Renyard, R., see Greenspoon, J., 1957.

Rescorla, R. A. Pavlovian conditioning and its proper control procedures. *Psychological Review,* 1967, *74,* 71–80. **717**

Rescorla, R. A., & LoLordo, V. M. Inhibition of avoidance behavior. *Journal of Comparative and Physiological Psychology,* 1965, *59,* 406–412. **709, 716, 717**

Rescorla, R. A., & Solomon, R. L. Two-process learning theory: Relationships between Pavlovian conditioning and instrumental learning. *Psychological Review.* 1967, *74,* 151–182. **569, 726, 809**

Restle, F. A theory of discrimination learning. *Psychological Review,* 1955, *62,* 11–19. (a) **949, 957**

Restle, F. Axioms of a theory of discrimination learning. *Psychometrika,* 1955, *20,* 201–208. (b) **949, 957**

Restle, F. Theory of selective learning with probable reinforcements. *Psychological Review,* 1957, *64,* 182–191. **948, 949, 957**

Restle, F. Toward a quantitative description of learning set data. *Psychological Review,* 1958, *65,* 77–91. **957**

Restle, F. Additivity of cues and transfer in discrimination of consonant clusters. *Journal of Experimental Psychology,* 1959, *57,* 9–14. **957**

Restle, F. *Psychology of judgment and choice: A theoretical essay.* New York: Wiley, 1961. **928, 934, 938, 1005**

Restle, F. The selection of strategies in cue learning. *Psychological Review,* 1962, *69,* 329–343. **949**

Restle, F. Sources of difficulty in learning paired-associates. In R. C. Atkinson (Ed.), *Studies in mathematical psychology.* Stanford: Stanford University Press, 1964. Pp. 116–172. **1005, 1006**

Restle, F. Significance of all-or-none learning. *Psychological Bulletin,* 1965, *64,* 313–325. **989**

Restle, F. Run structure and probability learning: Disproof of Restle's model. *Journal of Experimental Psychology,* 1966, *72,* 382–389. **935, 983**

Restle, F. Grammatical analysis of the prediction of binary events. *Journal of Verbal Learning and Verbal Behavior,* 1967, *6,* 17–25. **935**

Restle, F., & Emmerich, D. Memory in concept attainment: Effects of giving several problems concurrently. *Journal of Experimental Psychology,* 1966, *71,* 794–799. **972, 974**

Restle, F., see also Bourne, L. E., 1959; Polson, M., 1965.

Reynolds, B. Extinction of trace conditioned responses as a function of the spacing of trials during acquisition and extinction series. *Journal of Experimental Psychology,* 1945, *35,* 81–95. **570n**

Reynolds, B. The acquisition of a black-white discrimination habit under two levels of reinforcement. *Journal of Experimental Psychology,* 1949, *39,* 760–769. **637**

Reynolds, B. Acquisition of a simple spatial discrimination as a function of the amount of reinforcement. *Journal of Experimental Psychology,* 1950, *40,* 152–160. **637**

Reynolds, B., see also Grice, G. R., 1952.

Reynolds, E. G., see Hirsh, I. J., 1952, 1954.

Reynolds, G. S. Attention in the pigeon. *Journal of the Experimental Analysis of Behavior,* 1961, *4,* 203–208. **763, 777**

Reynolds, G. S. Behavioral contrast. *Journal of the Experimental Analysis of Behavior,* 1961, *4,* 57–71. **641**

Reynolds, G. S., & Limpo, A. J. Negative contrast after prolonged discrimination maintenance. *Psychonomic Science,* 1968, *10,* 323–324. **641**

Reynolds, H. V., see Gibson, J. J., 1969.

Reynolds, J. H., see Friedman, M. J., 1967.

Reynolds, W. F., Pavlik, W. B., & Goldstein, E. Secondary reinforcement effects as a function of reward magnitude training methods. *Psychological Reports,* 1964, *15,* 7–10. **666**

Reynolds, W. F., see also Besch, N. F., 1958.

Rice, C. E., & Kenshalo, D. R. Nociceptive threshold measurements in the cat. *Journal of Applied Physiology,* 1962, *17,* 1009–1012. **157**

Richardson, J. The relationship of stimulus similarity and number of responses. *Journal of Experimental Psychology,* 1958, *56,* 478–484. **892**

Richardson, J. Association among stimuli and the learning of verbal concept lists. *Journal of Experimental Psychology,* 1960, *60,* 290–298. **892**

Richardson, J. The learning of concept names mediated by concept examples. *Journal of Verbal Learning and Verbal Behavior,* 1962, *1,* 281–288. **1078**

Richardson, J. Facilitation of mediated transfer by instruction, B–C training and presentation of the mediating response. *Journal of Verbal Learning and Verbal Behavior,* 1966, *5,* 59–67. (a) **1078**

Richardson, J. The effect of B–C presentation and anticipation interval on mediated transfer. *Journal of Verbal Learning and Verbal Behavior,* 1966, *5,* 119–125. (b) **1078, 1079**

Richardson, J. The locus of mediation and the duration of the anticipation interval in a transfer paradigm. *Journal of Verbal Learning and Verbal Behavior,* 1967, *6,* 247–256. (a) **1078, 1079**

Richardson, J. Latencies of implicit verbal responses and the effect of the anticipation interval on mediated transfer. *Journal of Verbal Learning and Verbal Behavior,* 1967, *6,* 819–826. (b) **1058, 1079**

Richardson, J. Transfer and the *A–B* anticipation interval in the *A–B'*, *A–B* paradigm. *Journal of Verbal Learning and Verbal Behavior,* 1967, *6,* 897–902. (c) **1058**

Richardson, J. Implicit verbal chaining as the basis of transfer in paired-associate learning. *Journal of Experimental Psychology,* 1968, *76,* 109–115. (a) **1079**

Richardson, J. Latencies of implicit associative responses and positive transfer in paired-associate learning. *Journal of Verbal Learning and Verbal Behavior,* 1968, *7,* 638–646. (b) **1058, 1077**

Richardson, J., & Brown, B. L. Mediated transfer in paired-associate learning as a function of presentation rate and stimulus meaningfulness. *Journal of Experimental Psychology,* 1966, *72,* 820–828. **1062, 1079**

Richardson, J., & Erlebacher, A. Associative connection between paired verbal items. *Journal of Experimental Psychology,* 1958, *56,* 62–69. **899**

Richardson, J., & Gropper, M. S. Learning during recall trials. *Psychological Reports,* 1964, *15,* 551–560. **1096**

Richardson, J., see Underwood, B. J., 1956, 1956a, b, c.

Richter, C. P. Salt taste thresholds of normal and adrenalectomized rats. *Endocrinology,* 1939, *24,* 367–371. **627**

Richter, C. P., see also Pfaffmann, C., 1954; Wilkins, L., 1940.

Richter, M., see Levine, M., 1964.

Riese, W. see Goldstein, K., 1923.

Riesen, A. H. Delayed reward in discrimination learning by chimpanzees. *Comparative Psychology Monographs,* 1940, (No. 77) *15,* 1–53. **784**

Riesen, A. H. The development of visual perception in man and chimpanzee. *Science,* 1947, *106,* 107–108. **548**

Riesen, A. H. Studying perceptual development using the technique of sensory deprivation. *Journal of Nervous and Mental Disease,* 1961, *132,* 21–25. **548**

Riesen, A. H., & Aarons, L. Visual movement and intensity discrimination in cats after early deprivation of pattern vision. *Journal of Comparative and Physiological Psychology,* 1959, *52,* 142–149. **549**

Riesen, A. H., see also Hovland, C. I., 1940.

Rifkin, K. I., see McLaughlin, S. C., 1965.

Riggs, L. A. Continuous and reproducible records of the electrical activity of the human retina. *Proceedings of the Society for Experimental Biology and Medicine,* 1941, *48,* 204–207. **308**

Riggs, L. A. Electrophysiology of vision. In C. H. Graham

(Ed.), *Vision and visual perception.* New York: Wiley, 1965. Pp. 81-131. (a) **308**

Riggs, L. A. Light as a stimulus for vision. In C. H. Graham (Ed.), *Vision and visual perception.* New York: Wiley, 1965. Pp. 1-38. (b) **274, 278**

Riggs, L. A. Visual acuity. In C. H. Graham (Ed.), *Vision and visual perception.* New York: Wiley, 1965. Pp. 321-349. (c) **279, 298, 301, 304**

Riggs, L. A., Armington, J. C., & Ratliff, F. Motions of the retinal image during fixation. *Journal of the Optical Society of America,* 1954, *44,* 315-321. **305**

Riggs, L. A., & Graham, C. H. Some aspects of light adaptation in a single photo-receptor unit. *Journal of Cellular and Comparative Physiology,* 1940, *16,* 15-23. **311**

Riggs, L. A., Johnson, E. P., & Schick, A. M. L. Electrical responses of the human eye to moving stimulus patterns. *Science,* 1964, *144,* 567. **308**

Riggs, L. A., Johnson, E. P., & Schick, A. M. L. Electrical responses of the human eye to changes in wavelength of stimulating light. *Journal of the Optical Society of America,* 1966, *56,* 1621-1627. **308, 338**

Riggs, L. A., Mueller, C. G., Graham, C. H., & Mote, F. A. Photographic measurements of atmospheric "boil." *Journal of the Optical Society of America,* 1947, *37,* 415-420. **494**

Riggs, L. A., & Niehl, E. W. Eye movements recorded during convergence and divergence. *Journal of the Optical Society of America,* 1960, *50,* 913-920. **382, 387**

Riggs, L. A., & Ratliff, F. Visual acuity and the normal tremor of the eyes. *Science,* 1951, *41,* 139-147. **305**

Riggs, L. A., & Ratliff, F. The effects of counteracting the normal movements of the eye. *Journal of the Optical Society of America,* 1952, *42,* 872-873. **306, 375**

Riggs, L. A. Ratliff, F., Cornsweet, J. C., & Cornsweet, T. N. The disappearance of steadily fixated visual test objects. *Journal of the Optical Society of America,* 1953, *43,* 495-501. **306, 374, 375**

Riggs, L. A., & Schick, A. M. L. Accuracy of retinal image stabilization achieved with a plane mirror on a tightly fitting contact lens. *Vision Research,* 1968, *8,* 159-169. **306, 374, 375**

Riggs, L. A., & Tulunay, S. U. Visual effects of varying the extent of compensation for eye movements. *Journal of the Optical Society of America,* 1959, *49,* 741-745. **379**

Riggs, L. A., *see also* Armington, J. C., 1952; Berry, R. N., 1950; Graham, C. H., 1949; Johnson, E. P., 1951, 1964; Krauskopf, J., 1960; Ratliff, F., 1950.

Riley, D. A. Discrimination learning. In *Contemporary topics in experimental psychology.* Boston: Allyn and Bacon, 1968. **780**

Riley, D. A., *see also* Nealey, S. M., 1963; Postman, L., 1959.

Rinalducci, E., *see* Boynton, R. M., 1965.

Riopelle, A. J. Transfer suppression and learning sets. *Journal of Comparative and Physiological Psychology,* 1953, *46,* 108-114. **768**

Riopelle, A. J., Wunderlich, R. A., & Francisco, E. W. Discrimination of concentric-ring patterns by monkeys. *Journal of Comparative and Physiological Psychology,* 1958, *51,* 622. **768**

Riopelle, A., *see also* Fletcher, J. L., 1960.

Ritchie, B. F., Ebeling, E., & Roth, W. Evidence for continuity in the discrimination of vertical and horizontal patterns. *Journal of Comparative and Physiological Psychology,* 1950, 168-180. **767**

Ritchie, J. M., *see* Douglas, W. W., 1962.

Rittler, M. C., *see* Hardy, L. H., 1953.

Rivers, W. H. R. Vision. In A. C. Haddon (Ed.), *Reports of the Cambridge Anthropological Expedition to the Torres Straits.* Vol. II, Part 1. Cambridge: Cambridge University Press, 1901. **460**

Rivers, W. H. R. Observations on the senses of the Todas. *British Journal of Psychology,* 1905, *1,* 321-396. **460**

Rixon, R. H., *see* Stevenson, J. A. F., 1957.

Robbins, M. C., *see* Kilbride, P. L., 1968.

Roberts, C. L., *see* Premack, D., 1957.

Roberts, F. S., & Suppes, P. Some problems in the geometry of visual perception. *Synthese,* 1967, *17,* 173-201. **466n**

Roberts, W. A. The effects of shifts in magnitude of reward on runway performance in immature and adult rats. *Psychonomic Science,* 1966, *5,* 37-38. **634**

Roberts, W. H. The effect of delayed feeding on white rats in a problem cage. *Journal of Genetic Psychology,* 1930, *37,* 35-58. **678**

Roberts, W. W. Both rewarding and punishing effects from stimulation of hypothalamus of cat with same electrode at same intensity. *Journal of Comparative and Physiological Psychology,* 1958, *51,* 400-407. (a) **798**

Roberts, W. W. Rapid escape learning without avoidance learning motivated by hypothalamic stimulation in cats. *Journal of Comparative and Physiological Psychology,* 1958, *51,* 391-399. (b) **798**

Roberts, W. W. Fear-like behavior elicited from dorsomedial thalamus of cat. *Journal of Comparative and Physiological Psychology,* 1962, *55,* 191-197. **798**

Roberts, W. W., *see also* Delgado, J. M. R., 1954, 1954b.

Robinson, D., *see* Gibson, J. J., 1935.

Robinson, D. A. A method of measuring eye movement using a scleral search coil in a magnetic field. Institute of Electrical and Electronics Engineers, *Transactions on Bio-Medical Electronics,* 1963, *10,* 137-145. **305, 374**

Robinson, D. A. The mechanics of human smooth pursuit eye movements. *Journal of Physiology,* 1965, *180,* 569-591. **377, 378, 379, 380**

Robinson, D. E., & Jeffress, L. A. Effect of varying interaural noise correlation on the detectability of tonal signals. *Journal of the Acoustical Society of America,* 1963, *35,* 1947-1952. **242**

Robinson, D. E., *see also* Dolan, T. R., 1967.

Robinson, D. N. Disinhibition of visually masked stimuli. *Science,* 1966, *154,* 157-158. **431**

Robinson, D. W. The relation between the sone and phon scales of loudness. *Acustica,* 1953, *3,* 344-358. **247**

Robinson, D. W., & Dadson, R. S. A re-determination of the equal loudness relations for pure tones. *British Journal of Applied Physics,* 1956, *7,* 166-181. **246**

Robinson, E. S. Some factors determining the degree of retroactive inhibition. *Psychological Monographs,* 1920, *28,* No. 128. **1081, 1085**

Robinson, E. S. The "similarity" factor in retroaction. *American Journal of Psychology,* 1927, *39,* 297-312. **1081**

Robinson, E. S. *Association theory today.* New York: Century, 1932. **980**

Robinson, F. P. The role of eye movements in reading with an evaluation of the techniques for their improvement. *Iowa State University Aims Program Research,* 1933, *39.* **390**

Robinson, J., *see* Hayes, W. J., 1961.

Robinson, J. S. Stimulus substitution and response learning in the earthworm. *Journal of Comparative and Physiological Psychology,* 1953, *46,* 262-266. **698**

Robinson, J. S., & Higgins, K. S. The young child's ability to see a difference between mirror image forms. *Perceptual and Motor Skills,* 1967, *25,* 893-897. **450**

Robson, J. G., *see* Campbell, F. W., 1959.

Roby, T. B., *see* Sheffield, F. D., 1950, 1954.

Rochester, H., Holland, J. H., Haibt, L. H., & Duda, W. L. Tests on a cell assembly theory of the action of the brain, using a large digital computer. *IRE Transactions on Information Theory,* 1956, *2,* 80-93. **452**

Rock, I. The perception of the egocentric orientation of a line. *Journal of Experimental Psychology,* 1954, *48,* 367-374. **539**

Rock, I. The orientation of forms on the retina and in the

environment. *American Journal of Psychology,* 1956, 69, 513–528. **451**

Rock, I. The role of repetition in associative learning. *American Journal of Psychology,* 1957, 70, 186–193. **986**

Rock, I. Adaptation to a minified image. *Psychonomic Science,* 1965, 2, 105–106. **543**

Rock, I. *The nature of perceptual adaptation.* New York: Basic Books, 1966. **533, 534, 536, 540, 543, 544, 545**

Rock, I., & Brosgole, L. Grouping based on phenomenal proximity. *Journal of Experimental Psychology,* 1964, 67, 531–538. **434n**

Rock, I., & Ebenholtz, S. The relational determination of perceived size. *Psychological Review,* 1959, 66, 387–401. **508**

Rock, I., & Ebenholtz, S. Stroboscopic movement based on change of phenomenal rather than retinal location. *American Journal of Psychology,* 1962, 75, 193–207. **528**

Rock, I., & Fleck, F. A re-examination of the effect of monetary reward and punishment in figure–ground perception. *Journal of Experimental Psychology,* 1950, 40, 766–776. **440**

Rock, I., & Harris, C. Vision and touch. *Scientific American,* 1967, 216, 96–104. **536, 541**

Rock, I., & Heimer, W. The effect of retinal and phenomenal orientation on the perception of form. *American Journal of Psychology,* 1957, 70, 493–511. **451**

Rock, I., & Heimer, W. Further evidence of one-trial associative learning. *American Journal of Psychology,* 1959, 72, 1–16. **986**

Rock, I., & Kaufman, L. The moon illusion: II. *Science,* 1962, 136, 1023–1031. **511**

Rock, I., & McDermott, W. The perception of visual angle. *Acta Psychologica,* 1964, 22, 119–134. **509**

Rock, I., & Victor, J. Vision and touch: An experimentally created conflict between the two senses. *Science,* 1964, 143, 594–596. **536**

Rock, I., *see also* Epstein, W., 1960; Kaufman, L., 1962.

Rockway, M. R., & Duncan, C. P. Pre-recall warming up in verbal retention. *Journal of Experimental Psychology,* 1952, 43, 305–312. **1039**

Rodgers, R. S., *see* Landauer, A. A., 1964.

Rodrigues, J., *see* Bruner, J. S., 1951.

Rodwan, A., *see* Hake, H. W., 1966.

Roelofs, C. O. Die Optische Lokalisation. *Archiv für Augenheilkunde,* 1935, 109, 395–415. **534**

Roelofs, C. O., & Zeeman, W. P. C. Apparent size and apparent distance in binocular and monocular distance. *Ophthalmologica,* 1957, 133, 188–204. **513**

Roessler, E. B., *see* Amerine, M., 1965; Berg, H. W., 1963.

Roffler, S. K., & Butler, R. A. Factors that influence the localization of sound in the vertical plane. *Journal of the Acoustical Society of America,* 1968, 43, 1255–1259. **267**

Rogers, J. V., *see* Walters, G. C., 1963.

Rogers, R., *see* Sherrick, C. E., 1966.

Rogoff, I., *see* Winnick, W. A., 1965.

Rohles, F., *see* Helson, H., 1959.

Rohwer, W. D. Jr., *see* Jensen, A. R., 1965.

Rosanoff, A. J., *see* Kent, G. H., 1910.

Rose, J. Organization of frequency sensitive neurons in the cochlear nuclear complex of the cat. In G. Rasmussen & W. F. Windle (Eds.), *Neural mechanisms of the auditory and vestibular systems.* Springfield, Ill.: Charles C Thomas, 1960. **232**

Rose, J., Brugge, J. F., Anderson, D. J., & Hind, J. E. Phase-locked response to low-frequency tones in single auditory nerve fibers of the squirrel monkey. *Journal of Neurophysiology,* 1967, 30, 769–793. **232**

Rose, J. E., Greenwood, D. D., Goldberg, J. M., & Hind, J. E. Some discharge characteristics of single neurons in the inferior colliculus of the cat: I. Tonotopical organization, relation of spike counts to tone intensity, and firing patterns of single elements. *Journal of Neurophysiology,* 1963, 26, 294–320. **232**

Rose, J. E., Gross, N. B., Geisler, C. D., & Hind, J. E. Some effects of binaural stimulation on the activity of single neurons in the inferior colliculus of the cat. *Journal of Neurophysiology,* 1966, 29, 288–314. **265**

Rose, J. E., & Mountcastle, V. B. Touch and kinesthesis. In J. Field, H. W. Magoun, & V. E. Hall (Eds.), *Handbook of physiology.* Sec. 1, Vol. I. *Neurophysiology.* American Physiological Society, Washington D. C., 1959. Pp. 387–429. **128**

Rose, J. E., *see also* Brugge, J. F., 1964.

Rose, R. M., & Vitz, P. C. Role of runs in probability learning. *Journal of Experimental Psychology,* 1966, 72, 751–760. **936**

Rosen, E., & Russell, W. A. Frequency-characteristics of successive word-association. *American Journal of Psychology,* 1957, 70, 120–122. **872, 873**

Rosenberg, A. E. Effect of masking on periodic pulses. *Journal of the Acoustical Society of America,* 1965, 38, 747–758. **245**

Rosenblatt, F., *see* Gibson, J. J., 1955.

Rosenblith, J. F. Judgment of simple geometric figures by children. *Perceptual and Motor Skills,* 1965, 21, 947–990. **450**

Rosenblith, W. A., & Stevens, K. N. On the DL for frequency. *Journal of the Acoustical Society of America,* 1953, 25, 980–985. **249**

Rosenblith, W. A., *see also* Bekesy, Georg von, 1951.

Rosenblum, L. A., & Cross, H. A. Performance of neonatal monkeys in the visual-cliff situation. *American Journal of Psychology,* 1963, 76, 318–320. **549**

Rosenblum, L. A., *see also* Moltz, H., 1960.

Rosenthal, R. *Experimental effects in behavioral research.* New York: Appleton, 1966. **562n**

Rosenthal, S. R. Histamine as the chemical mediator for referred pain. In D. R. Kenshalo (Ed.), *The skin senses.* Springfield, Ill.: Charles C Thomas, 1968. Pp. 480–498. **162**

Rosenzweig, M. R. Cortical correlates of auditory localization and of related perceptual phenomena. *Journal of Comparative and Physiological Psychology,* 1954, 47, 269–276. **264**

Rosenzweig, M. R. Etudes sur l'association des mots. *Année Psychologique,* 1957, 57, 23–32. **875**

Rosenzweig, M. R. Comparisons among word-association responses in English, French, German, and Italian. *American Journal of Psychology,* 1961, 74, 347–360. **875**

Rosenzweig, M. R. The mechanisms of hunger and thirst. In L. Postman (Ed.), *Psychology in the making.* New York: Knopf, 1962. Pp. 73–143. **816**

Rosenzweig, M. R. Word associations of French workmen: Comparisons with associations of French students and American workmen and students. *Journal of Verbal Learning and Verbal Behavior,* 1964, 3, 57–69. **875**

Rosenzweig, M. R., & McNeill, D. Uses of the semantic count in experimental studies of verbal behavior. *American Journal of Psychology,* 1962, 75, 492–495. **895n**

Rosenzweig, M. R., & Manahem, R. Age, sexe et niveau d'instruction comme facteurs déterminants dans les associations de mots. *Année Psychologique,* 1962, 62, 45–61. **874**

Rosenzweig, M. R., & Postman, L. Intelligibility as a function of frequency of usage. *Journal of Experimental Psychology,* 1957, 54, 412–422. **255**

Rosenzweig, M. R., *see also* Wallach, H., 1949.

Rosner, B., *see* Kolers, P., 1960.

Rosner, B. S., & Goff, W. R. Electrical responses of the nervous system and subjective scales of intensity. In W. D. Neff (Ed.), *Contributions to sensory physiology.* New York: Academic Press, 1967. **82**

Ross, G. S., see Weitzman, E. D., 1961.

Ross, L., & Versace, J. The critical frequency for taste. *American Journal of Psychology*, 1953, 66, 496–497. **178**

Ross, L. E. Eyelid conditioning as a tool in psychological research: Some problems and prospects. In W. F. Prokasy (Ed.), *Classical conditioning*. New York: Appleton, 1965. **557**

Ross, L. E., see also Spence, K. W., 1959.

Ross, R. T., see Hull, C. L., 1940.

Ross, S. Matching functions and equal-sensation contours for loudness. *Journal of the Acoustical Society of America*, 1967, 42, 778–793. **247**

Rossi, P. J. Adaptation and negative aftereffect to lateral optical displacement in newly hatched chicks. *Science*, 1968, 160, 430–432. **549**

Rossi, G., & Cortesina, G. The efferent innervation of the inner ear: A historical–bibliographical survey. *Laryngoscope*, 1965, 75, 212–235. **233**

Rossman, E., see Posner, M. I., 1965.

Roth, S. R., Sterman, M. B., & Clemente, C. D. Comparison of EEG correlates of reinforcement, internal inhibition and sleep. *Electroencephalography and Clinical Neurophysiology*, 1967, 23, 509–520. **838**

Roth, W., see Ritchie, B. F., 1950.

Rothkopf, E. Z. Two predictors of stimulus equivalence in paired associate learning. *Psychological Reports*, 1960, 7, 241–250. **880**

Rothkopf, E. Z., & Coke, E. U. The prediction of free recall from word association measures. *Journal of Experimental Psychology*, 1961, 62, 433–438. (a) **879, 887**

Rothkopf, E. Z., & Coke, E. U. Intralist association data for 99 words of the Kent-Rosanoff word list. *Psychological Reports*, 1961, 8, 463–474. (b) **879**

Rothschild, H. Untersuchungen über die sogenannten anorthoskopischen Zerrbilder. *Zeitschrift für Psychologie*, 1922, 90, 137–166. **455**

Rouanet, H., see Suppes, P., 1964.

Rouse, R. O., & Verinis, J. S. Compound verbal stimuli and word association. *Psychological Report*, 1965, 17, 403–406. **871**

Rouse, R. O., see also Hull, C. L., 1951; Schwartz, F., 1961.

Roussel, J. Frustration effect as a function of repeated non-reinforcements and as a function of the consistency of reinforcement prior to the introduction of non-reinforcement. Unpublished master's thesis, Tulane University, 1952. Cited by Amsel, 1958. **810**

Roussel, J., see also Amsel, A., 1952.

Routtenberg, A. The two-arousal hypothesis: Reticular formation and limbic system. *Psychological Review*, 1968, 75, 51–80. **658**

Routtenberg, A., & Kuznesof, A. W. Self-starvation of rats living in activity wheels on a restricted feeding schedule. *Journal of Comparative and Physiological Psychology*, 1967, 64, 414–421. **653**

Routtenberg, A., & Lindy, J. Effects of the availability of rewarding septal and hypothalamic stimulation on bar pressing for food under conditions of deprivation. *Journal of Comparative and Physiological Psychology*, 1965, 60, 158–161. **651, 652**

Rowland, V., MacIntyre, W. J., & Bidder, T. G. The production of brain lesions with electric currents: II. Bidirectional currents. *Journal of Neurosurgery*, 1960, 17, 55–69. **644**

Rozin, P., see Smith, R. H., 1967.

Rubin, E. *Synoplevede Figurer*. Copenhagen: Gyldendalske, 1915. **432, 438**

Rubin, E. *Visuell wahrgenommene Figuren*. Copenhagen: Glydendalske, 1921. **432, 438**

Rubin, M., see Amoore, J. E., 1964.

Rubin, R., see Furchgott, E., 1953.

Rubinstein, H., see Pollack, I., 1959.

Ruch, T. C. The nervous system: Sensory functions. In J. F. Fulton (Ed.), *Howell's Textbook of Physiology*. (ed. 15) Philadelphia: Saunders, 1946. **81**

Ruch, T. C. Pathophysiology of pain. In T. C. Ruch, H. D. Patton, J. W. Woodbury, & A. L. Towe (Eds.), *Neurophysiology*. Philadelphia: Saunders, 1965. Pp. 345–363. **161**

Ruch, T. C., & Patton, H. D. (Eds.) *Physiology and biophysics*. Philadelphia: Saunders, 1965. **95**

Ruch, T. C., see also Mowrer, O. H., 1936.

Rudel, R. G., & Teuber, H. L. Decrement of visual and haptic Müller-Lyer illusion on repeated trials: A study of cross-modal transfer. *Quarterly Journal of Experimental Psychology*, 1963, 15, 125–131. **450, 465n, 471**

Rudy, J. W., see Patten, R. L., 1967.

Rump, E. E. The relationship between perceived size and perceived distance. *British Journal of Psychology*, 1961, 52, 111–124. **506**

Rundquist, E. A. Inheritance of spontaneous activity in rats. *Journal of Comparative Psychology*, 1933, 16, 415–438. **824**

Runge, P. S., see Thurlow, W. R., 1967.

Runquist, W. N. Retention of verbal associates as a function of strength. *Journal of Experimental Psychology*, 1957, 54, 369–374. **1086**

Runquist, W. N. Verbal learning. In J. B. Sidowski (Ed.), *Experimental methods and instrumentation in psychology*. New York: McGraw-Hill, 1966. **853n**

Runquist, W. N., see Johnson, P. A., 1968; Underwood, B. J., 1959.

Rupert, A., see Galambos, R., 1959; Hubel, D. H., 1959.

Rush, G. P. Visual grouping in relation to age. *Archives of Psychology*, 1937, 31. **434**

Rushton, W. A. H. Visual pigments in the colour blind. *Nature*, 1958, 182, 690–692. **323**

Rushton, W. A. H. Increment threshold and dark adaptation. *Journal of the Optical Society of America*, 1963, 3, 104–109. **287**

Rushton, W. A. H. Cone pigment dynamics in the deuteranope. *Journal of Physiology*, 1965, 176, 38–45. **288**

Rushton, W. A. H., & Westheimer, G. The effect upon the rod threshold of bleaching neighbouring rods. *Journal of Physiology*, 1962, 164, 318–329. **289**

Rushton, W. A. H., see also Campbell, F. W., 1954.

Russell, W. A. Assessment versus experimental acquisition of verbal habits. In C. N. Cofer (Ed.), *Verbal learning and verbal behavior*. New York: McGraw-Hill, 1961. Pp. 110–123. **850**

Russell, W. A., & Jenkins, J. J. The complete Minnesota norms for responses to 100 words from the Kent-Rosanoff Word Association Test. Tech. Rep. No. 11, Contract N8-Onr 66216, between the Office of Naval Research and the University of Minnesota, 1954. **875**

Russell, W. A., & Meseck, O. R. Der Einfluss der Assoziation auf das Erinnern von Worten in der Deutschen, Französischen, und Englischen Sprache. *Zeitschrift für experimentelle und angewandte Psychologie*, 1959, 6, 191–211. **875**

Russell, W. A., & Storms, L. H. Implicit verbal chaining in paired associate learning. *Journal of Experimental Psychology*, 1955, 49, 287–293. **781, 1078**

Russell, W. A., see also Jenkins, J. J., 1958, 1959, 1960, undated; Rosen, E., 1957.

Ryan, J. J. Comparison of verbal response transfer mediated by meaningfully similar and associated stimuli. *Journal of Experimental Psychology*, 1960, 60, 408–415. **1048, 1052**

Ryan, T., see Kamin, L., 1959.

Ryan, T. A., see Hochberg, J., 1955.

Sachs, M. B., & Kiang, N. Y. S. Two-tone inhibition in auditory-nerve fibers. *Journal of the Acoustical Society of America*, 1967, 43, 1120–1128. **233, 239**

Sadowski, B., & Longo, V. G. Electroencephalographic and

behavioural correlates of an instrumental reward conditioned response in rabbits. *Electroencephalography and Clinical Neurophysiology,* 1962, *14,* 465–476. **837**

Sadowsky, S. Discrimination learning as a function of stimulus location along an auditory intensity continuum. *Journal of the Experimental Analysis of Behavior,* 1966, *9,* 209–225. **715**

Sadowsky, S. Discriminative responding on associated mixed and multiple schedules as a function of food and ICS reinforcement. *Journal of the Experimental Analysis of Behavior,* 1969, *12,* 933–945. **607, 655, 694, 701**

Sagara, M., & Oyama, T. Experimental studies on figural aftereffects in Japan. *Psychological Bulletin,* 1957, *54,* 327–338. **469**

Sakai, M., *see* Gibson, W. E., 1965.

Sakoda, J. N., *see* Brand, H., 1956.

Salapatek, P., & Kesson, W. Visual scanning of triangles by the human newborn. *Journal of Experimental Child Psychology,* 1966, *3,* 155–167. **547**

Salk, L. Mother's heartbeat as an imprinting stimulus. *Transactions of the New York Academy of Science,* 1962, *24,* 753–763. **582**

Salk, L. Thoughts on the concept of imprinting and its place in early human development. *Canadian Psychiatric Association Journal,* 1966. *11* (Supplement), 295–305. **582**

Saltz, E. Response pretraining: Differentiation or availability? *Journal of Experimental Psychology.* 1961, *62,* 583–587. **1060**

Saltz, E., & Hamilton, H. Spontaneous recovery of List 1 responses in the *A–B, A'–C* paradigm. *Journal of Experimental Psychology,* 1967, *75,* 267–273. **1099**

Saltzman, D., *see* Peterson, L. R., 1962, 1963.

Saltzman, I. J. Maze learning in the absence of primary reinforcement: A study of secondary reinforcement. *Journal of Comparative and Physiological Psychology,* 1949, *42,* 161–173. **663, 664**

Saltzman, I., & Koch, S. The effect of low intensities of hunger on the behavior mediated by a habit of maximum strength. *Journal of Experimental Psychology,* 1948, *38,* 347–370. **826**

Salzen, E. A., & Sluckin, W. The incidence of the following response and the duration of responsiveness in domestic fowl. *Animal Behaviour,* 1959, *7,* 172–179. **585**

Sampson, H., & Spong, P. Binocular fixation and immediate memory. *British Journal of Psychology,* 1961, *52,* 239–248. **440**

Sandak, J. M., & Garskof, B. E. Associative unlearning as a function of degree of interpolated learning. *Psychonomic Science,* 1967, *7,* 215–216. **1096**

Sandak, J. M., *see also* Garskof, B. E., 1964.

Sandel, T. T., Teas, D. C., Feddersen, W. E., & Jeffress, L. A. Localization of sound from single and paired sources. *Journal of the Acoustical Society of America,* 1955, *27,* 842–852. **266**

Sandel, T. T., *see also* Feddersen, W. E., 1957; Jeffress, L., 1956.

Sanderson, W. R., *see* Vanderplas, J. M., 1965.

Sandström, C. I. *Orientation in the present space.* Stockholm: Almquist and Wiksell, 1951. **529**

Sanford, E. C. *A course in experimental psychology. Part I: Sensation and perception.* London: Heath, 1897. **462**

Sanford, E. C. *A course in experimental psychology.* Boston: Heath, 1898. **521**

Saslow, M. G. Latency for saccadic eye movement. *Journal of the Optical Society of America,* 1967, *57,* 1030–1033. **376**

Satinoff, E., *see* Smith, R. H., 1967.

Sato, M. The effect of temperature change on the response of taste receptors. In Y. Zotterman (Ed.), *Olfaction and taste.* Vol. I. New York: Pergamon, 1963. Pp. 151–164. **181**

Sato, M., *see also* Yamashita, S., 1967.

Sato, Y., *see* Ishiko, N., 1967.

Saunders, M. G., *see* Zubek, J. P., 1963.

Savage, C. W. Introspectionist and behaviorist interpretations of ratio scales of perceptual magnitudes. *Psychological Monographs,* 1966, *80,* Whole number 627. **84**

Savin, H. B., *see* Clayton, F. L., 1960.

Sawyer, C. H., & Kawakami, M. Characteristics of behavioral and electroencephalographic after-reactions to copulation and vaginal stimulation in the female rabbit. *Endocrinology,* 1959, *65,* 622–630. **838**

Sayers, B. McA. Acoustic-image lateralization judgments with binaural tones. *Journal of the Acoustical Society of America,* 1964, *36,* 923–926. **261**

Sayers, B. McA., & Toole, F. E. Acoustic-image lateralization judgments with binaural transients. *Journal of the Acoustical Society of America,* 1964, *36,* 1199–1205. **266**

Sayers, B. McA., *see also* Cherry, E. C., 1959; Leakey, D. M., 1958.

Scahill, G. H., *see* Dimmick, F. L., 1925.

Scandura, J. M., *see* Greeno, J. G., 1966.

Schachter, S. Obesity and eating. *Science,* 1968, *161,* 751–756. **817**

Schaefer, V. J., *see* Langmuir, I., 1944.

Schaeffer, R. W., & Premack, D. Licking rates in infant albino rats. *Science,* 1961, *134,* 1980–1981. **814**

Schafer, R., & Murphy, G. The role of autism in a visual figure-ground relationship. *Journal of Experimental Psychology,* 1943, *32,* 335–343. **439, 440**

Schafer, R., *see also* Rapaport, D., 1946.

Schafer, W., *see* Boynton, R. M., 1964.

Scharf, B. Complex sounds and critical bands. *Psychological Bulletin,* 1961, *58,* 205–217. **234, 240**

Scharf, B., & Stevens, J. C. The form of the loudness function near threshold. Vol. 1. *Proceedings of the 3rd International Congress on Acoustics, Stuttgart, 1959.* Amsterdam: Elsevier, 1961. Pp. 80–82. **80**

Scharf, B., *see also* Zwicker, E., 1965.

Scharlock, D. P., *see* Bugelski, B. R., 1952.

Schaub, R. E., *see* Kamin, L. J., 1963.

Scheible, H., & Underwood, B. J. The role of overt errors in serial rote learning. *Journal of Experimental Psychology,* 1954, *47,* 160–162. **1038**

Scheibner, H., *see* Boynton, R. M., 1965.

Scheibner, J. M. O., & Boynton, R. M. Residual red-green discrimination in dichromats. *Journal of the Optical Society of America,* 1968, *58,* 1151–1158. **367**

Schenkel, K. D. Accumulation-theory of binaural masked thresholds. *Journal of the Acoustical Society of America,* 1967, *41,* 20–31. **242**

Schick, A. M. L., *see* Johnson, E. P., 1964; Riggs, L. A., 1964, 1966, 1968.

Schiff, B. B., *see* Glickman, S. E., 1967.

Schiff, W. Perception of impending collision: A study of visually directed avoidance behavior. *Psychological Monographs: General and Applied,* 1965, *79,* 1–26. **505**

Schiff, W., Caviness, J., & Gibson, J. J. Persistent fear responses in rhesus monkeys to the optical stimulus of "looming." *Science,* 1962, *136,* 982–983. **505**

Schiffman, H., *see* Wynne, R. D., 1965.

Schiller, P., & Smith, M. Detection in metacontrast. *Journal of Experimental Psychology,* 1966, *71,* 32–46. **430**

Schlag-Rey, M., *see* Suppes, P., 1966.

Schlosberg, H. A study of the conditioned patellar reflex. *Journal of Experimental Psychology,* 1928, *11,* 468–494. **562, 563, 601**

Schlosberg, H. Conditioned responses in the white rat. *Journal of Genetic Psychology,* 1934, *45,* 303–335. **563, 571**

Schlosberg, H. Conditioned responses in the white rat: II. Conditioned responses based on shock to the foreleg. *Journal of Genetic Psychology,* 1936, *49,* 107–138. **563**

Schlosberg, H. The relationship between success and the laws of conditioning. *Psychological Review*, 1937, *44*, 379-394. **563, 726**

Schlosberg, H. The description of facial expression in terms of two dimensions. *Journal of Experimental Psychology*, 1952, *44*, 229-237. **55**

Schlosberg, H. Three dimensions of emotion. *Psychological Review*, 1954, *61*, 81-88. **55**

Schlosberg, H., & Heineman, C. The relationship between two measures of response strength. *Journal of Experimental Psychology*, 1950, *40*, 235-247. **861**

Schlosberg, H., & Pratt, C. H. The secondary reward value of inaccessible food for hungry and satiated rats. *Journal of Comparative and Physiological Psychology*, 1956, *49*, 149-152. **657, 669, 678n**

Schlosberg, H., *see also* Bilodeau, I. McD., 1951; Engen, T., 1958; White, C. T., 1952; Woodworth, R. S., 1954.

Schmidt, W. A. An experimental study in the psychology of reading. *Educational Monographs* (Supplement), *2*, 1917. **390**

Schneider, B., & Lane, H. Ratio scales, category scales, and variability in the production of loudness and softness. *Journal of the Acoustical Society of America*, 1963, *35*, 1953-1961. **248**

Schneider, R. A., Costiloe, J. P., Howard, R. P., & Wolf, S. Olfactory perception thresholds in hypogonadal women: Changes accompanying the administration of androgen and estrogen. *Journal of Clinical Endocrinology*, 1958, *18*, 379-390. **209**

Schneider, R. A., & Wolf, S. Olfactory perception thresholds for "citral" utilizing a new type of olfactorium. *Journal of Applied Physiology*, 1955, *8*, 337-342. **201, 208**

Schneider, R. A., & Wolf, S. Relation of olfactory acuity to nasal membrane function. *Journal of Applied Physiology*, 1960, *15*, 914-920. **209**

Schneiderman, N., *see* Vandercar, D. H., 1967.

Schober, H. A. W., & Hilz, R. Contrast sensitivity of the human eye for square-wave gratings. *Journal of the Optical Society of America*, 1965, *55*, 1086-1091. **304**

Schoeffler, M. S. Probability of response to compounds of discriminated stimuli. *Journal of Experimental Psychology*, 1956, *48*, 323-329. **927**

Schoenberg, K. M., *see* Mayzner, M. S., 1964.

Schoenfeld, W. N., Antonitis, J. J., & Bersh, P. J. A preliminary study of training conditions necessary for secondary reinforcement. *Journal of Experimental Psychology*, 1950, *40*, 40-45. **674**

Schoenfeld, W. N., *see also* Keller, F. S., 1950.

Scholl, K. Das räumliche Zusammenarbeiten von Auge und Hand. *Deutsche Zeitschrift für Nervenheilkunde*, 1926, *92*, 280-303. **537**

Schott, E. Ueber die Registrierung des Nystagmus und anderer Augenbewegungen vermittels des Saitengalvanometers. *Deutsche Archiv für klinische Medizin*, 1922. *140*, 79-90. **372**

Schouten, J. F. The perception of pitch. *Philips Technical Review*, 1940, *5*, 286-294. **245**

Schrier, A. M. Amount of incentive and performance on a black-white discrimination problem. *Journal of Comparative and Physiological Psychology*, 1956, *49*, 123-125. **637, 700**

Schrier, A. M. Comparison of two methods of investigating the effect of amount of reward on performance. *Journal of Comparative and Physiological Psychology*, 1958, *51*, 725-731. **637, 638, 639**

Schrier, A. M. A modified version of the Wisconsin General Test Apparatus. *Journal of Psychology*, 1961, *52*, 193-200. **750**

Schrier, A. M. Response latency of monkeys as a function of amount of reward. *Psychological Reports*, 1961, *8*, 283-289. **635, 638**

Schrier, A. M. Response latency of monkeys as a function of reward amount and trials within test days. *Psychological Reports*, 1962, *10*, 439-444. **638**

Schrier, A. M. Reinforcement variables and response rates of monkeys (Macaca mulatta). *Journal of Comparative and Physiological Psychology*, 1965, *59*, 378-384. **626, 630**

Schrier, A. M. Effects of an upward shift in amount of reinforcer on runway performance of rats. *Journal of Comparative and Physiological Psychology*, 1967, *64*, 490-492. **633, 635**

Schrier, A. M., & Harlow, H. F. Effect of amount of incentive on discrimination learning by monkeys. *Journal of Comparative and Physiological Psychology*, 1956, *49*, 117-122. **637, 639, 700**

Schrödinger, E. Theorie der Pigmente von grosster Leuchtkraft. *Annalen der Physik*, 1920, *62*, 603. **356**

Schriever, W. Experimentelle Studien über das Stereoskopische. *Sehen. Z. Psychol.*, 1925, *96*, 113-170. **502**

Schroeder, M. R., *see* Harvey, F. K., 1963.

Schuck, J. R., Brock, T. C., & Becker, L. A. Luminous figures: Factors affecting the reporting of disappearances. *Science*, 1964, *146*, 1598-1599. **454**

Schuck, J., & Leahy, W. R. A comparison of verbal and non-verbal reports of fragmenting visual images. *Perception and Psychophysics*, 1966, *1*, 191-192. **454**

Schulman, R. M. Paired-associate transfer following early stages of List I learning. *Journal of Experimental Psychology*, 1967, *73*, 589-594. **1069**

Schultz, D. P., *see* King, D. J., 1960.

Schultze, M. Zur Anatomie und Physiologie der Retina. *Archiv für Mikroshopische Anatomie*, 1866, *2*, 175-286 (also Plates 8-15). **283**

Schulz, R., *see* Spence, J., 1965.

Schulz, R. W., Liston, J. R., & Weaver, G. E. The A-B, B-C, A-C mediation paradigm: Recall of A-B following A-C learning. *Journal of Verbal Learning and Verbal Behavior*, 1968, *7*, 602-607. **1077**

Schulz, R., & Lovelace, E. Mediation in verbal paired-associate learning: The role of temporal factors. *Psychonomic Science*, 1964, *1*, 95-96. **1058, 1079**

Schulz, R. W., & Thysell, R. The effects of familiarization on meaningfulness. *Journal of Verbal Learning and Verbal Behavior*, 1965, *4*, 409-413. **866**

Schulz, R. W., & Weaver, G. E. The A-B, B-C, A-C mediation paradigm: The effects of variation in A-C study- and test-interval lengths and strength of A-B, B-C. *Journal of Experimental Psychology*, 1968, *76*, 303-311. **1075, 1079**

Schulz, R., Weaver, G., & Ginsberg, S. Mediation with pseudomediation controlled: Chaining is not an artifact! *Psychonomic Science*, 1965, *2*, 169-170. **1077**

Schulz, R. W., *see also* McGhee, N. E., 1961; Spreen, O., 1966; Underwood, B. J., 1959, 1960a, b, 1962.

Schumacher, G. A., Goodell, H., Hardy, J. D., & Wolff, H. G. Uniformity of the pain threshold in man. *Science*, 1940, *92*, 110. **158**

Schwartz, C. B. *Visual discrimination of camouflaged figures.* Unpublished doctoral dissertation, University of California at Berkeley, 1961. **440**

Schwartz, F., & Rouse, R. O. The activation and recovery of associations. *Psychological Issues*, 1961, *3*. **886**

Schwartz, M. Effect of stimulus class on transfer and RI in the A-B, C-B paradigm. *Journal of Verbal Learning and Verbal Behavior*, 1968, *7*, 189-195. **1064**

Schwartz, M., *see also* Postman, L., 1964.

Schwartzkopff, J., *see* Galambos, R., 1959.

Schwenn, E., & Postman, L. Studies of learning to learn: V. Gains in performance as a function of warm-up and associative practice. *Journal of Verbal Learning and Verbal Behavior*, 1967, *6*, 565-573. **1038**

Schwenn, E., & Underwood, B. J. Simulated similarity and

mediation time in transfer. *Journal of Verbal Learning and Verbal Behavior,* 1965, *4,* 476–483. **1058, 1079**

Scofield, E. H., *see* Foster, D., 1950.

Scott, E. D., & Wike, E. L. The effect of partially delayed reinforcement and trial-distribution on the extinction of an instrumental response. *American Journal of Psychology,* 1956, *69,* 264–268. **685**

Scott, H. H., Jr., *see* Kenshalo, D. R., 1966.

Scott, J. P. *Animal behavior.* Chicago: University of Chicago Press, 1958. **581**

Seagrim, G. N., *see* Day, R. H., 1959; Pollack, 1959.

Seaman, G., *see* Hochberg, J. E., 1951.

Searle, J. L., *see* Hoffman, H. S., 1966.

Sears, R. R. Effect of optic lobe ablation on the visuo-motor behavior of the goldfish. *Journal of Comparative Psychology,* 1934, *17,* 233–265. **578**

Seashore, E. C., Carter, E. A., Farnum, E. C., & Seis, R. W. The effect of practice on normal illusions. *Psychological Review* (Monograph Supplement), 1908, *9,* 103–104. **465**

Sechzer, J. A., & Brown, J. L. Color discrimination in the cat. *Science,* 1964, *144,* 427–429. **338**

Ségal, J., *see* Baumgardt, E., 1947.

Segall, M. H., Campbell, D. T., & Herskovits, M. J. Cultural differences in the perception of geometric illusions. *Science,* 1963, *139,* 769–771. **456, 460**

Segall, M. H., Campbell, D. T., & Herskovits, M. J. *The influence of culture on visual perception.* Indianapolis, Ind.: Bobbs-Merrill, 1966. **456, 460**

Seidel, R. J. A review of sensory preconditioning. *Psychological Bulletin,* 1959, *56,* 58–73. **564**

Seidel, R. J. The importance of the S-R role of the verbal mediator in mediate association. *Canadian Journal of Psychology,* 1962, *16,* 170–176. **1074**

Seidel, R. J. RTT paradigm: No panacea for theories of associative learning. *Psychological Review,* 1963, *70,* 565–572. **990**

Seis, R. W., *see* Seashore, E. C., 1908.

Seitz, W. C. *The responsive eye.* New York: Museum of Modern Art, 1965. **499**

Sekey, A. Short-term auditory frequency discrimination. *Journal of the Acoustical Society of America,* 1963, *35,* 682–690. **249**

Sekuler, R. W., & Ganz, L. Aftereffect of seen motion with a stabilized retinal image. *Science,* 1963, *139,* 419–420. **522**

Sekuler, R. W., *see also* Erlebacher, A., 1969.

Selfridge, J., *see* Miller, G. A., 1950.

Seligman, M. E. P. CS redundancy and secondary punishment. *Journal of Experimental Psychology,* 1966, *4,* 546–550. **676**

Seligman, M. E. P., *see also* Maier, S. F., 1968, 1969; Overmier, J. B., 1967.

Selkin, J., & Wertheimer, M. Disappearance of the Müller-Lyer Illusion under prolonged inspection. *Perceptual and Motor Skills,* 1957, *7,* 265–266. **465**

Sem-Jacobsen, C. W., & Torkildsen, A. Depth recording and electrical stimulation in the human brain. In E. R. Ramey & D. S. O'Doherty (Eds.), *Electrical studies on the unanesthetized brain.* New York: Hoeber, 1960. Pp. 280–288. **660**

Semmes, J., *see* Lashley, K. S., 1951.

Senden, M. von, *see* von Senden, M.

Sermat, V., *see* Abelson, R. P., 1962.

Sersen, E. A., *see* Warren, R. M., 1958; Weinstein, S., 1964.

Seward, J. P. An experimental test of Guthrie's theory of reinforcement. *Journal of Experimental Psychology,* 1942, *30,* 247–256. **568**

Seward, J. P., & Raskin, D. C. The role of fear in aversive behavior. *Journal of Comparative and Physiological Psychology,* 1960, *53,* 328–335. **725**

Seward, J. P., Uyeda, A. A., & Olds, J. Resistance to extinction

following cranial self-stimulation. *Journal of Comparative and Physiological Psychology,* 1959, *52,* 294–299. **675**

Sgro, F. J. Beta motion thresholds. *Journal of Experimental Psychology,* 1963, *66,* 281–285. **526**

Sgro, J. A., Dyal, J. A., & Anastasio, E. J. Effects of constant delay of reinforcement on acquisition asymptote and resistance to extinction. *Journal of Experimental Psychology,* 1967, *73,* 634–636. **685**

Sgro, J. A., & Weinstock, S. Effects of delay on subsequent running under immediate reinforcement. *Journal of Experimental Psychology,* 1963, *66,* 260–263. **685**

Shaffer, J. P. Effect of different stimulus frequencies on discrimination learning with probabilistic reinforcement. *Journal of Experimental Psychology,* 1963, *65,* 265–269. **926**

Shaffer, M. M., *see* Steiner, S. S., 1968.

Shaffer, O., & Wallach, H. Extent-of-motion thresholds under subject-relative and object-relative conditions. *Perception and Psychophysics,* 1966, *1,* 447–451. **521, 522**

Shagass, C., *see* Malmo, R. B., 1951.

Shanmugam, A. V., & Miron, M. S. Semantic effects in mediated transfer. *Journal of Verbal Learning and Verbal Behavior,* 1966, *5,* 361–368. **1074, 1075**

Shankweiler, D. P., *see* Liberman, A. M., 1967.

Shapiro, M. M. Salivary conditioning in dogs during fixed-interval reinforcement contingent upon lever pressing. *Journal of the Experimental Analysis of Behavior,* 1961, *4,* 361–364. **565**

Shapiro, M. M., & Miller, T. M. On the relationship between conditioned and discriminative stimuli and between instrumental and consummatory responses. In W. F. Prokasy (Ed.), *Classical conditioning.* New York: Appleton, 1965. **565, 622**

Shapiro, S. I. Response latencies in paired-associate learning as a function of free association strength, hierarchy, directionality, and mediation. Doctoral dissertation, Pennsylvania State University, 1966. **888**

Sharma, K. N., *see* Jacobs, H. L., 1968.

Sharma, K. N., *see also* Jacobs, H. L., 1969.

Sharpless, S., & Jasper, H. H. Habituation of the arousal reaction. *Brain,* 1956, *79,* 655–680. **591, 833, 834**

Shatel, R. B., *see* Kimble, G. A., 1952.

Shaw, J. G., *see* Newell, A., 1958.

Shaw, W. A., *see* Beck, J., 1961, 1963.

Shaxby, J. H., & Gage, F. H. The localization of sounds in the median plane. *Medical Research Council Special Report,* Series 166. London, 1932. **262**

Sheahan, D., *see* Peterson, M. J., 1964.

Sheeley, E. C. Temporal integration as a function of frequency. *Journal of the Acoustical Society of America,* 1964, *36,* 1850–1857. **234**

Sheer, D. E. (Ed.). *Electrical stimulation of the brain.* Austin: University of Texas Press, 1961. **644**

Sheffield, F. D. Relations between classical conditioning and instrumental learning. In W. F. Prokasy (Ed.), *Classical conditioning.* New York: Appleton, 1965. 302–322. **567n, 695, 696, 697n**

Sheffield, F. D. A drive-induction theory of reinforcement. In R. N. Haber (Ed.), *Current research in motivation.* New York: Holt, Rinehart and Winston, 1966. Pp. 98–111. **622, 657, 691, 695**

Sheffield, F. D., & Campbell, B. A. The role of experience in the "spontaneous" activity of hungry rats. *Journal of Comparative and Physiological Psychology,* 1954, *47,* 97–100. **808, 822**

Sheffield, F. D., & Roby, T. B. Reward value of a non-nutritive sweet taste. *Journal of Comparative and Physiological Psychology,* 1950, *43,* 471–481. **691, 817**

Sheffield, F. D., Roby, T. B., & Campbell, B. A. Drive reduction versus consummatory behavior as determinants of reinforcement. *Journal of Comparative and Physiological Psychology,* 1954, *47,* 349–355. **797**

Sheffield, F. D., & Temmer, H. W. Relative resistance to extinction of escape training and avoidance training. *Journal of Experimental Psychology*, 1950, *40*, 287-298. **724**

Sheffield, F. D., Wulff, J. J., & Backer, R. Reward value of copulation without sex drive reduction. *Journal of Comparative and Physiological Psychology*, 1951, *44*, 3-8. **691, 797**

Sheffield, F. D., see also Campbell, B. A., 1953.

Sheffield, V. F. Extinction as a function of partial reinforcement and distribution of practice. *Journal of Experimental Psychology*, 1949, *39*, 511-526. **576, 695**

Shelden, C. H. Depolarization in the treatment of trigeminal neuralgia: Evaluation of compression and electrical methods; clinical concept of neurophysiological mechanism. In R. S. Knighton & P. R. Dumke (Eds.), *Pain*. Boston: Little, Brown, 1966. Pp. 373-386. **165, 166**

Shelley, W. B., see Arthur, R. P., 1959.

Shelnutt, J., see Davis, H., 1967.

Shepard, R. N. Comments on Professor Underwood's paper. In C. N. Cofer & B. B. Musgrave (Eds.), *Verbal behavior and learning: Problems and processes*. New York: McGraw-Hill, 1963. Pp. 48-75. **1001**

Shepard, R. N. Attention and the metric structure of the stimulus. *Journal of Mathematical Psychology*, 1964, *1*, 54-87. **1001n**

Shepard, R. N. Approximation to uniform gradients of generalization by monotone transformations of scale. In D. I. Mostofsky (Ed.), *Stimulus generalization*. Stanford: Stanford University Press, 1965. **761**

Shepard, R. N., & Chang, J. Forced-choice of recognition memory under steady-state conditions. *Journal of Verbal Learning and Verbal Behavior*, 1963, *2*, 93-101. **1119**

Shepard, R. N., & Chang, J. J. Stimulus generalization and classification. *Journal of Experimental Psychology*, 1963, *65*, 94-102. **1001**

Shepard, R. N., Hovland, C. I., & Jenkins, H. M. Learning and memorization of classifications. *Psychological Monographs*, 1961, *75* (whole no. 517). **968, 969, 1001n**

Shepard, R. N., & Teghtsoonian, M. Retention of information under conditions approaching a steady state. *Journal of Experimental Psychology*, 1961, *62*, 202-222. **1118**

Shepard, W. O. Learning set in preschool children. *Journal of Comparative and Physiological Psychology*, 1957, *50*, 15-17. **768**

Shepp, B., & Zeaman, D. Discrimination learning of size and brightness by retardates. *Journal of Comparative and Physiological Psychology*, 1966, *62*, 55-59. **613**

Shepp, B. E., & Eimas, P. D. Intradimensional and extradimensional shifts in the rat. *Journal of Comparative and Physiological Psychology*, 1964, *57*, 357-361. **751**

Shepp, B. E., & Turrisi, F. D. Learning and transfer of mediating responses in discriminative learning. In N. R. Ellis (Ed.), *International review of research in mental retardation*. Vol. II. New York: Academic Press, 1966. Pp. 85-121. **767**

Sherlock, L., see Smith, O. W., 1957.

Sherrick, C. E. Studies of apparent tactile movement. In D. R. Kenshalo (Ed.), *The skin senses*. Springfield, Ill.: Charles C Thomas, 1968. Pp. 331-344. **139**

Sherrick, C., & Mangabeira-Albernaz, P. L. Auditory threshold shifts produced by simultaneously pulsed contralateral stimuli. *Journal of the Acoustical Society of America*, 1961, *33*, 1381-1385. **242**

Sherrick, C. E., & Rogers, R. Apparent haptic movement. *Perception and Psychophysics*, 1966, *1*, 175-180. **139**

Sherrington, C. S. The spinal cord. In E. A. (Sharpey-) Schaefer (Ed.), *Text-book of physiology*. Edinburgh: Pentland, 1900. Vol. 2. Cited by Brobeck, J. R., 1960. **796**

Sherrington, C. S. *Integrative action of the nervous system*. New Haven: Yale University Press, 1906. **121**

Shibuya, S., see Shibuya, T., 1963.

Shibuya, T. Dissociation of olfactory response and mucosal potential. *Science*, 1964, *143*, 1338-1340. **221**

Shibuya, T., & Shibuya, S. Olfactory epithelium: Unitary responses in the tortoise. *Science*, 1963, *140*, 495-496. **217**

Shibuya, T., see also Tucker, D., 1965.

Shiffrin, R. M., see Atkinson, R. C., 1965.

Shinno, T. Developmental studies on distance-constancy. In Y. Akishige (Ed.), *Experimental researches on the structure of the perceptual space*. Fukuoka, Japan: Kyushu University, 1967. **550**

Shipley, T. Convergence function in binocular visual space: I. A note on theory. *Journal of the Optical Society of America*, 1957, *47*, 795-803. **493**

Shipley, T. The frontal reference surface of visual space. *Documenta Opthalmologica*, 1959, *13*, 487-516. **493**

Shipley, T. E. Jr., see Wishner, J., 1957.

Shipley, W. C. Indirect conditioning. *Journal of General Psychology*, 1935, *12*, 337-357. **1073**

Shlaer, S. The relation between visual acuity and illumination. *Journal of General Physiology*, 1937, *21*, 165-188. **299**

Shlaer, S., see also Hecht, S., 1936, 1942.

Shortess, G. K., & Krauskopf, J. Role of involuntary eye movements in stereoscopic acuity. *Journal of the Optical Society of America*, 1961, *51*, 555-559. **306, 491n**

Shower, E. G., & Buddulph, R. Differential pitch sensitivity of the ear. *Journal of the Acoustical Society of America*, 1931, *3*, 275-287. **18, 249**

Shuell, P. J., & Keppel, J. A further test of the chaining hypothesis of serial learning. *Journal of Verbal Learning and Verbal Behavior*, 1967, *6*, 439-445. **1012**

Shuell, T. J. Retroactive inhibition in free-recall learning of categorized lists. *Journal of Verbal Learning and Verbal Behavior*, 1968, *7*, 797-805. **1102**

Shuell, T. J., & Keppel, G. Retroactive inhibition as a function of learning method. *Journal of Experimental Psychology*, 1967, *75*, 457-463. **1102**

Sickles, W. R. Experimental evidence for the electrical character of visual fields derived from quantitative analysis of the Ponzo Illusion. *Journal of Experimental Psychology*, 1942, *30*, 84-91. **458**

Sidman, M. A note on functional relations obtained from group data. *Psychological Bulletin*, 1952, *49*, 263-269. **609, 917**

Sidman, M. Two temporal parameters of the maintenance of avoidance behavior by the white rat. *Journal of Comparative and Physiological Psychology*, 1953, *46*, 253-261. **730, 731**

Sidman, M. *Tactics of scientific research*. New York: Basic Books, 1960. **598, 600, 620**

Sidman, M. Avoidance behavior. In W. K. Honig (Ed.), *Operant behavior: Areas of research and application*. New York: Appleton, 1966. Pp. 448-498. **730, 731**

Sidman, M., Herrnstein, R. J., & Conrad, D. G. Maintenance of avoidance behavior by unavoidable shocks. *Journal of Comparative and Physiological Psychology*, 1957, *50*, 553-557. **717**

Sidman, M., & Stebbins, W. C. Satiation effects under fixed-ratio schedules of reinforcement. *Journal of Comparative and Physiological Psychology*, 1954, *47*, 114-116. **605, 608**

Sidman, M., see also Stein, L., 1958.

Sieck, M. H., see Wenzell, B., 1966; Wenzel, B., 1966.

Siegel, A., see Kurtz, K. H., 1966.

Siegel, P. S. The relationship between voluntary water intake, body weight loss, and number of hours of water privation in the rat. *Journal of Comparative and Physiological Psychology*, 1947, *40*, 231-238. **813**

Siegel, P. S., & MacDonnell, M. F. A repetition of the Calvin-Bicknell-Sperling study of conditioned drive.

Journal of Comparative and Physiological Psychology, 1954, *47,* 250–252. **805**

Siegel, S. *Nonparametric statistics for the behavioral sciences.* New York: McGraw-Hill, 1956. **61**

Siipola, E., Walker, W. N., & Kolb, D. Task attitudes in word association, projective and nonprojective. *Journal of Personality,* 1955, *23,* 441–459. **863, 875**

Siipola, E., *see also* Dunn, S., 1958.

Silvar, S. D., & Pollack, R. H. Racial differences in pigmentation of the fundus oculi. *Psychonomic Science,* 1967, *7,* 159–160. **461**

Silvar, S. D., *see also* Pollack, R. H., 1967.

Silverman, S. R. Tolerance for pure tones and speech in normal and defective hearing. *Annals of Otolaryngology,* 1947, *56,* 658–677. **254**

Silverman, S. R., *see also* Davis, H., 1960; Hirsh, I. J., 1952.

Silverstein, A. The prediction of individual association hierarchies from cultural frequencies. *American Journal of Psychology,* 1967, *80,* 88–94. **876**

Silverstein, A. Unlearning, spontaneous recovery and the partial-reinforcement effect in paired-associate learning. *Journal of Experimental Psychology,* 1967, *73,* 15–21. **1099**

Silverstein, A., *see also* Hochberg, J., 1956; Paul, C., 1968.

Simmel, M., *see* Heider, F., 1944.

Simmons, F. B., Epley, J. M., Lummis, R. C., Guttman, N., Frishkopf, L. S., Harmon, L. D., & Zwicker, E. Auditory nerve: Electrical stimulation in man. *Science,* 1965, *148,* 104–106. **244, 245**

Simmons, F. B., Mongeon, C. J., Lewis, W. R., & Huntingdon, D. A. Electrical stimulation of acoustical nerve and inferior colliculus. *Archives of Otolaryngology,* 1964, *79,* 559–567. **245**

Simmons, M. W., *see* Weisberg, P., 1966.

Simmons, R. The relative effectiveness of certain incentives in animal learning. *Comparative Psychology Monographs,* 1924, *2,* No. 7. **617, 672**

Simon, H. A., & Feigenbaum, E. A. An information-processing theory of some effects of similarity, familiarization, and meaningfulness in verbal learning. *Journal of Verbal Learning and Verbal Behavior,* 1964, *3,* 385–396. **1008**

Simon, H. A., & Kotovsky, K. Human acquisition of concepts for sequential patterns. *Psychological Review,* 1963, *70,* 534–546. **979**

Simon, H. A., *see also* Feigenbaum, E. A., 1961, 1962, 1963; Gregg, L. W., 1967; Newell, A., 1958, 1961, 1963.

Simon, S., *see* Maltzman, I., 1959, 1960; Martin, R. B., 1966.

Sinclair, D., *see* Hagen, E., 1953.

Sinclair, D. C. Cutaneous sensation and the doctrine of specific energy. *Brain,* 1955, *78,* 584–614. **167**

Sinclair, D. C., & Hinshaw, J. R. Sensory changes in nerve blocks induced by cooling. *Brain,* 1951, *74,* 318–335. **160**

Sinclair, J. C., *see* Olds, J., 1957.

Singer, D., *see* Jones, F. N., 1962.

Singer, G., & Day, R. H. Spatial adaptation and aftereffect with optically transformed vision: Effects of active and passive responding and the relationship between test and exposure responses. *Journal of Experimental Psychology,* 1966, *71,* 725–731. **536**

Singh, D., *see* Meyer, D. S., 1966.

Siqueland, E. R. Basic learning processes: Instrumental conditioning in infants. In H. W. Reese & L. P. Lipsitt (Eds.), *Experimental child psychology: The scientific study of child behavior and development.* New York, Academic Press, 1970. **673**

Siskel, M., Jr., *see* Collier, G., 1959.

Sjöberg, L., *see* Ekman, G., 1965.

Skaggs, E. B. Further studies in retroactive inhibition. *Psychological Monographs,* 1925, *34.* **1081**

Skilling, A. K. Verbal association. Mimeographed report under Cooperative Research Program, U. S. Office of Education Contract N1073, with the University of Michigan,

S. A. and M. T. Mednick, principal investigators, 1962. **863***n*

Skinner, B. F. Drive and reflex strength: II. *Journal of General Psychology,* 1932, *6,* 38–48. **602**

Skinner, B. F. Two types of conditioned reflex and a pseudotype. *Journal of General Psychology,* 1935, *12,* 66–77. **563, 565, 594**

Skinner, B. F. Two types of conditioned reflex: A reply to Konorski and Miller. *Journal of General Psychology,* 1937, *16,* 272–279. **699**

Skinner, B. F. *The behavior of organisms.* New York: Appleton, 1938. **102, 565***n,* **594, 596, 662, 663, 679, 681, 684, 704, 738, 741, 752, 917**

Skinner, B. F. "Superstition" in the pigeon. *Journal of Experimental Psychology,* 1948, *38,* 168–172. **683, 692**

Skinner, B. F. Are theories of learning necessary? *Psychological Review,* 1950, *57,* 193–216. **907**

Skinner, B. F. *Science and human behavior.* New York: Macmillan, 1953. **553, 566***n,* **616***n,* **677, 697**

Skinner, B. F. A case history in scientific method. *American Psychologist,* 1956, *11,* 221–233. **602, 603**

Skinner, B. F. Pigeons in a pelican. *American Psychologist,* 1960, *15,* 28–37. **584**

Skinner, B. F. Operant behavior. In W. K. Honig (Ed.), *Operant behavior: Areas of research and application.* New York: Appleton, 1966. **697**

Skinner, B. F., & Campbell, S. L. An automatic shocking-grid apparatus for continuous use. *Journal of Comparative and Physiological Psychology,* 1947, *40,* 305–307. **706**

Skinner, B. F., *see also* Estes, W. K., 1941; Ferster, C. B., 1957; Heron, W. T., 1937; Morse, W. H., 1957.

Sklar, D. L., *see* Ward, W. D., 1959.

Skolnick, A. The role of eye-movements in the autokinetic phenomenon. *Journal of Experimental Psychology,* 1940, *26,* 373–393. **529**

Skude, G. Complexities of human taste variation. *Journal of Heredity,* 1960, *51,* 259–263. **182**

Slamecka, N. J. Retroactive inhibition of connected discourse as a function of practice level. *Journal of Experimental Psychology,* 1960, *59,* 104–108. (a) **1085, 1086**

Slamecka, N. J. Retroactive inhibition of connected discourse as a function of similarity of topic. *Journal of Experimental Psychology,* 1960, *60,* 245–249. (b) **1083**

Slamecka, N. J. Proactive inhibition of connected discourse. *Journal of Experimental Psychology,* 1961, *62,* 295–301. **1103, 1104**

Slamecka, N. J. An inquiry into the doctrine of remote associations. *Psychological Review,* 1964, *71,* 61–77. **1013**

Slamecka, N. J. Supplementary report: A search for spontaneous recovery of verbal associations. *Journal of Verbal Learning and Verbal Behavior,* 1966, *5,* 205–207. **1099**

Slamecka, N. J. Transfer with mixed and unmixed lists as a function of semantic relations. *Journal of Experimental Psychology,* 1967, *73,* 405–410. **1061, 1070**

Slamecka, N. J., & Ceraso, J. Retroactive and proactive inhibition of verbal learning. *Psychological Bulletin,* 1960, *57,* 449–475. **1084**

Sleight, W. G. Memory and formal training. *British Journal of Psychology,* 1911, *4,* 386–457. **1031**

Sluckin, W. *Imprinting and early learning.* Chicago: Aldine, 1965. **584, 587, 588, 746**

Sluckin, W., *see also* Salzen, E. A., 1959.

Small, A. M., Jr. Some parameters influencing the pitch of amplitude modulated signals. *Journal of the Acoustical Society of America,* 1955, *27,* 751–760. **245**

Small, A. M., Jr. Audition. In P. R. Farnsworth (Ed.), *Annual review of psychology.* Vol. 14. Palo Alto, Calif.: Annual Reviews, 1963. (a) **234**

Small, A. M., Jr. Auditory adaptation. In J. Jerger (Ed.), *Modern developments in audiology.* New York: Academic Press, 1963. (b) **235**

Small, A. M., Jr., & Campbell, R. A. Masking of pulsed tones

distance discrimination. *Journal of Experimental Psychology,* 1949, *39,* 73-83. **700**

Solomon, R. L. Punishment. *American Psychologist,* 1964, *19,* 239-253. **738n**

Solomon, R. L., & Brush, E. S. Experimentally derived conceptions of anxiety and aversion. In M. R. Jones (Ed.), *Nebraska symposium on motivation.* Vol. 4. Lincoln: University of Nebraska Press, 1956. Pp. 212-305. **726**

Solomon, R. L., & Howes, D. H. Word frequency, personal values and visual duration thresholds. *Psychological Review,* 1951, *58,* 256-270. **444**

Solomon, R. L., Kamin, L. J., & Wynne, L. C. Traumatic avoidance learning: The outcome of several extinction procedures with dogs. *Journal of Abnormal and Social Psychology,* 1953, *48,* 291-302. **727, 732**

Solomon, R. L., & Postman, L. Frequency of usage as a determinant of recognition thresholds for words. *Journal of Experimental Psychology,* 1952, *43,* 195-201. **255, 444**

Solomon, R. L., & Turner, L. H. Discriminative classical conditioning in dogs paralyzed by curare can later control discriminative avoidance responses in the normal state. *Psychological Review,* 1962, *69,* 202-219. **728, 818**

Solomon, R. L., & Wynne, L. C. Traumatic avoidance learning: Acquisition in normal dogs. *Psychological Monographs,* 1953, *67,* (Whole no. 354). **725, 726**

Solomon, R. L., *see also* Black, A. H., 1962; Brush, F. R., 1955; Church, R. M., 1956, 1966; Graham, C. H., 1949; Howes, D., 1951; Maier, S. F., 1968, 1969; Rescorla, R. A., 1967; Turner, L. H., 1962; Wynne, L. C., 1955.

Soltz, D. F., & Wertheimer, M. The retention of "good" and "bad" figures. *American Journal of Psychology,* 1959, *72,* 450-452. **445**

Sommer, R. The effects of rewards and punishments during perceptual organization. *Journal of Personality,* 1957, *25,* 550-559. **440**

Sommer, R., *see also* Ayllon, T., 1956.

Sonoda, G. Perceptual constancies observed in plane pictures. In Y. Akishige (Ed.), *Experimental research on the structure of the perceptual space.* Fukuoka, Japan: Kyushu University, 1961. **501**

Spalding, D. A. Instinct with original observations on young animals. *Macmillan's Magazine,* 1873, *27,* 282-293. Reprinted in *British Journal of Animal Behaviour,* 1954, *2,* 2-11. **548, 549, 581**

Sparrock, J. M. B., *see* Barlow, H. B., 1964.

Spear, N. E. Replication report: Absence of a successive contrast effect on instrumental running behavior after a shift in sucrose concentration. *Psychological Reports,* 1965, *16,* 393-394. **634**

Spear, N. E., & Hill, W. F. Adjustment to new reward: Simultaneous- and successive-contrast effects. *Journal of Experimental Psychology,* 1965, *70,* 510-519. **640**

Spear, N. E., Mikulka, P. J., & Podd, M. Transfer as a function of time to mediate. *Journal of Experimental Psychology,* 1966, *72,* 40-46. **1058**

Spear, N. E., & Spitzner, J. H. Simultaneous and successive contrast effects in selective learning. *Psychological Monographs,* 1966, *80,* (Whole no. 618). **640**

Spearman, C. The proof and measurement of association between two things. *American Journal of Psychology,* 1904, *15,* 72-101. **61**

Spearman, C. The method of "right and wrong cases" without Gauss' formula. *British Journal of Psychology,* 1908, *2,* 227-242. **26**

Speelman, R., *see* Sperling, G., 1965.

Spelt, D. K. The conditioning of the human fetus *in utero. Journal of Experimental Psychology,* 1948, *38,* 338-346. **556**

Spelt, D. K., *see also* Finger, F. W., 1947.

Spence, J., & Schulz, R. Negative transfer in paired-associate learning as a function of first-list trials. *Journal of Verbal Learning and Verbal Behavior,* 1965, *4,* 397-400. **1036, 1068**

Spence, J. T., *see* Spence, K. W., 1966.

Spence, K. W. The nature of discrimination learning in animals. *Psychological Review,* 1936, *43,* 427-449. **576, 596, 770, 774**

Spence, K. W. The differential response in animals to stimuli varying within a single dimension. *Psychological Review,* 1937, *44,* 430-444. **596, 751, 760, 764, 770**

Spence, K. W. An experimental test of the continuity and noncontinuity theories of discrimination learning. *Journal of Experimental Psychology,* 1945, *35,* 253-266. **766**

Spence, K. W. The role of secondary reinforcement in delayed reward learning. *Psychological Review,* 1947, *54,* 1-8. **679, 682**

Spence, K. W. Theoretical interpretations of learning. In S. S. Stevens (Ed.), *Handbook of experimental psychology.* New York: Wiley, 1951. Pp. 690-729. **559, 773, 801, 805**

Spence, K. W. The nature of response in discrimination learning. *Psychological Review,* 1952, *59,* 89-93. **774, 775**

Spence, K. W. *Behavior theory and conditioning.* New Haven: Yale University Press, 1956. **596n, 597, 621, 622, 632, 633, 635, 681, 741, 789, 805, 812, 984**

Spence, K. W. A theory of emotionally based drive (D) and its relation to performance in simple learning situations. *American Psychologist,* 1958, *13,* 131-141. **789**

Spence, K. W., & Ross, L. E. A methodological study of the form and latency of eyelid responses in conditioning. *Journal of Experimental Psychology,* 1959, *58,* 376-381. **557**

Spence, K. W., & Spence, J. T. The motivational components of manifest anxiety: Drive and drive stimuli. In C. D. Spielberger (Ed.), *Anxiety and behavior.* New York: Academic Press, 1966. Pp. 291-326. **790**

Spence, K. W., *see also* Bergman, G., 1944.

Spencer, W. A., Thompson, R. F. & Neilson, D. R., Jr. Response decrement of the flexion reflex in the acute spinal cat and transient restoration by strong stimuli. *Journal of Neurophysiology,* 1966, *29,* 221-239. **591**

Sperling, D. S., *see* Calvin, J. S., 1953.

Sperling, G. The information available in brief visual presentations. *Psychological Monographs,* 1960, *74,* (Whole No. 498). **444**

Sperling, G. A model for visual memory tasks. *Human Factors,* 1963, *5,* 19-31. **430, 444**

Sperling, G., & Speelman, R. Visual spatial localization during object motion, apparent object motion and image motion produced by eye movements. *Program of the 1965 annual meeting of the Optical Society of America, Journal of the Optical Society of America,* 1965, *55,* 1576 (abstract). **531**

Sperling, H. G., & Jolliffe, C. L. Intensity-time relationship at threshold for spectral stimuli in human vision. *Journal of the Optical Society of America,* 1965, *55,* 191-199. **303**

Sperry, R. W., & Miner, N. Pattern perception following insertion of mica plates into visual cortex. *Journal of Comparative and Physiological Psychology,* 1955, *48,* 463-469. **470**

Sperry, R. W., Miner, N., & Meyers, R. E. Visual pattern perception following subpial slicing and tantalum wire implantations in the visual cortex. *Journal of Comparative and Physiological Psychology,* 1955, *48,* 50-58. **470**

Spiegel, H. G. Ueber den Einfluss des Zwischenfeldes auf gesehene Abstaende. *Psychologische Forschung,* 1937, *21,* 327-383. **458**

Spigel, I. M. *Readings in the study of visually perceived movement.* New York: Harper and Row, 1965. **520**

Spiker, C. C. Experiments with children on the hypotheses of acquired distinctiveness and equivalence of cues. *Child Development,* 1956, *27,* 253-263. **751, 788**

Spiker, C. C. Associative transfer in paired-associate verbal learning. *Child Development*, 1960, *31*, 73–87. **1036**

Spiker, C. C. The hypothesis of stimulus interaction and an explanation of stimulus compounding. In L. P. Lipsitt & C. C. Spiker (Eds.), *Advances in child development and behavior.* Vol. 1. New York: Academic Press, 1963. Pp. 233–264. **782**

Spiker, C. C., see also Norcross, K. J., 1957, 1958.

Spitz, H. H. The present status of the Köhler-Wallach theory of satiation. *Psychological Bulletin*, 1958, *55*, 1–28. **469**

Spitzner, J. H., see Spear, N. E., 1966.

Spong, P., Haider, M., & Lindsley, D. B. Selective attentiveness and cortical evoked responses to visual and auditory stimuli. *Science*, 1965, *148*, 395–397. **233**

Spong, P., see also Sampson, H., 1961.

Spooner, A., & Kellogg, W. N. The backward conditioning curve. *American Journal of Psychology*, 1947, *60*, 321–334. **558, 561**

Spragg, S. D. S. Morphine addiction in chimpanzees. *Comparative Psychology Monographs*, 1940, *15*, No. 7. **557n**

Spreen, O., & Schulz, R. W. Parameters of abstraction, meaningfulness, and pronunciability for 329 nouns. *Journal of Verbal Learning and Verbal Behavior*, 1966, *5*, 459–468. **901**

Staats, A. W., & Staats, C. K. Meaning and *m*: Correlated but separate. *Psychological Review*, 1959, *66*, 136–144. **865**

Staats, C. K., see Staats, A. W., 1959.

Stainton, W. H. The phenomenon of Broca and Sulzer in foveal vision. *Journal of the Optical Society of America*, 1928, *16*, 26–39. **307**

Staner, B. J. Transfer as a function of simultaneous stimulus and response generalization. Unpublished master's thesis, Northwestern University, 1956. **1052, 1056**

Stanley, J. C., Jr., see Jenkins, W. O., 1950.

Stanley, W. C. Extinction as a function of the spacing of extinction trials. *Journal of Experimental Psychology*, 1952, *43*, 249–260. **576, 695**

Stanley, W. C., & Elliot, O. Differential human handling as reinforcing events and as treatments influencing later social behavior in basenji puppies. *Psychological Reports*, 1962, *10*, 775–788. **704**

Stark, K., see Postman, L., 1964, 1965, 1967, 1968, 1969.

Stark, L. Stability, oscillations, and noise in the human pupil servomechanism. *Proceedings of the Institute of Radio Engineers*, 1959, *47*, 1925–1939. **392**

Stavrianos, B. K. The relation of shape perception to explicit judgments of inclination. *Archives of Psychology*, 1945, *296*. **499, 515, 516**

Stearns, E. M. Reward value of saline and water for the rat. *Psychonomic Science*, 1965, *2*, 193–194. **190**

Stebbins, W. C. Auditory reaction time and the derivation of equal loudness contours for the monkey. *Journal of the Experimental Analysis of Behavior*, 1966, *9*, 135–142. **757**

Stebbins, W. C., see also Sidman, M., 1954.

Steele, W. M., see Cameron, E. H., 1905.

Steffy, R. A., see Eriksen, C. W., 1964.

Stein, L. Secondary reinforcement established with subcortical stimulation. *Science*, 1958, *127*, 466–467. **655, 674, 675**

Stein, L. Reciprocal action of reward and punishment mechanism. In R. Heath (Ed.), *The role of pleasure in behavior.* New York: Hoeber, 1964. Pp. 113–139. **647**

Stein, L., Sidman, M., & Brady, J. V. Some effects of two temporal variables on conditioned suppression. *Journal of the Experimental Analysis of Behavior*, 1958, *1*, 153–162. **713, 716**

Stein, L., see also Ray, O. S., 1959.

Steinberg, J. C., & Gardner, M. B. The dependence of hearing impairment on sound intensity. *Journal of the Acoustical Society of America*, 1937, *9*, 11–23. **240**

Steiner, S. S., Beer, B., & Shaffer, M. M. Escape from self-produced rates of brain-stimulation. *Science*, 1968, *163*, 90–91. **692**

Steiner, W. G. Electrical activity of rat brain as a correlate of primary drive. *Electroencephalography and Clinical Neurophysiology*, 1962, *14*, 233–243. **837**

Steinig, K. Untersuchungen über die Wahrnehmung der Bewegung durch das Auge: IV. *Zeitschrift für Psychologie*, 1929, *109*, 291–336. **527**

Steinmeyer, C. H., see Levine, M., 1967.

Stellar, E., & Hill, J. H. The rat's rate of drinking as a function of water deprivation. *Journal of Comparative and Physiological Psychology*, 1952, *45*, 96–102. **622, 813, 814, 818**

Stellar, E., see also Corbit, J. D., 1964; Pfaffmann, C., 1954.

Stellwagen, W. T., & Card, G. W. Human learning in multiple T-maze: An investigation of verbal and motor learning modes. *Psychonomic Science*, 1965, *2*, 227–228. **698**

Stenson, H. H. The physical factor structure of random forms and their judged complexity. *Perception and Psychophysics*, 1966, *1*, 303–310. **449**

Sterman, M. B., & Wyrwicka, W. EEG correlates of sleep: Evidence for separate forebrain substrates. *Brain Research*, 1967, *6*, 143–163. **838**

Sterman, M. B., see also Clemente, C. D., 1964; Roth, S. R., 1967; Wyrwicka, W., 1962.

Stern, J. A., see Gross, K., 1967; Hahn, W. W., 1962, 1964.

Sternbach, R. A. *Pain: A psychophysical analysis.* New York: Academic Press, 1968. **122, 155, 157**

Sternberg, S. Stochastic learning theory. In R. D. Luce, R. R. Bush, & E. Galanter (Eds.), *Handbook of mathematical psychology.* Vol. II. New York: Wiley, 1963. Pp. 9–120. **912n**

Stetson, R. H., & McDill, J. A. Mechanism of the different types of movement with a preliminary report of experimental data. *Psychological Monographs*, 1923, *32*, 18–40. **379**

Stettner, L. J., see Moltz, H., 1960.

Stevens, C. F. *Neurophysiology: A primer.* New York: Wiley, 1966. **95**

Stevens, C. F. Synaptic physiology. *Proceedings of the IEEE*, 1968, *56*, 915–930. **90**

Stevens, J. C., & Guirao, N. Individual loudness functions. *Journal of the Acoustical Society of America*, 1964, *36*, 2210–2213. **247**

Stevens, J. C., & Stevens, S. S. Warmth and cold: Dynamics of sensory intensity. *Journal of Experimental Psychology*, 1960, *60*, 183–192. **80**

Stevens, J. C., & Stevens, S. S. Brightness function: Effects of adaptation. *Journal of the Optical Society of America*, 1963, *53*, 375–385. **81**

Stevens, J. C., see also Marks, L. E., 1966; Scharf, B., 1959; Stevens, S. S., 1960.

Stevens, K. N., see Rosenblith, W. A., 1953.

Stevens, S. S. A scale for the measurement of a psychological magnitude: Loudness. *Psychological Review*, 1936, *43*, 405–416. **67**

Stevens, S. S. (Ed.). *Handbook of experimental psychology.* New York: Wiley, 1951. **17, 48, 316**

Stevens, S. S. Mathematics, measurement, and psychophysics. In S. S. Stevens (Ed.), *Handbook of experimental psychology.* New York: Wiley, 1951. Pp. 1–49. **833**

Stevens, S. S. The measurement of loudness. *Journal of the Acoustical Society of America*, 1955, *27*, 815–829. **247**

Stevens, S. S. On the averaging of data. *Science*, 1955, *121*, 113–116. **65**

Stevens, S. S. Calculation of the loudness of complex noises. *Journal of the Acoustical Society of America*, 1956, *28*, 807–832. (a) **248, 249**

Stevens, S. S. The direct estimation of sensory magnitudes—loudness. *American Journal of Psychology*, 1956, *69*, 1–25. (b) **247**

Stevens, S. S. On the psychophysical law. *Psychological Review*, 1957, *64*, 153–181. **69, 82, 928**

Stevens, S. S. Problems and methods of psychophysics. *Psychological Bulletin*, 1958, *54*, 177–196. **86**

Stevens, S. S. Cross-modality validation of subjective scales for loudness, vibration, and electric shock. *Journal of Experimental Psychology*, 1959, *57*, 201–209. **84**

Stevens, S. S. On the new psychophysics. *Scandinavian Journal of Psychology*, 1960, *1*, 27–35. **175**

Stevens, S. S. Is there a quantal threshold? In W. A. Rosenblith (Ed.), *Sensory communication*. New York: Wiley, 1961. **34**

Stevens, S. S. The psychophysics of sensory function. In W. A. Rosenblith (Ed.), *Sensory communication*. New York: Wiley, 1961. **79, 247**

Stevens, S. S. The basis of psychophysical judgments. *Journal of the Acoustical Society of America*, 1963, *35*, 611–612. **248**

Stevens, S. S. Matching functions between loudness and ten other continua. *Perception and Psychophysics*, 1966, *1*, 5–8. **84**

Stevens, S. S., & Davis, H. *Hearing*. New York: Wiley, 1938. **228, 230, 233, 244, 249**

Stevens, S. S., & Galanter, E. H. Ratio scales and category scales for dozen perceptual continua. *Journal of Experimental Psychology*, 1957, *54*, 377–411. **65, 82**

Stevens, S. S., & Greenbaum, H. B. Regression effects in psychophysical judgment. *Perception and Psychophysics*, 1966, *1*, 439–446. **84**

Stevens, S. S., & Guirao, N. Loudness, reciprocality, and partition scales. *Journal of the Acoustical Society of America*, 1962, *34*, 1466–1471. **248**

Stevens, S. S., Morgan, C. T., & Volkmann, J. Theory of neural quantum in the discrimination of loudness and pitch. *American Journal of Psychology*, 1941, *54*, 315–35. **33**

Stevens, S. S., & Newman, E. B. The localization of actual sources of sound. *American Journal of Psychology*, 1936, *48*, 297–306. **266**

Stevens, S. S., & Poulton, E. C. The estimation of loudness by unpracticed observers. *Journal of Experimental Psychology*, 1956, *51*, 71–78. **70**

Stevens, S. S., & Stevens, J. C. Brightness function: Parametric effects of adaptation and contrast. *Journal of the Optical Society of America*, 1960, *50*, 1139. **411**

Stevens, S. S., & Volkmann, J. The relation of pitch to frequency, a revised scale. *American Journal of Psychology*, 1940, *53*, 329–353. **67, 244**

Stevens, S. S., & Warshofsky, F. *Sound and hearing*. New York: Time, Inc., 1965. **270**

Stevens, S. S., *see also* Harper, R. S., 1948; Hawkins, J. E. Jr., 1950; Hudgins, C. V., 1947; Lane, H. L., 1961; Reese, T. S., 1960; Stevens, J. C., 1960, 1963.

Stevenson, H. W., & Bitterman, M. E. The distance-effect in the transposition of intermediate size by children. *American Journal of Psychology*, 1955, *68*, 274–279. **765**

Stevenson, H. W., Iscoe, I., & McConnell, C. A developmental study of transposition. *Journal of Experimental Psychology*, 1955, *49*, 278–280. **765**

Stevenson, J. A. F., & Rixon, R. H. Environmental temperature and deprivation of food and water on the spontaneous activity of rats. *Yale Journal of Biology and Medicine*, 1957, *29*, 575–584. **824**

Stevenson, J. A. F., *see also* Morgenson, G. J., 1966.

Stevenson, J. G. Reinforcing effects of chaffinch song. *Animal Behaviour*, 1967, *15*, 427–432. **693**

Stevenson, J. G. Song as a reinforcer. In R. A. Hinde (Ed.), *Bird vocalizations in relation to current problems in biology and psychology*. Cambridge: Cambridge University Press, 1969. **693**

Stevenson, J. G., & Reese, T. W. The effect of two schedules of primary and conditioned reinforcement. *Journal of the Experimental Analysis of Behavior*, 1962, *5*, 505–510. **671**

Steward, J. R., *see* Bousfield, W. A., 1961.

Stewart, E. C. The Gelb effect. *Journal of Experimental Psychology*, 1959, *57*, 235–242. **419**

Stewart, M. R., *see* Fagot, R. F., 1968.

Stigler, R. Chronophotische Studien über der Umgebungskontrast. *Pflügers Archiv für die gesamte Physiologie*, 1910, *134*, 365–435. **429**

Stiles, W. S. Visual properties studied by subjective measurements on the colour-adapted eye. *British Medical Bulletin*, 1953, *9*, 41–49. **342**

Stiles, W. S. Color vision: The approach through increment threshold sensitivity. *Proceedings of the National Academy of Science*, 1959, *45*, 100. **341**

Stiles, W. S., & Crawford, B. H. The luminous efficiency of rays entering the eye pupil at different points. *Proceedings of the Royal Society* (London), Ser. B, 1933, *112*, 428–450. **302**

Stiles, W. S., & Crawford, B. The luminal brightness increment as a function of wavelength for different conditions of the foveal and parafoveal retina. *Proceedings of the Royal Society* (London), Ser. B, 1934, *113*, 496–530. **334, 337**

Stiles, W. S., *see also* Wyszecki, G., 1967.

Stockwell, F. E., *see* Cieutat, V. J., 1958; Noble, C. E., 1957.

Stokes, L. W., *see* Bolles, R. C., 1965.

Stolurow, L. M. Rodent behavior in the presence of barriers: II. The metabolic maintenance method; A technique for caloric drive control and manipulation. *Journal of Genetic Psychology*, 1951, *79*, 289–335. **812, 826**

Stolwijk, J. A. J., *see* Hardy, J. D., 1968.

Stone, H. Determination of odor difference limens for three compounds. *Journal of Experimental Psychology*, 1963, *66*, 466–473. (a) **202**

Stone, H. Techniques for odor measurement: Olfactometric vs. sniffing. *Journal of Food Science*, 1963, *28*, 719–725. (b) **198, 201**

Stone, H. Behavioral aspects of absolute and differential olfactory sensitivity. *Annals of the New York Academy of Science*, 1964, *2*, 527–534. **18, 199**

Stone, H., & Bosley, J. Olfactory discrimination and Weber's Law. *Perceptual and Motor Skills*, 1965, *20*, 657–665. **202**

Stone, H., Ough, C. S., & Pangborn, R. M. Determination of odor difference thresholds. *Journal of Food Science*, 1962, *27*, 197–202. **202**

Stone, H., *see also* Ough, C. S., 1961.

Stone, L. J., & Dallenbach, K. M. Adaptation to the pain of radiant heat. *American Journal of Psychology*, 1934, *46*, 229–242. **159**

Stone, P. J., *see* Hunt, E. B., 1966.

Storms, L. H. Apparent backward association: A situational effect. *Journal of Experimental Psychology*, 1958, *55*, 390–395. **872**

Storms, L. H., *see also* Russell, W. A., 1955.

Story, A. Figural after-effects as a function of the perceived characteristics of the inspection figure. *American Journal of Psychology*, 1959, *72*, 46–56. **530**

Strassburger, F., & Wertheimer, M. The discrepancy hypothesis of affect and association values of nonsense syllables. *Psychological Reports*, 1959, *5*, 528. **900**

Stratton, G. M. Some preliminary experiments on vision without inversion of the retinal image. *Psychological Review*, 1896, *3*, 611–617. **533**

Stratton, G. M. Upright vision and the retinal image. *Psychological Review*, 1897, *4*, 182–187. **533**

Stratton, G. M. The psychology of change: How is the perception of movement related to that of succession? *Psychological Review*, 1911, *18*, 262–293. **527**

Straughan, J. H., *see* Estes, W. K., 1954.

Ström, L., see Borg, G., 1967; Diamant, H., 1963; Hensel, H., 1951.

Studdert-Kennedy, M., see Liberman, A. M., 1967.

Stuiver, M. Biophysics of the sense of smell. Doctoral dissertation, University of Groningen, Netherlands, 1958. **200, 202, 210, 211**

Su, J., Berkley, M. A., Terman, M., & Kling, J. W. Rate of intracranial self-stimulation as a function of stimulus waveform and intensity. Psychonomic Science, 1966, 5, 219-220. **646**

Suci, G. J., see Jenkins, J. J., 1958, 1959.

Sulzer, D., see Broca, A., 1903.

Sumby, W. H., & Pollack, I. Visual contribution to speech intelligibility. Journal of the Acoustical Society of America, 1954, 26, 212-215. **256**

Summers, D. A., see Hammond, K. R., 1965.

Supa, M., Cotzin, M., & Dallenbach, K. M. "Facial vision": The perception of obstacles by the blind. American Journal of Psychology, 1944, 57, 133-183. **270**

Suppes, P. Introduction to logic. Princeton, N.J.: Van Nostrand, 1957. **906, 943**

Suppes, P., & Atkinson, R. C. Markov learning models for multiperson interactions. Stanford: Stanford University Press, 1960. **934, 990**

Suppes, P. & Frankmann, R. W. Test of stimulus sampling theory for a continuum of responses with unimodal non-contingent determinant reinforcement. Journal of Experimental Psychology, 1961, 61, 122-132. **934**

Suppes, P., & Ginsberg, R. A fundamental property of all-or-none models, binominal distribution of responses prior to conditioning, with application to concept formation in children. Psychological Review, 1963, 70, 139-161. **951, 952, 996**

Suppes, P., Groen, G., & Schlag-Rey, M. A model for response latency in paired-associate learning. Journal of Mathematical Psychology, 1966, 3, 99-128. **957**

Suppes, P., Rouanet, H., Levine, M., & Frankmann, R. W. Empirical comparison of models for a continuum of responses with non-contingent bimodal reinforcement. In R. C. Atkinson (Ed.), Studies in mathematical psychology. Stanford: Stanford University Press, 1964. Pp. 358-379. **934**

Suppes, P., & Zinnes, J. L. Stochastic learning theories for a response continuum with nondeterminant reinforcement. Psychometrika, 1961, 26, 373-390. **934**

Suppes, P., & Zinnes, J. L. A continuous-response task with nondeterminant, contingent reinforcement. Journal of Mathematical Psychology, 1966, 3, 197-216. **934**

Suppes, P., see also Estes, W. K., 1959; Luce, R. D., 1965; Roberts, F. S., 1967.

Sutherland, N. S. Stimulus analyzing mechanisms. In Proceedings of a symposium on the mechanization of thought processes. Vol. II. London: Her Majesty's Stationery Office, 1959. Pp. 575-609. **1001**

Sutherland, N. S. Visual discrimination of horizontal and vertical rectangles by rats on a new discrimination training apparatus. Quarterly Journal of Experimental Psychology, 1961, 13, 117-121. **522**

Suydam, M. M., see Myers, J. L., 1963, 1966.

Svaetichin, G. The cone action potential. Acta Physiologica Scandinavica, 1956, 39, 17-46. **324**

Svaetichin, G., & MacNichol, E. F. Retinal mechanisms for chromatic and achromatic vision. Annals of the New York Academy of Science, 1958, 74, 385. **334**

Svaetichin, G., see also MacNichol, E. F., Jr., 1958.

Swanson, R., & Benton A. L. Some aspects of the genetic development of right-left discrimination. Child Development, 1955, 26, 123-133. **540**

Sweet, W. Pain. In J. Field (Ed.), Handbook of physiology: Neurophysiology. Sec. 1, Vol. 1. Washington, D.C.: American Physiological Society, 1959. Pp. 459-506. **162**

Sweet, W. H., see also Wall, P. D., 1967; White, J. C., 1955.

Swenson, E. J. Retroactive inhibition: A review of the literature. Minneapolis: University of Minnesota Press, 1941. **1088**

Swenson, H. A. The relative influence of accommodation and convergence in the judgment of distance. Journal of General Psychology, 1932, 7, 360-380. **480**

Swets, J. A. Central factors in auditory frequency selectivity. Psychological Bulletin, 1963, 60, 429-440. **240**

Swets, J. A. Is there a sensory threshold? Science, 1961, 134, 168-177. Also in J. A. Swets, Signal detection and recognition by human observers. New York: Wiley, 1964. **32**

Swets, J. A., Tanner, W. P., & Birdsall, T. G. Decision processes in perception. Psychological Review, 1961, 68, 301-340. **34**

Swets, J. A., see also Green, D. M., 1966.

Talbot, S. A., see Marshall, W. H., 1942.

Talbot, W. H., see Mountcastle, V. B., 1967.

Tallantis, B., see Grant, D. A., 1949.

Tallarico, R. B. Studies of visual depth perception: III. Choice behavior of newly hatched chicks on a visual cliff. Perceptual and Motor Skills, 1961, 12, 259-262. **549**

Tallarico, R. B., & Farrell, W. M. Studies of visual depth perception: An effect of early experience on chicks on a visual cliff. Journal of Comparative and Physiological Psychology, 1964, 57, 94-96. **549**

Tanaka, K. Developmental studies on size constancy. In Y. Akishige (Ed.), Experimental researches on the structure of the perceptual space. Bull. of the Faculty of Literature of Kyushu University, No. 10, Fukuoka, Japan, 1967. **550**

Tanner, W. P., see Swets, J. A., 1961.

Tasaki, I., Davis, H., & Eldredge, D. H. Exploration of cochlear potentials in guinea pig with a microelectrode. Journal of the Acoustical Society of America, 1954, 26, 765-773. **230**

Tasaki, I., Davis, H., & LeGouix, J. P. Space-time pattern of the cochlear microphonics (guinea pig) as recorded by differential electrodes. Journal of the Acoustical Society of America, 1952, 24, 502-519. **230**

Tasaki, I., see also Maruhashi, J., 1952.

Tateda, H., & Beidler, L. M. The receptor potential of the taste cell of the rat. Journal of General Physiology, 1964, 47, 479-486. **180**

Taub, E., & Berman, A. J. Movement and learning in the absence of sensory feedback. In S. J. Freedman (Ed.), The neuropsychology of spatially oriented behavior. Homewood, Ill.: Dorsey Press, 1968. **533**

Taub, T., see Glanzer, M., in press.

Tauc, L., see Bruner, J., 1966; Kandel, E. R., 1965.

Tausch, R. Optische Täuschungen als artifizielle Effekte der Gestaltungsprozesse von Grössen und Formenkonstanz in der natürlichen Raumwahrnehmung. Psychologische Forschung, 1954, 24, 299-348. **460, 462**

Taylor, E., see Smith, O. A. Jr., 1961.

Taylor, J. A. Drive theory and manifest anxiety. Psychological Bulletin, 1956, 53, 303-320. **789**

Taylor, J. G. The behavioral basis of perception. New Haven: Yale University Press, 1962. **453, 533, 542, 543n**

Taylor, R. W., see Jeffress, L. A., 1961.

Taylor, W. C., see Miller, G. A., 1948.

Teas, D. Lateralization of acoustic transients. Journal of the Acoustical Society of America, 1962, 34, 1460-1465. **263**

Teas, D. C., Eldredge, D. H., & Davis, H. Cochlear responses to acoustic transients: An interpretation of whole-nerve action potentials. Journal of the Acoustical Society of America, 1962, 34, 1438-1459. **230**

Teas, D. C., see also Feddersen, W. E., 1957; Sandel, T. T., 1955.

Tees, R. C., & More, L. K. Effect of amount of perceptual learning upon disappearances observed under reduced stimulation conditions. *Perception and Psychophysics,* 1967, *2,* 565–568. **454**

Teghtsoonian, M., & Teghtsoonian, R. Scaling apparent distance in natural indoor settings. *Psychonomic Science,* 1969, *16,* 281–283. **514**

Teghtsoonian, M., *see also* Shephard, R. N., 1961.

Teghtsoonian, R., & Campbell, B. A. Random activity of the rat during food deprivation as a function of environmental conditions. *Journal of Comparative and Physiological Psychology,* 1960, *53,* 242–244. **822**

Teghtsoonian, R., *see also* Campbell, B. A., 1958, 1961; Teghtsoonian, M., 1969.

Teichner, W. H. Experimental extinction as a function of the intertrial intervals during conditioning and extinction. *Journal of Experimental Psychology,* 1952, *44,* 170–178. **570**

Teitelbaum, P. Disturbances of feeding and drinking behavior after hypothalmic lesions. In M. R. Jones (Ed.), *Nebraska symposium on motivation.* Lincoln: University of Nebraska Press, 1961. **651**

Teitelbaum, P. The use of operant methods in the assessment and control of motivational states. In W. K. Honig (Ed.), *Operant behavior: Areas of research and application.* New York: Appleton, 1966. **697**

Teitelbaum, P., & Epstein, A. N. The lateral hypothalamic syndrome. *Psychological Review,* 1962, *69,* 74–90. **674, 651**

Teitelbaum, P., *see also* Epstein, A. N., 1962; Hoebel, B. G., 1962; Koh, S. D., 1961.

Temmer, H. W., *see* Sheffield, F. D., 1950.

Templeton, W. B., *see* Howard, I. P., 1964, 1965, 1966.

ten Doesschate, J., & Alpern, M. The effect of photoexcitation of the two retinas on pupil size. *Journal of Neurophysiology,* 1967, *30,* 562–576. **391, 392**

Terman, J. S. The control of interresponse times by brain-stimulation reinforcement. Unpublished doctoral dissertation, Brown University, 1968. **649, 650**

Terman, J. S., Terman, M., & Kling, J. W. Some temporal properties of intracranial self-stimulation. *Physiology and Behavior,* 1970, *5,* 183–191. **649**

Terman, M., & Kling, J. W. Discrimination of brightness differences by rats with food or brain-stimulation reinforcement. *Journal of the Experimental Analysis of Behavior,* 1968, *11,* 29–37. **619, 655, 701**

Terman, M., *see also* Su, J. 1966.

Terrace, H. S. The effects of retinal locus and attention on the perception of words. *Journal of Experimental Psychology,* 1959, *58,* 383–385. **444**

Terrace, H. S. Discrimination learning with and without errors. *Journal of the Experimental Analysis of Behavior,* 1963, *6,* 1–27. (a) **699, 778**

Terrace, H. S. Errorless discrimination learning in the pigeon: Effects of chlorpromazine and imipramine. *Science,* 1963, *140,* 318–319. (b) **779**

Terrace, H. S. Wavelength generalization after discrimination learning with and without errors. *Science,* 1964, *144,* 78–80. **778**

Terrace, H. S. Stimulus control. In W. K. Honig (Ed.), *Operant behavior: Areas of research and application.* New York: Appleton, 1966. Pp. 271–344. (a) **699, 700, 776, 777, 778**

Terrace, H. S. Behavioral contrast and the peak shift: Effects of extended discrimination training. *Journal of the Experimental Analysis of Behavior,* 1966, *9,* 613–617. (b) **641**

Terrace, H. S. Discrimination learning and inhibition. *Science,* 1966, *154,* 1677–1680. (c) **779**

Terwilliger, R. F. Retinal size as a determiner of the direction of size distortion in figural after-effects. *Quarterly Journal of Experimental Psychology,* 1961, *13,* 209–217. **471n**

Terwilliger, R. F. Evidence for a relationship between figural after-effects and after-images. *American Journal of Psychology,* 1963, *76,* 306–310. **473**

Teuber, H. L. Perception. In J. Field, H. W. Magoun, & V. E. Hall (Eds.), *Handbook of physiology: Section 1. Neurophysiology.* Vol. 3. Washington, D. C.: American Physiological Society, 1960. **530**

Teuber, H. L., *see also* Rudel, R. G., 1963.

Theios, H. J., & Brelsford, J., Jr. Theoretical interpretations of a Markov model for avoidance conditioning. *Journal of Mathematical Psychology,* 1966, *3,* 140–162. **996**

Theios, J., *see also* Bower, G. H., 1964.

Thiery, A. Ueber geometrisch-optische Täuschungen. *Philosophisches Studien,* 1895, *11,* 307–370. **458**

Thiery, A. Ueber geometrisch-optische Täuschungen. *Philosophisches Studien,* 1896, *12,* 67–126. **460**

Thompson, C. P. On the incompatibility of the Houston and Osgood transfer surfaces. *Psychological Review,* 1966, *73,* 586–588. **1056**

Thompson, H. S., *see* von Noorden, G. K., 1964.

Thompson, M. E. Learning as a function of the absolute and relative amounts of work. *Journal of Experimental Psychology,* 1944, *34,* 506–515. **574**

Thompson, P. O., Webster, J. C., & Gales, R. S. Liveness effects on the intelligibility of noise-masked speech. *Journal of the Acoustical Society of America,* 1961, *33,* 604–605. **257**

Thompson, P. O., *see also* Webster, J. C., 1954.

Thompson, R. & McConnell, J. V. Classical conditioning in the planarian, *Dugesia dorotocephala. Journal of Comparative and Physiological Psychology,* 1955, *48,* 65–68. **556**

Thompson, R. F. *Foundations of physiological psychology.* New York: Harper, 1967. **844**

Thompson, R. F., & Spencer, W. A. Habituation: A model phenomenon for the study of neuronal substrates of behavior. *Psychological Review,* 1966, 16–43. **591**

Thompson, R. F., *see also* Benjamin, R. M., 1959; Briggs, G. E., 1954; Hoffeld, D. R., 1960; Spencer, W. A., 1966.

Thompson, T. I. Visual reinforcement in fighting cocks. *Journal of the Experimental Analysis of Behavior,* 1964. *7,* 45–49. **696n**

Thompson, T. I., & Bloom, W. Aggressive behavior and extinction-induced response-rate increase. *Psychonomic Science,* 1966, *5,* 335–336. **695**

Thompson, W. E., *see* Besch, N. F., 1962.

Thomson, C. W., *see* Johnson, R. C., 1960.

Thomson, L. C., & Wright, W. D. The convergence of the tritanopic confusion loci and the derivation of the fundamental response functions. *Journal of the Optical Society of America,* 1953, *43,* 890–894. **329**

Thorkildsen, A., *see* Sem-Jacobsen, C. W., 1960.

Thorndike, E. L. Animal intelligence: An experimental study of the associative processes in animals. *Psychological Review* (Monograph Supplement), 1898, *2,* No. 8. **598, 609, 678, 734**

Thorndike, E. L. The instinctive reactions of young chicks. *Psychological Review,* 1899, *6,* 282–291. **548, 549**

Thorndike, E. L. *Educational psychology,* New York: Science Press, 1903. **1020**

Thorndike, E. L. *Animal intelligence.* New York: Macmillan, 1911. **609, 678, 690**

Thorndike, E. L. *Educational psychology: Vol. II. The psychology of learning.* New York: Teachers College, 1913. **597**

Thorndike, E. L. *Educational psychology: Vol. III. Mental work and fatigue.* New York: Teachers College, 1914. **1122**

Thorndike, E. L. Reward and punishment in animal learning. *Comparative Psychological Monographs,* 1932, *8,* (Whole No. 39). **734**

Thorndike, E. L., & Lorge, I. *The teacher's wordbook of 30,000 words.* New York: Teachers College, 1944. **862, 863, 894, 895**

Thorndike, E. L., & Woodworth, R. S. The influence of improvement in one mental function upon the efficiency of other functions. *Psychological Review,* 1901, *8,* 247–261, 384–395, 553–564. **1031**

Thornton, D. W., *see* Jones, A., 1967.

Thornton, G. B., *see* Tulving, E., 1959.

Thorpe, W. H. *Learning and instinct in animals.* 2nd ed. Cambridge: Harvard University Press, 1963. **556, 581, 584, 587, 588, 591, 592, 697**

Thorpe, W. H., *see also* Hinde, R. A., 1956.

Thouless, R. H. Phenomenal regression to the real object. *British Journal of Psychology,* 1931, *21,* 339–359; *22,* 1–30. **515**

Thumb, A., & Marbe, K. *Experimentelle Untersuchungen über die psychologischen Grundlagen der sprachlichen Analogiebildung.* Leipzig: W. Englemann, 1901. **861**

Thune, E. L. The effect of different types of preliminary activities on subsequent learning of paired-associate material. *Journal of Experimental Psychology,* 1950, *40,* 423–438. **1034, 1035**

Thune, L. E. Warm-up effect as a function of level of practice in verbal learning. *Journal of Experimental Psychology,* 1951, *42,* 250–256. **1034, 1036, 1037, 1045**

Thune, L. E., & Underwood, B. J. Retroactive inhibition as a function of degree of interpolated learning. *Journal of Experimental Psychology,* 1943, *32,* 185–200. **1086, 1090**

Thurlow, W. R. Studies in auditory theory: I. Binaural interaction and the perception of pitch. *Journal of Experimental Psychology,* 1943, *32,* 17–36. **244**

Thurlow, W. R. The perception of the pitch of high frequencies. *American Psychologist,* 1946, *1,* 255. **243**

Thurlow, W. R. Perception of low auditory pitch: A multicue, mediation theory. *Psychological Review,* 1963, *70,* 461–470. **246**

Thurlow, W. R. Audition. In P. Farnsworth (Ed.), *Annual review of psychology,* Vol. 16. Palo Alto, Calif.: Annual Reviews, 1965. **243**

Thurlow, W. R., & Bernstein, S. Simultaneous two-tone pitch discrimination. *Journal of the Acoustical Society of America,* 1957, *29,* 515–519. **250**

Thurlow, W. R., & Elfner, L. F. Pure-tone cross-ear localization effects. *Journal of the Acoustical Society of America,* 1959, *31,* 1606–1608. **263, 266**

Thurlow, W. R., & Elfner, L. F. Localization effects with steady thermal noise in one ear and pulsed thermal noise in the other. *Science,* 1961, *134,* 617–618. **263**

Thurlow, W. R., Gross, N. B., Kemp, E. H., & Lowy, K. Microelectrode studies of neural auditory activity of cat: I. Inferior colliculus. *Journal of Neurophysiology,* 1951, *14,* 289–304. **232**

Thurlow, W. R., & Hartman, T. F. The "missing fundamental" and related pitch effects. *Perceptual and Motor Skills,* 1959, *9,* 315–324. **246**

Thurlow, W. R., Mangels, J. W., & Runge, P. S. Head movements during sound localization. *Journal of the Acoustical Society of America,* 1967, *42,* 489–493. **267**

Thurlow, W. R., & Marten, A. E. Perception of steady and intermittent sound with alternating noise-burst stimuli. *Journal of the Acoustical Society of America,* 1962, *34,* 1853–1858. **265**

Thurlow, W. R., Marten, A. E., & Bhatt, B. J. Localization after-effects with pulse–tone and pulse–pulse stimuli. *Journal of the Acoustical Society of America,* 1965, *37,* 837–842. **265, 268**

Thurlow, W. R., & Melamed, L. E. Some new hypotheses on the mediation of loudness judgments. *Perception and Psychophysics,* 1967, *2,* 77–80. **248**

Thurlow, W. R., Parks, T. E. Precedence-suppression effects for two click sources. *Perceptual and Motor Skills,* 1961, *13,* 7–12. **268**

Thurlow, W. R., & Rawlings, I. L. Discrimination of number of simultaneously sounding tones. *Journal of the Acoustical Society of America,* 1959, *31,* 1332–1336. **250**

Thurlow, W. R., & Runge, P. S. Effect of induced head movements on localization of direction of sounds. *Journal of the Acoustical Society of America,* 1967, *42,* 480–488. **267, 268**

Thurlow, W. R., & Small, A. M., Jr. Pitch perception for certain periodic auditory stimuli. *Journal of the Acoustical Society of America,* 1955, *27,* 132–137. **245**

Thurlow, W. R., *see also* Small, A. M. Jr., 1954.

Thurston, E., *see* Washburn, M. F., 1934.

Thurstone, L. L. Psychophysical analysis. *American Journal of Psychology,* 1927, *38,* 368–389. (a). Also in L. L. Thurstone, *The measurement of values.* Chicago: University of Chicago Press, 1959. **51**

Thurstone, L. L. A law of comparative judgment. *Psychological Review,* 1927, *34,* 273–286. (b). Also in L. L. Thurstone, *The measurement of values.* Chicago: University of Chicago Press, 1959. **53**

Thurstone, L. L. The phi-gamma hypothesis. *Journal of Experimental Psychology,* 1928, *9,* 293–305. Also in L. L. Thurstone, *The measurement of values.* Chicago: University of Chicago Press, 1959. **32**

Thwing, E. J., *see* Egan, J. P., 1954.

Thysell, R., *see* Schulz, R. W., 1965.

Tighe, T. J., *see* Gibson, E. J., 1958, 1959; Walk, R. D., 1957.

Tilman, T. W., *see* Carhart, R., 1967.

Tinbergen, N. *The study of instinct.* Oxford: Clarendon Press, 1951. **745**

Tinbergen, N. The curious behavior of the stickleback. *Scientific American,* 1952, *187,* 22–26. **745**

Tinker, M. A. Reliability and validity of eye-movement measures of reading. *Journal of Experimental Psychology,* 1936, *19,* 732–746. **390**

Tinklepaugh, O. L. An experimental study of representative factors in monkeys. *Journal of Comparative Psychology,* 1928, *8,* 197–236. **689**

Titchener, E. B. *An outline of psychology.* New York: Macmillan, 1902. **403, 453, 527**

Titchener, E. B. *Experimental psychology:* Vol. II. *Quantitative.* New York: Macmillan, 1905. **14, 15**

Titchener, E. B. *Experimental psychology;* Vol. II. *Quantitative.* Part II. Instructors Manual. New York: Macmillan, 1905. **65, 66, 73**

Tobias, J. V., & Zerlin, S. Lateralization threshold as a function of stimulus duration. *Journal of the Acoustical Society of America,* 1959, *31,* 1591–1594. **263**

Todd, T. C., *see* Vitz, P. C., 1969.

Toffey, S., *see* Hoffman, H. S., 1966.

Tolman, E. C. *Purposive behavior in animals and men.* New York: Appleton, 1932. (Reprinted, University of California Press, 1949). **560n, 597, 662, 679, 681, 697, 741**

Tolman, E. C. Prediction of vicarious trial and error by means of the schematic sowbug. *Psychological Review,* 1939, *46,* 318–336. **749, 784**

Tolman, E. C. Discrimination versus learning and the schematic sowbug. *Psychological Review,* 1941, *48,* 367–382. **784**

Tolman, E. C. Cognitive maps in rats and men. *Psychological Review,* 1948, *55,* 189–208. **568**

Tolman, E. C. Principles of purposive behavior. In S. Koch (Ed.), *Psychology: A study of a science,* Vol 2. New York: McGraw-Hill, 1959. **560n**

Tolman, E. C., & Brunswik, E. The organism and the causal texture of the environment. *Psychological Review,* 1935, *42,* 43–77. **462**

Tolman, E. C., & Krechevsky, I. Means-end readiness and hypothesis: A contribution to comparative psychology. *Psychological Review,* 1933, *40,* 60–70. **765**

Tolman, E. C., & Minium, E. VTE in rats: Overlearning and

difficulty of discrimination. *Journal of Comparative Psychology*, 1942, *34*, 301–306. **784**

Toman, J. E. P., *see* Smith, S. M., 1947.

Tomita, T. Electrophysiological study of mechanisms subserving color coding in the fish retina. *Cold Spring Harbor Symposia on Quantitative Biology*, 1966, *30*, 559–566. **325**

Tomita, T., Kaneko, A., Murakami, M., & Pautler, E. L. Spectral response curves of single cones in the carp. *Vision Research*, 1967, *7*, 519–531. **308, 325**

Tomita, T., et al. Personal communication, 1968. **295**

Tonndorf, J. Harmonic distortion in cochlear models. *Journal of the Acoustical Society of America*, 1958, *30*, 929–937. **239**

Toole, F. E., *see* Sayers, B. McA., 1964.

Torgerson, W. S. *Theory and methods of scaling.* New York: Wiley, 1958. **53, 54, 57, 70, 71, 72**

Torgerson, W. S. Quantitative judgment scales. In H. Gulicksen & S. Messick (Eds.), *Psychological scaling.* New York: Wiley, 1960. **248**

Torgerson, W. S. Distances and ratios in psychophysical scaling. *Acta Psychologica* (Amsterdam), 1961, *19*, 201–205. **248**

Torii, S., *see* Oyama, T., 1955.

Trabasso, D., *see* Bower, G. H., 1963.

Trabasso, T. Additivity of cues in discrimination learning of letter patterns. *Journal of Experimental Psychology*, 1960, *60*, 83–88. **957**

Trabasso, T. Stimulus emphasis and all-or-none learning of concept identification. *Journal of Experimental Psychology*, 1963, *65*, 395–406. **957, 961**

Trabasso, T., & Bower, G. H. Component learning in the four-category concept problem. *Journal of Mathematical Psychology*, 1964, *1*, 143–169. (a) **958, 964, 975**

Trabasso, T., & Bower, G. H. Memory in concept identification. *Psychonomic Science*, 1964, *1*, 133–134. (b) **960, 973**

Trabasso, T., & Bower, G. H. Presolution dimensional shifts in concept identification: A test of the sampling with replacement axiom in all-or-none models. *Journal of Mathematical Psychology*, 1966, *3*, 163–173. **956, 957, 970, 978**

Trabasso, T. R., *see also* Bower, G. H., 1964; Friedman, M., 1967; Wonant, M. V., 1964.

Trapold, M. A. The effect of incentive motivation on an unrelated reflex response. *Journal of Comparative and Physiological Psychology*, 1962, *55*, 1034–1039. **808**

Trapold, M. A., & Fowler, H. Instrumental escape performance as a function of the intensity of noxious stimulation. *Journal of Experimental Psychology*, 1960, *60*, 323–326. **720, 721**

Trapold, M. A., *see also* Bower, G. H., 1959; Fowler, H., 1962.

Trattner, J., *see* Eisenberger, R., 1967.

Travis, A. M., & Woolsey, C. N. Motor performance of monkeys after bilateral partial and total cerebral decortications. *American Journal of Physical Medicine.* 1956, *35*, 273–310. **845**

Treichler, F. R., *see* Meyer, D. R., 1965.

Treisman, A. Contextual cues in selective listening. *Quarterly Journal of Experimental Psychology*, 1960, *12*, 242–248. **259**

Treisman, A. Binocular rivalry and stereoscopic depth perception. *Quarterly Journal of Experimental Psychology*, 1962, *14*, 23–37. **492**

Treisman, A. Monitoring and storage of irrelevant messages in selective attention. *Journal of Verbal Learning and Verbal Behavior*, 1964, *3*, 449–459. **259**

Treisman, M. Sensory scaling and the psychophysical law. *Quarterly Journal of Experimental Psychology*, 1964, *16*, 11–22. (a) **84**

Treisman, M. What do sensory scales measure? *Quarterly Journal of Experimental Psychology*, 1964, *16*, 385–391. (b) **84**

Tresselt, M. E., *see* Mayzner, M. S., 1962, 1964, 1965a, b, c.

Triebel, W., *see* Hochberg, J. E., 1951, 1955.

Triedman, M. H., *see* Boynton, R. M., 1953.

Troland, L. The "all or none law" in visual response. *Journal of the Optical Society of America*, 1920, *4*, 161–186. **286**

Trowill, J., *see* Gandelman, R., 1968.

Trumble, G., *see* Beer, B., 1965.

Trychin, S. Jr., *see* Walk, R. D., 1965.

Tschermak-Seysenegg, A. Über Parallaktoskopie. *Pflügers Archiv für Physiologie*, 1939, *241*, 455–469. **486**

Tucker, D. Physiology of olfaction. *Annual Symposium of American Society of Perfumers*, April 13, 1961. **208**

Tucker, D. Physical variables in the olfactory stimulation process. *Journal of General Physiology*, 1963, *46*, 453–489. (a) **200, 207**

Tucker, D. Olfactory, vomeronasal and trigeminal receptor responses to odorants. In Y. Zotterman (Ed.), *Olfaction and taste.* New York: Pergamon, 1963, 45–69. (b) **207**

Tucker, D., & Shibuya, T. A physiologic and pharmacologic study of olfactory receptors. *Cold Spring Harbor Symposia on Quantitative Biology*, 1965, *30*, 207–215. **194**

Tucker, D., *see also* Beidler, L. M., 1956; Henton, W. W., 1966.

Tulunay, S. U., *see* Riggs, L. A., 1959.

Tulunay, Ü., *see* Engen, T., 1956.

Tulving, E. Subjective organization in free recall of "unrelated" words. *Psychological Review*, 1962, *69*, 344–354. **855, 1043, 1045**

Tulving, E. Theoretical issues in free recall. In T. R. Dixon & D. L. Horton (Eds.), *Verbal behavior and general behavior theory.* Englewood Cliffs, N.J.: Prentice-Hall, 1968. **1043, 1101**

Tulving, E., & Arbuckle, T. Sources of intra-trial interference in immediate recall of paired associates. *Journal of Verbal Learning and Verbal Behavior*, 1963, *1*, 321–324. **1118**

Tulving, E., & Arbuckle, T. Input and output interference in short-term associative memory. *Journal of Experimental Psychology*, 1966, *72*, 145–150. **1118**

Tulving, E., McNulty, J. A., & Ozier, M. Vividness of words and learning to learn in free-recall learning. *Canadian Journal of Psychology*, 1965, *19*, 242–252. **1044, 1045**

Tulving, E., & Thornton, G. B. Interaction between proaction and retroaction in short-term retention. *Canadian Journal of Psychology*, 1959, *13*, 255–265. **1101**

Tulving, E., *see also* Freibergs, V., 1961; Heinemann, E. G., 1959.

Tunturi, A. R. Anatomy and physiology of the auditory cortex. In G. Rasmussen & W. F. Windle (Eds.), *Neural mechanisms of the auditory and vestibular systems.* Springfield, Ill.: Charles C Thomas, 1960. **232**

Turnage, T. W. Unit-sequence interference in short-term memory. *Journal of Verbal Learning and Verbal Behavior*, 1967, *6*, 61–65. **1128**

Turnage, T., & Anderson, N. Letter-frequency and associative probability as determinants of learning and retention. *Journal of Verbal Learning and Verbal Behavior*, 1965, *4*, 463–468. **1129**

Turnbull, W. W. Pitch discrimination as a function of tonal duration. *Journal of Experimental Psychology*, 1944, *34*, 302–316. **249**

Turner, L. H., & Solomon, R. L. Human traumatic avoidance learning: Theory and experiments on the operant-respondent distinction and failures to learn. *Psychological Monographs*, 1962, *76*, (Whole No. 559). **730**

Turner, L. H., *see also* Church, R. M., 1966; Solomon, R. L., 1962.

Turner, R. N., *see* Atkinson, R. C., 1959.

Turrisi, F. D., *see* Shepp, B. E., 1966.

Turvey, M. Analysis of augmented recall in short-term memory following a shift in connotation. *British Journal of Psychology*, 1968, *59*, 2, 131–137. **1117**

Twedt, H. M., & Underwood, B. J. Mixed vs. unmixed lists

in transfer studies. *Journal of Experimental Psychology*, 1959, *48*, 111–116. **1062, 1063, 1064, 1069, 1095**

Twelker, P. A., *see* Jones, F. N., 1962.

Twining, P. I. The relative importance of intervening activity and lapse of time in the production of forgetting. *Journal of Experimental Psychology*, 1940, *26*, 483–501. **1087**

Tyler, D. W., *see* Bitterman, M. E., 1955.

Ueda, T. Comparative and developmental studies on perceptual constancies. In Y. Akishige (Ed.), *Experimental researches on the structure of the perceptual space.* Fukuoka, Japan: Kyushu University, 1967. **548, 550**

Ugelow, A., *see* Hall, J. F., 1957.

Uhl, C. N. Effect of overlapping cues upon discrimination learning. *Journal of Experimental Psychology*, 1964, *67*, 91–97. **927**

Uhr, L. L. "Pattern recognition" computers as models for form perception. *Psychological Bulletin*, 1963, *60*, 40–73. **450, 452**

Uhr, L. L. (Ed.). *Pattern recognition.* New York: Wiley, 1966. **978**

Ullrich, J. Successive verbal discrimination learning as a function of free association strength. Unpublished master's thesis, Pennsylvania State University, 1966. **887**

Ulrich, P., *see* Ammons, R. B., 1959.

Underwood, B. J. The effect of successive interpolations on retroactive and proactive inhibition. *Psychological Monographs*, 1945, *59*, No. 3. **1068, 1087, 1090, 1103**

Underwood, B. J. Proactive and retroactive inhibition after five and forty-eight hours. *Journal of Experimental Psychology*, 1948, *38*, 29–38. (a) **1099, 1104, 1105**

Underwood, B. J. "Spontaneous" recovery of verbal associations. *Journal of Experimental Psychology*, 1948, *38*, 429–439. (b) **1092, 1099**

Underwood, B. J. Proactive inhibition as a function of time and degree of prior learning. *Journal of Experimental Psychology*, 1949, *39*, 24–34. **1035, 1036, 1090, 1103, 1104**

Underwood, B. J. Associative transfer in verbal learning as a function of response similarity and degree of first-list learning. *Journal of Experimental Psychology*, 1951, *42*, 44–53. **1056, 1057, 1058**

Underwood, B. J. An orientation for research on thinking. *Psychological Review*, 1952, *59*, 209–220. **975**

Underwood, B. J. Studies of distributed practice: VI. The influence of rest-interval activity in serial learning. *Journal of Experimental Psychology*, 1952, *43*, 329–340. **1038**

Underwood, B. J. Studies of distributed practice: VII. Learning and retention of serial nonsense lists as a function of intralist similarity. *Journal of Experimental Psychology*, 1952, *44*, 80–87. **894**

Underwood, B. J. Learning. *Annual Review of Psychology*, 1953, *4*, 31–58. **575**

Underwood, B. J. Studies of distributed practice: VIII. Learning and retention of paired nonsense syllables as a function of intralist similarity. *Journal of Experimental Psychology*, 1953, *45*, 133–142. (a) **1126**

Underwood, B. J. Studies of distributed practice: IX. Learning and retention of paired adjectives as a function of intralist similarity. *Journal of Experimental Psychology*, 1953, *45*, 143–149. (b) **1126**

Underwood, B. J. Speed of learning and amount retained: A consideration of methodology. *Psychological Bulletin*, 1954, *51*, 276–282. (a) **1124**

Underwood, B. J. Intralist similarity in verbal learning and retention. *Psychological Review*, 1954, *61*, 160–166. (b) **1126**

Underwood, B. J. Interference and forgetting. *Psychological Review*, 1957, *64*, 49–60. (a) **1102, 1106, 1107**

Underwood, B. J. Studies of distributed practice: XVI. Some evidence on the nature of the inhibition involved in massed learning of verbal materials. *Journal of Experimental Psychology*, 1957, *54*, 139–144. (b) **1121**

Underwood, B. J. An evaluation of the Gibson theory of verbal learning. In C. N. Cofer (Ed.), *Verbal learning and verbal behavior.* New York: McGraw-Hill, 1961. Pp. 197–216. **985, 1049, 1051**

Underwood, B. J. Stimulus selection in verbal learning. In C. N. Cofer & B. B. Musgrave (Eds.), *Verbal behavior and learning: Problems and processes.* New York: McGraw-Hill, 1963. Pp. 33–48. **982, 1001, 1011, 1021**

Underwood, B. J. Degree of learning and the measurement of forgetting. *Journal of Verbal Learning and Verbal Behavior*, 1964, *3*, 112–129. **1111, 1124**

Underwood, B. J. The representativeness of rote verbal learning. In A. W. Melton (Ed.), *Categories of human learning.* New York: Academic Press, 1964. Pp. 47–78. **891, 979**

Underwood, B. J. False recognition produced by implicit verbal responses. *Journal of Experimental Psychology*, 1965, *70*, 122–129. **886**

Underwood, B. J. *Experimental psychology.* 2nd ed. New York: Appleton, 1966. **907, 1061, 1124**

Underwood, B. J. Motor-skills learning and verbal learning: Some observations. In E. A. Bilodeau (Ed.), *Acquisition of skill.* New York: Academic Press, 1966. **575**

Underwood, B. J., & Ekstrand, B. R. An analysis of some shortcomings in the interference theory of forgetting. *Psychological Review*, 1966, *73*, 540–549. **1103, 1108, 1131**

Underwood, B. J., & Ekstrand, B. R. Word frequency and accumulative proactive inhibition. *Journal of Experimental Psychology*, 1967, *74*, 193–198. (a) **1106, 1129**

Underwood, B. J., & Ekstrand, B. R. Studies of distributed practice: XXIV. Differentiation and proactive inhibition. *Journal of Experimental Psychology*, 1967, *74*, 574–580. (b) **1109**

Underwood, B. J., & Ekstrand, B. R. Linguistic associations and retention. *Journal of Verbal Learning and Verbal Behavior*, 1968, *7*, 162–171. (a) **1130**

Underwood, B. J., & Ekstrand, B. R. Differentiation among stimuli as a factor in transfer performance. *Journal of Verbal Learning and Verbal Behavior*, 1968, *7*, 172–175. (b) **1062, 1063**

Underwood, B. J., Eckstrand, B. R., & Keppel, G. Studies of distributed practice: XXIII. Variations in response-term interference. *Journal of Experimental Psychology*, 1964, *68*, 201–212. **893**

Underwood, B. J., & Goad, D. Studies of distributed practice: I. The influence of intra-list similarity in serial learning. *Journal of Experimental Psychology*, 1951, *42*, 125–134. **893**

Underwood, B. J., Ham, M., & Ekstrand, B. R. Cue selection in paired-associate learning. *Journal of Experimental Psychology*, 1962, *64*, 405–409. **1021**

Underwood, B. J., & Keppel, G. An evaluation of two problems of method in the study of retention. *American Journal of Psychology*, 1962, *75*, 1–17. **1124**

Underwood, B. J., & Keppel, G. One-trial learning? *Journal of Verbal Learning and Verbal Behavior*, 1962, *1*, 1–13. **989**

Underwood, B. J., & Keppel, G. Retention as a function of degree of learning and letter-sequence interference. *Psychological Monographs*, 1963, *77*, No. 567. **1124, 1128**

Underwood, B. J., Keppel, G., & Schulz, R. W. Studies of distributed practice: XXII. Some conditions which enhance retention. *Journal of Experimental Psychology*, 1962, *64*, 355–363. **1108**

Underwood, B. J., & Postman, L. Extraexperimental sources of interference in forgetting. *Psychological Review*, 1960, *67*, 73–95. **885, 896, 1022, 1127**

Underwood, B. J., Rehula, R., & Keppel, G. Item selection

in paired-associate learning. *American Journal of Psychology*, 1962, *75*, 353–371. **897**

Underwood, B. J., & Richardson, J. Some verbal materials for the study of concept formation. *Psychological Bulletin*, 1956, *53*, 84–95. (a) **881, 889**

Underwood, B. J., & Richardson, J. Verbal concept learning as a function of instructions and dominance level. *Journal of Experimental Psychology*, 1956, *51*, 229–238. (b) **881, 889**

Underwood, B. J., & Richardson, J. Some verbal materials for the study of concept formation. *Psychological Bulletin*, 1956, *53*, 84–95. **1078**

Underwood, B. J., Runquist, W. N., & Schulz, R. W. Response learning in paired-associate lists as a function of intra-list similarity. *Journal of Experimental Psychology*, 1959, *58*, 70–78. **893, 1007, 1060**

Underwood, B. J., & Schulz, R. W. *Meaningfulness and verbal learning.* Chicago: Lippincott, 1960. (a) **852, 853, 854, 856, 858, 892, 896, 897, 899, 900, 982, 1007, 1050, 1059**

Underwood, B. J., & Schulz, R. W. Response dominance and rate of learning paired-associates. *Journal of General Psychology*, 1960, *62*, 153–158. (b) **889**

Underwood, B. J., *see also* Archer, E. J., 1951; Barnes, J. M., 1959; Ekstrand, B. R., 1965, 1966; Feldman, S. M., 1957; Greenberg, R., 1950; Keppel, G., 1962a, b, 1967; McGeoch, J. A., 1943; Morgan, R. I., 1950; Scheible, H., 1954; Schwenn, E., 1965; Thune, L. E., 1943; Twedt, H. M., 1959.

Unger, S. M., *see* Caron, A. J., 1963.

Upchurch, R. L., *see* Cormack, R. H., 1969.

Uyeda, A. A., *see* Fuster, J. M., 1962; Seward, J. P., 1959.

Vainstein, E., *see* Orbach, J., 1963.

Valenstein, E. S. The anatomical locus of reinforcement. In E. Stellar & J. M. Sprague (Eds.), *Progress in physiological psychology.* Vol. 1. New York: Academic Press, 1966. **644, 647**

Valenstein, E. S., & Beer, B. Unipolar and bipolar electrodes in self-stimulation experiments. *American Journal of Physiology*, 1961, *201*, 1181–1186. **644**

Valenstein, E. S., & Beer, B. Continuous opportunity for reinforcing brain stimulation. *Journal of the Experimental Analysis of Behavior*, 1964, *7*, 183–184. **654**

Valenstein, E. S., & Meyers, W. J. Rate-independent test of reinforcing consequences of brain stimulation. *Journal of Comparative and Physiological Psychology*, 1964, *57*, 52–60. **649, 650**

Valenstein, E. S., & Weber, M. L. Potentiation of insulin coma by saccharin. *Journal of Comparative and Physiological Psychology*, 1965, *60*, 443–446. **797**

Valenstein, E. S., *see also* Beer, B., 1960; Hodos, W., 1962; Meyers, W. J., 1963.

Valsi, E., *see* Bartley, S. H., 1957.

Van Allen, M. W., *see* von Noorden, G. K., 1964.

van Bergeijk, W. A. Variation on a theme of Békésy: A model of binaural interaction. *Journal of the Acoustical Society of America*, 1962, *34*, 1431–1437. **264**

van Bergeijk, W. A., Pierce, J. R., & David, E. E., Jr. *Waves and the ear.* Garden City, New York: Doubleday, 1960. **227**

van Bergeijk, W. A., *see also* Guttman, N., 1960; David, E. E., 1958, 1959.

Vandenbelt, D. J., *see* Bartoshuk, L. M., 1969.

Vandercar, D. H., & Schneiderman, N. Interstimulus interval functions in different response systems during classical discrimination conditioning of rabbits. *Psychonomic Science*, 1967, *9*, 9–10. **558, 559**

Vanderplas, J. M., Sanderson, W. R., & Vanderplas, J. N. Statistical and associational characteristics of 1,100 random shapes. *Perceptual and Motor Skills*, 1965, *21*, 339–348. **449**

Vanderplas, J. M., *see also* Crawford, J. L., 1959.

Vanderplas, J. N., *see* Vanderplas, J. M., 1965.

Van Mondfrans, A. P., *see* Johnson, T. J., 1965.

Van Ormer, E. B. Retention after intervals of sleep and waking. *Archives of Psychology*, 1932, *21*, No. 137. **1123**

Varga, M. E., & Pressman, Y. M. On conditioned connections in the forward and reverse directions. In A. A. Airapetyan et al. (Eds.), *Central and peripheral mechanisms of nervous activity.* Erevan, USSR: Akadamiya Nauk Armyanskoi SSR, 1966. (In Russian: English abstract by I. D. London in *Psychological Abstracts*, 1967, *41*, 1518.) **560n**

Varnadoe, K. W., *see* Clement, D. E., 1967.

Veer, R. A., *see* Jonkhees, L. B. W., 1958.

Vendrik, A. J. H., & Eijkman, E. G. Psychophysical properties determined with internal noise. In D. R. Kenshalo (Ed.), *The skin senses.* Springfield, Ill.: Charles C Thomas, 1968. Pp. 178–194. **147**

Vendrik, A. J. H., & Vos, J. J. Comparison of the stimulation of the warmth sense organ by microwave and infrared. *Journal of Applied Physiology*, 1958, *13*, 435–444. **153**

Veness, T. An experiment on slips of the tongue and word association faults. *Language and Speech*, 1962, *5*, 128–137. **866**

Verhoeff, F. H. The theory of binocular perspective. *American Journal of Physiological Optics*, 1925, *6*, 416. **466, 473**

Verhoeff, F. A new theory of binocular vision. *Archives of Ophthalmology*, 1935, *13*, 151–175. **488**

Verinis, J. S., *see* Rouse, R. O., 1965.

Vernon, M. D. The perception of inclined lines. *British Journal of Psychology*, 1934, *25*, 186–196. **466**

Verplanck, W. S. Burrhus F. Skinner. In W. K. Estes et al. (Eds.), *Modern learning theory.* New York: Appleton, 1954. **608**

Verplanck, W. S. The control of the content of conversation: Reinforcement of statements of opinion. *Journal of Abnormal and Social Psychology*, 1955, *51*, 668–676. **908n**

Verplanck, W. S., & Hayes, J. R. Eating and drinking as a function of maintenance schedule. *Journal of Comparative and Physiological Psychology*, 1953, *46*, 327–333. **669, 816**

Verrillo, R. T. Vibrotactile thresholds for hairy skin. *Journal of Experimental Psychology*, 1966, *72*, 47–50. **135**

Verrillo, R. T. A duplex mechanism of mechanoreception. In D. R. Kenshalo (Ed.), *The skin senses.* Springfield, Ill.: Charles C Thomas, 1968. Pp. 139–159. **135, 137**

Versace, J., *see* Ross, L., 1953.

Victor, J., *see* Rock, I., 1964.

Vierordt, K. *Der Zeitsinn nach Versuchen: Scheinbare Verzerrung bewegter Gegenstände.* Tübingen: H. Laupp, 1868.

Vilter, V. Nouvelle conception de relations synaptiques dans la photoperception par les cônes rétiniens. *Comptes Rendus ses Séances de la Société de Biologie* (Paris), 1949, *143*, 338–341. **303**

Vinacke, W. E. The investigation of concept formation. *Psychological Bulletin*, 1951, *48*, 1–31. **786**

Vince, M. A., *see* Hinde, R. A., 1956.

Vincent, R. J., Brown, B. R., Markley, R. P., & Arnoult, M. D. Distance discrimination in a simulated space environment. *Perception and Psychophysics*, 1969, *5*, 235–238. **494**

Vincent, S. B. The function of the vibrissae in the behavior of the white rat. *Behavioral Monographs*, 1912, 5. **612**

Virsu, V. Contrast and confluxion as components in geometric illusions. *Quarterly Journal of Experimental Psychology*, 1967, *19*, 198–207. **461, 463**

Vitz, P. C., & Todd, T. C. A coded element model of the

perceptual processing of sequential stimuli. *Psychological Review,* 1969, 76, 433–449. **448**

Vitz, P. C., *see also* Rose, R. M., 1966.

Voeks, V. Formalization and clarification of a theory of learning. *Journal of Psychology,* 1950, 30, 341–363. **567**

Volkmann, A. Über den Einflusss der Übung auf das Erkennen räumlicher Distanzen. *Berichte Sächsischer Gesellshaft der Wissenschaften, Mathematisch-Physische Klasse,* 1858, 10, 38–69. **1030**

Volkmann, F. C. Vision during voluntary saccadic eye movements. *Journal of the Optical Society of America,* 1962, 52, 571–578. **45, 377**

Volkmann, F. C., Schick, A. M. L., & Riggs, L. A. Time course of visual inhibition during voluntary saccades. *Journal of the Optical Society of America,* 1968, 58, 362–569. **377**

Volkmann, J., *see* Stevens, S. S., 1940, 1941.

von Békésy, G. Über das Fechner'sche Gesetz und seine akustischen Beobachtungsfehler und die Theorie des Hörens. *Annalen der Physik,* 1930, 7, 329–359. **33**

von Békésy, G. The variation of phase along the basilar membrane with sinusoidal vibration. *Journal of the Acoustical Society of America,* 1947, 19, 452–460. **230**

von Békésy, G. The moon illusion and similar auditory phenomena. *American Journal of Psychology,* 1949, 62, 540–552. **269**

von Békésy, G. Gross localization of the place of origin of the cochlear microphonics. *Journal of the Acoustical Society of America,* 1952, 24, 399–409. (a) **230**

von Békésy, G. Resting potentials inside the cochlear partition of the guinea pig. *Nature,* 1952, 169, 241–242. (b) **230**

von Békésy, G. Current status of theories of hearing. *Science,* 1956, 123, 779–783. **229**

von Békésy, G. Similarities between hearing and skin sensations. *Psychological Review,* 1959, 66, 1–22. **140, 268**

von Békésy, G. In E. G. Wever (Ed.), *Experiments in hearing.* New York: McGraw-Hill, 1960. **237, 238, 261, 265, 268, 269**

von Békésy, G. Hearing theories and complex sounds. *Journal of the Acoustical Society of America,* 1963, 35, 588–601. **244, 245**

von Békésy, G. Sweetness produced electrically on the tongue and its relation to taste theories. *Journal of Applied Physiology,* 1964, 19, 1105–1113. **178, 181**

von Békésy, G. Taste theories and the chemical stimulation of single papillae. *Journal of Applied Physiology,* 1966, 21, 1–9. **172, 175, 178**

von Békésy, G. *Sensory inhibition.* Princeton, N.J.: Princeton University Press, 1967. **231**

von Békésy, G., & Rosenblith, W. A. The mechanical properties of the ear. In S. S. Stevens (Ed.), *Handbook of experimental psychology.* New York: Wiley, 1951. **229**

von Fieandt, K. *Über Sehen von Tiefenbilden bei wechselnder Beleuchtungsrichtung.* Helsinki: Psychological Institute, University of Helsinki, 1938. **497**

von Frey, M. Beiträge zur Sinnesphysiologie der Haut. *Akademie der Wissenschaften Leipzig. Mathematisch-Naturwissenschaftlich Klasse Berichte.* 1895, 47, 166–184. **120, 121, 148, 155**

von Frey, M., & Kiesow, F. Über die Function der Tastkörperchen. *Zeitschrift für Psychologie,* 1899, 20, 126–163. **130**

von Frisch, K. *Bees, their vision, chemical senses and language.* Ithaca, New York: Cornell University Press, 1950. **745**

von Helmholtz, H., *see* Helmholtz, H. von

von Holzt, E. Relations between the central nervous system and the peripheral organs. *British Journal of Animal Behaviour,* 1954, 2, 89–94. **530, 535**

von Holzt, E. Aktive Leistungen der menschlichen Gesichtwahrnehmung. *Stadium Generale,* 1957, 10, 231–243. **460**

von Karpinska, L. Experimentelle Beiträge zur Analyse der Tiefenwahrnehmung. *Zeitschrift für Psychologie,* 1910, 57, 1–88. **491n**

von Kries, J. Normal and anomalous color systems. In Helmholtz, H. von, *Treatise on physiological optics,* English translation by J. P. C. Southall. Vol. II. Rochester, New York: Optical Society of America, 1924. Pp. 395–421. **336**

von Kries, J. Notes on perception of depth. 1925. In Helmholtz, H. von, *Treatise on physiological optics* J. P. C. Southall, (Ed.). Vol. 3. New York: Dover, 1962. **493**

von Lackum, W. J., *see* Melton, A. W., 1941.

von Noorden, G. K., Thompson, H. S., Van Allen, M. W. Eye movements in myotonic dystrophy. *Investigations in Ophthalmology,* 1964, 3, 313–324. **381**

von Senden, M. *Space and sight* (1932) (Transl. P. Heath). London: Methuen, 1960. **548**

von Skramlik, E. *Handbuch der Physiologie der niederen Sinne.* Leipzig: Georg Thieme, 1926. **182, 183, 184**

Vos, J. J., *see* Vendrik, A. J. H., 1958.

Voss, J. F., *see* Morning, N., 1964.

Voth, A. C., *see* Brown, J. F., 1937.

Waddell, D., *see* Beebe-Center, J. G., 1948.

Wade, M., *see* Lashley, K. S., 1946.

Wagner, A. R. The role of reinforcement and non-reinforcement in an "apparent frustration effect." *Journal of Experimental Psychology,* 1959, 57, 130–136. **576, 810**

Wagner, A. R. Conditioned frustration as a learned drive. *Journal of Experimental Psychology,* 1963, 66, 142–148. **811**

Wagner, A. R. Frustration and punishment. In R. N. Haber (Ed.), *Current research in motivation.* New York: Holt, Rinehart and Winston, 1966. Pp. 229–239. **811**

Wagner, A. R. Frustrative-nonreward: A variety of punishment? In B. A. Campbell & R. M. Church (Eds.), *Punishment.* New York: Appleton, 1969. **704**

Wagner, A. R., *see also* Logan, F. A., 1965.

Wagner, H. G., MacNichol, E. F., Jr., & Wolbarsht, M. L. The response properties of single ganglion cells in the goldfish retina. *Journal of General Physiology,* 1960, 43, Suppl. 2, 45–62. **295**

Wagner, H. G., *see also* Hartline, H. K., 1952, 1956.

Wagner, M., *see* Boynton, R. M., 1961.

Wagoner, K. S., *see* Nafe, J. P., 1941a, b.

Wainwright, A., *see* Gogel, W. C., 1961.

Wald, G. Human vision and the spectrum. *Science,* 1945, 101, 653–658. **275**

Wald, G. The chemistry of rod vision. *Science,* 1951, 113, 287–291. **286**

Wald, G. The receptors of human color vision. *Science,* 1964, 145, 1007–1016. **323, 337**

Wald, G., & Brown, P. K. Human color vision and color blindness. *Cold Spring Harbor Symposia on Quantitative Biology,* 1965, 30, 345–361. **364, 367**

Walk, R. D. The development of depth perception in animals and human infants. *Child Development Monographs,* 1966, 31, Serial 107, No. 5, 82–108. **548, 549**

Walk, R. D., & Gibson, E. J. A comparative and analytical study of visual depth perception. *Psychological Monographs,* 1961, 75, (Whole No. 519). **549**

Walk, R. D., Gibson, E. J., & Tighe, T. J. Behavior of light- and dark-reared rats on a visual cliff. *Science,* 1957, 126, 80–81. **549**

Walk, R. D., Trychin, S. Jr., & Karmel, B. Z. Depth perception in the dark-reared rat as a function of time in the dark. *Psychonomic Science,* 1965, 3, 9–10. **549**

Walk, R. D., *see* Gibson, E. J., 1956, 1958, 1959, 1960.

Walker, J., *see* Kamin, L., 1959.

Walker, R. Y. The eye-movements of good readers. *Psychological Monographs,* 1933, No. 199. **390**

Warren, H. C. *A history of the association psychology.* New York: Scribner's, 1921. **849**

Warren, J. M. Reversed discrimination as a function of the number of reinforcements during pre-training. *American Journal of Psychology,* 1954, *67,* 720. **768**

Warren, J. M., & Baron, A. The formation of learning sets by cats. *Journal of Comparative and Physiological Psychology,* 1956, *49,* 227–231. **768**

Warren, J. M., & Brookshire, K. H. Stimulus generalization and discrimination learning by primates. *Journal of Experimental Psychology,* 1959, *58,* 348–351. **772**

Warren, R. A., *see* Warren, R. M., 1963.

Warren, R. M. A basis for judgments of sensory intensity. *American Journal of Psychology,* 1958, *71,* 675–687. **244**

Warren, R. M., & Pfaffmann, C. Early experience and taste aversion. *Journal of Comparative and Physiological Psychology,* 1958, *52,* 263–266. **190**

Warren, R. M., & Pfaffmann, C. Suppression of sweet sensitivity by potassium gymnemate. *Journal of Applied Physiology,* 1959, *14,* 40–42. **177**

Warren, R. M., & Poulton, E. C. Lightness of grays: Effects of background reflectance. *Perception and Psychophysics,* 1966, *1,* 145–148. **414**

Warren, R. M., Sersen, E. A., & Pores, E. B. A basis for loudness judgments. *American Journal of Psychology,* 1958, *71,* 700–709. **248**

Warren, R. M., & Warren, R. A. A critique of Stevens' "new psychophysics." *Perceptual and Motor Skills,* 1963, *16,* 797–810. **84**

Warrington, E. K., *see* Kinsbourne, M., 1962.

Warshofsky, F., *see* Stevens, S. S., 1965.

Warter, P. J., Jr., *see* Smith, W. M., 1960.

Warwick, R. T. T., *see* Le Gros Clark, W. E., 1946.

Washburn, M. F. *Movement and mental imagery.* Boston: Houghton Mifflin, 1916. **453**

Washburn, M. F. Retinal rivalry as a neglected factor in stereoscopic vision. *Proceedings of the National Academy of Science,* 1933, *19,* 773–777. **491n**

Washburn, M. F., & Gillette, A. Motor factors in voluntary control of cube perspective fluctuations and retinal rivalry fluctuations. *American Journal of Psychology,* 1933, *45,* 315–319. **519**

Washburn, M. F., Mallay, H., & Naylor, A. The influence of the size of an outline cube on the fluctuations of its perspective. *American Journal of Psychology,* 1931, *43,* 484–489. **519**

Washburn, M. F., Reagan, C., & Thurston, E. The comparative controllability of the fluctuations of simple and complex ambiguous perspective figures. *American Journal of Psychology,* 1934, *46,* 636–638. **519**

Wason, P. C. The processing of positive and negative information. *Quarterly Journal of Experimental Psychology,* 1959, *11,* 92–107. **964**

Wason, P. C. On the failure to eliminate hypotheses in a conceptual task. *Quarterly Journal of Experimental Psychology,* 1960, *12,* 129–140. **964**

Wason, P. C. Response to a primitive and negative binary statement. *British Journal of Psychology,* 1961, *52,* 133–142. **964**

Watanabe, K., *see* Brown, K. T., 1965.

Watanobe, T., *see* Katsuki, Y., 1959.

Waters, J. E. A theoretical and developmental investigation of delayed speech feedback. *Genetic Psychology Monographs,* 1968, *78,* 3–54. **687**

Watson, J. B. The place of the conditioned-reflex in psychology. *Psychological Review,* 1916, *23,* 89–116. **562**

Watson, J. B. The effect of delayed feeding upon learning. *Psychobiology,* 1917, *1,* 51–60. **678**

Watson, J. B. *Psychology from the standpoint of a behaviorist.* Philadelphia: Lippincott, 1919. **562, 689**

Watson, J. B. *Psychological care of infant and child.* New York: Norton, 1928. **562**

Watson, J. B. *Behaviorism.* Chicago: University of Chicago Press, 1930. **621**

Watson, J. B., & Rayner, R. Conditioned emotional reactions. *Journal of Experimental Psychology,* 1920, *3,* 1–14. **562, 704**

Watson, J. B., *see also* Yerkes, R. M., 1911.

Waugh, N. C., & Norman, D. Primary memory. *Psychological Review,* 1965, *72,* 89–104. **1109, 1111**

Waugh, N. C., *see also* Loess, H., 1967.

Way, K. S., *see* Hastorf, A. H., 1952.

Wayner, M. J. Effects of intracarotid injections of hypertonic saline on spinal reflex excitability. In M. J. Wayner (Ed.), *Thirst.* Oxford: Pergamon, 1964, 335–360. **836**

Weale, R. A. Cone-monochromatism. *Journal of Physiology,* 1953, *121,* 548–569. **327**

Weasner, M. H., *see* Finger, F. W., 1960.

Weaver, G. E., *see* Schulz, R. W., 1965, 1968.

Webb, A. D., *see* Berg, H. W., 1963.

Webb, W. B. Drive stimuli as cues. *Psychological Reports,* 1955, *1,* 287–298. **795n**

Webb, W. B., *see also* Wipf, J. L., 1962.

Weber, E. Der Tastsinn und das Gemeingefühl. In Wagner (Ed.), *Handworterbuch der Physiologie,* 1846, *3,* 481–588. **129, 153**

Weber, M. L., *see* Valenstein, E. S., 1965.

Webster, D., *see* Quartermain, D., 1968.

Webster, H. The distortion of straight and curved lines in geometrical fields. *American Journal of Psychology,* 1948, *61,* 573. **460**

Webster, J. C. Speech communications as limited by ambient noise. *Journal of the Acoustical Society of America,* 1965, *37,* 692–699. **258**

Webster, J. C., & Thompson, P. O. Responding to both of two overlapping messages. *Journal of the Acoustical Society of America,* 1954, *26,* 396–402. **258**

Webster, J. C., *see also* Kryter, K. D., 1963; Thompson, P. O., 1961.

Webster, R. G., *see* McLaughlin, S. C., 1967.

Weddell, G. Somesthesis and the chemical senses. *Annual Review of Psychology,* 1955, *6,* 119–136. **154, 167**

Weddell, G., & Miller, S. Cutaneous sensibility. *Annual Review of Physiology,* 1962, *24,* 199–222. **124**

Weddell, G., & Pallie, W. Observations on the neurohistology of cutaneous blood vessels. In G. E. Wolstenholme & J. S. Freeman (Eds.), *Peripheral circulation in man* (A CIBA Foundation Symposium). London: J. & A. Churchill, 1954. Pp. 132–140. **124**

Weddell, G., Palmer, E., & Pallie, W. Nerve endings in mammalian skin. *Biological Review of the Cambridge Philosophical Society,* 1955, *30,* 159–195. **162**

Weddell, G., *see also* Hagen, E., 1953; Lele, P. P., 1954, 1956; Pattle, R. E., 1948.

Weeks, J. R. Experimental narcotics addiction. *Scientific American,* 1964, *210,* 46–52. **557n**

Weene, B., *see* Neisser, U., 1962.

Wegel, R. L., & Lane, C. E. The auditory masking of one pure tone by another and its probable relation to the dynamics of the inner ear. *Physiological Review,* 1924, *23,* 266–285. **239**

Weinberg, M., *see* Allen, F., 1925.

Weingartner, H. Associative structure and serial learning. *Journal of Verbal Learning and Verbal Behavior,* 1963, *2,* 476–478. **886**

Weinheimer, S., *see* Neimark, E., 1965.

Weinstein, S. The perception of depth in the absence of texture-gradient. *American Journal of Psychology,* 1957, *70,* 611–615. **501**

Weinstein, S. Intensive and extensive aspects of tactile sensitivity as a function of body part, sex, and laterality. In D. R. Kenshalo (Ed.), *The skin senses.* Springfield, Ill.: Charles C Thomas, 1968. Pp. 195–222. **133, 134, 138, 139**

Weinstein, S., Sersen, E. A., Fisher, L., & Weisinger, M. Is re-afference necessary for visual adaptation? *Perceptual and Motor Skills,* 1964, *18,* 641–648. **536**

Weinstock, S. Resistance to extinction of a running response following partial reinforcement under widely spaced trials. *Journal of Comparative and Physiological Psychology,* 1964, *47,* 318–322. **573**

Weinstock, S., *see also* Sgro, J. A., 1963.

Weintraub, D., *see* Hake, H. W., 1966.

Weisberg, P., & Fink, E. Fixed ratio and extinction performance of infants in the second year of life. *Journal of the Experimental Analysis of Behavior,* 1966, *9,* 105–109. **605, 608**

Weisberg, P., & Simmons, M. W. A modified WGTA for infants in their second year of life. *Journal of Psychology,* 1966, *63,* 99–104. **751**

Weise, P., & Bitterman, M. E. Response selection in discriminative learning. *Psychological Review,* 1951, *58,* 185–195. **774**

Weisinger, M., *see* Weinstein, S., 1964.

Weisman, R. G., Denny, M. R., Platt, S. A., & Zerbolio, D. J., Jr. Facilitation of extinction by a stimulus associated with long nonshock confinement periods. *Journal of Comparative and Physiological Psychology,* 1966, *62,* 26–30. **573**

Weiss, J. A tail electrode for unrestrained rats. *Journal of the Experimental Analysis of Behavior,* 1967, *10,* 85–86. **706**

Weiss, R. L., *see* Johnson, R. C., 1964.

Weiss, W. I., *see* Hovland, C. I., 1953.

Weisstein, N., & Haber, R. N. A U-shaped backward masking function in vision. *Psychonomic Science,* 1965, *2,* 75–76. **430**

Weisz, A., *see* Wallach, H., 1956; Gardner, W. J., 1960.

Weitz, J. Vibratory sensitivity as a function of skin temperature. *Journal of Experimental Psychology,* 1941, *28,* 21–36. **136**

Weitzman, E. D., Ross, G. S., Hodos, W., & Galambos, R. Behavioral method of study of pain in the monkey. *Science,* 1961, *133,* 37–38. **157**

Welch, G., *see* Zubek, J. P., 1963.

Welch, L. A preliminary study of the interaction of conflicting concepts of children between the ages of 3 and 5 years. *Psychological Review,* 1938, *2,* 439–459. **786**

Welch, L., & Long, L. The higher structural phases of concept formation of children. *Journal of Psychology,* 1940, *9,* 59–95. **786**

Weld, H. P., *see* Boring, E. G., 1948.

Wellman, B., *see* Hoffman, A. C., 1939.

Wells, C., *see* Diamant, H., 1965.

Wells, F. L. Practice effects in free association. *American Journal of Psychology,* 1911, *22,* 1–13. **866**

Wells, F. L. *Mental tests in clinical practice.* Yonkers, N. Y.: World Book, 1927. **877**

Wells, H. H. The effects of transfer in disjunctive concept formation. *Journal of Experimental Psychology,* 1963, *65,* 63–69. **963**

Wells, H. S. Temperature equilization for the relief of pain: An experimental study of the relation of thermal gradients to pain. *Archives of Physical Medicine and Rehabilitation,* 1947, *28,* 135–139. **156**

Wemple, L., *see* Zigler, M. J., 1930.

Wendt, G. R. An interpretation of inhibition and conditioned reflexes as competition between reaction systems. *Psychological Review,* 1936, *43,* 258–281. **571**

Wendt, R. H., Lindsley, D. F., Adey, W. R., & Fox S. S. Self-maintained visual stimulation in monkeys after long-term visual deprivation. *Science,* 1963, *139,* 336–338. **840**

Wenz, T. G., *see* McLaughlin, S. C., 1968.

Wenzel, B., & Sieck, M. H. Olfaction. *Annual Review of Physiology,* 1966, *28,* 381–434. **220**

Werblin, F. S. Functional organization of the vertebrate retina studied by intracellular recording from the retina of the mudpuppy, *Necturus maculosus.* Thesis, Johns Hopkins University, Baltimore, 1968. **308**

Werner, H. Studies on contour. *American Journal of Psychology,* 1935, *47,* 40–64. **429**

Werner, H. Dynamics in binocular depth perception. *Psychological Monographs,* 1937 (Whole No. 218). **492**

Werner, H. Studies on contour strobostereoscopic phenomena. *American Journal of Psychology,* 1940, *53,* 418–422. **429, 430**

Werner, H., & Wapner, S. Toward a general theory of perception. *Psychological Review,* 1952, *59,* 324–338. **437**

Werner, H., Wapner, S., & Bruell, J. H. Experiments on sensory-tonic field theory of perception: VI. Effect of position of head, eyes and of object on position of the apparent median plane. *Journal of Experimental Psychology,* 1953, *46,* 293–299. **534**

Werner, H., *see also* Wapner, S., 1957.

Wertheimer, M. Experimentelle Studien über das Sehen von Bewegung. *Zeitschrift für Psychologie,* 1912, *61,* 161–265. **525, 539**

Wertheimer, M. Untersuchungen zur Lehre von der Gestalt: II. *Psychologische Forschung,* 1923, *4,* 301–350. Abridged translation by M. Wertheimer: Principles of perceptual organization. In D. C. Beardslee & M. Wertheimer (Eds.), *Readings in perception.* Princeton, N.J.: Van Nostrand, 1958. **433**

Wertheimer, M. Psychomotor coordination of auditory and visual space at birth. *Science,* 1961, *134,* 1692. **547**

Wertheimer, M. *Drei Abhandlungen zur Gestalttheorie.* Erlangen: Philosophischen Akademie, 1925. **527**

Wertheimer, M., & Arena, A. J. Effect of exposure time on adaptation to disarranged hand-eye coordination. *Perceptual and Motor Skills,* 1959, *9,* 159–164. **536**

Wertheimer, M., *see also* Dinnerstein, D., 1957; Hornbostel, E. M. von, 1920; Selkin, J., 1957; Soltz, D. F., 1959; Strassburger, F., 1959.

Wesemann, A. F., *see* Meyer, D. R., 1960.

West, M. *A general service list of English words.* London: Longmans, 1953. **863, 895n**

Westheimer, G. H. Mechanism of saccadic eye movements. *Archives of Ophthalmology,* 1954, *52,* 710–724. (a) **376**

Westheimer, G. H. Eye movement responses to a horizontally moving visual stimulus. *Archives of Ophthalmology,* 1954, *52,* 932–943. (b) **378, 379**

Westheimer, G. H., & Mitchell, A. M. Eye movement responses to convergence stimuli. *Archives of Ophthalmology,* 1956, *55,* 848–856. **382**

Westheimer, G., *see* Campbell, F. W., 1960; Rashbass, C., 1961a, b; Rushton, W. A. H., 1962.

Wetzel, A. B., *see* Besch, N. F., 1962.

Wever, E. G. Beats and related phenomena resulting from the simultaneous sounding of two tones. *Psychological Review,* 1929, *36,* 402–418, 512–523. **237**

Wever, E. G. *Theory of hearing.* New York: Wiley, 1949. **228, 232, 233, 237, 244, 245**

Wever, E. G. Electrical potentials of the cochlea. *Physiological Review,* 1966, *46,* 102–127. **230**

Wever, E. G., & Bray, C. W. Action currents in the auditory nerve in response to acoustic stimulation. *Proceedings of the National Academy of Science,* 1930, *16,* 344–350. **230, 232**

Wever, E. G., & Lawrence, M. *Physiological acoustics.* Princeton, N.J.: Princeton University Press, 1954. **230, 238**

Wever, E. G., & Zener, K. E. The method of absolute judgment in psychophysics. *Psychological Review,* 1928, *35,* 466–493. **58**

Weymark, C., *see* Kenshalo, D. R., 1967.

Weymouth, F. W., *see* Andersen, E. E., 1923; Flom, M. C., 1963; Hirsch, M. J., 1948.

Whalen, P. M., *see* Brosgole, L., 1967.

Whalen, R. E. Effects of mounting without intromission and intromission without ejaculation on sexual behavior and maze learning. *Journal of Comparative and Physiological Psychology,* 1961, *54,* 409–415. **798**

Wham, D. S., *see* Irion, A. L., 1951.

Wheatstone, C., On some remarkable and hitherto unobserved phenomena of binocular vision: Part 2. *Philosophical Magazine,* 1852, series 4, 504–523. **479, 513**

Wheeler, K., *see* Gibson, J. J., 1969.

Wheeless, L. L., Jr., Boynton, R. M., & Cohen, G. H. Eye-movement responses to step and pulse-step stimuli. *Journal of the Optical Society of America,* 1966, *56,* 956–960. **379**

White, B., *see* Held, R., 1959.

White, B. L., *see* Haynes, H., 1965.

White, B. W. Stimulus conditions affecting a recently discovered stereoscopic effect. *American Journal of Psychology,* 1962, *75,* 411–420. **432**

White, C. T., & Schlosberg, H. Degree of conditioning of the GSR as a function of the period of delay. *Journal of Experimental Psychology,* 1952, *43,* 357–362. **558**

White, C. W., *see* Festinger, L., 1968.

White, G. C., *see* Bolles, R. C., 1968.

White, J. C., & Sweet, W. *Pain: Its mechanisms and neurosurgical control.* Springfield, Ill.: Charles C Thomas, 1955. **162, 164**

White, S. H., & Plum, G. E. Eye movement photography during children's discrimination learning. *Journal of Experimental Child Psychology,* 1965, *1,* 327–338. **784**

Whitely, P. L. The dependence of learning and recall upon prior intellectual activities. *Journal of Experimental Psychology,* 1927, *10,* 489–508. **1102**

Whitely, P. L., & Blankenship, A. B. The influence of certain conditions prior to learning upon subsequent recall. *Journal of Experimental Psychology,* 1936, *19,* 496–504. **1102**

Whitfield, I. C. *An introduction to electronics for physiological workers.* (2nd ed.) New York: Macmillan, 1959. **92**

Whitfield, I. C., & Evans, E. F. Responses of auditory cortical neurons to stimuli of changing frequency. *Journal of Neurophysiology,* 1965, *28,* 655–672. **232**

Whiting, J. W. M., & Mowrer, O. H. Habit progression and regression: A laboratory study of some factors relevant to human socialization. *Journal of Comparative Psychology,* 1943, *36,* 229–253, **740**

Whitmarsh, G. A., *see* Bousfield, W. A., 1958, 1960; Cohen, B. H., 1957.

Wickelgren, W. A. Acoustic similarity and intrusion errors in short-term memory. *Journal of Experimental Psychology,* 1965. *70,* 102–108. (a) **1001n, 1116**

Wickelgren, W. A. Distinctive features and errors in short-term memory for English vowels. *Journal of the Acoustical Society of America,* 1965, *38,* 583–588. (b) **1116**

Wickelgren, W. A. Acoustic similarity and retroactive interference in short-term memory. *Journal of Verbal Learning and Verbal Behavior,* 1965, *4,* 53–61. (c) **1119**

Wickelgren, W. A. Distinctive features and errors in short-term memory for English consonants. *Journal of the Acoustical Society of America,* 1966, *39,* 388–398. (a) **1116**

Wickelgren, W. A. Phonemic similarity and interference in short-term memory for single letters. *Journal of Experimental Psychology,* 1966, *71,* 396–404. (b) **1001n, 1116, 1118, 1119**

Wickelgren, W. A. Short-term recognition memory for single letters and phonemic similarity of retroactive interference. *Quarterly Journal of Experimental Psychology,* 1966, *18,* 55–62. (c) **1119**

Wickelgren, W. A., & Norman, D. A. Strength models and serial position in short-term recognition memory. *Journal of Mathematical Psychology,* 1966, *3,* 316–347. **998**

Wickens, C., *see* Wickens, D. D., 1940.

Wickens, D. D. The centrality of verbal learning. In A. W. Melton (Ed.), *Categories of human learning.* New York: Academic Press, 1964. Pp. 79–87. **979**

Wickens, D. D., Born, D., & Allen, C. Proactive inhibition and item similarity in short-term memory. *Journal of Verbal Learning and Verbal Behavior,* 1963, *2,* 440–445. **1114, 1116**

Wickens, D. D., & Cermak, L. S. Transfer effects of synonyms and antonyms in mixed and unmixed lists. *Journal of Verbal Learning and Verbal Behavior,* 1967, *6,* 832–839. **1070**

Wickens, D. D., & Wickens, C. A study of conditioning in the neonate. *Journal of Experimental Psychology,* 1940, *26,* 94–102. **553**

Wickens, D. D., *see also* Maher, W. B., 1954; Newton, J. M., 1956.

Wieland, B. A., *see* Cook, T. H., 1967; Mefferd, R. B. Jr., 1967, 1968.

Wiener, F. M., *see* Egan, J. P., 1946.

Wiesel, T. N., *see* Hubel, D. H., 1962.

Wigand, M. E., *see* Keidel, W. D., 1961.

Wiggins, J. S. Two determinants of associative reaction time. *Journal of Experimental Psychology,* 1957, *54,* 144–147. **862**

Wike, E. L. *Secondary reinforcement.* New York: Harper, 1966. **670, 671**

Wike, E. L., & Barrientos, G. Secondary reinforcement and multiple drive reduction. *Journal of Comparative and Physiological Psychology,* 1958, *51,* 640–643. **668**

Wike, E. L., & Kintsch, W. Delayed reinforcement and runway performance. *Psychological Review,* 1959, *9,* 179–187. **685**

Wike, E. L., & Remple, R. Delayed reinforcement, selective learning and habit reversal. *Psychological Record,* 1959, *9,* 179–187. **685**

Wike, E. L., *see also* Kintsch, W., 1957; Scott, E. D., 1956.

Wiley, R. E., *see* Horton, D. L., 1967a, b.

Wilkins, L., & Richter, C. P. A great craving for salt by a child with corticoadrenal insufficiency. *Journal of the American Medical Association,* 1940, *114,* 866–868. **188**

Wilkinson, H. J., *see* Jones, A., 1961.

Williams, C. E., *see* House, A. S., 1965.

Williams, C. M., *see* Lele, P. P., 1954.

Williams, D. R. Classical conditioning and incentive motivation. In W. F. Prokasy (Ed.), *Classical conditioning.* New York: Appleton, 1965. **622**

Williams, O. A study of the phenomenon of reminiscence. *Journal of Experimental Psychology,* 1926, *9,* 368–387. **1121**

Williams, R. A. Effects of repeated food deprivations and repeated feeding tests on feeding behavior. *Journal of Comparative and Physiological Psychology,* 1968, *65,* 222–226. **820, 821**

Williams, R. A., & Campbell, B. A. Weight loss and quinine-milk ingestion as measures of "hunger" in infant and adult rats. *Journal of Comparative and Physiological Psychology,* 1961, *54,* 220–222. **815, 817**

Williams, R. A., *see also* Campbell, B. A., 1961.

Willis, F. N., *see* Collier, G., 1961.

Wilson, A., *see* Flock, H. R., 1966.

Wilson, E. O. Chemical communication in the social insects. *Science,* 1965, *149,* 1064–1071. **194**

Wilson, G. T., & Radloff, W. P. Degree of arousal and performance: Effects of reticular stimulation on an operant task. *Psychonomic Science,* 1967, *7,* 13–14. **841**

Wilson, J. P. An auditory after-image. In *Symposium on frequency analysis and periodicity detection in hearing.* Driebergen, The Netherlands, 1969. **246**

Wilson, J. P., *see also* Kaess, D. W., 1964.

Wimer, C. An analysis of semantic stimulus factors in paired-associated learning. *Journal of Verbal Learning and Verbal Behavior,* 1963, *1,* 397–407. **900**

Wimer, R. Osgood's transfer surface: Extension and test.

Journal of Verbal Learning and Verbal Behavior, 1964, *3,* 274–279. **1052, 1056**

Winch, W. H. The transfer of improvement in memory in school children. *British Journal of Psychology,* 1908, *2,* 284–293. **1031**

Winch, W. H. The transfer of improvement in memory in school children. *British Journal of Psychology,* 1910, *3,* 386–405. **1031**

Windle, W. F., *see* Rasmussen, G. L., 1960.

Winkelmann, R. K. The sensory endings in the skin of the cat. *Journal of Comparative Neurology,* 1958, *109,* 221–232. **125**

Winnick, W. A., & Rogoff, I. Role of apparent slant in shape judgments. *Journal of Experimental Psychology,* 1965, *69,* 554–563. **516**

Winograd, E. Escape behavior under different fixed ratios and shock intensities. *Journal of the Experimental Analysis of Behavior,* 1965, *8,* 117–124. **723**

Winograd, E. List differentiation as a function of frequency and retention interval. *Journal of Experimental Psychology,* 1968, *76,* Monograph Supplement No. 2. **1091, 1103**

Winslow, C. N. Visual illusions in the chick. *Archives of Physiology,* 1933, *153,* 1–83. Cited in Zanforlin, M. Some observations of Gregory's theory of perceptual illusions. *Quarterly Journal of Experimental Psychology,* 1967, *19,* 193–197. **461**

Winzer, G. E., *see* Corliss, E. L. R., 1965.

Wipf, J. L., & Webb, W. B. Supplementary report: Proactive inhibition as a function of the method of reproduction. *Journal of Experimental Psychology,* 1962, *64,* 421. **1106**

Wirth, A., *see* Dodt, E., 1953.

Wisby, W. J., & Hasler, A. D. Effect of olfactory occlusion on migrating silver salmon (*O. kisutch*). *Journal of the Fisheries Research Board of Canada,* 1954, *11,* 472–478. **194**

Wischner, G. J. The effect of punishment on discrimination learning in a non-correction situation. *Journal of Experimental Psychology,* 1947, *37,* 271–284. **739**

Wischner, G. J., Fowler, H., & Kushnick, S. A. Effect of strength of punishment for "correct" or "incorrect" responses on visual discrimination performance. *Journal of Experimental Psychology,* 1963, *65,* 131–138. **740**

Wischner, G. J., *see also* Fowler, H., 1965, 1968.

Wishner, J., Shipley, T. E., Jr., & Hurvich, M. S. The serial-position curve as a function of organization. *American Journal of Psychology,* 1957, *70,* 258–262. **1016**

Wismer, B., & Lipsitt, L. P. Verbal mediation in paired-associate learning. *Journal of Experimental Psychology,* 1964, *68,* 441–448. **1077**

Witkin, H. A., & Asch, S. E. Studies in space orientation: III. Perception of the upright in the absence of a visual field. IV. Further experiments on perception of the upright with displaced visual fields. *Journal of Experimental Psychology,* 1948, *38,* 603–614, 762–782. **539**

Witkin, H. A., Lewis, H. B., Hertzman, M., Machover, K., Meissner, P. B., & Wapner, S. *Personality through perception.* New York: Harper, 1954. **470, 539n**

Witkin, H. A., Wapner, S., & Leventhal, T. Sound localization with conflicting visual and auditory cues. *Journal of Experimental Psychology,* 1952, *43,* 58–57. **269**

Witkin, H. A., *see also* Asch, S. E., 1948.

Witmer, L. R. The association value of three-place consonant syllables. *Journal of Genetic Psychology,* 1935, *47,* 337–360. **852, 982**

Witt, I., *see* Hensel, H., 1959.

Witte, R. S. Long-term effects of patterned reward schedules. *Journal of Experimental Psychology,* 1964, *68,* 588–594. **921, 934**

Wodinsky, J., *see* Bitterman, M. E., 1953.

Wohlgemuth, A. On the after-effect of seen movement. *British Journal of Psychology Monographs,* 1911, *1.* **522**

Wohlwill, J. F. Developmental studies of perception. *Psychological Bulletin,* 1960, *57,* 249–288. **550**

Wolbarsht, M. L., *see* Wagner, H. G., 1960.

Wolf, A. V. *Thirst: Physiology of the urge to drink and problems of water lack.* Springfield, Ill.: Charles C Thomas, 1958. **816**

Wolf, S., & Hardy, J. D. Studies on pain: Observations on pain due to local cooling. *Journal of Clinical Investigation,* 1941, *20,* 521–533. **159**

Wolf, S., *see also* Schneider, R. A., 1955, 1960.

Wolfe, J. B. The effect of delayed reward upon learning in the white rat. *Journal of Comparative Psychology,* 1943, *17,* 1–21. **679**

Wolfe, J. B. Effectiveness of token-rewards for chimpanzees. *Comparative Psychology Monographs,* 1936, *12,* No. 60. **665**

Wolfe, J. B., & Kaplon, M. D. Effect of amount of reward and consummative activity on learning in chickens. *Journal of Comparative Psychology,* 1941, *31,* 353–361. **617, 623**

Wolff, H. G., *see* Hardy, J. D., 1940, 1947, 1951; Schumacher, G. A., 1940.

Wolfle, H. M. Conditioning as a function of the interval between the conditioned and the original stimulus. *Journal of General Psychology,* 1932, *7,* 80–103. **558, 561**

Wolin, B. R., *see* Mayzner, M. S., 1965a, b, c.

Wood, C. L., III, *see* Jeffress, L., 1956.

Wood, P. B., *see* Kenshalo, D. R., 1968.

Woodburne, L. S. The effect of a constant visual angle upon the binocular discrimination of depth differences. *American Journal of Psychology,* 1934, *46,* 273–286. **486**

Woodrow, H. The effect of training upon transference. *Journal of Educational Psychology,* 1927, *18,* 159–172. **1032**

Woodrow, H., & Karpman, B. A new olfactometric technique and some results. *Journal of Experimental Psychology,* 1917, *2,* 431–447. **200, 211**

Woodrow, H., & Lowell, F. Children's association frequency tables. *Psychological Monographs,* 1916, *22,* (Whole No. 97). **864, 874**

Woods, P. J. The relationship between probability difference $(\pi_1-\pi_2)$ and learning rate in a contingent partial reinforcement situation. *Journal of Experimental Psychology,* 1959, *58,* 27–30. **932**

Woods, P. J., *see also* Brand, H., 1956.

Woodworth, R. S. *Dynamic psychology.* New York: Columbia University Press, 1918. **793, 794**

Woodworth, R. S. *Experimental psychology.* New York: Holt, 1938. **402, 438, 448, 491n, 492, 563, 794n, 850, 851n, 864, 877, 980**

Woodworth, R. S. *Dynamics of behavior.* New York: Holt, Rinehart & Winston, 1958. **793n**

Woodworth, R. S., & Schlosberg, H. *Experimental psychology.* New York: Holt, 1954. **212, 213, 399, 422, 508, 512, 522, 528, 558n, 559, 574, 575, 611, 619, 710, 794, 831, 850, 851n, 853n, 859n, 860, 861, 864, 868n, 877, 907, 945, 980**

Woodworth, R. S., *see also* Thorndike, E. L., 1901.

Woolsey, C. N. Organization of cortical auditory system: A review and synthesis. In G. Rasmussen & W. F. Windle (Eds.), *Neural mechanisms of the auditory and vestibular systems.* Springfield, Ill.: Charles C Thomas, 1960. **232**

Woolsey, C. N., *see also* Travis, A. M., 1956.

Worchel, P., & Berry, J. H. The perception of obstacles by the deaf. *Journal of Experimental Psychology,* 1952, *43,* 187–194. **270**

Worchel, P., & Dallenbach, K. M. "Facial vision": Perception of obstacles by the deaf-blind. *American Journal of Psychology,* 1947, *60,* 502–553. **270**

Worchel, P., *see also* Ammons, C. H., 1953.

Work, M. S., *see* Amsel, A., 1961, 1962.

Woskow, M. H., *see* Jones, F. N., 1964.

Wright, H. N. Temporal summation and backward masking. *Journal of the Acoustical Society of America,* 1964, *36,* 927–932. **241**

Wright, J. E., see Pliskoff, S. S., 1964.

Wright, J. H. Effects of formal interitem similarity and length of retention interval on proactive inhibition of short-term memory. *Journal of Experimental Psychology,* 1967, *75,* 386–395. **1115**

Wright, J. H., see also Dufort, R. H., 1962.

Wright, R. H., & Michels, K. M. Evaluation of far infrared relations to odor by a standards similarity method. *Annals of the New York Academy of Science,* 1964, *116,* 535–551. **220**

Wright, W. D. The functions and performance of the eye. *Journal of the Scientific Institute,* 1942, *19,* 161–165. **300**

Wright, W. D. *Researches in normal and defective colour vision.* London: Henry Kimpton, 1946. **362, 364, 365**

Wright, W. D., see also Thomson, L. C., 1953.

Wuest, F. J. *Psychophysical measurements from two theoretical viewpoints.* Unpublished doctoral dissertation, Brown University, 1961. **44**

Wulff, J. J., see Sheffield, F. D., 1951.

Wundt, W. *Beiträge zur Theorie der Sinneswahrnehmung.* Leipzig: C. F. Winter, 1862. **479**

Wundt, W. *Outlines of psychology* (4th German ed., transl. by C. H. Judd). Leipzig: Englemann, 1902. **403, 465, 466, 542**

Wyckoff, L. B., Jr. The role of observing responses in discrimination learning. *Psychological Review,* 1952, *59,* 431–442. **769, 948**

Wyckoff, L. B., & Page, H. A. A grid for administering shock. *American Journal of Psychology,* 1954, *67,* 154. **706**

Wyckoff, L. B., see also Ziegler, H., 1961.

Wylie, H. H. An experimental study of transfer of response in the white rat. *Behavior Monographs,* 1919, No. 16. **1045**

Wynne, L. C., see Solomon, R. L., 1953.

Wynne, R. D., Gerjuoy, H., & Schiffman, H. Association test antonym-response set. *Journal of Verbal Learning and Verbal Behavior,* 1965, *4,* 354–359. **871**

Wyrwicka, W., see Clemente, C. D., 1964; Sterman, M. B., 1967.

Wyszecki, G., & Stiles, W. S. *Color science: Concepts and methods, quantitative data and formulas.* New York: Wiley, 1967. **334, 352, 358, 359, 361, 362, 366, 367**

Yamaguchi, H. G. Drive (D) as a function of hours of hunger (h). *Journal of Experimental Psychology,* 1951, *42,* 108–117. **802, 825, 826**

Yamaguchi, H. G. Gradients of drive stimulus (S_D) intensity generalization. *Journal of Experimental Psychology,* 1952, *43,* 298–304. **830**

Yamaguchi, S. The synergistic taste effect of monosodium glutamate and disodium 5'-inosinate. *Journal of Food Science,* 1967, *32,* 473–478. **187**

Yamaguchi, S., see also Ikeda, S., 1962.

Yamashita, S., Ogawa, H., & Sato, M. Multimodal sensitivity of taste units in the rat. *Kumamoto Medical Journal,* 1967, *20,* 67–70. **181**

Yarbus, A. L. Motion of the eye on interchanging fixating points at rest in space. *Biophysics,* 1957, *2,* 679–683 (translated from *Biofizika 2,* 698–702). (a) **387**

Yarbus, A. L. The perception of an image fixed with respect to the retina. *Biophysics,* 1957, *2,* 683–690 (translated from *Biofizika 2,* 703–712). (b) **375**

Yarbus, A. L. *Eye movements and vision.* New York: Plenum Press, 1967. **374, 375, 379, 387, 459**

Yates, T., see Boynton, R. M., 1965.

Yellott, J. I., Jr. *Some effects of noncontingent success in human probability learning.* Technical Report No. 89, 1965. Stanford, Calif.: Institute for Mathematical Studies in the Social Sciences, Stanford University. **937**

Yensen, R. Some factors affecting taste sensitivity in man: II. Depletion of body salt. *Quarterly Journal of Experimental Psychology,* 1959, *11,* 230–238. **188**

Yensen, R. Taste sensitivity and food deprivation, blood sugar level and composition of meal. *Nature,* 1964, *203,* 327–328. **189**

Yerkes, D. N., see Yerkes, R. M., 1928.

Yerkes, R. M. The instincts, habits, and reactions of the frog: I. Associative processes of the green frog. *Harvard Psychology Studies,* 1903, *1,* 579–638. **704**

Yerkes, R. M. *The dancing mouse.* New York: Macmillan, 1907. **748**

Yerkes, R. M. The intelligence of earthworms. *Journal of Animal Behavior,* 1912, *2,* 332–352. **698**

Yerkes, R. M., & Dodson, J. D. The relation of strength of stimulus to rapidity of habit-formation. *Journal of Comparative Neurology and Psychology,* 1908, *18,* 459–482. **704, 829**

Yerkes, R. M., & Morgulis, S. The method of Pawlow in animal psychology. *Psychological Bulletin,* 1909, *6,* 257–273. **562**

Yerkes, R. M., & Watson, J. B. Methods of studying vision in animals. *Behavioral Monographs,* 1911, No. 2. **748**

Yerkes, R. M., & Yerkes, D. N. Concerning memory in the chimpanzee. *Journal of Comparative Psychology,* 1928, *8,* 237–271. **689**

Yoshida, M. Studies of psychometric classification of odors: 5. *Japanese Psychological Research,* 1964, *6,* 145–154. **216**

Yoshida, T. Figural aftereffect as a function of the brightness ratio between the inspection figure and its surrounding field. In *Studies in psychology in commemoration of Professor Matsusaburo Yokoyama's seventy-first birthday.* Tokyo: Keio University, 1960. **470**

Young, F. A. Boring's interpretation of Emmert's law. *American Journal of Psychology,* 1950, *63,* 277–280. **511**

Young, F. A. Concerning Emmert's law. *American Journal of Psychology,* 1951, *64,* 124–128. **511**

Young, P. T. Constancy of affective judgments to odor. *Journal of Experimental Psychology,* 1923, *6,* 182–191. **215**

Young, P. T. The role of head movements in auditory localization. *Journal of Experimental Psychology,* 1931, *14,* 95–124. **267**

Young, P. T., & Madsen, C. H., Jr. Individual isohedons in sucrose-sodium chloride and sucrose-saccharin gustatory areas. *Journal of Comparative and Physiological Psychology,* 1963, *56,* 903–909. **628**

Young, P. T., see also Kniep, E. H., 1931; Pfaffman, C., 1954.

Young, R. Paired-associate learning when the same items occur as stimuli and responses. *Journal of Experimental Psychology,* 1961, *61,* 315–318. **1012**

Young, R. K. Retroactive and proactive effects under varying conditions of response similarity. *Journal of Experimental Psychology,* 1955, *50,* 113–119. **1056, 1083, 1104**

Young, R. K. A comparison of two methods of learning serial associations. *American Journal of Psychology,* 1959, *72,* 554–559. **1012, 1023, 1064**

Young, R. K. Tests of three hypotheses about the stimulus in serial learning. *Journal of Experimental Psychology,* 1962, *63,* 307–313. **1012**

Young, R. K., & Casey, M. Transfer from serial to paired-associate learning. *Journal of Experimental Psychology,* 1964, *67,* 594–595. **1012**

Young, R. K., & Jennings, P. C. Backward learning when the same items serve as stimuli and responses. *Journal of Experimental Psychology,* 1964, *68,* 64–70. **1064**

Young, R. K., Milauckas, E. W., & Bryan, J. D. Serial learning as a function of prior paired-associate learning. *American Journal of Psychology,* 1963, *76,* 82–88. **1012**

Young, R. K., Patterson, J., & Benson, W. M. Backward serial learning. *Journal of Verbal Learning and Verbal Behavior,* 1963, *1,* 335–338. **1012**

Younger, M. S., *see* Bolles, R. C., 1967.

Yu, K. C., *see* King, D. J., 1962.

Yum, K. S. An experimental test of the law of assimilation. *Journal of Experimental Psychology,* 1931, *14,* 66–82. **1047**

Zachs, R., *see* Postman, L., 1968.

Zajaczkowska, A. Experimental test of Luneburg's theory: Horopter and alley experiments. *Journal of the Optical Society of America,* 1956, *46,* 514–527. **493**

Zajkowski, M. M., *see* Erickson, J. R., 1966, 1967.

Zanforlin, M. Some observations on Gregory's theory of perceptual illusions. *Quarterly Journal of Experimental Psychology,* 1967, *29,* 193–197. **456, 457, 461**

Zangwill, O. L., *see* Gregory, R. L., 1963.

Zaretsky, H., *see* Goodrich, K. P., 1962.

Zavortink, B. Retroactive inhibition in free-recall learning of conceptually related words as a function of change in context and interlist similarity. Unpublished doctoral dissertation, Univ. of California, Berkeley, 1968. **1085**

Zavortink, B., & Keppel, G. The influence of interpolated MMFR upon relearning in the *A–B, A–C* and *A–B, A–B'* paradigms. *Journal of Verbal Learning and Verbal Behavior,* 1968, *7,* 254–256. (a) **1062**

Zavortink, B., & Keppel, G. Retroactive inhibition in free-recall learning with alphabetical cues. *Journal of Experimental Psychology,* 1968. (b) **1044**

Zavortinck, B., *see also* Keppel, G., 1968.

Zeaman, D. Response latency as a function of the amount of reinforcement. *Journal of Experimental Psychology,* 1949, *39,* 466–483. **617, 618, 631, 795**

Zeaman, D., & House, P. J. The role of attention in retardate discrimination learning. In N. R. Ellis (Ed.), *Handbook in mental deficiency: Psychological theory and research.* New York: McGraw-Hill, 1963. Pp. 159–233. **949, 1001**

Zeaman, D., & Smith, R. W. Review of some recent findings in human cardiac conditioning. In W. F. Prokasy (Ed.), *Classical conditioning.* New York: Appleton, 1965. **567**

Zeaman, D., *see also* House, B. J., 1963; Shepp, B., 1966.

Zeeman, W. P. C., *see* Roelofs, C. O., 1957.

Zegers, R. T. The reversal illusion of the Ames trapezoid. *Transactions of the New York Academy of Sciences,* 1965, *26,* 377–400. **518**

Zeigler, H. P., *see* Megibow, M., 1968.

Zeigler, H. P., & Leibowitz, H. Apparent visual size as a function of distance for children and adults. *American Journal of Psychology,* 1957, *70,* 106–109. **513, 550**

Zeiler, M. D. The ratio theory of intermediate size discrimination. *Psychological Review,* 1963, *70,* 516–533. **765**

Zeiler, M. D. Stimulus definition and choice. In L. P. Lipsitt & C. C. Spiker (Eds.), *Advances in child development and behavior.* Vol. III. New York: Academic Press, 1967. Pp. 125–156. **765**

Zeiler, M. D., & Price, A. E. Discrimination with variable interval and continuous reinforcement schedules. *Psychonomic Science,* 1965, *3,* 299–300. **768**

Zelhart, P. F., *see* Johnson, R. C., 1964.

Zener, K. The significance of behavior accompanying conditioned salivary secretion for theories of the conditioned response. *American Journal of Psychology,* 1937, *50,* 384–403. **565**

Zener, K. E., *see* Wever, E. G., 1928.

Zerbolio, D. J., Jr., *see* Weisman, R. G., 1966.

Zerlin, S., *see* Davis, H., 1966; Tobias, J. V., 1959.

Zewi, M., *see* Granit, R., 1938.

Ziegler, H., & Wyckoff, L. B. Observing responses and discrimination learning. *Quarterly Journal of Experimental Psychology,* 1961, *13,* 129–140. **769**

Zigler, M. J., Cook, B., Miller, D., & Wemple, L. The perception of form in peripheral vision. *American Journal of Psychology,* 1930, *42,* 246–259. **443, 445**

Zimmerman, C., *see* Bruner, J. S., 1955.

Zimmerman, D. W. Durable secondary reinforcement. *Psychological Review,* 1957, *64,* 373–383. **670**

Zimmerman, D. W. Sustained performance in rats based on secondary reinforcement. *Journal of Comparative and Physiological Psychology,* 1959, *52,* 353–358. **672, 673**

Zimmerman, J. Technique for sustaining behavior with conditioned reinforcement. *Science,* 1963, *142,* 682–684. **665**

Zinnes, J. L., Suppes, P., 1961, 1966.

Zotterman, Y. Studies in the peripheral nervous mechanism of pain. *Acta Medica Scandinavica,* 1933, *80,* 185–242. **160**

Zotterman, Y. The water taste of the frog. *Experientia,* 1950, *6,* 57–58. **186**

Zotterman, Y. Species differences in the water taste. *Acta Physiologica Scandinavica,* 1956, *37,* 60–70. **186, 190**

Zotterman, Y., *see also* Andersen, H. T., 1963; Borg, G., 1967; Diamant, H., 1963, 1965; Hensel, H., 1951; Liljestrand, G., 1954.

Zubek, J. P., Welch, G., & Saunders, M. G. Electroencephalographic changes during and after 14 days of perceptual deprivation. *Science,* 1963, *139,* 490–492. **841**

Zuckerman, C., *see* Wallach, H., 1963.

Zusne, L., *see* Michels, K. M., 1965.

Zwaardemaker, H., *L'odorat.* Paris: Doin, 1925. **211, 212**

Zwicker, E. Der Ungewohnliche Amplitudengang der nichtlinearen Verzerrungen des Ohres. *Acustica,* 1955, *5,* 67–74. **237, 239**

Zwicker, E. "Negative after-image" in hearing. *Journal of the Acoustical Society of America,* 1964, *36,* 2413–2415. **244**

Zwicker, E., & Scharf, B. A model of loudness summation. *Psychological Review,* 1965, *72,* 3–26. **248**

Zwicker, E., *see also* Simmons, F. B., 1965.

Zwislocki, J. Theory of temporal auditory summation. *Journal of the Acoustical Society of America,* 1960, *32,* 1046–1060. **234**

Zwislocki, J., Damianopoulos, E. N., Buining, E., & Glanz, J. Central masking: Some steady-state and transient effects. *Perception and Psychophysics,* 1967, *2,* 59–64. **242**

Zwislocki, J., & Feldman, R. S. Just noticeable differences in dichotic phase. *Journal of the Acoustical Society of America,* 1956, *28,* 860–864. **266**

Zwislocki, J., *see also* Hellman, R. P., 1961.

SUBJECT
INDEX

REFERENCE TABLES AND FORMULAS

REFERENCE TABLE 1 p AND z VALUES

p	.01	.02	.03	.04	.05	.06	.07	.08	.09	.10
z	−2.33	−2.05	−1.88	−1.75	−1.64	−1.55	−1.48	−1.41	−1.34	−1.28
p	.11	.12	.13	.14	.15	.16	.17	.18	.19	.20
z	−1.23	−1.18	−1.13	−1.08	−1.04	−.99	−.95	−.92	−.88	−.84
p	.21	.22	.23	.24	.25	.26	.27	.28	.29	.30
z	−.81	−.77	−.74	−.71	−.67	−.64	−.61	−.58	−.55	−.52
p	.31	.32	.33	.34	.35	.36	.37	.38	.39	.40
z	−.50	−.47	−.44	−.41	−.39	−.36	−.33	−.31	−.28	−.25
p	.41	.42	.43	.44	.45	.46	.47	.48	.49	.50
z	−.23	−.20	−.18	−.15	−.13	−.10	−.08	−.05	−.03	00
p	.51	.52	.53	.54	.55	.56	.57	.58	.59	.60
z	+.03	+.05	+.08	+.10	+.13	+.15	+.18	+.20	+.23	+.25
p	.61	.62	.63	.64	.65	.66	.67	.68	.69	.70
z	+.28	+.31	+.33	+.36	+.39	+.41	+.44	+.47	+.50	+.52
p	.71	.72	.73	.74	.75	.76	.77	.78	.79	.80
z	+.55	+.58	+.61	+.64	+.67	+.71	+.74	+.77	+.81	+.84
p	.81	.82	.83	.84	.85	.86	.87	.88	.89	.90
z	+.88	+.92	+.95	+.99	+1.04	+1.08	+1.13	+1.18	+1.23	+1.28
p	.91	.92	.93	.94	.95	.96	.97	.98	.99	.995
z	+1.34	+1.41	+1.48	+1.55	+1.64	+1.75	+1.88	+2.05	+2.33	+2.58

REFERENCE TABLE 2 FOUR-PLACE LOGARITHMS

n	0	1	2	3	4	5	6	7	8	9
10	0000	0043	0086	0128	0170	0212	0253	0294	0334	0374
11	0414	0453	0492	0531	0569	0607	0645	0682	0719	0755
12	0792	0828	0864	0899	0934	0969	1004	1038	1072	1106
13	1139	1173	1206	1239	1271	1303	1335	1367	1399	1430
14	1461	1492	1523	1553	1584	1614	1644	1673	1703	1732
15	1761	1790	1818	1847	1875	1903	1931	1959	1987	2014
16	2041	2068	2095	2122	2148	2175	2201	2227	2253	2279
17	2304	2330	2355	2380	2405	2430	2455	2480	2504	2529
18	2553	2577	2601	2625	2648	2672	2695	2718	2742	2765
19	2788	2810	2833	2856	2878	2900	2923	2945	2967	2989
20	3010	3032	3054	3075	3096	3118	3139	3160	3181	3201
21	3222	3243	3263	3284	3304	3324	3345	3365	3385	3404
22	3424	3444	3464	3483	3502	3522	3541	3560	3579	3598
23	3617	3636	3655	3674	3692	3711	3729	3747	3766	3784
24	3802	3820	3838	3856	3874	3892	3909	3927	3945	3962
25	3979	3997	4014	4031	4048	4065	4082	4099	4116	4133
26	4150	4166	4183	4200	4216	4232	4249	4265	4281	4298
27	4314	4330	4346	4362	4378	4393	4409	4425	4440	4456
28	4472	4487	4502	4518	4533	4548	4564	4579	4594	4609
29	4624	4639	4654	4669	4683	4698	4713	4728	4742	4757
30	4771	4786	4800	4814	4829	4843	4857	4871	4886	4900
31	4914	4928	4942	4955	4969	4983	4997	5011	5024	5038
32	5051	5065	5079	5092	5105	5119	5132	5145	5159	5172
33	5185	5198	5211	5224	5237	5250	5263	5276	5289	5302
34	5315	5328	5340	5353	5366	5378	5391	5403	5416	5428
35	5441	5453	5465	5478	5490	5502	5514	5527	5539	5551
36	5563	5575	5587	5599	5611	5623	5635	5647	5658	5670
37	5682	5694	5705	5717	5729	5740	5752	5763	5775	5786
38	5798	5809	5821	5832	5843	5855	5866	5877	5888	5899
39	5911	5922	5933	5944	5955	5966	5977	5988	5999	6010
40	6021	6031	6042	6053	6064	6075	6085	6096	6107	6117
41	6128	6138	6149	6160	6170	6180	6191	6201	6212	6222
42	6232	6243	6253	6263	6274	6284	6294	6304	6314	6325
43	6335	6345	6355	6365	6375	6385	6395	6405	6415	6425
44	6435	6444	6454	6464	6474	6484	6493	6503	6513	6522
45	6532	6542	6551	6561	6571	6580	6590	6599	6609	6618
46	6628	6637	6646	6656	6665	6675	6684	6693	6702	6712
47	6721	6730	6739	6749	6758	6767	6776	6785	6794	6803
48	6812	6821	6830	6839	6848	6857	6866	6875	6884	6893
49	6902	6911	6920	6928	6937	6946	6955	6964	6972	6981
50	6990	6998	7007	7016	7024	7033	7042	7050	7059	7067
51	7076	7084	7093	7101	7110	7118	7126	7135	7143	7152
52	7160	7168	7177	7185	7193	7202	7210	7218	7226	7235
53	7243	7251	7259	7267	7275	7284	7292	7300	7308	7316
54	7324	7332	7340	7348	7356	7364	7372	7380	7388	7396

REFERENCE TABLE 2 FOUR-PLACE LOGARITHMS (*Continued*)

n	0	1	2	3	4	5	6	7	8	9
55	7404	7412	7419	7427	7435	7443	7451	7459	7466	7474
56	7482	7490	7497	7505	7513	7520	7528	7536	7543	7551
57	7559	7566	7574	7582	7589	7597	7604	7612	7619	7627
58	7634	7642	7649	7657	7664	7672	7679	7686	7694	7701
59	7709	7716	7723	7731	7738	7745	7752	7760	7767	7774
60	7782	7789	7796	7803	7810	7818	7825	7832	7839	7846
61	7853	7860	7868	7875	7882	7889	7896	7903	7910	7917
62	7924	7931	7938	7945	7952	7959	7966	7973	7980	7987
63	7993	8000	8007	8014	8021	8028	8035	8041	8048	8055
64	8062	8069	8075	8082	8089	8096	8102	8109	8116	8122
65	8129	8136	8142	8149	8156	8162	8169	8176	8182	8189
66	8195	8202	8209	8215	8222	8228	8235	8241	8248	8254
67	8261	8267	8274	8280	8287	8293	8299	8306	8312	8319
68	8325	8331	8338	8344	8351	8357	8363	8370	8376	8382
69	8388	8395	8401	8407	8414	8420	8426	8432	8439	8445
70	8451	8457	8463	8470	8476	8482	8488	8494	8500	8506
71	8513	8519	8525	8531	8537	8543	8549	8555	8561	8567
72	8573	8579	8585	8591	8597	8603	8609	8615	8621	8627
73	8633	8639	8645	8651	8657	8663	8669	8675	8681	8686
74	8692	8698	8704	8710	8716	8722	8727	8733	8739	8745
75	8751	8756	8762	8768	8774	8779	8785	8791	8797	8802
76	8808	8814	8820	8825	8831	8837	8842	8848	8854	8859
77	8865	8871	8876	8882	8887	8893	8899	8904	8910	8915
78	8921	8927	8932	8938	8943	8949	8954	8960	8965	8971
79	8976	8982	8987	8993	8998	9004	9009	9015	9020	9025
80	9031	9036	9042	9047	9053	9058	9063	9069	9074	9079
81	9085	9090	9096	9101	9106	9112	9117	9122	9128	9133
82	9138	9143	9149	9154	9159	9165	9170	9175	9180	9186
83	9191	9196	9201	9206	9212	9217	9222	9227	9232	9238
84	9243	9248	9253	9258	9263	9269	9274	9279	9284	9289
85	9294	9299	9304	9309	9315	9320	9325	9330	9335	9340
86	9345	9350	9355	9360	9365	9370	9375	9380	9385	9390
87	9395	9400	9405	9410	9415	9420	9425	9430	9435	9440
88	9445	9450	9455	9460	9465	9469	9474	9479	9484	9489
89	9494	9499	9504	9509	9513	9518	9523	9528	9533	9538
90	9542	9547	9552	9557	9562	9566	9571	9576	9581	9586
91	9590	9595	9600	9605	9609	9614	9619	9624	9628	9633
92	9638	9643	9647	9652	9657	9661	9666	9671	9675	9680
93	9685	9689	9694	9699	9703	9708	9713	9717	9722	9727
94	9731	9736	9741	9745	9750	9754	9759	9763	9768	9773
95	9777	9782	9786	9791	9795	9800	9805	9809	9814	9818
96	9823	9827	9832	9836	9841	9845	9850	9854	9859	9863
97	9868	9872	9877	9881	9886	9890	9894	9899	9903	9908
98	9912	9917	9921	9926	9930	9934	9939	9943	9948	9952
99	9956	9961	9965	9969	9974	9978	9983	9987	9991	9996

REFERENCE TABLE 3 RANDOM NUMBERS

Line \ Col.	(1)	(2)	(3)	(4)	(5)	(6)	(7)	(8)	(9)	(10)	(11)	(12)	(13)	(14)
1	10480	15011	01536	02011	81647	91646	69179	14194	62590	36207	20969	99570	91291	90700
2	22368	46573	25595	85393	30995	89198	27982	53402	93965	34095	52666	19174	39615	99505
3	24130	48360	22527	97265	76393	64809	15179	24830	49340	32081	30680	19655	63348	58629
4	42167	93093	06243	61680	07856	16376	39440	53537	71341	57004	00849	74917	97758	16379
5	37570	39975	81837	16656	06121	91782	60468	81305	49684	60672	14110	06927	01263	54613
6	77921	06907	11008	42751	27756	53498	18602	70659	90655	15053	21916	81825	44394	42880
7	99562	72905	56420	69994	98872	31016	71194	18738	44013	48840	63213	21069	10634	12952
8	96301	91977	05463	07972	18876	20922	94595	56869	69014	60045	18425	84903	42508	32307
9	89579	14342	63661	10281	17453	18103	57740	84378	25331	12566	58678	44947	05585	56941
10	85475	36857	53342	53988	53060	59533	38867	62300	08158	17983	16439	11458	18593	64952
11	28918	69578	88231	33276	70997	79936	56865	05859	90106	31595	01547	85590	91610	78188
12	63553	40961	48235	03427	49626	69445	18663	72695	52180	20847	12243	90511	33703	90322
13	09429	93969	52636	92737	88974	33488	36320	17617	30015	08272	84115	27156	30613	74952
14	10365	61129	87529	85689	48237	52267	67689	93394	01511	26358	85104	20285	29975	89868
15	07119	97336	71048	08178	77233	13916	47564	81056	97735	85977	29372	74461	28551	90707
16	51085	12765	51821	51259	77452	16308	60756	92144	49442	53900	70960	63990	75601	40719
17	02368	21382	52404	60268	89368	19885	55322	44819	01188	65255	64835	44919	05944	55157
18	01011	54092	33362	94904	31273	04146	18594	29852	71585	85030	51132	01915	92747	64951
19	52162	53916	46369	58586	23216	14513	83149	98736	23495	64350	94738	17752	35156	35749
20	07056	97628	33787	09998	42698	06691	76988	13602	51851	46104	88916	19509	25625	58104
21	48663	91245	85828	14346	09172	30168	90229	04734	59193	22178	30421	61666	99904	32812
22	54164	58492	22421	74103	47070	25306	76468	26384	58151	06646	21524	15227	96909	44592
23	32639	32363	05597	24200	13363	38005	94342	28728	35806	06912	17012	64161	18296	22851
24	29334	27001	87637	87308	58731	00256	45834	15398	46557	41135	10367	07684	36188	18510
25	02488	33062	28834	07351	19731	92420	60952	61280	50001	67658	32586	86679	50720	94953
26	81525	72295	04839	96423	24878	82651	66566	14778	76797	14780	13300	87074	79666	95725
27	29676	20591	68086	26432	46901	20849	89768	81536	86645	12659	92259	57102	80428	25280
28	00742	57392	39064	66432	84673	40027	32832	61362	98947	96067	64760	64584	96096	98253
29	05366	04213	25669	26422	44407	44048	37937	63904	45766	66134	75470	66520	34693	90449
30	91921	26418	64117	94305	26766	25940	39972	22209	71500	64568	91402	42416	07844	69618
31	00582	04711	87917	77341	42206	35126	74087	99547	81817	42607	43808	76655	62028	76630
32	00725	69884	62797	56170	86324	88072	76222	36086	84637	93161	76038	65855	77919	88006
33	69011	65795	95876	55293	18988	27354	26575	08615	40801	59920	29841	80150	12777	48501
34	25976	57948	29888	88604	67917	48708	18912	82271	65424	69774	33611	54262	85963	03547
35	09763	83473	73577	12908	30883	18317	28290	35797	05998	41688	34952	37888	38917	88050
36	91567	42595	27958	30134	04024	86385	29880	99730	55536	84855	29080	09250	79656	73211
37	17955	56349	90999	49127	20044	59931	06115	20542	18059	02008	73708	83517	36103	42791
38	46503	18584	18845	49618	02304	51038	20655	58727	28168	15475	56942	53389	20562	87338
39	92157	89634	94824	78171	84610	82834	09922	25417	44137	84813	25555	21246	35509	20468
40	14577	62765	35605	81263	39667	47358	56873	56307	61607	49518	89656	20103	77490	18062
41	98427	07523	33362	64270	01638	92477	66969	98420	04880	45585	46565	04102	46880	45709
42	34914	63976	88720	82765	34476	17032	87589	40836	32427	70002	70663	88863	77775	69348
43	70060	28277	39475	46473	23219	53416	94970	25832	69975	94884	19661	72828	00102	66794
44	53976	54914	06990	67245	68350	82948	11398	42878	80287	88267	47363	46634	06541	97809
45	76072	29515	40980	07391	58745	25774	22987	80059	39911	96189	41151	14222	60697	59583
46	90725	52210	83974	29992	65831	38857	50490	83765	55657	14361	31720	57375	56228	41546
47	64364	67412	33339	31926	14883	24413	59744	92351	97473	89286	35931	04110	23726	51900
48	08962	00358	31662	25388	61642	34072	81249	35648	56891	69352	48373	45578	78547	81788
49	95012	68379	93526	70765	10592	04542	76463	54328	02349	17247	28865	14777	62730	92277
50	15664	10493	20492	38391	91132	21999	59516	81652	27195	48223	46751	22923	32261	85653

Taken from the 30-page table of 105,000 random digits prepared by the Bureau of Transport Economics and Statistics of the Interstate Commerce Commission, Washington, D.C.

REFERENCE TABLE 4 SQUARES, SQUARE ROOTS, AND RECIPROCALS

n	n^2	$\sqrt{n}$	$\sqrt{10n}$	$1/n$	n	n^2	$\sqrt{n}$	$\sqrt{10n}$	$1/n$
1	1	1.000	3.162	1.00000	51	2601	7.141	22.583	.01961
2	4	1.414	4.472	.50000	52	2704	7.211	22.804	.01923
3	9	1.732	5.477	.33333	53	2809	7.280	23.022	.01887
4	16	2.000	6.325	.25000	54	2916	7.348	23.238	.01852
5	25	2.236	7.071	.20000	55	3025	7.416	23.452	.01818
6	36	2.449	7.746	.16667	56	3136	7.483	23.664	.01786
7	49	2.646	8.367	.14286	57	3249	7.550	23.875	.01754
8	64	2.828	8.944	.12500	58	3364	7.616	24.083	.01724
9	81	3.000	9.487	.11111	59	3481	7.681	24.290	.01695
10	100	3.162	10.000	.10000	60	3600	7.746	24.495	.01667
11	121	3.317	10.488	.09091	61	3721	7.810	24.698	.01639
12	144	3.464	10.954	.08333	62	3844	7.874	24.900	.01613
13	169	3.606	11.402	.07692	63	3969	7.937	25.100	.01587
14	196	3.742	11.832	.07143	64	4096	8.000	25.298	.01562
15	225	3.873	12.247	.06667	65	4225	8.062	25.495	.01538
16	256	4.000	12.649	.06250	66	4356	8.124	25.690	.01515
17	289	4.123	13.038	.05882	67	4489	8.185	25.884	.01493
18	324	4.243	13.416	.05556	68	4624	8.246	26.077	.01471
19	361	4.359	13.784	.05263	69	4761	8.307	26.268	.01449
20	400	4.472	14.142	.05000	70	4900	8.367	26.458	.01429
21	441	4.583	14.491	.04762	71	5041	8.426	26.646	.01408
22	484	4.690	14.832	.04545	72	5184	8.485	26.833	.01389
23	529	4.796	15.166	.04348	73	5329	8.544	27.019	.01370
24	576	4.899	15.492	.04167	74	5476	8.602	27.203	.01351
25	625	5.000	15.811	.04000	75	5625	8.660	27.386	.01333
26	676	5.099	16.125	.03846	76	5776	8.718	27.568	.01316
27	729	5.196	16.432	.03704	77	5929	8.775	27.749	.01299
28	784	5.292	16.733	.03571	78	6084	8.832	27.928	.01282
29	841	5.385	17.029	.03448	79	6241	8.888	28.107	.01266
30	900	5.477	17.321	.03333	80	6400	8.944	28.284	.01250
31	961	5.568	17.607	.03226	81	6561	9.000	28.460	.01235
32	1024	5.657	17.889	.03125	82	6724	9.055	28.636	.01220
33	1089	5.745	18.166	.03030	83	6889	9.110	28.810	.01205
34	1156	5.831	18.439	.02941	84	7056	9.165	28.983	.01190
35	1225	5.916	18.708	.02857	85	7225	9.220	29.155	.01176
36	1296	6.000	18.974	.02778	86	7396	9.274	29.326	.01163
37	1369	6.083	19.235	.02703	87	7569	9.327	29.496	.01149
38	1444	6.164	19.494	.02632	88	7744	9.381	29.665	.01136
39	1521	6.245	19.748	.02564	89	7921	9.434	29.833	.01124
40	1600	6.325	20.000	.02500	90	8100	9.487	30.000	.01111
41	1681	6.403	20.248	.02439	91	8281	9.539	30.166	.01099
42	1764	6.481	20.494	.02381	92	8464	9.592	30.332	.01087
43	1849	6.557	20.736	.02326	93	8649	9.644	30.496	.01075
44	1936	6.633	20.976	.02273	94	8836	9.695	30.659	.01064
45	2025	6.708	21.213	.02222	95	9025	9.747	30.822	.01053
46	2116	6.782	21.448	.02174	96	9216	9.798	30.984	.01042
47	2209	6.856	21.679	.02128	97	9409	9.849	31.145	.01031
48	2304	6.928	21.909	.02083	98	9604	9.899	31.305	.01020
49	2401	7.000	22.136	.02041	99	9801	9.950	31.464	.01010
50	2500	7.071	22.361	.02000	100	10000	10.000	31.623	.01000

REFERENCE TABLE 5 PERCENTILE VALUES
OF "STUDENT'S" DISTRIBUTION

n	$t_{.75}$	$t_{.90}$	$t_{.95}$	$t_{.99}$	$t_{.995}$
1	1.00	3.08	6.31	31.82	63.66
2	.82	1.89	2.92	6.96	9.92
3	.76	1.64	2.35	4.54	5.84
4	.74	1.53	2.13	3.75	4.60
5	.73	1.48	2.02	3.36	4.03
6	.72	1.44	1.94	3.14	3.71
7	.71	1.42	1.89	3.00	3.50
8	.71	1.40	1.86	2.90	3.36
9	.70	1.38	1.83	2.82	3.25
10	.70	1.37	1.81	2.76	3.17
11	.70	1.36	1.80	2.72	3.11
12	.70	1.36	1.78	2.68	3.05
13	.69	1.35	1.77	2.65	3.01
14	.69	1.34	1.76	2.62	2.98
15	.69	1.34	1.75	2.60	2.95
16	.69	1.34	1.75	2.58	2.92
17	.69	1.33	1.74	2.57	2.90
18	.69	1.33	1.73	2.55	2.88
19	.69	1.33	1.73	2.54	2.86
20	.69	1.32	1.72	2.53	2.85
21	.69	1.32	1.72	2.52	2.83
22	.69	1.32	1.72	2.51	2.82
23	.69	1.32	1.71	2.50	2.81
24	.68	1.32	1.71	2.49	2.80
25	.68	1.32	1.71	2.48	2.79
26	.68	1.32	1.71	2.48	2.78
27	.68	1.31	1.70	2.47	2.77
28	.68	1.31	1.70	2.47	2.76
29	.68	1.31	1.70	2.46	2.76
30	.68	1.31	1.70	2.46	2.75

Reprinted abridged from R. A. Fisher and F. Yates, *Statistical Tables for Biological, Agricultural, and Medical Research*, published by Oliver & Boyd Ltd., Edinburgh, 1963, by permission of the authors and publishers.

FORMULAS USEFUL IN LABORATORY WORK

Length

1 meter (m) = 3.28 feet (ft) = 39.37 inches (in.)
            = 100 centimeters (cm) = 1000 millimeters (mm)
            = 10^6 micrometers (μm), or microns (μ)
            = 10^9 nanometers (nm), or millimicrons (mμ)
            = 10^{10} Ångstrom units (Å)
1 foot = 12 in. = 30.48 cm
1 inch = 2.54 cm

Volume

1 liter (l) = 1.0567 quarts (qt) = 1000 milliliters (ml)
          = 1000.03 cubic centimeters (cc or cm^3)

Weight

1 gram (g) = .0022 pound (lb) = .035274 ounce (oz)
           = 1000 milligrams (mg) = 10^6 micrograms (μg)

Angle

1 degree (°, deg) = 60 minutes (min) = 3600 seconds (sec) = 0.0175 radian (rad)

Photometry

1 millilambert (mL) = 0.929 footlambert (ft L) = 3.183 candles per square meter (c/m^2)
                  = 10 apostilbs

Frequency

1 cycle per sec = 1 cps = 1 Hz = 360°/sec = 2 π rad/sec

Time

1 second (sec) = 1000 milliseconds (msec) = 10^6 microseconds (μsec)

Temperature

Degrees centigrade (°C) = 5/9(n°F − 32) = n°K − 273
Degrees fahrenheit (°F) = 9/5n°C + 32
Degrees kelvin (°K) = n°C + 273

π = 3.1416

e = 2.71828

DATE DUE

GAYLORD		PRINTED IN U.S.A.